Collins

SCRABBLE™
DICTIONARY

Published by Collins
An imprint of HarperCollins Publishers
Westerhill Road
Bishopbriggs
Glasgow G64 2QT

HarperCollins Publishers
1st Floor, Watermarque Building
Ringsend Road, Dublin 4, Ireland

Sixth Edition 2022

10 9 8 7 6 5 4 3 2 1

© HarperCollins Publishers 2006,
2010, 2011, 2013, 2015, 2019, 2022

HB ISBN 978-0-00-852392-3
PB ISBN 978-0-00-852391-6

Collins® is a registered trademark of
HarperCollins Publishers Limited

© 2022 Mattel. SCRABBLE™ and
SCRABBLE tiles, including S1 tiles,
are trademarks of Mattel.

www.collins.co.uk/scrabble

Typeset by Davidson Publishing
Solutions, Glasgow

Printed in the UK using 100% Renewable
Electricity at CPI Group (UK) Ltd

The contents of this publication are
believed correct at the time of printing.
Nevertheless the Publisher can accept no
responsibility for errors or omissions,
changes in the detail given or for any
expense or loss thereby caused.

HarperCollins does not warrant that any
website mentioned in this title will be
provided uninterrupted, that any website
will be error free, that defects will be
corrected, or that the website or the
server that makes it available are free of
viruses or bugs. For full terms and
conditions please refer to the site terms
provided on the website.

A catalogue record for this book is
available from the British Library.

If you would like to comment on any
aspect of this book, please contact us at
the given address or online.
E-mail: puzzles@harpercollins.co.uk
 facebook.com/collinsdictionary
 @collinsdict

MIX
Paper from
responsible sources
FSC™ C007454

Contents

Introduction

Collins Scrabble Dictionary is an invaluable tool for any competitive or club player, as well as for those who play with their friends and family.

This dictionary contains every word of between two and nine letters, with either a definition or a cross-reference to a defined root word.

It allows every Scrabble player, whether a beginner or veteran, access to the definitions of all the most useful words in Scrabble, enabling them to learn words by meaning rather than simply as combinations of letters. For many players, definitions are the key to remembering words, and to using them in Scrabble, and the ability to check meanings, inflections, and variant spellings will add interest to most social games.

The definitions are succinct and practical. In many cases, only a single definition is given, and in general only those parts of speech necessary for existing inflections are included. Cross-referred words include noun plurals, verb inflections, the comparative and superlative forms of adjectives, and variant spellings. Adjectives formed with obvious suffixes, such as *-like* and *-less*, are often also cross-referred to the root word when the meaning is easily deduced.

In any Scrabble game, most words will be between two and nine letters in length. Therefore, this book contains only those words, and does not include words between 10 and 15 letters in length. This accounts for the omission of some plurals and inflected forms of words that are themselves in the dictionary.

Unlike a conventional dictionary, every word in each section is listed in strict alphabetical order, regardless of the relationship between words. Thus there may be many words between the singular form of a noun and its plural. This strict alphabetization allows rapid checking of words – which is particularly important during Scrabble tournaments.

Rules for the Scrabble word list

- Does not include proper nouns, place names, or words with an initial capital letter, unless such words can also be spelt with a lower-case initial letter

- Does not include abbreviations, prefixes, suffixes, or words requiring apostrophes or hyphens

- Includes foreign words that are considered to have been absorbed into the English language

- Includes inflected forms, such as plurals and verb forms, eg plumb, plumbs, plumbed, plumbing

- Includes words that are old, obsolete, dialectal, historical and/or literary

- Includes World English, including spelling and variants from the US, South Africa, Australia, New Zealand, etc

- Includes words that are denoted contractions, short forms and slang

- Includes words that may be deemed rude or derogatory

Disclaimer
While every effort has been made to exclude words in the category of hate speech, no other word is excluded on the grounds of religion, gender, race, or for any reason other than that it is an invalid word form for the game of Scrabble. The presence or exclusion of any word does not in any way represent the views of the Publisher, HarperCollins.

Using the Scrabble Dictionary

This book includes all playable words of two to nine letters in length, in one straight alphabetical list. These words are either defined or cross-referred. Cross-referred words include noun plurals, verb inflections, the comparative and superlative forms of adjectives, and variant spellings. Adjectives formed with obvious suffixes such as *-like* and *-less* are often also cross-referred to the root word.

In *Collins Scrabble Dictionary*, only a single definition is given for each part of speech, and in general only those parts of speech necessary for existing inflections are included.

Main entry words   printed in bold capitals, eg:

AA

Accents   as English language Scrabble tiles are not accented, no accents are shown.

Parts of speech   shown in italics as an abbreviation, eg:

AA *n*

when more than one part of speech is given, the change of part of speech is shown after an arrow, eg:

ABANDON *vb* desert or leave
▷ *n* lack of inhibition

the abbreviated parts of speech are:

adj	adjective
adv	adverb
conj	conjunction
interj	interjection
n	noun
pl n	plural noun
prep	preposition
pron	pronoun
vb	verb

Definitions	definitions are succinct, with abbreviations sometimes used:

Brit	British
eg	for example
esp	especially
orig	originally
Scot	Scottish
sing	singular
usu	usually
E	East or eastern
N	North or northern
S	South or southern
W	West or western

Cross-references noun plurals, verb inflections, comparatives and superlatives, and derivatives are cross-referred to their root form, eg:

ABASH *vb* cause to feel ill at ease
ABASHES > ABASH
ABASHING > ABASH
ABASHLESS > ABASH
ABASHMENT > ABASH

Variant forms variant forms and synonyms are cross-referred to the most commonly used form of a word, eg:

CAFTAN *same as* **>** KAFTAN

noun plurals, verb inflections, comparatives and superlatives, and derivatives of the variant form are all cross-referred to the root form of that particular variant, eg:

CAFTAN *same as* **>** KAFTAN
CAFTANS > CAFTAN

Phrases when a word is most commonly used in a phrase, the phrase is given in italics and defined, eg:

BANGALORE as in *bangalore torpedo* explosive device in a long metal tube

Aa

AA *n* volcanic rock
AAH *vb* exclaim in pleasure
AAHED > AAH
AAHING > AAH
AAHS > AAH
AAL *n* small shrub or tree with yellow fruits
AALII *n* bushy shrub
AALIIS > AALII
AALS > AAL
AARDVARK *n* S African anteater with long ears and snout
AARDVARKS > AARDVARK
AARDWOLF *n* nocturnal mammal
AARGH *same as* > ARGH
AARRGH *same as* > ARGH
AARRGHH *same as* > ARGH
AARTI *n* Hindu ceremony
AARTIS > AARTI
AAS > AA
AASVOGEL *n* South African bird of prey
AASVOGELS > AASVOGEL
AB *n* abdominal muscle
ABA *n* type of Syrian cloth
ABAC *n* mathematical diagram
ABACA *n* species of banana
ABACAS > ABACA
ABACI > ABACUS
ABACK *adv* towards the back; backwards
ABACS > ABAC
ABACTINAL *adj* situated away from the mouth
ABACTOR *n* cattle thief
ABACTORS > ABACTOR
ABACUS *n* mathematical instrument
ABACUSES > ABACUS
ABAFT *adv* by the rear of (a ship) ▷ *adj* closer to the stern
ABAKA *n* abaca
ABAKAS > ABAKA
ABALONE *n* edible sea creature
ABALONES > ABALONE
ABAMP *same as* > ABAMPERE
ABAMPERE *n* cgs unit of current
ABAMPERES > ABAMPERE
ABAMPS > ABAMP
ABAND *vb* abandon
ABANDED > ABAND
ABANDING > ABAND

ABANDON *vb* desert or leave ▷ *n* lack of inhibition
ABANDONED *adj* deserted
ABANDONEE *n* person to whom something is relinquished
ABANDONER > ABANDON
ABANDONS > ABANDON
ABANDS > ABAND
ABAPICAL *adj* away from or opposite the apex
ABAS > ABA
ABASE *vb* humiliate or degrade (oneself)
ABASED > ABASE
ABASEDLY > ABASE
ABASEMENT > ABASE
ABASER > ABASE
ABASERS > ABASE
ABASES > ABASE
ABASH *vb* cause to feel ill at ease
ABASHED *adj* embarrassed and ashamed
ABASHEDLY > ABASHED
ABASHES > ABASH
ABASHING > ABASH
ABASHLESS > ABASH
ABASHMENT > ABASH
ABASIA *n* disorder affecting ability to walk
ABASIAS > ABASIA
ABASING > ABASE
ABASK *adv* in pleasant warmth
ABATABLE > ABATE
ABATE *vb* make or become less strong
ABATED > ABATE
ABATEMENT *n* diminution or alleviation
ABATER > ABATE
ABATERS > ABATE
ABATES > ABATE
ABATING > ABATE
ABATIS *n* rampart of felled trees
ABATISES > ABATIS
ABATOR *n* person who effects an abatement
ABATORS > ABATOR
ABATTIS *same as* > ABATIS
ABATTISES > ABATTIS
ABATTOIR *n* place where animals are killed for food
ABATTOIRS > ABATTOIR
ABATTU *adj* dejected
ABATURE *n* trail left by hunted stag
ABATURES > ABATURE

ABAXIAL *adj* facing away from the axis
ABAXILE *adj* away from the axis
ABAYA *n* Arab outer garment
ABAYAS > ABAYA
ABB *n* yarn used in weaving
ABBA *n* Coptic bishop
ABBACIES > ABBACY
ABBACY *n* office of abbot or abbess
ABBAS > ABBA
ABBATIAL *adj* relating to abbot, abbess, or abbey
ABBE *n* French abbot
ABBED *adj* displaying strong abdominal muscles
ABBES > ABBE
ABBESS *n* nun in charge of a convent
ABBESSES > ABBESS
ABBEY *n* dwelling place of monks or nuns
ABBEYS > ABBEY
ABBOT *n* head of an abbey of monks
ABBOTCIES > ABBOT
ABBOTCY > ABBOT
ABBOTS > ABBOT
ABBOTSHIP > ABBOT
ABBS > ABB
ABCEE *n* alphabet
ABCEES > ABCEE
ABCOULOMB *n* unit of electric charge
ABDABS *n* highly nervous state
ABDICABLE > ABDICATE
ABDICANT *n* one who abdicates
ABDICANTS > ABDICANT
ABDICATE *vb* give up a responsibility
ABDICATED > ABDICATE
ABDICATES > ABDICATE
ABDICATOR > ABDICATE
ABDOMEN *n* part of the body
ABDOMENS > ABDOMEN
ABDOMINA > ABDOMEN
ABDOMINAL > ABDOMEN
ABDUCE *vb* abduct
ABDUCED > ABDUCE
ABDUCENS *n* as in *abducens nerve* cranial nerve

ABDUCENT *adj* (of a muscle) abducting
ABDUCES > ABDUCE
ABDUCING > ABDUCE
ABDUCT *vb* carry off, kidnap
ABDUCTED > ABDUCT
ABDUCTEE > ABDUCT
ABDUCTEES > ABDUCT
ABDUCTING > ABDUCT
ABDUCTION *n* act of taking someone away
ABDUCTOR > ABDUCT
ABDUCTORS > ABDUCT
ABDUCTS > ABDUCT
ABEAM *adj* at right angles to a ship
ABEAR *vb* bear or behave
ABEARING > ABEAR
ABEARS > ABEAR
ABED *adv* in bed
ABEGGING *adj* in the act of begging
ABEIGH *adv* aloof
ABELE *n* white poplar tree
ABELES > ABELE
ABELIA *n* garden plant with pink or white flowers
ABELIAN > ABELIA
ABELIAS > ABELIA
ABELMOSK *n* tropical plant
ABELMOSKS > ABELMOSK
ABER *n* estuary
ABERNETHY *n* crisp unleavened biscuit
ABERRANCE > ABERRANT
ABERRANCY > ABERRANT
ABERRANT *adj* showing aberration ▷ *n* person whose behaviour is aberrant
ABERRANTS > ABERRANT
ABERRATE *vb* deviate from what is normal
ABERRATED > ABERRATE
ABERRATES > ABERRATE
ABERS > ABER
ABESSIVE *n* grammatical case indicating absence
ABESSIVES > ABESSIVE
ABET *vb* help in wrongdoing
ABETMENT > ABET
ABETMENTS > ABET
ABETS > ABET

a

ABETTAL > ABET
ABETTALS > ABET
ABETTED > ABET
ABETTER > ABET
ABETTERS > ABET
ABETTING > ABET
ABETTOR > ABET
ABETTORS > ABET
ABEYANCE *n* state of being suspended
ABEYANCES > ABEYANCE
ABEYANCY *n* abeyance
ABEYANT > ABEYANCE
ABFARAD *n* unit of capacitance
ABFARADS > ABFARAD
ABHENRIES > ABHENRY
ABHENRY *n* unit of inductance
ABHENRYS > ABHENRY
ABHOR *vb* detest utterly
ABHORRED > ABHOR
ABHORRENT *adj* hateful, loathsome
ABHORRER > ABHOR
ABHORRERS > ABHOR
ABHORRING > ABHOR
ABHORS > ABHOR
ABID > ABIDE
ABIDANCE > ABIDE
ABIDANCES > ABIDE
ABIDDEN > ABIDE
ABIDE *vb* endure, put up with
ABIDED > ABIDE
ABIDER > ABIDE
ABIDERS > ABIDE
ABIDES > ABIDE
ABIDING *adj* lasting ▷ *n* action of one who abides
ABIDINGLY > ABIDING
ABIDINGS > ABIDING
ABIES *n* fir tree
ABIETES > ABIES
ABIETIC *adj* as in *abietic acid* yellowish powder
ABIGAIL *n* a lady's maid
ABIGAILS > ABIGAIL
ABILITIES > ABILITY
ABILITY *n* competence, power
ABIOGENIC *adj* abiogenetic
ABIOSES > ABIOSIS
ABIOSIS *n* absence of life
ABIOTIC > ABIOSIS
ABITUR *n* German examination
ABITURS > ABITUR
ABJECT *adj* utterly miserable ▷ *vb* throw down
ABJECTED > ABJECT
ABJECTING > ABJECT
ABJECTION > ABJECT
ABJECTLY > ABJECT
ABJECTS > ABJECT
ABJOINT *vb* cut off
ABJOINTED > ABJOINT
ABJOINTS > ABJOINT
ABJURE *vb* deny or renounce on oath
ABJURED > ABJURE
ABJURER > ABJURE
ABJURERS > ABJURE
ABJURES > ABJURE

ABJURING > ABJURE
ABLATE *vb* remove by ablation
ABLATED > ABLATE
ABLATES > ABLATE
ABLATING > ABLATE
ABLATION *n* removal of an organ
ABLATIONS > ABLATION
ABLATIVAL > ABLATIVE
ABLATIVE *n* case of nouns ▷ *adj* relating to the ablative case
ABLATIVES > ABLATIVE
ABLATOR *n* heat shield of a space craft
ABLATORS > ABLATOR
ABLAUT *n* vowel gradation
ABLAUTS > ABLAUT
ABLAZE *adj* burning fiercely ▷ *adv* on fire
ABLE *adj* capable, competent ▷ *vb* enable
ABLED *adj* having physical powers
ABLEGATE *n* papal envoy
ABLEGATES > ABLEGATE
ABLEISM *n* discrimination against disabled people
ABLEISMS > ABLEISM
ABLEIST > ABLEISM
ABLEISTS > ABLEISM
ABLER > ABLE
ABLES > ABLE
ABLEST > ABLE
ABLET *n* freshwater fish
ABLETS > ABLET
ABLING > ABLE
ABLINGS *adv* possibly
ABLINS *adv* Scots word meaning perhaps
ABLOOM *adj* in flower
ABLOW *adj* blooming
ABLUENT *n* substance used for cleansing
ABLUENTS > ABLUENT
ABLUSH *adj* blushing
ABLUTED *adj* washed thoroughly
ABLUTION *n* ritual washing of a priest's hands
ABLUTIONS > ABLUTION
ABLY *adv* competently or skilfully
ABMHO *n* unit of electrical conductance
ABMHOS > ABMHO
ABNEGATE *vb* deny to oneself
ABNEGATED > ABNEGATE
ABNEGATES > ABNEGATE
ABNEGATOR > ABNEGATE
ABNORMAL *adj* not normal or usual ▷ *n* abnormal person or thing
ABNORMALS > ABNORMAL

ABNORMITY
> ABNORMAL
ABNORMOUS
> ABNORMAL
ABOARD *adv* onto a vehicle ▷ *adj* onto a vehicle
ABODE *n* home, dwelling ▷ *vb* forebode
ABODED > ABODE
ABODEMENT > ABODE
ABODES > ABODE
ABODING > ABODE
ABOHM *n* unit of resistance
ABOHMS > ABOHM
ABOIDEAU *n* dyke with sluicegate
ABOIDEAUS
> ABOIDEAU
ABOIDEAUX
> ABOIDEAU
ABOIL *adj* boiling
ABOITEAU *same as*
> ABOIDEAU
ABOITEAUS
> ABOITEAU
ABOITEAUX
> ABOITEAU
ABOLISH *vb* do away with
ABOLISHED > ABOLISH
ABOLISHER > ABOLISH
ABOLISHES > ABOLISH
ABOLITION *n* act of abolishing
ABOLLA *n* Roman cloak
ABOLLAE > ABOLLA
ABOLLAS > ABOLLA
ABOMA *n* South American snake
ABOMAS > ABOMA
ABOMASA > ABOMASUM
ABOMASAL > ABOMASUM
ABOMASI > ABOMASUS
ABOMASUM *n* compartment of a stomach
ABOMASUS *n* abomasum
ABOMINATE *vb* dislike intensely
ABONDANCE *same as*
> ABUNDANCE
ABOON *Scots word for*
> ABOVE
ABORAL *adj* away from the mouth
ABORALLY > ABORAL
ABORD *vb* accost
ABORDED > ABORD
ABORDING > ABORD
ABORDS > ABORD
ABORE > ABEAR
ABORIGEN *n* aborigine
ABORIGENS
> ABORIGEN
ABORIGIN *n* aborigine
ABORIGINE *n* original inhabitant
ABORIGINS
> ABORIGIN
ABORNE *adj* Shakespearean form of auburn
ABORNING > ABEAR
ABORT *vb* terminate ▷ *n* termination or failure
ABORTED > ABORT

ABORTEE *n* woman having an abortion
ABORTEES > ABORTEE
ABORTER > ABORT
ABORTERS > ABORT
ABORTING > ABORT
ABORTION *n* operation to end a pregnancy
ABORTIONS
> ABORTION
ABORTIVE *adj* unsuccessful
ABORTS > ABORT
ABORTUARY *n* place where abortions are performed
ABORTUS *n* aborted fetus
ABORTUSES > ABORTUS
ABOUGHT > ABY
ABOULIA *same as*
> ABULIA
ABOULIAS > ABOULIA
ABOULIC > ABOULIA
ABOUND *vb* be plentiful
ABOUNDED > ABOUND
ABOUNDING > ABOUND
ABOUNDS > ABOUND
ABOUT *adv* nearly, approximately
ABOUTS *prep* about
ABOVE *adv* higher (than) ▷ *n* something that is above
ABOVES > ABOVE
ABRACHIA *n* condition of having no arms
ABRACHIAS
> ABRACHIA
ABRADABLE > ABRADE
ABRADANT > ABRADE
ABRADANTS > ABRADE
ABRADE *vb* wear down by friction
ABRADED > ABRADE
ABRADER > ABRADE
ABRADERS > ABRADE
ABRADES > ABRADE
ABRADING > ABRADE
ABRAID *vb* awake
ABRAIDED > ABRAID
ABRAIDING > ABRAID
ABRAIDS > ABRAID
ABRAM *adj* auburn
ABRASAX *same as*
> ABRAXAS
ABRASAXES > ABRASAX
ABRASION *n* scraped area on the skin
ABRASIONS
> ABRASION
ABRASIVE *adj* harsh and unpleasant ▷ *n* substance for cleaning
ABRASIVES
> ABRASIVE
ABRAXAS *n* ancient charm composed of Greek letters
ABRAXASES > ABRAXAS
ABRAY *vb* awake
ABRAYED > ABRAY
ABRAYING > ABRAY
ABRAYS > ABRAY
ABRAZO *n* embrace
ABRAZOS > ABRAZO
ABREACT *vb* alleviate through abreaction
ABREACTED > ABREACT

ABREACTS > ABREACT
ABREAST adj side by side
ABREGE n abridgment
ABREGES > ABREGE
ABRI n shelter or place of refuge, esp in wartime
ABRICOCK n apricot
ABRICOCKS > ABRICOCK
ABRIDGE vb shorten by using fewer words
ABRIDGED > ABRIDGE
ABRIDGER > ABRIDGE
ABRIDGERS > ABRIDGE
ABRIDGES > ABRIDGE
ABRIDGING > ABRIDGE
ABRIM adj full to the brim
ABRIN n poisonous compound
ABRINS > ABRIN
ABRIS > ABRI
ABROACH adj (of a cask, barrel, etc) tapped
ABROAD adv in a foreign country ▷ adj in general circulation ▷ n foreign place
ABROADS > ABROAD
ABROGABLE adj able to be abrogated
ABROGATE vb cancel (a law or agreement) formally
ABROGATED > ABROGATE
ABROGATES > ABROGATE
ABROGATOR > ABROGATE
ABROOKE vb bear or tolerate
ABROOKED > ABROOKE
ABROOKES > ABROOKE
ABROOKING > ABROOKE
ABROSIA n condition involving refusal to eat
ABROSIAS > ABROSIA
ABRUPT adj sudden, unexpected ▷ n abyss
ABRUPTER > ABRUPT
ABRUPTEST > ABRUPT
ABRUPTION n breaking off of a part
ABRUPTLY > ABRUPT
ABRUPTS > ABRUPT
ABS > AB
ABSCESS n inflamed swelling ▷ vb form a swelling
ABSCESSED > ABSCESS
ABSCESSES > ABSCESS
ABSCIND vb cut off
ABSCINDED > ABSCIND
ABSCINDS > ABSCIND
ABSCISE vb separate or be separated by abscission
ABSCISED > ABSCISE
ABSCISES > ABSCISE
ABSCISIC adj as in abscisic acid type of acid
ABSCISIN n plant hormone
ABSCISING > ABSCISE
ABSCISINS > ABSCISIN
ABSCISS same as > ABSCISSA
ABSCISSA n cutting off

ABSCISSAE > ABSCISSA
ABSCISSAS > ABSCISSA
ABSCISSE same as > ABSCISSA
ABSCISSES > ABSCISSE
ABSCISSIN n plant hormone
ABSCOND vb leave secretly
ABSCONDED > ABSCOND
ABSCONDER > ABSCOND
ABSCONDS > ABSCOND
ABSEIL vb go down by a rope ▷ n instance of abseiling
ABSEILED > ABSEIL
ABSEILER n person who abseils
ABSEILERS > ABSEILER
ABSEILING > ABSEIL
ABSEILS > ABSEIL
ABSENCE n being away
ABSENCES > ABSENCE
ABSENT adj not present ▷ vb stay away
ABSENTED > ABSENT
ABSENTEE n person who is not present
ABSENTEES > ABSENTEE
ABSENTER > ABSENT
ABSENTERS > ABSENT
ABSENTING > ABSENT
ABSENTLY adv in an absent-minded manner
ABSENTS > ABSENT
ABSEY n alphabet
ABSEYS > ABSEY
ABSINTH same as > ABSINTHE
ABSINTHE n liqueur
ABSINTHES > ABSINTHE
ABSINTHS > ABSINTH
ABSIT n leave from college
ABSITS > ABSIT
ABSOLUTE adj complete, perfect ▷ n something absolute
ABSOLUTER > ABSOLUTE
ABSOLUTES > ABSOLUTE
ABSOLVE vb declare to be free from sin
ABSOLVED > ABSOLVE
ABSOLVENT n something that absolves
ABSOLVER > ABSOLVE
ABSOLVERS > ABSOLVE
ABSOLVES > ABSOLVE
ABSOLVING > ABSOLVE
ABSONANT adj unnatural and unreasonable
ABSORB vb soak up (a liquid)
ABSORBANT n absorbent substance
ABSORBATE n absorbed substance
ABSORBED adj engrossed
ABSORBENT adj able to absorb liquid ▷ n substance that absorbs

ABSORBER n thing that absorbs
ABSORBERS > ABSORBER
ABSORBING adj occupying one's attention
ABSORBS > ABSORB
ABSTAIN vb choose not to do something
ABSTAINED > ABSTAIN
ABSTAINER > ABSTAIN
ABSTAINS > ABSTAIN
ABSTERGE vb cleanse
ABSTERGED > ABSTERGE
ABSTERGES > ABSTERGE
ABSTINENT adj refraining from a certain activity
ABSTRACT adj existing as an idea ▷ n summary ▷ vb summarize
ABSTRACTS > ABSTRACT
ABSTRICT vb release
ABSTRICTS > ABSTRICT
ABSTRUSE adj not easy to understand
ABSTRUSER > ABSTRUSE
ABSURD adj incongruous or ridiculous ▷ n conception of the world
ABSURDER > ABSURD
ABSURDEST > ABSURD
ABSURDISM n belief that life is meaningless
ABSURDIST > ABSURDISM
ABSURDITY > ABSURD
ABSURDLY > ABSURD
ABSURDS > ABSURD
ABTHANE n ancient Scottish church territory
ABTHANES > ABTHANE
ABUBBLE adj bubbling
ABUILDING adj being built
ABULIA n pathological inability to take decisions
ABULIAS > ABULIA
ABULIC > ABULIA
ABUNA n male head of Ethiopian family
ABUNAS > ABUNA
ABUNDANCE n copious supply
ABUNDANCY n abundance
ABUNDANT adj plentiful
ABUNE Scots word for > ABOVE
ABURST adj bursting
ABUSABLE > ABUSE
ABUSAGE n wrong use
ABUSAGES > ABUSAGE
ABUSE vb use wrongly ▷ n prolonged ill-treatment
ABUSED > ABUSE
ABUSER > ABUSE
ABUSERS > ABUSE
ABUSES > ABUSE
ABUSING > ABUSE
ABUSION n wrong use or deception
ABUSIONS > ABUSION

ABUSIVE adj rude or insulting
ABUSIVELY > ABUSIVE
ABUT vb be next to or touching
ABUTILON n shrub
ABUTILONS > ABUTILON
ABUTMENT n construction supporting the end of a bridge
ABUTMENTS > ABUTMENT
ABUTS > ABUT
ABUTTAL same as > ABUTMENT
ABUTTALS > ABUTTAL
ABUTTED > ABUT
ABUTTER n owner of adjoining property
ABUTTERS > ABUTTER
ABUTTING > ABUT
ABUZZ adj noisy, busy with activity etc
ABVOLT n unit of potential difference in the electromagnetic system
ABVOLTS > ABVOLT
ABWATT n unit of power
ABWATTS > ABWATT
ABY vb pay the penalty for
ABYE same as > ABY
ABYEING > ABYE
ABYES > ABYE
ABYING > ABY
ABYS > ABY
ABYSM archaic word for > ABYSS
ABYSMAL adj extremely bad, awful
ABYSMALLY > ABYSMAL
ABYSMS > ABYSM
ABYSS n very deep hole or chasm
ABYSSAL adj of the ocean depths
ABYSSES > ABYSS
ACACIA n tree or shrub
ACACIAS > ACACIA
ACADEME n place of learning
ACADEMES > ACADEME
ACADEMIA n academic world
ACADEMIAS > ACADEMIA
ACADEMIC adj of a university ▷ n lecturer at a university
ACADEMICS > ACADEMIC
ACADEMIES > ACADEMY
ACADEMISM n adherence to rules
ACADEMIST > ACADEMY
ACADEMY n society for arts or sciences
ACAI n berry
ACAIS > ACAI
ACAJOU n type of mahogany
ACAJOUS > ACAJOU
ACALCULIA n inability to make calculations
ACALEPH n invertebrate
ACALEPHAE > ACALEPHE
ACALEPHAN > ACALEPH**

ACALEPHE n acaleph
ACALEPHES
> ACALEPHE
ACALEPHS > ACALEPH
ACANTH n acanthus
ACANTHA n thorn or prickle
ACANTHAE > ACANTHA
ACANTHAS > ACANTHA
ACANTHI > ACANTHUS
ACANTHIN n organic chemical
ACANTHINE adj of or resembling an acanthus
ACANTHINS
> ACANTHIN
ACANTHOID adj resembling a spine
ACANTHOUS adj of an acanthus
ACANTHS > ACANTH
ACANTHUS n prickly plant
ACAPNIA n lack of carbon dioxide
ACAPNIAS > ACAPNIA
ACARBOSE n diabetes medicine
ACARBOSES
> ACARBOSE
ACARI > ACARUS
ACARIAN > ACARUS
ACARIASES
> ACARIASIS
ACARIASIS n infestation of hair
ACARICIDE n any drug for killing acarids
ACARID n small arachnid ▷ adj of these arachnids
ACARIDAN same as
> ACARID
ACARIDANS
> ACARIDAN
ACARIDEAN > ACARID
ACARIDIAN > ACARID
ACARIDS > ACARID
ACARINE n acarid
ACARINES > ACARINE
ACAROID adj resembling a mite
ACAROLOGY n study of mites and ticks
ACARPOUS adj producing no fruit
ACARUS n type of mite
ACATER n buyer of provisions
ACATERS > ACATER
ACATES n provisions
ACATHISIA same as
> AKATHISIA
ACATOUR n buyer of provisions
ACATOURS > ACATOUR
ACAUDAL adj having no tail
ACAUDATE same as
> ACAUDAL
ACAULINE adj having no stem
ACAULOSE same as
> ACAULINE
ACAULOUS adj having a short stem
ACCA n academic
ACCABLE adj dejected or beaten
ACCAS > ACCA

ACCEDE vb consent or agree (to)
ACCEDED > ACCEDE
ACCEDENCE > ACCEDE
ACCEDER > ACCEDE
ACCEDERS > ACCEDE
ACCEDES > ACCEDE
ACCEDING > ACCEDE
ACCEND vb set alight
ACCENDED > ACCEND
ACCENDING > ACCEND
ACCENDS > ACCEND
ACCENSION > ACCEND
ACCENT n style of pronunciation ▷ vb place emphasis on
ACCENTED > ACCENT
ACCENTING > ACCENT
ACCENTOR n songbird
ACCENTORS
> ACCENTOR
ACCENTS > ACCENT
ACCENTUAL adj of accents
ACCEPT vb receive willingly
ACCEPTANT adj receiving willingly
ACCEPTED adj generally approved
ACCEPTEE n person who has been accepted
ACCEPTEES
> ACCEPTEE
ACCEPTER > ACCEPT
ACCEPTERS > ACCEPT
ACCEPTING > ACCEPT
ACCEPTIVE adj ready to accept
ACCEPTOR n person signing a bill of exchange
ACCEPTORS
> ACCEPTOR
ACCEPTS > ACCEPT
ACCESS n right to approach ▷ vb obtain data
ACCESSARY same as
> ACCESSORY
ACCESSED > ACCESS
ACCESSES > ACCESS
ACCESSING > ACCESS
ACCESSION n taking up of a position ▷ vb make a record of an addition to a collection
ACCESSORY n supplementary part ▷ adj supplementary
ACCIDENCE n inflectional morphology
ACCIDENT n mishap, often causing injury
ACCIDENTS
> ACCIDENT
ACCIDIA same as
> ACCIDIE
ACCIDIAS > ACCIDIA
ACCIDIE n spiritual sloth
ACCIDIES > ACCIDIE
ACCINGE vb put a belt around
ACCINGED > ACCINGE
ACCINGES > ACCINGE
ACCINGING > ACCINGE
ACCIPITER n hawk
ACCITE vb summon
ACCITED > ACCITE
ACCITES > ACCITE

ACCITING > ACCITE
ACCLAIM vb applaud, praise ▷ n enthusiastic approval
ACCLAIMED > ACCLAIM
ACCLAIMER > ACCLAIM
ACCLAIMS > ACCLAIM
ACCLIMATE vb adapt to a new climate
ACCLIVITY n upward slope
ACCLIVOUS
> ACCLIVITY
ACCLOY vb choke or clog
ACCLOYED > ACCLOY
ACCLOYING > ACCLOY
ACCLOYS > ACCLOY
ACCOAST vb accost
ACCOASTED > ACCOAST
ACCOASTS > ACCOAST
ACCOIED > ACCOY
ACCOIL n welcome ▷ vb gather together
ACCOILS > ACCOIL
ACCOLADE n award ▷ vb give an award
ACCOLADED
> ACCOLADE
ACCOLADES
> ACCOLADE
ACCOMPANY vb go along with
ACCOMPT vb account
ACCOMPTED > ACCOMPT
ACCOMPTS > ACCOMPT
ACCORAGE vb encourage
ACCORAGED
> ACCORAGE
ACCORAGES
> ACCORAGE
ACCORD n agreement, harmony ▷ vb fit in with
ACCORDANT adj in conformity or harmony
ACCORDED > ACCORD
ACCORDER > ACCORD
ACCORDERS > ACCORD
ACCORDING adj in proportion
ACCORDION n portable instrument
ACCORDS > ACCORD
ACCOST vb approach and speak to ▷ n greeting
ACCOSTED > ACCOST
ACCOSTING > ACCOST
ACCOSTS > ACCOST
ACCOUNT n report, description ▷ vb judge to be
ACCOUNTED > ACCOUNT
ACCOUNTS > ACCOUNT
ACCOURAGE vb encourage
ACCOURT vb entertain
ACCOURTED > ACCOURT
ACCOURTS > ACCOURT
ACCOUTER same as
> ACCOUTRE
ACCOUTERS
> ACCOUTER
ACCOUTRE vb provide with equipment
ACCOUTRED
> ACCOUTRE
ACCOUTRES
> ACCOUTRE
ACCOY vb soothe

ACCOYED > ACCOY
ACCOYING > ACCOY
ACCOYLD vb past tense of accoil
ACCOYS > ACCOY
ACCREDIT vb give official recognition to
ACCREDITS
> ACCREDIT
ACCRETE vb grow together
ACCRETED > ACCRETE
ACCRETES > ACCRETE
ACCRETING > ACCRETE
ACCRETION n gradual growth
ACCRETIVE
> ACCRETION
ACCREW vb accrue
ACCREWED > ACCREW
ACCREWING > ACCREW
ACCREWS > ACCREW
ACCROIDES n red alcohol-soluble resin
ACCRUABLE > ACCRUE
ACCRUAL n act of accruing
ACCRUALS > ACCRUAL
ACCRUE vb increase gradually
ACCRUED > ACCRUE
ACCRUES > ACCRUE
ACCRUING > ACCRUE
ACCUMBENT adj lying against
ACCURACY n representation of truth
ACCURATE adj exact, correct
ACCURSE vb curse
ACCURSED adj under a curse
ACCURSES > ACCURSE
ACCURSING > ACCURSE
ACCURST same as
> ACCURSED
ACCUSABLE > ACCUSE
ACCUSABLY > ACCUSE
ACCUSAL n accusation
ACCUSALS > ACCUSAL
ACCUSANT n person who accuses
ACCUSANTS
> ACCUSANT
ACCUSE vb charge with wrongdoing
ACCUSED n person accused of a crime
ACCUSER > ACCUSE
ACCUSERS > ACCUSE
ACCUSES > ACCUSE
ACCUSING > ACCUSE
ACCUSTOM vb make used to
ACCUSTOMS
> ACCUSTOM
ACE n playing card with one symbol on it ▷ adj excellent ▷ vb serve an ace in racquet sports
ACED > ACE
ACEDIA same as
> ACCIDIE
ACEDIAS > ACEDIA
ACELDAMA n place with ill feeling
ACELDAMAS
> ACELDAMA

ACELLULAR *adj* not made up of or containing cells
ACENTRIC *adj* without a centre ▷ *n* acentric chromosome or fragment
ACENTRICS > ACENTRIC
ACEPHALIC *adj* having no head or one that is reduced and indistinct, as certain insect larvae
ACEQUIA *n* irrigation ditch
ACEQUIAS > ACEQUIA
ACER *n* type of tree
ACERATE *same as* > ACERATED
ACERATED *adj* having sharp points
ACERB *adj* bitter
ACERBATE *vb* embitter or exasperate
ACERBATED > ACERBATE
ACERBATES > ACERBATE
ACERBER > ACERB
ACERBEST > ACERB
ACERBIC *adj* harsh or bitter
ACERBITY *n* bitter speech or temper
ACEROLA *n* cherry-like fruit
ACEROLAS > ACEROLA
ACEROSE *adj* shaped like a needle
ACEROUS *same as* > ACEROSE
ACERS > ACER
ACERVATE *adj* growing in heaps or clusters
ACERVULI > ACERVULUS
ACERVULUS *n* spore-producing part of plant
ACES > ACE
ACESCENCE > ACESCENT
ACESCENCY > ACESCENT
ACESCENT *adj* slightly sour or turning sour ▷ *n* something that is turning sour
ACESCENTS > ACESCENT
ACETA > ACETUM
ACETABULA *n* deep cuplike cavities on the side of the hipbones that receive the head of the thighbone
ACETAL *n* colourless liquid
ACETALS > ACETAL
ACETAMID *same as* > ACETAMIDE
ACETAMIDE *n* white or colourless soluble deliquescent crystalline compound
ACETAMIDS > ACETAMID
ACETATE *n* salt or ester of acetic acid
ACETATED *adj* combined with acetic acid

ACETATES > ACETATE
ACETIC *adj* of or involving vinegar
ACETIFIED > ACETIFY
ACETIFIER > ACETIFY
ACETIFIES > ACETIFY
ACETIFY *vb* become vinegar
ACETIN *n* type of acetate
ACETINS > ACETIN
ACETONE *n* colourless liquid used as a solvent
ACETONES > ACETONE
ACETONIC > ACETONE
ACETOSE *same as* > ACETOUS
ACETOUS *adj* containing acetic acid
ACETOXYL *n* medicine used to treat acne
ACETOXYLS > ACETOXYL
ACETUM *n* solution that has dilute acetic acid as solvent
ACETYL *n* type of monovalent radical
ACETYLATE *vb* introduce an acetyl group into (a chemical compound)
ACETYLENE *n* colourless flammable gas used in welding metals
ACETYLIC > ACETYL
ACETYLIDE *n* any of a class of carbides in which the carbon is present as a diatomic divalent ion
ACETYLS > ACETYL
ACH *interj* Scots expression of surprise
ACHAENIA > ACHAENIUM
ACHAENIUM *n* achene
ACHAGE *n* pain
ACHAGES > ACHAGE
ACHALASIA *n* failure of the cardiac sphincter of the oesophagus to relax, resulting in difficulty in swallowing
ACHAR *n* spicy pickle made from mango
ACHARNE *adj* furiously violent
ACHARS > ACHAR
ACHARYA *n* religious teacher and spiritual guide
ACHARYAS > ACHARYA
ACHATES *same as* > ACATES
ACHE *n* dull continuous pain ▷ *vb* be in or cause continuous dull pain
ACHED > ACHE
ACHENE *n* type of fruit
ACHENES > ACHENE
ACHENIA > ACHENIUM
ACHENIAL > ACHENE
ACHENIUM *n* achene
ACHENIUMS > ACHENIUM
ACHES > ACHE
ACHIER > ACHY
ACHIEST > ACHY
ACHIEVE *vb* gain by hard work or ability
ACHIEVED > ACHIEVE

ACHIEVER > ACHIEVE
ACHIEVERS > ACHIEVE
ACHIEVES > ACHIEVE
ACHIEVING > ACHIEVE
ACHILLEA *n* type of plant with white, yellow, or purple flowers, often grown in gardens
ACHILLEAS > ACHILLEA
ACHIMENES *n* tropical plant of the S America with showy red, blue, or white tubular flowers
ACHINESS > ACHY
ACHING > ACHE
ACHINGLY > ACHE
ACHINGS > ACHE
ACHIOTE *n* annatto
ACHIOTES > ACHIOTE
ACHIRAL *adj* of a tuber producing arrowroot
ACHKAN *n* man's coat in India
ACHKANS > ACHKAN
ACHOLIA *n* bile condition
ACHOLIAS > ACHOLIA
ACHOO *n* sound of a sneeze
ACHOOS > ACHOO
ACHROMAT *n* lens designed to bring light of two wavelengths to the same focal point
ACHROMATS > ACHROMAT
ACHROMIC *adj* colourless
ACHROMOUS *same as* > ACHROMIC
ACHY *adj* affected by a continuous dull pain
ACICLOVIR *same as* > ACYCLOVIR
ACICULA *n* needle-shaped part
ACICULAE > ACICULA
ACICULAR > ACICULA
ACICULAS > ACICULA
ACICULATE *adj* having aciculae
ACICULUM *n* bristle that supports the appendages of some polychaetes
ACICULUMS > ACICULUM
ACID *n* corrosive compound that combines with a base to form a salt ▷ *adj* containing acid
ACIDEMIA *n* abnormally high level of acid in blood
ACIDEMIAS > ACIDEMIA
ACIDER > ACID
ACIDEST > ACID
ACIDHEAD *n* person who uses LSD
ACIDHEADS > ACIDHEAD
ACIDIC *adj* containing acid
ACIDIER > ACIDY
ACIDIEST > ACIDY
ACIDIFIED > ACIDIFY
ACIDIFIER > ACIDIFY
ACIDIFIES > ACIDIFY
ACIDIFY *vb* convert into acid

ACIDITIES > ACIDITY
ACIDITY *n* quality of being acid
ACIDLY > ACID
ACIDNESS > ACID
ACIDOPHIL *adj* (of cells or cell contents) easily stained by acid dyes ▷ *n* acidophil organism
ACIDOSES > ACIDOSIS
ACIDOSIS *n* abnormal increase in the acidity of the blood and bodily fluids
ACIDOTIC > ACIDOSIS
ACIDS > ACID
ACIDULATE *vb* make slightly acid or sour
ACIDULENT *same as* > ACIDULOUS
ACIDULOUS *adj* rather sour
ACIDURIA *n* abnormally high level of acid in urine
ACIDURIAS > ACIDURIA
ACIDY *adj* resembling or containing acid
ACIERAGE *n* iron-plating of metal
ACIERAGES > ACIERAGE
ACIERATE *vb* change (iron) into steel
ACIERATED > ACIERATE
ACIERATES > ACIERATE
ACIFORM *adj* shaped like a needle
ACINAR *adj* of small sacs
ACING > ACE
ACINI > ACINUS
ACINIC > ACINUS
ACINIFORM *adj* shaped like a bunch of grapes
ACINOSE > ACINUS
ACINOUS > ACINUS
ACINUS *n* part of a gland
ACKEE *n* tropical tree
ACKEES > ACKEE
ACKER *same as* > ACCA
ACKERS > ACKER
ACKNEW > ACKNOW
ACKNOW *vb* recognize
ACKNOWING > ACKNOW
ACKNOWN > ACKNOW
ACKNOWNE *adj* aware
ACKNOWS > ACKNOW
ACLINIC *adj* unbending
ACMATIC *adj* highest or ultimate
ACME *n* highest point of achievement or excellence
ACMES > ACME
ACMIC *same as* > ACMATIC
ACMITE *n* chemical with pyramid-shaped crystals
ACMITES > ACMITE
ACNE *n* pimply skin disease
ACNED *adj* marked by acne
ACNES > ACNE
ACNODAL > ACNODE
ACNODE *n* isolated point on the graph of a curve
ACNODES > ACNODE
ACOCK *adv* cocked

ACOELOUS adj not having a stomach

ACOEMETI n order of monks

ACOLD adj feeling cold

ACOLUTHIC adj of an afterimage

ACOLYTE n follower or attendant

ACOLYTES > ACOLYTE

ACOLYTH n acolyte

ACOLYTHS > ACOLYTH

ACONITE n poisonous plant with hoodlike flowers

ACONITES > ACONITE

ACONITIC > ACONITE

ACONITINE n poison made from aconite

ACONITUM same as > ACONITE

ACONITUMS > ACONITUM

ACORN n nut of the oak tree

ACORNED adj covered with acorns

ACORNS > ACORN

ACOSMISM n belief that no world exists outside the mind

ACOSMISMS > ACOSMISM

ACOSMIST > ACOSMISM

ACOSMISTS > ACOSMISM

ACOUCHI n South American rodent with a white-tipped tail

ACOUCHIES > ACOUCHY

ACOUCHIS > ACOUCHI

ACOUCHY same as > ACOUCHI

ACOUSTIC adj of sound and hearing

ACOUSTICS n science of sounds

ACQUAINT vb make familiar, inform

ACQUAINTS > ACQUAINT

ACQUEST n something acquired

ACQUESTS > ACQUEST

ACQUIESCE vb agree to what someone wants

ACQUIGHT vb acquit

ACQUIGHTS > ACQUIGHT

ACQUIRAL > ACQUIRE

ACQUIRALS > ACQUIRE

ACQUIRE vb gain, get

ACQUIRED > ACQUIRE

ACQUIREE n one who acquires

ACQUIREES > ACQUIREE

ACQUIRER > ACQUIRE

ACQUIRERS > ACQUIRE

ACQUIRES > ACQUIRE

ACQUIRING > ACQUIRE

ACQUIS n as in acquis communautaire European Union laws

ACQUIST n acquisition

ACQUISTS > ACQUIST

ACQUIT vb pronounce (someone) innocent

ACQUITE vb acquit

ACQUITES > ACQUITE

ACQUITING > ACQUITE

ACQUITS > ACQUIT

ACQUITTAL n deliverance and release of a person appearing before a court on a charge of crime, as by a finding of not guilty

ACQUITTED > ACQUIT

ACQUITTER > ACQUIT

ACRASIA n lack of willpower

ACRASIAS > ACRASIA

ACRASIN n chemical

ACRASINS > ACRASIN

ACRATIC > ACRASIA

ACRAWL adv crawling

ACRE n measure of land, 4840 square yards (4046.86 square metres)

ACREAGE n land area in acres ▷ adj of or relating to a large allotment of land, esp in a rural area

ACREAGES > ACREAGE

ACRED adj having acres of land

ACRES > ACRE

ACRID adj pungent, bitter

ACRIDER > ACRID

ACRIDEST > ACRID

ACRIDIN n acridine

ACRIDINE n colourless crystalline solid

ACRIDINES > ACRIDINE

ACRIDINS > ACRIDIN

ACRIDITY > ACRID

ACRIDLY > ACRID

ACRIDNESS > ACRID

ACRIMONY n bitterness and resentment felt about something

ACRITARCH n type of fossil

ACRITICAL adj not critical

ACRO n event where acrobatic skiing moves are performed to music

ACROBAT n person skilled in gymnastic feats requiring agility and balance

ACROBATIC > ACROBAT

ACROBATS > ACROBAT

ACRODONT adj (of reptile teeth) fused at the base to the jawbones ▷ n acrodont reptile

ACRODONTS > ACRODONT

ACRODROME adj (of the veins of a leaf) running parallel to the edges of the leaf and fusing at the tip

ACROGEN n flowerless plant

ACROGENIC > ACROGEN

ACROGENS > ACROGEN

ACROLECT n most correct form of language

ACROLECTS > ACROLECT

ACROLEIN n colourless or yellowish flammable poisonous pungent liquid

ACROLEINS > ACROLEIN

ACROLITH n wooden sculpture with the head, hands, and feet in stone

ACROLITHS > ACROLITH

ACROMIA > ACROMION

ACROMIAL > ACROMION

ACROMION n outermost edge of the spine of the shoulder blade

ACRONIC adj occurring at sunset

ACRONICAL adj occurring at sunset

ACRONYCAL same as > ACRONICAL

ACRONYM n word formed from the initial letters of other words, such as NASA

ACRONYMIC > ACRONYM

ACRONYMS > ACRONYM

ACROPETAL adj (of leaves and flowers) produced in order from the base upwards so that the youngest are at the apex

ACROPHOBE n person afraid of heights

ACROPHONY n use of symbols to represent sounds

ACROPOLIS n citadel of an ancient Greek city

ACROS > ACRO

ACROSOMAL > ACROSOME

ACROSOME n structure in reproductive cell

ACROSOMES > ACROSOME

ACROSPIRE n first shoot developing from the plumule of a germinating grain seed

ACROSS adv from side to side (of)

ACROSTIC n lines of writing in which the first or last letters of each line spell a word or saying

ACROSTICS > ACROSTIC

ACROTER n plinth

ACROTERIA n acroters

ACROTERS > ACROTER

ACROTIC adj of a surface

ACROTISM n absence of pulse

ACROTISMS > ACROTISM

ACRYLATE n chemical compound in plastics and resins

ACRYLATES > ACRYLATE

ACRYLIC adj (synthetic fibre, paint, etc) made from acrylic acid ▷ n synthetic fibre used for clothes and blankets

ACRYLICS > ACRYLIC

ACRYLYL n type of monovalent group

ACRYLYLS > ACRYLYL

ACT n thing done ▷ vb do something

ACTA pl n minutes of meeting

ACTABLE > ACT

ACTANT n noun phrase functioning as the agent of a verb

ACTANTS > ACTANT

ACTED > ACT

ACTIN n protein

ACTINAL adj having tentacles

ACTINALLY > ACTINAL

ACTING n art of an actor ▷ adj temporarily performing the duties of an actor

ACTINGS > ACTING

ACTINIA n type of sea anemone

ACTINIAE > ACTINIA

ACTINIAN n sea anemone

ACTINIANS > ACTINIAN

ACTINIAS > ACTINIA

ACTINIC adj (of radiation) producing a photochemical effect

ACTINIDE n member of the actinide series

ACTINIDES > ACTINIDE

ACTINISM > ACTINIC

ACTINISMS > ACTINIC

ACTINIUM n radioactive chemical element

ACTINIUMS > ACTINIUM

ACTINOID adj having a radiate form, as a sea anemone or starfish ▷ n member of the actinide series

ACTINOIDS > ACTINOID

ACTINON same as > ACTINIDE

ACTINONS > ACTINON

ACTINOPOD n type of single-celled invertebrate

ACTINS > ACTIN

ACTION n process of doing something ▷ vb put into effect

ACTIONED > ACTION

ACTIONER n film with a fast-moving plot, usually containing scenes of violence

ACTIONERS > ACTIONER

ACTIONING > ACTION

ACTIONIST n activist

ACTIONS > ACTION

ACTIVATE vb make active

ACTIVATED > ACTIVATE

ACTIVATES > ACTIVATE

ACTIVATOR > ACTIVATE

ACTIVE adj moving, working ▷ n active form of a verb

ACTIVELY > ACTIVE

ACTIVES > ACTIVE

ACTIVISE same as > ACTIVIZE**

ACTIVISED
> ACTIVISE
ACTIVISES
> ACTIVISE
ACTIVISM *n* taking direct or militant action to achieve a political or social end
ACTIVISMS
> ACTIVISM
ACTIVIST > ACTIVISM
ACTIVISTS
> ACTIVISM
ACTIVITY *n* state of being active
ACTIVIZE *vb* make active
ACTIVIZED
> ACTIVIZE
ACTIVIZES
> ACTIVIZE
ACTON *n* jacket
ACTONS > ACTON
ACTOR *n* person who acts in a play, film, etc
ACTORISH > ACTOR
ACTORLIER > ACTORLY
ACTORLY *adj* characteristic of an actor
ACTORS > ACTOR
ACTRESS *n* woman who acts in a play, film, broadcast, etc
ACTRESSES > ACTRESS
ACTRESSY *adj* exaggerated and affected in manner
ACTS > ACT
ACTUAL *adj* existing in reality
ACTUALISE *same as* > ACTUALIZE
ACTUALIST *n* person dealing in hard fact
ACTUALITE *n* humorous word for truth
ACTUALITY *n* reality
ACTUALIZE *vb* make actual or real
ACTUALLY *adv* really, indeed
ACTUALS *pl n* commercial commodities that can be bought and used
ACTUARIAL > ACTUARY
ACTUARIES > ACTUARY
ACTUARY *n* statistician who calculates insurance risks
ACTUATE *vb* start up (a device)
ACTUATED > ACTUATE
ACTUATES > ACTUATE
ACTUATING > ACTUATE
ACTUATION > ACTUATE
ACTUATOR > ACTUATE
ACTUATORS > ACTUATE
ACTURE *n* action
ACTURES > ACTURE
ACUATE *adj* sharply pointed ▷ *vb* sharpen
ACUATED > ACUATE
ACUATES > ACUATE
ACUATING > ACUATE
ACUITIES > ACUITY
ACUITY *n* keenness of vision or thought
ACULEATE *adj* cutting ▷ *n* insect, such as a bee, with a sting

ACULEATED *same as* > ACULEATE
ACULEATES > ACULEATE
ACULEI > ACULEUS
ACULEUS *n* prickle or spine, such as the thorn of a rose
ACUMEN *n* ability to make good judgments
ACUMENS > ACUMEN
ACUMINATE *adj* narrowing to a sharp point, as some types of leaf ▷ *vb* make pointed or sharp
ACUMINOUS > ACUMEN
ACUPOINT *n* points on the body stimulated with acupuncture or acupressure
ACUPOINTS
> ACUPOINT
ACUSHLA *n* Irish endearment
ACUSHLAS > ACUSHLA
ACUTANCE *n* physical rather than subjective measure of the sharpness of a photographic image
ACUTANCES
> ACUTANCE
ACUTE *adj* severe ▷ *n* accent over a letter to indicate the quality or length of its sound, as over e in café
ACUTELY > ACUTE
ACUTENESS > ACUTE
ACUTER > ACUTE
ACUTES > ACUTE
ACUTEST > ACUTE
ACYCLIC *adj* not cyclic
ACYCLOVIR *n* antiviral drug
ACYL *n* member of the monovalent group of atoms RCO-
ACYLATE *vb* add acyl group to
ACYLATED > ACYLATE
ACYLATES > ACYLATE
ACYLATING > ACYLATE
ACYLATION *n* introduction into a chemical compound of an acyl group
ACYLOIN *n* organic chemical compound
ACYLOINS > ACYLOIN
ACYLS > ACYL
AD *n* advertisement
ADAGE *n* wise saying, proverb
ADAGES > ADAGE
ADAGIAL > ADAGE
ADAGIO *adv* (to be played) slowly and gracefully ▷ *n* movement or piece to be performed slowly
ADAGIOS > ADAGIO
ADAMANCE *n* being adamant
ADAMANCES
> ADAMANCE
ADAMANCY *n* being adamant

ADAMANT *adj* unshakable in determination or purpose ▷ *n* any extremely hard or apparently unbreakable substance
ADAMANTLY > ADAMANT
ADAMANTS > ADAMANT
ADAMSITE *n* yellow poisonous crystalline solid that readily sublimes
ADAMSITES
> ADAMSITE
ADAPT *vb* alter for new use or new conditions
ADAPTABLE > ADAPT
ADAPTED > ADAPT
ADAPTER *same as* > ADAPTOR
ADAPTERS > ADAPTER
ADAPTING > ADAPT
ADAPTION *n* adaptation
ADAPTIONS
> ADAPTION
ADAPTIVE > ADAPT
ADAPTOGEN *n* any of various natural substances used in herbal medicine to normalize and regulate the systems of the body
ADAPTOR *n* device for connecting several electrical appliances to a single socket
ADAPTORS > ADAPTOR
ADAPTS > ADAPT
ADAW *vb* subdue
ADAWED > ADAW
ADAWING > ADAW
ADAWS > ADAW
ADAXIAL *adj* facing the axis
ADAYS *adv* daily
ADBOT *n* spyware that collects information about a person to display targeted adverts
ADBOTS > ADBOT
ADD *vb* combine (numbers or quantities)
ADDABLE > ADD
ADDAX *n* antelope
ADDAXES > ADDAX
ADDEBTED *adj* indebted
ADDED > ADD
ADDEDLY > ADD
ADDEEM *vb* adjudge
ADDEEMED > ADDEEM
ADDEEMING > ADDEEM
ADDEEMS > ADDEEM
ADDEND *n* any of a set of numbers that is to be added
ADDENDA > ADDENDUM
ADDENDS > ADDEND
ADDENDUM *n* addition
ADDENDUMS
> ADDENDUM
ADDER *n* small poisonous snake
ADDERBEAD *n* type of prehistoric ornamental bead
ADDERS > ADDER
ADDERWORT *n* plant of the dock family
ADDIBLE *adj* addable

ADDICT *n* person who is unable to stop doing or taking something ▷ *vb* cause (someone or oneself) to become dependent (on something)
ADDICTED > ADDICT
ADDICTING > ADDICT
ADDICTION *n* condition of being abnormally dependent on some habit
ADDICTIVE *adj* causing addiction
ADDICTS > ADDICT
ADDIES > ADDY
ADDING *n* act or instance of addition ▷ *adj* of, for, or relating to addition
ADDINGS > ADDING
ADDIO *interj* farewell ▷ *n* cry of addio
ADDIOS > ADDIO
ADDITION *n* adding
ADDITIONS
> ADDITION
ADDITIVE *n* something added, esp to a foodstuff, to improve it or prevent deterioration ▷ *adj* characterized or produced by addition
ADDITIVES
> ADDITIVE
ADDITORY *adj* adding to something
ADDLE *vb* become muddled ▷ *adj* indicating a muddled state
ADDLED > ADDLE
ADDLEMENT > ADDLE
ADDLES > ADDLE
ADDLING > ADDLE
ADDOOM *vb* adjudge
ADDOOMED > ADDOOM
ADDOOMING > ADDOOM
ADDOOMS > ADDOOM
ADDORSED *adj* back to back
ADDRESS *n* place where a person lives ▷ *vb* mark the destination, as on an envelope
ADDRESSED > ADDRESS
ADDRESSEE *n* person addressed
ADDRESSER > ADDRESS
ADDRESSES > ADDRESS
ADDRESSOR > ADDRESS
ADDREST > ADDRESS
ADDS > ADD
ADDUCE *vb* mention something as evidence or proof
ADDUCED > ADDUCE
ADDUCENT > ADDUCE
ADDUCER > ADDUCE
ADDUCERS > ADDUCE
ADDUCES > ADDUCE
ADDUCIBLE > ADDUCE
ADDUCING > ADDUCE
ADDUCT *vb* draw towards medial axis ▷ *n* compound
ADDUCTED > ADDUCT
ADDUCTING > ADDUCT
ADDUCTION > ADDUCT
ADDUCTIVE > ADDUCE
ADDUCTOR *n* muscle that adducts

a

ADDUCTORS
> ADDUCTOR
ADDUCTS > ADDUCT
ADDY n email address
ADEEM vb cancel
ADEEMED > ADEEM
ADEEMING > ADEEM
ADEEMS > ADEEM
ADELGID n type of small sap-feeding insect
ADELGIDS > ADELGID
ADEMPTION n failure of a specific legacy, as by a testator disposing of the subject matter in their lifetime
ADENINE n chemical
ADENINES > ADENINE
ADENITIS n inflammation of a gland or lymph node
ADENOID adj of or resembling a gland
ADENOIDAL adj having a nasal voice caused by swollen adenoids
ADENOIDS pl n tissue at the back of the throat
ADENOMA n tumour occurring in glandular tissue
ADENOMAS > ADENOMA
ADENOMATA > ADENOMA
ADENOSES > ADENOSIS
ADENOSINE n nucleoside formed by the condensation of adenine and ribose
ADENOSIS n disease of glands
ADENYL n enzyme
ADENYLATE n type of enzyme
ADENYLIC adj as in adenylic acid nucleotide consisting of adenine, ribose or deoxyribose, and a phosphate group
ADENYLS > ADENYL
ADEPT n very skilful person ▷ adj proficient in something requiring skill
ADEPTER > ADEPT
ADEPTEST > ADEPT
ADEPTLY > ADEPT
ADEPTNESS > ADEPT
ADEPTS > ADEPT
ADEQUACY > ADEQUATE
ADEQUATE adj sufficient, enough
ADERMIN n vitamin
ADERMINS > ADERMIN
ADESPOTA n anonymous writings
ADESSIVE n grammatical case denoting place
ADESSIVES
> ADESSIVE
ADHAN n call to prayer
ADHANS > ADHAN
ADHARMA n wickedness
ADHARMAS > ADHARMA
ADHERABLE > ADHERE
ADHERE vb stick (to)
ADHERED > ADHERE
ADHERENCE > ADHERE

ADHEREND n something attached by adhesive
ADHERENDS
> ADHEREND
ADHERENT n devotee, follower ▷ adj sticking or attached
ADHERENTS
> ADHERENT
ADHERER > ADHERE
ADHERERS > ADHERE
ADHERES > ADHERE
ADHERING > ADHERE
ADHESION n sticking (to)
ADHESIONS
> ADHESION
ADHESIVE n substance used to stick things together ▷ adj able to stick to things
ADHESIVES
> ADHESIVE
ADHIBIT vb administer or apply
ADHIBITED > ADHIBIT
ADHIBITS > ADHIBIT
ADHOCRACY n management that responds to urgent problems rather than planning to avoid them
ADIABATIC adj (of a thermodynamic process) taking place without loss or gain of heat ▷ n curve or surface on a graph representing the changes in two or more characteristics (such as pressure and volume) of a system undergoing an adiabatic process
ADIAPHORA n matters of indifference
ADIEU n goodbye
ADIEUS > ADIEU
ADIEUX > ADIEU
ADIOS sentence substitute Spanish for goodbye ▷ n goodbye
ADIOSES > ADIOS
ADIPIC adj as in adipic acid crystalline solid used in the preparation of nylon
ADIPOCERE n waxlike substance formed during decomposition
ADIPOCYTE n fat cell that accumulates and stores fats
ADIPOSE adj of or containing fat ▷ n animal fat
ADIPOSES > ADIPOSIS
ADIPOSIS n obesity
ADIPOSITY > ADIPOSE
ADIPOUS adj made of fat
ADIPSIA n complete lack of thirst
ADIPSIAS > ADIPSIA
ADIT n shaft into a mine, for access or drainage
ADITS > ADIT
ADJACENCE
> ADJACENT
ADJACENCY
> ADJACENT
ADJACENT adj near or next (to) ▷ n side lying

between a specified angle and a right angle in a right-angled triangle
ADJACENTS
> ADJACENT
ADJECTIVE n word that adds information about a noun or pronoun ▷ adj additional or dependent
ADJIGO n SW Australian yam plant with edible tubers
ADJIGOS > ADJIGO
ADJOIN vb be next to
ADJOINED > ADJOIN
ADJOINING adj being in contact
ADJOINS > ADJOIN
ADJOINT n type of mathematical matrix
ADJOINTS > ADJOINT
ADJOURN vb close (a court) at the end of a session
ADJOURNED > ADJOURN
ADJOURNS > ADJOURN
ADJUDGE vb declare (to be)
ADJUDGED > ADJUDGE
ADJUDGES > ADJUDGE
ADJUDGING > ADJUDGE
ADJUNCT n something incidental added to something else
ADJUNCTLY > ADJUNCT
ADJUNCTS > ADJUNCT
ADJURE vb command (to do)
ADJURED > ADJURE
ADJURER > ADJURE
ADJURERS > ADJURE
ADJURES > ADJURE
ADJURING > ADJURE
ADJUROR > ADJURE
ADJURORS > ADJURE
ADJUST vb adapt to new conditions
ADJUSTED > ADJUST
ADJUSTER > ADJUST
ADJUSTERS > ADJUST
ADJUSTING > ADJUST
ADJUSTIVE > ADJUST
ADJUSTOR > ADJUST
ADJUSTORS > ADJUST
ADJUSTS > ADJUST
ADJUTAGE n nozzle
ADJUTAGES
> ADJUTAGE
ADJUTANCY
> ADJUTANT
ADJUTANT n army officer in charge of routine administration
ADJUTANTS
> ADJUTANT
ADJUVANCY
> ADJUVANT
ADJUVANT adj aiding or assisting ▷ n something that aids or assists
ADJUVANTS
> ADJUVANT
ADLAND n advertising industry and the people who work in it
ADLANDS > ADLAND
ADMAN n man who works in advertising

ADMASS n mass advertising
ADMASSES > ADMASS
ADMEASURE vb measure out (land, etc) as a share
ADMEN > ADMAN
ADMIN n administration
ADMINICLE n something contributing to prove a point without itself being complete proof
ADMINS > ADMIN
ADMIRABLE adj deserving or inspiring admiration
ADMIRABLY
> ADMIRABLE
ADMIRAL n highest naval rank
ADMIRALS > ADMIRAL
ADMIRALTY n office or jurisdiction of an admiral
ADMIRANCE n admiration
ADMIRE vb regard with esteem and approval
ADMIRED > ADMIRE
ADMIRER > ADMIRE
ADMIRERS > ADMIRE
ADMIRES > ADMIRE
ADMIRING > ADMIRE
ADMISSION n permission to enter
ADMISSIVE
> ADMISSION
ADMIT vb confess, acknowledge
ADMITS > ADMIT
ADMITTED > ADMIT
ADMITTEE n one who admits
ADMITTEES
> ADMITTEE
ADMITTER > ADMIT
ADMITTERS > ADMIT
ADMITTING > ADMIT
ADMIX vb mix or blend
ADMIXED > ADMIX
ADMIXES > ADMIX
ADMIXING > ADMIX
ADMIXT > ADMIX
ADMIXTURE n mixture
ADMONISH vb reprove sternly
ADMONITOR
> ADMONISH
ADNASCENT adj growing with something else
ADNATE adj growing closely attached to an adjacent part or organ
ADNATION > ADNATE
ADNATIONS > ADNATE
ADNEXA pl n organs adjoining the uterus
ADNEXAL > ADNEXA
ADNOMINAL n word modifying a noun ▷ adj of or relating to an adnoun
ADNOUN n adjective used as a noun
ADNOUNS > ADNOUN
ADO n fuss, trouble
ADOBE n sun-dried brick
ADOBELIKE > ADOBE
ADOBES > ADOBE
ADOBO n Philippine dish
ADOBOS > ADOBO

ADONIS *n* beautiful young man
ADONISE *vb* adorn
ADONISED > ADONISE
ADONISES > ADONISE
ADONISING > ADONISE
ADONIZE *vb* adorn
ADONIZED > ADONIZE
ADONIZES > ADONIZE
ADONIZING > ADONIZE
ADOORS *adv* at the door
ADOPT *vb* take (someone else's child) as one's own
ADOPTABLE > ADOPT
ADOPTED *adj* having been adopted
ADOPTEE *n* one who has been adopted
ADOPTEES > ADOPTEE
ADOPTER *n* person who adopts
ADOPTERS > ADOPTER
ADOPTING > ADOPT
ADOPTION > ADOPT
ADOPTIONS > ADOPT
ADOPTIOUS *adj* adopted
ADOPTIVE *adj* related by adoption
ADOPTS > ADOPT
ADORABLE *adj* very attractive
ADORABLY > ADORABLE
ADORATION *n* deep love or esteem
ADORE *vb* love intensely
ADORED > ADORE
ADORER > ADORE
ADORERS > ADORE
ADORES > ADORE
ADORING *adj* displaying intense love
ADORINGLY > ADORING
ADORKABLE *adj* charmingly unfashionable
ADORN *vb* decorate, embellish
ADORNED > ADORN
ADORNER > ADORN
ADORNERS > ADORN
ADORNING > ADORN
ADORNMENT > ADORN
ADORNS > ADORN
ADOS > ADO
ADOWN *adv* down
ADOZE *adv* asleep
ADPRESS *vb* press together
ADPRESSED > ADPRESS
ADPRESSES > ADPRESS
ADRAD *adj* afraid
ADRATE *n* price or tariff that businesses pay to advertise
ADRATES > ADRATE
ADREAD *vb* dread
ADREADED > ADREAD
ADREADING > ADREAD
ADREADS > ADREAD
ADRED *adj* filled with dread
ADRENAL *adj* near the kidneys ▷ *n* adrenal gland
ADRENALIN *n* hormone secreted by the adrenal glands in response to stress
ADRENALLY > ADRENAL

ADRENALS > ADRENAL
ADRIFT *adv* drifting
ADROIT *adj* quick and skilful
ADROITER > ADROIT
ADROITEST > ADROIT
ADROITLY > ADROIT
ADRY *adj* dry
ADS > AD
ADSCRIPT *n* serf
ADSCRIPTS > ADSCRIPT
ADSORB *vb* condense to form a thin film
ADSORBATE *n* substance that has been or is to be adsorbed on a surface
ADSORBED > ADSORB
ADSORBENT *adj* capable of adsorption ▷ *n* material, such as activated charcoal, on which adsorption can occur
ADSORBER > ADSORB
ADSORBERS > ADSORB
ADSORBING > ADSORB
ADSORBS > ADSORB
ADSPEAK *n* kind of language or jargon used in advertising or in advertisements
ADSPEAKS > ADSPEAK
ADSUKI *same as >* ADZUKI
ADSUKIS > ADSUKI
ADSUM *sentence substitute* I am present
ADUKI *same as >* ADZUKI
ADUKIS > ADUKI
ADULARIA *n* white or colourless glassy variety of orthoclase
ADULARIAS > ADULARIA
ADULATE *vb* flatter or praise obsequiously
ADULATED > ADULATE
ADULATES > ADULATE
ADULATING > ADULATE
ADULATION *n* uncritical admiration
ADULATOR > ADULATE
ADULATORS > ADULATE
ADULATORY *adj* expressing praise, esp obsequiously
ADULT *adj* fully grown, mature ▷ *n* adult person or animal
ADULTERER *n* person who has committed adultery
ADULTERY *n* sexual unfaithfulness of a spouse
ADULTHOOD > ADULT
ADULTLIKE > ADULT
ADULTLY > ADULT
ADULTNESS > ADULT
ADULTRESS *n* woman who has committed adultery
ADULTS > ADULT
ADUMBRAL *adj* shadowy
ADUMBRATE *vb* outline
ADUNC *adj* hooked
ADUNCATE *adj* hooked
ADUNCATED *adj* hooked
ADUNCITY *n* quality of being hooked

ADUNCOUS *adj* hooked
ADUST *vb* dry up or darken by heat
ADUSTED > ADUST
ADUSTING > ADUST
ADUSTS > ADUST
ADVANCE *vb* go or bring forward ▷ *n* forward movement ▷ *adj* done or happening before an event
ADVANCED *adj* at a late stage in development
ADVANCER > ADVANCE
ADVANCERS > ADVANCE
ADVANCES > ADVANCE
ADVANCING > ADVANCE
ADVANTAGE *n* more favourable position or state
ADVECT *vb* move horizontally in air
ADVECTED > ADVECT
ADVECTING > ADVECT
ADVECTION *n* transferring of heat in a horizontal stream of gas
ADVECTIVE > ADVECTION
ADVECTS > ADVECT
ADVENE *vb* add as extra
ADVENED > ADVENE
ADVENES > ADVENE
ADVENING > ADVENE
ADVENT *n* arrival
ADVENTIVE *adj* (of a species) introduced to a new area and not yet established there ▷ *n* such a plant or animal
ADVENTS > ADVENT
ADVENTURE *n* exciting and risky undertaking or exploit ▷ *vb* take a risk or put at risk
ADVERB *n* word that adds information about a verb, adjective, or other adverb
ADVERBIAL *n* word or group of words with the grammatical role of an adverb ▷ *adj* of or relating to an adverb
ADVERBS > ADVERB
ADVERSARY *n* opponent or enemy
ADVERSE *adj* unfavourable
ADVERSELY > ADVERSE
ADVERSER > ADVERSE
ADVERSEST > ADVERSE
ADVERSITY *n* very difficult or hard circumstances
ADVERT *n* advertisement ▷ *vb* draw attention (to)
ADVERTED > ADVERT
ADVERTENT *adj* heedful
ADVERTING > ADVERT
ADVERTISE *vb* present or praise (goods or services) to the public in order to encourage sales
ADVERTIZE *same as >* ADVERTISE
ADVERTS > ADVERT
ADVEW *vb* look at
ADVEWED > ADVEW
ADVEWING > ADVEW

ADVEWS > ADVEW
ADVICE *n* recommendation as to what to do
ADVICEFUL > ADVICE
ADVICES > ADVICE
ADVISABLE *adj* prudent, sensible
ADVISABLY > ADVISABLE
ADVISE *vb* offer advice to
ADVISED *adj* considered, thought-out
ADVISEDLY > ADVISED
ADVISEE *n* person receiving advice
ADVISEES > ADVISEE
ADVISER *n* person who offers advice, eg on careers to students or school pupils
ADVISERS > ADVISER
ADVISES > ADVISE
ADVISING > ADVISE
ADVISINGS > ADVISE
ADVISOR *same as >* ADVISER
ADVISORS > ADVISOR
ADVISORY *adj* giving advice ▷ *n* statement giving advice or a warning
ADVOCAAT *n* liqueur with a raw egg base
ADVOCAATS > ADVOCAAT
ADVOCACY *n* active support of a cause or course of action
ADVOCATE *vb* propose or recommend ▷ *n* person who publicly supports a cause
ADVOCATED > ADVOCATE
ADVOCATES > ADVOCATE
ADVOCATOR *n* person who advocates
ADVOUTRER *n* adulterer
ADVOUTRY *n* adultery
ADVOWSON *n* right of presentation to a vacant benefice
ADVOWSONS > ADVOWSON
ADWARD *vb* award
ADWARDED > ADWARD
ADWARDING > ADWARD
ADWARDS > ADWARD
ADWARE *n* computer software
ADWARES > ADWARE
ADWOMAN *n* woman working in advertising
ADWOMEN > ADWOMAN
ADYNAMIA *n* loss of vital power or strength, esp as the result of illness
ADYNAMIAS > ADYNAMIA
ADYNAMIC > ADYNAMIA
ADYTA > ADYTUM
ADYTUM *n* sacred place in ancient temples
ADZ *same as >* ADZE
ADZE *n* woodworking tool ▷ *vb* use an adze
ADZED > ADZE

a

ADZELIKE adj like an adze

ADZES > ADZE

ADZING > ADZE

ADZUKI n type of plant

ADZUKIS > ADZUKI

AE determiner one

AECIA > AECIUM

AECIAL > AECIUM

AECIDIA > AECIDIUM

AECIDIAL > AECIDIUM

AECIDIUM same as > AECIUM

AECIUM n area of some fungi

AEDES n type of mosquito which transmits yellow fever and dengue

AEDICULE n door or a window framed by columns and a pediment

AEDICULES > AEDICULE

AEDILE n magistrate of ancient Rome

AEDILES > AEDILE

AEDINE adj of a species of mosquito

AEFALD adj single

AEFAULD adj single

AEGIRINE n green mineral

AEGIRINES > AEGIRINE

AEGIRITE n green mineral

AEGIRITES > AEGIRITE

AEGIS n sponsorship, protection

AEGISES > AEGIS

AEGLOGUE n eclogue

AEGLOGUES > AEGLOGUE

AEGROTAT n certificate allowing a candidate to pass an examination missed through illness

AEGROTATS > AEGROTAT

AEMULE vb emulate

AEMULED > AEMULE

AEMULES > AEMULE

AEMULING > AEMULE

AENEOUS adj brass-coloured or greenish-gold

AENEUS n aquarium fish

AENEUSES > AENEUS

AEOLIAN adj of or relating to the wind

AEOLIPILE n device illustrating the reactive forces of a gas jet: usually a spherical vessel mounted so as to rotate and equipped with angled exit pipes from which steam within it escapes

AEOLIPYLE same as > AEOLIPILE

AEON n immeasurably long period of time

AEONIAN adj everlasting

AEONIC > AEON

AEONS > AEON

AEPYORNIS n type of large extinct flightless bird

whose remains have been found in Madagascar

AEQUORIN n type of protein

AEQUORINS > AEQUORIN

AERADIO n radio system for pilots

AERADIOS > AERADIO

AERATE vb put gas into (a liquid), as when making a fizzy drink

AERATED > AERATE

AERATES > AERATE

AERATING > AERATE

AERATION > AERATE

AERATIONS > AERATE

AERATOR > AERATE

AERATORS > AERATE

AERIAL adj in, from, or operating in the air ▷ n metal pole, wire, etc, for receiving or transmitting radio or TV signals

AERIALIST n trapeze artist or tightrope walker

AERIALITY > AERIAL

AERIALLY > AERIAL

AERIALS > AERIAL

AERIE variant spelling (esp US) of > EYRIE

AERIED adj in a very high place

AERIER > AERY

AERIES > AERIE

AERIEST > AERY

AERIFIED > AERIFY

AERIFIES > AERIFY

AERIFORM adj having the form of air

AERIFY vb change or cause to change into a gas

AERIFYING > AERIFY

AERILY > AERY

AERO n aerodynamic vehicle or component

AEROBAT n person who does stunt flying

AEROBATIC adj pertaining to stunt flying

AEROBATS > AEROBAT

AEROBE n organism that requires oxygen to survive

AEROBES > AEROBE

AEROBIA > AEROBIUM

AEROBIC adj designed for or relating to aerobics

AEROBICS n exercises designed to increase the amount of oxygen in the blood

AEROBIONT n organism needing oxygen to live

AEROBIUM same as > AEROBE

AEROBOMB n bomb dropped from aircraft

AEROBOMBS > AEROBOMB

AEROBOT n unmanned aircraft used esp in space exploration

AEROBOTS > AEROBOT

AEROBRAKE vb use airbrakes to slow aircraft

AEROBUS n monorail suspended by an overhead cable

AEROBUSES > AEROBUS

AERODART n metal arrow dropped from an aircraft as a weapon

AERODARTS > AERODART

AERODROME n small airport

AERODUCT n air duct

AERODUCTS > AERODUCT

AERODYNE n aircraft that derives its lift from aerodynamic forces

AERODYNES > AERODYNE

AEROFOIL n part of an aircraft, such as the wing, designed to give lift

AEROFOILS > AEROFOIL

AEROGEL n colloid

AEROGELS > AEROGEL

AEROGRAM n airmail letter on a single sheet of paper that seals to form an envelope

AEROGRAMS > AEROGRAM

AEROGRAPH n airborne instrument recording meteorological conditions

AEROLITE n stony meteorite consisting of silicate minerals

AEROLITES > AEROLITE

AEROLITH n meteorite

AEROLITHS > AEROLITH

AEROLITIC > AEROLITE

AEROLOGIC > AEROLOGY

AEROLOGY n study of the atmosphere, particularly its upper layers

AEROMANCY n using weather observation to foretell the future

AEROMETER n instrument for determining the mass or density of a gas, esp air

AEROMETRY n branch of physics concerned with the mechanical properties of gases, esp air

AEROMOTOR n aircraft engine

AERONAUT n person who flies in a lighter-than-air craft, esp the pilot or navigator

AERONAUTS > AERONAUT

AERONOMER n scientist studying atmosphere

AERONOMIC > AERONOMY

AERONOMY n science of the earth's upper atmosphere

AEROPAUSE n region of the upper atmosphere above which aircraft cannot fly

AEROPHAGY n spasmodic swallowing of air

AEROPHOBE n person with aerophobia

AEROPHONE n wind instrument

AEROPHORE n device for playing a wind instrument

AEROPHYTE another name for > EPIPHYTE

AEROPLANE n powered flying vehicle with fixed wings

AEROPULSE n type of jet engine

AEROS > AERO

AEROSAT n communications satellite

AEROSATS > AEROSAT

AEROSCOPE n device for observing the atmosphere

AEROSHELL n parachute used to slow spacecraft

AEROSOL n pressurized can from which a substance can be dispensed as a fine spray

AEROSOLS > AEROSOL

AEROSPACE n earth's atmosphere and space beyond ▷ adj of rockets or space vehicles

AEROSPIKE n type of rocket engine

AEROSTAT n lighter-than-air craft, such as a balloon

AEROSTATS > AEROSTAT

AEROTAXES > AEROTAXIS

AEROTAXIS n movement away from or towards oxygen

AEROTONE n bath incorporating air jets for massage

AEROTONES > AEROTONE

AEROTRAIN n train driven by a jet engine

AERUGO (esp of old bronze) another name for > VERDIGRIS

AERUGOS > AERUGO

AERY adj lofty, insubstantial, or visionary

AESC n rune

AESCES > AESC

AESCULIN n chemical in horse-chestnut bark

AESCULINS > AESCULIN

AESIR pl n Norse gods

AESTHESES > AESTHESIS

AESTHESIA n normal ability to experience sensation, perception, or sensitivity

AESTHESIS variant of > ESTHESIS

AESTHETE n person who has or affects an extravagant love of art

AESTHETES > AESTHETE

AESTHETIC adj relating to the appreciation of art and beauty ▷ n principle or set of principles relating to the appreciation of art and beauty

AESTIVAL *adj* of or occurring in summer

AESTIVATE *vb* pass the summer

AETATIS *adj* at the age of

AETHER *same as* > ETHER

AETHEREAL *variant spelling of* > ETHEREAL

AETHERIC > AETHER

AETHERS > AETHER

AETIOLOGY *n* philosophy or study of causation

AFALD *adj* single

AFAR *adv* at, from, or to a great distance ▷ *n* great distance

AFARA *n* African tree

AFARAS > AFARA

AFARS > AFAR

AFAWLD *adj* single

AFEAR *vb* frighten

AFEARD *an archaic or dialect word for* > AFRAID

AFEARED *same as* > AFEARD

AFEARING > AFEAR

AFEARS > AFEAR

AFEBRILE *adj* without fever

AFF *adv* off

AFFABLE *adj* friendly and easy to talk to

AFFABLY > AFFABLE

AFFAIR *n* event or happening

AFFAIRE *n* love affair

AFFAIRES > AFFAIRE

AFFAIRS *pl n* personal or business interests

AFFEAR *vb* frighten

AFFEARD > AFFEAR

AFFEARE *vb* frighten

AFFEARED > AFFEAR

AFFEARES > AFFEARE

AFFEARING > AFFEAR

AFFEARS > AFFEAR

AFFECT *vb* act on, influence ▷ *n* emotion associated with an idea or set of ideas

AFFECTED *adj* displaying affectation

AFFECTER > AFFECT

AFFECTERS > AFFECT

AFFECTING *adj* arousing feelings of pity

AFFECTION *n* fondness or love

AFFECTIVE *adj* relating to affects

AFFECTS > AFFECT

AFFEER *vb* assess

AFFEERED > AFFEER

AFFEERING > AFFEER

AFFEERS > AFFEER

AFFERENT *adj* directing inwards to a body part, esp the brain or spinal cord ▷ *n* nerve that conveys impulses towards an organ of the body

AFFERENTS > AFFERENT

AFFIANCE *vb* bind (a person or oneself) in a promise of marriage ▷ *n* solemn pledge, esp a marriage contract

AFFIANCED > AFFIANCE

AFFIANCES > AFFIANCE

AFFIANT *n* person who makes an affidavit

AFFIANTS > AFFIANT

AFFICHE *n* poster

AFFICHES > AFFICHE

AFFIDAVIT *n* written statement made on oath

AFFIED > AFFY

AFFIES > AFFY

AFFILIATE *vb* (of a group) link up with a larger group ▷ *n* person or organization that is affiliated with another

AFFINAL > AFFINE

AFFINE *adj* involving transformations which preserve collinearity ▷ *n* relation by marriage

AFFINED *adj* closely related

AFFINELY > AFFINE

AFFINES > AFFINE

AFFINITY *n* close connection or liking

AFFIRM *vb* declare to be true

AFFIRMANT > AFFIRM

AFFIRMED > AFFIRM

AFFIRMER > AFFIRM

AFFIRMERS > AFFIRM

AFFIRMING > AFFIRM

AFFIRMS > AFFIRM

AFFIX *vb* attach or fasten ▷ *n* word or syllable added to a word to change its meaning

AFFIXABLE > AFFIX

AFFIXAL > AFFIX

AFFIXED > AFFIX

AFFIXER > AFFIX

AFFIXERS > AFFIX

AFFIXES > AFFIX

AFFIXIAL > AFFIX

AFFIXING > AFFIX

AFFIXMENT > AFFIX

AFFIXTURE > AFFIX

AFFLATED *adj* inspired

AFFLATION *n* inspiration

AFFLATUS *n* supposed divine inspiration, esp in poetry

AFFLICT *vb* give pain or grief to

AFFLICTED > AFFLICT

AFFLICTER *n* one who afflicts

AFFLICTS > AFFLICT

AFFLUENCE *n* wealth

AFFLUENCY *n* affluence

AFFLUENT *adj* having plenty of money ▷ *n* tributary stream

AFFLUENTS > AFFLUENT

AFFLUENZA *n* guilt or lack of motivation experienced by people who have made or inherited large amounts of money

AFFLUX *n* flowing towards a point

AFFLUXES > AFFLUX

AFFLUXION *n* flow towards something

AFFOGATO *n* dessert made by pouring espresso over ice cream

AFFOGATOS > AFFOGATO

AFFOORD *vb* consent

AFFOORDED > AFFOORD

AFFOORDS > AFFOORD

AFFORCE *vb* strengthen

AFFORCED > AFFORCE

AFFORCES > AFFORCE

AFFORCING > AFFORCE

AFFORD *vb* have enough money to buy

AFFORDED > AFFORD

AFFORDING > AFFORD

AFFORDS > AFFORD

AFFOREST *vb* plant trees on

AFFORESTS > AFFOREST

AFFRAP *vb* strike

AFFRAPPED > AFFRAP

AFFRAPS > AFFRAP

AFFRAY *n* noisy fight, brawl ▷ *vb* frighten

AFFRAYED > AFFRAY

AFFRAYER > AFFRAY

AFFRAYERS > AFFRAY

AFFRAYING > AFFRAY

AFFRAYS > AFFRAY

AFFRENDED *adj* brought back into friendship

AFFRET *n* furious attack

AFFRETS > AFFRET

AFFRICATE *n* composite speech sound consisting of a stop and a fricative articulated at the same point

AFFRIGHT *vb* frighten ▷ *n* sudden terror

AFFRIGHTS > AFFRIGHT

AFFRONT *n* insult ▷ *vb* hurt someone's pride or dignity

AFFRONTE *adj* facing

AFFRONTED > AFFRONT

AFFRONTEE *adj* facing

AFFRONTS > AFFRONT

AFFUSION *n* baptizing of a person by pouring water onto his or her head

AFFUSIONS > AFFUSION

AFFY *vb* trust

AFFYDE > AFFY

AFFYING > AFFY

AFGHAN *n* type of blanket

AFGHANI *n* monetary unit of Afghanistan

AFGHANIS > AFGHANI

AFGHANS > AFGHAN

AFIELD *adj* away from one's usual surroundings or home

AFIRE *adj* on fire

AFLAJ > FALAJ

AFLAME *adj* burning

AFLATOXIN *n* toxin produced by a fungus growing on peanuts, maize, etc, which causes liver damage (esp cancer) in humans

AFLOAT *adj* floating ▷ *adv* floating

AFLUTTER *adv* in or into a nervous or excited state

AFOCAL *adj* relating to a method for transferring an image without bringing it into focus

AFOOT *adj* happening, in operation ▷ *adv* happening

AFORE *adv* before

AFOREHAND *adv* beforehand

AFORESAID *adj* referred to previously

AFORETIME *adv* formerly

AFOUL *adj* in or into a state of difficulty, confusion, or conflict (with)

AFRAID *adj* frightened

AFREET *n* powerful evil demon or giant monster

AFREETS > AFREET

AFRESH *adv* again, anew

AFRIT *same as* > AFREET

AFRITS > AFRIT

AFRO *n* full rounded hairstyle

AFRONT *adv* in front

AFROS > AFRO

AFT *adv* at or towards the rear of a ship or aircraft ▷ *adj* at or towards the rear of a ship or aircraft

AFTER *adv* at a later time

AFTERBODY *n* any discarded part that continues to trail a satellite, rocket, etc, in orbit

AFTERBURN *n* burning of calories after exercise

AFTERCARE *n* support given to a person discharged from a hospital or prison

AFTERCLAP *n* unexpected consequence

AFTERDAMP *n* poisonous gas formed after the explosion of firedamp in a coal mine

AFTERDECK *n* unprotected deck behind the bridge of a ship

AFTEREYE *vb* gaze at someone or something that has passed

AFTEREYED > AFTEREYE

AFTEREYES > AFTEREYE

AFTERGAME *n* second game that follows another

AFTERGLOW *n* glow left after a source of light has gone

AFTERHEAT *n* heat generated in a nuclear reactor after it has been shut down, produced by residual radioactivity in the fuel elements

AFTERINGS *n* last of the milk drawn in milking

AFTERLIFE n life after death

AFTERMAST n mast nearest the stern of a ship

AFTERMATH n results of an event considered together

AFTERMOST adj closer or closest to the rear or (in a vessel) the stern

AFTERNOON n time between noon and evening

AFTERPAIN n pain that comes after a while

AFTERPEAK n space behind the aftermost bulkhead, often used for storage

AFTERS n sweet course of a meal

AFTERSHOW n party held after a public performance of a play or film

AFTERSUN n moisturizing lotion applied to the skin to soothe sunburn and avoid peeling

AFTERSUNS
> AFTERSUN

AFTERTAX adj after tax has been paid

AFTERTIME n later period

AFTERWARD adv after an earlier event or time

AFTERWORD n epilogue or postscript in a book, etc

AFTMOST adj furthest towards rear

AFTOSA n foot-and-mouth disease

AFTOSAS > AFTOSA

AG n agriculture

AGA n title of respect

AGACANT adj irritating

AGACANTE adj irritating

AGACERIE n coquetry

AGACERIES
> AGACERIE

AGAIN adv once more

AGAINST prep in opposition or contrast to

AGALACTIA n absence or failure of secretion of milk

AGALLOCH another name for > EAGLEWOOD

AGALLOCHS
> AGALLOCH

AGALWOOD n eaglewood

AGALWOODS
> AGALWOOD

AGAMA n small lizard

AGAMAS > AGAMA

AGAMETE n reproductive cell

AGAMETES > AGAMETE

AGAMI n South American bird

AGAMIC adj asexual

AGAMID same as > AGAMA

AGAMIDS > AGAMID

AGAMIS > AGAMI

AGAMOGONY n asexual reproduction in protozoans that is characterized by multiple fission

AGAMOID n lizard of the agamid type

AGAMOIDS > AGAMOID

AGAMONT another name for > SCHIZONT

AGAMONTS > AGAMONT

AGAMOUS adj without sex

AGAPAE > AGAPE

AGAPAI > AGAPE

AGAPE adj (of the mouth) wide open ▷ n love feast among the early Christians

AGAPEIC > AGAPE

AGAPES > AGAPE

AGAR n jelly-like substance obtained from seaweed and used as a thickener in food

AGARIC n type of fungus

AGARICS > AGARIC

AGAROSE n gel used in chemistry

AGAROSES > AGAROSE

AGARS > AGAR

AGARWOOD n aromatic wood of an Asian tree

AGARWOODS
> AGARWOOD

AGAS > AGA

AGAST adj aghast ▷ vb terrify or be terrified

AGASTED > AGAST

AGASTING > AGAST

AGASTS > AGAST

AGATE n semiprecious form of quartz with striped colouring ▷ adv on the way

AGATES > AGATE

AGATEWARE n ceramic ware made to resemble agate or marble

AGATISE same as > AGATIZE

AGATISED > AGATISE

AGATISES > AGATISE

AGATISING > AGATISE

AGATIZE vb turn into agate

AGATIZED > AGATIZE

AGATIZES > AGATIZE

AGATIZING > AGATIZE

AGATOID adj like agate

AGAVE n tropical plant

AGAVES > AGAVE

AGAZE adj gazing at something

AGAZED adj amazed

AGE n length of time a person or thing has existed ▷ vb make or grow old

AGED adj old

AGEDLY > AGED

AGEDNESS > AGED

AGEE adj awry, crooked, or ajar ▷ adv awry

AGEING n fact or process of growing old ▷ adj becoming or appearing older

AGEINGS > AGEING

AGEISM n discrimination against people on the grounds of age

AGEISMS > AGEISM

AGEIST > AGEISM

AGEISTS > AGEISM

AGELAST n someone who never laughs

AGELASTIC > AGELAST

AGELASTS > AGELAST

AGELESS adj apparently never growing old

AGELESSLY > AGELESS

AGELONG adj lasting for a very long time

AGEMATE n person the same age as another person

AGEMATES > AGEMATE

AGEN archaic form of > AGAIN

AGENCIES > AGENCY

AGENCY n organization providing a service

AGENDA n list of things to be dealt with, esp at a meeting

AGENDAS > AGENDA

AGENDER adj of a person who does not identify with a gender

AGENDUM same as > AGENDA

AGENDUMS > AGENDUM

AGENE n chemical used to whiten flour

AGENES > AGENE

AGENESES > AGENESIS

AGENESIA n imperfect development

AGENESIAS
> AGENESIA

AGENESIS n (of an animal or plant) imperfect development

AGENETIC > AGENESIS

AGENISE same as > AGENIZE

AGENISED > AGENISE

AGENISES > AGENISE

AGENISING > AGENISE

AGENIZE vb whiten using agene

AGENIZED > AGENIZE

AGENIZES > AGENIZE

AGENIZING > AGENIZE

AGENT n person acting on behalf of another ▷ vb act as an agent

AGENTED > AGENT

AGENTIAL > AGENT

AGENTING > AGENT

AGENTINGS > AGENT

AGENTIVAL adj of the performer of an action

AGENTIVE adj denoting a case of noun etc indicating the agent described by the verb ▷ n agentive case

AGENTIVES
> AGENTIVE

AGENTRIES > AGENTRY

AGENTRY n activity of an agent

AGENTS > AGENT

AGER n something that ages

AGERATUM n tropical American plant with thick clusters of purplish-blue flowers

AGERATUMS
> AGERATUM

AGERS > AGER

AGES > AGE

AGEUSIA n lack of the sense of taste

AGEUSIAS > AGEUSIA

AGFLATION n inflation due to a rise in the demand for and price of agricultural products

AGGADA n explanation in Jewish literature

AGGADAH same as > AGGADA

AGGADAHS > AGGADAH

AGGADAS > AGGADA

AGGADIC adj of aggada

AGGADOT > AGGADA

AGGADOTH > AGGADA

AGGER n rampart

AGGERS adj aggressive

AGGIE n American agricultural student

AGGIES > AGGIE

AGGRACE vb add grace to

AGGRACED > AGGRACE

AGGRACES > AGGRACE

AGGRACING > AGGRACE

AGGRADE vb build up by the deposition of sediment

AGGRADED > AGGRADE

AGGRADES > AGGRADE

AGGRADING > AGGRADE

AGGRATE vb gratify

AGGRATED > AGGRATE

AGGRATES > AGGRATE

AGGRATING > AGGRATE

AGGRAVATE vb make worse

AGGREGATE n total ▷ adj gathered into a mass ▷ vb combine into a whole

AGGRESS vb attack first or begin a quarrel

AGGRESSED > AGGRESS

AGGRESSES > AGGRESS

AGGRESSOR n person or body that engages in aggressive behaviour

AGGRI adj of African beads

AGGRIEVE vb grieve

AGGRIEVED adj upset and angry

AGGRIEVES
> AGGRIEVE

AGGRO n aggressive behaviour

AGGROS > AGGRO

AGGRY adj of African beads

AGHA same as > AGA

AGHAS > AGHA

AGHAST adj overcome with amazement or horror

AGILA n eaglewood

AGILAS > AGILA

AGILE adj nimble, quick-moving

AGILELY > AGILE

AGILENESS > AGILE

AGILER > AGILE

AGILEST > AGILE

AGILITIES > AGILE

AGILITY > AGILE

AGIN prep against, opposed to

AGING same as > AGEING

AGINGS > AGING

AGINNER *n* someone who is against something
AGINNERS > AGINNER
AGIO *n* difference between the nominal and actual values of a currency
AGIOS > AGIO
AGIOTAGE *n* business of exchanging currencies
AGIOTAGES > AGIOTAGE
AGISM *same as* > AGEISM
AGISMS > AGISM
AGIST *vb* care for and feed (cattle or horses) for payment
AGISTED > AGIST
AGISTER *n* person who grazes cattle for money
AGISTERS > AGISTER
AGISTING > AGIST
AGISTMENT > AGEISM
AGISTOR *n* person who grazes cattle for money
AGISTORS > AGISTOR
AGISTS > AGIST
AGITA *n* acid indigestion
AGITABLE > AGITATE
AGITANS *adj* as in *paralysis agitans* Parkinson's disease
AGITAS > AGITA
AGITATE *vb* disturb or excite
AGITATED > AGITATE
AGITATES > AGITATE
AGITATING > AGITATE
AGITATION *n* state of excitement, disturbance, or worry
AGITATIVE > AGITATE
AGITATO *adv* (to be performed) in an agitated manner
AGITATOR *n* person who agitates for or against a cause, etc
AGITATORS > AGITATOR
AGITPOP *n* use of pop music to promote political propaganda
AGITPOPS > AGITPOP
AGITPROP *n* political agitation and propaganda
AGITPROPS > AGITPROP
AGLARE *adj* glaring
AGLEAM *adj* glowing
AGLEE *same as* > AGLEY
AGLET *n* metal tag
AGLETS > AGLET
AGLEY *adj* awry
AGLIMMER *adj* glimmering
AGLITTER *adj* sparkling, glittering
AGLOO *same as* > AGLU
AGLOOS > AGLOO
AGLOSSAL > AGLOSSIA
AGLOSSATE > AGLOSSIA
AGLOSSIA *n* congenital absence of the tongue
AGLOSSIAS > AGLOSSIA
AGLOW *adj* glowing

AGLU *n* breathing hole made in ice by a seal
AGLUS > AGLU
AGLY *Scots word for* > WRONG
AGLYCON *n* chemical compound
AGLYCONE *same as* > AGLYCON
AGLYCONES > AGLYCONE
AGLYCONS > AGLYCON
AGMA *n* symbol used to represent a velar nasal consonant
AGMAS > AGMA
AGMINATE *adj* gathered or clustered together
AGNAIL *another name for* > HANGNAIL
AGNAILS > AGNAIL
AGNAME *n* name additional to first name and surname
AGNAMED *adj* having an agname
AGNAMES > AGNAME
AGNATE *adj* related through a common male ancestor ▷ *n* descendant by male links from a common male ancestor
AGNATES > AGNATE
AGNATHAN *n* type of jawless eel-like aquatic vertebrate
AGNATHANS > AGNATHAN
AGNATHOUS *adj* (esp of lampreys and hagfishes) lacking jaws
AGNATIC > AGNATE
AGNATICAL > AGNATE
AGNATION > AGNATE
AGNATIONS > AGNATE
AGNISE *vb* acknowledge
AGNISED > AGNISE
AGNISES > AGNISE
AGNISING > AGNISE
AGNIZE *vb* acknowledge
AGNIZED > AGNIZE
AGNIZES > AGNIZE
AGNIZING > AGNIZE
AGNOLOTTI *n* small pasta shapes stuffed with fillings
AGNOMEN *n* name used by ancient Romans
AGNOMENS > AGNOMEN
AGNOMINA > AGNOMEN
AGNOMINAL > AGNOMEN
AGNOSIA *n* loss of power to recognize familiar objects
AGNOSIAS > AGNOSIA
AGNOSIC > AGNOSIA
AGNOSTIC *n* person who believes that it is impossible to know whether God exists ▷ *adj* of agnostics
AGNOSTICS > AGNOSTIC
AGO *adv* in the past
AGOG *adj* eager or curious
AGOGE *n* ancient Greek melodic form
AGOGES > AGOGE

AGOGIC *n* musical accent
AGOGICS > AGOGIC
AGOING *adj* moving
AGON *n* ancient Greek festival
AGONAL *adj* of agony
AGONE *an archaic word for* > AGO
AGONES > AGON
AGONIC *adj* forming no angle
AGONIES > AGONY
AGONISE *same as* > AGONIZE
AGONISED > AGONISE
AGONISES > AGONISE
AGONISING > AGONISE
AGONISM *n* struggle between opposing forces
AGONISMS > AGONISM
AGONIST *n* any muscle that is opposed in action by another muscle
AGONISTES *n* person suffering inner struggle
AGONISTIC *adj* striving for effect
AGONISTS > AGONIST
AGONIZE *vb* worry greatly
AGONIZED > AGONIZE
AGONIZES > AGONIZE
AGONIZING > AGONIZE
AGONS > AGON
AGONY *n* extreme physical or mental pain
AGOOD *adv* seriously or earnestly
AGORA *n* place of assembly in ancient Greece
AGORAE > AGORA
AGORAS > AGORA
AGOROT *pl n* Israeli coins
AGOROTH *same as* > AGOROT
AGOUTA *n* Haitian rodent
AGOUTAS > AGOUTA
AGOUTI *n* rodent
AGOUTIES > AGOUTI
AGOUTIS > AGOUTI
AGOUTY *same as* > AGOUTI
AGRAFE *same as* > AGRAFFE
AGRAFES > AGRAFE
AGRAFFE *n* loop and hook fastening
AGRAFFES > AGRAFFE
AGRAPHA > AGRAPHON
AGRAPHIA *n* loss of the ability to write, resulting from a brain lesion
AGRAPHIAS > AGRAPHIA
AGRAPHIC > AGRAPHIA
AGRAPHON *n* saying of Jesus not in Gospels
AGRARIAN *adj* of land or agriculture ▷ *n* person who favours the redistribution of landed property
AGRARIANS > AGRARIAN
AGRASTE > AGGRACE
AGRAVIC *adj* of zero gravity

AGREE *vb* be of the same opinion
AGREEABLE *adj* pleasant and enjoyable
AGREEABLY > AGREEABLE
AGREED *adj* determined by common consent
AGREEING > AGREE
AGREEMENT *n* agreeing
AGREES > AGREE
AGREGE *n* winner in examination for university teaching post
AGREGES > AGREGE
AGREMENS *n* amenities
AGREMENT *n* diplomatic approval of a country
AGREMENTS *n* amenities
AGRESTAL *adj* (of uncultivated plants such as weeds) growing on cultivated land
AGRESTIAL *adj* agrestal
AGRESTIC *adj* rural
AGRIA *n* appearance of pustules
AGRIAS > AGRIA
AGRIMONY *n* yellow-flowered plant with bitter-tasting fruits
AGRIN *adv* grinning ▷ *n* type of protein
AGRINS > AGRIN
AGRIOLOGY *n* study of primitive peoples
AGRISE *vb* fill with fear
AGRISED > AGRISE
AGRISES > AGRISE
AGRISING > AGRISE
AGRIZE *vb* fill with fear
AGRIZED > AGRIZE
AGRIZES > AGRIZE
AGRIZING > AGRIZE
AGRO *n* student of agriculture
AGRODOLCE *n* Italian sweet-and-sour sauce
AGROLOGIC > AGROLOGY
AGROLOGY *n* scientific study of soils and their potential productivity
AGRONOMIC > AGRONOMY
AGRONOMY *n* science of soil management and crop production
AGROS > AGRO
AGROUND *adv* onto the bottom of shallow water ▷ *adj* on the ground or bottom, as in shallow water
AGRYPNIA *n* inability to sleep
AGRYPNIAS > AGRYPNIA
AGRYZE *vb* fill with fear
AGRYZED > AGRYZE
AGRYZES > AGRYZE
AGRYZING > AGRYZE
AGS > AG
AGTERSKOT *n* final payment to a farmer for crops
AGUACATE *n* avocado
AGUACATES > AGUACATE

a

AGUE n periodic fever with shivering

AGUED adj suffering from fever

AGUELIKE > AGUE

AGUES > AGUE

AGUEWEED n N American plant with clusters of pale blue-violet or white flowers

AGUEWEEDS > AGUEWEED

AGUISE vb dress

AGUISED > AGUISE

AGUISES > AGUISE

AGUISH > AGUE

AGUISHLY > AGUE

AGUISING > AGUISE

AGUIZE vb dress

AGUIZED > AGUIZE

AGUIZES > AGUIZE

AGUIZING > AGUIZE

AGUNA n (in Jewish law) woman whose husband will not grant her a divorce

AGUNAH same as > AGUNA

AGUNOT > AGUNA

AGUNOTH > AGUNA

AGUTI n agouti

AGUTIS > AGUTI

AGYRIA n brain disease

AGYRIAS > AGYRIA

AH interj exclamation expressing surprise, joy etc ▷ vb say ah

AHA interj exclamation of triumph or surprise

AHCHOO interj sound made by someone sneezing

AHEAD adv in front

AHEAP adv in a heap

AHED > AH

AHEIGHT adv at height

AHEM interj clearing of the throat in order to attract attention

AHEMERAL adj not constituting a full 24-hour day

AHENT adv behind

AHI n yellowfin tuna

AHIGH adv at height

AHIMSA n the law of reverence for every form of life

AHIMSAS > AHIMSA

AHIND adv behind

AHING > AH

AHINT adv behind

AHIS > AHI

AHISTORIC adj not related to history; not historical

AHOLD adv holding

AHOLDS > AHOLD

AHORSE adv on horseback

AHOY interj hail used to call a ship

AHS > AH

AHULL adv with sails furled

AHUNGERED adj very hungry

AHUNGRY adj very hungry

AHURU n type of small pink cod of SW Pacific waters

AHURUHURU same as > AHURU

AHURUS > AHURU

AI n shaggy-coated slow-moving animal of South America

AIA n female servant in E Asia

AIAS > AIA

AIBLINS Scots word for > PERHAPS

AID n assistance or support ▷ vb help financially or in other ways

AIDA n cotton fabric with a natural mesh

AIDANCE n help

AIDANCES > AIDANCE

AIDANT adj helping ▷ n helper

AIDANTS > AIDANT

AIDAS > AIDA

AIDE n assistant

AIDED > AID

AIDER > AID

AIDES > AIDE

AIDFUL adj helpful

AIDING > AID

AIDLESS adj without help

AIDMAN n military medical assistant

AIDMEN > AIDMAN

AIDOI adj of the genitals

AIDOS Greek word for > SHAME

AIDS > AID

AIERIES > AIERY

AIERY n eyrie

AIGA n Māori word for family

AIGAS > AIGA

AIGHT adv all right

AIGLET same as > AGLET

AIGLETS > AIGLET

AIGRET same as > AIGRETTE

AIGRETS > AIGRET

AIGRETTE n long plume worn on hats or as a headdress, esp one of long egret feathers

AIGRETTES > AIGRETTE

AIGUILLE n rock mass or mountain peak shaped like a needle

AIGUILLES > AIGUILLE

AIKIDO n Japanese self-defence

AIKIDOS > AIKIDO

AIKONA interj South African expression meaning no

AIL vb trouble, afflict

AILANTHIC > AILANTHUS

AILANTHUS n type of deciduous tree with small greenish flowers and winged fruits, planted in Europe and N America

AILANTO n Asian tree

AILANTOS > AILANTO

AILED > AIL

AILERON n movable flap on an aircraft wing which controls rolling

AILERONS > AILERON

AILETTE n shoulder armour

AILETTES > AILETTE

AILING adj sickly

AILMENT n illness

AILMENTS > AILMENT

AILS > AIL

AIM vb point (a weapon or missile) or direct (a blow or remark) at a target ▷ n aiming

AIMED > AIM

AIMER > AIM

AIMERS > AIM

AIMFUL adj with purpose or intention

AIMFULLY > AIMFUL

AIMING > AIM

AIMLESS adj having no purpose

AIMLESSLY > AIMLESS

AIMS > AIM

AIN variant of > AYIN

AINE adj French word for elder (male)

AINEE adj French word for elder (female)

AINGA n Māori word for village

AINGAS > AINGA

AINS > AIN

AINSELL n Scots word meaning own self

AINSELLS > AINSELL

AIOLI n garlic mayonnaise

AIOLIS > AIOLI

AIR n mixture of gases forming the earth's atmosphere ▷ vb make known publicly

AIRBAG n safety device in a car

AIRBAGS > AIRBAG

AIRBALL n missed shot in basketball ▷ vb throw an airball

AIRBALLED > AIRBALL

AIRBALLS > AIRBALL

AIRBASE n centre from which military aircraft operate

AIRBASES > AIRBASE

AIRBOARD n inflatable body board

AIRBOARDS > AIRBOARD

AIRBOAT n boat for use in swamps

AIRBOATS > AIRBOAT

AIRBORNE adj carried by air

AIRBOUND adj heading into the air

AIRBRICK n brick with holes in it, put into the wall of a building for ventilation

AIRBRICKS > AIRBRICK

AIRBRUSH n atomizer that sprays paint by compressed air ▷ vb paint using an airbrush

AIRBURST n explosion of a bomb, shell, etc, in the air ▷ vb (of a bomb, shell, etc) to explode in the air

AIRBURSTS > AIRBURST

AIRBUS n commercial passenger aircraft

AIRBUSES > AIRBUS

AIRBUSSES > AIRBUS

AIRCHECK n recording of a radio broadcast

AIRCHECKS > AIRCHECK

AIRCOACH n bus travelling to and from an airport

AIRCON n air conditioner

AIRCONS > AIRCON

AIRCRAFT n any machine that flies, such as an aeroplane

AIRCREW n crew of an aircraft

AIRCREWS > AIRCREW

AIRDATE n date of a programme broadcast

AIRDATES > AIRDATE

AIRDRAWN adj imaginary

AIRDROME same as > AERODROME

AIRDROMES > AIRDROME

AIRDROP n delivery of supplies by parachute ▷ vb deliver (supplies, etc) by an airdrop

AIRDROPS > AIRDROP

AIRED > AIR

AIRER n device on which clothes are hung to dry

AIRERS > AIRER

AIREST > AIR

AIRFARE n money for an aircraft ticket

AIRFARES > AIRFARE

AIRFIELD n place where aircraft can land and take off

AIRFIELDS > AIRFIELD

AIRFLOW n flow of air past a moving object

AIRFLOWS > AIRFLOW

AIRFOIL same as > AEROFOIL

AIRFOILS > AIRFOIL

AIRFRAME n body of an aircraft, excluding its engines

AIRFRAMES > AIRFRAME

AIRGAP n gap between parts in an electrical machine

AIRGAPS > AIRGAP

AIRGLOW n faint light in the night sky

AIRGLOWS > AIRGLOW

AIRGRAPH n photographic reduction of a letter for sending airmail

AIRGRAPHS > AIRGRAPH

AIRGUN n gun fired by compressed air

AIRGUNS > AIRGUN

AIRHEAD n stupid person

AIRHEADED > AIRHEAD
AIRHEADS > AIRHEAD
AIRHOLE n hole that allows the passage of air
AIRHOLES > AIRHOLE
AIRIER > AIRY
AIRIEST > AIRY
AIRILY adv in a light-hearted and casual manner
AIRINESS n quality or condition of being fresh, light, or breezy
AIRING n exposure to air for drying or ventilation
AIRINGS > AIRING
AIRLESS adj stuffy
AIRLIFT n transport of troops or cargo by aircraft when other routes are blocked ▷ vb transport by airlift
AIRLIFTED > AIRLIFT
AIRLIFTS > AIRLIFT
AIRLIKE > AIR
AIRLINE n company providing scheduled flights for passengers and cargo
AIRLINER n large passenger aircraft
AIRLINERS > AIRLINER
AIRLINES > AIRLINE
AIRLOCK n air bubble blocking the flow of liquid in a pipe
AIRLOCKS > AIRLOCK
AIRMAIL n system of sending mail by aircraft ▷ adj of, used for, or concerned with airmail ▷ vb send by airmail
AIRMAILED > AIRMAIL
AIRMAILS > AIRMAIL
AIRMAN n member of an air force
AIRMEN > AIRMAN
AIRMOBILE adj using aircraft as transport
AIRN Scots word for > IRON
AIRNED > AIRN
AIRNING > AIRN
AIRNS > AIRN
AIRPARK n car park at airport
AIRPARKS > AIRPARK
AIRPLANE same as > AEROPLANE
AIRPLANES > AIRPLANE
AIRPLAY n broadcast performances of a record on radio
AIRPLAYS > AIRPLAY
AIRPORT n airfield for civilian aircraft, with facilities for aircraft maintenance and passengers
AIRPORTS > AIRPORT
AIRPOST n system of delivering mail by air
AIRPOSTS > AIRPOST
AIRPOWER n strength of a nation's air force
AIRPOWERS > AIRPOWER

AIRPROOF vb make something airtight
AIRPROOFS > AIRPROOF
AIRPROX n near collision involving aircraft
AIRPROXES > AIRPROX
AIRS pl n manners put on to impress people
AIRSCAPE n picture or view of sky
AIRSCAPES > AIRSCAPE
AIRSCREW n aircraft propeller
AIRSCREWS > AIRSCREW
AIRSHAFT n shaft for ventilation
AIRSHAFTS > AIRSHAFT
AIRSHED n air over a particular geographical area
AIRSHEDS > AIRSHED
AIRSHIP n lighter-than-air self-propelled aircraft
AIRSHIPS > AIRSHIP
AIRSHOT n shot that misses the ball completely
AIRSHOTS > AIRSHOT
AIRSHOW n occasion when an air base is open to the public
AIRSHOWS > AIRSHOW
AIRSICK adj nauseated from travelling in an aircraft
AIRSIDE n part of an airport nearest the aircraft
AIRSIDES > AIRSIDE
AIRSOME adj cold
AIRSPACE n atmosphere above a country, regarded as its territory
AIRSPACES > AIRSPACE
AIRSPEED n speed of an aircraft relative to the air in which it moves
AIRSPEEDS > AIRSPEED
AIRSTOP n helicopter landing-place
AIRSTOPS > AIRSTOP
AIRSTREAM n wind, esp at a high altitude
AIRSTRIKE n attack by military aircraft
AIRSTRIP n cleared area where aircraft can take off and land
AIRSTRIPS > AIRSTRIP
AIRT n point of the compass ▷ vb direct
AIRTED > AIRT
AIRTH same as > AIRT
AIRTHED > AIRTH
AIRTHING > AIRTH
AIRTHS > AIRTH
AIRTIGHT adj sealed so that air cannot enter
AIRTIME n time period on radio and TV
AIRTIMES > AIRTIME
AIRTING > AIRT
AIRTRAM n cable car

AIRTRAMS > AIRTRAM
AIRTS > AIRT
AIRVAC n evacuation by air ambulance
AIRVACS > AIRVAC
AIRWARD adj into air
AIRWARDS adv into air
AIRWAVE n radio wave used in radio and television broadcasting
AIRWAVES > AIRWAVE
AIRWAY n air route used regularly by aircraft
AIRWAYS > AIRWAY
AIRWISE adv towards the air
AIRWOMAN n member of an airforce
AIRWOMEN > AIRWOMAN
AIRWORTHY adj (of aircraft) fit to fly
AIRY adj well-ventilated
AIS > AI
AISLE n passageway separating seating areas, rows of shelves, etc
AISLED > AISLE
AISLELESS > AISLE
AISLES > AISLE
AISLEWAY n aisle
AISLEWAYS > AISLEWAY
AISLING Irish word for > DREAM
AISLINGS > AISLING
AIT n islet, esp in a river
AITCH n letter h or the sound represented by it
AITCHBONE n cut of beef from the rump bone
AITCHES > AITCH
AITS > AIT
AITU n half-human half-divine being
AITUS > AITU
AIVER n working horse
AIVERS > AIVER
AIYEE interj expressing alarm
AIZLE n Scots word for hot ashes
AIZLES > AIZLE
AJAR adv (of a door) partly open ▷ adj not in harmony
AJEE same as > AGEE
AJI n type of spicy pepper
AJIES > AJI
AJIS > AJI
AJIVA n Jainist term for a non-living thing
AJIVAS > AJIVA
AJOWAN n plant related to caraway
AJOWANS > AJOWAN
AJUGA n garden plant
AJUGAS > AJUGA
AJUTAGE n nozzle
AJUTAGES > AJUTAGE
AJWAN n plant related to caraway
AJWANS > AJWAN
AKA n type of New Zealand vine
AKARYOTE n cell without a nucleus
AKARYOTES > AKARYOTE

AKARYOTIC > AKARYOTE
AKAS > AKA
AKATEA n New Zealand vine with white flowers
AKATEAS > AKATEA
AKATHISIA n inability to sit still because of uncontrollable movement caused by reaction to drugs
AKE vb old spelling of ache
AKEAKE n New Zealand tree
AKEAKES > AKEAKE
AKEBIA n E Asian climbing plant
AKEBIAS > AKEBIA
AKED > AKE
AKEDAH n binding of Isaac in Bible
AKEDAHS > AKEDAH
AKEE same as > ACKEE
AKEES > AKEE
AKELA n adult leader of a pack of Cub Scouts
AKELAS > AKELA
AKENE same as > ACHENE
AKENES > AKENE
AKENIAL > AKENE
AKES > AKE
AKHARA n (in India) gymnasium
AKHARAS > AKHARA
AKIMBO adj as in with arms akimbo with hands on hips and elbows projecting outwards
AKIN adj related by blood
AKINESES > AKINESIS
AKINESIA n loss of power to move
AKINESIAS > AKINESIA
AKINESIS same as > AKINESIA
AKINETIC > AKINESIA
AKING > AKE
AKIRAHO n small New Zealand shrub with white flowers
AKIRAHOS > AKIRAHO
AKITA n large dog
AKITAS > AKITA
AKKAS slang word for > MONEY
AKOLUTHOS n leader of Byzantine Varangian Guard
AKRASIA n weakness of will
AKRASIAS > AKRASIA
AKRATIC > AKRASIA
AKVAVIT same as > AQUAVIT
AKVAVITS > AKVAVIT
AL same as > AAL
ALA n winglike structure
ALAAP n part of raga in Indian music
ALAAPS > ALAAP
ALABAMINE old name for > ASTATINE
ALABASTER n soft white translucent stone ▷ adj of or resembling alabaster
ALACHLOR n type of herbicide

ALACHLORS
> ALACHLOR

ALACK archaic or poetic word for > ALAS

ALACKADAY same as > ALACK

ALACRITY n speed, eagerness

ALAE > ALA

ALAIMENT old spelling of > ALLAYMENT

ALAIMENTS > ALAIMENT

ALALAGMOI > ALALAGMOS

ALALAGMOS n ancient Greek war cry

ALALIA n complete inability to speak

ALALIAS > ALALIA

ALAMEDA n public walk lined with trees

ALAMEDAS > ALAMEDA

ALAMO n poplar tree

ALAMODE n soft light silk used for shawls and dresses, esp in the 19th century

ALAMODES > ALAMODE

ALAMORT adj exhausted and downcast

ALAMOS > ALAMO

ALAN n member of ancient European nomadic people

ALAND vb come onto land

ALANDS > ALAND

ALANE Scots word for > ALONE

ALANG n type of grass in Malaysia

ALANGS > ALANG

ALANIN n alanine

ALANINE n chemical

ALANINES > ALANINE

ALANINS > ALANIN

ALANNAH interj term of endearment ▷ n cry of alannah

ALANNAHS > ALANNAH

ALANS > ALAN

ALANT n flowering plant used in herbal medicine

ALANTS > ALANT

ALANYL n chemical found in proteins

ALANYLS > ALANYL

ALAP n Indian vocal music without words

ALAPA n part of raga in Indian music

ALAPAS > ALAPA

ALAPS > ALAP

ALAR adj relating to, resembling, or having wings or alae

ALARM n sudden fear caused by awareness of danger ▷ vb fill with fear

ALARMABLE > ALARM

ALARMED > ALARM

ALARMEDLY > ALARM

ALARMING > ALARM

ALARMISM > ALARMIST

ALARMISMS > ALARMIST

ALARMIST n person who alarms others needlessly ▷ adj causing needless alarm

ALARMISTS > ALARMIST

ALARMS > ALARM

ALARUM n alarm, esp a call to arms ▷ vb raise the alarm

ALARUMED > ALARUM

ALARUMING > ALARUM

ALARUMS > ALARUM

ALARY adj of, relating to, or shaped like wings

ALAS adv unfortunately, regrettably

ALASKA n dessert made of cake and ice cream

ALASKAS > ALASKA

ALASTOR n avenging demon

ALASTORS > ALASTOR

ALASTRIM n form of smallpox

ALASTRIMS > ALASTRIM

ALATE adj having wings or winglike extensions ▷ n winged insect

ALATED adj having wings

ALATES > ALATE

ALATION n state of having wings

ALATIONS > ALATION

ALAY vb allay

ALAYED > ALAY

ALAYING > ALAY

ALAYS > ALAY

ALB n long white robe worn by a Christian priest

ALBA n song of lament

ALBACORE n tuna found in warm seas, eaten for food

ALBACORES > ALBACORE

ALBARELLI > ALBARELLO

ALBARELLO n storage jar

ALBAS > ALBA

ALBATA n variety of German silver consisting of nickel, copper, and zinc

ALBATAS > ALBATA

ALBATROSS n large sea bird with very long wings

ALBE old word for > ALBEIT

ALBEDO n measure of intensity of reflected light

ALBEDOES > ALBEDO

ALBEDOS > ALBEDO

ALBEE archaic form of > ALBEIT

ALBEIT conj even though

ALBERGHI > ALBERGO

ALBERGO n Italian word for inn

ALBERT n watch chain

ALBERTITE n black solid variety of bitumen that has a conchoidal fracture and occurs in veins in oil-bearing strata

ALBERTS > ALBERT

ALBESCENT adj shading into, growing, or becoming white

ALBESPINE old name for > HAWTHORN

ALBESPYNE old name for > HAWTHORN

ALBICORE n species of tuna

ALBICORES > ALBICORE

ALBINAL > ALBINO

ALBINESS n female albino

ALBINIC > ALBINO

ALBINISM > ALBINO

ALBINISMS > ALBINO

ALBINO n person or animal with white skin and hair and pink eyes

ALBINOISM > ALBINO

ALBINOS > ALBINO

ALBINOTIC > ALBINO

ALBITE n type of mineral

ALBITES > ALBITE

ALBITIC > ALBITE

ALBITICAL > ALBITE

ALBITISE same as > ALBITIZE

ALBITISED > ALBITISE

ALBITISES > ALBITISE

ALBITIZE vb turn into albite

ALBITIZED > ALBITIZE

ALBITIZES > ALBITIZE

ALBIZIA n mimosa

ALBIZIAS > ALBIZIA

ALBIZZIA n mimosa

ALBIZZIAS > ALBIZZIA

ALBRICIAS interj expression of joy

ALBS > ALB

ALBUGO n opacity of the cornea

ALBUGOS > ALBUGO

ALBUM n book with blank pages for keeping photographs or stamps in

ALBUMEN same as > ALBUMIN

ALBUMENS > ALBUMEN

ALBUMIN n protein found in blood plasma, egg white, milk, and muscle

ALBUMINS > ALBUMIN

ALBUMOSE the US name for > PROTEOSE

ALBUMOSES > ALBUMOSE

ALBUMS > ALBUM

ALBURNOUS > ALBURNUM

ALBURNUM former name for > SAPWOOD

ALBURNUMS > ALBURNUM

ALBUTEROL n drug used to treat lung diseases

ALCADE same as > ALCALDE

ALCADES > ALCADE

ALCAHEST same as > ALKAHEST

ALCAHESTS > ALCAHEST

ALCAIC n verse consisting of strophes with four tetrametric lines

ALCAICS > ALCAIC

ALCAIDE n commander of a fortress or castle

ALCAIDES > ALCAIDE

ALCALDE n (in Spain and Spanish America) the mayor or chief magistrate in a town

ALCALDES > ALCALDE

ALCARRAZA n Spanish water container

ALCATRAS n pelican

ALCAYDE n alcaide

ALCAYDES > ALCAYDE

ALCAZAR n Moorish palace or fortress

ALCAZARS > ALCAZAR

ALCHEMIC > ALCHEMY

ALCHEMIES > ALCHEMY

ALCHEMISE same as > ALCHEMIZE

ALCHEMIST n person who practises alchemy

ALCHEMIZE vb alter (an element, metal, etc) by alchemy

ALCHEMY n medieval form of chemistry

ALCHERA n mythical Golden Age

ALCHERAS > ALCHERA

ALCHYMIES > ALCHYMY

ALCHYMY old spelling of > ALCHEMY

ALCID n bird of the auk family

ALCIDINE adj relating to a family of sea birds including the auks, guillemots, and puffins

ALCIDS > ALCID

ALCO same as > ALKO

ALCOHOL n colourless flammable liquid present in intoxicating drinks

ALCOHOLIC adj of alcohol ▷ n person addicted to alcohol

ALCOHOLS > ALCOHOL

ALCOLOCK n breath-alcohol ignition-interlock device

ALCOLOCKS > ALCOLOCK

ALCOOL n form of pure grain spirit distilled in Quebec

ALCOOLS > ALCOOL

ALCOPOP n alcoholic drink that tastes like a soft drink

ALCOPOPS > ALCOPOP

ALCORZA n Spanish sweet

ALCORZAS > ALCORZA

ALCOS > ALCO

ALCOVE n recess in the wall of a room

ALCOVED adj with or in an alcove

ALCOVES > ALCOVE

ALDEA n Spanish village

ALDEAS > ALDEA

ALDEHYDE n one of a group of chemical compounds derived from alcohol by oxidation

ALDEHYDES > ALDEHYDE

ALDEHYDIC
> ALDEHYDE
ALDER n tree related to the birch
ALDERFLY n insect with large broad-based hind wings, which produces aquatic larvae
ALDERMAN n formerly, senior member of a local council
ALDERMEN > ALDERMAN
ALDERN adj made of alder wood
ALDERS > ALDER
ALDICARB n crystalline compound used as a pesticide
ALDICARBS
> ALDICARB
ALDOL n colourless or yellowish oily liquid
ALDOLASE n enzyme present in the body
ALDOLASES
> ALDOLASE
ALDOLS > ALDOL
ALDOSE n type of sugar
ALDOSES > ALDOSE
ALDOXIME n oxime formed by reaction between hydroxylamine and an aldehyde
ALDOXIMES
> ALDOXIME
ALDRIN n brown to white poisonous crystalline solid
ALDRINS > ALDRIN
ALE n kind of beer
ALEATORIC same as
> ALEATORY
ALEATORY adj dependent on chance
ALEBENCH n bench at alehouse
ALEC same as > ALECK
ALECITHAL adj (of an ovum) having little or no yolk
ALECK n irritatingly oversmart person
ALECKS > ALECK
ALECOST another name for
> COSTMARY
ALECOSTS > ALECOST
ALECS > ALEC
ALECTRYON n type of tree found in Australasia, SE Asia, and Micronesia
ALEE adj on or towards the lee
ALEF n first letter of Hebrew alphabet
ALEFS > ALEF
ALEFT adv at or to left
ALEGAR n malt vinegar
ALEGARS > ALEGAR
ALEGGE vb alleviate
ALEGGED > ALEGGE
ALEGGES > ALEGGE
ALEGGING > ALEGGE
ALEHOUSE n public house
ALEHOUSES
> ALEHOUSE
ALEMBIC n anything that distils
ALEMBICS > ALEMBIC

ALEMBROTH n mercury compound in alchemy
ALENCON n elaborate lace worked on a hexagonal mesh
ALENCONS > ALENCON
ALENGTH adv at length
ALEPH n first letter in the Hebrew alphabet
ALEPHS > ALEPH
ALEPINE n type of cloth
ALEPINES > ALEPINE
ALERCE n wood of the sandarac tree
ALERCES > ALERCE
ALERION n eagle in heraldry
ALERIONS > ALERION
ALERT adj watchful, attentive ▷ n warning of danger ▷ vb warn of danger
ALERTED > ALERT
ALERTER > ALERT
ALERTEST > ALERT
ALERTING > ALERT
ALERTLY > ALERT
ALERTNESS > ALERT
ALERTS > ALERT
ALES > ALE
ALETHIC adj of philosophical concepts
ALEURON n outer layer of seeds
ALEURONE same as
> ALEURON
ALEURONES
> ALEURONE
ALEURONIC > ALEURON
ALEURONS > ALEURON
ALEVIN n young fish, esp a young salmon or trout
ALEVINS > ALEVIN
ALEW n cry to call hunting hounds
ALEWASHED adj showing effects of beer drinking
ALEWIFE n North American fish
ALEWIVES > ALEWIFE
ALEWS > ALEW
ALEXANDER n cocktail made with creme de cacao
ALEXIA n disorder causing impaired ability to read
ALEXIAS > ALEXIA
ALEXIC > ALEXIA
ALEXIN n protein in blood serum
ALEXINE same as
> ALEXIN
ALEXINES > ALEXINE
ALEXINIC > ALEXIN
ALEXINS > ALEXIN
ALEYE vb allay
ALEYED > ALEYE
ALEYES > ALEYE
ALEYING > ALEYE
ALF n uncultivated Australian
ALFA n type of grass
ALFAKI same as
> ALFAQUI
ALFAKIS > ALFAKI
ALFALFA n kind of plant used to feed livestock
ALFALFAS > ALFALFA

ALFAQUI n expert in Muslim law
ALFAQUIN same as
> ALFAQUI
ALFAQUINS
> ALFAQUIN
ALFAQUIS > ALFAQUI
ALFAS > ALFA
ALFERECES > ALFEREZ
ALFEREZ n Spanish standard-bearer
ALFILARIA n plant with finely divided leaves and small pink or purplish flowers
ALFILERIA same as
> ALFILARIA
ALFORJA n saddlebag made of leather or canvas
ALFORJAS > ALFORJA
ALFREDO adj cooked with a cheese and egg sauce
ALFRESCO adj in the open air ▷ adv in the open air
ALFS > ALF
ALGA n multicellular organism
ALGAE > ALGA
ALGAECIDE n substance for killing algae
ALGAL > ALGA
ALGAROBA same as
> ALGARROBA
ALGAROBAS
> ALGARROBA
ALGARROBA n edible pod of these trees
ALGARROBO n carob
ALGAS > ALGA
ALGATE adv anyway
ALGATES adv anyway
ALGEBRA n branch of mathematics using symbols to represent numbers
ALGEBRAIC adj of or relating to algebra
ALGEBRAS > ALGEBRA
ALGERINE n soft striped woollen cloth
ALGERINES
> ALGERINE
ALGESES > ALGESIS
ALGESIA n capacity to feel pain
ALGESIAS > ALGESIA
ALGESIC > ALGESIA
ALGESIS n feeling of pain
ALGETIC > ALGESIA
ALGICIDAL
> ALGICIDE
ALGICIDE n any substance that kills algae
ALGICIDES
> ALGICIDE
ALGID adj chilly or cold
ALGIDITY > ALGID
ALGIDNESS > ALGID
ALGIN n seaweed solution
ALGINATE n salt or ester of alginic acid
ALGINATES
> ALGINATE
ALGINIC adj as in alginic acid powdery substance extracted from kelp

ALGINS > ALGIN
ALGOID adj resembling or relating to algae
ALGOLOGY n branch of biology concerned with the study of algae
ALGOMETER n instrument for measuring sensitivity to pressure or to pain
ALGOMETRY
> ALGOMETER
ALGOR n chill
ALGORISM n Arabic or decimal system of counting
ALGORISMS
> ALGORISM
ALGORITHM n logical arithmetical or computational procedure for solving a problem
ALGORS > ALGOR
ALGUACIL n Spanish law officer
ALGUACILS
> ALGUACIL
ALGUAZIL n Spanish law officer
ALGUAZILS
> ALGUAZIL
ALGUM n type of wood mentioned in Bible
ALGUMS > ALGUM
ALIAS adv also known as ▷ n false name ▷ vb give or assume an alias
ALIASED > ALIAS
ALIASES > ALIAS
ALIASING n error in a vision or sound signal
ALIASINGS
> ALIASING
ALIBI n plea of being somewhere else when a crime was committed ▷ vb provide someone with an alibi
ALIBIED > ALIBI
ALIBIES > ALIBI
ALIBIING > ALIBI
ALIBIS > ALIBI
ALIBLE adj nourishing
ALICANT n wine from Alicante in Spain
ALICANTS > ALICANT
ALICYCLIC adj (of an organic compound) having aliphatic properties, in spite of the presence of a ring of carbon atoms
ALIDAD same as
> ALIDADE
ALIDADE n surveying instrument
ALIDADES > ALIDADE
ALIDADS > ALIDAD
ALIEN adj foreign ▷ n foreigner ▷ vb transfer (property, etc) to another
ALIENABLE adj able to be transferred to another owner
ALIENAGE > ALIEN
ALIENAGES > ALIEN
ALIENATE vb cause to become hostile
ALIENATED > ALIENATE

ALIENATES
> ALIENATE
ALIENATOR n
> ALIENATE
ALIENED > ALIEN
ALIENEE n person to whom a transfer of property is made
ALIENEES > ALIENEE
ALIENER > ALIEN
ALIENERS > ALIEN
ALIENING > ALIEN
ALIENISM n old term for the study of mental illness
ALIENISMS
> ALIENISM
ALIENIST n old term for psychiatrist specializing in the legal aspects of mental illness
ALIENISTS
> ALIENIST
ALIENLY > ALIEN
ALIENNESS > ALIEN
ALIENOR n person who transfers property to another
ALIENORS > ALIENOR
ALIENS > ALIEN
ALIF n first letter of Arabic alphabet
ALIFORM adj wing-shaped
ALIFS > ALIF
ALIGARTA n alligator
ALIGARTAS
> ALIGARTA
ALIGHT vb step out of (a vehicle) ▷ adj on fire ▷ adv on fire
ALIGHTED > ALIGHT
ALIGHTING > ALIGHT
ALIGHTS > ALIGHT
ALIGN vb bring (a person or group) into agreement with the policy of another
ALIGNED > ALIGN
ALIGNER > ALIGN
ALIGNERS > ALIGN
ALIGNING > ALIGN
ALIGNMENT n arrangement in a straight line
ALIGNS > ALIGN
ALIKE adj like, similar ▷ adv in the same way
ALIKENESS > ALIKE
ALIMENT n something that nourishes the body ▷ vb support or sustain
ALIMENTAL > ALIMENT
ALIMENTED > ALIMENT
ALIMENTS > ALIMENT
ALIMONIED adj provided with alimony
ALIMONIES > ALIMONY
ALIMONY n allowance paid under a court order to a separated or divorced spouse
ALINE a rare spelling of
> ALIGN
ALINED > ALINE
ALINEMENT > ALINE
ALINER > ALINE
ALINERS > ALINE
ALINES > ALINE

ALINING > ALINE
ALIPED n bat-like creature ▷ adj having digits connected by a membrane
ALIPEDS > ALIPED
ALIPHATIC adj (of an organic compound) having an open chain structure
ALIQUANT adj denoting or belonging to a number that is not an exact divisor of a given number
ALIQUOT adj of or denoting an exact divisor of a number ▷ n exact divisor
ALIQUOTS > ALIQUOT
ALISMA n marsh plant
ALISMAS > ALISMA
ALISON same as
> ALYSSUM
ALISONS > ALISON
ALIST adj leaning over
ALIT rare past tense and past participle of
> ALIGHT
ALITERACY
> ALITERATE
ALITERATE n person who is able to read but disinclined to do so ▷ adj of or relating to aliterates
ALIUNDE adj from a source under consideration
ALIVE adj living, in existence
ALIVENESS > ALIVE
ALIYA same as > ALIYAH
ALIYAH n immigration to the Holy Land
ALIYAHS > ALIYAH
ALIYAS > ALIYA
ALIYOS n remission of sin in Jewish faith
ALIYOT > ALIYAH
ALIYOTH > ALIYAH
ALIZARI n madder plant from the Middle East
ALIZARIN n brownish-yellow powder or orange-red crystalline solid
ALIZARINE n alizarin
ALIZARINS
> ALIZARIN
ALIZARIS > ALIZARI
ALKAHEST n hypothetical universal solvent sought by alchemists
ALKAHESTS
> ALKAHEST
ALKALI n substance which combines with acid and neutralizes it to form a salt
ALKALIC adj (of rocks) containing large amounts of alkalis
ALKALIES > ALKALI
ALKALIFY vb make or become alkaline
ALKALIN adj alkaline
ALKALINE adj having the properties of or containing an alkali

ALKALIS > ALKALI
ALKALISE same as
> ALKALIZE
ALKALISED
> ALKALISE
ALKALISER
> ALKALISE
ALKALISES
> ALKALISE
ALKALIZE vb make alkaline
ALKALIZED
> ALKALIZE
ALKALIZER
> ALKALIZE
ALKALIZES
> ALKALIZE
ALKALOID n any of a group of organic compounds containing nitrogen
ALKALOIDS
> ALKALOID
ALKALOSES
> ALKALOSIS
ALKALOSIS n abnormal increase in the alkalinity of the blood and extracellular fluids
ALKALOTIC
> ALKALOSIS
ALKANE n saturated hydrocarbon
ALKANES > ALKANE
ALKANET n European plant whose roots yield a red dye
ALKANETS > ALKANET
ALKANNIN same as
> ALKANET
ALKANNINS
> ALKANNIN
ALKENE n unsaturated hydrocarbon
ALKENES > ALKENE
ALKIE same as > ALKY
ALKIES > ALKY
ALKINE n alkyne
ALKINES > ALKINE
ALKO n slang word for alcoholic
ALKOS > ALKO
ALKOXIDE n chemical compound containing oxygen
ALKOXIDES
> ALKOXIDE
ALKOXY adj of a type of chemical compound containing oxygen
ALKY n slang word for alcoholic
ALKYD n synthetic resin
ALKYDS > ALKYD
ALKYL n type of monovalent radical
ALKYLATE vb add alkyl group to a compound
ALKYLATED
> ALKYLATE
ALKYLATES
> ALKYLATE
ALKYLIC > ALKYL
ALKYLS > ALKYL
ALKYNE n any unsaturated aliphatic hydrocarbon
ALKYNES > ALKYNE

ALL adj whole quantity or number (of) ▷ adv wholly, entirely ▷ n entire being, effort, or property
ALLANITE n rare black or brown mineral
ALLANITES
> ALLANITE
ALLANTOIC
> ALLANTOIS
ALLANTOID adj relating to or resembling the allantois
ALLANTOIN n chemical used in cosmetics
ALLANTOIS n membranous sac growing out of the ventral surface of the hind gut of embryonic reptiles, birds, and mammals. It combines with the chorion to form the mammalian placenta
ALLATIVE n word in grammatical case denoting movement towards
ALLATIVES
> ALLATIVE
ALLAY vb reduce (fear or anger)
ALLAYED > ALLAY
ALLAYER > ALLAY
ALLAYERS > ALLAY
ALLAYING > ALLAY
ALLAYINGS > ALLAY
ALLAYMENT n mitigation
ALLAYS > ALLAY
ALLCOMERS n everyone who comes
ALLEDGE vb allege
ALLEDGED > ALLEDGE
ALLEDGES > ALLEDGE
ALLEDGING > ALLEDGE
ALLEE n avenue
ALLEES > ALLEE
ALLEGE vb state without proof
ALLEGED adj stated but not proved
ALLEGEDLY adv reportedly
ALLEGER > ALLEGE
ALLEGERS > ALLEGE
ALLEGES > ALLEGE
ALLEGGE vb alleviate
ALLEGGED > ALLEGGE
ALLEGGES > ALLEGGE
ALLEGGING > ALLEGGE
ALLEGIANT n loyalty
ALLEGING > ALLEGE
ALLEGORIC adj used in, containing, or characteristic of allegory
ALLEGORY n story with an underlying meaning as well as the literal one
ALLEGRO adv (to be played) in a brisk lively manner ▷ n piece or passage to be performed in a brisk lively manner
ALLEGROS > ALLEGRO
ALLEL n variant form of a gene
ALLELE n variant form of a gene

ALLELES > ALLELE
ALLELIC > ALLELE
ALLELISM > ALLELE
ALLELISMS > ALLELE
ALLELS > ALLEL
ALLELUIA n song of praise to God
ALLELUIAH interj alleluia
ALLELUIAS > ALLELUIA
ALLEMANDE n first movement of the classical suite, composed in a moderate tempo in a time signature of four-four
ALLENARLY adv solely
ALLERGEN n substance capable of causing an allergic reaction
ALLERGENS > ALLERGEN
ALLERGIC adj having or caused by an allergy ▷ n person with an allergy
ALLERGICS > ALLERGIC
ALLERGIES > ALLERGY
ALLERGIN n allergen
ALLERGINS > ALLERGIN
ALLERGIST n physician skilled in the diagnosis and treatment of diseases or conditions caused by allergy
ALLERGY n extreme sensitivity to a substance, which causes the body to react to it
ALLERION n eagle in heraldry
ALLERIONS > ALLERION
ALLETHRIN n clear viscous amber-coloured liquid
ALLEVIANT n medical treatment that reduces pain but does not cure the underlying problem
ALLEVIATE vb lessen (pain or suffering)
ALLEY n narrow street or path
ALLEYCAT n homeless cat that roams in back streets
ALLEYCATS > ALLEYCAT
ALLEYED adj having alleys
ALLEYS > ALLEY
ALLEYWAY n narrow passage with buildings or walls on both sides
ALLEYWAYS > ALLEYWAY
ALLHEAL n plant with reputed healing powers
ALLHEALS > ALLHEAL
ALLIABLE adj able to form an alliance
ALLIAK n Inuit sledge
ALLIAKS > ALLIAK
ALLIANCE n state of being allied
ALLIANCES > ALLIANCE
ALLICE n species of fish

ALLICES > ALLICE
ALLICHOLY n melancholy
ALLICIN n chemical found in garlic
ALLICINS > ALLICIN
ALLIED adj joined, as by treaty, agreement, or marriage
ALLIES > ALLY
ALLIGARTA n alligator
ALLIGATE vb join together
ALLIGATED > ALLIGATE
ALLIGATES > ALLIGATE
ALLIGATOR n reptile of the crocodile family, found in the southern US and China
ALLIS n species of fish
ALLISES > ALLIS
ALLIUM n type of plant
ALLIUMS > ALLIUM
ALLNESS n being all
ALLNESSES > ALLNESS
ALLNIGHT adj lasting all night
ALLOBAR n form of an element
ALLOBARS > ALLOBAR
ALLOCABLE > ALLOCATE
ALLOCARPY n production of fruit through cross-fertilization
ALLOCATE vb assign to someone or for a particular purpose
ALLOCATED > ALLOCATE
ALLOCATES > ALLOCATE
ALLOCATOR > ALLOCATE
ALLOD same as > ALLODIUM
ALLODIA > ALLODIUM
ALLODIAL adj (of land) held as an allodium
ALLODIUM n lands held free from rent or services due to an overlord
ALLODIUMS > ALLODIUM
ALLODS > ALLOD
ALLODYNIA n pain caused by a normally painless stimulus
ALLOGAMY n cross-fertilization in flowering plants
ALLOGENIC adj having different genes
ALLOGRAFT n tissue graft from a donor genetically unrelated to the recipient
ALLOGRAPH n document written by a person who is not a party to it
ALLOMERIC adj of similar crystalline structure
ALLOMETRY n study of the growth of part of an organism in relation to the growth of the entire organism

ALLOMONE n chemical substance secreted by certain animals
ALLOMONES > ALLOMONE
ALLOMORPH n any of the phonological representations of a single morpheme
ALLONGE n paper extension to bill of exchange ▷ vb (in fencing) lunge
ALLONGED > ALLONGE
ALLONGES > ALLONGE
ALLONGING > ALLONGE
ALLONS interj French word meaning let's go
ALLONYM n name assumed by a person
ALLONYMS > ALLONYM
ALLOPATH n person who practises or is skilled in allopathy
ALLOPATHS > ALLOPATH
ALLOPATHY n orthodox method of treating disease, by using drugs that produce an effect opposite to the effect of the disease being treated
ALLOPATRY n condition of taking place or existing in areas that are geographically separated from one another
ALLOPHANE n variously coloured amorphous mineral consisting of hydrated aluminium silicate and occurring in cracks in some sedimentary rocks
ALLOPHONE n any of several speech sounds that are regarded as contextual or environmental variants of the same phoneme
ALLOPLASM n part of the cytoplasm that is specialized to form cilia, flagella, and similar structures
ALLOSAUR n any large carnivorous bipedal dinosaur common in North America in late Jurassic times
ALLOSAURS > ALLOSAUR
ALLOSTERY n condition of an enzyme in which the structure and activity of the enzyme are modified by the binding of a metabolic molecule
ALLOT vb assign as a share or for a particular purpose
ALLOTMENT n distribution
ALLOTROPE n any of two or more physical forms in which an element can exist
ALLOTROPY n existence of an element in two or more physical forms

ALLOTS > ALLOT
ALLOTTED > ALLOT
ALLOTTEE n person to whom something is allotted
ALLOTTEES > ALLOTTEE
ALLOTTER n person who allots
ALLOTTERS > ALLOTTER
ALLOTTERY n something allotted
ALLOTTING > ALLOT
ALLOTYPE n type of specimen that differs from the original type
ALLOTYPES > ALLOTYPE
ALLOTYPIC > ALLOTYPE
ALLOTYPY n existence of allotypes
ALLOVER n fabric completely covered with a pattern
ALLOVERS > ALLOVER
ALLOW vb permit
ALLOWABLE adj permissible
ALLOWABLY > ALLOWABLE
ALLOWANCE n amount of money given at regular intervals
ALLOWED > ALLOW
ALLOWEDLY adv by general admission or agreement
ALLOWING > ALLOW
ALLOWS > ALLOW
ALLOXAN n chemical found in uric acid
ALLOXANS > ALLOXAN
ALLOY n mixture of two or more metals ▷ vb mix (metals)
ALLOYED > ALLOY
ALLOYING > ALLOY
ALLOYS > ALLOY
ALLOZYME n different form of an enzyme
ALLOZYMES > ALLOZYME
ALLS > ALL
ALLSEED n type of plant
ALLSEEDS > ALLSEED
ALLSORTS pl n assorted sweets
ALLSPICE n spice made from the berries of a tropical American tree
ALLSPICES > ALLSPICE
ALLUDE vb refer indirectly to
ALLUDED > ALLUDE
ALLUDES > ALLUDE
ALLUDING > ALLUDE
ALLURE n attractiveness ▷ vb entice or attract
ALLURED > ALLURE
ALLURER > ALLURE
ALLURERS > ALLURE
ALLURES > ALLURE
ALLURING adj extremely attractive
ALLUSION n indirect reference

ALLUSIONS
> ALLUSION

ALLUSIVE adj containing or full of allusions

ALLUVIA > ALLUVIUM

ALLUVIAL adj of or relating to alluvium ▷ n soil consisting of alluvium

ALLUVIALS
> ALLUVIAL

ALLUVION n wash of the sea or of a river

ALLUVIONS
> ALLUVION

ALLUVIUM n fertile soil deposited by flowing water

ALLUVIUMS
> ALLUVIUM

ALLY vb unite or be united, esp formally, as by treaty, confederation, or marriage ▷ n country, person, or group allied with another

ALLYING > ALLY

ALLYL n type of monovalent hydrocarbon

ALLYLIC > ALLYL

ALLYLS > ALLYL

ALLYOU pron all of you

ALMA same as > ALMAH

ALMAGEST n medieval treatise concerning alchemy or astrology

ALMAGESTS
> ALMAGEST

ALMAH n (in Egypt) female entertainer

ALMAHS > ALMAH

ALMAIN n German dance

ALMAINS > ALMAIN

ALMANAC n yearly calendar with detailed information on anniversaries, phases of the moon, etc

ALMANACK same as
> ALMANAC

ALMANACKS
> ALMANACK

ALMANACS > ALMANAC

ALMANDINE n deep violet-red garnet

ALMANDITE n form of garnet

ALMAS > ALMA

ALME same as > ALMEH

ALMEH n (in Egypt) female entertainer

ALMEHS > ALMEH

ALMEMAR n area in a synagogue

ALMEMARS > ALMEMAR

ALMERIES > ALMERY

ALMERY n cupboard for church vessels

ALMES > ALME

ALMIGHTY adj all-powerful ▷ adv extremely

ALMIRAH n cupboard

ALMIRAHS > ALMIRAH

ALMNER n almoner

ALMNERS > ALMNER

ALMOND n edible oval-shaped nut which grows on a small tree

ALMONDIER > ALMONDY

ALMONDITE n violet-red garnet

ALMONDS > ALMOND

ALMONDY adj containing or resembling almond

ALMONER n formerly, a hospital social worker

ALMONERS > ALMONER

ALMONRIES > ALMONRY

ALMONRY n house of an almoner, usually the place where alms were given

ALMOST adv very nearly

ALMOUS Scots word for
> ALMS

ALMS pl n gifts to the poor

ALMSGIVER n one who gives alms

ALMSHOUSE n (formerly) a house, financed by charity, which offered accommodation to the poor

ALMSMAN n man who gives or receives alms

ALMSMEN > ALMSMAN

ALMSWOMAN n woman who gives or receives alms

ALMSWOMEN
> ALMSWOMAN

ALMUCE n fur-lined hood or cape

ALMUCES > ALMUCE

ALMUD n Spanish unit of measure

ALMUDE same as > ALMUD

ALMUDES > ALMUDE

ALMUDS > ALMUD

ALMUG n type of wood mentioned in Bible

ALMUGS > ALMUG

ALNAGE n measurement in ells

ALNAGER n inspector of cloth

ALNAGERS > ALNAGER

ALNAGES > ALNAGE

ALNICO n alloy containing iron, nickel, and cobalt

ALNICOS > ALNICO

ALOCASIA n type of tropical plant

ALOCASIAS
> ALOCASIA

ALOD n feudal estate with no superior

ALODIA > ALODIUM

ALODIAL > ALODIUM

ALODIUM same as
> ALLODIUM

ALODIUMS > ALODIUM

ALODS > ALOD

ALOE n plant with fleshy spiny leaves

ALOED adj containing aloes

ALOES another name for
> EAGLEWOOD

ALOESWOOD n aromatic wood of an Asian tree

ALOETIC > ALOE

ALOETICS > ALOE

ALOFT adv in the air ▷ adj in or into a high or higher place

ALOGIA n inability to speak

ALOGIAS > ALOGIA

ALOGICAL adj without logic

ALOHA a Hawaiian word for
> HELLO

ALOHAS > ALOHA

ALOIN n crystalline compound

ALOINS > ALOIN

ALONE adv without anyone or anything else

ALONELY > ALONE

ALONENESS > ALONE

ALONG adv forward

ALONGSIDE adv beside (something)

ALONGST adv along

ALOO n (in Indian cookery) potato

ALOOF adj distant or haughty in manner

ALOOFLY > ALOOF

ALOOFNESS > ALOOF

ALOOS > ALOO

ALOPECIA n loss of hair

ALOPECIAS
> ALOPECIA

ALOPECIC > ALOPECIA

ALOPECOID n fox-like animal

ALOUD adv in an audible voice ▷ adj in a normal voice

ALOW adj in or into the lower rigging of a vessel, near the deck

ALOWE Scots word for
> ABLAZE

ALP n high mountain

ALPACA n Peruvian llama

ALPACAS > ALPACA

ALPACCA same as
> ALPACA

ALPACCAS > ALPACCA

ALPARGATA n Spanish sandal

ALPEEN n Irish cudgel

ALPEENS > ALPEEN

ALPENGLOW n reddish light on the summits of snow-covered mountain peaks at sunset or sunrise

ALPENHORN same as
> ALPHORN

ALPHA n first letter in the Greek alphabet

ALPHABET n set of letters used in writing a language

ALPHABETS
> ALPHABET

ALPHAS > ALPHA

ALPHASORT vb arrange in alphabetical order

ALPHATEST vb subject (an experimental product such as computer software) to an initial test

ALPHORN n wind instrument

ALPHORNS > ALPHORN

ALPHOSIS n absence of skin pigmentation, as in albinism

ALPHYL n univalent radical

ALPHYLS > ALPHYL

ALPINE adj of high mountains ▷ n mountain plant

ALPINELY > ALPINE

ALPINES > ALPINE

ALPINISM > ALPINIST

ALPINISMS
> ALPINIST

ALPINIST n mountain climber

ALPINISTS
> ALPINIST

ALPS > ALP

ALREADY adv before the present time

ALRIGHT adj all right

ALS > AL

ALSIKE n clover native to Europe and Asia

ALSIKES > ALSIKE

ALSO adv in addition, too

ALSOON same as
> ALSOONE

ALSOONE adv as soon

ALT n octave directly above the treble staff

ALTAR n table used for Communion in Christian churches

ALTARAGE n donations placed on altar for priest

ALTARAGES
> ALTARAGE

ALTARS > ALTAR

ALTARWISE adv in the position of an altar

ALTER vb make or become different

ALTERABLE > ALTER

ALTERABLY > ALTER

ALTERANT n alternative

ALTERANTS
> ALTERANT

ALTERCATE vb argue, esp heatedly

ALTERED > ALTER

ALTERER > ALTER

ALTERERS > ALTER

ALTERING > ALTER

ALTERITY n quality of being different

ALTERN adj alternate

ALTERNANT adj alternating

ALTERNAT n practice of deciding precedence by lot

ALTERNATE vb (cause to) occur by turns ▷ adj occurring by turns ▷ n person who substitutes for another in their absence

ALTERNATS
> ALTERNAT

ALTERNE n neighbouring but different plant group

ALTERNES > ALTERNE

ALTERS > ALTER

ALTESSE n French word for highness

ALTESSES > ALTESSE

ALTEZA n Spanish word for highness

ALTEZAS > ALTEZA

ALTEZZA n Italian word for highness

ALTEZZAS > ALTEZZA

ALTHAEA n type of plant

ALTHAEAS > ALTHAEA
ALTHEA same as
> ALTHAEA
ALTHEAS > ALTHAEA
ALTHO conj short form of
although
ALTHORN n valved brass
musical instrument
ALTHORNS > ALTHORN
ALTHOUGH conj despite
the fact that; even though
ALTIGRAPH n
instrument that measures
altitude
ALTIMETER n
instrument that measures
altitude
ALTIMETRY n science of
measuring altitudes, as
with an altimeter
ALTIPLANO n high
plateau
ALTISSIMO adj (of
music) very high in pitch
▷ n as in in altissimo the
octave commencing an
octave above the treble
clef
ALTITUDE n height
above sea level
ALTITUDES
> ALTITUDE
ALTO n (singer with) the
highest adult male voice
▷ adj denoting an
instrument, singer, or
voice with this range
ALTOIST n person who
plays the alto saxophone
ALTOISTS > ALTOIST
ALTOS > ALTO
ALTRICES pl n altricial
birds
ALTRICIAL adj (of the
young of some species of
birds after hatching)
naked, blind, and
dependent on the parents
for food ▷ n altricial bird,
such as a pigeon
ALTRUISM n unselfish
concern for the welfare of
others
ALTRUISMS
> ALTRUISM
ALTRUIST > ALTRUISM
ALTRUISTS
> ALTRUISM
ALTS > ALT
ALU same as > ALOO
ALUDEL n pear-shaped
vessel
ALUDELS > ALUDEL
ALULA n tuft of feathers
ALULAE > ALULA
ALULAR > ALULA
ALULAS > ALULA
ALUM n double sulphate of
aluminium and potassium
ALUMIN same as
> ALUMINA
ALUMINA n aluminium
oxide
ALUMINAS > ALUMINA
ALUMINATE n salt of the
ortho or meta acid forms
of aluminium hydroxide
ALUMINE n French word
for alumina

ALUMINES > ALUMINE
ALUMINIC adj of
aluminium
ALUMINIDE n type of
aluminium compound
ALUMINISE same as
> ALUMINIZE
ALUMINIUM n light
silvery-white metal that
does not rust
ALUMINIZE vb cover
with aluminium
ALUMINOUS adj
resembling aluminium
ALUMINS > ALUMIN
ALUMINUM same as
> ALUMINIUM
ALUMINUMS
> ALUMINUM
ALUMISH adj like alum
ALUMIUM old name for
> ALUMINIUM
ALUMIUMS > ALUMIUM
ALUMNA n female
graduate of a school,
college, etc
ALUMNAE > ALUMNA
ALUMNI > ALUMNUS
ALUMNUS n graduate of a
college
ALUMROOT n North
American plant
ALUMROOTS
> ALUMROOT
ALUMS > ALUM
ALUMSTONE same as
> ALUNITE
ALUNITE n white, grey,
or reddish mineral
ALUNITES > ALUNITE
ALURE n area behind
battlements
ALURES > ALURE
ALUS > ALU
ALVAR n area of exposed
limestone
ALVARS > ALVAR
ALVEARIES > ALVEARY
ALVEARY n beehive
ALVEATED adj with
vaults like beehive
ALVEOLAR adj
articulated with the
alveoli ▷ n alveolar
consonant
ALVEOLARS
> ALVEOLAR
ALVEOLATE adj having
many alveoli
ALVEOLE n alveolus
ALVEOLES > ALVEOLE
ALVEOLI > ALVEOLUS
ALVEOLUS n sockets in
which the roots of teeth
are embedded
ALVINE adj of or relating
to the intestines or
belly
ALWAY same as > ALWAYS
ALWAYS adv at all times
ALYSSUM n garden plant
with small yellow or white
flowers
ALYSSUMS > ALYSSUM
AM vb form of the present
tense of be
AMA n vessel for water
AMABILE adj sweet

AMADAVAT same as
> AVADAVAT
AMADAVATS
> AMADAVAT
AMADODA pl n South
African word meaning
grown men
AMADOU n spongy
substance made from
fungi
AMADOUS > AMADOU
AMAH n (in East Asia,
formerly) a nurse or
maidservant
AMAHS > AMAH
AMAIN adv with great
strength, speed, or haste
AMAKHOSI > INKHOSI
AMAKOSI > INKHOSI
AMALGAM n blend or
combination
AMALGAMS > AMALGAM
AMANDINE n almond
found in almonds
AMANDINES
> AMANDINE
AMANDLA n political
slogan calling for power to
the Black population
AMANDLAS > AMANDLA
AMANITA n type of
fungus
AMANITAS > AMANITA
AMANITIN n poison from
amanita
AMANITINS
> AMANITIN
AMARACUS n marjoram
AMARANT n amaranth
AMARANTH n imaginary
flower that never fades
AMARANTHS
> AMARANTH
AMARANTIN n protein
AMARANTS > AMARANT
AMARELLE n variety of
sour cherry that has pale
red fruit and colourless
juice
AMARELLES
> AMARELLE
AMARETTI > AMARETTO
AMARETTO n Italian
liqueur with a flavour of
almonds
AMARETTOS
> AMARETTO
AMARNA adj pertaining to
the reign of the Pharaoh
Akhenaton
AMARONE n strong dry red
Italian wine
AMARONES > AMARONE
AMARYLLID n plant of
the amaryllis family
AMARYLLIS n lily-like
plant with large red, pink,
or white flowers
AMAS > AMA
AMASS vb collect or
accumulate
AMASSABLE > AMASS
AMASSED > AMASS
AMASSER > AMASS
AMASSERS > AMASS
AMASSES > AMASS
AMASSING > AMASS
AMASSMENT > AMASS

AMATE vb match
AMATED > AMATE
AMATES > AMATE
AMATEUR n person who
engages in a sport or
activity as a pastime
rather than as a profession
▷ adj not professional
AMATEURS > AMATEUR
AMATING > AMATE
AMATION n lovemaking
AMATIONS > AMATION
AMATIVE a rare word for
> AMOROUS
AMATIVELY > AMATIVE
AMATOL n explosive
mixture
AMATOLS > AMATOL
AMATORIAL same as
> AMATORY
AMATORIAN > AMATORY
AMATORY adj relating to
love
AMAUROSES
> AMAUROSIS
AMAUROSIS n blindness,
esp when occurring
without observable
damage to the eye
AMAUROTIC
> AMAUROSIS
AMAUT n hooded coat
worn by Inuit women
AMAUTI same as > AMAUT
AMAUTIK same as
> AMAUT
AMAUTIKS > AMAUTIK
AMAUTIS > AMAUTI
AMAUTS > AMAUT
AMAZE vb surprise greatly,
astound
AMAZED > AMAZE
AMAZEDLY > AMAZE
AMAZEMENT n incredulity
or great astonishment
AMAZES > AMAZE
AMAZING adj causing
wonder or astonishment
AMAZINGLY > AMAZING
AMAZON n any tall, strong,
or aggressive woman
AMAZONIAN > AMAZON
AMAZONITE n green
variety of microcline used
as a gemstone
AMAZONS > AMAZON
AMBACH same as
> AMBATCH
AMBACHES > AMBACH
AMBAGE n ambiguity
AMBAGES > AMBAGE
AMBAGIOUS > AMBAGE
AMBAN n Chinese official
AMBANS > AMBAN
AMBARI same as
> AMBARY
AMBARIES > AMBARY
AMBARIS > AMBARI
AMBARY n tropical Asian
plant that yields a fibre
similar to jute
AMBASSAGE n embassy
AMBASSIES > AMBASSY
AMBASSY n embassy
AMBATCH n tree or shrub
AMBATCHES > AMBATCH
AMBEER n saliva coloured
by tobacco juice

AMBEERS > AMBEER
AMBER n clear yellowish fossil resin ▷ adj brownish-yellow
AMBERED adj fixed in amber
AMBERGRIS n waxy substance secreted by the sperm whale, used in making perfumes
AMBERIER > AMBERY
AMBERIES > AMBERY
AMBERIEST > AMBERY
AMBERINA n type of glassware
AMBERINAS > AMBERINA
AMBERITE n powder like amber
AMBERITES > AMBERITE
AMBERJACK n type of large fish with golden markings when young, found in Atlantic waters
AMBEROID n synthetic amber
AMBEROIDS > AMBEROID
AMBEROUS adj like amber
AMBERS > AMBER
AMBERY adj like amber ▷ n cupboard in the wall of a church
AMBIANCE same as > AMBIENCE
AMBIANCES > AMBIANCE
AMBIENCE n atmosphere of a place
AMBIENCES > AMBIENCE
AMBIENT adj surrounding ▷ n ambient music
AMBIENTS > AMBIENT
AMBIGUITY n possibility of interpreting an expression in more than one way
AMBIGUOUS adj having more than one possible meaning
AMBIPOLAR adj (of plasmas and semiconductors) involving both positive and negative charge carriers
AMBIT n limits or boundary
AMBITION n desire for success
AMBITIONS > AMBITION
AMBITIOUS adj having a strong desire for success
AMBITS > AMBIT
AMBITTY adj crystalline and brittle
AMBIVERT n person who is intermediate between an extrovert and an introvert
AMBIVERTS > AMBIVERT
AMBLE vb walk at a leisurely pace ▷ n leisurely walk or pace
AMBLED > AMBLE
AMBLER > AMBLE

AMBLERS > AMBLE
AMBLES > AMBLE
AMBLING n walking at a leisurely pace
AMBLINGS > AMBLING
AMBLYOPIA n impaired vision with no discernible damage to the eye or optic nerve
AMBLYOPIC > AMBLYOPIA
AMBO n early Christian pulpit
AMBOINA same as > AMBOYNA
AMBOINAS > AMBOINA
AMBONES > AMBO
AMBOS > AMBO
AMBOYNA n mottled curly-grained wood
AMBOYNAS > AMBOYNA
AMBRIES > AMBRY
AMBROID same as > AMBEROID
AMBROIDS > AMBROID
AMBROSIA n anything delightful to taste or smell
AMBROSIAL > AMBROSIA
AMBROSIAN > AMBROSIA
AMBROSIAS > AMBROSIA
AMBROTYPE n early type of glass negative that could be made to appear as a positive by backing it with black varnish or paper
AMBRY n cupboard in the wall of a church
AMBSACE n double ace, the lowest throw at dice
AMBSACES > AMBSACE
AMBULACRA n radial bands on the ventral surface of echinoderms, such as the starfish and sea urchin, on which the tube feet are situated
AMBULANCE n motor vehicle designed to carry sick or injured people
AMBULANT adj moving about from place to place
AMBULANTS > AMBULANT
AMBULATE vb wander about or move from one place to another
AMBULATED > AMBULATE
AMBULATES > AMBULATE
AMBULATOR n person who walks
AMBULETTE n motor vehicle designed for transporting ill or disabled people
AMBUSCADE n ambush ▷ vb ambush or lie in ambush
AMBUSCADO n ambuscade
AMBUSH n act of waiting in a concealed position to make a surprise attack ▷ vb attack from a concealed position

AMBUSHED > AMBUSH
AMBUSHER > AMBUSH
AMBUSHERS > AMBUSH
AMBUSHES > AMBUSH
AMBUSHING > AMBUSH
AME n soul
AMEARST old form of > AMERCE
AMEBA same as > AMOEBA
AMEBAE > AMEBA
AMEBAN > AMEBA
AMEBAS > AMEBA
AMEBEAN same as > AMOEBEAN
AMEBIASES > AMEBIASIS
AMEBIASIS n disease caused by amoeba
AMEBIC > AMEBA
AMEBOCYTE n any cell having properties similar to an amoeba, such as shape, mobility, and ability to engulf particles
AMEBOID same as > AMOEBOID
AMEER n (formerly) the ruler of Afghanistan
AMEERATE n country ruled by an ameer
AMEERATES > AMEERATE
AMEERS > AMEER
AMEIOSES > AMEIOSIS
AMEIOSIS n absence of pairing of chromosomes during meiosis
AMELCORN n variety of wheat
AMELCORNS > AMELCORN
AMELIA n congenital absence of arms or legs
AMELIAS > AMELIA
AMEN n term used at the end of a prayer or religious statement ▷ vb say amen
AMENABLE adj likely or willing to cooperate
AMENABLY > AMENABLE
AMENAGE vb tame
AMENAGED > AMENAGE
AMENAGES > AMENAGE
AMENAGING > AMENAGE
AMENAUNCE n person's bearing
AMEND vb make small changes
AMENDABLE > AMEND
AMENDE n public apology
AMENDED > AMEND
AMENDER > AMEND
AMENDERS > AMEND
AMENDES > AMENDE
AMENDING > AMEND
AMENDMENT n improvement or correction
AMENDS n recompense for injury, insult, etc
AMENE adj pleasant
AMENED > AMEN
AMENING > AMEN
AMENITIES > AMENITY
AMENITY n useful or enjoyable feature
AMENS > AMEN
AMENT n catkin

AMENTA > AMENTUM
AMENTAL > AMENTUM
AMENTIA n old word for congenital learning disability
AMENTIAS > AMENTIA
AMENTS > AMENT
AMENTUM same as > AMENT
AMERCE vb punish by a fine
AMERCED > AMERCE
AMERCER > AMERCE
AMERCERS > AMERCE
AMERCES > AMERCE
AMERCING > AMERCE
AMERICIUM n white metallic element artificially produced from plutonium
AMES > AME
AMESACE same as > AMBSACE
AMESACES > AMESACE
AMETHYST n bluish-violet variety of quartz used as a gemstone ▷ adj purple or violet
AMETHYSTS > AMETHYST
AMETROPIA n loss of ability to focus images on the retina, caused by an imperfection in the refractive function of the eye
AMETROPIC > AMETROPIA
AMI n male friend
AMIA n species of fish
AMIABLE adj friendly, pleasant-natured
AMIABLY > AMIABLE
AMIANTHUS n any of the fine silky varieties of asbestos
AMIANTUS n amianthus
AMIAS > AMIA
AMICABLE adj friendly
AMICABLY > AMICABLE
AMICE n item of clothing
AMICES > AMICE
AMICI > AMICUS
AMICUS n Latin for friend
AMID prep in the middle of, among
AMIDASE n enzyme
AMIDASES > AMIDASE
AMIDE n type of organic compound
AMIDES > AMIDE
AMIDIC > AMIDE
AMIDIN n form of starch
AMIDINE n crystalline compound
AMIDINES > AMIDINE
AMIDINS > AMIDIN
AMIDMOST adv in the middle
AMIDO adj containing amide
AMIDOGEN n chemical compound derived from ammonia
AMIDOGENS > AMIDOGEN
AMIDOL n chemical used in developing photographs

AMIDOLS > AMIDOL
AMIDONE *n* pain-killing drug
AMIDONES > AMIDONE
AMIDS *same as* > AMID
AMIDSHIP *adj* in the middle of a ship
AMIDSHIPS *adv* at or towards the middle of a ship ▷ *adj* at, near, or towards the middle of a ship
AMIDST *same as* > AMID
AMIE *n* female friend
AMIES > AMIE
AMIGA *n* female friend
AMIGAS > AMIGA
AMIGO *n* friend
AMIGOS > AMIGO
AMILDAR *n* manager in India
AMILDARS > AMILDAR
AMIN *same as* > AMINE
AMINE *n* chemical
AMINES > AMINE
AMINIC > AMINE
AMINITIES > AMINITY
AMINITY *n* amenity
AMINO *n* type of organic compound present in amino acids
AMINOS > AMINO
AMINS > AMIN
AMIR *n* (formerly) the ruler of Afghanistan
AMIRATE > AMIR
AMIRATES > AMIR
AMIRS > AMIR
AMIS *archaic form of* > AMICE
AMISES > AMIS
AMISS *adv* wrongly, badly ▷ *adj* wrong, faulty ▷ *n* evil deed
AMISSES > AMISS
AMISSIBLE *adj* likely to be lost
AMISSING *adj* missing
AMITIES > AMITY
AMITOSES > AMITOSIS
AMITOSIS *n* unusual form of cell division
AMITOTIC > AMITOSIS
AMITROLE *n* pesticide
AMITROLES > AMITROLE
AMITY *n* friendship
AMLA *n* species of Indian tree
AMLAS > AMLA
AMMAN *same as* > AMTMAN
AMMANS > AMMAN
AMMETER *n* instrument for measuring electric current
AMMETERS > AMMETER
AMMINE *n* chemical compound
AMMINES > AMMINE
AMMINO *adj* containing ammonia molecules
AMMIRAL *old word for* > ADMIRAL
AMMIRALS > AMMIRAL
AMMO *n* ammunition
AMMOCETE *n* ammocoete
AMMOCETES > AMMOCETE

AMMOCOETE *n* larva of primitive jawless vertebrates, such as the lamprey, that lives buried in mud and feeds on microorganisms
AMMOLITE *n* fossilized ammonite shell
AMMOLITES > AMMOLITE
AMMON *n* Asian wild sheep
AMMONAL *n* explosive
AMMONALS > AMMONAL
AMMONATE *same as* > AMMINE
AMMONATES > AMMONATE
AMMONIA *n* strong-smelling alkaline gas containing hydrogen and nitrogen
AMMONIAC *n* strong-smelling gum resin obtained from the stems of a N Asian plant
AMMONIACS > AMMONIAC
AMMONIAS > AMMONIA
AMMONIATE *vb* unite or treat with ammonia
AMMONIC *adj* of ammonia
AMMONICAL > AMMONIC
AMMONIFY *vb* treat or impregnate with ammonia or a compound of ammonia
AMMONITE *n* fossilized spiral shell of an extinct sea creature
AMMONITES > AMMONITE
AMMONITIC > AMMONITE
AMMONIUM *n* type of monovalent chemical group
AMMONIUMS > AMMONIUM
AMMONO *adj* using ammonia
AMMONOID *n* type of fossil
AMMONOIDS > AMMONOID
AMMONS > AMMON
AMMOS > AMMO
AMNESIA *n* loss of memory
AMNESIAC > AMNESIA
AMNESIACS > AMNESIA
AMNESIAS > AMNESIA
AMNESIC > AMNESIA
AMNESICS > AMNESIA
AMNESTIC *adj* relating to amnesia
AMNESTIED > AMNESTY
AMNESTIES > AMNESTY
AMNESTY *n* general pardon for offences against a government ▷ *vb* overlook or forget (an offence)
AMNIA > AMNION
AMNIC *adj* relating to amnion
AMNIO *n* amniocentesis
AMNION *n* innermost of two membranes enclosing an embryo

AMNIONIC > AMNION
AMNIONS > AMNION
AMNIOS > AMNIO
AMNIOTE *n* group of animals
AMNIOTES > AMNIOTE
AMNIOTIC *adj* of or relating to the amnion
AMNIOTOMY *n* breaking of the membrane surrounding a fetus to induce labour
AMOEBA *n* microscopic single-celled animal able to change its shape
AMOEBAE > AMOEBA
AMOEBAEAN *adj* of or relating to lines of verse dialogue that answer each other alternately
AMOEBAN > AMOEBA
AMOEBAS > AMOEBA
AMOEBEAN *same as* > AMOEBAEAN
AMOEBIC > AMOEBA
AMOEBOID *adj* of, related to, or resembling amoebae
AMOK *n* frenzied state
AMOKS > AMOK
AMOKURA *n* type of sea bird
AMOKURAS > AMOKURA
AMOLE *n* American plant
AMOLES > AMOLE
AMOMUM *n* plant of the ginger family
AMOMUMS > AMOMUM
AMONG *prep* in the midst of
AMONGST *same as* > AMONG
AMOOVE *vb* stir someone's emotions
AMOOVED > AMOOVE
AMOOVES > AMOOVE
AMOOVING > AMOOVE
AMORAL *adj* without moral standards
AMORALISM > AMORAL
AMORALIST > AMORAL
AMORALITY > AMORAL
AMORALLY > AMORAL
AMORANCE *n* condition of being in love
AMORANCES > AMORANCE
AMORANT > AMORANCE
AMORCE *n* small percussion cap
AMORCES > AMORCE
AMORET *n* sweetheart
AMORETS > AMORET
AMORETTI > AMORETTO
AMORETTO *n* (esp in painting) a small chubby naked boy representing a cupid
AMORETTOS > AMORETTO
AMORINI > AMORINO
AMORINO *same as* > AMORETTO
AMORISM > AMORIST
AMORISMS > AMORIST
AMORIST *n* lover or a writer about love
AMORISTIC > AMORIST
AMORISTS > AMORIST

AMORNINGS *adv* each morning
AMOROSA *n* lover
AMOROSAS > AMOROSA
AMOROSITY *n* quality of being amorous
AMOROSO *adv* (to be played) lovingly ▷ *n* sherry
AMOROSOS > AMOROSO
AMOROUS *adj* feeling, showing, or relating to love
AMOROUSLY > AMOROUS
AMORPHISM > AMORPHOUS
AMORPHOUS *adj* without distinct shape
AMORT *adj* in low spirits
AMORTISE *same as* > AMORTIZE
AMORTISED > AMORTIZE
AMORTISES > AMORTIZE
AMORTIZE *vb* pay off (a debt) gradually by periodic transfers to a sinking fund
AMORTIZED > AMORTIZE
AMORTIZES > AMORTIZE
AMOSITE *n* form of asbestos
AMOSITES > AMOSITE
AMOTION *n* act of removing
AMOTIONS > AMOTION
AMOUNT *n* extent or quantity ▷ *vb* be equal or add up to
AMOUNTED > AMOUNT
AMOUNTING > AMOUNT
AMOUNTS > AMOUNT
AMOUR *n* love affair
AMOURETTE *n* minor love affair
AMOURS > AMOUR
AMOVE *vb* stir someone's emotions
AMOVED > AMOVE
AMOVES > AMOVE
AMOVING > AMOVE
AMOWT *same as* > AMAUT
AMOWTS > AMOWT
AMP *n* ampere ▷ *vb* excite or become excited
AMPACITY *n* ampere capacity of a conductor
AMPASSIES > AMPASSY
AMPASSY *n* ampersand
AMPED > AMP
AMPERAGE *n* strength of an electric current measured in amperes
AMPERAGES > AMPERAGE
AMPERE *n* basic unit of electric current
AMPERES > AMPERE
AMPERSAND *n* character (&), meaning and
AMPERZAND *n* ampersand
AMPHIBIA *n* class of amphibians
AMPHIBIAN *n* type of animal that lives on land but breeds in water

a

AMPHIBOLE n any of a large group of minerals consisting of the silicates of calcium, iron, magnesium, sodium, and aluminium

AMPHIBOLY n ambiguity of expression, esp where due to a grammatical construction

AMPHIGORY n piece of nonsensical writing in verse or, less commonly, prose

AMPHIOXI
> AMPHIOXUS

AMPHIOXUS another name for the > LANCELET

AMPHIPATH adj of or relating to a molecule that possesses both hydrophobic and hydrophilic elements

AMPHIPOD n type of marine or freshwater crustacean with a flat body

AMPHIPODS
> AMPHIPOD

AMPHOLYTE n electrolyte that can be acid or base

AMPHORA n two-handled ancient Greek or Roman jar

AMPHORAE > AMPHORA

AMPHORAL > AMPHORA

AMPHORAS > AMPHORA

AMPHORIC adj resembling the sound of blowing into a bottle

AMPING > AMP

AMPLE adj more than sufficient

AMPLENESS > AMPLE

AMPLER > AMPLE

AMPLEST > AMPLE

AMPLEXUS n mating in amphibians

AMPLIDYNE n magnetic amplifier

AMPLIFIED > AMPLIFY

AMPLIFIER n device used to amplify a current or sound signal

AMPLIFIES > AMPLIFY

AMPLIFY vb increase the strength of (a current or sound signal)

AMPLITUDE n greatness of extent

AMPLOSOME n stocky body type

AMPLY adv fully or generously

AMPOULE n small sealed glass vessel

AMPOULES > AMPOULE

AMPS > AMP

AMPUL n ampoule

AMPULE same as
> AMPOULE

AMPULES > AMPULE

AMPULLA n dilated end part of certain tubes in the body

AMPULLAE > AMPULLA

AMPULLAR > AMPULLA

AMPULLARY > AMPULLA

AMPULS > AMPUL

AMPUTATE vb cut off (a limb or part of a limb) for medical reasons

AMPUTATED
> AMPUTATE

AMPUTATES
> AMPUTATE

AMPUTATOR
> AMPUTATE

AMPUTEE n person who has had a limb amputated

AMPUTEES > AMPUTEE

AMREETA same as
> AMRITA

AMREETAS > AMREETA

AMRIT n liquid used in the Amrit Ceremony

AMRITA n ambrosia of the gods that bestows immortality

AMRITAS > AMRITA

AMRITS > AMRIT

AMSINCKIA n Californian herb

AMTMAN n magistrate in parts of Europe

AMTMANS > AMTMAN

AMTRAC n amphibious tracked vehicle

AMTRACK same as
> AMTRAC

AMTRACKS > AMTRACK

AMTRACS > AMTRAC

AMTRAK same as
> AMTRAC

AMTRAKS > AMTRAK

AMU n unit of mass

AMUCK same as > AMOK

AMUCKS > AMUCK

AMULET n something carried or worn as a protection against evil

AMULETIC > AMULET

AMULETS > AMULET

AMUS > AMU

AMUSABLE adj capable of being amused

AMUSE vb cause to laugh or smile

AMUSEABLE same as
> AMUSABLE

AMUSED > AMUSE

AMUSEDLY > AMUSE

AMUSEMENT n state of being amused

AMUSER > AMUSE

AMUSERS > AMUSE

AMUSES > AMUSE

AMUSETTE n type of light cannon

AMUSETTES
> AMUSETTE

AMUSIA n inability to recognize musical tones

AMUSIAS > AMUSIA

AMUSIC > AMUSIA

AMUSING adj mildly entertaining

AMUSINGLY > AMUSING

AMUSIVE adj deceptive

AMYGDAL n almond

AMYGDALA n almond-shaped part, such as a tonsil or a lobe of the cerebellum

AMYGDALAE
> AMYGDALA

AMYGDALE n small hole in volcanic rock filled with minerals

AMYGDALES
> AMYGDALE

AMYGDALIN n white soluble bitter-tasting crystalline glycoside extracted from bitter almonds

AMYGDALS > AMYGDAL

AMYGDULE same as
> AMYGDALE

AMYGDULES
> AMYGDULE

AMYL n chemical compound

AMYLASE n enzyme

AMYLASES > AMYLASE

AMYLENE another name (no longer in technical usage) for > PENTENE

AMYLENES > AMYLENE

AMYLIC adj of or derived from amyl

AMYLOGEN n soluble part of starch

AMYLOGENS
> AMYLOGEN

AMYLOID n complex protein ▷ adj starchlike

AMYLOIDAL > AMYLOID

AMYLOIDS > AMYLOID

AMYLOPSIN n enzyme of the pancreatic juice that converts starch into sugar

AMYLOSE n type of chemical

AMYLOSES > AMYLOSE

AMYLS > AMYL

AMYLUM another name for > STARCH

AMYLUMS > AMYLUM

AMYOTONIA another name for > MYOTONIA

AMYTAL n as in sodium amytal type of sedative

AMYTALS > AMYTAL

AN adj form of a used before vowels ▷ n additional condition

ANA adv in equal quantities ▷ n collection of reminiscences

ANABAENA n type of freshwater alga

ANABAENAS
> ANABAENA

ANABANTID n type of spiny-finned fish of the family which includes the fighting fish, climbing perch, and gourami

ANABAS n type of fish

ANABASES > ANABASIS

ANABASIS n military expedition to the interior of a country

ANABATIC adj (of air currents) rising upwards, esp up slopes

ANABIOSES
> ANABIOSIS

ANABIOSIS n ability to return to life after apparent death

ANABIOTIC
> ANABIOSIS

ANABLEPS n type of tropical freshwater fish with eyes adapted for seeing both in air and water

ANABOLIC adj of or relating to anabolism

ANABOLISM n metabolic process in which body tissues are synthesized from food

ANABOLITE n product of anabolism

ANABRANCH n stream that leaves a river and enters it again further downstream

ANACHARIS n water plant

ANACLINAL adj (of valleys and similar formations) progressing in a direction opposite to the dip of the surrounding rock strata

ANACLISES
> ANACLITIC

ANACLISIS
> ANACLITIC

ANACLITIC adj of or relating to relationships that are characterized by the strong dependence of one person on others or another

ANACONDA n large S American snake

ANACONDAS
> ANACONDA

ANACRUSES
> ANACRUSIS

ANACRUSIS n one or more unstressed syllables at the beginning of a line of verse

ANADEM n garland for the head

ANADEMS > ANADEM

ANAEMIA n deficiency in the number of red blood cells

ANAEMIAS > ANAEMIA

ANAEMIC adj having anaemia

ANAEROBE n organism that does not require oxygen

ANAEROBES
> ANAEROBE

ANAEROBIA same as
> ANAEROBES

ANAEROBIC adj not requiring oxygen

ANAGEN n phase of hair growth

ANAGENS > ANAGEN

ANAGLYPH n type of stereoscopic picture

ANAGLYPHS
> ANAGLYPH

ANAGLYPHY
> ANAGLYPH

ANAGOGE n allegorical interpretation

ANAGOGES > ANAGOGE

ANAGOGIC > ANAGOGE

ANAGOGIES > ANAGOGY

ANAGOGY same as
> ANAGOGE

ANAGRAM n word or phrase made by rearranging the letters of another word or phrase

ANAGRAMS > ANAGRAM

ANAL adj of the anus

ANALCIME same as
> ANALCITE

ANALCIMES
> ANALCIME

ANALCIMIC
> ANALCIME

ANALCITE n white, grey, or colourless zeolite mineral

ANALCITES
> ANALCITE

ANALECTA same as
> ANALECTS

ANALECTIC
> ANALECTS

ANALECTS pl n selected literary passages from one or more works

ANALEMMA n scale shaped like a figure of eight

ANALEMMAS
> ANALEMMA

ANALEPTIC adj (of a drug, etc) stimulating the central nervous system ▷ n any drug, such as doxapram, that stimulates the central nervous system

ANALGESIA n absence of pain

ANALGESIC adj (drug) relieving pain ▷ n drug that relieves pain

ANALGETIC n painkilling drug

ANALGIA same as
> ANALGESIA

ANALGIAS > ANALGIA

ANALITIES > ANALITY

ANALITY n quality of being psychologically anal

ANALLY > ANAL

ANALOG same as
> ANALOGUE

ANALOGA > ANALOGON

ANALOGIC > ANALOGY

ANALOGIES > ANALOGY

ANALOGISE same as
> ANALOGIZE

ANALOGISM
> ANALOGIZE

ANALOGIST > ANALOGY

ANALOGIZE vb use analogy

ANALOGON n analogue

ANALOGONS
> ANALOGON

ANALOGOUS adj similar in some respects

ANALOGS > ANALOG

ANALOGUE n something that is similar in some respects to something else ▷ adj displaying information by means of a dial

ANALOGUES
> ANALOGUE

ANALOGY n similarity in some respects

ANALYSAND n any person who is undergoing psychoanalysis

ANALYSE vb make an analysis of (something)

ANALYSED > ANALYSE

ANALYSER > ANALYSE

ANALYSERS > ANALYSE

ANALYSES > ANALYSIS

ANALYSING > ANALYSE

ANALYSIS n separation of a whole into its parts for study and interpretation

ANALYST n person skilled in analysis

ANALYSTS > ANALYST

ANALYTE n substance that is being analysed

ANALYTES > ANALYTE

ANALYTIC adj relating to analysis ▷ n analytical logic

ANALYTICS
> ANALYTIC

ANALYZE same as
> ANALYSE

ANALYZED > ANALYZE

ANALYZER > ANALYZE

ANALYZERS > ANALYZE

ANALYZES > ANALYZE

ANALYZING > ANALYZE

ANAMNESES
> ANAMNESIS

ANAMNESIS n ability to recall past events

ANAMNIOTE n any vertebrate animal, such as a fish or amphibian, that lacks an amnion, chorion, and allantois during embryonic development

ANAN interj expression of failure to understand

ANANA n pineapple

ANANAS n plant related to the pineapple

ANANASES > ANANAS

ANANDA n Buddhist principle of extreme happiness

ANANDAS > ANANDA

ANANDROUS adj (of flowers) having no stamens

ANANKE n unalterable necessity

ANANKES > ANANKE

ANANTHOUS adj (of higher plants) having no flowers

ANAPAEST n metrical foot of three syllables, the first two short, the last long

ANAPAESTS
> ANAPAEST

ANAPEST same as
> ANAPAEST

ANAPESTIC > ANAPEST

ANAPESTS > ANAPEST

ANAPHASE n third stage of mitosis

ANAPHASES
> ANAPHASE

ANAPHASIC
> ANAPHASE

ANAPHOR n word referring back to a previous word

ANAPHORA n use of a word that has the same reference as a word used previously

ANAPHORAL
> ANAPHORA

ANAPHORAS
> ANAPHORA

ANAPHORIC adj of or relating to anaphorism

ANAPHORS > ANAPHOR

ANAPLASIA n reversion of plant or animal cells to a simpler less differentiated form

ANAPLASTY n plastic surgery

ANAPTYXES
> ANAPTYXIS

ANAPTYXIS n insertion of a short vowel between consonants in order to make a word more easily pronounceable

ANARCH n instigator or personification of anarchy

ANARCHAL > ANARCHY

ANARCHIAL > ANARCHY

ANARCHIC > ANARCHY

ANARCHIES > ANARCHY

ANARCHISE vb make anarchic

ANARCHISM n doctrine advocating the abolition of government

ANARCHIST n person who advocates the abolition of government

ANARCHIZE vb make anarchic

ANARCHS > ANARCH

ANARCHY n lawlessness and disorder

ANARTHRIA n loss of the ability to speak coherently

ANARTHRIC
> ANARTHRIA

-ANAS > ANA

ANASARCA n accumulation of fluid within subcutaneous connective tissue

ANASARCAS
> ANASARCA

ANASTASES
> ANASTASIS

ANASTASIS n Christ's harrowing of hell

ANASTATIC
> ANASTASIS

ANATA n Buddhist belief

ANATAS > ANATA

ANATASE n rare blue or black mineral

ANATASES > ANATASE

ANATEXES > ANATEXIS

ANATEXIS n partial melting of rocks

ANATHEMA n detested person or thing

ANATHEMAS
> ANATHEMA

ANATMAN same as
> ANATA

ANATMANS > ANATMAN

ANATOMIC > ANATOMY

ANATOMIES > ANATOMY

ANATOMISE same as
> ANATOMIZE

ANATOMIST n expert in anatomy

ANATOMIZE vb dissect (an animal or plant)

ANATOMY n science of the structure of the body

ANATOXIN n bacterial toxin used in inoculation

ANATOXINS
> ANATOXIN

ANATROPY n plant ovule inverted by a bending of the stalk

ANATTA n annatto

ANATTAS > ANATTA

ANATTO same as
> ANNATTO

ANATTOS > ANATTO

ANAXIAL adj asymmetrical

ANBURIES > ANBURY

ANBURY n soft spongy tumour occurring in horses and oxen

ANCE dialect form of > ONCE

ANCESTOR n person from whom one is descended

ANCESTORS
> ANCESTOR

ANCESTRAL adj of or inherited from ancestors ▷ n relation that holds between x and y if there is a chain of instances of a given relation leading from x to y

ANCESTRY n lineage or descent

ANCHO n chilli pepper

ANCHOR n heavy hooked device to fasten a ship to the sea bottom ▷ vb fasten with or as if with an anchor

ANCHORAGE n place where boats can be anchored

ANCHORED > ANCHOR

ANCHORESS
> ANCHORITE

ANCHORET n anchorite

ANCHORETS
> ANCHORET

ANCHORING > ANCHOR

ANCHORITE n religious recluse

ANCHORMAN n male presenter of a news programme on radio or television

ANCHORMEN
> ANCHORMAN

ANCHORS pl n brakes of a motor vehicle

ANCHOS > ANCHO

ANCHOVETA n type of small anchovy of the American Pacific, used as bait by tuna fishermen

ANCHOVIES > ANCHOVY

ANCHOVY n small strong-tasting fish

ANCHUSA n Eurasian plant

ANCHUSAS > ANCHUSA

ANCHUSIN same as
> ALKANET

ANCHUSINS
> ANCHUSIN
ANCHYLOSE same as
> ANKYLOSE
ANCIENT adj dating from very long ago ▷ n member of a civilized nation in the ancient world, esp a Greek, Roman, or Hebrew
ANCIENTER > ANCIENT
ANCIENTLY adv in ancient times
ANCIENTRY n quality of being ancient
ANCIENTS > ANCIENT
ANCILE n mythical Roman shield
ANCILIA > ANCILE
ANCILLA n Latin word for servant
ANCILLAE > ANCILLA
ANCILLARY adj supporting the main work of an organization ▷ n subsidiary or auxiliary thing or person
ANCILLAS > ANCILLA
ANCIPITAL adj flattened and having two edges
ANCLE old spelling of
> ANKLE
ANCLES > ANCLE
ANCOME n inflammation
ANCOMES > ANCOME
ANCON n projecting bracket
ANCONAL > ANCON
ANCONE same as > ANCON
ANCONEAL > ANCON
ANCONES > ANCON
ANCONOID > ANCON
ANCORA adv Italian for encore
ANCRESS n female anchorite
ANCRESSES > ANCRESS
AND n additional matter or problem
ANDANTE adv (to be played) moderately slowly ▷ n passage or piece to be performed moderately slowly
ANDANTES > ANDANTE
ANDANTINI
> ANDANTINO
ANDANTINO adv slightly faster or slower than andante ▷ n passage or piece to be performed in this way
ANDESINE n feldspar mineral of the plagioclase series
ANDESINES
> ANDESINE
ANDESITE n fine-grained tan or grey volcanic rock
ANDESITES
> ANDESITE
ANDESITIC
> ANDESITE
ANDESYTE n andesite
ANDESYTES
> ANDESYTE
ANDIRON n iron stand for supporting logs in a fireplace

ANDIRONS > ANDIRON
ANDOUILLE n spicy smoked pork sausage with a blackish skin
ANDRADITE n yellow, green, or brownish-black garnet
ANDRO n type of hormone
ANDROECIA n stamens of flowering plants collectively
ANDROGEN n type of steroid
ANDROGENS
> ANDROGEN
ANDROGYNE n person having both male and female characteristics
ANDROGYNY n state of being neither distinctly male nor distinctly female
ANDROID n robot resembling a human ▷ adj resembling a human being
ANDROIDS > ANDROID
ANDROLOGY n branch of medicine concerned with diseases and conditions specific to men
ANDROMEDA n type of shrub
ANDROS > ANDRO
ANDS > AND
ANDVILE old form of
> ANVIL
ANDVILES > ANDVILE
ANE Scots word for > ONE
ANEAR adv nearly ▷ vb approach
ANEARED > ANEAR
ANEARING > ANEAR
ANEARS > ANEAR
ANEATH Scots word for
> BENEATH
ANECDOTA pl n unpublished writings
ANECDOTAL adj containing or consisting exclusively of anecdotes rather than connected discourse or research conducted under controlled conditions
ANECDOTE n short amusing account of an incident
ANECDOTES
> ANECDOTE
ANECDOTIC
> ANECDOTE
ANECDYSES
> ANECDYSIS
ANECDYSIS n period between moults in arthropods
ANECHOIC adj having a low degree of reverberation of sound
ANELACE same as
> ANLACE
ANELACES > ANELACE
ANELASTIC adj not elastic
ANELE vb anoint, esp to give extreme unction to
ANELED > ANELE
ANELES > ANELE
ANELING > ANELE

ANELLI pl n pasta shaped like small rings
ANEMIA n anaemia
ANEMIAS > ANEMIA
ANEMIC same as
> ANAEMIC
ANEMOGRAM n record produced by anemograph
ANEMOLOGY n study of winds
ANEMONE n plant with white, purple, or red flowers
ANEMONES > ANEMONE
ANEMOSES > ANEMOSIS
ANEMOSIS n cracking in timber caused by wind affecting growing tree
ANENST dialect word for
> AGAINST
ANENT prep Scots word meaning alongside
ANERGIA n anergy
ANERGIAS > ANERGIA
ANERGIC > ANERGY
ANERGIES > ANERGY
ANERGY n lack of energy
ANERLY Scots word for
> ONLY
ANEROID adj not containing a liquid ▷ n barometer that does not contain liquid
ANEROIDS > ANEROID
ANES > ANE
ANESTRA > ANESTRUM
ANESTRI > ANESTRUS
ANESTROUS
> ANESTRUS
ANESTRUM n anestrus
ANESTRUS same as
> ANOESTRUS
ANETHOL n substance derived from oil of anise
ANETHOLE n white water-soluble crystalline substance with a liquorice-like odour
ANETHOLES
> ANETHOLE
ANETHOLS > ANETHOL
ANETIC adj medically soothing
ANEUPLOID adj (of polyploid cells or organisms) having a chromosome number that is not an exact multiple of the haploid number ▷ n cell or individual of this type
ANEURIN a less common name for > THIAMINE
ANEURINS > ANEURIN
ANEURISM same as
> ANEURYSM
ANEURISMS
> ANEURISM
ANEURYSM n permanent swelling of a blood vessel
ANEURYSMS
> ANEURYSM
ANEW adv once more
ANGA n part in Indian music
ANGAKOK n Inuit shaman
ANGAKOKS > ANGAKOK

ANGARIA n species of shellfish
ANGARIAS > ANGARIA
ANGARIES > ANGARY
ANGARY n right to use the property of a neutral state during a war
ANGAS > ANGA
ANGASHORE n miserable person given to complaining
ANGEKKOK n Inuit shaman
ANGEKKOKS
> ANGEKKOK
ANGEKOK n Inuit shaman
ANGEKOKS > ANGEKOK
ANGEL n spiritual being believed to be an attendant or messenger of God ▷ vb provide financial support for
ANGELED > ANGEL
ANGELFISH n South American aquarium fish with large fins
ANGELHOOD n state of being an angel
ANGELIC adj very kind, pure, or beautiful
ANGELICA n aromatic plant
ANGELICAL same as
> ANGELIC
ANGELICAS
> ANGELICA
ANGELING > ANGEL
ANGELS > ANGEL
ANGELUS n series of prayers
ANGELUSES > ANGELUS
ANGER n fierce displeasure or extreme annoyance ▷ vb make (someone) angry
ANGERED > ANGER
ANGERING > ANGER
ANGERLESS > ANGER
ANGERLY adv old form of angrily
ANGERS > ANGER
ANGICO n South American tree
ANGICOS > ANGICO
ANGINA n heart disorder causing sudden severe chest pains
ANGINAL > ANGINA
ANGINAS > ANGINA
ANGINOSE > ANGINA
ANGINOUS > ANGINA
ANGIOGRAM n X-ray picture obtained by angiography
ANGIOLOGY n branch of medical science concerned with the blood vessels and the lymphatic system
ANGIOMA n tumour consisting of a mass of blood vessels or lymphatic vessels
ANGIOMAS > ANGIOMA
ANGIOMATA > ANGIOMA
ANGISHORE same as
> ANGASHORE
ANGKLUNG n Asian musical instrument

ANGKLUNGS
> ANGKLUNG
ANGLE n space between or shape formed by two lines or surfaces that meet ▷ vb bend or place (something) at an angle
ANGLED > ANGLE
ANGLEDUG n earthworm
ANGLEDUGS
> ANGLEDUG
ANGLEPOD n American wild flower
ANGLEPODS
> ANGLEPOD
ANGLER n person who fishes with a hook and line
ANGLERS > ANGLER
ANGLES > ANGLE
ANGLESITE n white or grey secondary mineral
ANGLEWISE > ANGLE
ANGLEWORM n earthworm used as bait by anglers
ANGLICE adv in English
ANGLICISE same as
> ANGLICIZE
ANGLICISM n word, phrase, or idiom peculiar to the English language, esp as spoken in England
ANGLICIST n expert in or student of English literature or language
ANGLICIZE vb make or become English in outlook, form, etc
ANGLIFIED > ANGLIFY
ANGLIFIES > ANGLIFY
ANGLIFY same as
> ANGLICIZE
ANGLING n art or sport of fishing with a hook and line
ANGLINGS > ANGLING
ANGLIST same as
> ANGLICIST
ANGLISTS > ANGLIST
ANGLO n White inhabitant of the US not of Latin extraction
ANGLOPHIL n person having admiration for England or the English
ANGLOS > ANGLO
ANGOLA same as
> ANGORA
ANGOPHORA n Australian tree related to the eucalyptus
ANGORA n variety of goat, cat, or rabbit with long silky hair
ANGORAS > ANGORA
ANGOSTURA n bitter aromatic bark
ANGRIER > ANGRY
ANGRIES > ANGRY
ANGRIEST > ANGRY
ANGRILY > ANGRY
ANGRINESS > ANGRY
ANGRY adj full of anger ▷ n angry person
ANGST n feeling of anxiety
ANGSTIER > ANGSTY
ANGSTIEST > ANGSTY

ANGSTROM n unit of length used to measure wavelengths
ANGSTROMS
> ANGSTROM
ANGSTS > ANGST
ANGSTY adj displaying angst
ANGUIFORM adj shaped like a snake
ANGUINE adj of, relating to, or similar to a snake
ANGUIPED adj having snakes for legs ▷ n mythological Persian creature with snakes for legs
ANGUIPEDE n Persian mythological creature
ANGUIPEDS
> ANGUIPED
ANGUISH n great mental pain ▷ vb afflict or be afflicted with anguish
ANGUISHED adj feeling or showing great mental pain
ANGUISHES > ANGUISH
ANGULAR adj (of a person) lean and bony
ANGULARLY > ANGULAR
ANGULATE adj having angles or an angular shape ▷ vb make or become angular
ANGULATED
> ANGULATE
ANGULATES
> ANGULATE
ANGULOSE same as
> ANGULOUS
ANGULOUS adj having angles
ANHEDONIA n inability to feel pleasure
ANHEDONIC
> ANHEDONIA
ANHEDRAL n downward inclination of an aircraft wing in relation to the lateral axis
ANHEDRALS
> ANHEDRAL
ANHINGA n type of bird
ANHINGAS > ANHINGA
ANHUNGRED adj very hungry
ANHYDRASE n enzyme that catalyzes the removal of water
ANHYDRIDE n substance that combines with water to form an acid
ANHYDRITE n colourless or greyish-white mineral found in sedimentary rocks
ANHYDROUS adj containing no water
ANI n tropical bird
ANICCA n Buddhist belief
ANICCAS > ANICCA
ANICONIC adj (of images of deities, symbols, etc) not portrayed in a human or animal form
ANICONISM
> ANICONIC
ANICONIST > ANICONIC

ANICUT n dam in India
ANICUTS > ANICUT
ANIDROSES
> ANIDROSIS
ANIDROSIS n absence of sweating
ANIGH adv near
ANIGHT adv at night
ANIL n tropical shrub
ANILE adj of or like a feeble old woman
ANILIN n aniline
ANILINE n colourless oily liquid
ANILINES > ANILINE
ANILINGUS n oral stimulation of anus
ANILINS > ANILIN
ANILITIES > ANILE
ANILITY > ANILE
ANILS > ANIL
ANIMA n feminine principle as present in the male unconscious
ANIMACIES > ANIMACY
ANIMACY n state of being animate
ANIMAL n living creature capable of voluntary motion, esp one other than a human being ▷ adj of animals
ANIMALIAN > ANIMAL
ANIMALIC > ANIMAL
ANIMALIER n painter or sculptor of animal subjects, esp a member of a group of early 19th-century French sculptors who specialized in realistic figures of animals, usually in bronze
ANIMALISE same as
> ANIMALIZE
ANIMALISM n preoccupation with physical matters
ANIMALIST
> ANIMALISM
ANIMALITY n animal instincts of human beings
ANIMALIZE vb make (a person) brutal or sensual
ANIMALLY adv physically
ANIMALS > ANIMAL
ANIMAS > ANIMA
ANIMATE vb give life to ▷ adj having life
ANIMATED adj interesting and lively
ANIMATELY > ANIMATE
ANIMATER same as
> ANIMATOR
ANIMATERS
> ANIMATER
ANIMATES > ANIMATE
ANIMATEUR n active promoter of an artistic endeavour
ANIMATI > ANIMATO
ANIMATIC n animated film sequence
ANIMATICS
> ANIMATIC
ANIMATING > ANIMATE
ANIMATION n technique of making cartoon films

ANIMATISM n belief that inanimate objects have consciousness
ANIMATIST
> ANIMATISM
ANIMATO n piece of music performed in a lively manner
ANIMATOR n person who makes animated cartoons
ANIMATORS
> ANIMATOR
ANIMATOS > ANIMATO
ANIME n type of Japanese animation
ANIMES > ANIME
ANIMI > ANIMUS
ANIMIS > ANIMI
ANIMISM n belief that natural objects possess souls
ANIMISMS > ANIMISM
ANIMIST > ANIMISM
ANIMISTIC > ANIMISM
ANIMISTS > ANIMISM
ANIMOSITY n hostility, hatred
ANIMUS n hatred, animosity
ANIMUSES > ANIMUS
ANION n ion with negative charge
ANIONIC > ANION
ANIONS > ANION
ANIRIDIA n absence of the iris, due to a congenital condition or an injury
ANIRIDIAS
> ANIRIDIA
ANIRIDIC > ANIRIDIA
ANIS > ANI
ANISE n plant with liquorice-flavoured seeds
ANISEED n liquorice-flavoured seeds of the anise plant
ANISEEDS > ANISEED
ANISES > ANISE
ANISETTE n liquorice-flavoured liqueur made from aniseed
ANISETTES
> ANISETTE
ANISIC > ANISE
ANISOGAMY n type of reproduction in which the gametes are dissimilar
ANISOLE n colourless pleasant-smelling liquid used as a solvent
ANISOLES > ANISOLE
ANKER n old liquid measure for wine
ANKERITE n greyish to brown mineral that resembles dolomite
ANKERITES
> ANKERITE
ANKERS > ANKER
ANKH n ancient Egyptian symbol
ANKHS > ANKH
ANKLE n joint between the foot and leg ▷ vb move
ANKLEBONE the nontechnical name for
> TALUS

ANKLED > ANKLE

ANKLES > ANKLE

ANKLET *n* ornamental chain worn round the ankle

ANKLETS > ANKLET

ANKLING > ANKLE

ANKLONG *n* Asian musical instrument

ANKLONGS > ANKLONG

ANKLUNG *n* Asian musical instrument

ANKLUNGS > ANKLUNG

ANKUS *n* stick used for goading elephants

ANKUSES > ANKUS

ANKUSH *n* stick used for goading elephants

ANKUSHES > ANKUSH

ANKYLOSE *vb* (of bones in a joint, etc) to fuse or stiffen by ankylosis

ANKYLOSED
> ANKYLOSE

ANKYLOSES
> ANKYLOSE

ANKYLOSIS *n* abnormal immobility of a joint, caused by a fibrous growth

ANKYLOTIC
> ANKYLOSIS

ANLACE *n* medieval short dagger with a broad tapering blade

ANLACES > ANLACE

ANLAGE *n* organ or part in the earliest stage of development

ANLAGEN > ANLAGE

ANLAGES > ANLAGE

ANLAS *same as* > ANLACE

ANLASES > ANLAS

ANN *n* old Scots word for a widow's pension

ANNA *n* former Indian coin worth one sixteenth of a rupee

ANNAL *n* recorded events of one year

ANNALISE *vb* record in annals

ANNALISED
> ANNALISE

ANNALISES
> ANNALISE

ANNALIST > ANNAL

ANNALISTS > ANNAL

ANNALIZE *vb* record in annals

ANNALIZED
> ANNALIZE

ANNALIZES
> ANNALIZE

ANNALS > ANNAL

ANNAS > ANNA

ANNAT *n* old Scots word for a widow's pension

ANNATES *pl n* money paid to the Pope

ANNATS > ANNAT

ANNATTA *n* annatto

ANNATTAS > ANNATTA

ANNATTO *n* tropical tree

ANNATTOS > ANNATTO

ANNEAL *vb* toughen by heating and slow cooling ▷ *n* act of annealing

ANNEALED > ANNEAL

ANNEALER > ANNEAL

ANNEALERS > ANNEAL

ANNEALING > ANNEAL

ANNEALS > ANNEAL

ANNECTENT *adj* connecting

ANNELID *n* type of worm with a segmented body

ANNELIDAN > ANNELID

ANNELIDS > ANNELID

ANNEX *vb* seize (territory)

ANNEXABLE > ANNEX

ANNEXE *n* extension to a building

ANNEXED > ANNEX

ANNEXES > ANNEXE

ANNEXING > ANNEX

ANNEXION *n* old form of annexation

ANNEXIONS
> ANNEXION

ANNEXMENT > ANNEX

ANNEXURE *n* something that is added

ANNEXURES
> ANNEXURE

ANNICUT *n* dam in India

ANNICUTS > ANNICUT

ANNO *adv* Latin for in the year

ANNONA *n* American tree or shrub

ANNONAS > ANNONA

ANNOTATE *vb* add notes to (a written work)

ANNOTATED
> ANNOTATE

ANNOTATES
> ANNOTATE

ANNOTATOR
> ANNOTATE

ANNOUNCE *vb* make known publicly

ANNOUNCED
> ANNOUNCE

ANNOUNCER *n* person who introduces radio or television programmes

ANNOUNCES
> ANNOUNCE

ANNOY *vb* irritate or displease

ANNOYANCE *n* feeling of being annoyed

ANNOYED > ANNOY

ANNOYER > ANNOY

ANNOYERS > ANNOY

ANNOYING *adj* causing irritation or displeasure

ANNOYS > ANNOY

ANNS > ANN

ANNUAL *adj* happening once a year ▷ *n* plant that completes its life cycle in a year

ANNUALISE *same as*
> ANNUALIZE

ANNUALIZE *vb* calculate (a rate) for or as if for a year

ANNUALLY > ANNUAL

ANNUALS > ANNUAL

ANNUITANT *n* person in receipt of or entitled to an annuity

ANNUITIES > ANNUITY

ANNUITISE *same as*
> ANNUITIZE

ANNUITIZE *vb* convert a lump sum to a series of payments

ANNUITY *n* fixed sum paid every year

ANNUL *vb* declare (something, esp a marriage) invalid

ANNULAR *adj* ring-shaped ▷ *n* ring finger

ANNULARLY > ANNULAR

ANNULARS > ANNULAR

ANNULATE *adj* having, composed of, or marked with rings ▷ *n* annelid

ANNULATED
> ANNULATE

ANNULATES
> ANNULATE

ANNULET *n* moulding in the form of a ring

ANNULETS > ANNULET

ANNULI > ANNULUS

ANNULLED > ANNUL

ANNULLING > ANNUL

ANNULMENT *n* formal declaration that a contract or marriage is invalid

ANNULOSE *adj* having a body formed of a series of rings

ANNULS > ANNUL

ANNULUS *n* area between two concentric circles

ANNULUSES > ANNULUS

ANOA *n* type of small cattle

ANOAS > ANOA

ANOBIID *n* any type of beetle

ANOBIIDS > ANOBIID

ANODAL > ANODE

ANODALLY > ANODE

ANODE *n* positive electrode in a battery, valve, etc

ANODES > ANODE

ANODIC > ANODE

ANODISE *same as*
> ANODIZE

ANODISED > ANODISE

ANODISER *same as*
> ANODIZER

ANODISERS
> ANODISER

ANODISES > ANODISE

ANODISING > ANODISE

ANODIZE *vb* coat (metal) with a protective oxide film by electrolysis

ANODIZED > ANODIZE

ANODIZER *n* something that anodizes

ANODIZERS
> ANODIZER

ANODIZES > ANODIZE

ANODIZING > ANODIZE

ANODONTIA *n* congenital absence of teeth

ANODYNE *n* something that relieves pain or distress ▷ *adj* relieving pain or distress

ANODYNES > ANODYNE

ANODYNIC > ANODYNE

ANOESES > ANOESIS

ANOESIS *n* feeling without understanding

ANOESTRA
> ANOESTRUS

ANOESTRI
> ANOESTRUS

ANOESTRUM *same as*
> ANOESTRUS

ANOESTRUS *n* period between two periods of oestrus in many mammals

ANOETIC > ANOESIS

ANOINT *vb* smear with oil as a sign of consecration

ANOINTED > ANOINT

ANOINTER > ANOINT

ANOINTERS > ANOINT

ANOINTING *n* act of anointing

ANOINTS > ANOINT

ANOLE *n* type of lizard

ANOLES > ANOLE

ANOLYTE *n* part of an electrolyte around an anode

ANOLYTES > ANOLYTE

ANOMALIES > ANOMALY

ANOMALOUS *adj* different from the normal or usual order or type

ANOMALY *n* something that deviates from the normal, irregularity

ANOMIC > ANOMIE

ANOMIE *n* lack of social or moral standards

ANOMIES > ANOMIE

ANOMY *same as* > ANOMIE

ANON *adv* in a short time, soon

ANONYM *n* anonymous person or publication

ANONYMA *n* main vessel in the arterial network

ANONYMAS > ANONYMA

ANONYMISE *same as*
> ANONYMIZE

ANONYMITY
> ANONYMOUS

ANONYMIZE *vb* organize in a way that preserves anonymity

ANONYMOUS *adj* by someone whose name is unknown or withheld

ANONYMS > ANONYM

ANOOPSIA *n* squint in which the eye turns upwards

ANOOPSIAS
> ANOOPSIA

ANOPHELES *n* type of mosquito which transmits the malaria parasite to humans

ANOPIA *n* inability to see

ANOPIAS > ANOPIA

ANOPSIA *n* squint in which the eye turns upwards

ANOPSIAS > ANOPSIA

ANORAK *n* light waterproof hooded jacket

ANORAKS > ANORAK

ANORECTAL *adj* of the anus and rectum

ANORECTIC
> ANOREXIA

ANORETIC *n* anorectic

ANORETICS
> ANORETIC
ANOREXIA *n*
psychological disorder characterized by fear of becoming fat and refusal to eat
ANOREXIAS
> ANOREXIA
ANOREXIC > ANOREXIA
ANOREXICS
> ANOREXIA
ANOREXIES > ANOREXY
ANOREXY *old name for*
> ANOREXIA
ANORTHIC *another word for* > TRICLINIC
ANORTHITE *n* white to greyish-white or reddish-white mineral
ANOSMATIC > ANOSMIA
ANOSMIA *n* loss of the sense of smell
ANOSMIAS > ANOSMIA
ANOSMIC > ANOSMIA
ANOTHER *adj* one more
ANOUGH *adj* old form of enough
ANOUROUS *adj* having no tail
ANOVULANT *n* drug preventing ovulation
ANOVULAR *adj* without ovulation
ANOW *adj* old form of enough
ANOXAEMIA *n* deficiency in the amount of oxygen in the arterial blood
ANOXAEMIC
> ANOXAEMIA
ANOXEMIA *same as*
> ANOXAEMIA
ANOXEMIAS
> ANOXEMIA
ANOXEMIC > ANOXEMIA
ANOXIA *n* lack or absence of oxygen
ANOXIAS > ANOXIA
ANOXIC > ANOXIA
ANS *pl n* as in *ifs and ans* things that might have happened, but which did not
ANSA *n* either end of Saturn's rings
ANSAE > ANSA
ANSAPHONE *n* telephone answering machine
ANSATE *adj* having a handle or handle-like part
ANSATED *adj* ansate
ANSATZ *n* (in mathematics) assumption made to help solve a problem
ANSATZES > ANSATZ
ANSERINE *adj* of or resembling a goose ⊳ *n* chemical compound
ANSERINES
> ANSERINE
ANSEROUS *same as*
> ANSERINE
ANSWER *n* reply to a question, request, letter, etc ⊳ *vb* give an answer (to)
ANSWERED > ANSWER

ANSWERER > ANSWER
ANSWERERS > ANSWER
ANSWERING > ANSWER
ANSWERS > ANSWER
ANT *n* small insect living in highly organized colonies
ANTA *n* pilaster
ANTACID *n* substance that counteracts acidity ⊳ *adj* having the properties of this substance
ANTACIDS > ANTACID
ANTAE > ANTA
ANTALGIC *n* pain-relieving drug
ANTALGICS
> ANTALGIC
ANTALKALI *n* substance that neutralizes alkalis
ANTAR *old word for* > CAVE
ANTARA *n* South American panpipes
ANTARAS > ANTARA
ANTARCTIC *adj* relating to Antarctica
ANTARS > ANTAR
ANTAS > ANTA
ANTBEAR *n* aardvark
ANTBEARS > ANTBEAR
ANTBIRD *n* South American bird
ANTBIRDS > ANTBIRD
ANTE *n* player's stake in poker ⊳ *vb* place (one's stake) in poker
ANTEATER *n* mammal which feeds on ants by means of a long snout
ANTEATERS
> ANTEATER
ANTECEDE *vb* go before, as in time, order, etc
ANTECEDED
> ANTECEDE
ANTECEDES
> ANTECEDE
ANTECHOIR *n* part of a church in front of the choir, usually enclosed by screens, tombs, etc
ANTED > ANTE
ANTEDATE *vb* precede in time ⊳ *n* earlier date
ANTEDATED
> ANTEDATE
ANTEDATES
> ANTEDATE
ANTEED > ANTE
ANTEFIX *n* carved ornament
ANTEFIXA > ANTEFIX
ANTEFIXAE > ANTEFIX
ANTEFIXAL > ANTEFIX
ANTEFIXES > ANTEFIX
ANTEING > ANTE
ANTELOPE *n* deerlike mammal with long legs and horns
ANTELOPES
> ANTELOPE
ANTELUCAN *adj* before daylight
ANTENATAL *adj* during pregnancy, before birth ⊳ *n* examination during pregnancy
ANTENATI *pl n* people born before certain date

ANTENNA *n* insect's feeler
ANTENNAE > ANTENNA
ANTENNAL > ANTENNA
ANTENNARY > ANTENNA
ANTENNAS > ANTENNA
ANTENNULE *n* one of a pair of small mobile appendages on the heads of crustaceans in front of the antennae, usually having a sensory function
ANTEPAST *n* appetizer
ANTEPASTS
> ANTEPAST
ANTERIOR *adj* the front
ANTEROOM *n* small room leading into a larger one, often used as a waiting room
ANTEROOMS
> ANTEROOM
ANTES > ANTE
ANTETYPE *n* earlier form
ANTETYPES > ANTETYPE
ANTEVERT *vb* displace (an organ or part) by tilting it forward
ANTEVERTS
> ANTEVERT
ANTHELIA
> ANTHELION
ANTHELION *n* faint halo sometimes seen in polar or high altitude regions around the shadow of an object cast onto a thick cloud bank or fog
ANTHELIX *n* prominent curved fold of cartilage just inside the outer rim of the external ear
ANTHEM *n* song of loyalty, esp to a country ⊳ *vb* provide with an anthem
ANTHEMED > ANTHEM
ANTHEMIA
> ANTHEMION
ANTHEMIC > ANTHEM
ANTHEMING > ANTHEM
ANTHEMION *n* floral design, used esp in ancient Greek and Roman architecture and decoration, usually consisting of honeysuckle, lotus, or palmette leaf motifs
ANTHEMIS *n* genus of herbs of Mediterranean and SW Asia
ANTHEMS > ANTHEM
ANTHER *n* part of a flower's stamen containing pollen
ANTHERAL > ANTHER
ANTHERID *n* antheridium
ANTHERIDS
> ANTHERID
ANTHERS > ANTHER
ANTHESES > ANTHESIS
ANTHESIS *n* time when a flower begins reproductive cycle
ANTHILL *n* mound near an ants' nest
ANTHILLS > ANTHILL
ANTHOCARP *n* fruit developing from many flowers

ANTHOCYAN *n* any of a class of water-soluble glycosidic pigments
ANTHODIA
> ANTHODIUM
ANTHODIUM *another name for* > CAPITULUM
ANTHOID *adj* resembling a flower
ANTHOLOGY *n* collection of poems or other literary pieces by various authors
ANTHOTAXY *n* arrangement of flowers on a stem or parts on a flower
ANTHOZOAN *n* type of marine invertebrate with a body in the form of a polyp, such as corals, sea anemones, and sea pens
ANTHOZOIC
> ANTHOZOAN
ANTHRACES > ANTHRAX
ANTHRACIC *adj* of anthrax
ANTHRAX *n* dangerous disease of cattle and sheep, communicable to humans
ANTHRAXES > ANTHRAX
ANTHRO *n* short for anthropology
ANTHROPIC *adj* of or relating to human beings
ANTHROS > ANTHRO
ANTHURIUM *n* tropical American plant cultivated as a house plant for its showy foliage and flowers
ANTI *adj* opposed (to) ⊳ *n* opponent of a party, policy, or attitude
ANTIABUSE *adj* designed to prevent abuse
ANTIACNE *adj* inhibiting the development of acne
ANTIAGING *adj* resisting the effects of ageing
ANTIAIR *adj* countering attack by aircraft or missile
ANTIALIEN *adj* designed to prevent foreign animal or plant species from becoming established
ANTIAR *another name for* > UPAS
ANTIARIN *n* poison derived from antiar
ANTIARINS
> ANTIARIN
ANTIARMOR *adj* designed or equipped to combat armoured vehicles
ANTIARS > ANTIAR
ANTIATOM *n* atom composed of antiparticles
ANTIATOMS
> ANTIATOM
ANTIAUXIN *n* substance acting against auxin
ANTIBIAS *adj* countering bias
ANTIBLACK *adj* hostile to Black people
ANTIBODY *n* protein produced in the blood, which destroys bacteria

ANTIBOSS *adj* acting against bosses

ANTIBUG *adj* acting against computer bugs

ANTIBUSER *n* person who opposes the policy of transporting students to faraway schools to achieve racial balance

ANTIC *n* actor in a ludicrous or grotesque part ▷ *adj* fantastic

ANTICAL *adj* in front of or above another plant part

ANTICALLY > ANTICAL

ANTICAR *adj* opposed to cars

ANTICHLOR *n* substance used to remove chlorine from a material after bleaching or to neutralize the chlorine present

ANTICISE *same as* > ANTICIZE

ANTICISED > ANTICIZE

ANTICISES > ANTICIZE

ANTICITY *adj* opposed to cities

ANTICIVIC *adj* opposed to citizenship

ANTICIZE *vb* play absurdly

ANTICIZED > ANTICIZE

ANTICIZES > ANTICIZE

ANTICK *vb* perform antics

ANTICKE *archaic form of* > ANTIQUE

ANTICKED > ANTICK

ANTICKES > ANTICK

ANTICKING > ANTICK

ANTICKS > ANTICK

ANTICLINE *n* fold of rock raised up into a broad arch so that the strata slope down on both sides

ANTICLING *adj* acting against clinging

ANTICLY *adv* grotesquely

ANTICODON *n* element of RNA

ANTICOLD *adj* preventing or fighting the common cold

ANTICOUS *adj* on the part of a flower furthest from the stem

ANTICRACK *adj* protecting a computer against unauthorized access

ANTICRIME *adj* preventing or fighting crime

ANTICS *pl n* absurd acts or postures

ANTICULT *n* organization that is opposed to religious cults

ANTICULTS > ANTICULT

ANTIDORA > ANTIDORON

ANTIDORON *n* consecrated bread

ANTIDOTAL > ANTIDOTE

ANTIDOTE *n* substance that counteracts a poison ▷ *vb* counteract with an antidote

ANTIDOTED > ANTIDOTE

ANTIDOTES > ANTIDOTE

ANTIDRAFT *adj* opposed to conscription

ANTIDRUG *adj* intended to discourage illegal drug use

ANTIDUNE *n* type of sand hill or inclined bedding plane

ANTIDUNES > ANTIDUNE

ANTIELITE *adj* opposed to elitism

ANTIENT *old spelling of* > ANCIENT

ANTIENTS > ANTIENT

ANTIFA *n* antifascist organization

ANTIFAS > ANTIFA

ANTIFAT *adj* acting to remove or prevent fat

ANTIFLU *adj* acting against influenza

ANTIFOAM *adj* allowing gas to escape rather than form foam

ANTIFOG *adj* preventing the buildup of moisture on a surface

ANTIFRAUD *adj* acting against fraud

ANTIFUR *adj* opposed to the wearing of fur garments

ANTIGANG *adj* designed to restrict the activities of criminal gangs

ANTIGAY *adj* hostile to gay people

ANTIGEN *n* substance causing the blood to produce antibodies

ANTIGENE *n* antigen

ANTIGENES > ANTIGENE

ANTIGENIC > ANTIGEN

ANTIGENS > ANTIGEN

ANTIGLARE *adj* cutting down glare

ANTIGRAFT *adj* designed to reduce corruption

ANTIGUN *adj* opposed to the possession of guns

ANTIHELIX *same as* > ANTHELIX

ANTIHERO *n* central character in a book, film, etc, who lacks the traditional heroic virtues

ANTIHUMAN *adj* inhuman

ANTIJAM *adj* preventing jamming

ANTIKING *n* rival to an established king

ANTIKINGS > ANTIKING

ANTIKNOCK *n* substance added to motor fuel to reduce knocking in the engine caused by too rapid combustion

ANTILABOR *adj* opposed to labor interests

ANTILEAK *adj* preventing leaks

ANTILEFT *adj* opposed to the left wing in politics

ANTILIFE *adj* opposed to living in harmony with the natural order

ANTILIFER > ANTILIFE

ANTILOCK *adj* designed to prevent overbraking

ANTILOG *n* number whose logarithm to a given base is a given number

ANTILOGS > ANTILOG

ANTILOGY *n* contradiction in terms

ANTIMACHO *adj* opposed to macho attitudes

ANTIMALE *adj* opposed to men

ANTIMAN *adj* hostile to men

ANTIMASK *n* interlude in a masque

ANTIMASKS > ANTIMASK

ANTIMEN *adj* hostile to men

ANTIMERE *n* body part or organ that mirrors a similar structure on the other side

ANTIMERES > ANTIMERE

ANTIMERIC > ANTIMERE

ANTIMINE *adj* designed to counteract landmines

ANTIMONIC *adj* of or containing antimony in the pentavalent state

ANTIMONY *n* brittle silvery-white metallic element

ANTIMONYL *n* the monovalent group SbO–

ANTIMUON *n* antiparticle of a muon

ANTIMUONS > ANTIMUON

ANTIMUSIC *n* music intended to overthrow traditional conventions and expectations

ANTIMYCIN *n* antibiotic drug

ANTING *n* rubbing of ants by birds on their feathers

ANTINGS > ANTING

ANTINODAL > ANTINODE

ANTINODE *n* point of amplitude of displacement of opposite value to a node

ANTINODES > ANTINODE

ANTINOISE *n* sound generated so that it is out of phase with a noise, such as that made by an engine, in order to reduce the noise level by interference

ANTINOME *n* opposite

ANTINOMES > ANTINOME

ANTINOMIC > ANTINOMY

ANTINOMY *n* contradiction between two laws or principles that are reasonable in themselves

ANTINOVEL *n* type of prose fiction in which conventional elements of the novel are rejected

ANTINUKE *same as* > ANTINUKER

ANTINUKER *n* person who is opposed to nuclear weapons or energy

ANTINUKES > ANTINUKE

ANTIPAPAL *adj* opposed to the pope

ANTIPARTY *adj* opposed to a political party

ANTIPASTI > ANTIPASTO

ANTIPASTO *n* appetizer in an Italian meal

ANTIPATHY *n* dislike, hostility

ANTIPHON *n* hymn sung in alternate parts by two groups of singers

ANTIPHONS > ANTIPHON

ANTIPHONY *n* antiphonal singing of a musical composition by two choirs

ANTIPILL *adj* (of a material) not forming pills

ANTIPODAL *adj* of or relating to diametrically opposite points on the earth's surface

ANTIPODE *n* exact or direct opposite

ANTIPODES *pl n* any two places diametrically opposite one another on the earth's surface

ANTIPOLAR > ANTIPOLE

ANTIPOLE *n* opposite pole

ANTIPOLES > ANTIPOLE

ANTIPOPE *n* pope set up in opposition to the one chosen by church laws

ANTIPOPES > ANTIPOPE

ANTIPORN *adj* opposed to pornography

ANTIPOT *adj* opposed to illegal use of marijuana

ANTIPRESS *adj* hostile to the news media

ANTIPYIC *n* drug acting against suppuration

ANTIPYICS > ANTIPYIC

ANTIQUARK *n* antiparticle of a quark

ANTIQUARY *n* student or collector of antiques or ancient works of art

ANTIQUATE *vb* make obsolete or old-fashioned

ANTIQUE *n* object of an earlier period, valued for its beauty, workmanship, or age ▷ *adj* made in an earlier period ▷ *vb* give an antique appearance to

ANTIQUED > ANTIQUE

ANTIQUELY > ANTIQUE

ANTIQUER *n* collector of antiques

ANTIQUERS > ANTIQUER

ANTIQUES > ANTIQUE

ANTIQUEY *adj* having the appearance of an antique

ANTIQUIER > ANTIQUEY

ANTIQUING > ANTIQUE

ANTIQUITY *n* great age

ANTIRADAR *adj* preventing detection by radar

ANTIRAPE *adj* protecting against rape

ANTIRED *adj* of a particular colour of antiquark

ANTIRIOT *adj* designed for the control of crowds

ANTIROCK *adj* designed to prevent a vehicle from rocking

ANTIROLL *adj* designed to prevent a vehicle from tilting

ANTIROYAL *adj* opposed to the monarchy

ANTIRUST *adj* (of a product or procedure) effective against rust ▷ *n* substance or device that prevents rust

ANTIRUSTS > ANTIRUST

ANTIS > ANTI

ANTISAG *adj* preventing sagging

ANTISCIAN *n* person living on other side of equator

ANTISENSE *adj* acting in opposite way to RNA

ANTISERA > ANTISERUM

ANTISERUM *n* blood serum containing antibodies used to treat or provide immunity to a disease

ANTISEX *adj* opposed to sexual activity

ANTISHAKE *adj* (in photography) intended to reduce blurring caused by movement ▷ *n* antishake technology

ANTISHARK *adj* protecting against sharks

ANTISHIP *adj* designed for attacking ships

ANTISHOCK *n* one of a pair of walking poles designed to reduce stress on the knees

ANTISKID *adj* intended to prevent skidding

ANTISLEEP *adj* acting to prevent sleep

ANTISLIP *adj* acting to prevent slipping

ANTISMOG *adj* reducing smog

ANTISMOKE *adj* preventing smoke

ANTISMUT *adj* opposed to obscene material

ANTISNOB *n* person opposed to snobbery

ANTISNOBS > ANTISNOB

ANTISOLAR *adj* opposite to the sun

ANTISPAM *adj* intended to prevent spam

ANTISPAST *n* group of four syllables in poetic metre

ANTISTAT *n* substance preventing static electricity

ANTISTATE *adj* opposed to state authority

ANTISTATS > ANTISTAT

ANTISTICK *adj* preventing things from sticking to a surface

ANTISTORY *n* story without a plot

ANTISTYLE *n* style that rejects traditional aesthetics

ANTITANK *adj* (of weapons) designed to destroy military tanks

ANTITAX *adj* opposed to taxation

ANTITHEFT *adj* (of a device, campaign, system, etc) designed to prevent theft

ANTITHET *n* example of antithesis

ANTITHETS > ANTITHET

ANTITOXIC > ANTITOXIN

ANTITOXIN *n* (serum containing) an antibody that acts against a toxin

ANTITRADE *n* wind blowing in the opposite direction to a trade wind

ANTITRAGI *n* cartilaginous projections of the external ear opposite the tragus

ANTITRUST *adj* (of laws) opposing business monopolies ▷ *n* regulating or opposing trusts, monopolies, cartels, or similar organizations, esp in order to prevent unfair competition

ANTITUMOR *n* drug which acts against tumours

ANTITYPAL > ANTITYPE

ANTITYPE *n* something foreshadowed by a type or symbol

ANTITYPES > ANTITYPE

ANTITYPIC > ANTITYPE

ANTIULCER *adj* used to treat ulcers

ANTIUNION *adj* opposed to union

ANTIURBAN *adj* opposed to city life

ANTIVAX *adj* opposed to vaccination

ANTIVAXER *n* person opposed to vaccination

ANTIVENIN *n* antitoxin that counteracts a specific venom, esp snake venom

ANTIVENOM *n* venom antidote

ANTIVIRAL *adj* inhibiting the growth of viruses ▷ *n* any antiviral drug: used to treat diseases caused by viruses, such as herpes infections and AIDS

ANTIVIRUS *adj* relating to software designed to protect computer files from viruses ▷ *n* such a piece of software

ANTIWAR *adj* opposed to war

ANTIWEAR *adj* preventing wear

ANTIWEED *adj* killing or preventing weeds

ANTIWHITE *adj* hostile to White people

ANTIWOMAN *adj* hostile to women

ANTIWORLD *n* hypothetical or supposed world or universe composed of antimatter

ANTLER *n* branched horn of a male deer

ANTLERED *adj* having antlers

ANTLERS > ANTLER

ANTLIA *n* butterfly proboscis

ANTLIAE > ANTLIA

ANTLIATE *adj* relating to antlia

ANTLIKE *adj* of or like an ant or ants

ANTLION *n* type of insect resembling a dragonfly

ANTLIONS > ANTLION

ANTONYM *n* word that means the opposite of another

ANTONYMIC > ANTONYM

ANTONYMS > ANTONYM

ANTONYMY *n* use of antonyms

ANTPITTA *n* S American bird whose diet consists mainly of ants

ANTPITTAS > ANTPITTA

ANTRA > ANTRUM

ANTRAL > ANTRUM

ANTRE *n* cavern or cave

ANTRES > ANTRE

ANTRORSE *adj* directed or pointing upwards or forwards

ANTRUM *n* natural cavity, esp in a bone

ANTRUMS > ANTRUM

ANTS > ANT

ANTSIER > ANTSY

ANTSIEST > ANTSY

ANTSINESS > ANTSY

ANTSY *adj* restless, nervous, and impatient

ANTWACKIE *adj* old-fashioned

ANUCLEATE *adj* without a nucleus

ANURA *pl n* order of animals that comprises frogs and toads

ANURAL *adj* without a tail

ANURAN *n* type of amphibian

ANURANS > ANURAN

ANURESES > ANURESIS

ANURESIS *n* inability to urinate

ANURETIC > ANURESIS

ANURIA *n* result of a kidney disorder

ANURIAS > ANURIA

ANURIC > ANURIA

ANUROUS *adj* lacking a tail

ANUS *n* opening at the end of the alimentary canal, through which faeces are discharged

ANUSES > ANUS

ANVIL *n* heavy iron block on which metals are hammered into particular shapes ▷ *vb* forge on an anvil

ANVILED > ANVIL

ANVILING > ANVIL

ANVILLED > ANVIL

ANVILLING > ANVIL

ANVILS > ANVIL

ANVILTOP *n* type of cloud formation

ANVILTOPS > ANVILTOP

ANXIETIES > ANXIETY

ANXIETY *n* state of being anxious

ANXIOUS *adj* worried and tense

ANXIOUSLY > ANXIOUS

ANY *adj* one or some, no matter which ▷ *adv* at all

ANYBODIES > ANYBODY

ANYBODY *n* any person at random

ANYHOW *adv* anyway

ANYMORE *adv* at present

ANYON *n* type of elementary particle

ANYONE *pron* any person ▷ *n* any person at random

ANYONES > ANYONE

ANYONS > ANYON

ANYPLACE *adv* in, at, or to any unspecified place

ANYROAD *a northern English dialect word for* **> ANYWAY**

ANYTHING *pron* any object, event, or action whatever ▷ *n* any thing at random

ANYTHINGS > ANYTHING

ANYTIME *adv* at any time

ANYWAY *adv* at any rate, nevertheless

ANYWAYS nonstandard word for > ANYWAY

ANYWHEN adv at any time

ANYWHERE adv in, at, or to any place

ANYWHERES nonstandard word for > ANYWHERE

ANYWISE adv in any way or manner

ANZIANI pl n Italian word for councillors

AORIST n tense of the verb in classical Greek

AORISTIC > AORIST

AORISTS > AORIST

AORTA n main artery of the body, carrying oxygen-rich blood from the heart

AORTAE > AORTA

AORTAL > AORTA

AORTAS > AORTA

AORTIC > AORTA

AORTITIS n inflammation of the aorta

AOUDAD n wild mountain sheep

AOUDADS > AOUDAD

APACE adv swiftly

APACHE n Parisian gangster or ruffian

APACHES > APACHE

APADANA n ancient Persian palace hall

APADANAS > APADANA

APAGE interj Greek word meaning go away

APAGOGE n reduction to absurdity

APAGOGES > APAGOGE

APAGOGIC > APAGOGE

APAID > APAY

APANAGE same as > APPANAGE

APANAGED adj having apanage

APANAGES > APANAGE

APAREJO n kind of packsaddle made of stuffed leather cushions

APAREJOS > APAREJO

APART adv to pieces or in pieces

APARTHEID n former official government policy of racial segregation in S Africa

APARTMENT n room in a building

APARTNESS > APART

APATETIC adj of or relating to coloration that disguises and protects an animal

APATHATON old word for > EPITHET

APATHETIC adj having or showing little or no emotion

APATHIES > APATHY

APATHY n lack of interest or enthusiasm

APATITE n pale green to purple mineral, found in igneous rocks

APATITES > APATITE

APATOSAUR n long-necked dinosaur

APAY vb old word meaning satisfy

APAYD > APAY

APAYING > APAY

APAYS > APAY

APE n tailless monkey such as the chimpanzee or gorilla ▷ vb imitate

APEAK adj in a vertical or almost vertical position

APED > APE

APEDOM n state of being an ape

APEDOMS > APEDOM

APEEK adv nautical word meaning vertically

APEHOOD n state of being an ape

APEHOODS > APEHOOD

APELIKE > APE

APEMAN n primate thought to have been the forerunner of humans

APEMEN > APEMAN

APEPSIA n digestive disorder

APEPSIAS > APEPSIA

APEPSIES > APEPSY

APEPSY n apepsia

APER n person who apes

APERCU n outline

APERCUS > APERCU

APERIENT adj having a mild laxative effect ▷ n mild laxative

APERIENTS > APERIENT

APERIES > APERY

APERIODIC adj not periodic

APERITIF n alcoholic drink taken before a meal

APERITIFS > APERITIF

APERITIVE n laxative

APERS > APER

APERT adj open

APERTNESS > APERT

APERTURAL > APERTURE

APERTURE n opening or hole

APERTURED adj having an aperture

APERTURES > APERTURE

APERY n imitative behaviour

APES > APE

APESHIT adj vulgar slang word meaning crazy or furious

APETALIES > APETALOUS

APETALOUS adj (of flowering plants) having no petals

APETALY > APETALOUS

APEX n highest point

APEXES > APEX

APGAR n as in apgar score system for determining the condition of an infant at birth

APHAGIA n refusal or inability to swallow

APHAGIAS > APHAGIA

APHAKIA n absence of the lens of an eye

APHAKIAS > APHAKIA

APHANITE n type of fine-grained rock, such as a basalt

APHANITES > APHANITE

APHANITIC > APHANITE

APHASIA n disorder causing loss of ability to communicate

APHASIAC > APHASIA

APHASIACS > APHASIA

APHASIAS > APHASIA

APHASIC > APHASIA

APHASICS > APHASIA

APHELIA > APHELION

APHELIAN > APHELION

APHELION n point of a planet's orbit that is farthest from the sun

APHELIONS > APHELION

APHERESES > APHERESIS

APHERESIS n omission of a letter or syllable at the beginning of a word

APHERETIC > APHERESIS

APHESES > APHESIS

APHESIS n gradual disappearance of an unstressed vowel at the beginning of a word

APHETIC > APHESIS

APHETISE vb lose a vowel at the beginning of a word

APHETISED > APHETISE

APHETISES > APHETISE

APHETIZE vb lose a vowel at the beginning of a word

APHETIZED > APHETIZE

APHETIZES > APHETIZE

APHICIDE n substance for killing aphids

APHICIDES > APHICIDE

APHID n small insect which sucks the sap from plants

APHIDES > APHIS

APHIDIAN > APHID

APHIDIANS > APHID

APHIDIOUS > APHID

APHIDS > APHID

APHIS n type of aphid such as the blackfly

APHOLATE n type of pesticide

APHOLATES > APHOLATE

APHONIA n loss of the voice caused by damage to the vocal tract

APHONIAS > APHONIA

APHONIC adj affected with aphonia ▷ n person affected with aphonia

APHONICS > APHONIC

APHONIES > APHONY

APHONOUS > APHONIA

APHONY same as > APHONIA

APHORISE same as > APHORIZE

APHORISED > APHORISE

APHORISER > APHORISE

APHORISES > APHORISE

APHORISM n short clever saying expressing a general truth

APHORISMS > APHORISM

APHORIST > APHORISM

APHORISTS > APHORISM

APHORIZE vb write or speak in aphorisms

APHORIZED > APHORIZE

APHORIZER > APHORIZE

APHORIZES > APHORIZE

APHOTIC adj characterized by or growing in the absence of light

APHRODITE n North American butterfly

APHTHA n small ulceration

APHTHAE > APHTHA

APHTHOUS > APHTHA

APHYLLIES > APHYLLOUS

APHYLLOUS adj (of plants) having no leaves

APHYLLY > APHYLLOUS

APIACEOUS adj parsley-like

APIAN adj of, relating to, or resembling bees

APIARIAN adj of or relating to the breeding and care of bees ▷ n apiarist

APIARIANS > APIARIAN

APIARIES > APIARY

APIARIST n beekeeper

APIARISTS > APIARIST

APIARY n place where bees are kept

APICAL adj of, at, or being an apex ▷ n sound made with the tip of the tongue

APICALLY > APICAL

APICALS > APICAL

APICES plural of > APEX

APICIAN adj of fine or dainty food

APICULATE adj (of leaves) ending in a short sharp point

APICULI > APICULUS

APICULUS n short sharp point

APIECE adv each

APIEZON adj as in apiezon oil oil left by distillation

APIMANIA n extreme enthusiasm for bees
APIMANIAS
> APIMANIA
APING > APE
APIOL n substance derived from parsley seeds
APIOLOGY n study of bees
APIOLS > APIOL
APISH adj stupid or foolish
APISHLY > APISH
APISHNESS > APISH
APISM n behaviour like an ape
APISMS > APISM
APIVOROUS adj eating bees
APLANAT n aplanatic lens
APLANATIC adj (of a lens or mirror) free from spherical aberration
APLANATS > APLANAT
APLANETIC adj (esp of some algal and fungal spores) nonmotile or lacking a motile stage
APLASIA n congenital absence of an organ
APLASIAS > APLASIA
APLASTIC adj relating to or characterized by aplasia
APLENTY adv in plenty
APLITE n type of igneous rock
APLITES > APLITE
APLITIC > APLITE
APLOMB n calm self-possession
APLOMBS > APLOMB
APLUSTRE n stern ornament on an ancient Greek ship
APLUSTRES
> APLUSTRE
APNEA same as > APNOEA
APNEAL > APNEA
APNEAS > APNEA
APNEIC > APNEA
APNEUSES > APNEUSIS
APNEUSIS n gasping inhalation followed by short exhalation
APNEUSTIC adj of or relating to apneusis
APNOEA n temporary inability to breathe
APNOEAL > APNOEA
APNOEAS > APNOEA
APNOEIC > APNOEA
APO n type of protein
APOAPSES > APOAPSIS
APOAPSIS n point in an orbit furthest from the object orbited
APOCARP n apocarpous gynoecium or fruit
APOCARPS > APOCARP
APOCARPY n presence of many carpels
APOCOPATE vb omit the final sound or sounds of (a word)
APOCOPE n omission of the final sound or sounds of a word
APOCOPES > APOCOPE

APOCOPIC > APOCOPE
APOCRINE adj denoting a type of glandular secretion
APOCRYPHA n writings or statements of uncertain authority
APOD n animal without feet
APODAL adj (of snakes, eels, etc) without feet
APODE n animal without feet
APODES > APODE
APODICTIC adj unquestionably true by virtue of demonstration
APODOSES > APODOSIS
APODOSIS n consequent of a conditional statement
APODOUS same as > APODAL
APODS > APOD
APOENZYME n protein component that together with a coenzyme forms an enzyme
APOGAEIC > APOGEE
APOGAMIC > APOGAMY
APOGAMIES > APOGAMY
APOGAMOUS > APOGAMY
APOGAMY n type of reproduction in some ferns
APOGEAL > APOGEE
APOGEAN > APOGEE
APOGEE n point of moon's orbit
APOGEES > APOGEE
APOGEIC > APOGEE
APOGRAPH n exact copy
APOGRAPHS
> APOGRAPH
APOLLO n strikingly handsome youth
APOLLOS > APOLLO
APOLOG same as > APOLOGUE
APOLOGAL > APOLOGUE
APOLOGIA n formal written defence of a cause
APOLOGIAE
> APOLOGIA
APOLOGIAS
> APOLOGIA
APOLOGIES > APOLOGY
APOLOGISE same as > APOLOGIZE
APOLOGIST n person who formally defends a cause
APOLOGIZE vb make an apology
APOLOGS > APOLOG
APOLOGUE n allegory or moral fable
APOLOGUES
> APOLOGUE
APOLOGY n expression of regret for wrongdoing
APOLUNE n point in a lunar orbit
APOLUNES > APOLUNE
APOMICT n organism, esp a plant, produced by apomixis
APOMICTIC
> APOMIXIS

APOMICTS > APOMICT
APOMIXES > APOMIXIS
APOMIXIS n type of asexual reproduction
APOOP adv on the poop deck
APOPHASES
> APOPHASIS
APOPHASIS n device of mentioning a subject by stating that it will not be mentioned
APOPHATIC adj of theology that says God is indescribable
APOPHENIA n tendency to see patterns in random things
APOPHONY n change in the quality of vowels
APOPHYGE n outward curve at each end of the shaft of a column, adjoining the base or capital
APOPHYGES
> APOPHYGE
APOPHYSES
> APOPHYSIS
APOPHYSIS n process, outgrowth, or swelling from part of an animal or plant
APOPLAST n nonprotoplasmic component of a plant
APOPLASTS
> APOPLAST
APOPLEX vb afflict with apoplexy
APOPLEXED > APOPLEX
APOPLEXES > APOPLEX
APOPLEXY n extreme anger
APOPTOSES
> APOPTOSIS
APOPTOSIS n programmed death of some of an organism's cells as part of its natural growth and development
APOPTOTIC
> APOPTOSIS
APORETIC > APORIA
APORIA n doubt, real or professed, about what to do or say
APORIAS > APORIA
APORT adj on or towards the port side
APOS > APO
APOSITIA n unwillingness to eat
APOSITIAS
> APOSITIA
APOSITIC > APOSITIA
APOSPORIC
> APOSPORY
APOSPORY n development of the gametophyte from the sporophyte without the formation of spores
APOSTACY same as > APOSTASY
APOSTASY n abandonment of one's religious faith or other belief

APOSTATE n person who has abandoned his or her religion, political party, or cause ▷ adj guilty of apostasy
APOSTATES
> APOSTATE
APOSTATIC
> APOSTATE
APOSTIL n marginal note
APOSTILLE n apostil
APOSTILS > APOSTIL
APOSTLE n one of the twelve disciples chosen by Christ to preach His gospel
APOSTLES > APOSTLE
APOSTOLIC adj of or relating to the Apostles or their teachings
APOTHECE n obsolete word for shop
APOTHECES
> APOTHECE
APOTHECIA n cup-shaped structures that contain the asci, esp in lichens
APOTHEGM n short cryptic remark containing some general or generally accepted truth; maxim
APOTHEGMS
> APOTHEGM
APOTHEM n line from the centre of a polygon to one of its sides
APOTHEMS > APOTHEM
APOZEM n medicine dissolved in water
APOZEMS > APOZEM
APP n application program
APPAID > APPAY
APPAIR vb old form of impair
APPAIRED > APPAIR
APPAIRING > APPAIR
APPAIRS > APPAIR
APPAL vb dismay, terrify
APPALL same as > APPAL
APPALLED > APPALL
APPALLING adj dreadful, terrible
APPALLS > APPALL
APPALOOSA n North American horse breed
APPALS > APPAL
APPALTI > APPALTO
APPALTO n monopoly or contract
APPANAGE n land granted by a king for the support of a younger son
APPANAGED adj having appanage
APPANAGES
> APPANAGE
APPARAT n Communist Party organization
APPARATS > APPARAT
APPARATUS n equipment for a particular purpose
APPAREL n clothing ▷ vb clothe, adorn, etc
APPARELED > APPAREL
APPARELS > APPAREL
APPARENCY old word for > APPARENT

APPARENT adj readily seen, obvious ▷ n heir apparent

APPARENTS > APPARENT

APPARITOR n officer who summons witnesses and executes the orders of an ecclesiastical and (formerly) a civil court

APPAY old word for > SATISFY

APPAYD > APPAY

APPAYING > APPAY

APPAYS > APPAY

APPEACH old word for > ACCUSE

APPEACHED > APPEACH

APPEACHES > APPEACH

APPEAL vb make an earnest request ▷ n earnest request

APPEALED > APPEAL

APPEALER > APPEAL

APPEALERS > APPEAL

APPEALING adj attractive or pleasing

APPEALS > APPEAL

APPEAR vb become visible or present

APPEARED > APPEAR

APPEARER > APPEAR

APPEARERS > APPEAR

APPEARING > APPEAR

APPEARS > APPEAR

APPEASE vb pacify (a person) by yielding to his or her demands

APPEASED > APPEASE

APPEASER > APPEASE

APPEASERS > APPEASE

APPEASES > APPEASE

APPEASING > APPEASE

APPEL n stamp of the foot, used to warn of one's intent to attack

APPELLANT n person who makes an appeal to a higher court

APPELLATE adj of appeals

APPELLEE n person who is accused or appealed against

APPELLEES > APPELLEE

APPELLOR n person initiating a law case

APPELLORS > APPELLOR

APPELS > APPEL

APPEND vb join on, add

APPENDAGE n thing joined on or added

APPENDANT adj attached, affixed, or added ▷ n person or thing attached or added

APPENDED > APPEND

APPENDENT same as > APPENDANT

APPENDING > APPEND

APPENDIX n separate additional material at the end of a book

APPENDS > APPEND

APPERIL old word for > PERIL

APPERILL old word for > PERIL

APPERILLS > APPERILL

APPERILS > APPERIL

APPERTAIN vb belong to

APPESTAT n part of the brain that regulates hunger and satiety

APPESTATS > APPESTAT

APPETENCE n craving or desire

APPETENCY same as > APPETENCE

APPETENT adj eager

APPETIBLE adj old word meaning desirable

APPETISE vb stimulate the appetite

APPETISED > APPETISE

APPETISER same as > APPETIZER

APPETISES > APPETISE

APPETITE n desire for food or drink

APPETITES > APPETITE

APPETIZE vb stimulate the appetite

APPETIZED > APPETIZE

APPETIZER n thing eaten or drunk to stimulate the appetite

APPETIZES > APPETIZE

APPLAUD vb show approval of by clapping one's hands

APPLAUDED > APPLAUD

APPLAUDER > APPLAUD

APPLAUDS > APPLAUD

APPLAUSE n approval shown by clapping one's hands

APPLAUSES > APPLAUSE

APPLE n round firm fleshy fruit that grows on trees

APPLECART n cart used to carry apples

APPLEJACK n brandy made from apples

APPLES > APPLE

APPLET n computing program

APPLETINI n apple-flavoured alcoholic cocktail

APPLETS > APPLET

APPLEY adj resembling or tasting like an apple

APPLIABLE adj applicable

APPLIANCE n device with a specific function

APPLICANT n person who applies for something

APPLICATE adj applied practically

APPLIED adj (of a skill, science, etc) put to practical use

APPLIER > APPLY

APPLIERS > APPLY

APPLIES > APPLY

APPLIEST > APPLEY

APPLIQUE n decoration or trimming of one material sewn or otherwise fixed onto another ▷ vb sew or fix (a decoration) on as an appliqué

APPLIQUED > APPLIQUE

APPLIQUES > APPLIQUE

APPLY vb make a formal request

APPLYING > APPLY

APPOINT vb assign to a job or position

APPOINTED > APPOINT

APPOINTEE n person who is appointed

APPOINTER > APPOINT

APPOINTOR n person to whom a power to nominate persons to take property is given by deed or will

APPOINTS > APPOINT

APPORT n production of objects at a seance

APPORTION vb divide out in shares

APPORTS > APPORT

APPOSABLE adj capable of being apposed or brought into apposition

APPOSE vb place side by side or near to each other

APPOSED > APPOSE

APPOSER > APPOSE

APPOSES > APPOSE

APPOSING > APPOSE

APPOSITE adj suitable, apt

APPRAISAL n assessment of the worth or quality of a person or thing

APPRAISE vb estimate the value or quality of

APPRAISED > APPRAISE

APPRAISEE n person being appraised

APPRAISER > APPRAISE

APPRAISES > APPRAISE

APPREHEND vb arrest and take into custody

APPRESS vb press together

APPRESSED > APPRESS

APPRESSES > APPRESS

APPRISE vb make aware (of)

APPRISED > APPRISE

APPRISER > APPRISE

APPRISERS > APPRISE

APPRISES > APPRISE

APPRISING > APPRISE

APPRIZE same as > APPRISE

APPRIZED > APPRIZE

APPRIZER > APPRIZE

APPRIZERS > APPRIZE

APPRIZES > APPRIZE

APPRIZING > APPRIZE

APPRO n approval

APPROACH vb come near or nearer (to) ▷ n approaching or means of approaching

APPROBATE vb accept as valid

APPROOF old word for > TRIAL

APPROOFS > APPROOF

APPROS > APPRO

APPROVAL n consent

APPROVALS > APPROVAL

APPROVE vb consider good or right

APPROVED > APPROVE

APPROVER > APPROVE

APPROVERS > APPROVE

APPROVES > APPROVE

APPROVING > APPROVE

APPS > APP

APPUI n support

APPUIED > APPUY

APPUIS > APPUI

APPULSE n close approach of two celestial bodies

APPULSES > APPULSE

APPULSIVE > APPULSE

APPUY vb support

APPUYED > APPUY

APPUYING > APPUY

APPUYS > APPUY

APRACTIC > APRAXIA

APRAXIA n disorder impairing muscle movement

APRAXIAS > APRAXIA

APRAXIC > APRAXIA

APRES prep French word for after

APRICATE vb bask in sun

APRICATED > APRICATE

APRICATES > APRICATE

APRICOCK old word for > APRICOT

APRICOCKS > APRICOCK

APRICOT n yellowish-orange juicy fruit like a small peach ▷ adj yellowish-orange

APRICOTS > APRICOT

APRIORISM n philosophical doctrine that there may be genuine knowledge independent of experience

APRIORIST > APRIORISM

APRIORITY n condition of being innate in the mind

APRON n garment worn over the front of the body to protect the clothes ▷ vb equip with an apron

APRONED > APRON

APRONFUL n amount held in an apron

APRONFULS > APRONFUL

APRONING > APRON

APRONLIKE > APRON

APRONS > APRON
APROPOS *adv* appropriate(ly)
APROTIC *adj* (of solvents) neither accepting nor donating hydrogen ions
APSARAS *n* Hindu water sprite
APSARASES > APSARAS
APSE *n* arched or domed recess, esp in a church
APSES > APSE
APSIDAL > APSIS
APSIDES > APSIS
APSIDIOLE *n* small arch
APSIS *n* point in the elliptical orbit of a planet or satellite
APSO *n* Tibetan terrier
APSOS > APSO
APT *adj* having a specified tendency ▷ *vb* be fitting
APTAMER *n* artificially created DNA or RNA molecule
APTAMERS > APTAMER
APTED > APT
APTER > APT
APTERAL *adj* (esp of a classical temple) not having columns at the sides
APTERIA > APTERIUM
APTERISM > APTEROUS
APTERISMS > APTEROUS
APTERIUM *n* bare patch on the skin of a bird
APTEROUS *adj* (of insects) without wings, as silverfish and springtails
APTERYX *n* kiwi (the bird)
APTERYXES > APTERYX
APTEST > APT
APTING > APT
APTITUDE *n* natural ability
APTITUDES > APTITUDE
APTLY > APT
APTNESS > APT
APTNESSES > APT
APTOTE *n* noun without inflections
APTOTES > APTOTE
APTOTIC > APTOTE
APTS > APT
APYRASE *n* enzyme
APYRASES > APYRASE
APYRETIC > APYREXIA
APYREXIA *n* absence of fever
APYREXIAS > APYREXIA
AQUA *n* water
AQUABATIC *adj* of gymnastic feats in water
AQUABOARD *n* board used to ride on water
AQUACADE *same as* > AQUASHOW
AQUACADES > AQUACADE
AQUADROME *n* venue for water sports
AQUAE > AQUA
AQUAFABA *n* vegan substitute for egg whites

AQUAFABAS > AQUAFABA
AQUAFARM *vb* cultivate fish or shellfish
AQUAFARMS > AQUAFARM
AQUAFER *n* aquifer
AQUAFERS > AQUAFER
AQUAFIT *n* type of aerobic exercise done in water
AQUAFITS > AQUAFIT
AQUALUNG *n* mouthpiece attached to air cylinders, worn for underwater swimming
AQUALUNGS > AQUALUNG
AQUANAUT *n* person who lives and works underwater
AQUANAUTS > AQUANAUT
AQUAPHOBE *n* person afraid of water
AQUAPLANE *n* board on which a person stands to be towed by a motorboat ▷ *vb* ride on an aquaplane
AQUAPORIN *n* any one of a group of proteins in cell membranes that allow the passage of water across the membrane
AQUARELLE *n* method of watercolour painting in transparent washes
AQUARIA > AQUARIUM
AQUARIAL > AQUARIUM
AQUARIAN *n* person who keeps an aquarium
AQUARIANS > AQUARIAN
AQUARIIST *same as* > AQUARIST
AQUARIST *n* curator of an aquarium
AQUARISTS > AQUARIST
AQUARIUM *n* tank in which fish and other underwater creatures are kept
AQUARIUMS > AQUARIUM
AQUAROBIC *adj* pertaining to exercises performed standing up in a swimming pool
AQUAS > AQUA
AQUASCAPE *n* extensive view of a body of water seen from one place
AQUASHOW *n* exhibition of swimming and diving, often accompanied by music
AQUASHOWS > AQUASHOW
AQUATIC *adj* living in or near water ▷ *n* marine or freshwater animal or plant
AQUATICS *pl n* water sports
AQUATINT *n* print like a watercolour, produced by etching copper ▷ *vb* etch (a block, etc) in aquatint
AQUATINTA *n* aquatint

AQUATINTS > AQUATINT
AQUATONE *n* fitness exercise in water
AQUATONES > AQUATONE
AQUAVIT *n* grain- or potato-based spirit
AQUAVITS > AQUAVIT
AQUEDUCT *n* structure carrying water across a valley or river
AQUEDUCTS > AQUEDUCT
AQUEOUS *adj* of, like, or containing water
AQUEOUSLY > AQUEOUS
AQUIFER *n* deposit of rock containing water used to supply wells
AQUIFERS > AQUIFER
AQUILEGIA *another name for* > COLUMBINE
AQUILINE *adj* (of a nose) curved like an eagle's beak
AQUILON *n* name for the north wind
AQUILONS > AQUILON
AQUIVER *adv* quivering
AR *n* letter R
ARAARA *another name for* > TREVALLY
ARAARAS > ARAARA
ARABA *n* Asian carriage
ARABAS > ARABA
ARABESK *same as* > ARABESQUE
ARABESKS > ARABESK
ARABESQUE *n* ballet position in which one leg is raised behind and the arms are extended ▷ *adj* designating, of, or decorated in this style
ARABIC *adj* as in *gum arabic* gum exuded by certain acacia trees
ARABICA *n* high-quality coffee bean
ARABICAS > ARABICA
ARABICISE *same as* > ARABICIZE
ARABICIZE *vb* make or become Arabic
ARABILITY *n* suitability of land for growing crops
ARABIN *n* essence of gum arabic
ARABINOSE *n* pentose sugar in plant gums
ARABINS > ARABIN
ARABIS *n* type of plant
ARABISE *vb* make or become Arab
ARABISED > ARABISE
ARABISES > ARABISE
ARABISING > ARABISE
ARABIZE *vb* make or become Arab
ARABIZED > ARABIZE
ARABIZES > ARABIZE
ARABIZING > ARABIZE
ARABLE *adj* suitable for growing crops on ▷ *n* arable land or farming
ARABLES > ARABLE
ARACEOUS *same as* > AROID

ARACHIS *n* Brazilian plant
ARACHISES > ARACHIS
ARACHNID *n* eight-legged invertebrate, such as a spider, scorpion, tick, or mite
ARACHNIDS > ARACHNID
ARACHNOID *n* middle of the three membranes that cover the brain and spinal cord ▷ *adj* of or relating to the middle of the three meninges
ARAGONITE *n* generally white or grey mineral, found in sedimentary rocks
ARAHUANA *n* tropical freshwater fish
ARAHUANAS > ARAHUANA
ARAISE *vb* old form of raise
ARAISED > ARAISE
ARAISES > ARAISE
ARAISING > ARAISE
ARAK *same as* > ARRACK
ARAKS > ARAK
ARALIA *n* type of plant
ARALIAS > ARALIA
ARAME *n* Japanese edible seaweed
ARAMES > ARAME
ARAMID *n* synthetic fibre
ARAMIDS > ARAMID
ARANCINI *pl n* fried rice balls with a savoury filling
ARANEID *n* member of the spider family
ARANEIDAN > ARANEID
ARANEIDS > ARANEID
ARANEOUS *adj* like a spider's web
ARAPAIMA *n* very large primitive freshwater teleost fish that occurs in tropical S America
ARAPAIMAS > ARAPAIMA
ARAPONGA *n* South American bird with a bell-like call
ARAPONGAS > ARAPONGA
ARAPUNGA *same as* > ARAPONGA
ARAPUNGAS > ARAPUNGA
ARAR *n* African tree
ARAROBA *n* Brazilian leguminous tree
ARAROBAS > ARAROBA
ARARS > ARAR
ARAUCARIA *n* type of coniferous tree of S America, Australia, and Polynesia, such as the monkey puzzle and bunya-bunya
ARAWANA *n* tropical freshwater fish
ARAWANAS > ARAWANA
ARAYSE *vb* old form of raise
ARAYSED > ARAYSE
ARAYSES > ARAYSE

ARAYSING > ARAYSE
ARB short for
> ARBITRAGE
ARBA n Asian carriage
ARBALEST n large
medieval crossbow,
usually cocked by
mechanical means
ARBALESTS
> ARBALEST
ARBALIST same as
> ARBALEST
ARBALISTS
> ARBALIST
ARBAS > ARBA
ARBELEST n arbalest
ARBELESTS
> ARBELEST
ARBITER n person
empowered to judge in a
dispute
ARBITERS > ARBITER
ARBITRAGE n purchase
of currencies, securities,
or commodities in one
market for immediate
resale in others in order
to profit from unequal
prices
ARBITRAL adj of or
relating to arbitration
ARBITRARY adj based on
personal choice or chance,
rather than reason
ARBITRATE vb settle (a
dispute) by arbitration
ARBITRESS n female
arbitrator
ARBITRIUM n power to
decide
ARBLAST n arbalest
ARBLASTER > ARBLAST
ARBLASTS > ARBLAST
ARBOR n revolving shaft
or axle in a machine
ARBOREAL adj of or living
in trees
ARBORED adj having
arbors
ARBOREOUS adj thickly
wooded
ARBORES > ARBOR
ARBORET n old name for
an area planted with
shrubs
ARBORETA
> ARBORETUM
ARBORETS > ARBORET
ARBORETUM n place
where rare trees or shrubs
are cultivated
ARBORIO n as in arborio
rice variety of round-grain
rice used for making
risotto
ARBORIOS > ARBORIO
ARBORISE same as
> ARBORIZE
ARBORISED
> ARBORISE
ARBORISES
> ARBORISE
ARBORIST n specialist in
the cultivation of trees
ARBORISTS
> ARBORIST
ARBORIZE vb give or take
on a treelike branched
appearance

ARBORIZED
> ARBORIZE
ARBORIZES
> ARBORIZE
ARBOROUS adj of trees
ARBORS > ARBOR
ARBOUR n glade sheltered
by trees
ARBOURED adj having
arbours
ARBOURS > ARBOUR
ARBOVIRAL
> ARBOVIRUS
ARBOVIRUS n any one
of a group of viruses that
cause such diseases as
encephalitis and dengue
and are transmitted to
humans by arthropods,
esp insects and ticks
ARBS > ARB
ARBUSCLE n small tree
ARBUSCLES
> ARBUSCLE
ARBUTE old name for
> ARBUTUS
ARBUTEAN > ARBUTUS
ARBUTES > ARBUTE
ARBUTUS n evergreen
shrub with strawberry-like
berries
ARBUTUSES
> ARBUTUS
ARC n part of a circle or
other curve ▷ vb form an
arc
ARCADE n covered
passageway lined with
shops ▷ vb provide with
an arcade
ARCADED > ARCADE
ARCADES > ARCADE
ARCADIA n traditional
idealized rural setting
ARCADIAN n person who
leads a rural life
ARCADIANS
> ARCADIAN
ARCADIAS > ARCADIA
ARCADING > ARCADE
ARCADINGS > ARCADE
ARCANA n either of the
two divisions of a pack of
tarot cards
ARCANAS > ARCANA
ARCANE adj mysterious
and secret
ARCANELY > ARCANE
ARCANIST n person with
secret knowledge
ARCANISTS
> ARCANIST
ARCANUM n profound
secret or mystery known
only to initiates
ARCANUMS > ARCANUM
ARCATURE n small-scale
arcade
ARCATURES
> ARCATURE
ARCCOSINE n
trigonometric function
ARCED > ARC
ARCH n curved structure
supporting a bridge or roof
▷ vb (cause to) form an
arch ▷ adj superior,
knowing

ARCHAEA n order of
prokaryotic
microorganisms
ARCHAEAL same as
> ARCHAEAN
ARCHAEAN n type of
microorganism
ARCHAEANS
> ARCHAEAN
ARCHAEI > ARCHAEUS
ARCHAEON same as
> ARCHAEAN
ARCHAEUS n spirit
believed to inhabit a living
thing
ARCHAIC adj ancient
ARCHAICAL same as
> ARCHAIC
ARCHAISE same as
> ARCHAIZE
ARCHAISED
> ARCHAISE
ARCHAISER
> ARCHAISE
ARCHAISES
> ARCHAISE
ARCHAISM n archaic
word or phrase
ARCHAISMS
> ARCHAISM
ARCHAIST > ARCHAISM
ARCHAISTS
> ARCHAISM
ARCHAIZE vb give an
archaic appearance or
character to, as by the use
of archaisms
ARCHAIZED
> ARCHAIZE
ARCHAIZER
> ARCHAIZE
ARCHAIZES
> ARCHAIZE
ARCHANGEL n chief
angel
ARCHDRUID n chief or
principal druid
ARCHDUCAL adj of or
relating to an archduke,
archduchess, or archduchy
ARCHDUCHY n territory of
an archduke or
archduchess
ARCHDUKE n duke of
specially high rank
ARCHDUKES
> ARCHDUKE
ARCHEAN same as
> ARCHAEAN
ARCHED adj provided with
or spanned by an arch or
arches
ARCHEI > ARCHEUS
ARCHENEMY n chief
enemy
ARCHER n person who
shoots with a bow and
arrow
ARCHERESS n female
archer
ARCHERIES > ARCHERY
ARCHERS > ARCHER
ARCHERY n art or sport of
shooting with a bow and
arrow
ARCHES > ARCH
ARCHEST > ARCH
ARCHETYPE n perfect
specimen

ARCHEUS n spirit believed
to inhabit a living thing
ARCHFIEND n the chief
of fiends or devils
ARCHFOE n chief enemy
ARCHFOES > ARCHFOE
ARCHFOOL n very foolish
person
ARCHFOOLS
> ARCHFOOL
ARCHI > ARCO
ARCHICARP n female
reproductive structure in
some fungi
ARCHIL variant spelling of
> ORCHIL
ARCHILOWE n treat given
in return
ARCHILS > ARCHIL
ARCHIMAGE n great
magician or wizard
ARCHINE n Russian unit
of length
ARCHINES > ARCHINE
ARCHING n arched part
ARCHINGS > ARCHING
ARCHITECT n person
qualified to design and
supervise the construction
of buildings
ARCHITYPE n primitive
original from which others
derive
ARCHIVAL > ARCHIVE
ARCHIVE n collection of
records or documents ▷ vb
store (documents, data,
etc) in an archive or other
repository
ARCHIVED > ARCHIVE
ARCHIVES > ARCHIVE
ARCHIVING > ARCHIVE
ARCHIVIST n person in
charge of archives
ARCHIVOLT n moulding
around an arch,
sometimes decorated
ARCHLET n small arch
ARCHLETS > ARCHLET
ARCHLIKE adj like an
arch
ARCHLUTE n old bass
lute
ARCHLUTES
> ARCHLUTE
ARCHLY > ARCH
ARCHNESS > ARCH
ARCHOLOGY n study of
the origins of things
ARCHON n (in ancient
Athens) one of the nine
chief magistrates
ARCHONS > ARCHON
ARCHONTIC > ARCHON
ARCHOSAUR n early type
of dinosaur
ARCHRIVAL n chief rival
ARCHSTONE n
wedge-shaped stone
forming the curved part of
an arch
ARCHWAY n passageway
under an arch
ARCHWAYS > ARCHWAY
ARCHWISE adv like an
arch
ARCIFORM adj shaped
like an arch

ARCING n formation of an arc

ARCINGS > ARCING

ARCKED > ARC

ARCKING n formation of an arc

ARCKINGS > ARCKING

ARCMIN n 1/60 of a degree of an angle

ARCMINS > ARCMIN

ARCMINUTE n unit of angular measurement, 1/60 of a degree

ARCO adv musical direction meaning with bow ▷ n bow of a stringed instrument

ARCOGRAPH n instrument used for drawing arcs without using a central point

ARCOLOGY n architecture blending buildings with the natural environment

ARCOS > ARCO

ARCS > ARC

ARCSEC n 1/3600 of a degree of an angle

ARCSECOND n unit used in astronomy

ARCSECS > ARCSEC

ARCSINE n trigonometrical function

ARCSINES > ARCSINE

ARCTIC adj very cold ▷ n high waterproof overshoe with buckles

ARCTICS > ARCTIC

ARCTIID n type of moth

ARCTIIDS > ARCTIID

ARCTOID adj like a bear

ARCTOPHIL n arctophile

ARCUATE adj shaped or bent like an arc or bow

ARCUATED same as > ARCUATE

ARCUATELY > ARCUATE

ARCUATION n use of arches or vaults in buildings

ARCUS n circle around the cornea of the eye

ARCUSES > ARCUS

ARD n primitive plough

ARDEB n unit of dry measure

ARDEBS > ARDEB

ARDENCIES > ARDENT

ARDENCY > ARDENT

ARDENT adj passionate

ARDENTLY > ARDENT

ARDOR same as > ARDOUR

ARDORS > ARDOR

ARDOUR n passion

ARDOURS > ARDOUR

ARDRI n Irish high king

ARDRIGH n Irish high king

ARDRIGHS > ARDRIGH

ARDRIS > ARDRI

ARDS > ARD

ARDUOUS adj hard to accomplish, strenuous

ARDUOUSLY > ARDUOUS

ARE n unit of measure, 100 square metres ▷ vb form of the present tense of be

AREA n part or region

AREACH vb old form of reach

AREACHED > AREACH

AREACHES > AREACH

AREACHING > AREACH

AREAD vb old word meaning declare

AREADING > AREAD

AREADS > AREAD

AREAE > AREA

AREAL > AREA

AREALLY > AREA

AREAR n old form of arrear

AREARS > AREAR

AREAS > AREA

AREAWAY n passageway

AREAWAYS > AREAWAY

ARECA n type of palm tree

ARECAS > ARECA

ARECOLINE n drug derived from betel nut

ARED > AREAD

AREDD > AREAD

AREDE vb old word meaning declare

AREDES > AREDE

AREDING > AREDE

AREFIED > AREFY

AREFIES > AREFY

AREFY vb dry up

AREFYING > AREFY

AREG a plural of > ERG

AREIC adj relating to area

ARENA n seated enclosure for sports events

ARENAS > ARENA

ARENATION n use of hot sand as a medical poultice

ARENE n aromatic hydrocarbon

ARENES > ARENE

ARENITE n any arenaceous rock

ARENITES > ARENITE

ARENITIC > ARENITE

ARENOSE adj sandy

ARENOUS adj sandy

AREOLA n small circular area

AREOLAE > AREOLA

AREOLAR > AREOLA

AREOLAS > AREOLA

AREOLATE > AREOLA

AREOLATED adj areolate

AREOLE n space outlined on a surface

AREOLES > AREOLE

AREOLOGY n study of the planet Mars

AREOMETER n instrument for measuring the density of liquids

AREOMETRY n use of an araeometer

AREOSTYLE n building with widely spaced columns

AREPA n Colombian cornmeal cake

AREPAS > AREPA

ARERE adv old word meaning backwards

ARES > ARE

ARET vb old word meaning entrust

ARETE n sharp ridge separating two glacial valleys

ARETES > ARETE

ARETHUSA n N American orchid

ARETHUSAS > ARETHUSA

ARETS > ARET

ARETT vb old word meaning entrust

ARETTED > ARETT

ARETTING > ARETT

ARETTS > ARETT

AREW adv old word meaning in a row

ARF n barking sound

ARFS > ARF

ARGAL same as > ARGALI

ARGALA n Indian stork

ARGALAS > ARGALA

ARGALI n wild sheep

ARGALIS > ARGALI

ARGALS > ARGAL

ARGAN n Moroccan tree

ARGAND n lamp with a hollow circular wick

ARGANDS > ARGAND

ARGANS > ARGAN

ARGEMONE n prickly poppy

ARGEMONES > ARGEMONE

ARGENT n silver

ARGENTAL adj of or containing silver

ARGENTIC adj of or containing silver in the divalent or trivalent state

ARGENTINE adj of, relating to, or resembling silver ▷ n type of small silver fish

ARGENTITE n dark grey mineral

ARGENTOUS adj of or containing silver in the monovalent state

ARGENTS > ARGENT

ARGENTUM an obsolete name for > SILVER

ARGENTUMS > ARGENTUM

ARGH interj cry of pain

ARGHAN n agave plant

ARGHANS > ARGHAN

ARGIL n clay, esp potters' clay

ARGILLITE n any argillaceous rock, esp a hardened mudstone

ARGILS > ARGIL

ARGINASE n type of enzyme

ARGINASES > ARGINASE

ARGININE n essential amino acid

ARGININES > ARGININE

ARGLE vb quarrel

ARGLED > ARGLE

ARGLES > ARGLE

ARGLING > ARGLE

ARGOL n chemical compound

ARGOLS > ARGOL

ARGON n inert gas found in the air

ARGONAUT n paper nautilus

ARGONAUTS > ARGONAUT

ARGONON n inert gas

ARGONONS > ARGONON

ARGONS > ARGON

ARGOSIES > ARGOSY

ARGOSY n large merchant ship

ARGOT n slang or jargon

ARGOTIC > ARGOT

ARGOTS > ARGOT

ARGUABLE adj capable of being disputed

ARGUABLY adv it can be argued that

ARGUE vb try to prove by giving reasons

ARGUED > ARGUE

ARGUER > ARGUE

ARGUERS > ARGUE

ARGUES > ARGUE

ARGUFIED > ARGUFY

ARGUFIER > ARGUFY

ARGUFIERS > ARGUFY

ARGUFIES > ARGUFY

ARGUFY vb argue or quarrel, esp over something trivial

ARGUFYING > ARGUFY

ARGUING > ARGUE

ARGULI > ARGULUS

ARGULUS n parasite on fish

ARGUMENT n quarrel

ARGUMENTA n appeals to reason

ARGUMENTS > ARGUMENT

ARGUS n any of various brown butterflies

ARGUSES > ARGUS

ARGUTE adj shrill or keen

ARGUTELY > ARGUTE

ARGYLE adj with a diamond-shaped pattern ▷ n sock with this pattern

ARGYLES > ARGYLE

ARGYLL n sock with diamond pattern

ARGYLLS > ARGYLL

ARGYRIA n staining of skin by exposure to silver

ARGYRIAS > ARGYRIA

ARGYRITE n mineral containing silver sulphide

ARGYRITES > ARGYRITE

ARHAT n Buddhist who has achieved enlightenment

ARHATS > ARHAT

ARHATSHIP > ARHAT

ARHYTHMIA n irregular heartbeat

ARHYTHMIC > ARHYTHMIA

ARIA n elaborate song for solo voice, esp one from an opera

ARIARIES > ARIARY

ARIARY n currency of Madagascar

ARIAS > ARIA

ARID adj parched, dry

a

ARIDER > ARID
ARIDEST > ARID
ARIDITIES > ARID
ARIDITY > ARID
ARIDLY > ARID
ARIDNESS > ARID
ARIEL n type of Arabian gazelle
ARIELS > ARIEL
ARIETTA n short aria
ARIETTAS > ARIETTA
ARIETTE same as > ARIETTA
ARIETTES > ARIETTE
ARIGHT adv rightly
ARIKI n Polynesian chief
ARIKIS > ARIKI
ARIL n appendage on certain seeds
ARILED adj having an aril
ARILLARY adj having an aril
ARILLATE > ARILLATED
ARILLATED adj having an aril
ARILLI > ARILLUS
ARILLODE n structure in certain seeds
ARILLODES > ARILLODE
ARILLOID adj of or like an aril
ARILLUS n aril
ARILS > ARIL
ARIOSE adj songlike
ARIOSI > ARIOSO
ARIOSO n recitative with the lyrical quality of an aria
ARIOSOS > ARIOSO
ARIOT adv riotously
ARIPPLE adv in ripples
ARIS n Cockney slang for buttocks
ARISE vb come about
ARISEN > ARISE
ARISES > ARISE
ARISH n field that has been mown
ARISHES > ARISH
ARISING > ARISE
ARISTA n stiff bristle
ARISTAE > ARISTA
ARISTAS > ARISTA
ARISTATE > ARISTA
ARISTO n aristocrat
ARISTOS > ARISTO
ARISTOTLE n bottle
ARK n boat built by Noah, which survived the Flood ▷ vb place in an ark
ARKED > ARK
ARKING > ARK
ARKITE n passenger in ark
ARKITES > ARKITE
ARKOSE n type of sandstone
ARKOSES > ARKOSE
ARKOSIC > ARKOSE
ARKS > ARK
ARLE vb make a down payment
ARLED > ARLE
ARLES > ARLE
ARLING > ARLE

ARM n limbs from the shoulder to the wrist ▷ vb supply with weapons
ARMADA n large number of warships
ARMADAS > ARMADA
ARMADILLO n small S American mammal covered in strong bony plates
ARMAGNAC n dry brown brandy
ARMAGNACS > ARMAGNAC
ARMAMENT n military weapons
ARMAMENTS > ARMAMENT
ARMATURE n revolving structure in an electric motor or generator
ARMATURED > ARMATURE
ARMATURES > ARMATURE
ARMBAND n band worn on the arm
ARMBANDS > ARMBAND
ARMCHAIR n upholstered chair with side supports for the arms ▷ adj taking no active part
ARMCHAIRS > ARMCHAIR
ARMED adj equipped with or supported by arms, armour, etc
ARMER > ARM
ARMERIA n generic name for the plant thrift
ARMERIAS > ARMERIA
ARMERS > ARM
ARMET n close-fitting medieval visored helmet with a neck guard
ARMETS > ARMET
ARMFUL n as much as can be held in the arms
ARMFULS > ARMFUL
ARMGAUNT adj word in Shakespeare of uncertain meaning
ARMGUARD n covering to protect the arm
ARMGUARDS > ARMGUARD
ARMHOLE n opening in a garment through which the arm passes
ARMHOLES > ARMHOLE
ARMIES > ARMY
ARMIGER n person entitled to bear heraldic arms
ARMIGERAL > ARMIGER
ARMIGERO n armiger
ARMIGEROS > ARMIGERO
ARMIGERS > ARMIGER
ARMIL n bracelet
ARMILLA n bracelet
ARMILLAE > ARMILLA
ARMILLARY adj of or relating to bracelets
ARMILLAS > ARMILLA
ARMILS > ARMIL
ARMING n act of taking arms or providing with arms

ARMINGS > ARMING
ARMISTICE n agreed suspension of fighting
ARMLESS > ARM
ARMLET n band worn round the arm
ARMLETS > ARMLET
ARMLIKE > ARM
ARMLOAD n amount carried in the arms
ARMLOADS > ARMLOAD
ARMLOCK vb grip someone's arms
ARMLOCKED > ARMLOCK
ARMLOCKS > ARMLOCK
ARMOIRE n large cabinet
ARMOIRES > ARMOIRE
ARMONICA n glass harmonica
ARMONICAS > ARMONICA
ARMOR same as > ARMOUR
ARMORED same as > ARMOURED
ARMORER same as > ARMOURER
ARMORERS > ARMORER
ARMORIAL adj of or relating to heraldry or heraldic arms ▷ n book of coats of arms
ARMORIALS > ARMORIAL
ARMORIES > ARMORY
ARMORING > ARMOR
ARMORIST n heraldry expert
ARMORISTS > ARMORIST
ARMORLESS > ARMOR
ARMORS > ARMOR
ARMORY same as > ARMOURY
ARMOUR n metal clothing formerly worn to protect the body in battle ▷ vb equip or cover with armour
ARMOURED adj having a protective covering
ARMOURER n maker, repairer, or keeper of arms or armour
ARMOURERS > ARMOURER
ARMOURIES > ARMOURY
ARMOURING > ARMOUR
ARMOURS > ARMOUR
ARMOURY n place where weapons are stored
ARMOZEEN n material used for clerical gowns
ARMOZEENS > ARMOZEEN
ARMOZINE n material used for clerical gowns
ARMOZINES > ARMOZINE
ARMPIT n hollow under the arm at the shoulder
ARMPITS > ARMPIT
ARMREST n part of a chair or sofa that supports the arm
ARMRESTS > ARMREST
ARMS > ARM
ARMSFUL > ARMFUL

ARMURE n silk or wool fabric with a small cobbled pattern
ARMURES > ARMURE
ARMY n military land forces of a nation
ARMYWORM n caterpillar of a widely distributed noctuid moth
ARMYWORMS > ARMYWORM
ARNA n Indian water buffalo
ARNAS > ARNA
ARNATTO n annatto
ARNATTOS > ARNATTO
ARNICA n temperate or Arctic plant
ARNICAS > ARNICA
ARNOTTO n annatto
ARNOTTOS > ARNOTTO
ARNUT n plant with edible tubers
ARNUTS > ARNUT
AROBA n Asian carriage
AROBAS > AROBA
AROHA n love, compassion, or affection
AROHAS > AROHA
AROID n type of plant
AROIDS > AROID
AROINT vb drive away
AROINTED > AROINT
AROINTING > AROINT
AROINTS > AROINT
AROLLA n European pine tree
AROLLAS > AROLLA
AROMA n pleasant smell
AROMAS > AROMA
AROMATASE n enzyme involved in the production of oestrogen
AROMATIC adj having a distinctive pleasant smell ▷ n something, such as a plant or drug, that gives off a fragrant smell
AROMATICS > AROMATIC
AROMATISE same as > AROMATIZE
AROMATIZE vb make aromatic
AROSE > ARISE
AROUND adv on all sides (of)
AROUSABLE > AROUSE
AROUSAL > AROUSE
AROUSALS > AROUSE
AROUSE vb stimulate, make active
AROUSED > AROUSE
AROUSER > AROUSE
AROUSERS > AROUSE
AROUSES > AROUSE
AROUSING > AROUSE
AROW adv in a row
AROWANA n tropical freshwater fish
AROWANAS > AROWANA
AROYNT vb old word meaning to drive away
AROYNTED > AROYNT
AROYNTING > AROYNT
AROYNTS > AROYNT
ARPA n website concerned with structure of the internet

ARPAS > ARPA
ARPEGGIO n notes of a chord played or sung in quick succession
ARPEGGIOS > ARPEGGIO
ARPEN n former French unit of length
ARPENS > ARPEN
ARPENT n former French unit of length
ARPENTS > ARPENT
ARPILLERA n Peruvian wall-hanging
ARQUEBUS n portable long-barrelled gun dating from the 15th century
ARRACACHA n S American plant
ARRACK n alcoholic drink distilled from grain or rice
ARRACKS > ARRACK
ARRAH interj Irish exclamation
ARRAIGN vb bring (a prisoner) before a court to answer a charge
ARRAIGNED > ARRAIGN
ARRAIGNER > ARRAIGN
ARRAIGNS > ARRAIGN
ARRANGE vb plan
ARRANGED > ARRANGE
ARRANGER > ARRANGE
ARRANGERS > ARRANGE
ARRANGES > ARRANGE
ARRANGING > ARRANGE
ARRANT adj utter, downright
ARRANTLY > ARRANT
ARRAS n tapestry wall-hanging
ARRASED adj having an arras
ARRASENE n material used in embroidery
ARRASENES > ARRASENE
ARRASES > ARRAS
ARRAUGHT > AREACH
ARRAY n impressive display or collection ▷ vb arrange in order
ARRAYAL > ARRAY
ARRAYALS > ARRAY
ARRAYED > ARRAY
ARRAYER > ARRAY
ARRAYERS > ARRAY
ARRAYING > ARRAY
ARRAYMENT n act of arraying
ARRAYS > ARRAY
ARREAR n singular of arrears
ARREARAGE same as > ARREARS
ARREARS pl n money owed
ARRECT adj pricked up
ARREEDE vb old word meaning declare
ARREEDES > ARREEDE
ARREEDING > ARREEDE
ARREST vb take (a person) into custody ▷ n act of taking a person into custody
ARRESTANT n substance that stops a chemical reaction

ARRESTED > ARREST
ARRESTEE n arrested person
ARRESTEES > ARRESTEE
ARRESTER n person who arrests
ARRESTERS > ARRESTER
ARRESTING adj attracting attention, striking
ARRESTIVE adj making something stop
ARRESTOR n person or thing that arrests
ARRESTORS > ARRESTOR
ARRESTS > ARREST
ARRET n judicial decision
ARRETS > ARRET
ARRHIZAL adj without roots
ARRIAGE n Scottish feudal service
ARRIAGES > ARRIAGE
ARRIBA interj exclamation of pleasure or approval
ARRIDE vb old word meaning gratify
ARRIDED > ARRIDE
ARRIDES > ARRIDE
ARRIDING > ARRIDE
ARRIERE adj French word meaning old-fashioned
ARRIERO n mule driver
ARRIEROS > ARRIERO
ARRIS n sharp edge at the meeting of two surfaces
ARRISES > ARRIS
ARRISH n corn stubble
ARRISHES > ARRISH
ARRIVAL n arriving
ARRIVALS > ARRIVAL
ARRIVANCE n old word meaning people who have arrived
ARRIVANCY n arrivance
ARRIVE vb reach a place or destination
ARRIVED > ARRIVE
ARRIVER > ARRIVE
ARRIVERS > ARRIVE
ARRIVES > ARRIVE
ARRIVING > ARRIVE
ARRIVISME n unscrupulous ambition
ARRIVISTE n person who is unscrupulously ambitious
ARROBA n unit of weight in Spanish-speaking countries
ARROBAS > ARROBA
ARROCES > ARROZ
ARROGANCE > ARROGANT
ARROGANCY > ARROGANT
ARROGANT adj proud and overbearing
ARROGATE vb claim or seize without justification
ARROGATED > ARROGATE
ARROGATES > ARROGATE

ARROGATOR > ARROGATE
ARROW n pointed shaft shot from a bow
ARROWED adj having an arrow pattern
ARROWHEAD n pointed tip of an arrow
ARROWIER > ARROWY
ARROWIEST > ARROWY
ARROWING > ARROW
ARROWLESS > ARROW
ARROWLIKE > ARROW
ARROWROOT n nutritious starch obtained from the root of a Caribbean plant
ARROWS > ARROW
ARROWWOOD n any of various trees or shrubs, esp certain viburnums, having long straight tough stems formerly used by Native Americans to make arrows
ARROWWORM n type of small marine invertebrate with an elongated transparent body
ARROWY adj like an arrow
ARROYO n usually dry stream bed
ARROYOS > ARROYO
ARROZ n Spanish word for rice, used in name of various dishes
ARROZES > ARROZ
ARS > AR
ARSE n vulgar slang word for the buttocks or anus ▷ vb play the fool
ARSED > ARSE
ARSEHOLE n vulgar slang word for the anus
ARSEHOLED adj vulgar slang word for very drunk
ARSEHOLES > ARSEHOLE
ARSENAL n place where arms and ammunition are made or stored
ARSENALS > ARSENAL
ARSENATE n salt or ester of arsenic acid
ARSENATES > ARSENATE
ARSENIATE n arsenate
ARSENIC n toxic grey element ▷ adj of or containing arsenic
ARSENICAL adj of or containing arsenic ▷ n drug or insecticide containing arsenic
ARSENICS > ARSENIC
ARSENIDE n compound in which arsenic is the most electronegative element
ARSENIDES > ARSENIDE
ARSENIOUS adj of or containing arsenic in the trivalent state
ARSENITE n salt or ester of arsenous acid
ARSENITES > ARSENITE
ARSENO adj containing arsenic

ARSENOUS same as > ARSENIOUS
ARSES > ARSIS
ARSEY adj slang word meaning aggressive or irritable
ARSHEEN n old measure of length in Russia
ARSHEENS > ARSHEEN
ARSHIN n old measure of length in Russia
ARSHINE n old measure of length in Russia
ARSHINES > ARSHINE
ARSHINS > ARSHIN
ARSIER > ARSY
ARSIEST > ARSY
ARSINE n colourless poisonous gas
ARSINES > ARSINE
ARSING > ARSE
ARSINO adj containing arsine
ARSIS n long or stressed syllable in a metrical foot
ARSON n crime of intentionally setting property on fire
ARSONIST > ARSON
ARSONISTS > ARSON
ARSONITE n person committing arson
ARSONITES > ARSONITE
ARSONOUS adj of arson
ARSONS > ARSON
ARSY same as > ARSEY
ART n creation of works of beauty, esp paintings or sculpture
ARTAL a plural of > ROTL
ARTEFACT n something made by human beings
ARTEFACTS > ARTEFACT
ARTEL n cooperative union
ARTELS > ARTEL
ARTEMISIA n type of herbaceous plant of the N hemisphere, such as mugwort, sagebrush, and wormwood
ARTERIAL adj of an artery ▷ n major road
ARTERIALS > ARTERIAL
ARTERIES > ARTERY
ARTERIOLE n any of the small subdivisions of an artery that form thin-walled vessels ending in capillaries
ARTERITIS n inflammation of an artery
ARTERY n one of the tubes carrying blood from the heart
ARTESIAN adj as in artesian well sunken well receiving water from a higher altitude
ARTFUL adj cunning, wily
ARTFULLY > ARTFUL
ARTHOUSE n cinema which shows artistic films
ARTHOUSES > ARTHOUSE

ARTHRITIC
> ARTHRITIS

ARTHRITIS n painful inflammation of a joint or joints

ARTHRODIA n joint

ARTHROPOD n animal, such as a spider or insect, with jointed limbs and a segmented body

ARTHROSES
> ARTHROSIS

ARTHROSIS n disease of joint

ARTI n Hindu ritual performed in homes and temples

ARTIC n articulated vehicle

ARTICHOKE n flower head of a thistle-like plant, cooked as a vegetable

ARTICLE n written piece in a magazine or newspaper ▷ vb bind by a written contract

ARTICLED > ARTICLE

ARTICLES > ARTICLE

ARTICLING > ARTICLE

ARTICS > ARTIC

ARTICULAR adj of or relating to joints

ARTIER > ARTY

ARTIES > ARTY

ARTIEST > ARTY

ARTIFACT same as
> ARTEFACT

ARTIFACTS
> ARTIFACT

ARTIFICE n clever trick

ARTIFICER n craftsman or craftswoman

ARTIFICES
> ARTIFICE

ARTIGI n kind of hooded coat worn in Canada

ARTIGIS > ARTIGI

ARTILLERY n large-calibre guns

ARTILY > ARTY

ARTINESS > ARTY

ARTIS > ARTI

ARTISAN n skilled worker, craftsman or craftswoman

ARTISANAL > ARTISAN

ARTISANS > ARTISAN

ARTIST n person who produces works of art, esp paintings or sculpture

ARTISTE n professional entertainer such as a singer or dancer

ARTISTES > ARTISTE

ARTISTIC adj of or characteristic of art or artists

ARTISTRY n artistic skill

ARTISTS > ARTIST

ARTLESS adj free from deceit or cunning

ARTLESSLY > ARTLESS

ARTMAKER n person who creates art

ARTMAKERS
> ARTMAKER

ARTMAKING n process of making art

ARTS > ART

ARTSIE n arts student

ARTSIER > ARTSY

ARTSIES > ARTSY

ARTSIEST > ARTSY

ARTSINESS > ARTSY

ARTSMAN old word for
> CRAFTSMAN

ARTSMEN > ARTSMAN

ARTSY adj interested in the arts ▷ n person interested in the arts

ARTWORK n all the photographs and illustrations in a publication

ARTWORKS > ARTWORK

ARTY adj having an affected interest in art ▷ n person interested in art

ARUANA n tropical freshwater fish

ARUANAS > ARUANA

ARUGOLA same as
> ARUGULA

ARUGOLAS > ARUGOLA

ARUGULA n salad plant

ARUGULAS > ARUGULA

ARUHE n edible root of a fern

ARUHES > ARUHE

ARUM n type of plant

ARUMS > ARUM

ARUSPEX variant spelling of > HARUSPEX

ARUSPICES > ARUSPEX

ARVAL adj of ploughed land

ARVEE n short for recreational vehicle (RV)

ARVEES > ARVEE

ARVICOLE n water rat

ARVICOLES
> ARVICOLE

ARVO n afternoon

ARVOS > ARVO

ARY dialect form of > ANY

ARYBALLOS n ancient Greek flask

ARYL n (in chemistry) an aromatic group

ARYLS > ARYL

ARYTENOID adj denoting either of two small cartilages of the larynx that are attached to the vocal cords ▷ n arytenoid cartilage or muscle

ARYTHMIA n any variation

ARYTHMIAS
> ARYTHMIA

ARYTHMIC > ARYTHMIA

AS adv used to indicate amount or extent in comparisons ▷ n ancient Roman unit of weight

ASAFETIDA n bitter resin with an unpleasant onion-like smell

ASANA n any of various postures in yoga

ASANAS > ASANA

ASAR > AS

ASARUM n dried strong-scented root

ASARUMS > ASARUM

ASBESTIC > ASBESTOS

ASBESTINE
> ASBESTOS

ASBESTOS n fibrous mineral which does not burn

ASBESTOUS
> ASBESTOS

ASBESTUS n asbestos

ASCARED adj afraid

ASCARID n type of parasitic nematode

ASCARIDES > ASCARID

ASCARIDS > ASCARID

ASCARIS n ascarid

ASCARISES > ASCARIS

ASCAUNT adv old word meaning slantwise

ASCEND vb go or move up

ASCENDANT adj dominant or influential

ASCENDED > ASCEND

ASCENDENT same as
> ASCENDANT

ASCENDER n part of some lower-case letters that extends above the body of the letter

ASCENDERS
> ASCENDER

ASCENDEUR n metal grip that is threaded on a rope and can be alternately tightened and slackened as an aid to climbing the rope: used attached to slings for the feet and waist

ASCENDING adj moving upwards

ASCENDS > ASCEND

ASCENSION n act of ascending

ASCENSIVE adj moving upwards

ASCENT n act of ascending

ASCENTS > ASCENT

ASCERTAIN vb find out definitely

ASCESES > ASCESIS

ASCESIS n exercise of self-discipline

ASCETIC adj abstaining from worldly pleasures and comforts ▷ n person who abstains from worldly comforts and pleasures

ASCETICAL adj ascetic

ASCETICS > ASCETIC

ASCI > ASCUS

ASCIAN n person living in the tropics

ASCIANS > ASCIAN

ASCIDIA > ASCIDIUM

ASCIDIAN n type of minute marine invertebrate, such as the sea squirt

ASCIDIANS
> ASCIDIAN

ASCIDIATE
> ASCIDIUM

ASCIDIUM n part of a plant that is shaped like a pitcher

ASCITES n accumulation of serous fluid in the peritoneal cavity

ASCITIC > ASCITES

ASCITICAL > ASCITES

ASCLEPIAD n Greek verse form

ASCLEPIAS n type of plant often grown as a garden or greenhouse plant for its showy orange-scarlet or purple flowers

ASCOCARP n (in some ascomycetous fungi) a globular structure containing the asci

ASCOCARPS
> ASCOCARP

ASCOGONIA n female reproductive bodies in some fungi

ASCON n type of sponge having an oval shape and a thin body wall

ASCONCE adv old form of askance

ASCONOID adj like an ascon

ASCONS > ASCON

ASCORBATE n salt of ascorbic acid

ASCORBIC adj as in ascorbic acid vitamin present in citrus fruits, tomatoes, and green vegetables

ASCOSPORE n one of the spores (usually eight in number) that are produced in an ascus

ASCOT n type of cravat

ASCOTS > ASCOT

ASCRIBE vb attribute, as to a particular origin

ASCRIBED > ASCRIBE

ASCRIBES > ASCRIBE

ASCRIBING > ASCRIBE

ASCUS n saclike structure in fungi

ASDIC n early form of sonar

ASDICS > ASDIC

ASEA adv towards the sea

ASEISMIC adj denoting a region free of earthquakes

ASEITIES > ASEITY

ASEITY n existence derived from itself, having no other source

ASEMANTIC adj not semantic

ASEPALOUS adj (of a plant or flower) having no sepals

ASEPSES > ASEPSIS

ASEPSIS n aseptic condition

ASEPTATE adj not divided into cells or sections by septa

ASEPTIC adj free from harmful bacteria ▷ n aseptic substance

ASEPTICS > ASEPTIC

ASEXUAL adj without biological sex

ASEXUALLY > ASEXUAL

ASH n powdery substance left when something is burnt ▷ vb reduce to ashes

ASHAKE adv shaking

ASHAME vb make ashamed

ASHAMED *adj* feeling shame
ASHAMEDLY > ASHAMED
ASHAMES > ASHAME
ASHAMING > ASHAME
ASHCAKE *n* cornmeal bread
ASHCAKES > ASHCAKE
ASHCAN *n* large metal dustbin
ASHCANS > ASHCAN
ASHED > ASH
ASHEN *adj* pale with shock
ASHERIES > ASHERY
ASHERY *n* place where ashes are made
ASHES > ASH
ASHET *n* shallow oval dish or large plate
ASHETS > ASHET
ASHFALL *n* dropping of ash from a volcano
ASHFALLS > ASHFALL
ASHIER > ASHY
ASHIEST > ASHY
ASHINE *adv* old word meaning shining
ASHINESS > ASHY
ASHING > ASH
ASHIVER *adv* shivering
ASHKEY *n* winged fruit of the ash
ASHKEYS > ASHKEY
ASHLAR *n* block of hewn stone ▷ *vb* build with ashlars
ASHLARED > ASHLAR
ASHLARING > ASHLAR
ASHLARS > ASHLAR
ASHLER *same as* > ASHLAR
ASHLERED > ASHLER
ASHLERING > ASHLER
ASHLERS > ASHLER
ASHLESS > ASH
ASHMAN *n* man who shovels ashes
ASHMEN > ASHMAN
ASHORE *adv* towards or on land ▷ *adj* on land, having come from the water
ASHPAN *n* pan or tray to catch ashes
ASHPANS > ASHPAN
ASHPLANT *n* walking stick made from an ash sapling
ASHPLANTS > ASHPLANT
ASHRAF *pl n* descendants of Muhammad
ASHRAM *n* religious retreat where a Hindu holy man lives
ASHRAMA *n* stage in Hindu spiritual life
ASHRAMAS > ASHRAMA
ASHRAMITE *n* person living in an ashram
ASHRAMS > ASHRAM
ASHTANGA *n* type of yoga
ASHTANGAS > ASHTANGA
ASHTRAY *n* receptacle for tobacco ash and cigarette butts
ASHTRAYS > ASHTRAY

ASHY *adj* pale greyish
ASIAGO *n* type of cheese
ASIAGOS > ASIAGO
ASIDE *adv* one side ▷ *n* remark not meant to be heard by everyone present
ASIDES > ASIDE
ASINICO *n* old Spanish word for fool
ASINICOS > ASINICO
ASININE *adj* stupid, idiotic
ASININELY > ASININE
ASININITY > ASININE
ASK *vb* say (something) in a form that requires an answer
ASKANCE *adv* with an oblique glance ▷ *vb* turn aside
ASKANCED > ASKANCE
ASKANCES > ASKANCE
ASKANCING > ASKANCE
ASKANT *same as* > ASKANCE
ASKANTED > ASKANT
ASKANTING > ASKANT
ASKANTS > ASKANT
ASKARI *n* (in East Africa) a soldier or police officer
ASKARIS > ASKARI
ASKED > ASK
ASKER > ASK
ASKERS > ASK
ASKESES > ASKESIS
ASKESIS *n* practice of self-discipline
ASKEW *adj* one side, crooked
ASKEWNESS > ASKEW
ASKING > ASK
ASKINGS > ASK
ASKLENT *Scots word for* > ASLANT
ASKOI > ASKOS
ASKOS *n* ancient Greek vase
ASKS > ASK
ASLAKE *vb* slake
ASLAKED > ASLAKE
ASLAKES > ASLAKE
ASLAKING > ASLAKE
ASLANT *adv* at a slant (to), slanting (across)
ASLEEP *adj* sleeping
ASLOPE *adj* sloping
ASLOSH *adj* awash
ASMEAR *adj* smeared
ASMOULDER *adv* old word meaning smouldering
ASOCIAL *n* person who avoids social contact
ASOCIALS > ASOCIAL
ASP *n* small poisonous snake
ASPARAGUS *n* plant whose shoots are cooked as a vegetable
ASPARKLE *adv* sparkling
ASPARTAME *n* artificial sweetener
ASPARTATE *n* enzyme found in blood
ASPARTIC *adj* as in *aspartic acid* nonessential amino acid that is a component of proteins

ASPECT *n* feature or element ▷ *vb* look at
ASPECTED > ASPECT
ASPECTING > ASPECT
ASPECTS > ASPECT
ASPECTUAL *adj* of or relating to grammatical aspect
ASPEN *n* kind of poplar tree ▷ *adj* trembling
ASPENS > ASPEN
ASPER *n* former Turkish monetary unit
ASPERATE *adj* (of plant parts) having a rough surface due to a covering of short stiff hairs ▷ *vb* make rough
ASPERATED > ASPERATE
ASPERATES > ASPERATE
ASPERGE *vb* sprinkle
ASPERGED > ASPERGE
ASPERGER > ASPERGE
ASPERGES > ASPERGE
ASPERGILL *n* perforated instrument used to sprinkle holy water
ASPERGING > ASPERGE
ASPERITY *n* roughness of temper
ASPERMIA *n* failure to form or emit semen
ASPERMIAS > ASPERMIA
ASPEROUS *same as* > ASPERATE
ASPERS > ASPER
ASPERSE *vb* spread false rumours about
ASPERSED > ASPERSE
ASPERSER > ASPERSE
ASPERSERS > ASPERSE
ASPERSES > ASPERSE
ASPERSING > ASPERSE
ASPERSION *n* disparaging or malicious remark
ASPERSIVE > ASPERSE
ASPERSOIR *n* sprinkler for holy water
ASPERSOR > ASPERSE
ASPERSORS > ASPERSE
ASPERSORY *n* sprinkler for holy water
ASPHALT *n* black hard tar-like substance used for road surfaces etc ▷ *vb* cover with asphalt
ASPHALTED > ASPHALT
ASPHALTER *n* person who lays asphalt
ASPHALTIC > ASPHALT
ASPHALTS > ASPHALT
ASPHALTUM *n* asphalt
ASPHERIC *adj* not spherical ▷ *n* lens that is not completely spherical
ASPHERICS > ASPHERIC
ASPHODEL *n* plant with clusters of yellow or white flowers
ASPHODELS > ASPHODEL
ASPHYXIA *n* suffocation

ASPHYXIAL > ASPHYXIA
ASPHYXIAS > ASPHYXIA
ASPHYXIED > ASPHYXY
ASPHYXIES > ASPHYXY
ASPHYXY *vb* smother, suffocate
ASPIC *n* savoury jelly used to coat meat, eggs, fish, etc
ASPICK *old word for* > ASP
ASPICKS > ASPICK
ASPICS > ASPIC
ASPIDIA > ASPIDIUM
ASPIDIOID > ASPIDIUM
ASPIDIUM *n* variety of fern
ASPINE *old word for* > ASPEN
ASPINES > ASPINE
ASPIRANT *n* person who aspires ▷ *adj* aspiring or striving
ASPIRANTS > ASPIRANT
ASPIRATA *n* rough stop
ASPIRATAE > ASPIRATA
ASPIRATE *vb* pronounce with an *h* sound ▷ *n* *h* sound ▷ *adj* (of a stop) pronounced with a forceful and audible expulsion of breath
ASPIRATED > ASPIRATE
ASPIRATES > ASPIRATE
ASPIRATOR *n* device for removing fluids from a body cavity by suction
ASPIRE *vb* yearn (for), hope (to do or be)
ASPIRED > ASPIRE
ASPIRER > ASPIRE
ASPIRERS > ASPIRE
ASPIRES > ASPIRE
ASPIRIN *n* drug used to relieve pain and fever
ASPIRING > ASPIRE
ASPIRINS > ASPIRIN
ASPIS *n* horned viper
ASPISES > ASPIS
ASPISH *adj* like an asp
ASPLENIUM *n* type of fern
ASPORT *vb* old word meaning take away
ASPORTED > ASPORT
ASPORTING > ASPORT
ASPORTS > ASPORT
ASPOUT *adv* spouting
ASPRAWL *adv* sprawling
ASPREAD *adv* spreading
ASPRO *n* associate professor at an academic institution
ASPROS > ASPRO
ASPROUT *adv* sprouting
ASPS > ASP
ASQUAT *adv* squatting
ASQUINT *adj* with a glance from the corner of the eye
ASRAMA *n* stage in Hindu spiritual life

ASRAMAS > ASRAMA
ASS n donkey
ASSAGAI same as
> ASSEGAI
ASSAGAIED > ASSAGAI
ASSAGAIS > ASSAGAI
ASSAI adv (usually preceded by a musical direction) very ▷ n Brazilian palm tree
ASSAIL vb attack violently
ASSAILANT n person who attacks another, either physically or verbally
ASSAILED > ASSAIL
ASSAILER > ASSAIL
ASSAILERS > ASSAIL
ASSAILING > ASSAIL
ASSAILS > ASSAIL
ASSAIS > ASSAI
ASSAM n (in Malaysia) tamarind as used in cooking
ASSAMS > ASSAM
ASSART vb clear ground for cultivation
ASSARTED > ASSART
ASSARTING > ASSART
ASSARTS > ASSART
ASSASSIN n person who murders a prominent person
ASSASSINS
> ASSASSIN
ASSAULT n violent attack ▷ vb attack violently
ASSAULTED > ASSAULT
ASSAULTER > ASSAULT
ASSAULTS > ASSAULT
ASSAY n analysis of a substance ▷ vb make such an analysis
ASSAYABLE > ASSAY
ASSAYED > ASSAY
ASSAYER > ASSAY
ASSAYERS > ASSAY
ASSAYING > ASSAY
ASSAYINGS > ASSAY
ASSAYS > ASSAY
ASSEGAAI same as
> ASSEGAI
ASSEGAAIS
> ASSEGAAI
ASSEGAI n slender spear used in S Africa ▷ vb spear with an assegai
ASSEGAIED > ASSEGAI
ASSEGAIS > ASSEGAI
ASSEMBLE vb collect or congregate
ASSEMBLED
> ASSEMBLE
ASSEMBLER n person or thing that assembles
ASSEMBLES
> ASSEMBLE
ASSEMBLY n assembled group
ASSENT n agreement or consent ▷ vb agree or consent
ASSENTED > ASSENT
ASSENTER n person supporting another's nomination
ASSENTERS
> ASSENTER

ASSENTING > ASSENT
ASSENTIVE > ASSENT
ASSENTOR n voter legally required to endorse the nomination of a candidate
ASSENTORS
> ASSENTOR
ASSENTS > ASSENT
ASSERT vb declare forcefully
ASSERTED > ASSERT
ASSERTER > ASSERT
ASSERTERS > ASSERT
ASSERTING > ASSERT
ASSERTION n positive statement, usu made without evidence
ASSERTIVE adj confident and direct in dealing with others
ASSERTOR > ASSERT
ASSERTORS > ASSERT
ASSERTORY adj making affirmation
ASSERTS > ASSERT
ASSES > ASS
ASSESS vb judge the worth or importance of
ASSESSED > ASSESS
ASSESSES > ASSESS
ASSESSING > ASSESS
ASSESSOR n person who values property for taxation or insurance purposes
ASSESSORS
> ASSESSOR
ASSET n valuable or useful person or thing
ASSETLESS > ASSET
ASSETS > ASSET
ASSEVER vb old form of asseverate
ASSEVERED > ASSEVER
ASSEVERS > ASSEVER
ASSEZ adv (as part of a musical direction) fairly
ASSHOLE same as
> ARSEHOLE
ASSHOLES > ASSHOLE
ASSIDUITY n constant and close application
ASSIDUOUS adj hard-working
ASSIEGE vb old form of besiege
ASSIEGED > ASSIEGE
ASSIEGES > ASSIEGE
ASSIEGING > ASSIEGE
ASSIENTO n former slave trade treaty between Britain and Spain
ASSIENTOS > ASSIENTO
ASSIGN vb appoint (someone) to a job or task ▷ n person to whom property is assigned
ASSIGNAT n paper money issued in France by the Constituent Assembly in 1789
ASSIGNATS
> ASSIGNAT
ASSIGNED > ASSIGN
ASSIGNEE n person to whom some right, interest, or property is transferred

ASSIGNEES
> ASSIGNEE
ASSIGNER > ASSIGN
ASSIGNERS > ASSIGN
ASSIGNING > ASSIGN
ASSIGNOR n person who transfers or assigns property
ASSIGNORS
> ASSIGNOR
ASSIGNS > ASSIGN
ASSIST vb give help or support ▷ n pass by a player which enables another player to score a goal
ASSISTANT n helper ▷ adj junior or deputy
ASSISTED > ASSIST
ASSISTER > ASSIST
ASSISTERS > ASSIST
ASSISTING > ASSIST
ASSISTIVE adj providing a means of reducing a physical disability
ASSISTOR > ASSIST
ASSISTORS > ASSIST
ASSISTS > ASSIST
ASSIZE n sitting of a legislative assembly ▷ vb judge or assess
ASSIZED > ASSIZE
ASSIZER n weights and measures official
ASSIZERS > ASSIZER
ASSIZES > ASSIZE
ASSIZING > ASSIZE
ASSLIKE > ASS
ASSOCIATE vb connect in the mind ▷ n partner in business ▷ adj having partial rights or subordinate status
ASSOIL vb absolve
ASSOILED > ASSOIL
ASSOILING > ASSOIL
ASSOILS > ASSOIL
ASSOILZIE vb old Scots word meaning absolve
ASSONANCE n rhyming of vowel sounds but not consonants
ASSONANT
> ASSONANCE
ASSONANTS
> ASSONANCE
ASSONATE vb show assonance
ASSONATED
> ASSONATE
ASSONATES
> ASSONATE
ASSORT vb arrange or distribute equally
ASSORTED adj consisting of various types mixed together
ASSORTER > ASSORT
ASSORTERS > ASSORT
ASSORTING > ASSORT
ASSORTIVE > ASSORT
ASSORTS > ASSORT
ASSOT vb old word meaning make infatuated
ASSOTS > ASSOT
ASSOTT adj besotted
ASSOTTED > ASSOT

ASSOTTING > ASSOT
ASSUAGE vb relieve (pain, grief, thirst, etc)
ASSUAGED > ASSUAGE
ASSUAGER > ASSUAGE
ASSUAGERS > ASSUAGE
ASSUAGES > ASSUAGE
ASSUAGING > ASSUAGE
ASSUASIVE > ASSUAGE
ASSUETUDE n state of being accustomed
ASSUMABLE > ASSUME
ASSUMABLY > ASSUME
ASSUME vb take to be true without proof
ASSUMED adj false
ASSUMEDLY > ASSUME
ASSUMER > ASSUME
ASSUMERS > ASSUME
ASSUMES > ASSUME
ASSUMING adj expecting too much ▷ n action of one who assumes
ASSUMINGS
> ASSUMING
ASSUMPSIT n (before 1875) an action to recover damages for breach of an express or implied contract or agreement that was not under seal
ASSURABLE > ASSURE
ASSURANCE n assuring or being assured
ASSURE vb promise or guarantee
ASSURED adj confident ▷ n beneficiary under a life assurance policy
ASSUREDLY > ASSURED
ASSUREDS > ASSURED
ASSURER > ASSURE
ASSURERS > ASSURE
ASSURES > ASSURE
ASSURGENT adj (of leaves, stems, etc) curving or growing upwards
ASSURING > ASSURE
ASSUROR > ASSURE
ASSURORS > ASSURE
ASSWAGE old spelling of
> ASSUAGE
ASSWAGED > ASSWAGE
ASSWAGES > ASSWAGE
ASSWAGING > ASSWAGE
ASSWIPE n vulgar word for a contemptible person
ASSWIPES > ASSWIPE
ASTABLE adj not stable
ASTANGA same as
> ASHTANGA
ASTANGAS > ASTANGA
ASTARE adv staring
ASTART old word for
> START
ASTARTED > ASTART
ASTARTING > ASTART
ASTARTS > ASTART
ASTASIA n inability to stand
ASTASIAS > ASTASIA
ASTATIC adj not static
ASTATIDE n binary compound of astatine with a more electropositive element
ASTATIDES
> ASTATIDE

ASTATINE *n* radioactive nonmetallic element

ASTATINES
> ASTATINE

ASTATKI *n* fuel derived from petroleum

ASTATKIS > ASTATKI

ASTEISM *n* use of irony

ASTEISMS > ASTEISM

ASTELIC > ASTELY

ASTELIES > ASTELY

ASTELY *n* lack of central cylinder in plants

ASTER *n* plant with daisy-like flowers

ASTERIA *n* gemstone with starlike light effect

ASTERIAS > ASTERIA

ASTERID *n* variety of flowering plant

ASTERIDS > ASTERID

ASTERISK *n* star-shaped symbol (*) used in printing or writing to indicate a footnote, etc ▷ *vb* mark with an asterisk

ASTERISKS
> ASTERISK

ASTERISM *n* three asterisks arranged in a triangle to draw attention to the text that follows

ASTERISMS
> ASTERISM

ASTERN *adv* at or towards the stern of a ship ▷ *adj* at or towards the stern of a ship

ASTERNAL *adj* not connected or joined to the sternum

ASTEROID *n* any of the small planets that orbit the sun between Mars and Jupiter ▷ *adj* of, relating to, or belonging to the class *Asteroidea*

ASTEROIDS
> ASTEROID

ASTERS > ASTER

ASTERT *vb* start

ASTERTED > ASTERT

ASTERTING > ASTERT

ASTERTS > ASTERT

ASTHANGA *n* type of yoga

ASTHANGAS
> ASTHANGA

ASTHENIA *n* abnormal loss of strength

ASTHENIAS
> ASTHENIA

ASTHENIC *adj* of, relating to, or having asthenia ▷ *n* person having long limbs and a small trunk

ASTHENICS
> ASTHENIC

ASTHENIES > ASTHENY

ASTHENY *same as*
> ASTHENIA

ASTHMA *n* illness causing difficulty in breathing

ASTHMAS > ASTHMA

ASTHMATIC *adj* of, relating to, or having asthma ▷ *n* person who has asthma

ASTHORE *n* Irish endearment

ASTHORES > ASTHORE

ASTICHOUS *adj* not arranged in rows

ASTIGMIA *n* defect of a lens resulting in the formation of distorted images

ASTIGMIAS
> ASTIGMIA

ASTILBE *n* type of plant

ASTILBES > ASTILBE

ASTIR *adj* out of bed

ASTOMATAL *adj* having no stomata

ASTOMOUS *adj* having no mouth

ASTONE *old form of*
> ASTONISH

ASTONED > ASTONE

ASTONES > ASTONE

ASTONIED *adj* stunned

ASTONIES > ASTONY

ASTONING > ASTONE

ASTONISH *vb* surprise greatly

ASTONY *old form of*
> ASTONISH

ASTONYING > ASTONY

ASTOOP *adv* stooping

ASTOUND *vb* overwhelm with amazement

ASTOUNDED > ASTOUND

ASTOUNDS > ASTOUND

ASTRACHAN *same as*
> ASTRAKHAN

ASTRADDLE *adj* with a leg on either side of something

ASTRAGAL *n* small convex moulding, usually with a semicircular cross section

ASTRAGALI *n* bones of the ankles that articulate with the leg bones to form ankle joints

ASTRAGALS
> ASTRAGAL

ASTRAKHAN *n* dark curly fleece of lambs from Astrakhan in Russia

ASTRAL *adj* of stars ▷ *n* oil lamp

ASTRALLY > ASTRAL

ASTRALS > ASTRAL

ASTRAND *adv* on the shore

ASTRANTIA *n* flowering plant

ASTRAY *adv* off the right path

ASTRICT *vb* bind, confine, or constrict

ASTRICTED > ASTRICT

ASTRICTS > ASTRICT

ASTRIDE *adv* with a leg on either side (of) ▷ *adj* with a leg on either side

ASTRINGE *vb* cause contraction

ASTRINGED
> ASTRINGE

ASTRINGER *n* person who keeps goshawks

ASTRINGES
> ASTRINGE

ASTROCYTE *n* any of the star-shaped cells in the tissue supporting the brain and spinal cord (neuroglia)

ASTRODOME *n* transparent dome on the top of an aircraft, through which observations can be made, esp of the stars

ASTROFELL *n* plant in Spenser's poetry

ASTROID *n* hypocycloid having four cusps

ASTROIDS > ASTROID

ASTROLABE *n* instrument formerly used to measure the altitude of stars and planets

ASTROLOGY *n* study of the alleged influence of the stars, planets, and moon on human affairs

ASTRONAUT *n* person trained for travelling in space

ASTRONOMY *n* scientific study of heavenly bodies

ASTROPHEL *n* plant in Spenser's poetry

ASTRUT *adv* old word meaning in a protruding way

ASTUCIOUS *adj* old form of astute

ASTUCITY *n* quality of being astute

ASTUN *vb* old form of astonish

ASTUNNED > ASTUN

ASTUNNING > ASTUN

ASTUNS > ASTUN

ASTUTE *adj* perceptive or shrewd

ASTUTELY > ASTUTE

ASTUTER > ASTUTE

ASTUTEST > ASTUTE

ASTYLAR *adj* without columns or pilasters

ASUDDEN *adv* old form of suddenly

ASUNDER *adv* into parts or pieces ▷ *adj* into parts or pieces

ASURA *n* demon in Hindu mythology

ASURAS > ASURA

ASWARM *adj* filled, esp with moving things

ASWAY *adv* swaying

ASWIM *adv* floating

ASWING *adv* swinging

ASWIRL *adv* swirling

ASWOON *adv* swooning

ASYLA > ASYLUM

ASYLEE *n* person who is granted asylum

ASYLEES > ASYLEE

ASYLLABIC *adj* not functioning in the manner of a syllable

ASYLUM *n* refuge or sanctuary

ASYLUMS > ASYLUM

ASYMMETRY *n* lack of symmetry

ASYMPTOTE *n* straight line closely approached but never met by a curve

ASYNAPSES
> ASYNAPSIS

ASYNAPSIS *n* failure of pairing of chromosomes at meiosis

ASYNDETA
> ASYNDETON

ASYNDETIC *adj* (of a catalogue or index) without cross references

ASYNDETON *n* omission of a conjunction between the parts of a sentence

ASYNERGIA *n* lack of coordination between muscles or parts, as occurs in cerebellar disease

ASYNERGY *same as*
> ASYNERGIA

ASYSTOLE *n* absence of heartbeat

ASYSTOLES
> ASYSTOLE

ASYSTOLIC
> ASYSTOLE

AT *n* Laotian monetary unit worth one hundredth of a kip

ATAATA *n* grazing marine gastropod

ATAATAS > ATAATA

ATABAL *n* N African drum

ATABALS > ATABAL

ATABEG *n* Turkish ruler

ATABEGS > ATABEG

ATABEK *same as*
> ATABEG

ATABEKS > ATABEK

ATABRIN *n* drug formerly used for treating malaria

ATABRINE *same as*
> ATABRIN

ATABRINES
> ATABRINE

ATABRINS > ATABRIN

ATACAMITE *n* mineral containing copper

ATACTIC *adj* attribute of a polymer

ATAGHAN *variant of*
> YATAGHAN

ATAGHANS > ATAGHAN

ATALAYA *n* watchtower in Spain

ATALAYAS > ATALAYA

ATAMAN *n* elected leader of the Cossacks

ATAMANS > ATAMAN

ATAMASCO *n* N American lily

ATAMASCOS
> ATAMASCO

ATAP *n* palm tree of S Asia

ATAPS > ATAP

ATARACTIC *adj* able to calm or tranquillize ▷ *n* ataractic drug

ATARAXIA *n* calmness or peace of mind

ATARAXIAS
> ATARAXIA

ATARAXIC *same as*
> ATARACTIC

ATARAXICS
> ATARAXIC

ATARAXIES > ATARAXY

ATARAXY *same as*
> ATARAXIA

ATAVIC > ATAVISM
ATAVISM n recurrence of a trait present in distant ancestors
ATAVISMS > ATAVISM
ATAVIST > ATAVISM
ATAVISTIC adj of or relating to reversion to a former or more primitive type
ATAVISTS > ATAVISM
ATAXIA n lack of muscular coordination
ATAXIAS > ATAXIA
ATAXIC > ATAXIA
ATAXICS > ATAXIA
ATAXIES > ATAXY
ATAXY same as > ATAXIA
ATCHIEVE same as > ACHIEVE
ATCHIEVED > ATCHIEVE
ATCHIEVES > ATCHIEVE
ATE > EAT
ATEBRIN n drug formerly used to treat malaria
ATEBRINS > ATEBRIN
ATECHNIC adj without technical ability ▷ n person with no technical ability
ATECHNICS > ATECHNIC
ATELIC adj of action without end
ATELIER n workshop, artist's studio
ATELIERS > ATELIER
ATEMOYA n tropical fruit tree
ATEMOYAS > ATEMOYA
ATEMPORAL adj not governed by time
ATENOLOL n type of beta-blocker
ATENOLOLS > ATENOLOL
ATES n shop selling confectionery
ATHAME n witch's ceremonial knife
ATHAMES > ATHAME
ATHANASY n absence of death
ATHANOR n alchemist's furnace
ATHANORS > ATHANOR
ATHEISE vb speak atheistically
ATHEISED > ATHEISE
ATHEISES > ATHEISE
ATHEISING > ATHEISE
ATHEISM n belief that there is no God
ATHEISMS > ATHEISM
ATHEIST > ATHEISM
ATHEISTIC > ATHEISM
ATHEISTS > ATHEISM
ATHEIZE vb speak atheistically
ATHEIZED > ATHEIZE
ATHEIZES > ATHEIZE
ATHEIZING > ATHEIZE
ATHELING n (in Anglo-Saxon England) a prince of any of the royal dynasties

ATHELINGS > ATHELING
ATHEMATIC adj not based on themes
ATHENAEUM n institution for the promotion of learning
ATHENEUM same as > ATHENAEUM
ATHENEUMS > ATHENEUM
ATHEOLOGY n opposition to theology
ATHEOUS adj without a belief in god
ATHERINE n small fish
ATHERINES > ATHERINE
ATHEROMA n fatty deposit on or within an artery
ATHEROMAS > ATHEROMA
ATHETESES > ATHETESIS
ATHETESIS n dismissal of a text as not genuine
ATHETISE vb reject as not genuine
ATHETISED > ATHETISE
ATHETISES > ATHETISE
ATHETIZE vb reject as not genuine
ATHETIZED > ATHETIZE
ATHETIZES > ATHETIZE
ATHETOID > ATHETOSIS
ATHETOSES > ATHETOSIS
ATHETOSIC > ATHETOSIS
ATHETOSIS n condition characterized by uncontrolled rhythmic writhing movement, esp of fingers, hands, head, and tongue, caused by cerebral lesion
ATHETOTIC > ATHETOSIS
ATHIRST adj having an eager desire
ATHLETA same as > ATHLETE
ATHLETAS > ATHLETA
ATHLETE n person trained in or good at athletics
ATHLETES > ATHLETE
ATHLETIC adj physically fit or strong
ATHLETICS n track and field events
ATHODYD another name for > RAMJET
ATHODYDS > ATHODYD
ATHRILL adv feeling thrills
ATHROB adv throbbing
ATHROCYTE n cell able to store matter
ATHWART adv transversely
ATIGI n type of parka worn by the Inuit in Canada

ATIGIS > ATIGI
ATILT adj in a tilted or inclined position
ATIMIES > ATIMY
ATIMY n loss of honour
ATINGLE adv tingling
ATISHOO n sound of a sneeze
ATISHOOS > ATISHOO
ATLANTES > ATLAS
ATLAS n book of maps
ATLASES > ATLAS
ATLATL n Native American throwing stick
ATLATLS > ATLATL
ATMA same as > ATMAN
ATMAN n personal soul or self
ATMANS > ATMAN
ATMAS > ATMA
ATMOLOGY n study of aqueous vapour
ATMOLYSE vb separate gases by filtering
ATMOLYSED > ATMOLYSE
ATMOLYSES > ATMOLYSIS
ATMOLYSIS n method of separating gases that depends on their differential rates of diffusion through a porous substance
ATMOLYZE vb separate gases by filtering
ATMOLYZED > ATMOLYZE
ATMOLYZES > ATMOLYZE
ATMOMETER n instrument for measuring the rate of evaporation of water into the atmosphere
ATMOMETRY > ATMOMETER
ATMOS n (short for) atmosphere
ATMOSES > ATMOS
ATOC n skunk
ATOCIA n inability to have children
ATOCIAS > ATOCIA
ATOCS > ATOC
ATOK n skunk
ATOKAL adj having no children
ATOKE n part of a worm
ATOKES > ATOKE
ATOKOUS adj having no children
ATOKS > ATOK
ATOLL n ring-shaped coral reef enclosing a lagoon
ATOLLS > ATOLL
ATOM n smallest unit of matter which can take part in a chemical reaction
ATOMIC adj of or using atomic bombs or atomic energy
ATOMICAL > ATOMIC
ATOMICITY n state of being made up of atoms
ATOMICS n science of atoms

ATOMIES > ATOMY
ATOMISE same as > ATOMIZE
ATOMISED > ATOMISE
ATOMISER same as > ATOMIZER
ATOMISERS > ATOMISER
ATOMISES > ATOMISE
ATOMISING > ATOMISE
ATOMISM n ancient philosophical theory
ATOMISMS > ATOMISM
ATOMIST > ATOMISM
ATOMISTIC > ATOMISM
ATOMISTS > ATOMISM
ATOMIZE vb reduce to atoms or small particles
ATOMIZED > ATOMIZE
ATOMIZER n device for discharging a liquid in a fine spray
ATOMIZERS > ATOMIZER
ATOMIZES > ATOMIZE
ATOMIZING > ATOMIZE
ATOMS > ATOM
ATOMY n atom or minute particle
ATONABLE > ATONE
ATONAL adj (of music) not written in an established key
ATONALISM > ATONAL
ATONALIST > ATONAL
ATONALITY n absence of or disregard for an established musical key in a composition
ATONALLY > ATONAL
ATONE vb make amends (for sin or wrongdoing)
ATONEABLE > ATONE
ATONED > ATONE
ATONEMENT n something done to make amends for wrongdoing
ATONER > ATONE
ATONERS > ATONE
ATONES > ATONE
ATONIA n lack of normal muscle tone
ATONIAS > ATONIA
ATONIC adj carrying no stress ▷ n unaccented or unstressed syllable
ATONICITY > ATONIC
ATONICS > ATONIC
ATONIES > ATONY
ATONING > ATONE
ATONINGLY > ATONE
ATONY n lack of normal tone or tension, as in muscles
ATOP adv on top
ATOPIC adj of or relating to hypersensitivity to certain allergens
ATOPIES > ATOPY
ATOPY n tendency to be hypersensitive to certain allergens
ATRAMENT n old word meaning black liquid
ATRAMENTS > ATRAMENT
ATRAZINE n white crystalline compound

ATRAZINES
> ATRAZINE

ATREMBLE adv trembling

ATRESIA n absence of or unnatural narrowing of a body channel

ATRESIAS > ATRESIA

ATRESIC > ATRESIA

ATRETIC > ATRESIA

ATRIA > ATRIUM

ATRIAL > ATRIUM

ATRIP adj (of an anchor) no longer caught on the bottom

ATRIUM n upper chamber of either half of the heart

ATRIUMS > ATRIUM

ATROCIOUS adj extremely cruel or wicked

ATROCITY n wickedness

ATROPHIA n wasting disease

ATROPHIAS
> ATROPHIA

ATROPHIC > ATROPHY

ATROPHIED > ATROPHY

ATROPHIES > ATROPHY

ATROPHY n wasting away of an organ or part ▷ vb (cause to) waste away

ATROPIA same as
> ATROPINE

ATROPIAS > ATROPIA

ATROPIN same as
> ATROPINE

ATROPINE n poisonous alkaloid obtained from deadly nightshade

ATROPINES > ATROPINE

ATROPINS > ATROPIN

ATROPISM n condition caused by using belladonna

ATROPISMS
> ATROPISM

ATROPOUS adj growing straight

ATS > AT

ATT n old Siamese coin

ATTABOY sentence substitute expression of approval or exhortation

ATTABOYS > ATTABOY

ATTACH vb join, fasten, or connect

ATTACHE n specialist attached to a diplomatic mission

ATTACHED adj fond of

ATTACHER > ATTACH

ATTACHERS > ATTACH

ATTACHES > ATTACH

ATTACHING > ATTACH

ATTACK vb launch a physical assault (against) ▷ n act of attacking

ATTACKED > ATTACK

ATTACKER > ATTACK

ATTACKERS > ATTACK

ATTACKING > ATTACK

ATTACKMAN n attacking player in sport

ATTACKMEN
> ATTACKMAN

ATTACKS > ATTACK

ATTAGIRL humorous feminine version of
> ATTABOY

ATTAIN vb achieve or accomplish (a task or aim)

ATTAINDER n (formerly) the extinction of a person's civil rights resulting from a sentence of death or outlawry on conviction for treason or felony

ATTAINED > ATTAIN

ATTAINER > ATTAIN

ATTAINERS > ATTAIN

ATTAINING > ATTAIN

ATTAINS > ATTAIN

ATTAINT vb pass judgment of death ▷ n dishonour

ATTAINTED > ATTAINT

ATTAINTS > ATTAINT

ATTAP n palm tree of South Asia

ATTAPS > ATTAP

ATTAR n fragrant oil made from roses

ATTARS > ATTAR

ATTASK old word for
> CRITICIZE

ATTASKED > ATTASK

ATTASKING > ATTASK

ATTASKS > ATTASK

ATTASKT > ATTASK

ATTEMPER vb modify by blending

ATTEMPERS
> ATTEMPER

ATTEMPT vb try, make an effort ▷ n effort or endeavour

ATTEMPTED > ATTEMPT

ATTEMPTER > ATTEMPT

ATTEMPTS > ATTEMPT

ATTEND vb be present at

ATTENDANT n person who assists, guides, or provides a service ▷ adj accompanying

ATTENDED > ATTEND

ATTENDEE n person who is present at a specified event

ATTENDEES
> ATTENDEE

ATTENDER > ATTEND

ATTENDERS > ATTEND

ATTENDING > ATTEND

ATTENDS > ATTEND

ATTENT old word for
> ATTENTION

ATTENTAT n attempt

ATTENTATS
> ATTENTAT

ATTENTION n concentrated direction of the mind

ATTENTIVE adj giving attention

ATTENTS > ATTENT

ATTENUANT adj causing dilution or thinness, esp of the blood ▷ n attenuant drug or agent

ATTENUATE vb weaken or become weak ▷ adj diluted, weakened, slender, or reduced

ATTERCOP n spider

ATTERCOPS
> ATTERCOP

ATTEST vb affirm the truth of, be proof of

ATTESTANT > ATTEST

ATTESTED adj (of cattle) certified to be free from a disease, such as tuberculosis

ATTESTER > ATTEST

ATTESTERS > ATTEST

ATTESTING > ATTEST

ATTESTOR > ATTEST

ATTESTORS > ATTEST

ATTESTS > ATTEST

ATTIC n space or room within the roof of a house

ATTICISE same as
> ATTICIZE

ATTICISED
> ATTICISE

ATTICISES
> ATTICISE

ATTICISM n elegant, simple, and clear expression

ATTICISMS
> ATTICISM

ATTICIST > ATTICISM

ATTICISTS
> ATTICISM

ATTICIZE vb conform or adapt to the norms of Attica

ATTICIZED
> ATTICIZE

ATTICIZES
> ATTICIZE

ATTICS > ATTIC

ATTIRE n fine or formal clothes ▷ vb dress, esp in fine elegant clothes

ATTIRED > ATTIRE

ATTIRES > ATTIRE

ATTIRING > ATTIRE

ATTIRINGS > ATTIRE

ATTITUDE n way of thinking and behaving

ATTITUDES
> ATTITUDE

ATTOLASER n high-power laser capable of producing pulses with a duration measured in attoseconds

ATTOLLENS adj (of muscle) used to lift

ATTOLLENT adj muscle used in lifting

ATTOMETER same as
> ATTOMETRE

ATTOMETRE n ten to the power of minus eighteen metres

ATTONCE adv old word for at once

ATTONE vb old word meaning appease

ATTONED > ATTONE

ATTONES > ATTONE

ATTONING > ATTONE

ATTORN vb acknowledge a new owner of land as one's landlord

ATTORNED > ATTORN

ATTORNEY n person legally appointed to act for another

ATTORNEYS
> ATTORNEY

ATTORNING > ATTORN

ATTORNS > ATTORN

ATTOTESLA n ten to the power of minus eighteen teslas

ATTRACT vb arouse the interest or admiration of

ATTRACTED > ATTRACT

ATTRACTER > ATTRACT

ATTRACTOR > ATTRACT

ATTRACTS > ATTRACT

ATTRAHENS adj (of muscle) drawing towards

ATTRAHENT adj something that attracts

ATTRAP vb adorn

ATTRAPPED > ATTRAP

ATTRAPS > ATTRAP

ATTRIBUTE vb regard as belonging to or produced by ▷ n quality or feature representative of a person or thing

ATTRIST vb old word meaning to sadden

ATTRISTED > ATTRIST

ATTRISTS > ATTRIST

ATTRIT vb wear down or dispose of gradually

ATTRITE vb wear down

ATTRITED > ATTRITE

ATTRITES > ATTRITE

ATTRITING > ATTRITE

ATTRITION n constant wearing down to weaken or destroy

ATTRITIVE
> ATTRITION

ATTRITS > ATTRIT

ATTRITTED > ATTRIT

ATTUENT adj carrying out attuition

ATTUITE vb perceive by attuition

ATTUITED > ATTUITE

ATTUITES > ATTUITE

ATTUITING > ATTUITE

ATTUITION n way of mentally perceiving something

ATTUITIVE
> ATTUITION

ATTUNE vb adjust or accustom (a person or thing)

ATTUNED > ATTUNE

ATTUNES > ATTUNE

ATTUNING > ATTUNE

ATUA n spirit or demon

ATUAS > ATUA

ATWAIN adv old word meaning into two parts

ATWEEL Scots word for
> WELL

ATWEEN an archaic or Scots word for > BETWEEN

ATWITTER adv twittering

ATWIXT old word for
> BETWEEN

ATYPIC adj not typical

ATYPICAL adj not typical

AUA n yellow-eye mullet

AUAS > AUA

AUBADE n song or poem greeting the dawn

AUBADES > AUBADE

AUBERGE n inn or tavern

AUBERGES > AUBERGE

AUBERGINE n dark purple tropical fruit, cooked and eaten as a vegetable
AUBRETIA same as > AUBRIETIA
AUBRETIAS > AUBRETIA
AUBRIETA same as > AUBRIETIA
AUBRIETAS > AUBRIETIA
AUBRIETIA n trailing plant with purple flowers
AUBURN adj (of hair) reddish-brown ▷ n moderate reddish-brown colour
AUBURNS > AUBURN
AUCEPS n old word for a person who catches hawks
AUCEPSES > AUCEPS
AUCTION n public sale in which articles are sold to the highest bidder ▷ vb sell by auction
AUCTIONED > AUCTION
AUCTIONS > AUCTION
AUCTORIAL adj of or relating to an author
AUCUBA n Japanese laurel
AUCUBAS > AUCUBA
AUDACIOUS adj recklessly bold or daring
AUDACITY > AUDACIOUS
AUDAD n wild African sheep
AUDADS > AUDAD
AUDIAL adj of sound
AUDIBLE adj loud enough to be heard ▷ n play called in American football by a quarterback ▷ vb call an audible in American football
AUDIBLED > AUDIBLE
AUDIBLES > AUDIBLE
AUDIBLING > AUDIBLE
AUDIBLY > AUDIBLE
AUDIENCE n group of spectators or listeners
AUDIENCES > AUDIENCE
AUDIENCIA n court in South America
AUDIENT n person who hears
AUDIENTS > AUDIENT
AUDILE n person with a faculty for auditory imagery ▷ adj of or relating to such a person
AUDILES > AUDILE
AUDING n practice of listening to try to understand
AUDINGS > AUDING
AUDIO adj of sound or hearing ▷ n sound
AUDIOBOOK n recorded reading of a book
AUDIOGRAM n graphic record of the acuity of hearing of a person obtained by means of an audiometer

AUDIOLOGY n scientific study of hearing, often including the treatment of persons with hearing defects
AUDIOPHIL n audiophile
AUDIOS > AUDIO
AUDIOTAPE n (esp formerly) tape for recording sound
AUDIPHONE n type of hearing aid consisting of a diaphragm that, when placed against the upper teeth, conveys sound vibrations to the inner ear
AUDISM n prejudice against deaf people
AUDISMS > AUDISM
AUDIST n person prejudiced against deaf people
AUDISTS > AUDIST
AUDIT n official examination of business accounts ▷ vb examine (business accounts) officially
AUDITABLE > AUDIT
AUDITED > AUDIT
AUDITEE n one who is audited
AUDITEES > AUDITEE
AUDITING n act of auditing
AUDITINGS > AUDITING
AUDITION n test of a performer's ability to a particular role or job ▷ vb test or be tested in an audition
AUDITIONS > AUDITION
AUDITIVE n person who learns primarily by listening
AUDITIVES > AUDITIVE
AUDITOR n person qualified to audit accounts
AUDITORIA n areas of concert halls, theatres, schools, etc, in which audiences sit
AUDITORS > AUDITOR
AUDITORY adj of or relating to hearing
AUDITRESS n female auditor
AUDITS > AUDIT
AUE interj Māori exclamation
AUF old word for > OAF
AUFGABE n word used in psychology to mean task
AUFGABES > AUFGABE
AUFS > AUF
AUGEND n number to which a number is added
AUGENDS > AUGEND
AUGER n tool for boring holes
AUGERS > AUGER
AUGH interj expressing frustration
AUGHT adv in any least part ▷ n less common word for nought

AUGHTS > AUGHT
AUGITE n black or greenish-black mineral
AUGITES > AUGITE
AUGITIC > AUGITE
AUGMENT vb increase or enlarge ▷ n vowel prefix forming a past tense
AUGMENTED > AUGMENT
AUGMENTER > AUGMENT
AUGMENTOR > AUGMENT
AUGMENTS > AUGMENT
AUGUR vb be a sign of (future events) ▷ n religious official who interpreted omens
AUGURAL > AUGUR
AUGURED > AUGUR
AUGURER old word for > AUGUR
AUGURERS > AUGURER
AUGURIES > AUGURY
AUGURING > AUGUR
AUGURS > AUGUR
AUGURSHIP > AUGUR
AUGURY n foretelling of the future
AUGUST adj dignified and imposing ▷ n auguste
AUGUSTE n type of circus clown
AUGUSTER > AUGUST
AUGUSTES > AUGUSTE
AUGUSTEST > AUGUST
AUGUSTLY > AUGUST
AUGUSTS > AUGUST
AUK n sea bird with short wings
AUKLET n type of small auk
AUKLETS > AUKLET
AUKS > AUK
AULA n hall
AULARIAN n Oxford University student belonging to a hall
AULARIANS > AULARIAN
AULAS > AULA
AULD a Scots word for > OLD
AULDER > AULD
AULDEST > AULD
AULIC adj relating to a royal court
AULNAGE n measurement in ells
AULNAGER n inspector of cloth
AULNAGERS > AULNAGER
AULNAGES > AULNAGE
AULOI > AULOS
AULOS n ancient Greek pipe
AUMAIL old word for > ENAMEL
AUMAILED > AUMAIL
AUMAILING > AUMAIL
AUMAILS > AUMAIL
AUMBRIES > AUMBRY
AUMBRY same as > AMBRY
AUMIL n manager in India
AUMILS > AUMIL
AUNE n old French measure of length
AUNES > AUNE

AUNT n father's or mother's sister
AUNTER old word for > ADVENTURE
AUNTERS > AUNTER
AUNTHOOD > AUNT
AUNTHOODS > AUNT
AUNTIE n aunt
AUNTIES > AUNTIE
AUNTLIER > AUNTLY
AUNTLIEST > AUNTLY
AUNTLIKE > AUNT
AUNTLY adj of or like an aunt
AUNTS > AUNT
AUNTY same as > AUNTIE
AURA n distinctive air or quality of a person or thing
AURAE > AURA
AURAL adj of or using the ears or hearing
AURALITY > AURAL
AURALLY > AURAL
AURAR plural of > EYRIR
AURAS > AURA
AURATE n salt of auric acid
AURATED adj combined with auric acid
AURATES > AURATE
AUREATE adj covered with gold, gilded
AUREATELY > AUREATE
AUREI > AUREUS
AUREITIES > AUREITY
AUREITY n attributes of gold
AURELIA n large jellyfish
AURELIAN n person who studies butterflies and moths
AURELIANS > AURELIAN
AURELIAS > AURELIA
AUREOLA same as > AUREOLE
AUREOLAE > AUREOLA
AUREOLAS > AUREOLA
AUREOLE n halo ▷ vb encircle
AUREOLED > AUREOLE
AUREOLES > AUREOLE
AUREOLING > AUREOLE
AURES > AURIS
AUREUS n gold coin of the Roman Empire
AURIC adj of or containing gold in the trivalent state
AURICLE n upper chamber of the heart
AURICLED > AURICLE
AURICLES > AURICLE
AURICULA n alpine primrose with leaves shaped like a bear's ear
AURICULAE > AURICULA
AURICULAR adj of, relating to, or received by the sense or organs of hearing ▷ n auricular feather
AURICULAS > AURICULA
AURIFIED > AURIFY
AURIFIES > AURIFY

AURIFORM *adj* shaped like an ear
AURIFY *vb* turn into gold
AURIFYING > AURIFY
AURIS *n* medical word for ear
AURISCOPE *n* medical instrument for examining the external ear
AURIST *n* former name for an audiologist
AURISTS > AURIST
AUROCHS *n* recently extinct European wild ox
AUROCHSES > AUROCHS
AURORA *n* bands of light seen in the sky
AURORAE > AURORA
AURORAL > AURORA
AURORALLY > AURORA
AURORAS > AURORA
AUROREAN *adj* of dawn
AUROUS *adj* of or containing gold, esp in the monovalent state
AURUM *n* gold
AURUMS > AURUM
AUSFORM *vb* temper steel
AUSFORMED > AUSFORM
AUSFORMS > AUSFORM
AUSLANDER *n* German word meaning foreigner
AUSPEX *same as* > AUGUR
AUSPICATE *vb* inaugurate with a ceremony intended to bring good fortune
AUSPICE *n* patronage or guidance
AUSPICES > AUSPICE
AUSTENITE *n* solid solution of carbon in face-centred-cubic gamma iron, usually existing above 723°C
AUSTERE *adj* stern or severe
AUSTERELY > AUSTERE
AUSTERER > AUSTERE
AUSTEREST > AUSTERE
AUSTERITY *n* state of being austere
AUSTRAL *adj* southern ▷ *n* former monetary unit of Argentina
AUSTRALES > AUSTRAL
AUSTRALIS *adj* Australian
AUSTRALS > AUSTRAL
AUSUBO *n* tropical tree
AUSUBOS > AUSUBO
AUTACOID *n* any natural internal secretion, esp one that exerts an effect similar to a drug
AUTACOIDS > AUTACOID
AUTARCH *n* absolute ruler
AUTARCHIC > AUTARCHY
AUTARCHS > AUTARCH
AUTARCHY *n* absolute power or autocracy
AUTARKIC > AUTARKY
AUTARKIES > AUTARKY
AUTARKIST > AUTARKY
AUTARKY *n* policy of economic self-sufficiency

AUTECIOUS *adj* (of parasites, esp the rust fungi) completing the entire life cycle on a single species of host
AUTECISM > AUTECIOUS
AUTECISMS > AUTECIOUS
AUTEUR *n* director
AUTEURISM > AUTEUR
AUTEURIST > AUTEUR
AUTEURS > AUTEUR
AUTHENTIC *adj* known to be real, genuine
AUTHOR *n* writer of a book etc ▷ *vb* write or originate
AUTHORED > AUTHOR
AUTHORESS *n* female author
AUTHORIAL > AUTHOR
AUTHORING *n* creation of documents, esp multimedia documents
AUTHORISE *same as* > AUTHORIZE
AUTHORISH > AUTHOR
AUTHORISM *n* condition of being author
AUTHORITY *n* power to command or control others
AUTHORIZE *vb* give authority to
AUTHORS > AUTHOR
AUTISM *n* developmental condition characterized by difficulties with social communication and interaction
AUTISMS > AUTISM
AUTIST *n* autistic person
AUTISTIC > AUTISM
AUTISTICS > AUTISM
AUTISTS > AUTIST
AUTO *n* automobile ▷ *vb* travel in an automobile
AUTOBAHN *n* German motorway
AUTOBAHNS > AUTOBAHN
AUTOBANK *n* automated teller machine
AUTOBANKS > AUTOBANK
AUTOBODY *n* body of a motor vehicle
AUTOBUS *n* motor bus
AUTOBUSES > AUTOBUS
AUTOCADE *another name for* > MOTORCADE
AUTOCADES > AUTOCADE
AUTOCAR *n* motor car
AUTOCARP *n* fruit produced through self-fertilization
AUTOCARPS > AUTOCARP
AUTOCARS > AUTOCAR
AUTOCIDAL *adj* (of insect pest control) effected by the introduction of sterile or genetically altered individuals into the wild population
AUTOCLAVE *n* apparatus for sterilizing objects by

steam under pressure ▷ *vb* put in or subject to the action of an autoclave
AUTOCOID *n* hormone
AUTOCOIDS > AUTOCOID
AUTOCRACY *n* government by an autocrat
AUTOCRAT *n* ruler with absolute authority
AUTOCRATS > AUTOCRAT
AUTOCRIME *n* crime of stealing a car
AUTOCRINE *adj* relating to self-stimulation through production of a factor and its receptor
AUTOCROSS *n* motor-racing over a rough course
AUTOCUE *n* electronic television prompting device
AUTOCUES > AUTOCUE
AUTOCUTIE *n* young and attractive but inexperienced television presenter
AUTOCYCLE *n* bicycle powered or assisted by a small engine
AUTODIAL *vb* dial a telephone number automatically
AUTODIALS > AUTODIAL
AUTODROME *n* track for motor racing
AUTODYNE *adj* using the same elements and valves as oscillator and detector ▷ *n* autodyne circuit
AUTODYNES > AUTODYNE
AUTOECISM *n* (of a parasite) completion of an entire life cycle on a single species of host
AUTOED > AUTO
AUTOFLARE *n* automatic landing system in aircraft
AUTOFOCUS *n* camera system in which the lens is focused automatically
AUTOGAMIC > AUTOGAMY
AUTOGAMY *n* self-fertilization in flowering plants
AUTOGENIC *adj* produced from within
AUTOGENY *n* hypothetical process by which living organisms first arose on earth from nonliving matter
AUTOGIRO *n* self-propelled aircraft resembling a helicopter but with an unpowered rotor
AUTOGIROS > AUTOGIRO
AUTOGRAFT *n* tissue graft obtained from one part of a patient's body for use on another part

AUTOGRAPH *n* handwritten signature of a (famous) person ▷ *vb* write one's signature on or in
AUTOGUIDE *n* traffic information transmission system
AUTOGYRO *same as* > AUTOGIRO
AUTOGYROS > AUTOGYRO
AUTOHARP *n* zither-like musical instrument
AUTOHARPS > AUTOHARP
AUTOICOUS *adj* (of plants, esp mosses) having male and female reproductive organs on the same plant
AUTOING > AUTO
AUTOLATRY *n* self-worship
AUTOLOAD *vb* load automatically
AUTOLOADS > AUTOLOAD
AUTOLOGY *n* study of oneself
AUTOLYSE *vb* undergo or cause to undergo autolysis
AUTOLYSED > AUTOLYSE
AUTOLYSES > AUTOLYSE
AUTOLYSIN *n* any agent that produces autolysis
AUTOLYSIS *n* destruction of cells and tissues of an organism by enzymes produced by the cells themselves
AUTOLYTIC > AUTOLYSIS
AUTOLYZE *same as* > AUTOLYSE
AUTOLYZED > AUTOLYZE
AUTOLYZES > AUTOLYZE
AUTOMAGIC *adj* done with such ease and speed that it seems like magic
AUTOMAKER *n* car manufacturer
AUTOMAN *n* car manufacturer
AUTOMAT *n* vending machine
AUTOMATA > AUTOMATON
AUTOMATE *vb* make (a manufacturing process) automatic
AUTOMATED > AUTOMATE
AUTOMATES > AUTOMATE
AUTOMATIC *adj* (of a device) operating mechanically by itself ▷ *n* self-loading firearm
AUTOMATON *n* robot
AUTOMATS > AUTOMAT
AUTOMEN > AUTOMAN
AUTOMETER *n* small device inserted in a photocopier to enable the

process of copying to begin and to record the number of copies made

AUTONOMIC *adj* occurring involuntarily or spontaneously

AUTONOMY *n* self-government

AUTONYM *n* writing published under the real name of an author

AUTONYMS > AUTONYM

AUTOPEN *n* mechanical device used to produce imitation signatures

AUTOPENS > AUTOPEN

AUTOPHAGY *n* consumption of one's own tissue

AUTOPHOBY *n* reluctance to refer to oneself

AUTOPHONY *n* medical diagnosis by listening to vibration of one's own voice in patient

AUTOPHYTE *n* autotrophic plant, such as any green plant

AUTOPILOT *n* automatic pilot

AUTOPISTA *n* Spanish motorway

AUTOPOINT *n* point-to-point race in cars

AUTOPSIA *n* autopsy

AUTOPSIAS > AUTOPSIA

AUTOPSIC > AUTOPSY

AUTOPSIED > AUTOPSY

AUTOPSIES > AUTOPSY

AUTOPSIST > AUTOPSY

AUTOPSY *n* examination of a body to determine the cause of death

AUTOPTIC > AUTOPSY

AUTOPUT *n* motorway in the former Yugoslavia

AUTOPUTS > AUTOPUT

AUTOREPLY *n* email facility for sending automatic replies

AUTOROUTE *n* French motorway

AUTOS > AUTO

AUTOSAVE *n* computer facility for automatically saving data ▷ *vb* save (computer data) automatically

AUTOSAVED > AUTOSAVE

AUTOSAVES > AUTOSAVE

AUTOSCOPY *n* hallucination in which one sees oneself

AUTOSOMAL > AUTOSOME

AUTOSOME *n* type of chromosome

AUTOSOMES > AUTOSOME

AUTOSPORE *n* nonmotile algal spore that develops adult characteristics before being released

AUTOSPORT *n* sport of motor racing

AUTOTELIC *adj* justifying itself

AUTOTEST *n* motor race in which standard cars are driven round a circuit

AUTOTESTS > AUTOTEST

AUTOTIMER *n* device for turning a system on and off automatically at times predetermined by advance setting

AUTOTOMIC > AUTOTOMY

AUTOTOMY *n* casting off by an animal of a part of its body, to facilitate escape when attacked

AUTOTOXIC > AUTOTOXIN

AUTOTOXIN *n* any poison or toxin formed in the organism upon which it acts

AUTOTROPH *n* organism capable of manufacturing complex organic nutritive compounds from simple inorganic sources

AUTOTUNE *n* software that changes a recording of a vocal track

AUTOTUNES > AUTOTUNE

AUTOTYPE *n* photographic process for producing prints in black and white, using a carbon pigment ▷ *vb* process using autotype

AUTOTYPED > AUTOTYPE

AUTOTYPES > AUTOTYPE

AUTOTYPIC > AUTOTYPE

AUTOTYPY > AUTOTYPE

AUTOVAC *n* vacuum pump in a car petrol tank

AUTOVACS > AUTOVAC

AUTUMN *n* season between summer and winter

AUTUMNAL *adj* of, occurring in, or characteristic of autumn

AUTUMNIER > AUTUMNY

AUTUMNS > AUTUMN

AUTUMNY *adj* like autumn

AUTUNITE *n* yellowish fluorescent radioactive mineral

AUTUNITES > AUTUNITE

AUXESES > AUXESIS

AUXESIS *n* increase in cell size without division

AUXETIC *n* something that promotes growth

AUXETICS > AUXETIC

AUXILIAR *old word for* > AUXILIARY

AUXILIARS > AUXILIAR

AUXILIARY *adj* secondary or supplementary ▷ *n* person or thing that supplements or supports

AUXIN *n* plant hormone that promotes growth

AUXINIC > AUXIN

AUXINS > AUXIN

AUXOCYTE *n* any cell undergoing meiosis

AUXOCYTES > AUXOCYTE

AUXOMETER *n* instrument for measuring magnification

AUXOSPORE *n* diatom cell before its silicaceous cell wall is formed

AUXOTONIC *adj* (of muscle contraction) occurring against increasing force

AUXOTROPH *n* mutant strain of microorganism having nutritional requirements additional to those of the normal organism

AVA *n* Polynesian shrub

AVADAVAT *n* Asian weaverbird with usu red plumage, often kept as a cagebird

AVADAVATS > AVADAVAT

AVAIL *vb* be of use or advantage (to) ▷ *n* use or advantage

AVAILABLE *adj* obtainable or accessible

AVAILABLY > AVAILABLE

AVAILE *old word for* > LOWER

AVAILED > AVAIL

AVAILES > AVAILE

AVAILFUL *old word for* > USEFUL

AVAILING > AVAIL

AVAILS > AVAIL

AVAL *adj* of a grandparent

AVALANCHE *n* mass of snow or ice falling down a mountain ▷ *vb* come down overwhelmingly (upon)

AVALE *old word for* > LOWER

AVALED > AVALE

AVALEMENT *n* skiing technique where the knees are kept flexible

AVALES > AVALE

AVALING > AVALE

AVANT *prep* before

AVANTI *interj* forward!

AVANTIST *n* proponent of the avant-garde

AVANTISTS > AVANTIST

AVARICE *n* greed for wealth

AVARICES > AVARICE

AVAS > AVA

AVASCULAR *adj* (of certain tissues, such as cartilage) lacking blood vessels

AVAST *sentence substitute* stop! cease!

AVATAR *n* appearance of a god in animal or human form

AVATARS > AVATAR

AVAUNT *sentence substitute* go away! depart! ▷ *vb* go away; depart

AVAUNTED > AVAUNT

AVAUNTING > AVAUNT

AVAUNTS > AVAUNT

AVE *n* expression of welcome or farewell

AVEL *variant of* > OVEL

AVELLAN *adj* of hazelnuts

AVELLANE *same as* > AVELLAN

AVELS > AVEL

AVENGE *vb* take revenge in retaliation for (harm done) or on behalf of (a person harmed)

AVENGED > AVENGE

AVENGEFUL > AVENGE

AVENGER > AVENGE

AVENGERS > AVENGE

AVENGES > AVENGE

AVENGING > AVENGE

AVENIR *n* future

AVENIRS > AVENIR

AVENS *n* any of several temperate or Arctic rosaceous plants

AVENSES > AVENS

AVENTAIL *n* front flap of a helmet

AVENTAILE *n* aventail

AVENTAILS > AVENTAIL

AVENTRE *old word for* > THRUST

AVENTRED > AVENTRE

AVENTRES > AVENTRE

AVENTRING > AVENTRE

AVENTURE *old form of* > ADVENTURE

AVENTURES > AVENTURE

AVENTURIN *n* dark-coloured glass, usually green or brown, spangled with fine particles of gold, copper, or some other metal

AVENUE *n* wide street

AVENUES > AVENUE

AVER *vb* state to be true

AVERAGE *n* typical or normal amount or quality ▷ *adj* usual or typical ▷ *vb* calculate the average of

AVERAGED > AVERAGE

AVERAGELY > AVERAGE

AVERAGER *n* average adjuster

AVERAGERS > AVERAGER

AVERAGES > AVERAGE

AVERAGING > AVERAGE

AVERMENT > AVER

AVERMENTS > AVER

AVERRABLE > AVER

AVERRED > AVER

AVERRING > AVER

AVERS > AVER

AVERSE *adj* disinclined or unwilling

AVERSELY > AVERSE

AVERSION *n* strong dislike

AVERSIONS > AVERSION

AVERSIVE n tool or technique intended to repel animals etc

AVERSIVES > AVERSIVE

AVERT vb turn away

AVERTABLE > AVERT

AVERTED > AVERT

AVERTEDLY > AVERT

AVERTER > AVERT

AVERTERS > AVERT

AVERTIBLE > AVERT

AVERTING > AVERT

AVERTS > AVERT

AVES > AVE

AVGAS n aviation fuel

AVGASES > AVGAS

AVGASSES > AVGAS

AVIAN adj of or like a bird ▷ n bird

AVIANISE same as > AVIANIZE

AVIANISED > AVIANISE

AVIANISES > AVIANISE

AVIANIZE vb modify microorganisms in a chicken embryo

AVIANIZED > AVIANIZE

AVIANIZES > AVIANIZE

AVIANS > AVIAN

AVIARIES > AVIARY

AVIARIST n person who keeps an aviary

AVIARISTS > AVIARIST

AVIARY n large cage or enclosure for birds

AVIATE vb pilot or fly in an aircraft

AVIATED > AVIATE

AVIATES > AVIATE

AVIATIC adj pertaining to aviation

AVIATING > AVIATE

AVIATION n art of flying aircraft

AVIATIONS > AVIATION

AVIATOR n pilot of an aircraft

AVIATORS > AVIATOR

AVIATRESS n female aviator

AVIATRICE > AVIATOR

AVIATRIX > AVIATOR

AVICULAR adj of small birds

AVID adj keen or enthusiastic

AVIDER > AVID

AVIDEST > AVID

AVIDIN n protein found in egg white

AVIDINS > AVIDIN

AVIDITIES > AVIDITY

AVIDITY n quality or state of being avid

AVIDLY > AVID

AVIDNESS > AVID

AVIETTE n aeroplane driven by human strength

AVIETTES > AVIETTE

AVIFAUNA n all the birds in a particular region

AVIFAUNAE > AVIFAUNA

AVIFAUNAL > AVIFAUNA

AVIFAUNAS > AVIFAUNA

AVIFORM adj like a bird

AVIGATOR another word for > AVIATOR

AVIGATORS > AVIGATOR

AVINE adj of birds

AVION n aeroplane

AVIONIC > AVIONICS

AVIONICS n science and technology of electronics applied to aeronautics and astronautics

AVIONS > AVION

AVIRULENT adj (esp of bacteria) not virulent

AVISANDUM n consideration of a law case by a judge

AVISE old word for > ADVISE

AVISED > AVISE

AVISEMENT > AVISE

AVISES > AVISE

AVISING > AVISE

AVISO n boat carrying messages

AVISOS > AVISO

AVITAL adj of a grandfather

AVIZANDUM n judge's or court's decision to consider a case privately before giving judgment

AVIZE old word for > ADVISE

AVIZED > AVIZE

AVIZEFULL > AVIZE

AVIZES > AVIZE

AVIZING > AVIZE

AVO n Macao currency unit

AVOCADO n pear-shaped tropical fruit with a leathery green skin and yellowish-green flesh

AVOCADOES > AVOCADO

AVOCADOS > AVOCADO

AVOCATION n occupation

AVOCET n long-legged wading bird

AVOCETS > AVOCET

AVODIRE n African tree

AVODIRES > AVODIRE

AVOID vb prevent from happening

AVOIDABLE > AVOID

AVOIDABLY > AVOID

AVOIDANCE n act of keeping away from or preventing from happening

AVOIDANT adj (of behaviour) demonstrating a tendency to avoid intimacy or interaction with others

AVOIDED > AVOID

AVOIDER > AVOID

AVOIDERS > AVOID

AVOIDING > AVOID

AVOIDS > AVOID

AVOISION n nonpayment of tax

AVOISIONS > AVOISION

AVOPARCIN n type of antibiotic

AVOS > AVO

AVOSET n avocet

AVOSETS > AVOSET

AVOUCH vb vouch for

AVOUCHED > AVOUCH

AVOUCHER > AVOUCH

AVOUCHERS > AVOUCH

AVOUCHES > AVOUCH

AVOUCHING > AVOUCH

AVOURE old word for > AVOWAL

AVOURES > AVOURE

AVOUTERER old word for > ADULTERER

AVOUTRER old word for > ADULTERER

AVOUTRERS > AVOUTRER

AVOUTRIES > AVOUTRY

AVOUTRY old word for > ADULTERY

AVOW vb state or affirm

AVOWABLE > AVOW

AVOWABLY > AVOW

AVOWAL > AVOW

AVOWALS > AVOW

AVOWED adj openly declared

AVOWEDLY > AVOWED

AVOWER > AVOW

AVOWERS > AVOW

AVOWING > AVOW

AVOWRIES > AVOWRY

AVOWRY old word for > AVOWAL

AVOWS > AVOW

AVOYER n former Swiss magistrate

AVOYERS > AVOYER

AVRUGA n herring roe

AVRUGAS > AVRUGA

AVULSE vb take away by force

AVULSED > AVULSE

AVULSES > AVULSE

AVULSING > AVULSE

AVULSION n forcible tearing away of a bodily structure or part

AVULSIONS > AVULSION

AVUNCULAR adj (of a man) friendly, helpful, and caring towards someone younger

AVYZE old word for > ADVISE

AVYZED > AVYZE

AVYZES > AVYZE

AVYZING > AVYZE

AW variant of > ALL

AWA adv Scots word for away

AWAIT vb wait for

AWAITED > AWAIT

AWAITER > AWAIT

AWAITERS > AWAIT

AWAITING > AWAIT

AWAITS > AWAIT

AWAKE vb emerge or rouse from sleep ▷ adj not sleeping

AWAKED > AWAKE

AWAKEN vb awake

AWAKENED > AWAKEN

AWAKENER > AWAKEN

AWAKENERS > AWAKEN

AWAKENING n start of a feeling or awareness in someone

AWAKENS > AWAKEN

AWAKES > AWAKE

AWAKING n emergence from sleep

AWAKINGS > AWAKING

AWANTING adj missing

AWARD vb give (something, such as a prize) formally ▷ n something awarded, such as a prize

AWARDABLE > AWARD

AWARDED > AWARD

AWARDEE > AWARD

AWARDEES > AWARD

AWARDER > AWARD

AWARDERS > AWARD

AWARDING > AWARD

AWARDS > AWARD

AWARE adj having knowledge, informed

AWARENESS > AWARE

AWARER > AWARE

AWAREST > AWARE

AWARN vb old form of warn

AWARNED > AWARN

AWARNING > AWARN

AWARNS > AWARN

AWASH adv washed over by water ▷ adj washed over by water

AWATCH adv watching

AWATO n New Zealand caterpillar

AWATOS > AWATO

AWAVE adv in waves

AWAY adv from a place ▷ adj not present ▷ n game played or won at an opponent's ground

AWAYDAY n day trip taken for pleasure

AWAYDAYS > AWAYDAY

AWAYES old word for > AWAY

AWAYNESS > AWAY

AWAYS > AWAY

AWDL n traditional Welsh poem

AWDLS > AWDL

AWE n wonder and respect mixed with dread ▷ vb fill with awe

AWEARIED old word for > WEARY

AWEARY old form of > WEARY

AWEATHER adj towards the weather

AWED > AWE

AWEE adv Scots word meaning for a short time

AWEEL interj Scots word meaning well

AWEIGH adj (of an anchor) no longer hooked onto the bottom

AWEING > AWE

AWELESS > AWE

AWES > AWE
AWESOME adj inspiring awe
AWESOMELY > AWESOME
AWESTRIKE vb inspire great awe in
AWESTRUCK adj filled with awe
AWETO n New Zealand caterpillar
AWETOS > AWETO
AWFUL adj very bad or unpleasant ▷ adv very
AWFULLER > AWFUL
AWFULLEST > AWFUL
AWFULLY adv in an unpleasant way
AWFULNESS > AWFUL
AWFY adv (Scots) awfully, extremely
AWHAPE old word for > AMAZE
AWHAPED > AWHAPE
AWHAPES > AWHAPE
AWHAPING > AWHAPE
AWHATO n New Zealand caterpillar
AWHATOS > AWHATO
AWHEEL adv on wheels
AWHEELS same as > AWHEEL
AWHETO n New Zealand caterpillar
AWHETOS > AWHETO
AWHILE adv for a brief time
AWHIRL adv whirling
AWING > AWE
AWK n type of programming language
AWKS > AWK
AWKWARD adj clumsy or ungainly
AWKWARDER > AWKWARD
AWKWARDLY > AWKWARD
AWL n pointed tool for piercing wood, leather, etc
AWLBIRD n woodpecker
AWLBIRDS > AWLBIRD
AWLESS > AWE
AWLS > AWL
AWLWORT n type of aquatic plant
AWLWORTS > AWLWORT
AWMOUS Scots word for > ALMS
AWMRIE n cupboard for church vessels
AWMRIES > AWMRIE
AWMRY n cupboard for church vessels
AWN n bristle on certain grasses
AWNED > AWN
AWNER n machine for removing awns
AWNERS > AWNER
AWNIER > AWNY
AWNIEST > AWNY
AWNING n canvas roof supported by a frame to give protection against the weather
AWNINGED adj sheltered with an awning
AWNINGS > AWNING
AWNLESS > AWN
AWNS > AWN

AWNY adj having awns
AWOKE > AWAKE
AWOKEN > AWAKE
AWOL n person who is absent without leave
AWOLS > AWOL
AWORK adv old word meaning at work
AWRACK adv in wrecked condition
AWRONG adv old word meaning wrongly
AWRY adj with a twist to one side, askew
AWSOME adj old form of awesome
AX same as > AXE
AXAL adj of an axis
AXE n tool with a sharp blade for felling trees or chopping wood ▷ vb dismiss (employees), restrict (expenditure), or terminate (a project)
AXEBIRD n nightjar
AXEBIRDS > AXEBIRD
AXED > AXE
AXEL n ice-skating movement
AXELIKE adj like an axe in form
AXELS > AXEL
AXEMAN n man who wields an axe, esp to cut down trees
AXEMEN > AXEMAN
AXENIC adj (of a biological culture) free from other microorganisms
AXES > AXIS
AXIAL adj forming or of an axis
AXIALITY > AXIAL
AXIALLY > AXIAL
AXIL n angle where the stalk of a leaf joins a stem
AXILE adj of, relating to, or attached to the axis
AXILEMMA same as > AXOLEMMA
AXILEMMAS > AXILEMMA
AXILLA n area under a bird's wing
AXILLAE > AXILLA
AXILLAR same as > AXILLARY
AXILLARS > AXILLAR
AXILLARY adj of, relating to, or near the armpit ▷ n one of the feathers growing from the axilla of a bird's wing
AXILLAS > AXILLA
AXILS > AXIL
AXING > AXE
AXINITE n crystalline substance
AXINITES > AXINITE
AXIOLOGY n theory of values, moral or aesthetic
AXIOM n generally accepted principle
AXIOMATIC adj containing axioms
AXIOMS > AXIOM

AXION n type of hypothetical elementary particle
AXIONS > AXION
AXIS n imaginary line round which a body can rotate
AXISED adj having an axis
AXISES > AXIS
AXITE n type of gunpowder
AXITES > AXITE
AXLE n shaft on which a wheel or pair of wheels turns
AXLED adj having an axle
AXLES > AXLE
AXLETREE n bar fixed across the underpart of a wagon or carriage
AXLETREES > AXLETREE
AXLIKE > AX
AXMAN same as > AXEMAN
AXMEN > AXMAN
AXOID n type of curve
AXOIDS > AXOID
AXOLEMMA n membrane that encloses the axon of a nerve cell
AXOLEMMAS > AXOLEMMA
AXOLOTL n aquatic salamander of central America
AXOLOTLS > AXOLOTL
AXON n threadlike extension of a nerve cell
AXONAL > AXON
AXONE same as > AXON
AXONEMAL > AXONEME
AXONEME n part of a cell consisting of proteins
AXONEMES > AXONEME
AXONES > AXONE
AXONIC > AXON
AXONS > AXON
AXOPLASM n part of cell
AXOPLASMS > AXOPLASM
AXSEED n crown vetch
AXSEEDS > AXSEED
AY adv ever ▷ n expression of agreement
AYAH n Indian or Malay maidservant or nursemaid in former British Empire
AYAHS > AYAH
AYAHUASCA n type of Brazilian plant
AYAHUASCO n South American vine
AYATOLLAH n Islamic religious leader in Iran
AYAYA n type of Inuit singing
AYAYAS > AYAYA
AYE n affirmative vote or voter ▷ adv always
AYELP adv yelping
AYENBITE old word for > REMORSE
AYENBITES > AYENBITE
AYES > AYE
AYGRE old word for > EAGER

AYIN n 16th letter in the Hebrew alphabet
AYINS > AYIN
AYONT adv beyond
AYRE old word for > AIR
AYRES > AYRE
AYRIE old word for > EYRIE
AYRIES > AYRIE
AYS > AY
AYU n small Japanese fish
AYURVEDA n ancient medical treatise on the art of healing and prolonging life
AYURVEDAS > AYURVEDA
AYURVEDIC > AYURVEDA
AYUS > AYU
AYWORD n old word meaning byword
AYWORDS > AYWORD
AZALEA n garden shrub grown for its showy flowers
AZALEAS > AZALEA
AZAN n call to prayer
AZANS > AZAN
AZEDARACH n astringent bark of the chinaberry tree, formerly used as an emetic and cathartic
AZEOTROPE n mixture of liquids that boils at a constant temperature, at a given pressure, without a change in composition
AZEOTROPY > AZEOTROPE
AZERTY n European version of keyboard
AZIDE n type of chemical compound
AZIDES > AZIDE
AZIDO adj containing an azide
AZIMUTH n arc of the sky between the zenith and the horizon
AZIMUTHAL > AZIMUTH
AZIMUTHS > AZIMUTH
AZINE n organic compound
AZINES > AZINE
AZIONE n musical drama
AZIONES > AZIONE
AZLON n fibre made from protein
AZLONS > AZLON
AZO adj of the divalent group -N:N-
AZOIC adj without life
AZOLE n organic compound
AZOLES > AZOLE
AZOLLA n tropical water fern
AZOLLAS > AZOLLA
AZON n type of drawing paper
AZONAL adj not divided into zones
AZONIC adj not confined to a zone
AZONS > AZON

AZOTAEMIA *a less common name for* > URAEMIA
AZOTAEMIC > AZOTAEMIA
AZOTE *an obsolete name for* > NITROGEN
AZOTED *adj* old word meaning combined with nitrogen
AZOTEMIA *same as* > AZOTAEMIA
AZOTEMIAS > AZOTEMIA
AZOTEMIC > AZOTAEMIA
AZOTES > AZOTE
AZOTH *n* panacea postulated by Paracelsus
AZOTHS > AZOTH

AZOTIC *adj* of, containing, or concerned with nitrogen
AZOTISE *same as* > AZOTIZE
AZOTISED > AZOTISE
AZOTISES > AZOTISE
AZOTISING > AZOTISE
AZOTIZE *vb* combine or treat with nitrogen or a nitrogen compound
AZOTIZED > AZOTIZE
AZOTIZES > AZOTIZE
AZOTIZING > AZOTIZE
AZOTOUS *adj* containing nitrogen
AZOTURIA *n* presence of excess nitrogen in urine
AZOTURIAS > AZOTURIA
AZUKI *same as* > ADZUKI

AZUKIS > AZUKI
AZULEJO *n* Spanish porcelain tile
AZULEJOS > AZULEJO
AZURE *n* (of) the colour of a clear blue sky ▷ *adj* deep blue
AZUREAN *adj* azure
AZURES > AZURE
AZURIES > AZURY
AZURINE *n* blue dye
AZURINES > AZURINE
AZURITE *n* azure-blue mineral associated with copper deposits
AZURITES > AZURITE
AZURN *old word for* > AZURE
AZURY *adj* bluish ▷ *n* bluish colour

AZYGIES > AZYGY
AZYGOS *n* biological structure not in a pair
AZYGOSES > AZYGOS
AZYGOUS *adj* developing or occurring singly
AZYGOUSLY > AZYGOUS
AZYGY *n* state of not being joined in a pair
AZYM *n* unleavened bread
AZYME *same as* > AZYM
AZYMES > AZYME
AZYMITE *n* member of a church using unleavened bread in the Eucharist
AZYMITES > AZYMITE
AZYMOUS *adj* unleavened
AZYMS > AZYM

a

Bb

BA *n* symbol for the soul in Ancient Egyptian religion

BAA *vb* make the characteristic bleating sound of a sheep ▷ *n* cry made by a sheep

BAAED > BAA

BAAING > BAA

BAAINGS > BAA

BAAL *n* any false god or idol

BAALEBOS *n* master of the house

BAALIM > BAAL

BAALISM > BAAL

BAALISMS > BAAL

BAALS > BAAL

BAAS > BAA

BAASKAAP *same as* > BAASKAP

BAASKAAPS > BAASKAAP

BAASKAP *n* (formerly in South Africa) control by White people of other ethnic groups

BAASKAPS > BAASKAP

BAASSKAP *same as* > BAASKAP

BAASSKAPS > BAASSKAP

BABA *n* small cake of leavened dough

BABACO *n* greenish-yellow egg-shaped fruit

BABACOOTE *n* large lemur

BABACOS > BABACO

BABACU *n* type of Brazilian palm tree

BABACUS > BABACU

BABALAS *adj* South African word for drunk

BABAS > BABA

BABASSU *n* Brazilian palm tree with hard edible nuts

BABASSUS > BABASSU

BABBELAS *same as* > BABALAS

BABBITRY *same as* > BABBITTRY

BABBITT *vb* line (a bearing) or face (a surface) with a similar soft alloy

BABBITTED > BABBITT

BABBITTRY *n* narrow-minded materialism

BABBITTS > BABBITT

BABBLE *vb* talk excitedly or foolishly ▷ *n* muddled or foolish speech

BABBLED > BABBLE

BABBLER *n* person who babbles

BABBLERS > BABBLER

BABBLES > BABBLE

BABBLIER > BABBLE

BABBLIEST > BABBLE

BABBLING > BABBLE

BABBLINGS > BABBLE

BABBLY > BABBLE

BABE *n* baby

BABEL *n* confused mixture of noises or voices

BABELDOM > BABEL

BABELDOMS > BABEL

BABELISH > BABEL

BABELISM > BABEL

BABELISMS > BABEL

BABELS > BABEL

BABES > BABE

BABESIA *n* parasite causing infection in cattle

BABESIAE > BABESIA

BABESIAS > BABESIA

BABICHE *n* thongs or lacings of rawhide

BABICHES > BABICHE

BABIED > BABY

BABIER > BABY

BABIES > BABY

BABIEST > BABY

BABIRUSA *n* Indonesian wild pig with an almost hairless skin and huge curved canine teeth

BABIRUSAS > BABIRUSA

BABIRUSSA *same as* > BABIRUSA

BABKA *n* cake

BABKAS > BABKA

BABLAH *n* fruit rind used as a dye

BABLAHS > BABLAH

BABOO *same as* > BABU

BABOOL *n* type of acacia

BABOOLS > BABOOL

BABOON *n* large monkey with a pointed face and a long tail

BABOONERY *n* uncouth behaviour

BABOONISH *adj* uncouth

BABOONS > BABOON

BABOOS > BABOO

BABOOSH *same as* > BABOUCHE

BABOOSHES > BABOOSH

BABOUCHE *n* Middle-Eastern slipper

BABOUCHES > BABOUCHE

BABU *n* title or form of address used in India

BABUCHE *same as* > BABOUCHE

BABUCHES > BABUCHE

BABUDOM > BABU

BABUDOMS > BABU

BABUISM > BABU

BABUISMS > BABU

BABUL *n* N African and Indian tree with small yellow flowers

BABULS > BABUL

BABUS > BABU

BABUSHKA *n* headscarf tied under the chin, worn by Russian peasant women

BABUSHKAS > BABUSHKA

BABY *n* very young child or animal ▷ *adj* comparatively small of its type ▷ *vb* treat as a baby

BABYCCINO *n* drink of frothy milk with a chocolate topping, esp for young children

BABYCINO *same as* > BABYCCINO

BABYCINOS > BABYCINO

BABYDADDY *n* father of a child, who is not the current partner of the child's mother

BABYDOLL *n* woman's short nightdress

BABYDOLLS > BABYDOLL

BABYFOOD *n* puréed food for babies

BABYFOODS > BABYFOOD

BABYHOOD > BABY

BABYHOODS > BABY

BABYING > BABY

BABYISH > BABY

BABYISHLY > BABY

BABYLIKE *adj* like a baby

BABYMOON *n* early period of new parenthood

BABYMOONS > BABYMOON

BABYPROOF *adj* safe for babies to handle ▷ *vb* make babyproof

BABYSAT > BABYSIT

BABYSIT *vb* look after a child in its parents' absence

BABYSITS > BABYSIT

BAC *n* baccalaureate

BACALAO *n* dried salt cod

BACALAOS > BACALAO

BACALHAU *same as* > BACALAO

BACALHAUS > BACALHAU

BACCA *n* berry

BACCAE > BACCA

BACCALA *same as* > BACALAO

BACCALAS > BACCALA

BACCARA *same as* > BACCARAT

BACCARAS > BACCARA

BACCARAT *n* card game involving gambling

BACCARATS > BACCARAT

BACCARE *same as* > BACKARE

BACCAS > BACCA

BACCATE *adj* like a berry in form, texture, etc

BACCATED > BACCATE

BACCHANAL *n* follower of Bacchus ▷ *adj* of or relating to Bacchus

BACCHANT *n* priest or votary of Bacchus

BACCHANTE *n* priestess or female votary of Bacchus

BACCHANTS > BACCHANT

BACCHIAC > BACCHIUS

BACCHIAN *same as* > BACCHIC

BACCHIC *adj* riotously jovial

BACCHII > BACCHIUS

BACCHIUS *n* metrical foot of one short syllable followed by two long ones

BACCIES > BACCY

BACCIFORM *adj* shaped like a berry

BACCO *n* tobacco

BACCOES > BACCO

BACCOS > BACCO

BACCY *n* tobacco

BACH *same as* > BATCH

BACHA *n* Indian English word for a young child

BACHARACH *n* German wine

BACHAS > BACHA

BACHATA *n* type of dance music originating in the Dominican Republic

BACHATAS > BACHATA

BACHCHA *n* Indian English word for a young child

BACHCHAS > BACHCHA

BACHED > BACH

BACHELOR *n* unmarried man

BACHELORS > BACHELOR

BACHES > BACH

BACHING > BACH

BACHS > BACH

BACILLAR *same as* > BACILLARY

BACILLARY *adj* of or caused by bacilli

BACILLI > BACILLUS

BACILLUS *n* rod-shaped bacterium

BACK *n* rear part of the human body, from the neck to the pelvis ▷ *vb* (cause to) move backwards ▷ *adj* situated behind ▷ *adv* at, to, or towards the rear

BACKACHE *n* ache or pain in one's back

BACKACHES > BACKACHE

BACKACTER *n* mechanical excavator

BACKARE *interj* instruction to keep one's distance; back off

BACKBAND *n* back support

BACKBANDS > BACKBAND

BACKBAR *n* area behind a bar where bottles are stored

BACKBARS > BACKBAR

BACKBEAT *n* beat in music not usually accented

BACKBEATS > BACKBEAT

BACKBENCH *n* lower-ranking seats in Parliament

BACKBEND *n* gymnastic exercise in which the trunk is bent backwards until the hands touch the floor

BACKBENDS > BACKBEND

BACKBIT > BACKBITE

BACKBITE *vb* talk spitefully about an absent person

BACKBITER > BACKBITE

BACKBITES > BACKBITE

BACKBLOCK *n* singular of backblock: bush or remote farming area

BACKBOARD *n* board that is placed behind something to form or support its back

BACKBOND *n* legal document

BACKBONDS > BACKBOND

BACKBONE *n* spinal column

BACKBONED > BACKBONE

BACKBONES > BACKBONE

BACKBURN *vb* clear an area of bush by creating a fire ▷ *n* act or result of backburning

BACKBURNS > BACKBURN

BACKCAST *n* backward casting of fishing rod ▷ *vb* cast a fishing rod backwards

BACKCASTS > BACKCAST

BACKCHAT *n* impudent replies

BACKCHATS > BACKCHAT

BACKCHECK *vb* (in ice hockey) return from attack to defence

BACKCLOTH *n* painted curtain at the back of a stage set

BACKCOMB *vb* comb (the hair) towards the roots to give more bulk to a hairstyle

BACKCOMBS > BACKCOMB

BACKCOURT *n* part of the court between the service line and the baseline

BACKCROSS *vb* mate (a hybrid of the first generation) with one of its parents ▷ *n* offspring so produced

BACKDATE *vb* make (a document) effective from a date earlier than its completion

BACKDATED > BACKDATE

BACKDATES > BACKDATE

BACKDOOR *adj* secret, underhand, or obtained through influence

BACKDOWN *n* abandonment of an earlier claim

BACKDOWNS > BACKDOWN

BACKDRAFT *n* reverse movement of air

BACKDROP *vb* provide a backdrop to (something)

BACKDROPS > BACKDROP

BACKDROPT > BACKDROP

BACKED *adj* having a back or backing

BACKER *n* person who gives financial support

BACKERS > BACKER

BACKET *n* shallow box

BACKETS > BACKET

BACKFALL *n* fall onto the back

BACKFALLS > BACKFALL

BACKFAT *n* layer of fat in animals between the skin and muscle

BACKFATS > BACKFAT

BACKFIELD *n* quarterback and running backs in a team

BACKFILE *n* archives of a newspaper or magazine

BACKFILES > BACKFILE

BACKFILL *vb* refill an excavated trench, esp (in archaeology) at the end of an investigation ▷ *n* soil used to do this

BACKFILLS > BACKFILL

BACKFIRE *vb* (of a plan) fail to have the desired effect ▷ *n* (in an engine) explosion of unburnt gases in the exhaust system

BACKFIRED > BACKFIRE

BACKFIRES > BACKFIRE

BACKFISCH *n* teenage girl

BACKFIT *vb* overhaul a nuclear power plant

BACKFITS > BACKFIT

BACKFLIP *n* backwards somersault

BACKFLIPS > BACKFLIP

BACKFLOW *n* reverse flow

BACKFLOWS > BACKFLOW

BACKHAND *n* stroke played with the back of the hand facing the direction of the stroke ▷ *adv* with a backhand stroke ▷ *vb* play (a shot) backhand

BACKHANDS > BACKHAND

BACKHAUL *vb* transmit data

BACKHAULS > BACKHAUL

BACKHOE *n* digger ▷ *vb* dig with a backhoe

BACKHOED > BACKHOE

BACKHOES > BACKHOE

BACKHOUSE *n* toilet

BACKIE *n* ride on the back of someone's bicycle

BACKIES > BACKIE

BACKING *n* support

BACKINGS > BACKING

BACKLAND *n* undeveloped land behind a property

BACKLANDS > BACKLAND

BACKLASH *n* sudden and adverse reaction ▷ *vb* create a sudden and adverse reaction

BACKLESS *adj* (of a dress) low-cut at the back

BACKLIFT *n* backward movement of bat

BACKLIFTS > BACKLIFT

BACKLIGHT *vb* illuminate (something) from behind

BACKLINE *n* defensive players in a sports team as a unit

BACKLINER *n* defender in ice hockey

BACKLINES > BACKLINE

BACKLIST *n* publisher's previously published books that are still available ▷ *vb* put on a backlist

BACKLISTS > BACKLIST

BACKLIT *adj* illuminated from behind

BACKLOAD *n* load for lorry on return journey ▷ *vb* load a lorry for a return journey

BACKLOADS > BACKLOAD

BACKLOG *n* accumulation of things to be dealt with

BACKLOGS > BACKLOG

BACKLOT *n* area outside a film or television studio used for outdoor filming

BACKLOTS > BACKLOT

BACKMOST *adj* furthest back

BACKOUT *n* instance of withdrawing (from an agreement, etc)

BACKOUTS > BACKOUT

BACKPACK *n* large pack carried on the back ▷ *vb* go hiking with a backpack

BACKPACKS > BACKPACK

BACKPEDAL *vb* retract or modify a previous opinion, principle, etc

BACKPIECE *n* tattoo on the back

BACKPLANE *n* type of circuit board in a computer

BACKPLATE *n* plate of armour which guards the back

BACKREST *n* support for the back of something

BACKRESTS > BACKREST

BACKRONYM *n* contrived acronym using the initial letters of an existing word

BACKROOM *n* place where research or planning is done, esp secret research in wartime

BACKROOMS > BACKROOM

BACKRUSH *n* seaward return of wave

BACKS > BACK

BACKSAW *n* small handsaw

BACKSAWS > BACKSAW

BACKSEAT *n* seat at the back, esp of a vehicle

BACKSEATS > BACKSEAT

BACKSET *n* reversal ▷ *vb* attack from the rear

BACKSEY *n* sirloin

BACKSEYS > BACKSEY

BACKSHISH *same as* > BAKSHEESH

BACKSHORE *n* area of beach above high tide mark

BACKSIDE *n* buttocks

BACKSIDES > BACKSIDE

BACKSIGHT *n* sight of a rifle nearer the stock

b

b

BACKSLAP vb demonstrate effusive joviality

BACKSLAPS > BACKSLAP

BACKSLASH n slash which slopes to the left (\\)

BACKSLID > BACKSLIDE

BACKSLIDE vb relapse into former bad habits

BACKSPACE vb move a typewriter carriage or computer cursor backwards ▷ n typewriter key that effects such a movements

BACKSPEER same as > BACKSPEIR

BACKSPEIR vb interrogate

BACKSPIN n backward spin given to a ball to reduce its speed at impact

BACKSPINS > BACKSPIN

BACKSPLIT n house with a higher storey at the rear

BACKSTAB vb attack deceitfully

BACKSTABS > BACKSTAB

BACKSTAGE adj behind the stage in a theatre ▷ adv behind the stage in a theatre ▷ n area behind the stage in a theatre

BACKSTAIR adj underhand

BACKSTALL n backward flight of a kite ▷ vb execute a backstall in a kite

BACKSTAMP n mark stamped on the back of an envelope ▷ vb mark with a backstamp

BACKSTAY n stay leading aft from the upper part of a mast to the deck or stern

BACKSTAYS > BACKSTAY

BACKSTOP n screen or fence to prevent balls leaving the playing area ▷ vb provide with backing or support

BACKSTOPS > BACKSTOP

BACKSTORY n events assumed before a story begins

BACKSTRAP n cut of meat from the back of an animal

BACKSWEPT adj slanting backwards

BACKSWING n backward movement of a bat, etc

BACKSWORD n broad-bladed sword

BACKTALK n argumentative discourse

BACKTALKS > BACKTALK

BACKTRACK vb return by the same route by which one has come

BACKUP n support or reinforcement

BACKUPS > BACKUP

BACKVELD n (in South Africa) remote sparsely populated area

BACKVELDS > BACKVELD

BACKWALL n rear wall

BACKWALLS > BACKWALL

BACKWARD same as > BACKWARDS

BACKWARDS adv towards the rear

BACKWASH n water washed backwards by the motion of a boat ▷ vb remove oil from (combed wool)

BACKWATER n isolated or backward place or condition ▷ vb reverse the direction of a boat, esp to push the oars of a rowing boat

BACKWIND vb direct airflow into the back of a sail

BACKWINDS > BACKWIND

BACKWOOD > BACKWOODS

BACKWOODS pl n remote sparsely populated area

BACKWORD n act or an instance of failing to keep a promise or commitment

BACKWORDS > BACKWORD

BACKWORK n work carried out under the ground

BACKWORKS > BACKWORK

BACKWRAP n back support

BACKWRAPS > BACKWRAP

BACKYARD n yard at the back of a house, etc

BACKYARDS > BACKYARD

BACLAVA same as > BAKLAVA

BACLAVAS > BACLAVA

BACLOFEN n drug used to treat stroke patients

BACLOFENS > BACLOFEN

BACON n salted or smoked pig meat

BACONER n pig that weighs between 83 and 101 kg, from which bacon is cut

BACONERS > BACONER

BACONS > BACON

BACRONYM same as > BACKRONYM

BACRONYMS > BACRONYM

BACS > BAC

BACTERIA pl n large group of microorganisms

BACTERIAL > BACTERIA

BACTERIAN > BACTERIA

BACTERIAS > BACTERIA

BACTERIC > BACTERIA

BACTERIN n vaccine prepared from bacteria

BACTERINS > BACTERIN

BACTERISE same as > BACTERIZE

BACTERIUM n singular of bacteria

BACTERIZE vb subject to bacterial action

BACTEROID n type of rodlike bacterium occurring in the gut of humans and animals

BACULA > BACULUM

BACULINE adj relating to flogging

BACULITE n fossil

BACULITES > BACULITE

BACULUM n bony support in the penis of certain mammals

BACULUMS > BACULUM

BAD adj not good ▷ n unfortunate or unpleasant events collectively ▷ adv badly

BADASS n tough or aggressive person ▷ adj tough or aggressive

BADASSED > BADASS

BADASSES > BADASS

BADDER > BAD

BADDEST > BAD

BADDIE n bad character in a story, film, etc, esp an opponent of the hero

BADDIES > BADDIE

BADDISH > BAD

BADDY same as > BADDIE

BADE > BID

BADGE n emblem worn to show membership, rank, etc ▷ vb put a badge on

BADGED > BADGE

BADGELESS > BADGE

BADGER n nocturnal burrowing mammal ▷ vb pester or harass

BADGERED > BADGER

BADGERING > BADGER

BADGERLY adj resembling a badger

BADGERS > BADGER

BADGES > BADGE

BADGING > BADGE

BADINAGE n playful and witty conversation ▷ vb engage in badinage

BADINAGED > BADINAGE

BADINAGES > BADINAGE

BADINERIE n name given in the 18th century to a type of quick, light movement in a suite

BADIOUS adj chestnut; brownish-red

BADLAND > BADLANDS

BADLANDS pl n any deeply eroded barren area

BADLY adv poorly

BADMAN n hired gunman, outlaw, or criminal

BADMASH n evil-doer ▷ adj naughty or bad

BADMASHES > BADMASH

BADMEN > BADMAN

BADMINTON n game played with rackets and a shuttlecock, which is hit back and forth over a high net

BADMOUTH vb speak unfavourably about (someone or something)

BADMOUTHS > BADMOUTH

BADNESS > BAD

BADNESSES > BAD

BADS > BAD

BADWARE n software designed to harm a computer system

BADWARES > BADWARE

BAE n sweetheart

BAEL n type of spiny Indian tree

BAELS > BAEL

BAES > BAE

BAETYL n magical meteoric stone

BAETYLS > BAETYL

BAFF vb strike the ground with a golf club

BAFFED > BAFF

BAFFIES pl n slippers

BAFFING > BAFF

BAFFLE vb perplex or puzzle ▷ n device to limit or regulate the flow of fluid, light, or sound

BAFFLED > BAFFLE

BAFFLEGAB n insincere speech

BAFFLER > BAFFLE

BAFFLERS > BAFFLE

BAFFLES > BAFFLE

BAFFLING adj impossible to understand

BAFFS > BAFF

BAFFY n obsolete golf club

BAFT n coarse fabric

BAFTS > BAFT

BAG n flexible container with an opening at one end ▷ vb put into a bag

BAGARRE n brawl

BAGARRES > BAGARRE

BAGASS same as > BAGASSE

BAGASSE n pulp of sugar cane or similar plants

BAGASSES > BAGASSE

BAGATELLE n something of little value

BAGEL n hard ring-shaped bread roll ▷ vb win a tennis set by six games to love

BAGELED > BAGEL

BAGELING > BAGEL

BAGELLED > BAGEL

BAGELLING > BAGEL

BAGELS > BAGEL

BAGFUL n amount (of something) that can be held in a bag

BAGFULS > BAGFUL

BAGGAGE n suitcases packed for a journey

BAGGAGES > BAGGAGE
BAGGED > BAG
BAGGER n person who packs groceries
BAGGERS > BAGGER
BAGGIE n plastic bag
BAGGIER > BAGGY
BAGGIES > BAGGIE
BAGGIEST > BAGGY
BAGGILY > BAGGY
BAGGINESS > BAGGY
BAGGING n act of putting in a bag
BAGGINGS > BAGGING
BAGGIT n salmon which has not yet spawned
BAGGITS > BAGGIT
BAGGY adj hanging loosely
BAGH n (in India and Pakistan) a garden
BAGHOUSE n dust-filtering chamber
BAGHOUSES > BAGHOUSE
BAGHS > BAGH
BAGIE n turnip
BAGIES > BAGIE
BAGLESS adj (esp of a vacuum cleaner) not containing a bag
BAGLIKE > BAG
BAGMAN n travelling salesman
BAGMEN > BAGMAN
BAGNETTE variant of > BAGUETTE
BAGNETTES > BAGNETTE
BAGNIO n bathing-house
BAGNIOS > BAGNIO
BAGPIPE vb play the bagpipes
BAGPIPED > BAGPIPE
BAGPIPER > BAGPIPES
BAGPIPERS > BAGPIPES
BAGPIPES pl n musical wind instrument with reed pipes and an inflatable bag
BAGPIPING > BAGPIPE
BAGS > BAG
BAGSFUL > BAGFUL
BAGUET same as > BAGUETTE
BAGUETS > BAGUET
BAGUETTE n narrow French stick loaf
BAGUETTES > BAGUETTE
BAGUIO n hurricane
BAGUIOS > BAGUIO
BAGWASH n laundry that washes clothes without drying or pressing them
BAGWASHES > BAGWASH
BAGWIG n 18th-century wig with hair pushed back into a bag
BAGWIGS > BAGWIG
BAGWORM n type of moth
BAGWORMS > BAGWORM
BAH interj expression of contempt or disgust
BAHADA same as > BAJADA
BAHADAS > BAHADA

BAHADUR n title formerly conferred by the British on distinguished Indians
BAHADURS > BAHADUR
BAHOOKIE n Scottish informal word for the buttocks
BAHOOKIES > BAHOOKIE
BAHT n standard monetary unit of Thailand, divided into 100 satang
BAHTS > BAHT
BAHU n (in India) daughter-in-law
BAHUS > BAHU
BAHUT n decorative cabinet
BAHUTS > BAHUT
BAHUVRIHI n class of compound words consisting of two elements the first of which is a specific feature of the second
BAIDAR same as > BAIDARKA
BAIDARKA n narrow hunting boat
BAIDARKAS > BAIDARKA
BAIDARS > BAIDAR
BAIGNOIRE n low-level theatre box
BAIL n money deposited with a court as security for a person's reappearance ▷ vb pay bail for (a person)
BAILABLE adj eligible for release on bail
BAILBOND n document guaranteeing a prisoner released on bail will attend court
BAILBONDS > BAILBOND
BAILED > BAIL
BAILEE n person to whom the possession of goods is transferred under a bailment
BAILEES > BAILEE
BAILER > BAIL
BAILERS > BAIL
BAILEY n outermost wall or court of a castle
BAILEYS > BAILEY
BAILIE n (in Scotland) a municipal magistrate
BAILIES > BAILIE
BAILIFF n sheriff's officer who serves writs and summonses
BAILIFFS > BAILIFF
BAILING > BAIL
BAILIWICK n area a person is interested in or operates in
BAILLI same as > BAILIE
BAILLIAGE n magistrate's area of authority
BAILLIE same as > BAILIE
BAILLIES > BAILLIE
BAILLIS > BAILLI
BAILMENT n contractual delivery of goods in trust

to a person for a specific purpose
BAILMENTS > BAILMENT
BAILOR n owner of goods entrusted to another under a bailment
BAILORS > BAILOR
BAILOUT n instance of helping (a person, organization, etc) out of a predicament
BAILOUTS > BAILOUT
BAILS > BAIL
BAILSMAN n one standing bail for another
BAILSMEN > BAILSMAN
BAININ n Irish collarless jacket made of white wool
BAININS > BAININ
BAINITE n mixture of iron and iron carbide found in incompletely hardened steels
BAINITES > BAINITE
BAIRN n child
BAIRNISH > BAIRN
BAIRNLIER > BAIRN
BAIRNLIKE > BAIRN
BAIRNLY > BAIRN
BAIRNS > BAIRN
BAISA n small unit of currency in Oman
BAISAS > BAISA
BAISEMAIN n kissing of the hand
BAIT n piece of food on a hook or in a trap to attract fish or animals ▷ vb put a piece of food on or in (a hook or trap)
BAITED > BAIT
BAITER > BAIT
BAITERS > BAIT
BAITFISH n small fish used as bait
BAITH adj both
BAITING n act of placing bait
BAITINGS > BAITING
BAITS > BAIT
BAIZA n Omani unit of currency
BAIZAS > BAIZA
BAIZE n woollen fabric used to cover billiard and card tables ▷ vb line or cover with such fabric
BAIZED > BAIZE
BAIZES > BAIZE
BAIZING > BAIZE
BAJADA n sloping surface formed from rock deposits
BAJADAS > BAJADA
BAJAN n freshman at Aberdeen University
BAJANS > BAJAN
BAJILLION n extremely large but unspecified number, quantity, or amount
BAJRA n Indian millet
BAJRAS > BAJRA
BAJREE variant of > BAJRA
BAJREES > BAJREE
BAJRI variant of > BAJRA
BAJRIS > BAJRI

BAJU n Malay jacket
BAJUS > BAJU
BAKE vb cook by dry heat as in an oven ▷ n party at which the main dish is baked
BAKEAPPLE n cloudberry
BAKEBOARD n board for bread-making
BAKED > BAKE
BAKEHOUSE same as > BAKERY
BAKELITE n tradename for a class of resin
BAKELITES > BAKELITE
BAKEMEAT n pie
BAKEMEATS > BAKEMEAT
BAKEN > BAKE
BAKEOFF n baking competition
BAKEOFFS > BAKEOFF
BAKER n person whose business is to make or sell bread, cakes, etc
BAKERIES > BAKERY
BAKERS > BAKER
BAKERY n place where bread, cakes, etc are baked or sold
BAKES > BAKE
BAKESHOP n bakery
BAKESHOPS > BAKESHOP
BAKESTONE n flat stone in an oven
BAKEWARE n dishes for baking
BAKEWARES > BAKEWARE
BAKGAT adj fine, excellent, marvellous
BAKHSHISH same as > BAKSHEESH
BAKING n process of cooking bread, cakes, etc ▷ adj (esp of weather) very hot and dry
BAKINGS > BAKING
BAKKIE n small truck
BAKKIES > BAKKIE
BAKLAVA n rich pastry of Middle Eastern origin
BAKLAVAS > BAKLAVA
BAKLAWA same as > BAKLAVA
BAKLAWAS > BAKLAWA
BAKSHEESH n (in some Eastern countries) money given as a tip ▷ vb give such money to (a person)
BAKSHISH same as > BAKSHEESH
BAL n balmoral
BALACLAVA n close-fitting woollen hood that covers the ears and neck, as originally worn by soldiers in the Crimean War
BALADIN n dancer
BALADINE n female dancer
BALADINES > BALADINE
BALADINS > BALADIN
BALAFON n type of W African xylophone

BALAFONS > BALAFON

BALALAIKA *n* guitar-like musical instrument with a triangular body

BALANCE *n* stability of mind or body ▷ *vb* weigh in a balance

BALANCED *adj* having weight equally distributed

BALANCER *n* person or thing that balances

BALANCERS > BALANCER

BALANCES > BALANCE

BALANCING > BALANCE

BALANITIS *n* inflammation of the glans penis

BALAS *n* red variety of spinel, used as a gemstone

BALASES > BALAS

BALATA *n* tropical American tree yielding a latex-like sap

BALATAS > BALATA

BALAYAGE *vb* highlight hair by painting dye onto sections

BALAYAGED > BALAYAGE

BALAYAGES > BALAYAGE

BALBOA *n* standard currency unit of Panama

BALBOAS > BALBOA

BALCONET *n* small balcony

BALCONETS > BALCONET

BALCONIED > BALCONY

BALCONIES > BALCONY

BALCONY *n* platform on the outside of a building with a rail along the outer edge

BALD *adj* having little or no hair on the scalp ▷ *vb* make bald

BALDACHIN *n* richly ornamented silk and gold brocade

BALDAQUIN *same as* > BALDACHIN

BALDED > BALD

BALDER > BALD

BALDEST > BALD

BALDFACED *same as* > BALD

BALDHEAD *n* person with a bald head

BALDHEADS > BALDHEAD

BALDICOOT *another name for* > COOT

BALDIE *same as* > BALDY

BALDIER > BALDY

BALDIES > BALDIE

BALDIEST > BALDY

BALDING *adj* becoming bald

BALDISH > BALD

BALDLY > BALD

BALDMONEY *another name for* > SPIGNEL

BALDNESS > BALD

BALDPATE *n* type of duck

BALDPATED > BALDPATE

BALDPATES > BALDPATE

BALDRIC *n* wide silk sash or leather belt worn across the body

BALDRICK *same as* > BALDRIC

BALDRICKS > BALDRICK

BALDRICS > BALDRIC

BALDS > BALD

BALDY *adj* bald ▷ *n* bald person

BALE *same as* > BAIL

BALECTION *same as* > BOLECTION

BALED > BALE

BALEEN *n* whalebone

BALEENS > BALEEN

BALEFIRE *n* bonfire

BALEFIRES > BALEFIRE

BALEFUL *adj* vindictive or menacing

BALEFULLY > BALEFUL

BALER > BAIL

BALERS > BAIL

BALES > BALE

BALING *n* act of baling

BALINGS > BALING

BALISAUR *n* badger-like animal

BALISAURS > BALISAUR

BALISE *n* electronic beacon used on a railway

BALISES > BALISE

BALISTA *same as* > BALLISTA

BALISTAE > BALISTA

BALISTAS > BALISTA

BALK *vb* stop short, esp suddenly or unexpectedly ▷ *n* roughly squared heavy timber beam

BALKANISE *variant of* > BALKANIZE

BALKANIZE *vb* divide (a territory) into small warring states

BALKED > BALK

BALKER > BALK

BALKERS > BALK

BALKIER > BALKY

BALKIEST > BALKY

BALKILY > BALKY

BALKINESS > BALKY

BALKING > BALK

BALKINGLY > BALK

BALKINGS > BALKING

BALKLINE *n* line delimiting the balk area on a snooker table

BALKLINES > BALKLINE

BALKS > BALK

BALKY *adj* inclined to stop abruptly and unexpectedly

BALL *n* round or nearly round object, esp one used in games ▷ *vb* form into a ball

BALLABILE *n* part of ballet where all dancers perform

BALLABILI > BALLABILE

BALLAD *n* narrative poem or song ▷ *vb* sing or write a ballad

BALLADE *n* verse form

BALLADED > BALLAD

BALLADEER *n* singer of ballads ▷ *vb* perform as a balladeer

BALLADES > BALLADE

BALLADIC > BALLAD

BALLADIN *same as* > BALADIN

BALLADINE *same as* > BALADINE

BALLADING > BALLAD

BALLADINS > BALLADIN

BALLADIST > BALLAD

BALLADRY *n* ballad poetry or songs

BALLADS > BALLAD

BALLAN *n* species of fish

BALLANS > BALLAN

BALLANT *vb* write a ballad

BALLANTED > BALLANT

BALLANTS > BALLANT

BALLAST *n* substance used to stabilize a ship when it is not carrying cargo ▷ *vb* give stability to

BALLASTED > BALLAST

BALLASTER > BALLAST

BALLASTS > BALLAST

BALLAT *vb* write a ballad

BALLATED > BALLAT

BALLATING > BALLAT

BALLATS > BALLAT

BALLBOY *n* boy who retrieves balls during a tennis, football, etc, match

BALLBOYS > BALLBOY

BALLCLAY *n* clay suitable for ceramics

BALLCLAYS > BALLCLAY

BALLCOCK *n* device for regulating the flow of a liquid into a tank

BALLCOCKS > BALLCOCK

BALLED > BALL

BALLER *n* ball-game player

BALLERINA *n* female ballet dancer

BALLERINE > BALLERINA

BALLERS > BALLER

BALLET *n* classical style of expressive dancing based on conventional steps ▷ *vb* sing ballads

BALLETED > BALLET

BALLETIC > BALLET

BALLETING > BALLET

BALLETS > BALLET

BALLFIELD *n* baseball field

BALLGAME *n* any game played with a ball

BALLGAMES > BALLGAME

BALLGIRL *n* girl who retrieves balls during a tennis, football, etc, match

BALLGIRLS > BALLGIRL

BALLGOWN *n* long formal dress

BALLGOWNS > BALLGOWN

BALLHAWK *n* skilled basketball player ▷ *vb* act as a ballhawk

BALLHAWKS > BALLHAWK

BALLIER > BALLY

BALLIES > BALLY

BALLIEST > BALLY

BALLING *n* formation of a ball

BALLINGS > BALLING

BALLISTA *n* ancient catapult for hurling stones, etc

BALLISTAE > BALLISTA

BALLISTAS > BALLISTA

BALLISTIC *adj* of or relating to ballistics

BALLIUM *same as* > BAILEY

BALLIUMS > BALLIUM

BALLOCKS *same as* > BOLLOCKS

BALLON *n* light, graceful quality

BALLONET *n* air or gas compartment in a nonrigid airship

BALLONETS > BALLONET

BALLONNE *n* bouncing step

BALLONNES > BALLONNE

BALLONS > BALLON

BALLOON *n* inflatable rubber bag used as a plaything or decoration ▷ *vb* fly in a balloon

BALLOONED > BALLOON

BALLOONS > BALLOON

BALLOT *n* method of voting ▷ *vb* vote or ask for a vote from

BALLOTED > BALLOT

BALLOTEE > BALLOT

BALLOTEES > BALLOT

BALLOTER > BALLOT

BALLOTERS > BALLOT

BALLOTING *n* act of balloting

BALLOTINI *n* small glass beads

BALLOTS > BALLOT

BALLOW *n* heavy club

BALLOWS > BALLOW

BALLPARK *n* stadium used for baseball games

BALLPARKS > BALLPARK

BALLPEEN *adj* as in ballpeen hammer type of hammer

BALLPOINT *n* pen with a tiny ball bearing as a writing point

BALLROOM *n* large hall for dancing

BALLROOMS > BALLROOM

BALLS *n* plural of ball ▷ *vb* vulgar slang word meaning muddle or botch

BALLSED > BALLS

BALLSES > BALLS

BALLSIER > BALLSY

BALLSIEST > BALLSY

BALLSING > BALLS

BALLSY *adj* slang word meaning courageous and spirited

BALLUP *n* vulgar slang word for something botched or muddled

BALLUPS > BALLUP

BALLUTE *n* inflatable balloon parachute

BALLUTES > BALLUTE

BALLY *adj* euphemism for bloody ▷ *n* exaggerated fuss

BALLYARD *n* baseball ground

BALLYARDS > BALLYARD

BALLYHOO *n* exaggerated fuss ▷ *vb* advertise or publicize by sensational or blatant methods

BALLYHOOS > BALLYHOO

BALLYRAG *same as* > BULLYRAG

BALLYRAGS > BALLYRAG

BALM *n* aromatic substance used for healing and soothing ▷ *vb* apply balm to

BALMACAAN *n* man's knee-length loose flaring overcoat with raglan sleeves

BALMED > BALM

BALMIER > BALMY

BALMIEST > BALMY

BALMILY > BALMY

BALMINESS > BALMY

BALMING > BALM

BALMLIKE > BALM

BALMORAL *n* laced walking shoe

BALMORALS > BALMORAL

BALMS > BALM

BALMY *adj* (of weather) mild and pleasant

BALNEAL *adj* of or relating to baths or bathing

BALNEARY *same as* > BALNEAL

BALONEY *n* foolish talk; nonsense

BALONEYS > BALONEY

BALOO *n* bear

BALOOS > BALOO

BALS > BAL

BALSA *n* very light wood from a tropical American tree

BALSAM *n* type of fragrant balm ▷ *vb* embalm

BALSAMED > BALSAM

BALSAMIC > BALSAM

BALSAMIER > BALSAMY

BALSAMING > BALSAM

BALSAMS > BALSAM

BALSAMY *adj* sweet-smelling

BALSAS > BALSA

BALSAWOOD *same as* > BALSA

BALTHASAR *same as* > BALTHAZAR

BALTHAZAR *n* wine bottle holding the equivalent of sixteen normal bottles

BALTI *n* spicy Indian dish served in a metal dish

BALTIC *adj* very cold

BALTIS > BALTI

BALU *same as* > BALOO

BALUN *n* electrical device

BALUNS > BALUN

BALUS > BALU

BALUSTER *n* set of posts supporting a rail ▷ *adj* (of a shape) swelling at the base and rising in a concave curve to a narrow stem or neck

BALUSTERS > BALUSTER

BALZARINE *n* light fabric

BAM *vb* cheat

BAMBI *n* born-again middle-aged biker

BAMBINI > BAMBINO

BAMBINO *n* young child, esp an Italian one

BAMBINOS > BAMBINO

BAMBIS > BAMBI

BAMBOO *n* tall treelike tropical grass with hollow stems

BAMBOOS > BAMBOO

BAMBOOZLE *vb* cheat or mislead

BAMMED > BAM

BAMMER > BAM

BAMMERS > BAM

BAMMING > BAM

BAMPOT *n* fool

BAMPOTS > BAMPOT

BAMS > BAM

BAN *vb* prohibit or forbid officially ▷ *n* unit of currency in Romania and Moldova

BANAK *n* type of Central American tree

BANAKS > BANAK

BANAL *adj* ordinary and unoriginal

BANALER > BANAL

BANALEST > BANAL

BANALISE > BANAL

BANALISED > BANAL

BANALISES > BANAL

BANALITY > BANAL

BANALIZE > BANAL

BANALIZED > BANAL

BANALIZES > BANAL

BANALLY > BANAL

BANANA *n* yellow crescent-shaped fruit

BANANAS *adj* crazy

BANAUSIAN > BANAUSIC

BANAUSIC *adj* merely mechanical

BANC *n* as in *in banc* sitting as a full court

BANCO *n* call made in gambling games

BANCOS > BANCO

BANCS > BANC

BAND *n* group of musicians playing together ▷ *vb* unite

BANDA *n* African thatched hut

BANDAGE *n* piece of material used to cover a wound or wrap an injured limb ▷ *vb* cover with a bandage

BANDAGED > BANDAGE

BANDAGER > BANDAGE

BANDAGERS > BANDAGE

BANDAGES > BANDAGE

BANDAGING *n* act of bandaging

BANDAID *adj* (of a solution or remedy) temporary

BANDALORE *n* old-fashioned type of yo-yo

BANDANA *same as* > BANDANNA

BANDANAS > BANDANA

BANDANNA *n* large brightly coloured handkerchief or neckerchief

BANDANNAS > BANDANNA

BANDAR *n* species of monkey

BANDARI *n* Indian English word for female monkey

BANDARIS > BANDARI

BANDARS > BANDAR

BANDAS > BANDA

BANDBOX *n* lightweight usually cylindrical box for hats

BANDBOXES > BANDBOX

BANDBRAKE *n* type of brake

BANDEAU *n* narrow ribbon worn round the head

BANDEAUS > BANDEAU

BANDEAUX > BANDEAU

BANDED > BAND

BANDEIRA *n* 17th-century expedition in search of gold or slaves

BANDEIRAS > BANDEIRA

BANDELET *n* moulding round top of column

BANDELETS > BANDELET

BANDELIER *same as* > BANDOLEER

BANDER > BAND

BANDEROL *same as* > BANDEROLE

BANDEROLE *n* narrow flag usually with forked ends

BANDEROLS > BANDEROL

BANDH *n* (in India) a general strike

BANDHS > BANDH

BANDICOOT *n* ratlike Australian marsupial

BANDIED > BANDY

BANDIER > BANDY

BANDIES > BANDY

BANDIEST > BANDY

BANDINESS > BANDY

BANDING *n* practice of grouping schoolchildren according to ability

BANDINGS > BANDING

BANDIT *n* robber, esp a member of an armed gang

BANDITO *n* Mexican bandit

BANDITOS > BANDITO

BANDITRY > BANDIT

BANDITS > BANDIT

BANDITTI > BANDIT

BANDITTIS > BANDIT

BANDLIKE *adj* like a band

BANDMATE *n* fellow member of band

BANDMATES > BANDMATE

BANDOBAST *same as* > BANDOBUST

BANDOBUST *n* (in India and Pakistan) an arrangement

BANDOG *n* ferocious dog

BANDOGS > BANDOG

BANDOLEER *same as* > BANDOLIER

BANDOLEON *same as* > BANDONEON

BANDOLERO *n* highwayman

BANDOLIER *n* shoulder belt for holding cartridges

BANDOLINE *n* glutinous hair dressing, used (esp formerly) to keep the hair in place

BANDONEON *n* type of square concertina, esp used in Argentina

BANDONION *same as* > BANDONEON

BANDOOK *same as* > BUNDOOK

BANDOOKS > BANDOOK

BANDORA *same as* > BANDORE

BANDORAS > BANDORA

BANDORE *n* 16th-century musical instrument

BANDORES > BANDORE

BANDPASS *n* range of frequencies transmitted through a bandpass filter

BANDROL *same as* > BANDEROLE

BANDROLS > BANDROL

BANDS > BAND

BANDSAW *n* power saw with continuous blade ▷ *vb* cut with a bandsaw

BANDSAWED > BANDSAW

BANDSAWS > BANDSAW

BANDSHELL *n* bandstand concave at back

BANDSMAN *n* player in a musical band

BANDSMEN > BANDSMAN

b

b

BANDSTAND n roofed outdoor platform for a band

BANDSTER n binder of wheat sheaves

BANDSTERS > BANDSTER

BANDURA n type of lute

BANDURAS > BANDURA

BANDURIST n bandura player

BANDWAGON n type of wagon

BANDWIDTH n range of frequencies within a given waveband used for a particular transmission

BANDY adj having legs curved outwards at the knees ▷ vb exchange (words) in a heated manner

BANDYING > BANDY

BANDYINGS > BANDY

BANDYMAN n carriage or cart

BANDYMEN > BANDYMAN

BANE n person or thing that causes misery or distress ▷ vb cause harm or distress to (someone)

BANEBERRY n type of plant with small white flowers and red or white poisonous berries

BANED > BANE

BANEFUL adj destructive, poisonous, or fatal

BANEFULLY > BANEFUL

BANES > BANE

BANG vb make a short explosive noise

BANGALAY n Australian tree valued for its hard red wood

BANGALAYS > BANGALAY

BANGALORE adj as in bangalore torpedo explosive device in a long metal tube

BANGALOW n Australian palm tree native to New South Wales and Queensland

BANGALOWS > BANGALOW

BANGBELLY n dense cake with sweet and savoury ingredients

BANGED > BANG

BANGER n old decrepit car

BANGERS > BANGER

BANGING > BANG

BANGKOK n type of straw hat

BANGKOKS > BANGKOK

BANGLE n bracelet worn round the arm or the ankle

BANGLED > BANGLE

BANGLES > BANGLE

BANGS > BANG

BANGSRING same as > BANXRING

BANGSTER n ruffian

BANGSTERS > BANGSTER

BANGTAIL n horse's tail cut straight across but not through the bone

BANGTAILS > BANGTAIL

BANI > BAN

BANIA same as > BANYAN

BANIAN same as > BANYAN

BANIANS > BANIAN

BANIAS > BANIA

BANING > BANE

BANISH vb send (someone) into exile

BANISHED > BANISH

BANISHER > BANISH

BANISHERS > BANISH

BANISHES > BANISH

BANISHING > BANISH

BANISTER same as > BANNISTER

BANISTERS pl n railing supported by posts on a staircase

BANJAX vb ruin; destroy

BANJAXED > BANJAX

BANJAXES > BANJAX

BANJAXING > BANJAX

BANJO n guitar-like musical instrument with a circular body

BANJOES > BANJO

BANJOIST > BANJO

BANJOISTS > BANJO

BANJOLELE n musical instrument with a neck like a ukulele and a body like a banjo

BANJOS > BANJO

BANJULELE n small banjo

BANK n institution offering services such as the safekeeping and lending of money ▷ vb deposit (cash or cheques) in a bank

BANKABLE adj likely to ensure financial success

BANKBOOK n record of deposits, withdrawals, and interest held by depositors at certain banks

BANKBOOKS > BANKBOOK

BANKCARD n card guaranteeing payment of cheque

BANKCARDS > BANKCARD

BANKED > BANK

BANKER n manager or owner of a bank

BANKERLY adj like a banker

BANKERS > BANKER

BANKET n gold-bearing conglomerate found in South Africa

BANKETS > BANKET

BANKING > BANK

BANKINGS > BANKING

BANKIT same as > BANQUETTE

BANKITS > BANKIT

BANKNOTE n piece of paper money

BANKNOTES > BANKNOTE

BANKROLL n roll of currency notes ▷ vb provide the capital for

BANKROLLS > BANKROLL

BANKRUPT n person declared by a court to be unable to pay his or her debts ▷ vb make bankrupt

BANKRUPTS > BANKRUPT

BANKS > BANK

BANKSIA n Australian evergreen tree or shrub

BANKSIAS > BANKSIA

BANKSIDE n riverside

BANKSIDES > BANKSIDE

BANKSMAN n crane driver's helper

BANKSMEN > BANKSMAN

BANKSTER n banker whose illegal practices have been exposed

BANKSTERS > BANKSTER

BANLIEUE n suburb of a city

BANLIEUES > BANLIEUE

BANNABLE > BAN

BANNED > BAN

BANNER n long strip of cloth displaying a slogan, advertisement, etc ▷ vb (of a newspaper headline) to display (a story) prominently ▷ adj outstandingly successful

BANNERALL same as > BANDEROLE

BANNERED > BANNER

BANNERET n small banner

BANNERETS > BANNERET

BANNERING > BANNER

BANNEROL same as > BANDEROLE

BANNEROLS > BANNEROL

BANNERS > BANNER

BANNET n bonnet

BANNETS > BANNET

BANNING n act of banning

BANNINGS > BANNING

BANNISTER same as > BANISTERS

BANNOCK n round flat cake made from oatmeal or barley

BANNOCKS > BANNOCK

BANNS pl n public declaration, esp in a church, of an intended marriage

BANOFFEE n filling for a pie, consisting of toffee and banana

BANOFFEES > BANOFFEE

BANOFFI same as > BANOFFEE

BANOFFIS > BANOFFI

BANQUET n elaborate formal dinner ▷ vb hold or take part in a banquet

BANQUETED > BANQUET

BANQUETER > BANQUET

BANQUETS > BANQUET

BANQUETTE n upholstered bench

BANS same as > BANNS

BANSELA same as > BONSELA

BANSELAS > BANSELA

BANSHEE n (in Irish folklore) spirit whose wailing warns of a coming death

BANSHEES > BANSHEE

BANSHIE same as > BANSHEE

BANSHIES > BANSHIE

BANT n string ▷ vb tie with string

BANTAM n small breed of chicken

BANTAMS > BANTAM

BANTED > BANT

BANTENG n wild ox

BANTENGS > BANTENG

BANTER vb tease jokingly ▷ n teasing or joking conversation

BANTERED > BANTER

BANTERER > BANTER

BANTERERS > BANTER

BANTERING > BANTER

BANTERS > BANTER

BANTIES > BANTY

BANTING > BANT

BANTINGS > BANT

BANTLING n young child

BANTLINGS > BANTLING

BANTS > BANT

BANTY n bantam

BANXRING n tree-shrew

BANXRINGS > BANXRING

BANYA n traditional Russian steam bath

BANYAN n Indian tree

BANYANS > BANYAN

BANYAS > BANYA

BANZAI interj patriotic cheer, battle cry, or salutation

BANZAIS > BANZAI

BAO n steamed dumpling

BAOBAB n African tree with a thick trunk and angular branches

BAOBABS > BAOBAB

BAOS > BAO

BAP n large soft bread roll

BAPS > BAP

BAPTISE same as > BAPTIZE

BAPTISED > BAPTISE

BAPTISER > BAPTISE

BAPTISERS > BAPTISE

BAPTISES > BAPTISE

BAPTISIA n species of wild flower

BAPTISIAS > BAPTISIA

BAPTISING > BAPTISE

BAPTISM n Christian religious ceremony

BAPTISMAL > BAPTISM

BAPTISMS > BAPTISM

BAPTIST n one who baptizes

BAPTISTRY n part of a Christian church in which baptisms are carried out
BAPTISTS > BAPTIST
BAPTIZE vb perform baptism on
BAPTIZED > BAPTIZE
BAPTIZER > BAPTIZE
BAPTIZERS > BAPTIZE
BAPTIZES > BAPTIZE
BAPTIZING > BAPTIZE
BAPU n spiritual father
BAPUS > BAPU
BAR n rigid usually straight length of metal, wood, etc, longer than it is wide or thick ▷ vb fasten or secure with a bar
BARACAN same as
> BARRACAN
BARACANS > BARACAN
BARACHOIS n (in the Atlantic Provinces of Canada) a shallow lagoon formed by a sand bar
BARAGOUIN n incomprehensible language
BARASINGA n type of deer
BARATHEA n fabric made of silk and wool or cotton and rayon, used esp for coats
BARATHEAS
> BARATHEA
BARATHRUM n abyss
BARAZA n place where public meetings are held
BARAZAS > BARAZA
BARB n cutting remark ▷ vb provide with a barb or barbs
BARBAL adj of a beard
BARBARIAN n member of a primitive or uncivilized people ▷ adj uncivilized or brutal
BARBARIC adj cruel or brutal
BARBARISE same as
> BARBARIZE
BARBARISM n condition of being backward or ignorant
BARBARITY n state of being barbaric or barbarous
BARBARIZE vb make or become barbarous
BARBAROUS adj uncivilized
BARBASCO n S American plant
BARBASCOS
> BARBASCO
BARBASTEL n insectivorous forest bat
BARBATE adj having tufts of long hairs
BARBATED > BARBATE
BARBE n Waldensian missionary
BARBECUE n grill on which food is cooked over hot charcoal, usu outdoors ▷ vb cook (food) on a barbecue
BARBECUED > BARBECUE

BARBECUER
> BARBECUE
BARBECUES
> BARBECUE
BARBED > BARB
BARBEL n long thin growth that hangs from the jaws of certain fishes, such as the carp
BARBELL n long metal rod to which heavy discs are attached at each end for weightlifting
BARBELLS > BARBELL
BARBELS > BARBEL
BARBEQUE same as
> BARBECUE
BARBEQUED
> BARBEQUE
BARBEQUES
> BARBEQUE
BARBER n person who cuts men's hair and shaves beards ▷ vb cut the hair of
BARBERED > BARBER
BARBERING > BARBER
BARBERRY n shrub with orange or red berries
BARBERS > BARBER
BARBES > BARBE
BARBET n type of small tropical bird
BARBETS > BARBET
BARBETTE n earthen platform inside a parapet
BARBETTES
> BARBETTE
BARBICAN n walled defence to protect a gate or drawbridge of a fortification
BARBICANS
> BARBICAN
BARBICEL n minute hook on the barbule of a feather
BARBICELS > BARBICEL
BARBIE short for
> BARBECUE
BARBIES > BARBIE
BARBING > BARB
BARBITAL same as
> BARBITONE
BARBITALS
> BARBITAL
BARBITONE n long-acting barbiturate used medicinally, usually in the form of the sodium salt, as a sedative or hypnotic
BARBLESS > BARB
BARBOLA n creation of small models of flowers, etc from plastic paste
BARBOLAS > BARBOLA
BARBOT same as
> BURBOT
BARBOTINE n clay used in making decorated pottery
BARBOTS > BARBOT
BARBOTTE same as
> BURBOT
BARBOTTES
> BARBOTTE
BARBS > BARB
BARBULE n very small barb

BARBULES > BARBULE
BARBUT n open-faced helmet
BARBUTS > BARBUT
BARBWIRE n barbed wire
BARBWIRES
> BARBWIRE
BARBY short for
> BARBECUE
BARCA n boat
BARCAROLE n Venetian boat song
BARCAS > BARCA
BARCHAN n crescent-shaped shifting sand dune
BARCHANE same as
> BARCHAN
BARCHANES
> BARCHANE
BARCHANS > BARCHAN
BARCODE n machine-readable code printed on goods
BARCODED adj having a barcode
BARCODES > BARCODE
BARD n poet ▷ vb place a piece of pork fat on
BARDASH n kept boy in a homosexual relationship
BARDASHES > BARDASH
BARDE same as > BARD
BARDED > BARDE
BARDES > BARDE
BARDIC > BARD
BARDIE n type of Australian grub
BARDIER > BARD
BARDIES > BARDIE
BARDIEST > BARD
BARDING > BARD
BARDISM > BARD
BARDISMS > BARD
BARDLING n inferior poet
BARDLINGS
> BARDLING
BARDO n (in Tibetan Buddhism) the state of the soul between its death and its rebirth
BARDOS > BARDO
BARDS > BARD
BARDSHIP > BARD
BARDSHIPS > BARD
BARDY > BARD
BARE adj unclothed, naked ▷ vb uncover
BAREBACK adv (of horse-riding) without a saddle ▷ vb ride bareback
BAREBACKS
> BAREBACK
BAREBOAT n boat chartered without crew, provisions, etc
BAREBOATS
> BAREBOAT
BAREBONE n computer casing containing bare essentials
BAREBONED adj short of resources
BAREBONES
> BAREBONE
BARED > BARE
BAREFACED adj shameless or obvious

BAREFIT Scots word for
> BAREFOOT
BAREFOOT adv with the feet uncovered
BAREGE n light silky gauze fabric made of wool ▷ adj made of such a fabric
BAREGES > BAREGE
BAREGINE n curative ingredient in thermal waters
BAREGINES
> BAREGINE
BAREHAND vb handle with bare hands
BAREHANDS
> BAREHAND
BAREHEAD adv with head uncovered
BARELAND adj as in bareland croft refers to a croft with no croft house
BARELY adv only just
BARENESS > BARE
BARER > BARE
BARES > BARE
BARESARK another word for > BERSERK
BARESARKS
> BARESARK
BAREST > BARE
BARF vb vomit ▷ n act of vomiting
BARFED > BARF
BARFI n type of Indian dessert
BARFING > BARF
BARFIS > BARFI
BARFLIES > BARFLY
BARFLY n person who frequents bars
BARFS > BARF
BARFUL adj presenting difficulties
BARGAIN n agreement establishing what each party will give, receive, or perform in a transaction ▷ vb negotiate the terms of an agreement
BARGAINED > BARGAIN
BARGAINER > BARGAIN
BARGAINS > BARGAIN
BARGANDER same as
> BERGANDER
BARGE n flat-bottomed boat used to transport freight ▷ vb push violently
BARGED > BARGE
BARGEE n person in charge of a barge
BARGEES > BARGEE
BARGEESE > BARGOOSE
BARGELIKE adj like a barge
BARGELLO n zigzag tapestry stitch
BARGELLOS
> BARGELLO
BARGEMAN same as
> BARGEE
BARGEMEN > BARGEMAN
BARGEPOLE n long pole used to propel a barge
BARGES > BARGE
BARGEST same as
> BARGHEST
BARGESTS > BARGHEST

b

b

BARGHEST n mythical goblin in the shape of a dog
BARGHESTS > BARGHEST
BARGING > BARGE
BARGOON Canadian word for > BARGAIN
BARGOONS > BARGOON
BARGOOSE n type of goose; sheldrake
BARGUEST same as > BARGHEST
BARGUESTS > BARGUEST
BARHOP vb visit several bars in succession
BARHOPPED > BARHOP
BARHOPS > BARHOP
BARIATRIC adj of the treatment of obesity
BARIC adj of or containing barium
BARILLA n impure mixture of sodium carbonate and sodium sulphate
BARILLAS > BARILLA
BARING > BARE
BARISH adj quite thinly covered
BARISTA n person who makes and sells coffee in a coffee bar
BARISTAS > BARISTA
BARITE n colourless or white mineral
BARITES > BARITE
BARITONAL > BARITONE
BARITONE n (singer with) the second lowest adult male voice ▷ adj relating to or denoting a baritone
BARITONES > BARITONE
BARIUM n soft white metallic element
BARIUMS > BARIUM
BARK vb (of a dog) make its typical loud abrupt cry
BARKAN same as > BARCHAN
BARKANS > BARKAN
BARKED > BARK
BARKEEP n barkeeper
BARKEEPER another name (esp US) for > BARTENDER
BARKEEPS > BARKEEP
BARKEN vb become dry with a bark-like outer layer
BARKENED > BARKEN
BARKENING > BARKEN
BARKENS > BARKEN
BARKER n person at a fairground who calls loudly to passers-by in order to attract customers
BARKERS > BARKER
BARKHAN same as > BARCHAN
BARKHANS > BARKHAN
BARKIER > BARKY
BARKIEST > BARKY
BARKING > BARK
BARKLESS > BARK

BARKLIKE adj like a dog's bark
BARKS > BARK
BARKY adj having the texture or appearance of bark
BARLEDUC n French preserve made of currants
BARLEDUCS > BARLEDUC
BARLESS > BAR
BARLEY n tall grasslike plant cultivated for grain
BARLEYS > BARLEY
BARLOW n type of strong knife
BARLOWS > BARLOW
BARM n yeasty froth on fermenting malt liquors
BARMAID n woman who serves in a pub
BARMAIDS > BARMAID
BARMAN same as > BARTENDER
BARMBRACK n loaf of bread with currants in it
BARMEN > BARMAN
BARMIE same as > BARMY
BARMIER > BARMY
BARMIEST > BARMY
BARMILY > BARMY
BARMINESS > BARMY
BARMKIN n protective wall around castle
BARMKINS > BARMKIN
BARMPOT n foolish person
BARMPOTS > BARMPOT
BARMS > BARM
BARMY adj mad
BARN n large building on a farm used for storing grain ▷ vb keep in a barn
BARNACLE n shellfish that lives attached to rocks, ship bottoms, etc
BARNACLED > BARNACLE
BARNACLES > BARNACLE
BARNBOARD n softwood board for building barns
BARNBRACK same as > BARMBRACK
BARNED > BARN
BARNET n hair
BARNETS > BARNET
BARNEY n noisy fight or argument ▷ vb argue or quarrel
BARNEYED > BARNEY
BARNEYING > BARNEY
BARNEYS > BARNEY
BARNIER > BARNY
BARNIEST > BARNY
BARNING > BARN
BARNLIKE > BARN
BARNS > BARN
BARNSTORM vb tour rural districts putting on shows or making speeches in a political campaign
BARNWOOD n aged and weathered boards, esp those salvaged from dismantled barns
BARNWOODS > BARNWOOD

BARNY adj reminiscent of a barn
BARNYARD n yard adjoining a barn
BARNYARDS > BARNYARD
BAROCCO same as > BAROQUE
BAROCCOS > BAROCCO
BAROCK same as > BAROQUE
BAROCKS > BAROCK
BAROGRAM n record of atmospheric pressure traced by a barograph or similar instrument
BAROGRAMS > BAROGRAM
BAROGRAPH n barometer that automatically keeps a record of changes in atmospheric pressure
BAROLO n red Italian wine
BAROLOS > BAROLO
BAROMETER n instrument for measuring atmospheric pressure
BAROMETRY > BAROMETER
BAROMETZ n fern whose woolly rhizomes resemble a lamb
BARON n member of the lowest rank of nobility
BARONAGE n barons collectively
BARONAGES > BARONAGE
BARONESS n woman holding the rank of baron
BARONET n man who holds the lowest hereditary British title
BARONETCY n rank, position, or patent of a baronet
BARONETS > BARONET
BARONG n broad-bladed cleaver-like knife used in the Philippines
BARONGS > BARONG
BARONIAL adj of, relating to, or befitting a baron or barons
BARONIES > BARONY
BARONNE n baroness
BARONNES > BARONNE
BARONS > BARON
BARONY n domain or rank of a baron
BAROPHILE n living organism that grows best in conditions of high atmospheric pressure
BAROQUE n style of art, architecture, or music ▷ adj ornate in style
BAROQUELY > BAROQUE
BAROQUES > BAROQUE
BAROSAUR n large dinosaur
BAROSAURS > BAROSAUR
BAROSCOPE n any instrument for measuring atmospheric pressure, esp a manometer with one side open to the atmosphere

BAROSTAT n device for maintaining constant pressure, such as one used in an aircraft cabin
BAROSTATS > BAROSTAT
BAROTITIS n inflammation of the ear caused by a change in air pressure
BAROUCHE n type of horse-drawn carriage
BAROUCHES > BAROUCHE
BARP n hillock or bank of stones
BARPERSON n person who serves in a pub: used esp in advertisements
BARPS > BARP
BARQUE n sailing ship, esp one with three masts
BARQUES > BARQUE
BARQUETTE n boat-shaped pastry shell
BARRA n barramundi
BARRABLE > BAR
BARRACAN n thick, strong fabric
BARRACANS > BARRACAN
BARRACE n record of teams entering a sports contest
BARRACES > BARRACE
BARRACK vb criticize loudly or shout against (a team or speaker)
BARRACKED > BARRACK
BARRACKER > BARRACK
BARRACKS pl n building used to accommodate military personnel
BARRACOON n (formerly) a temporary place of confinement for slaves or convicts, esp those awaiting transportation
BARRACUDA n tropical sea fish
BARRAGE n continuous delivery of questions, complaints, etc ▷ vb attack or confront with a barrage
BARRAGED > BARRAGE
BARRAGES > BARRAGE
BARRAGING > BARRAGE
BARRANCA n ravine or precipice
BARRANCAS > BARRANCA
BARRANCO same as > BARRANCA
BARRANCOS > BARRANCO
BARRAS > BARRA
BARRASWAY n shallow lagoon by a sandbar
BARRAT n fraudulent dealings ▷ vb quarrel
BARRATED > BARRAT
BARRATER same as > BARRATOR
BARRATERS > BARRATER
BARRATING > BARRAT
BARRATOR n person guilty of barratry

BARRATORS
> BARRATOR

BARRATRY n (formerly) the vexatious stirring up of quarrels or bringing of lawsuits

BARRATS > BARRAT

BARRE n rail at hip height used for ballet practice ▷ vb execute guitar chords by laying the index finger over some or all of the strings ▷ adv by using the barre

BARRED > BAR

BARREED > BARREE

BARREFULL same as > BARFUL

BARREING > BARRE

BARREL n cylindrical container with rounded sides and flat ends ▷ vb put in a barrel

BARRELAGE > BARREL

BARRELED > BARREL

BARRELFUL same as > BARREL

BARRELING > BARREL

BARRELLED > BARREL

BARRELS > BARREL

BARREN adj incapable of producing offspring or fruit

BARRENER > BARREN

BARRENEST > BARREN

BARRENLY > BARREN

BARRENS pl n (in North America) a stretch of land that is sparsely vegetated

BARRES > BARRE

BARRET n small flat cap resembling a biretta

BARRETOR n quarrelsome person

BARRETORS > BARRETOR

BARRETRY same as > BARRATRY

BARRETS > BARRET

BARRETTE n clasp or pin for holding hair in place

BARRETTER same as > BARRETOR

BARRETTES > BARRETTE

BARRICADE n barrier, esp one erected hastily for defence ▷ vb erect a barricade across (an entrance)

BARRICADO same as > BARRICADE

BARRICO n small container for liquids

BARRICOES > BARRICO

BARRICOS > BARRICO

BARRIE adj dialect word for excellent

BARRIER n anything that prevents access, progress, or union ▷ vb create or form a barrier

BARRIERED > BARRIER

BARRIERS > BARRIER

BARRIES > BARRY

BARRIEST > BARRY

BARRING > BAR

BARRINGS > BAR

BARRIO n Spanish-speaking quarter in a town or city, esp in the US

BARRIOS > BARRIO

BARRIQUE n wine barrel made of oak

BARRIQUES > BARRIQUE

BARRISTER n lawyer qualified to plead in a higher court

BARRO adj embarrassing

BARROOM n room or building where alcoholic drinks are served over a counter

BARROOMS > BARROOM

BARROW n wheelbarrow

BARROWFUL same as > BARROW

BARROWS > BARROW

BARRULET n narrow band across heraldic shield

BARRULETS > BARRULET

BARRY n mistake or blunder ▷ adj dialect word for excellent

BARS > BAR

BARSTOOL n high stool in bar

BARSTOOLS > BARSTOOL

BARTEND vb serve drinks from a bar

BARTENDED > BARTEND

BARTENDER n person who serves in a bar

BARTENDS > BARTEND

BARTER vb trade (goods) in exchange for other goods ▷ n trade by the exchange of goods

BARTERED > BARTER

BARTERER > BARTER

BARTERERS > BARTER

BARTERING > BARTER

BARTERS > BARTER

BARTISAN same as > BARTIZAN

BARTISANS > BARTISAN

BARTIZAN n small turret projecting from a wall, parapet, or tower

BARTIZANS > BARTIZAN

BARTON n farmyard

BARTONS > BARTON

BARTSIA n type of semiparasitic plant

BARTSIAS > BARTSIA

BARWARE n glasses, etc used in a bar

BARWARES > BARWARE

BARWOOD n red wood from a small African tree

BARWOODS > BARWOOD

BARYE n unit of pressure

BARYES > BARYE

BARYON n elementary particle that has a mass greater than or equal to that of the proton

BARYONIC adj of or relating to a baryon

BARYONS > BARYON

BARYTA same as > BARITE

BARYTAS > BARYTA

BARYTE same as > BARITE

BARYTES > BARYTE

BARYTIC > BARYTA

BARYTON n bass viol with sympathetic strings as well as its six main strings

BARYTONE adj having the last syllable unaccented ▷ n word in which the last syllable is unaccented

BARYTONES > BARYTONE

BARYTONS > BARYTON

BAS > BA

BASAL adj of, at, or constituting a base

BASALLY > BASAL

BASALT n dark volcanic rock

BASALTES n unglazed black stoneware

BASALTIC > BASALT

BASALTINE adj resembling basalt ▷ n black or greenish-black mineral of the pyroxene group

BASALTS > BASALT

BASAN n sheepskin tanned in bark

BASANITE n black basaltic rock

BASANITES > BASANITE

BASANS > BASAN

BASANT n Pakistani spring festival

BASANTS > BASANT

BASCINET same as > BASINET

BASCINETS > BASCINET

BASCULE n drawbridge that operates by a counterbalanced weight

BASCULES > BASCULE

BASE n bottom or supporting part of anything ▷ vb use as a basis (for) ▷ adj dishonourable or immoral

BASEBALL n type of team ball game

BASEBALLS > BASEBALL

BASEBAND n transmission technique using a narrow range of frequencies

BASEBANDS > BASEBAND

BASEBOARD n board functioning as the base of anything

BASEBORN adj born of humble parents

BASED > BASE

BASEEJ pl n Iranian volunteer militia

BASEHEAD n habitual user of freebased cocaine

BASEHEADS > BASEHEAD

BASELARD n short sword

BASELARDS > BASELARD

BASELESS adj not based on fact

BASELINE n value or starting point on an imaginary scale with which other things are compared

BASELINER n tennis player who plays most of his or her shots from the back of the court

BASELINES > BASELINE

BASELOAD n constant part of an electrical power supply

BASELOADS > BASELOAD

BASELY > BASE

BASEMAN n fielder positioned near a base

BASEMEN > BASEMAN

BASEMENT n partly or wholly underground storey of a building

BASEMENTS > BASEMENT

BASEN Spenserian spelling of > BASIN

BASENESS > BASE

BASENJI n small breed of dog

BASENJIS > BASENJI

BASEPATH n diamond-shaped path between bases on a baseball field

BASEPATHS > BASEPATH

BASEPLATE n flat supporting plate or frame

BASER > BASE

BASES > BASIS

BASEST > BASE

BASH vb hit violently or forcefully ▷ n heavy blow

BASHAW n important or pompous person

BASHAWISM > BASHAW

BASHAWS > BASHAW

BASHED > BASH

BASHER > BASH

BASHERS > BASH

BASHES > BASH

BASHFUL adj shy or modest

BASHFULLY > BASHFUL

BASHING > BASH

BASHINGS > BASH

BASHLESS adj not ashamed

BASHLIK n Caucasian hood

BASHLIKS > BASHLIK

BASHLYK same as > BASHLIK

BASHLYKS > BASHLYK

BASHMENT same as > DANCEHALL

BASHMENTS > BASHMENT

BASHO n grand tournament in sumo wrestling

BASHTAG n (on Twitter) hashtag used for abusive comments

BASHTAGS > BASHTAG

BASIC adj of or forming a base or basis ▷ n fundamental principle, fact, etc

b

BASICALLY *adv* in a fundamental or elementary manner

BASICITY *n* state of being a base

BASICS > BASIC

BASIDIA > BASIDIUM

BASIDIAL > BASIDIUM

BASIDIUM *n* spore-forming structure in fungi

BASIFIED > BASIFY

BASIFIER > BASIFY

BASIFIERS > BASIFY

BASIFIES > BASIFY

BASIFIXED *adj* (of an anther) attached to the filament by its base

BASIFUGAL *a less common word for* > ACROPETAL

BASIFY *vb* make basic

BASIFYING > BASIFY

BASIJ *same as* > BASEEJ

BASIL *n* aromatic herb used in cooking

BASILAR *adj* of or situated at a base

BASILARY *same as* > BASILAR

BASILECT *n* debased dialect

BASILECTS > BASILECT

BASILIC > BASILICA

BASILICA *n* rectangular church with a rounded end and two aisles

BASILICAE > BASILICA

BASILICAL > BASILICA

BASILICAN > BASILICA

BASILICAS > BASILICA

BASILICON *n* healing ointment

BASILISK *n* legendary serpent said to kill by its breath or glance

BASILISKS > BASILISK

BASILS > BASIL

BASIN *n* round open container

BASINAL > BASIN

BASINED > BASIN

BASINET *n* close-fitting medieval helmet of light steel usually with a visor

BASINETS > BASINET

BASINFUL *n* amount a basin will hold

BASINFULS > BASINFUL

BASING > BASE

BASINLIKE > BASIN

BASINS > BASIN

BASION *n* (in anatomy) midpoint on the forward border of the foramen magnum

BASIONS > BASION

BASIPETAL *adj* (of leaves and flowers) produced in order from the apex downwards so that the youngest are at the base

BASIS *n* fundamental principles etc from which something is started or developed

BASK *vb* lie in or be exposed to something, esp pleasant warmth

BASKED > BASK

BASKET *n* container made of interwoven strips of wood or cane

BASKETFUL *n* as much as a basket will hold

BASKETRY *n* art or practice of making baskets

BASKETS > BASKET

BASKING > BASK

BASKS > BASK

BASMATI *n* variety of long-grain rice with slender aromatic grains

BASMATIS > BASMATI

BASNET *same as* > BASINET

BASNETS > BASNET

BASOCHE *n* society of medieval French lawyers who performed comic plays

BASOCHES > BASOCHE

BASON *same as* > BASIN

BASONS > BASON

BASOPHIL *adj* (of cells or cell contents) easily stained by basic dyes ▷ *n* basophil cell, esp a leucocyte

BASOPHILE *same as* > BASOPHIL

BASOPHILS > BASOPHIL

BASQUE *n* tight-fitting bodice

BASQUED > BASQUE

BASQUES > BASQUE

BASQUINE *n* tight-fitting bodice

BASQUINES > BASQUINE

BASS *n* (singer with) the lowest adult male voice ▷ *adj* relating to or denoting a bass ▷ *vb* speak or sing in a low pitch

BASSE *same as* > BASS

BASSED > BASS

BASSER *n* someone who plays bass guitar or double bass

BASSERS > BASSER

BASSES > BASS

BASSEST > BASS

BASSET *n* breed of hound ▷ *vb* (of rock) protrude through earth's surface

BASSETED > BASSET

BASSETING > BASSET

BASSETS > BASSET

BASSETT *same as* > BASSET

BASSETTED > BASSETT

BASSETTS > BASSETT

BASSI > BASSO

BASSIER > BASSY

BASSIEST > BASSY

BASSINET *n* wickerwork or wooden cradle or pram, usually hooded

BASSINETS > BASSINET

BASSING > BASS

BASSIST *n* player of a double bass, esp in a jazz band

BASSISTS > BASSIST

BASSLINE *n* (in jazz, rock, and pop music) part played by the bass guitar

BASSLINES > BASSLINE

BASSLY > BASS

BASSNESS > BASS

BASSO *n* singer with a bass voice

BASSOON *n* low-pitched woodwind instrument

BASSOONS > BASSOON

BASSOS > BASSO

BASSWOOD *n* N American linden tree

BASSWOODS > BASSWOOD

BASSY *adj* manifesting strong bass tones

BAST *n* fibrous material used for making rope, matting, etc

BASTA *interj* enough; stop

BASTARD *n* very difficult or unpleasant thing ▷ *adj* irregular in shape, size, or appearance

BASTARDLY *adj* cruel

BASTARDRY *n* malicious or cruel behaviour

BASTARDS > BASTARD

BASTARDY *n* archaic word meaning illegitimacy

BASTE *vb* moisten (meat) during cooking with hot fat

BASTED > BASTE

BASTER > BASTE

BASTERS > BASTE

BASTES > BASTE

BASTI *n* (in India) a slum inhabited by poor people

BASTIDE *n* small isolated house in France

BASTIDES > BASTIDE

BASTILE *same as* > BASTILLE

BASTILES > BASTILE

BASTILLE *n* prison

BASTILLES > BASTILLE

BASTINADE *same as* > BASTINADO

BASTINADO *n* punishment or torture by beating on the soles of the feet with a stick ▷ *vb* beat (a person) in this way

BASTING *n* loose temporary stitches

BASTINGS > BASTING

BASTION *n* projecting part of a fortification

BASTIONED > BASTION

BASTIONS > BASTION

BASTIS > BASTI

BASTLE *n* fortified house

BASTLES > BASTLE

BASTO *n* ace of clubs in certain card games

BASTOS > BASTO

BASTS > BAST

BASUCO *n* illegal cocaine-based drug

BASUCOS > BASUCO

BAT *n* any of various types of club used to hit the ball in certain sports ▷ *vb* strike with or as if with a bat

BATABLE > BAT

BATARD *n* canoe made of birchbark

BATARDS > BATARD

BATATA *n* sweet potato

BATATAS > BATATA

BATAVIA *n* variety of lettuce with smooth pale green leaves

BATAVIAS > BATAVIA

BATBOY *n* boy who works at baseball games

BATBOYS > BATBOY

BATCH *n* group of people or things dealt with at the same time ▷ *vb* group (items) for efficient processing

BATCHED > BATCH

BATCHER > BATCH

BATCHERS > BATCH

BATCHES > BATCH

BATCHING > BATCH

BATCHINGS > BATCH

BATE *vb* (of hawks) to jump violently from a perch or the falconer's fist

BATEAU *n* light flat-bottomed boat used on rivers in Canada and the northern US

BATEAUX > BATEAU

BATED > BATE

BATELESS > BATE

BATELEUR *n* African bird of prey with a short tail and long wings

BATELEURS > BATELEUR

BATEMENT *n* reduction

BATEMENTS > BATEMENT

BATES > BATE

BATFISH *n* type of angler fish with a flattened scaleless body

BATFISHES > BATFISH

BATFOWL *vb* catch birds by temporarily blinding them with light

BATFOWLED > BATFOWL

BATFOWLER > BATFOWL

BATFOWLS > BATFOWL

BATGIRL *n* girl who works at baseball games

BATGIRLS > BATGIRL

BATH *n* large container in which to wash the body ▷ *vb* wash in a bath

BATHCUBE *n* cube of soluble scented material for use in a bath

BATHCUBES > BATHCUBE

BATHE *vb* swim in open water for pleasure

BATHED > BATHE

BATHER > BATHE

BATHERS *pl n* swimming costume

BATHES > BATHE
BATHETIC *adj* containing or displaying bathos
BATHHOUSE *n* building containing baths, esp for public use
BATHING *n* act of bathing
BATHINGS > BATHING
BATHLESS > BATH
BATHMAT *n* mat to stand on after a bath
BATHMATS > BATHMAT
BATHMIC > BATHMISM
BATHMISM *n* growth-force
BATHMISMS > BATHMISM
BATHOLITE *same as* > BATHOLITH
BATHOLITH *n* very large irregular-shaped mass of igneous rock, esp granite, formed from an intrusion of magma at great depth, esp one exposed after erosion of less resistant overlying rocks
BATHORSE *n* officer's packhorse
BATHORSES > BATHORSE
BATHOS *n* sudden change from a serious subject to a trivial one
BATHOSES > BATHOS
BATHROBE *n* loose-fitting garment for wear before or after a bath or swimming
BATHROBES > BATHROBE
BATHROOM *n* room with a bath, sink, and usu a toilet
BATHROOMS > BATHROOM
BATHS > BATH
BATHTUB *n* bath, esp one not permanently fixed
BATHTUBS > BATHTUB
BATHWATER *n* used or unused water in a bathtub
BATHYAL *adj* relating to an ocean depth of between 200 and 2000 metres
BATHYBIUS *n* gelatinous substance on seabed
BATHYLITE *same as* > BATHOLITH
BATHYLITH *same as* > BATHOLITH
BATIK *n* process of printing fabric using wax to cover areas not to be dyed ▷ *vb* treat material with this process
BATIKED > BATIK
BATIKING > BATIK
BATIKS > BATIK
BATING > BATE
BATISTE *n* fine plain-weave cotton fabric
BATISTES > BATISTE
BATLER *n* flat piece of wood for beating clothes, etc before washing
BATLERS > BATLER
BATLET *same as* > BATLER

BATLETS > BATLET
BATLIKE > BAT
BATMAN *n* male servant in the armed forces
BATMEN > BATMAN
BATOLOGY *n* study of brambles
BATON *n* thin stick used by the conductor of an orchestra ▷ *vb* carry or wave a baton
BATONED > BATON
BATONING > BATON
BATONNIER *n* president of a Bar Association in Quebec
BATONS > BATON
BATOON *same as* > BATON
BATOONED > BATOON
BATOONING > BATOON
BATOONS > BATOON
BATRACHIA *n* group of amphibians including frogs and toads
BATS > BAT
BATSHIT *adj* slang word for eccentric or crazy
BATSMAN *n* man who bats or specializes in batting
BATSMEN > BATSMAN
BATSWING *adj* in the form of the wing of a bat
BATSWOMAN *n* woman who bats or specializes in batting
BATSWOMEN > BATSWOMAN
BATT *same as* > BAT
BATTA *n* soldier's allowance
BATTALIA *n* arrangement of army prepared for battle
BATTALIAS > BATTALIA
BATTALION *n* army unit consisting of three or more companies
BATTAS > BATTA
BATTEAU *same as* > BATEAU
BATTEAUX > BATTEAU
BATTED > BAT
BATTEL *vb* make fertile
BATTELED > BATTEL
BATTELER > BATTEL
BATTELERS > BATTEL
BATTELING > BATTEL
BATTELLED > BATTEL
BATTELS > BATTEL
BATTEMENT *n* extension of one leg forwards, sideways, or backwards, either once or repeatedly
BATTEN *n* strip of wood fixed to something, esp to hold it in place ▷ *vb* strengthen or fasten with battens
BATTENED > BATTEN
BATTENER > BATTEN
BATTENERS > BATTEN
BATTENING > BATTEN
BATTENS > BATTEN
BATTER *vb* hit repeatedly ▷ *n* mixture of flour, eggs, and milk, used in cooking

BATTERED *adj* subjected to persistent physical violence
BATTERER *n* person who batters someone
BATTERERS > BATTERER
BATTERIE *n* movement in ballet involving the legs beating together
BATTERIES > BATTERY
BATTERING *n* act or practice of battering someone
BATTERO *n* heavy club
BATTEROS > BATTERO
BATTERS > BATTER
BATTERY *n* device that produces electricity in a torch, radio, etc ▷ *adj* kept in series of cages for intensive rearing
BATTIER > BATTY
BATTIES > BATTY
BATTIEST > BATTY
BATTIK *same as* > BATIK
BATTIKS > BATTIK
BATTILL *vb* fatten an animal
BATTILLED > BATTILL
BATTILLS > BATTILL
BATTILY *adv* in an eccentric or crazy manner
BATTINESS > BATTY
BATTING *n* act of hitting with a bat
BATTINGS > BATTING
BATTLE *n* fight between large armed forces ▷ *vb* struggle
BATTLEAX *same as* > BATTLEAXE
BATTLEAXE *n* kind of axe formerly used in battle
BATTLEBUS *n* coach that transports politicians and their advisers round the country during an election campaign
BATTLED > BATTLE
BATTLER > BATTLE
BATTLERS > BATTLE
BATTLES > BATTLE
BATTLING > BATTLE
BATTOLOGY *n* unnecessary repetition of words
BATTS > BATT
BATTU *adj* (in ballet) involving a beating movement
BATTUE *n* beating of woodland or cover to force game to flee in the direction of hunters
BATTUES > BATTUE
BATTUTA *n* (in music) a beat
BATTUTAS > BATTUTA
BATTUTO *n* (in Italian cookery) selection of chopped herbs
BATTUTOS > BATTUTO
BATTY *adj* eccentric or crazy ▷ *n* person's bottom
BATWING *adj* shaped like the wings of a bat, as a black tie, collar, etc

BATWOMAN *n* female servant in any of the armed forces
BATWOMEN > BATWOMAN
BAUBEE *same as* > BAWBEE
BAUBEES > BAUBEE
BAUBLE *n* trinket of little value
BAUBLES > BAUBLE
BAUBLING > BAUBLE
BAUCHLE *vb* shuffle along
BAUCHLED > BAUCHLE
BAUCHLES > BAUCHLE
BAUCHLING > BAUCHLE
BAUD *n* unit used to measure the speed of transmission of electronic data
BAUDEKIN *old variant of* > BALDACHIN
BAUDEKINS > BAUDEKIN
BAUDRIC *same as* > BALDRIC
BAUDRICK *same as* > BALDRIC
BAUDRICKE *same as* > BALDRIC
BAUDRICKS > BAUDRICK
BAUDRICS > BAUDRIC
BAUDRONS *n* name for a cat
BAUDS > BAUD
BAUERA *n* small evergreen Australian shrub
BAUERAS > BAUERA
BAUHINIA *n* type of climbing or shrubby plant
BAUHINIAS > BAUHINIA
BAUK *same as* > BALK
BAUKED > BAUK
BAUKING > BAUK
BAUKS > BAUK
BAULK *same as* > BALK
BAULKED > BAULK
BAULKER > BAULK
BAULKERS > BAULK
BAULKIER > BAULKY
BAULKIEST > BAULKY
BAULKILY > BAULKY
BAULKING > BAULK
BAULKLINE *n* line across a pool table behind which the cue ball is placed at start of a game
BAULKS > BAULK
BAULKY *same as* > BALKY
BAUR *n* humorous anecdote; joke
BAURS > BAUR
BAUSOND *adj* (of animal) dappled with white spots
BAUXITE *n* claylike substance that is the chief source of aluminium
BAUXITES > BAUXITE
BAUXITIC > BAUXITE
BAVARDAGE *n* chattering
BAVAROIS *n* cold dessert consisting of a rich custard set with gelatine
BAVIN *n* bundle of brushwood or firewood ▷ *vb* bind (brushwood or firewood) into bavins

b

BAVINED > BAVIN
BAVINING > BAVIN
BAVINS > BAVIN
BAWBEE *n* former Scottish silver coin
BAWBEES > BAWBEE
BAWBLE *same as* > BAUBLE
BAWBLES > BAWBLE
BAWCOCK *n* fine fellow
BAWCOCKS > BAWCOCK
BAWD *n* person who runs a brothel, esp a woman
BAWDIER > BAWDY
BAWDIES > BAWDY
BAWDIEST > BAWDY
BAWDILY > BAWDY
BAWDINESS > BAWDY
BAWDKIN *same as* > BALDACHIN
BAWDKINS > BAWDKIN
BAWDRIC *n* heavy belt to support sword
BAWDRICS > BAWDRIC
BAWDRIES > BAWDRY
BAWDRY *n* obscene talk or language
BAWDS > BAWD
BAWDY *adj* (of writing etc) containing humorous references to sex ▷ *n* obscenity or eroticism, esp in writing or drama
BAWK *n* type of Atlantic seabird
BAWKS > BAWK
BAWL *vb* shout or weep noisily ▷ *n* loud shout or cry
BAWLED > BAWL
BAWLER > BAWL
BAWLERS > BAWL
BAWLEY *n* small fishing boat
BAWLEYS > BAWLEY
BAWLING > BAWL
BAWLINGS > BAWL
BAWLS > BAWL
BAWN *n* fortified enclosure
BAWNEEN *same as* > BAININ
BAWNEENS > BAWNEEN
BAWNS > BAWN
BAWR *same as* > BAUR
BAWRS > BAWR
BAWSUNT *adj* black and white in colour
BAWTIE *n* Scots word for a dog
BAWTIES > BAWTIE
BAWTY *same as* > BAWTIE
BAXTER *old variant of* > BAKER
BAXTERS > BAXTER
BAY *n* wide semicircular indentation of a shoreline ▷ *vb* howl in deep tones ▷ *adj* (esp of horses) of a reddish brown colour
BAYADEER *same as* > BAYADERE
BAYADEERS > BAYADERE
BAYADERE *n* female dancer, esp one serving in a Hindu temple ▷ *adj* (of fabric, etc) having horizontal stripes

BAYADERES > BAYADERE
BAYAMO *n* Cuban strong wind
BAYAMOS > BAYAMO
BAYARD *n* bay horse
BAYARDS > BAYARD
BAYBERRY *n* tropical American tree that yields an oil used in making bay rum
BAYE *vb* bathe
BAYED > BAY
BAYER > BAY
BAYES > BAYE
BAYEST > BAY
BAYFRONT *n* shoreline of a bay
BAYFRONTS > BAYFRONT
BAYING > BAY
BAYLE *n* barrier
BAYLES > BAYLE
BAYMAN *n* fisherman
BAYMEN > BAYMAN
BAYNODDY *n* person who fishes in a bay
BAYONET *n* sharp blade that can be fixed to the end of a rifle ▷ *vb* stab with a bayonet
BAYONETED > BAYONET
BAYONETS > BAYONET
BAYOU *n* (in the southern US) a sluggish marshy tributary of a lake or river
BAYOUS > BAYOU
BAYS > BAY
BAYSIDE *n* shore of a bay
BAYSIDES > BAYSIDE
BAYT *same as* > BATE
BAYTED > BAYT
BAYTING > BAYT
BAYTS > BAYT
BAYWOOD *n* light soft wood of a tropical American mahogany tree
BAYWOODS > BAYWOOD
BAYWOP *n* (in Newfoundland) derogatory term for a person from outport communities
BAYWOPS > BAYWOP
BAYYAN *n* Islamic declaration
BAYYANS > BAYYAN
BAZAAR *n* sale in aid of charity
BAZAARS > BAZAAR
BAZAR *same as* > BAZAAR
BAZARS > BAZAR
BAZAZZ *same as* > PIZZAZZ
BAZAZZES > BAZAZZ
BAZILLION *same as* > GAZILLION
BAZOO *a US slang word for* > MOUTH
BAZOOKA *n* portable rocket launcher that fires an armour-piercing projectile
BAZOOKAS > BAZOOKA
BAZOOM *n* woman's breast
BAZOOMS > BAZOOM
BAZOOS > BAZOO

BAZOUKI *same as* > BOUZOUKI
BAZOUKIS > BAZOUKI
BAZZ *vb* throw (an object)
BAZZAZZ *same as* > PIZZAZZ
BAZZAZZES > BAZZAZZ
BAZZED > BAZZ
BAZZES > BAZZ
BAZZING > BAZZ
BDELLIUM *n* African or W Asian tree that yields a gum resin
BDELLIUMS > BDELLIUM
BE *vb* exist or live
BEACH *n* area of sand or pebbles on a shore ▷ *vb* run or haul (a boat) onto a beach
BEACHBALL *n* light ball for playing on beach
BEACHBOY *n* male lifeguard on beach
BEACHBOYS > BEACHBOY
BEACHCOMB *vb* collect objects, seashells, etc on seashore
BEACHED > BEACH
BEACHES > BEACH
BEACHGOER *n* person who goes to the beach
BEACHHEAD *n* beach captured by an attacking army on which troops can be landed
BEACHIER > BEACHY
BEACHIEST > BEACHY
BEACHING > BEACH
BEACHSIDE *adj* situated near a beach
BEACHWEAR *n* clothes suitable for the beach
BEACHY *adj* with gentle sandy slopes
BEACON *n* fire or light on a hill or tower, used as a warning ▷ *vb* guide or warn
BEACONED > BEACON
BEACONING > BEACON
BEACONS > BEACON
BEAD *n* small piece of plastic, wood, etc, pierced for threading ▷ *vb* decorate with beads
BEADBLAST *n* jet of small glass beads blown from a nozzle under air or steam pressure ▷ *vb* clean or treat (a surface) with a beadblast
BEADED > BEAD
BEADER *n* person making things with beads
BEADERS > BEADER
BEADHOUSE *n* chapel
BEADIER > BEADY
BEADIEST > BEADY
BEADILY > BEADY
BEADINESS > BEADY
BEADING *n* strip of moulding used for edging furniture
BEADINGS > BEADING
BEADLE *n* (formerly) a minor parish official who acted as an usher

BEADLEDOM *n* petty officialdom
BEADLES > BEADLE
BEADLIKE > BEAD
BEADMAN *same as* > BEADSMAN
BEADMEN > BEADMAN
BEADROLL *n* list of persons for whom prayers are to be offered
BEADROLLS > BEADROLL
BEADS > BEAD
BEADSMAN *n* man who prays for another's soul
BEADSMEN > BEADSMAN
BEADWORK *same as* > BEADING
BEADWORKS > BEADWORK
BEADY *adj* small, round, and glittering
BEAGLE *n* small hound with short legs and drooping ears ▷ *vb* hunt with beagles, normally on foot
BEAGLED > BEAGLE
BEAGLER *n* person who hunts with beagles
BEAGLERS > BEAGLER
BEAGLES > BEAGLE
BEAGLING > BEAGLE
BEAGLINGS > BEAGLE
BEAK *n* projecting horny jaws of a bird
BEAKED > BEAK
BEAKER *n* large drinking cup
BEAKERFUL *n* amount of liquid in a full beaker
BEAKERS > BEAKER
BEAKIER > BEAK
BEAKIEST > BEAK
BEAKLESS > BEAK
BEAKLIKE > BEAK
BEAKS > BEAK
BEAKY > BEAK
BEAL *n* infected sore
BEALING *n* infected sore
BEALINGS > BEALING
BEALS > BEAL
BEAM *n* broad smile ▷ *vb* smile broadly
BEAMED > BEAM
BEAMER *n* full-pitched ball bowled at the batsman's head
BEAMERS > BEAMER
BEAMIER > BEAM
BEAMIEST > BEAM
BEAMILY > BEAM
BEAMINESS > BEAM
BEAMING > BEAM
BEAMINGLY > BEAM
BEAMINGS > BEAM
BEAMISH *adj* smiling
BEAMISHLY > BEAMISH
BEAMLESS > BEAM
BEAMLET *n* small beam
BEAMLETS > BEAMLET
BEAMLIKE > BEAM
BEAMS > BEAM
BEAMY > BEAM
BEAN *n* seed or pod of various plants, eaten as a vegetable or used to make

coffee etc ▷ *vb* strike on the head

BEANBAG *n* small cloth bag filled with dried beans and thrown in games

BEANBAGS > BEANBAG

BEANBALL *n* baseball intended to hit batter's head

BEANBALLS > BEANBALL

BEANED > BEAN

BEANERIES > BEANERY

BEANERY *n* cheap restaurant

BEANFEAST *n* any festive or merry occasion

BEANIE *n* close-fitting woollen hat

BEANIES > BEANIE

BEANING > BEAN

BEANLIKE > BEAN

BEANO *n* celebration or party

BEANOS > BEANO

BEANPOLE *n* pole used to support bean plants

BEANPOLES > BEANPOLE

BEANS > BEAN

BEANSTALK *n* stem of a bean plant

BEANY *same as* > BEANIE

BEAR *vb* support or hold up (something) ▷ *vb* lower the price of (a security) ▷ *n* type of omnivorous mammal

BEARABLE *adj* endurable

BEARABLY > BEARABLE

BEARBERRY *n* type of shrub

BEARBINE *n* type of bindweed

BEARBINES > BEARBINE

BEARCAT *n* lesser panda

BEARCATS > BEARCAT

BEARD *n* hair growing on the lower parts of a person's face ▷ *vb* oppose boldly

BEARDED > BEARD

BEARDIE *n* another name for bearded loach

BEARDIER > BEARDY

BEARDIES > BEARDIE

BEARDIEST > BEARDY

BEARDING > BEARD

BEARDLESS *adj* without a beard

BEARDLIKE *adj* like a beard

BEARDS > BEARD

BEARDY *adj* having a beard

BEARE *same as* > BEAR

BEARED > BEAR

BEARER *n* person who carries, presents, or upholds something

BEARERS > BEARER

BEARES > BEARE

BEARGRASS *n* North American plant

BEARHUG *n* wrestling hold in which the arms are locked tightly round an

opponent's chest and arms ▷ *vb* hold an opponent in a bearhug

BEARHUGS > BEARHUG

BEARING > BEAR

BEARINGS > BEAR

BEARISH *adj* like a bear

BEARISHLY > BEARISH

BEARLIKE > BEAR

BEARNAISE *n* rich sauce

BEARPAW *n* paw of a bear

BEARPAWS > BEARPAW

BEARS > BEAR

BEARSKIN *n* tall fur helmet worn by some British soldiers

BEARSKINS > BEARSKIN

BEARWARD *n* bear keeper

BEARWARDS > BEARWARD

BEARWOOD *another name for* > CASCARA

BEARWOODS > BEARWOOD

BEAST *n* large wild animal ▷ *vb* torture someone using excessive physical exercise

BEASTED > BEAST

BEASTHOOD > BEAST

BEASTIE *n* small animal

BEASTIES > BEASTIE

BEASTILY *same as* > BESTIALLY

BEASTING > BEAST

BEASTINGS *same as* > BEESTINGS

BEASTLIER > BEASTLY

BEASTLIKE > BEAST

BEASTLY *adj* unpleasant or disagreeable ▷ *adv* extremely

BEASTS > BEAST

BEAT *vb* strike with a series of violent blows ▷ *n* stroke or blow ▷ *adj* totally exhausted

BEATABLE > BEAT

BEATBOX *n* drum machine simulated by a human voice ▷ *vb* simulate a drum machine with a human voice

BEATBOXED > BEATBOX

BEATBOXER *n* person who practises beatboxing

BEATBOXES > BEATBOX

BEATDOWN *n* heavy defeat

BEATDOWNS > BEATDOWN

BEATEN > BEAT

BEATER *n* device used for beating

BEATERS > BEATER

BEATH *vb* dry; heat

BEATHED > BEATH

BEATHING > BEATH

BEATHS > BEATH

BEATIER > BEATY

BEATIEST > BEATY

BEATIFIC *adj* displaying great happiness

BEATIFIED > BEATIFY

BEATIFIES > BEATIFY

BEATIFY *vb* take first step towards making (a dead person) a saint

BEATING > BEAT

BEATINGS > BEAT

BEATITUDE *n* any of the blessings on the poor, meek, etc, in the Sermon on the Mount

BEATLESS > BEAT

BEATNIK *n* young person in the late 1950s who rebelled against conventional attitudes etc

BEATNIKS > BEATNIK

BEATS > BEAT

BEATY *adj* (of music) having a strong rhythm

BEAU *n* boyfriend or admirer

BEAUCOUP *n* large amount

BEAUCOUPS > BEAUCOUP

BEAUFET *same as* > BUFFET

BEAUFETS > BEAUFET

BEAUFFET *same as* > BUFFET

BEAUFFETS > BEAUFFET

BEAUFIN *same as* > BIFFIN

BEAUFINS > BEAUFIN

BEAUISH *adj* vain and showy

BEAUS > BEAU

BEAUT *n* person or thing that is outstanding or distinctive ▷ *adj* good or excellent ▷ *interj* exclamation of joy or pleasure

BEAUTEOUS *adj* beautiful

BEAUTER > BEAUT

BEAUTEST > BEAUT

BEAUTIED > BEAUTY

BEAUTIES > BEAUTY

BEAUTIFUL *adj* very attractive to look at

BEAUTIFY *vb* make beautiful

BEAUTS > BEAUT

BEAUTY *n* combination of all the qualities of a person or thing that delight the senses and mind ▷ *interj* expression of approval or agreement ▷ *vb* make beautiful

BEAUTYING > BEAUTY

BEAUX > BEAU

BEAUXITE *same as* > BAUXITE

BEAUXITES > BEAUXITE

BEAVER *n* amphibious rodent with a big flat tail ▷ *vb* work steadily or assiduously

BEAVERED > BEAVER

BEAVERIES > BEAVERY

BEAVERING > BEAVER

BEAVERS > BEAVER

BEAVERY *n* place for keeping beavers

BEBEERINE *n* alkaloid, resembling quinine, obtained from the bark of the greenheart and other plants

BEBEERU *n* tropical American tree

BEBEERUS > BEBEERU

BEBLOOD *vb* stain with blood

BEBLOODED > BEBLOOD

BEBLOODS > BEBLOOD

BEBOP *same as* > BOP

BEBOPPED > BEBOP

BEBOPPER > BEBOP

BEBOPPERS > BEBOP

BEBOPPING > BEBOP

BEBOPS > BEBOP

BEBUNG *n* vibrato effect on clavichord

BEBUNGS > BEBUNG

BECALL *vb* use insulting words about someone

BECALLED > BECALL

BECALLING > BECALL

BECALLS > BECALL

BECALM *vb* make calm

BECALMED *adj* (of a sailing ship) motionless through lack of wind

BECALMING > BECALM

BECALMS > BECALM

BECAME > BECOME

BECAP *vb* put a cap on

BECAPPED > BECAP

BECAPPING > BECAP

BECAPS > BECAP

BECARPET *vb* lay carpet on

BECARPETS > BECARPET

BECASSE *n* woodcock

BECASSES > BECASSE

BECAUSE *conj* on account of the fact that; on account of being; since

BECCACCIA *n* woodcock

BECCAFICO *n* European songbird, eaten as a delicacy in Italy and other countries

BECHALK *vb* mark with chalk

BECHALKED > BECHALK

BECHALKS > BECHALK

BECHAMEL *n* thick white sauce flavoured with onion and seasoning

BECHAMELS > BECHAMEL

BECHANCE *vb* happen (to)

BECHANCED > BECHANCE

BECHANCES > BECHANCE

BECHARM *vb* delight

BECHARMED > BECHARM

BECHARMS > BECHARM

BECK *n* stream ▷ *vb* attract someone's attention by nodding or gesturing

BECKE *same as* > BEAK

BECKED > BECK

BECKES > BECKE

BECKET *n* clevis forming part of one end of a sheave

BECKETS > BECKET

BECKING > BECK

BECKON *vb* summon with a gesture ▷ *n* summoning gesture

BECKONED > BECKON

BECKONER > BECKON

BECKONERS > BECKON

BECKONING > BECKON

BECKONS > BECKON

BECKS > BECK

BECLAMOR vb clamour excessively

BECLAMORS
> BECLAMOR

BECLAMOUR vb make a clamour

BECLASP vb embrace

BECLASPED > BECLASP

BECLASPS > BECLASP

BECLOAK vb dress in cloak

BECLOAKED > BECLOAK

BECLOAKS > BECLOAK

BECLOG vb put clogs on

BECLOGGED > BECLOG

BECLOGS > BECLOG

BECLOTHE vb put clothes on

BECLOTHED
> BECLOTHE

BECLOTHES
> BECLOTHE

BECLOUD vb cover or obscure with a cloud

BECLOUDED > BECLOUD

BECLOUDS > BECLOUD

BECLOWN vb clown around

BECLOWNED > BECLOWN

BECLOWNS > BECLOWN

BECOME vb come to be

BECOMES > BECOME

BECOMING adj attractive or pleasing ▷ n any process of change

BECOMINGS
> BECOMING

BECOWARD vb make cowardly

BECOWARDS
> BECOWARD

BECQUEREL n SI unit of radioactivity

BECRAWL vb crawl all over

BECRAWLED > BECRAWL

BECRAWLS > BECRAWL

BECRIME vb make someone guilty of a crime

BECRIMED > BECRIME

BECRIMES > BECRIME

BECRIMING > BECRIME

BECROWD vb crowd with something

BECROWDED > BECROWD

BECROWDS > BECROWD

BECRUST vb cover with crust

BECRUSTED > BECRUST

BECRUSTS > BECRUST

BECUDGEL vb arm with cudgel

BECUDGELS
> BECUDGEL

BECURL vb curl

BECURLED > BECURL

BECURLING > BECURL

BECURLS > BECURL

BECURSE vb curse

BECURSED > BECURSE

BECURSES > BECURSE

BECURSING > BECURSE

BECURST > BECURSE

BED n piece of furniture on which to sleep ▷ vb plant in a bed

BEDABBLE vb dabble; moisten

BEDABBLED
> BEDABBLE

BEDABBLES
> BEDABBLE

BEDAD interj exclamation of affirmation

BEDAGGLE vb soil by trailing through dirt

BEDAGGLED
> BEDAGGLE

BEDAGGLES
> BEDAGGLE

BEDAMN vb damn

BEDAMNED > BEDAMN

BEDAMNING > BEDAMN

BEDAMNS > BEDAMN

BEDARKEN vb make dark

BEDARKENS
> BEDARKEN

BEDASH vb sprinkle with liquid

BEDASHED > BEDASH

BEDASHES > BEDASH

BEDASHING > BEDASH

BEDAUB vb smear with something sticky or dirty

BEDAUBED > BEDAUB

BEDAUBING > BEDAUB

BEDAUBS > BEDAUB

BEDAWIN same as
> BEDOUIN

BEDAWINS > BEDAWIN

BEDAZE vb daze

BEDAZED > BEDAZE

BEDAZES > BEDAZE

BEDAZING > BEDAZE

BEDAZZLE vb dazzle or confuse, as with brilliance

BEDAZZLED
> BEDAZZLE

BEDAZZLES
> BEDAZZLE

BEDBATH n washing of a sick person in bed

BEDBATHS > BEDBATH

BEDBOARD n base of bed

BEDBOARDS
> BEDBOARD

BEDBUG n small blood-sucking wingless insect that infests dirty houses

BEDBUGS > BEDBUG

BEDCHAIR n adjustable chair to support invalid in bed

BEDCHAIRS
> BEDCHAIR

BEDCOVER n cover for bed

BEDCOVERS
> BEDCOVER

BEDDABLE adj sexually attractive

BEDDED > BED

BEDDER n (at some universities) college servant employed to keep students' rooms in order

BEDDERS > BEDDER

BEDDING > BED

BEDDINGS > BED

BEDE n prayer

BEDEAFEN vb deafen

BEDEAFENS
> BEDEAFEN

BEDECK vb cover with decorations

BEDECKED > BEDECK

BEDECKING > BEDECK

BEDECKS > BEDECK

BEDEGUAR n growth found on rosebushes

BEDEGUARS
> BEDEGUAR

BEDEHOUSE same as
> BEADHOUSE

BEDEL archaic spelling of
> BEADLE

BEDELL same as
> BEADLE

BEDELLS > BEDELL

BEDELS > BEDEL

BEDELSHIP > BEDEL

BEDEMAN same as
> BEADSMAN

BEDEMEN > BEDEMAN

BEDERAL same as
> BEDRAL

BEDERALS > BEDERAL

BEDES > BEDE

BEDESMAN same as
> BEADSMAN

BEDESMEN > BEDESMAN

BEDEVIL vb harass, confuse, or torment

BEDEVILED > BEDEVIL

BEDEVILS > BEDEVIL

BEDEW vb wet or cover with or as if with drops of dew

BEDEWED > BEDEW

BEDEWING > BEDEW

BEDEWS > BEDEW

BEDFAST an archaic word for > BEDRIDDEN

BEDFELLOW n temporary associate

BEDFRAME n framework of bed

BEDFRAMES
> BEDFRAME

BEDGOWN n night dress

BEDGOWNS > BEDGOWN

BEDHEAD n untidy state of the hair, esp caused by sleeping

BEDHEADS > BEDHEAD

BEDIAPER vb put a nappy on

BEDIAPERS
> BEDIAPER

BEDIDE > BEDYE

BEDIGHT vb array or adorn ▷ adj adorned or bedecked

BEDIGHTED > BEDIGHT

BEDIGHTS > BEDIGHT

BEDIM vb make dim

BEDIMMED > BEDIM

BEDIMMING > BEDIM

BEDIMPLE vb form dimples in

BEDIMPLED
> BEDIMPLE

BEDIMPLES
> BEDIMPLE

BEDIMS > BEDIM

BEDIRTIED > BEDIRTY

BEDIRTIES > BEDIRTY

BEDIRTY vb make dirty

BEDIZEN vb dress or decorate gaudily

BEDIZENED > BEDIZEN

BEDIZENS > BEDIZEN

BEDLAM n noisy confused situation

BEDLAMER n young harp seal

BEDLAMERS > BEDLAMER

BEDLAMISM > BEDLAM

BEDLAMITE n archaic word for a patient in a psychiatric hospital

BEDLAMP n bedside light

BEDLAMPS > BEDLAMP

BEDLAMS > BEDLAM

BEDLESS > BED

BEDLIKE adj like a bed

BEDLINER n lining for the bed of a truck

BEDLINERS
> BEDLINER

BEDMAKER n person who makes beds

BEDMAKERS
> BEDMAKER

BEDMATE n person who shares a bed

BEDMATES > BEDMATE

BEDOTTED adj scattered; strewn

BEDOUIN n member of any of the nomadic tribes of Arabs

BEDOUINS > BEDOUIN

BEDPAN n shallow bowl used as a toilet by bedridden people

BEDPANS > BEDPAN

BEDPLATE n heavy metal platform or frame to which an engine or machine is attached

BEDPLATES
> BEDPLATE

BEDPOST n vertical support on a bedstead

BEDPOSTS > BEDPOST

BEDQUILT n padded bed cover

BEDQUILTS
> BEDQUILT

BEDRAGGLE vb make (hair, clothing, etc) limp, untidy, or dirty, as with rain or mud

BEDRAIL n rail along the side of a bed connecting the headboard with the footboard

BEDRAILS > BEDRAIL

BEDRAL n minor church official

BEDRALS > BEDRAL

BEDRAPE vb adorn

BEDRAPED > BEDRAPE

BEDRAPES > BEDRAPE

BEDRAPING > BEDRAPE

BEDRENCH vb drench

BEDREST n rest in bed, eg to recover from illness

BEDRESTS > BEDREST

BEDRID same as
> BEDRIDDEN

BEDRIDDEN adj confined to bed because of illness or old age

BEDRIGHT *n* a right expected in the marital bed

BEDRIGHTS > BEDRIGHT

BEDRITE *same as* **>** BEDRIGHT

BEDRITES > BEDRITE

BEDRIVEL *vb* drivel around

BEDRIVELS **>** BEDRIVEL

BEDROCK *n* solid rock beneath the surface soil

BEDROCKS > BEDROCK

BEDROLL *n* portable roll of bedding

BEDROLLS > BEDROLL

BEDROOM *n* room used for sleeping

BEDROOMED *adj* containing specified number of bedrooms

BEDROOMS > BEDROOM

BEDROP *vb* drop on

BEDROPPED > BEDROP

BEDROPS > BEDROP

BEDROPT > BEDROP

BEDRUG *vb* drug excessively

BEDRUGGED > BEDRUG

BEDRUGS > BEDRUG

BEDS > BED

BEDSHEET *n* sheet for bed

BEDSHEETS **>** BEDSHEET

BEDSIDE *n* area beside a bed ▷ *adj* placed at or near the side of the bed

BEDSIDES > BEDSIDE

BEDSIT *n* furnished sitting room with a bed

BEDSITS > BEDSIT

BEDSITTER *same as* **>** BEDSIT

BEDSKIRT *n* drapery round the edge of a bed

BEDSKIRTS **>** BEDSKIRT

BEDSOCK *n* sock worn in bed

BEDSOCKS > BEDSOCK

BEDSONIA *n* bacterium causing diseases such as trachoma

BEDSONIAS **>** BEDSONIA

BEDSORE *n* ulcer on the skin, caused by a lengthy period of lying in bed due to illness

BEDSORES > BEDSORE

BEDSPREAD *n* top cover on a bed

BEDSPRING *vb* spring supporting mattress on bed

BEDSTAND *n* bedside table

BEDSTANDS **>** BEDSTAND

BEDSTEAD *n* framework of a bed

BEDSTEADS **>** BEDSTEAD

BEDSTRAW *n* plant with small white or yellow flowers

BEDSTRAWS **>** BEDSTRAW

BEDTICK *n* case containing stuffing in mattress

BEDTICKS > BEDTICK

BEDTIME *n* time when one usually goes to bed

BEDTIMES > BEDTIME

BEDU *adj* relating to beduins

BEDUCK *vb* duck under water

BEDUCKED > BEDUCK

BEDUCKING > BEDUCK

BEDUCKS > BEDUCK

BEDUIN *variant of* **>** BEDOUIN

BEDUINS > BEDUIN

BEDUMB *vb* make dumb

BEDUMBED > BEDUMB

BEDUMBING > BEDUMB

BEDUMBS > BEDUMB

BEDUNCE *vb* cause to look or feel foolish

BEDUNCED > BEDUNCE

BEDUNCES > BEDUNCE

BEDUNCING > BEDUNCE

BEDUNG *vb* spread with dung

BEDUNGED > BEDUNG

BEDUNGING > BEDUNG

BEDUNGS > BEDUNG

BEDUST *vb* cover with dust

BEDUSTED > BEDUST

BEDUSTING > BEDUST

BEDUSTS > BEDUST

BEDWARD *adj* towards bed

BEDWARDS *adv* towards bed

BEDWARF *vb* hamper growth of

BEDWARFED > BEDWARF

BEDWARFS > BEDWARF

BEDWARMER *n* metal pan containing hot coals, formerly used to warm a bed

BEDWETTER *n* person who urinates in bed

BEDYDE > BEDYE

BEDYE *vb* dye

BEDYED > BEDYE

BEDYEING > BEDYE

BEDYES > BEDYE

BEE *n* insect that makes wax and honey

BEEBEE *n* air rifle

BEEBEES > BEEBEE

BEEBREAD *n* mixture of pollen and nectar prepared by worker bees and fed to the larvae

BEEBREADS **>** BEEBREAD

BEECH *n* tree with a smooth greyish bark

BEECHEN > BEECH

BEECHES > BEECH

BEECHIER > BEECH

BEECHIEST > BEECH

BEECHMAST *n* nuts of beech tree

BEECHNUT *n* small brown triangular edible nut of the beech tree

BEECHNUTS > BEECHNUT

BEECHWOOD *n* wood of beech tree

BEECHY > BEECH

BEEDI *n* Indian cigarette

BEEDIE *same as* **>** BEEDI

BEEDIES > BEEDIE

BEEF *n* flesh of a cow, bull, or ox ▷ *vb* complain

BEEFALO *n* cross between cow and buffalo

BEEFALOES > BEEFALO

BEEFALOS > BEEFALO

BEEFCAKE *n* muscular man as displayed in photographs

BEEFCAKES **>** BEEFCAKE

BEEFEATER *n* yeoman warder at the Tower of London

BEEFED > BEEF

BEEFIER > BEEFY

BEEFIEST > BEEFY

BEEFILY > BEEFY

BEEFINESS > BEEFY

BEEFING > BEEF

BEEFLESS > BEEF

BEEFS > BEEF

BEEFSTEAK *n* piece of beef that can be grilled, fried, etc, cut from any lean part of the animal

BEEFWOOD *n* any of various trees that produce very hard wood

BEEFWOODS **>** BEEFWOOD

BEEFY *adj* like beef

BEEGAH *same as* **>** BIGHA

BEEGAHS > BEEGAH

BEEHIVE *n* structure in which bees live

BEEHIVED *adj* (esp of a hairstyle) shaped like a beehive

BEEHIVES > BEEHIVE

BEEKEEPER *n* person who keeps bees for their honey

BEELIKE > BEE

BEELINE *n* most direct route between two places ▷ *vb* make a beeline for (something)

BEELINED > BEELINE

BEELINES > BEELINE

BEELINING > BEELINE

BEEN *vb* past participle of be

BEENAH *n* understanding; insight

BEENAHS > BEENAH

BEENTO *n* W African word for a person who has lived in Britain ▷ *adj* of or relating to such a person

BEENTOS > BEENTO

BEEP *n* high-pitched sound, like that of a car horn ▷ *vb* (cause to) make this noise

BEEPED > BEEP

BEEPER > BEEP

BEEPERS > BEEP

BEEPING > BEEP

BEEPS > BEEP

BEER *n* alcoholic drink brewed from malt and hops

BEERAGE *n* brewing industry

BEERAGES > BEERAGE

BEERFEST *n* beer festival

BEERFESTS **>** BEERFEST

BEERHALL *n* large public room where beer is consumed

BEERHALLS **>** BEERHALL

BEERIER > BEERY

BEERIEST > BEERY

BEERILY > BEERY

BEERINESS > BEERY

BEERMAT *n* small mat put under a glass of beer

BEERMATS > BEERMAT

BEERNUT *n* coated peanut eaten as a snack

BEERNUTS > BEERNUT

BEERS > BEER

BEERSIES *pl n* New Zealand informal word for beers

BEERY *adj* smelling or tasting of beer

BEES > BEE

BEESOME *same as* **>** BISSON

BEESTING *adj* as in *beesting lips* of lips, pouting

BEESTINGS *n* first milk secreted by a cow or similar animal immediately after giving birth

BEESTUNG *adj* as in *beestung lips* of lips, pouting

BEESWAX *n* wax secreted by bees, used in polishes etc ▷ *vb* polish with such wax

BEESWAXED > BEESWAX

BEESWAXES > BEESWAX

BEESWING *n* light filmy crust that forms in port wine

BEESWINGS **>** BEESWING

BEET *n* plant with an edible root and leaves ▷ *vb* improve or make better

BEETED > BEET

BEETFLIES > BEETFLY

BEETFLY *n* type of fly which is a common pest of beets and mangel-wurzels

BEETING > BEET

BEETLE *n* insect with a hard wing cover on its back ▷ *vb* scuttle or scurry

BEETLED > BEETLE

BEETLER *n* one who operates a beetling machine

BEETLERS > BEETLER

BEETLES > BEETLE

BEETLING > BEETLE

BEETROOT *n* type of beet plant with a dark red root

BEETROOTS **>** BEETROOT

BEETS > BEET

BEEVES > BEEF

BEEYARD *n* place where bees are kept

b

BEEYARDS > BEEYARD

BEEZER n person or chap
▷ adj excellent

BEEZERS > BEEZER

BEFALL vb happen to
(someone)

BEFALLEN > BEFALL

BEFALLING > BEFALL

BEFALLS > BEFALL

BEFANA n Italian
gift-bearing good fairy

BEFANAS > BEFANA

BEFELD archaic past
participle of > BEFALL

BEFELL > BEFALL

BEFFANA same as
> BEFANA

BEFFANAS > BEFFANA

BEFINGER vb mark by
handling

BEFINGERS
> BEFINGER

BEFINNED adj with fins

BEFIT vb be appropriate
or suitable for

BEFITS > BEFIT

BEFITTED > BEFIT

BEFITTING > BEFIT

BEFLAG vb decorate with
flags

BEFLAGGED > BEFLAG

BEFLAGS > BEFLAG

BEFLEA vb infest with
fleas

BEFLEAED > BEFLEA

BEFLEAING > BEFLEA

BEFLEAS > BEFLEA

BEFLECK vb fleck

BEFLECKED > BEFLECK

BEFLECKS > BEFLECK

BEFLOWER vb decorate
with flowers

BEFLOWERS
> BEFLOWER

BEFLUM vb fool; deceive

BEFLUMMED > BEFLUM

BEFLUMS > BEFLUM

BEFOAM vb cover with
foam

BEFOAMED > BEFOAM

BEFOAMING > BEFOAM

BEFOAMS > BEFOAM

BEFOG vb surround with
fog

BEFOGGED > BEFOG

BEFOGGING > BEFOG

BEFOGS > BEFOG

BEFOOL vb make a fool of

BEFOOLED > BEFOOL

BEFOOLING > BEFOOL

BEFOOLS > BEFOOL

BEFORE adv indicating
something earlier in time,
in front of, or preferred to
▷ prep preceding in space
or time

BEFORTUNE vb happen
to

BEFOUL vb make dirty or
foul

BEFOULED > BEFOUL

BEFOULER > BEFOUL

BEFOULERS > BEFOUL

BEFOULING > BEFOUL

BEFOULS > BEFOUL

BEFRET vb fret about
something

BEFRETS > BEFRET

BEFRETTED > BEFRET

BEFRIEND vb become
friends with

BEFRIENDS
> BEFRIEND

BEFRINGE vb decorate
with fringe

BEFRINGED
> BEFRINGE

BEFRINGES
> BEFRINGE

BEFUDDLE vb confuse,
muddle, or perplex

BEFUDDLED
> BEFUDDLE

BEFUDDLES
> BEFUDDLE

BEG vb solicit (money,
food, etc), esp in the street

BEGAD interj emphatic
exclamation

BEGALL vb make sore by
rubbing

BEGALLED > BEGALL

BEGALLING > BEGALL

BEGALLS > BEGALL

BEGAN > BEGIN

BEGAR n compulsory
labour

BEGARS > BEGAR

BEGAT archaic past tense of
> BEGET

BEGAZE vb gaze about or
around

BEGAZED > BEGAZE

BEGAZES > BEGAZE

BEGAZING > BEGAZE

BEGEM vb decorate with
gems

BEGEMMED > BEGEM

BEGEMMING > BEGEM

BEGEMS > BEGEM

BEGET vb cause or create

BEGETS > BEGET

BEGETTER > BEGET

BEGETTERS > BEGET

BEGETTING > BEGET

BEGGAR n person who
begs, esp one who lives by
begging ▷ vb be beyond
the resources of

BEGGARDOM > BEGGAR

BEGGARED > BEGGAR

BEGGARIES > BEGGARY

BEGGARING > BEGGAR

BEGGARLY adj meanly
inadequate

BEGGARS > BEGGAR

BEGGARY n extreme
poverty or need

BEGGED > BEG

BEGGING > BEG

BEGGINGLY > BEG

BEGGINGS > BEG

BEGHARD n member of a
13th century Christian
brotherhood

BEGHARDS > BEGHARD

BEGIFT vb give a gift or
gifts to

BEGIFTED > BEGIFT

BEGIFTING > BEGIFT

BEGIFTS > BEGIFT

BEGILD vb gild

BEGILDED > BEGILD

BEGILDING > BEGILD

BEGILDS > BEGILD

BEGILT > BEGILD

BEGIN vb start

BEGINNE same as
> BEGINNING

BEGINNER n person who
has just started learning
to do something

BEGINNERS
> BEGINNER

BEGINNES > BEGINNE

BEGINNING n start

BEGINS > BEGIN

BEGIRD vb surround

BEGIRDED > BEGIRD

BEGIRDING > BEGIRD

BEGIRDLE vb surround
with girdle

BEGIRDLED > BEGIRDLE

BEGIRDLES
> BEGIRDLE

BEGIRDS > BEGIRD

BEGIRT > BEGIRD

BEGLAD vb make glad

BEGLADDED > BEGLAD

BEGLADS > BEGLAD

BEGLAMOR same as
> BEGLAMOUR

BEGLAMORS
> BEGLAMOR

BEGLAMOUR vb
glamourize

BEGLERBEG n governor
in the Ottoman empire

BEGLOOM vb make
gloomy

BEGLOOMED > BEGLOOM

BEGLOOMS > BEGLOOM

BEGNAW vb gnaw at

BEGNAWED > BEGNAW

BEGNAWING > BEGNAW

BEGNAWS > BEGNAW

BEGO vb harass; beset

BEGOES > BEGO

BEGOGGLED adj wearing
goggles

BEGOING > BEGO

BEGONE > BEGO

BEGONIA n tropical plant
with waxy flowers

BEGONIAS > BEGONIA

BEGORAH same as
> BEGORRA

BEGORED adj smeared
with gore

BEGORRA interj emphatic
exclamation, regarded as
a characteristic utterance
of Irish people

BEGORRAH same as
> BEGORRA

BEGOT > BEGET

BEGOTTEN > BEGET

BEGRIM same as
> BEGRIME

BEGRIME vb make dirty

BEGRIMED > BEGRIME

BEGRIMES > BEGRIME

BEGRIMING > BEGRIME

BEGRIMMED > BEGRIM

BEGRIMS > BEGRIM

BEGROAN vb groan at

BEGROANED > BEGROAN

BEGROANS > BEGROAN

BEGRUDGE vb envy
(someone) the possession
of something

BEGRUDGED
> BEGRUDGE

BEGRUDGER
> BEGRUDGE

BEGRUDGES
> BEGRUDGE

BEGS > BEG

BEGUILE vb cheat or
mislead

BEGUILED > BEGUILE

BEGUILER > BEGUILE

BEGUILERS > BEGUILE

BEGUILES > BEGUILE

BEGUILING adj
charming, often in a
deceptive way

BEGUIN another name for
> BEGHARD

BEGUINAGE n convent
for members of beguine
sisterhood

BEGUINE n S American
dance

BEGUINES > BEGUINE

BEGUINS > BEGUIN

BEGULF vb overwhelm

BEGULFED > BEGULF

BEGULFING > BEGULF

BEGULFS > BEGULF

BEGUM n Muslim woman
of high rank

BEGUMS > BEGUM

BEGUN > BEGIN

BEGUNK vb delude; trick

BEGUNKED > BEGUNK

BEGUNKING > BEGUNK

BEGUNKS > BEGUNK

BEHALF n interest, part,
benefit, or respect

BEHALVES > BEHALF

BEHAPPEN vb befall

BEHAPPENS
> BEHAPPEN

BEHATTED adj wearing a
hat

BEHAVE vb act or function
in a particular way

BEHAVED > BEHAVE

BEHAVER > BEHAVE

BEHAVERS > BEHAVE

BEHAVES > BEHAVE

BEHAVING > BEHAVE

BEHAVIOR same as
> BEHAVIOUR

BEHAVIORS
> BEHAVIOR

BEHAVIOUR n manner of
behaving

BEHEAD vb remove the
head from

BEHEADAL > BEHEAD

BEHEADALS > BEHEAD

BEHEADED > BEHEAD

BEHEADER > BEHEAD

BEHEADERS > BEHEAD

BEHEADING > BEHEAD

BEHEADS > BEHEAD

BEHELD > BEHOLD

BEHEMOTH n huge person
or thing

BEHEMOTHS
> BEHEMOTH

BEHEST n order or
earnest request

BEHESTS > BEHEST

BEHIGHT vb entrust

BEHIGHTED > BEHIGHT

BEHIGHTS > BEHIGHT

BEHIND adv indicating position to the rear, lateness, responsibility, etc ▷ n buttocks ▷ prep in or to a position further back than ▷ adj in a position further back

BEHINDS > BEHIND

BEHOLD vb look (at)

BEHOLDEN adj indebted or obliged

BEHOLDER > BEHOLD

BEHOLDERS > BEHOLD

BEHOLDING > BEHOLD

BEHOLDS > BEHOLD

BEHOOF n advantage or profit

BEHOOFS > BEHOOF

BEHOOVE same as > BEHOVE

BEHOOVED > BEHOOVE

BEHOOVES > BEHOOVE

BEHOOVING > BEHOOVE

BEHOTE same as > BEHIGHT

BEHOTES > BEHOTE

BEHOTING > BEHOTE

BEHOVE vb be necessary or fitting for

BEHOVED > BEHOVE

BEHOVEFUL adj useful; of benefit

BEHOVELY adj useful

BEHOVES > BEHOVE

BEHOVING > BEHOVE

BEHOWL vb howl at

BEHOWLED > BEHOWL

BEHOWLING > BEHOWL

BEHOWLS > BEHOWL

BEIGE adj pale brown ▷ n very light brown

BEIGEL same as > BAGEL

BEIGELS > BEIGEL

BEIGER > BEIGE

BEIGES > BEIGE

BEIGEST > BEIGE

BEIGIER > BEIGE

BEIGIEST > BEIGE

BEIGNE variant of > BEIGNET

BEIGNES > BEIGNE

BEIGNET n square deep-fried pastry served hot and sprinkled with icing sugar

BEIGNETS > BEIGNET

BEIGY > BEIGE

BEIN adj financially comfortable ▷ vb fill

BEINED > BEIN

BEING > BE

BEINGLESS > BE

BEINGNESS > BE

BEINGS > BEING

BEINING > BEIN

BEINKED adj daubed with ink

BEINNESS > BEIN

BEINS > BEIN

BEJABBERS same as > BEJABERS

BEJABERS interj exclamation of surprise

BEJADE vb jade; tire

BEJADED > BEJADE

BEJADES > BEJADE

BEJADING > BEJADE

BEJANT same as > BAJAN

BEJANTS > BEJANT

BEJASUS same as > BEJESUS

BEJASUSES > BEJASUS

BEJEEBERS same as > BEJABERS

BEJEEZUS same as > BEJESUS

BEJESUIT vb convert to Jesuitism

BEJESUITS > BEJESUIT

BEJESUS interj exclamation of surprise ▷ n as in the bejesus mild expletive

BEJESUSES > BEJESUS

BEJEWEL vb decorate with or as if with jewels

BEJEWELED > BEJEWEL

BEJEWELS > BEJEWEL

BEJUMBLE vb jumble up

BEJUMBLED > BEJUMBLE

BEJUMBLES > BEJUMBLE

BEKAH n half shekel

BEKAHS > BEKAH

BEKISS vb smother with kisses

BEKISSED > BEKISS

BEKISSES > BEKISS

BEKISSING > BEKISS

BEKNAVE vb treat as a knave

BEKNAVED > BEKNAVE

BEKNAVES > BEKNAVE

BEKNAVING > BEKNAVE

BEKNIGHT vb esteem

BEKNIGHTS > BEKNIGHT

BEKNOT vb tie a knot or knots in

BEKNOTS > BEKNOT

BEKNOTTED > BEKNOT

BEKNOWN adj known about

BEL n unit for comparing two power levels or measuring the intensity of a sound

BELABOR same as > BELABOUR

BELABORED > BELABOR

BELABORS > BELABOR

BELABOUR vb attack verbally or physically

BELABOURS > BELABOUR

BELACE vb decorate with lace

BELACED > BELACE

BELACES > BELACE

BELACING > BELACE

BELADIED > BELADY

BELADIES > BELADY

BELADY vb call a lady

BELADYING > BELADY

BELAH n Australian tree which yields a useful timber

BELAHS > BELAH

BELAMIES > BELAMY

BELAMOUR n beloved person

BELAMOURE n loved one

BELAMOURS > BELAMOUR

BELAMY n close friend

BELAR same as > BELAH

BELARS > BELAR

BELATE vb cause to be late

BELATED adj late or too late

BELATEDLY > BELATED

BELATES > BELATE

BELATING > BELATE

BELAUD vb praise highly

BELAUDED > BELAUD

BELAUDING > BELAUD

BELAUDS > BELAUD

BELAY vb secure a line to a pin or cleat ▷ n attachment (of a climber) to a mountain

BELAYED > BELAY

BELAYER > BELAY

BELAYERS > BELAY

BELAYING > BELAY

BELAYS > BELAY

BELCH vb expel wind from the stomach noisily through the mouth ▷ n act of belching

BELCHED > BELCH

BELCHER > BELCH

BELCHERS > BELCH

BELCHES > BELCH

BELCHING > BELCH

BELDAM n old woman, esp an ugly or malicious one

BELDAME same as > BELDAM

BELDAMES > BELDAME

BELDAMS > BELDAM

BELEAGUER vb trouble persistently

BELEAP vb leap over

BELEAPED > BELEAP

BELEAPING > BELEAP

BELEAPS > BELEAP

BELEAPT > BELEAP

BELEE vb put on sheltered side

BELEED > BELEE

BELEEING > BELEE

BELEES > BELEE

BELEMNITE n type of extinct marine mollusc related to the cuttlefish

BELEMNOID adj shaped like a dart

BELFRIED adj with a belfry

BELFRIES > BELFRY

BELFRY n part of a tower where bells are hung

BELGA n former Belgian monetary unit worth five francs

BELGARD n kind gaze

BELGARDS > BELGARD

BELGAS > BELGA

BELGICISM n word used by Belgians when speaking French or Dutch

BELIE vb show to be untrue

BELIED > BELIE

BELIEF n faith or confidence

BELIEFS > BELIEF

BELIER > BELIE

BELIERS > BELIE

BELIES > BELIE

BELIEVE vb accept as true or real

BELIEVED > BELIEVE

BELIEVER > BELIEVE

BELIEVERS > BELIEVE

BELIEVES > BELIEVE

BELIEVING > BELIEVE

BELIKE adv perhaps

BELIQUOR vb cause to be drunk

BELIQUORS > BELIQUOR

BELITTLE vb treat as having little value or importance

BELITTLED > BELITTLE

BELITTLER > BELITTLE

BELITTLES > BELITTLE

BELIVE adv speedily

BELL n hollow cup-shaped instrument that emits a ringing sound when struck ▷ vb utter (such a sound)

BELLBIND n bindweed-type climber

BELLBINDS > BELLBIND

BELLBIRD n Australasian bird with bell-like call

BELLBIRDS > BELLBIRD

BELLBOY n man or boy employed to carry luggage and answer calls for service

BELLBOYS > BELLBOY

BELLBUOY n buoy with a bell

BELLBUOYS > BELLBUOY

BELLCAST adj relating to a style of roof with a bell shape

BELLCOTE n small roofed structure for bell

BELLCOTES > BELLCOTE

BELLE n beautiful woman, esp the most attractive woman at a function

BELLED > BELL

BELLEEK n kind of thin fragile porcelain with a lustrous glaze

BELLEEKS > BELLEEK

BELLES > BELLE

BELLETER n person who makes bells

BELLETERS > BELLETER

BELLHOP same as > BELLBOY

BELLHOPS > BELLHOP

BELLIBONE n beautiful and good woman

BELLICOSE adj warlike and aggressive

BELLIED > BELLY

BELLIES > BELLY

BELLING > BELL

BELLINGS > BELL

BELLINI n Prosecco and peach cocktail

BELLINIS > BELLINI

BELLMAN n man who rings a bell, esp (formerly) a town crier

BELLMEN > BELLMAN

BELLOCK vb shout

BELLOCKED > BELLOCK

BELLOCKS > BELLOCK

BELLOW vb make a low deep cry like that of a bull ▷ n loud deep roar

BELLOWED > BELLOW

BELLOWER > BELLOW

BELLOWERS > BELLOW

BELLOWING n act of bellowing

BELLOWS pl n instrument for pumping a stream of air into something

BELLPULL n handle, rope, or cord pulled to operate a doorbell or servant's bell

BELLPULLS > BELLPULL

BELLS > BELL

BELLWORT n N American plant with slender bell-shaped yellow flowers

BELLWORTS > BELLWORT

BELLY n part of the body of a vertebrate which contains the intestines ▷ vb (cause to) swell out

BELLYACHE n pain in the abdomen ▷ vb complain repeatedly

BELLYBAND n strap around the belly of a draught animal, holding the shafts of a vehicle

BELLYBOAT n type of life jacket

BELLYFLOP vb perform a dive into water in which the body lands horizontally

BELLYFUL n more than one can tolerate

BELLYFULS > BELLYFUL

BELLYING > BELLY

BELLYINGS > BELLY

BELLYLIKE > BELLY

BELOMANCY n art of divination using arrows

BELON n type of oyster

BELONG vb be the property of

BELONGED > BELONG

BELONGER n native-born Caribbean

BELONGERS > BELONGER

BELONGING n secure relationship

BELONGS > BELONG

BELONS > BELON

BELOVE vb love

BELOVED adj dearly loved ▷ n person dearly loved

BELOVEDS > BELOVED

BELOVES > BELOVE

BELOVING > BELOVE

BELOW adv at or to a position lower than, under ▷ prep at or to a position lower than

BELOWS same as > BELLOWS

BELS > BEL

BELT n band of cloth, leather, etc, worn usu around the waist ▷ vb fasten with a belt

BELTED > BELT

BELTER n outstanding person or event

BELTERS > BELTER

BELTING n material used to make a belt or belts ▷ adj excellent

BELTINGS > BELTING

BELTLESS > BELT

BELTLIKE adj like a belt

BELTLINE n line separating car's windows from main body

BELTLINES > BELTLINE

BELTMAN n (formerly) a member of a beach life-saving team

BELTMEN > BELTMAN

BELTS > BELT

BELTWAY n people and institutions located in the area bounded by the Washington Beltway

BELTWAYS > BELTWAY

BELUGA n large white sturgeon

BELUGAS > BELUGA

BELVEDERE n building designed and situated to look out on pleasant scenery

BELYING > BELIE

BEMA n speaker's platform in the assembly in ancient Athens

BEMAD vb old word meaning cause to become mad

BEMADAM vb call a person madam

BEMADAMED > BEMADAM

BEMADAMS > BEMADAM

BEMADDED > BEMAD

BEMADDEN vb old word meaning cause to become mad

BEMADDENS > BEMADDEN

BEMADDING > BEMAD

BEMADS > BEMAD

BEMAS > BEMA

BEMATA > BEMA

BEMAUL vb maul

BEMAULED > BEMAUL

BEMAULING > BEMAUL

BEMAULS > BEMAUL

BEMAZED adj amazed

BEMBEX n type of wasp

BEMBEXES > BEMBEX

BEMBIX same as > BEMBEX

BEMBIXES > BEMBIX

BEMEAN a less common word for > DEMEAN

BEMEANED > BEMEAN

BEMEANING > BEMEAN

BEMEANS > BEMEAN

BEMEANT > BEMEAN

BEMEDAL vb decorate with medals

BEMEDALED > BEMEDAL

BEMEDALS > BEMEDAL

BEMETE vb measure

BEMETED > BEMETE

BEMETES > BEMETE

BEMETING > BEMETE

BEMINGLE vb mingle

BEMINGLED > BEMINGLE

BEMINGLES > BEMINGLE

BEMIRE vb soil with or as if with mire

BEMIRED > BEMIRE

BEMIRES > BEMIRE

BEMIRING > BEMIRE

BEMIST vb cloud with mist

BEMISTED > BEMIST

BEMISTING > BEMIST

BEMISTS > BEMIST

BEMIX vb mix thoroughly

BEMIXED > BEMIX

BEMIXES > BEMIX

BEMIXING > BEMIX

BEMIXT > BEMIX

BEMOAN vb express sorrow or dissatisfaction about

BEMOANED > BEMOAN

BEMOANER > BEMOAN

BEMOANERS > BEMOAN

BEMOANING > BEMOAN

BEMOANS > BEMOAN

BEMOCK vb mock

BEMOCKED > BEMOCK

BEMOCKING > BEMOCK

BEMOCKS > BEMOCK

BEMOIL vb soil with mud

BEMOILED > BEMOIL

BEMOILING > BEMOIL

BEMOILS > BEMOIL

BEMONSTER vb treat as monster

BEMOUTH vb endow with a mouth

BEMOUTHED > BEMOUTH

BEMOUTHS > BEMOUTH

BEMUD vb cover with mud

BEMUDDED > BEMUD

BEMUDDING > BEMUD

BEMUDDLE vb confound

BEMUDDLED > BEMUDDLE

BEMUDDLES > BEMUDDLE

BEMUDS > BEMUD

BEMUFFLE vb muffle up

BEMUFFLED > BEMUFFLE

BEMUFFLES > BEMUFFLE

BEMURMUR vb murmur at

BEMURMURS > BEMURMUR

BEMUSE vb confuse

BEMUSED adj puzzled or confused

BEMUSEDLY > BEMUSED

BEMUSES > BEMUSE

BEMUSING > BEMUSE

BEMUZZLE vb put muzzle on

BEMUZZLED > BEMUZZLE

BEMUZZLES > BEMUZZLE

BEN n mountain peak ▷ adv in ▷ adj inner

BENADRYL n tradename of an antihistamine drug used in sleeping tablets

BENADRYLS > BENADRYL

BENAME an archaic word for > NAME

BENAMED > BENAME

BENAMES > BENAME

BENAMING > BENAME

BENCH n long seat ▷ vb put a person on a bench

BENCHED > BENCH

BENCHER n member of the governing body of one of the Inns of Court

BENCHERS > BENCHER

BENCHES > BENCH

BENCHIER > BENCHY

BENCHIEST > BENCHY

BENCHING > BENCH

BENCHLAND n level ground at foot of mountains

BENCHLESS > BENCH

BENCHMARK n criterion by which to measure something ▷ vb measure or test against a benchmark

BENCHTOP adj for use at bench ▷ n flat surface area

BENCHTOPS > BENCHTOP

BENCHY adj (of a hillside) hollowed out in benches

BEND vb (cause to) form a curve ▷ n curved part

BENDABLE > BEND

BENDAY vb (printing) reproduce using the Benday technique

BENDAYED > BENDAY

BENDAYING > BENDAY

BENDAYS > BENDAY

BENDED > BEND

BENDEE same as > BENDY

BENDEES > BENDEE

BENDER n makeshift shelter

BENDERS > BENDER

BENDIER > BENDY

BENDIEST > BENDY

BENDINESS n state of being bendy

BENDING n curving action

BENDINGLY > BEND

BENDINGS > BENDING

BENDLET n narrow diagonal stripe on heraldic shield

BENDLETS > BENDLET

BENDS > BEND

BENDWAYS same as > BENDWISE

BENDWISE adv diagonally

BENDY adj flexible or pliable ▷ n okra

BENDYS > BENDY

BENE n blessing

BENEATH prep below ▷ adv below

BENEDICK n recently married man

BENEDICKS > BENEDICK

BENEDICT n newly married man

BENEDICTS > BENEDICT

BENEDIGHT adj blessed

BENEFACT vb be benefactor to

BENEFACTS > BENEFACT

BENEFIC adj rare word for beneficent

BENEFICE n church office providing its holder with an income ▷ vb provide with a benefice

BENEFICED > BENEFICE

BENEFICES > BENEFICE

BENEFIT n something that improves or promotes ▷ vb do or receive good

BENEFITED > BENEFIT

BENEFITER > BENEFIT

BENEFITS > BENEFIT

BENEMPT a past participle of > BENAME

BENEMPTED > BENEMPT

BENES > BENE

BENET vb trap (something) in a net

BENETS > BENET

BENETTED > BENET

BENETTING > BENET

BENGA n type of Kenyan popular music featuring guitars

BENGALINE n heavy corded fabric, esp silk with woollen or cotton cord

BENGAS > BENGA

BENI n sesame plant

BENIGHT vb shroud in darkness

BENIGHTED adj ignorant or uncultured

BENIGHTEN same as > BENIGHT

BENIGHTER > BENIGHT

BENIGHTS > BENIGHT

BENIGN adj showing kindliness

BENIGNANT adj kind or gracious

BENIGNER > BENIGN

BENIGNEST > BENIGN

BENIGNITY n kindliness

BENIGNLY > BENIGN

BENIS > BENI

BENISEED n sesame

BENISEEDS > BENISEED

BENISON n blessing, esp a spoken one

BENISONS > BENISON

BENITIER n basin for holy water

BENITIERS > BENITIER

BENJ another word for > BHANG

BENJAMIN same as > BENZOIN

BENJAMINS > BENJAMIN

BENJES > BENJ

BENNE another name for > SESAME

BENNES > BENNE

BENNET n Eurasian and N African plant with yellow flowers

BENNETS > BENNET

BENNI n sesame

BENNIES > BENNY

BENNIS > BENNI

BENNY n US word for a man's overcoat

BENOMYL n fungicide

BENOMYLS > BENOMYL

BENS > BEN

BENT adj not straight ▷ n personal inclination, propensity, or aptitude

BENTGRASS n variety of grass

BENTHAL > BENTHOS

BENTHIC > BENTHOS

BENTHOAL > BENTHOS

BENTHON same as > BENTHOS

BENTHONIC > BENTHOS

BENTHONS > BENTHON

BENTHOS n animals and plants living at the bottom of a sea or lake

BENTHOSES > BENTHOS

BENTIER > BENTY

BENTIEST > BENTY

BENTO n thin lightweight box used in Japanese cuisine

BENTONITE n valuable clay, formed by the decomposition of volcanic ash, that swells as it absorbs water: used as a filler in the building, paper, and pharmaceutical industries

BENTOS > BENTO

BENTS > BENT

BENTWOOD n wood bent in moulds, used mainly for furniture ▷ adj made from such wood

BENTWOODS > BENTWOOD

BENTY adj covered with bentgrass

BENUMB vb make numb or powerless

BENUMBED > BENUMB

BENUMBING > BENUMB

BENUMBS > BENUMB

BENZAL n transparent crystalline substance

BENZALS > BENZAL

BENZENE n flammable poisonous liquid used as a solvent, insecticide, etc

BENZENES > BENZENE

BENZENOID adj similar to benzene

BENZIDIN same as > BENZIDINE

BENZIDINE n grey or reddish poisonous crystalline powder

BENZIDINS > BENZIDIN

BENZIL n yellow compound radical

BENZILS > BENZIL

BENZIN same as > BENZINE

BENZINE n volatile liquid used as a solvent

BENZINES > BENZINE

BENZINS > BENZIN

BENZOATE n any salt or ester of benzoic acid

BENZOATES > BENZOATE

BENZOIC adj of, containing, or derived from benzoic acid or benzoin

BENZOIN n gum resin used in ointments, perfume, etc

BENZOINS > BENZOIN

BENZOL n crude form of benzene

BENZOLE same as > BENZOL

BENZOLES > BENZOLE

BENZOLINE n unpurified benzene

BENZOLS > BENZOL

BENZOYL n type of monovalent radical

BENZOYLS > BENZOYL

BENZYL n molecular fragment of certain alcohols and solvents

BENZYLIC > BENZYL

BENZYLS > BENZYL

BEPAINT vb dye; paint

BEPAINTED > BEPAINT

BEPAINTS > BEPAINT

BEPAT vb pat

BEPATCHED adj mended with or covered in patches

BEPATS > BEPAT

BEPATTED > BEPAT

BEPATTING > BEPAT

BEPEARL vb decorate with pearls

BEPEARLED > BEPEARL

BEPEARLS > BEPEARL

BEPELT vb pelt energetically

BEPELTED > BEPELT

BEPELTING > BEPELT

BEPELTS > BEPELT

BEPEPPER vb shower with small missiles

BEPEPPERS > BEPEPPER

BEPESTER vb pester persistently

BEPESTERS > BEPESTER

BEPIMPLE vb form pimples on

BEPIMPLED > BEPIMPLE

BEPIMPLES > BEPIMPLE

BEPITIED > BEPITY

BEPITIES > BEPITY

BEPITY vb feel great pity for

BEPITYING > BEPITY

BEPLASTER vb cover in thick plaster

BEPLUMED adj decorated with feathers

BEPOMMEL vb beat vigorously

BEPOMMELS > BEPOMMEL

BEPOWDER vb cover with powder

BEPOWDERS > BEPOWDER

BEPRAISE vb praise highly

BEPRAISED > BEPRAISE

BEPRAISES > BEPRAISE

BEPROSE vb (of poetry) reduce to prose

BEPROSED > BEPROSE

BEPROSES > BEPROSE

BEPROSING > BEPROSE

BEPUFF vb puff up

BEPUFFED > BEPUFF

BEPUFFING > BEPUFF

BEPUFFS > BEPUFF

BEQUEATH vb dispose of (property) as in a will

BEQUEATHS > BEQUEATH

BEQUEST n legal gift of money or property by someone who has died

BEQUESTS > BEQUEST

BERAKE vb rake thoroughly

BERAKED > BERAKE

BERAKES > BERAKE

BERAKING > BERAKE

BERASCAL vb accuse of being rascal

BERASCALS > BERASCAL

BERATE vb scold harshly

BERATED > BERATE

BERATES > BERATE

BERATING > BERATE

BERAY vb soil; defile

BERAYED > BERAY

BERAYING > BERAY

BERAYS > BERAY

BERBER same as > BERBERE

BERBERE n hot-tasting Ethiopian paste

BERBERES > BERBERE

BERBERIN same as > BERBERINE

BERBERINE n yellow bitter-tasting alkaloid obtained from barberry

BERBERINS > BERBERIN

BERBERIS n shrub with red berries

BERBERS > BERBER

BERBICE n as in berbice chair large armchair with long arms that can be folded inwards to act as leg rests

BERCEAU n arched trellis for climbing plants

BERCEAUX > BERCEAU

BERCEUSE n lullaby

BERCEUSES > BERCEUSE

BERDACHE n Native American man who adopts a female role

BERDACHES > BERDACHE

BERDASH same as
> BERDACHE
BERDASHES > BERDASH
BERE n barley
BEREAVE vb deprive (of)
something or someone
valued, esp through death
BEREAVED adj having
recently lost a close friend
or relative through death
BEREAVEN > BEREAVE
BEREAVER > BEREAVE
BEREAVERS > BEREAVE
BEREAVES > BEREAVE
BEREAVING > BEREAVE
BEREFT adj deprived
BERES > BERE
BERET n round flat
close-fitting brimless cap
BERETS > BERET
BERETTA n type of pistol
BERETTAS > BERETTA
BERG n iceberg
BERGALL n fish of the
wrasse family
BERGALLS > BERGALL
BERGAMA n type of
Turkish rug
BERGAMAS > BERGAMA
BERGAMASK n person
from Bergamo
BERGAMOT n small Asian
tree, the fruit of which
yields an oil used in
perfumery
BERGAMOTS
> BERGAMOT
BERGANDER n species of
duck
BERGEN n large rucksack
with a capacity of over
50 litres
BERGENIA n evergreen
ground-covering plant
BERGENIAS
> BERGENIA
BERGENS > BERGEN
BERGERE n type of French
armchair
BERGERES > BERGERE
BERGFALL n avalanche
BERGFALLS
> BERGFALL
BERGHAAN same as
> BERGMEHL
BERGHAANS
> BERGHAAN
BERGMEHL n light
powdery variety of calcite
BERGMEHLS
> BERGMEHL
BERGOMASK same as
> BERGAMASK
BERGS > BERG
BERGYLT n large
northern marine food
fish
BERGYLTS > BERGYLT
BERHYME vb mention in
poetry
BERHYMED > BERHYME
BERHYMES > BERHYME
BERHYMING > BERHYME
BERIBERI n disease
caused by dietary
deficiency of thiamine
BERIBERIS
> BERIBERI

BERIMBAU n Brazilian
single-stringed bowed
instrument, used to
accompany capoeira
BERIMBAUS
> BERIMBAU
BERIME same as
> BERHYME
BERIMED > BERIME
BERIMES > BERIME
BERIMING > BERIME
BERINGED adj wearing a
ring or rings
BERK n stupid person
BERKELIUM n
radioactive element
BERKO adj berserk
BERKS > BERK
BERLEY n bait scattered
on water to attract fish
▷ vb scatter (bait) on
water
BERLEYED > BERLEY
BERLEYING > BERLEY
BERLEYS > BERLEY
BERLIN n fine wool yarn
used for tapestry work, etc
BERLINE same as
> BERLIN
BERLINES > BERLINE
BERLINS > BERLIN
BERM n narrow grass strip
between the road and the
footpath in a residential
area ▷ vb create a berm
BERME same as > BERM
BERMED > BERM
BERMES > BERME
BERMING > BERM
BERMS > BERM
BERMUDAS pl n
close-fitting shorts that
come down to the knees
BERNICLE n barnacle
goose
BERNICLES
> BERNICLE
BEROB vb rob
BEROBBED > BEROB
BEROBBING > BEROB
BEROBED adj wearing a
robe
BEROBS > BEROB
BEROUGED adj wearing
rouge
BERRET same as > BERET
BERRETS > BERRET
BERRETTA same as
> BIRETTA
BERRETTAS
> BERRETTA
BERRIED > BERRY
BERRIES > BERRY
BERRIGAN n Australian
tree with hanging branches
BERRIGANS
> BERRIGAN
BERRY n small soft
stoneless fruit ▷ vb bear or
produce berries
BERRYING > BERRY
BERRYINGS > BERRY
BERRYLESS > BERRY
BERRYLIKE > BERRY
BERSEEM n
Mediterranean clover
grown as a forage crop and
to improve the soil

BERSEEMS > BERSEEM
BERSERK adj frenziedly
violent or destructive ▷ n
fearsome Norse warrior
BERSERKER same as
> BERSERK
BERSERKLY > BERSERK
BERSERKS > BERSERK
BERTH n bunk in a ship or
train ▷ vb dock (a ship)
BERTHA n type of lace
collar
BERTHAGE n place for
mooring boats
BERTHAGES
> BERTHAGE
BERTHAS > BERTHA
BERTHE n type of lace
collar
BERTHED > BERTH
BERTHES > BERTHE
BERTHING n act of
berthing
BERTHINGS
> BERTHING
BERTHS > BERTH
BERYL n hard transparent
mineral
BERYLINE > BERYL
BERYLLIA n beryllium
oxide
BERYLLIAS
> BERYLLIA
BERYLLIUM n toxic
silvery-white metallic
element
BERYLS > BERYL
BES variant of > BETH
BESAINT vb give saint
status to
BESAINTED > BESAINT
BESAINTS > BESAINT
BESANG > BESING
BESAT > BESIT
BESAW > BESEE
BESCATTER vb strew
BESCORCH vb scorch
badly
BESCOUR vb scour
thoroughly
BESCOURED > BESCOUR
BESCOURS > BESCOUR
BESCRAWL vb cover with
scrawls
BESCRAWLS
> BESCRAWL
BESCREEN vb conceal
with screen
BESCREENS
> BESCREEN
BESEE vb provide for;
mind
BESEECH vb ask earnestly
BESEECHED > BESEECH
BESEECHER > BESEECH
BESEECHES > BESEECH
BESEEING > BESEE
BESEEKE archaic form of
> BESEECH
BESEEKES > BESEEKE
BESEEKING > BESEEKE
BESEEM vb be suitable for
BESEEMED > BESEEM
BESEEMING > BESEEM
BESEEMLY adj becoming;
suitable
BESEEMS > BESEEM
BESEEN > BESEE

BESEES > BESEE
BESES > BES
BESET vb trouble or
harass constantly
BESETMENT > BESET
BESETS > BESET
BESETTER > BESET
BESETTERS > BESET
BESETTING adj
tempting, harassing, or
assailing
BESHADOW vb darken
with shadow
BESHADOWS
> BESHADOW
BESHAME vb cause to feel
shame
BESHAMED > BESHAME
BESHAMES > BESHAME
BESHAMING > BESHAME
BESHINE vb illuminate
BESHINES > BESHINE
BESHINING > BESHINE
BESHIVER vb shatter
BESHIVERS
> BESHIVER
BESHONE > BESHINE
BESHOUT vb shout about
BESHOUTED > BESHOUT
BESHOUTS > BESHOUT
BESHREW vb wish evil on
BESHREWED > BESHREW
BESHREWS > BESHREW
BESHROUD vb cover with
a shroud
BESHROUDS
> BESHROUD
BESIDE prep at, by, or to
the side of
BESIDES prep in addition
▷ adv in addition
BESIEGE vb surround
with military forces
BESIEGED > BESIEGE
BESIEGER > BESIEGE
BESIEGERS > BESIEGE
BESIEGES > BESIEGE
BESIEGING > BESIEGE
BESIGH vb sigh for
BESIGHED > BESIGH
BESIGHING > BESIGH
BESIGHS > BESIGH
BESING vb sing about
joyfully
BESINGING > BESING
BESINGS > BESING
BESIT vb suit; fit
BESITS > BESIT
BESITTING > BESIT
BESLAVE vb treat as slave
BESLAVED > BESLAVE
BESLAVER vb fawn over
BESLAVERS
> BESLAVER
BESLAVES > BESLAVE
BESLAVING > BESLAVE
BESLIME vb cover with
slime
BESLIMED > BESLIME
BESLIMES > BESLIME
BESLIMING > BESLIME
BESLOBBER vb slobber
over
BESLUBBER same as
> BESLOBBER
BESMEAR vb smear over
BESMEARED > BESMEAR

BESMEARER > BESMEAR
BESMEARS > BESMEAR
BESMILE *vb* smile on
BESMILED > BESMILE
BESMILES > BESMILE
BESMILING > BESMILE
BESMIRCH *vb* tarnish (someone's name or reputation)
BESMOKE *vb* blacken with smoke
BESMOKED > BESMOKE
BESMOKES > BESMOKE
BESMOKING > BESMOKE
BESMOOTH *vb* smooth
BESMOOTHS > BESMOOTH
BESMUDGE *vb* blacken
BESMUDGED > BESMUDGE
BESMUDGES > BESMUDGE
BESMUT *vb* blacken with smut
BESMUTCH *same as* > BESMIRCH
BESMUTS > BESMUT
BESMUTTED > BESMUT
BESNOW *vb* cover with snow
BESNOWED > BESNOW
BESNOWING > BESNOW
BESNOWS > BESNOW
BESOGNIO *n* worthless person
BESOGNIOS > BESOGNIO
BESOIN *n* need
BESOINS > BESOIN
BESOM *n* broom made of twigs ▷ *vb* sweep with a besom
BESOMED > BESOM
BESOMING > BESOM
BESOMS > BESOM
BESONIAN *same as* > BEZONIAN
BESONIANS > BESONIAN
BESOOTHE *vb* soothe
BESOOTHED > BESOOTHE
BESOOTHES > BESOOTHE
BESORT *vb* fit
BESORTED > BESORT
BESORTING > BESORT
BESORTS > BESORT
BESOT *vb* make stupid or muddled
BESOTS > BESOT
BESOTTED *adj* infatuated
BESOTTING > BESOT
BESOUGHT > BESEECH
BESOULED *adj* having a soul
BESPAKE > BESPEAK
BESPANGLE *vb* cover or adorn with or as if with spangles
BESPAT > BESPIT
BESPATE > BESPIT
BESPATTER *vb* splash, eg with dirty water
BESPEAK *vb* indicate or suggest
BESPEAKS > BESPEAK

BESPECKLE *vb* mark with speckles
BESPED > BESPEED
BESPEED *vb* get on with (doing something)
BESPEEDS > BESPEED
BESPICE *vb* flavour with spices
BESPICED > BESPICE
BESPICES > BESPICE
BESPICING > BESPICE
BESPIT *vb* cover with spittle
BESPITS > BESPIT
BESPOKE *adj* (esp of a suit) made to the customer's specifications
BESPOKEN > BESPEAK
BESPORT *vb* amuse oneself
BESPORTED > BESPORT
BESPORTS > BESPORT
BESPOT *vb* mark with spots
BESPOTS > BESPOT
BESPOTTED > BESPOT
BESPOUSE *vb* marry
BESPOUSED > BESPOUSE
BESPOUSES > BESPOUSE
BESPOUT *vb* speak pretentiously
BESPOUTED > BESPOUT
BESPOUTS > BESPOUT
BESPREAD *vb* cover (a surface) with something
BESPREADS > BESPREAD
BESPRENT *adj* sprinkled over
BEST *adj* most excellent of a particular group etc ▷ *adv* in a manner surpassing all others ▷ *n* utmost effort ▷ *vb* defeat
BESTAD *Spenserian form of* > BESTEAD
BESTADDE *Spenserian form of* > BESTEAD
BESTAIN *vb* stain
BESTAINED > BESTAIN
BESTAINS > BESTAIN
BESTAR *vb* decorate with stars
BESTARRED > BESTAR
BESTARS > BESTAR
BESTEAD *vb* serve; assist ▷ *adj* beset (by)
BESTEADED > BESTEAD
BESTEADS > BESTEAD
BESTED > BEST
BESTEST *adj* best
BESTI *Indian English word for* > SHAME
BESTIAL *adj* brutal or savage
BESTIALLY > BESTIAL
BESTIALS > BESTIAL
BESTIARY *n* medieval collection of descriptions of animals
BESTICK *vb* cover with sharp points
BESTICKS > BESTICK
BESTIE *n* best friend
BESTIES > BESTIE

BESTILL *vb* cause to be still
BESTILLED > BESTILL
BESTILLS > BESTILL
BESTING > BEST
BESTIR *vb* cause (oneself) to become active
BESTIRRED > BESTIR
BESTIRS > BESTIR
BESTIS > BESTI
BESTORM *vb* assault
BESTORMED > BESTORM
BESTORMS > BESTORM
BESTOW *vb* present (a gift) or confer (an honour)
BESTOWAL > BESTOW
BESTOWALS > BESTOW
BESTOWED > BESTOW
BESTOWER > BESTOW
BESTOWERS > BESTOW
BESTOWING > BESTOW
BESTOWS > BESTOW
BESTREAK *vb* streak
BESTREAKS > BESTREAK
BESTREW *vb* scatter or lie scattered over (a surface)
BESTREWED > BESTREW
BESTREWN > BESTREW
BESTREWS > BESTREW
BESTRID > BESTRIDE
BESTRIDE *vb* have or put a leg on either side of
BESTRIDES > BESTRIDE
BESTRODE > BESTRIDE
BESTROW *same as* > BESTREW
BESTROWED > BESTROW
BESTROWN > BESTROW
BESTROWS > BESTROW
BESTS > BEST
BESTUCK > BESTICK
BESTUD *vb* set with, or as with studs
BESTUDDED > BESTUD
BESTUDS > BESTUD
BESUITED *adj* wearing a suit
BESUNG > BESING
BESWARM *vb* swarm over
BESWARMED > BESWARM
BESWARMS > BESWARM
BET *n* wager between two parties predicting different outcomes of an event ▷ *vb* predict
BETA *n* second letter in the Greek alphabet, a consonant, transliterated as *b*
BETACISM *n* type of speech impediment
BETACISMS > BETACISM
BETAINE *n* sweet-tasting alkaloid that occurs in the sugar beet
BETAINES > BETAINE
BETAKE *vb* as in *betake oneself* go
BETAKEN > BETAKE
BETAKES > BETAKE
BETAKING > BETAKE
BETAS > BETA
BETATOPIC *adj* (of atoms) differing in proton

number by one, theoretically as a result of emission of a beta particle
BETATRON *n* type of particle accelerator for producing high-energy beams of electrons
BETATRONS > BETATRON
BETATTER *vb* make ragged
BETATTERS > BETATTER
BETAXED *adj* burdened with taxes
BETCHA *interj* bet you
BETE *same as* > BEET
BETED > BETE
BETEEM *vb* accord
BETEEME *same as* > BETEEM
BETEEMED > BETEEM
BETEEMES > BETEEME
BETEEMING > BETEEM
BETEEMS > BETEEM
BETEL *n* Asian climbing plant, the leaves and nuts of which can be chewed
BETELNUT *n* seed of the betel palm
BETELNUTS > BETELNUT
BETELS > BETEL
BETES > BETE
BETH *n* second letter of the Hebrew alphabet, transliterated as *b*
BETHANK *vb* thank
BETHANKED > BETHANK
BETHANKIT *n* grace spoken before meal
BETHANKS > BETHANK
BETHEL *n* seaman's chapel
BETHELS > BETHEL
BETHESDA *n* church building of certain Christian denominations
BETHESDAS > BETHESDA
BETHINK *vb* cause (oneself) to consider or meditate
BETHINKS > BETHINK
BETHORN *vb* cover with thorns
BETHORNED > BETHORN
BETHORNS > BETHORN
BETHOUGHT > BETHINK
BETHRALL *vb* make a slave of
BETHRALLS > BETHRALL
BETHS > BETH
BETHUMB *vb* (of books) wear by handling
BETHUMBED > BETHUMB
BETHUMBS > BETHUMB
BETHUMP *vb* thump hard
BETHUMPED > BETHUMP
BETHUMPS > BETHUMP
BETHWACK *vb* strike hard with flat object
BETHWACKS > BETHWACK
BETID > BETIDE
BETIDE *vb* happen (to)
BETIDED > BETIDE

b

BETIDES > BETIDE
BETIDING > BETIDE
BETIGHT > BETIDE
BETIME vb befall
BETIMED > BETIME
BETIMES > BETIME
BETIMING > BETIME
BETING > BETE
BETISE n folly or lack of perception
BETISES > BETISE
BETITTLE vb give title to
BETITLED > BETITLE
BETITLES > BETITLE
BETITTLING > BETITLE
BETOIL vb tire through hard work
BETOILED > BETOIL
BETOILING > BETOIL
BETOILS > BETOIL
BETOKEN vb indicate or signify
BETOKENED > BETOKEN
BETOKENS > BETOKEN
BETON n concrete
BETONIES > BETONY
BETONS > BETON
BETONY n North American plant
BETOOK > BETAKE
BETOSS vb toss about
BETOSSED > BETOSS
BETOSSES > BETOSS
BETOSSING > BETOSS
BETRAY vb hand over or expose (one's nation, friend, etc) treacherously to an enemy
BETRAYAL > BETRAY
BETRAYALS > BETRAY
BETRAYED > BETRAY
BETRAYER > BETRAY
BETRAYERS > BETRAY
BETRAYING > BETRAY
BETRAYS > BETRAY
BETREAD vb tread over
BETREADS > BETREAD
BETRIM vb decorate
BETRIMMED > BETRIM
BETRIMS > BETRIM
BETROD > BETREAD
BETRODDEN > BETREAD
BETROTH vb promise to marry or to give in marriage
BETROTHAL n engagement to be married
BETROTHED adj engaged to be married ▷ n person to whom one is engaged
BETROTHS > BETROTH
BETS > BET
BETTA n fighting fish
BETTAS > BETTA
BETTED > BET
BETTER adj more excellent than others ▷ adv in a more excellent manner ▷ vb improve upon
BETTERED > BETTER
BETTERING > BETTER
BETTERS > BETTER
BETTIES > BETTY
BETTING > BET
BETTINGS > BET

BETTONG n short-nosed rat kangaroo
BETTONGS > BETTONG
BETTOR n person who bets
BETTORS > BETTOR
BETTY n type of short crowbar
BETUMBLED adj thrown into disorder
BETWEEN adv indicating position in the middle, alternatives, etc ▷ prep at a point intermediate to two other points in space, time, etc
BETWEENS > BETWEEN
BETWIXT adv between
BEUNCLED adj having many uncles
BEURRE n butter
BEURRES > BEURRE
BEVATRON n proton synchrotron at the University of California
BEVATRONS > BEVATRON
BEVEL n slanting edge ▷ vb slope
BEVELED > BEVEL
BEVELER > BEVEL
BEVELERS > BEVEL
BEVELING > BEVEL
BEVELLED > BEVEL
BEVELLER > BEVEL
BEVELLERS > BEVEL
BEVELLING > BEVEL
BEVELMENT > BEVEL
BEVELS > BEVEL
BEVER n snack ▷ vb have a snack
BEVERAGE n drink
BEVERAGES > BEVERAGE
BEVERED > BEVER
BEVERING > BEVER
BEVERS > BEVER
BEVIES > BEVY
BEVOMIT vb vomit over
BEVOMITED > BEVOMIT
BEVOMITS > BEVOMIT
BEVOR n armour protecting lower part of face
BEVORS > BEVOR
BEVUE n careless error
BEVUES > BEVUE
BEVVIED > BEVVY
BEVVIES > BEVVY
BEVVY n alcoholic drink ▷ vb drink alcohol
BEVVYING > BEVVY
BEVY n flock or group
BEWAIL vb express great sorrow over
BEWAILED > BEWAIL
BEWAILER > BEWAIL
BEWAILERS > BEWAIL
BEWAILING > BEWAIL
BEWAILS > BEWAIL
BEWARE vb be on one's guard (against)
BEWARED > BEWARE
BEWARES > BEWARE
BEWARING > BEWARE
BEWEARIED > BEWEARY
BEWEARIES > BEWEARY

BEWEARY vb cause to be weary
BEWEEP vb express grief through weeping
BEWEEPING > BEWEEP
BEWEEPS > BEWEEP
BEWENT > BEGO
BEWEPT > BEWEEP
BEWET vb make wet
BEWETS > BEWET
BEWETTED > BEWET
BEWETTING > BEWET
BEWHORE vb treat as a whore
BEWHORED > BEWHORE
BEWHORES > BEWHORE
BEWHORING > BEWHORE
BEWIG vb adorn with a wig
BEWIGGED > BEWIG
BEWIGGING > BEWIG
BEWIGS > BEWIG
BEWILDER vb confuse utterly
BEWILDERS > BEWILDER
BEWINGED adj having wings
BEWITCH vb attract and fascinate
BEWITCHED > BEWITCH
BEWITCHER > BEWITCH
BEWITCHES > BEWITCH
BEWORM vb fill with worms
BEWORMED > BEWORM
BEWORMING > BEWORM
BEWORMS > BEWORM
BEWORRIED > BEWORRY
BEWORRIES > BEWORRY
BEWORRY vb beset with worry
BEWRAP vb wrap up
BEWRAPPED > BEWRAP
BEWRAPS > BEWRAP
BEWRAPT > BEWRAP
BEWRAY an obsolete word for > BETRAY
BEWRAYED > BEWRAY
BEWRAYER > BEWRAY
BEWRAYERS > BEWRAY
BEWRAYING > BEWRAY
BEWRAYS > BEWRAY
BEY n title in the Ottoman Empire
BEYLIC n province ruled over by a bey
BEYLICS > BEYLIC
BEYLIK same as > BEYLIC
BEYLIKS > BEYLIK
BEYOND prep at or to a point on the other side of ▷ adv at or to the far side of something ▷ n unknown, esp life after death
BEYONDS > BEYOND
BEYS > BEY
BEZ n part of a deer's horn
BEZANT n medieval Byzantine gold coin
BEZANTS > BEZANT
BEZAZZ another word for > PIZZAZZ
BEZAZZES > BEZAZZ
BEZEL n sloping edge of a cutting tool

BEZELLESS adj without a bezel
BEZELS > BEZEL
BEZES > BEZ
BEZIL archaic word for > ALCOHOLIC
BEZILS > BEZIL
BEZIQUE n card game for two or more players
BEZIQUES > BEZIQUE
BEZOAR n hard mass, such as a stone or hairball, in the stomach and intestines of animals
BEZOARDIC adj relating to bezoar
BEZOARS > BEZOAR
BEZONIAN n knave or rascal
BEZONIANS > BEZONIAN
BEZZANT same as > BEZANT
BEZZANTS > BEZZANT
BEZZAZZ same as > BEZAZZ
BEZZAZZES > BEZZAZZ
BEZZIE n best friend
BEZZIES > BEZZIE
BEZZLE vb waste (money)
BEZZLED > BEZZLE
BEZZLES > BEZZLE
BEZZLING > BEZZLE
BEZZY same as > BEZZIE
BHAGEE same as > BHAJI
BHAGEES > BHAGEE
BHAI n Indian form of address for a man
BHAIS > BHAI
BHAJAN n singing of devotional songs and hymns
BHAJANS > BHAJAN
BHAJEE same as > BHAJI
BHAJEES > BHAJEE
BHAJI n Indian deep-fried savoury of chopped vegetables in spiced batter
BHAJIA > BHAJI
BHAJIS > BHAJI
BHAKTA n Hindu term for a devotee of God
BHAKTAS > BHAKTA
BHAKTI n loving devotion to God leading to nirvana
BHAKTIS > BHAKTI
BHANG n preparation of Indian hemp
BHANGRA n Punjabi folk music combined with elements of Western pop music
BHANGRAS > BHANGRA
BHANGS > BHANG
BHARAL n wild Himalayan sheep
BHARALS > BHARAL
BHAT n currency of Thailand
BHATS > BHAT
BHAVAN n (in India) a large house or building
BHAVANS > BHAVAN
BHAWAN same as > BHAVAN
BHAWANS > BHAWAN

BHEESTIE *same as*
> BHISHTI
BHEESTIES > BHEESTY
BHEESTY *same as*
> BHISHTI
BHEL *same as* > BAEL
BHELPURI *n* Indian dish of puffed rice and vegetables
BHELPURIS
> BHELPURI
BHELS > BHEL
BHIKHU *n* fully ordained Buddhist monk
BHIKHUS > BHIKHU
BHIKKHUNI *n* fully ordained Buddhist nun
BHINDI *same as*
> BINDHI
BHINDIS > BHINDI
BHISHTI *n* (formerly in India) a water-carrier
BHISHTIS > BHISHTI
BHISTEE *same as*
> BHISHTI
BHISTEES > BHISTEE
BHISTI *same as*
> BHISHTI
BHISTIE *same as*
> BHISHTI
BHISTIES > BHISTIE
BHISTIS > BHISTI
BHOONA *same as* > BHUNA
BHOONAS > BHOONA
BHOOT *same as* > BHUT
BHOOTS > BHOOT
BHUNA *n* Indian sauce
BHUNAS > BHUNA
BHUT *n* Hindu term for a type of ghost
BHUTS > BHUT
BI *short for* > BISEXUAL
BIACETYL *n* liquid with strong odour
BIACETYLS
> BIACETYL
BIACH *n* slang term for a subordinate or inferior person
BIACHES > BIACH
BIALI *same as* > BIALY
BIALIES > BIALY
BIALIS > BIALI
BIALY *n* type of bagel
BIALYS > BIALY
BIANNUAL *adj* occurring twice a year ▷ *n* something that happens biannually
BIANNUALS
> BIANNUAL
BIAS *n* mental tendency, esp prejudice ▷ *vb* cause to have a bias ▷ *adj* slanting obliquely ▷ *adv* obliquely
BIASED > BIAS
BIASEDLY > BIAS
BIASES > BIAS
BIASING > BIAS
BIASINGS > BIAS
BIASNESS > BIAS
BIASSED *same as*
> BIASED
BIASSEDLY *same as*
> BIASEDLY
BIASSES *same as*
> BIASES

BIASSING *same as*
> BIASING
BIATCH *same as* > BIACH
BIATCHES > BIATCH
BIATHLETE *n* athlete taking part in biathlon
BIATHLON *n* contest combining skiing with rifle shooting
BIATHLONS
> BIATHLON
BIAXAL *same as*
> BIAXIAL
BIAXIAL *adj* (esp of a crystal) having two axes
BIAXIALLY > BIAXIAL
BIB *vb* drink
BIBACIOUS *adj* tending to drink to excess
BIBASIC *adj* with two bases
BIBATION *n* drinking to excess
BIBATIONS
> BIBATION
BIBB *n* wooden support on a mast for the trestletrees
BIBBED > BIB
BIBBER *n* drinker
BIBBERIES > BIBBERY
BIBBERS > BIBBER
BIBBERY *n* drinking to excess
BIBBING *n* act of bibbing
BIBBINGS > BIBBING
BIBBLE *n* pebble
BIBBLES > BIBBLE
BIBBS > BIBB
BIBCOCK *n* tap with a nozzle bent downwards
BIBCOCKS > BIBCOCK
BIBE *n* (in Newfoundland folklore) spirit whose wailing warns of a coming death
BIBELOT *n* attractive or curious trinket
BIBELOTS > BIBELOT
BIBES > BIBE
BIBFUL *n* as in *spill a bibful* divulge secrets
BIBFULS > BIBFUL
BIBIMBAP *n* Korean rice dish
BIBIMBAPS
> BIBIMBAP
BIBLE *n* any book containing the sacred writings of a religion
BIBLES > BIBLE
BIBLESS > BIB
BIBLICAL *adj* of, occurring in, or referring to the Bible
BIBLICISM *n* bible-learning
BIBLICIST
> BIBLICISM
BIBLIKE > BIB
BIBLIOTIC *n* study of books
BIBLIST *same as*
> BIBLICIST
BIBLISTS > BIBLIST
BIBS > BIB
BIBULOUS *adj* addicted to alcohol

BICAMERAL *adj* (of a legislature) consisting of two chambers
BICARB *n* bicarbonate of soda
BICARBS > BICARB
BICAUDAL *adj* having two tails
BICCIES > BICCY
BICCY *n* biscuit
BICE *n* medium blue colour
BICENTRIC *adj* having two centres
BICEP *same as* > BICEPS
BICEPS *n* muscle with two origins, esp the muscle that flexes the forearm
BICEPSES > BICEPS
BICES > BICE
BICHIR *n* African freshwater fish with an elongated body
BICHIRS > BICHIR
BICHORD *adj* having two strings for each note
BICHROME *adj* having two colours
BICIPITAL *adj* having two heads
BICKER *vb* argue over petty matters ▷ *n* petty squabble
BICKERED > BICKER
BICKERER > BICKER
BICKERERS > BICKER
BICKERING > BICKER
BICKERS > BICKER
BICKIE *short for*
> BISCUIT
BICKIES > BICKIE
BICOASTAL *adj* relating to both the east and west coasts of the US
BICOLOR *same as*
> BICOLOUR
BICOLORED *same as*
> BICOLOUR
BICOLORS > BICOLOR
BICOLOUR *adj* two-coloured
BICOLOURS
> BICOLOUR
BICONCAVE *adj* (of a lens) having concave faces on both sides
BICONVEX *adj* (of a lens) having convex faces on both sides
BICORN *adj* having two horns or hornlike parts
BICORNATE *same as*
> BICORN
BICORNE *same as*
> BICORN
BICORNES > BICORNE
BICORNS > BICORN
BICRON *n* billionth part of a metre
BICRONS > BICRON
BICURIOUS *adj* showing an interest in bisexuality
BICUSPID *adj* having two points ▷ *n* bicuspid tooth
BICUSPIDS
> BICUSPID

BICYCLE *n* vehicle with two wheels, one behind the other, pedalled by the rider ▷ *vb* ride a bicycle
BICYCLED > BICYCLE
BICYCLER > BICYCLE
BICYCLERS > BICYCLE
BICYCLES > BICYCLE
BICYCLIC *adj* of, forming, or formed by two circles, cycles, etc
BICYCLING > BICYCLE
BICYCLIST > BICYCLE
BID *vb* offer (an amount) in attempting to buy something ▷ *n* offer of a specified amount, as at an auction
BIDARKA *same as*
> BAIDARKA
BIDARKAS > BIDARKA
BIDARKEE *same as*
> BIDARKA
BIDARKEES
> BIDARKEE
BIDDABLE *adj* obedient
BIDDABLY > BIDDABLE
BIDDEN > BID
BIDDER > BID
BIDDERS > BID
BIDDIES > BIDDY
BIDDING > BID
BIDDINGS > BID
BIDDY *n* woman, esp an old gossipy one
BIDE *vb* stay or continue
BIDED > BIDE
BIDENT *n* instrument with two prongs
BIDENTAL *n* sacred place where lightning has struck
BIDENTALS
> BIDENTAL
BIDENTATE > BIDENT
BIDENTS > BIDENT
BIDER > BIDE
BIDERS > BIDE
BIDES > BIDE
BIDET *n* low basin for washing the genital area
BIDETS > BIDET
BIDI *same as* > BEEDI
BIDING > BIDE
BIDINGS > BIDE
BIDIS > BIDI
BIDON *n* oil drum
BIDONS > BIDON
BIDS > BID
BIELD *n* shelter ▷ *vb* shelter or take shelter
BIELDED > BIELD
BIELDIER > BIELDY
BIELDIEST > BIELDY
BIELDING > BIELD
BIELDS > BIELD
BIELDY *adj* sheltered
BIEN *adv* well
BIENNALE *n* event occurring every two years
BIENNALES
> BIENNALE
BIENNIA > BIENNIUM
BIENNIAL *adj* occurring every two years ▷ *n* plant that completes its life cycle in two years
BIENNIALS
> BIENNIAL

BIENNIUM n period of two years

BIENNIUMS > BIENNIUM

BIER n stand on which a body or coffin rests before burial

BIERS > BIER

BIERWURST n type of sausage

BIESTINGS same as > BEESTINGS

BIFACE n prehistoric stone tool

BIFACES > BIFACE

BIFACIAL adj having two faces or surfaces

BIFARIOUS adj having parts arranged in two rows on either side of a central axis

BIFF n blow with the fist ▷ vb give (someone) such a blow

BIFFED > BIFF

BIFFER n someone, such as a sportsperson, who has a reputation for hitting hard

BIFFERS > BIFFER

BIFFIES > BIFFY

BIFFIN n variety of red cooking apple

BIFFING > BIFF

BIFFINS > BIFFIN

BIFFO n fighting or aggressive behaviour ▷ adj aggressive

BIFFOS > BIFFO

BIFFS > BIFF

BIFFY n outdoor toilet

BIFID adj divided into two by a cleft in the middle

BIFIDA > BIFIDUM

BIFIDITY > BIFID

BIFIDLY > BIFID

BIFIDUM n type of bacterium

BIFIDUMS > BIFIDUM

BIFIDUS n bacterium of the human digestive system

BIFIDUSES > BIFIDUS

BIFILAR adj having two parallel threads, as in the suspension of certain measuring instruments

BIFILARLY > BIFILAR

BIFLEX adj bent or flexed in two places

BIFOCAL adj having two different focuses

BIFOCALED adj wearing bifocals

BIFOCALS pl n spectacles with lenses permitting near and distant vision

BIFOLD n something folded in two places

BIFOLDS > BIFOLD

BIFOLIATE adj having only two leaves

BIFORATE adj having two openings, pores, or perforations

BIFORKED adj two-pronged

BIFORM adj having or combining the characteristics of two forms, as a centaur

BIFORMED same as > BIFORM

BIFTAH same as > BIFTER

BIFTAHS > BIFTAH

BIFTER n cigarette

BIFTERS > BIFTER

BIFURCATE vb fork into two branches ▷ adj forked into two branches

BIG adj of considerable size, height, number, or capacity ▷ adv on a grand scale ▷ vb build

BIGA n chariot drawn by two horses

BIGAE > BIGA

BIGAMIES > BIGAMY

BIGAMIST > BIGAMY

BIGAMISTS > BIGAMY

BIGAMOUS > BIGAMY

BIGAMY n crime of marrying a person while still legally married to someone else

BIGARADE n Seville orange

BIGARADES > BIGARADE

BIGAROON same as > BIGARREAU

BIGAROONS > BIGAROON

BIGARREAU n any of several heart-shaped varieties of sweet cherry that have firm flesh

BIGEMINAL adj double; twinned

BIGEMINY n heart complaint

BIGENER n hybrid between individuals of different genera

BIGENERIC adj (of a hybrid plant) derived from parents of two different genera

BIGENERS > BIGENER

BIGEYE n type of red marine fish

BIGEYES > BIGEYE

BIGFEET > BIGFOOT

BIGFOOT n yeti ▷ vb throw one's weight around

BIGFOOTED > BIGFOOT

BIGFOOTS > BIGFOOT

BIGG n type of barley

BIGGED > BIG

BIGGER > BIG

BIGGEST > BIG

BIGGETIER > BIGGETY

BIGGETY adj conceited

BIGGIE n something big or important

BIGGIES > BIGGIE

BIGGIN n plain close-fitting cap

BIGGING > BIG

BIGGINGS > BIG

BIGGINS > BIGGIN

BIGGISH > BIG

BIGGITIER > BIGGITY

BIGGITY adj conceited

BIGGON same as > BIGGIN

BIGGONS > BIGGON

BIGGS > BIGG

BIGGY same as > BIGGIE

BIGHA n in India, unit for measuring land

BIGHAS > BIGHA

BIGHEAD n conceited person

BIGHEADED > BIGHEAD

BIGHEADS > BIGHEAD

BIGHORN n large wild mountain sheep

BIGHORNS > BIGHORN

BIGHT n long curved shoreline ▷ vb fasten or bind with a loop of rope

BIGHTED > BIGHT

BIGHTING > BIGHT

BIGHTS > BIGHT

BIGLY > BIG

BIGMOUTH n noisy, indiscreet, or boastful person

BIGMOUTHS > BIGMOUTH

BIGNESS > BIG

BIGNESSES > BIG

BIGNONIA n tropical American climbing shrub

BIGNONIAS > BIGNONIA

BIGOS n Polish stew

BIGOSES > BIGOS

BIGOT n person who is intolerant of ideas other than their own

BIGOTED > BIGOT

BIGOTEDLY > BIGOT

BIGOTRIES > BIGOTRY

BIGOTRY n attitudes, behaviour, or way of thinking of a bigot

BIGOTS > BIGOT

BIGS > BIG

BIGSTICK adj of or relating to irresistible military strength

BIGTIME adj important

BIGUANIDE n any of a class of compounds some of which are used in the treatment of certain forms of diabetes

BIGUINE same as > BEGUINE

BIGUINES > BIGUINE

BIGWIG n important person

BIGWIGS > BIGWIG

BIHOURLY adj occurring every two hours

BIJECTION n mathematical function or mapping that is both an injection and a surjection and therefore has an inverse

BIJECTIVE adj (of a function, relation, etc) associating two sets in such a way that every member of each set is uniquely paired with a member of the other

BIJOU adj (of a house) small but elegant ▷ n something small and delicately worked

BIJOUS > BIJOU

BIJOUX > BIJOU

BIJUGATE adj (of compound leaves) having two pairs of leaflets

BIJUGOUS same as > BIJUGATE

BIJURAL adj relating to two coexisting legal systems

BIJWONER same as > BYWONER

BIJWONERS > BIJWONER

BIKE same as > BICYCLE

BIKED > BIKE

BIKER n person who rides a motorcycle

BIKERS > BIKER

BIKES > BIKE

BIKEWAY n cycle lane

BIKEWAYS > BIKEWAY

BIKIE n member of a motorcycle gang

BIKIES > BIKIE

BIKING > BIKE

BIKINGS > BIKE

BIKINI n woman's brief two-piece swimming costume

BIKINIED > BIKINI

BIKINIS > BIKINI

BIKKIE short for > BISCUIT

BIKKIES > BIKKIE

BILABIAL adj of, relating to, or denoting a speech sound articulated using both lips ▷ n bilabial speech sound

BILABIALS > BILABIAL

BILABIATE adj divided into two lips

BILANDER n small two-masted cargo ship

BILANDERS > BILANDER

BILATERAL adj affecting or undertaken by two parties

BILAYER n part of a cell membrane

BILAYERS > BILAYER

BILBERRY n bluish-black edible berry

BILBIES > BILBY

BILBO n (formerly) a sword with a marked temper and elasticity

BILBOA same as > BILBO

BILBOAS > BILBOA

BILBOES > BILBO

BILBOS > BILBO

BILBY n Australian marsupial with long pointed ears and grey fur

BILE n bitter yellow fluid secreted by the liver ▷ vb Scots word for boil

BILECTION same as > BOLECTION

BILED > BILE

BILES > BILE

BILESTONE another name for > GALLSTONE

BILEVEL n hairstyle with two different lengths
BILEVELS > BILEVEL
BILGE n nonsense ▷ vb (of a vessel) to take in water at the bilge
BILGED > BILGE
BILGES > BILGE
BILGIER > BILGE
BILGIEST > BILGE
BILGING > BILGE
BILGY > BILGE
BILHARZIA n disease caused by infestation of the body with blood flukes
BILIAN n type of tree used for its wood
BILIANS > BILIAN
BILIARIES > BILIARY
BILIARY adj of bile, the ducts that convey bile, or the gall bladder ▷ n disease found in dogs
BILIMBI n type of fruit-bearing tree
BILIMBING same as > BILIMBI
BILIMBIS > BILIMBI
BILINEAR adj of or referring to two lines
BILING > BILE
BILINGUAL adj involving or using two languages ▷ n bilingual person
BILIOUS adj sick, nauseous
BILIOUSLY > BILIOUS
BILIRUBIN n orange-yellow pigment in the bile
BILITERAL adj relating to two letters
BILK vb cheat, esp by not paying ▷ n swindle or cheat
BILKED > BILK
BILKER > BILK
BILKERS > BILK
BILKING > BILK
BILKS > BILK
BILL n money owed for goods or services supplied ▷ vb send or present an account for payment to (a person)
BILLABLE adj that can be charged to a client
BILLABONG n stagnant pool in an intermittent stream
BILLBOARD n large outdoor board for displaying advertisements
BILLBOOK n business record of bills received, paid, etc
BILLBOOKS > BILLBOOK
BILLBUG n type of weevil
BILLBUGS > BILLBUG
BILLED > BILL
BILLER n stem of a plant
BILLERS > BILLER
BILLET vb assign a lodging to (a soldier) ▷ n accommodation for a soldier in civil lodgings
BILLETED > BILLET

BILLETEE > BILLET
BILLETEES > BILLET
BILLETER > BILLET
BILLETERS > BILLET
BILLETING n act of billeting
BILLETS > BILLET
BILLFISH n type of fish with elongated jaws, such as the spearfish and marlin
BILLFOLD n small folding case, usually of leather, for holding paper money, documents, etc
BILLFOLDS > BILLFOLD
BILLHEAD n printed form for making out bills
BILLHEADS > BILLHEAD
BILLHOOK n tool with a hooked blade, used for chopping etc
BILLHOOKS > BILLHOOK
BILLIARD n (modifier) of or relating to billiards
BILLIARDS n game played on a table with balls and a cue
BILLIE same as > BILLY
BILLIES > BILLY
BILLING n prominence given in programmes, advertisements, etc, to performers or acts
BILLINGS > BILLING
BILLION n one thousand million ▷ determiner amounting to a billion
BILLIONS > BILLION
BILLIONTH > BILLION
BILLMAN n person who uses a billhook
BILLMEN > BILLMAN
BILLON n alloy consisting of gold or silver and a base metal
BILLONS > BILLON
BILLOW n large sea wave ▷ vb rise up or swell out
BILLOWED > BILLOW
BILLOWIER > BILLOW
BILLOWING > BILLOW
BILLOWS > BILLOW
BILLOWY adj full of or forming billows
BILLS > BILL
BILLY n metal can or pot for cooking on a camp fire
BILLYBOY n type of river barge
BILLYBOYS > BILLYBOY
BILLYCAN same as > BILLY
BILLYCANS > BILLYCAN
BILLYCOCK n any of several round-crowned brimmed hats of felt, such as the bowler
BILLYO n as in like billyo phrase used to emphasize or intensify something
BILLYOH same as > BILLYO

BILLYOHS > BILLYOH
BILLYOS > BILLYO
BILOBAR same as > BILOBATE
BILOBATE adj divided into or having two lobes
BILOBATED same as > BILOBATE
BILOBED same as > BILOBATE
BILOBULAR adj having two lobules
BILOCULAR adj divided into two chambers or cavities
BILSTED n American gum tree
BILSTEDS > BILSTED
BILTONG n strips of dried meat
BILTONGS > BILTONG
BIMA same as > BEMA
BIMAH same as > BEMA
BIMAHS > BIMAH
BIMANAL same as > BIMANOUS
BIMANOUS adj having two hands as opposed to four feet
BIMANUAL adj using or requiring both hands
BIMAS > BIMA
BIMBASHI n Turkish military official
BIMBASHIS > BIMBASHI
BIMBETTE n derogatory term for an attractive but empty-headed young woman
BIMBETTES > BIMBETTE
BIMBLE n as in bimble box type of dense Australian tree
BIMBO n derogatory term for an attractive but empty-headed young person
BIMBOES > BIMBO
BIMBOS > BIMBO
BIMENSAL adj occurring every two months
BIMESTER n period of two months
BIMESTERS > BIMESTER
BIMETAL n material made from two sheets of metal
BIMETALS > BIMETAL
BIMETHYL another word for > ETHANE
BIMETHYLS > BIMETHYL
BIMINI n type of awning for a yacht
BIMINIS > BIMINI
BIMODAL adj having two modes
BIMONTHLY adj every two months ▷ adv every two months ▷ n periodical published every two months
BIMORPH n assembly of piezoelectric crystals
BIMORPHS > BIMORPH

BIN n container for rubbish or for storing grain, coal, etc ▷ vb put in a rubbish bin
BINAL adj twofold
BINARIES > BINARY
BINARISM n state of being binary
BINARISMS > BINARISM
BINARY adj composed of, relating to, or involving two ▷ n something composed of two parts or things
BINATE adj occurring in two parts or in pairs
BINATELY > BINATE
BINAURAL adj relating to, having, or hearing with both ears
BIND vb make secure with or as if with a rope ▷ n annoying situation
BINDABLE > BIND
BINDER n firm cover for holding loose sheets of paper together
BINDERIES > BINDERY
BINDERS > BINDER
BINDERY n bookbindery
BINDHI same as > BINDI
BINDHIS > BINDHI
BINDI n decorative dot worn in the middle of the forehead, esp by Hindu women
BINDING > BIND
BINDINGLY > BIND
BINDINGS > BIND
BINDIS > BINDI
BINDLE n small packet
BINDLES > BINDLE
BINDS > BIND
BINDWEED n plant that twines around a support
BINDWEEDS > BINDWEED
BINE n climbing or twining stem of various plants
BINER n clip used by climbers
BINERS > BINER
BINERVATE adj having two nerves
BINES > BINE
BING n heap or pile, esp of spoil from a mine
BINGE n bout of excessive indulgence ▷ vb indulge in a binge
BINGEABLE adj easy to consume in large quantities
BINGED > BINGE
BINGEING n act of indulging in a binge
BINGEINGS > BINGEING
BINGER > BINGE
BINGERS > BINGER
BINGES > BINGE
BINGIES > BINGY
BINGING n act of indulging in a binge
BINGINGS > BINGING

BINGLE *n* minor crash or upset, as in a car or on a surfboard ▷ *vb* layer (hair)
BINGLED > BINGLE
BINGLES > BINGLE
BINGLING > BINGLE
BINGO *n* gambling game ▷ *sentence substitute* cry by the winner of a game of bingo ▷ *vb* (in Scrabble) play all seven of one's tiles in a single turn
BINGOED > BINGO
BINGOES > BINGO
BINGOING > BINGO
BINGOS > BINGO
BINGS > BING
BINGY *Australian slang for* > STOMACH
BINIOU *n* small high-pitched Breton bagpipe
BINIOUS > BINIOU
BINIT *n* (computing) early form of bit
BINITS > BINIT
BINK *n* ledge
BINKS > BINK
BINMAN *another name for* > DUSTMAN
BINMEN > BINMAN
BINNACLE *n* box holding a ship's compass
BINNACLES > BINNACLE
BINNED > BIN
BINNING > BIN
BINOCLE *n* binocular-style telescope
BINOCLES > BINOCLE
BINOCS > BINOCULAR
BINOCULAR *adj* involving both eyes
BINOMIAL *adj* consisting of two terms ▷ *n* mathematical expression consisting of two terms, such as $3x + 2y$
BINOMIALS > BINOMIAL
BINOMINAL *adj* of or denoting the binomial nomenclature ▷ *n* two-part taxonomic name
BINOVULAR *adj* relating to or derived from two different ova
BINS > BIN
BINTURONG *n* arboreal SE Asian mammal with long shaggy black hair
BINUCLEAR *adj* having two nuclei
BIO *short for* > BIOGRAPHY
BIOACTIVE *adj* able to interact with living system
BIOASSAY *n* method of determining the effect of a change to substance ▷ *vb* subject to a bioassay
BIOASSAYS > BIOASSAY
BIOBANK *n* large store of human samples for medical research
BIOBANKS > BIOBANK

BIOBLAST *same as* > BIOPLAST
BIOBLASTS > BIOBLAST
BIOCENOSE *adj* living together in mutual dependence
BIOCHEMIC *adj* of or relating to chemical compounds, reactions, etc, occurring in living organisms
BIOCHIP *n* small glass or silicon plate containing an array of biochemical molecules or structures
BIOCHIPS > BIOCHIP
BIOCIDAL > BIOCIDE
BIOCIDE *n* substance used to destroy living things
BIOCIDES > BIOCIDE
BIOCLEAN *adj* free from harmful bacteria
BIOCYCLE *n* cycling of chemicals through the biosphere
BIOCYCLES > BIOCYCLE
BIODATA *n* information regarding an individual's education and work history
BIODIESEL *n* biofuel intended for use in diesel engines
BIODOT *n* temperature-sensitive device stuck to the skin in order to monitor stress
BIODOTS > BIODOT
BIOENERGY *n* energy derived from organic matter
BIOETHIC > BIOETHICS
BIOETHICS *n* study of ethical problems arising from biological research and its applications in such fields as organ transplantation, genetic engineering, or artificial insemination
BIOFACT *n* item of biological information
BIOFACTS > BIOFACT
BIOFIBERS *same as* > BIOFIBRES
BIOFIBRES *pl n* vegetable, animal, or mineral fibres existing in nature which are used by humans
BIOFILM *n* thin layer of living organisms
BIOFILMS > BIOFILM
BIOFOULER *n* animal that obstructs or pollutes the environment
BIOFUEL *n* gaseous, liquid, or solid substance of biological origin used as a fuel ▷ *vb* fuel (a vehicle, etc) using biofuel
BIOFUELED *adj* running on biofuel
BIOFUELS > BIOFUEL
BIOG *short form of* > BIOGRAPHY

BIOGAS *n* gaseous fuel produced by the fermentation of organic waste
BIOGASES > BIOGAS
BIOGASSES > BIOGAS
BIOGEN *n* hypothetical protein
BIOGENIC *adj* originating from a living organism
BIOGENIES > BIOGENY
BIOGENOUS > BIOGENY
BIOGENS > BIOGEN
BIOGENY *n* principle that a living organism must originate from a parent form similar to itself
BIOGRAPH *vb* write biography of
BIOGRAPHS > BIOGRAPH
BIOGRAPHY *n* account of a person's life by another person
BIOGS > BIOG
BIOHACKER *n* person who engages in biohacking
BIOHAZARD *n* material of biological origin that is hazardous to humans
BIOHERM *n* mound of material laid down by sedentary marine organisms
BIOHERMS > BIOHERM
BIOLOGIC *adj* of or relating to biology ▷ *n* drug that is derived from a living organism
BIOLOGICS > BIOLOGIC
BIOLOGIES > BIOLOGY
BIOLOGISM *n* explaining human behaviour through biology
BIOLOGIST > BIOLOGY
BIOLOGY *n* study of living organisms
BIOLYSES > BIOLYSIS
BIOLYSIS *n* death and dissolution of a living organism
BIOLYTIC > BIOLYSIS
BIOMARKER *n* substance, physiological characteristic, gene, etc that indicates, or may indicate, the presence of disease, a physiological abnormality, or a psychological condition
BIOMASS *n* total number of living organisms in a given area
BIOMASSES > BIOMASS
BIOME *n* major ecological community
BIOMES > BIOME
BIOMETER *n* device for measuring natural radiation
BIOMETERS > BIOMETER
BIOMETRIC *adj* of any automated system using physiological or behavioural traits as a means of identification

BIOMETRY *n* analysis of biological data
BIOMINING *n* using plants, etc to collect precious metals for extraction
BIOMORPH *n* form or pattern resembling living thing
BIOMORPHS > BIOMORPH
BIONIC *adj* having a part of the body that is operated electronically
BIONICS *n* study of biological functions to create electronic versions
BIONOMIC > BIONOMICS
BIONOMICS *a less common name for* > ECOLOGY
BIONOMIES > BIONOMY
BIONOMIST > BIONOMICS
BIONOMY *n* laws of life
BIONT *n* living thing
BIONTIC > BIONT
BIONTS > BIONT
BIOPARENT *n* biological parent
BIOPHILIA *n* innate love for the natural world, supposed to be felt universally by humankind
BIOPHOR *n* hypothetical material particle
BIOPHORE *same as* > BIOPHOR
BIOPHORES > BIOPHORE
BIOPHORS > BIOPHOR
BIOPIC *n* film based on the life of a famous person
BIOPICS > BIOPIC
BIOPIRACY *n* use of wild plants by international companies to develop medicines, without recompensing the countries from which they are taken
BIOPIRATE > BIOPIRACY
BIOPLASM *n* living matter
BIOPLASMS > BIOPLASM
BIOPLAST *n* very small unit of bioplasm
BIOPLASTS > BIOPLAST
BIOPLAY *n* play based on the life of a famous person
BIOPLAYS > BIOPLAY
BIOPSIC > BIOPSY
BIOPSIED > BIOPSY
BIOPSIES > BIOPSY
BIOPSY *n* examination of tissue from a living body ▷ *vb* perform a biopsy on
BIOPSYING > BIOPSY
BIOPTIC > BIOPSY
BIOREGION *n* area in which climate and environment are consistent
BIORHYTHM *n* complex recurring pattern of

physiological states, believed to affect physical, emotional, and mental states

BIOS > BIO

BIOSAFETY n precautions taken to control the cultivation and distribution of genetically modified crops and products

BIOSCOPE n kind of early film projector

BIOSCOPES > BIOSCOPE

BIOSCOPY n examination of a body to determine whether it is alive

BIOSENSOR n device used to monitor living systems

BIOSOCIAL adj relating to the interaction of biological and social elements

BIOSOLID n residue from treated sewage

BIOSOLIDS > BIOSOLID

BIOSPHERE n part of the earth's surface and atmosphere inhabited by living things

BIOSTABLE adj resistant to the effects of microorganisms

BIOSTATIC adj of or relating to the branch of biology that deals with the structure of organisms in relation to their function

BIOSTROME n rock layer consisting of a deposit of organic material, such as fossils

BIOTA n plant and animal life of a particular region or period

BIOTAS > BIOTA

BIOTECH n biotechnology

BIOTECHS > BIOTECH

BIOTERROR n use of biological weapons by terrorists

BIOTIC adj of or relating to living organisms ▷ n living organism

BIOTICAL same as > BIOTIC

BIOTICS > BIOTIC

BIOTIN n vitamin of the B complex, abundant in egg yolk and liver

BIOTINS > BIOTIN

BIOTITE n black or dark green mineral of the mica group

BIOTITES > BIOTITE

BIOTITIC > BIOTITE

BIOTOPE n small area that supports its own distinctive community

BIOTOPES > BIOTOPE

BIOTOXIN n toxic substance produced by a living organism

BIOTOXINS > BIOTOXIN

BIOTRON n climate-control chamber

BIOTRONS > BIOTRON

BIOTROPH n parasitic organism, esp a fungus

BIOTROPHS > BIOTROPH

BIOTURBED adj stirred by organisms

BIOTYPE n group of genetically identical plants within a species, produced by apomixis

BIOTYPES > BIOTYPE

BIOTYPIC > BIOTYPE

BIOVULAR adj (of twins) from two separate eggs

BIOWASTE n organic or biodegradable waste

BIOWASTES > BIOWASTE

BIOWEAPON n living organism or a toxic product manufactured from it, used to kill or incapacitate

BIPACK n obsolete filming process

BIPACKS > BIPACK

BIPAROUS adj producing offspring in pairs

BIPARTED adj divided into two parts

BIPARTITE adj consisting of two parts

BIPARTY adj involving two parties

BIPED n animal with two feet ▷ adj having two feet

BIPEDAL adj having two feet

BIPEDALLY > BIPEDAL

BIPEDS > BIPED

BIPHASIC adj having two phases

BIPHENYL n white or colourless crystalline solid used as a heat-transfer agent

BIPHENYLS > BIPHENYL

BIPINNATE adj (of pinnate leaves) having the leaflets themselves divided into smaller leaflets

BIPLANE n aeroplane with two sets of wings, one above the other

BIPLANES > BIPLANE

BIPOD n two-legged support or stand

BIPODS > BIPOD

BIPOLAR adj having two poles

BIPRISM n prism having a highly obtuse angle to facilitate beam splitting

BIPRISMS > BIPRISM

BIPYRAMID n geometrical form consisting of two pyramids with a common polygonal base

BIRACIAL adj involving two races or ethnic groups

BIRADIAL adj showing both bilateral and radial symmetry, as certain sea anemones

BIRADICAL n molecule with two centres

BIRAMOSE same as > BIRAMOUS

BIRAMOUS adj divided into two parts, as the appendages of crustaceans

BIRCH n tree with thin peeling bark ▷ vb flog with a birch

BIRCHBARK n as in birchbark biting Native Canadian craft in which designs are bitten onto bark from birch trees

BIRCHED > BIRCH

BIRCHEN > BIRCH

BIRCHES > BIRCH

BIRCHING n act of birching

BIRCHINGS > BIRCHING

BIRCHIR same as > BICHIR

BIRCHIRS > BIRCHIR

BIRCHWOOD n wood of the birch tree

BIRD n creature with feathers and wings, most types of which can fly ▷ vb hunt for birds

BIRDBATH n small basin or trough for birds to bathe in, usually in a garden

BIRDBATHS > BIRDBATH

BIRDBRAIN n stupid person

BIRDCAGE n wire or wicker cage in which captive birds are kept

BIRDCAGES > BIRDCAGE

BIRDCALL n characteristic call or song of a bird

BIRDCALLS > BIRDCALL

BIRDDOG n dog used or trained to retrieve game birds

BIRDDOGS > BIRDDOG

BIRDED > BIRD

BIRDER n birdwatcher

BIRDERS > BIRDER

BIRDFARM n place where birds are kept

BIRDFARMS > BIRDFARM

BIRDFEED n food for birds

BIRDFEEDS > BIRDFEED

BIRDHOUSE n small shelter or box for birds to nest in

BIRDIE n score of one stroke under par for a hole ▷ vb play (a hole) in one stroke under par

BIRDIED > BIRDIE

BIRDIEING > BIRDIE

BIRDIES > BIRDIE

BIRDING > BIRD

BIRDINGS > BIRD

BIRDLIFE n birds collectively

BIRDLIFES > BIRDLIFE

BIRDLIKE > BIRD

BIRDLIME n sticky substance smeared on twigs to catch small birds ▷ vb smear (twigs) with birdlime to catch (small birds)

BIRDLIMED > BIRDLIME

BIRDLIMES > BIRDLIME

BIRDMAN n man concerned with birds, such as a fowler or ornithologist

BIRDMEN > BIRDMAN

BIRDS > BIRD

BIRDSEED n mixture of various kinds of seeds for feeding cage birds

BIRDSEEDS > BIRDSEED

BIRDSEYE n type of primrose

BIRDSEYES > BIRDSEYE

BIRDSFOOT n type of plant with pods shaped like a bird's foot

BIRDSHOT n small pellets designed for shooting birds

BIRDSHOTS > BIRDSHOT

BIRDSONG n musical call of a bird or birds

BIRDSONGS > BIRDSONG

BIRDWATCH vb watch birds

BIRDWING n type of butterfly

BIRDWINGS > BIRDWING

BIREME n ancient galley having two banks of oars

BIREMES > BIREME

BIRETTA n stiff square cap worn by the Catholic clergy

BIRETTAS > BIRETTA

BIRIANI same as > BIRYANI

BIRIANIS > BIRIANI

BIRIYANI same as > BIRIANI

BIRIYANIS > BIRIANI

BIRK n birch tree ▷ adj consisting or made of birch

BIRKEN adj relating to the birch tree

BIRKIE n spirited or lively person ▷ adj lively

BIRKIER > BIRKIE

BIRKIES > BIRKIE

BIRKIEST > BIRKIE

BIRKS > BIRK

BIRL same as > BURL

BIRLE same as > BURL

BIRLED > BIRL

BIRLER > BIRL

BIRLERS > BIRL

BIRLES > BIRLE

BIRLIEMAN n judge dealing with local law

b

BIRLIEMEN
> BIRLIEMAN
BIRLING > BIRL
BIRLINGS > BIRL
BIRLINN n small Scottish book
BIRLINNS > BIRLINN
BIRLS > BIRL
BIRO n tradename of a kind of ballpoint pen
BIROS > BIRO
BIRR vb make or cause to make a whirring sound ▷ n whirring sound
BIRRED > BIRR
BIRRETTA same as > BIRETTA
BIRRETTAS > BIRRETTA
BIRRING > BIRR
BIRROTCH n plural of birr, Ethiopian monetary unit
BIRRS > BIRR
BIRSE n bristle ▷ vb bruise
BIRSED > BIRSE
BIRSES > BIRSE
BIRSIER > BIRSY
BIRSIEST > BIRSY
BIRSING > BIRSE
BIRSLE vb roast
BIRSLED > BIRSLE
BIRSLES > BIRSLE
BIRSLING > BIRSLE
BIRSY adj bristly
BIRTH n process of bearing young ▷ vb give birth to
BIRTHDATE n date on which a person was born
BIRTHDAY n anniversary of the day of one's birth
BIRTHDAYS
> BIRTHDAY
BIRTHDOM n birthright
BIRTHDOMS
> BIRTHDOM
BIRTHED > BIRTH
BIRTHER n person who believes Barack Obama was not born in the USA
BIRTHERS > BIRTHER
BIRTHING > BIRTH
BIRTHINGS > BIRTH
BIRTHMARK n blemish on the skin formed before birth
BIRTHNAME n name person was born with
BIRTHRATE n ratio of live births in a specified area, group, etc, to the population of that area, group, etc
BIRTHROOT n N American plant whose roots were formerly used by Native Americans as an aid in childbirth
BIRTHS > BIRTH
BIRTHWORT n type of climbing plant once believed to ease childbirth
BIRYANI n Indian rice-based dish
BIRYANIS > BIRYANI
BIS adv twice ▷ sentence substitute encore! again!

BISCACHA same as > VISCACHA
BISCACHAS
> BISCACHA
BISCOTTI > BISCOTTO
BISCOTTO n small Italian biscuit
BISCUIT n small flat dry sweet or plain cake ▷ adj pale brown
BISCUITS > BISCUIT
BISCUITY adj reminiscent of biscuit
BISE n cold dry northerly wind
BISECT vb divide into two equal parts
BISECTED > BISECT
BISECTING > BISECT
BISECTION > BISECT
BISECTOR n straight line or plane that bisects an angle
BISECTORS
> BISECTOR
BISECTRIX n bisector of the angle between the optic axes of a crystal
BISECTS > BISECT
BISERIAL adj in two rows
BISERIATE adj (of plant parts, such as petals) arranged in two whorls, cycles, rows, or series
BISERRATE adj (of leaf margins, etc) having serrations that are themselves serrate
BISES > BISE
BISEXUAL adj sexually attracted to both men and women ▷ n bisexual person
BISEXUALS
> BISEXUAL
BISH n mistake
BISHES > BISH
BISHOP n clergyman or clergywoman who governs a diocese ▷ vb make a bishop
BISHOPDOM n jurisdiction of bishop
BISHOPED > BISHOP
BISHOPESS > BISHOP
BISHOPING > BISHOP
BISHOPRIC n diocese or office of a bishop
BISHOPS > BISHOP
BISK a less common spelling of > BISQUE
BISKS > BISK
BISMAR n type of weighing scale
BISMARCK n type of pastry
BISMARCKS
> BISMARCK
BISMARS > BISMAR
BISMILLAH interj in the name of Allah, a preface to all except one of the surahs of the Koran, used by Muslims as a blessing before eating or some other action
BISMUTH n pinkish-white metallic element

BISMUTHAL > BISMUTH
BISMUTHIC adj of or containing bismuth in the pentavalent state
BISMUTHS > BISMUTH
BISNAGA n type of cactus
BISNAGAS > BISNAGA
BISOM same as > BESOM
BISOMS > BISOM
BISON same as > BUFFALO
BISONS > BISON
BISONTINE adj relating to bison
BISPHENOL n synthetic organic compound used to make plastics and resins
BISQUE n thick rich soup made from shellfish
BISQUES > BISQUE
BISSON adj blind ▷ vb cause to be blind
BISSONED > BISSON
BISSONING > BISSON
BISSONS > BISSON
BIST a form of the second person singular of > BE
BISTABLE adj (of an electronic system) having two stable states ▷ n bistable system
BISTABLES
> BISTABLE
BISTATE adj involving two states
BISTER same as > BISTRE
BISTERED > BISTER
BISTERS > BISTER
BISTORT n Eurasian plant with a spike of small pink flowers
BISTORTS > BISTORT
BISTOURY n long surgical knife with a narrow blade
BISTRE n water-soluble pigment
BISTRED > BISTRE
BISTRES > BISTRE
BISTRO n small restaurant
BISTROIC > BISTRO
BISTROS > BISTRO
BISULCATE adj marked by two grooves
BISULFATE n bisulphate
BISULFIDE n bisulphide
BISULFITE n bisulphite
BIT n small piece, portion, or quantity
BITABLE > BITE
BITCH n female dog, fox, or wolf ▷ vb complain or grumble
BITCHED > BITCH
BITCHEN same as > BITCHING
BITCHERY n spiteful talk
BITCHES > BITCH
BITCHFEST n malicious and spiteful discussion of people, events, etc
BITCHIER > BITCHY
BITCHIEST > BITCHY
BITCHILY > BITCHY
BITCHING adj wonderful or excellent

BITCHY adj spiteful or malicious
BITCOIN n type of digital currency
BITCOINS > BITCOIN
BITE vb grip, tear, or puncture the skin, as with the teeth or jaws ▷ n act of biting
BITEABLE > BITE
BITEPLATE n device used by dentists
BITER > BITE
BITERS > BITE
BITES > BITE
BITESIZE adj small enough to put in the mouth whole
BITEWING n dental X-ray film
BITEWINGS
> BITEWING
BITING > BITE
BITINGLY > BITE
BITINGS > BITE
BITLESS adj without a bit
BITMAP n picture created by colour or shading on a visual display unit ▷ vb create a bitmap of
BITMAPPED > BITMAP
BITMAPS > BITMAP
BITO n African and Asian tree
BITONAL adj consisting of black and white tones
BITOS > BITO
BITOU n as in bitou bush type of sprawling woody shrub
BITRATE n rate of data processing
BITRATES > BITRATE
BITS > BIT
BITSER n mongrel dog
BITSERS > BITSER
BITSIER > BITSY
BITSIEST > BITSY
BITSTOCK n handle or stock of a tool into which a drilling bit is fixed
BITSTOCKS
> BITSTOCK
BITSTREAM n sequence of digital data
BITSY adj very small
BITT n strong post on the deck of a ship for securing lines ▷ vb secure (a line) by means of a bitt
BITTACLE same as > BINNACLE
BITTACLES
> BITTACLE
BITTE interj you're welcome
BITTED > BITT
BITTEN > BITE
BITTER adj having a sharp unpleasant taste ▷ n beer with a slightly bitter taste ▷ adv very ▷ vb make or become bitter
BITTERED > BITTER
BITTERER > BITTER
BITTEREST > BITTER
BITTERING > BITTER

BITTERISH > BITTER
BITTERLY > BITTER
BITTERN *n* wading marsh bird with a booming call
BITTERNS > BITTERN
BITTERNUT *n* E North American hickory tree with thin-shelled nuts and bitter kernels
BITTERS *pl n* bitter-tasting spirits flavoured with plant extracts
BITTIE *n* small piece
BITTIER > BITTY
BITTIES > BITTIE
BITTIEST > BITTY
BITTILY *adv* in a disjointed way
BITTINESS > BITTY
BITTING > BITT
BITTINGS > BITT
BITTOCK *n* small amount
BITTOCKS > BITTOCK
BITTOR *n* bittern
BITTORS > BITTOR
BITTOUR *same as* **>** BITTOR
BITTOURS > BITTOUR
BITTS > BITT
BITTUR *same as* **>** BITTOR
BITTURS > BITTOR
BITTY *adj* lacking unity, disjointed
BITUMED *adj* covered with bitumen
BITUMEN *n* black sticky substance obtained from tar or petrol
BITUMENS > BITUMEN
BITURBO *n* engine with two turbochargers
BITURBOS > BITURBO
BITWISE *adj* relating to an operator in a programming language that manipulates bits
BIUNIQUE *adj* relating to a one-to-one correspondence
BIVALENCE *n* semantic principle that there are exactly two truth values, so that every meaningful statement is either true or false
BIVALENCY **>** BIVALENT
BIVALENT *adj* associated together in pairs *▷ n* structure consisting of two homologous chromosomes
BIVALENTS **>** BIVALENT
BIVALVATE *same as* **>** BIVALVE
BIVALVE *adj* (of a marine mollusc) with two hinged segments to its shell *▷ n* sea creature with a shell consisting of two hinged segments
BIVALVED > BIVALVE
BIVALVES > BIVALVE
BIVARIANT *same as* **>** BIVARIATE

BIVARIATE *adj* (of a distribution) involving two random variables, not necessarily independent of one another
BIVIA > BIVIUM
BIVINYL *another word for* **>** BUTADIENE
BIVINYLS > BIVINYL
BIVIOUS *adj* offering a choice of two different ways
BIVIUM *n* parting of ways
BIVOUAC *n* temporary camp in the open air *▷ vb* camp in a bivouac
BIVOUACKS > BIVOUAC
BIVOUACS > BIVOUAC
BIVVIED > BIVVY
BIVVIES > BIVVY
BIVVY *n* small tent or shelter *▷ vb* camp in a bivouac
BIVVYING > BIVVY
BIWEEKLY *adv* every two weeks *▷ n* periodical published every two weeks
BIYEARLY *adv* every two years
BIZ *n* business
BIZARRE *adj* odd or unusual *▷ n* bizarre thing
BIZARRELY > BIZARRE
BIZARRES > BIZARRE
BIZARRO *n* bizarre person
BIZARROS > BIZARRO
BIZAZZ *same as* **>** PIZAZZ
BIZAZZES > BIZAZZ
BIZCACHA *same as* **>** VISCACHA
BIZCACHAS **>** BIZCACHA
BIZE *n* dry, cold wind in France
BIZES > BIZE
BIZJET *n* small jet plane used by businesspeople
BIZJETS > BIZJET
BIZNAGA *same as* **>** BISNAGA
BIZNAGAS > BIZNAGA
BIZONAL > BIZONE
BIZONE *n* place comprising two zones
BIZONES > BIZONE
BIZZAZZ *n* combination of energy and style
BIZZAZZES > BIZZAZZ
BIZZES > BIZ
BIZZIES > BIZZY
BIZZO *n* empty and irrelevant talk or ideas
BIZZOS > BIZZO
BIZZY *n* slang word for a police officer
BLAB *vb* reveal (secrets) indiscreetly
BLABBED > BLAB
BLABBER *vb* talk without thinking *▷ n* person who blabs
BLABBERED > BLABBER
BLABBERS > BLABBER
BLABBIER > BLABBY
BLABBIEST > BLABBY

BLABBING > BLAB
BLABBINGS > BLAB
BLABBY *adj* talking too much; indiscreet
BLABS > BLAB
BLACK *adj* of the darkest colour, like coal *▷ n* darkest colour *▷ vb* make black
BLACKBALL *vb* exclude from a group *▷ n* hard boiled sweet with black-and-white stripes
BLACKBAND *n* type of iron ore
BLACKBIRD *n* common European thrush *▷ vb* (formerly) to capture and sell into slavery
BLACKBODY *n* hypothetical body that would be capable of absorbing all the electromagnetic radiation falling on it
BLACKBOY *n* grass tree
BLACKBOYS **>** BLACKBOY
BLACKBUCK *n* Indian antelope, the male of which has spiral horns, a dark back, and a white belly
BLACKBUTT *n* Australian eucalyptus tree with hard wood used as timber
BLACKCAP *n* brownish-grey warbler, the male of which has a black crown
BLACKCAPS **>** BLACKCAP
BLACKCOCK *n* male of the black grouse
BLACKDAMP *n* air that is low in oxygen content and high in carbon dioxide as a result of an explosion in a mine
BLACKED > BLACK
BLACKEN *vb* make or become black
BLACKENED > BLACKEN
BLACKENER > BLACKEN
BLACKENS > BLACKEN
BLACKER > BLACK
BLACKEST > BLACK
BLACKFACE *n* performer made up to imitate a Black person
BLACKFIN *n* type of tuna
BLACKFINS **>** BLACKFIN
BLACKFISH *n* small dark Australian estuary fish
BLACKFLY *n* type of black aphid that infests beans, sugar beet, and other plants
BLACKGAME *n* large N European grouse
BLACKGUM *n* US tree
BLACKGUMS **>** BLACKGUM
BLACKHEAD *n* black-tipped plug of fatty matter clogging a skin pore

BLACKING *n* preparation for giving a black finish to shoes, metals, etc
BLACKINGS **>** BLACKING
BLACKISH > BLACK
BLACKJACK *n* pontoon or a similar card game *▷ vb* hit with or as if with a kind of truncheon
BLACKLAND *n* dark soil
BLACKLEAD *n* graphite *▷ vb* colour with blacklead
BLACKLEG *n* person who continues to work during a strike *▷ vb* refuse to join a strike
BLACKLEGS **>** BLACKLEG
BLACKLIST *n* list of people or organizations considered untrustworthy etc *▷ vb* put on a blacklist
BLACKLY > BLACK
BLACKMAIL *n* act of attempting to extort money by threats *▷ vb* (attempt to) obtain money by blackmail
BLACKNESS > BLACK
BLACKOUT *n* extinguishing of all light as a precaution against an air attack
BLACKOUTS **>** BLACKOUT
BLACKPOLL *n* N American warbler, the male of which has a black-and-white head
BLACKS > BLACK
BLACKSPOT *n* as in *accident blackspot* spot where many accidents occur
BLACKTAIL *n* variety of mule deer having a black tail
BLACKTIP *n* shark of coastal tropical waters
BLACKTIPS **>** BLACKTIP
BLACKTOP *n* bituminous mixture used for paving
BLACKTOPS **>** BLACKTOP
BLACKWASH *n* wash for colouring a surface black
BLACKWOOD *n* tall Australian acacia tree which yields highly valued black timber
BLAD *same as* **>** BLAUD
BLADDED > BLAD
BLADDER *n* sac in the body where urine is held
BLADDERED *adj* intoxicated
BLADDERS > BLADDER
BLADDERY *adj* like a bladder
BLADDING > BLAD
BLADE *n* cutting edge of a weapon or tool
BLADED > BLADE
BLADELESS > BLADE
BLADELIKE > BLADE
BLADER *n* person skating with in-line skates**

BLADERS > BLADER
BLADES > BLADE
BLADEWORK n rowing technique
BLADIER > BLADY
BLADIEST > BLADY
BLADING n act or instance of skating with in-line skates
BLADINGS > BLADING
BLADS > BLAD
BLADY adj as in blady grass coarse leafy Australasian grass
BLAE adj bluish-grey
BLAEBERRY another name for > BILBERRY
BLAER > BLAE
BLAES n hardened clay or shale
BLAEST > BLAE
BLAFF n fish stew of the Caribbean ▷ vb make a barking noise
BLAFFED > BLAFF
BLAFFING > BLAFF
BLAFFS > BLAFF
BLAG vb obtain by wheedling or cadging ▷ n robbery, esp with violence
BLAGGED > BLAG
BLAGGER > BLAG
BLAGGERS > BLAG
BLAGGING > BLAG
BLAGGINGS > BLAG
BLAGS > BLAG
BLAGUE n pretentious but empty talk
BLAGUER > BLAGUE
BLAGUERS > BLAGUE
BLAGUES > BLAGUE
BLAGUEUR n bluffer
BLAGUEURS > BLAGUEUR
BLAH n worthless or silly talk ▷ adj uninteresting ▷ vb talk nonsense or boringly
BLAHED > BLAH
BLAHER > BLAH
BLAHEST > BLAH
BLAHING > BLAH
BLAHS > BLAH
BLAIN n blister, blotch, or sore on the skin
BLAINS > BLAIN
BLAISE same as > BLAES
BLAIZE same as > BLAES
BLAM n representation of the sound of a bullet being fired ▷ vb make the noise of a bullet being fired
BLAMABLE > BLAME
BLAMABLY > BLAME
BLAME vb consider (someone) responsible ▷ n responsibility for something that is wrong
BLAMEABLE > BLAME
BLAMEABLY > BLAME
BLAMED euphemistic word for > DAMNED
BLAMEFUL adj deserving blame
BLAMELESS adj free from blame
BLAMER > BLAME

BLAMERS > BLAME
BLAMES > BLAME
BLAMING > BLAME
BLAMMED > BLAM
BLAMMING > BLAM
BLAMS > BLAM
BLANCH vb become white or pale
BLANCHED > BLANCH
BLANCHER > BLANCH
BLANCHERS > BLANCH
BLANCHES > BLANCH
BLANCHING > BLANCH
BLANCO n whitening substance ▷ vb whiten (something) with blanco
BLANCOED > BLANCO
BLANCOING > BLANCO
BLANCOS > BLANCO
BLAND adj dull and uninteresting ▷ n bland thing ▷ vb as in bland out become bland
BLANDED > BLAND
BLANDER > BLAND
BLANDEST > BLAND
BLANDING > BLAND
BLANDISH vb persuade by mild flattery
BLANDLY > BLAND
BLANDNESS > BLAND
BLANDS > BLAND
BLANK adj not written on ▷ n empty space ▷ vb cross out, blot, or obscure
BLANKED > BLANK
BLANKER > BLANK
BLANKEST > BLANK
BLANKET n large thick cloth used as covering for a bed ▷ adj applying to a wide group of people, situations, conditions, etc ▷ vb cover as with a blanket
BLANKETED > BLANKET
BLANKETS > BLANKET
BLANKETY n euphemism for any taboo word
BLANKIE n child's security blanket
BLANKIES > BLANKIE
BLANKING > BLANK
BLANKINGS > BLANK
BLANKLY > BLANK
BLANKNESS > BLANK
BLANKS > BLANK
BLANKY same as > BLANKIE
BLANQUET n variety of pear
BLANQUETS > BLANQUET
BLARE vb sound loudly and harshly ▷ n loud harsh noise
BLARED > BLARE
BLARES > BLARE
BLARING > BLARE
BLARNEY n flattering talk ▷ vb cajole with flattery
BLARNEYED > BLARNEY
BLARNEYS > BLARNEY
BLART vb sound loudly and harshly
BLARTED > BLART
BLARTING > BLART
BLARTS > BLART

BLASE adj indifferent or bored through familiarity
BLASH n splash ▷ vb splash (something) with liquid
BLASHED > BLASH
BLASHES > BLASH
BLASHIER > BLASHY
BLASHIEST > BLASHY
BLASHING > BLASH
BLASHY adj windy and rainy
BLASPHEME vb speak disrespectfully of (God or sacred things)
BLASPHEMY n behaviour or language that shows disrespect for God or sacred things
BLAST n explosion ▷ vb blow up (a rock etc) with explosives ▷ interj expression of annoyance
BLASTED adv extreme or extremely ▷ adj blighted or withered
BLASTEMA n mass of animal cells that will regenerate a lost organ or tissue
BLASTEMAL > BLASTEMA
BLASTEMAS > BLASTEMA
BLASTEMIC > BLASTEMA
BLASTER > BLAST
BLASTERS > BLAST
BLASTHOLE n hole containing an explosive
BLASTIE n ugly creature
BLASTIER > BLASTY
BLASTIES > BLASTIE
BLASTIEST > BLASTY
BLASTING n distortion of sound caused by overloading certain components of a radio system
BLASTINGS > BLASTING
BLASTMENT n something that frustrates one's plans
BLASTOFF n launching of a rocket
BLASTOFFS > BLASTOFF
BLASTOID n extinct echinoderm found in fossil form
BLASTOIDS > BLASTOID
BLASTOMA n tumour composed of embryonic tissue that has not yet developed a specialized function
BLASTOMAS > BLASTOMA
BLASTOPOR n opening of the archenteron in the gastrula
BLASTS > BLAST
BLASTULA n early form of an animal embryo
BLASTULAE > BLASTULA
BLASTULAR > BLASTULA

BLASTULAS > BLASTULA
BLASTY adj gusty
BLAT vb cry out or bleat like a sheep
BLATANCY > BLATANT
BLATANT adj glaringly obvious
BLATANTLY > BLATANT
BLATE adj shy; ill at ease ▷ vb babble (something)
BLATED > BLATE
BLATER > BLATE
BLATES > BLATE
BLATEST > BLATE
BLATHER vb speak foolishly ▷ n foolish talk
BLATHERED > BLATHER
BLATHERER > BLATHER
BLATHERS > BLATHER
BLATING > BLATE
BLATS > BLAT
BLATT n newspaper
BLATTANT same as > BLATANT
BLATTED > BLAT
BLATTER vb prattle
BLATTERED > BLATTER
BLATTERS > BLATTER
BLATTING > BLAT
BLATTS > BLATT
BLAUBOK n South African antelope
BLAUBOKS > BLAUBOK
BLAUD vb slap
BLAUDED > BLAUD
BLAUDING > BLAUD
BLAUDS > BLAUD
BLAW vb Scots word for blow
BLAWED > BLAW
BLAWING > BLAW
BLAWN > BLAW
BLAWORT n harebell
BLAWORTS > BLAWORT
BLAWS > BLAW
BLAY n small river fish
BLAYS > BLAY
BLAZAR n type of active galaxy
BLAZARS > BLAZAR
BLAZE n strong fire or flame ▷ vb burn or shine brightly
BLAZED > BLAZE
BLAZER n lightweight jacket, often in the colours of a school etc
BLAZERED > BLAZER
BLAZERS > BLAZER
BLAZES pl n hell
BLAZING > BLAZE
BLAZINGLY > BLAZING
BLAZON vb proclaim publicly ▷ n coat of arms
BLAZONED > BLAZON
BLAZONER > BLAZON
BLAZONERS > BLAZON
BLAZONING > BLAZON
BLAZONRY n art or process of describing heraldic arms in proper form
BLAZONS > BLAZON
BLEACH vb make or become white or colourless ▷ n bleaching agent

BLEACHED > BLEACH
BLEACHER > BLEACH
BLEACHERS *pl n* tier of seats in a sports stadium, etc, that are unroofed and inexpensive
BLEACHERY *n* place where bleaching is carried out
BLEACHES > BLEACH
BLEACHING > BLEACH
BLEAK *adj* exposed and barren ▷ *n* type of fish found in slow-flowing rivers
BLEAKER > BLEAK
BLEAKEST > BLEAK
BLEAKISH > BLEAK
BLEAKLY > BLEAK
BLEAKNESS > BLEAK
BLEAKS > BLEAK
BLEAKY *same as* > BLEAK
BLEAR *vb* make (eyes or sight) dim with or as if with tears ▷ *adj* bleary
BLEARED > BLEAR
BLEARER > BLEAR
BLEAREST > BLEAR
BLEAREYED *adj* with eyes blurred, as with old age or after waking
BLEARIER > BLEARY
BLEARIEST > BLEARY
BLEARILY > BLEARY
BLEARING > BLEAR
BLEARS > BLEAR
BLEARY *adj* with eyes dimmed, as by tears or tiredness
BLEAT *vb* (of a sheep, goat, or calf) utter its plaintive cry ▷ *n* cry of sheep, goats, and calves
BLEATED > BLEAT
BLEATER > BLEAT
BLEATERS > BLEAT
BLEATING > BLEAT
BLEATINGS > BLEAT
BLEATS > BLEAT
BLEB *n* fluid-filled blister on the skin
BLEBBIER > BLEB
BLEBBIEST > BLEB
BLEBBING *n* formation of bleb
BLEBBINGS > BLEBBING
BLEBBY > BLEB
BLEBS > BLEB
BLECH *interj* expressing disgust
BLED > BLEED
BLEE *n* complexion; hue
BLEED *vb* lose or emit blood
BLEEDER *n* despicable person
BLEEDERS > BLEEDER
BLEEDING > BLEED
BLEEDINGS > BLEED
BLEEDS > BLEED
BLEEP *n* high-pitched signal or beep ▷ *vb* make such a noise
BLEEPED > BLEEP
BLEEPER *n* small portable radio receiver that makes a bleeping signal

BLEEPERS > BLEEPER
BLEEPING > BLEEP
BLEEPS > BLEEP
BLEES > BLEE
BLELLUM *n* babbler; blusterer
BLELLUMS > BLELLUM
BLEMISH *n* defect or stain ▷ *vb* spoil or tarnish
BLEMISHED > BLEMISH
BLEMISHER > BLEMISH
BLEMISHES > BLEMISH
BLENCH *vb* shy away, as in fear
BLENCHED > BLENCH
BLENCHER > BLENCH
BLENCHERS > BLENCH
BLENCHES > BLENCH
BLENCHING > BLENCH
BLEND *vb* mix or mingle (components or ingredients) ▷ *n* mixture
BLENDABLE *adj* capable of being blended
BLENDE *n* mineral consisting mainly of zinc sulphide
BLENDED > BLEND
BLENDER *n* electrical appliance for puréeing vegetables etc
BLENDERS > BLENDER
BLENDES > BLENDE
BLENDING > BLEND
BLENDINGS > BLEND
BLENDS > BLEND
BLENNIES > BLENNY
BLENNIOID *n* type of small, mainly marine spiny-finned fish with an elongated body, such as the blennies, butterfish, and gunnel
BLENNY *n* small fish with a tapering scaleless body
BLENT *a past participle of* > BLEND
BLEOMYCIN *n* drug used to treat cancer
BLERT *n* foolish person
BLERTS > BLERT
BLESBOK *n* S African antelope
BLESBOKS > BLESBOK
BLESBUCK *same as* > BLESBOK
BLESBUCKS > BLESBUCK
BLESS *vb* make holy by means of a religious rite
BLESSED *adj* made holy
BLESSEDER > BLESS
BLESSEDLY > BLESS
BLESSER > BLESS
BLESSERS > BLESS
BLESSES > BLESS
BLESSING > BLESS
BLESSINGS > BLESS
BLEST > BLESS
BLET *n* state of decay in certain fruits, due to overripening ▷ *vb* go soft
BLETHER *same as* > BLATHER
BLETHERED > BLETHER
BLETHERER > BLETHER
BLETHERS > BLETHER
BLETS > BLET

BLETTED > BLET
BLETTING > BLET
BLEUATRE *adj* blueish
BLEW > BLOW
BLEWART *same as* > BLAWORT
BLEWARTS > BLEWART
BLEWIT *same as* > BLEWITS
BLEWITS *n* type of edible fungus with a pale brown cap and a bluish stalk
BLEWITSES > BLEWITS
BLEY *same as* > BLAY
BLEYS > BLEY
BLIGHT *n* person or thing that spoils or prevents growth ▷ *vb* cause to suffer a blight
BLIGHTED > BLIGHT
BLIGHTER *n* irritating person
BLIGHTERS > BLIGHTER
BLIGHTIES > BLIGHTY
BLIGHTING > BLIGHT
BLIGHTS > BLIGHT
BLIGHTY *n* home country; home leave
BLIKSEM *interj* South African expression of surprise
BLIMBING *same as* > BILIMBI
BLIMBINGS > BLIMBING
BLIMEY *interj* exclamation of surprise or annoyance
BLIMP *n* small airship ▷ *vb* swell out
BLIMPED > BLIMP
BLIMPERY *n* complacent or reactionary behaviour
BLIMPING > BLIMP
BLIMPISH *adj* complacent and reactionary
BLIMPS > BLIMP
BLIMY *same as* > BLIMEY
BLIN *Scots word for* > BLIND
BLIND *adj* unable to see ▷ *vb* deprive of sight ▷ *n* covering for a window
BLINDAGE *n* (esp formerly) a protective screen or structure, as over a trench
BLINDAGES > BLINDAGE
BLINDED > BLIND
BLINDER *n* outstanding performance
BLINDERS > BLINDER
BLINDEST > BLIND
BLINDFISH *n* any of various small fishes, esp the cavefish, that have rudimentary or functionless eyes and occur in subterranean streams
BLINDFOLD *vb* prevent (a person) from seeing by covering the eyes ▷ *n* piece of cloth used to cover the eyes ▷ *adv* with the eyes covered by a cloth

BLINDGUT *same as* > CAECUM
BLINDGUTS > BLINDGUT
BLINDING *n* sand or grit spread over a road surface to fill up cracks ▷ *adj* making one blind or as if blind
BLINDINGS > BLINDING
BLINDLESS > BLIND
BLINDLY > BLIND
BLINDNESS > BLIND
BLINDS > BLIND
BLINDSIDE *vb* take (someone) by surprise
BLINDWORM *same as* > SLOWWORM
BLING *adj* flashy ▷ *n* ostentatious jewellery ▷ *vb* make ostentatious or flashy
BLINGED > BLING
BLINGER > BLING
BLINGEST > BLING
BLINGIER > BLINGY
BLINGIEST > BLINGY
BLINGING *adj* flashy and expensive
BLINGLISH *n* spoken English mixed with Black slang
BLINGS > BLING
BLINGY *same as* > BLING
BLINI *pl n* Russian pancakes made of buckwheat flour and yeast
BLINIS *same as* > BLINI
BLINK *vb* close and immediately reopen (the eyes) ▷ *n* act of blinking
BLINKARD *n* something that twinkles
BLINKARDS > BLINKARD
BLINKED > BLINK
BLINKER *vb* provide (a horse) with blinkers ▷ *n* flashing light for sending messages
BLINKERED *adj* considering only a narrow point of view
BLINKERS *same as* > BLINKER
BLINKING > BLINK
BLINKS > BLINK
BLINNED > BLIN
BLINNING > BLIN
BLINS > BLIN
BLINTZ *n* thin pancake folded over a filling usually of apple, cream cheese, or meat
BLINTZE *same as* > BLINTZ
BLINTZES > BLINTZE
BLINY *same as* > BLINI
BLIP *n* spot of light on a radar screen indicating the position of an object ▷ *vb* produce such a noise
BLIPPED > BLIP
BLIPPING > BLIP
BLIPS > BLIP

b

BLIPVERT *n* very short television advertisement

BLIPVERTS > BLIPVERT

BLISS *n* perfect happiness ▷ *vb* make or become perfectly happy

BLISSED > BLISS

BLISSES > BLISS

BLISSFUL *adj* serenely joyful or glad

BLISSING > BLISS

BLISSLESS > BLISS

BLIST *archaic form of* > BLESSED

BLISTER *n* small bubble on the skin ▷ *vb* (cause to) have blisters

BLISTERED > BLISTER

BLISTERS > BLISTER

BLISTERY > BLISTER

BLIT *vb* move (a block of data) in a computer's memory

BLITE *n* type of herb

BLITES > BLITE

BLITHE *adj* casual and indifferent

BLITHEFUL *same as* > BLITHE

BLITHELY > BLITHE

BLITHER *same as* > BLATHER

BLITHERED > BLITHER

BLITHERS > BLITHER

BLITHEST > BLITHE

BLITS > BLIT

BLITTED > BLIT

BLITTER *n* circuit that transfers large amounts of data within a computer's memory

BLITTERS > BLITTER

BLITTING > BLIT

BLITZ *n* violent and sustained attack by aircraft ▷ *vb* attack suddenly and intensively

BLITZED > BLITZ

BLITZER > BLITZ

BLITZERS > BLITZ

BLITZES > BLITZ

BLITZING > BLITZ

BLIVE *same as* > BELIVE

BLIZZARD *n* blinding storm of wind and snow ▷ *vb* (of weather) be stormy with wind and snow

BLIZZARDS > BLIZZARD

BLIZZARDY *adj* like a blizzard

BLOAT *vb* cause to swell, as with liquid or air ▷ *n* abnormal distention of the abdomen in cattle, sheep, etc

BLOATED *adj* swollen, as with a liquid, air, or wind

BLOATER *n* salted smoked herring

BLOATERS > BLOATER

BLOATING > BLOAT

BLOATINGS > BLOAT

BLOATS > BLOAT

BLOATWARE *n* software with more features than necessary

BLOB *n* soft mass or drop ▷ *vb* put blobs, as of ink or paint, on

BLOBBED > BLOB

BLOBBIER > BLOB

BLOBBIEST > BLOB

BLOBBING > BLOB

BLOBBY > BLOB

BLOBS > BLOB

BLOC *n* people or countries combined by a common interest

BLOCK *n* large solid piece of wood, stone, etc ▷ *vb* obstruct or impede by introducing an obstacle

BLOCKABLE > BLOCK

BLOCKADE *n* sealing off of a place to prevent the passage of goods ▷ *vb* impose a blockade on

BLOCKADED > BLOCKADE

BLOCKADER > BLOCKADE

BLOCKADES > BLOCKADE

BLOCKAGE *n* act of blocking or state of being blocked

BLOCKAGES > BLOCKAGE

BLOCKBUST *vb* bring about the sale of property at a low price by stirring up fears of racial change in an area

BLOCKED > BLOCK

BLOCKER *n* person or thing that blocks

BLOCKERS > BLOCKER

BLOCKHEAD *n* stupid person

BLOCKHOLE *n* lines marked near stumps on cricket pitch

BLOCKIE *n* owner of a small property, esp a farm

BLOCKIER > BLOCKY

BLOCKIES > BLOCKIE

BLOCKIEST > BLOCKY

BLOCKING *n* interruption of anode current in a valve

BLOCKINGS > BLOCKING

BLOCKISH *adj* lacking vivacity or imagination

BLOCKS > BLOCK

BLOCKSHIP *n* ship used to block a river or channel and prevent its being used

BLOCKWORK *n* wall-building style

BLOCKY *adj* like a block, esp in shape and solidity

BLOCS > BLOC

BLOG *n* journal written online and accessible to users of the internet ▷ *vb* write a blog

BLOGGABLE *adj* interesting enough to be a topic for a blog

BLOGGED > BLOG

BLOGGER > BLOG

BLOGGERS > BLOG

BLOGGIER > BLOGGY

BLOGGIEST > BLOGGY

BLOGGING > BLOG

BLOGGINGS > BLOG

BLOGGY *adj* characteristic of a blog

BLOGPOST *n* single posting made as part of a blog

BLOGPOSTS > BLOGPOST

BLOGRING *n* group of blogs joined in a ring

BLOGRINGS > BLOGRING

BLOGROLL *n* list of blogs

BLOGROLLS > BLOGROLL

BLOGS > BLOG

BLOKART *n* single-seat three-wheeled vehicle propelled by the wind

BLOKARTS > BLOKART

BLOKE *n* man

BLOKEDOM *n* state of being a bloke

BLOKEDOMS > BLOKEDOM

BLOKEISH *adj* denoting or exhibiting the characteristics believed typical of an ordinary man

BLOKES > BLOKE

BLOKEY *same as* > BLOKEISH

BLOKIER > BLOKEY

BLOKIEST > BLOKEY

BLOKISH *same as* > BLOKEISH

BLONCKET *adj* blue-grey

BLOND *adj* (of hair) light-coloured ▷ *n* person with light-coloured hair

BLONDE *adj* (of hair) light-coloured ▷ *n* person with light-coloured hair

BLONDER > BLONDE

BLONDES > BLONDE

BLONDEST > BLONDE

BLONDINE *vb* dye hair blonde

BLONDINED > BLONDINE

BLONDINES > BLONDINE

BLONDING *n* act or an instance of dyeing hair blonde

BLONDINGS > BLONDING

BLONDISH > BLOND

BLONDNESS > BLOND

BLONDS > BLOND

BLOOD *n* red fluid that flows around the body ▷ *vb* initiate (a person) to war or hunting

BLOODBATH *n* massacre

BLOODED *adj* (of horses, cattle, etc) of good breeding

BLOODFIN *n* silvery red-finned S American freshwater fish, popular in aquariums

BLOODFINS > BLOODFIN

BLOODIED > BLOODY

BLOODIER > BLOODY

BLOODIES > BLOODY

BLOODIEST > BLOODY

BLOODILY > BLOODY

BLOODING > BLOOD

BLOODINGS > BLOOD

BLOODLESS *adj* without blood or bloodshed

BLOODLIKE > BLOOD

BLOODLINE *n* all the members of a family group over generations, esp regarding characteristics common to that group

BLOODLUST *n* desire to see bloodshed

BLOODRED *adj* having a deep red colour

BLOODROOT *n* N American plant with a single whitish flower and a fleshy red root that yields a red dye

BLOODS > BLOOD

BLOODSHED *n* slaughter or killing

BLOODSHOT *adj* (of an eye) inflamed

BLOODWOOD *n* any of several species of Australian eucalyptus that exude a red sap

BLOODWORM *n* red wormlike aquatic larva of the midge

BLOODWORT *n* plant with red dye in roots

BLOODY *adj* covered with blood ▷ *adv* extreme or extremely ▷ *vb* stain with blood

BLOODYING > BLOODY

BLOOEY *adj* out of order; faulty

BLOOIE *same as* > BLOOEY

BLOOK *n* book published on a blog

BLOOKS > BLOOK

BLOOM *n* blossom on a flowering plant ▷ *vb* (of flowers) open

BLOOMED *adj* (of a lens) coated to reduce light lost by reflection

BLOOMER *n* stupid mistake

BLOOMERS *pl n* woman's baggy underwear

BLOOMERY *n* place in which malleable iron is produced directly from iron ore

BLOOMIER > BLOOMY

BLOOMIEST > BLOOMY

BLOOMING *n* act of blooming

BLOOMINGS > BLOOMING

BLOOMLESS > BLOOM

BLOOMS > BLOOM

BLOOMY *adj* having a fine whitish coating on the surface

BLOOP *vb* (baseball) hit a ball into the air beyond the infield

BLOOPED > BLOOP

BLOOPER *n* stupid mistake

BLOOPERS > BLOOPER
BLOOPIER > BLOOPY
BLOOPIEST > BLOOPY
BLOOPING > BLOOP
BLOOPS > BLOOP
BLOOPY *adj* (in baseball) relating to a ball hit into the air beyond the infield
BLOOSME *archaic form of* > BLOSSOM
BLOOSMED > BLOOSME
BLOOSMES > BLOOSME
BLOOSMING > BLOOSME
BLOOTERED *adj* Scots word meaning drunk
BLOQUISTE *n* supporter of autonomy for Quebec
BLORE *n* strong blast of wind
BLORES > BLORE
BLOSSOM *n* flowers of a plant ▷ *vb* (of plants) flower
BLOSSOMED > BLOSSOM
BLOSSOMS > BLOSSOM
BLOSSOMY *adj* full of blossoms
BLOT *n* spot or stain ▷ *vb* cause a blemish in or on
BLOTCH *n* discoloured area or stain ▷ *vb* become or cause to become marked by such discoloration
BLOTCHED > BLOTCH
BLOTCHES > BLOTCH
BLOTCHIER > BLOTCHY
BLOTCHILY > BLOTCHY
BLOTCHING > BLOTCH
BLOTCHY *adj* covered in or marked by blotches
BLOTLESS > BLOT
BLOTS > BLOT
BLOTTED > BLOT
BLOTTER *n* sheet of blotting paper
BLOTTERS > BLOTTER
BLOTTIER > BLOTTY
BLOTTIEST > BLOTTY
BLOTTING *n* blot analysis
BLOTTINGS > BLOTTING
BLOTTO *adj* extremely drunk
BLOTTY *adj* covered in blots
BLOUBOK *same as* > BLAUBOK
BLOUBOKS > BLOUBOK
BLOUSE *n* woman's shirtlike garment ▷ *vb* hang or cause to hang in full loose folds
BLOUSED > BLOUSE
BLOUSES > BLOUSE
BLOUSIER > BLOUSY
BLOUSIEST > BLOUSY
BLOUSILY > BLOUSY
BLOUSING > BLOUSE
BLOUSON *n* short loose jacket with a tight waist
BLOUSONS > BLOUSON
BLOUSY *adj* loose; blouse-like
BLOVIATE *vb* discourse at length
BLOVIATED > BLOVIATE

BLOVIATES > BLOVIATE
BLOW *vb* (of air, the wind, etc) move ▷ *n* hard hit
BLOWBACK *n* gases escaping to the rear
BLOWBACKS > BLOWBACK
BLOWBALL *n* dandelion seed head
BLOWBALLS > BLOWBALL
BLOWBY *n* leakage of gas past the piston of an engine at maximum pressure
BLOWBYS > BLOWBY
BLOWDART *n* dart from a blowpipe
BLOWDARTS > BLOWDART
BLOWDOWN *n* accidental burst of a cooling pipe in a nuclear reactor
BLOWDOWNS > BLOWDOWN
BLOWED > BLOW
BLOWER *n* mechanical device, such as a fan, that blows
BLOWERS > BLOWER
BLOWFISH *a popular name for* > PUFFER
BLOWFLIES > BLOWFLY
BLOWFLY *n* fly that lays its eggs in meat
BLOWGUN *same as* > BLOWPIPE
BLOWGUNS > BLOWGUN
BLOWHARD *n* boastful person ▷ *adj* blustering or boastful
BLOWHARDS > BLOWHARD
BLOWHOLE *n* nostril of a whale
BLOWHOLES > BLOWHOLE
BLOWIE *n* bluebottle
BLOWIER > BLOWY
BLOWIES > BLOWIE
BLOWIEST > BLOWY
BLOWINESS > BLOWY
BLOWING *n* moving of air
BLOWINGS > BLOWING
BLOWJOB *vulgar slang term for* > FELLATIO
BLOWJOBS > BLOWJOB
BLOWKART *n* land vehicle with a sail
BLOWKARTS > BLOWKART
BLOWLAMP *another name for* > BLOWTORCH
BLOWLAMPS > BLOWLAMP
BLOWN > BLOW
BLOWOFF *n* discharge of a surplus fluid
BLOWOFFS > BLOWOFF
BLOWOUT *n* sudden loss of air in a tyre
BLOWOUTS > BLOWOUT
BLOWPIPE *n* long tube from which darts etc are shot by blowing
BLOWPIPES > BLOWPIPE

BLOWS > BLOW
BLOWSE *n* large, red-faced woman
BLOWSED *same as* > BLOWSY
BLOWSES > BLOWSE
BLOWSIER > BLOWSY
BLOWSIEST > BLOWSY
BLOWSILY > BLOWSY
BLOWSY *adj* fat, untidy, and red-faced
BLOWTORCH *n* small burner producing a very hot flame
BLOWTUBE *n* tube for blowing air or oxygen into a flame to intensify its heat
BLOWTUBES > BLOWTUBE
BLOWUP *n* fit of temper
BLOWUPS > BLOWUP
BLOWY *adj* windy
BLOWZE *variant of* > BLOWSE
BLOWZED *same as* > BLOWSY
BLOWZES > BLOWZE
BLOWZIER > BLOWZY
BLOWZIEST > BLOWZY
BLOWZILY > BLOWZY
BLOWZY *same as* > BLOWSY
BLUB *a slang word for* > BLUBBER
BLUBBED > BLUB
BLUBBER *vb* sob without restraint ▷ *adj* swollen or fleshy ▷ *n* fat of whales, seals, etc
BLUBBERED > BLUBBER
BLUBBERER > BLUBBER
BLUBBERS > BLUBBER
BLUBBERY *adj* of, containing, or like blubber
BLUBBING > BLUB
BLUBS > BLUB
BLUCHER *n* high shoe with laces over the tongue
BLUCHERS > BLUCHER
BLUD *n* slang term for a friend
BLUDE *Scots form of* > BLOOD
BLUDES > BLUDE
BLUDGE *vb* evade work ▷ *n* easy task
BLUDGED > BLUDGE
BLUDGEON *n* short thick club ▷ *vb* hit with a bludgeon
BLUDGEONS > BLUDGEON
BLUDGER *n* person who scrounges
BLUDGERS > BLUDGER
BLUDGES > BLUDGE
BLUDGING > BLUDGE
BLUDIE *Scots form of* > BLOODY
BLUDIER > BLUDIE
BLUDIEST > BLUDIE
BLUDS > BLUD
BLUDY *same as* > BLUDIE
BLUE *n* colour of a clear unclouded sky ▷ *adj* of the colour blue ▷ *vb* make or become blue

BLUEBACK *n* type of salmon
BLUEBACKS > BLUEBACK
BLUEBALL *n* type of European herb
BLUEBALLS > BLUEBALL
BLUEBEARD *n* any man who murders his wife or wives
BLUEBEAT *n* type of Jamaican pop music of the 1960s
BLUEBEATS > BLUEBEAT
BLUEBELL *n* flower with blue bell-shaped flowers
BLUEBELLS > BLUEBELL
BLUEBERRY *n* very small blackish edible fruit that grows on a North American shrub
BLUEBILL *another name for* > SCAUP
BLUEBILLS > BLUEBILL
BLUEBIRD *n* North American songbird with a blue plumage
BLUEBIRDS > BLUEBIRD
BLUEBLOOD *n* royal or aristocratic person
BLUEBOOK *n* (in Britain) a government publication, usually the report of a commission
BLUEBOOKS > BLUEBOOK
BLUEBUCK *same as* > BLAUBOK
BLUEBUCKS > BLUEBUCK
BLUEBUSH *n* blue-grey herbaceous Australian shrub
BLUECAP *another name for* > BLUETIT
BLUECAPS > BLUECAP
BLUECOAT *n* person who wears blue uniform
BLUECOATS > BLUECOAT
BLUECURLS *n* North American plant
BLUED > BLUE
BLUEFIN *another name for* > TUNNY
BLUEFINS > BLUEFIN
BLUEFISH *n* type of bluish marine food and game fish
BLUEGILL *n* common N American sunfish, an important freshwater food and game fish
BLUEGILLS > BLUEGILL
BLUEGOWN *n* in past, pauper, recipient of blue gown on king's birthday
BLUEGOWNS > BLUEGOWN
BLUEGRASS *n* any of several North American bluish-green grasses
BLUEGUM *n* widely cultivated Australian tree

BLUEGUMS > BLUEGUM
BLUEHEAD n type of fish
BLUEHEADS
> BLUEHEAD
BLUEING > BLUE
BLUEINGS > BLUE
BLUEISH same as
> BLUISH
BLUEJACK n type of oak tree
BLUEJACKS
> BLUEJACK
BLUEJAY n N American jay
BLUEJAYS > BLUEJAY
BLUEJEANS n blue denim jeans
BLUELINE n blue-toned photographic proof
BLUELINER n machine for making blueprints
BLUELINES
> BLUELINE
BLUELY > BLUE
BLUEMOUTH n type of deepwater fish
BLUENESS > BLUE
BLUENOSE n puritanical or prudish person
BLUENOSED
> BLUENOSE
BLUENOSES
> BLUENOSE
BLUEPOINT n type of small oyster
BLUEPRINT n photographic print of a plan ▷ vb make a blueprint of (a plan)
BLUER > BLUE
BLUES pl n type of music
BLUESHIFT n shift in the spectral lines of a stellar spectrum
BLUESIER > BLUES
BLUESIEST > BLUES
BLUESMAN n blues musician
BLUESMEN > BLUESMAN
BLUEST > BLUE
BLUESTEM n type of tall grass
BLUESTEMS
> BLUESTEM
BLUESTONE n blue-grey sandstone containing much clay, used for building and paving
BLUESY > BLUES
BLUET n N American plant with small four-petalled blue flowers
BLUETICK n fast-running dog
BLUETICKS
> BLUETICK
BLUETIT n small European bird
BLUETITS > BLUETIT
BLUETS > BLUET
BLUETTE n short, brilliant piece of music
BLUETTES > BLUETTE
BLUEWEED n Eurasian weed with blue flowers and pink buds
BLUEWEEDS
> BLUEWEED

BLUEWING n type of duck
BLUEWINGS
> BLUEWING
BLUEWOOD n type of Mexican shrub
BLUEWOODS
> BLUEWOOD
BLUEY adj bluish ▷ n informal Australian word meaning blanket
BLUEYS > BLUEY
BLUFF vb pretend to be confident in order to influence (someone) ▷ n act of bluffing ▷ adj good-naturedly frank and hearty
BLUFFABLE > BLUFF
BLUFFED > BLUFF
BLUFFER > BLUFF
BLUFFERS > BLUFF
BLUFFEST > BLUFF
BLUFFING > BLUFF
BLUFFLY > BLUFF
BLUFFNESS > BLUFF
BLUFFS > BLUFF
BLUGGIER > BLUGGY
BLUGGIEST > BLUGGY
BLUGGY same as
> BLOODY
BLUID Scots word for
> BLOOD
BLUIDIER > BLUID
BLUIDIEST > BLUID
BLUIDS > BLUID
BLUIDY > BLUID
BLUIER > BLUEY
BLUIEST > BLUEY
BLUING > BLUE
BLUINGS > BLUE
BLUISH adj slightly blue
BLUME Scots word for
> BLOOM
BLUMED > BLUME
BLUMES > BLUME
BLUMING > BLUME
BLUNDER n clumsy mistake ▷ vb make a blunder
BLUNDERED > BLUNDER
BLUNDERER > BLUNDER
BLUNDERS > BLUNDER
BLUNGE vb mix clay with water
BLUNGED > BLUNGE
BLUNGER n large vat in which the contents are mixed by rotating arms
BLUNGERS > BLUNGER
BLUNGES > BLUNGE
BLUNGING > BLUNGE
BLUNK vb ruin; botch
BLUNKED > BLUNK
BLUNKER > BLUNK
BLUNKERS > BLUNK
BLUNKING > BLUNK
BLUNKS > BLUNK
BLUNT adj not having a sharp edge or point ▷ vb make less sharp
BLUNTED > BLUNT
BLUNTER > BLUNT
BLUNTEST > BLUNT
BLUNTHEAD n frequent user of marijuana
BLUNTING > BLUNT
BLUNTISH > BLUNT

BLUNTLY > BLUNT
BLUNTNESS > BLUNT
BLUNTS > BLUNT
BLUR vb make or become vague or less distinct ▷ n something vague, hazy, or indistinct
BLURB n promotional description, as on the jacket of a book ▷ vb describe or recommend in a blurb
BLURBED > BLURB
BLURBING > BLURB
BLURBIST n writer of blurbs
BLURBISTS
> BLURBIST
BLURBS > BLURB
BLURRED > BLUR
BLURREDLY > BLUR
BLURRIER > BLUR
BLURRIEST > BLUR
BLURRILY > BLUR
BLURRING > BLUR
BLURRY > BLUR
BLURS > BLUR
BLURT vb utter suddenly and involuntarily
BLURTED > BLURT
BLURTER > BLURT
BLURTERS > BLURT
BLURTING > BLURT
BLURTINGS > BLURT
BLURTS > BLURT
BLUSH vb become red in the face, esp from embarrassment or shame ▷ n reddening of the face
BLUSHED > BLUSH
BLUSHER n cosmetic for giving the cheeks a rosy colour
BLUSHERS > BLUSHER
BLUSHES > BLUSH
BLUSHET n modest young woman
BLUSHETS > BLUSHET
BLUSHFUL > BLUSH
BLUSHING > BLUSH
BLUSHINGS > BLUSH
BLUSHLESS > BLUSH
BLUSTER vb speak loudly or in a bullying way ▷ n empty threats or protests
BLUSTERED > BLUSTER
BLUSTERER > BLUSTER
BLUSTERS > BLUSTER
BLUSTERY adj (of wind) noisy or gusty
BLUSTROUS adj inclined to bluster
BLUTWURST n blood sausage
BLYPE n piece of skin peeled off after sunburn
BLYPES > BLYPE
BO interj exclamation uttered to startle or surprise someone ▷ n fellow, buddy
BOA n large nonvenomous snake
BOAB short for > BAOBAB
BOABS > BOAB
BOAK same as > BOKE
BOAKED > BOAK
BOAKING > BOAK

BOAKS > BOAK
BOAR n uncastrated male pig
BOARD n long flat piece of sawn timber ▷ vb go aboard (a train, aeroplane, etc)
BOARDABLE > BOARD
BOARDED > BOARD
BOARDER n person who pays rent for accommodation in someone else's home
BOARDERS > BOARDER
BOARDIES pl n board shorts
BOARDING n act of embarking on an aircraft, train, ship, etc
BOARDINGS
> BOARDING
BOARDLIKE > BOARD
BOARDMAN n man who carries a sandwich board
BOARDMEN > BOARDMAN
BOARDROOM n room where the board of a company meets
BOARDS > BOARD
BOARDWALK n promenade, esp along a beach, usually made of planks
BOARFISH n type of spiny-finned marine fish with a compressed body, a long snout, and large eyes
BOARHOUND n dog used to hunt boar
BOARISH adj coarse, cruel, or sensual
BOARISHLY > BOARISH
BOARS > BOAR
BOART same as > BORT
BOARTS > BOART
BOAS > BOA
BOAST vb speak too proudly about one's talents etc ▷ n bragging statement
BOASTED > BOAST
BOASTER > BOAST
BOASTERS > BOAST
BOASTFUL adj tending to boast
BOASTING > BOAST
BOASTINGS > BOAST
BOASTLESS > BOAST
BOASTS > BOAST
BOAT n small vehicle for travelling across water ▷ vb travel in a boat
BOATABLE adj able to be carried by boat
BOATBILL n nocturnal tropical American wading bird with a broad flattened bill
BOATBILLS
> BOATBILL
BOATED > BOAT
BOATEL n waterside hotel catering for boating people
BOATELS > BOATEL
BOATER n flat straw hat
BOATERS > BOATER
BOATFUL > BOAT

BOATFULS > BOAT

BOATHOOK *n* hooked pole used for fending off other vessels or obstacles

BOATHOOKS > BOATHOOK

BOATHOUSE *n* shelter by the edge of a river, lake, etc, for housing boats

BOATIE *n* boating enthusiast

BOATIES > BOATIE

BOATING *n* rowing, sailing, or cruising in boats as a form of recreation

BOATINGS > BOATING

BOATLIFT *n* evacuation by boat

BOATLIFTS > BOATLIFT

BOATLIKE > BOAT

BOATLOAD *n* amount of cargo or number of people held by a boat or ship

BOATLOADS > BOATLOAD

BOATMAN *n* man who works on, hires out, or repairs boats

BOATMEN > BOATMAN

BOATNECK *n* wide open neck on garment

BOATNECKS > BOATNECK

BOATPORT *n* enclosure for boats

BOATPORTS > BOATPORT

BOATS > BOAT

BOATSMAN *same as* **>** BOATMAN

BOATSMEN > BOATSMAN

BOATSWAIN *n* petty officer on a merchant ship or a warrant officer on a warship who is responsible for the maintenance of the ship and its equipment

BOATTAIL *n* type of blackbird

BOATTAILS > BOATTAIL

BOATYARD *n* place where boats are kept, repaired, etc

BOATYARDS > BOATYARD

BOB *vb* move or cause to move up and down repeatedly ▷ *n* short abrupt movement, as of the head

BOBA *n* type of Chinese tea

BOBAC *same as* **>** BOBAK

BOBACS > BOBAC

BOBAK *n* type of marmot

BOBAKS > BOBAK

BOBAS > BOBA

BOBBED > BOB

BOBBEJAAN *n* baboon

BOBBER *n* type of float for fishing

BOBBERIES > BOBBERY

BOBBERS > BOBBER

BOBBERY *n* mixed pack of hunting dogs ▷ *adj* noisy or excitable

BOBBIES > BOBBY

BOBBIN *n* reel on which thread is wound

BOBBINET *n* netted fabric of hexagonal mesh, made on a lace machine

BOBBINETS > BOBBINET

BOBBING > BOB

BOBBINS > BOBBIN

BOBBISH *adj* cheery

BOBBITT *vb* sever the penis of

BOBBITTED > BOBBITT

BOBBITTS > BOBBITT

BOBBLE *n* small ball of material, usu for decoration ▷ *vb* (of a ball) to bounce erratically because of an uneven playing surface

BOBBLED > BOBBLE

BOBBLES > BOBBLE

BOBBLIER > BOBBLY

BOBBLIEST > BOBBLY

BOBBLING > BOBBLE

BOBBLY *adj* (of fabric) covered in small balls; worn

BOBBY *n* slang word for a police officer

BOBBYSOCK *n* ankle-length sock worn esp by girls

BOBBYSOX *pl n* bobbysocks

BOBCAT *n* N American feline

BOBCATS > BOBCAT

BOBECHE *n* candle drip-catcher

BOBECHES > BOBECHE

BOBFLOAT *n* small buoyant float, usually consisting of a quill stuck through a piece of cork

BOBFLOATS > BOBFLOAT

BOBLET *n* two-person bobsleigh

BOBLETS > BOBLET

BOBO *n* rich person who holds bohemian values

BOBOL *n* type of fraud ▷ *vb* commit a bobol

BOBOLINK *n* American songbird

BOBOLINKS > BOBOLINK

BOBOLLED > BOBOL

BOBOLLING > BOBOL

BOBOLS > BOBOL

BOBOS > BOBO

BOBOTIE *n* dish of curried mince

BOBOTIES > BOBOTIE

BOBOWLER *n* large moth

BOBOWLERS > BOBOWLER

BOBS > BOB

BOBSKATE *n* child's skate with two parallel blades

BOBSKATES > BOBSKATE

BOBSLED *same as* **>** BOBSLEIGH

BOBSLEDS > BOBSLED

BOBSLEIGH *n* sledge for racing down an icy track ▷ *vb* ride on a bobsleigh

BOBSTAY *n* stay between a bowsprit and the stem of a vessel

BOBSTAYS > BOBSTAY

BOBTAIL *n* docked tail ▷ *adj* having the tail cut short ▷ *vb* dock the tail of

BOBTAILED > BOBTAIL

BOBTAILS > BOBTAIL

BOBWEIGHT *n* balance weight

BOBWHEEL *n* poetic device

BOBWHEELS > BOBWHEEL

BOBWHITE *n* brown N American quail

BOBWHITES > BOBWHITE

BOBWIG *n* type of short wig

BOBWIGS > BOBWIG

BOCACCIO *n* edible American fish

BOCACCIOS > BOCACCIO

BOCAGE *n* wooded countryside characteristic of northern France

BOCAGES > BOCAGE

BOCCA *n* round opening of a glass-furnace

BOCCAS > BOCCA

BOCCE *same as* **>** BOCCIE

BOCCES > BOCCE

BOCCI *same as* **>** BOCCIE

BOCCIA *same as* **>** BOCCIE

BOCCIAS > BOCCIA

BOCCIE *n* Italian version of bowls

BOCCIES > BOCCIE

BOCCIS > BOCCI

BOCK *variant spelling of* **>** BOKE

BOCKED > BOCK

BOCKEDY *adj* (of a structure, piece of furniture, etc) unsteady

BOCKING > BOCK

BOCKS > BOCK

BOCONCINI *pl n* small pieces of mozzarella

BOD *n* person

BODACH *n* old man

BODACHS > BODACH

BODACIOUS *adj* impressive or remarkable

BODDLE *same as* **>** BODLE

BODDLES > BODDLE

BODE *vb* portend or presage

BODED > BODE

BODEFUL *adj* portentous

BODEGA *n* shop in a Spanish-speaking country that sells wine

BODEGAS > BODEGA

BODEGUERO *n* wine seller or grocer

BODEMENT > BODE

BODEMENTS > BODE

BODES > BODE

BODGE *vb* make a mess of

BODGED > BODGE

BODGER *n* labourer who made chairs from felled trees

BODGERS > BODGER

BODGES > BODGE

BODGIE *n* unruly or uncouth young man, esp in the 1950s ▷ *adj* inferior

BODGIER > BODGIE

BODGIES > BODGIE

BODGIEST > BODGIE

BODGING > BODGE

BODHI *n* as in *bodhi tree* holy tree of Buddhists

BODHIS > BODHI

BODHRAN *n* shallow one-sided drum popular in Irish and Scottish folk music

BODHRANS > BODHRAN

BODICE *n* upper part of a dress

BODICES > BODICE

BODIED > BODY

BODIES > BODY

BODIKIN *n* little body

BODIKINS > BODIKIN

BODILESS *adj* having no body or substance

BODILY *adj* relating to the body ▷ *adv* by taking hold of the body

BODING > BODE

BODINGLY > BODE

BODINGS > BODE

BODKIN *n* blunt large-eyed needle

BODKINS > BODKIN

BODLE *n* small obsolete Scottish coin

BODLES > BODLE

BODRAG *n* enemy attack

BODRAGS > BODRAG

BODS > BOD

BODY *n* entire physical structure of an animal or human ▷ *vb* give form to

BODYBOARD *n* surfboard that is shorter and blunter than the standard board and on which the surfer lies rather than stands

BODYBUILD *vb* build up the muscles with exercises

BODYBUILT > BODYBUILD

BODYCHECK *n* obstruction of another player ▷ *vb* deliver a bodycheck to (an opponent)

BODYGUARD *n* person or group of people employed to protect someone

BODYING > BODY

BODYLINE *n* (in cricket) fast bowling aimed at the batsman's body

BODYLINES > BODYLINE

BODYMAN *n* person who repairs car bodies

BODYMEN > BODYMAN

BODYSHELL *n* external shell of a motor vehicle

BODYSIDE *n* side of a body of a vehicle

BODYSIDES > BODYSIDE

BODYSUIT n one-piece undergarment for a baby

BODYSUITS > BODYSUIT

BODYSURF vb ride a wave by lying on it without a surfboard

BODYSURFS > BODYSURF

BODYWASH n liquid soap for use in the shower or bath

BODYWORK n outer shell of a motor vehicle

BODYWORKS > BODYWORK

BOEHMITE n type of grey, red, or brown mineral

BOEHMITES > BOEHMITE

BOEP n South African word for a big belly

BOEPS > BOEP

BOERBUL n crossbred mastiff used esp as a watchdog

BOERBULL same as > BOERBUL

BOERBULLS > BOERBULL

BOERBULS > BOERBUL

BOEREWORS n spiced sausage

BOERTJIE South African word for > FRIEND

BOERTJIES > BOERTJIE

BOET n brother

BOETS > BOET

BOEUF n as in boeuf bourguignon type of beef casserole

BOEUFS > BOEUF

BOFF n boffin ▷ vb hit

BOFFED > BOFF

BOFFIN n scientist or expert

BOFFING > BOFF

BOFFINIER > BOFFINY

BOFFINS > BOFFIN

BOFFINY adj like a boffin

BOFFO n boffin

BOFFOLA n great success

BOFFOLAS > BOFFOLA

BOFFOS > BOFFO

BOFFS > BOFF

BOG n wet spongy ground ▷ vb mire or delay

BOGAN n youth who dresses and behaves rebelliously

BOGANS > BOGAN

BOGART vb monopolize or keep to oneself selfishly

BOGARTED > BOGART

BOGARTING > BOGART

BOGARTS > BOGART

BOGBEAN same as > BUCKBEAN

BOGBEANS > BOGBEAN

BOGEY n evil or mischievous spirit ▷ vb play (a hole) in one stroke over par

BOGEYED > BOGEY

BOGEYING > BOGEY

BOGEYISM n demonization

BOGEYISMS > BOGEYISM

BOGEYMAN n frightening person, real or imaginary, used as a threat, esp to children

BOGEYMEN > BOGEYMAN

BOGEYS > BOGEY

BOGGARD same as > BOGGART

BOGGARDS > BOGGARD

BOGGART n ghost or poltergeist

BOGGARTS > BOGGART

BOGGED > BOG

BOGGER n lavatory

BOGGERS > BOGGER

BOGGIER > BOG

BOGGIEST > BOG

BOGGINESS > BOG

BOGGING > BOG

BOGGISH > BOG

BOGGLE vb be surprised, confused, or alarmed

BOGGLED > BOGGLE

BOGGLER > BOGGLE

BOGGLERS > BOGGLE

BOGGLES > BOGGLE

BOGGLING > BOGGLE

BOGGY > BOG

BOGHEAD adj relating to variety of coal from which paraffin can be derived

BOGHOLE n natural hole of wet spongy ground

BOGHOLES > BOGHOLE

BOGIE same as > BOGEY

BOGIED > BOGIE

BOGIEING > BOGIE

BOGIES > BOGIE

BOGLAND n area of wetland

BOGLANDS > BOGLAND

BOGLE n rhythmic dance performed to ragga music ▷ vb perform such a dance

BOGLED > BOGLE

BOGLES > BOGLE

BOGLING > BOGLE

BOGMAN n body of a person found preserved in a peat bog

BOGMEN > BOGMAN

BOGOAK n oak or other wood found preserved in peat bogs

BOGOAKS > BOGOAK

BOGONG n large nocturnal Australian moth

BOGONGS > BOGONG

BOGS > BOG

BOGUE n type of Mediterranean fish

BOGUES > BOGUE

BOGUS adj not genuine

BOGUSLY > BOGUS

BOGUSNESS > BOGUS

BOGWOOD same as > BOGOAK

BOGWOODS > BOGWOOD

BOGY same as > BOGEY

BOGYISM same as > BOGEYISM

BOGYISMS > BOGYISM

BOGYMAN same as > BOGEYMAN

BOGYMEN > BOGYMAN

BOH same as > BO

BOHEA n black Chinese tea

BOHEAS > BOHEA

BOHEMIA n area frequented by unconventional (esp creative) people

BOHEMIAN adj unconventional in lifestyle or appearance ▷ n person, esp an artist or writer, who lives an unconventional life

BOHEMIANS > BOHEMIAN

BOHEMIAS > BOHEMIA

BOHO short for > BOHEMIAN

BOHOS > BOHO

BOHRIUM n element artificially produced in minute quantities

BOHRIUMS > BOHRIUM

BOHS > BOH

BOI n lesbian who dresses like a boy

BOIL vb change from a liquid to a vapour so quickly that bubbles are formed ▷ n state or action of boiling

BOILABLE > BOIL

BOILED > BOIL

BOILER n piece of equipment which provides hot water

BOILERIES > BOILERY

BOILERMAN n man who looks after boilers

BOILERMEN > BOILERMAN

BOILERS > BOILER

BOILERY n place where water is boiled to extract salt

BOILING adj very hot ▷ n sweet

BOILINGLY > BOILING

BOILINGS > BOILING

BOILOFF n quantity of liquefied gases lost in evaporation

BOILOFFS > BOILOFF

BOILOVER n surprising result in a sporting event, esp in a horse race

BOILOVERS > BOILOVER

BOILS > BOIL

BOING vb rebound making a noise

BOINGED > BOING

BOINGING > BOING

BOINGS > BOING

BOINK same as > BOING

BOINKED > BOINK

BOINKING > BOINK

BOINKS > BOINK

BOIS > BOI

BOISERIE n finely crafted wood-carving

BOISERIES > BOISERIE

BOITE n artist's portfolio

BOITES > BOITE

BOK n S African antelope

BOKE vb retch or vomit ▷ n retch

BOKED > BOKE

BOKEH n blurred area of an image

BOKEHS > BOKEH

BOKES > BOKE

BOKING > BOKE

BOKKEN n wooden practice sword in kendo

BOKKENS > BOKKEN

BOKO slang word for > NOSE

BOKOS > BOKO

BOKS > BOK

BOLA n missile used by gauchos and Indians of South America

BOLAR adj relating to clay

BOLAS same as > BOLA

BOLASES > BOLAS

BOLD adj confident and fearless ▷ n boldface ▷ vb be or make bold

BOLDED > BOLD

BOLDEN vb make bold

BOLDENED > BOLDEN

BOLDENING > BOLDEN

BOLDENS > BOLDEN

BOLDER > BOLD

BOLDEST > BOLD

BOLDFACE n weight of type characterized by thick heavy lines ▷ vb print in boldface

BOLDFACED > BOLDFACE

BOLDFACES > BOLDFACE

BOLDING > BOLD

BOLDLY > BOLD

BOLDNESS > BOLD

BOLDS > BOLD

BOLE n tree trunk

BOLECTION n stepped moulding covering and projecting beyond the joint between two members having surfaces at different levels

BOLERO n (music for) traditional Spanish dance

BOLEROS > BOLERO

BOLES > BOLE

BOLETE same as > BOLETUS

BOLETES > BOLETE

BOLETI > BOLETUS

BOLETUS n type of fungus

BOLETUSES > BOLETUS

BOLIDE n large exceptionally bright meteor that often explodes

BOLIDES > BOLIDE

BOLINE n (in Wicca) a knife

BOLINES > BOLINE

BOLIVAR n standard monetary unit of Venezuela, equal to 100 céntimos

BOLIVARES > BOLIVAR

BOLIVARS > BOLIVAR

BOLIVIA n type of woollen fabric

BOLIVIANO n (until 1963 and from 1987) the standard monetary unit of Bolivia, equal to 100 centavos

BOLIVIAS > BOLIVIA
BOLIX *same as* > BOLLOCKS
BOLIXED > BOLIX
BOLIXES > BOLIX
BOLIXING > BOLIX
BOLL *n* rounded seed capsule of cotton, flax, etc ▷ *vb* form into a boll
BOLLARD *n* short thick post used to prevent the passage of motor vehicles
BOLLARDS > BOLLARD
BOLLED > BOLL
BOLLEN > BOLL
BOLLETRIE *n* type of tree of the Caribbean
BOLLING > BOLL
BOLLIX *same as* > BOLLOCKS
BOLLIXED > BOLLIX
BOLLIXES > BOLLIX
BOLLIXING > BOLLIX
BOLLOCK *vb* vulgar slang word meaning rebuke severely
BOLLOCKED > BOLLOCK
BOLLOCKS *pl n* vulgar word for the testicles ▷ *interj* exclamation of annoyance, disbelief, etc ▷ *vb* rebuke severely
BOLLOX *same as* > BOLLOCKS
BOLLOXED > BOLLOX
BOLLOXES > BOLLOX
BOLLOXING > BOLLOX
BOLLS > BOLL
BOLLWORM *n* any of various moth caterpillars that feed on and destroy cotton bolls
BOLLWORMS > BOLLWORM
BOLO *n* large single-edged knife, originating in the Philippines
BOLOGNA *n* type of sausage
BOLOGNAS > BOLOGNA
BOLOGNESE *n* Italian meat and tomato sauce
BOLOGRAPH *n* record made by a bolometer
BOLOMETER *n* sensitive instrument for measuring radiant energy by the increase in the resistance of an electrical conductor
BOLOMETRY > BOLOMETER
BOLONEY *variant spelling of* > BALONEY
BOLONEYS > BOLONEY
BOLOS > BOLO
BOLSHEVIK *n* any political radical
BOLSHIE *adj* difficult or rebellious ▷ *n* any political radical
BOLSHIER > BOLSHIE
BOLSHIES > BOLSHIE
BOLSHIEST > BOLSHIE
BOLSHY *same as* > BOLSHIE
BOLSON *n* desert valley surrounded by mountains, with a shallow lake at the centre

BOLSONS > BOLSON
BOLSTER *vb* support or strengthen ▷ *n* long narrow pillow
BOLSTERED > BOLSTER
BOLSTERER > BOLSTER
BOLSTERS > BOLSTER
BOLT *n* sliding metal bar for fastening a door etc ▷ *vb* run away suddenly
BOLTED > BOLT
BOLTER > BOLT
BOLTERS > BOLT
BOLTHEAD *n* glass receptacle used in chemistry
BOLTHEADS > BOLTHEAD
BOLTHOLE *n* place of escape from danger
BOLTHOLES > BOLTHOLE
BOLTING > BOLT
BOLTINGS > BOLT
BOLTLESS > BOLT
BOLTLIKE > BOLT
BOLTONIA *n* N American plant with daisy-like flowers with white, violet, or pinkish rays
BOLTONIAS > BOLTONIA
BOLTROPE *n* rope sewn to the foot or luff of a sail to strengthen it
BOLTROPES > BOLTROPE
BOLTS > BOLT
BOLUS *same as* > BOLE
BOLUSES > BOLUS
BOMA *n* enclosure set up to protect a camp, herd of animals, etc
BOMAS > BOMA
BOMB *n* container fitted with explosive material ▷ *vb* attack with bombs
BOMBABLE > BOMB
BOMBARD *vb* attack with heavy gunfire or bombs ▷ *n* ancient type of cannon that threw stone balls
BOMBARDE *n* alto wind instrument similar to the oboe
BOMBARDED > BOMBARD
BOMBARDER > BOMBARD
BOMBARDES > BOMBARDE
BOMBARDON *n* brass instrument of the tuba type, similar to a sousaphone
BOMBARDS > BOMBARD
BOMBASINE *same as* > BOMBAZINE
BOMBAST *n* pompous language ▷ *vb* speak pompous language
BOMBASTED > BOMBAST
BOMBASTER > BOMBAST
BOMBASTIC > BOMBAST
BOMBASTS > BOMBAST
BOMBAX *n* type of S American tree
BOMBAXES > BOMBAX
BOMBAZINE *n* twill fabric, usually of silk and

worsted, formerly worn dyed black for mourning
BOMBE *n* dessert of ice cream lined or filled with custard, cake crumbs, etc ▷ *adj* (of furniture) having a projecting swollen shape
BOMBED > BOMB
BOMBER *n* aircraft that drops bombs
BOMBERS > BOMBER
BOMBES > BOMBE
BOMBESIN *n* hormone found in brain
BOMBESINS > BOMBESIN
BOMBILATE *same as* > BOMBINATE
BOMBINATE *vb* make a buzzing noise
BOMBING > BOMB
BOMBINGS > BOMB
BOMBLET *n* small bomb
BOMBLETS > BOMBLET
BOMBLOAD *n* quantity of bombs carried at one time
BOMBLOADS > BOMBLOAD
BOMBO *same as* > BUMBO
BOMBORA *n* submerged reef
BOMBORAS > BOMBORA
BOMBOS > BOMBO
BOMBPROOF *adj* able to withstand the impact of a bomb
BOMBS > BOMB
BOMBSHELL *n* shocking or unwelcome surprise
BOMBSIGHT *n* mechanical or electronic device in an aircraft for aiming bombs
BOMBSITE *n* area where the buildings have been destroyed by bombs
BOMBSITES > BOMBSITE
BOMBYCID *n* type of moth of the silkworm family
BOMBYCIDS > BOMBYCID
BOMBYCOID *adj* of or like bombycids
BOMBYX *n* type of moth
BOMBYXES > BOMBYX
BOMMIE *n* outcrop of coral reef
BOMMIES > BOMMIE
BON *adj* good
BONA *pl n* goods
BONACI *n* type of fish
BONACIS > BONACI
BONAMANI > BONAMANO
BONAMANO *n* gratuity
BONAMIA *n* parasite
BONAMIAS > BONAMIA
BONANZA *n* sudden good luck or wealth
BONANZAS > BONANZA
BONASSUS *same as* > BONASUS
BONASUS *n* European bison
BONASUSES > BONASUS
BONBON *n* sweet
BONBONS > BONBON

BONCE *n* head
BONCES > BONCE
BOND *n* something that binds, fastens or holds together ▷ *vb* bind
BONDABLE > BOND
BONDAGE *n* slavery
BONDAGER > BONDAGE
BONDAGERS > BONDAGE
BONDAGES > BONDAGE
BONDED *adj* consisting of, secured by, or operating under a bond or bonds
BONDER *same as* > BONDSTONE
BONDERS > BONDER
BONDING *n* process by which individuals become emotionally attached to one another
BONDINGS > BONDING
BONDLESS > BOND
BONDMAID *n* unmarried female servant
BONDMAIDS > BONDMAID
BONDMAN *same as* > BONDSMAN
BONDMEN > BONDMAN
BONDS > BOND
BONDSMAN *n* person bound by bond to act as surety for another
BONDSMEN > BONDSMAN
BONDSTONE *n* long stone or brick laid in a wall as a header
BONDUC *n* type of North American tree
BONDUCS > BONDUC
BONDWOMAN *n* female servant
BONDWOMEN > BONDWOMAN
BONE *n* any of the hard parts in the body that form the skeleton ▷ *vb* remove the bones from (meat for cooking etc)
BONEBED *n* site where dinosaur fossils are found
BONEBEDS > BONEBED
BONEBLACK *n* black residue from the destructive distillation of bones, containing about 10 per cent carbon and 80 per cent calcium phosphate, used as a decolorizing agent and pigment
BONED > BONE
BONEFISH *n* type of silvery marine game fish occurring in warm shallow waters
BONEHEAD *n* stupid or obstinate person
BONEHEADS > BONEHEAD
BONELESS > BONE
BONELIKE *adj* like bone
BONEMEAL *n* product of dried and ground animal bones, used as a fertilizer or in stock feeds
BONEMEALS > BONEMEAL
BONER *n* blunder

BONERS > BONER

BONES > BONE

BONESET n N American plant with flat clusters of small white flowers

BONESETS > BONESET

BONETIRED adj completely exhausted

BONEY same as > BONY

BONEYARD an informal name for a > CEMETERY

BONEYARDS > BONEYARD

BONEYER > BONEY

BONEYEST > BONEY

BONFIRE n large outdoor fire

BONFIRES > BONFIRE

BONG n deep reverberating sound, as of a large bell ▷ vb make a deep reverberating sound

BONGED > BONG

BONGING > BONG

BONGO n small drum played with the fingers

BONGOES > BONGO

BONGOIST n bongo player

BONGOISTS > BONGOIST

BONGOS > BONGO

BONGRACE n shade for face

BONGRACES > BONGRACE

BONGS > BONG

BONHAM n piglet

BONHAMS > BONHAM

BONHOMIE n cheerful friendliness

BONHOMIES > BONHOMIE

BONHOMMIE same as > BONHOMIE

BONHOMOUS adj exhibiting bonhomie

BONIATO n sweet potato

BONIATOS > BONIATO

BONIBELL same as > BONNIBELL

BONIBELLS > BONIBELL

BONIE same as > BONNY

BONIER > BONY

BONIEST > BONY

BONIFACE n pub landlord

BONIFACES > BONIFACE

BONILASSE n attractive young woman

BONINESS > BONY

BONING > BONE

BONINGS > BONE

BONISM n doctrine that the world is good, although not the best of all possible worlds

BONISMS > BONISM

BONIST > BONISM

BONISTS > BONISM

BONITA slang term for > HEROIN

BONITAS > BONITA

BONITO n small tuna-like marine food fish

BONITOES > BONITO

BONITOS > BONITO

BONJOUR interj hello

BONK vb hit

BONKED > BONK

BONKERS adj crazy

BONKING > BONK

BONKINGS > BONK

BONKS > BONK

BONNE n housemaid or female servant

BONNES > BONNE

BONNET n metal cover over a vehicle's engine ▷ vb place a bonnet on

BONNETED > BONNET

BONNETING > BONNET

BONNETS > BONNET

BONNIBELL n beautiful young woman

BONNIE same as > BONNY

BONNIER > BONNY

BONNIES > BONNY

BONNIEST > BONNY

BONNILY > BONNY

BONNINESS > BONNY

BONNOCK n thick oatmeal cake

BONNOCKS > BONNOCK

BONNY adj beautiful ▷ adv agreeably or well ▷ n beautiful person

BONOBO n type of anthropoid ape of central W Africa

BONOBOS > BONOBO

BONSAI n ornamental miniature tree or shrub

BONSELA n small gift of money

BONSELAS > BONSELA

BONSELLA same as > BONSELA

BONSELLAS > BONSELLA

BONSOIR interj good evening

BONSPELL same as > BONSPIEL

BONSPELLS > BONSPELL

BONSPIEL n curling match

BONSPIELS > BONSPIEL

BONTBOK n antelope found in S Africa

BONTBOKS > BONTBOK

BONTEBOK n S African antelope

BONTEBOKS > BONTEBOK

BONUS n something given, paid, or received above what is due or expected ▷ vb (in Scrabble) play all seven of one's tiles in a single turn

BONUSED > BONUS

BONUSES > BONUS

BONUSING n (in Scrabble) act of playing all seven of one's tiles in a single turn

BONUSINGS > BONUSING

BONUSSED > BONUS

BONUSSES > BONUS

BONUSSING > BONUS

BONXIE n great skua

BONXIES > BONXIE

BONY adj having many bones

BONZA same as > BONZER

BONZE n Chinese or Japanese Buddhist priest or monk

BONZER adj excellent

BONZES > BONZE

BOO interj shout of disapproval ▷ vb shout 'boo' to show disapproval

BOOAI same as > BOOHAI

BOOAIS > BOOAI

BOOAY same as > BOOHAI

BOOAYS > BOOAY

BOOB n foolish mistake ▷ vb make a foolish mistake ▷ adj of poor quality, similar to that provided in prison

BOOBED > BOOB

BOOBHEAD n repeat offender in a prison

BOOBHEADS > BOOBHEAD

BOOBIALLA n type of tree or shrub

BOOBIE same as > BOOBY

BOOBIES > BOOBY

BOOBING > BOOB

BOOBIRD n person who boos

BOOBIRDS > BOOBIRD

BOOBISH adj doltish

BOOBOISIE n group of people considered as stupid

BOOBOO n blunder

BOOBOOK n small spotted Australian brown owl

BOOBOOKS > BOOBOOK

BOOBOOS > BOOBOO

BOOBS > BOOB

BOOBY n foolish person

BOOBYISH > BOOBY

BOOBYISM > BOOBY

BOOBYISMS > BOOBY

BOOCOO same as > BEAUCOUP

BOOCOOS > BOOCOO

BOODIE n type of kangaroo

BOODIED > BOODY

BOODIES > BOODY

BOODLE n money or valuables that are counterfeit or used as a bribe ▷ vb give or receive money corruptly or illegally

BOODLED > BOODLE

BOODLER > BOODLE

BOODLERS > BOODLE

BOODLES > BOODLE

BOODLING > BOODLE

BOODY vb sulk

BOODYING > BOODY

BOOED > BOO

BOOFHEAD n stupid person

BOOFHEADS > BOOFHEAD

BOOFIER > BOOFY

BOOFIEST > BOOFY

BOOFY adj muscular and strong but stupid

BOOGALOO n type of dance performed to rock and roll music ▷ vb dance a boogaloo

BOOGALOOS > BOOGALOO

BOOGER n piece of dried mucus from the nose

BOOGERMAN American form of > BOGEYMAN

BOOGERMEN > BOOGERMAN

BOOGERS > BOOGER

BOOGEY same as > BOOGIE

BOOGEYED > BOOGEY

BOOGEYING > BOOGEY

BOOGEYMAN same as > BOGEYMAN

BOOGEYMEN > BOOGEYMAN

BOOGEYS > BOOGEY

BOOGIE vb dance to fast pop music ▷ n session of dancing to pop music

BOOGIED > BOOGIE

BOOGIEING > BOOGIE

BOOGIEMAN same as > BOGEYMAN

BOOGIEMEN > BOOGIEMAN

BOOGIES > BOOGIE

BOOGY same as > BOOGIE

BOOGYING > BOOGY

BOOGYMAN same as > BOGEYMAN

BOOGYMEN > BOOGYMAN

BOOH same as > BOO

BOOHAI n as in up the boohai thoroughly lost

BOOHAIS > BOOHAI

BOOHED > BOOH

BOOHING > BOOH

BOOHOO vb sob or pretend to sob noisily ▷ n distressed or pretended sobbing

BOOHOOED > BOOHOO

BOOHOOING > BOOHOO

BOOHOOS > BOOHOO

BOOHS > BOOH

BOOING n act of booing

BOOINGS > BOOING

BOOJUM n American tree

BOOJUMS > BOOJUM

BOOK n number of pages bound together between covers ▷ vb reserve (a place, passage, etc) in advance

BOOKABLE > BOOK

BOOKBAG n bag for books

BOOKBAGS > BOOKBAG

BOOKCASE n piece of furniture containing shelves for books

BOOKCASES > BOOKCASE

BOOKED > BOOK

BOOKEND n one of a pair of supports for holding books upright ▷ vb occur or be located on either side (of something)

BOOKENDED > BOOKEND

BOOKENDS > BOOKEND

BOOKER > BOOK

BOOKERS > BOOK

BOOKFUL > BOOK

BOOKFULS > BOOK

BOOKIE *short for*
> BOOKMAKER

BOOKIER > BOOKY

BOOKIES > BOOKIE

BOOKIEST > BOOKY

BOOKING *n* reservation,
as of a table or seat

BOOKINGS > BOOKING

BOOKISH *adj* fond of
reading

BOOKISHLY > BOOKISH

BOOKLAND *n* common
land given to private
owner

BOOKLANDS
> BOOKLAND

BOOKLESS > BOOK

BOOKLET *n* thin book
with paper covers

BOOKLETS > BOOKLET

BOOKLICE
> BOOKLOUSE

BOOKLIGHT *n* small light
that can be clipped onto a
book for reading by

BOOKLIKE *adj* like a book

BOOKLORE *n* knowledge
or beliefs gleaned from
books

BOOKLORES
> BOOKLORE

BOOKLOUSE *n* wingless
insect that feeds on
bookbinding paste, etc

BOOKMAKER *n* person
whose occupation is
taking bets

BOOKMAN *n* learned
person

BOOKMARK *n* address for a
website stored on a
computer so that the user
can easily return to the site
▷ *vb* identify and store (a
website) so that one can
return to it quickly and
easily

BOOKMARKS
> BOOKMARK

BOOKMEN > BOOKMAN

BOOKOO *same as*
> BOOCOO

BOOKOOS > BOOKOO

BOOKPLATE *n* label
bearing the owner's name
and an individual design or
coat of arms, pasted into a
book

BOOKRACK *n* rack for
holding books

BOOKRACKS
> BOOKRACK

BOOKREST *n* stand for
supporting open book

BOOKRESTS
> BOOKREST

BOOKS > BOOK

BOOKSHELF *n* shelf for
books

BOOKSHOP *n* shop where
books are sold

BOOKSHOPS
> BOOKSHOP

BOOKSIE *same as*
> BOOKSY

BOOKSIER > BOOKSY

BOOKSIEST > BOOKSY

BOOKSTALL *n* stall or
stand where periodicals,

newspapers, or books are
sold

BOOKSTAND *n* support
for open book

BOOKSTORE *same as*
> BOOKSHOP

BOOKSY *adj* inclined to be
bookish or literary

BOOKWORK *n* academic
study

BOOKWORKS
> BOOKWORK

BOOKWORM *n* person
devoted to reading

BOOKWORMS
> BOOKWORM

BOOKY *adj* bookish

BOOL *n* bowling ball ▷ *vb*
play bowls

BOOLED > BOOL

BOOLING > BOOL

BOOLS > BOOL

BOOM *vb* make a loud deep
echoing sound ▷ *n* loud
deep echoing sound

BOOMBOX *n* portable
stereo system

BOOMBOXES > BOOMBOX

BOOMBURB *n* large suburb
that is growing quickly

BOOMBURBS
> BOOMBURB

BOOMED > BOOM

BOOMER *n* large male
kangaroo

BOOMERANG *n* curved
wooden missile which can
be made to return to the
thrower ▷ *vb* (of a plan)
recoil unexpectedly

BOOMERS > BOOMER

BOOMIER > BOOMY

BOOMIEST > BOOMY

BOOMING > BOOM

BOOMINGLY > BOOM

BOOMINGS > BOOM

BOOMKIN *n* short boom
projecting from the deck
of a ship

BOOMKINS > BOOMKIN

BOOMLET *n* small boom in
business, birth rate, etc

BOOMLETS > BOOMLET

BOOMS > BOOM

BOOMSLANG *n* large
greenish venomous
tree-living snake of
southern Africa

BOOMSTICK *n* (in
logging) any of the larger
logs chained together to
create a floating boom

BOOMTOWN *n* town that is
enjoying sudden
prosperity or has grown
rapidly

BOOMTOWNS
> BOOMTOWN

BOOMY *adj* characterized
by heavy bass sound

BOON *n* something useful,
helpful, or beneficial ▷ *adj*
useful, helpful, or
beneficial

BOONDOCK *adj* of or
relating to the boondocks

BOONDOCKS *n* remote
rural area

BOONER *n* derogatory
term for a young
working-class person from
Canberra

BOONERS > BOONER

BOONEST > BOON

BOONGARY *n* tree
kangaroo of NE
Queensland, Australia

BOONIES *short form of*
> BOONDOCKS

BOONLESS > BOON

BOONS > BOON

BOOR *n* rude or insensitive
person

BOORD *obsolete spelling of*
> BOARD

BOORDE *obsolete spelling of*
> BOARD

BOORDES > BOORDE

BOORDS > BOORD

BOORISH *adj*
ill-mannered, clumsy, or
insensitive

BOORISHLY > BOORISH

BOORKA *same as* > BURKA

BOORKAS > BOORKA

BOORS > BOOR

BOORTREE *same as*
> BOURTREE

BOORTREES
> BOORTREE

BOOS > BOO

BOOSE *same as* > BOOZE

BOOSED > BOOSE

BOOSES > BOOSE

BOOSHIT *adj* slang word
for very good

BOOSING > BOOSE

BOOST *n* encouragement
or help ▷ *vb* improve

BOOSTED > BOOST

BOOSTER *n* small
additional injection of a
vaccine

BOOSTERS > BOOSTER

BOOSTING > BOOST

BOOSTS > BOOST

BOOT *n* outer covering for
the foot that extends
above the ankle ▷ *vb* kick

BOOTABLE > BOOT

BOOTBLACK *another word
for* > SHOEBLACK

BOOTCUT *adj* (of trousers)
slightly flared at the
bottom of the legs

BOOTED *adj* wearing boots

BOOTEE *n* baby's soft shoe

BOOTEES > BOOTEE

BOOTERIES > BOOTERY

BOOTERY *n* shop where
boots and shoes are sold

BOOTH *n* small partly
enclosed cubicle

BOOTHOSE *n* stocking
worn with boots

BOOTHS > BOOTH

BOOTIE *n* Royal Marine

BOOTIES > BOOTY

BOOTIKIN *n* small boot

BOOTIKINS
> BOOTIKIN

BOOTING > BOOT

BOOTJACK *n* device that
grips the heel of a boot to
enable the foot to be
withdrawn easily

BOOTJACKS
> BOOTJACK

BOOTLACE *n* strong lace
for fastening a boot

BOOTLACES
> BOOTLACE

BOOTLAST *n* foot shape
placed in boots or shoes to
keep their shape

BOOTLASTS
> BOOTLAST

BOOTLEG *adj* produced,
distributed, or sold illicitly
▷ *vb* make, carry, or sell
(illicit goods) ▷ *n*
something made or sold
illicitly

BOOTLEGS > BOOTLEG

BOOTLESS *adj* of little or
no use

BOOTLICK *vb* seek favour
by servile or ingratiating
behaviour

BOOTLICKS
> BOOTLICK

BOOTMAKER *n* person
who makes boots and
shoes

BOOTS > BOOT

BOOTSTRAP *n* leather or
fabric loop on the back or
side of a boot

BOOTY *n* valuable articles
obtained as plunder

BOOZE *n* alcoholic drink
▷ *vb* drink alcohol, esp in
excess

BOOZED > BOOZE

BOOZER *n* person who is
fond of drinking

BOOZERS > BOOZER

BOOZES > BOOZE

BOOZEY *same as* > BOOZY

BOOZIER > BOOZY

BOOZIEST > BOOZY

BOOZILY > BOOZY

BOOZINESS > BOOZY

BOOZING > BOOZE

BOOZINGS > BOOZE

BOOZY *adj* inclined to or
involving excessive
drinking of alcohol

BOP *vb* dance to pop music
▷ *n* form of jazz with
complex rhythms and
harmonies

BOPEEP *n* quick look;
peek

BOPEEPS > BOPEEP

BOPPED > BOP

BOPPER > BOP

BOPPERS > BOP

BOPPIER > BOPPY

BOPPIEST > BOPPY

BOPPING > BOP

BOPPISH *same as*
> BOPPY

BOPPY *adj* resembling or
suggesting bebop

BOPS > BOP

BOR *n* neighbour

BORA *n* Aboriginal
Australian initiation
ceremony

BORACES > BORAX

BORACHIO *n* pig's skin
wine carrier

BORACHIOS > BORACHIO

BORACIC same as
> BORIC

BORACITE n white mineral that forms salt deposits of magnesium borate

BORACITES
> BORACITE

BORAGE n Mediterranean plant with star-shaped blue flowers

BORAGES > BORAGE

BORAK n rubbish

BORAKS > BORAK

BORAL n type of fine powder

BORALS > BORAL

BORANE n any compound of boron and hydrogen

BORANES > BORANE

BORAS > BORA

BORATE n salt or ester of boric acid ▷ vb treat with borax, boric acid, or borate

BORATED > BORATE

BORATES > BORATE

BORATING > BORATE

BORAX n soluble white mineral occurring in alkaline soils and salt deposits

BORAXES > BORAX

BORAZON n extremely hard form of boron nitride

BORAZONS > BORAZON

BORD obsolete spelling of
> BOARD

BORDAR n smallholder who held cottage in return for menial work

BORDARS > BORDAR

BORDE obsolete spelling of
> BOARD

BORDEAUX n any of several wines produced around Bordeaux

BORDEL same as
> BORDELLO

BORDELLO n brothel

BORDELLOS
> BORDELLO

BORDELS > BORDEL

BORDER n dividing line between political or geographical regions ▷ vb provide with a border

BORDEREAU n memorandum or invoice prepared for a company by an underwriter, containing a list of reinsured risks

BORDERED > BORDER

BORDERER n person who lives in a border area, esp the border between England and Scotland

BORDERERS
> BORDERER

BORDERING > BORDER

BORDERS > BORDER

BORDES > BORDE

BORDS > BORD

BORDURE n outer edge of a shield, esp when decorated distinctively

BORDURES > BORDURE

BORE vb make (someone) weary by being dull

BOREAL adj of or relating to the north or the north wind

BOREALIS adj as in aurora borealis lights seen around the North Pole

BOREAS n name for the north wind

BOREASES > BOREAS

BORECOLE another name for > KALE

BORECOLES
> BORECOLE

BORED > BORE

BOREDOM n state of being bored

BOREDOMS > BOREDOM

BOREE same as > MYALL

BOREEN n country lane or narrow road

BOREENS > BOREEN

BOREES > BOREE

BOREHOLE n hole driven into the ground to obtain geological information, release water, etc

BOREHOLES
> BOREHOLE

BOREL adj unlearned ▷ n boring tool

BORELS > BOREL

BORER n machine or hand tool for boring holes

BORERS > BORER

BORES > BORE

BORESCOPE n long narrow device for inspection of, eg, boring

BORESOME adj boring

BORGHETTO n settlement outside city walls

BORGO n small attractive medieval village

BORGOS > BORGO

BORIC adj of or containing boron

BORIDE n compound in which boron is the most electronegative element

BORIDES > BORIDE

BORING n act or process of making or enlarging a hole ▷ adj dull

BORINGLY > BORING

BORINGS > BORING

BORK vb dismiss from a job unfairly

BORKED > BORK

BORKING n act of incorrectly configuring a device

BORKINGS > BORKING

BORKS > BORK

BORLOTTI pl n as in borlotti bean variety of kidney bean

BORM vb smear with paint, oil, etc

BORMED > BORM

BORMING > BORM

BORMS > BORM

BORN adj possessing certain qualities from birth

BORNA n as in borna disease viral disease found in mammals, esp horses

BORNE > BEAR

BORNEOL n white solid terpene alcohol

BORNEOLS > BORNEOL

BORNITE n type of mineral

BORNITES > BORNITE

BORNITIC > BORNITE

BORNYL n as in bornyl alcohol white solid alcohol from a Malaysian tree

BORNYLS > BORNYL

BORON n element used in hardening steel

BORONIA n Australian aromatic flowering shrub

BORONIAS > BORONIA

BORONIC > BORON

BORONS > BORON

BOROUGH n town or district with its own council

BOROUGHS > BOROUGH

BORREL adj ignorant

BORRELIA n type of bacterium

BORRELIAS
> BORRELIA

BORRELL same as
> BORREL

BORROW vb obtain (something) temporarily

BORROWED > BORROW

BORROWER > BORROW

BORROWERS > BORROW

BORROWING > BORROW

BORROWS > BORROW

BORS > BOR

BORSCH same as
> BORSCHT

BORSCHES > BORSCH

BORSCHT n Russian soup based on beetroot

BORSCHTS > BORSCHT

BORSHCH same as
> BORSCHT

BORSHCHES > BORSHCH

BORSHT same as
> BORSCHT

BORSHTS > BORSHT

BORSIC n composite material used in aviation

BORSICS > BORSIC

BORSTAL n (formerly in Britain) prison for young criminals

BORSTALL same as
> BORSTAL

BORSTALLS
> BORSTALL

BORSTALS > BORSTAL

BORT n inferior grade of diamond used for cutting and drilling

BORTIER > BORT

BORTIEST > BORT

BORTS > BORT

BORTSCH same as
> BORSCHT

BORTSCHES > BORTSCH

BORTY > BORT

BORTZ same as > BORT

BORTZES > BORTZ

BORZOI n tall dog with a long silky coat

BORZOIS > BORZOI

BOS > BO

BOSBERAAD n meeting in an isolated venue to break a political deadlock

BOSBOK same as
> BUSHBUCK

BOSBOKS > BOSBOK

BOSCAGE n mass of trees and shrubs

BOSCAGES > BOSCAGE

BOSCHBOK same as
> BUSHBUCK

BOSCHBOKS
> BOSCHBOK

BOSCHVARK same as
> BUSHPIG

BOSCHVELD same as
> BUSHVELD

BOSH n empty talk, nonsense

BOSHBOK same as
> BUSHBUCK

BOSHBOKS > BOSHBOK

BOSHES > BOSH

BOSHTA same as
> BOSHTER

BOSHTER adj excellent

BOSHVARK same as
> BOSCHVARK

BOSHVARKS
> BOSHVARK

BOSIE n (in cricket) another term for googly

BOSIES > BOSIE

BOSK n small wood of bushes and small trees

BOSKAGE same as
> BOSCAGE

BOSKAGES > BOSKAGE

BOSKER adj excellent

BOSKET n clump of small trees or bushes

BOSKETS > BOSKET

BOSKIER > BOSKY

BOSKIEST > BOSKY

BOSKINESS > BOSKY

BOSKS > BOSK

BOSKY adj containing or consisting of bushes or thickets

BOSOM n chest of a person ▷ adj very dear ▷ vb embrace

BOSOMED > BOSOM

BOSOMIER > BOSOMY

BOSOMIEST > BOSOMY

BOSOMING > BOSOM

BOSOMS > BOSOM

BOSOMY adj (of a woman) having large breasts

BOSON n type of elementary particle

BOSONIC > BOSON

BOSONS > BOSON

BOSQUE same as > BOSK

BOSQUES > BOSQUE

BOSQUET same as
> BOSKET

BOSQUETS > BOSQUET

BOSS n raised knob or stud ▷ vb employ, supervise, or be in charge of ▷ adj excellent

BOSSDOM n bosses collectively

BOSSDOMS > BOSSDOM

BOSSED > BOSS

BOSSER > BOSS
BOSSES > BOSS
BOSSEST > BOSS
BOSSET *n* either of the rudimentary antlers found in young deer
BOSSETS > BOSSET
BOSSIER > BOSSY
BOSSIES > BOSSY
BOSSIEST > BOSSY
BOSSILY > BOSSY
BOSSINESS > BOSSY
BOSSING *n* act of shaping malleable metal
BOSSINGS > BOSSING
BOSSISM *n* domination of political organizations by bosses
BOSSISMS > BOSSISM
BOSSY *adj* domineering or overbearing ▷ *n* US pet name for a cow
BOSTANGI *n* imperial Turkish guard
BOSTANGIS > BOSTANGI
BOSTHOON *n* boor
BOSTHOONS > BOSTHOON
BOSTON *n* card game for four, played with two packs
BOSTONS > BOSTON
BOSTRYX *n* phenomenon in which flowers develop on one side only
BOSTRYXES > BOSTRYX
BOSUN *same as* > BOATSWAIN
BOSUNS > BOSUN
BOT *vb* scrounge
BOTA *n* leather container
BOTANIC *same as* > BOTANICAL
BOTANICA *n* botany
BOTANICAL *adj* of or relating to botany or plants ▷ *n* any drug or pesticide that is made from parts of a plant
BOTANICAS > BOTANICA
BOTANICS > BOTANIC
BOTANIES > BOTANY
BOTANISE *same as* > BOTANIZE
BOTANISED > BOTANISE
BOTANISER > BOTANISE
BOTANISES > BOTANISE
BOTANIST > BOTANY
BOTANISTS > BOTANY
BOTANIZE *vb* collect or study plants
BOTANIZED > BOTANIZE
BOTANIZER > BOTANIZE
BOTANIZES > BOTANIZE
BOTANY *n* study of plants
BOTARGO *n* relish consisting of the roe of mullet or tuna, salted and pressed into rolls
BOTARGOES > BOTARGO

BOTARGOS > BOTARGO
BOTAS > BOTA
BOTCH *vb* spoil through clumsiness ▷ *n* badly done piece of work or repair
BOTCHED > BOTCH
BOTCHEDLY > BOTCH
BOTCHER > BOTCH
BOTCHERS > BOTCH
BOTCHERY *n* instance of botching
BOTCHES > BOTCH
BOTCHIER > BOTCHY
BOTCHIEST > BOTCHY
BOTCHILY > BOTCHY
BOTCHING > BOTCH
BOTCHINGS > BOTCH
BOTCHY *adj* clumsily done or made
BOTE *n* compensation given for injury or damage to property
BOTEL *same as* > BOATEL
BOTELS > BOTEL
BOTES > BOTE
BOTFLIES > BOTFLY
BOTFLY *n* type of stout-bodied hairy fly
BOTH *pron* two considered together ▷ *adj* two considered together ▷ *determiner* two
BOTHAN *n* unlicensed drinking house
BOTHANS > BOTHAN
BOTHER *vb* take the time or trouble ▷ *n* trouble, fuss, or difficulty ▷ *interj* exclamation of slight annoyance
BOTHERED > BOTHER
BOTHERING > BOTHER
BOTHERS > BOTHER
BOTHIE *same as* > BOTHY
BOTHIES > BOTHY
BOTHOLE *n* hole made by the larva of the botfly
BOTHOLES > BOTHOLE
BOTHRIA > BOTHRIUM
BOTHRIUM *n* groove-shaped sucker on tapeworm
BOTHRIUMS > BOTHRIUM
BOTHY *n* hut used for temporary shelter
BOTHYMAN *n* man who lives in bothy
BOTHYMEN > BOTHYMAN
BOTNET *n* network of infected computers
BOTNETS > BOTNET
BOTONE *adj* having lobes at the ends
BOTONEE *same as* > BOTONE
BOTONNEE *same as* > BOTONE
BOTOXED *adj* having had Botox treatment
BOTRYOID *adj* shaped like a bunch of grapes
BOTRYOSE *same as* > BOTRYOID
BOTRYTIS *n* type of fungus which causes plant diseases

BOTS *n* digestive disease of horses and some other animals
BOTT *same as* > BOT
BOTTARGA *same as* > BOTARGO
BOTTARGAS > BOTTARGA
BOTTE *n* thrust or hit
BOTTED > BOT
BOTTEGA *n* workshop; studio
BOTTEGAS > BOTTEGA
BOTTES > BOTTE
BOTTIES > BOTTY
BOTTINE *n* light boot for women or children
BOTTINES > BOTTINE
BOTTING > BOT
BOTTLE *n* container for holding liquids ▷ *vb* put in a bottle
BOTTLED > BOTTLE
BOTTLEFUL *same as* > BOTTLE
BOTTLER *n* exceptional person or thing
BOTTLERS > BOTTLER
BOTTLES > BOTTLE
BOTTLING > BOTTLE
BOTTLINGS > BOTTLE
BOTTOM *n* lowest, deepest, or farthest removed part of a thing ▷ *adj* lowest or last ▷ *vb* provide with a bottom
BOTTOMED > BOTTOM
BOTTOMER *n* pit worker
BOTTOMERS > BOTTOMER
BOTTOMING *n* lowest level of foundation material for a road or other structure
BOTTOMRY *n* loan in which a ship's owner pledges the ship as security
BOTTOMS > BOTTOM
BOTTOMSET *adj* as in *bottomset bed* fine sediment deposited at the front of a growing delta
BOTTONY *same as* > BOTONE
BOTTS > BOTT
BOTTY *n* diminutive for bottom
BOTULIN *n* potent toxin which causes botulism
BOTULINAL > BOTULIN
BOTULINS > BOTULIN
BOTULINUM *n* botulin-secreting bacterium
BOTULINUS *n* type of bacterium whose toxins (botulins) cause botulism
BOTULISM *n* severe food poisoning
BOTULISMS > BOTULISM
BOUBOU *n* long flowing garment
BOUBOUS > BOUBOU
BOUCHE *n* notch cut in the top corner of a shield

BOUCHEE *n* small pastry case filled with a savoury mixture
BOUCHEES > BOUCHEE
BOUCHES > BOUCHE
BOUCLE *n* looped yarn giving a knobbly effect ▷ *adj* of or designating such a yarn or fabric
BOUCLEE *n* support for a cue in billiards using the hand
BOUCLEES > BOUCLEE
BOUCLES > BOUCLE
BOUDERIE *n* sulkiness
BOUDERIES > BOUDERIE
BOUDIN *n* French version of a black pudding
BOUDINS > BOUDIN
BOUDOIR *n* woman's bedroom or private sitting room
BOUDOIRS > BOUDOIR
BOUFFANT *adj* (of a hairstyle) having extra height through backcombing ▷ *n* bouffant hairstyle
BOUFFANTS > BOUFFANT
BOUFFE *n* type of light or satirical opera common in France during the 19th century
BOUFFES > BOUFFE
BOUGE *vb* move
BOUGED > BOUGE
BOUGES > BOUGE
BOUGET *n* budget
BOUGETS > BOUGET
BOUGH *n* large branch of a tree
BOUGHED > BOUGH
BOUGHLESS > BOUGH
BOUGHPOT *n* container for displaying boughs
BOUGHPOTS > BOUGHPOT
BOUGHS > BOUGH
BOUGHT *n* curve
BOUGHTEN *archaic past participle of* > BUY
BOUGHTS > BOUGHT
BOUGIE *n* medical instrument
BOUGIES > BOUGIE
BOUGING > BOUGE
BOUILLI *n* stew
BOUILLIS > BOUILLI
BOUILLON *n* thin clear broth or stock
BOUILLONS > BOUILLON
BOUK *n* bulk; volume
BOUKS > BOUK
BOULDER *n* large rounded rock ▷ *vb* convert into boulders
BOULDERED > BOULDER
BOULDERER > BOULDER
BOULDERS > BOULDER
BOULDERY *adj* covered in boulders
BOULE *same as* > BOULLE
BOULES *n* game popular in France
BOULEVARD *n* wide, usu tree-lined, street**

b

BOULLE adj relating to a type of marquetry much used on French furniture from the 17th century ▷ n something ornamented with such marquetry

BOULLES > BOULLE

BOULT same as > BOLT

BOULTED > BOULT

BOULTER > BOULT

BOULTERS > BOULT

BOULTING > BOULT

BOULTINGS > BOULT

BOULTS > BOULT

BOUN vb prepare to go out

BOUNCE vb (of a ball etc) rebound from an impact ▷ n act of rebounding

BOUNCED > BOUNCE

BOUNCER n person employed at a nightclub etc to remove unwanted people

BOUNCERS > BOUNCER

BOUNCES > BOUNCE

BOUNCIER > BOUNCY

BOUNCIEST > BOUNCY

BOUNCILY > BOUNCY

BOUNCING adj vigorous and robust

BOUNCY adj lively, exuberant, or self-confident

BOUND vb jump suddenly ▷ n sudden jump ▷ adj certain

BOUNDABLE > BIND

BOUNDARY n dividing line that indicates the farthest limit

BOUNDED adj (of a set) having a bound

BOUNDEN adj morally obligatory

BOUNDER n morally reprehensible person

BOUNDERS > BOUNDER

BOUNDING > BOUND

BOUNDLESS adj unlimited

BOUNDNESS > BIND

BOUNDS pl n limit

BOUNED > BOUN

BOUNING > BOUN

BOUNS > BOUN

BOUNTEOUS adj giving freely

BOUNTIED > BOUNTY

BOUNTIES > BOUNTY

BOUNTIFUL adj plentiful

BOUNTREE another name for > BOURTREE

BOUNTREES > BOUNTREE

BOUNTY n generosity

BOUNTYHED n generosity

BOUQUET n bunch of flowers

BOUQUETS > BOUQUET

BOURASQUE n violent storm

BOURBON n whiskey made from maize

BOURBONS > BOURBON

BOURD n prank ▷ vb jest or joke

BOURDED > BOURD

BOURDER n prankster

BOURDERS > BOURDER

BOURDING > BOURD

BOURDON n 16-foot organ stop of the stopped diapason type

BOURDONS > BOURDON

BOURDS > BOURD

BOURG n French market town, esp one beside a castle

BOURGEOIS n middle-class (person) ▷ adj characteristic of or comprising the middle class

BOURGEON same as > BURGEON

BOURGEONS > BOURGEON

BOURGS > BOURG

BOURKHA same as > BURKA

BOURKHAS > BOURKHA

BOURLAW same as > BYRLAW

BOURLAWS > BOURLAW

BOURN n (in S Britain) stream

BOURNE same as > BOURN

BOURNES > BOURNE

BOURNS > BOURN

BOURREE n traditional French dance in fast duple time

BOURREES > BOURREE

BOURRIDE n Mediterranean fish soup

BOURRIDES > BOURRIDE

BOURSE n stock exchange of continental Europe, esp Paris

BOURSES > BOURSE

BOURSIER n stock-exchange worker

BOURSIERS > BOURSIER

BOURSIN n tradename of a smooth white creamy cheese, often flavoured with garlic

BOURSINS > BOURSIN

BOURTREE n elder tree

BOURTREES > BOURTREE

BOUSE vb raise or haul with a tackle

BOUSED > BOUSE

BOUSES > BOUSE

BOUSIER > BOUSY

BOUSIEST > BOUSY

BOUSING > BOUSE

BOUSOUKI same as > BOUZOUKI

BOUSOUKIA > BOUSOUKI

BOUSOUKIS > BOUSOUKI

BOUSY adj drunken; boozy

BOUT n period of activity or illness

BOUTADE n outburst

BOUTADES > BOUTADE

BOUTIQUE n small clothes shop

BOUTIQUES > BOUTIQUE

BOUTIQUEY adj typical of boutiques

BOUTON n knob-shaped contact between nerve fibres

BOUTONNE adj reserved or inhibited

BOUTONNEE same as > BOUTONNE

BOUTONS > BOUTON

BOUTS > BOUT

BOUVARDIA n flowering plant

BOUVIER n large powerful dog

BOUVIERS > BOUVIER

BOUZOUKI n Greek stringed musical instrument

BOUZOUKIA > BOUZOUKI

BOUZOUKIS > BOUZOUKI

BOVATE n obsolete measure of land

BOVATES > BOVATE

BOVID n type of ruminant

BOVIDS > BOVID

BOVINE n domesticated bovid mammal

BOVINELY > BOVINE

BOVINES > BOVINE

BOVINITY > BOVINE

BOVVER n rowdiness, esp caused by gangs of teenage youths

BOVVERS > BOVVER

BOW vb lower (one's head) or bend (one's knee or body) as a sign of respect or shame ▷ n movement made when bowing

BOWAT n lamp

BOWATS > BOWAT

BOWBENT adj bent; bow-like

BOWED adj lowered, bent forward, or curved

BOWEL n intestine, esp the large intestine ▷ vb remove the bowels

BOWELED > BOWEL

BOWELING > BOWEL

BOWELLED > BOWEL

BOWELLESS > BOWEL

BOWELLING > BOWEL

BOWELS > BOWEL

BOWER n shady leafy shelter ▷ vb surround as with a bower

BOWERBIRD n songbird of Australia and New Guinea, the males of which build bower-like display grounds to attract females

BOWERED > BOWER

BOWERIES > BOWERY

BOWERING > BOWER

BOWERS > BOWER

BOWERY n farm

BOWES poetic plural form of > BOUGH

BOWET same as > BOWAT

BOWETS > BOWET

BOWFIN n N American freshwater fish

BOWFINS > BOWFIN

BOWFRONT adj having a front that curves outwards

BOWGET obsolete variant of > BUDGET

BOWGETS > BOWGET

BOWHEAD n type of large-mouthed Arctic whale

BOWHEADS > BOWHEAD

BOWHUNT vb hunt using a bow and arrows

BOWHUNTED > BOWHUNT

BOWHUNTER n person hunting with bow and arrows

BOWHUNTS > BOWHUNT

BOWIE n as in bowie knife type of hunting knife

BOWING n musical technique

BOWINGLY > BOWING

BOWINGS > BOWING

BOWKNOT n decorative knot usually having two loops and two loose ends

BOWKNOTS > BOWKNOT

BOWL n round container with an open top ▷ vb roll smoothly along the ground

BOWLDER same as > BOULDER

BOWLDERS > BOWLDER

BOWLED > BOWL

BOWLEG n leg curving outwards like a bow between the ankle and the thigh

BOWLEGGED adj having legs that curve outwards like a bow

BOWLEGS > BOWLEG

BOWLER n player who sends a ball towards a batter

BOWLERS > BOWLER

BOWLESS > BOW

BOWLFUL same as > BOWL

BOWLFULS > BOWLFUL

BOWLIKE > BOW

BOWLINE n line used to keep the sail taut against the wind

BOWLINES > BOWLINE

BOWLING n game in which bowls are rolled at a group of pins

BOWLINGS > BOWLING

BOWLLIKE > BOWL

BOWLS n game involving biased wooden bowls and a small bowl (the jack)

BOWMAN n archer

BOWMEN > BOWMAN

BOWNE same as > BOUN

BOWNED > BOWNE

BOWNES > BOWNE

BOWNING > BOWNE

BOWPOT same as > BOUGHPOT

BOWPOTS > BOWPOT

BOWR n muscle

BOWRS > BOWR

BOWS > BOW

BOWSAW n saw with a thin blade in a bow-shaped frame

BOWSAWS > BOWSAW

BOWSE same as > BOUSE

BOWSED > BOWSE

BOWSER n tanker containing fuel for aircraft, military vehicles, etc
BOWSERS > BOWSER
BOWSES > BOWSE
BOWSEY same as > BOWSIE
BOWSEYS > BOWSEY
BOWSHOT n distance an arrow travels from the bow
BOWSHOTS > BOWSHOT
BOWSIE n low-class, mean or obstreperous person
BOWSIES > BOWSIE
BOWSING > BOWSE
BOWSMAN n man who hunts using a bow and arrows
BOWSMEN > BOWSMAN
BOWSPRIT n spar projecting from the bow of a sailing ship
BOWSPRITS > BOWSPRIT
BOWSTRING n string of an archer's bow
BOWSTRUNG > BOWSTRING
BOWWOOD n tree of the mulberry family, native to south-central US
BOWWOODS > BOWWOOD
BOWWOW n imitation of the bark of a dog ▷ vb make a noise like a dog
BOWWOWED > BOWWOW
BOWWOWING > BOWWOW
BOWWOWS > BOWWOW
BOWYANG n band worn round a trouser leg below the knee
BOWYANGS > BOWYANG
BOWYER n person who makes or sells archery bows
BOWYERS > BOWYER
BOX n container with a firm flat base and sides ▷ vb put into a box
BOXBALL n street ball game
BOXBALLS > BOXBALL
BOXBERRY n fruit of the partridgeberry or wintergreen
BOXBOARD n tough paperboard made from wood and wastepaper pulp: used for making boxes, etc
BOXBOARDS > BOXBOARD
BOXCAR n closed railway freight van
BOXCARS > BOXCAR
BOXED > BOX
BOXEN adj made of boxwood
BOXER n person who participates in the sport of boxing
BOXERCISE n system of sustained exercises combining boxing movements with aerobic activities
BOXERS > BOXER

BOXES > BOX
BOXFISH another name for > TRUNKFISH
BOXFISHES > BOXFISH
BOXFUL same as > BOX
BOXFULS > BOXFUL
BOXHAUL vb method for bringing a square-rigged ship onto a new tack
BOXHAULED > BOXHAUL
BOXHAULS > BOXHAUL
BOXIER > BOXY
BOXIEST > BOXY
BOXILY > BOXY
BOXINESS > BOXY
BOXING n sport of fighting with the fists
BOXINGS > BOXING
BOXKEEPER n person responsible for theatre boxes
BOXLA n type of lacrosse played indoors
BOXLAS > BOXLA
BOXLIKE > BOX
BOXPLOT n (in statistics) type of graph
BOXPLOTS > BOXPLOT
BOXROOM n small room in which boxes, cases, etc may be stored
BOXROOMS > BOXROOM
BOXTHORN n matrimony vine
BOXTHORNS > BOXTHORN
BOXTIES > BOXTY
BOXTY n type of Irish potato pancake
BOXWALLAH n derogatory Indian term for a salesperson
BOXWOOD n hard yellow wood of the box tree, used to make tool handles, etc
BOXWOODS > BOXWOOD
BOXY adj squarish or chunky
BOY n male child ▷ vb act the part of a boy in a play
BOYAR n member of an old order of Russian nobility
BOYARD same as > BOYAR
BOYARDS > BOYARD
BOYARISM > BOYAR
BOYARISMS > BOYAR
BOYARS > BOYAR
BOYAU n connecting trench
BOYAUX > BOYAU
BOYCHICK same as > BOYCHICK
BOYCHICKS > BOYCHICK
BOYCHIK n young boy
BOYCHIKS > BOYCHIK
BOYCOTT vb refuse to deal with (an organization or country) ▷ n instance of boycotting
BOYCOTTED > BOYCOTT
BOYCOTTER > BOYCOTT
BOYCOTTS > BOYCOTT
BOYED > BOY
BOYF n boyfriend
BOYFRIEND n male friend with whom a

person is romantically involved
BOYFS > BOYF
BOYG n troll-like mythical creature
BOYGS > BOYG
BOYHOOD n state or time of being a boy
BOYHOODS > BOYHOOD
BOYING > BOY
BOYISH adj of or like a boy in looks, behaviour, or character
BOYISHLY > BOYISH
BOYKIE n chap or fellow
BOYKIES > BOYKIE
BOYLA n Aboriginal Australian magician or medicine-man
BOYLAS > BOYLA
BOYO n boy or young man: often used in direct address
BOYOS > BOYO
BOYS > BOY
BOYSHORTS pl n women's underpants resembling close-fitting shorts
BOYSIER > BOYSY
BOYSIEST > BOYSY
BOYSY adj suited to or typical of boys or young men
BOZO n man, esp a stupid one
BOZOS > BOZO
BOZZETTI > BOZZETTO
BOZZETTO n small sketch of planned work
BRA n women's undergarment
BRAAI vb grill or roast (meat) over open coals
BRAAIED > BRAAI
BRAAIING > BRAAI
BRAAIS > BRAAI
BRAATA n small portion added to a purchase to encourage the customer to return
BRAATAS same as > BRAATA
BRAATASES > BRAATAS
BRABBLE rare word for > SQUABBLE
BRABBLED > BRABBLE
BRABBLER > BRABBLE
BRABBLERS > BRABBLE
BRABBLES > BRABBLE
BRABBLING > BRABBLE
BRACCATE adj (of birds) having feathered legs
BRACCIA > BRACCIO
BRACCIO n former unit of measurement of length
BRACE n object fastened to something to straighten or support it ▷ vb steady or prepare (oneself) for something unpleasant
BRACED > BRACE
BRACELET n ornamental chain or band for the wrist
BRACELETS pl n handcuffs

BRACER n person or thing that braces
BRACERO n Mexican World War II labourer
BRACEROS > BRACERO
BRACERS > BRACER
BRACES pl n pair of straps worn over the shoulders for holding up the trousers
BRACH n female dog
BRACHAH n blessing
BRACHAHS > BRACHAH
BRACHES > BRACH
BRACHET same as > BRACH
BRACHETS > BRACHET
BRACHIA > BRACHIUM
BRACHIAL adj of or relating to the arm or to an armlike part or structure ▷ n brachial part or structure
BRACHIALS > BRACHIAL
BRACHIATE adj having widely divergent paired branches ▷ vb (of some arboreal apes and monkeys) swing by the arms from one hold to the next
BRACHIUM n arm, esp the upper part
BRACHIUMS > BRACHIUM
BRACHOT > BRACHAH
BRACHS > BRACH
BRACING adj refreshing and invigorating ▷ n system of braces used to strengthen or support
BRACINGLY > BRACING
BRACINGS > BRACING
BRACIOLA n Italian meat roulade
BRACIOLAS > BRACIOLA
BRACIOLE > BRACIOLA
BRACIOLES > BRACIOLE
BRACK same as > BARMBRACK
BRACKEN n large fern
BRACKENS > BRACKEN
BRACKET n pair of characters used to enclose a section of writing ▷ vb put in brackets
BRACKETED > BRACKET
BRACKETS > BRACKET
BRACKISH adj (of water) slightly salty
BRACKS > BRACK
BRACONID n type of fly with parasitic larva
BRACONIDS > BRACONID
BRACT n leaf at the base of a flower
BRACTEAL > BRACT
BRACTEATE adj (of a plant) having bracts ▷ n fine decorated dish or plate of precious metal
BRACTED > BRACT
BRACTEOLE n secondary bract subtending a flower within an inflorescence

b

BRACTLESS > BRACT
BRACTLET *variant of* > BRACTEOLE
BRACTLETS > BRACTLET
BRACTS > BRACT
BRAD *n* small tapered nail with a small head
BRADAWL *n* small boring tool
BRADAWLS > BRADAWL
BRADDED > BRAD
BRADDING > BRAD
BRADOON *same as* > BRIDOON
BRADOONS > BRADOON
BRADS > BRAD
BRAE *n* hill or slope
BRAEHEID *n* summit of a hill or slope
BRAEHEIDS > BRAEHEID
BRAES > BRAE
BRAG *vb* speak arrogantly and boastfully ▷ *n* boastful talk or behaviour ▷ *adj* boastful
BRAGGART *n* person who boasts loudly ▷ *adj* boastful
BRAGGARTS > BRAGGART
BRAGGED > BRAG
BRAGGER > BRAG
BRAGGERS > BRAG
BRAGGEST > BRAG
BRAGGIER > BRAGGY
BRAGGIEST > BRAGGY
BRAGGING > BRAG
BRAGGINGS > BRAG
BRAGGY *adj* boastful
BRAGLY > BRAG
BRAGS > BRAG
BRAHMA *n* breed of domestic fowl
BRAHMAN *n* member of the highest Hindu caste
BRAHMANI *n* woman of the highest Hindu caste
BRAHMANIS > BRAHMANI
BRAHMANS > BRAHMAN
BRAHMAS > BRAHMA
BRAHMIN *same as* > BRAHMAN
BRAHMINS > BRAHMIN
BRAID *vb* interweave (hair, thread, etc) ▷ *n* length of hair etc that has been braided ▷ *adj* broad ▷ *adv* broadly
BRAIDE *adj* given to deceit
BRAIDED *adj* flowing in several shallow interconnected channels
BRAIDER > BRAID
BRAIDERS > BRAID
BRAIDEST > BRAID
BRAIDING *n* braids collectively
BRAIDINGS > BRAIDING
BRAIDS > BRAID
BRAIL *n* one of several lines fastened to a fore-and-aft sail to aid in furling it ▷ *vb* furl (a

fore-and-aft sail) using brails
BRAILED > BRAIL
BRAILING > BRAIL
BRAILLE *n* system of writing consisting of raised dots ▷ *vb* print or write using this method
BRAILLED > BRAILLE
BRAILLER *n* device for producing text in braille
BRAILLERS > BRAILLER
BRAILLES > BRAILLE
BRAILLING > BRAILLE
BRAILLIST *n* braille transcriber
BRAILS > BRAIL
BRAIN *n* soft mass of nervous tissue in the head ▷ *vb* hit (someone) hard on the head
BRAINBOX *n* skull
BRAINCASE *n* part of cranium that covers brain
BRAINDEAD *adj* having irreversible stoppage of breathing due to brain damage
BRAINED > BRAIN
BRAINFART *n* slang word for an idea expressed without much previous thought
BRAINFOOD *n* food containing nutrients that promote brain function
BRAINIAC *n* highly intelligent person
BRAINIACS > BRAINIAC
BRAINIER > BRAINY
BRAINIEST > BRAINY
BRAINILY > BRAINY
BRAINING > BRAIN
BRAINISH *adj* impulsive
BRAINLESS *adj* stupid
BRAINPAN *n* skull
BRAINPANS > BRAINPAN
BRAINS > BRAIN
BRAINSICK *adj* irrational; foolish
BRAINSTEM *n* stalklike part of the brain consisting of the medulla oblongata, the midbrain, and the pons Varolii
BRAINWASH *vb* cause (a person) to alter his or her beliefs, esp by methods based on isolation, sleeplessness, etc
BRAINWAVE *n* sudden idea
BRAINWORK *n* work done with the brain
BRAINY *adj* clever
BRAIRD *vb* appear as shoots
BRAIRDED > BRAIRD
BRAIRDING > BRAIRD
BRAIRDS > BRAIRD
BRAISE *vb* cook slowly in a covered pan with a little liquid
BRAISED > BRAISE

BRAISES > BRAISE
BRAISING > BRAISE
BRAIZE *n* sea bream
BRAIZES > BRAIZE
BRAK *n* crossbred dog ▷ *adj* (of water) slightly salty
BRAKE *n* device for slowing a vehicle ▷ *vb* apply a brake
BRAKEAGE > BRAKE
BRAKEAGES > BRAKE
BRAKED > BRAKE
BRAKELESS > BRAKE
BRAKEMAN *n* crew member of a goods or passenger train
BRAKEMEN > BRAKEMAN
BRAKES > BRAKE
BRAKESMAN *n* pithead winch operator
BRAKESMEN > BRAKESMAN
BRAKIER > BRAKY
BRAKIEST > BRAKY
BRAKING *n* act of braking
BRAKINGS > BRAKING
BRAKS > BRAK
BRAKY *adj* brambly
BRALESS > BRA
BRAMBLE *n* Scots word for blackberry ▷ *vb* pick blackberries
BRAMBLED > BRAMBLE
BRAMBLES > BRAMBLE
BRAMBLIER > BRAMBLE
BRAMBLING *n* Eurasian finch with a speckled head and back and, in the male, a reddish brown breast and darker wings and tail
BRAMBLY > BRAMBLE
BRAME *n* powerful feeling of emotion
BRAMES > BRAME
BRAN *n* husks of cereal grain ▷ *vb* clean with water in which bran has been boiled
BRANCARD *n* couch on shafts, carried between two horses
BRANCARDS > BRANCARD
BRANCH *n* secondary stem of a tree ▷ *vb* (of stems, roots, etc) divide, then develop in different directions
BRANCHED > BRANCH
BRANCHER *n* young bird learning to fly
BRANCHERS > BRANCHER
BRANCHERY *n* branches
BRANCHES > BRANCH
BRANCHIA *n* gill in aquatic animals
BRANCHIAE > BRANCHIA
BRANCHIAL *adj* of or relating to the gills of an aquatic animal, esp a fish
BRANCHIER > BRANCH
BRANCHING > BRANCH
BRANCHLET *n* small branch
BRANCHY > BRANCH

BRAND *n* particular product ▷ *vb* mark with a brand
BRANDADE *n* French puréed fish dish
BRANDADES > BRANDADE
BRANDED *adj* identifiable as being the product of a particular company
BRANDER > BRAND
BRANDERED > BRAND
BRANDERS > BRAND
BRANDIED > BRANDY
BRANDIES > BRANDY
BRANDING > BRAND
BRANDINGS > BRAND
BRANDISE *n* three-legged metal stand for cooking pots
BRANDISES > BRANDISE
BRANDISH *vb* wave (a weapon etc) in a threatening way ▷ *n* threatening or defiant flourish
BRANDLESS > BRAND
BRANDLING *n* type of small red earthworm found in manure and used as bait by anglers
BRANDRETH *n* framework of bars used for cooking meat over fire
BRANDS > BRAND
BRANDY *n* alcoholic spirit distilled from wine ▷ *vb* give brandy to
BRANDYING > BRANDY
BRANE *n* hypothetical component of string theory
BRANES > BRANE
BRANGLE *vb* quarrel noisily
BRANGLED > BRANGLE
BRANGLES > BRANGLE
BRANGLING > BRANGLE
BRANK *vb* walk with a swaggering gait
BRANKED > BRANK
BRANKIER > BRANKY
BRANKIEST > BRANKY
BRANKING > BRANK
BRANKS *pl n* (formerly) iron bridle used to restrain scolding women
BRANKY *adj* ostentatious
BRANLE *n* old French country dance performed in a linked circle
BRANLES > BRANLE
BRANNED > BRAN
BRANNER *n* person or machine that treats metal with bran
BRANNERS > BRANNER
BRANNIER > BRANNY
BRANNIEST > BRANNY
BRANNIGAN *n* noisy quarrel
BRANNING > BRAN
BRANNY *adj* having the appearance or texture of bran
BRANS > BRAN
BRANSLE *another word for* > BRANTLE

BRANSLES > BRANSLE
BRANT n type of small goose
BRANTAIL n singing bird with red tail
BRANTAILS > BRANTAIL
BRANTLE n French country dance
BRANTLES > BRANTLE
BRANTS > BRANT
BRAP interj exclamation used to imitate a burst of gunfire
BRAS archaic form of > BRASS
BRASCO n lavatory
BRASCOS > BRASCO
BRASERO n metal grid for burning coals
BRASEROS > BRASERO
BRASES > BRAS
BRASH adj offensively loud, showy, or self-confident ▷ n loose rubbish, such as broken rock, hedge clippings, etc ▷ vb assault
BRASHED > BRASH
BRASHER > BRASH
BRASHES > BRASH
BRASHEST > BRASH
BRASHIER > BRASHY
BRASHIEST > BRASHY
BRASHING > BRASH
BRASHLY > BRASH
BRASHNESS > BRASH
BRASHY adj loosely fragmented
BRASIER same as > BRAZIER
BRASIERS > BRASIER
BRASIL same as > BRAZIL
BRASILEIN same as > BRAZILEIN
BRASILIN same as > BRAZILIN
BRASILINS > BRASILIN
BRASILS > BRASIL
BRASS n alloy of copper and zinc ▷ vb make irritated or annoyed
BRASSAGE n amount charged by government for making coins
BRASSAGES > BRASSAGE
BRASSARD n identifying armband or badge
BRASSARDS > BRASSARD
BRASSART same as > BRASSARD
BRASSARTS > BRASSART
BRASSED > BRASS
BRASSERIE n restaurant serving drinks and cheap meals
BRASSES > BRASS
BRASSET same as > BRASSART
BRASSETS > BRASSET
BRASSICA n any plant of the cabbage and turnip family

BRASSICAS > BRASSICA
BRASSIE n former type of golf club
BRASSIER > BRASSY
BRASSIERE n bra
BRASSIES > BRASSIE
BRASSIEST > BRASSY
BRASSILY > BRASSY
BRASSING > BRASS
BRASSISH > BRASS
BRASSWARE n items made of brass
BRASSY adj showy and vulgar
BRAST same as > BURST
BRASTING > BRAST
BRASTS > BRAST
BRAT n unruly child
BRATCHET n hunting dog
BRATCHETS > BRATCHET
BRATLING n small badly behaved child
BRATLINGS > BRATLING
BRATPACK n group of precocious and successful young actors, writers, etc
BRATPACKS > BRATPACK
BRATS > BRAT
BRATTICE n partition of wood or treated cloth used to control ventilation in a mine ▷ vb fit with a brattice
BRATTICED > BRATTICE
BRATTICES > BRATTICE
BRATTIER > BRAT
BRATTIEST > BRAT
BRATTISH same as > BRATTICE
BRATTLE vb make a rattling sound
BRATTLED > BRATTLE
BRATTLES > BRATTLE
BRATTLING > BRATTLE
BRATTY > BRAT
BRATWURST n type of small pork sausage
BRAUNCH old variant of > BRANCH
BRAUNCHED > BRAUNCH
BRAUNCHES > BRAUNCH
BRAUNITE n brown or black mineral
BRAUNITES > BRAUNITE
BRAVA n professional assassin
BRAVADO n showy display of self-confidence ▷ vb behave with bravado
BRAVADOED > BRAVADO
BRAVADOES > BRAVADO
BRAVADOS > BRAVADO
BRAVAS > BRAVA
BRAVE adj having or showing courage, resolution, and daring ▷ n Native American warrior ▷ vb confront with resolution or courage
BRAVED > BRAVE
BRAVELY > BRAVE

BRAVENESS > BRAVE
BRAVER > BRAVE
BRAVERIES > BRAVE
BRAVERS > BRAVE
BRAVERY > BRAVE
BRAVES > BRAVE
BRAVEST > BRAVE
BRAVI > BRAVO
BRAVING > BRAVE
BRAVO interj well done! ▷ n cry of 'bravo' ▷ vb cry or shout 'bravo'
BRAVOED > BRAVO
BRAVOES > BRAVO
BRAVOING > BRAVO
BRAVOS > BRAVO
BRAVURA n display of boldness or daring
BRAVURAS > BRAVURA
BRAVURE > BRAVURA
BRAW adj fine or excellent, esp in appearance or dress
BRAWER > BRAW
BRAWEST > BRAW
BRAWL n noisy fight ▷ vb fight noisily
BRAWLED > BRAWL
BRAWLER > BRAWL
BRAWLERS > BRAWL
BRAWLIE adj in good health
BRAWLIER > BRAWLIE
BRAWLIEST > BRAWLIE
BRAWLING > BRAWL
BRAWLINGS > BRAWL
BRAWLS > BRAWL
BRAWLY > BRAW
BRAWN n physical strength
BRAWNED > BRAWN
BRAWNIER > BRAWNY
BRAWNIEST > BRAWNY
BRAWNILY > BRAWNY
BRAWNS > BRAWN
BRAWNY adj muscular and strong
BRAWS pl n fine apparel
BRAXIES > BRAXY
BRAXY n acute and usually fatal bacterial disease of sheep
BRAY vb (of a donkey) utter its loud harsh sound ▷ n donkey's loud harsh sound
BRAYED > BRAY
BRAYER > BRAY
BRAYERS > BRAY
BRAYING > BRAY
BRAYS > BRAY
BRAZA n Spanish unit of measurement
BRAZAS > BRAZA
BRAZE vb join (two metal surfaces) with brass ▷ n high-melting solder or alloy used in brazing
BRAZED > BRAZE
BRAZELESS > BRAZE
BRAZEN adj shameless and bold ▷ vb face and overcome boldly or shamelessly
BRAZENED > BRAZEN
BRAZENING > BRAZEN
BRAZENLY > BRAZEN
BRAZENRY n audacity
BRAZENS > BRAZEN

BRAZER > BRAZE
BRAZERS > BRAZE
BRAZES > BRAZE
BRAZIER n portable container for burning charcoal or coal
BRAZIERS > BRAZIER
BRAZIERY > BRAZIER
BRAZIL n red wood used for cabinetwork
BRAZILEIN n red crystalline solid
BRAZILIN n pale yellow soluble crystalline solid
BRAZILINS > BRAZILIN
BRAZILS > BRAZIL
BRAZING > BRAZE
BREACH n breaking of a promise, obligation, etc ▷ vb break (a promise, law, etc)
BREACHED > BREACH
BREACHER > BREACH
BREACHERS > BREACH
BREACHES > BREACH
BREACHING > BREACH
BREAD n food made by baking a mixture of flour and water or milk ▷ vb cover (food) with breadcrumbs before cooking
BREADBIN n container for bread
BREADBINS > BREADBIN
BREADBOX n airtight container for bread, cakes, etc
BREADED > BREAD
BREADHEAD n person solely concerned with money
BREADIER > BREADY
BREADIEST > BREADY
BREADING > BREAD
BREADLESS > BREAD
BREADLIKE adj like bread
BREADLINE n queue of people waiting for free food given as charity
BREADNUT n type of Central American and Caribbean tree
BREADNUTS > BREADNUT
BREADROOM n place where bread is kept on ship
BREADROOT n central N American leguminous plant with an edible starchy root
BREADS > BREAD
BREADTH n extent of something from side to side
BREADTHS > BREADTH
BREADY adj having the appearance or texture of bread
BREAK vb separate into pieces ▷ n act of breaking
BREAKABLE adj capable of being broken ▷ n fragile easily broken article

b

BREAKAGE n act or result of breaking
BREAKAGES > BREAKAGE
BREAKAWAY n dissenting group who have left a larger unit ▷ adj dissenting ▷ vb leave hastily or escape
BREAKBACK adj backbreaking; arduous
BREAKBEAT n type of electronic dance music
BREAKBONE adj as in breakbone fever dengue
BREAKDOWN n act or instance of breaking down
BREAKER n large wave
BREAKERS > BREAKER
BREAKEVEN n the level of commercial activity at which the total cost and total revenue of a business enterprise are equal
BREAKFAST n first meal of the day ▷ vb eat breakfast
BREAKING > BREAK
BREAKINGS > BRACKEN
BREAKNECK adj fast and dangerous
BREAKOFF n act or an instance of breaking off or stopping
BREAKOFFS > BREAKOFF
BREAKOUT n escape, esp from prison or confinement
BREAKOUTS > BREAKOUT
BREAKS > BREAK
BREAKTIME n period of rest or recreation, esp at school
BREAKUP n separation or disintegration
BREAKUPS > BREAKUP
BREAKWALL n breakwater
BREAM n Eurasian freshwater fish ▷ vb clean debris (from the bottom of a vessel)
BREAMED > BREAM
BREAMING > BREAM
BREAMS > BREAM
BREARE same as > BRIER
BREARES > BREARE
BREASKIT same as > BRISKET
BREASKITS > BREASKIT
BREAST n front part of the body from the neck to the abdomen ▷ vb reach the summit of
BREASTED > BREAST
BREASTFED adj fed at mother's breast
BREASTING > BREAST
BREASTPIN n brooch worn on the breast
BREASTS > BREAST
BREATH n taking in and letting out of air during breathing
BREATHE vb take in oxygen and give out carbon dioxide

BREATHED adj denoting a speech sound in which the vocal cords do not vibrate
BREATHER n short rest
BREATHERS > BREATHER
BREATHES > BREATHE
BREATHFUL > BREATH
BREATHIER > BREATHY
BREATHILY > BREATHY
BREATHING n passage of air into and out of the lungs to supply the body with oxygen
BREATHS > BREATH
BREATHY adj (of the speaking voice) accompanied by an audible emission of breath
BRECCIA n type of rock
BRECCIAL > BRECCIA
BRECCIAS > BRECCIA
BRECCIATE > BRECCIA
BRECHAM n straw horse-collar
BRECHAMS > BRECHAM
BRECHAN same as > BRECHAM
BRECHANS > BRECHAN
BRED n person who lives in a small remote place
BREDE archaic spelling of > BRAID
BREDED > BREDE
BREDES > BREDE
BREDIE n meat and vegetable stew
BREDIES > BREDIE
BREDING > BREDE
BREDREN same as > BRETHREN
BREDRENS > BREDREN
BREDRIN same as > BRETHREN
BREDRINS > BREDRIN
BREDS > BRED
BREE n broth, stock, or juice
BREECH n lower part ▷ vb fit (a gun) with a breech
BREECHED > BREECH
BREECHES pl n trousers extending to just below the knee
BREECHING n strap of a harness that passes behind a horse's haunches
BREED vb produce new or improved strains of (domestic animals or plants) ▷ n group of animals that within a species that have certain clearly defined characteristics
BREEDER n person who breeds plants or animals
BREEDERS > BREEDER
BREEDING > BREED
BREEDINGS > BREED
BREEDS > BREED
BREEKS pl n trousers
BREEM same as > BREME
BREENGE vb lunge forward ▷ n violent movement
BREENGED > BREENGE

BREENGES > BREENGE
BREENGING > BREENGE
BREER another word for > BRAIRD
BREERED > BREER
BREERING > BREER
BREERS > BREER
BREES > BREE
BREESE same as > BREEZE
BREESES > BREESE
BREEST Scot word for > BREAST
BREESTS > BREEST
BREEZE n gentle wind ▷ vb move quickly or casually
BREEZED > BREEZE
BREEZES > BREEZE
BREEZEWAY n roofed passageway connecting two buildings, sometimes with the sides enclosed
BREEZIER > BREEZY
BREEZIEST > BREEZY
BREEZILY > BREEZY
BREEZING > BREEZE
BREEZY adj windy
BREGMA n point on the top of the skull
BREGMAS > BREGMA
BREGMATA > BREGMA
BREGMATE > BREGMA
BREGMATIC > BREGMA
BREHON n (formerly) judge in Ireland
BREHONS > BREHON
BREI vb speak with a uvular r, esp in Afrikaans
BREID n bread
BREIDS > BREID
BREIING > BREI
BREINGE same as > BREENGE
BREINGED > BREINGE
BREINGES > BREINGE
BREINGING > BREINGE
BREIS > BREI
BREIST Scot word for > BREAST
BREISTS > BREIST
BREKKIE same as > BREKKY
BREKKIES > BREKKY
BREKKY slang word for > BREAKFAST
BRELOQUE n charm attached to watch chain
BRELOQUES > BRELOQUE
BREME adj well-known
BREN n type of machine gun ▷ vb burn
BRENNE vb burn
BRENNES > BRENNE
BRENNING > BREN
BRENS > BREN
BRENT n type of goose ▷ adj steep
BRENTER > BRENT
BRENTEST > BRENT
BRENTS > BRENT
BRER n brother: usually prefixed to a name
BRERE same as > BRIER
BRERES > BRERE
BRERS > BRER

BRESAOLA n (in Italian cookery) air-dried, salted beef
BRESAOLAS > BRESAOLA
BRETASCHE another word for > BRATTICE
BRETESSE another word for > BRATTICE
BRETESSES > BRETESSE
BRETHREN > BROTHER
BRETON n hat with an upturned brim and a rounded crown
BRETONS > BRETON
BRETTICE same as > BRATTICE
BRETTICED > BRETTICE
BRETTICES > BRETTICE
BREVE n accent placed over a vowel to indicate shortness
BREVES > BREVE
BREVET n document entitling a commissioned officer to hold temporarily a higher military rank ▷ vb promote by brevet
BREVETCY > BREVET
BREVETE adj patented
BREVETED > BREVET
BREVETING > BREVET
BREVETS > BREVET
BREVETTED > BREVET
BREVIARY n book of prayers to be recited daily by a Roman Catholic priest
BREVIATE n summary
BREVIATES > BREVIATE
BREVIER n (formerly) size of printer's type approximately equal to 8 point
BREVIERS > BREVIER
BREVIS same as > BREWIS
BREVISES > BREVIS
BREVITIES > BREVITY
BREVITY n shortness
BREW vb make (beer etc) by steeping, boiling, and fermentation ▷ n beverage produced by brewing
BREWAGE n product of brewing
BREWAGES > BREWAGE
BREWED > BREW
BREWER > BREW
BREWERIES > BREWERY
BREWERS > BREW
BREWERY n place where beer, etc is brewed
BREWHOUSE n brewery
BREWING n quantity of a beverage brewed at one time
BREWINGS > BREWING
BREWIS n bread soaked in broth, gravy, etc
BREWISES > BREWIS
BREWPUB n pub that incorporates a brewery on its premises

BREWPUBS > BREWPUB
BREWS > BREW
BREWSKI n beer
BREWSKIES > BREWSKI
BREWSKIS > BREWSKI
BREWSTER n person, particularly a woman, who brews
BREWSTERS > BREWSTER
BREY same as > BREI
BREYED > BREY
BREYING > BREY
BREYS > BREY
BRIAR n S European shrub with a hard woody root (briarroot)
BRIARD n medium-sized dog
BRIARDS > BRIARD
BRIARED > BRIAR
BRIARIER > BRIARY
BRIARIEST > BRIARY
BRIARROOT n hard woody root of the briar, used for making tobacco pipes
BRIARS > BRIAR
BRIARWOOD same as > BRIARROOT
BRIARY adj resembling or containing briar
BRIBABLE > BRIBE
BRIBE vb offer or give something to someone to gain favour, influence, etc ▷ n something given or offered as a bribe
BRIBEABLE > BRIBE
BRIBED > BRIBE
BRIBEE n one who is bribed
BRIBEES > BRIBEE
BRIBER > BRIBE
BRIBERIES > BRIBERY
BRIBERS > BRIBE
BRIBERY n process of giving or taking bribes
BRIBES > BRIBE
BRIBING > BRIBE
BRICABRAC n miscellaneous small objects, esp furniture and curios, kept because they are ornamental or rare
BRICHT Scot word for > BRIGHT
BRICHTER > BRICHT
BRICHTEST > BRICHT
BRICK n (rectangular block of) baked clay used in building ▷ vb build, enclose, or fill with bricks
BRICKBAT n blunt criticism
BRICKBATS > BRICKBAT
BRICKCLAY n clay for making bricks
BRICKED > BRICK
BRICKEN adj made of brick
BRICKIE n bricklayer
BRICKIER > BRICKY
BRICKIES > BRICKIE
BRICKIEST > BRICKY
BRICKING > BRICK
BRICKINGS > BRICK

BRICKKILN n kiln for making bricks
BRICKLE variant of > BRITTLE
BRICKLES > BRICKLE
BRICKLIKE > BRICK
BRICKS > BRICK
BRICKWALL same as > BRICOLE
BRICKWORK n structure, such as a wall, built of bricks
BRICKY adj resembling brick
BRICKYARD n place in which bricks are made, stored, or sold
BRICOLAGE n jumbled effect produced by the close proximity of buildings from different periods and in different architectural styles
BRICOLE n billiards shot
BRICOLES > BRICOLE
BRICOLEUR n person who practises bricolage
BRIDAL adj of a bride or a wedding ▷ n wedding or wedding feast
BRIDALLY > BRIDAL
BRIDALS > BRIDAL
BRIDE n woman who has just been or is about to be married ▷ vb act as a bride
BRIDECAKE n wedding cake
BRIDED > BRIDE
BRIDEMAID n old form of bridesmaid
BRIDEMAN n bridegroom's attendant
BRIDEMEN > BRIDEMAN
BRIDES > BRIDE
BRIDESMAN same as > BRIDEMAN
BRIDESMEN > BRIDESMAN
BRIDEWELL n house of correction
BRIDGABLE > BRIDGE
BRIDGE n structure for crossing a river etc ▷ vb build a bridge over (something)
BRIDGED > BRIDGE
BRIDGES > BRIDGE
BRIDGING n timber struts fixed between floor or roof joists
BRIDGINGS > BRIDGING
BRIDIE n semicircular pie containing meat and onions
BRIDIES > BRIDIE
BRIDING > BRIDE
BRIDLE n headgear for controlling a horse ▷ vb show anger or indignation
BRIDLED > BRIDLE
BRIDLER > BRIDLE
BRIDLERS > BRIDLE
BRIDLES > BRIDLE
BRIDLEWAY n path for riding horses
BRIDLING > BRIDLE
BRIDOON n horse's bit

BRIDOONS > BRIDOON
BRIE same as > BREE
BRIEF adj short in duration ▷ n condensed statement or written synopsis ▷ vb give information and instructions to (a person)
BRIEFCASE n small flat case for carrying papers, books, etc
BRIEFED > BRIEF
BRIEFER > BRIEF
BRIEFERS > BRIEF
BRIEFEST > BRIEF
BRIEFING n meeting for giving out detailed information or instructions
BRIEFINGS > BRIEFING
BRIEFLESS adj (of a barrister) without clients
BRIEFLY > BRIEF
BRIEFNESS > BRIEF
BRIEFS pl n men's or women's underpants without legs
BRIER same as > BRIAR
BRIERED > BRIER
BRIERIER > BRIER
BRIERIEST > BRIER
BRIERROOT same as > BRIARROOT
BRIERS > BRIER
BRIERWOOD same as > BRIARROOT
BRIERY > BRIER
BRIES > BRIE
BRIG n two-masted square-rigged ship
BRIGADE n army unit smaller than a division ▷ vb organize into a brigade
BRIGADED > BRIGADE
BRIGADES > BRIGADE
BRIGADIER n high-ranking army officer
BRIGADING > BRIGADE
BRIGALOW n type of acacia tree
BRIGALOWS > BRIGALOW
BRIGAND n bandit
BRIGANDRY > BRIGAND
BRIGANDS > BRIGAND
BRIGHT adj emitting or reflecting much light ▷ adv brightly
BRIGHTEN vb make or become bright or brighter
BRIGHTENS > BRIGHTEN
BRIGHTER > BRIGHT
BRIGHTEST > BRIGHT
BRIGHTISH > BRIGHT
BRIGHTLY > BRIGHT
BRIGHTS pl n high beam of the headlights of a motor vehicle
BRIGS > BRIG
BRIGUE vb solicit
BRIGUED > BRIGUE
BRIGUES > BRIGUE
BRIGUING > BRIGUE
BRIGUINGS > BRIGUE
BRIK n Tunisian pastry

BRIKI same as > CEZVE
BRIKIS > BRIKI
BRIKS > BRIK
BRILL n type of European flatfish popular as a food fish ▷ adj brilliant
BRILLER > BRILL
BRILLEST > BRILL
BRILLIANT adj shining with light ▷ n popular circular cut for diamonds and other gemstones in the form of two many-faceted pyramids (the top one truncated) joined at their bases
BRILLO n tradename for a type of scouring pad impregnated with a detergent
BRILLOS > BRILLO
BRILLS > BRILL
BRIM n upper rim of a vessel ▷ vb fill or be full to the brim
BRIMFUL adj completely filled with
BRIMFULL same as > BRIMFUL
BRIMFULLY > BRIMFUL
BRIMING n phosphorescence of sea
BRIMINGS > BRIMING
BRIMLESS > BRIM
BRIMMED > BRIM
BRIMMER n vessel, such as a glass or bowl, filled to the brim
BRIMMERS > BRIMMER
BRIMMING > BRIM
BRIMS > BRIM
BRIMSTONE n sulphur
BRIMSTONY adj like brimstone
BRIN n thread of silk from silkworm
BRINDED adj streaky or patchy
BRINDISI n song sung in celebration
BRINDISIS > BRINDISI
BRINDLE n brindled animal
BRINDLED adj brown or grey streaked with a darker colour
BRINDLES > BRINDLE
BRINE n salt water ▷ vb soak in or treat with brine
BRINED > BRINE
BRINELESS > BRINE
BRINER > BRINE
BRINERS > BRINE
BRINES > BRINE
BRING vb carry, convey, or take to a designated place or person
BRINGDOWN n comedown
BRINGER > BRING
BRINGERS > BRING
BRINGING > BRING
BRINGINGS > BRING
BRINGS > BRING
BRINIER > BRINY
BRINIES > BRINY
BRINIEST > BRINY

b

b

BRININESS > BRINY

BRINING > BRINE

BRINISH > BRINE

BRINJAL n dark purple tropical fruit, cooked and eaten as a vegetable

BRINJALS > BRINJAL

BRINJARRY n grain trader

BRINK n edge of a steep place

BRINKMAN n one who goes in for brinkmanship

BRINKMEN > BRINKMAN

BRINKS > BRINK

BRINNIES > BRINNY

BRINNY n stone, esp when thrown

BRINS > BRIN

BRINY adj very salty ▷ n sea

BRIO n liveliness

BRIOCHE n soft roll or loaf made from a very light yeast dough, sometimes mixed with currants

BRIOCHES > BRIOCHE

BRIOLETTE n pear-shaped gem cut with long triangular facets

BRIONIES > BRIONY

BRIONY same as > BRYONY

BRIOS > BRIO

BRIQUET same as > BRIQUETTE

BRIQUETS > BRIQUET

BRIQUETTE n block of compressed coal dust ▷ vb make into the form of a brick or bricks

BRIS n ritual circumcision of male babies

BRISANCE n shattering effect or power of an explosion or explosive

BRISANCES > BRISANCE

BRISANT > BRISANCE

BRISE n type of jump

BRISES > BRIS

BRISK adj lively and quick ▷ vb enliven

BRISKED > BRISK

BRISKEN vb make or become more lively or brisk

BRISKENED > BRISKEN

BRISKENS > BRISKEN

BRISKER > BRISK

BRISKEST > BRISK

BRISKET n beef from the breast of a cow

BRISKETS > BRISKET

BRISKIER > BRISKY

BRISKIEST > BRISKY

BRISKING > BRISK

BRISKISH > BRISK

BRISKLY > BRISK

BRISKNESS > BRISK

BRISKS > BRISK

BRISKY another word for > BRISK

BRISLING same as > SPRAT

BRISLINGS > BRISLING

BRISS same as > BRIS

BRISSES > BRIS

BRISTLE n short stiff hair ▷ vb (cause to) stand up like bristles

BRISTLED > BRISTLE

BRISTLES > BRISTLE

BRISTLIER > BRISTLE

BRISTLING > BRISTLE

BRISTLY > BRISTLE

BRISTOL n as in bristol board type of heavy cardboard

BRISTOLS pl n vulgar word for a woman's breasts

BRISURE n mark of cadency in heraldry

BRISURES > BRISURE

BRIT n young of a herring, sprat, or similar fish

BRITANNIA n coin bearing figure of Britannia

BRITCHES same as > BREECHES

BRITH same as > BRIS

BRITHS > BRITH

BRITS > BRIT

BRITSCHKA n light open carriage

BRITSKA same as > BRITZKA

BRITSKAS > BRITSKA

BRITT n young herring or sprat

BRITTANIA variant spelling of > BRITANNIA

BRITTLE adj hard but easily broken ▷ vb make brittle ▷ n crunchy sweet made with treacle and nuts

BRITTLED > BRITTLE

BRITTLELY > BRITTLE

BRITTLER > BRITTLE

BRITTLES > BRITTLE

BRITTLEST > BRITTLE

BRITTLING > BRITTLE

BRITTLY > BRITTLE

BRITTS > BRITT

BRITZKA n long horse-drawn carriage

BRITZKAS > BRITZKA

BRITZSKA same as > BRITZKA

BRITZSKAS > BRITZKA

BRIZE same as > BREEZE

BRIZES > BRIZE

BRO n close male associate

BROACH vb introduce (a topic) for discussion ▷ n spit for roasting meat

BROACHED > BROACH

BROACHER > BROACH

BROACHERS > BROACH

BROACHES > BROACH

BROACHING > BROACH

BROAD adj having great breadth or width ▷ n broad part of something

BROADAX same as > BROADAXE

BROADAXE n broad-bladed axe

BROADAXES > BROADAXE

BROADBAND n telecommunication transmission technique

using a wide range of frequencies

BROADBEAN n variety of bean

BROADBILL n tropical African and Asian bird with bright plumage and a short wide bill

BROADBRIM n broad-brimmed hat, esp one worn by the Quakers in the 17th century

BROADCAST n programme or announcement on radio or television ▷ vb transmit (a programme or announcement) on radio or television ▷ adj dispersed over a wide area ▷ adv far and wide

BROADEN vb make or become broad or broader

BROADENED > BROADEN

BROADENER > BROADEN

BROADENS > BROADEN

BROADER > BROAD

BROADEST > BROAD

BROADISH > BROAD

BROADLEAF n any tobacco plant having broad leaves, used esp in making cigars

BROADLINE n company dealing in large volumes of cheap products

BROADLOOM n a carpet woven on a wide loom

BROADLY > BROAD

BROADNESS > BROAD

BROADS > BROAD

BROADSIDE n strong verbal or written attack ▷ adv with a broader side facing an object

BROADTAIL n highly valued black wavy fur obtained from the skins of newly born karakul lambs

BROADWAY n wide road

BROADWAYS > BROADWAY

BROADWISE adv rare form of breadthwise

BROAST vb cook by broiling and roasting

BROASTED > BROAST

BROASTING > BROAST

BROASTS > BROAST

BROCADE n rich fabric woven with a raised design ▷ vb weave with such a design

BROCADED > BROCADE

BROCADES > BROCADE

BROCADING > BROCADE

BROCAGE another word for > BROKERAGE

BROCAGES > BROCAGE

BROCARD n basic principle of civil law

BROCARDS > BROCARD

BROCATEL n heavy upholstery brocade

BROCATELS > BROCATEL

BROCCOLI n type of cabbage with greenish flower heads

BROCCOLIS > BROCCOLI

BROCH n (in Scotland) a circular dry-stone tower large enough to serve as a fortified home

BROCHAN n type of thin porridge

BROCHANS > BROCHAN

BROCHE adj woven with a raised design, as brocade

BROCHED > BROCHE

BROCHES > BROCHE

BROCHETTE n skewer used for holding pieces of meat or vegetables while grilling

BROCHING > BROCHE

BROCHO same as > BRACHAH

BROCHOS > BROCHO

BROCHS > BROCH

BROCHURE n booklet that contains information about a product or service

BROCHURES > BROCHURE

BROCK n badger

BROCKAGE same as > BROKERAGE

BROCKAGES > BROCKAGE

BROCKED adj having different colours

BROCKET n small tropical American deer with small unbranched antlers

BROCKETS > BROCKET

BROCKIT same as > BROCKED

BROCKRAM another word for > BRECCIA

BROCKRAMS > BROCKRAM

BROCKS > BROCK

BROCOLI same as > BROCCOLI

BROCOLIS > BROCOLI

BROD vb prod

BRODDED > BROD

BRODDING > BROD

BRODDLE vb poke or pierce (something)

BRODDLED > BRODDLE

BRODDLES > BRODDLE

BRODDLING > BRODDLE

BRODEKIN another word for > BUSKIN

BRODEKINS > BRODEKIN

BRODKIN same as > BRODEKIN

BRODKINS > BRODKIN

BRODS > BROD

BROEKIES pl n underpants

BROG vb prick with an awl

BROGAN n heavy laced, usually ankle-high, work boot

BROGANS > BROGAN

BROGGED > BROG

BROGGING > BROG

BROGH same as > BROCH

BROGHS > BROGH

BROGS > BROG

BROGUE n gentle accent

BROGUEISH > BROGUE**

BROGUERY > BROGUE
BROGUES > BROGUE
BROGUISH > BROGUE
BROIDER *archaic word for* > EMBROIDER
BROIDERED > BROIDER
BROIDERER > BROIDER
BROIDERS > BROIDER
BROIDERY *n* old form of embroidery
BROIL *vb* cook by direct heat under a grill ▷ *n* process of broiling
BROILED > BROIL
BROILER *n* young tender chicken for roasting
BROILERS > BROILER
BROILING > BROIL
BROILS > BROIL
BROKAGE *another word for* > BROKERAGE
BROKAGES > BROKAGE
BROKE *vb* negotiate or deal
BROKED > BROKE
BROKEN > BREAK
BROKENLY > BREAK
BROKER *n* agent who buys or sells goods, securities, etc ▷ *vb* act as a broker (in)
BROKERAGE *n* commission charged by a broker
BROKERED > BROKER
BROKERIES > BROKERY
BROKERING > BROKER
BROKERS > BROKER
BROKERY *n* work done by a broker
BROKES > BROKE
BROKING > BROKE
BROKINGS > BROKE
BROLGA *n* large grey Australian crane with a trumpeting call
BROLGAS > BROLGA
BROLLIES > BROLLY
BROLLY *n* umbrella
BROMAL *n* synthetic liquid formerly used medicinally
BROMALS > BROMAL
BROMANCE *n* close friendship between two men
BROMANCES > BROMANCE
BROMANTIC *adj* pertaining to or indicating a bromance
BROMATE *same as* > BROMINATE
BROMATED > BROMATE
BROMATES > BROMATE
BROMATING > BROMATE
BROME *n* type of grass
BROMELAIN *n* enzyme in pineapples
BROMELIA *n* type of plant
BROMELIAD *n* tropical American plant with a rosette of fleshy leaves
BROMELIAS > BROMELIA
BROMELIN *n* protein-digesting enzyme found in pineapple

BROMELINS > BROMELIN
BROMEOSIN *another name for* > EOSIN
BROMES > BROME
BROMIC *adj* of or containing bromine in the trivalent or pentavalent state
BROMID *same as* > BROMIDE
BROMIDE *n* chemical compound used in medicine and photography
BROMIDES > BROMIDE
BROMIDIC *adj* ordinary
BROMIDS > BROMID
BROMIN *same as* > BROMINE
BROMINATE *vb* treat or react with bromine
BROMINE *n* dark red liquid element that gives off a pungent vapour
BROMINES > BROMINE
BROMINISM *same as* > BROMISM
BROMINS > BROMIN
BROMISE *same as* > BROMIZE
BROMISED > BROMISE
BROMISES > BROMISE
BROMISING > BROMIZE
BROMISM *n* bromine poisoning
BROMISMS > BROMISM
BROMIZE *vb* treat with bromine
BROMIZED > BROMIZE
BROMIZES > BROMIZE
BROMIZING > BROMIZE
BROMMER *n* S African word for bluebottle
BROMMERS > BROMMER
BROMO *n* something that contains bromide
BROMOFORM *n* heavy colourless liquid substance with a sweetish taste
BROMOS > BROMO
BRONC *same as* > BRONCO
BRONCHI > BRONCHUS
BRONCHIA *pl n* bronchial tubes
BRONCHIAL *adj* of the bronchi
BRONCHIUM *n* medium-sized bronchial tube
BRONCHO *same as* > BRONCO
BRONCHOS > BRONCHO
BRONCHUS *n* either of the two branches of the windpipe
BRONCO *n* (in the US) wild or partially tamed pony
BRONCOS > BRONCO
BRONCS > BRONC
BROND *n* piece of burning wood
BRONDE *adj* in a shade between blonde and brunette ▷ *n* woman with bronde hair
BRONDER > BRONDE

BRONDES > BRONDE
BRONDEST > BRONDE
BRONDS > BROND
BRONDYRON *n* sword
BRONZE *n* alloy of copper and tin ▷ *adj* made of, or coloured like, bronze ▷ *vb* (esp of the skin) make or become brown
BRONZED > BRONZE
BRONZEN *adj* made of or the colour of bronze
BRONZER *n* cosmetic applied to the skin to simulate a sun tan
BRONZERS > BRONZER
BRONZES > BRONZE
BRONZIER > BRONZE
BRONZIEST > BRONZE
BRONZIFY *vb* cause to become colour of bronze
BRONZING *n* blue pigment
BRONZINGS > BRONZING
BRONZITE *n* type of orthopyroxene often having a metallic or pearly sheen
BRONZITES > BRONZITE
BRONZY > BRONZE
BROO *n* brow of hill
BROOCH *n* ornament with a pin, worn fastened to clothes ▷ *vb* decorate with a brooch
BROOCHED > BROOCH
BROOCHES > BROOCH
BROOCHING > BROOCH
BROOD *n* number of birds produced at one hatching ▷ *vb* (of a bird) sit on or hatch eggs
BROODED > BROOD
BROODER *n* structure used for rearing young chickens or other fowl
BROODERS > BROODER
BROODIER > BROODY
BROODIEST > BROODY
BROODILY > BROODY
BROODING > BROOD
BROODINGS > BROOD
BROODLESS > BROOD
BROODMARE *n* mare for breeding
BROODS > BROOD
BROODY *adj* moody and sullen
BROOK *n* small stream ▷ *vb* bear or tolerate
BROOKABLE > BROOK
BROOKED > BROOK
BROOKIE *n* brook trout
BROOKIES > BROOKIE
BROOKING > BROOK
BROOKITE *n* reddish-brown to black mineral
BROOKITES > BROOKITE
BROOKLET *n* small brook
BROOKLETS > BROOKLET
BROOKLIKE > BROOK
BROOKLIME *n* type of blue-flowered trailing

plant of N America, Europe or Asia, which grows in moist places
BROOKS > BROOK
BROOKWEED *n* type of white-flowered plant of Europe or North America, growing in moist places
BROOL *n* low roar
BROOLS > BROOL
BROOM *n* long-handled sweeping brush ▷ *vb* sweep with a broom
BROOMBALL *n* type of ice hockey played with broom
BROOMCORN *n* variety of sorghum, the long stiff flower stalks of which can be used to make brooms
BROOMED > BROOM
BROOMIER > BROOMY
BROOMIEST > BROOMY
BROOMING > BROOM
BROOMRAPE *n* type of plant which grows as brownish small-flowered leafless parasites on the roots of other plants
BROOMS > BROOM
BROOMY *adj* covered with a growth of broom
BROOS > BROO
BROOSE *n* race at a country wedding
BROOSES > BROOSE
BROS > BRO
BROSE *n* oatmeal or pease porridge, sometimes with butter or fat added
BROSES > BROSE
BROSIER > BROSY
BROSIEST > BROSY
BROSY *adj* smeared with porridge
BROTH *n* soup, usu containing vegetables
BROTHA *n* informal term for an African-American man
BROTHAS > BROTHA
BROTHEL *n* house where people pay to have sex with sex workers
BROTHELS > BROTHEL
BROTHER *n* boy or man with the same parents as another person ▷ *interj* exclamation of amazement, surprise, disappointment, etc ▷ *vb* treat someone like a brother
BROTHERED > BROTHER
BROTHERLY *adj* of or like a brother, esp in showing loyalty and affection ▷ *adv* in a brotherly way
BROTHERS > BROTHER
BROTHIER > BROTHY
BROTHIEST > BROTHY
BROTHS > BROTH
BROTHY *adj* having the appearance or texture of broth
BROUGH *same as* > BROCH
BROUGHAM *n* horse-drawn closed carriage with a raised open driver's seat in front

b

BROUGHAMS
> BROUGHAM

BROUGHS > BROUGH

BROUGHT > BRING

BROUGHTA same as
> BRAATA

BROUGHTAS same as
> BRAATA

BROUHAHA n loud
confused noise

BROUHAHAS
> BROUHAHA

BROUZE same as > BROOSE

BROUZES > BROUZE

BROW n part of the face
(from the eyes to the
hairline)

BROWALLIA n flowering
plant

BROWBAND n strap of a
horse's bridle that goes
across the forehead

BROWBANDS
> BROWBAND

BROWBEAT vb frighten
(someone) with threats

BROWBEATS
> BROWBEAT

BROWBONE n bone of the
brow

BROWBONES
> BROWBONE

BROWED adj having a brow

BROWLESS > BROW

BROWN n colour of earth or
wood ▷ adj (of bread)
made from wheatmeal or
wholemeal flour ▷ vb
make or become brown

BROWNED > BROWN

BROWNER n brown object

BROWNERS > BROWNER

BROWNEST > BROWN

BROWNIE n small square
nutty chocolate cake

BROWNIER > BROWN

BROWNIES > BROWNIE

BROWNIEST > BROWN

BROWNING n substance
used to darken gravies

BROWNINGS
> BROWNING

BROWNISH > BROWN

BROWNNESS > BROWN

BROWNNOSE vb be
abjectly subservient

BROWNOUT n dimming or
reduction in the use of
electric lights in a city

BROWNOUTS
> BROWNOUT

BROWNS > BROWN

BROWNTAIL as in
browntail moth kind of
moth

BROWNY > BROWN

BROWRIDGE n ridge of
bone over eyes

BROWS > BROW

BROWSABLE > BROWSE

BROWSE vb look through
in a casual manner ▷ n
instance of browsing

BROWSED > BROWSE

BROWSER n software
package that enables a
user to read hypertext, esp
on the internet

BROWSERS > BROWSER

BROWSES > BROWSE

BROWSIER > BROWSE

BROWSIEST > BROWSE

BROWSING > BROWSE

BROWSINGS > BROWSE

BROWST n brewing (of ale,
tea)

BROWSTS > BROWST

BROWSY > BROWSE

BRR same as > BRRR

BRRR interj used to
suggest shivering

BRU South African word for
> FRIEND

BRUCELLA n type of
bacterium

BRUCELLAE
> BRUCELLA

BRUCELLAS
> BRUCELLA

BRUCHID n type of
beetle

BRUCHIDS > BRUCHID

BRUCIN same as
> BRUCINE

BRUCINE n bitter
poisonous alkaloid
resembling strychnine

BRUCINES > BRUCINE

BRUCINS > BRUCIN

BRUCITE n white
translucent mineral

BRUCITES > BRUCITE

BRUCKLE adj brittle

BRUGH n large house

BRUGHS > BRUGH

BRUHAHA same as
> BROUHAHA

BRUHAHAS > BRUHAHA

BRUILZIE same as
> BRULZIE

BRUILZIES
> BRUILZIE

BRUIN n name for a bear,
used in children's tales,
fables, etc

BRUINS > BRUIN

BRUISE n discoloured
area on the skin caused by
an injury ▷ vb cause a
bruise on

BRUISED > BRUISE

BRUISER n strong tough
person

BRUISERS > BRUISER

BRUISES > BRUISE

BRUISING adj causing
bruises, as by a blow ▷ n
bruise or bruises

BRUISINGS
> BRUISING

BRUIT vb report ▷ n
abnormal sound heard
within the body

BRUITED > BRUIT

BRUITER > BRUIT

BRUITERS > BRUIT

BRUITING > BRUIT

BRUITS > BRUIT

BRULE n person of Native
Canadian and French
Canadian ancestry

BRULES > BRULE

BRULOT n coffee-based
alcoholic drink, served
flaming

BRULOTS > BRULOT

BRULYIE same as
> BRULZIE

BRULYIES > BRULYIE

BRULZIE n noisy dispute

BRULZIES > BRULZIE

BRUMAL adj of,
characteristic of, or
relating to winter

BRUMBIES > BRUMBY

BRUMBY n wild horse

BRUME n heavy mist or fog

BRUMES > BRUME

BRUMMAGEM n something
that is cheap and flashy,
esp imitation jewellery

BRUMMER same as
> BROMMER

BRUMMERS > BRUMMER

BRUMOUS > BRUME

BRUNCH n breakfast and
lunch combined ▷ vb eat
brunch

BRUNCHED > BRUNCH

BRUNCHER > BRUNCH

BRUNCHERS > BRUNCH

BRUNCHES > BRUNCH

BRUNCHING > BRUNCH

BRUNET n boy or man
with dark brown hair

BRUNETS > BRUNET

BRUNETTE n girl or
woman with dark brown
hair

BRUNETTES > BRUNETTE

BRUNG > BRING

BRUNIZEM n prairie soil

BRUNIZEMS
> BRUNIZEM

BRUNT n main force or
shock of a blow, attack,
etc ▷ vb suffer the main
force or shock of a blow,
attack, etc

BRUNTED > BRUNT

BRUNTING > BRUNT

BRUNTS > BRUNT

BRUS > BRU

BRUSH n device made of
bristles, wires, etc ▷ vb
clean, scrub, or paint with
a brush

BRUSHABLE adj able to
be brushed

BRUSHBACK n (baseball)
ball intended to hit the
batter

BRUSHED adj treated with
a brushing process

BRUSHER > BRUSH

BRUSHERS > BRUSH

BRUSHES > BRUSH

BRUSHFIRE n fire in
bushes and scrub

BRUSHIER > BRUSHY

BRUSHIEST > BRUSHY

BRUSHING > BRUSH

BRUSHINGS > BRUSH

BRUSHLAND n land
characterized by patchy
shrubs

BRUSHLESS > BRUSH

BRUSHLIKE > BRUSH

BRUSHMARK n indented
lines sometimes left by the
bristles of a brush on a
painted surface

BRUSHOFF n abrupt
dismissal or rejection

BRUSHOFFS
> BRUSHOFF

BRUSHUP n the act or an
instance of tidying one's
appearance

BRUSHUPS > BRUSHUP

BRUSHWOOD n cut or
broken-off tree branches
and twigs

BRUSHWORK n
characteristic manner of
applying paint with a
brush

BRUSHY adj like a brush

BRUSK same as
> BRUSQUE

BRUSKER > BRUSK

BRUSKEST > BRUSK

BRUSQUE adj blunt or curt
in manner or speech

BRUSQUELY > BRUSQUE

BRUSQUER > BRUSQUE

BRUSQUEST > BRUSQUE

BRUSSELS adj as in
brussels sprout small
cabbage-like vegetable

BRUSSEN adj bold

BRUST same as > BURST

BRUSTING > BRUST

BRUSTS > BRUST

BRUT adj (of champagne
or sparkling wine) very dry
▷ n very dry champagne

BRUTAL adj cruel and
vicious

BRUTALISE same as
> BRUTALIZE

BRUTALISM n austere
architectural style of the
1950s on, characterized by
the use of exposed
concrete and angular
shapes

BRUTALIST
> BRUTALISM

BRUTALITY > BRUTAL

BRUTALIZE vb make or
become brutal

BRUTALLY > BRUTAL

BRUTE n brutal person
▷ adj wholly instinctive or
physical, like an animal

BRUTED > BRUTING

BRUTELIKE > BRUTE

BRUTELY > BRUTE

BRUTENESS > BRUTE

BRUTER n diamond cutter

BRUTERS > BRUTER

BRUTES > BRUTE

BRUTEST > BRUTE

BRUTIFIED > BRUTIFY

BRUTIFIES > BRUTIFY

BRUTIFY less common
word for > BRUTALIZE

BRUTING n diamond
cutting

BRUTINGS > BRUTING

BRUTISH adj of or like an
animal

BRUTISHLY > BRUTISH

BRUTISM n stupidity;
vulgarity

BRUTISMS > BRUTISM

BRUTS > BRUT

BRUX vb grind one's teeth

BRUXED > BRUX

BRUXES > BRUX

BRUXING > BRUX

BRUXISM n habit of grinding the teeth, esp unconsciously

BRUXISMS > BRUXISM

BRYOLOGY n branch of botany concerned with the study of bryophytes

BRYONIES > BRYONY

BRYONY n wild climbing hedge plant

BRYOPHYTE n type of plant such as mosses, liverworts, or hornworts, which has stems and leaves but lacks roots and reproduces by spores

BRYOZOAN n type of aquatic invertebrate which forms colonies of polyps

BRYOZOANS > BRYOZOAN

BUAT same as > BOWAT

BUATS > BUAT

BUAZE n fibrous African plant

BUAZES > BUAZE

BUB n youngster

BUBA another name for > YAWS

BUBAL n type of antelope

BUBALE n type of antelope

BUBALES > BUBALE

BUBALINE adj (of antelopes) related to or resembling the bubal

BUBALIS same as > BUBAL

BUBALISES > BUBALIS

BUBALS > BUBAL

BUBAS > BUBA

BUBBE n Yiddish word for grandmother

BUBBES > BUBBE

BUBBIE same as > BUBBE

BUBBIES > BUBBY

BUBBLE n ball of air in a liquid or solid ▷ vb form bubbles

BUBBLED > BUBBLE

BUBBLEGUM n type of chewing gum that can be blown into large bubbles

BUBBLER n drinking fountain

BUBBLERS > BUBBLER

BUBBLES > BUBBLE

BUBBLIER > BUBBLY

BUBBLIES > BUBBLY

BUBBLIEST > BUBBLY

BUBBLING > BUBBLE

BUBBLY adj excited and lively ▷ n champagne

BUBBY n old word for woman's breast

BUBINGA n reddish-brown wood from African tree

BUBINGAS > BUBINGA

BUBKES same as > BUBKIS

BUBKIS n nothing

BUBO n inflammation and swelling of a lymph node, esp in the armpit or groin

BUBOED > BUBO

BUBOES > BUBO

BUBONIC > BUBO

BUBS > BUB

BUBU same as > BOUBOU

BUBUKLE n red spot on skin

BUBUKLES > BUBUKLE

BUBUS > BUBU

BUCARDO n type of Spanish mountain goat, recently extinct

BUCARDOS > BUCARDO

BUCATINI pl n pasta in the shape of long tubes

BUCCAL adj of or relating to the cheek

BUCCALLY > BUCCAL

BUCCANEER n pirate ▷ vb be or act like a buccaneer

BUCCANIER same as > BUCCANEER

BUCCINA n curved Roman horn

BUCCINAS > BUCCINA

BUCELLAS n type of Portuguese white wine

BUCENTAUR n state barge of Venice from which the doge and other officials dropped a ring into the sea on Ascension Day to symbolize the ceremonial marriage of the state with the Adriatic

BUCHU n S African shrub whose leaves are used as an antiseptic and diuretic

BUCHUS > BUCHU

BUCK n male of the goat, hare, kangaroo, rabbit, and reindeer ▷ vb (of a horse etc) jump with legs stiff and back arched

BUCKAROO n cowboy

BUCKAROOS > BUCKAROO

BUCKAYRO same as > BUCKAROO

BUCKAYROS > BUCKAYRO

BUCKBEAN n type of marsh plant with white or pink flowers

BUCKBEANS > BUCKBEAN

BUCKBOARD n open four-wheeled horse-drawn carriage with the seat attached to a flexible board between the front and rear axles

BUCKBRUSH n American shrub

BUCKED > BUCK

BUCKEEN n (in Ireland) poor young man who aspires to the habits and dress of the wealthy

BUCKEENS > BUCKEEN

BUCKER > BUCK

BUCKEROO same as > BUCKAROO

BUCKEROOS > BUCKEROO

BUCKERS > BUCK

BUCKET n open-topped roughly cylindrical container ▷ vb rain heavily

BUCKETED > BUCKET

BUCKETFUL n amount that a bucket is able to hold

BUCKETING > BUCKET

BUCKETS > BUCKET

BUCKEYE n N American tree with erect clusters of white or red flowers and prickly fruits

BUCKEYES > BUCKEYE

BUCKHORN n horn from a buck, used for knife handles, etc

BUCKHORNS > BUCKHORN

BUCKHOUND n hound, smaller than a staghound, used for hunting the smaller breeds of deer, esp fallow deer

BUCKIE n whelk or its shell

BUCKIES > BUCKIE

BUCKING > BUCK

BUCKINGS > BUCK

BUCKISH > BUCK

BUCKISHLY > BUCK

BUCKLE n clasp for fastening a belt or strap ▷ vb fasten or be fastened with a buckle

BUCKLED > BUCKLE

BUCKLER n small round shield worn on the forearm ▷ vb defend

BUCKLERED > BUCKLER

BUCKLERS > BUCKLER

BUCKLES > BUCKLE

BUCKLING another name for > BLOATER

BUCKLINGS > BUCKLING

BUCKO n lively young fellow: often a term of address

BUCKOES > BUCKO

BUCKOS > BUCKO

BUCKRAKE n large rake attached to tractor

BUCKRAKES > BUCKRAKE

BUCKRAM n cotton or linen cloth stiffened with size, etc ▷ vb stiffen with buckram

BUCKRAMED > BUCKRAM

BUCKRAMS > BUCKRAM

BUCKS > BUCK

BUCKSAW n woodcutting saw

BUCKSAWS > BUCKSAW

BUCKSHEE adj free

BUCKSHEES > BUCKSHEE

BUCKSHISH n tip, present or gift

BUCKSHOT n large lead pellets used for shooting game

BUCKSHOTS > BUCKSHOT

BUCKSKIN n skin of a male deer ▷ adj greyish-yellow

BUCKSKINS pl n (in the US and Canada) breeches, shoes, or a suit of buckskin

BUCKSOM same as > BUXOM

BUCKTAIL n in fishing, fly with appearance of minnow

BUCKTAILS > BUCKTAIL

BUCKTEETH > BUCKTOOTH

BUCKTHORN n thorny shrub whose berries were formerly used as a purgative

BUCKTOOTH n projecting upper front tooth

BUCKU same as > BUCHU

BUCKUS > BUCKU

BUCKWHEAT n small black grain used for making flour

BUCKYBALL n ball-like polyhedral carbon molecule of the type found in buckminsterfullerene and other fullerenes

BUCKYTUBE n tube of carbon atoms structurally similar to buckminsterfullerene

BUCOLIC adj of the countryside or country life ▷ n pastoral poem

BUCOLICAL > BUCOLIC

BUCOLICS > BUCOLIC

BUD n swelling on a plant that develops into a leaf or flower ▷ vb produce buds

BUDA n sometimes derogatory Indian English word for an old man

BUDAS > BUDA

BUDDED > BUD

BUDDER > BUD

BUDDERS > BUD

BUDDHA n person who has achieved a state of perfect enlightenment

BUDDHAS > BUDDHA

BUDDIED > BUDDY

BUDDIER > BUDDY

BUDDIES > BUDDY

BUDDIEST > BUDDY

BUDDING > BUD

BUDDINGS > BUD

BUDDLE n sloping trough in which ore is washed ▷ vb wash (ore) in a buddle

BUDDLED > BUDDLE

BUDDLEIA n shrub with long spikes of purple flowers

BUDDLEIAS > BUDDLEIA

BUDDLES > BUDDLE

BUDDLING > BUDDLE

BUDDY n friend ▷ vb act as a friend to ▷ adj friendly

BUDDYING > BUDDY

BUDGE vb move slightly ▷ n lambskin dressed for the fur to be worn on the outer side

BUDGED > BUDGE

BUDGER > BUDGE

BUDGEREE adj good

BUDGERO same as > BUDGEROW

BUDGEROS > BUDGERO

BUDGEROW n barge used on the Ganges

BUDGEROWS
> BUDGEROW
BUDGERS > BUDGE
BUDGES > BUDGE
BUDGET n financial plan for a period of time ▷ vb plan the expenditure of (money or time) ▷ adj cheap
BUDGETARY > BUDGET
BUDGETED > BUDGET
BUDGETEER n one who prepares a budget
BUDGETER > BUDGET
BUDGETERS > BUDGET
BUDGETING n act of budgeting
BUDGETS > BUDGET
BUDGIE n short form of budgerigar
BUDGIES > BUDGIE
BUDGING > BUDGE
BUDI n sometimes derogatory Indian English word an for old woman
BUDIS > BUDI
BUDLESS > BUD
BUDLIKE > BUD
BUDMASH same as
> BADMASH
BUDMASHES
> BUDMASH
BUDO n combat and spirit in martial arts
BUDOS > BUDO
BUDS > BUD
BUDTENDER n person working in a shop where cannabis is sold
BUDWOOD n branch with buds that is used for grafting
BUDWOODS > BUDWOOD
BUDWORM n pest that eats tree leaves and buds
BUDWORMS > BUDWORM
BUFF n soft flexible undyed leather ▷ adj dull yellowish-brown ▷ vb clean or polish with soft material
BUFFA n female comic part in an opera
BUFFABLE > BUFF
BUFFALO n member of the cattle tribe ▷ vb confuse
BUFFALOED > BUFFALO
BUFFALOES > BUFFALO
BUFFALOS > BUFFALO
BUFFAS > BUFFA
BUFFE > BUFFO
BUFFED > BUFF
BUFFEL adj as in buffel grass grass used for pasture in Africa, India, and Australia
BUFFER vb protect from shock
BUFFERED > BUFFER
BUFFERING n act of buffering
BUFFERS > BUFFER
BUFFEST > BUFF
BUFFET n counter where drinks and snacks are served ▷ vb knock against or about

BUFFETED > BUFFET
BUFFETER > BUFFET
BUFFETERS > BUFFET
BUFFETING n response of an aircraft structure to buffet, esp an irregular oscillation of the tail
BUFFETS > BUFFET
BUFFI > BUFFO
BUFFIER > BUFFY
BUFFIEST > BUFFY
BUFFING n act of polishing
BUFFINGS > BUFFING
BUFFO n (in Italian opera of the 18th century) comic part, esp one for a bass
BUFFOON n clown or fool
BUFFOONS > BUFFOON
BUFFOS > BUFFO
BUFFS > BUFF
BUFFY adj having appearance or texture of buff
BUFO n type of toad
BUFOS > BUFO
BUFOTALIN n principal poisonous substance in the skin and saliva of the common European toad
BUG n insect ▷ vb irritate
BUGABOO n imaginary source of fear
BUGABOOS > BUGABOO
BUGBANE n European plant whose flowers are reputed to repel insects
BUGBANES > BUGBANE
BUGBEAR n thing that causes obsessive anxiety
BUGBEARS > BUGBEAR
BUGEYE n oyster-dredging boat
BUGEYES > BUGEYE
BUGGAN n evil spirit
BUGGANE same as
> BUGGAN
BUGGANES > BUGGANE
BUGGANS > BUGGAN
BUGGED > BUG
BUGGER n vulgar slang word for an unpleasant or difficult person or thing ▷ vb tire ▷ interj exclamation of annoyance or disappointment
BUGGERED > BUGGER
BUGGERIES > BUGGERY
BUGGERING > BUGGER
BUGGERS > BUGGER
BUGGERY n old term for anal intercourse
BUGGIER > BUGGY
BUGGIES > BUGGY
BUGGIEST > BUGGY
BUGGIN same as
> BUGGAN
BUGGINESS > BUGGY
BUGGING > BUG
BUGGINGS > BUG
BUGGINS > BUGGIN
BUGGY n light horse-drawn carriage ▷ adj infested with bugs
BUGHOUSE n slang term for a psychiatric hospital
BUGHOUSES
> BUGHOUSE

BUGLE n instrument like a small trumpet ▷ vb play or sound (on) a bugle
BUGLED > BUGLE
BUGLER > BUGLE
BUGLERS > BUGLE
BUGLES > BUGLE
BUGLET n small bugle
BUGLETS > BUGLET
BUGLEWEED same as
> BUGLE
BUGLING > BUGLE
BUGLOSS n hairy Eurasian plant with clusters of blue flowers
BUGLOSSES > BUGLOSS
BUGONG same as
> BOGONG
BUGONGS > BUGONG
BUGOUT n act of running away
BUGOUTS > BUGOUT
BUGS > BUG
BUGSEED n form of tumbleweed
BUGSEEDS > BUGSEED
BUGSHA same as
> BUQSHA
BUGSHAS > BUGSHA
BUGWORT another name for
> BUGBANE
BUGWORTS > BUGWORT
BUHL same as > BOULLE
BUHLS > BUHL
BUHLWORK n woodwork with decorative inlay
BUHLWORKS
> BUHLWORK
BUHR same as > BURR
BUHRS > BUHR
BUHRSTONE n hard tough rock containing silica, fossils, and cavities, formerly used as a grindstone
BUHUND n type of Norwegian dog
BUHUNDS > BUHUND
BUIBUI n black cloth worn as a shawl by Muslim women
BUIBUIS > BUIBUI
BUIK same as > BOOK
BUIKS > BUIK
BUILD vb make, construct, or form by joining parts or materials ▷ n shape of the body
BUILDABLE adj suitable for building on
BUILDDOWN n planned reduction
BUILDED > BUILD
BUILDER n person who constructs houses and other buildings
BUILDERS > BUILDER
BUILDING > BUILD
BUILDINGS > BUILD
BUILDOUT n expansion, development, or growth
BUILDOUTS
> BUILDOUT
BUILDS > BUILD
BUILDUP n gradual approach to a climax or critical point
BUILDUPS > BUILDUP

BUILT > BUILD
BUIRDLIER > BUIRDLY
BUIRDLY adj well-built
BUIST vb brand sheep with an identification mark
BUISTED > BUIST
BUISTING > BUIST
BUISTS > BUIST
BUKE same as > BOOK
BUKES > BUKE
BUKKAKE n type of sexual practice
BUKKAKES > BUKKAKE
BUKSHEE n person in charge of paying wages
BUKSHEES > BUKSHEE
BUKSHI same as
> BUKSHEE
BUKSHIS > BUKSHI
BULB n onion-shaped root which grows into a flower or plant ▷ vb form into the shape of a bulb
BULBAR adj of or relating to a bulb, esp the medulla oblongata
BULBED > BULB
BULBEL same as
> BULBIL
BULBELS > BULBEL
BULBIL n small bulblike organ growing on plants such as the onion and tiger lily
BULBILS > BULBIL
BULBING > BULB
BULBLET n small bulb at the base of a main bulb
BULBLETS > BULBLET
BULBOSITY > BULBOUS
BULBOUS adj round and fat
BULBOUSLY > BULBOUS
BULBS > BULB
BULBUL n songbird of tropical Africa and Asia
BULBULS > BULBUL
BULGAR same as
> BULGUR
BULGARS > BULGAR
BULGE n swelling on a normally flat surface ▷ vb swell outwards
BULGED > BULGE
BULGER > BULGE
BULGERS > BULGE
BULGES > BULGE
BULGHUR same as
> BULGUR
BULGHURS > BULGHUR
BULGIER > BULGE
BULGIEST > BULGE
BULGINE same as
> BULLGINE
BULGINES > BULGINE
BULGINESS > BULGE
BULGING adj curving outwards
BULGINGLY > BULGY
BULGUR n kind of dried cracked wheat
BULGURS > BULGUR
BULGY > BULGE
BULIMIA n eating disorder
BULIMIAC n person who has bulimia

BULIMIACS
> BULIMIAC

BULIMIAS > BULIMIA

BULIMIC > BULIMIA

BULIMICS > BULIMIA

BULIMIES > BULIMY

BULIMUS *n* terrestrial mollusc

BULIMUSES > BULIMIA

BULIMY *same as*
> BULIMIA

BULK *n* volume, size, or magnitude of something ▷ *vb* cohere or cause to cohere in a mass

BULKAGE > BULK

BULKAGES > BULK

BULKED > BULK

BULKER *n* ship that carries bulk cargo

BULKERS > BULKER

BULKHEAD *n* partition in a ship or aeroplane

BULKHEADS
> BULKHEAD

BULKIER > BULKY

BULKIEST > BULKY

BULKILY > BULKY

BULKINESS > BULKY

BULKING *n* expansion of excavated material to a greater volume

BULKINGS > BULKING

BULKS > BULK

BULKY *adj* very large and massive, esp so as to be unwieldy

BULL *n* male bovine animal ▷ *vb* raise the price of (a security)

BULLA *n* leaden seal affixed to a papal bull

BULLACE *n* small Eurasian tree of which the damson is the cultivated form

BULLACES > BULLACE

BULLAE > BULLA

BULLARIES > BULLARY

BULLARY *n* boilery for preparing salt

BULLATE *adj* puckered or blistered in appearance

BULLBARS *pl n* large protective metal grille on the front of some vehicles

BULLBAT *another name for*
> NIGHTHAWK

BULLBATS > BULLBAT

BULLBRIER *n* prickly American vine

BULLCOOK *n* casual or odd job worker in a camp

BULLCOOKS
> BULLCOOK

BULLDOG *n* thickset dog with a broad head and a muscular body

BULLDOGS > BULLDOG

BULLDOZE *vb* demolish or flatten with a bulldozer

BULLDOZED
> BULLDOZE

BULLDOZER *n* powerful tractor for moving earth

BULLDOZES
> BULLDOZE

BULLDUST *n* fine dust

BULLDUSTS
> BULLDUST

BULLED > BULL

BULLER *vb* make bubbling sound

BULLERED > BULLER

BULLERING > BULLER

BULLERS > BULLER

BULLET *n* small piece of metal fired from a gun ▷ *vb* move extremely quickly

BULLETED > BULLET

BULLETIN *n* short official report or announcement ▷ *vb* make known by bulletin

BULLETING > BULLET

BULLETINS
> BULLETIN

BULLETRIE *n* type of tree of the Caribbean

BULLETS > BULLET

BULLEY *n* fishing boat with two masts

BULLEYS > BULLEY

BULLFIGHT *n* public show in which a matador kills a bull

BULLFINCH *n* common European songbird

BULLFROG *n* large American frog with a deep croak

BULLFROGS
> BULLFROG

BULLGINE *n* steam locomotive

BULLGINES
> BULLGINE

BULLHEAD *n* type of small northern mainly marine fish

BULLHEADS
> BULLHEAD

BULLHORN *n* portable loudspeaker having a built-in amplifier and microphone

BULLHORNS
> BULLHORN

BULLIED > BULLY

BULLIER > BULLY

BULLIES > BULLY

BULLIEST > BULLY

BULLING *n* act of raising the price of a security

BULLINGS > BULLING

BULLION *n* gold or silver in the form of bars

BULLIONS > BULLION

BULLISH *adj* like a bull

BULLISHLY > BULLISH

BULLNECK *n* enlarged neck

BULLNECKS
> BULLNECK

BULLNOSE *n* rounded exterior angle, as where two walls meet

BULLNOSED *adj* having a rounded end

BULLNOSES
> BULLNOSE

BULLOCK *n* young bull ▷ *vb* work hard and long

BULLOCKED > BULLOCK

BULLOCKS > BULLOCK

BULLOCKY *n* driver of a team of bullocks ▷ *adj* resembling a bullock

BULLOSA *adj* as in epidermolysis bullosa type of genetic skin disorder

BULLOUS *adj* blistered

BULLPEN *n* large cell where prisoners are confined together temporarily

BULLPENS > BULLPEN

BULLPOUT *n* type of fish

BULLPOUTS
> BULLPOUT

BULLRING *n* arena for staging bullfights

BULLRINGS
> BULLRING

BULLRUSH *same as*
> BULRUSH

BULLS > BULL

BULLSEYE *n* central disc of a target

BULLSEYES
> BULLSEYE

BULLSHAT > BULLSHIT

BULLSHIT *n* vulgar word for exaggerated or foolish talk ▷ *vb* talk bullshit to

BULLSHITS
> BULLSHIT

BULLSHOT *n* cocktail of vodka and beef stock

BULLSHOTS
> BULLSHOT

BULLSNAKE *n* American burrowing snake

BULLWADDY *n* N Australian tree which grows in dense thickets

BULLWEED *n* knapweed

BULLWEEDS
> BULLWEED

BULLWHACK *vb* flog with short whip

BULLWHIP *n* long tapering heavy whip, esp one of plaited rawhide ▷ *vb* whip with a bullwhip

BULLWHIPS
> BULLWHIP

BULLY *n* person who repeatedly intimidates another person ▷ *vb* repeatedly intimidate another person ▷ *adj* dashing

BULLYBOY *n* ruffian or tough, esp a hired one

BULLYBOYS
> BULLYBOY

BULLYCIDE *n* suicide as a result of bullying

BULLYING *n* act of threatening another person

BULLYINGS
> BULLYING

BULLYISM > BULLY

BULLYISMS > BULLY

BULLYRAG *vb* bully, esp by means of cruel practical jokes

BULLYRAGS
> BULLYRAG

BULNBULN *another name for* > LYREBIRD

BULNBULNS > BULNBULN

BULRUSH *n* tall stiff reed

BULRUSHES > BULRUSH

BULRUSHY *adj* full of bulrushes

BULSE *n* purse or bag for diamonds

BULSES > BULSE

BULWADDEE *same as*
> BULLWADDY

BULWADDY *same as*
> BULLWADDY

BULWARK *n* wall used as a fortification ▷ *vb* defend or fortify with or as if with a bulwark

BULWARKED > BULWARK

BULWARKS > BULWARK

BUM *n* loafer or idler ▷ *vb* get by begging ▷ *adj* of poor quality

BUMALO *same as*
> BUMMALO

BUMALOTI *same as*
> BUMMALOTI

BUMALOTIS
> BUMMALOTI

BUMBAG *n* small bag attached to a belt and worn round the waist

BUMBAGS > BUMBAG

BUMBAZE *vb* confuse; bewilder

BUMBAZED > BUMBAZE

BUMBAZES > BUMBAZE

BUMBAZING > BUMBAZE

BUMBLE *vb* speak, do, or move in a clumsy way ▷ *n* blunder or botch

BUMBLEBEE *n* large hairy bee

BUMBLED > BUMBLE

BUMBLEDOM *n* self-importance in a minor office

BUMBLER > BUMBLE

BUMBLERS > BUMBLE

BUMBLES > BUMBLE

BUMBLING > BUMBLE

BUMBLINGS > BUMBLE

BUMBO *n* African tree

BUMBOAT *n* any small boat used for ferrying goods to a ship at anchor or at a mooring

BUMBOATS > BUMBOAT

BUMBOS > BUMBO

BUMELIA *n* thorny shrub

BUMELIAS > BUMELIA

BUMF *n* official documents or forms

BUMFLUFF *n* soft and fluffy growth of hair on the chin of an adolescent

BUMFLUFFS
> BUMFLUFF

BUMFS > BUMF

BUMFUCK *n* taboo slang for a remote or insignificant place

BUMFUCKS > BUMFUCK

BUMFUZZLE *vb* confuse

BUMKIN *same as*
> BUMPKIN

BUMKINS > BUMKIN

BUMMALO *n* Bombay duck

BUMMALOS > BUMMALO

BUMMALOTI *another word for* > BUMMALO

BUMMAREE n dealer at Billingsgate fish market
BUMMAREES > BUMMAREE
BUMMED > BUM
BUMMEL n stroll
BUMMELS > BUMMEL
BUMMER n unpleasant or disappointing experience
BUMMERS > BUMMER
BUMMEST > BUM
BUMMING > BUM
BUMMLE Scots variant of > BUMBLE
BUMMLED > BUMMLE
BUMMLES > BUMMLE
BUMMLING > BUMMLE
BUMMOCK n submerged mass of ice projecting downwards
BUMMOCKS > BUMMOCK
BUMP vb knock or strike with a jolt ▷ n dull thud from an impact or collision
BUMPED > BUMP
BUMPER n bar on the front and back of a vehicle ▷ adj unusually large or abundant ▷ vb toast with a full drinking glass
BUMPERED > BUMPER
BUMPERING > BUMPER
BUMPERS > BUMPER
BUMPH same as > BUMF
BUMPHS > BUMPH
BUMPIER > BUMPY
BUMPIEST > BUMPY
BUMPILY > BUMPY
BUMPINESS > BUMPY
BUMPING > BUMP
BUMPINGS > BUMP
BUMPKIN n awkward simple country person
BUMPKINLY adj like a bumpkin
BUMPKINS > BUMPKIN
BUMPOLOGY n humorous word for phrenology
BUMPS > BUMP
BUMPTIOUS adj offensively self-assertive
BUMPY adj having an uneven surface
BUMS > BUM
BUMSTER adj (of trousers) cut very low at the hips
BUMSTERS pl n trousers cut very low at the hips
BUMSUCKER n toady
BUMWAD n type of sketching paper
BUMWADS > BUMWAD
BUN n small sweet bread roll or cake
BUNA n synthetic rubber
BUNAS > BUNA
BUNBURIED > BUNBURY
BUNBURIES > BUNBURY
BUNBURY vb make up a story to avoid an unwanted engagement
BUNCE n windfall; boom ▷ vb charge someone too much money
BUNCED > BUNCE
BUNCES > BUNCE
BUNCH n number of things growing, fastened, or

grouped together ▷ vb group or be grouped together in a bunch
BUNCHED > BUNCH
BUNCHER n person who groups things together
BUNCHERS > BUNCHER
BUNCHES pl n hair tied into two sections
BUNCHIER > BUNCHY
BUNCHIEST > BUNCHY
BUNCHILY > BUNCHY
BUNCHING > BUNCH
BUNCHINGS > BUNCH
BUNCHY adj composed of or resembling bunches
BUNCING > BUNCE
BUNCO n swindle, esp one by confidence tricksters ▷ vb swindle
BUNCOED > BUNCO
BUNCOES > BUNCO
BUNCOING > BUNCO
BUNCOMBE same as > BUNKUM
BUNCOMBES > BUNCOMBE
BUNCOS > BUNCO
BUND n (in Germany) confederation ▷ vb form into an embankment
BUNDE > BUND
BUNDED > BUND
BUNDH same as > BANDH
BUNDHS > BUNDH
BUNDIED > BUNDY
BUNDIES > BUNDY
BUNDING > BUND
BUNDIST > BUND
BUNDISTS > BUND
BUNDLE n number of things gathered loosely together ▷ vb cause to go roughly or unceremoniously
BUNDLED > BUNDLE
BUNDLER > BUNDLE
BUNDLERS > BUNDLE
BUNDLES > BUNDLE
BUNDLING > BUNDLE
BUNDLINGS > BUNDLE
BUNDOBUST same as > BANDOBUST
BUNDOOK n rifle
BUNDOOKS > BUNDOOK
BUNDS > BUND
BUNDT n type of sweet cake
BUNDTS > BUNDT
BUNDU n largely uninhabited wild region far from towns
BUNDUS > BUNDU
BUNDWALL n concrete or earth wall surrounding a storage tank
BUNDWALLS > BUNDWALL
BUNDY n time clock at work ▷ vb register arrival or departure from work on a time clock
BUNDYING > BUNDY
BUNFIGHT n tea party
BUNFIGHTS > BUNFIGHT
BUNG n stopper for a cask etc ▷ vb close with a bung

BUNGALOID n bungalow-type house
BUNGALOW n one-storey house
BUNGALOWS > BUNGALOW
BUNGED > BUNG
BUNGEE n strong elastic cable
BUNGEES > BUNGEE
BUNGER n firework
BUNGERS > BUNGER
BUNGEY same as > BUNGEE
BUNGEYS > BUNGEY
BUNGHOLE n hole in a cask or barrel through which liquid can be drained
BUNGHOLES > BUNGHOLE
BUNGIE same as > BUNGEE
BUNGIES > BUNGIE
BUNGING > BUNG
BUNGLE vb spoil through incompetence ▷ n blunder or muddle
BUNGLED > BUNGLE
BUNGLER > BUNGLE
BUNGLERS > BUNGLE
BUNGLES > BUNGLE
BUNGLING > BUNGLE
BUNGLINGS > BUNGLE
BUNGS > BUNG
BUNGWALL n Australian fern with an edible rhizome
BUNGWALLS > BUNGWALL
BUNGY same as > BUNGEE
BUNHEAD n ballerina
BUNHEADS > BUNHEAD
BUNIA same as > BUNNIA
BUNIAS > BUNIA
BUNION n inflamed swelling on the big toe
BUNIONS > BUNION
BUNJE same as > BUNGEE
BUNJEE same as > BUNGEE
BUNJEES > BUNJEE
BUNJES > BUNJE
BUNJIE same as > BUNGEE
BUNJIES > BUNJIE
BUNJY same as > BUNGEE
BUNK n narrow shelflike bed ▷ vb prepare to sleep
BUNKED > BUNK
BUNKER n sand-filled hollow forming an obstacle on a golf course ▷ vb drive (the ball) into a bunker
BUNKERED > BUNKER
BUNKERING > BUNKER
BUNKERS > BUNKER
BUNKHOUSE n (in the US and Canada) building containing the sleeping quarters of workers on a ranch
BUNKIE n short for bunkhouse
BUNKIES > BUNKIE
BUNKING > BUNK

BUNKMATE n person who sleeps in the same quarters as another
BUNKMATES > BUNKMATE
BUNKO same as > BUNCO
BUNKOED > BUNKO
BUNKOING > BUNKO
BUNKOS > BUNKO
BUNKS > BUNK
BUNKUM n nonsense
BUNKUMS > BUNKUM
BUNN same as > BUN
BUNNET same as > BONNET
BUNNETS > BUNNET
BUNNIA n Hindu shopkeeper
BUNNIAS > BUNNIA
BUNNIES > BUNNY
BUNNS > BUNN
BUNNY n child's word for a rabbit
BUNODONT adj (of the teeth of certain mammals) having cusps that are separate and rounded
BUNRAKU n Japanese puppet theatre
BUNRAKUS > BUNRAKU
BUNS > BUN
BUNSEN n as in bunsen burner gas burner used in scientific labs
BUNSENS > BUNSEN
BUNT vb (of an animal) butt (something) with the head or horns ▷ n act or an instance of bunting
BUNTAL n straw obtained from leaves of the talipot palm
BUNTALS > BUNTAL
BUNTED > BUNT
BUNTER n batter who deliberately taps ball lightly
BUNTERS > BUNTER
BUNTIER > BUNT
BUNTIEST > BUNT
BUNTING n decorative flags
BUNTINGS > BUNTING
BUNTLINE n one of several lines fastened to the foot of a square sail
BUNTLINES > BUNTLINE
BUNTS > BUNT
BUNTY > BUNT
BUNYA n tall dome-shaped Australian coniferous tree
BUNYAS > BUNYA
BUNYIP n legendary monster said to live in swamps and lakes
BUNYIPS > BUNYIP
BUOY n floating marker anchored in the sea ▷ vb prevent from sinking
BUOYAGE n system of buoys
BUOYAGES > BUOYAGE
BUOYANCE same as > BUOYANCY
BUOYANCES > BUOYANCE

BUOYANCY n ability to float in a liquid or to rise in a fluid

BUOYANT adj able to float

BUOYANTLY > BUOYANT

BUOYED > BUOY

BUOYING > BUOY

BUOYS > BUOY

BUPKES same as > BUPKIS

BUPKIS n nothing

BUPKUS same as > BUPKIS

BUPLEVER n type of plant

BUPLEVERS > BUPLEVER

BUPPIE n affluent young Black person

BUPPIES > BUPPIE

BUPPY variant of > BUPPIE

BUPRESTID n type of mainly tropical beetle, the adults of which are brilliantly coloured

BUPROPION n antidepressant drug used to help people stop smoking

BUQSHA n former Yemeni coin

BUQSHAS > BUQSHA

BUR same as > BURR

BURA same as > BURAN

BURAN n blizzard, with the wind blowing from the north and reaching gale force

BURANS > BURAN

BURAS > BURA

BURB n suburb

BURBLE vb make a bubbling sound ▷ n bubbling or gurgling sound

BURBLED > BURBLE

BURBLER > BURBLE

BURBLERS > BURBLE

BURBLES > BURBLE

BURBLIER > BURBLY

BURBLIEST > BURBLY

BURBLING > BURBLE

BURBLINGS > BURBLE

BURBLY adj burbling

BURBOT n freshwater fish of the cod family that has barbels around its mouth

BURBOTS > BURBOT

BURBS > BURB

BURD Scots form of > BIRD

BURDASH n fringed sash worn over a coat

BURDASHES > BURDASH

BURDEN n heavy load ▷ vb put a burden on

BURDENED > BURDEN

BURDENER > BURDEN

BURDENERS > BURDEN

BURDENING > BURDEN

BURDENOUS > BURDEN

BURDENS > BURDEN

BURDIE Scots form of > BIRDIE

BURDIES > BURDIE

BURDIZZO n surgical instrument

BURDIZZOS > BURDIZZO

BURDOCK n weed with prickly burrs

BURDOCKS > BURDOCK

BURDS > BURD

BUREAU n office that provides a service

BUREAUS > BUREAU

BUREAUX > BUREAU

BURET same as > BURETTE

BURETS > BURET

BURETTE n glass tube for dispensing known volumes of fluids

BURETTES > BURETTE

BURFI same as > BARFI

BURFIS > BURFI

BURG n fortified town

BURGAGE n type of tenure of land or tenement in a town or city

BURGAGES > BURGAGE

BURGANET same as > BURGONET

BURGANETS > BURGANET

BURGEE n triangular or swallow-tailed flag flown from the mast of a merchant ship

BURGEES > BURGEE

BURGEON vb develop or grow rapidly ▷ n bud of a plant

BURGEONED > BURGEON

BURGEONS > BURGEON

BURGER n hamburger

BURGERS > BURGER

BURGESS n (in England) citizen of a borough

BURGESSES > BURGESS

BURGH n Scottish borough

BURGHAL > BURGH

BURGHER n citizen

BURGHERS > BURGHER

BURGHS > BURGH

BURGHUL same as > BULGUR

BURGHULS > BURGHUL

BURGLAR n person who enters a building to commit a crime, esp theft ▷ vb burgle

BURGLARED > BURGLAR

BURGLARS > BURGLAR

BURGLARY n crime of entering a building as a trespasser to commit theft or another offence

BURGLE vb break into (a house, shop, etc)

BURGLED > BURGLE

BURGLES > BURGLE

BURGLING > BURGLE

BURGONET n light 16th-century helmet, usually made of steel, with hinged cheekpieces

BURGONETS > BURGONET

BURGOO n porridge

BURGOOS > BURGOO

BURGOUT same as > BURGOO

BURGOUTS > BURGOUT

BURGRAVE n military governor of a German town or castle, esp in the 12th and 13th centuries

BURGRAVES > BURGRAVE

BURGS > BURG

BURGUNDY adj dark-purplish red

BURHEL same as > BHARAL

BURHELS > BURHEL

BURIAL n burying of a dead body

BURIALS > BURIAL

BURIED > BURY

BURIER n person or thing that buries

BURIERS > BURIER

BURIES > BURY

BURIN n steel chisel used for engraving metal, wood, or marble

BURINIST > BURIN

BURINISTS > BURIN

BURINS > BURIN

BURITI n type of palm tree

BURITIS > BURITI

BURK same as > BERK

BURKA same as > BURQA

BURKAS > BURKA

BURKE vb suppress or silence

BURKED > BURKE

BURKER > BURKE

BURKERS > BURKE

BURKES > BURKE

BURKHA same as > BURQA

BURKHAS > BURKHA

BURKING > BURKE

BURKINI n swimming costume covering the whole body apart from the face, hands, and feet

BURKINIS > BURKINI

BURKITE n murderer

BURKITES > BURKITE

BURKS > BURK

BURL n small knot or lump in wool ▷ vb remove the burls from (cloth)

BURLADERO n safe area for bull-fighter in bull ring

BURLAP n coarse fabric woven from jute, hemp, or the like

BURLAPS > BURLAP

BURLED > BURL

BURLER > BURL

BURLERS > BURL

BURLESK same as > BURLESQUE

BURLESKS > BURLESK

BURLESQUE n artistic work which satirizes a subject by caricature ▷ adj of or characteristic of a burlesque ▷ vb represent or imitate (a person or thing) in a ludicrous way

BURLETTA n type of comic opera

BURLETTAS > BURLETTA

BURLEY same as > BERLEY

BURLEYCUE same as > BURLESQUE

BURLEYED > BURLEY

BURLEYING > BURLEY

BURLEYS > BURLEY

BURLIER > BURLY

BURLIEST > BURLY

BURLIKE adj like a bur

BURLILY > BURLY

BURLINESS > BURLY

BURLING > BURL

BURLS > BURL

BURLY adj (of a person) broad and strong

BURN vb be or set on fire ▷ n injury or mark caused by fire or exposure to heat

BURNABLE > BURN

BURNABLES > BURN

BURNED > BURN

BURNER n part of a stove or lamp that produces the flame

BURNERS > BURNER

BURNET n type of rose

BURNETS > BURNET

BURNIE n sideburn

BURNIES > BURNIE

BURNING > BURN

BURNINGLY > BURN

BURNINGS > BURN

BURNISH vb make smooth and shiny by rubbing ▷ n shiny finish

BURNISHED > BURNISH

BURNISHER > BURNISH

BURNISHES > BURNISH

BURNOOSE same as > BURNOUS

BURNOOSED > BURNOUS

BURNOOSES > BURNOOSE

BURNOUS n long circular cloak with a hood, worn esp by Arabs

BURNOUSE same as > BURNOUS

BURNOUSED > BURNOUS

BURNOUSES > BURNOUSE

BURNOUT n failure of a mechanical device from excessive heating

BURNOUTS > BURNOUT

BURNS > BURN

BURNSIDE n land along side of burn

BURNSIDES > BURNSIDE

BURNT > BURN

BUROO n informal Scottish or Irish name for an unemployment benefit office

BUROOS > BUROO

BURP n belch ▷ vb belch

BURPED > BURP

BURPEE n type of physical exercise movement

BURPEES > BURPEE

BURPING > BURP

BURPS > BURP

BURQA n garment worn by some Muslim women in public

BURQAS > BURQA

BURQUINI n swimming costume covering the whole body apart from the face, hands, and feet

BURQUINIS > BURQUINI

b

BURR n small rotary file ▷ vb form a rough edge on (a workpiece)

BURRAMYS n very rare Australian mountain pigmy possum

BURRATA n type of Italian cheese

BURRATAS > BURRATA

BURRAWANG n Australian plant with fernlike leaves and an edible nut

BURRED > BURR

BURREL same as > BHARAL

BURRELL variant of > BHARAL

BURRELLS > BURRELL

BURRELS > BURREL

BURRER n person who removes burrs

BURRERS > BURRER

BURRFISH n type of fish with sharp spines

BURRHEL same as > BHARAL

BURRHELS > BURRHEL

BURRIER > BURRY

BURRIEST > BURRY

BURRING > BURR

BURRITO n tortilla folded over a filling of minced beef, chicken, cheese, or beans

BURRITOS > BURRITO

BURRO n donkey, esp one used as a pack animal

BURROS > BURRO

BURROW n hole dug in the ground by a rabbit etc ▷ vb dig holes in the ground

BURROWED > BURROW

BURROWER > BURROW

BURROWERS > BURROW

BURROWING > BURROW

BURROWS > BURROW

BURRS > BURR

BURRSTONE same as > BUHRSTONE

BURRY adj full of or covered in burs

BURS > BUR

BURSA n small fluid-filled sac that reduces friction between movable parts of the body

BURSAE > BURSA

BURSAL > BURSA

BURSAR n treasurer of a school, college, or university

BURSARIAL adj of, relating to, or paid by a bursar or bursary

BURSARIES > BURSARY

BURSARS > BURSAR

BURSARY n scholarship

BURSAS > BURSA

BURSATE > BURSA

BURSE n flat case used at Mass as a container for the corporal

BURSEED n type of plant

BURSEEDS > BURSEED

BURSERA adj of a type of gum tree

BURSES > BURSE

BURSICON n hormone produced by the insect brain

BURSICONS > BURSICON

BURSIFORM adj shaped like a pouch or sac

BURSITIS n inflammation of a bursa, esp one in the shoulder joint

BURST vb break or cause to break open or apart suddenly and noisily ▷ n sudden breaking open or apart ▷ adj broken apart

BURSTED > BURST

BURSTEN > BURST

BURSTER > BURST

BURSTERS > BURST

BURSTIER > BURSTY

BURSTIEST > BURSTY

BURSTING > BURST

BURSTONE same as > BUHRSTONE

BURSTONES > BURSTONE

BURSTS > BURST

BURSTY adj occurring or happening in sudden bursts; irregular

BURTHEN archaic word for > BURDEN

BURTHENED > BURTHEN

BURTHENS > BURTHEN

BURTON n type of hoisting tackle

BURTONS > BURTON

BURWEED n any of various plants that bear burs, such as the burdock

BURWEEDS > BURWEED

BURY vb place in a grave

BURYING > BURY

BUS n large motor vehicle for carrying passengers between stops ▷ vb travel by bus

BUSBAR n electrical conductor

BUSBARS > BUSBAR

BUSBIES > BUSBY

BUSBOY n waiter's assistant

BUSBOYS > BUSBOY

BUSBY n tall fur hat worn by some soldiers

BUSED > BUS

BUSERA n Ugandan alcoholic drink made from millet

BUSERAS > BUSERA

BUSES > BUS

BUSGIRL n waiter's assistant

BUSGIRLS > BUSGIRL

BUSH n dense woody plant, smaller than a tree ▷ vb fit a bush to (a casing or bearing)

BUSHBABY n small African tree-living mammal with large eyes

BUSHBUCK n small nocturnal spiral-horned antelope of Africa

BUSHBUCKS > BUSHBUCK

BUSHCRAFT n ability and experience in matters concerned with living in the bush

BUSHED adj extremely tired

BUSHEL n obsolete unit of measure equal to 8 gallons ▷ vb alter or mend (a garment)

BUSHELED > BUSHEL

BUSHELER > BUSHEL

BUSHELERS > BUSHEL

BUSHELFUL n amount equivalent to a bushel

BUSHELING > BUSHEL

BUSHELLED > BUSHEL

BUSHELLER > BUSHEL

BUSHELMAN > BUSHEL

BUSHELMEN > BUSHEL

BUSHELS > BUSHEL

BUSHER > BUSH

BUSHERS > BUSH

BUSHES > BUSH

BUSHFIRE n uncontrolled fire in the bush

BUSHFIRES > BUSHFIRE

BUSHFLIES > BUSHFLY

BUSHFLY n small black Australian fly

BUSHGOAT n S African antelope

BUSHGOATS > BUSHGOAT

BUSHIDO n feudal code of the Japanese samurai

BUSHIDOS > BUSHIDO

BUSHIE same as > BUSHY

BUSHIER > BUSHY

BUSHIES > BUSHY

BUSHIEST > BUSHY

BUSHILY > BUSHY

BUSHINESS > BUSHY

BUSHING same as > BUSH

BUSHINGS > BUSHING

BUSHLAND n land characterized by natural vegetation

BUSHLANDS > BUSHLAND

BUSHLESS > BUSH

BUSHLIKE > BUSH

BUSHLOT n small wooded area of land

BUSHLOTS > BUSHLOT

BUSHMAN n person who lives or travels in the bush

BUSHMEAT n meat taken from any animal native to African forests

BUSHMEATS > BUSHMEAT

BUSHMEN > BUSHMAN

BUSHPIG n wild brown or black forest pig of tropical Africa and Madagascar

BUSHPIGS > BUSHPIG

BUSHTIT n small grey active North American songbird

BUSHTITS > BUSHTIT

BUSHVELD n bushy countryside

BUSHVELDS > BUSHVELD

BUSHWA n nonsense

BUSHWAH same as > BUSHWA

BUSHWAHS > BUSHWAH

BUSHWALK vb hike through bushland

BUSHWALKS > BUSHWALK

BUSHWAS > BUSHWA

BUSHWHACK vb ambush

BUSHWOMAN > BUSHMAN

BUSHWOMEN > BUSHMAN

BUSHY adj (of hair) thick and shaggy ▷ n person who lives in the bush

BUSIED > BUSY

BUSIER > BUSY

BUSIES > BUSY

BUSIEST > BUSY

BUSILY adv in a busy manner

BUSINESS n purchase and sale of goods and services

BUSINESSY adj of, relating to, typical of, or suitable for the world of commercial or industrial business

BUSING n act of transporting by bus from one area to another

BUSINGS > BUSING

BUSK vb act as a busker ▷ n strip of whalebone, wood, steel, etc, inserted into the front of a corset

BUSKED > BUSK

BUSKER > BUSK

BUSKERS > BUSK

BUSKET n bouquet

BUSKETS > BUSKET

BUSKIN n (formerly) sandal-like covering

BUSKINED adj relating to tragedy

BUSKING > BUSK

BUSKINGS > BUSK

BUSKINS > BUSKIN

BUSKS > BUSK

BUSKY same as > BOSKY

BUSLOAD n number of people bus carries

BUSLOADS > BUSLOAD

BUSMAN n person who drives a bus

BUSMEN > BUSMAN

BUSS archaic or dialect word for > KISS

BUSSED > BUS

BUSSES > BUS

BUSSING n act of transporting by bus from one area to another

BUSSINGS > BUSSING

BUSSU n type of palm tree

BUSSUS > BUSSU

BUST n chest of a human being ▷ adj broken ▷ vb burst or break

BUSTARD n type of bird

BUSTARDS > BUSTARD

BUSTED > BUST

BUSTEE same as > BASTI

BUSTEES > BUSTEE

BUSTER n person or thing destroying something as specified

BUSTERS > BUSTER

BUSTI same as > BASTI

BUSTIC n type of small American tree

BUSTICATE vb break

BUSTICS > BUSTIC

BUSTIER n close-fitting strapless women's top

BUSTIERS > BUSTIER

BUSTIEST > BUSTY

BUSTINESS > BUSTY

BUSTING > BUST

BUSTINGS > BUST

BUSTIS > BUSTI

BUSTLE vb hurry with a show of activity or energy ▷ n energetic and noisy activity

BUSTLED > BUSTLE

BUSTLER > BUSTLE

BUSTLERS > BUSTLE

BUSTLES > BUSTLE

BUSTLINE n shape or size of woman's bust

BUSTLINES > BUSTLINE

BUSTLING > BUSTLE

BUSTS > BUST

BUSTY adj (of a woman) having a prominent bust

BUSULFAN n drug used to treat cancer

BUSULFANS > BUSULFAN

BUSUUTI n garment worn by Ugandan women

BUSUUTIS > BUSUUTI

BUSY adj actively employed ▷ vb keep (someone, esp oneself) busy

BUSYBODY n meddlesome or nosy person

BUSYING > BUSY

BUSYNESS > BUSY

BUSYWORK n unproductive work

BUSYWORKS > BUSYWORK

BUT prep except ▷ adv only ▷ n outer room of a two-roomed cottage: usually the kitchen

BUTADIENE n colourless easily liquefiable flammable gas

BUTANE n gas used for fuel

BUTANES > BUTANE

BUTANOIC adj as in butanoic acid kind of acid

BUTANOL n colourless substance

BUTANOLS > BUTANOL

BUTANONE n colourless soluble flammable liquid used mainly as a solvent for resins

BUTANONES > BUTANONE

BUTCH adj markedly or aggressively masculine ▷ n strong, rugged man

BUTCHER n person who slaughters animals or sells their meat ▷ vb kill and prepare (animals) for meat

BUTCHERED > BUTCHER

BUTCHERER > BUTCHER

BUTCHERLY adj like a butcher

BUTCHERS > BUTCHER

BUTCHERY n senseless slaughter

BUTCHES > BUTCH

BUTCHEST > BUTCH

BUTCHING n dialect word for butchering

BUTCHINGS > BUTCH

BUTCHNESS > BUTCH

BUTE n drug used in veterinary medicine

BUTENE n pungent colourless gas

BUTENES > BUTENE

BUTEO n type of American hawk

BUTEONINE adj of hawks

BUTEOS > BUTEO

BUTES > BUTE

BUTLE vb act as butler

BUTLED > BUTLE

BUTLER n chief male servant ▷ vb act as a butler

BUTLERAGE > BUTLER

BUTLERED > BUTLER

BUTLERIES > BUTLERY

BUTLERING > BUTLER

BUTLERS > BUTLER

BUTLERY n butler's room

BUTLES > BUTLE

BUTLING > BUTLE

BUTMENT same as > ABUTMENT

BUTMENTS > BUTMENT

BUTOH n style of contemporary Japanese dance

BUTOHS > BUTOH

BUTS > BUT

BUTSUDAN n (in Buddhism) small household altar

BUTSUDANS > BUTSUDAN

BUTT n thicker or blunt end of something, such as the end of the stock of a rifle ▷ vb strike or push with the head or horns

BUTTALS pl n abuttals

BUTTE n isolated steep flat-topped hill

BUTTED > BUTT

BUTTER n edible fatty yellow solid made form cream ▷ vb put butter on

BUTTERBUR n Eurasian plant with fragrant whitish or purple flowers and woolly stems

BUTTERCUP n small yellow flower

BUTTERED > BUTTER

BUTTERFAT n fatty substance of milk from which butter is made, consisting of a mixture of glycerides, mainly butyrin, olein, and palmitin

BUTTERFLY n insect with brightly coloured wings

BUTTERIER > BUTTERY

BUTTERIES > BUTTERY

BUTTERINE n artificial butter made partly from milk

BUTTERING > BUTTER

BUTTERNUT n E North American walnut tree

BUTTERS > BUTTER

BUTTERY n (in some universities) room in which food and drink are sold to students ▷ adj containing, like, or coated with butter

BUTTES > BUTTE

BUTTHEAD n stupid person

BUTTHEADS > BUTTHEAD

BUTTIES > BUTTY

BUTTING > BUTT

BUTTINSKI same as > BUTTINSKY

BUTTINSKY n busybody

BUTTLE vb act as butler

BUTTLED > BUTTLE

BUTTLES > BUTTLE

BUTTLING > BUTTLE

BUTTOCK n either of the two fleshy masses that form the human rump ▷ vb perform a kind of wrestling manoeuvre on a person

BUTTOCKED > BUTTOCK

BUTTOCKS > BUTTOCK

BUTTON n small disc or knob sewn to clothing ▷ vb fasten with buttons

BUTTONED > BUTTON

BUTTONER > BUTTON

BUTTONERS > BUTTON

BUTTONIER > BUTTONY

BUTTONING > BUTTON

BUTTONS n page boy

BUTTONY adj having a lot of buttons

BUTTRESS n structure to support a wall ▷ vb support with, or as if with, a buttress

BUTTS > BUTT

BUTTSTOCK n part of gun

BUTTY n sandwich

BUTTYMAN n coalmine worker

BUTTYMEN > BUTTYMAN

BUTUT n Gambian monetary unit worth one hundredth of a dalasi

BUTUTS > BUTUT

BUTYL n substituent group of a certain carbon compound

BUTYLATE vb introduce butyl into (compound)

BUTYLATED > BUTYLATE

BUTYLATES > BUTYLATE

BUTYLENE same as > BUTENE

BUTYLENES > BUTYLENE

BUTYLS > BUTYL

BUTYRAL n type of resin

BUTYRALS > BUTYRAL

BUTYRATE n any salt or ester of butyric acid

BUTYRATES > BUTYRATE

BUTYRIC adj as in butyric acid type of acid

BUTYRIN n colourless liquid found in butter

BUTYRINS > BUTYRIN

BUTYROUS adj butyraceous

BUTYRYL n radical of butyric acid

BUTYRYLS > BUTYRYL

BUVETTE n roadside café

BUVETTES > BUVETTE

BUXOM adj (of a woman) healthily plump

BUXOMER > BUXOM

BUXOMEST > BUXOM

BUXOMLY > BUXOM

BUXOMNESS > BUXOM

BUY vb acquire by paying money for ▷ n thing acquired through payment

BUYABLE > BUY

BUYABLES > BUY

BUYBACK n repurchase by a company of some or all of its shares from an early investor

BUYBACKS > BUYBACK

BUYER n customer

BUYERS > BUYER

BUYING n act or instance of purchasing something

BUYINGS > BUYING

BUYOFF n purchase

BUYOFFS > BUYOFF

BUYOUT n purchase of a company

BUYOUTS > BUYOUT

BUYS > BUY

BUZKASHI n team sport played in Afghanistan

BUZKASHIS > BUZKASHI

BUZUKI same as > BOUZOUKI

BUZUKIA > BUZUKI

BUZUKIS > BUZUKI

BUZZ n rapidly vibrating humming sound ▷ vb make a humming sound

BUZZARD n bird of prey of the hawk family

BUZZARDS > BUZZARD

BUZZBAIT n fishing lure with small blades that stir the water

BUZZBAITS > BUZZBAIT

BUZZCUT n very short haircut

BUZZCUTS > BUZZCUT

BUZZED > BUZZ

BUZZER n electronic device that produces a buzzing sound as a signal

BUZZERS > BUZZER

BUZZES > BUZZ

BUZZIER > BUZZY

BUZZIEST > BUZZY

BUZZING > BUZZ

BUZZINGLY > BUZZ

BUZZINGS > BUZZ

b

BUZZKILL n someone or something that spoils the enjoyment of others

BUZZKILLS
> BUZZKILL

BUZZSAW n power-operated circular saw

BUZZSAWS > BUZZSAW

BUZZWIG n bushy wig

BUZZWIGS > BUZZWIG

BUZZWORD n vogue word in a certain community or among a particular group

BUZZWORDS
> BUZZWORD

BUZZY adj making a buzzing sound

BWANA n (in E Africa) master, often used as a respectful form of address

BWANAS > BWANA

BWAZI same as > BUAZE

BWAZIS > BWAZI

BY prep indicating agent, nearness, movement past, etc ▷ adv near ▷ n pass to the next round

BYCATCH n unwanted fish and sea animals caught along with the desired kind

BYCATCHES > BYCATCH

BYCOKET n former Italian high-crowned hat

BYCOKETS > BYCOKET

BYDE same as > BIDE

BYDED > BYDE

BYDES > BYDE

BYDING > BYDE

BYE n situation where a player or team wins a round by having no opponent ▷ interj goodbye

BYELAW n rule made by a local authority

BYELAWS > BYELAW

BYES > BYE

BYGONE adj past ▷ n article from a former time

BYGONES > BYGONE

BYKE n wasp's nest ▷ vb swarm

BYKED > BYKE

BYKES > BYKE

BYKING > BYKE

BYLANDER same as
> BILANDER

BYLANDERS
> BYLANDER

BYLANE n side lane or alley off a road

BYLANES > BYLANE

BYLAW n rule made by a local authority

BYLAWS > BYLAW

BYLINE n line under the title of a newspaper or magazine article giving the author's name ▷ vb give a byline to

BYLINED > BYLINE

BYLINER > BYLINE

BYLINERS > BYLINE

BYLINES > BYLINE

BYLINING > BYLINE

BYLIVE same as
> BELIVE

BYNAME n nickname

BYNAMES > BYNAME

BYNEMPT archaic past participle of > BENAME

BYPASS n main road built to avoid a city ▷ vb go round or avoid

BYPASSED > BYPASS

BYPASSES > BYPASS

BYPASSING > BYPASS

BYPAST > BYPASS

BYPATH n little-used path or track, esp in the country

BYPATHS > BYPATH

BYPLACE n private place

BYPLACES > BYPLACE

BYPLAY n secondary action or talking carried on apart while the main action proceeds

BYPLAYS > BYPLAY

BYPRODUCT n secondary product

BYRE n shelter for cows

BYREMAN n man who works in a byre

BYREMEN > BYREMAN

BYRES > BYRE

BYREWOMAN n woman who works in a byre

BYREWOMEN
> BYREWOMAN

BYRL same as > BIRL

BYRLADY interj archaic exclamation of surprise

BYRLAKIN interj By Our Ladykin

BYRLAW same as > BYLAW

BYRLAWS > BYRLAW

BYRLED > BYRL

BYRLING > BYRL

BYRLS > BYRL

BYRNIE n archaic word for coat of mail

BYRNIES > BYRNIE

BYROAD n secondary or side road

BYROADS > BYROAD

BYROOM n private room

BYROOMS > BYROOM

BYS > BY

BYSSAL adj of mollusc's byssus

BYSSI > BYSSUS

BYSSINE adj made from flax

BYSSOID adj consisting of fine fibres

BYSSUS n mass of threads that attaches an animal to a hard surface

BYSSUSES > BYSSUS

BYSTANDER n person present but not involved

BYSTREET n obscure or secondary street

BYSTREETS
> BYSTREET

BYTALK n trivial conversation

BYTALKS > BYTALK

BYTE n group of bits processed as one unit of data

BYTES > BYTE

BYTOWNITE n rare mineral

BYWAY n minor road

BYWAYS > BYWAY

BYWONER n poor tenant-farmer

BYWONERS > BYWONER

BYWORD n person or thing regarded as a perfect example of something

BYWORDS > BYWORD

BYWORK n work done outside usual working hours

BYWORKS > BYWORK

BYZANT same as
> BEZANT

BYZANTINE adj of, characteristic of, or relating to Byzantium or the Byzantine Empire

BYZANTS > BYZANT

Cc

CAA a Scot word for > CALL
CAAED > CAA
CAAING > CAA
CAAS > CAA
CAATINGA n Brazilian semi-arid scrub forest
CAATINGAS > CAATINGA
CAB n taxi ▷ vb take a taxi
CABA same as > CABAS
CABAL n small group of political plotters ▷ vb form a cabal
CABALA variant spelling of > KABBALAH
CABALAS > CABALA
CABALETTA n final section of an aria
CABALETTE > CABALETTA
CABALISM > CABALA
CABALISMS > CABALA
CABALIST > CABALA
CABALISTS > CABALA
CABALLED > CABAL
CABALLER > CABAL
CABALLERO n Spanish gentleman
CABALLERS > CABAL
CABALLINE adj pertaining to a horse
CABALLING > CABAL
CABALS > CABAL
CABANA n tent used as a dressing room by the sea
CABANAS > CABANA
CABARET n dancing and singing show in a nightclub
CABARETS > CABARET
CABAS n small bag
CABBAGE n vegetable with a large head of green leaves ▷ vb steal
CABBAGED > CABBAGE
CABBAGES > CABBAGE
CABBAGEY > CABBAGE
CABBAGIER > CABBAGY
CABBAGING > CABBAGE
CABBAGY adj resembling cabbage
CABBALA variant spelling of > KABBALAH
CABBALAH same as > CABBALA
CABBALAHS > CABBALA
CABBALAS > CABBALA
CABBALISM > CABBALA
CABBALIST > CABBALA
CABBED > CAB
CABBIE n taxi driver
CABBIES > CABBIE
CABBING > CAB

CABBY same as > CABBIE
CABDRIVER n taxi-driver
CABER n tree trunk tossed in competition at Highland games
CABERNET n type of grape, or the red wine made from it
CABERNETS > CABERNET
CABERS > CABER
CABESTRO n halter made from horsehair
CABESTROS > CABESTRO
CABEZON n large fish
CABEZONE same as > CABEZON
CABEZONES > CABEZON
CABEZONS > CABEZON
CABILDO n Spanish municipal council
CABILDOS > CABILDO
CABIN n compartment in a ship or aircraft ▷ vb confine in a small space
CABINED > CABIN
CABINET n piece of furniture with drawers or shelves
CABINETRY n cabinetmaking
CABINETS > CABINET
CABINING > CABIN
CABINMATE n sharer of cabin
CABINS > CABIN
CABLE n strong thick rope; a wire or bundle of wires that conduct electricity ▷ vb (esp formerly) send (someone) a message by cable
CABLECAST n broadcast on cable
CABLED > CABLE
CABLEGRAM n message sent by cable
CABLER n cable broadcasting company
CABLERS > CABLER
CABLES > CABLE
CABLET n small cable
CABLETS > CABLET
CABLEWAY n transport system involving cars, buckets, etc, suspended on cables
CABLEWAYS > CABLEWAY
CABLING > CABLE
CABLINGS > CABLE
CABMAN n driver of a cab
CABMEN > CABMAN

CABOB vb roast on a skewer
CABOBBED > CABOB
CABOBBING > CABOB
CABOBS > CABOB
CABOC n type of Scottish cheese
CABOCEER n (formerly) African appointed to deal with European slave traders
CABOCEERS > CABOCEER
CABOCHED adj in heraldry, with the face exposed, but neck concealed
CABOCHON n smooth domed gem, polished but unfaceted
CABOCHONS > CABOCHON
CABOCS > CABOC
CABOMBA n type of aquatic plant
CABOMBAS > CABOMBA
CABOODLE n lot, bunch, or group
CABOODLES > CABOODLE
CABOOSE n guard's van on a train
CABOOSES > CABOOSE
CABOSHED same as > CABOCHED
CABOTAGE n coastal navigation or shipping, esp within the borders of one country
CABOTAGES > CABOTAGE
CABOVER n truck or lorry in which the cab is over the engine
CABOVERS > CABOVER
CABRE adj heraldic term designating an animal rearing
CABRESTA variant of > CABESTRO
CABRESTAS > CABRESTA
CABRESTO variant of > CABESTRO
CABRESTOS > CABRESTO
CABRETTA n soft leather obtained from the skins of certain South American or African sheep
CABRETTAS > CABRETTA
CABRIE n pronghorn antelope

CABRIES > CABRIE
CABRILLA n type of food fish occurring in warm seas around Florida and the Caribbean
CABRILLAS > CABRILLA
CABRIO short for > CABRIOLET
CABRIOLE n type of furniture leg featuring a tapering curve
CABRIOLES > CABRIOLE
CABRIOLET n small horse-drawn carriage with a folding hood
CABRIOS > CABRIO
CABRIT n pronghorn antelope
CABRITS > CABRIT
CABS > CAB
CABSTAND n taxi-rank
CABSTANDS > CABSTAND
CACA n heroin
CACAFOGO same as > CACAFUEGO
CACAFOGOS > CACAFUEGO
CACAFUEGO n spitfire
CACAO same as > COCOA
CACAOS > CACAO
CACAS > CACA
CACHACA n white Brazilian rum made from sugar cane
CACHACAS > CACHACA
CACHAEMIA n poisoned condition of the blood
CACHAEMIC > CACHAEMIA
CACHALOT n sperm whale
CACHALOTS > CACHALOT
CACHE n hidden store of weapons or treasure ▷ vb store in a cache
CACHECTIC > CACHEXIA
CACHED > CACHE
CACHEPOT n ornamental container for a flowerpot
CACHEPOTS > CACHEPOT
CACHES > CACHE
CACHET n prestige, distinction ▷ vb apply a commemorative design to an envelope, as a first-day cover
CACHETED > CACHET
CACHETING > CACHET

CACHETS > CACHET
CACHEXIA n generally weakened condition of body or mind
CACHEXIAS
> CACHEXIA
CACHEXIC > CACHEXIA
CACHEXIES
> CACHEXIA
CACHEXY same as
> CACHEXIA
CACHING > CACHE
CACHOLONG n type of opal
CACHOLOT same as
> CACHALOT
CACHOLOTS
> CACHALOT
CACHOU same as
> CATECHU
CACHOUS > CACHOU
CACHUCHA n graceful Spanish solo dance in triple time
CACHUCHAS
> CACHUCHA
CACIQUE n Native American chief in a Spanish-speaking region
CACIQUES > CACIQUE
CACIQUISM n (esp in Spanish America) government by local political bosses
CACK n slang word for nonsense ▷ vb slang word for defecate
CACKED > CACK
CACKIER > CACKY
CACKIEST > CACKY
CACKING > CACK
CACKLE vb laugh shrilly ▷ n cackling noise
CACKLED > CACKLE
CACKLER > CACKLE
CACKLERS > CACKLE
CACKLES > CACKLE
CACKLING > CACKLE
CACKS > CACK
CACKY adj dirty or worthless
CACODEMON n evil spirit or devil
CACODOXY n heterodoxy
CACODYL n oily poisonous liquid with a strong garlic smell
CACODYLIC > CACODYL
CACODYLS > CACODYL
CACOEPIES > CACOEPY
CACOEPY n bad or mistaken pronunciation
CACOETHES n uncontrollable urge or desire, esp for something harmful
CACOETHIC
> CACOETHES
CACOGENIC adj reducing the quality of the human race
CACOLET n seat fitted to the back of a mule
CACOLETS > CACOLET
CACOLOGY n bad choice of words
CACOMIXL n carnivorous mammal

CACOMIXLE same as
> CACOMIXL
CACOMIXLS
> CACOMIXL
CACONYM n erroneous name
CACONYMS > CACONYM
CACONYMY > CACONYM
CACOON n large seed of the sword-bean
CACOONS > CACOON
CACOPHONY n harsh discordant sound
CACOTOPIA n dystopia, the opposite of utopia
CACTI > CACTUS
CACTIFORM adj cactus-like
CACTOID adj resembling a cactus
CACTUS n fleshy desert plant with spines but no leaves
CACTUSES > CACTUS
CACUMEN n apex
CACUMENS > CACUMEN
CACUMINA > CACUMEN
CACUMINAL adj relating to or denoting a consonant articulated with the tip of the tongue turned back towards the hard palate ▷ n consonant articulated in this manner
CAD n dishonourable man
CADAGA n eucalyptus tree
CADAGAS > CADAGA
CADAGI same as
> CADAGA
CADAGIS > CADAGI
CADASTER n register of ownership, boundaries, and value of property
CADASTERS
> CADASTER
CADASTRAL
> CADASTER
CADASTRE same as
> CADASTER
CADASTRES
> CADASTER
CADAVER n corpse
CADAVERIC > CADAVER
CADAVERS > CADAVER
CADDICE same as
> CADDIS
CADDICES > CADDICE
CADDIE n person who carries a golfer's clubs ▷ vb act as a caddie
CADDIED > CADDIE
CADDIES > CADDIE
CADDIS n type of coarse woollen yarn, braid, or fabric
CADDISED adj trimmed with a type of ribbon
CADDISES > CADDIS
CADDISFLY n small fly
CADDISH > CAD
CADDISHLY > CAD
CADDY same as > CADDIE
CADDYING > CADDIE
CADDYSS same as
> CADDIS
CADDYSSES > CADDIS
CADE n juniper tree ▷ adj (of a young animal) left by

its mother and reared by humans
CADEAU n present
CADEAUX > CADEAU
CADEE old form of
> CADET
CADEES > CADEE
CADELLE n type of beetle that feeds on flour, grain, and other stored foods
CADELLES > CADELLE
CADENCE n rise and fall in the pitch of the voice ▷ vb modulate musically
CADENCED > CADENCE
CADENCES > CADENCE
CADENCIES > CADENCY
CADENCING > CADENCE
CADENCY same as
> CADENCE
CADENT adj having cadence
CADENTIAL > CADENT
CADENZA n complex solo passage in a piece of music
CADENZAS > CADENZA
CADES > CADE
CADET n young person training for the armed forces or police
CADETS > CADET
CADETSHIP > CADET
CADGE vb get (something) by taking advantage of someone's generosity
CADGED > CADGE
CADGER n person who cadges
CADGERS > CADGER
CADGES > CADGE
CADGIER > CADGY
CADGIEST > CADGY
CADGING > CADGE
CADGY adj cheerful
CADI n judge in a Muslim community
CADIE n messenger
CADIES > CADIE
CADIS > CADI
CADMIC > CADMIUM
CADMIUM n bluish-white metallic element used in alloys
CADMIUMS > CADMIUM
CADRANS n instrument used in gem cutting
CADRANSES > CADRANS
CADRE n group of people trained to form the core of a political or military unit
CADRES > CADRE
CADS > CAD
CADUAC n windfall
CADUACS > CADUAC
CADUCEAN > CADUCEUS
CADUCEI > CADUCEUS
CADUCEUS n mythical staff carried by Hermes (Mercury)
CADUCITY n perishableness
CADUCOUS adj (of parts of a plant or animal) shed during the life of the organism
CAECA > CAECUM
CAECAL > CAECUM
CAECALLY > CAECUM

CAECILIAN n type of tropical limbless amphibian resembling an earthworm
CAECITIS n inflammation of the caecum
CAECUM n pouch at the beginning of the large intestine
CAEOMA n aecium in some rust fungi that has no surrounding membrane
CAEOMAS > CAEOMA
CAERULE same as
> CERULE
CAERULEAN same as
> CERULEAN
CAESAR n any emperor, autocrat, dictator, or other powerful ruler
CAESAREAN n surgical incision through the abdominal and uterine walls in order to deliver a baby
CAESARIAN variant spelling of > CAESAREAN
CAESARISM n imperialism
CAESARS > CAESAR
CAESE interj Shakespearean interjection
CAESIOUS adj having a waxy bluish-grey coating
CAESIUM n silvery-white metallic element used in photocells
CAESIUMS > CAESIUM
CAESTUS same as
> CESTUS
CAESTUSES > CAESTUS
CAESURA n pause in a line of verse
CAESURAE > CAESURA
CAESURAL > CAESURA
CAESURAS > CAESURA
CAESURIC > CAESURA
CAF n short for cafeteria
CAFARD n feeling of severe depression
CAFARDS > CAFARD
CAFE n small or inexpensive restaurant serving light refreshments
CAFES > CAFE
CAFETERIA n self-service restaurant
CAFETIERE n kind of coffeepot in which boiling water is poured onto ground coffee and a plunger fitted with a metal filter is pressed down, forcing the grounds to the bottom
CAFETORIA variant of
> CAFETERIA
CAFF n café
CAFFEIN same as
> CAFFEINE
CAFFEINE n stimulant found in tea and coffee
CAFFEINES
> CAFFEINE
CAFFEINIC adj of or containing caffeine
CAFFEINS > CAFFEIN

CAFFEISM n addiction to caffeine

CAFFEISMS > CAFFEISM

CAFFILA n caravan train

CAFFILAS > CAFFILA

CAFFS > CAFF

CAFILA same as > CAFFILA

CAFILAS > CAFILA

CAFS > CAF

CAFTAN same as > KAFTAN

CAFTANED adj wearing caftan

CAFTANS > CAFTAN

CAG same as > CAGOULE

CAGANER n figure of a squatting defecating person

CAGANERS > CAGANER

CAGE n enclosure of bars or wires, for keeping animals or birds ▷ vb confine in a cage

CAGED > CAGE

CAGEFUL n amount which fills a cage to capacity

CAGEFULS > CAGEFUL

CAGELIKE > CAGE

CAGELING n bird kept in a cage

CAGELINGS > CAGELING

CAGER n basketball player

CAGERS > CAGER

CAGES > CAGE

CAGEWORK n something constructed as if from the bars of a cage

CAGEWORKS > CAGEWORK

CAGEY adj reluctant to go into details

CAGEYNESS > CAGEY

CAGIER > CAGEY

CAGIEST > CAGEY

CAGILY > CAGEY

CAGINESS > CAGY

CAGING > CAGE

CAGMAG adj done shoddily ▷ vb chat idly

CAGMAGGED > CAGMAG

CAGMAGS > CAGMAG

CAGOT n member of a class of French outcasts

CAGOTS > CAGOT

CAGOUL same as > CAGOULE

CAGOULE n lightweight hooded waterproof jacket

CAGOULES > CAGOULE

CAGOULS > CAGOUL

CAGS > CAG

CAGY same as > CAGEY

CAGYNESS > CAGY

CAHIER n notebook

CAHIERS > CAHIER

CAHOOT n partnership

CAHOOTS > CAHOOT

CAHOUN n type of S American palm tree

CAHOUNS > CAHOUN

CAHOW n Bermuda petrel

CAHOWS > CAHOW

CAID n Moroccan district administrator

CAIDS > CAID

CAILLACH same as > CAILLEACH

CAILLACHS > CAILLACH

CAILLE n quail

CAILLEACH n old woman

CAILLES > CAILLE

CAILLIACH same as > CAILLEACH

CAIMAC same as > CAIMACAM

CAIMACAM n Turkish governor of a sanjak

CAIMACAMS > CAIMACAM

CAIMACS > CAIMAC

CAIMAN same as > CAYMAN

CAIMANS > CAIMAN

CAIN n (in Scotland and Ireland) payment in kind

CAINS > CAIN

CAIQUE n long narrow light rowing skiff used on the Bosporus

CAIQUES > CAIQUE

CAIRD n travelling tinker

CAIRDS > CAIRD

CAIRN n mound of stones erected as a memorial or marker

CAIRNED adj marked by a cairn

CAIRNGORM n yellow or brownish quartz gemstone

CAIRNIER > CAIRNY

CAIRNIEST > CAIRNY

CAIRNS > CAIRN

CAIRNY adj covered with cairns

CAISSON n watertight enclosure pumped dry to enable construction work to be done

CAISSONS > CAISSON

CAITIFF n cowardly or base person ▷ adj cowardly

CAITIFFS > CAITIFF

CAITIVE n captive

CAITIVES > CAITIVE

CAJAPUT same as > CAJUPUT

CAJAPUTS > CAJAPUT

CAJEPUT same as > CAJUPUT

CAJEPUTS > CAJEPUT

CAJOLE vb persuade by flattery

CAJOLED > CAJOLE

CAJOLER > CAJOLE

CAJOLERS > CAJOLE

CAJOLERY > CAJOLE

CAJOLES > CAJOLE

CAJOLING > CAJOLE

CAJON n Peruvian wooden box used as a drum

CAJONES > CAJON

CAJUN n music of the Cajun people

CAJUPUT n small tree or shrub

CAJUPUTS > CAJUPUT

CAKE n sweet food baked from a mixture of flour, eggs, etc ▷ vb form into a hardened mass or crust

CAKEAGE n charge in a restaurant for serving cake brought in from outside

CAKEAGES > CAKEAGE

CAKEBOX n box for a cake

CAKEBOXES > CAKEBOX

CAKED > CAKE

CAKEHOLE n slang word for mouth

CAKEHOLES > CAKEHOLE

CAKES > CAKE

CAKEWALK n dance based on a march with the prize of a cake for the best performers ▷ vb perform the cakewalk

CAKEWALKS > CAKEWALK

CAKEY > CAKE

CAKIER > CAKE

CAKIEST > CAKE

CAKINESS > CAKE

CAKING > CAKE

CAKINGS > CAKE

CAKY > CAKE

CAL n short for calorie

CALABASH n type of large round gourd

CALABAZA n variety of squash

CALABAZAS > CALABAZA

CALABOGUS n mixed drink containing rum, spruce beer, and molasses

CALABOOSE n prison

CALABRESE n kind of green sprouting broccoli

CALADIUM n type of tropical plant

CALADIUMS > CALADIUM

CALALOO same as > CALALU

CALALOOS > CALALOO

CALALU n edible leaves of various plants

CALALUS > CALALU

CALAMANCO n glossy woollen fabric woven with a checked design that shows on one side only

CALAMANSI n hybrid citrus fruit from the Philippines

CALAMAR n any member of the squid family

CALAMARI n squid cooked for eating, esp cut into rings and fried in batter

CALAMARIS > CALAMARI

CALAMARS > CALAMAR

CALAMARY variant of > CALAMARI

CALAMATA same as > KALAMATA

CALAMATAS > CALAMATA

CALAMI > CALAMUS

CALAMINE n pink powder consisting chiefly of zinc oxide, used in skin lotions and ointments ▷ vb apply calamine

CALAMINED > CALAMINE

CALAMINES > CALAMINE

CALAMINT n aromatic Eurasian plant with clusters of purple or pink flowers

CALAMINTS > CALAMINT

CALAMITE n type of extinct treelike plant related to the horsetails

CALAMITES > CALAMITE

CALAMITY n disaster

CALAMUS n tropical Asian palm

CALAMUSES > CALAMUS

CALANDO adv (to be performed) with gradually decreasing tone and speed

CALANDRIA n cylindrical vessel through which vertical tubes pass, esp one forming part of an evaporator, heat exchanger, or nuclear reactor

CALANTHE n type of orchid

CALANTHES > CALANTHE

CALASH n horse-drawn carriage with low wheels and a folding top

CALASHES > CALASH

CALATHEA n S American plant often grown as a greenhouse or house plant for its variegated leaves

CALATHEAS > CALATHEA

CALATHI > CALATHUS

CALATHOS same as > CALATHUS

CALATHUS n vase-shaped basket represented in ancient Greek art, used as a symbol of fruitfulness

CALAVANCE n type of pulse

CALCANEA > CALCANEUM

CALCANEAL > CALCANEUS

CALCANEAN > CALCANEUS

CALCANEI > CALCANEUS

CALCANEUM same as > CALCANEUS

CALCANEUS n largest tarsal bone, forming the heel in human beings

CALCAR n spur or spurlike process

CALCARATE > CALCAR

CALCARIA > CALCAR

CALCARINE > CALCAR

CALCARS > CALCAR

CALCEATE vb to shoe

CALCEATED > CALCEATE

CALCEATES
> CALCEATE

CALCED *adj* wearing shoes

CALCEDONY *n* microcrystalline often greyish form of quartz with crystals arranged in parallel fibres: a gemstone

CALCES > CALX

CALCIC *adj* of, containing, or concerned with lime or calcium

CALCICOLE *n* any plant that thrives in lime-rich soils

CALCIFIC *adj* forming or causing to form lime or chalk

CALCIFIED > CALCIFY

CALCIFIES > CALCIFY

CALCIFUGE *n* any plant that thrives in acid soils but not in lime-rich soils

CALCIFY *vb* harden by the depositing of calcium salts

CALCIMINE *n* white or pale tinted wash for walls ▷ *vb* cover with calcimine

CALCINE *vb* oxidize (a substance) by heating

CALCINED > CALCINE

CALCINES > CALCINE

CALCINING > CALCINE

CALCITE *n* colourless or white form of calcium carbonate

CALCITES > CALCITE

CALCITIC > CALCITE

CALCIUM *n* silvery-white metallic element

CALCIUMS > CALCIUM

CALCRETE *another name for* > CALICHE

CALCRETES
> CALCRETE

CALCSPAR *another name for* > CALCITE

CALCSPARS
> CALCSPAR

CALCTUFA *another name for* > TUFA

CALCTUFAS
> CALCTUFA

CALCTUFF *another name for* > TUFA

CALCTUFFS
> CALCTUFF

CALCULAR *adj* relating to calculus

CALCULARY *adj* relating to stone

CALCULATE *vb* solve or find out by a mathematical procedure or by reasoning

CALCULI > CALCULUS

CALCULOSE *adj* relating to calculi

CALCULOUS *adj* of a stonelike accretion of minerals and salts found in ducts or hollow organs of the body

CALCULUS *n* branch of mathematics dealing with infinitesimal changes to a variable number or quantity

CALDARIA
> CALDARIUM

CALDARIUM *n* (in ancient Rome) a room for taking hot baths

CALDERA *n* large basin-shaped crater at the top of a volcano

CALDERAS > CALDERA

CALDRON *same as* > CAULDRON

CALDRONS > CALDRON

CALECHE *variant of* > CALASH

CALECHES > CALECHE

CALEFIED > CALEFY

CALEFIES > CALEFY

CALEFY *vb* make warm

CALEFYING > CALEFY

CALEMBOUR *n* pun

CALENDAL > CALENDS

CALENDAR *n* chart showing a year divided up into months, weeks, and days ▷ *vb* enter in a calendar

CALENDARS
> CALENDAR

CALENDER *n* machine in which paper or cloth is smoothed by passing it between rollers ▷ *vb* smooth in such a machine

CALENDERS
> CALENDER

CALENDRER
> CALENDER

CALENDRIC
> CALENDAR

CALENDRY *n* place where calendering is carried out

CALENDS *pl n* first day of each month in the ancient Roman calendar

CALENDULA *n* marigold

CALENTURE *n* mild fever of tropical climates, similar in its symptoms to sunstroke

CALESA *n* horse-drawn buggy

CALESAS > CALESA

CALESCENT *adj* increasing in heat

CALF *n* young cow, bull, elephant, whale, or seal

CALFDOZER *n* small bulldozer

CALFHOOD *n* state of being a calf

CALFHOODS
> CALFHOOD

CALFLESS > CALF

CALFLICK *another word for* > COWLICK

CALFLICKS
> CALFLICK

CALFLIKE > CALF

CALFS > CALF

CALFSKIN *n* fine leather made from the skin of a calf

CALFSKINS
> CALFSKIN

CALIATOUR *n* red sandalwood

CALIBER *same as* > CALIBRE

CALIBERED > CALIBER

CALIBERS > CALIBER

CALIBRATE *vb* mark the scale or check the accuracy of (a measuring instrument)

CALIBRE *n* person's ability or worth

CALIBRED > CALIBRE

CALIBRES > CALIBRE

CALICES > CALIX

CALICHE *n* bed of sand or clay in arid regions

CALICHES > CALICHE

CALICLE *same as* > CALYCLE

CALICLES > CALICLE

CALICO *n* white cotton fabric

CALICOES > CALICO

CALICOS > CALICO

CALICULAR > CALYCLE

CALID *adj* warm

CALIDITY > CALID

CALIF *same as* > CALIPH

CALIFATE *same as* > CALIPHATE

CALIFATES
> CALIFATE

CALIFONT *n* gas water heater

CALIFONTS
> CALIFONT

CALIFS > CALIF

CALIGO *n* speck on the cornea causing poor vision

CALIGOES > CALIGO

CALIGOS > CALIGO

CALIMA *n* Saharan dust-storm

CALIMAS > CALIMA

CALIMOCHO *n* Spanish cocktail consisting of cola and red wine

CALIOLOGY *n* the study of birds' nests

CALIPASH *n* greenish glutinous edible part of the turtle

CALIPEE *n* edible part of the turtle found next to the lower shell

CALIPEES > CALIPEE

CALIPER *same as* > CALLIPER

CALIPERED
> CALLIPER

CALIPERS > CALLIPER

CALIPH *n* Muslim ruler

CALIPHAL > CALIPH

CALIPHATE *n* office, jurisdiction, or reign of a caliph

CALIPHS > CALIPH

CALISAYA *n* bark of a type of tropical tree from which quinine is extracted

CALISAYAS
> CALISAYA

CALIVER *n* type of musket

CALIVERS > CALIVER

CALIX *n* cup

CALIXES > CALIX

CALK *same as* > CAULK

CALKED > CALK

CALKER > CALK

CALKERS > CALK

CALKIN *same as* > CALK

CALKING > CALK

CALKINGS > CALK

CALKINS > CALKIN

CALKS > CALK

CALL *vb* name ▷ *n* cry, shout

CALLA *n* S African plant with a white funnel-shaped spathe enclosing a yellow spadix

CALLABLE *adj* (of a security) subject to redemption before maturity

CALLAIDES > CALLAIS

CALLAIS *n* type of green stone

CALLALOO *n* leafy green vegetable

CALLALOOS
> CALLALOO

CALLALOU *n* crabmeat soup

CALLALOUS
> CALLALOU

CALLAN *same as* > CALLANT

CALLANS > CALLAN

CALLANT *n* youth

CALLANTS > CALLANT

CALLAS > CALLA

CALLBACK *n* telephone call made in response to an earlier call

CALLBACKS
> CALLBACK

CALLBOARD *n* notice board listing opportunities for performers

CALLBOY *n* person who notifies actors when it is time to go on stage

CALLBOYS > CALLBOY

CALLED > CALL

CALLEE *n* computer function being used

CALLEES > CALLEE

CALLER *n* person or thing that calls, esp a person who makes a brief visit ▷ *adj* (of food, esp fish) fresh

CALLERS > CALLER

CALLET *n* scold

CALLETS > CALLET

CALLID *adj* cunning

CALLIDITY > CALLID

CALLIGRAM *n* poem in which words are positioned so as to create a visual image of the subject on the page

CALLING *n* vocation, profession

CALLINGS > CALLING

CALLIOPE *n* steam organ

CALLIOPES
> CALLIOPE

CALLIPASH *same as* > CALIPASH

CALLIPEE *same as* > CALIPEE

CALLIPEES
> CALLIPEE

CALLIPER *n* metal splint for supporting the leg ▷ *vb*

measure the dimensions of (an object) with callipers

CALLIPERS > CALLIPER

CALLOP n edible Australian freshwater fish

CALLOPS > CALLOP

CALLOSE n carbohydrate found in plants

CALLOSES > CALLOSE

CALLOSITY same as > CALLUS

CALLOUS adj showing no concern for other people's feelings ▷ vb make or become callous

CALLOUSED > CALLOUS

CALLOUSES > CALLOUS

CALLOUSLY > CALLOUS

CALLOUT n inset text within a printed article

CALLOUTS > CALLOUT

CALLOW adj young and inexperienced ▷ n someone young and inexperienced

CALLOWER > CALLOW

CALLOWEST > CALLOW

CALLOWLY adv in a manner suggesting immaturity or inexperience

CALLOWS > CALLOW

CALLS > CALL

CALLTIME n time available for making calls on a mobile phone

CALLTIMES > CALLTIME

CALLUNA n type of heather

CALLUNAS > CALLUNA

CALLUS n area of thick hardened skin ▷ vb produce or cause to produce a callus

CALLUSED > CALLUS

CALLUSES > CALLUS

CALLUSING > CALLUS

CALM adj not agitated or excited ▷ n peaceful state ▷ vb make or become calm

CALMANT n sedative

CALMANTS > CALMANT

CALMATIVE adj (of a remedy or agent) sedative ▷ n sedative remedy or drug

CALMED > CALM

CALMER > CALM

CALMEST > CALM

CALMIER > CALMY

CALMIEST > CALMY

CALMING > CALM

CALMINGLY > CALM

CALMINGS > CALM

CALMLY > CALM

CALMNESS > CALM

CALMS > CALM

CALMSTANE same as > CAMSTONE

CALMSTONE same as > CAMSTONE

CALMY adj tranquil

CALO n military servant

CALOMEL n colourless tasteless powder

CALOMELS > CALOMEL

CALORIC adj of heat or calories ▷ n hypothetical fluid formerly postulated as the embodiment of heat

CALORICS > CALORIC

CALORIE n unit of measurement for the energy value of food

CALORIES > CALORIE

CALORIFIC adj of calories or heat

CALORISE same as > CALORIZE

CALORISED > CALORISE

CALORISES > CALORISE

CALORIST n believer in caloric theory

CALORISTS > CALORIST

CALORIZE vb coat (a ferrous metal) by spraying with aluminium powder and then heating

CALORIZED > CALORIZE

CALORIZES > CALORIZE

CALORY same as > CALORIE

CALOS > CALO

CALOTTE n skullcap worn by Roman Catholic clergy

CALOTTES > CALOTTE

CALOTYPE n early photographic process

CALOTYPES > CALOTYPE

CALOYER n monk of the Greek Orthodox Church, esp of the Basilian Order

CALOYERS > CALOYER

CALP n type of limestone

CALPA n Hindu unit of time

CALPAC n large black brimless hat

CALPACK same as > CALPAC

CALPACKS > CALPACK

CALPACS > CALPAC

CALPAIN n type of enzyme

CALPAINS > CALPAIN

CALPAS > CALPA

CALPS > CALP

CALQUE same as > CAULK

CALQUED > CALQUE

CALQUES > CALQUE

CALQUING > CALQUE

CALS > CAL

CALTHA n marsh marigold

CALTHAS > CALTHA

CALTHROP same as > CALTROP

CALTHROPS > CALTROP

CALTRAP same as > CALTROP

CALTRAPS > CALTRAP

CALTROP n floating Asian plant

CALTROPS > CALTROP

CALUMBA n Mozambiquan root used for medicinal purposes

CALUMBAS > CALUMBA

CALUMET n peace pipe

CALUMETS > CALUMET

CALUMNIED > CALUMNY

CALUMNIES > CALUMNY

CALUMNY n false or malicious statement ▷ vb make a false or malicious statement about (a person)

CALUTRON n device used for the separation of isotopes

CALUTRONS > CALUTRON

CALVADOS n type of apple brandy

CALVARIA n top part of the skull of vertebrates

CALVARIAE > CALVARIA

CALVARIAL > CALVARIA

CALVARIAN > CALVARIA

CALVARIAS > CALVARIA

CALVARIES > CALVARY

CALVARIUM same as > CALVARIA

CALVARY n representation of Christ's crucifixion

CALVE vb give birth to a calf

CALVED > CALVE

CALVER vb prepare fish for cooking

CALVERED > CALVER

CALVERING > CALVER

CALVERS > CALVER

CALVES > CALF

CALVING > CALVE

CALVITIES n baldness

CALX n powdery metallic oxide formed when an ore or mineral is roasted

CALXES > CALX

CALYCATE > CALYX

CALYCEAL adj resembling a calyx

CALYCES > CALYX

CALYCINAL same as > CALYCINE

CALYCINE adj relating to, belonging to, or resembling a calyx

CALYCLE n cup-shaped structure, as in the coral skeleton

CALYCLED > CALYCLE

CALYCLES > CALYCLE

CALYCOID adj resembling a calyx

CALYCULAR > CALYCLE

CALYCULE n bracts surrounding the base of the calyx

CALYCULES > CALYCLE

CALYCULI > CALYCULUS

CALYCULUS same as > CALYCLE

CALYPSO n Trinidadian song with improvised topical lyrics

CALYPSOES > CALYPSO

CALYPSOS > CALYPSO

CALYPTER n alula

CALYPTERA same as > CALYPTRA

CALYPTERS > CALYPTER

CALYPTRA n membranous hood covering the spore-bearing capsule of mosses and liverworts

CALYPTRAS > CALYPTRA

CALYX n outer leaves that protect a flower bud

CALYXES > CALYX

CALZONE n folded pizza filled with cheese, tomatoes, etc

CALZONES > CALZONE

CALZONI > CALZONE

CAM n device that converts a circular motion to a to-and-fro motion ▷ vb furnish (a machine) with a cam

CAMA n hybrid offspring of a camel and a llama

CAMAIEU n cameo

CAMAIEUX > CAMAIEU

CAMAIL n covering of chain mail

CAMAILED > CAMAIL

CAMAILS > CAMAIL

CAMAN n wooden stick used to hit the ball in shinty

CAMANACHD n shinty

CAMANS > CAMAN

CAMARILLA n group of confidential advisers, esp formerly, to the Spanish kings

CAMARON n shrimp

CAMARONS > CAMARON

CAMAS same as > CAMASS

CAMASES > CAMAS

CAMASH same as > CAMASS

CAMASHES > CAMASS

CAMASS n type of North American plant

CAMASSES > CAMASS

CAMBER n slight upward curve to the centre of a surface ▷ vb form or be formed with a surface that curves upwards to its centre

CAMBERED > CAMBER

CAMBERING > CAMBER

CAMBERS > CAMBER

CAMBIA > CAMBIUM

CAMBIAL > CAMBIUM

CAMBIFORM > CAMBIUM

CAMBISM > CAMBIST

CAMBISMS > CAMBIST

CAMBIST n dealer or expert in foreign exchange

CAMBISTRY > CAMBIST

CAMBISTS > CAMBIST

CAMBIUM n meristem that increases the girth of stems and roots

CAMBIUMS > CAMBIUM

CAMBOGE n type of gum resin

CAMBOGES > CAMBOGE

CAMBOGIA *another name for* > GAMBOGE

CAMBOGIAS > CAMBOGIA

CAMBOOSE *n* cabin built as living quarters for a gang of lumber workers

CAMBOOSES > CAMBOOSE

CAMBREL *variant of* > GAMBREL

CAMBRELS > CAMBREL

CAMBRIC *n* fine white linen fabric

CAMBRICS > CAMBRIC

CAMCORD *vb* film with a camcorder

CAMCORDED > CAMCORD

CAMCORDER *n* combined portable video camera and recorder

CAMCORDS > CAMCORD

CAME > COME

CAMEL *n* humped mammal

CAMELBACK *n* type of locomotive

CAMELEER *n* camel-driver

CAMELEERS > CAMELEER

CAMELEON *same as* > CHAMELEON

CAMELEONS > CAMELEON

CAMELHAIR *n* hair of camel

CAMELIA *same as* > CAMELLIA

CAMELIAS > CAMELIA

CAMELID *adj* of or relating to camels ▷ *n* any animal of the camel family

CAMELIDS > CAMELID

CAMELINE *n* material made from camel hair

CAMELINES > CAMELINE

CAMELISH > CAMEL

CAMELLIA *n* evergreen ornamental shrub with white, pink, or red flowers

CAMELLIAS > CAMELLIA

CAMELLIKE > CAMEL

CAMELOID *n* member of the camel family

CAMELOIDS > CAMELOID

CAMELOT *n* supposedly idyllic period or age

CAMELOTS > CAMELOT

CAMELRIES > CAMELRY

CAMELRY *n* troops mounted on camels

CAMELS > CAMEL

CAMEO *n* brooch or ring with a profile head carved in relief ▷ *vb* appear in a brief role

CAMEOED > CAMEO

CAMEOING > CAMEO

CAMEOS > CAMEO

CAMERA *n* apparatus used for taking still or moving images

CAMERAE > CAMERA

CAMERAL *adj* of or relating to a judicial or legislative chamber

CAMERAMAN *n* man who operates a camera for television or cinema

CAMERAMEN > CAMERAMAN

CAMERAS > CAMERA

CAMERATED *adj* vaulted

CAMES *pl n* pieces of lead used in lattice windows

CAMESE *same as* > CAMISE

CAMESES > CAMESE

CAMI *n* camisole

CAMION *n* lorry, or, esp formerly, a large dray

CAMIONS > CAMION

CAMIS *n* light robe

CAMISA *n* smock

CAMISADE *same as* > CAMISADO

CAMISADES > CAMISADE

CAMISADO *n* (formerly) an attack made under cover of darkness

CAMISADOS > CAMISADO

CAMISAS > CAMISA

CAMISE *n* loose light shirt, smock, or tunic originally worn in the Middle Ages

CAMISES > CAMISE

CAMISIA *n* surplice

CAMISIAS > CAMISIA

CAMISOLE *n* woman's bodice-like garment

CAMISOLES > CAMISOLE

CAMLET *n* tough waterproof cloth

CAMLETS > CAMLET

CAMMED > CAM

CAMMIE *n* webcam award

CAMMIES > CAMMIE

CAMMING > CAM

CAMO *n* short for camouflage

CAMOGIE *n* form of hurling played by women

CAMOGIES > CAMOGIE

CAMOMILE *n* aromatic plant, used to make herbal tea

CAMOMILES > CAMOMILE

CAMOODI *a Caribbean name for* > ANACONDA

CAMOODIS > CAMOODI

CAMORRA *n* secret criminal group

CAMORRAS > CAMORRA

CAMORRIST > CAMORRA

CAMOS > CAMO

CAMOTE *n* type of sweet potato

CAMOTES > CAMOTE

CAMOUFLET *n* type of bomb used in a siege to collapse an enemy's tunnel

CAMP *vb* stay in a camp ▷ *adj* consciously artificial ▷ *n* (place for) temporary lodgings consisting of tents, huts, or cabins

CAMPAGNA *same as* > CHAMPAIGN

CAMPAGNAS > CAMPAGNA

CAMPAGNE > CAMPAGNA

CAMPAIGN *n* series of coordinated activities designed to achieve a goal ▷ *vb* take part in a campaign

CAMPAIGNS > CAMPAIGN

CAMPANA *n* bell or bell shape

CAMPANAS > CAMPANA

CAMPANERO *n* South American bellbird

CAMPANILE *n* bell tower, usu one not attached to another building

CAMPANILI > CAMPANILE

CAMPANIST *n* expert on bells

CAMPANULA *n* plant with blue or white bell-shaped flowers

CAMPCRAFT *n* skills required when camping

CAMPEACHY *adj* as in *campeachy wood* kind of wood

CAMPEADOR *n* champion; term applied especially to El Cid

CAMPED > CAMP

CAMPER *n* person who lives or temporarily stays in a tent, cabin, etc

CAMPERIES > CAMPERY

CAMPERS > CAMPER

CAMPERY *n* campness

CAMPESINO *n* Latin American rural peasant

CAMPEST > CAMP

CAMPFIRE *n* outdoor fire in a camp

CAMPFIRES > CAMPFIRE

CAMPHANE *n* one of the terpene hydrocarbons

CAMPHANES > CAMPHANE

CAMPHENE *n* colourless crystalline insoluble terpene

CAMPHENES > CAMPHENE

CAMPHINE *n* type of solvent

CAMPHINES > CAMPHINE

CAMPHIRE *an archaic name for* > HENNA

CAMPHIRES > CAMPHIRE

CAMPHOL *another word for* > BORNEOL

CAMPHOLS > CAMPHOL

CAMPHONE *n* combined mobile phone and digital camera

CAMPHONES > CAMPHONE

CAMPHOR *n* aromatic crystalline substance

CAMPHORIC > CAMPHOR

CAMPHORS > CAMPHOR

CAMPI > CAMPO

CAMPIER > CAMPY

CAMPIEST > CAMPY

CAMPILY > CAMPY

CAMPINESS > CAMPY

CAMPING > CAMP

CAMPINGS > CAMP

CAMPION *n* red, pink, or white wild flower

CAMPIONS > CAMPION

CAMPLE *vb* argue

CAMPLED > CAMPLE

CAMPLES > CAMPLE

CAMPLING > CAMPLE

CAMPLY > CAMP

CAMPNESS > CAMP

CAMPO *n* level or undulating savanna country

CAMPODEID *n* member of the Campodea genus of bristle-tails

CAMPONG *n* in Malaysia, a village

CAMPONGS > CAMPONG

CAMPOREE *n* local meeting or assembly of Scouts

CAMPOREES > CAMPOREE

CAMPOS > CAMPO

CAMPOUT *n* camping trip

CAMPOUTS > CAMPOUT

CAMPS > CAMP

CAMPSHIRT *n* short-sleeved shirt

CAMPSITE *n* area on which holiday makers may pitch a tent

CAMPSITES > CAMPSITE

CAMPSTOOL *n* folding stool

CAMPUS *n* grounds of a university or college ▷ *vb* restrict a student to campus, as a punishment

CAMPUSED > CAMPUS

CAMPUSES > CAMPUS

CAMPUSING > CAMPUS

CAMPY *adj* consciously artificial

CAMS > CAM

CAMSHAFT *n* part of an engine consisting of a rod to which cams are fixed

CAMSHAFTS > CAMSHAFT

CAMSHO *adj* crooked

CAMSHOCH *same as* > CAMSHO

CAMSTAIRY *adj* perverse

CAMSTANE *same as* > CAMSTONE

CAMSTANES > CAMSTONE

CAMSTEARY *same as* > CAMSTAIRY

CAMSTONE *n* limestone used for whitening stone doorsteps

CAMSTONES > CAMSTONE

CAMUS *n* type of loose robe

CAMUSES > CAMUS

CAMWHORE *vb* perform sexual acts in front of a webcam for money

CAMWHORED
> CAMWHORE
CAMWHORES
> CAMWHORE
CAMWOOD n W African leguminous tree
CAMWOODS > CAMWOOD
CAN vb be able to ▷ vb put (food etc) into a can ▷ n metal container for food or liquids
CANADA n canada goose
CANADAS > CANADA
CANAIGRE n southern US dock, the root of which yields a substance used in tanning
CANAIGRES
> CANAIGRE
CANAILLE n masses or rabble
CANAILLES
> CANAILLE
CANAKIN same as
> CANNIKIN
CANAKINS > CANAKIN
CANAL n artificial waterway ▷ vb dig a canal through
CANALBOAT n boat made for canals
CANALED > CANAL
CANALING > CANAL
CANALISE same as
> CANALIZE
CANALISED
> CANALIZE
CANALISES
> CANALIZE
CANALIZE vb give direction to
CANALIZED
> CANALIZE
CANALIZES
> CANALIZE
CANALLED > CANAL
CANALLER n canal boat worker
CANALLERS
> CANALLER
CANALLING > CANAL
CANALS > CANAL
CANAPE n small piece of bread or toast with a savoury topping
CANAPES > CANAPE
CANARD n false report
CANARDS > CANARD
CANARIED > CANARY
CANARIES > CANARY
CANARY n small yellow songbird often kept as a pet ▷ vb perform a dance called the canary
CANARYING > CANARY
CANASTA n card game like rummy, played with two packs
CANASTAS > CANASTA
CANASTER n coarsely broken dried tobacco leaves
CANASTERS
> CANASTER
CANBANK n container for receiving cans for recycling
CANBANKS > CANBANK

CANCAN n lively high-kicking dance performed by a female group
CANCANS > CANCAN
CANCEL vb stop (something that has been arranged) from taking place ▷ n new leaf or section of a book replacing a defective one
CANCELBOT n computer program that deletes unwanted mailings to internet usergroups
CANCELED > CANCEL
CANCELEER vb (of a hawk) to turn in flight when a stoop fails, in order to re-attempt it
CANCELER > CANCEL
CANCELERS > CANCEL
CANCELIER variant of
> CANCELEER
CANCELING > CANCEL
CANCELLED > CANCEL
CANCELLER > CANCEL
CANCELLI pl n any lattice-like structures
CANCELS > CANCEL
CANCER n serious disease resulting from a malignant growth or tumour
CANCERATE vb become cancerous
CANCERED adj affected by cancer
CANCEROUS > CANCER
CANCERS > CANCER
CANCHA n toasted maize
CANCHAS > CANCHA
CANCRINE adj crab-like
CANCROID adj resembling a cancerous growth ▷ n skin cancer, esp one of only moderate malignancy
CANCROIDS
> CANCROID
CANDELA n unit of luminous intensity
CANDELAS > CANDELA
CANDENT adj emitting light as a result of being heated to a high temperature
CANDID adj honest and straightforward ▷ n unposed photograph
CANDIDA n yeastlike parasitic fungus
CANDIDACY
> CANDIDATE
CANDIDAL > CANDIDA
CANDIDAS > CANDIDA
CANDIDATE n person seeking a job or position
CANDIDER > CANDID
CANDIDEST > CANDID
CANDIDLY > CANDID
CANDIDS > CANDID
CANDIE n South Indian unit of weight
CANDIED adj coated with sugar
CANDIES > CANDY
CANDIRU n parasitic freshwater catfish of the Amazon region

CANDIRUS > CANDIRU
CANDLE n stick of wax enclosing a wick, burned to produce light ▷ vb test by holding up to a candle
CANDLED > CANDLE
CANDLELIT adj lit by the light of candles
CANDLENUT n tropical Asian and Polynesian tree
CANDLEPIN n bowling pin, as used in skittles, tenpin bowling, candlepins, etc
CANDLER > CANDLE
CANDLERS > CANDLE
CANDLES > CANDLE
CANDLING > CANDLE
CANDOCK n type of water lily
CANDOCKS > CANDOCK
CANDOR same as
> CANDOUR
CANDORS > CANDOR
CANDOUR n honesty and straightforwardness
CANDOURS > CANDOUR
CANDY n sweet or sweets ▷ vb make sweet
CANDYGRAM n message accompanied by sweets
CANDYING > CANDY
CANDYMAN n itinerant seller of toffee
CANDYMEN > CANDYMAN
CANDYTUFT n garden plant with clusters of white, pink, or purple flowers
CANE n stem of the bamboo or similar plant ▷ vb beat with a cane
CANEBRAKE n thicket of canes
CANED > CANE
CANEFRUIT n fruit, like the raspberry, which grows on woody-stemmed plants
CANEGRUB n Australian grub that feeds on sugarcane
CANEGRUBS
> CANEGRUB
CANEH n Hebrew unit of length
CANEHS > CANEH
CANELLA n fragrant cinnamon-like inner bark of a Caribbean tree
CANELLAS > CANELLA
CANELLINI n white kidney bean
CANEPHOR n sculpted figure carrying a basket on its head
CANEPHORA same as
> CANEPHOR
CANEPHORE same as
> CANEPHOR
CANEPHORS > CANEPHOR
CANER > CANE
CANERS > CANE
CANES > CANE
CANESCENT adj white or greyish due to the presence of numerous short white hairs

CANEWARE n type of unglazed stoneware
CANEWARES
> CANEWARE
CANFIELD n gambling game adapted from a type of patience
CANFIELDS
> CANFIELD
CANFUL n amount a can will hold
CANFULS > CANFUL
CANG same as > CANGUE
CANGLE vb wrangle
CANGLED > CANGLE
CANGLES > CANGLE
CANGLING > CANGLE
CANGS > CANG
CANGUE n (formerly in China) a wooden collar worn as a punishment
CANGUES > CANGUE
CANICULAR adj of or relating to the star Sirius or its rising
CANID n animal of the dog family
CANIDS > CANID
CANIER > CANY
CANIEST > CANY
CANIKIN same as
> CANNIKIN
CANIKINS > CANIKIN
CANINE adj of or like a dog ▷ n sharp pointed tooth between the incisors and the molars
CANINES > CANINE
CANING n beating with a cane as a punishment
CANINGS > CANING
CANINITY > CANINE
CANISTEL n Caribbean fruit
CANISTELS
> CANISTEL
CANISTER n metal container ▷ vb put into canisters
CANISTERS
> CANISTER
CANITIES n grey hair
CANKER n ulceration ▷ vb infect or become infected with or as if with canker
CANKERED > CANKER
CANKERIER > CANKERY
CANKERING > CANKER
CANKEROUS adj having cankers
CANKERS > CANKER
CANKERY adj like a canker
CANKLE n thickened ankle on an overweight person
CANKLES > CANKLE
CANN vb direct a ship's steering
CANNA n type of tropical plant
CANNABIC > CANNABIS
CANNABIN n greenish-black poisonous resin obtained from the Indian hemp plant
CANNABINS
> CANNABIN**

CANNABIS n Asian plant with tough fibres

CANNACH n cotton grass

CANNACHS > CANNACH

CANNAE vb Scottish form of 'cannot'

CANNAS > CANNA

CANNED > CAN

CANNEL n type of dull coal

CANNELON n type of meat loaf

CANNELONI pl n pasta in the shape of tubes, which are usually stuffed

CANNELONS
> CANNELON

CANNELS > CANNEL

CANNELURE n groove or fluting, esp one around the cylindrical part of a bullet

CANNER n person or organization whose job is to can foods

CANNERIES > CANNERY

CANNERS > CANNER

CANNERY n factory where food is canned

CANNIBAL n person who eats human flesh

CANNIBALS
> CANNIBAL

CANNIE same as > CANNY

CANNIER > CANNY

CANNIEST > CANNY

CANNIKIN n small can, esp one used as a drinking vessel

CANNIKINS
> CANNIKIN

CANNILY > CANNY

CANNINESS > CANNY

CANNING n act of putting food in a can

CANNINGS > CANNING

CANNISTER same as > CANISTER

CANNOLI n Sicilian pudding of pasta shells filled with sweetened ricotta

CANNOLIS > CANNOLI

CANNON n gun of large calibre ▷ vb collide (with)

CANNONADE n continuous heavy gunfire ▷ vb attack (a target) with cannon

CANNONED > CANNON

CANNONEER n (formerly) a soldier who served and fired a cannon

CANNONIER same as > CANNONEER

CANNONING > CANNON

CANNONRY n volley of artillery fire

CANNONS > CANNON

CANNOT vb can not

CANNS > CANN

CANNULA n narrow tube for insertion into a bodily cavity

CANNULAE > CANNULA

CANNULAR adj shaped like a cannula

CANNULAS > CANNULA

CANNULATE vb insert a cannula into ▷ adj shaped like a cannula

CANNY adj shrewd, cautious ▷ adv quite

CANOE n light narrow open boat propelled by a paddle or paddles ▷ vb use a canoe

CANOEABLE > CANOE

CANOED > CANOE

CANOEING > CANOE

CANOEINGS > CANOE

CANOEIST > CANOE

CANOEISTS > CANOE

CANOEMAN n man who canoes

CANOEMEN > CANOEMAN

CANOER > CANOE

CANOERS > CANOE

CANOES > CANOE

CANOEWOOD n type of tree

CANOLA n cooking oil extracted from a variety of rapeseed

CANOLAS > CANOLA

CANON n priest serving in a cathedral

CANONESS n woman belonging to any one of several religious orders

CANONIC same as > CANONICAL

CANONICAL adj conforming with canon law

CANONISE same as > CANONIZE

CANONISED
> CANONISE

CANONISER
> CANONISE

CANONISES
> CANONISE

CANONIST n specialist in canon law

CANONISTS
> CANONIST

CANONIZE vb declare (a person) officially to be a saint

CANONIZED
> CANONIZE

CANONIZER
> CANONIZE

CANONIZES
> CANONIZE

CANONRIES > CANONRY

CANONRY n office, benefice, or status of a canon

CANONS > CANON

CANOODLE vb kiss and cuddle

CANOODLED
> CANOODLE

CANOODLER
> CANOODLE

CANOODLES
> CANOODLE

CANOPIC adj of a type of ancient Egyptian vase

CANOPIED > CANOPY

CANOPIES > CANOPY

CANOPY n covering above a bed, door, etc ▷ vb cover with or as if with a canopy

CANOPYING > CANOPY

CANOROUS adj tuneful

CANS > CAN

CANSFUL > CANFUL

CANSO n love song

CANSOS > CANSO

CANST vb form of 'can' used with the pronoun thou or its relative form

CANSTICK n candlestick

CANSTICKS
> CANSTICK

CANT n insincere talk ▷ vb use cant ▷ adj oblique

CANTABANK n itinerant singer

CANTABILE adv flowing and melodious ▷ n piece or passage performed in this way

CANTAL n French cheese

CANTALA n tropical American plant, the agave

CANTALAS > CANTALA

CANTALOUP n type of melon

CANTALS > CANTAL

CANTAR variant form of > KANTAR

CANTARS > CANTAR

CANTATA n musical work consisting of arias, duets, and choruses

CANTATAS > CANTATA

CANTATE n 98th psalm sung as a nonmetrical hymn

CANTATES > CANTATE

CANTDOG same as > CANTHOOK

CANTDOGS > CANTDOG

CANTED > CANT

CANTEEN n restaurant attached to a workplace or school

CANTEENS > CANTEEN

CANTER vb move at gait between trot and gallop

CANTERED > CANTER

CANTERING > CANTER

CANTERS > CANTER

CANTEST > CANT

CANTHAL > CANTHUS

CANTHARI
> CANTHARUS

CANTHARID n type of beetle with a soft elongated body

CANTHARIS n type of soldier beetle

CANTHARUS n large two-handled pottery cup

CANTHI > CANTHUS

CANTHIC adj relating to the canthus

CANTHITIS n inflammation of canthus

CANTHOOK n wooden pole with a hook used for handling logs

CANTHOOKS
> CANTHOOK

CANTHUS n inner or outer corner or angle of the eye

CANTIC > CANT

CANTICLE n short hymn with words from the Bible

CANTICLES > CANTICLE

CANTICO vb dance as part of an act of worship

CANTICOED > CANTICO

CANTICOS > CANTICO

CANTICOY same as > CANTICO

CANTICOYS
> CANTICOY

CANTICUM n canticle

CANTICUMS
> CANTICUM

CANTIER > CANTY

CANTIEST > CANTY

CANTILENA n smooth flowing style in the writing of vocal music

CANTILLY > CANTY

CANTINA n bar or wine shop, esp in a Spanish-speaking country

CANTINAS > CANTINA

CANTINESS > CANTY

CANTING > CANT

CANTINGLY > CANT

CANTINGS > CANT

CANTION n song

CANTIONS > CANTION

CANTLE n back part of a saddle that slopes upwards ▷ vb set up, or stand, on high

CANTLED > CANTLE

CANTLES > CANTLE

CANTLET n piece

CANTLETS > CANTLET

CANTLING > CANTLE

CANTO same as > CANTUS

CANTON n political division of a country, esp Switzerland ▷ vb divide into cantons

CANTONAL > CANTON

CANTONED > CANTON

CANTONING > CANTON

CANTONISE vb divide into cantons

CANTONIZE same as > CANTONISE

CANTONS > CANTON

CANTOR n man employed to lead services in a synagogue

CANTORIAL adj of or relating to a precentor

CANTORIS adj (in antiphonal music) to be sung by the cantorial side of a choir

CANTORS > CANTOR

CANTOS > CANTO

CANTRAIP n witch's spell or charm

CANTRAIPS
> CANTRAIP

CANTRAP same as > CANTRAIP

CANTRAPS > CANTRAP

CANTRED n district comprising a hundred villages

CANTREDS > CANTRED

CANTREF same as > CANTRED

CANTREFS > CANTREF

CANTRIP n magic spell ▷ adj (of an effect) produced by black magic

CANTRIPS > CANTRIP

CANTS > CANT
CANTUS *n* medieval form of church singing
CANTUSES > CANTUS
CANTY *adj* lively
CANULA *same as* **>** CANNULA
CANULAE > CANULA
CANULAR *adj* shaped like a cannula
CANULAS > CANULA
CANULATE *same as* **>** CANNULATE
CANULATED **>** CANULATE
CANULATES **>** CANULATE
CANVAS *n* heavy coarse cloth ▷ *vb* cover with, or be applied to, canvas
CANVASED > CANVAS
CANVASER > CANVAS
CANVASERS > CANVAS
CANVASES > CANVAS
CANVASING > CANVAS
CANVASS *vb* try to get votes or support (from) ▷ *n* canvassing
CANVASSED > CANVASS
CANVASSER > CANVASS
CANVASSES > CANVASS
CANY *adj* cane-like
CANYON *n* deep narrow valley
CANYONEER *n* canyon explorer
CANYONING *n* sport of going down a canyon river by any of various means
CANYONS > CANYON
CANZONA *n* type of 16th- or 17th-century contrapuntal music
CANZONAS > CANZONA
CANZONE *n* Provençal or Italian lyric, often in praise of love or beauty
CANZONES > CANZONE
CANZONET *n* short, cheery, or lively Italian song
CANZONETS **>** CANZONET
CANZONI > CANZONE
CAP *n* soft close-fitting covering for the head ▷ *vb* cover or top with something
CAPA *n* type of Spanish cloak
CAPABLE *adj* having the ability (for)
CAPABLER > CAPABLE
CAPABLEST > CAPABLE
CAPABLY > CAPABLE
CAPACIOUS *adj* roomy
CAPACITOR *n* device for storing electrical charge
CAPACITY *n* ability to contain, absorb, or hold ▷ *adj* of the maximum amount or number possible
CAPARISON *n* decorated covering for a horse or other animal, esp (formerly) for a warhorse ▷ *vb* put a caparison on

CAPAS > CAPA
CAPCOM *n* flight controller who communicates with the crew of a spacecraft
CAPCOMS > CAPCOM
CAPE *n* short cloak ▷ *vb* cut and remove the hide of an animal
CAPED > CAPE
CAPEESH *same as* **>** CAPISCE
CAPELAN *another word for* **>** CAPELIN
CAPELANS > CAPELAN
CAPELET *n* small cape
CAPELETS > CAPELET
CAPELIKE *adj* like a cape
CAPELIN *n* type of small marine food fish
CAPELINE *n* cap-shaped bandage to cover the head or an amputation stump
CAPELINES **>** CAPELINE
CAPELINS > CAPELIN
CAPELLET *n* wen-like swelling on a horse
CAPELLETS **>** CAPELLET
CAPELLINE *same as* **>** CAPELINE
CAPELLINI *n* type of pasta
CAPER *n* high-spirited prank ▷ *vb* skip about
CAPERED > CAPER
CAPERER > CAPER
CAPERERS > CAPER
CAPERING > CAPER
CAPERS *pl n* pickled flower buds of a Mediterranean shrub used in sauces
CAPES > CAPE
CAPESKIN *n* soft leather obtained from the skins of a type of lamb or sheep having hairlike wool ▷ *adj* made of this leather
CAPESKINS > CAPESKIN
CAPEWORK *n* use of the cape by the matador in bullfighting
CAPEWORKS **>** CAPEWORK
CAPEX *n* capital expenditure
CAPEXES > CAPEX
CAPFUL *n* quantity held by a (usually bottle) cap
CAPFULS > CAPFUL
CAPH *n* letter of the Hebrew alphabet
CAPHS > CAPH
CAPI > CAPO
CAPIAS *n* (formerly) a writ directing the arrest of a named person
CAPIASES > CAPIAS
CAPICHE *interj* do you understand?
CAPICOLLA *n* Italian cut of pork
CAPICOLLO *same as* **>** CAPICOLLA
CAPILLARY *n* very fine blood vessel ▷ *adj* (of a tube) having a fine bore

CAPING > CAPE
CAPISCE *interj* expression meaning *do you understand?*
CAPISH *interj* do you understand?
CAPITA > CAPUT
CAPITAL *n* chief city of a country ▷ *adj* involving or punishable by death
CAPITALLY *adv* in an excellent manner
CAPITALS > CAPITAL
CAPITAN *another name for* **>** HOGFISH
CAPITANI > CAPITANO
CAPITANO *n* chief; captain
CAPITANOS **>** CAPITANO
CAPITANS > CAPITAN
CAPITATE *n* largest of the bones of the human wrist
CAPITATED *adj* having fixed upper limit
CAPITATES **>** CAPITATE
CAPITAYN *n* captain
CAPITAYNS **>** CAPITAYN
CAPITELLA *n* plural form of singular: capitellum, an enlarged knoblike structure at the end of a bone that forms an articulation with another bone
CAPITOL *n* (in America) building housing the state legislature
CAPITOLS > CAPITOL
CAPITULA **>** CAPITULUM
CAPITULAR *adj* of or associated with a cathedral chapter ▷ *n* member of a cathedral chapter
CAPITULUM *n* racemose inflorescence in the form of a disc of sessile flowers, the youngest at the centre. It occurs in the daisy and related plants
CAPIZ *n* bivalve shell of a mollusc
CAPIZES > CAPIZ
CAPLE *n* horse
CAPLESS > CAPLE
CAPLESS > CAP
CAPLET *n* medicinal tablet, usually oval in shape, coated in a soluble substance
CAPLETS > CAPLET
CAPLIKE *adj* like a cap
CAPLIN *same as* **>** CAPELIN
CAPLINS > CAPLIN
CAPMAKER > CAP
CAPMAKERS > CAP
CAPO *n* device used to raise the pitch of a stringed instrument
CAPOCCHIA *n* fool
CAPOEIRA *n* Brazilian combination of martial art and dance

CAPOEIRAS **>** CAPOEIRA
CAPON *n* cock fowl fattened for eating
CAPONATA *n* Sicilian antipasto relish
CAPONATAS **>** CAPONATA
CAPONIER *n* covered passageway built across a ditch as a military defence
CAPONIERE *same as* **>** CAPONIER
CAPONIERS **>** CAPONIER
CAPONISE *same as* **>** CAPONIZE
CAPONISED **>** CAPONISE
CAPONISES **>** CAPONISE
CAPONIZE *vb* make (a cock) into a capon
CAPONIZED **>** CAPONIZE
CAPONIZES **>** CAPONIZE
CAPONS > CAPON
CAPORAL *n* strong coarse dark tobacco
CAPORALS > CAPORAL
CAPOS > CAPO
CAPOT *n* winning of all the tricks by one player ▷ *vb* score a capot (against)
CAPOTASTO *same as* **>** CAPO
CAPOTE *n* long cloak or soldier's coat, usually with a hood
CAPOTES > CAPOTE
CAPOTS > CAPOT
CAPOTTED > CAPOT
CAPOTTING > CAPOT
CAPOUCH *same as* **>** CAPUCHE
CAPOUCHES > CAPOUCH
CAPPED > CAP
CAPPER > CAP
CAPPERS > CAP
CAPPING > CAP
CAPPINGS > CAP
CAPRATE *n* any salt of capric acid
CAPRATES > CAPRATE
CAPRESE *n* salad of mozzarella, basil, and tomatoes
CAPRESES > CAPRESE
CAPRI *adj* as in *capri pants* women's tight-fitting trousers
CAPRIC *adj* (of a type of acid) smelling of goats
CAPRICCI **>** CAPRICCIO
CAPRICCIO *n* lively piece composed freely and without adhering to the rules for any specific musical form
CAPRICE *n* whim
CAPRICES > CAPRICE
CAPRID *n* any member of the goat family
CAPRIDS > CAPRID
CAPRIFIED > CAPRIFY
CAPRIFIES > CAPRIFY

CAPRIFIG n wild variety of fig of S Europe and SW Asia

CAPRIFIGS > CAPRIFIG

CAPRIFOIL variant of > CAPRIFOLE

CAPRIFOLE n honeysuckle

CAPRIFORM adj goatlike

CAPRIFY vb induce figs to ripen

CAPRINE adj of or resembling a goat

CAPRIOLE n upward but not forward leap made by a horse ▷ vb perform a capriole

CAPRIOLED > CAPRIOLE

CAPRIOLES > CAPRIOLE

CAPRIS pl n women's tight-fitting trousers

CAPROATE n any salt of caproic acid

CAPROATES > CAPROATE

CAPROCK n layer of rock that overlies a salt dome

CAPROCKS > CAPROCK

CAPROIC adj as in caproic acid oily acid found in milk

CAPRYLATE n any salt of caprylic acid

CAPRYLIC variant of > CAPRIC

CAPS > CAP

CAPSAICIN n colourless crystalline bitter alkaloid

CAPSICIN n liquid or resin extracted from capsicum

CAPSICINS > CAPSICIN

CAPSICUM n kind of pepper used as a vegetable or as a spice

CAPSICUMS > CAPSICUM

CAPSID n outer protein coat of a mature virus

CAPSIDAL > CAPSID

CAPSIDS > CAPSID

CAPSIZAL > CAPSIZE

CAPSIZALS > CAPSIZE

CAPSIZE vb (of a boat) overturn accidentally

CAPSIZED > CAPSIZE

CAPSIZES > CAPSIZE

CAPSIZING > CAPSIZE

CAPSOMER n one of the units making up a viral capsid

CAPSOMERE n any of the protein units that together form the capsid of a virus

CAPSOMERS > CAPSOMER

CAPSTAN n rotating cylinder round which a ship's rope is wound

CAPSTANS > CAPSTAN

CAPSTONE n one of a set of slabs on the top of a wall, building, etc

CAPSTONES > CAPSTONE

CAPSULAR adj relating to a capsule

CAPSULARY same as > CAPSULAR

CAPSULATE adj within or formed into a capsule

CAPSULE n soluble gelatine case containing a dose of medicine ▷ adj very concise ▷ vb contain within a capsule

CAPSULED > CAPSULE

CAPSULES > CAPSULE

CAPSULING > CAPSULE

CAPSULISE same as > CAPSULIZE

CAPSULIZE vb state (information) in a highly condensed form

CAPTAIN n commander of a ship or civil aircraft ▷ vb be captain of

CAPTAINCY > CAPTAIN

CAPTAINED > CAPTAIN

CAPTAINRY n condition or skill of being a captain

CAPTAINS > CAPTAIN

CAPTAN n type of fungicide

CAPTANS > CAPTAN

CAPTCHA n test in which the user of a website has to decipher a distorted image

CAPTCHAS > CAPTCHA

CAPTION n title or explanation accompanying an illustration ▷ vb provide with a caption

CAPTIONED > CAPTION

CAPTIONS > CAPTION

CAPTIOUS adj tending to make trivial criticisms

CAPTIVATE vb attract and hold the attention of

CAPTIVE n person kept in confinement ▷ adj kept in confinement ▷ vb take prisoner

CAPTIVED > CAPTIVE

CAPTIVES > CAPTIVE

CAPTIVING > CAPTIVE

CAPTIVITY n state of being kept in confinement

CAPTOPRIL n drug used to treat high blood pressure and congestive heart failure

CAPTOR n person who captures a person or animal

CAPTORS > CAPTOR

CAPTURE vb take by force ▷ n capturing

CAPTURED > CAPTURE

CAPTURER > CAPTURE

CAPTURERS > CAPTURE

CAPTURES > CAPTURE

CAPTURING > CAPTURE

CAPUCCIO n hood

CAPUCCIOS > CAPUCCIO

CAPUCHE n large hood or cowl, esp that worn by Capuchin friars

CAPUCHED adj hooded

CAPUCHES > CAPUCHE

CAPUCHIN n S American monkey with thick hair on the top of its head

CAPUCHINS > CAPUCHIN

CAPUERA variant of > CAPOEIRA

CAPUERAS > CAPUERA

CAPUL same as > CAPLE

CAPULS > CAPUL

CAPUT n main or most prominent part of an organ or structure

CAPYBARA n very large S American rodent

CAPYBARAS > CAPYBARA

CAR n motor vehicle designed to carry a small number of people

CARABAO n water buffalo

CARABAOS > CARABAO

CARABID n type of beetle

CARABIDS > CARABID

CARABIN same as > CARBINE

CARABINE same as > CARBINE

CARABINER variant spelling of > KARABINER

CARABINES > CARABINE

CARABINS > CARABIN

CARACAL n lynx with reddish fur, which inhabits deserts of N Africa and S Asia

CARACALS > CARACAL

CARACARA n carrion-eating bird of S North, Central, and S America

CARACARAS > CARACARA

CARACK same as > CARRACK

CARACKS > CARACK

CARACOL same as > CARACOLE

CARACOLE n half turn to the right or left ▷ vb execute a half turn to the right or left

CARACOLED > CARACOLE

CARACOLER > CARACOLE

CARACOLES > CARACOLE

CARACOLS > CARACOL

CARACT n sign or symbol

CARACTS > CARACT

CARACUL n fur from the skins of newly born lambs of the karakul sheep

CARACULS > CARACUL

CARAFE n glass bottle

CARAFES > CARAFE

CARAGANA n pea tree

CARAGANAS > CARAGANA

CARAGEEN same as > CARRAGEEN

CARAGEENS > CARAGEEN

CARAMBA interj Spanish interjection similar to 'wow!'

CARAMBOLA n yellow edible star-shaped fruit that grows on a Brazilian tree

CARAMBOLE vb make a carom or carambola (shot in billiards)

CARAMEL n chewy sweet made from sugar and milk ▷ vb turn into caramel

CARAMELS > CARAMEL

CARANGID n type of marine fish

CARANGIDS > CARANGID

CARANGOID same as > CARANGID

CARANNA n gumlike substance

CARANNAS > CARANNA

CARAP n crabwood

CARAPACE n hard upper shell of tortoises and crustaceans

CARAPACED adj having carapace

CARAPACES > CARAPACE

CARAPAX n carapace

CARAPAXES > CARAPAX

CARAPS > CARAP

CARASSOW same as > CURASSOW

CARASSOWS > CARASSOW

CARAT n unit of weight of precious stones

CARATE n tropical disease

CARATES > CARATE

CARATS > CARAT

CARAUNA same as > CARANNA

CARAUNAS > CARAUNA

CARAVAN n large enclosed vehicle for living in ▷ vb travel or have a holiday in a caravan

CARAVANCE same as > CALAVANCE

CARAVANED > CARAVAN

CARAVANER n person who holidays in a caravan

CARAVANS > CARAVAN

CARAVEL n two- or three-masted sailing ship

CARAVELLE variant of > CARAVEL

CARAVELS > CARAVEL

CARAWAY n plant whose seeds are used as a spice

CARAWAYS > CARAWAY

CARB n carbohydrate

CARBACHOL n cholinergic agent

CARBAMATE n salt or ester of carbamic acid

CARBAMIC adj as in carbamic acid hypothetical compound known only in carbamate salts

CARBAMIDE another name for > UREA

CARBAMINO adj relating to the compound produced when carbon dioxide reacts with an amino group

CARBAMOYL same as > CARBAMYL

CARBAMYL n radical from carbamic acid
CARBAMYLS
> CARBAMYL
CARBANION n negatively charged organic ion in which most of the negative charge is localized on a carbon atom
CARBARN n streetcar depot
CARBARNS > CARBARN
CARBARYL n organic compound of the carbamate group
CARBARYLS
> CARBARYL
CARBAZOLE n colourless insoluble solid obtained from coal tar
CARBEEN n Australian eucalyptus tree
CARBEENS > CARBEEN
CARBENE n type of divalent free radical
CARBENES > CARBENE
CARBIDE n compound of carbon with a metal
CARBIDES > CARBIDE
CARBIDOPA n drug used to treat symptoms of Parkinson's disease
CARBIES > CARBY
CARBINE n light automatic rifle
CARBINEER n (formerly) a soldier equipped with a carbine
CARBINES > CARBINE
CARBINIER same as
> CARBINEER
CARBINOL same as
> METHANOL
CARBINOLS
> CARBINOL
CARBO n carbohydrate
CARBOLIC adj as in carbolic acid phenol, when it is used as a disinfectant
CARBOLICS
> CARBOLIC
CARBOLISE same as
> CARBOLIZE
CARBOLIZE another word for > PHENOLATE
CARBON n nonmetallic element
CARBONADE n stew of beef and onions cooked in beer
CARBONADO n piece of meat, fish, etc, scored and grilled ▷ vb score and grill (meat, fish, etc)
CARBONARA n pasta sauce containing cream, bacon and cheese
CARBONATE n salt or ester of carbonic acid ▷ vb form or turn into a carbonate
CARBONIC adj containing carbon
CARBONISE same as
> CARBONIZE
CARBONIUM n as in carbonium ion type of positively charged organic ion

CARBONIZE vb turn into carbon as a result of heating
CARBONOUS > CARBON
CARBONS > CARBON
CARBONYL n the divalent group =CO
CARBONYLS
> CARBONYL
CARBORA n former name for the koala
CARBORAS > CARBORA
CARBORNE adj travelling by car
CARBOS > CARBO
CARBOXYL adj as in carboxyl group functional group in organic acids
CARBOXYLS
> CARBOXYL
CARBOY n large bottle with a protective casing
CARBOYED > CARBOY
CARBOYS > CARBOY
CARBS > CARB
CARBUNCLE n inflamed boil
CARBURATE same as
> CARBURET
CARBURET vb combine with carbon
CARBURETS
> CARBURET
CARBURISE same as
> CARBONIZE
CARBURIZE same as
> CARBONIZE
CARBY n short for carburettor
CARCAJOU a North American name for
> WOLVERINE
CARCAJOUS
> CARCAJOU
CARCAKE n (formerly, in Scotland) a cake traditionally made for Shrove Tuesday
CARCAKES > CARCAKE
CARCANET n jewelled collar or necklace
CARCANETS
> CARCANET
CARCASE same as
> CARCASS
CARCASED > CARCASE
CARCASES > CARCASE
CARCASING > CARCASE
CARCASS n dead body of an animal ▷ vb make a carcass of
CARCASSED > CARCASS
CARCASSES > CARCASS
CARCEL n French unit of light
CARCELS > CARCEL
CARCERAL adj relating to prison
CARCINOID n small serotonin-secreting tumour
CARCINOMA n malignant tumour
CARD n piece of thick stiff paper or cardboard ▷ vb comb out fibres of wool or cotton before spinning
CARDAMINE n bittercress

CARDAMOM n spice obtained from the seeds of a tropical plant
CARDAMOMS
> CARDAMOM
CARDAMON same as
> CARDAMOM
CARDAMONS
> CARDAMON
CARDAMUM same as
> CARDAMOM
CARDAMUMS
> CARDAMUM
CARDAN n as in cardan joint type of universal joint
CARDBOARD n thin stiff board made from paper pulp ▷ adj without substance
CARDCASE n small case for holding business cards
CARDCASES
> CARDCASE
CARDECU n old French coin (a quarter of a crown)
CARDECUE same as
> CARDECU
CARDECUES
> CARDECUE
CARDECUS > CARDECU
CARDED > CARD
CARDER > CARD
CARDERS > CARD
CARDI n cardigan
CARDIA n lower oesophageal sphincter
CARDIAC adj of the heart ▷ n person with a heart disorder
CARDIACAL > CARDIAC
CARDIACS > CARDIAC
CARDIAE > CARDIA
CARDIALGY n pain in or near the heart
CARDIAS > CARDIA
CARDIE short for
> CARDIGAN
CARDIES > CARDIE
CARDIGAN n knitted jacket
CARDIGANS
> CARDIGAN
CARDINAL n high-ranking clergyman of the RC Church ▷ adj fundamentally important
CARDINALS
> CARDINAL
CARDING > CARD
CARDINGS > CARD
CARDIO adj exercising heart ▷ n cardiovascular exercise
CARDIOID n heart-shaped curve
CARDIOIDS
> CARDIOID
CARDIOS > CARDIO
CARDIS > CARDI
CARDITIC > CARDITIS
CARDITIS n inflammation of the heart
CARDON n variety of cactus
CARDONS > CARDON
CARDOON n thistle-like S European plant
CARDOONS > CARDOON

CARDPHONE n public telephone operated by the insertion of a phonecard instead of coins
CARDPUNCH n device for putting data from a CPU onto punched cards
CARDS > CARD
CARDSHARP n professional card player who cheats
CARDUUS n thistle
CARDUUSES > CARDUUS
CARDY short for
> CARDIGAN
CARE vb be concerned ▷ n careful attention, caution
CARED > CARE
CAREEN vb tilt over to one side
CAREENAGE > CAREEN
CAREENED > CAREEN
CAREENER > CAREEN
CAREENERS > CAREEN
CAREENING > CAREEN
CAREENS > CAREEN
CAREER n series of jobs that a person has through their life ▷ vb rush in an uncontrolled way ▷ adj having chosen to dedicate his or her life to a particular occupation
CAREERED > CAREER
CAREERER > CAREER
CAREERERS > CAREER
CAREERING > CAREER
CAREERISM
> CAREERIST
CAREERIST n person who seeks advancement by any possible means
CAREERS > CAREER
CAREFREE adj without worry or responsibility
CAREFUL adj cautious in attitude or action
CAREFULLY > CAREFUL
CAREGIVER same as
> CARER
CARELESS adj done or acting with insufficient attention
CARELINE n telephone service set up by a company or other organization
CARELINES
> CARELINE
CAREME n period of Lent
CAREMES > CAREME
CARER n person who looks after someone who is ill or old, often a relative
CARERS > CARER
CARES > CARE
CARESS n gentle affectionate touch or embrace ▷ vb touch gently and affectionately
CARESSED > CARESS
CARESSER > CARESS
CARESSERS > CARESS
CARESSES > CARESS
CARESSING > CARESS
CARESSIVE adj caressing

CARET n proofreading symbol

CARETAKE vb work as a caretaker

CARETAKEN > CARETAKE

CARETAKER n person employed to look after a place ▷ adj performing the duties of an office temporarily

CARETAKES > CARETAKE

CARETOOK > CARETAKE

CARETS > CARET

CAREWARE n computer software licensed in exchange for a donation to charity

CAREWARES > CAREWARE

CAREWORN adj showing signs of worry

CAREX n any member of the sedge family

CARFARE n fare that a passenger is charged for a ride on a bus, etc

CARFARES > CARFARE

CARFAX n place where principal roads or streets intersect

CARFAXES > CARFAX

CARFOX same as > CARFAX

CARFOXES > CARFOX

CARFUFFLE variant spelling of > KERFUFFLE

CARFUL n maximum number of people a car will hold

CARFULS > CARFUL

CARGEESE > CARGOOSE

CARGO n goods carried by a ship, aircraft, etc ▷ vb load

CARGOED > CARGO

CARGOES > CARGO

CARGOING > CARGO

CARGOOSE n crested grebe

CARGOS > CARGO

CARHOP n waiter or waitress at a drive-in restaurant ▷ vb work as a carhop

CARHOPPED > CARHOP

CARHOPS > CARHOP

CARIACOU n type of deer

CARIACOUS > CARIACOU

CARIAMA another word for > SERIEMA

CARIAMAS > CARIAMA

CARIBE n piranha

CARIBES > CARIBE

CARIBOO same as > CARIBOU

CARIBOOS > CARIBOO

CARIBOU n large N American reindeer

CARIBOUS > CARIBOU

CARICES > CAREX

CARIED adj (of teeth) decayed

CARIERE obsolete word for > CAREER

CARIERES > CARIERE

CARIES n tooth decay

CARILLON n set of bells played by keyboard or mechanically ▷ vb play a carillon

CARILLONS > CARILLON

CARINA n keel-like part or ridge

CARINAE > CARINA

CARINAL adj keel-like

CARINAS > CARINA

CARINATE adj having a keel or ridge

CARINATED same as > CARINATE

CARING adj feeling or showing care and compassion for other people ▷ n practice or profession of providing social or medical care

CARINGLY > CARING

CARINGS > CARING

CARIOCA n Brazilian dance similar to the samba

CARIOCAS > CARIOCA

CARIOLE n small open two-wheeled horse-drawn vehicle

CARIOLES > CARIOLE

CARIOSE same as > CARIOUS

CARIOSITY > CARIOUS

CARIOUS adj (of teeth or bone) affected with caries

CARITAS n divine love; charity

CARITASES > CARITAS

CARITATES > CARITAS

CARJACK vb attack (a car driver) to rob them or to steal the car

CARJACKED > CARJACK

CARJACKER > CARJACK

CARJACKS > CARJACK

CARJACOU variation of > CARIACOU

CARJACOUS > CARJACOUS

CARK vb break down

CARKED > CARK

CARKING > CARK

CARKS > CARK

CARL another word for > CHURL

CARLE same as > CARL

CARLES > CARLE

CARLESS > CAR

CARLIN same as > CARLING

CARLINE same as > CARLING

CARLINES > CARLINE

CARLING n fore-and-aft beam in a vessel

CARLINGS > CARLING

CARLINS > CARLIN

CARLISH adj churlish

CARLOAD n amount that can be carried by a car

CARLOADS > CARLOAD

CARLOCK n type of Russian isinglass

CARLOCKS > CARLOCK

CARLOT n boor

CARLOTS > CARLOT

CARLS > CARL

CARMAKER n car manufacturing company

CARMAKERS > CARMAKER

CARMAN n man who drives a car or cart

CARMELITE n member of an order of mendicant friars

CARMEN > CARMAN

CARMINE adj vivid red ▷ n vivid red colour, sometimes with a purplish tinge

CARMINES > CARMINE

CARN n cairn

CARNAGE n extensive slaughter of people

CARNAGES > CARNAGE

CARNAHUBA same as > CARNAUBA

CARNAL adj of a physical or sensual nature ▷ vb act in a carnal manner

CARNALISE vb make carnal

CARNALISM > CARNALISE

CARNALIST > CARNALISE

CARNALITY > CARNAL

CARNALIZE same as > CARNALISE

CARNALLED > CARNAL

CARNALLY > CARNAL

CARNALS > CARNAL

CARNAROLI n variety of short-grain rice used for risotto

CARNATION n cultivated plant with fragrant white, pink, or red flowers

CARNAUBA n Brazilian fan palm tree

CARNAUBAS > CARNAUBA

CARNELIAN n reddish-yellow gemstone

CARNEOUS adj fleshy

CARNET n type of customs licence

CARNETS > CARNET

CARNEY same as > CARNY

CARNEYED > CARNEY

CARNEYING > CARNEY

CARNEYS > CARNEY

CARNIE same as > CARNY

CARNIED > CARNY

CARNIER > CARNY

CARNIES > CARNY

CARNIEST > CARNY

CARNIFEX n executioner

CARNIFIED > CARNIFY

CARNIFIES > CARNIFY

CARNIFY vb be altered so as to resemble skeletal muscle

CARNITINE n type of white betaine

CARNIVAL n festive period with processions, music, and dancing in the street

CARNIVALS > CARNIVAL

CARNIVORA n members of a group of carnivorous mammals

CARNIVORE n meat-eating animal

CARNIVORY n state of being carnivore

CARNOSAUR n meat-eating dinosaur

CARNOSE adj fleshy

CARNOSITY n fleshy protrusion

CARNOTITE n radioactive yellow mineral

CARNS > CARN

CARNY vb coax or cajole or act in a wheedling manner ▷ n person who works in a carnival ▷ adj sly

CARNYING > CARNY

CARNYX n bronze Celtic war trumpet

CARNYXES > CARNYX

CAROACH same as > CAROCHE

CAROACHES > CAROACH

CAROB n pod of a Mediterranean tree, used as a chocolate substitute

CAROBS > CAROB

CAROCH same as > CAROCHE

CAROCHE n stately ceremonial carriage used in the 16th and 17th centuries

CAROCHES > CAROCHE

CAROL n joyful Christmas hymn ▷ vb sing carols

CAROLED > CAROL

CAROLER > CAROL

CAROLERS > CAROL

CAROLI > CAROLUS

CAROLING > CAROL

CAROLINGS > CAROL

CAROLLED > CAROL

CAROLLER > CAROL

CAROLLERS > CAROL

CAROLLING > CAROL

CAROLS > CAROL

CAROLUS n any of several coins struck in the reign of a king called Charles

CAROLUSES > CAROLUS

CAROM n shot in which the cue ball is caused to contact one object ball after another ▷ vb carambole

CAROMED > CAROM

CAROMEL vb turn into caramel

CAROMELS > CAROMEL

CAROMING > CAROM

CAROMS > CAROM

CARON n inverted circumflex

CARONS > CARON

CAROTENE n orange-red hydrocarbons found in many plants

CAROTENES > CAROTENE

CAROTID n either of the two arteries supplying blood to the head ▷ adj of either of these arteries

CAROTIDAL > CAROTID

CAROTIDS > CAROTID

CAROTIN same as > CAROTENE

CAROTINS > CAROTIN
CAROUSAL *n* merry drinking party
CAROUSALS > CAROUSAL
CAROUSE *vb* have a merry drinking party
CAROUSED > CAROUSE
CAROUSEL *n* revolving conveyor belt for luggage or photographic slides
CAROUSELS > CAROUSEL
CAROUSER > CAROUSE
CAROUSERS > CAROUSE
CAROUSES > CAROUSE
CAROUSING > CAROUSE
CARP *n* large freshwater fish ▷ *vb* complain, find fault
CARPACCIO *n* Italian dish of thin slices of raw meat or fish
CARPAL *n* wrist bone
CARPALE *same as* > CARPAL
CARPALES > CARPALE
CARPALIA > CARPAL
CARPALS > CARPAL
CARPED > CARP
CARPEL *n* female reproductive organ of a flowering plant
CARPELS > CARPEL
CARPENTER *n* person who makes or repairs wooden structures ▷ *vb* do the work of a carpenter
CARPENTRY *n* skill or work of a carpenter
CARPER > CARP
CARPERS > CARP
CARPET *n* heavy fabric for covering floors ▷ *vb* cover with a carpet
CARPETBAG *n* travelling bag made of carpeting
CARPETED > CARPET
CARPETING *n* carpet material or carpets in general
CARPETS > CARPET
CARPHONE *n* (formerly) phone designed for use in a car
CARPHONES > CARPHONE
CARPI > CARPUS
CARPING *adj* tending to make petty complaints ▷ *n* petty complaint
CARPINGLY > CARPING
CARPINGS > CARPING
CARPLIKE *adj* like a carp
CARPOLOGY *n* branch of botany concerned with the study of fruits and seeds
CARPOOL *vb* share the use of a single car to travel to work or school
CARPOOLED > CARPOOL
CARPOOLER > CARPOOL
CARPOOLS > CARPOOL
CARPORT *n* shelter for a car, consisting of a roof supported by posts
CARPORTS > CARPORT

CARPS > CARP
CARPUS *n* set of eight bones of the wrist
CARR *n* area of bog or fen in which scrub has become established
CARRACK *n* galleon used as a merchantman
CARRACKS > CARRACK
CARRACT *same as* > CARRACK
CARRACTS > CARRACT
CARRAGEEN *n* edible red seaweed of North America and N Europe
CARRAT *same as* > CARAT
CARRATS > CARRAT
CARRAWAY *same as* > CARAWAY
CARRAWAYS > CARRAWAY
CARRECT *same as* > CARRACK
CARRECTS > CARRECT
CARREFOUR *n* public square, esp one at the intersection of several roads
CARREL *n* small individual study room or private desk
CARRELL *same as* > CARREL
CARRELLS > CARRELL
CARRELS > CARREL
CARRIAGE *n* one of the sections of a train for passengers
CARRIAGES > CARRIAGE
CARRICK *n* as in *carrick bend* type of knot
CARRIED > CARRY
CARRIER *n* person or thing that carries something
CARRIERS > CARRIER
CARRIES > CARRY
CARRIOLE *same as* > CARIOLE
CARRIOLES > CARRIOLE
CARRION *n* dead and rotting flesh
CARRIONS > CARRION
CARRITCH *n* catechism
CARROCH *variant of* > CAROCHE
CARROCHES > CAROM
CARROM *same as* > CAROM
CARROMED > CARROM
CARROMING > CARROM
CARROMS > CARROM
CARRON *n* as in *carron oil* ointment of limewater and linseed oil
CARRONADE *n* obsolete naval gun of short barrel and large bore
CARROT *n* long tapering orange root vegetable
CARROTIER > CARROTY
CARROTIN *n* carotene
CARROTINS > CARROTIN
CARROTS > CARROT
CARROTTOP *n* facetious term for a person with red hair

CARROTY *adj* (of hair) reddish-orange
CARROUSEL *variant spelling of* > CAROUSEL
CARRS > CARR
CARRY *vb* take from one place to another
CARRYALL *n* light four-wheeled horse-drawn carriage usually designed to carry four passengers
CARRYALLS > CARRYALL
CARRYBACK *n* amount carried back in accounting
CARRYCOT *n* light portable bed for a baby, with handles and a hood
CARRYCOTS > CARRYCOT
CARRYING > CARRY
CARRYON *n* fuss or commotion
CARRYONS > CARRYON
CARRYOUT *n* hot cooked food bought in a shop for consumption elsewhere
CARRYOUTS > CARRYOUT
CARRYOVER *n* sum or balance carried forward in accounting
CARRYTALE *n* gossip
CARS > CAR
CARSE *n* riverside area of flat fertile alluvium
CARSES > CARSE
CARSEY *slang word for* > TOILET
CARSEYS > CARSEY
CARSHARE *same as* > CARPOOL
CARSHARED > CARSHARE
CARSHARES > CARSHARE
CARSICK *adj* nauseated from riding in a car
CARSPIEL *n* curling match which has a car as a prize
CARSPIELS > CARSPIEL
CART *n* open two-wheeled horse-drawn vehicle ▷ *vb* carry, usu with some effort
CARTA *n* charter
CARTABLE > CART
CARTAGE *n* process or cost of carting
CARTAGES > CARTAGE
CARTAS > CARTA
CARTE *n* fencing position
CARTED > CART
CARTEL *n* association of competing firms formed to fix prices
CARTELISE *same as* > CARTELIZE
CARTELISM > CARTEL
CARTELIST > CARTEL
CARTELIZE *vb* form or be formed into a cartel
CARTELS > CARTEL
CARTER > CART
CARTERS > CART

CARTES > CARTE
CARTFUL *n* amount a cart can hold
CARTFULS > CARTFUL
CARTHORSE *n* large heavily built horse
CARTILAGE *n* strong flexible tissue forming part of the skeleton
CARTING > CART
CARTLOAD *n* amount a cart can hold
CARTLOADS > CARTLOAD
CARTOGRAM *n* map showing statistical information in diagrammatic form
CARTOLOGY *n* theory of mapmaking
CARTON *n* container made of cardboard or waxed paper ▷ *vb* enclose (goods) in a carton
CARTONAGE *n* material from which mummy masks and coffins were made
CARTONED > CARTON
CARTONING > CARTON
CARTONS > CARTON
CARTOON *n* humorous or satirical drawing ▷ *vb* depict in a cartoon
CARTOONED > CARTOON
CARTOONS > CARTOON
CARTOONY *adj* of or like a cartoon
CARTOP *adj* designed to be transported on top of a vehicle
CARTOPPER *n* anything designed to be transported on top of a vehicle
CARTOUCH *same as* > CARTOUCHE
CARTOUCHE *n* ornamental tablet or panel in the form of a scroll
CARTRIDGE *n* casing containing an explosive charge and bullet for a gun
CARTROAD *n* road for carts to drive on
CARTROADS > CARTROAD
CARTS > CART
CARTULARY *n* collection of charters or records, esp relating to the title to an estate or monastery
CARTWAY *n* way by which carts travel
CARTWAYS > CARTWAY
CARTWHEEL *n* sideways somersault supported by the hands with legs outstretched ▷ *vb* perform a cartwheel movement
CARUCAGE *n* tax due on a carucate
CARUCAGES > CARUCAGE
CARUCATE *n* area of land an oxen team could plough in a year

CARUCATES
> CARUCATE
CARUNCLE n fleshy outgrowth on the heads of certain birds, such as a cock's comb
CARUNCLES
> CARUNCLE
CARVACROL n aromatic phenol found in oregano
CARVE vb cut to form an object
CARVED > CARVE
CARVEL same as
> CARAVEL
CARVELS > CARVEL
CARVEN an archaic or literary past participle of
> CARVE
CARVER n carving knife
CARVERIES > CARVERY
CARVERS > CARVER
CARVERY n restaurant where customers pay a set price for unrestricted helpings
CARVES > CARVE
CARVIES > CARVY
CARVING n figure or design produced by carving stone or wood
CARVINGS > CARVING
CARVY n caraway seed
CARWASH n drive-through structure containing automated equipment for washing cars
CARWASHES > CARWASH
CARYATIC > CARYATID
CARYATID n supporting column in the shape of a female figure
CARYATIDS
> CARYATID
CARYOPSES
> CARYOPSIS
CARYOPSIS n dry seedlike fruit having the pericarp fused to the seed coat of the single seed: produced by the grasses
CARYOTIN variant of
> KARYOTIN
CARYOTINS
> CARYOTIN
CASA n house
CASABA n kind of winter muskmelon
CASABAS > CASABA
CASAS > CASA
CASAVA same as
> CASSAVA
CASAVAS > CASAVA
CASBAH n citadel of a N African city
CASBAHS > CASBAH
CASCABEL n knoblike protrusion on a type of cannon
CASCABELS
> CASCABEL
CASCABLE same as
> CASCABEL
CASCABLES
> CASCABLE
CASCADE n waterfall ▷ vb flow or fall in a cascade
CASCADED > CASCADE

CASCADES > CASCADE
CASCADING > CASCADE
CASCADURA n Trinidadian fish
CASCARA n bark of a N American shrub, used as a laxative
CASCARAS > CASCARA
CASCHROM n wooden hand-plough
CASCHROMS
> CASCHROM
CASCO n Argentinian homestead
CASCOS > CASCO
CASE n instance, example ▷ vb inspect (a building) with the intention of burgling it
CASEASE n proteolytic enzyme
CASEASES > CASEASE
CASEATE vb undergo caseation
CASEATED > CASEATE
CASEATES > CASEATE
CASEATING > CASEATE
CASEATION n formation of cheese from casein during the coagulation of milk
CASEBOOK n book in which records of legal or medical cases are kept
CASEBOOKS
> CASEBOOK
CASEBOUND another word for > HARDBACK
CASED > CASE
CASEFIED > CASEFY
CASEFIES > CASEFY
CASEFY vb make or become similar to cheese
CASEFYING > CASEFY
CASEIC adj relating to cheese
CASEIN n phosphoprotein forming the basis of cheese
CASEINATE n protein found in milk
CASEINS > CASEIN
CASELAW n law established by previous cases
CASELAWS > CASELAW
CASELOAD n number of cases that a worker deals with at any one time
CASELOADS
> CASELOAD
CASEMAKER n in bookbinding, machine that makes stiff covers for hardbacks
CASEMAN n in printing, a person who sets and corrects type
CASEMATE n armoured compartment in a ship or fortification in which guns are mounted
CASEMATED
> CASEMATE
CASEMATES
> CASEMATE
CASEMEN > CASEMAN
CASEMENT n window that is hinged on one side

CASEMENTS
> CASEMENT
CASEMIX n mix or type of patients treated by a hospital or medical unit
CASEMIXES > CASEMIX
CASEOSE n peptide produced by the peptic digestion of casein
CASEOSES > CASEOSE
CASEOUS adj of or like cheese
CASERN n (formerly) a billet or accommodation for soldiers in a town
CASERNE same as
> CASERN
CASERNES > CASERNE
CASERNS > CASERN
CASES > CASE
CASETTE variant of
> CASSETTE
CASETTES > CASETTE
CASEVAC vb evacuate (a casualty) from a combat zone, usu by air
CASEVACED > CASEVAC
CASEVACS > CASEVAC
CASEWORK n social work based on close study
CASEWORKS
> CASEWORK
CASEWORM n caddis worm
CASEWORMS
> CASEWORM
CASH n banknotes and coins ▷ adj of, for, or paid in cash ▷ vb obtain cash for
CASHABLE > CASH
CASHAW n winter squash
CASHAWS > CASHAW
CASHBACK n discount offered in return for immediate payment
CASHBACKS
> CASHBACK
CASHBOOK n journal in which cash receipts and payments are recorded
CASHBOOKS
> CASHBOOK
CASHBOX n box for holding cash
CASHBOXES > CASHBOX
CASHED > CASH
CASHES > CASH
CASHEW n edible kidney-shaped nut
CASHEWS > CASHEW
CASHIER n person responsible for handling cash in a bank, shop, etc ▷ vb dismiss with dishonour from the armed forces
CASHIERED > CASHIER
CASHIERER > CASHIER
CASHIERS > CASHIER
CASHING > CASH
CASHLESS adj using credit cards or electronic money transfers instead of coins or banknotes
CASHMERE n fine soft wool obtained from goats
CASHMERES
> CASHMERE

CASHOO n catechu
CASHOOS > CASHOO
CASHPOINT n cash dispenser
CASHSPIEL n curling match with cash prizes
CASIMERE same as
> CASSIMERE
CASIMERES
> CASIMERE
CASIMIRE variant of
> CASSIMERE
CASIMIRES
> CASIMIRE
CASING n protective case, covering
CASINGS > CASING
CASINI > CASINO
CASINO n public building or room where gambling games are played
CASINOS > CASINO
CASITA n small house
CASITAS > CASITA
CASK n large barrel ▷ vb put into a cask
CASKED > CASK
CASKET n small box for valuables ▷ vb put into a casket
CASKETED > CASKET
CASKETING > CASKET
CASKETS > CASKET
CASKIER > CASKY
CASKIEST > CASKY
CASKING > CASK
CASKS > CASK
CASKSTAND n frame on which a cask rests
CASKY adj (of wine) having a musty smell due to resting too long in the cask
CASPASE n type of enzyme
CASPASES > CASPASE
CASQUE n helmet or a helmet-like process or structure
CASQUED > CASQUE
CASQUES > CASQUE
CASSABA same as
> CASABA
CASSABAS > CASSABA
CASSAREEP n juice of the bitter cassava root, boiled down to a syrup and used as a flavouring
CASSATA n ice cream usually containing nuts and candied fruit
CASSATAS > CASSATA
CASSATION n (esp in France) annulment, as of a judicial decision by a higher court
CASSAVA n starch obtained from the roots of a tropical American plant, used to make tapioca
CASSAVAS > CASSAVA
CASSENA same as
> CASSINA
CASSENAS > CASSENA
CASSENE same as
> CASSINA
CASSENES > CASSENE

CASSEROLE n covered dish in which food is cooked slowly, usu in an oven ▷ vb cook in a casserole

CASSETTE n (formerly) plastic container for magnetic tape

CASSETTES > CASSETTE

CASSIA n tropical plant whose pods yield a mild laxative

CASSIAS > CASSIA

CASSIE n type of thorny shrub

CASSIES > CASSIE

CASSIMERE n woollen suiting cloth of plain or twill weave

CASSINA n American tree

CASSINAS > CASSINA

CASSINE same as > CASSINA

CASSINES > CASSINE

CASSINGLE n (formerly) cassette single

CASSINO n card game for two to four players

CASSINOS > CASSINO

CASSIOPE n type of evergreen shrub

CASSIOPES > CASSIOPE

CASSIS n blackcurrant cordial

CASSISES > CASSIS

CASSOCK n long tunic, usu black, worn by priests

CASSOCKED > CASSOCK

CASSOCKS > CASSOCK

CASSONADE n raw sugar

CASSONE n highly decorated Italian dowry chest

CASSONES > CASSONE

CASSOULET n stew originating from France, made from haricot beans and goose, duck, pork, etc

CASSOWARY n large flightless bird of Australia and New Guinea

CASSPIR n armoured military vehicle

CASSPIRS > CASSPIR

CAST n actors in a play or film collectively ▷ vb select (an actor) to play a part in a play or film

CASTABLE adj able to be cast

CASTANET > CASTANETS

CASTANETS pl n musical instrument, used by Spanish dancers, consisting of curved pieces of hollow wood clicked together in the hand

CASTAWAY n shipwrecked person ▷ adj shipwrecked or put adrift ▷ vb cause (a ship, person, etc) to be shipwrecked or abandoned

CASTAWAYS > CASTAWAY

CASTE n any of the hereditary classes into which Hindu society is divided

CASTED adj having a caste

CASTEISM n belief in, and adherence to, the caste system

CASTEISMS > CASTEISM

CASTELESS adj having no caste

CASTELLA > CASTELLUM

CASTELLAN n keeper or governor of a castle

CASTELLUM n fort

CASTER n person or thing that casts

CASTERED adj having casters

CASTERS > CASTER

CASTES > CASTE

CASTIGATE vb reprimand severely

CASTING > CAST

CASTINGS > CAST

CASTLE n large fortified building ▷ vb (in chess) make a move involving king and rook

CASTLED adj like a castle in construction

CASTLES > CASTLE

CASTLING n (in chess) act of castling

CASTLINGS > CASTLING

CASTOCK n kale stalk

CASTOCKS > CASTOCK

CASTOFF n person or thing that has been discarded or abandoned

CASTOFFS > CASTOFF

CASTOR same as > CASTER

CASTOREUM n oil secreted from the beaver, used as bait by trappers

CASTORIES > CASTORY

CASTORS > CASTOR

CASTORY n dye derived from beaver pelts

CASTRAL adj relating to camps

CASTRATE vb remove the testicles of

CASTRATED > CASTRATE

CASTRATER > CASTRATE

CASTRATES > CASTRATE

CASTRATI > CASTRATO

CASTRATO n male singer who retains a soprano or alto voice

CASTRATOR > CASTRATE

CASTRATOS > CASTRATO

CASTS > CAST

CASUAL adj careless, nonchalant ▷ n occasional worker

CASUALISE vb make (a regular employee) into a casual worker

CASUALISM > CASUALISE

CASUALIZE same as > CASUALISE

CASUALLY > CASUAL

CASUALS > CASUAL

CASUALTY n person killed or injured in an accident or war

CASUARINA n Australian tree with jointed green branches

CASUIST n person who attempts to resolve moral dilemmas

CASUISTIC > CASUIST

CASUISTRY n reasoning that is misleading or oversubtle

CASUISTS > CASUIST

CASUS n event

CAT n small domesticated furry mammal ▷ vb flog with a cat-'o-nine-tails

CATABASES > CATABASIS

CATABASIS n descent or downward movement

CATABATIC > CATABASIS

CATABOLIC adj of a metabolic process in which complex molecules are broken down into simple ones with the release of energy

CATACLASM n breaking down

CATACLYSM n violent upheaval

CATACOMB n underground burial place

CATACOMBS > CATACOMB

CATAFALCO n temporary raised platform on which a body lies in state before or during a funeral

CATAGEN n phase of hair growth

CATAGENS > CATAGEN

CATALASE n enzyme that catalyses the decomposition of hydrogen peroxide

CATALASES > CATALASE

CATALATIC adj relating to catalase

CATALEPSY n trancelike state in which the body is rigid

CATALEXES > CATALEXIS

CATALEXIS n the state of lacking a syllable in the last foot of a line of poetry

CATALO same as > CATTALO

CATALOES > CATALO

CATALOG same as > CATALOGUE

CATALOGED > CATALOGUE

CATALOGER > CATALOGUE

CATALOGIC > CATALOG

CATALOGNE n type of weaving

CATALOGS > CATALOG

CATALOGUE n book containing details of items for sale ▷ vb enter (an item) in a catalogue

CATALOS > CATALO

CATALPA n tree of N America and Asia with bell-shaped whitish flowers

CATALPAS > CATALPA

CATALYSE vb speed up (a chemical reaction) by a catalyst

CATALYSED > CATALYSE

CATALYSER > CATALYSE

CATALYSES > CATALYSIS

CATALYSIS n acceleration of a chemical reaction by the action of a catalyst

CATALYST n substance that speeds up a chemical reaction without itself changing

CATALYSTS > CATALYST

CATALYTIC adj of or relating to catalysis

CATALYZE same as > CATALYSE

CATALYZED > CATALYZE

CATALYZER > CATALYZE

CATALYZES > CATALYZE

CATAMARAN n boat with twin parallel hulls

CATAMENIA another word for > MENSES

CATAMITE n boy kept as a homosexual partner

CATAMITES > CATAMITE

CATAMOUNT n any of various medium-sized felines, such as the puma or lynx

CATAPAN n governor in the Byzantine Empire

CATAPANS > CATAPAN

CATAPHOR n word that refers to or stands for another word used later

CATAPHORA n use of a word such as a pronoun that has the same reference as a word used subsequently in the same discourse

CATAPHORS > CATAPHOR

CATAPHYLL n simplified form of plant leaf, such as a scale leaf or cotyledon

CATAPLASM another name for > POULTICE

CATAPLEXY n sudden temporary paralysis, brought on by severe shock

CATAPULT n Y-shaped device with a loop of elastic, used by children for firing stones ▷ vb shoot forwards or upwards violently

CATAPULTS
> CATAPULT

CATARACT n eye disease in which the lens becomes opaque

CATARACTS
> CATARACT

CATARHINE n ape with nostrils close together

CATARRH n excessive mucus in the nose and throat, during or following a cold

CATARRHAL > CATARRH

CATARRHS > CATARRH

CATASTA n platform on which slaves were presented for sale

CATASTAS > CATASTA

CATATONIA n form of schizophrenia characterized by stupor, with outbreaks of excitement

CATATONIC
> CATATONIA

CATATONY another word for > CATATONIA

CATAWBA n type of red North American grape

CATAWBAS > CATAWBA

CATBIRD n North American songbird

CATBIRDS > CATBIRD

CATBOAT n sailing vessel

CATBOATS > CATBOAT

CATBRIAR same as
> CATBRIER

CATBRIARS same as
> CATBRIERS

CATBRIER n greenbrier

CATBRIERS
> CATBRIER

CATCALL n derisive whistle or cry ▷ vb utter such a call (at)

CATCALLED > CATCALL

CATCALLER > CATCALL

CATCALLS > CATCALL

CATCH vb seize, capture ▷ n device for fastening a door, window, etc

CATCHABLE > CATCH

CATCHALL n something designed to cover a variety of situations

CATCHALLS
> CATCHALL

CATCHCRY n well-known much-used phrase, perhaps associated with a particular group

CATCHED rarely used past tense of > CATCH

CATCHEN archaic form of
> CATCH

CATCHER n person or thing that catches, esp in a game or sport

CATCHERS > CATCHER

CATCHES > CATCH

CATCHFLY n type of plant with sticky calyxes and stems on which insects are trapped

CATCHIER > CATCHY

CATCHIEST > CATCHY

CATCHILY adv in a pleasant or catchy way

CATCHING > CATCH

CATCHINGS > CATCH

CATCHLINE n political or advertising slogan

CATCHMENT n structure in which water is collected

CATCHPOLE n (in medieval England) a sheriff's officer who arrested debtors

CATCHPOLL same as
> CATCHPOLE

CATCHT same as
> CATCHED

CATCHUP variant spelling (esp US) of > KETCHUP

CATCHUPS > CATCHUP

CATCHWEED n goosegrass

CATCHWORD n well-known and frequently used phrase

CATCHY adj (of a tune) pleasant and easily remembered

CATCLAW n type of shrub; black bead

CATCLAWS > CATCLAW

CATCON n catalytic converter

CATCONS > CATCON

CATE n delicacy

CATECHIN n soluble yellow solid substance found in mahogany wood

CATECHINS
> CATECHIN

CATECHISE same as
> CATECHIZE

CATECHISM n instruction on the doctrine of a Christian Church in a series of questions and answers

CATECHIST
> CATECHIZE

CATECHIZE vb instruct by using a catechism

CATECHOL n colourless crystalline phenol found in resins and lignins

CATECHOLS > CATECHOL

CATECHU n astringent resinous substance

CATECHUS > CATECHU

CATEGORIC adj unqualified

CATEGORY n class, group

CATELOG old form of
> CATALOGUE

CATELOGS > CATELOG

CATENA n connected series, esp of patristic comments on the Bible

CATENAE > CATENA

CATENANE n type of chemical compound

CATENANES
> CATENANE

CATENARY n curve assumed by a heavy uniform flexible cord hanging freely from two points ▷ adj of, resembling, relating to, or constructed using a catenary or suspended chain

CATENAS > CATENA

CATENATE vb arrange or be arranged in a series of chains or rings

CATENATED
> CATENATE

CATENATES
> CATENATE

CATENOID n geometrical surface generated by rotating a catenary about its axis

CATENOIDS
> CATENOID

CATER vb provide what is needed or wanted, esp food or services

CATERAN n (formerly) a member of a band of brigands in the Scottish highlands

CATERANS > CATERAN

CATERED > CATER

CATERER n person whose job is to provide food for social events

CATERERS > CATERER

CATERESS n female caterer

CATERING n supplying of food for a social event

CATERINGS
> CATERING

CATERS > CATER

CATERWAUL n wail, yowl ▷ vb make a yowling noise like a cat

CATES pl n choice dainty food

CATFACE n deformity of the surface of a tree trunk, caused by fire or disease

CATFACES > CATFACE

CATFACING n disorder that affects tomatoes, causing scarring of the fruit

CATFALL n line used as a tackle for hoisting an anchor to the cathead

CATFALLS > CATFALL

CATFIGHT n fight, especially between two women

CATFIGHTS
> CATFIGHT

CATFISH vb create a false identity online to lure someone into a relationship

CATFISHED > CATFISH

CATFISHES > CATFISH

CATFLAP n small flap in a door to let a cat go through

CATFLAPS > CATFLAP

CATFOOD n food for cats

CATFOODS > CATFOOD

CATGUT n strong cord used to string musical instruments and sports rackets

CATGUTS > CATGUT

CATHARISE vb purify

CATHARIZE same as
> CATHARISE

CATHARSES
> CATHARSIS

CATHARSIS n relief of strong suppressed emotions

CATHARTIC adj causing catharsis ▷ n drug that causes catharsis

CATHEAD n fitting at the bow of a vessel for securing the anchor when raised

CATHEADS > CATHEAD

CATHECT vb invest mental or emotional energy in

CATHECTED > CATHECT

CATHECTIC adj of or relating to cathexis

CATHECTS > CATHECT

CATHEDRA n bishop's throne

CATHEDRAE
> CATHEDRA

CATHEDRAL n principal church of a diocese

CATHEDRAS
> CATHEDRA

CATHEPSIN n proteolytic enzyme responsible for the autolysis of cells after death

CATHEPTIC
> CATHEPSIN

CATHETER n tube inserted into a body cavity to drain fluid

CATHETERS
> CATHETER

CATHETUS n straight line or radius perpendicular to another line or radius

CATHEXES > CATHEXIS

CATHEXIS n concentration of psychic energy on a single goal

CATHINONE n synthetic alkaloid compound found in certain stimulants

CATHISMA n short hymn used as a response

CATHISMAS
> CATHISMA

CATHODAL > CATHODE

CATHODE n negative electrode, by which electrons leave a circuit

CATHODES > CATHODE

CATHODIC > CATHODE

CATHOLE n hole in a ship through which ropes are passed

CATHOLES > CATHOLE

CATHOLIC adj (of tastes or interests) covering a wide range ▷ n member of the Roman Catholic Church

CATHOLICS
> CATHOLIC

CATHOLYTE same as
> CATOLYTE

CATHOOD n state of being a cat

CATHOODS > CATHOOD

CATHOUSE a slang word for
> BROTHEL

CATHOUSES
> CATHOUSE

CATION n positively charged ion

CATIONIC > CATION
CATIONS > CATION
CATJANG n tropical shrub
CATJANGS > CATJANG
CATKIN n drooping flower spike of certain trees
CATKINATE adj like catkin
CATKINS > CATKIN
CATLIKE > CAT
CATLIN same as > CATLING
CATLING n long double-edged surgical knife for amputations
CATLINGS > CATLING
CATLINITE n type of red-brown clay
CATLINS > CATLIN
CATMINT n Eurasian plant with scented leaves that attract cats
CATMINTS > CATMINT
CATNAP vb doze ▷ n short sleep or doze
CATNAPER > CATNAP
CATNAPERS > CATNAP
CATNAPPED > CATNAP
CATNAPPER > CATNAP
CATNAPS > CATNAP
CATNEP same as > CATMINT
CATNEPS > CATNEP
CATNIP same as > CATMINT
CATNIPS > CATNIP
CATOLYTE n part of the electrolyte that surrounds the cathode in an electrolytic cell
CATOLYTES > CATOLYTE
CATOPTRIC adj relating to reflection
CATRIGGED adj rigged like a catboat
CATS > CAT
CATSKIN n skin or fur of a cat
CATSKINS > CATSKIN
CATSPAW n person used by another as a tool
CATSPAWS > CATSPAW
CATSUIT n one-piece usually close-fitting trouser suit
CATSUITS > CATSUIT
CATSUP variant (esp US) of > KETCHUP
CATSUPS > CATSUP
CATTABU n cross between common cattle and zebu
CATTABUS > CATTABU
CATTAIL n reed mace
CATTAILS > CATTAIL
CATTALO n hardy breed of cattle
CATTALOES > CATTALO
CATTALOS > CATTALO
CATTED > CAT
CATTERIES > CATTERY
CATTERY n place where cats are bred or looked after
CATTIE same as > CATTY
CATTIER > CATTY

CATTIES > CATTY
CATTIEST > CATTY
CATTILY > CATTY
CATTINESS > CATTY
CATTING > CAT
CATTISH > CAT
CATTISHLY > CAT
CATTLE pl n domesticated cows and bulls
CATTLEMAN n person who breeds, rears, or tends cattle
CATTLEMEN > CATTLEMAN
CATTLEYA n tropical American orchid cultivated for its purplish-pink or white showy flowers
CATTLEYAS > CATTLEYA
CATTY adj spiteful ▷ n unit of weight, used esp in China
CATWALK n narrow pathway or platform
CATWALKS > CATWALK
CATWORKS n machinery on a drilling platform
CATWORM n type of carnivorous worm
CATWORMS > CATWORM
CAUCHEMAR n nightmare
CAUCUS n local committee or faction of a political party ▷ vb hold a caucus
CAUCUSED > CAUCUS
CAUCUSES > CAUCUS
CAUCUSING > CAUCUS
CAUCUSSED > CAUCUS
CAUCUSSES > CAUCUS
CAUDA n tail of an animal
CAUDAD adv towards the tail or posterior part
CAUDAE > CAUDA
CAUDAL adj at or near an animal's tail
CAUDALLY > CAUDAL
CAUDATE adj having a tail or a tail-like appendage ▷ n lizard-like amphibian
CAUDATED same as > CAUDATE
CAUDATES > CAUDATE
CAUDATION > CAUDATE
CAUDEX n thickened persistent stem base of some herbaceous perennial plants
CAUDEXES > CAUDEX
CAUDICES > CAUDEX
CAUDICLE n stalk to which an orchid's pollen masses are attached
CAUDICLES > CAUDICLE
CAUDILLO n (in Spanish-speaking countries) a military or political leader
CAUDILLOS > CAUDILLO
CAUDLE n hot spiced wine drink made with gruel, formerly used medicinally ▷ vb make such a drink

CAUDLED > CAUDLE
CAUDLES > CAUDLE
CAUDLING > CAUDLE
CAUDRON Spenserian spelling of > CAULDRON
CAUDRONS > CAUDRON
CAUF n cage for holding live fish in the water
CAUGHT > CATCH
CAUK n type of barite
CAUKER n one who caulks
CAUKERS > CAUKER
CAUKS > CAUK
CAUL n membrane sometimes covering a child's head at birth
CAULD a Scot word for > COLD
CAULDER > CAULD
CAULDEST > CAULD
CAULDRIFE adj susceptible to cold
CAULDRON n large pot used for boiling
CAULDRONS > CAULDRON
CAULDS > CAULD
CAULES > CAULIS
CAULICLE n small stalk or stem
CAULICLES > CAULICLE
CAULICULI n plural form of singular cauliculus: another word for caulicle
CAULIFORM adj resembling a caulis
CAULINARY another word for > CAULINE
CAULINE adj relating to or growing from a plant stem
CAULIS n main stem of a plant
CAULK vb fill in (cracks) with paste etc
CAULKED > CAULK
CAULKER > CAULK
CAULKERS > CAULK
CAULKING > CAULK
CAULKINGS > CAULK
CAULKS > CAULK
CAULOME n plant's stem structure, considered as a whole
CAULOMES > CAULOME
CAULS > CAUL
CAUM same as > CAM
CAUMED > CAUM
CAUMING > CAUM
CAUMS > CAUM
CAUMSTANE same as > CAMSTONE
CAUMSTONE same as > CAMSTONE
CAUP n type of quaich
CAUPS > CAUP
CAURI n former coin of Guinea
CAURIS > CAURI
CAUSA n reason or cause
CAUSABLE > CAUSE
CAUSAE > CAUSA
CAUSAL adj of or being a cause ▷ n something that suggests a cause

CAUSALGIA n burning sensation along the course of a peripheral nerve together with local changes in the appearance of the skin
CAUSALGIC > CAUSALGIA
CAUSALITY n relationship of cause and effect
CAUSALLY > CAUSAL
CAUSALS > CAUSAL
CAUSATION n relationship of cause and effect
CAUSATIVE adj producing an effect ▷ n causative form or class of verbs
CAUSE n something that produces a particular effect ▷ vb be the cause of
CAUSED > CAUSE
CAUSELESS > CAUSE
CAUSEN old infinitive of > CAUSE
CAUSER > CAUSE
CAUSERIE n informal talk or conversational piece of writing
CAUSERIES > CAUSERIE
CAUSERS > CAUSE
CAUSES > CAUSE
CAUSEWAY n raised path or road across water or marshland
CAUSEWAYS > CAUSEWAY
CAUSEY n cobbled street ▷ vb cobble
CAUSEYED > CAUSEY
CAUSEYS > CAUSEY
CAUSING > CAUSE
CAUSTIC adj capable of burning by chemical action ▷ n caustic substance
CAUSTICAL > CAUSTIC
CAUSTICS > CAUSTIC
CAUTEL n craftiness
CAUTELOUS > CAUTEL
CAUTELS > CAUTEL
CAUTER n cauterizing instrument
CAUTERANT same as > CAUTERY
CAUTERIES > CAUTERY
CAUTERISE same as > CAUTERIZE
CAUTERISM > CAUTERIZE
CAUTERIZE vb burn (a wound) with heat or a caustic agent to prevent infection
CAUTERS > CAUTER
CAUTERY n coagulation of blood or destruction of body tissue by cauterizing
CAUTION n care, esp in the face of danger ▷ vb warn, advise
CAUTIONED > CAUTION
CAUTIONER > CAUTION
CAUTIONRY n in Scots law, standing surety

CAUTIONS > CAUTION

CAUTIOUS adj showing caution

CAUVES > CAUF

CAVA n Spanish sparkling wine

CAVALCADE n procession of people on horseback or in cars

CAVALERO n cavalier

CAVALEROS > CAVALERO

CAVALETTI n bars supported on low stands used in dressage and horse jumping

CAVALIER adj showing haughty disregard ▷ n gallant gentleman

CAVALIERS > CAVALIER

CAVALLA n type of tropical fish

CAVALLAS > CAVALLA

CAVALLIES > CAVALLY

CAVALLY same as > CAVALLA

CAVALRIES > CAVALRY

CAVALRY n part of the army

CAVAS > CAVA

CAVASS n Turkish armed police officer

CAVASSES > CAVASS

CAVATINA n solo song resembling a simple aria

CAVATINAS > CAVATINA

CAVATINE > CAVATINA

CAVE n hollow in the side of a hill or cliff ▷ vb hollow out

CAVEAT n warning ▷ vb introduce a caveat

CAVEATED > CAVEAT

CAVEATING > CAVEAT

CAVEATOR n person who enters a caveat

CAVEATORS > CAVEATOR

CAVEATS > CAVEAT

CAVED > CAVE

CAVEFISH n small N American freshwater fish

CAVEL n drawing of lots among miners for an easy and profitable place at the coalface

CAVELIKE adj resembling a cave

CAVELS > CAVEL

CAVEMAN n prehistoric cave dweller

CAVEMEN > CAVEMAN

CAVENDISH n tobacco that has been sweetened and pressed into moulds to form bars

CAVEOLA n pit in a cell membrane

CAVEOLAE > CAVEOLA

CAVEOLAR > CAVEOLA

CAVER > CAVE

CAVERN n large cave ▷ vb shut in or as if in a cavern

CAVERNED > CAVERN

CAVERNING > CAVERN

CAVERNOUS adj like a cavern in vastness, depth, or hollowness

CAVERNS > CAVERN

CAVERS > CAVER

CAVES > CAVE

CAVESSON n kind of hard noseband, used (esp formerly) in breaking a horse in

CAVESSONS > CAVESSON

CAVETTI > CAVETTO

CAVETTO n concave moulding, shaped to a quarter circle in cross section

CAVETTOS > CAVETTO

CAVIAR n salted sturgeon roe, regarded as a delicacy

CAVIARE same as > CAVIAR

CAVIARES > CAVIARE

CAVIARIE same as > CAVIAR

CAVIARIES > CAVIARIE

CAVIARS > CAVIAR

CAVICORN adj (of sheep, goats, etc) having hollow horns as distinct from the solid antlers of deer ▷ n sheep, goat, etc with hollow horns

CAVICORNS > CAVICORN

CAVIE n hen coop

CAVIER same as > CAVIAR

CAVIERS > CAVIER

CAVIES > CAVY

CAVIL vb make petty objections ▷ n petty objection

CAVILED > CAVIL

CAVILER > CAVIL

CAVILERS > CAVIL

CAVILING > CAVIL

CAVILLED > CAVIL

CAVILLER > CAVIL

CAVILLERS > CAVIL

CAVILLING > CAVIL

CAVILS > CAVIL

CAVING n sport of exploring caves

CAVINGS > CAVING

CAVITARY adj containing cavities

CAVITATE vb form cavities or bubbles

CAVITATED > CAVITATE

CAVITATES > CAVITATE

CAVITIED > CAVITY

CAVITIES > CAVITY

CAVITY n hollow space

CAVORT vb skip about

CAVORTED > CAVORT

CAVORTER > CAVORT

CAVORTERS > CAVORT

CAVORTING > CAVORT

CAVORTS > CAVORT

CAVY n type of small rodent

CAW n cry of a crow, rook, or raven ▷ vb make this cry

CAWED > CAW

CAWING > CAW

CAWINGS > CAW

CAWK same as > CAUK

CAWKER n metal projection on a horse's shoe to prevent slipping

CAWKERS > CAWKER

CAWKS > CAWK

CAWS > CAW

CAXON n type of wig

CAXONS > CAXON

CAY n low island or bank composed of sand and coral fragments

CAYENNE n very hot condiment

CAYENNED adj seasoned with cayenne

CAYENNES > CAYENNE

CAYMAN n S American reptile similar to an alligator

CAYMANS > CAYMAN

CAYS > CAY

CAYUSE n small pony used by Native Americans

CAYUSES > CAYUSE

CAZ short for > CASUAL

CAZH adj casual

CAZIQUE same as > CACIQUE

CAZIQUES > CAZIQUE

CEANOTHUS n N American shrub grown for its ornamental, often blue, flower clusters

CEAS same as > CAESE

CEASE vb bring or come to an end

CEASED > CEASE

CEASEFIRE n temporary truce

CEASELESS adj without stopping

CEASES > CEASE

CEASING > CEASE

CEASINGS > CEASE

CEAZE obsolete spelling of > SEIZE

CEAZED > CEAZE

CEAZES > CEAZE

CEAZING > CEAZE

CEBADILLA same as > SABADILLA

CEBID n any member of the Cebidae family of New World monkeys

CEBIDS > CEBID

CEBOID same as > CEBID

CEBOIDS > CEBOID

CECA > CECUM

CECAL > CECUM

CECALLY > CECUM

CECILS pl n fried meatballs

CECITIES > CECITY

CECITIS n inflammation of the c(a)ecum

CECITISES > CECITIS

CECITY n rare word for blindness

CECROPIA n large North American moth

CECROPIAS > CECROPIA

CECROPIN n antimicrobial peptide originally derived from the cecropia moth

CECROPINS > CECROPIN

CECUM same as > CAECUM

CEDAR n evergreen coniferous tree ▷ adj made of the wood of a cedar tree

CEDARBIRD n type of waxwing

CEDARED adj covered with cedars

CEDARIER > CEDARY

CEDARIEST > CEDARY

CEDARN adj relating to cedar

CEDARS > CEDAR

CEDARWOOD n wood of any of the cedar trees

CEDARY adj like cedar

CEDE vb surrender (territory or legal rights)

CEDED > CEDE

CEDER > CEDE

CEDERS > CEDE

CEDES > CEDE

CEDI n standard monetary unit of Ghana, divided into 100 pesewas

CEDILLA n character placed under a c in some languages

CEDILLAS > CEDILLA

CEDING > CEDE

CEDIS > CEDI

CEDRATE n citron

CEDRATES > CEDRATE

CEDRINE adj relating to cedar

CEDULA n form of identification in Spanish-speaking countries

CEDULAS > CEDULA

CEE n third letter of the alphabet

CEES > CEE

CEIBA n type of tropical tree

CEIBAS > CEIBA

CEIL vb line (a ceiling) with plaster, boarding, etc

CEILED > CEIL

CEILER > CEIL

CEILERS > CEIL

CEILI variant spelling of > CEILIDH

CEILIDH n social gathering for singing and dancing

CEILIDHS > CEILIDH

CEILING n inner upper surface of a room ▷ vb make a ceiling

CEILINGED > CEILING

CEILINGS > CEILING

CEILIS > CEILI

CEILS > CEIL

CEINTURE n belt

CEINTURES > CEINTURE

CEL short for > CELLULOID

CELADON n type of porcelain having a greyish-green glaze: mainly Chinese

CELADONS > CELADON

CELANDINE n wild plant with yellow flowers

CELEB n celebrity

CELEBRANT n person who performs a religious ceremony

CELEBRATE vb hold festivities to mark (a happy event, anniversary, etc)

CELEBRITY n famous person

CELEBS > CELEB

CELECOXIB n type of anti-inflammatory drug

CELERIAC n variety of celery with a large turnip-like root

CELERIACS
> CELERIAC

CELERIES > CELERY

CELERITY n swiftness

CELERY n vegetable with long green crisp edible stalks

CELESTA n instrument like a small piano

CELESTAS > CELESTA

CELESTE same as
> CELESTA

CELESTES > CELESTE

CELESTIAL adj heavenly, divine

CELESTINE same as
> CELESTITE

CELESTITE n white, red, or blue mineral

CELIAC same as
> COELIAC

CELIACS > CELIAC

CELIBACY > CELIBATE

CELIBATE adj unmarried, esp because of a religious vow ▷ n celibate person

CELIBATES
> CELIBATE

CELIBATIC adj celibate

CELL n smallest unit of an organism that is able to function independently

CELLA n inner room of a classical temple

CELLAE > CELLA

CELLAR n underground room for storage ▷ vb store in a cellar

CELLARAGE n area of a cellar

CELLARED > CELLAR

CELLARER n monastic official responsible for food, drink, etc

CELLARERS
> CELLARER

CELLARET n case, cabinet, or sideboard with compartments for holding wine bottles

CELLARETS
> CELLARET

CELLARING > CELLAR

CELLARIST same as
> CELLARER

CELLARMAN n person in charge of a cellar

CELLARMEN
> CELLARMAN

CELLAROUS adj relating to a cellar

CELLARS > CELLAR

CELLARWAY n way into cellar

CELLBLOCK n group of prison cells

CELLED adj cellular

CELLI > CELLO

CELLING n formation of cells

CELLINGS > CELLING

CELLIST > CELLO

CELLISTS > CELLO

CELLMATE n person with whom a prisoner shares a prison cell

CELLMATES
> CELLMATE

CELLO n large low-pitched instrument of the violin family

CELLOIDIN n nitrocellulose compound

CELLOS > CELLO

CELLOSE n disaccharide obtained by the hydrolysis of cellulose by cellulase

CELLOSES > CELLOSE

CELLPHONE n portable telephone operated by cellular radio

CELLS > CELL

CELLULAR adj of or consisting of cells ▷ n cellular phone

CELLULARS
> CELLULAR

CELLULASE n any enzyme that converts cellulose to the disaccharide cellobiose

CELLULE n very small cell

CELLULES > CELLULE

CELLULITE n fat deposits under the skin alleged to resist dieting

CELLULOID n kind of plastic used to make toys and, formerly, photographic film

CELLULOSE n main constituent of plant cell walls, used in making paper, plastics, etc

CELLULOUS
> CELLULOSE

CELOM same as > COELOM

CELOMATA > CELOM

CELOMIC > CELOM

CELOMS > CELOM

CELOSIA same as
> COCKSCOMB

CELOSIAS > CELOSIA

CELOTEX n tradename for a type of insulation board

CELOTEXES > CELOTEX

CELS > CEL

CELSITUDE n loftiness

CELT n stone or metal axelike instrument with a bevelled edge

CELTS > CELT

CEMBALI > CEMBALO

CEMBALIST > CEMBALO

CEMBALO n harpsichord

CEMBALOS > CEMBALO

CEMBRA n Swiss pine

CEMBRAS > CEMBRA

CEMENT n powder mixed with water and sand to make mortar or concrete ▷ vb join, bind, or cover with cement

CEMENTA > CEMENTUM

CEMENTED > CEMENT

CEMENTER > CEMENT

CEMENTERS > CEMENT

CEMENTING > CEMENT

CEMENTITE n hard brittle compound of iron and carbon

CEMENTS > CEMENT

CEMENTUM n thin bonelike tissue that covers the dentine in the root of a tooth

CEMENTUMS
> CEMENTUM

CEMETERY n place where dead people are buried

CEMITARE obsolete spelling of > SCIMITAR

CEMITARES
> CEMITARE

CENACLE n supper room, esp one on an upper floor

CENACLES > CENACLE

CENDRE adj ash-blond

CENOBITE same as
> COENOBITE

CENOBITES
> CENOBITE

CENOBITIC
> CENOBITE

CENOTAPH n monument honouring soldiers who died in a war

CENOTAPHS
> CENOTAPH

CENOTE n natural well formed by the collapse of an overlying limestone crust

CENOTES > CENOTE

CENOZOIC adj of or relating to the most recent geological era

CENS n type of annual property rent

CENSE vb burn incense near or before (an altar, shrine, etc)

CENSED > CENSE

CENSER n container for burning incense

CENSERS > CENSER

CENSES > CENSE

CENSING > CENSE

CENSOR n person authorized to prohibit anything considered obscene or objectionable ▷ vb ban or cut parts of (a film, book, etc)

CENSORED > CENSOR

CENSORIAL > CENSOR

CENSORIAN > CENSOR

CENSORING > CENSOR

CENSORS > CENSOR

CENSUAL > CENSUS

CENSURE n severe disapproval ▷ vb criticize severely

CENSURED > CENSURE

CENSURER > CENSURE

CENSURERS > CENSURE

CENSURES > CENSURE

CENSURING > CENSURE

CENSUS n official count of a population ▷ vb conduct a census

CENSUSED > CENSUS

CENSUSES > CENSUS

CENSUSING > CENSUS

CENT n hundredth part of a monetary unit such as the dollar or euro

CENTAGE n rate per hundred

CENTAGES > CENTAGE

CENTAI > CENTAS

CENTAL n unit of weight equal to 100 pounds (45.3 kilograms)

CENTALS > CENTAL

CENTARE same as
> CENTIARE

CENTARES > CENTARE

CENTAS n former monetary unit of Lithuania

CENTAUR n mythical creature

CENTAUREA n type of plant of the genus which includes the cornflower and knapweed

CENTAURIC adj integrating mind and body

CENTAURS > CENTAUR

CENTAURY n plant with purplish-pink flowers

CENTAVO n monetary unit in many Latin American countries

CENTAVOS > CENTAVO

CENTENARY n 100th anniversary or its celebration ▷ adj of or relating to a period of 100 years

CENTENIER n in Jersey, a local police officer

CENTER same as
> CENTRE

CENTERED > CENTER

CENTERING same as
> CENTRING

CENTERS > CENTER

CENTESES > CENTESIS

CENTESIMI
> CENTESIMO

CENTESIMO n former monetary unit of Italy, San Marino, and the Vatican City worth one hundredth of a lira

CENTESIS n surgical puncturing of part of the body with a hollow needle, to extract fluid

CENTIARE n unit of area equal to one square metre

CENTIARES
> CENTIARE

CENTIGRAM n one hundredth of a gram

CENTILE n (in statistics) another word for percentile

CENTILES > CENTILE

CENTIME n monetary unit worth one hundredth of a franc

CENTIMES > CENTIME

CENTIMO n monetary unit of Costa Rica, Paraguay, Peru, and Venezuela

CENTIMOS > CENTIMO

CENTINEL obsolete variant of > SENTINEL

CENTINELL obsolete variant of > SENTINEL

CENTINELS > CENTINEL

CENTIPEDE n small wormlike creature with many legs

CENTNER n unit of weight equivalent to 100 pounds (45.3 kilograms)

CENTNERS > CENTNER

CENTO n piece of writing composed of quotations from other authors

CENTOIST n one who composes centos

CENTOISTS > CENTOIST

CENTONATE adj having many patches ▷ n Gregorian chant comprised of a patchwork of texts and melodies

CENTONEL obsolete variant of > SENTINEL

CENTONELL obsolete variant of > SENTINEL

CENTONELS > CENTONEL

CENTONES > CENTO

CENTONIST same as > CENTOIST

CENTOS > CENTO

CENTRA > CENTRUM

CENTRAL adj of, at, or forming the centre ▷ n workplace serving as a telecommunications facility

CENTRALER > CENTRAL

CENTRALLY > CENTRAL

CENTRALS > CENTRAL

CENTRE n middle point or part ▷ vb put in the centre of something

CENTRED adj mentally and emotionally confident, focused, and well-balanced

CENTREING same as > CENTRING

CENTREMAN n ice hockey player occupying a central position

CENTREMEN > CENTREMAN

CENTRES > CENTRE

CENTRIC adj being central or having a centre

CENTRICAL same as > CENTRIC

CENTRIES > CENTRY

CENTRING n temporary structure used to support an arch during construction

CENTRINGS > CENTRING

CENTRIOLE n either of two rodlike bodies in most animal cells that form the poles of the spindle during mitosis

CENTRISM > CENTRIST

CENTRISMS > CENTRIST

CENTRIST n person favouring political moderation

CENTRISTS > CENTRIST

CENTRODE n locus produced by plotting the course of two bodies in relative motion

CENTRODES > CENTRODE

CENTROID n centre of mass of an object of uniform density, esp of a geometric figure

CENTROIDS > CENTROID

CENTRUM n main part or body of a vertebra

CENTRUMS > CENTRUM

CENTRY obsolete variant of > SENTRY

CENTS > CENT

CENTU > CENTAS

CENTUM adj denoting or belonging to certain Indo-European languages ▷ n hundred

CENTUMS > CENTUM

CENTUMVIR n one of the Roman judges who sat in civil cases

CENTUPLE n one hundredfold

CENTUPLED > CENTUPLE

CENTUPLES > CENTUPLE

CENTURIAL adj of or relating to a Roman century

CENTURIES > CENTURY

CENTURION n (in ancient Rome) officer commanding 100 men

CENTURY n period of 100 years

CEORL n freeman of the lowest class in Anglo-Saxon England

CEORLISH > CEORL

CEORLS > CEORL

CEP another name for > PORCINO

CEPACEOUS adj having an onion-like smell or taste

CEPAGE n grape variety or type of wine

CEPAGES > CEPAGE

CEPE another spelling of > CEP

CEPES > CEPE

CEPHALAD adv towards the head or anterior part

CEPHALATE adj possessing a head

CEPHALIC adj of or relating to the head ▷ n remedy for pains in the head

CEPHALICS > CEPHALIC

CEPHALIN n phospholipid, similar to lecithin, that occurs in the nerve tissue and brain

CEPHALINS > CEPHALIN

CEPHALOUS adj with a head

CEPHEID n type of variable star with a regular cycle of variations in luminosity

CEPHEIDS > CEPHEID

CEPS > CEP

CERACEOUS adj waxlike or waxy

CERAMAL same as > CERMET

CERAMALS > CERAMAL

CERAMIC n hard brittle material ▷ adj made of ceramic

CERAMICS n art of producing ceramic objects

CERAMIDE n class of compounds used as moisturizers

CERAMIDES > CERAMIDE

CERAMIST > CERAMICS

CERAMISTS > CERAMICS

CERASIN n meta-arabinic acid

CERASINS > CERASIN

CERASTES n type of venomous snake, esp the horned viper

CERASTIUM n mouse-eared chickweed

CERATE n hard ointment or medicated paste

CERATED adj (of certain birds, such as the falcon) having a cere

CERATES > CERATE

CERATIN same as > KERATIN

CERATINS > CERATIN

CERATITIS same as > KERATITIS

CERATODUS n type of extinct lungfish common in Cretaceous and Triassic times

CERATOID adj having the shape or texture of animal horn

CERBEREAN adj of or resembling Cerberus, the three-headed dog that guarded the entrance to Hades in Greek mythology

CERBERIAN same as > CERBEREAN

CERCAL adj of or relating to a tail

CERCARIA n one of the larval forms of trematode worms

CERCARIAE > CERCARIA

CERCARIAL > CERCARIA

CERCARIAN > CERCARIA

CERCARIAS > CERCARIA

CERCI > CERCUS

CERCIS n type of tree or shrub

CERCISES > CERCIS

CERCLAGE n treatment of a malfunctioning cervix by means of a suture in early pregnancy

CERCLAGES > CERCLAGE

CERCOPID n froghopper or spittlebug

CERCOPIDS > CERCOPID

CERCUS n one of a pair of sensory appendages on some insects and other arthropods

CERE n soft waxy swelling at the base of the upper beak of a parrot ▷ vb wrap in a cerecloth

CEREAL n grass plant with edible grain, such as oat or wheat

CEREALIST n expert in cereals

CEREALS > CEREAL

CEREBELLA n plural of singular cerebellum: one of the major divisions of the vertebrate brain

CEREBRA > CEREBRUM

CEREBRAL same as > CACUMINAL

CEREBRALS > CEREBRAL

CEREBRATE vb use the mind

CEREBRIC > CEREBRUM

CEREBROID > CEREBRUM

CEREBRUM n main part of the brain

CEREBRUMS > CEREBRUM

CERECLOTH n waxed waterproof cloth of a kind formerly used as a shroud

CERED > CERE

CEREMENT n any burial clothes

CEREMENTS > CEREMENT

CEREMONY n formal act or ritual

CEREOUS adj waxlike

CERES > CERE

CERESIN n white wax extracted from ozocerite

CERESINE same as > CERESIN

CERESINES > CERESINE

CERESINS > CERESIN

CEREUS n type of tropical American cactus

CEREUSES > CEREUS

CERGE n large altar candle

CERGES > CERGE

CERIA n ceric oxide

CERIAS > CERIA

CERIC adj of or containing cerium in the tetravalent state

CERING > CERE

CERIPH same as > SERIF

CERIPHS > CERIPH

CERISE adj cherry-red ▷ n moderate to dark red colour

CERISES > CERISE

CERITE n hydrous silicate of cerium
CERITES > CERITE
CERIUM n steel-grey metallic element
CERIUMS > CERIUM
CERMET n material consisting of a metal matrix with ceramic particles disseminated through it
CERMETS > CERMET
CERNE obsolete variant of > ENCIRCLE
CERNED > CERNE
CERNES > CERNE
CERNING > CERNE
CERNUOUS adj (of some flowers or buds) drooping
CERO n type of large food fish
CEROC n dance combining many styles, including jive and salsa
CEROCS > CEROC
CEROGRAPH n writing on wax
CEROMANCY n divination by interpreting significance of shapes formed when melted wax is dropped into water
CEROON n hide-covered bale
CEROONS > CEROON
CEROS > CERO
CEROTIC adj as in cerotic acid white insoluble odourless wax
CEROTYPE n process for preparing a printing plate
CEROTYPES > CEROTYPE
CEROUS adj of or containing cerium in the trivalent state
CERRADO n vast area of tropical savanna in Brazil
CERRADOS > CERRADO
CERRIAL adj relating to the cerris
CERRIS n Turkey oak
CERRISES > CERRIS
CERT n certainty
CERTAIN adj positive and confident
CERTAINER > CERTAIN
CERTAINLY adv without doubt ▷ sentence substitute by all means
CERTAINTY n state of being sure
CERTES adv with certainty
CERTIE n as in by my certie assuredly
CERTIFIED > CERTIFY
CERTIFIER > CERTIFY
CERTIFIES > CERTIFY
CERTIFY vb confirm, attest to
CERTITUDE n confidence, certainty
CERTS > CERT
CERTY n as in by my certy assuredly
CERULE adj sky-blue
CERULEAN n deep blue colour

CERULEANS > CERULEAN
CERULEIN n type of dyestuff
CERULEINS > CERULEIN
CERULEOUS adj sky-blue
CERUMEN n wax secreted by glands in the external ear
CERUMENS > CERUMEN
CERUSE n white lead
CERUSES > CERUSE
CERUSITE same as > CERUSSITE
CERUSITES > CERUSITE
CERUSSITE n usually white mineral, found in veins
CERVELAS n French garlicky pork sausage
CERVELAT n smoked sausage made from pork and beef
CERVELATS > CERVELAT
CERVEZA n Spanish word for beer
CERVEZAS > CERVEZA
CERVICAL adj of or relating to the neck or cervix
CERVICES > CERVIX
CERVICUM n flexible region between the prothorax and head in insects
CERVICUMS > CERVICUM
CERVID n type of ruminant mammal characterized by the presence of antlers
CERVIDS > CERVID
CERVINE adj resembling or relating to a deer
CERVIX n narrow entrance of the womb
CERVIXES > CERVIX
CESAREAN variant of > CAESAREAN
CESAREANS > CESAREAN
CESAREVNA n wife of a Russian tsar's eldest son
CESARIAN US variant of > CAESAREAN
CESARIANS > CESARIAN
CESIOUS same as > CAESIOUS
CESIUM same as > CAESIUM
CESIUMS > CESIUM
CESPITOSE adj growing in dense tufts
CESS n any of several special taxes, such as a land tax in Scotland ▷ vb tax or assess for taxation
CESSATION n ceasing
CESSE obsolete variant of > CEASE
CESSED > CESS
CESSER n coming to an end of a term interest or annuity
CESSERS > CESSER

CESSES > CESS
CESSING > CESS
CESSION n ceding
CESSIONS > CESSION
CESSPIT same as > CESSPOOL
CESSPITS > CESSPIT
CESSPOOL n covered tank or pit for collecting and storing sewage or waste water
CESSPOOLS > CESSPOOL
CESTA n in jai alai, the basket used to throw and catch the pelota
CESTAS > CESTA
CESTI > CESTUS
CESTODE n type of parasitic flatworm such as the tapeworms
CESTODES > CESTODE
CESTOI > CESTOS
CESTOID adj (esp of tapeworms and similar animals) ribbon-like in form ▷ n ribbon-like worm
CESTOIDS > CESTOID
CESTOS same as > CESTUS
CESTOSES > CESTOS
CESTUI n legal term to designate a person
CESTUIS > CESTUI
CESTUS n girdle of Aphrodite
CESTUSES > CESTUS
CESURA variant spelling of > CAESURA
CESURAE > CESURA
CESURAL > CESURA
CESURAS > CESURA
CESURE same as > CAESURA
CESURES > CESURE
CETACEAN n fish-shaped sea mammal such as a whale or dolphin ▷ adj relating to these mammals
CETACEANS > CETACEAN
CETACEOUS same as > CETACEAN
CETANE n colourless liquid hydrocarbon, used as a solvent
CETANES > CETANE
CETE n group of badgers
CETERACH n scale-fern
CETERACHS > CETERACH
CETES > CETE
CETOLOGY n branch of zoology concerned with the study of whales (cetaceans)
CETRIMIDE n quaternary ammonium compound used as a detergent
CETUXIMAB n monoclonal antibody used to treat cancer
CETYL n univalent alcohol radical
CETYLS > CETYL
CETYWALL n valerian

CETYWALLS > CETYWALL
CEVADILLA same as > SABADILLA
CEVAPCICI n sausages made with beef and paprika
CEVICHE n Peruvian seafood dish
CEVICHES > CEVICHE
CEVITAMIC adj as in cevitamic acid ascorbic (acid)
CEYLANITE same as > CEYLONITE
CEYLONITE n pleonaste
CEZVE n small metal pot for brewing coffee
CEZVES > CEZVE
CH pron obsolete form of I
CHA n tea
CHABAZITE n pink, white, or colourless zeolite mineral
CHABLIS n dry white French wine
CHABOUK n type of whip
CHABOUKS > CHABOUK
CHABUK same as > CHABOUK
CHABUKS > CHABUK
CHACE obsolete variant of > CHASE
CHACED > CHACE
CHACES > CHACE
CHACHKA n cheap trinket
CHACHKAS > CHACHKA
CHACING > CHACE
CHACK vb bite
CHACKED > CHACK
CHACKING > CHACK
CHACKS > CHACK
CHACMA n type of baboon with coarse greyish hair, living in S and E Africa
CHACMAS > CHACMA
CHACO same as > SHAKO
CHACOES > CHACO
CHACONINE n toxic substance found in potatoes
CHACONNE n musical form consisting of a set of variations on a repeated melodic bass line
CHACONNES > CHACONNE
CHACOS > CHACO
CHAD n small pieces removed during the punching of holes in punch cards, printer paper, etc
CHADAR same as > CHUDDAR
CHADARIM > CHEDER
CHADARS > CHADAR
CHADDAR same as > CHUDDAR
CHADDARS > CHADDAR
CHADDOR same as > CHUDDAR
CHADDORS > CHADDOR
CHADLESS adj (of a keypunch) not producing chads
CHADO n Japanese tea ceremony
CHADOR same as > CHUDDAR

CHADORS > CHADOR

CHADOS > CHADO

CHADRI *n* shroud which covers the body from head to foot

CHADS > CHAD

CHAEBOL *n* large, usually family-owned, business group in South Korea

CHAEBOLS > CHAEBOL

CHAETA *n* a bristle on the body of an annelid

CHAETAE > CHAETA

CHAETAL > CHAETA

CHAETODON *n* butterfly fish

CHAETOPOD *n* type of annelid worm

CHAFE *vb* make sore or worn by rubbing

CHAFED > CHAFE

CHAFER *n* large beetle

CHAFERS > CHAFER

CHAFES > CHAFE

CHAFF *n* grain husks ▷ *vb* tease good-naturedly

CHAFFED > CHAFF

CHAFFER *vb* haggle

CHAFFERED > CHAFFER

CHAFFERER > CHAFFER

CHAFFERS > CHAFFER

CHAFFERY *n* bargaining

CHAFFIER > CHAFF

CHAFFIEST > CHAFF

CHAFFINCH *n* small European songbird

CHAFFING > CHAFF

CHAFFINGS > CHAFF

CHAFFRON *same as* > CHAMFRON

CHAFFRONS > CHAMFRON

CHAFFS > CHAFF

CHAFFY > CHAFF

CHAFING > CHAFE

CHAFT *n* jaw

CHAFTS > CHAFT

CHAGAN *n* Mongolian royal or imperial title

CHAGANS > CHAGAN

CHAGRIN *n* annoyance and disappointment ▷ *vb* embarrass and annoy

CHAGRINED > CHAGRIN

CHAGRINS > CHAGRIN

CHAI *n* tea, esp as made in India with added spices

CHAIN *n* flexible length of connected metal links ▷ *vb* restrict or fasten with or as if with a chain

CHAINE *adj* (of a dance turn) producing a full rotation for every two steps taken ▷ *vb* produce a full rotation for every two steps taken

CHAINED > CHAIN

CHAINER *n* person who chains

CHAINERS > CHAINER

CHAINES > CHAINE

CHAINFALL *n* type of hoist

CHAINING > CHAIN

CHAINLESS *adj* having no chain

CHAINLET *n* small chain

CHAINLETS > CHAINLET

CHAINMAN *n* person who does the chaining in a survey

CHAINMEN > CHAINMAN

CHAINS > CHAIN

CHAINSAW *n* motor-driven saw with teeth linked in a continuous chain ▷ *vb* operate a chainsaw

CHAINSAWS > CHAINSAW

CHAINSHOT *n* cannon shot of two balls joined by a chain

CHAINWORK *n* work linked or looped in the manner of a chain

CHAIR *n* seat with a back, for one person ▷ *vb* preside over (a meeting)

CHAIRBACK *n* back part of a chair

CHAIRDAYS *n* old age

CHAIRED > CHAIR

CHAIRING > CHAIR

CHAIRLIFT *n* series of chairs suspended from a moving cable for carrying people up a slope

CHAIRMAN *n* man in charge of a company or a meeting ▷ *vb* act as chairman of

CHAIRMANS > CHAIRMAN

CHAIRMEN > CHAIRMAN

CHAIRS > CHAIR

CHAIS > CHAI

CHAISE *n* light horse-drawn carriage

CHAISES > CHAISE

CHAKALAKA *n* relish made from tomatoes, onions, and spices

CHAKRA *n* (in yoga) any of the seven major energy centres in the body

CHAKRAS > CHAKRA

CHAL *n* in Romany, person or fellow

CHALAH *same as* > CHALLAH

CHALAHS > CHALAH

CHALAN *vb* (in India) to cause an accused person to appear before a magistrate ▷ *n* invoice, pass, or voucher

CHALANED > CHALAN

CHALANING > CHALAN

CHALANNED *same as* > CHALANED

CHALANS > CHALAN

CHALAZA *n* one of a pair of spiral threads holding the yolk of a bird's egg in position

CHALAZAE > CHALAZA

CHALAZAL > CHALAZA

CHALAZAS > CHALAZA

CHALAZIA > CHALAZION

CHALAZION *n* small cyst on the eyelid resulting from chronic inflammation of a meibomian gland

CHALCID *n* type of tiny insect

CHALCIDS > CHALCID

CHALCOGEN *n* any of the elements oxygen, sulphur, selenium, tellurium, or polonium, of group 6A of the periodic table

CHALDER *n* former Scottish dry measure

CHALDERS > CHALDER

CHALDRON *n* unit of capacity equal to 36 bushels

CHALDRONS > CHALDRON

CHALEH *same as* > CHALLAH

CHALEHS > CHALEH

CHALET *n* kind of Swiss wooden house with a steeply sloping roof

CHALETS > CHALET

CHALICE *n* large goblet

CHALICED *adj* (of plants) having cup-shaped flowers

CHALICES > CHALICE

CHALK *n* soft white rock consisting of calcium carbonate ▷ *vb* draw or mark with chalk

CHALKED > CHALK

CHALKFACE *n* work or art of teaching in a school

CHALKIER > CHALK

CHALKIEST > CHALK

CHALKING > CHALK

CHALKLAND *n* land largely composed of chalk

CHALKLIKE > CHALK

CHALKMARK *n* as in *walk the chalkmark* straight line drawn with chalk, used as a sobriety test

CHALKPIT *n* quarry for chalk

CHALKPITS > CHALKPIT

CHALKS > CHALK

CHALKY > CHALK

CHALLA *same as* > CHALLAH

CHALLAH *n* type of bread

CHALLAHS > CHALLAH

CHALLAN *same as* > CHALAN

CHALLANS > CHALLAN

CHALLAS > CHALLA

CHALLENGE *n* demanding or stimulating situation ▷ *vb* issue a challenge to

CHALLIE *same as* > CHALLIS

CHALLIES > CHALLIE

CHALLIS *n* lightweight plain-weave fabric

CHALLISES > CHALLIS

CHALLOT > CHALLAH

CHALLOTH > CHALLAH

CHALLY *same as* > CHALLIS

CHALONE *n* any internal secretion that inhibits a physiological process or function

CHALONES > CHALONE

CHALONIC > CHALONE

CHALOT > CHALAH

CHALOTH > CHALAH

CHALS > CHAL

CHALUMEAU *n* early type of reed instrument, precursor of the clarinet

CHALUPA *n* Mexican dish

CHALUPAS > CHALUPA

CHALUTZ *n* member of an organization of immigrants to Israeli agricultural settlements

CHALUTZES > CHALUTZ

CHALUTZIM > CHALUTZ

CHALYBEAN *adj* (of steel) of superior quality

CHALYBITE *another name for* > SIDERITE

CHAM *an archaic word for* > KHAN

CHAMADE *n* (formerly) a signal by drum or trumpet inviting an enemy to a parley

CHAMADES > CHAMADE

CHAMBER *n* hall used for formal meetings ▷ *vb* act lasciviously

CHAMBERED > CHAMBER

CHAMBERER *n* lascivious person

CHAMBERS *pl n* judge's room for hearing private cases not taken in open court

CHAMBRAY *n* smooth light fabric of cotton, linen, etc, with white weft and a coloured warp

CHAMBRAYS > CHAMBRAY

CHAMBRE *adj* (of wine) at room temperature

CHAMELEON *n* small lizard that changes colour to blend in with its surroundings

CHAMELOT *same as* > CAMLET

CHAMELOTS > CHAMELOT

CHAMETZ *n* leavened food which may not be eaten during Passover

CHAMETZES > CHAMETZ

CHAMFER *same as* > CHASE

CHAMFERED > CHAMFER

CHAMFERER > CHAMFER

CHAMFERS > CHAMFER

CHAMFRAIN *same as* > CHAMFRON

CHAMFRON *n* piece of armour for a horse's head

CHAMFRONS > CHAMFRON

CHAMISA *n* American shrub

CHAMISAL *n* place overgrown with chamiso

CHAMISALS > CHAMISAL

CHAMISAS > CHAMISA

CHAMISE *same as* > CHAMISO

CHAMISES > CHAMISE

CHAMISO *n* four-wing saltbush

CHAMISOS > CHAMISO
CHAMLET *same as*
> CAMLET
CHAMLETS > CHAMLET
CHAMMIED > CHAMMY
CHAMMIES > CHAMMY
CHAMMY *same as*
> CHAMOIS
CHAMMYING > CHAMMY
CHAMOIS *n* small
mountain antelope or a
piece of leather from its
skin, used for polishing
▷ *vb* polish with a chamois
CHAMOISED > CHAMOIS
CHAMOISES > CHAMOIS
CHAMOIX *same as*
> CHAMOIS
CHAMOMILE *same as*
> CAMOMILE
CHAMP *vb* chew noisily
CHAMPAC *n* type of tree
CHAMPACA *same as*
> CHAMPAC
CHAMPACAS > CHAMPACA
CHAMPACS > CHAMPAC
CHAMPAGNE *n* sparkling
white French wine ▷ *adj*
denoting a luxurious
lifestyle
CHAMPAIGN *n* expanse of
open level or gently
undulating country
CHAMPAK *same as*
> CHAMPAC
CHAMPAKS > CHAMPAK
CHAMPART *n* granting of
land to a person for a
portion of the crops
CHAMPARTS
> CHAMPART
CHAMPAS *n* champagne
CHAMPED > CHAMP
CHAMPER > CHAMP
CHAMPERS *n* champagne
CHAMPERTY *n* (formerly)
an illegal bargain between
a party to litigation and an
outsider whereby the
latter agrees to pay for the
action and thereby share
in any proceeds recovered
CHAMPIER > CHAMPY
CHAMPIEST > CHAMPY
CHAMPING > CHAMP
CHAMPION *n* overall
winner of a competition
▷ *vb* support ▷ *adj*
excellent ▷ *adv* very well
CHAMPIONS
> CHAMPION
CHAMPLEVE *adj* of or
relating to a process of
enamelling by which
grooves are cut into a
metal base and filled with
enamel colours ▷ *n* object
enamelled by this process
CHAMPS > CHAMP
CHAMPY *adj* (of earth)
churned up (by cattle, for
example)
CHAMS > CHAM
CHANA *n* (in Indian
cookery) chickpeas
CHANAS > CHANA
CHANCE *n* likelihood,
probability ▷ *vb* risk,
hazard

CHANCED > CHANCE
CHANCEFUL > CHANCE
CHANCEL *n* part of a
church containing the
altar and choir
CHANCELS > CHANCEL
CHANCER *n* unscrupulous
or dishonest opportunist
CHANCERS > CHANCER
CHANCERY *n* Lord
Chancellor's court, now a
division of the High Court
of Justice
CHANCES > CHANCE
CHANCEY *same as*
> CHANCY
CHANCIER > CHANCY
CHANCIEST > CHANCY
CHANCILY > CHANCY
CHANCING > CHANCE
CHANCRE *n* small hard
growth
CHANCRES > CHANCRE
CHANCROID *n* soft ulcer
caused by a bacterial
infection ▷ *adj* relating to
or resembling a chancroid
or chancre
CHANCROUS > CHANCRE
CHANCY *adj* uncertain,
risky
CHANDELLE *n* abrupt
climbing turn almost to
the point of stalling, in
which an aircraft's
momentum is used to
increase its rate of climb
▷ *vb* carry out a chandelle
CHANDLER *n* dealer, esp
in ships' supplies
CHANDLERS
> CHANDLER
CHANDLERY *n* business,
warehouse, or
merchandise of a
chandler
CHANFRON *same as*
> CHAMFRON
CHANFRONS
> CHANFRON
CHANG *n* loud discordant
noise
CHANGA *interj* in Indian
English, an expression of
approval or agreement
CHANGE *n* becoming
different ▷ *vb* make or
become different
CHANGED > CHANGE
CHANGEFUL *adj* often
changing
CHANGER > CHANGE
CHANGERS > CHANGE
CHANGES > CHANGE
CHANGEUP *n* type of
baseball pitch
CHANGEUPS
> CHANGEUP
CHANGING > CHANGE
CHANGS > CHANG
CHANK *n* shell of several
types of sea conch, used to
make bracelets
CHANKS > CHANK
CHANNEL *n* band of
broadcasting frequencies
▷ *vb* direct or convey
through a channel
CHANNELED > CHANNEL

CHANNELER > CHANNEL
CHANNELS > CHANNEL
CHANNER *n* gravel
CHANNERS > CHANNER
CHANOYO *variant of*
> CHADO
CHANOYOS > CHANOYO
CHANOYU *same as* > CHADO
CHANOYUS > CHANOYU
CHANSON *n* song
CHANSONS > CHANSON
CHANT *vb* utter or sing (a
slogan or psalm) ▷ *n*
rhythmic or repetitious
slogan
CHANTABLE > CHANT
CHANTAGE *n* blackmail
CHANTAGES
> CHANTAGE
CHANTED > CHANT
CHANTER *n* (on bagpipes)
pipe on which the melody
is played
CHANTERS > CHANTER
CHANTEUSE *n* female
singer, esp in a nightclub
or cabaret
CHANTEY *the usual US
spelling of* > SHANTY
CHANTEYS > CHANTEY
CHANTIE *n* chamber pot
CHANTIES > CHANTY
CHANTILLY *n* as in
chantilly lace delicate
ornamental lace
CHANTING > CHANT
CHANTINGS
> CHANTING
CHANTOR *same as*
> CHANTER
CHANTORS > CHANTOR
CHANTRESS *n* female
chanter
CHANTRIES > CHANTRY
CHANTRY *n* endowment
for the singing of Masses
for the founder
CHANTS > CHANT
CHANTY *same as*
> SHANTY
CHANUKIAH *variant of*
> HANUKIAH
CHAO *n* Vietnamese rice
porridge
CHAOLOGY *n* study of
chaos theory
CHAORDIC *adj* combining
elements of chaos and
order
CHAOS *n* complete
disorder or confusion
CHAOSES > CHAOS
CHAOTIC > CHAOS
CHAP *n* man or boy ▷ *vb*
(of the skin) to make or
become raw and cracked,
esp by exposure to cold
CHAPARRAL *n* (in the
southwestern US) a dense
growth of shrubs and
trees, esp evergreen oaks
CHAPATI *n* (in Indian
cookery) flat thin
unleavened bread
CHAPATIES > CHAPATI
CHAPATIS > CHAPATI
CHAPATTI *same as*
> CHAPATI

CHAPATTIS
> CHAPATTI
CHAPBOOK *n* book of
popular ballads, stories,
etc, formerly sold by
chapmen or pedlars
CHAPBOOKS
> CHAPBOOK
CHAPE *n* metal tip or
trimming for a scabbard
CHAPEAU *n* hat
CHAPEAUS > CHAPEAU
CHAPEAUX > CHAPEAU
CHAPEL *n* place of
worship with its own altar,
within a church
CHAPELESS > CHAPE
CHAPELRY *n* district
legally assigned to and
served by an Anglican
chapel
CHAPELS > CHAPEL
CHAPERON *n* older or
married woman who
supervises a young
unmarried woman ▷ *vb*
act as a chaperon to
CHAPERONE *same as*
> CHAPERON
CHAPERONS
> CHAPERON
CHAPES > CHAPE
CHAPESS *n* woman
CHAPESSES > CHAPESS
CHAPITER *same as*
> CAPITAL
CHAPITERS
> CHAPITER
CHAPKA *same as*
> CZAPKA
CHAPKAS > CHAPKA
CHAPLAIN *n* clergyman
or clergywoman attached
to a chapel, military body,
or institution
CHAPLAINS
> CHAPLAIN
CHAPLESS *adj* lacking a
lower jaw
CHAPLET *n* garland for
the head ▷ *vb* create a
garland
CHAPLETED > CHAPLET
CHAPLETS > CHAPLET
CHAPMAN *n* travelling
pedlar
CHAPMEN > CHAPMAN
CHAPPAL *n* one of a pair
of sandals, usually of
leather, worn in India
CHAPPALS > CHAPPAL
CHAPPATI *same as*
> CHAPATI
CHAPPATIS
> CHAPPATI
CHAPPED > CHAP
CHAPPESS *same as*
> CHAPESS
CHAPPIE *n* man or boy
CHAPPIER > CHAPPY
CHAPPIES > CHAPPIE
CHAPPIEST > CHAPPY
CHAPPING > CHAP
CHAPPY *adj* (of skin)
chapped
CHAPRASSI *n* in India,
during the British Empire,
an office messenger

CHAPS > CHAP
CHAPSTICK *n* cylinder of a substance for preventing or soothing chapped lips
CHAPT *adj* chapped
CHAPTER *n* division of a book ▷ *vb* divide into chapters
CHAPTERAL > CHAPTER
CHAPTERED > CHAPTER
CHAPTERS > CHAPTER
CHAPTREL *n* capital of a pillar supporting an arch
**CHAPTRELS
>** CHAPTREL
CHAQUETA *n* South American cowboy jacket
**CHAQUETAS
>** CHAQUETA
CHAR *vb* blacken by partial burning ▷ *n* charwoman
CHARA *n* type of green freshwater algae
CHARABANC *n* coach for sightseeing
CHARACID *same as*
> CHARACIN
**CHARACIDS
>** CHARACIN
CHARACIN *n* type of small carnivorous freshwater fish of Central and S America and Africa
**CHARACINS
>** CHARACIN
CHARACT *n* distinctive mark
CHARACTER *n* combination of qualities distinguishing a person, group, or place
CHARACTS > CHARACT
CHARADE *n* absurd pretence
CHARADES *n* game in which teams act out each syllable of a word or phrase
CHARANGA *n* type of orchestra used in performing traditional Cuban music
**CHARANGAS
>** CHARANGA
CHARANGO *n* Andean ten-stringed mandolin
**CHARANGOS
>** CHARANGO
CHARAS *another name for*
> HASHISH
CHARASES > CHARAS
CHARBROIL *vb* grill over charcoal
CHARCOAL *n* black substance formed by partially burning wood ▷ *adj* very dark grey ▷ *vb* write, draw, or blacken with charcoal
**CHARCOALS
>** CHARCOAL
CHARCOALY *adj* like charcoal
CHARD *n* variety of beet
CHARDS > CHARD
CHARE *same as >* CHAR
CHARED > CHARE
CHARES > CHARE

CHARET *obsolete variant of*
> CHARIOT
CHARETS > CHARET
CHARETTE *n* public brainstorming session
**CHARETTES
>** CHARETTE
CHARGE *vb* ask as a price ▷ *n* price charged
CHARGED > CHARGE
CHARGEFUL *adj* expensive
CHARGER *n* device for charging an accumulator
CHARGERS > CHARGER
CHARGES > CHARGE
CHARGING *n* act of charging
**CHARGINGS
>** CHARGING
CHARGRILL *vb* grill over charcoal
CHARIDEE *n* jocular spelling of charity, as pronounced in a mid-Atlantic accent
**CHARIDEES
>** CHARIDEE
CHARIER > CHARY
CHARIEST > CHARY
CHARILY *adv* cautiously
CHARINESS *n* state of being chary
CHARING > CHARE
CHARIOT *n* two-wheeled horse-drawn vehicle ▷ *vb* ride in a chariot
CHARIOTED > CHARIOT
CHARIOTS > CHARIOT
CHARISM *same as*
> CHARISMA
CHARISMA *n* person's power to attract or influence people
**CHARISMAS
>** CHARISMA
CHARISMS > CHARISM
CHARITIES > CHARITY
CHARITY *n* organization that gives help, such as money or food, to those in need
CHARIVARI *n* discordant mock serenade to newlyweds, made with pans, kettles, etc ▷ *vb* make such a serenade
CHARK *vb* char
CHARKA *same as*
> CHARKHA
CHARKAS > CHARKA
CHARKED > CHARK
CHARKHA *n* (in India) a spinning wheel, esp for cotton
CHARKHAS > CHARKHA
CHARKING > CHARK
CHARKS > CHARK
CHARLADY *same as*
> CHARWOMAN
CHARLATAN *n* person who claims expertise that he or she does not have
CHARLEY *n* as in *charley horse* muscle stiffness after strenuous exercise
CHARLEYS > CHARLEY
CHARLIE *n* fool

CHARLIER *n* as in *charlier shoe* special light horseshoe
CHARLIES > CHARLIE
CHARLOCK *n* weed with hairy leaves and yellow flowers
**CHARLOCKS
>** CHARLOCK
CHARLOTTE *n* dessert made with fruit and bread or cake crumbs
CHARM *n* attractive quality ▷ *vb* attract, delight
CHARMED *adj* delighted or fascinated
CHARMER *n* attractive person
CHARMERS > CHARMER
CHARMEUSE *n* trademark for a lightweight fabric with a satin-like finish
CHARMFUL *adj* highly charming or enchanting
CHARMING *adj* attractive
CHARMLESS *adj* devoid of charm
CHARMONIA *pl n* elementary particles containing an antiquark and a charm quark
CHARMS > CHARM
CHARNECO *n* type of sweet wine
**CHARNECOS
>** CHARNECO
CHARNEL *adj* ghastly ▷ *n* ghastly thing
CHARNELS > CHARNEL
CHAROSET *n* dish eaten at Passover
CHAROSETH *same as*
> CHAROSET
**CHAROSETS
>** CHAROSET
CHARPAI *same as*
> CHARPOY
CHARPAIS > CHARPAI
CHARPIE *n* lint pieces used to make surgical dressings
CHARPIES > CHARPIE
CHARPOY *n* type of bedstead
CHARPOYS > CHARPOY
CHARQUI *n* meat, esp beef, cut into strips and dried
CHARQUID > CHARQUI
CHARQUIS > CHARQUI
CHARR *same as >* CHAR
CHARREADA *n* Mexican display of skills similar to a rodeo
CHARRED > CHAR
CHARRIER > CHARRY
CHARRIEST > CHARRY
CHARRING > CHAR
CHARRO *n* Mexican cowboy
CHARROS > CHARRO
CHARRS > CHARR
CHARRY *adj* of or relating to charcoal
CHARS > CHAR
CHART *n* graph, table, or diagram showing information ▷ *vb* plot the course of

CHARTA *n* charter
CHARTABLE > CHART
CHARTAS > CHARTA
CHARTED > CHART
CHARTER *n* document granting or demanding certain rights ▷ *vb* hire by charter
CHARTERED *adj* officially qualified to practise a profession
CHARTERER > CHARTER
CHARTERS > CHARTER
CHARTING > CHART
CHARTISM *n* historical reform movement in Britain
**CHARTISMS
>** CHARTISM
CHARTIST *n* supporter of chartism
**CHARTISTS
>** CHARTIST
CHARTLESS *adj* not mapped
CHARTS > CHART
CHARVER *n* derogatory term for a young working-class person
CHARVERS > CHARVER
CHARWOMAN *n* woman whose job is to clean other people's homes
**CHARWOMEN
>** CHARWOMAN
CHARY *adj* wary, careful
CHAS > CHA
CHASE *vb* run after quickly in order to catch or drive away ▷ *n* chasing, pursuit
CHASEABLE > CHASE
CHASED > CHASE
CHASEPORT *n* porthole through which a chase gun is fired
CHASER > CHASE
CHASERS > CHASE
CHASES > CHASE
CHASING > CHASE
CHASINGS > CHASE
CHASM *n* deep crack in the earth
CHASMAL > CHASM
CHASMED > CHASM
CHASMIC > CHASM
CHASMIER > CHASMY
CHASMIEST > CHASMY
CHASMS > CHASM
CHASMY *adj* full of chasms
CHASSE *n* one of a series of gliding steps in ballet ▷ *vb* perform either of these steps
CHASSED > CHASSE
CHASSEED > CHASSE
CHASSEING > CHASSE
CHASSEPOT *n* breech-loading bolt-action rifle formerly used by the French Army
CHASSES > CHASSE
CHASSEUR *n* member of a unit specially trained and equipped for swift deployment ▷ *adj* designating or cooked in a sauce consisting of white wine and mushrooms

CHASSEURS
> CHASSEUR
CHASSIS n frame, wheels, and mechanical parts of a vehicle
CHASTE adj pure and modest
CHASTELY > CHASTE
CHASTEN vb subdue by criticism
CHASTENED > CHASTEN
CHASTENER > CHASTEN
CHASTENS > CHASTEN
CHASTER > CHASTE
CHASTEST > CHASTE
CHASTISE vb scold severely
CHASTISED
> CHASTISE
CHASTISER
> CHASTISE
CHASTISES
> CHASTISE
CHASTITY n state of being chaste
CHASUBLE n long sleeveless robe worn by a priest when celebrating Mass
CHASUBLES
> CHASUBLE
CHAT n informal conversation ▷ vb have an informal conversation
CHATBOT n computer program that simulates conversation with human users over the internet
CHATBOTS > CHATBOT
CHATCHKA variant of
> TCHOTCHKE
CHATCHKAS
> CHATCHKA
CHATCHKE same as
> TCHOTCHKE
CHATCHKES
> CHATCHKE
CHATEAU n French castle
CHATEAUS > CHATEAU
CHATEAUX > CHATEAU
CHATELAIN same as
> CASTELLAN
CHATLINE n telephone service enabling callers to join in general conversation with each other
CHATLINES
> CHATLINE
CHATON n in jewellery, a stone with a reflective metal foil backing
CHATONS > CHATON
CHATOYANT adj having changeable lustre ▷ n gemstone with a changeable lustre
CHATROOM n site on the internet where users have group discussions by email
CHATROOMS
> CHATROOM
CHATS > CHAT
CHATTA n umbrella
CHATTAS > CHATTA
CHATTED > CHAT
CHATTEL n item of movable personal property

CHATTELS > CHATTEL
CHATTER vb speak quickly and continuously about unimportant things ▷ n idle talk
CHATTERED > CHATTER
CHATTERER same as
> COTINGA
CHATTERS > CHATTER
CHATTERY adj tending to chatter
CHATTI n (in India) earthenware pot
CHATTIER > CHATTY
CHATTIES > CHATTY
CHATTIEST > CHATTY
CHATTILY > CHATTY
CHATTING > CHAT
CHATTIS > CHATTI
CHATTY adj (of a person) fond of friendly, informal conversation ▷ n (in India) earthenware pot
CHAUFE obsolete variant of
> CHAFE
CHAUFED > CHAUFE
CHAUFER same as
> CHAUFFER
CHAUFERS > CHAUFER
CHAUFES > CHAUFE
CHAUFF obsolete variant of
> CHAFE
CHAUFFED > CHAUFF
CHAUFFER n small portable heater or stove
CHAUFFERS
> CHAUFFER
CHAUFFEUR n person employed to drive a car for someone ▷ vb act as driver for (someone)
CHAUFFING > CHAUFF
CHAUFFS > CHAUFF
CHAUFING > CHAUFE
CHAUMER n chamber
CHAUMERS > CHAUMER
CHAUNCE archaic variant of
> CHANCE
CHAUNCED > CHAUNCE
CHAUNCES > CHAUNCE
CHAUNCING > CHAUNCE
CHAUNGE archaic variant of
> CHANGE
CHAUNGED > CHAUNGE
CHAUNGES > CHAUNGE
CHAUNGING > CHAUNGE
CHAUNT a less common variant of > CHANT
CHAUNTED > CHAUNT
CHAUNTER > CHAUNT
CHAUNTERS > CHAUNT
CHAUNTING > CHAUNT
CHAUNTRY same as
> CHANTRY
CHAUNTS > CHAUNT
CHAUSSES n tight-fitting medieval garment covering the feet and legs, usually made of chain mail
CHAUSSURE n any type of footwear
CHAUVIN n chauvinist
CHAUVINS > CHAUVIN
CHAV n insulting word for a young working-class person who wears casual sports clothes

CHAVE vb old dialect term for 'I have'
CHAVENDER n chub
CHAVETTE n insulting word for a young working-class woman who wears casual sports clothes
CHAVETTES
> CHAVETTE
CHAVISH > CHAV
CHAVS > CHAV
CHAVVIER > CHAVVY
CHAVVIEST > CHAVVY
CHAVVY adj relating to or like a chav
CHAW vb chew (tobacco), esp without swallowing it ▷ n something chewed, esp a plug of tobacco
CHAWBACON n bumpkin
CHAWDRON n entrails
CHAWDRONS
> CHAWDRON
CHAWED > CHAW
CHAWER > CHAW
CHAWERS > CHAW
CHAWING > CHAW
CHAWK n jackdaw
CHAWKS > CHAWK
CHAWS > CHAW
CHAY n plant of the madder family
CHAYA same as > CHAY
CHAYAS > CHAYA
CHAYOTE n tropical climbing plant
CHAYOTES > CHAYOTE
CHAYROOT n root of the chay plant
CHAYROOTS
> CHAYROOT
CHAYS > CHAY
CHAZAN n man employed to lead services in a synagogue
CHAZANIM > CHAZAN
CHAZANS > CHAZAN
CHAZZAN variant of
> CHAZAN
CHAZZANIM > CHAZZAN
CHAZZANS > CHAZZAN
CHAZZEN same as
> CHAZZAN
CHAZZENIM > CHAZZEN
CHAZZENS > CHAZZEN
CHE pron dialectal form meaning 'I'
CHEAP adj costing relatively little ▷ adv at very little cost ▷ n bargain ▷ vb take the cheapest option
CHEAPED > CHEAP
CHEAPEN vb lower the reputation of
CHEAPENED > CHEAPEN
CHEAPENER > CHEAPEN
CHEAPENS > CHEAPEN
CHEAPER > CHEAP
CHEAPEST > CHEAP
CHEAPIE n something inexpensive
CHEAPIES > CHEAPIE
CHEAPING > CHEAP
CHEAPISH > CHEAP
CHEAPJACK n person who sells cheap and

shoddy goods ▷ adj shoddy or inferior
CHEAPLY > CHEAP
CHEAPNESS > CHEAP
CHEAPO n very cheap and possibly shoddy thing
CHEAPOS > CHEAPO
CHEAPS > CHEAP
CHEAPSHOT n abusive remark
CHEAPY same as
> CHEAPIE
CHEAT vb act dishonestly to gain profit or advantage ▷ n person who cheats
CHEATABLE > CHEAT
CHEATED > CHEAT
CHEATER > CHEAT
CHEATERS > CHEAT
CHEATERY n cheating
CHEATING > CHEAT
CHEATINGS > CHEAT
CHEATS > CHEAT
CHEBEC n type of boat
CHEBECS > CHEBEC
CHECHAKO same as
> CHEECHAKO
CHECHAKOS
> CHECHAKO
CHECHAQUO same as
> CHEECHAKO
CHECHIA n Berber skullcap
CHECHIAS > CHECHIA
CHECK vb examine or investigate ▷ n control designed to ensure accuracy
CHECKABLE > CHECK
CHECKBOOK n American word for chequebook
CHECKBOX n small clickable box on a computer screen
CHECKED > CHECK
CHECKER same as
> CHEQUER
CHECKERED same as
> CHEQUERED
CHECKERS n game for two players using a checkerboard and small pieces
CHECKIER > CHECKY
CHECKIEST > CHECKY
CHECKING n act of checking
CHECKINGS
> CHECKING
CHECKLESS adj without check or restraint
CHECKLIST vb check items, facts, etc, against those in a list used for verification
CHECKMARK vb make a mark of approval or verification
CHECKMATE n winning position in which an opponent's king is under attack and unable to escape ▷ vb place the king of (one's opponent) in checkmate ▷ interj call made when placing an opponent's king in checkmate

CHECKOFF n paying of an employee's union dues straight from their salary

CHECKOFFS
> CHECKOFF

CHECKOUT n counter in a supermarket, where customers pay

CHECKOUTS
> CHECKOUT

CHECKRAIL another word for > GUARDRAIL

CHECKREIN n bearing rein

CHECKROOM n place at a railway station, airport, etc, where luggage may be left for a small charge with an attendant for safekeeping

CHECKROW n row of plants, esp corn ▷ vb plant in checkrows

CHECKROWS
> CHECKROW

CHECKS > CHECK

CHECKSTOP n roadside area where drivers are randomly breath-tested

CHECKSUM n digit attached to the end of a message to verify data

CHECKSUMS
> CHECKSUM

CHECKUP n thorough medical examination

CHECKUPS > CHECKUP

CHECKY adj having squares of alternating tinctures or furs

CHEDARIM same as
> CHADARIM

CHEDDAR n type of smooth hard yellow or whitish cheese

CHEDDARS > CHEDDAR

CHEDDARY adj like cheddar cheese

CHEDDITE n type of explosive

CHEDDITES
> CHEDDITE

CHEDER n Jewish religious education

CHEDERS > CHEDER

CHEDITE same as
> CHEDDITE

CHEDITES > CHEDITE

CHEECHAKO n local name for a newcomer to Alaska

CHEEK n either side of the face below the eye ▷ vb speak impudently to

CHEEKBONE n bone at the top of the cheek, just below the eye

CHEEKED > CHEEK

CHEEKFUL n quantity that can be held in a cheek

CHEEKFULS
> CHEEKFUL

CHEEKIER > CHEEKY

CHEEKIEST > CHEEKY

CHEEKILY > CHEEKY

CHEEKING > CHEEK

CHEEKLESS > CHEEK

CHEEKS > CHEEK

CHEEKY adj impudent, disrespectful

CHEEP n young bird's high-pitched cry ▷ vb utter a cheep

CHEEPED > CHEEP

CHEEPER > CHEEP

CHEEPERS > CHEEP

CHEEPING > CHEEP

CHEEPS > CHEEP

CHEER vb applaud or encourage with shouts ▷ n shout of applause or encouragement

CHEERED > CHEER

CHEERER > CHEER

CHEERERS > CHEER

CHEERFUL adj having a happy disposition

CHEERIER > CHEERY

CHEERIEST > CHEERY

CHEERILY > CHEERY

CHEERING n act of cheering

CHEERINGS
> CHEERING

CHEERIO interj goodbye ▷ n small red cocktail sausage ▷ sentence substitute farewell greeting

CHEERIOS > CHEERIO

CHEERLEAD vb lead a crowd in formal cheers at sports events

CHEERLED
> CHEERLEAD

CHEERLESS adj dreary, gloomy

CHEERLY adv cheerfully

CHEERO same as
> CHEERIO

CHEEROS > CHEERO

CHEERS interj drinking toast

CHEERY adj cheerful

CHEESE n food made from coagulated milk curd ▷ vb stop

CHEESED > CHEESE

CHEESES > CHEESE

CHEESEVAT n in cheese-making, vat in which curds are formed and cut

CHEESIER > CHEESY

CHEESIEST > CHEESY

CHEESILY > CHEESY

CHEESING > CHEESE

CHEESY adj like cheese

CHEETAH n large fast-running spotted African wild cat

CHEETAHS > CHEETAH

CHEEWINK same as
> CHEWINK

CHEEWINKS
> CHEEWINK

CHEF n cook in a restaurant ▷ vb work as a chef

CHEFDOM n state or condition of being a chef

CHEFDOMS > CHEFDOM

CHEFED > CHEF

CHEFFED > CHEF

CHEFFIER > CHEFFY

CHEFFIEST > CHEFFY

CHEFFING > CHEF

CHEFFY adj relating to or characteristic of chefs

CHEFING > CHEF

CHEFS > CHEF

CHEGOE same as
> CHIGGER

CHEGOES > CHEGOE

CHEILITIS n inflammation of the lip(s)

CHEKA n secret police set up in Russia in 1917

CHEKAS > CHEKA

CHEKIST n member of the cheka

CHEKISTS > CHEKIST

CHELA n disciple of a religious teacher

CHELAE > CHELA

CHELAS > CHELA

CHELASHIP > CHELA

CHELATE n coordination compound ▷ adj of or possessing chelae ▷ vb form a chelate

CHELATED > CHELATE

CHELATES > CHELATE

CHELATING > CHELATE

CHELATION n process by which a chelate is formed

CHELATOR > CHELATE

CHELATORS > CHELATE

CHELICERA n one of a pair of appendages on the head of spiders and other arachnids: often modified as food-catching claws

CHELIFORM adj shaped like a chela

CHELIPED n (on a arthropod) either of two legs which each carry a claw

CHELIPEDS
> CHELIPED

CHELLUP n noise

CHELLUPS > CHELLUP

CHELOID variant spelling of > KELOID

CHELOIDAL > CHELOID

CHELOIDS > CHELOID

CHELONE n hardy N American plant

CHELONES > CHELONE

CHELONIAN n type of reptile such as the tortoises and turtles, in which most of the body is enclosed in a protective bony capsule

CHELP vb to chatter or speak out of turn

CHELPED > CHELP

CHELPING > CHELP

CHELPS > CHELP

CHEM n chemistry

CHEMIC vb bleach ▷ n chemist

CHEMICAL n substance used in or resulting from a reaction involving changes to atoms or molecules ▷ adj of chemistry or chemicals

CHEMICALS
> CHEMICAL

CHEMICKED > CHEMIC

CHEMICS > CHEMIC

CHEMISE n woman's loose-fitting slip

CHEMISES > CHEMISE

CHEMISM n chemical action

CHEMISMS > CHEMISM

CHEMISORB vb take up (a substance) by chemisorption

CHEMIST n shop selling medicines and cosmetics

CHEMISTRY n science of the composition, properties, and reactions of substances

CHEMISTS > CHEMIST

CHEMITYPE n process by which a relief impression is obtained from an engraving

CHEMITYPY
> CHEMITYPE

CHEMMIES > CHEMMY

CHEMMY n gambling card game

CHEMO n short form of chemotherapy

CHEMOKINE n type of protein

CHEMOS > CHEMO

CHEMOSORB same as
> CHEMISORB

CHEMOSTAT n apparatus for growing bacterial cultures at a constant rate by controlling the supply of nutrient medium

CHEMPADUK n Malaysian evergreen tree

CHEMS > CHEM

CHEMSEX n sex while on drugs

CHEMSEXES > CHEMSEX

CHEMTRAIL n supposed vapour trail containing toxic chemicals

CHEMURGIC
> CHEMURGY

CHEMURGY n branch of chemistry

CHENAR n oriental plane tree

CHENARS > CHENAR

CHENET another word for
> GENIP

CHENETS > CHENET

CHENILLE n (fabric of) thick tufty yarn

CHENILLES
> CHENILLE

CHENIX n ancient measure, slightly more than a quart

CHENIXES > CHENIX

CHENOPOD n plant of the beetroot family

CHENOPODS
> CHENOPOD

CHEONGSAM n straight dress, usually of silk or cotton, with a stand-up collar and a slit in one side of the skirt, worn by Chinese women

CHEQUE n written order to one's bank to pay money from one's account

CHEQUER n piece used in Chinese chequers ▷ vb

make irregular in colour or character
CHEQUERED adj marked by varied fortunes
CHEQUERS n game of draughts
CHEQUES > CHEQUE
CHEQUIER > CHEQUY
CHEQUIEST > CHEQUY
CHEQUING adj as in chequing account (in Canada) account against which cheques can be drawn
CHEQUY same as > CHECKY
CHER adj dear or expensive
CHERALITE n rare phosphate-silicate of thorium and calcium
CHERE feminine variant of > CHER
CHERIMOYA n large tropical fruit with cream-coloured flesh
CHERISH vb cling to (an idea or feeling)
CHERISHED > CHERISH
CHERISHER > CHERISH
CHERISHES > CHERISH
CHERMOULA n type of marinade used in N African cookery
CHERNOZEM n black soil, rich in humus and carbonates, in cool or temperate semiarid regions, as the grasslands of Russia
CHEROOT n cigar with both ends cut flat
CHEROOTS > CHEROOT
CHERRIED > CHERRY
CHERRIER > CHERRY
CHERRIES > CHERRY
CHERRIEST > CHERRY
CHERRY n small red or black fruit with a stone ▷ adj deep red ▷ vb cheer
CHERRYING > CHERRY
CHERT n microcrystalline form of silica
CHERTIER > CHERT
CHERTIEST > CHERT
CHERTS > CHERT
CHERTY > CHERT
CHERUB n angel, often represented as a winged child
CHERUBIC > CHERUB
CHERUBIM > CHERUB
CHERUBIMS > CHERUB
CHERUBIN n cherub ▷ adj cherubic
CHERUBINS > CHERUBIN
CHERUBS > CHERUB
CHERUP same as > CHIRRUP
CHERUPED > CHERUP
CHERUPING > CHERUP
CHERUPS > CHERUP
CHERVIL n aniseed-flavoured herb
CHERVILS > CHERVIL
CHESHIRE n breed of American pig
CHESHIRES > CHESHIRE

CHESIL n gravel or shingle
CHESILS > CHESIL
CHESNUT rare variant of > CHESTNUT
CHESNUTS > CHESNUT
CHESS n board game for two players
CHESSEL n mould used in cheese-making
CHESSELS > CHESSEL
CHESSES > CHESS
CHESSMAN n piece used in chess
CHESSMEN > CHESSMAN
CHEST n front of the body, from neck to waist ▷ vb hit with the chest, as with a ball in football
CHESTED > CHEST
CHESTFUL n amount a chest will hold
CHESTFULS > CHESTFUL
CHESTIER > CHESTY
CHESTIEST > CHESTY
CHESTILY > CHESTY
CHESTING > CHEST
CHESTNUT n reddish-brown edible nut ▷ adj (of hair or a horse) reddish-brown
CHESTNUTS > CHESTNUT
CHESTS > CHEST
CHESTY adj symptomatic of chest disease
CHETAH same as > CHEETAH
CHETAHS > CHETAH
CHETH same as > HETH
CHETHS > CHETH
CHETNIK n member of a Serbian nationalist paramilitary group
CHETNIKS > CHETNIK
CHETRUM n monetary unit in Bhutan
CHETRUMS > CHETRUM
CHEVAL n as in cheval glass full-length mirror that can swivel
CHEVALET n bridge of a stringed musical instrument
CHEVALETS > CHEVALET
CHEVALIER n member of the French Legion of Honour
CHEVELURE n nebulous part of the tail of a comet
CHEVEN n chub
CHEVENS > CHEVEN
CHEVEREL n kid or goatskin leather
CHEVERELS > CHEVEREL
CHEVERIL same as > CHEVEREL
CHEVERILS > CHEVERIL
CHEVERON same as > CHEVRON
CHEVERONS > CHEVERON
CHEVERYE same as > CHIEFERY

CHEVERYES > CHEVERYE
CHEVET n semicircular or polygonal east end of a church
CHEVETS > CHEVET
CHEVIED > CHEVY
CHEVIES > CHEVY
CHEVILLE n peg of a stringed musical instrument
CHEVILLES > CHEVILLE
CHEVIN same as > CHEVEN
CHEVINS > CHEVIN
CHEVIOT n type of British sheep reared for its wool
CHEVIOTS > CHEVIOT
CHEVRE n any cheese made from goats' milk
CHEVRES > CHEVRE
CHEVRET n type of goats' cheese
CHEVRETS > CHEVRET
CHEVRETTE n skin of a young goat
CHEVRON n V-shaped pattern ▷ vb make a chevron
CHEVRONED > CHEVRON
CHEVRONS > CHEVRON
CHEVRONY adj in heraldry, bearing chevrons
CHEVROTIN n soft goat's cheese
CHEVY same as > CHIVY
CHEVYING > CHEVY
CHEW vb grind (food) between the teeth ▷ n act of chewing
CHEWABLE > CHEW
CHEWED > CHEW
CHEWER > CHEW
CHEWERS > CHEW
CHEWET n type of meat pie
CHEWETS > CHEWET
CHEWIE n chewing gum
CHEWIER > CHEWY
CHEWIES > CHEWY
CHEWIEST > CHEWY
CHEWINESS > CHEWY
CHEWING > CHEW
CHEWINK n towhee
CHEWINKS > CHEWINK
CHEWS > CHEW
CHEWY adj requiring a lot of chewing ▷ n dog's rubber toy
CHEZ prep at the home of
CHHERTUM same as > CHETRUM
CHI n 22nd letter of the Greek alphabet
CHIA n plant of the mint family
CHIACK vb tease or banter ▷ n good-humoured banter
CHIACKED > CHIACK
CHIACKING > CHIACK
CHIACKS > CHIACK
CHIANTI n dry red Italian wine
CHIANTIS > CHIANTI
CHIAO n Chinese coin equal to one tenth of one yuan

CHIAOS > CHIAO
CHIAREZZA n (in music) clarity
CHIAREZZE > CHIAREZZA
CHIAS > CHIA
CHIASM same as > CHIASMA
CHIASMA n crossing over of two anatomical structures
CHIASMAL > CHIASMA
CHIASMAS > CHIASMA
CHIASMATA > CHIASMA
CHIASMI > CHIASMUS
CHIASMIC > CHIASMA
CHIASMS > CHIASM
CHIASMUS n reversal of the order of words in the second of two parallel phrases
CHIASTIC > CHIASMUS
CHIAUS same as > CHOUSE
CHIAUSED > CHIAUS
CHIAUSES > CHIAUS
CHIAUSING > CHIAUS
CHIB vb in Scots English, stab or slash with a sharp weapon ▷ n sharp weapon
CHIBBED > CHIB
CHIBBING > CHIB
CHIBOL n spring onion
CHIBOLS > CHIBOL
CHIBOUK n Turkish tobacco pipe with an extremely long stem
CHIBOUKS > CHIBOUK
CHIBOUQUE same as > CHIBOUK
CHIBS > CHIB
CHIC adj stylish, elegant ▷ n stylishness, elegance
CHICA n Spanish girl or young woman
CHICALOTE n type of poppy of the southwestern US and Mexico with prickly leaves and white or yellow flowers
CHICANA n American female citizen of Mexican origin
CHICANAS > CHICANA
CHICANE n obstacle in a motor-racing circuit ▷ vb deceive or trick by chicanery
CHICANED > CHICANE
CHICANER > CHICANE
CHICANERS > CHICANE
CHICANERY n trickery, deception
CHICANES > CHICANE
CHICANING > CHICANE
CHICANO n American male citizen of Mexican origin
CHICANOS > CHICANO
CHICAS > CHICA
CHICCORY variant spelling of > CHICORY
CHICER > CHIC
CHICEST > CHIC
CHICH another word for > CHICKPEA

CHICHA n Andean drink made from fermented maize

CHICHAS > CHICHA

CHICHES > CHICH

CHICHI adj affectedly pretty or stylish ⊳ n quality of being affectedly pretty or stylish

CHICHIER > CHICHI

CHICHIEST > CHICHI

CHICHIS > CHICHI

CHICK n baby bird

CHICKADEE n small North American songbird

CHICKAREE n American red squirrel

CHICKEE n open-sided, thatched building on stilts

CHICKEES > CHICKEE

CHICKEN n domestic fowl ⊳ adj cowardly ⊳ vb lose one's nerve

CHICKENED > CHICKEN

CHICKENS > CHICKEN

CHICKLING n small chick

CHICKORY same as > CHICORY

CHICKPEA n edible yellow pealike seed

CHICKPEAS > CHICKPEA

CHICKS > CHICK

CHICKWEED n weed with small white flowers

CHICLE n gumlike substance obtained from the sapodilla

CHICLES > CHICLE

CHICLY > CHIC

CHICNESS > CHIC

CHICO n spiny chenopodiaceous shrub

CHICON same as > CHICORY

CHICONS > CHICON

CHICORIES > CHICORY

CHICORY n plant whose leaves are used in salads

CHICOS > CHICO

CHICOT n dead tree

CHICOTS > CHICOT

CHICS > CHIC

CHID > CHIDE

CHIDDEN > CHIDE

CHIDE vb rebuke, scold

CHIDED > CHIDE

CHIDER > CHIDE

CHIDERS > CHIDE

CHIDES > CHIDE

CHIDING > CHIDE

CHIDINGLY > CHIDE

CHIDINGS > CHIDE

CHIDLINGS n intestines of a pig prepared as a dish

CHIEF n head of a group of people ⊳ adj most important

CHIEFDOM n any tribal social group led by a chief

CHIEFDOMS > CHIEFDOM

CHIEFER > CHIEF

CHIEFERY n lands belonging to a chief

CHIEFESS n female chief

CHIEFEST > CHIEF

CHIEFLESS adj lacking a chief

CHIEFLING n petty chief

CHIEFLY adv especially ⊳ adj of or relating to a chief or chieftain

CHIEFRIES > CHIEFRY

CHIEFRY same as > CHIEFERY

CHIEFS > CHIEF

CHIEFSHIP n state of being a chief

CHIEFTAIN n leader of a tribe

CHIEL n young man

CHIELD same as > CHIEL

CHIELDS > CHIELD

CHIELS > CHIEL

CHIFFON n fine see-through fabric ⊳ adj made of chiffon

CHIFFONS > CHIFFON

CHIFFONY adj like chiffon

CHIGETAI n variety of the Asiatic wild ass of Mongolia

CHIGETAIS > CHIGETAI

CHIGGA n derogatory word for a young working-class Tasmanian

CHIGGAS > CHIGGA

CHIGGER n parasitic larva of various mites

CHIGGERS > CHIGGER

CHIGNON n knot of hair pinned up at the back of the head ⊳ vb make a chignon

CHIGNONED > CHIGNON

CHIGNONS > CHIGNON

CHIGOE same as > CHIGGER

CHIGOES > CHIGOE

CHIGRE same as > CHIGGER

CHIGRES > CHIGRE

CHIHUAHUA n tiny short-haired dog

CHIK n slatted blind

CHIKARA n Indian seven-stringed musical instrument

CHIKARAS > CHIKARA

CHIKHOR same as > CHUKAR

CHIKHORS > CHIKHOR

CHIKOR same as > CHUKAR

CHIKORS > CHIKOR

CHIKS > CHIK

CHILBLAIN n inflammation of the fingers or toes, caused by exposure to cold

CHILD n young human being ⊳ vb give birth

CHILDBED n condition of giving birth to a child

CHILDBEDS > CHILDBED

CHILDCARE n care provided for children without homes (or with a seriously disturbed home life) by a local authority

CHILDE n young man of noble birth

CHILDED > CHILD

CHILDER dialect variant of > CHILDREN

CHILDES > CHILDE

CHILDHOOD n time or condition of being a child

CHILDING > CHILD

CHILDISH adj immature, silly

CHILDLESS > CHILD

CHILDLIER > CHILD

CHILDLIKE adj innocent, trustful

CHILDLY > CHILD

CHILDNESS n nature of a child

CHILDREN > CHILD

CHILDS > CHILD

CHILE variant spelling of > CHILLI

CHILES > CHILE

CHILI same as > CHILLI

CHILIAD n group of one thousand

CHILIADAL > CHILIAD

CHILIADIC > CHILIAD

CHILIADS > CHILIAD

CHILIAGON n thousand-sided polygon

CHILIARCH n commander of a thousand men

CHILIASM n belief in the Second Coming of Christ

CHILIASMS > CHILIASM

CHILIAST > CHILIASM

CHILIASTS > CHILIASM

CHILIDOG n hot dog served with chilli sauce

CHILIDOGS > CHILIDOG

CHILIES > CHILI

CHILIS > CHILI

CHILL n feverish cold ⊳ vb make (something) cool or cold ⊳ adj unpleasantly cold

CHILLADA n spicy Mexican dish made of fried vegetables and pulses

CHILLADAS > CHILLADA

CHILLAX vb take rest or recreation, as from work

CHILLAXED > CHILLAX

CHILLAXES > CHILLAX

CHILLED > CHILL

CHILLER n cooling or refrigerating device

CHILLERS > CHILLER

CHILLEST > CHILL

CHILLI n small red or green hot-tasting capsicum pod, used in cooking

CHILLIER > CHILLY

CHILLIES > CHILLI

CHILLIEST > CHILLY

CHILLILY > CHILLY

CHILLING > CHILL

CHILLINGS > CHILL

CHILLIS > CHILLI

CHILLNESS > CHILL

CHILLS > CHILL

CHILLUM n short pipe used for smoking

CHILLUMS > CHILLUM

CHILLY adj moderately cold

CHILOPOD n type of arthropod of the class which includes the centipedes

CHILOPODS > CHILOPOD

CHILTEPIN n variety of chilli pepper

CHIMAERA same as > CHIMERA

CHIMAERAS > CHIMAERA

CHIMAERIC > CHIMAERA

CHIMAR same as > CHIMERE

CHIMARS > CHIMAR

CHIMB same as > CHIME

CHIMBLEY same as > CHIMNEY

CHIMBLEYS > CHIMBLEY

CHIMBLIES > CHIMBLY

CHIMBLY same as > CHIMNEY

CHIMBS > CHIMB

CHIME n musical ringing sound of a bell or clock ⊳ vb make a musical ringing sound

CHIMED > CHIME

CHIMENEA n freestanding outdoor fireplace

CHIMENEAS > CHIMENEA

CHIMER > CHIME

CHIMERA n unrealistic hope or idea

CHIMERAS > CHIMERA

CHIMERE n gown worn by bishops

CHIMERES > CHIMERE

CHIMERIC same as > CHIMERA

CHIMERID n fish of the genus Chimaera

CHIMERIDS > CHIMERID

CHIMERISM n medical condition in which a person possesses two genetically distinct sets of cells

CHIMERS > CHIME

CHIMES > CHIME

CHIMINEA n free-standing outdoor fireplace with a rounded body

CHIMINEAS > CHIMINEA

CHIMING > CHIME

CHIMLA same as > CHIMNEY

CHIMLAS > CHIMLA

CHIMLEY same as > CHIMNEY

CHIMLEYS > CHIMLEY

CHIMNEY n hollow vertical structure for carrying away smoke from a fire ⊳ vb climb two vertical, parallel, chimney-like rock faces

CHIMNEYED > CHIMNEY

CHIMNEYS > CHIMNEY
CHIMO *interj* Inuit greeting and toast
CHIMP *n* chimpanzee
CHIMPS > CHIMP
CHIN *n* part of the face below the mouth ▷ *vb* hit someone in the chin
CHINA *n* fine earthenware or porcelain
CHINAMAN *n* type of ball bowled in cricket
CHINAMEN > CHINAMAN
CHINAMPA *n* in Mesoamerican agriculture, an artificially created island used for growing crops
CHINAMPAS > CHINAMPA
CHINAR *same as* **>** CHENAR
CHINAROOT *n* bristly greenbrier
CHINARS > CHINAR
CHINAS > CHINA
CHINAWARE *n* articles made of china, esp those made for domestic use
CHINBONE *n* front part of the mandible which forms the chin
CHINBONES > CHINBONE
CHINCAPIN *n* dwarf chestnut tree
CHINCH *n* (S US) bedbug ▷ *vb* be frugal or miserly
CHINCHED > CHINCH
CHINCHES > CHINCH
CHINCHIER > CHINCHY
CHINCHING > CHINCH
CHINCHY *adj* tightfisted
CHINCOUGH *n* whooping cough
CHINDIT *n* Allied soldier fighting behind the Japanese lines in Burma during World War II
CHINDITS > CHINDIT
CHINE *same as* **>** CHIME
CHINED > CHINE
CHINES > CHINE
CHINESE *adj* of or relating to China
CHING *n* high-pitched ring or chime
CHINGS > CHING
CHINING > CHINE
CHINK *n* small narrow opening ▷ *vb* make a light ringing sound
CHINKAPIN *same as* **>** CHINCAPIN
CHINKARA *n* Indian gazelle
CHINKARAS > CHINKARA
CHINKED > CHINK
CHINKIER > CHINKY
CHINKIEST > CHINKY
CHINKING > CHINK
CHINKS > CHINK
CHINKY *adj* making a light ringing sound
CHINLESS *adj* having a receding chin
CHINNED > CHIN

CHINNING > CHIN
CHINO *n* durable cotton twill cloth
CHINOIS *n* conical sieve
CHINOISES > CHINOIS
CHINONE *n* benzoquinone
CHINONES > CHINONE
CHINOOK *n* wind found in the Rocky Mountains
CHINOOKS > CHINOOK
CHINOS *pl n* trousers made of a kind of hard-wearing cotton
CHINOVNIK *n* Russian official or bureaucrat
CHINS > CHIN
CHINSE *vb* fill the seams of a boat
CHINSED > CHINSE
CHINSES > CHINSE
CHINSING > CHINSE
CHINSTRAP *n* strap on a helmet which fastens under the chin
CHINTS *obsolete variant of* **>** CHINTZ
CHINTSES > CHINTS
CHINTZ *n* printed cotton fabric with a glazed finish
CHINTZES > CHINTZ
CHINTZIER > CHINTZY
CHINTZILY *adv* gaudily
CHINTZY *adj* of or covered with chintz
CHINWAG *n* chat
CHINWAGS > CHINWAG
CHIP *n* strip of potato, fried in deep fat ▷ *vb* break small pieces from
CHIPBOARD *n* thin board made of compressed wood particles
CHIPMAKER *n* maker of microchips
CHIPMUCK *another word for* **>** CHIPMUNK
CHIPMUCKS > CHIPMUCK
CHIPMUNK *n* small squirrel-like N American rodent with a striped back
CHIPMUNKS > CHIPMUNK
CHIPOCHIA *same as* **>** CAPOCCHIA
CHIPOLATA *n* small sausage
CHIPOTLE *n* dried chilli pepper
CHIPOTLES > CHIPOTLE
CHIPPABLE > CHIP
CHIPPED > CHIP
CHIPPER *vb* chirp or chatter ▷ *adj* cheerful, lively
CHIPPERED > CHIPPER
CHIPPERER > CHIPPER
CHIPPERS > CHIPPER
CHIPPIE *same as* **>** CHIPPY
CHIPPIER > CHIPPY
CHIPPIES > CHIPPY
CHIPPIEST > CHIPPY
CHIPPING > CHIP
CHIPPINGS > CHIP

CHIPPY *n* fish-and-chip shop ▷ *adj* resentful or oversensitive about being perceived as inferior
CHIPS > CHIP
CHIPSET *n* highly integrated circuit on the motherboard of a computer
CHIPSETS > CHIPSET
CHIRAGRA *n* gout occurring in the hands
CHIRAGRAS > CHIRAGRA
CHIRAGRIC > CHIRAGRA
CHIRAL > CHIRALITY
CHIRALITY *n* configuration or handedness (left or right) of an asymmetric, optically active chemical compound
CHIRIMOYA *same as* **>** CHERIMOYA
CHIRK *vb* creak, like a door ▷ *adj* high-spirited
CHIRKED > CHIRK
CHIRKER > CHIRK
CHIRKEST > CHIRK
CHIRKING > CHIRK
CHIRKS > CHIRK
CHIRL *vb* warble
CHIRLED > CHIRL
CHIRLING > CHIRL
CHIRLS > CHIRL
CHIRM *n* chirping of birds ▷ *vb* (esp of a bird) to chirp
CHIRMED > CHIRM
CHIRMING > CHIRM
CHIRMS > CHIRM
CHIRO *n* informal name for chiropractor
CHIROLOGY *n* palmistry
CHIRONOMY *n* art of hand movement in oratory or theatrical performance
CHIROPODY *n* treatment of the feet, esp the treatment of corns, verrucas, etc
CHIROPTER *n* type of bat
CHIROS > CHIRO
CHIRP *vb* (of a bird or insect) make a short high-pitched sound ▷ *n* chirping sound
CHIRPED > CHIRP
CHIRPER > CHIRP
CHIRPERS > CHIRP
CHIRPIER > CHIRPY
CHIRPIEST > CHIRPY
CHIRPILY > CHIRPY
CHIRPING *n* act of chirping
CHIRPINGS > CHIRPING
CHIRPS > CHIRP
CHIRPY *adj* lively and cheerful
CHIRR *vb* (esp of certain insects, such as crickets) to make a shrill trilled sound ▷ *n* sound of chirring
CHIRRE *same as* **>** CHIRR
CHIRRED > CHIRR

CHIRREN *pl n* dialect form of children
CHIRRES > CHIRRE
CHIRRING > CHIRR
CHIRRS > CHIRR
CHIRRUP *vb* (of some birds) to chirp repeatedly ▷ *n* chirruping sound
CHIRRUPED > CHIRRUP
CHIRRUPER > CHIRRUP
CHIRRUPS > CHIRRUP
CHIRRUPY *adj* making chirping sounds
CHIRT *vb* squirt
CHIRTED > CHIRT
CHIRTING > CHIRT
CHIRTS > CHIRT
CHIRU *n* Tibetan antelope
CHIRUS > CHIRU
CHIS > CHI
CHISEL *n* metal tool with a sharp end for shaping wood or stone ▷ *vb* carve or form with a chisel
CHISELED *same as* **>** CHISELLED
CHISELER > CHISEL
CHISELERS > CHISEL
CHISELING > CHISEL
CHISELLED *adj* finely or sharply formed
CHISELLER *n* person who uses a chisel
CHISELS > CHISEL
CHIT *n* short official note, such as a receipt ▷ *vb* sprout
CHITAL *n* type of deer
CHITALS > CHITAL
CHITCHAT *n* chat, gossip ▷ *vb* gossip
CHITCHATS > CHITCHAT
CHITIN *n* outer layer of the bodies of arthropods
CHITINOID > CHITIN
CHITINOUS > CHITIN
CHITINS > CHITIN
CHITLIN *n* pig intestine cooked and served as a dish
CHITLING > CHITLINGS
CHITLINGS *same as* **>** CHIDLINGS
CHITLINS > CHITLIN
CHITON *n* (in ancient Greece and Rome) a loose woollen tunic
CHITONS > CHITON
CHITOSAN *n* polysaccharide derived from chitin
CHITOSANS > CHITOSAN
CHITS > CHIT
CHITTED > CHIT
CHITTER *vb* twitter or chirp
CHITTERED > CHITTER
CHITTERS > CHITTER
CHITTIER > CHITTY
CHITTIES > CHITTY
CHITTIEST > CHIT
CHITTING > CHIT
CHITTY *adj* childish ▷ *vb* sprout
CHIV *n* knife ▷ *vb* stab (someone)

CHIVALRIC
> CHIVALRY

CHIVALRY n courteous behaviour, esp by men towards women

CHIVAREE n charivari
▷ vb perform a chivaree

CHIVAREED
> CHIVAREE

CHIVAREES
> CHIVAREE

CHIVARI same as
> CHARIVARI

CHIVARIED > CHIVARI

CHIVARIES > CHIVARI

CHIVE n small Eurasian plant ▷ vb file or cut off

CHIVED > CHIVE

CHIVES same as > CHIVE

CHIVIED > CHIVY

CHIVIES > CHIVY

CHIVING > CHIVE

CHIVS > CHIV

CHIVVED > CHIV

CHIVVIED > CHIVVY

CHIVVIES > CHIVVY

CHIVVING > CHIV

CHIVVY same as > CHIVY

CHIVVYING > CHIVVY

CHIVY vb harass or nag
▷ n hunt

CHIVYING > CHIVY

CHIWEENIE n cross between a chihuahua and a dachshund

CHIYOGAMI n type of highly decorated Japanese craft paper

CHIZ n cheat ▷ vb cheat

CHIZZ same as > CHIZ

CHIZZED > CHIZ

CHIZZES > CHIZ

CHIZZING > CHIZ

CHLAMYDES > CHLAMYS

CHLAMYDIA n type of bacteria

CHLAMYS n woollen cloak worn by ancient Greek soldiers

CHLAMYSES > CHLAMYS

CHLOASMA n patches of darker colour on a person's skin

CHLOASMAS
> CHLOASMA

CHLORACNE n disfiguring skin disease that results from contact with or ingestion or inhalation of certain chlorinated aromatic hydrocarbons

CHLORAL n colourless oily liquid with a pungent odour

CHLORALS > CHLORAL

CHLORATE n type of chemical salt

CHLORATES
> CHLORATE

CHLORDAN same as
> CHLORDANE

CHLORDANE n white insoluble toxic solid

CHLORDANS
> CHLORDAN

CHLORELLA n type of microscopic unicellular green alga, some species

of which are used in the preparation of human food

CHLORIC adj of or containing chlorine in the pentavalent state

CHLORID n type of chlorine compound

CHLORIDE n compound of chlorine and another substance

CHLORIDES
> CHLORIDE

CHLORIDIC
> CHLORIDE

CHLORIDS > CHLORID

CHLORIN same as
> CHLORINE

CHLORINE n strong-smelling greenish-yellow gaseous element, used to disinfect water

CHLORINES
> CHLORINE

CHLORINS > CHLORIN

CHLORITE n any of a group of green soft secondary minerals

CHLORITES
> CHLORITE

CHLORITIC
> CHLORITE

CHLOROSES
> CHLOROSIS

CHLOROSIS n disorder characterized by pale greenish-yellow skin, caused by insufficient iron in the body

CHLOROTIC
> CHLOROSIS

CHLOROUS adj of or containing chlorine in the trivalent state

CHOANA n posterior nasal aperture

CHOANAE > CHOANA

CHOBDAR n in India and Nepal, king's macebearer or attendant

CHOBDARS > CHOBDAR

CHOC short form of
> CHOCOLATE

CHOCCIER > CHOCCY

CHOCCIES > CHOCCY

CHOCCIEST > CHOCCY

CHOCCY n chocolate ▷ adj made of, tasting of, smelling of, or resembling chocolate

CHOCHO same as
> CHAYOTE

CHOCHOS > CHOCHO

CHOCK n block or wedge used to prevent a heavy object from moving ▷ vb secure by a chock ▷ adv as closely or tightly as possible

CHOCKED > CHOCK

CHOCKER adj full up

CHOCKERS adj Australian term meaning full up, packed

CHOCKFUL adj filled to capacity

CHOCKFULL variant of
> CHOCKFUL

CHOCKIE n chocolate
▷ adj like chocolate

CHOCKIER > CHOCKIE

CHOCKIES > CHOCKIE

CHOCKIEST > CHOCKIE

CHOCKING > CHOCK

CHOCKO same as > CHOCO

CHOCKOS > CHOCKO

CHOCKS > CHOCK

CHOCKY n chocolate ▷ adj like chocolate

CHOCO n member of the Australian army

CHOCOLATE n sweet food made from cacao seeds ▷ adj dark brown

CHOCOLATY
> CHOCOLATE

CHOCOS > CHOCO

CHOCS > CHOC

CHOCTAW n movement in ice-skating

CHOCTAWS > CHOCTAW

CHODE > CHIDE

CHOENIX same as
> CHENIX

CHOENIXES > CHOENIX

CHOG n core of a piece of fruit

CHOGS > CHOG

CHOICE n choosing ▷ adj of high quality

CHOICEFUL adj fickle

CHOICELY > CHOICE

CHOICER > CHOICE

CHOICES > CHOICE

CHOICEST > CHOICE

CHOIL n end of a knife blade next to the handle

CHOILS > CHOIL

CHOIR n organized group of singers, esp in church
▷ vb sing in chorus

CHOIRBOY n boy who sings in a church choir

CHOIRBOYS > CHOIRBOY

CHOIRED > CHOIR

CHOIRGIRL n girl who sings in a choir

CHOIRING > CHOIR

CHOIRLIKE > CHOIR

CHOIRMAN n man who sings in a choir

CHOIRMEN > CHOIRMAN

CHOIRS > CHOIR

CHOKE vb hinder or stop the breathing of (a person) by strangling or smothering ▷ n device found in a petrol engine

CHOKEABLE > CHOKE

CHOKEBORE n shotgun bore that becomes narrower towards the muzzle so that the shot is not scattered

CHOKECOIL n type of electronic inductor

CHOKED adj disappointed or angry

CHOKEDAMP another word for > BLACKDAMP

CHOKEHOLD n act of holding a person's neck across the windpipe, esp from behind

CHOKER n tight-fitting necklace

CHOKERMAN n person who attaches cables to logs

CHOKERMEN
> CHOKERMAN

CHOKERS > CHOKER

CHOKES > CHOKE

CHOKEY n slang word for prison ▷ adj involving, caused by, or causing choking

CHOKEYS > CHOKEY

CHOKIDAR n in India, a gatekeeper

CHOKIDARS
> CHOKIDAR

CHOKIER > CHOKEY

CHOKIES > CHOKY

CHOKIEST > CHOKEY

CHOKING > CHOKE

CHOKINGLY > CHOKE

CHOKO n pear-shaped fruit of a tropical American vine, eaten as a vegetable

CHOKOS > CHOKO

CHOKRA n in India, a boy or young man

CHOKRAS > CHOKRA

CHOKRI n in India, a girl or young woman

CHOKRIS > CHOKRI

CHOKY same as > CHOKEY

CHOLA n long, loose Sikh robe

CHOLAEMIA n toxic medical condition indicated by the presence of bile in the blood

CHOLAEMIC
> CHOLAEMIA

CHOLAS > CHOLA

CHOLATE n salt of cholic acid

CHOLATES > CHOLATE

CHOLECYST n gall bladder

CHOLELITH n gallstone

CHOLEMIA same as
> CHOLAEMIA

CHOLEMIAS
> CHOLEMIA

CHOLENT n meal prepared on Friday and left to cook until eaten for Sabbath lunch

CHOLENTS > CHOLENT

CHOLER n bad temper

CHOLERA n serious infectious disease

CHOLERAIC > CHOLERA

CHOLERAS > CHOLERA

CHOLERIC adj bad-tempered

CHOLEROID > CHOLERA

CHOLERS > CHOLER

CHOLI n short-sleeved bodice, as worn by Indian women

CHOLIAMB n imperfect iambic trimeter, with a spondee as the last foot

CHOLIAMBS
> CHOLIAMB

CHOLIC adj as in cholic acid crystalline acid found in bile

CHOLINE n colourless viscous soluble alkaline

substance present in animal tissues
CHOLINES > CHOLINE
CHOLIS > CHOLI
CHOLLA n type of spiny cactus
CHOLLAS > CHOLLA
CHOLLERS pl n jowls or cheeks
CHOLTRIES > CHOLTRY
CHOLTRY n caravanserai
CHOMETZ same as **>** CHAMETZ
CHOMETZES > CHOMETZ
CHOMMIE n (in informal South African English) friend
CHOMMIES > CHOMMIE
CHOMP vb chew noisily ▷ n act or sound of chewing in this manner
CHOMPED > CHOMP
CHOMPER > CHOMP
CHOMPERS > CHOMP
CHOMPING > CHOMP
CHOMPS > CHOMP
CHON n North and South Korean monetary unit
CHONDRAL adj of or relating to cartilage
CHONDRE another word for **>** CHONDRULE
CHONDRES > CHONDRE
CHONDRI > CHONDRUS
CHONDRIFY vb become or convert into cartilage
CHONDRIN n resilient translucent bluish-white substance that forms the matrix of cartilage
CHONDRINS > CHONDRIN
CHONDRITE n stony meteorite consisting mainly of silicate minerals in the form of chondrules
CHONDROID adj resembling cartilage
CHONDROMA n benign cartilaginous growth or neoplasm
CHONDRULE n one of the small spherical masses of mainly silicate minerals present in chondrites
CHONDRUS n cartilage
CHONS > CHON
CHOOF vb go away
CHOOFED > CHOOF
CHOOFING > CHOOF
CHOOFS > CHOOF
CHOOK n hen or chicken ▷ vb make the sound of a hen of chicken
CHOOKED > CHOOK
CHOOKIE same as **>** CHOOK
CHOOKIES > CHOOKIE
CHOOKING > CHOOK
CHOOKS > CHOOK
CHOOM n Englishman
CHOOMS > CHOOM
CHOON n slang term for music that one likes
CHOONS > CHOON
CHOOSE vb select from a number of alternatives
CHOOSER > CHOOSE

CHOOSERS > CHOOSE
CHOOSES > CHOOSE
CHOOSEY same as **>** CHOOSY
CHOOSIER > CHOOSY
CHOOSIEST > CHOOSY
CHOOSILY adv in a fussy or choosy way
CHOOSING > CHOOSE
CHOOSY adj fussy, hard to please
CHOP vb cut with a blow from an axe or knife ▷ n cutting or sharp blow
CHOPHOUSE n restaurant specializing in steaks, grills, chops, etc
CHOPIN same as **>** CHOPINE
CHOPINE n sandal-like shoe popular in the 18th century
CHOPINES > CHOPINE
CHOPINS > CHOPIN
CHOPLOGIC n person who uses excessively subtle or involved logic
CHOPPED > CHOP
CHOPPER n helicopter ▷ vb travel by helicopter
CHOPPERED > CHOPPER
CHOPPERS > CHOPPER
CHOPPIER > CHOPPY
CHOPPIEST > CHOPPY
CHOPPILY > CHOPPY
CHOPPING > CHOP
CHOPPINGS > CHOP
CHOPPY adj (of the sea) fairly rough
CHOPS > CHOP
CHOPSOCKY n genre of martial arts film
CHOPSTICK n one of a pair of thin sticks used as eating utensils
CHORAGI > CHORAGUS
CHORAGIC > CHORAGUS
CHORAGUS n leader of a chorus
CHORAL adj of a choir ▷ n slow stately hymn tune
CHORALE n slow stately hymn tune
CHORALES > CHORALE
CHORALIST n singer or composer of chorals
CHORALLY > CHORAL
CHORALS > CHORAL
CHORD n straight line joining two points on a curve ▷ vb provide (a melodic line) with chords
CHORDA n in anatomy, a cord
CHORDAE > CHORDA
CHORDAL > CHORD
CHORDATE n type of animal which includes the vertebrates
CHORDATES > CHORDATE
CHORDED > CHORD
CHORDEE n unusual bending downwards of the penis
CHORDEES > CHORDEE
CHORDING n distribution of chords throughout a piece of harmony

CHORDINGS > CHORDING
CHORDLIKE adj like a chord
CHORDS > CHORD
CHORDWISE adv in the direction of an aerofoil chord ▷ adj moving in this direction
CHORE n routine task ▷ vb carry out chores
CHOREA n disorder of the nervous system
CHOREAL > CHOREA
CHOREAS > CHOREA
CHOREATIC > CHOREA
CHOREBOY n boy who does chores
CHOREBOYS > CHOREBOY
CHORED > CHORE
CHOREE n trochee
CHOREES > CHOREE
CHOREGI > CHOREGUS
CHOREGIC > CHOREGUS
CHOREGUS n in ancient Greece, the producer and financier of a dramatist's works
CHOREIC > CHOREA
CHOREMAN n handyman
CHOREMEN > CHOREMAN
CHOREOID adj resembling chorea
CHORES > CHORE
CHOREUS same as **>** CHOREE
CHOREUSES > CHOREUS
CHORIA > CHORION
CHORIAL > CHORION
CHORIAMB n metrical foot used in classical verse
CHORIAMBI > CHORIAMB
CHORIAMBS > CHORIAMB
CHORIC adj in the manner of a chorus
CHORINE n young woman in a chorus line
CHORINES > CHORINE
CHORING > CHORE
CHORIOID same as **>** CHOROID
CHORIOIDS > CHORIOID
CHORION n outer membrane forming a sac around an embryo
CHORIONIC > CHORION
CHORIONS > CHORION
CHORISES > CHORISIS
CHORISIS n multiplication of leaves etc by branching or splitting
CHORISM > CHORISIS
CHORISMS > CHORISIS
CHORIST n choir member
CHORISTER n singer in a choir
CHORISTS > CHORIST
CHORIZO n kind of highly seasoned pork sausage of Spain or Mexico
CHORIZONT n person who challenges the authorship of a work

CHORIZOS > CHORIZO
CHOROID adj resembling the chorion, esp in being vascular ▷ n vascular membrane of the eyeball
CHOROIDAL > CHOROID
CHOROIDS > CHOROID
CHOROLOGY n study of the causal relations between geographical phenomena occurring within a particular region
CHORRIE n dilapidated old car
CHORRIES > CHORRIE
CHORTEN n Buddhist shrine
CHORTENS > CHORTEN
CHORTLE vb chuckle in amusement ▷ n amused chuckle
CHORTLED > CHORTLE
CHORTLER > CHORTLE
CHORTLERS > CHORTLE
CHORTLES > CHORTLE
CHORTLING > CHORTLE
CHORUS n large choir ▷ vb sing or say together
CHORUSED > CHORUS
CHORUSES > CHORUS
CHORUSING > CHORUS
CHORUSSED > CHORUS
CHORUSSES > CHORUS
CHOSE n item of property
CHOSEN > CHOOSE
CHOSES > CHOSE
CHOTA adj (in British Empire Indian usage) small
CHOTT variant spelling of **>** SHOTT
CHOTTS > CHOTT
CHOU n type of cabbage
CHOUGH n large black Eurasian and N African bird of the crow family
CHOUGHS > CHOUGH
CHOULTRY same as **>** CHOLTRY
CHOUNTER same as **>** CHUNTER
CHOUNTERS > CHOUNTER
CHOUSE vb cheat
CHOUSED > CHOUSE
CHOUSER > CHOUSE
CHOUSERS > CHOUSE
CHOUSES > CHOUSE
CHOUSH n Turkish messenger
CHOUSHES > CHOUSH
CHOUSING > CHOUSE
CHOUT n blackmail
CHOUTS > CHOUT
CHOUX > CHOU
CHOW n thick-coated dog with a curled tail, orig from China ▷ vb eat
CHOWCHOW same as **>** CHOW
CHOWCHOWS > CHOWCHOW
CHOWDER n thick soup containing clams or fish ▷ vb make a chowder of
CHOWDERED > CHOWDER
CHOWDERS > CHOWDER

CHOWDOWN n act of eating a lot of food

CHOWDOWNS > CHOWDOWN

CHOWED > CHOW

CHOWHOUND n person who loves eating

CHOWING > CHOW

CHOWK n marketplace or market area

CHOWKIDAR same as > CHOKIDAR

CHOWKS > CHOWK

CHOWRI n fly-whisk

CHOWRIES > CHOWRI

CHOWRIS > CHOWRI

CHOWRY same as > CHOWRI

CHOWS > CHOW

CHOWSE same as > CHOUSE

CHOWSED > CHOWSE

CHOWSES > CHOWSE

CHOWSING > CHOWSE

CHOWTIME n mealtime

CHOWTIMES > CHOWTIME

CHRESARD n amount of water present in the soil that is available to plants

CHRESARDS > CHRESARD

CHRISM n consecrated oil used for anointing in some churches

CHRISMA > CHRISMON

CHRISMAL n chrism container

CHRISMALS > CHRISMAL

CHRISMON n monogram and symbol of Christ's name

CHRISMONS > CHRISMON

CHRISMS > CHRISM

CHRISOM same as > CHRISM

CHRISOMS > CHRISOM

CHRISTEN vb baptize

CHRISTENS > CHRISTEN

CHRISTIAN adj exhibiting kindness or goodness

CHRISTIE same as > CHRISTY

CHRISTIES > CHRISTIE

CHRISTOM same as > CHRISOM

CHRISTOMS > CHRISTOM

CHRISTY n skiing turn for stopping or changing direction quickly

CHROMA n attribute of a colour

CHROMAKEY n (in colour television) a special effect in which a coloured background can be eliminated and a different background substituted

CHROMAS > CHROMA

CHROMATE n any salt or ester of chromic acid

CHROMATES > CHROMATE

CHROMATIC adj of colour or colours

CHROMATID n either of the two strands into which a chromosome divides during mitosis. They separate to form daughter chromosomes at anaphase

CHROMATIN n part of the nucleus of a cell that forms the chromosomes and can easily be dyed

CHROME n anything plated with chromium ▷ vb plate with chromium ▷ adj of or having the appearance of chrome

CHROMED > CHROME

CHROMEL n nickel-based alloy

CHROMELS > CHROMEL

CHROMENE n chemical compound

CHROMENES > CHROMENE

CHROMES > CHROME

CHROMIC adj of or containing chromium in the trivalent state

CHROMIDE n any member of the cichlid family of fish

CHROMIDES > CHROMIDE

CHROMIDIA n chromatins in cell cytoplasm

CHROMIER > CHROME

CHROMIEST > CHROMY

CHROMING > CHROME

CHROMINGS > CHROME

CHROMISE same as > CHROMIZE

CHROMISED > CHROMISE

CHROMISES > CHROMISE

CHROMITE n brownish-black mineral which is the only commercial source of chromium

CHROMITES > CHROMITE

CHROMIUM n grey metallic element used in steel alloys and for electroplating

CHROMIUMS > CHROMIUM

CHROMIZE vb chrome-plate

CHROMIZED > CHROMIZE

CHROMIZES > CHROMIZE

CHROMO n picture produced by lithography

CHROMOGEN n compound that forms coloured compounds on oxidation

CHROMOLY n type of steel alloy

CHROMOLYS > CHROMOLY

CHROMOS > CHROMO

CHROMOUS adj of or containing chromium in the divalent state

CHROMY > CHROME

CHROMYL n type of divalent radical

CHROMYLS > CHROMYL

CHRONAXIE n minimum time required for excitation of a nerve or muscle when the stimulus is double the minimum (threshold) necessary to elicit a basic response

CHRONAXY same as > CHRONAXIE

CHRONIC adj (of an illness) lasting a long time ▷ n chronically ill patient

CHRONICAL > CHRONIC

CHRONICLE n record of events in order of occurrence ▷ vb record in or as if in a chronicle

CHRONICS > CHRONIC

CHRONON n unit of time

CHRONONS > CHRONON

CHRYSALID adj of or relating to a chrysalis

CHRYSALIS n insect in the stage between larva and adult, when it is in a cocoon

CHRYSANTH n chrysanthemum

CHTHONIAN adj of or relating to the underworld

CHTHONIC same as > CHTHONIAN

CHUB n European freshwater fish of the carp family

CHUBASCO n in Mexico, a hurricane

CHUBASCOS > CHUBASCO

CHUBBIER > CHUBBY

CHUBBIEST > CHUBBY

CHUBBILY > CHUBBY

CHUBBY adj plump and round

CHUBS > CHUB

CHUCK vb throw ▷ n cut of beef from the neck to the shoulder

CHUCKED > CHUCK

CHUCKER n person who throws something

CHUCKERS > CHUCKER

CHUCKHOLE n pothole

CHUCKIE n small stone

CHUCKIES > CHUCKIE

CHUCKING > CHUCK

CHUCKLE vb laugh softly ▷ n soft laugh

CHUCKLED > CHUCKLE

CHUCKLER > CHUCKLE

CHUCKLERS > CHUCKLE

CHUCKLES > CHUCKLE

CHUCKLING > CHUCKLE

CHUCKS > CHUCK

CHUCKY same as > CHUCKIE

CHUDDAH same as > CHUDDAR

CHUDDAHS > CHUDDAH

CHUDDAR n large shawl or veil

CHUDDARS > CHUDDAR

CHUDDER same as > CHUDDAR

CHUDDERS > CHUDDER

CHUDDIES pl n underpants

CHUDDY n chewing gum

CHUFA n type of sedge

CHUFAS > CHUFA

CHUFF vb (of a steam engine) move while making a puffing sound ▷ n puffing sound of or as if of a steam engine ▷ adj boorish

CHUFFED adj very pleased

CHUFFER > CHUFF

CHUFFEST > CHUFF

CHUFFIER > CHUFFY

CHUFFIEST > CHUFFY

CHUFFING > CHUFF

CHUFFS > CHUFF

CHUFFY adj boorish and surly

CHUG n short dull sound like the noise of an engine ▷ vb operate or move with this sound

CHUGALUG vb gulp down a drink in one go

CHUGALUGS > CHUGALUG

CHUGGED > CHUG

CHUGGER > CHUG

CHUGGERS > CHUG

CHUGGING n act of drinking a liquid quickly

CHUGGINGS > CHUGGING

CHUGS > CHUG

CHUKAR n common Indian partridge

CHUKARS > CHUKAR

CHUKKA n period of play in polo

CHUKKAR same as > CHUKKA

CHUKKARS > CHUKKAR

CHUKKAS > CHUKKA

CHUKKER same as > CHUKKA

CHUKKERS > CHUKKER

CHUKOR same as > CHUKAR

CHUKORS > CHUKOR

CHUM n close friend ▷ vb be or become an intimate friend (of)

CHUMASH n printed book containing one of the Five Books of Moses

CHUMASHES > CHUMASH

CHUMASHIM > CHUMASH

CHUMLEY same as > CHIMNEY

CHUMLEYS > CHUMLEY

CHUMMAGE n formerly, fee paid by a prisoner for sole occupancy of a cell

CHUMMAGES > CHUMMAGE

CHUMMED > CHUM

CHUMMIER > CHUMMY

CHUMMIES > CHUMMY

CHUMMIEST > CHUMMY

CHUMMILY > CHUMMY

CHUMMING > CHUM

CHUMMY adj friendly ▷ n chum

CHUMP n stupid person ▷ vb chew noisily

CHUMPED > CHUMP
CHUMPING n collecting wood for bonfires on Guy Fawkes Day
CHUMPINGS > CHUMPING
CHUMPS > CHUMP
CHUMS > CHUM
CHUMSHIP n friendship
CHUMSHIPS > CHUMSHIP
CHUNDER vb slang word for vomit
CHUNDERED > CHUNDER
CHUNDERS > CHUNDER
CHUNK n thick solid piece ▷ vb break up into chunks
CHUNKED > CHUNK
CHUNKIER > CHUNKY
CHUNKIEST > CHUNKY
CHUNKILY > CHUNKY
CHUNKING n mnemonic technique involving grouping together of a number of items
CHUNKINGS > CHUNKING
CHUNKS > CHUNK
CHUNKY adj (of a person) broad and heavy
CHUNNEL n rail tunnel linking England and France
CHUNNELS > CHUNNEL
CHUNNER same as > CHUNTER
CHUNNERED > CHUNNER
CHUNNERS > CHUNNER
CHUNTER vb mutter or grumble incessantly in a meaningless fashion
CHUNTERED > CHUNTER
CHUNTERS > CHUNTER
CHUPATI same as > CHUPATTI
CHUPATIS > CHUPATI
CHUPATTI variant spelling of > CHAPATI
CHUPATTIS > CHUPATTI
CHUPATTY same as > CHUPATTI
CHUPPA variant of > CHUPPAH
CHUPPAH n canopy under which a marriage is performed
CHUPPAHS > CHUPPAH
CHUPPAS > CHUPPA
CHUPPOT > CHUPPAH
CHUPPOTH > CHUPPAH
CHUPRASSY same as > CHAPRASSI
CHUR interj expression of agreement
CHURCH n building for public Christian worship ▷ vb bring someone to church for special ceremonies
CHURCHED > CHURCH
CHURCHES > CHURCH
CHURCHIER > CHURCHY
CHURCHING > CHURCH
CHURCHISM n adherence to the principles of an established church

CHURCHLY adj appropriate to, associated with, or suggestive of church life and customs
CHURCHMAN n clergyman
CHURCHMEN > CHURCHMAN
CHURCHWAY n way or road that leads to a church
CHURCHY adj like a church, church service, etc
CHURIDAR n as in churidar pyjamas long tight-fitting trousers, worn by Indian men and women
CHURIDARS > CHURIDAR
CHURINGA n sacred amulet of the native Australians
CHURINGAS > CHURINGA
CHURL n surly ill-bred person
CHURLISH adj surly and rude
CHURLS > CHURL
CHURN n machine in which cream is shaken to make butter ▷ vb stir (cream) vigorously to make butter
CHURNED > CHURN
CHURNER > CHURN
CHURNERS > CHURN
CHURNING n quantity of butter churned at any one time
CHURNINGS > CHURNING
CHURNMILK n buttermilk
CHURNS > CHURN
CHURR same as > CHIRR
CHURRED > CHURR
CHURRING > CHURR
CHURRO n Spanish dough stick snack
CHURROS > CHURRO
CHURRS > CHURR
CHURRUS n hemp resin
CHURRUSES > CHURRUS
CHUSE obsolete variant of > CHOOSE
CHUSED > CHUSE
CHUSES > CHUSE
CHUSING > CHUSE
CHUT interj expression of surprise or annoyance ▷ n such an expression
CHUTE n steep slope down which things may be slid ▷ vb descend by a chute
CHUTED > CHUTE
CHUTES > CHUTE
CHUTING > CHUTE
CHUTIST > CHUTE
CHUTISTS > CHUTE
CHUTNEE same as > CHUTNEY
CHUTNEES > CHUTNEE
CHUTNEY n pickle made from fruit, vinegar, spices, and sugar
CHUTNEYS > CHUTNEY
CHUTS > CHUT
CHUTZPA same as > CHUTZPAH

CHUTZPAH n unashamed self-confidence
CHUTZPAHS > CHUTZPAH
CHUTZPAS > CHUTZPA
CHYACK same as > CHIACK
CHYACKED > CHYACK
CHYACKING > CHYACK
CHYACKS > CHYACK
CHYLDE archaic word for > CHILD
CHYLE n milky fluid formed in the small intestine during digestion
CHYLES > CHYLE
CHYLIFIED > CHYLIFY
CHYLIFIES > CHYLIFY
CHYLIFY vb be turned into chyle
CHYLOUS > CHYLE
CHYLURIA n presence of chyle in urine
CHYLURIAS > CHYLURIA
CHYME n partially digested food that leaves the stomach
CHYMES > CHYME
CHYMIC same as > CHEMIC
CHYMICS > CHYMIC
CHYMIFIED > CHYMIFY
CHYMIFIES > CHYMIFY
CHYMIFY vb form into chyme
CHYMIST same as > CHEMIST
CHYMISTRY same as > CHEMISTRY
CHYMISTS > CHYMIST
CHYMOSIN another name for > RENNIN
CHYMOSINS > CHYMOSIN
CHYMOUS > CHYME
CHYND adj chined
CHYPRE n perfume made from sandalwood
CHYPRES > CHYPRE
CHYRON n caption superimposed on a TV screen
CHYRONS > CHYRON
CHYTRID n variety of fungus
CHYTRIDS > CHYTRID
CIABATTA n type of bread made with olive oil
CIABATTAS > CIABATTA
CIABATTE > CIABATTA
CIAO an informal word for > HELLO
CIBATION n feeding
CIBATIONS > CIBATION
CIBOL same as > CHIBOL
CIBOLS > CIBOL
CIBORIA > CIBORIUM
CIBORIUM n goblet-shaped lidded vessel used to hold consecrated wafers in Holy Communion
CIBORIUMS > CIBORIUM

CIBOULE same as > CHIBOL
CIBOULES > CIBOULE
CICADA n large insect that makes a high-pitched drone
CICADAE > CICADA
CICADAS > CICADA
CICALA same as > CICADA
CICALAS > CICALA
CICALE > CICALA
CICATRICE n scar
CICATRISE same as > CICATRIZE
CICATRIX n scar
CICATRIZE vb (of a wound or defect in tissue) to close or be closed by scar formation
CICELIES > CICELY
CICELY n type of plant
CICERO n measure for type that is somewhat larger than the pica
CICERONE n person who guides and informs sightseers ▷ vb act as a cicerone
CICERONED > CICERONE
CICERONES > CICERONE
CICERONI > CICERONE
CICEROS > CICERO
CICHLID n type of tropical freshwater fish popular in aquariums
CICHLIDAE n cichlids
CICHLIDS > CICHLID
CICHLOID > CICHLID
CICINNUS n scorpioid cyme
CICISBEI > CICISBEO
CICISBEO n escort or lover of a married woman, esp in 18th-century Italy
CICISBEOS > CICISBEO
CICLATON n rich material of silk and gold
CICLATONS > CICLATON
CICLATOUN same as > CICLATON
CICOREE same as > CHICORY
CICOREES > CICOREE
CICUTA n spotted hemlock
CICUTAS > CICUTA
CICUTINE same as > CONIINE
CICUTINES > CICUTINE
CID n leader
CIDARIS n sea urchin
CIDARISES > CIDARIS
CIDE Shakespearean variant of > DECIDE
CIDED > CIDE
CIDER n alcoholic drink made from fermented apple juice
CIDERIER > CIDERY
CIDERIEST > CIDERY
CIDERKIN n weak type of cider

CIDERKINS
> CIDERKIN

CIDERS > CIDER

CIDERY adj like cider

CIDES > CIDE

CIDING > CIDE

CIDS > CID

CIEL same as > CEIL

CIELED > CIEL

CIELING same as
> CEILING

CIELINGS > CIEL

CIELS > CIEL

CIERGE same as > CERGE

CIERGES > CIERGE

CIG same as > CIGARETTE

CIGAR n roll of cured
tobacco leaves for
smoking

CIGARET same as
> CIGARETTE

CIGARETS > CIGARET

CIGARETTE n thin roll of
shredded tobacco in thin
paper, for smoking

CIGARILLO n small cigar
often only slightly larger
than a cigarette

CIGARLIKE > CIGAR

CIGARS > CIGAR

CIGGIE same as
> CIGARETTE

CIGGIES > CIGGIE

CIGGY same as
> CIGARETTE

CIGS > CIG

CIGUATERA n food
poisoning caused by a
toxin in seafood

CILANTRO same as
> CORIANDER

CILANTROS
> CILANTRO

CILIA > CILIUM

CILIARY adj of or
relating to cilia

CILIATE n type of
protozoan

CILIATED > CILIATE

CILIATELY > CILIATE

CILIATES > CILIATE

CILIATION > CILIATE

CILICE n haircloth fabric
or garment

CILICES > CILICE

CILICIOUS adj made of
hair

CILIOLATE adj covered
with minute hairs, as
some plants

CILIUM n short thread
projecting from a cell that
causes movement

CILL variant spelling (used
in the building industry) of
> SILL

CILLS > CILL

CIMAR same as > CYMAR

CIMARS > CIMAR

CIMBALOM n type of
dulcimer, esp of Hungary

CIMBALOMS
> CIMBALOM

CIMELIA pl n (especially,
ecclesiastical) treasures

CIMEX n type of
heteropterous insect, esp
the bedbug

CIMICES > CIMEX

CIMIER n crest of a
helmet

CIMIERS > CIMIER

CIMINITE n type of
igneous rock

CIMINITES
> CIMINITE

CIMMERIAN adj very dark
or gloomy

CIMOLITE n clayey,
whitish mineral

CIMOLITES
> CIMOLITE

CINCH n easy task ⊳ vb
fasten a girth around (a
horse)

CINCHED > CINCH

CINCHES > CINCH

CINCHING > CINCH

CINCHINGS > CINCH

CINCHONA same as
> CALISAYA

CINCHONAS
> CINCHONA

CINCHONIC
> CINCHONA

CINCINNUS same as
> CICINNUS

CINCT adj encircled

CINCTURE n something,
such as a belt or girdle,
that goes around another
thing ⊳ vb encircle

CINCTURED
> CINCTURE

CINCTURES
> CINCTURE

CINDER n piece of
material that will not
burn, left after burning
coal ⊳ vb burn to cinders

CINDERED > CINDER

CINDERIER > CINDERY

CINDERING > CINDER

CINDEROUS > CINDER

CINDERS > CINDER

CINDERY adj covered in
cinders

CINE n as in cine camera
camera able to film
moving pictures

CINEAST same as
> CINEASTE

CINEASTE n enthusiast
for films

CINEASTES
> CINEASTE

CINEASTS > CINEAST

CINEMA n place for
showing films

CINEMAS > CINEMA

CINEMATIC > CINEMA

CINEOL n colourless oily
liquid with a camphor-like
odour and a spicy taste

CINEOLE same as
> CINEOL

CINEOLES > CINEOLE

CINEOLS > CINEOL

CINEPHILE n film
enthusiast

CINEPLEX n large
cinema complex

CINERAMIC adj relating
to a cinematic process
producing widescreen
images

CINERARIA n garden
plant with daisy-like
flowers

CINERARY adj of
(someone's) ashes

CINERATOR same as
> CREMATOR

CINEREA n grey matter
of the brain and nervous
system

CINEREAL adj ashy

CINEREAS > CINEREA

CINEREOUS adj of a
greyish colour

CINERIN n either of two
organic compounds used
as insecticides

CINERINS > CINERIN

CINES > CINE

CINGULA > CINGULUM

CINGULAR adj
ring-shaped

CINGULATE
> CINGULUM

CINGULUM n girdle-like
part of certain structures

CINNABAR n heavy red
mineral containing
mercury

CINNABARS
> CINNABAR

CINNAMIC > CINNAMON

CINNAMON n spice
obtained from the bark of
an Asian tree

CINNAMONS
> CINNAMON

CINNAMONY adj like
cinnamon

CINNAMYL n univalent
radical of cinnamic
compounds

CINNAMYLS
> CINNAMYL

CINQ n number five

CINQS > CINQ

CINQUAIN n stanza of
five lines

CINQUAINS
> CINQUAIN

CINQUE n number five in
cards, dice, etc

CINQUES > CINQUE

CION same as > SCION

CIONS > CION

CIOPPINO n Italian rich
fish stew

CIOPPINOS
> CIOPPINO

CIPAILLE n type of pie
traditional in Quebec

CIPAILLES
> CIPAILLE

CIPHER n system of
secret writing ⊳ vb put (a
message) into secret
writing

CIPHERED > CIPHER

CIPHERER > CIPHER

CIPHERERS > CIPHER

CIPHERING > CIPHER

CIPHERS > CIPHER

CIPHONIES > CIPHONY

CIPHONY n ciphered
telephony

CIPOLIN n Italian marble
with alternating white
and green streaks

CIPOLINS > CIPOLIN

CIPOLLINO same as
> CIPOLIN

CIPPI > CIPPUS

CIPPUS n pillar bearing
an inscription

CIRCA prep
approximately, about

CIRCADIAN adj of
biological processes that
occur regularly at 24-hour
intervals

CIRCAR n in India, part of
a province

CIRCARS > CIRCAR

CIRCINATE adj (of part
of a plant, such as a young
fern) coiled so that the tip
is at the centre

CIRCITER prep around,
about

CIRCLE n perfectly round
geometric figure, line, or
shape ⊳ vb move in a circle
(round)

CIRCLED > CIRCLE

CIRCLER > CIRCLE

CIRCLERS > CIRCLE

CIRCLES > CIRCLE

CIRCLET n circular
ornament worn on the
head

CIRCLETS > CIRCLET

CIRCLING > CIRCLE

CIRCLINGS > CIRCLE

CIRCLIP n type of
fastener

CIRCLIPS > CIRCLIP

CIRCS pl n circumstances

CIRCUIT n complete
route or course, esp a
circular one ⊳ vb make or
travel in a circuit around
(something)

CIRCUITAL > CIRCUIT

CIRCUITED > CIRCUIT

CIRCUITRY n electrical
circuits

CIRCUITS > CIRCUIT

CIRCUITY n (of speech,
reasoning, etc) a
roundabout or devious
quality

CIRCULAR adj in the
shape of a circle ⊳ n letter
for general distribution

CIRCULARS
> CIRCULAR

CIRCULATE vb send, go,
or pass from place to place
or person to person

CIRCUS n travelling
company of acrobats,
clowns, performing
animals, etc

CIRCUSES > CIRCUS

CIRCUSIER > CIRCUSY

CIRCUSSY adj like a
circus

CIRCUSY adj like a circus

CIRE adj (of fabric)
treated with a heat or wax
process to make it smooth
⊳ n such a surface on a
fabric

CIRES > CIRE

CIRL n bird belonging to
the bunting family

CIRLS > CIRL

CIRQUE n steep-sided semicircular hollow found in mountainous areas
CIRQUES > CIRQUE
CIRRATE adj bearing or resembling cirri
CIRRHOSED > CIRRHOSIS
CIRRHOSES > CIRRHOSIS
CIRRHOSIS n serious liver disease
CIRRHOTIC > CIRRHOSIS
CIRRI > CIRRUS
CIRRIFORM adj cirrus-like
CIRRIPED same as > CIRRIPEDE
CIRRIPEDE n type of marine crustacean of the subclass including the barnacles
CIRRIPEDS > CIRRIPED
CIRROSE same as > CIRRATE
CIRROUS same as > CIRRATE
CIRRUS n high wispy cloud
CIRRUSES > CIRRUS
CIRSOID adj resembling a varix
CIS adj having two groups of atoms on the same side of a double bond
CISALPINE adj on this (the southern) side of the Alps, as viewed from Rome
CISCO n whitefish, esp the lake herring of cold deep lakes of North America
CISCOES > CISCO
CISCOS > CISCO
CISELEUR n person who is expert in ciselure
CISELEURS > CISELEUR
CISELURE n art or process of chasing metal
CISELURES > CISELURE
CISGENDER adj having an assigned birth gender and gender identity that are the same
CISLUNAR adj of or relating to the space between the earth and the moon
CISPADANE adj on this (the southern) side of the River Po, as viewed from Rome
CISPLATIN n cytotoxic drug used in the treatment of tumours
CISSIER > CISSY
CISSIES > CISSY
CISSIEST > CISSY
CISSIFIED another word for > SISSY
CISSING n appearance of pinholes, craters, etc, in paintwork
CISSINGS > CISSING

CISSOID n type of geometric curve
CISSOIDS > CISSOID
CISSUS n type of climbing plant
CISSUSES > CISSUS
CISSY same as > SISSY
CIST n wooden box for holding ritual objects used in ancient Rome and Greece
CISTED > CIST
CISTERN n water tank, esp one that holds water for flushing a toilet
CISTERNA n sac or partially closed space containing body fluid, esp lymph or cerebrospinal fluid
CISTERNAE > CISTERNA
CISTERNAL > CISTERN
CISTERNS > CISTERN
CISTIC adj cist-like
CISTRON n section of a chromosome that encodes a single polypeptide chain
CISTRONIC > CISTRON
CISTRONS > CISTRON
CISTS > CIST
CISTUS n type of plant
CISTUSES > CISTUS
CISTVAEN n pre-Christian stone coffin or burial chamber
CISTVAENS > CISTVAEN
CIT n pejorative term for a town dweller
CITABLE > CITE
CITADEL n fortress in a city
CITADELS > CITADEL
CITAL n court summons
CITALS > CITAL
CITATION n commendation for bravery
CITATIONS > CITATION
CITATOR n legal publication
CITATORS > CITATOR
CITATORY > CITATION
CITE vb quote, refer to
CITEABLE > CITE
CITED > CITE
CITER > CITE
CITERS > CITE
CITES > CITE
CITESS n female cit
CITESSES > CITESS
CITHARA n ancient stringed musical instrument
CITHARAS > CITHARA
CITHARIST n player of the cithara
CITHER same as > CITTERN
CITHERN same as > CITTERN
CITHERNS > CITHERN
CITHERS > CITHER
CITHREN same as > CITHARA

CITHRENS > CITHREN
CITIED adj having cities
CITIES > CITY
CITIFIED > CITIFY
CITIFIES > CITIFY
CITIFY vb cause to conform to or adopt the customs, habits, or dress of city people
CITIFYING > CITIFY
CITIGRADE adj relating to (fast-moving) wolf spiders
CITING > CITE
CITIZEN n native or naturalized member of a state or nation
CITIZENLY adj like a citizen
CITIZENRY n citizens collectively
CITIZENS > CITIZEN
CITO adv swiftly
CITOLA same as > CITOLE
CITOLAS > CITOLA
CITOLE n type of medieval stringed instrument
CITOLES > CITOLE
CITRAL n volatile liquid with a lemon-like odour
CITRALS > CITRAL
CITRANGE n type of acidic and aromatic orange
CITRANGES > CITRANGE
CITRATE n any salt or ester of citric acid
CITRATED adj treated with a citrate
CITRATES > CITRATE
CITREOUS adj of a greenish-yellow colour
CITRIC adj of or derived from citrus fruits or citric acid
CITRIN n vitamin P
CITRINE n brownish-yellow variety of quartz: a gemstone
CITRINES > CITRINE
CITRININ n type of mycotoxin
CITRININS > CITRININ
CITRINS > CITRIN
CITRON n lemon-like fruit of a small Asian tree
CITRONS > CITRON
CITROUS same as > CITRUS
CITRUS n type of tropical or subtropical tree or shrub
CITRUSES > CITRUS
CITRUSIER > CITRUSY
CITRUSSY adj having or resembling the taste or colour of a citrus fruit
CITRUSY same as > CITRUSSY
CITS > CIT
CITTERN n medieval stringed instrument
CITTERNS > CITTERN
CITY n large or important town

CITYFIED > CITYFY
CITYFIES > CITYFY
CITYFY same as > CITIFY
CITYFYING > CITYFY
CITYSCAPE n urban landscape
CITYWARD adv towards a city
CITYWIDE adj occurring throughout a city
CIVE same as > CHIVE
CIVES > CIVE
CIVET n spotted catlike African mammal
CIVETLIKE > CIVET
CIVETS > CIVET
CIVIC adj of a city or citizens
CIVICALLY > CIVIC
CIVICISM n principle of civil government
CIVICISMS > CIVICISM
CIVICS n study of the rights and responsibilities of citizenship
CIVIE same as > CIVVY
CIVIES > CIVIE
CIVIL adj relating to the citizens of a state
CIVILIAN adj not belonging to the armed forces ▷ n person who is not a member of the armed forces or police
CIVILIANS > CIVILIAN
CIVILISE same as > CIVILIZE
CIVILISED same as > CIVILIZED
CIVILISER > CIVILISE
CIVILISES > CIVILISE
CIVILIST n civilian
CIVILISTS > CIVILIST
CIVILITY n polite or courteous behaviour
CIVILIZE vb refine or educate (a person)
CIVILIZED adj having a high state of culture and social development
CIVILIZER > CIVILIZE
CIVILIZES > CIVILIZE
CIVILLY > CIVIL
CIVILNESS > CIVIL
CIVILS n civil engineering
CIVISM n good citizenship
CIVISMS > CIVISM
CIVVIES > CIVVY
CIVVY n civilian
CIZERS archaic spelling of > SCISSORS
CLABBER vb cover with mud
CLABBERED > CLABBER
CLABBERS > CLABBER
CLACH n stone ▷ vb kill by stoning
CLACHAN n small village

CLACHANS > CLACHAN
CLACHED > CLACH
CLACHES > CLACH
CLACHING > CLACH
CLACHS > CLACH
CLACK n sound made by two hard objects striking each other ▷ vb make this sound
CLACKBOX n casing enclosing a clack
CLACKDISH n formerly, a dish carried by a beggar
CLACKED > CLACK
CLACKER n object that makes a clacking sound
CLACKERS > CLACKER
CLACKING > CLACK
CLACKS > CLACK
CLAD vb bond a metal to (another metal), esp to form a protective coat
CLADDAGH n Irish ring
CLADDAGHS > CLADDAGH
CLADDED adj covered with cladding
CLADDER > CLAD
CLADDERS > CLAD
CLADDIE another name for > KORARI
CLADDIES > CLADDIE
CLADDING > CLAD
CLADDINGS > CLOTHE
CLADE n group of organisms sharing a common ancestor
CLADES > CLADE
CLADISM > CLADIST
CLADISMS > CLADIST
CLADIST n proponent of cladistics
CLADISTIC > CLADIST
CLADISTS > CLADIST
CLADODE n stem resembling and functioning as a leaf
CLADODES > CLADODE
CLADODIAL > CLADODE
CLADOGRAM n treelike diagram illustrating the development of a clade
CLADS > CLAD
CLAES Scots word for > CLOTHES
CLAFOUTI same as > CLAFOUTIS
CLAFOUTIS n French baked pudding
CLAG n sticky mud ▷ vb stick, as mud
CLAGGED > CLAG
CLAGGIER > CLAGGY
CLAGGIEST > CLAGGY
CLAGGING > CLAG
CLAGGY adj stickily clinging, as mud
CLAGS > CLAG
CLAIM vb assert as a fact ▷ n assertion that something is true
CLAIMABLE > CLAIM
CLAIMANT n person who makes a claim
CLAIMANTS > CLAIMANT
CLAIMED > CLAIM
CLAIMER > CLAIM

CLAIMERS > CLAIM
CLAIMING > CLAIM
CLAIMS > CLAIM
CLAM n edible shellfish with a hinged shell ▷ vb gather clams
CLAMANCY n urgency
CLAMANT adj noisy
CLAMANTLY > CLAMANT
CLAMBAKE n picnic, often by the sea, at which clams, etc, are baked
CLAMBAKES > CLAMBAKE
CLAMBE old variant of > CLIMB
CLAMBER vb climb awkwardly ▷ n climb performed in this manner
CLAMBERED > CLAMBER
CLAMBERER > CLAMBER
CLAMBERS > CLAMBER
CLAME archaic variant of > CLAIM
CLAMES > CLAME
CLAMLIKE > CLAM
CLAMMED > CLAM
CLAMMER n person who gathers clams
CLAMMERS > CLAMMER
CLAMMIER > CLAMMY
CLAMMIEST > CLAMMY
CLAMMILY > CLAMMY
CLAMMING > CLAM
CLAMMY adj unpleasantly moist and sticky
CLAMOR same as > CLAMOUR
CLAMORED > CLAMOR
CLAMORER > CLAMOR
CLAMORERS > CLAMOR
CLAMORING > CLAMOR
CLAMOROUS > CLAMOR
CLAMORS > CLAMOR
CLAMOUR n loud protest ▷ vb make a loud noise or outcry
CLAMOURED > CLAMOUR
CLAMOURER > CLAMOUR
CLAMOURS > CLAMOUR
CLAMP n tool with movable jaws for holding things together tightly ▷ vb fasten with a clamp
CLAMPDOWN n sudden restrictive measure
CLAMPED > CLAMP
CLAMPER n spiked metal frame fastened to the sole of a shoe ▷ vb tread heavily
CLAMPERED > CLAMPER
CLAMPERS > CLAMPER
CLAMPING n act of clamping
CLAMPINGS > CLAMPING
CLAMPS > CLAMP
CLAMS > CLAM
CLAMSHELL n dredging bucket that is hinged like the shell of a clam
CLAMWORM the US name for the > RAGWORM
CLAMWORMS > CLAMWORM
CLAN n group of families with a common ancestor

CLANG vb make a loud ringing metallic sound ▷ n ringing metallic sound
CLANGBOX n device fitted to a jet-engine to change the direction of thrust
CLANGED > CLANG
CLANGER n obvious mistake
CLANGERS > CLANGER
CLANGING > CLANG
CLANGINGS > CLANG
CLANGOR same as > CLANGOUR
CLANGORED > CLANGOR
CLANGORS > CLANGOR
CLANGOUR n loud continuous clanging sound ▷ vb make or produce a loud resonant noise
CLANGOURS > CLANGOUR
CLANGS > CLANG
CLANK n harsh metallic sound ▷ vb make such a sound
CLANKED > CLANK
CLANKIER > CLANKY
CLANKIEST > CLANKY
CLANKING > CLANK
CLANKINGS > CLANK
CLANKS > CLANK
CLANKY adj making clanking sounds
CLANNISH adj (of a group) tending to exclude outsiders
CLANS > CLAN
CLANSHIP n association of families under the leadership of a chieftain
CLANSHIPS > CLANSHIP
CLANSMAN n man belonging to a clan
CLANSMEN > CLANSMAN
CLAP vb applaud by hitting the palms of one's hands sharply together ▷ n act or sound of clapping
CLAPBOARD n long thin timber board with one edge thicker than the other, used esp in the US and Canada in wood-frame construction by lapping each board over the one below ▷ vb cover with such boards
CLAPBREAD n type of cake made from oatmeal
CLAPDISH same as > CLACKDISH
CLAPNET n net that can be closed instantly by pulling a string
CLAPNETS > CLAPNET
CLAPPED > CLAP
CLAPPER n piece of metal inside a bell ▷ vb make a sound like a clapper
CLAPPERED > CLAPPER
CLAPPERS > CLAPPER
CLAPPING > CLAP
CLAPPINGS > CLAP
CLAPS > CLAP

CLAPT > CLAP
CLAPTRAP n foolish or pretentious talk
CLAPTRAPS > CLAPTRAP
CLAQUE n group of people hired to applaud
CLAQUER same as > CLAQUEUR
CLAQUERS > CLAQUER
CLAQUES > CLAQUE
CLAQUEUR n member of a claque
CLAQUEURS > CLAQUEUR
CLARAIN n one of the four major lithotypes of banded coal
CLARAINS > CLARAIN
CLARENCE n closed four-wheeled horse-drawn carriage, having a glass front
CLARENCES > CLARENCE
CLARENDON n style of boldface roman type
CLARET n dry red wine from Bordeaux ▷ adj purplish-red ▷ vb drink claret
CLARETED > CLARET
CLARETING > CLARET
CLARETS > CLARET
CLARIES > CLARY
CLARIFIED > CLARIFY
CLARIFIER > CLARIFY
CLARIFIES > CLARIFY
CLARIFY vb make (a matter) clear and unambiguous
CLARINET n keyed woodwind instrument with a single reed
CLARINETS > CLARINET
CLARINI > CLARINO
CLARINO adj relating to a high passage for the trumpet in 18th-century music ▷ n high register of the trumpet
CLARINOS > CLARINO
CLARION n obsolete high-pitched trumpet ▷ adj clear and ringing ▷ vb proclaim loudly
CLARIONED > CLARION
CLARIONET same as > CLARINET
CLARIONS > CLARION
CLARITIES > CLARITY
CLARITY n clearness
CLARKIA n N American plant cultivated for its red, purple, or pink flowers
CLARKIAS > CLARKIA
CLARO n mild light-coloured cigar
CLAROES > CLARO
CLAROS > CLARO
CLARSACH n Celtic harp of Scotland and Ireland
CLARSACHS > CLARSACH
CLART vb to dirty
CLARTED > CLART

CLARTHEAD n slow-witted or stupid person

CLARTIER > CLARTY

CLARTIEST > CLARTY

CLARTING > CLART

CLARTS pl n lumps of mud, esp on shoes

CLARTY adj dirty, esp covered in mud

CLARY n European plant with aromatic leaves and blue flowers

CLASH vb come into conflict ▷ n fight, argument

CLASHED > CLASH

CLASHER > CLASH

CLASHERS > CLASH

CLASHES > CLASH

CLASHING > CLASH

CLASHINGS > CLASH

CLASP n device for fastening things ▷ vb grasp or embrace firmly

CLASPED > CLASP

CLASPER > CLASP

CLASPERS > CLASPER

CLASPING > CLASP

CLASPINGS > CLASP

CLASPS > CLASP

CLASPT old inflection of > CLASP

CLASS n group of people sharing a similar social position ▷ vb place in a class

CLASSABLE > CLASS

CLASSED > CLASS

CLASSER > CLASS

CLASSERS > CLASS

CLASSES > CLASSIS

CLASSIBLE adj able to be classed

CLASSIC adj being a typical example of something ▷ n author, artist, or work of art of recognized excellence

CLASSICAL adj of or in a restrained conservative style

CLASSICO adj (of Italian wines) coming from the centre of a specific wine-growing region

CLASSICS > CLASSIC

CLASSIER > CLASSY

CLASSIEST > CLASSY

CLASSIFIC adj relating to classification

CLASSIFY vb divide into groups with similar characteristics

CLASSILY > CLASSY

CLASSING > CLASS

CLASSINGS > CLASS

CLASSIS n governing body of elders or pastors

CLASSISM n belief that people from certain social or economic classes are superior to others

CLASSISMS > CLASSISM

CLASSIST > CLASSISM

CLASSISTS > CLASSISM

CLASSLESS adj not belonging to a class

CLASSMAN n graduate of Oxford University with a classed honours degree

CLASSMATE n friend or contemporary in the same class of a school

CLASSMEN > CLASSMAN

CLASSON n elementary atomic particle

CLASSONS > CLASSON

CLASSROOM n room in a school where lessons take place

CLASSWORK n school work done in class

CLASSY adj stylish and elegant

CLAST n fragment of a clastic rock

CLASTIC adj composed of fragments ▷ n clast

CLASTICS > CLASTIC

CLASTS > CLAST

CLAT n irksome or troublesome task ▷ vb scrape

CLATCH vb move making a squelching sound

CLATCHED > CLATCH

CLATCHES > CLATCH

CLATCHING > CLATCH

CLATHRATE adj resembling a net or lattice ▷ n solid compound in which molecules of one substance are physically trapped in the crystal lattice of another

CLATS > CLAT

CLATTED > CLAT

CLATTER n rattling noise ▷ vb make a rattling noise, as when hard objects hit each other

CLATTERED > CLATTER

CLATTERER > CLATTER

CLATTERS > CLATTER

CLATTERY adj making a clattering sound

CLATTING > CLAT

CLAUCHT vb seize by force

CLAUCHTED > CLAUCHT

CLAUCHTS > CLAUCHT

CLAUGHT same as > CLAUCHT

CLAUGHTED > CLAUGHT

CLAUGHTS > CLAUGHT

CLAUSAL > CLAUSE

CLAUSE n section of a legal document

CLAUSES > CLAUSE

CLAUSTRA > CLAUSTRUM

CLAUSTRAL same as > CLOISTRAL

CLAUSTRUM n thin layer of grey matter in the brain

CLAUSULA n type of cadence in polyphony

CLAUSULAE > CLAUSULA

CLAUSULAR > CLAUSE

CLAUT same as > CLAT

CLAUTED > CLAUT

CLAUTING > CLAUT

CLAUTS > CLAUT

CLAVATE adj shaped like a club with the thicker end uppermost

CLAVATED same as > CLAVATE

CLAVATELY > CLAVATE

CLAVATION > CLAVATE

CLAVE n one of a pair of hardwood sticks struck together to make a hollow sound

CLAVECIN n harpsichord

CLAVECINS > CLAVECIN

CLAVER vb talk idly ▷ n idle talk

CLAVERED > CLAVER

CLAVERING > CLAVER

CLAVERS > CLAVER

CLAVES > CLAVE

CLAVI > CLAVUS

CLAVICLE n bone connecting the shoulder blade to the breastbone

CLAVICLES > CLAVICLE

CLAVICORN n type of beetle such as the ladybirds, characterized by club-shaped antennae

CLAVICULA n clavicle

CLAVIE n tar-barrel traditionally set alight in Moray in Scotland on Hogmanay

CLAVIER n any keyboard instrument

CLAVIERS > CLAVIER

CLAVIES > CLAVIE

CLAVIFORM same as > CLAVATE

CLAVIGER n key- or club-bearer

CLAVIGERS > CLAVIGER

CLAVIS n key

CLAVULATE adj club-shaped

CLAVUS n corn on the toe

CLAW n sharp hooked nail of a bird or beast ▷ vb tear with claws or nails

CLAWBACK n recovery of a sum of money

CLAWBACKS > CLAWBACK

CLAWED > CLAW

CLAWER > CLAW

CLAWERS > CLAW

CLAWING > CLAW

CLAWLESS > CLAW

CLAWLIKE adj resembling a claw or claws

CLAWS > CLAW

CLAXON same as > KLAXON

CLAXONS > CLAXON

CLAY n fine-grained earth used to make bricks and pottery ▷ vb cover or mix with clay

CLAYBANK n dull brownish-orange colour

CLAYBANKS > CLAYBANK

CLAYED > CLAY

CLAYEY > CLAY

CLAYIER > CLAYEY

CLAYIEST > CLAYEY

CLAYING > CLAY

CLAYISH > CLAY

CLAYLIKE > CLAY

CLAYMORE n large two-edged sword formerly used by Scottish Highlanders

CLAYMORES > CLAYMORE

CLAYPAN n layer of stiff impervious clay situated just below the surface of the ground

CLAYPANS > CLAYPAN

CLAYS > CLAY

CLAYSTONE n compact very fine-grained rock consisting of consolidated clay particles

CLAYTONIA n low-growing N American succulent plant

CLAYWARE n pottery

CLAYWARES > CLAYWARE

CLEAN adj free from dirt or impurities ▷ vb make (something) free from dirt ▷ adv completely

CLEANABLE > CLEAN

CLEANED > CLEAN

CLEANER n person or thing that removes dirt

CLEANERS > CLEANER

CLEANEST > CLEAN

CLEANING n act of cleaning something

CLEANINGS > CLEANING

CLEANISH adj quite clean

CLEANLIER > CLEANLY

CLEANLILY > CLEANLY

CLEANLY adv easily or smoothly ▷ adj habitually clean or neat

CLEANNESS > CLEAN

CLEANOUT n act or instance of cleaning (something) out

CLEANOUTS > CLEANOUT

CLEANS > CLEAN

CLEANSE vb make clean

CLEANSED > CLEANSE

CLEANSER n cleansing agent, such as a detergent

CLEANSERS > CLEANSER

CLEANSES > CLEANSE

CLEANSING > CLEANSE

CLEANSKIN n unbranded animal

CLEANTECH n clean technology

CLEANUP n process of cleaning up or eliminating something

CLEANUPS > CLEANUP

CLEAR adj free from doubt or confusion ▷ adv in a clear or distinct manner ▷ vb make or become clear

CLEARABLE > CLEAR

CLEARAGE n clearance

CLEARAGES > CLEARAGE

CLEARANCE n clearing

CLEARCOLE n type of size containing whiting ▷ vb paint (a wall) with this size

CLEARCUT n act of felling all trees in area

CLEARCUTS > CLEARCUT

CLEARED > CLEAR

CLEARER > CLEAR

CLEARERS > CLEAR

CLEAREST > CLEAR

CLEAREYED adj having good judgment

CLEARING n treeless area in a wood

CLEARINGS > CLEARING

CLEARLY adv in a clear, distinct, or obvious manner

CLEARNESS > CLEAR

CLEAROUT n act or instance of removing (things or material)

CLEAROUTS > CLEAROUT

CLEARS > CLEAR

CLEARSKIN same as > CLEANSKIN

CLEARWAY n stretch of road on which motorists may stop in an emergency

CLEARWAYS > CLEARWAY

CLEARWEED n plant like nettle

CLEARWING n type of moth

CLEAT n wedge ▷ vb supply or support with a cleat or cleats

CLEATED > CLEAT

CLEATING > CLEAT

CLEATS > CLEAT

CLEAVABLE > CLEAVE

CLEAVAGE n division or split

CLEAVAGES > CLEAVAGE

CLEAVE vb split apart ▷ n split

CLEAVED > CLEAVE

CLEAVER n butcher's heavy knife with a square blade

CLEAVERS n plant with small white flowers and sticky fruits

CLEAVES > CLEAVE

CLEAVING > CLEAVE

CLEAVINGS > CLEAVE

CLECHE adj (in heraldry) voided so that only a narrow border is visible

CLECK vb (of birds) to hatch ▷ n piece of gossip

CLECKED > CLECK

CLECKIER > CLECK

CLECKIEST > CLECK

CLECKING > CLECK

CLECKINGS > CLECK

CLECKS > CLECK

CLECKY > CLECK

CLEEK n large hook, such as one used to land fish ▷ vb seize

CLEEKED > CLEEK

CLEEKING > CLEEK

CLEEKIT > CLEEK

CLEEKS > CLEEK

CLEEP same as > CLEPE

CLEEPED > CLEEP

CLEEPING > CLEEP

CLEEPS > CLEEP

CLEEVE n cliff

CLEEVES > CLEEVE

CLEF n symbol at the beginning of a stave to show the pitch

CLEFS > CLEF

CLEFT vb split ▷ n opening

CLEFTED > CLEFT

CLEFTING > CLEFT

CLEFTS > CLEFT

CLEG another name for a > HORSEFLY

CLEGS > CLEG

CLEIDOIC adj as in cleidoic egg egg of birds and insects

CLEIK same as > CLEEK

CLEIKS > CLEIK

CLEITHRAL adj covered with a roof

CLEM vb be hungry or cause to be hungry

CLEMATIS n climbing plant with large colourful flowers

CLEMENCY n kind or lenient treatment

CLEMENT adj (of weather) mild

CLEMENTLY > CLEMENT

CLEMMED > CLEM

CLEMMING > CLEM

CLEMS > CLEM

CLENCH vb close or squeeze (one's teeth or fist) tightly ▷ n firm grasp or grip

CLENCHED > CLENCH

CLENCHER > CLENCH

CLENCHERS > CLENCH

CLENCHES > CLENCH

CLENCHING > CLENCH

CLEOME n type of herbaceous or shrubby plant

CLEOMES > CLEOME

CLEOPATRA n type of yellow butterfly, the male of which has its wings flushed with orange

CLEPE vb call by the name of

CLEPED > CLEPE

CLEPES > CLEPE

CLEPING > CLEPE

CLEPSYDRA n ancient device for measuring time by the flow of water or mercury through a small aperture

CLEPT > CLEPE

CLERGIES > CLERGY

CLERGY n priests and ministers as a group

CLERGYMAN n member of the clergy

CLERGYMEN > CLERGYMAN

CLERIC n member of the clergy

CLERICAL adj of clerks or office work

CLERICALS pl n distinctive dress of a clergyman or clergywoman

CLERICATE n clerical post

CLERICITY n condition of being a clergyman or clergywoman

CLERICS > CLERIC

CLERID n beetle that preys on other insects

CLERIDS > CLERID

CLERIHEW n form of comic or satiric verse

CLERIHEWS > CLERIHEW

CLERISIES > CLERISY

CLERISY n learned or educated people

CLERK n employee who keeps records, files, and accounts ▷ vb work as a clerk

CLERKDOM > CLERK

CLERKDOMS > CLERK

CLERKED > CLERK

CLERKESS n female office clerk

CLERKING > CLERK

CLERKISH > CLERK

CLERKLIER > CLERKLY

CLERKLIKE adj acting in a scholarly manner

CLERKLING n young or inexperienced clerk

CLERKLY adj of or like a clerk ▷ adv in the manner of a clerk

CLERKS > CLERK

CLERKSHIP > CLERK

CLERUCH n settler in a cleruchy

CLERUCHIA same as > CLERUCHY

CLERUCHS > CLERUCH

CLERUCHY n type of colony of ancient Athens

CLEUCH same as > CLOUGH

CLEUCHS > CLEUCH

CLEUGH same as > CLOUGH

CLEUGHS > CLEUGH

CLEVE same as > CLEEVE

CLEVEITE n crystalline variety of the mineral uraninite

CLEVEITES > CLEVEITE

CLEVER adj intelligent, quick at learning

CLEVERER > CLEVER

CLEVEREST > CLEVER

CLEVERISH > CLEVER

CLEVERLY > CLEVER

CLEVES > CLEVE

CLEVIS n type of fastening used in agriculture

CLEVISES > CLEVIS

CLEW n ball of thread, yarn, or twine ▷ vb coil or roll into a ball

CLEWED > CLEW

CLEWING > CLEW

CLEWS > CLEW

CLIANTHUS n plant with slender scarlet flowers

CLICHE n expression or idea that is no longer effective because of overuse ▷ vb use a cliché (in speech or writing)

CLICHED > CLICHE

CLICHEED > CLICHE

CLICHES > CLICHE

CLICK n short sharp sound ▷ vb make this sound

CLICKABLE adj (of a website) having links that can be accessed by clicking a computer mouse

CLICKBAIT n hyperlink that entices one to click through to a new website

CLICKED > CLICK

CLICKER > CLICK

CLICKERS > CLICK

CLICKET vb make a click

CLICKETED > CLICKET

CLICKETS > CLICKET

CLICKING > CLICK

CLICKINGS > CLICK

CLICKLESS > CLICK

CLICKS > CLICK

CLICKWRAP adj (of agreement) consented to by user clicking computer button

CLIED > CLY

CLIENT n person who uses the services of a professional person or company

CLIENTAGE same as > CLIENTELE

CLIENTAL > CLIENT

CLIENTELE n clients collectively

CLIENTS > CLIENT

CLIES > CLY

CLIFF n steep rock face, esp along the sea shore ▷ vb scale a cliff

CLIFFED > CLIFF

CLIFFHANG vb (of a serial or film) to end on a note of suspense

CLIFFHUNG > CLIFFHANG

CLIFFIER > CLIFF

CLIFFIEST > CLIFF

CLIFFLIKE > CLIFF

CLIFFS > CLIFF

CLIFFSIDE n side of a cliff

CLIFFTOP n top of a cliff

CLIFFTOPS > CLIFFTOP

CLIFFY > CLIFF

CLIFT same as > CLIFF

CLIFTED > CLIFT

CLIFTIER > CLIFT

CLIFTIEST > CLIFT

CLIFTS > CLIFT

CLIFTY > CLIFT

CLIMACTIC adj consisting of, involving, or causing a climax

CLIMATAL > CLIMATE

CLIMATE n typical weather conditions of an area ▷ vb acclimatize

CLIMATED > CLIMATE
CLIMATES > CLIMATE
CLIMATIC > CLIMATE
CLIMATING > CLIMATE
CLIMATISE *vb* in Australia, adapt or become accustomed to a new climate or environment
CLIMATIZE *same as* > CLIMATISE
CLIMATURE *n* clime
CLIMAX *n* most intense point of an experience, series of events, or story ▷ *vb* reach a climax
CLIMAXED > CLIMAX
CLIMAXES > CLIMAX
CLIMAXING > CLIMAX
CLIMB *vb* go up, ascend ▷ *n* climbing
CLIMBABLE > CLIMB
CLIMBDOWN *n* act of backing down from opinion
CLIMBED > CLIMB
CLIMBER *n* person or thing that climbs
CLIMBERS > CLIMBER
CLIMBING > CLIMB
CLIMBINGS > CLIMB
CLIMBS > CLIMB
CLIME *n* place or its climate
CLIMES > CLIME
CLINAL > CLINE
CLINALLY > CLINE
CLINAMEN *n* bias
CLINAMENS > CLINAMEN
CLINCH *vb* settle (an argument or agreement) decisively ▷ *n* movement in which one competitor holds on to the other to avoid punches
CLINCHED > CLINCH
CLINCHER *n* something decisive
CLINCHERS > CLINCHER
CLINCHES > CLINCH
CLINCHING > CLINCH
CLINE *n* variation within a species
CLINES > CLINE
CLING *vb* hold tightly or stick closely ▷ *n* tendency of cotton fibres in a sample to stick to each other
CLINGED > CLING
CLINGER > CLING
CLINGERS > CLING
CLINGFILM *n* thin polythene material for wrapping food
CLINGFISH *n* type of small marine fish with a flattened elongated body and a sucking disc beneath the head for clinging to rocks, etc
CLINGIER > CLING
CLINGIEST > CLING
CLINGING > CLING
CLINGS > CLING
CLINGWRAP *same as* > CLINGFILM

CLINGY > CLING
CLINIC *n* building where outpatients receive medical treatment or advice
CLINICAL *adj* of a clinic
CLINICIAN *n* physician, psychiatrist, etc, who specializes in clinical work as opposed to one engaged in laboratory or experimental studies
CLINICS > CLINIC
CLINIQUE *same as* > CLINIC
CLINIQUES > CLINIC
CLINK *n* light sharp metallic sound ▷ *vb* make a light sharp metallic sound
CLINKED > CLINK
CLINKER *n* fused coal left over in a fire or furnace ▷ *vb* form clinker during burning
CLINKERED > CLINKER
CLINKERS > CLINKER
CLINKING > CLINK
CLINKS > CLINK
CLINOAXES > CLINOAXIS
CLINOAXIS *n* in a monoclinic crystal, the lateral axis which forms an oblique angle with the vertical axis
CLINOSTAT *n* apparatus for studying tropisms in plants, usually a rotating disc to which the plant is attached so that it receives an equal stimulus on all sides
CLINQUANT *adj* glittering, esp with tinsel ▷ *n* tinsel or imitation gold leaf
CLINT *n* section of a limestone pavement separated from others by fissures
CLINTONIA *n* type of temperate plant with white, greenish-yellow, or purplish flowers, broad ribbed leaves, and blue berries
CLINTS > CLINT
CLIOMETRY *n* study of economic history using statistics and computer analysis
CLIP *vb* cut with shears or scissors ▷ *n* short extract of a film
CLIPART *n* large collection of simple drawings stored in a computer
CLIPARTS > CLIPART
CLIPBOARD *n* portable writing board with a clip at the top for holding paper
CLIPE *same as* > CLYPE
CLIPED > CLIPE
CLIPES > CLIPE
CLIPING > CLIPE
CLIPPABLE > CLIP
CLIPPED > CLIP

CLIPPER *n* fast commercial sailing ship
CLIPPERS *pl n* tool for clipping
CLIPPIE *n* bus conductress
CLIPPIES > CLIPPIE
CLIPPING > CLIP
CLIPPINGS > CLIP
CLIPS > CLIP
CLIPSHEAR *n* earwig
CLIPSHEET *n* sheet of paper with text printed on one side only
CLIPT *old inflection of* > CLIP
CLIQUE *n* small exclusive group ▷ *vb* form a clique
CLIQUED > CLIQUE
CLIQUES > CLIQUE
CLIQUEY *adj* exclusive, confined to a small group
CLIQUIER > CLIQUEY
CLIQUIEST > CLIQUEY
CLIQUING > CLIQUE
CLIQUISH > CLIQUE
CLIQUISM > CLIQUE
CLIQUISMS > CLIQUE
CLIQUY *same as* > CLIQUEY
CLIT *slang word for* > CLITORIS
CLITELLA > CLITELLUM
CLITELLAR > CLITELLUM
CLITELLUM *n* thickened saddle-like region of epidermis in earthworms and leeches
CLITHRAL *same as* > CLEITHRAL
CLITIC *adj* (of a word) incapable of being stressed ▷ *n* clitic word
CLITICISE *same as* > CLITICIZE
CLITICIZE *vb* pronounce as part of following or preceding word
CLITICS > CLITIC
CLITORAL > CLITORIS
CLITORIC > CLITORIS
CLITORIS *n* small sensitive organ at the front of the vulva
CLITS > CLIT
CLITTER *vb* make a shrill noise
CLITTERED > CLITTER
CLITTERS > CLITTER
CLIVERS *same as* > CLEAVERS
CLIVIA *n* plant belonging to the Amaryllid family
CLIVIAS > CLIVIA
CLOACA *n* body cavity in most animals
CLOACAE > CLOACA
CLOACAL > CLOACA
CLOACAS > CLOACA
CLOACINAL > CLOACA
CLOACITIS *n* inflammation of the cloaca in birds, including domestic fowl, and other

animals with a common opening of the urinary and gastrointestinal tracts
CLOAK *n* loose sleeveless outer garment ▷ *vb* cover or conceal
CLOAKED > CLOAK
CLOAKING > CLOAK
CLOAKROOM *n* room where coats may be left temporarily
CLOAKS > CLOAK
CLOAM *adj* made of clay or earthenware ▷ *n* clay or earthenware pots, dishes, etc, collectively
CLOAMS > CLOAM
CLOBBER *vb* hit ▷ *n* belongings, esp clothes
CLOBBERED > CLOBBER
CLOBBERS > CLOBBER
CLOCHARD *n* tramp
CLOCHARDS > CLOCHARD
CLOCHE *n* cover to protect young plants
CLOCHES > CLOCHE
CLOCK *n* instrument for showing the time ▷ *vb* record (time) with a stopwatch
CLOCKED > CLOCK
CLOCKER > CLOCK
CLOCKERS > CLOCK
CLOCKFACE *n* face of a clock
CLOCKING > CLOCK
CLOCKINGS > CLOCK
CLOCKLIKE > CLOCK
CLOCKS > CLOCK
CLOCKWISE *adj* in the direction in which the hands of a clock rotate
CLOCKWORK *n* mechanism similar to the kind in a clock, used in wind-up toys
CLOD *n* lump of earth ▷ *vb* pelt with clods
CLODDED > CLOD
CLODDIER > CLOD
CLODDIEST > CLOD
CLODDING > CLOD
CLODDISH > CLOD
CLODDY > CLOD
CLODLY > CLOD
CLODPATE *n* dull or stupid person
CLODPATED *adj* stupid
CLODPATES > CLODPATE
CLODPOLE *same as* > CLODPATE
CLODPOLES > CLODPATE
CLODPOLL *same as* > CLODPATE
CLODPOLLS > CLODPOLL
CLODS > CLOD
CLOFF *n* cleft of a tree
CLOFFS > CLOFF
CLOG *vb* obstruct ▷ *n* wooden or wooden-soled shoe
CLOGDANCE *n* dance performed in clogs
CLOGGED > CLOG

CLOGGER n clogmaker

CLOGGERS > CLOGGER

CLOGGIER > CLOG

CLOGGIEST > CLOG

CLOGGILY > CLOG

CLOGGING > CLOG

CLOGGINGS > CLOG

CLOGGY > CLOG

CLOGMAKER n maker of clogs

CLOGS > CLOG

CLOISON n partition

CLOISONNE n design made by filling in a wire outline with coloured enamel ▷ adj of, relating to, or made by cloisonné

CLOISONS > CLOISON

CLOISTER n covered pillared arcade, usu in a monastery ▷ vb confine or seclude in or as if in a monastery

CLOISTERS > CLOISTER

CLOISTRAL adj of, like, or characteristic of a cloister

CLOKE same as > CLOAK

CLOKED > CLOKE

CLOKES > CLOKE

CLOKING > CLOKE

CLOMB a past tense and past participle of > CLIMB

CLOMP same as > CLUMP

CLOMPED > CLOMP

CLOMPING > CLOMP

CLOMPS > CLOMP

CLON same as > CLONE

CLONAL > CLONE

CLONALLY > CLONE

CLONE n animal or plant produced artificially from the cells of another animal or plant ▷ vb produce as a clone

CLONED > CLONE

CLONER > CLONE

CLONERS > CLONE

CLONES > CLONE

CLONIC > CLONUS

CLONICITY > CLONUS

CLONIDINE n anti-hypertensive drug

CLONING > CLONE

CLONINGS > CLONE

CLONISM n series of clonic spasms

CLONISMS > CLONISM

CLONK vb make a loud dull thud ▷ n loud thud

CLONKED > CLONK

CLONKIER > CLONKY

CLONKIEST > CLONKY

CLONKING > CLONK

CLONKS > CLONK

CLONKY same as > CLUNKY

CLONS > CLON

CLONUS n type of convulsion

CLONUSES > CLONUS

CLOOP n sound made when a cork is drawn from a bottle

CLOOPS > CLOOP

CLOOT n hoof

CLOOTIE adj as in clootie dumpling kind of dumpling

CLOOTS > CLOOT

CLOP vb make a sound as of a horse's hooves ▷ n sound of this nature

CLOPPED > CLOP

CLOPPING > CLOP

CLOPS > CLOP

CLOQUE n fabric with an embossed surface

CLOQUES > CLOQUE

CLOSABLE > CLOSE

CLOSE vb shut ▷ n end, conclusion ▷ adj near ▷ adv closely, tightly

CLOSEABLE > CLOSE

CLOSED > CLOSE

CLOSEDOWN n closure or stoppage of operations

CLOSEHEAD n entrance to a close

CLOSELY > CLOSE

CLOSENESS > CLOSE

CLOSEOUT n termination of an account on which the margin is exhausted

CLOSEOUTS
> CLOSEOUT

CLOSER > CLOSE

CLOSERS > CLOSE

CLOSES > CLOSE

CLOSEST > CLOSE

CLOSET n cupboard ▷ adj private, secret ▷ vb shut (oneself) away in private

CLOSETED > CLOSET

CLOSETFUL n quantity that may be contained in a closet

CLOSETING > CLOSET

CLOSETS > CLOSET

CLOSEUP n photo taken close to a subject

CLOSEUPS > CLOSEUP

CLOSING > CLOSE

CLOSINGS > CLOSE

CLOSURE n closing ▷ vb (in a deliberative body) to end (debate) by closure

CLOSURED > CLOSURE

CLOSURES > CLOSURE

CLOSURING > CLOSURE

CLOT n soft thick lump formed from liquid ▷ vb form soft thick lumps

CLOTBUR n burdock

CLOTBURS > CLOTBUR

CLOTE n burdock

CLOTES > CLOTE

CLOTH n (piece of) woven fabric

CLOTHE vb put clothes on

CLOTHED > CLOTHE

CLOTHES pl n garments

CLOTHIER n maker or seller of clothes or cloth

CLOTHIERS
> CLOTHIER

CLOTHING > CLOTHE

CLOTHINGS > CLOTHE

CLOTHLIKE > CLOTH

CLOTHS > CLOTH

CLOTPOLL same as
> CLODPOLL

CLOTPOLLS
> CLOTPOLL

CLOTS > CLOT

CLOTTED > CLOT

CLOTTER vb to clot

CLOTTERED > CLOTTER

CLOTTERS > CLOTTER

CLOTTIER > CLOTTY

CLOTTIEST > CLOTTY

CLOTTING > CLOT

CLOTTINGS > CLOT

CLOTTISH > CLOT

CLOTTY adj full of clots

CLOTURE n closure in the US Senate ▷ vb end (debate) in the US Senate by cloture

CLOTURED > CLOTURE

CLOTURES > CLOTURE

CLOTURING > CLOTURE

CLOU n crux; focus

CLOUD n mass of condensed water vapour floating in the sky ▷ vb become cloudy

CLOUDAGE n mass of clouds

CLOUDAGES
> CLOUDAGE

CLOUDED > CLOUD

CLOUDIER > CLOUDY

CLOUDIEST > CLOUDY

CLOUDILY > CLOUDY

CLOUDING > CLOUD

CLOUDINGS > CLOUD

CLOUDLAND n realm or fantasy or impractical notions

CLOUDLESS > CLOUD

CLOUDLET n small cloud

CLOUDLETS
> CLOUDLET

CLOUDLIKE > CLOUD

CLOUDS > CLOUD

CLOUDTOWN n cloudland

CLOUDY adj having a lot of clouds

CLOUGH n gorge or narrow ravine

CLOUGHS > CLOUGH

CLOUR vb to thump or dent

CLOURED > CLOUR

CLOURING > CLOUR

CLOURS > CLOUR

CLOUS > CLOU

CLOUT n hard blow ▷ vb hit hard

CLOUTED > CLOUT

CLOUTER > CLOUT

CLOUTERLY adj clumsy

CLOUTERS > CLOUT

CLOUTING > CLOUT

CLOUTS > CLOUT

CLOVE n tropical evergreen myrtaceous tree

CLOVEN > CLEAVE

CLOVER n plant with three-lobed leaves

CLOVERED adj covered with clover

CLOVERIER > CLOVERY

CLOVERS > CLOVER

CLOVERY adj like clover

CLOVES > CLOVE

CLOVIS n as in clovis point flint projectile dating from the 10th millennium BC

CLOW n clove ▷ vb rake with a fork

CLOWDER n collective term for a group of cats

CLOWDERS > CLOWDER

CLOWED > CLOW

CLOWING > CLOW

CLOWN n comic entertainer in a circus ▷ vb behave foolishly

CLOWNED > CLOWN

CLOWNERY > CLOWN

CLOWNFISH n small, brightly coloured tropical fish

CLOWNING > CLOWN

CLOWNINGS > CLOWN

CLOWNISH > CLOWN

CLOWNS > CLOWN

CLOWS > CLOW

CLOY vb cause weariness through an excess of something initially pleasurable

CLOYE vb to claw

CLOYED > CLOY

CLOYES > CLOYE

CLOYING adj sickeningly sweet

CLOYINGLY > CLOYING

CLOYLESS adj not cloying

CLOYMENT n satiety

CLOYMENTS
> CLOYMENT

CLOYS > CLOY

CLOYSOME adj cloying

CLOZAPINE n drug used to treat schizophrenia

CLOZE adj as in cloze test test of the ability to understand text

CLOZES > CLOZE

CLUB n association of people with common interests ▷ vb hit with a club

CLUBABLE same as
> CLUBBABLE

CLUBBABLE adj suitable to be a member of a club

CLUBBED > CLUB

CLUBBER n person who regularly frequents nightclubs

CLUBBERS > CLUBBER

CLUBBIER > CLUBBY

CLUBBIEST > CLUBBY

CLUBBILY > CLUBBY

CLUBBING > CLUB

CLUBBINGS > CLUB

CLUBBISH adj clubby

CLUBBISM n advantage gained through membership of a club or clubs

CLUBBISMS
> CLUBBISM

CLUBBIST > CLUBBISM

CLUBBISTS
> CLUBBISM

CLUBBY adj sociable, esp effusively so

CLUBFACE n face of golf club

CLUBFACES
> CLUBFACE

CLUBFEET > CLUBFOOT

CLUBFOOT n congenital deformity of the foot

CLUBHAND n congenital deformity of the hand
CLUBHANDS > CLUBHAND
CLUBHAUL vb force (a sailing vessel) onto a new tack, esp in an emergency
CLUBHAULS > CLUBHAUL
CLUBHEAD n head of golf club
CLUBHEADS > CLUBHEAD
CLUBHOUSE n premises of a sports or other club, esp a golf club
CLUBLAND n area of London which contains most of the famous clubs
CLUBLANDS > CLUBLAND
CLUBLIKE adj like a club
CLUBMAN n man who is an enthusiastic member of a club or clubs
CLUBMATE n friend or contemporary in the same club
CLUBMATES > CLUBMATE
CLUBMEN > CLUBMAN
CLUBMOSS n type of green moss-like plant
CLUBROOM n room in which a club meets
CLUBROOMS > CLUBROOM
CLUBROOT n disease of cabbages
CLUBROOTS > CLUBROOT
CLUBRUSH n any rush of the genus Scirpus
CLUBS > CLUB
CLUBWOMAN n woman who is an enthusiastic member of a club or clubs
CLUBWOMEN > CLUBWOMAN
CLUCK n low clicking noise made by a hen ▷ vb make this noise
CLUCKED > CLUCK
CLUCKER n chicken
CLUCKERS > CLUCKER
CLUCKIER > CLUCKY
CLUCKIEST > CLUCKY
CLUCKING > CLUCK
CLUCKS > CLUCK
CLUCKY adj wishing to have a baby
CLUDGIE n toilet
CLUDGIES > CLUDGIE
CLUE n something that helps to solve a mystery or puzzle ▷ vb help solve a mystery or puzzle
CLUED > CLUE
CLUEING > CLUE
CLUELESS adj stupid
CLUES > CLUE
CLUEY adj (Australian) well-informed and adroit
CLUIER > CLUEY
CLUIEST > CLUEY
CLUING > CLUE
CLUMBER n type of thickset spaniel

CLUMBERS > CLUMBER
CLUMP n small group of things or people ▷ vb walk heavily
CLUMPED > CLUMP
CLUMPER vb walk heavily
CLUMPERED > CLUMPER
CLUMPERS > CLUMP
CLUMPET n large chunk of floating ice
CLUMPETS > CLUMPET
CLUMPIER > CLUMP
CLUMPIEST > CLUMP
CLUMPING > CLUMP
CLUMPISH > CLUMP
CLUMPLIKE > CLUMP
CLUMPS > CLUMP
CLUMPY > CLUMP
CLUMSIER > CLUMSY
CLUMSIEST > CLUMSY
CLUMSILY > CLUMSY
CLUMSY adj lacking skill or physical coordination
CLUNCH n hardened clay
CLUNCHES > CLUNCH
CLUNG > CLING
CLUNK n dull metallic sound ▷ vb make such a sound
CLUNKED > CLUNK
CLUNKER n dilapidated old car or other machine
CLUNKERS > CLUNKER
CLUNKIER > CLUNKY
CLUNKIEST > CLUNKY
CLUNKING > CLUNK
CLUNKS > CLUNK
CLUNKY adj making a clunking noise
CLUPEID n type of fish
CLUPEIDS > CLUPEID
CLUPEOID n type of soft-finned fish
CLUPEOIDS > CLUPEOID
CLUSIA n tree of the tropical American genus Clusia
CLUSIAS > CLUSIA
CLUSTER n small close group ▷ vb gather in clusters
CLUSTERED > CLUSTER
CLUSTERS > CLUSTER
CLUSTERY adj full of clusters
CLUTCH vb grasp tightly ▷ n mechanical device
CLUTCHED > CLUTCH
CLUTCHES > CLUTCH
CLUTCHIER > CLUTCHY
CLUTCHING > CLUTCH
CLUTCHY adj (of a person) tending to cling
CLUTTER vb scatter objects about (a place) untidily ▷ n untidy mess
CLUTTERED > CLUTTER
CLUTTERS > CLUTTER
CLUTTERY adj full of clutter
CLY vb steal or seize
CLYING > CLY
CLYPE vb tell tales ▷ n person who tells tales
CLYPEAL > CLYPEUS
CLYPEATE > CLYPEUS

CLYPED > CLYPE
CLYPEI > CLYPEUS
CLYPES > CLYPE
CLYPEUS n cuticular plate on the head of some insects
CLYPING > CLYPE
CLYSTER a former name for an > ENEMA
CLYSTERS > CLYSTER
CNEMIAL > CNEMIS
CNEMIDES > CNEMIS
CNEMIS n shin or tibia
CNIDA n stinging organ in jellyfish
CNIDAE > CNIDA
CNIDARIAN n type of invertebrate of the phylum which comprises the coelenterates
COACH n long-distance bus ▷ vb train, teach
COACHABLE adj capable of being coached
COACHDOG n Dalmatian dog
COACHDOGS > COACHDOG
COACHED > COACH
COACHEE n person who receives training from a coach
COACHEES > COACHEE
COACHER > COACH
COACHERS > COACH
COACHES > COACH
COACHIER > COACHY
COACHIES > COACHY
COACHIEST > COACHY
COACHING > COACH
COACHINGS > COACH
COACHLINE n decorative line on the bodywork of a vehicle
COACHLOAD n quantity that a coach can carry
COACHMAN n driver of a horse-drawn coach or carriage
COACHMEN > COACHMAN
COACHROOF n raised part of yacht cabin roof
COACHWHIP n whipsnake
COACHWOOD n Australian tree yielding light aromatic wood used for furniture etc
COACHWORK n body of a car
COACHY n coachman ▷ adj resembling or pertaining to a coach
COACT vb act together
COACTED > COACT
COACTING > COACT
COACTION n any relationship between organisms within a community
COACTIONS > COACTION
COACTIVE > COACTION
COACTOR > COACT
COACTORS > COACT
COACTS > COACT
COADAPTED adj adapted to one another
COADIES > COADY

COADJUTOR n bishop appointed as assistant to a diocesan bishop
COADMIRE vb admire together
COADMIRED > COADMIRE
COADMIRES > COADMIRE
COADMIT vb admit together
COADMITS > COADMIT
COADUNATE same as > CONNATE
COADY n sauce made from molasses
COAEVAL n contemporary
COAEVALS > COAEVAL
COAGENCY n joint agency
COAGENT > COAGENCY
COAGENTS > COAGENCY
COAGULA > COAGULUM
COAGULANT n substance causing coagulation
COAGULASE n any enzyme that causes coagulation of blood
COAGULATE vb change from a liquid to a semisolid mass ▷ n solid or semisolid substance produced by coagulation
COAGULUM n any coagulated mass
COAGULUMS > COAGULUM
COAITA n spider monkey
COAITAS > COAITA
COAL n black rock consisting mainly of carbon, used as fuel ▷ vb take in, or turn into coal
COALA same as > KOALA
COALAS > COALA
COALBALL n in coal, nodule containing petrified plant or animal remains
COALBALLS > COALBALL
COALBIN n bin for holding coal
COALBINS > COALBIN
COALBOX n box for holding coal
COALBOXES > COALBOX
COALDUST n dust from coal
COALDUSTS > COALDUST
COALED > COAL
COALER n ship, train, etc, used to carry or supply coal
COALERS > COALER
COALESCE vb come together, merge
COALESCED > COALESCE
COALESCES > COALESCE
COALFACE n exposed seam of coal in a mine
COALFACES > COALFACE
COALFIELD n area with coal under the ground

COALFISH n type of dark-coloured food fish occurring in northern seas

COALHOLE n small coal cellar

COALHOLES > COALHOLE

COALHOUSE n shed or building for storing coal

COALIER > COAL

COALIEST > COAL

COALIFIED > COALIFY

COALIFIES > COALIFY

COALIFY vb turn into coal

COALING > COAL

COALISE vb form a coalition

COALISED > COALISE

COALISES > COALISE

COALISING > COALISE

COALITION n temporary alliance, esp between political parties

COALIZE same as > COALISE

COALIZED > COALIZE

COALIZES > COALIZE

COALIZING > COALIZE

COALLESS adj without coal

COALMAN n man who delivers coal

COALMEN > COALMAN

COALMINE n mine from which coal is extracted

COALMINER > COALMINE

COALMINES > COALMINE

COALPIT n pit from which coal is extracted

COALPITS > COALPIT

COALS > COAL

COALSACK n dark nebula near the constellation Cygnus

COALSACKS > COALSACK

COALSHED n shed in which coal is stored

COALSHEDS > COALSHED

COALY > COAL

COALYARD n yard in which coal is stored

COALYARDS > COALYARD

COAMING n raised frame round a ship's hatchway for keeping out water

COAMINGS > COAMING

COANCHOR vb co-present a TV programme

COANCHORS > COANCHOR

COANNEX vb annex with something else

COANNEXED > COANNEX

COANNEXES > COANNEX

COAPPEAR vb appear jointly

COAPPEARS > COAPPEAR

COAPT vb secure

COAPTED > COAPT

COAPTING > COAPT

COAPTS > COAPT

COARB n spiritual successor

COARBS > COARB

COARCTATE adj (of a pupa) enclosed in a hard barrel-shaped case (puparium), as in the housefly ▷ vb (esp of the aorta) to become narrower

COARSE adj rough in texture

COARSELY > COARSE

COARSEN vb make or become coarse

COARSENED > COARSEN

COARSENS > COARSEN

COARSER > COARSE

COARSEST > COARSE

COARSISH > COARSE

COASSIST vb assist jointly

COASSISTS > COASSIST

COASSUME vb assume jointly

COASSUMED > COASSUME

COASSUMES > COASSUME

COAST n place where the land meets the sea ▷ vb move by momentum, without the use of power

COASTAL > COAST

COASTALLY > COAST

COASTED > COAST

COASTER n small mat placed under a glass

COASTERS > COASTER

COASTING > COAST

COASTINGS > COAST

COASTLAND n land fringing a coast

COASTLINE n outline of a coast

COASTS > COAST

COASTWARD adv towards the coast

COASTWISE adv along the coast

COAT n outer garment with long sleeves ▷ vb cover with a layer

COATDRESS n garment that can be worn as a coat or a dress

COATE same as > QUOTE

COATED adj covered with an outer layer, film, etc

COATEE n short coat, esp for a baby

COATEES > COATEE

COATER n machine that applies a coating to something

COATERS > COATER

COATES > COATE

COATI n type of omnivorous mammal

COATING n covering layer

COATINGS > COATING

COATIS > COATI

COATLESS adj without a coat

COATLIKE adj like a coat

COATRACK n rack for hanging coats on

COATRACKS > COATRACK

COATROOM n cloakroom

COATROOMS > COATROOM

COATS > COAT

COATSTAND n stand for hanging coats on

COATTAIL n long tapering tail at the back of a man's tailored coat

COATTAILS > COATTAIL

COATTEND vb attend jointly

COATTENDS > COATTEND

COATTEST vb attest jointly

COATTESTS > COATTEST

COAUTHOR n person who shares the writing of a book, article, etc, with another ▷ vb be the joint author of (a book, article, etc)

COAUTHORS > COAUTHOR

COAX vb persuade gently

COAXAL same as > COAXIAL

COAXED > COAX

COAXER > COAX

COAXERS > COAX

COAXES > COAX

COAXIAL adj (of a cable) transmitting by means of two concentric conductors separated by an insulator

COAXIALLY > COAXIAL

COAXING n act of coaxing

COAXINGLY > COAX

COAXINGS > COAXING

COB n stalk of an ear of maize ▷ vb beat

COBAEA n tropical climbing shrub

COBAEAS > COBAEA

COBALAMIN n vitamin B12

COBALT n brittle silvery-white metallic element

COBALTIC adj of or containing cobalt, esp in the trivalent state

COBALTINE same as > COBALTITE

COBALTITE n rare silvery-white mineral

COBALTOUS adj of or containing cobalt in the divalent state

COBALTS > COBALT

COBB same as > COB

COBBED > COB

COBBER n friend

COBBERS > COBBER

COBBIER > COBBY

COBBIEST > COBBY

COBBING > COB

COBBLE n cobblestone ▷ vb pave (a road) with cobblestones

COBBLED > COBBLE

COBBLER n shoe mender

COBBLERS > COBBLER

COBBLERY n shoemaking or shoemending

COBBLES > COBBLE

COBBLING > COBBLE

COBBLINGS > COBBLE

COBBS > COBB

COBBY adj short and stocky

COBIA n large dark-striped game fish

COBIAS > COBIA

COBLE n small single-masted flat-bottomed fishing boat

COBLES > COBLE

COBLOAF n round loaf of bread

COBLOAVES > COBLOAF

COBNUT another name for > HAZELNUT

COBNUTS > COBNUT

COBRA n venomous hooded snake of Asia and Africa

COBRAS > COBRA

COBRIC > COBRA

COBRIFORM adj cobra-like

COBS > COB

COBURG n rounded loaf with a cross cut on the top

COBURGS > COBURG

COBWEB n spider's web

COBWEBBED > COBWEB

COBWEBBY > COBWEB

COBWEBS > COBWEB

COBZA n Romanian lute

COBZAS > COBZA

COCA n S American shrub

COCAIN same as > COCAINE

COCAINE n drug used illegally as a narcotic and as an anaesthetic

COCAINES > COCAINE

COCAINISE same as > COCAINIZE

COCAINISM n use of cocaine

COCAINIST n cocaine addict

COCAINIZE vb anaesthetize with cocaine

COCAINS > COCAIN

COCAPTAIN vb to captain jointly

COCAS > COCA

COCCAL > COCCUS

COCCI > COCCUS

COCCIC > COCCUS

COCCID n type of homopterous insect

COCCIDIA > COCCIDIUM

COCCIDIAN same as > COCCIDIUM

COCCIDIUM n any parasitic protozoan of the order Coccidia

COCCIDS > COCCID

COCCO n taro

COCCOID > COCCUS

COCCOIDAL > COCCUS

COCCOIDS > COCCUS

COCCOLITE n variety of pyroxene

COCCOLITH n any of the round calcareous plates in chalk formations: formed the outer layer of unicellular plankton

COCCOS > COCCO

COCCOUS > COCCUS

COCCUS n any spherical or nearly spherical bacterium

COCCYGEAL > COCCYX

COCCYGES > COCCYX

COCCYGIAN > COCCYX

COCCYX n bone at the base of the spinal column

COCCYXES > COCCYX

COCH obsolete variant of > COACH

COCHAIR vb chair jointly

COCHAIRED > COCHAIR

COCHAIRS > COCHAIR

COCHES > COCH

COCHIN n large breed of domestic fowl

COCHINEAL n red dye obtained from a Mexican insect, used for food colouring

COCHINS > COCHIN

COCHLEA n spiral tube in the internal ear

COCHLEAE > COCHLEA

COCHLEAR adj of or relating to the cochlea ▷ n spoonful

COCHLEARE variant of > COCHLEAR

COCHLEARS > COCHLEAR

COCHLEAS > COCHLEA

COCHLEATE adj shaped like a snail's shell

COCINERA n in Mexico, a female cook

COCINERAS > COCINERA

COCK n male bird, esp of domestic fowl ▷ vb draw back (the hammer of a gun) to firing position

COCKADE n feather or rosette worn on a hat as a badge

COCKADED > COCKADE

COCKADES > COCKADE

COCKAMAMY adj ridiculous or nonsensical

COCKAPOO n cross between a cocker spaniel and a poodle

COCKAPOOS > COCKAPOO

COCKATEEL same as > COCKATIEL

COCKATIEL n crested Australian parrot with a greyish-brown and yellow plumage

COCKATOO n crested parrot of Australia or Indonesia

COCKATOOS > COCKATOO

COCKBILL vb tilt up one end of

COCKBILLS > COCKBILL

COCKBIRD n male bird

COCKBIRDS > COCKBIRD

COCKBOAT n any small boat

COCKBOATS > COCKBOAT

COCKCROW n daybreak

COCKCROWS > COCKCROW

COCKED > COCK

COCKER n devotee of cockfighting ▷ vb pamper or spoil by indulgence

COCKERED > COCKER

COCKEREL n young domestic cock

COCKERELS > COCKEREL

COCKERING > COCKER

COCKERS > COCKER

COCKET n document issued by a customs officer

COCKETS > COCKET

COCKEYE n eye affected with strabismus or one that squints

COCKEYED adj crooked, askew

COCKEYES > COCKEYE

COCKFIGHT n fight between two gamecocks fitted with sharp metal spurs

COCKHORSE n rocking horse

COCKIER > COCKY

COCKIES > COCKY

COCKIEST > COCKY

COCKILY > COCKY

COCKINESS n conceited self-assurance

COCKING > COCK

COCKISH adj wanton

COCKLE n edible shellfish ▷ vb fish for cockles

COCKLEBUR n type of coarse weed with spiny burs

COCKLED > COCKLE

COCKLEERT a Southwest English dialect variant of > COCKCROW

COCKLEMAN n man who collects cockles

COCKLEMEN > COCKLEMAN

COCKLER n person employed to gather cockles

COCKLERS > COCKLER

COCKLES > COCKLE

COCKLIKE adj resembling a cock

COCKLING > COCKLE

COCKLINGS > COCKLING

COCKLOFT n small loft, garret, or attic

COCKLOFTS > COCKLOFT

COCKMATCH n cockfight

COCKNEY n native of London, esp of its East End ▷ adj characteristic of cockneys or their dialect

COCKNEYFY vb cause (one's speech, manners, etc) to fit the stereotyped idea of a cockney

COCKNEYS > COCKNEY

COCKNIFY same as > COCKNEYFY

COCKPIT n pilot's compartment in an aircraft

COCKPITS > COCKPIT

COCKROACH n beetle-like insect which is a household pest

COCKS > COCK

COCKSCOMB n comb of a domestic cock

COCKSFOOT n type of Eurasian grass, cultivated as a pasture grass in N America and S Africa

COCKSHIES > COCKSHY

COCKSHOT another name for > COCKSHY

COCKSHOTS > COCKSHOT

COCKSHUT n dusk

COCKSHUTS > COCKSHUT

COCKSHY n target aimed at in throwing games

COCKSIER > COCKSY

COCKSIEST > COCKSY

COCKSMAN n man reputed to be sexually accomplished

COCKSMEN > COCKSMAN

COCKSPUR n spur on the leg of a cock

COCKSPURS > COCKSPUR

COCKSURE adj overconfident, arrogant

COCKSWAIN same as > COXSWAIN

COCKSY adj cocky

COCKTAIL n mixed alcoholic drink

COCKTAILS > COCKTAIL

COCKUP n something done badly ▷ vb ruin or spoil

COCKUPS > COCKUP

COCKY adj conceited and overconfident ▷ n farmer whose farm is regarded as small or of little account

COCO n coconut palm

COCOA n powder made from the seed of the cacao tree

COCOANUT same as > COCONUT

COCOANUTS > COCONUT

COCOAS > COCOA

COCOBOLA n type of rosewood

COCOBOLAS > COCOBOLA

COCOBOLO same as > COCOBOLA

COCOBOLOS > COCOBOLO

COCOMAT n mat made from coconut fibre

COCOMATS > COCOMAT

COCONUT n large hard fruit of a type of palm tree

COCONUTS > COCONUT

COCONUTTY adj tasting of coconut

COCOON n silky protective covering of a silkworm ▷ vb wrap up tightly for protection

COCOONED > COCOON

COCOONER n person who retreats to a secure family environment

COCOONERS > COCOONER

COCOONERY n place where silkworms feed and make cocoons

COCOONING > COCOON

COCOONS > COCOON

COCOPAN n (in South Africa) a small wagon running on narrow-gauge railway lines used in mines

COCOPANS > COCOPAN

COCOPLUM n tropical shrub or its fruit

COCOPLUMS > COCOPLUM

COCOS > COCO

COCOTTE n small fireproof dish in which individual portions of food are cooked

COCOTTES > COCOTTE

COCOUNSEL vb to counsel jointly

COCOYAM n food plant of West Africa with edible underground stem

COCOYAMS > COCOYAM

COCOZELLE n variety of squash

COCREATE vb create jointly

COCREATED > COCREATE

COCREATES > COCREATE

COCREATOR > COCREATE

COCTILE adj made by exposing to heat

COCTION n boiling

COCTIONS > COCTION

COCULTURE vb to culture together

COCURATE vb curate jointly

COCURATED > COCURATE

COCURATES > COCURATE

COCURATOR n joint curator

COCUSWOOD n wood from a tropical American leguminous tree, used for inlaying, musical instruments, etc

COD n large food fish of the North Atlantic ▷ adj having the character of an imitation or parody ▷ vb make fun of

CODA n final part of a musical composition

CODABLE adj capable of being coded

CODAS > CODA

CODDED > COD

CODDER n cod fisherman or fishing boat

CODDERS > CODDER

CODDING > COD

CODDLE vb pamper, overprotect ▷ n stew made from ham and bacon scraps

CODDLED > CODDLE

CODDLER > CODDLE

CODDLERS > CODDLE

CODDLES > CODDLE

CODDLING > CODDLE

CODE n system by which messages can be communicated secretly or briefly ▷ vb put into code

CODEBOOK n book containing the means to decipher a code

CODEBOOKS > CODEBOOK

CODEBTOR n fellow debtor

CODEBTORS > CODEBTOR

CODEC n set of electrical equipment

CODECS > CODEC

CODED > CODE

CODEIA n codeine

CODEIAS > CODEIA

CODEIN same as > CODEINE

CODEINA obsolete variant of > CODEINE

CODEINAS > CODEINA

CODEINE n drug used as a painkiller

CODEINES > CODEINE

CODEINS > CODEIN

CODELESS adj lacking a code

CODEN n identification code assigned to a publication

CODENAME same as > CODEWORD

CODENAMES > CODEWORD

CODENS > CODEN

CODER n person or thing that codes

CODERIVE vb derive jointly

CODERIVED > CODERIVE

CODERIVES > CODERIVE

CODERS > CODER

CODES > CODE

CODESIGN vb design jointly

CODESIGNS > CODESIGN

CODETTA n short coda

CODETTAS > CODETTA

CODEVELOP vb to develop jointly

CODEWORD n (esp in military use) a word used to identify a classified plan, operation, etc

CODEWORDS > CODEWORD

CODEX n volume of manuscripts of an ancient text

CODEXES > CODEX

CODFISH n cod

CODFISHES > CODFISH

CODGER n old man

CODGERS > CODGER

CODICES > CODEX

CODICIL n addition to a will

CODICILS > CODICIL

CODIFIED > CODIFY

CODIFIER > CODIFY

CODIFIERS > CODIFY

CODIFIES > CODIFY

CODIFY vb organize (rules or procedures) systematically

CODIFYING > CODIFY

CODILLA n coarse tow of hemp and flax

CODILLAS > CODILLA

CODILLE n in the card game ombre, term indicating that the game is won

CODILLES > CODILLE

CODING > CODE

CODINGS > CODE

CODIRECT vb direct jointly

CODIRECTS > CODIRECT

CODIST n codifier

CODISTS > CODIST

CODLIN same as > CODLING

CODLING n young cod

CODLINGS > CODLING

CODLINS > CODLIN

CODOLOGY n art or practice of bluffing or deception

CODOMAIN n set of values that a function is allowed to take

CODOMAINS > CODOMAIN

CODON n part of a DNA molecule

CODONS > CODON

CODPIECE n bag covering the male genitals, attached to the breeches

CODPIECES > CODPIECE

CODRIVE vb take alternate turns driving a car with another person

CODRIVEN > CODRIVE

CODRIVER n one of two drivers who take turns to drive a car

CODRIVERS > CODRIVER

CODRIVES > CODRIVE

CODRIVING > CODRIVE

CODROVE > CODRIVE

CODS > COD

COECILIAN n tropical limbless amphibian resembling an earthworm

COED adj educating boys and girls together ▷ n school or college that educates boys and girls together

COEDIT vb edit (a book, newspaper, etc) jointly

COEDITED > COEDIT

COEDITING > COEDIT

COEDITOR > COEDIT

COEDITORS > COEDIT

COEDITS > COEDIT

COEDS > COED

COEFFECT n secondary effect

COEFFECTS > COEFFECT

COEHORN n type of small artillery mortar

COEHORNS > COEHORN

COELIAC adj of or relating to the abdomen ▷ n person who has coeliac disease

COELIACS > COELIAC

COELOM n body cavity of many multicellular animals

COELOMATA n animals possessing a coelom

COELOMATE adj possessing a coelom

COELOME same as > COELOM

COELOMES > COELOME

COELOMIC > COELOM

COELOMS > COELOM

COELOSTAT n astronomical instrument consisting of a plane mirror mounted parallel to the earth's axis and rotated about this axis once every two days so that light from a celestial body, esp the sun, is reflected onto a second mirror, which reflects the beam into a telescope

COEMBODY vb embody jointly

COEMPLOY vb employ together

COEMPLOYS > COEMPLOY

COEMPT vb buy up something in its entirety

COEMPTED > COEMPT

COEMPTING > COEMPT

COEMPTION n buying up of the complete supply of a commodity

COEMPTS > COEMPT

COENACLE same as > CENACLE

COENACLES > COENACLE

COENACT vb enact jointly

COENACTED > COENACT

COENACTS > COENACT

COENAMOR vb enamour jointly

COENAMORS > COENAMOR

COENAMOUR vb enamour jointly

COENDURE vb endure together

COENDURED > COENDURE

COENDURES > COENDURE

COENOBIA > COENOBIUM

COENOBITE n member of a religious order in a monastic community

COENOBIUM n monastery or convent

COENOCYTE n mass of protoplasm containing many nuclei and enclosed by a cell wall: occurs in many fungi and some algae

COENOSARC n system of protoplasmic branches connecting the polyps of colonial organisms such as corals

COENURE variant form of > COENURUS

COENURES > COENURE

COENURI > COENURUS

COENURUS n encysted larval form of a type of tapeworm with many encapsulated heads

COENZYME n type of nonprotein organic molecule

COENZYMES > COENZYME

COEQUAL n equal ▷ adj of the same size, rank, etc

COEQUALLY > COEQUAL

COEQUALS > COEQUAL

COEQUATE vb equate together

COEQUATED > COEQUATE

COEQUATES > COEQUATE

COERCE vb compel, force

COERCED > COERCE

COERCER > COERCE

COERCERS > COERCE

COERCES > COERCE

COERCIBLE > COERCE

COERCIBLY > COERCE

COERCING > COERCE

COERCION n act or power of coercing

COERCIONS > COERCION

COERCIVE > COERCE

COERECT vb erect together

COERECTED > COERECT

COERECTS > COERECT

COESITE n polymorph of silicon dioxide

COESITES > COESITE

COETERNAL adj existing together eternally

COEVAL n contemporary ▷ adj contemporary

COEVALITY > COEVAL

COEVALLY > COEVAL

COEVALS > COEVAL

COEVOLVE vb evolve together

COEVOLVED > COEVOLVE

COEVOLVES > COEVOLVE

COEXERT vb exert together

COEXERTED > COEXERT

COEXERTS > COEXERT

COEXIST vb exist together, esp peacefully despite differences

COEXISTED > COEXIST

COEXISTS > COEXIST

COEXTEND vb extend or cause to extend equally in space or time

COEXTENDS
> COEXTEND
COFACTOR n type of nonprotein substance
COFACTORS
> COFACTOR
COFEATURE vb to feature together
COFF vb buy
COFFED > COFF
COFFEE n drink made from the roasted and ground seeds of a tropical shrub ▷ adj medium-brown
COFFEEPOT n pot in which coffee is brewed or served
COFFEES > COFFEE
COFFER n chest, esp for storing valuables ▷ vb store
COFFERDAM n watertight enclosure pumped dry to enable construction work to be done
COFFERED > COFFER
COFFERING
> COFFERDAM
COFFERS > COFFER
COFFIN n box in which a corpse is buried or cremated ▷ vb place in or as in a coffin
COFFINED > COFFIN
COFFING > COFF
COFFINING > COFFIN
COFFINITE n uranium-bearing silicate mineral
COFFINS > COFFIN
COFFLE n (esp formerly) line of slaves, beasts, etc, fastened together ▷ vb fasten together in a coffle
COFFLED > COFFLE
COFFLES > COFFLE
COFFLING > COFFLE
COFFRET n small coffer
COFFRETS > COFFRET
COFFS > COFF
COFINANCE vb to finance jointly
COFIRING n combustion of two different types of fuel at the same time
COFIRINGS
> COFIRING
COFOUND vb found jointly
COFOUNDED > COFOUND
COFOUNDER > COFOUND
COFOUNDS > COFOUND
COFT > COFF
COG n one of the teeth on the rim of a gearwheel ▷ vb roll (cast-steel ingots) to convert them into blooms
COGENCE > COGENT
COGENCES > COGENT
COGENCIES > COGENT
COGENCY > COGENT
COGENER n thing of the same kind
COGENERS > COGENER
COGENT adj forcefully convincing

COGENTLY > COGENT
COGGED > COG
COGGER n deceiver
COGGERS > COGGER
COGGIE n quaich or drinking cup
COGGIES > COGGIE
COGGING > COG
COGGINGS > COG
COGGLE vb wobble or rock
COGGLED > COGGLE
COGGLES > COGGLE
COGGLIER > COGGLE
COGGLIEST > COGGLE
COGGLING > COGGLE
COGGLY > COGGLE
COGIE same as > COGGIE
COGIES > COGIE
COGITABLE adj conceivable
COGITATE vb think deeply about
COGITATED
> COGITATE
COGITATES
> COGITATE
COGITATOR
> COGITATE
COGITO n philosophical theory
COGITOS > COGITO
COGNAC n French brandy
COGNACS > COGNAC
COGNATE adj derived from a common original form ▷ n cognate word or language
COGNATELY > COGNATE
COGNATES > COGNATE
COGNATION > COGNATE
COGNISANT same as > COGNIZANT
COGNISE same as > COGNIZE
COGNISED > COGNISE
COGNISER > COGNISE
COGNISERS > COGNISE
COGNISES > COGNISE
COGNISING > COGNISE
COGNITION n act or experience of knowing or acquiring knowledge
COGNITIVE adj of or relating to cognition
COGNIZANT adj aware
COGNIZE vb perceive, become aware of, or know
COGNIZED > COGNIZE
COGNIZER > COGNIZE
COGNIZERS > COGNIZE
COGNIZES > COGNIZE
COGNIZING > COGNIZE
COGNOMEN n nickname
COGNOMENS
> COGNOMEN
COGNOMINA
> COGNOMEN
COGNOSCE vb in Scots law, to give judgment upon
COGNOSCED
> COGNOSCE
COGNOSCES
> COGNOSCE
COGNOVIT n in law, a defendant's confession that the case against him or her is just

COGNOVITS
> COGNOVIT
COGON n type of coarse tropical grass used for thatching
COGONS > COGON
COGS > COG
COGUE n wooden pail or drinking vessel
COGUES > COGUE
COGWAY n rack railway
COGWAYS > COGWAY
COGWHEEL same as > GEARWHEEL
COGWHEELS
> COGWHEEL
COHAB n cohabitor
COHABIT vb live together as spouses without being married
COHABITED > COHABIT
COHABITEE > COHABIT
COHABITER > COHABIT
COHABITOR n one who cohabits
COHABITS > COHABIT
COHABS > COHAB
COHEAD vb head jointly
COHEADED > COHEAD
COHEADING > COHEAD
COHEADS > COHEAD
COHEIR n person who inherits jointly with others
COHEIRESS > COHEIR
COHEIRS > COHEIR
COHEN same as > KOHEN
COHENS > COHEN
COHERE vb hold or stick together
COHERED > COHERE
COHERENCE n logical or natural connection or consistency
COHERENCY same as > COHERENCE
COHERENT adj logical and consistent
COHERER n electrical component
COHERERS > COHERER
COHERES > COHERE
COHERING > COHERE
COHERITOR n coheir
COHESIBLE adj capable of cohesion
COHESION n sticking together
COHESIONS
> COHESION
COHESIVE adj sticking together to form a whole
COHIBIT vb restrain
COHIBITED > COHIBIT
COHIBITS > COHIBIT
COHO n type of Pacific salmon
COHOBATE vb redistil (a distillate), esp by allowing it to mingle with the remaining matter
COHOBATED
> COHOBATE
COHOBATES
> COHOBATE
COHOE same as > COHO
COHOES > COHO
COHOG n quahog, an edible clam

COHOGS > COHOG
COHOLDER n joint holder
COHOLDERS
> COHOLDER
COHORN same as > COEHORN
COHORNS > COHORN
COHORT n band of associates
COHORTS > COHORT
COHOS > COHO
COHOSH n type of North American plant
COHOSHES > COHOSH
COHOST vb host jointly
COHOSTED > COHOST
COHOSTESS vb (of a woman) to host jointly
COHOSTING > COHOST
COHOSTS > COHOST
COHOUSING n type of housing with some shared facilities
COHUNE n tropical feather palm
COHUNES > COHUNE
COHYPONYM n word which is one of multiple hyponyms of another word
COIF vb arrange the hair of ▷ n close-fitting cap worn in the Middle Ages
COIFED adj wearing a coif
COIFFE vb coiffure
COIFFED > COIF
COIFFES > COIFFE
COIFFEUR n hairdresser
COIFFEURS
> COIFFEUR
COIFFEUSE
> COIFFEUR
COIFFING > COIF
COIFFURE n hairstyle ▷ vb dress or arrange (the hair)
COIFFURED
> COIFFURE
COIFFURES
> COIFFURE
COIFING > COIF
COIFS > COIF
COIGN vb wedge ▷ n quoin
COIGNE same as > COIGN
COIGNED > COIGN
COIGNES > COIGNE
COIGNING > COIGN
COIGNS > COIGN
COIL vb wind in loops ▷ n something coiled
COILED > COIL
COILER > COIL
COILERS > COIL
COILING > COIL
COILS > COIL
COIN n piece of metal money ▷ vb invent (a word or phrase)
COINABLE > COIN
COINAGE n coins collectively
COINAGES > COINAGE
COINCIDE vb happen at the same time
COINCIDED
> COINCIDE
COINCIDES > COINCIDE

COINED > COIN

COINER > COIN

COINERS > COIN

COINFECT vb infect at same time as other infection

COINFECTS > COINFECT

COINFER vb infer jointly

COINFERS > COINFER

COINHERE vb inhere together

COINHERED > COINHERE

COINHERES > COINHERE

COINING > COIN

COININGS > COIN

COINMATE n fellow inmate

COINMATES > COINMATE

COINOP adj (of a machine) operated by putting a coin in a slot

COINS > COIN

COINSURE vb insure jointly

COINSURED > COINSURE

COINSURER > COINSURE

COINSURES > COINSURE

COINTER vb inter together

COINTERS > COINTER

COINTREAU n tradename for a French orange liqueur

COINVENT vb invent jointly

COINVENTS > COINVENT

COINVEST vb invest jointly

COINVESTS > COINVEST

COIR n coconut fibre, used for matting

COIRS > COIR

COISTREL n knave

COISTRELS > COISTREL

COISTRIL same as > COISTREL

COISTRILS > COISTRIL

COIT n buttocks

COITAL > COITUS

COITALLY > COITUS

COITION same as > COITUS

COITIONAL > COITION

COITIONS > COITION

COITS > COIT

COITUS n sexual intercourse

COITUSES > COITUS

COJOIN vb conjoin

COJOINED > COJOIN

COJOINING > COJOIN

COJOINS > COJOIN

COJONES pl n manly courage

COKE n solid fuel left after gas has been distilled from coal ▷ vb become or convert into coke

COKED > COKE

COKEHEAD n cocaine addict

COKEHEADS > COKEHEAD

COKELIKE > COKE

COKERNUT same as > COCONUT

COKERNUTS > COKERNUT

COKES n fool

COKESES > COKES

COKIER > COKY

COKIEST > COKY

COKING n act of coking

COKINGS > COKING

COKULORIS n palette with irregular holes, placed between lighting and camera to prevent glare

COKY adj like coke

COL n high mountain pass

COLA n dark brown fizzy soft drink

COLANDER n perforated bowl for straining or rinsing foods

COLANDERS > COLANDER

COLAS > COLA

COLBIES > COLBY

COLBY n type of mild-tasting hard cheese

COLBYS > COLBY

COLCANNON n dish, originating in Ireland, of potatoes and cabbage or other greens boiled and mashed together

COLCHICA > COLCHICUM

COLCHICUM n type of Eurasian liliaceous plant, such as the autumn crocus

COLCOTHAR n finely powdered form of ferric oxide produced by heating ferric sulphate and used as a pigment and as jewellers' rouge

COLD adj lacking heat ▷ n lack of heat

COLDBLOOD n any heavy draught-horse

COLDCOCK vb knock to the ground

COLDCOCKS > COLDCOCK

COLDER > COLD

COLDEST > COLD

COLDHOUSE n unheated greenhouse

COLDIE n cold can or bottle of beer

COLDIES > COLDIE

COLDISH > COLD

COLDLY > COLD

COLDNESS > COLD

COLDS > COLD

COLE same as > CABBAGE

COLEAD vb lead together

COLEADER > COLEAD

COLEADERS > COLEAD

COLEADING > COLEAD

COLEADS > COLEAD

COLECTOMY n surgical removal of part or all of the colon

COLED > COLEAD

COLEOPTER n aircraft that has an annular wing with the fuselage and engine on the centre line

COLES > COLE

COLESEED n seeds or plants of the cole

COLESEEDS > COLESEED

COLESLAW n salad dish of shredded raw cabbage in a dressing

COLESLAWS > COLESLAW

COLESSEE n joint lessee

COLESSEES > COLESSEE

COLESSOR n joint lessor

COLESSORS > COLESSOR

COLEWORT same as > CABBAGE

COLEWORTS > CABBAGE

COLEY same as > COALFISH

COLEYS > COLEY

COLIBRI n hummingbird

COLIBRIS > COLIBRI

COLIC n severe pains in the stomach and bowels

COLICIN n bactericidal protein

COLICINE n antibacterial protein

COLICINES > COLICINE

COLICINS > COLICIN

COLICKIER > COLICKY

COLICKY adj relating to or suffering from colic

COLICROOT n N American plant with tubular white or yellow flowers and a bitter root formerly used to relieve colic

COLICS > COLIC

COLICWEED n type of plant such as the squirrel corn and Dutchman's-breeches

COLIES > COLY

COLIFORM n type of bacteria of the intestinal tract

COLIFORMS > COLIFORM

COLIN n quail

COLINEAR same as > COLLINEAR

COLINS > COLIN

COLIPHAGE n bacteriophage

COLISEUM n large building, such as a stadium or theatre, used for entertainments, sports, etc

COLISEUMS > COLISEUM

COLISTIN n polymyxin antibiotic

COLISTINS > COLISTIN

COLITIC > COLITIS

COLITIS n inflammation of the colon

COLITISES > COLITIS

COLL vb embrace

COLLAB n collaboration

COLLABS > COLLAB

COLLAGE n type of art form ▷ vb make a collage

COLLAGED > COLLAGE

COLLAGEN n protein found in cartilage and bone that yields gelatine when boiled

COLLAGENS > COLLAGEN

COLLAGES > COLLAGE

COLLAGING > COLLAGE

COLLAGIST > COLLAGE

COLLAPSAR n collapsed star, either a white dwarf, neutron star, or black hole

COLLAPSE vb fall down suddenly ▷ n collapsing

COLLAPSED > COLLAPSE

COLLAPSES > COLLAPSE

COLLAR n part of a garment round the neck ▷ vb seize, arrest

COLLARD n variety of cabbage with a crown of edible leaves

COLLARDS > COLLARD

COLLARED > COLLAR

COLLARET n small collar

COLLARETS > COLLARET

COLLARING > COLLAR

COLLARS > COLLAR

COLLATE vb gather together, examine, and put in order

COLLATED > COLLATE

COLLATES > COLLATE

COLLATING > COLLATE

COLLATION n collating

COLLATIVE adj involving collation

COLLATOR n person or machine that collates texts or manuscripts

COLLATORS > COLLATOR

COLLEAGUE n fellow worker, esp in a profession

COLLECT vb gather together ▷ n short prayer

COLLECTED adj calm and controlled

COLLECTOR n person who collects objects as a hobby

COLLECTS > COLLECT

COLLED > COLL

COLLEEN n girl or young woman

COLLEENS > COLLEEN

COLLEGE n place of higher education

COLLEGER n member of a college

COLLEGERS > COLLEGER

COLLEGES > COLLEGE

COLLEGIA
> COLLEGIUM
COLLEGIAL adj of or relating to a college
COLLEGIAN n member of a college
COLLEGIUM n (in the former Soviet Union) a board in charge of a department
COLLET n (in a jewellery setting) a band or coronet-shaped claw that holds an individual stone ▷ vb mount in a collet
COLLETED > COLLET
COLLETING > COLLET
COLLETS > COLLET
COLLICULI n plural form of singular colliculus: small elevation, as on the surface of the optic lobe of the brain
COLLIDE vb crash together violently
COLLIDED > COLLIDE
COLLIDER n particle accelerator in which beams of particles are made to collide
COLLIDERS
> COLLIDER
COLLIDES > COLLIDE
COLLIDING > COLLIDE
COLLIE n silky-haired sheepdog
COLLIED > COLLY
COLLIER n coal miner
COLLIERS > COLLIER
COLLIERY n coal mine
COLLIES > COLLY
COLLIGATE vb connect or link together
COLLIMATE vb adjust the line of sight of (an optical instrument)
COLLINEAR adj lying on the same straight line
COLLING n embrace
COLLINGS > COLLING
COLLINS n type of cocktail
COLLINSES > COLLINS
COLLINSIA n N American plant with blue, white, or purple flowers
COLLISION n violent crash between moving objects
COLLOCATE vb (of words) occur together regularly
COLLODION n colourless or yellow syrupy liquid that consists of a solution of pyroxylin in ether and alcohol
COLLODIUM same as
> COLLODION
COLLOGUE vb confer confidentially
COLLOGUED
> COLLOGUE
COLLOGUES
> COLLOGUE
COLLOID n suspension of particles in a solution ▷ adj relating to the gluelike material found

in certain degenerating tissues
COLLOIDAL adj of, denoting, or having the character of a colloid
COLLOIDS > COLLOID
COLLOP n small slice of meat
COLLOPS > COLLOP
COLLOQUE vb converse
COLLOQUED
> COLLOQUE
COLLOQUES
> COLLOQUE
COLLOQUIA n plural form of singular colloquium: informal gathering
COLLOQUY n conversation or conference
COLLOTYPE n method of lithographic printing from a flat surface of hardened gelatine: used mainly for fine-detail reproduction in monochrome or colour
COLLOTYPY
> COLLOTYPE
COLLS > COLL
COLLUDE vb act in collusion
COLLUDED > COLLUDE
COLLUDER > COLLUDE
COLLUDERS > COLLUDE
COLLUDES > COLLUDE
COLLUDING > COLLUDE
COLLUSION n secret or illegal cooperation
COLLUSIVE
> COLLUSION
COLLUVIA
> COLLUVIUM
COLLUVIAL
> COLLUVIUM
COLLUVIES n offscourings
COLLUVIUM n mixture of rock fragments from the bases of cliffs
COLLY n soot or grime, such as coal dust ▷ vb begrime
COLLYING > COLLY
COLLYRIA
> COLLYRIUM
COLLYRIUM a technical name for an > EYEWASH
COLOBI > COLOBUS
COLOBID n type of African monkey
COLOBIDS > COLOBID
COLOBOMA n structural defect of the eye, esp in the choroid, retina, or iris
COLOBOMAS
> COLOBOMA
COLOBUS n type of Old World monkey
COLOBUSES > COLOBUS
COLOCATE vb locate together
COLOCATED
> COLOCATE
COLOCATES
> COLOCATE
COLOCYNTH n type of Mediterranean and Asian climbing plant with bitter-tasting fruit

COLOG n logarithm of the reciprocal of a number
COLOGNE n mild perfume
COLOGNED > COLOGNE
COLOGNES > COLOGNE
COLOGS > COLOG
COLOMBARD n type of grape
COLON n punctuation mark (:)
COLONE variant of
> COLON
COLONEL n senior commissioned army or air-force officer
COLONELCY > COLONEL
COLONELS > COLONEL
COLONES > COLONE
COLONI > COLONUS
COLONIAL n inhabitant of a colony ▷ adj of or inhabiting a colony or colonies
COLONIALS
> COLONIAL
COLONIC adj of or relating to the colon ▷ n irrigation of the colon
COLONICS > COLONIC
COLONIES > COLONY
COLONISE same as
> COLONIZE
COLONISED
> COLONISE
COLONISER
> COLONISE
COLONISES
> COLONISE
COLONIST n settler in a colony
COLONISTS
> COLONIST
COLONITIS same as
> COLITIS
COLONIZE vb make into a colony
COLONIZED
> COLONIZE
COLONIZER
> COLONIZE
COLONIZES
> COLONIZE
COLONNADE n row of columns
COLONS > COLON
COLONUS n ancient Roman farmer
COLONY n people who settle in a new country but remain ruled by their homeland
COLOPHON n publisher's symbol on a book
COLOPHONS
> COLOPHON
COLOPHONY another name for > ROSIN
COLOR same as > COLOUR
COLORABLE > COLOR
COLORABLY > COLOR
COLORADO adj (of a cigar) of middling colour and strength
COLORANT n any substance that imparts colour, such as a pigment, dye, or ink
COLORANTS > COLORANT

COLORBRED adj (of animals) bred for their colour
COLORCAST vb broadcast in colour
COLORED same as
> COLOURED
COLOREDS same as
> COLOUREDS
COLORER > COLOR
COLORERS > COLOR
COLORFAST adj variant of colourfast: (of a fabric) having a colour that does not run when washed
COLORFUL > COLOR
COLORIER > COLORY
COLORIEST > COLORY
COLORIFIC adj relating to colour
COLORING same as
> COLOURING
COLORINGS > COLORING
COLORISE same as
> COLOURIZE
COLORISED
> COLORISE
COLORISER
> COLORISE
COLORISES > COLORISE
COLORISM > COLOR
COLORISMS > COLOR
COLORIST > COLOR
COLORISTS > COLOR
COLORIZE same as
> COLOURIZE
COLORIZED
> COLOURIZE
COLORIZER
> COLORIZE
COLORIZES
> COLORIZE
COLORLESS > COLOR
COLORMAN same as
> COLOURMAN
COLORMEN > COLORMAN
COLORS > COLOR
COLORWASH n cheap form of distemper ▷ vb paint with this
COLORWAY variant of
> COLOURWAY
COLORWAYS
> COLORWAY
COLORY adj full of color
COLOSSAL adj very large
COLOSSEUM same as
> COLISEUM
COLOSSI > COLOSSUS
COLOSSUS n huge statue
COLOSTOMY n operation to form an opening from the colon onto the surface of the body, for emptying the bowel
COLOSTRAL
> COLOSTRUM
COLOSTRIC
> COLOSTRUM
COLOSTRUM n thin milky secretion that precedes lactation
COLOTOMY n colonic incision
COLOUR n appearance of things as a result of reflecting light ▷ vb apply colour to

COLOURANT same as
> COLORANT
COLOURED adj having
colour
COLOUREDS pl n items of
laundry of any colour but
white
COLOURER > COLOUR
COLOURERS > COLOUR
COLOURFUL adj with
bright or varied colours
COLOURIER > COLOURY
COLOURING n
application of colour
COLOURISE same as
> COLOURIZE
COLOURISM n
discrimination in which
people are judged on the
basis of their skin colour
COLOURIST n person
who uses colour, esp an
artist
COLOURIZE vb add
colour electronically to (an
old black-and-white film)
COLOURMAN n person
who deals in paints
COLOURMEN
> COLOURMAN
COLOURS > COLOUR
COLOURWAY n one of
several different
combinations of colours in
which a given pattern is
printed on fabrics,
wallpapers, etc
COLOURY adj possessing
colour
COLPITIS another name
for > VAGINITIS
COLPOTOMY n surgical
incision into the wall of
the vagina
COLS > COL
COLT n young male horse
▷ vb to fool
COLTAN n metallic ore
COLTANS > COLTAN
COLTED > COLT
COLTER same as
> COULTER
COLTERS > COLTER
COLTHOOD n state of
being a colt
COLTHOODS
> COLTHOOD
COLTING > COLT
COLTISH adj
inexperienced
COLTISHLY > COLTISH
COLTS > COLT
COLTSFOOT n weed with
yellow flowers and
heart-shaped leaves
COLTWOOD n plant
mentioned in Spenser's
Faerie Queene
COLTWOODS
> COLTWOOD
COLUBRIAD n epic poem
about a snake
COLUBRID n type of
snake such as the grass
snake and whip snakes
COLUBRIDS
> COLUBRID
COLUBRINE adj of or
resembling a snake

COLUGO n flying lemur
COLUGOS > COLUGO
COLUMBARY n dovecote
COLUMBATE n niobate
COLUMBIC another word
for > NIOBIC
COLUMBINE n garden
flower with five petals
▷ adj of, relating to, or
resembling a dove
COLUMBITE n black
mineral occurring in
coarse granite
COLUMBIUM the former
name of > NIOBIUM
COLUMBOUS another word
for > NIOBOUS
COLUMEL n in botany, the
central column in a
capsule
COLUMELLA n central
part of the spore-
producing body of some
fungi and mosses
COLUMELS > COLUMEL
COLUMN n pillar ▷ vb
create a column
COLUMNAL n part of the
stem of a crinoid
COLUMNALS
> COLUMNAL
COLUMNAR > COLUMN
COLUMNEA n flowering
plant
COLUMNEAS
> COLUMNEA
COLUMNED > COLUMN
COLUMNIST n journalist
who writes a regular
feature in a newspaper
COLUMNS > COLUMN
COLURE n either of two
great circles on the
celestial sphere
COLURES > COLURE
COLY n S African arboreal
bird
COLZA n Eurasian plant
with bright yellow flowers
COLZAS > COLZA
COMA n state of deep
unconsciousness
COMADE > COMAKE
COMAE > COMA
COMAKE vb make
together
COMAKER > COMAKE
COMAKERS > COMAKE
COMAKES > COMAKE
COMAKING > COMAKE
COMAL > COMA
COMANAGE vb manage
jointly
COMANAGED
> COMANAGE
COMANAGER
> COMANAGE
COMANAGES
> COMANAGE
COMARB same as > COARB
COMARBS > COMARB
COMART n covenant
COMARTS > COMART
COMAS > COMA
COMATE adj having tufts
of hair ▷ n companion
COMATES > COMATE
COMATIC > COMA

COMATIK variant of
> KOMATIK
COMATIKS > COMATIK
COMATOSE adj in a coma
COMATULA same as
> COMATULID
COMATULAE
> COMATULID
COMATULID n any of a
group of crinoid
echinoderms, including
the feather stars, in which
the adults are
free-swimming
COMB n toothed
implement for arranging
the hair ▷ vb use a comb
on
COMBAT vb fight, struggle
▷ n fight or struggle
COMBATANT n fighter
▷ adj fighting
COMBATED > COMBAT
COMBATER > COMBAT
COMBATERS > COMBAT
COMBATING > COMBAT
COMBATIVE adj eager or
ready to fight, argue, etc
COMBATS > COMBAT
COMBATTED > COMBAT
COMBE same as > COMB
COMBED > COMB
COMBER n long curling
wave
COMBERS > COMBER
COMBES > COMBE
COMBI n combination
boiler
COMBIER > COMBY
COMBIES > COMBY
COMBIEST > COMBY
COMBINATE adj
betrothed
COMBINE vb join together
▷ n association of people
or firms for a common
purpose
COMBINED n competitive
event consisting of two
skiing competitions
COMBINEDS > COMBINE
COMBINER > COMBINE
COMBINERS > COMBINE
COMBINES > COMBINE
COMBING > COMB
COMBINGS pl n loose hair
or fibres removed by
combing, esp from
animals
COMBINING > COMBINE
COMBIS > COMBI
COMBLE n apex; zenith
COMBLES > COMBLE
COMBLESS adj without a
comb
COMBLIKE adj
resembling a comb
COMBO n small group of
jazz musicians
COMBOS > COMBO
COMBOVER n hairstyle in
which thinning hair is
combed over the scalp
COMBOVERS
> COMBOVER
COMBRETUM n any tree or
shrub belonging to the
genus Combretum

COMBS > COMB
COMBUST vb burn
COMBUSTED > COMBUST
COMBUSTOR n
combustion system of a
jet engine or ramjet,
comprising the
combustion chamber, the
fuel injection apparatus,
and the igniter
COMBUSTS > COMBUST
COMBWISE adv in the
manner of a comb
COMBY adj comb-like ▷ n
combination boiler
COME vb move towards a
place, arrive
COMEBACK n return to a
former position ▷ vb
return, esp to the memory
COMEBACKS
> COMEBACK
COMEDDLE vb mix
COMEDDLED
> COMEDDLE
COMEDDLES
> COMEDDLE
COMEDIAN n entertainer
who tells jokes
COMEDIANS
> COMEDIAN
COMEDIC adj of or
relating to comedy
COMEDIES > COMEDY
COMEDIST n writer of
comedies
COMEDISTS
> COMEDIST
COMEDO the technical name
for > BLACKHEAD
COMEDONES > COMEDO
COMEDOS > COMEDO
COMEDOWN n decline in
status ▷ vb come to a
place regarded as lower
COMEDOWNS
> COMEDOWN
COMEDY n humorous play,
film, or programme
COMELIER > COMELY
COMELIEST > COMELY
COMELILY > COMELY
COMELY adj nice-looking
COMEMBER n fellow
member
COMEMBERS
> COMEMBER
COMEOVER n person who
has come from Britain to
the Isle of Man to settle
COMEOVERS
> COMEOVER
COMER n person who
comes
COMERS > COMER
COMES > COME
COMET n heavenly body
with a long luminous tail
COMETARY > COMET
COMETH > COME
COMETHER n coaxing;
allure
COMETHERS
> COMETHER
COMETIC > COMET
COMETS > COMET
COMFIER > COMFY
COMFIEST > COMFY

COMFILY *adv* in a manner suggestive of or promoting comfort

COMFINESS > COMFY

COMFIT *n* sugar-coated sweet

COMFITS > COMFIT

COMFITURE *n* confiture

COMFORT *n* physical ease or wellbeing ▷ *vb* soothe, console

COMFORTED > COMFORT

COMFORTER *n* person or thing that comforts

COMFORTS > COMFORT

COMFREY *n* tall plant with bell-shaped flowers

COMFREYS > COMFREY

COMFY *adj* comfortable

COMIC *adj* humorous, funny ▷ *n* comedian

COMICAL *adj* amusing

COMICALLY > COMICAL

COMICE *n* kind of pear

COMICES > COMICE

COMICS > COMIC

COMING > COME

COMINGLE *same as* > COMMINGLE

COMINGLED > COMINGLE

COMINGLES > COMINGLE

COMINGS > COME

COMIQUE *n* comic actor

COMIQUES > COMIQUE

COMITADJI *n* Balkan guerrilla fighter

COMITAL *adj* relating to a count or earl

COMITATUS *n* leader's retinue

COMITIA *n* ancient Roman assembly

COMITIAL > COMITIA

COMITIAS > COMITIA

COMITIES > COMITY

COMITY *n* friendly politeness, esp between different countries

COMIX *n* comic books in general

COMM *n* as in *comm badge* small wearable badge-shaped radio transmitter and receiver

COMMA *n* punctuation mark (,)

COMMAND *vb* order ▷ *n* authoritative instruction that something must be done

COMMANDED > COMMAND

COMMANDER *n* military officer in command of a group or operation

COMMANDO *n* (member of) a military unit trained for swift raids in enemy territory

COMMANDOS > COMMANDO

COMMANDS > COMMAND

COMMAS > COMMA

COMMATA > COMMA

COMMENCE *vb* begin

COMMENCED > COMMENCE

COMMENCER > COMMENCE

COMMENCES > COMMENCE

COMMEND *vb* praise

COMMENDAM *n* temporary holding of an ecclesiastical benefice

COMMENDED > COMMEND

COMMENDER > COMMEND

COMMENDS > COMMEND

COMMENSAL *adj* (of two different species of plant or animal) living in close association, such that one species benefits without harming the other ▷ *n* commensal plant or animal

COMMENT *n* remark ▷ *vb* make a comment

COMMENTED > COMMENT

COMMENTER > COMMENT

COMMENTOR > COMMENT

COMMENTS > COMMENT

COMMER *same as* > COMER

COMMERCE *n* buying and selling, trade ▷ *vb* to trade

COMMERCED > COMMERCE

COMMERCES > COMMERCE

COMMERE *n* female compere

COMMERES > COMMERE

COMMERGE *vb* merge together

COMMERGED > COMMERGE

COMMERGES > COMMERGE

COMMERS > COMMER

COMMIE *n* communist

COMMIES > COMMIE

COMMINATE *vb* to anathematise

COMMINGLE *vb* mix or be mixed

COMMINUTE *vb* break (a bone) into several small fragments

COMMIS *n* apprentice waiter or chef ▷ *adj* (of a waiter or chef) apprentice

COMMISH *n* commissioner

COMMISHES > COMMISH

COMMISSAR *n* (formerly) official responsible for political education in Communist countries

COMMIT *vb* perform (a crime or error)

COMMITS > COMMIT

COMMITTAL *n* act of committing or pledging

COMMITTED > COMMIT

COMMITTEE *n* group of people appointed to perform a specified service or function

COMMITTER > COMMIT

COMMIX *a rare word for* > MIX

COMMIXED > COMMIX

COMMIXES > COMMIX

COMMIXING > COMMIX

COMMIXT > COMMIX

COMMO *short for* > COMMUNIST

COMMODE *n* seat with a hinged flap concealing a chamber pot

COMMODES > COMMODE

COMMODIFY *vb* to make into a commodity

COMMODITY *n* something that can be bought or sold

COMMODO *same as* > COMODO

COMMODORE *n* senior commissioned officer in the navy

COMMON *adj* occurring often ▷ *n* area of grassy land belonging to a community ▷ *vb* sit at table with strangers

COMMONAGE *n* use of something, esp a pasture, in common with others

COMMONED > COMMON

COMMONER *n* person who does not belong to the nobility

COMMONERS > COMMONER

COMMONEST > COMMON

COMMONEY *n* playing marble of a common sort

COMMONEYS > COMMONEY

COMMONING > COMMON

COMMONLY *adv* usually

COMMONS *n* people not of noble birth viewed as forming a political order

COMMORANT *n* resident

COMMOS > COMMO

COMMOT *n* in medieval Wales, a division of land

COMMOTE *same as* > COMMOT

COMMOTES > COMMOTE

COMMOTION *n* noisy disturbance

COMMOTS > COMMOT

COMMOVE *vb* disturb

COMMOVED > COMMOVE

COMMOVES > COMMOVE

COMMOVING > COMMOVE

COMMS *pl n* communications

COMMUNAL *adj* shared

COMMUNARD *n* member of a commune

COMMUNE *n* group of people who live together and share everything ▷ *vb* feel very close (to)

COMMUNED > COMMUNE

COMMUNER > COMMUNE

COMMUNERS > COMMUNE

COMMUNES > COMMUNE

COMMUNING > COMMUNE

COMMUNION *n* sharing of thoughts or feelings

COMMUNISE *same as* > COMMUNIZE

COMMUNISM *n* belief that all property and means of production should be shared by the community

COMMUNIST *n* supporter of any form of communism ▷ *adj* of, characterized by,

favouring, or relating to communism

COMMUNITY *n* all the people living in one district

COMMUNIZE *vb* make (property) public

COMMUTATE *vb* reverse the direction of (an electric current)

COMMUTE *vb* travel daily to and from work ▷ *n* journey made by commuting

COMMUTED > COMMUTE

COMMUTER *n* person who commutes to and from work

COMMUTERS > COMMUTER

COMMUTES > COMMUTE

COMMUTING *n* act of commuting

COMMUTUAL *adj* mutual

COMMY *same as* > COMMIE

COMODO *adv* (to be performed) at a convenient relaxed speed

COMONOMER *n* monomer that, with another, constitutes a copolymer

COMORBID *adj* (of illness) happening at same time as other illness

COMOSE *another word for* > COMATE

COMOUS *adj* hairy

COMP *n* person who sets and corrects type ▷ *vb* set or correct type

COMPACT *adj* closely packed ▷ *n* small flat case containing a mirror and face powder ▷ *vb* pack closely together

COMPACTED > COMPACT

COMPACTER > COMPACT

COMPACTLY > COMPACT

COMPACTOR *n* machine which compresses waste material for easier disposal

COMPACTS > COMPACT

COMPADRE *n* masculine friend

COMPADRES > COMPADRE

COMPAGE *obsolete form of* > COMPAGES

COMPAGES *n* structure or framework

COMPAND *vb* (of a transmitter signal) to compress before, and expand after, transmission

COMPANDED > COMPAND

COMPANDER *n* system for improving the signal-to-noise ratio of a signal at a transmitter or recorder by first compressing the volume range of the signal and then restoring it to its original amplitude level at the receiving or reproducing apparatus

COMPANDOR *same as* > COMPANDER

COMPANDS > COMPAND

COMPANIED > COMPANY
COMPANIES > COMPANY
COMPANING > COMPANY
COMPANION n person who associates with or accompanies someone ▷ vb accompany or be a companion to
COMPANY n business organization ▷ vb associate or keep company with someone
COMPARE vb examine (things) and point out the resemblances or differences
COMPARED > COMPARE
COMPARER > COMPARE
COMPARERS > COMPARE
COMPARES > COMPARE
COMPARING > COMPARE
COMPART vb divide into parts
COMPARTED > COMPART
COMPARTS > COMPART
COMPAS n rhythm in flamenco
COMPASS n instrument for showing direction ▷ vb encircle or surround
COMPASSED > COMPASS
COMPASSES > COMPASS
COMPAST adj rounded
COMPEAR vb in Scots law, to appear in court
COMPEARED > COMPEAR
COMPEARS > COMPEAR
COMPED > COMP
COMPEER n person of equal rank, status, or ability ▷ vb to equal
COMPEERED > COMPEER
COMPEERS > COMPEER
COMPEL vb force (to be or do)
COMPELLED > COMPEL
COMPELLER > COMPEL
COMPELS > COMPEL
COMPEND n compendium
COMPENDIA n plural form of singular compendium: book containing a collection of useful hints
COMPENDS > COMPEND
COMPER n person who regularly enters competitions
COMPERE n person who presents a stage, radio, or television show ▷ vb be the compere of
COMPERED > COMPERE
COMPERES > COMPERE
COMPERING > COMPERE
COMPERS > COMPER
COMPESCE vb curb
COMPESCED
 > COMPESCE
COMPESCES
 > COMPESCE
COMPETE vb try to win or achieve (a prize, profit, etc)
COMPETED > COMPETE
COMPETENT adj having the skill or knowledge to do something well

COMPETES > COMPETE
COMPETING > COMPETE
COMPILE vb collect and arrange (information), esp to make a book
COMPILED > COMPILE
COMPILER n person who compiles information
COMPILERS
 > COMPILER
COMPILES > COMPILE
COMPILING > COMPILE
COMPING n act of comping
COMPINGS > COMPING
COMPITAL adj pertaining to crossroads
COMPLAIN vb express resentment or displeasure
COMPLAINS
 > COMPLAIN
COMPLAINT n complaining
COMPLEAT an archaic spelling of **>** COMPLETE
COMPLEATS
 > COMPLEAT
COMPLECT vb interweave or entwine
COMPLECTS
 > COMPLECT
COMPLETE adj thorough, absolute ▷ vb finish
COMPLETED
 > COMPLETE
COMPLETER
 > COMPLETE
COMPLETES
 > COMPLETE
COMPLEX adj made up of parts ▷ n whole made up of parts ▷ vb form a complex
COMPLEXED > COMPLEX
COMPLEXER > COMPLEX
COMPLEXES > COMPLEX
COMPLEXLY > COMPLEX
COMPLEXUS n complex
COMPLIANT adj complying, obliging, or yielding
COMPLICE n associate or accomplice
COMPLICES
 > COMPLICE
COMPLICIT adj involved in a crime or questionable act
COMPLIED > COMPLY
COMPLIER > COMPLY
COMPLIERS > COMPLY
COMPLIES > COMPLY
COMPLIN same as
 > COMPLINE
COMPLINE n last service of the day in the Roman Catholic Church
COMPLINES
 > COMPLINE
COMPLINS > COMPLIN
COMPLISH vb accomplish
COMPLOT n plot or conspiracy ▷ vb plot together
COMPLOTS > COMPLOT
COMPLUVIA n plural form of singular compluvium: an unroofed

space over the atrium in a Roman house, though which rain fell and was collected
COMPLY vb act in accordance (with)
COMPLYING > COMPLY
COMPO n mixture of materials, such as mortar, plaster, etc ▷ adj intended to last for several days
COMPONE same as
 > COMPONY
COMPONENT adj (being) part of a whole ▷ n constituent part or feature of a whole
COMPONY adj made up of alternating metal and colour, colour and fur, or fur and metal
COMPORT vb behave (oneself) in a specified way
COMPORTED > COMPORT
COMPORTS > COMPORT
COMPOS > COMPO
COMPOSE vb put together
COMPOSED adj calm
COMPOSER n person who writes music
COMPOSERS
 > COMPOSER
COMPOSES > COMPOSE
COMPOSING > COMPOSE
COMPOSITE adj made up of separate parts ▷ n something composed of separate parts ▷ vb merge related motions from local branches of (a political party, trade union, etc) so as to produce a manageable number of proposals for discussion at national level
COMPOST n decayed plants used as a fertilizer ▷ vb make (vegetable matter) into compost
COMPOSTED > COMPOST
COMPOSTER n bin or other container used to turn garden waste into compost
COMPOSTS > COMPOST
COMPOSURE n calmness
COMPOT same as
 > COMPOTE
COMPOTE n fruit stewed with sugar
COMPOTES > COMPOTE
COMPOTIER n dish for holding compote
COMPOTS > COMPOT
COMPOUND adj (thing, esp chemical) made up of two or more combined parts or elements ▷ vb combine or make by combining ▷ n fenced enclosure containing buildings
COMPOUNDS
 > COMPOUND
COMPRADOR n (formerly in China and some other Asian countries) a native agent of a foreign enterprise

COMPRESS vb squeeze together ▷ n pad applied to stop bleeding or cool inflammation
COMPRINT vb print jointly
COMPRINTS
 > COMPRINT
COMPRISAL
 > COMPRISE
COMPRISE vb be made up of or make up
COMPRISED
 > COMPRISE
COMPRISES
 > COMPRISE
COMPRIZE same as
 > COMPRISE
COMPRIZED
 > COMPRIZE
COMPRIZES
 > COMPRIZE
COMPS > COMP
COMPT obsolete variant of
 > COUNT
COMPTABLE n countable
COMPTED > COMPT
COMPTER n formerly, a prison
COMPTERS > COMPTER
COMPTIBLE same as
 > COMPTABLE
COMPTING > COMPT
COMPTROLL obsolete variant of **>** CONTROL
COMPTS > COMPT
COMPULSE vb compel
COMPULSED
 > COMPULSE
COMPULSES
 > COMPULSE
COMPUTANT n calculator
COMPUTE vb calculate, esp using a computer ▷ n calculation
COMPUTED > COMPUTE
COMPUTER n electronic machine that stores and processes data
COMPUTERS
 > COMPUTER
COMPUTES > COMPUTE
COMPUTING n activity of using computers and writing programs for them ▷ adj of or relating to computers
COMPUTIST n one who computes
COMRADE n fellow member of a union or socialist political party
COMRADELY adj like a comrade
COMRADERY n comradeship
COMRADES > COMRADE
COMS pl n one-piece woollen undergarment with long sleeves and legs
COMSAT n communications satellite
COMSATS > COMSAT
COMSYMP n disparaging term for a person sympathetic to communism
COMSYMPS > COMSYMP

COMTE *n* European noble
COMTES > COMTE
COMUS *n* wild party
COMUSES > COMUS
CON *vb* deceive, swindle ▷ *n* convict ▷ *prep* with
CONACRE *n* farming land let for a season or for eleven months ▷ *vb* let conacre
CONACRED > CONACRE
CONACRES > CONACRE
CONACRING > CONACRE
CONARIA > CONARIUM
CONARIAL > CONARIUM
CONARIUM *n* pineal gland
CONATION *n* psychological element that tends towards activity or change
CONATIONS > CONATION
CONATIVE *adj* aspect of some verbs indicating the effort of the agent in performing the verb
CONATUS *n* effort or striving of natural impulse
CONCAUSE *n* shared cause
CONCAUSES > CONCAUSE
CONCAVE *adj* curving inwards ▷ *vb* make concave
CONCAVED > CONCAVE
CONCAVELY > CONCAVE
CONCAVES > CONCAVE
CONCAVING > CONCAVE
CONCAVITY *n* state or quality of being concave
CONCEAL *vb* cover and hide
CONCEALED > CONCEAL
CONCEALER > CONCEAL
CONCEALS > CONCEAL
CONCEDE *vb* admit to be true
CONCEDED > CONCEDE
CONCEDER > CONCEDE
CONCEDERS > CONCEDE
CONCEDES > CONCEDE
CONCEDING > CONCEDE
CONCEDO *interj* I allow; I concede (a point)
CONCEIT *n* too high an opinion of oneself ▷ *vb* like or be able to bear (something, such as food or drink)
CONCEITED *adj* having an excessively high opinion of oneself
CONCEITS > CONCEIT
CONCEITY *adj* full of conceit
CONCEIVE *vb* imagine, think
CONCEIVED > CONCEIVE
CONCEIVER > CONCEIVE
CONCEIVES > CONCEIVE
CONCENT *n* concord, as of sounds, voices, etc
CONCENTER *same as* > CONCENTRE

CONCENTRE *vb* converge or cause to converge on a common centre
CONCENTS > CONCENT
CONCENTUS *n* vocal harmony
CONCEPT *n* abstract or general idea
CONCEPTI > CONCEPTUS
CONCEPTS > CONCEPT
CONCEPTUS *n* any product of conception, including the embryo, foetus and surrounding tissue
CONCERN *n* anxiety, worry ▷ *vb* worry (someone)
CONCERNED *adj* interested, involved
CONCERNS > CONCERN
CONCERT *n* musical entertainment
CONCERTED *adj* done together
CONCERTI > CONCERTO
CONCERTO *n* large-scale composition for a solo instrument and orchestra
CONCERTOS > CONCERTO
CONCERTS > CONCERT
CONCETTI > CONCETTO
CONCETTO *n* conceit, ingenious thought
CONCH *same as* > CONCHA
CONCHA *n* any bodily organ or part resembling a shell in shape
CONCHAE > CONCHA
CONCHAL > CONCHA
CONCHAS > CONCHA
CONCHATE *adj* shell-shaped
CONCHE *n* machine used to make chocolate ▷ *vb* use a conche
CONCHED > CONCHE
CONCHES > CONCHE
CONCHIE *n* conscientious objector
CONCHIES > CONCHIE
CONCHING > CONCHE
CONCHITIS *n* inflammation of the outer ear
CONCHO *n* American metal ornament
CONCHOID *n* type of plane curve
CONCHOIDS > CONCHOID
CONCHOS > CONCHO
CONCHS > CONCH
CONCHY *same as* > CONCHIE

CONCIERGE *n* (in France) caretaker in a block of flats
CONCILIAR *adj* of, from, or by means of a council, esp an ecclesiastical one
CONCISE *adj* brief and to the point ▷ *vb* mutilate
CONCISED > CONCISE
CONCISELY > CONCISE
CONCISER > CONCISE
CONCISES > CONCISE

CONCISEST > CONCISE
CONCISING > CONCISE
CONCISION *n* quality of being concise
CONCLAVE *n* secret meeting
CONCLAVES > CONCLAVE
CONCLUDE *vb* decide by reasoning
CONCLUDED > CONCLUDE
CONCLUDER > CONCLUDE
CONCLUDES > CONCLUDE
CONCOCT *vb* make up (a story or plan)
CONCOCTED > CONCOCT
CONCOCTER > CONCOCT
CONCOCTOR > CONCOCT
CONCOCTS > CONCOCT
CONCOLOR *adj* of a single colour
CONCORD *n* state of peaceful agreement, harmony ▷ *vb* agree
CONCORDAL > CONCORD
CONCORDAT *n* pact or treaty
CONCORDED > CONCORD
CONCORDS > CONCORD
CONCOURS *n* contest
CONCOURSE *n* large open public place where people can gather
CONCREATE *vb* to create at the same time
CONCRETE *n* mixture of cement, sand, stone, and water, used in building ▷ *vb* cover with concrete ▷ *adj* made of concrete
CONCRETED > CONCRETE
CONCRETES > CONCRETE
CONCREW *vb* grow together
CONCREWED > CONCREW
CONCREWS > CONCREW
CONCUBINE *n* woman living in a man's house but not married to him and kept for his sexual pleasure
CONCUPIES > CONCUPY
CONCUPY *n* concupiscence
CONCUR *vb* agree
CONCURRED > CONCUR
CONCURS > CONCUR
CONCUSS *vb* injure (the brain) by a fall or blow
CONCUSSED > CONCUSS
CONCUSSES > CONCUSS
CONCYCLIC *adj* (of a set of geometric points) lying on a common circle
COND *old inflection of* > CON
CONDEMN *vb* express disapproval of
CONDEMNED > CONDEMN
CONDEMNER > CONDEMN
CONDEMNOR > CONDEMN
CONDEMNS > CONDEMN
CONDENSE *vb* make shorter

CONDENSED *adj* (of printers' type) narrower than usual for a particular height
CONDENSER *same as* > CAPACITOR
CONDENSES > CONDENSE
CONDER *n* person who directs the steering of a vessel
CONDERS > CONDER
CONDIDDLE *vb* to steal
CONDIE *n* culvert; tunnel
CONDIES > CONDIE
CONDIGN *adj* (esp of a punishment) fitting
CONDIGNLY > CONDIGN
CONDIMENT *n* seasoning for food, such as salt or pepper
CONDITION *n* particular state of being ▷ *vb* train or influence to behave in a particular way
CONDO *n* condominium
CONDOES > CONDO
CONDOLE *vb* express sympathy with someone in grief, pain, etc
CONDOLED > CONDOLE
CONDOLENT *adj* expressing sympathy with someone in grief
CONDOLER > CONDOLE
CONDOLERS > CONDOLE
CONDOLES > CONDOLE
CONDOLING > CONDOLE
CONDOM *n* contraceptive
CONDOMS > CONDOM
CONDONE *vb* overlook or forgive (wrongdoing)
CONDONED > CONDONE
CONDONER > CONDONE
CONDONERS > CONDONE
CONDONES > CONDONE
CONDONING > CONDONE
CONDOR *n* large vulture of S America
CONDORES > CONDOR
CONDORS > CONDOR
CONDOS > CONDO
CONDUCE *vb* lead or contribute (to a result)
CONDUCED > CONDUCE
CONDUCER > CONDUCE
CONDUCERS > CONDUCE
CONDUCES > CONDUCE
CONDUCING > CONDUCE
CONDUCIVE *adj* likely to lead (to)
CONDUCT *n* management of an activity ▷ *vb* carry out (a task)
CONDUCTED > CONDUCT
CONDUCTI > CONDUCTUS
CONDUCTOR *n* person who conducts musicians
CONDUCTS > CONDUCT
CONDUCTUS *n* medieval liturgical composition
CONDUIT *n* channel or tube for fluid or cables
CONDUITS > CONDUIT
CONDYLAR > CONDYLE
CONDYLE *n* rounded projection on the articulating end of a bone

CONDYLES > CONDYLE
CONDYLOID adj of or resembling a condyle
CONDYLOMA n skin tumour
CONE n object with a circular base, tapering to a point ▷ vb shape like a cone or part of a cone
CONED > CONE
CONELESS adj not bearing cones
CONELIKE adj like a cone
CONELRAD n US defence and information system for use in the event of air attack
CONELRADS > CONELRAD
CONENOSE n bloodsucking bug of the genus Triatoma
CONENOSES > CONENOSE
CONEPATE same as > CONEPATL
CONEPATES > CONEPATL
CONEPATL n skunk
CONEPATLS > CONEPATL
CONES > CONE
CONEY same as > CONY
CONEYS > CONEY
CONF n online forum
CONFAB n conversation ▷ vb converse
CONFABBED > CONFAB
CONFABS > CONFAB
CONFECT vb prepare by combining ingredients
CONFECTED > CONFECT
CONFECTS > CONFECT
CONFER vb discuss together
CONFEREE n person who takes part in a conference
CONFEREES > CONFEREE
CONFERRAL > CONFER
CONFERRED > CONFER
CONFERREE same as > CONFEREE
CONFERRER > CONFER
CONFERS > CONFER
CONFERVA n type of threadlike green alga typically occurring in fresh water
CONFERVAE > CONFERVA
CONFERVAL > CONFERVA
CONFERVAS > CONFERVA
CONFESS vb admit (a fault or crime)
CONFESSED > CONFESS
CONFESSES > CONFESS
CONFESSOR n priest who hears confessions
CONFEST adj admitted
CONFESTLY adv confessedly
CONFETTI n small pieces of coloured paper thrown at weddings
CONFETTO n sweetmeat

CONFIDANT n person confided in
CONFIDE vb tell someone (a secret)
CONFIDED > CONFIDE
CONFIDENT adj sure, esp of oneself
CONFIDER > CONFIDE
CONFIDERS > CONFIDE
CONFIDES > CONFIDE
CONFIDING adj trusting
CONFIGURE vb to design or set up
CONFINE vb keep within bounds ▷ n limit
CONFINED adj enclosed or restricted
CONFINER > CONFINE
CONFINERS > CONFINE
CONFINES > CONFINE
CONFINING > CONFINE
CONFIRM vb prove to be true
CONFIRMED adj firmly established in a habit or condition
CONFIRMEE n person to whom a confirmation is made
CONFIRMER > CONFIRM
CONFIRMOR n person who makes a confirmation
CONFIRMS > CONFIRM
CONFISEUR n confectioner
CONFIT n preserve
CONFITEOR n Catholic prayer asking for forgiveness
CONFITS > CONFIT
CONFITURE n confection, preserve of fruit, etc
CONFIX vb fasten
CONFIXED > CONFIX
CONFIXES > CONFIX
CONFIXING > CONFIX
CONFLATE vb combine or blend into a whole
CONFLATED > CONFLATE
CONFLATES > CONFLATE
CONFLICT n disagreement ▷ vb be incompatible
CONFLICTS > CONFLICT
CONFLUENT adj flowing together or merging ▷ n stream that flows into another, usually of approximately equal size
CONFLUX n merging or following together, especially of rivers
CONFLUXES > CONFLUX
CONFOCAL adj having a common focus or common foci
CONFORM vb comply with accepted standards or customs
CONFORMAL adj (of a transformation) preserving the angles of the depicted surface
CONFORMED > CONFORM

CONFORMER > CONFORM
CONFORMS > CONFORM
CONFOUND vb astound, bewilder
CONFOUNDS > CONFOUND
CONFRERE n colleague
CONFRERES > CONFRERE
CONFRERIE n brotherhood
CONFRONT vb come face to face with
CONFRONTE adj in heraldry, (of two animals) face to face
CONFRONTS > CONFRONT
CONFS > CONF
CONFUSE vb mix up
CONFUSED adj lacking a clear understanding of something
CONFUSES > CONFUSE
CONFUSING adj causing bewilderment
CONFUSION n mistaking one person or thing for another
CONFUTE vb prove wrong
CONFUTED > CONFUTE
CONFUTER > CONFUTE
CONFUTERS > CONFUTE
CONFUTES > CONFUTE
CONFUTING > CONFUTE
CONGA n dance performed by a number of people in single file ▷ vb dance the conga
CONGAED > CONGA
CONGAING > CONGA
CONGAS > CONGA
CONGE n permission to depart or dismissal, esp when formal ▷ vb take one's leave
CONGEAL vb (of a liquid) become thick and sticky
CONGEALED > CONGEAL
CONGEALER > CONGEAL
CONGEALS > CONGEAL
CONGED > CONGE
CONGEE same as > CONGE
CONGEED > CONGEE
CONGEEING > CONGEE
CONGEES > CONGEE
CONGEING > CONGE
CONGENER n member of a class, group, or other category, esp any animal of a specified genus
CONGENERS > CONGENER
CONGENIAL adj pleasant, agreeable
CONGENIC adj (of inbred animal cells) genetically identical except for a single gene locus
CONGER n large sea eel
CONGERIES n collection of objects or ideas
CONGERS > CONGER
CONGES > CONGE
CONGEST vb crowd or become crowded to excess
CONGESTED adj crowded to excess

CONGESTS > CONGEST
CONGIARY n Roman emperor's gift to the people or soldiers
CONGII > CONGIUS
CONGIUS n unit of liquid measure equal to 1 imperial gallon
CONGLOBE vb gather into a globe or ball
CONGLOBED > CONGLOBE
CONGLOBES > CONGLOBE
CONGO same as > CONGOU
CONGOES > CONGO
CONGOS > CONGO
CONGOU n kind of black tea from China
CONGOUS > CONGOU
CONGRATS sentence substitute congratulations
CONGREE vb agree
CONGREED > CONGREE
CONGREES > CONGREE
CONGREET vb (of two or more people) to greet one another
CONGREETS > CONGREET
CONGRESS n formal meeting for discussion
CONGRUE vb agree
CONGRUED > CONGRUE
CONGRUES > CONGRUE
CONGRUING > CONGRUE
CONGRUITY > CONGRUOUS
CONGRUOUS adj appropriate or in keeping
CONI > CONUS
CONIA same as > CONIINE
CONIAS > CONIA
CONIC adj having the shape of a cone
CONICAL adj cone-shaped
CONICALLY > CONIC
CONICINE same as > CONIINE
CONICINES > CONICINE
CONICITY > CONICAL
CONICS n branch of geometry
CONIDIA > CONIDIUM
CONIDIAL > CONIDIUM
CONIDIAN > CONIDIUM
CONIDIUM n asexual spore formed at the tip of a specialized filament in certain types of fungi
CONIES > CONY
CONIFER n cone-bearing tree, such as the fir or pine
CONIFERS > CONIFER
CONIFORM adj cone-shaped
CONIINE n colourless poisonous soluble liquid alkaloid found in hemlock
CONIINES > CONIINE
CONIMA n gum resin from the conium hemlock tree
CONIMAS > CONIMA

CONIN same as
> CONIINE
CONINE same as
> CONIINE
CONINES > CONINE
CONING > CONE
CONINS > CONIN
CONIOLOGY variant
spelling of > KONIOLOGY
CONIOSES > CONIOSIS
CONIOSIS n any disease
or condition caused by
dust inhalation
CONIUM n umbelliferous
plant, esp hemlock
CONIUMS > CONIUM
CONJECT vb conjecture
CONJECTED > CONJECT
CONJECTS > CONJECT
CONJEE n gruel of boiled
rice and water ▷ vb
prepare as, or in, a conjee
CONJEED > CONJEE
CONJEEING > CONJEE
CONJEES > CONJEE
CONJOIN vb join or
become joined
CONJOINED > CONJOIN
CONJOINER > CONJOIN
CONJOINS > CONJOIN
CONJOINT adj united,
joint, or associated
CONJUGAL adj of
marriage
CONJUGANT n either of
a pair of organisms or
gametes undergoing
conjugation
CONJUGATE vb inflect
(a verb) systematically
CONJUNCT adj joined
▷ n one of the propositions
or formulas in a
conjunction
CONJUNCTS
> CONJUNCT
CONJUNTO n style of
Mexican music
CONJUNTOS
> CONJUNTO
CONJURE vb perform
tricks that appear to be
magic
CONJURED > CONJURE
CONJURER same as
> CONJUROR
CONJURERS
> CONJUROR
CONJURES > CONJURE
CONJURIES > CONJURY
CONJURING n
performance of tricks that
appear to defy natural
laws ▷ adj denoting or
relating to such tricks or
entertainment
CONJUROR n person who
performs magic tricks for
people's entertainment
CONJURORS
> CONJUROR
CONJURY n magic
CONK n nose ▷ vb strike
(someone) on the head or
nose
CONKED > CONK
CONKER n nut of the horse
chestnut

CONKERS n game played
with conkers tied on
strings
CONKIER > CONKY
CONKIEST > CONKY
CONKING > CONK
CONKOUT n time when a
machine stops working
CONKOUTS > CONKOUT
CONKS > CONK
CONKY adj affected by the
timber disease, conk
CONLANG n artificially
constructed language
CONLANGER n person
who creates a conlang
CONLANGS > CONLANG
CONMAN n man who uses
confidence tricks to
swindle or defraud
CONMEN > CONMAN
CONN same as > CON
CONNATE adj existing
in a person or thing from
birth
CONNATELY > CONNATE
CONNATION n joining of
similar parts or organs
CONNATURE n sharing a
common nature or
character
CONNE same as > CON
CONNECT vb join together
CONNECTED adj joined or
linked together
CONNECTER > CONNECT
CONNECTOR > CONNECT
CONNECTS > CONNECT
CONNED > CON
CONNER same as
> CONDER
CONNERS > CONNER
CONNES > CONNE
CONNEXION n act or
state of connecting
CONNEXIVE adj
connective
CONNIE n tram or bus
conductor
CONNIES > CONNIE
CONNING > CON
CONNINGS > CON
CONNIVE vb allow
(wrongdoing) by ignoring
it
CONNIVED > CONNIVE
CONNIVENT adj (of parts
of plants and animals)
touching without being
fused, as some petals,
insect wings, etc
CONNIVER > CONNIVE
CONNIVERS > CONNIVE
CONNIVERY n act of
conniving
CONNIVES > CONNIVE
CONNIVING n act or
instance of allowing
(wrongdoing) by ignoring
it
CONNOR n type of
saltwater fish
CONNORS > CONNOR
CONNOTATE vb to
connote
CONNOTE vb imply or
suggest
CONNOTED > CONNOTE

CONNOTES > CONNOTE
CONNOTING > CONNOTE
CONNOTIVE adj act or
state of connecting
CONNS > CONN
CONNUBIAL adj of
marriage
CONODONT n toothlike
fossil derived from an
eel-like animal
CONODONTS
> CONODONT
CONOID n geometric
surface ▷ adj conical,
cone-shaped
CONOIDAL same as
> CONOID
CONOIDIC > CONOID
CONOIDS > CONOID
CONOMINEE n joint
nominee
CONQUER vb defeat
CONQUERED > CONQUER
CONQUERER variant of
> CONQUEROR
CONQUEROR > CONQUER
CONQUERS > CONQUER
CONQUEST n conquering
CONQUESTS
> CONQUEST
CONQUIAN same as
> COONCAN
CONQUIANS > COONCAN
CONS > CON
CONSCIENT adj
conscious
CONSCIOUS adj alert and
awake ▷ n conscious part
of the mind
CONSCRIBE vb to enrol
compulsorily
CONSCRIPT n person
enrolled for compulsory
military service ▷ vb enrol
(someone) for compulsory
military service
CONSEIL n advice
CONSEILS > CONSEIL
CONSENSUS n general
agreement
CONSENT n agreement,
permission ▷ vb permit,
agree to
CONSENTED > CONSENT
CONSENTER > CONSENT
CONSENTS > CONSENT
CONSERVE vb protect
from harm, decay, or loss
▷ n jam containing large
pieces of fruit
CONSERVED
> CONSERVE
CONSERVER
> CONSERVE
CONSERVES
> CONSERVE
CONSIDER vb regard as
CONSIDERS
> CONSIDER
CONSIGN vb put
somewhere
CONSIGNED > CONSIGN
CONSIGNEE n person,
agent, organization, etc,
to which merchandise is
consigned
CONSIGNER same as
> CONSIGNOR

CONSIGNOR n person,
enterprise, etc, that
consigns goods
CONSIGNS > CONSIGN
CONSIST vb be
composed (of)
CONSISTED > CONSIST
CONSISTS > CONSIST
CONSOCIES n natural
community with a single
dominant species
CONSOL n consolidated
annuity, a former British
government security
CONSOLATE vb to
console
CONSOLE vb comfort in
distress ▷ n panel of
controls for electronic
equipment
CONSOLED > CONSOLE
CONSOLER > CONSOLE
CONSOLERS > CONSOLE
CONSOLES > CONSOLE
CONSOLING > CONSOLE
CONSOLS > CONSOL
CONSOLUTE adj (of two
or more liquids) mutually
soluble in all proportions
CONSOMME n thin clear
meat soup
CONSOMMES
> CONSOMME
CONSONANT n speech
sound made by partially or
completely blocking the
breath stream ▷ adj
agreeing (with)
CONSONOUS adj
harmonious
CONSORT vb keep
company (with) ▷ n
spouse of a monarch
CONSORTED > CONSORT
CONSORTER > CONSORT
CONSORTIA n plural
form of singular
consortium: association
of financiers, companies
etc
CONSORTS > CONSORT
CONSPIRE vb plan a
crime together in secret
CONSPIRED
> CONSPIRE
CONSPIRER
> CONSPIRE
CONSPIRES
> CONSPIRE
CONSPUE vb spit on with
contempt
CONSPUED > CONSPUE
CONSPUES > CONSPUE
CONSPUING > CONSPUE
CONSTABLE n police
officer of the lowest rank
CONSTANCY n quality of
having a resolute mind,
purpose, or affection
CONSTANT adj
continuous ▷ n unvarying
quantity
CONSTANTS
> CONSTANT
CONSTATE vb affirm
CONSTATED
> CONSTATE
CONSTATES
> CONSTATE

CONSTER obsolete variant of > CONSTRUE

CONSTERED > CONSTRUE

CONSTERS > CONSTER

CONSTRAIN vb compel, force

CONSTRICT vb make narrower by squeezing

CONSTRUAL n act of construing

CONSTRUCT vb build or put together ▷ n complex idea resulting from the combination of simpler ideas

CONSTRUE vb interpret ▷ n something that is construed, such as a piece of translation

CONSTRUED > CONSTRUE

CONSTRUER > CONSTRUE

CONSTRUES > CONSTRUE

CONSUL n official representing a state in a foreign country

CONSULAGE n duty paid by merchants for a consul's protection of their goods while abroad

CONSULAR n anyone of consular rank

CONSULARS > CONSULAR

CONSULATE n workplace or position of a consul

CONSULS > CONSUL

CONSULT vb go to for advice or information

CONSULTA n official planning meeting

CONSULTAS > CONSULTA

CONSULTED > CONSULT

CONSULTEE n person who is consulted

CONSULTER > CONSULT

CONSULTOR > CONSULT

CONSULTS > CONSULT

CONSUME vb eat or drink

CONSUMED > CONSUME

CONSUMER n person who buys goods or uses services

CONSUMERS > CONSUMER

CONSUMES > CONSUME

CONSUMING > CONSUME

CONSUMPT n quantity used up; consumption

CONSUMPTS > CONSUMPT

CONTACT n communicating ▷ vb get in touch with ▷ interj (formerly) call made by the pilot to indicate the engine is ready for starting

CONTACTED > CONTACT

CONTACTEE n person contacted by aliens

CONTACTOR n type of switch for repeatedly opening and closing an electric circuit. Its operation can be mechanical, electromagnetic, or pneumatic

CONTACTS > CONTACT

CONTADINA n female Italian farmer

CONTADINE > CONTADINA

CONTADINI > CONTADINO

CONTADINO n Italian farmer

CONTAGIA > CONTAGIUM

CONTAGION n passing on of disease by contact

CONTAGIUM n specific virus or other direct cause of any infectious disease

CONTAIN vb hold or be capable of holding

CONTAINED > CONTAIN

CONTAINER n object used to hold or store things in

CONTAINS > CONTAIN

CONTANGO n postponement of payment for and delivery of stock ▷ vb arrange such a postponement of payment

CONTANGOS > CONTANGO

CONTE n tale or short story, esp of adventure

CONTECK n contention

CONTECKS > CONTECK

CONTEMN vb regard with contempt

CONTEMNED > CONTEMN

CONTEMNER > CONTEMN

CONTEMNOR > CONTEMN

CONTEMNS > CONTEMN

CONTEMPER vb to modify

CONTEMPO adj contemporary

CONTEMPT n dislike and disregard

CONTEMPTS > CONTEMPT

CONTEND vb deal with

CONTENDED > CONTEND

CONTENDER > CONTEND

CONTENDS > CONTEND

CONTENT n meaning or substance of a piece of writing ▷ adj satisfied with things as they are ▷ vb make (someone) content

CONTENTED adj satisfied with one's situation or life

CONTENTLY > CONTENT

CONTENTS > CONTENT

CONTES > CONTE

CONTESSA n Italian countess

CONTESSAS > CONTESSA

CONTEST n competition or struggle ▷ vb dispute, object to

CONTESTED > CONTEST

CONTESTER > CONTEST

CONTESTS > CONTEST

CONTEXT n circumstances of an event or fact

CONTEXTS > CONTEXT

CONTICENT adj silent

CONTINENT n one of the earth's large masses of land ▷ adj able to control one's bladder and bowels

CONTINUA > CONTINUUM

CONTINUAL adj constant

CONTINUE vb (cause to) remain in a condition or place

CONTINUED > CONTINUE

CONTINUER > CONTINUE

CONTINUES > CONTINUE

CONTINUO n continuous bass part, usu played on a keyboard instrument

CONTINUOS > CONTINUO

CONTINUUM n continuous series

CONTLINE n space between the bilges of stowed casks

CONTLINES > CONTLINE

CONTO n former Portuguese monetary unit worth 1000 escudos

CONTORNI > CONTORNO

CONTORNO n in Italy, side dish of salad or vegetables

CONTORNOS > CONTORNO

CONTORT vb twist out of shape

CONTORTED adj twisted out of shape

CONTORTS > CONTORT

CONTOS > CONTO

CONTOUR n outline ▷ vb shape so as to form or follow the contour of something

CONTOURED > CONTOUR

CONTOURS > CONTOUR

CONTRA n counter-argument

CONTRACT n (document setting out) a formal agreement ▷ vb make a formal agreement (to do something)

CONTRACTS > CONTRACT

CONTRAIL n aeroplane's vapour trail

CONTRAILS > CONTRAIL

CONTRAIR adj contrary

CONTRALTI > CONTRALTO

CONTRALTO n (singer with) the lowest female voice ▷ adj of or denoting a contralto

CONTRARY n complete opposite ▷ adj opposed, completely different ▷ adv in opposition

CONTRAS > CONTRA

CONTRAST n obvious difference ▷ vb compare in order to show differences

CONTRASTS > CONTRAST

CONTRASTY adj (of a photograph or subject) having sharp gradations in tone, esp between light and dark areas

CONTRAT old form of > CONTRACT

CONTRATE adj (of gears) having teeth set at a right angle to the axis

CONTRATS > CONTRAT

CONTRIST vb make sad

CONTRISTS > CONTRIST

CONTRITE adj sorry and apologetic

CONTRIVE vb make happen

CONTRIVED adj planned or artificial

CONTRIVER > CONTRIVE

CONTRIVES > CONTRIVE

CONTROL n power to direct something ▷ vb have power over

CONTROLE adj officially registered

CONTROLS > CONTROL

CONTROUL obsolete variant of > CONTROL

CONTROULS > CONTROUL

CONTUMACY n obstinate disobedience

CONTUMELY n scornful or insulting treatment

CONTUND vb pummel

CONTUNDED > CONTUND

CONTUNDS > CONTUND

CONTUSE vb injure (the body) without breaking the skin

CONTUSED > CONTUSE

CONTUSES > CONTUSE

CONTUSING > CONTUSE

CONTUSION n bruise

CONTUSIVE > CONTUSE

CONUNDRUM n riddle

CONURBAN adj relating to an urban region

CONURBIA n conurbations considered collectively

CONURBIAS > CONURBIA

CONURE n small American parrot

CONURES > CONURE

CONUS n any of several cone-shaped structures

CONVECT vb circulate hot air by convection

CONVECTED > CONVECT

CONVECTOR n heater that gives out hot air

CONVECTS > CONVECT

CONVENE vb gather or summon for a formal meeting

CONVENED > CONVENE

CONVENER n person who calls a meeting

CONVENERS > CONVENER

CONVENES > CONVENE

CONVENING n act of convening

CONVENOR same as
> CONVENER
CONVENORS
> CONVENOR
CONVENT n building
where nuns live ▷ vb
summon
CONVENTED > CONVENT
CONVENTS > CONVENT
CONVERGE vb meet or
join
CONVERGED
> CONVERGE
CONVERGES
> CONVERGE
CONVERSE vb have a
conversation ▷ n opposite
or contrary ▷ adj reversed
or opposite
CONVERSED
> CONVERSE
CONVERSER
> CONVERSE
CONVERSES
> CONVERSE
CONVERSO n medieval
Spanish Jew converting to
Catholicism
CONVERSOS
> CONVERSO
CONVERT vb change in
form, character, or
function ▷ n person
who has converted to
a different belief or
religion
CONVERTED > CONVERT
CONVERTER n person or
thing that converts
CONVERTOR same as
> CONVERTER
CONVERTS > CONVERT
CONVEX adj curving
outwards ▷ vb make
convex
CONVEXED > CONVEX
CONVEXES > CONVEX
CONVEXING > CONVEX
CONVEXITY n state or
quality of being convex
CONVEXLY > CONVEX
CONVEY vb communicate
(information)
CONVEYAL n act or
means of conveying
CONVEYALS
> CONVEYAL
CONVEYED > CONVEY
CONVEYER same as
> CONVEYOR
CONVEYERS
> CONVEYOR
CONVEYING > CONVEY
CONVEYOR n person or
thing that conveys
CONVEYORS
> CONVEYOR
CONVEYS > CONVEY
CONVICT vb declare
guilty ▷ n person serving a
prison sentence ▷ adj
convicted
CONVICTED > CONVICT
CONVICTS > CONVICT
CONVINCE vb persuade
by argument or evidence
CONVINCED
> CONVINCE

CONVINCER
> CONVINCE
CONVINCES
> CONVINCE
CONVIVE vb feast
together
CONVIVED > CONVIVE
CONVIVES > CONVIVE
CONVIVIAL adj sociable,
lively
CONVIVING > CONVIVE
CONVO n conversation
CONVOCATE vb call
together
CONVOKE vb call together
CONVOKED > CONVOKE
CONVOKER > CONVOKE
CONVOKERS > CONVOKE
CONVOKES > CONVOKE
CONVOKING > CONVOKE
CONVOLUTE vb form into
a twisted, coiled, or rolled
shape ▷ adj rolled
longitudinally upon itself
CONVOLVE vb wind or roll
together
CONVOLVED
> CONVOLVE
CONVOLVES
> CONVOLVE
CONVOS > CONVO
CONVOY n group of
vehicles or ships travelling
together ▷ vb escort while
in transit
CONVOYED > CONVOY
CONVOYING > CONVOY
CONVOYS > CONVOY
CONVULSE vb (of part of
the body) undergo violent
spasms
CONVULSED
> CONVULSE
CONVULSES
> CONVULSE
CONWOMAN n woman
who uses confidence
tricks to swindle or
defraud
CONWOMEN > CONWOMAN
CONY n rabbit
COO vb (of a dove or
pigeon) make a soft
murmuring sound ▷ n
sound of cooing ▷ interj
exclamation of surprise,
awe, etc
COOCH n vulgar word for
the vagina
COOCHES > COOCH
COOCOO old spelling of
> CUCKOO
COOED > COO
COOEE interj call to attract
attention ▷ vb utter this
call ▷ n calling distance
COOEED > COOEE
COOEEING > COOEE
COOEES > COOEE
COOER > COO
COOERS > COO
COOEY same as > COOEE
COOEYED > COOEY
COOEYING > COOEY
COOEYS > COOEY
COOF n unintelligent
person
COOFS > COOF

COOING > COO
COOINGLY > COO
COOINGS > COO
COOK vb prepare (food) by
heating ▷ n person who
cooks food
COOKABLE adj able to be
cooked ▷ n something
that can be cooked
COOKABLES
> COOKABLE
COOKBOOK n book
containing recipes and
instructions for cooking
COOKBOOKS
> COOKBOOK
COOKED > COOK
COOKER n apparatus for
cooking heated by gas or
electricity
COOKERIES > COOKERY
COOKERS > COOKER
COOKERY n art of cooking
COOKEY same as
> COOKIE
COOKEYS > COOKEY
COOKHOUSE n place for
cooking, esp a camp
kitchen
COOKIE n biscuit
COOKIES > COOKIE
COOKING > COOK
COOKINGS > COOK
COOKLESS adj devoid of a
cook
COOKMAID n maid who
assists a cook
COOKMAIDS
> COOKMAID
COOKOFF n cookery
competition
COOKOFFS > COOKOFF
COOKOUT n party where a
meal is cooked and eaten
out of doors
COOKOUTS > COOKOUT
COOKROOM n room in
which food is cooked
COOKROOMS
> COOKROOM
COOKS > COOK
COOKSHACK n makeshift
building in which food is
cooked
COOKSHOP n shop that
sells cookery equipment
COOKSHOPS
> COOKSHOP
COOKSTOVE n stove for
cooking
COOKTOP n flat unit for
cooking in saucepans or
the top part of a stove
COOKTOPS > COOKTOP
COOKWARE n cooking
utensils
COOKWARES
> COOKWARE
COOKY same as > COOKIE
COOL adj moderately cold
▷ vb make or become cool
▷ n coolness
COOLABAH n Australian
tree that grows along
rivers, with smooth bark
and long narrow leaves
COOLABAHS
> COOLABAH

COOLAMON n shallow dish
of wood or bark, used for
carrying water
COOLAMONS
> COOLAMON
COOLANT n fluid used to
cool machinery while it is
working
COOLANTS > COOLANT
COOLDOWN n gentle
stretching exercises after
strenuous activity
COOLDOWNS
> COOLDOWN
COOLED > COOL
COOLER n container for
making or keeping things
cool
COOLERS > COOLER
COOLEST > COOL
COOLHOUSE n
greenhouse in which a
cool temperature is
maintained
COOLIBAH same as
> COOLABAH
COOLIBAHS
> COOLIBAH
COOLIBAR same as
> COOLABAH
COOLIBARS
> COOLIBAR
COOLING n as in
regenerative cooling method
of cooling rocket
combustion chambers
COOLINGLY > COOL
COOLINGS > COOLING
COOLISH > COOL
COOLIST n person who
does not believe in global
warming
COOLISTS > COOLIST
COOLLY > COOL
COOLNESS > COOL
COOLS > COOL
COOLTH n coolness
COOLTHS > COOLTH
COOM n waste material
▷ vb blacken
COOMB n short valley or
deep hollow
COOMBE same as > COOMB
COOMBES > COOMBE
COOMBS > COOMB
COOMED > COOM
COOMIER > COOMY
COOMIEST > COOMY
COOMING > COOM
COOMS > COOM
COOMY adj grimy
COON n raccoon
COONCAN n card game for
two players, similar to
rummy
COONCANS > COONCAN
COONDOG n dog trained to
hunt raccoons
COONDOGS > COONDOG
COONHOUND n dog for
hunting raccoons
COONS > COON
COONSHIT n vulgar term
for a contemptible person
COONSHITS
> COONSHIT
COONSKIN n pelt of a
raccoon

COONSKINS
> COONSKIN
COONTIE n evergreen plant of S Florida
COONTIES > COONTIE
COONTY same as
> COONTIE
COOP n cage or pen for poultry ▷ vb confine in a restricted area
COOPED > COOP
COOPER n person who makes or repairs barrels ▷ vb make or mend (barrels, casks, etc)
COOPERAGE n craft, place of work, or products of a cooper
COOPERATE vb work or act together
COOPERED > COOPER
COOPERIES > COOPERY
COOPERING > COOPER
COOPERS > COOPER
COOPERY same as
> COOPERAGE
COOPING > COOP
COOPS > COOP
COOPT vb add (someone) to a group by the agreement of the existing members
COOPTED > COOPT
COOPTING > COOPT
COOPTION > COOPT
COOPTIONS > COOPT
COOPTS > COOPT
COORDINAL adj (of animals or plants) belonging to the same order
COORIE same as
> COURIE
COORIED > COORIE
COORIEING > COORIE
COORIES > COORIE
COOS > COO
COOSEN same as > COZEN
COOSENED > COOSEN
COOSENING > COOSEN
COOSENS > COOSEN
COOSER n stallion
COOSERS > COOSER
COOSIN same as > COZEN
COOSINED > COOSIN
COOSINING > COOSIN
COOSINS > COOSIN
COOST Scots form of
> CAST
COOT n small black water bird
COOTCH n hiding place ▷ vb hide
COOTCHED > COOTCH
COOTCHES > COOTCH
COOTCHING > COOTCH
COOTER n type of freshwater turtle
COOTERS > COOTER
COOTIE n body louse
COOTIES > COOTIE
COOTIKIN n gaiter
COOTIKINS
> COOTIKIN
COOTS > COOT
COOZE n vulgar word for the female genitals
COOZES > COOZE

COP same as > COPPER
COPACETIC adj very good
COPAIBA n resin obtained from certain tropical trees
COPAIBAS > COPAIBA
COPAIVA same as
> COPAIBA
COPAIVAS > COPAIVA
COPAL n resin used in varnishes
COPALM n aromatic resin
COPALMS > COPALM
COPALS > COPAL
COPARCENY n form of joint ownership of property
COPARENT n fellow parent
COPARENTS
> COPARENT
COPARTNER n partner or associate
COPASETIC same as
> COPACETIC
COPASTOR n fellow pastor
COPASTORS
> COPASTOR
COPATAINE adj (of a hat) high-crowned
COPATRIOT n fellow patriot
COPATRON n fellow patron
COPATRONS
> COPATRON
COPAY n amount payable for treatment by person with medical insurance
COPAYMENT n fee paid for medical insurance
COPAYS > COPAY
COPE vb deal successfully (with) ▷ n large ceremonial cloak worn by some Christian priests
COPECK same as
> KOPECK
COPECKS > COPECK
COPED > COPE
COPEMATE n partner
COPEMATES
> COPEMATE
COPEN n shade of blue
COPENS > COPEN
COPEPOD n type of minute crustacean
COPEPODS > COPEPOD
COPER n horse-dealer ▷ vb smuggle liquor to deep-sea fishermen
COPERED > COPER
COPERING > COPER
COPERS > COPER
COPES > COPE
COPESETIC same as
> COPACETIC
COPESTONE same as
> CAPSTONE
COPIABLE adj able to be copied
COPIED > COPY
COPIER n machine that copies
COPIERS > COPIER
COPIES > COPY

COPIHUE n Chilean bellflower
COPIHUES > COPIHUE
COPILOT n second pilot of an aircraft ▷ vb act as a copilot
COPILOTED > COPILOT
COPILOTS > COPILOT
COPING n sloping top row of a wall
COPINGS > COPING
COPIOUS adj abundant, plentiful
COPIOUSLY > COPIOUS
COPITA n tulip-shaped sherry glass
COPITAS > COPITA
COPLANAR adj lying in the same plane
COPLOT vb plot together
COPLOTS > COPLOT
COPLOTTED > COPLOT
COPOLYMER n chemical compound of high molecular weight formed by uniting the molecules of two or more different compounds (monomers)
COPOUT n act of avoiding responsibility
COPOUTS > COPOUT
COPPED > COP
COPPER n soft reddish-brown metal ▷ adj reddish-brown ▷ vb coat or cover with copper
COPPERAH same as
> COPRA
COPPERAHS
> COPPERAH
COPPERAS n ferrous sulphate
COPPERED > COPPER
COPPERIER > COPPERY
COPPERING > COPPER
COPPERISH adj copper-like
COPPERS > COPPER
COPPERY adj like copper
COPPICE n small group of trees growing close together ▷ vb trim back (trees or bushes) to form a coppice
COPPICED > COPPICE
COPPICES > COPPICE
COPPICING > COPPICE
COPPIES > COPPY
COPPIN n ball of thread
COPPING > COP
COPPINS > COPPIN
COPPLE n hill rising to a point
COPPLES > COPPLE
COPPRA same as > COPRA
COPPRAS > COPPRA
COPPY n small wooden stool
COPRA n dried oil-yielding kernel of the coconut
COPRAEMIA n type of poisoning caused by faecal matter entering the bloodstream
COPRAEMIC adj relating to or causing copraemia
COPRAH same as > COPRA
COPRAHS > COPRAH

COPRAS > COPRA
COPREMIA same as
> COPRAEMIA
COPREMIAS
> COPREMIA
COPREMIC same as
> COPRAEMIC
COPRESENT vb to present jointly
COPRINCE n fellow prince
COPRINCES
> COPRINCE
COPRODUCE vb to produce jointly
COPRODUCT n joint product
COPROLITE n rounded stony nodule thought to be fossilized faeces
COPROLITH n hard stony mass of dried faeces
COPROLOGY n preoccupation with excrement
COPROSMA n Australasian shrub sometimes planted for ornament
COPROSMAS
> COPROSMA
COPROZOIC adj (of animals) living in dung
COPS > COP
COPSE same as
> COPPICE
COPSED > COPSE
COPSES > COPSE
COPSEWOOD n brushwood
COPSHOP n police station
COPSHOPS > COPSHOP
COPSIER > COPSY
COPSIEST > COPSY
COPSING > COPSY
COPSY adj having copses
COPTER n helicopter
COPTERS > COPTER
COPUBLISH vb to publish jointly
COPULA n verb used to link the subject and complement of a sentence
COPULAE > COPULA
COPULAR > COPULA
COPULAS > COPULA
COPULATE vb have sexual intercourse
COPULATED
> COPULATE
COPULATES
> COPULATE
COPURIFY vb purify together
COPY n thing made to look exactly like another ▷ vb make a copy of
COPYABLE > COPY
COPYBOOK n book of specimens for imitation
COPYBOOKS
> COPYBOOK
COPYBOY n formerly, in journalism, young man who carried copy and ran errands
COPYBOYS > COPYBOY
COPYCAT n person who imitates or copies

COQUINA n soft limestone

COQUINAS > COQUINA

COQUIS > COQUI

COQUITO n Chilean palm tree yielding edible nuts and a syrup

COQUITOS > COQUITO

COR interj exclamation of surprise, amazement, or admiration ▷ n Hebrew measure of dry weight

CORACLE n small round boat of wicker covered with skins

CORACLES > CORACLE

CORACOID n paired ventral bone of the pectoral girdle in vertebrates

CORACOIDS > CORACOID

CORAGGIO interj exhortation to hold one's nerve

CORAL n hard substance formed from the skeletons of very small sea animals ▷ adj orange-pink

CORALLA > CORALLUM

CORALLINE n type of red alga impregnated with calcium carbonate

CORALLITE n skeleton of a coral polyp

CORALLOID same as **>** CORALLINE

CORALLUM n skeleton of any zoophyte

CORALROOT n N temperate leafless orchid with small yellow-green or purple flowers and branched roots resembling coral

CORALS > CORAL

CORALWORT n coralroot or toothwort

CORAM prep before, in the presence of

CORAMINE n type of stimulant

CORAMINES > CORAMINE

CORANACH same as **>** CORONACH

CORANACHS > CORONACH

CORANTO same as **>** COURANTE

CORANTOES > CORANTO

CORANTOS > CORANTO

CORBAN n gift to God

CORBANS > CORBAN

CORBE obsolete variant of **>** CORBEL

CORBEAU n blackish green colour

CORBEAUS > CORBEAU

CORBEIL n carved ornament in the form of a basket of fruit, flowers, etc

CORBEILLE same as **>** CORBEIL

CORBEILS > CORBEIL

CORBEL n stone or timber support sticking out of a wall ▷ vb lay (a stone or brick) so that it forms a corbel

CORBELED > CORBEL

CORBELING n set of corbels stepped outwards, one above another

CORBELLED > CORBEL

CORBELS > CORBEL

CORBES > CORBE

CORBICULA n pollen basket

CORBIE n raven or crow

CORBIES > CORBIE

CORBINA n type of North American whiting

CORBINAS > CORBINA

CORBY same as **>** CORBIE

CORCASS n in Ireland, marshland

CORCASSES > CORCASS

CORD n thin rope or thick string ▷ adj (of fabric) ribbed ▷ vb bind or furnish with a cord or cords

CORDAGE n lines and rigging of a vessel

CORDAGES > CORDAGE

CORDATE adj heart-shaped

CORDATELY > CORDATE

CORDED adj tied or fastened with cord

CORDELLE vb to tow

CORDELLED > CORDELLE

CORDELLES > CORDELLE

CORDER > CORD

CORDERS > CORD

CORDGRASS n type of coarse grass

CORDIAL adj warm and friendly ▷ n drink with a fruit base

CORDIALLY > CORDIAL

CORDIALS > CORDIAL

CORDIFORM adj heart-shaped

CORDINER n shoemaker

CORDINERS > CORDINER

CORDING > CORD

CORDINGS > CORD

CORDITE n explosive used in guns and bombs

CORDITES > CORDITE

CORDLESS adj powered by an internal battery rather than a power cable

CORDLIKE > CORD

CORDOBA n standard monetary unit of Nicaragua

CORDOBAS > CORDOBA

CORDON n chain of police, soldiers, etc, guarding an area ▷ vb put or form a cordon (around)

CORDONED > CORDON

CORDONING > CORDON

CORDONNET n type of thread

CORDONS > CORDON

CORDOTOMY n method of pain relief in which nerves are cut

CORDOVAN n fine leather made principally from horsehide

CORDOVANS > CORDOVAN

CORDS pl n trousers made of corduroy

CORDUROY n cotton fabric with a velvety ribbed surface

CORDUROYS pl n trousers made of corduroy

CORDWAIN an archaic name for **>** CORDOVAN

CORDWAINS > CORDWAIN

CORDWOOD n wood that has been cut into lengths of four feet so that it can be stacked in cords

CORDWOODS > CORDWOOD

CORDYLINE n any tree of the genus Cordyline

CORE n central part of certain fruits, containing the seeds ▷ vb remove the core from

CORED > CORE

COREDEEM vb redeem together

COREDEEMS > COREDEEM

COREGENT n joint regent

COREGENTS > COREGENT

COREIGN vb reign jointly

COREIGNS > COREIGN

CORELATE same as **>** CORRELATE

CORELATED > CORELATE

CORELATES > CORELATE

CORELESS > CORE

CORELLA n white Australian cockatoo

CORELLAS > CORELLA

COREMIA > COREMIUM

COREMIUM n spore-producing organ of certain fungi

COREOPSIS n American and tropical African plant cultivated for its yellow, brown, or yellow-and-red daisy-like flowers

CORER > CORE

CORERS > CORE

CORES > CORE

COREY n vulgar word for the penis

COREYS > COREY

CORF n wagon or basket used formerly in mines

CORFHOUSE n shed used for curing salmon and storing nets

CORGI n short-legged sturdy dog

CORGIS > CORGI

CORIA > CORIUM

CORIANDER n plant grown for its aromatic seeds and leaves

CORIES > CORY

CORING > CORE

CORIOUS adj leathery

CORIUM n deep inner layer of the skin

CORIUMS > CORIUM

CORIVAL same as **>** CORRIVAL

---

someone ▷ vb imitate with great attention to detail

COPYCATS > COPYCAT

COPYDESK n desk where newspaper copy is edited

COPYDESKS > COPYDESK

COPYEDIT vb prepare text for printing by styling, correcting, etc

COPYEDITS > COPYEDIT

COPYFIGHT n legal battle over the use of a copyright

COPYGIRL n formerly, in journalism, young woman who carried copy and ran errands

COPYGIRLS > COPYGIRL

COPYGRAPH n process for copying type

COPYHOLD n tenure less than freehold of land in England evidenced by a copy of the Court roll

COPYHOLDS > COPYHOLD

COPYING n act of copying

COPYINGS > COPYING

COPYISM n slavish copying

COPYISMS > COPYISM

COPYIST n person who makes written copies

COPYISTS > COPYIST

COPYLEFT n permission to use something free of charge ▷ vb use copyright law to make (work, esp software) free to use

COPYLEFTS > COPYLEFT

COPYREAD vb subedit

COPYREADS > COPYREAD

COPYRIGHT n exclusive legal right to reproduce a book, work of art, etc ▷ vb take out a copyright on ▷ adj protected by copyright

COPYTAKER n (esp in a newspaper office) a person employed to type reports as journalists dictate them over the telephone

COQUET vb behave flirtatiously

COQUETRY n flirtation

COQUETS > COQUET

COQUETTE n woman who flirts

COQUETTED > COQUET

COQUETTES > COQUETTE

COQUI n type of tree-dwelling frog

COQUILLA n type of South American nut

COQUILLAS > COQUILLA

COQUILLE n any dish, esp seafood, served in a scallop shell

COQUILLES > COQUILLE

CORIVALRY > CORIVAL

CORIVALS > CORIVAL

CORIXID n type of water bug

CORIXIDS > CORIXID

CORK n thick light bark of a Mediterranean oak ▷ vb seal with a cork ▷ adj made of cork

CORKAGE n restaurant's charge for serving wine bought elsewhere

CORKAGES > CORKAGE

CORKBOARD n thin slab made of granules of cork, used as a floor or wall finish and as an insulator

CORKBORER n tool for cutting a hole in a stopper to insert a glass tube

CORKED adj (of wine) spoiled through having a decayed cork

CORKER n splendid or outstanding person or thing

CORKERS > CORKER

CORKIER > CORKY

CORKIEST > CORKY

CORKINESS > CORKY

CORKING adj excellent

CORKIR n lichen from which red or purple dye is made

CORKIRS > CORKIR

CORKLIKE > CORK

CORKS > CORK

CORKSCREW n spiral metal tool for pulling corks from bottles ▷ adj like a corkscrew in shape ▷ vb move in a spiral or zigzag course

CORKTREE n type of evergreen oak tree

CORKTREES > CORKTREE

CORKWING n type of greenish or bluish European fish

CORKWINGS > CORKWING

CORKWOOD n type of small tree of the southeastern US, with very lightweight porous wood

CORKWOODS > CORKWOOD

CORKY same as > CORKED

CORM n bulblike underground stem of certain plants

CORMEL n new small corm arising from the base of a fully developed one

CORMELS > CORMEL

CORMIDIA > CORMIDIUM

CORMIDIUM n collection of polyps in a siphonophore

CORMLET n small corm

CORMLETS > CORMLET

CORMLIKE adj resembling a corm

CORMOID adj like a corm

CORMORANT n large dark-coloured long-necked sea bird

CORMOUS > CORM

CORMS > CORM

CORMUS n corm

CORMUSES > CORMUS

CORN n cereal plant such as wheat or oats ▷ vb feed (animals) with corn, esp oats

CORNACRE same as > CONACRE

CORNACRES > CORNACRE

CORNAGE n rent fixed according to the number of horned cattle pastured

CORNAGES > CORNAGE

CORNBALL n person given to mawkish or unsophisticated behaviour

CORNBALLS > CORNBALL

CORNBORER n larva of the pyralid moth

CORNBRAID vb braid hair in cornrows

CORNBRASH n type of limestone which produces good soil for growing corn

CORNBREAD n bread made from maize meal

CORNCAKE n kind of cornmeal flatbread

CORNCAKES > CORNCAKE

CORNCOB n core of an ear of maize, to which the kernels are attached

CORNCOBS > CORNCOB

CORNCRAKE n brown Eurasian bird with a harsh cry

CORNCRIB n ventilated building for the storage of unhusked maize

CORNCRIBS > CORNCRIB

CORNEA n transparent membrane covering the eyeball

CORNEAE > CORNEA

CORNEAL > CORNEA

CORNEAS > CORNEA

CORNED adj preserved in salt or brine

CORNEITIS n inflammation of cornea

CORNEL n type of plant such as the dogwood and dwarf cornel

CORNELIAN same as > CARNELIAN

CORNELS > CORNEL

CORNEMUSE n French bagpipe

CORNEOUS adj horny

CORNER n area or angle where two converging lines or surfaces meet ▷ vb force into a difficult or inescapable position

CORNERED > CORNER

CORNERING n act of cornering

CORNERMAN n in baseball, first baseman

CORNERMEN > CORNERMAN

CORNERS > CORNER

CORNET n former cavalry officer

CORNETCY n commission or rank of a cornet

CORNETIST n person who plays the cornet

CORNETS > CORNET

CORNETT n musical instrument

CORNETTI > CORNETTO

CORNETTO same as > CORNETT

CORNETTOS > CORNETTO

CORNETTS > CORNETT

CORNFED adj fed on corn

CORNFIELD n field planted with cereal crops

CORNFLAG n gladiolus

CORNFLAGS > CORNFLAG

CORNFLAKE n singular form of plural cornflakes: toasted flakes made from cornmeal, sold as a breakfast cereal

CORNFLIES > CORNFLY

CORNFLOUR n fine maize flour

CORNFLY n small fly

CORNHUSK n outer protective covering of an ear of maize

CORNHUSKS > CORNHUSK

CORNI > CORNO

CORNICE n decorative moulding round the top of a wall ▷ vb furnish or decorate with or as if with a cornice

CORNICED > CORNICE

CORNICES > CORNICE

CORNICHE n coastal road, esp one built into the face of a cliff

CORNICHES > CORNICHE

CORNICHON n type of small gherkin

CORNICING n act of cornicing

CORNICLE n wax-secreting organ on an aphid's abdomen

CORNICLES > CORNICLE

CORNICULA n plural form of singular corniculum: small horn

CORNIER > CORNY

CORNIEST > CORNY

CORNIFIC adj producing horns

CORNIFIED > CORNIFY

CORNIFIES > CORNIFY

CORNIFORM adj horn-shaped

CORNIFY vb turn soft tissue hard

CORNILY > CORNY

CORNINESS > CORNY

CORNING > CORN

CORNIST n horn-player

CORNISTS > CORNIST

CORNLAND n land suitable for growing corn or grain

CORNLANDS > CORNLAND

CORNLOFT n loft for storing corn

CORNLOFTS > CORNLOFT

CORNMEAL n meal made from maize

CORNMEALS > CORNMEAL

CORNMILL n flour mill

CORNMILLS > CORNMILL

CORNMOTH n moth whose larvae feed on grain

CORNMOTHS > CORNMOTH

CORNO n French horn

CORNOPEAN n cornet (the brass musical instrument)

CORNPIPE n musical instrument made from a stalk of corn etc

CORNPIPES > CORNPIPE

CORNPONE n American corn bread

CORNPONES > CORNPONE

CORNRENT n rent for land that is paid in corn

CORNRENTS > CORNRENT

CORNROW n hairstyle in which the hair is plaited in close parallel rows ▷ vb style the hair in a cornrow

CORNROWED > CORNROW

CORNROWS > CORNROW

CORNS > CORN

CORNSILK n threads on an ear of maize

CORNSILKS > CORNSILK

CORNSTALK n stalk or stem of corn

CORNSTONE n mottled green and red limestone

CORNU n part or structure resembling a horn or having a hornlike pattern

CORNUA > CORNU

CORNUAL > CORNU

CORNUS n any member of the genus Cornus, such as dogwood

CORNUSES > CORNUS

CORNUTE adj having or resembling cornua ▷ vb make a cuckold of

CORNUTED same as > CORNUTE

CORNUTES > CORNUTE

CORNUTING > CORNUTE

CORNUTO n cuckold

CORNUTOS > CORNUTO

CORNWORM n cornmoth larva

CORNWORMS > CORNWORM

CORNY adj unoriginal or excessively sentimental

COROCORE same as > COROCORO

COROCORES > COROCORE

COROCORO n South Asian vessel fitted with outriggers

COROCOROS > COROCORO

CORODIES > CORODY

CORODY n feudal law

COROLLA n petals of a flower collectively

COROLLARY n idea, fact, or proposition which is the natural result of something else ▷ adj consequent or resultant

COROLLAS > COROLLA

COROLLATE adj having a corolla

COROLLINE adj relating to a corolla

CORONA n ring of light round the moon or sun

CORONACH n dirge or lamentation for the dead

CORONACHS > CORONACH

CORONAE > CORONA

CORONAL n circlet for the head ▷ adj of or relating to a corona or coronal

CORONALLY > CORONAL

CORONALS > CORONAL

CORONARY adj of the arteries surrounding the heart ▷ n coronary thrombosis

CORONAS > CORONA

CORONATE vb to crown

CORONATED > CORONATE

CORONATES > CORONATE

CORONEL n iron head of a tilting spear

CORONELS > CORONEL

CORONER n official responsible for the investigation of deaths

CORONERS > CORONER

CORONET n small crown

CORONETED adj wearing a coronet

CORONETS > CORONET

CORONIAL adj relating to a coroner

CORONIS n symbol used in Greek writing

CORONISES > CORONIS

CORONIUM n highly ionized iron and nickel seen as a put a green line in the solar coronal spectrum

CORONIUMS > CORONIUM

CORONOID adj crown-shaped

COROTATE vb rotate together

COROTATED > COROTATE

COROTATES > COROTATE

COROZO n tropical American palm whose seeds yield a useful oil

COROZOS > COROZO

CORPORA > CORPUS

CORPORAL n noncommissioned officer in an army ▷ adj of the body

CORPORALE same as > CORPORAL

CORPORALS > CORPORAL

CORPORAS n communion cloth

CORPORATE adj of business corporations

CORPOREAL adj physical or tangible

CORPORIFY vb to embody

CORPOSANT n Saint Elmo's fire

CORPS n military unit with a specific function

CORPSE n dead body ▷ vb laugh or cause to laugh involuntarily or inopportunely while on stage

CORPSED > CORPSE

CORPSES > CORPSE

CORPSING > CORPSE

CORPSMAN n medical orderly or stretcher-bearer

CORPSMEN > CORPSMAN

CORPULENT adj fat or plump

CORPUS n collection of writings, esp by a single author

CORPUSCLE n red or white blood cell

CORPUSES > CORPUS

CORRADE vb erode by the abrasive action of rock particles

CORRADED > CORRADE

CORRADES > CORRADE

CORRADING > CORRADE

CORRAL n enclosure for cattle or horses ▷ vb put in a corral

CORRALLED > CORRAL

CORRALS > CORRAL

CORRASION n erosion of rocks caused by fragments transported over them by water, wind, or ice

CORRASIVE > CORRASION

CORREA n Australian evergreen shrub with large showy tubular flowers

CORREAS > CORREA

CORRECT adj free from error, true ▷ vb put right

CORRECTED > CORRECT

CORRECTER > CORRECT

CORRECTLY > CORRECT

CORRECTOR > CORRECT

CORRECTS > CORRECT

CORRELATE vb place or be placed in a mutual relationship ▷ n either of two things mutually related ▷ adj having a mutual, complementary, or reciprocal relationship

CORRETTO n espresso containing alcohol

CORRETTOS > CORRETTO

CORRIDA the Spanish word for > BULLFIGHT

CORRIDAS > CORRIDA

CORRIDOR n passage in a building or train

CORRIDORS > CORRIDOR

CORRIE same as > CIRQUE

CORRIES > CORRIE

CORRIGENT n corrective

CORRIVAL a rare word for > RIVAL

CORRIVALS > CORRIVAL

CORRODANT > CORRODE

CORRODE vb eat or be eaten away by chemical action or rust

CORRODED > CORRODE

CORRODENT > CORRODE

CORRODER > CORRODE

CORRODERS > CORRODE

CORRODES > CORRODE

CORRODIES > CORRODY

CORRODING > CORRODE

CORRODY same as > CORODY

CORROSION n process by which something, esp a metal, is corroded

CORROSIVE adj (esp of acids or alkalis) capable of destroying solid materials ▷ n corrosive substance, such as a strong acid or alkali

CORRUGATE vb fold into alternate grooves and ridges ▷ adj folded into furrows and ridges

CORRUPT adj open to or involving bribery ▷ vb make corrupt

CORRUPTED > CORRUPT

CORRUPTER > CORRUPT

CORRUPTLY > CORRUPT

CORRUPTOR > CORRUPT

CORRUPTS > CORRUPT

CORS > COR

CORSAC n type of fox of central Asia

CORSACS > CORSAC

CORSAGE n small bouquet worn on the bodice of a dress

CORSAGES > CORSAGE

CORSAIR n pirate

CORSAIRS > CORSAIR

CORSE n archaic word for corpse

CORSELET n one-piece undergarment combining a corset and bra

CORSELETS > CORSELET

CORSES > CORSE

CORSET n women's undergarment ▷ vb dress or enclose in, or as in, a corset

CORSETED > CORSET

CORSETIER n corset-maker

CORSETING > CORSET

CORSETRY n making of or dealing in corsets

CORSETS > CORSET

CORSEY n pavement or pathway

CORSEYS > CORSEY

CORSITE n type of rock

CORSITES > CORSITE

CORSIVE n corrodent

CORSIVES > CORSIVE

CORSLET same as > CORSELET

CORSLETED > CORSLET

CORSLETS > CORSLET

CORSNED n ordeal to discover innocence or guilt

CORSNEDS > CORSNED

CORSO n promenade

CORSOS > CORSO

CORTEGE n funeral procession

CORTEGES > CORTEGE

CORTEX n outer layer of the brain or other internal organ

CORTEXES > CORTEX

CORTICAL > CORTEX

CORTICATE adj (of plants, seeds, etc) having a bark, husk, or rind

CORTICES > CORTEX

CORTICOID n steroid hormone

CORTICOSE adj consisting of or like bark

CORTILE n open, internal courtyard

CORTILI > CORTILE

CORTIN n adrenal cortex extract

CORTINA n weblike part of certain mushrooms

CORTINAS > CORTINA

CORTINS > CORTIN

CORTISOL n principal glucocorticoid secreted by the adrenal cortex

CORTISOLS > CORTISOL

CORTISONE n steroid hormone used to treat various diseases

CORULER n joint ruler

CORULERS > CORULER

CORUNDUM n hard mineral used as an abrasive

CORUNDUMS > CORUNDUM

CORUSCANT adj giving off flashes of light

CORUSCATE vb sparkle

CORVEE n day's unpaid labour owed by a feudal vassal to their lord

CORVEES > CORVEE

CORVES > CORF

CORVET same as > CURVET

CORVETED > CORVET

CORVETING > CORVET

CORVETS > CORVET

CORVETTE n lightly armed escort warship ▷ vb participate in social activities with fellow Corvette car enthusiasts

CORVETTED > CORVETTE

CORVETTES > CORVETTE

CORVID n any member of the crow family

CORVIDS > CORVID

CORVINA same as > CORBINA

CORVINAS > CORVINA

CORVINE adj of, relating to, or resembling a crow

CORVUS n type of ancient hook

CORVUSES > CORVUS

CORY n catfish belonging to the South American Corydoras genus

CORYBANT n wild attendant of the goddess Cybele

CORYBANTS > CORYBANT

CORYDALIS n N temperate plant with finely lobed leaves and spurred yellow or pinkish flowers

CORYLUS n hazel genus

CORYLUSES > CORYLUS

CORYMB n flat-topped flower cluster

CORYMBED > CORYMB

CORYMBOSE > CORYMB

CORYMBOUS > CORYMB

CORYMBS > CORYMB

CORYPHAEI n plural form of singular coryphaeus: leader of the chorus

CORYPHE n leader of a Greek chorus

CORYPHEE n leading dancer of a corps de ballet

CORYPHEES > CORYPHEE

CORYPHENE n any fish of the genus Coryphaena

CORYPHES > CORYPHE

CORYZA n acute inflammation in the nose

CORYZAL > CORYZA

CORYZAS > CORYZA

COS same as > COSINE

COSCRIPT vb script jointly

COSCRIPTS > COSCRIPT

COSE vb get cosy

COSEC same as > COSECANT

COSECANT n ratio of the hypotenuse to the opposite side in a right-angled triangle

COSECANTS > COSECANT

COSECH n hyperbolic cosecant

COSECHS > COSECH

COSECS > COSEC

COSED > COSE

COSEISMAL adj of or designating points at which earthquake waves are felt at the same time ▷ n such a line on a map

COSEISMIC same as > COSEISMAL

COSES > COSE

COSET n mathematical set

COSETS > COSET

COSEY n tea cosy

COSEYS > COSEY

COSH n heavy blunt weapon ▷ vb hit with a cosh

COSHED > COSH

COSHER vb pamper or coddle

COSHERED > COSHER

COSHERER > COSHER

COSHERERS > COSHER

COSHERIES > COSHERY

COSHERING > COSHER

COSHERS > COSHER

COSHERY n Irish chief's right to lodge at their tenants' houses

COSHES > COSH

COSHING > COSH

COSIE same as > COSY

COSIED > COSY

COSIER n cobbler

COSIERS > COSIER

COSIES > COSY

COSIEST > COSY

COSIGN vb sign jointly

COSIGNED > COSIGN

COSIGNER > COSIGN

COSIGNERS > COSIGN

COSIGNING > COSIGN

COSIGNS > COSIGN

COSILY > COSY

COSINE n trigonometric function

COSINES > COSINE

COSINESS > COSY

COSING > COSE

COSMEA n plant of the genus Cosmos

COSMEAS > COSMEA

COSMESES > COSMESIS

COSMESIS n aesthetic covering on a prosthesis to make it look more natural

COSMETIC n preparation used to improve the appearance of a person's skin ▷ adj improving the appearance only

COSMETICS > COSMETIC

COSMIC adj of the whole universe

COSMICAL same as > COSMIC

COSMID n segment of DNA

COSMIDS > COSMID

COSMIN same as > COSMINE

COSMINE n substance resembling dentine

COSMINES > COSMINE

COSMINS > COSMIN

COSMISM n Russian cultural and philosophical movement

COSMISMS > COSMISM

COSMIST > COSMISM

COSMISTS > COSMISM

COSMOCRAT n ruler of the world

COSMOGENY same as > COSMOGONY

COSMOGONY n study of the origin of the universe

COSMOID adj having two inner bony layers and a cosmine outer layer

COSMOLINE n type of petroleum jelly ▷ vb to apply cosmoline to

COSMOLOGY n study of the origin and nature of the universe

COSMONAUT n Russian name for an astronaut

COSMORAMA n lifelike display, using mirrors and lenses, which shows reflections of various views of parts of the world

COSMOS n universe

COSMOSES > COSMOS

COSMOTRON n large type of particle accelerator

COSPHERED adj sharing the same sphere

COSPLAY n recreational activity in which people interact while dressed as fictional characters

COSPLAYS > COSPLAY

COSPONSOR vb to sponsor jointly

COSS another name for > KOS

COSSACK n Slavonic warrior-peasant

COSSACKS > COSSACK

COSSES > COSS

COSSET vb pamper ▷ n any pet animal, esp a lamb

COSSETED > COSSET

COSSETING > COSSET

COSSETS > COSSET

COSSETTED adj pampered, spoilt

COSSIE n informal name for a swimming costume

COSSIES > COSSIE

COST n amount of money, time, labour, etc, required for something ▷ vb have as its cost

COSTA n riblike part, such as the midrib of a plant leaf

COSTAE > COSTA

COSTAL n strengthening rib of an insect's wing

COSTALGIA n pain in the ribs

COSTALLY > COSTAL

COSTALS > COSTAL

COSTAR n actor who shares the billing with another ▷ vb share the billing with another actor

COSTARD n English variety of apple tree

COSTARDS > COSTARD

COSTARRED > COSTAR

COSTARS > COSTAR

COSTATE adj having ribs

COSTATED same as > COSTATE

COSTE vb draw near

COSTEAN vb mine for lodes

COSTEANED > COSTEAN

COSTEANS > COSTEAN

COSTED > COST

COSTER n person who sells fruit, vegetables etc from a barrow

COSTERS > COSTER

COSTES > COSTE

COSTING n as in marginal costing method of cost accounting

COSTINGS > COSTING

COSTIVE adj having or causing constipation

COSTIVELY > COSTIVE

COSTLESS > COST

COSTLIER > COSTLY

COSTLIEST > COSTLY

COSTLY adj expensive

COSTMARY n herbaceous Asian plant

COSTOTOMY n surgical incision into a rib

COSTREL n flask, usually of earthenware or leather

COSTRELS > COSTREL

COSTS > COST

COSTUME n style of dress of a particular place or time, or for a particular activity ▷ vb provide with a costume

COSTUMED > COSTUME

COSTUMER same as > COSTUMIER

COSTUMERS > COSTUMIER

COSTUMERY n collective term for costumes

COSTUMES > COSTUME

COSTUMEY adj (stage) costume-like; unrealistic

COSTUMIER n maker or seller of costumes

COSTUMING n act of providing (someone) with a costume

COSTUS n Himalayan herb with an aromatic root

COSTUSES > COSTUS

COSY adj warm and snug ▷ n cover for keeping things warm ▷ vb make oneself snug and warm

COSYING > COSY

COT n baby's bed with high sides ▷ vb entangle or become entangled

COTAN same as > COTANGENT

COTANGENT n (in trigonometry) the ratio of the length of the adjacent side to that of the opposite side in a right-angled triangle

COTANS > COTAN

COTE same as > COT

COTEAU n hillside

COTEAUS > COTEAU

COTEAUX > COTEAU

COTED > COTE

COTELETTE n cutlet

COTELINE n kind of muslin

COTELINES > COTELINE

COTENANCY > COTENANT

COTENANT n person who holds property jointly or in common with others

COTENANTS > COTENANT

COTERIE *n* exclusive group, clique
COTERIES > COTERIE
COTES > COTE
COTH *n* hyperbolic cotangent
COTHS > COTH
COTHURN *same as* > COTHURNUS
COTHURNAL > COTHURNUS
COTHURNI > COTHURNUS
COTHURNS > COTHURN
COTHURNUS *n* buskin worn in ancient Greek tragedy
COTICULAR *adj* relating to whetstones
COTIDAL *adj* (of a line on a tidal chart) joining points at which high tide occurs simultaneously
COTIJA *n* salty Mexican cheese
COTIJAS > COTIJA
COTILLION *n* French formation dance of the 18th century
COTILLON *same as* > COTILLION
COTILLONS > COTILLON
COTING > COTE
COTINGA *n* tropical bird
COTINGAS > COTINGA
COTININE *n* substance used to indicate presence of nicotine
COTININES > COTININE
COTISE *same as* > COTTISE
COTISED > COTISE
COTISES > COTISE
COTISING > COTISE
COTLAND *n* grounds that belong to a cotter
COTLANDS > COTLAND
COTQUEAN *n* coarse woman
COTQUEANS > COTQUEAN
COTRUSTEE *n* fellow trustee
COTS > COT
COTT *same as* > COT
COTTA *n* short surplice
COTTABUS *n* ancient Greek game involving throwing wine into a vessel
COTTAE > COTTA
COTTAGE *n* small house in the country ▷ *vb* engage in homosexual activity in a public lavatory
COTTAGED > COTTAGE
COTTAGER *n* person who lives in a cottage
COTTAGERS > COTTAGER
COTTAGES > COTTAGE
COTTAGEY *adj* resembling a cottage
COTTAGIER > COTTAGEY

COTTAGING *n* homosexual activity between men in a public lavatory
COTTAR *n* cottage-dwelling peasant
COTTARS > COTTAR
COTTAS > COTTA
COTTED > COT
COTTER *n* pin or wedge used to secure machine parts ▷ *vb* secure (two parts) with a cotter
COTTERED > COTTER
COTTERING > COTTER
COTTERS > COTTER
COTTID *n* type of fish typically with a large head, tapering body, and spiny fins
COTTIDS > COTTID
COTTIER *same as* > COTTAR
COTTIERS > COTTIER
COTTING > COT
COTTISE *n* type of heraldic decoration ▷ *vb* (in heraldry) decorate with a cottise
COTTISED > COTTISE
COTTISES > COTTISE
COTTISING > COTTISE
COTTOID *adj* resembling a fish of the genus Cottus
COTTON *n* white downy fibre covering the seeds of a tropical plant ▷ *vb* take a liking
COTTONADE *n* coarse fabric of cotton or mixed fibres, used for work clothes, etc
COTTONED > COTTON
COTTONIER > COTTONY
COTTONING > COTTON
COTTONS > COTTON
COTTONY *adj* like cotton
COTTOWN *Scots variant of* > COTTON
COTTOWNS > COTTOWN
COTTS > COTT
COTTUS *n* type of fish with four yellowish knobs on its head
COTTUSES > COTTUS
COTURNIX *n* variety of quail
COTWAL *n* Indian police officer
COTWALS > COTWAL
COTYLAE > COTYLE
COTYLE *n* cuplike cavity
COTYLEDON *n* first leaf of a plant embryo
COTYLES > COTYLE
COTYLOID *adj* shaped like a cup ▷ *n* small bone forming part of the acetabular cavity in some mammals
COTYLOIDS > COTYLOID
COTYPE *n* additional specimen in biological study
COTYPES > COTYPE
COUCAL *n* type of ground-living bird of

Africa, S Asia, and Australia, with long strong legs
COUCALS > COUCAL
COUCH *n* piece of upholstered furniture for seating more than one person ▷ *vb* express in a particular way
COUCHANT *adj* in a lying position
COUCHE *adj* in heraldry (of a shield), tilted
COUCHED > COUCH
COUCHEE *n* reception held late at night
COUCHEES > COUCHEE
COUCHER > COUCH
COUCHERS > COUCH
COUCHES > COUCH
COUCHETTE *n* bed converted from seats on a train or ship
COUCHING *n* method of embroidery
COUCHINGS > COUCHING
COUDE *adj* relating to the construction of a reflecting telescope ▷ *n* type of reflecting telescope
COUDES > COUDE
COUGAN *n* drunk and rowdy person
COUGANS > COUGAN
COUGAR *n* puma
COUGARS > COUGAR
COUGH *vb* expel air from the lungs abruptly and noisily ▷ *n* act or sound of coughing
COUGHED > COUGH
COUGHER > COUGH
COUGHERS > COUGH
COUGHING > COUGH
COUGHINGS > COUGH
COUGHS > COUGH
COUGUAR *same as* > COUGAR
COUGUARS > COUGUAR
COULD > CAN
COULDEST *same as* > COULDST
COULDST *vb* form of 'could' used with the pronoun *thou* or its relative form
COULEE *n* flow of molten lava
COULEES > COULEE
COULIBIAC *n* Russian fish pie
COULIS *n* thin purée of vegetables or fruit
COULISSE *n* timber grooved to take a sliding panel
COULISSES > COULISSE
COULOIR *n* deep gully on a mountain side, esp in the French Alps
COULOIRS > COULOIR
COULOMB *n* SI unit of electric charge
COULOMBIC > COULOMB
COULOMBS > COULOMB

COULTER *n* blade at the front of a ploughshare
COULTERS > COULTER
COUMARIC > COUMARIN
COUMARIN *n* white vanilla-scented crystalline ester
COUMARINS > COUMARIN
COUMARONE *n* colourless insoluble aromatic liquid obtained from coal tar and used in the manufacture of synthetic resins
COUMAROU *n* tonka bean tree, or its seed
COUMAROUS > COUMAROU
COUNCIL *n* group meeting for discussion or consultation ▷ *adj* of or by a council
COUNCILOR *n* member of a council
COUNCILS > COUNCIL
COUNSEL *n* advice or guidance ▷ *vb* give guidance to
COUNSELED > COUNSEL
COUNSELEE *n* one who is counselled
COUNSELOR *n* person who gives counsel
COUNSELS > COUNSEL
COUNT *vb* say numbers in order ▷ *n* counting
COUNTABLE *adj* capable of being counted
COUNTABLY > COUNTABLE
COUNTBACK *n* system of deciding the winner of a tied competition by comparing earlier points or scores
COUNTDOWN *n* counting backwards to zero of the seconds before an event ▷ *vb* count numbers backwards towards zero, esp in timing such a critical operation
COUNTED > COUNT
COUNTER *n* long flat surface in a bank or shop ▷ *vb* oppose, retaliate against ▷ *adv* in the opposite direction
COUNTERED > COUNTER
COUNTERS > COUNTER
COUNTESS *n* woman holding the rank of count or earl
COUNTIAN *n* dweller in a given county
COUNTIANS > COUNTIAN
COUNTIES > COUNTY
COUNTING *n* act or instance of saying numbers in order
COUNTINGS > COUNTING
COUNTLESS *adj* too many to count
COUNTLINE *n* (in confectionery marketing) a chocolate-based bar
COUNTRIES > COUNTRY

COUNTROL obsolete variant of > CONTROL
COUNTROLS > COUNTROL
COUNTRY n nation
COUNTS > COUNT
COUNTSHIP > COUNT
COUNTY n (in some countries) division of a country ▷ adj upper-class
COUP n successful action ▷ vb turn or fall over
COUPE n sports car with two doors and a sloping fixed roof
COUPED > COUP
COUPEE n dance movement
COUPEES > COUPEE
COUPER n dealer
COUPERS > COUPER
COUPES > COUPE
COUPING > COUP
COUPLE n two people who are married or romantically involved ▷ vb connect, associate
COUPLED > COUPLE
COUPLEDOM n state of living as a couple, esp when regarded as being interested in each other to the exclusion of the outside world
COUPLER n mechanical device
COUPLERS > COUPLER
COUPLES > COUPLE
COUPLET n two consecutive lines of verse
COUPLETS > COUPLET
COUPLING n device for connecting things, such as railway carriages
COUPLINGS > COUPLING
COUPON n piece of paper entitling the holder to a discount or gift
COUPONING n in marketing, distribution or redemption of promotional coupons
COUPONS > COUPON
COUPS > COUP
COUPURE n entrenchment made by besieged forces behind a breach
COUPURES > COUPURE
COUR obsolete variant of > COVER
COURAGE n ability to face danger or pain without fear
COURAGES > COURAGE
COURANT n old dance in quick triple time ▷ adj (of an animal) running
COURANTE n old dance in quick triple time
COURANTES > COURANTE
COURANTO same as > COURANTE
COURANTOS > COURANTO
COURANTS > COURANT

COURB vb to bend
COURBARIL n tropical American tree whose wood is a useful timber and whose gum is a source of copal
COURBED > COURB
COURBETTE same as > CURVET
COURBING > COURB
COURBS > COURB
COURD obsolete variant of > COVERED
COURE obsolete variant of > COVER
COURED > COURE
COURES > COURE
COURGETTE n type of small vegetable marrow
COURIE vb nestle or snuggle
COURIED > COURIE
COURIEING > COURIE
COURIER n person employed to look after holidaymakers ▷ vb send (a parcel, letter, etc) by courier
COURIERED > COURIER
COURIERS > COURIER
COURIES > COURIE
COURING > COUR
COURLAN another name for > LIMPKIN
COURLANS > COURLAN
COURS > COUR
COURSE n series of lessons or medical treatment ▷ vb (of liquid) run swiftly
COURSED > COURSE
COURSER n swift horse
COURSERS > COURSER
COURSES another word for > MENSES
COURSING n hunting with hounds trained to hunt game by sight
COURSINGS > COURSING
COURT n body which decides legal cases ▷ vb try to gain the love of
COURTED > COURT
COURTEOUS adj polite
COURTER n suitor
COURTERS > COURTER
COURTESAN n mistress or high-class prostitute
COURTESY n politeness, good manners
COURTEZAN same as > COURTESAN
COURTIER n attendant at a royal court
COURTIERS > COURTIER
COURTING > COURT
COURTINGS > COURT
COURTLET n small court
COURTLETS > COURTLET
COURTLIER > COURTLY
COURTLIKE adj courtly
COURTLING n fawning courtier
COURTLY adj ceremoniously polite

COURTROOM n room in which the sittings of a law court are held
COURTS > COURT
COURTSHIP n courting of an intended spouse or mate
COURTSIDE n in sport, area closest to the court
COURTYARD n paved space enclosed by buildings or walls
COUSCOUS n type of semolina used in North African cookery
COUSIN n child of one's uncle or aunt
COUSINAGE n kinship
COUSINLY > COUSIN
COUSINRY n collective term for cousins
COUSINS > COUSIN
COUTA n traditional Australian sailing boat
COUTAS > COUTA
COUTEAU n large two-edged knife used formerly as a weapon
COUTEAUX > COUTEAU
COUTER n armour designed to protect the elbow
COUTERS > COUTER
COUTH adj refined ▷ n refinement
COUTHER > COUTH
COUTHEST > COUTH
COUTHIE adj sociable
COUTHIER > COUTHIE
COUTHIEST > COUTHIE
COUTHS > COUTH
COUTHY same as > COUTHIE
COUTIL n type of tightly woven twill cloth
COUTILLE same as > COUTIL
COUTILLES > COUTILLE
COUTILS > COUTIL
COUTURE n high-fashion designing and dressmaking ▷ adj relating to high fashion design and dress-making
COUTURES > COUTURE
COUTURIER n person who designs women's fashion clothes
COUVADE n custom in certain cultures relating to childbirth
COUVADES > COUVADE
COUVERT another word for > COVER
COUVERTS > COUVERT
COUZIN n South African word for a friend
COUZINS > COUZIN
COVALENCE same as > COVALENCY
COVALENCY n ability to form a bond in which two atoms share a pair of electrons
COVALENT > COVALENCY

COVARIANT n variant that varies leaving certain mathematical relationships it has with another variant (its covariant) unchanged
COVARIATE n statistical variable
COVARIED > COVARY
COVARIES > COVARY
COVARY vb vary together maintaining a certain mathematical relationship
COVARYING > COVARY
COVE n small bay or inlet ▷ vb form an architectural cove in
COVED > COVE
COVELET n small cove
COVELETS > COVELET
COVELLINE same as > COVELLITE
COVELLITE n indigo copper (blue sulphide of copper)
COVEN n meeting of witches
COVENANT n contract ▷ vb agree by a covenant
COVENANTS > COVENANT
COVENS > COVEN
COVENT same as > CONVENT
COVENTS > COVENT
COVER vb place something over, to protect or conceal ▷ n anything that covers
COVERABLE > COVER
COVERAGE n amount or extent covered
COVERAGES > COVERAGE
COVERALL n thing that covers something entirely
COVERALLS > COVERALL
COVERED > COVER
COVERER > COVER
COVERERS > COVER
COVERING another word for > COVER
COVERINGS > COVERING
COVERLESS > COVER
COVERLET n bed cover
COVERLETS > COVERLET
COVERLID same as > COVERLET
COVERLIDS > COVERLID
COVERS > COVER
COVERSED adj as in coversed sine obsolete function in trigonometry
COVERSINE n function in trigonometry
COVERSLIP n very thin piece of glass placed over a specimen on a glass slide
COVERT adj concealed, secret ▷ n thicket giving shelter to game birds or animals
COVERTER > COVERT

COVERTEST > COVERT
COVERTLY > COVERT
COVERTS > COVERT
COVERTURE *n* condition or status of a married woman considered as being under the protection and influence of her husband
COVERUP *n* concealment of a mistake, crime, etc
COVERUPS > COVERUP
COVES > COVE
COVET *vb* long to possess (what belongs to someone else)
COVETABLE > COVET
COVETED > COVET
COVETER > COVET
COVETERS > COVET
COVETING > COVET
COVETISE *n* covetousness
COVETISES > COVETISE
COVETOUS *adj* jealously longing to possess something
COVETS > COVET
COVEY *n* small flock of grouse or partridge
COVEYS > COVEY
COVIN *n* conspiracy between two or more persons
COVINE *n* conspiracy between two or more persons
COVINES > COVINE
COVING *same as* > COVE
COVINGS > COVING
COVINOUS *adj* deceitful
COVINS > COVIN
COVYNE *same as* > COVIN
COVYNES > COVYNE
COW *n* mature female of certain mammals ▷ *vb* intimidate, subdue
COWABUNGA *interj* expression of enthusiasm or delight
COWAGE *n* tropical climbing plant
COWAGES > COWAGE
COWAL *n* shallow lake or swampy depression supporting vegetation
COWALS > COWAL
COWAN *n* drystone waller
COWANS > COWAN
COWARD *n* person who lacks courage ▷ *vb* show (someone) up to be a coward
COWARDED > COWARD
COWARDICE *n* lack of courage
COWARDING > COWARD
COWARDLY *adj* of or characteristic of a coward
COWARDRY *n* cowardice
COWARDS > COWARD
COWBANE *n* poisonous marsh plant
COWBANES > COWBANE
COWBELL *n* bell hung around a cow's neck
COWBELLS > COWBELL

COWBERRY *n* evergreen shrub of N temperate and Arctic regions
COWBIND *n* any of various bryony plants, esp the white bryony
COWBINDS > COWBIND
COWBIRD *n* American oriole with a dark plumage and short bill
COWBIRDS > COWBIRD
COWBOY *n* (in the US) man who herds and tends cattle on a ranch ▷ *vb* work or behave as a cowboy
COWBOYED > COWBOY
COWBOYING *n* act of working or behaving as a cowboy
COWBOYS > COWBOY
COWED > COW
COWEDLY > COW
COWER *vb* cringe in fear
COWERED > COWER
COWERING > COWER
COWERS > COWER
COWFEEDER *n* dairyman
COWFISH *n* type of trunkfish with hornlike spines over the eyes
COWFISHES > COWFISH
COWFLAP *n* cow dung
COWFLAPS > COWFLAP
COWFLOP *n* foxglove
COWFLOPS > COWFLOP
COWGIRL *n* (in the US) woman who herds and tends cattle on a ranch
COWGIRLS > COWGIRL
COWGRASS *n* red clover
COWHAGE *same as* > COWAGE
COWHAGES > COWHAGE
COWHAND *same as* > COWBOY
COWHANDS > COWHAND
COWHEARD *same as* > COWHERD
COWHEARDS > COWHEARD
COWHEEL *n* heel of a cow, used as a cooking ingredient
COWHEELS > COWHEEL
COWHERB *n* European plant with clusters of pink flowers
COWHERBS > COWHERB
COWHERD *n* person employed to tend cattle
COWHERDS > COWHERD
COWHIDE *n* hide of a cow ▷ *vb* lash with a cowhide whip
COWHIDED > COWHIDE
COWHIDES > COWHIDE
COWHIDING > COWHIDE
COWHOUSE *n* byre
COWHOUSES > COWHOUSE
COWIER > COWY
COWIEST > COWY
COWING > COW
COWINNER *n* joint winner
COWINNERS > COWINNER

COWISH *adj* cowardly ▷ *n* N American plant with an edible root
COWISHES > COWISH
COWITCH *another name for* > COWAGE
COWITCHES > COWITCH
COWK *vb* retch or feel nauseated
COWKED > COWK
COWKING > COWK
COWKS > COWK
COWL *same as* > COWLING
COWLED *adj* wearing a cowl
COWLICK *n* tuft of hair over the forehead
COWLICKS > COWLICK
COWLIKE *adj* like a cow
COWLING *n* cover on an engine
COWLINGS > COWLING
COWLS > COWL
COWLSTAFF *n* pole, used by two people, for carrying a vessel
COWMAN *n* man who owns cattle
COWMEN > COWMAN
COWORKER *n* fellow worker
COWORKERS > COWORKER
COWP *same as* > COUP
COWPAT *n* pool of cow dung
COWPATS > COWPAT
COWPEA *n* type of tropical climbing plant
COWPEAS > COWPEA
COWPED > COWP
COWPIE *n* cowpat
COWPIES > COWPIE
COWPING > COWP
COWPLOP *n* cow dung
COWPLOPS > COWPLOP
COWPOKE *n* cowboy
COWPOKES > COWPOKE
COWPOX *n* disease of cows
COWPOXES > COWPOX
COWPS > COWP
COWPUNK *n* music that combines country music and punk
COWPUNKS > COWPUNK
COWRIE *n* brightly marked sea shell
COWRIES > COWRIE
COWRITE *vb* write jointly
COWRITER > COWRITE
COWRITERS > COWRITE
COWRITES > COWRITE
COWRITING > COWRITE
COWRITTEN > COWRITE
COWROTE > COWRITE
COWRY *same as* > COWRIE
COWS > COW
COWSHED *n* byre
COWSHEDS > COWSHED
COWSKIN *same as* > COWHIDE
COWSKINS > COWSKIN
COWSLIP *n* small yellow European wild flower
COWSLIPS > COWSLIP
COWTOWN *n* rural town in a cattle-raising area

COWTOWNS > COWTOWN
COWTREE *n* South American tree that produces latex
COWTREES > COWTREE
COWY *adj* cowlike
COX *n* coxswain ▷ *vb* act as cox of (a boat)
COXA *n* technical name for the hipbone or hip joint
COXAE > COXA
COXAL > COXA
COXALGIA *n* pain in the hip joint
COXALGIAS > COXALGIA
COXALGIC > COXALGIA
COXALGIES > COXALGIA
COXALGY *same as* > COXALGIA
COXCOMB *same as* > COCKSCOMB
COXCOMBIC > COXCOMB
COXCOMBRY *n* conceited arrogance or foppishness
COXCOMBS > COXCOMB
COXED > COX
COXES > COX
COXIB *n* anti-inflammatory drug
COXIBS > COXIB
COXIER > COXY
COXIEST > COXY
COXINESS > COXY
COXING > COX
COXITIDES > COXITIS
COXITIS *n* inflammation of the hip joint
COXLESS > COX
COXSACKIE *adj* as in *coxsackie virus* type of virus
COXSWAIN *n* person who steers a rowing boat
COXSWAINS > COXSWAIN
COXY *adj* cocky
COY *adj* affectedly shy or modest ▷ *vb* caress
COYAU *n* type of steep roof
COYAUS > COYAU
COYDOG *n* cross between a coyote and a dog
COYDOGS > COYDOG
COYED > COY
COYER > COY
COYEST > COY
COYING > COY
COYISH > COY
COYISHLY > COY
COYLY > COY
COYNESS > COY
COYNESSES > COY
COYOTE *n* prairie wolf of N America
COYOTES > COYOTE
COYOTILLO *n* thorny poisonous shrub of Mexico and the southwestern US
COYPOU *same as* > COYPU
COYPOUS > COYPOU
COYPU *n* beaver-like aquatic rodent
COYPUS > COYPU
COYS > COY
COYSTREL *same as* > COISTREL

COYSTRELS
> COYSTREL
COYSTRIL *same as*
> COISTREL
COYSTRILS
> COYSTRIL
COZ *archaic word for*
> COUSIN
COZE *vb* to chat
COZED > COZE
COZEN *vb* cheat, trick
COZENAGE > COZEN
COZENAGES > COZEN
COZENED > COZEN
COZENER > COZEN
COZENERS > COZEN
COZENING > COZEN
COZENS > COZEN
COZES > COZE
COZEY *n* tea cosy
COZEYS > COZEY
COZIE *same as* > COZEY
COZIED > COZY
COZIER *n* cobbler
COZIERS > COZIER
COZIES > COZY
COZIEST > COZY
COZILY > COZY
COZINESS > COZY
COZING > COZE
COZY *same as* > COSY
COZYING > COZY
COZZES > COZ
COZZIE *n* swimming costume
COZZIES > COZZIE
CRAAL *n* enclosure for livestock ▷ *vb* enclose in a craal
CRAALED > CRAAL
CRAALING > CRAAL
CRAALS > CRAAL
CRAB *n* edible shellfish with ten legs, the first pair modified into pincers ▷ *vb* catch crabs
CRABAPPLE *n* tree bearing small sour apple-like fruit
CRABBED > CRAB
CRABBEDLY > CRAB
CRABBER *n* crab fisherman
CRABBERS > CRABBER
CRABBIER > CRABBY
CRABBIEST > CRABBY
CRABBILY > CRABBY
CRABBING > CRAB
CRABBIT *adj* Scots word meaning bad-tempered
CRABBY *adj* bad-tempered
CRABEATER *n* species of seal
CRABGRASS *n* type of coarse weedy grass
CRABLIKE *adj* resembling a crab
CRABMEAT *n* edible flesh of a crab
CRABMEATS
> CRABMEAT
CRABS > CRAB
CRABSTICK *n* stick, cane, or cudgel made of crabapple wood
CRABWISE *adv* (of motion) sideways

CRABWOOD *n* tropical American tree
CRABWOODS > CRABWOOD
CRACHACH *pl n* (in Wales) elitists
CRACK *vb* break or split partially ▷ *n* sudden sharp noise ▷ *adj* first-rate, excellent
CRACKBACK *n* in American football, illegal blocking of an opponent
CRACKDOWN *n* severe disciplinary measures
CRACKED *adj* damaged by cracking
CRACKER *n* thin dry biscuit
CRACKERS *adj* mad
CRACKET *n* low stool, often one with three legs
CRACKETS > CRACKET
CRACKHEAD *n* person addicted to the drug crack
CRACKIE *n* small mongrel dog
CRACKIER > CRACKY
CRACKIES > CRACKY
CRACKIEST > CRACKY
CRACKING *adj* very fast
CRACKINGS
> CRACKING
CRACKJAW *adj* difficult to pronounce ▷ *n* word or phrase that is difficult to pronounce
CRACKJAWS
> CRACKJAW
CRACKLE *vb* make small sharp popping noises ▷ *n* crackling sound
CRACKLED > CRACKLE
CRACKLES > CRACKLE
CRACKLIER > CRACKLY
CRACKLING *n* crackle
CRACKLY *adj* making a crackling sound
CRACKNEL *n* type of hard plain biscuit
CRACKNELS
> CRACKNEL
CRACKPOT *adj* eccentric ▷ *n* eccentric person
CRACKPOTS
> CRACKPOT
CRACKS > CRACK
CRACKSMAN *n* burglar, esp a safe-breaker
CRACKSMEN
> CRACKSMAN
CRACKUP *n* collapse
CRACKUPS > CRACKUP
CRACKY *adj* full of cracks ▷ *n* something that is full of cracks
CRACOWE *n* medieval shoe with a sharply pointed toe
CRACOWES > CRACOWE
CRADLE *n* baby's bed on rockers ▷ *vb* hold gently as if in a cradle
CRADLED > CRADLE
CRADLER > CRADLE
CRADLERS > CRADLE
CRADLES > CRADLE
CRADLING *n* framework of iron or wood, esp as

used in the construction of a ceiling
CRADLINGS
> CRADLING
CRAFT *n* occupation requiring skill with the hands ▷ *vb* make skilfully
CRAFTED > CRAFT
CRAFTER *n* person doing craftwork
CRAFTERS > CRAFTER
CRAFTIER > CRAFTY
CRAFTIEST > CRAFTY
CRAFTILY > CRAFTY
CRAFTING > CRAFT
CRAFTLESS *adj* guileless
CRAFTS > CRAFT
CRAFTSMAN *n* skilled worker
CRAFTSMEN
> CRAFTSMAN
CRAFTWORK *n* handicraft
CRAFTY *adj* skilled in deception
CRAG *n* steep rugged rock
CRAGFAST *adj* stranded on a crag
CRAGGED *same as*
> CRAGGY
CRAGGER *n* member of a carbon reduction action group
CRAGGERS > CRAGGER
CRAGGIER > CRAGGY
CRAGGIEST > CRAGGY
CRAGGILY > CRAGGY
CRAGGY *adj* having many crags
CRAGS > CRAG
CRAGSMAN *n* rock climber
CRAGSMEN > CRAGSMAN
CRAIC *n* Irish word meaning fun
CRAICS > CRAIC
CRAIG *a Scot word for*
> CRAG
CRAIGS > CRAIG
CRAKE *n* bird of the rail family, such as the corncrake ▷ *vb* to boast
CRAKED > CRAKE
CRAKES > CRAKE
CRAKING > CRAKE
CRAM *vb* force into too small a space ▷ *n* act or condition of cramming
CRAMBE *n* any plant of the genus Crambe
CRAMBES > CRAMBE
CRAMBO *n* word game
CRAMBOES > CRAMBO
CRAMBOS > CRAMBO
CRAME *n* merchant's booth or stall
CRAMES > CRAME
CRAMESIES > CRAMESY
CRAMESY *same as*
> CRAMOISY
CRAMFULL *adj* very full
CRAMMABLE *adj* able to be crammed or filled
CRAMMED > CRAM
CRAMMER *n* person or school that prepares pupils for an examination
CRAMMERS > CRAMMER
CRAMMING *n* act of cramming

CRAMMINGS
> CRAMMING
CRAMOISIE *same as*
> CRAMOISY
CRAMOISY *adj* of a crimson colour ▷ *n* crimson cloth
CRAMP *n* painful muscular contraction ▷ *vb* affect with a cramp
CRAMPBARK *n* guelder rose
CRAMPED *adj* closed in
CRAMPER *n* brace for the feet in the sport of curling
CRAMPERS > CRAMPER
CRAMPET *n* cramp iron
CRAMPETS > CRAMPET
CRAMPFISH *n* electric ray
CRAMPIER > CRAMPY
CRAMPIEST > CRAMPY
CRAMPING > CRAMP
CRAMPIT *same as*
> CRAMPET
CRAMPITS > CRAMPIT
CRAMPON *n* spiked plate strapped to a boot for climbing on ice ▷ *vb* climb using crampons
CRAMPONED > CRAMPON
CRAMPONS > CRAMPON
CRAMPOON *same as*
> CRAMPON
CRAMPOONS
> CRAMPOON
CRAMPS > CRAMP
CRAMPY *adj* affected with cramp
CRAMS > CRAM
CRAN *n* unit of capacity used for measuring fresh herring, equal to 37.5 gallons
CRANACHAN *n* Scottish dessert made with oatmeal, cream, and whisky
CRANAGE *n* use of a crane
CRANAGES > CRANAGE
CRANAPPLE *adj* (of juice) blended from cranberries and apples
CRANBERRY *n* sour edible red berry
CRANCH *vb* to crunch
CRANCHED > CRANCH
CRANCHES > CRANCH
CRANCHING > CRANCH
CRANE *n* machine for lifting and moving heavy weights ▷ *vb* stretch (one's neck) to see something
CRANED > CRANE
CRANEFLY *n* fly with long legs, slender wings, and a narrow body
CRANELIKE *adj* like a crane
CRANES > CRANE
CRANIA > CRANIUM
CRANIAL *adj* of or relating to the skull
CRANIALLY > CRANIAL
CRANIATE *adj* having a skull or cranium ▷ *n* vertebrate

CRANIATES
> CRANIATE
CRANING > CRANE
CRANIUM n skull
CRANIUMS > CRANIUM
CRANK n arm projecting at right angles from a shaft ▷ vb turn with a crank ▷ adj (of a sailing vessel) easily keeled over by the wind
CRANKBAIT n fishing lure shaped so that it stays under water
CRANKCASE n metal case that encloses the crankshaft in an internal-combustion engine
CRANKED > CRANK
CRANKER > CRANK
CRANKEST > CRANK
CRANKIER > CRANKY
CRANKIEST > CRANK
CRANKILY > CRANKY
CRANKING > CRANK
CRANKISH adj somewhat eccentric or bad-tempered
CRANKLE vb bend or wind
CRANKLED > CRANKLE
CRANKLES > CRANKLE
CRANKLING > CRANKLE
CRANKLY adj vigorously
CRANKNESS n (of a vessel) liability to capsize
CRANKOUS adj fretful
CRANKPIN n short cylindrical pin in a crankshaft, to which the connecting rod is attached
CRANKPINS
> CRANKPIN
CRANKS > CRANK
CRANKY same as
> CRANKISH
CRANNIED > CRANNY
CRANNIES > CRANNY
CRANNOG n ancient Celtic lake or bog dwelling
CRANNOGE same as
> CRANNOG
CRANNOGES
> CRANNOGE
CRANNOGS > CRANNOG
CRANNY n narrow opening ▷ vb become full of crannies
CRANNYING > CRANNY
CRANREUCH n hoarfrost
CRANS > CRAN
CRANTS n garland carried in front of a maiden's bier
CRANTSES > CRANTS
CRAP n slang word for rubbish, nonsense ▷ vb defecate
CRAPAUD n frog or toad
CRAPAUDS > CRAPAUD
CRAPE same as > CREPE
CRAPED > CRAPE
CRAPELIKE > CRAPE
CRAPES > CRAPE
CRAPIER > CRAPE
CRAPIEST > CRAPE
CRAPING > CRAPE
CRAPLE same as
> GRAPPLE

CRAPLES > CRAPLE
CRAPOLA n slang word for rubbish, nonsense
CRAPOLAS > CRAPOLA
CRAPPED > CRAP
CRAPPER n toilet
CRAPPERS > CRAPPER
CRAPPIE n N American freshwater fish
CRAPPIER > CRAPPY
CRAPPIES > CRAPPIE
CRAPPIEST > CRAPPY
CRAPPING > CRAP
CRAPPY adj slang word for worthless, of poor quality
CRAPS pl n game using two dice
CRAPSHOOT n dice game
CRAPULENT adj given to or resulting from excessive eating or drinking
CRAPULOUS same as
> CRAPULENT
CRAPY > CRAPE
CRARE n type of trading vessel
CRARES > CRARE
CRASES > CRASIS
CRASH n collision involving a vehicle or vehicles ▷ vb (cause to) collide violently with a vehicle, a stationary object, or the ground ▷ adj requiring or using great effort in order to achieve results quickly
CRASHED > CRASH
CRASHER > CRASH
CRASHERS > CRASH
CRASHES > CRASH
CRASHING adj extreme
CRASHPAD n place to sleep or live temporarily
CRASHPADS
> CRASHPAD
CRASIS n fusion or contraction of two adjacent vowels into one
CRASS adj stupid and insensitive
CRASSER > CRASS
CRASSEST > CRASS
CRASSLY > CRASS
CRASSNESS > CRASS
CRATCH n rack for holding fodder for cattle, etc
CRATCHES > CRATCH
CRATE n large wooden container for packing goods ▷ vb put in a crate
CRATED > CRATE
CRATEFUL > CRATE
CRATEFULS > CRATE
CRATER n bowl-shaped opening at the top of a volcano ▷ vb make or form craters
CRATERED > CRATER
CRATERING > CRATER
CRATERLET n small crater
CRATEROUS > CRATER
CRATERS > CRATER
CRATES > CRATE
CRATHUR same as
> CRATUR

CRATHURS > CRATHUR
CRATING > CRATE
CRATON n stable part of the earth's continental crust
CRATONIC > CRATON
CRATONS > CRATON
CRATUR n whisky or whiskey
CRATURS > CRATUR
CRAUNCH same as
> CRUNCH
CRAUNCHED > CRAUNCH
CRAUNCHES > CRAUNCH
CRAUNCHY > CRAUNCH
CRAVAT n man's scarf worn like a tie ▷ vb wear a cravat
CRAVATE same as
> CRAVAT
CRAVATES > CRAVATE
CRAVATS > CRAVAT
CRAVATTED > CRAVAT
CRAVE vb desire intensely
CRAVED > CRAVE
CRAVEN adj cowardly ▷ n coward ▷ vb make cowardly
CRAVENED > CRAVEN
CRAVENER > CRAVEN
CRAVENEST > CRAVEN
CRAVENING > CRAVEN
CRAVENLY > CRAVEN
CRAVENS > CRAVEN
CRAVER > CRAVE
CRAVERS > CRAVE
CRAVES > CRAVE
CRAVING n intense desire or longing
CRAVINGS > CRAVING
CRAW n pouchlike part of a bird's oesophagus
CRAWDAD n crayfish
CRAWDADDY n crayfish
CRAWDADS > CRAWDAD
CRAWFISH same as
> CRAYFISH
CRAWL vb move on one's hands and knees ▷ n crawling motion or pace
CRAWLED > CRAWL
CRAWLER n servile flatterer
CRAWLERS > CRAWLER
CRAWLIER > CRAWLY
CRAWLIEST > CRAWLY
CRAWLING n defect in freshly applied paint or varnish characterized by bare patches and ridging
CRAWLINGS
> CRAWLING
CRAWLS > CRAWL
CRAWLWAY n in a mine, low passageway that can only be negotiated by crawling
CRAWLWAYS
> CRAWLWAY
CRAWLY adj feeling like creatures are crawling on one's skin
CRAWS > CRAW
CRAY n crayfish ▷ adj crazy
CRAYER same as > CRARE
CRAYERS > CRAYER
CRAYEST > CRAY

CRAYFISH n edible shellfish like a lobster
CRAYON n stick or pencil of coloured wax or clay ▷ vb draw or colour with a crayon
CRAYONED > CRAYON
CRAYONER > CRAYON
CRAYONERS > CRAYON
CRAYONING > CRAYON
CRAYONIST > CRAYON
CRAYONS > CRAYON
CRAYS > CRAY
CRAYTHUR variant of
> CRATUR
CRAYTHURS
> CRAYTHUR
CRAZE n short-lived fashion or enthusiasm ▷ vb make mad
CRAZED adj wild and uncontrolled
CRAZES > CRAZE
CRAZIER > CRAZY
CRAZIES > CRAZY
CRAZIEST > CRAZY
CRAZILY > CRAZY
CRAZINESS > CRAZY
CRAZING n act of crazing
CRAZINGS > CRAZING
CRAZY adj ridiculous ▷ n crazy person
CRAZYWEED n locoweed
CREACH same as
> CREAGH
CREACHS > CREACH
CREAGH n foray
CREAGHS > CREAGH
CREAK n harsh squeaking sound ▷ vb make or move with a harsh squeaking sound
CREAKED > CREAK
CREAKIER > CREAK
CREAKIEST > CREAK
CREAKILY > CREAK
CREAKING > CREAK
CREAKS > CREAK
CREAKY > CREAK
CREAM n fatty part of milk ▷ vb beat to a creamy consistency
CREAMCUPS n Californian plant with small cream-coloured or yellow flowers on long stalks
CREAMED > CREAM
CREAMER n powdered milk substitute for use in coffee
CREAMERS > CREAMER
CREAMERY n place where dairy products are made or sold
CREAMIER > CREAMY
CREAMIEST > CREAMY
CREAMILY > CREAMY
CREAMING > CREAM
CREAMLAID adj (of laid paper) cream-coloured and of a ribbed appearance
CREAMLIKE > CREAM
CREAMPUFF n puff pastry filled with cream
CREAMS > CREAM

CREAMWARE n type of earthenware with a deep cream body developed about 1720 and widely produced

CREAMWOVE adj (of wove paper) cream-coloured and even-surfaced

CREAMY adj resembling cream in colour, taste, or consistency

CREANCE n long light cord used in falconry

CREANCES > CREANCE

CREANT adj formative

CREASE n line made by folding or pressing ▷ vb crush or line

CREASED > CREASE

CREASER > CREASE

CREASERS > CREASE

CREASES > CREASE

CREASIER > CREASE

CREASIEST > CREASE

CREASING > CREASE

CREASOTE same as > CREOSOTE

CREASOTED > CREASOTE

CREASOTES > CREASOTE

CREASY > CREASE

CREATABLE > CREATE

CREATE vb make, cause to exist

CREATED > CREATE

CREATES > CREATE

CREATIC adj relating to flesh or meat

CREATIN same as > CREATINE

CREATINE n metabolite involved in biochemical reactions

CREATINES > CREATINE

CREATING > CREATE

CREATINS > CREATIN

CREATION n creating or being created

CREATIONS > CREATION

CREATIVE adj imaginative or inventive ▷ n person who is creative professionally

CREATIVES > CREATIVE

CREATOR n person who creates

CREATORS > CREATOR

CREATRESS n female creator

CREATRIX > CREATOR

CREATURAL > CREATURE

CREATURE n animal, person, or other being

CREATURES > CREATURE

CRECHE n place where small children are looked after

CRECHES > CRECHE

CRED n short for credibility

CREDAL > CREED

CREDENCE n belief in the truth or accuracy of a statement

CREDENCES > CREDENCE

CREDENDA > CREDENDUM

CREDENDUM n article of faith

CREDENT adj believing or believable

CREDENZA n type of small sideboard

CREDENZAS > CREDENZA

CREDIBLE adj believable

CREDIBLY > CREDIBLE

CREDIT n system of allowing customers to receive goods and pay later ▷ vb enter as a credit in an account

CREDITED > CREDIT

CREDITING > CREDIT

CREDITOR n person to whom money is owed

CREDITORS > CREDITOR

CREDITS pl n list of people responsible for the production of a film or TV programme

CREDO n creed

CREDOS > CREDO

CREDS > CRED

CREDULITY n willingness to believe something on little evidence

CREDULOUS adj too willing to believe

CREE vb soften grain by boiling or soaking

CREED n statement or system of (Christian) beliefs or principles

CREEDAL > CREED

CREEDS > CREED

CREEING > CREE

CREEK n narrow inlet or bay

CREEKIER > CREEKY

CREEKIEST > CREEKY

CREEKS > CREEK

CREEKSIDE n side of a creek

CREEKY adj abounding in creeks

CREEL n wicker basket used by anglers ▷ vb to fish using creels

CREELED > CREEL

CREELING > CREEL

CREELS > CREEL

CREEP vb move quietly and cautiously ▷ n creeping movement

CREEPAGE n imperceptible movement

CREEPAGES > CREEPAGE

CREEPED > CREEP

CREEPER n creeping plant ▷ vb train a plant to creep

CREEPERED > CREEPER

CREEPERS > CREEPER

CREEPIE n low stool

CREEPIER > CREEPY

CREEPIES > CREEPIE

CREEPIEST > CREEPY

CREEPILY > CREEPY

CREEPING > CREEP

CREEPMICE n plural form of singular creepmouse: a term of endearment

CREEPS > CREEP

CREEPY adj causing a feeling of fear or disgust

CREES > CREE

CREESE same as > KRIS

CREESED > CREESE

CREESES > CREESE

CREESH vb lubricate

CREESHED > CREESH

CREESHES > CREESH

CREESHIER > CREESHY

CREESHING > CREESH

CREESHY adj greasy

CREESING > CREESE

CREM n crematorium

CREMAINS pl n cremated remains of a body

CREMANT adj (of wine) moderately sparkling

CREMASTER n muscle which raises and lowers the scrotum

CREMATE vb burn (a corpse) to ash

CREMATED > CREMATE

CREMATES > CREMATE

CREMATING > CREMATE

CREMATION > CREMATE

CREMATOR n furnace for cremating corpses

CREMATORS > CREMATOR

CREMATORY adj of or relating to cremation or crematoriums

CREME n cream

CREMES > CREME

CREMINI n variety of mushroom

CREMINIS > CREMINI

CREMOCARP n any fruit, such as anise or fennel, consisting of two united carpels

CREMONA same as > CROMORNA

CREMONAS > CREMONA

CREMOR n thick creamy liquid

CREMORNE n penis

CREMORNES > CREMORNE

CREMORS > CREMOR

CREMOSIN adj crimson

CREMS > CREM

CREMSIN same as > CREMOSIN

CRENA n cleft or notch

CRENAS > CRENA

CRENATE adj having a scalloped margin, as certain leaves

CRENATED same as > CRENATE

CRENATELY > CRENATE

CRENATION n any of the rounded teeth or the notches between them on a crenate structure

CRENATURE same as > CRENATION

CRENEL n opening formed in the top of a wall having slanting sides ▷ vb crenellate

CRENELATE vb supply with battlements

CRENELED > CRENEL

CRENELING > CRENEL

CRENELLE same as > CRENEL

CRENELLED > CRENEL

CRENELLES > CRENELLE

CRENELS > CRENEL

CRENSHAW n variety of melon

CRENSHAWS > CRENSHAW

CRENULATE adj having a margin very finely notched with rounded projections, as certain leaves

CREODONT n type of extinct Tertiary mammal, the ancestor of modern carnivores

CREODONTS > CREODONT

CREOLE n language developed from a mixture of languages ▷ adj of or relating to a creole

CREOLES > CREOLE

CREOLIAN n Creole

CREOLIANS > CREOLIAN

CREOLISE vb (of a pidgin language) to become the native language of a speech community

CREOLISED same as > CREOLIZED

CREOLISES > CREOLISE

CREOLIST n student of creole languages

CREOLISTS > CREOLIST

CREOLIZE same as > CREOLISE

CREOLIZED adj (of a language) incorporating a considerable range of features from one or more unrelated languages, as the result of contact between language communities

CREOLIZES > CREOLIZE

CREOPHAGY n act of eating meat

CREOSOL n insoluble oily liquid

CREOSOLS > CREOSOL

CREOSOTE n dark oily liquid made from coal tar and used for preserving wood ▷ vb treat with creosote

CREOSOTED > CREOSOTE

CREOSOTES > CREOSOTE

CREOSOTIC > CREOSOTE

CREPANCE n injury to a horse's hind leg caused by being struck by the shoe of the other hind foot

CREPANCES
> CREPANCE

CREPE *n* fabric or rubber with a crinkled texture ▷ *vb* crimp or frizz

CREPED > CREPE

CREPELIKE *adj* like crepe

CREPERIE *n* eating establishment that specializes in pancakes

CREPERIES
> CREPERIE

CREPES > CREPE

CREPEY *same as* > CREPY

CREPIER > CREPY

CREPIEST > CREPY

CREPINESS > CREPY

CREPING > CREPE

CREPITANT
> CREPITATE

CREPITATE *vb* make a rattling or crackling sound

CREPITUS *n* crackling chest sound heard in pneumonia and other lung diseases

CREPOLINE *n* light silk material used in dressmaking

CREPON *n* thin material made of fine wool and/or silk

CREPONS > CREPON

CREPS *pl n* slang term for training shoes

CREPT > CREEP

CREPUSCLE *n* twilight

CREPY *adj* (esp of the skin) having a dry wrinkled appearance like crepe

CRESCENDI
> CRESCENDO

CRESCENDO *n* gradual increase in loudness, esp in music ▷ *adv* gradually getting louder ▷ *vb* increase in loudness or force

CRESCENT *n* (curved shape of) the moon as seen in its first or last quarter ▷ *adj* crescent-shaped

CRESCENTS
> CRESCENT

CRESCIVE *adj* increasing

CRESOL *n* aromatic compound

CRESOLS > CRESOL

CRESS *n* plant with strong-tasting leaves, used in salads

CRESSES > CRESS

CRESSET *n* metal basket mounted on a pole

CRESSETS > CRESSET

CRESSIER > CRESSY

CRESSIEST > CRESSY

CRESSY > CRESS

CREST *n* top of a mountain, hill, or wave ▷ *vb* come to or be at the top of

CRESTA *adj* as in *cresta run* high-speed tobogganing down a steep narrow passage

CRESTAL > CRYSTAL

CRESTALS > CRESTAL

CRESTED > CREST

CRESTING *same as* > CREST

CRESTINGS > CREST

CRESTLESS > CREST

CRESTON *n* hogback

CRESTONS > CRESTON

CRESTS > CREST

CRESYL *n* tolyl

CRESYLIC *adj* of, concerned with, or containing creosote or cresol

CRESYLS > CRESYL

CRETIC *n* metrical foot

CRETICS > CRETIC

CRETIN *n* insulting term for a stupid person

CRETINISE *vb* make (someone) a cretin

CRETINISM *n* old-fashioned word for a condition arising from a deficiency of thyroid hormone

CRETINIZE *same as* > CRETINISE

CRETINOID > CRETIN

CRETINOUS > CRETIN

CRETINS > CRETIN

CRETISM *n* lying

CRETISMS > CRETISM

CRETONNE *n* heavy printed cotton fabric used in furnishings

CRETONNES
> CRETONNE

CRETONS *pl n* spread made from pork fat and onions

CREUTZER *n* former copper and silver coin of Germany or Austria

CREUTZERS
> CREUTZER

CREVALLE *n* any fish of the family Carangidae

CREVALLES
> CREVALLE

CREVASSE *n* deep open crack in a glacier ▷ *vb* make a break or fissure in (a dyke, wall, etc)

CREVASSED
> CREVASSE

CREVASSES
> CREVASSE

CREVETTE *n* shrimp

CREVETTES
> CREVETTE

CREVICE *n* narrow crack or gap in rock

CREVICED > CREVICE

CREVICES > CREVICE

CREW *n* people who work on a ship or aircraft ▷ *vb* serve as a crew member (on)

CREWCUT *n* very short haircut

CREWCUTS > CREWCUT

CREWE *n* type of pot

CREWED > CREW

CREWEL *n* fine worsted yarn used in embroidery ▷ *vb* embroider in crewel

CREWELIST > CREWEL

CREWELLED > CREWEL

CREWELS > CREWEL

CREWES > CREWE

CREWING > CREW

CREWLESS *adj* lacking a crew

CREWMAN *n* member of a ship's crew

CREWMATE *n* colleague on the crew of a boat or ship

CREWMATES > CREWMATE

CREWMEN > CREWMAN

CREWNECK *n* plain round neckline in sweaters

CREWNECKS
> CREWNECK

CREWS > CREW

CRIA *n* baby llama or alpaca

CRIANT *adj* garish

CRIAS > CRIA

CRIB *n* piece of writing stolen from elsewhere ▷ *vb* copy (someone's work) dishonestly

CRIBBAGE *n* card game for two to four players

CRIBBAGES
> CRIBBAGE

CRIBBED > CRIB

CRIBBER > CRIB

CRIBBERS > CRIB

CRIBBING > CRIB

CRIBBINGS > CRIB

CRIBBLE *vb* to sift

CRIBBLED > CRIBBLE

CRIBBLES > CRIBBLE

CRIBBLING > CRIBBLE

CRIBELLA
> CRIBELLUM

CRIBELLAR
> CRIBELLUM

CRIBELLUM *n* sievelike spinning organ in certain spiders that occurs between the spinnerets

CRIBLE *adj* dotted ▷ *n* method of engraving with holes or dots

CRIBLES > CRIBLE

CRIBRATE *adj* sievelike

CRIBROSE *adj* pierced with holes

CRIBROUS *same as* > CRIBROSE

CRIBS > CRIB

CRIBWORK *same as* > CRIB

CRIBWORKS
> CRIBWORK

CRICETID *n* any member of the family Cricetidae, such as the hamster and vole

CRICETIDS
> CRICETID

CRICK *n* muscle spasm or cramp in the back or neck ▷ *vb* cause a crick in

CRICKED > CRICK

CRICKET *n* outdoor sport ▷ *vb* play cricket

CRICKETED > CRICKET

CRICKETER > CRICKET

CRICKETS > CRICKET

CRICKEY *same as* > CRIKEY

CRICKING > CRICK

CRICKS > CRICK

CRICKY *same as* > CRIKEY

CRICOID *adj* of or relating to part of the larynx ▷ *n* this cartilage

CRICOIDS > CRICOID

CRIED > CRY

CRIER *n* (formerly) official who made public announcements

CRIERS > CRIER

CRIES > CRY

CRIKEY *interj* expression of surprise

CRIM *short for*
> CRIMINAL

CRIME *n* unlawful act ▷ *vb* charge with a crime

CRIMED > CRIME

CRIMEFUL *adj* criminal

CRIMELESS *adj* innocent

CRIMEN *n* crime

CRIMES > CRIME

CRIMEWAVE *n* period of increased criminal activity

CRIMINA > CRIMEN

CRIMINAL *n* person guilty of a crime ▷ *adj* of crime

CRIMINALS
> CRIMINAL

CRIMINATE *vb* charge with a crime

CRIMINE *interj* expression of surprise

CRIMING > CRIME

CRIMINI *same as*
> CRIMINE

CRIMINIS *n* as in *particeps criminis* accomplice in crime

CRIMINOUS *adj* criminal

CRIMINY *same as*
> CRIMINE

CRIMMER *variant spelling of* > KRIMMER

CRIMMERS > CRIMMER

CRIMP *vb* fold or press into ridges ▷ *n* act or result of crimping

CRIMPED > CRIMP

CRIMPER > CRIMP

CRIMPERS > CRIMP

CRIMPIER > CRIMP

CRIMPIEST > CRIMP

CRIMPING > CRIMP

CRIMPLE *vb* crumple, wrinkle, or curl

CRIMPLED > CRIMPLE

CRIMPLES > CRIMPLE

CRIMPLING > CRIMPLE

CRIMPS > CRIMP

CRIMPY > CRIMP

CRIMS > CRIM

CRIMSON *adj* deep purplish-red ▷ *n* deep or vivid red colour ▷ *vb* make or become crimson

CRIMSONED > CRIMSON

CRIMSONS > CRIMSON

CRINAL *adj* relating to the hair

CRINATE *adj* having hair

CRINATED *same as*
> CRINATE

CRINE *vb* to shrivel

CRINED > CRINE

CRINES > CRINE

CRINGE vb flinch in fear ▷ n act of cringing

CRINGED > CRINGE

CRINGER > CRINGE

CRINGERS > CRINGE

CRINGES > CRINGE

CRINGEY adj causing the urge to cringe

CRINGIER > CRINGEY

CRINGIEST > CRINGEY

CRINGING > CRINGE

CRINGINGS > CRINGE

CRINGLE n eye at the edge of a sail

CRINGLES > CRINGLE

CRINGY same as > CRINGEY

CRINING > CRINE

CRINITE adj covered with soft hairs or tufts ▷ n sedimentary rock

CRINITES > CRINITE

CRINKLE n wrinkle, crease, or fold ▷ vb become slightly creased or folded

CRINKLED > CRINKLE

CRINKLES > CRINKLE

CRINKLIER > CRINKLY

CRINKLIES > CRINKLY

CRINKLING > CRINKLE

CRINKLY adj wrinkled ▷ n derogatory term for an old person

CRINOID n type of primitive echinoderm

CRINOIDAL > CRINOID

CRINOIDS > CRINOID

CRINOLINE n hooped petticoat

CRINOSE adj hairy

CRINUM n type of mostly tropical plant

CRINUMS > CRINUM

CRIOLLO n native or inhabitant of Latin America of European descent ▷ adj of, relating to, or characteristic of a criollo or criollos

CRIOLLOS > CRIOLLO

CRIOS n multicoloured woven woollen belt

CRIOSES > CRIOS

CRIPE variant of > CRIPES

CRIPES interj expression of surprise

CRIPPLE vb make lame or disabled

CRIPPLED > CRIPPLE

CRIPPLER > CRIPPLE

CRIPPLERS > CRIPPLE

CRIPPLES > CRIPPLE

CRIPPLING adj damaging or injurious

CRIS variant of > KRIS

CRISE n crisis

CRISES > CRISIS

CRISIC adj relating to a crisis

CRISIS n crucial stage, turning point

CRISP adj fresh and firm ▷ n very thin slice of potato fried till crunchy ▷ vb make or become crisp

CRISPATE adj having a curled or waved appearance

CRISPATED same as > CRISPATE

CRISPED same as > CRISPATE

CRISPEN vb make crisp

CRISPENED > CRISPEN

CRISPENS > CRISPEN

CRISPER n compartment in a refrigerator

CRISPERS > CRISPER

CRISPEST > CRISP

CRISPHEAD n variety of lettuce

CRISPIER > CRISPY

CRISPIES pl n as in rice crispies puffed grains of rice, eaten esp as breakfast cereal

CRISPIEST > CRISPY

CRISPILY > CRISPY

CRISPIN n cobbler

CRISPING > CRISP

CRISPINS > CRISPIN

CRISPLY > CRISP

CRISPNESS > CRISP

CRISPS > CRISP

CRISPY adj hard and crunchy

CRISSA > CRISSUM

CRISSAL > CRISSUM

CRISSUM n area or feathers surrounding the cloaca of a bird

CRISTA n structure resembling a ridge or crest

CRISTAE > CRISTA

CRISTATE adj having a crest

CRISTATED same as > CRISTATE

CRIT short for > CRITICISM

CRITERIA > CRITERION

CRITERIAL > CRITERION

CRITERION n standard of judgment

CRITERIUM n type of bicycle race, involving many laps of a short course

CRITH n unit of weight for gases

CRITHS > CRITH

CRITIC n professional judge of any of the arts

CRITICAL adj very important or dangerous

CRITICISE same as > CRITICIZE

CRITICISM n fault-finding

CRITICIZE vb find fault with

CRITICS > CRITIC

CRITIQUE n critical essay ▷ vb review critically

CRITIQUED > CRITIQUE

CRITIQUES > CRITIQUE

CRITS > CRIT

CRITTER a dialect word for > CREATURE

CRITTERS > CRITTER

CRITTUR same as > CRITTER

CRITTURS > CRITTUR

CRIVENS interj expression of surprise

CRIVVENS same as > CRIVENS

CROAK vb (of a frog or crow) give a low hoarse cry ▷ n low hoarse sound

CROAKED > CROAK

CROAKER n animal, bird, etc, that croaks

CROAKERS > CROAKER

CROAKIER > CROAK

CROAKIEST > CROAK

CROAKILY > CROAK

CROAKING > CROAK

CROAKINGS > CROAK

CROAKS > CROAK

CROAKY > CROAK

CROC short for > CROCODILE

CROCEATE adj saffron-coloured

CROCEIN n any one of a group of red or orange acid azo dyes

CROCEINE same as > CROCEIN

CROCEINES > CROCEIN

CROCEINS > CROCEIN

CROCEOUS adj saffron-coloured

CROCHE n knob at the top of a deer's horn

CROCHES > CROCHE

CROCHET vb make by looping and intertwining yarn with a hooked needle ▷ n work made in this way

CROCHETED > CROCHET

CROCHETER > CROCHET

CROCHETS > CROCHET

CROCI > CROCUS

CROCINE adj relating to the crocus

CROCK n earthenware pot or jar ▷ vb injure or cause to become weak

CROCKED adj injured

CROCKERY n dishes

CROCKET n carved ornament in the form of a curled leaf or cusp

CROCKETED > CROCKET

CROCKETS > CROCKET

CROCKING > CROCK

CROCKPOT n tradename for a brand of slow cooker

CROCKPOTS > CROCKPOT

CROCKS > CROCK

CROCODILE n large amphibious tropical reptile

CROCOITE n rare orange secondary mineral

CROCOITES > CROCOITE

CROCOSMIA n type of S African plant

CROCS > CROC

CROCUS n flowering plant

CROCUSES > CROCUS

CROFT n small farm worked by one family in Scotland ▷ vb farm land as a croft

CROFTED > CROFT

CROFTER n owner or tenant of a small farm, esp in Scotland or northern England

CROFTERS > CROFTER

CROFTING n system or occupation of working land in crofts

CROFTINGS > CROFTING

CROFTS > CROFT

CROG vb ride on a bicycle as a passenger

CROGGED > CROG

CROGGIES > CROGGY

CROGGING > CROG

CROGGY n ride on a bicycle as a passenger

CROGS > CROG

CROISSANT n rich flaky crescent-shaped roll

CROJIK n triangular sail

CROJIKS > CROJIK

CROKINOLE n board game popular in Canada in which players flick wooden discs

CROMACK same as > CRUMMOCK

CROMACKS > CROMACK

CROMB same as > CROME

CROMBEC n African bird with colourful plumage

CROMBECS > CROMBEC

CROMBED > CROMB

CROMBING > CROMB

CROMBS > CROMB

CROME n hook ▷ vb use a crome

CROMED > CROME

CROMES > CROME

CROMING > CROME

CROMLECH n circle of prehistoric standing stones

CROMLECHS > CROMLECH

CROMORNA n one of the reed stops in an organ

CROMORNAS > CROMORNA

CROMORNE variant of > CROMORNA

CROMORNES > CROMORNE

CRON n computer application that schedules tasks chronologically

CRONE n witchlike old woman

CRONES > CRONE

CRONET n hair which grows over the top of a horse's hoof

CRONETS > CRONET

CRONIES > CRONY

CRONISH > CRONE

CRONK adj unfit

CRONKER > CRONK

CRONKEST > CRONK

CRONS > CRON

CRONY n close friend

CRONYISM n appointing friends to high-level posts

CRONYISMS
> CRONYISM
CROODLE vb nestle close
CROODLED > CROODLE
CROODLES > CROODLE
CROODLING > CROODLE
CROOK n dishonest person
▷ vb bend or curve ▷ adj
informal Australian word
meaning ill
CROOKBACK a rare word
for > HUNCHBACK
CROOKED adj bent or
twisted
CROOKEDER > CROOKED
CROOKEDLY > CROOKED
CROOKER > CROOK
CROOKERY n illegal or
dishonest activity
CROOKEST > CROOK
CROOKING > CROOK
CROOKNECK n any type
of summer squash
CROOKS > CROOK
CROOL vb spoil
CROOLED > CROOL
CROOLING > CROOL
CROOLS > CROOL
CROON vb sing, hum, or
speak in a soft low tone
▷ n soft low singing or
humming
CROONED > CROON
CROONER > CROON
CROONERS > CROON
CROONIER > CROONY
CROONIEST > CROONY
CROONING > CROON
CROONINGS > CROON
CROONS > CROON
CROONY adj singing like a
crooner
CROOVE n animal
enclosure
CROOVES > CROOVE
CROP n cultivated plant
▷ vb cut very short
CROPBOUND n poultry
disease causing a
pendulous crop
CROPFUL n quantity
that can be held in the
craw
CROPFULL adj satiated
▷ n amount that a crop
can take
CROPFULLS
> CROPFULL
CROPFULS > CROPFUL
CROPLAND n land on
which crops are grown
CROPLANDS
> CROPLAND
CROPLESS adj without
crops
CROPPED > CROP
CROPPER n person who
cultivates or harvests a
crop
CROPPERS > CROPPER
CROPPIE same as
> CROPPY
CROPPIES > CROPPY
CROPPING > CROP
CROPPINGS > CROP
CROPPY n rebel in the
Irish rising of 1798
CROPS > CROP

CROPSICK adj sick from
excessive food or drink
CROQUANTE n crisp
nut-filled chocolate or cake
CROQUET n game played
on a lawn in which balls
are hit through hoops ▷ vb
drive away a ball by hitting
one's own when the two
are in contact
CROQUETED > CROQUET
CROQUETS > CROQUET
CROQUETTE n fried cake
of potato, meat, or fish
CROQUIS n rough sketch
CRORE n (in Indian
English) ten million
CROREPATI n (in India)
person whose assets are
at least 10 million rupees
CRORES > CRORE
CROSIER n staff carried
by bishops as a symbol of
pastoral office ▷ vb bear or
carry such a staff
CROSIERED > CROSIER
CROSIERS > CROSIER
CROSS vb move or go
across (something) ▷ n
structure, symbol, or mark
of two intersecting lines
▷ adj angry, annoyed
CROSSABLE adj capable
of being crossed
CROSSARM n in mining,
horizontal bar on which a
drill is mounted
CROSSARMS
> CROSSARM
CROSSBAND vb to set the
grain of layers of wood at
right angles to one
another
CROSSBAR n horizontal
bar across goalposts or on
a bicycle ▷ vb provide with
crossbars
CROSSBARS
> CROSSBAR
CROSSBEAM n beam that
spans from one support to
another
CROSSBILL n finch that
has a bill with crossed tips
CROSSBIT
> CROSSBITE
CROSSBITE vb to trick
CROSSBOW n weapon
consisting of a bow fixed
across a wooden stock
CROSSBOWS
> CROSSBOW
CROSSBRED adj bred
from two different types of
animal or plant ▷ n
crossbred plant or animal,
esp an animal resulting
from a cross between two
pure breeds
CROSSBUCK n US
roadsign used at railroad
crossings
CROSSCUT vb cut across
▷ adj cut across ▷ n
transverse cut or course
CROSSCUTS
> CROSSCUT
CROSSE n light staff used
in playing lacrosse

CROSSED > CROSS
CROSSER > CROSS
CROSSERS > CROSS
CROSSES > CROSS
CROSSEST > CROSS
CROSSETTE n in
architecture, return in a
corner of the architrave of
a window or door
CROSSFALL n camber of
a road
CROSSFIRE n gunfire
crossing another line of
fire
CROSSFISH n starfish
CROSSHAIR n one of two
fine wires that cross in the
focal plane of a gunsight
or other optical
instrument, used to define
the line of sight
CROSSHEAD n subsection
or paragraph heading
printed within the body of
the text
CROSSING n place where
a street may be crossed
safely
CROSSINGS
> CROSSING
CROSSISH > CROSS
CROSSJACK n square sail
on a ship's mizzenmast
CROSSLET n cross having
a smaller cross near the
end of each arm
CROSSLETS
> CROSSLET
CROSSLIKE adj like a
cross
CROSSLY > CROSS
CROSSNESS > CROSS
CROSSOVER n place at
which a crossing is made
▷ adj (of music, fashion,
art, etc) combining two
distinct styles
CROSSPLY adj having
layers of fabric with cords
running diagonally
CROSSROAD n road that
crosses another road
CROSSRUFF n alternate
trumping of each other's
leads by two partners, or
by declarer and dummy
▷ vb trump alternately in
two hands of a
partnership
CROSSTALK n rapid or
witty talk
CROSSTIE n railway
sleeper
CROSSTIED adj tied with
ropes going across
CROSSTIES
> CROSSTIE
CROSSTOWN adj going
across town
CROSSTREE n either of a
pair of wooden or metal
braces on the head of a
mast to support the
topmast, etc
CROSSWALK n place
marked where pedestrians
may cross a road
CROSSWAY same as
> CROSSROAD

CROSSWAYS same as
> CROSSWISE
CROSSWIND n wind that
blows at right angles to
the direction of travel
CROSSWIRE n either of
the two lines that cross in
a gunsight
CROSSWISE adv across
▷ adj across
CROSSWORD n puzzle in
which the solver deduces
words suggested by clues
and writes them into a
grid
CROSSWORT n
herbaceous Eurasian plant
with pale yellow flowers
and whorls of hairy leaves
CROST > CROSS
CROSTATA n type of fruit
tart
CROSTATAS
> CROSTATA
CROSTINI > CROSTINO
CROSTINIS
> CROSTINO
CROSTINO n piece of
toasted bread served with
a savoury topping
CROTAL n any of various
lichens used in dyeing
wool
CROTALA > CROTALUM
CROTALE n type of small
cymbal
CROTALES > CROTALE
CROTALINE adj relating
to rattlesnakes
CROTALISM n poisoning
due to ingestion of plants
of the genus Crotalaria
CROTALS > CROTAL
CROTALUM n ancient
castanet-like percussion
instrument
CROTCH n part of the
body between the tops of
the legs
CROTCHED > CROTCH
CROTCHES > CROTCH
CROTCHET n musical
note half the length of a
minim
CROTCHETS
> CROTCHET
CROTCHETY adj
bad-tempered
CROTON n type of shrub or
tree, the seeds of which
yield croton oil
CROTONBUG n species of
cockroach
CROTONIC adj as in
crotonic acid type of
colourless acid
CROTONS > CROTON
CROTTLE same as
> CROTAL
CROTTLES > CROTTLE
CROUCH vb bend low with
the legs and body close ▷ n
this position
CROUCHED > CROUCH
CROUCHES > CROUCH
CROUCHING > CROUCH
CROUP n throat disease of
children, with a cough
▷ vb have croup

CROUPADE *n* leap by a horse, pulling the hind legs towards the belly

CROUPADES > CROUPADE

CROUPE *same as* > CROUP

CROUPED > CROUP

CROUPER *obsolete variant of* > CRUPPER

CROUPERS > CROUPER

CROUPES > CROUPE

CROUPIER *n* person who collects bets and pays out winnings at a gambling table in a casino

CROUPIERS > CROUPIER

CROUPIEST > CROUP

CROUPILY > CROUP

CROUPING > CROUP

CROUPON *n* type of highly polished flexible leather

CROUPONS > CROUPON

CROUPOUS > CROUP

CROUPS > CROUP

CROUPY > CROUP

CROUSE *adj* lively, confident, or saucy

CROUSELY > CROUSE

CROUSTADE *n* pastry case in which food is served

CROUT *n* sauerkraut

CROUTE *n* small round of toasted bread on which a savoury mixture is served

CROUTES > CROUTE

CROUTON *n* small piece of fried or toasted bread served in soup

CROUTONS > CROUTON

CROUTS > CROUT

CROW *n* large black bird with a harsh call ▷ *vb* (of a cock) make a shrill squawking sound

CROWBAIT *n* worn-out horse

CROWBAITS > CROWBAIT

CROWBAR *n* iron bar used as a lever ▷ *vb* use a crowbar to lever (something)

CROWBARS > CROWBAR

CROWBERRY *n* low-growing N temperate evergreen shrub with small purplish flowers and black berry-like fruit

CROWBOOT *n* type of Inuit boot made of fur and leather

CROWBOOTS > CROWBOOT

CROWD *n* large group of people or things ▷ *vb* gather together in large numbers

CROWDED > CROWD

CROWDEDLY > CROWD

CROWDER > CROWD

CROWDERS > CROWD

CROWDFUND *vb* fund a project via a large number of small donations

CROWDIE *n* porridge of meal and water

CROWDIES > CROWDIE

CROWDING > CROWD

CROWDS > CROWD

CROWDY *same as* > CROWDIE

CROWEA *n* Australian shrub with pink flowers

CROWEAS > CROWEA

CROWED > CROW

CROWER > CROW

CROWERS > CROW

CROWFEET > CROWFOOT

CROWFOOT *n* type of plant

CROWFOOTS > CROWFOOT

CROWING *n* act of crowing

CROWINGLY > CROW

CROWINGS > CROWING

CROWLIKE *adj* like a crow

CROWN *n* monarch's headdress of gold and jewels ▷ *vb* put a crown on the head of (someone) to proclaim him or her monarch

CROWNED > CROWN

CROWNER *n* promotional label

CROWNERS > CROWNER

CROWNET *n* coronet

CROWNETS > CROWNET

CROWNING *n* coronation

CROWNINGS > CROWNING

CROWNLAND *n* large administrative division of the former empire of Austria-Hungary

CROWNLESS > CROWN

CROWNLET *n* small crown

CROWNLETS > CROWNLET

CROWNLIKE *adj* like a crown

CROWNS > CROWN

CROWNWORK *n* manufacture of artificial crowns for teeth

CROWS > CROW

CROWSFEET > CROWSFOOT

CROWSFOOT *n* wrinkle at side of eye

CROWSTEP *n* set of steps to the top of a gable on a building

CROWSTEPS > CROWSTEP

CROZE *n* recess cut at the end of a barrel or cask to receive the head

CROZER *n* machine which cuts grooves in cask staves

CROZERS > CROZER

CROZES > CROZE

CROZIER *same as* > CROSIER

CROZIERS > CROZIER

CROZZLED *adj* blackened or burnt at the edges

CRU *n* (in France) a vineyard, group of vineyards, or wine-producing region

CRUBEEN *n* pig's trotter

CRUBEENS > CRUBEEN

CRUCES > CRUX

CRUCIAL *adj* very important

CRUCIALLY > CRUCIAL

CRUCIAN *n* European fish

CRUCIANS > CRUCIAN

CRUCIATE *adj* shaped or arranged like a cross ▷ *n* cruciate ligament

CRUCIATES > CRUCIATE

CRUCIBLE *n* pot in which metals are melted

CRUCIBLES > CRUCIBLE

CRUCIFER *n* type of plant with four petals arranged like a cross

CRUCIFERS > CRUCIFER

CRUCIFIED > CRUCIFY

CRUCIFIER > CRUCIFY

CRUCIFIES > CRUCIFY

CRUCIFIX *n* model of Christ on the Cross

CRUCIFORM *adj* cross-shaped ▷ *n* geometric curve, shaped like a cross, that has four similar branches asymptotic to two mutually perpendicular pairs of lines

CRUCIFY *vb* put to death by fastening to a cross

CRUCK *n* wooden timber supporting the end of certain roofs

CRUCKS > CRUCK

CRUD *n* sticky or encrusted substance ▷ *interj* expression of disgust, disappointment, etc ▷ *vb* cover with a sticky or encrusted substance

CRUDDED > CRUD

CRUDDIER > CRUDDY

CRUDDIEST > CRUDDY

CRUDDING > CRUD

CRUDDLE *vb* curdle

CRUDDLED > CRUDDLE

CRUDDLES > CRUDDLE

CRUDDLING > CRUDDLE

CRUDDY *adj* dirty or unpleasant

CRUDE *adj* rough and simple ▷ *n* crude oil

CRUDELY > CRUDE

CRUDENESS > CRUDE

CRUDER > CRUDE

CRUDES > CRUDE

CRUDEST > CRUDE

CRUDIER > CRUDY

CRUDIEST > CRUDY

CRUDITES *pl n* selection of raw vegetables often served with a variety of dips before a meal

CRUDITIES > CRUDE

CRUDITY > CRUDE

CRUDO *n* sliced raw seafood

CRUDOS > CRUDO

CRUDS > CRUD

CRUDY *adj* raw

CRUE *obsolete variant of* > CREW

CRUEL *adj* delighting in others' pain

CRUELER > CRUEL

CRUELEST > CRUEL

CRUELLER > CRUEL

CRUELLEST > CRUEL

CRUELLS *same as* > CRUELS

CRUELLY > CRUEL

CRUELNESS > CRUEL

CRUELS *n* disease of cattle and sheep

CRUELTIES > CRUELTY

CRUELTY *n* deliberate infliction of pain or suffering

CRUES > CRUE

CRUET *n* small container for salt, pepper, etc, at table

CRUETS > CRUET

CRUFT *n* redundant technical hardware

CRUFTS > CRUFT

CRUISE *n* sea trip for pleasure ▷ *vb* sail from place to place for pleasure

CRUISED > CRUISE

CRUISER *n* fast warship

CRUISERS > CRUISER

CRUISES > CRUISE

CRUISEWAY *n* canal used for recreational purposes

CRUISEY *same as* > CRUISY

CRUISIE *same as* > CRUIZIE

CRUISIER > CRUISY

CRUISIES > CRUISIE

CRUISIEST > CRUISY

CRUISING > CRUISE

CRUISINGS > CRUISE

CRUISY *adj* relaxed or easy-going

CRUIVE *n* animal enclosure

CRUIVES > CRUIVE

CRUIZIE *n* oil lamp

CRUIZIES > CRUIZIE

CRULLER *n* light sweet ring-shaped cake, fried in deep fat

CRULLERS > CRULLER

CRUMB *n* small fragment of bread or other dry food ▷ *vb* prepare or cover (food) with breadcrumbs ▷ *adj* (esp of pie crusts) made with a mixture of biscuit crumbs, sugar, etc

CRUMBED > CRUMB

CRUMBER > CRUMB

CRUMBERS > CRUMB

CRUMBIER > CRUMBY

CRUMBIEST > CRUMBY

CRUMBING > CRUMB

CRUMBLE *vb* break into fragments ▷ *n* pudding of stewed fruit with a crumbly topping

CRUMBLED > CRUMBLE

CRUMBLES > CRUMBLE

CRUMBLIER > CRUMBLY

CRUMBLIES *pl n* jocular or derogatory term for elderly people

CRUMBLING > CRUMBLE

CRUMBLY *adj* easily crumbled or crumbling

CRUMBS *interj* expression of dismay or surprise
CRUMBUM *n* rogue
CRUMBUMS > CRUMBUM
CRUMBY *adj* full of crumbs
CRUMEN *n* deer's larmier or tear-pit
CRUMENAL *n* purse
CRUMENALS > CRUMENAL
CRUMENS > CRUMEN
CRUMHORN *n* medieval woodwind instrument of bass pitch
CRUMHORNS > CRUMHORN
CRUMMACK *same as* > CRUMMOCK
CRUMMACKS > CRUMMACK
CRUMMIE *n* cow with a crumpled horn
CRUMMIER > CRUMMY
CRUMMIES > CRUMMY
CRUMMIEST > CRUMMY
CRUMMILY *adv* in a manner suggestive of or indicating poor quality
CRUMMOCK *n* stick with a crooked head
CRUMMOCKS > CRUMMOCK
CRUMMY *adj* of poor quality ▷ *n* lorry that carries loggers to work from their camp
CRUMP *vb* thud or explode with a loud dull sound ▷ *n* crunching, thudding, or exploding noise ▷ *adj* crooked
CRUMPED > CRUMP
CRUMPER > CRUMP
CRUMPEST > CRUMP
CRUMPET *n* round soft yeast cake, eaten buttered
CRUMPETS > CRUMPET
CRUMPIER > CRUMPY
CRUMPIEST > CRUMPY
CRUMPING > CRUMP
CRUMPLE *vb* crush, crease ▷ *n* untidy crease or wrinkle
CRUMPLED > CRUMPLE
CRUMPLES > CRUMPLE
CRUMPLIER > CRUMPLE
CRUMPLING > CRUMPLE
CRUMPLY > CRUMPLE
CRUMPS > CRUMP
CRUMPY *adj* crisp
CRUNCH *vb* bite or chew with a noisy crushing sound ▷ *n* crunching sound
CRUNCHED > CRUNCH
CRUNCHER > CRUNCH
CRUNCHERS > CRUNCH
CRUNCHES > CRUNCH
CRUNCHIE *n* type of crunchy oat biscuit
CRUNCHIER > CRUNCH
CRUNCHIES > CRUNCHIE
CRUNCHILY > CRUNCH
CRUNCHING > CRUNCH
CRUNCHY > CRUNCH
CRUNK *n* form of hip-hop music originating in the Southern US

CRUNKED *adj* excited or intoxicated
CRUNKLE *Scots variant of* > CRINKLE
CRUNKLED > CRUNKLE
CRUNKLES > CRUNKLE
CRUNKLING > CRUNKLE
CRUNKS > CRUNK
CRUNODAL > CRUNODE
CRUNODE *n* point at which two branches of a curve intersect
CRUNODES > CRUNODE
CRUOR *n* blood clot
CRUORES > CRUOR
CRUORS > CRUOR
CRUPPER *n* strap that passes from the back of a saddle under a horse's tail
CRUPPERS > CRUPPER
CRURA > CRUS
CRURAL *adj* of or relating to the leg or thigh
CRUS *n* leg, esp from the knee to the foot
CRUSADE *n* medieval Christian war to recover the Holy Land from the Muslims ▷ *vb* take part in a crusade
CRUSADED > CRUSADE
CRUSADER > CRUSADE
CRUSADERS > CRUSADE
CRUSADES > CRUSADE
CRUSADING > CRUSADE
CRUSADO *n* former gold or silver coin of Portugal
CRUSADOES > CRUSADO
CRUSADOS > CRUSADO
CRUSE *n* small earthenware jug or pot
CRUSES > CRUSE
CRUSET *n* goldsmith's crucible
CRUSETS > CRUSET
CRUSH *vb* compress so as to injure, break, or crumple ▷ *n* dense crowd
CRUSHABLE > CRUSH
CRUSHED > CRUSH
CRUSHER > CRUSH
CRUSHERS > CRUSH
CRUSHES > CRUSH
CRUSHING *n* act or instance of compressing so as to injure or break
CRUSHINGS > CRUSHING
CRUSIAN *variant of* > CRUCIAN
CRUSIANS > CRUSIAN
CRUSIE *same as* > CRUIZIE
CRUSIES > CRUSIE
CRUSILY *adj* (in heraldry) strewn with crosses
CRUST *n* hard outer part of something, esp bread ▷ *vb* cover with or form a crust
CRUSTA *n* hard outer layer
CRUSTACEA *n* members of the Crustacea class of arthropods including the lobster
CRUSTAE > CRUSTA
CRUSTAL *adj* of or relating to the earth's crust

CRUSTAS > CRUSTA
CRUSTATE *adj* covered with a crust
CRUSTATED *same as* > CRUSTATE
CRUSTED > CRUST
CRUSTIER > CRUSTY
CRUSTIES > CRUSTY
CRUSTIEST > CRUSTY
CRUSTILY > CRUSTY
CRUSTING > CRUST
CRUSTLESS *adj* lacking a crust
CRUSTLIKE *adj* like a crust
CRUSTOSE *adj* having a crustlike appearance
CRUSTS > CRUST
CRUSTY *adj* having a crust ▷ *n* scruffy type of punk or hippy whose lifestyle involves travelling and squatting
CRUSY *same as* > CRUIZIE
CRUTCH *n* long stick-like support with a rest for the armpit ▷ *vb* support or sustain (a person or thing) as with a crutch
CRUTCHED > CRUTCH
CRUTCHES > CRUTCH
CRUTCHING > CRUTCH
CRUVE *same as* > CRUIVE
CRUVES > CRUVE
CRUX *n* crucial or decisive point
CRUXES > CRUX
CRUZADO *same as* > CRUSADO
CRUZADOES > CRUZADO
CRUZADOS > CRUZADO
CRUZEIRO *n* former monetary unit of Brazil, replaced by the cruzeiro real
CRUZEIROS > CRUZEIRO
CRUZIE *same as* > CRUIZIE
CRUZIES > CRUZIE
CRWTH *n* ancient stringed instrument of Celtic origin
CRWTHS > CRWTH
CRY *vb* shed tears ▷ *n* fit of weeping
CRYBABIES > CRYBABY
CRYBABY *n* person, esp a child, who cries too readily
CRYER *same as* > CRIER
CRYERS > CRYER
CRYING > CRY
CRYINGLY > CRY
CRYINGS > CRY
CRYOBANK *n* place for storing genetic material at low temperature
CRYOBANKS > CRYOBANK
CRYOCABLE *n* highly conducting electrical cable cooled with a refrigerant such as liquid nitrogen
CRYOGEN *n* substance used to produce low temperatures

CRYOGENIC *adj* of the branch of physics concerned with the production of very low temperatures
CRYOGENS > CRYOGEN
CRYOGENY *n* cryogenic science
CRYOLITE *n* white or colourless mineral
CRYOLITES > CRYOLITE
CRYOMETER *n* thermometer for measuring low temperatures
CRYOMETRY > CRYOMETER
CRYONIC *adj* relating to or involving cryonics
CRYONICS *n* practice of freezing a human corpse in the hope of restoring it to life in the future
CRYOPHYTE *n* organism, esp an alga or moss, that grows on snow or ice
CRYOPROBE *n* supercooled instrument used in surgery
CRYOSCOPE *n* any instrument used to determine the freezing point of a substance
CRYOSCOPY *n* determination of freezing points, esp for the determination of molecular weights by measuring the lowering of the freezing point of a solvent when a known quantity of solute is added
CRYOSTAT *n* apparatus for maintaining a constant low temperature
CRYOSTATS > CRYOSTAT
CRYOTRON *n* switch working at the temperature of liquid helium
CRYOTRONS > CRYOTRON
CRYPT *n* vault under a church, esp one used as a burial place
CRYPTADIA *n* things to be kept hidden
CRYPTAL > CRYPT
CRYPTIC *adj* obscure in meaning, secret
CRYPTICAL *same as* > CRYPTIC
CRYPTO *n* person who is a secret member of an organization or sect
CRYPTOGAM *n* plant that reproduces by spores not seeds
CRYPTON *n* hypothetical particle
CRYPTONS > CRYPTON
CRYPTONYM *n* code name
CRYPTOS > CRYPTO
CRYPTS > CRYPT
CRYSTAL *n* symmetrically shaped solid formed naturally ▷ *adj* bright and clear

C

CRYSTALS > CRYSTAL

CSARDAS n type of Hungarian folk dance

CSARDASES > CSARDAS

CTENE n locomotor organ found in ctenophores (or comb jellies)

CTENES > CTENE

CTENIDIA > CTENIDIUM

CTENIDIUM n one of the comblike respiratory gills of molluscs

CTENIFORM adj comblike

CTENOID adj toothed like a comb, as the scales of perches

CUADRILLA n matador's assistants in a bullfight

CUATRO n four-stringed guitar

CUATROS > CUATRO

CUB n young wild animal such as a bear or fox ▷ adj young or inexperienced ▷ vb give birth to cubs

CUBAGE same as > CUBATURE

CUBAGES > CUBAGE

CUBANE n rare octahedral hydrocarbon

CUBANELLE n variety of pepper

CUBANES > CUBANE

CUBATURE n determination of the cubic contents of something

CUBATURES > CUBATURE

CUBBED > CUB

CUBBIER > CUBBY

CUBBIES > CUBBY

CUBBIEST > CUBBY

CUBBING > CUB

CUBBINGS > CUB

CUBBISH > CUB

CUBBISHLY > CUB

CUBBY n cubbyhole ▷ adj short and plump

CUBBYHOLE n small enclosed space or room

CUBE n object with six equal square sides ▷ vb cut into cubes

CUBEB n SE Asian woody climbing plant with brownish berries

CUBEBS > CUBEB

CUBED > CUBE

CUBELIKE adj like a cube

CUBER > CUBE

CUBERS > CUBE

CUBES > CUBE

CUBHOOD n state of being a cub

CUBHOODS > CUBHOOD

CUBIC adj having three dimensions ▷ n cubic equation

CUBICA n fine shalloon-like fabric

CUBICAL adj of or related to volume

CUBICALLY > CUBICAL

CUBICAS > CUBICA

CUBICITY n property of being cubelike

CUBICLE n enclosed part of a large room, screened for privacy

CUBICLES > CUBICLE

CUBICLY > CUBIC

CUBICS > CUBIC

CUBICULA > CUBICULUM

CUBICULUM n underground burial chamber in Imperial Rome, such as those found in the catacombs

CUBIFORM adj having the shape of a cube

CUBING > CUBE

CUBISM n style of art in which objects are represented by geometrical shapes

CUBISMS > CUBISM

CUBIST > CUBISM

CUBISTIC > CUBISM

CUBISTS > CUBISM

CUBIT n old measure of length based on the length of the forearm

CUBITAL adj of or relating to the forearm

CUBITI > CUBITUS

CUBITS > CUBIT

CUBITUS n elbow

CUBITUSES > CUBITUS

CUBLESS adj having no cubs

CUBOID adj shaped like a cube ▷ n geometric solid whose six faces are rectangles

CUBOIDAL same as > CUBOID

CUBOIDS > CUBOID

CUBS > CUB

CUCKING adj as in cucking stool stool in which suspected witches were tested

CUCKOLD n man whose spouse has been unfaithful ▷ vb be unfaithful to (one's husband)

CUCKOLDED > CUCKOLD

CUCKOLDLY adj possessing the qualities of a cuckold

CUCKOLDOM n state of being a cuckold

CUCKOLDRY > CUCKOLD

CUCKOLDS > CUCKOLD

CUCKOO n migratory bird ▷ vb repeat over and over

CUCKOOED > CUCKOO

CUCKOOING > CUCKOO

CUCKOOS > CUCKOO

CUCULLATE adj shaped like a hood or having a hoodlike part

CUCUMBER n long green-skinned fleshy fruit used in salads

CUCUMBERS > CUCUMBER

CUCURBIT n type of tropical or subtropical creeping plant

CUCURBITS > CUCURBIT

CUD n partially digested food chewed by a ruminant

CUDBEAR another name for > ORCHIL

CUDBEARS > CUDBEAR

CUDDEN n young coalfish

CUDDENS > CUDDEN

CUDDIE same as > CUDDY

CUDDIES > CUDDY

CUDDIN same as > CUDDEN

CUDDINS > CUDDIN

CUDDLE n hug ▷ vb hold close

CUDDLED > CUDDLE

CUDDLER > CUDDLE

CUDDLERS > CUDDLE

CUDDLES > CUDDLE

CUDDLIER > CUDDLE

CUDDLIEST > CUDDLE

CUDDLING > CUDDLE

CUDDLY > CUDDLE

CUDDY n small cabin in a boat

CUDGEL n short thick stick used as a weapon ▷ vb use a cudgel

CUDGELED > CUDGEL

CUDGELER > CUDGEL

CUDGELERS > CUDGEL

CUDGELING > CUDGEL

CUDGELLED > CUDGEL

CUDGELLER > CUDGEL

CUDGELS > CUDGEL

CUDGERIE n type of large tropical tree with light-coloured wood

CUDGERIES > CUDGERIE

CUDS > CUD

CUDWEED n type of temperate plant

CUDWEEDS > CUDWEED

CUE n signal to an actor or musician to begin speaking or playing ▷ vb give a cue to

CUED > CUE

CUEING > CUE

CUEINGS > CUEING

CUEIST n snooker or billiards player

CUEISTS > CUEIST

CUES > CUE

CUESTA n long low ridge with a steep scarp slope and a gentle back slope

CUESTAS > CUESTA

CUFF n end of a sleeve ▷ vb hit with an open hand

CUFFABLE adj able to be folded down at the ankle

CUFFED > CUFF

CUFFIN n man

CUFFING > CUFF

CUFFINS > CUFFIN

CUFFLE vb scuffle

CUFFLED > CUFFLE

CUFFLES > CUFFLE

CUFFLESS adj having no cuff(s)

CUFFLING > CUFFLE

CUFFLINK n detachable fastener for shirt cuff

CUFFLINKS > CUFFLINK

CUFFO adv free of charge

CUFFS > CUFF

CUFFUFFLE same as > KERFUFFLE

CUIF same as > COOF

CUIFS > CUIF

CUING > CUE

CUIRASS n piece of armour covering the chest and back ▷ vb equip with a cuirass

CUIRASSED > CUIRASS

CUIRASSES > CUIRASS

CUISH same as > CUISSE

CUISHES > CUISH

CUISINART n tradename for a type of food processor

CUISINE n style of cooking

CUISINES > CUISINE

CUISINIER n cook

CUISSE n piece of armour for the thigh

CUISSER same as > COOSER

CUISSERS > CUISSER

CUISSES > CUISSE

CUIT n ankle

CUITER vb pamper

CUITERED > CUITER

CUITERING > CUITER

CUITERS > CUITER

CUITIKIN n gaiter

CUITIKINS > CUITIKIN

CUITS > CUIT

CUITTLE vb wheedle

CUITTLED > CUITTLE

CUITTLES > CUITTLE

CUITTLING > CUITTLE

CUKE n cucumber

CUKES > CUKE

CULCH n the basis of an oyster bed

CULCHES > CULCH

CULCHIE n mildly derogatory Irish term for a country-dweller ▷ adj rough or unsophisticated

CULCHIER > CULCHIE

CULCHIES > CULCHIE

CULCHIEST > CULCHIE

CULET n flat face at the bottom of a gem

CULETS > CULET

CULEX n type of mosquito

CULEXES > CULEX

CULICES > CULEX

CULICID n type of dipterous insect

CULICIDS > CULICID

CULICINE n any member of the genus Culex containing mosquitoes

CULICINES > CULICINE

CULINARY adj of kitchens or cookery

CULL vb choose, gather ▷ n culling

CULLAY n soapbark tree

CULLAYS > CULLAY

CULLED > CULL

CULLENDER same as > COLANDER

CULLER n person employed to cull animals

CULLERS > CULLER
CULLET n waste glass for melting down to be reused
CULLETS > CULLET
CULLIED > CULLY
CULLIES > CULLY
CULLING > CULL
CULLINGS > CULL
CULLION n rascal
CULLIONLY > CULLION
CULLIONS > CULLION
CULLIS same as
> COULISSE
CULLISES > CULLIS
CULLS > CULL
CULLY n pal ▷ vb to trick
CULLYING > CULLY
CULLYISM n state of being a dupe
CULLYISMS
> CULLYISM
CULM n coal-mine waste ▷ vb form a stalk or stem
CULMED > CULM
CULMEN n summit
CULMINA > CULMEN
CULMINANT adj highest or culminating
CULMINATE vb reach the highest point or climax
CULMING > CULM
CULMS > CULM
CULOTTE > CULOTTES
CULOTTES pl n women's knee-length trousers cut to look like a skirt
CULPA n act of neglect
CULPABLE adj deserving blame
CULPABLY > CULPABLE
CULPAE > CULPA
CULPATORY adj expressing blame
CULPRIT n person guilty of an offence or misdeed
CULPRITS > CULPRIT
CULSHIE n mildly derogatory Irish term for a country-dweller ▷ adj rough or unsophisticated
CULSHIER > CULSHIE
CULSHIES > CULSHIE
CULSHIEST > CULSHIE
CULT n specific system of worship ▷ adj very popular among a limited group of people
CULTCH same as > CULCH
CULTCHES > CULTCH
CULTER same as
> COULTER
CULTERS > CULTER
CULTI > CULTUS
CULTIC adj of or relating to a religious cult
CULTIER > CULTY
CULTIEST > CULTY
CULTIGEN n cultivated species of plant that did not come from a wild type
CULTIGENS
> CULTIGEN
CULTISH adj intended to appeal to a small group of fashionable people
CULTISHLY > CULTISH
CULTISM > CULT
CULTISMS > CULT

CULTIST > CULT
CULTISTS > CULT
CULTIVAR n cultivated plant produced from a natural species
CULTIVARS
> CULTIVAR
CULTIVATE vb prepare (land) to grow crops
CULTLIKE adj resembling a cult
CULTRATE adj shaped like a knife blade
CULTRATED same as
> CULTRATE
CULTS > CULT
CULTURAL adj of or relating to artistic or social pursuits
CULTURATI n people interested in cultural activities
CULTURE n ideas, customs, and art of a particular society ▷ vb grow (bacteria) for study
CULTURED adj showing good taste or manners
CULTURES > CULTURE
CULTURING > CULTURE
CULTURIST > CULTURE
CULTUS another word for
> CULT
CULTUSES > CULTUS
CULTY same as
> CULTISH
CULVER an archaic or poetic name for > PIGEON
CULVERIN n long-range medium to heavy cannon used during the 15th, 16th, and 17th centuries
CULVERINS
> CULVERIN
CULVERS > CULVER
CULVERT n drain under a road or railway ▷ vb direct water through a culvert
CULVERTED > CULVERT
CULVERTS > CULVERT
CUM prep with ▷ n vulgar word for semen ▷ vb ejaculate sperm
CUMACEAN n type of small marine crustacean
CUMACEANS
> CUMACEAN
CUMARIC > CUMARIN
CUMARIN same as
> COUMARIN
CUMARINS > CUMARIN
CUMARONE variant spelling of > COUMARONE
CUMARONES
> CUMARONE
CUMBENT adj lying down
CUMBER vb obstruct or hinder ▷ n hindrance or burden
CUMBERED > CUMBER
CUMBERER > CUMBER
CUMBERERS > CUMBER
CUMBERING > CUMBER
CUMBERS > CUMBER
CUMBIA n Colombian style of music
CUMBIAS > CUMBIA

CUMBRANCE n burden, obstacle, or hindrance
CUMBROUS adj awkward because of size, weight, or height
CUMBUNGI n type of tall Australian marsh plant
CUMBUNGIS
> CUMBUNGI
CUMEC n unit of volumetric rate of flow
CUMECS > CUMEC
CUMIN n sweet-smelling seeds of a Mediterranean plant, used in cooking
CUMINS > CUMIN
CUMMED > CUM
CUMMER n gossip
CUMMERS > CUMMER
CUMMIN same as > CUMIN
CUMMING > CUM
CUMMINS > CUMMIN
CUMQUAT same as
> KUMQUAT
CUMQUATS > CUMQUAT
CUMS > CUM
CUMSHAW n (used, esp formerly, by beggars in Chinese ports) a present or tip
CUMSHAWS > CUMSHAW
CUMULATE vb accumulate ▷ adj heaped up
CUMULATED
> CUMULATE
CUMULATES
> CUMULATE
CUMULET n variety of domestic fancy pigeon
CUMULETS > CUMULET
CUMULI > CUMULUS
CUMULOSE adj full of heaps
CUMULOUS adj resembling or consisting of cumulus clouds
CUMULUS n thick white or dark grey cloud
CUMULUSES > CUMULUS
CUNABULA n cradle
CUNCTATOR n person in habit of being late
CUNDIES > CUNDY
CUNDUM n early form of condom
CUNDUMS > CUNDUM
CUNDY n sewer
CUNEAL same as
> CUNEIFORM
CUNEATE adj wedge-shaped
CUNEATED same as
> CUNEATE
CUNEATELY > CUNEATE
CUNEATIC adj cuneiform
CUNEI > CUNEUS
CUNEIFORM adj (written in) an ancient system of writing using wedge-shaped characters ▷ n ancient system of writing using wedge-shaped characters
CUNETTE n small trench dug in the main ditch of a fortification
CUNETTES > CUNETTE

CUNEUS n small wedge-shaped area of the cerebral cortex
CUNIFORM same as
> CUNEIFORM
CUNIFORMS
> CUNIFORM
CUNIT n one hundred cubic feet
CUNITS > CUNIT
CUNJEVOI n plant of tropical Asia and Australia
CUNJEVOIS
> CUNJEVOI
CUNNER n fish of the wrasse family
CUNNERS > CUNNER
CUNNING adj clever at deceiving ▷ n cleverness at deceiving
CUNNINGER > CUNNING
CUNNINGLY > CUNNING
CUNNINGS > CUNNING
CUNT n taboo word for the female genitals
CUNTS > CUNT
CUP n small bowl-shaped drinking container with a handle ▷ vb form (one's hands) into the shape of a cup
CUPBEARER n attendant who fills and serves cups
CUPBOARD n piece of furniture or alcove with a door, for storage ▷ vb store in a cupboard
CUPBOARDS
> CUPBOARD
CUPCAKE n small cake baked in a cup-shaped foil or paper case
CUPCAKES > CUPCAKE
CUPEL n refractory pot in which gold or silver is refined ▷ vb refine (gold or silver) by means of cupellation
CUPELED > CUPEL
CUPELER > CUPEL
CUPELERS > CUPEL
CUPELING > CUPEL
CUPELLED > CUPEL
CUPELLER > CUPEL
CUPELLERS > CUPEL
CUPELLING > CUPEL
CUPELS > CUPEL
CUPFERRON n compound used in chemical analysis
CUPFUL n amount a cup will hold
CUPFULS > CUPFUL
CUPGALL n gall found on oakleaves
CUPGALLS > CUPGALL
CUPHEAD n type of bolt or rivet with a cup-shaped head
CUPHEADS > CUPHEAD
CUPHOLDER n device in a car for holding a drinking cup
CUPID n figure representing the Roman god of love
CUPIDITY n greed for money or possessions
CUPIDS > CUPID

CUPLIKE > CUP
CUPMAN n drinking companion
CUPMEN > CUPMAN
CUPOLA n domed roof or ceiling ▷ vb provide with a cupola
CUPOLAED > CUPOLA
CUPOLAING > CUPOLA
CUPOLAR > CUPOLA
CUPOLAS > CUPOLA
CUPOLATED > CUPOLA
CUPPA n cup of tea
CUPPAS > CUPPA
CUPPED > CUP
CUPPER same as > CUPPA
CUPPERS > CUPPER
CUPPIER > CUPPY
CUPPIEST > CUPPY
CUPPING > CUP
CUPPINGS > CUP
CUPPY adj cup-shaped
CUPREOUS adj of copper
CUPRESSUS n type of tree
CUPRIC adj of or containing copper in the divalent state
CUPRITE n red secondary mineral
CUPRITES > CUPRITE
CUPROUS adj of or containing copper in the monovalent state
CUPRUM an obsolete name for > COPPER
CUPRUMS > CUPRUM
CUPS > CUP
CUPSFUL > CUPFUL
CUPULA n dome-shaped structure
CUPULAE > CUPULA
CUPULAR same as > CUPULATE
CUPULATE adj shaped like a small cup
CUPULE n cup-shaped part or structure
CUPULES > CUPULE
CUR n mongrel dog
CURABLE adj capable of being cured
CURABLY > CURABLE
CURACAO n orange-flavoured liqueur
CURACAOS > CURACAO
CURACIES > CURACY
CURACOA same as > CURACAO
CURACOAS > CURACOA
CURACY n work or position of a curate
CURAGH same as > CURRACH
CURAGHS > CURAGH
CURANDERA n female faith healer
CURANDERO n male faith healer
CURARA same as > CURARE
CURARAS > CURARA
CURARE n poisonous resin of a S American tree
CURARES > CURARE
CURARI same as > CURARE

CURARINE n alkaloid extracted from curare, used as a muscle relaxant in surgery
CURARINES > CURARINE
CURARIS > CURARI
CURARISE same as > CURARIZE
CURARISED > CURARISE
CURARISES > CURARISE
CURARIZE vb paralyse or treat with curare
CURARIZED > CURARIZE
CURARIZES > CURARIZE
CURASSOW n gallinaceous ground-nesting bird
CURASSOWS > CURASSOW
CURAT n cuirass
CURATE n clergyman or clergywoman who assists a parish priest ▷ vb be in charge of (an art exhibition or museum)
CURATED > CURATE
CURATES > CURATE
CURATING > CURATE
CURATION n work of a curator
CURATIONS > CURATION
CURATIVE n something able to cure ▷ adj able to cure
CURATIVES > CURATIVE
CURATOR n person in charge of a museum or art gallery
CURATORS > CURATOR
CURATORY > CURATOR
CURATRIX n female curator
CURATS > CURAT
CURB n something that restrains ▷ vb control, restrain
CURBABLE adj capable of being restrained
CURBED > CURB
CURBER > CURB
CURBERS > CURB
CURBING the US spelling of > KERBING
CURBINGS > CURBING
CURBLESS adj having no restraint
CURBS > CURB
CURBSIDE n pavement
CURBSIDES > CURBSIDE
CURBSTONE the US spelling of > KERBSTONE
CURCH n woman's plain cap or kerchief
CURCHEF same as > CURCH
CURCHEFS > CURCHEF
CURCHES > CURCH
CURCULIO n type of American weevil
CURCULIOS > CURCULIO

CURCUMA n type of tropical Asian tuberous plant
CURCUMAS > CURCUMA
CURCUMIN n yellow dye derived from turmeric
CURCUMINE same as > CURCUMIN
CURCUMINS > CURCUMIN
CURD n coagulated milk, used to make cheese ▷ vb turn into or become curd
CURDED > CURD
CURDIER > CURD
CURDIEST > CURD
CURDINESS > CURD
CURDING > CURD
CURDLE vb turn into curd, coagulate
CURDLED > CURDLE
CURDLER > CURDLE
CURDLERS > CURDLE
CURDLES > CURDLE
CURDLING > CURDLE
CURDS > CURD
CURDY > CURD
CURE vb get rid of (an illness or problem) ▷ n (treatment causing) curing of an illness or person
CURED > CURE
CURELESS > CURE
CURER > CURE
CURERS > CURE
CURES > CURE
CURET same as > CURETTE
CURETS > CURET
CURETTAGE n process of using a curette
CURETTE n surgical instrument for scraping tissue from body cavities ▷ vb scrape with a curette
CURETTED > CURETTE
CURETTES > CURETTE
CURETTING > CURETTE
CURF n type of limestone
CURFEW n law ordering people to stay inside after a specific time
CURFEWS > CURFEW
CURFS > CURF
CURFUFFLE vb make a kerfuffle
CURIA n papal court and government of the Roman Catholic Church
CURIAE > CURIA
CURIAL > CURIA
CURIALISM n ultramontanism
CURIALIST > CURIALISM
CURIAS > CURIA
CURIE n standard unit of radioactivity
CURIES > CURIE
CURIET n cuirass
CURIETS > CURIET
CURING n act of curing
CURINGS > CURING
CURIO n rare or unusual object valued as a collector's item
CURIOS > CURIO

CURIOSA pl n curiosities
CURIOSITY n eagerness to know or find out
CURIOUS adj eager to learn or know
CURIOUSER > CURIOUS
CURIOUSLY > CURIOUS
CURITE n oxide of uranium and lead
CURITES > CURITE
CURIUM n radioactive element artificially produced from plutonium
CURIUMS > CURIUM
CURL n curved piece of hair ▷ vb make (hair) into curls or (of hair) grow in curls
CURLED > CURL
CURLER n pin or small tube for curling hair
CURLERS > CURLER
CURLEW n long-billed wading bird
CURLEWS > CURLEW
CURLI pl n curled hairlike processes on the surface of the E. coli bacterium
CURLICUE n ornamental curl or twist ▷ vb curl or twist elaborately, as in curlicues
CURLICUED > CURLICUE
CURLICUES > CURLICUE
CURLIER > CURLY
CURLIES pl n as in have by the short and curlies have completely in one's power
CURLIEST > CURLY
CURLILY > CURLY
CURLINESS > CURLY
CURLING n game like bowls, played with heavy stones on ice
CURLINGS > CURLING
CURLPAPER n strip of paper used to roll up and set a section of hair, usually wetted, into a curl
CURLS > CURL
CURLY adj tending to curl
CURLYCUE same as > CURLICUE
CURLYCUES > CURLYCUE
CURN n grain (of corn etc)
CURNEY same as > CURNY
CURNIER > CURNY
CURNIEST > CURNY
CURNS > CURN
CURNY adj granular
CURPEL same as > CRUPPER
CURPELS > CURPEL
CURR vb purr
CURRACH a Scot or Irish name for > CORACLE
CURRACHS > CURRACH
CURRAGH same as > CURRACH
CURRAGHS > CURRAGH
CURRAJONG same as > KURRAJONG
CURRAN n black bun
CURRANS > CURRAN**

CURRANT *n* small dried grape
CURRANTS > CURRANT
CURRANTY > CURRANT
CURRAWONG *n* Australian songbird
CURRED > CURR
CURREJONG *same as* > KURRAJONG
CURRENCY *n* money in use in a particular country
CURRENT *adj* of the immediate present ▷ *n* flow of water or air in one direction
CURRENTLY > CURRENT
CURRENTS > CURRENT
CURRICLE *n* two-wheeled open carriage drawn by two horses side by side
CURRICLES > CURRICLE
CURRICULA *n* plural form of singular curriculum: course of study in one subject at school or college
CURRIE *same as* > CURRY
CURRIED > CURRY
CURRIER *n* person who curries leather
CURRIERS > CURRIER
CURRIERY *n* trade, work, or place of occupation of a currier
CURRIES > CURRY
CURRIJONG *same as* > KURRAJONG
CURRING > CURR
CURRISH *adj* of or like a cur
CURRISHLY > CURRISH
CURRS > CURR
CURRY *n* Indian dish of meat or vegetables in a hot spicy sauce ▷ *vb* prepare (food) with curry powder
CURRYCOMB *n* ridged comb used for grooming horses
CURRYING > CURRY
CURRYINGS > CURRY
CURS > CUR
CURSAL > CURSUS
CURSE *vb* swear (at) ▷ *n* swearword
CURSED > CURSE
CURSEDER > CURSED
CURSEDEST > CURSED
CURSEDLY > CURSE
CURSENARY *same as* > CURSORARY
CURSER > CURSE
CURSERS > CURSE
CURSES > CURSE
CURSI > CURSUS
CURSILLO *n* short religious retreat
CURSILLOS > CURSILLO
CURSING > CURSE
CURSINGS > CURSE
CURSITOR *n* clerk in the Court of Chancery
CURSITORS > CURSITOR

CURSITORY > CURSITOR
CURSIVE *n* handwriting done with joined letters ▷ *adj* of handwriting or print in which letters are joined in a flowing style
CURSIVELY > CURSIVE
CURSIVES > CURSIVE
CURSOR *n* movable point of light that shows a specific position on a visual display unit
CURSORARY *adj* cursory
CURSORES > CURSOR
CURSORIAL *adj* adapted for running
CURSORILY > CURSORY
CURSORS > CURSOR
CURSORY *adj* quick and superficial
CURST *same as* > CURSED
CURSTNESS *n* peevishness
CURSUS *n* Neolithic parallel earthworks
CURT *adj* brief and rather rude
CURTAIL *vb* cut short
CURTAILED > CURTAIL
CURTAILER > CURTAIL
CURTAILS > CURTAIL
CURTAIN *n* piece of cloth hung at a window or opening as a screen ▷ *vb* provide with curtains
CURTAINED > CURTAIN
CURTAINS *pl n* death or ruin
CURTAL *adj* cut short ▷ *n* animal whose tail has been docked
CURTALAX *same as* > CURTALAXE
CURTALAXE *n* cutlass
CURTALS > CURTAL
CURTANA *n* unpointed sword displayed at a coronation as an emblem of mercy
CURTANAS > CURTANA
CURTATE *adj* shortened
CURTATION > CURTATE
CURTAXE *same as* > CURTALAXE
CURTAXES > CURTAXE
CURTER > CURT
CURTESIES > CURTESY
CURTEST > CURT
CURTESY *n* widower's life interest in his wife's estate
CURTILAGE *n* enclosed area of land adjacent to a dwelling house
CURTLY > CURT
CURTNESS > CURT
CURTSEY *same as* > CURTSY
CURTSEYED > CURTSEY
CURTSEYS > CURTSEY
CURTSIED > CURTSY
CURTSIES > CURTSY
CURTSY *n* woman's gesture of respect ▷ *vb* make a curtsy
CURTSYING > CURTSY
CURULE *adj* (in ancient Rome) of the highest rank,

esp one entitled to use a curule chair
CURVATE *adj* curved
CURVATED *same as* > CURVATE
CURVATION > CURVATE
CURVATIVE *adj* having curved edges
CURVATURE *n* curved shape
CURVE *n* continuously bending line with no straight parts ▷ *vb* form or move in a curve
CURVEBALL *n* in baseball, a ball pitched in a curving path ▷ *vb* pitch a curveball
CURVED > CURVE
CURVEDLY > CURVE
CURVES > CURVE
CURVESOME *adj* curvaceous
CURVET *n* horse's low leap with all four feet off the ground ▷ *vb* make such a leap
CURVETED > CURVET
CURVETING > CURVET
CURVETS > CURVET
CURVETTED > CURVET
CURVEY *same as* > CURVY
CURVIER > CURVE
CURVIEST > CURVE
CURVIFORM *adj* having a curved form
CURVINESS > CURVY
CURVING > CURVE
CURVITAL *adj* relating to curvature
CURVITIES > CURVITY
CURVITY *n* curvedness
CURVY > CURVE
CUSCUS *n* large Australian nocturnal possum
CUSCUSES > CUSCUS
CUSEC *n* unit of flow equal to 1 cubic foot per second
CUSECS > CUSEC
CUSH *n* cushion
CUSHAT *n* wood pigeon
CUSHATS > CUSHAT
CUSHAW *same as* > CASHAW
CUSHAWS > CUSHAW
CUSHES > CUSH
CUSHIE *same as* > CUSHAT
CUSHIER > CUSHY
CUSHIES > CUSHIE
CUSHIEST > CUSHY
CUSHILY > CUSHY
CUSHINESS > CUSHY
CUSHION *n* bag filled with soft material, to make a seat more comfortable ▷ *vb* lessen the effects of
CUSHIONED > CUSHION
CUSHIONET *n* small cushion
CUSHIONS > CUSHION
CUSHIONY *adj* like a cushion
CUSHTY *interj* exclamation of pleasure, agreement, approval, etc
CUSHY *adj* easy
CUSK *n* type of food fish of

northern coastal waters, with a single long dorsal fin
CUSKS > CUSK
CUSP *n* pointed end, esp on a tooth
CUSPAL > CUSP
CUSPATE *adj* having a cusp or cusps
CUSPATED *same as* > CUSPATE
CUSPED *same as* > CUSPATE
CUSPID *n* tooth having one point
CUSPIDAL *same as* > CUSPIDATE
CUSPIDATE *adj* having a cusp or cusps
CUSPIDES > CUSPIS
CUSPIDOR *another word* (esp US) for > SPITTOON
CUSPIDORE *same as* > CUSPIDOR
CUSPIDORS > CUSPIDOR
CUSPIDS > CUSPID
CUSPIER > CUSPY
CUSPIEST > CUSPY
CUSPIS *n* in anatomy, a tapering structure
CUSPLIKE *adj* like a cusp
CUSPS > CUSP
CUSPY *adj* (of a computer program) well-designed and user-friendly
CUSS *n* curse, oath ▷ *vb* swear (at)
CUSSED *adj* obstinate
CUSSEDLY > CUSSED
CUSSER *same as* > COOSER
CUSSERS > CUSSER
CUSSES > CUSS
CUSSING > CUSS
CUSSO *n* tree of the rose family
CUSSOS > CUSSO
CUSSWORD *n* swearword
CUSSWORDS > CUSSWORD
CUSTARD *n* sweet yellow sauce made from milk and eggs
CUSTARDS > CUSTARD
CUSTARDY *adj* like custard
CUSTOCK *same as* > CASTOCK
CUSTOCKS > CUSTOCK
CUSTODE *n* custodian
CUSTODES > CUSTODE
CUSTODIAL > CUSTODY
CUSTODIAN *n* person in charge of a public building
CUSTODIER *n* custodian
CUSTODIES > CUSTODY
CUSTODY *n* protective care
CUSTOM *n* long-established activity or action ▷ *adj* made to the specifications of an individual customer
CUSTOMARY *adj* usual ▷ *n* statement in writing of customary laws and practices

CUSTOMED *adj* accustomed

CUSTOMER *n* person who buys goods or services

CUSTOMERS
> CUSTOMER

CUSTOMISE *same as*
> CUSTOMIZE

CUSTOMIZE *vb* make (something) according to a customer's individual requirements

CUSTOMS *n* duty charged on imports or exports

CUSTOS *n* superior in the Franciscan religious order

CUSTREL *n* knave

CUSTRELS > CUSTREL

CUSTUMAL *another word for* > CUSTOMARY

CUSTUMALS
> CUSTUMAL

CUSTUMARY *n* customary

CUSUM *n* analysis technique used in statistics

CUSUMS > CUSUM

CUT *vb* open up, penetrate, wound, or divide with a sharp instrument

CUTANEOUS *adj* of the skin

CUTAWAY *adj* (of a drawing or model) having part of the outside omitted to reveal the inside ▷ *n* man's coat cut diagonally from the front waist to the back of the knees

CUTAWAYS > CUTAWAY

CUTBACK *n* decrease or reduction

CUTBACKS > CUTBACK

CUTBANK *n* steep banking at a bend in a river

CUTBANKS > CUTBANK

CUTBLOCK *n* area where logging is permitted

CUTBLOCKS
> CUTBLOCK

CUTCH *same as*
> CATECHU

CUTCHA *adj* crude

CUTCHERRY *n* (formerly, in India) government offices and law courts collectively

CUTCHERY *same as*
> CUTCHERRY

CUTCHES > CUTCH

CUTDOWN *n* decrease

CUTDOWNS > CUTDOWN

CUTE *adj* appealing or attractive

CUTELY > CUTE

CUTENESS > CUTE

CUTER > CUTE

CUTES > CUTIS

CUTESIE *same as*
> CUTESY

CUTESIER > CUTESY

CUTESIEST > CUTESY

CUTEST > CUTE

CUTESY *adj* affectedly cute or coy

CUTEY *same as* > CUTIE

CUTEYS > CUTEY

CUTGLASS *adj* (of an accent) upper-class

CUTGRASS *n* any grass of the genus Leersia

CUTICLE *n* skin at the base of a fingernail or toenail

CUTICLES > CUTICLE

CUTICULA *n* cuticle

CUTICULAE
> CUTICULA

CUTICULAR > CUTICLE

CUTIE *n* person regarded as appealing or attractive

CUTIES > CUTIE

CUTIKIN *same as*
> CUITIKIN

CUTIKINS > CUTIKIN

CUTIN *n* waxy waterproof substance

CUTINISE *same as*
> CUTINIZE

CUTINISED
> CUTINISE

CUTINISES
> CUTINISE

CUTINIZE *vb* become or cause to become covered or impregnated with cutin

CUTINIZED
> CUTINIZE

CUTINIZES
> CUTINIZE

CUTINS > CUTIN

CUTIS *a technical name for the* > SKIN

CUTISES > CUTIS

CUTLAS *same as*
> CUTLASS

CUTLASES > CUTLAS

CUTLASS *n* curved one-edged sword formerly used by sailors

CUTLASSES > CUTLASS

CUTLER *n* maker of cutlery

CUTLERIES > CUTLERY

CUTLERS > CUTLER

CUTLERY *n* knives, forks, and spoons

CUTLET *n* small piece of meat like a chop

CUTLETS > CUTLET

CUTLETTE *n* flat croquette of minced meat

CUTLETTES
> CUTLETTE

CUTLINE *n* caption

CUTLINES > CUTLINE

CUTOFF *n* limit or termination

CUTOFFS > CUTOFF

CUTOUT *n* something that has been cut out from something else

CUTOUTS > CUTOUT

CUTOVER *n* transitional period in an IT system changeover

CUTOVERS > CUTOVER

CUTPURSE *n* pickpocket

CUTPURSES
> CUTPURSE

CUTS > CUT

CUTSCENE *n* non-interactive scene in a computer game

CUTSCENES
> CUTSCENE

CUTTABLE *adj* capable of being cut

CUTTAGE *n* propagation by using parts taken from growing plants

CUTTAGES > CUTTAGE

CUTTER *n* person or tool that cuts

CUTTERS > CUTTER

CUTTHROAT *n* person who cuts throats

CUTTIER > CUTTY

CUTTIES > CUTTY

CUTTIEST > CUTTY

CUTTING > CUT

CUTTINGLY > CUT

CUTTINGS > CUT

CUTTLE *vb* to whisper

CUTTLED > CUTTLE

CUTTLES > CUTTLE

CUTTLING > CUTTLE

CUTTO *n* large knife

CUTTOE *same as* > CUTTO

CUTTOES > CUTTO

CUTTY *adj* short or cut short ▷ *n* something cut short

CUTUP *n* joker or prankster

CUTUPS > CUTUP

CUTWATER *n* forward part of the stem of a vessel, which cuts through the water

CUTWATERS
> CUTWATER

CUTWORK *n* type of openwork embroidery

CUTWORKS > CUTWORK

CUTWORM *n* caterpillar of various types of moth

CUTWORMS > CUTWORM

CUVEE *n* individual batch or blend of wine

CUVEES > CUVEE

CUVETTE *n* shallow dish or vessel for holding liquid

CUVETTES > CUVETTE

CUZ *n* cousin

CUZES > CUZ

CUZZES > CUZ

CUZZIE *n* close friend or family member

CUZZIES > CUZZIE

CWM *same as* > CIRQUE

CWMS > CWM

CWTCH *vb* cuddle or be cuddled

CWTCHED > CWTCH

CWTCHES > CWTCH

CWTCHING > CWTCH

CYAN *n* highly saturated green-blue ▷ *adj* of this colour

CYANAMID *same as*
> CYANAMIDE

CYANAMIDE *n* white or colourless crystalline soluble weak dibasic acid, which can be hydrolysed to urea

CYANAMIDS
> CYANAMID

CYANATE *n* any salt or ester of cyanic acid

CYANATES > CYANATE

CYANIC *adj* as in *cyanic acid* colourless poisonous volatile liquid acid

CYANID *same as*
> CYANIDE

CYANIDE *n* extremely poisonous chemical compound ▷ *vb* treat with cyanide

CYANIDED > CYANIDE

CYANIDES > CYANIDE

CYANIDING > CYANIDE

CYANIDS > CYANID

CYANIN *same as*
> CYANINE

CYANINE *n* blue dye used in photography

CYANINES > CYANINE

CYANINS > CYANIN

CYANISE *same as*
> CYANIZE

CYANISED > CYANISE

CYANISES > CYANISE

CYANISING > CYANISE

CYANITE *variant spelling of* > KYANITE

CYANITES > CYANITE

CYANITIC > CYANITE

CYANIZE *vb* turn into cyanide

CYANIZED > CYANIZE

CYANIZES > CYANIZE

CYANIZING > CYANIZE

CYANO *adj* containing cyanogen

CYANOGEN *n* poisonous colourless flammable gas

CYANOGENS
> CYANOGEN

CYANOSE *same as*
> CYANOSIS

CYANOSED *adj* affected by cyanosis

CYANOSES > CYANOSIS

CYANOSIS *n* blueness of the skin, caused by a deficiency of oxygen in the blood

CYANOTIC > CYANOSIS

CYANOTYPE *another name for* > BLUEPRINT

CYANS > CYAN

CYANURATE *n* chemical derived from cyanide

CYANURET *n* cyanide

CYANURETS
> CYANURET

CYANURIC *adj* as in *cyanuric acid* type of acid

CYATHI > CYATHUS

CYATHIA > CYATHIUM

CYATHIUM *n* inflorescence of the type found in the poinsettia

CYATHUS *n* ancient measure of wine

CYBER *adj* involving computers

CYBERCAFE *n* café equipped with computer terminals which customers can use to access the internet

CYBERCAST *same as*
> WEBCAST

CYBERNATE *vb* control (a manufacturing process) with a servomechanism or (of a process) to be controlled by a servomechanism

CYBERNAUT n person using internet

CYBERPET n electronic toy that simulates the activities of a pet

CYBERPETS
> CYBERPET

CYBERPORN n pornography on the internet

CYBERPUNK n genre of science fiction that features rebellious computer hackers and is set in a dystopian society integrated by computer networks

CYBERSEX n exchanging of sexual messages or information via the internet

CYBERWAR n information warfare

CYBERWARS
> CYBERWAR

CYBORG n (in science fiction) a living being enhanced by computer implants

CYBORGS > CYBORG

CYBRARIAN n person in charge of computer archives

CYBRID n cytoplasmic hybrid

CYBRIDS > CYBRID

CYCAD n type of tropical or subtropical plant

CYCADEOID n (now extinct) plant with a woody stem and tough leaves

CYCADS > CYCAD

CYCAS n palm tree of the genus Cycas

CYCASES > CYCAS

CYCASIN n glucoside, toxic to mammals, occurring in cycads

CYCASINS > CYCASIN

CYCLAMATE n salt or ester of cyclamic acid. Certain of the salts have a very sweet taste and were formerly used as food additives and sugar substitutes

CYCLAMEN n plant with red, pink, or white flowers ▷ adj of a dark reddish-purple colour

CYCLAMENS
> CYCLAMEN

CYCLAMIC adj as in cyclamic acid type of acid

CYCLASE n enzyme which acts as a catalyst in the formation of a cyclic compound

CYCLASES > CYCLASE

CYCLE vb ride a bicycle ▷ n bicycle

CYCLECAR n any light car with an engine capacity of 1100cc or less

CYCLECARS > CYCLECAR

CYCLED > CYCLE

CYCLEPATH n special path for bicycles

CYCLER same as
> CYCLIST

CYCLERIES > CYCLERY

CYCLERS > CYCLER

CYCLERY n business dealing in bicycles and bicycle accessories

CYCLES > CYCLE

CYCLEWAY n path or way designed, and reserved for, cyclists

CYCLEWAYS
> CYCLEWAY

CYCLIC adj recurring or revolving in cycles

CYCLICAL n short-term trend, of which reversal is expected ▷ adj cyclic

CYCLICALS > CYCLIC

CYCLICISM > CYCLIC

CYCLICITY > CYCLIC

CYCLICLY > CYCLIC

CYCLIN n type of protein

CYCLING > CYCLE

CYCLINGS > CYCLE

CYCLINS > CYCLIN

CYCLISE same as
> CYCLIZE

CYCLISED > CYCLISE

CYCLISES > CYCLISE

CYCLISING > CYCLISE

CYCLIST n person who rides a bicycle

CYCLISTS > CYCLIST

CYCLITOL n alicyclic compound

CYCLITOLS
> CYCLITOL

CYCLIZE vb be cyclical

CYCLIZED > CYCLIZE

CYCLIZES > CYCLIZE

CYCLIZINE n drug used to relieve the symptoms of motion sickness

CYCLIZING > CYCLIZE

CYCLO n type of rickshaw

CYCLOGIRO n aircraft lifted and propelled by pivoted blades rotating parallel to roughly horizontal transverse axes

CYCLOID adj resembling a circle ▷ n mathematical curve

CYCLOIDAL > CYCLOID

CYCLOIDS > CYCLOID

CYCLOLITH n stone circle

CYCLONAL > CYCLONE

CYCLONE n violent wind moving round a central area

CYCLONES > CYCLONE

CYCLONIC > CYCLONE

CYCLONITE n white crystalline insoluble explosive prepared by the action of nitric acid on hexamethylenetetramine

CYCLOPEAN adj of or relating to the Cyclops

CYCLOPES > CYCLOPS

CYCLOPIAN > CYCLOPS

CYCLOPIC > CYCLOPS

CYCLOPS n type of copepod characterized by having one eye

CYCLORAMA n large picture, such as a battle scene, on the interior wall of a cylindrical room, designed to appear in natural perspective to a spectator in the centre

CYCLOS > CYCLO

CYCLOSES > CYCLOSIS

CYCLOSIS n circulation of cytoplasm or cell organelles, such as food vacuoles in some protozoans

CYCLOTRON n apparatus that accelerates charged particles by means of a strong vertical magnetic field

CYCLUS n cycle

CYCLUSES > CYCLUS

CYDER same as > CIDER

CYDERS > CYDER

CYESES > CYESIS

CYESIS the technical name for > PREGNANCY

CYGNET n young swan

CYGNETS > CYGNET

CYLICES > CYLIX

CYLIKES > CYLIX

CYLINDER n solid or hollow body with straight sides and circular ends

CYLINDERS
> CYLINDER

CYLINDRIC adj shaped like, or characteristic of a cylinder

CYLIX variant of > KYLIX

CYMA n moulding with a double curve, part concave and part convex

CYMAE > CYMA

CYMAGRAPH same as
> CYMOGRAPH

CYMAR n woman's short fur-trimmed jacket, popular in the 17th and 18th centuries

CYMARS > CYMAR

CYMAS > CYMA

CYMATIA > CYMATIUM

CYMATICS n therapy involving sound waves directed at the body

CYMATIUM n top moulding of a classical cornice or entablature

CYMBAL n percussion instrument

CYMBALEER > CYMBAL

CYMBALER > CYMBAL

CYMBALERS > CYMBAL

CYMBALIST > CYMBAL

CYMBALO another name for
> DULCIMER

CYMBALOES > CYMBALO

CYMBALOM same as
> CIMBALOM

CYMBALOMS
> CYMBALOM

CYMBALOS > CYMBALO

CYMBALS > CYMBAL

CYMBIDIA
> CYMBIDIUM

CYMBIDIUM n any orchid of the genus Cymbidium

CYMBIFORM adj shaped like a boat

CYMBLING same as
> CYMLING

CYMBLINGS > CYMLING

CYME n type of flower cluster

CYMENE n colourless insoluble liquid

CYMENES > CYMENE

CYMES > CYME

CYMLIN same as
> CYMLING

CYMLING n pattypan squash

CYMLINGS > CYMLING

CYMLINS > CYMLIN

CYMOGENE n mixture of volatile flammable hydrocarbons

CYMOGENES
> CYMOGENE

CYMOGRAPH n instrument for tracing the outline of an architectural moulding

CYMOID adj resembling a cyme or cyma

CYMOL same as > CYMENE

CYMOLS > CYMOL

CYMOPHANE n yellow or green opalescent variety of chrysoberyl

CYMOSE adj having the characteristics of a cyme

CYMOSELY > CYMOSE

CYMOUS adj relating to a cyme

CYNANCHE n any disease characterized by inflammation and swelling of the throat

CYNANCHES
> CYNANCHE

CYNEGETIC adj relating to hunting

CYNIC n person who believes that people always act selfishly ▷ adj of or relating to Sirius, the Dog Star

CYNICAL adj believing that people always act selfishly

CYNICALLY > CYNICAL

CYNICISM n attitude or beliefs of a cynic

CYNICISMS
> CYNICISM

CYNICS > CYNIC

CYNODONT n carnivorous mammal-like reptile

CYNODONTS
> CYNODONT

CYNOMOLGI n plural form of singular cynomolgus: type of monkey

CYNOSURAL
> CYNOSURE

CYNOSURE n centre of attention

CYNOSURES
> CYNOSURE

CYPHER same as
> CIPHER

CYPHERED > CYPHER

CYPHERING > CYPHER
CYPHERS > CYPHER
CYPRES n legal doctrine
CYPRESES > CYPRESS
CYPRESS n evergreen tree with dark green leaves
CYPRESSES > CYPRESS
CYPRIAN n licentious or profligate person
CYPRIANS > CYPRIAN
CYPRID n small bivalve freshwater crustacean
CYPRIDES > CYPRIS
CYPRIDS > CYPRID
CYPRINE adj relating to carp ▷ n type of silicate mineral
CYPRINES > CYPRINE
CYPRINID n type of mainly freshwater fish, usu with toothless jaws
CYPRINIDS > CYPRINID
CYPRINOID n type of fish belonging to the suborder which includes cyprinids, electric eels, and loaches
CYPRIS n small bivalve freshwater crustacean
CYPRUS same as > CYPRESS
CYPRUSES > CYPRUS
CYPSELA n dry one-seeded fruit of the daisy and related plants
CYPSELAE > CYPSELA
CYST n (abnormal) sac in the body containing fluid or soft matter
CYSTEIN same as > CYSTEINE
CYSTEINE n sulphur-containing amino acid
CYSTEINES > CYSTEINE
CYSTEINIC > CYSTEINE
CYSTEINS > CYSTEIN
CYSTIC adj of, relating to, or resembling a cyst
CYSTID n fossil echinoderm of an extinct order of sea lilies
CYSTIDEAN same as > CYSTID
CYSTIDS > CYSTID

CYSTIFORM adj having the form of a cyst
CYSTINE n sulphur-containing amino acid
CYSTINES > CYSTINE
CYSTITIS n inflammation of the bladder
CYSTOCARP n reproductive body in red algae, developed after fertilization and consisting of filaments bearing carpospores
CYSTOCELE n hernia of the urinary bladder
CYSTOID adj resembling a cyst or bladder ▷ n tissue mass that resembles a cyst but lacks an outer membrane
CYSTOIDS > CYSTOID
CYSTOLITH n knoblike deposit of calcium carbonate in the epidermal cells of such plants as the stinging nettle
CYSTOTOMY n surgical incision into the gall bladder or urinary bladder
CYSTS > CYST
CYTASE n cellulose-dissolving enzyme
CYTASES > CYTASE
CYTASTER another word for > ASTER
CYTASTERS > CYTASTER
CYTE n biological cell
CYTES > CYTE
CYTIDINE n nucleoside formed by the condensation of cytosine and ribose
CYTIDINES > CYTIDINE
CYTIDYLIC adj as in *cytidylic acid* nucleotide that is found in DNA
CYTISI > CYTISUS
CYTISINE n poisonous alkaloid found in laburnum seeds
CYTISINES > CYTISINE
CYTISUS n any plant of the broom genus, Cytisus

CYTODE n mass of protoplasm without a nucleus
CYTODES > CYTODE
CYTOGENY n origin and development of plant cells
CYTOID adj resembling a cell
CYTOKINE n type of protein that carries signals to neighbouring cells
CYTOKINES > CYTOKINE
CYTOKININ n any of a group of plant hormones that promote cell division and retard ageing in plants
CYTOLOGIC > CYTOLOGY
CYTOLOGY n study of plant and animal cells
CYTOLYSES > CYTOLYSIS
CYTOLYSIN n substance that can partially or completely destroy animal cells
CYTOLYSIS n dissolution of cells, esp by the destruction of their membranes
CYTOLYTIC > CYTOLYSIS
CYTOMETER n glass slide used to count and measure blood cells
CYTOMETRY n counting of blood cells using a cytometer
CYTON n main part of a neuron
CYTONS > CYTON
CYTOPATHY n disease of a cell
CYTOPENIA n blood disorder where there is a deficiency in the blood cells
CYTOPLASM n protoplasm of a cell excluding the nucleus
CYTOPLAST n intact cytoplasm of a single cell
CYTOSINE n white crystalline pyrimidine occurring in nucleic acids
CYTOSINES > CYTOSINE

CYTOSOL n solution in a biological cell
CYTOSOLIC > CYTOSOL
CYTOSOLS > CYTOSOL
CYTOSOME n body of a cell excluding its nucleus
CYTOSOMES > CYTOSOME
CYTOTAXES > CYTOTAXIS
CYTOTAXIS n movement of cells due to external stimulation
CYTOTOXIC adj poisonous to living cells: denoting certain drugs used in the treatment of leukaemia and other cancers
CYTOTOXIN n any substance that is poisonous to living cells
CZAPKA n leather and felt peaked military helmet of Polish origin
CZAPKAS > CZAPKA
CZAR n Russian emperor
CZARDAS n Hungarian national dance of alternating slow and fast sections
CZARDASES > CZARDAS
CZARDOM > CZAR
CZARDOMS > CZARDOM
CZAREVICH n son of a czar
CZAREVNA n daughter of a czar
CZAREVNAS > CZAREVNA
CZARINA n wife of a czar
CZARINAS > CZARINA
CZARISM n system of government by a czar
CZARISMS > CZARISM
CZARIST n supporter of a czar
CZARISTS > CZARIST
CZARITSA n wife of a czar
CZARITSAS > CZARITSA
CZARITZA same as > CZARITSA
CZARITZAS > CZARITZA
CZARS > CZAR

Dd

DA n Burmese knife
DAAL n (in Indian cookery) split pulses
DAALS > DAAL
DAB vb pat lightly ▷ n small amount of something soft or moist
DABBA n in Indian cookery, a round metal box used to transport hot food
DABBAS > DABBA
DABBED > DAB
DABBER n pad used by printers for applying ink by hand
DABBERS > DABBER
DABBING > DAB
DABBITIES > DABBITY
DABBITY n temporary tattoo
DABBLE vb be involved in something superficially
DABBLED > DABBLE
DABBLER > DABBLE
DABBLERS > DABBLE
DABBLES > DABBLE
DABBLING > DABBLE
DABBLINGS > DABBLE
DABCHICK n type of small grebe
DABCHICKS > DABCHICK
DABS > DAB
DABSTER n incompetent or amateurish worker
DABSTERS > DABSTER
DACE n small European freshwater fish
DACES > DACE
DACHA n country cottage in Russia
DACHAS > DACHA
DACHSHUND n dog with a long body and short legs
DACITE n volcanic rock
DACITES > DACITE
DACK vb remove the trousers from (someone) by force
DACKED > DACK
DACKER vb walk slowly
DACKERED > DACKER
DACKERING > DACKER
DACKERS > DACKER
DACKING > DACK
DACKS > DACK
DACOIT n (in India and Myanmar) a member of a gang of armed robbers
DACOITAGE n robbery by armed gang
DACOITIES > DACOITY

DACOITS > DACOIT
DACOITY n (in India and Myanmar) robbery by an armed gang
DACQUOISE n cake with meringue layers
DACRON n US tradename for a synthetic polyester fibre or fabric
DACRONS > DACRON
DACTYL n metrical foot of three syllables, one long followed by two short
DACTYLAR adj of or relating to a dactyl
DACTYLI > DACTYLUS
DACTYLIC same as **>** DACTYL
DACTYLICS > DACTYLIC
DACTYLIST n poet
DACTYLS > DACTYL
DACTYLUS n tip of a squid's tentacular club
DAD n father ▷ vb act or treat as a father
DADA n nihilistic artistic movement of the early 20th century
DADAH n illegal drugs
DADAHS > DADAH
DADAISM same as **>** DADA
DADAISMS > DADAISM
DADAIST > DADA
DADAISTIC > DADA
DADAISTS > DADA
DADAS > DADA
DADBOD n untoned male physique
DADBODS > DADBOD
DADCHELOR adj as in dadchelor party party held for a prospective father
DADDED > DAD
DADDIES > DADDY
DADDING > DAD
DADDLE vb walk unsteadily
DADDLED > DADDLE
DADDLES > DADDLE
DADDLING > DADDLE
DADDOCK n core of a dead tree
DADDOCKS > DADDOCK
DADDY n father
DADGUM mild form of **>** DAMNED
DADO n lower part of an interior wall decorated differently from the upper part ▷ vb provide with a dado
DADOED > DADO
DADOES > DADO

DADOING > DADO
DADOS > DADO
DADS > DAD
DAE a Scot word for **>** DO
DAEDAL adj skilful or intricate
DAEDALEAN same as **>** DAEDALIAN
DAEDALIAN adj of, relating to, or resembling the work of Daedalus, the Athenian architect and inventor of Greek mythology
DAEDALIC same as **>** DAEDALIAN
DAEING > DAE
DAEMON same as **>** DEMON
DAEMONES > DAEMON
DAEMONIC > DAEMON
DAEMONS > DAEMON
DAES > DAE
DAFF vb frolic
DAFFED > DAFF
DAFFIER > DAFFY
DAFFIES > DAFFY
DAFFIEST > DAFFY
DAFFILY > DAFFY
DAFFINESS > DAFFY
DAFFING > DAFF
DAFFINGS > DAFF
DAFFODIL n yellow trumpet-shaped flower that blooms in spring ▷ adj brilliant yellow
DAFFODILS > DAFFODIL
DAFFS > DAFF
DAFFY adj daft ▷ n daffodil
DAFT adj foolish or crazy
DAFTAR Indian word for **>** OFFICE
DAFTARS > DAFTAR
DAFTER > DAFT
DAFTEST > DAFT
DAFTIE n foolish person
DAFTIES > DAFTIE
DAFTLY > DAFT
DAFTNESS > DAFT
DAG n daglock ▷ vb cut daglocks from sheep
DAGABA n dome-shaped Buddhist shrine
DAGABAS > DAGABA
DAGGA n cannabis
DAGGAS > DAGGA
DAGGED > DAG
DAGGER n short weapon with pointed blade ▷ vb stab with a dagger
DAGGERED > DAGGER
DAGGERING > DAGGER

DAGGERS > DAGGER
DAGGIER > DAGGY
DAGGIEST > DAGGY
DAGGING > DAG
DAGGINGS > DAG
DAGGLE vb trail through water
DAGGLED > DAGGLE
DAGGLES > DAGGLE
DAGGLING > DAGGLE
DAGGY adj amusing
DAGLOCK n dung-caked lock of wool around the hindquarters of a sheep
DAGLOCKS > DAGLOCK
DAGOBA n dome-shaped Buddhist shrine
DAGOBAS > DAGOBA
DAGS > DAG
DAGWOOD n European shrub
DAGWOODS > DAGWOOD
DAH n long sound used in Morse code
DAHABEAH n houseboat used on the Nile
DAHABEAHS > DAHABEAH
DAHABEEAH n Egyptian houseboat
DAHABIAH same as **>** DAHABEAH
DAHABIAHS > DAHABIAH
DAHABIEH n Egyptian houseboat
DAHABIEHS > DAHABIEH
DAHABIYA n Egyptian houseboat
DAHABIYAH n Egyptian houseboat
DAHABIYAS > DAHABIYA
DAHABIYEH n Egyptian houseboat
DAHL same as **>** DHAL
DAHLIA n brightly coloured garden flower
DAHLIAS > DAHLIA
DAHLS > DAHL
DAHOON n evergreen shrub
DAHOONS > DAHOON
DAHS > DAH
DAIDLE vb waddle about
DAIDLED > DAIDLE
DAIDLES > DAIDLE
DAIDLING > DAIDLE
DAIDZEIN n type of protein
DAIDZEINS > DAIDZEIN

DAIKER vb walk slowly
DAIKERED > DAIKER
DAIKERING > DAIKER
DAIKERS > DAIKER
DAIKO n Japanese drum
DAIKON another name for
> MOOLI
DAIKONS > DAIKON
DAIKOS > DAIKO
DAILIES > DAILY
DAILINESS > DAILY
DAILY adj occurring every
day or every weekday
▷ adv every day ▷ n daily
newspaper
DAILYNESS > DAILY
DAIMEN adj occasional
DAIMIO same as
> DAIMYO
DAIMIOS > DAIMIO
DAIMOKU n Nichiren
Buddhist chant
DAIMOKUS > DAIMOKU
DAIMON same as
> DEMON
DAIMONES pl n
disembodied souls
DAIMONIC > DAIMON
DAIMONS > DAIMON
DAIMYO n magnate in
Japan from the 11th to the
19th century
DAIMYOS > DAIMYO
DAINE vb condescend
DAINED > DAINE
DAINES > DAINE
DAINING > DAINE
DAINT adj dainty ▷ n
dainty
DAINTIER > DAINTY
DAINTIES > DAINTY
DAINTIEST > DAINTY
DAINTILY > DAINTY
DAINTS > DAINT
DAINTY adj delicate or
elegant ▷ n small cake or
sweet
DAIQUIRI n iced drink
containing rum, lime juice,
and sugar
DAIQUIRIS
> DAIQUIRI
DAIRIES > DAIRY
DAIRY n place for the
processing or sale of milk
and its products ▷ adj of
milk or its products
DAIRYING n business of
producing, processing,
and selling dairy products
DAIRYINGS
> DAIRYING
DAIRYMAID n (formerly)
woman employed to milk
cows
DAIRYMAN n man
employed to look after
cows
DAIRYMEN > DAIRYMAN
DAIS n raised platform in
a hall, used by a speaker
DAISES > DAIS
DAISHIKI n upper
garment
DAISHIKIS
> DAISHIKI
DAISIED > DAISY
DAISIES > DAISY

DAISY n small wild flower
with a yellow centre and
white petals
DAISYLIKE adj like a
daisy
DAK n system of mail
delivery or passenger
transport
DAKER vb walk slowly
DAKERED > DAKER
DAKERHEN n European
bird
DAKERHENS
> DAKERHEN
DAKERING > DAKER
DAKERS > DAKER
DAKOIT same as
> DACOIT
DAKOITI same as
> DAKOIT
DAKOITIES > DAKOIT
DAKOITIS > DAKOITI
DAKOITS > DAKOIT
DAKOITY n armed
robbery
DAKS an informal name for
> TROUSERS
DAL same as > DECALITRE
DALAPON n herbicide
DALAPONS > DALAPON
DALASI n standard
monetary unit of The
Gambia, divided into 100
bututs
DALASIS > DALASI
DALE n (esp in N England)
valley
DALED same as > DALETH
DALEDH n letter of the
Hebrew alphabet
DALEDHS > DALEDH
DALEDS > DALED
DALES > DALE
DALESMAN n person
living in a dale, esp in the
dales of N England
DALESMEN > DALESMAN
DALETH n fourth letter of
the Hebrew alphabet
DALETHS > DALETH
DALGYTE another name for
> BILBY
DALGYTES > DALGYTE
DALI n type of tree
DALIS > DALI
DALLE > DALLES
DALLES pl n stretch of a
river between high rock
walls, with rapids and
dangerous currents
DALLIANCE n flirtation
DALLIED > DALLY
DALLIER > DALLY
DALLIERS > DALLY
DALLIES > DALLY
DALLOP n semisolid lump
DALLOPS > DALLOP
DALLY vb waste time
DALLYING > DALLY
DALMAHOY n bushy wig
DALMAHOYS
> DALMAHOY
DALMATIAN n breed of
dog characterized by its
striking spotted markings
DALMATIC n
wide-sleeved tunic-like
vestment open at the

sides, worn by deacons
and bishops
DALMATICS
> DALMATIC
DALS > DAL
DALT n foster child
DALTON n atomic mass
unit
DALTONIAN n
colour-blind person
DALTONIC
> DALTONISM
DALTONISM n colour
blindness, esp the
confusion of red and green
DALTONS > DALTON
DALTS > DALT
DAM n barrier built across a
river to create a lake ▷ vb
build a dam across (a river)
DAMAGE vb harm, spoil
▷ n harm to a person or
thing
DAMAGED > DAMAGE
DAMAGER > DAMAGE
DAMAGERS > DAMAGE
DAMAGES pl n money
awarded as compensation
for injury or loss
DAMAGING > DAMAGE
DAMAN n the Syrian rock
hyrax
DAMANS > DAMAN
DAMAR same as > DAMMAR
DAMARS > DAMAR
DAMASCENE vb
ornament (metal, esp
steel) by etching or by
inlaying, usually with gold
or silver ▷ n design or
article produced by this
process ▷ adj of or relating
to this process
DAMASK n fabric with a
pattern woven into it,
used for tablecloths etc
▷ vb ornament (metal) by
etching or inlaying, usually
with gold or silver
DAMASKED > DAMASK
DAMASKEEN vb decorate
metal
DAMASKIN vb decorate
metal
DAMASKING > DAMASK
DAMASKINS
> DAMASKIN
DAMASKS > DAMASK
DAMASQUIN vb decorate
metal
DAMASSIN n patterned
damask
DAMASSINS
> DAMASSIN
DAMBOARD n
draughtboard
DAMBOARDS
> DAMBOARD
DAMBROD n draughtboard
DAMBRODS > DAMBROD
DAME n woman
DAMEHOOD n state of
being a dame
DAMEHOODS
> DAMEHOOD
DAMES > DAME
DAMEWORT n
sweet-scented perennial

plant with mauve or white
flowers
DAMEWORTS
> DAMEWORT
DAMFOOL adj foolish ▷ n
foolish person
DAMFOOLS > DAMFOOL
DAMIANA n herbal
medicine
DAMIANAS > DAMIANA
DAMMAR n any of various
resins obtained from SE
Asian trees
DAMMARS > DAMMAR
DAMME interj exclamation
of surprise
DAMMED > DAM
DAMMER same as
> DAMMAR
DAMMERS > DAMMER
DAMMING > DAM
DAMMIT interj
exclamation of surprise
DAMN interj exclamation of
annoyance ▷ adj extreme
▷ adv extremely ▷ vb
condemn as bad or
worthless
DAMNABLE adj annoying
DAMNABLY adv in a
detestable manner
DAMNATION interj
exclamation of anger ▷ n
eternal punishment
DAMNATORY adj
threatening or
occasioning
condemnation
DAMNDEST n utmost
DAMNDESTS
> DAMNDEST
DAMNED adj condemned
to hell ▷ adv extremely
DAMNEDER > DAMNED
DAMNEDEST n utmost
DAMNER n person who
damns
DAMNERS > DAMNER
DAMNEST same as
> DAMNEDEST
DAMNESTS > DAMNEST
DAMNIFIED > DAMNIFY
DAMNIFIES > DAMNIFY
DAMNIFY vb cause loss or
damage to (a person)
DAMNING > DAMN
DAMNINGLY > DAMN
DAMNS > DAMN
DAMOISEL same as
> DAMSEL
DAMOISELS
> DAMOISEL
DAMOSEL same as
> DAMSEL
DAMOSELS > DAMOSEL
DAMOZEL n young
woman
DAMOZELS > DAMOZEL
DAMP adj slightly wet ▷ n
slight wetness, moisture
▷ vb make damp
DAMPED > DAMP
DAMPEN vb reduce the
intensity of
DAMPENED > DAMPEN
DAMPENER > DAMPEN
DAMPENERS > DAMPEN
DAMPENING > DAMPEN

DAMPENS > DAMPEN
DAMPER *n* movable plate to regulate the draught in a fire
DAMPERS > DAMPER
DAMPEST > DAMP
DAMPIER > DAMPY
DAMPIEST > DAMPY
DAMPING *n* act of moistening
DAMPINGS > DAMPING
DAMPISH > DAMP
DAMPLY > DAMP
DAMPNESS > DAMP
DAMPS > DAMP
DAMPY *adj* damp
DAMS > DAM
DAMSEL *n* young woman
DAMSELFLY *n* type of insect similar to but smaller than a dragonfly
DAMSELS > DAMSEL
DAMSON *n* small blue-black plumlike fruit
DAMSONS > DAMSON
DAN *n* in judo, any of the 10 black-belt grades of proficiency
DANAZOL *n* synthetic male hormone
DANAZOLS > DANAZOL
DANCE *vb* move the feet and body rhythmically in time to music ▷ *n* series of steps and movements in time to music
DANCEABLE > DANCE
DANCECORE *n* type of electronic dance music
DANCED > DANCE
DANCEHALL *n* style of dance-oriented reggae
DANCELIKE *adj* like a dance
DANCER > DANCE
DANCERS > DANCE
DANCES > DANCE
DANCETTE *another name for* > CHEVRON
DANCETTEE *adj* having a zigzag pattern
DANCETTES > DANCETTE
DANCETTY *adj* having a zigzag pattern
DANCEWEAR *n* clothing suitable for dance practice
DANCEY *adj* of, relating to, or resembling dance music
DANCICAL *n* type of dance show set to pop music
DANCICALS > DANCICAL
DANCIER > DANCEY
DANCIEST > DANCEY
DANCING > DANCE
DANCINGS > DANCE
DANCY *adj* (of music) appropriate for dancing
DANDELION *n* yellow-flowered wild plant
DANDER *n* stroll ▷ *vb* stroll
DANDERED > DANDER
DANDERING > DANDER
DANDERS > DANDER
DANDIACAL *adj* like a dandy

DANDIER > DANDY
DANDIES > DANDY
DANDIEST > DANDY
DANDIFIED > DANDIFY
DANDIFIES > DANDIFY
DANDIFY *vb* dress like or cause to resemble a dandy
DANDILY > DANDY
DANDIPRAT *n* small English coin minted in the 16th century
DANDLE *vb* move (a child) up and down on one's knee
DANDLED > DANDLE
DANDLER > DANDLE
DANDLERS > DANDLE
DANDLES > DANDLE
DANDLING > DANDLE
DANDRIFF *same as* > DANDRUFF
DANDRIFFS > DANDRIFF
DANDRUFF *n* loose scales of dry dead skin shed from the scalp
DANDRUFFS > DANDRUFF
DANDRUFFY *adj* like dandruff
DANDY *n* man who is overconcerned with the elegance of his appearance ▷ *adj* very good
DANDYFUNK *n* ship's biscuit
DANDYISH > DANDY
DANDYISM > DANDY
DANDYISMS > DANDY
DANDYPRAT *n* English coin
DANEGELD *n* tax levied in Anglo-Saxon England to provide protection from Viking invaders
DANEGELDS > DANEGELD
DANEGELT *same as* > DANEGELD
DANEGELTS > DANEGELT
DANELAGH *same as* > DANELAW
DANELAGHS > DANELAGH
DANELAW *n* Danish law in parts of Anglo-Saxon England
DANELAWS > DANELAW
DANEWEED *n* dwarf elder
DANEWEEDS > DANEWEED
DANEWORT *n* dwarf elder
DANEWORTS > DANEWORT
DANG *vb* euphemism for damn, meaning condemn ▷ *adj* euphemism for damn, meaning extreme
DANGED > DANG
DANGER *n* state of being vulnerable to injury, loss, or evil ▷ *vb* in archaic usage, endanger
DANGERED > DANGER
DANGERING > DANGER
DANGEROUS *adj* likely or able to cause injury or harm

DANGERS > DANGER
DANGEST > DANG
DANGING > DANG
DANGLE *vb* hang loosely ▷ *n* act of dangling or something that dangles
DANGLED > DANGLE
DANGLER > DANGLE
DANGLERS > DANGLE
DANGLES > DANGLE
DANGLIER > DANGLE
DANGLIEST > DANGLE
DANGLING > DANGLE
DANGLINGS > DANGLE
DANGLY > DANGLE
DANGS > DANG
DANIO *n* type of tropical freshwater fish
DANIOS > DANIO
DANISH *n* sweet pastry
DANISHES > DANISH
DANK *adj* unpleasantly damp and chilly ▷ *n* unpleasant damp and chilliness
DANKER > DANK
DANKEST > DANK
DANKISH > DANK
DANKLY > DANK
DANKNESS > DANK
DANKS > DANK
DANNEBROG *n* Danish flag
DANNIES > DANNY
DANNY *n* hand (used esp when addressing children)
DANS > DAN
DANSAK *n* type of Indian dish
DANSAKS > DANSAK
DANSEUR *n* male ballet dancer
DANSEURS > DANSEUR
DANSEUSE *n* female ballet dancer
DANSEUSES > DANSEUSE
DANT *vb* intimidate
DANTED > DANT
DANTHONIA *n* type of grass of N temperate regions and S America
DANTING > DANT
DANTON *same as* > DAUNTON
DANTONED > DANTON
DANTONING > DANTON
DANTONS > DANTON
DANTS > DANT
DAP *vb* engage in a type of fly fishing
DAPHNE *n* ornamental Eurasian shrub
DAPHNES > DAPHNE
DAPHNIA *n* type of water flea
DAPHNIAS > DAPHNIA
DAPHNID *n* water flea
DAPHNIDS > DAPHNID
DAPPED > DAP
DAPPER *adj* (of a man) neat in appearance ▷ *n* fisherman or -woman who uses a bobbing bait
DAPPEREST > DAPPER
DAPPERLY > DAPPER

DAPPERS > DAPPER
DAPPING > DAP
DAPPLE *vb* mark or become marked with spots or patches of a different colour ▷ *n* mottled or spotted markings ▷ *adj* marked with dapples or spots
DAPPLED > DAPPLE
DAPPLES > DAPPLE
DAPPLING > DAPPLE
DAPS > DAP
DAPSONE *n* antimicrobial drug
DAPSONES > DAPSONE
DAQUIRI *n* rum cocktail
DAQUIRIS > DAQUIRI
DARAF *n* unit of elastance equal to a reciprocal farad
DARAFS > DARAF
DARB *n* something excellent
DARBAR *n* hall in a Sikh temple
DARBARS > DARBAR
DARBIES *pl n* handcuffs
DARBS > DARB
DARCIES > DARCY
DARCY *n* unit expressing the permeability coefficient of rock
DARCYS > DARCY
DARE *vb* be courageous enough to try (to do something) ▷ *n* challenge to do something risky
DARED > DARE
DAREDEVIL *n* recklessly bold person ▷ *adj* recklessly bold or daring
DAREFUL *adj* daring
DARER > DARE
DARERS > DARE
DARES > DARE
DARESAY *vb* venture to say
DARG *n* day's work
DARGA *same as* > DARGAH
DARGAH *n* tomb of a Muslim saint
DARGAHS > DARGAH
DARGAS > DARGA
DARGLE *n* wooded hollow
DARGLES > DARGLE
DARGS > DARG
DARI *n* variety of sorghum
DARIC *n* gold coin of ancient Persia
DARICS > DARIC
DARING *adj* willing to take risks ▷ *n* courage to do dangerous things
DARINGLY > DARING
DARINGS > DARING
DARIOLE *n* small cup-shaped mould
DARIOLES > DARIOLE
DARIS > DARI
DARK *adj* having little or no light ▷ *n* absence of light ▷ *vb* in archaic usage, darken
DARKED > DARK
DARKEN *vb* make or become dark or darker
DARKENED > DARKEN
DARKENER > DARKEN

DARKENERS > DARKEN
DARKENING > DARKEN
DARKENS > DARKEN
DARKER > DARK
DARKEST > DARK
DARKFIELD *n* as in *darkfield microscope* kind of microscope
DARKING > DARK
DARKISH > DARK
DARKLE *vb* grow dark
DARKLED > DARKLE
DARKLES > DARKLE
DARKLIER > DARK
DARKLIEST > DARK
DARKLING *adj* in the dark or night
DARKLINGS *adv* in darkness
DARKLY > DARK
DARKMANS *n* slang term for night-time
DARKNESS > DARK
DARKNET *n* covert communication network on the internet
DARKNETS > DARKNET
DARKROOM *n* darkened room for processing photographic film
DARKROOMS > DARKROOM
DARKS > DARK
DARKSOME *adj* dark or darkish
DARLING *n* much-loved person ▷ *adj* much-loved
DARLINGLY > DARLING
DARLINGS > DARLING
DARN *vb* mend (a garment) with a series of interwoven stitches ▷ *n* patch of darned work
DARNATION mild form of > DAMNATION
DARNDEST *n* utmost
DARNDESTS > DARNDEST
DARNED *adj* damned
DARNEDER > DARNED
DARNEDEST *a euphemistic word for* > DAMNEDEST
DARNEL *n* weed that grows in grain fields
DARNELS > DARNEL
DARNER > DARN
DARNERS > DARN
DARNEST *same as* > DARNDEST
DARNESTS > DARNEST
DARNING > DARN
DARNINGS > DARN
DARNS > DARN
DAROGHA *n* in India, a manager
DAROGHAS > DAROGHA
DARRAIGN *same as* > DERAIGN
DARRAIGNE *vb* clear from guilt
DARRAIGNS > DARRAIGN
DARRAIN *vb* clear of guilt
DARRAINE *vb* clear of guilt
DARRAINED > DARRAINE
DARRAINES > DARRAINE

DARRAINS > DARRAIN
DARRAYN *vb* clear of guilt
DARRAYNED > DARRAYN
DARRAYNS > DARRAYN
DARRE *vb* archaic spelling of dare
DARRED > DARRE
DARRES > DARRE
DARRING > DARRE
DARSHAN *n* Hindu blessing
DARSHANS > DARSHAN
DART *n* small narrow pointed missile ▷ *vb* move or direct quickly and suddenly
DARTBOARD *n* circular board used as the target in the game of darts
DARTED > DART
DARTER *n* type of aquatic bird
DARTERS > DARTER
DARTING > DART
DARTINGLY > DART
DARTITIS *n* nervous twitching while playing darts
DARTLE *vb* move swiftly
DARTLED > DARTLE
DARTLES > DARTLE
DARTLING > DARTLE
DARTRE *n* skin disease
DARTRES > DARTRE
DARTROUS *adj* having a skin disease
DARTS *n* game in which darts are thrown at a dartboard
DARZI *n* tailor in India
DARZIS > DARZI
DAS > DA
DASH *vb* move quickly ▷ *n* sudden quick movement
DASHBOARD *n* instrument panel in a vehicle
DASHCAM *n* video camera on a vehicle's dashboard
DASHCAMS > DASHCAM
DASHED > DASH
DASHEEN *another name for* > TARO
DASHEENS > DASHEEN
DASHEKI *same as* > DASHIKI
DASHEKIS > DASHEKI
DASHER *n* one of the boards surrounding an ice-hockey rink
DASHERS > DASHER
DASHES > DASH
DASHI *n* clear stock made from dried fish and kelp
DASHIER > DASHY
DASHIEST > DASHY
DASHIKI *n* large loose-fitting buttonless upper garment
DASHIKIS > DASHIKI
DASHING *adj* stylish and attractive
DASHINGLY > DASHING
DASHIS > DASHI
DASHLIGHT *n* light illuminating the dashboard of an automobile

DASHPOT *n* device for damping vibrations
DASHPOTS > DASHPOT
DASHY *adj* showy
DASSIE *n* type of hoofed rodent-like animal
DASSIES > DASSIE
DASTARD *n* contemptible sneaking coward
DASTARDLY *adj* wicked and cowardly
DASTARDS > DASTARD
DASTARDY *n* cowardice
DASYMETER *n* device for measuring density of gases
DASYPOD *n* armadillo
DASYPODS > DASYPOD
DASYURE *n* small marsupial of Australia, New Guinea, and adjacent islands
DASYURES > DASYURE
DATA *n* information consisting of observations, measurements, or facts
DATABANK *n* store of a large amount of information
DATABANKS > DATABANK
DATABASE *n* store of information in a form that can be easily handled by a computer ▷ *vb* put data into a database
DATABASED > DATABASE
DATABASES > DATABASE
DATABLE > DATE
DATABUS *n* pathway transferring data between computer parts
DATABUSES > DATABUS
DATACARD *n* smart card
DATACARDS > DATACARD
DATACOMMS *n* transmission of data
DATAFLOW *n* as in *dataflow architecture* means of arranging computer data processing
DATAGLOVE *n* glove worn to manipulate virtual objects on a computer
DATAGRAM *n* (in computing) self-contained unit of data transmitted in a packet-switched network
DATAGRAMS > DATAGRAM
DATAL *adj* slow-witted ▷ *n* day labour
DATALLER *n* worker paid by the day
DATALLERS > DATALLER
DATALS > DATAL
DATARIA *n* Roman Catholic office
DATARIAS > DATARIA
DATARIES > DATARY
DATARY *n* head of the dataria

DATCHA *same as* > DACHA
DATCHAS > DATCHA
DATE *n* specified day of the month ▷ *vb* mark with the date
DATEABLE > DATE
DATEBOOK *n* list of forthcoming events
DATEBOOKS > DATEBOOK
DATED *adj* old-fashioned
DATEDLY > DATED
DATEDNESS > DATED
DATELESS > DATE
DATELINE *n* information about the place and time an article was written
DATELINED > DATELINE
DATELINES > DATELINE
DATER *n* person who dates
DATERS > DATER
DATES > DATE
DATING *n* any of several techniques for establishing the age of objects
DATINGS > DATING
DATIVAL > DATIVE
DATIVE *adj* denoting a grammatical case ▷ *n* grammatical case
DATIVELY > DATIVE
DATIVES > DATIVE
DATO *n* chief of any of certain Muslim tribes in the Philippine Islands
DATOLITE *n* colourless mineral
DATOLITES > DATOLITE
DATOS > DATO
DATTO *n* Datsun car
DATTOS > DATTO
DATUM *n* single piece of information in the form of a fact or statistic
DATUMS > DATUM
DATURA *n* type of plant
DATURAS > DATURA
DATURIC > DATURA
DATURINE *n* poisonous alkaloid
DATURINES > DATURINE
DAUB *vb* smear or spread quickly or clumsily ▷ *n* crude or badly done painting
DAUBE *n* braised meat stew
DAUBED > DAUB
DAUBER > DAUB
DAUBERIES > DAUBERY
DAUBERS > DAUB
DAUBERY *n* act or an instance of daubing
DAUBES > DAUBE
DAUBIER > DAUB
DAUBIEST > DAUB
DAUBING > DAUB
DAUBINGLY > DAUB
DAUBINGS > DAUB
DAUBRIES > DAUBRY
DAUBRY *n* unskilful painting

DAUBS > DAUB

DAUBY > DAUB

DAUD n lump or chunk of something ⊳ vb (in dialect) whack

DAUDED > DAUD

DAUDING > DAUD

DAUDS > DAUD

DAUGHTER n female child ⊳ adj denoting a cell, chromosome, etc produced by the division of one of its own kind

DAUGHTERS > DAUGHTER

DAULT n foster child

DAULTS > DAULT

DAUNDER vb stroll

DAUNDERED > DAUNDER

DAUNDERS > DAUNDER

DAUNER vb stroll

DAUNERED > DAUNER

DAUNERING > DAUNER

DAUNERS > DAUNER

DAUNT vb intimidate

DAUNTED > DAUNT

DAUNTER > DAUNT

DAUNTERS > DAUNT

DAUNTING adj intimidating or worrying

DAUNTLESS adj fearless

DAUNTON vb dishearten

DAUNTONED > DAUNTON

DAUNTONS > DAUNTON

DAUNTS > DAUNT

DAUPHIN n (formerly) eldest son of the king of France

DAUPHINE n wife of a dauphin

DAUPHINES > DAUPHINE

DAUPHINS > DAUPHIN

DAUR a Scot word for > DARE

DAURED > DAUR

DAURING > DAUR

DAURS > DAUR

DAUT vb fondle

DAUTED > DAUT

DAUTIE n darling

DAUTIES > DAUTIE

DAUTING > DAUT

DAUTS > DAUT

DAVEN vb pray

DAVENED > DAVEN

DAVENING > DAVEN

DAVENPORT n small writing table with drawers

DAVENS > DAVEN

DAVIDIA n Chinese shrub

DAVIDIAS > DAVIDIA

DAVIES > DAVY

DAVIT n crane, usu one of a pair, at a ship's side, for lowering and hoisting a lifeboat

DAVITS > DAVIT

DAVY n miner's safety lamp

DAW n archaic, dialect, or poetic name for a jackdaw ⊳ vb old word for dawn

DAWAH n practice of educating non-Muslims about the message of Islam

DAWAHS > DAWAH

DAWBAKE n foolish or slow-witted person

DAWBAKES > DAWBAKE

DAWBRIES > DAWBRY

DAWBRY n unskilful painting

DAWCOCK n male jackdaw

DAWCOCKS > DAWCOCK

DAWD vb thump

DAWDED > DAWD

DAWDING > DAWD

DAWDLE vb walk slowly, lag behind

DAWDLED > DAWDLE

DAWDLER > DAWDLE

DAWDLERS > DAWDLE

DAWDLES > DAWDLE

DAWDLING n act or instance of lagging behind

DAWDLINGS > DAWDLING

DAWDS > DAWD

DAWED > DAW

DAWEN > DAW

DAWING > DAW

DAWISH > DAW

DAWK same as > DAK

DAWKS > DAWK

DAWN n daybreak ⊳ vb begin to grow light

DAWNED > DAWN

DAWNER vb stroll

DAWNERED > DAWNER

DAWNERING > DAWNER

DAWNERS > DAWNER

DAWNEY adj (of a person) dull or slow

DAWNING > DAWN

DAWNINGS > DAWN

DAWNLIKE > DAWN

DAWNS > DAWN

DAWS > DAW

DAWSONITE n mineral

DAWT vb fondle

DAWTED > DAWT

DAWTIE n darling

DAWTIES > DAWTIE

DAWTING > DAWT

DAWTS > DAWT

DAY n period of 24 hours

DAYAN n senior rabbi, esp one who sits in a religious court

DAYANIM > DAYAN

DAYANS > DAYAN

DAYBED n narrow bed for day use

DAYBEDS > DAYBED

DAYBOAT n small sailing boat with no sleeping accommodation

DAYBOATS > DAYBOAT

DAYBOOK n book in which transactions are recorded as they occur

DAYBOOKS > DAYBOOK

DAYBOY n boy who attends a boarding school but returns home each evening

DAYBOYS > DAYBOY

DAYBREAK n time in the morning when light first appears

DAYBREAKS > DAYBREAK

DAYCARE n care provided during the working day for people who might be at risk if left on their own

DAYCARES > DAYCARE

DAYCATION n day trip to a place

DAYCENTRE n building used for daycare or other welfare services

DAYCH vb thatch

DAYCHED > DAYCH

DAYCHES > DAYCH

DAYCHING > DAYCH

DAYDREAM n pleasant fantasy indulged in while awake ⊳ vb indulge in idle fantasy

DAYDREAMS > DAYDREAM

DAYDREAMT > DAYDREAM

DAYDREAMY adj tending to daydream

DAYFLIES > DAYFLY

DAYFLOWER n type of tropical and subtropical plant with narrow pointed leaves and blue or purplish flowers which wilt quickly

DAYFLY another name for > MAYFLY

DAYGIRL n girl who attends a boarding school but returns home each evening

DAYGIRLS > DAYGIRL

DAYGLO n fluorescent colours

DAYGLOW n fluorescent colours

DAYGLOWS > DAYGLOW

DAYLIGHT n light from the sun

DAYLIGHTS pl n consciousness or wits

DAYLILIES > DAYLILY

DAYLILY n any of various plants having lily-like flowers

DAYLIT > DAYLIGHT

DAYLONG adv lasting the entire day

DAYMARE n bad dream during the day

DAYMARES > DAYMARE

DAYMARK n navigation aid

DAYMARKS > DAYMARK

DAYNT adj dainty ⊳ n thing or condition that is extravagant or best

DAYNTS > DAYNT

DAYPACK n small rucksack

DAYPACKS > DAYPACK

DAYROOM n communal living room in a residential institution

DAYROOMS > DAYROOM

DAYS adv during the day, esp regularly

DAYSACK n rucksack

DAYSACKS > DAYSACK

DAYSAIL vb take a day trip on a sailing boat or yacht

DAYSAILED > DAYSAIL

DAYSAILER same as > DAYSAILOR

DAYSAILOR n small sailing boat with no sleeping accommodation

DAYSAILS > DAYSAIL

DAYSHELL n thistle

DAYSHELLS > DAYSHELL

DAYSIDE n side of a planet nearest the sun

DAYSIDES > DAYSIDE

DAYSMAN n umpire

DAYSMEN > DAYSMAN

DAYSPRING a poetic word for > DAWN

DAYSTAR a poetic word for > SUN

DAYSTARS > DAYSTAR

DAYTALE n day labour

DAYTALER n worker paid by the day

DAYTALERS > DAYTALER

DAYTALES > DAYTALE

DAYTIME n time from sunrise to sunset

DAYTIMES > DAYTIME

DAYWEAR n clothes for everyday or informal wear

DAYWEARS > DAYWEAR

DAYWORK n daytime work

DAYWORKER > DAYWORK

DAYWORKS > DAYWORK

DAZE vb stun, by a blow or shock ⊳ n state of confusion or shock

DAZED > DAZE

DAZEDLY > DAZE

DAZEDNESS > DAZE

DAZER > DAZE

DAZERS > DAZE

DAZES > DAZE

DAZING > DAZE

DAZZLE vb impress greatly ⊳ n bright light that dazzles

DAZZLED > DAZZLE

DAZZLER > DAZZLE

DAZZLERS > DAZZLE

DAZZLES > DAZZLE

DAZZLING > DAZZLE

DAZZLINGS > DAZZLING

DE prep of or from

DEACIDIFY vb removal acid from

DEACON n ordained minister ranking immediately below a priest ⊳ vb make a deacon of

DEACONED > DEACON

DEACONESS n a female member of the laity with duties similar to those of a deacon

DEACONING > DEACON

DEACONRY n office or status of a deacon

DEACONS > DEACON

DEAD adj no longer alive ⊳ n period during which coldness or darkness is most intense ⊳ adv extremely ⊳ vb in archaic usage, die or kill

DEADBEAT n lazy useless person

DEADBEATS
> DEADBEAT

DEADBOLT n bolt operated without a spring

DEADBOLTS
> DEADBOLT

DEADBOY same as
> DEADMAN

DEADBOYS > DEADBOY

DEADED > DEAD

DEADEN vb make less intense

DEADENED > DEADEN

DEADENER > DEADEN

DEADENERS > DEADEN

DEADENING > DEADEN

DEADENS > DEADEN

DEADER n dead person

DEADERS > DEAD

DEADEST > DEAD

DEADEYE n either of two dislike blocks used to tighten a shroud on a boat

DEADEYES > DEADEYE

DEADFALL n type of trap using a heavy weight to crush prey

DEADFALLS
> DEADFALL

DEADHEAD n person who does not pay on a bus, at a game, etc ▷ vb cut off withered flowers from (a plant)

DEADHEADS
> DEADHEAD

DEADHOUSE n mortuary

DEADING > DEAD

DEADLIER > DEADLY

DEADLIEST > DEADLY

DEADLIFT vb lift a weight off the ground and stand up

DEADLIFTS
> DEADLIFT

DEADLIGHT n bull's-eye let into the deck or hull of a vessel to admit light to a cabin

DEADLINE n time limit ▷ vb put a time limit on an action, decision, etc

DEADLINED
> DEADLINE

DEADLINES
> DEADLINE

DEADLOCK n point in a dispute at which no agreement can be reached ▷ vb bring or come to a deadlock

DEADLOCKS
> DEADLOCK

DEADLY adj likely to cause death ▷ adv extremely

DEADMAN n item used in construction

DEADMEN > DEADMAN

DEADNESS > DEAD

DEADPAN adv showing no emotion or expression ▷ adj deliberately emotionless ▷ n deadpan expression or manner

DEADPANS > DEADPAN

DEADS > DEAD

DEADSTOCK n farm equipment

DEADWATER n still water

DEADWOOD n dead trees or branches

DEADWOODS
> DEADWOOD

DEAERATE vb remove air from

DEAERATED
> DEAERATE

DEAERATES
> DEAERATE

DEAERATOR
> DEAERATE

DEAF adj unable to hear

DEAFBLIND adj unable to hear or see

DEAFEN vb make deaf, esp temporarily

DEAFENED > DEAFEN

DEAFENING n excessively loud

DEAFENS > DEAFEN

DEAFER > DEAF

DEAFEST > DEAF

DEAFISH > DEAF

DEAFLY > DEAF

DEAFNESS > DEAF

DEAIR vb remove air from

DEAIRED > DEAIR

DEAIRING > DEAIR

DEAIRS > DEAIR

DEAL n agreement or transaction ▷ vb inflict (a blow) on ▷ adj of fir or pine

DEALATE adj (of insects) having lost their wings after mating ▷ n insect that has shed its wings

DEALATED same as
> DEALATE

DEALATES > DEALATE

DEALATION > DEALATE

DEALBATE adj bleached

DEALER n person whose business involves buying and selling

DEALERS > DEALER

DEALFISH n long thin fish

DEALIGN vb fall out of agreement with (a political party)

DEALIGNED > DEALIGN

DEALIGNS > DEALIGN

DEALING > DEAL

DEALINGS pl n transactions or business relations

DEALMAKER n person who makes deals

DEALS > DEAL

DEALT > DEAL

DEAMINASE n enzyme that breaks down amino compounds

DEAMINATE vb remove one or more amino groups from (a molecule)

DEAMINISE same as
> DEAMINATE

DEAMINIZE same as
> DEAMINATE

DEAN n chief administrative official of a college or university faculty ▷ vb punish (a student) by sending them to the dean

DEANED > DEAN

DEANER n shilling

DEANERIES > DEANERY

DEANERS > DEANER

DEANERY n office or residence of a dean

DEANING > DEAN

DEANS > DEAN

DEANSHIP > DEAN

DEANSHIPS > DEAN

DEAR n someone regarded with affection ▷ adj much-loved

DEARE vb harm

DEARED > DEARE

DEARER > DEAR

DEARES > DEARE

DEAREST n term of affection

DEARESTS > DEAREST

DEARIE same as > DEARY

DEARIES > DEARY

DEARING > DEARE

DEARLING n darling

DEARLINGS
> DEARLING

DEARLY adv very much

DEARN vb hide

DEARNED > DEARN

DEARNESS > DEAR

DEARNFUL adj secret

DEARNING > DEARN

DEARNLY > DEARN

DEARNS > DEARN

DEARS > DEAR

DEARTH n inadequate amount, scarcity

DEARTHS > DEARTH

DEARY n term of affection: now often sarcastic or facetious

DEASH vb remove ash from

DEASHED > DEASH

DEASHES > DEASH

DEASHING > DEASH

DEASIL n motion towards the sun

DEASILS > DEASIL

DEASIUL n motion towards the sun

DEASIULS > DEASIUL

DEASOIL n motion towards the sun

DEASOILS > DEASOIL

DEATH n permanent end of life in a person or animal

DEATHBED n bed where a person is about to die or has just died

DEATHBEDS
> DEATHBED

DEATHBLOW n thing or event that destroys hope

DEATHCARE adj relating to services helping arrange funerals

DEATHCUP n poisonous fungus

DEATHCUPS
> DEATHCUP

DEATHFUL adj murderous

DEATHIER > DEATH

DEATHIEST > DEATH

DEATHLESS adj everlasting, because of fine qualities

DEATHLIER > DEATHLY

DEATHLIKE > DEATH

DEATHLY adv like death ▷ adj resembling death

DEATHS > DEATH

DEATHSMAN n executioner

DEATHSMEN
> DEATHSMAN

DEATHTRAP n building, vehicle, etc, that is considered very unsafe

DEATHWARD adv heading towards death

DEATHY > DEATH

DEAVE vb deafen

DEAVED > DEAVE

DEAVES > DEAVE

DEAVING > DEAVE

DEAW n archaic spelling of dew ▷ vb cover with dew

DEAWED > DEAW

DEAWIE > DEAW

DEAWING > DEAW

DEAWS > DEAW

DEAWY > DEAW

DEB n debutante

DEBACLE n disastrous failure

DEBACLES > DEBACLE

DEBAG vb remove the trousers from (someone) by force

DEBAGGED > DEBAG

DEBAGGING > DEBAG

DEBAGS > DEBAG

DEBAR vb prevent, bar

DEBARK vb remove the bark from (a tree)

DEBARKED > DEBARK

DEBARKER > DEBARK

DEBARKERS > DEBARK

DEBARKING > DEBARK

DEBARKS > DEBARK

DEBARMENT > DEBAR

DEBARRASS vb relieve

DEBARRED > DEBAR

DEBARRING > DEBAR

DEBARS > DEBAR

DEBASE vb lower in value, quality, or character

DEBASED > DEBASE

DEBASER > DEBASE

DEBASERS > DEBASE

DEBASES > DEBASE

DEBASING > DEBASE

DEBATABLE adj not absolutely certain

DEBATABLY
> DEBATABLE

DEBATE n discussion ▷ vb discuss formally

DEBATED > DEBATE

DEBATEFUL adj quarrelsome

DEBATER > DEBATE

DEBATERS > DEBATE

DEBATES > DEBATE

DEBATING n act of debating

DEBATINGS
> DEBATING

DEBAUCH vb make (someone) bad or corrupt ▷ n instance or period of extreme dissipation

DEBAUCHED > DEBAUCH

DEBAUCHEE n man who leads a life of reckless dissipation
DEBAUCHES > DEBAUCH
DEBAUCHES > DEBAUCH
DEBBIER > DEBBY
DEBBIES > DEBBY
DEBBIEST > DEBBY
DEBBY n debutante ▷ adj of, or resembling a debutante
DEBE n tin
DEBEAK vb remove part of the beak of poultry
DEBEAKED > DEBEAK
DEBEAKING > DEBEAK
DEBEAKS > DEBEAK
DEBEARD vb remove the beard from a mussel
DEBEARDED > DEBEARD
DEBEARDS > DEBEARD
DEBEL vb beat in war
DEBELLED > DEBEL
DEBELLING > DEBEL
DEBELS > DEBEL
DEBENTURE n long-term bond bearing fixed interest, issued by a company or a government agency
DEBES > DEBE
DEBILE adj lacking strength
DEBILITY n weakness, infirmity
DEBIT n sum owing entered on the left side of an account ▷ vb charge (an account) with a debt
DEBITED > DEBIT
DEBITING > DEBIT
DEBITOR n person in debt
DEBITORS > DEBITOR
DEBITS > DEBIT
DEBONAIR adj charming and refined
DEBONAIRE adj suave and refined
DEBONE vb remove bones from
DEBONED > DEBONE
DEBONER > DEBONE
DEBONERS > DEBONE
DEBONES > DEBONE
DEBONING > DEBONE
DEBOSH vb debauch
DEBOSHED > DEBOSH
DEBOSHES > DEBOSH
DEBOSHING > DEBOSH
DEBOSS vb carve a design into
DEBOSSED > DEBOSS
DEBOSSES > DEBOSS
DEBOSSING > DEBOSS
DEBOUCH vb move out from a narrow place to a wider one ▷ n outlet or passage, as for the exit of troops
DEBOUCHE same as > DEBOUCH
DEBOUCHED > DEBOUCH
DEBOUCHES > DEBOUCH
DEBRIDE vb remove dead tissue from
DEBRIDED > DEBRIDE
DEBRIDES > DEBRIDE

DEBRIDING > DEBRIDE
DEBRIEF vb receive a report from (a soldier, diplomat, etc) after an event
DEBRIEFED > DEBRIEF
DEBRIEFER > DEBRIEF
DEBRIEFS > DEBRIEF
DEBRIS n fragments of something destroyed
DEBRUISE vb (in heraldry) overlay or partly cover
DEBRUISED > DEBRUISE
DEBRUISES > DEBRUISE
DEBS > DEB
DEBT n something owed, esp money
DEBTED adj in debt
DEBTEE n person owed a debt
DEBTEES > DEBTEE
DEBTLESS > DEBT
DEBTOR n person who owes money
DEBTORS > DEBTOR
DEBTS > DEBT
DEBUD same as > DISBUD
DEBUDDED > DEBUD
DEBUDDING > DEBUD
DEBUDS > DEBUD
DEBUG vb find and remove defects in (a computer program) ▷ n something that locates and removes defects in a device, system, etc
DEBUGGED > DEBUG
DEBUGGER > DEBUG
DEBUGGERS > DEBUG
DEBUGGING n act of debugging
DEBUGS > DEBUG
DEBUNK vb expose the falseness of
DEBUNKED > DEBUNK
DEBUNKER > DEBUNK
DEBUNKERS > DEBUNK
DEBUNKING > DEBUNK
DEBUNKS > DEBUNK
DEBUR vb remove burs from
DEBURR vb remove burrs from
DEBURRED > DEBURR
DEBURRING > DEBURR
DEBURRS > DEBURR
DEBURS > DEBUR
DEBUS vb unload (goods) or (esp of troops) to alight from a motor vehicle
DEBUSED > DEBUS
DEBUSES > DEBUS
DEBUSING > DEBUS
DEBUSSED > DEBUS
DEBUSSES > DEBUS
DEBUSSING > DEBUS
DEBUT n first public appearance of a performer ▷ vb make a debut
DEBUTANT n person making a first appearance in a particular capacity
DEBUTANTE n young upper-class woman being formally presented to society

DEBUTANTS > DEBUTANT
DEBUTED > DEBUT
DEBUTING > DEBUT
DEBUTS > DEBUT
DEBYE n unit of electric dipole moment
DEBYES > DEBYE
DECACHORD n instrument with ten strings
DECAD n ten years
DECADAL > DECADE
DECADE n period of ten years
DECADENCE n deterioration in morality or culture
DECADENCY same as > DECADENCE
DECADENT adj characterized by decay or decline, as in being self-indulgent or morally corrupt ▷ n decadent person
DECADENTS > DECADENT
DECADES > DECADE
DECADS > DECAD
DECAF n decaffeinated coffee ▷ adj decaffeinated
DECAFF n decaffeinated coffee
DECAFFS > DECAFF
DECAFS > DECAF
DECAGON n geometric figure with ten faces
DECAGONAL > DECAGON
DECAGONS > DECAGON
DECAGRAM n ten grams
DECAGRAMS > DECAGRAM
DECAHEDRA n plural form of singular decahedron: solid figure with ten plane faces
DECAL vb transfer (a design) by decalcomania
DECALCIFY vb remove calcium or lime from (bones, teeth, etc)
DECALED > DECAL
DECALING > DECAL
DECALITER same as > DECALITRE
DECALITRE n measure of volume equivalent to 10 litres
DECALLED > DECAL
DECALLING > DECAL
DECALOG same as > DECALOGUE
DECALOGS > DECALOG
DECALOGUE n Ten Commandments
DECALS > DECAL
DECAMETER same as > DECAMETRE
DECAMETRE n unit of length equal to ten metres
DECAMP vb depart secretly or suddenly
DECAMPED > DECAMP
DECAMPING > DECAMP
DECAMPS > DECAMP
DECAN n one of three divisions of a sign of the zodiac

DECANAL adj of or relating to a dean or deanery
DECANALLY > DECANAL
DECANE n liquid alkane hydrocarbon
DECANES > DECANE
DECANI adj to be sung by the decanal side of a choir
DECANOIC adj as in decanoic acid white crystalline insoluble carboxylic acid
DECANS > DECAN
DECANT vb pour (a liquid) from one container to another
DECANTATE vb decant
DECANTED > DECANT
DECANTER n stoppered bottle for wine or spirits
DECANTERS > DECANTER
DECANTING > DECANT
DECANTS > DECANT
DECAPOD n creature, such as a crab, with five pairs of walking limbs ▷ adj of, relating to, or belonging to these creatures
DECAPODAL > DECAPOD
DECAPODAN > DECAPOD
DECAPODS > DECAPOD
DECARB vb decarbonize
DECARBED > DECARB
DECARBING > DECARB
DECARBS > DECARB
DECARE n ten ares or 1000 square metres
DECARES > DECARE
DECASTERE n ten steres
DECASTICH n poem with ten lines
DECASTYLE n portico consisting of ten columns
DECATHLON n athletic contest with ten events
DECAUDATE vb remove the tail from
DECAY vb become weaker or more corrupt ▷ n process of decaying
DECAYABLE > DECAY
DECAYED > DECAY
DECAYER > DECAY
DECAYERS > DECAY
DECAYING > DECAY
DECAYLESS adj immortal
DECAYS > DECAY
DECCIE n decoration
DECCIES > DECCIE
DECEASE n death
DECEASED adj dead ▷ n dead person
DECEASEDS > DECEASED
DECEASES > DECEASE
DECEASING > DECEASE
DECEDENT n deceased person
DECEDENTS > DECEDENT
DECEIT n behaviour intended to deceive
DECEITFUL adj full of deceit

d

DECEITS > DECEIT

DECEIVE vb mislead by lying

DECEIVED > DECEIVE

DECEIVER > DECEIVE

DECEIVERS > DECEIVE

DECEIVES > DECEIVE

DECEIVING > DECEIVE

DECELERON n type of aileron

DECEMVIR n member of a board of ten magistrates in Ancient Rome

DECEMVIRI > DECEMVIR

DECEMVIRS > DECEMVIR

DECENARY adj of or relating to a tithing

DECENCIES pl n generally accepted standards of good behaviour

DECENCY n conformity to the prevailing standards of what is right

DECENNARY same as > DECENARY

DECENNIA > DECENNIUM

DECENNIAL adj lasting for ten years ▷ n tenth anniversary or its celebration

DECENNIUM a less common word for > DECADE

DECENT adj (of a person) polite and morally acceptable

DECENTER vb put out of centre

DECENTERS > DECENTER

DECENTEST > DECENT

DECENTLY > DECENT

DECENTRE vb put out of centre

DECENTRED > DECENTRE

DECENTRES > DECENTRE

DECEPTION n deceiving

DECEPTIVE adj likely or designed to deceive

DECEPTORY adj deceiving

DECERN vb decree or adjudge

DECERNED > DECERN

DECERNING > DECERN

DECERNS > DECERN

DECERTIFY vb withdraw or remove a certificate or certification from (a person, organization, or country)

DECESSION n departure

DECHEANCE n forfeiting

DECIARE n one tenth of an are or 10 square metres

DECIARES > DECIARE

DECIBEL n unit for measuring the intensity of sound

DECIBELS > DECIBEL

DECIDABLE adj able to be decided

DECIDE vb (cause to) reach a decision

DECIDED adj unmistakable

DECIDEDLY > DECIDED

DECIDER n thing that determines who wins a match or championship

DECIDERS > DECIDER

DECIDES > DECIDE

DECIDING > DECIDE

DECIDUA n membrane lining the uterus of some mammals during pregnancy

DECIDUAE > DECIDUA

DECIDUAL > DECIDUA

DECIDUAS > DECIDUA

DECIDUATE > DECIDUA

DECIDUOUS adj (of a tree) shedding its leaves annually

DECIGRAM n tenth of a gram

DECIGRAMS > DECIGRAM

DECILE n one of nine values of a variable divided into ten equal groups

DECILES > DECILE

DECILITER same as > DECILITRE

DECILITRE n measure of volume equivalent to one tenth of a litre

DECILLION n (in Britain, France, and Germany) the number represented as one followed by 60 zeros (10^{60})

DECIMAL n fraction written in the form of a dot followed by one or more numbers ▷ adj relating to or using powers of ten

DECIMALLY > DECIMAL

DECIMALS > DECIMAL

DECIMATE vb destroy or kill a large proportion of

DECIMATED > DECIMATE

DECIMATES > DECIMATE

DECIMATOR > DECIMATE

DECIME n former French coin

DECIMES > DECIME

DECIMETER same as > DECIMETRE

DECIMETRE n unit of length equal to one tenth of a metre

DECIPHER vb work out the meaning of (something illegible or in code)

DECIPHERS > DECIPHER

DECISION n judgment, conclusion, or resolution

DECISIONS > DECISION

DECISIVE adj having a definite influence

DECISORY adj deciding

DECISTERE n tenth of a stere

DECK n area of a ship that forms a floor ▷ vb dress or decorate

DECKCHAIR n folding wooden and canvas chair designed for use outside

DECKED adj having a wooden deck or platform

DECKEL same as > DECKLE

DECKELS > DECKEL

DECKER > DECK

DECKERS > DECK

DECKHAND n seafarer assigned various duties on the deck of a ship

DECKHANDS > DECKHAND

DECKHOUSE n houselike cabin on the deck of a ship

DECKING n wooden platform in a garden

DECKINGS > DECKING

DECKLE n frame used to contain pulp on the mould in the making of handmade paper

DECKLED > DECKLE

DECKLES > DECKLE

DECKLESS adj without a deck

DECKO n look ▷ vb have a look

DECKOED > DECKO

DECKOING > DECKO

DECKOS > DECKO

DECKS > DECK

DECLAIM vb speak loudly and dramatically

DECLAIMED > DECLAIM

DECLAIMER > DECLAIM

DECLAIMS > DECLAIM

DECLARANT n person who makes a declaration

DECLARE vb state firmly and forcefully

DECLARED > DECLARE

DECLARER n person who declares

DECLARERS > DECLARER

DECLARES > DECLARE

DECLARING > DECLARE

DECLASS vb lower in social status or position

DECLASSE adj having lost social standing or status

DECLASSED > DECLASS

DECLASSEE adj (of a woman) having lost social standing or status

DECLASSES > DECLASS

DECLAW vb remove claws from

DECLAWED > DECLAW

DECLAWING > DECLAW

DECLAWS > DECLAW

DECLINAL adj bending down ▷ n action of politely refusing or declining

DECLINALS > DECLINAL

DECLINANT adj heraldry term ▷ n person who is diminishing in luck or wealth

DECLINATE adj (esp of plant parts) descending from the horizontal in a curve

DECLINE vb become smaller, weaker, or less important ▷ n gradual weakening or loss

DECLINED > DECLINE

DECLINER > DECLINE

DECLINERS > DECLINE

DECLINES > DECLINE

DECLINING > DECLINE

DECLINIST n person believing something is in decline

DECLIVITY n downward slope

DECLIVOUS adj steep

DECLUTCH vb disengage the clutch of a motor vehicle

DECLUTTER vb simplify or get rid of mess, disorder, complications, etc

DECO adj as in art deco style of art, jewellery, design, etc

DECOCT vb extract the essence from (a substance) by boiling

DECOCTED > DECOCT

DECOCTING > DECOCT

DECOCTION n extraction by boiling

DECOCTIVE > DECOCT

DECOCTS > DECOCT

DECOCTURE n substance obtained by decoction

DECODABLE adj capable of being decoded

DECODE vb convert from code into ordinary language

DECODED > DECODE

DECODER > DECODE

DECODERS > DECODE

DECODES > DECODE

DECODING n act of decoding

DECODINGS > DECODING

DECOHERER n electrical device

DECOKE n decarbonize

DECOKED > DECOKE

DECOKES > DECOKE

DECOKING > DECOKE

DECOLLATE vb separate (continuous stationery, etc) into individual forms

DECOLLETE adj (of a woman's garment) low-cut ▷ n low-cut neckline

DECOLOR vb bleach

DECOLORED > DECOLOR

DECOLORS > DECOLOR

DECOLOUR vb deprive of colour, as by bleaching

DECOLOURS > DECOLOUR

DECOMMIT vb withdraw from a commitment or agreed course of action

DECOMMITS > DECOMMIT

DECOMPLEX adj repeatedly compound

DECOMPOSE vb be broken down through chemical or bacterial action

DECONGEST vb relieve congestion in

DECONTROL vb free of restraints or controls, esp government controls

DECOR n style in which a room or house is decorated

DECORATE vb make more attractive by adding something ornamental

DECORATED > DECORATE

DECORATES > DECORATE

DECORATOR n person whose profession is the painting and wallpapering of buildings

DECOROUS adj polite, calm, and sensible in behaviour

DECORS > DECOR

DECORUM n polite and socially correct behaviour

DECORUMS > DECORUM

DECOS pl n decorations

DECOUPAGE n art or process of decorating a surface with shapes or illustrations cut from paper, card, etc

DECOUPLE vb separate two joined entities or subsystems

DECOUPLED > DECOUPLE

DECOUPLER > DECOUPLE

DECOUPLES > DECOUPLE

DECOY n person or thing used to lure someone into danger ▷ vb lure away by means of a trick

DECOYED > DECOY

DECOYER > DECOY

DECOYERS > DECOY

DECOYING > DECOY

DECOYS > DECOY

DECREASE vb make or become less ▷ n lessening, reduction

DECREASED > DECREASE

DECREASES > DECREASE

DECREE n law made by someone in authority ▷ vb order by decree

DECREED > DECREE

DECREEING > DECREE

DECREER > DECREE

DECREERS > DECREE

DECREES > DECREE

DECREET n final judgment or sentence of a court

DECREETS > DECREET

DECREMENT n act of decreasing

DECREPIT adj weakened or worn out by age or long use

DECRETAL n papal decree ▷ adj of or relating to a decretal or a decree

DECRETALS > DECRETAL

DECRETIST n law student

DECRETIVE adj of a decree

DECRETORY adj of a decree

DECREW vb archaic word for decrease

DECREWED > DECREW

DECREWING > DECREW

DECREWS > DECREW

DECRIAL > DECRY

DECRIALS > DECRY

DECRIED > DECRY

DECRIER > DECRY

DECRIERS > DECRY

DECRIES > DECRY

DECROWN vb depose

DECROWNED > DECROWN

DECROWNS > DECROWN

DECRY vb express disapproval of

DECRYING > DECRY

DECRYPT vb decode (a message)

DECRYPTED > DECRYPT

DECRYPTS > DECRYPT

DECTET n group of ten musicians

DECTETS > DECTET

DECUBITAL > DECUBITUS

DECUBITI > DECUBITUS

DECUBITUS n posture adopted when lying down

DECUMAN n large wave

DECUMANS > DECUMAN

DECUMBENT adj lying down or lying flat

DECUPLE vb increase by ten times ▷ n amount ten times as large as a given reference ▷ adj increasing tenfold

DECUPLED > DECUPLE

DECUPLES > DECUPLE

DECUPLING > DECUPLE

DECURIA n group of ten

DECURIAS > DECURIA

DECURIES > DECURY

DECURION n local councillor

DECURIONS > DECURION

DECURRENT adj extending down the stem, esp (of a leaf) having the base of the blade extending down the stem as two wings

DECURSION n state of being decurrent

DECURSIVE adj extending downwards

DECURVE vb curve downwards

DECURVED adj bent or curved downwards

DECURVES > DECURVE

DECURVING > DECURVE

DECURY n (in ancient Rome) a body of ten men

DECUSSATE vb cross or cause to cross in the form of the letter X ▷ adj in the form of the letter X

DEDAL same as > DAEDAL

DEDALIAN adj of Daedalus

DEDANS n open gallery at the server's end of a real tennis court

DEDENDA > DEDENDUM

DEDENDUM n radial distance between the pitch circle and root of a gear tooth

DEDENDUMS > DEDENDUM

DEDICANT n person who dedicates

DEDICANTS > DEDICANT

DEDICATE vb commit (oneself or one's time) wholly to a special purpose or cause

DEDICATED adj devoted to a particular purpose or cause

DEDICATEE > DEDICATE

DEDICATES > DEDICATE

DEDICATOR > DEDICATE

DEDIMUS n document authorizing a person to act as a judge

DEDIMUSES > DEDIMUS

DEDUCE vb reach (a conclusion) by reasoning from evidence

DEDUCED > DEDUCE

DEDUCES > DEDUCE

DEDUCIBLE > DEDUCE

DEDUCIBLY > DEDUCE

DEDUCING > DEDUCE

DEDUCT vb subtract

DEDUCTED > DEDUCT

DEDUCTING > DEDUCT

DEDUCTION n deducting

DEDUCTIVE adj of or relating to deduction

DEDUCTS > DEDUCT

DEE a Scot word for > DIE

DEED n something that is done ▷ vb convey or transfer (property) by deed ▷ adj Scots form of dead

DEEDED > DEED

DEEDER > DEED

DEEDEST > DEED

DEEDFUL adj full of exploits

DEEDIER > DEEDY

DEEDIEST > DEEDY

DEEDILY > DEEDY

DEEDING > DEED

DEEDLESS adj without exploits

DEEDS > DEED

DEEDY adj hard-working

DEEING > DEE

DEEJAY n disc jockey ▷ vb work or act as a disc jockey

DEEJAYED > DEEJAY

DEEJAYING n act of deejaying

DEEJAYS > DEEJAY

DEEK interj look at!

DEELY adj as in deely boppers hairband with two bobbing antennae-like attachments

DEEM vb consider, judge

DEEMED > DEEM

DEEMING > DEEM

DEEMS > DEEM

DEEMSTER n title of one of the two justices in the Isle of Man

DEEMSTERS > DEEMSTER

DEEN n din

DEENS > DEEN

DEEP adj extending or situated far down, inwards, backwards, or sideways ▷ n any deep place on land or under water

DEEPEN vb make or become deeper or more intense

DEEPENED > DEEPEN

DEEPENER > DEEPEN

DEEPENERS > DEEPEN

DEEPENING n act of deepening

DEEPENS > DEEPEN

DEEPER > DEEP

DEEPEST > DEEP

DEEPFELT adj sincere

DEEPFROZE vb froze in a freezer

DEEPIE n 3D film

DEEPIES > DEEPIE

DEEPLY > DEEP

DEEPMOST adj deepest

DEEPNESS > DEEP

DEEPS > DEEP

DEEPWATER adj seagoing

DEER n large wild animal, the male of which has antlers

DEERBERRY n huckleberry

DEERE adj serious ▷ n deer

DEERES > DEERE

DEERFLIES > DEERFLY

DEERFLY n insect related to the horsefly

DEERGRASS n type of plant that grows in dense tufts in peat bogs of temperate regions

DEERHORN n horn of a deer

DEERHORNS > DEERHORN

DEERHOUND n very large rough-coated breed of dog of the greyhound type

DEERLET n small deer

DEERLETS > DEERLET

DEERLIKE adj like a deer

DEERS > DEER

DEERSKIN n hide of a deer

DEERSKINS > DEERSKIN

DEERWEED n forage plant

DEERWEEDS > DEERWEED

DEERYARD n gathering place for deer

DEERYARDS > DEERYARD

DEES > DEE

DEET n insect repellent

DEETS > DEET

DEEV n mythical monster

DEEVE vb deafen

DEEVED > DEEVE

DEEVES > DEEVE

DEEVING > DEEVE

DEEVS > DEEV

DEEWAN n chief of a village in India

DEEWANS > DEEWAN

DEF adj very good

DEFACE vb deliberately spoil the appearance of

DEFACED > DEFACE

DEFACER > DEFACE

DEFACERS > DEFACE

DEFACES > DEFACE

DEFACING > DEFACE

DEFAECATE same as > DEFECATE

DEFALCATE vb make wrong use of funds entrusted to one

DEFAME vb attack the good reputation of

DEFAMED > DEFAME

DEFAMER > DEFAME

DEFAMERS > DEFAME

DEFAMES > DEFAME

DEFAMING > DEFAME

DEFAMINGS > DEFAME

DEFANG vb remove the fangs of

DEFANGED > DEFANG

DEFANGING > DEFANG

DEFANGS > DEFANG

DEFAST adj old form of defaced

DEFASTE adj old form of defaced

DEFAT vb remove fat from

DEFATS > DEFAT

DEFATTED > DEFAT

DEFATTING > DEFAT

DEFAULT n failure to do something ▷ vb fail to fulfil an obligation

DEFAULTED > DEFAULT

DEFAULTER n person who defaults

DEFAULTS > DEFAULT

DEFEAT vb win a victory over ▷ n defeating

DEFEATED > DEFEAT

DEFEATER > DEFEAT

DEFEATERS > DEFEAT

DEFEATING > DEFEAT

DEFEATISM n ready acceptance or expectation of defeat

DEFEATIST > DEFEATISM

DEFEATS > DEFEAT

DEFEATURE vb deform

DEFECATE vb discharge waste from the body

DEFECATED > DEFECATE

DEFECATES > DEFECATE

DEFECATOR > DEFECATE

DEFECT n imperfection, blemish ▷ vb desert one's cause or country to join the opposing forces

DEFECTED > DEFECT

DEFECTING > DEFECT

DEFECTION n act or an instance of defecting

DEFECTIVE adj imperfect, faulty

DEFECTOR > DEFECT

DEFECTORS > DEFECT

DEFECTS > DEFECT

DEFENCE n resistance against attack ▷ vb provide with defence

DEFENCED > DEFENCE

DEFENCES > DEFENCE

DEFENCING > DEFENCE

DEFEND vb protect from harm or danger

DEFENDANT n person accused of a crime ▷ adj making a defence

DEFENDED > DEFEND

DEFENDER > DEFEND

DEFENDERS > DEFEND

DEFENDING > DEFEND

DEFENDS > DEFEND

DEFENSE same as > DEFENCE

DEFENSED > DEFENSE

DEFENSES > DEFENSE

DEFENSING > DEFENSE

DEFENSIVE adj intended for defence

DEFER vb delay (something) until a future time

DEFERABLE > DEFER

DEFERENCE n polite and respectful behaviour

DEFERENT adj conveying outwards, down, or away ▷ n type of circle in the Ptolemaic system

DEFERENTS > DEFERENT

DEFERMENT n act of deferring or putting off until another time

DEFERRAL same as > DEFERMENT

DEFERRALS > DEFERRAL

DEFERRED adj withheld over a certain period

DEFERRER > DEFER

DEFERRERS > DEFER

DEFERRING > DEFER

DEFERS > DEFER

DEFFER > DEF

DEFFEST > DEF

DEFFLY archaic form of > DEFTLY

DEFFO interj informal word meaning definitely

DEFI n challenge

DEFIANCE n open resistance or disobedience

DEFIANCES > DEFIANCE

DEFIANT adj marked by resistance or bold opposition, as to authority

DEFIANTLY > DEFIANT

DEFICIENT adj lacking some essential thing or quality

DEFICIT n amount by which a sum of money is too small

DEFICITS > DEFICIT

DEFIED > DEFY

DEFIER > DEFY

DEFIERS > DEFY

DEFIES > DEFY

DEFILADE n protection provided by obstacles against enemy crossfire from the rear, or observation ▷ vb provide protection for by defilade

DEFILADED > DEFILADE

DEFILADES > DEFILADE

DEFILE vb treat (something sacred or important) without respect ▷ n narrow valley or pass

DEFILED > DEFILE

DEFILER > DEFILE

DEFILERS > DEFILE

DEFILES > DEFILE

DEFILING > DEFILE

DEFINABLE > DEFINE

DEFINABLY > DEFINE

DEFINE vb state precisely the meaning of

DEFINED > DEFINE

DEFINER > DEFINE

DEFINERS > DEFINE

DEFINES > DEFINE

DEFINIENS n word or words used to define or give an account of the meaning of another word, as in a dictionary entry

DEFINING > DEFINE

DEFINITE adj firm, clear, and precise ▷ n something that is firm, clear, and precise

DEFINITES > DEFINITE

DEFIS > DEFI

DEFLATE vb (cause to) collapse through the release of air

DEFLATED > DEFLATE

DEFLATER > DEFLATE

DEFLATERS > DEFLATE

DEFLATES > DEFLATE

DEFLATING > DEFLATE

DEFLATION n reduction in economic activity resulting in lower output and investment

DEFLATOR > DEFLATE

DEFLATORS > DEFLATE

DEFLEA vb remove fleas from

DEFLEAED > DEFLEA

DEFLEAING > DEFLEA

DEFLEAS > DEFLEA

DEFLECT vb (cause to) turn aside from a course

DEFLECTED > DEFLECT

DEFLECTOR > DEFLECT

DEFLECTS > DEFLECT

DEFLEX vb turn downwards

DEFLEXED > DEFLEX

DEFLEXES > DEFLEX

DEFLEXING > DEFLEX

DEFLEXION n deflection

DEFLEXURE n act of deflecting

DEFLORATE vb deflower

DEFLOWER vb despoil of beauty, innocence, etc

DEFLOWERS > DEFLOWER

DEFLUENT adj running downwards

DEFLUXION n discharge

DEFO interj informal word meaning definitely

DEFOAM vb remove foam from

DEFOAMED > DEFOAM

DEFOAMER > DEFOAM

DEFOAMERS > DEFOAM

DEFOAMING > DEFOAM

DEFOAMS > DEFOAM

DEFOCUS vb put out of focus

DEFOCUSED > DEFOCUS

DEFOCUSES > DEFOCUS

DEFOG vb clear of vapour

DEFOGGED > DEFOG

DEFOGGER > DEFOG

DEFOGGERS > DEFOG

DEFOGGING > DEFOG

DEFOGS > DEFOG

DEFOLIANT n chemical sprayed or dusted onto trees to cause their leaves to fall, esp to remove cover from an enemy in warfare

DEFOLIATE vb deprive (a plant) of its leaves ▷ adj (of a plant) having shed its leaves

DEFORCE vb withhold (property, esp land) wrongfully or by force from the rightful owner

DEFORCED > DEFORCE

DEFORCER > DEFORCE

DEFORCERS > DEFORCE

DEFORCES > DEFORCE

DEFORCING > DEFORCE

DEFOREST vb clear of trees

DEFORESTS > DEFOREST

DEFORM vb put out of shape or spoil the appearance of

DEFORMED adj disfigured or misshapen

DEFORMER > DEFORM

DEFORMERS > DEFORM

DEFORMING > DEFORM

DEFORMITY n distortion of a body part

DEFORMS > DEFORM

DEFOUL vb defile

DEFOULED > DEFOUL

DEFOULING > DEFOUL

DEFOULS > DEFOUL

DEFRAG vb defragment

DEFRAGGED > DEFRAG

DEFRAGGER > DEFRAG

DEFRAGS > DEFRAG

DEFRAUD vb cheat out of money, property, etc

DEFRAUDED > DEFRAUD

DEFRAUDER > DEFRAUD

DEFRAUDS > DEFRAUD

DEFRAY vb provide money for (costs or expenses)

DEFRAYAL > DEFRAY

DEFRAYALS > DEFRAY

DEFRAYED > DEFRAY

DEFRAYER > DEFRAY
DEFRAYERS > DEFRAY
DEFRAYING > DEFRAY
DEFRAYS > DEFRAY
DEFREEZE *vb* defrost
DEFREEZES
> DEFREEZE
DEFRIEND *vb* remove (a person) from the list of one's friends on a social networking website
DEFRIENDS
> DEFRIEND
DEFROCK *vb* deprive (a priest) of priestly status
DEFROCKED > DEFROCK
DEFROCKS > DEFROCK
DEFROST *vb* make or become free of ice
DEFROSTED > DEFROST
DEFROSTER *n* device by which the de-icing process of a refrigerator is accelerated, usually by circulating the refrigerant without the expansion process
DEFROSTS > DEFROST
DEFROZE > DEFREEZE
DEFROZEN > DEFREEZE
DEFT *adj* quick and skilful in movement
DEFTER > DEFT
DEFTEST > DEFT
DEFTLY > DEFT
DEFTNESS > DEFT
DEFUEL *vb* remove fuel from
DEFUELED > DEFUEL
DEFUELING > DEFUEL
DEFUELLED > DEFUEL
DEFUELS > DEFUEL
DEFUNCT *adj* no longer existing or operative ▷ *n* deceased person
DEFUNCTS > DEFUNCT
DEFUND *vb* stop funds to
DEFUNDED > DEFUND
DEFUNDING > DEFUND
DEFUNDS > DEFUND
DEFUSE *vb* remove the fuse of (an explosive device)
DEFUSED > DEFUSE
DEFUSER > DEFUSE
DEFUSERS > DEFUSE
DEFUSES > DEFUSE
DEFUSING > DEFUSE
DEFUZE *same as* > DEFUSE
DEFUZED > DEFUZE
DEFUZES > DEFUZE
DEFUZING > DEFUZE
DEFY *vb* resist openly and boldly
DEFYING > DEFY
DEG *vb* water (a plant, etc)
DEGAGE *adj* unconstrained in manner
DEGAME *n* tree of South and Central America
DEGAMES > DEGAME
DEGAMI *same as* > DEGAME
DEGAMIS > DEGAMI
DEGARNISH *vb* remove ornament from
DEGAS *vb* remove gas from (a container, vacuum

tube, liquid, adsorbent, etc)
DEGASES > DEGAS
DEGASSED > DEGAS
DEGASSER > DEGAS
DEGASSERS > DEGAS
DEGASSES > DEGAS
DEGASSING > DEGAS
DEGAUSS *vb* demagnetize
DEGAUSSED > DEGAUSS
DEGAUSSER > DEGAUSS
DEGAUSSES > DEGAUSS
DEGEARING *n* process in which a company replaces some or all of its fixed-interest loan stock with ordinary shares
DEGENDER *vb* remove reference to gender from
DEGENDERS > DEGENDER
DEGERM *vb* remove germs from
DEGERMED > DEGERM
DEGERMING > DEGERM
DEGERMS > DEGERM
DEGGED > DEG
DEGGING > DEG
DEGLAZE *vb* dilute meat sediments in (a pan) in order to make a sauce or gravy
DEGLAZED > DEGLAZE
DEGLAZES > DEGLAZE
DEGLAZING > DEGLAZE
DEGOUT *n* disgust ▷ *vb* cover (something) with gouts or drops of something
DEGOUTED > DEGOUT
DEGOUTING > DEGOUT
DEGOUTS > DEGOUT
DEGRADE *vb* reduce to dishonour or disgrace
DEGRADED > DEGRADE
DEGRADER > DEGRADE
DEGRADERS > DEGRADE
DEGRADES > DEGRADE
DEGRADING *adj* causing humiliation
DEGRAS *n* emulsion used for dressing hides
DEGREASE *vb* remove grease from
DEGREASED
> DEGREASE
DEGREASER
> DEGREASE
DEGREASES
> DEGREASE
DEGREE *n* stage in a scale of relative amount or intensity
DEGREED *adj* having a degree
DEGREES > DEGREE
DEGS > DEG
DEGU *n* small S American rodent
DEGUM *vb* remove gum from
DEGUMMED > DEGUM
DEGUMMING > DEGUM
DEGUMS > DEGUM
DEGUS > DEGU
DEGUST *vb* taste, esp with care or relish
DEGUSTATE *same as* > DEGUST

DEGUSTED > DEGUST
DEGUSTING > DEGUST
DEGUSTS > DEGUST
DEHAIR *vb* remove hair
DEHAIRED > DEHAIR
DEHAIRING > DEHAIR
DEHAIRS > DEHAIR
DEHISCE *vb* (of the seed capsules of some plants) to burst open spontaneously
DEHISCED > DEHISCE
DEHISCENT *adj* (of fruits, anthers, etc) opening spontaneously to release seeds or pollen
DEHISCES > DEHISCE
DEHISCING > DEHISCE
DEHORN *vb* remove or prevent the growth of the horns of (cattle, sheep, or goats)
DEHORNED > DEHORN
DEHORNER > DEHORN
DEHORNERS > DEHORN
DEHORNING > DEHORN
DEHORNS > DEHORN
DEHORS *prep* apart from
DEHORT *vb* dissuade
DEHORTED > DEHORT
DEHORTER > DEHORT
DEHORTERS > DEHORT
DEHORTING > DEHORT
DEHORTS > DEHORT
DEHYDRATE *vb* remove water from (food) to preserve it
DEI > DEUS
DEICE *vb* free or be freed of ice
DEICED > DEICE
DEICER > DEICE
DEICERS > DEICE
DEICES > DEICE
DEICIDAL > DEICIDE
DEICIDE *n* act of killing a god
DEICIDES > DEICIDE
DEICING > DEICE
DEICTIC *adj* proving by direct argument ▷ *n* term whose reference depends on the context
DEICTICS > DEICTIC
DEID *a Scot word for* > DEAD
DEIDER > DEID
DEIDEST > DEID
DEIDS > DEID
DEIF *a Scot word for* > DEAF
DEIFER > DEIF
DEIFEST > DEIF
DEIFIC *adj* making divine or exalting to the position of a god
DEIFICAL *adj* divine
DEIFIED > DEIFY
DEIFIER > DEIFY
DEIFIERS > DEIFY
DEIFIES > DEIFY
DEIFORM *adj* having the form or appearance of a god
DEIFY *vb* treat or worship as a god
DEIFYING > DEIFY

DEIGN *vb* agree (to do something), but as if doing someone a favour
DEIGNED > DEIGN
DEIGNING > DEIGN
DEIGNS > DEIGN
DEIL *a Scot word for* > DEVIL
DEILS > DEIL
DEINDEX *vb* cause to become no longer index-linked
DEINDEXED > DEINDEX
DEINDEXES > DEINDEX
DEINOSAUR *n* dinosaur
DEIONISE *same as* > DEIONIZE
DEIONISED
> DEIONISE
DEIONISER
> DEIONISE
DEIONISES
> DEIONISE
DEIONIZE *vb* remove ions from (water, etc), esp by ion exchange
DEIONIZED
> DEIONIZE
DEIONIZER
> DEIONIZE
DEIONIZES
> DEIONIZE
DEIPAROUS *adj* giving birth to a god
DEISEAL *n* motion towards the sun
DEISEALS > DEISEAL
DEISHEAL *n* clockwise motion
DEISHEALS
> DEISHEAL
DEISM *n* belief in God but not in divine revelation
DEISMS > DEISM
DEIST > DEISM
DEISTIC > DEISM
DEISTICAL > DEISM
DEISTS > DEISM
DEITIES > DEITY
DEITY *n* god or goddess
DEIXES > DEIXIS
DEIXIS *n* use or reference of a deictic word
DEIXISES > DEIXIS
DEJECT *vb* dispirit; dishearten ▷ *adj* downcast
DEJECTA *pl n* waste products excreted from the body
DEJECTED *adj* unhappy
DEJECTING > DEJECT
DEJECTION *n* lowness of spirits
DEJECTORY *adj* causing dejection
DEJECTS > DEJECT
DEJEUNE *n* lunch
DEJEUNER *n* lunch
DEJEUNERS
> DEJEUNER
DEJEUNES > DEJEUNE
DEKAGRAM *n* ten grams
DEKAGRAMS > DEKAGRAM
DEKALITER *n* ten litres
DEKALITRE *n* ten litres
DEKALOGY *n* series of ten related works

DEKAMETER n ten meters

DEKAMETRE n ten metres

DEKARE n unit of measurement equal to ten ares

DEKARES > DEKARE

DEKE vb make a deceptive movement ▷ n deceptive movement

DEKED > DEKE

DEKEING > DEKE

DEKES > DEKE

DEKING > DEKE

DEKKO n look ▷ vb have a look

DEKKOED > DEKKO

DEKKOING > DEKKO

DEKKOS > DEKKO

DEL n differential operator

DELAINE n sheer wool or wool and cotton fabric

DELAINES > DELAINE

DELAPSE vb be inherited

DELAPSED > DELAPSE

DELAPSES > DELAPSE

DELAPSING > DELAPSE

DELAPSION n falling down

DELATE vb (formerly) to bring a charge against

DELATED > DELATE

DELATES > DELATE

DELATING > DELATE

DELATION > DELATE

DELATIONS > DELATE

DELATOR > DELATE

DELATORS > DELATE

DELAY vb put off to a later time ▷ n act of delaying

DELAYABLE > DELAY

DELAYED > DELAY

DELAYER > DELAY

DELAYERS > DELAY

DELAYING > DELAY

DELAYS > DELAY

DELE n sign indicating that typeset matter is to be deleted ▷ vb mark (matter to be deleted) with a dele

DELEAD vb remove lead from

DELEADED > DELEAD

DELEADING > DELEAD

DELEADS > DELEAD

DELEAVE vb separate copies

DELEAVED > DELEAVE

DELEAVES > DELEAVE

DELEAVING > DELEAVE

DELEBLE adj able to be deleted

DELECTATE vb delight

DELED > DELE

DELEGABLE > DELEGATE

DELEGACY n elected standing committee at some British universities

DELEGATE n person chosen to represent others, esp at a meeting ▷ vb entrust (duties or powers) to someone

DELEGATED > DELEGATE

DELEGATEE > DELEGATE

DELEGATES > DELEGATE

DELEGATOR > DELEGATE

DELEING > DELE

DELENDA pl n items for deleting

DELES > DELE

DELETABLE > DELETE

DELETE vb remove (something written or printed)

DELETED > DELETE

DELETES > DELETE

DELETING > DELETE

DELETION n act of deleting or fact of being deleted

DELETIONS > DELETION

DELETIVE > DELETE

DELETORY > DELETE

DELF n kind of earthenware

DELFS > DELF

DELFT n type of earthenware

DELFTS > DELFT

DELFTWARE same as > DELFT

DELI n delicatessen

DELIBATE vb taste

DELIBATED > DELIBATE

DELIBATES > DELIBATE

DELIBLE adj able to be deleted

DELICACY n being delicate

DELICATE adj fine or subtle in quality ▷ n delicacy

DELICATES > DELICATE

DELICE n delicacy

DELICES > DELICE

DELICIOUS adj very appealing to taste or smell

DELICT n wrongful act for which the person injured has the right to a civil remedy

DELICTS > DELICT

DELIGHT n (source of) great pleasure ▷ vb please greatly

DELIGHTED adj greatly pleased ▷ sentence substitute I should be delighted to!

DELIGHTER > DELIGHT

DELIGHTS > DELIGHT

DELIME vb remove lime from

DELIMED > DELIME

DELIMES > DELIME

DELIMING > DELIME

DELIMIT vb mark or lay down the limits of

DELIMITED > DELIMIT

DELIMITER > DELIMIT

DELIMITS > DELIMIT

DELINEATE vb show by drawing

DELINK vb remove or break a link

DELINKED > DELINK

DELINKING > DELINK

DELINKS > DELINK

DELIQUIUM n loss of consciousness

DELIRIA > DELIRIUM

DELIRIANT > DELIRIUM

DELIRIOUS adj wildly excited

DELIRIUM n state of excitement and confusion

DELIRIUMS > DELIRIUM

DELIS > DELI

DELISH adj delicious

DELIST vb remove from a list

DELISTED > DELIST

DELISTING > DELIST

DELISTS > DELIST

DELIVER vb carry (goods etc) to a destination

DELIVERED > DELIVER

DELIVERER > DELIVER

DELIVERLY adv quickly

DELIVERS > DELIVER

DELIVERY n delivering

DELL n small wooded hollow

DELLIER > DELLY

DELLIES > DELLY

DELLIEST > DELLY

DELLS > DELL

DELLY n delicatessen ▷ adj full of dells

DELO an informal word for > DELEGATE

DELOPE vb shoot into the air

DELOPED > DELOPE

DELOPES > DELOPE

DELOPING > DELOPE

DELOS > DELO

DELOUSE vb rid (a person or animal) of lice

DELOUSED > DELOUSE

DELOUSER > DELOUSE

DELOUSERS > DELOUSE

DELOUSES > DELOUSE

DELOUSING > DELOUSE

DELPH n kind of earthenware

DELPHIC adj obscure or ambiguous

DELPHIN n fatty substance from dolphin oil

DELPHINIA n plural form of singular delphinium: garden plant with blue, white or pink flowers

DELPHINS > DELPHIN

DELPHS > DELPH

DELS > DEL

DELT n deltoid muscle

DELTA n fourth letter in the Greek alphabet

DELTAIC > DELTA

DELTAS > DELTA

DELTIC > DELTA

DELTOID n muscle acting to raise the arm ▷ adj shaped like a Greek capital delta

DELTOIDEI n deltoid

DELTOIDS > DELTOID

DELTS > DELT

DELUBRA > DELUBRUM

DELUBRUM n shrine

DELUBRUMS > DELUBRUM

DELUDABLE > DELUDE

DELUDE vb deceive

DELUDED > DELUDE

DELUDER > DELUDE

DELUDERS > DELUDE

DELUDES > DELUDE

DELUDING > DELUDE

DELUGE n great flood ▷ vb flood

DELUGED > DELUGE

DELUGES > DELUGE

DELUGING > DELUGE

DELUNDUNG n spotted mammal

DELUSION n mistaken idea or belief

DELUSIONS > DELUSION

DELUSIVE > DELUSION

DELUSORY > DELUSION

DELUSTER same as > DELUSTRE

DELUSTERS > DELUSTER

DELUSTRE vb remove the lustre from

DELUSTRED > DELUSTRE

DELUSTRES > DELUSTRE

DELUXE adj rich, elegant, superior, or sumptuous

DELVE vb research deeply (for information)

DELVED > DELVE

DELVER > DELVE

DELVERS > DELVE

DELVES > DELVE

DELVING > DELVE

DEMAGOG same as > DEMAGOGUE

DEMAGOGED > DEMAGOG

DEMAGOGIC adj of, characteristic of, relating to, or resembling a demagogue

DEMAGOGS > DEMAGOG

DEMAGOGUE n political agitator who appeals to the prejudice and passions of the mob

DEMAGOGY n demagoguery

DEMAIN n demesne

DEMAINE n demesne

DEMAINES > DEMAINE

DEMAINS > DEMAIN

DEMAN vb reduce the workforce of (a plant, industry, etc)

DEMAND vb request forcefully ▷ n forceful request

DEMANDANT n (formerly) the plaintiff in an action relating to real property

DEMANDED > DEMAND

DEMANDER > DEMAND

DEMANDERS > DEMAND

DEMANDING adj requiring a lot of time or effort

DEMANDS > DEMAND

DEMANNED > DEMAN

DEMANNING > DEMAN

DEMANS > DEMAN
DEMANTOID n bright green variety of andradite garnet
DEMARCATE vb mark, fix, or draw the boundaries, limits, etc, of
DEMARCHE n move, step, or manoeuvre, esp in diplomatic affairs
DEMARCHES
> DEMARCHE
DEMARK vb demarcate
DEMARKED > DEMARK
DEMARKET vb discourage consumers from buying
DEMARKETS
> DEMARKET
DEMARKING > DEMARK
DEMARKS > DEMARK
DEMAST vb remove the mast from
DEMASTED > DEMAST
DEMASTING > DEMAST
DEMASTS > DEMAST
DEMAYNE n demesne
DEMAYNES > DEMAYNE
DEME n (in preclassical Greece) the territory inhabited by a tribe
DEMEAN vb lower (oneself) in dignity, status, or character
DEMEANE n demesne
DEMEANED > DEMEAN
DEMEANES > demesne
DEMEANING > DEMEAN
DEMEANOR same as
> DEMEANOUR
DEMEANORS
> DEMEANOUR
DEMEANOUR n way a person behaves
DEMEANS > DEMEAN
DEMENT vb deteriorate mentally, esp because of old age
DEMENTATE vb deteriorate mentally
DEMENTED adj driven mad
DEMENTI n denial
DEMENTIA n state of serious mental deterioration
DEMENTIAL
> DEMENTIA
DEMENTIAS
> DEMENTIA
DEMENTING > DEMENT
DEMENTIS > DEMENTI
DEMENTS > DEMENT
DEMERARA n brown crystallized cane sugar from the Caribbean and nearby countries
DEMERARAN adj from Demerara
DEMERARAS
> DEMERARA
DEMERGE vb separate a company from another
DEMERGED > DEMERGE
DEMERGER n separation of two or more companies which have previously been merged
DEMERGERS > DEMERGER

DEMERGES > DEMERGE
DEMERGING > DEMERGE
DEMERIT n fault, disadvantage ▷ vb deserve
DEMERITED > DEMERIT
DEMERITS > DEMERIT
DEMERSAL adj living or occurring on the bottom of a sea or a lake
DEMERSE vb immerse
DEMERSED > DEMERSE
DEMERSES > DEMERSE
DEMERSING > DEMERSE
DEMERSION > DEMERSE
DEMES > DEME
DEMESNE n land surrounding a house
DEMESNES > DEMESNE
DEMETON n insecticide
DEMETONS > DEMETON
DEMIC adj of population
DEMIES > DEMY
DEMIGOD n being who is part mortal, part god
DEMIGODS > DEMIGOD
DEMIJOHN n large bottle with a short neck, often encased in wicker
DEMIJOHNS
> DEMIJOHN
DEMILUNE n outwork in front of a fort, shaped like a crescent moon
DEMILUNES
> DEMILUNE
DEMIMONDE n (esp in the 19th century) class of women considered to be outside respectable society
DEMINER n person who removes mines
DEMINERS > DEMINER
DEMINING n act of removing mines
DEMININGS
> DEMINING
DEMIPIQUE n low pique on a saddle
DEMIREP n woman of bad repute, esp a prostitute
DEMIREPS > DEMIREP
DEMISABLE > DEMISE
DEMISE n eventual failure (of something successful) ▷ vb transfer for a limited period
DEMISED > DEMISE
DEMISES > DEMISE
DEMISING > DEMISE
DEMISS adj humble
DEMISSION n relinquishment of or abdication from an office, responsibility, etc
DEMISSIVE adj humble
DEMISSLY > DEMISS
DEMIST vb remove condensation from (a windscreen)
DEMISTED > DEMIST
DEMISTER n device in a motor vehicle to free the windscreen of condensation
DEMISTERS > DEMISTER

DEMISTING n act of removing condensation from (a windscreen)
DEMISTS > DEMIST
DEMIT vb resign (an office, position, etc)
DEMITASSE n small cup used to serve coffee, esp after a meal
DEMITS > DEMIT
DEMITTED > DEMIT
DEMITTING > DEMIT
DEMIURGE n (in the philosophy of Plato) the creator of the universe
DEMIURGES
> DEMIURGE
DEMIURGIC
> DEMIURGE
DEMIURGUS n demiurge
DEMIVEG n person who eats poultry and fish, but no red meat ▷ adj denoting a person who eats poultry and fish, but no red meat
DEMIVEGES > DEMIVEG
DEMIVOLT n half turn on the hind legs
DEMIVOLTE same as
> DEMIVOLT
DEMIVOLTS
> DEMIVOLT
DEMIWORLD n demimonde
DEMO n demonstration, organized expression of public opinion ▷ vb demonstrate
DEMOB vb demobilize
DEMOBBED > DEMOB
DEMOBBING > DEMOB
DEMOBS > DEMOB
DEMOCRACY n government by the people or their elected representatives
DEMOCRAT n advocate of democracy
DEMOCRATS
> DEMOCRAT
DEMOCRATY n democracy
DEMODE adj out of fashion
DEMODED adj out of fashion
DEMOED > DEMO
DEMOI > DEMOS
DEMOING > DEMO
DEMOLISH vb knock down or destroy (a building)
DEMOLOGY n demography
DEMON n evil spirit
DEMONESS n female demon
DEMONIAC adj appearing to be possessed by a devil ▷ n person possessed by an evil spirit or demon
DEMONIACS
> DEMONIAC
DEMONIAN adj of a demon
DEMONIC adj evil
DEMONICAL adj demonic

DEMONISE same as
> DEMONIZE
DEMONISED
> DEMONISE
DEMONISES
> DEMONISE
DEMONISM n study of demons
DEMONISMS
> DEMONISM
DEMONIST > DEMONISM
DEMONISTS
> DEMONISM
DEMONIZE vb make into a demon
DEMONIZED
> DEMONIZE
DEMONIZES
> DEMONIZE
DEMONRIES > DEMON
DEMONRY > DEMON
DEMONS > DEMON
DEMONYM n name for the inhabitants of a place
DEMONYMS > DEMONYM
DEMOS n people of a nation regarded as a political unit
DEMOSCENE n computer art subculture
DEMOSES > DEMOS
DEMOTE vb reduce in status or rank
DEMOTED > DEMOTE
DEMOTES > DEMOTE
DEMOTIC adj of the common people ▷ n demotic script of ancient Egypt
DEMOTICS > DEMOTIC
DEMOTING > DEMOTE
DEMOTION > DEMOTE
DEMOTIONS > DEMOTE
DEMOTIST > DEMOTIC
DEMOTISTS > DEMOTIC
DEMOUNT vb remove (a motor, gun, etc) from its mounting or setting
DEMOUNTED > DEMOUNT
DEMOUNTS > DEMOUNT
DEMPSTER same as
> DEEMSTER
DEMPSTERS
> DEMPSTER
DEMPT > DEEM
DEMULCENT adj soothing ▷ n drug or agent that soothes the irritation of inflamed or injured skin surfaces
DEMULSIFY vb undergo or cause to undergo a process in which an emulsion is permanently broken down into its constituents
DEMUR vb raise objections or show reluctance ▷ n act of demurring
DEMURE adj quiet, reserved, and rather shy ▷ vb archaic word meaning to look demure
DEMURED > DEMURE
DEMURELY > DEMURE
DEMURER > DEMURE
DEMURES > DEMURE
DEMUREST > DEMURE

d

DEMURING > DEMURE

DEMURRAGE n delaying of a ship, railway wagon, etc, caused by the charterer's failure to load, unload, etc, before the time of scheduled departure

DEMURRAL n act of demurring

DEMURRALS > DEMURRAL

DEMURRED > DEMUR

DEMURRER n any objection raised

DEMURRERS > DEMURRER

DEMURRING > DEMUR

DEMURS > DEMUR

DEMY n size of printing paper, 17½ by 22½ inches (444.5 × 571.5 mm)

DEMYSHIP n scholarship at Oxford University

DEMYSHIPS > DEMY

DEMYSTIFY vb remove the mystery from

DEMYTHIFY vb remove the mythical characteristics from

DEN n home of a wild animal ▷ vb live in or as if in a den

DENAR n monetary unit of North Macedonia, divided into 100 deni

DENARI > DENAR

DENARIES > DENARY

DENARII > DENARIUS

DENARIUS n ancient Roman silver coin, often called a penny in translation

DENARS > DENAR

DENARY same as > DENARIUS

DENATURE vb change the nature of

DENATURED > DENATURE

DENATURES > DENATURE

DENAY vb old form of deny

DENAYED > DENAY

DENAYING > DENAY

DENAYS > DENAY

DENAZIFY vb free or declare (people, institutions, etc) freed from Nazi influence or ideology

DENCH adj excellent

DENDRIMER n chemical compound with treelike molecular structure

DENDRITE n threadlike extension of a nerve cell

DENDRITES > DENDRITE

DENDRITIC > DENDRITE

DENDROID adj freely branching ▷ n something that branches freely

DENDROIDS > DENDROID

DENDRON same as > DENDRITE

DENDRONS > DENDRON

DENE n narrow wooded valley

DENERVATE vb deprive (a tissue or organ) of its nerve supply

DENES > DENE

DENET vb remove from the former Net Book Agreement

DENETS > DENET

DENETTED > DENET

DENETTING > DENET

DENGUE n viral disease transmitted by mosquitoes

DENGUES > DENGUE

DENI n monetary unit of North Macedonia

DENIABLE adj able to be denied

DENIABLY > DENIABLE

DENIAL n statement that something is not true

DENIALIST n person who refuses to believe an established fact

DENIALS > DENIAL

DENIED > DENY

DENIER n unit of weight used to measure the fineness of nylon or silk

DENIERS > DENIER

DENIES > DENY

DENIGRATE vb criticize unfairly

DENIM n hard-wearing cotton fabric, usu blue

DENIMED adj wearing denim

DENIMS pl n jeans or overalls made of denim

DENIS > DENI

DENITRATE vb undergo or cause to undergo a process in which a compound loses a nitro or nitrate group, nitrogen dioxide, or nitric acid

DENITRIFY vb undergo or cause to undergo loss or removal of nitrogen compounds or nitrogen

DENIZEN n inhabitant ▷ vb make a denizen

DENIZENED > DENIZEN

DENIZENS > DENIZEN

DENNED > DEN

DENNET n carriage for one horse

DENNETS > DENNET

DENNING > DEN

DENOMINAL adj formed from a noun

DENOTABLE > DENOTE

DENOTATE vb denote

DENOTATED > DENOTATE

DENOTATES > DENOTATE

DENOTE vb be a sign of

DENOTED > DENOTE

DENOTES > DENOTE

DENOTING > DENOTE

DENOTIVE > DENOTE

DENOUNCE vb speak vehemently against

DENOUNCED > DENOUNCE

DENOUNCER > DENOUNCE

DENOUNCES > DENOUNCE

DENS > DEN

DENSE adj closely packed

DENSELY > DENSE

DENSENESS > DENSE

DENSER > DENSE

DENSEST > DENSE

DENSIFIED > DENSIFY

DENSIFIER > DENSIFY

DENSIFIES > DENSIFY

DENSIFY vb make or become dense

DENSITIES > DENSITY

DENSITY n degree to which something is filled or occupied

DENT n hollow in the surface of something, made by hitting it ▷ vb make a dent in

DENTAL adj of teeth or dentistry ▷ n dental consonant

DENTALIA > DENTALIUM

DENTALISE same as > DENTALIZE

DENTALITY n use of teeth in pronouncing words

DENTALIUM n type of mollusc

DENTALIZE vb pronounce (a consonant) with the tip of one's tongue against the upper front teeth

DENTALLY > DENTAL

DENTALS > DENTAL

DENTARIA n plant of the crucifer family

DENTARIAS > DENTARIA

DENTARIES > DENTARY

DENTARY n lower jawbone with teeth

DENTATE adj having teeth or toothlike notches

DENTATED adj having teeth

DENTATELY > DENTATE

DENTATION n state or condition of being dentate

DENTED > DENT

DENTEL n architectural ornament

DENTELLE n lacelike ornamentation on a book

DENTELLES > DENTELLE

DENTELS > DENTEL

DENTEX n large predatory fish

DENTEXES > DENTEX

DENTICARE n publicly funded dental care

DENTICLE n small tooth or toothlike part, such as any of the placoid scales of sharks

DENTICLES > DENTICLE

DENTIFORM adj shaped like a tooth

DENTIL n architectural ornament

DENTILED > DENTIL

DENTILS > DENTIL

DENTIN same as > DENTINE

DENTINAL > DENTINE

DENTINE n hard dense tissue forming the bulk of a tooth

DENTINES > DENTINE

DENTING > DENT

DENTINS > DENTIN

DENTIST n person qualified to practise dentistry

DENTISTRY n branch of medicine concerned with the teeth and gums

DENTISTS > DENTIST

DENTITION n typical arrangement of teeth in a species

DENTOID adj resembling a tooth

DENTS > DENT

DENTULOUS adj having teeth

DENTURAL > DENTURE

DENTURE n false tooth

DENTURES > DENTURE

DENTURISM n practice of making and fitting dentures

DENTURIST n person who makes dentures

DENUDATE adj denuded ▷ vb denude

DENUDATED > DENUDATE

DENUDATES > DENUDATE

DENUDE vb remove the covering or protection from

DENUDED > DENUDE

DENUDER > DENUDE

DENUDERS > DENUDE

DENUDES > DENUDE

DENUDING > DENUDE

DENY vb declare to be untrue

DENYING > DENY

DENYINGLY > DENY

DEODAND n thing forfeited to charity because it has caused a death

DEODANDS > DEODAND

DEODAR n Himalayan cedar with drooping branches

DEODARA same as > DEODAR

DEODARAS > DEODARA

DEODARS > DEODAR

DEODATE n offering to God

DEODATES > DEODATE

DEODORANT n substance applied to the body to mask the smell of perspiration

DEODORISE same as > DEODORIZE

DEODORIZE vb remove or disguise the smell of

DEONTIC *n* ethical concept such as obligation or permissibility
DEONTICS > DEONTIC
DEORBIT *vb* go out of orbit
DEORBITED > DEORBIT
DEORBITS > DEORBIT
DEOXIDATE *vb* remove oxygen atoms from
DEOXIDISE *same as* > DEOXIDIZE
DEOXIDIZE *vb* remove oxygen atoms from (a compound, molecule, etc)
DEOXY *adj* having less oxygen than a specified related compound
DEP *n* small shop where newspapers, sweets, soft drinks, etc are sold
DEPAINT *vb* depict
DEPAINTED > DEPAINT
DEPAINTS > DEPAINT
DEPANNEUR *n* (in Quebec) a convenience store
DEPART *vb* leave
DEPARTED *adj* dead ▷ *n* dead person
DEPARTEDS > DEPARTED
DEPARTEE > DEPART
DEPARTEES > DEPART
DEPARTER > DEPART
DEPARTERS > DEPART
DEPARTING > DEPART
DEPARTS > DEPART
DEPARTURE *n* act of departing
DEPASTURE *vb* graze or denude by grazing (a pasture, esp a meadow specially grown for the purpose)
DEPECHE *n* message ▷ *vb* dispatch; rid oneself of
DEPECHED > DEPECHE
DEPECHES > DEPECHE
DEPECHING > DEPECHE
DEPEINCT *vb* paint
DEPEINCTS > DEPEINCT
DEPEND *vb* put trust (in)
DEPENDANT *same as* > DEPENDENT
DEPENDED > DEPEND
DEPENDENT *adj* depending on someone or something ▷ *n* element in a phrase or clause that is not the governor
DEPENDING > DEPEND
DEPENDS > DEPEND
DEPEOPLE *vb* reduce population
DEPEOPLED > DEPEOPLE
DEPEOPLES > DEPEOPLE
DEPERM *vb* demagnetize (a ship or submarine)
DEPERMED > DEPERM
DEPERMING > DEPERM
DEPERMS > DEPERM
DEPICT *vb* produce a picture of

DEPICTED > DEPICT
DEPICTER > DEPICT
DEPICTERS > DEPICT
DEPICTING > DEPICT
DEPICTION > DEPICT
DEPICTIVE > DEPICT
DEPICTOR > DEPICT
DEPICTORS > DEPICT
DEPICTS > DEPICT
DEPICTURE *a less common word for* > DEPICT
DEPIGMENT *vb* reduce or remove the normal pigmentation of (the skin)
DEPILATE *vb* remove the hair from
DEPILATED > DEPILATE
DEPILATES > DEPILATE
DEPILATOR > DEPILATE
DEPLANE *vb* disembark from an aeroplane
DEPLANED > DEPLANE
DEPLANES > DEPLANE
DEPLANING > DEPLANE
DEPLENISH *vb* deprive of contents, such as furniture, stock, etc
DEPLETE *vb* use up
DEPLETED > DEPLETE
DEPLETER > DEPLETE
DEPLETERS > DEPLETE
DEPLETES > DEPLETE
DEPLETING > DEPLETE
DEPLETION > DEPLETE
DEPLETIVE > DEPLETE
DEPLETORY > DEPLETE
DEPLORE *vb* condemn strongly
DEPLORED > DEPLORE
DEPLORER > DEPLORE
DEPLORERS > DEPLORE
DEPLORES > DEPLORE
DEPLORING > DEPLORE
DEPLOY *vb* get (troops or resources) ready for immediate action
DEPLOYED > DEPLOY
DEPLOYER > DEPLOY
DEPLOYERS > DEPLOY
DEPLOYING > DEPLOY
DEPLOYS > DEPLOY
DEPLUME *vb* deprive of feathers
DEPLUMED > DEPLUME
DEPLUMES > DEPLUME
DEPLUMING > DEPLUME
DEPOLISH *vb* remove the polish from
DEPONE *vb* declare (something) under oath
DEPONED > DEPONE
DEPONENT *n* person who makes a statement on oath ▷ *adj* having a passive form but active meaning
DEPONENTS > DEPONENT
DEPONES > DEPONE
DEPONING > DEPONE
DEPORT *vb* remove forcibly from a country
DEPORTED > DEPORT

DEPORTEE *n* person deported or awaiting deportation
DEPORTEES > DEPORTEE
DEPORTER > DEPORT
DEPORTERS > DEPORT
DEPORTING > DEPORT
DEPORTS > DEPORT
DEPOSABLE > DEPOSE
DEPOSAL *n* deposition; giving of testimony under oath
DEPOSALS > DEPOSAL
DEPOSE *vb* remove from an office or position of power
DEPOSED > DEPOSE
DEPOSER > DEPOSE
DEPOSERS > DEPOSE
DEPOSES > DEPOSE
DEPOSING > DEPOSE
DEPOSIT *vb* put down ▷ *n* sum of money paid into a bank account
DEPOSITED > DEPOSIT
DEPOSITOR *n* person who places or has money on deposit in a bank or similar organization
DEPOSITS > DEPOSIT
DEPOT *n* building where goods or vehicles are kept when not in use ▷ *adj* (of a drug) designed for gradual release
DEPOTS > DEPOT
DEPRAVE *vb* make morally bad
DEPRAVED *adj* morally bad
DEPRAVER > DEPRAVE
DEPRAVERS > DEPRAVE
DEPRAVES > DEPRAVE
DEPRAVING > DEPRAVE
DEPRAVITY *n* moral corruption
DEPRECATE *vb* express disapproval of
DEPREDATE *vb* plunder or destroy
DEPREHEND *vb* apprehend
DEPRENYL *n* drug combating effects of ageing
DEPRENYLS > DEPRENYL
DEPRESS *vb* make sad
DEPRESSED *adj* lower than the surrounding surface
DEPRESSES > DEPRESS
DEPRESSOR *n* person or thing that depresses
DEPRIME *vb* remove the primer from a device
DEPRIMED > DEPRIME
DEPRIMES > DEPRIME
DEPRIMING > DEPRIME
DEPRIVAL > DEPRIVE
DEPRIVALS > DEPRIVE
DEPRIVE *vb* prevent from (having or enjoying)
DEPRIVED *adj* lacking adequate living conditions, education, etc
DEPRIVER > DEPRIVE

DEPRIVERS > DEPRIVE
DEPRIVES > DEPRIVE
DEPRIVING > DEPRIVE
DEPROGRAM *vb* free someone from indoctrination
DEPS > DEP
DEPSIDE *n* organic chemical compound
DEPSIDES > DEPSIDE
DEPTH *n* distance downwards, backwards, or inwards
DEPTHLESS *adj* immeasurably deep
DEPTHS > DEPTH
DEPURANT *adj* purifying
DEPURANTS > DEPURANT
DEPURATE *vb* cleanse or purify or to be cleansed or purified
DEPURATED > DEPURATE
DEPURATES > DEPURATE
DEPURATOR > DEPURATE
DEPUTABLE > DEPUTE
DEPUTE *vb* appoint (someone) to act on one's behalf ▷ *n* deputy
DEPUTED > DEPUTE
DEPUTES > DEPUTE
DEPUTIES > DEPUTY
DEPUTING > DEPUTE
DEPUTISE *same as* > DEPUTIZE
DEPUTISED > DEPUTISE
DEPUTISES > DEPUTISE
DEPUTIZE *vb* act as deputy
DEPUTIZED > DEPUTIZE
DEPUTIZES > DEPUTIZE
DEPUTY *n* person appointed to act on behalf of another
DEQUEUE *vb* remove (an item) from a queue of computing tasks
DEQUEUED > DEQUEUE
DEQUEUES > DEQUEUE
DEQUEUING > DEQUEUE
DERACINE *adj* uprooted from their usual environment ▷ *n* person who has been uprooted from their usual environment
DERACINES > DERACINE
DERAIGN *vb* contest (a claim, suit, etc)
DERAIGNED > DERAIGN
DERAIGNS > DERAIGN
DERAIL *vb* cause (a train) to go off the rails
DERAILED > DERAIL
DERAILER *same as* > DERAIL
DERAILERS > DERAILER
DERAILING > DERAIL
DERAILS > DERAIL

DERANGE vb disturb the order or arrangement of
DERANGED > DERANGE
DERANGER > DERANGE
DERANGERS > DERANGE
DERANGES > DERANGE
DERANGING > DERANGE
DERAT vb remove rats from
DERATE vb assess the value of some types of property at a lower rate than others for local taxation
DERATED > DERATE
DERATES > DERATE
DERATING > DERATE
DERATINGS > DERATE
DERATION vb end rationing of (food, petrol, etc)
DERATIONS > DERATION
DERATS > DERAT
DERATTED > DERAT
DERATTING > DERAT
DERAY vb old word meanng go mad
DERAYED > DERAY
DERAYING > DERAY
DERAYS > DERAY
DERBIES > DERBY
DERBY n bowler hat
DERE vb injure
DERECHO n long, fast-moving line of severe storms
DERECHOS > DERECHO
DERED > DERE
DERELICT adj unused and falling into ruins ▷ n social outcast, vagrant
DERELICTS
  > DERELICT
DEREPRESS vb induce operation of gene
DERES > DERE
DERHAM same as
  > DIRHAM
DERHAMS > DERHAM
DERIDE vb treat with contempt or ridicule
DERIDED > DERIDE
DERIDER > DERIDE
DERIDERS > DERIDE
DERIDES > DERIDE
DERIDING > DERIDE
DERIG vb remove equipment from
DERIGGED > DERIG
DERIGGING > DERIG
DERIGS > DERIG
DERING > DERE
DERINGER same as
  > DERRINGER
DERINGERS
  > DERRINGER
DERISIBLE adj subject to or deserving of derision
DERISION n act of deriding
DERISIONS
  > DERISION
DERISIVE adj mocking, scornful
DERISORY adj too small or inadequate to be considered seriously

DERIVABLE > DERIVE
DERIVABLY > DERIVE
DERIVATE n derivative ▷ vb derive (something)
DERIVATED
  > DERIVATE
DERIVATES
  > DERIVATE
DERIVE vb take or develop (from)
DERIVED > DERIVE
DERIVER > DERIVE
DERIVERS > DERIVE
DERIVES > DERIVE
DERIVING > DERIVE
DERM same as > DERMA
DERMA n beef or fowl intestine used as a casing for certain dishes, esp kishke
DERMAL adj of or relating to the skin
DERMAS > DERMA
DERMATIC adj of skin
DERMATOID adj resembling skin
DERMATOME n surgical instrument for cutting thin slices of skin, esp for grafting
DERMESTID n type of beetle whose larva and adult is destructive to many stored organic materials, such as wool and meat
DERMIC > DERMIS
DERMIS another name for > CORIUM
DERMISES > DERMIS
DERMOID adj of or resembling skin ▷ n congenital cystic tumour whose walls are lined with epithelium
DERMOIDS > DERMOID
DERMS > DERM
DERN n concealment ▷ vb keep hidden
DERNED > DERN
DERNFUL adj sorrowful
DERNIER adj last
DERNIES > DERNY
DERNING > DERN
DERNLY adv sorrowfully
DERNS > DERN
DERNY n bicycle with a small motor
DERNYS > DERNY
DERO n vagrant or derelict
DEROGATE vb detract from ▷ adj debased or degraded
DEROGATED
  > DEROGATE
DEROGATES
  > DEROGATE
DEROS > DERO
DERRICK n simple crane ▷ vb raise or lower the jib of (a crane)
DERRICKED > DERRICK
DERRICKS > DERRICK
DERRIERE n backside
DERRIERES
  > DERRIERE
DERRIES > DERRY

DERRINGER n small large-bored pistol
DERRIS n woody climbing plant
DERRISES > DERRIS
DERRO n vagrant or derelict
DERROS > DERRO
DERRY n derelict house, esp one used by tramps
DERTH same as > DEARTH
DERTHS > DERTH
DERV n diesel oil, when used for road transport
DERVISH n member of a Muslim religious order noted for a frenzied whirling dance
DERVISHES > DERVISH
DERVS > DERV
DESALT vb desalinate
DESALTED > DESALT
DESALTER > DESALT
DESALTERS > DESALT
DESALTING > DESALT
DESALTS > DESALT
DESAND vb remove sand from
DESANDED > DESAND
DESANDING > DESAND
DESANDS > DESAND
DESCALE vb remove a hard coating from inside (a kettle or pipe)
DESCALED > DESCALE
DESCALER n something that removes limescale
DESCALERS
  > DESCALER
DESCALES > DESCALE
DESCALING > DESCALE
DESCANT n tune played or sung above a basic melody ▷ adj denoting the highest member in a family of musical instruments ▷ vb compose or perform a descant (for a piece of music)
DESCANTED > DESCANT
DESCANTER > DESCANT
DESCANTS > DESCANT
DESCEND vb move down (a slope etc)
DESCENDED > DESCEND
DESCENDER > DESCEND
DESCENDS > DESCEND
DESCENT n descending
DESCENTS > DESCENT
DESCHOOL vb educate by means other than a school
DESCHOOLS
  > DESCHOOL
DESCRIBE vb give an account of (something or someone) in words
DESCRIBED
  > DESCRIBE
DESCRIBER
  > DESCRIBE
DESCRIBES
  > DESCRIBE
DESCRIED > DESCRY
DESCRIER > DESCRY
DESCRIERS > DESCRY
DESCRIES > DESCRY
DESCRIVE vb describe

DESCRIVED
  > DESCRIVE
DESCRIVES
  > DESCRIVE
DESCRY vb catch sight of
DESCRYING > DESCRY
DESECRATE vb damage or insult (something sacred)
DESEED vb remove the seeds from (eg a fruit)
DESEEDED > DESEED
DESEEDER n person who deseeds
DESEEDERS
  > DESEEDER
DESEEDING > DESEED
DESEEDS > DESEED
DESELECT vb refuse to select (an MP) for re-election
DESELECTS
  > DESELECT
DESERT n region with little or no vegetation because of low rainfall ▷ vb abandon (a person or place) without intending to return
DESERTED > DESERT
DESERTER > DESERT
DESERTERS > DESERT
DESERTIC adj (of soil) developing in hot climates
DESERTIFY vb turn into desert
DESERTING > DESERT
DESERTION n act of deserting or abandoning or the state of being deserted or abandoned
DESERTS > DESERT
DESERVE vb be entitled to or worthy of
DESERVED > DESERVE
DESERVER > DESERVE
DESERVERS > DESERVE
DESERVES > DESERVE
DESERVING adj worthy of help, praise, or reward ▷ n merit or demerit
DESEX vb desexualize
DESEXED > DESEX
DESEXES > DESEX
DESEXING > DESEX
DESHI same as > DESI
DESHIS > DESHI
DESI adj (in Indian English) indigenous or local ▷ n (in Indian English) indigenous or local person
DESICCANT adj desiccating or drying ▷ n substance, such as calcium oxide, that absorbs water and is used to remove moisture
DESICCATE vb remove most of the water from
DESIGN vb work out the structure or form of (something), by making a sketch or plans ▷ n preliminary drawing
DESIGNATE vb give a name to ▷ adj appointed but not yet in office
DESIGNED > DESIGN

DESIGNEE *n* person designated to do something

DESIGNEES > DESIGNEE

DESIGNER *n* person who draws up original sketches or plans from which things are made ▷ *adj* designed by a well-known designer

DESIGNERS > DESIGNER

DESIGNFUL *adj* scheming

DESIGNING *adj* cunning and scheming

DESIGNS > DESIGN

DESILVER *vb* remove silver from

DESILVERS > DESILVER

DESINE *same as* > DESIGN

DESINED > DESINE

DESINENCE *n* ending or termination, esp an inflectional ending of a word

DESINENT > DESINENCE

DESINES > DESINE

DESINING > DESINE

DESIPIENT *adj* foolish

DESIRABLE *adj* worth having ▷ *n* person or thing that is the object of desire

DESIRABLY > DESIRABLE

DESIRE *vb* want very much ▷ *n* wish, longing

DESIRED > DESIRE

DESIRER > DESIRE

DESIRERS > DESIRE

DESIRES > DESIRE

DESIRING > DESIRE

DESIROUS *adj* having a desire for

DESIS > DESI

DESIST *vb* stop (doing something)

DESISTED > DESIST

DESISTING > DESIST

DESISTS > DESIST

DESK *n* piece of furniture with a writing surface and drawers

DESKBOUND *adj* engaged in or involving sedentary work, as at an office desk

DESKFAST *n* breakfast eaten at one's desk at work

DESKFASTS > DESKFAST

DESKILL *vb* mechanize or computerize (a job) thereby reducing the skill required to do it

DESKILLED > DESKILL

DESKILLS > DESKILL

DESKING *n* desks and related furnishings in a given space, eg an office

DESKINGS > DESKING

DESKMAN *n* police officer in charge in police station

DESKMEN > DESKMAN

DESKNOTE *n* small computer

DESKNOTES > DESKNOTE

DESKS > DESK

DESKTOP *adj* (of a computer) small enough to use at a desk ▷ *n* computer small enough to use at a desk

DESKTOPS > DESKTOP

DESMAN *n* either of two molelike amphibious mammals

DESMANS > DESMAN

DESMID *n* type of mainly unicellular freshwater green alga

DESMIDIAN > DESMID

DESMIDS > DESMID

DESMINE *n* type of mineral

DESMINES > DESMINE

DESMODIUM *n* type of plant

DESMOID *adj* resembling a tendon or ligament ▷ *n* very firm tumour of connective tissue

DESMOIDS > DESMOID

DESMOSOME *n* structure in the cell membranes of adjacent cells that binds them together

DESNOOD *vb* remove the snood of a turkey poult to reduce the risk of cannibalism

DESNOODED > DESNOOD

DESNOODS > DESNOOD

DESOEUVRE *adj* with nothing to do

DESOLATE *adj* uninhabited and bleak ▷ *vb* deprive of inhabitants

DESOLATED > DESOLATE

DESOLATER > DESOLATE

DESOLATES > DESOLATE

DESOLATOR > DESOLATE

DESORB *vb* change from an adsorbed state to a gaseous or liquid state

DESORBED > DESORB

DESORBER *n* something that desorbs

DESORBERS > DESORBER

DESORBING > DESORB

DESORBS > DESORB

DESOXY *same as* > DEOXY

DESPAIR *n* total loss of hope ▷ *vb* lose hope

DESPAIRED > DESPAIR

DESPAIRER *n* one who despairs

DESPAIRS > DESPAIR

DESPATCH *same as* > DISPATCH

DESPERADO *n* reckless person ready to commit any violent illegal act

DESPERATE *adj* in despair and reckless

DESPIGHT *obsolete form of* > DESPITE

DESPIGHTS > DESPIGHT

DESPISAL > DESPISE

DESPISALS > DESPISE

DESPISE *vb* regard with contempt

DESPISED > DESPISE

DESPISER > DESPISE

DESPISERS > DESPISE

DESPISES > DESPISE

DESPISING > DESPISE

DESPITE *prep* in spite of ▷ *n* contempt ▷ *vb* show contempt for

DESPITED > DESPITE

DESPITES > DESPITE

DESPITING > DESPITE

DESPOIL *vb* plunder

DESPOILED > DESPOIL

DESPOILER > DESPOIL

DESPOILS > DESPOIL

DESPOND *vb* lose heart or hope

DESPONDED > DESPOND

DESPONDS > DESPOND

DESPOT *n* person in power who acts unfairly or cruelly

DESPOTAT *n* despot's domain

DESPOTATE *same as* > DESPOTAT

DESPOTATS > DESPOTAT

DESPOTIC > DESPOT

DESPOTISM *n* unfair or cruel government or behaviour

DESPOTS > DESPOT

DESPUMATE *vb* clarify or purify (a liquid) by skimming a scum from its surface

DESSE *n* old word for desk

DESSERT *n* sweet course served at the end of a meal

DESSERTS > DESSERT

DESSES > DESSE

DESSYATIN *n* Russian measure of land

DESTAIN *vb* remove stain from

DESTAINED > DESTAIN

DESTAINS > DESTAIN

DESTEMPER *same as* > DISTEMPER

DESTINATE *same as* > DESTINE

DESTINE *vb* set apart or appoint

DESTINED *adj* certain to be or to do something

DESTINES > DESTINE

DESTINIES > DESTINY

DESTINING > DESTINE

DESTINY *n* future marked out for a person or thing

DESTITUTE *adj* having no money or possessions

DESTOCK *vb* reduce the amount of stock

DESTOCKED > DESTOCK

DESTOCKS > DESTOCK

DESTREAM *vb* take (pupils) out of classes that are organized by ability

DESTREAMS > DESTREAM

DESTRESS *vb* make or become less stressed

DESTRIER *an archaic word for* > WARHORSE

DESTRIERS > DESTRIER

DESTROY *vb* ruin, demolish

DESTROYED > DESTROY

DESTROYER *n* small heavily armed warship

DESTROYS > DESTROY

DESTRUCT *vb* destroy intentionally for safety ▷ *n* act of destructing ▷ *adj* capable of self-destruction

DESTRUCTO *n* person who causes havoc or destruction

DESTRUCTS > DESTRUCT

DESUETUDE *n* condition of not being in use

DESUGAR *vb* remove sugar from

DESUGARED > DESUGAR

DESUGARS > DESUGAR

DESULFUR *same as* > DESULPHUR

DESULFURS > DESULFUR

DESULPHUR *vb* remove sulphur from

DESULTORY *adj* jumping from one thing to another, disconnected

DESYATIN *n* Russian unit of area

DESYATINS > DESYATIN

DESYNE *same as* > DESIGN

DESYNED > DESYNE

DESYNES > DESYNE

DESYNING > DESYNE

DETACH *vb* disengage and separate

DETACHED *adj* (of a house) not joined to another house

DETACHER > DETACH

DETACHERS > DETACH

DETACHES > DETACH

DETACHING > DETACH

DETAIL *n* individual piece of information ▷ *vb* list fully

DETAILED *adj* having many details

DETAILER > DETAIL

DETAILERS > DETAIL

DETAILING > DETAIL

DETAILS > DETAIL

DETAIN *vb* delay (someone)

DETAINED > DETAIN

DETAINEE > DETAIN

DETAINEES > DETAIN

DETAINER *n* wrongful withholding of the property of another person

DETAINERS > DETAINER

DETAINING > DETAIN

DETAINS > DETAIN

d

DETANGLE vb remove tangles from (esp hair)
DETANGLED > DETANGLE
DETANGLER n cosmetic product used to detangle hair
DETANGLES > DETANGLE
DETASSEL vb remove top part of corn plant
DETASSELS > DETASSEL
DETECT vb notice
DETECTED > DETECT
DETECTER > DETECT
DETECTERS > DETECT
DETECTING > DETECT
DETECTION n act of noticing, discovering, or sensing something
DETECTIVE n police officer or private agent who investigates crime ▷ adj used in or serving for detection
DETECTOR n instrument used to find something
DETECTORS > DETECTOR
DETECTS > DETECT
DETENT n mechanism to check movement in one direction only
DETENTE n easing of tension between nations
DETENTES > DETENTE
DETENTION n imprisonment
DETENTIST n supporter of detente
DETENTS > DETENT
DETENU n prisoner
DETENUE n female prisoner
DETENUES > DETENUE
DETENUS > DETENU
DETER vb discourage (someone) from doing something by instilling fear or doubt
DETERGE vb wash or wipe away
DETERGED > DETERGE
DETERGENT n chemical substance for washing clothes or dishes ▷ adj having cleansing power
DETERGER n detergent
DETERGERS > DETERGER
DETERGES > DETERGE
DETERGING > DETERGE
DETERMENT > DETER
DETERMINE vb settle (an argument or a question) conclusively
DETERRED > DETER
DETERRENT n something that deters ▷ adj tending to deter
DETERRER > DETER
DETERRERS > DETERRER
DETERRING > DETER
DETERS > DETER
DETERSION n act of cleansing

DETERSIVE same as > DETERGENT
DETEST vb dislike intensely
DETESTED > DETEST
DETESTER > DETEST
DETESTERS > DETEST
DETESTING > DETEST
DETESTS > DETEST
DETHATCH vb remove dead grass from lawn
DETHRONE vb remove from a throne or position of power
DETHRONED > DETHRONE
DETHRONER > DETHRONE
DETHRONES > DETHRONE
DETICK vb remove ticks from
DETICKED > DETICK
DETICKER > DETICK
DETICKERS > DETICK
DETICKING > DETICK
DETICKS > DETICK
DETINUE n action brought by a plaintiff to recover goods wrongfully detained
DETINUES > DETINUE
DETONABLE adj that can be detonated
DETONATE vb explode
DETONATED > DETONATE
DETONATES > DETONATE
DETONATOR n small amount of explosive, or a device, used to set off an explosion
DETORSION > DETORT
DETORT vb twist or distort
DETORTED > DETORT
DETORTING > DETORT
DETORTION > DETORT
DETORTS > DETORT
DETOUR n route that is not the most direct one ▷ vb deviate or cause to deviate from a direct route or course of action
DETOURED > DETOUR
DETOURING > DETOUR
DETOURS > DETOUR
DETOX n treatment to rid the body of poisonous substances ▷ vb undergo treatment to rid the body of poisonous substances
DETOXED > DETOX
DETOXES > DETOX
DETOXIFY vb remove poison from
DETOXING > DETOX
DETRACT vb make (something) seem less good
DETRACTED > DETRACT
DETRACTOR > DETRACT
DETRACTS > DETRACT
DETRAIN vb leave or cause to leave a railway train, as passengers, etc
DETRAINED > DETRAIN

DETRAINS > DETRAIN
DETRAQUE n insane person
DETRAQUEE n female insane person
DETRAQUES > DETRAQUE
DETRIMENT n disadvantage or damage
DETRITAL > DETRITUS
DETRITION n act of rubbing or wearing away by friction
DETRITUS n loose mass of stones and silt worn away from rocks
DETRUDE vb force down or thrust away or out
DETRUDED > DETRUDE
DETRUDES > DETRUDE
DETRUDING > DETRUDE
DETRUSION > DETRUDE
DETRUSOR n muscle in the wall of the bladder
DETRUSORS > DETRUSOR
DETUNE vb change pitch of (stringed instrument)
DETUNED > DETUNE
DETUNES > DETUNE
DETUNING > DETUNE
DEUCE vb score deuce in tennis ▷ n score of forty all
DEUCED adj damned
DEUCEDLY > DEUCED
DEUCES > DEUCE
DEUCING > DEUCE
DEUDDARN n two-tiered Welsh dresser
DEUDDARNS > DEUDDARN
DEUS n god
DEUTERATE vb treat or combine with deuterium
DEUTERIC adj (of mineral) formed by metasomatic changes
DEUTERIDE n compound of deuterium with some other element. It is analogous to a hydride
DEUTERIUM n isotope of hydrogen twice as heavy as the normal atom
DEUTERON n nucleus of a deuterium atom, consisting of one proton and one neutron
DEUTERONS > DEUTERON
DEUTON old form of > DEUTERON
DEUTONS > DEUTON
DEUTZIA n shrub with clusters of pink or white flowers
DEUTZIAS > DEUTZIA
DEV same as > DEVA
DEVA n (in Hinduism and Buddhism) divine being or god
DEVALL vb Scots word meaning stop
DEVALLED > DEVALL
DEVALLING > DEVALL
DEVALLS > DEVALL
DEVALUATE same as > DEVALUE

DEVALUE vb reduce the exchange value of (a currency)
DEVALUED > DEVALUE
DEVALUES > DEVALUE
DEVALUING > DEVALUE
DEVAS > DEVA
DEVASTATE vb destroy
DEVEIN vb remove vein from
DEVEINED > DEVEIN
DEVEINING > DEVEIN
DEVEINS > DEVEIN
DEVEL same as > DEVVEL
DEVELED > DEVEL
DEVELING > DEVEL
DEVELLED > DEVEL
DEVELLING > DEVEL
DEVELOP vb grow or bring to a later, more elaborate, or more advanced stage
DEVELOPE old form of > DEVELOP
DEVELOPED > DEVELOP
DEVELOPER n person who develops property
DEVELOPES > DEVELOPE
DEVELOPPE n ballet position
DEVELOPS > DEVELOP
DEVELS > DEVEL
DEVERBAL n word deriving from verb
DEVERBALS > DEVERBAL
DEVEST variant spelling of > DIVEST
DEVESTED > DEVEST
DEVESTING > DEVEST
DEVESTS > DEVEST
DEVI n Hindu goddess
DEVIANCE n act or state of being deviant
DEVIANCES > DEVIANCE
DEVIANCY same as > DEVIANCE
DEVIANT adj (person) deviating from what is considered acceptable behaviour ▷ n person whose behaviour deviates from what is considered to be acceptable
DEVIANTS > DEVIANT
DEVIATE vb differ from others in belief or thought
DEVIATED > DEVIATE
DEVIATES > DEVIATE
DEVIATING > DEVIATE
DEVIATION n act or result of deviating
DEVIATIVE adj tending to deviate
DEVIATOR > DEVIATE
DEVIATORS > DEVIATE
DEVIATORY > DEVIATE
DEVICE n machine or tool used for a specific task
DEVICEFUL adj full of devices
DEVICES > DEVICE
DEVIL n evil spirit ▷ vb prepare (food) with a highly flavoured spiced mixture

DEVILDOM n domain of evil spirits

DEVILDOMS
> DEVILDOM

DEVILED > DEVIL

DEVILESS n female devil

DEVILET n young devil

DEVILETS > DEVILET

DEVILFISH n manta fish

DEVILING > DEVIL

DEVILINGS > DEVIL

DEVILISH adj cruel or unpleasant ▷ adv extremely

DEVILISM n doctrine of devil

DEVILISMS
> DEVILISM

DEVILKIN n small devil

DEVILKINS
> DEVILKIN

DEVILLED > DEVIL

DEVILLING > DEVIL

DEVILMENT n mischievous conduct

DEVILRIES > DEVILRY

DEVILRY n mischievousness

DEVILS > DEVIL

DEVILSHIP n character of devil

DEVILTRY same as
> DEVILRY

DEVILWOOD n small US tree

DEVIOUS adj insincere and dishonest

DEVIOUSLY > DEVIOUS

DEVIS > DEVI

DEVISABLE adj (of property, esp realty) capable of being transferred by will

DEVISAL n act of inventing, contriving, or devising

DEVISALS > DEVISAL

DEVISE vb work out (something) in one's mind ▷ n disposition of property by will

DEVISED > DEVISE

DEVISEE n person to whom property, esp realty, is devised by will

DEVISEES > DEVISEE

DEVISER > DEVISE

DEVISERS > DEVISE

DEVISES > DEVISE

DEVISING > DEVISE

DEVISOR n person who devises property, esp realty, by will

DEVISORS > DEVISOR

DEVITRIFY vb change from a vitreous state to a crystalline state

DEVLING n young devil

DEVLINGS > DEVLING

DEVO n short for devolution

DEVOICE vb make (a voiced speech sound) voiceless

DEVOICED > DEVOICE

DEVOICES > DEVOICE

DEVOICING n act of devoicing

DEVOID adj completely lacking (in)

DEVOIR n duty

DEVOIRS > DEVOIR

DEVOLVE vb pass to a successor or substitute

DEVOLVED > DEVOLVE

DEVOLVES > DEVOLVE

DEVOLVING > DEVOLVE

DEVON n bland processed meat in sausage form, eaten cold in slices

DEVONIAN adj denoting the fourth period of the Palaeozoic era

DEVONPORT same as
> DAVENPORT

DEVONS > DEVON

DEVORE n velvet fabric with a raised pattern

DEVORES > DEVORE

DEVOS > DEVO

DEVOT n devotee

DEVOTE vb apply or dedicate to a particular purpose

DEVOTED adj showing loyalty or devotion

DEVOTEDLY > DEVOTED

DEVOTEE n person who is very enthusiastic about something

DEVOTEES > DEVOTEE

DEVOTES > DEVOTE

DEVOTING > DEVOTE

DEVOTION n strong affection for or loyalty to someone or something

DEVOTIONS
> DEVOTION

DEVOTS > DEVOT

DEVOUR vb eat greedily

DEVOURED > DEVOUR

DEVOURER > DEVOUR

DEVOURERS > DEVOUR

DEVOURING > DEVOUR

DEVOURS > DEVOUR

DEVOUT adj deeply religious

DEVOUTER > DEVOUT

DEVOUTEST > DEVOUT

DEVOUTLY > DEVOUT

DEVS > DEV

DEVVEL vb strike with blow

DEVVELLED > DEVVEL

DEVVELS > DEVVEL

DEW n drops of water that form on the ground at night from vapour in the air ▷ vb moisten with or as with dew

DEWAN n (formerly in India) the chief or finance minister of a state ruled by an Indian prince

DEWANI n post of a dewan

DEWANIS > DEWANI

DEWANNIES > DEWANNY

DEWANNY same as
> DEWANI

DEWANS > DEWAN

DEWAR n type of vacuum flask

DEWARS > DEWAR

DEWATER vb remove water from

DEWATERED > DEWATER

DEWATERER > DEWATER

DEWATERS > DEWATER

DEWAX vb remove wax from

DEWAXED > DEWAX

DEWAXES > DEWAX

DEWAXING > DEWAX

DEWBERRY n type of bramble with blue-black fruits

DEWCLAW n nonfunctional claw on a dog's leg

DEWCLAWED > DEWCLAW

DEWCLAWS > DEWCLAW

DEWDROP n drop of dew

DEWDROPS > DEWDROP

DEWED > DEW

DEWFALL n formation of dew

DEWFALLS > DEWFALL

DEWFULL obsolete form of
> DUE

DEWIER > DEWY

DEWIEST > DEWY

DEWILY > DEWY

DEWINESS > DEWY

DEWING > DEW

DEWITT vb kill, esp hang unlawfully

DEWITTED > DEWITT

DEWITTING > DEWITT

DEWITTS > DEWITT

DEWLAP n loose fold of skin hanging under the throat in dogs, cattle, etc

DEWLAPPED > DEWLAP

DEWLAPS > DEWLAP

DEWLAPT > DEWLAP

DEWLESS > DEW

DEWOOL vb remove wool from

DEWOOLED > DEWOOL

DEWOOLING > DEWOOL

DEWOOLS > DEWOOL

DEWORM vb rid of worms

DEWORMED > DEWORM

DEWORMER > DEWORM

DEWORMERS > DEWORM

DEWORMING > DEWORM

DEWORMS > DEWORM

DEWPOINT n temperature at which water droplets form in the air

DEWPOINTS
> DEWPOINT

DEWS > DEW

DEWY adj moist with or as with dew

DEX n dextroamphetamine

DEXES > DEX

DEXIE n pill containing dextroamphetamine

DEXIES > DEXIE

DEXTER adj of or on the right side of a shield, etc, from the bearer's point of view ▷ n small breed of beef cattle

DEXTERITY n skill in using one's hands

DEXTEROUS adj possessing or done with dexterity

DEXTERS > DEXTER

DEXTRAL n right-handed person

DEXTRALLY > DEXTRAL

DEXTRALS > DEXTRAL

DEXTRAN n polysaccharide compound

DEXTRANS > DEXTRAN

DEXTRIN n sticky substance obtained from starch

DEXTRINE same as
> DEXTRIN

DEXTRINES
> DEXTRINE

DEXTRINS > DEXTRIN

DEXTRO adj dextrorotatory or rotating to the right

DEXTRORSE adj (of some climbing plants) growing upwards in a helix from left to right or anticlockwise

DEXTROSE n glucose occurring in fruit, honey, and the blood of animals

DEXTROSES
> DEXTROSE

DEXTROUS same as
> DEXTEROUS

DEXY same as > DEXIE

DEY n title given to commanders or governors of the Janissaries of Algiers

DEYS > DEY

DEZINC vb remove zinc from

DEZINCED > DEZINC

DEZINCING > DEZINC

DEZINCKED > DEZINC

DEZINCS > DEZINC

DHABA n roadside café in India

DHABAS > DHABA

DHAK n tropical Asian tree

DHAKS > DHAK

DHAL n curry made from lentils or beans

DHALS > DHAL

DHAMMA variant of
> DHARMA

DHAMMAS > DHAMMA

DHANSAK n any of a variety of Indian dishes

DHANSAKS > DHANSAK

DHARMA n moral law or behaviour

DHARMAS > DHARMA

DHARMIC > DHARMA

DHARMSALA n Indian hostel

DHARNA n (in India) a method of obtaining justice

DHARNAS > DHARNA

DHIKR n Sufi religious ceremony

DHIKRS > DHIKR

DHIMMI n non-Muslim living in a state governed by sharia law

DHIMMIS > DHIMMI

DHOBI n (in India, Malaya, East Africa, etc, esp formerly) a washerman

DHOBIS > DHOBI

DHOL n type of Indian drum

d

DHOLAK n type of two-headed drum
DHOLAKS > DHOLAK
DHOLE n fierce canine mammal
DHOLES > DHOLE
DHOLL same as > DHAL
DHOLLS > DHOLL
DHOLS > DHOL
DHOOLIES > DHOOLY
DHOOLY same as > DOOLIE
DHOORA same as > DURRA
DHOORAS > DHOORA
DHOOTI same as > DHOTI
DHOOTIE same as > DHOTI
DHOOTIES > DHOOTIE
DHOOTIS > DHOOTI
DHOTI n long loincloth worn by men in India
DHOTIS > DHOTI
DHOURRA same as > DURRA
DHOURRAS > DHOURRA
DHOW n Arab sailing ship
DHOWS > DHOW
DHURNA same as > DHARNA
DHURNAS > DHURNA
DHURRA same as > DURRA
DHURRAS > DHURRA
DHURRIE same as > DURRIE
DHURRIES > DHURRIE
DHUTI same as > DHOTI
DHUTIS > DHUTI
DHYANA n type of Hindu meditation
DHYANAS > DHYANA
DI > DEUS
DIABASE n altered dolerite
DIABASES > DIABASE
DIABASIC > DIABASE
DIABETES n disorder in which an abnormal amount of urine containing an excess of sugar is excreted
DIABETIC n person who has diabetes ▷ adj of or having diabetes
DIABETICS > DIABETIC
DIABLE n type of sauce
DIABLERIE n magic or witchcraft connected with devils
DIABLERY same as > DIABLERIE
DIABLES > DIABLE
DIABOLIC adj of the Devil
DIABOLISE same as > DIABOLIZE
DIABOLISM n witchcraft, devil worship
DIABOLIST > DIABOLISM
DIABOLIZE vb make (someone or something) diabolical
DIABOLO n game using a spinning top and a cord fastened to two sticks
DIABOLOGY n study of devils

DIABOLOS > DIABOLO
DIACETYL n aromatic compound
DIACETYLS > DIACETYL
DIACHRONY n change over time
DIACHYLON n acid or salt that contains two acidic hydrogen atoms
DIACHYLUM n plaster containing glycerin with lead salts
DIACID n lead plaster
DIACIDIC adj capable of neutralizing two protons with one molecule
DIACIDS > DIACID
DIACODION n herbal remedy aiding sleep
DIACODIUM n syrup of poppies
DIACONAL adj of or associated with a deacon or the diaconate
DIACONATE n position or period of office of a deacon
DIACRITIC n sign above or below a character to indicate phonetic value or stress
DIACT same as > DIACTINE
DIACTINAL adj having two pointed ends
DIACTINE adj two-rayed ▷ n two-rayed sponge spicule
DIACTINES > DIACTINE
DIACTINIC adj able to transmit photochemically active radiation
DIACTS > DIACT
DIADEM n crown ▷ vb adorn or crown with or as with a diadem
DIADEMED > DIADEM
DIADEMING > DIADEM
DIADEMS > DIADEM
DIADOCHI pl n six generals who fought for control of the Alexandrian Empire
DIADOCHY n replacement of one element in a crystal by another
DIADROM n complete course of pendulum
DIADROMS > DIADROM
DIAERESES > DIAERESIS
DIAERESIS n mark placed over a vowel to show that it is pronounced separately from the preceding one, for example in Noël
DIAERETIC > DIAERESIS
DIAGLYPH n figure cut into stone
DIAGLYPHS > DIAGLYPH
DIAGNOSE vb determine by diagnosis
DIAGNOSED > DIAGNOSE

DIAGNOSES > DIAGNOSIS
DIAGNOSIS n discovery and identification of diseases from the examination of symptoms
DIAGONAL adj from corner to corner ▷ n diagonal line
DIAGONALS > DIAGONAL
DIAGRAM n sketch showing the form or workings of something ▷ vb show in or as if in a diagram
DIAGRAMED > DIAGRAM
DIAGRAMS > DIAGRAM
DIAGRAPH n device for enlarging or reducing maps, plans, etc
DIAGRAPHS > DIAGRAPH
DIAGRID n diagonal structure network
DIAGRIDS > DIAGRID
DIAL n face of a clock or watch ▷ vb operate the dial or buttons on a telephone in order to contact (a number)
DIALECT n form of a language spoken in a particular area
DIALECTAL > DIALECT
DIALECTIC n logical debate by question and answer to resolve differences between two views ▷ adj of or relating to logical disputation
DIALECTS > DIALECT
DIALED > DIAL
DIALER > DIAL
DIALERS > DIAL
DIALING > DIAL
DIALINGS > DIAL
DIALIST n dial-maker
DIALISTS > DIALIST
DIALLAGE n green or brownish-black variety of the mineral augite
DIALLAGES > DIALLAGE
DIALLAGIC > DIALLAGE
DIALLED > DIAL
DIALLEL n interbreeding among a group of parents ▷ adj (of lines) not parallel, meeting, or intersecting
DIALLELS > DIALLEL
DIALLER > DIAL
DIALLERS > DIAL
DIALLING > DIAL
DIALLINGS > DIAL
DIALLIST same as > DIALIST
DIALLISTS > DIALLIST
DIALOG same as > DIALOGUE
DIALOGED > DIALOG
DIALOGER > DIALOG
DIALOGERS > DIALOG
DIALOGIC > DIALOGUE
DIALOGING > DIALOG

DIALOGISE same as > DIALOGIZE
DIALOGISM n deduction with one premise and a disjunctive conclusion
DIALOGIST n person who writes or takes part in a dialogue
DIALOGITE n carbonate mineral
DIALOGIZE vb carry on a dialogue
DIALOGS > DIALOG
DIALOGUE n conversation between two people, esp in a book, film, or play ▷ vb put into the form of a dialogue
DIALOGUED > DIALOGUE
DIALOGUER > DIALOGUE
DIALOGUES > DIALOGUE
DIALS > DIAL
DIALYSATE n liquid used in dialysis
DIALYSE vb separate by dialysis
DIALYSED > DIALYSE
DIALYSER n machine that performs dialysis
DIALYSERS > DIALYSER
DIALYSES > DIALYSIS
DIALYSING > DIALYSE
DIALYSIS n filtering of blood through a membrane to remove waste products
DIALYTIC > DIALYSIS
DIALYZATE same as > DIALYSATE
DIALYZE same as > DIALYSE
DIALYZED > DIALYZE
DIALYZER same as > DIALYSER
DIALYZERS > DIALYZER
DIALYZES > DIALYZE
DIALYZING > DIALYZE
DIAMAGNET n substance exhibiting diamagnetism
DIAMANTE adj decorated with artificial jewels or sequins ▷ n fabric so covered
DIAMANTES > DIAMANTE
DIAMETER n (length of) a straight line through the centre of a circle or sphere
DIAMETERS > DIAMETER
DIAMETRAL same as > DIAMETRIC
DIAMETRIC adj of a diameter
DIAMIDE n compound containing two amido groups
DIAMIDES > DIAMIDE
DIAMIN same as > DIAMINE
DIAMINE n any chemical compound containing two amino groups in its molecules

DIAMINES > DIAMINE

DIAMINS > DIAMIN

DIAMOND *n* exceptionally hard precious stone ▷ *adj* (of an anniversary) the sixtieth ▷ *vb* stud or decorate with diamonds

DIAMONDED > DIAMOND

DIAMONDS > DIAMOND

DIAMYL *adj* with two amyl groups

DIANDRIES > DIANDRY

DIANDROUS *adj* (of some flowers or flowering plants) having two stamens

DIANDRY *n* practice of having two husbands

DIANE *adj* as in *steak diane* steak served in a rich sauce

DIANODAL *adj* going through a node

DIANOETIC *adj* of or relating to thought, esp to discursive reasoning rather than intuition

DIANOIA *n* perception and experience regarded as lower modes of knowledge

DIANOIAS > DIANOIA

DIANTHUS *n* type of widely cultivated Eurasian plant

DIAPASE *same as* > DIAPASON

DIAPASES > DIAPASE

DIAPASON *n* either of two stops found throughout the range of a pipe organ

DIAPASONS > DIAPASON

DIAPAUSE *vb* undergo diapause ▷ *n* period of suspended development and growth

DIAPAUSED > DIAPAUSE

DIAPAUSES > DIAPAUSE

DIAPENTE *n* (in classical Greece) the interval of a perfect fifth

DIAPENTES > DIAPENTE

DIAPER *n* nappy ▷ *vb* decorate with a geometric pattern

DIAPERED > DIAPER

DIAPERING > DIAPER

DIAPERS > DIAPER

DIAPHONE *n* set of all realizations of a given phoneme in a language

DIAPHONES > DIAPHONE

DIAPHONIC > DIAPHONY

DIAPHONY *n* style of two-part polyphonic singing

DIAPHRAGM *n* muscular partition that separates the abdominal cavity and chest cavity

DIAPHYSES > DIAPHYSIS

DIAPHYSIS *n* shaft of a long bone

DIAPIR *n* type of geological formation

DIAPIRIC > DIAPIR

DIAPIRISM > DIAPIR

DIAPIRS > DIAPIR

DIAPSID *n* reptile with two holes in rear of skull

DIAPSIDS > DIAPSID

DIAPYESES > DIAPYESIS

DIAPYESIS *n* discharge of pus

DIAPYETIC > DIAPYESIS

DIARCH *adj* (of a vascular bundle) having two strands of xylem

DIARCHAL > DIARCHY

DIARCHIC > DIARCHY

DIARCHIES > DIARCHY

DIARCHY *n* government by two states, individuals, etc

DIARIAL > DIARY

DIARIAN > DIARY

DIARIES > DIARY

DIARISE *same as* > DIARIZE

DIARISED > DIARISE

DIARISES > DIARISE

DIARISING > DIARISE

DIARIST *n* person who writes a diary

DIARISTIC > DIARIST

DIARISTS > DIARIST

DIARIZE *vb* record in diary

DIARIZED > DIARIZE

DIARIZES > DIARIZE

DIARIZING > DIARIZE

DIARRHEA *same as* > DIARRHOEA

DIARRHEAL > DIARRHEA

DIARRHEAS > DIARRHEA

DIARRHEIC > DIARRHEA

DIARRHOEA *n* frequent discharge of abnormally liquid faeces

DIARY *n* (book for) a record of daily events, appointments, or observations

DIASCIA *n* S African plant, usu with pink flowers

DIASCIAS > DIASCIA

DIASCOPE *n* optical projector used to display transparencies

DIASCOPES > DIASCOPE

DIASPORA *n* dispersion or spreading of a people

DIASPORAS > DIASPORA

DIASPORE *n* white, yellowish, or grey mineral

DIASPORES > DIASPORE

DIASPORIC > DIASPORA

DIASTASE *n* enzyme that converts starch into sugar

DIASTASES > DIASTASIS

DIASTASIC > DIASTASE

DIASTASIS *n* separation of an epiphysis from the long bone to which it is normally attached without fracture of the bone

DIASTATIC > DIASTASIS

DIASTEM *same as* > DIASTEMA

DIASTEMA *n* abnormal space, fissure, or cleft in a bodily organ or part

DIASTEMAS > DIASTEMA

DIASTEMS > DIASTEM

DIASTER *n* stage in cell division

DIASTERS > DIASTER

DIASTOLE *n* dilation of the chambers of the heart

DIASTOLES > DIASTOLE

DIASTOLIC > DIASTOLE

DIASTRAL > DIASTER

DIASTYLE *adj* having columns about three diameters apart ▷ *n* diastyle building

DIASTYLES > DIASTYLE

DIATHERMY *n* local heating of the body tissues with an electric current for medical or surgical purposes

DIATHESES > DIATHESIS

DIATHESIS *n* hereditary or acquired susceptibility of the body to one or more diseases

DIATHETIC > DIATHESIS

DIATOM *n* microscopic unicellular alga

DIATOMIC *adj* containing two atoms

DIATOMIST *n* specialist in diatoms

DIATOMITE *n* soft very fine-grained whitish rock consisting of the siliceous remains of diatoms deposited in the ocean or in ponds or lakes. It is used as an absorbent, filtering medium, insulator, filler, etc

DIATOMS > DIATOM

DIATONIC *adj* of a regular major or minor scale

DIATREME *n* volcanic vent produced by an eruption of gas

DIATREMES > DIATREME

DIATRETA > DIATRETUM

DIATRETUM *n* Roman glass bowl

DIATRIBE *n* bitter critical attack

DIATRIBES > DIATRIBE

DIATRON *n* circuit that uses diodes

DIATRONS > DIATRON

DIATROPIC *adj* relating to a type of response in plants to an external stimulus

DIAXON *n* bipolar cell

DIAXONS > DIAXON

DIAZEPAM *n* minor tranquillizer used to treat epilepsy

DIAZEPAMS > DIAZEPAM

DIAZEUXES > DIAZEUXIS

DIAZEUXIS *n* separation of two tetrachords by interval of a tone

DIAZIN *same as* > DIAZINE

DIAZINE *n* organic compound

DIAZINES > DIAZINE

DIAZINON *n* type of insecticide

DIAZINONS > DIAZINON

DIAZINS > DIAZIN

DIAZO *adj* relating to a method for reproducing documents ▷ *n* document produced by this method

DIAZOES > DIAZO

DIAZOLE *n* type of organic compound

DIAZOLES > DIAZOLE

DIAZONIUM *n* type of chemical group

DIAZOS > DIAZO

DIAZOTISE *same as* > DIAZOTIZE

DIAZOTIZE *vb* cause (an aryl amine) to react with nitrous acid to produce a diazonium salt

DIB *vb* fish by allowing the bait to bob and dip on the surface

DIBASIC *adj* (of an acid) containing two acidic hydrogen atoms

DIBBED > DIB

DIBBER *same as* > DIBBLE

DIBBERS > DIBBER

DIBBING > DIB

DIBBLE *n* small gardening tool ▷ *vb* make a hole in (the ground) with a dibble

DIBBLED > DIBBLE

DIBBLER > DIBBLE

DIBBLERS > DIBBLE

DIBBLES > DIBBLE

DIBBLING > DIBBLE

DIBBS *n* money

DIBBUK *variant spelling of* > DYBBUK

DIBBUKIM > DIBBUK

DIBBUKKIM > DIBBUK

DIBBUKS > DIBBUK

DIBROMIDE *n* chemical compound that contains two bromine atoms per molecule

DIBS > DIB

DIBUTYL adj with two butyl groups

DICACIOUS adj teasing

DICACITY n playful teasing

DICACODYL n oily slightly water-soluble poisonous liquid with garlic-like odour

DICALCIUM n two atoms of calcium in a compound

DICAMBA n type of weedkiller

DICAMBAS > DICAMBA

DICAST n juror in ancient Athens

DICASTERY n congregation

DICASTIC > DICAST

DICASTS > DICAST

DICE n small cube with numbered sides ⊳ vb cut (food) into small cubes

DICED > DICE

DICELIKE adj like dice

DICENTRA n Asian or N American ornamental plant

DICENTRAS > DICENTRA

DICENTRIC n abnormal chromosome with two centromeres

DICER > DICE

DICERS > DICE

DICES > DICE

DICEY adj dangerous or risky

DICH interj archaic expression meaning 'may it do'

DICHASIA > DICHASIUM

DICHASIAL > DICHASIUM

DICHASIUM n cymose inflorescence in which each branch bearing a flower gives rise to two other flowering branches, as in the stitchwort

DICHOGAMY n maturation of male and female parts of a flower at different times, preventing automatic self-pollination

DICHONDRA n creeping perennial herb

DICHOPTIC adj having the eyes distinctly separate

DICHORD n two-stringed musical instrument

DICHORDS > DICHORD

DICHOTIC adj relating to or involving the stimulation of each ear simultaneously by different sounds

DICHOTOMY n division into two opposed groups or parts

DICHROIC adj having or consisting of only two colours

DICHROISM n property of a uniaxial crystal, such as tourmaline, of showing a perceptible difference in colour when viewed along two different axes in transmitted white light

DICHROITE n grey or violet-blue dichroic material

DICHROMAT n person able to distinguish only two colours

DICHROMIC adj of or involving only two colours

DICHT vb wipe

DICHTED > DICHT

DICHTING > DICHT

DICHTS > DICHT

DICIER > DICEY

DICIEST > DICEY

DICING > DICE

DICINGS > DICE

DICK n fellow ⊳ vb vulgar word meaning penetrate with a penis

DICKED > DICK

DICKENS n euphemism for devil

DICKENSES > DICKENS

DICKER vb trade (goods) by bargaining ⊳ n petty bargain or barter

DICKERED > DICKER

DICKERER n person who dickers

DICKERERS > DICKERER

DICKERING > DICKER

DICKERS > DICKER

DICKEY same as > DICKY

DICKEYS > DICKEY

DICKHEAD n vulgar word for a stupid or despicable man

DICKHEADS > DICKHEAD

DICKIE same as > DICKY

DICKIER > DICKY

DICKIES > DICKY

DICKIEST > DICKY

DICKING > DICK

DICKINGS > DICKING

DICKS > DICK

DICKTIER > DICKTY

DICKTIEST > DICKTY

DICKTY same as > DICTY

DICKY n false shirt front ⊳ adj shaky or weak

DICKYBIRD same as > DICKY

DICLINIES > DICLINOUS

DICLINISM > DICLINOUS

DICLINOUS adj (of flowering plants) bearing unisexual flowers

DICLINY > DICLINOUS

DICOT n type of flowering plant

DICOTS > DICOT

DICOTYL n type of flowering plant

DICOTYLS > DICOTYL

DICROTAL same as > DICROTIC

DICROTIC adj having or relating to a double pulse for each heartbeat

DICROTISM > DICROTIC

DICROTOUS same as > DICROTIC

DICT vb dictate

DICTA > DICTUM

DICTATE vb say aloud for someone else to write down ⊳ n authoritative command

DICTATED > DICTATE

DICTATES > DICTATE

DICTATING > DICTATE

DICTATION n act of dictating words to be taken down in writing

DICTATOR n ruler who has complete power

DICTATORS > DICTATOR

DICTATORY adj tending to dictate

DICTATRIX n female dictator

DICTATURE n dictatorship

DICTED > DICT

DICTIER > DICTY

DICTIEST > DICTY

DICTING > DICT

DICTION n manner of pronouncing words and sounds

DICTIONAL > DICTION

DICTIONS > DICTION

DICTS > DICT

DICTUM n formal statement

DICTUMS > DICTUM

DICTY adj conceited; snobbish

DICTYOGEN n plant with net-veined leaves

DICUMAROL n anticoagulant drug

DICYCLIC adj having the perianth arranged in two whorls

DICYCLIES > DICYCLIC

DICYCLY > DICYCLIC

DID > DO

DIDACT n instructive person

DIDACTIC adj intended to instruct

DIDACTICS n art or science of teaching

DIDACTS > DIDACT

DIDACTYL adj having only two toes on each foot ⊳ n animal with only two toes on each foot

DIDACTYLS > DIDACTYL

DIDAKAI same as > DIDICOY

DIDAKAIS > DIDAKAI

DIDAKEI same as > DIDICOY

DIDAKEIS > DIDAKEI

DIDAPPER n small grebe

DIDAPPERS > DIDAPPER

DIDDER vb shake with fear

DIDDERED > DIDDER

DIDDERING > DIDDER

DIDDERS > DIDDER

DIDDICOY same as > DIDICOY

DIDDICOYS > DIDDICOY

DIDDIER > DIDDY

DIDDIES > DIDDY

DIDDIEST > DIDDY

DIDDLE vb swindle

DIDDLED > DIDDLE

DIDDLER > DIDDLE

DIDDLERS > DIDDLE

DIDDLES > DIDDLE

DIDDLEY n worthless amount

DIDDLEYS > DIDDLEY

DIDDLIES > DIDDLY

DIDDLING > DIDDLE

DIDDLY n worthless amount

DIDDUMS interj expression of sympathy, esp to a child

DIDDY n Scots word for a foolish person ⊳ adj foolish

DIDELPHIC adj with two genital tubes or ovaries

DIDELPHID n marsupial

DIDICOI same as > DIDICOY

DIDICOIS > DIDICOI

DIDICOY n (in Britain) a person who lives like a Roma but is not a true one

DIDICOYS > DIDICOY

DIDIE same as > DIDY

DIDIES > DIDY

DIDJERIDU n Aboriginal Australian wind instrument

DIDO n antic

DIDOES > DIDO

DIDOS > DIDO

DIDRACHM n two-drachma piece

DIDRACHMA same as > DIDRACHM

DIDRACHMS > DIDRACHM

DIDST form of the past tense of > DO

DIDY n (US) child's word for nappy

DIDYMIUM n metallic mixture once thought to be an element

DIDYMIUMS > DIDYMIUM

DIDYMO n class of algae

DIDYMOS > DIDYMO

DIDYMOUS adj in pairs or in two parts

DIDYNAMY n (of stamens) being in two unequal pairs

DIE vb cease all biological activity permanently ⊳ n shaped block used to cut or form metal

DIEB n N African jackal

DIEBACK n disease of trees and shrubs ⊳ vb (of plants) to suffer from dieback

DIEBACKS > DIEBACK

DIEBS > DIEB

DIECIOUS same as > DIOECIOUS

DIED > DIE

DIEDRAL same as > DIHEDRAL

DIEDRALS > DIEDRAL
DIEDRE *n* large shallow groove or corner in a rock face
DIEDRES > DIEDRE
DIEGESES > DIEGESIS
DIEGESIS *n* utterance of fact
DIEGETIC *adj* relating to a factual narrative
DIEHARD *n* person who resists change
DIEHARDS > DIEHARD
DIEING > DIE
DIEL *n* 24-hour period ▷ *adj* of or lasting for any 24-hour period
DIELDRIN *n* highly toxic insecticide
DIELDRINS > DIELDRIN
DIELS > DIEL
DIELYTRA *n* genus of herbaceous plants
DIELYTRAS > DIELYTRA
DIEMAKER *n* one who makes dies
DIEMAKERS > DIEMAKER
DIENE *n* type of hydrocarbon
DIENES > DIENE
DIEOFF *n* process of dying in large numbers
DIEOFFS > DIEOFF
DIERESES > DIERESIS
DIERESIS *same as* > DIAERESIS
DIERETIC > DIERESIS
DIES > DIE
DIESEL *vb* drive diesel-fuelled vehicle ▷ *n* diesel engine
DIESELED > DIESEL
DIESELING > DIESEL
DIESELISE *same as* > DIESELIZE
DIESELIZE *vb* be equipped with diesel engine
DIESELS > DIESEL
DIESES > DIESIS
DIESINKER *n* person who engraves dies
DIESIS *n* printed symbol indicating a footnote
DIESTER *n* synthetic lubricant
DIESTERS > DIESTER
DIESTOCK *n* device holding the dies used to cut an external screw thread
DIESTOCKS > DIESTOCK
DIESTROUS *same as* > DIOESTRUS
DIESTRUM *another word for* > DIOESTRUS
DIESTRUMS > DIESTRUM
DIESTRUS *same as* > DIOESTRUS
DIET *n* food that a person or animal regularly eats ▷ *vb* follow a special diet so as to lose weight ▷ *adj*

(of food) suitable for a weight-reduction diet
DIETARIAN *n* dieter
DIETARIES > DIETARY
DIETARILY > DIETARY
DIETARY *adj* of or relating to a diet ▷ *n* regulated diet
DIETED > DIET
DIETER > DIET
DIETERS > DIET
DIETETIC *adj* prepared for special dietary requirements
DIETETICS *n* study of diet and nutrition
DIETHER *n* chemical compound
DIETHERS > DIETHER
DIETHYL *adj* as in *diethyl ether* ether
DIETHYLS > DIETHYL
DIETICIAN *n* person who specializes in dietetics
DIETINE *n* low-ranking diet or assembly
DIETINES > DIETINE
DIETING > DIET
DIETINGS > DIET
DIETIST *another word for* > DIETITIAN
DIETISTS > DIETIST
DIETITIAN *same as* > DIETICIAN
DIETS > DIET
DIF *same as* > DIFF
DIFF *n* informal word meaning difference
DIFFER *vb* be unlike
DIFFERED > DIFFER
DIFFERENT *adj* unlike
DIFFERING > DIFFER
DIFFERS > DIFFER
DIFFICILE *adj* difficult
DIFFICULT *adj* requiring effort or skill to do or understand
DIFFIDENT *adj* lacking self-confidence
DIFFLUENT *adj* flowing; not fixed
DIFFORM *adj* irregular in form
DIFFRACT *vb* cause to undergo diffraction
DIFFRACTS > DIFFRACT
DIFFS > DIFF
DIFFUSE *vb* spread over a wide area ▷ *adj* widely spread
DIFFUSED > DIFFUSE
DIFFUSELY > DIFFUSE
DIFFUSER *n* person or thing that diffuses
DIFFUSERS > DIFFUSER
DIFFUSES > DIFFUSE
DIFFUSING > DIFFUSE
DIFFUSION *n* act of diffusing or the fact of being diffused
DIFFUSIVE *adj* characterized by diffusion
DIFFUSOR *same as* > DIFFUSER
DIFFUSORS > DIFFUSOR

DIFS > DIF
DIG *vb* cut into, break up, and turn over or remove (earth), esp with a spade ▷ *n* digging
DIGAMIES > DIGAMY
DIGAMIST > DIGAMY
DIGAMISTS > DIGAMY
DIGAMMA *n* obsolete letter of the Greek alphabet
DIGAMMAS > DIGAMMA
DIGAMOUS > DIGAMY
DIGAMY *n* second marriage
DIGASTRIC *adj* (of certain muscles) having two fleshy portions joined by a tendon ▷ *n* muscle of the mandible that assists in lowering the lower jaw
DIGENESES > DIGENESIS
DIGENESIS *n* ability to alternate between means of reproduction
DIGENETIC *adj* of or relating to digenesis
DIGERATI *pl n* people who earn large amounts of money through internet-related business
DIGEST *vb* subject to a process of digestion ▷ *n* shortened version of a book, report, or article
DIGESTANT *same as* > DIGESTIVE
DIGESTED > DIGEST
DIGESTER *n* apparatus or vessel, such as an autoclave, in which digestion is carried out
DIGESTERS > DIGESTER
DIGESTIF *n* something, esp a drink, taken as an aid to digestion, either before or after a meal
DIGESTIFS > DIGESTIF
DIGESTING > DIGEST
DIGESTION *n* (body's system for) breaking down food into easily absorbed substances
DIGESTIVE *adj* relating to digestion
DIGESTOR *same as* > DIGESTER
DIGESTORS > DIGESTOR
DIGESTS > DIGEST
DIGGABLE *adj* that can be dug
DIGGED *a past tense of* > DIG
DIGGER *n* machine used for digging
DIGGERS > DIGGER
DIGGING > DIG
DIGGINGS *pl n* material that has been dug out
DIGHT *vb* adorn or equip, as for battle
DIGHTED > DIGHT
DIGHTING > DIGHT
DIGHTS > DIGHT

DIGICAM *n* digital camera
DIGICAMS > DIGICAM
DIGIPACK *n* (esp formerly) type of packaging for a CD or DVD
DIGIPACKS > DIGIPACK
DIGIT *n* finger or toe
DIGITAL *adj* displaying information as numbers ▷ *n* one of the keys on the manuals of an organ or piano, etc
DIGITALIN *n* poisonous amorphous crystalline mixture of glycosides extracted from digitalis leaves and formerly used in treating heart disease
DIGITALIS *n* drug made from foxglove leaves, used as a heart stimulant
DIGITALLY > DIGITAL
DIGITALS > DIGITAL
DIGITATE *adj* (of leaves) having leaflets in the form of a spread hand
DIGITATED *same as* > DIGITATE
DIGITISE *same as* > DIGITIZE
DIGITISED > DIGITISE
DIGITISER > DIGITIZE
DIGITISES > DIGITISE
DIGITIZE *vb* transcribe (data) into a digital form for processing by a computer
DIGITIZED *adj* recorded or stored in digital form
DIGITIZER > DIGITIZE
DIGITIZES > DIGITIZE
DIGITONIN *n* type of glycoside
DIGITOXIN *same as* > DIGOXIN
DIGITRON *n* type of tube for displaying information
DIGITRONS > DIGITRON
DIGITS > DIGIT
DIGITULE *n* any small finger-like process
DIGITULES > DIGITULE
DIGLOSSIA *n* existence in a language of a high, or socially prestigious, and a low, or everyday, form, as German and Swiss German in Switzerland
DIGLOSSIC > DIGLOSSIA
DIGLOT *n* bilingual book
DIGLOTS > DIGLOT
DIGLOTTIC > DIGLOT
DIGLYPH *n* ornament in a Doric frieze with two grooves
DIGLYPHS > DIGLYPH
DIGNIFIED *adj* calm, impressive, and worthy of respect

DIGNIFIES > DIGNIFY

DIGNIFY vb add distinction to

DIGNITARY n person of high official position

DIGNITIES > DIGNITY

DIGNITY n serious, calm, and controlled behaviour or manner

DIGONAL adj of or relating to a symmetry operation

DIGOXIN n glycoside extracted from the leaves of the woolly foxglove

DIGOXINS > DIGOXIN

DIGRAPH n two letters used to represent a single sound

DIGRAPHIC > DIGRAPH

DIGRAPHS > DIGRAPH

DIGRESS vb depart from the main subject in speech or writing

DIGRESSED > DIGRESS

DIGRESSER > DIGRESS

DIGRESSES > DIGRESS

DIGS > DIG

DIGYNIAN adj relating to plant class Digynia

DIGYNOUS another word for > DIGYNIAN

DIHEDRA > DIHEDRON

DIHEDRAL adj having or formed by two intersecting planes ▷ n figure formed by two intersecting planes

DIHEDRALS > DIHEDRAL

DIHEDRON n figure formed by two intersecting planes

DIHEDRONS > DIHEDRON

DIHYBRID n offspring of two individuals that differ with respect to two pairs of genes

DIHYBRIDS > DIHYBRID

DIHYDRIC adj (of an alcohol) containing two hydroxyl groups per molecule

DIKA n wild mango

DIKAS > DIKA

DIKAST same as > DICAST

DIKASTS > DIKAST

DIKDIK n small African antelope

DIKDIKS > DIKDIK

DIKE same as > DYKE

DIKED > DIKE

DIKER n builder of dikes

DIKERS > DIKER

DIKES > DIKE

DIKETONE n as in diphenylene diketone compound used in dye manufacture, aka anthraquinone

DIKETONES > DIKETONE

DIKING > DIKE

DIKKOP n type of brownish shore bird with a large head and eyes

DIKKOPS > DIKKOP

DIKTAT n dictatorial decree

DIKTATS > DIKTAT

DILATABLE > DILATE

DILATABLY > DILATE

DILATANCY n phenomenon caused by the nature of the stacking or fitting together of particles or granules in a heterogeneous system, such as the solidification of certain sols under pressure, and the thixotropy of certain gels

DILATANT adj tending to dilate ▷ n something, such as a catheter, that causes dilation

DILATANTS > DILATANT

DILATATE same as > DILATE

DILATATOR same as > DILATOR

DILATE vb make or become wider or larger

DILATED > DILATE

DILATER same as > DILATOR

DILATERS > DILATER

DILATES > DILATE

DILATING > DILATE

DILATION > DILATE

DILATIONS > DILATE

DILATIVE > DILATE

DILATOR n something that dilates an object

DILATORS > DILATOR

DILATORY adj tending or intended to waste time

DILDO n object used as a substitute for an erect penis

DILDOE same as > DILDO

DILDOES > DILDOE

DILDOS > DILDO

DILEMMA n situation offering a choice between two undesirable alternatives

DILEMMAS > DILEMMA

DILEMMIC > DILEMMA

DILIGENCE n steady and careful application

DILIGENT adj careful and persevering in carrying out duties

DILL n sweet-smelling herb ▷ vb flavour with dill

DILLED > DILL

DILLI n small bag, esp one made of plaited grass

DILLIER > DILLY

DILLIES > DILLY

DILLIEST > DILLY

DILLING > DILL

DILLINGS > DILL

DILLIS > DILLI

DILLS > DILL

DILLWEED n dill plant or its foliage

DILLWEEDS > DILLWEED

DILLY adj foolish ▷ n person or thing that is remarkable

DILSCOOP n type of shot in cricket in which the ball goes over the wicketkeeper's head

DILSCOOPS > DILSCOOP

DILTIAZEM n drug used to treat angina

DILUENT adj causing dilution or serving to dilute ▷ n substance used for or causing dilution

DILUENTS > DILUENT

DILUTABLE > DILUTE

DILUTE vb make (a liquid) less concentrated, esp by adding water ▷ adj (of a liquid) thin and watery

DILUTED > DILUTE

DILUTEE > DILUTE

DILUTEES > DILUTE

DILUTER > DILUTE

DILUTERS > DILUTE

DILUTES > DILUTE

DILUTING > DILUTE

DILUTION n act of diluting or state of being diluted

DILUTIONS > DILUTION

DILUTIVE adj having effect of decreasing earnings per share

DILUTOR n thing intended to have a diluting effect

DILUTORS > DILUTOR

DILUVIA > DILUVIUM

DILUVIAL adj of a flood, esp the great Flood described in the Old Testament

DILUVIAN same as > DILUVIAL

DILUVION same as > DILUVIUM

DILUVIONS > DILUVION

DILUVIUM n glacial drift

DILUVIUMS > DILUVIUM

DIM adj badly lit ▷ vb make or become dim

DIMBLE n wooded hollow; dingle

DIMBLES > DIMBLE

DIMBO n unintelligent person

DIMBOES > DIMBO

DIMBOS > DIMBO

DIME n coin of the US and Canada, worth ten cents

DIMENSION n measurement of the size of something in a particular direction ▷ vb shape or cut to specified dimensions

DIMER n type of molecule

DIMERIC adj of a dimer

DIMERISE same as > DIMERIZE

DIMERISED > DIMERISE

DIMERISES > DIMERISE

DIMERISM > DIMEROUS

DIMERISMS > DIMEROUS

DIMERIZE vb react or cause to react to form a dimer

DIMERIZED > DIMERIZE

DIMERIZES > DIMERIZE

DIMEROUS adj consisting of or divided into two segments, as the tarsi of some insects

DIMERS > DIMER

DIMES > DIME

DIMETER n type of verse

DIMETERS > DIMETER

DIMETHYL n ethane

DIMETHYLS > DIMETHYL

DIMETRIC adj of, relating to, or shaped like a quadrilateral

DIMIDIATE adj divided in halves ▷ vb halve (two bearings) so that they can be represented on the same shield

DIMINISH vb make or become smaller, fewer, or less

DIMISSORY adj granting permission to be ordained

DIMITIES > DIMITY

DIMITY n light strong cotton fabric with woven stripes or squares

DIMLY > DIM

DIMMABLE adj that can be dimmed

DIMMED > DIM

DIMMER > DIM

DIMMERS > DIM

DIMMEST > DIM

DIMMING n as in global dimming decrease in the amount of sunlight reaching the earth

DIMMINGS > DIMMING

DIMMISH > DIM

DIMNESS > DIM

DIMNESSES > DIM

DIMORPH n either of two forms of a substance that exhibits dimorphism

DIMORPHIC adj having two distinct forms

DIMORPHS > DIMORPH

DIMOUT n reduction of lighting

DIMOUTS > DIMOUT

DIMP n in Northern English dialect, a cigarette butt

DIMPLE n small natural dent, esp in the cheeks or chin ▷ vb produce dimples by smiling

DIMPLED > DIMPLE

DIMPLES > DIMPLE

DIMPLIER > DIMPLE

DIMPLIEST > DIMPLE

DIMPLING > DIMPLE

DIMPLY > DIMPLE

DIMPS > DIMP

DIMPSIES > DIMPSY

DIMPSY n twilight

DIMS > DIM

DIMWIT n stupid person

DIMWITS > DIMWIT

d

DIMWITTED > DIMWIT
DIMYARIAN adj with two adductor muscles
DIMYARY adj with two adductor muscles
DIN n loud unpleasant confused noise ▷ vb instil (something) into someone by constant repetition
DINAR n monetary unit
DINARCHY same as > DIARCHY
DINARS > DINAR
DINDLE another word for > DINNLE
DINDLED > DINDLE
DINDLES > DINDLE
DINDLING > DINDLE
DINE vb eat dinner
DINED > DINE
DINER n person eating a meal
DINERIC adj of or concerned with the interface between immiscible liquids
DINERO n money
DINEROS > DINERO
DINERS > DINER
DINES > DINE
DINETTE n alcove or small area for use as a dining room
DINETTES > DINETTE
DINFUL adj noisy
DING n small dent in a vehicle ▷ vb ring or cause to ring, esp with tedious repetition
DINGBAT n any unnamed object
DINGBATS > DINGBAT
DINGDONG n sound of a bell or bells ▷ vb make such a sound
DINGDONGS > DINGDONG
DINGE n dent ▷ vb make a dent in (something)
DINGED > DINGE
DINGER n (in baseball) home run
DINGERS > DINGER
DINGES n jocular word for something whose name is unknown or forgotten
DINGESES > DINGES
DINGEY same as > DINGHY
DINGEYS > DINGEY
DINGHIES > DINGHY
DINGHY n small boat, powered by sails, oars, or a motor ▷ vb ignore or avoid a person or event
DINGIED > DINGY
DINGIER > DINGY
DINGIES > DINGY
DINGIEST > DINGY
DINGILY > DINGY
DINGINESS > DINGY
DINGING > DINGE
DINGLE n small wooded hollow or valley
DINGLES > DINGLE
DINGO n Australian wild dog ▷ vb act in a cowardly manner

DINGOED > DINGO
DINGOES > DINGO
DINGOING > DINGO
DINGOS > DINGO
DINGUS same as > DINGES
DINGUSES > DINGUS
DINGY adj lacking light ▷ vb ignore or avoid a person or event
DINGYING > DINGY
DINIC n remedy for vertigo
DINICS > DINIC
DINING n act of dining
DININGS > DINING
DINITRO adj containing two nitro groups
DINK adj neat or neatly dressed ▷ vb carry (a second person) on a horse, bicycle, etc ▷ n ball struck delicately
DINKED > DINK
DINKER > DINK
DINKEST > DINK
DINKEY n small locomotive
DINKEYS > DINKEY
DINKIE n affluent married childless person ▷ adj designed for or appealing to dinkies
DINKIER > DINKY
DINKIES > DINKIE
DINKIEST > DINKY
DINKING > DINK
DINKLIER > DINKLY
DINKLIEST > DINKLY
DINKLY adj neat
DINKS > DINK
DINKUM n truth or genuineness
DINKUMS > DINKUM
DINKY adj small and neat
DINMONT n neutered sheep
DINMONTS > DINMONT
DINNA vb a Scots word for do not
DINNAE vb (Scots) do not
DINNED > DIN
DINNER vb dine ▷ n main meal of the day
DINNERED > DINNER
DINNERING > DINNER
DINNERS > DINNER
DINNING > DIN
DINNLE vb shake
DINNLED > DINNLE
DINNLES > DINNLE
DINNLING > DINNLE
DINO n dinosaur
DINOCERAS n uintathere, a gigantic fossil ungulate
DINOMANIA n strong interest in dinosaurs
DINOS > DINO
DINOSAUR n type of extinct reptile, many of which were of gigantic size
DINOSAURS > DINOSAUR
DINOTHERE n type of extinct elephant-like

mammal with tusks curving downwards and backwards
DINS > DIN
DINT variant of > DENT
DINTED > DINT
DINTING > DINT
DINTLESS > DINT
DINTS > DINT
DIOBOL n ancient Greek coin
DIOBOLON same as > DIOBOL
DIOBOLONS > DIOBOLON
DIOBOLS > DIOBOL
DIOCESAN adj of or relating to a diocese ▷ n bishop of a diocese
DIOCESANS > DIOCESAN
DIOCESE n district over which a bishop has control
DIOCESES > DIOCESE
DIODE n semiconductor device
DIODES > DIODE
DIOECIES > DIOECY
DIOECIOUS adj (of plants) having the male and female reproductive organs on separate plants
DIOECISM > DIOECIOUS
DIOECISMS > DIOECIOUS
DIOECY n state of being dioecious
DIOESTRUS n period in mammal's oestral cycle
DIOICOUS same as > DIOECIOUS
DIOL n any of a class of alcohols that have two hydroxyl groups in each molecule
DIOLEFIN n type of polymer
DIOLEFINS > DIOLEFIN
DIOLS > DIOL
DIONYSIAC same as > DIONYSIAN
DIONYSIAN adj relating to the set of creative qualities that encompasses spontaneity and irrationality
DIOPSIDE n colourless or pale-green pyroxene mineral
DIOPSIDES > DIOPSIDE
DIOPSIDIC > DIOPSIDE
DIOPTASE n green glassy mineral
DIOPTASES > DIOPTASE
DIOPTER same as > DIOPTRE
DIOPTERS > DIOPTER
DIOPTRAL > DIOPTRE
DIOPTRATE adj (of compound eye) divided by transverse line
DIOPTRE n unit for measuring the refractive power of a lens

DIOPTRES > DIOPTRE
DIOPTRIC adj of or concerned with dioptrics
DIOPTRICS n branch of geometrical optics concerned with the formation of images by lenses
DIORAMA n miniature three-dimensional scene
DIORAMAS > DIORAMA
DIORAMIC > DIORAMA
DIORISM n definition; clarity
DIORISMS > DIORISM
DIORISTIC > DIORISM
DIORITE n dark coarse-grained igneous plutonic rock
DIORITES > DIORITE
DIORITIC > DIORITE
DIOSGENIN n yam-based substance used in hormone therapy
DIOTA n type of ancient vase
DIOTAS > DIOTA
DIOXAN n colourless insoluble toxic liquid
DIOXANE same as > DIOXAN
DIOXANES > DIOXANE
DIOXANS > DIOXAN
DIOXID same as > DIOXIDE
DIOXIDE n oxide containing two oxygen atoms per molecule
DIOXIDES > DIOXIDE
DIOXIDS > DIOXID
DIOXIN n poisonous chemical by-product of certain weedkillers
DIOXINS > DIOXIN
DIP vb plunge quickly or briefly into a liquid ▷ n dipping
DIPCHICK same as > DABCHICK
DIPCHICKS > DIPCHICK
DIPEPTIDE n compound consisting of two linked amino acids
DIPHASE adj of, having, or concerned with two phases
DIPHASIC same as > DIPHASE
DIPHENYL another name for > BIPHENYL
DIPHENYLS > DIPHENYL
DIPHONE n combination of two speech sounds
DIPHONES > DIPHONE
DIPHTHONG n union of two vowel sounds in a single compound sound
DIPHYSITE n belief in Christ having both divine and human natures
DIPLEGIA n paralysis of corresponding parts on both sides of the body
DIPLEGIAS > DIPLEGIA
DIPLEGIC > DIPLEGIA

DIPLEX *adj* permitting simultaneous transmission in both directions

DIPLEXER *n* device that enables the simultaneous transmission of more than one signal

DIPLEXERS > DIPLEXER

DIPLOE *n* spongy bone separating the two layers of compact bone of the skull

DIPLOES > DIPLOE

DIPLOGEN *n* heavy hydrogen

DIPLOGENS > DIPLOGEN

DIPLOIC *adj* relating to a diploe

DIPLOID *adj* denoting a cell or organism with pairs of homologous chromosomes ▷ *n* diploid cell or organism

DIPLOIDIC > DIPLOID

DIPLOIDS > DIPLOID

DIPLOIDY > DIPLOID

DIPLOMA *vb* bestow diploma on ▷ *n* qualification awarded by a college on successful completion of a course

DIPLOMACY *n* conduct of the relations between nations by peaceful means

DIPLOMAED > DIPLOMA

DIPLOMAS > DIPLOMA

DIPLOMAT *n* official engaged in diplomacy

DIPLOMATA > DIPLOMA

DIPLOMATE *n* any person who has been granted a diploma, esp a physician certified as a specialist

DIPLOMATS > DIPLOMAT

DIPLON another name for > DEUTERON

DIPLONEMA a less common name for > DIPLOTENE

DIPLONS > DIPLON

DIPLONT *n* animal or plant that has the diploid number of chromosomes in its somatic cells

DIPLONTIC > DIPLONT

DIPLONTS > DIPLONT

DIPLOPIA *n* visual defect in which a single object is seen in duplicate

DIPLOPIAS > DIPLOPIA

DIPLOPIC > DIPLOPIA

DIPLOPOD *n* type of arthropod such as the millipede

DIPLOPODS > DIPLOPOD

DIPLOSES > DIPLOSIS

DIPLOSIS *n* doubling of the haploid number of chromosomes

DIPLOTENE *n* fourth stage in the prophase of meiosis, during which the paired homologous chromosomes separate except at the places where genetic exchange has occurred

DIPLOZOA *n* type of parasitic worm

DIPLOZOIC *adj* (of certain animals) bilaterally symmetrical

DIPLOZOON *n* type of parasitic worm

DIPNET *vb* fish using a fishing net on a pole

DIPNETS > DIPNET

DIPNETTED > DIPNET

DIPNOAN *n* lungfish

DIPNOANS > DIPNOAN

DIPNOOUS *adj* having lungs and gills

DIPODIC > DIPODY

DIPODIES > DIPODY

DIPODY *n* metrical unit consisting of two feet

DIPOLAR > DIPOLE

DIPOLE *n* two equal but opposite electric charges or magnetic poles separated by a small distance

DIPOLES > DIPOLE

DIPPABLE > DIP

DIPPED > DIP

DIPPER *n* ladle used for dipping

DIPPERFUL *n* amount held by scoop

DIPPERS > DIPPER

DIPPIER > DIPPY

DIPPIEST > DIPPY

DIPPINESS > DIPPY

DIPPING > DIP

DIPPINGS > DIP

DIPPY *adj* odd, eccentric, or crazy

DIPROTIC *adj* having two hydrogen atoms

DIPS > DIP

DIPSADES > DIPSAS

DIPSAS *n* type of snake

DIPSHIT *n* vulgar word for a stupid person

DIPSHITS > DIPSHIT

DIPSO *n* dipsomaniac

DIPSOS > DIPSO

DIPSTICK *n* notched rod dipped into a container to measure the level of a liquid

DIPSTICKS > DIPSTICK

DIPSWITCH *n* switch for dipping a vehicle's headlights

DIPT > DIP

DIPTERA *n* order of insects with two wings

DIPTERAL *adj* having a double row of columns

DIPTERAN *n* dipterous insect ▷ *adj* having two wings or winglike parts

DIPTERANS > DIPTERAN

DIPTERAS > DIPTERA

DIPTERIST *n* fly expert

DIPTEROI > DIPTEROS

DIPTERON same as > DIPTERAN

DIPTERONS > DIPTERON

DIPTEROS *n* Greek building with double columns

DIPTEROUS *adj* having two wings or winglike parts

DIPTYCA same as > DIPTYCH

DIPTYCAS > DIPTYCA

DIPTYCH *n* painting on two hinged panels

DIPTYCHS > DIPTYCH

DIQUARK *n* particle in physics

DIQUARKS > DIQUARK

DIQUAT *n* type of herbicide

DIQUATS > DIQUAT

DIRAM *n* money unit of Tajikistan

DIRAMS > DIRAM

DIRDAM same as > DIRDUM

DIRDAMS > DIRDAM

DIRDUM *n* tumult

DIRDUMS > DIRDUM

DIRE *adj* disastrous, urgent, or terrible

DIRECT *adj* (of a route) shortest, straight ▷ *adv* in a direct manner ▷ *vb* lead and organize

DIRECTED > DIRECT

DIRECTER > DIRECT

DIRECTEST > DIRECT

DIRECTING > DIRECT

DIRECTION *n* course or line along which a person or thing moves, points, or lies

DIRECTIVE *n* instruction, order ▷ *adj* tending to direct

DIRECTLY *adv* in a direct manner

DIRECTOR *n* person or thing that directs or controls

DIRECTORS > DIRECTOR

DIRECTORY *n* book listing names, addresses, and telephone numbers ▷ *adj* directing

DIRECTRIX *n* fixed reference line, situated on the convex side of a conic section, that is used when defining or calculating its eccentricity

DIRECTS > DIRECT

DIREFUL same as > DIRE

DIREFULLY > DIREFUL

DIRELY > DIRE

DIREMPT *vb* separate with force

DIREMPTED > DIREMPT

DIREMPTS > DIREMPT

DIRENESS > DIRE

DIRER > DIRE

DIREST > DIRE

DIRGE *n* slow sad song of mourning

DIRGEFUL > DIRGE

DIRGELIKE > DIRGE

DIRGES > DIRGE

DIRHAM *n* standard monetary unit of Morocco

DIRHAMS > DIRHAM

DIRHEM same as > DIRHAM

DIRHEMS > DIRHEM

DIRIGE *n* dirge

DIRIGENT *adj* directing

DIRIGES > DIRIGE

DIRIGIBLE *adj* able to be steered ▷ *n* airship

DIRIGISM same as > DIRIGISME

DIRIGISME *n* control by the state of economic and social matters

DIRIGISMS > DIRIGISM

DIRIGISTE > DIRIGISME

DIRIMENT *adj* (of an impediment to marriage in canon law) totally invalidating

DIRK *n* dagger, formerly worn by Scottish Highlanders ▷ *vb* stab with a dirk

DIRKE variant of > DIRK

DIRKED > DIRK

DIRKES > DIRKE

DIRKING > DIRK

DIRKS > DIRK

DIRL *vb* tingle; vibrate

DIRLED > DIRL

DIRLING > DIRL

DIRLS > DIRL

DIRNDL *n* full gathered skirt

DIRNDLS > DIRNDL

DIRT *vb* soil ▷ *n* unclean substance, filth

DIRTBAG *n* filthy person

DIRTBAGS > DIRTBAG

DIRTBALL *n* insulting word for a contemptible person

DIRTBALLS > DIRTBALL

DIRTED > DIRT

DIRTIED > DIRTY

DIRTIER > DIRTY

DIRTIES > DIRTY

DIRTIEST > DIRTY

DIRTILY > DIRTY

DIRTINESS > DIRTY

DIRTING > DIRT

DIRTS > DIRT

DIRTY *adj* covered or marked with dirt ▷ *vb* make dirty

DIRTYING > DIRTY

DIS same as > DISS

DISA *n* type of orchid

DISABLE *vb* make ineffective, unfit, or incapable

DISABLED *adj* restricted in ability to move or use a sense

DISABLER > DISABLE

DISABLERS > DISABLE

DISABLES > DISABLE

DISABLING > DISABLE

DISABLISM *n* discrimination against disabled people

DISABLIST > DISABLISM

DISABUSAL
> DISABUSE
DISABUSE vb rid
(someone) of a mistaken
idea
DISABUSED
> DISABUSE
DISABUSES
> DISABUSE
DISACCORD n lack of
agreement or harmony
▷ vb be out of agreement
DISADORN vb deprive of
ornamentation
DISADORNS
> DISADORN
DISAFFECT vb cause to
lose loyalty or affection
DISAFFIRM vb deny or
contradict (a statement)
DISAGREE vb argue or
have different opinions
DISAGREED
> DISAGREE
DISAGREES
> DISAGREE
DISALLIED > DISALLY
DISALLIES > DISALLY
DISALLOW vb reject as
untrue or invalid
DISALLOWS
> DISALLOW
DISALLY vb separate
DISANCHOR vb raise
anchor of
DISANNEX vb disunite
DISANNUL vb cancel
DISANNULS
> DISANNUL
DISANOINT vb invalidate
anointment of
DISAPPEAR vb cease to
be visible
DISAPPLY vb make (law)
invalid
DISARM vb deprive of
weapons
DISARMED > DISARM
DISARMER > DISARM
DISARMERS > DISARM
DISARMING adj
removing hostility or
suspicion
DISARMS > DISARM
DISARRAY n confusion
and lack of discipline ▷ vb
throw into confusion
DISARRAYS
> DISARRAY
DISAS > DISA
DISASTER n occurrence
that causes great distress
or destruction
DISASTERS
> DISASTER
DISATTIRE vb remove
clothes from
DISATTUNE vb render
out of tune
DISAVOUCH archaic form
of > DISAVOW
DISAVOW vb deny
connection with or
responsibility for
DISAVOWAL > DISAVOW
DISAVOWED > DISAVOW
DISAVOWER > DISAVOW
DISAVOWS > DISAVOW

DISBAND vb (cause to)
cease to function as a
group
DISBANDED > DISBAND
DISBANDS > DISBAND
DISBAR vb deprive (a
barrister) of the right to
practise
DISBARK same as
> DISEMBARK
DISBARKED > DISBARK
DISBARKS > DISBARK
DISBARRED > DISBAR
DISBARS > DISBAR
DISBELIEF n refusal or
reluctance to believe
DISBENCH vb remove
from bench
DISBODIED adj
disembodied
DISBOSOM vb disclose
DISBOSOMS
> DISBOSOM
DISBOUND adj unbound
DISBOWEL vb
disembowel
DISBOWELS
> DISBOWEL
DISBRANCH vb remove
or cut a branch or
branches from (a tree)
DISBUD vb remove
superfluous buds from (a
plant, esp a fruit tree)
DISBUDDED > DISBUD
DISBUDS > DISBUD
DISBURDEN vb remove a
load from (a person or
animal)
DISBURSAL
> DISBURSE
DISBURSE vb pay out
DISBURSED
> DISBURSE
DISBURSER
> DISBURSE
DISBURSES
> DISBURSE
DISC n flat circular object
▷ vb work (land) with a
disc harrow
DISCAGE vb release from
cage
DISCAGED > DISCAGE
DISCAGES > DISCAGE
DISCAGING > DISCAGE
DISCAL adj relating to or
resembling a disc
DISCALCED adj
barefooted: used to
denote friars and nuns
who wear sandals
DISCANDIE same as
> DISCANDY
DISCANDY vb melt;
dissolve
DISCANT same as
> DESCANT
DISCANTED > DISCANT
DISCANTER > DISCANT
DISCANTS > DISCANT
DISCARD vb get rid of
(something or someone)
as useless or undesirable
▷ n person or thing that
has been cast aside
DISCARDED > DISCARD
DISCARDER > DISCARD

DISCARDS > DISCARD
DISCASE vb remove the
case from
DISCASED > DISCASE
DISCASES > DISCASE
DISCASING > DISCASE
DISCED > DISC
DISCEPT vb discuss
DISCEPTED > DISCEPT
DISCEPTS > DISCEPT
DISCERN vb see or be
aware of (something)
clearly
DISCERNED > DISCERN
DISCERNER > DISCERN
DISCERNS > DISCERN
DISCERP vb divide
DISCERPED > DISCERP
DISCERPS > DISCERP
DISCHARGE vb release,
allow to go ▷ n substance
that comes out from a
place
DISCHURCH vb deprive of
church membership
DISCI > DISCUS
DISCIDE vb split
DISCIDED > DISCIDE
DISCIDES > DISCIDE
DISCIDING > DISCIDE
DISCIFORM adj
disc-shaped
DISCINCT adj loosely
dressed, without belt
DISCING > DISC
DISCIPLE vb teach ▷ n
follower of the doctrines
of a teacher, esp Jesus
Christ
DISCIPLED
> DISCIPLE
DISCIPLES
> DISCIPLE
DISCLAIM vb deny
(responsibility for or
knowledge of something)
DISCLAIMS
> DISCLAIM
DISCLESS adj having no
disc
DISCLIKE > DISC
DISCLIMAX n climax
community resulting from
the activities of human
beings or domestic
animals in climatic and
other conditions that
would otherwise support
a different type of
community
DISCLOSE vb make
known
DISCLOSED
> DISCLOSE
DISCLOSER
> DISCLOSE
DISCLOSES
> DISCLOSE
DISCLOST > DISCLOSE
DISCO vb go to a disco ▷ n
nightclub where people
dance to amplified pop
records
DISCOBOLI pl n discus
throwers
DISCOED > DISCO
DISCOER > DISCO
DISCOERS > DISCO

DISCOES > DISCO
DISCOID adj like a disc
▷ n dislike object
DISCOIDAL adj like a
disc
DISCOIDS > DISCOID
DISCOING > DISCO
DISCOLOGY n study of
gramophone records
DISCOLOR same as
> DISCOLOUR
DISCOLORS
> DISCOLOR
DISCOLOUR vb change in
colour, fade
DISCOMFIT vb make
uneasy or confused
DISCOMMON vb deprive
(land) of the character and
status of common, as by
enclosure
DISCORD n lack of
agreement or harmony
between people ▷ vb
disagree
DISCORDED > DISCORD
DISCORDS > DISCORD
DISCOS > DISCO
DISCOUNT vb take no
account of something ▷ n
deduction from the full
price of something
DISCOUNTS
> DISCOUNT
DISCOURE vb discover
DISCOURED
> DISCOURE
DISCOURES
> DISCOURE
DISCOURSE n
conversation ▷ vb speak
or write (about) at length
DISCOVER vb be the first
to find or to find out about
DISCOVERS
> DISCOVER
DISCOVERT adj (of a
woman) not under the
protection of a husband
DISCOVERY n
discovering
DISCREDIT vb damage
the reputation of ▷ n
damage to someone's
reputation
DISCREET adj careful to
avoid embarrassment, esp
by keeping confidences
secret
DISCRETE adj separate,
distinct
DISCRETER
> DISCRETE
DISCROWN vb deprive of a
crown
DISCROWNS
> DISCROWN
DISCS > DISC
DISCUMBER vb
disencumber
DISCURE old form of
> DISCOVER
DISCURED > DISCURE
DISCURES > DISCURE
DISCURING > DISCURE
DISCURSUS n discursive
reasoning
DISCUS n object thrown
in sports competitions

DISCUSES > DISCUS

DISCUSS vb consider (something) by talking it over

DISCUSSED > DISCUSS

DISCUSSER > DISCUSS

DISCUSSES > DISCUSS

DISDAIN n feeling of superiority and dislike ▷ vb refuse with disdain

DISDAINED > DISDAIN

DISDAINS > DISDAIN

DISEASE vb make uneasy ▷ n illness, sickness

DISEASED adj having or affected with disease

DISEASES > DISEASE

DISEASING > DISEASE

DISEDGE vb render blunt

DISEDGED > DISEDGE

DISEDGES > DISEDGE

DISEDGING > DISEDGE

DISEMBARK vb get off a ship, aircraft, or bus

DISEMBODY vb free from the body or from physical form

DISEMPLOY vb dismiss from employment

DISENABLE vb cause to become incapable

DISENDOW vb take away an endowment from

DISENDOWS > DISENDOW

DISENGAGE vb release from a connection

DISENROL vb remove from register

DISENROLS > DISENROL

DISENTAIL vb free (an estate) from entail ▷ n act of disentailing

DISENTOMB vb disinter

DISESTEEM vb think little of ▷ n lack of esteem

DISEUR n (esp formerly) an actor who presents dramatic recitals

DISEURS > DISEUR

DISEUSE n (esp formerly) an actress who presents dramatic recitals

DISEUSES > DISEUSE

DISFAME n discredit ▷ vb throw into disrepute or remove fame (from)

DISFAMED > DISFAME

DISFAMES > DISFAME

DISFAMING > DISFAME

DISFAVOR same as > DISFAVOUR

DISFAVORS > DISFAVOR

DISFAVOUR n disapproval or dislike ▷ vb regard or treat with disapproval or dislike

DISFIGURE vb spoil the appearance of

DISFLESH vb reduce flesh of

DISFLUENT adj lacking fluency in speech

DISFOREST same as > DEFOREST

DISFORM vb change form of

DISFORMED > DISFORM

DISFORMS > DISFORM

DISFROCK another word for > UNFROCK

DISFROCKS > DISFROCK

DISGAVEL vb deprive of quality of gavelkind

DISGAVELS > DISGAVEL

DISGEST vb digest

DISGESTED > DISGEST

DISGESTS > DISGEST

DISGODDED adj deprived of religion

DISGORGE vb empty out, discharge

DISGORGED > DISGORGE

DISGORGER n thin notched metal implement for removing hooks from a fish

DISGORGES > DISGORGE

DISGOWN vb remove a gown from

DISGOWNED > DISGOWN

DISGOWNS > DISGOWN

DISGRACE n condition of shame, loss of reputation, or dishonour ▷ vb bring shame upon (oneself or others)

DISGRACED > DISGRACE

DISGRACER > DISGRACE

DISGRACES > DISGRACE

DISGRADE vb degrade

DISGRADED > DISGRADE

DISGRADES > DISGRADE

DISGUISE vb change the appearance to conceal the identity ▷ n mask, costume, or manner that disguises

DISGUISED > DISGUISE

DISGUISER > DISGUISE

DISGUISES > DISGUISE

DISGUST n great loathing or distaste ▷ vb sicken, fill with loathing

DISGUSTED > DISGUST

DISGUSTS > DISGUST

DISH n shallow container used for holding or serving food ▷ vb put into a dish

DISHABIT vb dislodge

DISHABITS > DISHABIT

DISHABLE obsolete form of > DISABLE

DISHABLED > DISHABLE

DISHABLES > DISHABLE

DISHALLOW vb make unholy

DISHCLOTH n cloth for washing dishes

DISHCLOUT same as > DISHCLOTH

DISHDASH same as > DISHDASHA

DISHDASHA n long-sleeved collarless white garment worn by some Muslim men

DISHED adj shaped like a dish

DISHELM vb remove a helmet from

DISHELMED > DISHELM

DISHELMS > DISHELM

DISHERIT vb disinherit

DISHERITS > DISHERIT

DISHES > DISH

DISHEVEL vb disarrange (the hair or clothes) of (someone)

DISHEVELS > DISHEVEL

DISHFUL n the amount that a dish is able to hold

DISHFULS > DISHFUL

DISHIER > DISHY

DISHIEST > DISHY

DISHING > DISH

DISHINGS > DISH

DISHLIKE > DISH

DISHMOP n mop for cleaning dishes

DISHMOPS > DISHMOP

DISHOARD vb put previously withheld (money) into circulation

DISHOARDS > DISHOARD

DISHOME vb deprive of home

DISHOMED > DISHOME

DISHOMES > DISHOME

DISHOMING > DISHOME

DISHONEST adj not honest or fair

DISHONOR same as > DISHONOUR

DISHONORS > DISHONOR

DISHONOUR vb treat with disrespect ▷ n lack of respect

DISHORN vb remove the horns from

DISHORNED > DISHORN

DISHORNS > DISHORN

DISHORSE vb dismount

DISHORSED > DISHORSE

DISHORSES > DISHORSE

DISHOUSE vb deprive of home

DISHOUSED > DISHOUSE

DISHOUSES > DISHOUSE

DISHPAN n large pan for washing dishes, pots, etc

DISHPANS > DISHPAN

DISHRAG n dishcloth

DISHRAGS > DISHRAG

DISHTOWEL n towel for drying dishes and kitchen utensils

DISHUMOUR vb upset; offend

DISHWARE n tableware

DISHWARES > DISHWARE

DISHWATER n water in which dishes and kitchen utensils are or have been washed

DISHY adj good-looking

DISILLUDE vb remove illusions from

DISIMMURE vb release

DISINFECT vb rid of harmful germs, chemically

DISINFEST vb rid of vermin

DISINFORM vb give wrong information

DISINHUME vb dig up

DISINTER vb dig up

DISINTERS > DISINTER

DISINURE vb render unaccustomed

DISINURED > DISINURE

DISINURES > DISINURE

DISINVENT vb undo the invention or existence of

DISINVEST vb remove investment (from)

DISINVITE vb retract invitation to

DISJASKIT adj fatigued

DISJECT vb break apart

DISJECTED > DISJECT

DISJECTS > DISJECT

DISJOIN vb disconnect or become disconnected

DISJOINED > DISJOIN

DISJOINS > DISJOIN

DISJOINT vb take apart or come apart at the joints ▷ adj (of two sets) having no members in common

DISJOINTS > DISJOINT

DISJUNCT adj not united or joined ▷ n one of the propositions or formulas in a disjunction

DISJUNCTS > DISJUNCT

DISJUNE n breakfast ▷ vb breakfast

DISJUNED > DISJUNE

DISJUNES > DISJUNE

DISJUNING > DISJUNE

DISK same as > DISC

DISKED > DISK

DISKER n person who breaks up earth with a type of farm implement

DISKERS > DISKER

DISKETTE n floppy disk

DISKETTES > DISKETTE

DISKING > DISK

DISKLESS > DISK

DISKLIKE > DISK

DISKS > DISK

DISLEAF vb remove a leaf or leaves from

DISLEAFED > DISLEAF

DISLEAFS > DISLEAF

DISLEAL archaic form of > DISLOYAL

DISLEAVE variant of > DISLEAF

DISLEAVED
> DISLEAVE
DISLEAVES
> DISLEAVE
DISLIKE vb consider unpleasant or disagreeable ▷ n feeling of not liking something or someone
DISLIKED > DISLIKE
DISLIKEN vb render dissimilar to
DISLIKENS
> DISLIKEN
DISLIKER > DISLIKE
DISLIKERS > DISLIKE
DISLIKES > DISLIKE
DISLIKING > DISLIKE
DISLIMB vb remove limbs from
DISLIMBED > DISLIMB
DISLIMBS > DISLIMB
DISLIMN vb efface
DISLIMNED > DISLIMN
DISLIMNS > DISLIMN
DISLINK vb disunite
DISLINKED > DISLINK
DISLINKS > DISLINK
DISLOAD vb unload
DISLOADED > DISLOAD
DISLOADS > DISLOAD
DISLOCATE vb displace (a bone or joint) from its normal position
DISLODGE vb remove (something) from a previously fixed position
DISLODGED
> DISLODGE
DISLODGES
> DISLODGE
DISLOIGN vb put at a distance
DISLOIGNS
> DISLOIGN
DISLOYAL adj not loyal, deserting one's allegiance
DISLUSTRE vb remove lustre from
DISMAL adj gloomy
DISMALER > DISMAL
DISMALEST > DISMAL
DISMALITY > DISMAL
DISMALLER > DISMAL
DISMALLY > DISMAL
DISMALS pl n gloomy state of mind
DISMAN vb remove men from
DISMANNED > DISMAN
DISMANS > DISMAN
DISMANTLE vb take apart piece by piece
DISMASK vb remove a mask from
DISMASKED > DISMASK
DISMASKS > DISMASK
DISMAST vb break off the mast or masts of (a sailing vessel)
DISMASTED > DISMAST
DISMASTS > DISMAST
DISMAY vb fill with alarm or sadness ▷ n alarm mixed with sadness
DISMAYD adj word used by Spenser meaning misshapen

DISMAYED > DISMAY
DISMAYFUL > DISMAY
DISMAYING > DISMAY
DISMAYL vb remove a coat of mail from
DISMAYLED > DISMAYL
DISMAYLS > DISMAYL
DISMAYS > DISMAY
DISME old form of
> DIME
DISMEMBER vb remove the limbs of
DISMES > DISME
DISMISS vb remove (an employee) from a job ▷ sentence substitute order to end an activity or give permission to disperse
DISMISSAL n official notice of discharge from employment or service
DISMISSED > DISMISS
DISMISSES > DISMISS
DISMODED adj no longer fashionable
DISMOUNT vb get off a horse or bicycle ▷ n act of dismounting
DISMOUNTS
> DISMOUNT
DISNATURE vb cause to be in an unnatural condition
DISNEST vb remove from a nest
DISNESTED > DISNEST
DISNESTS > DISNEST
DISOBEY vb neglect or refuse to obey
DISOBEYED > DISOBEY
DISOBEYER > DISOBEY
DISOBEYS > DISOBEY
DISOBLIGE vb disregard the desires of
DISODIUM n compound containing two sodium atoms
DISOMIC adj having an extra chromosome in the haploid state
DISOMIES > DISOMIC
DISOMY > DISOMIC
DISORBED adj thrown out of orbit
DISORDER n state of untidiness and disorganization ▷ vb upset the order of
DISORDERS
> DISORDER
DISORIENT vb cause (someone) to lose their bearings
DISOWN vb deny any connection with (someone)
DISOWNED > DISOWN
DISOWNER > DISOWN
DISOWNERS > DISOWN
DISOWNING > DISOWN
DISOWNS > DISOWN
DISPACE vb move or travel about
DISPACED > DISPACE
DISPACES > DISPACE
DISPACING > DISPACE
DISPARAGE vb speak contemptuously of

DISPARATE adj completely different ▷ n unlike things or people
DISPARITY n inequality or difference
DISPARK vb release
DISPARKED > DISPARK
DISPARKS > DISPARK
DISPART vb separate
DISPARTED > DISPART
DISPARTS > DISPART
DISPATCH vb send off to a destination or to perform a task ▷ n official communication or report, sent in haste
DISPATHY obsolete spelling of > DYSPATHY
DISPAUPER vb state that someone is no longer a pauper
DISPEACE n absence of peace
DISPEACES
> DISPEACE
DISPEL vb destroy or remove
DISPELLED > DISPEL
DISPELLER > DISPEL
DISPELS > DISPEL
DISPENCE same as
> DISPENSE
DISPENCED
> DISPENCE
DISPENCES
> DISPENCE
DISPEND vb spend
DISPENDED > DISPEND
DISPENDS > DISPEND
DISPENSE vb distribute in portions
DISPENSED
> DISPENSE
DISPENSER n device, such as a vending machine, that automatically dispenses a single item or a measured quantity
DISPENSES
> DISPENSE
DISPEOPLE vb remove inhabitants from
DISPERSAL n act of dispersing or the condition of being dispersed
DISPERSE vb scatter over a wide area ▷ adj of or consisting of the particles in a colloid or suspension
DISPERSED
> DISPERSE
DISPERSER
> DISPERSE
DISPERSES
> DISPERSE
DISPIRIT vb make downhearted
DISPIRITS
> DISPIRIT
DISPLACE vb move from the usual location
DISPLACED
> DISPLACE
DISPLACER
> DISPLACE
DISPLACES
> DISPLACE
DISPLANT vb displace

DISPLANTS
> DISPLANT
DISPLAY vb make visible or noticeable ▷ n displaying
DISPLAYED > DISPLAY
DISPLAYER > DISPLAY
DISPLAYS > DISPLAY
DISPLE vb punish
DISPLEASE vb annoy or upset
DISPLED > DISPLE
DISPLES > DISPLE
DISPLING > DISPLE
DISPLODE obsolete word for > EXPLODE
DISPLODED
> DISPLODE
DISPLODES
> DISPLODE
DISPLUME vb remove feathers from
DISPLUMED
> DISPLUME
DISPLUMES
> DISPLUME
DISPONDEE n (poetry) double foot of two long syllables
DISPONE vb transfer ownership
DISPONED > DISPONE
DISPONEE vb person whom something is disponed to
DISPONEES
> DISPONEE
DISPONER > DISPONE
DISPONERS > DISPONE
DISPONES > DISPONE
DISPONGE same as
> DISPUNGE
DISPONGED
> DISPONGE
DISPONGES
> DISPONGE
DISPONING > DISPONE
DISPORT vb indulge (oneself) in pleasure ▷ n amusement
DISPORTED > DISPORT
DISPORTS > DISPORT
DISPOSAL n getting rid of something
DISPOSALS
> DISPOSAL
DISPOSE vb place in a certain order
DISPOSED adj willing or eager
DISPOSER > DISPOSE
DISPOSERS > DISPOSE
DISPOSES > DISPOSE
DISPOSING > DISPOSE
DISPOST vb remove from a post
DISPOSTED > DISPOST
DISPOSTS > DISPOST
DISPOSURE a rare word for > DISPOSAL
DISPRAD old form of
> DISPREAD
DISPRAISE vb express disapproval or condemnation of ▷ n disapproval, etc, expressed
DISPREAD vb spread out

DISPREADS
> DISPREAD

DISPRED old spelling of
> DISPREAD

DISPREDS > DISPRED

DISPRISON vb release
from captivity

DISPRIZE vb scorn

DISPRIZED
> DISPRIZE

DISPRIZES
> DISPRIZE

DISPROFIT n loss ▷ vb
(cause to) fail to profit

DISPROOF n facts that
disprove something

DISPROOFS
> DISPROOF

DISPROOVE vb
disapprove of

DISPROVAL
> DISPROVE

DISPROVE vb show (an
assertion or claim) to be
incorrect

DISPROVED
> DISPROVE

DISPROVEN
> DISPROVE

DISPROVER
> DISPROVE

DISPROVES
> DISPROVE

DISPUNGE vb expunge

DISPUNGED
> DISPUNGE

DISPUNGES
> DISPUNGE

DISPURSE another word
for > DISBURSE

DISPURSED
> DISPURSE

DISPURSES
> DISPURSE

DISPURVEY vb strip of
equipment, provisions, etc

DISPUTANT n person
who argues ▷ adj engaged
in argument

DISPUTE n
disagreement, argument
▷ vb argue about
(something)

DISPUTED > DISPUTE

DISPUTER > DISPUTE

DISPUTERS > DISPUTE

DISPUTES > DISPUTE

DISPUTING > DISPUTE

DISQUIET n feeling of
anxiety ▷ vb make
(someone) anxious ▷ adj
uneasy or anxious

DISQUIETS
> DISQUIET

DISRANK vb demote

DISRANKED > DISRANK

DISRANKS > DISRANK

DISRATE vb punish (an
officer) by lowering in rank

DISRATED > DISRATE

DISRATES > DISRATE

DISRATING > DISRATE

DISREGARD vb give little
or no attention to ▷ n lack
of attention or respect

DISRELISH vb have a
feeling of aversion for ▷ n
such a feeling

DISREPAIR n condition
of being worn out or in
poor working order

DISREPUTE n loss or lack
of good reputation

DISROBE vb undress

DISROBED > DISROBE

DISROBER > DISROBE

DISROBERS > DISROBE

DISROBES > DISROBE

DISROBING > DISROBE

DISROOT vb uproot

DISROOTED > DISROOT

DISROOTS > DISROOT

DISRUPT vb interrupt the
progress of

DISRUPTED > DISRUPT

DISRUPTER > DISRUPT

DISRUPTOR > DISRUPT

DISRUPTS > DISRUPT

DISS vb treat (a person)
with contempt

DISSAVE vb spend
savings

DISSAVED > DISSAVE

DISSAVER n person who
dissaves

DISSAVERS
> DISSAVER

DISSAVES > DISSAVE

DISSAVING > DISSAVE

DISSEAT vb unseat

DISSEATED > DISSEAT

DISSEATS > DISSEAT

DISSECT vb cut
something open to
examine it

DISSECTED adj in the
form of narrow lobes or
segments

DISSECTOR > DISSECT

DISSECTS > DISSECT

DISSED > DISS

DISSEISE vb deprive of
seisin

DISSEISED
> DISSEISE

DISSEISEE n person
who is disseised

DISSEISES
> DISSEISE

DISSEISIN n act of
disseising or state of being
disseised

DISSEISOR
> DISSEISE

DISSEIZE same as
> DISSEISE

DISSEIZED
> DISSEIZE

DISSEIZEE n person
who is disseized

DISSEIZES
> DISSEIZE

DISSEIZIN same as
> DISSEISIN

DISSEIZOR
> DISSEIZE

DISSEMBLE vb conceal
one's real motives or
emotions by pretence

DISSEMBLY n
dismantling

DISSENSUS n
disagreement within
group

DISSENT vb disagree ▷ n
disagreement

DISSENTED > DISSENT

DISSENTER > DISSENT

DISSENTS > DISSENT

DISSERT vb give or make
a dissertation; dissertate

DISSERTED > DISSERT

DISSERTS > DISSERT

DISSERVE vb do a
disservice to

DISSERVED
> DISSERVE

DISSERVES
> DISSERVE

DISSES > DISS

DISSEVER vb break off or
become broken off

DISSEVERS
> DISSEVER

DISSHIVER vb break in
pieces

DISSIDENT n person
who disagrees with and
criticizes the government
▷ adj disagreeing with the
government

DISSIGHT n eyesore

DISSIGHTS
> DISSIGHT

DISSIMILE n
comparison using
contrast

DISSING > DISS

DISSIPATE vb waste or
squander

DISSOCIAL adj
incongruous or
irreconcilable

DISSOLUTE adj leading
an immoral life

DISSOLVE vb (cause to)
become liquid ▷ n scene
filmed or televised by
dissolving

DISSOLVED
> DISSOLVE

DISSOLVER
> DISSOLVE

DISSOLVES
> DISSOLVE

DISSONANT adj
discordant

DISSUADE vb deter
(someone) by persuasion
from doing something

DISSUADED
> DISSUADE

DISSUADER
> DISSUADE

DISSUADES
> DISSUADE

DISSUNDER vb separate

DISTAFF n rod on which
wool etc is wound for
spinning

DISTAFFS > DISTAFF

DISTAIN vb stain;
tarnish

DISTAINED > DISTAIN

DISTAINS > DISTAIN

DISTAL adj (of a bone,
limb, etc) situated farthest
from the point of
attachment

DISTALLY > DISTAL

DISTANCE n space
between two points

DISTANCED
> DISTANCE

DISTANCES
> DISTANCE

DISTANT adj far apart

DISTANTLY > DISTANT

DISTASTE n dislike,
disgust

DISTASTED
> DISTASTE

DISTASTES
> DISTASTE

DISTAVES > DISTAFF

DISTEMPER n highly
contagious viral disease of
dogs ▷ vb paint with
distemper

DISTEND vb (of part of
the body) swell

DISTENDED > DISTEND

DISTENDER > DISTEND

DISTENDS > DISTEND

DISTENT adj bloated;
swollen ▷ n breadth;
distension

DISTENTS > DISTENT

DISTHENE n
bluish-green mineral

DISTHENES
> DISTHENE

DISTHRONE vb remove
from throne

DISTICH n unit of two
verse lines

DISTICHAL > DISTICH

DISTICHS > DISTICH

DISTIL vb subject to or
obtain by distillation

DISTILL same as
> DISTIL

DISTILLED > DISTIL

DISTILLER n person or
company that makes
strong alcoholic drink, esp
whisky

DISTILLS > DISTILL

DISTILS > DISTIL

DISTINCT adj not the
same

DISTINGUE adj
distinguished or noble

DISTOME n parasitic
flatworm

DISTOMES > DISTOME

DISTORT vb
misrepresent (the truth or
facts)

DISTORTED > DISTORT

DISTORTER > DISTORT

DISTORTS > DISTORT

DISTRACT vb draw the
attention of (a person)
away from something

DISTRACTS
> DISTRACT

DISTRAIL n trail made
by aircraft flying through
cloud

DISTRAILS
> DISTRAIL

DISTRAIN vb seize
(personal property) to
enforce payment of a debt

DISTRAINS
> DISTRAIN

DISTRAINT n act or
process of distraining

DISTRAIT adj
absent-minded or
preoccupied

DISTRAITE *feminine form of* > DISTRAIT
DISTRESS *n* extreme unhappiness ▷ *vb* upset badly
DISTRICT *n* area of land regarded as an administrative or geographical unit ▷ *vb* divide into districts
DISTRICTS > DISTRICT
DISTRIX *n* splitting of the ends of hairs
DISTRIXES > DISTRIX
DISTRUST *vb* regard as untrustworthy ▷ *n* feeling of suspicion or doubt
DISTRUSTS > DISTRUST
DISTUNE *vb* cause to be out of tune
DISTUNED > DISTUNE
DISTUNES > DISTUNE
DISTUNING > DISTUNE
DISTURB *vb* intrude on
DISTURBED *adj* emotionally upset or maladjusted
DISTURBER > DISTURB
DISTURBS > DISTURB
DISTYLE *n* temple with two columns
DISTYLES > DISTYLE
DISULFATE *n* chemical compound containing two sulfate ions
DISULFID *same as* > DISULFIDE
DISULFIDE *n* compound of a base with two atoms of sulfur
DISULFIDS > DISULFID
DISUNION > DISUNITE
DISUNIONS > DISUNITE
DISUNITE *vb* cause disagreement among
DISUNITED > DISUNITE
DISUNITER > DISUNITE
DISUNITES > DISUNITE
DISUNITY *n* dissension or disagreement
DISUSAGE *n* disuse
DISUSAGES > DISUSAGE
DISUSE *vb* stop using ▷ *n* state of being no longer used
DISUSED *adj* no longer used
DISUSES > DISUSE
DISUSING > DISUSE
DISVALUE *vb* belittle
DISVALUED > DISVALUE
DISVALUES > DISVALUE
DISVOUCH *vb* dissociate oneself from
DISYOKE *vb* unyoke
DISYOKED > DISYOKE
DISYOKES > DISYOKE
DISYOKING > DISYOKE

DIT *vb* stop something happening ▷ *n* short sound used in the spoken representation of telegraphic codes
DITA *n* tropical shrub
DITAL *n* key for raising the pitch of a lute string
DITALS > DITAL
DITAS > DITA
DITCH *n* narrow channel dug in the earth for drainage or irrigation ▷ *vb* abandon
DITCHED > DITCH
DITCHER > DITCH
DITCHERS > DITCH
DITCHES > DITCH
DITCHING > DITCH
DITCHLESS > DITCH
DITE *vb* set down in writing
DITED > DITE
DITES > DITE
DITHECAL *adj* having two thecae
DITHECOUS *another word for* > DITHECAL
DITHEISM *n* belief in two equal gods
DITHEISMS > DITHEISM
DITHEIST > DITHEISM
DITHEISTS > DITHEISM
DITHELETE *n* one believing that Christ had two wills
DITHELISM *n* belief that Christ had two wills
DITHER *vb* be uncertain or indecisive ▷ *n* state of indecision or agitation
DITHERED > DITHER
DITHERER > DITHER
DITHERERS > DITHER
DITHERIER > DITHER
DITHERING *n* instance of being uncertain or indecisive
DITHERS > DITHER
DITHERY > DITHER
DITHIOL *n* chemical compound
DITHIOLS > DITHIOL
DITHIONIC *adj* as in dithionic acid type of acid
DITHYRAMB *n* (in ancient Greece) a passionate choral hymn in honour of Dionysus
DITING > DITE
DITOKOUS *adj* producing two eggs
DITONE *n* interval of two tones
DITONES > DITONE
DITROCHEE *n* double metrical foot
DITS > DIT
DITSIER > DITSY
DITSIEST > DITSY
DITSINESS > DITSY
DITSY *same as* > DITZY
DITT *same as* > DIT
DITTANDER *n* type of plant of coastal Europe, N Africa, and SW Asia, with

clusters of small white flowers
DITTANIES > DITTANY
DITTANY *n* aromatic plant
DITTAY *n* accusation; charge
DITTAYS > DITTAY
DITTED > DIT
DITTIED > DITTY
DITTIES > DITTY
DITTING > DIT
DITTIT > DIT
DITTO *n* same ▷ *adv* in the same way ▷ *sentence substitute* used to avoid repeating or to confirm agreement with an immediately preceding sentence ▷ *vb* copy
DITTOED > DITTO
DITTOING > DITTO
DITTOLOGY *n* interpretation in two ways
DITTOS > DITTO
DITTS > DITT
DITTY *vb* set to music ▷ *n* short simple poem or song
DITTYING > DITTY
DITZ *n* silly scatterbrained person
DITZES > DITZ
DITZIER > DITZY
DITZIEST > DITZY
DITZINESS > DITZY
DITZY *adj* silly and scatterbrained
DIURESES > DIURESIS
DIURESIS *n* excretion of an unusually large quantity of urine
DIURETIC *n* drug that increases the flow of urine ▷ *adj* acting to increase the flow of urine
DIURETICS > DIURETIC
DIURNAL *adj* happening during the day or daily ▷ *n* service book containing all the canonical hours except matins
DIURNALLY > DIURNAL
DIURNALS > DIURNAL
DIURON *n* type of herbicide
DIURONS > DIURON
DIUTURNAL *adj* long-lasting
DIV *n* dividend
DIVA *n* distinguished female singer
DIVAGATE *vb* digress or wander
DIVAGATED > DIVAGATE
DIVAGATES > DIVAGATE
DIVALENCE > DIVALENT
DIVALENCY > DIVALENT
DIVALENT *n* element that can unite with two atoms ▷ *adj* having two valencies or a valency of two

DIVALENTS > DIVALENT
DIVAN *n* low backless bed
DIVANS > DIVAN
DIVAS > DIVA
DIVE *vb* plunge headfirst into water ▷ *n* diving
DIVEBOMB *vb* bomb while making steep dives
DIVEBOMBS > DIVEBOMB
DIVED > DIVE
DIVELLENT *adj* separating
DIVER *n* person who works or explores underwater
DIVERGE *vb* separate and go in different directions
DIVERGED > DIVERGE
DIVERGENT *adj* diverging or causing divergence
DIVERGES > DIVERGE
DIVERGING > DIVERGE
DIVERS *adj* various ▷ *determiner* various
DIVERSE *vb* turn away ▷ *adj* having variety, assorted
DIVERSED > DIVERSE
DIVERSELY > DIVERSE
DIVERSES > DIVERSE
DIVERSIFY *vb* create different forms of
DIVERSING > DIVERSE
DIVERSION *n* official detour used by traffic when a main route is closed
DIVERSITY *n* quality of being different or varied
DIVERSLY > DIVERS
DIVERT *vb* change the direction of
DIVERTED > DIVERT
DIVERTER > DIVERT
DIVERTERS > DIVERT
DIVERTING > DIVERT
DIVERTIVE > DIVERT
DIVERTS > DIVERT
DIVES > DIVE
DIVEST *vb* strip (of clothes)
DIVESTED > DIVEST
DIVESTING > DIVEST
DIVESTS > DIVEST
DIVESTURE > DIVEST
DIVI *alternative spelling of* > DIVVY
DIVIDABLE > DIVIDE
DIVIDANT *adj* distinct
DIVIDE *vb* separate into parts ▷ *n* division, split
DIVIDED *adj* split
DIVIDEDLY > DIVIDED
DIVIDEND *n* sum of money representing part of the profit made, paid by a company to its shareholders
DIVIDENDS > DIVIDEND
DIVIDER *n* screen used to divide a room into separate areas
DIVIDERS *pl n* compasses with two

d

pointed arms, used for measuring or dividing lines

DIVIDES > DIVIDE

DIVIDING > DIVIDE

DIVIDINGS > DIVIDE

DIVIDIVI n tropical tree

DIVIDIVIS > DIVIDIVI

DIVIDUAL adj divisible

DIVIDUOUS adj divided

DIVIED > DIVI

DIVINABLE > DIVINE

DIVINATOR n diviner

DIVINE adj of God or a god ▷ vb discover (something) by intuition or guessing ▷ n priest who is learned in theology

DIVINED > DIVINE

DIVINELY > DIVINE

DIVINER > DIVINE

DIVINERS > DIVINE

DIVINES > DIVINE

DIVINEST > DIVINE

DIVING > DIVE

DIVINGS > DIVE

DIVINIFY vb give divine status to

DIVINING > DIVINE

DIVINISE same as > DIVINIZE

DIVINISED > DIVINISE

DIVINISES > DIVINISE

DIVINITY n study of religion

DIVINIZE vb make divine

DIVINIZED > DIVINIZE

DIVINIZES > DIVINIZE

DIVIS > DIVI

DIVISIBLE adj capable of being divided

DIVISIBLY > DIVISIBLE

DIVISIM adv separately

DIVISION n dividing, sharing out

DIVISIONS > DIVISION

DIVISIVE adj tending to cause disagreement

DIVISOR n number to be divided into another number

DIVISORS > DIVISOR

DIVNA vb do not

DIVO n male diva

DIVORCE n legal ending of a marriage ▷ vb legally end one's marriage (to)

DIVORCED > DIVORCE

DIVORCEE n person who is divorced

DIVORCEES > DIVORCEE

DIVORCER > DIVORCE

DIVORCERS > DIVORCE

DIVORCES > DIVORCE

DIVORCING > DIVORCE

DIVORCIVE > DIVORCE

DIVOS > DIVO

DIVOT n small piece of turf

DIVOTS > DIVOT

DIVS > DIV

DIVULGATE vb make publicly known

DIVULGE vb make known, disclose

DIVULGED > DIVULGE

DIVULGER > DIVULGE

DIVULGERS > DIVULGE

DIVULGES > DIVULGE

DIVULGING > DIVULGE

DIVULSE vb tear apart

DIVULSED > DIVULSE

DIVULSES > DIVULSE

DIVULSING > DIVULSE

DIVULSION n tearing or pulling apart

DIVULSIVE > DIVULSION

DIVVIED > DIVVY

DIVVIER > DIVVY

DIVVIERS > DIVVY

DIVVIEST > DIVVY

DIVVY vb divide and share ▷ adj dialect word for stupid

DIVVYING > DIVVY

DIVYING alternative present participle of > DIVVY

DIWAN same as > DEWAN

DIWANS > DIWAN

DIXI interj I have spoken

DIXIE n large metal pot for cooking, brewing tea, etc

DIXIES > DIXIE

DIXIT n statement

DIXITS > DIXIT

DIXY same as > DIXIE

DIYA n small oil lamp, usu made from clay

DIYAS > DIYA

DIZAIN n ten-line poem

DIZAINS > DIZAIN

DIZEN archaic word for > BEDIZEN

DIZENED > DIZEN

DIZENING > DIZEN

DIZENMENT > DIZEN

DIZENS > DIZEN

DIZYGOTIC adj developed from two separately fertilized eggs

DIZYGOUS another word for > DIZYGOTIC

DIZZARD n dunce

DIZZARDS > DIZZARD

DIZZIED > DIZZY

DIZZIER > DIZZY

DIZZIES > DIZZY

DIZZIEST > DIZZY

DIZZILY > DIZZY

DIZZINESS > DIZZY

DIZZY adj having or causing a whirling sensation ▷ vb make dizzy

DIZZYING > DIZZY

DJEBEL variant spelling of > JEBEL

DJEBELS > DJEBEL

DJELLABA n kind of loose cloak with a hood, worn by men esp in North Africa and the Middle East

DJELLABAH same as > DJELLABA

DJELLABAS > DJELLABA

DJEMBE n W African drum

DJEMBES > DJEMBE

DJIBBA same as > JUBBAH

DJIBBAH same as > JUBBAH

DJIBBAHS > DJIBBAH

DJIBBAS > DJIBBA

DJIN same as > JINN

DJINN > DJINNI

DJINNI same as > JINNI

DJINNS > DJINNI

DJINNY same as > JINNI

DJINS > DJIN

DO vb perform or complete (a deed or action) ▷ n party, celebration

DOAB n alluvial land between two converging rivers

DOABLE adj capable of being done

DOABS > DOAB

DOAT same as > DOTE

DOATED > DOAT

DOATER > DOAT

DOATERS > DOAT

DOATING > DOAT

DOATINGS > DOAT

DOATS > DOAT

DOB vb as in dob in inform against or report

DOBBED > DOB

DOBBER n informant or traitor

DOBBERS > DOBBER

DOBBIE same as > DOBBY

DOBBIES > DOBBY

DOBBIN n name for a horse

DOBBING > DOB

DOBBINS > DOBBIN

DOBBY n attachment to a loom, used in weaving small figures

DOBCHICK same as > DABCHICK

DOBCHICKS > DOBCHICK

DOBE same as > ADOBE

DOBES > DOBE

DOBHASH n interpreter

DOBHASHES > DOBHASH

DOBIE n cannabis

DOBIES > DOBIE

DOBLA n medieval Spanish gold coin, probably worth 20 maravedis

DOBLAS > DOBLA

DOBLON variant spelling of > DOUBLOON

DOBLONES > DOBLON

DOBLONS > DOBLON

DOBRA n standard monetary unit of São Tomé e Principe

DOBRAS > DOBRA

DOBRO n type of acoustic guitar

DOBROS > DOBRO

DOBS > DOB

DOBSON n larva of a dobsonfly

DOBSONFLY n large North American insect

DOBSONS > DOBSON

DOBY same as > DOBIE

DOC same as > DOCTOR

DOCENT n voluntary worker who acts as a guide

DOCENTS > DOCENT

DOCETIC adj believing that the humanity of Christ was apparent and not real

DOCHMIAC > DOCHMIUS

DOCHMIACS > DOCHMIAC

DOCHMII > DOCHMIUS

DOCHMIUS n five-syllable foot

DOCHT > DOW

DOCIBLE adj easily tamed

DOCILE adj (of a person or animal) easily controlled

DOCILELY > DOCILE

DOCILER > DOCILE

DOCILEST > DOCILE

DOCILITY > DOCILE

DOCIMASY n close examination

DOCK n enclosed area of water where ships are loaded, unloaded, or repaired ▷ vb bring or be brought into dock

DOCKAGE n charge levied upon a vessel for using a dock

DOCKAGES > DOCKAGE

DOCKED > DOCK

DOCKEN n something of no value or importance

DOCKENS > DOCKEN

DOCKER n person employed to load and unload ships

DOCKERS > DOCKER

DOCKET n label on a delivery, stating contents, delivery instructions, etc ▷ vb fix a docket to (a package or other delivery)

DOCKETED > DOCKET

DOCKETING > DOCKET

DOCKETS > DOCKET

DOCKHAND n dock labourer

DOCKHANDS > DOCKHAND

DOCKING > DOCK

DOCKINGS > DOCK

DOCKISE same as > DOCKIZE

DOCKISED > DOCKISE

DOCKISES > DOCKISE

DOCKISING > DOCKISE

DOCKIZE vb convert into docks

DOCKIZED > DOCKIZE

DOCKIZES > DOCKIZE

DOCKIZING > DOCKIZE

DOCKLAND n area around the docks

DOCKLANDS > DOCKLAND

DOCKS > DOCK

DOCKSIDE n area next to dock

DOCKSIDES > DOCKSIDE

DOCKYARD *n* place where ships are built or repaired

DOCKYARDS > DOCKYARD

DOCO *n* documentary

DOCOS > DOCO

DOCQUET *same as* > DOCKET

DOCQUETED > DOCQUET

DOCQUETS > DOCQUET

DOCS > DOC

DOCTOR *n* person licensed to practise medicine ▷ *vb* alter in order to deceive

DOCTORAL > DOCTOR

DOCTORAND *n* student working towards doctorate

DOCTORATE *n* highest academic degree in any field of knowledge

DOCTORED > DOCTOR

DOCTORESS *n* female doctor

DOCTORIAL > DOCTOR

DOCTORING *n* act of doctoring

DOCTORLY > DOCTOR

DOCTORS > DOCTOR

DOCTRESS *same as* > DOCTORESS

DOCTRINAL > DOCTRINE

DOCTRINE *n* body of teachings of a religious, political, or philosophical group

DOCTRINES > DOCTRINE

DOCU *n* documentary film

DOCUDRAMA *n* film or television programme based on true events, presented in a dramatized form

DOCUMENT *n* piece of paper providing an official record of something ▷ *vb* record or report (something) in detail

DOCUMENTS > DOCUMENT

DOCUS > DOCU

DOCUSOAP *n* reality television programme in the style of a documentary

DOCUSOAPS > DOCUSOAP

DOD *vb* clip

DODDARD *adj* archaic word for missing branches; rotten ▷ *n* tree missing its top branches through rot

DODDARDS > DODDARD

DODDED > DOD

DODDER *vb* move unsteadily ▷ *n* type of rootless parasitic plant

DODDERED > DODDER

DODDERER > DODDER

DODDERERS > DODDER

DODDERIER > DODDER

DODDERING *adj* shaky, feeble, or infirm, esp from old age

DODDERS > DODDER

DODDERY > DODDER

DODDIER > DODDY

DODDIES > DODDY

DODDIEST > DODDY

DODDING > DOD

DODDIPOLL *same as* > DODDYPOLL

DODDLE *n* something easily accomplished

DODDLES > DODDLE

DODDY *n* bad mood ▷ *adj* sulky

DODDYPOLL *n* dunce

DODECAGON *n* geometric figure with twelve sides

DODGE *vb* avoid (a blow, being seen, etc) by moving suddenly ▷ *n* cunning or deceitful trick

DODGEBALL *n* game in which the players form a circle and try to hit opponents in the circle with a large ball

DODGED > DODGE

DODGEM *n* bumper car

DODGEMS > DODGEM

DODGER *n* person who evades a responsibility or duty

DODGERIES > DODGERY

DODGERS > DODGER

DODGERY *n* deception

DODGES > DODGE

DODGIER > DODGY

DODGIEST > DODGY

DODGINESS > DODGY

DODGING > DODGE

DODGINGS > DODGE

DODGY *adj* dangerous, risky

DODKIN *n* coin of little value

DODKINS > DODKIN

DODMAN *n* snail

DODMANS > DODMAN

DODO *n* large flightless extinct bird

DODOES > DODO

DODOISM > DODO

DODOISMS > DODO

DODOS > DODO

DODS > DOD

DOE *n* female deer, hare, or rabbit

DOEK *n* square of cloth worn on the head by some African women

DOEKS > DOEK

DOEN > DO

DOER *n* active or energetic person

DOERS > DOER

DOES > DO

DOESKIN *n* skin of a deer, lamb, or sheep

DOESKINS > DOESKIN

DOEST > DO

DOETH > DO

DOF *informal South African word for* > STUPID

DOFF *vb* take off or lift (one's hat) in polite greeting

DOFFED > DOFF

DOFFER > DOFF

DOFFERS > DOFF

DOFFING > DOFF

DOFFS > DOFF

DOG *n* domesticated four-legged mammal ▷ *vb* follow (someone) closely

DOGARESSA *n* wife of doge

DOGATE *n* office of doge

DOGATES > DOGATE

DOGBANE *n* N American plant

DOGBANES > DOGBANE

DOGBERRY *n* any of certain plants that have berry-like fruits

DOGBOLT *n* bolt on a cannon

DOGBOLTS > DOGBOLT

DOGCART *n* light horse-drawn two-wheeled cart

DOGCARTS > DOGCART

DOGDOM *n* world of dogs

DOGDOMS > DOGDOM

DOGE *n* (formerly) chief magistrate of Venice or Genoa

DOGEAR *vb* fold down the corner of (a page) ▷ *n* folded-down corner of a page

DOGEARED > DOGEAR

DOGEARING > DOGEAR

DOGEARS > DOGEAR

DOGEATE *n* office of doge

DOGEATES > DOGEATE

DOGEDOM *n* domain of a doge

DOGEDOMS > DOGEDOM

DOGES > DOGE

DOGESHIP > DOGE

DOGESHIPS > DOGE

DOGEY *same as* > DOGIE

DOGEYS > DOGEY

DOGFACE *n* WW2 US soldier

DOGFACES > DOGFACE

DOGFIGHT *vb* fight in confused way ▷ *n* close-quarters combat between fighter aircraft

DOGFIGHTS > DOGFIGHT

DOGFISH *n* small shark

DOGFISHES > DOGFISH

DOGFOOD *n* food for a dog

DOGFOODS > DOGFOOD

DOGFOUGHT > DOGFIGHT

DOGFOX *n* male fox

DOGFOXES > DOGFOX

DOGGED *adj* stubbornly determined

DOGGEDER > DOGGED

DOGGEDEST > DOGGED

DOGGEDLY > DOGGED

DOGGER *n* Dutch fishing vessel with two masts

DOGGEREL *n* poorly written poetry, usu comic

DOGGERELS > DOGGEREL

DOGGERIES > DOGGERY

DOGGERMAN *n* sailor on dogger

DOGGERMEN > DOGGERMAN

DOGGERS > DOGGER

DOGGERY *n* surly behaviour

DOGGESS *n* female dog

DOGGESSES > DOGGESS

DOGGIE *same as* > DOGGY

DOGGIER > DOGGY

DOGGIES > DOGGY

DOGGIEST > DOGGY

DOGGINESS > DOGGY

DOGGING > DOG

DOGGINGS > DOG

DOGGISH *adj* of or like a dog

DOGGISHLY > DOGGISH

DOGGO *adv* in hiding and keeping quiet

DOGGONE *interj* exclamation of annoyance, disappointment, etc ▷ *vb* damn ▷ *adj* damnedest

DOGGONED > DOGGONE

DOGGONER > DOGGONE

DOGGONES > DOGGONE

DOGGONEST > DOGGONE

DOGGONING > DOGGONE

DOGGREL *same as* > DOGGEREL

DOGGRELS > DOGGREL

DOGGY *n* child's word for a dog ▷ *adj* of or like a dog

DOGHANGED *same as* > HANGDOG

DOGHOLE *n* squalid dwelling place

DOGHOLES > DOGHOLE

DOGHOUSE *n* kennel

DOGHOUSES > DOGHOUSE

DOGIE *n* motherless calf

DOGIES > DOGIE

DOGLEG *n* sharp bend ▷ *vb* go off at an angle ▷ *adj* of or with the shape of a dogleg

DOGLEGGED > DOGLEG

DOGLEGS > DOGLEG

DOGLIKE > DOG

DOGMA *n* doctrine or system of doctrines proclaimed by authority as true

DOGMAN *n* person who directs a crane whilst riding on an object being lifted by it

DOGMAS > DOGMA

DOGMATA > DOGMA

DOGMATIC *adj* habitually stating one's opinions forcefully or arrogantly

DOGMATICS *n* study of religious dogmas and doctrines

DOGMATISE *same as* > DOGMATIZE

DOGMATISM > DOGMATIZE

DOGMATIST *n* dogmatic person

DOGMATIZE *vb* say or state (something) in a dogmatic manner

DOGMATORY > DOGMA

DOGMEN > DOGMAN

DOGNAP *vb* carry off and hold (a dog), usually for ransom

DOGNAPED > DOGNAP

DOGNAPER > DOGNAP

d

DOGNAPERS > DOGNAP
DOGNAPING > DOGNAP
DOGNAPPED > DOGNAP
DOGNAPPER > DOGNAP
DOGNAPS > DOGNAP
DOGPILE n pile of bodies formed by people jumping on top of each other
DOGPILES > DOGPILE
DOGREL n doggerel
DOGRELS > DOGREL
DOGROBBER n army cook
DOGS > DOG
DOGSBODY n person who carries out boring tasks for others ▷ vb act as a dogsbody
DOGSHIP n condition of being a dog
DOGSHIPS > DOGSHIP
DOGSHORES n pieces of wood to prop up boat
DOGSHOW n competition in which dogs are judged
DOGSHOWS > DOGSHOW
DOGSKIN n leather from a dog's skin
DOGSKINS > DOGSKIN
DOGSLED n sleigh drawn by dogs
DOGSLEDS > DOGSLED
DOGSLEEP n feigned sleep
**DOGSLEEPS
>** DOGSLEEP
DOGSTAIL n type of grass
**DOGSTAILS
>** DOGSTAIL
DOGTAIL same as
> DOGSTAIL
DOGTAILS > DOGTAIL
DOGTEETH > DOGTOOTH
DOGTOOTH n medieval carved ornament
DOGTOWN n community of prairie dogs
DOGTOWNS > DOGTOWN
DOGTROT n gently paced trot
DOGTROTS > DOGTROT
DOGVANE n light windvane mounted on the side of a vessel
DOGVANES > DOGVANE
DOGWATCH n either of two watches aboard ship, from four to six pm or from six to eight pm
DOGWOOD n type of tree or shrub
DOGWOODS > DOGWOOD
DOGY same as **>** DOGIE
DOH n in tonic sol-fa, the first degree of any major scale ▷ interj exclamation of annoyance when something goes wrong
DOHS > DOH
DOHYO n sumo wrestling ring
DOHYOS > DOHYO
DOILED same as **>** DOILT
DOILIED adj having a doily
DOILIES > DOILY
DOILT adj foolish
DOILTER > DOILT
DOILTEST > DOILT

DOILY n decorative lacy paper mat, laid on a plate
DOING > DO
DOINGS pl n deeds or actions
DOIT n former small copper coin of the Netherlands
DOITED adj foolish or childish, as from senility
DOITIT same as **>** DOITED
DOITKIN same as **>** DOIT
DOITKINS > DOITKIN
DOITS > DOIT
DOJO n room or hall for the practice of martial arts
DOJOS > DOJO
DOL n unit of pain intensity, as measured by dolorimetry
DOLABRATE adj shaped like a hatchet or axe head
DOLCE n dessert ▷ adv (to be performed) gently and sweetly
DOLCES > DOLCE
DOLCETTO n variety of grape
**DOLCETTOS
>** DOLCETTO
DOLCI > DOLCE
DOLDRUMS pl n unhappy state of mind
DOLE n money received from the state while unemployed ▷ vb distribute in small quantities
DOLED > DOLE
DOLEFUL adj dreary, unhappy
DOLEFULLY > DOLEFUL
DOLENT adj sad
DOLENTE adv (to be performed) in a sorrowful manner
DOLERITE n dark igneous rock such as augite
**DOLERITES
>** DOLERITE
**DOLERITIC
>** DOLERITE
DOLES > DOLE
DOLESOME same as **>** DOLEFUL
DOLIA > DOLIUM
DOLICHOS n tropical vine
DOLICHURI n plural of dolichurus, a dactylic hexameter
DOLINA same as **>** DOLINE
DOLINAS > DOLINA
DOLINE n depression of the ground surface formed in limestone regions
DOLINES > DOLINE
DOLING > DOLE
DOLIUM n genus of molluscs
DOLL n small model of a human being, used as a toy ▷ vb as in doll up dress up
DOLLAR n standard monetary unit of many countries

DOLLARED adj flagged with a dollar sign
DOLLARISE same as **>** DOLLARIZE
DOLLARIZE vb replace a country's currency with US dollar
DOLLARS > DOLLAR
DOLLDOM > DOLL
DOLLDOMS > DOLL
DOLLED > DOLL
DOLLHOOD > DOLL
DOLLHOODS > DOLL
DOLLHOUSE n toy house in which dolls and miniature furniture can be put
DOLLIED > DOLLY
DOLLIER n person who operates a dolly
DOLLIERS > DOLLIER
DOLLIES > DOLLY
DOLLINESS > DOLLY
DOLLING > DOLL
DOLLISH > DOLL
DOLLISHLY > DOLL
DOLLOP n lump (of food) ▷ vb serve out (food)
DOLLOPED > DOLLOP
DOLLOPING > DOLLOP
DOLLOPS > DOLLOP
DOLLS > DOLL
DOLLY adj attractive and unintelligent ▷ n wheeled support for a camera ▷ vb wheel a camera on a dolly
DOLLYBIRD n pretty and fashionable young woman
DOLLYING > DOLLY
DOLMA n vine leaf stuffed with a filling of meat and rice
DOLMADES > DOLMA
DOLMAN n long Turkish outer robe
DOLMANS > DOLMAN
DOLMAS > DOLMA
DOLMEN n prehistoric monument
DOLMENIC > DOLMEN
DOLMENS > DOLMEN
DOLOMITE n mineral consisting of calcium magnesium carbonate
**DOLOMITES
>** DOLOMITE
**DOLOMITIC
>** DOLOMITE
DOLOR same as **>** DOLOUR
DOLORIFIC adj causing pain or sadness
DOLOROSO adv (to be performed) in a sorrowful manner
DOLOROUS adj sad, mournful
DOLORS > DOLOR
DOLOS n knucklebone of a sheep, buck, etc, used esp by diviners
DOLOSSE > DOLOS
DOLOSTONE n rock composed of the mineral dolomite
DOLOUR n grief or sorrow
DOLOURS > DOLOUR
DOLPHIN n sea mammal of the whale family

DOLPHINET n female dolphin
DOLPHINS > DOLPHIN
DOLS > DOL
DOLT n stupid person
DOLTISH > DOLT
DOLTISHLY > DOLT
DOLTS > DOLT
DOM n title given to various monks and to certain of the canons regular
DOMAIN n field of knowledge or activity
DOMAINAL > DOMAIN
DOMAINE n French estate
DOMAINES > DOMAINE
DOMAINS > DOMAIN
DOMAL adj of a house
DOMANIAL > DOMAIN
DOMATIA > DOMATIUM
DOMATIUM n plant cavity inhabited by commensal insects or mites or, occasionally, microorganisms
DOME n rounded roof built on a circular base ▷ vb cover with or as if with a dome
DOMED > DOME
DOMELIKE > DOME
DOMES > DOME
DOMESDAY same as **>** DOOMSDAY
**DOMESDAYS
>** DOMESDAY
DOMESTIC adj of one's own country or a specific country ▷ n person whose job is to do housework in someone else's house
**DOMESTICS
>** DOMESTIC
DOMETT n wool and cotton cloth
DOMETTS > DOMETT
DOMIC adj dome-shaped
DOMICAL > DOME
DOMICALLY > DOME
DOMICIL same as **>** DOMICILE
DOMICILE n place where one lives ▷ vb establish or be established in a dwelling place
**DOMICILED
>** DOMICILE
**DOMICILES
>** DOMICILE
DOMICILS > DOMICIL
DOMIER > DOMY
DOMIEST > DOMY
DOMINANCE n control
**DOMINANCY
>** DOMINANCE
DOMINANT adj having authority or influence ▷ n dominant allele or character
**DOMINANTS
>** DOMINANT
DOMINATE vb control or govern
**DOMINATED
>** DOMINATE
**DOMINATES
>** DOMINATE

DOMINATOR
> DOMINATE

DOMINE n clergyman or clergywoman

DOMINEE n minister of the Dutch Reformed Church

DOMINEER vb act with arrogance or tyranny

DOMINEERS
> DOMINEER

DOMINEES > DOMINEE

DOMINES > DOMINE

DOMING > DOME

DOMINICAL adj of, relating to, or emanating from Jesus Christ as Lord

DOMINICK n breed of chicken

DOMINICKS
> DOMINICK

DOMINIE n minister, clergyman or clergywoman: also used as a term of address

DOMINIES > DOMINIE

DOMINION same as
> DOMINIUM

DOMINIONS same as
> DOMINION

DOMINIQUE n type of chicken

DOMINIUM n ownership or right to possession of property, esp realty

DOMINIUMS
> DOMINIUM

DOMINO n small rectangular block marked with dots, used in dominoes

DOMINOES n game in which dominoes with matching halves are laid together

DOMINOS > DOMINO

DOMOIC adj as in domoic acid kind of amino acid

DOMS > DOM

DOMY adj having a dome or domes

DON vb put on (clothing)
▷ n member of the teaching staff at a university or college

DONA n Spanish woman

DONAH n woman

DONAHS > DONAH

DONAIR same as > DONER

DONAIRS > DONAIR

DONARIES > DONARY

DONARY n thing given for holy use

DONAS > DONA

DONATARY n recipient

DONATE vb give, esp to a charity or organization

DONATED > DONATE

DONATES > DONATE

DONATING > DONATE

DONATION n donating

DONATIONS
> DONATION

DONATISM n doctrine and beliefs relating to an early Christian sect

DONATISMS
> DONATISM

DONATIVE n gift or donation ▷ adj of or like a donation

DONATIVES
> DONATIVE

DONATOR > DONATE

DONATORS > DONATE

DONATORY n recipient

DONDER vb beat (someone) up ▷ n wretch

DONDERED > DONDER

DONDERING > DONDER

DONDERS > DONDER

DONE > DO

DONEE n person who receives a gift

DONEES > DONEE

DONEGAL n type of tweed

DONEGALS > DONEGAL

DONENESS n extent to which something is cooked

DONEPEZIL n drug used to treat dementia

DONER n kebab of grilled meat served in pitta bread

DONERS > DONER

DONG n deep reverberating sound of a large bell ▷ vb (of a bell) to make a deep reverberating sound

DONGA n steep-sided gully created by soil erosion

DONGAS > DONGA

DONGED > DONG

DONGING > DONG

DONGLE n electronic device

DONGLES > DONGLE

DONGOLA n leather tanned using a particular method

DONGOLAS > DONGOLA

DONGS > DONG

DONING n act of giving blood

DONINGS > DONING

DONJON n heavily fortified central tower of a castle

DONJONS > DONJON

DONKEY n long-eared member of the horse family

DONKEYMAN n person working in a ship's engine room

DONKEYMEN
> DONKEYMAN

DONKEYS > DONKEY

DONKO n tearoom or cafeteria in a factory, wharf area, etc

DONKOS > DONKO

DONNA n Italian woman

DONNARD same as
> DONNERT

DONNART same as
> DONNERT

DONNAS > DONNA

DONNAT n lazy person

DONNATS > DONNAT

DONNE same as > DONNEE

DONNED > DON

DONNEE n subject or theme

DONNEES > DONNEE

DONNERD adj stunned

DONNERED same as
> DONNERT

DONNERT adj stunned

DONNES > DONNE

DONNICKER n toilet

DONNIES > DONNY

DONNIKER same as
> DONNICKER

DONNIKERS
> DONNIKER

DONNING > DON

DONNISH adj serious and academic

DONNISHLY > DONNISH

DONNISM n loftiness

DONNISMS > DONNISM

DONNOT n lazy person

DONNOTS > DONNOT

DONNY same as > DANNY

DONOR n person who gives blood or organs for medical use

DONORS > DONOR

DONORSHIP > DONOR

DONS > DON

DONSHIP n state or condition of being a don

DONSHIPS > DONSHIP

DONSIE adj rather unwell

DONSIER > DONSIE

DONSIEST > DONSIE

DONSY same as > DONSIE

DONUT same as
> DOUGHNUT

DONUTS > DONUT

DONUTTED > DONUT

DONUTTING > DONUT

DONZEL n man of high birth

DONZELS > DONZEL

DOO a Scot word for > DOVE

DOOB n type of Indian grass

DOOBIE same as > DOOB

DOOBIES > DOOBIE

DOOBREY n thingumabob

DOOBREYS > DOOBREY

DOOBRIE same as
> DOOBREY

DOOBRIES > DOOBRIE

DOOBRY n thing whose name is unknown or forgotten

DOOBS > DOOB

DOOCE vb dismiss (an employee) because of comments they have posted on the internet

DOOCED > DOOCE

DOOCES > DOOCE

DOOCING > DOOCE

DOOCOT n dovecote

DOOCOTS > DOOCOT

DOODAD same as
> DOODAH

DOODADS > DOODAD

DOODAH n unnamed thing

DOODAHS > DOODAH

DOODIES > DOODY

DOODLE vb scribble or draw aimlessly ▷ n shape or picture drawn aimlessly

DOODLEBUG n diviner's rod

DOODLED > DOODLE

DOODLER > DOODLE

DOODLERS > DOODLE

DOODLES > DOODLE

DOODLING > DOODLE

DOODOO n excrement

DOODOOS > DOODOO

DOODY same as > DOODOO

DOOFER n thingamajig

DOOFERS > DOOFER

DOOFUS n slow-witted or stupid person

DOOFUSES > DOOFUS

DOOHICKEY another name for > DOODAH

DOOK n wooden plug driven into a wall to hold a nail, screw, etc ▷ vb dip or plunge

DOOKED > DOOK

DOOKET n dovecote

DOOKETS > DOOKET

DOOKING > DOOK

DOOKS > DOOK

DOOL n boundary marker

DOOLALLY adj out of one's mind

DOOLAN n New Zealand informal term for a Roman Catholic

DOOLANS > DOOLAN

DOOLE same as > DOOL

DOOLEE same as
> DOOLIE

DOOLEES > DOOLEE

DOOLES > DOOLE

DOOLIE n enclosed couch on poles for carrying passengers

DOOLIES > DOOLIE

DOOLS > DOOL

DOOLY same as > DOOLIE

DOOM n death or a terrible fate ▷ vb destine or condemn to death or a terrible fate

DOOMED > DOOM

DOOMFUL > DOOM

DOOMFULLY > DOOM

DOOMIER > DOOMY

DOOMIEST > DOOMY

DOOMILY > DOOMY

DOOMING > DOOM

DOOMS > DOOM

DOOMSAYER n pessimist

DOOMSDAY n day on which the Last Judgment will occur

DOOMSDAYS
> DOOMSDAY

DOOMSMAN n pessimist

DOOMSMEN > DOOMSMAN

DOOMSTER n person habitually given to predictions of impending disaster or doom

DOOMSTERS
> DOOMSTER

DOOMWATCH n surveillance of the environment to warn of and prevent harm to it from human factors such as pollution or overpopulation

DOOMY adj despondent or pessimistic

DOON same as > DOWN

DOONA n large quilt used as a bed cover

DOONAS > DOONA

DOOR n hinged or sliding panel for closing the

entrance to a building, room, etc

DOORBELL n device for visitors to announce presence at a door

DOORBELLS > DOORBELL

DOORCASE same as > DOORFRAME

DOORCASES > DOORCASE

DOORED adj having a door

DOORFRAME n frame that supports a door

DOORJAMB n vertical post forming one side of a door frame

DOORJAMBS > DOORJAMB

DOORKNOB n knob for opening and closing a door

DOORKNOBS > DOORKNOB

DOORKNOCK n fund-raising campaign for charity conducted by seeking donations from door to door

DOORLESS > DOOR

DOORLIKE adj like a door

DOORMAN n man employed to be on duty at the entrance to a large public building

DOORMAT n mat for wiping dirt from shoes before going indoors

DOORMATS > DOORMAT

DOORMEN > DOORMAN

DOORN n thorn

DOORNAIL n as in dead as a doornail dead beyond any doubt

DOORNAILS > DOORNAIL

DOORNBOOM n S African tree with yellow or white flowers

DOORNS > DOORN

DOORPLATE n name-plate on door

DOORPOST same as > DOORJAMB

DOORPOSTS > DOORPOST

DOORS > DOOR

DOORSILL n horizontal member of wood, stone, etc, forming the bottom of a doorframe

DOORSILLS > DOORSILL

DOORSMAN n doorkeeper

DOORSMEN > DOORSMAN

DOORSTEP n step in front of a door

DOORSTEPS > DOORSTEP

DOORSTONE n stone of threshold

DOORSTOP n object which prevents a door from closing or striking a wall

DOORSTOPS > DOORSTOP

DOORWAY n opening into a building or room

DOORWAYS > DOORWAY

DOORWOMAN n woman employed to be on duty at the entrance to a large public building

DOORWOMEN > DOORWOMAN

DOORYARD n yard in front of the front or back door of a house

DOORYARDS > DOORYARD

DOOS > DOO

DOOSES > DOOS

DOOSRA n type of delivery in cricket

DOOSRAS > DOOSRA

DOOWOP n style of singing in harmony

DOOWOPS > DOOWOP

DOOZER same as > DOOZY

DOOZERS > DOOZER

DOOZIE same as > DOOZY

DOOZIES > DOOZIE

DOOZY n something excellent

DOP n small drink ▷ vb fail to reach the required standard in (an examination, course, etc)

DOPA n precursor to dopamine

DOPAMINE n chemical found in the brain that acts as a neurotransmitter

DOPAMINES > DOPAMINE

DOPANT n element or compound used to produce an effect in a semiconductor

DOPANTS > DOPANT

DOPAS > DOPA

DOPATTA n headscarf

DOPATTAS > DOPATTA

DOPE n additive used to improve the properties of something ▷ vb apply a dopant ▷ adj excellent

DOPED > DOPE

DOPEHEAD n habitual drug user

DOPEHEADS > DOPEHEAD

DOPER n person who administers dope

DOPERS > DOPER

DOPES > DOPE

DOPESHEET n document giving information on horse races

DOPEST > DOPE

DOPESTER n person who makes predictions, esp in sport or politics

DOPESTERS > DOPESTER

DOPEY adj half-asleep, drowsy

DOPEYNESS > DOPEY

DOPIAZA n Indian meat or fish dish cooked in onion sauce

DOPIAZAS > DOPIAZA

DOPIER > DOPEY

DOPIEST > DOPEY

DOPILY > DOPEY

DOPINESS > DOPEY

DOPING > DOPE

DOPINGS > DOPE

DOPPED > DOP

DOPPER n member of an Afrikaner church which practises a strict Calvinism

DOPPERS > DOPPER

DOPPIE n cartridge case

DOPPIES > DOPPIE

DOPPING > DOP

DOPPINGS > DOP

DOPPIO n double measure, esp of espresso coffee

DOPPIOS > DOPPIO

DOPS > DOP

DOPY same as > DOPEY

DOR n European dung beetle ▷ vb mock

DORAD n South American river fish

DORADO n large marine percoid fish

DORADOS > DORADO

DORADS > DORAD

DORB same as > DORBA

DORBA n stupid, inept, or clumsy person

DORBAS > DORBA

DORBEETLE same as > DOR

DORBS > DORB

DORBUG n type of beetle

DORBUGS > DORBUG

DORE n walleye fish

DOREE n walleye fish

DOREES > DOREE

DORES > DORE

DORHAWK n nightjar

DORHAWKS > DORHAWK

DORIC adj rustic

DORIDOID n shell-less mollusc

DORIDOIDS > DORIDOID

DORIES > DORY

DORIS n woman

DORISE same as > DORIZE

DORISED > DORISE

DORISES > DORISE

DORISING > DORISE

DORIZE vb become Doric

DORIZED > DORIZE

DORIZES > DORIZE

DORIZING > DORIZE

DORK n stupid person

DORKIER > DORK

DORKIEST > DORK

DORKINESS > DORK

DORKISH adj stupid or contemptible

DORKS > DORK

DORKY > DORK

DORLACH n quiver of arrows

DORLACHS > DORLACH

DORM same as > DORMITORY

DORMANCY > DORMANT

DORMANT n supporting beam ▷ adj temporarily quiet, inactive, or not being used

DORMANTS > DORMANT

DORMER n window that sticks out from a sloping roof

DORMERED adj having dormer windows

DORMERS > DORMER

DORMICE > DORMOUSE

DORMIE adj (in golf) leading by as many holes as there are left

DORMIENT adj dormant

DORMIN n hormone found in plants

DORMINS > DORMIN

DORMITION n process of falling asleep

DORMITIVE adj sleep-inducing

DORMITORY n large room, esp at a school, containing several beds ▷ adj (of a town or suburb) having many inhabitants who travel to work in a nearby city

DORMOUSE n small mouselike rodent with a furry tail

DORMS > DORM

DORMY same as > DORMIE

DORNECK same as > DORNICK

DORNECKS > DORNECK

DORNICK n heavy damask cloth

DORNICKS > DORNICK

DORNOCK same as > DORNICK

DORNOCKS > DORNOCK

DORONICUM n Eurasian and N African plant with yellow daisy-like flowers

DORP n small town

DORPER n breed of sheep

DORPERS > DORPER

DORPS > DORP

DORR same as > DOR

DORRED > DOR

DORRING > DOR

DORRS > DORR

DORS > DOR

DORSA > DORSUM

DORSAD adj towards the back or dorsal aspect

DORSAL adj of or on the back ▷ n dorsal fin

DORSALLY > DORSAL

DORSALS > DORSAL

DORSE n type of small fish

DORSEL another word for > DOSSAL

DORSELS > DORSEL

DORSER n hanging tapestry

DORSERS > DORSER

DORSES > DORSE

DORSIFLEX adj bending towards the back ▷ vb bend towards the back or dorsal

DORSUM n the back

DORT vb sulk

DORTED > DORT

DORTER n dormitory

DORTERS > DORTER

DORTIER > DORTY

DORTIEST > DORTY

DORTINESS > DORTY

DORTING > DORT

DORTOUR same as > DORTER

DORTOURS > DORTOUR

DORTS > DORT

DORTY *adj* haughty, or sullen

DORY *n* spiny-finned edible sea fish

DORYMAN *n* person who fishes from a small boat called a dory

DORYMEN > DORYMAN

DOS > DO

DOSA *n* Indian pancake made from rice flour

DOSAGE *same as* > DOSE

DOSAGES > DOSAGE

DOSAI > DOSA

DOSAS > DOSA

DOSE *n* specific quantity of a medicine taken at one time ▷ *vb* give a dose to

DOSED > DOSE

DOSEH *n* former Egyptian religious ceremony

DOSEHS > DOSEH

DOSEMETER *same as* > DOSIMETER

DOSER > DOSE

DOSERS > DOSE

DOSES > DOSE

DOSH *n* money

DOSHA *n* (in Hinduism) any of the three energies believed to be in the body

DOSHAS > DOSHA

DOSHES > DOSH

DOSIMETER *n* instrument for measuring the dose of X-rays or other radiation absorbed by matter or the intensity of a source of radiation

DOSIMETRY > DOSIMETER

DOSING > DOSE

DOSIOLOGY *n* study of doses

DOSOLOGY *same as* > DOSIOLOGY

DOSS *vb* sleep, esp in a dosshouse ▷ *n* bed, esp in a dosshouse

DOSSAL *n* ornamental hanging used in churches

DOSSALS > DOSSAL

DOSSED > DOSS

DOSSEL *same as* > DOSSAL

DOSSELS > DOSSEL

DOSSER *n* bag or basket for carrying objects on the back

DOSSERET *n* stone above column supporting an arch

DOSSERETS > DOSSERET

DOSSERS > DOSSER

DOSSES > DOSS

DOSSHOUSE *n* cheap lodging house for homeless people

DOSSIER *n* collection of documents about a subject or person

DOSSIERS > DOSSIER

DOSSIL *n* lint for dressing wound

DOSSILS > DOSSIL

DOSSING > DOSS

DOST *a singular form of the present tense (indicative mood) of* > DO

DOT *n* small round mark ▷ *vb* mark with a dot

DOTAGE *n* weakness as a result of old age

DOTAGES > DOTAGE

DOTAL *adj* of a dowry

DOTANT *another word for* > DOTARD

DOTANTS > DOTANT

DOTARD *n* person who is feeble-minded through old age

DOTARDLY *adj* like a dotard

DOTARDS > DOTARD

DOTATION *n* act of giving a dowry

DOTATIONS > DOTATION

DOTCOM *n* company that does most of its business on the internet

DOTCOMMER *n* person who carries out business on the internet

DOTCOMS > DOTCOM

DOTE *vb* love to an excessive or foolish degree

DOTED > DOTE

DOTER > DOTE

DOTERS > DOTE

DOTES > DOTE

DOTH *a singular form of the present tense of* > DO

DOTIER > DOTY

DOTIEST > DOTY

DOTING > DOTE

DOTINGLY > DOTE

DOTINGS > DOTE

DOTISH *adj* foolish

DOTS > DOT

DOTTED > DOT

DOTTEL *same as* > DOTTLE

DOTTELS > DOTTEL

DOTTER > DOT

DOTTEREL *n* rare kind of plover

DOTTERELS > DOTTEREL

DOTTERS > DOT

DOTTIER > DOTTY

DOTTIEST > DOTTY

DOTTILY > DOTTY

DOTTINESS > DOTTY

DOTTING > DOT

DOTTLE *n* tobacco left in a pipe after smoking ▷ *adj* relating to dottle

DOTTLED *adj* foolish

DOTTLER > DOTTLE

DOTTLES > DOTTLE

DOTTLEST > DOTTLE

DOTTREL *same as* > DOTTREL

DOTTRELS > DOTTREL

DOTTY *adj* rather eccentric

DOTY *adj* (of wood) rotten

DOUANE *n* customs house

DOUANES > DOUANE

DOUANIER *n* customs officer

DOUANIERS > DOUANIER

DOUAR *same as* > DUAR

DOUARS > DOUAR

DOUBLE *adj* as much again in number, amount, size, etc ▷ *adv* twice over ▷ *n* twice the number, amount, size, etc ▷ *vb* make or become twice as much or as many

DOUBLED > DOUBLE

DOUBLER > DOUBLE

DOUBLERS > DOUBLE

DOUBLES > DOUBLE

DOUBLET *n* man's close-fitting jacket, with or without sleeves

DOUBLETON *n* original holding of two cards only in a suit

DOUBLETS > DOUBLET

DOUBLING > DOUBLE

DOUBLINGS > DOUBLE

DOUBLOON *n* former Spanish gold coin

DOUBLOONS > DOUBLOON

DOUBLURE *n* decorative lining of vellum or leather, etc, on the inside of a book cover

DOUBLURES > DOUBLURE

DOUBLY *adv* in a greater degree, quantity, or measure

DOUBT *n* uncertainty about the truth, facts, or existence of something ▷ *vb* question the truth of

DOUBTABLE > DOUBT

DOUBTABLY > DOUBT

DOUBTED > DOUBT

DOUBTER > DOUBT

DOUBTERS > DOUBT

DOUBTFUL *adj* unlikely ▷ *n* person who is undecided or uncertain about an issue

DOUBTFULS > DOUBTFUL

DOUBTING > DOUBT

DOUBTINGS > DOUBT

DOUBTLESS *adv* probably or certainly ▷ *adj* certain

DOUBTS > DOUBT

DOUC *n* Old World monkey

DOUCE *adj* quiet

DOUCELY > DOUCE

DOUCENESS > DOUCE

DOUCEPERE *same as* > DOUZEPER

DOUCER > DOUCE

DOUCEST > DOUCE

DOUCET *n* former flute-like instrument

DOUCETS > DOUCET

DOUCEUR *n* gratuity, tip, or bribe

DOUCEURS > DOUCEUR

DOUCHE *n* stream of water onto or into the body ▷ *vb* cleanse or treat by means of a douche

DOUCHEBAG *n* despicable person

DOUCHED > DOUCHE

DOUCHES > DOUCHE

DOUCHING *n* act of douching

DOUCHINGS > DOUCHING

DOUCINE *n* type of moulding for a cornice

DOUCINES > DOUCINE

DOUCS > DOUC

DOUGH *n* thick mixture used for making bread etc

DOUGHBALL *n* ball of bread used as bait in carp fishing

DOUGHBOY *n* infantryman, esp in World War I

DOUGHBOYS > DOUGHBOY

DOUGHFACE *n* Northern Democrat who sided with the South in the American Civil War

DOUGHIER > DOUGHY

DOUGHIEST > DOUGHY

DOUGHLIKE > DOUGH

DOUGHNUT *n* small cake of sweetened dough fried in deep fat ▷ *vb* surround a speaker to give the impression that Parliament is crowded

DOUGHNUTS > DOUGHNUT

DOUGHS > DOUGH

DOUGHT > DOW

DOUGHTIER > DOUGHTY

DOUGHTILY > DOUGHTY

DOUGHTY *adj* brave and determined

DOUGHY *adj* resembling dough in consistency, colour, etc

DOUK *same as* > DOOK

DOUKED > DOUK

DOUKING > DOUK

DOUKS > DOUK

DOULA *n* woman who supports families during pregnancy and childbirth

DOULAS > DOULA

DOULEIA *same as* > DULIA

DOULEIAS > DOULEIA

DOUM *n* as in *doum palm* variety of palm tree

DOUMA *same as* > DUMA

DOUMAS > DOUMA

DOUMS > DOUM

DOUN *same as* > DOWN

DOUP *n* bottom

DOUPIONI *n* type of fabric

DOUPIONIS > DOUPIONI

DOUPPIONI *n* type of silk yarn

DOUPS > DOUP

DOUR *adj* sullen and unfriendly

DOURA *same as* > DURRA

DOURAH *same as* > DURRA

DOURAHS > DOURAH

DOURAS > DOURA

DOURER > DOUR

DOUREST > DOUR

DOURINE *n* infectious disease of horses

DOURINES > DOURINE
DOURLY > DOUR
DOURNESS > DOUR
DOUSE vb drench with water or other liquid ▷ n immersion
DOUSED > DOUSE
DOUSER > DOUSE
DOUSERS > DOUSE
DOUSES > DOUSE
DOUSING > DOUSE
DOUT vb extinguish
DOUTED > DOUT
DOUTER > DOUT
DOUTERS > DOUT
DOUTING > DOUT
DOUTS > DOUT
DOUX adj sweet
DOUZEPER n distinguished person
DOUZEPERS > DOUZEPER
DOVE vb be semiconscious ▷ n bird with a heavy body, small head, and short legs
DOVECOT same as > DOVECOTE
DOVECOTE n structure for housing pigeons
DOVECOTES > DOVECOTE
DOVECOTS > DOVECOT
DOVED > DOVE
DOVEISH adj dovelike
DOVEISHLY > DOVEISH
DOVEKEY same as > DOVEKIE
DOVEKEYS > DOVEKEY
DOVEKIE n small short-billed auk
DOVEKIES > DOVEKIE
DOVELET n small dove
DOVELETS > DOVELET
DOVELIKE > DOVE
DOVEN vb pray
DOVENED > DOVEN
DOVENING > DOVEN
DOVENS > DOVEN
DOVER vb doze ▷ n doze
DOVERED > DOVER
DOVERING > DOVER
DOVERS > DOVER
DOVES > DOVE
DOVETAIL n joint containing wedge-shaped tenons ▷ vb fit together neatly
DOVETAILS > DOVETAIL
DOVIE Scots word for > STUPID
DOVIER > DOVIE
DOVIEST > DOVIE
DOVING > DOVE
DOVISH > DOVE
DOVISHLY > DOVISH
DOW vb archaic word meaning be of worth
DOWABLE adj capable of being endowed
DOWAGER n widow possessing property or a title obtained from her husband
DOWAGERS > DOWAGER
DOWAR same as > DUAR

DOWARS > DOWAR
DOWD n person who wears unfashionable clothes
DOWDIER > DOWDY
DOWDIES > DOWDY
DOWDIEST > DOWDY
DOWDILY > DOWDY
DOWDINESS > DOWDY
DOWDS > DOWD
DOWDY adj dull and old-fashioned ▷ n dowdy person
DOWDYISH > DOWDY
DOWDYISM > DOWDY
DOWDYISMS > DOWD
DOWED > DOW
DOWEL n wooden or metal peg used as a fastener ▷ vb join pieces of wood using dowels
DOWELED > DOWEL
DOWELING n joining of two pieces of wood using dowels
DOWELINGS > DOWELING
DOWELLED > DOWEL
DOWELLING same as > DOWELING
DOWELS > DOWEL
DOWER n life interest in a part of her husband's estate allotted to a widow by law ▷ vb endow
DOWERED > DOWER
DOWERIES > DOWERY
DOWERING > DOWER
DOWERLESS > DOWER
DOWERS > DOWER
DOWERY same as > DOWRY
DOWF adj dull; listless
DOWFNESS > DOWF
DOWIE adj dull and dreary
DOWIER > DOWIE
DOWIEST > DOWIE
DOWING > DOW
DOWITCHER n type of snipelike shore bird of arctic and subarctic N America
DOWL n fluff
DOWLAS n coarse fabric
DOWLASES > DOWLAS
DOWLE same as > DOWL
DOWLES > DOWLE
DOWLIER > DOWLY
DOWLIEST > DOWLY
DOWLNE n obsolete word meaning down (feathers)
DOWLNES > DOWLNE
DOWLNEY > DOWLNE
DOWLS > DOWL
DOWLY adj dull
DOWN adv indicating movement to or position in a lower place ▷ adj unhappy ▷ vb drink quickly ▷ n soft fine feathers
DOWNA obsolete Scots form of > CANNOT
DOWNBEAT adj gloomy ▷ n first beat of a bar
DOWNBEATS > DOWNBEAT
DOWNBOUND adj travelling south

DOWNBOW n (in music) a downward stroke of the bow across the strings
DOWNBOWS > DOWNBOW
DOWNBURST n very high-speed downward movement of turbulent air in a limited area for a short time. Near the ground it spreads out from its centre with high horizontal velocities
DOWNCAST adj sad, dejected ▷ n ventilation shaft
DOWNCASTS > DOWNCAST
DOWNCOME same as > DOWNCOMER
DOWNCOMER n pipe that connects a cistern to a WC, wash basin, etc
DOWNCOMES > DOWNCOME
DOWNCOURT adv in or to the far end of a basketball court
DOWNCRIED > DOWNCRY
DOWNCRIES > DOWNCRY
DOWNCRY vb denigrate or disparage
DOWNDRAFT n downward air current
DOWNED > DOWN
DOWNER n dispiriting experience
DOWNERS > DOWNER
DOWNFALL n sudden loss of success or power
DOWNFALLS > DOWNFALL
DOWNFIELD adj at far end of field
DOWNFLOW n something that flows down
DOWNFLOWS > DOWNFLOW
DOWNFORCE n force produced by air resistance plus gravity that increases the stability of an aircraft or motor vehicle by pressing it downwards
DOWNGRADE vb reduce in importance or value
DOWNHAUL n line for hauling down a sail or for increasing the tension at its luff
DOWNHAULS > DOWNHAUL
DOWNHILL adj going or sloping down ▷ adv towards the bottom of a hill ▷ n downward slope
DOWNHILLS > DOWNHILL
DOWNHOLE adj (in the oil industry) denoting any piece of equipment that is used in the well itself
DOWNIER > DOWNY
DOWNIES > DOWNY
DOWNIEST > DOWNY
DOWNILY adv in a manner resembling or indicating a layer of soft fine feathers or hairs
DOWNINESS > DOWNY

DOWNING > DOWN
DOWNLAND same as > DOWNS
DOWNLANDS > DOWNLAND
DOWNLESS > DOWN
DOWNLIGHT n lamp shining downwards
DOWNLIKE > DOWN
DOWNLINK n satellite transmission channel
DOWNLINKS > DOWNLINK
DOWNLOAD vb transfer data from one computer to another ▷ n file transferred in such a way
DOWNLOADS > DOWNLOAD
DOWNLOW n as in on the downlow not widely known
DOWNLOWS > DOWNLOW
DOWNMOST adj lowest
DOWNPIPE n pipe for carrying rainwater from a roof gutter to the ground or to a drain
DOWNPIPES > DOWNPIPE
DOWNPLAY vb play down
DOWNPLAYS > DOWNPLAY
DOWNPOUR n heavy fall of rain
DOWNPOURS > DOWNPOUR
DOWNRANGE adv in the direction of the intended flight path of a rocket or missile
DOWNRATE vb reduce in value or importance
DOWNRATED > DOWNRATE
DOWNRATES > DOWNRATE
DOWNRIGHT adv extreme(ly) ▷ adj absolute
DOWNRIVER adv in direction of current
DOWNRUSH n instance of rushing down
DOWNS pl n low grassy hills, esp in S England
DOWNSCALE vb reduce in scale
DOWNSHIFT vb reduce work hours
DOWNSIDE n disadvantageous aspect of a situation
DOWNSIDES > DOWNSIDE
DOWNSIZE vb reduce the number of people employed by (a company)
DOWNSIZED > DOWNSIZE
DOWNSIZER > DOWNSIZE
DOWNSIZES > DOWNSIZE
DOWNSLIDE n downward trend
DOWNSLOPE adv towards the bottom of a slope ▷ n downward slope
DOWNSPIN n sudden downturn

DOWNSPINS
> DOWNSPIN
DOWNSPOUT same as
> DOWNPIPE
DOWNSTAGE adj or at the front part of the stage ▷ adv at or towards the front of the stage ▷ n front half of the stage
DOWNSTAIR adj situated on lower floor
DOWNSTATE adj in, or relating to the part of the state away from large cities, esp the southern part ▷ adv towards the southern part of a state ▷ n southern part of a state
DOWNSWEPT adj curved downwards
DOWNSWING n statistical downward trend in business activity, the death rate, etc
DOWNTHROW n state of throwing down or being thrown down
DOWNTICK n small decrease
DOWNTICKS
> DOWNTICK
DOWNTIME n time during which a computer or other machine is not working
DOWNTIMES
> DOWNTIME
DOWNTOWN n central or lower part of a city, esp the main commercial area ▷ adv towards, to, or into this area ▷ adj of, relating to, or situated in the downtown area
DOWNTOWNS
> DOWNTOWN
DOWNTREND n downward trend
DOWNTROD adj downtrodden
DOWNTURN n drop in the success of an economy or a business
DOWNTURNS
> DOWNTURN
DOWNVOTE vb publicly disapprove of a social media post
DOWNVOTED
> DOWNVOTE
DOWNVOTES
> DOWNVOTE
DOWNWARD same as
> DOWNWARDS
DOWNWARDS adv from a higher to a lower level, condition, or position
DOWNWARP n wide depression in the earth's surface
DOWNWARPS
> DOWNWARP
DOWNWASH n downward deflection of an airflow, esp one caused by an aircraft wing
DOWNWIND adj in the same direction towards which the wind is blowing

DOWNY adj covered with soft fine hair or feathers ▷ n bed
DOWNZONE vb reduce density of housing in area
DOWNZONED
> DOWNZONE
DOWNZONES
> DOWNZONE
DOWP same as > DOUP
DOWPS > DOWP
DOWRIES > DOWRY
DOWRY n property brought by a woman to her husband at marriage
DOWS > DOW
DOWSABEL n sweetheart
DOWSABELS
> DOWSABEL
DOWSE same as > DOUSE
DOWSED > DOWSE
DOWSER > DOWSE
DOWSERS > DOWSE
DOWSES > DOWSE
DOWSET same as
> DOUCET
DOWSETS > DOWSET
DOWSING n act of dowsing
DOWSINGS > DOWSING
DOWT n cigarette butt
DOWTS > DOWT
DOX vb publish someone's personal information on the internet
DOXAPRAM n drug used to stimulate the respiration
DOXAPRAMS
> DOXAPRAM
DOXASTIC adj of or relating to belief ▷ n branch of logic that studies the concept of belief
DOXASTICS
> DOXASTIC
DOXED > DOX
DOXES > DOX
DOXIE same as > DOXY
DOXIES > DOXY
DOXING > DOX
DOXOLOGY n short hymn of praise to God
DOXY n opinion or doctrine, esp concerning religious matters
DOY n beloved person: used esp as an endearment
DOYEN n senior member of a group, profession, or society
DOYENNE > DOYEN
DOYENNES > DOYEN
DOYENS > DOYEN
DOYLEY same as > DOILY
DOYLEYS > DOYLEY
DOYLIES > DOYLY
DOYLY same as > DOILY
DOYS > DOY
DOZE vb sleep lightly or briefly ▷ n short sleep
DOZED adj (of timber or rubber) rotten or decayed
DOZEN n set of twelve ▷ vb stun
DOZENED > DOZEN
DOZENING > DOZEN

DOZENS > DOZEN
DOZENTH > DOZEN
DOZENTHS > DOZEN
DOZER > DOZE
DOZERS > DOZE
DOZIER > DOZY
DOZIEST > DOZY
DOZILY > DOZY
DOZINESS > DOZY
DOZING > DOZE
DOZINGS > DOZE
DOZY adj feeling sleepy
DRAB adj dull and dreary ▷ n light olive-brown colour ▷ vb consort with prostitutes
DRABBED > DRAB
DRABBER n one who frequents prostitutes ▷ adj more drab
DRABBERS > DRABBER
DRABBEST > DRAB
DRABBET n yellowish-brown fabric of coarse linen
DRABBETS > DRABBET
DRABBIER > DRABBY
DRABBIEST > DRABBY
DRABBING > DRAB
DRABBISH adj slightly drab
DRABBLE vb make or become wet or dirty
DRABBLED > DRABBLE
DRABBLER n part fixed to bottom of sail
DRABBLERS
> DRABBLER
DRABBLES > DRABBLE
DRABBLING > DRABBLE
DRABBY adj slightly drab
DRABETTE n type of rough linen fabric
DRABETTES
> DRABETTE
DRABLER same as
> DRABBLER
DRABLERS > DRABLER
DRABLY > DRAB
DRABNESS > DRAB
DRABS > DRAB
DRAC same as > DRACK
DRACAENA n type of tropical plant often cultivated as a house plant for its decorative foliage
DRACAENAS
> DRACAENA
DRACENA same as
> DRACAENA
DRACENAS > DRACENA
DRACHM n unit of liquid measure
DRACHMA n former monetary unit of Greece
DRACHMAE > DRACHMA
DRACHMAI > DRACHMA
DRACHMAS > DRACHMA
DRACHMS > DRACHM
DRACK adj unattractive
DRACO n as in draco lizard flying lizard
DRACONE n large container towed by a ship
DRACONES > DRACONE
DRACONIAN adj severe, harsh

DRACONIC same as
> DRACONIAN
DRACONISM
> DRACONIAN
DRACONTIC same as
> DRACONIC
DRAD archaic past of
> DREAD
DRAFF n residue of husks used as a food for cattle
DRAFFIER > DRAFF
DRAFFIEST > DRAFF
DRAFFISH adj worthless
DRAFFS > DRAFF
DRAFFY > DRAFF
DRAFT same as
> DRAUGHT
DRAFTABLE > DRAFT
DRAFTED > DRAFT
DRAFTEE n conscript
DRAFTEES > DRAFTEE
DRAFTER > DRAFT
DRAFTERS > DRAFT
DRAFTIER > DRAFTY
DRAFTIEST > DRAFTY
DRAFTILY > DRAFTY
DRAFTING > DRAFT
DRAFTINGS > DRAFT
DRAFTS > DRAFT
DRAFTSMAN adj person skilled in drawing
DRAFTSMEN
> DRAFTSMAN
DRAFTY same as
> DRAUGHTY
DRAG vb pull with force, esp along the ground ▷ n person or thing that slows up progress
DRAGEE n sweet made of a nut, fruit, etc, coated with a hard sugar icing
DRAGEES > DRAGEE
DRAGGED > DRAG
DRAGGER > DRAG
DRAGGERS > DRAG
DRAGGIER > DRAGGY
DRAGGIEST > DRAGGY
DRAGGING > DRAG
DRAGGINGS
> DRAGGING
DRAGGLE vb make or become wet or dirty by trailing on the ground
DRAGGLED > DRAGGLE
DRAGGLES > DRAGGLE
DRAGGLING > DRAGGLE
DRAGGY adj slow or boring
DRAGHOUND n hound used to follow an artificial trail of scent in a drag hunt
DRAGLINE same as
> DRAGROPE
DRAGLINES
> DRAGLINE
DRAGNET n net used to scour the bottom of a pond or river
DRAGNETS > DRAGNET
DRAGOMAN n (in some Middle Eastern countries) professional interpreter or guide
DRAGOMANS
> DRAGOMAN
DRAGOMEN > DRAGOMAN

DRAGON n mythical fire-breathing monster like a huge lizard

DRAGONESS > DRAGON

DRAGONET n type of small spiny-finned fish with a flat head and a slender brightly coloured body

DRAGONETS > DRAGONET

DRAGONFLY n brightly coloured insect with a long slender body and two pairs of wings

DRAGONISE same as > DRAGONIZE

DRAGONISH > DRAGON

DRAGONISM n vigilance

DRAGONIZE vb turn into dragon

DRAGONNE adj dragonlike

DRAGONS > DRAGON

DRAGOON n heavily armed cavalryman ▷ vb coerce, force

DRAGOONED > DRAGOON

DRAGOONS > DRAGOON

DRAGROPE n rope used to drag military equipment, esp artillery

DRAGROPES > DRAGROPE

DRAGS > DRAG

DRAGSMAN n carriage driver

DRAGSMEN > DRAGSMAN

DRAGSTER n car specially built or modified for drag racing

DRAGSTERS > DRAGSTER

DRAGSTRIP n track for drag racing

DRAGWAY n race course for drag racing

DRAGWAYS > DRAGWAY

DRAIL n weighted hook used in trolling ▷ vb fish with a drail

DRAILED > DRAIL

DRAILING > DRAIL

DRAILS > DRAIL

DRAIN n pipe or channel that carries off water or sewage ▷ vb draw off or remove liquid from

DRAINABLE > DRAIN

DRAINAGE n system of drains

DRAINAGES > DRAINAGE

DRAINED > DRAIN

DRAINER n person or thing that drains

DRAINERS > DRAINER

DRAINING > DRAIN

DRAINPIPE same as > DOWNPIPE

DRAINS > DRAIN

DRAISENE same as > DRAISINE

DRAISENES > DRAISENE

DRAISINE n light rail vehicle

DRAISINES > DRAISINE

DRAKE n male duck

DRAKES > DRAKE

DRAM n small amount of a strong alcoholic drink, esp whisky ▷ vb drink a dram

DRAMA n serious play for theatre, television, or radio

DRAMADIES > DRAMEDY

DRAMADY same as > DRAMEDY

DRAMAS > DRAMA

DRAMATIC adj of or like drama

DRAMATICS n art of acting or producing plays

DRAMATISE same as > DRAMATIZE

DRAMATIST n person who writes plays

DRAMATIZE vb rewrite (a book) in the form of a play

DRAMATURG n literary adviser at a theatre

DRAMEDIES > DRAMEDY

DRAMEDY n television or film drama in which there are important elements of comedy

DRAMMACH n oatmeal mixed with cold water

DRAMMACHS > DRAMMACH

DRAMMED > DRAM

DRAMMING > DRAM

DRAMMOCK same as > DRAMMACH

DRAMMOCKS > DRAMMOCK

DRAMS > DRAM

DRAMSHOP n bar

DRAMSHOPS > DRAMSHOP

DRANGWAY n narrow lane

DRANGWAYS > DRANGWAY

DRANK > DRINK

DRANT vb drone

DRANTED > DRANT

DRANTING > DRANT

DRANTS > DRANT

DRAP a Scot word for > DROP

DRAPABLE > DRAPE

DRAPE vb cover with material, usu in folds ▷ n piece of cloth hung at a window or opening as a screen

DRAPEABLE > DRAPE

DRAPED > DRAPE

DRAPER n person who sells fabrics and sewing materials

DRAPERIED > DRAPERY

DRAPERIES > DRAPERY

DRAPERS > DRAPER

DRAPERY n fabric or clothing arranged and draped

DRAPES pl n material hung at an opening or window to shut out light or to provide privacy

DRAPET n cloth

DRAPETS > DRAPET

DRAPEY adj hanging in loose folds

DRAPIER n draper

DRAPIERS > DRAPIER

DRAPIEST > DRAPEY

DRAPING > DRAPE

DRAPPED > DRAP

DRAPPIE n little drop

DRAPPIES > DRAPPIE

DRAPPING > DRAP

DRAPPY n drop (of liquid)

DRAPS > DRAP

DRASTIC n strong purgative ▷ adj strong and severe

DRASTICS > DRASTIC

DRAT interj exclamation of annoyance ▷ vb curse

DRATCHELL n dialect word meaning a scruffy woman

DRATS > DRAT

DRATTED adj wretched

DRATTING > DRAT

DRAUGHT vb make preliminary plan ▷ n current of cold air, esp in an enclosed space ▷ adj (of an animal) used for pulling heavy loads

DRAUGHTED > DRAUGHT

DRAUGHTER > DRAUGHT

DRAUGHTS n game for two players using a draughtboard and 12 draughtsmen each

DRAUGHTY adj exposed to draughts of air

DRAUNT same as > DRANT

DRAUNTED > DRAUNT

DRAUNTING > DRAUNT

DRAUNTS > DRAUNT

DRAVE archaic past of > DRIVE

DRAW vb sketch (a figure, picture, etc) with a pencil or pen ▷ n attraction

DRAWABLE > DRAW

DRAWBACK n disadvantage ▷ vb move backwards

DRAWBACKS > DRAWBACK

DRAWBAR n strong metal bar on a tractor, locomotive, etc

DRAWBARS > DRAWBAR

DRAWBORE n hole bored through tenon

DRAWBORES > DRAWBORE

DRAWCARD n performer certain to attract a large audience

DRAWCARDS > DRAWCARD

DRAWCORD n cord for drawing tight eg round a hood

DRAWCORDS > DRAWCORD

DRAWDOWN n decrease

DRAWDOWNS > DRAWDOWN

DRAWEE n person or organization on which payment is drawn

DRAWEES > DRAWEE

DRAWER n sliding box-shaped part of a piece of furniture, used for storage

DRAWERFUL n amount contained in drawer

DRAWERS pl n undergarment worn on the lower part of the body

DRAWING > DRAW

DRAWINGS > DRAW

DRAWKNIFE n woodcutting tool with two handles at right angles to the blade, used to shave wood

DRAWL vb speak slowly, with long vowel sounds ▷ n drawling manner of speech

DRAWLED > DRAWL

DRAWLER > DRAWL

DRAWLERS > DRAWL

DRAWLIER > DRAWL

DRAWLIEST > DRAWL

DRAWLING > DRAWL

DRAWLS > DRAWL

DRAWLY > DRAWL

DRAWN > DRAW

DRAWNWORK n type of ornamental needlework

DRAWPLATE n plate used to reduce the diameter of wire by drawing it through conical holes

DRAWS > DRAW

DRAWSHAVE same as > DRAWKNIFE

DRAWTUBE n type of tube used in a telescope

DRAWTUBES > DRAWTUBE

DRAY vb pull using cart ▷ n low cart used for carrying heavy loads

DRAYAGE n act of transporting something a short distance

DRAYAGES > DRAYAGE

DRAYED > DRAY

DRAYHORSE n large powerful horse used for drawing a dray

DRAYING > DRAY

DRAYMAN n driver of a dray

DRAYMEN > DRAYMAN

DRAYS > DRAY

DRAZEL n woman considered dirty or immoral

DRAZELS > DRAZEL

DREAD vb anticipate with apprehension or fear ▷ n great fear ▷ adj awesome

DREADED > DREAD

DREADER > DREAD

DREADERS > DREAD

DREADEST > DREAD

DREADFUL n cheap, often lurid or sensational book or magazine ▷ adj very disagreeable or shocking

DREADFULS > DREADFUL

DREADING > DREAD

DREADLESS > DREAD

DREADLOCK n Rastafarian hair braid

DREADLY > DREAD

DREADS > DREAD

DREAM *n* imagined events experienced while asleep ▷ *vb* see imaginary pictures in the mind while asleep ▷ *adj* ideal

DREAMBOAT *n* exceptionally attractive person or thing

DREAMED > DREAM

DREAMER *n* person who dreams habitually

DREAMERS > DREAMER

DREAMERY *n* dream world

DREAMFUL > DREAM

DREAMHOLE *n* light-admitting hole in a tower

DREAMIER > DREAMY

DREAMIEST > DREAMY

DREAMILY > DREAMY

DREAMING > DREAM

DREAMINGS > DREAM

DREAMLAND *n* ideal land existing in dreams or in the imagination

DREAMLESS > DREAM

DREAMLIKE > DREAM

DREAMS > DREAM

DREAMT > DREAM

DREAMTIME *n* time when the world was new and fresh

DREAMY *adj* vague or impractical

DREAR *same as* > DREARY

DREARE *obsolete form of* > DREAR

DREARER > DREAR

DREARES > DREARE

DREAREST > DREAR

DREARIER > DREARY

DREARIES > DREARY

DREARIEST > DREARY

DREARILY > DREARY

DREARING *n* sorrow

DREARINGS > DREARING

DREARS > DREAR

DREARY *adj* dull, boring ▷ *n* dreary thing or person

DRECK *n* rubbish

DRECKIER > DRECK

DRECKIEST > DRECK

DRECKISH *adj* like rubbish

DRECKS > DRECK

DRECKSILL *n* doorstep

DRECKY > DRECK

DREDGE *vb* clear or search (a river bed or harbour) by removing silt or mud

DREDGED > DREDGE

DREDGER *n* machine used to remove mud from a river bed or harbour

DREDGERS > DREDGER

DREDGES > DREDGE

DREDGING > DREDGE

DREDGINGS > DREDGE

DREE *vb* endure ▷ *adj* dreary

DREED > DREE

DREEING > DREE

DREER > DREE

DREES > DREE

DREEST > DREE

DREG *n* small quantity

DREGGIER > DREGGY

DREGGIEST > DREGGY

DREGGISH *adj* foul

DREGGY *adj* like or full of dregs

DREGS *pl n* solid particles that settle at the bottom of some liquids

DREICH *adj* dreary

DREICHER > DREICH

DREICHEST > DREICH

DREIDEL *n* spinning top

DREIDELS > DREIDEL

DREIDL *same as* > DREIDEL

DREIDLS > DREIDL

DREIGH *same as* > DREICH

DREIGHER > DREIGH

DREIGHEST > DREIGH

DREK *same as* > DRECK

DREKKIER > DREKKY

DREKKIEST > DREKKY

DREKKY > DREK

DREKS > DREK

DRENCH *vb* make completely wet ▷ *n* act or an instance of drenching

DRENCHED > DRENCH

DRENCHER > DRENCH

DRENCHERS > DRENCH

DRENCHES > DRENCH

DRENCHING > DRENCH

DRENT *obsolete word for* > DRENCHED

DREPANID *n* type of moth of the superfamily which comprises the hook-tip moths

DREPANIDS > DREPANID

DREPANIUM *n* type of flower cluster

DRERE *obsolete form of* > DREAR

DRERES > DRERE

DRERIHEAD *n* obsolete word for dreary

DRESS *n* one-piece consisting of a skirt and bodice ▷ *vb* put clothes on ▷ *adj* suitable for a formal occasion

DRESSAGE *n* training of a horse to perform manoeuvres in response to the rider's body signals

DRESSAGES > DRESSAGE

DRESSED > DRESS

DRESSER *n* piece of furniture with shelves and cupboards

DRESSERS > DRESSER

DRESSES > DRESS

DRESSIER > DRESSY

DRESSIEST > DRESSY

DRESSILY > DRESSY

DRESSING *n* sauce for salad

DRESSINGS *pl n* dressed stonework, mouldings, and carved ornaments used to form quoins, keystones, sills, and similar features

DRESSMADE > DRESSMAKE

DRESSMAKE *vb* make clothes

DRESSY *adj* (of clothes) elegant

DREST > DRESS

DREVILL *n* offensive person

DREVILLS > DREVILL

DREW > DRAW

DREY *n* squirrel's nest

DREYS > DREY

DRIB *vb* flow in drops

DRIBBED > DRIB

DRIBBER > DRIB

DRIBBERS > DRIB

DRIBBING > DRIB

DRIBBLE *vb* (allow to) flow in drops ▷ *n* small quantity of liquid falling in drops

DRIBBLED > DRIBBLE

DRIBBLER > DRIBBLE

DRIBBLERS > DRIBBLE

DRIBBLES > DRIBBLE

DRIBBLET *same as* > DRIBLET

DRIBBLETS > DRIBLET

DRIBBLIER > DRIBBLE

DRIBBLING *n* act of dribbling

DRIBBLY > DRIBBLE

DRIBLET *n* small amount

DRIBLETS > DRIBLET

DRIBS > DRIB

DRICE *n* pellets of frozen carbon dioxide

DRICES > DRICE

DRICKSIE *same as* > DRUXY

DRICKSIER > DRICKSIE

DRIED > DRY

DRIEGH *adj* dreary

DRIER > DRY

DRIERS > DRY

DRIES > DRY

DRIEST > DRY

DRIFT *vb* be carried along by currents of air or water ▷ *n* something piled up by the wind or current

DRIFTAGE *n* act of drifting

DRIFTAGES > DRIFTAGE

DRIFTED > DRIFT

DRIFTER *n* person who moves aimlessly from place to place or job to job

DRIFTERS > DRIFTER

DRIFTIER > DRIFT

DRIFTIEST > DRIFT

DRIFTING *n* act of drifting

DRIFTINGS > DRIFTING

DRIFTLESS > DRIFT

DRIFTNET *n* fishing net that drifts with the tide

DRIFTNETS > DRIFTNET

DRIFTPIN *same as* > DRIFT

DRIFTPINS > DRIFTPIN

DRIFTS > DRIFT

DRIFTWOOD *n* wood floating on or washed ashore by the sea

DRIFTY > DRIFT

DRILL *n* tool or machine for boring holes ▷ *vb* bore a hole in (something) with or as if with a drill

DRILLABLE > DRILL

DRILLED > DRILL

DRILLER > DRILL

DRILLERS > DRILL

DRILLHOLE *n* hole drilled in the ground, usu for exploratory purposes

DRILLING *n* type of hard-wearing cloth

DRILLINGS > DRILL

DRILLS > DRILL

DRILLSHIP *n* floating drilling platform

DRILY *adv* in a dry manner

DRINK *vb* swallow (a liquid) ▷ *n* (portion of) a liquid suitable for drinking

DRINKABLE > DRINK

DRINKABLY > DRINK

DRINKER *n* person who drinks

DRINKERS > DRINKER

DRINKING > DRINK

DRINKINGS > DRINK

DRINKS > DRINK

DRIP *vb* (let) fall in drops ▷ *n* falling of drops of liquid

DRIPLESS > DRIP

DRIPPED > DRIP

DRIPPER > DRIP

DRIPPERS > DRIP

DRIPPIER > DRIPPY

DRIPPIEST > DRIPPY

DRIPPILY > DRIPPY

DRIPPING > DRIP

DRIPPINGS > DRIP

DRIPPY *adj* mawkish, insipid, or inane

DRIPS > DRIP

DRIPSTONE *n* form of calcium carbonate existing in stalactites or stalagmites

DRIPT > DRIP

DRISHEEN *n* pudding made of sheep's intestines filled with meal and sheep's blood

DRISHEENS > DRISHEEN

DRIVABLE > DRIVE

DRIVE *vb* guide the movement of (a vehicle) ▷ *n* journey by car, van, etc

DRIVEABLE > DRIVE

DRIVEL *n* foolish talk ▷ *vb* speak foolishly

DRIVELED > DRIVEL

DRIVELER > DRIVEL

DRIVELERS > DRIVEL

DRIVELINE *n* transmission line from engine to wheels of vehicle

DRIVELING > DRIVEL

DRIVELLED > DRIVEL

DRIVELLER > DRIVEL

DRIVELS > DRIVEL

DRIVEN > DRIVE

DRIVER n person who drives a vehicle
DRIVERS > DRIVER
DRIVES > DRIVE
DRIVEWAY n path for vehicles connecting a building to a public road
DRIVEWAYS > DRIVEWAY
DRIVING > DRIVE
DRIVINGLY > DRIVE
DRIVINGS > DRIVE
DRIZZLE n very light rain ▷ vb rain lightly
DRIZZLED > DRIZZLE
DRIZZLES > DRIZZLE
DRIZZLIER > DRIZZLE
DRIZZLING > DRIZZLE
DRIZZLY > DRIZZLE
DROGER n long-masted boat
DROGERS > DROGER
DROGHER same as > DROGER
DROGHERS > DROGHER
DROGUE n any funnel-like device used as a sea anchor
DROGUES > DROGUE
DROGUET n woollen fabric
DROGUETS > DROGUET
DROICH n dwarf
DROICHIER > DROICHY
DROICHS > DROICH
DROICHY adj dwarfish
DROID same as > ANDROID
DROIDS > DROID
DROIL vb carry out boring menial work
DROILED > DROIL
DROILING > DROIL
DROILS > DROIL
DROIT n legal or moral right or claim
DROITS > DROIT
DROKE n small group of trees
DROKES > DROKE
DROLE adj amusing ▷ n scoundrel
DROLER > DROLE
DROLES > DROLE
DROLEST > DROLE
DROLL vb speak wittily ▷ adj quaintly amusing
DROLLED > DROLL
DROLLER > DROLL
DROLLERY n humour
DROLLEST > DROLL
DROLLING > DROLL
DROLLINGS > DROLL
DROLLISH adj somewhat droll
DROLLNESS > DROLL
DROLLS > DROLL
DROLLY > DROLL
DROME same as > AERODROME
DROMEDARE obsolete form of > DROMEDARY
DROMEDARY n camel with a single hump
DROMES > DROME
DROMIC adj relating to a running track

DROMICAL same as > DROMIC
DROMOI > DROMOS
DROMON same as > DROMOND
DROMOND n sailing vessel of the 12th to 15th centuries
DROMONDS > DROMOND
DROMONS > DROMON
DROMOS n Greek passageway
DRONE n male bee ▷ vb make a monotonous low dull sound
DRONED > DRONE
DRONER > DRONE
DRONERS > DRONE
DRONES > DRONE
DRONGO n tropical songbird
DRONGOES > DRONGO
DRONGOS > DRONGO
DRONIER > DRONY
DRONIEST > DRONY
DRONING > DRONE
DRONINGLY > DRONE
DRONISH > DRONE
DRONISHLY > DRONE
DRONKLAP n South African word for a drunkard
DRONKLAPS > DRONKLAP
DRONY adj monotonous
DROOB n pathetic person
DROOBS > DROOB
DROOG n ruffian
DROOGISH > DROOG
DROOGS > DROOG
DROOK same as > DROUK
DROOKED > DROOK
DROOKING > DROOK
DROOKINGS > DROOK
DROOKIT same as > DROUKIT
DROOKS > DROOK
DROOL vb show excessive enthusiasm (for)
DROOLED > DROOL
DROOLIER > DROOLY
DROOLIEST > DROOLY
DROOLING > DROOL
DROOLS > DROOL
DROOLY adj tending to drool
DROOME obsolete form of > DRUM
DROOMES > DROOME
DROOP vb hang downwards loosely ▷ n act or state of drooping
DROOPED > DROOP
DROOPIER > DROOPY
DROOPIEST > DROOPY
DROOPILY > DROOPY
DROOPING > DROOP
DROOPS > DROOP
DROOPY adj hanging or sagging downwards
DROP vb (allow to) fall vertically ▷ n small quantity of liquid forming a round shape
DROPCLOTH n cloth spread on floor to catch drips while painting

DROPDOWN n menu on a computer screen, beneath a selected item
DROPDOWNS > DROPDOWN
DROPFLIES > DROPFLY
DROPFLY n (in angling) an artificial fly
DROPFORGE vb forge metal between two dies
DROPHEAD adj as in drophead coupe two-door car with a folding roof and sloping back
DROPHEADS > DROPHEAD
DROPKICK n kick in which a ball is dropped and then kicked
DROPKICKS > DROPKICK
DROPLET n very small drop of liquid
DROPLETS > DROPLET
DROPLIGHT n electric light that may be raised or lowered by means of a pulley or other mechanism
DROPLIKE adj like a drop
DROPLOCK adj as in droplock loan type of bank loan ▷ n type of bank loan
DROPLOCKS > DROPLOCK
DROPOUT n person who rejects conventional society
DROPOUTS > DROPOUT
DROPPABLE > DROP
DROPPED > DROP
DROPPER n small tube with a rubber part at one end
DROPPERS > DROPPER
DROPPING > DROP
DROPPINGS pl n faeces of certain animals, such as rabbits or birds
DROPPLE n trickle
DROPPLES > DROPPLE
DROPS > DROP
DROPSEED n type of grass
DROPSEEDS > DROPSEED
DROPSHOT n type of tennis shot
DROPSHOTS > DROPSHOT
DROPSICAL > DROPSY
DROPSIED > DROPSY
DROPSIES > DROPSY
DROPSONDE n radiosonde dropped by parachute
DROPSTONE n calcium carbonate in stalactites
DROPSY n illness in which watery fluid collects in the body
DROPT > DROP
DROPTOP n convertible car
DROPTOPS > DROPTOP
DROPWISE adv in form of a drop
DROPWORT n Eurasian plant with cream-coloured flowers, related to the rose

DROPWORTS > DROPWORT
DROSERA n insectivorous plant
DROSERAS > DROSERA
DROSHKIES > DROSHKY
DROSHKY n four-wheeled carriage, formerly used in Russia
DROSKIES > DROSKY
DROSKY same as > DROSHKY
DROSS n scum formed on the surfaces of molten metals
DROSSES > DROSS
DROSSIER > DROSS
DROSSIEST > DROSS
DROSSY > DROSS
DROSTDIES > DROSTDY
DROSTDY n office of landdrost
DROSTDYS > DROSTDY
DROUGHT n prolonged shortage of rainfall
DROUGHTS > DROUGHT
DROUGHTY > DROUGHT
DROUK vb drench
DROUKED > DROUK
DROUKING > DROUK
DROUKINGS > DROUK
DROUKIT adj drenched
DROUKS > DROUK
DROUTH same as > DROUGHT
DROUTHIER > DROUTHY
DROUTHS > DROUTH
DROUTHY adj thirsty or dry
DROVE vb drive livestock ▷ n moving crowd
DROVED > DROVE
DROVER n person who drives sheep or cattle
DROVERS > DROVER
DROVES > DROVE
DROVING > DROVE
DROVINGS > DROVE
DROW n sea fog
DROWN vb die or kill by immersion in liquid
DROWND dialect form of > DROWN
DROWNDED > DROWND
DROWNDING > DROWND
DROWNDS > DROWND
DROWNED > DROWN
DROWNER > DROWN
DROWNERS > DROWN
DROWNING > DROWN
DROWNINGS > DROWN
DROWNS > DROWN
DROWS > DROW
DROWSE vb be sleepy, dull, or sluggish ▷ n state of being drowsy
DROWSED > DROWSE
DROWSES > DROWSE
DROWSIER > DROWSY
DROWSIEST > DROWSY
DROWSIHED adj old form of drowsy
DROWSILY > DROWSY
DROWSING > DROWSE
DROWSY adj feeling sleepy
DRUB vb beat as with a stick ▷ n blow, as from a stick

DRUBBED > DRUB
DRUBBER > DRUB
DRUBBERS > DRUB
DRUBBING > DRUB
DRUBBINGS > DRUB
DRUBS > DRUB
DRUCKEN *adj* old word meaning drunken
DRUDGE *n* person who works hard at uninteresting tasks ▷ *vb* work at such tasks
DRUDGED > DRUDGE
DRUDGER > DRUDGE
DRUDGERS > DRUDGE
DRUDGERY *n* uninteresting work that must be done
DRUDGES > DRUDGE
DRUDGING > DRUDGE
DRUDGISM > DRUDGE
DRUDGISMS > DRUDGE
DRUG *n* substance used in the treatment or prevention of disease ▷ *vb* give a drug to (a person or animal) to cause sleepiness or unconsciousness
DRUGGED > DRUG
DRUGGER *n* druggist
DRUGGERS > DRUGGER
DRUGGET *n* coarse fabric used as a protective floor-covering, etc
DRUGGETS > DRUGGET
DRUGGIE *n* drug addict
DRUGGIER > DRUG
DRUGGIES > DRUGGIE
DRUGGIEST > DRUG
DRUGGING > DRUG
DRUGGIST *n* pharmacist
DRUGGISTS
> DRUGGIST
DRUGGY > DRUG
DRUGLESS *adj* having no drugs
DRUGLORD *n* criminal who controls the distribution and sale of large quantities of illegal drugs
DRUGLORDS
> DRUGLORD
DRUGMAKER *n* manufacturer of drugs
DRUGS > DRUG
DRUGSTER *n* drug addict
DRUGSTERS
> DRUGSTER
DRUGSTORE *n* pharmacy where a wide range of goods are available
DRUID *n* member of an ancient order of priests in the pre-Christian era
DRUIDESS > DRUID
DRUIDIC > DRUID
DRUIDICAL > DRUID
DRUIDISM > DRUID
DRUIDISMS > DRUID
DRUIDRIES > DRUID
DRUIDRY > DRUID
DRUIDS > DRUID
DRUM *n* percussion instrument ▷ *vb* play (music) on a drum
DRUMBEAT *n* sound made by beating a drum

DRUMBEATS
> DRUMBEAT
DRUMBLE *vb* be inactive
DRUMBLED > DRUMBLE
DRUMBLES > DRUMBLE
DRUMBLING > DRUMBLE
DRUMFIRE *n* heavy, rapid, and continuous gunfire, the sound of which resembles rapid drumbeats
DRUMFIRES
> DRUMFIRE
DRUMFISH *n* one of several types of fish that make a drumming sound
DRUMHEAD *n* part of a drum that is struck
DRUMHEADS
> DRUMHEAD
DRUMLIER > DRUMLY
DRUMLIEST > DRUMLY
DRUMLIKE > DRUM
DRUMLIN *n* streamlined mound of glacial drift
DRUMLINS > DRUMLIN
DRUMLY *adj* dismal; dreary
DRUMMED > DRUM
DRUMMER *n* person who plays a drum or drums
DRUMMERS > DRUMMER
DRUMMIES > DRUMMY
DRUMMING *n* act of drumming
DRUMMINGS
> DRUMMING
DRUMMOCK *same as*
> DRAMMOCK
DRUMMOCKS
> DRUMMOCK
DRUMMY *n* (in South Africa) drum majorette
DRUMROLL *n* continued repeated sound of drum
DRUMROLLS
> DRUMROLL
DRUMS > DRUM
DRUMSTICK *n* stick used for playing a drum
DRUNK *adj* intoxicated with alcoholic drink ▷ *n* drunk person
DRUNKARD *n* person who frequently gets drunk
DRUNKARDS
> DRUNKARD
DRUNKEN *adj* drunk or frequently drunk
DRUNKENLY > DRUNKEN
DRUNKER > DRUNK
DRUNKEST > DRUNK
DRUNKISH *adj* rather drunk
DRUNKS > DRUNK
DRUPE *n* fleshy fruit with a stone, such as the peach or cherry
DRUPEL *same as*
> DRUPELET
DRUPELET *n* small drupe, usually one of a number forming a compound fruit
DRUPELETS
> DRUPELET
DRUPELS > DRUPEL
DRUPES > DRUPE

DRUSE *n* aggregate of small crystals within a cavity
DRUSEN *pl n* small deposits of material on the retina
DRUSES > DRUSE
DRUSIER > DRUSY
DRUSIEST > DRUSY
DRUSY *adj* made of tiny crystals
DRUTHER *n* preference
DRUTHERS *n* preference
DRUXIER > DRUXY
DRUXIEST > DRUXY
DRUXY *adj* (of wood) having decayed white spots
DRY *adj* lacking moisture ▷ *vb* make or become dry
DRYABLE > DRY
DRYAD *n* wood nymph
DRYADES > DRYAD
DRYADIC > DRYAD
DRYADS > DRYAD
DRYAS *n* alpine plant with white flowers
DRYASDUST *adj* boringly bookish
DRYBEAT *vb* beat severely
DRYBEATEN > DRYBEAT
DRYBEATS > DRYBEAT
DRYER > DRY
DRYERS > DRY
DRYEST > DRY
DRYING > DRY
DRYINGS > DRY
DRYISH *adj* fairly dry
DRYLAND *n* arid area
DRYLANDS > DRYLAND
DRYLOT *n* livestock enclosure
DRYLOTS > DRYLOT
DRYLY *same as* > DRILY
DRYMOUTH *n* condition of insufficient saliva
DRYMOUTHS
> DRYMOUTH
DRYNESS > DRY
DRYNESSES > DRY
DRYPOINT *n* copper engraving technique using a hard steel needle
DRYPOINTS
> DRYPOINT
DRYS > DRY
DRYSALTER *n* dealer in certain chemical products, such as dyestuffs and gums, and in dried, tinned, or salted foods and edible oils
DRYSTONE *adj* (of a wall) made without mortar
DRYSUIT *n* waterproof rubber suit worn by divers
DRYSUITS > DRYSUIT
DRYWALL *n* wall built without mortar ▷ *vb* build a wall without mortar
DRYWALLED > DRYWALL
DRYWALLER *n* person who builds drystone walls
DRYWALLS > DRYWALL
DRYWELL *n* type of sewage disposal system
DRYWELLS > DRYWELL
DSO *same as* > ZHO

DSOBO *same as* > ZOBO
DSOBOS > DSOBO
DSOMO *same as* > ZHOMO
DSOMOS > DSOMO
DSOS > DSO
DUAD *a rare word for* > PAIR
DUADS > DUAD
DUAL *adj* having two parts, functions, or aspects ▷ *n* dual number ▷ *vb* make (a road) into a dual carriageway
DUALIN *n* explosive substance
DUALINS > DUALIN
DUALISE *same as*
> DUALIZE
DUALISED > DUALISE
DUALISES > DUALISE
DUALISING > DUALISE
DUALISM *n* state of having two distinct parts
DUALISMS > DUALISM
DUALIST > DUALISM
DUALISTIC > DUALISM
DUALISTS > DUALISM
DUALITIES > DUALITY
DUALITY *n* state or quality of being two or in two parts
DUALIZE *vb* cause to have two parts
DUALIZED > DUALIZE
DUALIZES > DUALIZE
DUALIZING > DUALIZE
DUALLED > DUAL
DUALLIE *n* pickup truck with dual rear tyres
DUALLIES > DUALLIE
DUALLING > DUAL
DUALLY > DUAL
DUALS > DUAL
DUAN *n* poem
DUANS > DUAN
DUAR *n* Arab camp
DUARCHIES > DUARCHY
DUARCHY *same as*
> DIARCHY
DUARS > DUAR
DUATHLETE *n* athlete who competes in duathlons
DUATHLON *n* athletic contest in which each athlete competes in running and cycling events
DUATHLONS
> DUATHLON
DUB *vb* give (a person or place) a name or nickname ▷ *n* style of reggae record production
DUBBED > DUB
DUBBER > DUB
DUBBERS > DUB
DUBBIN *n* thick grease applied to leather to soften and waterproof it ▷ *vb* apply dubbin to
DUBBINED > DUBBIN
DUBBING > DUB
DUBBINGS > DUB
DUBBINING > DUBBIN
DUBBINS > DUBBIN
DUBBO *adj* stupid ▷ *n* stupid person
DUBBOS > DUBBO
DUBIETIES > DUBIETY

DUBIETY n state of being doubtful

DUBIOSITY same as > DUBIETY

DUBIOUS adj feeling or causing doubt

DUBIOUSLY > DUBIOUS

DUBITABLE adj open to doubt

DUBITABLY > DUBITABLE

DUBITANCY > DUBITATE

DUBITATE vb doubt

DUBITATED > DUBITATE

DUBITATES > DUBITATE

DUBNIUM n chemical element

DUBNIUMS > DUBNIUM

DUBONNET n dark purplish-red colour

DUBONNETS > DUBONNET

DUBS > DUB

DUBSTEP n genre of electronic music

DUBSTEPS > DUBSTEP

DUCAL adj of a duke

DUCALLY > DUCAL

DUCAT n former European gold or silver coin

DUCATOON n former silver coin

DUCATOONS > DUCATOON

DUCATS > DUCAT

DUCDAME interj Shakespearean nonsense word

DUCE n leader

DUCES > DUCE

DUCHESS n woman who holds the rank of duke ▷ vb overwhelm with flattering attention

DUCHESSE n type of satin

DUCHESSED > DUCHESS

DUCHESSES > DUCHESS

DUCHIES > DUCHY

DUCHY n territory of a duke or duchess

DUCI > DUCE

DUCK n water bird ▷ vb move (the head or body) quickly downwards

DUCKBILL n duck-billed platypus

DUCKBILLS > DUCKBILL

DUCKBOARD n board or boards laid so as to form a floor or path over wet or muddy ground

DUCKED > DUCK

DUCKER > DUCK

DUCKERS > DUCK

DUCKFOOT adj as in duckfoot quote chevron-shaped quotation mark

DUCKIE same as > DUCKY

DUCKIER > DUCKY

DUCKIES > DUCKY

DUCKIEST > DUCKY

DUCKING > DUCK

DUCKINGS > DUCK

DUCKISH n twilight

DUCKISHES > DUCKISH

DUCKLING n baby duck

DUCKLINGS > DUCKLING

DUCKMOLE another word for > DUCKBILL

DUCKMOLES > DUCKMOLE

DUCKPIN n short bowling pin

DUCKPINS > DUCKPIN

DUCKS > DUCK

DUCKSHOVE vb evade responsibility

DUCKTAIL n Teddy boy's hairstyle

DUCKTAILS > DUCKTAIL

DUCKWALK vb walk in a squatting posture

DUCKWALKS > DUCKWALK

DUCKWEED n type of small stemless aquatic plant

DUCKWEEDS > DUCKWEED

DUCKY n darling or dear ▷ adj delightful

DUCT vb convey via a duct ▷ n tube, pipe, or channel through which liquid or gas is conveyed

DUCTAL > DUCT

DUCTED > DUCT

DUCTILE adj (of a metal) able to be shaped into sheets or wires

DUCTILELY > DUCTILE

DUCTILITY > DUCTILE

DUCTING > DUCT

DUCTINGS > DUCT

DUCTLESS > DUCT

DUCTS > DUCT

DUCTULE n small duct

DUCTULES > DUCTULE

DUCTWORK n system of ducts

DUCTWORKS > DUCTWORK

DUD n ineffectual person or thing ▷ adj bad or useless

DUDDER n door-to-door salesperson ▷ vb tremble or shudder

DUDDERED > DUDDER

DUDDERIES > DUDDERY

DUDDERING > DUDDER

DUDDERS > DUDDER

DUDDERY n place where old clothes are sold

DUDDIE adj ragged ▷ n friend or a chum

DUDDIER > DUDDIE

DUDDIES > DUDDIE

DUDDIEST > DUDDIE

DUDDY same as > DUDDIE

DUDE vb dress fashionably ▷ n man

DUDED > DUDE

DUDEEN n clay pipe with a short stem

DUDEENS > DUDEEN

DUDENESS n state of being a dude

DUDES > DUDE

DUDETTE n woman who behaves like a dude

DUDETTES > DUDETTE

DUDGEON n anger or resentment

DUDGEONS > DUDGEON

DUDHEEN n type of pipe

DUDHEENS > DUDHEEN

DUDING > DUDE

DUDISH > DUDE

DUDISHLY > DUDE

DUDISM n being a dude

DUDISMS > DUDISM

DUDS > DUD

DUE vb supply with ▷ adj expected or scheduled to be present or arrive ▷ n something that is owed or required ▷ adv directly or exactly

DUECENTO n thirteenth century (in Italian art)

DUECENTOS > DUECENTO

DUED > DUE

DUEFUL adj proper

DUEL n formal fight with deadly weapons between two people ▷ vb fight in a duel

DUELED > DUEL

DUELER > DUEL

DUELERS > DUELER

DUELING > DUEL

DUELINGS > DUELING

DUELIST > DUEL

DUELISTS > DUELIST

DUELLED > DUEL

DUELLER > DUEL

DUELLERS > DUELLER

DUELLI > DUELLO

DUELLING > DUEL

DUELLINGS > DUELLING

DUELLIST > DUEL

DUELLISTS > DUELLIST

DUELLO n art of duelling

DUELLOS > DUELLO

DUELS > DUEL

DUELSOME adj given to duelling

DUENDE n Spanish goblin

DUENDES > DUENDE

DUENESS > DUE

DUENESSES > DUE

DUENNA n (esp in Spain) woman acting as a chaperone to a young woman

DUENNAS > DUENNA

DUES pl n membership fees

DUET n piece of music for two performers ▷ vb perform a duet

DUETED > DUET

DUETING > DUET

DUETS > DUET

DUETT same as > DUET

DUETTED > DUET

DUETTI > DUETTO

DUETTING > DUET

DUETTINO n simple duet

DUETTINOS > DUETTINO

DUETTIST > DUET

DUETTISTS > DUET

DUETTO same as > DUET

DUETTOS > DUETTO

DUETTS > DUETT

DUFF adj broken or useless ▷ vb change the appearance of or give a false appearance to (old or stolen goods) ▷ n mishit golf shot

DUFFED > DUFF

DUFFEL n heavy woollen cloth with a thick nap

DUFFELS > DUFFEL

DUFFER n dull or incompetent person

DUFFERDOM n condition of being a duffer

DUFFERISM same as > DUFFERDOM

DUFFERS > DUFFER

DUFFEST > DUFF

DUFFING > DUFF

DUFFINGS > DUFF

DUFFLE same as > DUFFEL

DUFFLES > DUFFLE

DUFFS > DUFF

DUFUS same as > DOOFUS

DUFUSES > DUFUS

DUG Scottish word for > DOG

DUGITE n medium-sized Australian venomous snake

DUGITES > DUGITE

DUGONG n whalelike mammal of tropical waters

DUGONGS > DUGONG

DUGOUT n (at a sports ground) covered bench where managers and substitutes sit

DUGOUTS > DUGOUT

DUGS > DUG

DUH interj ironic response to a question or statement

DUHKHA same as > DUKKHA

DUHKHAS > DUHKHA

DUI > DUO

DUIKER n small African antelope

DUIKERBOK same as > DUIKER

DUIKERS > DUIKER

DUING > DUE

DUIT n former Dutch coin

DUITS > DUIT

DUKA n shop

DUKAS > DUKA

DUKE vb fight with fists ▷ n nobleman of the highest rank

DUKED > DUKE

DUKEDOM n title, rank, or position of a duke

DUKEDOMS > DUKEDOM

DUKELING n low-ranking duke

DUKELINGS > DUKELING

DUKERIES > DUKERY

DUKERY n duke's domain

DUKES pl n fists

DUKESHIP > DUKE

DUKESHIPS > DUKE

DUKING > DUKE

DUKKA *n* mix of ground roast nuts and spices
DUKKAH *same as* > DUKKA
DUKKAHS > DUKKAH
DUKKAS > DUKKA
DUKKHA *n* Buddhist belief that all things are suffering
DUKKHAS > DUKKHA
DULCAMARA *n* orange-fruited vine
DULCE *n* sweet food or drink
DULCES > DULCE
DULCET *adj* (of a sound) soothing or pleasant ▷ *n* soft organ stop
DULCETLY > DULCET
DULCETS > DULCET
DULCIAN *n* precursor to the bassoon
DULCIANA *n* sweet-toned organ stop, controlling metal pipes of narrow scale
DULCIANAS > DULCIANA
DULCIANS > DULCIAN
DULCIFIED > DULCIFY
DULCIFIES > DULCIFY
DULCIFY *vb* make pleasant or agreeable
DULCIMER *n* tuned percussion instrument
DULCIMERS > DULCIMER
DULCIMORE *former name for* > DULCIMER
DULCINEA *n* female sweetheart
DULCINEAS > DULCINEA
DULCITE *n* sweet substance
DULCITES > DULCITE
DULCITOL *another word for* > DULCITE
DULCITOLS > DULCITOL
DULCITUDE *n* sweetness
DULCOSE *another word for* > DULCITE
DULCOSES > DULCOSE
DULE *n* suffering; misery
DULES > DULE
DULIA *n* veneration accorded to saints
DULIAS > DULIA
DULL *adj* not interesting ▷ *vb* make or become dull
DULLARD *n* dull or stupid person
DULLARDS > DULLARD
DULLED > DULL
DULLER > DULL
DULLEST > DULL
DULLIER > DULL
DULLIEST > DULL
DULLING > DULL
DULLISH > DULL
DULLISHLY > DULL
DULLNESS > DULL
DULLS > DULL
DULLY > DULL
DULNESS > DULL
DULNESSES > DULL
DULOCRACY *n* rule by slaves

DULOSES > DULOSIS
DULOSIS *n* behaviour where one species of ant forces members of another to work for them
DULOTIC > DULOSIS
DULSE *n* seaweed with large red edible fronds
DULSES > DULSE
DULY *adv* in a proper manner
DUM *adj* steamed
DUMA *n* elective legislative assembly established by Tsar Nicholas II
DUMAIST *n* member of duma
DUMAISTS > DUMAIST
DUMAS > DUMA
DUMB *vb* silence ▷ *adj* temporarily bereft of speech
DUMBBELL *n* short bar with a heavy ball or disc at each end, used for physical exercise
DUMBBELLS > DUMBBELL
DUMBCANE *n* tropical aroid plant
DUMBCANES > DUMBCANE
DUMBED > DUMB
DUMBER > DUMB
DUMBEST > DUMB
DUMBFOUND *vb* make silent with astonishment
DUMBHEAD *n* dunce
DUMBHEADS > DUMBHEAD
DUMBING > DUMB
DUMBLY > DUMB
DUMBNESS > DUMB
DUMBO *n* unintelligent person
DUMBOS > DUMBO
DUMBS > DUMB
DUMBSHIT *n* vulgar word for a stupid person
DUMBSHITS > DUMBSHIT
DUMBSHOW *n* actions performed without words in a play
DUMBSHOWS > DUMBSHOW
DUMBSIZE *vb* reduce the number in a workforce to the point it becomes ineffective
DUMBSIZED > DUMBSIZE
DUMBSIZES > DUMBSIZE
DUMDUM *n* soft-nosed bullet
DUMDUMS > DUMDUM
DUMELA *sentence substitute* hello
DUMFOUND *same as* > DUMBFOUND
DUMFOUNDS > DUMFOUND
DUMKA *n* Slavonic lyrical song
DUMKAS > DUMKA
DUMKY > DUMKA

DUMMERER *n* archaic word for a person who pretends they cannot speak
DUMMERERS > DUMMERER
DUMMIED > DUMMY
DUMMIER > DUMMY
DUMMIES > DUMMY
DUMMIEST > DUMMY
DUMMINESS > DUMMY
DUMMKOPF *n* stupid person
DUMMKOPFS > DUMMKOPF
DUMMY *n* figure representing the human form ▷ *adj* imitation, substitute ▷ *vb* prepare an imitation of (a proposed book, page, etc)
DUMMYING > DUMMY
DUMOSE *adj* bushlike
DUMOSITY > DUMOSE
DUMOUS *same as* > DUMOSE
DUMP *vb* drop or let fall in a careless manner ▷ *n* place where waste materials are left
DUMPBIN *n* unit in a bookshop displaying a particular publisher's books
DUMPBINS > DUMPBIN
DUMPCART *n* cart for dumping without handling
DUMPCARTS > DUMPCART
DUMPED > DUMP
DUMPEE *n* person dumped from a relationship
DUMPEES > DUMPEE
DUMPER > DUMP
DUMPERS > DUMP
DUMPIER > DUMPY
DUMPIES > DUMPY
DUMPIEST > DUMPY
DUMPILY > DUMPY
DUMPINESS > DUMPY
DUMPING > DUMP
DUMPINGS > DUMP
DUMPISH *same as* > DUMPY
DUMPISHLY > DUMPISH
DUMPLE *vb* form into a dumpling shape
DUMPLED > DUMPLE
DUMPLES > DUMPLE
DUMPLING *n* small ball of dough cooked and served with stew
DUMPLINGS > DUMPLING
DUMPS *pl n* state of melancholy
DUMPSITE *n* location of dump
DUMPSITES > DUMPSITE
DUMPSTER *n* refuse skip
DUMPSTERS > DUMPSTER
DUMPTRUCK *n* lorry with a tipping container
DUMPY *adj* short and plump ▷ *n* short, plump person

DUN *adj* brownish-grey ▷ *vb* demand payment from (a debtor) ▷ *n* demand for payment
DUNAM *n* unit of area measurement
DUNAMS > DUNAM
DUNCE *n* person who is stupid or slow to learn
DUNCEDOM > DUNCE
DUNCEDOMS > DUNCE
DUNCELIKE > DUNCE
DUNCERIES > DUNCERY
DUNCERY *n* duncelike behaviour
DUNCES > DUNCE
DUNCH *vb* push against gently
DUNCHED > DUNCH
DUNCHES > DUNCH
DUNCHING > DUNCH
DUNCICAL *adj* duncelike
DUNCISH *adj* duncelike
DUNCISHLY > DUNCE
DUNDER *n* cane juice lees
DUNDERS > DUNDER
DUNE *n* mound or ridge of drifted sand
DUNELAND *n* land characterized by dunes
DUNELANDS > DUNELAND
DUNELIKE > DUNE
DUNES > DUNE
DUNG *n* faeces from animals such as cattle ▷ *vb* cover (ground) with manure
DUNGAREE *n* coarse cotton fabric used chiefly for work clothes, etc
DUNGAREED *adj* wearing dungarees
DUNGAREES > DUNGAREE
DUNGED > DUNG
DUNGEON *vb* hold captive in dungeon ▷ *n* underground prison cell
DUNGEONED > DUNGEON
DUNGEONER *n* jailer
DUNGEONS > DUNGEON
DUNGER *n* old decrepit car
DUNGERS > DUNGER
DUNGHEAP *n* pile of dung
DUNGHEAPS > DUNGHEAP
DUNGHILL *n* heap of dung
DUNGHILLS > DUNGHILL
DUNGIER > DUNG
DUNGIEST > DUNG
DUNGING > DUNG
DUNGMERE *n* cesspool
DUNGMERES > DUNGMERE
DUNGS > DUNG
DUNGY > DUNG
DUNITE *n* ultrabasic igneous rock
DUNITES > DUNITE
DUNITIC > DUNITE
DUNK *vb* dip (a biscuit or bread) in a drink or soup before eating it
DUNKED > DUNK
DUNKER > DUNK

d

DUNKERS > DUNK
DUNKING n act of dunking
DUNKINGS > DUNKING
DUNKS > DUNK
DUNLIN n small sandpiper
DUNLINS > DUNLIN
DUNNAGE n loose material used for packing cargo
DUNNAGES > DUNNAGE
DUNNAKIN n lavatory
DUNNAKINS > DUNNAKIN
DUNNART n type of insectivorous marsupial
DUNNARTS > DUNNART
DUNNED > DUN
DUNNER > DUN
DUNNESS > DUN
DUNNESSES > DUN
DUNNEST > DUN
DUNNIER > DUNNY
DUNNIES > DUNNY
DUNNIEST > DUNNY
DUNNING > DUN
DUNNINGS > DUNNING
DUNNISH > DUN
DUNNITE n explosive containing ammonium picrate
DUNNITES > DUNNITE
DUNNO vb slang for don't know
DUNNOCK n hedge sparrow
DUNNOCKS > DUNNOCK
DUNNY n in Australia, toilet ▷ adj like or relating to a dunny
DUNS > DUN
DUNSH same as > DUNCH
DUNSHED > DUNSH
DUNSHES > DUNSH
DUNSHING > DUNSH
DUNT n blow ▷ vb strike or hit
DUNTED > DUNT
DUNTING > DUNT
DUNTS > DUNT
DUO same as > DUET
DUOBINARY adj denoting a communications system for coding digital data in which three data bands are used, 0, +1, −1
DUODECIMO n book size resulting from folding a sheet of paper into twelve leaves
DUODENA > DUODENUM
DUODENAL > DUODENUM
DUODENARY adj of or relating to the number 12
DUODENUM n first part of the small intestine, just below the stomach
DUODENUMS > DUODENUM
DUOLOG same as > DUOLOGUE
DUOLOGS > DUOLOG
DUOLOGUE n (in drama) conversation between only two speakers
DUOLOGUES > DUOLOGUE

DUOMI > DUOMO
DUOMO n cathedral in Italy
DUOMOS > DUOMO
DUOPOLIES > DUOPOLY
DUOPOLIST n either of the two suppliers in a duopoly
DUOPOLY n situation when control of a commodity is vested in two producers or suppliers
DUOPSONY n two rival buyers controlling sellers
DUOS > DUO
DUOTONE n process for producing halftone illustrations
DUOTONES > DUOTONE
DUP vb open
DUPABLE > DUPE
DUPATTA n scarf worn in India
DUPATTAS > DUPATTA
DUPE vb deceive or cheat ▷ n person who is easily deceived
DUPED > DUPE
DUPER > DUPE
DUPERIES > DUPERY
DUPERS > DUPE
DUPERY > DUPE
DUPES > DUPE
DUPING n act of duping
DUPINGS > DUPING
DUPION n silk fabric made from the threads of double cocoons
DUPIONS > DUPION
DUPLE adj having two beats in a bar
DUPLET n pair of electrons shared between two atoms in a covalent bond
DUPLETS > DUPLET
DUPLEX vb duplicate ▷ n apartment on two floors ▷ adj having two parts
DUPLEXED > DUPLEX
DUPLEXER n telecommunications system
DUPLEXERS > DUPLEXER
DUPLEXES > DUPLEX
DUPLEXING n act of duplicating
DUPLEXITY > DUPLEX
DUPLICAND n feu duty doubled
DUPLICATE adj copied exactly from an original ▷ n exact copy ▷ vb make an exact copy of
DUPLICITY n deceitful behaviour
DUPLIED > DUPLY
DUPLIES > DUPLY
DUPLY vb give a second reply
DUPLYING > DUPLY
DUPONDII > DUPONDIUS
DUPONDIUS n brass coin of ancient Rome worth half a sesterce
DUPPED > DUP
DUPPIES > DUPPY

DUPPING > DUP
DUPPY n spirit or ghost
DUPS > DUP
DURA same as > DURRA
DURABLE adj long-lasting
DURABLES pl n goods that require infrequent replacement
DURABLY > DURABLE
DURAL n alloy of aluminium and copper
DURALS > DURAL
DURALUMIN n light and strong aluminium alloy containing copper, silicon, magnesium, and manganese
DURAMEN another name for > HEARTWOOD
DURAMENS > DURAMEN
DURANCE n imprisonment
DURANCES > DURANCE
DURANT n tough, leathery cloth
DURANTS > DURANT
DURAS > DURA
DURATION n length of time that something lasts
DURATIONS > DURATION
DURATIVE adj denoting an aspect of verbs that includes the imperfective and the progressive ▷ n durative aspect of a verb
DURATIVES > DURATIVE
DURBAR n (formerly) the court of a native ruler or a governor in India
DURBARS > DURBAR
DURDUM same as > DIRDUM
DURDUMS > DURDUM
DURE vb endure
DURED > DURE
DUREFUL adj lasting
DURES > DURE
DURESS n compulsion by use of force or threats
DURESSE same as > DURESS
DURESSES > DURESS
DURGAH same as > DARGAH
DURGAHS > DURGAH
DURGAN n dwarf
DURGANS > DURGAN
DURGIER > DURGY
DURGIEST > DURGY
DURGY adj dwarflike
DURIAN n SE Asian tree with very large oval fruits
DURIANS > DURIAN
DURICRUST another name for > CALICHE
DURING prep throughout or within the limit of (a period of time)
DURION same as > DURIAN
DURIONS > DURION
DURMAST n large Eurasian oak tree with lobed leaves
DURMASTS > DURMAST
DURN same as > DARN
DURNDEST same as > DARNEDEST

DURNED > DURN
DURNEDER > DURNED
DURNEDEST > DURN
DURNING > DURN
DURNS > DURN
DURO n silver peso of Spain or Spanish America
DUROC n breed of pig
DUROCS > DUROC
DUROMETER n instrument for measuring hardness
DUROS > DURO
DUROY n coarse woollen fabric
DUROYS > DUROY
DURR same as > DURRA
DURRA n Old World variety of sorghum
DURRAS > DURRA
DURRIE n cotton carpet made in India, often in rectangular pieces fringed at the ends
DURRIES > DURRY
DURRS > DURR
DURRY n cigarette
DURST a past tense of > DARE
DURUKULI n S American monkey
DURUKULIS > DURUKULI
DURUM n variety of wheat
DURUMS > DURUM
DURZI n Indian tailor
DURZIS > DURZI
DUSH vb strike hard
DUSHED > DUSH
DUSHES > DUSH
DUSHING > DUSH
DUSK n time just before nightfall, when it is almost dark ▷ adj shady ▷ vb make or become dark
DUSKED > DUSK
DUSKEN vb grow dark
DUSKENED > DUSKEN
DUSKENING > DUSKEN
DUSKENS > DUSKEN
DUSKER > DUSK
DUSKEST > DUSK
DUSKIER > DUSKY
DUSKIEST > DUSKY
DUSKILY > DUSKY
DUSKINESS > DUSKY
DUSKING > DUSK
DUSKISH > DUSK
DUSKISHLY > DUSK
DUSKLY > DUSK
DUSKNESS > DUSK
DUSKS > DUSK
DUSKY adj dark in colour
DUST n small dry particles of earth, sand, or dirt ▷ vb remove dust from (furniture) by wiping
DUSTBALL n ball of dust
DUSTBALLS > DUSTBALL
DUSTBIN n large container for household rubbish
DUSTBINS > DUSTBIN
DUSTCART n truck for collecting household rubbish

d

DUSTCARTS
> DUSTCART
DUSTCLOTH *n* cloth used for dusting
DUSTCOAT *n* light, loose-fitting long coat
DUSTCOATS
> DUSTCOAT
DUSTCOVER *same as*
> DUSTSHEET
DUSTED > DUST
DUSTER *n* cloth used for dusting
DUSTERS > DUSTER
DUSTHEAP *n* accumulation of refuse
DUSTHEAPS
> DUSTHEAP
DUSTIER > DUSTY
DUSTIEST > DUSTY
DUSTILY > DUSTY
DUSTINESS > DUSTY
DUSTING > DUST
DUSTINGS > DUST
DUSTLESS > DUST
DUSTLIKE > DUST
DUSTMAN *n* man whose job is to collect household rubbish
DUSTMEN > DUSTMAN
DUSTOFF *n* casualty evacuation helicopter
DUSTOFFS > DUSTOFF
DUSTPAN *n* short-handled shovel
DUSTPANS > DUSTPAN
DUSTPROOF *adj* repelling dust
DUSTRAG *n* cloth for dusting
DUSTRAGS > DUSTRAG
DUSTS > DUST
DUSTSHEET *n* large cloth cover to protect furniture from dust
DUSTSTORM *n* storm with whirling column of dust
DUSTUP *n* quarrel, fight, or argument
DUSTUPS > DUSTUP
DUSTY *adj* covered with dust
DUTCH *n* wife
DUTCHES > DUTCH
DUTCHMAN *n* piece of wood, metal, etc, used to repair or patch faulty workmanship
DUTCHMEN > DUTCHMAN
DUTEOUS *adj* dutiful or obedient
DUTEOUSLY > DUTEOUS
DUTIABLE *adj* (of goods) requiring payment of duty
DUTIED *adj* liable for duty
DUTIES > DUTY
DUTIFUL *adj* doing what is expected
DUTIFULLY > DUTIFUL
DUTY *n* work or a task performed as part of one's job
DUUMVIR *n* one of two coequal magistrates or officers
DUUMVIRAL > DUUMVIR
DUUMVIRI > DUUMVIR

DUUMVIRS > DUUMVIR
DUVET *n* large quilt used as a bed cover
DUVETINE *same as*
> DUVETYN
DUVETINES
> DUVETINE
DUVETS > DUVET
DUVETYN *n* soft napped velvety fabric of cotton, silk, wool, or rayon
DUVETYNE *same as*
> DUVETYN
DUVETYNES
> DUVETYNE
DUVETYNS > DUVETYN
DUX *n* (in Scottish and certain other schools) the top pupil in a class or school
DUXELLES *n* paste of mushrooms and onions
DUXES > DUX
DUYKER *same as*
> DUIKER
DUYKERS > DUYKER
DVANDVA *n* class of compound words
DVANDVAS > DVANDVA
DVORNIK *n* Russian doorkeeper
DVORNIKS > DVORNIK
DWAAL *n* state of absent-mindedness
DWAALS > DWAAL
DWALE *n* deadly nightshade
DWALES > DWALE
DWALM *same as* > DWAM
DWALMED > DWALM
DWALMING > DWALM
DWALMS > DWALM
DWAM *n* stupor or daydream ▷ *vb* faint or fall ill
DWAMMED > DWAM
DWAMMING > DWAM
DWAMS > DWAM
DWANG *n* short piece of wood inserted in a timber-framed wall
DWANGS > DWANG
DWARF *adj* undersized ▷ *n* person who is smaller than average ▷ *vb* cause (someone or something) to seem small by being much larger
DWARFED > DWARF
DWARFER > DWARF
DWARFEST > DWARF
DWARFING > DWARF
DWARFISH > DWARF
DWARFISM *n* condition of being a dwarf
DWARFISMS
> DWARFISM
DWARFLIKE > DWARF
DWARFNESS > DWARF
DWARFS > DWARF
DWARVES > DWARF
DWAUM *same as* > DWAM
DWAUMED > DWAUM
DWAUMING > DWAUM
DWAUMS > DWAUM
DWEEB *n* stupid or uninteresting person
DWEEBIER > DWEEBY

DWEEBIEST > DWEEBY
DWEEBISH > DWEEB
DWEEBS > DWEEB
DWEEBY *adj* like or typical of a dweeb
DWELL *vb* live, reside ▷ *n* regular pause in the operation of a machine
DWELLED > DWELL
DWELLER > DWELL
DWELLERS > DWELL
DWELLING > DWELL
DWELLINGS > DWELL
DWELLS > DWELL
DWELT > DWELL
DWILE *n* floor cloth
DWILES > DWILE
DWINDLE *vb* grow less in size, strength, or number
DWINDLED > DWINDLE
DWINDLES > DWINDLE
DWINDLING > DWINDLE
DWINE *vb* languish
DWINED > DWINE
DWINES > DWINE
DWINING > DWINE
DYABLE > DYE
DYAD *n* operator that is the unspecified product of two vectors
DYADIC *adj* of or relating to a dyad ▷ *n* sum of a particular number of dyads
DYADICS > DYADIC
DYADS > DYAD
DYARCHAL > DYARCHY
DYARCHIC > DYARCHY
DYARCHIES > DYARCHY
DYARCHY *same as*
> DIARCHY
DYBBUK *n* (in Jewish folklore) the soul of a dead sinner possessing a living person's body
DYBBUKIM > DYBBUK
DYBBUKKIM > DYBBUK
DYBBUKS > DYBBUK
DYE *n* colouring substance ▷ *vb* colour (hair or fabric) by applying a dye
DYEABLE > DYE
DYED > DYE
DYEING > DYE
DYEINGS > DYE
DYELINE *same as*
> DIAZO
DYELINES > DYELINE
DYER > DYE
DYERS > DYE
DYES > DYE
DYESTER *n* dyer
DYESTERS > DYESTER
DYESTUFF *n* substance that can be used as a dye or from which a dye can be obtained
DYESTUFFS
> DYESTUFF
DYEWEED *n* plant that produces dye
DYEWEEDS > DYEWEED
DYEWOOD *n* any wood from which dyes and pigments can be obtained
DYEWOODS > DYEWOOD
DYEWORKS *n* place where dye is made

DYING > DIE
DYINGLY > DIE
DYINGNESS > DIE
DYINGS > DIE
DYKE *n* wall built to prevent flooding ▷ *vb* protect with a dyke
DYKED > DYKE
DYKES > DYKE
DYKING > DYKE
DYKON *n* celebrity admired by lesbians
DYKONS > DYKON
DYNAMETER *n* instrument for determining the magnifying power of telescopes
DYNAMIC *adj* full of energy, ambition, and new ideas ▷ *n* energetic or driving force
DYNAMICAL *same as*
> DYNAMIC
DYNAMICS *n* branch of mechanics concerned with motions of bodies
DYNAMISE *same as*
> DYNAMIZE
DYNAMISED
> DYNAMISE
DYNAMISES
> DYNAMISE
DYNAMISM *n* great energy and enthusiasm
DYNAMISMS
> DYNAMISM
DYNAMIST > DYNAMISM
DYNAMISTS
> DYNAMISM
DYNAMITE *n* explosive made of nitroglycerine ▷ *vb* blow (something) up with dynamite
DYNAMITED
> DYNAMITE
DYNAMITER
> DYNAMITE
DYNAMITES
> DYNAMITE
DYNAMITIC
> DYNAMITE
DYNAMIZE *vb* cause to be dynamic
DYNAMIZED
> DYNAMIZE
DYNAMIZES
> DYNAMIZE
DYNAMO *n* device for converting mechanical energy into electrical energy
DYNAMOS > DYNAMO
DYNAMOTOR *n* electrical machine having a single magnetic field and two independent armature windings of which one acts as a motor and the other a generator: used to convert direct current from a battery into alternating current
DYNAST *n* hereditary ruler
DYNASTIC > DYNASTY
DYNASTIES > DYNASTY
DYNASTS > DYNAST
DYNASTY *n* sequence of hereditary rulers

DYNATRON *n* as in
dynatron oscillator type of
oscillator
DYNATRONS
> DYNATRON
DYNE *n* unit of force
DYNEIN *n* class of proteins
DYNEINS > DYNEIN
DYNEL *n* trade name for a
synthetic fibre
DYNELS > DYNEL
DYNES > DYNE
DYNODE *n* electrical
component
DYNODES > DYNODE
DYNORPHIN *n* drug used
to treat cocaine addiction
DYSBINDIN *n* gene
associated with
schizophrenia
DYSCHROA *n*
discolouration of skin
DYSCHROAS
> DYSCHROA
DYSCHROIA *same as*
> DYSCHROA
DYSCRASIA *n* any
abnormal physiological
condition, esp of the blood
DYSCRASIC
> DYSCRASIA
DYSCRATIC
> DYSCRASIA
DYSENTERY *n* infection
of the intestine causing
severe diarrhoea
DYSFLUENT *adj* not
fluent
DYSGENIC *adj* referring
to the degeneration of the
human race
DYSGENICS *n* study of
factors capable of
reducing the quality of the
human race
DYSLALIA *n* defective
speech
DYSLALIAS
> DYSLALIA
DYSLECTIC
> DYSLEXIA

DYSLEXIA *n* disorder
causing impaired ability to
read
DYSLEXIAS > DYSLEXIA
DYSLEXIC > DYSLEXIA
DYSLEXICS
> DYSLEXIA
DYSLOGIES > DYSLOGY
DYSLOGY *n*
uncomplimentary
remarks
DYSMELIA *n* condition of
missing or stunted limbs
DYSMELIAS
> DYSMELIA
DYSMELIC > DYSMELIA
DYSODIL *n* yellow or
green mineral
DYSODILE *same as*
> DYSODIL
DYSODILES
> DYSODILE
DYSODILS > DYSODIL
DYSODYLE *same as*
> DYSODIL
DYSODYLES
> DYSODYLE
DYSPATHY *n* dislike
DYSPEPSIA *n*
indigestion
DYSPEPSY *same as*
> DYSPEPSIA
DYSPEPTIC *adj* relating
to dyspepsia ▷ *n* person
with dyspepsia
DYSPHAGIA *n* difficulty
in swallowing, caused by
obstruction or spasm of
the oesophagus
DYSPHAGIC
> DYSPHAGIA
DYSPHAGY *same as*
> DYSPHAGIA
DYSPHASIA *n* disorder of
language caused by a
brain lesion
DYSPHASIC
> DYSPHASIA
DYSPHONIA *n* any
impairment in the ability
to speak normally, as from

spasm or strain of the
vocal cords
DYSPHONIC
> DYSPHONIA
DYSPHORIA *n* feeling of
being ill at ease
DYSPHORIC
> DYSPHORIA
DYSPLASIA *n* abnormal
development of an organ
or part of the body,
including congenital
absence
DYSPNEA *same as*
> DYSPNOEA
DYSPNEAL > DYSPNEA
DYSPNEAS > DYSPNEA
DYSPNEIC > DYSPNEA
DYSPNOEA *n* difficulty in
breathing or in catching
the breath
DYSPNOEAL
> DYSPNOEA
DYSPNOEAS
> DYSPNOEA
DYSPNOEIC
> DYSPNOEA
DYSPNOIC > DYSPNOEA
DYSPRAXIA *n*
impairment in the control
of the motor system
DYSPRAXIC *adj* having
dyspraxia
DYSTAXIA *n* lack of
muscular coordination
resulting in shaky limb
movements and unsteady
gait
DYSTAXIAS
> DYSTAXIA
DYSTAXIC *adj* relating to
or affected by dystaxia
DYSTECTIC *adj* difficult
to fuse together
DYSTHESIA *n*
unpleasant skin sensation
DYSTHETIC
> DYSTHESIA
DYSTHYMIA *n* tendency
to psychological
depression

DYSTHYMIC
> DYSTHYMIA
DYSTOCIA *n* abnormal,
slow, or difficult childbirth
DYSTOCIAL
> DYSTOCIA
DYSTOCIAS
> DYSTOCIA
DYSTONIA *n* neurological
disorder
DYSTONIAS
> DYSTONIA
DYSTONIC > DYSTONIA
DYSTOPIA *n* imaginary
place where everything is
as bad as it can be
DYSTOPIAN
> DYSTOPIA
DYSTOPIAS
> DYSTOPIA
DYSTROPHY *n* any of
various bodily disorders,
characterized by wasting
of tissues
DYSURIA *n* difficult or
painful urination
DYSURIAS > DYSURIA
DYSURIC > DYSURIA
DYSURIES > DYSURY
DYSURY *same as*
> DYSURIA
DYTISCID *n* type of
carnivorous aquatic beetle
with large flattened back
legs used for swimming
DYTISCIDS
> DYTISCID
DYVOUR *n* debtor
DYVOURIES > DYVOURY
DYVOURS > DYVOUR
DYVOURY *n* bankruptcy
DZEREN *n* Chinese yellow
antelope
DZERENS > DZEREN
DZHO *same as* > ZHO
DZHOS > DZHO
DZIGGETAI *variant of*
> CHIGETAI
DZO *variant spelling of* > ZO
DZOS > DZO

Ee

EA n river

EACH pron every (one) taken separately ▷ determiner every (one) of two or more considered individually ▷ adv for, to, or from each one

EACHWHERE adv everywhere

EADISH n aftermath

EADISHES > EADISH

EAGER adj showing or feeling great desire, keen ▷ n eagre

EAGERER > EAGER

EAGEREST > EAGER

EAGERLY > EAGER

EAGERNESS > EAGER

EAGERS > EAGER

EAGLE n bird of prey ▷ vb in golf, score two strokes under par for a hole

EAGLED > EAGLE

EAGLEHAWK n large Australian eagle

EAGLES > EAGLE

EAGLET n young eagle

EAGLETS > EAGLET

EAGLEWOOD n Asian thymelaeaceous tree with fragrant wood that yields a resin used as a perfume

EAGLING > EAGLE

EAGRE n tidal bore, esp of the Humber or Severn estuaries

EAGRES > EAGRE

EALDORMAN n official of Anglo-Saxon England, appointed by the king, who was responsible for law, order, and justice in his shire and for leading his local fyrd in battle

EALDORMEN > EALDORMAN

EALE n beast in Roman legend ▷ vb to ail

EALED > EALE

EALES > EALE

EALING > EALE

EAN vb give birth

EANED > EAN

EANING > EAN

EANLING n newborn lamb

EANLINGS > EANLING

EANS > EAN

EAR n organ of hearing, esp the external part of it ▷ vb (of cereal plants) to develop such parts

EARACHE n pain in the ear

EARACHES > EARACHE

EARBALL n device used in acupressure

EARBALLS > EARBALL

EARBASH vb talk incessantly

EARBASHED > EARBASH

EARBASHER > EARBASH

EARBASHES > EARBASH

EARBOB n earring

EARBOBS > EARBOB

EARBUD n small earphone

EARBUDS > EARBUD

EARCON n sound representing an object or event

EARCONS > EARCON

EARD vb bury

EARDED > EARD

EARDING > EARD

EARDROP n pendant earring

EARDROPS pl n liquid medication for inserting into the external ear

EARDRUM n part of the ear which enables one to hear sounds

EARDRUMS > EARDRUM

EARDS > EARD

EARED adj having an ear or ears

EARFLAP n either of two pieces of fabric or fur attached to a cap

EARFLAPS > EARFLAP

EARFUL n scolding or telling-off

EARFULS > EARFUL

EARHOLE n the external opening of the ear

EARHOLES > EARHOLE

EARING n line fastened to a corner of a sail for reefing

EARINGS > EARING

EARL n British nobleman ranking next below a marquess

EARLAP same as > EARFLAP

EARLAPS > EARLAP

EARLDOM n rank, title, or dignity of an earl or countess

EARLDOMS > EARLDOM

EARLESS > EAR

EARLIER > EARLY

EARLIES > EARLY

EARLIEST > EARLY

EARLIKE > EAR

EARLINESS > EARLY

EARLOBE n fleshy lower part of the outer ear

EARLOBES > EARLOBE

EARLOCK n curl of hair close to ear

EARLOCKS > EARLOCK

EARLS > EARL

EARLSHIP n title or position of earl

EARLSHIPS > EARLSHIP

EARLY adv before the expected or usual time ▷ adj occurring or arriving before the correct or expected time ▷ n something which is early

EARLYWOOD n light wood made by tree in spring

EARMARK vb set (something) aside for a specific purpose ▷ n distinguishing mark

EARMARKED > EARMARK

EARMARKS > EARMARK

EARMUFF n item of clothing for keeping the ears warm

EARMUFFS > EARMUFF

EARN vb obtain by work or merit

EARNED > EARN

EARNER > EARN

EARNERS > EARN

EARNEST adj serious and sincere ▷ n part payment given in advance

EARNESTLY > EARNEST

EARNESTS > EARNEST

EARNING > EARN

EARNINGS pl n money earned

EARNS > EARN

EARNT > EARN

EARPHONE n receiver for a radio etc, held to or put in the ear

EARPHONES > EARPHONE

EARPICK n instrument for removing ear wax

EARPICKS > EARPICK

EARPIECE n earphone in a telephone receiver

EARPIECES > EARPIECE

EARPLUG n piece of soft material placed in the ear to keep out water or noise

EARPLUGS > EARPLUG

EARRING n ornament for the lobe of the ear

EARRINGED adj wearing earrings

EARRINGS > EARRING

EARS > EAR

EARSHOT n hearing range

EARSHOTS > EARSHOT

EARST adv first; previously

EARSTONE n calcium carbonate crystal in the ear

EARSTONES > EARSTONE

EARTH n planet that we live on ▷ vb connect (a circuit) to earth

EARTHBORN adj of earthly origin

EARTHED > EARTH

EARTHEN adj made of baked clay or earth

EARTHFALL n landslide

EARTHFAST adj method of building

EARTHFLAX n type of asbestos

EARTHIER > EARTHY

EARTHIEST > EARTHY

EARTHILY > EARTHY

EARTHING > EARTH

EARTHLIER > EARTHLY

EARTHLIES > EARTHLY

EARTHLIKE > EARTH

EARTHLING n (esp in poetry or science fiction) an inhabitant of the earth

EARTHLY adj conceivable or possible ▷ n chance

EARTHMAN n (esp in science fiction) an inhabitant or native of the earth

EARTHMEN > EARTHMAN

EARTHNUT n perennial umbelliferous plant of Europe and Asia, with edible dark brown tubers

EARTHNUTS > EARTHNUT

EARTHPEA n peanut; groundnut

EARTHPEAS > EARTHPEA

EARTHRISE n rising of the earth above the lunar horizon, as seen from a spacecraft emerging from the lunar farside

EARTHS > EARTH

EARTHSET n setting of the earth below the lunar horizon

EARTHSETS > EARTHSET

EARTHSTAR n type of woodland fungus

EARTHWARD adv towards the earth

EARTHWAX n ozocerite

EARTHWOLF n aardvark

EARTHWORK n fortification made of earth

EARTHWORM n worm which burrows in the soil

EARTHY adj coarse or crude

EARWAX nontechnical name for > CERUMEN

EARWAXES > EARWAX

EARWIG n small insect with a pincer-like tail ▷ vb eavesdrop

EARWIGGED > EARWIG

EARWIGGY adj like an earwig

EARWIGS > EARWIG

EARWORM n irritatingly catchy tune

EARWORMS > EARWORM

EAS > EA

EASE n freedom from difficulty, discomfort, or worry ▷ vb give bodily or mental ease to

EASED > EASE

EASEFUL adj characterized by or bringing ease

EASEFULLY > EASEFUL

EASEL n frame to support an artist's canvas or a blackboard

EASELED adj mounted on an easel

EASELESS > EASE

EASELS > EASEL

EASEMENT n right of a landowner to make limited use of a neighbour's land

EASEMENTS > EASEMENT

EASER > EASE

EASERS > EASE

EASES > EASE

EASIED > EASY

EASIER > EASY

EASIES > EASY

EASIEST > EASY

EASILY adv without difficulty

EASINESS n quality or condition of being easy to accomplish, do, obtain, etc

EASING n as in quantitative easing increasing the supply of money to stimulate the economy

EASINGS > EASING

EASLE n hot ash

EASLES > EASLE

EASSEL adv easterly

EASSIL adv easterly

EAST n (direction towards) the part of the horizon where the sun rises ▷ adj in the east ▷ adv in, to, or towards the east ▷ vb move or turn east

EASTABOUT adv in, to, or towards the east

EASTBOUND adj going towards the east

EASTED > EAST

EASTER n most important festival of the Christian Church

EASTERLY adj of or in the east ▷ adv towards the east ▷ n wind from the east

EASTERN adj situated in or towards the east

EASTERNER n person from the east of a country or area

EASTERS > EASTER

EASTING n net distance eastwards made by a vessel moving towards the east

EASTINGS > EASTING

EASTLAND n land in east

EASTLANDS > EASTLAND

EASTLIN adj easterly

EASTLING adj easterly

EASTLINGS adv eastward

EASTLINS adv eastward

EASTMOST adj furthest east

EASTS > EAST

EASTWARD same as > EASTWARDS

EASTWARDS adv towards the east

EASY adj not needing much work or effort ▷ vb stop rowing

EASYGOING adj relaxed in manner

EASYING > EASY

EAT vb take (food) into the mouth and swallow it

EATABLE adj fit or suitable for eating

EATABLES pl n food

EATAGE n grazing rights

EATAGES > EATAGE

EATCHE n adze

EATCHES > EATCHE

EATEN > EAT

EATER > EAT

EATERIE same as > EATERY

EATERIES > EATERY

EATERS > EAT

EATERY n restaurant or eating house

EATH adj easy

EATHE same as > EATH

EATHLY > EATH

EATING > EAT

EATINGS > EAT

EATS > EAT

EAU same as > EA

EAUS > EAU

EAUX > EAU

EAVE vb give cover under the eaves of a building

EAVED adj having eaves

EAVES > EAVE

EAVESDRIP n water dropping from eaves

EAVESDROP vb listen secretly to a private conversation

EAVING > EAVE

EBAUCHE n rough sketch

EBAUCHES > EBAUCHE

EBAYER n any person who uses eBay

EBAYERS > EBAYER

EBAYING n buying or selling using eBay

EBAYINGS > EBAYING

EBB vb (of tide water) flow back ▷ n flowing back of the tide

EBBED > EBB

EBBET n type of newt

EBBETS > EBBET

EBBING > EBB

EBBLESS > EBB

EBBS > EBB

EBENEZER n chapel

EBENEZERS > EBENEZER

EBENISTE n cabinetmaker

EBENISTES > EBENISTE

EBIONISE same as > EBIONIZE

EBIONISED > EBIONISE

EBIONISES > EBIONISE

EBIONISING > EBIONISE

EBIONISM n doctrine that the poor shall be saved

EBIONISMS > EBIONISM

EBIONITIC > EBIONISM

EBIONIZE vb preach ebionism

EBIONIZED > EBIONIZE

EBIONIZES > EBIONIZE

EBON poetic word for > EBONY

EBONICS n dialect used by African-Americans

EBONIES > EBONY

EBONISE same as > EBONIZE

EBONISED > EBONISE

EBONISES > EBONISE

EBONISING > EBONISE

EBONIST n carver of ebony

EBONISTS > EBONIST

EBONITE another name for > VULCANITE

EBONITES > EBONITE

EBONIZE vb stain or otherwise finish in imitation of ebony

EBONIZED > EBONIZE

EBONIZES > EBONIZE

EBONIZING > EBONIZE

EBONS > EBON

EBONY n hard black wood ▷ adj deep black

EBOOK n book in electronic form

EBOOKS > EBOOK

EBRIATE adj drunk

EBRIATED same as > EBRIATE

EBRIETIES > EBRIETY

EBRIETY n drunkenness

EBRILLADE n jerk on rein, when horse refuses to turn

EBRIOSE adj drunk

EBRIOSITY > EBRIOSE

EBULLIENT adj full of enthusiasm or excitement

EBURNEAN adj made of ivory

EBURNEOUS adj like ivory

ECAD n organism whose form has been affected by its environment

ECADS > ECAD

ECARINATE adj having no carina or keel

ECARTE n card game for two, played with 32 cards and king high

ECARTES > ECARTE

ECAUDATE adj tailless

ECBOLE n digression

ECBOLES > ECBOLE

ECBOLIC adj inducing labour ▷ n drug or agent that induces labour

ECBOLICS > ECBOLIC

ECCE interj behold

ECCENTRIC adj odd or unconventional ▷ n eccentric person

ECCLESIA n (in formal Church usage) a congregation

ECCLESIAE > ECCLESIA

ECCLESIAL adj ecclesiastical

ECCO interj look there

ECCRINE adj of or denoting glands that secrete externally

ECCRISES > ECCRISIS

ECCRISIS n excrement

ECCRITIC n purgative

ECCRITICS > ECCRITIC

ECDEMIC adj not indigenous or endemic

ECDYSES > ECDYSIS

ECDYSIAL > ECDYSIS

ECDYSIAST facetious word for > STRIPPER

ECDYSIS n shedding of the cuticle in arthropods or the outer epidermal layer in reptiles

ECDYSISES > ECDYSIS

ECDYSON same as > ECDYSONE

ECDYSONE n hormone secreted by the prothoracic gland of insects

ECDYSONES > ECDYSONE

ECDYSONS > ECDYSON

ECESIC > ECESIS

ECESIS n establishment of a plant in a new environment

ECESISES > ECESIS

ECH same as > ECHE

ECHAPPE n leap in ballet

ECHAPPES > ECHAPPE

ECHARD n water that is present in the soil but cannot be utilized by plants

ECHARDS > ECHARD

ECHE vb eke out

ECHED > ECHE

ECHELLE n ladder; scale

ECHELLES > ECHELLE**

ECHELON *n* level of power or responsibility ▷ *vb* assemble soldiers in rows

ECHELONED > ECHELON

ECHELONS > ECHELON

ECHES > ECHE

ECHEVERIA *n* tropical American plant cultivated for its colourful foliage

ECHIDNA *n* spiny egg-laying mammal

ECHIDNAE > ECHIDNA

ECHIDNAS > ECHIDNA

ECHIDNINE *n* snake poison

ECHINACEA *n* N American plant with purple and black flowers

ECHINATE *adj* covered with spines, bristles, or bristle-like outgrowths

ECHINATED *same as* > ECHINATE

ECHING > ECHE

ECHINI > ECHINUS

ECHINOID *n* type of echinoderm of the class which includes the sea urchins and sand dollars

ECHINOIDS > ECHINOID

ECHINUS *n* ovolo moulding between the shaft and the abacus of a Doric column

ECHINUSES > ECHINUS

ECHIUM *n* type of Eurasian and African plant

ECHIUMS > ECHIUM

ECHIURAN *n* spoonworm

ECHIURANS > ECHIURAN

ECHIUROID *n* marine worm

ECHO *n* repetition of sounds by reflection of sound waves off a surface ▷ *vb* repeat or be repeated as an echo

ECHOED > ECHO

ECHOER > ECHO

ECHOERS > ECHO

ECHOES > ECHO

ECHOEY *adj* producing echoes

ECHOGRAM *n* record made by echography

ECHOGRAMS > ECHOGRAM

ECHOGRAPH *n* device that uses sonic waves to measure the depth of water

ECHOIC *adj* characteristic of or resembling an echo

ECHOIER > ECHOEY

ECHOIEST > ECHOEY

ECHOING > ECHO

ECHOISE *same as* > ECHOIZE

ECHOISED > ECHOISE

ECHOISES > ECHOISE

ECHOISING > ECHOISE

ECHOISM *n* onomatopoeia as a source of word formation

ECHOISMS > ECHOISM

ECHOIST > ECHOISM

ECHOISTS > ECHOISM

ECHOIZE *vb* repeat like an echo

ECHOIZED > ECHOIZE

ECHOIZES > ECHOIZE

ECHOIZING > ECHOIZE

ECHOLALIA *n* tendency to repeat mechanically words just spoken by another person

ECHOLALIC > ECHOLALIA

ECHOLESS > ECHO

ECHOS > ECHO

ECHOVIRUS *n* any of a group of viruses that can cause symptoms of mild meningitis, the common cold, or infections of the intestinal and respiratory tracts

ECHT *adj* real

ECLAIR *n* finger-shaped pastry filled with cream and covered with chocolate

ECLAIRS > ECLAIR

ECLAMPSIA *n* serious condition that can develop towards the end of a pregnancy, causing high blood pressure, swelling, and convulsions

ECLAMPSY *same as* > ECLAMPSIA

ECLAMPTIC > ECLAMPSIA

ECLAT *n* brilliant success

ECLATS > ECLAT

ECLECTIC *adj* selecting from various styles, ideas, or sources ▷ *n* person who takes an eclectic approach

ECLECTICS > ECLECTIC

ECLIPSE *n* temporary obscuring of one star or planet by another ▷ *vb* surpass or outclass

ECLIPSED > ECLIPSE

ECLIPSER > ECLIPSE

ECLIPSERS > ECLIPSE

ECLIPSES > ECLIPSIS

ECLIPSING > ECLIPSE

ECLIPSIS *same as* > ELLIPSIS

ECLIPTIC *n* apparent path of the sun ▷ *adj* of or relating to an eclipse

ECLIPTICS > ECLIPTIC

ECLOGITE *n* rare coarse-grained basic rock

ECLOGITES > ECLOGITE

ECLOGUE *n* pastoral or idyllic poem, usually in the form of a conversation or soliloquy

ECLOGUES > ECLOGUE

ECLOSE *vb* emerge

ECLOSED > ECLOSE

ECLOSES > ECLOSE

ECLOSING > ECLOSE

ECLOSION *n* emergence of an insect larva from the egg or an adult from the pupal case

ECLOSIONS > ECLOSION

ECO *n* ecology activist

ECOCIDAL > ECOCIDE

ECOCIDE *n* total destruction of an area of the natural environment

ECOCIDES > ECOCIDE

ECOD *same as* > EGAD

ECOFREAK *n* environmentalist

ECOFREAKS > ECOFREAK

ECOGIFT *n* donation of land for environmental purposes

ECOGIFTS > ECOGIFT

ECOLODGE *n* eco-friendly tourist accommodation

ECOLODGES > ECOLODGE

ECOLOGIC > ECOLOGY

ECOLOGIES > ECOLOGY

ECOLOGIST > ECOLOGY

ECOLOGY *n* study of the links between living things and their environment

ECOMAP *n* diagram showing the links between an individual and their community

ECOMAPS > ECOMAP

ECOMMERCE *n* business transactions conducted on the internet

ECOMUSEUM *n* museum exploring the history, culture, and environment of a region

ECONOBOX *n* fuel efficient utility vehicle

ECONOMIC *adj* of economics

ECONOMICS *n* social science concerned with the production and consumption of goods and services

ECONOMIES > ECONOMY

ECONOMISE *same as* > ECONOMIZE

ECONOMISM *n* political theory that regards economics as the main factor in society, ignoring or reducing to simplistic economic terms other factors such as culture, nationality, etc

ECONOMIST *n* specialist in economics

ECONOMIZE *vb* reduce expense or waste

ECONOMY *n* system of interrelationship of money, industry, and employment in a country ▷ *adj* denoting a class of air travel that is cheaper than first-class

ECONUT *n* derogatory term for a keen environmentalist

ECONUTS > ECONUT

ECOPHOBIA *n* fear of home

ECORCHE *n* anatomical figure without the skin

ECORCHES > ECORCHE

ECOREGION *n* area defined by its environmental conditions,

esp climate, landforms, and soil characteristics

ECOS > ECO

ECOSPHERE *n* planetary ecosystem, consisting of all living organisms and their environment

ECOSSAISE *n* lively dance in two-four time

ECOSTATE *adj* with no ribs or nerves

ECOSYSTEM *n* system involving interactions between a community and its environment

ECOTAGE *n* sabotage for ecological motives

ECOTAGES > ECOTAGE

ECOTARIAN *n* person who eats only eco-friendly food

ECOTONAL > ECOTONE

ECOTONE *n* zone between two major ecological communities

ECOTONES > ECOTONE

ECOTOPIA *n* ecologically ideal area or society

ECOTOPIAS > ECOTOPIA

ECOTOUR *n* holiday taking care not to damage environment ▷ *vb* take an ecotour

ECOTOURED > ECOTOUR

ECOTOURS > ECOTOUR

ECOTOXIC *adj* harmful to animals, plants or the environment

ECOTYPE *n* group of organisms in a species that have adapted to a particular environment

ECOTYPES > ECOTYPE

ECOTYPIC > ECOTYPE

ECOZONE *n* large area with an ecosystem

ECOZONES > ECOZONE

ECPHRASES > ECPHRASIS

ECPHRASIS *same as* > EKPHRASIS

ECRASEUR *n* surgical device consisting of a heavy wire loop

ECRASEURS > ECRASEUR

ECRITOIRE *n* writing desk with compartments and drawers

ECRU *n* greyish-yellow colour

ECRUS > ECRU

ECSTASES > ECSTASIS

ECSTASIED > ECSTASY

ECSTASIES > ECSTASY

ECSTASIS *same as* > ECSTASY

ECSTASISE *same as* > ECSTASIZE

ECSTASIZE *vb* make or become ecstatic

ECSTASY *n* state of intense delight

ECSTATIC *adj* in a trancelike state of great rapture or delight ▷ *n* person who has periods of intense trancelike joy

ECSTATICS pl n fits of delight or rapture

ECTASES > ECTASIS

ECTASIA n distension or dilation of a duct, vessel, or hollow viscus

ECTASIAS > ECTASIA

ECTASIS same as > ECTASIA

ECTATIC > ECTASIS

ECTHYMA n local inflammation of the skin

ECTHYMAS > ECTHYMA

ECTHYMATA > ECTHYMA

ECTOBLAST same as > EPIBLAST

ECTOCRINE n substance that is released by an organism into the external environment and influences the development, behaviour, etc, of members of the same or different species

ECTODERM n outer germ layer of an animal embryo

ECTODERMS > ECTODERM

ECTOGENE n type of gene

ECTOGENES > ECTOGENE

ECTOGENIC adj capable of developing outside the host

ECTOGENY n (of bacteria, etc) development outside the host

ECTOMERE n any of the blastomeres that later develop into ectoderm

ECTOMERES > ECTOMERE

ECTOMERIC > ECTOMERE

ECTOMORPH n person with a thin body build: said to be correlated with cerebrotonia

ECTOPHYTE n parasitic plant that lives on the surface of its host

ECTOPIA n congenital displacement of an organ or part

ECTOPIAS > ECTOPIA

ECTOPIC > ECTOPIA

ECTOPIES > ECTOPY

ECTOPLASM n substance that supposedly is emitted from the body of a medium during a trance

ECTOPROCT another word for > BRYOZOAN

ECTOPY same as > ECTOPIA

ECTOSARC n ectoplasm of an amoeba or any other protozoan

ECTOSARCS > ECTOSARC

ECTOTHERM n animal whose body temperature is determined by ambient temperature

ECTOZOA > ECTOZOON

ECTOZOAN same as > ECTOZOON

ECTOZOANS > ECTOZOON

ECTOZOIC > ECTOZOON

ECTOZOON n parasitic organism that lives on the outside of its host

ECTROPIC > ECTROPION

ECTROPION n condition in which the eyelid turns over exposing some of the inner lid

ECTROPIUM same as > ECTROPION

ECTYPAL > ECTYPE

ECTYPE n copy

ECTYPES > ECTYPE

ECU n any of various former French gold or silver coins

ECUELLE n covered soup bowl with handles

ECUELLES > ECUELLE

ECUMENE n inhabited area of the world

ECUMENES > ECUMENE

ECUMENIC adj tending to promote unity among Churches

ECUMENICS > ECUMENIC

ECUMENISM n aim of unity among Christian churches throughout the world

ECUMENIST n believer in ecumenicism

ECURIE n team of motor-racing cars

ECURIES > ECURIE

ECUS > ECU

ECZEMA n skin disease causing intense itching

ECZEMAS > ECZEMA

ED n editor

EDACIOUS adj devoted to eating

EDACITIES > EDACIOUS

EDACITY > EDACIOUS

EDAMAME n Japanese dish of salted green soya beans

EDAMAMES > EDAMAME

EDAPHIC adj of or relating to the physical and chemical conditions of the soil

EDDIED > EDDY

EDDIES > EDDY

EDDISH n pasture grass

EDDISHES > EDDISH

EDDO same as > TARO

EDDOES > EDDO

EDDY n circular movement of air, water, etc ▷ vb move with a circular motion

EDDYING > EDDY

EDELWEISS n alpine plant with white flowers

EDEMA same as > OEDEMA

EDEMAS > EDEMA

EDEMATA > EDEMA

EDEMATOSE > EDEMA

EDEMATOUS > EDEMA

EDENIC adj delightful, like the Garden of Eden

EDENTAL adj having few or no teeth

EDENTATE n mammal with few or no teeth, such as an armadillo or a sloth ▷ adj denoting such a mammal

EDENTATES > EDENTATE

EDGE n border or line where something ends or begins ▷ vb provide an edge or border for

EDGEBONE n aitchbone

EDGEBONES > EDGEBONE

EDGED > EDGE

EDGELESS > EDGE

EDGER > EDGE

EDGERS > EDGE

EDGES > EDGE

EDGEWAYS adv with the edge forwards or uppermost

EDGEWISE same as > EDGEWAYS

EDGIER > EDGY

EDGIEST > EDGY

EDGILY > EDGY

EDGINESS > EDGY

EDGING n anything placed along an edge to finish it ▷ adj relating to or used for making an edge

EDGINGS > EDGING

EDGY adj nervous or irritable

EDH n character of the runic alphabet

EDHS > EDH

EDIBILITY > EDIBLE

EDIBLE adj fit to be eaten

EDIBLES pl n articles fit to eat

EDICT n order issued by an authority

EDICTAL > EDICT

EDICTALLY > EDICT

EDICTS > EDICT

EDIFICE n large building

EDIFICES > EDIFICE

EDIFICIAL > EDIFICE

EDIFIED > EDIFY

EDIFIER > EDIFY

EDIFIERS > EDIFY

EDIFIES > EDIFY

EDIFY vb improve morally by instruction

EDIFYING > EDIFY

EDILE variant spelling of > AEDILE

EDILES > EDILE

EDIT vb prepare (a book, film, etc) for publication or broadcast ▷ n act of editing

EDITABLE > EDIT

EDITED > EDIT

EDITING > EDIT

EDITINGS > EDIT

EDITION n number of copies of a new publication printed at one time ▷ vb produce multiple copies of (an original work of art)

EDITIONED > EDITION

EDITIONS > EDITION

EDITOR n person who edits

EDITORIAL n newspaper article stating the opinion of the editor ▷ adj of editing or editors

EDITORS > EDITOR

EDITRESS n female editor

EDITRICES > EDITRIX

EDITRIX n female editor

EDITRIXES > EDITRIX

EDITS > EDIT

EDS > ED

EDUCABLE adj capable of being trained or educated ▷ n person who is capable of being educated

EDUCABLES > EDUCABLE

EDUCATE vb teach

EDUCATED adj having had an education

EDUCATES > EDUCATE

EDUCATING > EDUCATE

EDUCATION n process of acquiring knowledge and understanding

EDUCATIVE adj educating

EDUCATOR n person who educates

EDUCATORS > EDUCATOR

EDUCATORY adj educative or educational

EDUCE vb evolve or develop

EDUCED > EDUCE

EDUCEMENT > EDUCE

EDUCES > EDUCE

EDUCIBLE > EDUCE

EDUCING > EDUCE

EDUCT n substance separated from a mixture without chemical change

EDUCTION n something educed

EDUCTIONS > EDUCTION

EDUCTIVE > EDUCE

EDUCTOR > EDUCE

EDUCTORS > EDUCE

EDUCTS > EDUCT

EE Scots word for > EYE

EECH same as > ECHE

EECHED > EECH

EECHES > EECH

EECHING > EECH

EEEW interj exclamation of disgust

EEJIT Scots and Irish word for > IDIOT

EEJITS > EEJIT

EEK interj indicating shock or fright

EEL n snakelike fish

EELFARE n young eel

EELFARES > EELFARE

EELGRASS n type of submerged marine plant with grasslike leaves

EELIER > EEL

EELIEST > EEL

EELING n practice of catching eels

EELINGS > EELING

EELLIKE adj resembling an eel

EELPOUT n marine eel-like blennioid fish

EELPOUTS > EELPOUT
EELS > EEL
EELWORM n any of various nematode worms
EELWORMS > EELWORM
EELWRACK n grasslike plant growing in seawater
EELWRACKS > EELWRACK
EELY > EEL
EEN > EE
EENSIER > EENSY
EENSIEST > EENSY
EENSY adj very small
EERIE adj uncannily frightening or disturbing
EERIER > EERIE
EERIEST > EERIE
EERILY > EERIE
EERINESS > EERIE
EERY same as > EERIE
EEVEN n old form of evening
EEVENS > EEVEN
EEVN same as > EEVEN
EEVNING n old form of evening
EEVNINGS > EEVNING
EEVNS > EEVN
EEW interj exclamation of disgust
EF n letter F
EFF vb use bad language
EFFABLE adj capable of being expressed in words
EFFACE vb remove by rubbing
EFFACED > EFFACE
EFFACER > EFFACE
EFFACERS > EFFACE
EFFACES > EFFACE
EFFACING > EFFACE
EFFECT n change or result caused by someone or something ▷ vb cause to happen, accomplish
EFFECTED > EFFECT
EFFECTER > EFFECT
EFFECTERS > EFFECT
EFFECTING > EFFECT
EFFECTIVE adj producing a desired result ▷ n soldier who is equipped and prepared for action
EFFECTOR n nerve ending that terminates in a muscle or gland
EFFECTORS > EFFECTOR
EFFECTS pl n personal belongings
EFFECTUAL adj producing the intended result
EFFED > EFF
EFFEIR vb suit
EFFEIRED > EFFEIR
EFFEIRING > EFFEIR
EFFEIRS > EFFEIR
EFFENDI n (in the Ottoman Empire) a title of respect
EFFENDIS > EFFENDI
EFFERE same as > EFFEIR
EFFERED > EFFERE
EFFERENCE > EFFERENT

EFFERENT adj carrying or conducting outwards ▷ n type of nerve
EFFERENTS > EFFERENT
EFFERES > EFFERE
EFFERING > EFFERE
EFFETE adj powerless, feeble
EFFETELY > EFFETE
EFFICACY n quality of being successful in producing an intended result
EFFICIENT adj functioning effectively with little waste of effort
EFFIERCE vb archaic word meaning make fierce
EFFIERCED > EFFIERCE
EFFIERCES > EFFIERCE
EFFIGIAL > EFFIGY
EFFIGIES > EFFIGY
EFFIGY n image or likeness of a person
EFFING > EFF
EFFINGS > EFF
EFFLUENCE n act or process of flowing out
EFFLUENT n liquid discharged as waste ▷ adj flowing out or forth
EFFLUENTS > EFFLUENT
EFFLUVIA > EFFLUVIUM
EFFLUVIAL > EFFLUVIUM
EFFLUVIUM n unpleasant smell, as of decaying matter or gaseous waste
EFFLUX same as > EFFLUENCE
EFFLUXES > EFFLUX
EFFLUXION same as > EFFLUX
EFFORCE vb old word for force
EFFORCED > EFFORCE
EFFORCES > EFFORCE
EFFORCING > EFFORCE
EFFORT n physical or mental exertion
EFFORTFUL > EFFORT
EFFORTS > EFFORT
EFFRAIDE archaic form of > AFRAID
EFFRAY archaic form of > AFFRAY
EFFRAYS > EFFRAY
EFFS > EFF
EFFULGE vb radiate
EFFULGED > EFFULGE
EFFULGENT adj radiant
EFFULGES > EFFULGE
EFFULGING > EFFULGE
EFFUSE vb pour or flow out ▷ adj (esp of an inflorescence) spreading out loosely
EFFUSED > EFFUSE
EFFUSES > EFFUSE
EFFUSING > EFFUSE
EFFUSION n unrestrained outburst

EFFUSIONS > EFFUSION
EFFUSIVE adj openly emotional, demonstrative
EFS > EF
EFT n dialect or archaic name for a newt ▷ adv again
EFTEST adj nearest at hand
EFTS > EFT
EFTSOON > EFTSOONS
EFTSOONS adv soon afterwards
EGAD n mild oath or expression of surprise
EGADS > EGAD
EGAL adj equal
EGALITE n equality
EGALITES > EGALITE
EGALITIES > EGALITY
EGALITY n equality
EGALLY > EGAL
EGAREMENT n confusion
EGENCE n need
EGENCES > EGENCE
EGENCIES > EGENCY
EGENCY same as > EGENCE
EGER same as > EAGRE
EGERS > EGER
EGEST vb excrete (waste material)
EGESTA pl n anything egested, as waste material from the body
EGESTED > EGEST
EGESTING > EGEST
EGESTION > EGEST
EGESTIONS > EGEST
EGESTIVE > EGEST
EGESTS > EGEST
EGG n object laid by birds and other creatures, containing a developing embryo ▷ vb urge or incite, esp to daring or foolish acts
EGGAR same as > EGGER
EGGARS > EGGAR
EGGBEATER n kitchen utensil for beating eggs, whipping cream, etc
EGGCORN n misspelling caused by the mishearing of a word
EGGCORNS > EGGCORN
EGGCUP n cup for holding a boiled egg
EGGCUPS > EGGCUP
EGGED > EGG
EGGER n moth with brown body and wings
EGGERIES > EGGERY
EGGERS > EGGER
EGGERY n place where eggs are laid
EGGFRUIT n fruit of eggplant
EGGFRUITS > EGGFRUIT
EGGHEAD n intellectual person
EGGHEADED > EGGHEAD
EGGHEADS > EGGHEAD
EGGIER > EGGY
EGGIEST > EGGY
EGGING > EGG

EGGLER n egg dealer: sometimes itinerant
EGGLERS > EGGLER
EGGLESS > EGG
EGGLIKE adj like an egg
EGGMASS n intelligentsia
EGGMASSES > EGGMASS
EGGNOG n drink made of raw eggs, milk, sugar, spice, and brandy or rum
EGGNOGS > EGGNOG
EGGPLANT n dark purple tropical fruit, cooked and eaten as a vegetable
EGGPLANTS > EGGPLANT
EGGS > EGG
EGGSHELL n hard covering round the egg of a bird or animal ▷ adj (of paint) having a very slight sheen
EGGSHELLS > EGGSHELL
EGGWASH n beaten egg for brushing on pastry
EGGWASHES > EGGWASH
EGGWHISK same as > EGGBEATER
EGGWHISKS > EGGWHISK
EGGY adj soaked in or tasting of egg
EGIS rare spelling of > AEGIS
EGISES > EGIS
EGLANTINE n Eurasian rose
EGLATERE archaic name for > EGLANTINE
EGLATERES > EGLATERE
EGLOMISE n gilding
EGLOMISES > EGLOMISE
EGMA mispronunciation of > ENIGMA
EGMAS > EGMA
EGO n conscious mind of an individual
EGOISM n excessive concern for one's own interests
EGOISMS > EGOISM
EGOIST n person who is preoccupied with their own interests
EGOISTIC > EGOIST
EGOISTS > EGOIST
EGOITIES > EGOITY
EGOITY n essence of the ego
EGOLESS adj without an ego
EGOMANIA n obsessive concern with one's own needs and desires
EGOMANIAC > EGOMANIA
EGOMANIAS > EGOMANIA
EGOS > EGO
EGOSURF vb search for one's own name on the internet
EGOSURFED > EGOSURF
EGOSURFS > EGOSURF
EGOTHEISM n making god of oneself

e

EGOTISE same as
> EGOTIZE
EGOTISED > EGOTISE
EGOTISES > EGOTISE
EGOTISING > EGOTISE
EGOTISM n concern only
for one's own interests and
feelings
EGOTISMS > EGOTISM
EGOTIST n conceited
boastful person
EGOTISTIC > EGOTIST
EGOTISTS > EGOTIST
EGOTIZE vb talk or write
in a self-important way
EGOTIZED > EGOTIZE
EGOTIZES > EGOTIZE
EGOTIZING > EGOTIZE
EGREGIOUS adj
outstandingly bad
EGRESS same as
> EMERSION
EGRESSED > EGRESS
EGRESSES > EGRESS
EGRESSING > EGRESS
EGRESSION same as
> EGRESS
EGRESSIVE n speech
sound produced with an
exhalation of breath
EGRET n lesser white
heron
EGRETS > EGRET
EGYPTIAN n type of
typeface
EGYPTIANS
> EGYPTIAN
EH interj exclamation of
surprise or inquiry ▷ vb say
'eh'
EHED > EH
EHING > EH
EHS > EH
EIDE > EIDOS
EIDENT adj diligent
EIDER n Arctic duck
EIDERDOWN n quilt (orig
stuffed with eider
feathers)
EIDERS > EIDER
EIDETIC adj (of images)
exceptionally vivid,
allowing detailed recall of
something ▷ n person
with eidetic ability
EIDETICS > EIDETIC
EIDOGRAPH n device for
copying drawings
EIDOLA > EIDOLON
EIDOLIC > EIDOLON
EIDOLON n unsubstantial
image
EIDOLONS > EIDOLON
EIDOS n intellectual
character of a culture or a
social group
EIGENMODE n
characteristic vibration
pattern
EIGENTONE n
characteristic acoustic
resonance frequency of a
system
EIGHT n one more than
seven
EIGHTBALL n black ball
in pool
EIGHTEEN n eight and ten

EIGHTEENS
> EIGHTEEN
EIGHTFOIL n eight
leaved flower shape in
heraldry
EIGHTFOLD adj having
eight times as many or as
much ▷ adv by eight times
as many or as much
EIGHTFOOT adj
measuring eight feet
EIGHTH n number eight
in a series ▷ adj coming
after the seventh and
before the ninth
EIGHTHLY adv in the
eighth place or position
EIGHTHS > EIGHTH
EIGHTIES > EIGHTY
EIGHTIETH n one of 80
approximately equal parts
of something
EIGHTS > EIGHT
EIGHTSMAN n member of
an eight-man team
EIGHTSMEN
> EIGHTSMAN
EIGHTSOME n group of
eight people
EIGHTVO another word for
> OCTAVO
EIGHTVOS > EIGHTVO
EIGHTY n eight times ten
EIGNE adj firstborn
EIK variant form of > EKE
EIKED > EIK
EIKING > EIK
EIKON variant spelling of
> ICON
EIKONES > EIKON
EIKONS > EIKON
EIKS > EIK
EILD n old age
EILDING n fuel
EILDINGS > EILDING
EILDS > EILD
EINA interj exclamation of
pain
EINE pl n eyes
EINKORN n variety of
wheat of Greece and SW
Asia
EINKORNS > EINKORN
EINSTEIN n scientific
genius
EINSTEINS
> EINSTEIN
EIRACK n young hen
EIRACKS > EIRACK
EIRENIC variant spelling
of > IRENIC
EIRENICAL same as
> IRENIC
EIRENICON n
proposition that attempts
to harmonize conflicting
viewpoints
EIRENICS n theology
concerned with unity
among churches
EISEGESES
> EISEGESIS
EISEGESIS n
interpretation of a text,
esp a biblical text, using
one's own ideas
EISEL n vinegar
EISELL same as > EISEL

EISELLS > EISELL
EISELS > EISEL
EISH interj South African
exclamation
EISWEIN n wine made
from grapes frozen on the
vine
EISWEINS > EISWEIN
EITHER pron one or the
other (of two) ▷ adv
likewise ▷ determiner one
or the other (of two)
EJACULATE vb utter
abruptly
EJECT vb force out, expel
EJECTA pl n matter
thrown out by a volcano
or during a meteorite
impact
EJECTABLE > EJECT
EJECTED > EJECT
EJECTING > EJECT
EJECTION > EJECT
EJECTIONS > EJECT
EJECTIVE adj relating to
or causing ejection ▷ n
ejective consonant
EJECTIVES
> EJECTIVE
EJECTMENT n (formerly)
an action brought by a
wrongfully dispossessed
owner seeking to recover
possession of their land
EJECTOR n person or
thing that ejects
EJECTORS > EJECTOR
EJECTS > EJECT
EJIDO n communal
farmland in Mexico
EJIDOS > EJIDO
EKE vb increase, enlarge,
or lengthen
EKED > EKE
EKES > EKE
EKING > EKE
EKISTIC > EKISTICS
EKISTICAL
> EKISTICS
EKISTICS n science or
study of human
settlements
EKKA n type of one-horse
carriage
EKKAS > EKKA
EKLOGITE same as
> ECLOGITE
EKLOGITES
> EKLOGITE
EKPHRASES
> EKPHRASIS
EKPHRASIS n
description of a visual
work of art
EKPWELE n former
monetary unit of
Equatorial Guinea
EKPWELES > EKPWELE
EKTEXINE n in pollen
and spores, the outer of
the two layers that make
up the exine
EKTEXINES
> EKTEXINE
EKUELE same as
> EKPWELE
EL n American elevated
railway

ELABORATE adj with a
lot of fine detail ▷ vb
expand upon
ELAEAGNUS n Eurasian
ornamental shrub or small
tree
ELAEOLITE n nephelite
ELAIN same as
> TRIOLEIN
ELAINS > ELAIN
ELAIOSOME n oil-rich
body on seeds or fruits
that attracts ants, which
act as dispersal agents
ELAN n style and vigour
ELANCE vb throw a lance
ELANCED > ELANCE
ELANCES > ELANCE
ELANCING > ELANCE
ELAND n large antelope of
southern Africa
ELANDS > ELAND
ELANET n bird of prey
ELANETS > ELANET
ELANS > ELAN
ELAPHINE adj of or like a
red deer
ELAPID n mostly tropical
type of venomous snake
ELAPIDS > ELAPID
ELAPINE adj of or like an
elapid
ELAPSE vb (of time) pass
by
ELAPSED > ELAPSE
ELAPSES > ELAPSE
ELAPSING > ELAPSE
ELASTANCE n reciprocal
of capacitance
ELASTANE n synthetic
fibre that is able to return
to its original shape after
being stretched
ELASTANES
> ELASTANE
ELASTASE n enzyme
that digests elastin
ELASTASES
> ELASTASE
ELASTIC adj resuming
normal shape after
distortion ▷ n tape or
fabric containing
interwoven strands of
flexible rubber
ELASTICS > ELASTIC
ELASTIN n fibrous
scleroprotein
ELASTINS > ELASTIN
ELASTOMER n any
material, such as natural
or synthetic rubber, that is
able to resume its original
shape when a deforming
force is removed
ELATE vb fill with high
spirits, exhilaration, pride
or optimism
ELATED adj extremely
happy and excited
ELATEDLY > ELATED
ELATER n elaterid beetle
ELATERID n type of
beetle of the family which
constitutes the click
beetles
ELATERIDS
> ELATERID

ELATERIN n white crystalline substance found in elaterium, used as a purgative
ELATERINS > ELATERIN
ELATERITE n dark brown naturally occurring bitumen resembling rubber
ELATERIUM n greenish sediment found from the juice of the squirting cucumber, used as a purgative
ELATERS > ELATER
ELATES > ELATE
ELATING > ELATE
ELATION n feeling of great happiness and excitement
ELATIONS > ELATION
ELATIVE adj denoting a grammatical case in Finnish and other languages ▷ n elative case
ELATIVES > ELATIVE
ELBOW n joint between the upper arm and the forearm ▷ vb shove or strike with the elbow
ELBOWED > ELBOW
ELBOWING n act of elbowing
ELBOWINGS > ELBOWING
ELBOWROOM n sufficient scope to move or function
ELBOWS > ELBOW
ELCHEE n ambassador
ELCHEES > ELCHEE
ELCHI same as > ELCHEE
ELCHIS > ELCHI
ELD n old age
ELDER adj older ▷ n older person
ELDERCARE n care of elderly
ELDERLIES > ELDERLY
ELDERLY adj (fairly) old
ELDERS > ELDER
ELDERSHIP > ELDER
ELDEST n oldest child
ELDESTS > ELDEST
ELDIN n fuel
ELDING same as > ELDIN
ELDINGS > ELDING
ELDINS > ELDIN
ELDORADO n place of great riches or fabulous opportunity
ELDORADOS > ELDORADO
ELDRESS n woman elder
ELDRESSES > ELDRESS
ELDRICH same as > ELDRITCH
ELDRITCH adj weird, uncanny
ELDS > ELD
ELECT vb choose by voting ▷ adj appointed but not yet in office
ELECTABLE > ELECT
ELECTED > ELECT
ELECTEE n someone who is elected
ELECTEES > ELECTEE

ELECTING > ELECT
ELECTION n choosing of representatives by voting
ELECTIONS > ELECTION
ELECTIVE adj chosen by election ▷ n optional course or hospital placement undertaken by a medical student
ELECTIVES > ELECTIVE
ELECTOR n someone who has the right to vote in an election
ELECTORAL adj of or relating to elections
ELECTORS > ELECTOR
ELECTRESS n female elector
ELECTRET n permanently polarized dielectric material
ELECTRETS > ELECTRET
ELECTRIC adj produced by, transmitting, or powered by electricity ▷ n electric train, car, etc
ELECTRICS > ELECTRIC
ELECTRIFY vb adapt for operation by electric power
ELECTRISE same as > ELECTRIZE
ELECTRIZE vb electrify
ELECTRO vb (in printing) make a metallic copy of a page
ELECTRODE n conductor through which an electric current enters or leaves a battery, vacuum tube, etc
ELECTROED > ELECTRO
ELECTRON n elementary particle in all atoms that has a negative electrical charge
ELECTRONS > ELECTRON
ELECTROS > ELECTRO
ELECTRUM n alloy of gold (55–88 per cent) and silver used for jewellery and ornaments
ELECTRUMS > ELECTRUM
ELECTS > ELECT
ELECTUARY n paste taken orally, containing a drug mixed with syrup or honey
ELEDOISIN n substance extracted from the salivary glands of a small octopus for medical applications
ELEGANCE n dignified grace in appearance, movement, or behaviour
ELEGANCES > ELEGANCE
ELEGANCY same as > ELEGANCE
ELEGANT adj pleasing or graceful in dress, style, or design
ELEGANTLY > ELEGANT

ELEGIAC adj mournful or plaintive ▷ n elegiac couplet or stanza
ELEGIACAL > ELEGIAC
ELEGIACS > ELEGIAC
ELEGIAST n writer of elegies
ELEGIASTS > ELEGIAST
ELEGIES > ELEGY
ELEGISE same as > ELEGIZE
ELEGISED > ELEGISE
ELEGISES > ELEGISE
ELEGISING > ELEGISE
ELEGIST > ELEGIZE
ELEGISTS > ELEGIZE
ELEGIT n writ delivering debtor's property to plaintiff
ELEGITS > ELEGIT
ELEGIZE vb compose an elegy or elegies (in memory of)
ELEGIZED > ELEGIZE
ELEGIZES > ELEGIZE
ELEGIZING > ELEGIZE
ELEGY n mournful poem, esp a lament for the dead
ELEMENT n component part
ELEMENTAL adj of primitive natural forces or passions ▷ n spirit or force that is said to appear in physical form
ELEMENTS > ELEMENT
ELEMI n fragrant resin obtained from various tropical trees
ELEMIS > ELEMI
ELENCH n refutation in logic
ELENCHI > ELENCHUS
ELENCHIC > ELENCHUS
ELENCHS > ELENCH
ELENCHTIC same as > ELENCTIC
ELENCHUS n refutation of an argument by proving the contrary of its conclusion
ELENCTIC adj refuting an argument by proving the falsehood of its conclusion
ELEOPTENE n liquid part of a volatile oil
ELEPHANT n huge four-footed thick-skinned animal with ivory tusks and a long trunk
ELEPHANTS > ELEPHANT
ELEPIDOTE n large rhododendron with leathery leaves
ELEUTHERI pl n secret society
ELEVATE vb raise in rank or status
ELEVATED adj higher than normal ▷ n railway that runs on an elevated structure
ELEVATEDS > ELEVATED
ELEVATES > ELEVATE

ELEVATING > ELEVATE
ELEVATION n raising
ELEVATOR n lift for carrying people
ELEVATORS > ELEVATOR
ELEVATORY > ELEVATE
ELEVEN n one more than ten
ELEVENS > ELEVEN
ELEVENSES n mid-morning snack
ELEVENTH n number eleven in a series ▷ adj coming after the tenth in numbering or counting order, position, time, etc
ELEVENTHS > ELEVENTH
ELEVON n aircraft control surface usually fitted to tailless or delta-wing aircraft
ELEVONS > ELEVON
ELF n (in folklore) small mischievous fairy ▷ vb entangle (esp hair)
ELFED > ELF
ELFHOOD > ELF
ELFHOODS > ELF
ELFIN adj small and delicate ▷ n young elf
ELFING > ELF
ELFINS > ELFIN
ELFISH adj of, relating to, or like an elf or elves ▷ n supposed language of elves
ELFISHES > ELFISH
ELFISHLY > ELFISH
ELFLAND another name for > FAIRYLAND
ELFLANDS > ELFLAND
ELFLIKE > ELF
ELFLOCK n lock of hair
ELFLOCKS > ELFLOCK
ELFS > ELF
ELHI adj informal US word meaning relating to elementary or high school
ELIAD n glance
ELIADS > ELIAD
ELICHE n pasta in the form of spirals
ELICHES > ELICHE
ELICIT vb bring about (a response or reaction)
ELICITED > ELICIT
ELICITING > ELICIT
ELICITOR > ELICIT
ELICITORS > ELICIT
ELICITS > ELICIT
ELIDE vb omit (a vowel or syllable) from a word
ELIDED > ELIDE
ELIDES > ELIDE
ELIDIBLE > ELIDE
ELIDING > ELIDE
ELIGIBLE adj meeting the requirements or qualifications needed ▷ n eligible person or thing
ELIGIBLES > ELIGIBLE
ELIGIBLY > ELIGIBLE
ELIMINANT > ELIMINATE
ELIMINATE vb get rid of

ELINT n electronic intelligence

ELINTS > ELINT

ELISION n omission of a vowel or syllable from a word

ELISIONS > ELISION

ELITE n most powerful, rich, or gifted members of a group ▷ adj of, relating to, or suitable for an elite

ELITES > ELITE

ELITISM n belief that society should be ruled by a small group of superior people

ELITISMS > ELITISM

ELITIST > ELITISM

ELITISTS > ELITISM

ELIXIR n legendary liquid

ELIXIRS > ELIXIR

ELK n large deer of N Europe and Asia

ELKHORN n as in elkhorn fern fern with a large leaf like an elk's horn

ELKHOUND n powerful breed of dog

ELKHOUNDS > ELKHOUND

ELKS > ELK

ELL n obsolete unit of length

ELLAGIC adj as in ellagic acid derived from gallnuts

ELLIPSE n oval shape

ELLIPSES > ELLIPSIS

ELLIPSIS n omission of letters or words in a sentence

ELLIPSOID n surface whose plane sections are ellipses or circles

ELLIPTIC adj relating to or having the shape of an ellipse

ELLOPS same as > ELOPS

ELLOPSES > ELLOPS

ELLS > ELL

ELLWAND n stick for measuring lengths

ELLWANDS > ELLWAND

ELM n tree with serrated leaves

ELMEN adj of or relating to elm trees

ELMIER > ELMY

ELMIEST > ELMY

ELMS > ELM

ELMWOOD n wood from an elm tree

ELMWOODS > ELMWOOD

ELMY adj of or relating to elm trees

ELOCUTE vb speak as if practising elocution

ELOCUTED > ELOCUTE

ELOCUTES > ELOCUTE

ELOCUTING > ELOCUTE

ELOCUTION n art of speaking clearly in public

ELOCUTORY > ELOCUTION

ELODEA n type of American plant

ELODEAS > ELODEA

ELOGE same as > EULOGY

ELOGES > ELOGE

ELOGIES > ELOGY

ELOGIST > ELOGY

ELOGISTS > ELOGY

ELOGIUM same as > EULOGY

ELOGIUMS > ELOGIUM

ELOGY same as > EULOGY

ELOIGN vb remove (oneself, one's property, etc) to a distant place

ELOIGNED > ELOIGN

ELOIGNER > ELOIGN

ELOIGNERS > ELOIGN

ELOIGNING > ELOIGN

ELOIGNS > ELOIGN

ELOIN same as > ELOIGN

ELOINED > ELOIN

ELOINER > ELOIN

ELOINERS > ELOINER

ELOINING > ELOIN

ELOINMENT > ELOIGN

ELOINS > ELOIN

ELONGATE vb make or become longer ▷ adj long and narrow

ELONGATED > ELONGATE

ELONGATES > ELONGATE

ELOPE vb (of two people) run away secretly to get married

ELOPED > ELOPE

ELOPEMENT > ELOPE

ELOPER > ELOPE

ELOPERS > ELOPE

ELOPES > ELOPE

ELOPING > ELOPE

ELOPS n type of fish

ELOPSES > ELOPS

ELOQUENCE n fluent powerful use of language

ELOQUENT adj (of speech or writing) fluent and persuasive

ELPEE n LP, long-playing record

ELPEES > ELPEE

ELS > EL

ELSE adv in addition or more

ELSEWHERE adv in or to another place

ELSEWISE adv otherwise

ELSHIN n cobbler's awl

ELSHINS > ELSHIN

ELSIN variant of > ELSHIN

ELSINS > ELSIN

ELT n young female pig

ELTCHI variant of > ELCHEE

ELTCHIS > ELTCHI

ELTS > ELT

ELUANT same as > ELUENT

ELUANTS > ELUANT

ELUATE n solution of adsorbed material obtained during the process of elution

ELUATES > ELUATE

ELUCIDATE vb make (something difficult) clear

ELUDE vb escape from by cleverness or quickness

ELUDED > ELUDE

ELUDER > ELUDE

ELUDERS > ELUDE

ELUDES > ELUDE

ELUDIBLE adj able to be eluded

ELUDING > ELUDE

ELUENT n solvent used for eluting

ELUENTS > ELUENT

ELUSION > ELUDE

ELUSIONS > ELUDE

ELUSIVE adj difficult to catch or remember

ELUSIVELY > ELUSIVE

ELUSORY adj avoiding the issue

ELUTE vb wash out (a substance) by the action of a solvent

ELUTED > ELUTE

ELUTES > ELUTE

ELUTING > ELUTE

ELUTION > ELUTE

ELUTIONS > ELUTE

ELUTOR > ELUTE

ELUTORS > ELUTE

ELUTRIATE vb purify or separate (a substance or mixture) by washing and straining or decanting

ELUVIA > ELUVIUM

ELUVIAL > ELUVIUM

ELUVIATE vb remove material suspended in water in a layer of soil by the action of rainfall

ELUVIATED > ELUVIATE

ELUVIATES > ELUVIATE

ELUVIUM n mass of sand, silt, etc

ELUVIUMS > ELUVIUM

ELVAN n type of rock

ELVANITE variant of > ELVAN

ELVANITES > ELVANITE

ELVANS > ELVAN

ELVEN adj like an elf

ELVER n young eel

ELVERS > ELVER

ELVES > ELF

ELVISH same as > ELFISH

ELVISHES > ELVISH

ELVISHLY > ELVISH

ELYSIAN adj delightful, blissful

ELYTRA > ELYTRON

ELYTRAL > ELYTRON

ELYTROID > ELYTRON

ELYTRON n either of the horny front wings of beetles and some other insects

ELYTROUS > ELYTRON

ELYTRUM same as > ELYTRON

EM n square of a body of any size of type, used as a unit of measurement

EMACIATE vb become or cause to become abnormally thin

EMACIATED adj abnormally thin

EMACIATES > EMACIATE

EMACS n powerful computer program

EMACSEN > EMACS

EMAIL n electronic mail ▷ vb send a message by electronic mail

EMAILABLE adj capable of being emailed

EMAILED > EMAIL

EMAILER > EMAIL

EMAILERS > EMAILER

EMAILING > EMAIL

EMAILINGS > EMAILING

EMAILS > EMAIL

EMANANT > EMANATE

EMANATE vb issue, proceed from a source

EMANATED > EMANATE

EMANATES > EMANATE

EMANATING > EMANATE

EMANATION n act or instance of emanating

EMANATIST > EMANATE

EMANATIVE > EMANATE

EMANATOR > EMANATE

EMANATORS > EMANATE

EMANATORY > EMANATE

EMBACE variant of > EMBASE

EMBACES > EMBACE

EMBACING > EMBACE

EMBAIL vb enclose in a circle

EMBAILED > EMBAIL

EMBAILING > EMBAIL

EMBAILS > EMBAIL

EMBALE vb bind

EMBALED > EMBALE

EMBALES > EMBALE

EMBALING > EMBALE

EMBALL vb enclose in a circle

EMBALLED > EMBALL

EMBALLING > EMBALL

EMBALLS > EMBALL

EMBALM vb preserve (a corpse) from decay by the use of chemicals etc

EMBALMED > EMBALM

EMBALMER > EMBALM

EMBALMERS > EMBALM

EMBALMING > EMBALM

EMBALMS > EMBALM

EMBANK vb protect, enclose, or confine with an embankment

EMBANKED > EMBANK

EMBANKER > EMBANK

EMBANKERS > EMBANK

EMBANKING > EMBANK

EMBANKS > EMBANK

EMBAR vb close in with bars

EMBARGO n order by a government prohibiting trade with a country ▷ vb put an embargo on

EMBARGOED > EMBARGO

EMBARGOES > EMBARGO

EMBARK vb board a ship or aircraft

EMBARKED > EMBARK

EMBARKING > EMBARK

EMBARKS > EMBARK

EMBARRAS n
embarrassment
EMBARRASS vb cause to
feel self-conscious or
ashamed
EMBARRED > EMBAR
EMBARRING > EMBAR
EMBARS > EMBAR
EMBASE vb degrade or
debase
EMBASED > EMBASE
EMBASES > EMBASE
EMBASING > EMBASE
EMBASSADE n embassy
EMBASSAGE n work of an
embassy
EMBASSIES > EMBASSY
EMBASSY n offices or
official residence of an
ambassador
EMBASTE > EMBASTE
EMBATHE vb bathe with
water
EMBATHED > EMBATHE
EMBATHES > EMBATHE
EMBATHING > EMBATHE
EMBATTLE vb deploy
(troops) for battle
EMBATTLED adj having a
lot of difficulties
EMBATTLES
> EMBATTLE
EMBAY vb form into a bay
EMBAYED > EMBAY
EMBAYING > EMBAY
EMBAYLD archaic past form
of **>** EMBAIL
EMBAYMENT n shape
resembling a bay
EMBAYS > EMBAY
EMBED vb fix firmly in
something solid ▷ n
journalist accompanying
an active military unit
EMBEDDED > EMBED
EMBEDDING n practice of
assigning or being
assigned a journalist to
accompany an active
military unit
EMBEDMENT > EMBED
EMBEDS > EMBED
EMBELLISH vb decorate
EMBER n glowing piece of
wood or coal in a dying fire
EMBERS > EMBER
EMBEZZLE vb steal
money that has been
entrusted to one
EMBEZZLED
> EMBEZZLE
EMBEZZLER
> EMBEZZLE
EMBEZZLES
> EMBEZZLE
EMBIGGEN vb make
bigger
EMBIGGENS
> EMBIGGEN
EMBITTER vb make (a
person) resentful or bitter
EMBITTERS
> EMBITTER
EMBLAZE vb cause to
light up
EMBLAZED > EMBLAZE
EMBLAZER > EMBLAZE
EMBLAZERS > EMBLAZE

EMBLAZES > EMBLAZE
EMBLAZING > EMBLAZE
EMBLAZON vb decorate
with bright colours
EMBLAZONS
> EMBLAZON
EMBLEM n object or
design that symbolizes a
quality, type, or group ▷ vb
represent or signify
EMBLEMA n mosaic
decoration
EMBLEMATA > EMBLEMA
EMBLEMED > EMBLEM
EMBLEMING > EMBLEM
EMBLEMISE same as
> EMBLEMIZE
EMBLEMIZE vb function
as an emblem of
EMBLEMS > EMBLEM
EMBLIC n type of Indian
tree
EMBLICS > EMBLIC
EMBLOOM vb adorn with
blooms
EMBLOOMED > EMBLOOM
EMBLOOMS > EMBLOOM
EMBLOSSOM vb adorn
with blossom
EMBODIED > EMBODY
EMBODIER > EMBODY
EMBODIERS > EMBODY
EMBODIES > EMBODY
EMBODY vb be an example
or expression of
EMBODYING > EMBODY
EMBOG vb sink down into a
bog
EMBOGGED > EMBOG
EMBOGGING > EMBOG
EMBOGS > EMBOG
EMBOGUE vb go out
through a narrow channel
or passage
EMBOGUED > EMBOGUE
EMBOGUES > EMBOGUE
EMBOGUING > EMBOGUE
EMBOIL vb enrage or be
enraged
EMBOILED > EMBOIL
EMBOILING > EMBOIL
EMBOILS > EMBOIL
EMBOLDEN vb encourage
(someone)
EMBOLDENS
> EMBOLDEN
EMBOLI > EMBOLUS
EMBOLIC adj of or
relating to an embolus or
embolism
EMBOLIES > EMBOLY
EMBOLISE same as
> EMBOLIZE
EMBOLISED
> EMBOLISE
EMBOLISES
> EMBOLISE
EMBOLISM n blocking of
a blood vessel by a blood
clot or air bubble
EMBOLISMS
> EMBOLISM
EMBOLIZE vb cause
embolism in (a blood
vessel)
EMBOLIZED
> EMBOLIZE
EMBOLIZES > EMBOLIZE

EMBOLUS n material that
blocks a blood vessel
EMBOLUSES > EMBOLUS
EMBOLY n infolding of an
outer layer of cells so as to
form a pocket in the
surface
EMBORDER vb edge or
border
EMBORDERS
> EMBORDER
EMBOSCATA n sudden
attack or raid
EMBOSK vb hide or cover
EMBOSKED > EMBOSK
EMBOSKING > EMBOSK
EMBOSKS > EMBOSK
EMBOSOM vb enclose or
envelop, esp protectively
EMBOSOMED > EMBOSOM
EMBOSOMS > EMBOSOM
EMBOSS vb create a
decoration that stands
out on (a surface)
EMBOSSED adj (of a
design or pattern)
standing out from a
surface
EMBOSSER > EMBOSS
EMBOSSERS > EMBOSS
EMBOSSES > EMBOSS
EMBOSSING n decoration
that stands out on (a
surface)
EMBOST > EMBOSS
EMBOUND vb surround or
encircle
EMBOUNDED > EMBOUND
EMBOUNDS > EMBOUND
EMBOW vb design or create
(a structure) in the form of
an arch or vault
EMBOWED > EMBOW
EMBOWEL vb bury or
embed deeply
EMBOWELED > EMBOWEL
EMBOWELS > EMBOWEL
EMBOWER vb enclose in or
as in a bower
EMBOWERED > EMBOWER
EMBOWERS > EMBOWER
EMBOWING > EMBOW
EMBOWMENT > EMBOW
EMBOWS > EMBOW
EMBOX vb put in a box
EMBOXED > EMBOX
EMBOXES > EMBOX
EMBOXING > EMBOX
EMBRACE vb clasp in the
arms, hug ▷ n act of
embracing
EMBRACED > EMBRACE
EMBRACEOR n person
guilty of embracery
EMBRACER > EMBRACE
EMBRACERS > EMBRACE
EMBRACERY n offence of
attempting to corrupt
means to influence a jury
or juror, as by bribery or
threats
EMBRACES > EMBRACE
EMBRACING > EMBRACE
EMBRACIVE > EMBRACE
EMBRAID vb braid or
interweave
EMBRAIDED > EMBRAID
EMBRAIDS > EMBRAID

EMBRANGLE vb confuse
or entangle
EMBRASOR n one who
embraces
EMBRASORS
> EMBRASOR
EMBRASURE n door or
window having splayed
sides so that the opening
is larger on the inside
EMBRAVE vb adorn or
decorate
EMBRAVED > EMBRAVE
EMBRAVES > EMBRAVE
EMBRAVING > EMBRAVE
EMBRAZURE variant of
> EMBRASURE
EMBREAD vb braid
EMBREADED > EMBREAD
EMBREADS > EMBREAD
EMBREATHE vb breathe
in air
EMBRITTLE vb become
brittle
EMBROCATE vb apply a
liniment or lotion to (a
part of the body)
EMBROGLIO same as
> IMBROGLIO
EMBROIDER vb decorate
with needlework
EMBROIL vb involve (a
person) in problems
EMBROILED > EMBROIL
EMBROILER > EMBROIL
EMBROILS > EMBROIL
EMBROWN vb make or
become brown
EMBROWNED > EMBROWN
EMBROWNS > EMBROWN
EMBRUE variant spelling of
> IMBRUE
EMBRUED > EMBRUE
EMBRUES > EMBRUE
EMBRUING > EMBRUE
EMBRUTE variant of
> IMBRUTE
EMBRUTED > EMBRUTE
EMBRUTES > EMBRUTE
EMBRUTING > EMBRUTE
EMBRYO n unborn
creature in the early
stages of development
EMBRYOID > EMBRYO
EMBRYOIDS > EMBRYO
EMBRYON variant of
> EMBRYO
EMBRYONAL same as
> EMBRYONIC
EMBRYONIC adj at an
early stage
EMBRYONS > EMBRYON
EMBRYOS > EMBRYO
EMBRYOTIC variant of
> EMBRYONIC
EMBUS vb cause (troops)
to board a transport
vehicle
EMBUSED > EMBUS
EMBUSES > EMBUS
EMBUSIED > EMBUSY
EMBUSIES > EMBUSY
EMBUSING > EMBUS
EMBUSQUE n man who
avoids military
conscription by obtaining
a government job
EMBUSQUES > EMBUSQUE

e

EMBUSSED > EMBUS

EMBUSSES > EMBUS

EMBUSSING > EMBUS

EMBUSY *vb* keep occupied

EMBUSYING > EMBUSY

EMCEE *n* master of ceremonies ▷ *vb* act as master of ceremonies (for or at)

EMCEED > EMCEE

EMCEEING > EMCEE

EMCEES > EMCEE

EMDASH *n* long dash in punctuation

EMDASHES > EMDASH

EME *n* uncle

EMEER *variant of* > EMIR

EMEERATE *variant of* > EMIRATE

EMEERATES > EMEERATE

EMEERS > EMEER

EMEND *vb* remove errors from

EMENDABLE > EMEND

EMENDALS *pl n* funds put aside for repairs

EMENDATE *vb* make corrections

EMENDATED > EMENDATE

EMENDATES > EMENDATE

EMENDATOR *n* one who emends a text

EMENDED > EMEND

EMENDER > EMEND

EMENDERS > EMEND

EMENDING > EMEND

EMENDS > EMEND

EMERALD *n* bright green precious stone ▷ *adj* bright green

EMERALDS > EMERALD

EMERAUDE *archaic variant of* > EMERALD

EMERAUDES > EMERAUDE

EMERG *n* part of a hospital dealing with emergencies

EMERGE *vb* come into view

EMERGED > EMERGE

EMERGENCE *n* act or process of emerging

EMERGENCY *n* sudden unforeseen occurrence needing immediate action

EMERGENT *adj* coming into being or notice ▷ *n* aquatic plant with stem and leaves above the water

EMERGENTS > EMERGENT

EMERGES > EMERGE

EMERGING > EMERGE

EMERGS > EMERG

EMERIED > EMERY

EMERIES > EMERY

EMERITA *adj* retired, but retaining an honorary title ▷ *n* woman who is retired, but retains an honorary title

EMERITAE > EMERITA

EMERITAS > EMERITA

EMERITI > EMERITUS

EMERITUS *adj* retired, but retaining an honorary title ▷ *n* person who is retired, but retains an honorary title

EMEROD *n* haemorrhoid

EMERODS > EMEROD

EMEROID *variant of* > EMEROD

EMEROIDS > EMEROID

EMERSE *same as* > EMERSED

EMERSED *adj* protruding above the surface of the water

EMERSION *n* act or an instance of emerging

EMERSIONS > EMERSION

EMERY *n* hard mineral used for smoothing and polishing ▷ *vb* apply emery to

EMERYING > EMERY

EMES > EME

EMESES > EMESIS

EMESIS *technical name for* > VOMITING

EMESISES > EMESIS

EMETIC *n* substance that causes vomiting ▷ *adj* causing vomiting

EMETICAL *same as* > EMETIC

EMETICS > EMETIC

EMETIN *same as* > EMETINE

EMETINE *n* white bitter poisonous alkaloid

EMETINES > EMETINE

EMETINS > EMETIN

EMEU *variant of* > EMU

EMEUS > EMEU

EMEUTE *n* uprising or rebellion

EMEUTES > EMEUTE

EMIC *adj* of or relating to a significant linguistic unit ▷ *n* emic viewpoint or approach

EMICANT > EMICATE

EMICATE *vb* twinkle

EMICATED > EMICATE

EMICATES > EMICATE

EMICATING > EMICATE

EMICATION > EMICATE

EMICS > EMIC

EMICTION *n* passing of urine

EMICTIONS > EMICTION

EMICTORY > EMICTION

EMIGRANT *n* person who leaves one place or country, esp a native country, to settle in another

EMIGRANTS > EMIGRANT

EMIGRATE *vb* go and settle in another country

EMIGRATED > EMIGRATE

EMIGRATES > EMIGRATE

EMIGRE *n* someone who has left his or her native country for political reasons

EMIGREE *n* female emigre

EMIGREES > EMIGREE

EMIGRES > EMIGRE

EMINENCE *n* position of superiority or fame

EMINENCES > EMINENCE

EMINENCY *same as* > EMINENCE

EMINENT *adj* distinguished, well-known

EMINENTLY > EMINENT

EMIR *n* Muslim ruler

EMIRATE *n* emir's country

EMIRATES > EMIRATE

EMIRS > EMIR

EMISSARY *n* agent sent on a mission by a government ▷ *adj* (of veins) draining blood from sinuses in the dura mater to veins outside the skull

EMISSILE *adj* able to be emitted

EMISSION *n* act of giving out heat, light, a smell, etc

EMISSIONS > EMISSION

EMISSIVE > EMISSION

EMIT *vb* give out

EMITS > EMIT

EMITTANCE > EMIT

EMITTED > EMIT

EMITTER *n* person or thing that emits

EMITTERS > EMITTER

EMITTING > EMIT

EMLETS *pl n* as in *blood-drop emlets* Chilean plant

EMMA *n* former communications code for the letter M

EMMARBLE *vb* decorate with marble

EMMARBLED > EMMARBLE

EMMARBLES > EMMARBLE

EMMAS > EMMA

EMMER *n* variety of wheat

EMMERS > EMMER

EMMESH *variant of* > ENMESH

EMMESHED > EMMESH

EMMESHES > EMMESH

EMMESHING > EMMESH

EMMET *n* tourist or holidaymaker

EMMETROPE *n* person whose vision is normal

EMMETS > EMMET

EMMEW *vb* restrict

EMMEWED > EMMEW

EMMEWING > EMMEW

EMMEWS > EMMEW

EMMOVE *vb* cause emotion in

EMMOVED > EMMOVE

EMMOVES > EMMOVE

EMMOVING > EMMOVE

EMMY *n* award for outstanding television performances and productions

EMMYS > EMMY

EMO *n* type of music combining rock with emotional lyrics

EMOCORE *same as* > EMO

EMOCORES > EMOCORE

EMODIN *n* chemical compound obtained from rhubarb root

EMODINS > EMODIN

EMOJI *n* digital icon used in electronic communication

EMOJIS > EMOJI

EMOLLIATE *vb* make soft or smooth

EMOLLIENT *adj* softening, soothing ▷ *n* substance which softens or soothes the skin

EMOLUMENT *n* fees or wages from employment

EMONG *variant of* > AMONG

EMONGES *variant of* > AMONG

EMONGEST *variant of* > AMONGST

EMONGST *variant of* > AMONGST

EMOS > EMO

EMOTE *vb* display exaggerated emotion, as if acting

EMOTED > EMOTE

EMOTER > EMOTE

EMOTERS > EMOTE

EMOTES > EMOTE

EMOTICON *n* any of several combinations of symbols used in email and texting

EMOTICONS > EMOTICON

EMOTING > EMOTE

EMOTION *n* strong feeling

EMOTIONAL *adj* readily affected by or appealing to the emotions

EMOTIONS > EMOTION

EMOTIVE *adj* tending to arouse emotion

EMOTIVELY > EMOTIVE

EMOTIVISM *n* theory that moral utterances do not have a truth value but express the feelings of the speaker, so that *murder is wrong* is equivalent to *down with murder*

EMOTIVITY > EMOTIVE

EMOVE *vb* cause to feel emotion

EMOVED > EMOVE

EMOVES > EMOVE

EMOVING > EMOVE

EMPACKET *vb* wrap up

EMPACKETS > EMPACKET

EMPAESTIC *adj* embossed

EMPAIRE *variant of* > IMPAIR

EMPAIRED > EMPAIRE

EMPAIRES > EMPAIRE

EMPAIRING > EMPAIRE

EMPALE *less common spelling of* > IMPALE

EMPALED > EMPALE

EMPALER > EMPALE

EMPALERS > EMPALE
EMPALES > EMPALE
EMPALING > EMPALE
EMPANADA n Spanish meat-filled pastry
EMPANADAS > EMPANADA
EMPANEL vb enter on a list (names of persons to be summoned for jury service)
EMPANELED > EMPANEL
EMPANELS > EMPANEL
EMPANOPLY vb put armour on
EMPARE archaic variant of > IMPAIR
EMPARED > EMPARE
EMPARES > EMPARE
EMPARING > EMPARE
EMPARL variant of > IMPARL
EMPARLED > EMPARL
EMPARLING > EMPARL
EMPARLS > EMPARL
EMPART variant of > IMPART
EMPARTED > EMPART
EMPARTING > EMPART
EMPARTS > EMPART
EMPATHIC adj of or relating to empathy
EMPATHIES > EMPATHY
EMPATHISE same as > EMPATHIZE
EMPATHIST > EMPATHY
EMPATHIZE vb sense and understand someone else's feelings as if they were one's own
EMPATHY n ability to understand someone else's feelings
EMPATRON vb treat in the manner of a patron
EMPATRONS > EMPATRON
EMPAYRE archaic variant of > IMPAIR
EMPAYRED > EMPAYRE
EMPAYRES > EMPAYRE
EMPAYRING > EMPAYRE
EMPEACH variant of > IMPEACH
EMPEACHED > EMPEACH
EMPEACHES > EMPEACH
EMPENNAGE n rear part of an aircraft, comprising the fin, rudder, and tailplane
EMPEOPLE vb bring people into
EMPEOPLED > EMPEOPLE
EMPEOPLES > EMPEOPLE
EMPERCE archaic variant of > EMPIERCE
EMPERCED > EMPERCE
EMPERCES > EMPERCE
EMPERCING > EMPERCE
EMPERIES > EMPERY
EMPERISE variant of > EMPERIZE
EMPERISED > EMPERISE
EMPERISES > EMPERISE

EMPERISH vb damage or harm
EMPERIZE vb act like an emperor
EMPERIZED > EMPERIZE
EMPERIZES > EMPERIZE
EMPEROR n ruler of an empire
EMPERORS > EMPEROR
EMPERY n dominion or power
EMPHASES > EMPHASIS
EMPHASIS n special importance or significance
EMPHASISE same as > EMPHASIZE
EMPHASIZE vb give emphasis or prominence to
EMPHATIC adj showing emphasis ▷ n emphatic consonant, as used in Arabic
EMPHATICS > EMPHATIC
EMPHLYSES > EMPHLYSIS
EMPHLYSIS n outbreak of blisters on the body
EMPHYSEMA n condition in which the air sacs of the lungs are grossly enlarged, causing breathlessness
EMPIERCE vb pierce or cut
EMPIERCED > EMPIERCE
EMPIERCES > EMPIERCE
EMPIGHT adj attached or positioned ▷ vb attach or position
EMPIGHTED > EMPIGHT
EMPIGHTS > EMPIGHT
EMPIRE n group of territories under the rule of one state or person
EMPIRES > EMPIRE
EMPIRIC n person who relies on empirical methods
EMPIRICAL adj relying on experiment or experience, not on theory ▷ n posterior probability of an event derived on the basis of its observed frequency in a sample
EMPIRICS > EMPIRIC
EMPLACE vb put in place or position
EMPLACED > EMPLACE
EMPLACES > EMPLACE
EMPLACING > EMPLACE
EMPLANE vb board or put on board an aeroplane
EMPLANED > EMPLANE
EMPLANES > EMPLANE
EMPLANING > EMPLANE
EMPLASTER vb cover with plaster
EMPLASTIC adj sticky
EMPLASTRA n plural of emplastrum, a medicated plaster
EMPLEACH variant of > IMPLEACH

EMPLECTON n type of masonry filled with rubbish
EMPLECTUM variant of > EMPLECTON
EMPLONGE variant of > IMPLUNGE
EMPLONGED > EMPLONGE
EMPLONGES > EMPLONGE
EMPLOY vb engage or make use of the services of (a person) in return for money ▷ n state of being employed
EMPLOYE same as > EMPLOYEE
EMPLOYED > EMPLOY
EMPLOYEE n person who is hired to work for someone in return for payment
EMPLOYEES > EMPLOYEE
EMPLOYER n person or organization that employs someone
EMPLOYERS > EMPLOYER
EMPLOYES > EMPLOYE
EMPLOYING > EMPLOY
EMPLOYS > EMPLOY
EMPLUME vb put a plume on
EMPLUMED > EMPLUME
EMPLUMES > EMPLUME
EMPLUMING > EMPLUME
EMPOISON vb embitter or corrupt
EMPOISONS > EMPOISON
EMPOLDER variant spelling of > IMPOLDER
EMPOLDERS > EMPOLDER
EMPORIA > EMPORIUM
EMPORIUM n large general shop
EMPORIUMS > EMPORIUM
EMPOWER vb enable, authorize
EMPOWERED > EMPOWER
EMPOWERS > EMPOWER
EMPRESS n woman who rules an empire
EMPRESSE adj keen; zealous
EMPRESSES > EMPRESS
EMPRISE n chivalrous or daring enterprise
EMPRISES > EMPRISE
EMPRIZE variant of > EMPRISE
EMPRIZES > EMPRIZE
EMPT vb empty
EMPTED > EMPT
EMPTIABLE > EMPTY
EMPTIED > EMPTY
EMPTIER > EMPTY
EMPTIERS > EMPTY
EMPTIES > EMPTY
EMPTIEST > EMPTY
EMPTILY > EMPTY
EMPTINESS > EMPTY
EMPTING > EMPT
EMPTINGS variant of > EMPTINS

EMPTINS pl n liquid leavening agent made from potatoes
EMPTION n process of buying something
EMPTIONAL > EMPTION
EMPTIONS > EMPTION
EMPTS > EMPT
EMPTY adj containing nothing ▷ vb make or become empty ▷ n empty container, esp a bottle
EMPTYING > EMPTY
EMPTYINGS > EMPTY
EMPTYSES > EMPTYSIS
EMPTYSIS n act of spitting up blood
EMPURPLE vb make or become purple
EMPURPLED > EMPURPLE
EMPURPLES > EMPURPLE
EMPUSA n goblin in Greek mythology
EMPUSAS > EMPUSA
EMPUSE variant of > EMPUSA
EMPUSES > EMPUSE
EMPYEMA n collection of pus in a body cavity
EMPYEMAS > EMPYEMA
EMPYEMATA > EMPYEMA
EMPYEMIC > EMPYEMA
EMPYESES > EMPYESIS
EMPYESIS n pus-filled boil on the skin
EMPYREAL variant of > EMPYREAN
EMPYREAN n heavens or sky ▷ adj of or relating to the sky or the heavens
EMPYREANS > EMPYREAN
EMPYREUMA n smell and taste associated with burning vegetable and animal matter
EMS > EM
EMU n large Australian flightless bird with long legs
EMULATE vb attempt to equal or surpass by imitating
EMULATED > EMULATE
EMULATES > EMULATE
EMULATING > EMULATE
EMULATION n act of emulating or imitating
EMULATIVE > EMULATE
EMULATOR > EMULATE
EMULATORS > EMULATE
EMULE variant of > EMULATE
EMULED > EMULE
EMULES > EMULE
EMULGE vb remove liquid from
EMULGED > EMULGE
EMULGENCE > EMULGE
EMULGENT > EMULGE
EMULGES > EMULGE
EMULGING > EMULGE
EMULING > EMULE
EMULOUS adj desiring or aiming to equal or surpass another

EMULOUSLY > EMULOUS
EMULSIBLE
> EMULSIFY
EMULSIFY *vb* (of two liquids) join together
EMULSIN *n* enzyme that is found in almonds
EMULSINS > EMULSIN
EMULSION *n* light-sensitive coating on photographic film ▷ *vb* paint with emulsion paint
EMULSIONS
> EMULSION
EMULSIVE > EMULSION
EMULSOID *n* sol with a liquid disperse phase
EMULSOIDS
> EMULSOID
EMULSOR *n* device that emulsifies
EMULSORS > EMULSOR
EMUNCTION
> EMUNCTORY
EMUNCTORY *adj* relating to a bodily organ or duct with an excretory function ▷ *n* excretory organ or duct
EMUNGE *vb* clean or clear out
EMUNGED > EMUNGE
EMUNGES > EMUNGE
EMUNGING > EMUNGE
EMURE *variant of*
> IMMURE
EMURED > EMURE
EMURES > EMURE
EMURING > EMURE
EMUS > EMU
EMYD *n* freshwater tortoise or terrapin
EMYDE *same as* > EMYD
EMYDES > EMYDE
EMYDS > EMYD
EMYS *n* freshwater tortoise or terrapin
EN *n* unit of measurement, half the width of an em
ENABLE *vb* provide (a person) with the means (to do something)
ENABLED > ENABLE
ENABLER > ENABLE
ENABLERS > ENABLE
ENABLES > ENABLE
ENABLING > ENABLE
ENACT *vb* establish by law
ENACTABLE > ENACT
ENACTED > ENACT
ENACTING > ENACT
ENACTION > ENACT
ENACTIONS > ENACT
ENACTIVE > ENACT
ENACTMENT > ENACT
ENACTOR > ENACT
ENACTORS > ENACT
ENACTORY > ENACT
ENACTS > ENACT
ENACTURE > ENACT
ENACTURES > ENACT
ENALAPRIL *n* ACE inhibitor used to treat high blood pressure and congestive heart failure
ENALLAGE *n* act of using one grammatical form in the place of another

ENALLAGES
> ENALLAGE
ENAMEL *n* glasslike coating applied to metal etc to preserve the surface ▷ *vb* cover with enamel
ENAMELED > ENAMEL
ENAMELER > ENAMEL
ENAMELERS > ENAMEL
ENAMELING > ENAMEL
ENAMELIST > ENAMEL
ENAMELLED > ENAMEL
ENAMELLER > ENAMEL
ENAMELS > ENAMEL
ENAMINE *n* type of unsaturated compound
ENAMINES > ENAMINE
ENAMOR *same as*
> ENAMOUR
ENAMORADO *n* beloved one
ENAMORED *same as*
> ENAMOURED
ENAMORING > ENAMOR
ENAMORS > ENAMOR
ENAMOUR *vb* inspire with love
ENAMOURED *adj* inspired with love
ENAMOURS > ENAMOUR
ENANTHEMA *n* ulcer on a mucous membrane
ENARCH *variant of*
> INARCH
ENARCHED > ENARCH
ENARCHES > ENARCH
ENARCHING > ENARCH
ENARGITE *n* sulphide of copper and arsenic
ENARGITES
> ENARGITE
ENARM *vb* provide with arms
ENARMED > ENARM
ENARMING > ENARM
ENARMS > ENARM
ENATE *adj* growing out or outwards ▷ *n* relative on the mother's side
ENATES > ENATE
ENATIC *adj* related on one's mother's side
ENATION > ENATE
ENATIONS > ENATE
ENAUNTER *conj* in case that
ENCAENIA *n* festival of dedication or commemoration
ENCAENIAS
> ENCAENIA
ENCAGE *vb* confine in or as in a cage
ENCAGED > ENCAGE
ENCAGES > ENCAGE
ENCAGING > ENCAGE
ENCALM *vb* becalm, settle
ENCALMED > ENCALM
ENCALMING > ENCALM
ENCALMS > ENCALM
ENCAMP *vb* set up in a camp
ENCAMPED > ENCAMP
ENCAMPING > ENCAMP
ENCAMPS > ENCAMP
ENCANTHIS *n* tumour of the eye

ENCAPSULE *vb* enclose or be enclosed in or as if in a capsule
ENCARPUS *n* decoration of fruit or flowers on a frieze
ENCASE *vb* enclose or cover completely
ENCASED > ENCASE
ENCASES > ENCASE
ENCASH *vb* exchange (a cheque) for cash
ENCASHED > ENCASH
ENCASHES > ENCASH
ENCASHING > ENCASH
ENCASING > ENCASE
ENCASTRE *adj* (of a beam) fixed at the ends
ENCAUSTIC *adj* decorated by any process involving burning in colours, esp by inlaying coloured clays and baking or by fusing wax colours to the surface ▷ *n* process of burning in colours
ENCAVE *variant of*
> INCAVE
ENCAVED > ENCAVE
ENCAVES > ENCAVE
ENCAVING > ENCAVE
ENCEINTE *n* boundary wall enclosing a defended area
ENCEINTES
> ENCEINTE
ENCEPHALA *n* brains
ENCHAFE *vb* heat up
ENCHAFED > ENCHAFE
ENCHAFES > ENCHAFE
ENCHAFING > ENCHAFE
ENCHAIN *vb* bind with chains
ENCHAINED > ENCHAIN
ENCHAINS > ENCHAIN
ENCHANT *vb* delight and fascinate
ENCHANTED > ENCHANT
ENCHANTER > ENCHANT
ENCHANTS > ENCHANT
ENCHARGE *vb* give into the custody of
ENCHARGED > ENCHARGE
ENCHARGES
> ENCHARGE
ENCHARM *vb* enchant
ENCHARMED > ENCHARM
ENCHARMS > ENCHARM
ENCHASE *less common word for* > CHASE
ENCHASED > ENCHASE
ENCHASER > ENCHASE
ENCHASERS > ENCHASE
ENCHASES > ENCHASE
ENCHASING > ENCHASE
ENCHEASON *n* reason
ENCHEER *vb* cheer up
ENCHEERED > ENCHEER
ENCHEERS > ENCHEER
ENCHILADA *n* Mexican dish of a tortilla filled with meat, served with chilli sauce
ENCHORIAL *adj* of or used in a particular country: used esp of the popular (demotic) writing of the ancient Egyptians

ENCHORIC *same as*
> ENCHORIAL
ENCIERRO *n* Spanish bull run
ENCIERROS
> ENCIERRO
ENCINA *n* type of oak
ENCINAL > ENCINA
ENCINAS > ENCINA
ENCIPHER *vb* convert (a message, document, etc) from plain text into code or cipher
ENCIPHERS
> ENCIPHER
ENCIRCLE *vb* form a circle around
ENCIRCLED
> ENCIRCLE
ENCIRCLES
> ENCIRCLE
ENCLASP *vb* clasp
ENCLASPED > ENCLASP
ENCLASPS > ENCLASP
ENCLAVE *n* part of a country entirely surrounded by another ▷ *vb* hold in an enclave
ENCLAVED > ENCLAVE
ENCLAVES > ENCLAVE
ENCLAVING > ENCLAVE
ENCLISES > ENCLISIS
ENCLISIS *n* state of being enclitic
ENCLITIC *adj* relating to a monosyllabic word treated as a suffix ▷ *n* enclitic word or linguistic form
ENCLITICS
> ENCLITIC
ENCLOSE *vb* surround completely
ENCLOSED > ENCLOSE
ENCLOSER > ENCLOSE
ENCLOSERS > ENCLOSE
ENCLOSES > ENCLOSE
ENCLOSING > ENCLOSE
ENCLOSURE *n* area of land enclosed by a fence, wall, or hedge
ENCLOTHE *vb* clothe
ENCLOTHED
> ENCLOTHE
ENCLOTHES
> ENCLOTHE
ENCLOUD *vb* hide with clouds
ENCLOUDED > ENCLOUD
ENCLOUDS > ENCLOUD
ENCODABLE > ENCODE
ENCODE *vb* convert (a message) into code
ENCODED > ENCODE
ENCODER > ENCODE
ENCODERS > ENCODE
ENCODES > ENCODE
ENCODING *n* act of encoding
ENCODINGS
> ENCODING
ENCOLOUR *vb* give a colour to
ENCOLOURS > ENCOLOUR
ENCOLPIA
> ENCOLPION
ENCOLPION *n* religious symbol worn on the breast

ENCOLPIUM *variant of*
> ENCOLPION

ENCOLURE *n* mane of a horse

ENCOLURES
> ENCOLURE

ENCOMIA > ENCOMIUM

ENCOMIAST *n* person who speaks or writes an encomium

ENCOMION *variant of*
> ENCOMIUM

ENCOMIUM *n* formal expression of praise

ENCOMIUMS
> ENCOMIUM

ENCOMPASS *vb* surround

ENCORE *interj* again, once more ▷ *n* extra performance due to enthusiastic demand ▷ *vb* demand an extra or repeated performance

ENCORED > ENCORE

ENCORES > ENCORE

ENCORING > ENCORE

ENCOUNTER *vb* meet unexpectedly ▷ *n* unexpected meeting

ENCOURAGE *vb* inspire with confidence

ENCRADLE *vb* put in a cradle

ENCRADLED
> ENCRADLE

ENCRADLES
> ENCRADLE

ENCRATIES > ENCRATY

ENCRATY *n* control of one's desires, actions, etc

ENCREASE *variant form of*
> INCREASE

ENCREASED
> ENCREASE

ENCREASES
> ENCREASE

ENCRIMSON *vb* make crimson

ENCRINAL
> ENCRINITE

ENCRINIC
> ENCRINITE

ENCRINITE *n* sedimentary rock formed almost exclusively from the skeletal plates of crinoids

ENCROACH *vb* intrude gradually on a person's rights or land

ENCRUST *vb* cover with a layer of something

ENCRUSTED > ENCRUST

ENCRUSTS > ENCRUST

ENCRYPT *vb* put (a message) into code

ENCRYPTED > ENCRYPT

ENCRYPTS > ENCRYPT

ENCUMBER *vb* hinder or impede

ENCUMBERS
> ENCUMBER

ENCURTAIN *vb* cover or surround with curtains

ENCYCLIC *n* letter sent by the Pope to all bishops

ENCYCLICS
> ENCYCLIC

ENCYST *vb* enclose or become enclosed by a cyst, thick membrane, or shell

ENCYSTED > ENCYST

ENCYSTING > ENCYST

ENCYSTS > ENCYST

END *n* furthest point or part ▷ *vb* bring or come to a finish

ENDAMAGE *vb* cause injury to

ENDAMAGED
> ENDAMAGE

ENDAMAGES
> ENDAMAGE

ENDAMEBA *same as*
> ENDAMOEBA

ENDAMEBAE
> ENDAMEBA

ENDAMEBAS
> ENDAMEBA

ENDAMEBIC
> ENDAMEBA

ENDAMOEBA *same as*
> ENTAMOEBA

ENDANGER *vb* put in danger

ENDANGERS
> ENDANGER

ENDARCH *adj* having the first-formed xylem internal to that formed later

ENDARCHY *n* state of being endarch

ENDART *variant of*
> INDART

ENDARTED > ENDART

ENDARTING > ENDART

ENDARTS > ENDART

ENDASH *n* short dash in punctuation

ENDASHES > ENDASH

ENDBRAIN *n* part of the brain

ENDBRAINS
> ENDBRAIN

ENDCAP *n* display placed at the end of a shop aisle

ENDCAPS > ENDCAP

ENDEAR *vb* cause to be liked

ENDEARED > ENDEAR

ENDEARING *adj* giving rise to love or esteem

ENDEARS > ENDEAR

ENDEAVOR *same as*
> ENDEAVOUR

ENDEAVORS
> ENDEAVOR

ENDEAVOUR *vb* try ▷ *n* effort

ENDECAGON *n* figure with eleven sides

ENDED > END

ENDEICTIC
> ENDEIXIS

ENDEIXES > ENDEIXIS

ENDEIXIS *n* sign or mark

ENDEMIAL *same as*
> ENDEMIC

ENDEMIC *adj* present within a particular area or group of people ▷ *n* endemic disease or plant

ENDEMICAL *adj* endemic

ENDEMICS > ENDEMIC

ENDEMISM > ENDEMIC

ENDEMISMS > ENDEMIC

ENDENIZEN *vb* make a denizen

ENDER > END

ENDERMIC *adj* (of a medicine) acting by absorption through the skin

ENDERON *variant of*
> ANDIRON

ENDERONS > ENDERON

ENDERS > END

ENDEW *variant of* > ENDUE

ENDEWED > ENDEW

ENDEWING > ENDEW

ENDEWS > ENDEW

ENDEXINE *n* inner layer of an exine

ENDEXINES
> ENDEXINE

ENDGAME *n* closing stage of a game of chess

ENDGAMES > ENDGAME

ENDGATE *n* tailboard of a vehicle

ENDGATES > ENDGATE

ENDING *n* last part or conclusion of something

ENDINGS > ENDING

ENDIRON *variant of*
> ANDIRON

ENDIRONS > ENDIRON

ENDITE *variant of*
> INDICT

ENDITED > ENDITE

ENDITES > ENDITE

ENDITING > ENDITE

ENDIVE *n* curly-leaved plant used in salads

ENDIVES > ENDIVE

ENDLANG *variant of*
> ENDLONG

ENDLEAF *n* endpaper in a book

ENDLEAFS > ENDLEAF

ENDLEAVES > ENDLEAF

ENDLESS *adj* having no end

ENDLESSLY > ENDLESS

ENDLONG *adv* lengthways or on end

ENDMOST *adj* nearest the end

ENDNOTE *n* note at the end of a section of writing

ENDNOTES > ENDNOTE

ENDOBLAST *less common name for* > ENDODERM

ENDOCARP *n* inner layer of a fruit

ENDOCARPS
> ENDOCARP

ENDOCAST *n* cast made of the inside of a cranial cavity to show the size and shape of a brain

ENDOCASTS
> ENDOCAST

ENDOCRINE *adj* relating to the glands which secrete hormones directly into the bloodstream ▷ *n* endocrine gland

ENDOCYTIC *adj* involving absorption of cells

ENDODERM *n* inner germ layer of an animal embryo

ENDODERMS
> ENDODERM

ENDODYNE *same as*
> AUTODYNE

ENDOERGIC *adj* (of a nuclear reaction) occurring with absorption of energy

ENDOGAMIC
> ENDOGAMY

ENDOGAMY *n* marriage within one's own tribe or similar unit

ENDOGEN *n* plant that increases in size by internal growth

ENDOGENIC *adj* formed or occurring inside the earth

ENDOGENS > ENDOGEN

ENDOGENY *n* development by internal growth

ENDOLYMPH *n* fluid that fills the membranous labyrinth of the internal ear

ENDOMIXES
> ENDOMIXIS

ENDOMIXIS *n* reorganization of certain nuclei with some protozoa

ENDOMORPH *n* person with a fat and heavy body build: said to be correlated with viscerotonia

ENDOPHAGY *n* cannibalism within the same group or tribe

ENDOPHYTE *n* fungus, or occasionally an alga or other organism, that lives within a plant

ENDOPLASM *n* inner cytoplasm in some cells, esp protozoa, which is more granular and fluid than the outer cytoplasm

ENDOPOD *n* inner branch of a two-branched crustacean

ENDOPODS > ENDOPOD

ENDOPROCT *n* small animal living in water

ENDORPHIN *n* chemical occurring in the brain, which has a similar effect to morphine

ENDORSE *vb* give approval to

ENDORSED > ENDORSE

ENDORSEE *n* person in whose favour a negotiable instrument is endorsed

ENDORSEES
> ENDORSEE

ENDORSER > ENDORSE

ENDORSERS > ENDORSE

ENDORSES > ENDORSE

ENDORSING > ENDORSE

ENDORSIVE > ENDORSE

ENDORSOR > ENDORSE

ENDORSORS > ENDORSE

ENDOSARC *same as*
> ENDOPLASM

ENDOSARCS
> ENDOSARC

ENDOSCOPE *n* long slender medical

instrument used for examining the interior of hollow organs including the lung, stomach, bladder and bowel

ENDOSCOPY
> ENDOSCOPE

ENDOSMOS *same as*
> ENDOSMOSE

ENDOSMOSE *n* osmosis in which water enters a cell or organism from the surrounding solution

ENDOSOME *n* sac within a biological cell

ENDOSOMES
> ENDOSOME

ENDOSPERM *n* tissue within the seed of a flowering plant that surrounds and nourishes the developing embryo

ENDOSPORE *n* small asexual spore produced by some bacteria and algae

ENDOSS *vb* endorse

ENDOSSED > ENDOSS

ENDOSSES > ENDOSS

ENDOSSING > ENDOSS

ENDOSTEA
> ENDOSTEUM

ENDOSTEAL
> ENDOSTEUM

ENDOSTEUM *n* highly vascular membrane lining the marrow cavity of long bones, such as the femur and humerus

ENDOSTYLE *n* groove or fold in the pharynx of various chordates

ENDOTHERM *n* animal with warm blood

ENDOTOXIC
> ENDOTOXIN

ENDOTOXIN *n* toxin contained within the protoplasm of an organism, esp a bacterium, and liberated only at death

ENDOW *vb* provide permanent income for

ENDOWED > ENDOW

ENDOWER > ENDOW

ENDOWERS > ENDOW

ENDOWING > ENDOW

ENDOWMENT *n* money given to an institution, such as a hospital

ENDOWS > ENDOW

ENDOZOA > ENDOZOON

ENDOZOIC *adj* (of a plant) living within an animal

ENDOZOON *variant of*
> ENTOZOON

ENDPAPER *n* either of two leaves pasted to the inside of the cover of a book

ENDPAPERS
> ENDPAPER

ENDPLATE *n* any usually flat platelike structure at the end of something

ENDPLATES
> ENDPLATE

ENDPLAY *n* technique in card games ▷ *vb* force (an opponent) to make a particular lead near the end of a hand

ENDPLAYED > ENDPLAY

ENDPLAYS > ENDPLAY

ENDPOINT *n* point at which anything is complete

ENDPOINTS
> ENDPOINT

ENDRIN *n* type of insecticide

ENDRINS > ENDRIN

ENDS > END

ENDSHIP *n* small village

ENDSHIPS > ENDSHIP

ENDUE *vb* invest or provide, as with some quality or trait

ENDUED > ENDUE

ENDUES > ENDUE

ENDUING > ENDUE

ENDUNGEON *vb* put in a dungeon

ENDURABLE > ENDURE

ENDURABLY > ENDURE

ENDURANCE *n* act or power of enduring

ENDURE *vb* bear (hardship) patiently

ENDURED > ENDURE

ENDURER > ENDURE

ENDURERS > ENDURE

ENDURES > ENDURE

ENDURING *adj* long-lasting

ENDURO *n* long-distance race for vehicles

ENDUROS > ENDURO

ENDWAYS *adv* having the end forwards or upwards ▷ *adj* vertical or upright

ENDWISE *same as*
> ENDWAYS

ENDYSES > ENDYSIS

ENDYSIS *n* formation of new layers of integument after ecdysis

ENDZONE *n* (in American football) area at either end of the playing field

ENDZONES > ENDZONE

ENE *variant of* > EVEN

ENEMA *n* medicine that helps to empty the bowels

ENEMAS > ENEMA

ENEMATA > ENEMA

ENEMIES > ENEMY

ENEMY *n* hostile person or nation, opponent ▷ *adj* of or belonging to an enemy

ENERGETIC *adj* having or showing energy and enthusiasm

ENERGIC > ENERGY

ENERGID *n* nucleus and cytoplasm in a syncytium

ENERGIDS > ENERGID

ENERGIES > ENERGY

ENERGISE *same as*
> ENERGIZE

ENERGISED
> ENERGISE

ENERGISER
> ENERGISE

ENERGISES
> ENERGISE

ENERGIZE *vb* give vigour to

ENERGIZED
> ENERGIZE

ENERGIZER
> ENERGIZE

ENERGIZES
> ENERGIZE

ENERGUMEN *n* person thought to be possessed by an evil spirit

ENERGY *n* capacity for intense activity

ENERVATE *vb* deprive of strength or vitality ▷ *adj* deprived of strength or vitality

ENERVATED
> ENERVATE

ENERVATES
> ENERVATE

ENERVATOR
> ENERVATE

ENERVE *vb* enervate

ENERVED > ENERVE

ENERVES > ENERVE

ENERVING > ENERVE

ENES > ENE

ENEW *vb* force a bird into water

ENEWED > ENEW

ENEWING > ENEW

ENEWS > ENEW

ENFACE *vb* write, print, or stamp (something) on the face of (a document)

ENFACED > ENFACE

ENFACES > ENFACE

ENFACING > ENFACE

ENFANT *n* French child

ENFANTS > ENFANT

ENFEEBLE *vb* weaken

ENFEEBLED
> ENFEEBLE

ENFEEBLER
> ENFEEBLE

ENFEEBLES
> ENFEEBLE

ENFELON *vb* infuriate

ENFELONED > ENFELON

ENFELONS > ENFELON

ENFEOFF *vb* invest (a person) with possession of a freehold estate in land

ENFEOFFED > ENFEOFF

ENFEOFFS > ENFEOFF

ENFESTED *adj* made bitter

ENFETTER *vb* fetter

ENFETTERS
> ENFETTER

ENFEVER *vb* make feverish

ENFEVERED > ENFEVER

ENFEVERS > ENFEVER

ENFIERCE *vb* make ferocious

ENFIERCED
> ENFIERCE

ENFIERCES
> ENFIERCE

ENFILADE *n* burst of gunfire sweeping from end to end along a line of troops ▷ *vb* attack with an enfilade

ENFILADED
> ENFILADE

ENFILADES
> ENFILADE

ENFILED *adj* passed through

ENFIRE *vb* set alight

ENFIRED > ENFIRE

ENFIRES > ENFIRE

ENFIRING > ENFIRE

ENFIX *variant of* > INFIX

ENFIXED > ENFIX

ENFIXES > ENFIX

ENFIXING > ENFIX

ENFLAME *variant of*
> INFLAME

ENFLAMED > ENFLAME

ENFLAMES > ENFLAME

ENFLAMING > ENFLAME

ENFLESH *vb* make flesh

ENFLESHED > ENFLESH

ENFLESHES > ENFLESH

ENFLOWER *vb* put flowers on

ENFLOWERS
> ENFLOWER

ENFOLD *vb* cover by wrapping something around

ENFOLDED > ENFOLD

ENFOLDER > ENFOLD

ENFOLDERS > ENFOLD

ENFOLDING > ENFOLD

ENFOLDS > ENFOLD

ENFORCE *vb* impose obedience (to a law etc)

ENFORCED > ENFORCE

ENFORCER > ENFORCE

ENFORCERS > ENFORCE

ENFORCES > ENFORCE

ENFORCING > ENFORCE

ENFOREST *vb* make into a forest

ENFORESTS
> ENFOREST

ENFORM *variant of*
> INFORM

ENFORMED > ENFORM

ENFORMING > ENFORM

ENFORMS > ENFORM

ENFRAME *vb* put inside a frame

ENFRAMED > ENFRAME

ENFRAMES > ENFRAME

ENFRAMING > ENFRAME

ENFREE *vb* release, make free

ENFREED > ENFREE

ENFREEDOM *variant of*
> ENFREE

ENFREEING > ENFREE

ENFREES > ENFREE

ENFREEZE *vb* freeze

ENFREEZES
> ENFREEZE

ENFROSEN *archaic past participle of* > ENFREEZE

ENFROZE > ENFREEZE

ENFROZEN > ENFREEZE

ENG *another name for*
> AGMA

ENGAGE *vb* take part, participate ▷ *adj* (of an artist) morally or politically committed to some ideology

ENGAGED *adj* pledged to be married

ENGAGEDLY > ENGAGED

ENGAGEE *adj* (of a female artist) morally or politically committed to some ideology
ENGAGER > ENGAGE
ENGAGERS > ENGAGE
ENGAGES > ENGAGE
ENGAGING *adj* charming
ENGAOL *vb* put into gaol
ENGAOLED > ENGAOL
ENGAOLING > ENGAOL
ENGAOLS > ENGAOL
ENGARLAND *vb* cover with garlands
ENGENDER *vb* produce, cause to occur
ENGENDERS > ENGENDER
ENGENDURE > ENGENDER
ENGILD *vb* cover with or as if with gold
ENGILDED > ENGILD
ENGILDING > ENGILD
ENGILDS > ENGILD
ENGILT > ENGILD
ENGINE *n* any machine which converts energy into mechanical work ▷ *vb* put an engine in
ENGINED > ENGINE
ENGINEER *n* person trained in any branch of engineering ▷ *vb* plan in a clever manner
ENGINEERS > ENGINEER
ENGINER > ENGINE
ENGINERS > ENGINE
ENGINERY *n* collection or assembly of engines
ENGINES > ENGINE
ENGINING > ENGINE
ENGINOUS *adj* ingenious or clever
ENGIRD *vb* surround
ENGIRDED > ENGIRD
ENGIRDING > ENGIRD
ENGIRDLE *variant of* > ENGIRD
ENGIRDLED > ENGIRDLE
ENGIRDLES > ENGIRDLE
ENGIRDS > ENGIRD
ENGIRT > ENGIRD
ENGLACIAL *adj* embedded in, carried by, or running through a glacier
ENGLISH *vb* put spin on a billiard ball
ENGLISHED > ENGLISH
ENGLISHES > ENGLISH
ENGLOBE *vb* surround as if in a globe
ENGLOBED > ENGLOBE
ENGLOBES > ENGLOBE
ENGLOBING > ENGLOBE
ENGLOOM *vb* make dull or dismal
ENGLOOMED > ENGLOOM
ENGLOOMS > ENGLOOM
ENGLUT *vb* devour ravenously
ENGLUTS > ENGLUT
ENGLUTTED > ENGLUT
ENGOBE *n* liquid put on pottery before glazing

ENGOBES > ENGOBE
ENGORE *vb* pierce or wound
ENGORED > ENGORE
ENGORES > ENGORE
ENGORGE *vb* clog with blood
ENGORGED > ENGORGE
ENGORGES > ENGORGE
ENGORGING > ENGORGE
ENGORING > ENGORE
ENGOULED *adj* (in heraldry) with ends coming from the mouths of animals
ENGOUMENT *n* obsessive liking
ENGRACE *vb* give grace to
ENGRACED > ENGRACE
ENGRACES > ENGRACE
ENGRACING > ENGRACE
ENGRAFF *variant of* > ENGRAFT
ENGRAFFED > ENGRAFF
ENGRAFFS > ENGRAFF
ENGRAFT *vb* graft (a shoot, bud, etc) onto a stock
ENGRAFTED > ENGRAFT
ENGRAFTS > ENGRAFT
ENGRAIL *vb* decorate or mark with small carved notches
ENGRAILED > ENGRAIL
ENGRAILS > ENGRAIL
ENGRAIN *variant spelling of* > INGRAIN
ENGRAINED > ENGRAIN
ENGRAINER > ENGRAIN
ENGRAINS > ENGRAIN
ENGRAM *n* physical basis of an individual memory in the brain
ENGRAMMA *variant of* > ENGRAM
ENGRAMMAS > ENGRAMMA
ENGRAMME *variant of* > ENGRAM
ENGRAMMES > ENGRAMME
ENGRAMMIC > ENGRAM
ENGRAMS > ENGRAM
ENGRASP *vb* grasp or seize
ENGRASPED > ENGRASP
ENGRASPS > ENGRASP
ENGRAVE *vb* carve (a design) onto a hard surface
ENGRAVED > ENGRAVE
ENGRAVEN > ENGRAVE
ENGRAVER > ENGRAVE
ENGRAVERS > ENGRAVE
ENGRAVERY > ENGRAVE
ENGRAVES > ENGRAVE
ENGRAVING *n* print made from an engraved plate
ENGRENAGE *n* act of putting into gear
ENGRIEVE *vb* grieve
ENGRIEVED > ENGRIEVE
ENGRIEVES > ENGRIEVE
ENGROOVE *vb* put a groove in

ENGROOVED > ENGROOVE
ENGROOVES > ENGROOVE
ENGROSS *vb* occupy the attention of (a person) completely
ENGROSSED > ENGROSS
ENGROSSER > ENGROSS
ENGROSSES > ENGROSS
ENGS > ENG
ENGUARD *vb* protect or defend
ENGUARDED > ENGUARD
ENGUARDS > ENGUARD
ENGULF *vb* cover or surround completely
ENGULFED > ENGULF
ENGULFING > ENGULF
ENGULFS > ENGULF
ENGULPH *variant of* > ENGULF
ENGULPHED > ENGULPH
ENGULPHS > ENGULPH
ENGYSCOPE *n* microscope
ENHALO *vb* surround with or as if with a halo
ENHALOED > ENHALO
ENHALOES > ENHALO
ENHALOING > ENHALO
ENHALOS > ENHALO
ENHANCE *vb* increase in quality, value, or attractiveness
ENHANCED > ENHANCE
ENHANCER > ENHANCE
ENHANCERS > ENHANCE
ENHANCES > ENHANCE
ENHANCING > ENHANCE
ENHANCIVE > ENHANCE
ENHEARSE *variant of* > INHEARSE
ENHEARSED > ENHEARSE
ENHEARSES > ENHEARSE
ENHEARTEN *vb* give heart to, encourage
ENHUNGER *vb* cause to be hungry
ENHUNGERS > ENHUNGER
ENHYDRITE *n* type of mineral
ENHYDROS *n* piece of chalcedony that contains water
ENHYDROUS > ENHYDROS
ENIAC *n* early type of computer built in the 1940s
ENIACS > ENIAC
ENIGMA *n* puzzling thing or person
ENIGMAS > ENIGMA
ENIGMATA > ENIGMA
ENIGMATIC > ENIGMA
ENISLE *vb* put on or make into an island
ENISLED > ENISLE
ENISLES > ENISLE
ENISLING > ENISLE
ENJAMB *vb* (of a line of verse) run over into the next line
ENJAMBED > ENJAMB

ENJAMBING > ENJAMB
ENJAMBS > ENJAMB
ENJOIN *vb* order (someone) to do something
ENJOINDER *n* order
ENJOINED > ENJOIN
ENJOINER > ENJOIN
ENJOINERS > ENJOIN
ENJOINING > ENJOIN
ENJOINS > ENJOIN
ENJOY *vb* take joy in
ENJOYABLE > ENJOY
ENJOYABLY > ENJOY
ENJOYED > ENJOY
ENJOYER > ENJOY
ENJOYERS > ENJOY
ENJOYING > ENJOY
ENJOYMENT *n* act or condition of receiving pleasure from something
ENJOYS > ENJOY
ENKERNEL *vb* put inside a kernel
ENKERNELS > ENKERNEL
ENKINDLE *vb* set on fire
ENKINDLED > ENKINDLE
ENKINDLER > ENKINDLE
ENKINDLES > ENKINDLE
ENLACE *vb* bind or encircle with or as with laces
ENLACED > ENLACE
ENLACES > ENLACE
ENLACING > ENLACE
ENLARD *vb* put lard on
ENLARDED > ENLARD
ENLARDING > ENLARD
ENLARDS > ENLARD
ENLARGE *vb* make or grow larger
ENLARGED > ENLARGE
ENLARGEN *variant of* > ENLARGE
ENLARGENS > ENLARGEN
ENLARGER *n* optical instrument for making enlarged photographs
ENLARGERS > ENLARGER
ENLARGES > ENLARGE
ENLARGING > ENLARGE
ENLEVE *adj* having been abducted
ENLIGHT *vb* light up
ENLIGHTED > ENLIGHT
ENLIGHTEN *vb* give information to
ENLIGHTS > ENLIGHT
ENLINK *vb* link together
ENLINKED > ENLINK
ENLINKING > ENLINK
ENLINKS > ENLINK
ENLIST *vb* enter the armed forces
ENLISTED > ENLIST
ENLISTEE > ENLIST
ENLISTEES > ENLIST
ENLISTER > ENLIST
ENLISTERS > ENLIST
ENLISTING > ENLIST
ENLISTS > ENLIST

e

ENLIT > ENLIGHT
ENLIVEN vb make lively or cheerful
ENLIVENED > ENLIVEN
ENLIVENER > ENLIVEN
ENLIVENS > ENLIVEN
ENLOCK vb lock or secure
ENLOCKED > ENLOCK
ENLOCKING > ENLOCK
ENLOCKS > ENLOCK
ENLUMINE vb illuminate
**ENLUMINED
> ENLUMINE**
**ENLUMINES
> ENLUMINE**
ENMESH vb catch or involve in or as if in a net or snare
ENMESHED > ENMESH
ENMESHES > ENMESH
ENMESHING > ENMESH
ENMEW variant of **> EMMEW**
ENMEWED > ENMEW
ENMEWING > ENMEW
ENMEWS > ENMEW
ENMITIES > ENMITY
ENMITY n ill will, hatred
ENMOSSED adj having a covering of moss
ENMOVE variant of **> EMMOVE**
ENMOVED > ENMOVE
ENMOVES > ENMOVE
ENMOVING > ENMOVE
ENNAGE n number of ens in printed matter
ENNAGES > ENNAGE
ENNEAD n group or series of nine
ENNEADIC > ENNEAD
ENNEADS > ENNEAD
ENNEAGON another name for **>** NONAGON
**ENNEAGONS
> ENNEAGON**
ENNEAGRAM n personality system involving nine distinct but interconnected personality types
ENNOBLE vb make noble, elevate
ENNOBLED > ENNOBLE
ENNOBLER > ENNOBLE
ENNOBLERS > ENNOBLE
ENNOBLES > ENNOBLE
ENNOBLING > ENNOBLE
ENNOG n back alley
ENNOGS > ENNOG
ENNUI n boredom, dissatisfaction ▷ vb bore
ENNUIED > ENNUI
ENNUIS > ENNUI
ENNUYE adj bored
ENNUYED > ENNUI
ENNUYEE same as **> ENNUYE**
ENNUYING > ENNUI
ENODAL adj having no nodes
ENOKI variant of **> ENOKITAKE**
ENOKIDAKE variant of **> ENOKITAKE**
ENOKIS > ENOKI
ENOKITAKE n Japanese mushroom

ENOL n type of organic compound
ENOLASE n type of enzyme
ENOLASES > ENOLASE
ENOLIC > ENOL
ENOLOGIES > ENOLOGY
ENOLOGIST n wine expert
ENOLOGY usual US spelling of **>** OENOLOGY
ENOLS > ENOL
ENOMOTIES > ENOMOTY
ENOMOTY n division of the Spartan army in ancient Greece
ENOPHILE n lover of wine
**ENOPHILES
> ENOPHILE**
ENORM variant of **> ENORMOUS**
ENORMITY n great wickedness
ENORMOUS adj very big, vast
ENOSES > ENOSIS
ENOSIS n union of Greece and Cyprus
ENOSISES > ENOSIS
ENOUGH adj as much or as many as necessary ▷ n sufficient quantity ▷ adv sufficiently
ENOUGHS > ENOUGH
ENOUNCE vb enunciate
ENOUNCED > ENOUNCE
ENOUNCES > ENOUNCE
ENOUNCING > ENOUNCE
ENOW archaic word for **> ENOUGH**
ENOWS > ENOW
ENPLANE vb board an aircraft
ENPLANED > ENPLANE
ENPLANES > ENPLANE
ENPLANING > ENPLANE
ENPRINT n standard photographic print
ENPRINTS > ENPRINT
ENQUEUE vb add (an item) to a queue of computing tasks
ENQUEUED > ENQUEUE
ENQUEUES > ENQUEUE
ENQUEUING > ENQUEUE
ENQUIRE same as **> INQUIRE**
ENQUIRED > ENQUIRE
ENQUIRER > ENQUIRE
ENQUIRERS > ENQUIRE
ENQUIRES > ENQUIRE
ENQUIRIES > ENQUIRE
ENQUIRING > ENQUIRE
ENQUIRY > ENQUIRE
ENRACE vb archaic word meaning to bring into a race (of people)
ENRACED > ENRACE
ENRACES > ENRACE
ENRACING > ENRACE
ENRAGE vb make extremely angry
ENRAGED > ENRAGE
ENRAGEDLY > ENRAGE
ENRAGES > ENRAGE
ENRAGING > ENRAGE
ENRANCKLE vb upset, make irate

ENRANGE vb arrange, organize
ENRANGED > ENRANGE
ENRANGES > ENRANGE
ENRANGING > ENRANGE
ENRANK vb put in a row
ENRANKED > ENRANK
ENRANKING > ENRANK
ENRANKS > ENRANK
ENRAPT > ENRAPTURE
ENRAPTURE vb fill with delight
ENRAUNGE archaic variant of **>** ENRANGE
**ENRAUNGED
> ENRAUNGE**
**ENRAUNGES
> ENRAUNGE**
ENRAVISH vb enchant
ENRHEUM vb pass a cold on to
ENRHEUMED > ENRHEUM
ENRHEUMS > ENRHEUM
ENRICH vb improve in quality
ENRICHED > ENRICH
ENRICHER > ENRICH
ENRICHERS > ENRICH
ENRICHES > ENRICH
ENRICHING > ENRICH
ENRIDGED adj ridged
ENRING vb put a ring round
ENRINGED > ENRING
ENRINGING > ENRING
ENRINGS > ENRING
ENRIVEN adj ripped
ENROBE vb dress in or as if in a robe
ENROBED > ENROBE
ENROBER > ENROBE
ENROBERS > ENROBE
ENROBES > ENROBE
ENROBING > ENROBE
ENROL vb (cause to) become a member
ENROLL same as **>** ENROL
ENROLLED > ENROLL
ENROLLEE > ENROL
ENROLLEES > ENROL
ENROLLER > ENROL
ENROLLERS > ENROL
ENROLLING > ENROLL
ENROLLS > ENROLL
ENROLMENT n act of enrolling or state of being enrolled
ENROLS > ENROL
ENROOT vb establish (plants) by fixing their roots in the earth
ENROOTED > ENROOT
ENROOTING > ENROOT
ENROOTS > ENROOT
ENROUGH vb roughen
ENROUGHED > ENROUGH
ENROUGHS > ENROUGH
ENROUND vb encircle
ENROUNDED > ENROUND
ENROUNDS > ENROUND
ENS n entity
ENSAMPLE n example ▷ vb make an example
**ENSAMPLED
> ENSAMPLE**
**ENSAMPLES
> ENSAMPLE**

ENSATE adj shaped like a sword
ENSCONCE vb settle firmly or comfortably
**ENSCONCED
> ENSCONCE**
**ENSCONCES
> ENSCONCE**
ENSCROLL variant of **> INSCROLL**
**ENSCROLLS
> INSCROLL**
ENSEAL vb seal up
ENSEALED > ENSEAL
ENSEALING > ENSEAL
ENSEALS > ENSEAL
ENSEAM vb put a seam on
ENSEAMED > ENSEAM
ENSEAMING > ENSEAM
ENSEAMS > ENSEAM
ENSEAR vb dry
ENSEARED > ENSEAR
ENSEARING > ENSEAR
ENSEARS > ENSEAR
ENSEMBLE n all the parts of something taken together ▷ adv all together or at once ▷ adj (of a film or play) involving several separate but often interrelated story lines
**ENSEMBLES
> ENSEMBLE**
ENSERF vb enslave
ENSERFED > ENSERF
ENSERFING > ENSERF
ENSERFS > ENSERF
ENSEW variant of **>** ENSUE
ENSEWED > ENSEW
ENSEWING > ENSEW
ENSEWS > ENSEW
ENSHEATH variant of **> INSHEATHE**
ENSHEATHE variant of **> INSHEATHE**
**ENSHEATHS
> ENSHEATH**
ENSHELL variant of **> INSHELL**
ENSHELLED > ENSHELL
ENSHELLS > ENSHELL
ENSHELTER vb shelter
ENSHIELD vb protect
**ENSHIELDS
> ENSHIELD**
ENSHRINE vb cherish or treasure
**ENSHRINED
> ENSHRINE**
**ENSHRINEE
> ENSHRINE**
**ENSHRINES
> ENSHRINE**
ENSHROUD vb cover or hide as with a shroud
**ENSHROUDS
> ENSHROUD**
ENSIFORM adj shaped like a sword blade
ENSIGN n military officer ▷ vb mark with a sign
ENSIGNCY > ENSIGN
ENSIGNED > ENSIGN
ENSIGNING > ENSIGN
ENSIGNS > ENSIGN
ENSILAGE n process of ensiling green fodder ▷ vb make into silage

ENSILAGED
> ENSILAGE
ENSILAGES
> ENSILAGE
ENSILE vb store and preserve (green fodder) in an enclosed pit or silo
ENSILED > ENSILE
ENSILES > ENSILE
ENSILING > ENSILE
ENSKIED > ENSKY
ENSKIES > ENSKY
ENSKY vb put in the sky
ENSKYED > ENSKY
ENSKYING > ENSKY
ENSLAVE vb make a slave of (someone)
ENSLAVED > ENSLAVE
ENSLAVER > ENSLAVE
ENSLAVERS > ENSLAVE
ENSLAVES > ENSLAVE
ENSLAVING > ENSLAVE
ENSNARE vb catch in or as if in a snare
ENSNARED > ENSNARE
ENSNARER > ENSNARE
ENSNARERS > ENSNARE
ENSNARES > ENSNARE
ENSNARING > ENSNARE
ENSNARL vb catch in or as if in a snarl
ENSNARLED > ENSNARL
ENSNARLS > ENSNARL
ENSORCEL vb enchant
ENSORCELL variant of
> ENSORCEL
ENSORCELS
> ENSORCEL
ENSOUL vb endow with a soul
ENSOULED > ENSOUL
ENSOULING > ENSOUL
ENSOULS > ENSOUL
ENSPHERE vb enclose in or as if in a sphere
ENSPHERED
> ENSPHERE
ENSPHERES
> ENSPHERE
ENSTAMP vb imprint with a stamp
ENSTAMPED > ENSTAMP
ENSTAMPS > ENSTAMP
ENSTATITE n grey, green, yellow, or brown pyroxene mineral consisting of magnesium silicate in orthorhombic crystalline form
ENSTEEP vb soak in water
ENSTEEPED > ENSTEEP
ENSTEEPS > ENSTEEP
ENSTYLE vb give a name to
ENSTYLED > ENSTYLE
ENSTYLES > ENSTYLE
ENSTYLING > ENSTYLE
ENSUE vb come next, result
ENSUED > ENSUE
ENSUES > ENSUE
ENSUING adj following subsequently or in order
ENSUITE n bathroom attached to another room
ENSUITES > ENSUITE

ENSURE vb make certain or sure
ENSURED > ENSURE
ENSURER > ENSURE
ENSURERS > ENSURE
ENSURES > ENSURE
ENSURING > ENSURE
ENSWATHE vb bind or wrap
ENSWATHED
> ENSWATHE
ENSWATHES
> ENSWATHE
ENSWEEP vb sweep across
ENSWEEPS > ENSWEEP
ENSWEPT > ENSWEEP
ENTAIL vb bring about or impose inevitably ▷ n restriction imposed by entailing an estate
ENTAILED > ENTAIL
ENTAILER > ENTAIL
ENTAILERS > ENTAIL
ENTAILING > ENTAIL
ENTAILS > ENTAIL
ENTAME vb make tame
ENTAMEBA same as
> ENTAMOEBA
ENTAMEBAE
> ENTAMEBA
ENTAMEBAS
> ENTAMEBA
ENTAMED > ENTAME
ENTAMES > ENTAME
ENTAMING > ENTAME
ENTAMOEBA n parasitic amoeba that lives in the intestines of humans and causes amoebic dysentery
ENTANGLE vb catch or involve in or as if in a tangle
ENTANGLED
> ENTANGLE
ENTANGLER
> ENTANGLE
ENTANGLES
> ENTANGLE
ENTASES > ENTASIS
ENTASIA same as
> ENTASIS
ENTASIAS > ENTASIA
ENTASIS n slightly convex curve given to the shaft of a structure
ENTASTIC adj (of a disease) characterized by spasms
ENTAYLE variant of
> ENTAIL
ENTAYLED > ENTAYLE
ENTAYLES > ENTAYLE
ENTAYLING > ENTAYLE
ENTELECHY n (in the philosophy of Aristotle) actuality as opposed to potentiality
ENTELLUS n langur of S Asia
ENTENDER vb make more tender
ENTENDERS
> ENTENDER
ENTENTE n friendly understanding between nations
ENTENTES > ENTENTE

ENTER vb come or go in
ENTERA > ENTERON
ENTERABLE > ENTER
ENTERAL same as
> ENTERIC
ENTERALLY > ENTERIC
ENTERATE adj with an intestine separate from the outer wall of the body
ENTERED > ENTER
ENTERER > ENTER
ENTERERS > ENTER
ENTERIC adj intestinal ▷ n infectious disease of the intestines
ENTERICS > ENTERIC
ENTERING > ENTER
ENTERINGS > ENTER
ENTERITIS n inflammation of the intestine
ENTERON n alimentary canal
ENTERONS > ENTERON
ENTERS > ENTER
ENTERTAIN vb amuse
ENTERTAKE vb entertain
ENTERTOOK
> ENTERTAKE
ENTETE adj obsessed
ENTETEE variant of
> ENTETE
ENTHALPY n property of a thermodynamic system
ENTHETIC adj (esp of infectious diseases) introduced into the body from without
ENTHRAL vb hold the attention of
ENTHRALL same as
> ENTHRAL
ENTHRALLS
> ENTHRALL
ENTHRALS > ENTHRAL
ENTHRONE vb place (someone) on a throne
ENTHRONED
> ENTHRONE
ENTHRONES
> ENTHRONE
ENTHUSE vb (cause to) show enthusiasm
ENTHUSED > ENTHUSE
ENTHUSES > ENTHUSE
ENTHUSING > ENTHUSE
ENTHYMEME n incomplete syllogism, in which one or more premises are unexpressed as their truth is considered to be self-evident
ENTIA > ENS
ENTICE vb attract by exciting hope or desire, tempt
ENTICED > ENTICE
ENTICER > ENTICE
ENTICERS > ENTICE
ENTICES > ENTICE
ENTICING > ENTICE
ENTICINGS > ENTICE
ENTIRE adj including every detail, part, or aspect of something ▷ n state of being entire
ENTIRELY adv without reservation or exception

ENTIRES > ENTIRE
ENTIRETY n state of being entire or whole
ENTITIES > ENTITY
ENTITLE vb give a right to
ENTITLED > ENTITLE
ENTITLES > ENTITLE
ENTITLING > ENTITLE
ENTITY n separate distinct thing
ENTOBLAST less common name for > ENDODERM
ENTODERM same as
> ENDODERM
ENTODERMS
> ENTODERM
ENTOIL archaic word for
> ENSNARE
ENTOILED > ENTOIL
ENTOILING > ENTOIL
ENTOILS > ENTOIL
ENTOMB vb place (a corpse) in a tomb
ENTOMBED > ENTOMB
ENTOMBING > ENTOMB
ENTOMBS > ENTOMB
ENTOMIC adj denoting or relating to insects
ENTOPHYTE variant of
> ENDOPHYTE
ENTOPIC adj situated in its normal place or position
ENTOPROCT n type of marine animal
ENTOPTIC adj (of visual sensation) resulting from structures within the eye itself
ENTOPTICS n study of entoptic visions
ENTOTIC adj of or relating to the inner ear
ENTOURAGE n group of people who assist an important person
ENTOZOA > ENTOZOON
ENTOZOAL > ENTOZOON
ENTOZOAN same as
> ENTOZOON
ENTOZOANS
> ENTOZOON
ENTOZOIC adj of or relating to an entozoon
ENTOZOON n internal parasite
ENTRAIL vb twist or entangle
ENTRAILED > ENTRAIL
ENTRAILS pl n intestines
ENTRAIN vb board or put aboard a train
ENTRAINED > ENTRAIN
ENTRAINER > ENTRAIN
ENTRAINS > ENTRAIN
ENTRALL old variant of
> ENTRAILS
ENTRALLES old variant of
> ENTRAILS
ENTRAMMEL vb hamper or obstruct by entangling
ENTRANCE n way into a place ▷ vb delight ▷ adj necessary in order to enter something
ENTRANCED
> ENTRANCE

e

ENTRANCES
> ENTRANCE
ENTRANT n person who enters a university, contest, etc
ENTRANTS > ENTRANT
ENTRAP vb trick into difficulty etc
ENTRAPPED > ENTRAP
ENTRAPPER > ENTRAP
ENTRAPS > ENTRAP
ENTREAT vb ask earnestly
ENTREATED > ENTREAT
ENTREATS > ENTREAT
ENTREATY n earnest request
ENTRECHAT n leap in ballet during which the dancer repeatedly crosses their feet or beats them together
ENTRECOTE n beefsteak cut from between the ribs
ENTREE n dish served before a main course
ENTREES > ENTREE
ENTREMES variant of > ENTREMETS
ENTREMETS n dessert
ENTRENCH vb establish firmly
ENTREPOT n warehouse for commercial goods
ENTREPOTS
> ENTREPOT
ENTRESOL another name for > MEZZANINE
ENTRESOLS
> ENTRESOL
ENTREZ interj enter
ENTRIES > ENTRY
ENTRISM variant of > ENTRYISM
ENTRISMS > ENTRISM
ENTRIST > ENTRISM
ENTRISTS > ENTRIST
ENTROLD adj word used by Spenser meaning surrounded
ENTROPIC > ENTROPY
ENTROPIES > ENTROPY
ENTROPION n turning inwards of the edge of the eyelid
ENTROPIUM variant of > ENTROPION
ENTROPY n lack of organization
ENTRUST vb put into the care or protection of
ENTRUSTED > ENTRUST
ENTRUSTS > ENTRUST
ENTRY n entrance ▷ adj necessary in order to enter something
ENTRYISM n joining a political party to change its principles
ENTRYISMS
> ENTRYISM
ENTRYIST > ENTRYISM
ENTRYISTS
> ENTRYISM
ENTRYWAY n entrance passage
ENTRYWAYS
> ENTRYWAY

ENTS pl n (college) entertainments
ENTWINE vb twist together around
ENTWINED > ENTWINE
ENTWINES > ENTWINE
ENTWINING > ENTWINE
ENTWIST vb twist together or around
ENTWISTED > ENTWIST
ENTWISTS > ENTWIST
ENUCLEATE vb remove the nucleus from (a cell) ▷ adj (of cells) deprived of their nuclei
ENUF common intentional literary misspelling of > ENOUGH
ENUMERATE vb name one by one
ENUNCIATE vb pronounce clearly
ENURE variant spelling of > INURE
ENURED > ENURE
ENUREMENT > ENURE
ENURES > ENURE
ENURESES > ENURESIS
ENURESIS n involuntary discharge of urine, esp during sleep
ENURETIC > ENURESIS
ENURETICS
> ENURESIS
ENURING > ENURE
ENURN same as > INURN
ENURNED same as > INURNED
ENURNING same as > INURNING
ENURNS same as > INURNS
ENVASSAL vb make a vassal of
ENVASSALS
> ENVASSAL
ENVAULT vb enclose in a vault; entomb
ENVAULTED > ENVAULT
ENVAULTS > ENVAULT
ENVEIGLE same as > INVEIGLE
ENVEIGLED
> ENVEIGLE
ENVEIGLES
> ENVEIGLE
ENVELOP vb wrap up, enclose
ENVELOPE n folded gummed paper cover for a letter
ENVELOPED > ENVELOP
ENVELOPER > ENVELOP
ENVELOPES
> ENVELOPE
ENVELOPS > ENVELOP
ENVENOM vb fill or impregnate with venom
ENVENOMED > ENVENOM
ENVENOMS > ENVENOM
ENVERMEIL vb dye vermilion
ENVIABLE adj arousing envy, fortunate
ENVIABLY > ENVIABLE
ENVIED > ENVY
ENVIER > ENVY
ENVIERS > ENVY

ENVIES > ENVY
ENVIOUS adj full of envy
ENVIOUSLY > ENVIOUS
ENVIRO n environmentalist
ENVIRON vb encircle or surround
ENVIRONED > ENVIRON
ENVIRONS pl n surrounding area, esp of a town
ENVIROS > ENVIRO
ENVISAGE vb conceive of as a possibility
ENVISAGED
> ENVISAGE
ENVISAGES
> ENVISAGE
ENVISION vb conceive of as a possibility, esp in the future
ENVISIONS
> ENVISION
ENVOI same as > ENVOY
ENVOIS > ENVOI
ENVOY n messenger
ENVOYS > ENVOY
ENVOYSHIP > ENVOY
ENVY n feeling of discontent aroused by another's good fortune ▷ vb grudge (another's good fortune, success, or qualities)
ENVYING > ENVY
ENVYINGLY > ENVY
ENVYINGS > ENVY
ENWALL vb wall in
ENWALLED > ENWALL
ENWALLING > ENWALL
ENWALLOW vb sink or plunge
ENWALLOWS
> ENWALLOW
ENWALLS > ENWALL
ENWHEEL archaic word for > ENCIRCLE
ENWHEELED > ENWHEEL
ENWHEELS > ENWHEEL
ENWIND vb wind or coil around
ENWINDING > ENWIND
ENWINDS > ENWIND
ENWOMB vb enclose in or as if in a womb
ENWOMBED > ENWOMB
ENWOMBING > ENWOMB
ENWOMBS > ENWOMB
ENWOUND > ENWIND
ENWRAP vb wrap or cover up
ENWRAPPED > ENWRAP
ENWRAPS > ENWRAP
ENWRAPT > ENWRAP
ENWREATH vb surround or encircle with or as with a wreath or wreaths
ENWREATHE same as > ENWREATH
ENWREATHS
> ENWREATH
ENZIAN n gentian violet
ENZIANS > ENZIAN
ENZONE vb enclose in a zone
ENZONED > ENZONE
ENZONES > ENZONE
ENZONING > ENZONE

ENZOOTIC adj (of diseases) affecting animals within a limited region ▷ n enzootic disease
ENZOOTICS
> ENZOOTIC
ENZYM same as > ENZYME
ENZYMATIC same as > ENZYME
ENZYME n complex protein that acts as a catalyst
ENZYMES > ENZYME
ENZYMIC > ENZYME
ENZYMS > ENZYM
EOAN adj of or relating to the dawn
EOBIONT n hypothetical chemical precursor of a living cell
EOBIONTS > EOBIONT
EOCENE adj of, denoting, or formed in the second epoch of the Tertiary period
EOHIPPUS n extinct dog-sized ancestor of the horse
EOLIAN adj of or relating to the wind
EOLIENNE n type of fine cloth
EOLIENNES
> EOLIENNE
EOLIPILE variant of > AEOLIPILE
EOLIPILES
> EOLIPILE
EOLITH n stone used as a primitive tool in Eolithic times
EOLITHIC > EOLITH
EOLITHS > EOLITH
EOLOPILE variant of > AEOLIPILE
EOLOPILES
> EOLOPILE
EON n immeasurably long period of time
EONIAN adj everlasting
EONISM n adoption of female dress and behaviour by a male
EONISMS > EONISM
EONS > EON
EORL n Anglo-Saxon nobleman
EORLS > EORL
EOSIN n red crystalline water-insoluble derivative of fluorescein
EOSINE same as > EOSIN
EOSINES > EOSINE
EOSINIC > EOSIN
EOSINS > EOSIN
EOTHEN adv from the East
EPACRID n type of heath-like plant
EPACRIDS > EPACRID
EPACRIS n genus of the epacrids
EPACRISES > EPACRIS
EPACT n difference in time between the solar year and the lunar year
EPACTS > EPACT
EPAENETIC adj eulogistic

EPAGOGE *n* inductive reasoning

EPAGOGES > EPAGOGE

EPAGOGIC > EPAGOGE

EPANODOS *n* return to main theme after a digression

EPARCH *n* bishop or metropolitan in charge of an eparchy

EPARCHATE *same as* > EPARCHY

EPARCHIAL > EPARCHY

EPARCHIES > EPARCHY

EPARCHS > EPARCH

EPARCHY *n* diocese of the Eastern Christian Church

EPATANT *adj* startling or shocking

EPATER *vb* startle or shock

EPATERED > EPATER

EPATERING > EPATER

EPATERS > EPATER

EPAULE *n* shoulder of a fortification

EPAULES > EPAULE

EPAULET *same as* > EPAULETTE

EPAULETED *adj* wearing an epaulet

EPAULETS > EPAULET

EPAULETTE *n* shoulder ornament on a uniform

EPAXIAL *adj* above the axis

EPAZOTE *n* type of herb

EPAZOTES > EPAZOTE

EPEDAPHIC *adj* of or relating to atmospheric conditions

EPEE *n* straight-bladed sword used in fencing

EPEEIST *n* one who uses or specializes in using an epee

EPEEISTS > EPEEIST

EPEES > EPEE

EPEIRA *same as* > EPEIRID

EPEIRAS > EPEIRA

EPEIRIC *adj* in, of, or relating to a continent

EPEIRID *n* type of spider

EPEIRIDS > EPEIRID

EPENDYMA *n* membrane lining the ventricles of the brain and the central canal of the spinal cord

EPENDYMAL > EPENDYMA

EPENDYMAS > EPENDYMA

EPEOLATRY *n* worship of words

EPERDU *adj* distracted

EPERDUE *adj* distracted

EPERGNE *n* ornamental centrepiece for a table

EPERGNES > EPERGNE

EPHA *same as* > EPHAH

EPHAH *n* Hebrew unit of dry measure

EPHAHS > EPHAH

EPHAS > EPHA

EPHEBE *n* (in ancient Greece) youth about to enter full citizenship

EPHEBES > EPHEBE

EPHEBI > EPHEBUS

EPHEBIC > EPHEBE

EPHEBOI > EPHEBOS

EPHEBOS *same as* > EPHEBE

EPHEBUS *same as* > EPHEBE

EPHEDRA *n* gymnosperm shrub

EPHEDRAS > EPHEDRA

EPHEDRIN *same as* > EPHEDRINE

EPHEDRINE *n* alkaloid used for treatment of asthma and hay fever

EPHEDRINS > EPHEDRIN

EPHELIDES > EPHELIS

EPHELIS *n* freckle

EPHEMERA *n* something transitory or short-lived

EPHEMERAE > EPHEMERA

EPHEMERAL *adj* short-lived ▷ *n* short-lived organism, such as the mayfly

EPHEMERAS > EPHEMERA

EPHEMERID *n* mayfly

EPHEMERIS *n* table giving the future positions of a planet, comet, or satellite

EPHEMERON *n* an insect that lives for only one day; anything short-lived

EPHIALTES *n* incubus

EPHOD *n* embroidered vestment worn by priests

EPHODS > EPHOD

EPHOR *n* one of a board of senior magistrates in several ancient Greek states

EPHORAL > EPHOR

EPHORALTY > EPHOR

EPHORATE > EPHOR

EPHORATES > EPHOR

EPHORI > EPHOR

EPHORS > EPHOR

EPIBIOSES > EPIBIOSIS

EPIBIOSIS *n* any relationship between two organisms in which one grows on the other but is not parasitic on it

EPIBIOTIC > EPIBIOSIS

EPIBLAST *n* outermost layer of an embryo, which becomes the ectoderm at gastrulation

EPIBLASTS > EPIBLAST

EPIBLEM *n* outermost cell layer of a root

EPIBLEMS > EPIBLEM

EPIBOLIC > EPIBOLY

EPIBOLIES > EPIBOLY

EPIBOLY *n* process that occurs during gastrulation in vertebrates

EPIC *n* long poem, book, or film about heroic events or actions ▷ *adj* very impressive or ambitious

EPICAL > EPIC

EPICALLY > EPIC

EPICALYX *n* small sepal-like bracts in some flowers

EPICANTHI *n* folds of skin extending vertically over the inner angles of the eyes

EPICARDIA *n* layers of pericardia in direct contact with the heart

EPICARP *n* outermost layer of the pericarp of fruits

EPICARPS > EPICARP

EPICEDE *same as* > EPICEDIUM

EPICEDES > EPICEDE

EPICEDIA > EPICEDIUM

EPICEDIAL > EPICEDIUM

EPICEDIAN > EPICEDIUM

EPICEDIUM *n* funeral ode

EPICENE *adj* having the characteristics of both sexes; hermaphroditic ▷ *n* epicene person or creature

EPICENES > EPICENE

EPICENISM > EPICENE

EPICENTER *same as* > EPICENTRE

EPICENTRA *n* epicentres

EPICENTRE *n* point on the earth's surface immediately above the origin of an earthquake

EPICIER *n* grocer

EPICIERS > EPICIER

EPICISM *n* style or trope characteristic of epics

EPICISMS > EPICISM

EPICIST *n* writer of epics

EPICISTS > EPICIST

EPICLESES > EPICLESIS

EPICLESIS *n* invocation of the Holy Spirit to consecrate the bread and wine of the Eucharist

EPICLIKE *adj* resembling or reminiscent of an epic

EPICORMIC *adj* (of a tree shoot or branch) growing from a dormant bud below the bark

EPICOTYL *n* part of an embryo plant stem above the cotyledons but beneath the terminal bud

EPICOTYLS > EPICOTYL

EPICRANIA *n* tissue covering the cranium

EPICRISES > EPICRISIS

EPICRISIS *n* secondary crisis occurring in the course of a disease

EPICRITIC *adj* (of certain nerve fibres of the skin) serving to perceive and distinguish fine variations of temperature or touch

EPICS > EPIC

EPICURE *n* person who enjoys good food and drink

EPICUREAN *adj* devoted to sensual pleasures, esp food and drink ▷ *n* epicure

EPICURES > EPICURE

EPICURISE *same as* > EPICURIZE

EPICURISM > EPICURE

EPICURIZE *vb* act as an epicure

EPICYCLE *n* (in the Ptolemaic system) a small circle, around which a planet was thought to revolve

EPICYCLES > EPICYCLE

EPICYCLIC > EPICYCLE

EPIDEMIC *n* widespread occurrence of a disease ▷ *adj* (esp of a disease) affecting many people in an area

EPIDEMICS > EPIDEMIC

EPIDERM *same as* > EPIDERMIS

EPIDERMAL > EPIDERMIS

EPIDERMIC > EPIDERMIS

EPIDERMIS *n* outer layer of the skin

EPIDERMS > EPIDERM

EPIDICTIC *adj* designed to display something, esp the skill of the speaker in rhetoric

EPIDOSITE *n* rock formed of quartz and epidote

EPIDOTE *n* green mineral

EPIDOTES > EPIDOTE

EPIDOTIC > EPIDOTE

EPIDURAL *n* spinal anaesthetic injected to relieve pain during childbirth ▷ *adj* on or over the outermost membrane covering the brain and spinal cord

EPIDURALS > EPIDURAL

EPIFAUNA *n* animals that live on the surface of the seabed

EPIFAUNAE > EPIFAUNA

EPIFAUNAL > EPIFAUNA

EPIFAUNAS > EPIFAUNA

EPIFOCAL *adj* situated or occurring at an epicentre

EPIGAEAL *same as* > EPIGEAL

EPIGAEAN *same as* > EPIGEAL

EPIGAEOUS *same as* > EPIGEAL

EPIGAMIC *adj* denoting an animal feature that attracts the opposite sex

EPIGEAL *adj* of or relating to a form of seed germination

e

EPIGEAN *same as*
> EPIGEAL

EPIGEIC *same as*
> EPIGEAL

EPIGENE *adj* formed or taking place at or near the surface of the earth

EPIGENIC *adj* pertaining to the theory of the gradual development of the embryo

EPIGENIST *n* one who studies or espouses the theory of the gradual development of the embryo

EPIGENOME *n* group of chemical compounds that modify a genome

EPIGENOUS *adj* growing on the surface, esp the upper surface, of an organism or part

EPIGEOUS *same as*
> EPIGEAL

EPIGON *same as*
> EPIGONE

EPIGONE *n* inferior follower or imitator

EPIGONES > EPIGONE

EPIGONI > EPIGONE

EPIGONIC > EPIGONE

EPIGONISM > EPIGONE

EPIGONOUS > EPIGONE

EPIGONS > EPIGON

EPIGONUS *same as*
> EPIGONE

EPIGRAM *n* short witty remark or poem

EPIGRAMS > EPIGRAM

EPIGRAPH *n* quotation at the start of a book

EPIGRAPHS
> EPIGRAPH

EPIGRAPHY *n* study of ancient inscriptions

EPIGYNIES
> EPIGYNOUS

EPIGYNOUS *adj* (of flowers) having the receptacle enclosing and fused with the gynoecium so that the other floral parts arise above it

EPIGYNY > EPIGYNOUS

EPILATE *vb* remove hair from

EPILATED > EPILATE

EPILATES > EPILATE

EPILATING > EPILATE

EPILATION > EPILATE

EPILATOR *n* electrical appliance for plucking unwanted hair

EPILATORS
> EPILATOR

EPILEPSY *n* disorder of the nervous system causing loss of consciousness and sometimes convulsions

EPILEPTIC *adj* of or having epilepsy ▷ *n* person who has epilepsy

EPILIMNIA *n* upper layers of water in lakes

EPILITHIC *adj* (of plants) growing on the surface of rock

EPILOBIUM *n* willow-herb

EPILOG *same as*
> EPILOGUE

EPILOGIC > EPILOGUE

EPILOGISE *same as*
> EPILOGIZE

EPILOGIST
> EPILOGUE

EPILOGIZE *vb* write or deliver epilogues

EPILOGS > EPILOG

EPILOGUE *n* short speech or poem at the end of a literary work, esp a play

EPILOGUED *adj* followed by an epilogue

EPILOGUES
> EPILOGUE

EPIMER *n* isomer

EPIMERASE *n* enzyme that interconverts epimers

EPIMERE *n* dorsal part of the mesoderm of a vertebrate embryo

EPIMERES > EPIMERE

EPIMERIC
> EPIMERISM

EPIMERISE *same as*
> EPIMERIZE

EPIMERISM *n* optical isomerism in which isomers can form about asymmetric atoms within the molecule

EPIMERIZE *vb* change (a chemical compound) into an epimer

EPIMERS > EPIMER

EPIMYSIA
> EPIMYSIUM

EPIMYSIUM *n* sheath of connective tissue that encloses a skeletal muscle

EPINAOI > EPINAOS

EPINAOS *n* rear vestibule

EPINASTIC
> EPINASTY

EPINASTY *n* increased growth of the upper surface of a plant part

EPINEURAL *adj* outside a nerve trunk

EPINEURIA *n* sheaths of connective tissue around bundles of nerve fibres

EPINICIAN
> EPINICION

EPINICION *n* victory song

EPINIKIAN
> EPINICION

EPINIKION *same as*
> EPINICION

EPINOSIC *adj* unhealthy

EPIPHANIC
> EPIPHANY

EPIPHANY *n* moment of great or sudden revelation

EPIPHRAGM *n* disc of calcium phosphate and mucilage secreted by snails over the aperture of their shells before hibernation

EPIPHYSES
> EPIPHYSIS

EPIPHYSIS *n* end of a long bone, initially separated from the shaft (diaphysis) by a section of cartilage that eventually ossifies so that the two portions fuse together

EPIPHYTAL
> EPIPHYTE

EPIPHYTE *n* plant that grows on another plant but is not parasitic on it

EPIPHYTES
> EPIPHYTE

EPIPHYTIC
> EPIPHYTE

EPIPLOA > EPIPLOON

EPIPLOIC > EPIPLOON

EPIPLOON *n* greater omentum

EPIPLOONS
> EPIPLOON

EPIPOLIC
> EPIPOLISM

EPIPOLISM *n* fluorescence

EPIROGENY *n* formation and submergence of continents by broad, relatively slow, displacements of the earth's crust

EPIRRHEMA *n* address in Greek comedy

EPISCIA *n* creeping plant

EPISCIAS > EPISCIA

EPISCOPAL *adj* of or governed by bishops

EPISCOPE *n* optical device that projects an enlarged image

EPISCOPES
> EPISCOPE

EPISCOPY *n* area overseen

EPISEMON *n* emblem

EPISEMONS
> EPISEMON

EPISODAL *same as*
> EPISODIC

EPISODE *n* incident in a series of incidents

EPISODES > EPISODE

EPISODIAL *same as*
> EPISODIC

EPISODIC *adj* occurring at irregular intervals

EPISOMAL *adj* of or like an episome

EPISOME *n* unit of genetic material (DNA) in bacteria that can be replicated

EPISOMES > EPISOME

EPISPERM *n* protective outer layer of certain seeds

EPISPERMS
> EPISPERM

EPISPORE *n* outer layer of certain spores

EPISPORES
> EPISPORE

EPISTASES
> EPISTASIS

EPISTASIS *n* scum on the surface of a liquid, esp on an old specimen of urine

EPISTASY *same as*
> EPISTASIS

EPISTATIC
> EPISTASIS

EPISTAXES
> EPISTAXIS

EPISTAXIS *technical name for* > NOSEBLEED

EPISTEMIC *adj* of or relating to knowledge or epistemology

EPISTERNA *n* parts of the sternums of mammals

EPISTLE *n* letter, esp of an apostle ▷ *vb* preface

EPISTLED > EPISTLE

EPISTLER *n* writer of an epistle or epistles

EPISTLERS
> EPISTLER

EPISTLES > EPISTLE

EPISTLING > EPISTLE

EPISTOLER *same as*
> EPISTLER

EPISTOLET *n* short letter

EPISTOLIC > EPISTLE

EPISTOME *n* area between the mouth and antennae of crustaceans

EPISTOMES
> EPISTOME

EPISTYLE *n* lowest part of an entablature that bears on the columns

EPISTYLES
> EPISTYLE

EPITAPH *n* commemorative inscription on a tomb ▷ *vb* compose an epitaph

EPITAPHED > EPITAPH

EPITAPHER > EPITAPH

EPITAPHIC > EPITAPH

EPITAPHS > EPITAPH

EPITASES > EPITASIS

EPITASIS *n* (in classical drama) part of a play in which the main action develops

EPITAXES > EPITAXIS

EPITAXIAL > EPITAXY

EPITAXIC > EPITAXY

EPITAXIES > EPITAXY

EPITAXIS *same as*
> EPITAXY

EPITAXY *n* growth of a thin layer on the surface of a crystal

EPITHECA *n* outer and older layer of the cell wall of a diatom

EPITHECAE
> EPITHECA

EPITHELIA *n* animal tissues consisting of one or more layers of closely packed cells covering the external and internal surfaces of the body

EPITHEM *n* external topical application

EPITHEMA > EPITHEM

EPITHEMS > EPITHEM

EPITHESES
> EPITHESIS

EPITHESIS *n* addition of a letter to the end of a word, so that its sense does not change

EPITHET n descriptive word or name ▷ vb name
EPITHETED > EPITHET
EPITHETIC > EPITHET
EPITHETON same as > EPITHET
EPITHETS > EPITHET
EPITOME n typical example
EPITOMES > EPITOME
EPITOMIC > EPITOME
EPITOMISE same as > EPITOMIZE
EPITOMIST > EPITOMIZE
EPITOMIZE vb be the epitome of
EPITONIC adj undergoing too great a strain
EPITOPE n site on an antigen at which a specific antibody becomes attached
EPITOPES > EPITOPE
EPITRITE n metrical foot with three long syllables and one short one
EPITRITES > EPITRITE
EPIZEUXES > EPIZEUXIS
EPIZEUXIS n deliberate repetition of a word
EPIZOA > EPIZOON
EPIZOAN same as > EPIZOON
EPIZOANS > EPIZOAN
EPIZOIC adj (of an animal or plant) growing or living on the exterior of a living animal
EPIZOISM > EPIZOIC
EPIZOISMS > EPIZOIC
EPIZOITE n organism that lives on an animal but is not parasitic on it
EPIZOITES > EPIZOITE
EPIZOON n animal that lives on the body of another animal
EPIZOOTIC adj (of a disease) suddenly and temporarily affecting a large number of animals over a large area ▷ n epizootic disease
EPIZOOTY n animal disease
EPOCH n period of notable events
EPOCHA same as > EPOCH
EPOCHAL > EPOCH
EPOCHALLY > EPOCH
EPOCHAS > EPOCHA
EPOCHS > EPOCH
EPODE n part of a lyric ode that follows the strophe and the antistrophe
EPODES > EPODE
EPODIC > EPODE
EPONYM n name derived from the name of a real or mythical person
EPONYMIC > EPONYM
EPONYMIES > EPONYMY

EPONYMOUS adj after whom a book, play, etc is named
EPONYMS > EPONYM
EPONYMY n derivation of names of places, etc, from those of persons
EPOPEE n epic poem
EPOPEES > EPOPEE
EPOPOEIA same as > EPOPEE
EPOPOEIAS > EPOPOEIA
EPOPT n one initiated into the Eleusinian mysteries, an ancient Greek festival
EPOPTS > EPOPT
EPOS n body of poetry in which the tradition of a people is conveyed
EPOSES > EPOS
EPOXIDE n chemical compound
EPOXIDES > EPOXIDE
EPOXIDISE same as > EPOXIDIZE
EPOXIDIZE vb form an epoxide
EPOXIED > EPOXY
EPOXIES > EPOXY
EPOXY adj of or containing a specific type of chemical compound ▷ n epoxy resin ▷ vb glue with epoxy resin
EPOXYED > EPOXY
EPOXYING > EPOXY
EPRIS adj enamoured
EPRISE feminine form of > EPRIS
EPSILON n fifth letter of the Greek alphabet
EPSILONIC adj of or relating to an arbitrary small quantity
EPSILONS > EPSILON
EPSOMITE n sulphate of magnesium
EPSOMITES > EPSOMITE
EPUISE adj exhausted
EPUISEE feminine form of > EPUISE
EPULARY adj of or relating to feasting
EPULATION n feasting
EPULIDES > EPULIS
EPULIS n swelling of the gum
EPULISES > EPULIS
EPULOTIC n scarring
EPULOTICS > EPULOTIC
EPURATE vb purify
EPURATED > EPURATE
EPURATES > EPURATE
EPURATING > EPURATE
EPURATION > EPURATE
EPYLLIA > EPYLLION
EPYLLION n miniature epic
EPYLLIONS > EPYLLION
EQUABLE adj even-tempered
EQUABLY > EQUABLE
EQUAL adj identical in size, quantity, degree, etc

▷ n person or thing equal to another ▷ vb be equal to
EQUALED > EQUAL
EQUALI pl n pieces for a group of instruments of the same kind
EQUALING > EQUAL
EQUALISE same as > EQUALIZE
EQUALISED > EQUALIZE
EQUALISER same as > EQUALIZER
EQUALISES > EQUALIZE
EQUALITY n state of being equal
EQUALIZE vb make or become equal
EQUALIZED > EQUALIZE
EQUALIZER n person or thing that equalizes, esp a device to counterbalance opposing forces
EQUALIZES > EQUALIZE
EQUALLED > EQUAL
EQUALLING > EQUAL
EQUALLY > EQUAL
EQUALNESS n equality
EQUALS > EQUAL
EQUANT n circle in which a planet was formerly believed to move
EQUANTS > EQUANT
EQUATABLE > EQUATE
EQUATE vb make or regard as equivalent
EQUATED > EQUATE
EQUATES > EQUATE
EQUATING > EQUATE
EQUATION n mathematical statement that two expressions are equal
EQUATIONS > EQUATION
EQUATIVE adj (in grammar) denoting the equivalence or identity of two terms
EQUATOR n imaginary circle round the earth
EQUATORS > EQUATOR
EQUERRIES > EQUERRY
EQUERRY n attendant to a member of a royal family
EQUES n (in ancient Rome) horseman
EQUID n any animal of the horse family
EQUIDS > EQUID
EQUIFINAL adj having the same end or result
EQUIMOLAL adj having an equal number of moles
EQUIMOLAR same as > EQUIMOLAL
EQUINAL same as > EQUINE
EQUINE adj of or like a horse ▷ n any animal of the horse family
EQUINELY > EQUINE
EQUINES > EQUINE
EQUINIA n glanders

EQUINIAS > EQUINIA
EQUINITY n horse-like nature
EQUINOX n time of year when day and night are of equal length
EQUINOXES > EQUINOX
EQUIP vb provide with supplies, components, etc
EQUIPAGE n horse-drawn carriage, esp one elegantly equipped and attended by liveried footmen ▷ vb equip
EQUIPAGED > EQUIPAGE
EQUIPAGES > EQUIPAGE
EQUIPE n (esp in motor racing) team
EQUIPES > EQUIPE
EQUIPMENT n set of tools or devices used for a particular purpose
EQUIPOISE n perfect balance ▷ vb offset or balance in weight or force
EQUIPPED > EQUIP
EQUIPPER > EQUIP
EQUIPPERS > EQUIP
EQUIPPING > EQUIP
EQUIPS > EQUIP
EQUISETA > EQUISETUM
EQUISETIC > EQUISETUM
EQUISETUM n type of plant such as the horsetail
EQUITABLE adj fair and reasonable
EQUITABLY > EQUITABLE
EQUITANT adj having the base folded around the stem
EQUITES pl n cavalry
EQUITIES > EQUITY
EQUITY n fairness
EQUIVALVE adj equipped with identical valves
EQUIVOCAL adj ambiguous
EQUIVOKE same as > EQUIVOQUE
EQUIVOKES > EQUIVOKE
EQUIVOQUE n play on words
ER interj sound made when hesitating in speech
ERA n period of time considered as distinctive
ERADIATE less common word for > RADIATE
ERADIATED > ERADIATE
ERADIATES > ERADIATE
ERADICANT > ERADICATE
ERADICATE vb destroy completely
ERAS > ERA
ERASABLE > ERASE
ERASE vb destroy all traces of
ERASED > ERASE
ERASEMENT > ERASE**

ERASER n object for erasing something written

ERASERS > ERASER

ERASES > ERASE

ERASING > ERASE

ERASION n act of erasing

ERASIONS > ERASION

ERASURE n erasing

ERASURES > ERASURE

ERATHEM n stratum of rocks representing a specific geological era

ERATHEMS > ERATHEM

ERBIA n oxide of erbium

ERBIAS > ERBIA

ERBIUM n metallic element of the lanthanide series

ERBIUMS > ERBIUM

ERE prep before ▷ vb plough

ERECT vb build ▷ adj upright

ERECTABLE > ERECT

ERECTED > ERECT

ERECTER same as > ERECTOR

ERECTERS > ERECTER

ERECTILE adj capable of becoming erect

ERECTING > ERECT

ERECTION n act of erecting or the state of being erected

ERECTIONS > ERECTION

ERECTIVE adj tending to erect

ERECTLY > ERECT

ERECTNESS > ERECT

ERECTOR n any muscle that raises a part or makes it erect

ERECTORS > ERECTOR

ERECTS > ERECT

ERED > ERE

ERELONG adv before long

EREMIC adj of or relating to deserts

EREMITAL > EREMITE

EREMITE n Christian hermit

EREMITES > EREMITE

EREMITIC > EREMITE

EREMITISH > EREMITE

EREMITISM > EREMITE

EREMURI > EREMURUS

EREMURUS n type of herb

ERENOW adv long before the present

EREPSIN n mixture of proteolytic enzymes secreted by the small intestine

EREPSINS > EREPSIN

ERES > ERE

ERETHIC > ERETHISM

ERETHISM n abnormally high degree of irritability or sensitivity in any part of the body

ERETHISMS > ERETHISM

ERETHITIC > ERETHISM

EREV n day before

EREVS > EREV

EREWHILE adv short time ago

EREWHILES same as > EREWHILE

ERF n plot of land marked off for building purposes

ERG same as > ERGOMETER

ERGASTIC adj consisting of the non-living by-products of protoplasmic activity

ERGATANER n wingless male ant

ERGATE n worker ant

ERGATES > ERGATE

ERGATIVE adj denoting a verb that takes the same noun as either direct object or subject ▷ n ergative verb

ERGATIVES > ERGATIVE

ERGATOID > ERGATE

ERGATOIDS > ERGATOID

ERGO same as > ERGOMETER

ERGODIC adj of or relating to the probability that any state will recur

ERGOGENIC adj giving energy

ERGOGRAM n tracing produced by an ergograph

ERGOGRAMS > ERGOGRAM

ERGOGRAPH n instrument that measures and records the amount of work a muscle does during contraction, its rate of fatigue, etc

ERGOMANIA n excessive desire to work

ERGOMETER n dynamometer

ERGOMETRY n measurement of work done

ERGON n work

ERGONOMIC adj designed to minimize effort

ERGONS > ERGON

ERGOS > ERGO

ERGOT n fungal disease of cereal

ERGOTIC > ERGOT

ERGOTISE same as > ERGOTIZE

ERGOTISED > ERGOTISE

ERGOTISES > ERGOTISE

ERGOTISM n ergot poisoning

ERGOTISMS > ERGOTISM

ERGOTIZE vb inflict ergotism upon

ERGOTIZED > ERGOTIZE

ERGOTIZES > ERGOTIZE

ERGOTS > ERGOT

ERGS > ERG

ERHU n Chinese two-stringed violin

ERHUS > ERHU

ERIACH same as > ERIC

ERIACHS > ERIACH

ERIC n (in old Irish law) fine paid by a murderer to the family of his or her victim

ERICA n genus of plants including heathers

ERICAS > ERICA

ERICK same as > ERIC

ERICKS > ERICK

ERICOID adj (of leaves) small and tough, resembling those of heather

ERICS > ERIC

ERIGERON n type of plant

ERIGERONS > ERIGERON

ERING > ERE

ERINGO same as > ERYNGO

ERINGOES > ERINGO

ERINGOS > ERINGO

ERINITE n arsenate of copper

ERINITES > ERINITE

ERINUS n type of plant

ERINUSES > ERINUS

ERIOMETER n device for measuring the diameters of minute particles or fibres

ERIONITE n common form of zeolite

ERIONITES > ERIONITE

ERIOPHYID n type of mite

ERISTIC adj of, relating, or given to controversy or logical disputation ▷ n person who engages in logical disputes

ERISTICAL same as > ERISTIC

ERISTICS > ERISTIC

ERK n aircraftman or naval rating

ERKS > ERK

ERLANG n unit of traffic intensity in a telephone system

ERLANGS > ERLANG

ERLKING n malevolent spirit who carries off children

ERLKINGS > ERLKING

ERM interj expression of hesitation

ERMELIN n ermine

ERMELINS > ERMELIN

ERMINE n stoat in northern regions

ERMINED adj clad in the fur of the ermine

ERMINES > ERMINE

ERN archaic variant of > EARN

ERNE n fish-eating (European) sea eagle

ERNED > ERN

ERNES > ERNE

ERNING > ERN

ERNS > ERN

ERODABLE > ERODE

ERODE vb wear away

ERODED > ERODE

ERODENT > ERODE

ERODENTS > ERODE

ERODES > ERODE

ERODIBLE > ERODE

ERODING > ERODE

ERODIUM n type of geranium

ERODIUMS > ERODIUM

EROGENIC same as > EROGENOUS

EROGENOUS adj sensitive to sexual stimulation

EROS n love

EROSE adj jagged or uneven, as though gnawed or bitten

EROSELY > EROSE

EROSES > EROS

EROSIBLE adj able to be eroded

EROSION n wearing away of rocks or soil

EROSIONAL > EROSION

EROSIONS > EROSION

EROSIVE > EROSION

EROSIVITY > EROSION

EROSTRATE adj without a beak

EROTEMA n rhetorical question

EROTEMAS > EROTEMA

EROTEME same as > EROTEMA

EROTEMES > EROTEME

EROTESES > EROTESIS

EROTESIS same as > EROTEMA

EROTETIC adj pertaining to a rhetorical question

EROTIC adj relating to sexual pleasure or desire ▷ n person who has strong sexual desires

EROTICA n sexual literature or art

EROTICAL adj erotic

EROTICAS > EROTICA

EROTICISE same as > EROTICIZE

EROTICISM n erotic quality or nature

EROTICIST > EROTICISM

EROTICIZE vb regard or present in a sexual way

EROTICS > EROTIC

EROTISE same as > EROTIZE

EROTISED > EROTISE

EROTISES > EROTISE

EROTISING > EROTISE

EROTISM same as > EROTICISM

EROTISMS > EROTISM

EROTIZE vb make erotic

EROTIZED > EROTIZE

EROTIZES > EROTIZE

EROTIZING > EROTIZE

EROTOLOGY n study of erotic stimuli and sexual behaviour

ERR vb make a mistake

ERRABLE adj capable of making a mistake

ERRANCIES > ERRANCY

ERRANCY n state or an instance of erring or a tendency to err

ERRAND n short trip to do something for someone
ERRANDS > ERRAND
ERRANT adj behaving in a manner considered to be unacceptable ▷ n knight-errant
ERRANTLY > ERRANT
ERRANTRY n way of life of a knight errant
ERRANTS > ERRANT
ERRATA > ERRATUM
ERRATAS informal variant of > ERRATA
ERRATIC adj irregular or unpredictable ▷ n rock that has been transported by glacial action
ERRATICAL adj erratic
ERRATICS > ERRATIC
ERRATUM n error in writing or printing
ERRED > ERR
ERRHINE adj causing nasal secretion ▷ n errhine drug or agent
ERRHINES > ERRHINE
ERRING > ERR
ERRINGLY > ERR
ERRINGS > ERRING
ERRONEOUS adj incorrect, mistaken
ERROR n mistake, inaccuracy, or misjudgment
ERRORIST n one who makes errors
ERRORISTS > ERRORIST
ERRORLESS > ERROR
ERRORS > ERROR
ERRS > ERR
ERS same as > ERVIL
ERSATZ adj made in imitation ▷ n ersatz substance or article
ERSATZES > ERSATZ
ERSES > ERS
ERST adv long ago
ERSTWHILE adj former ▷ adv formerly
ERUCIC adj as in erucic acid crystalline fatty acid
ERUCIFORM adj resembling a caterpillar
ERUCT vb belch
ERUCTATE same as > ERUCT
ERUCTATED > ERUCTATE
ERUCTATES > ERUCTATE
ERUCTED > ERUCT
ERUCTING > ERUCT
ERUCTS > ERUCT
ERUDITE adj having great academic knowledge ▷ n erudite person
ERUDITELY > ERUDITE
ERUDITES > ERUDITE
ERUDITION > ERUDITE
ERUGO n verdigris
ERUGOS > ERUGO
ERUMPENT adj bursting out or developing as though bursting through

ERUPT vb eject (steam, water, or volcanic material) violently
ERUPTED > ERUPT
ERUPTIBLE > ERUPT
ERUPTING > ERUPT
ERUPTION > ERUPT
ERUPTIONS > ERUPT
ERUPTIVE adj erupting or tending to erupt ▷ n type of volcanic rock
ERUPTIVES > ERUPTIVE
ERUPTS > ERUPT
ERUV n area within which certain activities forbidden to be done on the Sabbath are permitted
ERUVIM > ERUV
ERUVIN > ERUV
ERUVS > ERUV
ERVALENTA n health food made from lentil and barley flour
ERVEN > ERF
ERVIL n type of vetch
ERVILS > ERVIL
ERYNGIUM n type of temperate and subtropical plant
ERYNGIUMS > ERYNGIUM
ERYNGO n type of plant with toothed or lobed leaves
ERYNGOES > ERYNGO
ERYNGOS > ERYNGO
ERYTHEMA n patchy inflammation of the skin
ERYTHEMAL > ERYTHEMA
ERYTHEMAS > ERYTHEMA
ERYTHEMIC > ERYTHEMA
ERYTHRINA n tropical tree with red flowers
ERYTHRISM n abnormal red coloration, as in plumage or hair
ERYTHRITE n sweet crystalline compound extracted from certain algae and lichens
ERYTHROID adj red or reddish
ERYTHRON n red blood cells and their related tissues
ERYTHRONS > ERYTHRON
ES n letter S
ESCABECHE n (in Mexican cookery) pickled vegetables and peppers, served as a condiment for fish
ESCALADE n assault by the use of ladders, esp on a fortification ▷ vb gain access to (a place) by the use of ladders
ESCALADED > ESCALADE
ESCALADER > ESCALADE
ESCALADES > ESCALADE
ESCALADO n escalade

ESCALATE vb increase in extent or intensity
ESCALATED > ESCALATE
ESCALATES > ESCALATE
ESCALATOR n moving staircase
ESCALIER n staircase
ESCALIERS > ESCALIER
ESCALLOP another word for > SCALLOP
ESCALLOPS > ESCALLOP
ESCALOP another word for > SCALLOP
ESCALOPE n thin slice of meat, esp veal
ESCALOPED > ESCALOP
ESCALOPES > ESCALOPE
ESCALOPS > ESCALOP
ESCAPABLE > ESCAPE
ESCAPADE n mischievous adventure
ESCAPADES > ESCAPADE
ESCAPADO n escaped criminal
ESCAPADOS > ESCAPADO
ESCAPE vb get free (of) ▷ n act of escaping
ESCAPED > ESCAPE
ESCAPEE n person who has escaped
ESCAPEES > ESCAPEE
ESCAPER > ESCAPE
ESCAPERS > ESCAPE
ESCAPES > ESCAPE
ESCAPING > ESCAPE
ESCAPISM n taking refuge in fantasy to avoid unpleasant reality
ESCAPISMS > ESCAPISM
ESCAPIST > ESCAPISM
ESCAPISTS > ESCAPISM
ESCAR same as > ESKER
ESCARGOT n variety of edible snail, usually eaten with a sauce made of melted butter and garlic
ESCARGOTS > ESCARGOT
ESCAROLE n variety of endive with broad leaves, used in salads
ESCAROLES > ESCAROLE
ESCARP n inner side of a ditch separating besiegers and besieged ▷ vb make into a slope
ESCARPED > ESCARP
ESCARPING > ESCARP
ESCARPS > ESCARP
ESCARS > ESCAR
ESCHALOT another name for a > SHALLOT
ESCHALOTS > ESCHALOT
ESCHAR n dry scab or slough
ESCHARS > ESCHAR
ESCHEAT n possessions that become state

property in the absence of an heir ▷ vb take such property
ESCHEATED > ESCHEAT
ESCHEATOR > ESCHEAT
ESCHEATS > ESCHEAT
ESCHEW vb abstain from, avoid
ESCHEWAL > ESCHEW
ESCHEWALS > ESCHEW
ESCHEWED > ESCHEW
ESCHEWER > ESCHEW
ESCHEWERS > ESCHEW
ESCHEWING > ESCHEW
ESCHEWS > ESCHEW
ESCLANDRE n scandal or notoriety
ESCOLAR n slender spiny-finned fish
ESCOLARS > ESCOLAR
ESCOPETTE n carbine
ESCORT n people following another person for protection or as an honour ▷ vb act as an escort to
ESCORTAGE > ESCORT
ESCORTED > ESCORT
ESCORTING > ESCORT
ESCORTS > ESCORT
ESCOT vb maintain
ESCOTED > ESCOT
ESCOTING > ESCOT
ESCOTS > ESCOT
ESCOTTED > ESCOT
ESCOTTING > ESCOT
ESCRIBANO n clerk
ESCRIBE vb make a mathematical drawing
ESCRIBED > ESCRIBE
ESCRIBES > ESCRIBE
ESCRIBING > ESCRIBE
ESCROC n conman
ESCROCS > ESCROC
ESCROL same as > ESCROLL
ESCROLL n scroll
ESCROLLS > ESCROLL
ESCROLS > ESCROL
ESCROW n item delivered to a third party pending fulfilment of a condition ▷ vb place (money, a document, etc) in escrow
ESCROWED > ESCROW
ESCROWING > ESCROW
ESCROWS > ESCROW
ESCUAGE (in medieval Europe) another word for > SCUTAGE
ESCUAGES > ESCUAGE
ESCUDO n former monetary unit of Portugal
ESCUDOS > ESCUDO
ESCULENT adj edible ▷ n any edible substance
ESCULENTS > ESCULENT
ESEMPLASY n unification
ESERINE n crystalline alkaloid
ESERINES > ESERINE
ESES > ES
ESILE n vinegar
ESILES > ESILE
ESKAR same as > ESKER
ESKARS > ESKAR

ESKER n long ridge of gravel, sand, etc

ESKERS > ESKER

ESKIES > ESKY

ESKY n portable insulated container

ESLOIN same as > ELOIGN

ESLOINED > ESLOIN

ESLOINING > ESLOIN

ESLOINS > ESLOIN

ESLOYNE same as > ELOIGN

ESLOYNED > ESLOYNE

ESLOYNES > ESLOYNE

ESLOYNING > ESLOYNE

ESNE n household slave

ESNECIES > ESNECY

ESNECY n inheritance law

ESNES > ESNE

ESOPHAGI > ESOPHAGUS

ESOPHAGUS n part of the alimentary canal between the pharynx and the stomach

ESOTERIC adj understood by only a small number of people with special knowledge

ESOTERICA n (collection of) esoteric things

ESOTERIES > ESOTERIC

ESOTERISM > ESOTERIC

ESOTERY > ESOTERIC

ESOTROPIA n condition in which eye turns inwards

ESOTROPIC > ESOTROPIA

ESPADA n sword

ESPADAS > ESPADA

ESPAGNOLE n tomato and sherry sauce

ESPALIER n shrub or fruit tree trained to grow flat ▷ vb train (a plant) on an espalier

ESPALIERS > ESPALIER

ESPANOL n Spanish person

ESPANOLES > ESPANOL

ESPARTO n grass of S Europe and N Africa

ESPARTOS > ESPARTO

ESPECIAL adj special

ESPERANCE n hope or expectation

ESPIAL n act or fact of being seen or discovered

ESPIALS > ESPIAL

ESPIED > ESPY

ESPIEGLE adj playful

ESPIER > ESPY

ESPIERS > ESPY

ESPIES > ESPY

ESPIONAGE n spying

ESPLANADE n wide open road used as a public promenade

ESPOIR n category of wrestler

ESPOIRS > ESPOIR

ESPOUSAL n adoption or support

ESPOUSALS > ESPOUSAL

ESPOUSE vb adopt or give support to (a cause etc)

ESPOUSED > ESPOUSE

ESPOUSER > ESPOUSE

ESPOUSERS > ESPOUSE

ESPOUSES > ESPOUSE

ESPOUSING > ESPOUSE

ESPRESSO n strong coffee made by forcing steam or boiling water through ground coffee beans

ESPRESSOS > ESPRESSO

ESPRIT n spirit, liveliness, or wit

ESPRITS > ESPRIT

ESPUMOSO n sparkling wine

ESPUMOSOS > ESPUMOSO

ESPY vb catch sight of

ESPYING > ESPY

ESQUIRE n courtesy title placed after a man's name ▷ vb escort

ESQUIRED > ESQUIRE

ESQUIRES > ESQUIRE

ESQUIRESS feminine form of > ESQUIRE

ESQUIRING > ESQUIRE

ESQUISSE n sketch

ESQUISSES > ESQUISSE

ESS n letter S

ESSAY n short literary composition ▷ vb attempt

ESSAYED > ESSAY

ESSAYER > ESSAY

ESSAYERS > ESSAY

ESSAYETTE n short essay

ESSAYING > ESSAY

ESSAYISH > ESSAY

ESSAYIST n person who writes essays

ESSAYISTS > ESSAYIST

ESSAYS > ESSAY

ESSE n existence

ESSENCE n most important feature of a thing which determines its identity

ESSENCES > ESSENCE

ESSENTIAL adj vitally important ▷ n something fundamental or indispensable

ESSES > ESS

ESSIVE n grammatical case

ESSIVES > ESSIVE

ESSOIN n excuse ▷ vb excuse for not appearing in court

ESSOINED > ESSOIN

ESSOINER > ESSOIN

ESSOINERS > ESSOIN

ESSOINING > ESSOIN

ESSOINS > ESSOIN

ESSONITE variant spelling of > HESSONITE

ESSONITES > ESSONITE

ESSOYNE same as > ESSOIN

ESSOYNES > ESSOYNE

EST n treatment intended to help people towards psychological growth

ESTABLISH vb set up on a permanent basis

ESTACADE n defensive arrangement of stakes

ESTACADES > ESTACADE

ESTAFETTE n mounted courier

ESTAMINET n small café, bar, or bistro, esp a shabby one

ESTANCIA n (in Spanish America) a large estate or cattle ranch

ESTANCIAS > ESTANCIA

ESTATE n landed property ▷ vb provide with an estate

ESTATED > ESTATE

ESTATES > ESTATE

ESTATING > ESTATE

ESTEEM n high regard ▷ vb think highly of

ESTEEMED > ESTEEM

ESTEEMING > ESTEEM

ESTEEMS > ESTEEM

ESTER n chemical compound

ESTERASE n any of a group of enzymes that hydrolyse esters

ESTERASES > ESTERASE

ESTERIFY vb change or cause to change into an ester

ESTERS > ESTER

ESTHESES > ESTHESIS

ESTHESIA US spelling of > AESTHESIA

ESTHESIAS > ESTHESIA

ESTHESIS n esthesia

ESTHETE US spelling of > AESTHETE

ESTHETES > ESTHETE

ESTHETIC > ESTHETE

ESTHETICS > ESTHETE

ESTIMABLE adj worthy of respect

ESTIMABLY > ESTIMABLE

ESTIMATE vb calculate roughly ▷ n approximate calculation

ESTIMATED > ESTIMATE

ESTIMATES > ESTIMATE

ESTIMATOR n person or thing that estimates

ESTIVAL usual US spelling of > AESTIVAL

ESTIVATE usual US spelling of > AESTIVATE

ESTIVATED > ESTIVATE

ESTIVATES > ESTIVATE

ESTIVATOR > ESTIVATE

ESTOC n short stabbing sword

ESTOCS > ESTOC

ESTOILE n heraldic star with wavy points

ESTOILES > ESTOILE

ESTOP vb preclude by estoppel

ESTOPPAGE > ESTOP

ESTOPPED > ESTOP

ESTOPPEL n rule precluding a person from denying the truth of a statement of facts

ESTOPPELS > ESTOPPEL

ESTOPPING > ESTOP

ESTOPS > ESTOP

ESTOVER same as > ESTOVERS

ESTOVERS pl n right allowed by law to tenants of land to cut timber, esp for fuel and repairs

ESTRADE n dais or raised platform

ESTRADES > ESTRADE

ESTRADIOL n most potent estrogenic hormone secreted by the mammalian ovary

ESTRAGON another name for > TARRAGON

ESTRAGONS > ESTRAGON

ESTRAL US spelling of > OESTRAL

ESTRANGE vb separate and live apart from (one's spouse)

ESTRANGED adj no longer living with one's spouse

ESTRANGER > ESTRANGE

ESTRANGES > ESTRANGE

ESTRAPADE n attempt by a horse to throw its rider

ESTRAY n stray domestic animal of unknown ownership ▷ vb stray

ESTRAYED > ESTRAY

ESTRAYING > ESTRAY

ESTRAYS > ESTRAY

ESTREAT n extract from a court record ▷ vb send an extract of a court record

ESTREATED > ESTREAT

ESTREATS > ESTREAT

ESTREPE vb lay waste

ESTREPED > ESTREPE

ESTREPES > ESTREPE

ESTREPING > ESTREPE

ESTRICH n obsolete word for ostrich

ESTRICHES > ESTRICH

ESTRIDGE same as > ESTRICH

ESTRIDGES > ESTRIDGE

ESTRILDID n weaver finch

ESTRIN US spelling of > OESTRIN

ESTRINS > ESTRIN

ESTRIOL usual US spelling of > OESTRIOL

ESTRIOLS > ESTRIOL

ESTRO n poetic inspiration
ESTROGEN usual US spelling of > OESTROGEN
ESTROGENS > ESTROGEN
ESTRONE usual US spelling of > OESTRONE
ESTRONES > ESTRONE
ESTROS > ESTRO
ESTROUS > ESTRUS
ESTRUAL > ESTRUS
ESTRUM usual US spelling of > OESTRUM
ESTRUMS > ESTRUM
ESTRUS usual US spelling of > OESTRUS
ESTRUSES > ESTRUS
ESTS > EST
ESTUARIAL > ESTUARY
ESTUARIAN > ESTUARY
ESTUARIES > ESTUARY
ESTUARINE adj formed or deposited in an estuary
ESTUARY n mouth of a river
ESURIENCE > ESURIENT
ESURIENCY > ESURIENT
ESURIENT adj greedy
ET dialect past tense of > EAT
ETA n seventh letter in the Greek alphabet
ETACISM n pronunciation of eta as a long vowel sound
ETACISMS > ETACISM
ETAERIO n aggregate fruit
ETAERIOS > ETAERIO
ETAGE n floor in a multi-storey building
ETAGERE n stand with open shelves for displaying ornaments, etc
ETAGERES > ETAGERE
ETAGES > ETAGE
ETALAGE n display
ETALAGES > ETALAGE
ETALON n device used in spectroscopy
ETALONS > ETALON
ETAMIN same as > ETAMINE
ETAMINE n cotton or worsted fabric of loose weave
ETAMINES > ETAMINE
ETAMINS > ETAMIN
ETAPE n public storehouse
ETAPES > ETAPE
ETAS > ETA
ETAT n state
ETATISM same as > ETATISME
ETATISME n authoritarian control by the state
ETATISMES > ETATISME
ETATISMS > ETATISM
ETATIST > ETATISME
ETATISTE > ETATISME
ETATISTES > ETATISME

ETATS > ETAT
ETCETERA n number of other items
ETCETERAS pl n miscellaneous extra things or people
ETCH vb wear away or cut the surface of (metal, glass, etc) with acid
ETCHANT n any acid or corrosive used for etching
ETCHANTS > ETCHANT
ETCHED > ETCH
ETCHER > ETCH
ETCHERS > ETCH
ETCHES > ETCH
ETCHING n picture printed from an etched metal plate
ETCHINGS > ETCHING
ETEN n giant
ETENS > ETEN
ETERNAL adj without beginning or end ▷ n eternal thing
ETERNALLY > ETERNAL
ETERNALS > ETERNAL
ETERNE archaic or poetic word for > ETERNAL
ETERNISE same as > ETERNIZE
ETERNISED > ETERNISE
ETERNISES > ETERNISE
ETERNITY n infinite time
ETERNIZE vb make eternal
ETERNIZED > ETERNIZE
ETERNIZES > ETERNIZE
ETESIAN adj (of NW winds) recurring annually in the summer in the E Mediterranean ▷ n etesian wind
ETESIANS > ETESIAN
ETH same as > EDH
ETHAL n cetyl alcohol
ETHALS > ETHAL
ETHANAL n colourless volatile pungent liquid
ETHANALS > ETHANAL
ETHANE n odourless flammable gas
ETHANES > ETHANE
ETHANOATE same as > ACETATE
ETHANOIC adj as in ethanoic acid acetic acid
ETHANOL same as > ALCOHOL
ETHANOLS > ETHANOL
ETHANOYL n type of acyl group or radical
ETHANOYLS > ETHANOYL
ETHE adj easy
ETHENE same as > ETHYLENE
ETHENES > ETHENE
ETHEPHON n synthetic plant-growth regulator
ETHEPHONS > ETHEPHON
ETHER n colourless anaesthetic

ETHERCAP n spider
ETHERCAPS > ETHERCAP
ETHEREAL adj extremely delicate
ETHEREOUS same as > ETHEREAL
ETHERIAL same as > ETHEREAL
ETHERIC > ETHER
ETHERICAL > ETHER
ETHERIFY vb change (a compound, such as an alcohol) into an ether
ETHERION n gas formerly believed to exist in air
ETHERIONS > ETHERION
ETHERISE same as > ETHERIZE
ETHERISED > ETHERISE
ETHERISER > ETHERISE
ETHERISES > ETHERISE
ETHERISH > ETHER
ETHERISM n addiction to ether
ETHERISMS > ETHERISM
ETHERIST > ETHERISM
ETHERISTS > ETHERISM
ETHERIZE vb subject (a person) to the anaesthetic influence of ether fumes
ETHERIZED > ETHERIZE
ETHERIZER > ETHERIZE
ETHERIZES > ETHERIZE
ETHERS > ETHER
ETHIC n moral principle
ETHICAL adj of or based on a system of moral beliefs ▷ n drug available only on prescription
ETHICALLY > ETHICAL
ETHICALS > ETHICAL
ETHICIAN > ETHICS
ETHICIANS > ETHICS
ETHICISE same as > ETHICIZE
ETHICISED > ETHICISE
ETHICISES > ETHICISE
ETHICISM > ETHICS
ETHICISMS > ETHICS
ETHICIST > ETHICS
ETHICISTS > ETHICS
ETHICIZE vb make or consider as ethical
ETHICIZED > ETHICIZE
ETHICIZES > ETHICIZE
ETHICS n code of behaviour
ETHINYL same as > ETHYNYL
ETHINYLS > ETHINYL
ETHION n type of pesticide
ETHIONINE n type of amino acid

ETHIONS > ETHION
ETHIOPS n dark-coloured chemical compound
ETHIOPSES > ETHIOPS
ETHMOID adj denoting or relating to a specific bone of the skull ▷ n ethmoid bone
ETHMOIDAL same as > ETHMOID
ETHMOIDS > ETHMOID
ETHNARCH n ruler of a people or province, as in parts of the Roman and Byzantine Empires
ETHNARCHS > ETHNARCH
ETHNARCHY > ETHNARCH
ETHNE > ETHNOS
ETHNIC adj relating to a people or group that shares a culture, religion, or language ▷ n member of an ethnic group
ETHNICAL same as > ETHNIC
ETHNICISM n paganism
ETHNICITY > ETHNIC
ETHNICS > ETHNIC
ETHNOCIDE n extermination of an ethnic group
ETHNOGENY n branch of ethnology that deals with the origins of ethnic groups
ETHNOLOGY n study of the origins and characteristics of peoples
ETHNONYM n name of ethnic group
ETHNONYMS > ETHNONYM
ETHNOS n ethnic group
ETHNOSES > ETHNOS
ETHOGRAM n description of animal's behaviour
ETHOGRAMS > ETHOGRAM
ETHOLOGIC > ETHOLOGY
ETHOLOGY n study of the behaviour of animals in their normal environment
ETHONONE another name for > KETENE
ETHONONES > ETHONONE
ETHOS n distinctive spirit and attitudes of a people, culture, etc
ETHOSES > ETHOS
ETHOXIDE n any of a class of saltlike compounds
ETHOXIDES > ETHOXIDE
ETHOXIES > ETHOXY
ETHOXY same as > ETHOXYL
ETHOXYL n univalent radical
ETHOXYLS > ETHOXYL
ETHS > ETH
ETHYL adj type of chemical hydrocarbon group

e

ETHYLATE *same as*
> ETHOXIDE
ETHYLATED > ETHYLATE
ETHYLATES > ETHYLATE
ETHYLENE *n* poisonous gas used as an anaesthetic and as fuel
ETHYLENES
> ETHYLENE
ETHYLENIC
> ETHYLENE
ETHYLIC > ETHYL
ETHYLS > ETHYL
ETHYNE *another name for*
> ACETYLENE
ETHYNES > ETHYNE
ETHYNYL *n* univalent radical
ETHYNYLS > ETHYNYL
ETIC *adj* relating to linguistic terms analysed without regard to structural function ▷ *n* etic approach or viewpoint
ETICS > ETIC
ETIOLATE *vb* become pale and weak
ETIOLATED
> ETIOLATE
ETIOLATES
> ETIOLATE
ETIOLIN *n* yellow pigment
ETIOLINS > ETIOLIN
ETIOLOGIC
> ETIOLOGY
ETIOLOGY *n* study of the causes of diseases
ETIQUETTE *n* conventional code of conduct
ETNA *n* container used to heat liquids
ETNAS > ETNA
ETOILE *n* star
ETOILES > ETOILE
ETOUFFEE *n* spicy Cajun stew
ETOUFFEES
> ETOUFFEE
ETOURDI *adj* foolish
ETOURDIE *feminine form of* > ETOURDI
ETRANGER *n* foreigner
ETRANGERE *feminine form of* > ETRANGER
ETRANGERS
> ETRANGER
ETRENNE *n* New Year's gift
ETRENNES > ETRENNE
ETRIER *n* short portable ladder or set of webbing loops
ETRIERS > ETRIER
ETTERCAP *n* spider
ETTERCAPS
> ETTERCAP
ETTIN *n* giant
ETTINS > ETTIN
ETTLE *vb* intend
ETTLED > ETTLE
ETTLES > ETTLE
ETTLING > ETTLE
ETUDE *n* short musical composition for a solo instrument
ETUDES > ETUDE

ETUI *n* small usually ornamented case
ETUIS > ETUI
ETWEE *same as* > ETUI
ETWEES > ETWEE
ETYMA > ETYMON
ETYMIC > ETYMON
ETYMOLOGY *n* study of the sources and development of words
ETYMON *n* earliest form of a word or morpheme from which another is derived
ETYMONS > ETYMON
ETYPIC *adj* unable to conform to type
ETYPICAL *same as* > ETYPIC
EUCAIN *same as* > EUCAINE
EUCAINE *n* crystalline optically active substance
EUCAINES > EUCAINE
EUCAINS > EUCAIN
EUCALYPT *n* myrtaceous tree
EUCALYPTI *n* eucalypts
EUCALYPTS
> EUCALYPT
EUCARYON *same as* > EUKARYOTE
EUCARYONS
> EUCARYON
EUCARYOT *same as* > EUKARYOTE
EUCARYOTE *same as* > EUKARYOTE
EUCARYOTS
> EUCARYOT
EUCHARIS *n* S American plant cultivated for its large white fragrant flowers
EUCHLORIC
> EUCHLORIN
EUCHLORIN *n* explosive gaseous mixture of chlorine and chlorine dioxide
EUCHOLOGY *n* prayer formulary
EUCHRE *n* US and Canadian card game ▷ *vb* prevent (a player) from making their contracted tricks
EUCHRED > EUCHRE
EUCHRES > EUCHRE
EUCHRING > EUCHRE
EUCLASE *n* brittle green gem
EUCLASES > EUCLASE
EUCLIDEAN *adj* of or relating to Euclid (Greek mathematician of Alexandria, 3rd century BC), esp his system of geometry
EUCLIDIAN *same as* > EUCLIDEAN
EUCRITE *n* type of stony meteorite
EUCRITES > EUCRITE
EUCRITIC > EUCRITE
EUCRYPHIA *n* Australian and S American tree or shrub, mostly evergreen, with dark lustrous green leaves and white flowers

EUCYCLIC *adj* (of plants) having the same number of leaves in each whorl
EUDAEMON *same as* > EUDEMON
EUDAEMONS
> EUDAEMON
EUDAEMONY *same as* > EUDEMONIA
EUDAIMON *same as* > EUDAEMON
EUDAIMONS
> EUDAIMON
EUDEMON *n* benevolent spirit or demon
EUDEMONIA *n* happiness, esp (in the philosophy of Aristotle) that resulting from a rational active life
EUDEMONIC
> EUDEMONIA
EUDEMONS > EUDEMON
EUDIALYTE *n* brownish-red mineral
EUGARIE *another name for* > PIPI
EUGARIES > EUGARIE
EUGE *interj* well done!
EUGENIA *n* plant of the clove family
EUGENIAS > EUGENIA
EUGENIC > EUGENICS
EUGENICAL
> EUGENICS
EUGENICS *n* study of methods of improving the human race
EUGENISM > EUGENICS
EUGENISMS
> EUGENICS
EUGENIST > EUGENICS
EUGENISTS
> EUGENICS
EUGENOL *n* oily liquid used in perfumery
EUGENOLS > EUGENOL
EUGH *archaic form of* > YEW
EUGHEN *archaic form of* > YEW
EUGHS > EUGH
EUGLENA *n* type of freshwater unicellular organism
EUGLENAS > EUGLENA
EUGLENID *same as* > EUGLENA
EUGLENIDS
> EUGLENID
EUGLENOID > EUGLENA
EUK *vb* itch
EUKARYON *same as* > EUKARYOTE
EUKARYONS
> EUKARYON
EUKARYOT *same as* > EUKARYOTE
EUKARYOTE *n* type of organism whose cells each have a distinct nucleus within which the genetic material is contained
EUKARYOTS
> EUKARYOT
EUKED > EUK
EUKING > EUK
EUKS > EUK
EULACHAN *same as* > EULACHON

EULACHANS
> EULACHAN
EULACHON *n* salmonoid food fish
EULACHONS
> EULACHON
EULOGIA *n* blessed bread
EULOGIAE > EULOGIA
EULOGIAS > EULOGIA
EULOGIES > EULOGY
EULOGISE *same as* > EULOGIZE
EULOGISED
> EULOGISE
EULOGISER
> EULOGISE
EULOGISES
> EULOGISE
EULOGIST > EULOGIZE
EULOGISTS
> EULOGIZE
EULOGIUM *same as* > EULOGY
EULOGIUMS
> EULOGIUM
EULOGIZE *vb* praise (a person or thing) highly in speech or writing
EULOGIZED
> EULOGIZE
EULOGIZER
> EULOGIZE
EULOGIZES
> EULOGIZE
EULOGY *n* speech or writing in praise of a person
EUMELANIN *n* dark melanin
EUMERISM *n* collection of similar parts
EUMERISMS
> EUMERISM
EUMONG *same as* > EUMUNG
EUMONGS > EUMONG
EUMUNG *n* any of various Australian acacias
EUMUNGS > EUMUNG
EUNUCH *n* castrated man
EUNUCHISE *same as* > EUNUCHIZE
EUNUCHISM > EUNUCH
EUNUCHIZE *vb* castrate
EUNUCHOID *n* person resembling a eunuch
EUNUCHS > EUNUCH
EUOI *n* cry of Bacchic frenzy
EUONYMIN *n* extract derived from the bark of the euonymus
EUONYMINS
> EUONYMIN
EUONYMUS *n* type of N temperate tree or shrub
EUOUAE *n* mnemonic used in medieval music
EUOUAES > EUOUAE
EUPAD *n* antiseptic powder
EUPADS > EUPAD
EUPATRID *n* (in ancient Greece) hereditary noble or landowner
EUPATRIDS
> EUPATRID

EUPEPSIA n good digestion

EUPEPSIAS
> EUPEPSIA

EUPEPSIES > EUPEPSY

EUPEPSY same as
> EUPEPSIA

EUPEPTIC > EUPEPSIA

EUPHAUSID n small pelagic shrimplike crustacean

EUPHEMISE same as
> EUPHEMIZE

EUPHEMISM n inoffensive word or phrase substituted for one considered offensive or upsetting

EUPHEMIST
> EUPHEMISM

EUPHEMIZE vb speak in euphemisms or refer to by means of a euphemism

EUPHENIC adj of or pertaining to biological improvement

EUPHENICS n science of biological improvement

EUPHOBIA n fear of good news

EUPHOBIAS
> EUPHOBIA

EUPHON n glass harmonica

EUPHONIA same as
> EUPHONY

EUPHONIAS
> EUPHONIA

EUPHONIC adj denoting or relating to euphony

EUPHONIES > EUPHONY

EUPHONISE same as
> EUPHONIZE

EUPHONISM n use of pleasant-sounding words

EUPHONIUM n brass musical instrument, tenor tuba

EUPHONIZE vb make pleasant to hear

EUPHONS > EUPHON

EUPHONY n pleasing sound

EUPHORBIA n type of plant such as the spurge or poinsettia

EUPHORIA n sense of elation

EUPHORIAS
> EUPHORIA

EUPHORIC > EUPHORIA

EUPHORIES > EUPHORY

EUPHORY same as
> EUPHORIA

EUPHOTIC adj denoting the part of a sea or lake with enough light to enable photosynthesis

EUPHRASIA n eyebright

EUPHRASY same as
> EYEBRIGHT

EUPHROE n wooden block through which the lines of a crowfoot are rove

EUPHROES > EUPHROE

EUPHUISE same as
> EUPHUIZE

EUPHUISED
> EUPHUISE

EUPHUISES
> EUPHUISE

EUPHUISM n artificial prose style of the Elizabethan period

EUPHUISMS
> EUPHUISM

EUPHUIST > EUPHUISM

EUPHUISTS
> EUPHUISM

EUPHUIZE vb write in euphuism

EUPHUIZED
> EUPHUIZE

EUPHUIZES > EUPHUIZE

EUPLASTIC adj healing quickly and well

EUPLOID adj having chromosomes in an exact multiple of the haploid number ▷ n euploid cell or individual

EUPLOIDS > EUPLOID

EUPLOIDY > EUPLOID

EUPNEA same as
> EUPNOEA

EUPNEAS > EUPNEA

EUPNEIC > EUPNEA

EUPNOEA n normal relaxed breathing

EUPNOEAS > EUPNOEA

EUPNOEIC > EUPNOEA

EUREKA n exclamation of triumph at finding something

EUREKAS > EUREKA

EURHYTHMY n rhythmic movement

EURIPI > EURIPUS

EURIPUS n strait or channel with a strong current or tide

EURIPUSES > EURIPUS

EURO n unit of the single currency of the European Union

EUROBOND n bond issued in a eurocurrency

EUROBONDS
> EUROBOND

EUROCRAT n member, esp a senior member, of the administration of the European Union

EUROCRATS
> EUROCRAT

EUROCREEP n gradual introduction of the euro into use in Britain

EUROKIES > EUROKY

EUROKOUS > EUROKY

EUROKY n ability of an organism to live under different conditions

EUROLAND n area containing the countries using the euro

EUROLANDS
> EUROLAND

EURONOTE n form of euro-commercial paper consisting of short-term negotiable bearer notes

EURONOTES
> EURONOTE

EUROPHILE n person who admires Europe, Europeans, or the European Union

EUROPIUM n silvery-white element of the lanthanide series

EUROPIUMS
> EUROPIUM

EUROPOP n type of pop music by European artists

EUROPOPS > EUROPOP

EUROS > EURO

EUROZONE n area containing the countries using the euro

EUROZONES
> EUROZONE

EURYBATH n organism that can live at different depths underwater

EURYBATHS
> EURYBATH

EURYOKIES > EURYOKY

EURYOKOUS > EURYOKY

EURYOKY same as
> EUROKY

EURYTHERM n organism that can tolerate widely differing temperatures

EURYTHMIC adj having a pleasing and harmonious rhythm, order, or structure

EURYTHMY n dancing style in which the rhythm of music is expressed through body movements

EURYTOPIC adj (of a species) able to tolerate a wide range of environments

EUSOCIAL adj using division of labour

EUSOL n solution of eupad in water

EUSOLS > EUSOL

EUSTACIES
> EUSTATIC

EUSTACY > EUSTATIC

EUSTASIES
> EUSTATIC

EUSTASY > EUSTATIC

EUSTATIC adj denoting worldwide changes in sea level

EUSTELE n central cylinder of a seed plant

EUSTELES > EUSTELE

EUSTRESS n type of stress that is beneficial

EUSTYLE n building with columns optimally spaced

EUSTYLES > EUSTYLE

EUTAXIA n condition of being easily melted

EUTAXIAS > EUTAXIA

EUTAXIES > EUTAXY

EUTAXITE n banded volcanic rock

EUTAXITES
> EUTAXITE

EUTAXITIC
> EUTAXITE

EUTAXY n good order

EUTECTIC adj having the lowest freezing point possible for the mixture ▷ n eutectic mixture

EUTECTICS
> EUTECTIC

EUTECTOID n mixture of substances similar to a eutectic, but forming two

or three constituents from a solid instead of from a melt ▷ adj concerned with or suitable for eutectoid mixtures

EUTEXIA same as
> EUTAXIA

EUTEXIAS > EUTEXIA

EUTHANASE same as
> EUTHANIZE

EUTHANASY n the act of killing someone painlessly

EUTHANAZE same as
> EUTHANIZE

EUTHANISE same as
> EUTHANIZE

EUTHANIZE vb end the life of (a person or animal with an incurable condition)

EUTHENICS n study of the control of the environment, esp with a view to improving the health and living standards of the human race

EUTHENIST
> EUTHENICS

EUTHERIAN n type of mammal with a placenta, whose young reach an advanced state of development before birth

EUTHYMIA n pleasant state of mind

EUTHYMIAS > EUTHYMIA

EUTHYROID n condition of having thyroid glands that function normally

EUTRAPELY n conversational skill

EUTROPHIC adj (of lakes and similar habitats) rich in organic and mineral nutrients and supporting an abundant plant life, which in the process of decaying depletes the oxygen supply for animal life

EUTROPHY
> EUTROPHIC

EUTROPIC > EUTROPY

EUTROPIES > EUTROPY

EUTROPOUS > EUTROPY

EUTROPY n chemical structure

EUXENITE n rare brownish-black mineral

EUXENITES
> EUXENITE

EVACUANT adj serving to promote excretion ▷ n evacuant agent

EVACUANTS
> EVACUANT

EVACUATE vb send (someone) away from a place of danger

EVACUATED
> EVACUATE

EVACUATES
> EVACUATE

EVACUATOR
> EVACUATE

EVACUEE n person evacuated from a place of danger

EVACUEES > EVACUEE
EVADABLE > EVADE
EVADE vb get away from or avoid
EVADED > EVADE
EVADER > EVADE
EVADERS > EVADE
EVADES > EVADE
EVADIBLE > EVADE
EVADING > EVADE
EVADINGLY > EVADE
EVAGATION n digression
EVAGINATE vb turn (an organ or part) inside out
EVALUABLE
> EVALUATE
EVALUATE vb find or judge the value of
EVALUATED
> EVALUATE
EVALUATES
> EVALUATE
EVALUATOR
> EVALUATE
EVANESCE vb fade gradually from sight
EVANESCED
> EVANESCE
EVANESCES
> EVANESCE
EVANGEL n gospel of Christianity
EVANGELIC adj of, based upon, or following from the gospels
EVANGELS > EVANGEL
EVANGELY n gospel
EVANISH poetic word for
> VANISH
EVANISHED > EVANISH
EVANISHES > EVANISH
EVANITION > EVANISH
EVAPORATE vb change from a liquid or solid to a vapour
EVAPORITE n any sedimentary rock formed by evaporation of former seas or salt-water lakes
EVASIBLE > EVASION
EVASION n act of evading something by cunning or illegal means
EVASIONAL > EVASION
EVASIONS > EVASION
EVASIVE adj not straightforward
EVASIVELY > EVASIVE
EVE n evening or day before some special event
EVECTION n irregularity in the moon's motion caused by perturbations of the sun and planets
EVECTIONS
> EVECTION
EVEJAR n nightjar
EVEJARS > EVEJAR
EVEN adj flat or smooth
▷ adv equally ▷ vb make even ▷ n eve
EVENED > EVEN
EVENEMENT n event
EVENER > EVEN
EVENERS > EVEN
EVENEST > EVEN
EVENFALL n early evening

EVENFALLS
> EVENFALL
EVENING n end of the day or early part of the night
▷ adj of or in the evening
EVENINGS adv in the evening, esp regularly
EVENLY > EVEN
EVENNESS > EVEN
EVENS adv (of a bet) winning the same as the amount staked if successful
EVENSONG n evening prayer
EVENSONGS
> EVENSONG
EVENT n anything that takes place ▷ vb take part or ride (a horse) in eventing
EVENTED > EVENT
EVENTER > EVENTING
EVENTERS > EVENTING
EVENTFUL adj full of exciting incidents
EVENTIDE n evening
EVENTIDES
> EVENTIDE
EVENTING n riding competitions, usu involving cross-country, jumping, and dressage
EVENTINGS
> EVENTING
EVENTIVE adj relating to an event
EVENTLESS > EVENT
EVENTRATE vb open the belly of
EVENTS > EVENT
EVENTUAL adj ultimate
EVENTUATE vb result ultimately (in)
EVER adv at any time
EVERGLADE n large area of submerged marshland
EVERGREEN adj (tree or shrub) having leaves throughout the year ▷ n evergreen tree or shrub
EVERMORE adv for all time to come
EVERNET n hypothetical form of internet
EVERNETS > EVERNET
EVERSIBLE > EVERT
EVERSION > EVERT
EVERSIONS > EVERT
EVERT vb turn (some bodily part) outwards or inside out
EVERTED > EVERT
EVERTING > EVERT
EVERTOR n any muscle that turns a part outwards
EVERTORS > EVERTOR
EVERTS > EVERT
EVERWHERE adv to or in all parts or places
EVERWHICH dialect version of > WHICHEVER
EVERY adj each without exception
EVERYBODY pron every person
EVERYDAY adj usual or ordinary ▷ n ordinary day

EVERYDAYS
> EVERYDAY
EVERYMAN n ordinary person; common person
EVERYMEN > EVERYMAN
EVERYONE pron every person
EVERYWAY adv in every way
EVERYWHEN adv to or in all parts or places
EVES > EVE
EVET n eft
EVETS > EVET
EVHOE interj cry of Bacchic frenzy
EVICT vb legally expel (someone) from his or her home
EVICTED > EVICT
EVICTEE > EVICT
EVICTEES > EVICT
EVICTING > EVICT
EVICTION > EVICT
EVICTIONS > EVICT
EVICTOR > EVICT
EVICTORS > EVICT
EVICTS > EVICT
EVIDENCE n ground for belief ▷ vb demonstrate, prove
EVIDENCED
> EVIDENCE
EVIDENCES
> EVIDENCE
EVIDENT adj easily seen or understood ▷ n item of evidence
EVIDENTLY adv without question
EVIDENTS > EVIDENT
EVIL n wickedness ▷ adj harmful ▷ adv in an evil manner
EVILDOER n wicked person
EVILDOERS
> EVILDOER
EVILDOING
> EVILDOER
EVILER > EVIL
EVILEST > EVIL
EVILLER > EVIL
EVILLEST > EVIL
EVILLY > EVIL
EVILNESS > EVIL
EVILS > EVIL
EVINCE vb make evident
EVINCED > EVINCE
EVINCES > EVINCE
EVINCIBLE > EVINCE
EVINCIBLY > EVINCE
EVINCING > EVINCE
EVINCIVE > EVINCE
EVIRATE vb deprive of strength or vigour
EVIRATED > EVIRATE
EVIRATES > EVIRATE
EVIRATING > EVIRATE
EVITABLE adj able to be avoided
EVITATE archaic word for
> AVOID
EVITATED > EVITATE
EVITATES > EVITATE
EVITATING > EVITATE
EVITATION > EVITATE

EVITE archaic word for
> AVOID
EVITED > EVITE
EVITERNAL adj eternal
EVITES > EVITE
EVITING > EVITE
EVO informal word for
> EVENING
EVOCABLE > EVOKE
EVOCATE vb evoke
EVOCATED > EVOCATE
EVOCATES > EVOCATE
EVOCATING > EVOCATE
EVOCATION n act of evoking
EVOCATIVE adj tending or serving to evoke
EVOCATOR n person or thing that evokes
EVOCATORS
> EVOCATOR
EVOCATORY adj evocative
EVOE interj cry of Bacchic frenzy
EVOHE interj cry of Bacchic frenzy
EVOKE vb call or summon up (a memory, feeling, etc)
EVOKED > EVOKE
EVOKER > EVOKE
EVOKERS > EVOKE
EVOKES > EVOKE
EVOKING > EVOKE
EVOLUE n colonial term for an African educated according to European principles
EVOLUES > EVOLUE
EVOLUTE n geometric curve ▷ adj having the margins rolled outwards ▷ vb evolve
EVOLUTED > EVOLUTE
EVOLUTES > EVOLUTE
EVOLUTING > EVOLUTE
EVOLUTION n gradual change in the characteristics of living things over successive generations, esp to a more complex form
EVOLUTIVE adj relating to, tending to, or promoting evolution
EVOLVABLE > EVOLVE
EVOLVE vb develop gradually
EVOLVED > EVOLVE
EVOLVENT adj evolving ▷ n involute curve
EVOLVENTS
> EVOLVENT
EVOLVER > EVOLVE
EVOLVERS > EVOLVE
EVOLVES > EVOLVE
EVOLVING > EVOLVE
EVONYMUS same as
> EUONYMUS
EVOS > EVO
EVOVAE n mnemonic used in medieval music
EVOVAES > EVOVAE
EVULGATE vb make public
EVULGATED
> EVULGATE
EVULGATES > EVULGATE

EVULSE *vb* extract by force
EVULSED > EVULSE
EVULSES > EVULSE
EVULSING > EVULSE
EVULSION *n* act of extracting by force
EVULSIONS > EVULSION
EVZONE *n* soldier in an elite Greek infantry regiment
EVZONES > EVZONE
EW *interj* expression of disgust
EWE *n* female sheep
EWER *n* large jug with a wide mouth
EWERS > EWER
EWES > EWE
EWEST *Scots word for* > NEAR
EWFTES *Spenserian plural of* > EFT
EWGHEN *archaic form of* > YEW
EWHOW *interj* expression of pity or regret
EWK *vb* itch
EWKED > EWK
EWKING > EWK
EWKS > EWK
EWT *archaic form of* > NEWT
EWTS > EWT
EX *prep* not including ▷ *n* former spouse, significant other, etc ▷ *vb* cross out or delete
EXABYTE *n* very large unit of computer memory
EXABYTES > EXABYTE
EXACT *adj* correct and complete in every detail ▷ *vb* demand (payment or obedience)
EXACTA *n* horse-racing bet
EXACTABLE > EXACT
EXACTAS > EXACTA
EXACTED > EXACT
EXACTER > EXACT
EXACTERS > EXACT
EXACTEST > EXACT
EXACTING *adj* making rigorous or excessive demands
EXACTION *n* act of obtaining or demanding money as a right
EXACTIONS > EXACTION
EXACTLY *adv* precisely, in every respect ▷ *interj* just so! precisely!
EXACTMENT *n* condition of being exact
EXACTNESS > EXACT
EXACTOR > EXACT
EXACTORS > EXACT
EXACTRESS > EXACT
EXACTS > EXACT
EXACUM *n* type of tropical plant
EXACUMS > EXACUM
EXAHERTZ *n* very large unit of frequency
EXALT *vb* praise highly
EXALTED *adj* high or elevated in rank, position, dignity, etc

EXALTEDLY > EXALTED
EXALTER > EXALT
EXALTERS > EXALT
EXALTING > EXALT
EXALTS > EXALT
EXAM *n* examination
EXAMEN *n* examination of conscience
EXAMENS > EXAMEN
EXAMETRE *n* ten to the power of eighteen metres
EXAMETRES > EXAMETRE
EXAMINANT *n* examiner
EXAMINATE *n* examinee
EXAMINE *vb* look at closely
EXAMINED > EXAMINE
EXAMINEE *n* person who sits an exam
EXAMINEES > EXAMINEE
EXAMINER > EXAMINE
EXAMINERS > EXAMINE
EXAMINES > EXAMINE
EXAMINING > EXAMINE
EXAMPLAR *archaic form of* > EXEMPLAR
EXAMPLARS > EXAMPLAR
EXAMPLE *n* specimen typical of its group
EXAMPLED > EXAMPLE
EXAMPLES > EXAMPLE
EXAMPLING > EXAMPLE
EXAMS > EXAM
EXANIMATE *adj* lacking life
EXANTHEM *same as* > EXANTHEMA
EXANTHEMA *n* skin eruption or rash occurring as a symptom in a disease such as measles or scarlet fever
EXANTHEMS > EXANTHEM
EXAPTED *adj* biologically adapted
EXAPTIVE *adj* involving biological adaptation
EXARATE *adj* (of the pupa of some insects) having legs, wings, antennae, etc, free and movable
EXARATION *n* writing
EXARCH *n* head of certain autonomous Orthodox Christian Churches ▷ *adj* (of a xylem strand) having the first-formed xylem external to that formed later
EXARCHAL > EXARCH
EXARCHATE *n* office, rank, or jurisdiction of an exarch
EXARCHIES > EXARCHY
EXARCHIST *n* supporter of an exarch
EXARCHS > EXARCH
EXARCHY *same as* > EXARCHATE
EXCAMB *vb* exchange
EXCAMBED > EXCAMB
EXCAMBING > EXCAMB
EXCAMBION *n* exchange, esp of land

EXCAMBIUM *same as* > EXCAMBION
EXCAMBS > EXCAMB
EXCARNATE *vb* remove flesh from
EXCAUDATE *adj* having no tail or tail-like process
EXCAVATE *vb* unearth buried objects from (a piece of land) methodically to learn about the past
EXCAVATED > EXCAVATE
EXCAVATES > EXCAVATE
EXCAVATOR *n* large machine used for digging
EXCEED *vb* be greater than
EXCEEDED > EXCEED
EXCEEDER > EXCEED
EXCEEDERS > EXCEED
EXCEEDING *adj* very great
EXCEEDS > EXCEED
EXCEL *vb* be superior to
EXCELLED > EXCEL
EXCELLENT *adj* exceptionally good
EXCELLING > EXCEL
EXCELS > EXCEL
EXCELSIOR *n* excellent: used as a motto and as a trademark for various products, esp in the US for fine wood shavings used for packing breakable objects
EXCENTRIC *same as* > ECCENTRIC
EXCEPT *prep* other than, not including ▷ *vb* leave out; omit; exclude
EXCEPTANT *n* person taking exception
EXCEPTED > EXCEPT
EXCEPTING *prep* except
EXCEPTION *n* excepting
EXCEPTIVE *adj* relating to or forming an exception
EXCEPTOR > EXCEPT
EXCEPTORS > EXCEPT
EXCEPTS > EXCEPT
EXCERPT *n* passage taken from a book, speech, etc ▷ *vb* take a passage from a book, speech, etc
EXCERPTA > EXCERPTUM
EXCERPTED > EXCERPT
EXCERPTER > EXCERPT
EXCERPTOR > EXCERPT
EXCERPTS > EXCERPT
EXCERPTUM *n* excerpt
EXCESS *n* state or act of exceeding the permitted limits ▷ *vb* make (a position) redundant
EXCESSED > EXCESS
EXCESSES > EXCESS
EXCESSING > EXCESS
EXCESSIVE *adj* exceeding the normal or permitted extents or limits
EXCHANGE *vb* give or receive (something) in return for something else ▷ *n* act of exchanging

EXCHANGED > EXCHANGE
EXCHANGER *n* person or thing that exchanges
EXCHANGES > EXCHANGE
EXCHEAT *same as* > ESCHEAT
EXCHEATS > EXCHEAT
EXCHEQUER *n* (in Britain and certain other countries) accounting department of the Treasury, responsible for receiving and issuing funds
EXCIDE *vb* cut out
EXCIDED > EXCIDE
EXCIDES > EXCIDE
EXCIDING > EXCIDE
EXCIMER *n* excited dimer which would remain dissociated in the ground state
EXCIMERS > EXCIMER
EXCIPIENT *n* substance, such as sugar or gum, used to prepare a drug or drugs in a form suitable for administration
EXCIPLE *n* part of a lichen
EXCIPLES > EXCIPLE
EXCISABLE > EXCISE
EXCISE *n* tax on goods produced for the home market ▷ *vb* cut out or away
EXCISED > EXCISE
EXCISEMAN *n* (formerly) a government agent who collected excise and prevented smuggling
EXCISEMEN > EXCISEMAN
EXCISES > EXCISE
EXCISING > EXCISE
EXCISION > EXCISE
EXCISIONS > EXCISE
EXCITABLE *adj* easily excited
EXCITABLY > EXCITABLE
EXCITANCY *n* ability to excite
EXCITANT *adj* able to excite or stimulate ▷ *n* something able to excite
EXCITANTS > EXCITANT
EXCITE *vb* arouse to strong emotion
EXCITED *adj* emotionally aroused, esp to pleasure or agitation
EXCITEDLY > EXCITED
EXCITER *n* person or thing that excites
EXCITERS > EXCITER
EXCITES > EXCITE
EXCITING *adj* causing excitement
EXCITON *n* excited electron bound to the hole produced by its excitation
EXCITONIC > EXCITON
EXCITONS > EXCITON
EXCITOR *n* type of nerve

EXCITORS > EXCITOR
EXCLAIM vb speak suddenly, cry out
EXCLAIMED > EXCLAIM
EXCLAIMER > EXCLAIM
EXCLAIMS > EXCLAIM
EXCLAVE n territory owned by a country, but surrounded by another
EXCLAVES > EXCLAVE
EXCLOSURE n area of land, esp in a forest, fenced round to keep out unwanted animals
EXCLUDE vb keep out, leave out
EXCLUDED > EXCLUDE
EXCLUDEE > EXCLUDE
EXCLUDEES > EXCLUDE
EXCLUDER > EXCLUDE
EXCLUDERS > EXCLUDE
EXCLUDES > EXCLUDE
EXCLUDING prep excepting
EXCLUSION n act or an instance of excluding or the state of being excluded
EXCLUSIVE adj excluding everything else ▷ n story reported in only one newspaper
EXCLUSORY > EXCLUDE
EXCORIATE vb censure severely
EXCREMENT n waste matter discharged from the body
EXCRETA pl n excrement
EXCRETAL > EXCRETA
EXCRETE vb discharge (waste matter) from the body
EXCRETED > EXCRETE
EXCRETER > EXCRETE
EXCRETERS > EXCRETE
EXCRETES > EXCRETE
EXCRETING > EXCRETE
EXCRETION > EXCRETE
EXCRETIVE > EXCRETE
EXCRETORY > EXCRETE
EXCUBANT adj keeping guard
EXCUDIT sentence substitute (named person) made this
EXCULPATE vb free from blame or guilt
EXCURRENT adj having an outward flow, as certain pores in sponges, ducts, etc
EXCURSE vb wander
EXCURSED > EXCURSE
EXCURSES > EXCURSE
EXCURSING > EXCURSE
EXCURSION n short journey, esp for pleasure
EXCURSIVE adj tending to digress
EXCURSUS n incidental digression from the main topic
EXCUSABLE > EXCUSE
EXCUSABLY > EXCUSE
EXCUSAL > EXCUSE
EXCUSALS > EXCUSE
EXCUSE n explanation offered to justify (a fault

etc) ▷ vb put forward a reason or justification for (a fault etc)
EXCUSED > EXCUSE
EXCUSER > EXCUSE
EXCUSERS > EXCUSE
EXCUSES > EXCUSE
EXCUSING > EXCUSE
EXCUSIVE adj excusing
EXEAT n leave of absence from school or some other institution
EXEATS > EXEAT
EXEC n executive
EXECRABLE adj of very poor quality
EXECRABLY > EXECRABLE
EXECRATE vb feel and express loathing and hatred of (someone or something)
EXECRATED > EXECRATE
EXECRATES > EXECRATE
EXECRATOR > EXECRATE
EXECS > EXEC
EXECUTANT n performer, esp of musical works
EXECUTARY n person whose job comprises tasks appropriate to a middle-management executive as well as those traditionally carried out by a secretary
EXECUTE vb put (a condemned person) to death
EXECUTED > EXECUTE
EXECUTER > EXECUTE
EXECUTERS > EXECUTE
EXECUTES > EXECUTE
EXECUTING > EXECUTE
EXECUTION n act of executing
EXECUTIVE n person or group in an administrative position ▷ adj having the function of carrying out plans, orders, laws, etc
EXECUTOR n person appointed to perform the instructions of a will
EXECUTORS > EXECUTOR
EXECUTORY adj (of a law, agreement, etc) coming into operation at a future date
EXECUTRIX n female executor
EXECUTRY n condition of being an executor
EXED > EX
EXEDRA n building, room, portico, or apse containing a continuous bench
EXEDRAE > EXEDRA
EXEDRAS > EXEDRA
EXEEM same as > EXEME
EXEEMED > EXEEM
EXEEMING > EXEEM
EXEEMS > EXEEM
EXEGESES > EXEGESIS

EXEGESIS n explanation of a text, esp of the Bible
EXEGETE n person who practises exegesis
EXEGETES > EXEGETE
EXEGETIC adj of or relating to exegesis
EXEGETICS n scientific study of exegesis and exegetical methods
EXEGETIST same as > EXEGETE
EXEME vb set free
EXEMED > EXEME
EXEMES > EXEME
EXEMING > EXEME
EXEMPLA > EXEMPLUM
EXEMPLAR n person or thing to be copied, model
EXEMPLARS > EXEMPLAR
EXEMPLARY adj being a good example
EXEMPLE same as > EXAMPLE
EXEMPLES > EXEMPLE
EXEMPLIFY vb show an example of
EXEMPLUM n anecdote that supports a moral point
EXEMPT adj not subject to an obligation etc ▷ vb release from an obligation etc ▷ n person who is exempt from an obligation, tax, etc
EXEMPTED > EXEMPT
EXEMPTING > EXEMPT
EXEMPTION > EXEMPT
EXEMPTIVE > EXEMPT
EXEMPTS > EXEMPT
EXEQUATUR n official authorization issued by a host country to a consular agent, permitting them to perform their official duties
EXEQUIAL > EXEQUY
EXEQUIES > EXEQUY
EXEQUY n funeral rite
EXERCISE n activity to train the body or mind ▷ vb make use of
EXERCISED > EXERCISE
EXERCISER n device with springs or elasticated cords for muscular exercise
EXERCISES > EXERCISE
EXERCYCLE n exercise bicycle
EXERGIES > EXERGY
EXERGONIC adj (of a biochemical reaction) producing energy and therefore occurring spontaneously
EXERGUAL > EXERGUE
EXERGUE n space on the reverse of a coin or medal
EXERGUES > EXERGUE
EXERGY n maximum amount of useful work obtainable from a system
EXERT vb use (influence, authority, etc) forcefully or effectively

EXERTED > EXERT
EXERTING > EXERT
EXERTION > EXERT
EXERTIONS > EXERT
EXERTIVE > EXERT
EXERTS > EXERT
EXES > EX
EXEUNT vb (they) go out
EXFIL vb exfiltrate
EXFILLED > EXFIL
EXFILLING > EXFIL
EXFILS > EXFIL
EXFOLIANT n cosmetic removing dead skin
EXFOLIATE vb peel in scales or layers
EXHALABLE > EXHALE
EXHALANT adj emitting a vapour or liquid ▷ n organ or vessel that emits a vapour or liquid
EXHALANTS > EXHALANT
EXHALE vb breathe out
EXHALED > EXHALE
EXHALENT same as > EXHALANT
EXHALENTS > EXHALANT
EXHALES > EXHALE
EXHALING > EXHALE
EXHAUST vb tire out ▷ n gases ejected from an engine as waste products
EXHAUSTED > EXHAUST
EXHAUSTER > EXHAUST
EXHAUSTS > EXHAUST
EXHEDRA same as > EXEDRA
EXHEDRAE > EXHEDRA
EXHIBIT vb display to the public ▷ n object exhibited to the public
EXHIBITED > EXHIBIT
EXHIBITER > EXHIBIT
EXHIBITOR n person or thing that exhibits
EXHIBITS > EXHIBIT
EXHORT vb urge earnestly
EXHORTED > EXHORT
EXHORTER > EXHORT
EXHORTERS > EXHORT
EXHORTING > EXHORT
EXHORTS > EXHORT
EXHUMATE same as > EXHUME
EXHUMATED > EXHUMATE
EXHUMATES > EXHUMATE
EXHUME vb dig up (something buried, esp a corpse)
EXHUMED > EXHUME
EXHUMER > EXHUME
EXHUMERS > EXHUME
EXHUMES > EXHUME
EXHUMING > EXHUME
EXIES n hysterics
EXIGEANT adj exacting
EXIGEANTE same as > EXIGEANT
EXIGENCE same as > EXIGENCY
EXIGENCES > EXIGENCE

EXIGENCY n urgent demand or need
EXIGENT adj urgent ▷ n emergency
EXIGENTLY > EXIGENT
EXIGENTS > EXIGENT
EXIGIBLE adj liable to be exacted or required
EXIGUITY > EXIGUOUS
EXIGUOUS adj scanty or meagre
EXILABLE > EXILE
EXILE n prolonged, usu enforced, absence from one's country ▷ vb expel from one's country
EXILED > EXILE
EXILEMENT same as > EXILE
EXILER > EXILE
EXILERS > EXILE
EXILES > EXILE
EXILIAN > EXILE
EXILIC > EXILE
EXILING > EXILE
EXILITIES > EXILITY
EXILITY n poverty or meagreness
EXIMIOUS adj select and distinguished
EXINE n outermost coat of a pollen grain or a spore
EXINES > EXINE
EXING > EX
EXIST vb have being or reality
EXISTED > EXIST
EXISTENCE n fact or state of being real, live, or actual
EXISTENT adj in existence ▷ n person or a thing that exists
EXISTENTS > EXISTENT
EXISTING > EXIST
EXISTS > EXIST
EXIT n way out ▷ vb go out
EXITANCE n measure of the ability of a surface to emit radiation
EXITANCES > EXITANCE
EXITED > EXIT
EXITING > EXIT
EXITLESS > EXIT
EXITS > EXIT
EXO informal word for > EXCELLENT
EXOCARP same as > EPICARP
EXOCARPS > EXOCARP
EXOCRINE adj relating to a gland, such as the sweat gland, that secretes externally through a duct ▷ n exocrine gland
EXOCRINES > EXOCRINE
EXOCYCLIC adj (of a cyclic compound) situated outside the ring
EXOCYTIC adj outside biological cell
EXOCYTOSE vb secrete substance from within cell
EXODE n exodus

EXODERM same as > ECTODERM
EXODERMAL > EXODERM
EXODERMIS same as > ECTODERM
EXODERMS > EXODERM
EXODES > EXODE
EXODIC > EXODUS
EXODIST > EXODUS
EXODISTS > EXODUS
EXODOI > EXODOS
EXODONTIA n branch of dental surgery concerned with the extraction of teeth
EXODOS n (in Greek drama) concluding scene
EXODUS n departure of a large number of people
EXODUSES > EXODUS
EXOENZYME n extracellular enzyme
EXOERGIC adj (of a nuclear reaction) occurring with evolution of energy
EXOGAMIC > EXOGAMY
EXOGAMIES > EXOGAMY
EXOGAMOUS > EXOGAMY
EXOGAMY n act of marrying a person from another tribe, clan, etc
EXOGEN n type of plant
EXOGENIC adj formed or occurring on the earth's surface
EXOGENISM > EXOGENOUS
EXOGENOUS adj having an external origin
EXOGENS > EXOGEN
EXOME n part of the genome consisting of exons
EXOMES > EXOME
EXOMION same as > EXOMIS
EXOMIONS > EXOMION
EXOMIS n sleeveless jacket
EXOMISES > EXOMIS
EXON n one of the officers who command the Yeomen of the Guard
EXONERATE vb free from blame or a criminal charge
EXONEREE n person who has been exonerated
EXONEREES > EXONEREE
EXONIC > EXON
EXONS > EXON
EXONUMIA n objects of interest to numismatists that are not coins, such as medals and tokens
EXONUMIST n collector of medals and tokens
EXONYM n name given to a place by foreigners
EXONYMS > EXONYM
EXOPHAGY n (among cannibals) custom of eating only members of other tribes
EXOPHORIC adj denoting or relating to a pronoun

such as 'I' or 'you', the meaning of which is determined by reference outside the discourse rather than by a preceding or following expression
EXOPLANET n planet that orbits a star in a solar system other than that of Earth
EXOPLASM another name for > ECTOPLASM
EXOPLASMS > EXOPLASM
EXOPOD same as > EXOPODITE
EXOPODITE n outer projection on the hind legs of some crustaceans
EXOPODS > EXOPOD
EXORABLE adj able to be persuaded or moved by pleading
EXORATION n plea
EXORCISE same as > EXORCIZE
EXORCISED > EXORCIZE
EXORCISER > EXORCIZE
EXORCISES > EXORCIZE
EXORCISM > EXORCIZE
EXORCISMS > EXORCIZE
EXORCIST > EXORCIZE
EXORCISTS > EXORCIZE
EXORCIZE vb expel (evil spirits) by prayers and religious rites
EXORCIZED > EXORCIZE
EXORCIZER > EXORCIZE
EXORCIZES > EXORCIZE
EXORDIA > EXORDIUM
EXORDIAL > EXORDIUM
EXORDIUM n introductory part or beginning, esp of an oration or discourse
EXORDIUMS > EXORDIUM
EXOSMIC > EXOSMOSIS
EXOSMOSE same as > EXOSMOSIS
EXOSMOSES > EXOSMOSIS
EXOSMOSIS n osmosis in which water flows from a cell or organism into the surrounding solution
EXOSMOTIC > EXOSMOSIS
EXOSPHERE n outermost layer of the earth's atmosphere
EXOSPORAL > EXOSPORE
EXOSPORE n outer layer of the spores of some algae and fungi
EXOSPORES > EXOSPORE
EXOSPORIA n exospores
EXOSTOSES > EXOSTOSIS

EXOSTOSIS n abnormal bony outgrowth from the surface of a bone
EXOTERIC adj intelligible to or intended for more than a select or initiated minority
EXOTIC adj having a strange allure or beauty ▷ n non-native plant
EXOTICA pl n (collection of) exotic objects
EXOTICISE same as > EXOTICIZE
EXOTICISM > EXOTIC
EXOTICIST > EXOTIC
EXOTICIZE vb regard or present as exotic
EXOTICS > EXOTIC
EXOTISM n something exotic
EXOTISMS > EXOTISM
EXOTOXIC > EXOTOXIN
EXOTOXIN n toxin produced by a microorganism and secreted into the surrounding medium
EXOTOXINS > EXOTOXIN
EXOTROPIA n condition in which eye turns outwards
EXOTROPIC > EXOTROPIA
EXPAND vb make or become larger
EXPANDED adj (of printer's type) wider than usual for a particular height
EXPANDER n device for exercising and developing the muscles of the body
EXPANDERS > EXPANDER
EXPANDING > EXPAND
EXPANDOR same as > EXPANDER
EXPANDORS > EXPANDER
EXPANDS > EXPAND
EXPANSE n uninterrupted wide area
EXPANSES > EXPANSE
EXPANSILE adj able to expand or cause expansion
EXPANSION n act of expanding
EXPANSIVE adj wide or extensive
EXPAT n short for expatriate
EXPATIATE vb speak or write at great length (on)
EXPATS > EXPAT
EXPECT vb regard as probable
EXPECTANT adj expecting or hopeful ▷ n person who expects something
EXPECTED > EXPECT
EXPECTER n person who expects
EXPECTERS > EXPECTER
EXPECTING adj pregnant

EXPECTS > EXPECT

EXPEDIENT n something that achieves a particular purpose ▷ adj suitable to the circumstances, appropriate

EXPEDITE vb hasten the progress of ▷ adj unimpeded or prompt

EXPEDITED > EXPEDITE

EXPEDITER n person who expedites something, esp a person employed in an industry to ensure that work on each job progresses efficiently

EXPEDITES > EXPEDITE

EXPEDITOR same as > EXPEDITER

EXPEL vb drive out with force

EXPELLANT adj forcing out or having the capacity to force out ▷ n medicine used to expel undesirable substances or organisms from the body, esp worms from the digestive tract

EXPELLED > EXPEL

EXPELLEE > EXPEL

EXPELLEES > EXPEL

EXPELLENT same as > EXPELLANT

EXPELLER > EXPEL

EXPELLERS pl n residue remaining after an oilseed has been crushed to expel the oil, used for animal fodder

EXPELLING > EXPEL

EXPELS > EXPEL

EXPEND vb spend, use up

EXPENDED > EXPEND

EXPENDER > EXPEND

EXPENDERS > EXPEND

EXPENDING > EXPEND

EXPENDS > EXPEND

EXPENSE n cost ▷ vb treat as an expense

EXPENSED > EXPENSE

EXPENSES > EXPENSE

EXPENSING > EXPENSE

EXPENSIVE adj high-priced

EXPERT n person with extensive skill or knowledge in a particular field ▷ adj skilful or knowledgeable ▷ vb experience

EXPERTED > EXPERT

EXPERTING > EXPERT

EXPERTISE same as > EXPERTIZE

EXPERTISM > EXPERTIZE

EXPERTIZE vb act as an expert or give an expert opinion (on)

EXPERTLY > EXPERT

EXPERTS > EXPERT

EXPIABLE adj capable of being expiated or atoned for

EXPIATE vb make amends for

EXPIATED > EXPIATE

EXPIATES > EXPIATE

EXPIATING > EXPIATE

EXPIATION n act, process, or a means of expiating

EXPIATOR > EXPIATE

EXPIATORS > EXPIATE

EXPIATORY adj capable of making expiation

EXPIRABLE > EXPIRE

EXPIRANT n one who expires

EXPIRANTS > EXPIRANT

EXPIRE vb finish or run out

EXPIRED > EXPIRE

EXPIRER > EXPIRE

EXPIRERS > EXPIRE

EXPIRES > EXPIRE

EXPIRIES > EXPIRY

EXPIRING > EXPIRE

EXPIRY n end, esp of a contract period

EXPISCATE vb find; fish out

EXPLAIN vb make clear and intelligible

EXPLAINED > EXPLAIN

EXPLAINER > EXPLAIN

EXPLAINS > EXPLAIN

EXPLANT vb transfer (living tissue) from its natural site to a new site or to a culture medium ▷ n piece of tissue treated in this way

EXPLANTED > EXPLANT

EXPLANTS > EXPLANT

EXPLETIVE n swearword ▷ adj expressing no particular meaning, esp when filling out a line of verse

EXPLETORY adj expletive

EXPLICATE vb explain

EXPLICIT adj precisely and clearly expressed ▷ n word used to indicate the end of a book

EXPLICITS > EXPLICIT

EXPLODE vb burst with great violence, blow up

EXPLODED > EXPLODE

EXPLODER > EXPLODE

EXPLODERS > EXPLODE

EXPLODES > EXPLODE

EXPLODING > EXPLODE

EXPLOIT vb take advantage of for one's own purposes ▷ n notable feat or deed

EXPLOITED > EXPLOIT

EXPLOITER > EXPLOIT

EXPLOITTS > EXPLOIT

EXPLORE vb investigate

EXPLORED > EXPLORE

EXPLORER > EXPLORE

EXPLORERS > EXPLORE

EXPLORES > EXPLORE

EXPLORING > EXPLORE

EXPLOSION n exploding

EXPLOSIVE adj tending to explode ▷ n substance that causes explosions

EXPO n exposition, large public exhibition

EXPONENT n person who advocates an idea, cause, etc ▷ adj offering a declaration, explanation, or interpretation

EXPONENTS > EXPONENT

EXPONIBLE adj able to be explained

EXPORT n selling or shipping of goods to a foreign country ▷ vb sell or ship (goods) to a foreign country

EXPORTED > EXPORT

EXPORTER > EXPORT

EXPORTERS > EXPORT

EXPORTING > EXPORT

EXPORTS > EXPORT

EXPOS > EXPO

EXPOSABLE > EXPOSE

EXPOSAL > EXPOSE

EXPOSALS > EXPOSE

EXPOSE vb uncover or reveal ▷ n bringing of a crime, scandal, etc to public notice

EXPOSED adj not concealed

EXPOSER > EXPOSE

EXPOSERS > EXPOSE

EXPOSES > EXPOSE

EXPOSING > EXPOSE

EXPOSIT vb state

EXPOSITED > EXPOSIT

EXPOSITOR n person who expounds

EXPOSITS > EXPOSIT

EXPOSOME n collection of environmental factors which can affect a person's health

EXPOSOMES > EXPOSOME

EXPOSTURE n exposure

EXPOSURE n exposing

EXPOSURES > EXPOSURE

EXPOUND vb explain in detail

EXPOUNDED > EXPOUND

EXPOUNDER > EXPOUND

EXPOUNDS > EXPOUND

EXPRESS vb put into words ▷ adj explicitly stated ▷ n fast train or bus stopping at only a few stations ▷ adv by express delivery

EXPRESSED > EXPRESS

EXPRESSER > EXPRESS

EXPRESSES > EXPRESS

EXPRESSLY adv definitely

EXPRESSO variant of > ESPRESSO

EXPRESSOS > ESPRESSO

EXPUGN vb storm

EXPUGNED > EXPUGN

EXPUGNING > EXPUGN

EXPUGNS > EXPUGN

EXPULSE vb expel

EXPULSED > EXPULSE

EXPULSES > EXPULSE

EXPULSING > EXPULSE

EXPULSION n act of expelling or the fact of being expelled

EXPULSIVE adj tending or serving to expel

EXPUNCT vb expunge

EXPUNCTED > EXPUNCT

EXPUNCTS > EXPUNCT

EXPUNGE vb delete, erase, blot out

EXPUNGED > EXPUNGE

EXPUNGER > EXPUNGE

EXPUNGERS > EXPUNGE

EXPUNGES > EXPUNGE

EXPUNGING > EXPUNGE

EXPURGATE vb remove objectionable parts from (a book etc)

EXPURGE vb purge

EXPURGED > EXPURGE

EXPURGES > EXPURGE

EXPURGING > EXPURGE

EXQUISITE adj of extreme beauty or delicacy ▷ n dandy

EXSCIND vb cut off or out

EXSCINDED > EXSCIND

EXSCINDS > EXSCIND

EXSECANT n trigonometric function

EXSECANTS > EXSECANT

EXSECT vb cut out

EXSECTED > EXSECT

EXSECTING > EXSECT

EXSECTION > EXSECT

EXSECTS > EXSECT

EXSERT vb thrust out ▷ adj protruded or stretched out from (something)

EXSERTED > EXSERT

EXSERTILE > EXSERT

EXSERTING > EXSERT

EXSERTION > EXSERT

EXSERTS > EXSERT

EXSICCANT n medicine which causes drying or desiccation

EXSICCATE vb dry up

EXSTROPHY n congenital eversion of a hollow organ, esp the urinary bladder

EXSUCCOUS adj without sap or juice

EXTANT adj still existing

EXTASIES > EXTASY

EXTASY same as > ECSTASY

EXTATIC same as > ECSTATIC

EXTEMPORE adj without planning or preparation ▷ adv without planning or preparation

EXTEND vb draw out or be drawn out, stretch

EXTENDANT adj (in heraldry) with wings spread

EXTENDED > EXTEND

EXTENDER n person or thing that extends

EXTENDERS > EXTENDER

EXTENDING > EXTEND

EXTENDS > EXTEND

EXTENSE adj extensive ▷ n extension; expanse

EXTENSES > EXTENSE

EXTENSILE adj capable of being extended

EXTENSION n room or rooms added to an existing building ▷ adj denoting something that can be extended or that extends another object

EXTENSITY n that part of sensory perception relating to the spatial aspect of objects

EXTENSIVE adj having a large extent, widespread

EXTENSOR n muscle that extends a part of the body

EXTENSORS > EXTENSOR

EXTENT n range over which something extends, area

EXTENTS > EXTENT

EXTENUATE vb make (an offence or fault) less blameworthy

EXTERIOR n part or surface on the outside ▷ adj of, on, or coming from the outside

EXTERIORS > EXTERIOR

EXTERMINE vb exterminate

EXTERN n person with an official connection to an institution but not residing in it

EXTERNAL adj of, situated on, or coming from the outside ▷ n external circumstance or aspect, esp one that is superficial or inessential

EXTERNALS > EXTERNAL

EXTERNAT n day school

EXTERNATS > EXTERNAT

EXTERNE same as > EXTERN

EXTERNES > EXTERNE

EXTERNS > EXTERN

EXTINCT adj having died out ▷ vb extinguish

EXTINCTED > EXTINCT

EXTINCTS > EXTINCT

EXTINE same as > EXINE

EXTINES > EXTINE

EXTIRP vb extirpate

EXTIRPATE vb destroy utterly

EXTIRPED > EXTIRP

EXTIRPING > EXTIRP

EXTIRPS > EXTIRP

EXTOL vb praise highly

EXTOLD archaic past participle of > EXTOL

EXTOLL same as > EXTOL

EXTOLLED > EXTOLL

EXTOLLER > EXTOL

EXTOLLERS > EXTOL

EXTOLLING > EXTOLL

EXTOLLS > EXTOLL

EXTOLMENT > EXTOL

EXTOLS > EXTOL

EXTORSIVE adj intended or tending to extort

EXTORT vb get (something) by force or threats

EXTORTED > EXTORT

EXTORTER > EXTORT

EXTORTERS > EXTORT

EXTORTING > EXTORT

EXTORTION n act of securing money, favours, etc by intimidation or violence

EXTORTIVE > EXTORT

EXTORTS > EXTORT

EXTRA adj more than is usual, expected or needed ▷ n additional person or thing ▷ adv unusually or exceptionally

EXTRABOLD n very bold typeface

EXTRACT vb pull out by force ▷ n something extracted, such as a passage from a book etc

EXTRACTED > EXTRACT

EXTRACTOR n person or thing that extracts

EXTRACTS > EXTRACT

EXTRADITE vb send (an accused person) back to his or her own country for trial

EXTRADOS n outer curve or surface of an arch or vault

EXTRAIT n extract

EXTRAITS > EXTRAIT

EXTRALITY n diplomatic immunity

EXTRANET n intranet modified to allow outside access

EXTRANETS > EXTRANET

EXTRAPOSE vb move (a word or words) to the end of a clause or sentence

EXTRAS > EXTRA

EXTRAUGHT old past participle of > EXTRACT

EXTRAVERT same as > EXTROVERT

EXTREAT n extraction ▷ vb extract or eliminate (something)

EXTREATED > EXTREAT

EXTREATS > EXTREAT

EXTREMA > EXTREMUM

EXTREMAL n clause in a recursive definition

EXTREMALS > EXTREMAL

EXTREME adj of a high or the highest degree or intensity ▷ n either of the two limits of a scale or range

EXTREMELY > EXTREME

EXTREMER > EXTREME

EXTREMES > EXTREME

EXTREMEST > EXTREME

EXTREMISM > EXTREMIST

EXTREMIST n person who favours immoderate methods ▷ adj holding extreme opinions

EXTREMITY n farthest point

EXTREMUM n extreme point

EXTREMUMS > EXTREMUM

EXTRICATE vb free from complication or difficulty

EXTRINSIC adj not contained or included within

EXTROPIAN n believer in extropy

EXTROPIES > EXTROPY

EXTROPY n supposition that human life will expand throughout the universe via technology

EXTRORSAL same as > EXTRORSE

EXTRORSE adj turned or opening outwards or away from the axis

EXTROVERT adj lively and outgoing ▷ n extrovert person

EXTRUDE vb squeeze or force out

EXTRUDED > EXTRUDE

EXTRUDER > EXTRUDE

EXTRUDERS > EXTRUDE

EXTRUDES > EXTRUDE

EXTRUDING > EXTRUDE

EXTRUSILE adj being thrust or forced out

EXTRUSION n act or process of extruding

EXTRUSIVE adj tending to extrude

EXTRUSORY > EXTRUDE

EXTUBATE vb remove tube from hollow organ

EXTUBATED > EXTUBATE

EXTUBATES > EXTUBATE

EXUBERANT adj high-spirited

EXUBERATE vb be exuberant

EXUDATE same as > EXUDATION

EXUDATES > EXUDATE

EXUDATION n act of exuding or oozing out

EXUDATIVE > EXUDATION

EXUDE vb (of a liquid or smell) seep or flow out slowly and steadily

EXUDED > EXUDE

EXUDES > EXUDE

EXUDING > EXUDE

EXUL vb exile; banish

EXULLED > EXUL

EXULLING > EXUL

EXULS > EXUL

EXULT vb be joyful or jubilant

EXULTANCE > EXULTANT

EXULTANCY > EXULTANT

EXULTANT adj elated or jubilant, esp because of triumph or success

EXULTED > EXULT

EXULTING > EXULT

EXULTS > EXULT

EXURB n residential area beyond suburbs

EXURBAN > EXURBIA

EXURBIA n region outside the suburbs of a city

EXURBIAS > EXURBIA

EXURBS > EXURB

EXUVIA n something cast off

EXUVIAE > EXUVIA

EXUVIAL > EXUVIA

EXUVIATE vb shed (a skin or similar outer covering)

EXUVIATED > EXUVIATE

EXUVIATES > EXUVIATE

EXUVIUM n something cast off

EYALET n province of Ottoman Empire

EYALETS > EYALET

EYAS n nestling hawk or falcon

EYASES > EYAS

EYASS same as > EYAS

EYASSES > EYASS

EYE n organ of sight ▷ vb look at carefully or warily

EYEABLE adj pleasant to look at

EYEBALL n ball-shaped part of the eye ▷ vb eye

EYEBALLED > EYEBALL

EYEBALLS > EYEBALL

EYEBANK n place in which corneas are stored

EYEBANKS > EYEBANK

EYEBAR n bar with flattened ends with holes for connecting pins

EYEBARS > EYEBAR

EYEBATH n small cup for applying medication to the eye

EYEBATHS > EYEBATH

EYEBEAM n glance

EYEBEAMS > EYEBEAM

EYEBLACK another name for > MASCARA

EYEBLACKS > EYEBLACK

EYEBLINK n very small amount of time

EYEBLINKS > EYEBLINK

EYEBOLT n type of threaded bolt

EYEBOLTS > EYEBOLT

EYEBRIGHT n type of plant with small white-and-purple flowers, formerly used to treat eye disorders

EYEBROW n line of hair on the bony ridge above the eye ▷ vb equip with artificial eyebrows

EYEBROWED > EYEBROW

EYEBROWS > EYEBROW

EYECUP same as > EYEBATH

EYECUPS > EYECUP

EYED > EYE

EYEDNESS > EYE

EYEDROPS n medicine applied to the eyes in drops

EYEFOLD n fold of skin above eye

EYEFOLDS > EYEFOLD

EYEFUL n view

EYEFULS > EYEFUL

EYEGLASS n lens for aiding defective vision

EYEHOLE n hole through which something is passed

EYEHOLES > EYEHOLE

EYEHOOK n hook attached to a ring at the extremity of a rope or chain

EYEHOOKS > EYEHOOK

EYEING > EYE

EYELASH n short hair that grows out from the eyelid

EYELASHES > EYELASH

EYELESS > EYE

EYELET n small hole for a lace or cord to be passed through ▷ vb supply with an eyelet or eyelets

EYELETED > EYELET

EYELETEER n small bodkin or other pointed tool for making eyelet holes

EYELETING > EYELET

EYELETS > EYELET

EYELETTED > EYELET

EYELEVEL adj level with a person's eyes

EYELIAD same as > OEILLADE

EYELIADS > EYELIAD

EYELID n fold of skin that covers the eye when it is closed

EYELIDS > EYELID

EYELIFT n cosmetic surgery for eyes

EYELIFTS > EYELIFT

EYELIKE > EYE

EYELINE n line of sight

EYELINER n cosmetic used to outline the eyes

EYELINERS > EYELINER

EYELINES > EYELINE

EYEN pl n eyes

EYEOPENER n something surprising

EYEPATCH n material worn over an injured eye

EYEPIECE n lens in a microscope, telescope, etc, into which the person using it looks

EYEPIECES > EYEPIECE

EYEPOINT n position of a lens at which the sharpest image is obtained

EYEPOINTS > EYEPOINT

EYEPOPPER n something that excites the eye

EYER n someone who eyes

EYERS > EYER

EYES > EYE

EYESHADE n opaque or tinted translucent visor

EYESHADES > EYESHADE

EYESHADOW n coloured cosmetic put around the eyes so as to enhance their colour or shape

EYESHINE n reflection of light from animal eye at night

EYESHINES > EYESHINE

EYESHOT n range of vision

EYESHOTS > EYESHOT

EYESIGHT n ability to see

EYESIGHTS > EYESIGHT

EYESOME adj attractive

EYESORE n ugly object

EYESORES > EYESORE

EYESPOT n small area of pigment

EYESPOTS > EYESPOT

EYESTALK n movable stalk bearing a compound eye at its tip

EYESTALKS > EYESTALK

EYESTONE n device for removing foreign body from eye

EYESTONES > EYESTONE

EYESTRAIN n fatigue or irritation of the eyes, caused by tiredness or a failure to wear glasses

EYETEETH > EYETOOTH

EYETOOTH n either of the two canine teeth in the upper jaw

EYEWASH n nonsense

EYEWASHES > EYEWASH

EYEWATER n lotion for the eyes

EYEWATERS > EYEWATER

EYEWEAR n spectacles; glasses

EYEWEARS > EYEWEAR

EYEWINK n wink of the eye; instant

EYEWINKS > EYEWINK

EYING > EYE

EYLIAD same as > OEILLADE

EYLIADS > EYLIAD

EYNE poetic plural of > EYE

EYOT n island

EYOTS > EYOT

EYRA n reddish-brown variety of the jaguarondi

EYRAS > EYRA

EYRE n obsolete circuit court

EYRES > EYRE

EYRIE n nest of an eagle

EYRIES > EYRIE

EYRIR n Icelandic monetary unit

EYRY same as > EYRIE

EZINE n magazine available only in electronic form

EZINES > EZINE

Ff

FA *same as* > FAH
FAA *Scot word for* > FALL
FAAING > FAA
FAAN > FAA
FAAS > FAA
FAB *adj* excellent ▷ *n* fabrication
FABACEOUS *adj* belonging to the legume family of flowering plants which includes peas and beans
FABBER > FAB
FABBEST > FAB
FABBIER > FABBY
FABBIEST > FABBY
FABBY *same as* > FAB
FABLE *n* story with a moral ▷ *vb* relate or tell (fables)
FABLED *adj* made famous in legend
FABLER > FABLE
FABLERS > FABLE
FABLES > FABLE
FABLET *n* large smartphone able to perform many of the functions of a tablet computer
FABLETS > FABLET
FABLIAU *n* comic, usually ribald verse tale
FABLIAUX > FABLIAU
FABLING > FABLE
FABLINGS > FABLE
FABRIC *n* knitted or woven cloth ▷ *vb* build
FABRICANT *n* manufacturer
FABRICATE *vb* make up (a story or lie)
FABRICKED > FABRIC
FABRICS > FABRIC
FABRIQUE *n* (in Quebec) group of laypersons who hold church property in trust for the parish
FABRIQUES > FABRIQUE
FABS > FAB
FABULAR *adj* relating to fables
FABULATE *vb* make up fables
FABULATED > FABULATE
FABULATES > FABULATE
FABULATOR > FABULATE
FABULISE *vb* make up fables
FABULISED > FABULISE

FABULISES > FABULISE
FABULISM *n* literary technique of placing fantastical elements in mundane settings
FABULISMS > FABULISM
FABULIST *n* person who invents or recounts fables
FABULISTS > FABULIST
FABULIZE *vb* make up fables
FABULIZED > FABULIZE
FABULIZES > FABULIZE
FABULOUS *adj* excellent
FABURDEN *n* early form of counterpoint
FABURDENS > FABURDEN
FACADE *n* front of a building
FACADES > FACADE
FACE *n* front of the head ▷ *vb* look or turn towards
FACEABLE > FACE
FACEBAR *n* wrestling hold
FACEBARS > FACEBAR
FACEBOOK *vb* search for (someone) on the Facebook website
FACEBOOKS > FACEBOOK
FACECLOTH *n* small piece of cloth used to wash the face and hands
FACED > FACE
FACEDOWN *vb* confront and force (someone or something) to back down
FACEDOWNS > FACEDOWN
FACELESS *adj* impersonal, anonymous
FACELIFT *n* cosmetic surgery for the face
FACELIFTS > FACELIFT
FACEMAIL *n* computer-generated face that delivers messages on screen
FACEMAILS > FACEMAIL
FACEMAN *n* miner who works at the coalface
FACEMASK *n* protective mask for the face
FACEMASKS > FACEMASK

FACEMEN > FACEMAN
FACEOFF *n* confrontation
FACEOFFS > FACEOFF
FACEPALM *vb* bring one's palm to one's face in dismay
FACEPALMS > FACEPALM
FACEPLANT *vb* fall on one's face
FACEPLATE *n* perforated circular metal plate that can be attached to the headstock of a lathe in order to hold flat or irregularly shaped workpieces
FACEPRINT *n* digitally recorded representation of a person's face that can be used for security purposes because it is as individual as a fingerprint
FACER *n* difficulty or problem
FACERS > FACER
FACES > FACE
FACET *n* aspect ▷ *vb* cut facets in (a gemstone)
FACETE *adj* witty and humorous
FACETED > FACET
FACETELY > FACETE
FACETIAE *pl n* humorous or witty sayings
FACETIME *vb* talk with (someone) via the FaceTime application
FACETIMED > FACETIME
FACETIMES > FACETIME
FACETING *n* act of faceting
FACETINGS > FACETING
FACETIOUS *adj* funny or trying to be funny, esp at inappropriate times
FACETS > FACET
FACETTED > FACET
FACETTING > FACET
FACEUP *adj* with the face or surface exposed
FACIA *same as* > FASCIA
FACIAE > FACIA
FACIAL *adj* of or relating to the face ▷ *n* beauty treatment for the face
FACIALIST *n* beautician who specializes in treatments for the face
FACIALLY > FACIAL
FACIALS > FACIAL

FACIAS > FACIA
FACIEND *n* multiplicand
FACIENDS > FACIEND
FACIES *n* general form and appearance
FACILE *adj* (of a remark, argument, etc) lacking depth
FACILELY > FACILE
FACILITY *n* skill
FACING *n* lining or covering for decoration or reinforcement
FACINGS > FACING
FACONNE *adj* denoting a fabric with the design woven in ▷ *n* such a fabric
FACONNES > FACONNE
FACSIMILE *n* exact copy ▷ *vb* make an exact copy of
FACT *n* event or thing known to have happened or existed
FACTA > FACTUM
FACTFUL > FACT
FACTICE *n* soft rubbery material
FACTICES > FACTICE
FACTICITY *n* philosophical process
FACTION *n* (dissenting) minority group within a larger body
FACTIONAL > FACTION
FACTIONS > FACTION
FACTIOUS *adj* of or producing factions
FACTIS *variant of* > FACTICE
FACTISES > FACTIS
FACTITIVE *adj* denoting a verb taking a direct object as well as a noun in apposition, as for example *elect* in *They elected John president*, where *John* is the direct object and *president* is the complement
FACTIVE *adj* giving rise to the presupposition that a sentence is true
FACTOID *n* piece of unreliable information believed to be true
FACTOIDAL > FACTOID
FACTOIDS > FACTOID
FACTOR *n* element contributing to a result ▷ *vb* engage in the business of a factor
FACTORAGE *n* commission payable to a factor
FACTORED > FACTOR

FACTORIAL n product of all the integers from one to a given number ▷ adj of factorials or factors

FACTORIES > FACTORY

FACTORING n business of a factor

FACTORISE same as > FACTORIZE

FACTORIZE vb calculate the factors of (a number)

FACTORS > FACTOR

FACTORY n building where goods are manufactured

FACTOTUM n person employed to do all sorts of work

FACTOTUMS > FACTOTUM

FACTS > FACT

FACTSHEET n printed sheet containing information relating to items covered in a television or radio programme

FACTUAL adj concerning facts rather than opinions or theories

FACTUALLY > FACTUAL

FACTUM n something done, deed

FACTUMS > FACTUM

FACTURE n construction

FACTURES > FACTURE

FACULA n any of the bright areas on the sun's surface

FACULAE > FACULA

FACULAR > FACULA

FACULTIES > FACULTY

FACULTY n physical or mental ability

FACUNDITY n eloquence, fluency of speech

FAD n short-lived fashion

FADABLE > FADE

FADAISE n silly remark

FADAISES > FADAISE

FADDIER > FADDY

FADDIEST > FADDY

FADDINESS n excessive fussiness

FADDISH > FAD

FADDISHLY > FAD

FADDISM > FAD

FADDISMS > FAD

FADDIST > FAD

FADDISTS > FAD

FADDLE vb mess around, toy with

FADDLED > FADDLE

FADDLES > FADDLE

FADDLING > FADDLE

FADDY adj unreasonably fussy, particularly about food

FADE vb (cause to) lose brightness, colour, or strength ▷ n act or an instance of fading

FADEAWAY n fading to the point of disappearance

FADEAWAYS > FADEAWAY

FADED > FADE

FADEDLY > FADE

FADEDNESS > FADE

FADEIN n gradual appearance of an image on film

FADEINS > FADEIN

FADELESS adj not subject to fading

FADEOUT n gradual disappearance of an image on film

FADEOUTS > FADEOUT

FADER > FADE

FADERS > FADE

FADES > FADE

FADEUR n blandness, insipidness

FADEURS > FADEUR

FADGE vb agree ▷ n package of wool in a wool-bale

FADGED > FADGE

FADGES > FADGE

FADGING > FADGE

FADIER > FADY

FADIEST > FADY

FADING n variation in strength of received radio signals

FADINGS > FADING

FADLIKE > FAD

FADO n type of melancholy Portuguese folk song

FADOMETER n instrument used to determine the resistance to fading of a pigment or dye

FADOS > FADO

FADS > FAD

FADY adj faded

FAE Scot word for > FROM

FAECAL adj of, relating to, or consisting of faeces

FAECES pl n waste matter discharged from the body

FAENA n matador's final actions before the kill

FAENAS > FAENA

FAERIE n land of fairies

FAERIES > FAERIE

FAERY same as > FAERIE

FAFF vb dither or fuss

FAFFED > FAFF

FAFFIER > FAFFY

FAFFIEST > FAFFY

FAFFING > FAFF

FAFFS > FAFF

FAFFY adj awkward and time-consuming to do or use

FAG n tiresome work ▷ vb work hard

FAGACEOUS adj relating to a family of trees, including beech, oak, and chestnut, whose fruit is enclosed in a husk

FAGGED > FAG

FAGGING > FAG

FAGGINGS > FAG

FAGGOT n ball of chopped liver, herbs, and bread ▷ vb collect into a bundle or bundles

FAGGOTED > FAGGOT

FAGGOTING n decorative needlework done by tying vertical threads together in bundles

FAGGOTS > FAGGOT

FAGIN n criminal

FAGINS > FAGIN

FAGOT same as > FAGGOT

FAGOTED > FAGOT

FAGOTER > FAGOT

FAGOTERS > FAGOT

FAGOTING same as > FAGGOTING

FAGOTINGS > FAGOTING

FAGOTS > FAGOT

FAGOTTI > FAGOTTO

FAGOTTIST n bassoon player

FAGOTTO n bassoon

FAGOTTOS > FAGOTTO

FAGS > FAG

FAH n (in tonic sol-fa) fourth degree of any major scale

FAHLBAND n thin bed of schistose rock impregnated with metallic sulphides

FAHLBANDS > FAHLBAND

FAHLERZ n copper ore

FAHLERZES > FAHLERZ

FAHLORE n copper ore

FAHLORES > FAHLORE

FAHS > FAH

FAIBLE variant of > FOIBLE

FAIBLES > FAIBLE

FAIENCE n tin-glazed earthenware

FAIENCES > FAIENCE

FAIK vb Scots word meaning fold

FAIKED > FAIK

FAIKES n sandy rock

FAIKING > FAIK

FAIKS > FAIK

FAIL vb be unsuccessful ▷ n instance of not passing an exam or test

FAILED > FAIL

FAILING n weak point ▷ prep in the absence of

FAILINGLY > FAILING

FAILINGS > FAILING

FAILLE n soft light ribbed fabric of silk, rayon, or taffeta

FAILLES > FAILLE

FAILOVER n automatic transfer to a backup computer system in the event of a primary system failure

FAILOVERS > FAILOVER

FAILS > FAIL

FAILURE n act or instance of failing

FAILURES > FAILURE

FAIN adv gladly ▷ adj willing or eager ▷ vb desire

FAINE variant of > FAIN

FAINEANCE > FAINEANT

FAINEANCY > FAINEANT

FAINEANT n lazy person ▷ adj indolent

FAINEANTS > FAINEANT

FAINED > FAIN

FAINER > FAIN

FAINES > FAINE

FAINEST > FAIN

FAINING > FAIN

FAINITES interj cry for truce or respite from the rules of a game

FAINLY > FAIN

FAINNE n badge worn by advocates of the Irish language

FAINNES > FAINNE

FAINNESS > FAIN

FAINS > FAIN

FAINT adj lacking clarity, brightness, or volume ▷ vb lose consciousness temporarily ▷ n temporary loss of consciousness

FAINTED > FAINT

FAINTER > FAINT

FAINTERS > FAINT

FAINTEST > FAINT

FAINTIER > FAINTY

FAINTIEST > FAINTY

FAINTING > FAINT

FAINTINGS > FAINT

FAINTISH > FAINT

FAINTLY > FAINT

FAINTNESS > FAINT

FAINTS > FAINT

FAINTY > FAINT

FAIR adj unbiased and reasonable ▷ adv fairly ▷ n travelling entertainment ▷ vb join together to form a smooth shape

FAIRED > FAIR

FAIRER > FAIR

FAIREST > FAIR

FAIRFACED adj (of brickwork) having a neat smooth unplastered surface

FAIRGOER n person attending fair

FAIRGOERS > FAIRGOER

FAIRIER > FAIRY

FAIRIES > FAIRY

FAIRIEST > FAIRY

FAIRILY > FAIRY

FAIRING n structure fitted round part of a vehicle to reduce drag

FAIRINGS > FAIRING

FAIRISH adj moderately good, well, etc

FAIRISHLY > FAIRISH

FAIRLEAD n block or ring through which a line is rove

FAIRLEADS > FAIRLEAD

FAIRLY adv moderately

FAIRNESS > FAIR

FAIRS > FAIR

FAIRWAY n area between the tee and the green

FAIRWAYS > FAIRWAY

FAIRY n imaginary small creature ▷ adj of or relating to a fairy or fairies

FAIRYDOM > FAIRY

FAIRYDOMS > FAIRY

FAIRYHOOD > FAIRY

FAIRYISM > FAIRY
FAIRYISMS > FAIRY
FAIRYLAND n imaginary place where fairies live
FAIRYLIKE > FAIRY
FAIRYTALE n story about fairies or other mythical or magical beings, esp one of traditional origin told to children
FAITH n strong belief, esp without proof
FAITHCURE n supposed cure or healing through prayer or faith in God
FAITHED adj having faith or a faith
FAITHER Scot word for > FATHER
FAITHERS > FAITHER
FAITHFUL adj loyal
FAITHFULS > FAITHFUL
FAITHING n practising a faith
FAITHINGS > FAITHING
FAITHLESS adj disloyal or dishonest
FAITHS > FAITH
FAITOR n impostor
FAITORS > FAITOR
FAITOUR n impostor
FAITOURS > FAITOUR
FAIX interj have faith
FAJITA > FAJITAS
FAJITAS pl n Mexican dish
FAKE vb cause something not genuine to appear so by fraud ▷ n person, thing, or act that is not genuine ▷ adj not genuine
FAKED > FAKE
FAKEER same as > FAKIR
FAKEERS > FAKEER
FAKEMENT n something false, counterfeit
FAKEMENTS > FAKEMENT
FAKER > FAKE
FAKERIES > FAKERY
FAKERS > FAKE
FAKERY > FAKE
FAKES > FAKE
FAKEST > FAKE
FAKEY adj (of a skateboarding manoeuvre) travelling backwards ▷ n skateboarding position in which the skateboarder faces backwards
FAKEYS > FAKEY
FAKIE same as > FAKEY
FAKIER > FAKEY
FAKIES > FAKIE
FAKIEST > FAKEY
FAKING > FAKE
FAKIR n Muslim who spurns worldly possessions
FAKIRISM > FAKIR
FAKIRISMS > FAKIR
FAKIRS > FAKIR
FALAFEL n ball or cake made from chickpeas

FALAFELS > FALAFEL
FALAJ n kind of irrigation channel in ancient Oman
FALANGISM > FALANGIST
FALANGIST n member of the Fascist movement founded in Spain in 1933
FALBALA n gathered flounce, frill, or ruffle
FALBALAS > FALBALA
FALCADE n movement of a horse
FALCADES > FALCADE
FALCATE adj shaped like a sickle
FALCATED same as > FALCATE
FALCATION > FALCATE
FALCES > FALX
FALCHION n short and slightly curved medieval sword broader towards the point
FALCHIONS > FALCHION
FALCIFORM same as > FALCATE
FALCON n small bird of prey
FALCONER n person who breeds or trains hawks or who follows the sport of falconry
FALCONERS > FALCONER
FALCONET n type of small falcon
FALCONETS > FALCONET
FALCONINE adj of, relating to, or resembling a falcon
FALCONOID n chemical thought to resist cancer
FALCONRY n art of training falcons
FALCONS > FALCON
FALCULA n sharp curved claw, esp of a bird
FALCULAE > FALCULA
FALCULAS > FALCULA
FALCULATE > FALCULA
FALDAGE n feudal right
FALDAGES > FALDAGE
FALDERAL n showy but worthless trifle ▷ vb sing nonsense words
FALDERALS > FALDERAL
FALDEROL same as > FALDERAL
FALDEROLS > FALDEROL
FALDETTA n Maltese woman's garment with a stiffened hood
FALDETTAS > FALDETTA
FALDSTOOL n backless seat, sometimes capable of being folded, used by bishops and certain other prelates
FALL vb drop through the force of gravity ▷ n falling
FALLACIES > FALLACY
FALLACY n false belief

FALLAL n showy ornament, trinket, or article of dress
FALLALERY > FALLAL
FALLALISH adj foppish
FALLALS > FALLAL
FALLAWAY n friendship that has been withdrawn
FALLAWAYS > FALLAWAY
FALLBACK n something that recedes or retreats
FALLBACKS > FALLBACK
FALLBOARD n cover for piano keyboard
FALLEN > FALL
FALLER n any device that falls or operates machinery by falling
FALLERS > FALLER
FALLFISH n large N American freshwater fish resembling the chub
FALLIBLE adj (of a person) liable to make mistakes
FALLIBLY > FALLIBLE
FALLING > FALL
FALLINGS > FALL
FALLOFF n decline or drop
FALLOFFS > FALLOFF
FALLOUT n descent of solid material in the atmosphere onto the earth
FALLOUTS > FALLOUT
FALLOW adj (of land) ploughed but left unseeded to regain fertility ▷ n land treated in this way ▷ vb leave (land) unseeded after ploughing and harrowing it
FALLOWED > FALLOW
FALLOWER > FALLOW
FALLOWEST > FALLOW
FALLOWING > FALLOW
FALLOWS > FALLOW
FALLS > FALL
FALSE adj not true or correct ▷ adv in a false or dishonest manner ▷ vb falsify
FALSED > FALSE
FALSEFACE n mask
FALSEHOOD n quality of being untrue
FALSELY > FALSE
FALSENESS > FALSE
FALSER > FALSE
FALSERS pl n colloquial term for false teeth
FALSES > FALSE
FALSEST > FALSE
FALSETTO n voice pitched higher than one's natural range
FALSETTOS > FALSETTO
FALSEWORK n framework supporting something under construction
FALSIE n pad used to enlarge breast shape

FALSIES > FALSIE
FALSIFIED > FALSIFY
FALSIFIER > FALSIFY
FALSIFIES > FALSIFY
FALSIFY vb alter fraudulently
FALSING > FALSE
FALSISH > FALSE
FALSISM > FALSE
FALSISMS > FALSE
FALSITIES > FALSITY
FALSITY n state of being false
FALTBOAT n collapsible boat made of waterproof material stretched over a light framework
FALTBOATS > FALTBOAT
FALTER vb be hesitant, weak, or unsure ▷ n uncertainty or hesitancy in speech or action
FALTERED > FALTER
FALTERER > FALTER
FALTERERS > FALTER
FALTERING > FALTER
FALTERS > FALTER
FALX n sickle-shaped anatomical structure
FAME n state of being widely recognized ▷ vb make known or famous
FAMED > FAME
FAMELESS > FAME
FAMES > FAME
FAMILIAL adj of or relating to the family
FAMILIAR adj well-known ▷ n demon supposed to attend a witch
FAMILIARS n attendant demons
FAMILIES > FAMILY
FAMILISM n beliefs of a mystical Christian religious sect
FAMILISMS > FAMILISM
FAMILIST adj relating to familism
FAMILLE n type of Chinese porcelain
FAMILLES > FAMILLE
FAMILY n group of parents and their children ▷ adj suitable for parents and children together
FAMINE n severe shortage of food
FAMINES > FAMINE
FAMING > FAME
FAMISH vb be or make very hungry or weak
FAMISHED adj very hungry
FAMISHES > FAMISH
FAMISHING > FAMISH
FAMOUS adj very well-known ▷ vb make famous
FAMOUSED > FAMOUS
FAMOUSES > FAMOUS
FAMOUSING > FAMOUS
FAMOUSLY adv excellently
FAMULI > FAMULUS

FAMULUS *n* (formerly) the attendant of a sorcerer or scholar

FAN *n* object used to create a current of air ▷ *vb* blow or cool with a fan

FANAL *n* lighthouse

FANALS > FANAL

FANATIC *n* person who is excessively enthusiastic about something ▷ *adj* excessively enthusiastic

FANATICAL *adj* surpassing what is normal or accepted in enthusiasm for or belief in something

FANATICS > FANATIC

FANBASE *n* body of admirers

FANBASES > FANBASE

FANBOY *n* obsessive fan of a subject or hobby

FANBOYS > FANBOY

FANCIABLE *adj* physically attractive

FANCIED *adj* imaginary

FANCIER *n* person interested in plants or animals

FANCIERS > FANCIER

FANCIES > FANCY

FANCIEST > FANCY

FANCIFIED > FANCIFY

FANCIFIES > FANCIFY

FANCIFUL *adj* not based on fact

FANCIFY *vb* make more beautiful

FANCILESS > FANCY

FANCILY > FANCY

FANCINESS > FANCY

FANCY *adj* elaborate, not plain ▷ *n* sudden irrational liking or desire ▷ *vb* suppose; imagine

FANCYING > FANCY

FANCYWORK *n* ornamental needlework

FAND *vb* old word meaning try

FANDANGLE *n* elaborate ornament

FANDANGO *n* lively Spanish dance

FANDANGOS > FANDANGO

FANDED > FAND

FANDING > FAND

FANDOM *n* collectively, the fans of a sport, pastime or person

FANDOMS > FANDOM

FANDS > FAND

FANE *n* temple or shrine

FANEGA *n* Spanish unit of measurement

FANEGADA *n* Spanish unit of land area

FANEGADAS > FANEGADA

FANEGAS > FANEGA

FANES > FANE

FANFARADE *n* fanfare

FANFARE *n* tune played on brass instruments ▷ *vb* perform a fanfare

FANFARED > FANFARE

FANFARES > FANFARE

FANFARING > FANFARE

FANFARON *n* braggart

FANFARONA *n* gold chain

FANFARONS > FANFARON

FANFIC *n* fiction based on work by other authors

FANFICS > FANFIC

FANFOLD *vb* fold (paper) like a fan

FANFOLDED > FANFOLD

FANFOLDS > FANFOLD

FANG *n* snake's tooth which injects poison ▷ *vb* dialect word meaning seize

FANGA *same as* > FANEGA

FANGAS > FANGA

FANGED > FANG

FANGING > FANG

FANGIRL *n* enthusiastic female devotee of something

FANGIRLS > FANGIRL

FANGLE *vb* fashion

FANGLED > FANGLE

FANGLES > FANGLE

FANGLESS > FANG

FANGLIKE > FANG

FANGLING > FANGLE

FANGO *n* mud from thermal springs in Italy

FANGOS > FANGO

FANGS > FANG

FANION *n* small flag used by surveyors

FANIONS > FANION

FANJET *same as* > TURBOFAN

FANJETS > FANJET

FANK *n* sheep pen ▷ *vb* put sheep in a pen

FANKED > FANK

FANKING > FANK

FANKLE *vb* entangle ▷ *n* tangle

FANKLED > FANKLE

FANKLES > FANKLE

FANKLING > FANKLE

FANKS > FANK

FANLIGHT *n* semicircular window over a door or window

FANLIGHTS > FANLIGHT

FANLIKE > FAN

FANNED > FAN

FANNEL *n* ecclesiastical vestment

FANNELL *variant of* > FANNEL

FANNELLS > FANNELL

FANNELS > FANNELL

FANNER > FAN

FANNERS > FAN

FANNIED > FANNY

FANNIES > FANNY

FANNING > FAN

FANNINGS > FAN

FANNY *n* vulgar word for the female genitals ▷ *vb* waste time; misbehave

FANNYING > FANNY

FANO *same as* > FANON

FANON *n* collar-shaped vestment

FANONS > FANON

FANOS > FANO

FANS > FAN

FANSITE *n* website aimed at fans of a celebrity, film, etc

FANSITES > FANSITE

FANSUB *n* fan-produced subtitling of films

FANSUBS > FANSUB

FANTAD *n* nervous, agitated state

FANTADS > FANTAD

FANTAIL *n* small New Zealand bird with a tail like a fan

FANTAILED *adj* having a tail like a fan

FANTAILS > FANTAIL

FANTASIA *n* musical composition of an improvised nature

FANTASIAS > FANTASIA

FANTASIE *same as* > FANTASY

FANTASIED > FANTASY

FANTASIES > FANTASY

FANTASISE *same as* > FANTASIZE

FANTASIST *n* person who indulges in fantasies

FANTASIZE *vb* indulge in daydreams

FANTASM *archaic spelling of* > PHANTASM

FANTASMAL > FANTASM

FANTASMIC > FANTASM

FANTASMS > FANTASM

FANTASQUE *n* fantasy

FANTAST *n* dreamer or visionary

FANTASTIC *adj* very good ▷ *n* person who dresses or behaves eccentrically

FANTASTRY *n* condition of being fantastic

FANTASTS > FANTAST

FANTASY *n* far-fetched notion ▷ *adj* of a type of competition ▷ *vb* fantasize

FANTEEG *n* nervous, agitated state

FANTEEGS > FANTEEG

FANTIGUE *variant of* > FANTEEG

FANTIGUES > FANTIGUE

FANTOD *n* crotchety or faddish behaviour

FANTODS > FANTOD

FANTOM *archaic spelling of* > PHANTOM

FANTOMS > FANTOM

FANTOOSH *adj* pretentious

FANUM *n* temple

FANUMS > FANUM

FANWISE *adj* like a fan

FANWORT *n* aquatic plant

FANWORTS > FANWORT

FANZINE *n* magazine produced by fans

FANZINES > FANZINE

FAP *adj* drunk

FAQIR *same as* > FAKIR

FAQIRS > FAQIR

FAQUIR *variant of* > FAQIR

FAQUIRS > FAQUIR

FAR *adv* at, to, or from a great distance ▷ *adj* remote in space or time ▷ *vb* go far

FARAD *n* unit of electrical capacitance

FARADAIC *same as* > FARADIC

FARADAY *n* quantity of electricity

FARADAYS > FARADAY

FARADIC *adj* of an intermittent asymmetric alternating current

FARADISE *same as* > FARADIZE

FARADISED > FARADISE

FARADISER > FARADISE

FARADISES > FARADISE

FARADISM *n* therapeutic use of faradic currents

FARADISMS > FARADISM

FARADIZE *vb* treat (an organ or part) with faradic currents

FARADIZED > FARADIZE

FARADIZER > FARADIZE

FARADIZES > FARADIZE

FARADS > FARAD

FARAND *adj* pleasant or attractive in manner or appearance

FARANDINE *n* silk and wool cloth

FARANDOLE *n* lively dance in six-eight or four-four time from Provence

FARANG *n* (in Thailand) a foreigner

FARANGS > FARANG

FARAWAY *adj* very distant

FARAWAYS *same as* > FARAWAY

FARCE *n* boisterous comedy ▷ *vb* enliven (a speech, etc) with jokes

FARCED > FARCE

FARCEMEAT *same as* > FORCEMEAT

FARCER *same as* > FARCEUR

FARCERS > FARCER

FARCES > FARCE

FARCEUR *n* writer of or performer in farces

FARCEURS > FARCEUR

FARCEUSE *n* female farceur

FARCEUSES > FARCEUSE

FARCI *adj* (of food) stuffed

FARCICAL *adj* ludicrous

FARCIE *same as* > FARCI

FARCIED *adj* afflicted with farcy

FARCIES > FARCY

FARCIFIED > FARCIFY
FARCIFIES > FARCIFY
FARCIFY vb turn into a farce
FARCIN n bacterial disease of horses
FARCING > FARCE
FARCINGS > FARCE
FARCINS > FARCIN
FARCY n bacterial disease of horses
FARD n paint for the face, esp white paint ▷ vb paint (the face) with fard
FARDAGE n material laid beneath or between cargo
FARDAGES > FARDAGE
FARDED > FARD
FARDEL n bundle or burden
FARDELS > FARDEL
FARDEN n farthing
FARDENS > FARDEN
FARDING > FARD
FARDINGS > FARD
FARDS > FARD
FARE n charge for a passenger's journey ▷ vb get on (as specified)
FAREBOX n box where money for bus fares is placed
FAREBOXES > FAREBOX
FARED > FARE
FARER > FARE
FARERS > FARE
FARES > FARE
FAREWELL interj goodbye ▷ n act of saying goodbye and leaving ▷ vb say goodbye ▷ adj parting or closing
FAREWELLS
> FAREWELL
FARFAL same as
> FALAFEL
FARFALLE n pasta in bow shapes
FARFALLES
> FARFALLE
FARFALS > FARFAL
FARFEL same as
> FALAFEL
FARFELS > FARFEL
FARFET adj far-fetched
FARINA n flour or meal made from any kind of cereal grain
FARINAS > FARINA
FARING > FARE
FARINHA n cassava meal
FARINHAS > FARINHA
FARINOSE adj similar to or yielding farina
FARL n thin cake of oatmeal, often triangular in shape
FARLE same as > FARL
FARLES > FARLE
FARLS > FARL
FARM n area of land for growing crops or rearing livestock ▷ vb cultivate (land)
FARMABLE > FARM
FARMED adj (of fish or game) reared on a farm
FARMER n person who

owns or runs a farm
FARMERESS n female farmer
FARMERIES > FARMERY
FARMERS > FARMER
FARMERY n farm buildings
FARMHAND n person who is hired to work on a farm
FARMHANDS
> FARMHAND
FARMHOUSE n house attached to a farm
FARMING n business or skill of agriculture
FARMINGS > FARMING
FARMLAND n land that is used for or suitable for farming
FARMLANDS
> FARMLAND
FARMOST adj most distant
FARMS > FARM
FARMSTEAD n farm and its buildings
FARMWIFE n woman who works on a farm
FARMWIVES
> FARMWIFE
FARMWORK n tasks carried out on a farm
FARMWORKS
> FARMWORK
FARMYARD n small area of land enclosed by or around the farm buildings
FARMYARDS
> FARMYARD
FARNARKEL vb spend time or act in a careless or inconsequential manner
FARNESOL n type of alcohol
FARNESOLS
> FARNESOL
FARNESS > FAR
FARNESSES > FAR
FARO n gambling game
FAROLITO n votive candle
FAROLITOS
> FAROLITO
FAROS > FARO
FAROUCHE adj sullen or shy
FARRAGO n jumbled mixture of things
FARRAGOES > FARRAGO
FARRAGOS > FARRAGO
FARRAND variant of
> FARAND
FARRANT variant of
> FARAND
FARRED > FAR
FARREN n allotted ground
FARRENS > FARREN
FARRIER n person who shoes horses
FARRIERS > FARRIER
FARRIERY n art, work, or establishment of a farrier
FARRING > FAR
FARRO n variety of wheat
FARROS > FARRO
FARROW n litter of piglets ▷ vb (of a sow) give birth ▷ adj (of a cow) not calving

in a given year
FARROWED > FARROW
FARROWING n (of a sow) act of giving birth
FARROWS > FARROW
FARRUCA n flamenco dance performed by men
FARRUCAS > FARRUCA
FARS > FAR
FARSE vb insert into
FARSED > FARSE
FARSEEING adj having shrewd judgment
FARSES > FARSE
FARSIDE n part of the Moon facing away from the Earth
FARSIDES > FARSIDE
FARSING > FARSE
FART n emission of gas from the anus ▷ vb emit gas from the anus
FARTED > FART
FARTHEL same as > FARL
FARTHELS > FARTHEL
FARTHER > FAR
FARTHEST > FAR
FARTHING n former British coin equivalent to a quarter of a penny
FARTHINGS
> FARTHING
FARTING > FART
FARTLEK n in sport, another name for interval training
FARTLEKS > FARTLEK
FARTS > FART
FAS > FA
FASCES pl n (in ancient Rome) a bundle of rods containing an axe
FASCI > FASCIO
FASCIA n outer surface of a dashboard
FASCIAE > FASCIA
FASCIAL > FASCIA
FASCIAS > FASCIA
FASCIATE adj (of stems and branches) abnormally flattened due to coalescence
FASCIATED same as
> FASCIATE
FASCICLE same as
> FASCICULE
FASCICLED adj in instalments
FASCICLES
> FASCICLE
FASCICULE n one part of a printed work that is published in instalments
FASCICULI
> FASCICULE
FASCIITIS n inflammation of the fascia of a muscle
FASCINATE vb attract and interest strongly
FASCINE n bundle of long sticks used in construction
FASCINES > FASCINE
FASCIO n political group
FASCIOLA n band
FASCIOLAS
> FASCIOLA

FASCIOLE n band
FASCIOLES
> FASCIOLE
FASCIS > FASCI
FASCISM n right-wing totalitarian political system
FASCISMI > FASCISMO
FASCISMO Italian word for
> FASCISM
FASCISMS > FASCISM
FASCIST n adherent or practitioner of fascism ▷ adj characteristic of or relating to fascism
FASCISTA Italian word for
> FASCIST
FASCISTI > FASCISTA
FASCISTIC > FASCIST
FASCISTS > FASCIST
FASCITIS same as
> FASCIITIS
FASH n worry ▷ vb trouble
FASHED > FASH
FASHERIES > FASHERY
FASHERY n difficulty, trouble
FASHES > FASH
FASHING > FASH
FASHION n style popular at a particular time ▷ vb form or make into a particular shape
FASHIONED > FASHION
FASHIONER > FASHION
FASHIONS > FASHION
FASHIONY adj fashionable, trendy
FASHIOUS adj troublesome
FAST adj (capable of) acting or moving quickly ▷ adv quickly ▷ vb go without food, esp for religious reasons ▷ n period of fasting
FASTBACK n car having a back that forms one continuous slope from roof to rear
FASTBACKS
> FASTBACK
FASTBALL n ball pitched at the pitcher's top speed
FASTBALLS
> FASTBALL
FASTED > FAST
FASTEN vb make or become firmly fixed or joined
FASTENED > FASTEN
FASTENER > FASTEN
FASTENERS > FASTEN
FASTENING n something that fastens something, such as a clasp or lock
FASTENS > FASTEN
FASTER > FAST
FASTERS > FAST
FASTEST > FAST
FASTI pl n in ancient Rome, business days
FASTIE n deceitful act
FASTIES > FASTIE
FASTIGIUM n highest point
FASTING > FAST
FASTINGS > FAST

FASTISH > FAST
FASTLY > FAST
FASTNESS n fortress, safe place
FASTS > FAST
FASTUOUS adj arrogant
FAT adj having excess flesh on the body ▷ n extra flesh on the body ▷ vb fatten
FATAL adj causing death or ruin
FATALISM n belief that all events are predetermined
FATALISMS > FATALISM
FATALIST > FATALISM
FATALISTS > FATALISM
FATALITY n death caused by an accident or disaster
FATALLY adv resulting in death or disaster
FATALNESS > FATAL
FATBACK n fat from the upper part of a side of pork
FATBACKS > FATBACK
FATBERG n large mass of fat in a sewer
FATBERGS > FATBERG
FATBIRD n nocturnal bird
FATBIRDS > FATBIRD
FATE n power supposed to predetermine events ▷ vb predetermine
FATED adj destined
FATEFUL adj having important, usu disastrous, consequences
FATEFULLY > FATEFUL
FATES > FATE
FATHEAD n stupid person
FATHEADED adj stupid
FATHEADS > FATHEAD
FATHER n male parent ▷ vb be the father of (offspring)
FATHERED > FATHER
FATHERING > FATHER
FATHERLY adj kind or protective, like a father
FATHERS > FATHER
FATHOM n unit of length ▷ vb understand
FATHOMED > FATHOM
FATHOMER > FATHOM
FATHOMERS > FATHOM
FATHOMING > FATHOM
FATHOMS > FATHOM
FATIDIC adj prophetic
FATIDICAL same as > FATIDIC
FATIGABLE > FATIGUE
FATIGATE vb fatigue
FATIGATED > FATIGATE
FATIGATES > FATIGATE
FATIGUE n extreme physical or mental tiredness ▷ vb tire out
FATIGUED > FATIGUE
FATIGUES > FATIGUE
FATIGUING > FATIGUE
FATING > FATE

FATISCENT adj having the appearance of being cracked
FATLESS > FAT
FATLIKE > FAT
FATLING n young farm animal fattened for killing
FATLINGS > FATLING
FATLY > FAT
FATNESS > FAT
FATNESSES > FAT
FATS > FAT
FATSIA n type of shrub
FATSIAS > FATSIA
FATSO n disparaging term for a fat person
FATSOES > FATSO
FATSOS > FATSO
FATSTOCK n livestock fattened and ready for market
FATSTOCKS > FATSTOCK
FATTED > FAT
FATTEN vb (cause to) become fat
FATTENED > FATTEN
FATTENER > FATTEN
FATTENERS > FATTEN
FATTENING > FATTEN
FATTENS > FATTEN
FATTER > FAT
FATTEST > FAT
FATTIER > FATTY
FATTIES > FATTY
FATTIEST > FATTY
FATTILY > FATTY
FATTINESS > FATTY
FATTING > FAT
FATTISH > FAT
FATTISM n discrimination on the basis of weight
FATTISMS > FATTISM
FATTIST > FATTISM
FATTISTS > FATTISM
FATTRELS n ends of ribbon
FATTY adj containing fat ▷ n insulting word for a fat person
FATUITIES > FATUITY
FATUITOUS > FATUITY
FATUITY n foolish thoughtlessness
FATUOUS adj foolish
FATUOUSLY > FATUOUS
FATWA n religious decree issued by a Muslim leader ▷ vb issue a fatwa
FATWAED > FATWA
FATWAH same as > FATWA
FATWAHED > FATWAH
FATWAHING > FATWAH
FATWAHS > FATWAH
FATWAING > FATWA
FATWAS > FATWA
FATWOOD n wood used for kindling
FATWOODS > FATWOOD
FAUBOURG n suburb or quarter, esp of a French city
FAUBOURGS > FAUBOURG
FAUCAL adj of or relating to the fauces

FAUCALS > FAUCAL
FAUCES n area of the mouth
FAUCET n tap
FAUCETRY n art or practice of making faucets
FAUCETS > FAUCET
FAUCHION n short sword
FAUCHIONS > FAUCHION
FAUCHON variant of > FAUCHION
FAUCHONS > FAUCHON
FAUCIAL same as > FAUCAL
FAUGH interj exclamation of disgust, scorn, etc
FAULCHION variant of > FAUCHION
FAULD n piece of armour
FAULDS > FAULD
FAULT n responsibility for something wrong ▷ vb criticize or blame
FAULTED > FAULT
FAULTFUL > FAULT
FAULTIER > FAULTY
FAULTIEST > FAULTY
FAULTILY > FAULTY
FAULTING > FAULT
FAULTLESS adj without fault
FAULTLINE n surface of a fault fracture
FAULTS > FAULT
FAULTY adj badly designed or not working properly
FAUN n (in Roman legend) mythological creature
FAUNA n animals of a given place or time
FAUNAE > FAUNA
FAUNAL > FAUNA
FAUNALLY > FAUNA
FAUNAS > FAUNA
FAUNIST > FAUNA
FAUNISTIC > FAUNA
FAUNISTS > FAUNA
FAUNLIKE > FAUN
FAUNS > FAUN
FAUNULA n fauna of a small single environment
FAUNULAE > FAUNULA
FAUNULE same as > FAUNULA
FAUNULES > FAUNULE
FAUR Scot word for > FAR
FAURD adj favoured
FAURER > FAUR
FAUREST > FAUR
FAUSTIAN adj of or relating to Faust, esp reminiscent of his bargain with the devil
FAUT Scot word for > FAULT
FAUTED > FAUT
FAUTEUIL n armchair, the sides of which are not upholstered
FAUTEUILS > FAUTEUIL
FAUTING > FAUT
FAUTOR n patron
FAUTORS > FAUTOR
FAUTS > FAUT

FAUVE adj of the style of the Fauve art movement ▷ n member of the Fauve art movement
FAUVES > FAUVE
FAUVETTE n singing bird, warbler
FAUVETTES > FAUVETTE
FAUVISM > FAUVE
FAUVISMS > FAUVISM
FAUVIST n artist following the Fauve style of painting
FAUVISTS > FAUVIST
FAUX adj false
FAUXMANCE n fake romance between two celebrities to gain media coverage
FAVA n type of bean
FAVAS > FAVA
FAVE short for > FAVOURITE
FAVEL adj (of a horse) fallow-coloured ▷ n fallow-coloured horse
FAVELA n (in Brazil) a shanty or shantytown
FAVELAS > FAVELA
FAVELL variant of > FAVEL
FAVELLA n group of spores
FAVELLAS > FAVELLA
FAVELS > FAVEL
FAVEOLATE adj pitted with cell-like cavities
FAVER > FAVE
FAVES > FAVE
FAVEST > FAVE
FAVICON n icon displayed before a website's URL
FAVICONS > FAVICON
FAVISM n type of anaemia
FAVISMS > FAVISM
FAVONIAN adj of or relating to the west wind
FAVOR same as > FAVOUR
FAVORABLE adj favourable
FAVORABLY adv favourably
FAVORED > FAVOR
FAVORER > FAVOUR
FAVORERS > FAVOUR
FAVORING > FAVOR
FAVORITE same as > FAVOURITE
FAVORITES > FAVORITE
FAVORLESS > FAVOR
FAVORS > FAVOR
FAVOSE same as > FAVEOLATE
FAVOUR n approving attitude ▷ vb prefer
FAVOURED > FAVOUR
FAVOURER > FAVOUR
FAVOURERS > FAVOUR
FAVOURING > FAVOUR
FAVOURITE adj most liked ▷ n preferred person or thing
FAVOURS > FAVOUR
FAVOUS adj resembling honeycomb

FAVRILE n type of iridescent glass
FAVRILES > FAVRILE
FAVUS n infectious fungal skin disease
FAVUSES > FAVUS
FAW n old word for an itinerant person
FAWN n young deer ▷ adj light yellowish-brown ▷ vb seek attention from (someone) by insincere flattery
FAWNED > FAWN
FAWNER > FAWN
FAWNERS > FAWN
FAWNIER > FAWNY
FAWNIEST > FAWNY
FAWNING > FAWN
FAWNINGLY > FAWN
FAWNINGS > FAWN
FAWNLIKE > FAWN
FAWNS > FAWN
FAWNY adj of a fawn colour
FAWS > FAW
FAX n electronic system ▷ vb send (a document) by this system
FAXABLE adj able to be faxed
FAXED > FAX
FAXES > FAX
FAXING > FAX
FAY n fairy or sprite ▷ adj of or resembling a fay ▷ vb fit or be fitted closely or tightly
FAYALITE n rare brown or black mineral
FAYALITES > FAYALITE
FAYED > FAY
FAYENCE variant of > FAIENCE
FAYENCES > FAYENCE
FAYER > FAY
FAYEST > FAY
FAYING > FAY
FAYNE archaic spelling of > FEIGN
FAYNED > FAYNE
FAYNES > FAYNE
FAYNING > FAYNE
FAYRE pseudo-archaic spelling of > FAIR
FAYRES > FAYRE
FAYS > FAY
FAZE vb disconcert or fluster
FAZED > FAZE
FAZENDA n large estate or ranch
FAZENDAS > FAZENDA
FAZES > FAZE
FAZING > FAZE
FE n variant of Hebrew letter pe, transliterated as f
FEAGUE vb whip or beat
FEAGUED > FEAGUE
FEAGUES > FEAGUE
FEAGUING > FEAGUE
FEAL vb conceal
FEALED > FEAL
FEALING > FEAL
FEALS > FEAL
FEALTIES > FEALTY

FEALTY n (in feudal society) subordinate's loyalty
FEAR n distress or alarm caused by impending danger or pain ▷ vb be afraid of (something or someone)
FEARE n companion
FEARED > FEAR
FEARER > FEAR
FEARERS > FEAR
FEARES > FEARE
FEARFUL adj feeling fear
FEARFULLY adv in a fearful manner
FEARING > FEAR
FEARLESS > FEAR
FEARS > FEAR
FEARSOME adj terrifying
FEART adj (Scots) afraid
FEASANCE n performance of an act
FEASANCES > FEASANCE
FEASE vb perform an act
FEASED > FEASE
FEASES > FEASE
FEASIBLE adj able to be done, possible
FEASIBLY > FEASIBLE
FEASING > FEASE
FEAST n lavish meal ▷ vb eat a feast
FEASTED > FEAST
FEASTER > FEAST
FEASTERS > FEAST
FEASTFUL adj festive
FEASTING > FEAST
FEASTINGS > FEAST
FEASTLESS > FEAST
FEASTS > FEAST
FEAT n remarkable, skilful, or daring action ▷ adj neat ▷ vb make neat
FEATED > FEAT
FEATEOUS adj neat
FEATER > FEAT
FEATEST > FEAT
FEATHER n one of the barbed shafts forming the plumage of birds ▷ vb fit or cover with feathers
FEATHERED > FEATHER
FEATHERS > FEATHER
FEATHERY > FEATHER
FEATING > FEAT
FEATLIER > FEAT
FEATLIEST > FEAT
FEATLY > FEAT
FEATOUS variant of > FEATEOUS
FEATS > FEAT
FEATUOUS variant of > FEATEOUS
FEATURE n part of the face, such as the eyes ▷ vb have as a feature or be a feature in
FEATURED adj having features as specified
FEATURELY adj handsome
FEATURES > FEATURE
FEATURING > FEATURE
FEAZE same as > FEEZE
FEAZED > FEAZE

FEAZES > FEAZE
FEAZING > FEAZE
FEBLESSE n feebleness
FEBLESSES > FEBLESSE
FEBRICITY n condition of having a fever
FEBRICULA n slight transient fever
FEBRICULE variant of > FEBRICULA
FEBRIFIC adj causing or having a fever
FEBRIFUGE n any drug or agent for reducing fever ▷ adj serving to reduce fever
FEBRILE adj very active and nervous
FEBRILITY > FEBRILE
FECAL same as > FAECAL
FECES same as > FAECES
FECHT Scot word for > FIGHT
FECHTER > FECHT
FECHTERS > FECHT
FECHTING > FECHT
FECHTS > FECHT
FECIAL adj heraldic
FECIALS > FECIAL
FECIT vb (he or she) made it
FECK vb euphemism for an expletive
FECKED > FECK
FECKIN same as > FECKING
FECKING > FECK
FECKLESS adj ineffectual or irresponsible
FECKLY adv dialect word meaning mostly
FECKS > FECK
FECULA n type of starch
FECULAE > FECULA
FECULAS > FECULA
FECULENCE > FECULENT
FECULENCY > FECULENT
FECULENT adj filthy, scummy, muddy, or foul
FECUND adj fertile
FECUNDATE vb make fruitful
FECUNDITY n fertility
FED n FBI agent
FEDARIE n old word for an accomplice
FEDARIES > FEDARIE
FEDAYEE n (in Arab states) a commando
FEDAYEEN > FEDAYEE
FEDELINI n type of pasta
FEDELINIS > FEDELINI
FEDERACY n alliance
FEDERAL adj of a system of governance ▷ n supporter of federal union or federation
FEDERALLY > FEDERAL
FEDERALS > FEDERAL
FEDERARIE variant of > FEDARIE
FEDERARY variant of > FEDARIE

FEDERATE vb unite in a federation ▷ adj federal
FEDERATED > FEDERATE
FEDERATES > FEDERATE
FEDERATOR > FEDERATE
FEDEX vb send by FedEx
FEDEXED > FEDEX
FEDEXES > FEDEX
FEDEXING > FEDEX
FEDORA n soft hat with a brim
FEDORAS > FEDORA
FEDS > FED
FEE n charge paid to be allowed to do something ▷ vb pay a fee to
FEEB n contemptible person
FEEBLE adj lacking physical or mental power ▷ vb make feeble
FEEBLED > FEEBLE
FEEBLER > FEEBLE
FEEBLES > FEEBLE
FEEBLEST > FEEBLE
FEEBLING > FEEBLE
FEEBLISH > FEEBLE
FEEBLY > FEEBLE
FEEBS > FEEB
FEED vb give food to ▷ n act of feeding
FEEDABLE > FEED
FEEDBACK n information received in response to something done
FEEDBACKS > FEEDBACK
FEEDBAG n any bag in which feed for livestock is sacked
FEEDBAGS > FEEDBAG
FEEDBOX n trough, manger
FEEDBOXES > FEEDBOX
FEEDER n baby's bib
FEEDERS > FEEDER
FEEDGRAIN n cereal grown to feed livestock
FEEDHOLE n small hole through which cable etc is inserted
FEEDHOLES > FEEDHOLE
FEEDING > FEED
FEEDINGS > FEED
FEEDLOT n area where livestock are fattened rapidly
FEEDLOTS > FEEDLOT
FEEDPIPE n pipe through which something is supplied to a machine or system
FEEDPIPES > FEEDPIPE
FEEDS > FEED
FEEDSTOCK n main raw material used in the manufacture of a product
FEEDSTUFF n any material used as a food, esp for animals
FEEDWATER n water, previously purified to prevent scale deposit or

corrosion, that is fed to boilers for steam generation

FEEDYARD n place where cattle are kept and fed

FEEDYARDS > FEEDYARD

FEEING > FEE

FEEL vb have a physical or emotional sensation of ▷ n act of feeling

FEELBAD adj inducing feelings of unhappiness

FEELER n organ of touch in some animals

FEELERS > FEELER

FEELESS > FEE

FEELGOOD adj causing or characterized by a feeling of self-satisfaction

FEELING > FEEL

FEELINGLY > FEEL

FEELINGS > FEEL

FEELS > FEEL

FEEN n in Irish dialect, an informal word for 'man'

FEENS > FEEN

FEER vb make a furrow

FEERED > FEER

FEERIE n fairyland

FEERIES > FEERIE

FEERIN n furrow

FEERING > FEER

FEERINGS > FEER

FEERINS > FEERIN

FEERS > FEER

FEES > FEE

FEESE vb perturb

FEESED > FEESE

FEESES > FEESE

FEESING > FEESE

FEET > FOOT

FEETFIRST adv with the feet coming first

FEETLESS > FOOT

FEEZE vb beat ▷ n rush

FEEZED > FEEZE

FEEZES > FEEZE

FEEZING > FEEZE

FEG same as > FIG

FEGARIES > FEGARY

FEGARY variant of > VAGARY

FEGS > FEG

FEH same as > FE

FEHM n medieval German court

FEHME > FEHM

FEHMIC > FEHM

FEHS > FEH

FEIGN vb pretend

FEIGNED > FEIGN

FEIGNEDLY > FEIGN

FEIGNER > FEIGN

FEIGNERS > FEIGN

FEIGNING > FEIGN

FEIGNINGS > FEIGN

FEIGNS > FEIGN

FEIJOA n evergreen myrtaceous shrub of S America

FEIJOADA n Brazilian stew of black beans, meat and vegetables

FEIJOADAS > FEIJOADA

FEIJOAS > FEIJOA

FEINT n sham attack meant to distract an opponent ▷ vb make a feint ▷ adj printing term meaning ruled with faint lines

FEINTED > FEINT

FEINTER > FEINT

FEINTEST > FEINT

FEINTING > FEINT

FEINTS pl n leavings of the second distillation of Scotch malt whisky

FEIRIE adj nimble

FEIRIER > FEIRIE

FEIRIEST > FEIRIE

FEIS n Irish music and dance festival

FEISEANNA > FEIS

FEIST n small aggressive dog

FEISTIER > FEISTY

FEISTIEST > FEISTY

FEISTILY > FEISTY

FEISTS > FEIST

FEISTY adj showing courage or spirit

FELAFEL same as > FALAFEL

FELAFELS > FELAFEL

FELCH vb taboo word meaning to suck semen from the vagina or anus of (a sexual partner)

FELCHED > FELCH

FELCHES > FELCH

FELCHING > FELCH

FELDGRAU n ordinary German soldier (from uniform colour)

FELDGRAUS > FELDGRAU

FELDSCHAR same as > FELDSHER

FELDSCHER same as > FELDSHER

FELDSHER n (in Russia) a medical doctor's assistant

FELDSHERS > FELDSHER

FELDSPAR n hard mineral that is the main constituent of igneous rocks

FELDSPARS > FELDSPAR

FELDSPATH variant of > FELDSPAR

FELICIA n type of African herb

FELICIAS > FELICIA

FELICIFIC adj making or tending to make happy

FELICITER adj happily, successfully

FELICITY n happiness

FELID n any animal belonging to the cat family

FELIDS > FELID

FELINE adj of cats ▷ n member of the cat family

FELINELY > FELINE

FELINES > FELINE

FELINITY > FELINE

FELL vb cut or knock down ▷ adj cruel or deadly

FELLA nonstandard variant of > FELLOW

FELLABLE > FELL

FELLAH n peasant in Arab countries

FELLAHEEN > FELLAH

FELLAHIN > FELLAH

FELLAHS > FELLAH

FELLAS > FELLA

FELLATE vb perform fellatio on (a person)

FELLATED > FELLATE

FELLATES > FELLATE

FELLATING > FELLATE

FELLATIO n sexual activity in which the penis is stimulated by the partner's mouth

FELLATION same as > FELLATIO

FELLATIOS > FELLATIO

FELLATOR > FELLATIO

FELLATORS > FELLATIO

FELLATRIX > FELLATIO

FELLED > FELL

FELLER n person or thing that fells

FELLERS > FELLER

FELLEST > FELL

FELLFIELD n stony tundra area with little vegetation

FELLIES > FELLY

FELLING > FELL

FELLINGS > FELLING

FELLNESS > FELL

FELLOE n (segment of) the rim of a wheel

FELLOES > FELLOE

FELLOW n man or boy ▷ adj in the same group or condition ▷ vb join as a companion

FELLOWED > FELLOW

FELLOWING > FELLOW

FELLOWLY adj friendly, companionable

FELLOWMAN n companion

FELLOWMEN > FELLOWMAN

FELLOWS > FELLOW

FELLS > FELL

FELLY same as > FELLOE

FELON n (formerly) person guilty of a felony ▷ adj evil

FELONIES > FELONY

FELONIOUS adj of, involving, or constituting a felony

FELONOUS adj wicked

FELONRIES > FELONRY

FELONRY n felons collectively

FELONS > FELON

FELONY n serious crime

FELQUISTE n member of paramilitary group seeking independence for Quebec

FELSIC adj relating to igneous rock

FELSITE n any fine-grained igneous rock

FELSITES > FELSITE

FELSITIC > FELSITE

FELSPAR same as > FELDSPAR

FELSPARS > FELSPAR

FELSTONE same as > FELSITE

FELSTONES > FELSTONE

FELT n matted fabric ▷ vb become matted

FELTED > FELT

FELTER vb mat together

FELTERED > FELTER

FELTERING > FELTER

FELTERS > FELTER

FELTIER > FELT

FELTIEST > FELT

FELTING n felted material

FELTINGS > FELTING

FELTLIKE > FELT

FELTS > FELT

FELTY > FELT

FELUCCA n narrow lateen-rigged vessel

FELUCCAS > FELUCCA

FELWORT n type of plant

FELWORTS > FELWORT

FEM n type of igneous rock

FEMAL archaic variant of > FEMALE

FEMALE adj of the sex which bears offspring ▷ n female person or animal

FEMALES > FEMALE

FEMALITY > FEMALE

FEMALS > FEMAL

FEME n woman or wife

FEMERALL n ventilator or smoke outlet on a roof

FEMERALLS > FEMERALL

FEMERELL n ventilator or smoke outlet in a roof

FEMERELLS > FEMERELL

FEMES > FEME

FEMETARY variant of > FUMITORY

FEMICIDAL > FEMICIDE

FEMICIDE n killing of a woman or girl

FEMICIDES > FEMICIDE

FEMINACY n feminine character

FEMINAL adj feminine, female

FEMINAZI n offensive term for a militant feminist

FEMINAZIS > FEMINAZI

FEMINETTY n quality of being feminine

FEMINIE n women collectively

FEMINIES > FEMINIE

FEMININE adj relating to females ▷ n short for feminine noun

FEMININES > FEMININE

FEMINISE same as > FEMINIZE

FEMINISED > FEMINISE

FEMINISES > FEMINISE

FEMINISM n advocacy of equal rights for women

FEMINISMS > FEMINISM

FEMINIST n person who advocates equal rights for women ▷ adj of, relating to, or advocating feminism

FEMINISTS > FEMINIST

FEMINITY > FEMINAL

FEMINIZE vb make or become feminine

FEMINIZED > FEMINIZE

FEMINIZES > FEMINIZE

FEMITER variant of > FUMITORY

FEMITERS > FEMITER

FEMME n woman or wife

FEMMES > FEMME

FEMMIER > FEMMY

FEMMIEST > FEMMY

FEMMY adj markedly or exaggeratedly feminine

FEMORA > FEMUR

FEMORAL adj of the thigh

FEMS > FEM

FEMUR n thighbone

FEMURS > FEMUR

FEN n low-lying flat marshy land

FENAGLE variant of > FINAGLE

FENAGLED > FENAGLE

FENAGLES > FENAGLE

FENAGLING > FENAGLE

FENCE n barrier of posts linked by wire or wood ▷ vb enclose with or as if with a fence

FENCED > FENCE

FENCELESS > FENCE

FENCELIKE > FENCE

FENCELINE n continuous extent of fence encompassing a tract of farmland

FENCER n person who fights with a sword

FENCEROW n uncultivated land flanking a fence

FENCEROWS > FENCEROW

FENCERS > FENCER

FENCES > FENCE

FENCEWIRE n wire used in making fences

FENCIBLE n person who undertook military service in defence of their homeland only

FENCIBLES > FENCIBLE

FENCING n sport of fighting with swords

FENCINGS > FENCING

FEND vb give support (to someone, esp oneself) ▷ n shift or effort

FENDED > FEND

FENDER n low metal frame in front of a fireplace

FENDERED adj having a fender

FENDERS > FENDER

FENDIER > FENDY

FENDIEST > FENDY

FENDING > FEND

FENDS > FEND

FENDY adj thrifty

FENESTRA n small opening in or between bones

FENESTRAE > FENESTRA

FENESTRAL > FENESTRA

FENESTRAS > FENESTRA

FENI n Goan alcoholic drink

FENING n small currency unit of Bosnia-Herzegovina

FENINGA > FENING

FENINGS > FENING

FENIS > FENI

FENITAR variant of > FUMITORY

FENITARS > FENITAR

FENKS n whale blubber

FENLAND > FEN

FENLANDS > FEN

FENMAN > FEN

FENMEN > FEN

FENNEC n type of nocturnal desert fox

FENNECS > FENNEC

FENNEL n fragrant plant

FENNELS > FENNEL

FENNIER > FENNY

FENNIES > FENNY

FENNIEST > FENNY

FENNING same as > FENING

FENNISH > FEN

FENNY adj boggy or marshy ▷ n feni

FENS > FEN

FENT n piece of waste fabric

FENTANYL n narcotic drug used in medicine to relieve pain

FENTANYLS > FENTANYL

FENTHION n type of pesticide

FENTHIONS > FENTHION

FENTS > FENT

FENUGREEK n Mediterranean plant grown for its heavily scented seeds

FENURON n type of herbicide

FENURONS > FENURON

FEOD same as > FEUD

FEODAL > FEOD

FEODARIES > FEOD

FEODARY > FEOD

FEODS > FEOD

FEOFF same as > FIEF

FEOFFED > FEOFF

FEOFFEE n (in feudal society) a vassal granted a fief by their lord

FEOFFEES > FEOFFEE

FEOFFER > FEOFF

FEOFFERS > FEOFF

FEOFFING > FEOFF

FEOFFMENT n (in medieval Europe) a lord's act of granting a fief to his man

FEOFFOR > FEOFF

FEOFFORS > FEOFF

FEOFFS > FEOFF

FER same as > FAR

FERACIOUS adj fruitful

FERACITY > FERACIOUS

FERAL adj wild ▷ n person who displays such tendencies and appearance

FERALISED same as > FERALIZED

FERALIZED adj once domesticated, but now wild

FERALS > FERAL

FERBAM n powder used as a fungicide

FERBAMS > FERBAM

FERE n companion ▷ adj fierce

FERER > FERE

FERES > FERE

FEREST > FERE

FERETORY n shrine, usually portable, for a saint's relics

FERIA n weekday on which no feast occurs

FERIAE > FERIA

FERIAL adj of or relating to a feria

FERIAS > FERIA

FERINE same as > FERAL

FERITIES > FERAL

FERITY > FERAL

FERLIE same as > FERLY

FERLIED > FERLY

FERLIER > FERLY

FERLIES > FERLY

FERLIEST > FERLY

FERLY adj wonderful ▷ n wonder ▷ vb wonder

FERLYING > FERLY

FERM variant of > FARM

FERMATA another word for > PAUSE

FERMATAS > FERMATA

FERMATE > FERMATA

FERMENT n any agent that causes fermentation ▷ vb (cause to) undergo fermentation

FERMENTED > FERMENT

FERMENTER > FERMENT

FERMENTOR > FERMENT

FERMENTS > FERMENT

FERMI n unit of length

FERMION n type of particle

FERMIONIC > FERMION

FERMIONS > FERMION

FERMIS > FERMI

FERMIUM n chemical element

FERMIUMS > FERMIUM

FERMS > FERM

FERN n flowerless plant with fine fronds

FERNALLY n seedless plant that is not a true fern

FERNBIRD n small brown and white New Zealand swamp bird with a fernlike tail

FERNBIRDS > FERNBIRD

FERNERIES > FERNERY

FERNERY n place where ferns are grown

FERNIER > FERN

FERNIEST > FERN

FERNING n production of a fern-like pattern

FERNINGS > FERNING

FERNINST same as > FORNENST

FERNLESS > FERN

FERNLIKE > FERN

FERNS > FERN

FERNSHAW n fern thicket

FERNSHAWS > FERNSHAW

FERNTICLE n freckle

FERNY > FERN

FEROCIOUS adj savagely fierce or cruel

FEROCITY > FEROCIOUS

FERRATE n type of salt

FERRATES > FERRATE

FERREL variant of > FERRULE

FERRELED > FERREL

FERRELING > FERREL

FERRELLED > FERREL

FERRELS > FERREL

FERREOUS adj containing or resembling iron

FERRET n tamed polecat ▷ vb hunt with ferrets

FERRETED > FERRET

FERRETER > FERRET

FERRETERS > FERRET

FERRETIER > FERRETY

FERRETING > FERRET

FERRETS > FERRET

FERRETY adj like a ferret

FERRIAGE n transportation by ferry

FERRIAGES > FERRIAGE

FERRIC adj of or containing iron

FERRIED > FERRY

FERRIES > FERRY

FERRITE n type of ceramic compound

FERRITES > FERRITE

FERRITIC > FERRITE

FERRITIN n type of protein

FERRITINS > FERRITIN

FERROCENE n reddish-orange insoluble crystalline compound

FERROGRAM n slide used to illustrate suspended iron particles in the lubricant of a machine

FERROTYPE n photographic print produced directly in a camera by exposing a sheet of iron or tin coated with a sensitized enamel

FERROUS adj of or containing iron in the divalent state

FERRUGO n disease affecting plants

FERRUGOS > FERRUGO
FERRULE *n* metal cap to strengthen the end of a stick ▷ *vb* equip (a stick, etc) with a ferrule
FERRULED > FERRULE
FERRULES > FERRULE
FERRULING > FERRULE
FERRUM *Latin word for* > IRON
FERRUMS > FERRUM
FERRY *n* boat for transporting people and vehicles ▷ *vb* carry by ferry
FERRYBOAT *same as* > FERRY
FERRYING > FERRY
FERRYMAN *n* someone who provides a ferry service
FERRYMEN > FERRYMAN
FERTIGATE *vb* fertilize and irrigate at the same time
FERTILE *adj* capable of producing young, crops, or vegetation
FERTILELY > FERTILE
FERTILER > FERTILE
FERTILEST > FERTILE
FERTILISE *same as* > FERTILIZE
FERTILITY *n* ability to produce offspring, esp abundantly
FERTILIZE *vb* to supply (soil or water) with mineral and organic nutrients to aid the growth of plants
FERULA *n* large Mediterranean plant
FERULAE > FERULA
FERULAS > FERULA
FERULE *same as* > FERRULE
FERULED > FERULE
FERULES > FERULE
FERULING > FERULE
FERVENCY *another word for* > FERVOUR
FERVENT *adj* intensely passionate and sincere
FERVENTER > FERVENT
FERVENTLY > FERVENT
FERVID *same as* > FERVENT
FERVIDER > FERVID
FERVIDEST > FERVID
FERVIDITY > FERVID
FERVIDLY > FERVID
FERVOR *same as* > FERVOUR
FERVOROUS > FERVOUR
FERVORS > FERVOR
FERVOUR *n* intensity of feeling
FERVOURS > FERVOUR
FES > FE
FESCUE *n* pasture and lawn grass with stiff narrow leaves
FESCUES > FESCUE
FESS *vb* confess
FESSE *n* horizontal band across a shield
FESSED > FESS
FESSES > FESSE

FESSING > FESS
FESSWISE *adv* in heraldry, with a horizontal band across the shield
FEST *n* event at which the emphasis is on a particular activity
FESTA *n* festival
FESTAL *adj* festive ▷ *n* festivity
FESTALLY > FESTAL
FESTALS > FESTAL
FESTAS > FESTA
FESTER *vb* grow worse and increasingly hostile ▷ *n* small ulcer or sore containing pus
FESTERED > FESTER
FESTERING > FESTER
FESTERS > FESTER
FESTIER > FESTY
FESTIEST > FESTY
FESTILOGY *n* treatise about church festivals
FESTINATE *vb* hurry
FESTIVAL *n* organized series of special events or performances
FESTIVALS > FESTIVAL
FESTIVE *adj* of or like a celebration
FESTIVELY > FESTIVE
FESTIVITY *n* happy celebration
FESTIVOUS > FESTIVE
FESTOLOGY *variant of* > FESTILOGY
FESTOON *vb* hang decorations in loops ▷ *n* decorative chain
FESTOONED > FESTOON
FESTOONS > FESTOON
FESTS > FEST
FESTY *adj* dirty
FET *vb* fetch
FETA *n* white salty Greek cheese
FETAL *adj* of, relating to, or resembling a fetus
FETAS > FETA
FETATION *n* state of pregnancy
FETATIONS > FETATION
FETCH *vb* go after and bring back ▷ *n* ghost or apparition of a living person
FETCHED > FETCH
FETCHER *n* person or animal that fetches
FETCHERS > FETCHER
FETCHES > FETCH
FETCHING *adj* attractive
FETE *n* gala, bazaar, etc, usu held outdoors ▷ *vb* honour or entertain regally
FETED > FETE
FETERITA *n* type of sorghum
FETERITAS > FETERITA
FETES > FETE
FETIAL *n* ancient Roman herald
FETIALES > FETIAL

FETIALIS *n* priest in ancient Rome
FETIALS > FETIAL
FETICH *same as* > FETISH
FETICHE *variant of* > FETICH
FETICHES > FETICH
FETICHISE *variant of* > FETICHIZE
FETICHISM *same as* > FETISHISM
FETICHIST > FETISHISM
FETICHIZE *vb* be excessively or irrationally devoted to an object, activity, etc
FETICIDAL > FETICIDE
FETICIDE *n* destruction of a fetus in the uterus
FETICIDES > FETICIDE
FETID *adj* stinking
FETIDER > FETID
FETIDEST > FETID
FETIDITY > FETID
FETIDLY > FETID
FETIDNESS > FETID
FETING > FETE
FETISH *n* irrational devotion (to an object, activity, etc)
FETISHES > FETISH
FETISHISE *same as* > FETISHIZE
FETISHISM *n* excessive attention or attachment to something
FETISHIST > FETISHISM
FETISHIZE *vb* be excessively or irrationally devoted to (an object, activity, etc)
FETLOCK *n* projection behind and above a horse's hoof
FETLOCKED *adj* having fetlocks
FETLOCKS > FETLOCK
FETOLOGY *n* branch of medicine concerned with the fetus in the uterus
FETOR *n* stale or putrid odour
FETORS > FETOR
FETOSCOPE *n* fibreoptic instrument that enables examination of a fetus
FETOSCOPY > FETOSCOPE
FETS > FET
FETT *variant of* > FET
FETTA *variant of* > FETA
FETTAS > FETTA
FETTED > FET
FETTER *n* chain or shackle for the foot ▷ *vb* restrict
FETTERED > FETTER
FETTERER > FETTER
FETTERERS > FETTER
FETTERING > FETTER
FETTERS > FETTER
FETTING > FET
FETTLE *same as* > FETTLING

FETTLED > FETTLE
FETTLER *n* person employed to maintain railway tracks
FETTLERS > FETTLER
FETTLES > FETTLE
FETTLING *n* refractory material used to line the hearth of puddling furnaces
FETTLINGS > FETTLING
FETTS > FETT
FETTUCINE *n* type of pasta in the form of narrow ribbons
FETTUCINI *same as* > FETTUCINE
FETUS *n* embryo of a mammal in the later stages of development
FETUSES > FETUS
FETWA *variant of* > FATWA
FETWAS > FETWA
FEU *n* (in Scotland) type of rent ▷ *vb* grant land to a person who pays a feu
FEUAR *n* tenant of a feu
FEUARS > FEUAR
FEUD *n* long bitter hostility between two people or groups ▷ *vb* carry on a feud
FEUDAL *adj* of or like feudalism
FEUDALISE *same as* > FEUDALIZE
FEUDALISM *n* medieval system in which people held land from a lord, and in return worked and fought for him
FEUDALIST > FEUDALISM
FEUDALITY *n* state or quality of being feudal
FEUDALIZE *vb* make feudal
FEUDALLY > FEUDAL
FEUDARIES > FEUDARY
FEUDARY *n* holder of land through feudal right
FEUDATORY *n* person holding a fief ▷ *adj* relating to or characteristic of the relationship between lord and vassal
FEUDED > FEUD
FEUDING > FEUD
FEUDINGS > FEUD
FEUDIST *n* person who takes part in a feud or quarrel
FEUDISTS > FEUDIST
FEUDS > FEUD
FEUED > FEU
FEUILLETE *n* puff pastry
FEUING > FEU
FEUS > FEU
FEUTRE *vb* place in a resting position
FEUTRED > FEUTRE
FEUTRES > FEUTRE
FEUTRING > FEUTRE
FEVER *n* (illness causing) high body temperature ▷ *vb* affect with or as if with fever

FEVERED > FEVER
FEVERFEW n bushy European plant with white flower heads, formerly used medicinally
FEVERFEWS > FEVERFEW
FEVERING > FEVER
FEVERISH adj suffering from fever
FEVERLESS > FEVER
FEVEROUS same as > FEVERISH
FEVERROOT n American wild plant
FEVERS > FEVER
FEVERWEED n plant thought to be medicinal
FEVERWORT n any of several plants considered to have medicinal properties, such as horse gentian and boneset
FEW adj not many ▷ n as in the few small number of people considered as a class
FEWER > FEW
FEWEST > FEW
FEWMET variant of > FUMET
FEWMETS > FEWMET
FEWNESS > FEW
FEWNESSES > FEW
FEWS > FEW
FEWTER variant of > FEUTRE
FEWTERED > FEWTER
FEWTERING > FEUTRE
FEWTERS > FEWTER
FEWTRILS n trifles, trivia
FEY adj whimsically strange ▷ vb clean out
FEYED > FEY
FEYER > FEY
FEYEST > FEY
FEYING > FEY
FEYLY > FEY
FEYNESS > FEY
FEYNESSES > FEY
FEYS > FEY
FEZ n brimless tasselled cap, orig from Turkey
FEZES > FEZ
FEZZED adj wearing a fez
FEZZES > FEZ
FEZZY > FEZ
FIACRE n small four-wheeled horse-drawn carriage
FIACRES > FIACRE
FIANCE n man engaged to be married
FIANCEE n woman who is engaged to be married
FIANCEES > FIANCEE
FIANCES > FIANCE
FIAR n property owner
FIARS n legally fixed price of corn
FIASCHI > FIASCO
FIASCO n ridiculous or humiliating failure
FIASCOES > FIASCO
FIASCOS > FIASCO
FIAT n arbitrary order ▷ vb issue a fiat
FIATED > FIAT

FIATING > FIAT
FIATS > FIAT
FIAUNT n warrant issued to the Irish Court of Chancery
FIAUNTS > FIAUNT
FIB n trivial lie ▷ vb tell a lie
FIBBED > FIB
FIBBER > FIB
FIBBERIES > FIB
FIBBERS > FIB
FIBBERY > FIB
FIBBING > FIB
FIBER same as > FIBRE
FIBERED > FIBRE
FIBERFILL same as > FIBREFILL
FIBERISE same as > FIBERIZE
FIBERISED > FIBERISE
FIBERISES > FIBERISE
FIBERIZE vb break into fibres
FIBERIZED > FIBERIZE
FIBERIZES > FIBERIZE
FIBERLESS > FIBRE
FIBERLIKE > FIBER
FIBERS > FIBER
FIBRANNE n synthetic fabric
FIBRANNES > FIBRANNE
FIBRATE n drug used to lower fat levels in the body
FIBRATES > FIBRATE
FIBRE n thread that can be spun into yarn
FIBRED > FIBRE
FIBREFILL n synthetic fibre used as a filling for pillows, quilted materials, etc
FIBRELESS > FIBRE
FIBRELIKE adj like a fibre
FIBRES > FIBRE
FIBRIFORM adj having the form of a fibre or fibres
FIBRIL n small fibre
FIBRILAR > FIBRIL
FIBRILLA same as > FIBRIL
FIBRILLAE > FIBRILLA
FIBRILLAR > FIBRIL
FIBRILLIN n kind of protein
FIBRILS > FIBRIL
FIBRIN n white insoluble elastic protein
FIBRINOID > FIBRIN
FIBRINOUS adj of, containing, or resembling fibrin
FIBRINS > FIBRIN
FIBRO n mixture of cement and asbestos fibre
FIBROCYTE n type of fibroblast
FIBROID adj (of structures or tissues) containing or resembling fibres ▷ n benign tumour

composed of fibrous connective tissue
FIBROIDS > FIBROID
FIBROIN n tough elastic protein
FIBROINS > FIBROIN
FIBROLINE n type of yarn
FIBROLITE n trademark name for a type of building board containing asbestos and cement
FIBROMA n type of benign tumour
FIBROMAS > FIBROMA
FIBROMATA > FIBROMA
FIBROS > FIBRO
FIBROSE vb become fibrous
FIBROSED > FIBROSE
FIBROSES > FIBROSE
FIBROSING > FIBROSE
FIBROSIS n formation of an abnormal amount of fibrous tissue
FIBROTIC > FIBROSIS
FIBROUS adj consisting of, containing, or resembling fibres
FIBROUSLY > FIBROUS
FIBS > FIB
FIBSTER n fibber
FIBSTERS > FIBSTER
FIBULA n slender outer bone of the lower leg
FIBULAE > FIBULA
FIBULAR > FIBULA
FIBULAS > FIBULA
FICAIN n cysteine proteinase isolated from the latex of figs
FICAINS > FICAIN
FICE n small aggressive dog
FICES > FICE
FICHE n film for storing publications in miniature
FICHES > FICHE
FICHU n woman's shawl or scarf
FICHUS > FICHU
FICIN n enzyme
FICINS > FICIN
FICKLE adj changeable, inconstant ▷ vb puzzle
FICKLED > FICKLE
FICKLER > FICKLE
FICKLES > FICKLE
FICKLEST > FICKLE
FICKLING > FICKLE
FICKLY > FICKLE
FICO n worthless trifle
FICOES > FICO
FICOS > FICO
FICTILE adj moulded or capable of being moulded from clay
FICTION n literary works of the imagination
FICTIONAL > FICTION
FICTIONS > FICTION
FICTIVE adj of, relating to, or able to create fiction
FICTIVELY > FICTIVE
FICTOR n sculptor
FICTORS > FICTOR
FICUS n type of plant

FICUSES > FICUS
FID n spike for separating strands of rope in splicing
FIDDIOUS vb treat someone as Coriolanus, in the eponymous play, dealt with Aufidius
FIDDLE n violin ▷ vb play the violin
FIDDLED > FIDDLE
FIDDLER n person who plays the fiddle
FIDDLERS > FIDDLER
FIDDLES > FIDDLE
FIDDLEY n vertical space above a vessel's engine room
FIDDLEYS > FIDDLEY
FIDDLIER > FIDDLY
FIDDLIEST > FIDDLY
FIDDLING adj trivial ▷ n act of fiddling
FIDDLINGS > FIDDLING
FIDDLY adj awkward to do or use
FIDEISM n theological doctrine
FIDEISMS > FIDEISM
FIDEIST > FIDEISM
FIDEISTIC > FIDEISM
FIDEISTS > FIDEISM
FIDELISMO n belief in the principles of Fidel Castro, Cuban Communist statesman
FIDELISTA n advocate of fidelismo
FIDELITY n faithfulness
FIDES n faith or trust
FIDGE obsolete word for > FIDGET
FIDGED > FIDGE
FIDGES > FIDGE
FIDGET vb move about restlessly ▷ n person who fidgets
FIDGETED > FIDGET
FIDGETER > FIDGET
FIDGETERS > FIDGET
FIDGETIER > FIDGET
FIDGETING > FIDGET
FIDGETS > FIDGET
FIDGETY > FIDGET
FIDGING > FIDGE
FIDIBUS n spill for lighting a candle or pipe
FIDIBUSES > FIDIBUS
FIDO n generic term for a dog
FIDOS > FIDO
FIDS > FID
FIDUCIAL adj used as a standard of reference or measurement
FIDUCIARY n person bound to act for someone else's benefit, as a trustee ▷ adj of a trust or trustee
FIE same as > FEY
FIEF n land granted by a lord in return for war service
FIEFDOM n (in Feudal Europe) the property owned by a lord
FIEFDOMS > FIEFDOM
FIEFS > FIEF

FIELD n piece of land used for pasture or growing crops ▷ vb stop, catch, or return (the ball) as a fielder

FIELDBOOT n knee-length boot

FIELDED > FIELD

FIELDER n (in certain sports) player whose task is to field the ball

FIELDERS > FIELDER

FIELDFARE n type of large Old World thrush

FIELDING > FIELD

FIELDINGS > FIELD

FIELDMICE pl n nocturnal mice

FIELDS > FIELD

FIELDSMAN n fielder

FIELDSMEN > FIELDSMAN

FIELDVOLE n small rodent

FIELDWARD adv towards a field or fields

FIELDWORK n investigation made in the field as opposed to the classroom or the laboratory

FIEND n evil spirit

FIENDISH adj of or like a fiend

FIENDLIKE adj > FIEND

FIENDS > FIEND

FIENT n fiend

FIENTS > FIENT

FIER same as > FERE

FIERCE adj wild or aggressive

FIERCELY > FIERCE

FIERCER > FIERCE

FIERCEST > FIERCE

FIERE same as > FERE

FIERES > FIERE

FIERIER > FIERY

FIERIEST > FIERY

FIERILY > FIERY

FIERINESS > FIERY

FIERS > FIER

FIERY adj consisting of or like fire

FIEST > FIE

FIESTA n religious festival, carnival

FIESTAS > FIESTA

FIFE n small high-pitched flute ▷ vb play (music) on a fife

FIFED > FIFE

FIFER > FIFE

FIFERS > FIFE

FIFES > FIFE

FIFI n mountaineering hook

FIFING > FIFE

FIFIS > FIFI

FIFTEEN n five and ten

FIFTEENER n fifteen-syllable line of poetry

FIFTEENS > FIFTEEN

FIFTEENTH adj coming after the fourteenth in order, position, time, etc ▷ n one of 15 equal or nearly equal parts of something

FIFTH n number five in a series ▷ adj of or being number five in a series

FIFTHLY adv in the fifth place or position

FIFTHS > FIFTH

FIFTIES > FIFTY

FIFTIETH adj being the number of fifty in order ▷ n one of 50 equal or parts

FIFTIETHS > FIFTIETH

FIFTY n five times ten

FIFTYFOLD adj multiplied fifty times

FIFTYISH > FIFTY

FIG n soft pear-shaped fruit ▷ vb dress (up) or rig (out)

FIGEATER n large beetle

FIGEATERS > FIGEATER

FIGGED > FIG

FIGGERIES > FIGGERY

FIGGERY n adornment, ornament

FIGGIER > FIGGY

FIGGIEST > FIGGY

FIGGING > FIG

FIGGY adj tasting like figs

FIGHT vb struggle (against) in battle or physical combat ▷ n aggressive conflict between two (groups of) people

FIGHTABLE > FIGHT

FIGHTBACK n act or campaign of resistance

FIGHTER n boxer

FIGHTERS > FIGHTER

FIGHTING > FIGHT

FIGHTINGS > FIGHT

FIGHTS > FIGHT

FIGJAM n very conceited person

FIGJAMS > FIGJAM

FIGLIKE adj like a fig

FIGMENT n fantastic notion, invention, or fabrication

FIGMENTS > FIGMENT

FIGO variant of > FICO

FIGOS > FIGO

FIGS > FIG

FIGTREE n tree that produces figs

FIGTREES > FIGTREE

FIGULINE adj of or resembling clay ▷ n article made of clay

FIGULINES > FIGULINE

FIGURABLE > FIGURE

FIGURAL adj composed of or relating to human or animal figures

FIGURALLY > FIGURAL

FIGURANT n ballet dancer who does group work but no solo roles

FIGURANTE n female figurant

FIGURANTS > FIGURANT

FIGURATE adj exhibiting or produced by figuration

FIGURE n numerical symbol ▷ vb calculate (sums or amounts)

FIGURED adj decorated with a design

FIGUREDLY > FIGURED

FIGURER > FIGURE

FIGURERS > FIGURE

FIGURES > FIGURE

FIGURINE n statuette

FIGURINES > FIGURINE

FIGURING > FIGURE

FIGURIST n user of numbers

FIGURISTS > FIGURIST

FIGWORT n plant with small brown or greenish flowers

FIGWORTS > FIGWORT

FIKE vb fidget

FIKED > FIKE

FIKERIES > FIKERY

FIKERY n fuss

FIKES > FIKE

FIKIER > FIKY

FIKIEST > FIKY

FIKING > FIKE

FIKISH adj fussy

FIKY adj fussy

FIL same as > FILS

FILA > FILUM

FILABEG variant of > FILIBEG

FILABEGS > FILABEG

FILACEOUS adj made of threads

FILACER n formerly, English legal officer

FILACERS > FILACER

FILAGGRIN n protein found in skin cells

FILAGREE same as > FILIGREE

FILAGREED > FILIGREE

FILAGREES > FILIGREE

FILAMENT n fine wire in a light bulb that gives out light

FILAMENTS > FILAMENT

FILANDER n species of kangaroo

FILANDERS > FILANDER

FILAR adj of thread

FILAREE n type of storksbill, a weed

FILAREES > FILAREE

FILARIA n type of parasitic nematode worm

FILARIAE > FILARIA

FILARIAL > FILARIA

FILARIAN > FILARIA

FILARIID adj of or relating to a family of threadlike roundworms

FILARIIDS > FILARIID

FILASSE n vegetable fibre such as jute

FILASSES > FILASSE

FILATORY n machine for making threads

FILATURE n act or process of spinning silk, etc, into threads

FILATURES > FILATURE

FILAZER variant of > FILACER

FILAZERS > FILAZER

FILBERD variant of > FILBERT

FILBERDS > FILBERD

FILBERT n hazelnut

FILBERTS > FILBERT

FILCH vb steal (small amounts)

FILCHED > FILCH

FILCHER > FILCH

FILCHERS > FILCH

FILCHES > FILCH

FILCHING > FILCH

FILCHINGS > FILCH

FILE n box or folder used to keep documents in order ▷ vb place (a document) in a file

FILEABLE > FILE

FILECARD n type of brush with sharp steel bristles, used for cleaning the teeth of a file

FILECARDS > FILECARD

FILED > FILE

FILEFISH n tropical fish with a narrow body

FILEMOT n type of brown colour

FILEMOTS > FILEMOT

FILENAME n codified name of a file a computer system

FILENAMES > FILENAME

FILER > FILE

FILERS > FILE

FILES > FILE

FILET variant of > FILLET

FILETED > FILET

FILETING > FILET

FILETS > FILET

FILFOT variant of > FYLFOT

FILFOTS > FILFOT

FILIAL adj of or befitting a son or daughter

FILIALLY > FILIAL

FILIATE vb fix judicially the paternity of (a child)

FILIATED > FILIATE

FILIATES > FILIATE

FILIATING > FILIATE

FILIATION n line of descent

FILIBEG n kilt worn by Scottish Highlanders

FILIBEGS > FILIBEG

FILICIDAL > FILICIDE

FILICIDE n act of killing one's own son or daughter

FILICIDES > FILICIDE

FILIFORM adj having the form of a thread

FILIGRAIN n filigree

FILIGRANE variant of > FILIGRAIN

FILIGREE n delicate ornamental work of gold or silver wire ▷ adj made of filigree ▷ vb decorate with or as if with filigree
FILIGREED
> FILIGREE
FILIGREES
> FILIGREE
FILII > FILIUS
FILING > FILE
FILINGS pl n shavings removed by a file
FILIOQUE n theological term found in the Nicene Creed
FILIOQUES
> FILIOQUE
FILISTER same as
> FILLISTER
FILISTERS
> FILISTER
FILIUS n son
FILK n parodic type of folk music with science fiction lyrics
FILKS > FILK
FILL vb make or become full
FILLABLE > FILL
FILLAGREE same as
> FILIGREE
FILLE n girl
FILLED > FILL
FILLER n substance that fills a gap or increases bulk
FILLERS > FILLER
FILLES > FILLE
FILLESTER same as
> FILLISTER
FILLET n boneless piece of meat or fish ▷ vb remove the bones from
FILLETED > FILLET
FILLETER n person who fillets
FILLETERS
> FILLETER
FILLETING > FILLET
FILLETS > FILLET
FILLIBEG same as
> FILIBEG
FILLIBEGS
> FILIBEG
FILLIES > FILLY
FILLING n substance that fills a gap or cavity ▷ adj (of food) substantial and satisfying
FILLINGS > FILLING
FILLIP n something that adds stimulation or enjoyment ▷ vb stimulate or excite
FILLIPED > FILLIP
FILLIPEEN n philopoena
FILLIPING > FILLIP
FILLIPS > FILLIP
FILLISTER n adjustable plane for cutting rabbets, grooves, etc
FILLO variant of > FILO
FILLOS > FILLO
FILLS > FILL
FILLY n young female horse

FILM n projected images creating the illusion of movement ▷ vb photograph with a video camera ▷ adj connected with films or the cinema
FILMABLE > FILM
FILMCARD n cinema loyalty card
FILMCARDS
> FILMCARD
FILMDOM n cinema industry
FILMDOMS > FILMDOM
FILMED > FILM
FILMER n film-maker
FILMERS > FILMER
FILMFEST n film festival
FILMFESTS
> FILMFEST
FILMGOER n person who goes regularly to the cinema
FILMGOERS
> FILMGOER
FILMGOING n activity of going to see films
FILMI adj of or relating to Indian films
FILMIC adj of or suggestive of films or the cinema
FILMIER > FILMY
FILMIEST > FILMY
FILMILY > FILMY
FILMINESS > FILMY
FILMING n act of photographing with a video camera
FILMINGS > FILMING
FILMIS > FILMI
FILMISH > FILM
FILMLAND n cinema industry
FILMLANDS
> FILMLAND
FILMLESS > FILM
FILMLIKE > FILM
FILMMAKER n person who makes films
FILMS > FILM
FILMSET vb set (type matter) by filmsetting
FILMSETS > FILMSET
FILMSTRIP n strip of film composed of different images projected separately as slides
FILMY adj very thin, delicate
FILO n type of flaky Greek pastry in very thin sheets
FILOPLUME n any of the hairlike feathers that lack vanes and occur between the contour feathers
FILOPODIA n plural form of singular filopodium: ectoplasmic pseudopodium
FILOS > FILO
FILOSE adj resembling a thread or threadlike process
FILOSELLE n soft silk thread, used esp for embroidery

FILOVIRUS n any member of a family of viruses that includes the agents responsible for Ebola virus disease and Marburg disease
FILS n monetary unit of Bahrain, Iraq, Jordan, and Kuwait
FILTER n device permitting fluid to pass but retaining solids ▷ vb remove impurities from (a substance) with a filter
FILTERED > FILTER
FILTERER > FILTER
FILTERERS > FILTER
FILTERING > FILTER
FILTERS > FILTER
FILTH n disgusting dirt
FILTHIER > FILTHY
FILTHIEST > FILTHY
FILTHILY > FILTHY
FILTHS > FILTH
FILTHY adj characterized by or full of filth ▷ adv extremely
FILTRABLE adj capable of being filtered
FILTRATE n filtered gas or liquid ▷ vb remove impurities with a filter
FILTRATED
> FILTRATE
FILTRATES
> FILTRATE
FILTRE adj as in cafe filtre a strong black filtered coffee
FILUM n any threadlike structure or part
FIMBLE n male plant of the hemp
FIMBLES > FIMBLE
FIMBRIA n fringe or fringelike margin or border
FIMBRIAE > FIMBRIA
FIMBRIAL > FIMBRIA
FIMBRIATE adj having a fringed margin, as some petals, antennae, etc
FIN n any of the appendages of some aquatic animals ▷ vb provide with fins
FINABLE adj liable to a fine
FINAGLE vb get or achieve by craftiness or trickery
FINAGLED > FINAGLE
FINAGLER > FINAGLE
FINAGLERS > FINAGLE
FINAGLES > FINAGLE
FINAGLING n use of trickery to achieve aims
FINAL adj at the end ▷ n deciding contest
FINALE n concluding part of a performance
FINALES > FINALE
FINALIS n musical finishing note
FINALISE same as
> FINALIZE
FINALISED
> FINALISE
FINALISER > FINALISE

FINALISES
> FINALISE
FINALISM n doctrine that final causes determine the course of all events
FINALISMS
> FINALISM
FINALIST n competitor in a final
FINALISTS
> FINALIST
FINALITY n condition or quality of being final or settled
FINALIZE vb put into final form
FINALIZED
> FINALIZE
FINALIZER
> FINALIZE
FINALIZES
> FINALIZE
FINALLY adv after a long delay
FINALS pl n deciding part of a competition
FINANCE vb provide or obtain funds for ▷ n system of money, credit, and investment
FINANCED > FINANCE
FINANCES > FINANCE
FINANCIAL adj of or relating to finance, finances, or people who manage money ▷ n financial institution or report
FINANCIER n person involved in large-scale financial business
FINANCING > FINANCE
FINBACK another name for
> RORQUAL
FINBACKS > FINBACK
FINCA n Spanish villa
FINCAS > FINCA
FINCH n small songbird with a short strong beak
FINCHED adj with streaks or spots on the back
FINCHES > FINCH
FINCHLIKE adj like a finch
FIND vb discover by chance ▷ n person or thing found, esp when valuable
FINDABLE > FIND
FINDER n small telescope fitted to a larger one
FINDERS > FINDER
FINDING > FIND
FINDINGS > FIND
FINDRAM variant of
> FINNAN
FINDRAMS > FINDRAM
FINDS > FIND
FINE adj very good ▷ n payment imposed as a penalty ▷ vb impose a fine on
FINEABLE same as
> FINABLE
FINED > FINE
FINEER variant of
> VENEER
FINEERED > FINEER

FINEERING > FINEER
FINEERS > FINEER
FINEISH > FINE
FINELESS > FINE
FINELY *adv* into small pieces
FINENESS *n* state or quality of being fine
FINER > FINE
FINERIES > FINERY
FINERS > FINE
FINERY *n* showy clothing
FINES > FINE
FINESPUN *adj* spun or drawn out to a fine thread
FINESSE *n* delicate skill ▷ *vb* bring about with finesse
FINESSED > FINESSE
FINESSER > FINESSE
FINESSERS > FINESSE
FINESSES > FINESSE
FINESSING > FINESSE
FINEST *n* (in the US) police of a particular city
FINESTS > FINEST
FINFISH *n* fish with fins, as opposed to shellfish
FINFISHES > FINFISH
FINFOOT *n* type of aquatic bird
FINFOOTS > FINFOOT
FINGAN *variant of* > FINJAN
FINGANS > FINGAN
FINGER *n* one of the four long jointed parts of the hand ▷ *vb* touch or handle with the fingers
FINGERED *adj* marked or dirtied by handling
FINGERER > FINGER
FINGERERS > FINGER
FINGERING *n* technique of using the fingers in playing a musical instrument
FINGERS > FINGER
FINGERTIP *n* end joint or tip of a finger
FINI *n* end; finish
FINIAL *n* ornament at the apex of a gable or spire
FINIALED *adj* having a finial or finials
FINIALS > FINIAL
FINICAL *another word for* > FINICKY
FINICALLY > FINICAL
FINICKETY *adj* fussy or tricky
FINICKIER > FINICKY
FINICKIN *variant of* > FINICKY
FINICKING *same as* > FINICKY
FINICKY *adj* excessively particular, fussy
FINIKIN *variant of* > FINICKY
FINIKING *variant of* > FINICKY
FINING *n* process of removing bubbles from molten glass
FININGS > FINING
FINIS *n* end; finish
FINISES > FINIS

FINISH *vb* bring to an end, stop ▷ *n* end, last part
FINISHED *adj* perfected
FINISHER *n* craftsperson who carries out the final tasks in a manufacturing process
FINISHERS > FINISHER
FINISHES > FINISH
FINISHING *n* act or skill of goal scoring
FINITE *adj* having limits in space, time, or size ▷ *n* verb limited by person, number, tense or mood
FINITELY > FINITE
FINITES > FINITE
FINITISM *n* mathematical philosophy which rejects infinite quantities
FINITISMS > FINITISM
FINITIST *n* one who believes in or advocates finitism
FINITISTS > FINITIST
FINITO *adj* finished
FINITUDE > FINITE
FINITUDES > FINITE
FINJAN *n* small, handleless coffee cup
FINJANS > FINJAN
FINK *n* strikebreaker ▷ *vb* inform (on someone), as to the police
FINKED > FINK
FINKING > FINK
FINKS > FINK
FINLESS > FIN
FINLIKE > FIN
FINLIT *n* understanding of the concepts associated with finance
FINLITS > FINLIT
FINMARK *n* former monetary unit of Finland
FINMARKS > FINMARK
FINNAC *variant of* > FINNOCK
FINNACK *variant of* > FINNOCK
FINNACKS > FINNACK
FINNACS > FINNAC
FINNAN *n* smoked haddock
FINNANS > FINNAN
FINNED > FIN
FINNER *another name for* > RORQUAL
FINNERS > FINNER
FINNESKO *n* reindeer-skin boot
FINNICKY *variant of* > FINICKY
FINNIER > FINNY
FINNIEST > FINNY
FINNING > FIN
FINNMARK *n* former Finnish monetary unit
FINNMARKS > FINNMARK
FINNOCHIO *variant of* > FINOCCHIO

FINNOCK *n* young sea trout on its first return to fresh water
FINNOCKS > FINNOCK
FINNSKO *variant of* > FINNESKO
FINNY *adj* relating to or containing many fishes
FINO *n* very dry sherry
FINOCCHIO *n* variety of fennel with celery-like stalks which are eaten as a vegetable
FINOCHIO *same as* > FINOCCHIO
FINOCHIOS > FINOCHIO
FINOS > FINO
FINS > FIN
FINSKO *variant of* > FINNESKO
FINTECH *n* financial services technology
FINTECHS > FINTECH
FIORATURA *same as* > FIORITURA
FIORD *same as* > FJORD
FIORDS > FIORD
FIORIN *n* type of temperate perennial grass
FIORINS > FIORIN
FIORITURA *n* embellishment, esp ornamentation added by the performer
FIORITURE > FIORITURA
FIPPENCE *n* fivepence
FIPPENCES > FIPPENCE
FIPPLE *n* wooden plug forming a flue in the end of a pipe
FIPPLES > FIPPLE
FIQH *n* Islamic jurisprudence
FIQHS > FIQH
FIQUE *n* hemp
FIQUES > FIQUE
FIR *n* pyramid-shaped tree
FIRE *n* state of combustion producing heat, flames, and smoke ▷ *vb* operate (a weapon) so that a bullet or missile is released
FIREABLE > FIRE
FIREARM *n* rifle, pistol, or shotgun
FIREARMED *adj* carrying firearm
FIREARMS > FIREARM
FIREBACK *n* ornamental iron slab against the back wall of a hearth
FIREBACKS > FIREBACK
FIREBALL *n* ball of fire at the centre of an explosion
FIREBALLS > FIREBALL
FIREBASE *n* artillery base from which heavy fire is directed at the enemy
FIREBASES > FIREBASE

FIREBIRD *n* any of various songbirds having a bright red plumage, esp the Baltimore oriole
FIREBIRDS > FIREBIRD
FIREBOARD *n* mantelpiece
FIREBOAT *n* motor vessel with fire-fighting apparatus
FIREBOATS > FIREBOAT
FIREBOMB *n* bomb that is designed to cause fires ▷ *vb* detonate such a bomb
FIREBOMBS > FIREBOMB
FIREBOX *n* furnace chamber of a boiler in a steam locomotive
FIREBOXES > FIREBOX
FIREBRAND *n* person who causes unrest
FIREBRAT *n* type of small primitive wingless insect
FIREBRATS > FIREBRAT
FIREBREAK *n* strip of cleared land to stop the advance of a fire
FIREBRICK *n* heat-resistant brick used for lining furnaces, fireplaces, etc
FIREBUG *n* person who deliberately sets fire to property
FIREBUGS > FIREBUG
FIREBUSH *n* as in Chilean firebush South American shrub with scarlet flowers
FIRECLAY *n* heat-resistant clay used in the making of firebricks, furnace linings, etc
FIRECLAYS > FIRECLAY
FIRECREST *n* small European warbler with a crown striped with yellow, black, and white
FIRED > FIRE
FIREDAMP *n* explosive gas, composed mainly of methane, formed in mines
FIREDAMPS > FIREDAMP
FIREDOG *n* either of two metal stands supporting logs in a fire
FIREDOGS > FIREDOG
FIREDRAKE *n* fire-breathing dragon
FIREFANG *vb* become overheated through decomposition
FIREFANGS > FIREFANG
FIREFIGHT *n* brief small-scale engagement between opposing military ground forces using short-range light weapons
FIREFLIES > FIREFLY
FIREFLOAT *n* boat used for firefighting

FIREFLOOD n method of extracting oil from a well by burning some of the oil to increase the rate of flow

FIREFLY n beetle that glows in the dark

FIREGUARD same as > FIREBREAK

FIREHALL n US and Canadian word for fire station

FIREHALLS > FIREHALL

FIREHOSE n hose used to extinguish fires

FIREHOSES > FIREHOSE

FIREHOUSE n fire station

FIRELESS > FIRE

FIRELIGHT n light from a fire

FIRELIT adj lit by firelight

FIRELOCK n obsolete type of gunlock with a priming mechanism ignited by sparks

FIRELOCKS > FIRELOCK

FIREMAN n a male firefighter

FIREMANIC > FIREMAN

FIREMARK n plaque indicating that a building is insured

FIREMARKS > FIREMARK

FIREMEN > FIREMAN

FIREPAN n metal container for a fire in a room

FIREPANS > FIREPAN

FIREPINK n wildflower belonging to the pink family

FIREPINKS > FIREPINK

FIREPIT n hole dug in the ground for a fire

FIREPITS > FIREPIT

FIREPLACE n recess in a room for a fire

FIREPLUG n US and New Zealand name for a fire hydrant

FIREPLUGS > FIREPLUG

FIREPOT n Chinese fondue-like cooking pot

FIREPOTS > FIREPOT

FIREPOWER n amount of fire that may be delivered by a unit or weapon

FIREPROOF adj capable of resisting damage by fire ▷ vb make resistant to fire

FIRER > FIRE

FIREREEL n fire engine

FIREREELS > FIREREEL

FIREROOM n stokehold

FIREROOMS > FIREROOM

FIRERS > FIRE

FIRES > FIRE

FIRESCAPE vb arrange a garden so that fire cannot spread easily

FIRESHIP n vessel set alight and directed among enemy warships

FIRESHIPS > FIRESHIP

FIRESIDE n hearth

FIRESIDES > FIRESIDE

FIRESTONE n sandstone that withstands intense heat, esp one used for lining kilns, furnaces, etc

FIRESTORM n uncontrollable blaze sustained by violent winds that are drawn into the column of rising hot air over the burning area: often the result of heavy bombing

FIRETHORN n type of evergreen spiny shrub of SE Europe and Asia with bright red or orange fruits, cultivated for ornament

FIRETRAP n building that would burn easily or one without fire escapes

FIRETRAPS > FIRETRAP

FIRETRUCK n fire engine

FIREWALL n appliance that prevents unauthorized access to a computer network from the internet ▷ vb protect (a computer system) or block (unwanted access) with a firewall

FIREWALLS > FIREWALL

FIREWATER n any alcoholic spirit

FIREWEED n first vegetation growing in burnt-over areas

FIREWEEDS > FIREWEED

FIREWOMAN n female firefighter

FIREWOMEN > FIREWOMAN

FIREWOOD n wood for burning

FIREWOODS > FIREWOOD

FIREWORK n device ignited to produce colourful sparks and explosions

FIREWORKS pl n show in which fireworks are let off

FIREWORM n cranberry worm

FIREWORMS > FIREWORM

FIRIE n in Australian English, informal word for a firefighter

FIRIES > FIRIE

FIRING n discharge of a firearm

FIRINGS > FIRING

FIRK vb beat

FIRKED > FIRK

FIRKIN n small wooden barrel or similar container

FIRKING > FIRK

FIRKINS > FIRKIN

FIRKS > FIRK

FIRLOT n unit of measurement for grain

FIRLOTS > FIRLOT

FIRM adj not soft or yielding ▷ adv in an unyielding manner ▷ vb make or become firm ▷ n business company

FIRMAMENT n sky or the heavens

FIRMAN n edict of a sultan

FIRMANS > FIRMAN

FIRMED > FIRM

FIRMER > FIRM

FIRMERS > FIRM

FIRMEST > FIRM

FIRMING > FIRM

FIRMLESS adj unstable

FIRMLY > FIRM

FIRMNESS > FIRM

FIRMS > FIRM

FIRMWARE n fixed form of software programmed into a read-only memory

FIRMWARES > FIRMWARE

FIRN another name for > NEVE

FIRNS > FIRN

FIRRIER > FIRRY

FIRRIEST > FIRRY

FIRRING n wooden battens used in building construction

FIRRINGS > FIRRING

FIRRY adj of, relating to, or made from fir trees

FIRS > FIR

FIRST adj earliest in time or order ▷ n person or thing coming before all others ▷ adv before anything else

FIRSTBORN adj eldest of the children in a family ▷ n eldest child in a family

FIRSTHAND adj from the original source

FIRSTLING n first, esp the first offspring

FIRSTLY adv coming before other points, questions, etc

FIRSTNESS > FIRST

FIRSTS pl n saleable goods of the highest quality

FIRTH n narrow inlet of the sea, esp in Scotland

FIRTHS > FIRTH

FIRWOOD n wood of the fir tree

FIRWOODS > FIRWOOD

FISC n state or royal treasury

FISCAL adj of government finances, esp taxes ▷ n (in some countries) a public prosecutor

FISCALIST > FISCAL

FISCALLY > FISCAL

FISCALS > FISCAL

FISCS > FISC

FISGIG variant of > FISHGIG

FISGIGS > FISGIG

FISH n cold-blooded vertebrate with gills, that lives in water ▷ vb try to catch fish

FISHABLE > FISH

FISHBALL n fried ball of flaked fish and mashed potato

FISHBALLS > FISHBALL

FISHBOAT n boat used for fishing

FISHBOATS > FISHBOAT

FISHBOLT n bolt used for fastening a fishplate to a rail

FISHBOLTS > FISHBOLT

FISHBONE n bone of a fish

FISHBONES > FISHBONE

FISHBOWL n goldfish bowl

FISHBOWLS > FISHBOWL

FISHCAKE n mixture of flaked fish and mashed potatoes formed into a flat circular shape

FISHCAKES > FISHCAKE

FISHED > FISH

FISHER n fisherman

FISHERIES > FISHERY

FISHERMAN n person who catches fish for a living or for pleasure

FISHERMEN > FISHERMAN

FISHERS > FISHER

FISHERY n area of the sea used for fishing

FISHES > FISH

FISHEYE n type of lens

FISHEYES > FISHEYE

FISHFUL adj teeming with fish

FISHGIG n pole with barbed prongs for impaling fish

FISHGIGS > FISHGIG

FISHHOOK n sharp hook used in angling, esp one with a barb

FISHHOOKS > FISHHOOK

FISHIER > FISHY

FISHIEST > FISHY

FISHIFIED > FISHIFY

FISHIFIES > FISHIFY

FISHIFY vb change into fish

FISHILY > FISHY

FISHINESS > FISHY

FISHING n job or pastime of catching fish

FISHINGS > FISHING

FISHKILL n mass killing of fish by pollution

FISHKILLS > FISHKILL

FISHLESS > FISH

FISHLIKE > FISH

FISHLINE n line used on a fishing-rod

FISHLINES > FISHLINE

FISHMEAL n ground dried fish used as feed for farm animals or as a fertilizer
FISHMEALS > FISHMEAL
FISHNET n open mesh fabric resembling netting
FISHNETS > FISHNET
FISHPLATE n metal plate holding rails together
FISHPOLE n boom arm for a microphone
FISHPOLES > FISHPOLE
FISHPOND > FISH
FISHPONDS > FISH
FISHSKIN n skin of a fish
FISHSKINS > FISHSKIN
FISHTAIL n nozzle placed over a Bunsen burner to produce a fanlike flame ▷ vb slow an aeroplane by swerving the tail
FISHTAILS > FISHTAIL
FISHWAY n fish ladder
FISHWAYS > FISHWAY
FISHWIFE n derogatory term for a coarse scolding woman
FISHWIVES > FISHWIFE
FISHWORM n worm used as fishing bait
FISHWORMS > FISHWORM
FISHY adj of or like fish
FISHYBACK n goods supply chain involving container transfer from lorry to ship
FISK vb frisk
FISKED > FISK
FISKING > FISK
FISKS > FISK
FISNOMIE n physiognomy
FISNOMIES > FISNOMIE
FISSATE > FISSILE
FISSILE adj capable of undergoing nuclear fission
FISSILITY > FISSILE
FISSION n splitting
FISSIONAL > FISSION
FISSIONED adj split or broken into parts
FISSIONS > FISSION
FISSIPED adj having toes separated from one another ▷ n fissiped animal
FISSIPEDE > FISSIPED
FISSIPEDS > FISSIPED
FISSIVE > FISSILE
FISSLE vb rustle
FISSLED > FISSLE
FISSLES > FISSLE
FISSLING > FISSLE
FISSURAL > FISSURE
FISSURE n long narrow cleft or crack ▷ vb crack or split apart

FISSURED > FISSURE
FISSURES > FISSURE
FISSURING > FISSURE
FIST n clenched hand ▷ vb hit with the fist
FISTED > FIST
FISTFIGHT n fight using bare fists
FISTFUL n quantity that can be held in a fist or hand
FISTFULS > FISTFUL
FISTIANA n world of boxing
FISTIANAS > FISTIANA
FISTIC adj of or relating to fisticuffs or boxing
FISTICAL > FISTIC
FISTICUFF n cuff or blow ▷ vb fight or strike with the fists
FISTIER > FIST
FISTIEST > FIST
FISTING n act of fisting
FISTINGS > FISTING
FISTMELE n measurement of the height of the string of a braced bow
FISTMELES > FISTMELE
FISTNOTE n note in printed text preceded by the fist symbol
FISTNOTES > FISTNOTE
FISTS > FIST
FISTULA n long narrow ulcer
FISTULAE > FISTULA
FISTULAR same as > FISTULOUS
FISTULAS > FISTULA
FISTULATE same as > FISTULOUS
FISTULOSE variant of > FISTULOUS
FISTULOUS adj containing, relating to, or resembling a fistula
FISTY > FIST
FIT vb be appropriate or suitable for ▷ adj appropriate ▷ n way in which something fits
FITCH n fur of the polecat or ferret
FITCHE adj pointed
FITCHEE variant of > FITCHE
FITCHES > FITCH
FITCHET same as > FITCH
FITCHETS > FITCHET
FITCHEW archaic name for > POLECAT
FITCHEWS > FITCHEW
FITCHY variant of > FITCHE
FITFUL adj occurring in irregular spells
FITFULLY > FITFUL
FITLIER > FITLY
FITLIEST > FITLY
FITLY adv in a proper manner or place or at a proper time
FITMENT n accessory attached to a machine

FITMENTS > FITMENT
FITNA n state of trouble or chaos
FITNAS > FITNA
FITNESS n state of being fit
FITNESSES > FITNESS
FITS > FIT
FITT n song
FITTABLE > FIT
FITTE variant of > FITT
FITTED > FIT
FITTER > FIT
FITTERS > FIT
FITTES > FITTE
FITTEST > FIT
FITTING > FIT
FITTINGLY > FIT
FITTINGS > FIT
FITTS > FITT
FIVE n one more than four
FIVEFOLD adj having five times as many or as much ▷ adv by five times as many or as much
FIVEPENCE n five-penny coin
FIVEPENNY adj (of a nail) one and three-quarters of an inch in length
FIVEPIN > FIVEPINS
FIVEPINS n bowling game played esp in Canada
FIVER n five-pound note
FIVERS > FIVER
FIVES n ball game resembling squash
FIX vb make or become firm, stable, or secure ▷ n difficult situation
FIXABLE > FIX
FIXATE vb become or cause to become fixed
FIXATED > FIXATE
FIXATES > FIXATE
FIXATIF variant of > FIXATIVE
FIXATIFS > FIXATIF
FIXATING > FIXATE
FIXATION n obsessive interest in something
FIXATIONS > FIXATION
FIXATIVE n liquid used to preserve or hold things in place ▷ adj serving or tending to fix
FIXATIVES > FIXATIVE
FIXATURE n something that holds an object in place
FIXATURES > FIXATURE
FIXED adj attached or placed so as to be immovable
FIXEDLY > FIXED
FIXEDNESS > FIXED
FIXER n solution used to make a photographic image permanent
FIXERS > FIXER
FIXES > FIX
FIXING n means of attaching one thing to another

FIXINGS pl n apparatus or equipment
FIXIT n solution to a complex problem ▷ adj that fixes things
FIXITIES > FIXITY
FIXITS > FIXIT
FIXITY n state of being fixed
FIXIVE > FIX
FIXT adj fixed
FIXTURE n permanently fitted piece of household equipment
FIXTURES > FIXTURE
FIXURE n firmness
FIXURES > FIXURE
FIZ variant of > FIZZ
FIZGIG vb inform on someone to the police
FIZGIGGED > FIZGIG
FIZGIGS > FIZGIG
FIZZ vb make a hissing or bubbling noise ▷ n hissing or bubbling noise
FIZZED > FIZZ
FIZZEN variant of > FOISON
FIZZENS > FIZZEN
FIZZER n anything that fizzes
FIZZERS > FIZZER
FIZZES > FIZZ
FIZZGIG variant of > FISHGIG
FIZZGIGS > FIZZGIG
FIZZIER > FIZZ
FIZZIEST > FIZZ
FIZZILY adv in a fizzy manner
FIZZINESS > FIZZ
FIZZING > FIZZ
FIZZINGS > FIZZ
FIZZLE vb make a weak hissing or bubbling sound ▷ n hissing or bubbling sound
FIZZLED > FIZZLE
FIZZLES > FIZZLE
FIZZLING > FIZZLE
FIZZY > FIZZ
FJELD n high rocky plateau
FJELDS > FJELD
FJORD n long narrow inlet of the sea between cliffs
FJORDIC > FJORD
FJORDS > FJORD
FLAB n unsightly body fat
FLABBIER > FLABBY
FLABBIEST > FLABBY
FLABBILY > FLABBY
FLABBY adj having flabby flesh
FLABELLA > FLABELLUM
FLABELLUM n fan-shaped organ or part, such as the tip of the proboscis of a honeybee
FLABS > FLAB
FLACCID adj soft and limp
FLACCIDER > FLACCID
FLACCIDLY > FLACCID
FLACK vb flap
FLACKED > FLACK
FLACKER vb flap

FLACKERED > FLACKER
FLACKERS > FLACKER
FLACKERY > FLACK
FLACKET n flagon ▷ vb
flap or flutter about
FLACKETED > FLACKET
FLACKETS > FLACKET
FLACKING > FLACK
FLACKS > FLACK
FLACON n small
stoppered bottle or flask
FLACONS > FLACON
FLAFF vb flap
FLAFFED > FLAFF
FLAFFER vb flutter
FLAFFERED > FLAFFER
FLAFFERS > FLAFFER
FLAFFING > FLAFF
FLAFFS > FLAFF
FLAG n piece of cloth
attached to a pole as an
emblem or signal ▷ vb
mark with a flag or sticker
FLAGELLA
> FLAGELLUM
FLAGELLAR
> FLAGELLUM
FLAGELLIN n structural
protein of bacterial
flagella
FLAGELLUM n whiplike
outgrowth from a cell that
acts as an organ of
movement
FLAGEOLET n small
instrument like a recorder
FLAGGED > FLAG
FLAGGER > FLAG
FLAGGERS > FLAG
FLAGGIER > FLAGGY
FLAGGIEST > FLAGGY
FLAGGING > FLAG
FLAGGINGS > FLAG
FLAGGY adj drooping
FLAGITATE vb
importune
FLAGLESS > FLAG
FLAGMAN n person who
has charge of a flag
FLAGMEN > FLAGMAN
FLAGON n wide bottle
FLAGONS > FLAGON
FLAGPOLE n pole for a
flag
FLAGPOLES
> FLAGPOLE
FLAGRANCE
> FLAGRANT
FLAGRANCY
> FLAGRANT
FLAGRANT adj openly
outrageous
FLAGS > FLAG
FLAGSHIP n admiral's
ship
FLAGSHIPS
> FLAGSHIP
FLAGSTAFF same as
> FLAGPOLE
FLAGSTICK n in golf,
pole used to indicate
position of hole
FLAGSTONE n flat slab of
hard stone for paving
FLAIL vb wave about
wildly ▷ n tool formerly
used for threshing grain by
hand

FLAILED > FLAIL
FLAILING > FLAIL
FLAILS > FLAIL
FLAIR n natural ability
FLAIRS > FLAIR
FLAK n anti-aircraft fire
FLAKE n small thin piece,
esp chipped off something
▷ vb peel off in flakes
FLAKED > FLAKE
FLAKER > FLAKE
FLAKERS > FLAKE
FLAKES > FLAKE
FLAKEY same as > FLAKY
FLAKIER > FLAKY
FLAKIES pl n dandruff
FLAKIEST > FLAKY
FLAKILY > FLAKY
FLAKINESS > FLAKY
FLAKING > FLAKE
FLAKS > FLAK
FLAKY adj like or made of
flakes
FLAM n falsehood,
deception, or sham ▷ vb
cheat or deceive
FLAMBE vb cook or serve
(food) in flaming brandy
▷ adj (of food) served in
flaming brandy
FLAMBEAU n burning
torch, as used in night
processions
FLAMBEAUS
> FLAMBEAU
FLAMBEAUX
> FLAMBEAU
FLAMBEE same as
> FLAMBE
FLAMBEED > FLAMBEE
FLAMBEES > FLAMBEE
FLAMBEING > FLAMBE
FLAMBES > FLAMBE
FLAME n luminous
burning gas coming from
burning material ▷ vb
burn brightly
FLAMED > FLAME
FLAMELESS > FLAME
FLAMELET > FLAME
FLAMELETS > FLAME
FLAMELIKE > FLAME
FLAMEN n (in ancient
Rome) type of priest
FLAMENCO n rhythmical
Spanish dance
accompanied by a guitar
and vocalist
FLAMENCOS
> FLAMENCO
FLAMENS > FLAMEN
FLAMEOUT n failure of an
aircraft jet engine in flight
due to extinction of the
flame ▷ vb (of a jet engine)
to fail in flight or to cause
(a jet engine) to fail in
flight
FLAMEOUTS
> FLAMEOUT
FLAMER > FLAME
FLAMERS > FLAME
FLAMES > FLAME
FLAMFEW n fantastic trifle
FLAMFEWS > FLAMFEW
FLAMIER > FLAMY
FLAMIEST > FLAMY
FLAMINES > FLAMEN

FLAMING adj burning
with flames ▷ adv
extremely
FLAMINGLY > FLAMING
FLAMINGO n large pink
wading bird with a long
neck and legs
FLAMINGOS > FLAMINGO
FLAMM variant of > FLAM
FLAMMABLE adj easily set
on fire
FLAMMED > FLAM
FLAMMING > FLAM
FLAMMS > FLAMM
FLAMMULE n small flame
FLAMMULES
> FLAMMULE
FLAMS > FLAM
FLAMY > FLAME
FLAN n open sweet or
savoury tart
FLANCARD n armour
covering a horse's flank
FLANCARDS
> FLANCARD
FLANCH variant of
> FLAUNCH
FLANCHED > FLANCH
FLANCHES > FLANCH
FLANCHING > FLANCH
FLANE vb walk idly,
saunter
FLANED > FLANE
FLANERIE n aimless
strolling or lounging
FLANERIES
> FLANERIE
FLANES > FLANE
FLANEUR n idler or loafer
FLANEURS > FLANEUR
FLANGE n projecting rim
or collar ▷ vb attach or
provide (a component)
with a flange
FLANGED > FLANGE
FLANGER > FLANGE
FLANGERS > FLANGE
FLANGES > FLANGE
FLANGING n act of
flanging
FLANGINGS
> FLANGING
FLANING > FLANE
FLANK n part of the side
between the hips and ribs
▷ vb be at or move along
the side of
FLANKED > FLANK
FLANKEN n cut of beef
FLANKENS > FLANKEN
FLANKER n one of a
detachment of soldiers
guarding the flanks
FLANKERED > FLANKER
FLANKERS > FLANKER
FLANKING > FLANK
FLANKS > FLANK
FLANNEL n small piece of
cloth for washing the face
▷ vb talk evasively
FLANNELED > FLANNEL
FLANNELET n cotton
imitation of flannel
FLANNELLY adj like
flannel
FLANNELS > FLANNEL
FLANNEN adj made of
flannel

FLANNENS > FLANNEN
FLANNIE same as
> FLANNY
FLANNIES > FLANNIE
FLANNY n shirt made of
flannel
FLANS > FLAN
FLAP vb move back and
forwards or up and down
▷ n action or sound of
flapping
FLAPERON n control flap
on aircraft wing
FLAPERONS
> FLAPERON
FLAPJACK n chewy
biscuit made with oats
FLAPJACKS
> FLAPJACK
FLAPLESS > FLAP
FLAPLIKE adj like a
flap
FLAPPABLE > FLAP
FLAPPED > FLAP
FLAPPER n (in the 1920s)
an unconventional young
woman
FLAPPERS > FLAPPER
FLAPPIER > FLAPPY
FLAPPIEST > FLAPPY
FLAPPING > FLAP
FLAPPINGS > FLAP
FLAPPY adj loose
FLAPS > FLAP
FLAPTRACK n
component in an aircraft
wing
FLARE vb blaze with a
sudden unsteady flame
▷ n sudden unsteady
flame
FLAREBACK n flame in
the breech of a gun when
fired
FLARED > FLARE
FLARES pl n trousers with
legs that widen below the
knee
FLAREUP n outbreak of
something
FLAREUPS > FLAREUP
FLARIER > FLARY
FLARIEST > FLARY
FLARING > FLARE
FLARINGLY > FLARE
FLARY adj flare-like
FLASER n type of
sedimentary structure in
rock
FLASERS > FLASER
FLASH n sudden burst of
light or flame ▷ vb emit
or reflect light suddenly or
intermittently
FLASHBACK n scene in a
book, play, or film, that
shows earlier events ▷ vb
return in a novel, film, etc,
to a past event
FLASHBANG n stun
grenade
FLASHBULB n small light
bulb that produces a
bright flash of light
FLASHCARD n card
shown briefly as a
memory test

FLASHCUBE n in photography, a cube with a bulb that is attached to a camera

FLASHED > FLASH

FLASHER > FLASH

FLASHERS > FLASHER

FLASHES > FLASH

FLASHEST > FLASH

FLASHGUN n type of electronic flash for a camera

FLASHGUNS > FLASHGUN

FLASHIER > FLASHY

FLASHIEST > FLASHY

FLASHILY > FLASHY

FLASHING n watertight material used to cover joins in a roof

FLASHINGS > FLASHING

FLASHLAMP n electric lamp producing a flash of intense light

FLASHOVER n electric discharge over or around the surface of an insulator

FLASHTUBE n tube used in a flashlamp

FLASHY adj showy in a vulgar way

FLASK n flat bottle

FLASKET n long shallow basket

FLASKETS > FLASKET

FLASKS > FLASK

FLAT adj level and horizontal ▷ adv in or into a flat position ▷ n flat surface ▷ vb live in a flat

FLATBACK n flat-backed ornament, designed for viewing from front

FLATBACKS > FLATBACK

FLATBED n type of printing machine

FLATBEDS > FLATBED

FLATBOAT n flat-bottomed boat for transporting goods on a canal

FLATBOATS > FLATBOAT

FLATBREAD n type of thin unleavened bread

FLATBROD n flatbread made with rye

FLATBRODS > FLATBROD

FLATCAP n Elizabethan man's hat

FLATCAPS > FLATCAP

FLATCAR n railway goods wagon without raised sides

FLATCARS > FLATCAR

FLATETTE n very small flat

FLATETTES > FLATETTE

FLATFEET > FLATFOOT

FLATFISH n sea fish, such as the sole, which has a flat body

FLATFOOT n flattening of the instep arch

FLATFOOTS > FLATFOOT

FLATFORM n thick, level sole on a shoe

FLATFORMS > FLATFORM

FLATHEAD n common Australian flatfish

FLATHEADS > FLATHEAD

FLATIRON n (formerly) an iron for pressing clothes that was heated by being placed on a stove

FLATIRONS > FLATIRON

FLATLAND n land notable for its levelness

FLATLANDS > FLATLAND

FLATLET n small flat

FLATLETS > FLATLET

FLATLINE vb have flat line displaying on medical equipment monitoring one's vital signs

FLATLINED > FLATLINE

FLATLINER > FLATLINE

FLATLINES > FLATLINE

FLATLING adv in a flat or prostrate position ▷ adj with the flat side, as of a sword

FLATLINGS same as > FLATLING

FLATLONG adv prostrate

FLATLY > FLAT

FLATMATE n person with whom one shares a flat

FLATMATES > FLATMATE

FLATNESS > FLAT

FLATPACK n pieces packed into a flat box for home assembly

FLATPACKS > FLATPACK

FLATPICK vb play (a guitar, etc) by plucking individual strings with a plectrum

FLATPICKS > FLATPICK

FLATS > FLAT

FLATSHARE n state of living in a flat where each occupant shares the facilities and expenses ▷ vb live in a flat with other people who are not relatives

FLATSTICK adv with great speed or effort

FLATTED > FLAT

FLATTEN vb make or become flat or flatter

FLATTENED > FLATTEN

FLATTENER > FLATTEN

FLATTENS > FLATTEN

FLATTER vb praise insincerely

FLATTERED > FLATTER

FLATTERER > FLATTER

FLATTERS > FLATTER

FLATTERY n excessive or insincere praise

FLATTEST > FLAT

FLATTIE n flat tyre

FLATTIES > FLATTIE

FLATTING > FLAT

FLATTINGS > FLAT

FLATTISH adj somewhat flat

FLATTOP n informal name for an aircraft carrier

FLATTOPS > FLATTOP

FLATTY n flat shoe

FLATULENT adj having too much gas in the intestines

FLATUOUS > FLATUS

FLATUS n gas generated in the alimentary canal

FLATUSES > FLATUS

FLATWARE n cutlery

FLATWARES > FLATWARE

FLATWASH n laundry that can be ironed mechanically

FLATWATER n slowly moving water in a river

FLATWAYS adv with the flat or broad side down or in contact with another surface

FLATWISE same as > FLATWAYS

FLATWORK n laundry that can be ironed mechanically

FLATWORKS > FLATWORK

FLATWORM n worm, such as a tapeworm, with a flattened body

FLATWORMS > FLATWORM

FLAUGHT vb flutter

FLAUGHTED > FLAUGHT

FLAUGHTER vb cut peat

FLAUGHTS > FLAUGHT

FLAUNCH n cement or mortar slope to throw off water ▷ vb cause to slope in this manner

FLAUNCHED > FLAUNCH

FLAUNCHES > FLAUNCH

FLAUNE variant of > FLAM

FLAUNES > FLAUNE

FLAUNT vb display (oneself or one's possessions) arrogantly ▷ n act of flaunting

FLAUNTED > FLAUNT

FLAUNTER > FLAUNT

FLAUNTERS > FLAUNT

FLAUNTIER > FLAUNTY

FLAUNTILY > FLAUNTY

FLAUNTING > FLAUNT

FLAUNTS > FLAUNT

FLAUNTY adj characterized by or inclined to ostentatious display

FLAUTA n tortilla rolled around a filling

FLAUTAS > FLAUTA

FLAUTIST n flute player

FLAUTISTS > FLAUTIST

FLAVA n individual style

FLAVANOL n type of flavonoid

FLAVANOLS > FLAVANOL

FLAVANONE n flavone-derived compound

FLAVAS > FLAVA

FLAVIN n heterocyclic ketone

FLAVINE same as > FLAVIN

FLAVINES > FLAVINE

FLAVINS > FLAVIN

FLAVONE n crystalline compound occurring in plants

FLAVONES > FLAVONE

FLAVONOID n any of a group of organic compounds that occur as pigments in fruit and flowers

FLAVONOL n flavonoid said to offer protection against heart disease

FLAVONOLS > FLAVONOL

FLAVOR same as > FLAVOUR

FLAVORED > FLAVOR

FLAVORER > FLAVOR

FLAVORERS > FLAVOR

FLAVORFUL adj flavourful

FLAVORIER > FLAVORY

FLAVORING n flavouring

FLAVORIST n blender of ingredients, to create or enhance flavours

FLAVOROUS adj having flavour

FLAVORS > FLAVOR

FLAVORY adj flavoursome

FLAVOUR n distinctive taste ▷ vb give flavour to

FLAVOURED > FLAVOUR

FLAVOURER > FLAVOUR

FLAVOURS > FLAVOUR

FLAVOURY adj flavoursome

FLAW n imperfection or blemish ▷ vb make or become blemished, defective, or imperfect

FLAWED > FLAW

FLAWIER > FLAW

FLAWIEST > FLAW

FLAWING > FLAW

FLAWLESS > FLAW

FLAWN variant of > FLAM

FLAWNS > FLAWN

FLAWS > FLAW

FLAWY > FLAW

FLAX n plant grown for its stem fibres and seeds

FLAXEN adj (of hair) pale yellow

FLAXES > FLAX

FLAXIER > FLAXY

FLAXIEST > FLAXY

FLAXLIKE adj like flax

FLAXSEED n seed of the flax plant, which yields linseed oil

FLAXSEEDS > FLAXSEED

FLAXY same as > FLAXEN

FLAY vb remove the skin from

FLAYED > FLAY
FLAYER n FLAY
FLAYERS > FLAY
FLAYING > FLAY
FLAYS > FLAY
FLAYSOME adj frightening
FLEA n small bloodsucking insect
FLEABAG n dirty or unkempt person, esp a woman
FLEABAGS > FLEABAG
FLEABANE n as in Canadian fleabane small plant thought to ward off fleas
FLEABANES > FLEABANE
FLEABITE n bite of a flea
FLEABITES > FLEABITE
FLEADH n festival of Irish music, dancing, and culture
FLEADHS > FLEADH
FLEAM n lancet used for letting blood
FLEAMS > FLEAM
FLEAPIT n shabby cinema or theatre
FLEAPITS > FLEAPIT
FLEAS > FLEA
FLEASOME adj having fleas
FLEAWORT n type of plant
FLEAWORTS > FLEAWORT
FLECHE n slender spire
FLECHES > FLECHE
FLECHETTE n steel dart or missile dropped from an aircraft, as in World War I
FLECK n small mark, streak, or speck ▷ vb speckle
FLECKED > FLECK
FLECKER same as > FLECK
FLECKERED > FLECKER
FLECKERS > FLECKER
FLECKIER > FLECKY
FLECKIEST > FLECKY
FLECKING > FLECK
FLECKLESS > FLECK
FLECKS > FLECK
FLECKY > FLECK
FLECTION n act of bending or the state of being bent
FLECTIONS > FLECTION
FLED > FLEE
FLEDGE vb feed and care for (a young bird) until it is able to fly
FLEDGED > FLEDGE
FLEDGES > FLEDGE
FLEDGIER > FLEDGY
FLEDGIEST > FLEDGY
FLEDGING > FLEDGE
FLEDGLING n young bird ▷ adj new or inexperienced
FLEDGY adj feathery or feathered
FLEE vb run away (from)
FLEECE n sheep's coat of wool ▷ vb defraud or overcharge

FLEECED > FLEECE
FLEECER > FLEECE
FLEECERS > FLEECE
FLEECES > FLEECE
FLEECH vb flatter
FLEECHED > FLEECH
FLEECHES > FLEECH
FLEECHING > FLEECH
FLEECIE n person who collects fleeces for baling
FLEECIER > FLEECY
FLEECIES > FLEECIE
FLEECIEST > FLEECY
FLEECILY > FLEECY
FLEECING > FLEECE
FLEECY adj made of or like fleece ▷ n person who collects fleeces for baling
FLEEING > FLEE
FLEEK n as in on fleek stylish, on trend
FLEEKS same as > FLEEK
FLEER vb grin or laugh at ▷ n derisory glance or grin
FLEERED > FLEER
FLEERER > FLEER
FLEERERS > FLEER
FLEERING > FLEER
FLEERINGS > FLEER
FLEERS > FLEER
FLEES > FLEE
FLEET n number of warships organized as a unit ▷ adj swift in movement ▷ vb move rapidly
FLEETED > FLEET
FLEETER n person who sails with a fleet of ships
FLEETERS > FLEETER
FLEETEST > FLEET
FLEETING adj rapid and soon passing
FLEETLY > FLEET
FLEETNESS > FLEET
FLEETS > FLEET
FLEG vb scare
FLEGGED > FLEG
FLEGGING > FLEG
FLEGS > FLEG
FLEHMEN vb (of mammal) grimace
FLEHMENED > FLEHMEN
FLEHMENS > FLEHMEN
FLEISHIG same as > FLEISHIK
FLEISHIK adj containing or derived from meat or meat products
FLEME vb drive out
FLEMED > FLEME
FLEMES > FLEME
FLEMING n inhabitant of Flanders or a Flemish-speaking Belgian
FLEMISH vb stow (a rope) in a Flemish coil
FLEMISHED > FLEMISH
FLEMISHES > FLEMISH
FLEMIT > FLEME
FLENCH same as > FLENSE
FLENCHED > FLENCH
FLENCHER > FLENCH
FLENCHERS > FLENCH
FLENCHES > FLENCH
FLENCHING > FLENCH

FLENSE vb strip (a whale, seal, etc) of (its blubber or skin)
FLENSED > FLENSE
FLENSER > FLENSE
FLENSERS > FLENSE
FLENSES > FLENSE
FLENSING > FLENSE
FLEROVIUM n transuranic element
FLESH n soft part of a human or animal body ▷ vb remove flesh from
FLESHED > FLESH
FLESHER n person or machine that fleshes hides or skins
FLESHERS > FLESHER
FLESHES > FLESH
FLESHHOOD n incarnation
FLESHIER > FLESHY
FLESHIEST > FLESHY
FLESHILY > FLESHY
FLESHING > FLESH
FLESHINGS pl n tights of the colour of the wearer's skin
FLESHLESS > FLESH
FLESHLIER > FLESHLY
FLESHLING n voluptuary
FLESHLY adj fleshy; fat
FLESHMENT n act of fleshing
FLESHPOT n pot in which meat is cooked
FLESHPOTS pl n places, such as brothels and strip clubs, where sexual desires are catered to
FLESHWORM n flesh-eating worm
FLESHY adj plump
FLETCH same as > FLEDGE
FLETCHED > FLETCH
FLETCHER n person who makes arrows
FLETCHERS > FLETCHER
FLETCHES > FLETCH
FLETCHING > FLETCH
FLETTON n type of brick
FLETTONS > FLETTON
FLEUR n flower emblem used in heraldry
FLEURET same as > FLEURETTE
FLEURETS > FLEURET
FLEURETTE n ornament resembling a flower
FLEURON n decorative piece of pastry
FLEURONS > FLEURON
FLEURS > FLEUR
FLEURY same as > FLORY
FLEW > FLY
FLEWED adj having large flews
FLEWS pl n upper lip of a bloodhound or similar dog
FLEX n flexible insulated electric cable ▷ vb bend
FLEXAGON n hexagon made from a single pliable strip of triangles
FLEXAGONS > FLEXAGON

FLEXED > FLEX
FLEXES > FLEX
FLEXI n flexitime
FLEXIBLE adj easily bent
FLEXIBLY > FLEXIBLE
FLEXILE same as > FLEXIBLE
FLEXING > FLEX
FLEXION n act of bending a joint or limb
FLEXIONAL > FLEXION
FLEXIONS > FLEXION
FLEXIS > FLEXI
FLEXITIME n system permitting variation in starting and finishing times of work
FLEXO n flexography
FLEXOR n type of muscle
FLEXORS > FLEXOR
FLEXOS > FLEXO
FLEXTIME same as > FLEXITIME
FLEXTIMER > FLEXTIME
FLEXTIMES > FLEXTIME
FLEXUOSE same as > FLEXUOUS
FLEXUOUS adj full of bends or curves
FLEXURAL > FLEXURE
FLEXURE n act of flexing or the state of being flexed
FLEXURES > FLEXURE
FLEXWING n collapsible fabric wing used in hang gliding
FLEXWINGS > FLEXWING
FLEY vb be afraid or cause to be afraid
FLEYED > FLEY
FLEYING > FLEY
FLEYS > FLEY
FLIBBERT n small piece or bit
FLIBBERTS > FLIBBERT
FLIC n French police officer
FLICHTER vb flutter
FLICHTERS > FLICHTER
FLICK vb touch or move in a quick movement ▷ n tap or quick stroke
FLICKABLE > FLICK
FLICKED > FLICK
FLICKER vb shine unsteadily or intermittently ▷ n unsteady brief light
FLICKERED > FLICKER
FLICKERS > FLICKER
FLICKERY adj flickering
FLICKING > FLICK
FLICKS > FLICK
FLICS > FLIC
FLIED > FLY
FLIER > FLY
FLIERS > FLY
FLIES > FLY
FLIEST > FLY
FLIGHT n journey by air ▷ vb cause (a ball, dart, etc) to float slowly or deceptively towards its target

FLIGHTED > FLIGHT
FLIGHTIER > FLIGHTY
FLIGHTILY > FLIGHTY
FLIGHTING > FLIGHT
FLIGHTS > FLIGHT
FLIGHTY *adj* frivolous and fickle
FLIM *n* five-pound note
FLIMFLAM *n* nonsense ▷ *vb* deceive
FLIMFLAMS > FLIMFLAM
FLIMP *vb* steal
FLIMPED > FLIMP
FLIMPING > FLIMP
FLIMPS > FLIMP
FLIMS > FLIM
FLIMSIER > FLIMSY
FLIMSIES > FLIMSY
FLIMSIEST > FLIMSY
FLIMSILY > FLIMSY
FLIMSY *adj* not strong or substantial ▷ *n* thin paper used for making carbon copies
FLINCH *vb* draw back suddenly
FLINCHED > FLINCH
FLINCHER > FLINCH
FLINCHERS > FLINCH
FLINCHES > FLINCH
FLINCHING > FLINCH
FLINDER *n* fragment ▷ *vb* scamper about flutteringly
FLINDERED > FLINDER
FLINDERS > FLINDER
FLING *vb* throw, send, or move forcefully or hurriedly ▷ *n* spell of self-indulgent enjoyment
FLINGER > FLING
FLINGERS > FLING
FLINGING > FLING
FLINGS > FLING
FLINKITE *n* anhydrous phosphate
FLINKITES > FLINKITE
FLINT *n* hard grey stone ▷ *vb* fit or provide with a flint
FLINTED > FLINT
FLINTHEAD *n* American wading bird
FLINTIER > FLINTY
FLINTIEST > FLINTY
FLINTIFY *vb* turn to flint
FLINTILY > FLINTY
FLINTING > FLINT
FLINTLIKE > FLINT
FLINTLOCK *n* obsolete gun in which the powder was lit by a spark from a flint
FLINTS > FLINT
FLINTY *adj* cruel
FLIP *vb* throw (something small or light) carelessly ▷ *n* snap or tap ▷ *adj* flippant
FLIPBOARD *n* piece of office equipment consisting of a board to which a flipchart, etc can be attached
FLIPBOOK *n* book of drawings made to seem animated by flipping pages
FLIPBOOKS > FLIPBOOK
FLIPCHART *n* pad containing large sheets of paper, mounted on a stand and used to present reports, etc
FLIPFLOP *n* rubber sandal
FLIPFLOPS > FLIPFLOP
FLIPPANCY > FLIPPANT
FLIPPANT *adj* treating serious things lightly
FLIPPED > FLIP
FLIPPER *n* limb of a sea animal adapted for swimming
FLIPPERS > FLIPPER
FLIPPEST > FLIP
FLIPPIER > FLIPPY
FLIPPIEST > FLIPPY
FLIPPING *n* act or instance of flipping
FLIPPINGS > FLIPPING
FLIPPY *adj* (of clothes) moving to and fro as the wearer walks
FLIPS > FLIP
FLIPSIDE *n* reverse or opposite side
FLIPSIDES > FLIPSIDE
FLIR *n* forward looking infrared radar
FLIRS > FLIR
FLIRT *vb* behave as if physically attracted to someone ▷ *n* person who flirts
FLIRTED > FLIRT
FLIRTER > FLIRT
FLIRTERS > FLIRT
FLIRTIER > FLIRT
FLIRTIEST > FLIRT
FLIRTING > FLIRT
FLIRTINGS > FLIRT
FLIRTISH > FLIRT
FLIRTS > FLIRT
FLIRTY > FLIRT
FLISK *vb* skip
FLISKED > FLISK
FLISKIER > FLISK
FLISKIEST > FLISK
FLISKING > FLISK
FLISKS > FLISK
FLISKY > FLISK
FLIT *vb* move lightly and rapidly ▷ *n* act of flitting
FLITCH *n* side of pork salted and cured ▷ *vb* cut (a tree trunk) into pieces of timber
FLITCHED > FLITCH
FLITCHES > FLITCH
FLITCHING > FLITCH
FLITE *vb* scold or rail at ▷ *n* dispute or scolding
FLITED > FLITE
FLITES > FLITE
FLITING > FLITE
FLITS > FLIT
FLITT *adj* fleet ▷ *vb* to flit
FLITTED > FLIT

FLITTER > FLIT
FLITTERED > FLIT
FLITTERN *n* bark of young oak tree
FLITTERNS > FLITTERN
FLITTERS > FLIT
FLITTING > FLIT
FLITTINGS > FLIT
FLITTS > FLITT
FLIVVER *n* old, cheap, or battered car
FLIVVERS > FLIVVER
FLIX *n* fur ▷ *vb* have fur
FLIXED > FLIX
FLIXES > FLIX
FLIXING > FLIX
FLIXWEED *n* plant of the mustard family
FLIXWEEDS > FLIXWEED
FLOAT *vb* rest on the surface of a liquid ▷ *n* object used to help someone or something float
FLOATABLE > FLOAT
FLOATAGE *same as* > FLOTAGE
FLOATAGES > FLOATAGE
FLOATANT *n* substance used in fly-fishing, to help dry flies to float
FLOATANTS > FLOATANT
FLOATBASE *n* place where seaplanes dock
FLOATCUT *adj* as in *floatcut file* file with rows of parallel teeth
FLOATED > FLOAT
FLOATEL *same as* > FLOTEL
FLOATELS > FLOATEL
FLOATER *n* person or thing that floats
FLOATERS > FLOATER
FLOATIER > FLOATY
FLOATIEST > FLOATY
FLOATING *adj* moving about, changing
FLOATINGS > FLOATING
FLOATS *pl n* footlights
FLOATY *adj* filmy and light
FLOB *vb* spit
FLOBBED > FLOB
FLOBBING > FLOB
FLOBS > FLOB
FLOC *same as* > FLOCK
FLOCCED > FLOC
FLOCCI > FLOCCUS
FLOCCING > FLOC
FLOCCOSE *adj* consisting of or covered with woolly tufts or hairs
FLOCCULAR > FLOCCUS
FLOCCULE *n* small aggregate of flocculent material
FLOCCULES > FLOCCULE
FLOCCULI > FLOCCULUS
FLOCCULUS *same as* > FLOCCULE

FLOCCUS *n* downy or woolly covering ▷ *adj* (of a cloud) having the appearance of woolly tufts
FLOCK *n* number of animals of one kind together ▷ *vb* gather in a crowd ▷ *adj* (of wallpaper) with a velvety raised pattern
FLOCKED > FLOCK
FLOCKIER > FLOCK
FLOCKIEST > FLOCK
FLOCKING > FLOCK
FLOCKINGS > FLOCK
FLOCKLESS > FLOCK
FLOCKS > FLOCK
FLOCKY > FLOCK
FLOCS > FLOC
FLOE *n* sheet of floating ice
FLOES > FLOE
FLOG *vb* beat with a whip or stick
FLOGGABLE > FLOG
FLOGGED > FLOG
FLOGGER > FLOG
FLOGGERS > FLOG
FLOGGING > FLOG
FLOGGINGS > FLOG
FLOGS > FLOG
FLOKATI *n* Greek hand-woven shaggy woollen rug
FLOKATIS > FLOKATI
FLONG *n* material used for making moulds in stereotyping
FLONGS > FLONG
FLOOD *n* overflow of water onto a normally dry area ▷ *vb* cover or become covered with water
FLOODABLE > FLOOD
FLOODED > FLOOD
FLOODER > FLOOD
FLOODERS > FLOOD
FLOODGATE *n* gate used to control the flow of water
FLOODING *n* submerging of land under water
FLOODINGS > FLOODING
FLOODLESS > FLOOD
FLOODLIT *adj* illuminated with a floodlight
FLOODMARK *n* high-water mark
FLOODS > FLOOD
FLOODTIDE *n* rising tide
FLOODWALL *n* wall built as a defence against floods
FLOODWAY *n* conduit for floodwater
FLOODWAYS > FLOODWAY
FLOOEY *adj* awry
FLOOIE *same as* > FLOOEY
FLOOR *n* lower surface of a room ▷ *vb* knock down
FLOORAGE *n* area of floor
FLOORAGES > FLOORAGE
FLOORED > FLOOR
FLOORER *n* coup de grâce

FLOORERS > FLOORER
FLOORHEAD n upper side of a floor timber
FLOORING > FLOOR
FLOORINGS > FLOOR
FLOORLESS > FLOOR
FLOORPAN n bottom part of a motor vehicle's interior
FLOORPANS > FLOORPAN
FLOORS > FLOOR
FLOORSHOW n entertainment on floor of nightclub
FLOOSIE same as > FLOOZY
FLOOSIES > FLOOSIE
FLOOSY variant of > FLOOSIE
FLOOZIE same as > FLOOZY
FLOOZIES > FLOOZY
FLOOZY n derogatory term for a woman considered immodest
FLOP vb bend, fall, or collapse loosely or carelessly ▷ n failure
FLOPHOUSE n cheap lodging house, esp one used by tramps
FLOPOVER n TV visual effect of page being turned
FLOPOVERS > FLOPOVER
FLOPPED > FLOP
FLOPPER > FLOP
FLOPPERS > FLOP
FLOPPIER > FLOPPY
FLOPPIES > FLOPPY
FLOPPIEST > FLOPPY
FLOPPILY > FLOPPY
FLOPPING > FLOP
FLOPPY adj hanging downwards, loose ▷ n floppy disk
FLOPS > FLOP
FLOPTICAL n type of floppy disk
FLOR n type of yeast
FLORA n plants of a given place or time
FLORAE > FLORA
FLORAL adj consisting of or decorated with flowers ▷ n class of perfume
FLORALLY > FLORAL
FLORALS > FLORAL
FLORAS > FLORA
FLOREANT > FLOREAT
FLOREAT vb may (a person, institution, etc) flourish
FLOREATED same as > FLORIATED
FLORENCE n type of fennel
FLORENCES > FLORENCE
FLORET n part of a composite flower head
FLORETS > FLORET
FLORIATED adj having ornamentation based on flowers and leaves
FLORICANE n fruiting stem of plant

FLORID adj with a red or flushed complexion
FLORIDEAN n member of the red seaweed family
FLORIDER > FLORID
FLORIDEST > FLORID
FLORIDITY > FLORID
FLORIDLY > FLORID
FLORIER > FLORY
FLORIEST > FLORY
FLORIFORM adj flower-shaped
FLORIGEN n hypothetical plant hormone
FLORIGENS > FLORIGEN
FLORIN n former British and Australian coin
FLORINS > FLORIN
FLORIST n seller of flowers
FLORISTIC adj of or relating to flowers or a flora
FLORISTRY > FLORIST
FLORISTS > FLORIST
FLORS > FLOR
FLORUIT prep (he or she) flourished in ▷ n such a period in a person's life
FLORUITS > FLORUIT
FLORULA n flora of a small single environment
FLORULAE > FLORULA
FLORULE same as > FLORULA
FLORULES > FLORULE
FLORY adj containing a fleur-de-lys
FLOSCULAR > FLOSCULE
FLOSCULE n floret
FLOSCULES > FLOSCULE
FLOSH n hopper-shaped box
FLOSHES > FLOSH
FLOSS n fine silky fibres ▷ vb clean (between the teeth) with dental floss
FLOSSED > FLOSS
FLOSSER > FLOSS
FLOSSERS > FLOSS
FLOSSES > FLOSS
FLOSSIE variant of > FLOSSY
FLOSSIER > FLOSSY
FLOSSIES > FLOSSY
FLOSSIEST > FLOSSY
FLOSSILY > FLOSSY
FLOSSING > FLOSS
FLOSSINGS > FLOSS
FLOSSY adj consisting of or resembling floss ▷ n floozy
FLOTA n formerly, Spanish commercial fleet
FLOTAGE n act or state of floating
FLOTAGES > FLOTAGE
FLOTANT adj in heraldry, flying in the air
FLOTAS > FLOTA
FLOTATION n launching or financing of a business enterprise

FLOTE n aquatic perennial grass ▷ vb skim (eg milk)
FLOTED > FLOTE
FLOTEL n (in the oil industry) rig or boat used as accommodation
FLOTELS > FLOTEL
FLOTES > FLOTE
FLOTILLA n small fleet or fleet of small ships
FLOTILLAS > FLOTILLA
FLOTING > FLOTE
FLOTSAM n floating wreckage
FLOTSAMS > FLOTSAM
FLOUNCE vb go with emphatic movements ▷ n flouncing movement
FLOUNCED > FLOUNCE
FLOUNCES > FLOUNCE
FLOUNCIER > FLOUNCE
FLOUNCING n material, such as lace or embroidered fabric, used for making flounces
FLOUNCY > FLOUNCE
FLOUNDER vb move with difficulty, as in mud ▷ n edible flatfish
FLOUNDERS > FLOUNDER
FLOUR n powder made by grinding grain, esp wheat ▷ vb sprinkle with flour
FLOURED > FLOUR
FLOURIER > FLOUR
FLOURIEST > FLOUR
FLOURING > FLOUR
FLOURISH vb be active, successful, or widespread ▷ n dramatic waving motion
FLOURISHY adj full of flourishes
FLOURLESS > FLOUR
FLOURS > FLOUR
FLOURY > FLOUR
FLOUSE vb splash
FLOUSED > FLOUSE
FLOUSES > FLOUSE
FLOUSH variant of > FLOUSE
FLOUSHED > FLOUSH
FLOUSHES > FLOUSH
FLOUSHING > FLOUSH
FLOUSING > FLOUSE
FLOUT vb deliberately disobey (a rule, law, etc)
FLOUTED > FLOUT
FLOUTER > FLOUT
FLOUTERS > FLOUT
FLOUTING > FLOUT
FLOUTS > FLOUT
FLOW vb (of liquid) move in a stream ▷ n act, rate, or manner of flowing
FLOWABLE adj capable of flowing
FLOWAGE n act of overflowing or the state of having overflowed
FLOWAGES > FLOWAGE
FLOWCHART n diagrammatic representation of the sequence of operations or

equipment in an industrial process, computer program, etc
FLOWED > FLOW
FLOWER n part of a plant that produces seeds ▷ vb produce flowers, bloom
FLOWERAGE n mass of flowers
FLOWERBED n piece of ground for growing flowers
FLOWERED adj decorated with a floral design
FLOWERER n plant that flowers at a specified time or in a specified way
FLOWERERS > FLOWERER
FLOWERET another name for > FLORET
FLOWERETS > FLOWERET
FLOWERFUL adj having plentiful flowers
FLOWERIER > FLOWERY
FLOWERILY > FLOWERY
FLOWERING adj (of certain species of plants) capable of producing conspicuous flowers
FLOWERPOT n pot in which plants are grown
FLOWERS > FLOWER
FLOWERY adj decorated with a floral design
FLOWING > FLOW
FLOWINGLY > FLOW
FLOWMETER n instrument that measures the rate of flow of a liquid or gas within a pipe or tube
FLOWN > FLY
FLOWS > FLOW
FLOWSTONE n type of speleothem
FLOX adj as in flox silk type of silk
FLU n any of various viral infections
FLUATE n fluoride
FLUATES > FLUATE
FLUB vb bungle
FLUBBED > FLUB
FLUBBER > FLUB
FLUBBERS > FLUB
FLUBBING > FLUB
FLUBDUB n bunkum
FLUBDUBS > FLUBDUB
FLUBS > FLUB
FLUCTUANT adj inclined to vary or fluctuate
FLUCTUATE vb change frequently and erratically
FLUE n passage or pipe for smoke or hot air
FLUED adj having a flue
FLUELLEN n type of plant
FLUELLENS > FLUELLEN
FLUELLIN same as > FLUELLEN
FLUELLINS > FLUELLIN
FLUENCE vb particle or energy density
FLUENCES > FLUENCE

FLUENCIES > FLUENCY
FLUENCY n quality of being fluent
FLUENT adj able to speak or write with ease ▷ n variable quantity in fluxions
FLUENTLY > FLUENT
FLUENTS > FLUENT
FLUERIC adj of or relating to fluidics
FLUERICS pl n fluidics
FLUES > FLUE
FLUEWORK n collectively, organ stops
FLUEWORKS > FLUEWORK
FLUEY adj involved in, caused by, or like influenza
FLUFF n soft fibres ▷ vb make or become soft and puffy
FLUFFBALL n ball of fluff
FLUFFED > FLUFF
FLUFFER n person employed on a railway to clear the tracks
FLUFFERS > FLUFFER
FLUFFIER > FLUFFY
FLUFFIEST > FLUFFY
FLUFFILY > FLUFFY
FLUFFING > FLUFF
FLUFFS > FLUFF
FLUFFY adj of, resembling, or covered with fluff
FLUGEL n grand piano or harpsichord
FLUGELMAN variant of > FUGLEMAN
FLUGELMEN > FLUGELMAN
FLUGELS > FLUGEL
FLUID n substance able to flow and change its shape ▷ adj able to flow or change shape easily
FLUIDAL > FLUID
FLUIDALLY > FLUID
FLUIDIC > FLUIDICS
FLUIDICS n study and use of the flow of fluids in tubes
FLUIDIFY vb make fluid
FLUIDISE same as > FLUIDIZE
FLUIDISED > FLUIDIZE
FLUIDISER > FLUIDIZE
FLUIDISES > FLUIDIZE
FLUIDITY n state of being fluid
FLUIDIZE vb make fluid
FLUIDIZED > FLUIDIZE
FLUIDIZER > FLUIDIZE
FLUIDIZES > FLUIDIZE
FLUIDLIKE > FLUID
FLUIDLY > FLUID
FLUIDNESS > FLUID
FLUIDRAM n British imperial measure
FLUIDRAMS > FLUIDRAM

FLUIDS > FLUID
FLUIER > FLUEY
FLUIEST > FLUEY
FLUISH > FLU
FLUKE n accidental stroke of luck ▷ vb gain, make, or hit by a fluke
FLUKED > FLUKE
FLUKES > FLUKE
FLUKEY same as > FLUKY
FLUKIER > FLUKY
FLUKIEST > FLUKY
FLUKILY > FLUKY
FLUKINESS > FLUKY
FLUKING > FLUKE
FLUKY adj done or gained by an accident
FLUME n narrow sloping channel for water ▷ vb transport (logs) in a flume
FLUMED > FLUME
FLUMES > FLUME
FLUMING > FLUME
FLUMMERY n silly or trivial talk
FLUMMOX vb puzzle or confuse
FLUMMOXED > FLUMMOX
FLUMMOXES > FLUMMOX
FLUMP vb move or fall heavily
FLUMPED > FLUMP
FLUMPING > FLUMP
FLUMPS > FLUMP
FLUNG > FLING
FLUNK vb fail ▷ n low grade below the pass standard
FLUNKED > FLUNK
FLUNKER > FLUNK
FLUNKERS > FLUNK
FLUNKEY same as > FLUNKY
FLUNKEYS > FLUNKEY
FLUNKIE same as > FLUNKY
FLUNKIES > FLUNKY
FLUNKING > FLUNK
FLUNKS > FLUNK
FLUNKY n servile person
FLUNKYISM > FLUNKY
FLUOR same as > FLUORSPAR
FLUORENE n white insoluble crystalline solid
FLUORENES > FLUORENE
FLUORESCE vb exhibit fluorescence
FLUORIC adj of, concerned with, or produced from fluorine or fluorspar
FLUORID same as > FLUORIDE
FLUORIDE n compound containing fluorine
FLUORIDES > FLUORIDE
FLUORIDS > FLUORID
FLUORIN same as > FLUORINE
FLUORINE n toxic yellow gas: most reactive of all the elements
FLUORINES > FLUORINE
FLUORINS > FLUORIN

FLUORITE same as > FLUORSPAR
FLUORITES > FLUORITE
FLUOROSES > FLUOROSIS
FLUOROSIS n fluoride poisoning, due to ingestion of too much fluoride in drinking water over a long period or to ingestion of pesticides containing fluoride salts. Chronic fluorosis results in mottling of the teeth of children
FLUOROTIC > FLUOROSIS
FLUORS > FLUOR
FLUORSPAR n white or colourless mineral, consisting of calcium fluoride in crystalline form: the chief ore of fluorine
FLURR vb scatter
FLURRED > FLURR
FLURRIED > FLURRY
FLURRIES > FLURRY
FLURRING > FLURR
FLURRS > FLURR
FLURRY n sudden commotion ▷ vb confuse
FLURRYING > FLURRY
FLUS > FLU
FLUSH vb blush or cause to blush ▷ n blush ▷ adj level with the surrounding surface ▷ adv so as to be level
FLUSHABLE > FLUSH
FLUSHED > FLUSH
FLUSHER > FLUSH
FLUSHERS > FLUSH
FLUSHES > FLUSH
FLUSHEST > FLUSH
FLUSHIER > FLUSHY
FLUSHIEST > FLUSHY
FLUSHING n extra feeding given to ewes before mating to increase the lambing percentage
FLUSHINGS > FLUSHING
FLUSHNESS > FLUSH
FLUSHWORK n decorative treatment of the surface of an outside wall with flints split to show their smooth black surface, combined with dressed stone to form patterns such as tracery or initials
FLUSHY adj ruddy
FLUSTER vb make nervous or upset ▷ n nervous or upset state
FLUSTERED > FLUSTER
FLUSTERS > FLUSTER
FLUSTERY adj flustered
FLUSTRATE vb fluster
FLUTE n wind instrument ▷ vb utter in a high-pitched tone
FLUTED adj having decorative grooves
FLUTELIKE > FLUTE
FLUTER n craftsperson who makes flutes or fluting

FLUTERS > FLUTER
FLUTES > FLUTE
FLUTEY adj resembling a flute in sound
FLUTEYER > FLUTEY
FLUTEYEST > FLUTEY
FLUTIER > FLUTEY
FLUTIEST > FLUTEY
FLUTINA n type of accordion
FLUTINAS > FLUTINA
FLUTING n design of decorative grooves
FLUTINGS > FLUTING
FLUTIST same as > FLAUTIST
FLUTISTS > FLUTIST
FLUTTER vb flap ▷ n flapping movement
FLUTTERED > FLUTTER
FLUTTERER > FLUTTER
FLUTTERS > FLUTTER
FLUTTERY adj flapping rapidly
FLUTY > FLUTE
FLUVIAL adj of rivers
FLUVIATIC > FLUVIAL
FLUX n constant change or instability ▷ vb make or become fluid
FLUXED > FLUX
FLUXES > FLUX
FLUXGATE n type of magnetometer
FLUXGATES > FLUXGATE
FLUXING > FLUX
FLUXION n rate of change of a function
FLUXIONAL > FLUXION
FLUXIONS > FLUXION
FLUXIVE > FLUX
FLUXMETER n any instrument for measuring magnetic flux, usually by measuring the charge that flows through a coil when the flux changes
FLUYT n Dutch sailing ship
FLUYTS > FLUYT
FLY vb move through the air on wings or in an aircraft ▷ n fastening at the front of trousers ▷ adj sharp and cunning
FLYABLE > FLY
FLYAWAY adj (of hair) very fine and soft ▷ n person who is frivolous or flighty
FLYAWAYS > FLYAWAY
FLYBACK n item of electrical equipment
FLYBACKS > FLYBACK
FLYBANE n type of campion
FLYBANES > FLYBANE
FLYBELT n strip of tsetse-infested land
FLYBELTS > FLYBELT
FLYBLEW > FLYBLOW
FLYBLOW vb contaminate ▷ n egg or young larva of a blowfly
FLYBLOWN adj covered with blowfly eggs
FLYBLOWS > FLYBLOW

FLYBOAT n any small swift boat

FLYBOATS > FLYBOAT

FLYBOOK n small case or wallet for storing artificial flies

FLYBOOKS > FLYBOOK

FLYBOY n air force pilot

FLYBOYS > FLYBOY

FLYBRIDGE n highest navigational bridge on a ship

FLYBY n flight past a particular position or target

FLYBYS > FLYBY

FLYER > FLY

FLYERS > FLY

FLYEST > FLY

FLYFISHER n angler who fishes with a fly

FLYHAND n device on a printing press

FLYHANDS > FLYHAND

FLYING > FLY

FLYINGS > FLY

FLYLEAF n blank leaf at the beginning or end of a book

FLYLEAVES > FLYLEAF

FLYLESS > FLY

FLYLINE n type of line used in fly fishing

FLYLINES > FLYLINE

FLYMAKER n person who makes fishing flies

FLYMAKERS
> FLYMAKER

FLYMAN n stagehand

FLYMEN > FLYMAN

FLYOFF n all water transferred from the earth to the atmosphere

FLYOFFS > FLYOFF

FLYOVER n road passing over another by a bridge

FLYOVERS > FLYOVER

FLYPAPER n paper with a sticky poisonous coating, used to kill flies

FLYPAPERS
> FLYPAPER

FLYPAST n ceremonial flight of aircraft over a given area

FLYPASTS > FLYPAST

FLYPE vb fold back

FLYPED > FLYPE

FLYPES > FLYPE

FLYPING > FLYPE

FLYPITCH n area for unlicensed stalls at markets

FLYPOSTER n person who puts up posters illegally

FLYRODDER n angler using artificial fly

FLYSCH n type of marine sedimentary facies

FLYSCHES > FLYSCH

FLYSCREEN n wire-mesh screen over a window to prevent flies from entering a room

FLYSHEET n part of tent

FLYSHEETS
> FLYSHEET

FLYSPECK n small speck of the excrement of a fly ▷ vb mark with flyspecks

FLYSPECKS
> FLYSPECK

FLYSPRAY n insecticide sprayed from an aerosol

FLYSPRAYS
> FLYSPRAY

FLYSTRIKE n infestation of wounded sheep by blowflies or maggots

FLYTE same as > FLITE

FLYTED > FLYTE

FLYTES > FLYTE

FLYTIER n person who makes their own fishing flies

FLYTIERS > FLYTIER

FLYTING > FLYTE

FLYTINGS > FLYTE

FLYTRAP n any of various insectivorous plants

FLYTRAPS > FLYTRAP

FLYWAY n usual route used by birds when migrating

FLYWAYS > FLYWAY

FLYWEIGHT n boxer weighing up to 112lb (professional) or 51kg (amateur)

FLYWHEEL n heavy wheel regulating the speed of a machine

FLYWHEELS
> FLYWHEEL

FOAL n young of a horse or related animal ▷ vb give birth to a foal

FOALED > FOAL

FOALFOOT n coltsfoot

FOALFOOTS
> FOALFOOT

FOALING n act of giving birth to a foal

FOALINGS > FOALING

FOALS > FOAL

FOAM n mass of small bubbles on a liquid ▷ vb produce foam

FOAMABLE > FOAM

FOAMED > FOAM

FOAMER n (possibly obsessive) enthusiast

FOAMERS > FOAMER

FOAMIER > FOAMY

FOAMIEST > FOAMY

FOAMILY > FOAMY

FOAMINESS > FOAMY

FOAMING > FOAM

FOAMINGLY > FOAM

FOAMINGS > FOAM

FOAMLESS > FOAM

FOAMLIKE > FOAM

FOAMS > FOAM

FOAMY adj of, resembling, consisting of, or covered with foam

FOB n short watch chain ▷ vb cheat

FOBBED > FOB

FOBBING > FOB

FOBS > FOB

FOCACCIA n flat Italian bread made with olive oil and yeast

FOCACCIAS > FOCACCIA

FOCAL adj of or at a focus

FOCALISE same as
> FOCALIZE

FOCALISED
> FOCALIZE

FOCALISES
> FOCALIZE

FOCALIZE less common word for > FOCUS

FOCALIZED
> FOCALIZE

FOCALIZES
> FOCALIZE

FOCALLY > FOCAL

FOCI > FOCUS

FOCIMETER n photographic focusing device

FOCOMETER n instrument for measuring the focal length of a lens

FOCUS n point at which light or sound waves converge ▷ vb bring or come into focus

FOCUSABLE > FOCUS

FOCUSED > FOCUS

FOCUSER > FOCUS

FOCUSERS > FOCUS

FOCUSES > FOCUS

FOCUSING > FOCUS

FOCUSINGS > FOCUS

FOCUSLESS > FOCUS

FOCUSSED > FOCUS

FOCUSSES > FOCUS

FOCUSSING > FOCUS

FODDER n feed for livestock ▷ vb supply (livestock) with fodder

FODDERED > FODDER

FODDERER > FODDER

FODDERERS > FODDER

FODDERING > FODDER

FODDERS > FODDER

FODGEL adj buxom

FOE n enemy, opponent

FOEDARIE variant of
> FEDARIE

FOEDARIES
> FOEDARIE

FOEDERATI pl n (in ancient Rome) tribes bound by treaty to support the Roman Empire

FOEFIE adj as in foefie slide rope along which a person may traverse on a pulley

FOEHN same as > FOHN

FOEHNS > FOEHN

FOEMAN n enemy in war

FOEMEN > FOEMAN

FOEN same as > FOE

FOES > FOE

FOETAL same as > FETAL

FOETATION same as
> FETATION

FOETICIDE same as
> FETICIDE

FOETID same as
> FETID

FOETIDER > FOETID

FOETIDEST > FOETID

FOETIDLY > FOETID

FOETOR same as > FETOR

FOETORS > FOETOR

FOETUS same as > FETUS

FOETUSES > FOETUS

FOG n mass of condensed water vapour in the lower air ▷ vb cover with steam

FOGASH n type of Hungarian pikeperch

FOGASHES > FOGASH

FOGBOUND adj prevented from operating by fog

FOGBOW n faint arc of light sometimes seen in a fog bank

FOGBOWS > FOGBOW

FOGDOG n spot sometimes seen in fog near the horizon

FOGDOGS > FOGDOG

FOGEY n old-fashioned person

FOGEYDOM > FOGEY

FOGEYDOMS > FOGEY

FOGEYISH > FOGEY

FOGEYISM > FOGEY

FOGEYISMS > FOGEY

FOGEYS > FOGEY

FOGFRUIT n wildflower of the verbena family

FOGFRUITS > FOGFRUIT

FOGGAGE n grass grown for winter grazing

FOGGAGES > FOGGAGE

FOGGED > FOG

FOGGER n device that generates a fog

FOGGERS > FOGGER

FOGGIER > FOG

FOGGIEST > FOG

FOGGILY > FOG

FOGGINESS > FOG

FOGGING n act of fogging

FOGGINGS > FOGGING

FOGGY > FOG

FOGHORN n large horn sounded to warn ships in fog

FOGHORNS > FOGHORN

FOGIE variant of > FOGEY

FOGIES > FOGIE

FOGLE n silk handkerchief

FOGLES > FOGLE

FOGLESS > FOG

FOGLIGHT n motor-vehicle light used in fog

FOGLIGHTS
> FOGLIGHT

FOGMAN n person in charge of railway fog-signals

FOGMEN > FOGMAN

FOGOU n subterranean building found in Cornwall

FOGOUS > FOGOU

FOGRAM n fogey

FOGRAMITE > FOGRAM

FOGRAMITY > FOGRAM

FOGRAMS > FOGRAM

FOGS > FOG

FOGY same as > FOGEY

FOGYDOM > FOGY

FOGYDOMS > FOGY

FOGYISH > FOGY

FOGYISM > FOGY

FOGYISMS > FOGY

FOH interj expression of disgust

FOHN n type of warm dry wind

FOHNS > FOHN

FOIBLE n minor weakness or slight peculiarity

FOIBLES > FOIBLE

FOID n rock-forming mineral similar to feldspar

FOIDS > FOID

FOIL vb ruin (someone's plan) ▷ n metal in a thin sheet, esp for wrapping food

FOILABLE > FOIL

FOILBORNE adj moving by means of hydrofoils

FOILED > FOIL

FOILING > FOIL

FOILINGS > FOIL

FOILIST n person who fences with a foil

FOILISTS > FOILIST

FOILS > FOIL

FOILSMAN n person who uses or specializes in using a foil

FOILSMEN > FOILSMAN

FOIN n thrust or lunge with a weapon ▷ vb thrust with a weapon

FOINED > FOIN

FOINING > FOIN

FOININGLY > FOIN

FOINS > FOIN

FOISON n plentiful supply or yield

FOISONS > FOISON

FOIST vb force or impose on

FOISTED > FOIST

FOISTER > FOIST

FOISTERS > FOIST

FOISTING > FOIST

FOISTS > FOIST

FOLACIN n folic acid

FOLACINS > FOLACIN

FOLATE n folic acid

FOLATES > FOLATE

FOLD vb bend so that one part covers another ▷ n folded piece or part

FOLDABLE > FOLD

FOLDAWAY adj (of a bed) able to be folded and put away when not in use

FOLDAWAYS > FOLDAWAY

FOLDBACK n (in multitrack recording) a process for returning a signal to a performer instantly

FOLDBACKS > FOLDBACK

FOLDBOAT another name for > FALTBOAT

FOLDBOATS > FOLDBOAT

FOLDED > FOLD

FOLDER n piece of folded cardboard for holding loose papers

FOLDEROL same as > FALDERAL

FOLDEROLS > FOLDEROL

FOLDERS > FOLDER

FOLDING > FOLD

FOLDINGS > FOLDING

FOLDOUT another name for > GATEFOLD

FOLDOUTS > FOLDOUT

FOLDS > FOLD

FOLDUP n something that folds up

FOLDUPS > FOLDUP

FOLEY n footsteps editor

FOLEYS > FOLEY

FOLIA > FOLIUM

FOLIAGE n leaves

FOLIAGED adj having foliage

FOLIAGES > FOLIAGE

FOLIAR adj of or relating to a leaf or leaves

FOLIATE adj relating to, possessing, or resembling leaves ▷ vb ornament with foliage or with leaf forms such as foils

FOLIATED adj ornamented with or made up of foliage or foils

FOLIATES > FOLIATE

FOLIATING > FOLIATE

FOLIATION n process of producing leaves

FOLIATURE > FOLIATION

FOLIC adj as in folic acid any of a group of vitamins of the B complex

FOLIE n madness

FOLIES > FOLIE

FOLIO n sheet of paper folded in half to make two leaves of a book ▷ adj of or made in the largest book size ▷ vb number the leaves of (a book) consecutively

FOLIOED > FOLIO

FOLIOING > FOLIO

FOLIOLATE adj possessing or relating to leaflets

FOLIOLE n part of a compound leaf

FOLIOLES > FOLIOLE

FOLIOLOSE > FOLIOLE

FOLIOS > FOLIO

FOLIOSE adj leaf-bearing

FOLIOUS adj leaf-bearing

FOLIUM n plane geometrical curve

FOLIUMS > FOLIUM

FOLK n people in general ▷ adj traditional to the common people of a country

FOLKIE n devotee of folk music ▷ adj of or relating to folk music

FOLKIER > FOLKIE

FOLKIES > FOLKIE

FOLKIEST > FOLKIE

FOLKINESS n quality of being folky

FOLKISH > FOLK

FOLKLAND n former type of land tenure

FOLKLANDS > FOLKLAND

FOLKLIFE n traditional customs, arts, crafts, and other forms of cultural expression of a people

FOLKLIFES > FOLKLIFE

FOLKLIKE > FOLK

FOLKLIVES > FOLKLIFE

FOLKLORE n traditional beliefs and stories of a people

FOLKLORES > FOLKLORE

FOLKLORIC > FOLKLORE

FOLKMOOT n (in early medieval England) an assembly of the people of a district, town, or shire

FOLKMOOTS > FOLKMOOT

FOLKMOT same as > FOLKMOOT

FOLKMOTE same as > FOLKMOOT

FOLKMOTES > FOLKMOTE

FOLKMOTS > FOLKMOT

FOLKS > FOLK

FOLKSIER > FOLKSY

FOLKSIEST > FOLKSY

FOLKSILY > FOLKSY

FOLKSONG n traditional song

FOLKSONGS > FOLKSONG

FOLKSY adj simple and unpretentious

FOLKTALE n tale or legend from an oral tradition

FOLKTALES > FOLKTALE

FOLKWAY singular form of > FOLKWAYS

FOLKWAYS pl n traditional and customary ways of living

FOLKY same as > FOLKIE

FOLLES > FOLLIS

FOLLICLE n small cavity in the body, esp one from which a hair grows

FOLLICLES > FOLLICLE

FOLLIED > FOLLY

FOLLIES > FOLLY

FOLLIS n Roman coin

FOLLOW vb go or come after

FOLLOWED > FOLLOW

FOLLOWER n disciple or supporter

FOLLOWERS > FOLLOWER

FOLLOWING adj about to be mentioned ▷ n group of supporters ▷ prep as a result of

FOLLOWS > FOLLOW

FOLLOWUP n further action

FOLLOWUPS > FOLLOWUP

FOLLY n foolishness ▷ vb behave foolishly

FOLLYING > FOLLY

FOMENT vb encourage or stir up (trouble)

FOMENTED > FOMENT

FOMENTER > FOMENT

FOMENTERS > FOMENT

FOMENTING > FOMENT

FOMENTS > FOMENT

FOMES n any material that may harbour pathogens

FOMITE same as > FOMES

FOMITES > FOMES

FON vb compel

FOND adj tender, loving ▷ n background of a design, as in lace ▷ vb dote

FONDA n Spanish hotel

FONDANT n (sweet made from) flavoured paste of sugar and water ▷ adj (of a colour) soft

FONDANTS > FONDANT

FONDAS > FONDA

FONDED > FOND

FONDER > FOND

FONDEST > FOND

FONDING > FOND

FONDLE vb caress

FONDLED > FONDLE

FONDLER > FONDLE

FONDLERS > FONDLE

FONDLES > FONDLE

FONDLING > FONDLE

FONDLINGS > FONDLE

FONDLY > FOND

FONDNESS > FOND

FONDS > FOND

FONDU n ballet movement

FONDUE n Swiss dish ▷ vb cook and serve (food) as a fondue

FONDUED > FONDUE

FONDUEING > FONDUE

FONDUES > FONDUE

FONDUING > FONDUE

FONDUS > FONDU

FONE n informal spelling of telephone

FONES > FONE

FONLY adv foolishly

FONNED > FON

FONNING > FON

FONS > FON

FONT n bowl in a church for baptismal water

FONTAL > FONT

FONTANEL n soft membraneous gap in an infant's skull

FONTANELS > FONTANEL

FONTANGE n type of tall headdress

FONTANGES > FONTANGE

FONTICULI pl n fontanelles

FONTINA n mild Italian cheese

FONTINAS > FONTINA

FONTLET n > FONT

FONTLETS > FONT

FONTS > FONT

FOO n temporary computer variable or file

FOOBAR same as > FUBAR

FOOD n what one eats; solid nourishment

FOODBANK n charity which distributes food to the needy

FOODBANKS > FOODBANK

FOODBORNE *adj* (of illness) caused by contaminated food
FOODERIES > FOODERY
FOODERY *n* restaurant
FOODFUL *adj* supplying abundant food
FOODIE *n* gourmet
FOODIES > FOODIE
FOODISM *n* enthusiasm for and interest in good food
FOODISMS > FOODISM
FOODLAND *n* land on which food is produced
FOODLANDS > FOODLAND
FOODLESS > FOOD
FOODOIR *n* book or blog that combines a personal memoir with recipes
FOODOIRS > FOODOIR
FOODS > FOOD
FOODSHED *n* the area through which food is transported from farm to consumer
FOODSHEDS > FOODSHED
FOODSTUFF *n* substance used as food
FOODWAYS *pl n* customs and traditions relating to food and its preparation
FOODY *same as* > FOODIE
FOOFARAW *n* vulgar ornamentation
FOOFARAWS > FOOFARAW
FOOL *n* person lacking sense or judgment ▷ *vb* deceive (someone)
FOOLED > FOOL
FOOLERIES > FOOLERY
FOOLERY *n* foolish behaviour
FOOLFISH *n* orange filefish or winter flounder
FOOLHARDY *adj* recklessly adventurous
FOOLING > FOOL
FOOLINGS > FOOL
FOOLISH *adj* unwise, silly, or absurd
FOOLISHER > FOOLISH
FOOLISHLY > FOOLISH
FOOLPROOF *adj* unable to fail
FOOLS > FOOL
FOOLSCAP *n* size of paper, 34.3 × 43.2 centimetres
FOOLSCAPS > FOOLSCAP
FOOS > FOO
FOOSBALL *n* US and Canadian name for table football
FOOSBALLS > FOOSBALL
FOOT *n* part of the leg below the ankle ▷ *vb* kick
FOOTAGE *n* amount of film used
FOOTAGES > FOOTAGE
FOOTBAG *n* sport of keeping a beanbag off the ground by kicking it

FOOTBAGS > FOOTBAG
FOOTBALL *n* game played by two teams kicking a ball in an attempt to score goals
FOOTBALLS > FOOTBALL
FOOTBAR *n* any bar used by the foot
FOOTBARS > FOOTBAR
FOOTBATH *n* vessel for bathing the feet
FOOTBATHS > FOOTBATH
FOOTBED *n* insole in a boot or shoe
FOOTBEDS > FOOTBED
FOOTBOARD *n* treadle or foot-operated lever on a machine
FOOTBOY *n* boy servant
FOOTBOYS > FOOTBOY
FOOTBRAKE *n* brake operated with the foot
FOOTCLOTH *obsolete word for* > CAPARISON
FOOTED > FOOT
FOOTER *n* person who goes on foot ▷ *vb* potter
FOOTERED > FOOTER
FOOTERING > FOOTER
FOOTERS > FOOTER
FOOTFALL *n* sound of a footstep
FOOTFALLS > FOOTFALL
FOOTFAULT *n* fault that occurs when the server fails to keep both feet behind the baseline until he/she has served
FOOTGEAR *another name for* > FOOTWEAR
FOOTGEARS > FOOTGEAR
FOOTHILL *n* lower slope of a mountain or a relatively low hill at the foot of a mountain
FOOTHILLS > FOOTHILL
FOOTHOLD *n* secure position from which progress may be made
FOOTHOLDS > FOOTHOLD
FOOTIE *same as* > FOOTY
FOOTIER > FOOTY
FOOTIES > FOOTIE
FOOTIEST > FOOTY
FOOTING *n* basis or foundation
FOOTINGS > FOOTING
FOOTLE *vb* loiter aimlessly ▷ *n* foolishness
FOOTLED > FOOTLE
FOOTLER > FOOTLE
FOOTLERS > FOOTLE
FOOTLESS > FOOTLE
FOOTLIGHT *n* light illuminating the front of a stage
FOOTLIKE > FOOT
FOOTLING *adj* trivial ▷ *n* trifle
FOOTLINGS > FOOTLING

FOOTLONG *n* type of extra-long frankfurter
FOOTLONGS > FOOTLONG
FOOTLOOSE *adj* free from ties
FOOTMAN *n* male servant in uniform
FOOTMARK *n* mark or trace of mud, wetness, etc, left by a person's foot on a surface
FOOTMARKS > FOOTMARK
FOOTMEN > FOOTMAN
FOOTMUFF *n* muff used to keep the feet warm
FOOTMUFFS > FOOTMUFF
FOOTNOTE *n* note printed at the foot of a page ▷ *vb* supply (a page, book, etc) with footnotes
FOOTNOTED > FOOTNOTE
FOOTNOTES > FOOTNOTE
FOOTPACE *n* normal or walking pace
FOOTPACES > FOOTPACE
FOOTPAD *n* highwayman, on foot rather than horseback
FOOTPADS > FOOTPAD
FOOTPAGE *n* errand-boy
FOOTPAGES > FOOTPAGE
FOOTPATH *n* narrow path for walkers only
FOOTPATHS > FOOTPATH
FOOTPLATE *n* platform in the cab of a locomotive for the driver
FOOTPOST *n* post delivered on foot
FOOTPOSTS > FOOTPOST
FOOTPRINT *n* mark left by a foot
FOOTPUMP *n* pump operated with the foot
FOOTPUMPS > FOOTPUMP
FOOTRA *variant of* > FOUTRA
FOOTRACE *n* race run on foot
FOOTRACES > FOOTRACE
FOOTRAS > FOOTRA
FOOTREST *n* something that provides a support for the feet, such as a low stool, rail, etc
FOOTRESTS > FOOTREST
FOOTROPE *n* part of a boltrope to which the foot of a sail is stitched
FOOTROPES > FOOTROPE
FOOTRULE *n* rigid measure, one foot in length
FOOTRULES > FOOTRULE
FOOTS *pl n* sediment that accumulates at the bottom of a vessel

FOOTSAL *n* type of indoor football with five players on each side
FOOTSALS > FOOTSAL
FOOTSIE *n* flirtation involving the touching together of feet
FOOTSIES > FOOTSIE
FOOTSLOG *vb* march
FOOTSLOGS > FOOTSLOG
FOOTSORE *adj* having sore or tired feet, esp from much walking
FOOTSTALK *n* small supporting stalk in animals and plants
FOOTSTALL *n* pedestal, plinth, or base of a column, pier, or statue
FOOTSTEP *n* step in walking
FOOTSTEPS > FOOTSTEP
FOOTSTOCK *another name for* > TAILSTOCK
FOOTSTONE *n* memorial stone at the foot of a grave
FOOTSTOOL *n* low stool used to rest the feet on while sitting
FOOTSY *variant of* > FOOTSIE
FOOTWALL *n* rocks on the lower side of an inclined fault plane or mineral vein
FOOTWALLS > FOOTWALL
FOOTWAY *n* way or path for pedestrians
FOOTWAYS > FOOTWAY
FOOTWEAR *n* anything worn to cover the feet
FOOTWEARS > FOOTWEAR
FOOTWEARY *adj* tired from walking
FOOTWELL *n* part of a car in which the foot pedals are located
FOOTWELLS > FOOTWELL
FOOTWORK *n* skilful use of the feet, as in sport or dancing
FOOTWORKS > FOOTWORK
FOOTWORN *adj* footsore
FOOTY *n* football ▷ *adj* mean
FOOZLE *vb* bungle (a shot) ▷ *n* bungled shot
FOOZLED > FOOZLE
FOOZLER > FOOZLE
FOOZLERS > FOOZLE
FOOZLES > FOOZLE
FOOZLING > FOOZLE
FOOZLINGS > FOOZLE
FOP *n* man excessively concerned with fashion ▷ *vb* act like a fop
FOPLING *n* vain affected dandy
FOPLINGS > FOPLING
FOPPED > FOP
FOPPERIES > FOPPERY
FOPPERY *n* clothes, affectations, etc of or befitting a fop

FOPPING > FOP
FOPPISH > FOP
FOPPISHLY > FOP
FOPS > FOP
FOR prep indicating benefit, receipt, timespan, distance, etc
FORA > FORUM
FORAGE vb search about (for) ▷ n food for cattle or horses
FORAGED > FORAGE
FORAGER > FORAGE
FORAGERS > FORAGE
FORAGES > FORAGE
FORAGING > FORAGE
FORAM n marine protozoan
FORAMEN n natural hole
FORAMENS > FORAMEN
FORAMINA > FORAMEN
FORAMINAL > FORAMEN
FORAMS > FORAM
FORANE adj as in vicar forane type of Roman Catholic priest
FORASMUCH conj since
FORAY n brief raid or attack ▷ vb raid or ravage (a town, district, etc)
FORAYED > FORAY
FORAYER > FORAY
FORAYERS > FORAY
FORAYING > FORAY
FORAYS > FORAY
FORB n any herbaceous plant that is not a grass
FORBAD > FORBID
FORBADE > FORBID
FORBARE > FORBEAR
FORBEAR vb cease or refrain (from doing something)
FORBEARER > FORBEAR
FORBEARS > FORBEAR
FORBID vb prohibit, refuse to allow
FORBIDAL > FORBID
FORBIDALS > FORBIDAL
FORBIDDAL n prohibition
FORBIDDEN adj not permitted by order or law
FORBIDDER > FORBID
FORBIDS > FORBID
FORBODE vb obsolete word meaning forbid ▷ n obsolete word meaning forbidding
FORBODED > FORBODE
FORBODES > FORBODE
FORBODING > FORBODE
FORBORE past tense of > FORBEAR
FORBORNE > FORBEAR
FORBS > FORB
FORBY adv besides
FORBYE same as > FORBY
FORCAT n convict or galley slave
FORCATS > FORCAT
FORCE n strength or power ▷ vb compel, make (someone) do something
FORCEABLE > FORCE
FORCEABLY adv in a forcible manner

FORCED adj compulsory
FORCEDLY > FORCED
FORCEFUL adj emphatic and confident
FORCELESS > FORCE
FORCEMEAT n mixture of chopped ingredients used for stuffing
FORCEOUT n play in baseball in which a runner is forced to run to next base and is put out
FORCEOUTS > FORCEOUT
FORCEPS pl n surgical pincers
FORCEPSES > FORCEPS
FORCER > FORCE
FORCERS > FORCE
FORCES > FORCE
FORCIBLE adj involving physical force or violence
FORCIBLY > FORCIBLE
FORCING > FORCE
FORCINGLY > FORCE
FORCIPATE > FORCEPS
FORCIPES > FORCEPS
FORD n shallow place where a river may be crossed ▷ vb cross (a river) at a ford
FORDABLE > FORD
FORDED > FORD
FORDID > FORDO
FORDING > FORD
FORDLESS > FORD
FORDO vb destroy
FORDOES > FORDO
FORDOING > FORDO
FORDONE > FORDO
FORDONNE vb as in from fordonne fordone
FORDS > FORD
FORE adj in, at, or towards the front ▷ n front part ▷ interj golfer's shouted warning
FOREANENT prep opposite
FOREARM n arm from the wrist to the elbow ▷ vb prepare beforehand
FOREARMED > FOREARM
FOREARMS > FOREARM
FOREBAY n reservoir or canal
FOREBAYS > FOREBAY
FOREBEAR n ancestor
FOREBEARS > FOREBEAR
FOREBITT n post at a ship's foremast for securing cables
FOREBITTS > FOREBITT
FOREBODE vb warn of or indicate (an event, result, etc) in advance
FOREBODED > FOREBODE
FOREBODER > FOREBODE
FOREBODES > FOREBODE
FOREBODY n part of a ship forward of the foremast
FOREBOOM n boom of a foremast

FOREBOOMS > FOREBOOM
FOREBRAIN n the part of the brain that develops from the anterior portion of the neural tube
FOREBY variant of > FORBY
FOREBYE variant of > FORBY
FORECABIN n forward cabin on a vessel
FORECADDY n caddy who goes ahead of the golfer to point out the ball's location
FORECAR n vehicle attached to a motorcycle
FORECARS > FORECAR
FORECAST vb predict (weather, events, etc) ▷ n prediction
FORECASTS > FORECAST
FORECHECK vb in ice-hockey, to try to gain control of the puck while at opponents' end of rink
FORECLOSE vb take possession of (property bought with borrowed money which has not been repaid)
FORECLOTH n cloth hung over the front of something, especially an altar
FORECOURT n courtyard or open space in front of a building
FOREDATE vb antedate
FOREDATED > FOREDATE
FOREDATES > FOREDATE
FOREDECK n deck between the bridge and the forecastle
FOREDECKS > FOREDECK
FOREDID > FOREDO
FOREDO same as > FORDO
FOREDOES > FOREDO
FOREDOING > FOREDO
FOREDONE > FOREDO
FOREDOOM vb doom or condemn beforehand
FOREDOOMS > FOREDOOM
FOREFACE n muzzle of an animal
FOREFACES > FOREFACE
FOREFEEL vb have a premonition of
FOREFEELS > FOREFEEL
FOREFEET > FOREFOOT
FOREFELT > FOREFEEL
FOREFEND same as > FORFEND
FOREFENDS > FOREFEND
FOREFOOT n either of the front feet of an animal
FOREFRONT n most active or prominent position

FOREGLEAM n early or premonitory inkling or indication
FOREGO same as > FORGO
FOREGOER > FOREGO
FOREGOERS > FOREGO
FOREGOES > FOREGO
FOREGOING adj going before, preceding
FOREGONE adj gone or completed
FOREGUT n anterior part of the digestive tract of vertebrates
FOREGUTS > FOREGUT
FOREHAND n stroke played with the palm of the hand facing forward ▷ adj (of a stroke) made with the wrist facing the direction of play ▷ adv with a forehand stroke ▷ vb play (a shot) forehand
FOREHANDS > FOREHAND
FOREHEAD n part of the face above the eyebrows
FOREHEADS > FOREHEAD
FOREHENT vb seize in advance
FOREHENTS > FOREHENT
FOREHOCK n foreleg cut of bacon or pork
FOREHOCKS > FOREHOCK
FOREHOOF n front hoof
FOREHOOFS > FOREHOOF
FOREIGN adj not of, or in, one's own country
FOREIGNER n person from a foreign country
FOREIGNLY > FOREIGN
FOREJUDGE same as > FORJUDGE
FOREKING n previous king
FOREKINGS > FOREKING
FOREKNEW > FOREKNOW
FOREKNOW vb know in advance
FOREKNOWN > FOREKNOW
FOREKNOWS > FOREKNOW
FOREL vb cover (a book) with parchment
FORELADY n forewoman of a jury
FORELAID > FORELAY
FORELAIN > FORELIE
FORELAND n headland, cape, or coastal promontory
FORELANDS > FORELAND
FORELAY archaic word for > AMBUSH
FORELAYS > FORELAY
FORELEG n either of the front legs of an animal
FORELEGS > FORELEG
FORELEND vb give up
FORELENDS > FORELEND

FORELENT > FORELEND
FORELIE vb lie in front of
FORELIES > FORELIE
FORELIFT vb lift up in front
FORELIFTS
> FORELIFT
FORELIMB n front or anterior limb
FORELIMBS
> FORELIMB
FORELLED > FOREL
FORELLING > FOREL
FORELOCK n lock of hair over the forehead ▷ vb secure (a bolt) by means of a forelock
FORELOCKS
> FORELOCK
FORELS > FOREL
FORELYING > FORELIE
FOREMAN n person in charge of a group of workers
FOREMAST n mast nearest the bow of a ship
FOREMASTS
> FOREMAST
FOREMEAN vb intend in advance
FOREMEANS
> FOREMEAN
FOREMEANT
> FOREMEAN
FOREMEN > FOREMAN
FOREMILK n first milk drawn from a cow's udder prior to milking
FOREMILKS
> FOREMILK
FOREMOST adv first in time, place, or importance ▷ adj first in time, place, or importance
FORENAME n first name
FORENAMED adj named or mentioned previously
FORENAMES > FORENAME
FORENIGHT n evening
FORENOON n morning
FORENOONS
> FORENOON
FORENSIC adj used in or connected with courts of law
FORENSICS n art or study of formal debating
FOREPART n first or front part in place, order, or time
FOREPARTS > FOREPART
FOREPAST adj bygone
FOREPAW n either of the front feet of a land mammal
FOREPAWS > FOREPAW
FOREPEAK n interior part of a vessel that is furthest forward
FOREPEAKS
> FOREPEAK
FOREPLAN vb plan in advance
FOREPLANS
> FOREPLAN
FOREPLAY n sexual stimulation before intercourse

FOREPLAYS
> FOREPLAY
FOREPOINT vb predetermine or indicate in advance
FORERAN > FORERUN
FORERANK n first rank
FORERANKS
> FORERANK
FOREREACH vb keep moving under momentum without engine or sails
FOREREAD vb foretell
FOREREADS
> FOREREAD
FORERUN vb serve as a herald for
FORERUNS > FORERUN
FORES > FORE
FORESAID less common word for > AFORESAID
FORESAIL n main sail on the foremast of a ship
FORESAILS
> FORESAIL
FORESAW > FORESEE
FORESAY vb foretell
FORESAYS > FORESAY
FORESEE vb see or know beforehand
FORESEEN > FORESEE
FORESEER > FORESEE
FORESEERS > FORESEE
FORESEES > FORESEE
FORESHANK n top of the front leg of an animal
FORESHEET n sheet of a foresail
FORESHEW variant of
> FORESHOW
FORESHEWN
> FORESHEW
FORESHEWS
> FORESHEW
FORESHIP n fore part of a ship
FORESHIPS
> FORESHIP
FORESHOCK n relatively small earthquake heralding the arrival of a much larger one. Some large earthquakes are preceded by a series of foreshocks
FORESHORE n part of the shore between high- and low-tide marks
FORESHOW vb indicate in advance
FORESHOWN
> FORESHOW
FORESHOWS
> FORESHOW
FORESIDE n front or upper side or part
FORESIDES
> FORESIDE
FORESIGHT n ability to anticipate and provide for future needs
FORESKIN n fold of skin covering the tip of the penis
FORESKINS
> FORESKIN
FORESKIRT n front skirt of a garment (as opposed to the train)

FORESLACK variant of
> FORSLACK
FORESLOW variant of
> FORSLOW
FORESLOWS
> FORESLOW
FORESPAKE
> FORESPEAK
FORESPEAK vb predict
FORESPEND variant of
> FORSPEND
FORESPENT
> FORESPEND
FORESPOKE
> FORESPEAK
FOREST n large area with a thick growth of trees ▷ vb create a forest (in)
FORESTAGE n part of a stage in front of the curtain
FORESTAIR n external stair
FORESTAL > FOREST
FORESTALL vb prevent or guard against in advance
FORESTAY n adjustable stay used on ships
FORESTAYS
> FORESTAY
FORESTEAL > FOREST
FORESTED > FOREST
FORESTER n person skilled in forestry
FORESTERS
> FORESTER
FORESTIAL > FOREST
FORESTINE > FOREST
FORESTING > FOREST
FORESTRY n science of planting and caring for trees
FORESTS > FOREST
FORESWEAR vb forgo
FORESWORE
> FORESWEAR
FORESWORN
> FORESWEAR
FORETASTE n early limited experience of something to come ▷ vb have a foretaste of
FORETEACH vb teach beforehand
FORETEETH
> FORETOOTH
FORETELL vb tell or indicate beforehand
FORETELLS
> FORETELL
FORETHINK vb have prescience
FORETIME n time already gone
FORETIMES
> FORETIME
FORETOKEN n sign of a future event ▷ vb foreshadow
FORETOLD > FORETELL
FORETOOTH another word for an > INCISOR
FORETOP n platform at the top of the foremast
FORETOPS > FORETOP
FOREVER adv without end ▷ n very long time

FOREVERS > FOREVER
FOREWARD n vanguard ▷ vb guard (something) in front
FOREWARDS
> FOREWARD
FOREWARN vb warn beforehand
FOREWARNS
> FOREWARN
FOREWEIGH vb assess in advance
FOREWENT past tense of
> FOREGO
FOREWIND n favourable wind
FOREWINDS
> FOREWIND
FOREWING n either wing of the anterior pair of an insect's two pairs of wings
FOREWINGS
> FOREWING
FOREWOMAN n woman in charge of a group of workers
FOREWOMEN
> FOREWOMAN
FOREWORD n introduction to a book
FOREWORDS
> FOREWORD
FOREWORN same as
> FORWORN
FOREX n foreign exchange
FOREXES > FOREX
FOREYARD n yard for supporting the foresail of a square-rigger
FOREYARDS
> FOREYARD
FORFAIR vb perish
FORFAIRED > FORFAIR
FORFAIRN adj worn out
FORFAIRS > FORFAIR
FORFAITER n someone who purchases receivables from exporters
FORFAULT variant of
> FORFEIT
FORFAULTS
> FORFAULT
FORFEIT n thing lost or given up as a penalty for a fault or mistake ▷ vb lose as a forfeit ▷ adj lost as a forfeit
FORFEITED > FORFEIT
FORFEITER > FORFEIT
FORFEITS > FORFEIT
FORFEND vb protect or secure
FORFENDED > FORFEND
FORFENDS > FORFEND
FORFEX n pair of pincers, esp the paired terminal appendages of an earwig
FORFEXES > FORFEX
FORFICATE adj (esp of the tails of certain birds) deeply forked
FORFOCHEN Scots word for
> EXHAUSTED
FORGAT past tense of
> FORGET
FORGATHER vb gather together
FORGAVE > FORGIVE**

f

FORGE n place where metal is worked, smithy ▷ vb make a fraudulent imitation of (something)

FORGEABLE > FORGE

FORGED > FORGE

FORGEMAN > FORGE

FORGEMEN > FORGE

FORGER > FORGE

FORGERIES > FORGERY

FORGERS > FORGE

FORGERY n illegal copy of something

FORGES > FORGE

FORGET vb fail to remember

FORGETFUL adj tending to forget

FORGETIVE adj imaginative and inventive

FORGETS > FORGET

FORGETTER > FORGET

FORGING n process of producing a metal component by hammering

FORGINGS > FORGING

FORGIVE vb cease to blame or hold resentment against, pardon

FORGIVEN > FORGIVE

FORGIVER > FORGIVE

FORGIVERS > FORGIVE

FORGIVES > FORGIVE

FORGIVING adj willing to forgive

FORGO vb do without or give up

FORGOER > FORGO

FORGOERS > FORGO

FORGOES > FORGO

FORGOING > FORGO

FORGONE > FORGO

FORGOT past tense of > FORGET

FORGOTTEN past participle of > FORGET

FORHAILE vb distress

FORHAILED > FORHAILE

FORHAILES > FORHAILE

FORHENT variant of > FOREHENT

FORHENTS > FORHENT

FORHOO vb forsake

FORHOOED > FORHOO

FORHOOIE variant of > FORHOO

FORHOOIED > FORHOOIE

FORHOOIES > FORHOOIE

FORHOOING > FORHOO

FORHOOS > FORHOO

FORHOW variant of > FORHOO

FORHOWED > FORHOW

FORHOWING > FORHOW

FORHOWS > FORHOW

FORINSEC adj foreign

FORINT n standard monetary unit of Hungary

FORINTS > FORINT

FORJASKIT adj exhausted

FORJESKIT variant of > FORJASKIT

FORJUDGE vb deprive of a right by the judgment of a court

FORJUDGED > FORJUDGE

FORJUDGES > FORJUDGE

FORK n tool for eating food ▷ vb pick up, dig, etc with a fork

FORKBALL n method of pitching in baseball

FORKBALLS > FORKBALL

FORKED adj having a fork or forklike parts

FORKEDLY > FORKED

FORKER > FORK

FORKERS > FORK

FORKFUL > FORK

FORKFULS > FORK

FORKHEAD n forked head of a rod

FORKHEADS > FORKHEAD

FORKIER > FORKY

FORKIEST > FORKY

FORKINESS > FORKY

FORKING > FORK

FORKLESS > FORK

FORKLIFT n vehicle for loading goods on wooden pallets

FORKLIFTS > FORKLIFT

FORKLIKE > FORK

FORKS > FORK

FORKSFUL > FORK

FORKTAIL n bird belonging to the flycatcher family

FORKTAILS > FORKTAIL

FORKY adj forked

FORLANA n Venetian dance

FORLANAS > FORLANA

FORLEND variant of > FORELEND

FORLENDS > FORLEND

FORLENT > FORLEND

FORLESE vb lose, forsake

FORLESES > FORLESE

FORLESING > FORLESE

FORLORE > FORLESE

FORLORN adj lonely and unhappy ▷ n forsaken person

FORLORNER > FORLORN

FORLORNLY > FORLORN

FORLORNS > FORLORN

FORM n shape or appearance ▷ vb give a (particular) shape to or take a (particular) shape

FORMABLE > FORM

FORMABLY > FORM

FORMAL adj of or characterized by conventions of behaviour ▷ n woman's evening gown

FORMALIN n solution of formaldehyde in water

FORMALINE n forty per cent solution of formaldehyde in water, used as a disinfectant

FORMALINS > FORMALIN

FORMALISE same as > FORMALIZE

FORMALISM n concern with outward appearances and structure at the expense of content

FORMALIST > FORMALISM

FORMALITY n requirement of custom or etiquette

FORMALIZE vb make official or formal

FORMALLY > FORMAL

FORMALS > FORMAL

FORMAMIDE n amide derived from formic acid

FORMANT n any of several frequency ranges

FORMANTS > FORMANT

FORMAT n size and shape of a publication ▷ vb arrange in a format

FORMATE n type of salt or ester of formic acid ▷ vb fly aircraft in formation

FORMATED > FORMAT

FORMATES > FORMATE

FORMATING > FORMAT

FORMATION n forming

FORMATIVE adj of or relating to development ▷ n inflectional or derivational affix

FORMATS > FORMAT

FORMATTED > FORMAT

FORMATTER > FORMAT

FORME n type matter assembled and ready for printing

FORMED > FORM

FORMEE n type of heraldic cross

FORMEES > FORMEE

FORMER adj of an earlier time, previous ▷ n person or thing that forms or shapes

FORMERLY adv in the past

FORMERS > FORMER

FORMES > FORME

FORMFUL adj imaginative

FORMIATE variant of > FORMATE

FORMIATES > FORMIATE

FORMIC adj of, relating to, or derived from ants

FORMICA n tradename for any of various laminated plastic sheets

FORMICANT adj low-tension (of pulse)

FORMICARY n ant hill

FORMICAS > FORMICA

FORMICATE vb crawl around like ants

FORMING > FORM

FORMINGS > FORM

FORMLESS adj without a definite shape or form

FORMOL same as > FORMALIN

FORMOLS > FORMOL

FORMS > FORM

FORMULA n written form of a scientific or mathematical rule

FORMULAE > FORMULA

FORMULAIC > FORMULA

FORMULAR adj of or relating to formulas ▷ n model or set form

FORMULARS > FORMULAR

FORMULARY n book of prescribed formulas ▷ adj of, relating to, or of the nature of a formula

FORMULAS > FORMULA

FORMULATE vb plan or describe precisely and clearly

FORMULISE vb express in a formula

FORMULISM n adherence to or belief in formulas

FORMULIST > FORMULISM

FORMULIZE variant of > FORMULISE

FORMWORK n arrangement of wooden boards to shape concrete

FORMWORKS > FORMWORK

FORMYL n the monovalent group CHO-

FORMYLS > FORMYL

FORNENST prep situated against or facing towards

FORNENT variant of > FORNENST

FORNICAL > FORNIX

FORNICATE vb have sexual intercourse without being married ▷ adj arched or hoodlike in form

FORNICES > FORNIX

FORNIX n any archlike structure

FORPET n quarter of a peck (measure)

FORPETS > FORPET

FORPINE vb waste away

FORPINED > FORPINE

FORPINES > FORPINE

FORPINING > FORPINE

FORPIT variant of > FORPET

FORPITS > FORPIT

FORRAD adv Scots word for forward ▷ n forward

FORRADER > FORRAD

FORRADS > FORRAD

FORRARDER adv further forward

FORRAY archaic variant of > FORAY

FORRAYED > FORRAY

FORRAYING > FORRAY

FORRAYS > FORRAY

FORREN adj old word for foreign

FORRIT adv Scots word for forward(s)

FORSAID > FORSAY

FORSAKE vb withdraw support or friendship from

FORSAKEN adj completely deserted or helpless

FORSAKER > FORSAKE
FORSAKERS > FORSAKE
FORSAKES > FORSAKE
FORSAKING > FORSAKE
FORSAY vb renounce
FORSAYING > FORSAY
FORSAYS > FORSAY
FORSLACK vb be neglectful
FORSLACKS > FORSLACK
FORSLOE variant of > FORSLOW
FORSLOED > FORSLOE
FORSLOES > FORSLOE
FORSLOW vb hinder
FORSLOWED > FORSLOW
FORSLOWS > FORSLOW
FORSOOK past tense of > FORSAKE
FORSOOTH adv indeed
FORSPEAK vb bewitch
FORSPEAKS > FORSPEAK
FORSPEND vb exhaust
FORSPENDS > FORSPEND
FORSPENT > FORSPEND
FORSPOKE > FORSPEAK
FORSPOKEN > FORSPEAK
FORSWATT adj sweat-covered
FORSWEAR vb renounce or reject
FORSWEARS > FORSWEAR
FORSWINK vb exhaust through toil
FORSWINKS > FORSWINK
FORSWONCK variant of > FORSWUNK
FORSWORE > FORSWEAR
FORSWORN past participle of > FORSWEAR
FORSWUNK adj overworked
FORSYTHIA n shrub with yellow flowers in spring
FORT n fortified building or place ▷ vb fortify
FORTALICE n small fort or outwork of a fortification
FORTE n thing at which a person excels ▷ adv loudly
FORTED > FORT
FORTES > FORTIS
FORTH adv forwards, out, or away ▷ prep out of
FORTHCAME > FORTHCOME
FORTHCOME vb come forth
FORTHINK vb regret
FORTHINKS > FORTHINK
FORTHWITH adv at once
FORTHY adv old word for therefore
FORTIES > FORTY
FORTIETH adj being the number of forty in order ▷ n one of 40 equal parts
FORTIETHS > FORTIETH
FORTIFIED > FORTIFY

FORTIFIER > FORTIFY
FORTIFIES > FORTIFY
FORTIFY vb make (a place) defensible, as by building walls
FORTILAGE n small fort
FORTING > FORT
FORTIS adj (of a consonant) articulated with considerable muscular tension ▷ n type of consonantal pronunciation
FORTITUDE n courage in adversity or pain
FORTLET > FORT
FORTLETS > FORT
FORTNIGHT n two weeks
FORTRESS n large fort or fortified town ▷ vb protect with or as if with a fortress
FORTS > FORT
FORTUITY n chance or accidental occurrence
FORTUNATE adj having good luck
FORTUNE n luck, esp when favourable ▷ vb befall
FORTUNED > FORTUNE
FORTUNES > FORTUNE
FORTUNING > FORTUNE
FORTUNISE same as > FORTUNIZE
FORTUNIZE vb make happy
FORTY n four times ten
FORTYFOLD adj multiplied forty times
FORTYISH > FORTY
FORUM n meeting or medium for open discussion or debate
FORUMS > FORUM
FORWANDER vb wander far
FORWARD same as > FORWARDS
FORWARDED > FORWARD
FORWARDER n person or thing that forwards
FORWARDLY > FORWARD
FORWARDS adv towards or at a place further ahead in space or time
FORWARN archaic word for > FORBID
FORWARNED > FORWARN
FORWARNS > FORWARN
FORWASTE vb lay waste
FORWASTED > FORWASTE
FORWASTES > FORWASTE
FORWEARY vb exhaust
FORWENT past tense of > FORGO
FORWHY adv for what reason
FORWORN adj weary
FORZA n force
FORZANDI > FORZANDO
FORZANDO another word for > SFORZANDO
FORZANDOS > FORZANDO
FORZATI > FORZATO
FORZATO variant of > FORZANDO

FORZATOS > FORZATO
FORZE > FORZA
FOSCARNET n antiviral medication
FOSS same as > FOSSE
FOSSA n anatomical depression, trench, or hollow area
FOSSAE > FOSSA
FOSSAS > FOSSA
FOSSATE adj having cavities or depressions
FOSSE n ditch or moat, esp one dug as a fortification
FOSSED adj having a ditch or moat
FOSSES > FOSSE
FOSSETTE n small depression or fossa, as in a bone
FOSSETTES > FOSSETTE
FOSSICK vb search, esp for gold or precious stones
FOSSICKED > FOSSICK
FOSSICKER > FOSSICK
FOSSICKS > FOSSICK
FOSSIL n hardened remains of an animal or plant preserved in rock ▷ adj of, like, or being a fossil
FOSSILISE same as > FOSSILIZE
FOSSILIZE vb turn into a fossil
FOSSILS > FOSSIL
FOSSOR n grave digger
FOSSORIAL adj (of the forelimbs and skeleton of burrowing animals) adapted for digging
FOSSORS > FOSSOR
FOSSULA n small fossa
FOSSULAE > FOSSULA
FOSSULATE adj hollowed
FOSTER vb promote the growth or development of ▷ adj of or involved in fostering a child
FOSTERAGE n act of caring for or bringing up a foster child
FOSTERED > FOSTER
FOSTERER > FOSTER
FOSTERERS > FOSTER
FOSTERING > FOSTER
FOSTERS > FOSTER
FOSTRESS n female fosterer
FOTHER vb stop a leak in a ship's hull
FOTHERED > FOTHER
FOTHERING > FOTHER
FOTHERS > FOTHER
FOU adj full ▷ n bushel
FOUAT n succulent pink-flowered plant
FOUATS > FOUAT
FOUD n sheriff in Orkney and Shetland
FOUDRIE n foud's district or office
FOUDRIES > FOUDRIE
FOUDS > FOUD
FOUER > FOU
FOUEST > FOU

FOUET n archaic word for a whip
FOUETS > FOUET
FOUETTE n step in ballet
FOUETTES > FOUETTE
FOUGADE n booby-trapped pit or type of mine
FOUGADES > FOUGADE
FOUGASSE n type of bread made with olive oil
FOUGASSES > FOUGASSE
FOUGHT > FIGHT
FOUGHTEN > FIGHT
FOUGHTIER > FOUGHTY
FOUGHTY adj musty
FOUL adj loathsome or offensive ▷ n violation of the rules ▷ vb make dirty or polluted
FOULARD n soft light fabric
FOULARDS > FOULARD
FOULBROOD n disease of honeybees
FOULDER vb flash like lightning
FOULDERED > FOULDER
FOULDERS > FOULDER
FOULE n type of woollen cloth
FOULED > FOUL
FOULER > FOUL
FOULES > FOULE
FOULEST > FOUL
FOULIE n bad mood
FOULIES > FOULIE
FOULING > FOUL
FOULINGS > FOUL
FOULLY > FOUL
FOULMART n polecat
FOULMARTS > FOULMART
FOULNESS n state or quality of being foul
FOULS > FOUL
FOUMART former name for the > POLECAT
FOUMARTS > FOUMART
FOUND vb set up or establish (an institution, etc)
FOUNDED > FOUND
FOUNDER vb break down or fail ▷ n person who establishes an institution, etc
FOUNDERED > FOUNDER
FOUNDERS > FOUNDER
FOUNDING > FOUND
FOUNDINGS > FOUND
FOUNDLING n abandoned baby
FOUNDRESS n female founder
FOUNDRIES > FOUNDRY
FOUNDRY n place where metal is melted and cast
FOUNDS > FOUND
FOUNT same as > FONT
FOUNTAIN n jet of water
FOUNTAINS > FOUNTAIN
FOUNTFUL adj full of springs
FOUNTS > FOUNT
FOUR n one more than three

FOURBALL n type of golf match for two pairs
FOURBALLS > FOURBALL
FOURCHEE n type of heraldic cross
FOURCHEES > FOURCHEE
FOUREYED adj wearing spectacles
FOURFOLD adj having four times as many or as much ▷ adv by four times as many or as much
FOURGON n long covered wagon
FOURGONS > FOURGON
FOURPENCE n former English silver coin then worth four pennies
FOURPENNY adj blow, esp with the fist
FOURPLAY n supply of television, internet, landline and mobile phone services by one provider
FOURPLAYS > FOURPLAY
FOURPLEX n building that contains four separate dwellings
FOURS > FOUR
FOURSCORE adj eighty
FOURSES n snack eaten at four o'clock
FOURSOME n group of four people
FOURSOMES > FOURSOME
FOURTEEN n four and ten
FOURTEENS > FOURTEEN
FOURTH n number four in a series ▷ adj of or being number four in a series
FOURTHLY adv in the fourth place or position
FOURTHS > FOURTH
FOUS > FOU
FOUSSA n Madagascan civet-like animal
FOUSSAS > FOUSSA
FOUSTIER > FOUSTY
FOUSTIEST > FOUSTY
FOUSTY archaic variant of > FUSTY
FOUTER same as > FOOTER
FOUTERED > FOUTER
FOUTERING > FOUTER
FOUTERS > FOUTER
FOUTH n abundance
FOUTHS > FOUTH
FOUTRA n fig; expression of contempt
FOUTRAS > FOUTRA
FOUTRE same as > FOOTER
FOUTRED > FOUTRE
FOUTRES > FOUTRE
FOUTRING > FOUTRE
FOVEA n any small pit in the surface of a bodily organ or part
FOVEAE > FOVEA
FOVEAL > FOVEA
FOVEAS > FOVEA
FOVEATE > FOVEA

FOVEATED > FOVEA
FOVEIFORM adj shaped like small pit
FOVEOLA n small fovea
FOVEOLAE > FOVEOLA
FOVEOLAR > FOVEOLA
FOVEOLAS > FOVEOLA
FOVEOLATE > FOVEOLA
FOVEOLE same as > FOVEOLA
FOVEOLES > FOVEOLE
FOVEOLET same as > FOVEOLA
FOVEOLETS > FOVEOLET
FOWL n domestic cock or hen ▷ vb hunt or snare wild birds
FOWLED > FOWL
FOWLER > FOWLING
FOWLERS > FOWLING
FOWLING n shooting or trapping of birds for sport or as a livelihood
FOWLINGS > FOWLING
FOWLPOX n viral infection of poultry and other birds
FOWLPOXES > FOWLPOX
FOWLS > FOWL
FOWTH variant of > FOUTH
FOWTHS > FOWTH
FOX n reddish-brown bushy-tailed animal of the dog family ▷ vb perplex or deceive
FOXBERRY n lingonberry
FOXED > FOX
FOXES > FOX
FOXFIRE n glow emitted by certain fungi
FOXFIRES > FOXFIRE
FOXFISH n type of shark
FOXFISHES > FOXFISH
FOXGLOVE n tall plant with purple or white flowers
FOXGLOVES > FOXGLOVE
FOXHOLE n small pit dug for protection
FOXHOLES > FOXHOLE
FOXHOUND n dog bred for hunting foxes
FOXHOUNDS > FOXHOUND
FOXHUNT n hunting of foxes with hounds ▷ vb hunt foxes with hounds
FOXHUNTED > FOXHUNT
FOXHUNTER > FOXHUNT
FOXHUNTS > FOXHUNT
FOXIE n fox terrier
FOXIER > FOXY
FOXIES > FOXIE
FOXIEST > FOXY
FOXILY > FOXY
FOXINESS > FOXY
FOXING n piece of leather used on part of the upper of a shoe
FOXINGS > FOXING
FOXLIKE > FOX
FOXSHARK n thresher shark
FOXSHARKS > FOXSHARK
FOXSHIP n cunning
FOXSHIPS > FOXSHIP

FOXSKIN adj made from the skin of a fox ▷ n skin of a fox
FOXSKINS > FOXSKIN
FOXTAIL n type of grass
FOXTAILS > FOXTAIL
FOXTROT n ballroom dance with slow and quick steps ▷ vb perform this dance
FOXTROTS > FOXTROT
FOXY adj of or like a fox, esp in craftiness
FOY n loyalty
FOYBOAT n small rowing boat
FOYBOATS > FOYBOAT
FOYER n entrance hall in a theatre, cinema, or hotel
FOYERS > FOYER
FOYLE variant of > FOIL
FOYLED > FOYLE
FOYLES > FOYLE
FOYLING > FOYLE
FOYNE variant of > FOIN
FOYNED > FOYNE
FOYNES > FOYNE
FOYNING > FOYNE
FOYS > FOY
FOZIER > FOZY
FOZIEST > FOZY
FOZINESS > FOZY
FOZY adj spongy
FRA n brother: a title given to an Italian monk or friar
FRAB vb nag
FRABBED > FRAB
FRABBING > FRAB
FRABBIT adj peevish
FRABJOUS adj splendid
FRABS > FRAB
FRACAS n noisy quarrel
FRACASES > FRACAS
FRACK adj bold ▷ vb release oil or gas from rock by fracking
FRACKED > FRACK
FRACKER n individual or company which engages in fracking
FRACKERS > FRACKER
FRACKING n method of releasing oil or gas from rock
FRACKINGS > FRACKING
FRACKS > FRACK
FRACT vb break
FRACTAL n mathematically repeating structure ▷ adj relating to or involving fractals
FRACTALS > FRACTAL
FRACTED > FRACT
FRACTI > FRACTUS
FRACTING > FRACT
FRACTION n numerical quantity that is not a whole number ▷ vb divide
FRACTIONS > FRACTION
FRACTIOUS adj easily upset and angered
FRACTS > FRACT
FRACTUR variant of > FRAKTUR
FRACTURAL > FRACTURE

FRACTURE n breaking, esp of a bone ▷ vb break
FRACTURED > FRACTURE
FRACTURER > FRACTURE
FRACTURES > FRACTURE
FRACTURS > FRACTUR
FRACTUS n ragged-shaped cloud formation
FRAE Scot word for > FROM
FRAENA > FRAENUM
FRAENUM n fold of membrane or skin that supports an organ
FRAENUMS > FRAENUM
FRAG vb kill or wound (a fellow soldier or superior officer) deliberately
FRAGGED > FRAG
FRAGGING > FRAG
FRAGGINGS > FRAG
FRAGILE adj easily broken or damaged
FRAGILELY > FRAGILE
FRAGILER > FRAGILE
FRAGILEST > FRAGILE
FRAGILITY > FRAGILE
FRAGMENT n piece broken off ▷ vb break into pieces
FRAGMENTS > FRAGMENT
FRAGOR n sudden sound
FRAGORS > FRAGOR
FRAGRANCE n pleasant smell
FRAGRANCY same as > FRAGRANCE
FRAGRANT adj sweet-smelling
FRAGS > FRAG
FRAICHEUR n freshness
FRAIL adj physically weak ▷ n rush basket for figs or raisins
FRAILER > FRAIL
FRAILEST > FRAIL
FRAILISH > FRAIL
FRAILLY > FRAIL
FRAILNESS > FRAIL
FRAILS > FRAIL
FRAILTEE variant of > FRAILTY
FRAILTEES > FRAILTEE
FRAILTIES > FRAILTY
FRAILTY n physical or moral weakness
FRAIM n stranger
FRAIMS > FRAIM
FRAISE n neck ruff worn during the 16th century ▷ vb provide a rampart with a palisade
FRAISED > FRAISE
FRAISES > FRAISE
FRAISING > FRAISE
FRAKTUR n style of typeface
FRAKTURS > FRAKTUR
FRAMABLE > FRAME
FRAMBESIA n infectious disease
FRAMBOISE n brandy distilled from raspberries in the Alsace-Lorraine region

FRAME *n* structure giving shape or support ▷ *vb* put together, construct
FRAMEABLE > FRAME
FRAMED > FRAME
FRAMELESS > FRAME
FRAMER > FRAME
FRAMERS > FRAME
FRAMES > FRAME
FRAMEWORK *n* supporting structure
FRAMING *n* frame, framework, or system of frames
FRAMINGS > FRAMING
FRAMPAL *same as* > FRAMPOLD
FRAMPLER *n* quarrelsome person
FRAMPLERS > FRAMPLER
FRAMPOLD *adj* peevish
FRANC *n* monetary unit
FRANCHISE *n* right to vote ▷ *vb* grant (a person, firm, etc) a franchise
FRANCISE *same as* > FRANCIZE
FRANCISED > FRANCISE
FRANCISES > FRANCISE
FRANCIUM *n* radioactive metallic element
FRANCIUMS > FRANCIUM
FRANCIZE *vb* make French
FRANCIZED > FRANCIZE
FRANCIZES > FRANCIZE
FRANCO *adj* post-free
FRANCOLIN *n* African or Asian partridge
FRANCS > FRANC
FRANGER *n* condom
FRANGERS > FRANGER
FRANGIBLE *adj* breakable or fragile
FRANGLAIS *n* informal French containing a high proportion of words of English origin
FRANION *n* lover, paramour
FRANIONS > FRANION
FRANK *adj* honest and straightforward in speech or attitude ▷ *n* official mark on a letter permitting delivery ▷ *vb* put such a mark on (a letter)
FRANKABLE > FRANK
FRANKED > FRANK
FRANKER > FRANK
FRANKERS > FRANK
FRANKEST > FRANK
FRANKFORT *same as* > FRANKFURT
FRANKFURT *n* light brown smoked sausage
FRANKING > FRANK
FRANKLIN *n* (in 14th- and 15th-century England) a landholder of free but not noble birth

FRANKLINS > FRANKLIN
FRANKLY *adv* in truth
FRANKNESS > FRANK
FRANKS > FRANK
FRANKUM *n* spruce resin
FRANKUMS > FRANKUM
FRANSERIA *n* American shrub
FRANTIC *adj* distracted with rage, grief, joy, etc
FRANTICLY > FRANTIC
FRANZIER > FRANZY
FRANZIEST > FRANZY
FRANZY *adj* irritable
FRAP *vb* lash down or together
FRAPE *adj* tightly bound ▷ *vb* alter information on a person's social networking profile
FRAPEAGE *n* act of altering information on a person's social networking profile
FRAPEAGES > FRAPEAGE
FRAPED > FRAPE
FRAPES > FRAPE
FRAPING > FRAPE
FRAPPANT *adj* striking, vivid
FRAPPE *adj* (of drinks) chilled ▷ *n* type of drink
FRAPPED > FRAP
FRAPPEE *same as* > FRAPPE
FRAPPES > FRAPPE
FRAPPING > FRAP
FRAPS > FRAP
FRAS > FRA
FRASCATI *n* dry or semisweet white wine from the Lazio region of Italy
FRASCATIS > FRASCATI
FRASS *n* refuse left by insects and insect larvae
FRASSES > FRASS
FRAT *n* member of a fraternity
FRATCH *n* quarrel
FRATCHES > FRATCH
FRATCHETY *adj* quarrelsome
FRATCHIER > FRATCHY
FRATCHING > FRATCH
FRATCHY *adj* quarrelsome
FRATE *n* friar
FRATER *n* mendicant friar or a lay brother in a monastery or priory
FRATERIES > FRATER
FRATERNAL *adj* of a brother, brotherly
FRATERS > FRATER
FRATERY > FRATER
FRATI > FRATE
FRATRIES > FRATER
FRATRY > FRATER
FRATS > FRAT
FRAU *n* married German woman
FRAUD *n* (criminal) deception, swindle
FRAUDFUL > FRAUD

FRAUDS > FRAUD
FRAUDSMAN *n* practitioner of criminal fraud
FRAUDSMEN > FRAUDSMAN
FRAUDSTER *n* person who commits a fraud
FRAUGHAN *n* small shrub
FRAUGHANS > FRAUGHAN
FRAUGHT *adj* tense or anxious ▷ *vb* archaic word for load ▷ *n* archaic word for freight
FRAUGHTED > FRAUGHT
FRAUGHTER > FRAUGHT
FRAUGHTS > FRAUGHT
FRAULEIN *n* unmarried German woman
FRAULEINS > FRAULEIN
FRAUS > FRAU
FRAUTAGE *n* cargo
FRAUTAGES > FRAUTAGE
FRAWZEY *n* celebration
FRAWZEYS > FRAWZEY
FRAY *n* noisy quarrel or conflict ▷ *vb* make or become ragged at the edge
FRAYED > FRAY
FRAYING > FRAY
FRAYINGS > FRAY
FRAYS > FRAY
FRAZIL *n* small pieces of ice that form in turbulently moving water
FRAZILS > FRAZIL
FRAZZLE *n* exhausted state ▷ *vb* tire out
FRAZZLED > FRAZZLE
FRAZZLES > FRAZZLE
FRAZZLING > FRAZZLE
FREAK *n* abnormal person or thing ▷ *adj* abnormal ▷ *vb* streak with colour
FREAKED > FREAK
FREAKERY *n* as in *control freakery* obsessive need to be in control of events
FREAKFUL *variant of* > FREAKISH
FREAKIER > FREAKY
FREAKIEST > FREAKY
FREAKILY > FREAKY
FREAKING > FREAK
FREAKISH *adj* of, related to, or characteristic of a freak
FREAKOUT *n* heightened emotional state
FREAKOUTS > FREAKOUT
FREAKS > FREAK
FREAKY *adj* weird, peculiar
FRECKLE *n* small brown spot on the skin ▷ *vb* mark or become marked with freckles
FRECKLED > FRECKLE
FRECKLES > FRECKLE
FRECKLIER > FRECKLE
FRECKLING > FRECKLE
FRECKLY > FRECKLE
FREDAINE *n* escapade

FREDAINES > FREDAINE
FREE *adj* able to act at will, not compelled or restrained ▷ *vb* release, liberate
FREEBASE *n* cocaine that has been refined by heating it in ether or some other solvent ▷ *vb* refine (cocaine) in this way
FREEBASED > FREEBASE
FREEBASER > FREEBASE
FREEBASES > FREEBASE
FREEBEE *variant of* > FREEBIE
FREEBEES > FREEBEE
FREEBIE *n* something provided without charge ▷ *adj* without charge
FREEBIES > FREEBIE
FREEBOARD *n* space or distance between the deck of a vessel and the water line
FREEBOOT *vb* act as a freebooter
FREEBOOTS > FREEBOOT
FREEBOOTY > FREEBOOT
FREEBORN *adj* not born in slavery
FREECYCLE *vb* recycle an unwanted item by donating it
FREED > FREE
FREEDIVER *n* person who dives without breathing apparatus
FREEDMAN *n* man freed from slavery
FREEDMEN > FREEDMAN
FREEDOM *n* right of unrestricted use or access
FREEDOMS > FREEDOM
FREEFALL *n* as in *freefall parachuting* parachuting in which the jumper manoeuvres in free fall before opening the parachute
FREEFORM *n* irregular flowing shape, often used in industrial or fabric design ▷ *adj* freely flowing, spontaneous
FREEGAN *n* person who avoids buying consumer goods
FREEGANS > FREEGAN
FREEHAND *adj* drawn without guiding instruments
FREEHOLD *n* tenure of land for life without restrictions ▷ *adj* of or held by freehold
FREEHOLDS > FREEHOLD
FREEING > FREE
FREEKEH *n* type of cereal
FREEKEHS > FREEKEH
FREELANCE *n* self-employed person doing specific pieces of

work for various employers ▷ *vb* work as a freelance ▷ *adv* of or as a freelance

FREELOAD *vb* act as a freeloader

FREELOADS
> FREELOAD

FREELY > FREE

FREEMAN *n* person who has been given the freedom of a city

FREEMASON *n* member of a guild of itinerant skilled stonemasons, who had a system of secret signs and passwords with which they recognized each other

FREEMEN > FREEMAN

FREEMIUM *n* free service with paid additional options

FREEMIUMS
> FREEMIUM

FREENESS > FREE

FREEPHONE *n* system of telephone use in which the cost of calls in response to an advertisement is borne by the advertiser

FREEPOST *adj* (of post) able to be posted without charge

FREEPOSTS
> FREEPOST

FREER *n* liberator

FREERIDE *n* extreme form of skiing, snowboarding, or mountain biking

FREERIDES
> FREERIDE

FREERS > FREER

FREES > FREE

FREESHEET *n* newspaper that is distributed free, paid for by its advertisers

FREESIA *n* plant with fragrant tubular flowers

FREESIAS > FREESIA

FREEST > FREE

FREESTONE *n* any fine-grained stone, esp sandstone or limestone, that can be cut and worked in any direction without breaking

FREESTYLE *n* competition, such as in swimming, in which each participant may use a style of his or her choice ▷ *vb* perform (music, a sport, etc) in a freestyle manner

FREET *n* omen or superstition

FREETIER > FREETY

FREETIEST > FREETY

FREETS > FREET

FREETY *adj* superstitious

FREEWARE *n* computer software that may be distributed and used without payment

FREEWARES
> FREEWARE

FREEWAY *n* motorway

FREEWAYS > FREEWAY

FREEWHEEL *vb* travel downhill on a bicycle without pedalling ▷ *n* device in the rear hub of a bicycle wheel that permits it to rotate freely while the pedals are stationary

FREEWILL *n* apparent human ability to make choices that are not externally determined

FREEWOMAN *n* woman who is free or at liberty

FREEWOMEN
> FREEWOMAN

FREEWRITE *vb* write freely without stopping or thinking

FREEWROTE
> FREEWRITE

FREEZABLE > FREEZE

FREEZE *vb* turn from liquid to solid by the reduction of temperature ▷ *n* period of very cold weather

FREEZER *n* insulated cabinet for cold-storage of perishable foods

FREEZERS > FREEZER

FREEZES > FREEZE

FREEZING > FREEZE

FREEZINGS > FREEZE

FREIGHT *n* commercial transport of goods ▷ *vb* send by freight

FREIGHTED > FREIGHT

FREIGHTER *n* ship or aircraft for transporting goods

FREIGHTS > FREIGHT

FREIT *variant of* > FREET

FREITIER > FREITY

FREITIEST > FREITY

FREITS > FREIT

FREITY *adj* superstitious

FREMD *n* strange person or thing

FREMDS > FREMD

FREMIT *same as* > FREMD

FREMITS > FREMIT

FREMITUS *n* vibration felt by a hand placed on the body

FRENA > FRENUM

FRENCH *vb* cut (food) into thin strips

FRENCHED > FRENCH

FRENCHES > FRENCH

FRENCHIFY *vb* make or become French in appearance, behaviour, etc

FRENCHING > FRENCH

FRENEMIES > FRENEMY

FRENEMY *n* supposed friend who behaves in a treacherous manner

FRENETIC *adj* uncontrolled, excited ▷ *n* madman

FRENETICS
> FRENETIC

FRENNE *variant of*
> FREMD

FRENNES > FRENNE

FRENULA > FRENULUM

FRENULAR > FRENULUM

FRENULUM *n* group of bristles on the hind wing of some moths

FRENULUMS
> FRENULUM

FRENUM *same as*
> FRAENUM

FRENUMS > FRENUM

FRENZICAL > FRENZY

FRENZIED *adj* filled with or as if with frenzy

FRENZIES > FRENZY

FRENZILY > FRENZY

FRENZY *n* wild excitement or agitation ▷ *vb* make frantic

FRENZYING > FRENZY

FREON *n* tradename for an aerosol refrigerant

FREONS > FREON

FREQUENCE *same as*
> FREQUENCY

FREQUENCY *n* rate of occurrence

FREQUENT *adj* happening often ▷ *vb* visit habitually

FREQUENTS
> FREQUENT

FRERE *n* friar

FRERES > FRERE

FRESCADE *n* shady place or cool walk

FRESCADES
> FRESCADE

FRESCO *n* watercolour painting done on wet plaster ▷ *vb* paint a fresco

FRESCOED > FRESCO

FRESCOER > FRESCO

FRESCOERS > FRESCO

FRESCOES > FRESCO

FRESCOING > FRESCO

FRESCOIST > FRESCO

FRESCOS > FRESCO

FRESH *adj* newly made, acquired, etc ▷ *adv* recently ▷ *vb* freshen

FRESHED > FRESH

FRESHEN *vb* make or become fresh or fresher

FRESHENED > FRESHEN

FRESHENER > FRESHEN

FRESHENS > FRESHEN

FRESHER *n* first-year student

FRESHERS > FRESHER

FRESHES > FRESH

FRESHEST > FRESH

FRESHET *n* sudden overflowing of a river

FRESHETS > FRESHET

FRESHIE *n* (in Australia) freshwater crocodile

FRESHIES > FRESHIE

FRESHING > FRESH

FRESHISH > FRESH

FRESHLY > FRESH

FRESHMAN *same as*
> FRESHER

FRESHMEN > FRESHMAN

FRESHNESS > FRESH

FRESNEL *n* unit of frequency

FRESNELS > FRESNEL

FRET *vb* be worried ▷ *n* worried state

FRETBOARD *n* fingerboard with frets on a stringed musical instrument

FRETFUL *adj* irritable

FRETFULLY > FRETFUL

FRETLESS > FRET

FRETS > FRET

FRETSAW *n* fine saw with a narrow blade, used for fretwork

FRETSAWS > FRETSAW

FRETSOME *adj* vexing

FRETTED > FRET

FRETTER > FRET

FRETTERS > FRET

FRETTIER > FRETTY

FRETTIEST > FRETTY

FRETTING > FRET

FRETTINGS > FRET

FRETTY *adj* decorated with frets

FRETWORK *n* decorative carving in wood

FRETWORKS
> FRETWORK

FRIABLE *adj* easily crumbled

FRIAND *n* small almond cake

FRIANDE *variant of*
> FRIAND

FRIANDES > FRIANDE

FRIANDS > FRIAND

FRIAR *n* member of a male Roman Catholic religious order

FRIARBIRD *n* Australian honeyeater with a naked head

FRIARIES > FRIARY

FRIARLY > FRIAR

FRIARS > FRIAR

FRIARY *n* house of friars

FRIB *n* piece of wool removed from a fleece during classing

FRIBBLE *vb* fritter away ▷ *n* wasteful or frivolous person or action ▷ *adj* frivolous

FRIBBLED > FRIBBLE

FRIBBLER > FRIBBLE

FRIBBLERS > FRIBBLE

FRIBBLES > FRIBBLE

FRIBBLING > FRIBBLE

FRIBBLISH *adj* trifling

FRIBS > FRIB

FRICADEL *variant of*
> FRIKKADEL

FRICADELS
> FRICADEL

FRICANDO *n* larded and braised veal fillet

FRICASSEE *n* stewed meat served in a thick white sauce ▷ *vb* prepare (meat) as a fricassee

FRICATIVE *n* consonant produced by friction of the breath through a partially open mouth, such as (f) or (z) ▷ *adj* relating to or being a fricative

FRICHT *vb* Scots word for frighten

FRICHTED > FRICHT

FRICHTING > FRICHT

FRICHTS > FRICHT
FRICKING *adj* slang word for absolute
FRICOT *n* Acadian stew of potatoes and meat or fish
FRICOTS > FRICOT
FRICTION *n* resistance met with by a body moving over another
FRICTIONS > FRICTION
FRIDGE *n* apparatus in which food and drinks are kept cool ▷ *vb* archaic word for chafe
FRIDGED > FRIDGE
FRIDGES > FRIDGE
FRIDGING > FRIDGE
FRIED > FRY
FRIEDCAKE *n* type of doughnut
FRIEND *n* person whom one knows well and likes ▷ *vb* befriend
FRIENDED > FRIEND
FRIENDING > FRIEND
FRIENDLY *adj* showing or expressing liking ▷ *n* match played for its own sake and not as part of a competition
FRIENDS > FRIEND
FRIER *same as* **>** FRYER
FRIERS > FRIER
FRIES > FRY
FRIEZE *n* ornamental band on a wall ▷ *vb* give a nap to (cloth)
FRIEZED > FRIEZE
FRIEZES > FRIEZE
FRIEZING > FRIEZE
FRIG *vb* behave foolishly or aimlessly ▷ *n* fridge
FRIGATE *n* medium-sized fast warship
FRIGATES > FRIGATE
FRIGATOON *n* Venetian sailing ship
FRIGES > FRIG
FRIGGED > FRIG
FRIGGER > FRIG
FRIGGERS > FRIG
FRIGGING > FRIG
FRIGGINGS > FRIG
FRIGHT *n* sudden fear or alarm
FRIGHTED > FRIGHT
FRIGHTEN *vb* scare or terrify
FRIGHTENS > FRIGHTEN
FRIGHTFUL *adj* horrifying
FRIGHTING > FRIGHT
FRIGHTS > FRIGHT
FRIGID *adj* formal or stiff in temperament
FRIGIDER > FRIGID
FRIGIDEST > FRIGID
FRIGIDITY > FRIGID
FRIGIDLY > FRIGID
FRIGOT *variant of* **>** FRIGATE
FRIGOTS > FRIGOT
FRIGS > FRIG
FRIJOL *n* variety of bean
FRIJOLE *variant of* **>** FRIJOL

FRIJOLES > FRIJOL
FRIKKADEL *n* South African meatball
FRILL *n* gathered strip of fabric attached at one edge ▷ *vb* adorn or fit with a frill or frills
FRILLED > FRILL
FRILLER > FRILL
FRILLERS > FRILL
FRILLERY *n* fabric or clothing arranged in frills
FRILLIER > FRILLY
FRILLIES *pl n* flimsy women's underwear
FRILLIEST > FRILLY
FRILLING > FRILL
FRILLINGS > FRILL
FRILLS > FRILL
FRILLY *adj* with a frill or frills
FRINGE *n* hair cut short and hanging over the forehead ▷ *vb* decorate with a fringe ▷ *adj* (of theatre) unofficial or unconventional
FRINGED > FRINGE
FRINGES > FRINGE
FRINGIER > FRINGY
FRINGIEST > FRINGY
FRINGING *n* act of fringing
FRINGINGS > FRINGING
FRINGY *adj* having a fringe
FRIPON *n* rogue
FRIPONS > FRIPON
FRIPPER *n* dealer in old clothes
FRIPPERER *same as* **>** FRIPPER
FRIPPERS > FRIPPER
FRIPPERY *n* useless ornamentation
FRIPPET *n* frivolous or flamboyant young woman
FRIPPETS > FRIPPET
FRIS *n* fine frieze-like fabric
FRISBEE *n* tradename of a light plastic disc for throwing in a game
FRISBEES > FRISBEE
FRISE *n* fabric with a long nap used for upholstery and rugs
FRISEE *n* endive
FRISEES > FRISEE
FRISES > FRIS
FRISETTE *n* curly or frizzed fringe, often an artificial hairpiece, worn by women on the forehead
FRISETTES > FRISETTE
FRISEUR *n* hairdresser
FRISEURS > FRISEUR
FRISK *vb* move or leap playfully ▷ *n* playful movement
FRISKA *n* (in Hungarian music) the fast movement of a piece
FRISKAS > FRISKA
FRISKED > FRISK
FRISKER > FRISK

FRISKERS > FRISK
FRISKET *n* part of a hand printing press
FRISKETS > FRISKET
FRISKFUL > FRISK
FRISKIER > FRISKY
FRISKIEST > FRISKY
FRISKILY > FRISKY
FRISKING > FRISK
FRISKINGS > FRISK
FRISKS > FRISK
FRISKY *adj* lively or high-spirited
FRISSON *n* shiver of fear or excitement
FRISSONS > FRISSON
FRIST *archaic word for* **>** POSTPONE
FRISTED > FRIST
FRISTING > FRIST
FRISTS > FRIST
FRISURE *n* styling the hair into curls
FRISURES > FRISURE
FRIT *n* basic materials for making glass, glazes for pottery, etc ▷ *vb* fuse (materials) in making frit
FRITES *pl n* chipped potatoes
FRITFLIES > FRITFLY
FRITFLY *n* type of small black fly
FRITH *same as* **>** FIRTH
FRITHBORH *n* type of pledge
FRITHS > FRITH
FRITS > FRIT
FRITT *same as* **>** FRIT
FRITTATA *n* flat thick Italian omelette
FRITTATAS > FRITTATA
FRITTED > FRIT
FRITTER *n* piece of food fried in batter ▷ *vb* waste or squander
FRITTERED > FRITTER
FRITTERER > FRITTER
FRITTERS > FRITTER
FRITTING > FRIT
FRITTS > FRITT
FRITURE *archaic word for* **>** FRITTER
FRITURES > FRITURE
FRITZ *n* as in *on the fritz* in a state of disrepair ▷ *vb* (of an appliance, etc) become broken or start malfunctioning
FRITZED > FRITZ
FRITZES > FRITZ
FRITZING > FRITZ
FRIULANO *n* type of Italian cheese
FRIULANOS > FRIULANO
FRIVOL *vb* behave frivolously
FRIVOLED > FRIVOL
FRIVOLER > FRIVOL
FRIVOLERS > FRIVOL
FRIVOLING > FRIVOL
FRIVOLITY > FRIVOLOUS
FRIVOLLED > FRIVOL
FRIVOLLER > FRIVOL
FRIVOLOUS *adj* not serious or sensible

FRIVOLS > FRIVOL
FRIZ *variant of* **>** FRIZZ
FRIZADO *n* fine frieze-like fabric
FRIZADOS > FRIZADO
FRIZE *n* coarse woollen fabric ▷ *vb* freeze
FRIZED > FRIZE
FRIZER *n* person who gives nap to cloth
FRIZERS > FRIZER
FRIZES > FRIZE
FRIZETTE *same as* **>** FRISETTE
FRIZETTES > FRIZETTE
FRIZING > FRIZE
FRIZZ *vb* form (hair) into stiff wiry curls ▷ *n* hair that has been frizzed
FRIZZANTE *adj* (of wine) slightly effervescent
FRIZZED > FRIZZ
FRIZZER > FRIZZ
FRIZZERS > FRIZZ
FRIZZES > FRIZZ
FRIZZIER > FRIZZY
FRIZZIES *pl n* condition of having frizzy hair
FRIZZIEST > FRIZZY
FRIZZILY > FRIZZY
FRIZZING > FRIZZ
FRIZZLE *vb* cook or heat until crisp and shrivelled ▷ *n* tight curl
FRIZZLED > FRIZZLE
FRIZZLER > FRIZZLE
FRIZZLERS > FRIZZLE
FRIZZLES > FRIZZLE
FRIZZLIER > FRIZZLE
FRIZZLING > FRIZZLE
FRIZZLY > FRIZZLE
FRIZZY *adj* (of the hair) in tight crisp wiry curls
FRO *adv* away ▷ *n* afro
FROCK *n* dress ▷ *vb* invest (a person) with the office or status of a cleric
FROCKED > FROCK
FROCKING *n* coarse material suitable for making frocks or work clothes
FROCKINGS > FROCKING
FROCKLESS > FROCK
FROCKS > FROCK
FROE *n* cutting tool
FROES > FROE
FROG *n* type of amphibian
FROGBIT *n* floating aquatic Eurasian plant
FROGBITS > FROGBIT
FROGEYE *n* plant disease
FROGEYED *adj* affected by frogeye
FROGEYES > FROGEYE
FROGFISH *n* type of angler fish
FROGGED *adj* decorated with frogging
FROGGERY *n* place where frogs are kept
FROGGIER > FROGGY
FROGGIEST > FROGGY
FROGGING *n* decorative fastening of looped braid on a coat

FROGGINGS
> FROGGING
FROGGY adj like a frog
FROGLET n young frog
FROGLETS > FROGLET
FROGLIKE > FROG
FROGLING n young frog
FROGLINGS
> FROGLING
FROGMAN n swimmer with equipment for working under water
FROGMARCH vb force (a resisting person) to move by holding their arms ▷ n method of carrying a resisting person in which each limb is held
FROGMEN > FROGMAN
FROGMOUTH n type of nocturnal insectivorous bird of SE Asia and Australia
FROGS > FROG
FROGSPAWN n jelly-like substance containing frog's eggs
FROIDEUR n coldness
FROIDEURS
> FROIDEUR
FROING n as in toing and froing going back and forth
FROINGS > FROING
FROISE n kind of pancake
FROISES > FROISE
FROLIC vb run and play in a lively way ▷ n lively and merry behaviour ▷ adj full of merriment or fun
FROLICKED > FROLIC
FROLICKER > FROLIC
FROLICKY adj frolicsome
FROLICS > FROLIC
FROM prep indicating the point of departure, source, etc
FROMAGE n as in fromage frais low-fat soft cheese
FROMAGES > FROMAGE
FROMENTY same as
> FRUMENTY
FROND n long leaf or leaflike part of a fern, palm, or seaweed
FRONDAGE n fronds collectively
FRONDAGES
> FRONDAGE
FRONDED adj having fronds
FRONDENT adj leafy
FRONDEUR n 17th-century French rebel
FRONDEURS
> FRONDEUR
FRONDLESS > FROND
FRONDOSE adj leafy or like a leaf
FRONDOUS adj leafy or like a leaf
FRONDS > FROND
FRONS n plate on the head of some insects
FRONT n fore part ▷ adj of or at the front ▷ vb face (onto)
FRONTAGE n facade of a building

FRONTAGER n owner of a building or land on the front of a street
FRONTAGES
> FRONTAGE
FRONTAL adj of, at, or in the front ▷ n decorative hanging for the front of an altar
FRONTALLY > FRONTAL
FRONTALS > FRONTAL
FRONTED > FRONT
FRONTENIS n racket used in Basque ball game
FRONTER n front side
FRONTERS > FRONTER
FRONTES > FRONS
FRONTEST > FRONT
FRONTIER n area of a country bordering on another
FRONTIERS
> FRONTIER
FRONTING > FRONT
FRONTLESS > FRONT
FRONTLET n small decorative loop worn on a woman's forehead
FRONTLETS
> FRONTLET
FRONTLINE adj of, relating to, or suitable for the front line of a military formation
FRONTLIST n list of books about to be published
FRONTMAN n nominal leader who lacks real power or authority
FRONTMEN > FRONTMAN
FRONTON n wall against which pelota or jai alai is played
FRONTONS > FRONTON
FRONTOON variant of
> FRONTON
FRONTOONS
> FRONTOON
FRONTPAGE adj on or suitable for the front page of a newspaper ▷ vb place something on the front page of a newspaper
FRONTS > FRONT
FRONTWARD adv towards the front
FRONTWAYS adv with the front forward
FRONTWISE variant of
> FRONTWAYS
FRORE adj very cold or frosty
FROREN variant of
> FRORE
FRORN variant of > FRORE
FRORNE variant of
> FRORE
FRORY variant of > FRORE
FROS > FRO
FROSH n freshman
FROSHES > FROSH
FROST n white frozen dew or mist ▷ vb become covered with frost
FROSTBIT
> FROSTBITE

FROSTBITE n destruction of tissue, esp of the fingers or ears, by cold ▷ vb affect with frostbite
FROSTED adj (of glass) having a rough surface to make it opaque ▷ n type of ice cream dish
FROSTEDS > FROSTED
FROSTFISH n American fish appearing in frosty weather
FROSTIER > FROSTY
FROSTIEST > FROSTY
FROSTILY > FROSTY
FROSTING n sugar icing
FROSTINGS
> FROSTING
FROSTLESS > FROST
FROSTLIKE > FROST
FROSTLINE n depth to which ground freezes in winter
FROSTNIP n milder form of frostbite
FROSTNIPS
> FROSTNIP
FROSTS > FROST
FROSTWORK n patterns made by frost on glass, metal, etc
FROSTY adj characterized or covered by frost
FROTH n mass of small bubbles ▷ vb foam
FROTHED > FROTH
FROTHER > FROTH
FROTHERS > FROTH
FROTHERY n anything insubstantial, like froth
FROTHIER > FROTH
FROTHIEST > FROTH
FROTHILY > FROTH
FROTHING n act of frothing
FROTHINGS
> FROTHING
FROTHLESS > FROTH
FROTHS > FROTH
FROTHY > FROTH
FROTTAGE n act or process of taking a rubbing from a rough surface for a work of art
FROTTAGES
> FROTTAGE
FROTTEUR n person who rubs against another person's body for a sexual thrill
FROTTEURS
> FROTTEUR
FROUFROU n swishing sound, as made by a long silk dress
FROUFROUS
> FROUFROU
FROUGHIER > FROUGHY
FROUGHY adj rancid
FROUNCE vb wrinkle
FROUNCED > FROUNCE
FROUNCES > FROUNCE
FROUNCING > FROUNCE
FROUZIER > FROUZY
FROUZIEST > FROUZY
FROUZILY adv in a frouzy manner

FROUZY same as
> FROWZY
FROW same as > FROE
FROWARD adj obstinate
FROWARDLY > FROWARD
FROWARDS same as
> FROWARD
FROWIE variant of
> FROUGHY
FROWIER > FROWIE
FROWIEST > FROWIE
FROWN vb wrinkle one's brows in worry, anger, or thought ▷ n frowning expression
FROWNED > FROWN
FROWNER > FROWN
FROWNERS > FROWN
FROWNIER > FROWNY
FROWNIEST > FROWNY
FROWNING > FROWN
FROWNS > FROWN
FROWNY adj displaying a frown
FROWS > FROW
FROWSIER > FROWSY
FROWSIEST > FROWSY
FROWSILY adv in a frowsy manner
FROWST n hot and stale atmosphere ▷ vb abandon oneself to such an atmosphere
FROWSTED > FROWST
FROWSTER > FROWST
FROWSTERS > FROWST
FROWSTIER > FROWSTY
FROWSTING > FROWST
FROWSTS > FROWST
FROWSTY adj stale or musty
FROWSY same as
> FROWZY
FROWY variant of
> FROUGHY
FROWZIER > FROWZY
FROWZIEST > FROWZY
FROWZILY > FROWZY
FROWZY adj dirty or unkempt
FROZE > FREEZE
FROZEN > FREEZE
FROZENLY > FREEZE
FRUCTAN n type of polymer of fructose
FRUCTANS > FRUCTAN
FRUCTED adj fruit-bearing
FRUCTIFY vb (cause to) bear fruit
FRUCTIVE adj fruitful
FRUCTOSE n crystalline sugar occurring in many fruits
FRUCTOSES
> FRUCTOSE
FRUCTUARY n archaic word for a person who enjoys the fruits of something
FRUCTUATE vb bear fruit
FRUCTUOUS adj productive or fruitful
FRUG vb perform the frug, a 1960s dance
FRUGAL adj thrifty, sparing
FRUGALIST > FRUGAL

FRUGALITY > FRUGAL
FRUGALLY > FRUGAL
FRUGGED > FRUG
FRUGGING > FRUG
FRUGIVORE *adj* fruit-eating
FRUGS > FRUG
FRUICT *obsolete variant of* > FRUIT
FRUICTS > FRUICT
FRUIT *n* part of a plant containing seeds ▷ *vb* bear fruit
FRUITAGE *n* process, state, or season of producing fruit
FRUITAGES > FRUITAGE
FRUITCAKE *n* cake containing dried fruit
FRUITED > FRUIT
FRUITER *n* fruit grower
FRUITERER *n* person who sells fruit
FRUITERS > FRUITER
FRUITERY *n* fruitage
FRUITFUL *adj* useful or productive
FRUITIER > FRUITY
FRUITIEST > FRUITY
FRUITILY > FRUITY
FRUITING > FRUIT
FRUITINGS > FRUIT
FRUITION *n* fulfilment of something worked for or desired
FRUITIONS > FRUITION
FRUITIVE *adj* enjoying
FRUITLESS *adj* useless or unproductive
FRUITLET *n* small fruit
FRUITLETS > FRUITLET
FRUITLIKE > FRUIT
FRUITS > FRUIT
FRUITWOOD *n* wood of a fruit tree
FRUITWORM *n* insect larva that feeds on fruit
FRUITY *adj* of or like fruit
FRUMENTY *n* kind of porridge made from hulled wheat boiled with milk, sweetened, and spiced
FRUMP *n* dowdy person ▷ *vb* mock or taunt
FRUMPED > FRUMP
FRUMPIER > FRUMPY
FRUMPIEST > FRUMPY
FRUMPILY > FRUMPY
FRUMPING > FRUMP
FRUMPISH *same as* > FRUMPY
FRUMPLE *vb* wrinkle or crumple
FRUMPLED > FRUMPLE
FRUMPLES > FRUMPLE
FRUMPLING > FRUMPLE
FRUMPS > FRUMP
FRUMPY *adj* (of a person, clothes, etc) dowdy or unattractive
FRUSEMIDE *n* diuretic used to relieve oedema, for example caused by heart or kidney disease
FRUSH *vb* break into pieces

FRUSHED > FRUSH
FRUSHES > FRUSH
FRUSHING > FRUSH
FRUST *n* fragment
FRUSTA > FRUSTUM
FRUSTRATE *vb* upset or anger ▷ *adj* frustrated or thwarted
FRUSTS > FRUST
FRUSTULE *n* hard siliceous cell wall of a diatom
FRUSTULES > FRUSTULE
FRUSTUM *n* part of a solid between the base and a plane parallel to the base
FRUSTUMS > FRUSTUM
FRUTEX *n* shrub
FRUTICES > FRUTEX
FRUTICOSE *adj* shrubby
FRUTIFIED > FRUTIFY
FRUTIFIES > FRUTIFY
FRUTIFY *vb* malapropism for notify
FRY *vb* cook or be cooked in fat or oil ▷ *n* dish of fried food
FRYABLE > FRY
FRYBREAD *n* Native American fried bread
FRYBREADS > FRYBREAD
FRYER *n* person or thing that fries
FRYERS > FRYER
FRYING > FRY
FRYINGS > FRY
FRYPAN *n* long-handled shallow pan used for frying
FRYPANS > FRYPAN
FUB *vb* cheat
FUBAR *adj* irreparably damaged or bungled
FUBBED > FUB
FUBBERIES > FUBBERY
FUBBERY *n* cheating
FUBBIER > FUBBY
FUBBIEST > FUBBY
FUBBING > FUB
FUBBY *adj* short and stout
FUBS > FUB
FUBSIER > FUBSY
FUBSIEST > FUBSY
FUBSY *adj* short and stout
FUCHSIA *n* ornamental shrub
FUCHSIAS > FUCHSIA
FUCHSIN *n* greenish crimson substance
FUCHSINE *same as* > FUCHSIN
FUCHSINES > FUCHSINE
FUCHSINS > FUCHSIN
FUCHSITE *n* form of mica
FUCHSITES > FUCHSITE
FUCI > FUCUS
FUCK *vb* taboo word meaning have sexual intercourse (with) ▷ *n* act of sexual intercourse
FUCKED > FUCK
FUCKER *n* taboo word for a despicable or obnoxious person

FUCKERS > FUCKER
FUCKFACE *n* taboo word for a stupid or contemptible person
FUCKFACES > FUCKFACE
FUCKHEAD *n* taboo word for a stupid or contemptible person
FUCKHEADS > FUCKHEAD
FUCKING > FUCK
FUCKINGS > FUCK
FUCKOFF *n* taboo word for an annoying or unpleasant person
FUCKOFFS > FUCKOFF
FUCKS > FUCK
FUCKUP *vb* taboo word meaning to damage or bungle ▷ *n* taboo word meaning an act or an instance of bungling
FUCKUPS > FUCKUP
FUCKWIT *n* taboo word for a fool or idiot
FUCKWITS > FUCKWIT
FUCOID *n* type of seaweed
FUCOIDAL *adj* of or relating to fucoid
FUCOIDS > FUCOID
FUCOSE *n* aldose
FUCOSES > FUCOSE
FUCOUS *same as* > FUCOIDAL
FUCUS *n* type of seaweed
FUCUSED *adj* archaic word meaning made up with cosmetics
FUCUSES > FUCUS
FUD *n* rabbit's tail
FUDDIER > FUDDY
FUDDIES > FUDDY
FUDDIEST > FUDDY
FUDDLE *vb* cause to be intoxicated or confused ▷ *n* confused state
FUDDLED > FUDDLE
FUDDLER > FUDDLE
FUDDLERS > FUDDLE
FUDDLES > FUDDLE
FUDDLING > FUDDLE
FUDDLINGS > FUDDLE
FUDDY *n* old-fashioned person ▷ *adj* old-fashioned
FUDGE *n* soft caramel-like sweet ▷ *vb* make (an issue) less clear deliberately ▷ *interj* mild exclamation of annoyance
FUDGED > FUDGE
FUDGES > FUDGE
FUDGIER > FUDGY
FUDGIEST > FUDGY
FUDGING > FUDGE
FUDGY *adj* resembling or containing fudge
FUDS > FUD
FUEHRER *n* leader: applied esp to Adolf Hitler
FUEHRERS > FUEHRER
FUEL *n* substance burned or treated to produce heat or power ▷ *vb* provide with fuel
FUELED > FUEL

FUELER > FUEL
FUELERS > FUEL
FUELING > FUEL
FUELLED > FUEL
FUELLER > FUEL
FUELLERS > FUEL
FUELLING > FUEL
FUELS > FUEL
FUELWOOD *n* any wood used as a fuel
FUELWOODS > FUELWOOD
FUERO *n* Spanish code of laws
FUEROS > FUERO
FUFF *vb* puff
FUFFED > FUFF
FUFFIER > FUFFY
FUFFIEST > FUFFY
FUFFING > FUFF
FUFFS > FUFF
FUFFY *adj* puffy
FUG *n* hot stale atmosphere ▷ *vb* sit in a fug
FUGACIOUS *adj* passing quickly away
FUGACITY *n* property of a gas that expresses its tendency to escape or expand
FUGAL *adj* of, relating to, or in the style of a fugue
FUGALLY > FUGAL
FUGATO *adj* in the manner or style of a fugue ▷ *n* movement, section, or piece in this style
FUGATOS > FUGATO
FUGGED > FUG
FUGGIER > FUG
FUGGIEST > FUG
FUGGILY > FUG
FUGGINESS *n* state or condition of being fuggy
FUGGING > FUG
FUGGY > FUG
FUGHETTA *n* short fugue
FUGHETTAS > FUGHETTA
FUGIE *n* runaway
FUGIES > FUGIE
FUGIO *n* former US copper coin
FUGIOS > FUGIO
FUGITIVE *n* person who flees, esp from arrest or pursuit ▷ *adj* fleeing
FUGITIVES > FUGITIVE
FUGLE *vb* act as a fugleman
FUGLED > FUGLE
FUGLEMAN *n* (formerly) a soldier used as an example for those learning drill
FUGLEMEN > FUGLEMAN
FUGLES > FUGLE
FUGLIER > FUGLY
FUGLIEST > FUGLY
FUGLING > FUGLE
FUGLY *adj* vulgar slang word for very ugly
FUGS > FUG
FUGU *n* pufferfish
FUGUE *n* type of musical composition ▷ *vb* be in a dreamlike, altered state of consciousness

FUGUED > FUGUE
FUGUELIKE > FUGUE
FUGUES > FUGUE
FUGUING > FUGUE
FUGUIST n composer of fugues
FUGUISTS > FUGUIST
FUGUS > FUGU
FUHRER same as > FUEHRER
FUHRERS > FUHRER
FUJI n type of African music
FUJIS > FUJI
FULCRA > FULCRUM
FULCRATE > FULCRUM
FULCRUM n pivot about which a lever turns
FULCRUMS > FULCRUM
FULFIL vb achieve (a desire or promise)
FULFILL same as > FULFIL
FULFILLED > FULFILL
FULFILLER > FULFILL
FULFILLS > FULFILL
FULFILS > FULFIL
FULGENCY > FULGENT
FULGENT adj shining brilliantly
FULGENTLY > FULGENT
FULGID same as > FULGENT
FULGOR n brilliance
FULGOROUS > FULGOR
FULGORS > FULGOR
FULGOUR variant of > FULGOR
FULGOURS > FULGOUR
FULGURAL > FULGURATE
FULGURANT > FULGURATE
FULGURATE vb flash like lightning
FULGURITE n tube of glassy mineral matter found in sand and rock, formed by the action of lightning
FULGUROUS adj flashing like or resembling lightning
FULHAM n loaded die
FULHAMS > FULHAM
FULL adj containing as much or as many as possible ▷ adv completely ▷ vb clean, shrink, and press cloth
FULLAGE n price charged for fulling cloth
FULLAGES > FULLAGE
FULLAM variant of > FULHAM
FULLAMS > FULLAM
FULLAN variant of > FULHAM
FULLANS > FULLAN
FULLBACK n defensive player
FULLBACKS > FULLBACK
FULLBLOOD n person or animal with unmixed ancestry
FULLED > FULL
FULLER n person who fulls cloth for a living ▷ vb

forge (a groove) or caulk (a riveted joint)
FULLERED > FULLER
FULLERENE n any of various carbon molecules with a polyhedral structure similar to that of buckminsterfullerene
FULLERIDE n compound of a fullerene in which atoms are trapped inside the cage of carbon atoms
FULLERIES > FULLERY
FULLERING > FULLER
FULLERITE n crystalline form of a fullerene
FULLERS > FULLER
FULLERY n place where fulling is carried out
FULLEST > FULL
FULLFACE n in printing, a letter that takes up full body size
FULLFACES > FULLFACE
FULLING > FULL
FULLISH > FULL
FULLNESS > FULL
FULLS > FULL
FULLY adv greatest degree or extent
FULMAR n Arctic sea bird
FULMARS > FULMAR
FULMINANT adj sudden and violent
FULMINATE vb criticize or denounce angrily ▷ n any salt or ester of fulminic acid, esp the mercury salt, which is used as a detonator
FULMINE vb fulminate
FULMINED > FULMINE
FULMINES > FULMINE
FULMINIC adj as in fulminic acid, unstable volatile acid
FULMINING > FULMINE
FULMINOUS adj harshly critical
FULNESS > FULL
FULNESSES > FULL
FULSOME adj distastefully excessive or insincere
FULSOMELY > FULSOME
FULSOMER > FULSOME
FULSOMEST > FULSOME
FULVID variant of > FULVOUS
FULVOUS adj of a dull brownish-yellow colour
FUM n phoenix, in Chinese mythology
FUMADO n salted, smoked fish
FUMADOES > FUMADO
FUMADOS > FUMADO
FUMAGE n tax on hearths
FUMAGES > FUMAGE
FUMARASE n enzyme
FUMARASES > FUMARASE
FUMARATE n salt of fumaric acid
FUMARATES > FUMARATE
FUMARIC adj as in fumaric acid colourless crystalline acid

FUMAROLE n vent in or near a volcano from which hot gases, esp steam, are emitted
FUMAROLES > FUMAROLE
FUMAROLIC > FUMAROLE
FUMATORIA pl n small airtight chambers for fumigating insects or fungi
FUMATORY n chamber where insects and fungi are destroyed by fumigation
FUMBLE vb handle awkwardly ▷ n act of fumbling
FUMBLED > FUMBLE
FUMBLER > FUMBLE
FUMBLERS > FUMBLE
FUMBLES > FUMBLE
FUMBLING > FUMBLE
FUME vb be very angry
FUMED adj (of wood) having been exposed to ammonia fumes
FUMELESS > FUME
FUMELIKE > FUME
FUMER > FUME
FUMEROLE variant of > FUMAROLE
FUMEROLES > FUMEROLE
FUMERS > FUME
FUMES > FUME
FUMET n liquor from cooking fish, meat, or game
FUMETS > FUMET
FUMETTE variant of > FUMET
FUMETTES > FUMETTE
FUMETTI > FUMETTO
FUMETTO n speech balloon in a comic or cartoon
FUMETTOS > FUMETTO
FUMIER > FUME
FUMIEST > FUME
FUMIGANT n substance used for fumigating
FUMIGANTS > FUMIGANT
FUMIGATE vb disinfect with fumes
FUMIGATED > FUMIGATE
FUMIGATES > FUMIGATE
FUMIGATOR > FUMIGATE
FUMING > FUME
FUMINGLY > FUME
FUMITORY n chiefly European plant with spurred flowers, formerly used medicinally
FUMOSITY > FUME
FUMOUS > FUME
FUMS > FUM
FUMULI > FUMULUS
FUMULUS n smokelike cloud
FUMY > FUME
FUN n enjoyment or amusement ▷ vb trick

▷ adj providing amusement or entertainment
FUNBOARD n type of surfboard
FUNBOARDS > FUNBOARD
FUNCKIA n ornamental plant
FUNCKIAS > FUNCKIA
FUNCTION n purpose something exists for ▷ vb operate or work
FUNCTIONS > FUNCTION
FUNCTOR n performer of a function
FUNCTORS > FUNCTOR
FUND n stock of money for a special purpose ▷ vb provide money to
FUNDABLE > FUND
FUNDAMENT n buttocks
FUNDED > FUND
FUNDER > FUND
FUNDERS > FUND
FUNDI n expert or boffin
FUNDIC > FUNDUS
FUNDIE n fundamentalist
FUNDIES > FUNDIE
FUNDING > FUND
FUNDINGS > FUND
FUNDIS > FUNDI
FUNDLESS > FUND
FUNDRAISE vb raise money for a cause
FUNDS pl n money that is readily available
FUNDUS n base of an organ
FUNDY n fundamentalist
FUNEBRAL variant of > FUNEBRIAL
FUNEBRE adj funereal or mournful
FUNEBRIAL same as > FUNEREAL
FUNERAL n ceremony of burying or cremating a dead person
FUNERALS > FUNERAL
FUNERARY adj of or for a funeral
FUNEREAL adj gloomy or sombre
FUNEST adj lamentable
FUNFAIR n entertainment with machines to ride on and stalls
FUNFAIRS > FUNFAIR
FUNFEST n enjoyable time
FUNFESTS > FUNFEST
FUNG same as > FUNK
FUNGAL adj of, derived from, or caused by a fungus or fungi ▷ n fungus or fungal infection
FUNGALS > FUNGAL
FUNGI > FUNGUS
FUNGIBLE n goods replaceable by similar goods of equal quantity or weight ▷ adj having the quality of fungibles
FUNGIBLES > FUNGIBLE

FUNGIC > FUNGUS
FUNGICIDE *n* substance that destroys fungi
FUNGIFORM *adj* shaped like a mushroom or similar fungus
FUNGISTAT *n* substance that inhibits the growth of fungi
FUNGO *n* in baseball, act of tossing and hitting the ball ▷ *vb* toss and hit a ball
FUNGOED > FUNGO
FUNGOES > FUNGO
FUNGOID *adj* resembling a fungus
FUNGOIDAL > FUNGOID
FUNGOIDS > FUNGOID
FUNGOING > FUNGO
FUNGOS > FUNGO
FUNGOSITY > FUNGOUS
FUNGOUS *adj* appearing and spreading quickly like a fungus
FUNGS > FUNG
FUNGUS *n* plant such as a mushroom or mould
FUNGUSES > FUNGUS
FUNHOUSE *n* amusing place at fairground
FUNHOUSES > FUNHOUSE
FUNICLE *n* stalk that attaches an ovule to the wall of the ovary
FUNICLES > FUNICLE
FUNICULAR *n* cable railway on a mountainside or cliff ▷ *adj* relating to or operated by a rope, cable, etc
FUNICULI > FUNICULUS
FUNICULUS *same as* **>** FUNICLE
FUNK *n* style of dance music with a strong beat ▷ *vb* avoid (doing something) through fear
FUNKED > FUNK
FUNKER > FUNK
FUNKERS > FUNK
FUNKHOLE *n* dugout
FUNKHOLES > FUNKHOLE
FUNKIA *n* ornamental plant
FUNKIAS > FUNKIA
FUNKIER > FUNKY
FUNKIEST > FUNKY
FUNKILY > FUNKY
FUNKINESS > FUNKY
FUNKING > FUNK
FUNKS > FUNK
FUNKSTER *n* performer or fan of funk music
FUNKSTERS > FUNKSTER
FUNKY *adj* (of music) having a strong beat
FUNNED > FUN
FUNNEL *n* cone-shaped tube ▷ *vb* (cause to) move through or as if through a funnel
FUNNELED > FUNNEL
FUNNELING > FUNNEL
FUNNELLED > FUNNEL

FUNNELS > FUNNEL
FUNNER > FUN
FUNNEST > FUN
FUNNIER > FUNNY
FUNNIES *pl n* comic strips in a newspaper
FUNNIEST > FUNNY
FUNNILY > FUNNY
FUNNINESS > FUNNY
FUNNING > FUN
FUNNY *adj* comical, humorous ▷ *n* joke or witticism
FUNNYMAN *n* comedian
FUNNYMEN > FUNNYMAN
FUNPLEX *n* large amusement centre
FUNPLEXES > FUNPLEX
FUNS > FUN
FUNSTER *n* funnyman or funnywoman
FUNSTERS > FUNSTER
FUR *n* soft hair of a mammal ▷ *vb* cover or become covered with fur
FURACIOUS *adj* thievish
FURACITY > FURACIOUS
FURAL *same as* **>** FURFURAL
FURALS > FURAL
FURAN *n* colourless liquid used as a solvent
FURANE *variant of* **>** FURAN
FURANES > FURANE
FURANOSE *n* simple sugar containing a furan ring
FURANOSES > FURANOSE
FURANS > FURAN
FURBALL *n* ball of fur regurgitated by an animal
FURBALLS > FURBALL
FURBEARER *n* mammal hunted for its pelt or fur
FURBELOW *n* flounce, ruffle, or other ornamental trim ▷ *vb* put a furbelow on (a garment)
FURBELOWS > FURBELOW
FURBISH *vb* smarten up
FURBISHED > FURBISH
FURBISHER > FURBISH
FURBISHES > FURBISH
FURCA *n* any forklike structure, esp in insects
FURCAE > FURCA
FURCAL > FURCA
FURCATE *vb* divide into two parts ▷ *adj* forked, branching
FURCATED > FURCATE
FURCATELY > FURCATE
FURCATES > FURCATE
FURCATING > FURCATE
FURCATION > FURCATE
FURCRAEA *n* plant belonging to the Agave family
FURCRAEAS > FURCRAEA
FURCULA *n* any forklike part or organ
FURCULAE > FURCULA
FURCULAR > FURCULA

FURCULUM *same as* **>** FURCULA
FURDER *same as* **>** FURTHER
FUREUR *n* rage or anger
FUREURS > FUREUR
FURFAIR *variant of* **>** FURFUR
FURFAIRS > FURFAIR
FURFUR *n* scurf or scaling of the skin
FURFURAL *n* colourless liquid used as a solvent
FURFURALS > FURFURAL
FURFURAN *same as* **>** FURAN
FURFURANS > FURFURAN
FURFURES > FURFUR
FURFUROL *variant of* **>** FURFURAL
FURFUROLE *variant of* **>** FURFURAL
FURFUROLS > FURFUROL
FURFUROUS > FURFUR
FURFURS > FURFUR
FURIBUND *adj* furious
FURIES > FURY
FURIOSITY > FURIOUS
FURIOSO *adv* in a frantically rushing manner ▷ *n* passage or piece to be performed in this way
FURIOSOS > FURIOSO
FURIOUS *adj* very angry
FURIOUSLY > FURIOUS
FURKID *n* companion animal
FURKIDS > FURKID
FURL *vb* roll up and fasten (a sail, umbrella, or flag) ▷ *n* act or an instance of furling
FURLABLE > FURL
FURLANA *variant of* **>** FORLANA
FURLANAS > FURLANA
FURLED > FURL
FURLER > FURL
FURLERS > FURL
FURLESS > FUR
FURLIKE *adj* like fur
FURLING > FURL
FURLONG *n* unit of length
FURLONGS > FURLONG
FURLOUGH *n* leave of absence ▷ *vb* grant a furlough to
FURLOUGHS > FURLOUGH
FURLS > FURL
FURMENTY *same as* **>** FRUMENTY
FURMETIES > FURMETY
FURMETY *same as* **>** FRUMENTY
FURMITIES > FURMITY
FURMITY *same as* **>** FRUMENTY
FURNACE *n* enclosed chamber containing a very hot fire ▷ *vb* burn in a furnace
FURNACED > FURNACE
FURNACES > FURNACE
FURNACING > FURNACE

FURNIMENT *n* furniture
FURNISH *vb* provide with furniture
FURNISHED > FURNISH
FURNISHER > FURNISH
FURNISHES > FURNISH
FURNITURE *n* large movable articles such as chairs and wardrobes
FUROL *variant of* **>** FURAL
FUROLE *variant of* **>** FURAL
FUROLES > FUROLE
FUROLS > FUROL
FUROR *same as* **>** FURORE
FURORE *n* very excited or angry reaction
FURORES > FURORE
FURORS > FUROR
FURPHIES > FURPHY
FURPHY *n* rumour or fictitious story
FURPIECE *n* item of clothing made of or decorated with fur
FURPIECES > FURPIECE
FURR *vb* old word meaning furrow
FURRED *same as* **>** FURRY
FURRIER *n* dealer in furs
FURRIERS > FURRIER
FURRIERY *n* occupation of a furrier
FURRIES > FURRY
FURRIEST > FURRY
FURRILY > FURRY
FURRINER *n* dialect rendering of foreigner
FURRINERS > FURRINER
FURRINESS > FURRY
FURRING > FUR
FURRINGS > FUR
FURROW *n* trench made by a plough ▷ *vb* make or become wrinkled
FURROWED > FURROW
FURROWER > FURROW
FURROWERS > FURROW
FURROWIER > FURROWY
FURROWING > FURROW
FURROWS > FURROW
FURROWY *adj* having furrows
FURRS > FURR
FURRY *adj* like or covered with fur or something furlike ▷ *n* child's fur-covered toy animal
FURS > FUR
FURTH *adv* Scots word meening out
FURTHER *adv* in addition ▷ *adj* more distant ▷ *vb* promote
FURTHERED > FURTHER
FURTHERER > FURTHER
FURTHERS > FURTHER
FURTHEST *adv* to the greatest degree ▷ *adj* most distant
FURTIVE *adj* sly and secretive
FURTIVELY > FURTIVE
FURUNCLE *technical name for* **>** BOIL
FURUNCLES > FURUNCLE

FURY *n* wild anger
FURZE *n* gorse
FURZES > FURZE
FURZIER > FURZE
FURZIEST > FURZE
FURZY > FURZE
FUSAIN *n* fine charcoal pencil
FUSAINS > FUSAIN
FUSARIA > FUSARIUM
FUSARIUM *n* type of fungus
FUSARIUMS > FUSARIUM
FUSAROL *variant of* > FUSAROLE
FUSAROLE *n* type of architectural moulding
FUSAROLES > FUSAROLE
FUSAROLS > FUSAROL
FUSBALL *same as* > FOOSBALL
FUSBALLS > FUSBALL
FUSC *adj* dark brown
FUSCOUS *adj* of a brownish-grey colour
FUSE *n* cord containing an explosive for detonating a bomb ▷ *vb* (cause to) fail as a result of a blown fuse
FUSED > FUSE
FUSEE *n* (in early clocks and watches) a spirally grooved spindle
FUSEES > FUSEE
FUSEL *n* mixture of amyl alcohols, propanol, and butanol
FUSELAGE *n* body of an aircraft
FUSELAGES > FUSELAGE
FUSELESS > FUSE
FUSELIKE > FUSE
FUSELS > FUSEL
FUSES > FUSE
FUSHION *n* spirit
FUSHIONS > FUSHION
FUSIBLE *adj* capable of being melted
FUSIBLY > FUSIBLE
FUSIDIC *adj* as in *fusidic acid* kind of acid
FUSIFORM *adj* elongated and tapering at both ends
FUSIL *n* light flintlock musket
FUSILE *adj* easily melted
FUSILEER *same as* > FUSILIER
FUSILEERS > FUSILEER
FUSILIER *n* soldier of certain regiments

FUSILIERS > FUSILIER
FUSILLADE *n* continuous discharge of firearms ▷ *vb* attack with a fusillade
FUSILLI *n* spiral-shaped pasta
FUSILLIS > FUSILLI
FUSILS > FUSIL
FUSING > FUSE
FUSION *n* melting ▷ *adj* of a style of cooking
FUSIONAL > FUSION
FUSIONISM *n* favouring of coalitions among political groups
FUSIONIST > FUSIONISM
FUSIONS > FUSION
FUSK *vb* obtain data from (a website) by using hacking software
FUSKED > FUSK
FUSKER *vb* obtain data from (a website) by using hacking software
FUSKERED > FUSKER
FUSKERING > FUSKER
FUSKERS > FUSKER
FUSKING > FUSK
FUSKS > FUSK
FUSS *n* needless activity or worry ▷ *vb* make a fuss
FUSSBALL *same as* > FOOSBALL
FUSSBALLS > FUSSBALL
FUSSED > FUSS
FUSSER > FUSS
FUSSERS > FUSS
FUSSES > FUSS
FUSSIER > FUSSY
FUSSIEST > FUSSY
FUSSILY > FUSSY
FUSSINESS > FUSSY
FUSSING > FUSS
FUSSPOT *n* person who is difficult to please and complains often
FUSSPOTS > FUSSPOT
FUSSY *adj* inclined to fuss
FUST *vb* become mouldy
FUSTED > FUST
FUSTET *n* wood of the Venetian sumach shrub
FUSTETS > FUSTET
FUSTIAN *n* (formerly) a hard-wearing fabric of cotton mixed with flax or wool ▷ *adj* cheap
FUSTIANS > FUSTIAN
FUSTIC *n* large tropical American tree
FUSTICS > FUSTIC

FUSTIER > FUSTY
FUSTIEST > FUSTY
FUSTIGATE *vb* beat
FUSTILUGS *n* fat person
FUSTILY > FUSTY
FUSTINESS > FUSTY
FUSTING > FUST
FUSTOC *variant of* > FUSTIC
FUSTOCS > FUSTOC
FUSTS > FUST
FUSTY *adj* stale-smelling
FUSULINID *n* any of various extinct foraminifers
FUSUMA *n* Japanese sliding door
FUSUMAS > FUSUMA
FUTCHEL *n* timber support in a carriage
FUTCHELS > FUTCHEL
FUTHARC *same as* > FUTHARK
FUTHARCS > FUTHARC
FUTHARK *n* phonetic alphabet consisting of runes
FUTHARKS > FUTHARK
FUTHORC *same as* > FUTHORK
FUTHORCS > FUTHORC
FUTHORK *same as* > FUTHORK
FUTHORKS > FUTHORK
FUTILE *adj* unsuccessful or useless
FUTILELY > FUTILE
FUTILER > FUTILE
FUTILEST > FUTILE
FUTILITY *n* lack of effectiveness or success
FUTON *n* Japanese-style bed
FUTONS > FUTON
FUTSAL *n* form of association football
FUTSALS > FUTSAL
FUTTOCK *n* one of the ribs in the frame of a wooden vessel
FUTTOCKS > FUTTOCK
FUTURAL *adj* relating to the future
FUTURE *n* time to come ▷ *adj* yet to come or be
FUTURES *pl n* type of commodity trading
FUTURISM *n* early 20th-century artistic movement
FUTURISMS > FUTURISM
FUTURIST > FUTURISM
FUTURISTS > FUTURISM

FUTURITY *n* future
FUTZ *vb* fritter time away
FUTZED > FUTZ
FUTZES > FUTZ
FUTZING > FUTZ
FUZE *same as* > FUSE
FUZED > FUZE
FUZEE *same as* > FUSEE
FUZEES > FUZEE
FUZELESS *adj* without a fuze
FUZES > FUZE
FUZIL *variant of* > FUSIL
FUZILS > FUZIL
FUZING > FUZE
FUZZ *n* mass of fine or curly hairs or fibres ▷ *vb* make or become fuzzy
FUZZBALL *n* ball of fuzz
FUZZBALLS > FUZZBALL
FUZZBOX *n* device that distorts sound
FUZZBOXES > FUZZBOX
FUZZED > FUZZ
FUZZES > FUZZ
FUZZIER > FUZZY
FUZZIEST > FUZZY
FUZZILY > FUZZY
FUZZINESS > FUZZY
FUZZING > FUZZ
FUZZLE *vb* make drunk
FUZZLED > FUZZLE
FUZZLES > FUZZLE
FUZZLING > FUZZLE
FUZZTONE *n* device distorting electric guitar sound
FUZZTONES > FUZZTONE
FUZZY *adj* of, like, or covered with fuzz
FY *interj* exclamation of disapproval
FYCE *variant of* > FICE
FYCES > FYCE
FYKE *n* fish trap ▷ *vb* catch fish in this manner
FYKED > FYKE
FYKES > FYKE
FYKING > FYKE
FYLE *variant of* > FILE
FYLES > FYLE
FYLFOT *rare word for* > SWASTIKA
FYLFOTS > FYLFOT
FYNBOS *n* area of low-growing, evergreen vegetation
FYNBOSES > FYNBOS
FYRD *n* militia of an Anglo-Saxon shire
FYRDS > FYRD
FYTTE *n* section of a song
FYTTES > FYTTE

Gg

GAB *vb* talk or chatter ▷ *n* mechanical device

GABARDINE *n* strong twill cloth used esp for raincoats

GABBA *n* type of electronic dance music

GABBARD *same as* > GABBART

GABBARDS > GABBARD

GABBART *n* Scottish sailing barge

GABBARTS > GABBART

GABBAS > GABBA

GABBED > GAB

GABBER > GAB

GABBERS > GAB

GABBIER > GABBY

GABBIEST > GABBY

GABBINESS > GABBY

GABBING > GAB

GABBLE *vb* speak rapidly and indistinctly ▷ *n* rapid indistinct speech

GABBLED > GABBLE

GABBLER > GABBLE

GABBLERS > GABBLE

GABBLES > GABBLE

GABBLING > GABBLE

GABBLINGS > GABBLE

GABBRO *n* dark basic plutonic igneous rock

GABBROIC > GABBRO

GABBROID *adj* gabbro-like

GABBROS > GABBRO

GABBY *adj* talkative

GABELLE *n* salt tax levied until 1790

GABELLED > GABELLE

GABELLER *n* person who collects the gabelle

GABELLERS > GABELLER

GABELLES > GABELLE

GABERDINE *same as* > GABARDINE

GABFEST *n* prolonged gossiping or conversation

GABFESTS > GABFEST

GABIES > GABY

GABION *n* cylindrical metal container filled with stones

GABIONADE *n* row of gabions submerged in a waterway, stream, river, etc, to control the flow of water

GABIONAGE *n* structure composed of gabions

GABIONED > GABION

GABIONS > GABION

GABLE *n* triangular upper part of a wall between sloping roofs

GABLED > GABLE

GABLELIKE > GABLE

GABLES > GABLE

GABLET *n* small gable

GABLETS > GABLET

GABLING > GABLE

GABNASH *n* chatter

GABNASHES > GABNASH

GABOON *n* dark wood

GABOONS > GABOON

GABS > GAB

GABY *n* unintelligent person

GACH *vb* behave boastfully

GACHED > GACH

GACHER *n* person who boasts

GACHERS > GACHER

GACHES > GACH

GACHING > GACH

GAD *vb* go about in search of pleasure ▷ *n* carefree adventure

GADABOUT *n* pleasure-seeker

GADABOUTS > GADABOUT

GADARENE *adj* headlong

GADDED > GAD

GADDER > GAD

GADDERS > GAD

GADDI *n* cushioned Indian throne

GADDING > GAD

GADDIS > GADDI

GADE *same as* > GAD

GADES > GADE

GADFLIES > GADFLY

GADFLY *n* fly that bites cattle

GADGE *n* man

GADGES > GADGE

GADGET *n* small mechanical device or appliance

GADGETEER *n* person who delights in gadgetry

GADGETIER > GADGETY

GADGETRY *n* gadgets

GADGETS > GADGET

GADGETY *adj* characterized by gadgets

GADGIE *n* fellow

GADGIES > GADGIE

GADI *n* cushioned Indian throne

GADID *n* type of marine fish

GADIDS > GADID

GADIS > GADI

GADJE *same as* > GADGIE

GADJES > GADJE

GADJO *same as* > GORGIO

GADJOS > GADJO

GADLING *n* vagabond

GADLINGS > GADLING

GADMAN *n* person who drives animals

GADMEN > GADMAN

GADOID *adj* of the cod family of marine fishes ▷ *n* gadoid fish

GADOIDS > GADOID

GADOLINIC *adj* relating to gadolinium, a silvery white metallic element

GADROON *n* type of decorative moulding

GADROONED > GADROON

GADROONS > GADROON

GADS > GAD

GADSMAN *n* person who drives animals

GADSMEN > GADSMAN

GADSO *n* archaic expression of surprise

GADWALL *n* type of duck related to the mallard

GADWALLS > GADWALL

GADZOOKS *interj* mild oath

GAE *Scot word for* > GO

GAED > GAE

GAEING > GAE

GAELICISE *vb* adapt to conform to Gaelic spelling and pronunciation

GAELICISM > GAELICISE

GAELICIZE *same as* > GAELICISE

GAEN > GAE

GAES > GAE

GAFF *n* stick with an iron hook for landing large fish ▷ *vb* hook or land (a fish) with a gaff

GAFFE *n* social blunder

GAFFED > GAFF

GAFFER *n* foreman or boss

GAFFERS > GAFFER

GAFFES > GAFFE

GAFFING > GAFF

GAFFINGS > GAFF

GAFFS > GAFF

GAFFSAIL *n* quadrilateral fore-and-aft sail on a sailing vessel

GAFFSAILS > GAFFSAIL

GAG *vb* choke or retch ▷ *n* cloth etc put into or tied across the mouth

GAGA *adj* senile

GAGAKU *n* type of traditional Japanese music

GAGAKUS > GAGAKU

GAGE *vb* gauge ▷ *n* (formerly) an object thrown down as a challenge to fight

GAGEABLE > GAGE

GAGEABLY > GAGE

GAGED > GAGE

GAGER *same as* > GAUGER

GAGERS > GAGER

GAGES > GAGE

GAGGED > GAG

GAGGER *n* person or thing that gags

GAGGERIES > GAGGERY

GAGGERS > GAGGER

GAGGERY *n* practice of telling jokes

GAGGING > GAG

GAGGLE *n* disorderly crowd ▷ *vb* (of geese) to cackle

GAGGLED > GAGGLE

GAGGLES > GAGGLE

GAGGLING > GAGGLE

GAGGLINGS > GAGGLE

GAGING > GAGE

GAGMAN *n* person who writes gags for a comedian

GAGMEN > GAGMAN

GAGS > GAG

GAGSTER *n* standup comedian

GAGSTERS > GAGSTER

GAHNITE *n* dark green mineral

GAHNITES > GAHNITE

GAID *same as* > GAD

GAIDS > GAID

GAIETIES > GAIETY

GAIETY *n* cheerfulness

GAIJIN *n* (in Japan) a foreigner

GAILLARD *same as* > GALLIARD

GAILLARDE *same as* > GAILLARD

GAILY *adv* merrily

GAIN *vb* acquire or obtain ▷ *n* profit or advantage ▷ *adj* straight or near

GAINABLE > GAIN

GAINED > GAIN

GAINER *n* person or thing that gains

GAINERS > GAINER

GAINEST > GAIN

GAINFUL *adj* useful or profitable

GAINFULLY > GAINFUL

GAINING > GAIN

GAININGS pl n profits or earnings

GAINLESS > GAIN

GAINLIER > GAINLY

GAINLIEST > GAINLY

GAINLY adj graceful or well-formed ▷ adv conveniently or suitably

GAINS pl n profits or winnings

GAINSAID > GAINSAY

GAINSAY vb deny or contradict

GAINSAYER > GAINSAY

GAINSAYS > GAINSAY

GAINST short for > AGAINST

GAIR n strip of green grass on a hillside

GAIRFOWL same as > GAREFOWL

GAIRFOWLS > GAIRFOWL

GAIRS > GAIR

GAIT n manner of walking ▷ vb teach (a horse) a particular gait

GAITA n type of bagpipe

GAITAS > GAITA

GAITED > GAIT

GAITER n cloth or leather covering for the lower leg

GAITERED adj wearing gaiters

GAITERS > GAITER

GAITING > GAIT

GAITS > GAIT

GAITT Scots word for > GATE

GAITTS > GAITT

GAJO same as > GORGIO

GAJOS > GAJO

GAK n cocaine

GAKS > GAK

GAL n girl

GALA n festival

GALABEA same as > DJELLABA

GALABEAH same as > DJELLABA

GALABEAHS > GALABEAH

GALABEAS > GALABEA

GALABIA same as > DJELLABA

GALABIAH same as > DJELLABA

GALABIAHS > GALABIAH

GALABIAS > GALABIA

GALABIEH same as > DJELLABA

GALABIEHS > GALABIEH

GALABIYA same as > DJELLABA

GALABIYAH same as > DJELLABA

GALABIYAS > GALABIYA

GALACTIC adj of the Galaxy or other galaxies

GALACTICO n famous and highly paid footballer

GALACTOSE n white water-soluble monosaccharide found in lactose

GALAGE same as > GALOSH

GALAGES > GALAGE

GALAGO another name for > BUSHBABY

GALAGOS > GALAGO

GALAH n Australian cockatoo

GALAHS > GALAH

GALANGA same as > GALINGALE

GALANGAL same as > GALINGALE

GALANGALS > GALANGAL

GALANGAS > GALANGA

GALANT n 18th-century style of music

GALANTINE n cold dish of meat or poultry, which is boned, cooked, stuffed, then pressed into a neat shape and glazed

GALANTS > GALANT

GALANTY n as in galanty show pantomime shadow play

GALAPAGO n tortoise

GALAPAGOS > GALAPAGO

GALAS > GALA

GALATEA n strong twill-weave cotton fabric

GALATEAS > GALATEA

GALAVANT same as > GALLIVANT

GALAVANTS > GALAVANT

GALAX n coltsfoot

GALAXES > GALAX

GALAXIES > GALAXY

GALAXY n system of stars

GALBANUM n bitter aromatic gum resin

GALBANUMS > GALBANUM

GALDRAGON old Scots word for a > SORCERESS

GALE n strong wind ▷ vb be very stormy

GALEA n part or organ shaped like a helmet

GALEAE > GALEA

GALEAS > GALEA

GALEATE > GALEA

GALEATED > GALEA

GALED > GALE

GALEIFORM > GALEA

GALENA n soft bluish-grey mineral

GALENAS > GALENA

GALENGALE same as > GALINGALE

GALENIC > GALENA

GALENICAL n any drug prepared from plant or animal tissue, esp vegetables, rather than being chemically synthesized ▷ adj denoting or belonging to this group of drugs

GALENITE same as > GALENA

GALENITES > GALENITE

GALENOID adj pertaining to galena

GALERE n group of people having a common interest

GALERES > GALERE

GALES > GALE

GALETTE n type of savoury pancake

GALETTES > GALETTE

GALILEE n type of porch or chapel

GALILEES > GALILEE

GALING > GALE

GALINGALE n European plant with rough-edged leaves, reddish spikelets of flowers, and aromatic roots

GALIONGEE n sailor

GALIOT n small swift galley

GALIOTS > GALIOT

GALIPOT n resin obtained from several species of pine

GALIPOTS > GALIPOT

GALIVANT same as > GALLIVANT

GALIVANTS > GALIVANT

GALL n impudence ▷ vb annoy

GALLABEA same as > DJELLABA

GALLABEAH same as > DJELLABA

GALLABEAS > GALLABEA

GALLABIA same as > DJELLABA

GALLABIAH same as > DJELLABA

GALLABIAS > GALLABIA

GALLABIEH same as > DJELLABA

GALLABIYA same as > DJELLABA

GALLAMINE n muscle relaxant used in anaesthesia

GALLANT adj brave and noble ▷ n man who tried to impress with fashionable clothes or daring acts ▷ vb court or flirt (with)

GALLANTED > GALLANT

GALLANTER > GALLANT

GALLANTLY > GALLANT

GALLANTRY n showy, attentive treatment of women

GALLANTS > GALLANT

GALLATE n salt of gallic acid

GALLATES > GALLATE

GALLED > GALL

GALLEIN n type of dyestuff

GALLEINS > GALLEIN

GALLEON n large three-masted sailing ship

GALLEONS > GALLEON

GALLERIA n central court through several storeys of a shopping centre

GALLERIAS > GALLERIA

GALLERIED adj having a gallery or galleries

GALLERIES > GALLERY

GALLERIST n person who owns or runs an art gallery

GALLERY n room or building for displaying works of art ▷ vb tunnel; form an underground gallery

GALLET vb use mixture to support a roof-slate

GALLETA n low-growing, coarse grass

GALLETAS > GALLETA

GALLETED > GALLET

GALLETING > GALLET

GALLETS > GALLET

GALLEY n kitchen of a ship or aircraft

GALLEYS > GALLEY

GALLFLIES > GALLFLY

GALLFLY n any of several small insects

GALLIARD n spirited dance in triple time for two persons, popular in the 16th and 17th centuries ▷ adj lively

GALLIARDS > GALLIARD

GALLIASS same as > GALLEASS

GALLIC adj of or containing gallium

GALLICA n variety of rose

GALLICAN adj favouring restriction of papal control of the French church

GALLICAS > GALLICA

GALLICISE same as > GALLICIZE

GALLICISM n word or idiom borrowed from French

GALLICIZE vb make or become French in attitude, language, etc

GALLIED > GALLY

GALLIER > GALLY

GALLIES > GALLY

GALLIEST > GALLY

GALLINAZO n black vulture

GALLING adj annoying or bitterly humiliating

GALLINGLY > GALLING

GALLINULE n moorhen

GALLIOT same as > GALIOT

GALLIOTS > GALLIOT

GALLIPOT same as > GALIPOT

GALLIPOTS > GALLIPOT

GALLISE same as > GALLIZE

GALLISED > GALLISE

GALLISES > GALLISE

GALLISING > GALLISE

GALLISISE vb gallise

GALLISIZE same as > GALLISE

GALLIUM n soft grey metallic element

GALLIUMS > GALLIUM
GALLIVANT *vb* go about in search of pleasure
GALLIVAT *n* armed vessel formerly used in Asian waters
GALLIVATS > GALLIVAT
GALLIWASP *n* type of Central American lizard
GALLIZE *vb* add water and sugar to increase the quantity of wine produced
GALLIZED > GALLIZE
GALLIZES > GALLIZE
GALLIZING > GALLIZE
GALLNUT *n* type of plant gall that resembles a nut
GALLNUTS > GALLNUT
GALLOCK *adj* left-handed
GALLON *n* liquid measure of eight pints, equal to 4.55 litres
GALLONAGE *n* capacity measured in gallons
GALLONS > GALLON
GALLOON *n* narrow band of cord, gold braid, etc
GALLOONED > GALLOON
GALLOONS > GALLOON
GALLOOT *same as* > GALOOT
GALLOOTS > GALLOOT
GALLOP *n* horse's fastest pace ▷ *vb* go or ride at a gallop
GALLOPADE *n* gallop ▷ *vb* perform a gallopade
GALLOPED > GALLOP
GALLOPER > GALLOP
GALLOPERS > GALLOP
GALLOPING *adj* progressing at or as if at a gallop
GALLOPS > GALLOP
GALLOUS *adj* of or containing gallium in the divalent state
GALLOW *vb* frighten
GALLOWAY *n* breed of hornless beef cattle
GALLOWAYS > GALLOWAY
GALLOWED > GALLOW
GALLOWING > GALLOW
GALLOWS *n* wooden structure used for hanging criminals
GALLOWSES > GALLOWS
GALLS > GALL
GALLSTONE *n* hard mass formed in the gall bladder or its ducts
GALLUMPH *same as* > GALUMPH
GALLUMPHS > GALLUMPH
GALLUS *adj* bold
GALLUSED *adj* held up by galluses
GALLUSES *pl n* suspenders for trousers
GALLY *vb* frighten ▷ *adj* (of land) damp or barren
GALLYING > GALLY
GALOCHE *same as* > GALOSH
GALOCHED > GALOCHE

GALOCHES > GALOCHE
GALOCHING > GALOCHE
GALOOT *n* clumsy or uncouth person
GALOOTS > GALOOT
GALOP *n* 19th-century dance in quick duple time ▷ *vb* dance a galop
GALOPADE *same as* > GALOP
GALOPADES > GALOP
GALOPED > GALOP
GALOPIN *n* boy who ran errands for a cook
GALOPING > GALOP
GALOPINS > GALOPIN
GALOPPED > GALOP
GALOPPING > GALOP
GALOPS > GALOP
GALORE *adj* in abundance ▷ *n* abundance
GALORES > GALORE
GALOSH *n* waterproof overshoe ▷ *vb* cover with galoshes
GALOSHE *same as* > GALOSH
GALOSHED > GALOSH
GALOSHES > GALOSH
GALOSHING > GALOSH
GALOWSES *Shakespearean plural for* > GALLOWS
GALRAVAGE *same as* > GILRAVAGE
GALS > GAL
GALTONIA *n* type of bulbous plant with waxy white flowers and a fragrant scent
GALTONIAS > GALTONIA
GALUMPH *vb* leap or move about clumsily
GALUMPHED > GALUMPH
GALUMPHER > GALUMPH
GALUMPHS > GALUMPH
GALUT *same as* > GALUTH
GALUTH *n* exile of Jews from Palestine
GALUTHS > GALUTH
GALUTS > GALUT
GALVANIC *adj* of or producing an electric current generated by chemical means
GALVANISE *same as* > GALVANIZE
GALVANISM *n* electricity, esp when produced by chemical means as in a cell or battery
GALVANIST > GALVANISM
GALVANIZE *vb* stimulate into action ▷ *n* galvanized iron, usually in the form of corrugated sheets as used in roofing
GALVO *n* instrument for measuring electric current
GALVOS > GALVO
GALYAC *same as* > GALYAK
GALYACS > GALYAC
GALYAK *n* smooth glossy fur
GALYAKS > GALYAK

GAM *n* school of whales ▷ *vb* (of whales) form a school
GAMA *n* tall perennial grass
GAMAHUCHE *n* vulgar word for cunnilingus or fellatio ▷ *vb* practise cunnilingus or fellatio on
GAMARUCHE *same as* > GAMAHUCHE
GAMAS > GAMA
GAMASH *n* type of gaiter
GAMASHES > GAMASH
GAMAY *n* red grape variety
GAMAYS > GAMAY
GAMB *n* in heraldry, the whole foreleg of a beast
GAMBA *n* second-largest member of the viol family
GAMBADE *same as* > GAMBADO
GAMBADES > GAMBADE
GAMBADO *n* leap or gambol; caper ▷ *vb* perform a gambado
GAMBADOED > GAMBADO
GAMBADOES > GAMBADO
GAMBADOS > GAMBADO
GAMBAS > GAMBA
GAMBE *same as* > GAMB
GAMBES > GAMBE
GAMBESON *n* garment worn under mail in the Middle Ages
GAMBESONS > GAMBESON
GAMBET *n* tattler
GAMBETS > GAMBET
GAMBETTA *n* redshank
GAMBETTAS > GAMBETTA
GAMBIA *same as* > GAMBIER
GAMBIAS > GAMBIA
GAMBIER *n* astringent resinous substance
GAMBIERS > GAMBIER
GAMBIR *same as* > GAMBIER
GAMBIRS > GAMBIR
GAMBIST *n* person who plays the (viola da) gamba
GAMBISTS > GAMBIST
GAMBIT *n* opening move intended to secure an advantage ▷ *vb* sacrifice a chess piece to gain a better position
GAMBITED > GAMBIT
GAMBITING > GAMBIT
GAMBITS > GAMBIT
GAMBLE *vb* play games of chance to win money ▷ *n* risky undertaking
GAMBLED > GAMBLE
GAMBLER > GAMBLE
GAMBLERS > GAMBLE
GAMBLES > GAMBLE
GAMBLING > GAMBLE
GAMBLINGS > GAMBLE
GAMBO *n* farm cart
GAMBOES > GAMBO
GAMBOGE *n* gum resin
GAMBOGES > GAMBOGE
GAMBOGIAN > GAMBOGE
GAMBOGIC > GAMBOGE
GAMBOL *vb* jump about playfully, frolic ▷ *n* frolic

GAMBOLED > GAMBOL
GAMBOLING > GAMBOL
GAMBOLLED > GAMBOL
GAMBOLS > GAMBOL
GAMBOS > GAMBO
GAMBREL *n* hock of a horse or similar animal
GAMBRELS > GAMBREL
GAMBROON *n* type of linen cloth
GAMBROONS > GAMBROON
GAMBS > GAMB
GAMBUSIA *n* small fish that feeds on mosquito larvae
GAMBUSIAS > GAMBUSIA
GAME *n* amusement or pastime ▷ *vb* play games ▷ *adj* brave
GAMEBAG *n* bag for carrying hunted game birds
GAMEBAGS > GAMEBAG
GAMEBOOK *n* book containing a range of possible strategies for a game
GAMEBOOKS > GAMEBOOK
GAMECOCK *n* cock bred and trained for fighting
GAMECOCKS > GAMECOCK
GAMED > GAME
GAMEFISH *n* fish caught for sport
GAMEFOWL *n* cock bred for cockfighting
GAMEFOWLS > GAMEFOWL
GAMELAN *n* type of percussion orchestra
GAMELANS > GAMELAN
GAMELIKE > GAME
GAMELY *adv* in a brave or sporting manner
GAMENESS *n* courage or bravery
GAMEPLAY *n* plot of a computer or video game or the way that it is played
GAMEPLAYS > GAMEPLAY
GAMER *n* person who plays computer games
GAMERS > GAMER
GAMES > GAME
GAMESHOW *n* TV show in which games are played by contestants
GAMESHOWS > GAMESHOW
GAMESIER > GAMESY
GAMESIEST > GAMESY
GAMESMAN *n* one who practises gamesmanship
GAMESMEN > GAMESMAN
GAMESOME *adj* full of merriment
GAMEST > GAME
GAMESTER *n* someone who plays games
GAMESTERS > GAMESTER
GAMESY *adj* sporty
GAMETAL > GAMETE

g

GAMETE n reproductive cell

GAMETES > GAMETE

GAMETIC > GAMETE

GAMEY adj having the smell or flavour of game

GAMEYNESS n quality of being gamey

GAMGEE n as in gamgee tissue type of wound-dressing

GAMIC adj (esp of reproduction) requiring the fusion of gametes

GAMIER > GAMEY

GAMIEST > GAMEY

GAMIFIED > GAMIFY

GAMIFIES > GAMIFY

GAMIFY vb add gamelike elements to a task to encourage participation

GAMIFYING > GAMIFY

GAMILY > GAMEY

GAMIN n street urchin

GAMINE n slim boyish young woman

GAMINERIE n impish behaviour

GAMINES > GAMINE

GAMINESS > GAMEY

GAMING n playing games

GAMINGS > GAMING

GAMINS > GAMIN

GAMMA n third letter of the Greek alphabet

GAMMADIA > GAMMADION

GAMMADION n decorative figure composed of a number of Greek capital gammas, esp radiating from a centre, as in a swastika

GAMMAS > GAMMA

GAMMATIA > GAMMATION

GAMMATION same as > GAMMADION

GAMME n musical scale

GAMMED > GAM

GAMMER n dialect word for an old woman

GAMMERS > GAMMER

GAMMES > GAMME

GAMMIER > GAMMY

GAMMIEST > GAMMY

GAMMING > GAM

GAMMOCK vb clown around

GAMMOCKED > GAMMOCK

GAMMOCKS > GAMMOCK

GAMMON n cured or smoked ham ▷ vb score a double victory in backgammon over

GAMMONED > GAMMON

GAMMONER > GAMMON

GAMMONERS > GAMMON

GAMMONING > GAMMON

GAMMONS > GAMMON

GAMMY adj (of the leg) lame

GAMODEME n isolated breeding population

GAMODEMES > GAMODEME

GAMONE n chemical used by gametes

GAMONES > GAMONE

GAMP n umbrella

GAMPISH adj bulging

GAMPS > GAMP

GAMS > GAM

GAMUT n whole range or scale (of music, emotions, etc)

GAMUTS > GAMUT

GAMY same as > GAMEY

GAMYNESS > GAMY

GAN vb go

GANACHE n rich icing or filling

GANACHES > GANACHE

GANCH vb impale

GANCHED > GANCH

GANCHES > GANCH

GANCHING > GANCH

GANDER n male goose ▷ vb look

GANDERED > GANDER

GANDERING > GANDER

GANDERISM > GANDER

GANDERS > GANDER

GANDY adj as in gandy dancer railway track maintenance worker

GANE > GO

GANEF n unscrupulous opportunist

GANEFS > GANEF

GANEV same as > GANEF

GANEVS > GANEV

GANG n (criminal) group ▷ vb become or act as a gang

GANGBANG n sexual intercourse with several men one after the other ▷ vb force to take part in a gangbang

GANGBANGS > GANGBANG

GANGBO n order restricting the activities of a gang member

GANGBOARD n gangway

GANGBOS > GANGBO

GANGED > GANG

GANGER n foreman of a gang of labourers

GANGERS > GANGER

GANGING > GANG

GANGINGS > GANG

GANGLAND n criminal underworld

GANGLANDS > GANGLAND

GANGLE vb move awkwardly

GANGLED > GANGLE

GANGLES > GANGLE

GANGLIA > GANGLION

GANGLIAL > GANGLION

GANGLIAR > GANGLION

GANGLIATE vb form a ganglion

GANGLIER > GANGLY

GANGLIEST > GANGLY

GANGLING adj lanky and awkward

GANGLION n group of nerve cells

GANGLIONS > GANGLION

GANGLY same as > GANGLING

GANGPLANK n portable bridge for boarding or leaving a ship

GANGPLOW n plough designed to produce parallel furrows

GANGPLOWS > GANGPLOW

GANGREL n wandering beggar

GANGRELS > GANGREL

GANGRENE n decay of body tissue as a result of disease or injury ▷ vb become or cause to become affected with gangrene

GANGRENED > GANGRENE

GANGRENES > GANGRENE

GANGS > GANG

GANGSHAG vb participate in group sex with

GANGSHAGS > GANGSHAG

GANGSMAN n foreman

GANGSMEN > GANGSMAN

GANGSTA n member of a street gang

GANGSTAS > GANGSTA

GANGSTER n member of a criminal gang

GANGSTERS > GANGSTER

GANGUE n valueless material in an ore

GANGUES > GANGUE

GANGWAY same as > GANGPLANK

GANGWAYS > GANGWAY

GANISTER n type of sedimentary rock

GANISTERS > GANISTER

GANJA n highly potent form of cannabis

GANJAH same as > GANJA

GANJAHS > GANJAH

GANJAS > GANJA

GANNED > GAN

GANNET n large sea bird

GANNETRY n gannets' breeding-place

GANNETS > GANNET

GANNING > GAN

GANNISTER same as > GANISTER

GANOF same as > GANEF

GANOFS > GANOF

GANOID adj of the scales of certain fishes ▷ n ganoid fish

GANOIDS > GANOID

GANOIN n outer layer of fish scales

GANOINE same as > GANOIN

GANOINES > GANOINE

GANOINS > GANOIN

GANS > GAN

GANSEY n jersey or pullover

GANSEYS > GANSEY

GANT vb yawn

GANTED > GANT

GANTELOPE same as > GAUNTLET

GANTING > GANT

GANTLET n section of a railway where two tracks overlap ▷ vb make railway tracks form a gantlet

GANTLETED > GANTLET

GANTLETS > GANTLET

GANTLINE n line rove through a sheave for hoisting men or gear

GANTLINES > GANTLINE

GANTLOPE same as > GAUNTLET

GANTLOPES > GANTLOPE

GANTRIES > GANTRY

GANTRY n structure supporting something

GANTS > GANT

GANYMEDE n potboy

GANYMEDES > GANYMEDE

GANZFELD n type of experiment used in parapsychology

GANZFELDS > GANZFELD

GAOL same as > JAIL

GAOLBIRD n person who is or has been confined to gaol, esp repeatedly

GAOLBIRDS > GAOLBIRD

GAOLBREAK less common spelling of > JAILBREAK

GAOLBROKE > GAOLBREAK

GAOLED > GAOL

GAOLER > GAOL

GAOLERESS n female gaoler

GAOLERS > GAOL

GAOLING > GAOL

GAOLLESS adj without a gaol

GAOLS > GAOL

GAP n break or opening

GAPE vb stare in wonder ▷ n act of gaping

GAPED > GAPE

GAPER n person or thing that gapes

GAPERS > GAPER

GAPES n disease of young domestic fowl

GAPESEED n person who stares, mouth agape, at something

GAPESEEDS > GAPESEED

GAPEWORM n type of parasitic worm that lives in the trachea of birds

GAPEWORMS > GAPEWORM

GAPIER > GAPE

GAPIEST > GAPE

GAPING adj wide open ▷ n state of having a gaping mouth

GAPINGLY > GAPING

GAPINGS > GAPING

GAPLESS > GAP

GAPO n (in S America) forest near a river

GAPOS > GAPO

GAPOSIS n gap between closed fastenings on a garment
GAPOSISES >GAPOSIS
GAPPED >GAP
GAPPER n person taking a year out of education
GAPPERS >GAPPER
GAPPIER >GAP
GAPPIEST >GAP
GAPPING n the act of taking a gap year
GAPPINGS >GAPPING
GAPPY >GAP
GAPS >GAP
GAPY >GAPE
GAR vb Scots word meaning compel
GARAGE n building used to house cars ▷ vb put or keep a car in a garage
GARAGED >GARAGE
GARAGEMAN n car mechanic
GARAGEMEN
 >GARAGEMAN
GARAGES >GARAGE
GARAGEY adj (of music) in a garage style
GARAGIER >GARAGEY
GARAGIEST >GARAGEY
GARAGING n accommodation for housing a motor vehicle
GARAGINGS
 >GARAGING
GARAGIST n person who runs a garage
GARAGISTE n small-scale wine-maker
GARAGISTS
 >GARAGIST
GARB n clothes ▷ vb clothe
GARBAGE n rubbish
GARBAGES >GARBAGE
GARBAGEY >GARBAGE
GARBAGIER >GARBAGY
GARBAGY adj like garbage
GARBANZO another name for >CHICKPEA
GARBANZOS
 >GARBANZO
GARBE n in heraldry, a wheat-sheaf
GARBED >GARB
GARBES >GARBE
GARBING >GARB
GARBLE vb jumble (a story, quotation, etc), esp unintentionally ▷ n act of garbling
GARBLED adj (of a story etc) jumbled and confused
GARBLER >GARBLE
GARBLERS >GARBLE
GARBLES >GARBLE
GARBLESS >GARB
GARBLING >GARBLE
GARBLINGS >GARBLE
GARBO n dustman
GARBOARD n bottommost plank of a vessel's hull
GARBOARDS
 >GARBOARD
GARBOIL n confusion or disturbance

GARBOILS >GARBOIL
GARBOLOGY n study of the contents of domestic dustbins to analyse the consumption patterns of households
GARBOS >GARBO
GARBS >GARB
GARBURE n thick soup from France
GARBURES >GARBURE
GARCINIA n tropical tree
GARCINIAS
 >GARCINIA
GARCON n waiter
GARCONS >GARCON
GARDA n member of the Irish police force
GARDAI >GARDA
GARDANT same as >GUARDANT
GARDANTS >GARDANT
GARDEN n piece of land for growing flowers, fruit, or vegetables ▷ vb cultivate a garden
GARDENED >GARDEN
GARDENER n person who works in or takes care of a garden as an occupation or pastime
GARDENERS
 >GARDENER
GARDENFUL n quantity that will fill a garden
GARDENIA n large fragrant white waxy flower
GARDENIAS
 >GARDENIA
GARDENING n planning and cultivation of a garden
GARDENS >GARDEN
GARDEROBE n wardrobe or the contents of a wardrobe
GARDYLOO n act of throwing slops from a window
GARDYLOOS
 >GARDYLOO
GARE n filth ▷ adj greedy; covetous
GAREFOWL n great auk
GAREFOWLS
 >GAREFOWL
GARES >GARE
GARFISH same as >GARPIKE
GARFISHES >GARFISH
GARGANEY n small Eurasian duck, closely related to the mallard
GARGANEYS
 >GARGANEY
GARGANTUA n monster in Japanese film
GARGARISE vb gargle
GARGARISM n gargle
GARGARIZE same as >GARGARISE
GARGET n inflammation of the mammary gland
GARGETS >GARGET
GARGETY >GARGET
GARGLE vb wash the throat ▷ n liquid used for gargling

GARGLED >GARGLE
GARGLER >GARGLE
GARGLERS >GARGLE
GARGLES >GARGLE
GARGLING >GARGLE
GARGOYLE n waterspout carved in the form of a grotesque face, esp on a church ▷ vb provide with gargoyles
GARGOYLED >GARGOYLE
GARGOYLES
 >GARGOYLE
GARI n thinly sliced pickled ginger
GARIAL same as >GAVIAL
GARIALS >GARIAL
GARIBALDI n loose blouse with long sleeves popular in the 1860s
GARIGUE n open shrubby vegetation of dry Mediterranean regions
GARIGUES >GARIGUE
GARIS >GARI
GARISH adj crudely bright or colourful ▷ vb heal
GARISHED >GARISH
GARISHES >GARISH
GARISHING >GARISH
GARISHLY >GARISH
GARJAN same as >GURJUN
GARJANS >GARJAN
GARLAND n wreath of flowers worn or hung as a decoration ▷ vb decorate with garlands
GARLANDED >GARLAND
GARLANDRY n collective term for garlands
GARLANDS >GARLAND
GARLIC n pungent bulb of a plant of the onion family
GARLICKED adj flavoured with garlic
GARLICKY adj containing or resembling the taste or odour of garlic
GARLICS >GARLIC
GARMENT n article of clothing ▷ vb cover or clothe
GARMENTED >GARMENT
GARMENTS >GARMENT
GARMS pl n clothing
GARNER vb collect or store ▷ n place for storage or safekeeping
GARNERED >GARNER
GARNERING >GARNER
GARNERS >GARNER
GARNET n red semiprecious stone
GARNETS >GARNET
GARNI adj garnished
GARNISH vb decorate (food) ▷ n decoration for food
GARNISHED >GARNISH
GARNISHEE n person upon whom a notice of warning has been served ▷ vb attach (a debt or other property) by a notice of warning

GARNISHER >GARNISH
GARNISHES >GARNISH
GARNISHOR n person who or thing that garnishes
GARNISHRY n decoration
GARNITURE n decoration or embellishment
GAROTE same as >GARROTTE
GAROTED >GAROTE
GAROTES >GAROTE
GAROTING >GAROTE
GAROTTE same as >GARROTTE
GAROTTED >GAROTTE
GAROTTER >GAROTTE
GAROTTERS >GAROTTE
GAROTTES >GAROTTE
GAROTTING >GAROTTE
GAROUPA same as >GROPER
GAROUPAS >GAROUPA
GARPIKE n primitive freshwater bony fish
GARPIKES >GARPIKE
GARRAN same as >GARRON
GARRANS >GARRAN
GARRE vb compel
GARRED >GAR
GARRES >GARRE
GARRET n attic in a house
GARRETED adj living in a garret
GARRETEER n person who lives in a garret
GARRETS >GARRET
GARRIGUE same as >GARIGUE
GARRIGUES
 >GARRIGUE
GARRING >GAR
GARRISON n troops stationed in a town or fort ▷ vb station troops in
GARRISONS
 >GARRISON
GARRON n small sturdy pony
GARRONS >GARRON
GARROT n goldeneye duck
GARROTE same as >GARROTTE
GARROTED >GARROTE
GARROTER >GARROTE
GARROTERS >GARROTE
GARROTES >GARROTE
GARROTING >GARROTE
GARROTS >GARROT
GARROTTE n Spanish method of execution by strangling ▷ vb kill by this method
GARROTTED
 >GARROTTE
GARROTTER
 >GARROTTE
GARROTTES
 >GARROTTE
GARRULITY
 >GARRULOUS
GARRULOUS adj talkative
GARRYA n catkin-bearing evergreen shrub
GARRYAS >GARRYA
GARRYOWEN n (in rugby union) high kick forwards

followed by a charge to the place where the ball lands

GARS > GAR

GART *a past tense of* > GAR

GARTER *n* band used to hold up a sock or stocking ▷ *vb* secure with a garter

GARTERED > GARTER

GARTERING > GARTER

GARTERS > GARTER

GARTH *n* courtyard surrounded by a cloister

GARTHS > GARTH

GARUDA *n* Hindu god

GARUDAS > GARUDA

GARUM *n* fermented fish sauce

GARUMS > GARUM

GARVEY *n* small flat-bottomed yacht

GARVEYS > GARVEY

GARVIE *n* sprat

GARVIES > GARVIE

GARVOCK *n* sprat

GARVOCKS > GARVOCK

GAS *n* airlike substance that is not liquid or solid ▷ *vb* poison or render unconscious with gas

GASAHOL *n* mixture of petrol and alcohol used as fuel

GASAHOLS > GASAHOL

GASALIER *same as* > GASOLIER

GASALIERS > GASALIER

GASBAG *n* person who talks too much ▷ *vb* talk in a voluble way

GASBAGGED > GASBAG

GASBAGS > GASBAG

GASCON *n* boaster

GASCONADE *n* boastful talk, bragging, or bluster ▷ *vb* boast, brag, or bluster

GASCONISM > GASCON

GASCONS > GASCON

GASEITIES > GASEITY

GASEITY *n* state of being gaseous

GASELIER *same as* > GASOLIER

GASELIERS > GASELIER

GASEOUS *adj* of or like gas

GASES > GAS

GASFIELD *n* area in which natural gas is found underground

GASFIELDS > GASFIELD

GASH *vb* make a long deep cut in ▷ *n* long deep cut ▷ *adj* witty

GASHED > GASH

GASHER > GASH

GASHES > GASH

GASHEST > GASH

GASHFUL *adj* full of gashes

GASHING > GASH

GASHLIER > GASHLY

GASHLIEST > GASHLY

GASHLY *adv* wittily ▷ *adj* hideous; ghastly

GASHOLDER *n* large tank for storing gas

GASHOUSE *n* gasworks

GASHOUSES > GASHOUSE

GASIFIED > GASIFY

GASIFIER > GASIFY

GASIFIERS > GASIFY

GASIFIES > GASIFY

GASIFORM *adj* in a gaseous form

GASIFY *vb* change into a gas

GASIFYING > GASIFY

GASKET *n* type of seal

GASKETED *adj* having a gasket

GASKETS > GASKET

GASKIN *n* lower part of a horse's thigh

GASKING *same as* > GASKIN

GASKINGS > GASKING

GASKINS > GASKIN

GASLESS > GAS

GASLIGHT *vb* manipulate (a person) by presenting them with lies until they doubt their sanity

GASLIGHTS > GASLIGHT

GASLIT *adj* lit by gas

GASMAN *n* man employed by a gas company

GASMEN > GASMAN

GASOGENE *n* siphon bottle

GASOGENES > GASOGENE

GASOHOL *n* mixture of petrol and alcohol used as fuel

GASOHOLS > GASOHOL

GASOLENE *same as* > GASOLINE

GASOLENES > GASOLENE

GASOLIER *n* branched hanging fitting for gaslights

GASOLIERS > GASOLIER

GASOLINE *n* petrol

GASOLINES > GASOLINE

GASOLINIC > GASOLINE

GASOMETER *same as* > GASHOLDER

GASOMETRY *n* measurement of quantities of gases

GASP *vb* draw in breath sharply or with difficulty ▷ *n* convulsive intake of breath

GASPED > GASP

GASPER *n* person who gasps

GASPEREAU *another name for* > ALEWIFE

GASPERS > GASPER

GASPIER > GASP

GASPIEST > GASP

GASPINESS > GASP

GASPING > GASP

GASPINGLY > GASP

GASPINGS > GASP

GASPS > GASP

GASPY > GASP

GASSED > GAS

GASSER *n* drilling or well that yields natural gas

GASSERS > GASSER

GASSES > GAS

GASSIER > GASSY

GASSIEST > GASSY

GASSILY > GASSY

GASSINESS > GASSY

GASSING > GAS

GASSINGS > GAS

GASSY *adj* filled with gas

GAST *vb* old word for frighten

GASTED > GAST

GASTER *vb* old word for frighten

GASTERED > GASTER

GASTERING > GASTER

GASTERS > GASTER

GASTFULL *adj* dismal

GASTHAUS *n* guest house

GASTIGHT *adj* not allowing gas to enter or escape

GASTING > GAST

GASTNESS *n* dread

GASTNESSE *same as* > GASTNESS

GASTRAEA *n* hypothetical primeval form posited by Haeckel

GASTRAEAS > GASTRAEA

GASTRAEUM *n* underside of the body

GASTRAL *adj* relating to the stomach

GASTREA *same as* > GASTRAEA

GASTREAS > GASTREA

GASTRIC *adj* of the stomach

GASTRIN *n* polypeptide hormone

GASTRINS > GASTRIN

GASTRITIC > GASTRITIS

GASTRITIS *n* inflammation of the stomach lining

GASTROPOD *n* type of mollusc, such as a snail, with a single flattened muscular foot

GASTROPUB *n* pub specializing in high-quality food

GASTRULA *n* saclike animal embryo

GASTRULAE > GASTRULA

GASTRULAR > GASTRULA

GASTRULAS > GASTRULA

GASTS > GAST

GASWORKS *n* plant where coal gas is made

GAT *n* pistol or revolver

GATCH *vb* behave boastfully

GATCHED > GATCH

GATCHER *n* person who boasts

GATCHERS > GATCHER

GATCHES > GATCH

GATCHING > GATCH

GATE *n* movable barrier, usu hinged, in a wall or fence ▷ *vb* provide with a gate or gates

GATEAU *n* rich elaborate cake

GATEAUS > GATEAU

GATEAUX > GATEAU

GATECRASH *vb* gain entry to (a party, concert, etc) without invitation or payment

GATED > GATE

GATEFOLD *n* oversize page in a book or magazine that is folded in

GATEFOLDS > GATEFOLD

GATEHOUSE *n* building at or above a gateway

GATELEG *n* table having hinged legs that swing out

GATELEGS > GATELEG

GATELESS > GATE

GATELIKE > GATE

GATEMAN *n* gatekeeper

GATEMEN > GATEMAN

GATEPOST *n* post on which a gate is hung

GATEPOSTS > GATEPOST

GATER *variant of* > GATOR

GATERS > GATER

GATES > GATE

GATEWAY *n* entrance with a gate

GATEWAYS > GATEWAY

GATH *n* (in Indian music) second section of a raga

GATHER *vb* assemble ▷ *n* act of gathering

GATHERED > GATHER

GATHERER > GATHER

GATHERERS > GATHER

GATHERING *n* assembly

GATHERS > GATHER

GATHS > GATH

GATING > GATE

GATINGS > GATING

GATLING *n* as in *gatling gun* kind of machine-gun

GATOR *short form of* > ALLIGATOR

GATORS > GATOR

GATS > GAT

GATVOL *adj* in South African English, fed up

GAU *n* district set up by the Nazi Party

GAUCH *vb* behave boastfully

GAUCHE *adj* socially awkward ▷ *vb* make gauche

GAUCHED > GAUCHE

GAUCHELY > GAUCHE

GAUCHER *n* gauche person

GAUCHERIE *n* quality of being gauche

GAUCHERS > GAUCHER

GAUCHES > GAUCHE

GAUCHESCO *adj* relating to the folk traditions of the gauchos

GAUCHEST > GAUCHE

GAUCHING > GAUCHE

GAUCHO *n* S American cowboy
GAUCHOS > GAUCHO
GAUCIE *variant of* > GAUCY
GAUCIER > GAUCY
GAUCIEST > GAUCY
GAUCY *adj* plump or jolly
GAUD *n* article of cheap finery ▷ *vb* decorate gaudily
GAUDEAMUS *n* first word of a traditional graduation song, hence the song itself
GAUDED > GAUD
GAUDERIES > GAUDERY
GAUDERY *n* cheap finery or display
GAUDGIE *same as* > GADGIE
GAUDGIES > GAUDGIE
GAUDIER > GAUDY
GAUDIES > GAUDY
GAUDIEST > GAUDY
GAUDILY > GAUDY
GAUDINESS > GAUDY
GAUDING > GAUD
GAUDS > GAUD
GAUDY *adj* vulgarly bright or colourful ▷ *n* festival held at some schools and colleges
GAUFER *n* wafer
GAUFERS > GAUFER
GAUFFER *same as* > GOFFER
GAUFFERED > GAUFFER
GAUFFERS > GAUFFER
GAUFRE *same as* > GAUFER
GAUFRES > GAUFRE
GAUGE *vb* estimate or judge ▷ *n* measuring instrument ▷ *adj* of a pressure measurement
GAUGEABLE > GAUGE
GAUGEABLY > GAUGE
GAUGED > GAUGE
GAUGER *n* person or thing that gauges
GAUGERS > GAUGER
GAUGES > GAUGE
GAUGING > GAUGE
GAUGINGS > GAUGE
GAUJE *same as* > GADGIE
GAUJES > GAUJE
GAULEITER *n* person in a position of authority who behaves in an overbearing authoritarian manner
GAULT *n* stiff compact clay or thick heavy clayey soil
GAULTER *n* person who digs gault
GAULTERS > GAULTER
GAULTS > GAULT
GAUM *vb* understand
GAUMED > GAUM
GAUMIER > GAUMY
GAUMIEST > GAUMY
GAUMING > GAUM
GAUMLESS *variant spelling of* > GORMLESS
GAUMS > GAUM
GAUMY *adj* clogged
GAUN > GO
GAUNCH *same as* > GANCH

GAUNCHED > GAUNCH
GAUNCHES > GAUNCH
GAUNCHING > GAUNCH
GAUNT *adj* lean and haggard ▷ *vb* yawn
GAUNTED > GAUNT
GAUNTER > GAUNT
GAUNTEST > GAUNT
GAUNTING > GAUNT
GAUNTLET *n* heavy glove with a long cuff ▷ *vb* run (or cause to run) the gauntlet
GAUNTLETS > GAUNTLET
GAUNTLY > GAUNT
GAUNTNESS > GAUNT
GAUNTREE *same as* > GANTRY
GAUNTREES > GAUNTREE
GAUNTRIES > GAUNTRY
GAUNTRY *same as* > GANTRY
GAUNTS > GAUNT
GAUP *same as* > GAWP
GAUPED > GAUP
GAUPER > GAUP
GAUPERS > GAUP
GAUPING > GAUP
GAUPS > GAUP
GAUPUS *same as* > GAWPUS
GAUPUSES > GAUPUS
GAUR *n* large wild member of the cattle tribe
GAURS > GAUR
GAUS > GAU
GAUSS *n* unit of magnetic flux density
GAUSSES > GAUSS
GAUSSIAN *adj* denoting the mathematical principles of K F Gauss
GAUZE *n* transparent loosely woven fabric
GAUZELIKE > GAUZE
GAUZES > GAUZE
GAUZIER > GAUZY
GAUZIEST > GAUZY
GAUZILY > GAUZY
GAUZINESS > GAUZY
GAUZY *adj* resembling gauze
GAVAGE *n* forced feeding by means of a tube
GAVAGES > GAVAGE
GAVE > GIVE
GAVEL *n* small hammer banged on a table ▷ *vb* use a gavel to restore order
GAVELED > GAVEL
GAVELING > GAVEL
GAVELKIND *n* former system of land tenure peculiar to Kent based on the payment of rent to the lord instead of the performance of services by the tenant
GAVELLED > GAVEL
GAVELLING > GAVEL
GAVELMAN *n* gavelkind tenant
GAVELMEN > GAVELMAN
GAVELOCK *n* iron crowbar
GAVELOCKS > GAVELOCK

GAVELS > GAVEL
GAVIAL *n* as in *false gavial* small crocodile
GAVIALOID *adj* of or like gavials
GAVIALS > GAVIAL
GAVOT *same as* > GAVOTTE
GAVOTS > GAVOT
GAVOTTE *n* old formal dance ▷ *vb* dance a gavotte
GAVOTTED > GAVOTTE
GAVOTTES > GAVOTTE
GAVOTTING > GAVOTTE
GAW *n* as in *weather gaw* partial rainbow
GAWCIER > GAWCY
GAWCIEST > GAWCY
GAWCY *same as* > GAUCY
GAWD *same as* > GAUD
GAWDS > GAWD
GAWK *vb* stare stupidly
GAWKED > GAWK
GAWKER > GAWK
GAWKERS > GAWK
GAWKIER > GAWKY
GAWKIES > GAWKY
GAWKIEST > GAWKY
GAWKIHOOD *n* state of being gawky
GAWKILY > GAWKY
GAWKINESS > GAWKY
GAWKING > GAWK
GAWKISH *same as* > GAWKY
GAWKISHLY > GAWKY
GAWKS > GAWK
GAWKY *adj* clumsy or awkward ▷ *n* clumsy or awkward person
GAWMOGE *n* clownish person
GAWMOGES > GAWMOGE
GAWP *vb* stare stupidly
GAWPED > GAWP
GAWPER > GAWP
GAWPERS > GAWP
GAWPING > GAWP
GAWPS > GAWP
GAWPUS *n* silly person
GAWPUSES > GAWPUS
GAWS > GAW
GAWSIE *same as* > GAUCY
GAWSIER > GAWSIE
GAWSIEST > GAWSIE
GAWSY *same as* > GAUCY
GAY *adj* carefree and merry ▷ *n* homosexual person
GAYAL *n* type of ox
GAYALS > GAYAL
GAYCATION *n* holiday designed for the gay market
GAYDAR *n* supposed ability to recognize if another person is gay
GAYDARS > GAYDAR
GAYER > GAY
GAYEST > GAY
GAYETIES > GAYETY
GAYETY *same as* > GAIETY
GAYLY > GAY
GAYNESS > GAY
GAYNESSES > GAY
GAYS > GAY

GAYSOME *adj* full of merriment
GAYWINGS *n* flowering wintergreen
GAZABO *n* fellow or companion
GAZABOES > GAZABO
GAZABOS > GAZABO
GAZAL *same as* > GHAZAL
GAZALS > GAZAL
GAZANG *vb* inconvenience a buyer by declining to sell a house just before the purchase is completed
GAZANGED > GAZANG
GAZANGING > GAZANG
GAZANGS > GAZANG
GAZANIA *n* S African plant
GAZANIAS > GAZANIA
GAZAR *n* type of silk cloth
GAZARS > GAZAR
GAZE *vb* look fixedly ▷ *n* fixed look
GAZEBO *n* summerhouse with a good view
GAZEBOES > GAZEBO
GAZEBOS > GAZEBO
GAZED > GAZE
GAZEFUL *adj* gazing
GAZEHOUND *n* hound such as a greyhound that hunts by sight rather than by scent
GAZELLE *n* small graceful antelope
GAZELLES > GAZELLE
GAZEMENT *n* view
GAZEMENTS > GAZEMENT
GAZER > GAZE
GAZERS > GAZE
GAZES > GAZE
GAZETTE *n* official publication containing announcements ▷ *vb* announce or report (facts or an event) in a gazette
GAZETTED > GAZETTE
GAZETTEER *n* (part of) a book that lists and describes places ▷ *vb* list in a gazetteer
GAZETTES > GAZETTE
GAZETTING > GAZETTE
GAZIER > GAZY
GAZIEST > GAZY
GAZILLION *n* in informal English, an extremely large but unspecified number, quantity, or amount
GAZING > GAZE
GAZINGS > GAZE
GAZOGENE *same as* > GASOGENE
GAZOGENES > GAZOGENE
GAZON *n* sod used to cover a parapet in a fortification
GAZONS > GAZON
GAZOO *n* kazoo
GAZOOKA *same as* > GAZOO
GAZOOKAS > GAZOOKA
GAZOON *same as* > GAZON
GAZOONS > GAZOON
GAZOOS > GAZOO

g

g

GAZPACHO n Spanish soup made from tomatoes, peppers, etc, and served cold
GAZPACHOS > GAZPACHO
GAZUMP vb raise the price of a property after verbally agreeing it with (a prospective buyer) ▷ n act or an instance of gazumping
GAZUMPED > GAZUMP
GAZUMPER > GAZUMP
GAZUMPERS > GAZUMP
GAZUMPING n act of gazumping
GAZUMPS > GAZUMP
GAZUNDER vb reduce an offer on a property immediately before purchase ▷ n act or instance of gazundering
GAZUNDERS > GAZUNDER
GAZY adj prone to gazing
GEAL vb congeal
GEALED > GEAL
GEALING > GEAL
GEALOUS Spenserian spelling of > JEALOUS
GEALOUSY Spenserian spelling of > JEALOUSY
GEALS > GEAL
GEAN n white-flowered tree
GEANS > GEAN
GEAR n set of toothed wheels used to change direction or speed ▷ vb prepare or organize for something
GEARBOX n case enclosing a set of gears in a motor vehicle
GEARBOXES > GEARBOX
GEARCASE n protective casing for gears
GEARCASES > GEARCASE
GEARE Spenserian spelling of > JEER
GEARED > GEAR
GEARES > GEARE
GEARHEAD n part in engine gear system
GEARHEADS > GEARHEAD
GEARING n system of gears designed to transmit motion
GEARINGS > GEARING
GEARLESS > GEAR
GEARS > GEAR
GEARSHIFT n lever used to move gearwheels relative to each other, esp in a motor vehicle
GEARSTICK n lever used to move gear wheels in a motor vehicle
GEARWHEEL n one of the toothed wheels in the gears of a motor vehicle
GEASON adj wonderful
GEAT n in casting, the channel which leads to a mould
GEATS > GEAT

GEBUR n tenant farmer
GEBURS > GEBUR
GECK vb beguile
GECKED > GECK
GECKING > GECK
GECKO n small tropical lizard
GECKOES > GECKO
GECKOS > GECKO
GECKS > GECK
GED Scots word for > PIKE
GEDACT n flutelike stopped metal diapason organ pipe
GEDACTS > GEDACT
GEDDIT interj exclamation meaning do you understand it?
GEDECKT same as > GEDACT
GEDECKTS > GEDECKT
GEDS > GED
GEE interj mild exclamation of surprise, admiration, etc ▷ vb move (an animal, esp a horse) ahead
GEEBAG n in Irish slang, a disagreeable woman
GEEBAGS > GEEBAG
GEEBUNG n Australian tree or shrub
GEEBUNGS > GEEBUNG
GEECHEE n speaker of a dialect found in an area of the southern US
GEECHEES > GEECHEE
GEED > GEE
GEEGAW same as > GEWGAW
GEEGAWS > GEEGAW
GEEING > GEE
GEEK n person skilled in a specific subject
GEEKDOM > GEEK
GEEKDOMS > GEEK
GEEKED adj highly excited
GEEKERIES > GEEKERY
GEEKERY n preoccupation with, or great knowledge about, a specialized subject
GEEKIER > GEEKY
GEEKIEST > GEEKY
GEEKINESS > GEEK
GEEKISH adj of or like a geek
GEEKISM n preoccupation with subjects generally considered unfashionable or boring
GEEKISMS > GEEKISM
GEEKS > GEEK
GEEKSPEAK n slang word for jargon used by geeks, esp computer enthusiasts
GEEKY adj of or like a geek
GEELBEK n edible marine fish
GEELBEKS > GEELBEK
GEEP n cross between a goat and a sheep
GEEPOUND another name for > SLUG
GEEPOUNDS > GEEPOUND

GEEPS > GEEP
GEES > GEE
GEESE > GOOSE
GEEST n area of heathland in N Germany and adjacent areas
GEESTS > GEEST
GEEZ interj expression of surprise
GEEZAH variant spelling of > GEEZER
GEEZAHS > GEEZAH
GEEZER n man
GEEZERS > GEEZER
GEFILTE adj as in gefilte fish dish of fish stuffed with various ingredients
GEFUFFLE same as > KERFUFFLE
GEFUFFLED > GEFUFFLE
GEFUFFLES > GEFUFFLE
GEFULLTE adj as in gefullte fish dish of fish stuffed with various ingredients
GEGGIE Scottish slang word for > MOUTH
GEGGIES > GEGGIE
GEHLENITE n green mineral consisting of calcium aluminium silicate in tetragonal crystalline form
GEISHA n (in Japan) professional female companion for men
GEISHAS > GEISHA
GEIST n spirit
GEISTS > GEIST
GEIT n border on clothing ▷ vb put a border on (an article of clothing)
GEITED > GEIT
GEITING > GEIT
GEITS > GEIT
GEL n jelly-like substance ▷ vb form a gel
GELABLE adj capable of forming a gel
GELADA n NE African baboon
GELADAS > GELADA
GELANDE adj as in gelande jump jump made in downhill skiing
GELANT same as > GELLANT
GELANTS > GELANT
GELASTIC adj relating to laughter
GELATE vb form a gel
GELATED > GELATE
GELATES > GELATE
GELATI n layered dessert
GELATIN same as > GELATINE
GELATINE n substance made by boiling animal bones
GELATINES > GELATINE
GELATING > GELATE
GELATINS > GELATIN
GELATION n act or process of freezing a liquid
GELATIONS > GELATION

GELATIS > GELATI
GELATO n Italian ice cream
GELATOS > GELATO
GELCAP n medicine enclosed in gelatine
GELCAPS > GELCAP
GELCOAT n thin layer of gel or resin applied to a surface
GELCOATS > GELCOAT
GELD vb emasculate; weaken ▷ n tax on land in Anglo-Saxon and Norman England
GELDED > GELD
GELDER > GELD
GELDERS > GELD
GELDING > GELD
GELDINGS > GELD
GELDS > GELD
GELEE n jelly
GELEES > GELEE
GELID adj very cold, icy, or frosty
GELIDER > GELID
GELIDEST > GELID
GELIDITY > GELID
GELIDLY > GELID
GELIDNESS > GELID
GELIGNITE n type of dynamite used for blasting
GELLANT n substance that causes gelling
GELLANTS > GELLANT
GELLED > GEL
GELLIES > GELLY
GELLING > GEL
GELLY same as > GELIGNITE
GELOSIES > GELOSY
GELOSY Spenserian spelling of > JEALOUSY
GELS > GEL
GELSEMIA > GELSEMIUM
GELSEMINE n alkaloid obtained from gelsemium
GELSEMIUM n type of climbing shrub of SE Asia and North America, esp the yellow jasmine
GELT n money
GELTS > GELT
GEM n precious stone or jewel ▷ vb set or ornament with gems
GEMATRIA n numerology of the Hebrew language and alphabet
GEMATRIAS > GEMATRIA
GEMCLIP n paperclip
GEMCLIPS > GEMCLIP
GEMEL n in heraldry, either of a pair of parallel bars
GEMELS > GEMEL
GEMFISH n Australian food fish with a delicate flavour
GEMFISHES > GEMFISH
GEMINAL adj occurring in pairs
GEMINALLY > GEMINAL
GEMINATE adj combined in pairs ▷ vb arrange or be arranged in pairs

GEMINATED
> GEMINATE

GEMINATES
> GEMINATE

GEMINI n expression of surprise

GEMINIES > GEMINY

GEMINOUS adj in pairs

GEMINY n pair

GEMLIKE > GEM

GEMMA n reproductive structure in liverworts, mosses, etc

GEMMAE > GEMMA

GEMMAN dialect form of > GENTLEMAN

GEMMATE adj (of some plants and animals) having gemmae ▷ vb produce or reproduce by gemmae

GEMMATED > GEMMATE

GEMMATES > GEMMATE

GEMMATING > GEMMATE

GEMMATION > GEMMATE

GEMMATIVE adj relating to gemmation

GEMMED > GEM

GEMMEN > GEMMAN

GEMMEOUS adj gem-like

GEMMERIES > GEMMERY

GEMMERY n gems collectively

GEMMIER > GEM

GEMMIEST > GEM

GEMMILY > GEM

GEMMINESS > GEM

GEMMING > GEM

GEMMOLOGY same as > GEMOLOGY

GEMMULE n bud

GEMMULES > GEMMULE

GEMMY > GEM

GEMOLOGY n branch of mineralogy that is concerned with gems and gemstones

GEMONY same as > JIMINY

GEMOT n (in Anglo-Saxon England) a legal or administrative assembly

GEMOTE same as > GEMOT

GEMOTES > GEMOTE

GEMOTS > GEMOT

GEMS > GEM

GEMSBOK same as > ORYX

GEMSBOKS > GEMSBOK

GEMSBUCK same as > ORYX

GEMSBUCKS > GEMSBUCK

GEMSHORN n type of medieval flute

GEMSHORNS > GEMSHORN

GEMSTONE n precious or semiprecious stone, esp one which has been cut and polished

GEMSTONES > GEMSTONE

GEMUTLICH adj having a feeling or atmosphere of warmth and friendliness

GEN n information ▷ vb gain information

GENA n cheek

GENAL > GENA

GENAPPE n smooth worsted yarn used for braid, etc

GENAPPES > GENAPPE

GENAS > GENA

GENDARME n member of the French police force

GENDARMES > GENDARME

GENDER n state of being male or female in relation to social and cultural roles ▷ vb assign a gender to

GENDERED > GENDER

GENDERING > GENDER

GENDERISE same as > GENDERIZE

GENDERIZE vb make distinctions according to gender in or among

GENDERS > GENDER

GENE n part of a cell

GENEALOGY n (study of) the history and descent of a family or families

GENERA > GENUS

GENERABLE adj able to be generated

GENERAL adj common or widespread ▷ n very senior army officer ▷ vb act as a general

GENERALCY n rank of general

GENERALE singular form of > GENERALIA

GENERALIA n generalities

GENERALLY adv usually

GENERALS > GENERAL

GENERANT n something that generates

GENERANTS > GENERANT

GENERATE vb produce or bring into being

GENERATED > GENERATE

GENERATES > GENERATE

GENERATOR n machine for converting mechanical energy into electrical energy

GENERIC adj of a class, group, or genus ▷ n drug, food product, etc that does not have a trademark

GENERICAL same as > GENERIC

GENERICS > GENERIC

GENEROUS adj free in giving

GENES > GENE

GENESES > GENESIS

GENESIS n beginning or origin

GENET n type of agile catlike mammal

GENETIC adj of genes or genetics

GENETICAL same as > GENETIC

GENETICS n study of heredity and variation in organisms

GENETRIX n female progenitor

GENETS > GENET

GENETTE same as > GENET

GENETTES > GENETTE

GENEVA n gin

GENEVAS > GENEVA

GENIAL adj cheerful and friendly

GENIALISE vb make genial

GENIALITY > GENIAL

GENIALIZE same as > GENIALISE

GENIALLY > GENIAL

GENIC adj of or relating to a gene or genes

GENICALLY > GENIC

GENICULAR adj of or relating to the knee

GENIE n (in fairy tales) magical wish-granting servant

GENIES > GENIE

GENII > GENIUS

GENIP same as > GENIPAP

GENIPAP n evergreen Caribbean tree

GENIPAPO n tropical American tree

GENIPAPOS > GENIPAPO

GENIPAPS > GENIPAP

GENIPS > GENIP

GENISTA n any member of the broom family

GENISTAS > GENISTA

GENISTEIN n substance found in plants, thought to fight cancer

GENITAL adj of the reproductive organs

GENITALIA same as > GENITALS

GENITALIC > GENITALIA

GENITALLY > GENITAL

GENITALS pl n external reproductive organs

GENITIVAL > GENITIVE

GENITIVE n grammatical case indicating possession ▷ adj denoting such a grammatical case

GENITIVES > GENITIVE

GENITOR n biological father

GENITORS > GENITOR

GENITRIX same as > GENETRIX

GENITURE n birth

GENITURES > GENITURE

GENIUS n (person with) an exceptional ability

GENIUSES > GENIUS

GENIZAH n repository for sacred objects which may not be destroyed

GENIZAHS > GENIZAH

GENIZOT > GENIZAH

GENIZOTH > GENIZAH

GENLOCK n generator locking device ▷ vb activate a genlock

GENLOCKED > GENLOCK

GENLOCKS > GENLOCK

GENNAKER n type of sail for boats

GENNAKERS > GENNAKER

GENNED > GEN

GENNEL same as > GINNEL

GENNELS > GENNEL

GENNET n female donkey or ass

GENNETS > GENNET

GENNIES > GENNY

GENNING > GEN

GENNY same as > GENOA

GENOA n large triangular jib sail

GENOAS > GENOA

GENOCIDAL > GENOCIDE

GENOCIDE n deliberate killing of an ethnic group

GENOCIDES > GENOCIDE

GENOGRAM n expanded family tree

GENOGRAMS > GENOGRAM

GENOISE n rich sponge cake

GENOISES > GENOISE

GENOM same as > GENOME

GENOME n all the genetic material in an organism

GENOMES > GENOME

GENOMIC > GENOME

GENOMICS n branch of molecular genetics concerned with the study of genomes

GENOMS > GENOM

GENOTOXIC adj harmful to genetic material

GENOTYPE n genetic constitution of an organism ▷ vb determine the genotype of

GENOTYPED > GENOTYPE

GENOTYPES > GENOTYPE

GENOTYPIC > GENOTYPE

GENRE n style of literary, musical, or artistic work

GENRES > GENRE

GENRO n group of Japanese statesmen

GENROS > GENRO

GENS n (in ancient Rome) a group of aristocratic families

GENSENG same as > GINSENG

GENSENGS > GENSENG

GENT n gentleman

GENTEEL adj affectedly proper and polite

GENTEELER > GENTEEL

GENTEELLY > GENTEEL

GENTES > GENS

GENTIAN n mountain plant with deep blue flowers

GENTIANS > GENTIAN

GENTIER > GENTY

GENTIEST > GENTY

GENTIL *adj* gentle

GENTILE *n* non-Jewish person ▷ *adj* used to designate a place or the inhabitants of a place

GENTILES > GENTILE

GENTILIC *adj* tribal

GENTILISE *vb* live like a gentile

GENTILISH *adj* heathenish

GENTILISM *n* heathenism

GENTILITY *n* noble birth or ancestry

GENTILIZE *same as* > GENTILISE

GENTLE *adj* mild or kindly ▷ *vb* tame or subdue (a horse) ▷ *n* maggot, esp when used as bait in fishing

GENTLED > GENTLE

GENTLEMAN *n* a cultured and courteous man

GENTLEMEN > GENTLEMAN

GENTLER > GENTLE

GENTLES > GENTLE

GENTLEST > GENTLE

GENTLING > GENTLE

GENTLY > GENTLE

GENTOO *n* grey-backed penguin

GENTOOS > GENTOO

GENTRICE *n* high birth

GENTRICES > GENTRICE

GENTRIES > GENTRY

GENTRIFY *vb* cause a neighbourhood to appeal to the middle classes

GENTRY *n* term for people just below the nobility in social rank

GENTS *n* men's public toilet

GENTY *adj* neat

GENU *n* any knee-like bend in a structure or part

GENUA > GENU

GENUFLECT *vb* bend the knee as a sign of reverence or deference

GENUINE *adj* not fake, authentic

GENUINELY > GENUINE

GENUS *n* group of animals or plants

GENUSES > GENUS

GEO *n* (esp in Shetland) a small fjord or gully

GEOBOTANY *n* study of plants in relation to their geological habitat

GEOCACHE *vb* search for hidden containers using GPS as a recreational activity

GEOCACHED > GEOCACHE

GEOCACHER *n* person who participates in geocaching

GEOCACHES > GEOCACHE

GEOCARPIC > GEOCARPY

GEOCARPY *n* ripening of fruits below ground, as occurs in the peanut

GEOCODE *vb* assign geographical coordinates to a physical location using a digital code

GEOCODED > GEOCODE

GEOCODES > GEOCODE

GEOCODING > GEOCODE

GEOCORONA *n* outer layer of earth's atmosphere

GEODATA *n* information about geographical location held in a digital format

GEODE *n* cavity within a rock mass or nodule

GEODES > GEODE

GEODESIC *adj* of the geometry of curved surfaces ▷ *n* shortest line between two points on a curve

GEODESICS > GEODESIC

GEODESIES > GEODESY

GEODESIST > GEODESY

GEODESY *n* study of the shape and size of the earth

GEODETIC *same as* > GEODESIC

GEODETICS *same as* > GEODETIC

GEODIC > GEODE

GEODUCK *n* king clam

GEODUCKS > GEODUCK

GEOFACT *n* rock shaped by natural forces

GEOFACTS > GEOFACT

GEOGENIES > GEOGENY

GEOGENY *same as* > GEOGONY

GEOGNOSES > GEOGNOSY

GEOGNOSIS *same as* > GEOGNOSY

GEOGNOST > GEOGNOSY

GEOGNOSTS > GEOGNOSY

GEOGNOSY *n* early form of geology

GEOGONIC > GEOGONY

GEOGONIES > GEOGONY

GEOGONY *n* science of the earth's formation

GEOGRAPHY *n* study of the earth's physical features, climate, population, etc

GEOID *n* hypothetical surface

GEOIDAL > GEOID

GEOIDS > GEOID

GEOLATRY *n* worship of the earth

GEOLOGER > GEOLOGY

GEOLOGERS > GEOLOGY

GEOLOGIAN > GEOLOGY

GEOLOGIC > GEOLOGY

GEOLOGIES > GEOLOGY

GEOLOGISE *same as* > GEOLOGIZE

GEOLOGIST > GEOLOGY

GEOLOGIZE *vb* study the geological features of (an area)

GEOLOGY *n* study of the earth

GEOMANCER > GEOMANCY

GEOMANCY *n* prophecy made from casting down a handful of earth

GEOMANT *n* geomancer

GEOMANTIC > GEOMANCY

GEOMANTS > GEOMANT

GEOMATICS *n* branch of science dealing with the collection, storage, and analysis of geographical data

GEOMETER *n* person who is practised in or who studies geometry

GEOMETERS > GEOMETER

GEOMETRIC *adj* of geometry

GEOMETRID *n* type of moth, the larvae of which are called measuring worms, inchworms, or loopers

GEOMETRY *n* branch of mathematics dealing with points, lines, curves, and surfaces

GEOMYOID *adj* relating to burrowing rodents of the genus Geomys

GEONOMICS *n* doctrine holding that those things found in nature belong to no one person but instead belong equally to all

GEOPHAGIA *same as* > GEOPHAGY

GEOPHAGY *n* practice of eating earth, clay, chalk, etc, found in some primitive tribes

GEOPHILIC *adj* soil-loving

GEOPHONE *n* device for recording seismic movement

GEOPHONES > GEOPHONE

GEOPHYTE *n* perennial plant that propagates by means of buds below the soil surface

GEOPHYTES > GEOPHYTE

GEOPHYTIC > GEOPHYTE

GEOPONIC *adj* of or relating to agriculture, esp as a science

GEOPONICS *n* science of agriculture

GEOPROBE *n* probing device used for sampling soil

GEOPROBES > GEOPROBE

GEORGETTE *n* fine silky fabric

GEORGIC *adj* agricultural ▷ *n* poem about rural or agricultural life

GEORGICAL *same as* > GEORGIC

GEORGICS > GEORGIC

GEOS > GEO

GEOSPHERE *n* the rigid outer layer of the earth

GEOSTATIC *adj* denoting or relating to the pressure exerted by a mass of rock or a similar substance

GEOTACTIC > GEOTAXIS

GEOTAG *n* geographical co-ordinates digitally applied to data ▷ *vb* apply a geotag to data

GEOTAGGED > GEOTAG

GEOTAGS > GEOTAG

GEOTAXES > GEOTAXIS

GEOTAXIS *n* movement of an organism in response to the stimulus of gravity

GEOTHERM *n* line or surface within or on the earth connecting points of equal temperature

GEOTHERMS > GEOTHERM

GEOTROPIC *adj* of geotropism: the response of a plant to the stimulus of gravity

GER *n* portable Mongolian dwelling

GERAH *n* ancient Hebrew unit of weight

GERAHS > GERAH

GERANIAL *n* cis-isomer of citral

GERANIALS > GERANIAL

GERANIOL *n* type of alcohol with an odour of roses

GERANIOLS > GERANIOL

GERANIUM *n* cultivated plant with red, pink, or white flowers

GERANIUMS > GERANIUM

GERARDIA *n* any plant of the genus Gerardia

GERARDIAS > GERARDIA

GERBE *same as* > GARBE

GERBERA *n* type of plant

GERBERAS > GERBERA

GERBES > GERBE

GERBIL *n* burrowing desert rodent of Asia and Africa

GERBILLE *same as* > GERBIL

GERBILLES > GERBILLE

GERBILS > GERBIL

GERE *Spenserian spelling of* > GEAR

GERENT *n* person who rules or manages

GERENTS > GERENT

GERENUK *n* slender antelope

GERENUKS > GERENUK

GERES > GERE

GERFALCON *same as* > GYRFALCON

GERIATRIC *adj* of elderly people

GERLE *Spenserian spelling of* > GIRL

GERLES > GERLE

GERM *n* microbe, esp one causing disease ▷ *vb* sprout

GERMAIN same as
> GERMEN
GERMAINE same as
> GERMEN
GERMAINES > GERMAINE
GERMAINS > GERMAIN
GERMAN n type of dance
▷ adj having the same
parents as oneself
GERMANDER n type of
plant
GERMANE adj relevant
GERMANELY > GERMANE
GERMANIC adj of or
containing germanium in
the tetravalent state
GERMANISE same as
> GERMANIZE
GERMANITE n mineral
consisting of a complex
copper arsenic sulphide
containing germanium,
gallium, iron, zinc, and
lead: an ore of germanium
and gallium
GERMANIUM n brittle grey
element that is a
semiconductor
GERMANIZE vb adopt or
cause to adopt German
customs, speech,
institutions, etc
GERMANOUS adj of or
containing germanium in
the divalent state
GERMANS > GERMAN
GERMED > GERM
GERMEN n cells that gives
rise to the germ cells
GERMENS > GERMEN
GERMFREE > GERM
GERMICIDE n substance
that kills germs
GERMIER > GERMY
GERMIEST > GERMY
GERMIN same as > GERMEN
GERMINA > GERMEN
GERMINAL adj of or in
the earliest stage of
development
GERMINANT adj in the
process of germinating
GERMINATE vb (cause to)
sprout or begin to grow
GERMINESS > GERMY
GERMING > GERM
GERMINS > GERMIN
GERMLIKE > GERM
GERMPLASM n plant
genetic material
GERMPROOF adj
protected against the
penetration of germs
GERMS > GERM
GERMY adj full of germs
GERNE vb grin
GERNED > GERNE
GERNES > GERNE
GERNING > GERNE
GERONIMO interj shout
given by US paratroopers
as they jump into battle
GERONTIC adj of or
relating to the senescence
of an organism
GEROPIGA n grape syrup
used to sweeten inferior
port wines

GEROPIGAS
> GEROPIGA
GERS > GER
GERT adv in dialect, great
or very big
GERTCHA interj get out of
here!
GERUND n noun formed
from a verb
GERUNDIAL > GERUND
GERUNDIVE n (in Latin
grammar) an adjective
formed from a verb,
expressing the desirability
of the activity denoted by
the verb ▷ adj of or
relating to the gerund or
gerundive
GERUNDS > GERUND
GESNERIA n S American
plant grown for its bright
flowers
GESNERIAD
> GESNERIA
GESNERIAS
> GESNERIA
GESSAMINE another word
for > JASMINE
GESSE Spenserian spelling
of > GUESS
GESSED > GESSE
GESSES > GESSE
GESSING > GESSE
GESSO n plaster used for
painting or in sculpture
▷ vb apply gesso to
GESSOED > GESSO
GESSOES > GESSO
GEST n notable deed or
exploit
GESTALT n perceptual
pattern or structure
GESTALTEN > GESTALT
GESTALTS > GESTALT
GESTANT adj laden
GESTAPO n any secret
state police organization
GESTAPOS > GESTAPO
GESTATE vb carry
(young) in the uterus
during pregnancy
GESTATED > GESTATE
GESTATES > GESTATE
GESTATING > GESTATE
GESTATION n (period of)
carrying of young in the
womb between
conception and birth
GESTATIVE
> GESTATION
GESTATORY
> GESTATION
GESTE same as > GEST
GESTES > GESTE
GESTIC adj consisting of
gestures
GESTICAL > GESTIC
GESTS > GEST
GESTURAL > GESTURE
GESTURE n movement to
convey meaning ▷ vb
gesticulate
GESTURED > GESTURE
GESTURER > GESTURE
GESTURERS > GESTURE
GESTURES > GESTURE
GESTURING > GESTURE
GET vb obtain or receive

GETA n type of Japanese
wooden sandal
GETABLE > GET
GETAS > GETA
GETATABLE adj
accessible
GETAWAY n used in
escape
GETAWAYS > GETAWAY
GETOUT n excuse to get
out of doing something
GETOUTS > GETOUT
GETS > GET
GETTABLE > GET
GETTER n person or thing
that gets ▷ vb remove (a
gas) by the action of a
getter
GETTERED > GETTER
GETTERING > GETTER
GETTERS > GETTER
GETTING > GET
GETTINGS > GET
GETUP n outfit
GETUPS > GETUP
GEUM n type of herbaceous
plant
GEUMS > GEUM
GEWGAW n showy but
valueless trinket ▷ adj
showy and valueless
GEWGAWED adj decorated
gaudily
GEWGAWS > GEWGAW
GEY adv extremely ▷ adj
gallant
GEYAN adv somewhat
GEYER > GEY
GEYEST > GEY
GEYSER n spring that
discharges steam and hot
water ▷ vb erupt like a
geyser
GEYSERED > GEYSER
GEYSERING > GEYSER
GEYSERITE n mineral
form of hydrated silica
resembling opal,
deposited from the waters
of geysers and hot springs
GEYSERS > GEYSER
GHARIAL same as
> GAVIAL
GHARIALS > GHARIAL
GHARRI same as
> GHARRY
GHARRIES > GHARRY
GHARRIS > GHARRI
GHARRY n (in India)
horse-drawn vehicle
GHAST vb terrify
GHASTED > GHAST
GHASTFUL adj dismal
GHASTING > GHAST
GHASTLIER > GHASTLY
GHASTLY adj unpleasant
▷ adv unhealthily
GHASTNESS n dread
GHASTS > GHAST
GHAT n (in India) set of
steps leading down to a
river
GHATS > GHAT
GHAUT n small cleft in a
hill
GHAUTS > GHAUT
GHAZAL n Arabic love
poem

GHAZALS > GHAZAL
GHAZEL same as
> GHAZAL
GHAZELS > GHAZEL
GHAZI n Muslim fighter
against infidels
GHAZIES > GHAZI
GHAZIS > GHAZI
GHEE n (in Indian cookery)
clarified butter
GHEES > GHEE
GHERAO n form of
industrial action in India
▷ vb trap an employer in
his or her office, to indicate
the workforce's discontent
GHERAOED > GHERAO
GHERAOES > GHERAO
GHERAOING > GHERAO
GHERAOS > GHERAO
GHERKIN n small pickled
cucumber
GHERKINS > GHERKIN
GHESSE Spenserian spelling
of > GUESS
GHESSED > GHESSE
GHESSES > GHESSE
GHESSING > GHESSE
GHEST > GHESSE
GHETTO n slum area
inhabited by a deprived
minority ▷ vb ghettoize
GHETTOED > GHETTO
GHETTOES > GHETTO
GHETTOING > GHETTO
GHETTOISE same as
> GHETTOIZE
GHETTOIZE vb confine
(someone or something)
to a particular area or
category
GHETTOS > GHETTO
GHI same as > GHEE
GHIBLI n fiercely hot
wind of North Africa
GHIBLIS > GHIBLI
GHILGAI same as
> GILGAI
GHILGAIS > GHILGAI
GHILLIE n (in Scotland)
attendant for hunting or
fishing ▷ vb act as a ghillie
GHILLIED > GHILLIE
GHILLIES > GHILLIE
GHILLYING > GHILLIE
GHIS > GHI
GHOST n disembodied
spirit of a dead person ▷ vb
ghostwrite
GHOSTED > GHOST
GHOSTIER > GHOSTY
GHOSTIEST > GHOSTY
GHOSTING > GHOST
GHOSTINGS > GHOST
GHOSTLIER > GHOSTLY
GHOSTLIKE > GHOST
GHOSTLY adj frightening
in appearance or effect
GHOSTS > GHOST
GHOSTY adj pertaining to
ghosts
GHOUL n person with
morbid interests
GHOULIE n goblin
GHOULIES > GHOULIE
GHOULISH adj of or
relating to ghouls
GHOULS > GHOUL

g

GHRELIN n hormone that stimulates appetite
GHRELINS > GHRELIN
GHUBAR adj as in ghubar numeral type of numeral
GHYLL same as > GILL
GHYLLS > GHYLL
GI n white suit worn in martial arts
GIAMBEUX n jambeaux; leg armour
GIANT n mythical being of superhuman size ▷ adj huge
GIANTESS same as > GIANT
GIANTHOOD n condition of being a giant
GIANTISM same as > GIGANTISM
GIANTISMS > GIANTISM
GIANTLIER > GIANTLY
GIANTLIKE > GIANT
GIANTLY adj giantlike
GIANTRIES > GIANTRY
GIANTRY n collective term for giants
GIANTS > GIANT
GIANTSHIP n style of address for a giant
GIAOUR n archaic derogatory term for a non-Muslim, esp a Christian, used esp by the Turks
GIAOURS > GIAOUR
GIARDIA n species of parasite
GIARDIAS > GIARDIA
GIB n metal wedge, pad, or thrust bearing ▷ vb fasten or supply with a gib
GIBBED > GIB
GIBBER vb speak or utter rapidly and unintelligibly ▷ n boulder
GIBBERED > GIBBER
GIBBERING n rapid, unintelligible speech
GIBBERISH n rapid unintelligible talk
GIBBERS > GIBBER
GIBBET n gallows for displaying executed criminals ▷ vb put to death by hanging on a gibbet
GIBBETED > GIBBET
GIBBETING > GIBBET
GIBBETS > GIBBET
GIBBETTED > GIBBET
GIBBING > GIB
GIBBON n agile tree-dwelling ape of S Asia
GIBBONS > GIBBON
GIBBOSE same as > GIBBOUS
GIBBOSITY n state of being gibbous
GIBBOUS adj (of the moon) between half and fully illuminated
GIBBOUSLY > GIBBOUS
GIBBSITE n mineral consisting of hydrated aluminium oxide
GIBBSITES > GIBBSITE

GIBE vb make jeering or scoffing remarks (at) ▷ n derisive or provoking remark
GIBED > GIBE
GIBEL n Prussian carp
GIBELS > GIBEL
GIBER > GIBE
GIBERS > GIBE
GIBES > GIBE
GIBING > GIBE
GIBINGLY > GIBE
GIBLET > GIBLETS
GIBLETS pl n gizzard, liver, heart, and neck of a fowl
GIBLI same as > GHIBLI
GIBLIS > GIBLI
GIBS > GIB
GIBSON n martini garnished with onion
GIBSONS > GIBSON
GIBUS n collapsible top hat
GIBUSES > GIBUS
GID n disease of sheep
GIDDAP interj exclamation used to make a horse go faster
GIDDAY interj expression of greeting
GIDDIED > GIDDY
GIDDIER > GIDDY
GIDDIES > GIDDY
GIDDILY > GIDDY
GIDDINESS > GIDDY
GIDDUP same as > GIDDYUP
GIDDY adj having or causing a feeling of dizziness ▷ vb make giddy
GIDDYAP same as > GIDDYUP
GIDDYING > GIDDY
GIDDYUP interj exclamation used to make a horse go faster
GIDGEE n small acacia tree
GIDGEES > GIDGEE
GIDJEE same as > GIDGEE
GIDJEES > GIDJEE
GIDS > GID
GIE Scot word for > GIVE
GIED > GIE
GIEING > GIE
GIEN > GIE
GIES > GIE
GIF n file held in GIF format
GIFS > GIF
GIFT n present ▷ vb make a present of
GIFTABLE adj suitable as gift ▷ n something suitable as gift
GIFTABLES > GIFTABLE
GIFTED adj talented
GIFTEDLY > GIFTED
GIFTEE n person given a gift
GIFTEES > GIFTEE
GIFTING n act of gifting
GIFTINGS > GIFTING
GIFTLESS > GIFT

GIFTS > GIFT
GIFTSHOP n shop selling articles suitable for gifts
GIFTSHOPS > GIFTSHOP
GIFTWARE n anything that may be given as a present
GIFTWARES > GIFTWARE
GIFTWRAP vb wrap (a gift) in decorative wrapping paper
GIFTWRAPS > GIFTWRAP
GIG n single performance by pop or jazz musicians ▷ vb play a gig or gigs
GIGA same as > GIGUE
GIGABIT n unit of information in computing
GIGABITS > GIGABIT
GIGABYTE n one thousand and twenty-four megabytes
GIGABYTES > GIGABYTE
GIGACYCLE same as > GIGAHERTZ
GIGAFLOP n measure of computer processing speed
GIGAFLOPS > GIGAFLOP
GIGAHERTZ n unit of frequency equal to 10^9 hertz
GIGANTEAN adj gigantic
GIGANTIC adj enormous
GIGANTISM n excessive growth of the entire body, caused by overproduction of growth hormone by the pituitary gland during childhood or adolescence
GIGAS > GIGA
GIGATON n unit of explosive force
GIGATONS > GIGATON
GIGAVOLT n billion volts
GIGAVOLTS > GIGAVOLT
GIGAWATT n unit of power equal to 1 billion watts
GIGAWATTS > GIGAWATT
GIGGED > GIG
GIGGING > GIG
GIGGIT vb move quickly
GIGGITED > GIGGIT
GIGGITING > GIGGIT
GIGGITS > GIGGIT
GIGGLE vb laugh nervously or foolishly ▷ n such a laugh
GIGGLED > GIGGLE
GIGGLER > GIGGLE
GIGGLERS > GIGGLE
GIGGLES > GIGGLE
GIGGLIER > GIGGLE
GIGGLIEST > GIGGLE
GIGGLING > GIGGLE
GIGGLINGS > GIGGLE
GIGGLY > GIGGLE
GIGHE > GIGA
GIGLET n flighty girl
GIGLETS > GIGLET

GIGLOT same as > GIGLET
GIGLOTS > GIGLOT
GIGMAN n one who places great importance on respectability
GIGMANITY > GIGMAN
GIGMEN > GIGMAN
GIGOLO n man paid to be an escort
GIGOLOS > GIGOLO
GIGOT n leg of lamb or mutton
GIGOTS > GIGOT
GIGS > GIG
GIGUE n piece of music incorporated into the classical suite
GIGUES > GIGUE
GILA n large venomous brightly coloured lizard
GILAS > GILA
GILBERT n unit of magnetomotive force
GILBERTS > GILBERT
GILCUP same as > GILTCUP
GILCUPS > GILCUP
GILD vb put a thin layer of gold on
GILDED > GILD
GILDEN adj gilded
GILDER > GILD
GILDERS > GILD
GILDHALL same as > GUILDHALL
GILDHALLS > GILDHALL
GILDING > GILD
GILDINGS > GILD
GILDS > GILD
GILDSMAN > GILD
GILDSMEN > GILD
GILET n waist- or hip-length garment
GILETS > GILET
GILGAI n natural water hole
GILGAIS > GILGAI
GILGIE n type of freshwater crayfish
GILGIES > GILGIE
GILL n radiating structure beneath the cap of a mushroom ▷ vb catch (fish) or (of fish) to be caught in a gill net
GILLAROO n type of brown trout
GILLAROOS > GILLAROO
GILLED > GILL
GILLER > GILL
GILLERS > GILL
GILLET n mare
GILLETS > GILLET
GILLFLIRT n flirtatious woman
GILLIE n (in Scotland) attendant for hunting or fishing ▷ vb act as a gillie
GILLIED > GILLIE
GILLIES > GILLIE
GILLING > GILL
GILLION n (no longer in technical use) one thousand million
GILLIONS > GILLION

GILLNET n net designed to catch fish by the gills ▷ vb fish using a gillnet
GILLNETS > GILLNET
GILLS pl n breathing organs in fish and other water creatures
GILLY same as > GILLIE
GILLYING > GILLY
GILLYVOR n type of carnation
GILLYVORS > GILLYVOR
GILPEY n mischievous, frolicsome boy or girl
GILPEYS > GILPEY
GILPIES > GILPY
GILPY same as > GILPEY
GILRAVAGE vb make merry, especially to excess
GILSONITE n very pure form of asphalt found in Utah and Colorado
GILT n young sow
GILTCUP n buttercup
GILTCUPS > GILTCUP
GILTHEAD n type of fish
GILTHEADS > GILTHEAD
GILTS > GILT
GILTWOOD adj made of wood and gilded
GIMBAL vb support on gimbals
GIMBALED > GIMBAL
GIMBALING > GIMBAL
GIMBALLED > GIMBAL
GIMBALS pl n set of pivoted rings
GIMCRACK adj showy but cheap ▷ n cheap showy trifle or gadget
GIMCRACKS > GIMCRACK
GIMEL n third letter of the Hebrew alphabet
GIMELS > GIMEL
GIMLET n small tool ▷ adj penetrating or piercing ▷ vb make holes in (wood) using a gimlet
GIMLETED > GIMLET
GIMLETING > GIMLET
GIMLETS > GIMLET
GIMMAL n ring composed of interlocking rings ▷ vb provide with gimmals
GIMMALLED > GIMMAL
GIMMALS > GIMMAL
GIMME interj give me! ▷ n something easily obtained
GIMMER n year-old ewe
GIMMERS > GIMMER
GIMMES > GIMME
GIMMICK n something designed to attract attention ▷ vb make gimmicky
GIMMICKED > GIMMICK
GIMMICKRY > GIMMICK
GIMMICKS > GIMMICK
GIMMICKY > GIMMICK
GIMMIE n very short putt in golf
GIMMIES > GIMMIE
GIMMOR n mechanical device
GIMMORS > GIMMOR

GIMP n tapelike trimming of silk, wool, or cotton, often stiffened with wire ▷ vb slang term for limp
GIMPED > GIMP
GIMPIER > GIMPY
GIMPIEST > GIMPY
GIMPING > GIMP
GIMPS > GIMP
GIMPY same as > GAMMY
GIN n spirit flavoured with juniper berries ▷ vb free (cotton) of seeds with an engine
GINCH same as > GITCH
GINCHES > GINCH
GING n child's catapult
GINGAL n type of musket mounted on a swivel
GINGALL same as > GINGAL
GINGALLS > GINGALL
GINGALS > GINGAL
GINGE n person with ginger hair
GINGELEY same as > GINGILI
GINGELEYS > GINGELEY
GINGELI same as > GINGILI
GINGELIES > GINGELY
GINGELIS > GINGELI
GINGELLI same as > GINGILI
GINGELLIS > GINGILI
GINGELLY same as > GINGILI
GINGELY same as > GINGILI
GINGER n root of a tropical plant, used as a spice ▷ adj light reddish-brown ▷ vb add the spice ginger to (a dish)
GINGERADE n fizzy drink flavoured with ginger
GINGERED > GINGER
GINGERIER > GINGERY
GINGERING > GINGER
GINGERLY adv cautiously ▷ adj cautious
GINGEROUS adj reddish
GINGERS > GINGER
GINGERY adj like or tasting of ginger
GINGES > GINGE
GINGHAM n cotton cloth, usu checked or striped
GINGHAMS > GINGHAM
GINGILI n oil obtained from sesame seeds
GINGILIS > GINGILI
GINGILLI same as > GINGILI
GINGILLIS > GINGILI
GINGIVA same as > GUM
GINGIVAE > GINGIVA
GINGIVAL > GINGIVA
GINGKO same as > GINKGO
GINGKOES > GINGKO
GINGKOS > GINGKO
GINGLE same as > JINGLE
GINGLES > GINGLE
GINGLYMI > GINGLYMUS

GINGLYMUS n hinge joint
GINGS > GING
GINHOUSE n building where cotton is ginned
GINHOUSES > GINHOUSE
GINK n man or boy
GINKGO n ornamental Chinese tree
GINKGOES > GINKGO
GINKGOS > GINKGO
GINKS > GINK
GINN same as > JINN
GINNED > GIN
GINNEL n narrow passageway between buildings
GINNELS > GINNEL
GINNER > GIN
GINNERIES > GINHOUSE
GINNERS > GIN
GINNERY another word for > GINHOUSE
GINNIER > GINNY
GINNIEST > GINNY
GINNING > GIN
GINNINGS > GIN
GINNY adj relating to the spirit gin
GINORMOUS adj very large
GINS > GIN
GINSENG n (root of) a plant
GINSENGS > GINSENG
GINSHOP n tavern
GINSHOPS > GINSHOP
GIO same as > GEO
GIOCOSO adv (of music) to be expressed joyfully or playfully
GIOS > GIO
GIP vb clean fish before curing
GIPON another word for > JUPON
GIPONS > GIPON
GIPPED > GIP
GIPPER > GIP
GIPPERS > GIPPER
GIPPIES > GIPPY
GIPPING > GIP
GIPPY n starling
GIPS > GIP
GIPSEN obsolete word for > GYPSY
GIPSENS > GIPSEN
GIPSIED > GIPSY
GIPSIES > GIPSY
GIPSY n member of a nomadic people ▷ vb live like a gipsy
GIPSYDOM > GIPSY
GIPSYDOMS > GIPSY
GIPSYHOOD > GIPSY
GIPSYING > GIPSY
GIPSYISH > GIPSY
GIPSYISM n gipsy custom
GIPSYISMS > GIPSYISM
GIPSYWORT n hairy Eurasian plant with two-lipped white flowers with purple dots on the lower lip

GIRAFFE n African ruminant mammal
GIRAFFES > GIRAFFE
GIRAFFID adj giraffe-like ▷ n member of the Giraffidae family
GIRAFFIDS > GIRAFFID
GIRAFFINE adj relating to a giraffe
GIRAFFISH > GIRAFFE
GIRAFFOID adj giraffe-like
GIRANDOLA same as > GIRANDOLE
GIRANDOLE n ornamental branched wall candleholder, usually incorporating a mirror
GIRASOL n type of opal
GIRASOLE same as > GIRASOL
GIRASOLES > GIRASOLE
GIRASOLS > GIRASOL
GIRD vb put a belt round ▷ n blow or stroke
GIRDED > GIRD
GIRDER n large metal beam
GIRDERS > GIRDER
GIRDING > GIRD
GIRDINGLY > GIRD
GIRDINGS > GIRD
GIRDLE n woman's elastic corset ▷ vb surround or encircle
GIRDLED > GIRDLE
GIRDLER n person or thing that girdles
GIRDLERS > GIRDLER
GIRDLES > GIRDLE
GIRDLING > GIRDLE
GIRDS > GIRD
GIRKIN same as > GHERKIN
GIRKINS > GIRKIN
GIRL n female child
GIRLHOOD n state or time of being a girl
GIRLHOODS > GIRLHOOD
GIRLIE adj suited to young women ▷ n little girl
GIRLIER > GIRLY
GIRLIES > GIRLIE
GIRLIEST > GIRLY
GIRLISH adj of or like a girl in looks, behaviour, etc
GIRLISHLY > GIRLISH
GIRLOND obsolete word for > GARLAND
GIRLONDS > GIRLOND
GIRLS > GIRL
GIRLY same as > GIRLIE
GIRN vb grimace or snarl
GIRNED > GIRN
GIRNEL n large chest for storing meal
GIRNELS > GIRNEL
GIRNER > GIRN
GIRNERS > GIRN
GIRNIE adj peevish
GIRNIER > GIRNIE
GIRNIEST > GIRNIE
GIRNING > GIRN
GIRNS > GIRN

g

GIRO n system of transferring money

GIROLLE n chanterelle mushroom

GIROLLES > GIROLLE

GIRON n part of a heraldic shield

GIRONIC > GIRON

GIRONNY adj divided into segments from the fesse point

GIRONS > GIRON

GIROS > GIRO

GIROSOL same as > GIRASOL

GIROSOLS > GIROSOL

GIRR same as > GIRD

GIRRS > GIRR

GIRSH n currency unit of Saudi Arabia

GIRSHES > GIRSH

GIRT vb gird; bind

GIRTED > GIRT

GIRTH n measurement round something ▷ vb fasten a girth on (a horse)

GIRTHED > GIRTH

GIRTHING > GIRTH

GIRTHLINE same as > GIRTLINE

GIRTHS > GIRTH

GIRTING > GIRT

GIRTLINE n gantline

GIRTLINES > GIRTLINE

GIRTS > GIRT

GIS > GI

GISARME n long-shafted battle-axe

GISARMES > GISARME

GISM n vulgar word for semen

GISMO same as > GIZMO

GISMOLOGY same as > GIZMOLOGY

GISMOS > GISMO

GISMS > GISM

GIST n substance or main point of a matter

GISTS > GIST

GIT vb dialect version of get

GITANA n Romany woman from Spain

GITANAS > GITANA

GITANO n Romany man from Spain

GITANOS > GITANO

GITCH n underwear

GITCHES > GITCH

GITE n self-catering holiday cottage for let in France

GITES > GITE

GITS > GIT

GITTARONE n acoustic bass guitar

GITTED > GIT

GITTERN n obsolete medieval instrument ▷ vb play the gittern

GITTERNED > GITTERN

GITTERNS > GITTERN

GITTIN n Jewish divorce

GITTING > GIT

GIUST same as > JOUST

GIUSTED > GIUST

GIUSTING > GIUST

GIUSTO adv as observed strictly

GIUSTS > GIUST

GIVABLE > GIVE

GIVE vb present (something) to another person ▷ n resilience or elasticity

GIVEABLE > GIVE

GIVEAWAY n something that reveals hidden feelings or intentions ▷ adj very cheap or free

GIVEAWAYS > GIVEAWAY

GIVEBACK n reduction in wages in return for some other benefit, in time of recession

GIVEBACKS > GIVEBACK

GIVED same as > GYVED

GIVEN n assumed fact

GIVENNESS n condition of being given

GIVENS > GIVEN

GIVER > GIVE

GIVERS > GIVE

GIVES > GIVE

GIVING > GIVE

GIVINGS > GIVE

GIZMO n device

GIZMOLOGY n study of gadgets

GIZMOS > GIZMO

GIZZ n wig

GIZZARD n part of a bird's stomach

GIZZARDS > GIZZARD

GIZZEN vb (of wood) to warp

GIZZENED > GIZZEN

GIZZENING > GIZZEN

GIZZENS > GIZZEN

GIZZES > GIZZ

GJETOST n type of Norwegian cheese

GJETOSTS > GJETOST

GJU n type of violin used in Shetland

GJUS > GJU

GLABELLA n elevation of the frontal bone above the nose

GLABELLAE > GLABELLA

GLABELLAR > GLABELLA

GLABRATE same as > GLABROUS

GLABROUS adj without hair or a similar growth

GLACE adj preserved in a thick sugary syrup ▷ vb ice or candy (cakes, fruits, etc)

GLACED > GLACE

GLACEED > GLACE

GLACEING > GLACE

GLACES > GLACE

GLACIAL adj of ice or glaciers ▷ n ice age

GLACIALLY > GLACIAL

GLACIALS > GLACIAL

GLACIATE vb cover or become covered with glaciers or masses of ice

GLACIATED > GLACIATE

GLACIATES > GLACIATE

GLACIER n slow-moving mass of ice

GLACIERED adj having a glacier or glaciers

GLACIERS > GLACIER

GLACIS n slight incline

GLACISES > GLACIS

GLAD adj pleased and happy ▷ vb become glad ▷ n gladiolus

GLADDED > GLAD

GLADDEN vb make glad

GLADDENED > GLADDEN

GLADDENER > GLADDEN

GLADDENS > GLADDEN

GLADDER > GLAD

GLADDEST > GLAD

GLADDIE n gladiolus

GLADDIES > GLADDIE

GLADDING > GLAD

GLADDON n stinking iris

GLADDONS > GLADDON

GLADE n open space in a forest

GLADELIKE > GLADE

GLADES > GLADE

GLADFUL adj full of gladness

GLADIATE adj shaped like a sword

GLADIATOR n (in ancient Rome) man trained to fight in arenas to provide entertainment

GLADIER > GLADE

GLADIEST > GLADE

GLADIOLA same as > GLADIOLUS

GLADIOLAR > GLADIOLUS

GLADIOLAS > GLADIOLA

GLADIOLE same as > GLADIOLUS

GLADIOLES > GLADIOLE

GLADIOLI > GLADIOLUS

GLADIOLUS n garden plant with sword-shaped leaves

GLADIUS n short sword used by Roman legionaries

GLADIUSES > GLADIUS

GLADLIER > GLAD

GLADLIEST > GLAD

GLADLY > GLAD

GLADNESS > GLAD

GLADS > GLAD

GLADSOME adj joyous or cheerful

GLADSOMER > GLADSOME

GLADSTONE n light four-wheeled horse-drawn vehicle

GLADWRAP n in New Zealand English, thin film for wrapping food ▷ vb cover with gladwrap

GLADWRAPS > GLADWRAP

GLADY > GLADE

GLAIK n prank

GLAIKET same as > GLAIKIT

GLAIKIT adj foolish

GLAIKS > GLAIK

GLAIR n white of egg ▷ vb apply glair to (something)

GLAIRE same as > GLAIR

GLAIRED > GLAIR

GLAIREOUS > GLAIR

GLAIRES > GLAIRE

GLAIRIER > GLAIR

GLAIRIEST > GLAIR

GLAIRIN n viscous mineral deposit

GLAIRING > GLAIR

GLAIRINS > GLAIRIN

GLAIRS > GLAIR

GLAIRY > GLAIR

GLAIVE archaic word for > SWORD

GLAIVED adj armed with a sword

GLAIVES > GLAIVE

GLAM n magical illusion ▷ vb make oneself look glamorous ▷ adj glamorous

GLAMMED > GLAM

GLAMMER > GLAM

GLAMMEST > GLAM

GLAMMIER > GLAMMY

GLAMMIEST > GLAMMY

GLAMMING > GLAM

GLAMMY adj glamorous

GLAMOR same as > GLAMOUR

GLAMORED > GLAMOR

GLAMORING > GLAMOR

GLAMORISE same as > GLAMORIZE

GLAMORIZE vb cause to be or seem glamorous

GLAMOROUS adj alluring

GLAMORS > GLAMOR

GLAMOUR n alluring charm or fascination ▷ vb bewitch

GLAMOURED adj bewitched

GLAMOURS > GLAMOUR

GLAMPING n camping with luxurious physical comforts

GLAMPINGS > GLAMPING

GLAMS > GLAM

GLANCE vb look rapidly or briefly ▷ n brief look

GLANCED > GLANCE

GLANCER n log or pole used to protect trees from damage

GLANCERS > GLANCER

GLANCES > GLANCE

GLANCING > GLANCE

GLANCINGS > GLANCE

GLAND n organ that produces and secretes substances

GLANDERED > GLANDERS

GLANDERS n highly infectious bacterial disease of horses, sometimes transmitted to humans

GLANDES > GLANS

GLANDLESS > GLAND

GLANDLIKE > GLAND

GLANDS > GLAND

GLANDULAR *adj* of or affecting a gland or glands

GLANDULE *n* small gland

GLANDULES
> GLANDULE

GLANS *n* any small rounded body or glandlike mass

GLARE *vb* stare angrily ▷ *n* angry stare ▷ *adj* smooth and glassy

GLAREAL *adj* (of a plant) growing in cultivated land

GLARED > GLARE

GLARELESS > GLARE

GLAREOUS *adj* resembling the white of an egg

GLARES > GLARE

GLARIER > GLARE

GLARIEST > GLARE

GLARINESS > GLARE

GLARING *adj* conspicuous

GLARINGLY > GLARING

GLARY > GLARE

GLASNOST *n* policy of openness and accountability, esp, formerly, in the USSR

GLASNOSTS
> GLASNOST

GLASS *n* hard brittle substance ▷ *vb* cover with, enclose in, or fit with glass

GLASSED > GLASS

GLASSEN *adj* glassy

GLASSES *pl n* pair of lenses for correcting faulty vision

GLASSFUL *n* amount held by a full glass

GLASSFULS
> GLASSFUL

GLASSIE *same as*
> GLASSY

GLASSIER > GLASSY

GLASSIES > GLASSY

GLASSIEST > GLASSY

GLASSIFY *vb* turn into glass

GLASSILY > GLASSY

GLASSINE *n* glazed translucent paper used for book jackets

GLASSINES
> GLASSINE

GLASSING > GLASS

GLASSLESS > GLASS

GLASSLIKE > GLASS

GLASSMAN *n* man whose work is making or selling glassware

GLASSMEN > GLASSMAN

GLASSWARE *n* articles made of glass

GLASSWORK *n* production of glassware

GLASSWORM *n* larva of gnat

GLASSWORT *n* type of plant of salt marshes, with fleshy stems and scalelike leaves, formerly used in glass-making

GLASSY *adj* like glass ▷ *n* glass marble

GLAUCOMA *n* eye disease

GLAUCOMAS
> GLAUCOMA

GLAUCOUS *adj* covered with a bluish waxy or powdery bloom

GLAUM *vb* snatch

GLAUMED > GLAUM

GLAUMING > GLAUM

GLAUMS > GLAUM

GLAUR *n* mud or mire

GLAURIER > GLAUR

GLAURIEST > GLAUR

GLAURS > GLAUR

GLAURY > GLAUR

GLAZE *vb* fit or cover with glass ▷ *n* transparent coating

GLAZED > GLAZE

GLAZEN *adj* glazed

GLAZER > GLAZE

GLAZERS > GLAZE

GLAZES > GLAZE

GLAZIER *n* person who fits windows with glass

GLAZIERS > GLAZIER

GLAZIERY > GLAZIER

GLAZIEST > GLAZE

GLAZILY > GLAZE

GLAZINESS > GLAZE

GLAZING *n* surface of a glazed object

GLAZINGS > GLAZING

GLAZY > GLAZE

GLEAM *n* small beam or glow of light ▷ *vb* emit a gleam

GLEAMED > GLEAM

GLEAMER *n* mirror used to cheat in card games

GLEAMERS > GLEAMER

GLEAMIER > GLEAM

GLEAMIEST > GLEAM

GLEAMING > GLEAM

GLEAMINGS > GLEAM

GLEAMS > GLEAM

GLEAMY > GLEAM

GLEAN *vb* gather (facts etc) bit by bit

GLEANABLE > GLEAN

GLEANED > GLEAN

GLEANER > GLEAN

GLEANERS > GLEAN

GLEANING > GLEAN

GLEANINGS *pl n* pieces of information that have been gleaned

GLEANS > GLEAN

GLEAVE *archaic word for*
> SWORD

GLEAVES > GLEAVE

GLEBA *n* mass of spores

GLEBAE > GLEBA

GLEBE *n* land granted to a member of the clergy

GLEBELESS > GLEBE

GLEBES > GLEBE

GLEBIER > GLEBY

GLEBIEST > GLEBY

GLEBOUS *adj* gleby

GLEBY *adj* relating to a glebe

GLED *n* red kite (bird)

GLEDE *same as* > GLED

GLEDES > GLEDE

GLEDGE *vb* glance sideways

GLEDGED > GLEDGE

GLEDGES > GLEDGE

GLEDGING > GLEDGE

GLEDS > GLED

GLEE *n* triumph and delight ▷ *vb* be full of glee

GLEED *n* burning ember or hot coal

GLEEDS > GLEED

GLEEFUL *adj* merry or joyful

GLEEFULLY > GLEEFUL

GLEEING > GLEE

GLEEK *vb* jeer

GLEEKED > GLEEK

GLEEKING > GLEEK

GLEEKS > GLEEK

GLEEMAN *n* minstrel

GLEEMEN > GLEEMAN

GLEENIE *n* guinea fowl

GLEENIES > GLEENIE

GLEES > GLEE

GLEESOME *adj* full of glee

GLEET *n* inflammation of the urethra ▷ *vb* discharge pus

GLEETED > GLEET

GLEETIER > GLEET

GLEETIEST > GLEET

GLEETING > GLEET

GLEETS > GLEET

GLEETY > GLEET

GLEG *adj* quick

GLEGGER > GLEG

GLEGGEST > GLEG

GLEGLY > GLEG

GLEGNESS > GLEG

GLEI *same as* > GLEY

GLEIS > GLEI

GLEN *n* deep narrow valley, esp in Scotland

GLENGARRY *n* brimless Scottish cap with a crease down the crown

GLENLIKE > GLEN

GLENOID *adj* resembling or having a shallow cavity ▷ *n* shallow cavity

GLENOIDAL > GLENOID

GLENOIDS > GLENOID

GLENS > GLEN

GLENT *same as* > GLINT

GLENTED > GLENT

GLENTING > GLENT

GLENTS > GLENT

GLEY *n* bluish-grey compact sticky soil ▷ *vb* squint

GLEYED > GLEY

GLEYING > GLEY

GLEYINGS > GLEYING

GLEYS > GLEY

GLIA *n* web of tissue that supports nerve cells

GLIADIN *n* protein of cereals with a high proline content

GLIADINE *same as*
> GLIADIN

GLIADINES > GLIADIN

GLIADINS > GLIADIN

GLIAL > GLIA

GLIAS > GLIA

GLIB *adj* fluent but insincere or superficial ▷ *vb* render glib, smooth, or slippery

GLIBBED > GLIB

GLIBBER > GLIB

GLIBBERY *adj* slippery

GLIBBEST > GLIB

GLIBBING > GLIB

GLIBLY > GLIB

GLIBNESS > GLIB

GLIBS > GLIB

GLID *adj* moving smoothly and easily

GLIDDER > GLID

GLIDDERY *adj* slippery

GLIDDEST > GLID

GLIDE *vb* move easily and smoothly ▷ *n* smooth easy movement

GLIDED > GLIDE

GLIDEPATH *n* path followed by aircraft coming in to land

GLIDER *n* flying phalanger

GLIDERS > GLIDER

GLIDES > GLIDE

GLIDING *n* sport of flying gliders

GLIDINGLY > GLIDE

GLIDINGS > GLIDING

GLIFF *n* slap

GLIFFING > GLIFF

GLIFFINGS > GLIFF

GLIFFS > GLIFF

GLIFT *n* moment

GLIFTS > GLIFT

GLIKE *same as* > GLEEK

GLIKES > GLIKE

GLIM *n* light or lamp

GLIME *vb* glance sideways

GLIMED > GLIME

GLIMES > GLIME

GLIMING > GLIME

GLIMMER *vb* shine faintly, flicker ▷ *n* faint gleam

GLIMMERED > GLIMMER

GLIMMERS > GLIMMER

GLIMMERY *adj* glimmering, shimmery

GLIMPSE *n* brief or incomplete view ▷ *vb* catch a glimpse of

GLIMPSED > GLIMPSE

GLIMPSER > GLIMPSE

GLIMPSERS > GLIMPSE

GLIMPSES > GLIMPSE

GLIMPSING > GLIMPSE

GLIMS > GLIM

GLINT *vb* gleam brightly ▷ *n* bright gleam

GLINTED > GLINT

GLINTIER > GLINT

GLINTIEST > GLINT

GLINTING > GLINT

GLINTS > GLINT

GLINTY > GLINT

GLIOMA *n* tumour of the brain and spinal cord

GLIOMAS > GLIOMA

GLIOMATA > GLIOMA

GLIOSES > GLIOSIS

GLIOSIS *n* process leading to scarring in the nervous system

GLISK *n* glimpse

GLISKS > GLISK

GLISSADE *n* gliding step in ballet ▷ *vb* perform a glissade

g

GLISSADED > GLISSADE
GLISSADER > GLISSADE
GLISSADES
> GLISSADE
GLISSANDI
> GLISSANDO
GLISSANDO *n* slide between two notes in which all intermediate notes are played
GLISSE *n* type of dance step
GLISSES > GLISSE
GLISTEN *vb* gleam by reflecting light ▷ *n* gleam or gloss
GLISTENED > GLISTEN
GLISTENS > GLISTEN
GLISTER *archaic word for* > GLITTER
GLISTERED > GLISTER
GLISTERS > GLISTER
GLIT *n* slimy matter
GLITCH *n* small problem that stops something from working
GLITCHES > GLITCH
GLITCHIER > GLITCH
GLITCHY > GLITCH
GLITS > GLIT
GLITTER *vb* shine with bright flashes ▷ *n* sparkle or brilliance
GLITTERED > GLITTER
GLITTERS > GLITTER
GLITTERY > GLITTER
GLITZ *n* ostentatious showiness ▷ *vb* make something more attractive
GLITZED > GLITZ
GLITZES > GLITZ
GLITZIER > GLITZY
GLITZIEST > GLITZY
GLITZILY > GLITZY
GLITZING > GLITZ
GLITZY *adj* showily attractive
GLOAM *n* dusk
GLOAMING *n* twilight
GLOAMINGS
> GLOAMING
GLOAMS > GLOAM
GLOAT *vb* regard one's own good fortune with pleasure ▷ *n* act of gloating
GLOATED > GLOAT
GLOATER > GLOAT
GLOATERS > GLOAT
GLOATING *n* act of gloating
GLOATINGS
> GLOATING
GLOATS > GLOAT
GLOB *n* rounded mass of thick fluid
GLOBAL *adj* worldwide
GLOBALISE *same as*
> GLOBALIZE
GLOBALISM *n* policy which is worldwide in scope
GLOBALIST
> GLOBALISM
GLOBALIZE *vb* put (something) into effect worldwide

GLOBALLY > GLOBAL
GLOBATE *adj* shaped like a globe
GLOBATED *same as*
> GLOBATE
GLOBBIER > GLOBBY
GLOBBIEST > GLOBBY
GLOBBY *adj* thick and lumpy
GLOBE *n* sphere with a map of the earth on it ▷ *vb* form or cause to form into a globe
GLOBED > GLOBE
GLOBEFISH *n* type of fish that can inflate its body
GLOBELIKE > GLOBE
GLOBES > GLOBE
GLOBESITY *n* informal word for obesity seen as a worldwide social problem
GLOBETROT *vb* regularly travel internationally
GLOBI > GLOBUS
GLOBIER > GLOBY
GLOBIEST > GLOBY
GLOBIN *n* protein component of haemoglobin
GLOBING > GLOBE
GLOBINS > GLOBIN
GLOBOID *adj* shaped approximately like a globe ▷ *n* globoid body
GLOBOIDS > GLOBOID
GLOBOSE *adj* spherical or approximately spherical ▷ *n* globose object
GLOBOSELY > GLOBOSE
GLOBOSITY > GLOBOSE
GLOBOUS *same as*
> GLOBOSE
GLOBS > GLOB
GLOBULAR *adj* shaped like a globe or globule ▷ *n* globular star cluster
GLOBULARS
> GLOBULAR
GLOBULE *n* small round drop
GLOBULES > GLOBULE
GLOBULET *n* small globule
GLOBULETS
> GLOBULET
GLOBULIN *n* simple protein found in living tissue
GLOBULINS
> GLOBULIN
GLOBULITE *n* spherical form of crystallite
GLOBULOUS *same as*
> GLOBULAR
GLOBUS *n* any spherelike structure
GLOBY *adj* round
GLOCHID *n* barbed spine on a plant
GLOCHIDIA *n* plural form of singular glochidium, a barbed hair on some plants
GLOCHIDS > GLOCHID
GLODE > GLIDE
GLOGG *n* hot alcoholic mixed drink
GLOGGS > GLOGG

GLOIRE *n* glory
GLOIRES > GLOIRE
GLOM *vb* attach oneself to or associate oneself with
GLOMERA > GLOMUS
GLOMERATE *adj* gathered into a compact rounded mass ▷ *vb* wind into a ball
GLOMERULE *n* cymose inflorescence in the form of a ball-like cluster of flowers
GLOMERULI *n* plural of singular glomerulus: a knot of blood vessels in the kidney
GLOMMED > GLOM
GLOMMING > GLOM
GLOMS > GLOM
GLOMUS *n* small anastomosis in an artery or vein
GLONOIN *n* nitroglycerin
GLONOINS > GLONOIN
GLOOM *n* melancholy ▷ *vb* look sullen or unhappy
GLOOMED > GLOOM
GLOOMFUL > GLOOM
GLOOMIER > GLOOMY
GLOOMIEST > GLOOMY
GLOOMILY > GLOOMY
GLOOMING > GLOOM
GLOOMINGS > GLOOM
GLOOMLESS > GLOOM
GLOOMS > GLOOM
GLOOMSTER *n* person with gloomy outlook
GLOOMY *adj* despairing or sad
GLOOP *vb* cover with a viscous substance
GLOOPED > GLOOP
GLOOPIER > GLOOP
GLOOPIEST > GLOOP
GLOOPING > GLOOP
GLOOPS > GLOOP
GLOOPY > GLOOP
GLOP *vb* cover with a viscous substance
GLOPPED > GLOP
GLOPPIER > GLOP
GLOPPIEST > GLOP
GLOPPING > GLOP
GLOPPY > GLOP
GLOPS > GLOP
GLORIA *n* silk, wool, cotton, or nylon fabric
GLORIAS > GLORIA
GLORIED > GLORY
GLORIES > GLORY
GLORIFIED > GLORIFY
GLORIFIER > GLORIFY
GLORIFIES > GLORIFY
GLORIFY *vb* make (something) seem more worthy than it is
GLORIOLE *another name for a* > HALO
GLORIOLES
> GLORIOLE
GLORIOSA *n* bulbous African tropical plant
GLORIOSAS
> GLORIOSA
GLORIOUS *adj* brilliantly beautiful
GLORY *n* praise or honour ▷ *vb* triumph or exalt

GLORYING > GLORY
GLOSS *n* surface shine or lustre ▷ *vb* make glossy
GLOSSA *n* paired tonguelike lobe in the labium of an insect
GLOSSAE > GLOSSA
GLOSSAL > GLOSSA
GLOSSARY *n* list of special or technical words with definitions
GLOSSAS > GLOSSA
GLOSSATOR *n* writer of glosses and commentaries, esp (in the Middle Ages) an interpreter of Roman and Canon Law
GLOSSED > GLOSS
GLOSSEME *n* smallest meaningful unit of a language, such as stress, form, etc
GLOSSEMES
> GLOSSEME
GLOSSER > GLOSS
GLOSSERS > GLOSS
GLOSSES > GLOSS
GLOSSIER > GLOSSY
GLOSSIES > GLOSSY
GLOSSIEST > GLOSSY
GLOSSILY > GLOSSY
GLOSSINA *n* tsetse fly
GLOSSINAS
> GLOSSINA
GLOSSING > GLOSS
GLOSSIST *same as*
> GLOSSATOR
GLOSSISTS
> GLOSSIST
GLOSSITIC
> GLOSSITIS
GLOSSITIS *n* inflammation of the tongue
GLOSSLESS > GLOSS
GLOSSY *adj* smooth and shiny ▷ *n* expensively produced magazine
GLOST *n* lead glaze used for pottery
GLOSTS > GLOST
GLOTTAL *adj* of the glottis
GLOTTIC *adj* of or relating to the tongue or the glottis
GLOTTIDES > GLOTTIS
GLOTTIS *n* vocal cords and the space between them
GLOTTISES > GLOTTIS
GLOUT *vb* look sullen
GLOUTED > GLOUT
GLOUTING > GLOUT
GLOUTS > GLOUT
GLOVE *n* covering for the hand
GLOVEBOX *n* small compartment in a car for miscellaneous articles
GLOVED > GLOVE
GLOVELESS > GLOVE
GLOVELIKE *adj* like a glove
GLOVER *n* person who makes or sells gloves
GLOVERS > GLOVER

GLOVES > GLOVE
GLOVING > GLOVE
GLOVINGS > GLOVING
GLOW *vb* emit light and heat without flames ▷ *n* glowing light
GLOWED > GLOW
GLOWER *n* scowl ▷ *vb* stare angrily
GLOWERED > GLOWER
GLOWERING > GLOWER
GLOWERS > GLOWER
GLOWFLIES > GLOWFLY
GLOWFLY *n* firefly
GLOWING *adj* full of praise
GLOWINGLY > GLOWING
GLOWLAMP *n* small light consisting of two or more electrodes in an inert gas
**GLOWLAMPS
> GLOWLAMP**
GLOWS > GLOW
GLOWSTICK *n* plastic tube containing a luminescent material, waved or held aloft esp at gigs, raves, etc
GLOWWORM *n* European beetle which produces a greenish light
**GLOWWORMS
> GLOWWORM**
GLOXINIA *n* tropical plant with large bell-shaped flowers
**GLOXINIAS
> GLOXINIA**
GLOZE *vb* explain away ▷ *n* flattery or deceit
GLOZED > GLOZE
GLOZES > GLOZE
GLOZING > GLOZE
GLOZINGS > GLOZE
GLUCAGON *n* hormone that releases glucose into the blood
**GLUCAGONS
> GLUCAGON**
GLUCAN *n* any polysaccharide consisting of a polymer of glucose
GLUCANS > GLUCAN
GLUCINA *n* oxide of glucinum
GLUCINAS > GLUCINA
**GLUCINIC
> GLUCINIUM**
GLUCINIUM *former name of >* BERYLLIUM
GLUCINUM *same as* **> GLUCINIUM**
**GLUCINUMS
> GLUCINIUM**
GLUCONATE *n* compound formed when a mineral is bound to gluconic acid
GLUCONIC *adj* as in *gluconic acid* acid that occurs naturally in fruit
GLUCOSE *n* kind of sugar found in fruit
GLUCOSES > GLUCOSE
GLUCOSIC > GLUCOSE
GLUCOSIDE *n* any of a large group of glycosides that yield glucose on hydrolysis

GLUE *n* natural or synthetic sticky substance ▷ *vb* fasten with glue
GLUEBALL *n* hypothetical composite subatomic particle
**GLUEBALLS
> GLUEBALL**
GLUED > GLUE
GLUEING > GLUE
GLUEISH *same as* **> GLUISH**
GLUELIKE > GLUE
GLUEPOT *n* container for holding glue
GLUEPOTS > GLUEPOT
GLUER > GLUE
GLUERS > GLUE
GLUES > GLUE
GLUEY > GLUE
GLUEYNESS > GLUE
GLUG *n* word representing a gurgling sound ▷ *vb* drink noisily, taking big gulps
GLUGGABLE *adj* (of wine) easy and pleasant to drink
GLUGGED > GLUG
GLUGGING > GLUG
GLUGS > GLUG
GLUHWEIN *n* mulled wine
**GLUHWEINS
> GLUHWEIN**
GLUIER > GLUE
GLUIEST > GLUE
GLUILY > GLUE
GLUINESS > GLUE
GLUING > GLUE
GLUISH *adj* having the properties of glue
GLUM *adj* sullen or gloomy
GLUME *n* one of a pair of dry membranous bracts in grasses
GLUMELIKE > GLUME
GLUMELLA *n* palea
**GLUMELLAS
> GLUMELLA**
GLUMES > GLUME
GLUMLY > GLUM
GLUMMER > GLUM
GLUMMEST > GLUM
GLUMNESS > GLUM
GLUMPIER > GLUMPY
GLUMPIEST > GLUMPY
GLUMPILY > GLUMPY
GLUMPISH > GLUMPY
GLUMPS *n* state of sulking
GLUMPY *adj* sullen
GLUMS *n* gloomy feelings
GLUNCH *vb* look sullen
GLUNCHED > GLUNCH
GLUNCHES > GLUNCH
GLUNCHING > GLUNCH
GLUON *n* hypothetical particle
GLUONS > GLUON
GLURGE *n* stories supposed to be true but often fabricated
GLURGES > GLURGE
GLUT *n* excessive supply ▷ *vb* oversupply
GLUTAEAL > GLUTAEUS
GLUTAEI > GLUTAEUS
GLUTAEUS *same as* **> GLUTEUS**

GLUTAMATE *n* any salt of glutamic acid, esp its sodium salt
GLUTAMIC *adj* as in *glutamic acid* nonessential amino acid that plays a part in nitrogen metabolism
GLUTAMINE *n* nonessential amino acid occurring in proteins: plays an important role in protein metabolism
GLUTCH *vb* swallow
GLUTCHED > GLUTCH
GLUTCHES > GLUTCH
GLUTCHING > GLUTCH
GLUTE *same as* **> GLUTEUS**
GLUTEAL > GLUTEUS
GLUTEI > GLUTEUS
GLUTELIN *n* water-insoluble plant protein found in cereals
**GLUTELINS
> GLUTELIN**
GLUTEN *n* protein found in cereal grain
GLUTENIN *n* type of protein
**GLUTENINS
> GLUTENIN**
GLUTENOUS > GLUTEN
GLUTENS > GLUTEN
GLUTES > GLUTE
GLUTEUS *n* any of the three muscles of the buttock
GLUTINOUS *adj* sticky or gluey
GLUTS > GLUT
GLUTTED > GLUT
GLUTTING > GLUT
GLUTTON *n* greedy person
GLUTTONS > GLUTTON
GLUTTONY *n* practice of eating too much
GLYCAEMIA *n* presence of glucose in blood
**GLYCAEMIC
> GLYCAEMIA**
GLYCAN *n* polysaccharide
GLYCANS > GLYCAN
GLYCATION *n* the bonding of a sugar molecule to a protein or lipid
GLYCEMIA *US spelling of* **> GLYCAEMIA**
**GLYCEMIAS
> GLYCEMIA**
GLYCEMIC > GLYCEMIA
GLYCERIA *n* manna grass
**GLYCERIAS
> GLYCERIA**
GLYCERIC *adj* of, containing, or derived from glycerol
GLYCERIDE *n* any fatty-acid ester of glycerol
GLYCERIN *same as* **> GLYCEROL**
GLYCERINE *same as* **> GLYCEROL**
**GLYCERINS
> GLYCERIN**

GLYCEROL *n* colourless odourless syrupy liquid
**GLYCEROLS
> GLYCEROL**
GLYCERYL *n* (something) derived from glycerol
**GLYCERYLS
> GLYCERYL**
GLYCIN *same as* **> GLYCINE**
GLYCINE *n* nonessential amino acid
GLYCINES > GLYCINE
GLYCINS > GLYCIN
GLYCOCOLL *n* glycine
GLYCOGEN *n* starchlike carbohydrate stored in the liver and muscles of humans and animals
**GLYCOGENS
> GLYCOGEN**
GLYCOL *n* another name (not in technical usage) for a diol
GLYCOLIC > GLYCOL
GLYCOLLIC > GLYCOL
GLYCOLS > GLYCOL
GLYCONIC *n* verse consisting of a spondee, choriamb and pyrrhic
**GLYCONICS
> GLYCONIC**
GLYCOSE *n* any of various monosaccharides
GLYCOSES > GLYCOSE
GLYCOSIDE *n* any of a group of substances, such as digitoxin, derived from monosaccharides by replacing the hydroxyl group by another group
GLYCOSYL *n* glucose-derived radical
**GLYCOSYLS
> GLYCOSYL**
GLYCYL *n* radical of glycine
GLYCYLS > GLYCYL
GLYPH *n* carved channel or groove
GLYPHIC > GLYPH
GLYPHS > GLYPH
GLYPTAL *n* alkyd resin
GLYPTALS > GLYPTAL
GLYPTIC *adj* of or relating to engraving or carving
GLYPTICS *n* art of engraving precious stones
GMELINITE *n* zeolitic mineral
GNAMMA *variant of* **> NAMMA**
GNAR *same as* **> GNARL**
GNARL *n* any knotty protuberance or swelling on a tree ▷ *vb* knot or cause to knot
GNARLED *adj* rough, twisted, and knobbly
GNARLIER > GNARLY
GNARLIEST > GNARLY
GNARLING > GNARL
GNARLS > GNARL
GNARLY *adj* good
GNARR *same as* **> GNARL**
GNARRED > GNAR
GNARRING > GNAR

g

g

GNARRS > GNARR

GNARS > GNAR

GNASH vb grind (the teeth) together ▷ n act of gnashing the teeth

GNASHED > GNASH

GNASHER n tooth

GNASHERS pl n teeth, esp false ones

GNASHES > GNASH

GNASHING > GNASH

GNASHINGS > GNASHING

GNAT n small biting two-winged fly

GNATHAL same as > GNATHIC

GNATHIC adj of or relating to the jaw

GNATHION n lowest point of the midline of the lower jaw: a reference point in craniometry

GNATHIONS > GNATHION

GNATHITE n appendage of an arthropod that is specialized for grasping or chewing

GNATHITES > GNATHITE

GNATHONIC adj deceitfully flattering

GNATLIKE > GNAT

GNATLING n small gnat

GNATLINGS > GNATLING

GNATS > GNAT

GNATTIER > GNATTY

GNATTIEST > GNATTY

GNATTY adj infested with gnats

GNATWREN n small bird of the gnatcatcher family

GNATWRENS > GNATWREN

GNAW vb bite or chew steadily ▷ n act or an instance of gnawing

GNAWABLE > GNAW

GNAWED > GNAW

GNAWER > GNAW

GNAWERS > GNAW

GNAWING > GNAW

GNAWINGLY > GNAW

GNAWINGS > GNAW

GNAWN > GNAW

GNAWS > GNAW

GNEISS n coarse-grained metamorphic rock

GNEISSES > GNEISS

GNEISSIC > GNEISS

GNEISSOID > GNEISS

GNEISSOSE > GNEISS

GNOCCHI n dumplings

GNOMAE > GNOME

GNOME n imaginary creature like a little old man

GNOMELIKE > GNOME

GNOMES > GNOME

GNOMIC adj of pithy sayings

GNOMICAL same as > GNOMIC

GNOMISH > GNOME

GNOMIST n writer of pithy sayings

GNOMISTS > GNOMIST

GNOMON n stationary arm on a sundial

GNOMONIC > GNOMON

GNOMONICS > GNOMON

GNOMONS > GNOMON

GNOSES > GNOSIS

GNOSIS n supposedly revealed knowledge of spiritual truths

GNOSTIC adj of, relating to, or possessing knowledge ▷ n one who knows

GNOSTICAL same as > GNOSTIC

GNOSTICS > GNOSTIC

GNOW n Australian wild bird

GNOWS > GNOW

GNU n ox-like S African antelope

GNUS > GNU

GO vb move to or from a place ▷ n attempt

GOA n Tibetan gazelle

GOAD vb provoke (someone) to take some kind of action, usu in anger ▷ n spur or provocation

GOADED > GOAD

GOADING > GOAD

GOADLIKE > GOAD

GOADS > GOAD

GOADSMAN n person who uses a goad

GOADSMEN > GOADSMAN

GOADSTER n goadsman

GOADSTERS > GOADSTER

GOAF n waste left in old mine workings

GOAFS > GOAF

GOAL n posts through which the ball or puck has to move to score ▷ vb in rugby, to convert a try into a goal

GOALBALL n game played with a ball that emits sound

GOALBALLS > GOALBALL

GOALED > GOAL

GOALIE n goalkeeper

GOALIES > GOALIE

GOALING > GOAL

GOALLESS > GOAL

GOALMOUTH n area in front of the goal

GOALPOST n one of the two posts marking the limit of a goal

GOALPOSTS > GOALPOST

GOALS > GOAL

GOALWARD adv towards a goal

GOALWARDS same as > GOALWARD

GOANNA n large Australian lizard

GOANNAS > GOANNA

GOARY variant spelling of > GORY

GOAS > GOA

GOAT n sure-footed ruminant animal with horns

GOATEE n pointed tuft-like beard

GOATEED > GOATEE

GOATEES > GOATEE

GOATFISH n red mullet

GOATHERD n person who looks after a herd of goats

GOATHERDS > GOATHERD

GOATIER > GOATY

GOATIES > GOATY

GOATIEST > GOATY

GOATISH adj of, like, or relating to a goat

GOATISHLY > GOATISH

GOATLIKE > GOAT

GOATLING n young goat

GOATLINGS > GOATLING

GOATS > GOAT

GOATSE n deliberately offensive image placed maliciously into a website

GOATSES > GOATSE

GOATSKIN n leather made from the skin of a goat

GOATSKINS > GOATSKIN

GOATWEED n plant of the genus Capraria

GOATWEEDS > GOATWEED

GOATY n pointed tuft-like beard ▷ adj resembling a goat

GOB n lump of a soft substance ▷ vb spit

GOBAN n board on which go is played

GOBANG n Japanese board-game

GOBANGS > GOBANG

GOBANS > GOBAN

GOBAR adj as in gobar numeral kind of numeral

GOBBED > GOB

GOBBELINE same as > GOBLIN

GOBBET n lump, esp of food

GOBBETS > GOBBET

GOBBI > GOBBO

GOBBIER > GOBBY

GOBBIEST > GOBBY

GOBBING > GOB

GOBBLE vb eat hastily and greedily ▷ n rapid gurgling cry of the male turkey ▷ interj imitation of this sound

GOBBLED > GOBBLE

GOBBLER n turkey

GOBBLERS > GOBBLER

GOBBLES > GOBBLE

GOBBLING > GOBBLE

GOBBO n hunchback

GOBBY adj loudmouthed and offensive

GOBI n (in Indian cookery) cauliflower

GOBIES > GOBY

GOBIID n small spiny-finned fish

GOBIIDS > GOBIID

GOBIOID n type of spiny-finned fish

GOBIOIDS > GOBIOID

GOBIS > GOBI

GOBLET n drinking cup without handles

GOBLETS > GOBLET

GOBLIN n (in folklore) small malevolent creature

GOBLINS > GOBLIN

GOBO n shield placed around a microphone

GOBOES > GOBO

GOBONEE same as > GOBONY

GOBONY adj in heraldry, composed of a row of small, alternately coloured, squares

GOBOS > GOBO

GOBS > GOB

GOBSHITE n vulgar Irish slang for a stupid person

GOBSHITES > GOBSHITE

GOBURRA n kookaburra

GOBURRAS > GOBURRA

GOBY n small spiny-finned fish

GOCHUJANG n spicy paste used in Korean cuisine

GOD n spirit or being worshipped as having supernatural power ▷ vb deify

GODAWFUL adj very bad or unpleasant

GODCHILD n child for whom a person stands as godparent

GODDAM vb damn

GODDAMMED > GODDAM

GODDAMMIT interj an oath expressing anger, surprise, irritation, etc

GODDAMN interj oath expressing anger, surprise, etc ▷ adj extremely ▷ vb damn

GODDAMNED > GODDAMN

GODDAMNIT interj god damn it

GODDAMNS > GODDAMN

GODDAMS > GODDAM

GODDED > GOD

GODDEN n evening greeting

GODDENS > GODDEN

GODDESS n female divinity

GODDESSES > GODDESS

GODDING > GOD

GODET n triangular piece of material inserted into a garment

GODETIA n plant with showy flowers

GODETIAS > GODETIA

GODETS > GODET

GODFATHER n male godparent ▷ vb be a godfather to

GODHEAD n essential nature and condition of being a god

GODHEADS > GODHEAD

GODHOOD n state of being divine

GODHOODS > GODHOOD

GODLESS adj wicked or unprincipled

GODLESSLY > GODLESS

GODLIER > GODLY

GODLIEST > GODLY

GODLIKE adj resembling or befitting a god or God

GODLILY > GODLY

GODLINESS > GODLY

GODLING n little god

GODLINGS > GODLING

GODLY adj devout or pious

GODMOTHER n female godparent

GODOWN n (in East Asia and India) a warehouse

GODOWNS > GODOWN

GODPARENT n person who promises at a child's baptism to bring the child up as a Christian

GODROON same as > GADROON

GODROONED > GODROON

GODROONS > GODROON

GODS > GOD

GODSEND n something unexpected but welcome

GODSENDS > GODSEND

GODSHIP n divinity

GODSHIPS > GODSHIP

GODSLOT n time in a schedule for religious broadcasts

GODSLOTS > GODSLOT

GODSO same as > GADSO

GODSON n male godchild

GODSONS > GODSON

GODSPEED n expression of one's good wishes for a person's success and safety

GODSPEEDS > GODSPEED

GODSQUAD n derogatory word for evangelical Christians

GODSQUADS > GODSQUAD

GODWARD adv towards God

GODWARDS same as > GODWARD

GODWIT n shore bird with long legs and an upturned bill

GODWITS > GODWIT

GOE same as > GO

GOEL n in Jewish law, a blood-avenger

GOELS > GOEL

GOER n person who attends something regularly

GOERS > GOER

GOES > GO

GOEST vb archaic 2nd person sing present of go

GOETH vb archaic 3rd person sing present of go

GOETHITE n black, brown, or yellow mineral

GOETHITES > GOETHITE

GOETIC > GOETY

GOETIES > GOETY

GOETY n witchcraft

GOEY adj go-ahead

GOFER n employee or assistant performing menial tasks

GOFERS > GOFER

GOFF obsolete variant of > GOLF

GOFFED > GOFF

GOFFER vb press pleats into (a frill) ▷ n ornamental frill made by pressing pleats

GOFFERED > GOFFER

GOFFERING > GOFFER

GOFFERS > GOFFER

GOFFING > GOFF

GOFFS > GOFF

GOGGA n any small insect

GOGGAS > GOGGA

GOGGLE vb (of the eyes) bulge ▷ n fixed or bulging stare

GOGGLEBOX n television set

GOGGLED > GOGGLE

GOGGLER n big-eyed scad

GOGGLERS > GOGGLER

GOGGLES > GOGGLE

GOGGLIER > GOGGLE

GOGGLIEST > GOGGLE

GOGGLING > GOGGLE

GOGGLINGS > GOGGLE

GOGGLY > GOGGLE

GOGLET n long-necked water-cooling vessel

GOGLETS > GOGLET

GOGO n disco

GOGOS > GOGO

GOHONZON n (in Nichiren Buddhism) paper scroll to which devotional chanting is directed

GOHONZONS > GOHONZON

GOIER > GOEY

GOIEST > GOEY

GOING > GO

GOINGS > GO

GOITER same as > GOITRE

GOITERED > GOITER

GOITERS > GOITER

GOITRE n swelling of the thyroid gland in the neck

GOITRED > GOITRE

GOITRES > GOITRE

GOITROGEN n substance that induces the formation of a goitre

GOITROUS > GOITRE

GOJI same as > WOLFBERRY

GOJIS > GOJI

GOLCONDA n source of wealth or riches, esp a mine

GOLCONDAS > GOLCONDA

GOLD n yellow precious metal ▷ adj made of gold

GOLDARN euphemistic variant of > GODDAMN

GOLDARNED > GOLDARN

GOLDARNS > GOLDARN

GOLDBRICK vb swindle

GOLDBUG n American beetle with a bright metallic lustre

GOLDBUGS > GOLDBUG

GOLDCREST n small bird with a yellow crown

GOLDEN adj made of gold ▷ vb gild

GOLDENED > GOLDEN

GOLDENER > GOLDEN

GOLDENEST > GOLDEN

GOLDENEYE n type of black-and-white diving duck of northern regions

GOLDENING > GOLDEN

GOLDENLY > GOLDEN

GOLDENROD n tall plant with spikes of small yellow flowers

GOLDENS > GOLDEN

GOLDER > GOLD

GOLDEST > GOLD

GOLDEYE n N American fish

GOLDEYES > GOLDEYE

GOLDFIELD n area in which there are gold deposits

GOLDFINCH n kind of finch, the male of which has yellow-and-black wings

GOLDFINNY same as > GOLDSINNY

GOLDFISH n orange fish kept in ponds or aquariums

GOLDIER > GOLDY

GOLDIES > GOLDY

GOLDIEST > GOLDY

GOLDISH > GOLD

GOLDLESS > GOLD

GOLDMINER n miner who works in a gold mine

GOLDS > GOLD

GOLDSINNY n small European fish

GOLDSIZE n adhesive used to fix gold leaf to a surface

GOLDSIZES > GOLDSIZE

GOLDSMITH n dealer in or maker of gold articles

GOLDSPINK n goldfinch

GOLDSTICK n colonel in the Life Guards who carries out ceremonial duties

GOLDSTONE n dark-coloured glass, usually green or brown, spangled with fine particles of gold, copper, or some other metal

GOLDTAIL n as in goldtail moth European moth with white wings and a soft white furry body with a yellow tail tuft

GOLDTONE adj gold-coloured ▷ n photographic image printed on a glass-plate with a painted golden backing

GOLDTONES > GOLDTONE

GOLDURN variant of > GODDAMN

GOLDURNS > GOLDURN

GOLDWORK n gold objects collectively

GOLDWORKS > GOLDWORK

GOLDY adj gold-like ▷ n goldfinch

GOLE obsolete spelling of > GOAL

GOLEM n (in Jewish legend) artificially created human

GOLEMS > GOLEM

GOLES > GOLE

GOLF n outdoor sport ▷ vb play golf

GOLFED > GOLF

GOLFER n person who plays golf

GOLFERS > GOLFER

GOLFIANA n collection of golfing memorabilia

GOLFIANAS > GOLFIANA

GOLFING > GOLF

GOLFINGS > GOLF

GOLFS > GOLF

GOLGOTHA n place of burial

GOLGOTHAS > GOLGOTHA

GOLIARD n one of a number of wandering scholars

GOLIARDIC > GOLIARD

GOLIARDS > GOLIARD

GOLIARDY > GOLIARD

GOLIAS vb behave outrageously

GOLIASED > GOLIAS

GOLIASES > GOLIAS

GOLIASING > GOLIAS

GOLIATH n giant

GOLIATHS > GOLIATH

GOLLAN n yellow flower

GOLLAND same as > GOLLAN

GOLLANDS > GOLLAND

GOLLANS > GOLLAN

GOLLAR same as > GOLLER

GOLLARED > GOLLAR

GOLLARING > GOLLAR

GOLLARS > GOLLAR

GOLLER vb roar

GOLLERED > GOLLER

GOLLERING > GOLLER

GOLLERS > GOLLER

GOLLIED > GOLLY

GOLLIES > GOLLY

GOLLOP vb eat or drink (something) quickly or greedily

GOLLOPED > GOLLOP

GOLLOPER > GOLLOP

GOLLOPERS > GOLLOP

GOLLOPING > GOLLOP

GOLLOPS > GOLLOP

GOLLY interj exclamation of mild surprise ▷ vb spit

GOLLYING > GOLLY

GOLOMYNKA n oily fish found only in Lake Baikal

GOLOSH same as > GALOSH

GOLOSHE same as > GALOSH

GOLOSHED > GOLOSH

GOLOSHES > GOLOSH

GOLOSHING > GOLOSH

GOLOSHOES > GOLOSH

GOLP same as > GOLPE

GOLPE n in heraldry, a purple circle

GOLPES > GOLPE
GOLPS > GOLP
GOMBEEN n usury
GOMBEENS > GOMBEEN
GOMBO same as > GUMBO
GOMBOS > GOMBO
GOMBRO same as > GUMBO
GOMBROON n Persian and Chinese pottery and porcelain wares
GOMBROONS > GOMBROON
GOMBROS > GOMBRO
GOMER n unwanted hospital patient
GOMERAL same as > GOMERIL
GOMERALS > GOMERAL
GOMEREL same as > GOMERIL
GOMERELS > GOMEREL
GOMERIL n Scots word for a slow-witted person
GOMERILS > GOMERIL
GOMERS > GOMER
GOMOKU another word for > GOBANG
GOMOKUS > GOMOKU
GOMPA n Tibetan monastery
GOMPAS > GOMPA
GOMPHOSES > GOMPHOSIS
GOMPHOSIS n form of immovable articulation in which a peglike part fits into a cavity, as in the setting of a tooth in its socket
GOMUTI n feather palm tree
GOMUTIS > GOMUTI
GOMUTO same as > GOMUTI
GOMUTOS > GOMUTO
GON n geometrical grade
GONAD n organ producing reproductive cells
GONADAL > GONAD
GONADIAL > GONAD
GONADIC > GONAD
GONADS > GONAD
GONCH same as > GITCH
GONCHES > GONCH
GONDELAY same as > GONDOLA
GONDELAYS > GONDELAY
GONDOLA n long narrow boat used in Venice
GONDOLAS > GONDOLA
GONDOLIER n person who propels a gondola
GONE > GO
GONEF same as > GANEF
GONEFS > GONEF
GONENESS n faintness from hunger
GONER n person or thing beyond help or recovery
GONERS > GONER
GONFALON n banner hanging from a crossbar
GONFALONS > GONFALON
GONFANON same as > GONFALON
GONFANONS > GONFANON

GONG n rimmed metal disc ▷ vb sound a gong
GONGED > GONG
GONGING > GONG
GONGLIKE > GONG
GONGS > GONG
GONGSTER n person who strikes a gong
GONGSTERS > GONGSTER
GONGYO n Buddhist ceremony
GONGYOS > GONGYO
GONIA > GONION
GONIATITE n type of extinct cephalopod mollusc similar to an ammonite
GONIDIA > GONIDIUM
GONIDIAL > GONIDIUM
GONIDIC > GONIDIUM
GONIDIUM n green algal cell in the thallus of a lichen
GONIF same as > GANEF
GONIFF same as > GANEF
GONIFFS > GONIFF
GONIFS > GONIF
GONION n point or apex of the angle of the lower jaw
GONIUM n immature reproductive cell
GONK n stuffed toy, often used as a mascot
GONKS > GONK
GONNA vb going to
GONOCOCCI n plural of singular gonococcus
GONOCYTE n any cell which may potentially undergo meiosis
GONOCYTES > GONOCYTE
GONODUCT n duct leading from a gonad to the exterior, through which gametes pass
GONODUCTS > GONODUCT
GONOF same as > GANEF
GONOFS > GONOF
GONOPH same as > GANEF
GONOPHORE n polyp in certain coelenterates that bears gonads
GONOPHS > GONOPH
GONOPOD n either of the reproductive organs of insects
GONOPODS > GONOPOD
GONOPORE n external pore in insects, earthworms, etc, through which the gametes are extruded
GONOPORES > GONOPORE
GONORRHEA n infectious venereal disease
GONOSOME n individuals, collectively, in a colonial animal that are involved with reproduction
GONOSOMES > GONOSOME
GONS > GON
GONYS n lower outline of a bird's bill

GONYSES > GONYS
GONZO adj wild or crazy ▷ n wild or crazy person
GONZOS > GONZO
GOO n sticky substance
GOOBER another name for > PEANUT
GOOBERS > GOOBER
GOOBIES > GOOBY
GOOBY n spittle
GOOD adj giving pleasure ▷ n benefit
GOODBY same as > GOODBYE
GOODBYE n expression used on parting ▷ interj expression used on parting ▷ sentence substitute farewell
GOODBYES > GOODBYE
GOODBYS > GOODBY
GOODFACED adj with a handsome face
GOODFELLA n gangster, esp one in the Mafia
GOODIE same as > GOODY
GOODIER > GOODY
GOODIES > GOODY
GOODIEST > GOODY
GOODINESS > GOODY
GOODISH > GOOD
GOODLIER > GOODLY
GOODLIEST > GOODLY
GOODLY adj considerable
GOODMAN n husband
GOODMEN > GOODMAN
GOODNESS n quality of being good ▷ interj exclamation of surprise
GOODNIGHT n conventional expression of farewell used in the evening or at night
GOODS > GOOD
GOODSIRE n grandfather
GOODSIRES > GOODSIRE
GOODTIME adj wildly seeking pleasure
GOODWIFE n mistress of a household
GOODWILL n kindly feeling
GOODWILLS > GOODWILL
GOODWIVES > GOODWIFE
GOODY n hero in a book or film ▷ interj child's exclamation of pleasure ▷ adj smug and sanctimonious
GOODYEAR n euphemistic term for the Devil
GOODYEARS > GOODYEAR
GOOEY adj sticky and soft
GOOEYNESS > GOOEY
GOOF n mistake ▷ vb make a mistake
GOOFBALL n barbiturate sleeping pill
GOOFBALLS > GOOFBALL
GOOFED > GOOF
GOOFIER > GOOFY
GOOFIEST > GOOFY
GOOFILY > GOOFY

GOOFINESS > GOOFY
GOOFING > GOOF
GOOFS > GOOF
GOOFUS n slow-witted or stupid person
GOOFUSES > GOOFUS
GOOFY adj silly or ridiculous
GOOG n egg
GOOGLE vb search on the internet using a search engine
GOOGLED > GOOGLE
GOOGLES > GOOGLE
GOOGLIES > GOOGLY
GOOGLING > GOOGLE
GOOGLY n ball that spins unexpectedly on the bounce
GOOGOL n number shown as one followed by 100 zeros
GOOGOLS > GOOGOL
GOOGS > GOOG
GOOIER > GOOEY
GOOIEST > GOOEY
GOOILY > GOOEY
GOOINESS n quality of being gooey
GOOK n sticky, messy substance
GOOKIER > GOOKY
GOOKIEST > GOOKY
GOOKS > GOOK
GOOKY adj sticky and messy
GOOL n corn marigold
GOOLD Scots word for > GOLD
GOOLDS > GOOLD
GOOLEY same as > GOOLIE
GOOLEYS > GOOLEY
GOOLIE n vulgar word for a testicle
GOOLIES > GOOLIE
GOOLS > GOOL
GOOLY same as > GOOLIE
GOOMBAH n patron or mentor
GOOMBAHS > GOOMBAH
GOOMBAY n Bahamian soft drink
GOOMBAYS > GOOMBAY
GOON n person hired to commit violent acts
GOONDA n (in India) habitual criminal
GOONDAS > GOONDA
GOONERIES > GOONERY
GOONERY n behaviour typical of goons
GOONEY n albatross
GOONEYS > GOONEY
GOONIE Scots word for a > GOWN
GOONIER > GOON
GOONIES > GOONIE
GOONIEST > GOON
GOONS > GOON
GOONY > GOON
GOOP n sticky or semiliquid substance
GOOPED adj as in gooped up sticky with goop
GOOPIER > GOOP
GOOPIEST > GOOP

GOOPINESS *n* quality of being goopy
GOOPS > GOOP
GOOPY > GOOP
GOOR *same as* > GUR
GOORAL *same as* > GORAL
GOORALS > GOORAL
GOORIE *same as* > KURI
GOORIES > GOORIE
GOOROO *same as* > GURU
GOOROOS > GOOROO
GOORS > GOOR
GOORY *same as* > KURI
GOOS > GOO
GOOSANDER *n* type of duck
GOOSE *n* web-footed bird like a large duck ▷ *vb* prod (someone) playfully in the bottom
GOOSED > GOOSE
GOOSEFISH *another name for* > MONKFISH
GOOSEFOOT *n* type of usu weedy plant with leaves shaped like a goose's foot
GOOSEGOB *n* gooseberry
GOOSEGOBS > GOOSEGOB
GOOSEGOG *n* gooseberry
GOOSEGOGS > GOOSEGOG
GOOSEHERD *n* person who herds geese
GOOSELIKE *adj* like a goose
GOOSENECK *n* pivot between the forward end of a boom and a mast, to allow the boom to swing freely
GOOSERIES > GOOSERY
GOOSERY *n* place for keeping geese
GOOSES > GOOSE
GOOSEY *same as* > GOOSY
GOOSEYS > GOOSEY
GOOSIER > GOOSY
GOOSIES > GOOSY
GOOSIEST > GOOSY
GOOSINESS > GOOSY
GOOSING > GOOSE
GOOSY *adj* of or like a goose ▷ *n* goose
GOPAK *n* Russian peasant dance
GOPAKS > GOPAK
GOPHER *n* American burrowing rodent ▷ *vb* burrow
GOPHERED > GOPHER
GOPHERING > GOPHER
GOPHERS > GOPHER
GOPIK *n* money unit of Azerbaijan
GOPIKS > GOPIK
GOPURA *n* gateway tower of an Indian temple
GOPURAM *same as* > GOPURA
GOPURAMS > GOPURAM
GOPURAS > GOPURA
GOR *interj* God! ▷ *n* seagull
GORA *n* (in Indian English) White or fair-skinned male
GORAL *n* small S Asian goat antelope

GORALS > GORAL
GORAMIES > GORAMY
GORAMY *same as* > GOURAMI
GORAS > GORA
GORBELLY *n* large belly
GORBLIMEY *interj* exclamation of surprise or annoyance ▷ *n* instance of having uttered this exclamation
GORBLIMY *same as* > GORBLIMEY
GORCOCK *n* male of the red grouse
GORCOCKS > GORCOCK
GORCROW *n* carrion crow
GORCROWS > GORCROW
GORDITA *n* small thick tortilla
GORDITAS > GORDITA
GORE *n* blood from a wound ▷ *vb* pierce with horns
GORED > GORE
GOREFEST *n* film featuring excessive depictions of bloodshed
GOREFESTS > GOREFEST
GOREHOUND *n* enthusiast of gory horror films
GORES > GORE
GORGE *n* deep narrow valley ▷ *vb* eat greedily
GORGEABLE > GORGE
GORGED > GORGE
GORGEDLY > GORGE
GORGEOUS *adj* strikingly beautiful or attractive
GORGER > GORGE
GORGERIN *another name for* > NECKING
GORGERINS > GORGERIN
GORGERS > GORGE
GORGES > GORGE
GORGET *n* collar-like piece of armour
GORGETED > GORGET
GORGETS > GORGET
GORGIA *n* improvised sung passage
GORGIAS > GORGIA
GORGING > GORGE
GORGIO *n* word used by Roma people for a non-Roma
GORGIOS > GORGIO
GORGON *n* terrifying or repulsive woman
GORGONEIA *n* plural of gorgoneion: representation of a Gorgon's head
GORGONIAN *n* type of coral with a horny or chalky branching skeleton, such as the sea fan and red coral
GORGONISE *vb* turn to stone
GORGONIZE *same as* > GORGONISE
GORGONS > GORGON
GORHEN *n* female red grouse
GORHENS > GORHEN

GORI *n* (in Indian English) White or fair-skinned female
GORIER > GORY
GORIEST > GORY
GORILLA *n* largest of the apes, found in Africa
GORILLAS > GORILLA
GORILLIAN > GORILLA
GORILLINE > GORILLA
GORILLOID > GORILLA
GORILY > GORY
GORINESS > GORY
GORING > GORE
GORINGS > GORE
GORIS > GORI
GORM *n* foolish person ▷ *vb* understand
GORMAND *same as* > GOURMAND
GORMANDS > GORMAND
GORMED > GORM
GORMIER > GORMY
GORMIEST > GORMY
GORMING > GORM
GORMLESS *adj* stupid
GORMS > GORM
GORMY *adj* gormless
GORP *same as* > GAWP
GORPED > GORP
GORPING > GORP
GORPS > GORP
GORS > GOR
GORSE *n* prickly yellow-flowered shrub
GORSEDD *n* meeting held daily before an eisteddfod
GORSEDDS > GORSEDD
GORSES > GORSE
GORSIER > GORSE
GORSIEST > GORSE
GORSOON *n* young boy
GORSOONS > GORSOON
GORSY > GORSE
GORY *adj* horrific or bloodthirsty
GOS > GO
GOSH *interj* exclamation of mild surprise or wonder
GOSHAWK *n* large hawk
GOSHAWKS > GOSHAWK
GOSHT *n* Indian meat dish
GOSHTS > GOSHT
GOSLARITE *n* hydrated zinc sulphate
GOSLET *n* pygmy goose
GOSLETS > GOSLET
GOSLING *n* young goose
GOSLINGS > GOSLING
GOSPEL *n* any of the first four books of the New Testament ▷ *adj* denoting a kind of religious music ▷ *vb* teach the gospel
GOSPELER *same as* > GOSPELLER
GOSPELERS > GOSPELER
GOSPELISE *vb* evangelise
GOSPELIZE *same as* > GOSPELISE
GOSPELLED > GOSPEL
GOSPELLER *n* person who reads or chants the Gospel in a religious service

GOSPELLY *adj* like gospel music
GOSPELS > GOSPEL
GOSPODA > GOSPODIN
GOSPODAR *n* hospodar
GOSPODARS > GOSPODAR
GOSPODIN *n* Russian title of address, often indicating respect
GOSPORT *n* aeroplane communication device
GOSPORTS > GOSPORT
GOSS *vb* spit
GOSSAMER *n* very fine fabric
GOSSAMERS > GOSSAMER
GOSSAMERY *adj* like gossamer
GOSSAN *n* oxidized portion of a mineral vein in rock
GOSSANS > GOSSAN
GOSSE *variant of* > GORSE
GOSSED > GOSS
GOSSES > GOSSE
GOSSIB *n* gossip
GOSSIBS > GOSSIB
GOSSING > GOSS
GOSSIP *n* idle talk, esp about other people ▷ *vb* engage in gossip
GOSSIPED > GOSSIP
GOSSIPER > GOSSIP
GOSSIPERS > GOSSIP
GOSSIPIER > GOSSIPY
GOSSIPING > GOSSIP
GOSSIPPED > GOSSIP
GOSSIPPER > GOSSIP
GOSSIPRY *n* idle talk
GOSSIPS > GOSSIP
GOSSIPY *adj* tending to gossip
GOSSOON *n* young boy
GOSSOONS > GOSSOON
GOSSYPINE *adj* cottony
GOSSYPOL *n* toxic crystalline pigment that is a constituent of cottonseed oil
GOSSYPOLS > GOSSYPOL
GOSTER *vb* laugh uncontrollably
GOSTERED > GOSTER
GOSTERING > GOSTER
GOSTERS > GOSTER
GOT > GET
GOTCH *same as* > GITCH
GOTCHA *adj* as in *gotcha lizard* Australian name for a crocodile
GOTCHAS > GOTCHA
GOTCHES > GOTCH
GOTCHIES *pl n* underwear
GOTH *n* aficionado of goth music and fashion
GOTHIC *adj* of or relating to a literary style ▷ *n* family of heavy script typefaces
GOTHICISE *same as* > GOTHICIZE
GOTHICISM > GOTHIC
GOTHICIZE *vb* make gothic in style

g

GOTHICS > GOTHIC
GOTHIER > GOTHY
GOTHIEST > GOTHY
GOTHITE *same as*
> GOETHITE
GOTHITES > GOTHITE
GOTHS > GOTH
GOTHY *adj* characteristic
of goth music and fashion
GOTTA *vb* got to
GOTTEN *a past participle of*
> GET
GOUACHE *n* (painting
using) watercolours mixed
with glue
GOUACHES > GOUACHE
GOUCH *vb* become drowsy
or lethargic under the
influence of narcotics
GOUCHED > GOUCH
GOUCHES > GOUCH
GOUCHING > GOUCH
GOUGE *vb* scoop or force
out ▷ *n* hole or groove
GOUGED > GOUGE
GOUGER *n* person or tool
that gouges
GOUGERE *n* choux pastry
flavoured with cheese
GOUGERES > GOUGERE
GOUGERS > GOUGER
GOUGES > GOUGE
GOUGING > GOUGE
GOUJEERS *same as*
> GOODYEAR
GOUJON *n* small strip of
food
GOUJONS > GOUJON
GOUK *same as* > GOWK
GOUKS > GOUK
GOULASH *n* rich stew
seasoned with paprika
GOULASHES > GOULASH
GOURA *n* large, crested
ground pigeon found in
New Guinea
GOURAMI *n* large SE Asian
labyrinth fish
GOURAMIES > GOURAMI
GOURAMIS > GOURAMI
GOURAS > GOURA
GOURD *n* fleshy fruit of a
climbing plant
GOURDE *n* standard
monetary unit of Haiti
GOURDES > GOURDE
GOURDFUL *n* as much as a
gourd will hold
GOURDFULS
> GOURDFUL
GOURDIER > GOURDY
GOURDIEST > GOURDY
GOURDLIKE > GOURD
GOURDS > GOURD
GOURDY *adj* (of horses)
swollen-legged
GOURMAND *n* person who
is very keen on food and
drink
GOURMANDS
> GOURMAND
GOURMET *n* connoisseur
of food and drink
GOURMETS > GOURMET
GOUSTIER > GOUSTY
GOUSTIEST > GOUSTY
GOUSTROUS *adj* stormy
GOUSTY *adj* dismal

GOUT *n* drop or splash (of
something)
GOUTFLIES > GOUTFLY
GOUTFLY *n* fly whose
larvae infect crops
GOUTIER > GOUTY
GOUTIEST > GOUTY
GOUTILY > GOUTY
GOUTINESS > GOUTY
GOUTS > GOUT
GOUTTE *n* (in heraldry)
the shape of a drop of
liquid
GOUTTES > GOUTTE
GOUTWEED *n* Eurasian
plant with white flowers
and creeping underground
stems
GOUTWEEDS > GOUTWEED
GOUTWORT *n* bishop's
weed
GOUTWORTS
> GOUTWORT
GOUTY *adj* having the
disease gout
GOV *n* boss
GOVERN *vb* rule, direct, or
control ▷ *n* ability to be
governed
GOVERNALL *n*
government
GOVERNED > GOVERN
GOVERNESS *n* woman
teacher in a private
household ▷ *vb* act as a
governess
GOVERNING > GOVERN
GOVERNOR *n* official
governing a province or
state
GOVERNORS
> GOVERNOR
GOVERNS > GOVERN
GOVS > GOV
GOWAN *n* any of various
yellow or white field
flowers
GOWANED > GOWAN
GOWANS > GOWAN
GOWANY > GOWAN
GOWD *Scots word for* > GOLD
GOWDER > GOWD
GOWDEST > GOWD
GOWDS > GOWD
GOWDSPINK *n* goldfinch
GOWF *vb* strike
GOWFED > GOWF
GOWFER > GOWF
GOWFERS > GOWF
GOWFING > GOWF
GOWFS > GOWF
GOWK *n* stupid person
GOWKS > GOWK
GOWL *n* substance in the
corner of the eyes after
sleep ▷ *vb* howl
GOWLAN *same as*
> GOLLAN
GOWLAND *same as*
> GOLLAN
GOWLANDS > GOWLAND
GOWLANS > GOWLAN
GOWLED > GOWL
GOWLING > GOWL
GOWLS > GOWL
GOWN *n* woman's long
formal dress ▷ *vb* supply
with or dress in a gown

GOWNBOY *n* foundationer
schoolboy who wears a
gown
GOWNBOYS > GOWNBOY
GOWNED > GOWN
GOWNING > GOWN
GOWNMAN *n* professional
person who wears a gown
GOWNMEN > GOWNMAN
GOWNS > GOWN
GOWNSMAN *same as*
> GOWNMAN
GOWNSMEN > GOWNSMAN
GOWPEN *n* pair of cupped
hands
GOWPENFUL *n* amount
that can be contained in
cupped hands
GOWPENS > GOWPEN
GOX *n* gaseous oxygen
GOXES > GOX
GOYLE *n* ravine
GOYLES > GOYLE
GOZZAN *same as*
> GOSSAN
GOZZANS > GOZZAN
GRAAL *n* holy grail
GRAALS > GRAAL
GRAB *vb* grasp suddenly,
snatch ▷ *n* sudden snatch
GRABBABLE > GRAB
GRABBED > GRAB
GRABBER > GRAB
GRABBERS > GRAB
GRABBIER > GRABBY
GRABBIEST > GRABBY
GRABBING > GRAB
GRABBLE *vb* scratch or
feel about with the hands
GRABBLED > GRABBLE
GRABBLER > GRABBLE
GRABBLERS > GRABBLE
GRABBLES > GRABBLE
GRABBLING > GRABBLE
GRABBY *adj* greedy or
selfish
GRABEN *n* elongated
trough of land
GRABENS > GRABEN
GRABS > GRAB
GRACE *n* beauty and
elegance ▷ *vb* honour
GRACED > GRACE
GRACEFUL *adj* having
beauty of movement,
style, or form
GRACELESS *adj* lacking
elegance
GRACES > GRACE
GRACILE *adj* gracefully
thin or slender
GRACILES > GRACILIS
GRACILIS *n* thin muscle
on the inner thigh
GRACILITY > GRACILE
GRACING > GRACE
GRACIOSO *n* clown in
Spanish comedy
GRACIOSOS
> GRACIOSO
GRACIOUS *adj* kind and
courteous ▷ *interj*
expression of mild surprise
or wonder
GRACKLE *n* American
songbird with a dark
iridescent plumage
GRACKLES > GRACKLE

GRAD *n* graduate
GRADABLE *adj* capable of
being graded ▷ *n* word of
this kind
GRADABLES
> GRADABLE
GRADATE *vb* change or
cause to change
imperceptibly
GRADATED > GRADATE
GRADATES > GRADATE
GRADATIM *adv* step by
step
GRADATING > GRADATE
GRADATION *n* (stage in) a
series of degrees or steps
GRADATORY *adj* moving
step by step ▷ *n* flight of
stairs
GRADDAN *vb* dress corn
GRADDANED > GRADDAN
GRADDANS > GRADDAN
GRADE *n* place on a scale
of quality, rank, or size
▷ *vb* arrange in grades
GRADED > GRADE
GRADELESS > GRADE
GRADELIER > GRADELY
GRADELY *adj* fine
GRADER *n* person or thing
that grades
GRADERS > GRADER
GRADES > GRADE
GRADIENT *n* (degree of)
slope ▷ *adj* sloping
uniformly
GRADIENTS
> GRADIENT
GRADIN *n* ledge above or
behind an altar
GRADINE *same as*
> GRADIN
GRADINES > GRADINE
GRADING > GRADE
GRADINGS > GRADING
GRADINI > GRADINO
GRADINO *n* work of art
that decorates an altar
gradin
GRADINS > GRADIN
GRADS > GRAD
GRADUAL *adj* occurring or
moving in small stages ▷ *n*
antiphon or group of
several antiphons
GRADUALLY > GRADUAL
GRADUALS > GRADUAL
GRADUAND *n* person who
is about to graduate
GRADUANDS
> GRADUAND
GRADUATE *vb* receive a
degree or diploma ▷ *n*
holder of a degree
GRADUATED
> GRADUATE
GRADUATES
> GRADUATE
GRADUATOR
> GRADUATE
GRADUS *n* book of études
or other musical exercises
GRADUSES > GRADUS
GRAECISE *same as*
> GRAECIZE
GRAECISED
> GRAECISE
GRAECISES > GRAECISE

GRAECIZE *vb* make or become like the ancient Greeks
GRAECIZED > GRAECIZE
GRAECIZES > GRAECIZE
GRAFF *same as* > GRAFT
GRAFFED > GRAFF
GRAFFING > GRAFF
GRAFFITI *pl n* words or drawings scribbled or sprayed on walls etc
GRAFFITIS > GRAFFITI
GRAFFITO *n* instance of graffiti
GRAFFS > GRAFF
GRAFT *n* surgical transplant of skin or tissue ▷ *vb* transplant (living tissue) surgically
GRAFTAGE *n* in horticulture, the art of grafting
GRAFTAGES > GRAFTAGE
GRAFTED > GRAFT
GRAFTER > GRAFT
GRAFTERS > GRAFT
GRAFTING > GRAFT
GRAFTINGS > GRAFT
GRAFTS > GRAFT
GRAHAM *n* cracker made of graham flour
GRAHAMS > GRAHAM
GRAIL *n* any desired ambition or goal
GRAILE *same as* > GRAIL
GRAILES > GRAILE
GRAILS > GRAIL
GRAIN *n* seedlike fruit of a cereal plant ▷ *vb* paint in imitation of the grain of wood or leather
GRAINAGE *n* duty paid on grain
GRAINAGES > GRAINAGE
GRAINE *n* eggs of the silkworm
GRAINED > GRAIN
GRAINER > GRAIN
GRAINERS > GRAIN
GRAINES > GRAINE
GRAINIER > GRAINY
GRAINIEST > GRAINY
GRAINING *n* pattern or texture of the grain of wood, leather, etc
GRAININGS > GRAINING
GRAINLESS > GRAIN
GRAINS > GRAIN
GRAINY *adj* resembling, full of, or composed of grain
GRAIP *n* long-handled gardening fork
GRAIPS > GRAIP
GRAITH *vb* clothe
GRAITHED > GRAITH
GRAITHING > GRAITH
GRAITHLY > GRAITH
GRAITHS > GRAITH
GRAKLE *same as* > GRACKLE
GRAKLES > GRAKLE

GRALLOCH *n* entrails of a deer ▷ *vb* disembowel (a deer killed in a hunt)
GRALLOCHS > GRALLOCH
GRAM *n* metric unit of mass
GRAMA *n* type of grass
GRAMARIES > GRAMARY
GRAMARY *same as* > GRAMARYE
GRAMARYE *n* magic, necromancy, or occult learning
GRAMARYES > GRAMARYE
GRAMAS > GRAMA
GRAMASH *n* type of gaiter
GRAMASHES > GRAMASH
GRAME *n* sorrow
GRAMERCY *interj* many thanks
GRAMMA *n* pasture grass of the South American plains
GRAMMAGE *n* weight of paper expressed as grams per square metre
GRAMMAGES > GRAMMAGE
GRAMMAR *n* branch of linguistics
GRAMMARS > GRAMMAR
GRAMMAS > GRAMMA
GRAMMATIC *adj* of or relating to grammar
GRAMME *same as* > GRAM
GRAMMES > GRAMME
GRAMOCHE *same as* > GRAMASH
GRAMOCHES > GRAMOCHE
GRAMP *n* grandfather
GRAMPA *variant of* > GRANDPA
GRAMPAS > GRAMPA
GRAMPIES > GRAMPY
GRAMPS > GRAMP
GRAMPUS *n* dolphin-like mammal
GRAMPUSES > GRAMPUS
GRAMPY *n* grandfather
GRAMS > GRAM
GRAN *n* grandmother
GRANA > GRANUM
GRANARIES > GRANARY
GRANARY *n* storehouse for grain
GRAND *adj* large or impressive, imposing ▷ *n* thousand pounds or dollars
GRANDAD *n* grandfather
GRANDADDY *same as* > GRANDAD
GRANDADS > GRANDAD
GRANDAM *n* archaic word for grandmother
GRANDAME *same as* > GRANDAM
GRANDAMES > GRANDAME
GRANDAMS > GRANDAM
GRANDAUNT *n* great-aunt
GRANDBABY *n* very young grandchild
GRANDDAD *same as* > GRANDAD

GRANDDADS > GRANDAD
GRANDDAM *same as* > GRANDAM
GRANDDAMS > GRANDDAM
GRANDE *feminine form of* > GRAND
GRANDEE *n* Spanish nobleman of the highest rank
GRANDEES > GRANDEE
GRANDER > GRAND
GRANDEST > GRAND
GRANDEUR *n* magnificence
GRANDEURS > GRANDEUR
GRANDIOSE *adj* imposing
GRANDIOSO *adv* (to be played) in a grand manner
GRANDKID *n* grandchild
GRANDKIDS > GRANDKID
GRANDLY > GRAND
GRANDMA *n* grandmother
GRANDMAMA *same as* > GRANDMA
GRANDMAS > GRANDMA
GRANDNESS > GRAND
GRANDPA *n* grandfather
GRANDPAPA *same as* > GRANDPA
GRANDPAS > GRANDPA
GRANDS > GRAND
GRANDSIR *same as* > GRANDSIRE
GRANDSIRE *n* grandfather
GRANDSIRS > GRANDSIR
GRANDSON *n* male grandchild
GRANDSONS > GRANDSON
GRANFER *n* grandfather
GRANFERS > GRANFER
GRANGE *n* country house with farm buildings
GRANGER *n* keeper or member of a grange
GRANGERS > GRANGER
GRANGES > GRANGE
GRANITA *n* Italian iced drink
GRANITAS > GRANITA
GRANITE *n* very hard igneous rock
GRANITES > GRANITE
GRANITIC > GRANITE
GRANITISE *vb* form granite
GRANITITE *n* any granite with a high content of biotite
GRANITIZE *same as* > GRANITISE
GRANITOID *n* rock that contains or resembles granite
GRANIVORE *n* animal that feeds on seeds and grain
GRANNAM *n* old woman
GRANNAMS > GRANNAM
GRANNIE *same as* > GRANNY
GRANNIED > GRANNY
GRANNIES > GRANNY

GRANNOM *n* type of caddis fly used as a bait by anglers
GRANNOMS > GRANNOM
GRANNY *n* grandmother ▷ *vb* defeat without conceding a single point
GRANNYING > GRANNY
GRANNYISH *adj* typical of or suitable for an elderly woman
GRANOLA *n* muesli-like breakfast cereal
GRANOLAS > GRANOLA
GRANOLITH *n* paving material consisting of a mixture of cement and crushed granite or granite chippings
GRANS > GRAN
GRANT *vb* consent to fulfil (a request) ▷ *n* money provided by a government for a specific purpose
GRANTABLE > GRANT
GRANTED > GRANT
GRANTEE *n* person to whom a grant is made
GRANTEES > GRANTEE
GRANTER > GRANT
GRANTERS > GRANT
GRANTING > GRANT
GRANTOR *n* person who makes a grant
GRANTORS > GRANTOR
GRANTS > GRANT
GRANTSMAN *n* student who specializes in obtaining grants
GRANTSMEN > GRANTSMAN
GRANULAR *adj* of or like grains
GRANULARY *adj* granular
GRANULATE *vb* make into grains
GRANULE *n* small grain
GRANULES > GRANULE
GRANULITE *n* granular foliated metamorphic rock in which the minerals form a mosaic of equal-sized granules
GRANULOMA *n* tumour composed of granulation tissue produced in response to chronic infection, inflammation, a foreign body, or to unknown causes
GRANULOSE *less common word for* > GRANULAR
GRANULOUS *adj* consisting of grains or granules
GRANUM *n* membrane layer in a chloroplast
GRANUMS > GRANUM
GRAPE *n* small juicy green or purple berry ▷ *vb* grope
GRAPED > GRAPE
GRAPELESS > GRAPE
GRAPELICE *pl n* lice that are destructive to grape plants
GRAPELIKE > GRAPE
GRAPERIES > GRAPERY
GRAPERY *n* building where grapes are grown

g

GRAPES n abnormal growth on the fetlock of a horse

GRAPESEED n seed of the grape

GRAPESHOT n bullets which scatter when fired

GRAPETREE n sea grape, a shrubby plant resembling a grapevine

GRAPEVINE n grape-bearing vine

GRAPEY > GRAPE

GRAPH n type of graph ▷ vb draw or represent in a graph

GRAPHED > GRAPH

GRAPHEME n smallest meaningful contrastive unit in a writing system

GRAPHEMES > GRAPHEME

GRAPHEMIC > GRAPHEME

GRAPHENE n layer of graphite one atom thick

GRAPHENES > GRAPHENE

GRAPHIC adj vividly descriptive

GRAPHICAL same as > GRAPHIC

GRAPHICLY > GRAPHIC

GRAPHICS pl n diagrams, graphs, etc, esp as used on a television programme or computer screen

GRAPHING > GRAPH

GRAPHITE n soft black form of carbon, used in pencil leads

GRAPHITES > GRAPHITE

GRAPHITIC > GRAPHITE

GRAPHIUM n stylus (for writing)

GRAPHIUMS > GRAPHIUM

GRAPHS > GRAPH

GRAPIER > GRAPE

GRAPIEST > GRAPE

GRAPINESS > GRAPE

GRAPING > GRAPE

GRAPLE same as > GRAPPLE

GRAPLES > GRAPLE

GRAPLIN same as > GRAPNEL

GRAPLINE same as > GRAPNEL

GRAPLINES > GRAPLINE

GRAPLINS > GRAPLIN

GRAPNEL n device with several hooks

GRAPNELS > GRAPNEL

GRAPPA n type of Italian brandy

GRAPPAS > GRAPPA

GRAPPLE vb try to cope with (something difficult) ▷ n grapnel

GRAPPLED > GRAPPLE

GRAPPLER > GRAPPLE

GRAPPLERS > GRAPPLE

GRAPPLES > GRAPPLE

GRAPPLING n act of gripping or seizing, as in wrestling

GRASP vb grip something firmly ▷ n grip or clasp

GRASPABLE > GRASP

GRASPED > GRASP

GRASPER > GRASP

GRASPERS > GRASP

GRASPING adj greedy or avaricious

GRASPLESS adj relaxed

GRASPS > GRASP

GRASS n common type of plant ▷ vb cover with grass

GRASSBIRD n type of warbler found in long grass and reed beds

GRASSED > GRASS

GRASSER n police informant

GRASSERS > GRASSER

GRASSES > GRASS

GRASSHOOK another name for > SICKLE

GRASSIER > GRASSY

GRASSIEST > GRASSY

GRASSILY > GRASSY

GRASSING > GRASS

GRASSINGS > GRASS

GRASSLAND n land covered with grass

GRASSLESS > GRASS

GRASSLIKE > GRASS

GRASSPLOT n plot of ground overgrown with grass

GRASSQUIT n tropical American finch

GRASSROOT adj relating to the ordinary people, especially as part of the electorate

GRASSUM n in Scots law, sum paid when taking a lease

GRASSUMS > GRASSUM

GRASSY adj covered with, containing, or resembling grass

GRASTE archaic past participle of > GRACE

GRAT > GREET

GRATE vb rub into small bits on a rough surface ▷ n framework of metal bars for holding fuel in a fireplace

GRATED > GRATE

GRATEFUL adj feeling or showing gratitude

GRATELESS > GRATE

GRATER n tool with a sharp surface for grating food

GRATERS > GRATER

GRATES > GRATE

GRATICULE n grid of intersecting lines, esp of latitude and longitude on which a map is drawn

GRATIFIED > GRATIFY

GRATIFIER > GRATIFY

GRATIFIES > GRATIFY

GRATIFY vb satisfy or please ▷ adj giving one satisfaction or pleasure

GRATIN n crust of browned breadcrumbs

GRATINATE vb cook until the juice is absorbed and the surface crisps

GRATINE adj cooked au gratin

GRATINEE vb cook au gratin

GRATINEED > GRATINEE

GRATINEES > GRATINEE

GRATING adj harsh or rasping ▷ n framework of metal bars covering an opening

GRATINGLY > GRATING

GRATINGS > GRATING

GRATINS > GRATIN

GRATIS adj free, for nothing

GRATITUDE n feeling of being thankful for a favour or gift

GRATTOIR n scraper made of flint

GRATTOIRS > GRATTOIR

GRATUITY n money given for services rendered, tip

GRATULANT > GRATULATE

GRATULATE vb greet joyously

GRAUNCH vb crush or destroy

GRAUNCHED > GRAUNCH

GRAUNCHER > GRAUNCH

GRAUNCHES > GRAUNCH

GRAUPEL n soft hail or snow pellets

GRAUPELS > GRAUPEL

GRAV n unit of acceleration

GRAVADLAX same as > GRAVLAX

GRAVAMEN n that part of an accusation weighing most heavily against an accused

GRAVAMENS > GRAVAMEN

GRAVAMINA > GRAVAMEN

GRAVE n hole for burying a corpse ▷ adj causing concern ▷ vb cut, carve, sculpt, or engrave ▷ adv to be performed in a solemn manner

GRAVED > GRAVE

GRAVEL n mixture of small stones and coarse sand ▷ vb cover with gravel

GRAVELED > GRAVEL

GRAVELESS > GRAVE

GRAVELIKE > GRAVE

GRAVELING > GRAVEL

GRAVELISH > GRAVEL

GRAVELLED > GRAVEL

GRAVELLY adj like gravel

GRAVELS > GRAVEL

GRAVELY > GRAVE

GRAVEN > GRAVE

GRAVENESS > GRAVE

GRAVER n tool for engraving

GRAVERS > GRAVER

GRAVES > GRAVE

GRAVESIDE n area surrounding a grave

GRAVESITE n site of grave

GRAVEST > GRAVE

GRAVEWARD adj moving towards grave

GRAVEYARD n cemetery

GRAVID adj pregnant

GRAVIDA n pregnant woman

GRAVIDAE > GRAVIDA

GRAVIDAS > GRAVIDA

GRAVIDITY > GRAVID

GRAVIDLY > GRAVID

GRAVIES > GRAVY

GRAVING > GRAVE

GRAVINGS > GRAVE

GRAVIS adj as in myasthenia gravis chronic muscle-weakening disease

GRAVITAS n seriousness or solemnity

GRAVITATE vb be influenced or drawn towards

GRAVITIES > GRAVITY

GRAVITINO n hypothetical subatomic particle

GRAVITON n postulated quantum of gravitational energy

GRAVITONS > GRAVITON

GRAVITY n force of attraction

GRAVLAKS same as > GRAVLAX

GRAVLAX n dry-cured salmon

GRAVLAXES > GRAVLAX

GRAVS > GRAV

GRAVURE n method of intaglio printing

GRAVURES > GRAVURE

GRAVY n juices from meat in cooking

GRAWLIX n sequence of symbols used in text to replace profanity

GRAWLIXES > GRAWLIX

GRAY same as > GREY

GRAYBACK same as > GREYBACK

GRAYBACKS > GRAYBACK

GRAYBEARD same as > GREYBEARD

GRAYED > GRAY

GRAYER > GRAY

GRAYEST > GRAY

GRAYFISH n dogfish

GRAYFLIES > GRAYFLY

GRAYFLY n trumpet fly

GRAYHEAD n one with grey hair

GRAYHEADS > GRAYHEAD

GRAYHEN n female of the black grouse

GRAYHENS > GRAYHEN

GRAYHOUND US spelling of > GREYHOUND

GRAYING > GRAY

g

GRAYISH > GRAY

GRAYLAG same as > GREYLAG

GRAYLAGS > GRAYLAG

GRAYLE n holy grail

GRAYLES > GRAYLE

GRAYLING n fish of the salmon family

GRAYLINGS > GRAYLING

GRAYLIST vb hold (someone) in suspicion, without actually excluding him or her from a particular activity

GRAYLISTS > GRAYLIST

GRAYLY > GRAY

GRAYMAIL n tactic to avoid prosecution in an espionage case

GRAYMAILS > GRAYMAIL

GRAYNESS > GREY

GRAYOUT n impairment of vision due to lack of oxygen

GRAYOUTS > GRAYOUT

GRAYS > GRAY

GRAYSCALE adj in shades of grey

GRAYSTONE n grey igneous rock of volcanic origin

GRAYWACKE same as > GREYWACKE

GRAYWATER n water that has been used

GRAZABLE > GRAZE

GRAZE vb feed on grass ▷ n slight scratch or scrape

GRAZEABLE > GRAZE

GRAZED > GRAZE

GRAZER > GRAZE

GRAZERS > GRAZE

GRAZES > GRAZE

GRAZIER n person who feeds cattle for market

GRAZIERS > GRAZIER

GRAZING n land on which grass for livestock is grown

GRAZINGLY > GRAZE

GRAZINGS > GRAZING

GRAZIOSO adv (of music) to be played gracefully

GREASE n soft melted animal fat ▷ vb apply grease to

GREASED > GREASE

GREASER n mechanic, esp of motor vehicles

GREASERS > GREASER

GREASES > GREASE

GREASIER > GREASY

GREASIES > GREASY

GREASIEST > GREASY

GREASILY > GREASY

GREASING > GREASE

GREASY adj covered with or containing grease ▷ n shearer

GREAT adj large in size or number ▷ n distinguished person

GREATCOAT n heavy overcoat

GREATEN vb make or become great

GREATENED > GREATEN

GREATENS > GREATEN

GREATER > GREAT

GREATEST n most outstanding individual in a given field

GREATESTS > GREATEST

GREATLY > GREAT

GREATNESS > GREAT

GREATS > GREAT

GREAVE n piece of armour for the shin ▷ vb grieve

GREAVED > GREAVE

GREAVES pl n residue left after the rendering of tallow

GREAVING > GREAVE

GREBE n diving water bird

GREBES > GREBE

GREBO same as > GREEBO

GREBOES > GREBO

GREBOS > GREBO

GRECE n flight of steps

GRECES > GRECE

GRECIAN same as > GRECE

GRECIANS > GRECIAN

GRECISE same as > GRAECIZE

GRECISED > GRECISE

GRECISES > GRECISE

GRECISING > GRECISE

GRECIZE same as > GRAECIZE

GRECIZED > GRECIZE

GRECIZES > GRECIZE

GRECIZING > GRECIZE

GRECQUE n ornament of Greek origin

GRECQUES > GRECQUE

GREE n superiority or victory ▷ vb come or cause to come to agreement or harmony

GREEBO n unkempt or dirty-looking rock music fan

GREEBOES > GREEBO

GREEBOS > GREEBO

GREECE same as > GRECE

GREECES > GRECE

GREED n excessive desire for food, wealth, etc

GREEDHEAD n avaricious person

GREEDIER > GREEDY

GREEDIEST > GREEDY

GREEDILY > GREEDY

GREEDLESS > GREED

GREEDS > GREED

GREEDSOME same as > GREEDY

GREEDY adj having an excessive desire for something

GREEGREE same as > GRIGRI

GREEGREES > GREEGREE

GREEING > GREE

GREEK vb represent text as grey lines on a computer screen

GREEKED > GREEK

GREEKING > GREEK

GREEKINGS > GREEK

GREEN adj of a colour between blue and yellow ▷ n colour between blue and yellow ▷ vb make or become green

GREENBACK n inconvertible legal-tender US currency note originally issued during the Civil War in 1862

GREENBELT n zone of farmland, parks, and open country surrounding a town or city

GREENBONE n an eel-like food fish

GREENBUG n common name for Schizaphis graminum

GREENBUGS > GREENBUG

GREENED > GREEN

GREENER n recent immigrant

GREENERS > GREENER

GREENERY n vegetation

GREENEST > GREEN

GREENEYE n small slender fish with pale green eyes

GREENEYES > GREENEYE

GREENFLY n green aphid, a common garden pest

GREENGAGE n sweet green plum

GREENHAND n greenhorn

GREENHEAD n male mallard

GREENHORN n novice

GREENIE n conservationist

GREENIER > GREEN

GREENIES > GREENIE

GREENIEST > GREEN

GREENING n process of making or becoming more aware of environmental considerations

GREENINGS > GREENING

GREENISH > GREEN

GREENLET n type of insectivorous songbird

GREENLETS > GREENLET

GREENLING n type of food fish of the N Pacific Ocean

GREENLIT adj given permission to proceed

GREENLY > GREEN

GREENMAIL n practice of a company buying sufficient shares in another company to threaten takeover and making a quick profit as a result of the threatened company buying back its shares at a higher price ▷ vb carry out the practice of greenmail

GREENNESS > GREEN

GREENROOM n backstage room in a theatre where performers rest or receive visitors

GREENS > GREEN

GREENSAND n olive-green sandstone consisting mainly of quartz and glauconite

GREENSICK adj having greensickness: same as chlorosis

GREENSOME n match for two pairs in which each of the four players tees off and after selecting the better drive the partners of each pair play that ball alternately

GREENTH n greenness

GREENTHS > GREENTH

GREENWASH n superficial or insincere display of concern for the environment that is shown by an organization ▷ vb adopt a 'greenwash' policy

GREENWAY n linear open space, with pedestrian and cycle paths

GREENWAYS > GREENWAY

GREENWEED n woodwaxen

GREENWING n teal

GREENWOOD n forest or wood when the leaves are green

GREENY > GREEN

GREES > GREE

GREESE same as > GRECE

GREESES > GREESE

GREESING > GREESE

GREESINGS > GREESE

GREET vb meet with expressions of welcome ▷ n weeping

GREETE same as > GREET

GREETED > GREET

GREETER n person who greets people

GREETERS > GREETER

GREETES > GREETE

GREETING n act or words of welcoming on meeting

GREETINGS > GREETING

GREETS > GREET

GREFFIER n registrar

GREFFIERS > GREFFIER

GREGALE n northeasterly wind occurring in the Mediterranean

GREGALES > GREGALE

GREGARIAN adj gregarious

GREGARINE n type of parasitic protozoan typically occurring in other invertebrates

GREGATIM adv in flocks or crowds

GREGE vb make heavy

GREGED > GREGE

GREGES > GREGE

GREGING > GREGE

GREGO n short, thick jacket

GREGOS > GREGO

GREIGE adj (of a fabric or material) not yet dyed ▷ n unbleached or undyed cloth or yarn

g

GREIGES > GREIGE
GREIN vb desire fervently
GREINED > GREIN
GREINING > GREIN
GREINS > GREIN
GREISEN n light-coloured metamorphic rock
GREISENS > GREISEN
GREISLY same as > GRISLY
GREMIAL n cloth spread on the lap of a bishop during Mass
GREMIALS > GREMIAL
GREMLIN n imaginary being
GREMLINS > GREMLIN
GREMMIE n young surfer
GREMMIES > GREMMIE
GREMMY same as > GREMMIE
GREMOLATA n garnish of finely chopped parsley, garlic and lemon
GREN same as > GRIN
GRENACHE n variety of grape
GRENACHES > GRENACHE
GRENADE n small bomb
GRENADES > GRENADE
GRENADIER n soldier of a regiment formerly trained to throw grenades
GRENADINE n syrup made from pomegranates
GRENNED > GREN
GRENNING > GREN
GRENS > GREN
GRESE same as > GRECE
GRESES > GRESE
GRESSING same as > GRECE
GRESSINGS > GRESSING
GREVE same as > GREAVE
GREVES > GREVE
GREVILLEA n any of various Australian evergreen trees and shrubs
GREW vb shudder
GREWED > GREW
GREWHOUND n greyhound
GREWING > GREW
GREWS > GREW
GREWSOME archaic or US spelling of > GRUESOME
GREWSOMER > GREWSOME
GREX n group of plants
GREXES > GREX
GREY adj of a colour between black and white ▷ n grey colour ▷ vb become or make grey
GREYBACK n any of various animals having a grey back, such as the grey whale and the hooded crow
GREYBACKS > GREYBACK
GREYBEARD n old man, esp a sage
GREYED > GREY
GREYER > GREY

GREYEST > GREY
GREYHEAD n one having grey hair
GREYHEADS > GREYHEAD
GREYHEN n female of the black grouse
GREYHENS > GREYHEN
GREYHOUND n swift slender dog used in racing
GREYING > GREY
GREYINGS > GREY
GREYISH > GREY
GREYLAG n large grey goose
GREYLAGS > GREYLAG
GREYLIST vb hold (someone) in suspicion, without actually excluding him or her from a particular activity
GREYLISTS > GREYLIST
GREYLY > GREY
GREYNESS > GREY
GREYS > GREY
GREYSCALE n range of grey shades from white to black
GREYSTONE n type of grey rock
GREYWACKE n any dark sandstone or grit having a matrix of clay minerals
GRIBBLE n type of small marine crustacean
GRIBBLES > GRIBBLE
GRICE vb collect objects concerned with railways ▷ n object collected or place visited by a railway enthusiast
GRICED > GRICE
GRICER > GRICE
GRICERS > GRICE
GRICES > GRICE
GRICING > GRICE
GRICINGS > GRICE
GRID n network of horizontal and vertical lines, bars, etc ▷ vb form a grid pattern
GRIDDED > GRID
GRIDDER n American football player
GRIDDERS > GRIDDER
GRIDDING > GRID
GRIDDLE n flat iron plate for cooking ▷ vb cook (food) on a griddle
GRIDDLED > GRIDDLE
GRIDDLES > GRIDDLE
GRIDDLING > GRIDDLE
GRIDE vb grate or scrape harshly ▷ n harsh or piercing sound
GRIDED > GRIDE
GRIDELIN n greyish violet colour
GRIDELINS > GRIDELIN
GRIDES > GRIDE
GRIDING > GRIDE
GRIDIRON n frame of metal bars for grilling food ▷ vb cover with parallel lines
GRIDIRONS > GRIDIRON

GRIDLOCK n situation where traffic is not moving ▷ vb (of traffic) to obstruct (an area)
GRIDLOCKS > GRIDLOCK
GRIDS > GRID
GRIECE same as > GRECE
GRIECED > GRIECE
GRIECES > GRIECE
GRIEF n deep sadness
GRIEFER n online gamer who spoils the game for others on purpose
GRIEFERS > GRIEFER
GRIEFFUL adj stricken with grief
GRIEFLESS > GRIEF
GRIEFS > GRIEF
GRIESIE same as > GRISY
GRIESLY same as > GRISY
GRIESY same as > GRISY
GRIEVANCE n real or imaginary cause for complaint
GRIEVANT n any person with a grievance
GRIEVANTS > GRIEVANT
GRIEVE vb (cause to) feel grief ▷ n farm manager or overseer
GRIEVED > GRIEVE
GRIEVER > GRIEVE
GRIEVERS > GRIEVE
GRIEVES > GRIEVE
GRIEVING > GRIEVE
GRIEVINGS > GRIEVE
GRIEVOUS adj very severe or painful
GRIFF n information
GRIFFE n carved ornament at the base of a column
GRIFFES > GRIFFE
GRIFFIN n mythical monster
GRIFFINS > GRIFFIN
GRIFFON same as > GRIFFIN
GRIFFONS > GRIFFON
GRIFFS > GRIFF
GRIFT vb swindle
GRIFTED > GRIFT
GRIFTER > GRIFT
GRIFTERS > GRIFT
GRIFTING > GRIFT
GRIFTS > GRIFT
GRIG n young eel ▷ vb fish for grigs
GRIGGED > GRIG
GRIGGING > GRIG
GRIGRI n African talisman, amulet, or charm
GRIGRIS > GRIGRI
GRIGS > GRIG
GRIKE n fissure in rock
GRIKES > GRIKE
GRILL n device on a cooker ▷ vb cook under a grill
GRILLADE n grilled food
GRILLADES > GRILLADE

GRILLAGE n arrangement of beams and crossbeams used as a foundation on soft ground
GRILLAGES > GRILLAGE
GRILLE n grating over an opening
GRILLED adj cooked on a grill or gridiron
GRILLER > GRILL
GRILLERS > GRILL
GRILLERY n place where food is grilled
GRILLES > GRILLE
GRILLING > GRILL
GRILLINGS > GRILL
GRILLION n extremely large but unspecified number, quantity, or amount ▷ determiner amounting to a grillion
GRILLIONS > GRILLION
GRILLROOM n restaurant serving grilled foods
GRILLS > GRILL
GRILLWORK same as > GRILL
GRILSE n salmon on its first return from the sea to fresh water
GRILSES > GRILSE
GRIM adj stern
GRIMACE n ugly or distorted facial expression ▷ vb make a grimace
GRIMACED > GRIMACE
GRIMACER > GRIMACE
GRIMACERS > GRIMACE
GRIMACES > GRIMACE
GRIMACING > GRIMACE
GRIMALKIN n old cat, esp an old female cat
GRIME n ingrained dirt ▷ vb make very dirty
GRIMED > GRIME
GRIMES > GRIME
GRIMIER > GRIME
GRIMIEST > GRIME
GRIMILY > GRIME
GRIMINESS > GRIME
GRIMING > GRIME
GRIMLY > GRIM
GRIMMER > GRIM
GRIMMEST > GRIM
GRIMNESS > GRIM
GRIMOIRE n textbook of sorcery and magic
GRIMOIRES > GRIMOIRE
GRIMY > GRIME
GRIN vb smile broadly, showing the teeth ▷ n broad smile
GRINCH n person whose attitude has a dispiriting effect
GRINCHES > GRINCH
GRIND vb crush or rub to a powder ▷ n hard work
GRINDED obsolete past participle of > GRIND
GRINDELIA n type of coarse American plant with yellow daisy-like flower heads
GRINDER n device for grinding substances

GRINDERS > GRINDER
GRINDERY n place in which tools and cutlery are sharpened
GRINDING > GRIND
GRINDINGS > GRIND
GRINDS > GRIND
GRINNED > GRIN
GRINNER > GRIN
GRINNERS > GRIN
GRINNING > GRIN
GRINNINGS > GRIN
GRINS > GRIN
GRIOT n (in W Africa) member of a caste recording tribal history
GRIOTS > GRIOT
GRIP n firm hold or grasp ▷ vb grasp or hold tightly
GRIPE vb complain persistently ▷ n complaint
GRIPED > GRIPE
GRIPER > GRIPE
GRIPERS > GRIPE
GRIPES > GRIPE
GRIPEY adj causing gripes
GRIPIER > GRIPEY
GRIPIEST > GRIPEY
GRIPING n act of griping
GRIPINGLY > GRIPE
GRIPINGS > GRIPING
GRIPLE same as > GRIPPLE
GRIPMAN n cable-car operator
GRIPMEN > GRIPMAN
GRIPPE former name for > INFLUENZA
GRIPPED > GRIP
GRIPPER > GRIP
GRIPPERS > GRIP
GRIPPES > GRIPPE
GRIPPIER > GRIPPY
GRIPPIEST > GRIPPY
GRIPPING > GRIP
GRIPPLE adj greedy ▷ n hook
GRIPPLES > GRIPPLE
GRIPPY adj having grip
GRIPS > GRIP
GRIPSACK n travel bag
GRIPSACKS > GRIPSACK
GRIPT archaic variant of > GRIPPED
GRIPTAPE n rough tape for sticking to a surface to provide a greater grip
GRIPTAPES > GRIPTAPE
GRIPY same as > GRIPEY
GRIS same as > GRECE
GRISAILLE n technique of monochrome painting in shades of grey, as in an oil painting or a wall decoration, imitating the effect of relief
GRISE vb shudder
GRISED > GRISE
GRISELY same as > GRISLY
GRISEOUS adj streaked or mixed with grey
GRISES > GRISE
GRISETTE n (formerly) a young French working-class woman

GRISETTES > GRISETTE
GRISGRIS same as > GRIGRI
GRISING > GRISE
GRISKIN n lean part of a loin of pork
GRISKINS > GRISKIN
GRISLED another word for > GRIZZLED
GRISLIER > GRISLY
GRISLIES > GRISLY
GRISLIEST > GRISLY
GRISLY adj horrifying or ghastly ▷ n large American bear
GRISON n type of mammal
GRISONS > GRISON
GRISSINI pl n thin crisp breadsticks
GRISSINO n Italian breadstick
GRIST n grain for grinding
GRISTER n device for grinding grain
GRISTERS > GRISTER
GRISTLE n tough stringy animal tissue found in meat
GRISTLES > GRISTLE
GRISTLIER > GRISTLE
GRISTLY > GRISTLE
GRISTMILL n mill, esp one equipped with large grinding stones for grinding grain
GRISTS > GRIST
GRISY adj grim
GRIT n rough particles of sand ▷ vb spread grit on (an icy road etc) ▷ adj great
GRITH n security or peace guaranteed for a period of time
GRITHS > GRITH
GRITLESS > GRIT
GRITS > GRIT
GRITSTONE same as > GRIT
GRITTED > GRIT
GRITTER n vehicle that spreads grit on the roads
GRITTERS > GRITTER
GRITTEST > GRIT
GRITTIER > GRITTY
GRITTIEST > GRITTY
GRITTILY > GRITTY
GRITTING n spreading grit on road surfaces
GRITTINGS > GRITTING
GRITTY adj courageous and tough
GRIVATION n (in navigation) grid variation
GRIVET n E African monkey
GRIVETS > GRIVET
GRIZ n grizzly bear
GRIZE same as > GRECE
GRIZES > GRIZE
GRIZZES > GRIZ
GRIZZLE vb whine or complain ▷ n grey colour
GRIZZLED adj grey-haired

GRIZZLER > GRIZZLE
GRIZZLERS > GRIZZLE
GRIZZLES > GRIZZLE
GRIZZLIER > GRIZZLY
GRIZZLIES > GRIZZLY
GRIZZLING > GRIZZLE
GRIZZLY n large American bear ▷ adj somewhat grey
GROAN n deep sound of grief or pain ▷ vb utter a groan
GROANED > GROAN
GROANER n person or thing that groans
GROANERS > GROANER
GROANFUL adj sad
GROANING > GROAN
GROANINGS > GROAN
GROANS > GROAN
GROAT n fourpenny piece
GROATS pl n hulled and crushed grain of various cereals
GROCER n shopkeeper selling foodstuffs
GROCERIES pl n food and other household supplies
GROCERS > GROCER
GROCERY n business or premises of a grocer
GROCKED same as > GROKKED
GROCKING same as > GROKKING
GROCKLE n tourist in SW England
GROCKLES > GROCKLE
GRODIER > GRODY
GRODIEST > GRODY
GRODY adj unpleasant
GROG n spirit, usu rum, and water ▷ vb drink grog
GROGGED > GROG
GROGGERY n grogshop
GROGGIER > GROGGY
GROGGIEST > GROGGY
GROGGILY > GROGGY
GROGGING > GROG
GROGGY adj faint, shaky, or dizzy
GROGRAM n coarse fabric
GROGRAMS > GROGRAM
GROGS > GROG
GROGSHOP n drinking place, esp one of disreputable character
GROGSHOPS > GROGSHOP
GROIN n place where the legs join the abdomen ▷ vb construct with curved arrises
GROINED > GROIN
GROINING > GROIN
GROININGS > GROIN
GROINS > GROIN
GROK vb understand completely and intuitively
GROKED > GROK
GROKING > GROK
GROKKED > GROK
GROKKING > GROK
GROKS > GROK
GROMA n Roman surveying instrument
GROMAS > GROMA

GROMET same as > GROMMET
GROMETS > GROMET
GROMMET n ring or eyelet
GROMMETED adj having grommets
GROMMETS > GROMMET
GROMWELL n hairy flowering plant
GROMWELLS > GROMWELL
GRONE obsolete word for > GROAN
GRONED > GRONE
GRONEFULL same as > GROANFUL
GRONES > GRONE
GRONING > GRONE
GROOF n face, or front of the body
GROOFS > GROOF
GROOLIER > GROOLY
GROOLIEST > GROOLY
GROOLY adj gruesome
GROOM n person who looks after horses ▷ vb make or keep one's clothes and appearance neat and tidy
GROOMED > GROOM
GROOMER > GROOM
GROOMERS > GROOM
GROOMING > GROOM
GROOMINGS > GROOM
GROOMS > GROOM
GROOMSMAN n man who attends the bridegroom at a wedding, usually the best man
GROOMSMEN > GROOMSMAN
GROOVE n long narrow channel in a surface
GROOVED > GROOVE
GROOVER n device that makes grooves
GROOVERS > GROOVER
GROOVES > GROOVE
GROOVIER > GROOVY
GROOVIEST > GROOVY
GROOVILY > GROOVY
GROOVING > GROOVE
GROOVY adj attractive or exciting
GROPE vb feel about or search uncertainly ▷ n instance of groping
GROPED > GROPE
GROPER n type of large fish of warm and tropical seas
GROPERS > GROPER
GROPES > GROPE
GROPING > GROPE
GROPINGLY > GROPE
GROSBEAK n finch with a large powerful bill
GROSBEAKS > GROSBEAK
GROSCHEN n former Austrian monetary unit worth one hundredth of a schilling
GROSCHENS > GROSCHEN
GROSER n gooseberry
GROSERS > GROSER
GROSERT another word for > GROSER

GROSERTS > GROSERT

GROSET another word for > GROSER

GROSETS > GROSET

GROSGRAIN n heavy ribbed silk or rayon fabric

GROSS adj flagrant ▷ n twelve dozen ▷ vb make as total revenue before deductions ▷ interj exclamation indicating disgust

GROSSART another word for > GROSER

GROSSARTS > GROSSART

GROSSED > GROSS

GROSSER > GROSS

GROSSERS > GROSS

GROSSES > GROSS

GROSSEST > GROSS

GROSSING > GROSS

GROSSLY > GROSS

GROSSNESS > GROSS

GROSSULAR n type of garnet

GROSZ n Polish monetary unit

GROSZE > GROSZ

GROSZY > GROSZ

GROT n rubbish

GROTESQUE adj strangely distorted ▷ n grotesque person or thing

GROTS > GROT

GROTTIER > GROTTY

GROTTIEST > GROTTY

GROTTO n small picturesque cave

GROTTOED adj having a grotto

GROTTOES > GROTTO

GROTTOS > GROTTO

GROTTY adj nasty or in bad condition

GROUCH vb grumble or complain ▷ n person who is always complaining

GROUCHED > GROUCH

GROUCHES > GROUCH

GROUCHIER > GROUCHY

GROUCHILY > GROUCHY

GROUCHING > GROUCH

GROUCHY adj bad-tempered

GROUF same as > GROOF

GROUFS > GROUF

GROUGH n natural channel or fissure in a peat moor

GROUGHS > GROUGH

GROUND n surface of the earth ▷ adj on or of the ground ▷ vb base or establish

GROUNDAGE n fee levied on a vessel entering a port or anchored off a shore

GROUNDED adj sensible and down-to-earth

GROUNDEN obsolete variant of > GROUND

GROUNDER n (in baseball) ball that travels along the ground

GROUNDERS > GROUNDER

GROUNDHOG another name for > WOODCHUCK

GROUNDING n basic knowledge of a subject

GROUNDMAN n groundsman

GROUNDMEN > GROUNDMAN

GROUNDNUT n peanut

GROUNDOUT n (in baseball) being put out after hitting a grounder that is fielded and thrown to first base

GROUNDS > GROUND

GROUNDSEL n yellow-flowered weed

GROUP n number of people or things regarded as a unit ▷ vb place or form into a group

GROUPABLE > GROUP

GROUPAGE n gathering people or objects into a group or groups

GROUPAGES > GROUPAGE

GROUPED > GROUP

GROUPER n large edible sea fish

GROUPERS > GROUPER

GROUPIE n ardent fan of a celebrity or of a sport or activity

GROUPIES > GROUPIE

GROUPING n set of people or organizations who act or work together to achieve a shared aim

GROUPINGS > GROUPING

GROUPIST n follower of a group

GROUPISTS > GROUPIST

GROUPLET n small group

GROUPLETS > GROUPLET

GROUPOID n magma

GROUPOIDS > GROUPOID

GROUPS > GROUP

GROUPWARE n software that enables computers within a group or organization to work together, allowing users to exchange electronic-mail messages, access shared files and databases, use video conferencing, etc

GROUPWORK n work done by a group acting together

GROUPY same as > GROUPIE

GROUSE n stocky game bird ▷ vb grumble or complain ▷ adj fine or excellent

GROUSED > GROUSE

GROUSER > GROUSE

GROUSERS > GROUSE

GROUSES > GROUSE

GROUSEST > GROUSE

GROUSING > GROUSE

GROUT n thin mortar ▷ vb fill up with grout

GROUTED > GROUT

GROUTER > GROUT

GROUTERS > GROUT

GROUTIER > GROUTY

GROUTIEST > GROUTY

GROUTING > GROUT

GROUTINGS > GROUT

GROUTS pl n sediment or grounds

GROUTY adj sullen or surly

GROVE n small group of trees

GROVED > GROVE

GROVEL vb behave humbly in order to win a superior's favour

GROVELED > GROVEL

GROVELER > GROVEL

GROVELERS > GROVEL

GROVELESS > GROVE

GROVELING > GROVEL

GROVELLED > GROVEL

GROVELLER > GROVEL

GROVELS > GROVEL

GROVES > GROVE

GROVET n wrestling hold

GROVETS > GROVET

GROVIER > GROVY

GROVIEST > GROVY

GROVY adj like a grove

GROW vb develop physically

GROWABLE adj able to be cultivated

GROWER n person who grows plants

GROWERS > GROWER

GROWING > GROW

GROWINGLY > GROW

GROWINGS > GROW

GROWL vb make a low rumbling sound ▷ n growling sound

GROWLED > GROWL

GROWLER n person, animal, or thing that growls

GROWLERS > GROWLER

GROWLERY n place to retreat to, alone, when ill-humoured

GROWLIER > GROWL

GROWLIEST > GROWL

GROWLING > GROWL

GROWLINGS > GROWL

GROWLS > GROWL

GROWLY > GROWL

GROWN > GROW

GROWNUP n adult

GROWNUPS > GROWNUP

GROWS > GROW

GROWTH n growing ▷ adj of or relating to growth

GROWTHIER > GROWTHY

GROWTHIST n advocate of the importance of economic growth

GROWTHS > GROWTH

GROWTHY adj rapid-growing

GROYNE n wall built out from the shore to control erosion

GROYNES > GROYNE

GROZING adj as in grozing iron iron for smoothing joints between lead pipes

GRR interj expressing anger or annoyance

GRRL n as in riot grrl young woman who enjoys feminist punk rock

GRRLS > GRRL

GRRRL same as > GRRL

GRRRLS > GRRRL

GRUB n legless insect larva ▷ vb search carefully for something

GRUBBED > GRUB

GRUBBER n person who grubs

GRUBBERS > GRUBBER

GRUBBIER > GRUBBY

GRUBBIEST > GRUBBY

GRUBBILY > GRUBBY

GRUBBING > GRUB

GRUBBLE same as > GRABBLE

GRUBBLED > GRUBBLE

GRUBBLES > GRUBBLE

GRUBBLING > GRUBBLE

GRUBBY adj dirty

GRUBS > GRUB

GRUBSTAKE n supplies provided for a prospector on the condition that the donor has a stake in any finds ▷ vb furnish with such supplies

GRUBWORM another word for > GRUB

GRUBWORMS > GRUBWORM

GRUDGE vb be unwilling to give or allow ▷ n resentment ▷ adj planned or carried out in order to settle a grudge

GRUDGED > GRUDGE

GRUDGEFUL adj envious

GRUDGER > GRUDGE

GRUDGERS > GRUDGE

GRUDGES > GRUDGE

GRUDGING > GRUDGE

GRUDGINGS > GRUDGE

GRUE n shiver or shudder ▷ vb shiver or shudder

GRUED > GRUE

GRUEING > GRUE

GRUEL n thin porridge ▷ vb subject to exhausting experiences

GRUELED > GRUEL

GRUELER > GRUEL

GRUELERS > GRUEL

GRUELING same as > GRUELLING

GRUELINGS > GRUELING

GRUELLED > GRUEL

GRUELLER > GRUEL

GRUELLERS > GRUEL

GRUELLING adj exhausting or severe ▷ n severe experience, esp punishment

GRUELS > GRUEL

GRUES > GRUE

GRUESOME adj causing horror and disgust

GRUESOMER > GRUESOME

GRUFE same as > GROOF

GRUFES > GRUFE

GRUFF adj rough or surly in manner or voice ▷ vb talk gruffly

GRUFFED > GRUFF
GRUFFER > GRUFF
GRUFFEST > GRUFF
GRUFFIER > GRUFFY
GRUFFIEST > GRUFFY
GRUFFILY > GRUFFY
GRUFFING > GRUFF
GRUFFISH > GRUFF
GRUFFLY > GRUFF
GRUFFNESS > GRUFF
GRUFFS > GRUFF
GRUFFY *adj* gruff
GRUFTED *adj* dirty
GRUGRU *n* tropical
American palm
GRUGRUS > GRUGRU
GRUIFORM *adj* relating to
an order of birds, including
cranes and bustards
GRUING > GRUE
GRUM *adj* surly
GRUMBLE *vb* complain
▷ *n* complaint
GRUMBLED > GRUMBLE
GRUMBLER > GRUMBLE
GRUMBLERS > GRUMBLE
GRUMBLES > GRUMBLE
GRUMBLIER > GRUMBLE
GRUMBLING > GRUMBLE
GRUMBLY > GRUMBLE
GRUME *n* clot
GRUMES > GRUME
GRUMLY > GRUM
GRUMMER > GRUM
GRUMMEST > GRUM
GRUMMET *same as*
> GROMMET
GRUMMETED *adj* having
grummets
GRUMMETS > GRUMMET
GRUMNESS > GRUM
GRUMOSE *same as*
> GRUMOUS
GRUMOUS *adj* (esp of plant
parts) consisting of
granular tissue
GRUMP *n* surly or
bad-tempered person
▷ *vb* complain or grumble
GRUMPED > GRUMP
GRUMPH *vb* grunt
GRUMPHED > GRUMPH
GRUMPHIE *n* pig
GRUMPHIES
> GRUMPHIE
GRUMPHING > GRUMPH
GRUMPHS > GRUMPH
GRUMPHY *same as*
> GRUMPHIE
GRUMPIER > GRUMPY
GRUMPIES > GRUMPY
GRUMPIEST > GRUMPY
GRUMPILY > GRUMPY
GRUMPING > GRUMP
GRUMPISH *same as*
> GRUMPY
GRUMPS > GRUMP
GRUMPY *adj* bad-
tempered ▷ *n*
bad-tempered person
GRUND *n* as in *grund mail*
payment for right of
burial
GRUNDIES *pl n* men's
underpants
GRUNDLE *n* perineum
GRUNDLES > GRUNDLE

GRUNGE *n* style of rock
music with a distorted
guitar sound
GRUNGER *n* fan of grunge
music
GRUNGERS > GRUNGER
GRUNGES > GRUNGE
GRUNGEY *adj* messy or
dirty
GRUNGIER > GRUNGY
GRUNGIEST > GRUNGY
GRUNGY *adj* messy or dirty
GRUNION *n* Californian
marine fish that spawns
on beaches
GRUNIONS > GRUNION
GRUNT *vb* make a low
short gruff sound, like a
pig ▷ *n* pig's sound
GRUNTED > GRUNT
GRUNTER *n* person or
animal that grunts, esp a
pig
GRUNTERS > GRUNTER
GRUNTING > GRUNT
GRUNTINGS > GRUNT
GRUNTLE *vb* grunt or
groan
GRUNTLED > GRUNTLE
GRUNTLES > GRUNTLE
GRUNTLING > GRUNTLE
GRUNTS > GRUNT
GRUPPETTI
> GRUPPETTO
GRUPPETTO *n* turn
GRUSHIE *adj* healthy and
strong
GRUTCH *vb* grudge
GRUTCHED > GRUTCH
GRUTCHES > GRUTCH
GRUTCHING > GRUTCH
GRUTTEN > GREET
GRUYERE *n* hard flat
whole-milk cheese with
holes
GRUYERES > GRUYERE
GRYCE *same as* > GRICE
GRYCES > GRYCE
GRYDE *same as* > GRIDE
GRYDED > GRYDE
GRYDES > GRYDE
GRYDING > GRYDE
GRYESY *adj* grey
GRYFON *same as*
> GRIFFIN
GRYFONS > GRYFON
GRYKE *same as* > GRIKE
GRYKES > GRYKE
GRYPE *same as* > GRIPE
GRYPES > GRYPE
GRYPHON *same as*
> GRIFFIN
GRYPHONS > GRYPHON
GRYPT *archaic form of*
> GRIPPED
GRYSBOK *n* small
antelope
GRYSBOKS > GRYSBOK
GRYSELY *same as*
> GRISLY
GRYSIE *same as* > GRISY
GU *same as* > GJU
GUACAMOLE *n* spread of
mashed avocado, tomato
pulp, mayonnaise, and
seasoning
GUACHARO *another name
for* > OILBIRD

GUACHAROS > GUACHARO
GUACO *n* any of several
plants used as an antidote
to snakebite
GUACOS > GUACO
GUAIAC *same as*
> GUAIACUM
GUAIACOL *n* yellowish
creosote-like liquid
GUAIACOLS
> GUAIACOL
GUAIACS > GUAIAC
GUAIACUM *n* tropical
American evergreen tree
GUAIACUMS
> GUAIACUM
GUAIOCUM *same as*
> GUAIACUM
GUAIOCUMS
> GUAIOCUM
GUAN *n* type of bird of
Central and S America
GUANA *another word for*
> IGUANA
GUANABANA *n* tropical
tree or its fruit
GUANACO *n* S American
animal related to the
llama
GUANACOS > GUANACO
GUANAS > GUANA
GUANASE *n* type of
enzyme
GUANASES > GUANASE
GUANAY *n* type of
cormorant
GUANAYS > GUANAY
GUANAZOLO *n* form of
guanine
GUANGO *n* rain tree
GUANGOS > GUANGO
GUANIDIN *same as*
> GUANIDINE
GUANIDINE *n* strongly
alkaline crystalline
substance, soluble in
water and found in plant
and animal tissues
GUANIDINS
> GUANIDIN
GUANIN *same as*
> GUANINE
GUANINE *n* white almost
insoluble compound
GUANINES > GUANINE
GUANINS > GUANIN
GUANO *n* dried sea-bird
manure
GUANOS > GUANO
GUANOSINE *n* nucleoside
consisting of guanine and
ribose
GUANS > GUAN
GUANXI *n* Chinese social
concept
GUANXIS > GUANXI
GUANYLIC *adj* as in
guanylic acid nucleotide
consisting of guanine,
ribose or deoxyribose, and
a phosphate group
GUAR *n* Indian plant
GUARACHA *same as*
> HUARACHE
GUARACHAS
> GUARACHA
GUARACHE *same as*
> HUARACHE

GUARACHES
> GUARACHE
GUARACHI *same as*
> HUARACHE
GUARACHIS
> GUARACHI
GUARANA *n* type of shrub
native to Venezuela
GUARANAS > GUARANA
GUARANI *n* standard
monetary unit of Paraguay
GUARANIES > GUARANI
GUARANIS > GUARANI
GUARANTEE *n* formal
assurance, esp in writing,
that a product will meet
certain standards ▷ *vb*
give a guarantee
GUARANTOR *n* person
who gives or is bound by a
guarantee
GUARANTY *n* pledge of
responsibility for fulfilling
another person's
obligations in case of
default
GUARD *vb* watch over to
protect or to prevent
escape ▷ *n* person or
group that guards
GUARDABLE > GUARD
GUARDAGE *n* state of
being in the care of a
guardian
GUARDAGES
> GUARDAGE
GUARDANT *adj* (of a
beast) shown full face ▷ *n*
guardian
GUARDANTS
> GUARDANT
GUARDDOG *n* dog trained
to protect premises
GUARDDOGS
> GUARDDOG
GUARDED *adj* cautious or
noncommittal
GUARDEDLY > GUARDED
GUARDEE *n* guardsman
GUARDEES > GUARDEE
GUARDER > GUARD
GUARDERS > GUARD
GUARDIAN *n* keeper or
protector ▷ *adj* protecting
or safeguarding
GUARDIANS
> GUARDIAN
GUARDING > GUARD
GUARDLESS > GUARD
GUARDLIKE > GUARD
GUARDRAIL *n* railing at
the side of a staircase,
road, etc, as a safety
barrier
GUARDROOM *n* room used
by guards
GUARDS > GUARD
GUARDSHIP *n* warship
responsible for the safety
of other ships in its
company
GUARDSMAN *n* member of
the Guards
GUARDSMEN
> GUARDSMAN
GUARISH *vb* heal
GUARISHED > GUARISH
GUARISHES > GUARISH
GUARS > GUAR

GUAVA n yellow-skinned tropical American fruit
GUAVAS > GUAVA
GUAYABERA n type of embroidered men's shirt
GUAYULE n bushy shrub of the southwestern US
GUAYULES > GUAYULE
GUB n Scots word for mouth ▷ vb hit or defeat
GUBBAH same as > GUB
GUBBAHS > GUBBAH
GUBBED > GUB
GUBBING > GUB
GUBBINS n object of little or no value
GUBBINSES > GUBBINS
GUBERNIYA n territorial division of imperial Russia
GUBS > GUB
GUCK n slimy matter
GUCKIER > GUCKY
GUCKIEST > GUCKY
GUCKS > GUCK
GUCKY adj slimy and mucky
GUDDLE vb catch (fish) with the hands ▷ n muddle
GUDDLED > GUDDLE
GUDDLES > GUDDLE
GUDDLING > GUDDLE
GUDE Scots word for > GOOD
GUDEMAN n male householder
GUDEMEN > GUDEMAN
GUDES n goods
GUDESIRE n grandfather
GUDESIRES > GUDESIRE
GUDEWIFE n female householder
GUDEWIVES > GUDEWIFE
GUDGEON n small freshwater fish ▷ vb trick or cheat
GUDGEONED > GUDGEON
GUDGEONS > GUDGEON
GUE same as > GJU
GUELDER adj as in guelder rose kind of shrub
GUENON n slender Old World monkey
GUENONS > GUENON
GUERDON n reward or payment ▷ vb give a guerdon to
GUERDONED > GUERDON
GUERDONER > GUERDON
GUERDONS > GUERDON
GUEREZA n handsome colobus monkey
GUEREZAS > GUEREZA
GUERIDON n small ornately carved table
GUERIDONS > GUERIDON
GUERILLA same as > GUERRILLA
GUERILLAS > GUERILLA
GUERITE n turret used by a sentry
GUERITES > GUERITE
GUERNSEY n seaman's knitted woollen sweater
GUERNSEYS > GUERNSEY

GUERRILLA n member of an unofficial armed force fighting regular forces
GUES > GUE
GUESS vb estimate or draw a conclusion without proper knowledge ▷ n estimate or conclusion reached by guessing
GUESSABLE > GUESS
GUESSED > GUESS
GUESSER > GUESS
GUESSERS > GUESS
GUESSES > GUESS
GUESSING > GUESS
GUESSINGS > GUESS
GUESSWORK n process or results of guessing
GUEST n person entertained at another's expense ▷ vb appear as a visiting player or performer
GUESTBOOK n page on a website where users leave comments
GUESTED > GUEST
GUESTEN vb stay as a guest in someone's house
GUESTENED > GUESTEN
GUESTENS > GUESTEN
GUESTING > GUEST
GUESTS > GUEST
GUESTWISE adv as, or in the manner of, a guest
GUFF n nonsense
GUFFAW n crude noisy laugh ▷ vb laugh in this way
GUFFAWED > GUFFAW
GUFFAWING > GUFFAW
GUFFAWS > GUFFAW
GUFFIE Scots word for > PIG
GUFFIES > GUFFIE
GUFFS > GUFF
GUGA n gannet chick
GUGAS > GUGA
GUGGLE vb drink making a gurgling sound
GUGGLED > GUGGLE
GUGGLES > GUGGLE
GUGGLING > GUGGLE
GUGLET same as > GOGLET
GUGLETS > GUGLET
GUICHET n grating, hatch, or small opening in a wall
GUICHETS > GUICHET
GUID Scot word for > GOOD
GUIDABLE > GUIDE
GUIDAGE n guidance
GUIDAGES > GUIDAGE
GUIDANCE n leadership, instruction, or advice
GUIDANCES > GUIDANCE
GUIDE n person who conducts tour expeditions ▷ vb act as a guide for
GUIDEBOOK n handbook with information for visitors to a place
GUIDED > GUIDE
GUIDELESS > GUIDE
GUIDELINE n set principle for doing something

GUIDEPOST n sign on a post by a road indicating directions
GUIDER > GUIDE
GUIDERS > GUIDE
GUIDES > GUIDE
GUIDESHIP n supervision
GUIDEWAY n track controlling the motion of something
GUIDEWAYS > GUIDEWAY
GUIDEWORD n word at top of dictionary page indicating first entry on page
GUIDING > GUIDE
GUIDINGS > GUIDE
GUIDON n small pennant
GUIDONS > GUIDON
GUIDS pl n Scots word for possessions
GUILD n organization or club
GUILDER n former monetary unit of the Netherlands
GUILDERS > GUILDER
GUILDHALL n hall where members of a guild meet
GUILDRIES > GUILDRY
GUILDRY n in Scotland, corporation of merchants
GUILDS > GUILD
GUILDSHIP n condition of being a member of a guild
GUILDSMAN n man who is a member of a guild
GUILDSMEN > GUILDSMAN
GUILE n cunning or deceit ▷ vb deceive
GUILED > GUILE
GUILEFUL > GUILE
GUILELESS adj free from guile
GUILER n deceiver
GUILERS > GUILER
GUILES > GUILE
GUILING > GUILE
GUILLEMET n (in printing) a duckfoot quote
GUILLEMOT n black-and-white diving sea bird of N hemisphere
GUILLOCHE n ornamental band or border with a repeating pattern of two or more interwoven wavy lines, as in architecture ▷ vb decorate with guilloches
GUILT n fact or state of having done wrong ▷ vb make (a person) feel guilty
GUILTED > GUILT
GUILTIER > GUILTY
GUILTIEST > GUILTY
GUILTILY > GUILTY
GUILTING > GUILT
GUILTLESS adj innocent
GUILTS > GUILT
GUILTY adj responsible for an offence or misdeed
GUIMBARD n Jew's harp
GUIMBARDS > GUIMBARD

GUIMP same as > GUIMPE
GUIMPE n short blouse worn under a pinafore dress ▷ vb make with gimp
GUIMPED > GUIMPE
GUIMPES > GUIMPE
GUIMPING > GUIMPE
GUIMPS > GUIMP
GUINEA n former British monetary unit
GUINEAS > GUINEA
GUINEP n type of tropical American tree
GUINEPS > GUINEP
GUIPURE n heavy lace
GUIPURES > GUIPURE
GUIRO n percussion instrument made from a hollow gourd
GUIROS > GUIRO
GUISARD n guiser
GUISARDS > GUISARD
GUISE n false appearance ▷ vb disguise or be disguised in fancy dress
GUISED > GUISE
GUISER n mummer, esp at Christmas or Halloween revels
GUISERS > GUISER
GUISES > GUISE
GUISING > GUISE
GUISINGS > GUISE
GUITAR n stringed instrument
GUITARIST > GUITAR
GUITARS > GUITAR
GUITGUIT n bird belonging to the family Coerebidae
GUITGUITS > GUITGUIT
GUIZER same as > GUISER
GUIZERS > GUIZER
GUL n design used in Turkoman carpets
GULA n gluttony
GULAG n forced-labour camp
GULAGS > GULAG
GULAR adj of or situated in the throat or oesophagus ▷ n throat or oesophagus
GULARS > GULAR
GULAS > GULA
GULCH n deep narrow valley ▷ vb swallow fast
GULCHED > GULCH
GULCHES > GULCH
GULCHING > GULCH
GULDEN same as > GUILDER
GULDENS > GULDEN
GULE Scots word for > MARIGOLD
GULES n red in heraldry
GULET n wooden Turkish sailing boat
GULETS > GULET
GULF n large deep bay ▷ vb swallow up
GULFED > GULF
GULFIER > GULF
GULFIEST > GULF
GULFING > GULF
GULFLIKE > GULF

GULFS > GULF
GULFWEED n type of brown seaweed
GULFWEEDS > GULFWEED
GULFY > GULF
GULL n long-winged sea bird ▷ vb cheat or deceive
GULLABLE same as > GULLIBLE
GULLABLY > GULLABLE
GULLED > GULL
GULLER n deceiver
GULLERIES > GULLERY
GULLERS > GULLER
GULLERY n breeding-place for gulls
GULLET n muscular tube from the mouth to the stomach
GULLETS > GULLET
GULLEY same as > GULLY
GULLEYED > GULLEY
GULLEYING > GULLEY
GULLEYS > GULLEY
GULLIBLE adj easily tricked
GULLIBLY > GULLIBLE
GULLIED > GULLY
GULLIES > GULLY
GULLING > GULL
GULLISH adj stupid
GULLS > GULL
GULLWING adj (of vehicle door) opening upwards
GULLY n channel cut by running water ▷ vb make (channels) in (the ground, sand, etc)
GULLYING > GULLY
GULOSITY n greed or gluttony
GULP vb swallow hastily ▷ n gulping
GULPED > GULP
GULPER > GULP
GULPERS > GULP
GULPH archaic word for > GULF
GULPHS > GULPH
GULPIER > GULP
GULPIEST > GULP
GULPING > GULP
GULPINGLY > GULP
GULPS > GULP
GULPY > GULP
GULS > GUL
GULY adj relating to gules
GUM n firm flesh in which the teeth are set ▷ vb stick with gum
GUMBALL n round piece of chewing gum
GUMBALLS > GUMBALL
GUMBO n soup or stew thickened with okra pods
GUMBOIL n abscess on the gum
GUMBOILS > GUMBOIL
GUMBOOT n long rubber boot
GUMBOOTS > GUMBOOT
GUMBOS > GUMBO
GUMBOTIL n sticky clay formed by the weathering of glacial drift
GUMBOTILS > GUMBOTIL

GUMDROP n hard jelly-like sweet
GUMDROPS > GUMDROP
GUMLANDS pl n infertile land where kauri once grew
GUMLESS > GUM
GUMLIKE > GUM
GUMLINE n line where gums meet teeth
GUMLINES > GUMLINE
GUMMA n rubbery tumour
GUMMAS > GUMMA
GUMMATA > GUMMA
GUMMATOUS > GUMMA
GUMMED > GUM
GUMMER n punch-cutting tool
GUMMERS > GUMMER
GUMMI n gelatin-based flavoured sweet
GUMMIER > GUMMY
GUMMIES > GUMMY
GUMMIEST > GUMMY
GUMMILY > GUMMY
GUMMINESS > GUMMY
GUMMING > GUM
GUMMINGS > GUM
GUMMIS > GUMMI
GUMMITE n orange or yellowish amorphous secondary mineral
GUMMITES > GUMMITE
GUMMOSE same as > GUMMOUS
GUMMOSES > GUMMOSE
GUMMOSIS n abnormal production of gum in trees
GUMMOSITY > GUMMOUS
GUMMOUS adj resembling or consisting of gum
GUMMY adj toothless ▷ n type of small crustacean-eating shark
GUMNUT n hardened seed container of the gumtree
GUMNUTS > GUMNUT
GUMP vb guddle
GUMPED > GUMP
GUMPHION n funeral banner
GUMPHIONS > GUMPHION
GUMPING > GUMP
GUMPS > GUMP
GUMPTION n resourcefulness
GUMPTIONS > GUMPTION
GUMPTIOUS > GUMPTION
GUMS > GUM
GUMSHIELD n plate or strip of soft waxy substance used by boxers to protect the teeth and gums
GUMSHOE n waterproof overshoe ▷ vb act stealthily
GUMSHOED > GUMSHOE
GUMSHOES > GUMSHOE
GUMSUCKER n native-born Australian
GUMTREE n any of various trees that yield gum
GUMTREES > GUMTREE
GUMWEED n any of several yellow-flowered plants

GUMWEEDS > GUMWEED
GUMWOOD same as > GUMTREE
GUMWOODS > GUMWOOD
GUN n weapon with a tube from which missiles are fired ▷ vb cause (an engine) to run at high speed
GUNBOAT n small warship
GUNBOATS > GUNBOAT
GUNCOTTON n form of cellulose nitrate used as an explosive
GUNDIES > GUNDY
GUNDOG n dog trained to work with a hunter or gamekeeper
GUNDOGS > GUNDOG
GUNDY n toffee
GUNFIGHT n fight between persons using firearms ▷ vb fight with guns
GUNFIGHTS > GUNFIGHT
GUNFIRE n repeated firing of guns
GUNFIRES > GUNFIRE
GUNFLINT n piece of flint in a flintlock's hammer used to strike the spark that ignites the charge
GUNFLINTS > GUNFLINT
GUNFOUGHT > GUNFIGHT
GUNG adj as in gung ho extremely or excessively enthusiastic about something
GUNGE n sticky unpleasant substance ▷ vb block or encrust with gunge
GUNGED > GUNGE
GUNGES > GUNGE
GUNGIER > GUNGE
GUNGIEST > GUNGE
GUNGING > GUNGE
GUNGY > GUNGE
GUNHOUSE n on a warship, an armoured rotatable enclosure for guns
GUNHOUSES > GUNHOUSE
GUNITE n mortar sprayed in a very dense concrete layer
GUNITES > GUNITE
GUNK n slimy or filthy substance ▷ vb cover with gunk
GUNKED > GUNK
GUNKHOLE vb make a series of short boat excursions
GUNKHOLED > GUNKHOLE
GUNKHOLES > GUNKHOLE
GUNKIER > GUNK
GUNKIEST > GUNK
GUNKING > GUNK
GUNKS > GUNK
GUNKY > GUNK
GUNLAYER n person who aims a ship's gun

GUNLAYERS > GUNLAYER
GUNLESS > GUN
GUNLOCK n mechanism in some firearms
GUNLOCKS > GUNLOCK
GUNMAKER n person who makes guns
GUNMAKERS > GUNMAKER
GUNMAN n armed criminal
GUNMEN > GUNMAN
GUNMETAL n alloy of copper, tin, and zinc ▷ adj dark grey
GUNMETALS > GUNMETAL
GUNNAGE n number of guns carried by a warship
GUNNAGES > GUNNAGE
GUNNED > GUN
GUNNEL same as > GUNWALE
GUNNELS > GUNNEL
GUNNEN > GUN
GUNNER n artillery soldier
GUNNERA n type of herbaceous plant
GUNNERAS > GUNNERA
GUNNERIES > GUNNERY
GUNNERS > GUNNER
GUNNERY n use or science of large guns
GUNNIES > GUNNY
GUNNING > GUN
GUNNINGS > GUN
GUNNY n strong coarse fabric used for sacks
GUNNYBAG same as > GUNNYSACK
GUNNYBAGS > GUNNYBAG
GUNNYSACK n sack made from gunny
GUNPAPER n cellulose nitrate explosive made by treating paper with nitric acid
GUNPAPERS > GUNPAPER
GUNPLAY n use of firearms, as by criminals
GUNPLAYS > GUNPLAY
GUNPOINT n muzzle of a gun
GUNPOINTS > GUNPOINT
GUNPORT n porthole or other opening for a gun
GUNPORTS > GUNPORT
GUNPOWDER n explosive mixture of potassium nitrate, sulphur, and charcoal
GUNROOM n room where guns are stored
GUNROOMS > GUNROOM
GUNRUNNER n person who smuggles guns and ammunition
GUNS > GUN
GUNSEL n criminal who carries a gun
GUNSELS > GUNSEL
GUNSHIP n ship or helicopter armed with heavy guns
GUNSHIPS > GUNSHIP

g

GUNSHOT n shot or range of a gun
GUNSHOTS > GUNSHOT
GUNSIGHT n device on a gun which helps the user to aim
GUNSIGHTS > GUNSIGHT
GUNSMITH n person who manufactures or repairs firearms, esp portable guns
GUNSMITHS > GUNSMITH
GUNSTICK n ramrod
GUNSTICKS > GUNSTICK
GUNSTOCK n wooden handle to which the barrel of a rifle is attached
GUNSTOCKS > GUNSTOCK
GUNSTONE n cannonball
GUNSTONES > GUNSTONE
GUNTER n type of gaffing
GUNTERS > GUNTER
GUNWALE n top of a ship's side
GUNWALES > GUNWALE
GUNYAH n hut or shelter in the bush
GUNYAHS > GUNYAH
GUP n gossip
GUPPIES > GUPPY
GUPPY n small colourful aquarium fish
GUPS > GUP
GUQIN n type of Chinese zither
GUQINS > GUQIN
GUR n unrefined cane sugar
GURAMI same as > GOURAMI
GURAMIS > GURAMI
GURDIES > GURDY
GURDWARA n Sikh place of worship
GURDWARAS > GURDWARA
GURDY n winch on a fishing boat
GURGE vb swallow up
GURGED > GURGE
GURGES > GURGE
GURGING > GURGE
GURGLE n bubbling noise ▷ vb (of water) to make low bubbling noises when flowing
GURGLED > GURGLE
GURGLES > GURGLE
GURGLET same as > GOGLET
GURGLETS > GURGLET
GURGLIER > GURGLY
GURGLIEST > GURGLY
GURGLING > GURGLE
GURGLY adj making gurgling sounds
GURGOYLE same as > GARGOYLE
GURGOYLES > GURGOYLE
GURJUN n S or SE Asian tree that yields a resin
GURJUNS > GURJUN

GURL vb snarl
GURLED > GURL
GURLET n type of pickaxe
GURLETS > GURLET
GURLIER > GURLY
GURLIEST > GURLY
GURLING > GURL
GURLS > GURL
GURLY adj stormy
GURN variant spelling of > GIRN
GURNARD n spiny armour-headed sea fish
GURNARDS > GURNARD
GURNED > GURN
GURNET same as > GURNARD
GURNETS > GURNET
GURNEY n wheeled stretcher for transporting hospital patients
GURNEYS > GURNEY
GURNING > GURN
GURNS > GURN
GURRAH n type of coarse muslin
GURRAHS > GURRAH
GURRIER n tough, ill-mannered person
GURRIERS > GURRIER
GURRIES > GURRY
GURRY n dog-fight
GURS > GUR
GURSH n unit of currency in Saudi Arabia
GURSHES > GURSH
GURU n Hindu or Sikh religious teacher or leader
GURUDOM n state of being a guru
GURUDOMS > GURUDOM
GURUISM > GURU
GURUISMS > GURU
GURUS > GURU
GURUSHIP > GURU
GURUSHIPS > GURU
GUS > GU
GUSH vb flow out suddenly and profusely ▷ n sudden copious flow
GUSHED > GUSH
GUSHER n spurting oil well
GUSHERS > GUSHER
GUSHES > GUSH
GUSHIER > GUSHY
GUSHIEST > GUSHY
GUSHILY > GUSHY
GUSHINESS > GUSHY
GUSHING > GUSH
GUSHINGLY > GUSH
GUSHY adj displaying excessive sentimentality
GUSLA n Balkan single-stringed musical instrument
GUSLAR n player of the gusla
GUSLARS > GUSLAR
GUSLAS > GUSLA
GUSLE same as > GUSLA
GUSLES > GUSLE
GUSLI n Russian harp-like musical instrument
GUSLIS > GUSLI

GUSSET n piece of material sewn into a garment to strengthen it ▷ vb put a gusset in (a garment)
GUSSETED > GUSSET
GUSSETING > GUSSET
GUSSETS > GUSSET
GUSSIE n young pig
GUSSIED > GUSSY
GUSSIES > GUSSY
GUSSY vb dress elaborately
GUSSYING > GUSSY
GUST n sudden blast of wind ▷ vb blow in gusts
GUSTABLE n anything that can be tasted
GUSTABLES > GUSTABLE
GUSTATION n act of tasting or the faculty of taste
GUSTATIVE > GUSTATION
GUSTATORY > GUSTATION
GUSTED > GUST
GUSTFUL adj tasty
GUSTIE adj tasty
GUSTIER > GUSTY
GUSTIEST > GUSTY
GUSTILY > GUSTY
GUSTINESS > GUSTY
GUSTING > GUST
GUSTLESS adj tasteless
GUSTO n enjoyment or zest
GUSTOES > GUSTO
GUSTOS > GUSTO
GUSTS > GUST
GUSTY adj windy and blustery
GUT n intestine ▷ vb remove the guts from ▷ adj basic or instinctive
GUTBUCKET n highly emotional style of jazz playing
GUTCHER n grandfather
GUTCHERS > GUTCHER
GUTFUL n bellyful
GUTFULS > GUTFUL
GUTLESS adj cowardly
GUTLESSLY > GUTLESS
GUTLIKE > GUT
GUTROT n upset stomach
GUTROTS > GUTROT
GUTS vb devour greedily
GUTSED > GUTS
GUTSER n as in come a gutser fall heavily to the ground
GUTSERS > GUTSER
GUTSES > GUTS
GUTSFUL n bellyful
GUTSFULS > GUTSFUL
GUTSIER > GUTSY
GUTSIEST > GUTSY
GUTSILY > GUTSY
GUTSINESS > GUTSY
GUTSING > GUTS
GUTSY adj courageous
GUTTA n small drop-like ornament
GUTTAE > GUTTA
GUTTAS > GUTTA

GUTTATE adj covered with small drops or drop-like markings ▷ vb exude droplets of liquid
GUTTATED same as > GUTTATE
GUTTATES > GUTTATE
GUTTATING > GUTTATE
GUTTATION > GUTTATE
GUTTED > GUT
GUTTER n shallow channel for carrying away water ▷ vb (of a candle) burn unsteadily
GUTTERED > GUTTER
GUTTERIER > GUTTERY
GUTTERING n material for gutters
GUTTERS > GUTTER
GUTTERY adj vulgar
GUTTIER > GUTTY
GUTTIES > GUTTY
GUTTIEST > GUTTY
GUTTING > GUT
GUTTLE vb eat greedily
GUTTLED > GUTTLE
GUTTLER > GUTTLE
GUTTLERS > GUTTLE
GUTTLES > GUTTLE
GUTTLING > GUTTLE
GUTTURAL adj (of a sound) produced at the back of the throat ▷ n guttural consonant
GUTTURALS > GUTTURAL
GUTTY n urchin or delinquent ▷ adj courageous
GUTZER n bad fall
GUTZERS > GUTZER
GUV informal name for > GOVERNOR
GUVS > GUV
GUY n man or boy ▷ vb make fun of
GUYED > GUY
GUYING > GUY
GUYLE same as > GUILE
GUYLED > GUYLE
GUYLER > GUYLE
GUYLERS > GUYLE
GUYLES > GUYLE
GUYLINE n guy rope
GUYLINER n eyeliner worn by men
GUYLINERS > GUYLINER
GUYLINES > GUYLINE
GUYLING > GUYLE
GUYOT n flat-topped submarine mountain
GUYOTS > GUYOT
GUYS > GUY
GUYSE same as > GUISE
GUYSES > GUYSE
GUZZLE vb eat or drink greedily
GUZZLED > GUZZLE
GUZZLER n person or thing that guzzles
GUZZLERS > GUZZLER
GUZZLES > GUZZLE
GUZZLING > GUZZLE
GWEDUC same as > GEODUCK
GWEDUCK same as > GEODUCK

GWEDUCKS > GWEDUCK
GWEDUCS > GWEDUC
GWINE *dialect form of*
> GOING
GWINIAD *n* type of
freshwater white fish
GWINIADS > GWINIAD
GWYNIAD *n* type of
freshwater white fish
GWYNIADS > GWYNIAD
GYAL *same as* > GAYAL
GYALS > GYAL
GYAN *n* (in Indian English)
knowledge
GYANS > GYAN
GYBE *vb* (of a sail) swing
suddenly from one side to
the other ▷ *n* instance of
gybing
GYBED > GYBE
GYBES > GYBE
GYBING > GYBE
GYELD *old form of*
> GUILD
GYELDS > GYELD
GYLDEN *old form of*
> GOLDEN
GYM *n* gymnasium
GYMBAL *same as*
> GIMBAL
GYMBALS > GYMBAL
GYMKHANA *n* horse-riding
competition
GYMKHANAS
> GYMKHANA
GYMMAL *same as*
> GIMMAL
GYMMALS > GYMMAL
GYMNASIA
> GYMNASIUM
GYMNASIAL
> GYMNASIUM
GYMNASIC
> GYMNASIUM
GYMNASIEN
> GYMNASIUM
GYMNASIUM *n* large room
with equipment for
physical training
GYMNAST *n* expert in
gymnastics
GYMNASTIC *adj* of,
relating to, like, or
involving gymnastics
GYMNASTS > GYMNAST
GYMNIC *adj* gymnastic
GYMNOSOPH *n* adherent
of gymnosophy: belief
that food and clothing are
detrimental to purity of
thought
GYMP *same as* > GIMP
GYMPED > GYMP
GYMPIE *n* tall tree with
stinging hairs on its leaves
GYMPIES > GYMPIE
GYMPING > GYMP

GYMPS > GYMP
GYMS > GYM
GYMSLIP *n* tunic or
pinafore formerly worn by
schoolgirls
GYMSLIPS > GYMSLIP
GYMSUIT *n* costume
worn for gymnastics
GYMSUITS > GYMSUIT
GYNAE *adj* gynaecological
▷ *n* gynaecology
GYNAECEA
> GYNAECEUM
GYNAECEUM *same as*
> GYNAECIA
GYNAECIA
> GYNAECIUM
GYNAECIUM *same as*
> GYNOECIUM
GYNAECOID *adj*
resembling, relating to, or
like a woman
GYNAES > GYNAE
GYNANDRY *n*
hermaphroditism
GYNARCHIC
> GYNARCHY
GYNARCHY *n* government
by women
GYNECIA > GYNECIUM
GYNECIC *adj* relating to
the female sex
GYNECIUM *same as*
> GYNOECIUM
GYNECOID *same as*
> GYNAECOID
GYNIATRY *n*
gynaecology: medicine
concerned with diseases
in women
GYNIE *n* gynaecology
GYNIES > GYNIE
GYNNEY *n* guinea hen
GYNNEYS > GYNNEY
GYNNIES > GYNNY
GYNNY *same as* > GYNNEY
GYNO *n* gynaecologist
GYNOCRACY *n*
government by women
GYNOECIA
> GYNOECIUM
GYNOECIUM *n* carpels of
a flowering plant
collectively
GYNOPHOBE *n* person
who hates or fears women
GYNOPHORE *n* stalk in
some plants that bears the
gynoecium above the level
of the other flower parts
GYNOS > GYNO
GYNY *n* gynaecology
GYOZA *n* Japanese fried
dumpling
GYOZAS > GYOZA
GYP *n* slang word for
severe pain

GYPLURE *n* synthetic
version of a gypsy moth
pheromone
GYPLURES > GYPLURE
GYPO *n* small-scale
independent logger
GYPOS > GYPO
GYPPIE *same as* > GIPPY
GYPPIES > GYPPY
GYPPY *same as* > GIPPY
GYPS > GYP
GYPSEIAN *adj* relating to
gypsies
GYPSEOUS > GYPSUM
GYPSIED > GYPSY
GYPSIES > GYPSY
GYPSUM *n* chalklike
mineral
GYPSUMS > GYPSUM
GYPSY *n* member of a
nomadic people ▷ *vb* live
like a gypsy
GYPSYDOM > GYPSY
GYPSYDOMS
> GYPSYDOM
GYPSYHOOD > GYPSY
GYPSYING > GYPSY
GYPSYISH > GYPSY
GYPSYISM *n* state of
being a gypsy
GYPSYISMS
> GYPSYISM
GYPSYWORT *n* type of
Eurasian herb with white
flowers
GYRAL *adj* having a
circular, spiral, or rotating
motion
GYRALLY > GYRAL
GYRANT *adj* gyrating
GYRASE *n* topoisomerase
enzyme
GYRASES > GYRASE
GYRATE *vb* rotate or spiral
about a point or axis ▷ *adj*
curved or coiled into a
circle
GYRATED > GYRATE
GYRATES > GYRATE
GYRATING > GYRATE
GYRATION *n* act or
process of gyrating
GYRATIONS
> GYRATION
GYRATOR *n* electronic
circuit that inverts the
impedance
GYRATORS > GYRATOR
GYRATORY > GYRATE
GYRE *n* circular or spiral
movement or path ▷ *vb*
whirl
GYRED > GYRE
GYRENE *n* nickname for a
member of the US Marine
Corps
GYRENES > GYRENE

GYRES > GYRE
GYRFALCON *n* very large
rare falcon of northern
regions
GYRI > GYRUS
GYRING > GYRE
GYRO *n* gyrocompass
GYROCAR *n* two-wheeled
car
GYROCARS > GYROCAR
GYRODYNE *n* aircraft with
rotor
GYRODYNES
> GYRODYNE
GYROIDAL *adj* spiral
GYROLITE *n* silicate
GYROLITES
> GYROLITE
GYROMANCY *n* divination
by spinning in a circle,
then falling on any of
various letters that have
been written on the
ground
GYRON *same as* > GIRON
GYRONIC > GYRON
GYRONNY *same as*
> GIRONNY
GYRONS > GYRON
GYROPILOT *n* type of
automatic pilot
GYROPLANE *another name*
for > AUTOGIRO
GYROS > GYRO
GYROSCOPE *n* disc
rotating on an axis that
can turn in any direction,
so the disc maintains the
same position regardless
of the movement of the
surrounding structure
GYROSE *adj* marked with
sinuous lines
GYROSTAT *same as*
> GYROSCOPE
GYROSTATS
> GYROSTAT
GYROUS *adj* marked with
sinuous lines
GYROVAGUE *n* peripatetic
monk
GYRUS *n* convolution
GYRUSES > GYRUS
GYTE *n* Scots word for a
spoilt child
GYTES > GYTE
GYTRASH *n* spirit that
haunts lonely roads
GYTRASHES > GYTRASH
GYTTJA *n* sediment on a
lake bottom
GYTTJAS > GYTTJA
GYVE *vb* shackle or fetter
▷ *n* fetter
GYVED > GYVE
GYVES > GYVE
GYVING > GYVE

g

Hh

HA *interj* exclamation of triumph, surprise, or scorn
HAAF *n* fishing ground off the Shetland and Orkney Islands
HAAFS > HAAF
HAANEPOOT *n* variety of grape
HAAR *n* cold sea mist or fog off the North Sea
HAARS > HAAR
HABANERA *n* slow Cuban dance in duple time
HABANERAS > HABANERA
HABANERO *n* variety of chilli pepper
HABANEROS > HABANERO
HABDABS *n* highly nervous state
HABDALAH *n* prayer at end of Jewish sabbath
HABDALAHS > HABDALAH
HABENDUM *n* part of a deed defining the limits of ownership
HABENDUMS > HABENDUM
HABERDINE *n* dried cod
HABERGEON *n* light sleeveless coat of mail worn in the 14th century under the plated hauberk
HABILABLE *adj* able to wear clothes
HABILE *adj* skilful
HABIT *n* established way of behaving ▷ *vb* clothe
HABITABLE *adj* fit to be lived in
HABITABLY > HABITABLE
HABITAN *same as* > HABITANT
HABITANS > HABITANT
HABITANT *n* person who lives in a place
HABITANTS > HABITANT
HABITAT *n* natural home of an animal or plant
HABITATS > HABITAT
HABITED *adj* dressed in a habit
HABITING > HABIT
HABITS > HABIT
HABITUAL *adj* done regularly and repeatedly ▷ *n* person with a habit
HABITUALS > HABITUAL
HABITUATE *vb* accustom

HABITUDE *n* habit or tendency
HABITUDES > HABITUDE
HABITUE *n* frequent visitor to a place
HABITUES > HABITUE
HABITUS *n* general physical state
HABITUSES > HABITUS
HABLE *old form of* > ABLE
HABOOB *n* sandstorm
HABOOBS > HABOOB
HABU *n* large venomous snake
HABUS > HABU
HACEK *n* pronunciation symbol in Slavonic language
HACEKS > HACEK
HACENDADO *n* owner of a hacienda
HACHIS *n* hash (the dish)
HACHURE *n* shading drawn on a map to indicate steepness of a hill ▷ *vb* mark or show by hachures
HACHURED > HACHURE
HACHURES > HACHURE
HACHURING > HACHURE
HACIENDA *n* ranch or large estate in Latin America
HACIENDAS > HACIENDA
HACK *vb* cut or chop violently ▷ *n* (inferior) writer or journalist ▷ *adj* unoriginal or of a low standard
HACKABLE > HACK
HACKAMORE *n* rope or rawhide halter used for unbroken foals
HACKBERRY *n* American tree or shrub with edible cherry-like fruits
HACKBOLT *n* shearwater
HACKBOLTS > HACKBOLT
HACKBUT *another word for* > ARQUEBUS
HACKBUTS > HACKBUT
HACKED > HACK
HACKEE *n* chipmunk
HACKEES > HACKEE
HACKER *n* computer enthusiast
HACKERIES > HACKERY
HACKERS > HACKER
HACKERY *n* journalism
HACKETTE *n* informal, derogatory term for female journalist

HACKETTES > HACKETTE
HACKIE *n* US word meaning cab driver
HACKIES > HACKIE
HACKING > HACK
HACKINGS > HACK
HACKLE *same as* > HECKLE
HACKLED > HACKLE
HACKLER > HACKLE
HACKLERS > HACKLE
HACKLES *pl n* hairs which rise in response to emotion
HACKLET *n* kittiwake
HACKLETS > HACKLET
HACKLIER > HACKLY
HACKLIEST > HACKLY
HACKLING > HACKLE
HACKLY *adj* rough or jagged
HACKMAN *n* taxi driver
HACKMEN > HACKMAN
HACKNEY *n* taxi ▷ *vb* make commonplace and banal by too frequent use
HACKNEYED *adj* (of a word or phrase) unoriginal and overused
HACKNEYS > HACKNEY
HACKS > HACK
HACKSAW *n* small saw for cutting metal ▷ *vb* cut with a hacksaw
HACKSAWED > HACKSAW
HACKSAWN > HACKSAW
HACKSAWS > HACKSAW
HACKWORK *n* dull repetitive work
HACKWORKS > HACKWORK
HACQUETON *n* padded jacket worn under chain mail
HAD *vb* Scots form of hold
HADAL *adj* denoting very deep zones of the oceans
HADARIM > HEDER
HADAWAY *sentence substitute* exclamation urging the hearer to refrain from delay
HADDEN > HAD
HADDEST *same as* > HADST
HADDIE *n* finnan haddock
HADDIES > HADDIE
HADDING > HAD
HADDOCK *n* edible sea fish of N Atlantic
HADDOCKS > HADDOCK
HADE *n* angle made to the vertical by the plane of a

fault or vein ▷ *vb* incline from the vertical
HADED > HADE
HADEDAH *n* large grey-green S African ibis
HADEDAHS > HADEDAH
HADES > HADE
HADING > HADE
HADITH *n* body of tradition about Muhammad and his followers
HADITHS > HADITH
HADJ *same as* > HAJJ
HADJEE *same as* > HADJI
HADJEES > HADJEE
HADJES > HADJ
HADJI *same as* > HAJJI
HADJIS > HADJI
HADROME *n* part of xylem
HADROMES > HADROME
HADRON *n* type of elementary particle
HADRONIC > HADRON
HADRONS > HADRON
HADROSAUR *n* any one of a large group of duck-billed partly aquatic bipedal dinosaurs
HADS > HAD
HADST *singular form of the past tense (indicative mood) of* > HAVE
HAE *Scot variant of* > HAVE
HAECCEITY *n* property that uniquely identifies an object
HAED > HAE
HAEING > HAE
HAEM *n* red organic pigment containing ferrous iron
HAEMAL *adj* of the blood
HAEMATAL *same as* > HAEMAL
HAEMATEIN *n* dark purple water-insoluble crystalline substance obtained from logwood and used as an indicator and biological stain
HAEMATIC *n* agent that stimulates the production of red blood cells
HAEMATICS > HAEMATIC
HAEMATIN *n* dark bluish or brownish pigment
HAEMATINS > HAEMATIN
HAEMATITE *same as* > HEMATITE
HAEMATOID *adj* resembling blood

HAEMATOMA n tumour of clotted or partially clotted blood
HAEMIC same as > HAEMATIC
HAEMIN n haematin chloride
HAEMINS > HAEMIN
HAEMOCOEL n body cavity of many invertebrates, including arthropods and molluscs, developed from part of the blood system
HAEMOCYTE n any blood cell, esp a red blood cell
HAEMOID same as > HAEMATOID
HAEMOLYSE same as > HAEMOLYZE
HAEMOLYZE vb break down red blood cells
HAEMONIES > HAEMONY
HAEMONY n plant mentioned in Milton's poetry
HAEMOSTAT n surgical instrument that stops bleeding by compression of a blood vessel
HAEMS > HAEM
HAEN > HAE
HAEREDES > HAERES
HAEREMAI interj Māori expression of welcome ▷ n act of saying 'haeremai'
HAEREMAIS > HAEREMAI
HAERES same as > HERES
HAES > HAE
HAET n whit
HAETS > HAET
HAFF n lagoon
HAFFET n side of head
HAFFETS > HAFFET
HAFFIT same as > HAFFET
HAFFITS > HAFFIT
HAFFLIN same as > HALFLING
HAFFLINS > HAFFLIN
HAFFS > HAFF
HAFIZ n title for a person who knows the Koran by heart
HAFIZES > HAFIZ
HAFNIUM n metallic element found in zirconium ores
HAFNIUMS > HAFNIUM
HAFT n handle of an axe, knife, or dagger ▷ vb provide with a haft
HAFTARA same as > HAFTARAH
HAFTARAH n short reading from the Prophets
HAFTARAHS > HAFTARAH
HAFTARAS > HAFTARA
HAFTAROS > HAFTARAH
HAFTAROT > HAFTARAH
HAFTAROTH > HAFTARAH
HAFTED > HAFT
HAFTER > HAFT
HAFTERS > HAFT
HAFTING > HAFT

HAFTORAH same as > HAFTARAH
HAFTORAHS > HAFTORAH
HAFTOROS > HAFTORAH
HAFTOROT > HAFTORAH
HAFTOROTH > HAFTORAH
HAFTS > HAFT
HAG n ugly old woman ▷ vb hack
HAGADIC same as > HAGGADIC
HAGADIST same as > HAGGADIST
HAGADISTS > HAGADIST
HAGBERRY same as > HACKBERRY
HAGBOLT same as > HACKBOLT
HAGBOLTS > HAGBOLT
HAGBORN adj born of a witch
HAGBUSH same as > ARQUEBUS
HAGBUSHES > HAGBUSH
HAGBUT same as > ARQUEBUS
HAGBUTEER > HAGBUT
HAGBUTS > HAGBUT
HAGBUTTER > HAGBUT
HAGDEN same as > HACKBOLT
HAGDENS > HAGDEN
HAGDON same as > HACKBOLT
HAGDONS > HAGDON
HAGDOWN same as > HACKBOLT
HAGDOWNS > HAGDOWN
HAGFISH n any of various primitive eel-like vertebrates
HAGFISHES > HAGFISH
HAGG n a boggy place
HAGGADA same as > HAGGADAH
HAGGADAH n book containing the order of service of the traditional Jewish Passover meal
HAGGADAHS > HAGGADAH
HAGGADAS > HAGGADA
HAGGADIC > HAGGADAH
HAGGADIST n writer of Aggadoth
HAGGADOT > HAGGADAH
HAGGADOTH > HAGGADAH
HAGGARD adj looking tired and ill ▷ n hawk that has reached maturity before being caught
HAGGARDLY > HAGGARD
HAGGARDS > HAGGARD
HAGGED > HAG
HAGGING > HAG
HAGGIS n Scottish dish
HAGGISES > HAGGIS
HAGGISH > HAG
HAGGISHLY > HAG
HAGGLE vb bargain or wrangle over a price
HAGGLED > HAGGLE
HAGGLER > HAGGLE
HAGGLERS > HAGGLE

HAGGLES > HAGGLE
HAGGLING n act of haggling
HAGGLINGS > HAGGLING
HAGGS > HAGG
HAGIARCHY n government by saints, holy people, or those in holy orders
HAGIOLOGY n literature about the lives and legends of saints
HAGLET same as > HACKLET
HAGLETS > HAGLET
HAGLIKE > HAG
HAGRIDDEN > HAGRIDE
HAGRIDE vb torment or obsess
HAGRIDER > HAGRIDE
HAGRIDERS > HAGRIDE
HAGRIDES > HAGRIDE
HAGRIDING > HAGRIDE
HAGRODE > HAGRIDE
HAGS > HAG
HAH same as > HA
HAHA n wall or other boundary marker that is set in a ditch
HAHAS > HAHA
HAHNIUM n transuranic element
HAHNIUMS > HAHNIUM
HAHS > HAH
HAICK same as > HAIK
HAICKS > HAICK
HAIDUK n rural brigand
HAIDUKS > HAIDUK
HAIK n Arab's outer garment
HAIKA > HAIK
HAIKAI same as > HAIKU
HAIKS > HAIK
HAIKU n Japanese verse form in 17 syllables
HAIKUS > HAIKU
HAIL n (shower of) small pellets of ice ▷ vb fall as or like hail ▷ sentence substitute exclamation of greeting
HAILED > HAIL
HAILER > HAIL
HAILERS > HAIL
HAILIER > HAIL
HAILIEST > HAIL
HAILING > HAIL
HAILS > HAIL
HAILSHOT n small scattering shot
HAILSHOTS > HAILSHOT
HAILSTONE n pellet of hail
HAILSTORM n storm during which hail falls
HAILY > HAIL
HAIMISH same as > HEIMISH
HAIN vb Scots word meaning save
HAINCH Scots form of > HAUNCH
HAINCHED > HAINCH
HAINCHES > HAINCH
HAINCHING > HAINCH
HAINED > HAIN

HAINING > HAIN
HAININGS > HAIN
HAINS > HAIN
HAINT same as > HAUNT
HAINTS > HAINT
HAIQUE same as > HAIK
HAIQUES > HAIQUE
HAIR n threadlike growth on the skin ▷ vb provide with hair
HAIRBALL n mass of hair that forms in the stomach an animal
HAIRBALLS > HAIRBALL
HAIRBAND n band worn around head to control hair
HAIRBANDS > HAIRBAND
HAIRBELL same as > HAREBELL
HAIRBELLS > HAIRBELL
HAIRBRUSH n brush for grooming the hair
HAIRCAP n type of moss
HAIRCAPS > HAIRCAP
HAIRCLOTH n cloth woven from horsehair, used in upholstery
HAIRCUT n act or an instance of cutting the hair
HAIRCUTS > HAIRCUT
HAIRDO n hairstyle
HAIRDOS > HAIRDO
HAIRDRIER same as > HAIRDRYER
HAIRDRYER n hand-held electric device that blows out hot air and is used to dry and, sometimes, assist in styling the hair, as in blow-drying
HAIRED adj with hair
HAIRGRIP n small bent clasp used to fasten the hair
HAIRGRIPS > HAIRGRIP
HAIRIER > HAIRY
HAIRIEST > HAIRY
HAIRIF another name for > CLEAVERS
HAIRIFS > HAIRIF
HAIRILY adv in a hairy manner
HAIRINESS > HAIRY
HAIRING > HAIR
HAIRLESS adj having little or no hair ▷ n as in Mexican hairless small breed of hairless dog
HAIRLIKE > HAIR
HAIRLINE n edge of hair at the top of the forehead ▷ adj very fine or narrow
HAIRLINES > HAIRLINE
HAIRLOCK n lock of hair
HAIRLOCKS > HAIRLOCK
HAIRNET n any of several kinds of light netting worn over the hair
HAIRNETS > HAIRNET

h

HAIRPIECE *n* section of false hair added to a person's real hair

HAIRPIN *n* U-shaped wire used to hold the hair in place

HAIRPINS > HAIRPIN

HAIRS > HAIR

HAIRSPRAY *n* fixative solution sprayed onto the hair to keep a hairstyle in shape

HAIRST *Scots form of* > HARVEST

HAIRSTED > HAIRST

HAIRSTING > HAIRST

HAIRSTS > HAIRST

HAIRSTYLE *n* cut and arrangement of a person's hair

HAIRTAIL *n* spiny-finned fish

HAIRTAILS > HAIRTAIL

HAIRWING *n* fishing lure tied with hair

HAIRWINGS > HAIRWING

HAIRWORK *n* thing made from hair

HAIRWORKS > HAIRWORK

HAIRWORM *n* any of various hairlike nematode worms

HAIRWORMS > HAIRWORM

HAIRY *adj* covered with hair

HAIRYBACK *n* minute bristly aquatic worm

HAITH *interj* Scots oath

HAJ *same as* > HADJ

HAJES > HAJ

HAJI *same as* > HAJJI

HAJIS > HAJI

HAJJ *n* pilgrimage a Muslim makes to Mecca

HAJJAH *n* Muslim woman who has made a pilgrimage to Mecca

HAJJAHS > HAJJAH

HAJJES > HAJJ

HAJJI *n* Muslim who has made a pilgrimage to Mecca

HAJJIS > HAJJI

HAKA *n* ceremonial Māori dance with chanting

HAKAM *n* text written by a rabbi

HAKAMS > HAKAM

HAKARI *n* Māori ritual feast

HAKARIS > HAKARI

HAKAS > HAKA

HAKE *n* edible sea fish of N hemisphere

HAKEA *n* Australian tree or shrub with hard woody fruit

HAKEAS > HAKEA

HAKEEM *same as* > HAKIM

HAKEEMS > HAKEEM

HAKES > HAKE

HAKIM *n* Muslim judge, ruler, or administrator

HAKIMS > HAKIM

HAKU *in New Zealand English, same as* > KINGFISH

HAKUS > HAKU

HALACHA *n* Jewish religious law

HALACHAS > HALACHA

HALACHIC > HALACHA

HALACHIST > HALACHA

HALACHOT > HALACHA

HALACHOTH > HALACHA

HALAKAH *same as* > HALACHA

HALAKAHS > HALAKAH

HALAKHA *same as* > HALACHA

HALAKHAH *same as* > HALACHA

HALAKHAHS > HALAKHAH

HALAKHAS > HALAKHA

HALAKHIC > HALAKHAH

HALAKHIST > HALAKHAH

HALAKHOT > HALAKHA

HALAKHOTH > HALAKHAH

HALAKIC > HALAKHA

HALAKIST > HALAKHA

HALAKISTS > HALAKHA

HALAKOTH > HALAKHA

HALAL *n* meat from animals slaughtered according to Muslim law ▷ *adj* of or relating to such meat ▷ *vb* kill (animals) in this way

HALALA *n* money unit in Saudi Arabia

HALALAH *same as* > HALALA

HALALAHS > HALALAH

HALALAS > HALALA

HALALLED > HALAL

HALALLING > HALAL

HALALS > HALAL

HALATION *n* bright ring surrounding a light source

HALATIONS > HALATION

HALAVAH *same as* > HALVAH

HALAVAHS > HALAVAH

HALAZONE *n* type of disinfectant

HALAZONES > HALAZONE

HALBERD *n* spear with an axe blade

HALBERDS > HALBERD

HALBERT *same as* > HALBERD

HALBERTS > HALBERT

HALCYON *adj* peaceful and happy ▷ *n* mythological bird

HALCYONIC *adj* peaceful and happy

HALCYONS > HALCYON

HALE *adj* healthy, robust ▷ *vb* pull or drag

HALED > HALE

HALENESS > HALE

HALER *same as* > HELLER

HALERS > HALER

HALERU > HALER

HALES > HALE

HALEST > HALE

HALF *n* either of two equal parts ▷ *adj* denoting one of two equal parts ▷ *adv* to the extent of half

HALFA *n* African grass

HALFAS > HALFA

HALFBACK *n* position in some team sports

HALFBACKS > HALFBACK

HALFBEAK *n* type of fish with a short upper jaw and a protruding lower jaw

HALFBEAKS > HALFBEAK

HALFEN *same as* > HALF

HALFLIFE *n* time taken for half of the atoms in a radioactive material to undergo decay

HALFLIN *same as* > HALFLING

HALFLING *n* person only half-grown

HALFLINGS > HALFLING

HALFLINS > HALFLIN

HALFLIVES > HALFLIFE

HALFNESS > HALF

HALFPACE *n* landing on staircase

HALFPACES > HALFPACE

HALFPENCE > HALFPENNY

HALFPENNY *n* former British coin worth half an old penny

HALFPIPE *n* U-shaped object used in skateboarding stunts

HALFPIPES > HALFPIPE

HALFS > HALF

HALFTIME *n* rest period between the two halves of a game

HALFTIMES > HALFTIME

HALFTONE *n* illustration showing lights and shadows by means of very small dots ▷ *adj* relating to, used in, or made by halftone

HALFTONES > HALFTONE

HALFTRACK *n* vehicle with caterpillar tracks and wheels

HALFWAY *adj* at or to half the distance

HALFWIT *n* foolish or stupid person

HALFWITS > HALFWIT

HALIBUT *n* large edible flatfish of N Atlantic

HALIBUTS > HALIBUT

HALICORE *n* dugong

HALICORES > HALICORE

HALID *same as* > HALIDE

HALIDE *n* binary compound

HALIDES > HALIDE

HALIDOM *n* holy place or thing

HALIDOME *same as* > HALIDOM

HALIDOMES > HALIDOME

HALIDOMS > HALIDOM

HALIDS > HALID

HALIER *n* former currency unit of Slovakia

HALIEROV > HALIER

HALIERS > HALIER

HALIEUTIC *adj* of fishing

HALIMOT *n* court held by lord

HALIMOTE *same as* > HALIMOT

HALIMOTES > HALIMOTE

HALIMOTS > HALIMOT

HALING > HALE

HALIOTIS *n* type of shellfish

HALITE *n* colourless or white mineral

HALITES > HALITE

HALITOSES > HALITOSIS

HALITOSIS *n* unpleasant-smelling breath

HALITOTIC > HALITUS

HALITOUS > HALITUS

HALITUS *n* vapour

HALITUSES > HALITUS

HALL *n* entrance passage

HALLAH *variant spelling of* > CHALLAH

HALLAHS > HALLAH

HALLAL *same as* > HALAL

HALLALI *n* bugle call

HALLALIS > HALLALI

HALLALLED > HALLAL

HALLALOO *same as* > HALLOO

HALLALOOS > HALLALOO

HALLALS > HALLAL

HALLAN *n* partition in cottage

HALLANS > HALLAN

HALLEL *n* (in Judaism) section of the liturgy

HALLELS > HALLEL

HALLIAN *same as* > HALLION

HALLIANS > HALLIAN

HALLIARD *same as* > HALYARD

HALLIARDS > HALLIARD

HALLING *n* Norwegian country dance

HALLINGS > HALLING

HALLION *n* lout

HALLIONS > HALLION

HALLMARK *n* typical feature ▷ *vb* stamp with a hallmark

HALLMARKS > HALLMARK

HALLO *same as* > HALLOO

HALLOA *same as* > HALLOO

HALLOAED > HALLOA

HALLOAING > HALLOA

HALLOAS > HALLOA

HALLOED > HALLO

HALLOES > HALLO

HALLOING > HALLO

HALLOO *interj* shout used to call hounds at a hunt

▷ *n* shout of 'halloo' ▷ *vb* shout (something) to (someone)
HALLOOED > HALLOO
HALLOOING > HALLOO
HALLOOS > HALLOO
HALLOS > HALLO
HALLOT > HALLAH
HALLOTH *same as* > CHALLAH
HALLOUMI *n* salty white sheep's cheese from Greece or Turkey, usually eaten grilled
HALLOUMIS > HALLOUMI
HALLOW *vb* consecrate or set apart as being holy
HALLOWED *adj* regarded as holy
HALLOWER > HALLOW
HALLOWERS > HALLOW
HALLOWING > HALLOW
HALLOWS > HALLOW
HALLS > HALL
HALLSTAND *n* piece of furniture on which are hung coats, hats, etc
HALLUCAL > HALLUX
HALLUCES > HALLUX
HALLUX *n* first digit on the hind foot of an animal
HALLWAY *n* entrance area
HALLWAYS > HALLWAY
HALLYON *same as* > HALLION
HALLYONS > HALLYON
HALM *same as* > HAULM
HALMA *n* board game
HALMAS > HALMA
HALMS > HALM
HALO *n* ring of light round the head of a sacred figure ▷ *vb* surround with a halo
HALOBIONT *n* plant or animal that lives in a salty environment such as the sea
HALOCLINE *n* gradient in salinity of sea
HALOED > HALO
HALOES > HALO
HALOGEN *n* any of a group of nonmetallic elements
HALOGENIC *adj* of or relating to halogens
HALOGENS > HALOGEN
HALOGETON *n* herbaceous plant
HALOID *adj* resembling or derived from a halogen ▷ *n* compound containing halogen atoms in its molecules
HALOIDS > HALOID
HALOING > HALO
HALOLIKE > HALO
HALON *n* any of a class of chemical compounds
HALONS > HALON
HALOPHILE *n* organism that thrives in an extremely salty environment, such as the Dead Sea
HALOPHILY *n* ability to live in salty environment
HALOPHOBE *n* plant unable to live in salty soil

HALOPHYTE *n* plant that grows in very salty soil, as in a salt marsh
HALOS > HALO
HALOSERE *n* plant community that originates and develops in conditions of high salinity
HALOSERES > HALOSERE
HALOTHANE *n* colourless volatile slightly soluble liquid with an odour resembling that of chloroform
HALOUMI *same as* > HALLOUMI
HALOUMIS > HALOUMI
HALSE *vb* embrace
HALSED > HALSE
HALSER > HALSE
HALSERS > HALSE
HALSES > HALSE
HALSING > HALSE
HALT *vb* come or bring to a stop ▷ *n* temporary stop ▷ *adj* lame
HALTED > HALT
HALTER *n* strap round a horse's head with a rope to lead it with ▷ *vb* put a halter on (a horse)
HALTERE *n* one of a pair of modified hind wings in dipterous insects
HALTERED > HALTER
HALTERES > HALTERE
HALTERING > HALTER
HALTERS > HALTER
HALTING > HALT
HALTINGLY > HALT
HALTINGS > HALT
HALTLESS > HALT
HALTS > HALT
HALUTZ *variant spelling of* > CHALUTZ
HALUTZIM > HALUTZ
HALVA *same as* > HALVAH
HALVAH *n* E Mediterranean, Middle Eastern, or Indian sweetmeat
HALVAHS > HALVAH
HALVAS > HALVA
HALVE *vb* divide in half
HALVED > HALVE
HALVER > HALVE
HALVERS > HALVE
HALVES > HALVE
HALVING *n* act of halving
HALVINGS > HALVING
HALWA *n* type of sweet Indian dish
HALWAS > HALWA
HALYARD *n* rope for raising a ship's sail or flag
HALYARDS > HALYARD
HAM *n* smoked or salted meat from a pig's thigh ▷ *vb* overact
HAMADA *n* rocky plateau in desert
HAMADAS > HAMADA
HAMADRYAD *n* one of a class of nymphs, each of which inhabits a tree and dies with it
HAMADRYAS *n* type of baboon

HAMAL *n* (in Middle Eastern countries) a porter or servant
HAMALS > HAMAL
HAMAMELIS *n* any of several trees or shrubs native to E Asia and North America and cultivated as ornamentals
HAMARTIA *n* flaw in character which leads to the downfall of the protagonist in a tragedy
HAMARTIAS > HAMARTIA
HAMATE *adj* hook-shaped ▷ *n* small bone in the wrist
HAMATES > HAMATE
HAMATSA *n* Native Canadian dance
HAMATSAS > HAMATSA
HAMAUL *same as* > HAMAL
HAMAULS > HAMAUL
HAMBA *interj* South African slang meaning 'go away'
HAMBLE *vb* mutilate
HAMBLED > HAMBLE
HAMBLES > HAMBLE
HAMBLING > HAMBLE
HAMBONE *vb* strike body to provide percussion
HAMBONED > HAMBONE
HAMBONES > HAMBONE
HAMBONING > HAMBONE
HAMBURG *same as* > HAMBURGER
HAMBURGER *n* minced beef shaped into a flat disc, cooked and usually served in a bread roll
HAMBURGS > HAMBURG
HAME *n* Scots word for home ▷ *vb* to home
HAMED > HAME
HAMES > HAME
HAMEWITH *adv* Scots word meaning homewards
HAMFAT *n* mediocre performer
HAMFATS > HAMFAT
HAMFATTER *n* inferior actor or musician
HAMING > HAME
HAMLET *n* small village
HAMLETS > HAMLET
HAMMADA *same as* > HAMADA
HAMMADAS > HAMMADA
HAMMAL *same as* > HAMAL
HAMMALS > HAMMAL
HAMMAM *n* bathing establishment
HAMMAMS > HAMMAM
HAMMED > HAM
HAMMER *n* tool ▷ *vb* hit (as if) with a hammer
HAMMERED > HAMMER
HAMMERER > HAMMER
HAMMERERS > HAMMER
HAMMERING > HAMMER
HAMMERKOP *n* shark with hammer-shaped head
HAMMERMAN *n* person working with hammer
HAMMERMEN > HAMMERMAN
HAMMERS > HAMMER

HAMMERTOE *n* condition in which the toe is permanently bent at the joint
HAMMIER > HAMMY
HAMMIES > HAMMY
HAMMIEST > HAMMY
HAMMILY > HAMMY
HAMMINESS > HAMMY
HAMMING > HAM
HAMMOCK *same as* > HUMMOCK
HAMMOCKS > HAMMOCK
HAMMY *adj* (of an actor) overacting or tending to overact ▷ *n* hamstring
HAMOSE *adj* shaped like a hook
HAMOUS *same as* > HAMOSE
HAMPER *vb* make it difficult for (someone or something) to move or progress ▷ *n* large basket with a lid
HAMPERED > HAMPER
HAMPERER > HAMPER
HAMPERERS > HAMPER
HAMPERING > HAMPER
HAMPERS > HAMPER
HAMPSTER *same as* > HAMSTER
HAMPSTERS > HAMPSTER
HAMS > HAM
HAMSTER *n* small rodent with a short tail and cheek pouches
HAMSTERS > HAMSTER
HAMSTRING *n* tendon at the back of the knee ▷ *vb* make it difficult for (someone) to take any action
HAMSTRUNG > HAMSTRING
HAMULAR > HAMULUS
HAMULATE > HAMULUS
HAMULI > HAMULUS
HAMULOSE > HAMULUS
HAMULOUS > HAMULUS
HAMULUS *n* biological attribute
HAMZA *n* sign used in Arabic to represent the glottal stop
HAMZAH *same as* > HAMZA
HAMZAHS > HAMZAH
HAMZAS > HAMZA
HAN *archaic inflected form of* > HAVE
HANAP *n* medieval drinking cup
HANAPER *n* small wickerwork basket
HANAPERS > HANAPER
HANAPS > HANAP
HANCE *same as* > HAUNCH
HANCES > HANCE
HANCH *vb* try to bite
HANCHED > HANCH
HANCHES > HANCH
HANCHING > HANCH
HAND *n* part of the body at the end of the arm ▷ *vb* pass, give
HANDAX *n* small axe held in one hand

h

HANDAXE same as > HANDAX

HANDAXES > HANDAX

HANDBAG n woman's small bag

HANDBAGS pl n incident in which people threaten to fight

HANDBALL n game in which two teams try to throw a ball into their opponent's goal ▷ vb pass (the ball) with a blow of the fist

HANDBALLS > HANDBALL

HANDBELL n bell rung by hand, esp one of a tuned set used in musical performance

HANDBELLS > HANDBELL

HANDBILL n small printed notice

HANDBILLS > HANDBILL

HANDBLOWN adj (of glass) made by hand

HANDBOOK n small reference or instruction book

HANDBOOKS > HANDBOOK

HANDBRAKE n brake in a motor vehicle operated by a hand lever

HANDCAR n small railway vehicle

HANDCARS > HANDCAR

HANDCART n simple cart pushed or pulled by hand, used for transporting goods

HANDCARTS > HANDCART

HANDCLAP n act of clapping hands

HANDCLAPS > HANDCLAP

HANDCLASP another word for > HANDSHAKE

HANDCRAFT n handicraft

HANDCUFF n one of a linked pair of metal rings for locking round wrists ▷ vb put handcuffs on

HANDCUFFS > HANDCUFF

HANDED > HAND

HANDER > HAND

HANDERS > HAND

HANDFAST n agreement, esp of marriage, confirmed by a handshake ▷ vb betroth or marry (two persons or another person) by joining the hands

HANDFASTS > HANDFAST

HANDFED > HANDFEED

HANDFEED vb feed (a person or an animal) by hand

HANDFEEDS > HANDFEED

HANDFUL n amount that can be held in the hand

HANDFULS > HANDFUL

HANDGLASS n hand-held magnifying glass

HANDGRIP n covering on the handle of a racket or club

HANDGRIPS > HANDGRIP

HANDGUN n firearm such as a pistol

HANDGUNS > HANDGUN

HANDHELD adj held in position by the hand ▷ n computer that can be held in the hand

HANDHELDS > HANDHELD

HANDHOLD n object, crevice, etc, that can be used as a grip or support, as in climbing

HANDHOLDS > HANDHOLD

HANDICAP n hindrance or disadvantage ▷ vb make it difficult for (someone) to do something

HANDICAPS > HANDICAP

HANDIER > HANDY

HANDIEST > HANDY

HANDILY adv in a handy way or manner

HANDINESS > HANDY

HANDING > HAND

HANDISM n discrimination against left- or right-handed people

HANDISMS > HANDISM

HANDIWORK n result of someone's work or activity

HANDJAR n Persian dagger

HANDJARS > HANDJAR

HANDJOB n vulgar word for manual stimulation of another person's penis

HANDJOBS > HANDJOB

HANDKNIT n garment knitted by hand

HANDKNITS > HANDKNIT

HANDLE n part of an object that is held so that it can be used ▷ vb hold, feel, or move with the hands

HANDLEBAR adj as in handlebar moustache bushy extended moustache with curled ends that resembles the handlebars of a bicycle

HANDLED > HANDLE

HANDLER n person who controls an animal

HANDLERS > HANDLER

HANDLES > HANDLE

HANDLESS > HAND

HANDLIKE > HAND

HANDLINE n hand-operated fishing line

HANDLINER n fisherman who fishes with a handline

HANDLINES > HANDLINE

HANDLING n act or an instance of picking up, turning over, or touching something

HANDLINGS > HANDLING

HANDLIST n rough list

HANDLISTS > HANDLIST

HANDLOOM n weaving device operated by hand

HANDLOOMS > HANDLOOM

HANDMADE adj made by hand, not by machine

HANDMAID n person or thing that serves as a useful but subordinate purpose

HANDMAIDS > HANDMAID

HANDOFF n (in rugby) act of warding off an opposing player

HANDOFFS > HANDOFF

HANDOUT n clothing, food, or money given to a needy person

HANDOUTS > HANDOUT

HANDOVER n transfer or surrender

HANDOVERS > HANDOVER

HANDPASS vb pass the ball by striking it with the hand

HANDPHONE n in SE Asian English, mobile phone

HANDPICK vb choose or select with great care, as for a special job or purpose

HANDPICKS > HANDPICK

HANDPLAY n fighting with fists

HANDPLAYS > HANDPLAY

HANDPRESS n printing press operated by hand

HANDPRINT n print of hand

HANDRAIL n rail alongside a stairway, to provide support

HANDRAILS > HANDRAIL

HANDROLL n large dried-seaweed cone filled with cold rice and other ingredients

HANDROLLS > HANDROLL

HANDS > HAND

HANDSAW n any saw for use in one hand only

HANDSAWS > HANDSAW

HANDSEL n gift for good luck ▷ vb give a handsel to (a person)

HANDSELED > HANDSEL

HANDSELS > HANDSEL

HANDSET n telephone mouth- and earpiece in a single unit

HANDSETS > HANDSET

HANDSEWN adj sewn by hand

HANDSFUL > HANDFUL

HANDSHAKE n act of grasping and shaking a person's hand, such as in greeting or when agreeing on a deal

HANDSIER > HANDSY

HANDSIEST > HANDSY

HANDSOME adj (esp of a man) good-looking ▷ n term of endearment for a beloved person

HANDSOMER > HANDSOME

HANDSOMES > HANDSOME

HANDSPIKE n bar or length of pipe used as a lever

HANDSTAFF n staff held in hand

HANDSTAMP vb stamp by hand

HANDSTAND n act of supporting the body on the hands in an upside-down position

HANDSTURN n slightest amount of work

HANDSY adj engaging in unwanted physical contact

HANDTOWEL n towel for drying hands

HANDWHEEL n wheel operated by hand

HANDWORK n work done by hand rather than by machine

HANDWORKS > HANDWORK

HANDWOVEN adj woven by hand

HANDWRIT > HANDWRITE

HANDWRITE vb write by hand

HANDWROTE > HANDWRITE

HANDY adj convenient, useful

HANDYMAN n man who is good at making or repairing things

HANDYMEN > HANDYMAN

HANDYWORK same as > HANDIWORK

HANEPOOT n variety of muscat grape

HANEPOOTS > HANEPOOT

HANG vb attach or be attached at the top with the lower part free

HANGABLE adj suitable for hanging

HANGAR n large shed for storing aircraft ▷ vb put in a hangar

HANGARAGE n combined hangar and garage

HANGARED > HANGAR

HANGARING > HANGAR

HANGARS > HANGAR

HANGBIRD n any bird, esp the Baltimore oriole, that builds a hanging nest

HANGBIRDS > HANGBIRD

HANGDOG adj guilty, ashamed ▷ n furtive or sneaky person

HANGDOGS > HANGDOG

HANGED > HANG

HANGER n curved piece of wood, wire, etc with a hook
HANGERS > HANGER
HANGFIRE n failure to fire
HANGFIRES
> HANGFIRE
HANGI n Māori oven
HANGING > HANG
HANGINGS > HANG
HANGIS > HANGI
HANGMAN n man who executes people by hanging
HANGMEN > HANGMAN
HANGNAIL n piece of skin partly torn away from the base or side of a fingernail
HANGNAILS
> HANGNAIL
HANGNEST same as
> HANGBIRD
HANGNESTS
> HANGNEST
HANGOUT n place where one lives or that one frequently visits
HANGOUTS > HANGOUT
HANGOVER n headache and nausea as a result of drinking too much alcohol
HANGOVERS
> HANGOVER
HANGRIER > HANGRY
HANGRIEST > HANGRY
HANGRY adj irritable as a result of feeling hungry
HANGS > HANG
HANGTAG n attached label
HANGTAGS > HANGTAG
HANGUL n alphabetic scheme used in Korean
HANGULS > HANGUL
HANGUP n emotional or psychological problem
HANGUPS > HANGUP
HANIWA n Japanese funeral offering
HANIWAS > HANIWA
HANJAR same as
> HANDJAR
HANJARS > HANJAR
HANK n coil, esp of yarn ▷ vb attach (a sail) to a stay by hanks
HANKED > HANK
HANKER vb desire intensely
HANKERED > HANKER
HANKERER > HANKER
HANKERERS > HANKER
HANKERING > HANKER
HANKERS > HANKER
HANKIE same as > HANKY
HANKIES > HANKY
HANKING > HANK
HANKS > HANK
HANKY n handkerchief
HANSA same as > HANSE
HANSAS > HANSA
HANSE n medieval guild of merchants
HANSEATIC > HANSA
HANSEL same as
> HANDSEL
HANSELED > HANSEL

HANSELING > HANSEL
HANSELLED > HANSEL
HANSELS > HANSEL
HANSES > HANSE
HANSOM n two-wheeled one-horse carriage
HANSOMS > HANSOM
HANT same as > HAUNT
HANTED > HANT
HANTING > HANT
HANTLE n good deal
HANTLES > HANTLE
HANTS > HANT
HANUKIAH n candelabrum having nine branches that is lit during the festival of Hanukkah
HANUKIAHS
> HANUKIAH
HANUMAN n type of monkey
HANUMANS > HANUMAN
HAO n monetary unit of Vietnam
HAOMA n type of ritual drink
HAOMAS > HAOMA
HAOS > HAO
HAP n luck ▷ vb cover up
HAPAX n word that appears once in a work of literature
HAPAXES > HAPAX
HAPHAZARD adj not organized or planned ▷ n chance
HAPHTARA same as
> HAFTARAH
HAPHTARAH same as
> HAFTARAH
HAPHTARAS
> HAPHTARA
HAPHTAROT
> HAPHTARA
HAPKIDO n Korean martial art
HAPKIDOS > HAPKIDO
HAPLESS adj unlucky
HAPLESSLY > HAPLESS
HAPLITE variant of
> APLITE
HAPLITES > HAPLITE
HAPLITIC > HAPLITE
HAPLOID adj denoting a cell or organism with unpaired chromosomes ▷ n haploid cell or organism
HAPLOIDIC adj denoting a cell or organism with unpaired chromosomes
HAPLOIDS > HAPLOID
HAPLOIDY > HAPLOID
HAPLOLOGY n omission of a repeated occurrence of a sound or syllable in fluent speech
HAPLONT n organism with a haploid number of chromosomes
HAPLONTIC > HAPLONT
HAPLONTS > HAPLONT
HAPLOPIA n normal single vision
HAPLOPIAS
> HAPLOPIA
HAPLOSES > HAPLOSIS

HAPLOSIS n production of a haploid number of chromosomes during meiosis
HAPLOTYPE n collection of genetic markers usually inherited together
HAPLY archaic word for
> PERHAPS
HAPPED > HAP
HAPPEN vb take place, occur
HAPPENED > HAPPEN
HAPPENING n event, occurrence ▷ adj fashionable and up-to-the-minute
HAPPENS > HAPPEN
HAPPI n type of loose Japanese coat
HAPPIED > HAPPY
HAPPIER > HAPPY
HAPPIES > HAPPY
HAPPIEST > HAPPY
HAPPILY > HAPPY
HAPPINESS > HAPPY
HAPPING > HAP
HAPPIS > HAPPI
HAPPOSHU n beer-like Japanese drink
HAPPOSHUS > HAPPOSHU
HAPPY adj feeling or causing joy ▷ vb make happy
HAPPYING > HAPPY
HAPS > HAP
HAPTEN n incomplete antigen
HAPTENE same as
> HAPTEN
HAPTENES > HAPTENE
HAPTENIC > HAPTENE
HAPTENS > HAPTEN
HAPTERON n organ of attachment in some aquatic plants
HAPTERONS
> HAPTERON
HAPTIC adj relating to or based on the sense of touch
HAPTICAL same as
> HAPTIC
HAPTICS n science of sense of touch
HAPU n subtribe
HAPUKA another name for
> GROPER
HAPUKAS > HAPUKA
HAPUKU same as
> HAPUKA
HAPUKUS > HAPUKU
HAPUS > HAPU
HAQUETON same as
> HACQUETON
HAQUETONS
> HAQUETON
HARAAM same as > HARAM
HARAKEKE in New Zealand English, another name for
> FLAX
HARAKEKES
> HARAKEKE
HARAM n anything that is forbidden by Islamic law
HARAMBEE n work chant used on the E African coast ▷ interj cry of harambee

HARAMBEES
> HARAMBEE
HARAMDA same as
> HARAMZADA
HARAMDAS > HARAMDA
HARAMDI same as
> HARAMZADI
HARAMDIS > HARAMDI
HARAMS > HARAM
HARAMZADA n in Indian English, slang word for a male whose parents are not married
HARAMZADI n in Indian English, slang word for a female whose parents are not married
HARANGUE vb address angrily or forcefully ▷ n angry or forceful speech
HARANGUED
> HARANGUE
HARANGUER
> HARANGUE
HARANGUES
> HARANGUE
HARASS vb annoy or trouble constantly
HARASSED > HARASS
HARASSER > HARASS
HARASSERS > HARASS
HARASSES > HARASS
HARASSING > HARASS
HARBINGER n someone or something that announces the approach of something ▷ vb announce the approach or arrival of
HARBOR same as
> HARBOUR
HARBORAGE n shelter or refuge, as for a ship
HARBORED > HARBOR
HARBORER > HARBOR
HARBORERS > HARBOR
HARBORFUL n amount a harbour can hold
HARBORING > HARBOR
HARBOROUS adj hospitable
HARBORS > HARBOR
HARBOUR n sheltered port ▷ vb maintain secretly in the mind
HARBOURED > HARBOUR
HARBOURER > HARBOUR
HARBOURS > HARBOUR
HARD adj firm, solid, or rigid ▷ adv with great energy or effort
HARDASS n tough person
HARDASSES > HARDASS
HARDBACK n book with a stiff cover ▷ adj of or denoting a hardback
HARDBACKS
> HARDBACK
HARDBAG n rigid container on a motorcycle
HARDBAGS > HARDBAG
HARDBAKE n almond toffee
HARDBAKES
> HARDBAKE
HARDBALL n as in play hardball act in a ruthless or uncompromising way

HARDBALLS
> HARDBALL

HARDBEAM same as
> HORNBEAM

HARDBEAMS
> HARDBEAM

HARDBOARD n thin stiff
board made of
compressed sawdust and
wood chips

HARDBODY n attractive
person with a muscular
physique

HARDBOOT n type of
skiing boot

HARDBOOTS
> HARDBOOT

HARDBOUND same as
> HARDBACK

HARDCASE n tough
person ▷ adj relating to a
container that has a rigid
structure

HARDCASES
> HARDCASE

HARDCORE n style of rock
music with short fast
songs and little melody

HARDCORES
> HARDCORE

HARDCOURT adj (of
tennis) played on hard
surface

HARDCOVER same as
> HARDBACK

HARDEDGE n style of
painting in which vividly
coloured subjects are
clearly delineated ▷ adj of,
relating to, or denoting
this style of painting

HARDEDGES
> HARDEDGE

HARDEN vb make or
become hard ▷ n rough
fabric made from hards

HARDENED adj
toughened by experience

HARDENER n person or
thing that hardens

HARDENERS
> HARDENER

HARDENING n act or
process of becoming or
making hard

HARDENS > HARDEN

HARDER > HARD

HARDEST > HARD

HARDFACE n
uncompromising person

HARDFACES
> HARDFACE

HARDGOODS same as
> HARDWARE

HARDGRASS n coarse
grass

HARDHACK n woody plant

HARDHACKS
> HARDHACK

HARDHAT n hat made of a
hard material for
protection ▷ adj typical of
construction workers

HARDHATS > HARDHAT

HARDHEAD same as
> HARDHEADS

HARDHEADS n thistle-like
plant

HARDIER > HARDY

HARDIES > HARDY

HARDIEST > HARDY

HARDIHEAD same as
> HARDIHOOD

HARDIHOOD n courage or
daring

HARDILY adv in a hardy
manner

HARDIMENT same as
> HARDIHOOD

HARDINESS n condition
or quality of being hardy,
robust, or bold

HARDISH > HARD

HARDLINE adj
uncompromising

HARDLINER
> HARDLINE

HARDLY adv scarcely or
not at all

HARDMAN n tough,
ruthless, or violent man

HARDMEN > HARDMAN

HARDNESS n quality
or condition of being
hard

HARDNOSE n tough
person

HARDNOSED adj tough,
shrewd, and practical

HARDNOSES
> HARDNOSE

HARDOKE n burdock

HARDOKES > HARDOKE

HARDPACK n rigid
backpack

HARDPACKS
> HARDPACK

HARDPAN n hard
impervious layer of clay
below the soil

HARDPANS > HARDPAN

HARDPARTS n skeleton

HARDROCK adj concerned
with extracting minerals
other than coal ▷ n tough
uncompromising man

HARDROCKS
> HARDROCK

HARDS pl n coarse fibres
and other refuse from flax
and hemp

HARDSCAPE n artificial
features used in landscape
architecture

HARDSET adj in
difficulties

HARDSHELL adj having a
shell or carapace that is
thick, heavy, or hard

HARDSHIP n suffering

HARDSHIPS
> HARDSHIP

HARDSTAND n hard
surface on which vehicles
may be parked

HARDTACK n kind of hard
saltless biscuit, formerly
eaten by sailors

HARDTACKS
> HARDTACK

HARDTAIL n mountain
bike with no rear
suspension

HARDTAILS
> HARDTAIL

HARDTOP n car equipped
with a metal or plastic roof

HARDTOPS > HARDTOP

HARDWARE n metal tools
or implements

HARDWARES
> HARDWARE

HARDWIRE vb instal
permanently in computer

HARDWIRED adj (of a
circuit or instruction)
permanently wired into a
computer, replacing
separate software

HARDWIRES
> HARDWIRE

HARDWOOD n wood of a
broad-leaved tree such as
oak or ash

HARDWOODS
> HARDWOOD

HARDY adj able to stand
difficult conditions ▷ n
any blacksmith's tool
made with a square shank

HARE n animal like a large
rabbit, with longer ears
and legs ▷ vb run (away)
quickly

HAREBELL n blue
bell-shaped flower

HAREBELLS
> HAREBELL

HARED > HARE

HAREEM same as > HAREM

HAREEMS > HAREEM

HARELD n long-tailed
duck

HARELDS > HARELD

HARELIKE > HARE

HAREM n (formerly)
Muslim man's wives and
concubines

HAREMS > HAREM

HARES > HARE

HARESTAIL n species of
cotton grass

HAREWOOD n sycamore
wood that has been
stained for use in furniture
making

HAREWOODS
> HAREWOOD

HARIANA n Indian breed
of cattle

HARIANAS > HARIANA

HARICOT n variety of
French bean

HARICOTS > HARICOT

HARIGALDS pl n
intestines

HARIGALS same as
> HARIGALDS

HARIJAN n member of an
Indian caste

HARIJANS > HARIJAN

HARIM same as > HAREM

HARIMS > HARIM

HARING > HARE

HARIOLATE vb practise
divination

HARIRA n Moroccan soup

HARIRAS > HARIRA

HARISH adj like hare

HARISSA n hot paste

HARISSAS > HARISSA

HARK vb listen

HARKED > HARK

HARKEN same as
> HEARKEN

HARKENED > HARKEN

HARKENER > HARKEN

HARKENERS > HARKEN

HARKENING > HARKEN

HARKENS > HARKEN

HARKING > HARK

HARKS > HARK

HARL same as > HERL

HARLED > HARL

HARLEQUIN n stock
comic character with a
diamond-patterned
costume and mask ▷ adj
in many colours

HARLING > HARL

HARLINGS > HARL

HARLOT n old-fashioned
word for a prostitute ▷ adj
of or like a harlot

HARLOTRY > HARLOT

HARLOTS > HARLOT

HARLS > HARL

HARM vb injure physically,
mentally, or morally ▷ n
physical, mental, or moral
injury

HARMALA n African plant

HARMALAS > HARMALA

HARMALIN n chemical
derived from harmala

HARMALINE same as
> HARMALIN

HARMALINS
> HARMALIN

HARMAN n constable

HARMANS > HARMAN

HARMATTAN n dry dusty
wind from the Sahara
blowing towards the W
African coast, esp from
November to March

HARMDOING n doing of
harm

HARMED > HARM

HARMEL same as
> HARMALA

HARMELS > HARMEL

HARMER > HARM

HARMERS > HARM

HARMFUL adj causing or
tending to cause harm

HARMFULLY > HARMFUL

HARMIN same as
> HARMALIN

HARMINE same as
> HARMALIN

HARMINES > HARMINE

HARMING > HARM

HARMINS > HARMIN

HARMLESS adj safe to
use, touch, or be near

HARMONIC adj of
harmony ▷ n overtone of
a musical note produced
when that note is played

HARMONICA n small wind
instrument played by
sucking and blowing

HARMONICS n science of
musical sounds

HARMONIES > HARMONY

HARMONISE same as
> HARMONIZE

HARMONIST n person
skilled in the art and
techniques of harmony

HARMONIUM n keyboard
instrument like a small
organ

HARMONIZE vb sing or play in harmony
HARMONY n peaceful agreement and cooperation
HARMOST n Spartan governor
HARMOSTS > HARMOST
HARMOSTY n office of a harmost
HARMOTOME n mineral of the zeolite group
HARMS > HARM
HARN n coarse linen
HARNESS n arrangement of straps for attaching a horse to a cart or plough ▷ vb put a harness on
HARNESSED > HARNESS
HARNESSER > HARNESS
HARNESSES > HARNESS
HARNS > HARN
HARO interj cry meaning alas ▷ n cry of 'haro'
HAROS > HARO
HAROSET n Jewish dish eaten at Passover
HAROSETH same as > HAROSET
HAROSETHS > HAROSETH
HAROSETS > HAROSET
HARP n large triangular stringed instrument ▷ vb play the harp
HARPED > HARP
HARPER > HARP
HARPERS > HARP
HARPIES > HARPY
HARPIN n type of protein
HARPING > HARP
HARPINGS pl n wooden members used for strengthening the bow of a vessel
HARPINS same as > HARPINGS
HARPIST > HARP
HARPISTS > HARP
HARPOON n barbed spear attached to a rope for hunting whales ▷ vb spear with a harpoon
HARPOONED > HARPOON
HARPOONER > HARPOON
HARPOONS > HARPOON
HARPS > HARP
HARPY n nasty or bad-tempered woman
HARPYLIKE > HARPY
HARQUEBUS variant of > ARQUEBUS
HARRIDAN n nagging or vicious woman
HARRIDANS > HARRIDAN
HARRIED > HARRY
HARRIER n cross-country runner
HARRIERS > HARRIER
HARRIES > HARRY
HARROW n implement used to break up lumps of soil ▷ vb draw a harrow over
HARROWED > HARROW
HARROWER > HARROW
HARROWERS > HARROW

HARROWING > HARROW
HARROWS > HARROW
HARRUMPH vb clear or make the noise of clearing the throat
HARRUMPHS > HARRUMPH
HARRY vb keep asking (someone) to do something
HARRYING > HARRY
HARSH adj severe and difficult to cope with ▷ vb ruin or end a state of elation
HARSHED > HARSH
HARSHEN vb make harsh
HARSHENED > HARSHEN
HARSHENS > HARSHEN
HARSHER > HARSH
HARSHES > HARSH
HARSHEST > HARSH
HARSHING > HARSH
HARSHLY > HARSH
HARSHNESS > HARSH
HARSLET same as > HASLET
HARSLETS > HARSLET
HART n adult male deer
HARTAL n (in India) closing shops or suspending work
HARTALS > HARTAL
HARTBEES same as > HARTBEEST
HARTBEEST n African antelope
HARTELY archaic spelling of > HEARTILY
HARTEN same as > HEARTEN
HARTENED > HARTEN
HARTENING > HARTEN
HARTENS > HARTEN
HARTLESSE same as > HEARTLESS
HARTS > HART
HARTSHORN n sal volatile
HARUMPH same as > HARRUMPH
HARUMPHED > HARUMPH
HARUMPHS > HARUMPH
HARUSPEX n priest in ancient Rome
HARUSPICY > HARUSPEX
HARVEST n (season for) the gathering of crops ▷ vb gather (a ripened crop)
HARVESTED > HARVEST
HARVESTER n harvesting machine, esp a combine harvester
HARVESTS > HARVEST
HAS > HAVE
HASH n dish of diced cooked meat and vegetables reheated ▷ vb chop into small pieces
HASHED > HASH
HASHEESH same as > HASHISH
HASHES > HASH
HASHHEAD n regular marijuana user
HASHHEADS > HASHHEAD
HASHIER > HASH

HASHIEST > HASH
HASHING > HASH
HASHINGS > HASHING
HASHISH n illegal drug made from the cannabis plant
HASHISHES > HASHISH
HASHMARK n character (#)
HASHMARKS > HASHMARK
HASHTAG n word or phrase used to denote the topic of a Twitter post
HASHTAGS > HASHTAG
HASHY > HASH
HASK n archaic name for a basket for transporting fish
HASKS > HASK
HASLET n loaf of cooked minced pig's offal, eaten cold
HASLETS > HASLET
HASP n type of fastening ▷ vb secure (a door, window, etc) with a hasp
HASPED > HASP
HASPING > HASP
HASPS > HASP
HASS n as in white hass oatmeal pudding made with sheep's gullet
HASSAR n South American catfish
HASSARS > HASSAR
HASSEL variant of > HASSLE
HASSELS > HASSEL
HASSES > HASS
HASSIUM n chemical element
HASSIUMS > HASSIUM
HASSLE n trouble, bother ▷ vb bother or annoy
HASSLED > HASSLE
HASSLES > HASSLE
HASSLING > HASSLE
HASSOCK n cushion for kneeling on in church
HASSOCKS > HASSOCK
HASSOCKY adj full of hassocks
HAST singular form of the present tense (indicative mood) of > HAVE
HASTA Spanish for > UNTIL
HASTATE adj shaped like a spear
HASTATED same as > HASTATE
HASTATELY > HASTATE
HASTE n (excessive) quickness ▷ vb hasten
HASTED > HASTE
HASTEFUL > HASTE
HASTEN vb (cause to) hurry
HASTENED > HASTEN
HASTENER > HASTEN
HASTENERS > HASTEN
HASTENING > HASTEN
HASTENS > HASTEN
HASTES > HASTE
HASTIER > HASTY
HASTIEST > HASTY
HASTILY > HASTY

HASTINESS > HASTY
HASTING > HASTE
HASTINGS > HASTE
HASTY adj (too) quick
HAT n covering for the head, often with a brim ▷ vb supply (a person) with a hat or put a hat on (someone)
HATABLE > HATE
HATBAND n band or ribbon around a hat
HATBANDS > HATBAND
HATBOX n box or case for a hat or hats
HATBOXES > HATBOX
HATBRUSH n brush for hats
HATCH vb (cause to) emerge from an egg ▷ n hinged door covering an opening in a floor or wall
HATCHABLE > HATCH
HATCHBACK n car with a lifting door at the back
HATCHECK n cloakroom
HATCHECKS > HATCHECK
HATCHED > HATCH
HATCHEL same as > HECKLE
HATCHELED > HATCHEL
HATCHELS > HATCHEL
HATCHER > HATCH
HATCHERS > HATCH
HATCHERY n place where eggs are hatched under artificial conditions
HATCHES > HATCH
HATCHET n small axe
HATCHETS > HATCHET
HATCHETY adj like a hatchet
HATCHING > HATCH
HATCHINGS > HATCH
HATCHLING n young animal that has newly hatched from an egg
HATCHMENT n diamond-shaped tablet displaying the coat of arms of a dead person
HATCHWAY n opening in the deck of a ship
HATCHWAYS > HATCHWAY
HATE vb dislike intensely ▷ n intense dislike
HATEABLE > HATE
HATED > HATE
HATEFUL adj causing or deserving hate
HATEFULLY > HATEFUL
HATELESS > HATE
HATER > HATE
HATERENT same as > HATRED
HATERENTS > HATERENT
HATERS > HATE
HATES > HATE
HATFUL n amount a hat will hold
HATFULS > HATFUL
HATGUARD n string to keep a hat from blowing off
HATGUARDS > HATGUARD

HATH form of the present tense (indicative mood) of > HAVE

HATHA n as in hatha yoga form of yoga

HATINATOR n small fancy hat

HATING > HATE

HATLESS > HAT

HATLIKE > HAT

HATMAKER n maker of hats

HATMAKERS > HATMAKER

HATPEG n peg to hang hat on

HATPEGS > HATPEG

HATPIN n pin used to secure a woman's hat to her hair

HATPINS > HATPIN

HATRACK n rack for hanging hats on

HATRACKS > HATRACK

HATRED n intense dislike

HATREDS > HATRED

HATS > HAT

HATSFUL > HATFUL

HATSTAND n frame or pole equipped with hooks or arms for hanging up hats, coats, etc

HATSTANDS > HATSTAND

HATTED > HAT

HATTER n person who makes and sells hats ▷ vb annoy

HATTERED > HATTER

HATTERIA n species of reptile

HATTERIAS > HATTERIA

HATTERING > HATTER

HATTERS > HATTER

HATTING > HAT

HATTINGS > HAT

HATTOCK n small hat

HATTOCKS > HATTOCK

HAUBERK n long sleeveless coat of mail

HAUBERKS > HAUBERK

HAUBOIS same as > HAUTBOY

HAUD Scot word for > HOLD

HAUDING > HAUD

HAUDS > HAUD

HAUF Scot word for > HALF

HAUFS > HAUF

HAUGH n low-lying often alluvial riverside meadow

HAUGHS > HAUGH

HAUGHT same as > HAUGHTY

HAUGHTIER > HAUGHTY

HAUGHTILY > HAUGHTY

HAUGHTY adj proud, arrogant

HAUL vb pull or drag with effort ▷ n hauling

HAULAGE n (charge for) transporting goods

HAULAGES > HAULAGE

HAULBACK n (in lumbering) line used to bring a cable back

HAULBACKS > HAULBACK

HAULD Scots word for > HOLD

HAULDS > HAULD

HAULED > HAUL

HAULER same as > HAULIER

HAULERS > HAULER

HAULIER n firm or person that transports goods by road

HAULIERS > HAULIER

HAULING n act of hauling

HAULINGS > HAULING

HAULM n stalks of beans, peas, or potatoes collectively

HAULMIER > HAULMY

HAULMIEST > HAULMY

HAULMS > HAULM

HAULMY adj having haulms

HAULOUT n act of hauling a boat out of water

HAULOUTS > HAULOUT

HAULS > HAUL

HAULST same as > HALSE

HAULT same as > HAUGHTY

HAULYARD same as > HALYARD

HAULYARDS > HAULYARD

HAUN n Scot word for hand

HAUNCH n human hip or fleshy hindquarter of an animal ▷ vb cause (an animal) to come down on its haunches

HAUNCHED > HAUNCH

HAUNCHES > HAUNCH

HAUNCHING > HAUNCH

HAUNS > HAUN

HAUNT vb visit in the form of a ghost ▷ n place visited frequently

HAUNTED adj frequented by ghosts

HAUNTER > HAUNT

HAUNTERS > HAUNT

HAUNTING adj memorably beautiful or sad

HAUNTINGS > HAUNT

HAUNTS > HAUNT

HAURIANT adj rising

HAURIENT same as > HAURIANT

HAUSE same as > HALSE

HAUSED > HAUSE

HAUSEN n variety of sturgeon

HAUSENS > HAUSEN

HAUSES > HAUSE

HAUSFRAU n German housewife

HAUSFRAUS > HAUSFRAU

HAUSING > HAUSE

HAUSTELLA n plural of haustellum: tip of the proboscis of an insect

HAUSTORIA n plural of haustorium: organ of a parasitic plant that absorbs food and water from host tissues

HAUT same as > HAUGHTY

HAUTBOIS same as > HAUTBOY

HAUTBOY n type of strawberry

HAUTBOYS > HAUTBOY

HAUTE adj French word meaning high

HAUTER > HAUT

HAUTEST > HAUT

HAUTEUR n haughtiness

HAUTEURS > HAUTEUR

HAUYNE n blue mineral containing calcium

HAUYNES > HAUYNE

HAVARTI n Danish cheese

HAVARTIS > HAVARTI

HAVDALAH n ceremony at the end of the Sabbath

HAVDALAHS > HAVDALAH

HAVDOLOH same as > HAVDALAH

HAVDOLOHS > HAVDOLOH

HAVE vb possess, hold ▷ n person possessing wealth, security, etc

HAVELOCK n cap flap covering the back of the neck

HAVELOCKS > HAVELOCK

HAVEN n place of safety ▷ vb secure or shelter in or as if in a haven

HAVENED > HAVEN

HAVENING > HAVEN

HAVENLESS > HAVEN

HAVENS > HAVEN

HAVEOUR same as > HAVIOR

HAVEOURS > HAVEOUR

HAVER vb talk nonsense ▷ n nonsense

HAVERED > HAVER

HAVEREL n fool

HAVERELS > HAVEREL

HAVERING > HAVER

HAVERINGS > HAVER

HAVERS > HAVER

HAVERSACK n canvas bag carried on the back or shoulder

HAVERSINE n half the value of the versed sine

HAVES > HAVE

HAVILDAR n noncommissioned officer in the Indian army, equivalent in rank to sergeant

HAVILDARS > HAVILDAR

HAVING > HAVE

HAVINGS > HAVE

HAVIOR same as > HAVIOUR

HAVIORS > HAVIOR

HAVIOUR n possession

HAVIOURS > HAVIOUR

HAVOC n disorder and confusion ▷ vb lay waste

HAVOCKED > HAVOC

HAVOCKER > HAVOC

HAVOCKERS > HAVOC

HAVOCKING > HAVOC

HAVOCS > HAVOC

HAW n hawthorn berry ▷ vb make an inarticulate utterance

HAWALA n Middle Eastern system of money transfer

HAWALAS > HAWALA

HAWBUCK n bumpkin

HAWBUCKS > HAWBUCK

HAWEATER n resident of Manitoulin Island, Ontario

HAWEATERS > HAWEATER

HAWED > HAW

HAWFINCH n European finch with a stout bill and brown plumage with black-and-white wings

HAWING > HAW

HAWK n bird of prey ▷ vb offer (goods) for sale in the street or door-to-door

HAWKBELL n bell fitted to a hawk's leg

HAWKBELLS > HAWKBELL

HAWKBILL same as > HAWKSBILL

HAWKBILLS > HAWKBILL

HAWKBIT n any of three perennial plants

HAWKBITS > HAWKBIT

HAWKED > HAWK

HAWKER n travelling salesperson

HAWKERS > HAWKER

HAWKEY same as > HOCKEY

HAWKEYED adj having extremely keen sight

HAWKEYS > HAWKEY

HAWKIE n cow with white stripe on face

HAWKIES > HAWKIE

HAWKING another name for > FALCONRY

HAWKINGS > HAWKING

HAWKISH adj favouring the use of force rather than diplomacy

HAWKISHLY > HAWKISH

HAWKIT adj having a white streak

HAWKLIKE > HAWK

HAWKMOTH n narrow-winged moth

HAWKMOTHS > HAWKMOTH

HAWKNOSE n hooked nose

HAWKNOSES > HAWKNOSE

HAWKS > HAWK

HAWKSBILL n type of turtle

HAWKSHAW n private detective

HAWKSHAWS > HAWKSHAW

HAWKWEED n hairy plant with clusters of dandelion-like flowers

HAWKWEEDS > HAWKWEED

HAWM vb be idle and relaxed

HAWMED > HAWM

HAWMING > HAWM

HAWMS > HAWM

HAWS > HAW

HAWSE vb of boats, pitch violently when at anchor

HAWSED > HAWSE
HAWSEHOLE n one of the holes in the upper part of the bows of a vessel through which the anchor ropes pass
HAWSEPIPE n strong metal pipe through which an anchor rope passes
HAWSER n large rope used on a ship
HAWSERS > HAWSER
HAWSES > HAWSE
HAWSING > HAWSE
HAWTHORN n thorny shrub or tree
HAWTHORNS
> HAWTHORN
HAWTHORNY adj resembling hawthorns
HAY n grass cut and dried as fodder ▷ vb cut, dry, and store (grass, clover, etc) as fodder
HAYBAND n rope made by twisting hay together
HAYBANDS > HAYBAND
HAYBOX n airtight box used to keep partially cooked food warm
HAYBOXES > HAYBOX
HAYCATION n working holiday at a farm
HAYCOCK n pile of hay left until dry enough to move
HAYCOCKS > HAYCOCK
HAYED > HAY
HAYER n person who makes hay
HAYERS > HAYER
HAYEY > HAY
HAYFIELD n field of hay
HAYFIELDS
> HAYFIELD
HAYFORK n long-handled fork
HAYFORKS > HAYFORK
HAYIER > HAYEY
HAYIEST > HAYEY
HAYING > HAY
HAYINGS > HAY
HAYLAGE n type of hay for animal fodder
HAYLAGES > HAYLAGE
HAYLE n welfare
HAYLES > HAYLE
HAYLOFT n loft for storing hay
HAYLOFTS > HAYLOFT
HAYMAKER n person who helps to cut, turn, toss, spread, or carry hay
HAYMAKERS
> HAYMAKER
HAYMAKING
> HAYMAKER
HAYMOW n part of a barn where hay is stored
HAYMOWS > HAYMOW
HAYRACK n rack for holding hay for feeding to animals
HAYRACKS > HAYRACK
HAYRAKE n large rake used to collect hay
HAYRAKES > HAYRAKE
HAYRICK same as
> HAYSTACK

HAYRICKS > HAYRICK
HAYRIDE n pleasure trip in hay wagon
HAYRIDES > HAYRIDE
HAYS > HAY
HAYSEED n seeds or fragments of grass or straw
HAYSEEDS > HAYSEED
HAYSEL n season for making hay
HAYSELS > HAYSEL
HAYSTACK n large pile of stored hay
HAYSTACKS
> HAYSTACK
HAYWARD n parish officer in charge of enclosures and fences
HAYWARDS > HAYWARD
HAYWIRE adj (of things) not functioning properly ▷ n wire for binding hay
HAYWIRES > HAYWIRE
HAZAN n man employed to lead services in a synagogue
HAZANIM > HAZAN
HAZANS > HAZAN
HAZARD n something that could be dangerous ▷ vb put in danger
HAZARDED > HAZARD
HAZARDER > HAZARD
HAZARDERS > HAZARD
HAZARDING > HAZARD
HAZARDIZE same as
> HAZARD
HAZARDOUS adj involving great risk
HAZARDRY n taking of risks
HAZARDS > HAZARD
HAZE n mist, often caused by heat ▷ vb make or become hazy
HAZED > HAZE
HAZEL n small tree producing edible nuts ▷ adj (of eyes) greenish-brown
HAZELHEN n type of grouse
HAZELHENS
> HAZELHEN
HAZELLY > HAZEL
HAZELNUT n nut of a hazel shrub, which has a smooth shiny hard shell
HAZELNUTS
> HAZELNUT
HAZELS > HAZEL
HAZELWOOD n the wood of the hazel
HAZER > HAZE
HAZERS > HAZE
HAZES > HAZE
HAZIER > HAZY
HAZIEST > HAZY
HAZILY > HAZY
HAZINESS > HAZY
HAZING > HAZE
HAZINGS > HAZE
HAZMAT n hazardous material
HAZMATS > HAZMAT
HAZY adj not clear, misty
HAZZAN same as > HAZAN

HAZZANIM > HAZZAN
HAZZANS > HAZZAN
HE pron male person or animal ▷ n male person or animal ▷ interj expression of amusement or derision
HEAD n upper or front part of the body ▷ adj chief, principal ▷ vb be at the top or front of
HEADACHE n continuous pain in the head
HEADACHES
> HEADACHE
HEADACHEY same as
> HEADACHY
HEADACHY adj suffering from, caused by, or likely to cause a headache
HEADAGE n payment to farmer based on animals owned
HEADAGES > HEADAGE
HEADBAND n ribbon or band worn around the head
HEADBANDS
> HEADBAND
HEADBANG vb nod one's head violently to the beat of loud rock music
HEADBANGS
> HEADBANG
HEADBOARD n vertical board at the top end of a bed
HEADCASE n foolish or crazy person
HEADCASES
> HEADCASE
HEADCHAIR n chair with support for the head
HEADCLOTH n kerchief worn on the head
HEADCOUNT n count of number of people present
HEADDRESS n decorative head covering
HEADED adj having a head or heads
HEADEND n facility from which cable television is transmitted
HEADENDS > HEADEND
HEADER n striking a ball with the head
HEADERS > HEADER
HEADFAST n mooring rope at the bows of a ship
HEADFASTS
> HEADFAST
HEADFIRST adv with the head foremost
HEADFISH same as
> SUNFISH
HEADFRAME n structure supporting winding machinery at mine
HEADFUCK n taboo slang for experience that is wildly exciting or impressive
HEADFUCKS
> HEADFUCK
HEADFUL n amount head will hold
HEADFULS > HEADFUL
HEADGATE n gate used to control the flow of water

at the upper end of a lock or conduit
HEADGATES
> HEADGATE
HEADGEAR n hats collectively
HEADGEARS
> HEADGEAR
HEADGUARD n padded helmet worn to protect the head in contact sports
HEADHUNT vb recruit employee from another company
HEADHUNTS > HEADHUNT
HEADIER > HEADY
HEADIEST > HEADY
HEADILY > HEADY
HEADINESS > HEADY
HEADING same as > HEAD
HEADINGS > HEADING
HEADLAMP same as
> HEADLIGHT
HEADLAMPS
> HEADLAMP
HEADLAND n area of land jutting out into the sea
HEADLANDS
> HEADLAND
HEADLEASE n main lease often subdivided
HEADLESS adj without a head
HEADLIGHT n powerful light on the front of a vehicle
HEADLIKE > HEAD
HEADLINE n title at the top of a newspaper article, esp on the front page
HEADLINED
> HEADLINE
HEADLINER n performer given prominent billing
HEADLINES
> HEADLINE
HEADLOCK n wrestling hold
HEADLOCKS
> HEADLOCK
HEADLONG adj with the head first ▷ adv with the head foremost
HEADMAN n chief or leader
HEADMARK n characteristic
HEADMARKS
> HEADMARK
HEADMEN > HEADMAN
HEADMOST less common word for > FOREMOST
HEADNOTE n note at book chapter head
HEADNOTES
> HEADNOTE
HEADPEACE archaic form of > HEADPIECE
HEADPHONE n small loudspeaker held against the ear
HEADPIECE n decorative band at the top of a page, chapter, etc
HEADPIN another word for
> KINGPIN
HEADPINS > HEADPIN
HEADPOND n artificial pond behind a dam

h

HEADPONDS
> HEADPOND
HEADRACE n channel that carries water to a water wheel, turbine, etc
HEADRACES
> HEADRACE
HEADRAIL n end of a snooker table from which play is started
HEADRAILS
> HEADRAIL
HEADREACH n distance made to windward while tacking ▷ vb gain distance over (another boat) when tacking
HEADREST n support for the head, as on a dentist's chair or car seat
HEADRESTS
> HEADREST
HEADRIG n edge of ploughed field
HEADRIGS > HEADRIG
HEADRING n African head decoration
HEADRINGS
> HEADRING
HEADROOM n space above person's head in a vehicle
HEADROOMS
> HEADROOM
HEADROPE n rope round an animal's head
HEADROPES
> HEADROPE
HEADS adv with the side of a coin with a head on it uppermost
HEADSAIL n any sail set forward of the foremast
HEADSAILS
> HEADSAIL
HEADSCARF n scarf for the head, often worn tied under the chin
HEADSET n pair of headphones
HEADSETS > HEADSET
HEADSHAKE n gesture of shaking head
HEADSHIP n position or state of being a leader, esp the head teacher of a school
HEADSHIPS
> HEADSHIP
HEADSHOT n photo of person's head
HEADSHOTS
> HEADSHOT
HEADSMAN n (formerly) an executioner who beheaded condemned persons
HEADSMEN > HEADSMAN
HEADSPACE n space between bolt and cartridge in a rifle
HEADSTALL n part of a bridle that fits round a horse's head
HEADSTAND n act or an instance of balancing on the head, usually with the hands as support
HEADSTAY n rope from mast to bow on ship

HEADSTAYS
> HEADSTAY
HEADSTICK n piece of wood formerly used in typesetting
HEADSTOCK n part of a machine that supports and transmits the drive to the chuck
HEADSTONE n memorial stone on a grave
HEADWALL n steep slope at the head of a glacial cirque
HEADWALLS
> HEADWALL
HEADWARD same as
> HEADWARDS
HEADWARDS adv backwards beyond the original source
HEADWATER n highest part of river
HEADWAY same as
> HEADROOM
HEADWAYS > HEADWAY
HEADWIND n wind blowing against the course of an aircraft or ship
HEADWINDS
> HEADWIND
HEADWORD n key word placed at the beginning of a line, paragraph, etc, as in a dictionary entry
HEADWORDS
> HEADWORD
HEADWORK n intellectual labour
HEADWORKS
> HEADWORK
HEADY adj intoxicating or exciting
HEAL vb make or become well
HEALABLE > HEAL
HEALD same as > HEDDLE
HEALDED > HEALD
HEALDING > HEALD
HEALDS > HEALD
HEALED > HEAL
HEALEE n person who is being healed
HEALEES > HEALEE
HEALER > HEAL
HEALERS > HEAL
HEALING > HEAL
HEALINGLY > HEAL
HEALINGS > HEAL
HEALS > HEAL
HEALSOME Scots word for
> WHOLESOME
HEALTH n normal (good) condition of someone's body ▷ interj exclamation wishing someone good health as part of a toast
HEALTHFUL same as
> HEALTHY
HEALTHIER > HEALTHY
HEALTHILY > HEALTHY
HEALTHISM n lifestyle that prioritizes health and fitness over anything else
HEALTHS > HEALTH
HEALTHY adj having good health

HEAME old form of > HOME
HEAP n pile of things one on top of another ▷ vb gather into a pile
HEAPED > HEAP
HEAPER > HEAP
HEAPERS > HEAP
HEAPIER > HEAPY
HEAPIEST > HEAPY
HEAPING adj (of a spoonful) heaped
HEAPS > HEAP
HEAPSTEAD n buildings at mine
HEAPY adj having many heaps
HEAR vb perceive (a sound) by ear
HEARABLE > HEAR
HEARD same as > HERD
HEARDS > HEARD
HEARE old form of > HAIR
HEARER > HEAR
HEARERS > HEAR
HEARES > HEARE
HEARIE old form of
> HAIRY
HEARING > HEAR
HEARINGS > HEAR
HEARKEN vb listen
HEARKENED > HEARKEN
HEARKENER > HEARKEN
HEARKENS > HEARKEN
HEARS > HEAR
HEARSAY n gossip, rumour
HEARSAYS > HEARSAY
HEARSE n funeral car used to carry a coffin ▷ vb put in hearse
HEARSED > HEARSE
HEARSES > HEARSE
HEARSIER > HEARSY
HEARSIEST > HEARSY
HEARSING > HEARSE
HEARSY adj like a hearse
HEART n organ that pumps blood round the body ▷ vb (of vegetables) form a heart
HEARTACHE n intense anguish
HEARTBEAT n one complete pulsation of the heart
HEARTBURN n burning sensation in the chest caused by indigestion
HEARTED > HEART
HEARTEN vb encourage, make cheerful
HEARTENED > HEARTEN
HEARTENER > HEARTEN
HEARTENS > HEARTEN
HEARTFELT adj felt sincerely or strongly
HEARTFREE adj not in love
HEARTH n floor of a fireplace
HEARTHRUG n rug laid before a fireplace
HEARTHS > HEARTH
HEARTIER > HEARTY
HEARTIES > HEARTY
HEARTIEST > HEARTY
HEARTIKIN n little heart

HEARTILY adv thoroughly or vigorously
HEARTING > HEART
HEARTLAND n central region of a country or continent
HEARTLESS adj cruel, unkind
HEARTLET n little heart
HEARTLETS > HEART
HEARTLING n little heart
HEARTLY adv vigorously
HEARTPEA same as
> HEARTSEED
HEARTPEAS
> HEARTPEA
HEARTS n card game
HEARTSEED n type of vine
HEARTSICK adj deeply dejected or despondent
HEARTSINK n patient who visits a doctor with multiple non-specific symptoms that are impossible to treat
HEARTSOME adj cheering or encouraging
HEARTSORE adj greatly distressed ▷ n cause of pain in the heart or the pain itself
HEARTWOOD n central core of dark hard wood in tree trunks
HEARTWORM n parasitic nematode worm that lives in the heart and bloodstream of vertebrates
HEARTY adj substantial, nourishing ▷ n comrade, esp a sailor
HEAST same as > HEST
HEASTE same as > HEST
HEASTES > HEASTE
HEASTS > HEAST
HEAT vb make or become hot ▷ n state of being hot
HEATABLE > HEAT
HEATED adj angry and excited
HEATEDLY > HEATED
HEATER n device for supplying heat
HEATERS > HEATER
HEATH n area of open uncultivated land
HEATHBIRD n black grouse
HEATHCOCK same as
> BLACKCOCK
HEATHEN n person who does not believe in an established religion ▷ adj of or relating to heathen peoples
HEATHENRY > HEATHEN
HEATHENS > HEATHEN
HEATHER n low-growing plant ▷ adj of a heather colour
HEATHERED > HEATHER
HEATHERS > HEATHER
HEATHERY > HEATHER
HEATHFOWL n black grouse
HEATHIER > HEATH**

HEATHIEST > HEATH
HEATHLAND *n* area of heath
HEATHLESS > HEATH
HEATHLIKE > HEATH
HEATHS > HEATH
HEATHY > HEATH
HEATING *n* device or system for supplying heat
HEATINGS > HEATING
HEATLESS > HEAT
HEATPROOF > HEAT
HEATS > HEAT
HEATSPOT *n* spot on skin produced by heat
HEATSPOTS > HEATSPOT
HEATWAVE *n* prolonged period of unusually hot weather
HEATWAVES
> HEATWAVE
HEAUME *n* large helmet reaching the shoulders
HEAUMES > HEAUME
HEAVE *vb* lift with effort ▷ *n* heaving
HEAVED > HEAVE
HEAVEN *n* place believed to be the home of God
HEAVENLY *adj* of or like heaven
HEAVENS > HEAVEN
HEAVER > HEAVE
HEAVERS > HEAVE
HEAVES > HEAVE
HEAVIER > HEAVY
HEAVIES > HEAVY
HEAVIEST > HEAVY
HEAVILY > HEAVY
HEAVINESS > HEAVY
HEAVING > HEAVE
HEAVINGS > HEAVE
HEAVY *adj* of great weight ▷ *n* person hired to threaten violence
HEAVYISH *adj* rather heavy
HEAVYSET *adj* stockily built
HEBDOMAD *n* number seven or a group of seven
HEBDOMADS > HEBDOMAD
HEBE *n* any of various flowering shrubs
HEBEN *old form of >* EBONY
HEBENON *n* source of poison
HEBENONS > HEBENON
HEBENS > HEBEN
HEBES > HEBE
HEBETANT *adj* causing dullness
HEBETATE *adj* (of plant parts) having a blunt or soft point ▷ *vb* make or become blunted
HEBETATED
> HEBETATE
HEBETATES
> HEBETATE
HEBETIC *adj* of or relating to puberty
HEBETUDE *n* mental dullness or lethargy
HEBETUDES
> HEBETUDE
HEBONA *same as*
> HEBENON

HEBONAS > HEBONA
HEBRAISE *same as*
> HEBRAIZE
HEBRAISED
> HEBRAISE
HEBRAISES
> HEBRAISE
HEBRAIZE *vb* become or cause to become Hebrew or Hebraic
HEBRAIZED
> HEBRAIZE
HEBRAIZES
> HEBRAIZE
HECATOMB *n* sacrifice of 100 oxen
HECATOMBS
> HECATOMB
HECH *interj* expression of surprise
HECHT *same as >* HIGHT
HECHTING > HECHT
HECHTS > HECHT
HECK *interj* mild exclamation of surprise, irritation, etc ▷ *n* frame for obstructing the passage of fish in a river
HECKLE *vb* interrupt with comments, questions, or taunts ▷ *n* instrument for combing flax or hemp
HECKLED > HECKLE
HECKLER > HECKLE
HECKLERS > HECKLE
HECKLES > HECKLE
HECKLING > HECKLE
HECKLINGS > HECKLE
HECKS > HECK
HECKUVA *adj* heck of a
HECOGENIN *n* plant chemical
HECTARE *n* one hundred ares
HECTARES > HECTARE
HECTIC *adj* rushed or busy ▷ *n* hectic fever or flush
HECTICAL *same as*
> HECTIC
HECTICLY > HECTIC
HECTICS > HECTIC
HECTOGRAM *n* one hundred grams. 1 hectogram is equivalent to 3.527 ounces
HECTOR *vb* bully ▷ *n* blustering bully
HECTORED > HECTOR
HECTORER > HECTOR
HECTORERS > HECTOR
HECTORING > HECTOR
HECTORISM > HECTOR
HECTORLY > HECTOR
HECTORS > HECTOR
HEDARIM *same as*
> HADARIM
HEDDLE *n* frame on a loom ▷ *vb* pass thread through a heddle
HEDDLED > HEDDLE
HEDDLES > HEDDLE
HEDDLING > HEDDLE
HEDER *variant spelling of*
> CHEDER
HEDERA *n* ivy
HEDERAL > HEDERA
HEDERAS > HEDERA

HEDERATED *adj* honoured with crown of ivy
HEDERS > HEDER
HEDGE *n* row of bushes forming a barrier or boundary ▷ *vb* be evasive or noncommittal
HEDGEBILL *n* tool for pruning a hedge
HEDGED > HEDGE
HEDGEHOG *n* small mammal with a protective covering of spines
HEDGEHOGS
> HEDGEHOG
HEDGEHOP *vb* (of an aircraft) to fly close to the ground, as in crop spraying
HEDGEHOPS
> HEDGEHOP
HEDGEPIG *same as*
> HEDGEHOG
HEDGEPIGS
> HEDGEPIG
HEDGER > HEDGE
HEDGEROW *n* bushes forming a hedge
HEDGEROWS
> HEDGEROW
HEDGERS > HEDGE
HEDGES > HEDGE
HEDGIER > HEDGE
HEDGIEST > HEDGE
HEDGING > HEDGE
HEDGINGLY > HEDGE
HEDGINGS > HEDGE
HEDGY > HEDGE
HEDONIC > HEDONISM
HEDONICS *n* branch of psychology concerned with the study of pleasant and unpleasant sensations
HEDONISM *n* doctrine that pleasure is the most important thing in life
HEDONISMS
> HEDONISM
HEDONIST > HEDONISM
HEDONISTS
> HEDONISM
HEDYPHANE *n* variety of lead ore
HEDYSARUM *n* leguminous plant of the genus Hedysarum
HEED *n* careful attention ▷ *vb* pay careful attention to
HEEDED > HEED
HEEDER > HEED
HEEDERS > HEED
HEEDFUL > HEED
HEEDFULLY > HEED
HEEDIER > HEEDY
HEEDIEST > HEEDY
HEEDINESS > HEED
HEEDING > HEED
HEEDLESS *adj* taking no notice
HEEDS > HEED
HEEDY *adj* heedful; attentive
HEEHAW *interj* representation of the braying sound of a donkey ▷ *vb* make braying sound

HEEHAWED > HEEHAW
HEEHAWING > HEEHAW
HEEHAWS > HEEHAW
HEEL *n* back part of the foot ▷ *vb* repair the heel of (a shoe)
HEELBALL *n* mixture of beeswax and lampblack used by shoemakers
HEELBALLS
> HEELBALL
HEELBAR *n* small shop where shoes are repaired
HEELBARS > HEELBAR
HEELED > HEEL
HEELER *n* dog that herds cattle by biting at their heels
HEELERS > HEELER
HEELING > HEEL
HEELINGS > HEEL
HEELLESS > HEEL
HEELPIECE *n* piece of a shoe, stocking, etc, designed to fit the heel
HEELPLATE *n* reinforcing piece of metal
HEELPOST *n* post for carrying the hinges of a door or gate
HEELPOSTS
> HEELPOST
HEELS > HEEL
HEELTAP *n* layer of leather, etc, in the heel of a shoe
HEELTAPS > HEELTAP
HEEZE *Scots word for*
> HOIST
HEEZED > HEEZE
HEEZES > HEEZE
HEEZIE *n* act of lifting
HEEZIES > HEEZIE
HEEZING > HEEZE
HEFT *vb* assess the weight of (something) by lifting ▷ *n* weight
HEFTE *same as >* HEAVE
HEFTED > HEFT
HEFTER > HEFT
HEFTERS > HEFT
HEFTIER > HEFTY
HEFTIEST > HEFTY
HEFTILY > HEFTY
HEFTINESS > HEFTY
HEFTING > HEFT
HEFTS > HEFT
HEFTY *adj* large, heavy, or strong
HEGARI *n* African sorghum
HEGARIS > HEGARI
HEGEMON *n* person in authority
HEGEMONIC
> HEGEMONY
HEGEMONS > HEGEMON
HEGEMONY *n* political domination
HEGIRA *n* emigration escape or flight
HEGIRAS > HEGIRA
HEGUMEN *n* head of a monastery of the Eastern Church
HEGUMENE *n* head of Greek nunnery
HEGUMENES > HEGUMENE

HEGUMENOI
> HEGUMENOS
HEGUMENOS *same as*
> HEGUMEN
HEGUMENS > HEGUMEN
HEGUMENY *n* office of
hegumen
HEH *interj* exclamation of
surprise or inquiry
HEHS > HEH
HEID *Scot word for* > HEAD
HEIDS > HEID
HEIDUC *n* Hungarian
guerilla warrior
HEIDUCS > HEIDUC
HEIFER *n* young cow
HEIFERS > HEIFER
HEIGH *same as* > HEY
HEIGHT *n* distance from
base to top
HEIGHTEN *vb* make or
become higher or more
intense
HEIGHTENS
> HEIGHTEN
HEIGHTH *obsolete form of*
> HEIGHT
HEIGHTHS > HEIGHTH
HEIGHTISM *n*
discrimination based on
people's heights
HEIGHTS > HEIGHT
HEIL *vb* give a German
greeting
HEILED > HEIL
HEILING > HEIL
HEILS > HEIL
HEIMISH *adj* comfortable
HEINIE *n* buttocks
HEINIES > HEINIE
HEINOUS *adj* evil and
shocking
HEINOUSLY > HEINOUS
HEIR *n* person entitled to
inherit property or rank
▷ *vb* inherit
HEIRDOM *n* succession by
right of blood
HEIRDOMS > HEIRDOM
HEIRED > HEIR
HEIRESS *n* woman who
inherits or expects to
inherit great wealth
HEIRESSES > HEIRESS
HEIRING > HEIR
HEIRLESS > HEIR
HEIRLOOM *n* object that
has belonged to a family
for generations
HEIRLOOMS
> HEIRLOOM
HEIRS > HEIR
HEIRSHIP *n* state or
condition of being an heir
HEIRSHIPS
> HEIRSHIP
HEISHI *n* Native
American shell jewellery
HEIST *n* robbery ▷ *vb*
steal or burgle
HEISTED > HEIST
HEISTER > HEIST
HEISTERS > HEIST
HEISTING > HEIST
HEISTS > HEIST
HEITIKI *n* Māori neck
ornament of greenstone
HEITIKIS > HEITIKI

HEJAB *same as* > HIJAB
HEJABS > HEJAB
HEJIRA *same as*
> HEGIRA
HEJIRAS > HEJIRA
HEJRA *same as* > HEGIRA
HEJRAS > HEJRA
HEKETARA *n* small shrub
that has flowers with
white petals and yellow
centres
HEKETARAS
> HEKETARA
HEKTARE *same as*
> HECTARE
HEKTARES > HEKTARE
HEKTOGRAM *same as*
> HECTOGRAM
HELCOID *adj* having
ulcers
HELD > HOLD
HELE *vb* as in *hele in* insert
(cuttings, etc) into soil
HELED > HELE
HELENIUM *n* plant with
daisy-like yellow or
variegated flowers
HELENIUMS
> HELENIUM
HELES > HELE
HELIAC *same as*
> HELIACAL
HELIACAL *adj* as in
heliacal rising rising of a
celestial object at
approximately the same
time as the rising of the
sun
HELIAST *n* ancient Greek
juror
HELIASTS > HELIAST
HELIBORNE *adj* carried in
helicopter
HELIBUS *n* helicopter
carrying passengers
HELIBUSES > HELIBUS
HELICAL *adj* spiral
HELICALLY > HELICAL
HELICASE *n* enzyme
vital to all living organisms
HELICASES
> HELICASE
HELICES > HELIX
HELICITY *n* projection
of the spin of an
elementary particle on the
direction of propagation
HELICLINE *n*
spiral-shaped ramp
HELICOID *adj* shaped
like a spiral ▷ *n* any surface
resembling that of a screw
thread
HELICOIDS
> HELICOID
HELICON *n* bass tuba
HELICONIA *n* tropical
flowering plant
HELICONS > HELICON
HELICOPT *vb* transport
using a helicopter
HELICOPTS
> HELICOPT
HELICTITE *n* twisted
stalactite
HELIDECK *n* landing
deck for helicopters on
ships, oil platforms, etc

HELIDECKS
> HELIDECK
HELIDROME *n* small
airport for helicopters
HELILIFT *vb* transport
by helicopter
HELILIFTS
> HELILIFT
HELIMAN *n* helicopter
pilot
HELIMEN > HELIMAN
HELING > HELE
HELIO *n* instrument for
sending messages in
Morse code
HELIODOR *n* clear yellow
form of beryl used as a
gemstone
HELIODORS
> HELIODOR
HELIOGRAM *n* message
sent by reflecting the sun's
rays in a mirror
HELIOLOGY *n* study of
sun
HELIOPSES
> HELIOPSIS
HELIOPSIS *n* type of
flowering plant
HELIOS > HELIO
HELIOSES > HELIOSIS
HELIOSIS *n* bad effect of
overexposure to the sun
HELIOSTAT *n*
astronomical instrument
used to reflect the light of
the sun in a constant
direction
HELIOTYPE *n* printing
process in which an
impression is taken in ink
from a gelatine surface
that has been exposed
under a negative and
prepared for printing
HELIOTYPY *same as*
> HELIOTYPE
HELIOZOAN *n* type of
protozoan, typically
having a siliceous shell and
stiff radiating cytoplasmic
projections
HELIOZOIC
> HELIOZOAN
HELIPAD *n* place for
helicopters to land and
take off
HELIPADS > HELIPAD
HELIPILOT *n* helicopter
pilot
HELIPORT *n* airport for
helicopters
HELIPORTS
> HELIPORT
HELISKI *vb* ski down a
mountain after ascending
it by helicopter
HELISKIED > HELISKI
HELISKIS > HELISKI
HELISTOP *n* landing
place for helicopter
HELISTOPS > HELISTOP
HELITACK *n* use of
helicopters to extinguish a
forest fire
HELITACKS
> HELITACK
HELIUM *n* very light
colourless odourless gas

HELIUMS > HELIUM
HELIX *n* spiral
HELIXES > HELIX
HELL *n* believed to be
where wicked people go
when they die ▷ *vb* act
wildly
HELLBENT *adj* intent
HELLBOX *n* (in printing)
container for broken type
HELLBOXES > HELLBOX
HELLBROTH *n* evil
concoction
HELLCAT *n* spiteful
fierce-tempered woman
HELLCATS > HELLCAT
HELLDIVER *n* small
greyish-brown North
American grebe
HELLEBORE *n* plant with
white flowers that bloom
in winter
HELLED > HELL
HELLENISE *same as*
> HELLENIZE
HELLENIZE *vb* make or
become like the ancient
Greeks
HELLER *n* monetary unit
of the Czech Republic
HELLERI *n* Central
American fish
HELLERIES > HELLERY
HELLERIS > HELLERI
HELLERS > HELLER
HELLERY *n* wild or
mischievous behaviour
HELLFIRE *n* torment of
hell, imagined as eternal
fire
HELLFIRES
> HELLFIRE
HELLHOLE *n* unpleasant
or evil place
HELLHOLES
> HELLHOLE
HELLHOUND *n* hound of
hell
HELLICAT *n* evil creature
HELLICATS
> HELLICAT
HELLIER *n* slater
HELLIERS > HELLIER
HELLING > HELL
HELLION *n* rough or
rowdy person, esp a child
HELLIONS > HELLION
HELLISH *adj* very
unpleasant ▷ *adv*
(intensifier) extremely
HELLISHLY > HELLISH
HELLKITE *n* bird of prey
from hell
HELLKITES
> HELLKITE
HELLO *interj* expression of
greeting or surprise ▷ *n*
act of saying 'hello'
▷ *sentence substitute*
expression of greeting ▷ *vb*
say hello
HELLOED > HELLO
HELLOES > HELLO
HELLOING > HELLO
HELLOS > HELLO
HELLOVA *same as*
> HELLUVA
HELLS > HELL

HELLSCAPE n harshly unpleasant environment
HELLUVA adj phonetic representation of 'hell of a'
HELLWARD adj towards hell
HELLWARDS adv towards hell
HELM n tiller or wheel for steering a ship ▷ vb direct or steer
HELMED > HELM
HELMER n film director
HELMERS > HELMER
HELMET n hard hat worn for protection
HELMETED > HELMET
HELMETING n wearing or provision of a helmet
HELMETS > HELMET
HELMING > HELM
HELMINTH n any parasitic worm, esp a nematode or fluke
HELMINTHS > HELMINTH
HELMLESS > HELM
HELMS > HELM
HELMSMAN n person at the helm who steers the ship
HELMSMEN > HELMSMAN
HELO n helicopter
HELOPHYTE n any perennial marsh plant that bears its overwintering buds in the mud below the surface
HELOS > HELO
HELOT n serf or slave
HELOTAGE same as > HELOTISM
HELOTAGES > HELOTAGE
HELOTISM n condition or quality of being a helot
HELOTISMS > HELOTISM
HELOTRIES > HELOTRY
HELOTRY n serfdom or slavery
HELOTS > HELOT
HELP vb make something easier, better, or quicker for (someone) ▷ n assistance or support
HELPABLE > HELP
HELPDESK n place where advice is given by telephone
HELPDESKS > HELPDESK
HELPED > HELP
HELPER > HELP
HELPERS > HELP
HELPFUL adj giving help
HELPFULLY > HELPFUL
HELPING n single portion of food
HELPINGS > HELPING
HELPLESS adj weak or incapable
HELPLINE n telephone line set aside for callers to contact an organization for help with a problem
HELPLINES > HELPLINE

HELPMATE n companion and helper, esp a spouse
HELPMATES > HELPMATE
HELPMEET less common word for > HELPMATE
HELPMEETS > HELPMEET
HELPS > HELP
HELVE n handle of a hand tool such as an axe or pick ▷ vb fit a helve to (a tool)
HELVED > HELVE
HELVES > HELVE
HELVETIUM same as > ASTATINE
HELVING > HELVE
HEM n bottom edge of a garment ▷ vb provide with a hem
HEMAGOG same as > HEMAGOGUE
HEMAGOGS > HEMAGOG
HEMAGOGUE n haemagogue: drug that promotes the flow of blood
HEMAL same as > HAEMAL
HEMATAL same as > HEMAL
HEMATEIN same as > HAEMATEIN
HEMATEINS > HEMATEIN
HEMATIC same as > HAEMATIC
HEMATICS > HEMATIC
HEMATIN same as > HAEMATIN
HEMATINE n red dye
HEMATINES > HEMATINE
HEMATINIC same as > HAEMATIC
HEMATINS > HEMATIN
HEMATITE n red, grey, or black mineral
HEMATITES > HEMATITE
HEMATITIC > HEMATITE
HEMATOID same as > HAEMATOID
HEMATOMA same as > HAEMATOMA
HEMATOMAS > HEMATOMA
HEMATOSES > HEMATOSIS
HEMATOSIS n haematosis: oxygenation of venous blood in the lungs
HEMATOZOA n plural of hematozoon: protozoan that is parasitic in the blood
HEMATURIA n the presence of blood or red blood cells in the urine
HEMATURIC > HEMATURIA
HEME same as > HAEM
HEMELYTRA n plural of hemelytron: forewing of plant bugs
HEMES > HEME
HEMIALGIA n pain limited to one side of the body

HEMIC same as > HAEMATIC
HEMICYCLE n semicircular structure, room, arena, wall, etc
HEMIHEDRA n plural of hemihedron, a hemihedral solid
HEMIHEDRY n hemihedral property of crystals
HEMIN same as > HAEMIN
HEMINA n old liquid measure
HEMINAS > HEMINA
HEMINS > HEMIN
HEMIOLA n rhythmic device
HEMIOLAS > HEMIOLA
HEMIOLIA same as > HEMIOLA
HEMIOLIAS > HEMIOLIA
HEMIOLIC > HEMIOLA
HEMIONE same as > HEMIONUS
HEMIONES > HEMIONE
HEMIONUS n Asian wild ass
HEMIOPIA n defective vision seeing only halves of things
HEMIOPIAS > HEMIOPIA
HEMIOPIC > HEMIOPIA
HEMIOPSIA same as > HEMIOPIA
HEMIPOD same as > HEMIPODE
HEMIPODE n button quail
HEMIPODES > HEMIPODE
HEMIPODS > HEMIPOD
HEMIPTER n insect with beaklike mouthparts
HEMIPTERS > HEMIPTER
HEMISPACE n area in brain
HEMISTICH n half line of verse
HEMITROPE another name for > TWIN
HEMITROPY n state of being a twin
HEMLINE n level to which the hem of a skirt hangs
HEMLINES > HEMLINE
HEMLOCK n poisonous plant
HEMLOCKS > HEMLOCK
HEMMED > HEM
HEMMER n attachment on a sewing machine for hemming
HEMMERS > HEMMER
HEMMING > HEM
HEMOCOEL same as > HAEMOCOEL
HEMOCOELS > HEMOCOEL
HEMOCONIA n the small particles of matter, thought to be particles of the structure of red blood cells, that are present in blood that is flowing around the body

HEMOCYTE same as > HAEMOCYTE
HEMOCYTES > HEMOCYTE
HEMOID same as > HAEMATOID
HEMOLYMPH n blood-like fluid in invertebrates
HEMOLYSE vb break down so that haemoglobin is released
HEMOLYSED > HEMOLYSE
HEMOLYSES > HEMOLYSIS
HEMOLYSIN n haemolysin: substance that breaks down red blood cells
HEMOLYSIS n haemolysis: disintegration of red blood cells
HEMOLYTIC adj destroying red blood corpuscles
HEMOLYZE vb undergo or make undergo hemolysis
HEMOLYZED > HEMOLYZE
HEMOLYZES > HEMOLYZE
HEMOPHILE n haemophile: person with haemophilia
HEMOSTAT same as > HAEMOSTAT
HEMOSTATS > HEMOSTAT
HEMOTOXIC > HEMOTOXIN
HEMOTOXIN n substance that destroys red blood cells
HEMP n Asian plant with tough fibres
HEMPEN > HEMP
HEMPIE variant of > HEMPY
HEMPIER > HEMPY
HEMPIES > HEMPY
HEMPIEST > HEMPY
HEMPLIKE > HEMP
HEMPS > HEMP
HEMPSEED n seed of hemp
HEMPSEEDS > HEMPSEED
HEMPWEED n climbing weed
HEMPWEEDS > HEMPWEED
HEMPY adj of or like hemp ▷ n rogue
HEMS > HEM
HEMSTITCH n decorative edging stitch, usually for a hem, in which the cross threads are stitched in groups ▷ vb decorate (a hem, etc) with hemstitches
HEN n female domestic fowl ▷ vb lose one's courage
HENBANE n poisonous plant with sticky hairy leaves
HENBANES > HENBANE

h

HENBIT *n* European plant with small dark red flowers

HENBITS > HENBIT

HENCE *adv* from this time ▷ *interj* begone! away!

HENCH *adj* fit and muscular

HENCHER > HENCH

HENCHEST > HENCH

HENCHMAN *n* person employed by someone powerful to carry out orders

HENCHMEN > HENCHMAN

HENCOOP *n* cage for poultry

HENCOOPS > HENCOOP

HEND *vb* seize

HENDED > HEND

HENDIADYS *n* rhetorical device by which two nouns joined by a conjunction are used instead of a noun and modifier

HENDING > HEND

HENDS > HEND

HENEQUEN *n* agave plant native to Yucatán

HENEQUENS > HENEQUEN

HENEQUIN *same as* > HENEQUEN

HENEQUINS > HENEQUIN

HENGE *n* monument from the Neolithic and Bronze Ages

HENGES > HENGE

HENHOUSE *n* coop for hens

HENHOUSES > HENHOUSE

HENIQUEN *same as* > HENEQUEN

HENIQUENS > HENIQUEN

HENIQUIN *same as* > HENIQUIN

HENIQUINS > HENIQUIN

HENLEY *n* type of sweater

HENLEYS > HENLEY

HENLIKE > HEN

HENNA *n* reddish dye made from a shrub or tree ▷ *vb* dye (the hair) with henna

HENNAED > HENNA

HENNAING > HENNA

HENNAS > HENNA

HENNED > HEN

HENNER *n* challenge

HENNERIES > HENNERY

HENNERS > HENNER

HENNERY *n* place or farm for keeping poultry

HENNIER > HENNY

HENNIES > HENNY

HENNIEST > HENNY

HENNIN *n* former women's hat

HENNING > HEN

HENNINS > HENNIN

HENNISH > HEN

HENNISHLY > HEN

HENNY *adj* like a hen ▷ *n* cock that looks like a hen

HENOTIC *adj* acting to reconcile

HENPECK *vb* (of a woman) to harass or torment (a man)

HENPECKED *adj* (of a man) dominated by his wife

HENPECKS > HENPECK

HENRIES > HENRY

HENRY *n* unit of electrical inductance

HENRYS > HENRY

HENS > HEN

HENT *vb* seize ▷ *n* anything that has been grasped, esp by the mind

HENTED > HENT

HENTING > HENT

HENTS > HENT

HEP *adj* aware of or following the latest trends ▷ *n* fact of being hep

HEPAR *n* compound containing sulphur

HEPARIN *n* polysaccharide present in most body tissues

HEPARINS > HEPARIN

HEPARS > HEPAR

HEPATIC *adj* of the liver ▷ *n* any of various drugs for use in treating diseases of the liver

HEPATICA *n* woodland plant with white, mauve, or pink flowers

HEPATICAE > HEPATICA

HEPATICAL *same as* > HEPATIC

HEPATICAS > HEPATICA

HEPATICS > HEPATIC

HEPATISE *same as* > HEPATIZE

HEPATISED > HEPATISE

HEPATISES > HEPATISE

HEPATITE *n* mineral containing sulphur

HEPATITES > HEPATITE

HEPATITIS *n* inflammation of the liver

HEPATIZE *vb* turn into liver

HEPATIZED > HEPATIZE

HEPATIZES > HEPATIZE

HEPATOMA *n* cancer of liver

HEPATOMAS > HEPATOMA

HEPCAT *n* person who is hep

HEPCATS > HEPCAT

HEPPER > HEP

HEPPEST > HEP

HEPS > HEP

HEPSTER *same as* > HIPSTER

HEPSTERS > HEPSTER

HEPT *archaic spelling of* > HEAPED

HEPTAD *n* group or series of seven

HEPTADS > HEPTAD

HEPTAGLOT *n* book written in seven languages

HEPTAGON *n* geometric figure with seven sides

HEPTAGONS > HEPTAGON

HEPTANE *n* alkane found in petroleum

HEPTANES > HEPTANE

HEPTAPODY *n* verse with seven beats in rhythm

HEPTARCH > HEPTARCHY

HEPTARCHS > HEPTARCHY

HEPTARCHY *n* government by seven rulers

HEPTOSE *n* any monosaccharide with seven carbon atoms per molecule

HEPTOSES > HEPTOSE

HER *pron* refers to anything personified as feminine ▷ *adj* belonging to her ▷ *determiner* of, belonging to, or associated with her

HERALD *n* person who announces important news ▷ *vb* signal the approach of

HERALDED > HERALD

HERALDIC *adj* of or relating to heraldry

HERALDING > HERALD

HERALDIST > HERALDRY

HERALDRY *n* study of coats of arms and family trees

HERALDS > HERALD

HERB *n* plant used for flavouring in cookery, and in medicine

HERBAGE *n* herbaceous plants collectively

HERBAGED *adj* with grass growing on it

HERBAGES > HERBAGE

HERBAL *adj* of or relating to herbs, usually culinary or medicinal herbs ▷ *n* book describing and listing the properties of plants

HERBALISM *n* use of herbal medicine

HERBALIST *n* person who grows or specializes in the use of medicinal herbs

HERBALS > HERBAL

HERBAR *same as* > HERBARY

HERBARIA > HERBARIUM

HERBARIAL > HERBARIUM

HERBARIAN *same as* > HERBALIST

HERBARIES > HERBARY

HERBARIUM *n* collection of dried plants that are mounted and classified systematically

HERBARS > HERBAR

HERBARY *n* herb garden

HERBED *adj* flavoured with herbs

HERBELET *same as* > HERBLET

HERBELETS > HERBLET

HERBICIDE *n* chemical used to destroy plants, esp weeds

HERBIER > HERBY

HERBIEST > HERBY

HERBIST *same as* > HERBALIST

HERBISTS > HERBIST

HERBIVORA *n* animals that eat grass

HERBIVORE *n* animal that eats only plants

HERBIVORY > HERBIVORE

HERBLESS > HERB

HERBLET *n* little herb

HERBLETS > HERBLET

HERBLIKE > HERB

HERBOLOGY *n* use or study of herbal medicine

HERBORISE *same as* > HERBORIZE

HERBORIST *same as* > HERBALIST

HERBORIZE *vb* collect herbs

HERBOSE *same as* > HERBOUS

HERBOUS *adj* with abundance of herbs

HERBS > HERB

HERBY *adj* abounding in herbs

HERCOGAMY *n* prevention of flower pollination

HERCULEAN *adj* requiring great strength or effort

HERCULES *n* as in *hercules beetle* very large tropical American beetle

HERCYNITE *n* mineral containing iron

HERD *n* group of animals feeding and staying together ▷ *vb* collect into a herd

HERDBOY *n* boy who looks after herd

HERDBOYS > HERDBOY

HERDED > HERD

HERDEN *n* type of coarse cloth

HERDENS > HERDEN

HERDER *same as* > HERDSMAN

HERDERS > HERDER

HERDESS *n* female herder

HERDESSES > HERDESS

HERDIC *n* small horse-drawn carriage

HERDICS > HERDIC

HERDING *n* act of herding

HERDINGS > HERDING

HERDLIKE > HERD

HERDMAN *same as* > HERDSMAN

HERDMEN > HERDMAN

HERDS > HERD

HERDSMAN *n* man who looks after a herd of animals

HERDSMEN > HERDSMAN
HERDWICK *n* hardy breed of sheep
HERDWICKS > HERDWICK
HERE *adv* in, at, or to this place or point
HEREABOUT *adv* hereabouts
HEREAFTER *adv* after this point or time ▷ *n* life after death
HEREAT *adv* because of this
HEREAWAY *same as* > HEREABOUT
HEREAWAYS *dialect form of* > HERE
HEREBY *adv* by means of or as a result of this
HEREDES > HERES
HEREDITY *n* passing on of characteristics from one generation to another
HEREFROM *adv* from here
HEREIN *adv* in this place, matter, or document
HEREINTO *adv* into this place, circumstance, etc
HERENESS *n* state of being here
HEREOF *adv* of or concerning this
HEREON *archaic word for* > HEREUPON
HERES *n* heir
HERESIES > HERESY
HERESY *n* opinion contrary to accepted opinion or belief
HERETIC *n* person who holds unorthodox opinions
HERETICAL > HERETIC
HERETICS > HERETIC
HERETO *adv* this place, matter, or document
HERETRIX *n* in Scots law, female inheritor
HEREUNDER *adv* (in documents, etc) below this
HEREUNTO *archaic word for* > HERETO
HEREUPON *adv* following immediately after this
HEREWITH *adv* with this
HERIED > HERY
HERIES > HERY
HERIOT *n* (in medieval England) a death duty paid to the lord
HERIOTS > HERIOT
HERISSE *adj* with bristles
HERISSON *n* spiked beam used as fortification
HERISSONS > HERISSON
HERITABLE *adj* capable of being inherited
HERITABLY > HERITABLE
HERITAGE *n* something inherited
HERITAGES > HERITAGE
HERITOR *n* person who inherits

HERITORS > HERITOR
HERITRESS *n* female heritor
HERITRIX *n* female heritor
HERKOGAMY *same as* > HERCOGAMY
HERL *n* barb or barbs of a feather
HERLING *n* Scots word for a type of fish
HERLINGS > HERLING
HERLS > HERL
HERM *n* (in ancient Greece) a stone head of Hermes
HERMA *same as* > HERM
HERMAE > HERMA
HERMAEAN *adj* type of statue
HERMAI > HERMA
HERMANDAD *n* organization of middle classes in Spain
HERMETIC *adj* sealed so as to be airtight
HERMETICS *n* alchemy
HERMETISM *n* belief in pagan mystical knowledge
HERMETIST > HERMETISM
HERMIT *n* person living in solitude, esp for religious reasons
HERMITAGE *n* home of a hermit
HERMITESS *n* female hermit
HERMITIC > HERMIT
HERMITISM *n* act of living as hermit
HERMITRY *n* life as hermit
HERMITS > HERMIT
HERMS > HERM
HERN *archaic or dialect word for* > HERON
HERNIA *n* medical problem
HERNIAE > HERNIA
HERNIAL > HERNIA
HERNIAS > HERNIA
HERNIATE *vb* form a hernia
HERNIATED > HERNIA
HERNIATES > HERNIATE
HERNS > HERN
HERNSHAW *same as* > HERONSHAW
HERNSHAWS > HERNSHAW
HERO *n* principal character in a film, book, etc
HEROES > HERO
HEROIC *adj* courageous
HEROICAL *same as* > HEROIC
HEROICISE *same as* > HEROICIZE
HEROICIZE *same as* > HEROIZE
HEROICLY > HEROIC
HEROICS *pl n* extravagant behaviour
HEROIN *n* highly addictive illegal drug derived from morphine

HEROINE *n* principal female character in a novel, play, etc
HEROINES > HEROINE
HEROINISM *n* addiction to heroin
HEROINS > HEROIN
HEROISE *same as* > HEROIZE
HEROISED > HEROISE
HEROISES > HEROISE
HEROISING > HEROISE
HEROISM *n* great courage and bravery
HEROISMS > HEROISM
HEROIZE *vb* make into hero
HEROIZED > HEROIZE
HEROIZES > HEROIZE
HEROIZING > HEROIZE
HERON *n* long-legged wading bird
HERONRIES > HERONRY
HERONRY *n* colony of breeding herons
HERONS > HERON
HERONSEW *same as* > HERONSHAW
HERONSEWS > HERONSEW
HERONSHAW *n* young heron
HEROON *n* temple or monument dedicated to a hero
HEROONS > HEROON
HEROS > HERO
HEROSHIP > HERO
HEROSHIPS > HERO
HERPES *n* any of several inflammatory skin diseases
HERPESES > HERPES
HERPETIC *adj* of or relating to herpes ▷ *n* person with herpes
HERPETICS > HERPETIC
HERPETOID *adj* like reptile
HERPTILE *adj* denoting, relating to, or characterizing both reptiles and amphibians
HERRIED > HERRY
HERRIES > HERRY
HERRIMENT *n* act of plundering
HERRING *n* important food fish of northern seas
HERRINGER *n* person or boat catching herring
HERRINGS > HERRING
HERRY *vb* harry
HERRYING > HERRY
HERRYMENT *same as* > HERRIMENT
HERS *pron* something belonging to her
HERSALL *n* rehearsal
HERSALLS > HERSALL
HERSE *n* harrow
HERSED *adj* arranged like a harrow
HERSELF *pron* feminine singular reflexive form
HERSES > HERSE
HERSHIP *n* act of plundering

HERSHIPS > HERSHIP
HERSTORY *n* history from a female point of view or as it relates to women
HERTZ *n* unit of frequency
HERTZES > HERTZ
HERY *vb* praise
HERYE *same as* > HERY
HERYED > HERYE
HERYES > HERYE
HERYING > HERY
HES > HE
HESITANCE > HESITANT
HESITANCY > HESITANT
HESITANT *adj* undecided or wavering
HESITATE *vb* be slow or uncertain in doing something
HESITATED > HESITATE
HESITATER > HESITATE
HESITATES > HESITATE
HESITATOR > HESITATE
HESP *same as* > HASP
HESPED > HESP
HESPERID *n* species of butterfly
HESPERIDS > HESPERID
HESPING > HESP
HESPS > HESP
HESSIAN *n* coarse jute fabric
HESSIANS > HESSIAN
HESSITE *n* black or grey metallic mineral
HESSITES > HESSITE
HESSONITE *n* orange-brown variety of grossularite garnet
HEST *archaic word for* > BEHEST
HESTERNAL *adj* belonging to yesterday
HESTS > HEST
HET *n* short for heterosexual ▷ *adj* Scots word for hot
HETAERA *n* (esp in ancient Greece) a female prostitute
HETAERAE > HETAERA
HETAERAS > HETAERA
HETAERIC > HETAERA
HETAERISM *n* state of being a concubine
HETAERIST > HETAERISM
HETAIRA *same as* > HETAERA
HETAIRAI > HETAIRA
HETAIRAS > HETAIRA
HETAIRIA *n* society
HETAIRIAS > HETAIRIA
HETAIRIC > HETAIRIA
HETAIRISM *same as* > HETAERISM
HETAIRIST > HETAERISM
HETE *same as* > HIGHT
HETERO *n* short for heterosexual

HETERODOX *adj* differing from accepted doctrines or beliefs

HETERONYM *n* one of two or more words pronounced differently but spelt alike

HETEROPOD *n* marine invertebrate with a foot for swimming

HETEROS > HETERO

HETEROSES > HETEROSIS

HETEROSIS *n* increased size, strength, etc, of a hybrid as compared to either of its parents

HETEROTIC > HETEROSIS

HETES > HETE

HETH *n* eighth letter of the Hebrew alphabet

HETHER *same as* > HITHER

HETHS > HETH

HETING > HETE

HETMAN *another word for* > ATAMAN

HETMANATE > HETMAN

HETMANS > HETMAN

HETMEN > HETMAN

HETS > HET

HETTIE *n* slang term for a heterosexual

HETTIES > HETTIE

HEUCH *Scots word for* > CRAG

HEUCHERA *n* N American plant with heart-shaped leaves and mostly red flowers

HEUCHERAS > HEUCHERA

HEUCHS > HEUCH

HEUGH *same as* > HEUCH

HEUGHS > HEUGH

HEUREKA *same as* > EUREKA

HEUREKAS > HEUREKA

HEURETIC *same as* > HEURISTIC

HEURETICS *n* use of logic

HEURISM *n* use of logic

HEURISMS > HEURISM

HEURISTIC *adj* involving learning by investigation ▷ *n* science of heuristic procedure

HEVEA *n* rubber-producing South American tree

HEVEAS > HEVEA

HEW *vb* cut with an axe

HEWABLE > HEW

HEWED > HEW

HEWER > HEW

HEWERS > HEW

HEWGH *interj* sound made to imitate the flight of an arrow

HEWING > HEW

HEWINGS > HEW

HEWN > HEW

HEWS > HEW

HEX *adj* of or relating to hexadecimal notation ▷ *n* evil spell ▷ *vb* bewitch

HEXACHORD *n* (in medieval musical theory) any of three diatonic scales based upon C, F, and G, each consisting of six notes, from which solmization was developed

HEXACT *n* part of a sponge with six rays

HEXACTS > HEXACT

HEXAD *n* group or series of six

HEXADE *same as* > HEXAD

HEXADECYL *n* univalent radical derived from hexadecane

HEXADES > HEXADE

HEXADIC > HEXAD

HEXADS > HEXAD

HEXAFOIL *n* pattern with six lobes

HEXAFOILS > HEXAFOIL

HEXAGLOT *n* book written in six languages

HEXAGLOTS > HEXAGLOT

HEXAGON *n* geometrical figure with six sides

HEXAGONAL *adj* having six sides and six angles

HEXAGONS > HEXAGON

HEXAGRAM *n* star formed by extending the sides of a regular hexagon to meet at six points

HEXAGRAMS > HEXAGRAM

HEXAHEDRA *n* plural of hexahedron: solid figure with six plane faces

HEXAMERAL *adj* arranged in six groups

HEXAMETER *n* verse line consisting of six metrical feet

HEXAMINE *n* fuel for camping stoves

HEXAMINES > HEXAMINE

HEXANE *n* liquid alkane existing in five isomeric forms

HEXANES > HEXANE

HEXANOIC *adj* as in hexanoic acid insoluble oily carboxylic acid found in coconut and palm oils and in milk

HEXAPLA *n* edition of the Old Testament

HEXAPLAR > HEXAPLA

HEXAPLAS > HEXAPLA

HEXAPLOID *adj* with six times the normal number of chromosomes

HEXAPOD *n* six-footed arthropod

HEXAPODAL *adj* relating to the Hexapoda, ie insects

HEXAPODIC > HEXAPODY

HEXAPODS > HEXAPOD

HEXAPODY *n* verse measure consisting of six metrical feet

HEXARCH *adj* (of a plant) with six veins

HEXARCHY *n* alliance of six states

HEXASTICH *n* poem, stanza, or strophe that consists of six lines

HEXASTYLE *n* portico or facade with six columns ▷ *adj* having six columns

HEXATHLON *n* athletic contest comprising six events

HEXED > HEX

HEXENE *same as* > HEXYLENE

HEXENES > HEXENE

HEXER > HEX

HEXEREI *n* witchcraft

HEXEREIS > HEXEREI

HEXERS > HEX

HEXES > HEX

HEXING > HEX

HEXINGS > HEX

HEXONE *n* colourless insoluble liquid ketone

HEXONES > HEXONE

HEXOSAN *n* form of polysaccharide

HEXOSANS > HEXOSAN

HEXOSE *n* monosaccharide, such as glucose

HEXOSES > HEXOSE

HEXYL *n* chemical compound

HEXYLENE *n* chemical compound similar to ethylene

HEXYLENES > HEXYLENE

HEXYLIC > HEXYL

HEXYLS > HEXYL

HEY *interj* expression of surprise or for catching attention ▷ *vb* perform a country dance

HEYDAY *n* time of greatest success, prime

HEYDAYS > HEYDAY

HEYDEY *variant of* > HEYDAY

HEYDEYS > HEYDEY

HEYDUCK *same as* > HAIDUK

HEYDUCKS > HEYDUCK

HEYED > HEY

HEYING > HEY

HEYS > HEY

HI *interj* hello

HIANT *adj* gaping

HIATAL > HIATUS

HIATUS *n* pause or interruption in continuity

HIATUSES > HIATUS

HIBACHI *n* portable brazier for heating and cooking food

HIBACHIS > HIBACHI

HIBAKUSHA *n* survivor of either of the atomic-bomb attacks on Hiroshima and Nagasaki in 1945

HIBERNAL *adj* of or occurring in winter

HIBERNATE *vb* (of an animal) pass the winter as if in a deep sleep

HIBERNISE *same as* > HIBERNIZE

HIBERNIZE *vb* make Irish

HIBISCUS *n* tropical plant with large brightly coloured flowers

HIC *interj* representation of the sound of a hiccup

HICATEE *same as* > HICCATEE

HICATEES > HICATEE

HICCATEE *n* tortoise native to the Caribbean

HICCATEES > HICCATEE

HICCOUGH *same as* > HICCUP

HICCOUGHS > HICCOUGH

HICCUP *n* spasm of the breathing organs ▷ *vb* make a hiccup

HICCUPED > HICCUP

HICCUPIER > HICCUPY

HICCUPING > HICCUP

HICCUPPED > HICCUP

HICCUPS > HICCUP

HICCUPY *adj* tending to hiccup

HICK *n* unsophisticated country person ▷ *adj* unsophisticated

HICKER > HICK

HICKEST > HICK

HICKEY *n* object or gadget

HICKEYS > HICKEY

HICKIE *same as* > HICKEY

HICKIES > HICKIE

HICKISH > HICK

HICKORIES > HICKORY

HICKORY *n* N American nut-bearing tree

HICKS > HICK

HICKWALL *n* green woodpecker

HICKWALLS > HICKWALL

HICKYMAL *n* titmouse

HICKYMALS > HICKYMAL

HID > HIDE

HIDABLE > HIDE

HIDAGE *n* former tax on land

HIDAGES > HIDAGE

HIDALGA *n* Spanish noblewoman

HIDALGAS > HIDALGA

HIDALGO *n* member of the lower nobility in Spain

HIDALGOS > HIDALGO

HIDDEN > HIDE

HIDDENITE *n* green transparent variety of the mineral spodumene, used as a gemstone

HIDDENLY > HIDE

HIDDER *n* young ram

HIDDERS > HIDDER

HIDE *vb* put (oneself or an object) somewhere difficult to see or find ▷ *n* place of concealment, esp for a bird-watcher

HIDEAWAY *n* private place

HIDEAWAYS > HIDEAWAY

HIDEBOUND *adj* unwilling to accept new ideas
HIDED > HIDE
HIDELESS > HIDE
HIDEOSITY > HIDEOUS
HIDEOUS *adj* ugly, revolting
HIDEOUSLY > HIDEOUS
HIDEOUT *n* hiding place
HIDEOUTS > HIDEOUT
HIDER > HIDE
HIDERS > HIDE
HIDES > HIDE
HIDING > HIDE
HIDINGS > HIDE
HIDLING *n* hiding place
HIDLINGS *adv* in secret
HIDLINS *same as*
> HIDLINGS
HIDROSES > HIDROSIS
HIDROSIS *n* any skin disease affecting the sweat glands
HIDROTIC > HIDROSIS
HIDROTICS
> HIDROSIS
HIE *vb* hurry
HIED > HIE
HIEING > HIE
HIELAMAN *n* Aboriginal Australian shield
HIELAMANS
> HIELAMAN
HIELAND *adj* characteristic of Highlanders
HIEMAL *less common word for* **>** HIBERNAL
HIEMS *n* winter
HIERACIUM *n* plant of hawkweed family
HIERARCH *n* person in a position of high-priestly authority
HIERARCHS
> HIERARCH
HIERARCHY *n* system of people or things arranged in a graded order
HIERATIC *adj* of or relating to priests ▷ *n* hieratic script of ancient Egypt
HIERATICA *n* type of papyrus
HIERATICS
> HIERATIC
HIEROCRAT *n* person who believes in government by religious leaders
HIERODULE *n* (in ancient Greece) a temple slave
HIEROGRAM *n* sacred symbol
HIEROLOGY *n* sacred literature
HIERURGY *n* performance of religious drama or music
HIES > HIE
HIFALUTIN *adj* pompous or pretentious
HIGGLE *less common word for* **>** HAGGLE
HIGGLED > HIGGLE
HIGGLER > HIGGLE

HIGGLERS > HIGGLE
HIGGLES > HIGGLE
HIGGLING > HIGGLE
HIGGLINGS > HIGGLE
HIGH *adj* being a relatively great distance from top to bottom; tall ▷ *adv* at or to a height ▷ *n* high place or level ▷ *vb* hie
HIGHBALL *n* tall drink of whisky with soda water or ginger ale and ice ▷ *vb* move at great speed
HIGHBALLS
> HIGHBALL
HIGHBORN *adj* of noble or aristocratic birth
HIGHBOY *n* tall chest of drawers in two sections
HIGHBOYS > HIGHBOY
HIGHBRED *adj* of noble breeding
HIGHBROW *n* intellectual and serious person ▷ *adj* concerned with serious, intellectual subjects
HIGHBROWS
> HIGHBROW
HIGHBUSH *adj* (of bush) growing tall ▷ *n* tall-growing bush
HIGHCHAIR *n* long-legged chair with a tray attached, used by a very young child at mealtimes
HIGHED > HIGH
HIGHER *n* advanced level of the Scottish Certificate of Education ▷ *vb* raise up
HIGHERED > HIGHER
HIGHERING > HIGHER
HIGHERS > HIGHER
HIGHEST > HIGH
HIGHFLIER *same as*
> HIGHFLYER
HIGHFLYER *n* person who is extreme in aims, ambition, etc
HIGHING > HIGH
HIGHISH > HIGH
HIGHJACK *same as*
> HIJACK
HIGHJACKS
> HIGHJACK
HIGHJINKS *n* lively enjoyment
HIGHLAND *n* relatively high ground
HIGHLANDS
> HIGHLAND
HIGHLIFE *n* African music genre
HIGHLIFES
> HIGHLIFE
HIGHLIGHT *n* outstanding part or feature ▷ *vb* give emphasis to
HIGHLY *adv* extremely
HIGHMAN *n* dice weighted to make it fall in particular way
HIGHMEN > HIGHMAN
HIGHMOST *adj* highest
HIGHNESS *n* condition of being high or lofty
HIGHRISE *n* tall building
HIGHRISES > HIGHRISE

HIGHROAD *n* main road
HIGHROADS
> HIGHROAD
HIGHS > HIGH
HIGHSPOT *n* highlight
HIGHSPOTS
> HIGHSPOT
HIGHT *vb* archaic word for name or call
HIGHTAIL *vb* go or move in a great hurry
HIGHTAILS
> HIGHTAIL
HIGHTED > HIGHT
HIGHTH *old form of*
> HEIGHT
HIGHTHS > HIGHTH
HIGHTING *n* oath
HIGHTINGS
> HIGHTING
HIGHTOP *n* top of ship's mast
HIGHTOPS > HIGHTOP
HIGHTS > HIGHT
HIGHVELD *n* high-altitude grassland region of E South Africa
HIGHVELDS
> HIGHVELD
HIGHWAY *n* main road
HIGHWAYS > HIGHWAY
HIJAB *n* covering for the head and face
HIJABS > HIJAB
HIJACK *vb* seize control of (an aircraft or other vehicle) while travelling ▷ *n* instance of hijacking
HIJACKED > HIJACK
HIJACKER > HIJACK
HIJACKERS > HIJACK
HIJACKING > HIJACK
HIJACKS > HIJACK
HIJINKS *n* lively enjoyment
HIJRA *same as* **>** HIJRAH
HIJRAH *same as*
> HEGIRA
HIJRAHS > HIJRAH
HIJRAS > HIJRA
HIKE *n* long walk in the country, esp for pleasure ▷ *vb* go for a long walk
HIKED > HIKE
HIKER > HIKE
HIKERS > HIKE
HIKES > HIKE
HIKING *n* sport of taking long walks in the country
HIKINGS > HIKING
HIKOI *n* walk or march, esp a Māori protest march ▷ *vb* take part in such a march
HIKOIED > HIKOI
HIKOIING > HIKOI
HIKOIS > HIKOI
HILA > HILUM
HILAR > HILUS
HILARIOUS *adj* very funny
HILARITY *n* mirth and merriment
HILCH *vb* hobble
HILCHED > HILCH
HILCHES > HILCH
HILCHING > HILCH
HILD *same as* **>** HOLD

HILDING *n* coward
HILDINGS > HILDING
HILI > HILUS
HILL *n* raised part of the earth's surface ▷ *vb* form into a hill or mound
HILLBILLY *n* usually disparaging term for an unsophisticated country person
HILLCREST *n* crest of hill
HILLED > HILL
HILLER > HILL
HILLERS > HILL
HILLFOLK *n* people living in the hills
HILLFORT *n* fortified hilltop
HILLFORTS
> HILLFORT
HILLIER > HILL
HILLIEST > HILL
HILLINESS > HILL
HILLING > HILL
HILLINGS > HILLING
HILLMEN *same as*
> HILLFOLK
HILLO *same as* **>** HELLO
HILLOA *same as*
> HALLOA
HILLOAED > HILLOA
HILLOAING > HILLOA
HILLOAS > HILLOA
HILLOCK *n* small hill
HILLOCKED > HILLOCK
HILLOCKS > HILLOCK
HILLOCKY *adj* having hillocks
HILLOED > HILLO
HILLOES > HILLO
HILLOING > HILLO
HILLOS > HILLO
HILLS > HILL
HILLSIDE *n* side of a hill
HILLSIDES
> HILLSIDE
HILLSLOPE *same as*
> HILLSIDE
HILLTOP *n* top of hill
HILLTOPS > HILLTOP
HILLY *adj* full of hills
HILT *n* handle of a sword or knife ▷ *vb* supply with a hilt
HILTED > HILT
HILTING > HILT
HILTLESS > HILT
HILTS > HILT
HILUM *n* scar on a seed
HILUS *rare word for*
> HILUM
HIM *pron* refers to a male person or animal ▷ *n* male person
HIMATIA > HIMATION
HIMATION *n* (in ancient Greece) a cloak draped around the body
HIMATIONS
> HIMATION
HIMBO *n* derogatory term for an attractive but empty-headed man
HIMBOS > HIMBO
HIMS > HIM
HIMSELF *pron* masculine singular reflexive form

h

HIN *n* Hebrew unit of capacity
HINAHINA *same as* >MAHOE
HINAHINAS >HINAHINA
HINAU *n* New Zealand tree
HINAUS >HINAU
HIND *adj* situated at the back ▷ *n* female deer
HINDBERRY *n* raspberry
HINDBRAIN *n* part of the brain comprising the cerebellum, pons and medulla oblongata
HINDCAST *vb* test (a mathematical model)
HINDCASTS >HINDCAST
HINDER *vb* get in the way of ▷ *adj* situated at the back
HINDERED >HINDER
HINDERER >HINDER
HINDERERS >HINDER
HINDERING >HINDER
HINDERS >HINDER
HINDFEET >HINDFOOT
HINDFOOT *n* back foot
HINDGUT *n* part of the vertebrate digestive tract
HINDGUTS >HINDGUT
HINDHEAD *n* back of head
HINDHEADS >HINDHEAD
HINDLEG *n* back leg
HINDLEGS >HINDLEG
HINDMILK *n* breast milk produced after the first part of feeding
HINDMILKS >HINDMILK
HINDMOST >HIND
HINDRANCE *n* obstruction or snag
HINDS >HIND
HINDSHANK *n* meat from animal's hind leg
HINDSIGHT *n* ability to understand, after something has happened, what should have been done
HINDWARD *adj* at back
HINDWING *n* back wing
HINDWINGS >HINDWING
HING *n* asafoetida
HINGE *n* device for holding two parts so one can swing freely ▷ *vb* depend (on)
HINGED >HINGE
HINGELESS >HINGE
HINGELIKE >HINGE
HINGER *n* tool for making hinges
HINGERS >HINGER
HINGES >HINGE
HINGING >HINGE
HINGS >HING
HINKIER >HINKY
HINKIEST >HINKY
HINKY *adj* strange
HINNIE *n* sweetheart
HINNIED >HINNY

HINNIES >HINNY
HINNY *n* offspring of a male horse and a female donkey ▷ *vb* whinny
HINNYING >HINNY
HINS >HIN
HINT *n* indirect suggestion ▷ *vb* suggest indirectly
HINTED >HINT
HINTER >HINT
HINTERS >HINT
HINTING >HINT
HINTINGLY >HINT
HINTINGS >HINT
HINTS >HINT
HIOI *n* New Zealand plant of the mint family
HIOIS >HIOI
HIP *n* either side of the body between the pelvis and the thigh ▷ *adj* aware of or following the latest trends ▷ *interj* exclamation used to introduce cheers
HIPBONE *n* either of the bones that form the sides of the pelvis
HIPBONES >HIPBONE
HIPHUGGER *adj* (of trousers) having a low waist
HIPLESS >HIP
HIPLIKE >HIP
HIPLINE *n* widest part of a person's hips
HIPLINES >HIPLINE
HIPLY >HIP
HIPNESS >HIP
HIPNESSES >HIP
HIPPARCH *n* (in ancient Greece) a cavalry commander
HIPPARCHS >HIPPARCH
HIPPED *adj* having a hip or hips
HIPPEN *n* baby's nappy
HIPPENS >HIPPEN
HIPPER >HIP
HIPPEST >HIP
HIPPIATRY *n* treatment of disease in horses
HIPPIC *adj* of horses
HIPPIE *same as* >HIPPY
HIPPIEDOM >HIPPIE
HIPPIEISH >HIPPIE
HIPPIER >HIPPY
HIPPIES >HIPPY
HIPPIEST >HIPPY
HIPPIN *same as* >HIPPEN
HIPPINESS >HIPPY
HIPPING *same as* >HIPPEN
HIPPINGS >HIPPING
HIPPINS >HIPPIN
HIPPISH *adj* in low spirits
HIPPO *n* hippopotamus
HIPPOCRAS *n* old English drink of wine flavoured with spices
HIPPODAME *n* sea horse
HIPPOLOGY *n* study of horses
HIPPOS >HIPPO

HIPPURIC *adj* as in hippuric acid crystalline solid excreted in the urine of mammals
HIPPURITE *n* type of fossil
HIPPUS *n* spasm of eye
HIPPUSES >HIPPUS
HIPPY *n* person whose behaviour implies a rejection of values ▷ *adj* having large hips
HIPPYDOM >HIPPY
HIPPYDOMS >HIPPY
HIPPYISH *adj* pertaining to or like a hippy
HIPS >HIP
HIPSHOT *adj* having a dislocated hip
HIPSTER *n* enthusiast of modern jazz
HIPSTERS *pl n* trousers cut so that the top encircles the hips
HIPT *old form of* >HIPPED
HIRABLE >HIRE
HIRAGANA *n* Japanese system of writing
HIRAGANAS >HIRAGANA
HIRAGE *n* fee for hiring
HIRAGES >HIRAGE
HIRCINE *adj* of or like a goat, esp in smell
HIRCOSITY *n* quality of being like a goat
HIRE *vb* pay to have temporary use of ▷ *n* hiring
HIREABLE >HIRE
HIREAGE *same as* >HIRAGE
HIREAGES >HIREAGE
HIRED >HIRE
HIREE *n* hired person
HIREES >HIREE
HIRELING *n* derogatory term for a person who works only for wages
HIRELINGS >HIRELING
HIRER >HIRE
HIRERS >HIRE
HIRES >HIRE
HIRING >HIRE
HIRINGS >HIRE
HIRLING *n* Scots word for a type of fish
HIRLINGS >HIRLING
HIRPLE *vb* limp ▷ *n* limping gait
HIRPLED >HIRPLE
HIRPLES >HIRPLE
HIRPLING >HIRPLE
HIRRIENT *n* trilled sound
HIRRIENTS >HIRRIENT
HIRSEL *vb* sort into groups
HIRSELED >HIRSEL
HIRSELING >HIRSEL
HIRSELLED >HIRSEL
HIRSELS >HIRSEL
HIRSLE *vb* wriggle or fidget
HIRSLED >HIRSLE
HIRSLES >HIRSLE
HIRSLING >HIRSLE

HIRSTIE *adj* dry
HIRSUTE *adj* hairy
HIRSUTISM >HIRSUTE
HIRUDIN *n* anticoagulant
HIRUDINS >HIRUDIN
HIRUDINE *adj* of or resembling a swallow
HIS *adj* belonging to him
HISH *same as* >HISS
HISHED >HISH
HISHES >HISH
HISHING >HISH
HISN *dialect form of* >HIS
HISPANISM *n* Spanish turn of phrase
HISPID *adj* covered with stiff hairs or bristles
HISPIDITY >HISPID
HISS *n* sound like that of a long s (as an expression of contempt) ▷ *vb* utter a hiss ▷ *interj* exclamation of derision or disapproval
HISSED >HISS
HISSELF *dialect form of* >HIMSELF
HISSER >HISS
HISSERS >HISS
HISSES >HISS
HISSIER >HISSY
HISSIES >HISSY
HISSIEST >HISSY
HISSING >HISS
HISSINGLY >HISS
HISSINGS >HISS
HISSY *n* temper tantrum ▷ *adj* having the sound of a hiss
HIST *interj* exclamation used to attract attention ▷ *vb* make hist sound
HISTAMIN *variant of* >HISTAMINE
HISTAMINE *n* substance released by the body tissues in allergic reactions
HISTAMINS >HISTAMIN
HISTED >HIST
HISTIDIN *variant of* >HISTIDINE
HISTIDINE *n* nonessential amino acid that occurs in most proteins: a precursor of histamine
HISTIDINS >HISTIDIN
HISTIE *same as* >HIRSTIE
HISTING >HIST
HISTIOID *same as* >HISTOID
HISTOGEN *n* obsolete term for part of a plant stem
HISTOGENS >HISTOGEN
HISTOGENY >HISTOGEN
HISTOGRAM *n* statistical graph in which the frequency of values is represented by vertical bars of varying heights and widths

HISTOID adj (esp of a tumour)

HISTOLOGY n study of the tissues of an animal or plant

HISTONE n any of a group of proteins present in cell nuclei

HISTONES > HISTONE

HISTORIAN n writer of history

HISTORIC adj famous or significant in history

HISTORIED adj recorded in history

HISTORIES > HISTORY

HISTORIFY vb make part of history

HISTORISM n idea that history influences present

HISTORY n (record or account of) past events

HISTRIO n actor

HISTRION same as > HISTRIO

HISTRIONS > HISTRION

HISTRIOS > HISTRIO

HISTS > HIST

HIT vb strike, touch forcefully ▷ n hitting

HITCH n minor problem ▷ vb obtain (a lift) by hitchhiking

HITCHED > HITCH

HITCHER > HITCH

HITCHERS > HITCH

HITCHES > HITCH

HITCHHIKE vb travel by obtaining free lifts

HITCHIER > HITCH

HITCHIEST > HITCH

HITCHILY > HITCH

HITCHING > HITCH

HITCHY > HITCH

HITHE n small harbour

HITHER adv or towards this place ▷ vb come

HITHERED > HITHER

HITHERING > HITHER

HITHERS > HITHER

HITHERTO adv until this time

HITHES > HITHE

HITLESS > HIT

HITMAKER n successful performer or producer of popular music

HITMAKERS > HITMAKER

HITMAN n professional killer

HITMEN > HITMAN

HITS > HIT

HITTABLE > HIT

HITTER n boxer who has a hard punch rather than skill or finesse

HITTERS > HITTER

HITTING > HIT

HIVE n structure in which social bees live and rear their young ▷ vb cause (bees) to collect or (of bees) to collect inside a hive

HIVED > HIVE

HIVELESS > HIVE

HIVELIKE > HIVE

HIVEMIND n people who share their knowledge with one another, producing either collective intelligence or conformity

HIVEMINDS > HIVEMIND

HIVER n person who keeps beehives

HIVERS > HIVER

HIVES n allergic reaction

HIVEWARD adj towards hive

HIVEWARDS adv towards hive

HIVING > HIVE

HIYA sentence substitute informal term of greeting

HIZEN n type of Japanese porcelain

HIZENS > HIZEN

HIZZ same as > HISS

HIZZED > HIZZ

HIZZES > HIZZ

HIZZING > HIZZ

HIZZONER n nickname for mayor

HIZZONERS > HIZZONER

HM interj sound made to express hesitation or doubt

HMM same as > HM

HMMM interj expressing thoughtful consideration

HO interj imitation or representation of the sound of a deep laugh ▷ n cry of 'ho' ▷ vb halt

HOA same as > HO

HOACTZIN same as > HOATZIN

HOACTZINS > HOACTZIN

HOAED > HOA

HOAGIE n sandwich made with long bread roll

HOAGIES > HOAGIE

HOAGY same as > HOAGIE

HOAING > HOA

HOAR adj covered with hoarfrost ▷ vb make hoary

HOARD n store hidden away for future use ▷ vb save or store

HOARDED > HOARD

HOARDER > HOARD

HOARDERS > HOARD

HOARDING n large board for displaying advertisements

HOARDINGS > HOARDING

HOARDS > HOARD

HOARED > HOAR

HOARFROST n white ground frost

HOARHEAD n person with white hair

HOARHEADS > HOARHEAD

HOARHOUND same as > HOREHOUND

HOARIER > HOARY

HOARIEST > HOARY

HOARILY > HOARY

HOARINESS > HOARY

HOARING > HOAR

HOARS > HOAR

HOARSE adj (of a voice) rough and unclear

HOARSELY > HOARSE

HOARSEN vb make or become hoarse

HOARSENED > HOARSEN

HOARSENS > HOARSEN

HOARSER > HOARSE

HOARSEST > HOARSE

HOARY adj grey or white(-haired)

HOAS > HOA

HOAST n cough ▷ vb cough

HOASTED > HOAST

HOASTING > HOAST

HOASTMAN n shipper of coal

HOASTMEN > HOASTMAN

HOASTS > HOAST

HOATCHING adj infested

HOATZIN n South American bird

HOATZINES > HOATZIN

HOATZINS > HOATZIN

HOAX n deception or trick ▷ vb deceive or play a trick upon

HOAXED > HOAX

HOAXER > HOAX

HOAXERS > HOAX

HOAXES > HOAX

HOAXING > HOAX

HOB n flat top part of a cooker ▷ vb cut or form with a hob

HOBBED > HOB

HOBBER n machine used in making gears

HOBBERS > HOBBER

HOBBIES > HOBBY

HOBBING > HOB

HOBBISH adj like a clown

HOBBIT n one of an imaginary race of half-size people

HOBBITRY > HOBBIT

HOBBITS > HOBBIT

HOBBLE vb walk lamely ▷ n strap, rope, etc, used to hobble a horse

HOBBLED > HOBBLE

HOBBLER > HOBBLE

HOBBLERS > HOBBLE

HOBBLES > HOBBLE

HOBBLING > HOBBLE

HOBBLINGS > HOBBLE

HOBBY n activity pursued in one's spare time

HOBBYISM > HOBBY

HOBBYISMS > HOBBY

HOBBYIST > HOBBY

HOBBYISTS > HOBBY

HOBBYLESS > HOBBY

HOBDAY vb alleviate a breathing problem in certain horses

HOBDAYED > HOBDAY

HOBDAYING > HOBDAY

HOBDAYS > HOBDAY

HOBGOBLIN n mischievous goblin

HOBJOB vb do odd jobs

HOBJOBBED > HOBJOB

HOBJOBBER > HOBJOB

HOBJOBS > HOBJOB

HOBLIKE > HOB

HOBNAIL n short nail with a large head for protecting soles ▷ vb provide with hobnails

HOBNAILED > HOBNAIL

HOBNAILS > HOBNAIL

HOBNOB vb be on friendly terms (with)

HOBNOBBED > HOBNOB

HOBNOBBER > HOBNOB

HOBNOBBY adj tending to hobnob

HOBNOBS > HOBNOB

HOBO n tramp or vagrant ▷ vb live as hobo

HOBODOM > HOBO

HOBODOMS > HOBO

HOBOED > HOBO

HOBOES > HOBO

HOBOING > HOBO

HOBOISM > HOBO

HOBOISMS > HOBO

HOBOS > HOBO

HOBS > HOB

HOC adj Latin for this

HOCK n joint in the leg of an animal corresponding to a human ankle ▷ vb pawn

HOCKED > HOCK

HOCKER > HOCK

HOCKERS > HOCK

HOCKEY n team sport

HOCKEYS > HOCKEY

HOCKING > HOCK

HOCKLE vb spit

HOCKLED > HOCKLE

HOCKLES > HOCKLE

HOCKLING > HOCKLE

HOCKS > HOCK

HOCKSHOP n pawnshop

HOCKSHOPS > HOCKSHOP

HOCUS vb take in

HOCUSED > HOCUS

HOCUSES > HOCUS

HOCUSING > HOCUS

HOCUSSED > HOCUS

HOCUSSES > HOCUS

HOCUSSING > HOCUS

HOD n open wooden box attached to a pole ▷ vb bob up and down

HODAD n person who pretends to be a surfer

HODADDIES > HODADDY

HODADDY same as > HODAD

HODADS > HODAD

HODDED > HOD

HODDEN n coarse homespun cloth

HODDENS > HODDEN

HODDIN same as > HODDEN

HODDING > HOD

HODDINS > HODDIN

HODDLE vb waddle

HODDLED > HODDLE

HODDLES > HODDLE

HODDLING > HODDLE

HODIERNAL adj of the present day

HODJA n respectful Turkish form of address

h

HODJAS > HODJA
HODMAN n hod carrier
HODMANDOD n snail
HODMEN > HODMAN
HODOGRAPH n curve of which the radius vector represents the velocity of a moving particle
HODOMETER another name for > ODOMETER
HODOMETRY > HODOMETER
HODOSCOPE n any device for tracing the path of a charged particle, esp a particle found in cosmic rays
HODS > HOD
HOE n long-handled tool used for loosening soil or weeding ▷ vb scrape or weed with a hoe
HOECAKE n maize cake
HOECAKES > HOECAKE
HOED > HOE
HOEDOWN n boisterous square dance
HOEDOWNS > HOEDOWN
HOEING > HOE
HOELIKE > HOE
HOER > HOE
HOERS > HOE
HOES > HOE
HOG n castrated male pig ▷ vb take more than one's share of
HOGAN n wooden dwelling covered with earth
HOGANS > HOGAN
HOGBACK n narrow ridge of steeply inclined rock strata
HOGBACKS > HOGBACK
HOGEN n strong alcoholic drink
HOGENS > HOGEN
HOGFISH n type of fish
HOGFISHES > HOGFISH
HOGG same as > HOG
HOGGED > HOG
HOGGER > HOG
HOGGEREL n year-old sheep
HOGGERELS > HOGGEREL
HOGGERIES > HOGGERY
HOGGERS > HOG
HOGGERY n hogs collectively
HOGGET n young sheep that has yet to be sheared
HOGGETS > HOGGET
HOGGIN n finely sifted gravel
HOGGING same as > HOGGIN
HOGGINGS > HOGGING
HOGGINS > HOGGIN
HOGGISH adj selfish, gluttonous, or dirty
HOGGISHLY > HOGGISH
HOGGS > HOGG
HOGH n ridge of land
HOGHOOD n condition of being hog
HOGHOODS > HOGHOOD
HOGHS > HOGH
HOGLIKE > HOG

HOGMANAY n New Year's Eve
HOGMANAYS > HOGMANAY
HOGMANE n short stiff mane
HOGMANES > HOGMANE
HOGMENAY variant of > HOGMANAY
HOGMENAYS > HOGMENAY
HOGNOSE n as in hognose snake puff adder
HOGNOSED adj as in hognosed skunk any of several American skunks having a broad snoutlike nose
HOGNOSES > HOGNOSE
HOGNUT another name for > PIGNUT
HOGNUTS > HOGNUT
HOGS > HOG
HOGSHEAD n large cask
HOGSHEADS > HOGSHEAD
HOGTIE vb tie together the legs or the arms and legs of
HOGTIED > HOGTIE
HOGTIEING > HOGTIE
HOGTIES > HOGTIE
HOGTYING > HOGTIE
HOGWARD n person looking after hogs
HOGWARDS > HOGWARD
HOGWASH n nonsense
HOGWASHES > HOGWASH
HOGWEED n any of several umbelliferous plants
HOGWEEDS > HOGWEED
HOH same as > HO
HOHA adj bored or annoyed
HOHED > HOH
HOHING > HOH
HOHS > HOH
HOI same as > HOY
HOICK vb raise abruptly and sharply
HOICKED > HOICK
HOICKING > HOICK
HOICKS interj cry used to encourage hounds to hunt ▷ vb shout hoicks
HOICKSED > HOICKS
HOICKSES > HOICKS
HOICKSING > HOICKS
HOIDEN same as > HOYDEN
HOIDENED > HOIDEN
HOIDENING > HOIDEN
HOIDENISH > HOIDEN
HOIDENS > HOIDEN
HOIED > HOI
HOIING > HOI
HOIK same as > HOICK
HOIKED > HOIK
HOIKING > HOIK
HOIKS > HOIK
HOING > HO
HOIS > HOI
HOISE same as > HOIST
HOISED > HOISE
HOISES > HOISE
HOISIN n Chinese sweet spicy sauce

HOISING > HOISE
HOISINS > HOISIN
HOIST vb raise or lift up ▷ n device for lifting things
HOISTED > HOIST
HOISTER > HOIST
HOISTERS > HOIST
HOISTING > HOIST
HOISTINGS > HOIST
HOISTMAN n person operating a hoist
HOISTMEN > HOISTMAN
HOISTS > HOIST
HOISTWAY n shaft for a hoist
HOISTWAYS > HOISTWAY
HOKA n red cod
HOKAS > HOKA
HOKE vb overplay (a part, etc)
HOKED > HOKE
HOKES > HOKE
HOKEY adj corny
HOKEYNESS > HOKEY
HOKI n fish of New Zealand waters
HOKIER > HOKEY
HOKIEST > HOKEY
HOKILY > HOKEY
HOKINESS > HOKEY
HOKING > HOKE
HOKIS > HOKI
HOKKU same as > HAIKU
HOKONUI n illicit whisky
HOKONUIS > HOKONUI
HOKUM n rubbish, nonsense
HOKUMS > HOKUM
HOKYPOKY n trickery
HOLANDRIC adj relating to Y-chromosomal genes
HOLARCHY n system composed of interacting holons
HOLARD n amount of water contained in soil
HOLARDS > HOLARD
HOLD vb keep or support in or with the hands or arms ▷ n act or way of holding
HOLDABLE > HOLD
HOLDALL n large strong travelling bag
HOLDALLS > HOLDALL
HOLDBACK n part of a horse harness
HOLDBACKS > HOLDBACK
HOLDDOWN n control function in a computer
HOLDDOWNS > HOLDDOWN
HOLDEN past participle of > HOLD
HOLDER n person or thing that holds
HOLDERBAT n part of pipe used as fastening
HOLDERS > HOLDER
HOLDFAST n act of gripping strongly
HOLDFASTS > HOLDFAST
HOLDING > HOLD
HOLDINGS > HOLD

HOLDOUT n (in US English) person who refuses to change
HOLDOUTS > HOLDOUT
HOLDOVER n official who continues in office after his or her term has expired
HOLDOVERS > HOLDOVER
HOLDS > HOLD
HOLDUP n robbery, esp an armed one
HOLDUPS > HOLDUP
HOLE n area hollowed out in a solid ▷ vb make holes in
HOLED > HOLE
HOLELESS > HOLE
HOLES > HOLE
HOLESOM same as > HOLESOME
HOLESOME same as > WHOLESOME
HOLEY adj full of holes
HOLEYER > HOLEY
HOLEYEST > HOLEY
HOLIBUT same as > HALIBUT
HOLIBUTS > HOLIBUT
HOLIDAY n time spent away from home for rest or recreation ▷ vb spend a holiday
HOLIDAYED > HOLIDAY
HOLIDAYER > HOLIDAY
HOLIDAYS > HOLIDAY
HOLIER > HOLY
HOLIES > HOLY
HOLIEST > HOLY
HOLILY adv in a holy, devout, or sacred manner
HOLINESS n state of being holy
HOLING > HOLE
HOLINGS > HOLE
HOLISM n view that a whole is greater than the sum of its parts
HOLISMS > HOLISM
HOLIST > HOLISM
HOLISTIC adj considering the complete person, physically and mentally
HOLISTS > HOLISM
HOLK vb dig
HOLKED > HOLK
HOLKING > HOLK
HOLKS > HOLK
HOLLA same as > HOLLO
HOLLAED > HOLLA
HOLLAING > HOLLA
HOLLAND n coarse linen cloth, used esp for furnishing
HOLLANDS > HOLLAND
HOLLAS > HOLLA
HOLLER n shout, yell ▷ vb shout or yell
HOLLERED > HOLLER
HOLLERING > HOLLER
HOLLERS > HOLLER
HOLLIDAM same as > HALIDOM
HOLLIDAMS > HOLLIDAM
HOLLIES > HOLLY

HOLLO *interj* cry for attention, or of encouragement ▷ *vb* shout
HOLLOA *same as* ▷ HOLLO
HOLLOAED ▷ HOLLOA
HOLLOAING ▷ HOLLOA
HOLLOAS ▷ HOLLOA
HOLLOED ▷ HOLLO
HOLLOES ▷ HOLLO
HOLLOING ▷ HOLLO
HOLLOO *same as* ▷ HALLOO
HOLLOOED ▷ HOLLOO
HOLLOOING ▷ HOLLOO
HOLLOOS ▷ HOLLOO
HOLLOS ▷ HOLLO
HOLLOW *adj* having a hole or space inside ▷ *n* cavity or space ▷ *vb* form a hollow in
HOLLOWARE *n* hollow utensils such as cups
HOLLOWED ▷ HOLLOW
HOLLOWER ▷ HOLLOW
HOLLOWEST ▷ HOLLOW
HOLLOWING ▷ HOLLOW
HOLLOWLY ▷ HOLLOW
HOLLOWS ▷ HOLLOW
HOLLY *n* evergreen tree with prickly leaves and red berries
HOLLYHOCK *n* tall garden plant with spikes of colourful flowers
HOLM *n* island in a river, lake, or estuary
HOLME *same as* ▷ HOLM
HOLMES ▷ HOLME
HOLMIA *n* oxide of holmium
HOLMIAS ▷ HOLMIA
HOLMIC *adj* of or containing holmium
HOLMIUM *n* silver-white metallic element
HOLMIUMS ▷ HOLMIUM
HOLMS ▷ HOLM
HOLO *n* short for hologram
HOLOCAINE *n* type of anaesthetic for the eye
HOLOCAUST *n* destruction or loss of life on a massive scale
HOLOCENE *adj* of the most recent epoch of the Quaternary period
HOLOCRINE *adj* (of the secretion of glands) characterized by disintegration of the entire glandular cell in releasing its product, as in sebaceous glands
HOLOGAMY *n* condition of having gametes like ordinary cells
HOLOGRAM *n* three-dimensional photographic image
HOLOGRAMS ▷ HOLOGRAM
HOLOGRAPH *n* document handwritten by the author
HOLOGYNIC *adj* passed down through females
HOLOGYNY *n* inheritance of genetic traits through females only

HOLOHEDRA *n* geometrical forms with particular symmetry
HOLON *n* autonomous self-reliant unit, esp in manufacturing
HOLONIC ▷ HOLON
HOLONS ▷ HOLON
HOLOPHOTE *n* device for directing light from lighthouse
HOLOPHYTE *n* plant capable of synthesizing food from inorganic molecules
HOLOPTIC *adj* with eyes meeting at the front
HOLOS ▷ HOLO
HOLOTYPE *n* original specimen from which a description of a new species is made
HOLOTYPES ▷ HOLOTYPE
HOLOTYPIC ▷ HOLOTYPE
HOLOZOIC *adj* (of animals) obtaining nourishment by feeding on plants or other animals
HOLP *past tense of* ▷ HELP
HOLPEN *past participle of* ▷ HELP
HOLS *pl n* holidays
HOLSTEIN *n* breed of cattle
HOLSTEINS ▷ HOLSTEIN
HOLSTER *n* leather case for a pistol, hung from a belt ▷ *vb* return (a pistol) to its holster
HOLSTERED ▷ HOLSTER
HOLSTERS ▷ HOLSTER
HOLT *n* otter's lair
HOLTS ▷ HOLT
HOLUBTSI *pl n* cabbage rolls
HOLY *adj* of God or a god ▷ *n* sacred place
HOLYDAM *same as* ▷ HALIDOM
HOLYDAME *same as* ▷ HALIDOM
HOLYDAMES ▷ HOLYDAME
HOLYDAMS ▷ HOLYDAM
HOLYDAY *n* day on which a religious festival is observed
HOLYDAYS ▷ HOLYDAY
HOLYSTONE *n* soft sandstone used for scrubbing the decks of a vessel ▷ *vb* scrub (a vessel's decks) with a holystone
HOLYTIDE *n* time for special religious observance
HOLYTIDES ▷ HOLYTIDE
HOM *n* sacred plant of the Parsees and ancient Persians
HOMA *same as* ▷ HOM
HOMAGE *n* show of respect or honour towards someone or something ▷ *vb* render homage to

HOMAGED ▷ HOMAGE
HOMAGER ▷ HOMAGE
HOMAGERS ▷ HOMAGE
HOMAGES ▷ HOMAGE
HOMAGING ▷ HOMAGE
HOMALOID *n* geometrical plane
HOMALOIDS ▷ HOMALOID
HOMAS ▷ HOMA
HOMBRE *slang word for* ▷ MAN
HOMBRES ▷ HOMBRE
HOMBURG *n* man's soft felt hat
HOMBURGS ▷ HOMBURG
HOME *n* place where one lives ▷ *adj* of one's home, birthplace, or native country ▷ *adv* to or at home ▷ *vb* direct towards (a point or target)
HOMEBIRD *n* person who is reluctant to leave their home
HOMEBIRDS ▷ HOMEBIRD
HOMEBIRTH *n* act of giving birth to a child in one's own home
HOMEBODY *n* person whose life and interests are centred on the home
HOMEBOUND *adj* heading for home
HOMEBOY *n* close friend
HOMEBOYS ▷ HOMEBOY
HOMEBRED *adj* raised or bred at home ▷ *n* animal bred at home
HOMEBREDS ▷ HOMEBRED
HOMEBREW *n* home-made beer
HOMEBREWS ▷ HOMEBREW
HOMEBUILT *adj* built at home
HOMEBUYER *n* person buying a home
HOMECOMER *n* person coming home
HOMECRAFT *n* skills used in the home
HOMED ▷ HOME
HOMEFELT *adj* felt personally
HOMEGIRL ▷ HOMEBOY
HOMEGIRLS ▷ HOMEBOY
HOMEGROWN *adj* (esp of fruit and vegetables) produced in one's own country, district, estate, or garden
HOMELAND *n* country from which a person's ancestors came
HOMELANDS ▷ HOMELAND
HOMELESS *adj* having nowhere to live ▷ *pl n* people who have nowhere to live
HOMELIER ▷ HOMELY
HOMELIEST ▷ HOMELY
HOMELIKE ▷ HOME
HOMELILY ▷ HOMELY
HOMELY *adj* simple, ordinary, and comfortable

HOMELYN *n* species of ray
HOMELYNS ▷ HOMELYN
HOMEMADE *adj* made at home
HOMEMAKER *n* person, esp a housewife, who manages a home
HOMEOBOX *adj* of genes that regulate cell development
HOMEOMERY *n* condition of being made up of similar parts
HOMEOPATH *n* person who treats disease by the use of small amounts of a drug that produces symptoms like those of the disease being treated
HOMEOSES ▷ HOMEOSIS
HOMEOSIS *n* process of one part coming to resemble another
HOMEOTIC ▷ HOMEOSIS
HOMEOWNER *n* person who owns the home in which he or she lives
HOMEPAGE *n* main page of website
HOMEPAGES ▷ HOMEPAGE
HOMEPLACE *n* person's home
HOMEPORT *n* port where vessel is registered
HOMEPORTS ▷ HOMEPORT
HOMER *n* homing pigeon ▷ *vb* score a home run in baseball
HOMERED ▷ HOMER
HOMERIC *adj* grand or heroic
HOMERING ▷ HOMER
HOMEROOM *n* common room at school
HOMEROOMS ▷ HOMEROOM
HOMERS ▷ HOMER
HOMES ▷ HOME
HOMESICK *adj* sad because missing one's home and family
HOMESITE *n* site for building house
HOMESITES ▷ HOMESITE
HOMESPUN *adj* (of philosophies or opinions) plain and unsophisticated ▷ *n* cloth made at home or made of yarn spun at home
HOMESPUNS ▷ HOMESPUN
HOMESTALL *same as* ▷ HOMESTEAD
HOMESTAND *n* series of games played at a team's home ground
HOMESTAY *n* period spent living as a guest in someone's home
HOMESTAYS ▷ HOMESTAY
HOMESTEAD *n* farmhouse plus the adjoining land
HOMESTYLE *adj* (of cooking) simple and unfussy

HOMETOWN n town where one lives or was born
HOMETOWNS
> HOMETOWN
HOMEWARD adj going home ▷ adv towards home
HOMEWARDS adv towards home
HOMEWARE n crockery, furniture, and furnishings with which a house, room, etc, is furnished
HOMEWARES
> HOMEWARE
HOMEWORK n school work done at home
HOMEWORKS
> HOMEWORK
HOMEY same as > HOMY
HOMEYNESS > HOMEY
HOMEYS > HOMEY
HOMICIDAL adj of, involving, or characterized by homicide
HOMICIDE n killing of a human being
HOMICIDES
> HOMICIDE
HOMIE short for
> HOMEBOY
HOMIER > HOMY
HOMIES > HOMIE
HOMIEST > HOMY
HOMILETIC adj of or relating to a homily or sermon
HOMILIES > HOMILY
HOMILIST > HOMILY
HOMILISTS > HOMILY
HOMILY n speech telling people how they should behave
HOMINES > HOMO
HOMINESS > HOMY
HOMING adj relating to the ability to return home after travelling ▷ n ability to return home after travelling
HOMINGS > HOMING
HOMINIAN same as
> HOMINID
HOMINIANS
> HOMINIAN
HOMINID n humankind or any extinct forerunner of humankind ▷ adj of or belonging to this family
HOMINIDS > HOMINID
HOMINIES > HOMINY
HOMININ n member of a zoological family
HOMININE adj characteristic of humans
HOMININS > HOMININ
HOMINISE same as
> HOMINIZE
HOMINISED
> HOMINISE
HOMINISES
> HOMINISE
HOMINIZE vb make suitable for humans
HOMINIZED
> HOMINIZE
HOMINIZES
> HOMINIZE

HOMINOID n humanlike animal ▷ adj of or like a human
HOMINOIDS > HOMINOID
HOMINY n coarsely ground maize
HOMME French word for
> MAN
HOMMES > HOMME
HOMMOCK same as
> HUMMOCK
HOMMOCKS > HOMMOCK
HOMMOS same as
> HUMMUS
HOMMOSES > HOMMOS
HOMO n homogenized milk
HOMOCERCY n condition in fish of having a symmetrical tail
HOMODONT adj (of most nonmammalian vertebrates) having teeth that are all of the same type
HOMODYNE adj of strengthened radio waves
HOMOEOBOX same as
> HOMEOBOX
HOMOEOSES
> HOMOEOSIS
HOMOEOSIS n condition of controlling a system from within
HOMOEOTIC
> HOMOEOSIS
HOMOGAMIC
> HOMOGAMY
HOMOGAMY n simultaneous maturation of all the anthers and stigmas of a flower
HOMOGENY n similarity in structure of individuals or parts because of common ancestry
HOMOGONY n condition in a plant of having stamens and styles of the same length in all the flowers
HOMOGRAFT n tissue graft obtained from an organism of the same species as the recipient
HOMOGRAPH n word spelt the same as another, but with a different meaning
HOMOLOG same as
> HOMOLOGUE
HOMOLOGIC adj having a related or similar position, structure, etc
HOMOLOGS > HOMOLOG
HOMOLOGUE n homologous part or organ
HOMOLOGY n condition of being homologous
HOMOLYSES
> HOMOLYSIS
HOMOLYSIS n dissociation of a molecule into two neutral fragments
HOMOLYTIC
> HOMOLYSIS
HOMOMORPH n thing same in form as something else
HOMONYM n word that is spelt the same as another

HOMONYMIC > HOMONYM
HOMONYMS > HOMONYM
HOMONYMY n the quality of being pronounced or spelt the same way
HOMOPHILE n rare word for homosexual
HOMOPHOBE n person who hates homosexuality
HOMOPHONE n word pronounced the same as another, but with a different meaning or spelling
HOMOPHONY n linguistic phenomenon whereby words of different origins become identical in pronunciation
HOMOPHYLY n resemblance due to common ancestry
HOMOPLASY n state of being derived from an individual of the same species as the recipient
HOMOPOLAR adj of uniform charge
HOMOS > HOMO
HOMOSEX n sexual activity between homosexual people
HOMOSEXES > HOMOSEX
HOMOSPORY n state of producing spores of one kind only
HOMOSTYLY n (in flowers) existence of styles of only one length
HOMOTAXES
> HOMOTAXIS
HOMOTAXIC
> HOMOTAXIS
HOMOTAXIS n similarity of composition and arrangement in rock strata of different ages or in different regions
HOMOTONIC adj of same tone
HOMOTONY
> HOMOTONIC
HOMOTYPAL adj of normal type
HOMOTYPE n something with same structure as something else
HOMOTYPES
> HOMOTYPE
HOMOTYPIC same as
> HOMOTYPAL
HOMOTYPY > HOMOTYPE
HOMOUSIAN adj believing God the Son and God the Father to be of the same essence
HOMS > HOM
HOMUNCLE n homunculus
HOMUNCLES
> HOMUNCLE
HOMUNCULE n homunculus
HOMUNCULI n plural of homunculus: miniature man
HOMY adj like a home
HON short for > HONEY
HONAN n silk fabric of rough weave

HONANS > HONAN
HONCHO n person in charge ▷ vb supervise or be in charge of
HONCHOED > HONCHO
HONCHOES > HONCHO
HONCHOING > HONCHO
HONCHOS > HONCHO
HOND old form of > HAND
HONDA n loop used to make a lasso
HONDAS > HONDA
HONDLE vb negotiate on price
HONDLED > HONDLE
HONDLES > HONDLE
HONDLING > HONDLE
HONDS > HOND
HONE vb sharpen ▷ n fine whetstone used for sharpening edged tools and knives
HONED > HONE
HONER > HONE
HONERS > HONE
HONES > HONE
HONEST adj truthful and moral
HONESTER > HONEST
HONESTEST > HONEST
HONESTIES > HONESTY
HONESTLY adv in an honest manner ▷ interj expression of disgust, surprise, etc
HONESTY n quality of being honest
HONEWORT n European plant that has clusters of small white flowers
HONEWORTS
> HONEWORT
HONEY n edible substance made by bees; term of endearment ▷ vb sweeten with or as if with honey
HONEYBEE n bee widely domesticated as a source of honey and beeswax
HONEYBEES
> HONEYBEE
HONEYBELL n hybrid citrus fruit
HONEYBUN n term of endearment
HONEYBUNS
> HONEYBUN
HONEYCOMB n waxy structure of six-sided cells in which honey is stored by bees in a beehive ▷ vb pierce or fill with holes, cavities, etc
HONEYDEW n sugary substance produced by aphids and similar insects
HONEYDEWS
> HONEYDEW
HONEYED > HONEY
HONEYEDLY > HONEY
HONEYFUL adj full of honey
HONEYING > HONEY
HONEYLESS > HONEY
HONEYMOON n holiday taken by a newly married couple ▷ vb take a honeymoon

HONEYPOT n container for honey
HONEYPOTS > HONEYPOT
HONEYS > HONEY
HONEYTRAP n scheme in which a victim is lured into a compromising situation by an attractive person
HONG n (in China) a factory, warehouse, etc ▷ vb archaic form of hang
HONGI n Māori greeting in which people touch noses ▷ vb touch noses
HONGIED > HONGI
HONGIES > HONGI
HONGIING > HONGI
HONGING > HONG
HONGIS > HONGI
HONGS > HONG
HONIED same as > HONEYED
HONIEDLY > HONEY
HONING > HONE
HONK n sound made by a car horn ▷ vb (cause to) make this sound
HONKED > HONK
HONKER n person or thing that honks
HONKERS > HONKER
HONKING > HONK
HONKS > HONK
HONOR same as > HONOUR
HONORABLE adj possessing high principles
HONORABLY adv in an honourable way
HONORAND n person being honoured
HONORANDS > HONORAND
HONORARIA n fee pain for a nominally free service
HONORARY adj held or given only as an honour
HONORED > HONOR
HONOREE same as > HONORAND
HONOREES > HONOREE
HONORER > HONOUR
HONORERS > HONOUR
HONORIFIC adj showing respect
HONORING > HONOR
HONORLESS > HONOUR
HONORS same as > HONOURS
HONOUR n sense of honesty and fairness ▷ vb give praise and attention to
HONOURARY less common spelling of > HONORARY
HONOURED > HONOUR
HONOUREE n person who is honoured
HONOUREES > HONOUREE
HONOURER > HONOUR
HONOURERS > HONOUR
HONOURING > HONOUR
HONOURS > HONOUR
HONS > HON
HOO interj expression of joy, excitement, etc
HOOCH n alcoholic drink, esp illicitly distilled spirits

HOOCHES > HOOCH
HOOCHIE n immoral woman
HOOCHIES > HOOCHIE
HOOD n head covering, often attached to a coat or jacket ▷ vb cover with or as if with a hood
HOODED adj (of a garment) having a hood
HOODIA n any of several southern African succulent plants
HOODIAS > HOODIA
HOODIE n hooded sweatshirt
HOODIER > HOOD
HOODIES > HOODIE
HOODIEST > HOOD
HOODING > HOOD
HOODLESS > HOOD
HOODLIKE > HOOD
HOODLUM n violent criminal, gangster
HOODLUMS > HOODLUM
HOODMAN n man wearing a hood
HOODMEN > HOODMAN
HOODMOLD n moulding over door or window
HOODMOLDS > HOODMOLD
HOODOO n (cause of) bad luck ▷ vb bring bad luck to
HOODOOED > HOODOO
HOODOOING > HOODOO
HOODOOISM > HOODOO
HOODOOS > HOODOO
HOODS > HOOD
HOODWINK vb trick, deceive
HOODWINKS > HOODWINK
HOODY > HOOD
HOOEY n nonsense ▷ interj nonsense
HOOEYS > HOOEY
HOOF n horny covering of the foot of a horse, deer, etc ▷ vb kick or trample with the hooves
HOOFBEAT n sound made by hoof on the ground
HOOFBEATS > HOOFBEAT
HOOFBOUND adj (of a horse) having dry contracted hooves, with resultant pain and lameness
HOOFED adj having a hoof or hoofs
HOOFER n professional dancer
HOOFERS > HOOFER
HOOFING > HOOF
HOOFLESS > HOOF
HOOFLIKE > HOOF
HOOFPRINT n mark made by hoof on ground
HOOFROT n disease of hoof
HOOFROTS > HOOFROT
HOOFS > HOOF
HOOK n curved object used to hang, hold, or pull something ▷ vb fasten or catch (as if) with a hook

HOOKA same as > HOOKAH
HOOKAH n water-pipe for smoking tobacco
HOOKAHS > HOOKAH
HOOKAS > HOOKA
HOOKCHECK n in ice hockey, act of hooking an opposing player
HOOKED adj bent like a hook
HOOKER n person or thing that hooks
HOOKERS > HOOKER
HOOKEY same as > HOOKY
HOOKEYS > HOOKEY
HOOKIER > HOOKY
HOOKIES > HOOKY
HOOKIEST > HOOKY
HOOKING n act of hooking
HOOKINGS > HOOKING
HOOKLESS > HOOK
HOOKLET n little hook
HOOKLETS > HOOKLET
HOOKLIKE > HOOK
HOOKNOSE n nose with a pronounced outward and downward curve
HOOKNOSED > HOOKNOSE
HOOKNOSES > HOOKNOSE
HOOKS > HOOK
HOOKUP n contact of an aircraft with the hose of a tanker aircraft
HOOKUPS > HOOKUP
HOOKWORM n blood-sucking worm with hooked mouthparts
HOOKWORMS > HOOKWORM
HOOKY n truancy, usually from school ▷ adj hooklike
HOOLACHAN n Highland reel
HOOLEY n lively party
HOOLEYS > HOOLEY
HOOLICAN same as > HOOLACHAN
HOOLICANS > HOOLICAN
HOOLIE same as > HOOLEY
HOOLIER > HOOLY
HOOLIES > HOOLIE
HOOLIEST > HOOLY
HOOLIGAN n rowdy young person
HOOLIGANS > HOOLIGAN
HOOLOCK n Indian gibbon
HOOLOCKS > HOOLOCK
HOOLY adj careful or gentle
HOON n loutish youth who drives irresponsibly ▷ vb drive irresponsibly
HOONED > HOON
HOONING > HOON
HOONS > HOON
HOOP n rigid circular band ▷ vb surround with or as if with a hoop
HOOPED > HOOP
HOOPER rare word for > COOPER
HOOPERS > HOOPER

HOOPING > HOOP
HOOPLA n fairground game
HOOPLAS > HOOPLA
HOOPLESS > HOOP
HOOPLIKE > HOOP
HOOPOE n bird with a pinkish-brown plumage
HOOPOES > HOOPOE
HOOPOO same as > HOOPOE
HOOPOOS > HOOPOO
HOOPS > HOOP
HOOPSKIRT n skirt stiffened by hoops
HOOPSTER n basketball player
HOOPSTERS > HOOPSTER
HOOR n unpleasant or difficult thing
HOORAH same as > HURRAH
HOORAHED > HOORAH
HOORAHING > HOORAH
HOORAHS > HOORAH
HOORAY same as > HURRAH
HOORAYED > HOORAY
HOORAYING > HOORAY
HOORAYS > HOORAY
HOORD same as > HOARD
HOORDS > HOORD
HOOROO n cheer of joy or victory ▷ vb shout 'hooroo'
HOOROOED > HOOROO
HOOROOING > HOOROO
HOOROOS > HOOROO
HOORS > HOOR
HOOSEGOW slang word for > JAIL
HOOSEGOWS > HOOSEGOW
HOOSGOW same as > JAIL
HOOSGOWS > HOOSGOW
HOOSH vb shoo away
HOOSHED > HOOSH
HOOSHES > HOOSH
HOOSHING > HOOSH
HOOT n sound of a car horn ▷ vb sound (a car horn) ▷ interj exclamation of impatience or dissatisfaction
HOOTCH same as > HOOCH
HOOTCHES > HOOTCH
HOOTED > HOOT
HOOTER n device that hoots
HOOTERS > HOOTER
HOOTIER > HOOT
HOOTIEST > HOOT
HOOTING > HOOT
HOOTNANNY n informal performance by folk singers
HOOTS same as > HOOT
HOOTY > HOOT
HOOVE same as > HEAVE
HOOVED > HOOVE
HOOVEN > HOOVE
HOOVER vb vacuum-clean (a carpet, furniture, etc)
HOOVERED > HOOVER
HOOVERING n act of hoovering
HOOVERS > HOOVER

HOOVES > HOOF

HOOVING > HOOVE

HOP *vb* jump on one foot ▷ *n* instance of hopping

HOPAK *n* type of Ukrainian dance

HOPAKS > HOPAK

HOPBIND *n* stalk of the hop

HOPBINDS > HOPBIND

HOPBINE *same as* **>** HOPBIND

HOPBINES > HOPBINE

HOPDOG *n* species of caterpillar

HOPDOGS > HOPDOG

HOPE *vb* want (something) to happen or be true ▷ *n* expectation of something desired

HOPED > HOPE

HOPEFUL *adj* having, expressing, or inspiring hope ▷ *n* person considered to be on the brink of success

HOPEFULLY *adv* in a hopeful manner

HOPEFULS > HOPEFUL

HOPELESS *adj* having or offering no hope

HOPER > HOPE

HOPERS > HOPE

HOPES > HOPE

HOPFIELD *n* field where hops are grown

HOPFIELDS > HOPFIELD

HOPHEAD *n* heroin or opium addict

HOPHEADS > HOPHEAD

HOPING > HOPE

HOPINGLY > HOPE

HOPLITE *n* (in ancient Greece) a heavily armed infantryman

HOPLITES > HOPLITE

HOPLITIC > HOPLITE

HOPLOLOGY *n* study of weapons or armour

HOPPED > HOP

HOPPER *n* container for storing substances

HOPPERCAR *same as* **>** HOPPER

HOPPERS > HOPPER

HOPPIER > HOPPY

HOPPIEST > HOPPY

HOPPINESS *n* state of tasting or smelling of hops

HOPPING > HOP

HOPPINGS > HOP

HOPPLE *same as* **>** HOBBLE

HOPPLED > HOPPLE

HOPPLER > HOPPLE

HOPPLERS > HOPPLE

HOPPLES > HOPPLE

HOPPLING > HOPPLE

HOPPUS *adj* as in *hoppus foot* unit of volume for round timber

HOPPY *adj* tasting of hops

HOPS > HOP

HOPSACK *n* roughly woven fabric

HOPSACKS > HOPSACK

HOPSCOTCH *n* children's game of hopping in a pattern drawn on the ground

HOPTOAD *n* toad

HOPTOADS > HOPTOAD

HORA *n* traditional Israeli or Romanian circle dance

HORAH *same as* **>** HORA

HORAHS > HORAH

HORAL *less common word for* **>** HOURLY

HORARY *adj* relating to the hours

HORAS > HORA

HORDE *n* large crowd ▷ *vb* form, move in, or live in a horde

HORDED > HORDE

HORDEIN *n* simple protein, rich in proline, that occurs in barley

HORDEINS > HORDEIN

HORDEOLA > HORDEOLUM

HORDEOLUM *n* (in medicine) stye

HORDES > HORDE

HORDING > HORDE

HORDOCK *same as* **>** HARDOKE

HORDOCKS > HORDOCK

HORE *same as* **>** HOAR

HOREHOUND *n* plant that produces a bitter juice formerly used as a cough medicine

HORIATIKI *n* traditional Greek salad consisting of tomatoes, cucumber, onion, olives, and feta cheese

HORIZON *n* apparent line that divides the earth and the sky

HORIZONAL > HORIZON

HORIZONS > HORIZON

HORK *vb* spit

HORKED > HORK

HORKEY *same as* **>** HOCKEY

HORKEYS > HORKEY

HORKING > HORK

HORKS > HORK

HORLICKS *n* as in *make a horlicks* make a mistake or a mess

HORME *n* (in Jungian psychology) fundamental vital energy

HORMES > HORME

HORMESES > HORMESIS

HORMESIS *n* beneficial effect of exposure to a very small amount of a toxic substance

HORMETIC *adj* relating to hormesis

HORMIC > HORME

HORMONAL > HORMONE

HORMONE *n* substance secreted by certain glands

HORMONES > HORMONE

HORMONIC > HORMONE

HORN *n* one of a pair of bony growths ▷ *vb* provide with a horn or horns

HORNBAG *n* in Australian slang, an attractive person

HORNBAGS > HORNBAG

HORNBEAK *n* garfish

HORNBEAKS **>** HORNBEAK

HORNBEAM *n* tree with smooth grey bark

HORNBEAMS **>** HORNBEAM

HORNBILL *n* bird with a bony growth on its large beak

HORNBILLS **>** HORNBILL

HORNBOOK *n* page of religious text with flattened cow horn over it

HORNBOOKS **>** HORNBOOK

HORNBUG *n* stag beetle

HORNBUGS > HORNBUG

HORNDOG *n* sexually aggressive man

HORNDOGS > HORNDOG

HORNED *adj* having a horn, horns, or hornlike parts

HORNER *n* dealer in horn

HORNERS > HORNER

HORNET *n* large wasp with a severe sting

HORNETS > HORNET

HORNFELS *n* hard fine-grained metamorphic rock

HORNFISH *n* fish of the needlefish family

HORNFUL *n* amount a horn will hold

HORNFULS > HORNFUL

HORNGELD *n* feudal rent based on number of cattle

HORNGELDS **>** HORNGELD

HORNIER > HORNY

HORNIEST > HORNY

HORNILY > HORNY

HORNINESS > HORNY

HORNING > HORN

HORNINGS > HORN

HORNISH *adj* like horn

HORNIST *n* horn player

HORNISTS > HORNIST

HORNITO *n* small vent in volcano

HORNITOS > HORNITO

HORNLESS > HORN

HORNLET *n* small horn

HORNLETS > HORNLET

HORNLIKE > HORN

HORNPIPE *n* (music for) a solo dance, traditionally performed by sailors

HORNPIPES **>** HORNPIPE

HORNPOUT *n* catfish

HORNPOUTS **>** HORNPOUT

HORNS > HORN

HORNSTONE *same as* **>** HORNFELS

HORNTAIL *n* wasplike insect

HORNTAILS **>** HORNTAIL

HORNWORK *n* bastion in fortifications

HORNWORKS **>** HORNWORK

HORNWORM *n* caterpillar of the hawk moth

HORNWORMS **>** HORNWORM

HORNWORT *n* aquatic plant

HORNWORTS **>** HORNWORT

HORNWRACK *n* yellowish bryozoan or sea mat sometimes found on beaches after a storm

HORNY *adj* of or like horn

HORNYHEAD *n* species of fish

HORNYWINK *n* lapwing

HOROEKA *n* New Zealand tree

HOROEKAS > HOROEKA

HOROKAKA *n* low-growing New Zealand plant with fleshy leaves and pink or white flowers

HOROKAKAS **>** HOROKAKA

HOROLOGE *rare word for* **>** TIMEPIECE

HOROLOGER *n* an expert maker of timepieces

HOROLOGES **>** HOROLOGE

HOROLOGIA *n* plural of horologium: clocktower

HOROLOGIC **>** HOROLOGY

HOROLOGY *n* art of making clocks and watches or of measuring time

HOROMETRY *n* measurement of time

HOROPITO *n* New Zealand plant

HOROPITOS **>** HOROPITO

HOROPTER *n* locus of points in space that have the same disparity as fixation

HOROPTERS > HOROPTER

HOROSCOPE *n* prediction of a person's future based on the positions of the planets, sun, and moon at his or her birth

HOROSCOPY *n* casting and interpretation of horoscopes

HORRENT *adj* bristling

HORRIBLE *adj* disagreeable, unpleasant ▷ *n* horrible thing

HORRIBLES **>** HORRIBLE

HORRIBLY *adv* in a horrible manner

HORRID *adj* disagreeable, unpleasant

HORRIDER > HORRID

HORRIDEST > HORRID

HORRIDLY > HORRID

HORRIFIC *adj* causing horror

HORRIFIED *adj* terrified

HORRIFIES > HORRIFY

HORRIFY *vb* cause to feel horror or shock

HORROR n (thing or person causing) terror or hatred ▷ adj having a frightening subject

HORRORS pl n fit of misery or anxiety ▷ interj expression of dismay, sometimes facetious

HORS prep as in hors d'oeuvre appetizer

HORSE n large animal with hooves, a mane, and a tail ▷ vb provide with a horse

HORSEBACK n horse's back

HORSEBEAN n broad bean

HORSEBOX n trailer used for transporting horses

HORSECAR n streetcar drawn by horses

HORSECARS > HORSECAR

HORSED > HORSE

HORSEFLY n large bloodsucking fly

HORSEHAIR n hair from the tail or mane of a horse

HORSEHEAD n head of a horse

HORSEHIDE n hide of a horse

HORSELESS > HORSE

HORSELIKE > HORSE

HORSEMAN n person skilled in riding

HORSEMEAT n flesh of the horse used as food

HORSEMEN > HORSEMAN

HORSEMINT n European mint plant

HORSEPLAY n rough or rowdy play

HORSEPOND n pond where horses drink

HORSEPOX n viral infection of horses

HORSERACE n race for horses

HORSES > HORSE

HORSESHIT n vulgar word for nonsense, rubbish

HORSESHOD > HORSESHOE

HORSESHOE n protective U-shaped piece of iron nailed to a horse's hoof, regarded as a symbol of good luck ▷ vb fit with a horseshoe

HORSETAIL n plant with small dark toothlike leaves

HORSEWAY n road for horses

HORSEWAYS > HORSEWAY

HORSEWEED n US name for Canadian fleabane

HORSEWHIP n whip with a long thong, used for managing horses ▷ vb beat (a person or animal) with such a whip

HORSEY adj very keen on horses

HORSIE n child's word for a horse

HORSIER > HORSEY

HORSIES > HORSIE

HORSIEST > HORSEY

HORSILY > HORSEY

HORSINESS > HORSEY

HORSING > HORSE

HORSINGS > HORSE

HORSON same as > WHORESON

HORSONS > HORSON

HORST n ridge of land

HORSTE variant of > HORST

HORSTES > HORSTE

HORSTS > HORST

HORSY same as > HORSEY

HORTATION > HORTATORY

HORTATIVE same as > HORTATORY

HORTATORY adj encouraging

HORTENSIA n type of hydrangea

HOS > HO

HOSANNA interj exclamation of praise to God ▷ n act of crying 'hosanna' ▷ vb cry hosanna

HOSANNAED > HOSANNA

HOSANNAH same as > HOSANNA

HOSANNAHS > HOSANNAH

HOSANNAS > HOSANNA

HOSE n flexible pipe for conveying liquid ▷ vb water with a hose

HOSED > HOSE

HOSEL n socket in head of golf club

HOSELIKE > HOSEL

HOSELS > HOSEL

HOSEMAN n firefighter in charge of a hose

HOSEMEN > HOSEMAN

HOSEN > HOSE

HOSEPIPE n hose

HOSEPIPES > HOSEPIPE

HOSER n person who swindles or deceives others

HOSERS > HOSER

HOSES > HOSE

HOSEY vb claim possession

HOSEYED > HOSEY

HOSEYING > HOSEY

HOSEYS > HOSEY

HOSIER n person who sells stockings, etc

HOSIERIES > HOSIERY

HOSIERS > HOSIER

HOSIERY n stockings, socks, and tights collectively

HOSING > HOSE

HOSPICE n nursing home for the terminally ill

HOSPICES > HOSPICE

HOSPITAGE n behaviour of guest

HOSPITAL n place where people who are ill are looked after and treated

HOSPITALE n lodging

HOSPITALS > HOSPITAL

HOSPITIA > HOSPITIUM

HOSPITIUM same as > HOSPICE

HOSPODAR n (formerly) the governor or prince of Moldavia or Wallachia under Ottoman rule

HOSPODARS > HOSPODAR

HOSS n horse

HOSSES > HOSS

HOST n person who entertains guests ▷ vb be the host of

HOSTA n ornamental plant

HOSTAGE n person who is illegally held prisoner

HOSTAGES > HOSTAGE

HOSTAS > HOSTA

HOSTED > HOST

HOSTEL n building providing accommodation ▷ vb stay in hostels

HOSTELED > HOSTEL

HOSTELER same as > HOSTELLER

HOSTELERS > HOSTELER

HOSTELING n hostelling

HOSTELLED > HOSTEL

HOSTELLER n person who stays at youth hostels

HOSTELRY n inn, pub

HOSTELS > HOSTEL

HOSTESS n woman who receives and entertains guests ▷ vb act as hostess

HOSTESSED > HOSTESS

HOSTESSES > HOSTESS

HOSTIE n informal Australian word for an air hostess

HOSTIES > HOSTIE

HOSTILE adj unfriendly ▷ n hostile person

HOSTILELY > HOSTILE

HOSTILES > HOSTILE

HOSTILITY n unfriendly and aggressive feelings or behaviour

HOSTING > HOST

HOSTINGS > HOST

HOSTLER another name (esp Brit) for > OSTLER

HOSTLERS > HOSTLER

HOSTLESS adj lacking a host

HOSTLESSE adj inhospitable

HOSTLY > HOST

HOSTRIES > HOSTRY

HOSTRY n lodging

HOSTS > HOST

HOT adj having a high temperature ▷ vb make or become hot

HOTBED n any place encouraging a particular activity

HOTBEDS > HOTBED

HOTBLOOD n type of horse

HOTBLOODS > HOTBLOOD

HOTBOX n container maintained at a high temperature to heat its contents ▷ vb smoke marijuana in a closed room

HOTBOXED > HOTBOX

HOTBOXES > HOTBOX

HOTBOXING > HOTBOX

HOTCAKE n pancake

HOTCAKES > HOTCAKE

HOTCH vb jog

HOTCHED > HOTCH

HOTCHES > HOTCH

HOTCHING > HOTCH

HOTCHPOT n collecting of property so that it may be redistributed in equal shares

HOTCHPOTS > HOTCHPOT

HOTDOG vb perform a series of manoeuvres in skiing, etc

HOTDOGGED > HOTDOG

HOTDOGGER > HOTDOG

HOTDOGS > HOTDOG

HOTE > HIGHT

HOTEL n establishment providing lodging and meals

HOTELDOM n hotel business

HOTELDOMS > HOTELDOM

HOTELIER n owner or manager of a hotel

HOTELIERS > HOTELIER

HOTELING n office practice in which desk space is booked in advance by an employee as required

HOTELINGS > HOTELING

HOTELLING same as > HOTELING

HOTELMAN n hotel owner

HOTELMEN > HOTELMAN

HOTELS > HOTEL

HOTEN > HIGHT

HOTFOOT adv quickly and eagerly ▷ vb move quickly

HOTFOOTED > HOTFOOT

HOTFOOTS > HOTFOOT

HOTHEAD n excitable or fiery person

HOTHEADED adj impetuous, rash, or hot-tempered

HOTHEADS > HOTHEAD

HOTHOUSE n greenhouse

HOTHOUSED adj taught intensively

HOTHOUSES > HOTHOUSE

HOTLINE n direct telephone link for emergency use

HOTLINER n person running a phone-in radio programme

HOTLINERS > HOTLINER

HOTLINES > HOTLINE

HOTLINK n area on website connecting to another site

h

HOTLINKS > HOTLINK
HOTLY > HOT
HOTNESS > HOT
HOTNESSES > HOT
HOTPLATE n heated metal surface on an electric cooker
HOTPLATES > HOTPLATE
HOTPOT n casserole topped with potatoes
HOTPOTS > HOTPOT
HOTPRESS vb subject (paper, cloth, etc) to heat and pressure
HOTROD n car with a modified engine for increased power
HOTRODS > HOTROD
HOTS > HOT
HOTSHOT n important person or expert, esp when showy
HOTSHOTS > HOTSHOT
HOTSPOT n place where wireless broadband is provided
HOTSPOTS > HOTSPOT
HOTSPUR n impetuous or fiery person
HOTSPURS > HOTSPUR
HOTTED > HOT
HOTTENTOT n as in hottentot fig perennial plant with fleshy leaves, showy yellow or purple flowers, and edible fruits
HOTTER vb simmer
HOTTERED > HOTTER
HOTTERING > HOTTER
HOTTERS > HOTTER
HOTTEST > HOT
HOTTIE n attractive person
HOTTIES > HOTTIE
HOTTING n stealing fast cars to put on a show of skilful driving
HOTTINGS > HOTTING
HOTTISH adj fairly hot
HOTTY same as > HOTTIE
HOUDAH same as > HOWDAH
HOUDAHS > HOUDAH
HOUDAN n breed of light domestic fowl
HOUDANS > HOUDAN
HOUF same as > HOWF
HOUFED > HOUF
HOUFF same as > HOWF
HOUFFED > HOUFF
HOUFFING > HOUFF
HOUFFS > HOUFF
HOUFING > HOUF
HOUFS > HOUF
HOUGH n in Scotland, a cut of meat corresponding to shin ▷ vb hamstring (cattle, horses, etc)
HOUGHED > HOUGH
HOUGHING > HOUGH
HOUGHS > HOUGH
HOUHERE n small evergreen New Zealand tree
HOUHERES > HOUHERE
HOUMMOS same as > HUMMUS

HOUMMOSES > HOUMMOS
HOUMOUS same as > HUMMUS
HOUMOUSES > HOUMOUS
HOUMUS same as > HUMMUS
HOUMUSES > HOUMUS
HOUND n hunting dog ▷ vb pursue relentlessly
HOUNDED > HOUND
HOUNDER > HOUND
HOUNDERS > HOUND
HOUNDFISH n name given to various small sharks or dogfish
HOUNDING > HOUND
HOUNDS > HOUND
HOUNGAN n voodoo priest
HOUNGANS > HOUNGAN
HOUR n twenty-fourth part of a day, sixty minutes
HOURGLASS n device with two glass compartments, containing a quantity of sand that takes an hour to trickle from the top section to the bottom one
HOURI n any of the nymphs of paradise
HOURIS > HOURI
HOURLIES > HOURLY
HOURLONG adj lasting an hour
HOURLY adv (happening) every hour ▷ adj of, occurring, or done once every hour ▷ n something that is done by the hour
HOURPLATE n dial of clock
HOURS pl n indefinite time
HOUSE n building used as a home ▷ vb give accommodation to
HOUSEBOAT n stationary boat used as a home
HOUSEBOY n male domestic servant
HOUSEBOYS > HOUSEBOY
HOUSECARL n (in medieval Europe) a household warrior of Danish kings and nobles
HOUSECOAT n woman's long loose coat-shaped garment for wearing at home
HOUSED > HOUSE
HOUSEFLY n common fly often found in houses
HOUSEFUL n full amount or number that can be accommodated in a particular house
HOUSEFULS > HOUSEFUL
HOUSEHOLD n all the people living in a house ▷ adj relating to the running of a household
HOUSEKEEP vb run household
HOUSEKEPT > HOUSEKEEP
HOUSEL vb give the Eucharist to (someone)
HOUSELED > HOUSEL

HOUSELEEK n plant that has a rosette of succulent leaves and pinkish flowers and grows on walls
HOUSELESS > HOUSE
HOUSELIKE adj like a house
HOUSELINE n tarred marline
HOUSELING > HOUSEL
HOUSELLED > HOUSEL
HOUSELS > HOUSEL
HOUSEMAID n female servant employed to do housework
HOUSEMAN n junior hospital doctor
HOUSEMATE n person who is not part of the same family, but with whom one shares a house
HOUSEMEN > HOUSEMAN
HOUSER > HOUSE
HOUSEROOM n room for storage or lodging
HOUSERS > HOUSE
HOUSES > HOUSE
HOUSESAT > HOUSESIT
HOUSESIT vb live in and look after a house during the absence of its owner or owners
HOUSESITS > HOUSESIT
HOUSETOP n rooftop
HOUSETOPS > HOUSETOP
HOUSEWIFE n woman who runs her own household and does not have a job
HOUSEWORK n work of running a home, such as cleaning, cooking, and shopping
HOUSEWRAP n shawl or loose robe worn indoors
HOUSEY adj of or like house music
HOUSIER > HOUSEY
HOUSIEST > HOUSEY
HOUSING n (providing of) houses
HOUSINGS > HOUSING
HOUSLING adj of sacrament ▷ n growing of the climbing stem of the hop into a dense mass
HOUSLINGS > HOUSLING
HOUSTONIA n small North American plant with blue, white or purple flowers
HOUT same as > HOOT
HOUTED > HOUT
HOUTING n type of fish
HOUTINGS > HOUTING
HOUTS > HOUT
HOVE vb swell
HOVEA n Australian plant with purple flowers
HOVEAS > HOVEA
HOVED > HOVE
HOVEL n small dirty house or hut ▷ vb shelter or be sheltered in a hovel
HOVELED > HOVEL

HOVELING > HOVEL
HOVELLED > HOVEL
HOVELLER n person working on boat
HOVELLERS > HOVELLER
HOVELLING > HOVEL
HOVELS > HOVEL
HOVEN > HEAVE
HOVER vb (of a bird etc) remain suspended in one place in the air ▷ n act of hovering
HOVERED > HOVER
HOVERER > HOVER
HOVERERS > HOVER
HOVERFLY n hovering wasp-like fly
HOVERING > HOVER
HOVERPORT n port for hovercraft
HOVERS > HOVER
HOVES > HOVE
HOVING > HOVE
HOW adv in what way, by what means ▷ n the way a thing is done ▷ sentence substitute supposed Native American greeting
HOWBE same as > HOWBEIT
HOWBEIT adv in archaic usage, however
HOWDAH n canopied seat on an elephant's back
HOWDAHS > HOWDAH
HOWDIE n midwife
HOWDIED > HOWDY
HOWDIES > HOWDY
HOWDY vb greet someone
HOWDYING > HOWDY
HOWE n depression in the earth's surface
HOWES > HOWE
HOWEVER adv nevertheless
HOWF n haunt, esp a public house ▷ vb visit a place frequently
HOWFED > HOWF
HOWFF vb visit a place frequently
HOWFFED > HOWFF
HOWFFING > HOWFF
HOWFFS > HOWFF
HOWFING > HOWF
HOWFS > HOWF
HOWITZER n large gun firing shells at a steep angle
HOWITZERS > HOWITZER
HOWK vb dig (out or up)
HOWKED > HOWK
HOWKER > HOWK
HOWKERS > HOWK
HOWKING > HOWK
HOWKS > HOWK
HOWL n loud wailing cry ▷ vb utter a howl
HOWLBACK same as > HOWLROUND
HOWLBACKS > HOWLBACK
HOWLED > HOWL
HOWLER n stupid mistake
HOWLERS > HOWLER
HOWLET another word for > OWL

HOWLETS > HOWLET
HOWLING adj great ▷ n act of wailing
HOWLINGLY > HOWLING
HOWLINGS > HOWLING
HOWLROUND n condition, resulting in a howling noise, when sound from a loudspeaker is fed back into the microphone of a public-address or recording system
HOWLS > HOWL
HOWRE same as > HOUR
HOWRES > HOWRE
HOWS > HOW
HOWSO same as > HOWSOEVER
HOWSOEVER less common word for > HOWEVER
HOWTOWDIE n Scottish dish of boiled chicken with poached eggs and spinach
HOWZAT interj cry in cricket appealing for dismissal of batsman
HOWZIT informal word for > HELLO
HOX vb hamstring
HOXED > HOX
HOXES > HOX
HOXING > HOX
HOY interj cry used to attract someone's attention ▷ n freight barge ▷ vb drive animal with cry
HOYA n any of various E Asian or Australian plants
HOYAS > HOYA
HOYDEN n wild or boisterous girl ▷ vb behave like a hoyden
HOYDENED > HOYDEN
HOYDENING > HOYDEN
HOYDENISH > HOYDEN
HOYDENISM > HOYDEN
HOYDENS > HOYDEN
HOYED > HOY
HOYING > HOY
HOYLE n archer's mark used as a target
HOYLES > HOYLE
HOYS > HOY
HRYVNA n standard monetary unit of Ukraine
HRYVNAS > HRYVNA
HRYVNIA same as > HRYVNA
HRYVNIAS > HRYVNIA
HRYVNYA same as > HRYVNA
HRYVNYAS > HRYVNYA
HUANACO same as > GUANACO
HUANACOS > HUANACO
HUAQUERO n Central American tomb robber
HUAQUEROS > HUAQUERO
HUARACHE n Mexican sandal
HUARACHES > HUARACHE
HUARACHO same as > HUARACHE
HUARACHOS > HUARACHO

HUB n centre of a wheel, through which the axle passes
HUBBIES > HUBBY
HUBBLIER > HUBBLY
HUBBLIEST > HUBBLY
HUBBLY adj having an irregular surface
HUBBUB n confused noise of many voices
HUBBUBOO same as > HUBBUB
HUBBUBOOS > HUBBUBOO
HUBBUBS > HUBBUB
HUBBY n husband
HUBCAP n metal disc that protects the hub of a wheel
HUBCAPS > HUBCAP
HUBLESS adj without a hub
HUBRIS n pride, arrogance
HUBRISES > HUBRIS
HUBRISTIC > HUBRIS
HUBS > HUB
HUCK same as > HUCKABACK
HUCKABACK n coarse absorbent linen or cotton fabric used for towels and informal shirts, etc
HUCKED > HUCK
HUCKERY adj ugly
HUCKING > HUCK
HUCKLE n hip or haunch ▷ vb force out or arrest roughly
HUCKLED > HUCKLE
HUCKLES > HUCKLE
HUCKLING > HUCKLE
HUCKS > HUCK
HUCKSTER n person using aggressive methods of selling ▷ vb peddle
HUCKSTERS > HUCKSTER
HUCKSTERY > HUCKSTER
HUDDEN > HAUD
HUDDLE vb hunch (oneself) through cold or fear ▷ n small group
HUDDLED > HUDDLE
HUDDLER > HUDDLE
HUDDLERS > HUDDLE
HUDDLES > HUDDLE
HUDDLING > HUDDLE
HUDDUP interj get up
HUDNA n truce or ceasefire for a fixed duration
HUDNAS > HUDNA
HUDUD n set of laws and punishments in the Koran
HUDUDS > HUDUD
HUE n colour, shade
HUED adj having a hue or colour as specified
HUELESS > HUE
HUER n pilchard fisherman
HUERS > HUER
HUES > HUE
HUFF n passing mood of anger or resentment ▷ vb blow or puff heavily
HUFFED > HUFF
HUFFER > HUFFING

HUFFERS > HUFFING
HUFFIER > HUFF
HUFFIEST > HUFF
HUFFILY > HUFF
HUFFINESS > HUFF
HUFFING n practice of inhaling fumes for intoxicating effects
HUFFINGS > HUFFING
HUFFISH > HUFF
HUFFISHLY > HUFF
HUFFKIN n type of muffin
HUFFKINS > HUFFKIN
HUFFS > HUFF
HUFFY > HUFF
HUG vb clasp tightly in the arms, usu with affection ▷ n tight or fond embrace
HUGE adj very big
HUGELY adv very much
HUGENESS > HUGE
HUGEOUS same as > HUGE
HUGEOUSLY > HUGEOUS
HUGER > HUGE
HUGEST > HUGE
HUGGABLE > HUG
HUGGED > HUG
HUGGER > HUG
HUGGERS > HUG
HUGGIER > HUGGY
HUGGIEST > HUGGY
HUGGING > HUG
HUGGY adj sensitive and caring
HUGS > HUG
HUGY same as > HUGE
HUH interj exclamation of derision or inquiry
HUHU n type of hairy New Zealand beetle
HUHUS > HUHU
HUI n meeting of Māori people
HUIA n extinct bird of New Zealand
HUIAS > HUIA
HUIC interj in hunting, a call to hounds
HUIPIL n Mayan woman's blouse
HUIPILES > HUIPIL
HUIPILS > HUIPIL
HUIS > HUI
HUISACHE n American tree
HUISACHES > HUISACHE
HUISSIER n doorkeeper
HUISSIERS > HUISSIER
HUITAIN n verse of eighteen lines
HUITAINS > HUITAIN
HULA n swaying Hawaiian dance
HULAS > HULA
HULE same as > ULE
HULES > HULE
HULK n body of an abandoned ship ▷ vb move clumsily
HULKED > HULK
HULKIER > HULKY
HULKIEST > HULKY
HULKING adj bulky, unwieldy
HULKS > HULK

HULKY same as > HULKING
HULL n main body of a boat ▷ vb remove the hulls from
HULLED > HULL
HULLER > HULL
HULLERS > HULL
HULLIER > HULLY
HULLIEST > HULLY
HULLING > HULL
HULLO same as > HELLO
HULLOA same as > HALLOA
HULLOAED > HULLOA
HULLOAING > HULLOA
HULLOAS > HULLOA
HULLOED > HULLO
HULLOES > HULLO
HULLOING > HULLO
HULLOO same as > HALLOO
HULLOOED > HULLOO
HULLOOING > HULLOO
HULLOOS > HULLOO
HULLOS > HULLO
HULLS > HULL
HULLY adj having husks
HUM vb make a low continuous vibrating sound ▷ n humming sound
HUMA n mythical bird
HUMAN adj of or typical of people ▷ n human being
HUMANE adj kind or merciful
HUMANELY > HUMANE
HUMANER > HUMANE
HUMANEST > HUMANE
HUMANHOOD n state of being human
HUMANISE same as > HUMANIZE
HUMANISED > HUMANISE
HUMANISER > HUMANISE
HUMANISES > HUMANISE
HUMANISM n belief in human effort rather than religion
HUMANISMS > HUMANISM
HUMANIST > HUMANISM
HUMANISTS > HUMANISM
HUMANITY n human race
HUMANIZE vb make human or humane
HUMANIZED > HUMANIZE
HUMANIZER > HUMANIZE
HUMANIZES > HUMANIZE
HUMANKIND n human race
HUMANLIKE > HUMAN
HUMANLY adv by human powers or means
HUMANNESS > HUMAN
HUMANOID adj resembling a human being in appearance ▷ n (in science fiction) a robot or creature resembling a human being
HUMANOIDS > HUMANOID
HUMANS > HUMAN
HUMAS > HUMA
HUMATE n decomposed plants used as fertilizer

h

HUMATES > HUMATE
HUMBLE adj conscious of one's failings ▷ vb cause to feel humble, humiliate
HUMBLEBEE another name for the > BUMBLEBEE
HUMBLED > HUMBLE
HUMBLER > HUMBLE
HUMBLERS > HUMBLE
HUMBLES > HUMBLE
HUMBLESSE n quality of being humble
HUMBLEST > HUMBLE
HUMBLING > HUMBLE
HUMBLINGS > HUMBLE
HUMBLY > HUMBLE
HUMBUCKER n twin-coil guitar pick-up
HUMBUG n hard striped peppermint sweet ▷ vb cheat or deceive (someone)
HUMBUGGED > HUMBUG
HUMBUGGER > HUMBUG
HUMBUGS > HUMBUG
HUMBUZZ n type of beetle
HUMBUZZES > HUMBUZZ
HUMDINGER n excellent person or thing
HUMDRUM adj ordinary, dull ▷ n monotonous routine, task, or person
HUMDRUMS > HUMDRUM
HUMECT vb make moist
HUMECTANT adj producing moisture ▷ n substance added to another substance to keep it moist
HUMECTATE vb produce moisture
HUMECTED > HUMECT
HUMECTING > HUMECT
HUMECTIVE > HUMECT
HUMECTS > HUMECT
HUMEFIED > HUMEFY
HUMEFIES > HUMEFY
HUMEFY same as > HUMIFY
HUMEFYING > HUMEFY
HUMERAL adj of or relating to the humerus ▷ n silk shawl worn by a priest at High Mass; humeral veil
HUMERALS > HUMERAL
HUMERI > HUMERUS
HUMERUS n bone from the shoulder to the elbow
HUMF same as > HUMPH
HUMFED > HUMF
HUMFING > HUMF
HUMFS > HUMF
HUMHUM n Indian cotton cloth
HUMHUMS > HUMHUM
HUMIC adj of, derived from, or resembling humus
HUMICOLE n any plant that thrives on humus
HUMICOLES > HUMICOLE
HUMID adj damp and hot
HUMIDER > HUMID
HUMIDEST > HUMID
HUMIDEX n system of measuring discomfort

HUMIDEXES > HUMIDEX
HUMIDICES > HUMIDEX
HUMIDIFY vb make the air in (a room) more humid or damp
HUMIDITY n dampness
HUMIDLY > HUMID
HUMIDNESS > HUMID
HUMIDOR n humid place for storing cigars, tobacco, etc
HUMIDORS > HUMIDOR
HUMIFIED > HUMIFY
HUMIFIES > HUMIFY
HUMIFY vb convert or be converted into humus
HUMIFYING > HUMIFY
HUMILIANT adj humiliating
HUMILIATE vb lower the dignity or hurt the pride of
HUMILITY n quality of being humble
HUMINT n human intelligence
HUMINTS > HUMINT
HUMITE n mineral containing magnesium
HUMITES > HUMITE
HUMITURE n measure of both humidity and temperature
HUMITURES > HUMITURE
HUMLIE n hornless cow
HUMLIES > HUMLIE
HUMMABLE > HUM
HUMMAUM same as > HAMMAM
HUMMAUMS > HUMMAUM
HUMMED > HUM
HUMMEL adj (of cattle) hornless ▷ vb remove horns from
HUMMELLED > HUMMEL
HUMMELLER > HUMMEL
HUMMELS > HUMMEL
HUMMER > HUM
HUMMERS > HUM
HUMMING > HUM
HUMMINGS > HUM
HUMMLE adj as in humble bonnet type of Scottish cap
HUMMOCK n very small hill ▷ vb form into a hummock or hummocks
HUMMOCKED > HUMMOCK
HUMMOCKS > HUMMOCK
HUMMOCKY adj having hummocks
HUMMUM same as > HAMMAM
HUMMUMS > HUMMUM
HUMMUS n creamy dip
HUMMUSES > HUMMUS
HUMOGEN n type of fertilizer
HUMOGENS > HUMOGEN
HUMONGOUS same as > HUMUNGOUS
HUMOR same as > HUMOUR
HUMORAL adj denoting or relating to a type of immunity
HUMORALLY > HUMORAL
HUMORED > HUMOR
HUMORESK n humorous musical composition

HUMORESKS > HUMORESK
HUMORFUL > HUMOR
HUMORING > HUMOR
HUMORIST n writer or entertainer who uses humour in his or her work
HUMORISTS > HUMORIST
HUMORLESS > HUMOR
HUMOROUS adj amusing, esp in a witty or clever way
HUMORS > HUMOR
HUMORSOME adj capricious
HUMOUR n ability to say or perceive things that are amusing ▷ vb be kind and indulgent to
HUMOURED > HUMOUR
HUMOURFUL > HUMOUR
HUMOURING > HUMOUR
HUMOURS > HUMOUR
HUMOUS same as > HUMUS
HUMOUSES > HUMOUS
HUMP n raised piece of ground ▷ vb carry or heave
HUMPBACK same as > HUNCHBACK
HUMPBACKS > HUMPBACK
HUMPED > HUMP
HUMPEN n old German drinking glass
HUMPENS > HUMPEN
HUMPER > HUMP
HUMPERS > HUMP
HUMPH interj exclamation of annoyance or scepticism ▷ vb exclaim humph
HUMPHED > HUMPH
HUMPHING > HUMPH
HUMPHS > HUMPH
HUMPIER > HUMPY
HUMPIES > HUMPY
HUMPIEST > HUMPY
HUMPINESS > HUMPY
HUMPING > HUMP
HUMPLESS > HUMP
HUMPLIKE > HUMP
HUMPS > HUMP
HUMPTIES > HUMPTY
HUMPTY n low padded seat
HUMPY adj full of humps ▷ n primitive hut
HUMS > HUM
HUMSTRUM n medieval musical instrument
HUMSTRUMS > HUMSTRUM
HUMUNGOUS adj very large
HUMUS n decomposing matter in the soil
HUMUSES > HUMUS
HUMUSIER > HUMUSY
HUMUSIEST > HUMUSY
HUMUSY adj like humus
HUMVEE n military vehicle
HUMVEES > HUMVEE
HUN n member of any of several nomadic peoples
HUNCH n feeling or suspicion not based on facts ▷ vb draw (one's shoulders) up or together

HUNCHBACK n abnormal curvature of the spine
HUNCHED > HUNCH
HUNCHES > HUNCH
HUNCHING > HUNCH
HUNDRED n ten times ten ▷ adj amounting to a hundred
HUNDREDER n inhabitant of a hundred
HUNDREDOR same as > HUNDREDER
HUNDREDS > HUNDRED
HUNDREDTH adj being the ordinal number of 100 in numbering or counting order, position, time, etc ▷ n one of 100 approximately equal parts of something
HUNG > HANG
HUNGAN same as > HOUNGAN
HUNGANS > HUNGAN
HUNGER n discomfort or weakness from lack of food ▷ vb want very much
HUNGERED > HUNGER
HUNGERFUL adj hungry
HUNGERING > HUNGER
HUNGERLY adj hungry
HUNGERS > HUNGER
HUNGOVER adj suffering from hangover
HUNGRIER > HUNGRY
HUNGRIEST > HUNGRY
HUNGRILY > HUNGRY
HUNGRY adj desiring food
HUNH same as > HUH
HUNK n large piece
HUNKER vb squat
HUNKERED > HUNKER
HUNKERING > HUNKER
HUNKERS pl n haunches
HUNKIER > HUNKY
HUNKIEST > HUNKY
HUNKS n grumpy person
HUNKSES > HUNKS
HUNKY adj excellent
HUNNISH > HUN
HUNS > HUN
HUNT vb seek out and kill (wild animals) for food or sport ▷ n hunting
HUNTABLE > HUNT
HUNTAWAY n sheepdog trained to drive sheep by barking
HUNTAWAYS > HUNTAWAY
HUNTED adj harassed and worn
HUNTEDLY > HUNT
HUNTER n person or animal that hunts wild animals
HUNTERS > HUNTER
HUNTING n pursuit and killing or capture of wild animals
HUNTINGS > HUNTING
HUNTRESS n female hunter
HUNTS > HUNT
HUNTSMAN n man who hunts wild animals, esp foxes
HUNTSMEN > HUNTSMAN

HUP vb cry hup to get a horse to move

HUPIRO in New Zealand English, same as > STINKWOOD

HUPIROS > HUPIRO

HUPPAH variant spelling of > CHUPPAH

HUPPAHS > HUPPAH

HUPPED > HUP

HUPPING > HUP

HUPPOT > HUPPAH

HUPPOTH same as > HUPPOT

HUPS > HUP

HURCHEON same as > URCHIN

HURCHEONS > HURCHEON

HURDEN same as > HARDEN

HURDENS > HURDEN

HURDIES pl n buttocks or haunches

HURDLE n light barrier for jumping over in some races ▷ vb jump over (something)

HURDLED > HURDLE

HURDLER > HURDLE

HURDLERS > HURDLE

HURDLES > HURDLE

HURDLING > HURDLE

HURDLINGS > HURDLE

HURDS same as > HARDS

HURL vb throw or utter forcefully ▷ n act or an instance of hurling

HURLBAT same as > WHIRLBAT

HURLBATS > HURLBAT

HURLED > HURL

HURLER > HURL

HURLERS > HURL

HURLEY n another word for the game of hurling

HURLEYS > HURLEY

HURLIES > HURLY

HURLING n Irish game like hockey

HURLINGS > HURLING

HURLS > HURL

HURLY n wheeled barrow

HURRA same as > HURRAH

HURRAED > HURRA

HURRAH interj exclamation of joy or applause ▷ n cheer of joy or victory ▷ vb shout 'hurrah'

HURRAHED > HURRAH

HURRAHING > HURRAH

HURRAHS > HURRAH

HURRAING > HURRA

HURRAS > HURRA

HURRAY same as > HURRAH

HURRAYED > HURRAY

HURRAYING > HURRAY

HURRAYS > HURRAY

HURRICANE n very strong, often destructive, wind or storm

HURRICANO same as > HURRICANE

HURRIED adj done quickly or too quickly

HURRIEDLY > HURRIED

HURRIER > HURRY

HURRIERS > HURRY

HURRIES > HURRY

HURRY vb (cause to) move or act very quickly ▷ n doing something or the need to do something quickly

HURRYING > HURRY

HURRYINGS > HURRY

HURST n wood

HURSTS > HURST

HURT vb cause physical or mental pain to ▷ n physical or mental pain ▷ adj injured or pained

HURTER > HURT

HURTERS > HURT

HURTFUL adj unkind

HURTFULLY > HURTFUL

HURTING > HURT

HURTLE vb move quickly or violently

HURTLED > HURTLE

HURTLES > HURTLE

HURTLESS adj uninjured

HURTLING > HURTLE

HURTS > HURT

HUSBAND n man to whom one is married ▷ vb use economically

HUSBANDED > HUSBAND

HUSBANDER > HUSBAND

HUSBANDLY adj of or like a husband

HUSBANDRY n farming

HUSBANDS > HUSBAND

HUSH vb make or be silent ▷ n stillness or silence ▷ interj plea or demand for silence

HUSHABIED > HUSHABY

HUSHABIES > HUSHABY

HUSHABY interj used in quietening a baby or child to sleep ▷ n lullaby ▷ vb quieten to sleep

HUSHABYE same as > HUSHABY

HUSHED > HUSH

HUSHEDLY > HUSH

HUSHER same as > USHER

HUSHERED > HUSHER

HUSHERING > HUSHER

HUSHERS > HUSHER

HUSHES > HUSH

HUSHFUL adj quiet

HUSHIER > HUSHY

HUSHIEST > HUSHY

HUSHING > HUSH

HUSHPUPPY n snack of deep-fried dough

HUSHY adj secret

HUSK n outer covering of certain seeds and fruits ▷ vb remove the husk from

HUSKED > HUSK

HUSKER > HUSK

HUSKERS > HUSK

HUSKIER > HUSKY

HUSKIES > HUSKY

HUSKIEST > HUSKY

HUSKILY > HUSKY

HUSKINESS > HUSKY

HUSKING > HUSK

HUSKINGS > HUSK

HUSKLIKE > HUSK

HUSKS > HUSK

HUSKY adj slightly hoarse ▷ n Arctic sledge dog with thick hair and a curled tail

HUSO n sturgeon

HUSOS > HUSO

HUSS n flesh of the European dogfish

HUSSAR n lightly armed cavalry soldier

HUSSARS > HUSSAR

HUSSES > HUSS

HUSSIES > HUSSY

HUSSIF n sewing kit

HUSSIFS > HUSSIF

HUSSY n derogatory term for a woman considered immodest

HUSTINGS pl n political campaigns and speeches before an election

HUSTLE vb push about, jostle ▷ n lively activity or bustle

HUSTLED > HUSTLE

HUSTLER > HUSTLE

HUSTLERS > HUSTLE

HUSTLES > HUSTLE

HUSTLING > HUSTLE

HUSTLINGS > HUSTLE

HUSWIFE same as > HOUSEWIFE

HUSWIFES > HUSWIFE

HUSWIVES > HUSWIFE

HUT n small house, shelter, or shed ▷ vb equip with huts

HUTCH n cage for pet rabbits etc ▷ vb store or keep in or as if in a hutch

HUTCHED > HUTCH

HUTCHES > HUTCH

HUTCHIE n temporary shelter

HUTCHIES > HUTCHIE

HUTCHING > HUTCH

HUTIA n rodent native to the Caribbean

HUTIAS > HUTIA

HUTLIKE > HUT

HUTMENT n number or group of huts

HUTMENTS > HUTMENT

HUTS > HUT

HUTTED > HUT

HUTTING > HUT

HUTTINGS > HUT

HUTZPA same as > HUTZPAH

HUTZPAH variant spelling of > CHUTZPAH

HUTZPAHS > HUTZPAH

HUTZPAS > HUTZPA

HUZOOR n person of rank in India

HUZOORS > HUZOOR

HUZZA same as > HUZZAH

HUZZAED > HUZZA

HUZZAH archaic word for > HURRAH

HUZZAHED > HUZZAH

HUZZAHING > HUZZAH

HUZZAHS > HUZZAH

HUZZAING > HUZZA

HUZZAS > HUZZA

HUZZIES > HUZZY

HUZZY same as > HUSSY

HWAN another name for > WON

HWYL n emotional fervour, as in the recitation of poetry

HWYLS > HWYL

HYACINE same as > HYACINTH

HYACINES > HYACINE

HYACINTH n sweet-smelling spring flower that grows from a bulb

HYACINTHS > HYACINTH

HYAENA same as > HYENA

HYAENAS > HYAENA

HYAENIC > HYAENA

HYALIN n glassy translucent substance

HYALINE adj clear and translucent, with no fibres or granules ▷ n glassy transparent surface

HYALINES > HYALINE

HYALINISE same as > HYALINIZE

HYALINIZE vb give a glassy consistency to

HYALINS > HYALIN

HYALITE n clear and colourless variety of opal in globular form

HYALITES > HYALITE

HYALOGEN n insoluble substance in body structures

HYALOGENS > HYALOGEN

HYALOID adj clear and transparent ▷ n delicate transparent membrane

HYALOIDS > HYALOID

HYALONEMA n species of sponge

HYBRID n offspring of two plants or animals of different species ▷ adj of mixed origin

HYBRIDISE same as > HYBRIDIZE

HYBRIDISM > HYBRID

HYBRIDIST > HYBRID

HYBRIDITY > HYBRID

HYBRIDIZE vb produce or cause (species) to produce hybrids

HYBRIDOMA n hybrid cell formed by the fusion of two different types of cell, esp one capable of producing antibodies, but of limited lifespan, fused with an immortal tumour cell

HYBRIDOUS > HYBRID

HYBRIDS > HYBRID

HYBRIS same as > HUBRIS

HYBRISES > HYBRIS

HYBRISTIC > HYBRIS

HYDANTOIN n colourless odourless crystalline compound present in beet molasses and used in the manufacture of pharmaceuticals and synthetic resins

HYDATHODE n pore in plants, esp on the leaves, specialized for discharging water

HYDATID n cyst containing tapeworm larvae

HYDATIDS > HYDATID

HYDATOID adj watery

HYDRA n mythical many-headed water serpent

HYDRACID n acid, such as hydrochloric acid, that does not contain oxygen

HYDRACIDS > HYDRACID

HYDRAE > HYDRA

HYDRAEMIA n wateriness of blood

HYDRAGOG n drug that removes water

HYDRAGOGS > HYDRAGOG

HYDRANGEA n ornamental shrub with clusters of pink, blue, or white flowers

HYDRANT n outlet from a water main with a nozzle for a hose

HYDRANTH n polyp in a colony of hydrozoan coelenterates

HYDRANTHS > HYDRANTH

HYDRANTS > HYDRANT

HYDRAS > HYDRA

HYDRASE n enzyme that removes water

HYDRASES > HYDRASE

HYDRASTIS n any of various Japanese and E North American plants, such as goldenseal, having showy foliage and ornamental red fruits

HYDRATE n chemical compound of water with another substance ▷ vb treat or impregnate with water

HYDRATED adj (of a compound) chemically bonded to water molecules

HYDRATES > HYDRATE

HYDRATING > HYDRATE

HYDRATION > HYDRATE

HYDRATOR > HYDRATE

HYDRATORS > HYDRATE

HYDRAULIC adj operated by pressure forced through a pipe by a liquid such as water or oil

HYDRAZIDE n any of a class of chemical compounds that result when hydrogen in hydrazine or any of its derivatives is replaced by an acid radical

HYDRAZINE n colourless basic liquid made from sodium hypochlorite and ammonia: a strong reducing agent, used chiefly as a rocket fuel

HYDRAZOIC adj as in hydrazoic acid colourless highly explosive liquid

HYDREMIA same as > HYDRAEMIA

HYDREMIAS > HYDRAEMIA

HYDRIA n (in ancient Greece and Rome) a large water jar

HYDRIAE > HYDRIA

HYDRIC adj of or containing hydrogen

HYDRID same as > HYDROID

HYDRIDE n compound of hydrogen with another element

HYDRIDES > HYDRIDE

HYDRIDS > HYDRID

HYDRILLA n aquatic plant used as an oxygenator in aquaria and pools

HYDRILLAS > HYDRILLA

HYDRIODIC adj as in hydriodic acid colourless or pale yellow aqueous solution of hydrogen iodide: a strong acid

HYDRO n hotel offering facilities for hydropathy ▷ adj short for hydroelectric

HYDROCAST n gathering of water samples for analysis

HYDROCELE n abnormal collection of fluid in any saclike space

HYDROFOIL n fast light boat with its hull raised out of the water on one or more pairs of fins

HYDROGEL n gel in which the liquid constituent is water

HYDROGELS > HYDROGEL

HYDROGEN n light flammable colourless gas that combines with oxygen to form water

HYDROGENS > HYDROGEN

HYDROID adj of an order of colonial hydrozoan coelenterates ▷ n hydroid colony or individual

HYDROIDS > HYDROID

HYDROLASE n enzyme, such as an esterase, that controls hydrolysis

HYDROLOGY n study of the distribution, conservation, and use of the water of the earth and its atmosphere

HYDROLYSE vb subject to or undergo hydrolysis

HYDROLYTE n substance subjected to hydrolysis

HYDROLYZE same as > HYDROLYSE

HYDROMA same as > HYGROMA

HYDROMAS > HYDROMA

HYDROMATA > HYDROMA

HYDROMEL n another word for mead (the drink)

HYDROMELS > HYDROMEL

HYDRONAUT n person trained to operate deep submergence vessels

HYDRONIC adj using hot water in heating system

HYDRONIUM n as in hydronium ion positive ion formed by the attachment of a proton to a water molecule

HYDROPATH n exponent of treating disease using large quantities of water

HYDROPIC > HYDROPSY

HYDROPS n anaemia in a fetus

HYDROPSES > HYDROPS

HYDROPSY same as > DROPSY

HYDROPTIC > HYDROPSY

HYDROPULT n type of water pump

HYDROS > HYDRO

HYDROSERE n sere that begins in an aquatic environment

HYDROSKI n hydrofoil used on some seaplanes to provide extra lift when taking off

HYDROSKIS > HYDROSKI

HYDROSOL n sol that has water as its liquid phase

HYDROSOLS > HYDROSOL

HYDROSOMA same as > HYDROSOME

HYDROSOME n body of a colonial hydrozoan

HYDROSTAT n device that detects the presence of water as a prevention against drying out, overflow, etc, esp one used as a warning in a steam boiler

HYDROUS adj containing water

HYDROVANE n vane on a seaplane conferring stability on water (a sponson) or facilitating take-off (a hydrofoil)

HYDROXIDE n compound containing a hydroxyl group or ion

HYDROXIUM n type of positive ion

HYDROXY adj of a type of chemical compound

HYDROXYL n the monovalent group –OH or the ion OH^-

HYDROXYLS > HYDROXYL

HYDROZOA > HYDROZOON

HYDROZOAN n type of invertebrate of the class which includes the hydra and Portuguese man-of-war

HYDROZOON same as > HYDROZOAN

HYDYNE n type of rocket fuel

HYDYNES > HYDYNE

HYE same as > HIE

HYED > HYE

HYEING > HYE

HYEN same as > HYENA

HYENA n scavenging doglike mammal of Africa and S Asia

HYENAS > HYENA

HYENIC > HYENA

HYENINE adj of hyenas

HYENOID adj of or like hyenas

HYENS > HYEN

HYES > HYE

HYETAL adj of or relating to rain, rainfall, or rainy regions

HYETOLOGY n study of rainfall

HYGEIST same as > HYGIENIST

HYGEISTS > HYGEIST

HYGGE n Danish practice that promotes wellbeing

HYGGES > HYGGE

HYGIEIST same as > HYGIENIST

HYGIEISTS > HYGIEIST

HYGIENE n principles of health and cleanliness

HYGIENES > HYGIENE

HYGIENIC adj promoting health or cleanliness

HYGIENICS same as > HYGIENE

HYGIENIST n person skilled in the practice of hygiene

HYGRISTOR n electronic component the resistance of which varies with humidity

HYGRODEIK n type of thermometer

HYGROLOGY n study of humidity of air

HYGROMA n swelling soft tissue that occurs over a joint

HYGROMAS > HYGROMA

HYGROMATA > HYGROMA

HYGROPHIL adj moisture-loving

HYGROSTAT n device for maintaining constant humidity

HYING > HIE

HYKE same as > HAIK

HYKES > HYKE

HYLA n type of tropical American tree frog

HYLAS > HYLA

HYLDING same as > HILDING

HYLDINGS > HYLDING

HYLE n wood

HYLEG n dominant planet when someone is born

HYLEGS > HYLEG

HYLES > HYLE

HYLIC adj solid

HYLICISM n materialism

HYLICISMS > HYLICISM
HYLICIST > HYLICISM
HYLICISTS
> HYLICISM
HYLISM same as
> HYLICISM
HYLISMS > HYLISM
HYLIST > HYLISM
HYLISTS > HYLISM
HYLOBATE n gibbon
HYLOBATES
> HYLOBATE
HYLOIST n materialist
HYLOISTS > HYLOIST
HYLOPHYTE n plant that grows in woods
HYLOZOIC
> HYLOZOISM
HYLOZOISM n philosophical doctrine that life is one of the properties of matter
HYLOZOIST
> HYLOZOISM
HYLOZOISTS
> HYLOZOISM
HYMEN n membrane partly covering the vaginal opening
HYMENAEAL same as
> HYMENEAL
HYMENAEAN n person who believes there will be no resurrection
HYMENAL > HYMEN
HYMENEAL adj of or relating to marriage ▷ n wedding song or poem
HYMENEALS
> HYMENEAL
HYMENEAN n wedding song
HYMENEANS
> HYMENEAN
HYMENIA > HYMENIUM
HYMENIAL > HYMENIUM
HYMENIUM n (in some fungi) a layer of cell-producing spores
HYMENIUMS
> HYMENIUM
HYMENS > HYMEN
HYMN n Christian song of praise sung to God or a saint ▷ vb express (praises, thanks, etc) by singing hymns
HYMNAL n book of hymns ▷ adj of, relating to, or characteristic of hymns
HYMNALS > HYMNAL
HYMNARIES > HYMNARY
HYMNARY same as
> HYMNAL
HYMNBOOK n book containing the words and music of hymns
HYMNBOOKS
> HYMNBOOK
HYMNED > HYMN
HYMNIC > HYMN
HYMNING > HYMN
HYMNIST n person who composes hymns
HYMNISTS > HYMNIST
HYMNLESS > HYMN
HYMNLIKE > HYMN
HYMNODIES > HYMNODY
HYMNODIST same as
> HYMNIST

HYMNODY n composition or singing of hymns
HYMNOLOGY same as
> HYMNODY
HYMNS > HYMN
HYNDE same as > HIND
HYNDES > HYNDE
HYOID adj of or relating to the hyoid bone ▷ n horseshoe-shaped bone
HYOIDAL adj of or relating to the hyoid bone
HYOIDEAN same as
> HYOIDAL
HYOIDS > HYOID
HYOSCINE n colourless viscous liquid alkaloid
HYOSCINES
> HYOSCINE
HYP n short for hypotenuse ▷ vb offend
HYPALGIA n reduced ability to feel pain
HYPALGIAS
> HYPALGIA
HYPALLAGE n figure of speech in which the natural relations of two words in a statement are interchanged, as in the fire spread the wind
HYPANTHIA n plural of hypanthium: cup-shaped receptacle of perigynous or epigynous flowers
HYPATE n string of lyre
HYPATES > HYPATE
HYPE n intensive or exaggerated publicity or sales promotion ▷ vb promote (a product) using intensive or exaggerated publicity
HYPED > HYPE
HYPER n excitable person ▷ adj excitable
HYPERACID adj having excess acidity
HYPERARID adj extremely dry
HYPERBOLA n curve produced when a cone is cut by a plane at a steeper angle to its base than its side
HYPERBOLE n deliberate exaggeration for effect
HYPERCUBE n figure in a space of four or more dimensions having all its sides equal and all its angles right angles
HYPEREMIA n excessive blood in an organ or part
HYPEREMIC
> HYPEREMIA
HYPERER > HYPER
HYPEREST > HYPER
HYPERFINE adj as in hyperfine structure splitting of a spectral line of an atom or molecule into two or more closely spaced components as a result of interaction of the electrons with the magnetic moments of the nuclei

HYPERGAMY n marriage with a partner of higher social status
HYPERGOL n type of fuel
HYPERGOLS
> HYPERGOL
HYPERICIN n antidepressant and antiviral compound
HYPERICUM n herbaceous plant or shrub
HYPERLINK n link from a hypertext file that gives users instant access to related material in another file ▷ vb link (files) in this way
HYPERMART n very large supermarket
HYPERNOVA n exploding star that produces even more energy and light than a supernova
HYPERNYM n superordinate
HYPERNYMS
> HYPERNYM
HYPERNYMY
> HYPERNYM
HYPERON n any baryon that is not a nucleon
HYPERONS > HYPERON
HYPEROPE n person with hyperopia
HYPEROPES
> HYPEROPE
HYPEROPIA n inability to see near objects clearly because the images received by the eye are focused behind the retina
HYPEROPIC
> HYPEROPIA
HYPERPNEA n increase in breathing rate
HYPERPURE adj extremely pure
HYPERREAL adj involving or characterized by particularly realistic graphic representation ▷ n that which constitutes hyperreality
HYPERS > HYPER
HYPERTEXT n computer software and hardware that allows users to store and view text and move between related items easily
HYPES > HYPE
HYPESTER n person who gives a product intense publicity
HYPESTERS
> HYPESTER
HYPETHRAL adj having no roof
HYPHA n any of the filaments in the mycelium of a fungus
HYPHAE > HYPHA
HYPHAL > HYPHA
HYPHEMIA n bleeding inside eye
HYPHEMIAS
> HYPHEMIA
HYPHEN n punctuation mark (-) ▷ vb hyphenate

HYPHENATE vb separate (words) with a hyphen
HYPHENED > HYPHEN
HYPHENIC > HYPHEN
HYPHENING > HYPHEN
HYPHENISE same as
> HYPHENIZE
HYPHENISM > HYPHEN
HYPHENIZE same as
> HYPHENATE
HYPHENS > HYPHEN
HYPHIES > HYPHY
HYPHY n type of hip-hop music
HYPING > HYPE
HYPINGS > HYPE
HYPINOSES
> HYPINOSIS
HYPINOSIS n protein deficiency in blood
HYPNIC n sleeping drug
HYPNICS > HYPNIC
HYPNOGENY n hypnosis
HYPNOID adj of or relating to a state resembling sleep
HYPNOIDAL same as
> HYPNOID
HYPNOLOGY n study of sleep and hypnosis
HYPNONE n sleeping drug
HYPNONES > HYPNONE
HYPNOSES > HYPNOSIS
HYPNOSIS n artificially induced state of relaxation
HYPNOTEE n person being hypnotized
HYPNOTEES
> HYPNOTEE
HYPNOTIC adj of or (as if) producing hypnosis ▷ n drug that induces sleep
HYPNOTICS
> HYPNOTIC
HYPNOTISE same as
> HYPNOTIZE
HYPNOTISM n inducing hypnosis in someone
HYPNOTIST n person skilled in the theory and practice of hypnosis
HYPNOTIZE vb induce hypnosis in (a person)
HYPNOTOID adj like hypnosis
HYPNUM n species of moss
HYPNUMS > HYPNUM
HYPO vb inject with a hypodermic syringe
HYPOACID adj abnormally acidic
HYPOBARIC adj below normal pressure
HYPOBLAST n inner layer of an embryo at an early stage of development that becomes the endoderm at gastrulation
HYPOBOLE n act of anticipating objection
HYPOBOLES
> HYPOBOLE
HYPOCAUST n ancient Roman heating system in which hot air circulated under the floor and between double walls
HYPOCIST n type of juice

HYPOCISTS > HYPOCIST

HYPOCOTYL *n* part of an embryo plant between the cotyledons and the radicle

HYPOCRISY *n* (instance of) pretence of having standards or beliefs that are contrary to one's real character or actual behaviour

HYPOCRITE *n* person who pretends to be what he or she is not

HYPODERM *n* layer of thick-walled tissue in some plants

HYPODERMA *n* layer of skin tissue

HYPODERMS > HYPODERM

HYPOED > HYPO

HYPOGAEA > HYPOGAEUM

HYPOGAEAL > HYPOGAEUM

HYPOGAEAN > HYPOGAEUM

HYPOGAEUM *same as* > HYPOGEUM

HYPOGEA > HYPOGEUM

HYPOGEAL *adj* occurring or living below the surface of the ground

HYPOGEAN > HYPOGEUM

HYPOGENE *adj* formed, taking place, or originating beneath the surface of the earth

HYPOGENIC > HYPOGENE

HYPOGEOUS *same as* > HYPOGEAL

HYPOGEUM *n* underground vault, esp one used for burials

HYPOGYNY *adj* having the gynoecium above the other floral parts

HYPOID *adj* as in *hypoid gear* type of gear ▷ *n* hypoid gear

HYPOIDS > HYPOID

HYPOING > HYPO

HYPOMANIA *n* abnormal condition of extreme excitement, milder than mania but characterized by great optimism and overactivity and often by reckless spending of money

HYPOMANIC > HYPOMANIA

HYPOMORPH *n* mutant gene

HYPONASTY *n* increased growth of the lower surface of a plant part, resulting in an upward bending of the part

HYPONEA *same as* > HYPOPNEA

HYPONEAS > HYPONEA

HYPONOIA *n* underlying meaning

HYPONOIAS > HYPONOIA

HYPONYM *n* word whose meaning is included as part of another

HYPONYMS > HYPONYM

HYPONYMY > HYPONYM

HYPOPHYGE *another name for* > APOPHYGE

HYPOPLOID *adj* having or designating a chromosome number that is less than a multiple of the haploid number

HYPOPNEA *same as* > HYPOPNOEA

HYPOPNEAS > HYPOPNOEA

HYPOPNEIC > HYPOPNEA

HYPOPNOEA *n* abnormally shallow breathing, usually accompanied by a decrease in the breathing rate

HYPOPYON *n* pus in eye

HYPOPYONS > HYPOPYON

HYPOS > HYPO

HYPOSTOME *n* invertebrate body part

HYPOSTYLE *adj* having a roof supported by columns ▷ *n* building constructed in this way

HYPOTAXES > HYPOTAXIS

HYPOTAXIS *n* subordination of one clause to another by a conjunction

HYPOTHEC *n* charge on property in favour of a creditor

HYPOTHECA *n* inner and younger layer of the cell wall of a diatom

HYPOTHECS > HYPOTHEC

HYPOTONIA *n* state of being hypnotized

HYPOTONIC *adj* (of muscles) lacking normal tone or tension

HYPOXEMIA *n* lack of oxygen in blood

HYPOXEMIC > HYPOXEMIA

HYPOXIA *n* deficiency in oxygen delivery

HYPOXIAS > HYPOXIA

HYPOXIC > HYPOXIA

HYPPED > HYP

HYPPING > HYP

HYPS > HYP

HYPURAL *adj* below the tail

HYRACES > HYRAX

HYRACOID *n* hyrax

HYRACOIDS > HYRACOID

HYRAX *n* type of hoofed rodent-like animal of Africa and Asia

HYRAXES > HYRAX

HYSON *n* Chinese green tea

HYSONS > HYSON

HYSSOP *n* sweet-smelling herb used in folk medicine

HYSSOPS > HYSSOP

HYSTERIA *n* state of uncontrolled excitement, anger, or panic

HYSTERIAS > HYSTERIA

HYSTERIC *adj* of or suggesting hysteria

HYSTERICS *pl n* attack of hysteria

HYSTEROID *adj* resembling hysteria

HYTE *adj* crazy

HYTHE *same as* > HITHE

HYTHES > HYTHE

Ii

IAMB n metrical foot of two syllables
IAMBI > IAMBUS
IAMBIC adj written in a type of metrical unit ▷ n iambic foot, line, or stanza
IAMBICS > IAMBIC
IAMBIST n one who writes iambs
IAMBISTS > IAMBIST
IAMBS > IAMB
IAMBUS same as > IAMB
IAMBUSES > IAMBUS
IANTHINE adj violet
IATRIC adj relating to medicine or physicians
IATRICAL same as > IATRIC
IATROGENY n disease caused by medical intervention
IBADAH n following of Islamic beliefs and practices
IBADAT > IBADAH
IBERIS n plant with white or purple flowers
IBERISES > IBERIS
IBEX n wild goat
IBEXES > IBEX
IBICES > IBEX
IBIDEM adv in the same place
IBIS n large wading bird with long legs
IBISES > IBIS
IBOGAINE n dopamine blocker
IBOGAINES > IBOGAINE
IBRIK same as > CEZVE
IBRIKS > IBRIK
IBUPROFEN n drug that relieves pain and reduces inflammation
ICE n water in the solid state, formed by freezing liquid water ▷ vb form or cause to form ice
ICEBALL n ball of ice
ICEBALLS > ICEBALL
ICEBERG n large floating mass of ice
ICEBERGS > ICEBERG
ICEBLINK n yellowish-white reflected glare in the sky over an ice field
ICEBLINKS > ICEBLINK
ICEBOAT n boat that breaks up bodies of ice in water ▷ vb pilot an iceboat

ICEBOATED > ICEBOAT
ICEBOATER > ICEBOAT
ICEBOATS > ICEBOAT
ICEBOUND adj covered or made immobile by ice
ICEBOX n refrigerator
ICEBOXES > ICEBOX
ICECAP n mass of ice permanently covering an area
ICECAPPED adj having an icecap
ICECAPS > ICECAP
ICED adj covered with icing
ICEFALL n part of a glacier
ICEFALLS > ICEFALL
ICEFIELD n very large flat expanse of ice floating in the sea; large ice floe
ICEFIELDS > ICEFIELD
ICEFISH vb fish through a hole in the ice on a lake
ICEFISHED > ICEFISH
ICEFISHES > ICEFISH
ICEHOUSE n building for storing ice
ICEHOUSES > ICEHOUSE
ICEKHANA n motor race on a frozen lake
ICEKHANAS > ICEKHANA
ICELESS > ICE
ICELIKE > ICE
ICEMAKER n device for making ice
ICEMAKERS > ICEMAKER
ICEMAN n person who sells or delivers ice
ICEMEN > ICEMAN
ICEPACK n bag or folded cloth containing ice
ICEPACKS > ICEPACK
ICER n person who ices cakes
ICERS > ICER
ICES > ICE
ICESCAPE n landscape covered in ice
ICESCAPES > ICESCAPE
ICESTONE n cryolite
ICESTONES > ICESTONE
ICEWINE n dessert wine made from grapes that have frozen before being harvested
ICEWINES > ICEWINE
ICEWORM n small worm found in glaciers

ICEWORMS > ICEWORM
ICH archaic form of > EKE
ICHABOD interj the glory has departed
ICHED > ICH
ICHES > ICH
ICHING > ICH
ICHNEUMON n greyish-brown mongoose
ICHNITE n trace fossil
ICHNITES > ICHNITE
ICHNOLITE same as > ICHNITE
ICHNOLOGY n study of trace fossils
ICHOR n fluid said to flow in the veins of the gods
ICHOROUS > ICHOR
ICHORS > ICHOR
ICHS > ICH
ICHTHIC same as > ICHTHYIC
ICHTHYIC adj of, relating to, or characteristic of fishes
ICHTHYOID adj resembling a fish ▷ n fishlike vertebrate
ICHTHYS n early Christian emblem
ICHTHYSES > ICHTHYS
ICICLE n tapering spike of ice
ICICLED adj covered with icicles
ICICLES > ICICLE
ICIER > ICY
ICIEST > ICY
ICILY adv in an icy or reserved manner
ICINESS n condition of being icy or very cold
ICINESSES > ICINESS
ICING n mixture used to decorate cakes
ICINGS > ICING
ICK interj expression of disgust ▷ n something sticky
ICKER n ear of corn
ICKERS > ICKER
ICKIER > ICKY
ICKIEST > ICKY
ICKILY > ICKY
ICKINESS > ICKY
ICKLE ironically childish word for > LITTLE
ICKLER > ICKLE
ICKLEST > ICKLE
ICKS > ICK
ICKY adj sticky
ICON n picture of Christ or another religious figure

ICONES archaic form of > ICONS
ICONIC adj relating to the character of an icon
ICONICAL same as > ICONIC
ICONICITY > ICONIC
ICONIFIED > ICONIFY
ICONIFIES > ICONIFY
ICONIFY vb render as an icon
ICONISE same as > ICONIZE
ICONISED > ICONISE
ICONISES > ICONISE
ICONISING > ICONISE
ICONIZE vb render as an icon
ICONIZED > ICONIZE
ICONIZES > ICONIZE
ICONIZING > ICONIZE
ICONOLOGY n study or field of art history concerning icons
ICONOSTAS n screen with doors and icons set in tiers, which separates the from the nave
ICONS > ICON
ICTAL > ICTUS
ICTERIC > ICTERUS
ICTERICAL > ICTERUS
ICTERICS > ICTERUS
ICTERID n bird of the oriole family
ICTERIDS > ICTERID
ICTERINE > ICTERID
ICTERUS n yellowing of plant leaves
ICTERUSES > ICTERUS
ICTIC > ICTUS
ICTUS n metrical or rhythmic stress in verse feet
ICTUSES > ICTUS
ICY adj very cold
ID n mind's instinctive unconscious energies
IDANT n chromosome
IDANTS > IDANT
IDE n silver orfe fish
IDEA n plan or thought formed in the mind
IDEAED adj expressing a particular idea
IDEAL adj most suitable ▷ n conception of something that is perfect
IDEALESS > IDEA
IDEALISE same as > IDEALIZE
IDEALISED > IDEALISE
IDEALISER > IDEALISE

IDEALISES > IDEALISE
IDEALISM n tendency to seek perfection in everything
IDEALISMS > IDEALISM
IDEALIST > IDEALISM
IDEALISTS > IDEALISM
IDEALITY > IDEAL
IDEALIZE vb regard or portray as perfect or nearly perfect
IDEALIZED > IDEALIZE
IDEALIZER > IDEALIZE
IDEALIZES > IDEALIZE
IDEALLESS > IDEAL
IDEALLY > IDEAL
IDEALNESS > IDEAL
IDEALOGUE corruption of > IDEOLOGUE
IDEALOGY corruption of > IDEOLOGY
IDEALS > IDEAL
IDEAS > IDEA
IDEATA > IDEATUM
IDEATE vb form or have an idea of
IDEATED > IDEATE
IDEATES > IDEATE
IDEATING > IDEATE
IDEATION > IDEATE
IDEATIONS > IDEATE
IDEATIVE > IDEATE
IDEATUM n objective reality
IDEE n idea
IDEES > IDEE
IDEM adj same
IDENT n short visual image that works as a logo
IDENTIC adj having the same intention regarding another power
IDENTICAL adj exactly the same
IDENTIFY vb prove or recognize as being a certain person or thing
IDENTIKIT n trademark name for a set of transparencies of various typical facial characteristics that can be superimposed on one another to build up a picture of a person sought by the police
IDENTITY n state of being a specified person or thing
IDENTS > IDENT
IDEOGRAM n symbol that directly represents a concept or thing
IDEOGRAMS > IDEOGRAM
IDEOGRAPH same as > IDEOGRAM
IDEOLOGIC > IDEOLOGY
IDEOLOGUE n ideologist
IDEOLOGY n body of ideas and beliefs of a group, nation, etc

IDEOMOTOR adj designating automatic muscular movements stimulated by ideas
IDEOPHONE n sound that represents a complete idea
IDEOPOLIS n city whose economy mainly consists of intellectual enterprises
IDES n specific date of each month in the Roman calendar
IDIOBLAST n plant cell that differs from those around it in the same tissue
IDIOCIES > IDIOCY
IDIOCY n utter stupidity
IDIOGRAM another name for > KARYOGRAM
IDIOGRAMS > IDIOGRAM
IDIOGRAPH n trademark
IDIOLECT n variety or form of a language used by an individual
IDIOLECTS > IDIOLECT
IDIOM n group of words with special meaning
IDIOMATIC > IDIOM
IDIOMS > IDIOM
IDIOPATHY n any disease of unknown cause
IDIOPHONE n percussion instrument, such as a cymbal or xylophone, made of naturally sonorous material
IDIOPLASM n germ plasm
IDIOT n foolish or stupid person
IDIOTCIES > IDIOTCY
IDIOTCY same as > IDIOCY
IDIOTIC adj of or resembling an idiot
IDIOTICAL same as > IDIOTIC
IDIOTICON n dictionary of dialect
IDIOTISH same as > IDIOTIC
IDIOTISM archaic word for > IDIOCY
IDIOTISMS > IDIOTISM
IDIOTS > IDIOT
IDIOTYPE n unique part of antibody
IDIOTYPES > IDIOTYPE
IDIOTYPIC > IDIOTYPE
IDLE adj not doing anything ▷ vb spend (time) doing very little
IDLED > IDLE
IDLEHOOD > IDLE
IDLEHOODS > IDLE
IDLENESS > IDLE
IDLER n person who idles
IDLERS > IDLER
IDLES > IDLE
IDLESSE poetic word for > IDLENESS

IDLESSES > IDLESSE
IDLEST > IDLE
IDLING > IDLE
IDLY > IDLE
IDOCRASE n green, brown, or yellow mineral
IDOCRASES > IDOCRASE
IDOL n object of excessive devotion
IDOLA > IDOLUM
IDOLATER > IDOLATRY
IDOLATERS > IDOLATRY
IDOLATOR n one who worships idols
IDOLATORS > IDOLATRY
IDOLATRY n worship of idols
IDOLISE same as > IDOLIZE
IDOLISED > IDOLISE
IDOLISER > IDOLISE
IDOLISERS > IDOLISE
IDOLISES > IDOLISE
IDOLISING > IDOLISE
IDOLISM > IDOL
IDOLISMS > IDOL
IDOLIST > IDOLIZE
IDOLISTS > IDOLIZE
IDOLIZE vb love or admire excessively
IDOLIZED > IDOLIZE
IDOLIZER > IDOLIZE
IDOLIZERS > IDOLIZE
IDOLIZES > IDOLIZE
IDOLIZING > IDOLIZE
IDOLON n mental picture
IDOLS > IDOL
IDOLUM n mental picture
IDONEITY > IDONEOUS
IDONEOUS adj appropriate
IDS > ID
IDYL same as > IDYLL
IDYLIST same as > IDYLLIST
IDYLISTS > IDYLIST
IDYLL n scene or time of great peace and happiness
IDYLLIAN same as > IDYLLIC
IDYLLIC adj of or relating to an idyll
IDYLLIST n writer of idylls
IDYLLISTS > IDYLLIST
IDYLLS > IDYLL
IDYLS > IDYL
IF n uncertainty or doubt
IFF conj in logic, a shortened form of if and only if
IFFIER > IFFY
IFFIEST > IFFY
IFFILY adv in an iffy manner
IFFINESS > IFFY
IFFY adj doubtful, uncertain
IFS > IF
IFTAR n meal eaten by Muslims
IFTARS > IFTAR
IGAD same as > EGAD

IGAPO n flooded forest
IGAPOS > IGAPO
IGARAPE n canoe route
IGARAPES > IGARAPE
IGG vb antagonize
IGGED > IGG
IGGING > IGG
IGGS > IGG
IGLOO n Inuit house
IGLOOS > IGLOO
IGLU same as > IGLOO
IGLUS > IGLU
IGNARO n ignoramus
IGNAROES > IGNARO
IGNAROS > IGNARO
IGNATIA n dried seed
IGNATIAS > IGNATIA
IGNEOUS adj (of rock) formed as molten rock cools
IGNESCENT adj giving off sparks when struck, as a flint ▷ n ignescent substance
IGNIFIED > IGNIFY
IGNIFIES > IGNIFY
IGNIFY vb turn into fire
IGNIFYING > IGNIFY
IGNITABLE > IGNITE
IGNITE vb catch fire or set fire to
IGNITED > IGNITE
IGNITER n person or thing that ignites
IGNITERS > IGNITER
IGNITES > IGNITE
IGNITIBLE > IGNITE
IGNITING > IGNITE
IGNITION n system that ignites the fuel-and-air mixture to start an engine
IGNITIONS > IGNITION
IGNITOR same as > IGNITER
IGNITORS > IGNITER
IGNITRON n mercury-arc rectifier controlled by a subsidiary electrode
IGNITRONS > IGNITRON
IGNOBLE adj dishonourable
IGNOBLER > IGNOBLE
IGNOBLEST > IGNOBLE
IGNOBLY > IGNOBLE
IGNOMIES > IGNOMY
IGNOMINY n humiliating disgrace
IGNOMY Shakespearean variant of > IGNOMINY
IGNORABLE > IGNORE
IGNORAMI > IGNORAMUS
IGNORAMUS n ignorant person
IGNORANCE n lack of knowledge or education
IGNORANT adj lacking knowledge ▷ n ignorant person
IGNORANTS > IGNORANT
IGNORE vb refuse to notice, disregard deliberately ▷ n disregard
IGNORED > IGNORE
IGNORER > IGNORE

IGNORERS > IGNORE
IGNORES > IGNORE
IGNORING > IGNORE
IGUANA n large tropical American lizard
IGUANAS > IGUANA
IGUANIAN n IGUANA
IGUANIANS > IGUANA
IGUANID same as > IGUANA
IGUANIDS > IGUANID
IGUANODON n massive herbivorous long-tailed bipedal dinosaur
IHRAM n white robes worn by Muslim pilgrims to Mecca
IHRAMS > IHRAM
IJTIHAD n effort of deriving a legal ruling from the Koran
IJTIHADS > IJTIHAD
IKAN n (in Malaysia) fish
IKANS > IKAN
IKAT n method of creating patterns in fabric
IKATS > IKAT
IKEBANA n Japanese art of flower arrangement
IKEBANAS > IKEBANA
IKON same as > ICON
IKONS > IKON
ILEA > ILEUM
ILEAC adj of or relating to the ileum
ILEAL same as > ILEAC
ILEITIDES > ILEITIS
ILEITIS n inflammation of the ileum
ILEITISES > ILEITIS
ILEOSTOMY n surgical formation of a permanent opening through the abdominal wall into the ileum
ILEUM n lowest part of the small intestine
ILEUS n obstruction of the intestine
ILEUSES > ILEUS
ILEX n any of a genus of trees or shrubs that includes holly
ILEXES > ILEX
ILIA > ILIUM
ILIAC adj of or relating to the ilium
ILIACI > ILIACUS
ILIACUS n muscle near the ilium
ILIACUSES > ILIACUS
ILIAD n epic poem
ILIADS > ILIAD
ILIAL > ILIUM
ILICES > ILEX
ILIUM n part of the hipbone
ILK n type
ILKA determiner Scots word meaning each
ILKADAY n Scots word for a weekday
ILKADAYS > ILKADAY
ILKS > ILK
ILL adj not in good health ▷ n evil, harm ▷ adv badly
ILLAPSE vb slide in
ILLAPSED > ILLAPSE

ILLAPSES > ILLAPSE
ILLAPSING > ILLAPSE
ILLATION rare word for > INFERENCE
ILLATIONS > ILLATION
ILLATIVE adj of or relating to illation ▷ n illative case
ILLATIVES > ILLATIVE
ILLAWARRA n Australian breed of shorthorn dairy cattle
ILLEGAL adj against the law ▷ n person who entered or attempted to enter a country illegally
ILLEGALLY > ILLEGAL
ILLEGALS > ILLEGAL
ILLEGIBLE adj unable to be read or deciphered
ILLEGIBLY > ILLEGIBLE
ILLER > ILL
ILLEST > ILL
ILLIAD n wink
ILLIADS > ILLIAD
ILLIBERAL adj narrow-minded, intolerant
ILLICIT adj illegal
ILLICITLY > ILLICIT
ILLIMITED adj infinite
ILLINIUM n type of radioactive element
ILLINIUMS > ILLINIUM
ILLIPE n Asian tree
ILLIPES > ILLIPE
ILLIQUID adj (of an asset) not easily convertible into cash
ILLISION n act of striking against
ILLISIONS > ILLISION
ILLITE n clay mineral of the mica group
ILLITES > ILLITE
ILLITIC > ILLITE
ILLNESS n disease or indisposition
ILLNESSES > ILLNESS
ILLOGIC n reasoning characterized by lack of logic
ILLOGICAL adj unreasonable
ILLOGICS > ILLOGIC
ILLS > ILL
ILLTH n condition of poverty or misery
ILLTHS > ILLTH
ILLUDE vb trick or deceive
ILLUDED > ILLUDE
ILLUDES > ILLUDE
ILLUDING > ILLUDE
ILLUME vb illuminate
ILLUMED > ILLUME
ILLUMES > ILLUME
ILLUMINE vb throw light in or into
ILLUMINED > ILLUMINE
ILLUMINER n illuminator

ILLUMINES > ILLUMINE
ILLUMING > ILLUME
ILLUPI same as > ILLIPE
ILLUPIS > ILLUPI
ILLUSION n deceptive appearance or belief
ILLUSIONS > ILLUSION
ILLUSIVE same as > ILLUSORY
ILLUSORY adj seeming to be true, but actually false
ILLUVIA > ILLUVIUM
ILLUVIAL > ILLUVIUM
ILLUVIATE vb deposit illuvium
ILLUVIUM n material washed down from one soil layer to a lower one
ILLUVIUMS > ILLUVIUM
ILLY adv badly
ILMENITE n black mineral found in igneous rocks as layered deposits and in veins
ILMENITES > ILMENITE
IMAGE n mental picture of someone or something ▷ vb picture in the mind
IMAGEABLE > IMAGE
IMAGED > IMAGE
IMAGELESS > IMAGE
IMAGER n device that produces images
IMAGERIES > IMAGERY
IMAGERS > IMAGER
IMAGERY n images collectively, esp in the arts
IMAGES > IMAGE
IMAGINAL adj of, relating to, or resembling an imago
IMAGINARY adj existing only in the imagination
IMAGINE vb form a mental image of ▷ sentence substitute exclamation of surprise
IMAGINED > IMAGINE
IMAGINEER n person skilled in devising or implementing creative ideas ▷ vb devise and implement (a creative idea)
IMAGINER > IMAGINE
IMAGINERS > IMAGINE
IMAGINES > IMAGO
IMAGING > IMAGE
IMAGINGS > IMAGE
IMAGINING > IMAGINE
IMAGINIST n imaginative person
IMAGISM n poetic movement
IMAGISMS > IMAGISM
IMAGIST > IMAGISM
IMAGISTIC > IMAGISM
IMAGISTS > IMAGISM
IMAGO n mature adult insect
IMAGOES > IMAGO
IMAGOS > IMAGO
IMAM n leader of prayers in a mosque

IMAMATE n region or territory governed by an imam
IMAMATES > IMAMATE
IMAMS > IMAM
IMARET n (in Turkey) a hospice for pilgrims or travellers
IMARETS > IMARET
IMARI n Japanese porcelain
IMARIS > IMARI
IMAUM same as > IMAM
IMAUMS > IMAUM
IMBALANCE n lack of balance or proportion
IMBALM same as > EMBALM
IMBALMED > IMBALM
IMBALMER > IMBALM
IMBALMERS > IMBALM
IMBALMING > IMBALM
IMBALMS > IMBALM
IMBAR vb bar in
IMBARK vb cover in bark
IMBARKED > IMBARK
IMBARKING > IMBARK
IMBARKS > IMBARK
IMBARRED > IMBAR
IMBARRING > IMBAR
IMBARS > IMBAR
IMBASE vb degrade
IMBASED > IMBASE
IMBASES > IMBASE
IMBASING > IMBASE
IMBATHE vb bathe
IMBATHED > IMBATHE
IMBATHES > IMBATHE
IMBATHING > IMBATHE
IMBECILE n stupid person ▷ adj stupid or senseless
IMBECILES > IMBECILE
IMBECILIC > IMBECILE
IMBED same as > EMBED
IMBEDDED > IMBED
IMBEDDING > IMBED
IMBEDS > IMBED
IMBIBE vb drink (alcoholic drinks)
IMBIBED > IMBIBE
IMBIBER > IMBIBE
IMBIBERS > IMBIBE
IMBIBES > IMBIBE
IMBIBING > IMBIBE
IMBITTER same as > EMBITTER
IMBITTERS > IMBITTER
IMBIZO n meeting in S Africa
IMBIZOS > IMBIZO
IMBLAZE vb depict heraldically
IMBLAZED > IMBLAZE
IMBLAZES > IMBLAZE
IMBLAZING > IMBLAZE
IMBODIED > IMBODY
IMBODIES > IMBODY
IMBODY same as > EMBODY
IMBODYING > IMBODY
IMBOLDEN same as > EMBOLDEN
IMBOLDENS > IMBOLDEN

IMBORDER *vb* enclose in a border

IMBORDERS > IMBORDER

IMBOSK *vb* conceal

IMBOSKED > IMBOSK

IMBOSKING > IMBOSK

IMBOSKS > IMBOSK

IMBOSOM *vb* hold in one's heart

IMBOSOMED > IMBOSOM

IMBOSOMS > IMBOSOM

IMBOSS *same as* > EMBOSS

IMBOSSED > IMBOSS

IMBOSSES > IMBOSS

IMBOSSING > IMBOSS

IMBOWER *vb* enclose in a bower

IMBOWERED > IMBOWER

IMBOWERS > IMBOWER

IMBRANGLE *vb* entangle

IMBRAST *Spenserian past participle of* > EMBRACE

IMBREX *n* curved tile

IMBRICATE *adj* having tiles or slates that overlap ⊳ *vb* decorate with a repeating pattern resembling scales or overlapping tiles

IMBRICES > IMBREX

IMBROGLIO *n* confusing and complicated situation

IMBROWN *vb* make brown

IMBROWNED > IMBROWN

IMBROWNS > IMBROWN

IMBRUE *vb* stain, esp with blood

IMBRUED > IMBRUE

IMBRUES > IMBRUE

IMBRUING > IMBRUE

IMBRUTE *vb* reduce to a bestial state

IMBRUTED > IMBRUTE

IMBRUTES > IMBRUTE

IMBRUTING > IMBRUTE

IMBUE *vb* fill or inspire with (ideals or principles)

IMBUED > IMBUE

IMBUEMENT > IMBUE

IMBUES > IMBUE

IMBUING > IMBUE

IMBURSE *vb* pay

IMBURSED > IMBURSE

IMBURSES > IMBURSE

IMBURSING > IMBURSE

IMID *n* immunomodulatory drug

IMIDAZOLE *n* white crystalline basic heterocyclic compound

IMIDE *n* any of a class of organic compounds

IMIDES > IMIDE

IMIDIC > IMIDE

IMIDO > IMIDE

IMIDS > IMID

IMINAZOLE *same as* > IMIDAZOLE

IMINE *n* any of a class of organic compounds

IMINES > IMINE

IMINO > IMINE

IMINOUREA *another name for* > GUANIDINE

IMIPENEM *n* drug used to destroy bacteria

IMIPENEMS > IMIPENEM

IMITABLE > IMITATE

IMITANCY *n* tendency to imitate

IMITANT *same as* > IMITATION

IMITANTS > IMITANT

IMITATE *vb* take as a model

IMITATED > IMITATE

IMITATES > IMITATE

IMITATING > IMITATE

IMITATION *n* copy of an original ⊳ *adj* made to look like a material of superior quality

IMITATIVE *adj* imitating or tending to copy

IMITATOR > IMITATE

IMITATORS > IMITATE

IMMANACLE *vb* fetter

IMMANE *adj* monstrous

IMMANELY > IMMANE

IMMANENCE > IMMANENT

IMMANENCY > IMMANENT

IMMANENT *adj* present within and throughout something

IMMANITY > IMMANE

IMMANTLE *vb* cover with a mantle

IMMANTLED > IMMANTLE

IMMANTLES > IMMANTLE

IMMASK *vb* disguise

IMMASKED > IMMASK

IMMASKING > IMMASK

IMMASKS > IMMASK

IMMATURE *n* young animal ⊳ *adj* not fully developed

IMMATURER > IMMATURE

IMMATURES > IMMATURE

IMMEDIACY > IMMEDIATE

IMMEDIATE *adj* occurring at once

IMMENSE *adj* extremely large

IMMENSELY > IMMENSE

IMMENSER > IMMENSE

IMMENSEST > IMMENSE

IMMENSITY *n* state or quality of being immense

IMMERGE *archaic word for* > IMMERSE

IMMERGED > IMMERGE

IMMERGES > IMMERGE

IMMERGING > IMMERGE

IMMERSE *vb* involve deeply, engross

IMMERSED *adj* sunk or submerged

IMMERSER > IMMERSE

IMMERSERS > IMMERSE

IMMERSES > IMMERSE

IMMERSING > IMMERSE

IMMERSION *n* form of baptism in which part or the whole of a person's body is submerged in the water

IMMERSIVE *adj* providing information or stimulation for a number of senses, not only sight and sound

IMMESH *variant of* > ENMESH

IMMESHED > IMMESH

IMMESHES > IMMESH

IMMESHING > IMMESH

IMMEW *vb* confine

IMMEWED > IMMEW

IMMEWING > IMMEW

IMMEWS > IMMEW

IMMIES > IMMY

IMMIGRANT *n* person who comes to a foreign country in order to settle there

IMMIGRATE *vb* come to a place or country of which one is not a native in order to settle there

IMMINENCE > IMMINENT

IMMINENCY > IMMINENT

IMMINENT *adj* about to happen

IMMINGLE *vb* blend or mix together

IMMINGLED > IMMINGLE

IMMINGLES > IMMINGLE

IMMINUTE *adj* reduced

IMMISSION *n* insertion

IMMIT *vb* insert

IMMITS > IMMIT

IMMITTED > IMMIT

IMMITTING > IMMIT

IMMIX *vb* mix in

IMMIXED > IMMIX

IMMIXES > IMMIX

IMMIXING > IMMIX

IMMIXTURE > IMMIX

IMMOBILE *adj* not moving

IMMODEST *adj* behaving in an indecent or improper manner

IMMODESTY > IMMODEST

IMMOLATE *vb* kill as a sacrifice

IMMOLATED > IMMOLATE

IMMOLATES > IMMOLATE

IMMOLATOR > IMMOLATE

IMMOMENT *adj* of no value

IMMORAL *adj* morally wrong, corrupt

IMMORALLY > IMMORAL

IMMORTAL *adj* living forever ⊳ *n* person whose fame will last for all time

IMMORTALS > IMMORTAL

IMMOTILE *adj* not capable of moving spontaneously and independently

IMMOVABLE *adj* unable to be moved

IMMOVABLY > IMMOVABLE

IMMUNE *adj* protected against a specific disease ⊳ *n* immune person or animal

IMMUNER > IMMUNE

IMMUNES > IMMUNE

IMMUNEST > IMMUNE

IMMUNISE *same as* > IMMUNIZE

IMMUNISED > IMMUNISE

IMMUNISER > IMMUNISE

IMMUNISES > IMMUNISE

IMMUNITY *n* ability to resist disease

IMMUNIZE *vb* make immune to a disease

IMMUNIZED > IMMUNIZE

IMMUNIZER > IMMUNIZE

IMMUNIZES > IMMUNIZE

IMMUNOGEN *n* any substance that evokes an immune response

IMMURE *vb* imprison

IMMURED > IMMURE

IMMURES > IMMURE

IMMURING > IMMURE

IMMUTABLE *adj* unchangeable

IMMUTABLY > IMMUTABLE

IMMY *n* image-orthicon camera

IMP *n* (in folklore) creature with magical powers ⊳ *vb* method of repairing the wing of a hawk or falcon

IMPACABLE *adj* incapable of being placated or pacified

IMPACT *n* strong effect ⊳ *vb* have a strong effect on

IMPACTED > IMPACT

IMPACTER > IMPACT

IMPACTERS > IMPACT

IMPACTFUL > IMPACT

IMPACTING > IMPACT

IMPACTION > IMPACT

IMPACTITE *n* glassy rock formed in a meteor collision

IMPACTIVE *adj* of or relating to a physical impact

IMPACTOR > IMPACT

IMPACTORS > IMPACT

IMPACTS > IMPACT

IMPAINT *vb* paint

IMPAINTED > IMPAINT

IMPAINTS > IMPAINT

IMPAIR *vb* weaken or damage

IMPAIRED > IMPAIR

IMPAIRER > IMPAIR

IMPAIRERS > IMPAIR

IMPAIRING > IMPAIR

IMPAIRS > IMPAIR

IMPALA *n* southern African antelope

IMPALAS > IMPALA

IMPALE *vb* pierce with a sharp object

IMPALED > IMPALE

IMPALER > IMPALE

IMPALERS > IMPALE

IMPALES > IMPALE

IMPALING > IMPALE

IMPANATE *adj* embodied in bread

IMPANEL variant spelling (esp US) of > EMPANEL

IMPANELED > IMPANEL

IMPANELS > IMPANEL

IMPANNEL same as > IMPANEL

IMPANNELS > IMPANNEL

IMPARITY less common word for > DISPARITY

IMPARK vb make into a park

IMPARKED > IMPARK

IMPARKING > IMPARK

IMPARKS > IMPARK

IMPARL vb parley

IMPARLED > IMPARL

IMPARLING > IMPARL

IMPARLS > IMPARL

IMPART vb communicate (information)

IMPARTED > IMPART

IMPARTER > IMPART

IMPARTERS > IMPART

IMPARTIAL adj not favouring one side or the other

IMPARTING > IMPART

IMPARTS > IMPART

IMPASSE n situation in which progress is impossible

IMPASSES > IMPASSE

IMPASSION vb arouse the passions of

IMPASSIVE adj showing no emotion, calm

IMPASTE vb apply paint thickly to

IMPASTED > IMPASTE

IMPASTES > IMPASTE

IMPASTING > IMPASTE

IMPASTO n technique of applying paint thickly ▷ vb apply impasto

IMPASTOED > IMPASTO

IMPASTOS > IMPASTO

IMPATIENS n plant such as balsam, touch-me-not, and busy Lizzie

IMPATIENT adj irritable at any delay or difficulty

IMPAVE vb set in a pavement

IMPAVED > IMPAVE

IMPAVES > IMPAVE

IMPAVID adj fearless

IMPAVIDLY > IMPAVID

IMPAVING > IMPAVE

IMPAWN vb pawn

IMPAWNED > IMPAWN

IMPAWNING > IMPAWN

IMPAWNS > IMPAWN

IMPEACH vb charge with a serious crime against the state

IMPEACHED > IMPEACH

IMPEACHER > IMPEACH

IMPEACHES > IMPEACH

IMPEARL vb adorn with pearls

IMPEARLED > IMPEARL

IMPEARLS > IMPEARL

IMPECCANT adj not sinning

IMPED > IMP

IMPEDANCE n measure of the opposition to the flow of an alternating current

IMPEDE vb hinder in action or progress

IMPEDED > IMPEDE

IMPEDER > IMPEDE

IMPEDERS > IMPEDE

IMPEDES > IMPEDE

IMPEDING > IMPEDE

IMPEDOR n component that offers impedance

IMPEDORS > IMPEDOR

IMPEL vb push or force (someone) to do something

IMPELLED > IMPEL

IMPELLENT > IMPEL

IMPELLER n vaned rotating disc of a centrifugal pump, compressor, etc

IMPELLERS > IMPELLER

IMPELLING > IMPEL

IMPELLOR same as > IMPELLER

IMPELLORS > IMPELLOR

IMPELS > IMPEL

IMPEND vb be about to happen

IMPENDED > IMPEND

IMPENDENT adj impending; threatening

IMPENDING > IMPEND

IMPENDS > IMPEND

IMPENNATE adj (of birds) lacking true functional wings or feathers

IMPERATOR n (in imperial Rome) a title of the emperor

IMPERFECT adj having faults or mistakes ▷ n imperfect tense

IMPERIA > IMPERIUM

IMPERIAL adj of or like an empire or emperor ▷ n wine bottle holding the equivalent of eight normal bottles

IMPERIALS > IMPERIAL

IMPERIL vb put in danger

IMPERILED > IMPERIL

IMPERILS > IMPERIL

IMPERIOUS adj proud and domineering

IMPERIUM n supreme power of Roman consuls and emperors

IMPERIUMS > IMPERIUM

IMPETICOS vb put in a pocket

IMPETIGO n contagious skin disease

IMPETIGOS > IMPETIGO

IMPETRATE vb supplicate or entreat for, esp by prayer

IMPETUOUS adj done or acting without thought, rash

IMPETUS n incentive, impulse

IMPETUSES > IMPETUS

IMPHEE n African sorghum plant

IMPHEES > IMPHEE

IMPI n group of Zulu warriors

IMPIES > IMPI

IMPIETIES > IMPIETY

IMPIETY n lack of respect or religious reverence

IMPING > IMP

IMPINGE vb affect or restrict

IMPINGED > IMPINGE

IMPINGENT adj striking against or upon

IMPINGER > IMPINGE

IMPINGERS > IMPINGE

IMPINGES > IMPINGE

IMPINGING > IMPINGE

IMPINGS > IMP

IMPIOUS adj showing a lack of respect or reverence

IMPIOUSLY > IMPIOUS

IMPIS > IMPI

IMPISH adj mischievous

IMPISHLY > IMPISH

IMPLANT n something put into someone's body ▷ vb put (something) into someone's body

IMPLANTED > IMPLANT

IMPLANTER > IMPLANT

IMPLANTS > IMPLANT

IMPLATE vb sheathe

IMPLATED > IMPLATE

IMPLATES > IMPLATE

IMPLATING > IMPLATE

IMPLEACH vb intertwine

IMPLEAD vb sue or prosecute

IMPLEADED > IMPLEAD

IMPLEADER > IMPLEAD

IMPLEADS > IMPLEAD

IMPLED > IMPLEAD

IMPLEDGE vb pledge

IMPLEDGED > IMPLEDGE

IMPLEDGES > IMPLEDGE

IMPLEMENT vb carry out (instructions etc) ▷ n tool, instrument

IMPLETE vb fill

IMPLETED > IMPLETE

IMPLETES > IMPLETE

IMPLETING > IMPLETE

IMPLETION > IMPLETE

IMPLEX n part of an arthropod

IMPLEXES > IMPLEX

IMPLEXION n complication

IMPLICATE vb show to be involved, esp in a crime

IMPLICIT adj expressed indirectly

IMPLICITY > IMPLICIT

IMPLIED adj hinted at or suggested

IMPLIEDLY > IMPLIED

IMPLIES > IMPLY

IMPLODE vb collapse inwards

IMPLODED > IMPLODE

IMPLODENT n sound of an implosion

IMPLODES > IMPLODE

IMPLODING > IMPLODE

IMPLORE vb beg earnestly

IMPLORED > IMPLORE

IMPLORER > IMPLORE

IMPLORERS > IMPLORE

IMPLORES > IMPLORE

IMPLORING > IMPLORE

IMPLOSION n act or process of imploding

IMPLOSIVE adj consonant pronounced in a particular way

IMPLUNGE vb submerge

IMPLUNGED > IMPLUNGE

IMPLUNGES > IMPLUNGE

IMPLUVIA > IMPLUVIUM

IMPLUVIUM n rain-filled water tank

IMPLY vb indicate by hinting, suggest

IMPLYING > IMPLY

IMPOCKET vb put in a pocket

IMPOCKETS > IMPOCKET

IMPOLDER vb make into a polder

IMPOLDERS > IMPOLDER

IMPOLICY n act or an instance of being injudicious or impolitic

IMPOLITE adj showing bad manners

IMPOLITER > IMPOLITE

IMPOLITIC adj unwise or inadvisable

IMPONE vb impose

IMPONED > IMPONE

IMPONENT n person who imposes a duty, etc

IMPONENTS > IMPONENT

IMPONES > IMPONE

IMPONING > IMPONE

IMPOROUS adj not porous

IMPORT vb bring in (goods) from another country ▷ n something imported

IMPORTANT adj of great significance or value

IMPORTED > IMPORT

IMPORTER > IMPORT

IMPORTERS > IMPORT

IMPORTING > IMPORT

IMPORTS > IMPORT

IMPORTUNE vb harass with persistent requests

IMPOSABLE > IMPOSE

IMPOSE vb force the acceptance of

IMPOSED > IMPOSE

IMPOSER > IMPOSE

IMPOSERS > IMPOSE

IMPOSES > IMPOSE

IMPOSEX n acquisition by female organisms of male characteristics

IMPOSEXES > IMPOSEX
IMPOSING adj grand, impressive
IMPOST n tax, esp a customs duty ▷ vb classify (imported goods) according to the duty payable on them
IMPOSTED > IMPOST
IMPOSTER > IMPOST
IMPOSTERS > IMPOST
IMPOSTING > IMPOST
IMPOSTOR n person who cheats or swindles by pretending to be someone else
IMPOSTORS > IMPOSTOR
IMPOSTS > IMPOST
IMPOSTUME archaic word for > ABSCESS
IMPOSTURE n deception, esp by pretending to be someone else
IMPOT n slang term for the act of imposing
IMPOTENCE > IMPOTENT
IMPOTENCY > IMPOTENT
IMPOTENT adj powerless ▷ n one who is impotent
IMPOTENTS > IMPOTENT
IMPOTS > IMPOT
IMPOUND vb take legal possession of, confiscate
IMPOUNDED > IMPOUND
IMPOUNDER > IMPOUND
IMPOUNDS > IMPOUND
IMPOWER less common spelling of > EMPOWER
IMPOWERED > IMPOWER
IMPOWERS > IMPOWER
IMPRECATE vb swear, curse, or blaspheme
IMPRECISE adj inexact or inaccurate
IMPREGN vb impregnate
IMPREGNED > IMPREGN
IMPREGNS > IMPREGN
IMPRESA n heraldic device
IMPRESARI n impresarios
IMPRESAS > IMPRESA
IMPRESE same as > IMPRESA
IMPRESES > IMPRESE
IMPRESS vb affect strongly, usu favourably ▷ n impressing
IMPRESSE n heraldic device
IMPRESSED > IMPRESS
IMPRESSER > IMPRESS
IMPRESSES > IMPRESS
IMPREST n fund of cash used to pay incidental expenses
IMPRESTS > IMPREST
IMPRIMIS adv in the first place
IMPRINT n mark made by printing or stamping ▷ vb produce (a mark) by printing or stamping
IMPRINTED > IMPRINT

IMPRINTER > IMPRINT
IMPRINTS > IMPRINT
IMPRISON vb put in prison
IMPRISONS > IMPRISON
IMPRO n short for improvisation
IMPROBITY n dishonesty or wickedness
IMPROMPTU adj without planning or preparation ▷ adv in a spontaneous or improvised way ▷ n short piece of instrumental music resembling improvisation
IMPROPER adj indecent
IMPROS > IMPRO
IMPROV n improvisational comedy
IMPROVE vb make or become better
IMPROVED > IMPROVE
IMPROVER > IMPROVE
IMPROVERS > IMPROVE
IMPROVES > IMPROVE
IMPROVING > IMPROVE
IMPROVISE vb make use of whatever materials are available
IMPROVS > IMPROV
IMPRUDENT adj not sensible or wise
IMPS > IMP
IMPSONITE n asphaltite compound
IMPUDENCE n quality of being impudent
IMPUDENCY same as > IMPUDENCE
IMPUDENT adj cheeky, disrespectful
IMPUGN vb challenge the truth or validity of
IMPUGNED > IMPUGN
IMPUGNER > IMPUGN
IMPUGNERS > IMPUGN
IMPUGNING > IMPUGN
IMPUGNS > IMPUGN
IMPULSE vb give an impulse to ▷ n sudden urge to do something
IMPULSED > IMPULSE
IMPULSES > IMPULSE
IMPULSING > IMPULSE
IMPULSION n act of impelling or the state of being impelled
IMPULSIVE adj acting or done without careful consideration
IMPUNDULU n mythical bird associated with witchcraft, frequently manifested as the secretary bird
IMPUNITY n exemption or immunity from punishment or recrimination
IMPURE adj having dirty or unwanted substances mixed in
IMPURELY > IMPURE
IMPURER > IMPURE
IMPUREST > IMPURE
IMPURITY n impure element or thing

IMPURPLE vb colour purple
IMPURPLED > IMPURPLE
IMPURPLES > IMPURPLE
IMPUTABLE adj capable of being imputed
IMPUTABLY > IMPUTABLE
IMPUTE vb attribute responsibility to
IMPUTED > IMPUTE
IMPUTER > IMPUTE
IMPUTERS > IMPUTE
IMPUTES > IMPUTE
IMPUTING > IMPUTE
IMSHI interj go away!
IMSHY same as > IMSHI
IN prep indicating position inside, state or situation, etc ▷ adv indicating position inside, entry into, etc ▷ adj fashionable ▷ n way of approaching or befriending a person ▷ vb take in
INABILITY n lack of means or skill to do something
INACTION n act of doing nothing
INACTIONS > INACTION
INACTIVE adj idle
INAIDABLE adj beyond help
INAMORATA n woman with whom one is in love
INAMORATI > INAMORATO
INAMORATO n man with whom one is in love
INANE adj senseless, silly ▷ n something that is inane
INANELY > INANE
INANENESS > INANE
INANER > INANE
INANES > INANE
INANEST > INANE
INANGA n common type of New Zealand grass tree
INANGAS > INANGA
INANIMATE adj not living
INANITIES > INANITY
INANITION n exhaustion or weakness, as from lack of food
INANITY n lack of intelligence or imagination
INAPT adj not apt or fitting
INAPTER > INAPT
INAPTEST > INAPT
INAPTLY > INAPT
INAPTNESS > INAPT
INARABLE adj not arable
INARCH vb graft (a plant)
INARCHED > INARCH
INARCHES > INARCH
INARCHING > INARCH
INARM vb embrace
INARMED > INARM
INARMING > INARM
INARMS > INARM

INASMUCH conj as in inasmuch as , in view of the fact that
INAUDIBLE adj not loud enough to be heard
INAUDIBLY > INAUDIBLE
INAUGURAL adj of or for an inauguration ▷ n speech made at an inauguration
INAURATE adj gilded ▷ vb cover in gold
INAURATED > INAURATE
INAURATES > INAURATE
INBEING n existence in something else
INBEINGS > INBEING
INBENT adj bent inwards
INBOARD adj (of a boat's engine) inside the hull ▷ adv within the sides of or towards the centre of a vessel or aircraft
INBOARDS same as > INBOARD
INBORN adj existing from birth, natural
INBOUND vb pass into the playing area from outside it ▷ adj coming in
INBOUNDED > INBOUND
INBOUNDS > INBOUND
INBOX n folder which stores incoming email messages
INBOXES > INBOX
INBREAK n breaking in
INBREAKS > INBREAK
INBREATHE vb infuse or imbue
INBRED n inbred animal ▷ adj produced as a result of inbreeding
INBREDS > INBRED
INBREED vb breed from closely related individuals
INBREEDER > INBREED
INBREEDS > INBREED
INBRING vb bring in
INBRINGS > INBRING
INBROUGHT > INBRING
INBUILT adj present from the start
INBURNING adj burning within
INBURST n irruption ▷ vb burst in
INBURSTS > INBURST
INBY adv into the house or an inner room ▷ adj located near or nearest to the house
INBYE adv near the house
INCAGE vb confine in or as in a cage
INCAGED > INCAGE
INCAGES > INCAGE
INCAGING > INCAGE
INCANT vb chant (a spell)
INCANTED > INCANT
INCANTING > INCANT
INCANTS > INCANT
INCAPABLE adj unable (to do something)
INCAPABLY > INCAPABLE

INCARNATE *adj* in human form ▷ *vb* give a bodily or concrete form to

INCASE *variant spelling of* > ENCASE

INCASED > INCASE

INCASES > INCASE

INCASING > INCASE

INCAUTION *n* act of not being cautious

INCAVE *vb* hide

INCAVED > INCAVE

INCAVES > INCAVE

INCAVI > INCAVO

INCAVING > INCAVE

INCAVO *n* incised part of a carving

INCEDE *vb* advance

INCEDED > INCEDE

INCEDES > INCEDE

INCEDING > INCEDE

INCEL *n* involuntary celibate

INCELS > INCEL

INCENSE *vb* make very angry ▷ *n* substance that gives off a perfume when burned

INCENSED > INCENSE

INCENSER *n* incense burner

INCENSERS > INCENSER

INCENSES > INCENSE

INCENSING > INCENSE

INCENSOR *n* incense burner

INCENSORS > INCENSOR

INCENSORY *less common name for* > CENSER

INCENT *vb* provide incentive

INCENTED > INCENT

INCENTER *same as* > INCENTRE

INCENTERS > INCENTER

INCENTING > INCENT

INCENTIVE *n* something that encourages effort or action ▷ *adj* encouraging greater effort

INCENTRE *n* centre of an inscribed circle

INCENTRES > INCENTRE

INCENTS > INCENT

INCEPT *vb* (of organisms) to ingest (food) ▷ *n* rudimentary organ

INCEPTED > INCEPT

INCEPTING > INCEPT

INCEPTION *n* beginning

INCEPTIVE *adj* beginning ▷ *n* type of verb

INCEPTOR > INCEPT

INCEPTORS > INCEPT

INCEPTS > INCEPT

INCERTAIN *archaic form of* > UNCERTAIN

INCESSANT *adj* never stopping

INCEST *n* sexual intercourse between two closely related people

INCESTS > INCEST

INCH *n* unit of length ▷ *vb* move slowly and gradually

INCHASE *same as* > ENCHASE

INCHASED > INCHASE

INCHASES > INCHASE

INCHASING > INCHASE

INCHED > INCH

INCHER *n* something measuring given amount of inches

INCHERS > INCHER

INCHES > INCH

INCHING > INCH

INCHMEAL *adv* gradually

INCHOATE *adj* just begun and not yet properly developed ▷ *vb* begin

INCHOATED > INCHOATE

INCHOATES > INCHOATE

INCHPIN *n* cervine sweetbread

INCHPINS > INCHPIN

INCHTAPE *n* measuring tape marked out in inches

INCHTAPES > INCHTAPE

INCHWORM *n* larva of a type of moth

INCHWORMS > INCHWORM

INCIDENCE *n* extent or frequency of occurrence

INCIDENT *n* something that happens ▷ *adj* related (to) or dependent (on)

INCIDENTS > INCIDENT

INCIPIENT *adj* just starting to appear or happen

INCIPIT *n* Latin introductory phrase

INCIPITS > INCIPIT

INCISAL *adj* relating to the cutting edge of incisors and cuspids

INCISE *vb* cut into with a sharp tool

INCISED > INCISE

INCISES > INCISE

INCISING > INCISE

INCISION *n* cut, esp one made during a surgical operation

INCISIONS > INCISION

INCISIVE *adj* direct and forceful

INCISOR *n* front tooth, used for biting into food

INCISORS > INCISOR

INCISORY > INCISOR

INCISURAL > INCISURE

INCISURE *n* incision or notch in an organ or part

INCISURES > INCISURE

INCITABLE > INCITE

INCITANT *n* something that incites

INCITANTS > INCITANT

INCITE *vb* stir up, provoke

INCITED > INCITE

INCITER > INCITE

INCITERS > INCITE

INCITES > INCITE

INCITING > INCITE

INCIVIL *archaic form of* > UNCIVIL

INCIVISM *n* neglect of a citizen's duties

INCIVISMS > INCIVISM

INCLASP *vb* clasp

INCLASPED > INCLASP

INCLASPS > INCLASP

INCLE *same as* > INKLE

INCLEMENT *adj* (of weather) stormy or severe

INCLES > INCLE

INCLINE *vb* lean, slope ▷ *n* slope

INCLINED *adj* having a disposition

INCLINER > INCLINE

INCLINERS > INCLINE

INCLINES > INCLINE

INCLINING > INCLINE

INCLIP *vb* embrace

INCLIPPED > INCLIP

INCLIPS > INCLIP

INCLOSE *less common spelling of* > ENCLOSE

INCLOSED > INCLOSE

INCLOSER > INCLOSE

INCLOSERS > INCLOSE

INCLOSES > INCLOSE

INCLOSING > INCLOSE

INCLOSURE > INCLOSE

INCLUDE *vb* have as part of the whole

INCLUDED *adj* (of the stamens or pistils of a flower) not protruding beyond the corolla

INCLUDES > INCLUDE

INCLUDING > INCLUDE

INCLUSION *n* including or being included

INCLUSIVE *adj* including everything (specified)

INCOG *n* incognito

INCOGNITA *n* female who is in disguise or unknown

INCOGNITO *adv* having adopted a false identity ▷ *n* false identity ▷ *adj* under an assumed name or appearance

INCOGS > INCOG

INCOME *n* amount of money earned

INCOMER *n* person who comes to a place in which they were not born

INCOMERS > INCOMER

INCOMES > INCOME

INCOMING *adj* coming in ▷ *n* act of coming in

INCOMINGS > INCOMING

INCOMMODE *vb* cause inconvenience to

INCOMPACT *adj* not compact

INCONDITE *adj* poorly constructed or composed

INCONIE *adj* fine or delicate

INCONNU *n* whitefish of Arctic waters

INCONNUE *n* unknown woman

INCONNUES > INCONNUE

INCONNUS > INCONNU

INCONY *adj* fine or delicate

INCORPSE *vb* incorporate

INCORPSED > INCORPSE

INCORPSES > INCORPSE

INCORRECT *adj* wrong

INCORRUPT *adj* free from corruption

INCREASE *vb* make or become greater in size, number, etc ▷ *n* rise in number, size, etc

INCREASED > INCREASE

INCREASER > INCREASE

INCREASES > INCREASE

INCREATE *adj* (esp of gods) never having been created

INCREMATE *vb* cremate

INCREMENT *n* increase in money or value, esp a regular salary increase

INCRETION *n* direct secretion into the bloodstream, esp of a hormone from an endocrine gland

INCRETORY > INCRETION

INCROSS *n* variation produced by inbreeding ▷ *vb* produce by inbreeding

INCROSSED > INCROSS

INCROSSES > INCROSS

INCRUST *same as* > ENCRUST

INCRUSTED > INCRUST

INCRUSTS > INCRUST

INCUBATE *vb* (of a bird) hatch (eggs) by sitting on them

INCUBATED > INCUBATE

INCUBATES > INCUBATE

INCUBATOR *n* heated enclosed apparatus for rearing premature babies

INCUBI > INCUBUS

INCUBOUS *adj* having overlapping leaves

INCUBUS *n* (in folklore) type of demon

INCUBUSES > INCUBUS

INCUDAL > INCUS

INCUDATE > INCUS

INCUDES > INCUS

INCULCATE *vb* fix in someone's mind by constant repetition

INCULPATE *vb* cause (someone) to be blamed for a crime

INCULT *adj* (of land) uncultivated

INCUMBENT *n* person who holds a particular

office or position ▷ *adj* morally binding as a duty

INCUMBER *less common spelling of* > ENCUMBER

INCUMBERS > INCUMBER

INCUNABLE *n* early printed book

INCUR *vb* cause (something unpleasant) to happen

INCURABLE *adj* not able to be cured ▷ *n* person with an incurable disease

INCURABLY > INCURABLE

INCURIOUS *adj* showing no curiosity or interest

INCURRED > INCUR

INCURRENT *adj* (of anatomical ducts, tubes, channels, etc) having an inward flow

INCURRING > INCUR

INCURS > INCUR

INCURSION *n* sudden brief invasion

INCURSIVE > INCURSION

INCURVATE *vb* curve or cause to curve inwards ▷ *adj* curved inwards

INCURVE *vb* curve or cause to curve inwards

INCURVED > INCURVE

INCURVES > INCURVE

INCURVING > INCURVE

INCURVITY > INCURVE

INCUS *n* bone in the ear of mammals

INCUSE *n* design stamped or hammered onto a coin ▷ *vb* impress (a design) in a coin ▷ *adj* stamped or hammered onto a coin

INCUSED > INCUSE

INCUSES > INCUSE

INCUSING > INCUSE

INCUT *adj* cut or etched in ▷ *n* indent in rock used as a foothold

INCUTS > INCUT

INDABA *n* (among South Africans) a meeting to discuss a serious topic

INDABAS > INDABA

INDAGATE *vb* investigate

INDAGATED > INDAGATE

INDAGATES > INDAGATE

INDAGATOR > INDAGATE

INDAMIN *same as* > INDAMINE

INDAMINE *n* organic base used in the production of the dye safranine

INDAMINES > INDAMINE

INDAMINS > INDAMIN

INDART *vb* dart in

INDARTED > INDART

INDARTING > INDART

INDARTS > INDART

INDEBTED *adj* owing gratitude for help or favours

INDECENCY *n* state or quality of being indecent

INDECENT *adj* morally offensive

INDECORUM *n* indecorous behaviour or speech

INDEED *adv* really, certainly ▷ *interj* expression of indignation or surprise

INDEEDY *interj* indeed

INDELIBLE *adj* impossible to erase or remove

INDELIBLY > INDELIBLE

INDEMNIFY *vb* secure against loss, damage, or liability

INDEMNITY *n* insurance against loss or damage

INDENE *n* colourless liquid hydrocarbon

INDENES > INDENE

INDENT *vb* make a dent in

INDENTED > INDENT

INDENTER > INDENT

INDENTERS > INDENT

INDENTING > INDENT

INDENTION *n* space between a margin and the start of the line of text

INDENTOR > INDENT

INDENTORS > INDENT

INDENTS > INDENT

INDENTURE *n* contract, esp one binding an apprentice to his or her employer ▷ *vb* bind (an apprentice) by indenture

INDEVOUT *adj* not devout

INDEW *same as* > INDUE

INDEWED > INDEW

INDEWING > INDEW

INDEWS > INDEW

INDEX *n* alphabetical list of subjects dealt with in a book ▷ *vb* provide (a book) with an index

INDEXABLE > INDEX

INDEXAL > INDEX

INDEXED > INDEX

INDEXER > INDEX

INDEXERS > INDEX

INDEXES > INDEX

INDEXICAL *adj* arranged as or relating to an index or indexes ▷ *n* term whose reference depends on the context of utterance

INDEXING > INDEX

INDEXINGS > INDEX

INDEXLESS > INDEX

INDIA *n* code word for the letter I

INDIAS > INDIA

INDICAN *n* compound secreted in the urine

INDICANS > INDICAN

INDICANT *n* something that indicates

INDICANTS > INDICANT

INDICATE *vb* be a sign or symptom of

INDICATED > INDICATE

INDICATES > INDICATE

INDICATOR *n* something acting as a sign or indication

INDICES *plural of* > INDEX

INDICIA > INDICIUM

INDICIAL > INDICIUM

INDICIAS > INDICIUM

INDICIUM *n* notice

INDICIUMS > INDICIUM

INDICT *vb* formally charge with a crime

INDICTED > INDICT

INDICTEE > INDICT

INDICTEES > INDICT

INDICTER > INDICT

INDICTERS > INDICT

INDICTING > INDICT

INDICTION *n* recurring fiscal period of 15 years, often used as a unit for dating events

INDICTOR > INDICT

INDICTORS > INDICT

INDICTS > INDICT

INDIE *adj* (of rock music) released by an independent record label ▷ *n* independent record company

INDIES > INDIE

INDIGEN *same as* > INDIGENE

INDIGENCE > INDIGENT

INDIGENCY > INDIGENT

INDIGENE *n* indigenous person, animal, or thing

INDIGENES > INDIGENE

INDIGENS > INDIGEN

INDIGENT *adj* extremely poor ▷ *n* impoverished person

INDIGENTS > INDIGENT

INDIGEST *n* undigested mass ▷ *vb* suffer indigestion

INDIGESTS > INDIGEST

INDIGN *adj* undeserving

INDIGNANT *adj* feeling or showing indignation

INDIGNIFY *vb* treat in a humiliating manner

INDIGNITY *n* embarrassing or humiliating treatment

INDIGNLY > INDIGN

INDIGO *adj* deep violet-blue ▷ *n* dye of this colour

INDIGOES > INDIGO

INDIGOID *adj* of, concerned with, or resembling indigo or its blue colour ▷ *n* any of a number of synthetic dyes or pigments related in chemical structure to indigo

INDIGOIDS > INDIGOID

INDIGOS > INDIGO

INDIGOTIC > INDIGO

INDIGOTIN *same as* > INDIGO

INDINAVIR *n* drug used to treat AIDS

INDIRECT *adj* done or caused by someone or something else

INDIRUBIN *n* isomer of indigotin

INDISPOSE *vb* make unwilling or opposed

INDITE *vb* write

INDITED > INDITE

INDITER > INDITE

INDITERS > INDITE

INDITES > INDITE

INDITING > INDITE

INDIUM *n* soft silvery-white metallic element

INDIUMS > INDIUM

INDIVIDUA *pl n* indivisible entities

INDOCIBLE *same as* > INDOCILE

INDOCILE *adj* difficult to discipline or instruct

INDOL *same as* > INDOLE

INDOLE *n* crystalline heterocyclic compound

INDOLENCE > INDOLENT

INDOLENCY *n* laziness

INDOLENT *adj* lazy

INDOLES > INDOLE

INDOLS > INDOL

INDOOR *adj* inside a building

INDOORS *adv* inside or into a building

INDORSE *variant spelling of* > ENDORSE

INDORSED > INDORSE

INDORSEE *n* the person to whom a note or bill is indorsed

INDORSEES > INDORSE

INDORSER > INDORSE

INDORSERS > INDORSE

INDORSES > INDORSE

INDORSING > INDORSE

INDORSOR > INDORSE

INDORSORS > INDORSE

INDOW *archaic variant of* > ENDOW

INDOWED > INDOW

INDOWING > INDOW

INDOWS > INDOW

INDOXYL *n* water-soluble crystalline compound

INDOXYLS > INDOXYL

INDRAFT *same as* > INDRAUGHT

INDRAFTS > INDRAFT

INDRAUGHT *n* act of drawing or pulling in

INDRAWN *adj* drawn or pulled in

INDRENCH *vb* submerge

INDRI *same as* > INDRIS

INDRIS *n* large lemuroid primate

INDRISES > INDRIS

INDUBIOUS adj certain

INDUCE vb persuade or influence

INDUCED > INDUCE

INDUCER > INDUCE

INDUCERS > INDUCE

INDUCES > INDUCE

INDUCIAE n time limit for a defendant to appear in court

INDUCIBLE > INDUCE

INDUCING > INDUCE

INDUCT vb formally install (someone) in office

INDUCTED > INDUCT

INDUCTEE n military conscript

INDUCTEES > INDUCTEE

INDUCTILE adj not ductile, pliant, or yielding

INDUCTING > INDUCT

INDUCTION n the act of inducing

INDUCTIVE adj of or using induction

INDUCTOR n device designed to create inductance in an electrical circuit

INDUCTORS > INDUCTOR

INDUCTS > INDUCT

INDUE variant spelling of > ENDUE

INDUED > INDUE

INDUES > INDUE

INDUING > INDUE

INDULGE vb allow oneself pleasure

INDULGED > INDULGE

INDULGENT adj kind or lenient, often to excess

INDULGER > INDULGE

INDULGERS > INDULGE

INDULGES > INDULGE

INDULGING > INDULGE

INDULIN same as > INDULINE

INDULINE n any of a class of blue dyes obtained from aniline and aminoazobenzene

INDULINES > INDULINE

INDULINS > INDULIN

INDULT n type of faculty granted by the Holy See

INDULTS > INDULT

INDUMENTA pl n coverings of feather, fur, etc

INDUNA n (in South Africa) a Black African overseer

INDUNAS > INDUNA

INDURATE vb make or become hard or callous ▷ adj hardened, callous, or unfeeling

INDURATED > INDURATE

INDURATES > INDURATE

INDUSIA > INDUSIUM

INDUSIAL > INDUSIUM

INDUSIATE adj covered in indusia

INDUSIUM n outgrowth on the undersurface of fern leaves

INDUSTRY n manufacture of goods

INDUVIAE pl n withered leaves

INDUVIAL > INDUVIAE

INDUVIATE > INDUVIAE

INDWELL vb (of a spirit, principle, etc) to inhabit

INDWELLER > INDWELL

INDWELLS > INDWELL

INDWELT > INDWELL

INDYREF n independence referendum

INDYREFS > INDYREF

INEARTH poetic word for > BURY

INEARTHED > INEARTH

INEARTHS > INEARTH

INEBRIANT adj causing intoxication, esp drunkenness ▷ n something that inebriates

INEBRIATE adj habitually drunk ▷ n person who is habitually drunk ▷ vb make drunk

INEBRIETY > INEBRIATE

INEBRIOUS adj drunk

INEDIBLE adj not fit to be eaten

INEDIBLY > INEDIBLE

INEDITA pl n unpublished writings

INEDITED adj not edited

INEFFABLE adj too great for words

INEFFABLY > INEFFABLE

INELASTIC adj not elastic

INELEGANT adj lacking elegance or refinement

INEPT adj clumsy, lacking skill

INEPTER > INEPT

INEPTEST > INEPT

INEPTLY > INEPT

INEPTNESS > INEPT

INEQUABLE adj unfair

INEQUITY n injustice or unfairness

INERM adj without thorns

INERMOUS same as > INERM

INERRABLE adj not liable to error ▷ n person or thing that is incapable of error

INERRABLY > INERRABLE

INERRANCY > INERRABLE

INERRANT same as > INERRABLE

INERT n inert thing ▷ adj without the power of motion or resistance

INERTER > INERT

INERTEST > INERT

INERTIA n feeling of unwillingness to do anything

INERTIAE > INERTIA

INERTIAL > INERTIA

INERTIAS > INERTIA

INERTLY > INERT

INERTNESS > INERT

INERTS > INERT

INERUDITE adj not erudite

INESSIVE n grammatical case in Finnish

INESSIVES > INESSIVE

INEXACT adj not exact or accurate

INEXACTLY > INEXACT

INEXPERT n unskilled person ▷ adj lacking skill

INEXPERTS > INEXPERT

INFALL vb move towards (something) under the influence of gravity

INFALLING > INFALL

INFALLS > INFALL

INFAME vb defame

INFAMED > INFAME

INFAMES > INFAME

INFAMIES > INFAMY

INFAMING > INFAME

INFAMISE same as > INFAMIZE

INFAMISED > INFAMISE

INFAMISES > INFAMISE

INFAMIZE vb make infamous

INFAMIZED > INFAMIZE

INFAMIZES > INFAMIZE

INFAMOUS adj well-known for something bad

INFAMY n state of being infamous

INFANCIES > INFANCY

INFANCY n early childhood

INFANT n very young child ▷ adj of, relating to, or designed for young children

INFANTA n (formerly) daughter of a king of Spain or Portugal

INFANTAS > INFANTA

INFANTE n (formerly) any son of a king of Spain or Portugal, except the heir to the throne

INFANTEER n soldier belonging to the infantry

INFANTES > INFANTE

INFANTILE adj childish

INFANTINE adj infantile

INFANTRY n soldiers who fight on foot

INFANTS > INFANT

INFARCT n localized area of dead tissue ▷ vb obstruct the blood supply to part of a body

INFARCTED > INFARCT

INFARCTS > INFARCT

INFARE vb enter

INFARES > INFARE

INFATUATE vb inspire or fill with an intense and unreasoning passion ▷ n person who is infatuated

INFAUNA n fauna that lives in ocean and river beds

INFAUNAE > INFAUNA

INFAUNAL > INFAUNA

INFAUNAS > INFAUNA

INFAUST adj unlucky

INFECT vb affect with a disease ▷ adj contaminated or polluted with or as if with a disease

INFECTANT adj causing infection ▷ n thing that infects or causes infection

INFECTED > INFECT

INFECTER > INFECT

INFECTERS > INFECT

INFECTING > INFECT

INFECTION n infectious disease

INFECTIVE adj capable of causing infection

INFECTOR > INFECT

INFECTORS > INFECT

INFECTS > INFECT

INFECUND less common word for > INFERTILE

INFEED n action of supplying a machine with a material

INFEEDS > INFEED

INFEFT vb give possession of heritable property

INFEFTED > INFEFT

INFEFTING > INFEFT

INFEFTS > INFEFT

INFELT adj heartfelt

INFEOFF same as > ENFEOFF

INFEOFFED > INFEOFF

INFEOFFS > INFEOFF

INFER vb work out from evidence

INFERABLE > INFER

INFERABLY > INFER

INFERE adv together

INFERENCE n act or process of reaching a conclusion by reasoning from evidence

INFERIAE pl n offerings made to the spirits of the dead

INFERIBLE > INFER

INFERIOR adj lower in quality, position, or status ▷ n person of lower position or status

INFERIORS > INFERIOR

INFERNAL adj of hell

INFERNO n intense raging fire

INFERNOS > INFERNO

INFERRED > INFER

INFERRER > INFER

INFERRERS > INFER

INFERRING > INFER

INFERS > INFER

INFERTILE adj unable to produce offspring

INFEST vb inhabit or overrun in unpleasantly large numbers

INFESTANT n parasite
INFESTED > INFEST
INFESTER > INFEST
INFESTERS > INFEST
INFESTING > INFEST
INFESTS > INFEST
INFICETE adj not witty
INFIDEL n person with no religion ▷ adj of unbelievers or unbelief
INFIDELIC > INFIDEL
INFIDELS > INFIDEL
INFIELD n area of the field near the pitch
INFIELDER n player positioned in the infield
INFIELDS > INFIELD
INFIGHT vb box at close quarters
INFIGHTER > INFIGHT
INFIGHTS > INFIGHT
INFILL vb fill in ▷ n act of filling or closing gaps in something
INFILLED > INFILL
INFILLING > INFILL
INFILLS > INFILL
INFIMA > INFIMUM
INFIMUM n greatest lower bound
INFIMUMS > INFIMUM
INFINITE adj without any limit or end ▷ n something without any limit or end
INFINITES > INFINITE
INFINITY n endless space, time, or number
INFIRM vb make infirm ▷ adj physically or mentally weak
INFIRMARY n hospital
INFIRMED > INFIRM
INFIRMER > INFIRM
INFIRMEST > INFIRM
INFIRMING > INFIRM
INFIRMITY n state of being infirm
INFIRMLY > INFIRM
INFIRMS > INFIRM
INFIX vb fix firmly in ▷ n affix inserted into the middle of a word
INFIXED > INFIX
INFIXES > INFIX
INFIXING > INFIX
INFIXION > INFIX
INFIXIONS > INFIX
INFLAME vb make angry or excited
INFLAMED > INFLAME
INFLAMER > INFLAME
INFLAMERS > INFLAME
INFLAMES > INFLAME
INFLAMING > INFLAME
INFLATE vb expand by filling with air or gas
INFLATED > INFLATE
INFLATER > INFLATE
INFLATERS > INFLATE
INFLATES > INFLATE
INFLATING > INFLATE
INFLATION n act of inflating
INFLATIVE adj causing inflation
INFLATOR > INFLATE

INFLATORS > INFLATE
INFLATUS n act of breathing in
INFLECT vb change (the voice) in tone or pitch
INFLECTED > INFLECT
INFLECTOR > INFLECT
INFLECTS > INFLECT
INFLEXED adj curved or bent inwards and downwards towards the axis
INFLEXION n modulation of the voice
INFLEXURE same as > INFLEXION
INFLICT vb impose (something unpleasant) on
INFLICTED > INFLICT
INFLICTER > INFLICT
INFLICTOR > INFLICT
INFLICTS > INFLICT
INFLIGHT adj provided during flight in an aircraft
INFLOW n something, such as liquid or gas, that flows in ▷ vb flow in
INFLOWING same as > INFLOW
INFLOWS > INFLOW
INFLUENCE n effect of one person or thing on another ▷ vb have an effect on
INFLUENT adj flowing in ▷ n something flowing in, esp a tributary
INFLUENTS > INFLUENT
INFLUENZA n contagious viral disease causing headaches, muscle pains, and fever
INFLUX n arrival or entry of many people or things
INFLUXES > INFLUX
INFLUXION same as > INFLUX
INFO n information
INFOBAHN same as > INTERNET
INFOBAHNS > INFOBAHN
INFOLD variant spelling of > ENFOLD
INFOLDED > INFOLD
INFOLDER > INFOLD
INFOLDERS > INFOLD
INFOLDING > INFOLD
INFOLDS > INFOLD
INFOMANIA n obsessive devotion to gathering information
INFORCE same as > ENFORCE
INFORCED > INFORCE
INFORCES > INFORCE
INFORCING > INFORCE
INFORM vb tell ▷ adj without shape
INFORMAL adj relaxed and friendly
INFORMANT n person who gives information
INFORMED > INFORM
INFORMER n person who informs to the police

INFORMERS > INFORMER
INFORMING > INFORM
INFORMS > INFORM
INFORTUNE n misfortune
INFOS > INFO
INFOTECH n information technology
INFOTECHS > INFOTECH
INFOUGHT > INFIGHT
INFRA adv (esp in textual annotation) below
INFRACT vb violate or break (a law, an agreement, etc)
INFRACTED > INFRACT
INFRACTOR > INFRACT
INFRACTS > INFRACT
INFRARED adj of or using rays below the red end of the visible spectrum ▷ n infrared part of the spectrum
INFRAREDS > INFRARED
INFRINGE vb break (a law or agreement)
INFRINGED > INFRINGE
INFRINGER > INFRINGE
INFRINGES > INFRINGE
INFRUGAL adj wasteful
INFULA same as > INFULAE
INFULAE pl n two ribbons hanging from a bishop's mitre
INFURIATE vb make very angry ▷ adj furious
INFUSCATE adj (esp of the wings of an insect) tinged with brown
INFUSE vb fill (with an emotion or quality)
INFUSED > INFUSE
INFUSER n any device used to make an infusion
INFUSERS > INFUSER
INFUSES > INFUSE
INFUSIBLE adj unable to be fused or melted
INFUSING > INFUSE
INFUSION n infusing
INFUSIONS > INFUSION
INFUSIVE > INFUSION
INFUSORIA pl n tiny water-dwelling animals
INFUSORY adj containing infusoria ▷ n infusorian, a tiny water-dwelling mammal
ING n meadow near a river
INGAN Scots word for > ONION
INGANS > INGAN
INGATE n entrance
INGATES > INGATE
INGATHER vb gather together or in (a harvest)
INGATHERS > INGATHER
INGENER Shakespearean form of > ENGINEER

INGENERS > INGENER
INGENIOUS adj showing cleverness and originality
INGENIUM n genius
INGENIUMS > INGENIUM
INGENU n artless or inexperienced boy or young man
INGENUE n inexperienced girl or young woman
INGENUES > INGENUE
INGENUITY n cleverness at inventing things
INGENUOUS adj unsophisticated and trusting
INGENUS > INGENU
INGEST vb take (food or liquid) into the body
INGESTA pl n nourishment taken through the mouth
INGESTED > INGEST
INGESTING > INGEST
INGESTION > INGEST
INGESTIVE > INGEST
INGESTS > INGEST
INGINE n genius
INGINES > INGINE
INGLE n fire in a room or a fireplace
INGLENEUK same as > INGLENOOK
INGLENOOK n corner by a fireplace
INGLES > INGLE
INGLOBE vb shape as a sphere
INGLOBED > INGLOBE
INGLOBES > INGLOBE
INGLOBING > INGLOBE
INGLUVIAL > INGLUVIES
INGLUVIES n bird's craw
INGO n revelation
INGOES > INGO
INGOING same as > INGO
INGOINGS > INGOING
INGOT n oblong block of cast metal ▷ vb shape (metal) into ingots
INGOTED > INGOT
INGOTING > INGOT
INGOTS > INGOT
INGRAFT variant spelling of > ENGRAFT
INGRAFTED > INGRAFT
INGRAFTS > INGRAFT
INGRAIN vb impress deeply on the mind or nature ▷ adj (of carpets) made of fibre that is dyed before being spun ▷ n carpet made from ingrained yarn
INGRAINED > INGRAIN
INGRAINER n person who ingrains
INGRAINS > INGRAIN
INGRAM adj ignorant ▷ n ignorant person
INGRAMS > INGRAM
INGRATE n ungrateful person ▷ adj ungrateful
INGRATELY > INGRATE
INGRATES > INGRATE
INGRESS n entrance

INGRESSES > INGRESS
INGROOVE vb cut a groove into
INGROOVED > INGROOVE
INGROOVES > INGROOVE
INGROSS archaic form of **> ENGROSS**
INGROSSED > INGROSS
INGROSSES > INGROSS
INGROUND adj sunk into ground ▷ vb fix (something) in the ground or in a foundation
INGROUNDS > INGROUND
INGROUP n highly cohesive and relatively closed social group
INGROUPS > INGROUP
INGROWING adj (of a toenail) growing abnormally into the flesh
INGROWN adj grown abnormally into the flesh
INGROWTH n act of growing inwards
INGROWTHS > INGROWTH
INGRUM adj ignorant ▷ n ignorant person
INGRUMS > INGRUM
INGS > ING
INGUINAL adj of or relating to the groin
INGULF variant spelling of **> ENGULF**
INGULFED > INGULF
INGULFING > INGULF
INGULFS > INGULF
INGULPH archaic form of **> ENGULF**
INGULPHED > INGULPH
INGULPHS > INGULPH
INHABIT vb live in
INHABITED > INHABIT
INHABITER n inhabitant
INHABITOR n inhabitant
INHABITS > INHABIT
INHALABLE adj that can be inhaled
INHALANT n medical preparation inhaled to help breathing problems ▷ adj inhaled for its soothing or therapeutic effect
INHALANTS > INHALANT
INHALATOR n device for converting drugs into a fine spray for inhaling
INHALE vb breathe in (air, smoke, etc)
INHALED > INHALE
INHALER n container for an inhalant
INHALERS > INHALER
INHALES > INHALE
INHALING > INHALE
INHARMONY n discord
INHAUL n line for hauling in a sail
INHAULER same as **> INHAUL**
INHAULERS > INHAULER

INHAULS > INHAUL
INHAUST vb drink in
INHAUSTED > INHAUST
INHAUSTS > INHAUST
INHEARSE vb bury
INHEARSED > INHEARSE
INHEARSES > INHEARSE
INHERCE same as **> INHEARSE**
INHERCED > INHERCE
INHERCES > INHERCE
INHERCING > INHERCE
INHERE vb be an inseparable part (of)
INHERED > INHERE
INHERENCE n state or condition of being inherent
INHERENCY same as **> INHERENCE**
INHERENT adj existing as an inseparable part
INHERES > INHERE
INHERING > INHERE
INHERIT vb receive (money etc) from someone who has died
INHERITED > INHERIT
INHERITOR > INHERIT
INHERITS > INHERIT
INHESION less common word for **> INHERENCE**
INHESIONS > INHESION
INHIBIN n peptide hormone
INHIBINS > INHIBIN
INHIBIT vb restrain (an impulse or desire)
INHIBITED > INHIBIT
INHIBITER same as **> INHIBITOR**
INHIBITOR n person or thing that inhibits
INHIBITS > INHIBIT
INHOLDER n inhabitant
INHOLDERS > INHOLDER
INHOLDING n privately owned land inside a federal reserve
INHOOP vb confine
INHOOPED > INHOOP
INHOOPING > INHOOP
INHOOPS > INHOOP
INHUMAN adj cruel or brutal
INHUMANE adj not humane
INHUMANER > INHUMANE
INHUMANLY > INHUMAN
INHUMATE vb bury
INHUMATED > INHUMATE
INHUMATES > INHUMATE
INHUME vb inter
INHUMED > INHUME
INHUMER > INHUME
INHUMERS > INHUME
INHUMES > INHUME
INHUMING > INHUME
INIA > INION
INIMICAL adj unfavourable or hostile

INION n most prominent point at the back of the head
INIONS > INION
INIQUITY n injustice or wickedness
INISLE vb put on or make into an island
INISLED > INISLE
INISLES > INISLE
INISLING > INISLE
INITIAL adj first, at the beginning ▷ n first letter, esp of a person's name ▷ vb sign with one's initials
INITIALED > INITIAL
INITIALER > INITIAL
INITIALLY > INITIAL
INITIALS > INITIAL
INITIATE vb begin or set going ▷ n recently initiated person ▷ adj initiated
INITIATED > INITIATE
INITIATES > INITIATE
INITIATOR n person or thing that initiates
INJECT vb put (a fluid) into the body with a syringe
INJECTANT n injected substance
INJECTED > INJECT
INJECTING > INJECT
INJECTION n fluid injected into the body, esp for medicinal purposes
INJECTIVE > INJECTION
INJECTOR > INJECT
INJECTORS > INJECT
INJECTS > INJECT
INJELLIED > INJELLY
INJELLIES > INJELLY
INJELLY vb place in jelly
INJERA n white Ethiopian flatbread, similar to a crepe
INJERAS > INJERA
INJOINT vb join
INJOINTED > INJOINT
INJOINTS > INJOINT
INJUNCT vb issue a legal injunction against (a person)
INJUNCTED > INJUNCT
INJUNCTS > INJUNCT
INJURABLE > INJURE
INJURE vb hurt physically or mentally
INJURED > INJURE
INJURER > INJURE
INJURERS > INJURE
INJURES > INJURE
INJURIES > INJURY
INJURING > INJURE
INJURIOUS adj causing harm
INJURY n physical hurt
INJUSTICE n unfairness
INK n coloured liquid used for writing or printing ▷ vb mark in ink (something already marked in pencil)
INKBERRY n North American holly tree

INKBLOT n abstract patch of ink
INKBLOTS > INKBLOT
INKED > INK
INKER > INK
INKERS > INK
INKHOLDER same as **> INKHORN**
INKHORN n (formerly) a small portable container for ink
INKHORNS > INKHORN
INKHOSI n Zulu clan chief
INKHOSIS > INKHOSI
INKIER > INKY
INKIEST > INKY
INKINESS > INKY
INKING > INK
INKJET adj of a method of printing ▷ n inkjet printer
INKJETS > INKJET
INKLE n kind of linen tape used for trimmings ▷ vb hint
INKLED > INKLE
INKLES > INKLE
INKLESS > INK
INKLIKE > INK
INKLING n slight idea or suspicion
INKLINGS > INKLING
INKOSI same as **> INKHOSI**
INKOSIS > INKOSI
INKPAD n pad used for rubber-stamping or fingerprinting
INKPADS > INKPAD
INKPOT n ink-bottle
INKPOTS > INKPOT
INKS > INK
INKSPOT n ink stain
INKSPOTS > INKSPOT
INKSTAIN n stain made by ink
INKSTAINS > INKSTAIN
INKSTAND n stand or tray for holding writing tools and containers for ink
INKSTANDS > INKSTAND
INKSTONE n stone used in making ink
INKSTONES > INKSTONE
INKWELL n small container for ink
INKWELLS > INKWELL
INKWOOD n type of tree
INKWOODS > INKWOOD
INKY adj dark or black
INLACE variant spelling of **> ENLACE**
INLACED > INLACE
INLACES > INLACE
INLACING > INLACE
INLAID > INLAY
INLAND adv in or towards the interior of a country ▷ adj of or in the interior of a country or region ▷ n interior of a country or region
INLANDER > INLAND

INLANDERS > INLAND

INLANDS > INLAND

INLAY n inlaid substance or pattern ▷ vb decorate by inserting wooden pieces

INLAYER > INLAY

INLAYERS > INLAY

INLAYING > INLAY

INLAYINGS > INLAY

INLAYS > INLAY

INLET n water extending from the sea into the land ▷ vb insert or inlay

INLETS > INLET

INLETTING > INLET

INLIER n outcrop of rocks surrounded by younger rocks

INLIERS > INLIER

INLOCK vb lock up

INLOCKED > INLOCK

INLOCKING > INLOCK

INLOCKS > INLOCK

INLY adv inwardly

INLYING adj situated within or inside

INMATE n person living in an institution such as a prison

INMATES > INMATE

INMESH variant spelling of > ENMESH

INMESHED > INMESH

INMESHES > INMESH

INMESHING > INMESH

INMIGRANT adj coming in from another area of the same country ▷ n immigrant person or animal

INMOST adj innermost

INN n pub or small hotel, esp in the country ▷ vb stay at an inn

INNAGE n type of measurement

INNAGES > INNAGE

INNARDS pl n internal organs

INNATE adj being part of someone's nature, inborn

INNATELY > INNATE

INNATIVE adj native

INNED > IN

INNER adj happening or located inside ▷ n red innermost ring on a target

INNERLY > INNER

INNERMOST adj furthest inside

INNERNESS > INNER

INNERS > INNER

INNERSOLE same as > INSOLE

INNERVATE vb supply nerves to (a bodily organ or part)

INNERVE vb supply with nervous energy

INNERVED > INNERVE

INNERVES > INNERVE

INNERVING > INNERVE

INNERWEAR n underwear

INNING n division of baseball match

INNINGS > INNING

INNINGSES > INNINGS

INNIT interj isn't it

INNKEEPER n owner or manager of an inn

INNLESS adj without inns

INNOCENCE n quality or state of being innocent

INNOCENCY same as > INNOCENCE

INNOCENT adj not guilty of a crime ▷ n innocent person, esp a child

INNOCENTS > INNOCENT

INNOCUITY > INNOCUOUS

INNOCUOUS adj not harmful

INNOVATE vb introduce new ideas or methods

INNOVATED > INNOVATE

INNOVATES > INNOVATE

INNOVATOR > INNOVATE

INNOXIOUS adj not noxious

INNS > INN

INNUENDO n indirect reference to something rude or unpleasant

INNUENDOS > INNUENDO

INNYARD n courtyard of an inn

INNYARDS > INNYARD

INOCULA > INOCULUM

INOCULANT same as > INOCULUM

INOCULATE vb protect against disease by injecting with a vaccine

INOCULUM n substance used in giving an inoculation

INOCULUMS > INOCULUM

INODOROUS adj odourless

INOPINATE adj unexpected

INORB vb enclose in or as if in an orb

INORBED > INORB

INORBING > INORB

INORBS > INORB

INORGANIC adj not having the characteristics of living organisms ▷ n material not made from living organisms

INORNATE adj simple

INOSINE n type of molecule making up cell

INOSINES > INOSINE

INOSITE same as > INOSITOL

INOSITES > INOSITE

INOSITOL n cyclic alcohol

INOSITOLS > INOSITOL

INOTROPE n drug for controlling muscular contractions

INOTROPES > INOTROPE

INOTROPIC adj affecting or controlling the contraction of muscles, esp those of the heart

INPATIENT n patient who stays in a hospital for treatment

INPAYMENT n money paid into a bank account

INPHASE adj in the same phase

INPOUR vb pour in

INPOURED > INPOUR

INPOURING > INPOUR

INPOURS > INPOUR

INPUT n resources put into a project etc ▷ vb enter (data) in a computer

INPUTS > INPUT

INPUTTED > INPUT

INPUTTER > INPUT

INPUTTERS > INPUT

INPUTTING > INPUT

INQILAB n (in India, Pakistan, etc) revolution

INQILABS > INQILAB

INQUERE Spenserian form of > INQUIRE

INQUERED > INQUERE

INQUERES > INQUERE

INQUERING > INQUERE

INQUEST n official inquiry into a sudden death

INQUESTS > INQUEST

INQUIET vb disturb

INQUIETED > INQUIET

INQUIETLY > INQUIET

INQUIETS > INQUIET

INQUILINE n animal that lives in close association with another animal without harming it ▷ adj of or living as an inquiline

INQUINATE vb corrupt

INQUIRE vb seek information or ask (about)

INQUIRED > INQUIRE

INQUIRER > INQUIRE

INQUIRERS > INQUIRE

INQUIRES > INQUIRE

INQUIRIES > INQUIRY

INQUIRING > INQUIRE

INQUIRY n question

INQUORATE adj without enough people present to make a quorum

INRO n Japanese seal-box

INROAD n invasion or hostile attack

INROADS > INROAD

INRUN n slope down which ski jumpers ski

INRUNS > INRUN

INRUSH n sudden and overwhelming inward flow

INRUSHES > INRUSH

INRUSHING same as > INRUSH

INS > IN

INSANE adj severely mentally ill

INSANELY > INSANE

INSANER > INSANE

INSANEST > INSANE

INSANIE n insanity

INSANIES > INSANIE

INSANITY n state of being insane

INSATIATE adj not able to be satisfied

INSATIETY n insatiability

INSCAPE n essential inner nature of a person, etc

INSCAPES > INSCAPE

INSCIENCE n ignorance

INSCIENT adj ignorant

INSCONCE vb fortify

INSCONCED > INSCONCE

INSCONCES > INSCONCE

INSCRIBE vb write or carve words on

INSCRIBED > INSCRIBE

INSCRIBER > INSCRIBE

INSCRIBES > INSCRIBE

INSCROLL vb write on a scroll

INSCROLLS > INSCROLL

INSCULP vb engrave

INSCULPED > INSCULP

INSCULPS > INSCULP

INSCULPT adj engraved

INSEAM vb contain

INSEAMED > INSEAM

INSEAMING > INSEAM

INSEAMS > INSEAM

INSECT n small animal with six legs

INSECTAN > INSECT

INSECTARY n place where insects are kept

INSECTEAN > INSECT

INSECTILE > INSECT

INSECTION n incision

INSECTS > INSECT

INSECURE adj anxious, not confident

INSECURER > INSECURE

INSEEM vb cover with grease

INSEEMED > INSEEM

INSEEMING > INSEEM

INSEEMS > INSEEM

INSELBERG n isolated rocky hill rising abruptly from a flat plain

INSENSATE adj without sensation, unconscious

INSERT vb put inside or include ▷ n something inserted

INSERTED adj (of a muscle) attached to the bone that it moves

INSERTER > INSERT

INSERTERS > INSERT

INSERTING > INSERT

INSERTION n act of inserting

INSERTS > INSERT

INSET n small picture inserted within a larger one ▷ vb place in or within ▷ adj decorated with something inserted

INSETS > INSET
INSETTED > INSET
INSETTER > INSET
INSETTERS > INSET
INSETTING > INSET
INSHALLAH *sentence substitute* if Allah wills it
INSHEATH *vb* sheathe
INSHEATHE *vb* sheathe
INSHEATHS > INSHEATH
INSHELL *vb* retreat, as into a shell
INSHELLED > INSHELL
INSHELLS > INSHELL
INSHELTER *vb* put in a shelter
INSHIP *vb* travel or send by ship
INSHIPPED > INSHIP
INSHIPS > INSHIP
INSHORE *adj* close to the shore ▷ *adv* towards the shore
INSHRINE *variant spelling of* > ENSHRINE
INSHRINED > INSHRINE
INSHRINES > INSHRINE
INSIDE *prep* in or to the interior of ▷ *adj* on or of the inside ▷ *adv* on, in, or to the inside, indoors ▷ *n* inner side, surface, or part
INSIDER *n* someone who has privileged knowledge
INSIDERS > INSIDER
INSIDES > INSIDE
INSIDIOUS *adj* subtle or unseen but dangerous
INSIGHT *n* deep understanding
INSIGHTS > INSIGHT
INSIGNE *same as* > INSIGNIA
INSIGNIA *n* badge or emblem of honour or office
INSIGNIAS > INSIGNIA
INSINCERE *adj* showing false feelings, not genuine
INSINEW *vb* connect or strengthen, as with sinews
INSINEWED > INSINEW
INSINEWS > INSINEW
INSINUATE *vb* suggest indirectly
INSIPID *adj* lacking interest, spirit, or flavour
INSIPIDER > INSIPID
INSIPIDLY > INSIPID
INSIPIENT *adj* lacking wisdom
INSIST *vb* demand or state firmly
INSISTED > INSIST
INSISTENT *adj* making persistent demands
INSISTER > INSIST
INSISTERS > INSIST
INSISTING > INSIST
INSISTS > INSIST
INSNARE *less common spelling of* > ENSNARE

INSNARED > INSNARE
INSNARER > INSNARE
INSNARERS > INSNARE
INSNARES > INSNARE
INSNARING > INSNARE
INSOFAR *adv* to the extent
INSOLATE *vb* expose to sunlight, as for bleaching
INSOLATED > INSOLATE
INSOLATES > INSOLATE
INSOLE *n* inner sole of a shoe or boot
INSOLENCE > INSOLENT
INSOLENT *n* insolent person ▷ *adj* rude and disrespectful
INSOLENTS > INSOLENT
INSOLES > INSOLE
INSOLUBLE *adj* incapable of being solved
INSOLUBLY > INSOLUBLE
INSOLVENT *adj* unable to pay one's debts ▷ *n* person who is insolvent
INSOMNIA *n* inability to sleep
INSOMNIAC *adj* exhibiting or causing insomnia ▷ *n* person experiencing insomnia
INSOMNIAS > INSOMNIA
INSOMUCH *adv* such an extent
INSOOTH *adv* indeed
INSOUL *variant of* > ENSOUL
INSOULED > INSOUL
INSOULING > INSOUL
INSOULS > INSOUL
INSOURCE *vb* subcontract work to a company under the same general ownership
INSOURCED > INSOURCE
INSOURCES > INSOURCE
INSPAN *vb* harness (animals) to (a vehicle)
INSPANNED > INSPAN
INSPANS > INSPAN
INSPECT *vb* check closely or officially
INSPECTED > INSPECT
INSPECTOR *n* person who inspects
INSPECTS > INSPECT
INSPHERE *variant spelling of* > ENSPHERE
INSPHERED > INSPHERE
INSPHERES > INSPHERE
INSPIRE *vb* fill with enthusiasm, stimulate
INSPIRED *adj* brilliantly creative
INSPIRER > INSPIRE
INSPIRERS > INSPIRE
INSPIRES > INSPIRE
INSPIRING > INSPIRE

INSPIRIT *vb* fill with vigour
INSPIRITS > INSPIRIT
INSPO *n* source of inspiration
INSPOS > INSPO
INSTABLE *less common word for* > UNSTABLE
INSTAGRAM *vb* share (a photo) using the Instagram app
INSTAL *same as* > INSTALL
INSTALL *vb* put in and prepare (equipment) for use
INSTALLED > INSTALL
INSTALLER > INSTALL
INSTALLS > INSTALL
INSTALS > INSTAL
INSTANCE *n* particular example ▷ *vb* mention as an example
INSTANCED > INSTANCE
INSTANCES > INSTANCE
INSTANCY *n* quality of being urgent or imminent
INSTANT *n* very brief time ▷ *adj* happening at once
INSTANTER *adv* without delay
INSTANTLY *adv* immediately
INSTANTS > INSTANT
INSTAR *vb* decorate with stars ▷ *n* stage in the development of an insect
INSTARRED > INSTAR
INSTARS > INSTAR
INSTATE *vb* place in a position or office
INSTATED > INSTATE
INSTATES > INSTATE
INSTATING > INSTATE
INSTEAD *adv* as a replacement or substitute
INSTEP *n* part of the foot
INSTEPS > INSTEP
INSTIGATE *vb* cause to happen
INSTIL *vb* introduce (an idea etc) gradually into someone's mind
INSTILL *same as* > INSTIL
INSTILLED > INSTILL
INSTILLER > INSTIL
INSTILLS > INSTILL
INSTILS > INSTIL
INSTINCT *n* inborn tendency to behave in a certain way ▷ *adj* animated or impelled (by)
INSTINCTS > INSTINCT
INSTITUTE *n* organization set up for a specific purpose, esp research or teaching ▷ *vb* start or establish
INSTRESS *vb* create or sustain
INSTROKE *n* inward stroke

INSTROKES > INSTROKE
INSTRUCT *vb* order to do something
INSTRUCTS > INSTRUCT
INSUCKEN *adj* of a sucken
INSULA *n* pyramid-shaped area of the brain
INSULAE > INSULA
INSULANT *n* insulation
INSULANTS > INSULANT
INSULAR *adj* not open to new ideas, narrow-minded ▷ *n* islander
INSULARLY > INSULAR
INSULARS > INSULAR
INSULATE *vb* reduce the transfer of electricity, heat, or sound by lining with nonconducting material
INSULATED > INSULATE
INSULATES > INSULATE
INSULATOR *n* any material or device that insulates
INSULIN *n* hormone produced in the pancreas
INSULINS > INSULIN
INSULSE *adj* stupid
INSULSITY *n* stupidity
INSULT *vb* behave rudely to, offend ▷ *n* insulting remark or action
INSULTANT *adj* insulting
INSULTED > INSULT
INSULTER > INSULT
INSULTERS > INSULT
INSULTING > INSULT
INSULTS > INSULT
INSURABLE > INSURE
INSURANCE *n* agreement by which one makes regular payments to a company who pay an agreed sum if damage, loss, or death occurs
INSURANT *n* holder of an insurance policy
INSURANTS > INSURANT
INSURE *vb* protect by insurance
INSURED *adj* covered by insurance ▷ *n* those covered by an insurance policy
INSUREDS > INSURED
INSURER *n* person or company that sells insurance
INSURERS > INSURER
INSURES > INSURE
INSURGENT *adj* in revolt against an established authority ▷ *n* person who takes part in a rebellion
INSURING > INSURE
INSWATHE *vb* bind or wrap
INSWATHED > INSWATHE
INSWATHES > INSWATHE
INSWEPT *adj* narrowed towards the front

INSWING n type of movement of a bowled cricket ball

INSWINGER n ball bowled so as to move from off to leg through the air

INSWINGS > INSWING

INTACT adj not changed or damaged in any way

INTACTLY > INTACT

INTAGLI > INTAGLIO

INTAGLIO n (gem carved with) an engraved design

INTAGLIOS > INTAGLIO

INTAKE n amount or number taken in

INTAKES > INTAKE

INTARSIA n mosaic of inlaid wood

INTARSIAS > INTARSIA

INTEGER n positive or negative whole number or zero

INTEGERS > INTEGER

INTEGRAL adj being an essential part of a whole ▷ n sum of a large number of very small quantities

INTEGRALS > INTEGRAL

INTEGRAND n mathematical function to be integrated

INTEGRANT adj part of a whole ▷ n integrant thing or part

INTEGRATE vb combine into a whole ▷ adj made up of parts

INTEGRIN n protein that acts as a signal receptor between cells

INTEGRINS > INTEGRIN

INTEGRITY n quality of having high moral principles

INTEL n US military intelligence

INTELLECT n power of thinking and reasoning

INTELS > INTEL

INTENABLE adj untenable

INTEND vb propose or plan (to do something)

INTENDANT n provincial or colonial official of France, Spain, or Portugal

INTENDED adj planned or future ▷ n person whom one is to marry

INTENDEDS > INTENDED

INTENDER > INTEND

INTENDERS > INTEND

INTENDING > INTEND

INTENDS > INTEND

INTENIBLE adj incapable of holding

INTENSATE vb intensify

INTENSE adj of great strength or degree

INTENSELY > INTENSE

INTENSER > INTENSE

INTENSEST > INTENSE

INTENSIFY vb make or become more intense

INTENSION n set of characteristics or properties by which the referent or referents of a given word are determined

INTENSITY n state or quality of being intense

INTENSIVE adj using or needing concentrated effort or resources ▷ n intensifier or intensive pronoun or grammatical construction

INTENT n intention ▷ adj paying close attention

INTENTION n something intended

INTENTIVE adj intent

INTENTLY > INTENT

INTENTS > INTENT

INTER vb bury (a dead body)

INTERACT vb act on or in close relation with each other

INTERACTS > INTERACT

INTERAGE adj between different ages

INTERARCH vb have intersecting arches

INTERBANK adj conducted between or involving two or more banks

INTERBED vb lie between strata of different minerals

INTERBEDS > INTERBED

INTERBRED adj having been bred within a single family or strain so as to produce particular characteristics

INTERCEDE vb try to end a dispute between two people or groups

INTERCELL adj occurring between cells

INTERCEPT vb seize or stop in transit ▷ n point at which two figures intersect

INTERCITY adj (in Britain) denoting a fast train or passenger rail service, esp between main towns

INTERCLAN adj occurring between clans

INTERCLUB adj of, relating to, or conducted between two or more clubs

INTERCOM n internal communication system with loudspeakers

INTERCOMS > INTERCOM

INTERCOOL vb cool a car engine by means of an intercooler

INTERCROP n crop grown between the rows of another crop ▷ vb grow (one crop) between the rows of (another)

INTERCUT another word for > CROSSCUT

INTERCUTS > INTERCUT

INTERDASH vb dash between

INTERDEAL vb intrigue or plot

INTERDICT n official prohibition or restraint ▷ vb prohibit or forbid

INTERDINE vb eat together

INTERESS vb interest

INTERESSE vb interest

INTEREST n desire to know or hear more about something ▷ vb arouse the interest of

INTERESTS > INTEREST

INTERFACE n area where two things interact or link ▷ vb connect or be connected with by interface

INTERFERE vb try to influence other people's affairs where one is not involved or wanted

INTERFILE vb place (one or more items) among other items in a file or arrangement

INTERFIRM adj occurring between companies

INTERFLOW vb flow together

INTERFOLD vb fold together

INTERFUSE vb mix or become mixed

INTERGANG adj occurring between gangs

INTERGREW > INTERGROW

INTERGROW vb grow among

INTERIM adj temporary, provisional, or intervening ▷ n intervening time ▷ adv meantime

INTERIMS > INTERIM

INTERIOR n inside ▷ adj inside, inner

INTERIORS > INTERIOR

INTERJECT vb make (a remark) suddenly or as an interruption

INTERJOIN vb join together

INTERKNIT vb knit together

INTERKNOT vb knot together

INTERLACE vb join together as if by weaving

INTERLAID > INTERLAY

INTERLAP less common word for > OVERLAP

INTERLAPS > INTERLAP

INTERLARD vb insert in or occur throughout

INTERLAY vb insert (layers) between ▷ n

material, such as paper, placed between a printing plate and its base

INTERLAYS > INTERLAY

INTERLEAF n extra leaf which is inserted

INTERLEND vb lend between libraries

INTERLENT > INTERLEND

INTERLINE vb write or print (matter) between the lines of (a text or book)

INTERLINK vb connect together

INTERLOAN n loan between one library and another

INTERLOCK vb join firmly together ▷ n device used to prevent a mechanism from operating independently or unsafely ▷ adj (of fabric) closely knitted

INTERLOOP vb loop together

INTERLOPE vb intrude

INTERLUDE n short rest or break in an activity or event

INTERMALE adj occurring between males

INTERMAT n patch of seabed devoid of vegetation

INTERMATS > INTERMAT

INTERMENT n burial

INTERMESH vb net together

INTERMIT vb suspend (activity) or (of activity) to be suspended temporarily or at intervals

INTERMITS > INTERMIT

INTERMIX vb mix together

INTERMONT adj located between mountains

INTERMURE vb wall in

INTERN vb imprison, esp during a war ▷ n trainee doctor in a hospital

INTERNAL adj of or on the inside ▷ n medical examination of the inside of the body

INTERNALS > INTERNAL

INTERNE same as > INTERN

INTERNED > INTERN

INTERNEE n person who is interned

INTERNEES > INTERNEE

INTERNES > INTERNE

INTERNET n worldwide computer network

INTERNETS > INTERNET

INTERNING > INTERN

INTERNIST n physician who specializes in internal medicine

INTERNODE n part of a plant stem between two nodes

INTERNS > INTERN

INTERPAGE vb print (matter) on intervening pages

INTERPLAY n action and reaction of two things upon each other

INTERPLED adj having instituted a particular type of proceedings

INTERPONE vb interpose

INTERPOSE vb insert between or among things

INTERPRET vb explain the meaning of

INTERRACE adj involving different races or ethnic groups

INTERRAIL vb travel on an international rail pass

INTERRED > INTER

INTERREX n person who governs during an interregnum

INTERRING > INTER

INTERROW adj occurring between rows

INTERRUPT vb break into (a conversation etc) ▷ n signal to initiate the stopping of the running of one computer program in order to run another

INTERS > INTER

INTERSECT vb (of roads) meet and cross

INTERSERT vb insert between

INTERSEX n person with characteristics that are not uniquely male or female

INTERTERM adj occurring between terms ▷ n intersession

INTERTEXT adj text seen as modifying another text in literary theory

INTERTIE n short roofing timber

INTERTIES > INTERTIE

INTERTILL vb cultivate between rows of crops

INTERUNIT adj occurring between units

INTERVAL n time between two particular moments or events

INTERVALE dialect form of > INTERVAL

INTERVALS > INTERVAL

INTERVEIN vb intersect

INTERVENE vb involve oneself in a situation, esp to prevent conflict

INTERVIEW n formal discussion, esp between a job-seeker and an employer ▷ vb conduct an interview with

INTERWAR adj of or happening in the period between World War I and World War II

INTERWEB same as > INTERNET

INTERWEBS > INTERWEB

INTERWIND vb wind together

INTERWORD adj between words

INTERWORK vb interweave

INTERWOVE adj having been woven together

INTERZONE n area between two occupied zones

INTESTACY > INTESTATE

INTESTATE adj not having made a will ▷ n person who dies without having made a will

INTESTINE n lower part of the alimentary canal

INTHRAL archaic form of > ENTHRAL

INTHRALL archaic form of > ENTHRAL

INTHRALLS > INTHRALL

INTHRALS > INTHRAL

INTHRONE archaic form of > ENTHRONE

INTHRONED > INTHRONE

INTHRONES > INTHRONE

INTI n former monetary unit of Peru

INTIFADA n Palestinian uprising against Israel in the West Bank and Gaza Strip

INTIFADAH same as > INTIFADA

INTIFADAS > INTIFADA

INTIFADEH same as > INTIFADA

INTIL Scot form of > INTO

INTIMA n innermost layer of an organ or part

INTIMACY n close or warm friendship

INTIMAE > INTIMA

INTIMAL > INTIMA

INTIMAS > INTIMA

INTIMATE adj having a close personal relationship ▷ n close friend ▷ vb hint at or suggest

INTIMATED > INTIMATE

INTIMATER > INTIMATE

INTIMATES > INTIMATE

INTIME adj intimate

INTIMISM n school of impressionist painting

INTIMISMS > INTIMISM

INTIMIST > INTIMISM

INTIMISTE > INTIMISM

INTIMISTS > INTIMISM

INTIMITY n intimacy

INTINE n inner wall of a pollen grain or a spore

INTINES > INTINE

INTIRE archaic form of > ENTIRE

INTIS ≥ INTI

INTITLE archaic form of > ENTITLE

INTITLED > INTITLE

INTITLES > INTITLE

INTITLING > INTITLE

INTITULE vb (in Britain) to entitle (an act of parliament)

INTITULED > INTITULE

INTITULES > INTITULE

INTO prep indicating motion towards the centre, result of a change, etc

INTOED adj having inward-turning toes

INTOMB same as > ENTOMB

INTOMBED > INTOMB

INTOMBING > INTOMB

INTOMBS > INTOMB

INTONACO n wet plaster surface on which frescoes are painted

INTONACOS > INTONACO

INTONATE vb pronounce with a rise and fall of the voice

INTONATED > INTONATE

INTONATES > INTONATE

INTONATOR > INTONATE

INTONE vb speak or recite in an unvarying tone of voice

INTONED > INTONE

INTONER > INTONE

INTONERS > INTONE

INTONES > INTONE

INTONING > INTONE

INTONINGS > INTONE

INTORSION n spiral twisting in plant stems or other parts

INTORT vb twist inward

INTORTED > INTORT

INTORTING > INTORT

INTORTION > INTORT

INTORTS > INTORT

INTOWN adj infield

INTRA prep within

INTRACITY same as > INTERCITY

INTRADA n prelude

INTRADAS > INTRADA

INTRADAY adj occurring within one day

INTRADOS n inner curve or surface of an arch or vault

INTRANET n internal network that makes use of internet technology

INTRANETS > INTRANET

INTRANT n one who enters

INTRANTS > INTRANT

INTREAT archaic spelling of > ENTREAT

INTREATED > INTREAT

INTREATS > INTREAT

INTRENCH less common spelling of > ENTRENCH

INTREPID adj fearless, bold

INTRICACY > INTRICATE

INTRICATE adj involved or complicated

INTRIGANT n person who intrigues

INTRIGUE vb make interested or curious ▷ n secret plotting

INTRIGUED > INTRIGUE

INTRIGUER > INTRIGUE

INTRIGUES > INTRIGUE

INTRINCE adj intricate

INTRINSIC adj essential to the basic nature of something

INTRO n introduction

INTRODUCE vb present (someone) by name (to another person)

INTROFIED > INTROFY

INTROFIES > INTROFY

INTROFY vb increase the wetting properties

INTROIT n short prayer said or sung

INTROITAL > INTROIT

INTROITS > INTROIT

INTROITUS n entrance to a body cavity

INTROJECT vb (esp of a child) to incorporate ideas of others, or (in fantasy) of objects

INTROLD variant of > ENTROLD

INTROMIT vb enter or insert or allow to enter or be inserted

INTROMITS > INTROMIT

INTRON n stretch of DNA

INTRONIC adj of or like an intron

INTRONS > INTRON

INTRORSE adj turned inwards or towards the axis

INTROS > INTRO

INTROVERT n person concerned more with his or her thoughts and feelings than with the outside world ▷ adj shy and quiet ▷ vb turn (a hollow organ or part) inside out

INTRUDE vb come in or join in without being invited

INTRUDED > INTRUDE

INTRUDER n person who enters a place without permission

INTRUDERS > INTRUDER

INTRUDES > INTRUDE

INTRUDING > INTRUDE

INTRUSION n act of intruding

INTRUSIVE adj characterized by intrusion or tending to intrude

INTRUST same as > ENTRUST

INTRUSTED > INTRUST

INTRUSTS > INTRUST

INTUBATE vb insert a tube or cannula into (a hollow organ)

INTUBATED > INTUBATE

INTUBATES > INTUBATE

INTUIT vb know or discover by intuition

INTUITED > INTUIT

INTUITING > INTUIT

INTUITION n instinctive knowledge or insight without conscious reasoning

INTUITIVE adj of, possessing, or resulting from intuition

INTUITS > INTUIT

INTUMESCE vb swell or become swollen

INTURN n inward turn

INTURNED adj turned inward

INTURNS > INTURN

INTUSE n contusion

INTUSES > INTUSE

INTWINE less common spelling of > ENTWINE

INTWINED > INTWINE

INTWINES > INTWINE

INTWINING > INTWINE

INTWIST vb twist together

INTWISTED > INTWIST

INTWISTS > INTWIST

INUKSHUIT > INUKSHUK

INUKSHUK n stone used by Inuit people to mark a location

INUKSHUKS > INUKSHUK

INUKSUIT > INUKSUK

INUKSUK same as > INUKSHUK

INUKSUKS > INUKSUK

INULA n plant of the elecampane genus

INULAS > INULA

INULASE n enzyme

INULASES > INULASE

INULIN n fructose polysaccharide

INULINS > INULIN

INUMBRATE vb shade

INUNCTION n application of an ointment to the skin, esp by rubbing

INUNDANT > INUNDATE

INUNDATE vb flood

INUNDATED > INUNDATE

INUNDATES > INUNDATE

INUNDATOR > INUNDATE

INURBANE adj not urbane

INURE vb cause to accept or become hardened to

INURED > INURE

INUREMENT > INURE

INURES > INURE

INURING > INURE

INURN vb place (esp cremated ashes) in an urn

INURNED > INURN

INURNING > INURN

INURNMENT > INURN

INURNS > INURN

INUSITATE adj out of use

INUST adj burnt in

INUSTION > INUST

INUSTIONS > INUST

INUTILE adj useless

INUTILELY > INUTILE

INUTILITY > INUTILE

INVADABLE > INVADE

INVADE vb enter (a country) by military force

INVADED > INVADE

INVADER > INVADE

INVADERS > INVADE

INVADES > INVADE

INVADING > INVADE

INVALID n injured or chronically ill person ▷ vb dismiss from active service because of illness or injury ▷ adj having no legal force

INVALIDED > INVALID

INVALIDER > INVALID

INVALIDLY > INVALID

INVALIDS > INVALID

INVAR n alloy made from iron and nickel

INVARIANT n entity, quantity, etc, that is unaltered by a particular transformation of coordinates

INVARS > INVAR

INVASION n invading

INVASIONS > INVASION

INVASIVE adj of or relating to an invasion, intrusion, etc

INVEAGLE archaic form of > INVEIGLE

INVEAGLED > INVEAGLE

INVEAGLES > INVEAGLE

INVECKED same as > INVECTED

INVECTED adj bordered with small convex curves

INVECTIVE n abusive speech or writing ▷ adj characterized by or using abusive language, bitter sarcasm, etc

INVEIGH vb criticize strongly

INVEIGHED > INVEIGH

INVEIGHER > INVEIGH

INVEIGHS > INVEIGH

INVEIGLE vb coax by cunning or trickery

INVEIGLED > INVEIGLE

INVEIGLER > INVEIGLE

INVEIGLES > INVEIGLE

INVENIT sentence substitute (he or she) designed it

INVENT vb think up or create (something new)

INVENTED > INVENT

INVENTER same as > INVENTOR

INVENTERS > INVENTER

INVENTING > INVENT

INVENTION n something invented

INVENTIVE adj creative and resourceful

INVENTOR n person who invents, esp as a profession

INVENTORS > INVENTOR

INVENTORY n detailed list of goods or furnishings ▷ vb make a list of

INVENTS > INVENT

INVERITY n untruth

INVERNESS n type of cape

INVERSE vb make something opposite or contrary in effect ▷ adj reversed in effect, sequence, direction, etc ▷ n exact opposite

INVERSED > INVERSE

INVERSELY > INVERSE

INVERSES > INVERSE

INVERSING > INVERSE

INVERSION n act of inverting or state of being inverted

INVERSIVE > INVERSION

INVERT vb turn upside down or inside out

INVERTASE n enzyme, occurring in the intestinal juice of animals and in yeasts

INVERTED > INVERT

INVERTER n any device for converting a direct current into an alternating current

INVERTERS > INVERTER

INVERTIN same as > INVERTASE

INVERTING > INVERT

INVERTINS > INVERTIN

INVERTOR same as > INVERTER

INVERTORS > INVERTOR

INVERTS > INVERT

INVEST vb spend (money, time, etc) with the expectation of profit

INVESTED > INVEST

INVESTING > INVEST

INVESTOR > INVEST

INVESTORS > INVEST

INVESTS > INVEST

INVEXED adj concave

INVIABLE adj not viable, esp financially

INVIABLY > INVIABLE

INVIDIOUS adj likely to cause resentment

INVIOLACY > INVIOLATE

INVIOLATE adj unharmed, unaffected

INVIOUS adj without paths or roads

INVIRILE adj unmanly

INVISCID adj not viscid

INVISIBLE adj not able to be seen ▷ n invisible item of trade

INVISIBLY > INVISIBLE

INVITAL adj not vital

INVITE vb request the company of ▷ n invitation

INVITED > INVITE

INVITEE n one who is invited

INVITEES > INVITEE

INVITER > INVITE

INVITERS > INVITE

INVITES > INVITE

INVITING adj tempting, attractive ▷ n old word for invitation

INVITINGS > INVITING

INVOCABLE > INVOKE

INVOCATE archaic word for > INVOKE

INVOCATED > INVOCATE

INVOCATES > INVOCATE

INVOCATOR > INVOCATE

INVOICE n bill for goods or services ▷ vb present (a customer) with an invoice

INVOICED > INVOICE

INVOICES > INVOICE

INVOICING n act of presenting an invoice for payment

INVOKE vb put (a law or penalty) into operation

INVOKED > INVOKE

INVOKER > INVOKE

INVOKERS > INVOKE

INVOKES > INVOKE

INVOKING > INVOKE

INVOLUCEL n ring of bracts at the base of the florets of a compound umbel

INVOLUCRA n involucres

INVOLUCRE n ring of bracts at the base of an inflorescence in such plants as the composites

INVOLUTE adj complex, intricate, or involved ▷ n curve described by the free end of a thread as it is wound around another curve ▷ vb become involute

INVOLUTED > INVOLUTE

INVOLUTES > INVOLUTE

INVOLVE vb include as a necessary part

INVOLVED > INVOLVE

INVOLVER > INVOLVE

INVOLVERS > INVOLVE

INVOLVES > INVOLVE

INVOLVING > INVOLVE
INWALL vb surround with a wall
INWALLED > INWALL
INWALLING > INWALL
INWALLS > INWALL
INWARD adj directed towards the middle ▷ adv towards the inside or middle ▷ n inward part
INWARDLY adv within the private thoughts or feelings
INWARDS adv towards the inside or middle of something
INWEAVE vb weave together
INWEAVED > INWEAVE
INWEAVES > INWEAVE
INWEAVING > INWEAVE
INWICK vb perform a type of curling stroke
INWICKED > INWICK
INWICKING > INWICK
INWICKS > INWICK
INWIND vb wind or coil around
INWINDING > INWIND
INWINDS > INWIND
INWIT n conscience
INWITH adv within
INWITS > INWIT
INWORK vb work in
INWORKED > INWORK
INWORKING > INWORK
INWORKS > INWORK
INWORN adj worn in
INWOUND > INWIND
INWOVE > INWEAVE
INWOVEN > INWEAVE
INWRAP less common spelling of > ENWRAP
INWRAPPED > INWRAP
INWRAPS > INWRAP
INWRAPT > INWRAP
INWREATHE same as > ENWREATHE
INWROUGHT adj worked or woven into material, esp decoratively
INYALA n antelope
INYALAS > INYALA
IO interj exclamation of triumph ▷ n cry of 'io'
IODATE same as > IODIZE
IODATED > IODATE
IODATES > IODATE
IODATING > IODATE
IODATION > IODATE
IODATIONS > IODATE
IODIC adj of or containing iodine
IODID same as > IODIDE
IODIDE n chemical compound
IODIDES > IODIDE
IODIDS > IODID
IODIN same as > IODINE
IODINATE vb cause to combine with iodine
IODINATED > IODINATE
IODINATES > IODINATE
IODINE n bluish-black element

IODINES > IODINE
IODINS > IODIN
IODISE same as > IODIZE
IODISED > IODISE
IODISER > IODISE
IODISERS > IODISE
IODISES > IODISE
IODISING > IODISE
IODISM n poisoning caused by iodine or its compounds
IODISMS > IODISM
IODIZE vb treat with iodine
IODIZED > IODIZE
IODIZER > IODIZE
IODIZERS > IODIZE
IODIZES > IODIZE
IODIZING > IODIZE
IODOFORM n yellow crystalline insoluble volatile solid
IODOFORMS > IODOFORM
IODOMETRY n procedure used in volumetric analysis for determining the quantity of substance present that contains iodine
IODOPHILE adj taking an intense iodine stain
IODOPHOR n substance in which iodine is combined with an agent that renders it soluble
IODOPHORS > IODOPHOR
IODOPSIN n violet light-sensitive pigment in the retina
IODOPSINS > IODOPSIN
IODOUS adj of or containing iodine
IODURET n iodide
IODURETS > IODURET
IODYRITE n silver iodide
IODYRITES > IODYRITE
IOLITE n grey or violet-blue dichroic mineral
IOLITES > IOLITE
ION n electrically charged atom
IONIC adj of or in the form of ions
IONICALLY adv in an ionic manner
IONICITY n ionic character
IONICS pl n study of ions
IONISABLE > IONISE
IONISE same as > IONIZE
IONISED > IONISE
IONISER same as > IONIZER
IONISERS > IONISER
IONISES > IONISE
IONISING > IONISE
IONIUM n naturally occurring radioisotope of thorium
IONIUMS > IONIUM
IONIZABLE > IONIZE

IONIZE vb change into ions
IONIZED > IONIZE
IONIZER n person or thing that ionizes
IONIZERS > IONIZER
IONIZES > IONIZE
IONIZING > IONIZE
IONOGEN n compound that exists as ions when dissolved
IONOGENIC adj forming ions
IONOGENS > IONOGEN
IONOMER n type of thermoplastic
IONOMERS > IONOMER
IONONE n yellowish liquid mixture
IONONES > IONONE
IONOPAUSE n transitional zone in the atmosphere between the ionosphere and the exosphere
IONOPHORE n chemical compound capable of forming a complex with an ion and transporting it through a biological membrane
IONOSONDE n instrument measuring ionization
IONOTROPY n reversible interconversion of a pair of organic isomers as a result of the migration of an ionic part of the molecule
IONS > ION
IOPANOIC adj as in iopanoic acid type of acid containing iodine
IOS > IO
IOTA n ninth letter in the Greek alphabet
IOTACISM n pronunciation tendency in Modern Greek
IOTACISMS > IOTACISM
IOTAS > IOTA
IPECAC n type of S American shrub
IPECACS > IPECAC
IPOMOEA n convolvulaceous plant
IPOMOEAS > IPOMOEA
IPPON n winning point awarded in a judo or karate competition
IPPONS > IPPON
IPRINDOLE n antidepressant
IRACUND adj easily angered
IRADE n written edict of a Muslim ruler
IRADES > IRADE
IRASCIBLE adj easily angered
IRASCIBLY > IRASCIBLE
IRATE adj very angry
IRATELY > IRATE
IRATENESS > IRATE
IRATER > IRATE
IRATEST > IRATE

IRE vb anger ▷ n anger
IRED > IRE
IREFUL > IRE
IREFULLY > IRE
IRELESS > IRE
IRENIC adj tending to conciliate or promote peace
IRENICAL same as > IRENIC
IRENICISM > IRENICS
IRENICON variant spelling of > EIRENICON
IRENICONS > IRENICON
IRENICS n branch of theology
IRENOLOGY n study of peace
IRES > IRE
IRID n type of iris
IRIDAL > IRID
IRIDEAL > IRID
IRIDES > IRIS
IRIDIAL > IRID
IRIDIAN > IRID
IRIDIC adj of or containing iridium
IRIDISE vb make iridescent
IRIDISED > IRIDISE
IRIDISES > IRIDISE
IRIDISING > IRIDISE
IRIDIUM n very hard corrosion-resistant metal
IRIDIUMS > IRIDIUM
IRIDIZE vb make iridescent
IRIDIZED > IRIDIZE
IRIDIZES > IRIDIZE
IRIDIZING > IRIDIZE
IRIDOCYTE n cell in the skin of fish that gives them iridescence
IRIDOLOGY n technique used in complementary medicine to diagnose illness by studying a patient's eyes
IRIDOTOMY n surgical incision into the iris, esp to create an artificial pupil
IRIDS > IRID
IRING > IRE
IRIS n part of the eye ▷ vb display iridescence
IRISATE vb make iridescent
IRISATED > IRISATE
IRISATES > IRISATE
IRISATING > IRISATE
IRISATION > IRISATE
IRISCOPE n instrument that displays the prismatic colours
IRISCOPES > IRISCOPE
IRISED > IRIS
IRISES > IRIS
IRISING > IRIS
IRITIC > IRITIS
IRITIS n inflammation of the iris of the eye
IRITISES > IRITIS
IRK vb irritate, annoy
IRKED > IRK
IRKING > IRK
IRKS > IRK

IRKSOME adj irritating, annoying
IRKSOMELY > IRKSOME
IROKO n tropical African hardwood tree
IROKOS > IROKO
IRON n strong silvery-white metallic element ▷ adj made of iron ▷ vb smooth (clothes or fabric) with an iron
IRONBARK n Australian eucalyptus with hard rough bark
IRONBARKS > IRONBARK
IRONBOUND adj bound with iron
IRONCLAD adj covered or protected with iron ▷ n large wooden 19th-century warship with armoured plating
IRONCLADS > IRONCLAD
IRONE n fragrant liquid
IRONED > IRON
IRONER > IRON
IRONERS > IRON
IRONES > IRONE
IRONIC adj using irony
IRONICAL same as > IRONIC
IRONIER > IRONY
IRONIES > IRONY
IRONIEST > IRONY
IRONING n clothes to be ironed
IRONINGS > IRONING
IRONISE same as > IRONIZE
IRONISED > IRONISE
IRONISES > IRONISE
IRONISING > IRONISE
IRONIST > IRONIZE
IRONISTS > IRONIZE
IRONIZE vb use or indulge in irony
IRONIZED > IRONIZE
IRONIZES > IRONIZE
IRONIZING > IRONIZE
IRONLESS > IRON
IRONLIKE > IRON
IRONMAN n very strong man
IRONMEN > IRONMAN
IRONNESS > IRON
IRONS > IRON
IRONSIDE n person with great stamina or resistance
IRONSIDES > IRONSIDE
IRONSMITH adj blacksmith
IRONSTONE n rock consisting mainly of iron ore
IRONWARE n domestic articles made of iron
IRONWARES > IRONWARE
IRONWEED n plant with purplish leaves
IRONWEEDS > IRONWEED
IRONWOMAN n very strong woman

IRONWOMEN > IRONWOMAN
IRONWOOD n any of various trees, such as hornbeam, with exceptionally hard wood
IRONWOODS > IRONWOOD
IRONWORK n work done in iron, esp decorative work
IRONWORKS n building in which iron is smelted, cast, or wrought
IRONY n grammatical device ▷ adj of, resembling, or containing iron
IRRADIANT adj radiating light
IRRADIATE vb subject to or treat with radiation
IRREAL adj unreal
IRREALITY n unreality
IRREDENTA same as > IRRIDENTA
IRREGULAR adj not regular or even ▷ n soldier not in a regular army
IRRELATED adj irrelevant
IRRIDENTA n region that is ethnically or historically tied to one country, but which is ruled by another
IRRIGABLE > IRRIGATE
IRRIGABLY > IRRIGATE
IRRIGATE vb supply (land) with water by artificial channels or pipes
IRRIGATED > IRRIGATE
IRRIGATES > IRRIGATE
IRRIGATOR > IRRIGATE
IRRIGUOUS adj well-watered
IRRISION n mockery
IRRISIONS > IRRISION
IRRISORY adj mocking
IRRITABLE adj easily annoyed
IRRITABLY > IRRITABLE
IRRITANCY > IRRITANT
IRRITANT adj causing irritation ▷ n something that annoys or irritates
IRRITANTS > IRRITANT
IRRITATE vb annoy, anger
IRRITATED > IRRITATE
IRRITATES > IRRITATE
IRRITATOR > IRRITATE
IRRUPT vb enter forcibly or suddenly
IRRUPTED > IRRUPT
IRRUPTING > IRRUPT
IRRUPTION > IRRUPT

IRRUPTIVE adj irrupting or tending to irrupt
IRRUPTS > IRRUPT
IRUKANDJI n tiny but highly venomous Australian jellyfish
IS vb form of the present tense of be
ISABEL n brown yellow colour
ISABELLA same as > ISABEL
ISABELLAS > ISABELLA
ISABELS > ISABEL
ISAGOGE n academic introduction
ISAGOGES > ISAGOGE
ISAGOGIC > ISAGOGICS
ISAGOGICS n introductory studies, esp in the history of the Bible
ISALLOBAR n line on a map connecting places with equal pressure changes
ISARITHM n line on a map connecting places with the same population density
ISARITHMS > ISARITHM
ISATIN n yellowish-red crystalline compound
ISATINE same as > ISATIN
ISATINES > ISATINE
ISATINIC > ISATIN
ISATINS > ISATIN
ISBA n log hut
ISBAS > ISBA
ISCHAEMIA n inadequate supply of blood to an organ or part, as from an obstructed blood flow
ISCHAEMIC > ISCHAEMIA
ISCHEMIA same as > ISCHAEMIA
ISCHEMIAS > ISCHEMIA
ISCHEMIC > ISCHAEMIA
ISCHIA > ISCHIUM
ISCHIADIC > ISCHIUM
ISCHIAL > ISCHIUM
ISCHIATIC > ISCHIUM
ISCHIUM n part of the hipbone
ISCHURIA n retention of urine
ISCHURIAS > ISCHURIA
ISEIKONIA n seeing of same image in both eyes
ISEIKONIC > ISEIKONIA
ISENERGIC adj of equal energy
ISH n issue
ISHES > ISH
ISINGLASS n kind of gelatine obtained from some freshwater fish
ISIT sentence substitute expression used in response to a statement

ISLAND n piece of land surrounded by water ▷ vb cause to become an island
ISLANDED > ISLAND
ISLANDER n person who lives on an island
ISLANDERS > ISLANDER
ISLANDING > ISLAND
ISLANDS > ISLAND
ISLE vb make an isle of ▷ n island
ISLED > ISLE
ISLELESS adj without islands
ISLEMAN n islander
ISLEMEN > ISLEMAN
ISLES > ISLE
ISLESMAN same as > ISLEMAN
ISLESMEN > ISLESMAN
ISLET n small island
ISLETED adj having islets
ISLETS > ISLET
ISLING > ISLE
ISLOMANIA n obsessional enthusiasm or partiality for islands
ISM n doctrine, system, or practice
ISMATIC adj following fashionable doctrines
ISMATICAL same as > ISMATIC
ISMS > ISM
ISNA vb is not
ISNAE same as > ISNA
ISO n short segment of film that can be replayed easily
ISOAMYL n as in isoamyl acetate colourless volatile compound
ISOAMYLS > ISOAMYL
ISOBAR n line on a map connecting areas of equal atmospheric pressure
ISOBARE same as > ISOBAR
ISOBARES > ISOBARE
ISOBARIC adj having equal atmospheric pressure
ISOBARISM > ISOBAR
ISOBARS > ISOBAR
ISOBASE n line connecting points of equal land upheaval
ISOBASES > ISOBASE
ISOBATH n line on a map connecting points of equal depth of water
ISOBATHIC > ISOBATH
ISOBATHS > ISOBATH
ISOBRONT n line connecting points of simultaneous storm development
ISOBRONTS > ISOBRONT
ISOBUTANE n form of butane
ISOBUTENE n isomer of butene
ISOBUTYL n as in methyl isobutyl ketone colourless insoluble liquid ketone used as a solvent for organic compounds

ISOBUTYLS > ISOBUTYL
ISOCHASM *n* line connecting points of equal aurorae frequency
ISOCHASMS > ISOCHASM
ISOCHEIM *n* line on a map connecting places with the same mean winter temperature
ISOCHEIMS > ISOCHEIM
ISOCHIMAL > ISOCHIME
ISOCHIME *same as* > ISOCHEIM
ISOCHIMES > ISOCHIME
ISOCHOR *n* line on a graph showing variation of a fluid's temperature and pressure
ISOCHORE *same as* > ISOCHOR
ISOCHORES > ISOCHORE
ISOCHORIC > ISOCHOR
ISOCHORS > ISOCHORE
ISOCHRON *n* line on an isotope ratio diagram
ISOCHRONE *n* line on a map or diagram connecting places from which it takes the same time to travel to a certain point
ISOCHRONS > ISOCHRON
ISOCLINAL *adj* sloping in the same direction and at the same angle ▷ *n* imaginary line connecting points on the earth's surface having equal angles of dip
ISOCLINE *same as* > ISOCLINAL
ISOCLINES > ISOCLINE
ISOCLINIC *same as* > ISOCLINAL
ISOCRACY *n* form of government in which all people have equal powers
ISOCRATIC > ISOCRACY
ISOCRYMAL *same as* > ISOCRYME
ISOCRYME *n* line connecting points of equal winter temperature
ISOCRYMES > ISOCRYME
ISOCYANIC *adj* as in *isocyanic acid* hypothetical acid known only in the form of its compounds
ISOCYCLIC *adj* containing a closed ring of atoms of the same kind, esp carbon atoms
ISODICA > ISODICON
ISODICON *n* short anthem
ISODOMA > ISODOMON
ISODOMON *n* masonry formed of uniform blocks, with courses are of equal height

ISODOMOUS > ISODOMON
ISODOMUM *same as* > ISODOMON
ISODONT *n* animal in which the teeth are of similar size
ISODONTAL *same as* > ISODONT
ISODONTS > ISODONT
ISODOSE *n* dose of radiation applied in radiotherapy
ISODOSES > ISODOSE
ISOENZYME *same as* > ISOZYME
ISOETES *n* quillwort
ISOFORM *n* protein similar in function but not form to another
ISOFORMS > ISOFORM
ISOGAMETE *n* gamete that is similar in size and form to the one with which it unites in fertilization
ISOGAMIC > ISOGAMY
ISOGAMIES > ISOGAMY
ISOGAMOUS > ISOGAMY
ISOGAMY *n* fusion of similar gametes
ISOGENEIC *same as* > ISOGENIC
ISOGENIC *same as* > ISOGENOUS
ISOGENIES > ISOGENOUS
ISOGENOUS *adj* of similar origin, as parts derived from the same embryonic tissue
ISOGENY > ISOGENOUS
ISOGLOSS *n* line drawn on a linguistic map
ISOGON *n* equiangular polygon
ISOGONAL *same as* > ISOGONIC
ISOGONALS > ISOGONAL
ISOGONE *same as* > ISOGONIC
ISOGONES > ISOGONE
ISOGONIC *adj* having, making, or involving equal angles ▷ *n* imaginary line connecting points on the earth's surface having equal magnetic declination
ISOGONICS > ISOGONIC
ISOGONIES > ISOGONIC
ISOGONS > ISOGON
ISOGONY > ISOGONIC
ISOGRAFT *vb* grafting tissue from a donor genetically identical to the recipient
ISOGRAFTS > ISOGRAFT
ISOGRAM *same as* > ISOPLETH
ISOGRAMS > ISOGRAM
ISOGRAPH *n* line connecting points of the same linguistic usage
ISOGRAPHS > ISOGRAPH

ISOGRIV *n* line on a map connecting points of equal angular bearing
ISOGRIVS > ISOGRIV
ISOHEL *n* line on a map connecting places with equal sunshine
ISOHELS > ISOHEL
ISOHYDRIC *adj* having the same acidity or hydrogen-ion concentration
ISOHYET *n* line on a map connecting places with equal rainfall
ISOHYETAL *same as* > ISOHYET
ISOHYETS > ISOHYET
ISOKONT *same as* > ISOKONTAN
ISOKONTAN *n* alga whose zoospores have equal cilia
ISOKONTS > ISOKONT
ISOLABLE > ISOLATE
ISOLATE *vb* place apart or alone ▷ *n* isolated person or group
ISOLATED > ISOLATE
ISOLATES > ISOLATE
ISOLATING > ISOLATE
ISOLATION > ISOLATE
ISOLATIVE *adj* concerned with isolation
ISOLATOR > ISOLATE
ISOLATORS > ISOLATE
ISOLEAD *n* line on a ballistic graph
ISOLEADS > ISOLEAD
ISOLEX *n* line on map showing where a particular word is used
ISOLEXES > ISOLEX
ISOLINE *same as* > ISOPLETH
ISOLINES > ISOLINE
ISOLOG > ISOLOGOUS
ISOLOGOUS *adj* (of two or more organic compounds) having a similar structure but containing different atoms of the same valency
ISOLOGS > ISOLOGOUS
ISOLOGUE > ISOLOGOUS
ISOLOGUES > ISOLOGOUS
ISOMER *n* compound that has the same molecular formula as another
ISOMERASE *n* any enzyme that catalyses the conversion of one isomeric form of a compound to another
ISOMERE *same as* > ISOMER
ISOMERES > ISOMERE
ISOMERIC > ISOMER
ISOMERISE *same as* > ISOMERIZE
ISOMERISM *n* existence of two or more compounds having the same molecular formula but a different arrangement of atoms within the molecule

ISOMERIZE *vb* change or cause to change from one isomer to another
ISOMEROUS *adj* having an equal number of parts or markings
ISOMERS > ISOMER
ISOMETRIC *adj* relating to muscular contraction without shortening of the muscle ▷ *n* drawing made in this way
ISOMETRY *n* distance-preserving injective map between metric spaces
ISOMORPH *n* substance or organism that exhibits isomorphism
ISOMORPHS > ISOMORPH
ISONIAZID *n* soluble colourless crystalline compound used to treat tuberculosis
ISONOME *n* line on a map showing equal abundance of a species
ISONOMES > ISONOME
ISONOMIC > ISONOMY
ISONOMIES > ISONOMY
ISONOMOUS > ISONOMY
ISONOMY *n* equality before the law of the citizens of a state
ISOOCTANE *n* colourless liquid alkane hydrocarbon produced from petroleum
ISOPACH *n* line on a map connecting places with equal rock thickness
ISOPACHS > ISOPACH
ISOPHONE *n* isogloss marking off an area in which a particular feature of pronunciation is found
ISOPHONES > ISOPHONE
ISOPHOTAL > ISOPHOTE
ISOPHOTE *n* line on a diagram of a celestial object joining points of equal brightness
ISOPHOTES > ISOPHOTE
ISOPLETH *n* line on a map connecting places with the same amount of some geographical phenomenon
ISOPLETHS > ISOPLETH
ISOPOD *n* type of crustacean ▷ *adj* of this type of crustacean
ISOPODAN > ISOPOD
ISOPODANS > ISOPOD
ISOPODOUS > ISOPOD
ISOPODS > ISOPOD
ISOPOLITY *n* equality of political rights
ISOPRENE *n* colourless volatile liquid with a penetrating odour
ISOPRENES > ISOPRENE
ISOPROPYL *n* group of atoms

ISOPTERAN n termite
ISOPYCNAL n line on a map connecting points of equal atmospheric density
ISOPYCNIC same as > ISOPYCNAL
ISOS > ISO
ISOSCELES adj (of a triangle) having two sides of equal length
ISOSMOTIC same as > ISOTONIC
ISOSPIN n number used to classify elementary particles
ISOSPINS > ISOSPIN
ISOSPORY n condition of having spores of only one kind
ISOSTACY n state of balance in earth's crust
ISOSTASY same as > ISOSTACY
ISOSTATIC > ISOSTASY
ISOSTERIC adj (of two different molecules) having the same number of atoms and the same number and configuration of valency electrons
ISOTACH n line on a map connecting points of equal wind speed
ISOTACHS > ISOTACH
ISOTACTIC adj (of a stereospecific polymer) having identical steric configurations of the groups on each asymmetric carbon atom on the chain
ISOTHERAL > ISOTHERE
ISOTHERE n line on a map linking places with the same mean summer temperature
ISOTHERES > ISOTHERE
ISOTHERM n line on a map connecting points of equal temperature
ISOTHERMS > ISOTHERM
ISOTONE n atom with same number of neutrons as another
ISOTONES > ISOTONE
ISOTONIC adj (of two or more muscles) having equal tension
ISOTOPE n atom with same atomic number as another
ISOTOPES > ISOTOPE
ISOTOPIC > ISOTOPE
ISOTOPIES > ISOTOPE
ISOTOPY > ISOTOPE
ISOTRON n device for separating small quantities of isotopes
ISOTRONS > ISOTRON

ISOTROPIC adj having uniform physical properties, such as elasticity or conduction in all directions
ISOTROPY > ISOTROPIC
ISOTYPE n pictorial presentation of statistical information
ISOTYPES > ISOTYPE
ISOTYPIC > ISOTYPE
ISOZYME n variant of an enzyme
ISOZYMES > ISOZYME
ISOZYMIC > ISOZYME
ISPAGHULA n dietary fibre derived from seed husks and used as a thickener or stabilizer in the food industry
ISSEI n first-generation Japanese immigrant
ISSEIS > ISSEI
ISSUABLE adj capable of issuing or being issued
ISSUABLY > ISSUABLE
ISSUANCE n act of issuing
ISSUANCES > ISSUANCE
ISSUANT adj emerging or issuing
ISSUE n topic of interest or discussion ▷ vb make (a statement etc) publicly
ISSUED > ISSUE
ISSUELESS > ISSUE
ISSUER > ISSUE
ISSUERS > ISSUE
ISSUES > ISSUE
ISSUING > ISSUE
ISTANA n (in Malaysia) a royal palace
ISTANAS > ISTANA
ISTHMI > ISTHMUS
ISTHMIAN n inhabitant of an isthmus ▷ adj relating to or situated in an isthmus
ISTHMIANS > ISTHMIAN
ISTHMIC > ISTHMUS
ISTHMOID > ISTHMUS
ISTHMUS n narrow strip of land connecting two areas of land
ISTHMUSES > ISTHMUS
ISTLE n fibre obtained from various agave and yucca trees
ISTLES > ISTLE
IT pron refers to a nonhuman, animal, plant, or inanimate object ▷ n player whose turn it is to catch the others in children's games
ITA n type of palm
ITACISM n pronunciation of the Greek letter eta
ITACISMS > ITACISM

ITACONIC adj as in itaconic acid white colourless crystalline carboxylic acid
ITALIC adj (of printing type) sloping to the right ▷ n style of printing type
ITALICISE same as > ITALICIZE
ITALICIZE vb put in italics
ITALICS > ITALIC
ITAS > ITA
ITCH n skin irritation causing a desire to scratch ▷ vb have an itch
ITCHED > ITCH
ITCHES > ITCH
ITCHIER > ITCH
ITCHIEST > ITCH
ITCHILY > ITCH
ITCHINESS > ITCH
ITCHING > ITCH
ITCHINGS > ITCH
ITCHWEED n white hellebore
ITCHWEEDS > ITCHWEED
ITCHY > ITCH
ITEM n single thing in a list or collection ▷ adv likewise ▷ vb itemize
ITEMED > ITEM
ITEMING > ITEM
ITEMISE same as > ITEMIZE
ITEMISED > ITEMISE
ITEMISER > ITEMISE
ITEMISERS > ITEMISE
ITEMISES > ITEMISE
ITEMISING > ITEMISE
ITEMIZE vb make a list of
ITEMIZED > ITEMIZE
ITEMIZER > ITEMIZE
ITEMIZERS > ITEMIZER
ITEMIZES > ITEMIZE
ITEMIZING > ITEMIZE
ITEMS > ITEM
ITERANCE > ITERATE
ITERANCES > ITERATE
ITERANT > ITERATE
ITERATE vb repeat
ITERATED > ITERATE
ITERATES > ITERATE
ITERATING > ITERATE
ITERATION > ITERATE
ITERATIVE adj repetitious or frequent
ITERUM adv again
ITHER Scot word for > OTHER
ITINERACY n travelling from place to place
ITINERANT adj travelling from place to place ▷ n itinerant worker or other person
ITINERARY n detailed plan of a journey ▷ adj of or relating to travel or routes of travel

ITINERATE vb travel from place to place
ITS pron belonging to it ▷ adj of or belonging to it
ITSELF pron reflexive form of it
IURE adv by law
IVIED adj covered with ivy
IVIES > IVY
IVORIED > IVORY
IVORIER > IVORY
IVORIES pl n keys of a piano
IVORIEST > IVORY
IVORIST n worker in ivory
IVORISTS > IVORIST
IVORY n bony substance forming the tusks of elephants ▷ adj yellowish-white
IVORYBILL n large American woodpecker
IVORYLIKE > IVORY
IVORYWOOD n yellowish-white wood of an Australian tree, used for engraving, inlaying, and turnery
IVRESSE n drunkenness
IVRESSES > IVRESSE
IVY n evergreen climbing plant
IVYLEAF adj as in ivyleaf geranium type of geranium plant
IVYLIKE > IVY
IWI n Māori tribe
IWIS archaic word for > CERTAINLY
IXIA n southern African plant
IXIAS > IXIA
IXNAY interj nix
IXODIASES > IXODIASIS
IXODIASIS n disease transmitted by ticks
IXODID n hard-bodied tick
IXODIDS > IXODID
IXORA n flowering shrub
IXORAS > IXORA
IXTLE same as > ISTLE
IXTLES > IXTLE
IZAR n long garment worn by Muslim women
IZARD n type of goat-antelope
IZARDS > IZARD
IZARS > IZAR
IZVESTIA n news
IZVESTIAS > IZVESTIA
IZVESTIYA same as > IZVESTIA
IZZARD n letter Z
IZZARDS > IZZARD
IZZAT n honour or prestige
IZZATS > IZZAT

Jj

JA *interj* yes ▷ *sentence substitute* yes

JAAP *n* S African derogatory word for an unsophisticated person

JAAPS > JAAP

JAB *vb* poke sharply ▷ *n* quick punch or poke

JABBED > JAB

JABBER *vb* talk rapidly or incoherently ▷ *n* rapid or incoherent talk

JABBERED > JABBER

JABBERER > JABBER

JABBERERS > JABBER

JABBERING > JABBER

JABBERS > JABBER

JABBING > JAB

JABBINGLY > JAB

JABBLE *vb* ripple

JABBLED > JABBLE

JABBLES > JABBLE

JABBLING > JABBLE

JABERS *interj* Irish exclamation

JABIRU *n* large white-and-black Australian stork

JABIRUS > JABIRU

JABORANDI *n* any of several tropical American rutaceous shrubs

JABOT *n* frill or ruffle on the front of a blouse or shirt

JABOTS > JABOT

JABS > JAB

JACAL *n* Mexican daub hut

JACALES > JACAL

JACALS > JACAL

JACAMAR *n* tropical American bird with an iridescent plumage

JACAMARS > JACAMAR

JACANA *n* long-legged long-toed bird

JACANAS > JACANA

JACARANDA *n* tropical tree with sweet-smelling wood

JACARE *another name for* > CAYMAN

JACARES > JACARE

JACCHUS *n* small monkey

JACCHUSES > JACCHUS

JACENT *adj* lying

JACINTH *another name for* > HYACINTH

JACINTHE *n* hyacinth

JACINTHES > JACINTHE

JACINTHS > JACINTH

JACK *n* device for raising a motor vehicle or other heavy object ▷ *vb* lift or push (an object) with a jack

JACKAL *n* doglike wild animal of Africa and Asia ▷ *vb* behave like a jackal

JACKALLED > JACKAL

JACKALOPE *n* mythical animal of the western US

JACKALS > JACKAL

JACKAROO *same as* > JACKEROO

JACKAROOS > JACKAROO

JACKASS *n* fool

JACKASSES > JACKASS

JACKBOOT *n* high military boot ▷ *vb* oppress

JACKBOOTS > JACKBOOT

JACKDAW *n* Eurasian bird of the crow family

JACKDAWS > JACKDAW

JACKED > JACK

JACKEEN *n* slick self-assertive lower-class Dubliner

JACKEENS > JACKEEN

JACKER *n* labourer

JACKEROO *n* young male management trainee on a sheep or cattle station ▷ *vb* work as a jackeroo

JACKEROOS > JACKEROO

JACKERS > JACKER

JACKET *n* short coat ▷ *vb* put a jacket on (someone or something)

JACKETED > JACKET

JACKETING > JACKET

JACKETS > JACKET

JACKFISH *n* small pike fish

JACKFRUIT *n* tropical Asian tree

JACKIES > JACKY

JACKING > JACK

JACKINGS > JACK

JACKKNIFE *vb* (of an articulated truck) go out of control so that the trailer swings round at a sharp angle to the cab ▷ *n* large clasp knife

JACKLEG *n* unskilled worker

JACKLEGS > JACKLEG

JACKLIGHT *vb* hunt (fish or game) by dazzling them with a light

JACKLING *n* particular way of winning the ball in rugby

JACKLINGS > JACKLING

JACKMAN *n* retainer

JACKMEN > JACKMAN

JACKPLANE *n* large woodworking plane

JACKPOT *n* largest prize that may be won in a game ▷ *vb* accumulate stake money in a prize fund

JACKPOTS > JACKPOT

JACKROLL *vb* gang-rape

JACKROLLS > JACKROLL

JACKS *n* type of game

JACKSCREW *n* lifting device

JACKSHAFT *n* short length of shafting that transmits power from an engine or motor to a machine

JACKSIE *n* buttocks or anus

JACKSIES > JACKSIE

JACKSMELT *n* food fish of the North Pacific

JACKSMITH *n* smith who makes jacks

JACKSNIPE *n* small Eurasian short-billed snipe

JACKSTAFF *n* staff on a ship's bow, for flying the jack

JACKSTAY *n* object to which a sail edge is fastened along a yard

JACKSTAYS > JACKSTAY

JACKSTONE *n* small round pebble

JACKSTRAW *n* straw mannequin

JACKSY *same as* > JACKSIE

JACKY *n* old slang word for gin

JACOBIN *n* variety of fancy pigeon

JACOBINS > JACOBIN

JACOBUS *n* former English gold coin

JACOBUSES > JACOBUS

JACONET *n* light cotton fabric

JACONETS > JACONET

JACQUARD *n* fabric in which the design is incorporated into the weave

JACQUARDS > JACQUARD

JACQUERIE *n* peasant rising or revolt

JACTATION *n* act of boasting

JACULATE *vb* hurl

JACULATED > JACULATE

JACULATES > JACULATE

JACULATOR > JACULATE

JACUZZI *n* type of bath or pool

JACUZZIS > JACUZZI

JADE *n* semiprecious stone ▷ *adj* bluish-green ▷ *vb* exhaust or make exhausted from work or use

JADED *adj* tired and unenthusiastic

JADEDLY > JADED

JADEDNESS > JADED

JADEITE *n* usually green or white mineral

JADEITES > JADEITE

JADELIKE > JADE

JADERIES > JADERY

JADERY *n* shrewishness

JADES > JADE

JADING > JADE

JADISH > JADE

JADISHLY > JADE

JADITIC > JADE

JAEGER *n* German or Austrian marksman

JAEGERS > JAEGER

JAFA *n* New Zealand derogatory name for a person from Auckland

JAFAS > JAFA

JAFFA *n* (in cricket) well-bowled ball

JAFFAS > JAFFA

JAG *n* period of uncontrolled indulgence in an activity ▷ *vb* cut unevenly

JAGA *n* guard ▷ *vb* guard or watch

JAGAED > JAGA

JAGAING > JAGA

JAGAS > JAGA

JAGDWURST *n* type of cured German sausage

JAGER *same as* > JAEGER

JAGERS > JAGER

JAGG *same as* > JAG

JAGGARIES > JAGGARY

JAGGARY *same as* > JAGGERY

JAGGED > JAG

JAGGEDER > JAGGED
JAGGEDEST > JAG
JAGGEDLY > JAG
JAGGER n pedlar
JAGGERIES > JAGGERY
JAGGERS > JAGGER
JAGGERY n coarse brown sugar
JAGGHERY same as > JAGGERY
JAGGIER > JAGGY
JAGGIES > JAGGY
JAGGIEST > JAGGY
JAGGING > JAG
JAGGS > JAGG
JAGGY adj prickly ▷ n jagged computer image
JAGHIR n Indian regional governance
JAGHIRDAR n Indian regional governor
JAGHIRE n Indian regional governance
JAGHIRES > JAGHIRE
JAGHIRS > JAGHIR
JAGIR n Indian regional governance
JAGIRS > JAGIR
JAGLESS > JAG
JAGRA n Hindu festival
JAGRAS > JAGRA
JAGS > JAG
JAGUAR n large S American spotted cat
JAGUARS > JAGUAR
JAI interj victory (to)
JAIL n prison ▷ vb send to prison
JAILABLE > JAIL
JAILBAIT n young women collectively, considered sexually attractive but below the age of consent
JAILBAITS > JAILBAIT
JAILBIRD n person who has often been in prison
JAILBIRDS > JAILBIRD
JAILBREAK n escape from jail ▷ vb adapt an electronic device to use unauthorized software
JAILBROKE > JAILBREAK
JAILED > JAIL
JAILER n person in charge of a jail
JAILERESS n female jailer
JAILERS > JAILER
JAILHOUSE n jail
JAILING > JAIL
JAILLESS > JAIL
JAILOR same as > JAILER
JAILORESS n female jailor
JAILORS > JAILOR
JAILS > JAIL
JAK same as > JACK
JAKE adj slang word meaning all right
JAKER > JAKE
JAKES n toilet; lavatory
JAKESES > JAKES
JAKEST > JAKE

JAKEY n derogatory Scots word for a homeless alcoholic person
JAKEYS > JAKEY
JAKFRUIT same as > JACKFRUIT
JAKFRUITS > JAKFRUIT
JAKS > JAK
JALABIB > JILBAB
JALAP n Mexican convolvulaceous plant
JALAPENO n very hot type of green chilli pepper, used esp in Mexican cookery
JALAPENOS > JALAPENO
JALAPIC > JALAP
JALAPIN n purgative resin
JALAPINS > JALAPIN
JALAPS > JALAP
JALEBI n type of Asian sweet fried snack
JALEBIS > JALEBI
JALFREZI adj (in Indian cookery) stir-fried with green peppers, onions, and green chillies ▷ n curry made with green peppers, onions, and green chillies
JALFREZIS > JALFREZI
JALLEBI same as > JALEBI
JALLEBIS > JALLEBI
JALOP same as > JALAP
JALOPIES > JALOPY
JALOPPIES > JALOPPY
JALOPPY same as > JALOPY
JALOPS > JALOP
JALOPY n old car
JALOUSE vb suspect
JALOUSED > JALOUSE
JALOUSES > JALOUSE
JALOUSIE n window blind or shutter constructed from angled slats of wood, plastic, etc
JALOUSIED > JALOUSIE
JALOUSIES > JALOUSIE
JALOUSING > JALOUSE
JAM vb pack tightly into a place ▷ n fruit preserve or hold-up of traffic
JAMAAT n Islamic council
JAMAATS > JAMAAT
JAMADAR n Indian army officer
JAMADARS > JAMADAR
JAMB n side post of a door or window frame ▷ vb climb up a crack in rock
JAMBALAYA n Creole dish made of shrimps, ham, rice, onions, etc
JAMBART same as > GREAVE
JAMBARTS > JAMBART
JAMBE same as > JAMB
JAMBEAU another word for > GREAVE
JAMBEAUS > JAMBEAU

JAMBEAUX > JAMBEAU
JAMBED > JAMB
JAMBEE n light cane
JAMBEES > JAMBEE
JAMBER same as > GREAVE
JAMBERS > JAMBER
JAMBES > JAMBE
JAMBEUX > JAMBEAU
JAMBIER n greave
JAMBIERS > JAMBIER
JAMBING > JAMB
JAMBIYA n curved dagger
JAMBIYAH same as > JAMBIYA
JAMBIYAHS > JAMBIYAH
JAMBIYAS > JAMBIYA
JAMBO sentence substitute E African salutation
JAMBOK same as > SJAMBOK
JAMBOKKED > JAMBOK
JAMBOKS > JAMBOK
JAMBOLAN n Asian tree
JAMBOLANA same as > JAMBOLAN
JAMBOLANS > JAMBOLAN
JAMBONE n type of play in the card game euchre
JAMBONES > JAMBONE
JAMBOOL same as > JAMBOLAN
JAMBOOLS > JAMBOOL
JAMBOREE n large gathering or celebration
JAMBOREES > JAMBOREE
JAMBS > JAMB
JAMBU same as > JAMBOLAN
JAMBUL same as > JAMBOLAN
JAMBULS > JAMBUL
JAMBUS > JAMBU
JAMBUSTER n (in Canada) jam-filled doughnut
JAMDANI n patterned muslin
JAMDANIS > JAMDANI
JAMES n jemmy
JAMESES > JAMES
JAMJAR n container for preserves
JAMJARS > JAMJAR
JAMLIKE > JAM
JAMMABLE > JAM
JAMMED > JAM
JAMMER > JAM
JAMMERS > JAM
JAMMIER > JAMMY
JAMMIES informal word for > PYJAMAS
JAMMIEST > JAMMY
JAMMING > JAM
JAMMINGS > JAM
JAMMY adj lucky
JAMON n as in jamon serrano cured ham from Spain
JAMPACKED adj very crowded
JAMPAN n type of sedan chair used in India

JAMPANEE n jampan bearer
JAMPANEES > JAMPANEE
JAMPANI same as > JAMPANEE
JAMPANIS > JAMPANI
JAMPANS > JAMPAN
JAMPOT n container for preserves
JAMPOTS > JAMPOT
JAMS > JAM
JANE n girl or woman
JANES > JANE
JANGLE vb (cause to) make a harsh ringing noise ▷ n harsh ringing noise
JANGLED > JANGLE
JANGLER > JANGLE
JANGLERS > JANGLE
JANGLES > JANGLE
JANGLIER > JANGLY
JANGLIEST > JANGLY
JANGLING > JANGLE
JANGLINGS > JANGLE
JANGLY adj making a jangling sound
JANIFORM adj with two faces
JANISARY same as > JANISSARY
JANISSARY n infantryman in the Turkish army, originally a member of the sovereign's personal guard, from the 14th to the early 19th century
JANITOR n caretaker of a school or other building
JANITORS > JANITOR
JANITRESS n female janitor
JANITRIX n female janitor
JANIZAR same as > JANISSARY
JANIZARS > JANIZAR
JANIZARY same as > JANISSARY
JANKER n device for transporting logs
JANKERS > JANKER
JANN n lesser jinn
JANNEY vb act as a disguised reveller at Christmas
JANNEYED > JANNEY
JANNEYING > JANNEY
JANNEYS > JANNEY
JANNIED > JANNY
JANNIES > JANNY
JANNOCK same as > JONNOCK
JANNOCKS > JANNOCK
JANNS > JANN
JANNY n janitor ▷ vb work as a janitor
JANNYING > JANNY
JANNYINGS > JANNYING
JANSKY n unit of flux density
JANSKYS > JANSKY
JANTEE archaic version of > JAUNTY
JANTIER > JANTY
JANTIES > JANTY
JANTIEST > JANTY

JANTY n petty officer ▷ adj (in archaic usage) jaunty

JAP vb Scots word meaning splash

JAPAN n very hard varnish, usu black ▷ vb cover with this varnish ▷ adj relating to or varnished with japan

JAPANISE same as > JAPANIZE

JAPANISED > JAPANIZE

JAPANISES > JAPANIZE

JAPANIZE vb make Japanese

JAPANIZED > JAPANIZE

JAPANIZES > JAPANIZE

JAPANNED > JAPAN

JAPANNER > JAPAN

JAPANNERS > JAPAN

JAPANNING > JAPAN

JAPANS > JAPAN

JAPE n joke or prank ▷ vb joke or jest (about)

JAPED > JAPE

JAPER > JAPE

JAPERIES > JAPE

JAPERS > JAPE

JAPERY > JAPE

JAPES > JAPE

JAPING > JAPE

JAPINGLY > JAPE

JAPINGS > JAPING

JAPONICA n shrub with red flowers

JAPONICAS > JAPONICA

JAPPED > JAP

JAPPING > JAP

JAPS > JAP

JAR n wide-mouthed container ▷ vb have a disturbing or unpleasant effect

JARARACA n South American snake

JARARACAS > JARARACA

JARARAKA same as > JARARACA

JARARAKAS > JARARACA

JARFUL same as > JAR

JARFULS > JARFUL

JARGON n specialized technical language ▷ vb use or speak in jargon

JARGONED > JARGON

JARGONEER n user of jargon

JARGONEL n pear

JARGONELS > JARGONEL

JARGONIER > JARGONY

JARGONING > JARGON

JARGONISE same as > JARGONIZE

JARGONISH > JARGON

JARGONIST > JARGON

JARGONIZE vb render into jargon

JARGONS > JARGON

JARGONY adj full of jargon

JARGOON same as > JARGON

JARGOONS > JARGOON

JARHEAD n US Marine

JARHEADS > JARHEAD

JARINA n South American palm tree

JARINAS > JARINA

JARK n seal or pass

JARKMAN n forger of passes or licences

JARKMEN > JARKMAN

JARKS > JARK

JARL n Scandinavian chieftain or noble

JARLDOM > JARL

JARLDOMS > JARL

JARLS > JARL

JARLSBERG n Norwegian cheese

JAROOL n Indian tree

JAROOLS > JAROOL

JAROSITE n yellow to brown mineral

JAROSITES > JAROSITE

JAROVISE same as > JAROVIZE

JAROVISED > JAROVISE

JAROVISES > JAROVISE

JAROVIZE vb vernalize

JAROVIZED > JAROVIZE

JAROVIZES > JAROVIZE

JARP vb strike or smash

JARPED > JARP

JARPING > JARP

JARPS > JARP

JARRAH n Australian eucalypt yielding valuable timber

JARRAHS > JARRAH

JARRED > JAR

JARRING > JAR

JARRINGLY > JAR

JARRINGS > JAR

JARS > JAR

JARSFUL > JARFUL

JARTA n heart

JARTAS > JARTA

JARUL variant of > JAROOL

JARULS > JARUL

JARVEY n hackney coachman

JARVEYS > JARVEY

JARVIE same as > JARVEY

JARVIES > JARVIE

JASEY n wig

JASEYS > JASEY

JASIES > JASY

JASMIN same as > JASMINE

JASMINE n shrub with sweet-smelling yellow or white flowers

JASMINES > JASMINE

JASMINS > JASMIN

JASMONATE n plant hormone that regulates growth

JASP another word for > JASPER

JASPE adj resembling jasper ▷ n subtly striped woven fabric

JASPER n variety of quartz

JASPERIER > JASPERY

JASPERISE same as > JASPERIZE

JASPERIZE vb turn into jasper

JASPEROUS > JASPER

JASPERS > JASPER

JASPERY adj resembling jasper

JASPES > JASPE

JASPIDEAN > JASPER

JASPILITE n rock like jasper

JASPIS archaic word for > JASPER

JASPISES > JASPIS

JASPS > JASP

JASS obsolete variant of > JAZZ

JASSES > JASS

JASSID n leafhopper

JASSIDS > JASSID

JASY n wig

JATAKA n text describing the birth of Buddha

JATAKAS > JATAKA

JATO n jet-assisted takeoff

JATOS > JATO

JATROPHA n poisonous shrub of C America used primarily as a biofuel

JATROPHAS > JATROPHA

JAUK vb dawdle

JAUKED > JAUK

JAUKING > JAUK

JAUKS > JAUK

JAUNCE vb prance

JAUNCED > JAUNCE

JAUNCES > JAUNCE

JAUNCING > JAUNCE

JAUNDICE n disease marked by yellowness of the skin ▷ vb distort (the judgment, etc) adversely

JAUNDICED > JAUNDICE

JAUNDICES > JAUNDICE

JAUNSE same as > JAUNCE

JAUNSED > JAUNSE

JAUNSES > JAUNSE

JAUNSING > JAUNSE

JAUNT n short journey for pleasure ▷ vb make such a journey

JAUNTED > JAUNT

JAUNTEE old spelling of > JAUNTY

JAUNTIE old spelling of > JAUNTY

JAUNTIER > JAUNTY

JAUNTIES > JAUNTY

JAUNTIEST > JAUNTY

JAUNTILY > JAUNTY

JAUNTING > JAUNT

JAUNTS > JAUNT

JAUNTY adj sprightly and cheerful ▷ n master-at-arms on a naval ship

JAUP same as > JARP

JAUPED > JAUP

JAUPING > JAUP

JAUPS > JAUP

JAVA n coffee or a variety of it

JAVAS > JAVA

JAVEL adj as in javel water bleach or disinfectant

JAVELIN n light spear thrown in sports competitions ▷ vb spear with a javelin

JAVELINA n collared peccary

JAVELINAS > JAVELINA

JAVELINED > JAVELIN

JAVELINS > JAVELIN

JAVELLE adj as in javelle water bleach or disinfectant

JAVELS > JAVEL

JAW n one of the bones in which the teeth are set ▷ vb talk lengthily

JAWAN n (in India) a soldier

JAWANS > JAWAN

JAWARI n variety of sorghum

JAWARIS > JAWARI

JAWBATION n scolding

JAWBONE n lower jaw of a person or animal ▷ vb try to persuade by virtue of one's high office or position

JAWBONED > JAWBONE

JAWBONER > JAWBONE

JAWBONERS > JAWBONE

JAWBONES > JAWBONE

JAWBONING > JAWBONE

JAWBOX n metal sink

JAWBOXES > JAWBOX

JAWED > JAW

JAWFALL n dejection

JAWFALLS > JAWFALL

JAWHOLE n cesspit

JAWHOLES > JAWHOLE

JAWING > JAW

JAWINGS > JAW

JAWLESS > JAW

JAWLIKE > JAW

JAWLINE n outline of the jaw

JAWLINES > JAWLINE

JAWS > JAW

JAXIE same as > JACKSIE

JAXIES > JAXIE

JAXY same as > JACKSIE

JAY n type of bird

JAYBIRD n jay

JAYBIRDS > JAYBIRD

JAYCEE n member of a Junior Chamber of Commerce

JAYCEES > JAYCEE

JAYGEE n lieutenant junior grade in the US army

JAYGEES > JAYGEE

JAYHAWKER n Unionist guerrilla in US Civil War

JAYS > JAY

JAYVEE n junior varsity sports team

JAYVEES > JAYVEE

JAYWALK vb cross or walk in a street recklessly or illegally

JAYWALKED > JAYWALK

JAYWALKER > JAYWALK

JAYWALKS > JAYWALK

JAZERANT n coat of metal plates sewn onto cloth

JAZERANTS > JAZERANT

JAZIES > JAZY

JAZY n wig

JAZZ n kind of music ▷ vb play or dance to jazz music

JAZZBO n jazz musician or fan

JAZZBOS > JAZZBO

JAZZED > JAZZ

JAZZER > JAZZ

JAZZERS > JAZZ

JAZZES > JAZZ

JAZZIER > JAZZY

JAZZIEST > JAZZY

JAZZILY > JAZZY

JAZZINESS > JAZZY

JAZZING > JAZZ

JAZZLIKE > JAZZ

JAZZMAN > JAZZ

JAZZMEN > JAZZ

JAZZY adj flashy or showy

JEALOUS adj fearful of losing (something) to a rival

JEALOUSE vb be jealous of

JEALOUSED > JEALOUSE

JEALOUSER > JEALOUS

JEALOUSES > JEALOUSE

JEALOUSLY > JEALOUS

JEALOUSY n state of or an instance of feeling jealous

JEAN n tough twill-weave cotton fabric

JEANED adj wearing jeans

JEANETTE n light jean cloth

JEANETTES > JEANETTE

JEANS pl n casual denim trousers

JEANSWEAR n clothing made from denim

JEAT n jet

JEATS > JEAT

JEBEL n hill or mountain in an Arab country

JEBELS > JEBEL

JEDI n person claiming to live according to the Jedi philosophy

JEDIS > JEDI

JEE variant of > GEE

JEED > JEE

JEEING > JEE

JEEL vb make into jelly

JEELED > JEEL

JEELIE same as > JEELY

JEELIED > JEELY

JEELIEING > JEELIE

JEELIES > JEELY

JEELING > JEEL

JEELS > JEEL

JEELY n jelly ▷ vb make into jelly

JEELYING > JEELY

JEEP n small military four-wheel drive road vehicle ▷ vb travel in a jeep

JEEPED > JEEP

JEEPERS interj mild exclamation of surprise

JEEPING > JEEP

JEEPNEY n Filipino bus converted from a jeep

JEEPNEYS > JEEPNEY

JEEPS > JEEP

JEER vb scoff or deride ▷ n cry of derision

JEERED > JEER

JEERER > JEER

JEERERS > JEER

JEERING > JEER

JEERINGLY > JEER

JEERINGS > JEER

JEERS > JEER

JEES > JEE

JEESLY same as > JEEZLY

JEEZ interj expression of surprise or irritation

JEEZE same as > JEEZ

JEEZELY same as > JEEZLY

JEEZLY adj used as an intensifier

JEFE n (in Spanish-speaking countries) a military or political leader

JEFES > JEFE

JEFF vb downsize or close down (an organization)

JEFFED > JEFF

JEFFING > JEFF

JEFFS > JEFF

JEGGINGS pl n women's leggings designed to look like tight denim jeans

JEHAD same as > JIHAD

JEHADEEN same as > JIHADEEN

JEHADI same as > JIHADI

JEHADIS > JEHADI

JEHADISM same as > JIHADISM

JEHADISMS > JEHADISM

JEHADIST > JEHADISM

JEHADISTS > JEHADISM

JEHADS > JEHAD

JEHU n fast driver

JEHUS > JEHU

JEJUNA > JEJUNUM

JEJUNAL > JEJUNUM

JEJUNE adj simple or naive

JEJUNELY > JEJUNE

JEJUNITY > JEJUNE

JEJUNUM n part of the small intestine

JEJUNUMS > JEJUNUM

JELAB same as > JELLABA

JELABS > JELAB

JELL vb form into a jelly-like substance

JELLABA n loose robe with a hood

JELLABAH same as > JELLABA

JELLABAHS > JELLABAH

JELLABAS > JELLABA

JELLED > JELL

JELLIED > JELLY

JELLIES > JELLY

JELLIFIED > JELLIFY

JELLIFIES > JELLIFY

JELLIFY vb make into or become jelly

JELLING > JELL

JELLO n (in US English) type of dessert

JELLOS > JELLO

JELLS > JELL

JELLY n fruit-flavoured clear dessert set with gelatine ▷ vb jellify

JELLYBEAN n bean-shaped sweet with a brightly coloured coating around a gelatinous filling

JELLYFISH n small jelly-like sea animal

JELLYING > JELLY

JELLYLIKE > JELLY

JELLYROLL n type of cake

JELUTONG n Malaysian tree

JELUTONGS > JELUTONG

JEMADAR n native officer serving as a mercenary in India

JEMADARS > JEMADAR

JEMBE n hoe

JEMBES > JEMBE

JEMIDAR same as > JEMADAR

JEMIDARS > JEMIDAR

JEMIMA n boot with elastic sides

JEMIMAS > JEMIMA

JEMMIED > JEMMY

JEMMIER > JEMMY

JEMMIES > JEMMY

JEMMIEST > JEMMY

JEMMINESS > JEMMY

JEMMY n short steel crowbar used by burglars ▷ vb prise (something) open with a jemmy ▷ adj neat

JEMMYING > JEMMY

JENNET n female donkey or ass

JENNETING n early-season apple

JENNETS > JENNET

JENNIES > JENNY

JENNY same as > JENNET

JEOFAIL n oversight in legal pleading

JEOFAILS > JEOFAIL

JEON n Korean pancake

JEONS > JEON

JEOPARD vb put in jeopardy

JEOPARDED > JEOPARD

JEOPARDER > JEOPARD

JEOPARDS > JEOPARD

JEOPARDY n danger ▷ vb put in jeopardy

JEQUERITY same as > JEQUIRITY

JEQUIRITY n seed of the Indian liquorice

JERBIL variant spelling of > GERBIL

JERBILS > JERBIL

JERBOA n small mouselike rodent with long hind legs

JERBOAS > JERBOA

JEREED same as > JERID

JEREEDS > JEREED

JEREMIAD n long mournful complaint

JEREMIADS > JEREMIAD

JEREPIGO n sweet fortified wine similar to port

JEREPIGOS > JEREPIGO

JERFALCON variant of > GYRFALCON

JERID n wooden javelin

JERIDS > JERID

JERK vb move or throw abruptly ▷ n sharp or abruptly stopped movement

JERKED > JERK

JERKER > JERK

JERKERS > JERK

JERKIER > JERKY

JERKIES > JERKY

JERKIEST > JERKY

JERKILY > JERKY

JERKIN n sleeveless jacket

JERKINESS > JERKY

JERKING > JERK

JERKINGLY > JERK

JERKINGS > JERK

JERKINS > JERKIN

JERKS > JERK

JERKWATER adj inferior and insignificant ▷ n railway locomotive

JERKY adj characterized by jerks ▷ n type of cured meat

JEROBOAM n wine bottle holding the equivalent of four normal bottles

JEROBOAMS > JEROBOAM

JERQUE vb search for contraband

JERQUED > JERQUE

JERQUER > JERQUE

JERQUERS > JERQUE

JERQUES > JERQUE

JERQUING > JERQUE

JERQUINGS > JERQUE

JERREED variant spelling of > JERID

JERREEDS > JERREED

JERRICAN n five-gallon fuel can

JERRICANS > JERRICAN

JERRID n blunt javelin

JERRIDS > JERRID

JERRIES > JERRY

JERRY short for > JEROBOAM

JERRYCAN n flat-sided can used for storing or transporting liquids, esp motor fuel

JERRYCANS
> JERRYCAN
JERSEY n knitted jumper
JERSEYED > JERSEY
JERSEYS > JERSEY
JESS n short leather strap used in falconry ▷ vb put jesses on (a hawk or falcon)
JESSAMIES > JESSAMY
JESSAMINE same as
> JASMINE
JESSAMY n fop
JESSANT adj emerging
JESSE same as > JESS
JESSED > JESS
JESSERANT n coat of metal plates sewn onto cloth
JESSES > JESS
JESSIE n derogatory term for a weak or cowardly boy or man
JESSIES > JESSIE
JESSING > JESS
JEST vb joke ▷ n something done or said for amusement
JESTBOOK n book of amusing stories
JESTBOOKS
> JESTBOOK
JESTED > JEST
JESTEE n person about whom a joke is made
JESTEES > JESTEE
JESTER n professional clown at court
JESTERS > JESTER
JESTFUL > JEST
JESTING > JEST
JESTINGLY > JEST
JESTINGS > JEST
JESTS > JEST
JESUS n French paper size
JET n aircraft driven by jet propulsion ▷ vb fly by jet aircraft
JETBEAD n ornamental shrub
JETBEADS > JETBEAD
JETE n dance step
JETES > JETE
JETFOIL n type of hydrofoil that is propelled by water jets
JETFOILS > JETFOIL
JETLAG n tiredness caused by crossing timezones in jet flight
JETLAGS > JETLAG
JETLIKE > JET
JETLINER n commercial airliner powered by jet engines
JETLINERS
> JETLINER
JETON n gambling chip
JETONS > JETON
JETPACK n wearable harness with jets, used for transport
JETPACKS > JETPACK
JETPORT n airport for jet planes
JETPORTS > JETPORT
JETS > JET

JETSAM n goods thrown overboard to lighten a ship
JETSAMS > JETSAM
JETSOM same as
> JETSAM
JETSOMS > JETSOM
JETSON archaic form of
> JETSAM
JETSONS > JETSON
JETSTREAM n narrow belt of high-altitude winds moving east at high speeds)
JETTATURA n evil eye
JETTED > JET
JETTIED > JETTY
JETTIER > JETTY
JETTIES > JETTY
JETTIEST > JETTY
JETTINESS > JETTY
JETTING > JET
JETTISON vb abandon
JETTISONS
> JETTISON
JETTON n counter or token
JETTONS > JETTON
JETTY n small pier ▷ adj of or resembling jet, esp in colour or polish ▷ vb equip with a cantilevered floor
JETTYING > JETTY
JETWAY n tradename of device used in airports
JETWAYS > JETWAY
JEU n game
JEUNE adj young
JEUX > JEU
JEWEL n precious or semiprecious stone ▷ vb fit or decorate with a jewel or jewels
JEWELED > JEWEL
JEWELER same as
> JEWELLER
JEWELERS > JEWELER
JEWELFISH n beautifully coloured fish popular in aquaria
JEWELING > JEWEL
JEWELLED > JEWEL
JEWELLER n dealer in jewels
JEWELLERS
> JEWELLER
JEWELLERY n objects decorated with precious stones
JEWELLIKE > JEWEL
JEWELLING > JEWEL
JEWELRIES > JEWELRY
JEWELRY same as
> JEWELLERY
JEWELS > JEWEL
JEWELWEED n small bushy plant
JEWFISH n old-fashioned name for a type of freshwater catfish
JEWFISHES > JEWFISH
JEWIE n informal Australian word for a jewfish
JEWIES > JEWIE
JEZAIL n Afghan musket
JEZAILS > JEZAIL
JEZEBEL n shameless or scheming woman

JEZEBELS > JEZEBEL
JHALA n Indian musical style
JHALAS > JHALA
JHATKA n slaughter of animals for food according to Sikh law
JHATKAS > JHATKA
JIAO n Chinese currency unit
JIAOS > JIAO
JIB same as > JIBE
JIBB same as > JIBE
JIBBA n long, loose coat worn by Muslim men
JIBBAH same as
> JUBBAH
JIBBAHS > JIBBAH
JIBBAS > JIBBA
JIBBED > JIBB
JIBBER variant of
> GIBBER
JIBBERED > JIBBER
JIBBERING > JIBBER
JIBBERS > JIBBER
JIBBING > JIBB
JIBBINGS > JIBB
JIBBONS pl n spring onions
JIBBOOM n spar forming an extension of the bowsprit
JIBBOOMS > JIBBOOM
JIBBS > JIBB
JIBE vb taunt or jeer ▷ n insulting or taunting remark
JIBED > JIBE
JIBER > JIBE
JIBERS > JIBE
JIBES > JIBE
JIBING > JIBE
JIBINGLY > JIBE
JIBS > JIB
JICAMA n pale brown turnip
JICAMAS > JICAMA
JICKAJOG vb engage in sexual intercourse
JICKAJOGS
> JICKAJOG
JIFF same as > JIFFY
JIFFIES > JIFFY
JIFFS > JIFF
JIFFY n very short period of time
JIG n type of lively dance ▷ vb dance a jig
JIGAJIG vb engage in sexual intercourse
JIGAJIGS > JIGAJIG
JIGAJOG variant of
> JIGAJIG
JIGAJOGS > JIGAJOG
JIGAMAREE n thing
JIGGED > JIG
JIGGER n small whisky glass ▷ vb interfere or alter
JIGGERED > JIGGER
JIGGERING > JIGGER
JIGGERS > JIGGER
JIGGIER > JIGGY
JIGGIEST > JIGGY
JIGGING > JIG
JIGGINGS > JIG
JIGGISH > JIG

JIGGLE vb move up and down with short jerky movements ▷ n short jerky motion
JIGGLED > JIGGLE
JIGGLES > JIGGLE
JIGGLIER > JIGGLE
JIGGLIEST > JIGGLE
JIGGLING > JIGGLE
JIGGLY > JIGGLE
JIGGUMBOB n thing
JIGGY adj resembling a jig
JIGJIG variant of
> JIGAJIG
JIGJIGS > JIGJIG
JIGLIKE > JIG
JIGOT same as > GIGOT
JIGOTS > JIGOT
JIGS > JIG
JIGSAW n type of game ▷ vb cut with a jigsaw
JIGSAWED > JIGSAW
JIGSAWING > JIGSAW
JIGSAWN > JIGSAW
JIGSAWS > JIGSAW
JIHAD n Islamic holy war against unbelievers
JIHADEEN pl n jihadists
JIHADI n person who takes part in a jihad
JIHADIS > JIHADI
JIHADISM n Islamic fundamentalist movement that favours jihads
JIHADISMS
> JIHADISM
JIHADIST > JIHADISM
JIHADISTS
> JIHADISM
JIHADS > JIHAD
JILBAB n long robe worn by Muslim women
JILBABS > JILBAB
JILGIE n freshwater crayfish
JILGIES > JILGIE
JILL variant spelling of
> GILL
JILLAROO n young female management trainee on a sheep or cattle station
JILLAROOS
> JILLAROO
JILLET n flighty or capricious woman
JILLETS > JILLET
JILLFLIRT same as
> JILLET
JILLION n extremely large number or amount
JILLIONS > JILLION
JILLIONTH > JILLION
JILLS > JILL
JILT vb leave or reject (one's lover) ▷ n woman who jilts a lover
JILTED > JILT
JILTER > JILT
JILTERS > JILT
JILTING > JILT
JILTS > JILT
JIMCRACK same as
> GIMCRACK
JIMCRACKS
> JIMCRACK

JIMINY *interj* expression of surprise
JIMJAM > JIMJAMS
JIMJAMS *pl n* state of nervous tension, excitement, or anxiety
JIMMIE *same as* > JIMMY
JIMMIED > JIMMY
JIMMIES > JIMMY
JIMMINY *interj* expression of surprise
JIMMY *same as* > JEMMY
JIMMYING > JIMMY
JIMP *adj* handsome
JIMPER > JIMP
JIMPEST > JIMP
JIMPIER > JIMPY
JIMPIEST > JIMPY
JIMPLY *adv* neatly
JIMPNESS > JIMP
JIMPSON *same as* > JIMSON
JIMPY *adj* neat and tidy
JIMSON *n* as in *jimson weed* type of poisonous plant
JIMSONS > JIMSON
JIN *n* Chinese unit of weight
JINGAL *n* swivel-mounted gun
JINGALL *same as* > JINGAL
JINGALLS > JINGALL
JINGALS > JINGAL
JINGBANG *n* entirety of something
JINGBANGS > JINGBANG
JINGKO *same as* > GINGKO
JINGKOES > JINGKO
JINGLE *n* catchy verse or song used in an advert ▷ *vb* (cause to) make a gentle ringing sound
JINGLED > JINGLE
JINGLER > JINGLE
JINGLERS > JINGLE
JINGLES > JINGLE
JINGLET *n* sleigh-bell clapper
JINGLETS > JINGLET
JINGLIER > JINGLE
JINGLIEST > JINGLE
JINGLING > JINGLE
JINGLY > JINGLE
JINGO *n* loud and bellicose patriot; chauvinism
JINGOES > JINGO
JINGOISH > JINGO
JINGOISM *n* aggressive nationalism
JINGOISMS > JINGOISM
JINGOIST > JINGOISM
JINGOISTS > JINGOISM
JINJILI *n* type of sesame
JINJILIS > JINJILI
JINK *vb* move quickly or jerkily in order to dodge someone ▷ *n* jinking movement
JINKED > JINK

JINKER *n* vehicle for transporting timber ▷ *vb* carry or transport in a jinker
JINKERED > JINKER
JINKERING > JINKER
JINKERS > JINKER
JINKING > JINK
JINKS > JINK
JINN *n* spirit in Muslim mythology
JINNE *interj* South African exclamation
JINNEE *same as* > JINNI
JINNI *n* spirit in Muslim mythology
JINNIS > JINNI
JINNS > JINN
JINRIKSHA *same as* > RICKSHAW
JINS > JIN
JINX *n* person or thing bringing bad luck ▷ *vb* be or put a jinx on
JINXED > JINX
JINXES > JINX
JINXING > JINX
JIPIJAPA *n* plant whose leaves are used for making panama hats
JIPIJAPAS > JIPIJAPA
JIPYAPA *same as* > JIPIJAPA
JIPYAPAS > JIPYAPA
JIRBLE *vb* pour carelessly
JIRBLED > JIRBLE
JIRBLES > JIRBLE
JIRBLING > JIRBLE
JIRD *n* gerbil
JIRDS > JIRD
JIRGA *n* Afghan council
JIRGAS > JIRGA
JIRKINET *n* bodice
JIRKINETS > JIRKINET
JIRRE *same as* > JINNE
JISM *n* vulgar word for semen
JISMS > JISM
JISSOM *same as* > JISM
JISSOMS > JISSOM
JITNEY *n* small cheap bus
JITNEYS > JITNEY
JITTER *vb* be anxious or nervous
JITTERBUG *n* fast jerky American dance that was popular in the 1940s ▷ *vb* dance the jitterbug
JITTERED > JITTER
JITTERIER > JITTERY
JITTERING > JITTER
JITTERS > JITTER
JITTERY *adj* nervous
JIUJITSU *variant spelling of* > JUJITSU
JIUJITSUS > JIUJITSU
JIUJUTSU *same as* > JUJITSU
JIUJUTSUS > JIUJUTSU
JIVE *n* lively dance of the 1940s and 1950s ▷ *vb* dance the jive ▷ *adj*

pertaining to or indicative of jive
JIVEASS *adj* misleading or phoney ▷ *n* person who loves fun and excitement
JIVEASSES > JIVEASS
JIVED > JIVE
JIVER > JIVE
JIVERS > JIVE
JIVES > JIVE
JIVEST > JIVE
JIVEY *adj* jazzy; lively
JIVIER > JIVEY
JIVIEST > JIVEY
JIVING > JIVE
JIVY *same as* > JIVEY
JIZ *n* wig
JIZZ *n* term for the characteristics that identify a particular species of bird or plant
JIZZES > JIZZ
JNANA *n* type of yoga
JNANAS > JNANA
JO *n* Scots word for sweetheart
JOANNA *n* piano
JOANNAS > JOANNA
JOANNES *same as* > JOHANNES
JOANNESES > JOANNES
JOB *n* occupation or paid employment ▷ *vb* work at casual jobs
JOBATION *n* scolding
JOBATIONS > JOBATION
JOBBED > JOB
JOBBER *n* person who jobs
JOBBERIES > JOBBERY
JOBBERS > JOBBER
JOBBERY *n* practice of making private profit out of a public office
JOBBIE *n* referring to a thing usually specified in the preceding part of a sentence
JOBBIES > JOBBIE
JOBBING *adj* doing individual jobs for payment ▷ *n* act of seeking work
JOBBINGS > JOBBING
JOBCENTRE *n* office where unemployed people can find out about job vacancies
JOBE *vb* scold
JOBED > JOBE
JOBERNOWL *n* stupid person
JOBES > JOBE
JOBHOLDER *n* person who has a job
JOBING > JOBE
JOBLESS *pl n* as in *the jobless* unemployed people ▷ *adj* unemployed
JOBNAME *n* title of position
JOBNAMES > JOBNAME
JOBS > JOB
JOBSEEKER *n* person looking for employment
JOBSHARE *n* arrangement in which two

people divide the duties for one job between them
JOBSHARES > JOBSHARE
JOBSWORTH *n* person in a position of minor authority who invokes the letter of the law in order to avoid any action requiring initiative, cooperation, etc
JOCK *n* athlete
JOCKDOM *n* world of male athletes
JOCKDOMS > JOCKDOM
JOCKETTE *n* female athlete
JOCKETTES > JOCKETTE
JOCKEY *n* person who rides horses in races ▷ *vb* ride (a horse) in a race
JOCKEYED > JOCKEY
JOCKEYING > JOCKEY
JOCKEYISH > JOCKEY
JOCKEYISM *n* skills and practices of jockeys
JOCKEYS > JOCKEY
JOCKIER > JOCKY
JOCKIEST > JOCKY
JOCKISH *adj* macho
JOCKNEY *n* the Scots dialect influenced by cockney speech patterns
JOCKNEYS > JOCKNEY
JOCKO *n* chimpanzee
JOCKOS > JOCKO
JOCKS > JOCK
JOCKSTRAP *n* support worn by male athletes
JOCKTELEG *n* clasp knife
JOCKY *adj* indicating or appropriate to a male athlete
JOCO *adj* relaxed ▷ *n* joke
JOCOS > JOCO
JOCOSE *adj* playful or humorous
JOCOSELY > JOCOSE
JOCOSER > JOCOSE
JOCOSEST > JOCOSE
JOCOSITY > JOCOSE
JOCULAR *adj* fond of joking
JOCULARLY > JOCULAR
JOCULATOR *n* joker
JOCUND *adj* merry or cheerful
JOCUNDER > JOCUND
JOCUNDEST > JOCUND
JOCUNDITY > JOCUND
JOCUNDLY > JOCUND
JODEL *same as* > YODEL
JODELLED > JODEL
JODELLING > JODEL
JODELS > JODEL
JODHPUR *n* as in *jodhpur boots* ankle-length leather riding boots
JODHPURS *pl n* riding breeches
JOE *same as* > JO
JOES > JOE
JOEY *n* young kangaroo
JOEYS > JOEY
JOG *vb* run at a gentle pace, esp for exercise ▷ *n* slow run
JOGGED > JOG

JOGGER n person who runs at a jog for exercise
JOGGERS > JOGGER
JOGGING > JOG
JOGGINGS > JOG
JOGGLE vb shake or move jerkily ▷ n act of joggling
JOGGLED > JOGGLE
JOGGLER > JOGGLE
JOGGLERS > JOGGLE
JOGGLES > JOGGLE
JOGGLING > JOGGLE
JOGPANTS pl n trousers worn for jogging
JOGS > JOG
JOGTROT n easy bouncy gait ▷ vb move at a jogtrot
JOGTROTS > JOGTROT
JOHANNES n Portuguese gold coin minted in the early 18th century
JOHN n toilet
JOHNBOAT n small flat-bottomed boat
JOHNBOATS > JOHNBOAT
JOHNNIE same as > JOHNNY
JOHNNIES > JOHNNY
JOHNNY n chap
JOHNS > JOHN
JOHNSON slang word for > PENIS
JOHNSONS > JOHNSON
JOIN vb become a member (of) ▷ n place where two things are joined
JOINABLE > JOIN
JOINDER n act of joining, esp in legal contexts
JOINDERS > JOINDER
JOINED > JOIN
JOINER n maker of finished woodwork
JOINERIES > JOINERY
JOINERS > JOINER
JOINERY n joiner's work
JOINING > JOIN
JOININGS > JOIN
JOINS > JOIN
JOINT adj shared by two or more ▷ n place where bones meet but can move ▷ vb divide meat into joints
JOINTED adj having a joint or joints
JOINTEDLY > JOINTED
JOINTER n tool for pointing mortar joints
JOINTERS > JOINTER
JOINTING > JOINT
JOINTINGS > JOINTING
JOINTLESS > JOINT
JOINTLY > JOINT
JOINTNESS > JOINT
JOINTRESS n woman entitled to a jointure
JOINTS > JOINT
JOINTURE n provision made by a husband for his spouse after his death
JOINTURED > JOINTURE
JOINTURES > JOINTURE

JOINTWEED n American wild plant
JOINTWORM n larva of chalcid flies which form galls on the stems of cereal plants
JOIST n horizontal beam ▷ vb construct (a floor, roof, etc) with joists
JOISTED > JOIST
JOISTING > JOIST
JOISTS > JOIST
JOJOBA n shrub of SW North America
JOJOBAS > JOJOBA
JOKE n thing said or done to cause laughter ▷ vb make jokes
JOKED > JOKE
JOKER n person who jokes
JOKERS > JOKER
JOKES > JOKE
JOKESMITH n comedian
JOKESOME > JOKE
JOKESTER n person who makes jokes
JOKESTERS > JOKESTER
JOKEY adj intended as a joke
JOKIER > JOKEY
JOKIEST > JOKEY
JOKILY > JOKE
JOKINESS > JOKE
JOKING n act of joking
JOKINGLY > JOKE
JOKINGS > JOKING
JOKOL Shetland word for > YES
JOKY same as > JOKEY
JOL n party ▷ vb have a good time
JOLE vb knock
JOLED > JOLE
JOLES > JOLE
JOLING > JOLE
JOLIOTIUM n former name proposed for dubnium
JOLL variant of > JOLE
JOLLED > JOL
JOLLER n person who has a good time
JOLLERS > JOLLER
JOLLEY same as > JOLLY
JOLLEYER > JOLLEY
JOLLEYERS > JOLLEY
JOLLEYING > JOLLEY
JOLLEYS > JOLLEY
JOLLIED > JOLLY
JOLLIER n joker
JOLLIERS > JOLLIER
JOLLIES > JOLLY
JOLLIEST > JOLLY
JOLLIFIED > JOLLIFY
JOLLIFIES > JOLLIFY
JOLLIFY vb be or cause to be jolly
JOLLILY > JOLLY
JOLLIMENT > JOLLY
JOLLINESS > JOLLY
JOLLING > JOL
JOLLITIES > JOLLITY
JOLLITY n condition of being jolly

JOLLOF adj as in jollof rice W African dish made from rice and meat or fish
JOLLOP n cream or unguent
JOLLOPS > JOLLOP
JOLLS > JOLL
JOLLY adj full of good humour ▷ adv extremely ▷ vb try to make or keep (someone) cheerful ▷ n festivity or celebration
JOLLYBOAT n small boat used as a utility tender for a vessel
JOLLYER > JOLLY
JOLLYERS > JOLLY
JOLLYHEAD same as > JOLLITY
JOLLYING > JOLLY
JOLLYINGS > JOLLY
JOLS > JOL
JOLT n unpleasant surprise or shock ▷ vb surprise or shock
JOLTED > JOLT
JOLTER > JOLT
JOLTERS > JOLT
JOLTHEAD n fool
JOLTHEADS > JOLTHEAD
JOLTIER > JOLT
JOLTIEST > JOLT
JOLTILY > JOLT
JOLTING n act of jolting
JOLTINGLY > JOLT
JOLTINGS > JOLTING
JOLTS > JOLT
JOLTY > JOLT
JOMO same as > ZO
JOMON n particular era in Japanese history
JOMONS > JOMON
JOMOS > JOMO
JONCANOE n Jamaican ceremony
JONCANOES > JONCANOE
JONES vb desire
JONESED > JONES
JONESES > JONES
JONESING > JONES
JONG n friend, often used in direct address
JONGLEUR n (in medieval France) an itinerant minstrel
JONGLEURS > JONGLEUR
JONGS > JONG
JONNOCK adj genuine ▷ adv honestly
JONNYCAKE n type of flat bread
JONQUIL n fragrant narcissus
JONQUILS > JONQUIL
JONTIES > JONTY
JONTY n petty officer
JOOK vb poke or puncture (the skin) ▷ n jab or the resulting wound
JOOKED > JOOK
JOOKERIES > JOOKERY
JOOKERY n mischief
JOOKING > JOOK
JOOKS > JOOK

JOR n movement in Indian music
JORAM same as > JORUM
JORAMS > JORAM
JORDAN n chamber pot
JORDANS > JORDAN
JORDELOO same as > GARDYLOO
JORDELOOS > JORDELOO
JORS > JOR
JORUM n large drinking bowl or vessel or its contents
JORUMS > JORUM
JOSEPH n woman's floor-length riding coat
JOSEPHS > JOSEPH
JOSH vb tease ▷ n teasing or bantering joke
JOSHED > JOSH
JOSHER > JOSH
JOSHERS > JOSH
JOSHES > JOSH
JOSHING n act of joshing
JOSHINGLY > JOSH
JOSHINGS > JOSHING
JOSKIN n bumpkin
JOSKINS > JOSKIN
JOSS n Chinese deity
JOSSER n unintelligent person
JOSSERS > JOSSER
JOSSES > JOSS
JOSTLE vb knock or push against ▷ n act of jostling
JOSTLED > JOSTLE
JOSTLER > JOSTLE
JOSTLERS > JOSTLE
JOSTLES > JOSTLE
JOSTLING > JOSTLE
JOSTLINGS > JOSTLE
JOT vb write briefly ▷ n very small amount
JOTA n Spanish dance
JOTAS > JOTA
JOTS > JOT
JOTTED > JOT
JOTTER n notebook
JOTTERS > JOTTER
JOTTIER > JOTTY
JOTTIEST > JOTTY
JOTTING > JOT
JOTTINGS > JOT
JOTTY > JOT
JOTUN n giant
JOTUNN same as > JOTUN
JOTUNNS > JOTUNN
JOTUNS > JOTUN
JOUAL n nonstandard variety of Canadian French
JOUALS > JOUAL
JOUGS pl n iron ring for restraining an offender
JOUISANCE n joy
JOUK vb duck or dodge ▷ n sudden evasive movement
JOUKED > JOUK
JOUKERIES > JOUKERY
JOUKERY same as > JOOKERY
JOUKING > JOUK
JOUKS > JOUK
JOULE n unit of work or energy ▷ vb knock
JOULED > JOULE
JOULES > JOULE

JOUNCE *vb* shake or jolt or cause to shake or jolt ▷ *n* jolting movement
JOUNCED > JOUNCE
JOUNCES > JOUNCE
JOUNCIER > JOUNCE
JOUNCIEST > JOUNCE
JOUNCING > JOUNCE
JOUNCY > JOUNCE
JOUR *n* day
JOURNAL *n* daily newspaper or magazine ▷ *vb* record in a journal
JOURNALED > JOURNAL
JOURNALS > JOURNAL
JOURNEY *n* act of travelling from one place to another ▷ *vb* travel
JOURNEYED > JOURNEY
JOURNEYER > JOURNEY
JOURNEYS > JOURNEY
JOURNO *n* journalist
JOURNOS > JOURNO
JOURS > JOUR
JOUST *n* combat between two knights ▷ *vb* fight on horseback using lances
JOUSTED > JOUST
JOUSTER > JOUST
JOUSTERS > JOUST
JOUSTING *n* act of jousting
JOUSTINGS > JOUSTING
JOUSTS > JOUST
JOVIAL *adj* happy and cheerful
JOVIALITY > JOVIAL
JOVIALLY > JOVIAL
JOVIALTY > JOVIAL
JOW *vb* ring (a bell)
JOWAR *n* variety of sorghum
JOWARI *same as* > JOWAR
JOWARIS > JOWARI
JOWARS > JOWAR
JOWED > JOW
JOWING > JOW
JOWL *n* lower jaw ▷ *vb* knock
JOWLED > JOWL
JOWLER *n* dog with prominent jowls
JOWLERS > JOWLER
JOWLIER > JOWL
JOWLIEST > JOWL
JOWLINESS > JOWL
JOWLING > JOWL
JOWLS > JOWL
JOWLY > JOWL
JOWS > JOW
JOY *n* feeling of great delight or pleasure ▷ *vb* feel joy
JOYANCE *n* joyous feeling or festivity
JOYANCES > JOYANCE
JOYED > JOY
JOYFUL *adj* feeling or bringing great joy
JOYFULLER > JOYFUL
JOYFULLY > JOYFUL
JOYING > JOY
JOYLESS *adj* feeling or bringing no joy
JOYLESSLY > JOYLESS

JOYOUS *adj* extremely happy and enthusiastic
JOYOUSLY > JOYOUS
JOYPAD *n* computer games console
JOYPADS > JOYPAD
JOYPOP *vb* take addictive drugs occasionally
JOYPOPPED > JOYPOP
JOYPOPPER > JOYPOP
JOYPOPS > JOYPOP
JOYRIDDEN > JOYRIDE
JOYRIDE *n* drive in a car one has stolen ▷ *vb* take such a ride
JOYRIDER > JOYRIDE
JOYRIDERS > JOYRIDE
JOYRIDES > JOYRIDE
JOYRIDING > JOYRIDE
JOYRODE > JOYRIDE
JOYS > JOY
JOYSTICK *n* control device for an aircraft or computer
JOYSTICKS > JOYSTICK
JUBA *n* lively African-American dance
JUBAS > JUBA
JUBATE *adj* possessing a mane
JUBBAH *n* long loose outer garment with wide sleeves
JUBBAHS > JUBBAH
JUBE *n* part of a church or cathedral
JUBES > JUBE
JUBHAH *same as* > JUBBAH
JUBHAHS > JUBHAH
JUBILANCE > JUBILANT
JUBILANCY > JUBILANT
JUBILANT *adj* feeling or expressing great joy
JUBILATE *vb* have or express great joy
JUBILATED > JUBILATE
JUBILATES > JUBILATE
JUBILE *same as* > JUBILEE
JUBILEE *n* special anniversary, esp 25th or 50th
JUBILEES > JUBILEE
JUBILES > JUBILE
JUCO *n* junior college in America
JUCOS > JUCO
JUD *n* large block of coal
JUDAS *n* peephole
JUDASES > JUDAS
JUDDER *vb* vibrate violently ▷ *n* violent vibration
JUDDERED > JUDDER
JUDDERIER > JUDDERY
JUDDERING > JUDDER
JUDDERS > JUDDER
JUDDERY *adj* shaky
JUDGE *n* public official ▷ *vb* act as a judge
JUDGEABLE > JUDGE
JUDGED > JUDGE

JUDGELESS > JUDGE
JUDGELIKE > JUDGE
JUDGEMENT *same as* > JUDGMENT
JUDGER > JUDGE
JUDGERS > JUDGE
JUDGES > JUDGE
JUDGESHIP *n* position, office, or function of a judge
JUDGEY *adj* tending to be judgmental
JUDGIER > JUDGY
JUDGIEST > JUDGY
JUDGING *n* act of judging
JUDGINGLY > JUDGE
JUDGINGS > JUDGING
JUDGMATIC *adj* judicious
JUDGMENT *n* opinion reached after careful thought
JUDGMENTS > JUDGMENT
JUDGY *adj* tending to be judgmental
JUDICABLE *adj* capable of being judged, esp in a court of law
JUDICARE *n* (in Canada) state-paid legal services
JUDICARES > JUDICARE
JUDICATOR *n* person who acts as a judge
JUDICIAL *adj* of or by a court or judge
JUDICIARY *n* system of courts and judges ▷ *adj* of or relating to courts of law, judgment, or judges
JUDICIOUS *adj* well-judged and sensible
JUDIES > JUDY
JUDO *n* type of sport
JUDOGI *n* white two-piece cotton costume
JUDOGIS > JUDOGI
JUDOIST > JUDO
JUDOISTS > JUDO
JUDOKA *n* competitor or expert in judo
JUDOKAS > JUDOKA
JUDOS > JUDO
JUDS > JUD
JUDY *n* woman
JUG *n* container for liquids ▷ *vb* stew or boil (meat, esp hare) in an earthenware container
JUGA > JUGUM
JUGAAD *n* (in Indian English) problem-solving
JUGAADS > JUGAAD
JUGAL *adj* of or relating to the zygomatic bone ▷ *n* cheekbone
JUGALS > JUGAL
JUGATE *adj* having parts arranged in pairs
JUGFUL *same as* > JUG
JUGFULS > JUGFUL
JUGGED > JUG
JUGGING > JUG
JUGGINGS > JUG
JUGGINS *n* silly person
JUGGINSES > JUGGINS
JUGGLE *vb* throw and catch (objects) to keep

them in the air ▷ *n* act of juggling
JUGGLED > JUGGLE
JUGGLER *n* person who juggles, esp a professional entertainer
JUGGLERS > JUGGLER
JUGGLERY > JUGGLE
JUGGLES > JUGGLE
JUGGLING > JUGGLE
JUGGLINGS > JUGGLE
JUGHEAD *n* clumsy person
JUGHEADS > JUGHEAD
JUGLET *n* small jug
JUGLETS > JUGLET
JUGS > JUG
JUGSFUL > JUGFUL
JUGULA > JUGULUM
JUGULAR *n* one of three large veins of the neck
JUGULARS > JUGULAR
JUGULATE *vb* check (a disease) by extreme measures or remedies
JUGULATED > JUGULATE
JUGULATES > JUGULATE
JUGULUM *n* lower throat
JUGUM *n* part of an insect's forewing
JUGUMS > JUGUM
JUICE *n* liquid part of vegetables, fruit, or meat ▷ *vb* extract juice from fruits and vegetables
JUICED > JUICE
JUICEHEAD *n* alcoholic
JUICELESS > JUICE
JUICER *n* kitchen appliance
JUICERS > JUICER
JUICES > JUICE
JUICIER > JUICY
JUICIEST > JUICY
JUICILY > JUICY
JUICINESS > JUICY
JUICING > JUICE
JUICY *adj* full of juice
JUJITSU *n* Japanese martial art
JUJITSUS > JUJITSU
JUJU *n* W African magic charm or fetish
JUJUBE *n* chewy sweet made of flavoured gelatine
JUJUBES > JUJUBE
JUJUISM > JUJU
JUJUISMS > JUJU
JUJUIST > JUJU
JUJUISTS > JUJU
JUJUS > JUJU
JUJUTSU *same as* > JUJITSU
JUJUTSUS > JUJUTSU
JUKE *vb* dance or play dance music
JUKEBOX *n* coin-operated music box
JUKEBOXES > JUKEBOX
JUKED > JUKE
JUKES > JUKE
JUKING > JUKE
JUKSKEI *n* type of game
JUKSKEIS > JUKSKEI

JUKU n Japanese martial art

JUKUS > JUKU

JULEP n sweet alcoholic drink

JULEPS > JULEP

JULIENNE adj (of vegetables or meat) cut into thin shreds ▷ n clear soup containing thinly shredded vegetables ▷ vb cut into thin pieces

JULIENNED > JULIENNE

JULIENNES > JULIENNE

JULIET n code word for the letter J

JULIETS > JULIET

JUMAR n climbing tool ▷ vb climb (up a fixed rope) using jumars

JUMARED > JUMAR

JUMARING > JUMAR

JUMARRED > JUMAR

JUMARRING > JUMAR

JUMARS > JUMAR

JUMART n mythical offspring of a bull and a mare

JUMARTS > JUMART

JUMBAL same as > JUMBLE

JUMBALS > JUMBAL

JUMBIE n Caribbean ghost

JUMBIES > JUMBIE

JUMBLE n confused heap or state ▷ vb mix in a disordered way

JUMBLED > JUMBLE

JUMBLER > JUMBLE

JUMBLERS > JUMBLE

JUMBLES > JUMBLE

JUMBLIER > JUMBLE

JUMBLIEST > JUMBLE

JUMBLING > JUMBLE

JUMBLY > JUMBLE

JUMBO adj very large ▷ n large jet airliner

JUMBOISE same as > JUMBOIZE

JUMBOISED > JUMBOIZE

JUMBOISES > JUMBOIZE

JUMBOIZE vb extend (a ship) by inserting a part between the bow and stern

JUMBOIZED > JUMBOIZE

JUMBOIZES > JUMBOIZE

JUMBOS > JUMBO

JUMBUCK n sheep

JUMBUCKS > JUMBUCK

JUMBY n Caribbean ghost

JUMELLE n paired objects

JUMELLES > JUMELLE

JUMP vb leap or spring into the air using the leg muscles ▷ n act of jumping

JUMPABLE > JUMP

JUMPED > JUMP

JUMPER n sweater or pullover

JUMPERS > JUMPER

JUMPIER > JUMPY

JUMPIEST > JUMPY

JUMPILY > JUMPY

JUMPINESS > JUMPY

JUMPING > JUMP

JUMPINGLY > JUMP

JUMPINGS > JUMP

JUMPOFF n round in a showjumping contest

JUMPOFFS > JUMPOFF

JUMPROPE n rope held in the hands and jumped over

JUMPROPES > JUMPROPE

JUMPS > JUMP

JUMPSHOT n type of shot in basketball in which a player jumps to reach the basket

JUMPSHOTS > JUMPSHOT

JUMPSIES pl n game involving jumping over a straight rope

JUMPSUIT n one-piece garment of combined trousers and jacket or shirt

JUMPSUITS > JUMPSUIT

JUMPY adj nervous

JUN variant of > CHON

JUNCATE same as > JUNKET

JUNCATES > JUNCATE

JUNCO n North American bunting

JUNCOES > JUNCO

JUNCOS > JUNCO

JUNCTION n place where routes, railway lines, or roads meet

JUNCTIONS > JUNCTION

JUNCTURAL > JUNCTURE

JUNCTURE n point in time, esp a critical one

JUNCTURES > JUNCTURE

JUNCUS n type of rush

JUNCUSES > JUNCUS

JUNEATING n early-season apple

JUNGLE n tropical forest of dense tangled vegetation

JUNGLED adj covered with jungle

JUNGLEGYM n climbing frame for children

JUNGLES > JUNGLE

JUNGLI n uncultured person

JUNGLIER > JUNGLE

JUNGLIEST > JUNGLE

JUNGLIS > JUNGLI

JUNGLIST n jungle-music enthusiast

JUNGLISTS > JUNGLIST

JUNGLY > JUNGLE

JUNIOR adj of lower standing ▷ n junior person ▷ vb work as a junior

JUNIORATE n preparatory course for candidates for religious orders

JUNIORED > JUNIOR

JUNIORING > JUNIOR

JUNIORITY n condition of being junior

JUNIORS > JUNIOR

JUNIPER n evergreen shrub with purple berries

JUNIPERS > JUNIPER

JUNK n discarded or useless objects ▷ vb discard as junk

JUNKANOO n Bahamian ceremony

JUNKANOOS > JUNKANOO

JUNKED > JUNK

JUNKER n (formerly) young German nobleman

JUNKERDOM n condition of being a junker

JUNKERS > JUNKER

JUNKET n excursion by public officials ▷ vb (of a public official, committee, etc) to go on a junket

JUNKETED > JUNKET

JUNKETEER > JUNKET

JUNKETER > JUNKET

JUNKETERS > JUNKET

JUNKETING > JUNKET

JUNKETS > JUNKET

JUNKETTED > JUNKET

JUNKETTER > JUNKET

JUNKIE n slang word for person addicted to something

JUNKIER > JUNKY

JUNKIES > JUNKIE

JUNKIEST > JUNKY

JUNKINESS > JUNKY

JUNKING > JUNK

JUNKMAN n man who trades in discarded items

JUNKMEN > JUNKMAN

JUNKS > JUNK

JUNKY adj of low quality

JUNKYARD n place where junk is stored or collected for sale

JUNKYARDS > JUNKYARD

JUNTA n military officers holding power in a country

JUNTAS > JUNTA

JUNTO same as > JUNTA

JUNTOS > JUNTO

JUPATI n type of palm tree

JUPATIS > JUPATI

JUPE n sleeveless jacket

JUPES > JUPE

JUPON n short sleeveless padded garment

JUPONS > JUPON

JURA > JUS

JURAL adj of or relating to law or to the administration of justice

JURALLY > JURAL

JURANT n person taking oath

JURANTS > JURANT

JURASSIC adj of the second period of the Mesozoic era

JURAT n statement at the foot of an affidavit

JURATORY adj of, relating to, or expressed in an oath

JURATS > JURAT

JURE adv by legal right ▷ n legal right

JUREL n edible fish

JURELS > JUREL

JURES > JURE

JURIDIC same as > JURIDICAL

JURIDICAL adj of law or the administration of justice

JURIED > JURY

JURIES > JURY

JURIST n expert in law

JURISTIC adj of or relating to jurists

JURISTS > JURIST

JUROR n member of a jury

JURORS > JUROR

JURY n group of people sworn to deliver a verdict in a court of law ▷ adj makeshift ▷ vb evaluate by jury

JURYING > JURY

JURYLESS > JURY

JURYMAN n member of a jury, esp a man

JURYMAST n replacement mast

JURYMASTS > JURYMAST

JURYMEN > JURYMAN

JURYWOMAN n female member of a jury

JURYWOMEN > JURYWOMAN

JUS n right, power, or authority

JUSSIVE n mood of verbs used for giving orders; imperative

JUSSIVES > JUSSIVE

JUST adv very recently ▷ adj fair or impartial in action or judgment ▷ vb joust

JUSTED > JUST

JUSTER > JUST

JUSTERS > JUST

JUSTEST > JUST

JUSTICE n quality of being just

JUSTICER n magistrate

JUSTICERS > JUSTICER

JUSTICES > JUSTICE

JUSTICIAR n chief political and legal officer from the time of William I to that of Henry III, who deputized for the king in his absence and presided over the kings' courts

JUSTIFIED > JUSTIFY

JUSTIFIER > JUSTIFY

JUSTIFIES > JUSTIFY

JUSTIFY vb prove right or reasonable

JUSTING > JUST

JUSTLE less common word for > JOSTLE

JUSTLED > JUSTLE
JUSTLES > JUSTLE
JUSTLING > JUSTLE
JUSTLY > JUST
JUSTNESS > JUST
JUSTS *same as* **>** JOUST
JUT *vb* project or stick out
▷ *n* something that juts
out
JUTE *n* plant fibre, used
for rope, canvas, etc
JUTELIKE > JUTE

JUTES > JUTE
JUTS > JUT
JUTTED > JUT
JUTTIED > JUTTY
JUTTIER > JUTTY
JUTTIES > JUTTY
JUTTIEST > JUTTY
JUTTING > JUT
JUTTINGLY > JUT
JUTTY *vb* project beyond
▷ *adj* characterized by
jutting

JUTTYING > JUTTY
JUVE *same as*
> JUVENILE
JUVENAL *variant spelling*
(esp US) of **>** JUVENILE
JUVENALS > JUVENAL
JUVENILE *adj* young
▷ *n* young person or c
hild
JUVENILES
> JUVENILE
JUVENILIA *pl n* works

produced in an author's
youth
JUVES > JUVE
JUVIE *n* juvenile
detention centre
JUVIES > JUVIE
JUXTAPOSE *vb* put side
by side
JYMOLD *adj* having a
hinge
JYNX *n* wryneck
JYNXES > JYNX

j

Kk

KA *n* (in ancient Egypt) type of spirit ▷ *vb* (in archaic usage) help
KAAL *adj* naked
KAAMA *n* large African antelope with lyre-shaped horns
KAAMAS ▷ KAAMA
KAAS *n* Dutch cabinet or wardrobe
KAB *variant spelling of* ▷ CAB
KABAB *same as* ▷ KEBAB
KABABBED ▷ KABAB
KABABBING ▷ KABAB
KABABS ▷ KABAB
KABADDI *n* type of game
KABADDIS ▷ KABADDI
KABAKA *n* any of the former rulers of the Baganda people
KABAKAS ▷ KABAKA
KABALA *same as* ▷ KABBALAH
KABALAS ▷ KABALA
KABALISM ▷ KABALA
KABALISMS ▷ KABALA
KABALIST ▷ KABALA
KABALISTS ▷ KABALA
KABAR *archaic form of* ▷ CABER
KABARS ▷ KABAR
KABAYA *n* tunic
KABAYAS ▷ KABAYA
KABBALA *same as* ▷ KABBALAH
KABBALAH *n* ancient Jewish mystical tradition
KABBALAHS ▷ KABBALAH
KABBALAS ▷ KABBALA
KABBALISM ▷ KABBALAH
KABBALIST ▷ KABBALAH
KABELE *same as* ▷ KEBELE
KABELES ▷ KABELE
KABELJOU *n* large fish that is an important food fish of South African waters
KABELJOUS ▷ KABELJOU
KABELJOUW *same as* ▷ KABELJOU
KABIKI *n* fruit tree found in India
KABIKIS ▷ KABIKI
KABLOOEY *interj* expressing alarming or surprising abruptness
KABLOOIE *same as* ▷ KABLOOEY

KABLOONA *n* (among Canadian Inuits) person who is not Inuit
KABLOONAS ▷ KABLOONA
KABLOONAT ▷ KABLOONA
KABOB *same as* ▷ KEBAB
KABOBBED ▷ KABOB
KABOBBING ▷ KABOB
KABOBS ▷ KABOB
KABOCHA *n* type of Japanese pumpkin
KABOCHAS ▷ KABOCHA
KABOODLE *same as* ▷ CABOODLE
KABOODLES ▷ KABOODLE
KABOOM *n* loud echoing explosive sound
KABOOMS ▷ KABOOM
KABS ▷ KAB
KABUKI *n* form of Japanese drama
KABUKIS ▷ KABUKI
KACCHA *n* trousers worn traditionally by Sikhs
KACCHAS ▷ KACCHA
KACHA *adj* crude
KACHAHRI *n* Indian courthouse
KACHAHRIS ▷ KACHAHRI
KACHCHA *same as* ▷ KACHA
KACHERI *same as* ▷ KACHAHRI
KACHERIS ▷ KACHERI
KACHINA *n* type of supernatural being
KACHINAS ▷ KACHINA
KACHORI *n* balls of fried dough with various fillings, eaten as a snack
KACHORIS ▷ KACHORI
KACHUMBER *n* salad of onion, tomato, and cucumber
KACK *same as* ▷ CACK
KACKS ▷ KACK
KADAI *same as* ▷ KARAHI
KADAIS ▷ KADAI
KADAITCHA *n* (in certain Aboriginal Australian tribes) man with the mission of avenging the death of a tribesman
KADDISH *n* ancient Jewish liturgical prayer
KADDISHES ▷ KADDISH
KADDISHIM ▷ KADDISH
KADE *same as* ▷ KED
KADES ▷ KADE

KADI *variant spelling of* ▷ CADI
KADIS ▷ KADI
KAE *n* dialect word for jackdaw or jay ▷ *vb* (in archaic usage) help
KAED ▷ KAE
KAEING ▷ KAE
KAES ▷ KAE
KAF *n* letter of the Hebrew alphabet
KAFFIYAH *same as* ▷ KAFFIYEH
KAFFIYAHS ▷ KAFFIYAH
KAFFIYEH *same as* ▷ KEFFIYEH
KAFFIYEHS ▷ KAFFIYEH
KAFILA *n* caravan
KAFILAS ▷ KAFILA
KAFS ▷ KAF
KAFTAN *n* long loose garment
KAFTANS ▷ KAFTAN
KAFUFFLE *n* commotion or disorder
KAFUFFLES ▷ KAFUFFLE
KAGO *n* Japanese sedan chair
KAGOOL *variant spelling of* ▷ CAGOULE
KAGOOLS ▷ KAGOOL
KAGOS ▷ KAGO
KAGOUL *variant spelling of* ▷ CAGOULE
KAGOULE *same as* ▷ KAGOUL
KAGOULES ▷ KAGOULE
KAGOULS ▷ KAGOUL
KAGU *n* crested nocturnal bird
KAGUS ▷ KAGU
KAHAL *n* Jewish community
KAHALS ▷ KAHAL
KAHAWAI *n* food and game fish of New Zealand
KAHAWAIS ▷ KAHAWAI
KAHIKATEA *n* tall New Zealand coniferous tree
KAHIKATOA *n* tall New Zealand coniferous tree
KAHUNA *n* Hawaiian priest, shaman, or expert
KAHUNAS ▷ KAHUNA
KAI *n* food
KAIAK *same as* ▷ KAYAK
KAIAKED ▷ KAIAK
KAIAKING ▷ KAIAK
KAIAKS ▷ KAIAK
KAID *n* North African chieftain or leader

KAIDS ▷ KAID
KAIE *archaic form of* ▷ KEY
KAIES ▷ KAIE
KAIF *same as* ▷ KIF
KAIFS ▷ KAIF
KAIK *same as* ▷ KAINGA
KAIKA *same as* ▷ KAINGA
KAIKAI *n* food
KAIKAIS ▷ KAIKAI
KAIKAS ▷ KAIKA
KAIKAWAKA *n* small pyramid-shaped New Zealand conifer
KAIKOMAKO *n* small New Zealand tree with white flowers and black fruit
KAIKS ▷ KAIK
KAIL *same as* ▷ KALE
KAILS ▷ KAIL
KAILYAIRD *same as* ▷ KALEYARD
KAILYARD *same as* ▷ KALEYARD
KAILYARDS ▷ KAILYARD
KAIM *same as* ▷ KAME
KAIMAKAM *n* Turkish governor
KAIMAKAMS ▷ KAIMAKAM
KAIMS ▷ KAIM
KAIN *variant spelling of* ▷ CAIN
KAING ▷ KA
KAINGA *n* (in New Zealand) a Māori village or small settlement
KAINGAS ▷ KAINGA
KAINIT *same as* ▷ KAINITE
KAINITE *n* white mineral
KAINITES ▷ KAINITE
KAINITS ▷ KAINIT
KAINS ▷ KAIN
KAIROMONE *n* substance secreted by animal
KAIS ▷ KAI
KAISER *n* German or Austro-Hungarian emperor
KAISERDOM ▷ KAISER
KAISERIN *n* empress
KAISERINS ▷ KAISERIN
KAISERISM ▷ KAISER
KAISERS ▷ KAISER
KAIZEN *n* type of philosophy
KAIZENS ▷ KAIZEN
KAJAWAH *n* type of seat or pannier used on a camel
KAJAWAHS ▷ KAJAWAH

KAJEPUT n variety of Australian melaleuca
KAJEPUTS > KAJEPUT
KAK n South African vulgar slang word for faeces
KAKA n parrot of New Zealand
KAKAPO n nocturnal New Zealand parrot
KAKAPOS > KAKAPO
KAKARIKI n green-feathered New Zealand parrot
KAKARIKIS > KAKARIKI
KAKAS > KAKA
KAKEMONO n Japanese wall hanging
KAKEMONOS > KAKEMONO
KAKI n Asian persimmon tree
KAKIEMON n type of 17th century Japanese porcelain
KAKIEMONS > KAKIEMON
KAKIS > KAKI
KAKIVAK n fish spear used by Inuit people
KAKIVAKS > KAKIVAK
KAKODYL variant spelling of > CACODYL
KAKODYLS > KAKODYL
KAKS > KAK
KAKURO n crossword-style puzzle with numbers
KAKUROS > KAKURO
KALAM n discussion and debate
KALAMANSI n hybrid citrus fruit from the Philippines
KALAMATA n as in kalamata olive aubergine-coloured Greek olive
KALAMATAS > KALAMATA
KALAMDAN n Persian box in which to keep pens
KALAMDANS > KALAMDAN
KALAMKARI n Indian cloth printing and printed Indian cloth
KALAMS > KALAM
KALANCHOE n tropical succulent plant having small brightly coloured flowers and dark shiny leaves
KALE n cabbage with crinkled leaves
KALENDAR variant form of > CALENDAR
KALENDARS > KALENDAR
KALENDS same as > CALENDS
KALES > KALE
KALEWIFE n Scots word for a female vegetable or cabbage seller
KALEWIVES > KALEWIFE
KALEYARD n vegetable garden
KALEYARDS > KALEYARD

KALI another name for > SALTWORT
KALIAN another name for > HOOKAH
KALIANS > KALIAN
KALIF variant spelling of > CALIPH
KALIFATE same as > CALIPHATE
KALIFATES > KALIFATE
KALIFS > KALIF
KALIMBA n musical instrument
KALIMBAS > KALIMBA
KALINITE n alum
KALINITES > KALINITE
KALIPH variant spelling of > CALIPH
KALIPHATE same as > CALIPHATE
KALIPHS > KALIPH
KALIS > KALI
KALIUM n Latin for potassium
KALIUMS > KALIUM
KALLIDIN n type of peptide
KALLIDINS > KALLIDIN
KALLITYPE n old printing process
KALMIA n evergreen ericaceous shrub
KALMIAS > KALMIA
KALONG n fruit bat
KALONGS > KALONG
KALOOKI n card game
KALOOKIE same as > KALOOKI
KALOOKIES > KALOOKIE
KALOOKIS > KALOOKI
KALOTYPE variant spelling of > CALOTYPE
KALOTYPES > KALOTYPE
KALPA n period in Hindu cosmology
KALPAC variant spelling of > CALPAC
KALPACS > KALPAC
KALPAK variant spelling of > CALPAC
KALPAKS > KALPAK
KALPAS > KALPA
KALPIS n Greek water jar
KALPISES > KALPIS
KALSOMINE variant of > CALCIMINE
KALUKI same as > KALOOKI
KALUKIS > KALUKI
KALUMPIT n type of Filipino fruit tree or its fruit
KALUMPITS > KALUMPIT
KALYPTRA n Greek veil
KALYPTRAS > KALYPTRA
KAM Shakespearean word for > CROOKED
KAMA n large African antelope with lyre-shaped horns
KAMAAINA n Hawaiian local

KAMAAINAS > KAMAAINA
KAMACITE n alloy of iron and nickel, occurring in meteorites
KAMACITES > KAMACITE
KAMAHI n hardwood tree
KAMAHIS > KAMAHI
KAMALA n S Asian tree
KAMALAS > KAMALA
KAMAS > KAMA
KAME n irregular mound of gravel, sand, etc
KAMEES same as > KAMEEZ
KAMEESES > KAMEES
KAMEEZ n long tunic
KAMEEZES > KAMEEZ
KAMELA same as > KAMALA
KAMELAS > KAMELA
KAMERAD interj shout of surrender ▷ vb surrender
KAMERADED > KAMERAD
KAMERADS > KAMERAD
KAMES > KAME
KAMI n divine being or spiritual being in Shinto
KAMICHI n South American bird
KAMICHIS > KAMICHI
KAMIK n traditional Inuit boot
KAMIKAZE n Japanese pilot who performed a suicide mission ▷ adj undertaken in the knowledge that it will kill the person performing it
KAMIKAZES > KAMIKAZE
KAMIKS > KAMIK
KAMILA same as > KAMALA
KAMILAS > KAMILA
KAMIS same as > KAMEEZ
KAMISES > KAMIS
KAMME same as > KAM
KAMOKAMO n kind of marrow found in New Zealand
KAMOKAMOS > KAMOKAMO
KAMOTIK n type of Inuit sledge
KAMOTIKS > KAMOTIK
KAMOTIQ same as > KAMOTIK
KAMOTIQS > KAMOTIQ
KAMPONG n (in Malaysia) village
KAMPONGS > KAMPONG
KAMSEEN same as > KHAMSIN
KAMSEENS > KAMSEEN
KAMSIN same as > KAMSEEN
KAMSINS > KAMSIN
KANA n Japanese syllabary
KANAE n grey mullet
KANAES > KANAE
KANAMYCIN n type of antibiotic
KANAS > KANA
KANBAN n just-in-time manufacturing process
KANBANS > KANBAN

KANDIES > KANDY
KANDY same as > CANDIE
KANE n Hawaiian man or boy
KANEH n 6-cubit Hebrew measure
KANEHS > KANEH
KANES > KANE
KANG n Chinese heatable platform
KANGA n piece of gaily decorated thin cotton cloth
KANGAROO n Australian marsupial ▷ vb (of a car) move forward with sudden jerks
KANGAROOS > KANGAROO
KANGAS > KANGA
KANGHA n comb traditionally worn by Sikhs
KANGHAS > KANGHA
KANGS > KANG
KANJI n Japanese writing system
KANJIS > KANJI
KANS n Indian wild sugar cane
KANSES > KANS
KANT archaic spelling of > CANT
KANTAR n unit of weight
KANTARS > KANTAR
KANTED > KANT
KANTELA same as > KANTELE
KANTELAS > KANTELA
KANTELE n Finnish stringed instrument
KANTELES > KANTELE
KANTEN same as > AGAR
KANTENS > KANTEN
KANTHA n Bengali embroidered quilt
KANTHAS > KANTHA
KANTIKOY vb dance ceremonially
KANTIKOYS > KANTIKOY
KANTING > KANT
KANTS > KANT
KANUKA n New Zealand myrtaceous tree
KANUKAS > KANUKA
KANZU n long garment
KANZUS > KANZU
KAOLIANG n any of various E Asian varieties of sorghum
KAOLIANGS > KAOLIANG
KAOLIN n fine white clay
KAOLINE same as > KAOLIN
KAOLINES > KAOLINE
KAOLINIC > KAOLIN
KAOLINISE same as > KAOLINIZE
KAOLINITE n white or grey clay mineral consisting of hydrated aluminium silicate in triclinic crystalline form, the main constituent of kaolin
KAOLINIZE vb change into kaolin

KAOLINS > KAOLIN
KAON n type of meson
KAONIC > KAON
KAONS > KAON
KAPA n Hawaiian cloth made from beaten mulberry bark
KAPAS > KAPA
KAPEEK > KAPEYKA
KAPEYKA n small currency unit of Belarus
KAPH n 11th letter of the Hebrew alphabet
KAPHS > KAPH
KAPOK n fluffy fibre
KAPOKS > KAPOK
KAPOW n sharp explosive sound
KAPOWS > KAPOW
KAPPA n tenth letter in the Greek alphabet
KAPPAS > KAPPA
KAPU n (in Hawaii) system of rules for daily life
KAPUKA same as > BROADLEAF
KAPUKAS > KAPUKA
KAPUS > KAPU
KAPUT adj ruined or broken
KAPUTT same as > KAPUT
KARA n steel bangle traditionally worn by Sikhs
KARABINER n metal clip with a spring for attaching to a piton, belay, etc
KARAHI n type of wok
KARAHIS > KARAHI
KARAISM n beliefs and doctrines of a Jewish sect
KARAISMS > KARAISM
KARAIT same as > KRAIT
KARAITS > KARAIT
KARAKA n New Zealand tree
KARAKAS > KARAKA
KARAKIA n prayer
KARAKIAS > KARAKIA
KARAKUL n sheep of central Asia
KARAKULS > KARAKUL
KARAMU n small New Zealand tree
KARAMUS > KARAMU
KARANGA n call or chant of welcome, sung by a female elder ▷ vb perform a karanga
KARANGAED > KARANGA
KARANGAS > KARANGA
KARAOKE n form of entertainment
KARAOKES > KARAOKE
KARAS > KARA
KARAT n measure of the proportion of gold in an alloy
KARATE n Japanese system of unarmed combat
KARATEIST same as > KARATEKA
KARATEKA n competitor or expert in karate
KARATEKAS > KARATEKA
KARATES > KARATE
KARATS > KARAT

KAREAREA n New Zealand falcon
KAREAREAS > KAREAREA
KARENGO n edible type of Pacific seaweed
KARENGOS > KARENGO
KARITE n shea tree
KARITES > KARITE
KARK variant spelling of > CARK
KARKED > KARK
KARKING > KARK
KARKS > KARK
KARMA n person's actions affecting his or her fate in the next reincarnation
KARMAS > KARMA
KARMIC > KARMA
KARN old word for > CAIRN
KARNS > KARN
KARO n small New Zealand tree or shrub
KAROO n high arid plateau
KAROOS > KAROO
KARORO n large seagull
KAROROS > KARORO
KAROS > KARO
KAROSHI n (in Japan) death caused by overwork
KAROSHIS > KAROSHI
KAROSS n type of blanket
KAROSSES > KAROSS
KARRI n Australian eucalypt
KARRIS > KARRI
KARROO same as > KAROO
KARROOS > KARROO
KARSEY variant spelling of > KHAZI
KARSEYS > KARSEY
KARSIES > KARSY
KARST n characteristic scenery of a limestone region
KARSTIC > KARST
KARSTIFY vb become karstic
KARSTS > KARST
KARSY variant spelling of > KHAZI
KART n light low-framed vehicle
KARTER > KART
KARTERS > KART
KARTING > KART
KARTINGS > KART
KARTS > KART
KARYOGAMY n fusion of two gametic nuclei during fertilization
KARYOGRAM n diagram or photograph of the chromosomes of a cell, arranged in homologous pairs and in a numbered sequence
KARYOLOGY n study of cell nuclei, esp with reference to the number and shape of the chromosomes
KARYON n nucleus of a cell
KARYONS > KARYON
KARYOSOME n any of the dense aggregates of chromatin in the nucleus of a cell

KARYOTIN less common word for > CHROMATIN
KARYOTINS > KARYOTIN
KARYOTYPE n appearance of the chromosomes in a somatic cell of an individual or species, with reference to their number, size, shape, etc ▷ vb determine the karyotype of (a cell)
KARZIES > KARZY
KARZY variant spelling of > KHAZI
KAS > KA
KASBAH n citadel of any of various North African cities
KASBAHS > KASBAH
KASHA n dish originating in Eastern Europe
KASHAS > KASHA
KASHER vb make fit for use
KASHERED > KASHER
KASHERING > KASHER
KASHERS > KASHER
KASHMIR variant spelling of > CASHMERE
KASHMIRS > KASHMIR
KASHRUS same as > KASHRUTH
KASHRUSES > KASHRUS
KASHRUT same as > KASHRUTH
KASHRUTH n condition of being fit for ritual use in general
KASHRUTHS > KASHRUTH
KASHRUTS > KASHRUT
KASME interj (in Indian English) I swear
KAT same as > KHAT
KATA n form of exercise
KATABASES > KATABASIS
KATABASIS n retreat of the Greek mercenaries of Cyrus the Younger, after his death at Cunaxa, from the Euphrates to the Black Sea in 401–400 BC under the leadership of Xenophon
KATABATIC adj (of winds) blowing downhill through having become denser with cooling, esp at night when heat is lost from the earth's surface
KATABOLIC same as > CATABOLIC
KATAKANA n system of Japanese syllabic writing
KATAKANAS > KATAKANA
KATAL n SI unit of catalytic activity
KATALS > KATAL
KATANA n Japanese samurai sword
KATANAS > KATANA
KATAS > KATA
KATCHINA variant spelling of > KACHINA
KATCHINAS > KATCHINA

KATCINA variant spelling of > KACHINA
KATCINAS > KATCINA
KATHAK n form of dancing
KATHAKALI n form of dance drama of S India using mime and based on Hindu literature
KATHAKS > KATHAK
KATHARSES > KATHARSIS
KATHARSIS variant spelling of > CATHARSIS
KATHODAL > KATHODE
KATHODE variant spelling of > CATHODE
KATHODES > KATHODE
KATHODIC > KATHODE
KATHUMP n sound of a dull heavy blow
KATHUMPS > KATHUMP
KATI variant spelling of > CATTY
KATION variant spelling of > CATION
KATIONS > KATION
KATIPO n small poisonous New Zealand spider
KATIPOS > KATIPO
KATIS > KATI
KATORGA n type of labour camp
KATORGAS > KATORGA
KATS > KAT
KATSINA n (among the Hopi) doll representing spirit messengers
KATSINAM > KATSINA
KATSINAS > KATSINA
KATSURA n Asian tree
KATSURAS > KATSURA
KATTI variant spelling of > CATTY
KATTIS > KATTI
KATYDID n large green grasshopper of N America
KATYDIDS > KATYDID
KAUGH same as > KIAUGH
KAUGHS > KAUGH
KAUMATUA n senior member of a tribe
KAUMATUAS > KAUMATUA
KAUPAPA n strategy, policy, or cause
KAUPAPAS > KAUPAPA
KAURI n large New Zealand conifer
KAURIES > KAURY
KAURIS > KAURI
KAURU n edible stem of the cabbage tree
KAURUS > KAURU
KAURY variant spelling of > KAURI
KAVA n Polynesian shrub
KAVAKAVA same as > KAVA
KAVAKAVAS > KAVAKAVA
KAVAL n type of flute played in the Balkans
KAVALS > KAVAL
KAVAS > KAVA
KAVASS n armed Turkish constable
KAVASSES > KAVASS**

KAW variant spelling of > CAW

KAWA n protocol or etiquette

KAWAII n (in Japan) quality of being lovable or cute

KAWAIIS > KAWAII

KAWAKAWA n aromatic shrub or small tree of New Zealand

KAWAKAWAS > KAWAKAWA

KAWAS > KAWA

KAWAU n New Zealand name for black shag

KAWAUS > KAWAU

KAWED > KAW

KAWING > KAW

KAWS > KAW

KAY n name of the letter K

KAYAK n Inuit canoe ▷ vb travel by kayak

KAYAKED > KAYAK

KAYAKER > KAYAK

KAYAKERS > KAYAK

KAYAKING > KAYAK

KAYAKINGS > KAYAK

KAYAKS > KAYAK

KAYLE n one of a set of ninepins

KAYLES pl n ninepins

KAYLIED adj intoxicated or drunk

KAYO another term for > KNOCKOUT

KAYOED > KAYO

KAYOES > KAYO

KAYOING > KAYO

KAYOINGS > KAYO

KAYOS > KAYO

KAYS > KAY

KAZACHKI same as > KAZACHOK

KAZACHOC n Ukrainian folk dance

KAZACHOCS > KAZACHOC

KAZACHOK n Russian folk dance

KAZACHOKS > KAZACHOK

KAZATSKI same as > KAZACHOK

KAZATSKY same as > KAZACHOK

KAZATZKA same as > KAZACHOK

KAZATZKAS > KAZACHOK

KAZI variant spelling of > KHAZI

KAZILLION same as > GAZILLION

KAZIS > KAZI

KAZOO n musical instrument

KAZOOS > KAZOO

KBAR n kilobar

KBARS > KBAR

KEA n large brownish-green parrot of New Zealand

KEAS > KEA

KEASAR archaic variant of > KAISER

KEASARS > KEASAR

KEAVIE n archaic or dialect word for a type of crab

KEAVIES > KEAVIE

KEB vb Scots word meaning miscarry or reject a lamb

KEBAB n food grilled on a skewer ▷ vb skewer

KEBABBED > KEBAB

KEBABBING > KEBAB

KEBABS > KEBAB

KEBAR n Scots word for beam or rafter

KEBARS > KEBAR

KEBBED > KEB

KEBBIE n Scots word for shepherd's crook

KEBBIES > KEBBIE

KEBBING > KEB

KEBBOCK n Scots word for a cheese

KEBBOCKS > KEBBOCK

KEBBUCK same as > KEBBOCK

KEBBUCKS > KEBBUCK

KEBELE n Ethiopian local council

KEBELES > KEBELE

KEBLAH same as > KIBLAH

KEBLAHS > KEBLAH

KEBOB same as > KEBAB

KEBOBBED > KEBOB

KEBOBBING > KEBOB

KEBOBS > KEBOB

KEBS > KEB

KECK vb retch or feel nausea

KECKED > KECK

KECKING > KECK

KECKLE Scots variant of > CACKLE

KECKLED > KECKLE

KECKLES > KECKLE

KECKLING > KECKLE

KECKLINGS > KECKLE

KECKS n trousers

KECKSES > KECKS

KECKSIES > KECKSY

KECKSY n dialect word meaning hollow plant stalk

KED n as in sheep ked sheep tick

KEDDAH same as > KHEDA

KEDDAHS > KEDDAH

KEDGE vb move (a ship) using cable attached to an anchor ▷ n light anchor used for kedging

KEDGED > KEDGE

KEDGER n small anchor

KEDGEREE n dish of fish with rice and eggs

KEDGEREES > KEDGEREE

KEDGERS > KEDGER

KEDGES > KEDGE

KEDGIER > KEDGY

KEDGIEST > KEDGY

KEDGING > KEDGE

KEDGY adj dialect word for happy or lively

KEDS > KED

KEECH n old word for lump of fat

KEECHES > KEECH

KEEF same as > KIF

KEEFS > KEEF

KEEK Scot word for > PEEP

KEEKED > KEEK

KEEKER > KEEK

KEEKERS > KEEK

KEEKING > KEEK

KEEKS > KEEK

KEEL n part of a ship ▷ vb mark with a stain

KEELAGE n fee charged by certain ports

KEELAGES > KEELAGE

KEELBOAT n river boat with a shallow draught and a keel

KEELBOATS > KEELBOAT

KEELED > KEEL

KEELER n bargeman

KEELERS > KEELER

KEELHALE same as > KEELHAUL

KEELHALED > KEELHALE

KEELHALES > KEELHALE

KEELHAUL vb reprimand (someone) harshly

KEELHAULS > KEELHAUL

KEELIE n kestrel

KEELIES > KEELIE

KEELING > KEEL

KEELINGS > KEEL

KEELIVINE Scots word for > PENCIL

KEELLESS > KEEL

KEELMAN n bargeman

KEELMEN > KEELMAN

KEELS > KEEL

KEELSON n part of a ship

KEELSONS > KEELSON

KEELYVINE same as > KEELIVINE

KEEMA n (in Indian cookery) minced meat

KEEMAS > KEEMA

KEEN adj eager or enthusiastic ▷ vb wail over the dead ▷ n lament for the dead

KEENED > KEEN

KEENER > KEEN

KEENERS > KEEN

KEENEST > KEEN

KEENING > KEEN

KEENINGS > KEEN

KEENLY > KEEN

KEENNESS > KEEN

KEENO same as > KENO

KEENOS > KEENO

KEENS > KEEN

KEEP vb have or retain possession of ▷ n cost of food and everyday expenses

KEEPABLE > KEEP

KEEPER n person who looks after animals in a zoo

KEEPERS > KEEPER

KEEPING > KEEP

KEEPINGS > KEEP

KEEPNET n cylindrical net used to keep fish alive

KEEPNETS > KEEPNET

KEEPS > KEEP

KEEPSAKE n gift treasured for the sake of the giver

KEEPSAKES > KEEPSAKE

KEEPSAKY adj superficially attractive

KEESHOND n breed of dog of the spitz type

KEESHONDS > KEESHOND

KEESTER same as > KEISTER

KEESTERS > KEESTER

KEET short for > PARAKEET

KEETS > KEET

KEEVE n tub or vat

KEEVES > KEEVE

KEF same as > KIF

KEFFEL dialect word for > HORSE

KEFFELS > KEFFEL

KEFFIYAH same as > KAFFIYEH

KEFFIYAHS > KEFFIYAH

KEFFIYEH n cotton headdress worn by Arabs

KEFFIYEHS > KEFFIYEH

KEFIR n effervescent drink

KEFIRS > KEFIR

KEFS > KEF

KEFTEDES n Greek dish of meatballs cooked with herbs and onions

KEFUFFLE same as > KERFUFFLE

KEFUFFLED > KEFUFFLE

KEFUFFLES > KEFUFFLE

KEG n small metal beer barrel ▷ vb put in kegs

KEGELER same as > KEGLER

KEGELERS > KEGELER

KEGGED > KEG

KEGGER > KEG

KEGGERS > KEG

KEGGING > KEG

KEGLER n participant in a game of tenpin bowling

KEGLERS > KEGLER

KEGLING n bowling

KEGLINGS > KEGLING

KEGS > KEG

KEHUA n ghost or spirit

KEHUAS > KEHUA

KEIGHT > KETCH

KEIR same as > KIER

KEIREN n type of track cycling event

KEIRENS > KEIREN

KEIRETSU n group of Japanese businesses

KEIRETSUS > KEIRETSU

KEIRIN n cycling race originating in Japan

KEIRINS > KEIRIN

KEIRS > KEIR

KEISTER n rump

KEISTERS > KEISTER**

KEITLOA n type of rhinoceros
KEITLOAS > KEITLOA
KEKENO n New Zealand fur seal
KEKENOS > KEKENO
KEKERENGU n Māori bug
KEKS same as > KECKS
KEKSYE same as > KEX
KEKSYES > KEKSYE
KELEP n large ant found in Central and South America
KELEPS > KELEP
KELIM same as > KILIM
KELIMS > KELIM
KELL dialect word for > HAIRNET
KELLAUT same as > KHILAT
KELLAUTS > KELLAUT
KELLIES > KELLY
KELLS > KELL
KELLY n part of a drill system
KELOID n type of scar tissue
KELOIDAL > KELOID
KELOIDS > KELOID
KELP n large brown seaweed ▷ vb burn seaweed to make a type of ash
KELPED > KELP
KELPER n Falkland Islander
KELPERS > KELPER
KELPFISH n type of fish that lives among kelp
KELPIE n Australian sheepdog
KELPIES > KELPIE
KELPING > KELP
KELPS > KELP
KELPY same as > KELPIE
KELSON same as > KEELSON
KELSONS > KELSON
KELT n salmon that has recently spawned
KELTER same as > KILTER
KELTERS > KELTER
KELTIE variant spelling of > KELTY
KELTIES > KELTY
KELTS > KELT
KELTY n old Scots word for a drink imposed on someone not thought to be drinking enough
KELVIN n SI unit of temperature
KELVINS > KELVIN
KEMB old word for > COMB
KEMBED > KEMB
KEMBING > KEMB
KEMBLA n small change
KEMBLAS > KEMBLA
KEMBO same as > KIMBO
KEMBOED > KEMBO
KEMBOING > KEMBO
KEMBOS > KEMBO
KEMBS > KEMB
KEMP n coarse hair or strand of hair ▷ vb dialect word meaning to compete or try to come first

KEMPED > KEMP
KEMPER > KEMP
KEMPERS > KEMP
KEMPIER > KEMPY
KEMPIEST > KEMPY
KEMPING > KEMP
KEMPINGS > KEMP
KEMPLE n variable Scottish measure for hay or straw
KEMPLES > KEMPLE
KEMPS > KEMP
KEMPT adj (of hair) tidy
KEMPY > KEMP
KEN vb know ▷ n range of knowledge or perception
KENAF another name for > AMBARY
KENAFS > KENAF
KENCH n bin for salting and preserving fish
KENCHES > KENCH
KENDO n Japanese sport of fencing using wooden staves
KENDOIST n person who practises kendo
KENDOISTS > KENDOIST
KENDOS > KENDO
KENNED > KEN
KENNEL n hutlike shelter for a dog ▷ vb put or go into a kennel
KENNELED > KENNEL
KENNELING > KENNEL
KENNELLED > KENNEL
KENNELMAN n man who works in a kennels
KENNELMEN > KENNELMAN
KENNELS > KENNEL
KENNER > KEN
KENNERS > KEN
KENNET n old word for a small hunting dog
KENNETS > KENNET
KENNETT vb spoil or destroy ruthlessly
KENNETTED > KENNETT
KENNETTS > KENNETT
KENNING > KEN
KENNINGS > KEN
KENO n game of chance similar to bingo
KENOS > KENO
KENOSES > KENOSIS
KENOSIS n Christ's renunciation of certain divine attributes
KENOSISES > KENOSIS
KENOTIC > KENOSIS
KENOTICS > KENOSIS
KENOTRON n signal-amplifying device
KENOTRONS > KENOTRON
KENS > KEN
KENSPECK adj Scots for easily seen or recognized
KENT dialect word for > PUNT
KENTE n brightly coloured handwoven cloth
KENTED > KENT
KENTES > KENTE
KENTIA n plant name

KENTIAS > KENTIA
KENTING > KENT
KENTLEDGE n scrap metal used as ballast in a vessel
KENTS > KENT
KEP vb catch
KEPHALIC variant spelling of > CEPHALIC
KEPHALICS > KEPHALIC
KEPHALIN same as > CEPHALIN
KEPHALINS > KEPHALIN
KEPHIR same as > KEFIR
KEPHIRS > KEPHIR
KEPI n French military cap with a flat top and a horizontal peak
KEPIS > KEPI
KEPPED > KEP
KEPPEN > KEP
KEPPING > KEP
KEPPIT > KEP
KEPS > KEP
KEPT > KEEP
KERAMIC rare variant of > CERAMIC
KERAMICS rare variant of > CERAMICS
KERATIN n fibrous protein found in the hair and nails
KERATINS > KERATIN
KERATITIS n inflammation of the cornea
KERATOID adj resembling horn
KERATOMA n horny growth on the skin
KERATOMAS > KERATOMA
KERATOSE adj (esp of certain sponges) having a horny skeleton
KERATOSES > KERATOSIS
KERATOSIC > KERATOSE
KERATOSIS n any skin condition marked by a horny growth, such as a wart
KERATOTIC > KERATOSIS
KERB n edging to a footpath ▷ vb provide with or enclose with a kerb
KERBAYA n blouse worn by Malay women
KERBAYAS > KERBAYA
KERBED > KERB
KERBING n material used for a kerb
KERBINGS > KERBING
KERBLOOEY n sound of an explosion
KERBS > KERB
KERBSIDE n edge of a pavement where it drops to the level of the road
KERBSIDES > KERBSIDE
KERBSTONE n one of a series of stones that form a kerb

KERCHIEF n piece of cloth worn over the head or round the neck
KERCHIEFS > KERCHIEF
KERCHOO interj atishoo
KEREL n chap or fellow
KERELS > KEREL
KERERU n New Zealand pigeon
KERERUS > KERERU
KERF n cut made by a saw, an axe, etc ▷ vb cut
KERFED > KERF
KERFING > KERF
KERFLOOEY adv into state of destruction or malfunction
KERFS > KERF
KERFUFFLE n commotion or disorder ▷ vb put into disorder or disarray
KERKIER > KERKY
KERKIEST > KERKY
KERKY adj stupid
KERMA n quantity of radiation
KERMAS > KERMA
KERMES n dried bodies of female scale insects
KERMESES > KERMES
KERMESITE n red antimony
KERMESS same as > KERMIS
KERMESSE same as > KERMIS
KERMESSES > KERMESSE
KERMIS n (formerly) annual country festival or carnival
KERMISES > KERMIS
KERMODE n type of black bear found in Canada
KERMODES > KERMODE
KERN n projection of a printed character ▷ vb furnish (a typeface) with a kern
KERNE same as > KERN
KERNED > KERNE
KERNEL n seed of a nut, cereal, or fruit stone ▷ vb form kernels
KERNELED > KERNEL
KERNELING > KERNEL
KERNELLED > KERNEL
KERNELLY adj with or like kernels
KERNELS > KERNEL
KERNES > KERNE
KERNING n provision of kerns in printing
KERNINGS > KERNING
KERNISH adj resembling an armed foot soldier or peasant
KERNITE n light soft colourless or white mineral
KERNITES > KERNITE
KERNS > KERN
KERO short for > KEROSENE
KEROGEN n material that produces hydrocarbons when heated

k

KEROGENS > KEROGEN

KEROS > KERO

KEROSENE n liquid mixture distilled from petroleum and used as a fuel or solvent

KEROSENES > KEROSENE

KEROSINE same as > KEROSENE

KEROSINES > KEROSENE

KERPLUNK vb land noisily

KERPLUNKS > KERPLUNK

KERRIA n type of shrub with yellow flowers

KERRIAS > KERRIA

KERRIES > KERRY

KERRY n breed of dairy cattle

KERSEY n smooth woollen cloth

KERSEYS > KERSEY

KERVE dialect word for > CARVE

KERVED > KERVE

KERVES > KERVE

KERVING > KERVE

KERYGMA n Christian gospel

KERYGMAS > KERYGMA

KERYGMATA > KERYGMA

KESAR old variant of > KAISER

KESARS > KESAR

KESH n beard and uncut hair traditionally worn by Sikhs

KESHES > KESH

KEST old form of > CAST

KESTING > KEST

KESTREL n type of small falcon

KESTRELS > KESTREL

KESTS > KEST

KET n dialect word for carrion

KETA n type of salmon

KETAINE adj in poor taste

KETAMINE n drug used in medicine as an anaesthetic

KETAMINES > KETAMINE

KETAS > KETA

KETCH n two-masted sailing vessel ▷ vb (in archaic usage) catch

KETCHES > KETCH

KETCHING > KETCH

KETCHUP n thick cold sauce, usu made of tomatoes

KETCHUPS > KETCHUP

KETCHUPY adj like ketchup

KETE n basket woven from flax

KETENE n colourless irritating toxic gas

KETENES > KETENE

KETES > KETE

KETMIA n as in bladder ketmia plant with pale yellow flowers

KETMIAS > KETMIA

KETO adj as in keto form form of tautomeric compounds

KETOGENIC adj forming or able to stimulate the production of ketone bodies

KETOL n nitrogenous substance

KETOLS > KETOL

KETONE n type of organic solvent

KETONEMIA n excess of ketone bodies in the blood

KETONES > KETONE

KETONIC > KETONE

KETONURIA n presence of ketone bodies in the urine

KETOSE n any monosaccharide that contains a ketone group

KETOSES > KETOSIS

KETOSIS n high concentration of ketone bodies in the blood

KETOTIC > KETOSIS

KETOXIME n oxime formed by reaction between hydroxylamine and a ketone

KETOXIMES > KETOXIME

KETS > KET

KETTLE n container used for boiling water ▷ vb contain a public protest in an enclosed space

KETTLED > KETTLE

KETTLEFUL > KETTLE

KETTLES > KETTLE

KETTLING > KETTLE

KETUBAH n Jewish marriage contract

KETUBAHS > KETUBAH

KETUBOT > KETUBAH

KETUBOTH > KETUBAH

KEVEL n strong bitt or bollard for securing heavy hawsers

KEVELS > KEVEL

KEVIL old variant of > KEVEL

KEVILS > KEVIL

KEWL nonstandard variant spelling of > COOL

KEWLER > KEWL

KEWLEST > KEWL

KEWPIE n type of brightly coloured doll

KEWPIES > KEWPIE

KEX n any of several hollow-stemmed umbelliferous plants

KEXES > KEX

KEY n device for operating a lock by moving a bolt ▷ adj of great importance ▷ vb enter (text) using a keyboard

KEYBOARD n set of keys on a piano, computer, etc ▷ vb enter (text) using a keyboard

KEYBOARDS > KEYBOARD

KEYBUGLE n bugle with keys

KEYBUGLES > KEYBUGLE

KEYBUTTON n on a keyboard, an object which, when pressed, causes the letter, number, or symbol shown on it to be printed in a document

KEYCARD n electronic card used as a key

KEYCARDS > KEYCARD

KEYED > KEY

KEYER n device that keys signals or information into a device or computing system

KEYERS > KEYER

KEYEST > KEY

KEYFRAME n image used to show the start and end of animation sequence

KEYFRAMES > KEYFRAME

KEYHOLE n opening for inserting a key into a lock

KEYHOLES > KEYHOLE

KEYING > KEY

KEYINGS > KEY

KEYLESS > KEY

KEYLINE n outline image on artwork or plans to show where it is to be placed

KEYLINES > KEYLINE

KEYLOGGER n device or software application used for covertly recording and monitoring keystrokes made on a remote computer

KEYNOTE adj central or dominating ▷ n dominant idea of a speech etc ▷ vb deliver a keynote address to (a political convention, etc)

KEYNOTED > KEYNOTE

KEYNOTER n person delivering a keynote address

KEYNOTERS > KEYNOTER

KEYNOTES > KEYNOTE

KEYNOTING > KEYNOTE

KEYPAD n small panel with a set of buttons

KEYPADS > KEYPAD

KEYPAL n person one regularly exchanges emails with for fun

KEYPALS > KEYPAL

KEYPRESS n single depression of a keyboard key

KEYPUNCH n keyboard device to transfer data onto punched cards ▷ vb transfer (data) onto punched cards

KEYRING n metal ring for keeping keys together

KEYRINGS > KEYRING

KEYS interj children's cry for truce

KEYSET n set of computer keys used for a particular purpose

KEYSETS > KEYSET

KEYSTER same as > KEISTER

KEYSTERS > KEYSTER

KEYSTONE n most important part of a process, organization, etc ▷ vb project or provide with a distorted image

KEYSTONED > KEYSTONE

KEYSTONES > KEYSTONE

KEYSTROKE n single operation of the mechanism of a typewriter or keyboard-operated typesetting machine by the action of a key ▷ vb enter or cause to be recorded by pressing a key

KEYWAY n engineering device

KEYWAYS > KEYWAY

KEYWORD n word or phrase used to find something on a computer

KEYWORDS > KEYWORD

KEYWORKER n public sector worker regarded as providing an essential service

KGOTLA n (in South African English) meeting place

KGOTLAS > KGOTLA

KHADDAR n cotton cloth

KHADDARS > KHADDAR

KHADI same as > KHADDAR

KHADIS > KHADI

KHAF n letter of the Hebrew alphabet

KHAFS > KHAF

KHAKI adj dull yellowish-brown ▷ n fabric of this colour used for military uniforms

KHAKILIKE > KHAKI

KHAKIS > KHAKI

KHALAT same as > KHILAT

KHALATS > KHALAT

KHALIF variant spelling of > CALIPH

KHALIFA same as > CALIPH

KHALIFAH same as > CALIPH

KHALIFAHS > KHALIFAH

KHALIFAS > KHALIFA

KHALIFAT same as > CALIPHATE

KHALIFATE same as > CALIPHATE

KHALIFATS > KHALIFAT

KHALIFS > KHALIF

KHAMSEEN same as > KHAMSIN

KHAMSEENS > KHAMSEEN

KHAMSIN n hot southerly wind

KHAMSINS > KHAMSIN

KHAN n title of respect in Afghanistan and central Asia

KHANATE *n* territory ruled by a khan
KHANATES > KHANATE
KHANDA *n* double-edged sword
KHANDAS > KHANDA
KHANGA *same as* > KANGA
KHANGAS > KHANGA
KHANJAR *n* type of dagger
KHANJARS > KHANJAR
KHANS > KHAN
KHANSAMA *same as* > KHANSAMAH
KHANSAMAH *n* Indian cook or other male servant
KHANSAMAS > KHANSAMA
KHANUM *feminine form of* > KHAN
KHANUMS > KHANUM
KHAPH *n* letter of the Hebrew alphabet
KHAPHS > KHAPH
KHARIF *n* crop harvested at the beginning of winter
KHARIFS > KHARIF
KHAT *n* white-flowered evergreen shrub
KHATS > KHAT
KHAYA *n* type of African tree
KHAYAL *n* kind of Indian classical vocal music
KHAYALS > KHAYAL
KHAYAS > KHAYA
KHAZEN *same as* > CHAZAN
KHAZENIM > KHAZEN
KHAZENS > KHAZEN
KHAZI *n* lavatory
KHAZIS > KHAZI
KHEDA *n* enclosure used to capture wild elephants
KHEDAH *same as* > KHEDA
KHEDAHS > KHEDAH
KHEDAS > KHEDA
KHEDIVA *n* khedive's wife
KHEDIVAL > KHEDIVE
KHEDIVAS > KHEDIVA
KHEDIVATE > KHEDIVE
KHEDIVE *n* viceroy of Egypt under Ottoman suzerainty
KHEDIVES > KHEDIVE
KHEDIVIAL > KHEDIVE
KHET *n* Thai district
KHETH *same as* > HETH
KHETHS > KHETH
KHETS > KHET
KHI *n* letter of the Greek alphabet
KHILAFAT *same as* > CALIPHATE
KHILAFATS > KHILAFAT
KHILAT *n* (in the Middle East) gift given to someone as a mark of honour
KHILATS > KHILAT
KHILIM *same as* > KILIM
KHILIMS > KHILIM
KHIMAR *n* type of headscarf worn by Muslim women
KHIMARS > KHIMAR

KHIRKAH *n* dervish's woollen or cotton outer garment
KHIRKAHS > KHIRKAH
KHIS > KHI
KHODJA *same as* > KHOJA
KHODJAS > KHODJA
KHOJA *n* teacher in a Muslim school
KHOJAS > KHOJA
KHOR *n* watercourse
KHORS > KHOR
KHOTBAH *same as* > KHUTBAH
KHOTBAHS > KHOTBAH
KHOTBEH *same as* > KHUTBAH
KHOTBEHS > KHOTBEH
KHOUM *n* Mauritanian monetary unit
KHOUMS > KHOUM
KHUD *n* Indian ravine
KHUDS > KHUD
KHURTA *same as* > KURTA
KHURTAS > KHURTA
KHUSKHUS *n* aromatic perennial Indian grass whose roots are woven into mats, fans, and baskets
KHUTBAH *n* sermon in a Mosque, especially on a Friday
KHUTBAHS > KHUTBAH
KI *n* vital energy
KIAAT *n* tropical African leguminous tree
KIAATS > KIAAT
KIACK *n* N American fish of the herring family
KIACKS > KIACK
KIANG *n* variety of wild ass
KIANGS > KIANG
KIAUGH *n* (in Scots) anxiety
KIAUGHS > KIAUGH
KIBBE *n* Middle Eastern dish
KIBBEH *same as* > KIBBE
KIBBEHS > KIBBEH
KIBBES > KIBBE
KIBBI *same as* > KIBBE
KIBBIS > KIBBI
KIBBITZ *same as* > KIBITZ
KIBBITZED > KIBBITZ
KIBBITZER > KIBBITZ
KIBBITZES > KIBBITZ
KIBBLE *n* bucket used in wells or in mining for hoisting ▷ *vb* grind into small pieces
KIBBLED > KIBBLE
KIBBLES > KIBBLE
KIBBLING > KIBBLE
KIBBUTZ *n* communal farm or factory in Israel
KIBBUTZIM > KIBBUTZ
KIBE *n* chilblain
KIBEI *n* someone of Japanese ancestry born in the US and educated in Japan
KIBEIS > KIBEI
KIBES > KIBE
KIBIBYTE *n* two to the power of ten bytes

KIBIBYTES > KIBIBYTE
KIBITKA *n* (in Russia) covered sledge or wagon
KIBITKAS > KIBITKA
KIBITZ *vb* interfere or offer unwanted advice
KIBITZED > KIBITZ
KIBITZER > KIBITZ
KIBITZERS > KIBITZ
KIBITZES > KIBITZ
KIBITZING > KIBITZ
KIBLA *same as* > KIBLAH
KIBLAH *n* direction of Mecca
KIBLAHS > KIBLAH
KIBLAS > KIBLA
KIBOSH *vb* put a stop to
KIBOSHED > KIBOSH
KIBOSHES > KIBOSH
KIBOSHING > KIBOSH
KICK *vb* drive, push, or strike with the foot ▷ *n* thrust or blow with the foot
KICKABLE > KICK
KICKABOUT *n* informal game of soccer
KICKBACK *n* money paid illegally for favours done ▷ *vb* have a strong reaction
KICKBACKS > KICKBACK
KICKBALL *n* children's ball game or the large ball used in it
KICKBALLS > KICKBALL
KICKBOARD *n* type of float held on to by a swimmer when practising leg strokes
KICKBOX *vb* box with hands and feet
KICKBOXED > KICKBOX
KICKBOXER *n* someone who practises kickboxing, a martial art that resembles boxing but in which kicks are permitted
KICKBOXES > KICKBOX
KICKDOWN *n* method of changing gear in a car with automatic transmission
KICKDOWNS > KICKDOWN
KICKED > KICK
KICKER *n* person or thing that kicks
KICKERS > KICKER
KICKFLIP *n* type of skateboarding manoeuvre ▷ *vb* perform a kickflip in skateboarding
KICKFLIPS > KICKFLIP
KICKIER > KICKY
KICKIEST > KICKY
KICKING *n* act of kicking
KICKINGS > KICKING
KICKOFF *n* kick that starts a game of football
KICKOFFS > KICKOFF
KICKOUT *n* (in basketball) instance of kicking the ball
KICKOUTS > KICKOUT

KICKPLATE *n* metal plate at the base of a door
KICKS > KICK
KICKSHAW *n* valueless trinket
KICKSHAWS *same as* > KICKSHAW
KICKSTAND *n* short metal bar on a motorcycle, which when kicked into a vertical position holds the cycle upright when stationary
KICKSTART *vb* start by kicking pedal
KICKUP *n* fuss
KICKUPS > KICKUP
KICKY *adj* excitingly unusual and different
KID *n* child ▷ *vb* tease or deceive (someone) ▷ *adj* younger
KIDDED > KID
KIDDER > KID
KIDDERS > KID
KIDDIE *same as* > KIDDY
KIDDIED > KIDDY
KIDDIER *n* old word for a market trader
KIDDIERS > KIDDIER
KIDDIES > KIDDY
KIDDING *n* act of kidding
KIDDINGLY > KID
KIDDINGS > KIDDING
KIDDISH > KID
KIDDLE *n* device for catching fish in a river or in the sea
KIDDLES > KIDDLE
KIDDO *n* very informal term of address for a young person
KIDDOES > KIDDO
KIDDOS > KIDDO
KIDDUSH *n* (in Judaism) special blessing
KIDDUSHES > KIDDUSH
KIDDY *n* affectionate word for a child ▷ *vb* tease or deceive
KIDDYING > KIDDY
KIDDYWINK *n* humorous word for a child
KIDEL *same as* > KIDDLE
KIDELS > KIDEL
KIDGE *dialect word for* > LIVELY
KIDGIE *adj* dialect word for friendly and welcoming
KIDGIER > KIDGIE
KIDGIEST > KIDGIE
KIDGLOVE *adj* overdelicate or overrefined
KIDLET *n* humorous word for small child
KIDLETS > KIDLET
KIDLIKE > KID
KIDLING *n* young kid
KIDLINGS > KIDLING
KIDLIT *n* children's literature
KIDLITS > KIDLIT
KIDNAP *vb* seize and hold (a person) to ransom
KIDNAPED > KIDNAP
KIDNAPEE > KIDNAP
KIDNAPEES > KIDNAP
KIDNAPER > KIDNAP

k

KIDNAPERS > KIDNAP
KIDNAPING > KIDNAP
KIDNAPPED > KIDNAP
KIDNAPPEE > KIDNAP
KIDNAPPER > KIDNAP
KIDNAPS > KIDNAP
KIDNEY n either of the pair of organs that produce urine
KIDNEYS > KIDNEY
KIDOLOGY n practice of bluffing or deception
KIDS > KID
KIDSKIN n soft smooth leather
KIDSKINS > KIDSKIN
KIDSTAKES pl n pretence
KIDULT n adult interested in entertainments intended for children ▷ adj aimed at or suitable for kidults, or both children and adults
KIDULTS > KIDULT
KIDVID n informal word for children's video or television
KIDVIDS > KIDVID
KIEF same as > KIF
KIEFS > KIEF
KIEKIE n climbing bush plant of New Zealand
KIEKIES > KIEKIE
KIELBASA n Polish sausage
KIELBASAS > KIELBASA
KIELBASI same as > KIELBASA
KIELBASY same as > KIELBASA
KIER n vat in which cloth is bleached
KIERIE n South African cudgel
KIERIES > KIERIE
KIERS > KIER
KIESELGUR n type of mineral
KIESERITE n white mineral consisting of hydrated magnesium sulphate
KIESTER same as > KEISTER
KIESTERS > KIESTER
KIEV n type of chicken dish
KIEVE same as > KEEVE
KIEVES > KIEVE
KIEVS > KIEV
KIF n marijuana
KIFF adj South African slang for excellent
KIFS > KIF
KIGHT n archaic spelling of kite, the bird of prey
KIGHTS > KIGHT
KIKOI n piece of cotton cloth
KIKOIS > KIKOI
KIKUMON n emblem of the imperial family of Japan
KIKUMONS > KIKUMON
KIKUYU n type of grass
KIKUYUS > KIKUYU
KILD old spelling of > KILLED

KILDERKIN n obsolete unit of capacity
KILERG n 1000 ergs
KILERGS > KILERG
KILEY same as > KYLIE
KILEYS > KILEY
KILIKITI n Polynesian version of cricket
KILIKITIS > KILIKITI
KILIM n pileless woven rug
KILIMS > KILIM
KILL vb cause the death of ▷ n act of killing
KILLABLE > KILL
KILLADAR n fort commander or governor
KILLADARS > KILLADAR
KILLAS n Cornish clay slate
KILLASES > KILLAS
KILLCOW n important person
KILLCOWS > KILLCOW
KILLCROP n ever-hungry baby, thought to be a fairy changeling
KILLCROPS > KILLCROP
KILLDEE same as > KILLDEER
KILLDEER n large brown-and-white North American plover with a noisy cry
KILLDEERS > KILLDEER
KILLDEES > KILLDEE
KILLED > KILL
KILLER n person or animal that kills, esp habitually
KILLERS > KILLER
KILLICK n small anchor, esp one made of a heavy stone
KILLICKS > KILLICK
KILLIE same as > KILLIFISH
KILLIES > KILLIE
KILLIFISH n any of various chiefly American minnow-like fishes
KILLING adj very tiring ▷ n sudden financial success
KILLINGLY > KILLING
KILLINGS > KILLING
KILLJOY n person who spoils others' pleasure
KILLJOYS > KILLJOY
KILLOCK same as > KILLICK
KILLOCKS > KILLOCK
KILLOGIE n sheltered place in front of a kiln
KILLOGIES > KILLOGIE
KILLS > KILL
KILLUT same as > KHILAT
KILLUTS > KILLUT
KILN n type of oven ▷ vb fire or process in a kiln
KILNED > KILN
KILNING > KILN

KILNS > KILN
KILO n code word for the letter k
KILOBAR n 1000 bars
KILOBARS > KILOBAR
KILOBASE n unit of measurement for DNA and RNA equal to 1000 base pairs
KILOBASES > KILOBASE
KILOBAUD n 1000 baud
KILOBAUDS > KILOBAUD
KILOBIT n 1024 bits
KILOBITS > KILOBIT
KILOBYTE n 1024 units of information
KILOBYTES > KILOBYTE
KILOCURIE n unit of thousand curies
KILOCYCLE n short for kilocycle per second: a former unit of frequency equal to 1 kilohertz
KILOGAUSS n 1000 gauss
KILOGRAM n one thousand grams
KILOGRAMS > KILOGRAM
KILOGRAY n 1000 gray
KILOGRAYS > KILOGRAY
KILOHERTZ n one thousand hertz
KILOJOULE n 1000 joules
KILOLITER US spelling of > KILOLITRE
KILOLITRE n 1000 litres
KILOMETER same as > KILOMETRE
KILOMETRE n one thousand metres
KILOMOLE n 1000 moles
KILOMOLES > KILOMOLE
KILOPOND n informal unit of gravitational force
KILOPONDS > KILOPOND
KILORAD n 1000 rads
KILORADS > KILORAD
KILOS > KILO
KILOTON n one thousand tons
KILOTONNE same as > KILOTON
KILOTONS > KILOTON
KILOVOLT n one thousand volts
KILOVOLTS > KILOVOLT
KILOWATT n one thousand watts
KILOWATTS > KILOWATT
KILP dialect form of > KELP
KILPS > KILP
KILT n knee-length pleated tartan skirt-like garment ▷ vb put pleats in (cloth)
KILTED > KILT
KILTER n working order or alignment

KILTERS > KILTER
KILTIE n someone wearing a kilt
KILTIES > KILTIE
KILTING > KILT
KILTINGS > KILT
KILTLIKE > KILT
KILTS > KILT
KILTY same as > KILTIE
KIMBO vb place akimbo
KIMBOED > KIMBO
KIMBOING > KIMBO
KIMBOS > KIMBO
KIMCHEE same as > KIMCHI
KIMCHEES > KIMCHEE
KIMCHI n Korean dish
KIMCHIS > KIMCHI
KIMMER same as > CUMMER
KIMMERS > KIMMER
KIMONO n loose wide-sleeved Japanese robe
KIMONOED > KIMONO
KIMONOS > KIMONO
KIN n person's relatives collectively ▷ adj related by blood
KINA n standard monetary unit of Papua New Guinea
KINAKINA same as > QUININE
KINAKINAS > KINAKINA
KINARA n African candle holder
KINARAS > KINARA
KINAS > KINA
KINASE n type of enzyme
KINASES > KINASE
KINCHIN old slang word for > CHILD
KINCHINS > KINCHIN
KINCOB n fine silk fabric
KINCOBS > KINCOB
KIND adj considerate, friendly, and helpful ▷ n class or group with common characteristics ▷ vb old word for beget or father
KINDA adv very informal shortening of kind of
KINDED > KIND
KINDER adj more kind ▷ n kindergarten or nursery school
KINDERS > KINDER
KINDEST > KIND
KINDIE same as > KINDY
KINDIES > KINDY
KINDING > KIND
KINDLE vb set (a fire) alight
KINDLED > KINDLE
KINDLER > KINDLE
KINDLERS > KINDLE
KINDLES > KINDLE
KINDLESS adj heartless
KINDLIER > KINDLY
KINDLIEST > KINDLY
KINDLILY > KINDLY
KINDLING n dry wood or straw for starting fires
KINDLINGS > KINDLING

KINDLY adj having a warm-hearted nature ▷ adv in a considerate way

KINDNESS n quality of being kind

KINDRED adj having similar qualities ▷ n blood relationship

KINDREDS > KINDRED

KINDS > KIND

KINDY n kindergarten

KINE pl n cows or cattle ▷ n Japanese pestle

KINEMA same as > CINEMA

KINEMAS > KINEMA

KINEMATIC adj of or relating to the study of the motion of bodies without reference to mass or force

KINES > KINE

KINESCOPE n US name for a television tube ▷ vb record on film

KINESES > KINESIS

KINESIC adj of or relating to kinesics

KINESICS n study of the role of body movements in communication

KINESIS n movement of an organism

KINESISES > KINESIS

KINETIC adj relating to or caused by motion

KINETICAL same as > KINETIC

KINETICS n branch of mechanics concerned with the study of bodies in motion

KINETIN n plant hormone

KINETINS > KINETIN

KINFOLK another word for > KINSFOLK

KINFOLKS > KINFOLK

KING n male ruler of a monarchy ▷ vb make king

KINGBIRD n any of several large American flycatchers

KINGBIRDS > KINGBIRD

KINGBOLT n pivot bolt that connects the body of a horse-drawn carriage to the front axle

KINGBOLTS > KINGBOLT

KINGCRAFT n art of ruling as a king, esp by diplomacy and cunning

KINGCUP n yellow-flowered plant

KINGCUPS > KINGCUP

KINGDOM n state ruled by a king or queen

KINGDOMED adj old word for with a kingdom

KINGDOMS > KINGDOM

KINGED > KING

KINGFISH n food and game fish occurring in warm American Atlantic coastal waters

KINGHOOD > KING

KINGHOODS > KING

KINGING > KING

KINGKLIP n edible eel-like marine fish of S Africa

KINGKLIPS > KINGKLIP

KINGLE n Scots word for a type of hard rock

KINGLES > KINGLE

KINGLESS > KING

KINGLET n king of a small or insignificant territory

KINGLETS > KINGLET

KINGLIER > KINGLY

KINGLIEST > KINGLY

KINGLIKE > KING

KINGLING n minor king

KINGLINGS > KINGLING

KINGLY adj appropriate to a king ▷ adv in a manner appropriate to a king

KINGMAKER n person who has control over appointments to positions of authority

KINGPIN n most important person in an organization

KINGPINS > KINGPIN

KINGPOST n vertical post connecting the apex of a triangular roof truss to the tie beam

KINGPOSTS > KINGPOST

KINGS > KING

KINGSHIP n position or authority of a king

KINGSHIPS > KINGSHIP

KINGSIDE n side of the chessboard on which a particular king is at the start of a game

KINGSIDES > KINGSIDE

KINGSNAKE n North American snake

KINGWOOD n hard fine-grained violet-tinted wood of a Brazilian leguminous tree

KINGWOODS > KINGWOOD

KININ n type of polypeptide

KININS > KININ

KINK n twist or bend in rope, wire, hair, etc ▷ vb form or cause to form a kink

KINKAJOU n arboreal mammal of Central and South America

KINKAJOUS > KINKAJOU

KINKED > KINK

KINKIER > KINKY

KINKIEST > KINKY

KINKILY > KINKY

KINKINESS > KINKY

KINKING > KINK

KINKLE n little kink

KINKLES > KINKLE

KINKS > KINK

KINKY adj tightly curled or looped

KINLESS adj without any relatives

KINO same as > KENO

KINONE n benzoquinone

KINONES > KINONE

KINOS > KINO

KINRED old form of > KINDRED

KINREDS > KINRED

KINS > KIN

KINSFOLK pl n one's family or relatives

KINSFOLKS > KINSFOLK

KINSHIP n blood relationship

KINSHIPS > KINSHIP

KINSMAN n relative

KINSMEN > KINSMAN

KINSWOMAN > KINSMAN

KINSWOMEN > KINSMAN

KINTLEDGE same as > KENTLEDGE

KIORE n small brown rat native to New Zealand

KIORES > KIORE

KIOSK n small booth

KIOSKS > KIOSK

KIP vb sleep ▷ n sleep or slumber

KIPE n dialect word for a basket for catching fish

KIPES > KIPE

KIPP uncommon variant of > KIP

KIPPA n skullcap worn by male Jews

KIPPAGE n Scots word for a state of anger or excitement

KIPPAGES > KIPPAGE

KIPPAH same as > KIPPA

KIPPAHS > KIPPAH

KIPPAS > KIPPA

KIPPED > KIP

KIPPEN > KEP

KIPPER n cleaned, salted, and smoked herring ▷ vb cure (a herring) by salting and smoking it

KIPPERED adj (of fish, esp herring) having been cleaned, salted, and smoked

KIPPERER > KIPPER

KIPPERERS > KIPPER

KIPPERING > KIPPER

KIPPERS > KIPPER

KIPPING > KIP

KIPPS > KIPP

KIPS > KIP

KIPSKIN same as > KIP

KIPSKINS > KIPSKIN

KIPUNJI n Tanzanian species of monkey

KIPUNJIS > KIPUNJI

KIR n drink made from dry white wine and cassis

KIRANA n small family-owned shop in India

KIRANAS > KIRANA

KIRBEH n leather bottle

KIRBEHS > KIRBEH

KIRBIGRIP n hairgrip

KIRBY n as in kirby grip type of hairgrip

KIRIGAMI n art, originally Japanese, of folding and cutting paper into decorative shapes

KIRIGAMIS > KIRIGAMI

KIRIMON n Japanese imperial crest

KIRIMONS > KIRIMON

KIRK Scot word for > CHURCH

KIRKED > KIRK

KIRKING > KIRK

KIRKINGS > KIRK

KIRKMAN n member or strong upholder of the Kirk

KIRKMEN > KIRKMAN

KIRKS > KIRK

KIRKTON n village or town with a parish church

KIRKTONS > KIRKTON

KIRKWARD adv towards the church

KIRKYAIRD same as > KIRKYARD

KIRKYARD n churchyard

KIRKYARDS > KIRKYARD

KIRMESS same as > KERMIS

KIRMESSES > KIRMESS

KIRN dialect word for > CHURN

KIRNED > KIRN

KIRNING > KIRN

KIRNS > KIRN

KIRPAN n short sword traditionally carried by Sikhs

KIRPANS > KIRPAN

KIRRI n South African cudgel

KIRRIS > KIRRI

KIRS > KIR

KIRSCH n cherry brandy

KIRSCHES > KIRSCH

KIRTAN n devotional singing

KIRTANS > KIRTAN

KIRTLE n woman's skirt or dress ▷ vb dress with a kirtle

KIRTLED > KIRTLE

KIRTLES > KIRTLE

KIS > KI

KISAN n peasant or farmer

KISANS > KISAN

KISH n graphite formed on the surface of molten iron

KISHES > KISH

KISHKA same as > KISHKE

KISHKAS > KISHKA

KISHKE n stuffed beef or fowl intestine, boiled and roasted

KISHKES > KISHKE

KISKADEE n large flycatcher of tropical America

KISKADEES > KISKADEE

KISMAT same as > KISMET

KISMATS > KISMAT

KISMET n fate or destiny

k

KISMETIC > KISMET
KISMETS > KISMET
KISS vb touch with the lips in affection or greeting ▷ n touch with the lips
KISSABLE > KISS
KISSABLY > KISS
KISSAGRAM n greetings service in which a messenger kisses the person celebrating
KISSED > KISS
KISSEL n Russian dessert
KISSELS > KISSEL
KISSER n mouth or face
KISSERS > KISSER
KISSES > KISS
KISSIER > KISSY
KISSIEST > KISSY
KISSING > KISS
KISSINGS > KISSING
KISSOGRAM same as > KISSAGRAM
KISSY adj showing exaggerated affection
KIST n large wooden chest ▷ vb place in a coffin
KISTED > KIST
KISTFUL > KIST
KISTFULS > KIST
KISTING > KIST
KISTS > KIST
KISTVAEN n stone tomb
KISTVAENS > KISTVAEN
KIT n outfit or equipment for a specific purpose ▷ vb fit or provide
KITBAG n bag for a soldier's or traveller's belongings
KITBAGS > KITBAG
KITCHEN n room used for cooking ▷ vb (in archaic usage) provide with food
KITCHENED > KITCHEN
KITCHENER n someone employed in kitchen work
KITCHENET n small kitchen or part of another room equipped for use as a kitchen
KITCHENS > KITCHEN
KITE n light frame covered with a thin material ▷ vb soar and glide
KITEBOARD n board like a windsurfing board, towed by a large kite
KITED > KITE
KITELIKE > KITE
KITENGE n thick cotton cloth
KITENGES > KITENGE
KITER > KITE
KITERS > KITE
KITES > KITE
KITH n one's friends and acquaintances
KITHARA variant of > CITHARA
KITHARAS > KITHARA
KITHE same as > KYTHE
KITHED > KITHE
KITHES > KITHE
KITHING > KITHE

KITHS > KITH
KITING > KITE
KITINGS > KITE
KITLING dialect word for > KITTEN
KITLINGS > KITLING
KITS > KIT
KITSCH n tawdry or vulgarized art or literature with popular sentimental appeal ▷ adj having this quality
KITSCHES > KITSCH
KITSCHIER > KITSCH
KITSCHIFY vb make kitsch
KITSCHILY > KITSCH
KITSCHY > KITSCH
KITSET n New Zealand word for furniture supplied in pieces
KITSETS > KITSET
KITTED > KIT
KITTEL n white garment worn for certain Jewish rituals or burial
KITTELS > KITTEL
KITTEN n young cat ▷ vb (of cats) give birth
KITTENED > KITTEN
KITTENIER > KITTENY
KITTENING > KITTEN
KITTENISH adj lively and flirtatious
KITTENS > KITTEN
KITTENY adj like a kitten
KITTIES > KITTY
KITTING > KIT
KITTIWAKE n type of seagull
KITTLE adj capricious and unpredictable ▷ vb be troublesome or puzzling to (someone)
KITTLED > KITTLE
KITTLER > KITTLE
KITTLES > KITTLE
KITTLEST > KITTLE
KITTLIER > KITTLY
KITTLIEST > KITTLY
KITTLING > KITTLE
KITTLY Scots word for > TICKLISH
KITTUL n type of palm from which jaggery sugar comes
KITTULS > KITTUL
KITTY n communal fund
KITUL same as > KITTUL
KITULS > KITUL
KIVA n large room in a Pueblo village
KIVAS > KIVA
KIWI n New Zealand flightless bird with a long beak and no tail
KIWIFRUIT n edible oval fruit of the kiwi plant
KIWIS > KIWI
KLANG n (in music) kind of tone
KLANGS > KLANG
KLAP vb slap or spank
KLAPPED > KLAP
KLAPPING > KLAP
KLAPS > KLAP
KLATCH n gathering, especially over coffee

KLATCHES > KLATCH
KLATSCH same as > KLATCH
KLATSCHES > KLATSCH
KLAVERN n local Ku Klux Klan group
KLAVERNS > KLAVERN
KLAVIER same as > CLAVIER
KLAVIERS > KLAVIER
KLAXON n loud horn used on emergency vehicles ▷ vb hoot with a klaxon
KLAXONED > KLAXON
KLAXONING > KLAXON
KLAXONS > KLAXON
KLEAGLE n person with a particular rank in the Ku Klux Klan
KLEAGLES > KLEAGLE
KLEENEX n tradename for a kind of tissue
KLEENEXES > KLEENEX
KLEFTIKO n type of Greek lamb dish
KLEFTIKOS > KLEFTIKO
KLENDUSIC adj disease-resistant
KLEPHT n group of Greeks
KLEPHTIC > KLEPHT
KLEPHTISM > KLEPHT
KLEPHTS > KLEPHT
KLEPTO n compulsive thief
KLEPTOS > KLEPTO
KLETT n lightweight climbing boot
KLETTS > KLETT
KLEZMER n Jewish folk musician
KLEZMERS > KLEZMER
KLEZMORIM > KLEZMER
KLICK n kilometre
KLICKS > KLICK
KLIEG n as in klieg light intense carbon-arc light
KLIEGS > KLIEG
KLIK US military slang word for > KILOMETRE
KLIKS > KLIK
KLINKER n type of brick used in paving
KLINKERS > KLINKER
KLINOSTAT n rotating and tilting plant holder for studying and experimenting with plant growth
KLIPDAS n rock hyrax
KLIPDASES > KLIPDAS
KLISTER n type of ski dressing for improving grip on snow
KLISTERS > KLISTER
KLONDIKE same as > KLONDYKE
KLONDIKED > KLONDIKE
KLONDIKER same as > KLONDYKER
KLONDIKES > KLONDIKE
KLONDYKE n rich source of something ▷ vb transfer (bulk loads of fish) to factory ships at sea for processing

KLONDYKED > KLONDYKE
KLONDYKER n East European factory ship
KLONDYKES > KLONDYKE
KLONG n type of canal in Thailand
KLONGS > KLONG
KLOOCH same as > KLOOCHMAN
KLOOCHES > KLOOCH
KLOOCHMAN n Native American woman
KLOOCHMEN > KLOOCHMAN
KLOOF n mountain pass or gorge
KLOOFS > KLOOF
KLOOTCH same as > KLOOCHMAN
KLOOTCHES > KLOOTCH
KLUDGE n untidy solution ▷ vb cobble something together
KLUDGED > KLUDGE
KLUDGES > KLUDGE
KLUDGEY > KLUDGE
KLUDGIER > KLUDGE
KLUDGIEST > KLUDGE
KLUDGING > KLUDGE
KLUDGY > KLUDGE
KLUGE same as > KLUDGE
KLUGED > KLUGE
KLUGES > KLUGE
KLUGING > KLUGE
KLUTZ n clumsy or stupid person
KLUTZES > KLUTZ
KLUTZIER > KLUTZ
KLUTZIEST > KLUTZ
KLUTZY > KLUTZ
KLYSTRON n electron tube for the amplification of microwaves
KLYSTRONS > KLYSTRON
KNACK n skilful way of doing something ▷ vb dialect word for crack or snap
KNACKED adj broken or worn out
KNACKER n buyer of old horses for killing ▷ vb exhaust
KNACKERED adj extremely tired
KNACKERS > KNACKER
KNACKERY n slaughterhouse for horses
KNACKIER > KNACKY
KNACKIEST > KNACKY
KNACKING > KNACK
KNACKISH adj old word meaning cunning or artful
KNACKS > KNACK
KNACKY adj old or dialect word for cunning or artful
KNAG n knot in wood
KNAGGIER > KNAGGY
KNAGGIEST > KNAGGY
KNAGGY adj knotty
KNAGS > KNAG
KNAIDEL same as > KNEIDEL
KNAIDELS > KNAIDEL
KNAIDLACH > KNAIDEL

KNAP n crest of a hill ▷ vb hit, hammer, or chip
KNAPPED > KNAP
KNAPPER > KNAP
KNAPPERS > KNAP
KNAPPING > KNAP
KNAPPLE old word for > NIBBLE
KNAPPLED > KNAPPLE
KNAPPLES > KNAPPLE
KNAPPLING > KNAPPLE
KNAPS > KNAP
KNAPSACK n soldier's or traveller's bag worn strapped on the back
KNAPSACKS > KNAPSACK
KNAPWEED n plant with purplish thistle-like flowers
KNAPWEEDS > KNAPWEED
KNAR old spelling of > GNAR
KNARL old spelling of > GNARL
KNARLIER > KNARLY
KNARLIEST > KNARLY
KNARLS > KNARL
KNARLY same as > GNARLY
KNARRED > KNAR
KNARRIER > KNAR
KNARRIEST > KNAR
KNARRING > KNAR
KNARRY > KNAR
KNARS > KNAR
KNAUR variant form of > KNUR
KNAURS > KNAUR
KNAVE n jack at cards
KNAVERIES > KNAVERY
KNAVERY n dishonest behaviour
KNAVES > KNAVE
KNAVESHIP n old Scottish legal term for the small proportion of milled grain due to the person doing the milling
KNAVISH > KNAVE
KNAVISHLY > KNAVE
KNAWE same as > KNAWEL
KNAWEL n type of Old World plant
KNAWELS > KNAWEL
KNAWES > KNAWE
KNEAD vb work (dough) into a smooth mixture with the hands
KNEADABLE > KNEAD
KNEADED > KNEAD
KNEADER > KNEAD
KNEADERS > KNEAD
KNEADING > KNEAD
KNEADS > KNEAD
KNEE n joint between thigh and lower leg ▷ vb strike or push with the knee
KNEEBOARD vb surfboard ridden in kneeling position ▷ vb ride a kneeboard
KNEECAP nontechnical name for > PATELLA
KNEECAPS > KNEECAP
KNEED > KNEE
KNEEHOLE n space for the knees, esp under a desk

KNEEHOLES > KNEEHOLE
KNEEING > KNEE
KNEEJERK adj (of a reply or reaction) automatic and predictable
KNEEL vb fall or rest on one's knees ▷ n act or position of kneeling
KNEELED > KNEEL
KNEELER > KNEEL
KNEELERS > KNEEL
KNEELIKE adj like a knee
KNEELING > KNEEL
KNEELS > KNEEL
KNEEPAD n protective covering for the knee
KNEEPADS > KNEEPAD
KNEEPAN another word for > PATELLA
KNEEPANS > KNEEPAN
KNEEPIECE n knee-shaped piece of timber in ship
KNEEROOM n space to put one's knees
KNEEROOMS > KNEEROOM
KNEES > KNEE
KNEESIES n flirtatious touching of knees under table
KNEESOCK n type of sock that comes up to the knee
KNEESOCKS > KNEESOCK
KNEIDEL n (in Jewish cookery) small dumpling
KNEIDELS > KNEIDEL
KNEIDLACH > KNEIDEL
KNELL n sound of a bell, esp at a funeral or death ▷ vb ring a knell
KNELLED > KNELL
KNELLING > KNELL
KNELLS > KNELL
KNELT > KNEEL
KNESSET n parliament or assembly
KNESSETS > KNESSET
KNEVELL vb old Scots word meaning beat
KNEVELLED > KNEVELL
KNEVELLS > KNEVELL
KNEW > KNOW
KNICKER adj of or relating to knickers
KNICKERED adj wearing knickers
KNICKERS pl n woman's or girl's undergarment
KNICKS pl n knickers
KNIFE n sharp-edged blade with a handle ▷ vb cut or stab with a knife
KNIFED > KNIFE
KNIFELESS > KNIFE
KNIFELIKE > KNIFE
KNIFEMAN n man who is armed with a knife
KNIFEMEN > KNIFEMAN
KNIFER > KNIFE
KNIFEREST n support on which a carving knife or carving fork is placed at the table
KNIFERS > KNIFE
KNIFES > KNIFE

KNIFING > KNIFE
KNIFINGS > KNIFE
KNIGHT n man who has been given a knighthood ▷ vb award a knighthood to
KNIGHTAGE n group of knights or knights collectively
KNIGHTED > KNIGHT
KNIGHTING > KNIGHT
KNIGHTLY adj of, resembling, or appropriate for a knight
KNIGHTS > KNIGHT
KNIPHOFIA n any of several perennial southern African flowering plants
KNISH n type of dish
KNISHES > KNISH
KNIT vb make (a garment) by interlocking a series of loops in wool or other yarn ▷ n fabric made by knitting
KNITBONE n comfrey
KNITBONES > KNITBONE
KNITCH dialect word for > BUNDLE
KNITCHES > KNITCH
KNITS > KNIT
KNITTABLE > KNIT
KNITTED > KNIT
KNITTER > KNIT
KNITTERS > KNIT
KNITTING > KNIT
KNITTINGS > KNIT
KNITTLE n old word for string or cord
KNITTLES > KNITTLE
KNITWEAR n knitted clothes, such as sweaters
KNITWEARS > KNITWEAR
KNIVE rare variant of > KNIFE
KNIVED > KNIVE
KNIVES > KNIFE
KNIVING > KNIVE
KNOB n rounded projection, such as a switch on a radio ▷ vb supply with knobs
KNOBBED > KNOB
KNOBBER n two-year-old male deer
KNOBBERS > KNOBBER
KNOBBIER > KNOB
KNOBBIEST > KNOB
KNOBBING > KNOB
KNOBBLE n small knob ▷ vb dialect word meaning strike
KNOBBLED same as > KNOBBLY
KNOBBLES > KNOBBLE
KNOBBLIER > KNOBBLY
KNOBBLING > KNOBBLE
KNOBBLY adj covered with small bumps
KNOBBY > KNOB
KNOBHEAD n stupid person
KNOBHEADS > KNOBHEAD
KNOBLIKE > KNOB
KNOBS > KNOB

KNOBSTICK n stick with a round knob at the end, used as a club or missile by South African tribespeople
KNOCK vb give a blow or push to ▷ n blow or rap
KNOCKBACK n rejection, esp of a job application or invitation to go on a date
KNOCKDOWN adj (of a price) very low
KNOCKED > KNOCK
KNOCKER n metal fitting for knocking on a door
KNOCKERS > KNOCKER
KNOCKING > KNOCK
KNOCKINGS > KNOCK
KNOCKLESS > KNOCK
KNOCKOFF n informal word for a cheap, often illegal, copy of something
KNOCKOFFS > KNOCKOFF
KNOCKOUT n blow that renders an opponent unconscious ▷ vb render (someone) unconscious
KNOCKOUTS > KNOCKOUT
KNOCKS > KNOCK
KNOLL n small rounded hill ▷ vb (in archaic or dialect usage) knell
KNOLLED > KNOLL
KNOLLER > KNOLL
KNOLLERS > KNOLL
KNOLLIER > KNOLL
KNOLLIEST > KNOLL
KNOLLING > KNOLL
KNOLLS > KNOLL
KNOLLY > KNOLL
KNOP n knob, esp an ornamental one
KNOPPED > KNOP
KNOPS > KNOP
KNOSP n budlike architectural feature
KNOSPS > KNOSP
KNOT n type of fastening ▷ vb tie with or into a knot
KNOTGRASS n polygonaceous weedy plant whose small green flowers produce numerous seeds
KNOTHEAD n stupid person
KNOTHEADS > KNOTHEAD
KNOTHOLE n hole in a piece of wood where a knot has been
KNOTHOLES > KNOTHOLE
KNOTLESS > KNOT
KNOTLIKE > KNOT
KNOTS > KNOT
KNOTTED > KNOT
KNOTTER > KNOT
KNOTTERS > KNOT
KNOTTIER > KNOTTY
KNOTTIEST > KNOTTY
KNOTTILY > KNOTTY
KNOTTING > KNOT
KNOTTINGS > KNOT
KNOTTY adj full of knots
KNOTWEED n type of plant with small flowers and jointed stems

k

KNOTWEEDS
> KNOTWEED

KNOTWORK *n*
ornamentation consisting of a mass of intertwined and knotted cords

KNOTWORKS
> KNOTWORK

KNOUT *n* stout whip ▷ *vb* whip

KNOUTED > KNOUT

KNOUTING > KNOUT

KNOUTS > KNOUT

KNOW *vb* be or feel certain of the truth of (information etc)

KNOWABLE > KNOW

KNOWE *same as* > KNOLL

KNOWER > KNOW

KNOWERS > KNOW

KNOWES > KNOWE

KNOWHOW *n* ingenuity, knack, or skill

KNOWHOWS > KNOWHOW

KNOWING > KNOW

KNOWINGER > KNOW

KNOWINGLY > KNOW

KNOWINGS > KNOW

KNOWLEDGE *n* facts, feelings or experiences known by a person or group of people ▷ *vb* (in archaic usage) acknowledge

KNOWN *n* fact or something that is known

KNOWNS > KNOWN

KNOWS > KNOW

KNUB *dialect word for* > KNOB

KNUBBIER > KNUBBY

KNUBBIEST > KNUB

KNUBBLE *vb* dialect word for beat or pound using one's fists

KNUBBLED > KNUBBLE

KNUBBLES > KNUBBLE

KNUBBLIER > KNUBBLY

KNUBBLING > KNUBBLE

KNUBBLY *adj* having small lumps or protuberances

KNUBBY *adj* knub

KNUBS > KNUB

KNUCKLE *n* bone at the finger joint ▷ *vb* rub with the knuckles

KNUCKLED > KNUCKLE

KNUCKLER *n* type of pitch in baseball

KNUCKLERS
> KNUCKLER

KNUCKLES > KNUCKLE

KNUCKLIER > KNUCKLE

KNUCKLING > KNUCKLE

KNUCKLY > KNUCKLE

KNUR *n* knot or protuberance in a tree trunk or in wood

KNURL *n* small ridge, often one of a series ▷ *vb* impress with a series of fine ridges or serrations

KNURLED > KNURL

KNURLIER > KNURLY

KNURLIEST > KNURLY

KNURLING > KNURL

KNURLINGS > KNURL

KNURLS > KNURL

KNURLY *rare word for* > GNARLED

KNURR *same as for* > KNUR

KNURRS > KNURR

KNURS > KNUR

KNUT *n* dandy

KNUTS > KNUT

KO *n* (in New Zealand) traditional digging tool

KOA *n* Hawaiian leguminous tree

KOALA *n* tree-dwelling Australian marsupial with dense grey fur

KOALAS > KOALA

KOAN *n* (in Zen Buddhism) problem that admits no logical solution

KOANS > KOAN

KOAP *n* (in Papua New Guinean slang) sexual intercourse

KOAPS > KOAP

KOAS > KOA

KOB *n* any of several species of antelope

KOBAN *n* old oval-shaped Japanese gold coin

KOBANG *same as* > KOBAN

KOBANGS > KOBANG

KOBANS > KOBAN

KOBO *n* Nigerian monetary unit

KOBOLD *n* mischievous household sprite

KOBOLDS > KOBOLD

KOBOS > KOBO

KOBS > KOB

KOCHIA *n* any of several plants whose foliage turns dark red

KOCHIAS > KOCHIA

KOEKOEA *n* long-tailed cuckoo of New Zealand

KOEKOEAS > KOEKOEA

KOEL *n* any of several parasitic cuckoos

KOELS > KOEL

KOFF *n* Dutch masted merchant vessel

KOFFS > KOFF

KOFTA *n* Indian dish

KOFTAS > KOFTA

KOFTGAR *n* (in India) person skilled at inlaying steel with gold

KOFTGARI *n* ornamental Indian metalwork

KOFTGARIS
> KOFTGARI

KOFTGARS > KOFTGAR

KOFTWORK *same as*
> KOFTGARI

KOFTWORKS
> KOFTWORK

KOGAL *n* (in Japan) trendy teenage girl

KOGALS > KOGAL

KOHA *n* gift or donation, esp of cash

KOHANIM > KOHEN

KOHAS > KOHA

KOHEKOHE *n* New Zealand tree with large glossy leaves and reddish wood

KOHEKOHES > KOHEKOHE

KOHEN *n* member of the Jewish priestly caste

KOHL *n* cosmetic powder

KOHLRABI *n* type of cabbage with an edible stem

KOHLRABIS
> KOHLRABI

KOHLS > KOHL

KOI *n* any of various ornamental forms of the common carp

KOINE *n* common language among speakers of different languages

KOINES > KOINE

KOIS > KOI

KOJI *n* Japanese steamed rice

KOJIS > KOJI

KOKA *n* former type of score in judo

KOKAKO *n* type of crow

KOKAKOS > KOKAKO

KOKAM *same as* > KOKUM

KOKAMS > KOKAM

KOKANEE *n* type of freshwater salmon

KOKANEES > KOKANEE

KOKAS > KOKA

KOKER *n* Guyanese sluice

KOKERS > KOKER

KOKIRI *n* type of rough-skinned New Zealand triggerfish

KOKIRIS > KOKIRI

KOKOBEH *adj* (of certain fruit) having a rough skin

KOKOPU *n* any of several small freshwater fish of New Zealand

KOKOPUS > KOKOPU

KOKOWAI *n* type of clay

KOKOWAIS > KOKOWAI

KOKRA *n* type of wood

KOKRAS > KOKRA

KOKUM *n* tropical tree

KOKUMS > KOKUM

KOLA *n* as in kola nut caffeine-containing seed used in medicine and soft drinks

KOLACKIES > KOLACKY

KOLACKY *n* sweet bun with a fruit, jam, or nut filling

KOLAS > KOLA

KOLBASI *same as*
> KOLBASSI

KOLBASIS > KOLBASI

KOLBASSA *same as*
> KIELBASA

KOLBASSAS
> KOLBASSA

KOLBASSI *n* type of sausage

KOLBASSIS
> KOLBASSI

KOLHOZ *same as*
> KOLKHOZ

KOLHOZES > KOLHOZ

KOLHOZY > KOLHOZ

KOLINSKI *same as*
> KOLINSKY

KOLINSKY *n* Asian mink

KOLKHOS *same as*
> KOLKHOZ

KOLKHOSES > KOLKHOS

KOLKHOSY > KOLKHOS

KOLKHOZ *n* (formerly) collective farm in the Soviet Union

KOLKHOZES > KOLKHOZ

KOLKHOZY > KOLKHOZ

KOLKOZ *same as*
> KOLKHOZ

KOLKOZES > KOLKOZ

KOLKOZY > KOLKOZ

KOLO *n* Serbian folk dance

KOLOS > KOLO

KOMATIK *n* type of sledge

KOMATIKS > KOMATIK

KOMBU *n* dark brown seaweed

KOMBUS > KOMBU

KOMISSAR *same as*
> COMMISSAR

KOMISSARS
> KOMISSAR

KOMITAJI *n* rebel or revolutionary

KOMITAJIS
> KOMITAJI

KOMONDOR *n* large powerful dog of an ancient Hungarian breed, originally used for sheep herding

KOMONDORS
> KOMONDOR

KOMPROMAT *n* potentially damaging documents, photographs, etc kept for blackmail

KON *old word for* > KNOW

KONAKI *same as*
> KONEKE

KONAKIS > KONAKI

KONBU *same as* > KOMBU

KONBUS > KONBU

KOND > KON

KONDO *n* (in Uganda) thief or armed robber

KONDOS > KONDO

KONEKE *n* type of farm vehicle

KONEKES > KONEKE

KONFYT *n* South African fruit preserve

KONFYTS > KONFYT

KONGONI *n* E African hartebeest

KONIMETER *n* device for measuring airborne dust concentration in which samples are obtained by sucking the air through a hole and allowing it to pass over a glass plate coated with grease on which the particles collect

KONINI *n* edible dark purple berry

KONINIS > KONINI

KONIOLOGY *n* study of atmospheric dust and its effects

KONISCOPE *n* device for detecting and measuring dust in the air

KONK *same as* > CONK

KONKED > KONK

KONKING > KONK

KONKS > KONK

KONNING > KON

KONS > KON

KOODOO *same as* > KUDU
KOODOOS > KOODOO
KOOK *n* eccentric person ▷ *vb* dialect word for vanish
KOOKED > KOOK
KOOKIE *same as* > KOOKY
KOOKIER > KOOKY
KOOKIEST > KOOKY
KOOKILY > KOOKY
KOOKINESS > KOOKY
KOOKING > KOOK
KOOKS > KOOK
KOOKUM *same as* > KOKUM
KOOKUMS > KOOKUM
KOOKY *adj* crazy, eccentric, or foolish
KOOLAH *old form of* > KOALA
KOOLAHS > KOOLAH
KOORI *n* Aboriginal Australian
KOORIES > KOORI
KOORIS > KOORI
KOP *n* prominent isolated hill or mountain in southern Africa
KOPASETIC *same as* > COPACETIC
KOPECK *n* former Russian monetary unit
KOPECKS > KOPECK
KOPEK *same as* > KOPECK
KOPEKS > KOPEK
KOPH *n* 19th letter in the Hebrew alphabet
KOPHS > KOPH
KOPIYKA *n* monetary unit of Ukraine
KOPIYKAS > KOPIYKA
KOPIYKY > KOPIYKA
KOPIYOK > KOPIYKA
KOPJE *n* small hill
KOPJES > KOPJE
KOPPA *n* consonantal letter in the Greek alphabet
KOPPAS > KOPPA
KOPPIE *same as* > KOPJE
KOPPIES > KOPPIE
KOPS > KOP
KOR *n* ancient Hebrew unit of capacity
KORA *n* West African instrument
KORAI > KORE
KORARI *n* native New Zealand flax plant
KORARIS > KORARI
KORAS > KORA
KORAT *n* as in *korat cat* rare blue-grey breed of cat
KORATS > KORAT
KORE *n* ancient Greek statue of a young woman wearing clothes
KORERO *n* talk or discussion ▷ *vb* speak or converse
KOREROED > KORERO
KOREROING > KORERO
KOREROS > KORERO
KORES > KORE
KORFBALL *n* game similar to basketball, in which each team consists of six men and six women
KORFBALLS > KORFBALL

KORIMAKO *another name for* > BELLBIRD
KORIMAKOS > KORIMAKO
KORKIR *n* variety of lichen used in dyeing
KORKIRS > KORKIR
KORMA *n* type of mild Indian dish
KORMAS > KORMA
KORO *n* elderly Māori man
KOROMIKO *n* flowering New Zealand shrub
KOROMIKOS > KOROMIKO
KORORA *n* small New Zealand penguin
KORORAS > KORORA
KOROS > KORO
KOROWAI *n* decorative woven cloak worn by a Māori chief
KOROWAIS > KOROWAI
KORS > KOR
KORU *n* stylized curved pattern used esp in carving
KORUN > KORUNA
KORUNA *n* standard monetary unit of the Czech Republic
KORUNAS > KORUNA
KORUNY > KORUNA
KORUS > KORU
KOS *n* Indian unit of distance
KOSES > KOS
KOSHER *adj* conforming to Jewish religious law ▷ *n* kosher food ▷ *vb* prepare in accordance with Jewish dietary rules
KOSHERED > KOSHER
KOSHERING > KOSHER
KOSHERS > KOSHER
KOSMOS *variant form of* > COSMOS
KOSMOSES > KOSMOS
KOSS *same as* > KOS
KOSSES > KOSS
KOTARE *n* small greenish-blue kingfisher
KOTARES > KOTARE
KOTCH *vb* South African slang for vomit
KOTCHED > KOTCH
KOTCHES > KOTCH
KOTCHING > KOTCH
KOTO *n* Japanese stringed instrument
KOTOS > KOTO
KOTOW *same as* > KOWTOW
KOTOWED > KOTOW
KOTOWER > KOTOW
KOTOWERS > KOTOW
KOTOWING > KOTOW
KOTOWS > KOTOW
KOTTABOS *same as* > COTTABUS
KOTUKU *n* type of white heron
KOTUKUS > KOTUKU
KOTWAL *n* senior police officer or magistrate in an Indian town
KOTWALS > KOTWAL
KOULAN *same as* > KULAN
KOULANS > KOULAN

KOUMIS *same as* > KUMISS
KOUMISES > KOUMIS
KOUMISS *same as* > KUMISS
KOUMISSES > KOUMISS
KOUMYS *same as* > KUMISS
KOUMYSES > KOUMYS
KOUMYSS *same as* > KUMISS
KOUMYSSES > KOUMYSS
KOUPREY *n* large wild SE Asian ox
KOUPREYS > KOUPREY
KOURA *n* New Zealand freshwater crayfish
KOURAS > KOURA
KOURBASH *same as* > KURBASH
KOUROI > KOUROS
KOUROS *n* ancient Greek statue of a young man
KOUSKOUS *same as* > COUSCOUS
KOUSSO *n* Abyssinian tree
KOUSSOS > KOUSSO
KOW *old variant of* > COW
KOWHAI *n* New Zealand tree
KOWHAIS > KOWHAI
KOWS > KOW
KOWTOW *vb* be servile (towards) ▷ *n* act of kowtowing
KOWTOWED > KOWTOW
KOWTOWER > KOWTOW
KOWTOWERS > KOWTOW
KOWTOWING > KOWTOW
KOWTOWS > KOWTOW
KRAAL *n* S African village surrounded by a strong fence ▷ *adj* denoting or relating to the tribal aspects of the Black African way of life ▷ *vb* enclose (livestock) in a kraal
KRAALED > KRAAL
KRAALING > KRAAL
KRAALS > KRAAL
KRAB *same as* > KARABINER
KRABS > KRAB
KRAFT *n* strong wrapping paper
KRAFTS > KRAFT
KRAI *n* administrative division of Russia
KRAIS > KRAI
KRAIT *n* brightly coloured venomous snake of S and SE Asia
KRAITS > KRAIT
KRAKEN *n* legendary sea monster
KRAKENS > KRAKEN
KRAKOWIAK *n* Polish dance
KRAMERIA *another name for* > RHATANY
KRAMERIAS > KRAMERIA
KRANG *n* dead whale from which the blubber has been removed
KRANGS > KRANG
KRANS *n* sheer rock face

KRANSES > KRANS
KRANTZ *same as* > KRANS
KRANTZES > KRANTZ
KRANZ *same as* > KRANS
KRANZES > KRANZ
KRATER *same as* > CRATER
KRATERS > KRATER
KRAUT *n* sauerkraut
KRAUTROCK *n* experimental German rock music
KRAUTS > KRAUT
KRAY *same as* > KRAI
KRAYS > KRAY
KREASOTE *same as* > CREOSOTE
KREASOTED > KREASOTE
KREASOTES > KREASOTE
KREATINE *same as* > CREATINE
KREATINES > KREATINE
KREEP *n* lunar substance
KREEPS > KREEP
KREESE *same as* > KRIS
KREESED > KREESE
KREESES > KREESE
KREESING > KREESE
KREMLIN *n* citadel of any Russian city
KREMLINS > KREMLIN
KRENG *same as* > KRANG
KRENGS > KRENG
KREOSOTE *same as* > CREOSOTE
KREOSOTED > KREOSOTE
KREOSOTES > KREOSOTE
KREPLACH *pl n* small filled dough casings usually served in soup
KREPLECH *same as* > KREPLACH
KREUTZER *n* any of various former copper and silver coins of Germany or Austria
KREUTZERS > KREUTZER
KREUZER *same as* > KREUTZER
KREUZERS > KREUZER
KREWE *n* club taking part in New Orleans carnival parade
KREWES > KREWE
KRILL *n* small shrimplike sea creature
KRILLS > KRILL
KRIMMER *n* tightly curled light grey fur
KRIMMERS > KRIMMER
KRIS *n* type of Malayan and Indonesian knife ▷ *vb* stab or slash with a kris
KRISED > KRIS
KRISES > KRIS
KRISING > KRIS
KROMESKY *n* croquette consisting of a piece of bacon wrapped round minced meat or fish
KRONA *n* standard monetary unit of Sweden

k

KRONE n standard monetary unit of Norway and Denmark
KRONEN > KRONE
KRONER > KRONE
KRONOR > KRONA
KRONUR > KRONA
KROON n former monetary unit of Estonia
KROONI > KROON
KROONS > KROON
KRUBI n aroid plant with an unpleasant smell
KRUBIS > KRUBI
KRUBUT same as > KRUBI
KRUBUTS > KRUBUT
KRULLER variant spelling of > CRULLER
KRULLERS > KRULLER
KRUMHORN variant spelling of > CRUMHORN
KRUMHORNS > KRUMHORN
KRUMKAKE n Scandinavian biscuit
KRUMKAKES > KRUMKAKE
KRUMMHOLZ n zone of stunted wind-blown trees growing at high altitudes just above the timberline on tropical mountains
KRUMMHORN variant spelling of > CRUMHORN
KRUMPER > KRUMPING
KRUMPERS > KRUMPING
KRUMPING n type of aggressive dance
KRUMPINGS > KRUMPING
KRUNK n style of hip-hop music
KRUNKED same as > CRUNKED
KRUNKS > KRUNK
KRYOLITE variant spelling of > CRYOLITE
KRYOLITES > KRYOLITE
KRYOLITH same as > CRYOLITE
KRYOLITHS > KRYOLITH
KRYOMETER same as > CRYOMETER
KRYPSES > KRYPSIS
KRYPSIS n idea that Christ made secret use of his divine attributes
KRYPTON n colourless gas
KRYPTONS > KRYPTON
KRYTRON n type of fast electronic gas-discharge switch
KRYTRONS > KRYTRON
KSAR old form of > TSAR
KSARS > KSAR
KUBASA same as > KIELBASA
KUBASAS > KUBASA
KUBIE n Ukrainian roll filled with kielbasa
KUBIES > KUBIE
KUCCHA same as > KACCHA
KUCCHAS > KUCCHA
KUCHCHA same as > KACHA

KUCHEN n breadlike cake
KUCHENS > KUCHEN
KUDLIK n Inuit soapstone seal-oil lamp
KUDLIKS > KUDLIK
KUDO variant of > KUDOS
KUDOS n fame or credit
KUDOSES > KUDOS
KUDU n African antelope with spiral horns
KUDUS > KUDU
KUDZU n hairy leguminous climbing plant
KUDZUS > KUDZU
KUE n name of the letter Q
KUEH n (in Malaysia) any cake of Malay, Chinese, or Indian origin
KUES > KUE
KUFI n cap for Muslim man
KUFIS > KUFI
KUFIYAH same as > KEFFIYEH
KUFIYAHS > KUFIYAH
KUGEL n baked pudding in traditional Jewish cooking
KUGELS > KUGEL
KUIA n Māori female elder or elderly woman
KUIAS > KUIA
KUKRI n heavy, curved knife used by Gurkhas
KUKRIS > KUKRI
KUKU n mussel
KUKUS > KUKU
KULA n ceremonial gift exchange among islanders in the W Pacific
KULAK n (formerly) property-owning Russian peasant
KULAKI > KULAK
KULAKS > KULAK
KULAN n Asiatic wild ass
KULANS > KULAN
KULAS > KULA
KULBASA same as > KIELBASA
KULBASAS > KULBASA
KULFI n Indian dessert
KULFIS > KULFI
KULTUR n German civilization
KULTURS > KULTUR
KUMARA n tropical root vegetable with yellow flesh
KUMARAHOU n New Zealand shrub
KUMARAS > KUMARA
KUMARI n (in Indian English) maiden
KUMARIS > KUMARI
KUMBALOI pl n worry beads
KUMERA same as > KUMARA
KUMERAS > KUMERA
KUMIKUMI same as > KAMOKAMO
KUMIKUMIS > KUMIKUMI
KUMIS same as > KUMISS
KUMISES > KUMIS
KUMISS n drink made from fermented mare's or other milk

KUMISSES > KUMISS
KUMITE n freestyle sparring or fighting
KUMITES > KUMITE
KUMKUM n red pigment used by Hindu women to make a mark on the forehead
KUMKUMS > KUMKUM
KUMMEL n German liqueur
KUMMELS > KUMMEL
KUMQUAT n citrus fruit resembling a tiny orange
KUMQUATS > KUMQUAT
KUMYS same as > KUMISS
KUMYSES > KUMYS
KUNA n standard monetary unit of Croatia
KUNDALINI n (in yoga) life force that resides at the base of the spine
KUNE > KUNA
KUNEKUNE n feral pig
KUNEKUNES > KUNEKUNE
KUNJOOS adj (in Indian English) mean or stingy
KUNKAR n type of limestone
KUNKARS > KUNKAR
KUNKUR same as > KUNKAR
KUNKURS > KUNKUR
KUNZITE n variety of the mineral spodumene
KUNZITES > KUNZITE
KURBASH vb whip with a hide whip
KURBASHED > KURBASH
KURBASHES > KURBASH
KURFUFFLE same as > KERFUFFLE
KURGAN n Russian burial mound
KURGANS > KURGAN
KURI n mongrel dog
KURIS > KURI
KURRAJONG n Australian tree or shrub with tough fibrous bark
KURRE old variant of > CUR
KURRES > KURRE
KURSAAL n public room at a health resort
KURSAALS > KURSAAL
KURTA n long loose garment
KURTAS > KURTA
KURTOSES > KURTOSIS
KURTOSIS n measure of the concentration of a distribution around its mean
KURU n degenerative disease of the nervous system
KURUS > KURU
KURUSH n small currency unit of Turkey
KURUSHES > KURUSH
KURVEY vb (in old South African English) transport goods by ox cart
KURVEYED > KURVEY
KURVEYING > KURVEY
KURVEYOR > KURVEY
KURVEYORS > KURVEY
KURVEYS > KURVEY

KUSSO variant spelling of > KOUSSO
KUSSOS > KUSSO
KUTA n (in Indian English) male dog
KUTAS > KUTA
KUTCH same as > CATECHU
KUTCHA adj makeshift or not solid
KUTCHES > KUTCH
KUTI n (in Indian English) female dog
KUTIS > KUTI
KUTU n body louse
KUTUS > KUTU
KUVASZ n breed of dog from Hungary
KUVASZOK > KUVASZ
KUZU same as > KUDZU
KUZUS > KUZU
KVAS same as > KVASS
KVASES > KVAS
KVASS n alcoholic drink
KVASSES > KVASS
KVELL vb US word meaning be happy
KVELLED > KVELL
KVELLING > KVELL
KVELLS > KVELL
KVETCH vb complain or grumble
KVETCHED > KVETCH
KVETCHER > KVETCH
KVETCHERS > KVETCH
KVETCHES > KVETCH
KVETCHIER > KVETCHY
KVETCHILY > KVETCHY
KVETCHING n act of grumbling or complaining
KVETCHY adj tending to grumble or complain
KWACHA n standard monetary unit of Zambia
KWACHAS > KWACHA
KWAITO n type of South African pop music
KWAITOS > KWAITO
KWANZA n standard monetary unit of Angola
KWANZAS > KWANZA
KWELA n type of pop music
KWELAS > KWELA
KY pl n Scots word for cows
KYACK n type of pannier
KYACKS > KYACK
KYAK same as > KAYAK
KYAKS > KYAK
KYANG same as > KIANG
KYANGS > KYANG
KYANISE same as > KYANIZE
KYANISED > KYANISE
KYANISES > KYANISE
KYANISING > KYANISE
KYANITE n grey, green, or blue mineral
KYANITES > KYANITE
KYANITIC > KYANITE
KYANIZE vb treat (timber) with corrosive sublimate
KYANIZED > KYANIZE
KYANIZES > KYANIZE
KYANIZING > KYANIZE
KYAR same as > COIR

KYARS > KYAR
KYAT n standard monetary unit of Myanmar
KYATS > KYAT
KYBO n temporary lavatory used when camping
KYBOS > KYBO
KYBOSH same as > KIBOSH
KYBOSHED > KYBOSH
KYBOSHES > KYBOSH
KYBOSHING > KYBOSH
KYDST > KYTHE
KYE n Korean fundraising meeting
KYES > KYE
KYLE n narrow strait or channel
KYLES > KYLE
KYLICES > KYLIX

KYLIE n type of boomerang
KYLIES > KYLIE
KYLIKES > KYLIX
KYLIN n (in Chinese art) mythical animal
KYLINS > KYLIN
KYLIX n drinking vessel used in ancient Greece
KYLIXES > KYLIX
KYLLOSES > KYLLOSIS
KYLLOSIS n club foot
KYLOE n breed of beef cattle
KYLOES > KYLOE
KYMOGRAM n image or other visual record created by a kymograph
KYMOGRAMS > KYMOGRAM
KYMOGRAPH n rotatable drum for holding paper on

which a tracking stylus continuously records variations in blood pressure, respiratory movements, etc
KYND old variant of > KIND
KYNDE old variant of > KIND
KYNDED > KYNDE
KYNDES > KYNDE
KYNDING > KYND
KYNDS > KYND
KYNE pl n archaic word for cows
KYOGEN n type of Japanese drama
KYOGENS > KYOGEN
KYPE n hook on the lower jaw of a mature male salmon
KYPES > KYPE

KYPHOSES > KYPHOSIS
KYPHOSIS n backward curvature of the thoracic spine
KYPHOTIC > KYPHOSIS
KYRIE n type of prayer
KYRIELLE n verse form of French origin characterized by repeated lines or words
KYRIELLES > KYRIELLE
KYRIES > KYRIE
KYTE n belly
KYTES > KYTE
KYTHE vb appear
KYTHED > KYTHE
KYTHES > KYTHE
KYTHING > KYTHE
KYU n (in judo) one of the five student grades
KYUS > KYU

k

LI

LA n the sixth note of the musical scale

LAAGER n (in Africa) a camp defended by a circular formation of wagons ▷ vb form (wagons) into a laager

LAAGERED > LAAGER

LAAGERING > LAAGER

LAAGERS > LAAGER

LAARI same as > LARI

LAARIS > LAARI

LAB n laboratory

LABARA > LABARUM

LABARUM n standard carried in Christian processions

LABARUMS > LABARUM

LABDA same as > LAMBDA

LABDACISM n excessive use or idiosyncratic pronunciation of (l)

LABDANUM n dark resinous juice obtained from various rockroses

LABDANUMS > LABDANUM

LABDAS > LABDA

LABEL n piece of card fixed to an object ▷ vb give a label to

LABELABLE > LABEL

LABELED > LABEL

LABELER > LABEL

LABELERS > LABEL

LABELING > LABEL

LABELLA > LABELLUM

LABELLATE > LABELLUM

LABELLED > LABEL

LABELLER > LABEL

LABELLERS > LABEL

LABELLING > LABEL

LABELLIST n person who wears only clothes with fashionable brand names

LABELLOID > LABELLUM

LABELLUM n lip-like part of certain plants

LABELMATE n musician or singer who records for the same company as another

LABELS > LABEL

LABIA > LABIUM

LABIAL adj of the lips ▷ n speech sound that involves the lips

LABIALISE same as > LABIALIZE

LABIALISM > LABIALIZE

LABIALITY > LABIAL

LABIALIZE vb pronounce with articulation involving rounded lips

LABIALLY > LABIAL

LABIALS > LABIAL

LABIATE n plant with a two-lipped flower

LABIATED adj having a lip

LABIATES > LABIATE

LABILE adj (of a compound) prone to chemical change

LABILITY > LABILE

LABIS n spoon used to give the Eucharist to communicants

LABISES > LABIS

LABIUM n lip or liplike structure

LABLAB n twining leguminous plant

LABLABS > LABLAB

LABNEH n Mediterranean soft cheese

LABNEHS > LABNEH

LABOR same as > LABOUR

LABORED same as > LABOURED

LABOREDLY > LABOURED

LABORER same as > LABOURER

LABORERS > LABORER

LABORING > LABOR

LABORIOUS adj involving great prolonged effort

LABORISM same as > LABOURISM

LABORISMS > LABOURISM

LABORIST same as > LABOURIST

LABORISTS > LABOURIST

LABORITE n adherent of the Labour party

LABORITES > LABORITE

LABORS > LABOR

LABORSOME adj requiring hard work

LABOUR n physical work or exertion ▷ vb work hard

LABOURED adj uttered or done with difficulty

LABOURER n person who labours, esp someone doing manual work for wages

LABOURERS > LABOURER

LABOURING > LABOUR

LABOURISM n dominance of the working classes

LABOURIST n person who supports workers' rights

LABOURITE n person who supports workers' rights

LABOURS > LABOUR

LABRA > LABRUM

LABRADOR n large retriever dog with a usu gold or black coat

LABRADORS > LABRADOR

LABRAL adj of or like a lip

LABRET n piece of bone or shell

LABRETS > LABRET

LABRID same as > LABROID

LABRIDS > LABRID

LABROID n type of fish ▷ adj of or relating to such fish

LABROIDS > LABROID

LABROSE adj thick-lipped

LABRUM n lip or liplike part

LABRUMS > LABRUM

LABRUSCA n grape variety

LABRUSCAS > LABRUSCA

LABRYS n type of axe

LABRYSES > LABRYS

LABS > LAB

LABURNUM n ornamental tree with yellow hanging flowers

LABURNUMS > LABURNUM

LABYRINTH n complicated network of passages

LAC same as > LAKH

LACCOLITE same as > LACCOLITH

LACCOLITH n dome-shaped body of igneous rock between two layers of older sedimentary rock

LACE n delicate fabric ▷ vb fasten with shoelaces, cords, etc

LACEBARK n small evergreen tree

LACEBARKS > LACEBARK

LACED > LACE

LACELESS > LACE

LACELIKE > LACE

LACEMAKER n one who makes lace

LACER > LACE

LACERABLE > LACERATE

LACERANT adj painfully distressing

LACERATE vb tear (flesh) ▷ adj having edges that are jagged or torn

LACERATED > LACERATE

LACERATES > LACERATE

LACERS > LACE

LACERTIAN n type of reptile

LACERTID n type of lizard

LACERTIDS > LACERTID

LACERTINE adj relating to lacertids ▷ n lacertid lizard

LACES > LACE

LACET n braided work in lace

LACETS > LACET

LACEWING n any of various neuropterous insects

LACEWINGS > LACEWING

LACEWOOD n wood of sycamore tree

LACEWOODS > LACEWOOD

LACEWORK n work made from lace

LACEWORKS > LACEWORK

LACEY same as > LACY

LACHES n unreasonable delay in pursuing a legal remedy

LACHESES > LACHES

LACHRYMAL same as > LACRIMAL

LACIER > LACY

LACIEST > LACY

LACILY > LACY

LACINESS > LACY

LACING > LACE

LACINGS > LACE

LACINIA n narrow fringe on petal

LACINIAE > LACINIA

LACINIATE adj jagged

LACK n shortage of something needed ▷ vb need

LACKADAY another word for > ALAS

LACKED > LACK
LACKER *variant spelling of* > LACQUER
LACKERED > LACKER
LACKERING > LACKER
LACKERS > LACKER
LACKEY *n servile follower* ▷ *vb* act as a lackey (to)
LACKEYED > LACKEY
LACKEYING > LACKEY
LACKEYS > LACKEY
LACKING > LACK
LACKLAND *n* fool
LACKLANDS > LACKLAND
LACKS > LACK
LACMUS *n* old form of litmus
LACMUSES > LACMUS
LACONIC *adj* using only a few words, terse
LACONICAL *same as* > LACONIC
LACONISM *n* economy of expression
LACONISMS > LACONISM
LACQUER *n* hard varnish for wood or metal ▷ *vb* apply lacquer to
LACQUERED > LACQUER
LACQUERER > LACQUER
LACQUERS > LACQUER
LACQUEY *same as* > LACKEY
LACQUEYED > LACQUEY
LACQUEYS > LACQUEY
LACRIMAL *adj* of tears or the glands which produce them ▷ *n* bone near tear gland
LACRIMALS > LACRIMAL
LACRIMARY *adj* of or relating to tears or to the glands that secrete tears
LACRIMOSO *adj* tearful
LACROSSE *n* sport in which teams catch and throw a ball using long sticks with a pouched net
LACROSSES > LACROSSE
LACRYMAL *same as* > LACRIMAL
LACRYMALS > LACRYMAL
LACS > LAC
LACTAM *n* any of a group of inner amides
LACTAMS > LACTAM
LACTARIAN *n* vegetarian who eats dairy products
LACTARY *adj* relating to milk
LACTASE *n* any of a group of enzymes that hydrolyse lactose to glucose and galactose
LACTASES > LACTASE
LACTATE *vb* secrete milk ▷ *n* ester or salt of lactic acid
LACTATED > LACTATE
LACTATES > LACTATE
LACTATING > LACTATE
LACTATION *n* secretion of milk by female mammals to feed young

LACTEAL *adj* of or like milk ▷ *n* any of the lymphatic vessels that convey chyle from the small intestine to the blood
LACTEALLY > LACTEAL
LACTEALS > LACTEAL
LACTEAN *another word for* > LACTEOUS
LACTEOUS *adj* milky
LACTIC *adj* of or derived from milk
LACTIFIC *adj* yielding milk
LACTITOL *n* type of artificial sweetener
LACTITOLS > LACTITOL
LACTIVISM > LACTIVIST
LACTIVIST *n* person who advocates breast-feeding
LACTONE *n* any of a class of organic compounds
LACTONES > LACTONE
LACTONIC > LACTONE
LACTOSE *n* white crystalline sugar found in milk
LACTOSES > LACTOSE
LACTULOSE *n* synthetic sugar used as a laxative
LACUNA *n* gap or missing part, esp in a document or series
LACUNAE > LACUNA
LACUNAL > LACUNA
LACUNAR *n* ceiling, soffit, or vault having coffers ▷ *adj* having a lacuna
LACUNARIA > LACUNAR
LACUNARS > LACUNAR
LACUNARY > LACUNA
LACUNAS > LACUNA
LACUNATE > LACUNA
LACUNE *n* hiatus
LACUNES > LACUNE
LACUNOSE > LACUNA
LACY *adj* fine, like lace
LAD *n* boy or young man
LADANUM *same as* > LABDANUM
LADANUMS > LADANUM
LADDER *n* frame of two poles connected by horizontal steps for climbing ▷ *vb* cause to have a line of undone stitches
LADDERED > LADDER
LADDERIER > LADDERY
LADDERING > LADDER
LADDERS > LADDER
LADDERY *adj* (of tights) laddered
LADDIE *n* familiar term for a male, esp a young man
LADDIER > LADDY
LADDIES > LADDIE
LADDIEST > LADDY
LADDISH *adj* behaving in a macho or immature manner
LADDISHLY *adv* in a laddish manner

LADDISM *n* laddish attitudes and behaviour
LADDISMS > LADDISM
LADDY *adj* laddish
LADE *vb* put cargo on board ▷ *n* watercourse
LADED > LADE
LADEN *adj* loaded ▷ *vb* load with cargo
LADENED > LADEN
LADENING > LADEN
LADENS > LADEN
LADER > LADE
LADERS > LADE
LADES > LADE
LADETTE *n* young woman who behaves in ways considered typical of young men
LADETTES > LADETTE
LADHOOD > LAD
LADHOODS > LAD
LADIES *n* women's public toilet
LADIFIED > LADIFY
LADIFIES > LADIFY
LADIFY *same as* > LADYFY
LADIFYING > LADIFY
LADING > LADE
LADINGS > LADE
LADINO *n* Italian variety of white clover
LADINOS > LADINO
LADLE *n* long-handled spoon with a large bowl ▷ *vb* serve out
LADLED > LADLE
LADLEFUL > LADLE
LADLEFULS > LADLE
LADLER *n* person who serves with a ladle
LADLERS > LADLER
LADLES > LADLE
LADLING > LADLE
LADRON *same as* > LADRONE
LADRONE *n* thief
LADRONES > LADRONE
LADRONS > LADRON
LADS > LAD
LADY *n* woman ▷ *adj* female
LADYBIRD *n* small red beetle with black spots
LADYBIRDS > LADYBIRD
LADYBOY *n* (esp in Thailand) a transsexual or transgender person
LADYBOYS > LADYBOY
LADYBUG *same as* > LADYBIRD
LADYBUGS > LADYBUG
LADYCOW *another word for* > LADYBIRD
LADYCOWS > LADYCOW
LADYFIED > LADYFY
LADYFIES > LADYFY
LADYFISH *n* type of game fish
LADYFLIES > LADYFLY
LADYFLY *another word for* > LADYBIRD
LADYFY *vb* make a lady of (someone)
LADYFYING > LADYFY

LADYHOOD > LADY
LADYHOODS > LADY
LADYISH > LADY
LADYISM > LADY
LADYISMS > LADY
LADYKIN *n* endearing form of 'lady'
LADYKINS > LADYKIN
LADYLIKE *adj* polite and dignified
LADYLOVE *n* beloved woman
LADYLOVES > LADYLOVE
LADYNESS *n* state of being a lady
LADYPALM *n* small palm, grown indoors
LADYPALMS > LADYPALM
LADYSHIP *n* title of a peeress
LADYSHIPS > LADYSHIP
LAER *another word for* > LAAGER
LAERED > LAER
LAERING > LAER
LAERS > LAER
LAESIE *old form of* > LAZY
LAETARE *n* fourth Sunday of Lent
LAETARES > LAETARE
LAETRILE *n* drug used to treat cancer
LAETRILES > LAETRILE
LAEVIGATE *same as* > LEVIGATE
LAEVO *adj* on the left
LAEVULIN *n* polysaccharide occurring in the tubers of certain helianthus plants
LAEVULINS > LAEVULIN
LAEVULOSE *n* fructose
LAG *vb* go too slowly, fall behind ▷ *n* delay between events
LAGAN *n* goods or wreckage on the sea bed
LAGANS > LAGAN
LAGENA *n* bottle with a narrow neck
LAGENAS > LAGENA
LAGEND *same as* > LAGAN
LAGENDS > LAGEND
LAGER *n* light-bodied beer ▷ *vb* ferment into lager
LAGERED > LAGER
LAGERING > LAGER
LAGERS > LAGER
LAGGARD *n* person who lags behind ▷ *adj* sluggish, slow
LAGGARDLY *adj* like a laggard
LAGGARDS > LAGGARD
LAGGED > LAG
LAGGEN *n* spar of a barrel
LAGGENS > LAGGEN
LAGGER *n* person who lags pipes
LAGGERS > LAGGER
LAGGIN *same as* > LAGGEN
LAGGING > LAG

LAGGINGLY > LAG

LAGGINGS > LAG

LAGGINS > LAGGIN

LAGNAPPE same as
> LAGNIAPPE

LAGNAPPES
> LAGNIAPPE

LAGNIAPPE n small gift,
esp one given to a
customer who makes a
purchase

LAGOMORPH n type of
placental mammal of the
order which includes
rabbits and hares

LAGOON n water cut off
from the sea by reefs or
sand bars

LAGOONAL > LAGOON

LAGOONS > LAGOON

LAGRIMOSO adj
mournful

LAGS > LAG

LAGUNA n lagoon

LAGUNAS > LAGUNA

LAGUNE same as
> LAGOON

LAGUNES > LAGUNE

LAH n (in tonic sol-fa) sixth
degree of any major scale

LAHAL n game played by
native peoples of the
Pacific Northwest

LAHALS > LAHAL

LAHAR n landslide of
volcanic debris and water

LAHARS > LAHAR

LAHS > LAH

LAIC adj laical ⊳ n layman

LAICAL adj secular

LAICALLY > LAIC

LAICH n low-lying piece
of land

LAICHS > LAICH

LAICISE same as
> LAICIZE

LAICISED > LAICISE

LAICISES > LAICISE

LAICISING > LAICISE

LAICISM > LAIC

LAICISMS > LAIC

LAICITIES > LAICITY

LAICITY n state of being
laical

LAICIZE vb remove
ecclesiastical status from

LAICIZED > LAICIZE

LAICIZES > LAICIZE

LAICIZING > LAICIZE

LAICS > LAIC

LAID Scots form of > LOAD

LAIDED > LAID

LAIDING > LAID

LAIDLIER > LAIDLY

LAIDLIEST > LAIDLY

LAIDLY adj very ugly

LAIDS > LAID

LAIGH adj low-lying ⊳ n
area of low-lying ground

LAIGHER > LAIGH

LAIGHEST > LAIGH

LAIGHS > LAIGH

LAIK vb play (a game, etc)

LAIKA n type of small dog

LAIKAS > LAIKA

LAIKED > LAIK

LAIKER > LAIK

LAIKERS > LAIK

LAIKING > LAIK

LAIKS > LAIK

LAIN > LAY

LAIPSE vb beat soundly

LAIPSED > LAIPSE

LAIPSES > LAIPSE

LAIPSING > LAIPSE

LAIR n resting place of an
animal ⊳ vb retreat to or
rest in a lair

LAIRAGE n
accommodation for farm
animals

LAIRAGES > LAIRAGE

LAIRD n Scottish
landowner

LAIRDLIER > LAIRDLY

LAIRDLY adj pertaining
to lairds

LAIRDS > LAIRD

LAIRDSHIP n state of
being laird

LAIRED > LAIR

LAIRIER > LAIRY

LAIRIEST > LAIRY

LAIRING > LAIR

LAIRISE same as
> LAIRIZE

LAIRISED > LAIRISE

LAIRISES > LAIRISE

LAIRISING > LAIRISE

LAIRIZE vb show off

LAIRIZED > LAIRIZE

LAIRIZES > LAIRIZE

LAIRIZING > LAIRIZE

LAIRS > LAIR

LAIRY adj gaudy or flashy

LAISSE n type of rhyme
scheme

LAISSES > LAISSE

LAITANCE n white film
forming on drying
concrete

LAITANCES
> LAITANCE

LAITH Scots form of
> LOATH

LAITHLY same as
> LAIDLY

LAITIES > LAITY

LAITY n non-clergy

LAKE n expanse of water
entirely surrounded by
land ⊳ vb take time away
from work

LAKEBED n bed of lake

LAKEBEDS > LAKEBED

LAKED > LAKE

LAKEFILL n area of land
on a filled lake

LAKEFILLS
> LAKEFILL

LAKEFRONT n area at
edge of lake

LAKEHEAD n shore of a
lake farthest from the
outlet

LAKEHEADS
> LAKEHEAD

LAKELAND n countryside
with a lot of lakes

LAKELANDS
> LAKELAND

LAKELET n small lake

LAKELETS > LAKELET

LAKELIKE > LAKE

LAKEPORT n port on lake

LAKEPORTS
> LAKEPORT

LAKER n lake cargo
vessel

LAKERS > LAKER

LAKES > LAKE

LAKESHORE n area at
edge of lake

LAKESIDE n area at edge
of lake

LAKESIDES
> LAKESIDE

LAKEVIEW adj having a
view of a lake

LAKEWARD same as
> LAKEWARDS

LAKEWARDS adj towards
a lake

LAKH n (in India) 100 000,
esp referring to this sum of
rupees

LAKHS > LAKH

LAKIER > LAKY

LAKIEST > LAKY

LAKIN short form of
> LADYKIN

LAKING > LAKE

LAKINGS > LAKE

LAKINS > LAKIN

LAKISH adj similar to
poetry of Lake poets

LAKSA n (in Malaysia)
Chinese dish of rice
noodles in curry or hot
soup

LAKSAS > LAKSA

LAKY adj of the reddish
colour of the pigment
lake

LALANG n coarse weedy
Malaysian grass

LALANGS > LALANG

LALDIE n great gusto

LALDIES > LALDIE

LALDY same as > LALDIE

LALIQUE n ornamental
glass

LALIQUES > LALIQUE

LALL vb make imperfect 'l'
or 'r' sounds

LALLAN n literary version
of the English spoken in
Lowland Scotland

LALLAND same as
> LALLAN

LALLANDS > LALLAND

LALLANS > LALLAN

LALLATION n defect of
speech consisting of the
pronunciation of 'r' as 'l'

LALLED > LALL

LALLING > LALL

LALLINGS > LALL

LALLS > LALL

LALLYGAG vb loiter
aimlessly

LALLYGAGS
> LALLYGAG

LAM vb attack vigorously

LAMA n Buddhist priest in
Tibet or Mongolia

LAMAISTIC adj relating
to the Mahayana form of
Buddhism

LAMANTIN another word
for > MANATEE

LAMANTINS
> LAMANTIN

LAMAS > LAMA

LAMASERAI same as
> LAMASERY

LAMASERY n monastery
of lamas

LAMB n young sheep ⊳ vb
give birth to a lamb or
lambs

LAMBADA n type of
Brazilian dance

LAMBADAS > LAMBADA

LAMBAST vb beat or
thrash

LAMBASTE same as
> LAMBAST

LAMBASTED > LAMBAST

LAMBASTES
> LAMBASTE

LAMBASTS > LAMBAST

LAMBDA n 11th letter of
the Greek alphabet

LAMBDAS > LAMBDA

LAMBDOID adj having the
shape of the Greek letter
lambda

LAMBED > LAMB

LAMBENCY > LAMBENT

LAMBENT adj (of a flame)
flickering softly

LAMBENTLY > LAMBENT

LAMBER n person that
attends to lambing ewes

LAMBERS > LAMBER

LAMBERT n cgs unit of
illumination, equal to 1
lumen per square
centimetre

LAMBERTS > LAMBERT

LAMBIE same as
> LAMBKIN

LAMBIER > LAMBY

LAMBIES > LAMBIE

LAMBIEST > LAMBY

LAMBING n birth of lambs
at the end of winter

LAMBINGS > LAMBING

LAMBITIVE n medicine
taken by licking

LAMBKILL n N American
dwarf shrub

LAMBKILLS
> LAMBKILL

LAMBKIN n young lamb

LAMBKINS > LAMBKIN

LAMBLIKE > LAMB

LAMBLING n small lamb

LAMBLINGS
> LAMBLING

LAMBOYS n skirt-like
piece of armour made
from metal strips

LAMBRUSCO n Italian
sparkling wine

LAMBS > LAMB

LAMBSKIN n skin of a
lamb, usually with the
wool still on, used to make
coats, slippers, etc

LAMBSKINS
> LAMBSKIN

LAMBSWOOL n wool from
a lamb's first shearing

LAMBY adj lamb-like

LAME adj having an injured
or disabled leg or foot ⊳ vb
make lame ⊳ n fabric
interwoven with gold or
silver threads

LAMEBRAIN n stupid or slow-witted person

LAMED n 12th letter in the Hebrew alphabet

LAMEDH same as > LAMED

LAMEDHS > LAMEDH

LAMEDS > LAMED

LAMELLA n thin layer, plate, etc, like the calcified layers of which bone is formed

LAMELLAE > LAMELLA

LAMELLAR > LAMELLA

LAMELLAS > LAMELLA

LAMELLATE > LAMELLA

LAMELLOID another word for > LAMELLA

LAMELLOSE > LAMELLA

LAMELY > LAME

LAMENESS > LAME

LAMENT vb feel or express sorrow (for) ▷ n passionate expression of grief

LAMENTED adj grieved for

LAMENTER > LAMENT

LAMENTERS > LAMENT

LAMENTING > LAMENT

LAMENTS > LAMENT

LAMER > LAME

LAMES > LAME

LAMEST > LAME

LAMETER Scots form of > LAMIGER

LAMETERS > LAMETER

LAMIA n female monster with a snake's body and a woman's head

LAMIAE > LAMIA

LAMIAS > LAMIA

LAMIGER n disabled person

LAMIGERS > LAMIGER

LAMINA n thin plate, esp of bone or mineral

LAMINABLE > LAMINATE

LAMINAE > LAMINA

LAMINAL n consonant articulated with blade of tongue

LAMINALS > LAMINAL

LAMINAR > LAMINA

LAMINARIA n type of brown seaweed

LAMINARIN n carbohydrate, consisting of repeated glucose units, that is the main storage product of brown algae

LAMINARY > LAMINA

LAMINAS > LAMINA

LAMINATE vb make (a sheet of material) by sticking together thin sheets ▷ n laminated sheet ▷ adj composed of lamina

LAMINATED adj composed of many layers stuck together

LAMINATES > LAMINATE

LAMINATOR > LAMINATE

LAMING > LAME

LAMINGTON n sponge cake coated with a sweet coating

LAMININ n type of protein

LAMININS > LAMININ

LAMINITIS n (in animals with hooves) inflammation of the tissue to which the hoof is attached

LAMINOSE > LAMINA

LAMINOUS > LAMINA

LAMISH adj rather lame

LAMISTER n fugitive

LAMISTERS > LAMISTER

LAMITER same as > LAMETER

LAMITERS > LAMITER

LAMMED > LAM

LAMMER Scots word for > AMBER

LAMMERS > LAMMER

LAMMIE same as > LAMMY

LAMMIES > LAMMY

LAMMIGER same as > LAMIGER

LAMMIGERS > LAMIGER

LAMMING > LAM

LAMMINGS > LAM

LAMMY n thick woollen jumper

LAMP n device which produces light from electricity, oil, or gas ▷ vb go quickly with long steps

LAMPAD n candlestick

LAMPADARY n person who lights the lamps in an Orthodox Greek Church

LAMPADIST n prize-winner in race run by young men with torches

LAMPADS > LAMPAD

LAMPAS n swelling of the mucous membrane of the hard palate of horses

LAMPASES > LAMPAS

LAMPASSE same as > LAMPAS

LAMPASSES > LAMPASSE

LAMPBLACK n fine black soot used as a pigment in paint and ink ▷ vb blacken with fine black soot

LAMPBRUSH n as in lampbrush chromosome type of chromosome

LAMPED > LAMP

LAMPER n lamprey

LAMPERN n migratory European lamprey

LAMPERNS > LAMPERN

LAMPERS > LAMPER

LAMPERSES > LAMPERS

LAMPHOLE n hole in ground for lowering lamp into sewer

LAMPHOLES > LAMPHOLE

LAMPING > LAMP

LAMPINGS > LAMP

LAMPION n oil-burning lamp

LAMPIONS > LAMPION

LAMPLESS adj without a lamp

LAMPLIGHT n light produced by lamp

LAMPLIT adj lit by lamps

LAMPOON n humorous satire ridiculing someone ▷ vb satirize or ridicule

LAMPOONED > LAMPOON

LAMPOONER > LAMPOON

LAMPOONS > LAMPOON

LAMPPOST n post supporting a lamp in the street

LAMPPOSTS > LAMPPOST

LAMPREY n eel-like fish with a round sucking mouth

LAMPREYS > LAMPREY

LAMPS > LAMP

LAMPSHADE n shade used to reduce light shed by light bulb

LAMPSHELL n brachiopod

LAMPSTAND n stand for a lamp

LAMPUKA same as > LAMPUKI

LAMPUKAS > LAMPUKA

LAMPUKI n type of fish

LAMPUKIS > LAMPUKI

LAMPYRID n firefly

LAMPYRIDS > LAMPYRID

LAMS > LAM

LAMSTER n fugitive

LAMSTERS > LAMSTER

LANA n wood from genipap tree

LANAI Hawaiian word for > VERANDA

LANAIS > LANAI

LANAS > LANA

LANATE adj having or consisting of a woolly covering of hairs

LANATED same as > LANATE

LANCE n long spear used by a mounted soldier ▷ vb pierce (a boil or abscess) with a lancet

LANCED > LANCE

LANCEGAY n kind of ancient spear

LANCEGAYS > LANCEGAY

LANCEJACK n lance corporal

LANCELET n type of marine invertebrate

LANCELETS > LANCELET

LANCELIKE adj like a lance

LANCEOLAR adj narrow and tapering to a point at each end

LANCER n formerly, cavalry soldier armed with a lance

LANCERS n quadrille for eight or sixteen couples

LANCES > LANCE

LANCET n pointed two-edged surgical knife

LANCETED adj having one or more lancet arches or windows

LANCETS > LANCET

LANCEWOOD n New Zealand tree with slender leaves

LANCH obsolete form of > LAUNCH

LANCHED > LANCH

LANCHES > LANCH

LANCHING > LANCH

LANCIERS pl n type of dance

LANCIFORM adj in the form of a lance

LANCINATE adj (esp of pain) sharp or cutting

LANCING > LANCE

LAND n solid part of the earth's surface ▷ vb come or bring to earth after a flight, jump, or fall

LANDAMMAN n chairman of the governing council in some Swiss cantons

LANDAU n four-wheeled carriage with two folding hoods

LANDAULET n small landau

LANDAUS > LANDAU

LANDBOARD n narrow board, with wheels larger than those on a skateboard, usually ridden while standing

LANDDAMNE vb Shakespearian word for make (a person's life) unbearable

LANDDROS n sheriff

LANDDROST n South African magistrate

LANDE n type of moorland in SW France

LANDED adj possessing or consisting of lands

LANDER n spacecraft which lands on a planet or other body

LANDERS > LANDER

LANDES > LANDE

LANDFALL n ship's first landing after a voyage

LANDFALLS > LANDFALL

LANDFAST adj (of ice) attached to the shore

LANDFILL n disposing of rubbish by covering it with earth

LANDFILLS > LANDFILL

LANDFORCE n body of people trained for land warfare

LANDFORM n any natural feature of the earth's surface, such as valleys and mountains

LANDFORMS > LANDFORM

LANDGRAB n sudden attempt to establish ownership of something

LANDGRABS > LANDGRAB

LANDGRAVE n (from the 13th century to 1806) a count who ruled over a specified territory

LANDING n floor area at the top of a flight of stairs

LANDINGS > LANDING

LANDLADY n woman who owns and leases property

LANDLER n Austrian country dance

LANDLERS > LANDLER

LANDLESS > LAND

LANDLINE n telecommunications cable laid over land

LANDLINES > LANDLINE

LANDLOPER n vagabond or vagrant

LANDLORD n person who rents out land, houses, etc

LANDLORDS > LANDLORD

LANDMAN n person who lives and works on land

LANDMARK n prominent object in or feature of a landscape

LANDMARKS > LANDMARK

LANDMASS n large continuous area of land

LANDMEN > LANDMAN

LANDMINE n type of bomb laid on or just under the surface of the ground ▷ vb lay (an area) with landmines

LANDMINED > LANDMINE

LANDMINES > LANDMINE

LANDOWNER n person who owns land

LANDRACE n white very long-bodied lop-eared breed of pork pig

LANDRACES > LANDRACE

LANDRAIL n type of bird

LANDRAILS > LANDRAIL

LANDS pl n holdings in land

LANDSCAPE n extensive piece of inland scenery seen from one place ▷ vb improve natural features of (a piece of land) ▷ adj (of a publication or an illustration in a publication) of greater width than height

LANDSHARK n person who makes inordinate profits by buying and selling land

LANDSIDE n part of an airport farthest from the aircraft

LANDSIDES > LANDSIDE

LANDSKIP another word for > LANDSCAPE

LANDSKIPS > LANDSKIP

LANDSLEIT > LANDSMAN

LANDSLID > LANDSLIDE

LANDSLIDE vb cause land or rock to fall from hillside

LANDSLIP same as > LANDSLIDE

LANDSLIPS > LANDSLIP

LANDSMAN n person who works or lives on land, as distinguished from a seaman

LANDSMEN > LANDSMAN

LANDWARD same as > LANDWARDS

LANDWARDS adv towards land

LANDWASH n part of the shore between the high-water mark and the sea

LANDWIND n wind that comes from the land

LANDWINDS > LANDWIND

LANE n narrow road

LANELY Scots form of > LONELY

LANES > LANE

LANEWAY n lane

LANEWAYS > LANEWAY

LANG Scot word for > LONG

LANGAHA n type of Madagascan snake

LANGAHAS > LANGAHA

LANGAR n dining hall in a gurdwara

LANGARS > LANGAR

LANGER n Irish slang word for penis ▷ adj comparative form of lang

LANGERED adj drunk

LANGERS > LANGER

LANGEST > LANG

LANGLAUF n cross-country skiing

LANGLAUFS > LANGLAUF

LANGLEY n unit of solar radiation

LANGLEYS > LANGLEY

LANGOUSTE n spiny lobster

LANGRAGE n shot consisting of scrap iron packed into a case, formerly used in naval warfare

LANGRAGES > LANGRAGE

LANGREL same as > LANGRAGE

LANGRELS > LANGREL

LANGRIDGE same as > LANGRAGE

LANGSHAN n breed of chicken

LANGSHANS > LANGSHAN

LANGSPEL n type of Scandinavian stringed instrument

LANGSPELS > LANGSPEL

LANGSPIEL same as > LANGSPEL

LANGSPIL n type of Scandinavian stringed instrument

LANGSPILS > LANGSPIL

LANGSYNE adv long ago ▷ n times long past, esp those fondly remembered

LANGSYNES > LANGSYNE

LANGUAGE n system of sounds, symbols, etc for communicating thought ▷ vb express in language

LANGUAGED > LANGUAGE

LANGUAGES > LANGUAGE

LANGUE n language considered as an abstract system

LANGUED adj having a tongue

LANGUES > LANGUE

LANGUET n anything resembling a tongue

LANGUETS > LANGUET

LANGUETTE same as > LANGUET

LANGUID adj lacking energy

LANGUIDLY > LANGUID

LANGUISH vb suffer neglect or hardship

LANGUOR n dreamy relaxation

LANGUORS > LANGUOR

LANGUR n type of arboreal Old World monkey

LANGURS > LANGUR

LANIARD same as > LANYARD

LANIARDS > LANIARD

LANIARIES > LANIARY

LANIARY adj adapted for tearing ▷ n tooth adapted for tearing

LANITAL n fibre used in production of synthetic wool

LANITALS > LANITAL

LANK adj straight and limp ▷ vb become lank

LANKED > LANK

LANKER > LANK

LANKEST > LANK

LANKIER > LANKY

LANKIEST > LANKY

LANKILY > LANKY

LANKINESS > LANKY

LANKING > LANK

LANKLY > LANK

LANKNESS > LANK

LANKS > LANK

LANKY adj tall and thin

LANNER n large falcon

LANNERET n male or tercel of the lanner falcon

LANNERETS > LANNERET

LANNERS > LANNER

LANOLATED > LANOLIN

LANOLIN n grease from sheep's wool used in ointments etc

LANOLINE same as > LANOLIN

LANOLINES > LANOLINE

LANOLINS > LANOLIN

LANOSE same as > LANATE

LANOSITY > LANOSE

LANT n stale urine

LANTANA n shrub with orange or yellow flowers

LANTANAS > LANTANA

LANTERLOO n old card game

LANTERN n light in a transparent protective case ▷ vb supply with a lantern

LANTERNED > LANTERN

LANTERNS > LANTERN

LANTHANON n one of a group of chemical elements

LANTHANUM n silvery-white metallic element

LANTHORN archaic word for > LANTERN

LANTHORNS > LANTHORN

LANTS > LANT

LANTSKIP another word for > LANDSCAPE

LANTSKIPS > LANTSKIP

LANUGO n layer of fine hairs, esp the covering of the human fetus before birth

LANUGOS > LANUGO

LANX n dish; plate

LANYARD n neck cord to hold a knife or whistle

LANYARDS > LANYARD

LAODICEAN adj indifferent, esp in religious matters ▷ n person having a lukewarm attitude towards religious matters

LAOGAI n forced labour camp in China

LAOGAIS > LAOGAI

LAP n part between the waist and knees when sitting ▷ vb overtake so as to be one or more circuits ahead

LAPBOARD n flat board that can be used on the lap as a makeshift table or desk

LAPBOARDS > LAPBOARD

LAPDOG n small pet dog

LAPDOGS > LAPDOG

LAPEL n part of the front of a coat or jacket folded back towards the shoulders

LAPELED > LAPEL

LAPELLED > LAPEL

LAPELS > LAPEL

LAPFUL same as > LAP

LAPFULS > LAPFUL

LAPHELD adj small enough to be used on one's lap

LAPIDARY adj of or relating to stones ▷ n person who cuts, polishes, sets, or deals in gemstones

LAPIDATE vb pelt with stones

LAPIDATED > LAPIDATE

LAPIDATES
> LAPIDATE
LAPIDEOUS *adj* having appearance or texture of stone
LAPIDES > LAPIS
LAPIDIFIC *adj* transforming into stone
LAPIDIFY *vb* change into stone
LAPIDIST *n* cutter and engraver of precious stones
LAPIDISTS
> LAPIDIST
LAPILLI > LAPILLUS
LAPILLUS *n* small piece of lava thrown from a volcano
LAPIN *n* rabbit fur
LAPINS > LAPIN
LAPIS *n* as in *lapis lazuli* brilliant blue mineral gemstone
LAPISES > LAPIS
LAPJE *same as* > LAPPIE
LAPJES > LAPJE
LAPPED > LAP
LAPPEL *same as*
> LAPEL
LAPPELS > LAPPEL
LAPPER *n* one that laps
▷ *vb* curdle
LAPPERED > LAPPER
LAPPERING > LAPPER
LAPPERS > LAPPER
LAPPET *n* small hanging flap
LAPPETED > LAPPET
LAPPETS > LAPPET
LAPPIE *n* rag
LAPPIES > LAPPIE
LAPPING > LAP
LAPPINGS > LAP
LAPS > LAP
LAPSABLE > LAPSE
LAPSANG *n* Chinese tea
LAPSANGS > LAPSANG
LAPSE *n* temporary drop in a standard ▷ *vb* drop in standard
LAPSED > LAPSE
LAPSER > LAPSE
LAPSERS > LAPSE
LAPSES > LAPSE
LAPSIBLE > LAPSE
LAPSING > LAPSE
LAPSTONE *n* device used by a cobbler on which leather is beaten
LAPSTONES
> LAPSTONE
LAPSTRAKE *n* clinker-built boat
LAPSTREAK *same as*
> LAPSTRAKE
LAPSUS *n* lapse or error
LAPTOP *adj* small enough to fit on a user's lap ▷ *n* small computer
LAPTOPS > LAPTOP
LAPTRAY *n* tray with a cushioned underside
LAPTRAYS > LAPTRAY
LAPWING *n* plover with a tuft of feathers on the head
LAPWINGS > LAPWING

LAPWORK *n* work with lapping edges
LAPWORKS > LAPWORK
LAQUEARIA *n* ceiling made of panels
LAR *n* boy or young man
LARBOARD *n* port (side of a ship)
LARBOARDS
> LARBOARD
LARCENER > LARCENY
LARCENERS > LARCENY
LARCENIES > LARCENY
LARCENIST > LARCENY
LARCENOUS > LARCENY
LARCENY *n* theft
LARCH *n* deciduous coniferous tree
LARCHEN *adj* of larch
LARCHES > LARCH
LARCHWOOD *n* wood of the larch
LARD *n* soft white pig fat
▷ *vb* insert strips of bacon in before cooking
LARDALITE *n* type of mineral
LARDED > LARD
LARDER *n* storeroom for food
LARDERER *n* person in charge of larder
LARDERERS
> LARDERER
LARDERS > LARDER
LARDIER > LARDY
LARDIEST > LARDY
LARDING > LARD
LARDLIKE > LARD
LARDON *n* strip or cube of fat or bacon used in larding meat
LARDONS > LARDON
LARDOON *same as*
> LARDON
LARDOONS > LARDOON
LARDS > LARD
LARDY *adj* fat
LARE *another word for*
> LORE
LAREE *n* Asian fish-hook
LAREES > LAREE
LARES > LARE
LARGANDO *adv* (music) growing slower and more marked
LARGE *adj* great in size, number ▷ *n* formerly, musical note
LARGELY *adv* principally
LARGEN *another word for*
> ENLARGE
LARGENED > LARGEN
LARGENESS > LARGE
LARGENING > LARGEN
LARGENS > LARGEN
LARGER > LARGE
LARGES > LARGE
LARGESS *same as*
> LARGESSE
LARGESSE *n* generous giving, esp of money
LARGESSES
> LARGESSE
LARGEST > LARGE
LARGHETTO *adv* be performed moderately slowly ▷ *n* piece or

passage to be performed in this way
LARGISH *adj* fairly large
LARGITION *n* act of being generous
LARGO *adv* in a slow and dignified manner ▷ *n* performance piece in a slow manner
LARGOS > LARGO
LARI *n* monetary unit of Georgia
LARIAT *n* lasso ▷ *vb* tether with lariat
LARIATED > LARIAT
LARIATING > LARIAT
LARIATS > LARIAT
LARIGAN *n* type of tanned moccasin boot
LARIGANS > LARIGAN
LARINE *adj* of, relating to, or resembling a gull
LARIS > LARI
LARK *n* small brown songbird ▷ *vb* frolic
LARKED > LARK
LARKER > LARK
LARKERS > LARK
LARKIER > LARKY
LARKIEST > LARKY
LARKINESS > LARKY
LARKING > LARK
LARKISH > LARK
LARKS > LARK
LARKSOME *adj* mischievous
LARKSPUR *n* plant with spikes of blue, pink, or white flowers with spurs
LARKSPURS
> LARKSPUR
LARKY *adj* frolicsome
LARMIER *n* pouch under lower eyelid of deer
LARMIERS > LARMIER
LARN *vb* learn
LARNAKES > LARNAX
LARNAX *n* terracotta coffin
LARNED > LARN
LARNEY *n* South African word for a rich person
▷ *adj* (of clothes) smart
LARNEYS > LARNEY
LARNIER > LARNEY
LARNIEST > LARNEY
LARNING > LARN
LARNS > LARN
LARNT > LARN
LAROID *adj* relating to Larus genus of gull family
LARRIGAN *n* knee-high oiled leather moccasin boot worn by trappers, etc
LARRIGANS
> LARRIGAN
LARRIKIN *n* mischievous or unruly person
LARRIKINS
> LARRIKIN
LARRUP *vb* beat or flog
LARRUPED > LARRUP
LARRUPER > LARRUP
LARRUPERS > LARRUP
LARRUPING > LARRUP
LARRUPS > LARRUP
LARS > LAR

LARUM *archaic word for*
> ALARM
LARUMS > LARUM
LARVA *n* immature insect
LARVAE > LARVA
LARVAL > LARVA
LARVAS > LARVA
LARVATE *adj* masked; concealed
LARVATED *same as*
> LARVATE
LARVICIDE *vb* kill larvae with a chemical
LARVIFORM *adj* in the form of a larva
LARVIKITE *n* type of mineral
LARYNGAL *adj* laryngeal
▷ *n* sound articulated in the larynx
LARYNGALS
> LARYNGAL
LARYNGEAL *adj* of or relating to the larynx
LARYNGES > LARYNX
LARYNX *n* part of the throat containing the vocal cords
LARYNXES > LARYNX
LAS > LA
LASAGNA *same as*
> LASAGNE
LASAGNAS > LASAGNA
LASAGNE *n* sheet pasta
LASAGNES > LASAGNE
LASCAR *n* Indian or SE Asian sailor
LASCARS > LASCAR
LASE *vb* be capable of acting as a laser
LASED > LASE
LASER *n* device producing a very narrow intense beam of light ▷ *vb* use a laser on (something), esp as part of medical treatment
LASERDISC *n* disk similar in size to a long-playing record, on which data is stored in pits in a similar way to data storage on a compact disk
LASERDISK *same as*
> LASERDISC
LASERED > LASER
LASERING > LASER
LASERS > LASER
LASERWORT *n* type of plant
LASES > LASE
LASH *n* eyelash ▷ *vb* hit with a whip
LASHED > LASH
LASHER > LASH
LASHERS > LASH
LASHES > LASH
LASHING > LASH
LASHINGLY > LASH
LASHINGS *pl n* great amount of
LASHINS *variant of*
> LASHINGS
LASHKAR *n* troop of Indian men with weapons
LASHKARS > LASHKAR
LASHLESS *adj* (of a whip) without a lash

LASING > LASE

LASINGS > LASE

LASKET n loop at the foot of a sail onto which an extra sail may be fastened

LASKETS > LASKET

LASQUE n flat-cut diamond

LASQUES > LASQUE

LASS n girl or young woman

LASSES > LASS

LASSI n cold drink made of yoghurt or buttermilk, flavoured with sugar, salt, or spice

LASSIE n little lass

LASSIES > LASSIE

LASSIS > LASSI

LASSITUDE n physical or mental weariness

LASSLORN adj abandoned by a young woman

LASSO n rope with a noose ▷ vb catch with a lasso

LASSOCK another word for > LASS

LASSOCKS > LASSOCK

LASSOED > LASSO

LASSOER > LASSO

LASSOERS > LASSO

LASSOES > LASSO

LASSOING n act of lassoing

LASSOINGS > LASSOING

LASSOS > LASSO

LASSU n slow part of csárdás folk dance

LASSUS > LASSU

LASSY n short for molasses

LAST adv coming at the end or after all others ▷ adj only remaining ▷ n last person or thing ▷ vb continue

LASTAGE n space for storing goods in ship

LASTAGES > LASTAGE

LASTBORN n last child to be born

LASTBORNS > LASTBORN

LASTED > LAST

LASTER > LAST

LASTERS > LAST

LASTING adj remaining effective for a long time ▷ n strong durable fabric used for shoe uppers, etc

LASTINGLY > LASTING

LASTINGS > LASTING

LASTLY adv at the end or at the last point

LASTS > LAST

LAT n former coin of Latvia

LATAH n psychological condition

LATAHS > LATAH

LATAKIA n Turkish tobacco

LATAKIAS > LATAKIA

LATCH n fastening for a door with a bar and lever ▷ vb fasten with a latch

LATCHED > LATCH

LATCHES > LATCH

LATCHET n shoe fastening

LATCHETS > LATCHET

LATCHING > LATCH

LATCHKEY n key for an outside door or gate, esp one that lifts a latch

LATCHKEYS > LATCHKEY

LATE adj after the normal or expected time ▷ adv after the normal or expected time

LATECOMER n person or thing that comes late

LATED archaic word for > BELATED

LATEEN adj of a rig with a triangular sail bent to a yard hoisted to the head of a low mast

LATEENER n lateen-rigged ship

LATEENERS > LATEEN

LATEENS > LATEEN

LATELY adv in recent times

LATEN vb become or cause to become late

LATENCE > LATENT

LATENCES > LATENCE

LATENCIES > LATENT

LATENCY > LATENT

LATENED > LATEN

LATENESS > LATE

LATENING > LATEN

LATENS > LATEN

LATENT adj hidden and not yet developed ▷ n fingerprint that is not visible to the eye

LATENTLY > LATENT

LATENTS > LATENT

LATER adv afterwards

LATERAD adv towards the side

LATERAL adj of or relating to the side or sides ▷ n lateral object, part, passage, or movement ▷ vb pass laterally

LATERALED > LATERAL

LATERALLY > LATERAL

LATERALS > LATERAL

LATERBORN adj born later ▷ n one born later

LATERISE same as > LATERIZE

LATERISED > LATERISE

LATERISES > LATERISE

LATERITE n any of a group of deposits consisting of residual insoluble ferric and aluminium oxides

LATERITES > LATERITE

LATERITIC > LATERITE

LATERIZE vb develop into a laterite

LATERIZED > LATERIZE

LATERIZES > LATERIZE

LATESCENT n becoming latent

LATEST n the most recent news

LATESTS > LATEST

LATEWAKE n vigil held over a dead body

LATEWAKES > LATEWAKE

LATEWOOD n wood formed later in tree's growing season

LATEWOODS > LATEWOOD

LATEX n milky fluid found in some plants

LATEXES > LATEX

LATH n thin strip of wood ▷ vb attach laths to

LATHE n machine for turning wood or metal while it is being shaped ▷ vb shape, bore, or cut a screw thread in or on (a workpiece) on a lathe

LATHED > LATHE

LATHEE same as > LATHI

LATHEES > LATHEE

LATHEN adj covered with laths

LATHER n froth of soap and water ▷ vb make frothy

LATHERED > LATHER

LATHERER > LATHER

LATHERERS > LATHER

LATHERIER > LATHER

LATHERING > LATHER

LATHERS > LATHER

LATHERY > LATHER

LATHES > LATHE

LATHI n long heavy wooden stick used as a weapon in India

LATHIER > LATHY

LATHIEST > LATHY

LATHING > LATHE

LATHINGS > LATHE

LATHIS > LATHI

LATHLIKE > LATH

LATHS > LATH

LATHWORK n work made of laths

LATHWORKS > LATHWORK

LATHY adj resembling a lath, esp in being tall and thin

LATHYRISM n neurological disease often resulting in weakness and paralysis of the legs

LATHYRUS n genus of climbing plant

LATI > LAT

LATICES > LATEX

LATICIFER n cell or group of cells in a plant that contains latex

LATICLAVE n broad stripe on Roman senator's tunic

LATIFONDI > LATIFONDO

LATIFONDO n large agricultural estate in ancient Rome

LATIGO n strap on horse's saddle

LATIGOES > LATIGO

LATIGOS > LATIGO

LATILLA n stick making up part of ceiling

LATILLAS > LATILLA

LATIMERIA n type of coelacanth fish

LATINA n American female citizen of Latin American origin

LATINAS > LATINA

LATINISE same as > LATINIZE

LATINISED > LATINISE

LATINISES > LATINISE

LATINITY n facility in the use of Latin

LATINIZE vb translate into Latin

LATINIZED > LATINIZE

LATINIZES > LATINIZE

LATINO n American male citizen of Latin American origin

LATINOS > LATINO

LATISH adv rather late ▷ adj rather late

LATITANCY > LATITANT

LATITANT adj concealed

LATITAT n writ presuming that person accused was hiding

LATITATS > LATITAT

LATITUDE n angular distance measured in degrees N or S of the equator

LATITUDES > LATITUDE

LATKE n crispy Jewish pancake

LATKES > LATKE

LATOSOL n type of deep, well-drained soil

LATOSOLIC > LATOSOL

LATOSOLS > LATOSOL

LATRANT adj barking

LATRATION n instance of barking

LATRIA n adoration that may be offered to God alone

LATRIAS > LATRIA

LATRINE n toilet in a barracks

LATRINES > LATRINE

LATROCINY n banditry

LATRON n bandit

LATRONS > LATRON

LATS > LAT

LATTE n coffee with hot milk

LATTEN n metal or alloy, esp brass, made in thin sheets

LATTENS > LATTEN

LATTER adj second of two ▷ n second of two people or things

LATTERLY adv recently

LATTERS > LATTER

LATTES > LATTE
LATTICE n framework of intersecting strips of wood ▷ vb adorn with a lattice
LATTICED > LATTICE
LATTICES > LATTICE
LATTICING > LATTICE
LATTICINI > LATTICINO
LATTICINO n type of Italian glass
LATTIN n brass alloy beaten into a thin sheet
LATTINS > LATTIN
LATU n type of edible Asian seaweed
LATUS > LATU
LAUAN n type of wood used in furniture-making
LAUANS > LAUAN
LAUCH Scots form of > LAUGH
LAUCHING > LAUCH
LAUCHS > LAUCH
LAUD vb praise or glorify ▷ n praise or glorification
LAUDABLE adj praiseworthy
LAUDABLY > LAUDABLE
LAUDANUM n opium-based sedative
LAUDANUMS > LAUDANUM
LAUDATION formal word for > PRAISE
LAUDATIVE same as > LAUDATORY
LAUDATOR n one who praises highly
LAUDATORS > LAUDATOR
LAUDATORY adj praising or glorifying
LAUDED > LAUD
LAUDER > LAUD
LAUDERS > LAUD
LAUDING > LAUD
LAUDS n traditional morning prayer of the Western Church
LAUF n run in bobsleighing
LAUFS > LAUF
LAUGH vb make sounds with the voice expressing amusement ▷ n act of laughing
LAUGHABLE adj ridiculously inadequate
LAUGHABLY > LAUGHABLE
LAUGHED > LAUGH
LAUGHER > LAUGH
LAUGHERS > LAUGH
LAUGHFUL > LAUGH
LAUGHIER > LAUGHY
LAUGHIEST > LAUGHY
LAUGHING > LAUGH
LAUGHINGS > LAUGH
LAUGHLINE n funny line in dialogue
LAUGHS > LAUGH
LAUGHSOME adj causing laughter
LAUGHTER n sound or action of laughing
LAUGHTERS > LAUGHTER

LAUGHY adj laughing a lot
LAUNCE old form of > LANCE
LAUNCED > LAUNCE
LAUNCES > LAUNCE
LAUNCH vb put into the water for the first time ▷ n launching
LAUNCHED > LAUNCH
LAUNCHER n device for launching projectiles
LAUNCHERS > LAUNCHER
LAUNCHES > LAUNCH
LAUNCHING n act of launching
LAUNCHPAD n platform from which a spacecraft is launched
LAUNCING > LAUNCE
LAUND n open grassy space
LAUNDER vb wash and iron ▷ n water trough
LAUNDERED > LAUNDER
LAUNDERER > LAUNDER
LAUNDERS > LAUNDER
LAUNDRESS n woman who launders clothes, sheets, etc, for a living
LAUNDRIES > LAUNDRY
LAUNDRY n clothes for washing
LAUNDS > LAUND
LAURA n group of monastic cells
LAURAE > LAURA
LAURAS > LAURA
LAUREATE adj crowned with laurel leaves as a sign of honour ▷ n person honoured with an award for art or science ▷ vb crown with laurel
LAUREATED > LAUREATE
LAUREATES > LAUREATE
LAUREL n glossy-leaved shrub, bay tree ▷ vb crown with laurel
LAURELED > LAUREL
LAURELING > LAUREL
LAURELLED > LAUREL
LAURELS > LAUREL
LAURIC adj as in lauric acid dodecanoic acid
LAURYL n as in lauryl alcohol crystalline solid used to make detergents
LAURYLS > LAURYL
LAUWINE n avalanche
LAUWINES > LAUWINE
LAV short for > LAVATORY
LAVA n molten rock thrown out by volcanoes
LAVABO n ritual washing of priest's hands at Mass
LAVABOES > LAVABO
LAVABOS > LAVABO
LAVAFORM n in form of lava
LAVAGE n washing out of a hollow organ
LAVAGES > LAVAGE
LAVAL adj of or relating to lava

LAVALAVA n draped skirtlike garment worn by Polynesians
LAVALAVAS > LAVALAVA
LAVALIER n decorative pendant worn on chain
LAVALIERE same as > LAVALIER
LAVALIERS > LAVALIER
LAVALIKE > LAVA
LAVANDIN n hybrid of two varieties of the lavender plant
LAVANDINS > LAVANDIN
LAVAS > LAVA
LAVASH n Armenian flat bread
LAVASHES > LAVASH
LAVATERA n type of plant closely resembling the mallow
LAVATERAS > LAVATERA
LAVATION n act or process of washing
LAVATIONS > LAVATION
LAVATORY n toilet
LAVE archaic word for > WASH
LAVED > LAVE
LAVEER vb (in sailing) tack
LAVEERED > LAVEER
LAVEERING > LAVEER
LAVEERS > LAVEER
LAVEMENT n washing with injections of water
LAVEMENTS > LAVEMENT
LAVENDER n shrub with fragrant flowers ▷ adj bluish-purple
LAVENDERS > LAVENDER
LAVER n priest's basin for ritual ablutions
LAVEROCK Scot and northern English dialect word for > SKYLARK
LAVEROCKS > LAVEROCK
LAVERS > LAVER
LAVES > LAVE
LAVING > LAVE
LAVISH adj prolific ▷ vb give or spend generously
LAVISHED > LAVISH
LAVISHER > LAVISH
LAVISHERS > LAVISH
LAVISHES > LAVISH
LAVISHEST > LAVISH
LAVISHING > LAVISH
LAVISHLY > LAVISH
LAVOLT same as > LAVOLTA
LAVOLTA n old Italian dance ▷ vb dance the lavolta
LAVOLTAED > LAVOLTA
LAVOLTAS > LAVOLTA
LAVOLTED > LAVOLT
LAVOLTING > LAVOLT
LAVOLTS > LAVOLT
LAVRA same as > LAURA

LAVRAS > LAVRA
LAVROCK same as > LAVEROCK
LAVROCKS > LAVROCK
LAVS > LAV
LAVVIES > LAVVY
LAVVY n lavatory
LAW n rule binding on a community ▷ vb prosecute ▷ adj (in archaic usage) low
LAWBOOK n book on subject of law
LAWBOOKS > LAWBOOK
LAWCOURT n court of law
LAWCOURTS > LAWCOURT
LAWED > LAW
LAWER > LAW
LAWEST > LAW
LAWFARE n use of the law by a country against its enemies
LAWFARES > LAWFARE
LAWFUL adj allowed by law
LAWFULLY > LAWFUL
LAWGIVER n giver of a code of laws
LAWGIVERS > LAWGIVER
LAWGIVING > LAWGIVER
LAWIN n bill or reckoning
LAWINE n avalanche
LAWINES > LAWINE
LAWING same as > LAWIN
LAWINGS > LAWING
LAWINS > LAWIN
LAWK interj used to show surprise
LAWKS same as > LAWK
LAWLAND same as > LOWLAND
LAWLANDS > LAWLAND
LAWLESS adj breaking the law
LAWLESSLY > LAWLESS
LAWLIKE > LAW
LAWMAKER same as > LAWGIVER
LAWMAKERS > LAWMAKER
LAWMAKING n process of legislating
LAWMAN n officer of the law
LAWMEN > LAWMAN
LAWMONGER n inferior lawyer
LAWN n area of tended and mown grass ▷ vb create or make into a lawn
LAWNED adj having a lawn
LAWNIER > LAWN
LAWNIEST > LAWN
LAWNING > LAWN
LAWNMOWER n machine for cutting grass on lawns
LAWNS > LAWN
LAWNY > LAWN
LAWS > LAW
LAWSUIT n court case
LAWSUITS > LAWSUIT
LAWYER n professional legal expert ▷ vb act as lawyer
LAWYERED > LAWYER

LAWYERING > LAWYER
LAWYERLY adj like a lawyer
LAWYERS > LAWYER
LAX adj not strict ▷ vb make lax, loosen
LAXATION n act of making lax or the state of being lax
LAXATIONS > LAXATION
LAXATIVE adj (medicine) inducing the emptying of the bowels ▷ n medicine that induces the emptying of the bowels
LAXATIVES > LAXATIVE
LAXATOR n muscle that loosens body part
LAXATORS > LAXATOR
LAXED > LAX
LAXER > LAX
LAXES > LAX
LAXEST > LAX
LAXING > LAX
LAXISM > LAXIST
LAXISMS > LAXIST
LAXIST n lenient or tolerant person
LAXISTS > LAXIST
LAXITIES > LAX
LAXITY > LAX
LAXLY > LAX
LAXNESS > LAX
LAXNESSES > LAX
LAY vb put in horizontal position
LAYABOUT n lazy person ▷ vb hit out with violent and repeated blows in all directions
LAYABOUTS > LAYABOUT
LAYAWAY n merchandise reserved for future delivery
LAYAWAYS > LAYAWAY
LAYBACK n technique for climbing cracks ▷ vb use layback technique
LAYBACKED > LAYBACK
LAYBACKS > LAYBACK
LAYDEEZ pl n jocular spelling of ladies
LAYED > LAY
LAYER n single thickness of some substance ▷ vb form a layer
LAYERAGE n covering stem or branch with soil to encourage new roots
LAYERAGES > LAYERAGE
LAYERED > LAYER
LAYERING n act of arranging something in layers
LAYERINGS > LAYERING
LAYERS > LAYER
LAYETTE n clothes for a newborn baby
LAYETTES > LAYETTE
LAYIN n basketball score
LAYING > LAY
LAYINGS > LAY
LAYINS > LAYIN

LAYLOCK old form of > LILAC
LAYLOCKS > LAYLOCK
LAYMAN n person who is not a member of the clergy
LAYMANISE same as > LAYMANIZE
LAYMANIZE vb make (information) easier to understand
LAYMEN > LAYMAN
LAYOFF n act of suspending employees
LAYOFFS > LAYOFF
LAYOUT n arrangement, esp of printing matter
LAYOUTS > LAYOUT
LAYOVER n break in a journey
LAYOVERS > LAYOVER
LAYPEOPLE > LAYPERSON
LAYPERSON n person who is not a member of the clergy
LAYS > LAY
LAYSHAFT n auxiliary shaft in a gearbox
LAYSHAFTS > LAYSHAFT
LAYSTALL n place where waste is deposited
LAYSTALLS > LAYSTALL
LAYTIME n time allowed for loading cargo
LAYTIMES > LAYTIME
LAYUP n period of incapacity through illness
LAYUPS > LAYUP
LAYWOMAN n woman who is not a member of the clergy
LAYWOMEN > LAYWOMAN
LAZAR n archaic word for a person with leprosy
LAZARET same as > LAZARETTO
LAZARETS > LAZARET
LAZARETTE same as > LAZARETTO
LAZARETTO n small locker at the stern of a boat or a storeroom between decks of a ship
LAZARS > LAZAR
LAZE vb be idle or lazy ▷ n time spent lazing
LAZED > LAZE
LAZES > LAZE
LAZIED > LAZY
LAZIER > LAZY
LAZIES > LAZY
LAZIEST > LAZY
LAZILY > LAZY
LAZINESS > LAZY
LAZING > LAZE
LAZO another word for > LASSO
LAZOED > LAZO
LAZOES > LAZO
LAZOING > LAZO
LAZOS > LAZO
LAZULI n lapis lazuli
LAZULIS > LAZULI
LAZULITE n blue mineral
LAZULITES > LAZULITE

LAZURITE n rare blue mineral consisting of a sodium-calcium-aluminium silicate
LAZURITES > LAZURITE
LAZY vb laze ▷ adj not inclined to work or exert oneself
LAZYBONES n lazy person
LAZYING > LAZY
LAZYISH > LAZY
LAZZARONE n Italian street beggar
LAZZARONI > LAZZARONE
LAZZI > LAZZO
LAZZO n comic routine in the commedia dell'arte
LEA n meadow
LEACH vb remove by passing a liquid through ▷ n act or process of leaching
LEACHABLE > LEACH
LEACHATE n water that carries salts dissolved out of materials through which it has percolated
LEACHATES > LEACHATE
LEACHED > LEACH
LEACHER > LEACH
LEACHERS > LEACH
LEACHES > LEACH
LEACHIER > LEACHY
LEACHIEST > LEACHY
LEACHING > LEACH
LEACHINGS > LEACH
LEACHOUR old form of > LECHER
LEACHOURS > LEACHOUR
LEACHY adj porous
LEAD vb guide or conduct ▷ n first or most prominent place ▷ adj acting as a leader or lead
LEADABLE n able to be led
LEADED adj (of windows) made from many small panes of glass held together by lead strips
LEADEN adj heavy or sluggish ▷ vb become or cause to become leaden
LEADENED > LEADEN
LEADENING > LEADEN
LEADENLY > LEADEN
LEADENS > LEADEN
LEADER n person who leads
LEADERENE n strong female leader
LEADERS > LEADER
LEADIER > LEADY
LEADIEST > LEADY
LEADING > LEAD
LEADINGLY > LEAD
LEADINGS > LEAD
LEADLESS adj without lead
LEADMAN n man who leads
LEADMEN > LEADMAN
LEADOFF n initial move

LEADOFFS > LEADOFF
LEADPLANT n N American shrub
LEADS > LEAD
LEADSCREW n threaded rod in a lathe
LEADSMAN n sailor who takes soundings with a lead line
LEADSMEN > LEADSMAN
LEADWORK n maintenance work involving lead pipes, etc
LEADWORKS > LEADWORK
LEADWORT n type of tropical or subtropical shrub with red, blue, or white flowers
LEADWORTS > LEADWORT
LEADY adj like lead
LEAF n flat usu green blade attached to the stem of a plant ▷ vb turn (pages) cursorily
LEAFAGE n leaves of plants
LEAFAGES > LEAFAGE
LEAFBUD n bud producing leaves rather than flowers
LEAFBUDS > LEAFBUD
LEAFED > LEAF
LEAFERIES > LEAFERY
LEAFERY n foliage
LEAFIER > LEAFY
LEAFIEST > LEAFY
LEAFINESS > LEAFY
LEAFING > LEAF
LEAFLESS > LEAF
LEAFLET n sheet of printed matter for distribution ▷ vb distribute leaflets (to)
LEAFLETED > LEAFLET
LEAFLETER > LEAFLET
LEAFLETS > LEAFLET
LEAFLIKE > LEAF
LEAFMOLD n fungus on decayed leaves
LEAFMOLDS > LEAFMOLD
LEAFROLL n viral disease of potatoes
LEAFROLLS > LEAFROLL
LEAFS > LEAF
LEAFSTALK n stalk attaching a leaf to a stem or branch
LEAFWORM n cotton plant pest
LEAFWORMS > LEAFWORM
LEAFY adj covered with leaves
LEAGUE n association promoting the interests of its members
LEAGUED > LEAGUE
LEAGUER vb harass; beset ▷ n encampment, esp of besiegers
LEAGUERED > LEAGUER
LEAGUERS > LEAGUER
LEAGUES > LEAGUE
LEAGUING > LEAGUE

LEAK n hole or defect that allows the escape or entrance of liquid, gas, radiation, etc ▷ vb let liquid etc in or out
LEAKAGE n act or instance of leaking
LEAKAGES > LEAKAGE
LEAKED > LEAK
LEAKER > LEAK
LEAKERS > LEAK
LEAKIER > LEAKY
LEAKIEST > LEAKY
LEAKILY > LEAKY
LEAKINESS > LEAKY
LEAKING > LEAK
LEAKLESS > LEAK
LEAKPROOF adj not likely to leak
LEAKS > LEAK
LEAKY adj leaking
LEAL adj loyal
LEALER > LEAL
LEALEST > LEAL
LEALLY > LEAL
LEALTIES > LEAL
LEALTY > LEAL
LEAM vb shine
LEAMED > LEAM
LEAMING > LEAM
LEAMS > LEAM
LEAN vb rest (against) ▷ adj thin but healthy-looking ▷ n lean part of meat
LEANED > LEAN
LEANER > LEAN
LEANERS > LEAN
LEANEST > LEAN
LEANING > LEAN
LEANINGS > LEAN
LEANLY > LEAN
LEANNESS > LEAN
LEANS > LEAN
LEANT > LEAN
LEANY old form of > LEAN
LEAP vb make a sudden powerful jump ▷ n sudden powerful jump
LEAPED > LEAP
LEAPER > LEAP
LEAPEROUS old form of > LEPROUS
LEAPERS > LEAP
LEAPFROG n game in which a player vaults over another bending down ▷ vb play leapfrog
LEAPFROGS > LEAPFROG
LEAPING > LEAP
LEAPOROUS old form of > LEPROUS
LEAPROUS old form of > LEPROUS
LEAPS > LEAP
LEAPT > LEAP
LEAR vb instruct
LEARE same as > LEAR
LEARED > LEARE
LEARES > LEARE
LEARIER > LEARY
LEARIEST > LEARY
LEARINESS > LEARY
LEARING > LEAR
LEARN vb gain skill or knowledge by study, practice, or teaching

LEARNABLE > LEARN
LEARNED > LEARN
LEARNEDLY > LEARN
LEARNER n someone who is learning something
LEARNERS > LEARNER
LEARNING > LEARN
LEARNINGS > LEARN
LEARNS > LEARN
LEARNT > LEARN
LEARS > LEAR
LEARY same as > LEERY
LEAS > LEA
LEASABLE > LEASE
LEASE n contract by which land or property is rented for a stated time ▷ vb let or rent by lease
LEASEBACK n property transaction in which the buyer leases the property to the seller
LEASED > LEASE
LEASEHOLD adj (land or property) held on lease ▷ n land or property held under a lease
LEASER > LEASE
LEASERS > LEASE
LEASES > LEASE
LEASH n lead for a dog ▷ vb control by a leash
LEASHED > LEASH
LEASHES > LEASH
LEASHING > LEASH
LEASING > LEASE
LEASINGS > LEASE
LEASOW vb pasture
LEASOWE same as > LEASOW
LEASOWED > LEASOW
LEASOWES > LEASOWE
LEASOWING > LEASOW
LEASOWS > LEASOW
LEAST n smallest amount ▷ adj smallest ▷ n smallest one ▷ adv in the smallest degree
LEASTS > LEAST
LEASTWAYS adv at least
LEASTWISE same as > LEASTWAYS
LEASURE old form of > LEISURE
LEASURES > LEASURE
LEAT n trench or ditch that conveys water to a mill wheel
LEATHER n material made from treated animal skins ▷ n of leather ▷ vb beat or thrash
LEATHERED > LEATHER
LEATHERN adj made of or resembling leather
LEATHERS > LEATHER
LEATHERY adj like leather, tough
LEATS > LEAT
LEAVE vb go away from ▷ n permission to be absent
LEAVED adj with leaves
LEAVEN n substance that causes dough to rise ▷ vb raise with leaven
LEAVENED > LEAVEN

LEAVENER n person or thing that leavens
LEAVENERS > LEAVENER
LEAVENING > LEAVEN
LEAVENOUS adj containing leaven
LEAVENS > LEAVEN
LEAVER > LEAVE
LEAVERS > LEAVE
LEAVES > LEAF
LEAVIER > LEAVY
LEAVIEST > LEAVY
LEAVING > LEAVE
LEAVINGS pl n something remaining, such as refuse
LEAVY same as > LEAFY
LEAZE same as > LEASE
LEAZES > LEAZE
LEBBEK n type of timber tree
LEBBEKS > LEBBEK
LEBEN n semiliquid food made from curdled milk
LEBENS > LEBEN
LEBKUCHEN n biscuit, originating from Germany, usually containing honey, spices, etc
LECANORA n type of lichen
LECANORAS > LECANORA
LECCIES > LECCY
LECCY n electricity
LECH vb behave lecherously ▷ n lecherous act
LECHAIM interj drinking toast ▷ n drink for a toast
LECHAIMS > LECHAIM
LECHAYIM same as > LECHAIM
LECHAYIMS > LECHAYIM
LECHED > LECH
LECHER n man who has or shows excessive sexual desire ▷ vb behave lecherously
LECHERED > LECHER
LECHERIES > LECHERY
LECHERING > LECHER
LECHEROUS adj (of a man) having or showing excessive sexual desire
LECHERS > LECHER
LECHERY n unrestrained and promiscuous sexuality
LECHES > LECH
LECHING > LECH
LECHWE n African antelope
LECHWES > LECHWE
LECITHIN n yellow-brown compound found in plant and animal tissues
LECITHINS > LECITHIN
LECTERN n reading desk
LECTERNS > LECTERN
LECTIN n type of protein
LECTINS > LECTIN
LECTION n variant reading of a passage in a text

LECTIONS > LECTION
LECTOR n university lecturer
LECTORATE > LECTOR
LECTORS > LECTOR
LECTOTYPE n specimen designated by author after the publication of a species name
LECTRESS n female reader
LECTURE n informative talk ▷ vb give a talk
LECTURED > LECTURE
LECTURER n person who lectures, esp in a university or college
LECTURERS > LECTURER
LECTURES > LECTURE
LECTURING > LECTURE
LECTURN old form of > LECTERN
LECTURNS > LECTURN
LECYTHI > LECYTHUS
LECYTHIS n genus of very tall trees
LECYTHUS n (in ancient Greece) a vase with a narrow neck
LED > LEAD
LEDDEN n language; speech
LEDDENS > LEDDEN
LEDE n introductory part of a news story
LEDES > LEDE
LEDGE n narrow shelf
LEDGED > LEDGE
LEDGER n book of debit and credit accounts ▷ vb fish using a wire trace while the bait floats freely and the weight sinks
LEDGERED > LEDGER
LEDGERING > LEDGER
LEDGERS > LEDGER
LEDGES > LEDGE
LEDGIER > LEDGE
LEDGIEST > LEDGE
LEDGY > LEDGE
LEDUM n evergreen shrub
LEDUMS > LEDUM
LEE n sheltered side ▷ vb (Scots) lie
LEEAR Scots form of > LIAR
LEEARS > LEEAR
LEEBOARD n board lowered along the lee side of a vessel to reduce drift
LEEBOARDS > LEEBOARD
LEECH n bloodsucking worm ▷ vb use leeches to suck the blood of
LEECHDOM n remedy
LEECHDOMS > LEECHDOM
LEECHED > LEECH
LEECHEE same as > LITCHI
LEECHEES > LEECHEE
LEECHES > LEECH
LEECHING > LEECH
LEECHLIKE > LEECH
LEED > LEE
LEEING > LEE

LEEK n vegetable with a long bulb and thick stem
LEEKS > LEEK
LEEP vb boil; scald
LEEPED > LEEP
LEEPING > LEEP
LEEPS > LEEP
LEER vb look or grin at in a sneering manner ▷ n sneering look or grin
LEERED > LEER
LEERIER > LEERY
LEERIEST > LEERY
LEERILY > LEERY
LEERINESS > LEERY
LEERING > LEER
LEERINGLY > LEER
LEERINGS > LEER
LEERS > LEER
LEERY adj suspicious or wary (of)
LEES pl n sediment of wine
LEESE old form of > LOOSE
LEESES > LEESE
LEESING > LEESE
LEET n shortlist
LEETLE form of > LITTLE
LEETS > LEET
LEETSPEAK n jargon used by some internet groups
LEEWARD n lee side ▷ adv towards this side ▷ adj towards where the wind blows
LEEWARDLY > LEEWARD
LEEWARDS adv towards the lee side
LEEWAY n room for free movement within limits
LEEWAYS > LEEWAY
LEEZE adj as in leeze me Scots for lief is me, an expression of affection
LEFT adj on the opposite side from right ▷ n left side
LEFTE old past tense of > LIFT
LEFTER > LEFT
LEFTEST > LEFT
LEFTIE same as > LEFTY
LEFTIES > LEFTY
LEFTISH > LEFT
LEFTISM > LEFTIST
LEFTISMS > LEFTIST
LEFTIST adj of the political left ▷ n supporter of the political left
LEFTISTS > LEFTIST
LEFTMOST > LEFT
LEFTMOSTS > LEFT
LEFTOVER n unused portion of food or material ▷ adj left as an unused portion
LEFTOVERS > LEFTOVER
LEFTS > LEFT
LEFTWARD same as > LEFTWARDS
LEFTWARDS adv towards or on the left
LEFTWING adj of or relating to the leftist faction of a party, etc
LEFTY n left-winger

LEG n limb on which a person or animal walks, runs, or stands
LEGACIES > LEGACY
LEGACY n thing left in a will
LEGAL adj established or permitted by law ▷ n legal expert
LEGALESE n conventional language in which legal documents are written
LEGALESES > LEGALESE
LEGALISE same as > LEGALIZE
LEGALISED > LEGALISE
LEGALISER > LEGALISE
LEGALISES > LEGALISE
LEGALISM n strict adherence to the letter of the law
LEGALISMS > LEGALISM
LEGALIST > LEGALISM
LEGALISTS > LEGALISM
LEGALITY n state or quality of being legal or lawful
LEGALIZE vb make legal
LEGALIZED > LEGALIZE
LEGALIZER > LEGALIZE
LEGALIZES > LEGALIZE
LEGALLY > LEGAL
LEGALS > LEGAL
LEGATARY n legatee
LEGATE n messenger or representative, esp from the Pope ▷ vb leave as legacy
LEGATED > LEGATE
LEGATEE n recipient of a legacy
LEGATEES > LEGATEE
LEGATES > LEGATE
LEGATINE > LEGATE
LEGATING > LEGATE
LEGATION n diplomatic minister and his or her staff
LEGATIONS > LEGATION
LEGATO adv smoothly ▷ n playing with no gaps between notes
LEGATOR n person who gives a legacy or makes a bequest
LEGATORS > LEGATOR
LEGATOS > LEGATO
LEGEND n traditional story
LEGENDARY adj famous
LEGENDISE same as > LEGENDIZE
LEGENDIST n writer of legends
LEGENDIZE vb make into legend
LEGENDRY > LEGEND

LEGENDS > LEGEND
LEGER variant of > LEDGER
LEGERING > LEGER
LEGERINGS > LEGER
LEGERITY n agility
LEGERS > LEGER
LEGES > LEX
LEGGE vb lighten or lessen
LEGGED > LEG
LEGGER n person who moves barge through tunnel using legs
LEGGERS > LEGGER
LEGGES > LEGGE
LEGGIE n leg spin bowler
LEGGIER > LEGGY
LEGGIERO adj light; delicate
LEGGIES > LEGGIE
LEGGIEST > LEGGY
LEGGIN same as > LEGGING
LEGGINESS > LEGGY
LEGGING n extra outer covering for the lower leg
LEGGINGED > LEGGING
LEGGINGS > LEGGING
LEGGINS > LEGGIN
LEGGISM n blacklegging
LEGGISMS > LEGGISM
LEGGO sentence substitute let go!
LEGGY adj having long legs
LEGHOLD n type of animal trap that clamps down on the animal's leg
LEGHOLDS > LEGHOLD
LEGHORN n Italian wheat straw woven into hats
LEGHORNS > LEGHORN
LEGIBLE adj easily read
LEGIBLY > LEGIBLE
LEGION n large military force ▷ adj very large or numerous
LEGIONARY adj of or relating to a legion ▷ n soldier belonging to a legion
LEGIONED adj arranged in legions
LEGIONS > LEGION
LEGISLATE vb make laws
LEGIST n legal mind
LEGISTS > LEGIST
LEGIT n legitimate drama ▷ adj legitimate
LEGITIM n inheritance due to children from father
LEGITIMS > LEGITIM
LEGITS > LEGIT
LEGLAN same as > LEGLIN
LEGLANS > LEGLAN
LEGLEN same as > LEGLIN
LEGLENS > LEGLEN
LEGLESS adj without legs
LEGLET n leg jewellery
LEGLETS > LEGLET
LEGLIKE > LEG
LEGLIN n milk-pail
LEGLINS > LEGLIN

LEGMAN n newsman who reports from the scene
LEGMEN > LEGMAN
LEGONG n Indonesian dance
LEGONGS > LEGONG
LEGROOM n space to put one's legs
LEGROOMS > LEGROOM
LEGS > LEG
LEGSIDE n part of a cricket field to the left of a right-handed batsman as they face the bowler
LEGSIDES > LEGSIDE
LEGUAAN n S African lizard
LEGUAANS > LEGUAAN
LEGUAN same as > LEGUAAN
LEGUANS > LEGUAN
LEGUME n pod of a plant of the pea or bean family
LEGUMES > LEGUME
LEGUMIN n protein from leguminous plants
LEGUMINS > LEGUMIN
LEGWARMER n one of a pair of garments resembling stockings without feet
LEGWEAR n clothing for legs
LEGWEARS > LEGWEAR
LEGWORK n work that involves travelling on foot or as if on foot
LEGWORKS > LEGWORK
LEHAIM same as > LECHAIM
LEHAIMS > LEHAIM
LEHAYIM same as > LEHAIM
LEHAYIMS > LEHAYIM
LEHR n long tunnel-shaped oven used for annealing glass
LEHRJAHRE n apprenticeship
LEHRS > LEHR
LEHUA n flower of Hawaii
LEHUAS > LEHUA
LEI n Hawaiian garland
LEIDGER same as > LEDGER
LEIDGERS > LEIDGER
LEIGER same as > LEDGER
LEIGERS > LEIGER
LEIOMYOMA same as > FIBROID
LEIPOA n Australian bird
LEIPOAS > LEIPOA
LEIR same as > LEAR
LEIRED > LEIR
LEIRING > LEIR
LEIRS > LEIR
LEIS > LEI
LEISH adj agile
LEISHER > LEISH
LEISHEST > LEISH
LEISLER n small bat
LEISLERS > LEISLER
LEISTER n pronged fishing spear ▷ vb spear with a leister
LEISTERED > LEISTER
LEISTERS > LEISTER

LEISURE n time for relaxation or hobbies ▷ vb have leisure
LEISURED > LEISURE
LEISURELY adj deliberate, unhurried ▷ adv slowly
LEISURES > LEISURE
LEISURING > LEISURE
LEITMOTIF n recurring theme associated with a person, situation, or thought
LEITMOTIV same as > LEITMOTIF
LEK n bird display area ▷ vb gather at lek
LEKE old form of > LEAK
LEKGOTLA n meeting place for village assemblies, court cases, and meetings of village leaders
LEKGOTLAS > LEKGOTLA
LEKKED > LEK
LEKKER adj attractive or nice
LEKKING > LEK
LEKKINGS > LEK
LEKS > LEK
LEKU > LEK
LEKVAR n prune or apricot pie filling
LEKVARS > LEKVAR
LEKYTHI > LEKYTHOS
LEKYTHOI > LEKYTHOS
LEKYTHOS n Greek flask
LEKYTHUS same as > LEKYTHOS
LEMAN n beloved
LEMANS > LEMAN
LEME same as > LEAM
LEMED > LEME
LEMEL n metal filings
LEMELS > LEMEL
LEMES > LEME
LEMING > LEME
LEMMA n word in its citation form
LEMMAS > LEMMA
LEMMATA > LEMMA
LEMMATISE same as > LEMMATIZE
LEMMATIZE vb group together the inflected forms of (a word) for analysis as a single item
LEMME vb (short for) let me
LEMMING n rodent of Arctic regions
LEMMINGS > LEMMING
LEMNISCAL adj relating to a type of closed plane curve
LEMNISCI > LEMNISCUS
LEMNISCUS technical name for > FILLET
LEMON n yellow oval fruit ▷ adj pale-yellow ▷ vb flavour with lemon
LEMONADE n lemon-flavoured soft drink, often fizzy
LEMONADES > LEMONADE

LEMONED > LEMON
LEMONFISH n type of game fish
LEMONIER > LEMONY
LEMONIEST > LEMONY
LEMONING > LEMON
LEMONISH > LEMON
LEMONLIKE > LEMON
LEMONS > LEMON
LEMONWOOD n small tree of New Zealand
LEMONY adj like a lemon
LEMPIRA n monetary unit of Honduras
LEMPIRAS > LEMPIRA
LEMUR n animal like a small monkey
LEMURES pl n spirits of the dead
LEMURIAN same as > LEMUROID
LEMURIANS > LEMURIAN
LEMURINE same as > LEMUROID
LEMURINES > LEMURINE
LEMURLIKE > LEMUR
LEMUROID adj relating to the superfamily which includes the lemurs ▷ n animal that resembles or is closely related to a lemur
LEMUROIDS > LEMUROID
LEMURS > LEMUR
LEND vb give temporary use of
LENDABLE > LEND
LENDER > LEND
LENDERS > LEND
LENDING > LEND
LENDINGS > LEND
LENDS > LEND
LENES > LENIS
LENG vb linger ▷ adj long
LENGED > LENG
LENGER > LENG
LENGEST > LENG
LENGING > LENG
LENGS > LENG
LENGTH n extent or measurement from end to end
LENGTHEN vb make or become longer
LENGTHENS > LENGTHEN
LENGTHFUL > LENGTH
LENGTHIER > LENGTHY
LENGTHILY > LENGTHY
LENGTHMAN n person whose job it is to maintain a particular length of road or railway line
LENGTHMEN > LENGTHMAN
LENGTHS > LENGTH
LENGTHY adj very long
LENIENCE > LENIENT
LENIENCES > LENIENT
LENIENCY > LENIENT,
LENIENT adj tolerant, not strict or severe ▷ n lenient person
LENIENTLY > LENIENT
LENIENTS > LENIENT
LENIFIED > LENIFY

LENIFIES > LENIFY
LENIFY vb make lenient
LENIFYING > LENIFY
LENIS adj pronounced with little muscular tension ▷ n consonant like this
LENITE vb undergo lenition
LENITED > LENITE
LENITES > LENITE
LENITIES > LENITY
LENITING > LENITE
LENITION n weakening of consonant sound
LENITIONS > LENITION
LENITIVE adj soothing or alleviating of pain or distress ▷ n lenitive drug
LENITIVES > LENITIVE
LENITY n mercy or clemency
LENO n weave in which the warp yarns are twisted in pairs between the weft
LENOS > LENO
LENS n piece of glass or similar material with one or both sides curved
LENSE same as > LENS
LENSED adj incorporating a lens
LENSES > LENS
LENSING n materials which colour and diffuse light
LENSINGS > LENSING
LENSLESS > LENS
LENSLIKE adj like a lens
LENSMAN n camera operator
LENSMEN > LENSMAN
LENT > LEND
LENTANDO adv slowing down
LENTEN adj of or relating to Lent
LENTI > LENTO
LENTIC adj of, relating to, or inhabiting still water
LENTICEL n any of numerous pores in the stem of a woody plant
LENTICELS > LENTICEL
LENTICLE n lens-shaped layer of mineral or rock embedded in a matrix of different constitution
LENTICLES > LENTICLE
LENTICULE n small lentil
LENTIFORM adj shaped like a biconvex lens
LENTIGO technical name for a > FRECKLE
LENTIL n edible seed
LENTILS > LENTIL
LENTISC same as > LENTISK
LENTISCS > LENTISC
LENTISK n mastic tree
LENTISKS > LENTISK
LENTO adv slowly ▷ n movement or passage performed slowly

LENTOID adj lentiform ▷ n lentiform object
LENTOIDS > LENTOID
LENTOR n lethargy
LENTORS > LENTOR
LENTOS > LENTO
LENTOUS adj lethargic
LENVOY another word for > ENVOY
LENVOYS > LENVOY
LEONE n monetary unit of Sierra Leone
LEONES > LEONE
LEONINE adj like a lion
LEOPARD n large spotted animal of the cat family
LEOPARDS > LEOPARD
LEOTARD n tight-fitting garment covering the upper body
LEOTARDED adj wearing a leotard
LEOTARDS > LEOTARD
LEP dialect word for > LEAP
LEPER n person who is ignored or despised
LEPERS > LEPER
LEPID adj amusing
LEPIDOTE adj covered with scales, scaly leaves, or spots ▷ n lepidote person, creature, or thing
LEPIDOTES > LEPIDOTE
LEPORID adj of the family of mammals including rabbits and hares ▷ n any animal belonging to this family
LEPORIDAE > LEPORID
LEPORIDS > LEPORID
LEPORINE adj of, relating to, or resembling a hare
LEPPED > LEP
LEPPING > LEP
LEPRA n leprosy
LEPRAS > LEPRA
LEPROSE adj having or denoting a whitish scurfy surface
LEPROSERY n a hospital for people with leprosy
LEPROSIES > LEPROSY
LEPROSITY n state of being leprous
LEPROSY n disease attacking the nerves and skin
LEPROTIC adj relating to leprosy
LEPROUS adj having leprosy
LEPROUSLY > LEPROUS
LEPS > LEP
LEPT > LEP
LEPTA > LEPTON
LEPTIN n protein that regulates the amount of fat in the body
LEPTINS > LEPTIN
LEPTOME n tissue of plant conducting food
LEPTOMES > LEPTOME
LEPTON n any of a group of elementary particles with weak interactions
LEPTONIC > LEPTON
LEPTONS > LEPTON

LEPTOPHOS n type of pesticide

LEPTOSOME n person with a small bodily frame and a slender physique

LEPTOTENE n (in reproduction) early stage in cell division

LEQUEAR same as > LACUNAR

LEQUEARS > LEQUEAR

LERE same as > LEAR

LERED > LERE

LERES > LERE

LERING > LERE

LERNAEAN adj relating to Lerna, the swamp in which dwelt the Hydra

LERP n crystallized honeydew

LERPS > LERP

LESBIAN n homosexual woman ▷ adj of homosexual women

LESBIANS > LESBIAN

LESBIC adj relating to lesbians

LESBIGAY n characteristic of or intended for the lesbian, bisexual, and gay community

LESBIGAYS > LESBIGAY

LESION n change in an organ of the body caused by injury ▷ vb cause lesions

LESIONED > LESION

LESIONING > LESION

LESIONS > LESION

LESPEDEZA n bush clover

LESS n smaller amount ▷ adj smaller in extent, degree, or duration ▷ pron smaller part or quantity ▷ adv smaller extent or degree ▷ prep after deducting, minus

LESSEE n person to whom a lease is granted

LESSEES > LESSEE

LESSEN vb make or become smaller or not as much

LESSENED > LESSEN

LESSENING n act of lessening

LESSENS > LESSEN

LESSER adj not as great in quantity, size, or worth

LESSES > LESS

LESSON n class or single period of instruction in a subject ▷ vb censure or punish

LESSONED > LESSON

LESSONING > LESSON

LESSONS > LESSON

LESSOR n person who grants a lease of property

LESSORS > LESSOR

LEST conj so as to prevent any possibility that ▷ vb listen

LESTED > LEST

LESTING > LEST

LESTS > LEST

LESULA n species of monkey inhabiting forests in DR Congo

LESULAS > LESULA

LET n act of letting property ▷ vb obstruct

LETCH same as > LECH

LETCHED > LETCH

LETCHES > LETCH

LETCHING > LETCH

LETCHINGS > LETCH

LETDOWN n disappointment

LETDOWNS > LETDOWN

LETHAL adj deadly ▷ n weapon, etc capable of causing death

LETHALITY > LETHAL

LETHALLY > LETHAL

LETHALS > LETHAL

LETHARGIC > LETHARGY

LETHARGY n sluggishness or dullness

LETHE n forgetfulness

LETHEAN > LETHE

LETHEE n life-blood

LETHEES > LETHEE

LETHES > LETHE

LETHIED adj forgetful

LETOUT n circumstance that serves as an excuse not to do something

LETOUTS > LETOUT

LETROZOLE n drug used to treat breast cancer

LETS > LET

LETTABLE > LET

LETTED > LET

LETTER n written message ▷ vb put letters on

LETTERBOX n slot through which letters are delivered into a building

LETTERED adj learned

LETTERER > LETTER

LETTERERS > LETTER

LETTERING n act, art, or technique of inscribing letters on to something

LETTERMAN n successful college sportsman

LETTERMEN > LETTERMAN

LETTERN another word for > LECTERN

LETTERNS > LETTERN

LETTERS pl n literary knowledge

LETTERSET n method of rotary printing in which ink is transferred from raised surfaces to paper via a rubber-covered cylinder

LETTING > LET

LETTINGS > LET

LETTRE n letter

LETTRES > LETTRE

LETTUCE n plant with large green leaves used in salads

LETTUCES > LETTUCE

LETUP n lessening or abatement

LETUPS > LETUP

LEU n monetary unit of Romania

LEUCAEMIA same as > LEUKAEMIA

LEUCAEMIC > LEUCAEMIA

LEUCEMIA same as > LEUKAEMIA

LEUCEMIAS > LEUCEMIA

LEUCEMIC adj of or like leucemia

LEUCH > LAUCH

LEUCHEN > LAUCH

LEUCIN same as > LEUCINE

LEUCINE n essential amino acid

LEUCINES > LEUCINE

LEUCINS > LEUCIN

LEUCISM n condition causing pale discoloration of hair or skin

LEUCISMS > LEUCISM

LEUCISTIC adj having reduced pigmentation in the skin but normally coloured eyes

LEUCITE n grey or white mineral

LEUCITES > LEUCITE

LEUCITIC > LEUCITE

LEUCO n as in leuco base colourless compound

LEUCOCYTE n white blood cell

LEUCOMA n white opaque scar of the cornea

LEUCOMAS > LEUCOMA

LEUCON n type of sponge

LEUCONS > LEUCON

LEUCOSES > LEUCOSIS

LEUCOSIN n albumin in cereal grains

LEUCOSINS > LEUCOSIN

LEUCOSIS same as > LEUKAEMIA

LEUCOTIC adj of or relating to leucosis

LEUCOTOME n needle used in leucotomy

LEUCOTOMY n surgical operation of cutting some of the nerve fibres in the frontal lobes of the brain

LEUD Scots word for > BREADTH

LEUDES > LEUD

LEUDS > LEUD

LEUGH > LAUCH

LEUGHEN > LAUCH

LEUKAEMIA n disease caused by uncontrolled overproduction of white blood cells

LEUKAEMIC adj of or relating to leukaemia

LEUKEMIA same as > LEUKAEMIA

LEUKEMIAS > LEUKEMIA

LEUKEMIC > LEUKEMIA

LEUKEMICS > LEUKEMIA

LEUKEMOID adj resembling leukaemia

LEUKOCYTE same as > LEUCOCYTE

LEUKOMA same as > LEUCOMA

LEUKOMAS > LEUKOMA

LEUKON n white blood cell count

LEUKONS > LEUKON

LEUKOSES > LEUKOSIS

LEUKOSIS n abnormal growth of white blood cells

LEUKOTIC > LEUKOSIS

LEUKOTOME same as > LEUCOTOME

LEUKOTOMY n lobotomy

LEV n monetary unit of Bulgaria

LEVA > LEV

LEVANT n leather made from the skins of goats, sheep, or seals ▷ vb bolt or abscond

LEVANTED > LEVANT

LEVANTER n easterly wind in the W Mediterranean area, esp in the late summer

LEVANTERS > LEVANTER

LEVANTINE n cloth of twilled silk

LEVANTING > LEVANT

LEVANTS > LEVANT

LEVAS > LEV

LEVATOR n muscle that raises a part of the body

LEVATORES > LEVATOR

LEVATORS > LEVATOR

LEVE same as > LIEF

LEVEE n natural or artificial river embankment ▷ vb go to the reception of

LEVEED > LEVEE

LEVEEING > LEVEE

LEVEES > LEVEE

LEVEL adj horizontal ▷ vb make even or horizontal ▷ n horizontal line or surface

LEVELED > LEVEL

LEVELER same as > LEVELLER

LEVELERS > LEVELER

LEVELING > LEVEL

LEVELLED > LEVEL

LEVELLER n person or thing that levels

LEVELLERS > LEVELLER

LEVELLEST > LEVEL

LEVELLING > LEVEL

LEVELLY > LEVEL

LEVELNESS > LEVEL

LEVELS > LEVEL

LEVER n handle used to operate machinery ▷ vb prise or move with a lever

LEVERAGE n action or power of a lever ▷ vb borrow capital required

LEVERAGED > LEVERAGE

LEVERAGES > LEVERAGE

LEVERED > LEVER

LEVERET n young hare

LEVERETS > LEVERET
LEVERING > LEVER
LEVERS > LEVER
LEVES > LEVE
LEVIABLE adj (of taxes, tariffs, etc) liable to be levied
LEVIATHAN n sea monster
LEVIED > LEVY
LEVIER > LEVY
LEVIERS > LEVY
LEVIES > LEVY
LEVIGABLE > LEVIGATE
LEVIGATE vb grind into a fine powder or a smooth paste ▷ adj having a smooth polished surface
LEVIGATED > LEVIGATE
LEVIGATES > LEVIGATE
LEVIGATOR > LEVIGATE
LEVIN archaic word for > LIGHTNING
LEVINS > LEVIN
LEVIRATE n practice, required by Old Testament law, of marrying the widow of one's brother
LEVIRATES > LEVIRATE
LEVIRATIC > LEVIRATE
LEVIS pl n jeans
LEVITATE vb rise or cause to rise into the air
LEVITATED > LEVITATE
LEVITATES > LEVITATE
LEVITATOR > LEVITATE
LEVITE n Christian clergyman or clergywoman
LEVITES > LEVITE
LEVITIC > LEVITE
LEVITICAL > LEVITE
LEVITIES > LEVITY
LEVITY n fickleness
LEVO adj anticlockwise
LEVODOPA n substance occurring naturally in the body and used to treat Parkinson's disease
LEVODOPAS > LEVODOPA
LEVOGYRE n counterclockwise spiral
LEVOGYRES > LEVOGYRE
LEVS > LEV
LEVULIN n substance obtained from certain bulbs
LEVULINS > LEVULIN
LEVULOSE n fructose
LEVULOSES > LEVULOSE
LEVY vb impose and collect (a tax) ▷ n imposition or collection of taxes
LEVYING > LEVY
LEW adj tepid

LEWD adj lustful or indecent
LEWDER > LEWD
LEWDEST > LEWD
LEWDLY > LEWD
LEWDNESS > LEWD
LEWDSBIES > LEWDSBY
LEWDSBY another word for > LEWDSTER
LEWDSTER n lewd person
LEWDSTERS > LEWDSTER
LEWIS n lifting device for heavy stone or concrete blocks
LEWISES > LEWIS
LEWISIA n type of herb
LEWISIAS > LEWISIA
LEWISITE n colourless oily poisonous liquid
LEWISITES > LEWISITE
LEWISSON same as > LEWIS
LEWISSONS > LEWISSON
LEX n system or body of laws
LEXEME n minimal meaningful unit of language
LEXEMES > LEXEME
LEXEMIC > LEXEME
LEXES > LEX
LEXICA > LEXICON
LEXICAL adj relating to the vocabulary of a language
LEXICALLY > LEXICAL
LEXICON n dictionary
LEXICONS > LEXICON
LEXIGRAM n figure or symbol that represents a word
LEXIGRAMS > LEXIGRAM
LEXIS n totality of vocabulary in a language
LEXISES > LEXIS
LEY n land under grass
LEYLANDI same as > LEYLANDII
LEYLANDII n type of fast-growing cypress tree
LEYLANDIS > LEYLANDI
LEYS > LEY
LI n Chinese measurement of distance
LIABILITY n hindrance or disadvantage
LIABLE adj legally obliged or responsible
LIAISE vb establish and maintain communication
LIAISED > LIAISE
LIAISES > LIAISE
LIAISING > LIAISE
LIAISON n communication and contact between groups
LIAISONS > LIAISON
LIANA n climbing plant
LIANAS > LIANA
LIANE same as > LIANA
LIANES > LIANE
LIANG n Chinese unit of weight

LIANGS > LIANG
LIANOID > LIANA
LIAR n person who tells lies
LIARD adj grey ▷ n former small coin
LIARDS > LIARD
LIARS > LIAR
LIART Scots form of > LIARD
LIAS n lowest series of rocks of the Jurassic system
LIASES > LIAS
LIASSIC adj relating to the earliest epoch of the Jurassic period
LIATRIS n North American plant with white flowers
LIATRISES > LIATRIS
LIB n informal word for liberation ▷ vb geld
LIBANT adj touching lightly
LIBATE vb offer as gift to the gods
LIBATED > LIBATE
LIBATES > LIBATE
LIBATING > LIBATE
LIBATION n drink poured as an offering to the gods
LIBATIONS > LIBATION
LIBATORY > LIBATE
LIBBARD another word for > LEOPARD
LIBBARDS > LIBBARD
LIBBED > LIB
LIBBER n liberationist
LIBBERS > LIBBER
LIBBING > LIB
LIBECCHIO same as > LIBECCIO
LIBECCIO n strong westerly or southwesterly wind blowing onto the W coast of Corsica
LIBECCIOS > LIBECCIO
LIBEL n published statement falsely damaging a person's reputation ▷ vb falsely damage the reputation of
LIBELANT same as > LIBELLANT
LIBELANTS > LIBELANT
LIBELED > LIBEL
LIBELEE same as > LIBELLEE
LIBELEES > LIBELEE
LIBELER > LIBEL
LIBELERS > LIBEL
LIBELING > LIBEL
LIBELINGS > LIBEL
LIBELIST > LIBEL
LIBELISTS > LIBEL
LIBELLANT n party who brings an action in the ecclesiastical courts by presenting a libel
LIBELLED > LIBEL
LIBELLEE n person against whom a libel has been filed in an ecclesiastical court

LIBELLEES > LIBELLEE
LIBELLER > LIBEL
LIBELLERS > LIBEL
LIBELLING > LIBEL
LIBELLOUS > LIBEL
LIBELOUS > LIBEL
LIBELS > LIBEL
LIBER n tome or book
LIBERAL adj having social and political views that favour progress and reform ▷ n person with such views
LIBERALLY > LIBERAL
LIBERALS > LIBERAL
LIBERATE vb set free
LIBERATED adj not bound by traditional social roles
LIBERATES > LIBERATE
LIBERATOR > LIBERATE
LIBERO another name for > SWEEPER
LIBEROS > LIBERO
LIBERS > LIBER
LIBERTIES > LIBERTY
LIBERTINE n immoral person ▷ adj unscrupulous
LIBERTY n freedom
LIBIDINAL > LIBIDO
LIBIDO n psychic energy
LIBIDOS > LIBIDO
LIBKEN n lodging
LIBKENS > LIBKEN
LIBLAB n 19th century British liberal
LIBLABS > LIBLAB
LIBRA n ancient Roman unit of weight
LIBRAE > LIBRA
LIBRAIRE n bookseller
LIBRAIRES > LIBRAIRE
LIBRAIRIE n bookshop
LIBRARIAN n keeper of or worker in a library
LIBRARIES > LIBRARY
LIBRARY n room or building where books are kept
LIBRAS > LIBRA
LIBRATE vb oscillate or waver
LIBRATED > LIBRATE
LIBRATES > LIBRATE
LIBRATING > LIBRATE
LIBRATION n act or an instance of oscillating
LIBRATORY > LIBRATE
LIBRETTI > LIBRETTO
LIBRETTO n words of an opera
LIBRETTOS > LIBRETTO
LIBRI > LIBER
LIBRIFORM adj (of a fibre of woody tissue) elongated and having a pitted thickened cell wall
LIBS > LIB
LICE > LOUSE
LICENCE n document giving official permission ▷ vb (in the US) give permission to

LICENCED > LICENCE
LICENCEE same as
  > LICENSEE
LICENCEES
  > LICENCEE
LICENCER > LICENCE
LICENCERS > LICENCE
LICENCES > LICENCE
LICENCING > LICENCE
LICENSE vb grant or give a licence for
LICENSED > LICENSE
LICENSEE n holder of a licence
LICENSEES
  > LICENSEE
LICENSER > LICENSE
LICENSERS > LICENSE
LICENSES > LICENSE
LICENSING > LICENSE
LICENSOR > LICENSE
LICENSORS > LICENSE
LICENSURE n act of conferring licence
LICENTE adj permitted; allowed
LICH n dead body
LICHANOS n note played using forefinger
LICHEE same as
  > LITCHI
LICHEES > LICHEE
LICHEN n small flowerless plant forming a crust on rocks, trees, etc ▷ vb cover with lichen
LICHENED > LICHEN
LICHENIN n complex polysaccharide occurring in certain species of moss
LICHENING > LICHEN
LICHENINS
  > LICHENIN
LICHENISM n an association of fungus and alga as lichen
LICHENIST n person who studies lichens
LICHENOID > LICHEN
LICHENOSE > LICHEN
LICHENOUS > LICHEN
LICHENS > LICHEN
LICHES > LICH
LICHGATE n roofed gate to a churchyard
LICHGATES
  > LICHGATE
LICHI same as **> LITCHI**
LICHIS > LICHI
LICHT Scot word for
  > LIGHT
LICHTED > LICHT
LICHTER > LICHT
LICHTEST > LICHT
LICHTING > LICHT
LICHTLIED > LICHTLY
LICHTLIES > LICHTLY
LICHTLY vb Scots word meaning treat discourteously
LICHTS > LICHT
LICHWAKE n night vigil over a dead body
LICHWAKES
  > LICHWAKE
LICHWAY n path used to carry coffin into church
LICHWAYS > LICHWAY

LICIT adj lawful, permitted
LICITLY > LICIT
LICITNESS > LICIT
LICK vb pass the tongue over ▷ n licking
LICKED > LICK
LICKER > LICK
LICKERISH adj lecherous or lustful
LICKERS > LICK
LICKING n beating
LICKINGS > LICKING
LICKPENNY n something that uses up large amounts of money
LICKS > LICK
LICKSPIT n flattering or servile person
LICKSPITS
  > LICKSPIT
LICORICE same as
  > LIQUORICE
LICORICES
  > LICORICE
LICTOR n one of a group of ancient Roman officials
LICTORIAN > LICTOR
LICTORS > LICTOR
LID n movable cover
LIDAR n radar-type instrument
LIDARS > LIDAR
LIDDED > LID
LIDDING n lids
LIDDINGS > LIDDING
LIDGER variant form of
  > LEDGER
LIDGERS > LIDGER
LIDLESS adj having no lid or top
LIDO n open-air centre for swimming and water sports
LIDOCAINE n powerful local anaesthetic administered by injection
LIDOS > LIDO
LIDS > LID
LIE vb make a false statement ▷ n falsehood
LIED n setting for solo voice and piano of a poem
LIEDER > LIED
LIEF adv gladly ▷ adj ready ▷ n beloved person
LIEFER > LIEF
LIEFEST > LIEF
LIEFLY > LIEF
LIEFS > LIEF
LIEGE adj bound to give or receive feudal service ▷ n lord
LIEGEDOM > LIEGE
LIEGEDOMS > LIEGE
LIEGELESS > LIEGE
LIEGEMAN n (formerly) the subject of a sovereign or feudal lord
LIEGEMEN > LIEGEMAN
LIEGER same as
  > LEDGER
LIEGERS > LIEGER
LIEGES > LIEGE
LIEN n right to hold another's property until a debt is paid

LIENABLE adj that can be subject of a lien
LIENAL adj of or relating to the spleen
LIENEE n person against whom a lien has been placed
LIENEES > LIENEE
LIENOR n person who holds a lien
LIENORS > LIENOR
LIENS > LIEN
LIENTERIC
  > LIENTERY
LIENTERY n passage of undigested food in the faeces
LIER n person who lies down
LIERNE n short secondary rib that connects intersections of the primary ribs
LIERNES > LIERNE
LIERS > LIER
LIES > LIE
LIEU n stead
LIEUS > LIEU
LIEVE same as **> LEVE**
LIEVER > LIEVE
LIEVES > LIEVE
LIEVEST > LIEVE
LIFE n state of living beings
LIFEBELT n ring filled with air, used to keep a person afloat when in danger of drowning
LIFEBELTS
  > LIFEBELT
LIFEBLOOD n blood vital to life
LIFEBOAT n boat used for rescuing people at sea
LIFEBOATS
  > LIFEBOAT
LIFEBUOY n any of various kinds of buoyant device for keeping people afloat
LIFEBUOYS
  > LIFEBUOY
LIFECARE n care of person's health and welfare
LIFECARES
  > LIFECARE
LIFEFUL adj full of life
LIFEGUARD n person who saves people from drowning ▷ vb work as lifeguard
LIFEHACK n action that simplifies a task or reduces frustration in everyday life ▷ vb perform a lifehack
LIFEHACKS
  > LIFEHACK
LIFEHOLD adj (of land) held while one is alive
LIFELESS adj dead
LIFELIKE adj closely resembling or representing life
LIFELINE n means of contact or support
LIFELINES
  > LIFELINE

LIFELONG adj lasting all of a person's life
LIFER n prisoner sentenced to imprisonment for life
LIFERS > LIFER
LIFES pl n as in still lifes paintings or drawings of inanimate objects
LIFESAVER n saver of a person's life
LIFESOME adj full of life
LIFESPAN n period of time during which a person or animal may be expected to live
LIFESPANS > LIFESPAN
LIFESTYLE n particular attitudes, habits, etc ▷ adj suggestive of a fashionable or desirable lifestyle
LIFETIME n length of time a person is alive
LIFETIMES
  > LIFETIME
LIFEWAY n way of life
LIFEWAYS > LIFEWAY
LIFEWORK n work to which a person has devoted their life
LIFEWORKS
  > LIFEWORK
LIFEWORLD n way individual experiences world
LIFT vb move upwards in position, status, volume, etc ▷ n cage raised and lowered in a vertical shaft
LIFTABLE > LIFT
LIFTBACK n hatchback
LIFTBACKS
  > LIFTBACK
LIFTBOY n person who operates a lift
LIFTBOYS > LIFTBOY
LIFTED > LIFT
LIFTER > LIFT
LIFTERS > LIFT
LIFTGATE n rear opening of hatchback
LIFTGATES
  > LIFTGATE
LIFTING > LIFT
LIFTMAN same as
  > LIFTBOY
LIFTMEN > LIFTMAN
LIFTOFF n moment a rocket leaves the ground ▷ vb (of a rocket) to leave its launch pad
LIFTOFFS > LIFTOFF
LIFTS > LIFT
LIFULL obsolete form of
  > LIFEFUL
LIG n function with free entertainment and refreshments ▷ vb attend such a function
LIGAMENT n band of tissue joining bones
LIGAMENTS
  > LIGAMENT
LIGAN same as **> LAGAN**
LIGAND n atom, molecule, radical, or ion forming a complex with a central atom

LIGANDS > LIGAND

LIGANS > LIGAN

LIGASE n any of a class of enzymes

LIGASES > LIGASE

LIGATE vb tie up or constrict (something) with a ligature

LIGATED > LIGATE

LIGATES > LIGATE

LIGATING > LIGATE

LIGATION > LIGATE

LIGATIONS > LIGATE

LIGATIVE > LIGATE

LIGATURE n link, bond, or tie ▷ vb bind with a ligature

LIGATURED > LIGATURE

LIGATURES > LIGATURE

LIGER n hybrid offspring of a female tiger and a male lion

LIGERS > LIGER

LIGGE obsolete form of > LIE

LIGGED > LIG

LIGGER > LIG

LIGGERS > LIG

LIGGES > LIGGE

LIGGING > LIG

LIGGINGS > LIG

LIGHT n electromagnetic radiation by which things are visible ▷ adj bright ▷ vb ignite ▷ adv with little luggage

LIGHTBULB n glass bulb containing gas that emits light when a current is passed through it

LIGHTED > LIGHT

LIGHTEN vb make less dark

LIGHTENED > LIGHTEN

LIGHTENER > LIGHTEN

LIGHTENS > LIGHTEN

LIGHTER n device for lighting cigarettes etc ▷ vb convey in a type of flat-bottomed barge

LIGHTERED > LIGHTER

LIGHTERS > LIGHTER

LIGHTEST > LIGHT

LIGHTFACE n weight of type in printing

LIGHTFAST adj (of a dye) unaffected by light

LIGHTFUL adj full of light

LIGHTING > LIGHT

LIGHTINGS > LIGHT

LIGHTISH > LIGHT

LIGHTLESS > LIGHT

LIGHTLIED > LIGHTLY

LIGHTLIES > LIGHTLY

LIGHTLY adv in a light way ▷ vb belittle

LIGHTNESS n quality of being light

LIGHTNING n visible discharge of electricity in the atmosphere ▷ adj fast and sudden

LIGHTS > LIGHT

LIGHTSHIP n moored ship used as a lighthouse

LIGHTSOME adj lighthearted

LIGHTWAVE adj using light waves

LIGHTWOOD n Australian acacia

LIGNAGE another word for > LINEAGE

LIGNAGES > LIGNAGE

LIGNALOES another name for > EAGLEWOOD

LIGNAN n beneficial substance found in plants

LIGNANS > LIGNAN

LIGNE n unit of measurement

LIGNEOUS adj of or like wood

LIGNES > LIGNE

LIGNICOLE adj growing or living in wood

LIGNIFIED > LIGNIFY

LIGNIFIES > LIGNIFY

LIGNIFORM adj having the appearance of wood

LIGNIFY vb become woody with the deposition of lignin in cell walls

LIGNIN n complex polymer occurring in certain plant cell walls making the plant rigid

LIGNINS > LIGNIN

LIGNITE n woody textured rock used as fuel

LIGNITES > LIGNITE

LIGNITIC > LIGNITE

LIGNOSE n explosive compound

LIGNOSES > LIGNOSE

LIGNUM n wood

LIGNUMS > LIGNUM

LIGROIN n volatile fraction of petroleum

LIGROINE same as > LIGROIN

LIGROINES > LIGROINE

LIGROINS > LIGROIN

LIGS > LIG

LIGULA same as > LIGULE

LIGULAE > LIGULA

LIGULAR > LIGULA

LIGULAS > LIGULA

LIGULATE adj having the shape of a strap

LIGULATED same as > LIGULATE

LIGULE n membranous outgrowth between the leaf blade and sheath

LIGULES > LIGULE

LIGULOID > LIGULA

LIGURE n any of the 12 precious stones used in the breastplates of high priests

LIGURES > LIGURE

LIGUSTRUM n plant of a genus comprising the privets

LIKABLE adj easy to like

LIKABLY > LIKABLE

LIKE adj similar ▷ vb find enjoyable ▷ n favourable feeling, desire, or preference

LIKEABLE same as > LIKABLE

LIKEABLY same as > LIKABLY

LIKED > LIKE

LIKELIER > LIKELY

LIKELIEST > LIKELY

LIKELY adj tending or inclined ▷ adv probably

LIKEN vb compare

LIKENED > LIKEN

LIKENESS n resemblance

LIKENING > LIKEN

LIKENS > LIKEN

LIKER > LIKE

LIKES > LIKE

LIKEST > LIKE

LIKEWAKE same as > LYKEWAKE

LIKEWAKES > LIKEWAKE

LIKEWALK same as > LYKEWAKE

LIKEWALKS > LIKEWALK

LIKEWISE adv similarly

LIKIN n historically, Chinese tax

LIKING n fondness

LIKINGS > LIKING

LIKINS > LIKIN

LIKUTA n coin in the former Zaire

LILAC n shrub with pale mauve flowers ▷ adj light-purple

LILACS > LILAC

LILANGENI n standard monetary unit of eSwatini, divided into 100 cents

LILIED adj decorated with lilies

LILIES > LILY

LILL obsolete form of > LOLL

LILLED > LILL

LILLING > LILL

LILLIPUT adj tiny ▷ n tiny person or being

LILLIPUTS > LILLIPUT

LILLS > LILL

LILO n inflatable mattress

LILOS > LILO

LILT n musical quality in speech ▷ vb speak with a lilt

LILTED > LILT

LILTING > LILT

LILTINGLY > LILT

LILTS > LILT

LILY n plant which has large, often white, flowers

LILYLIKE adj resembling a lily

LIMA n type of edible bean

LIMACEL n small shell inside some kinds of slug

LIMACELS > LIMACEL

LIMACEOUS adj relating to the slug

LIMACES > LIMAX

LIMACINE adj relating to slugs

LIMACON n heart-shaped curve

LIMACONS > LIMACON

LIMAIL same as > LEMEL

LIMAILS > LIMAIL

LIMAN n lagoon

LIMANS > LIMAN

LIMAS > LIMA

LIMATION n polishing

LIMATIONS > LIMATION

LIMAX n slug

LIMB n arm, leg, or wing ▷ vb dismember

LIMBA n type of African tree

LIMBAS > LIMBA

LIMBATE adj having an edge or border of a different colour from the rest

LIMBEC obsolete form of > ALEMBIC

LIMBECK obsolete form of > ALEMBIC

LIMBECKS > LIMBECK

LIMBECS > LIMBEC

LIMBED > LIMB

LIMBER vb loosen stiff muscles by exercising ▷ adj pliant or supple ▷ n part of a gun carriage

LIMBERED > LIMBER

LIMBERER > LIMBER

LIMBEREST > LIMBER

LIMBERING > LIMBER

LIMBERLY > LIMBER

LIMBERS > LIMBER

LIMBI > LIMBUS

LIMBIC > LIMBUS

LIMBIER > LIMBY

LIMBIEST > LIMBY

LIMBING > LIMB

LIMBLESS > LIMB

LIMBMEAL adv piece by piece

LIMBO n region between Heaven and Hell for the unbaptized ▷ vb perform a Caribbean dance that entails passing under a bar while leaning backwards

LIMBOED > LIMBO

LIMBOES > LIMBO

LIMBOING > LIMBO

LIMBOS > LIMBO

LIMBOUS adj with overlapping edges

LIMBS > LIMB

LIMBUS n border

LIMBUSES > LIMBUS

LIMBY adj with long legs, stem, branches, etc

LIME n calcium compound used as a fertilizer or in making cement ▷ vb spread a calcium compound upon (land) ▷ adj having the flavour of lime fruit

LIMEADE n drink made from sweetened lime juice and plain or carbonated water

LIMEADES > LIMEADE

LIMED > LIME

LIMEKILN n kiln in which calcium carbonate is

burned to produce quicklime

LIMEKILNS > LIMEKILN

LIMELESS > LIME

LIMELIGHT n glare of publicity ▷ vb illuminate with limelight

LIMELIT > LIMELIGHT

LIMEN another term for > THRESHOLD

LIMENS > LIMEN

LIMEPIT n pit containing lime in which hides are placed to remove the hair

LIMEPITS > LIMEPIT

LIMERENCE n psychological state resulting from romantic attraction

LIMERICK n humorous verse of five lines

LIMERICKS > LIMERICK

LIMES n fortified boundary of the Roman Empire

LIMESCALE n flaky deposit left in containers such as kettles by the action of heat on water containing calcium salts

LIMESTONE n sedimentary rock used in building

LIMEWASH n mixture of lime and water used to whitewash walls, ceilings, etc

LIMEWATER n clear colourless solution of calcium hydroxide in water

LIMEY n British person ▷ adj British

LIMEYS > LIMEY

LIMIER > LIMY

LIMIEST > LIMY

LIMINA > LIMEN

LIMINAL adj relating to the point beyond which a sensation becomes too faint to be experienced

LIMINESS > LIMY

LIMING > LIME

LIMINGS > LIME

LIMIT n ultimate extent, degree, or amount of something ▷ vb restrict or confine

LIMITABLE > LIMIT

LIMITARY adj of, involving, or serving as a limit

LIMITED adj having a limit ▷ n limited train, bus, etc

LIMITEDLY > LIMITED

LIMITEDS > LIMITED

LIMITER n thing that limits something

LIMITERS > LIMITER

LIMITES > LIMES

LIMITING > LIMIT

LIMITINGS > LIMIT

LIMITLESS > LIMIT

LIMITS > LIMIT

LIMMA n semitone

LIMMAS > LIMMA

LIMMER n scoundrel

LIMMERS > LIMMER

LIMN vb represent in drawing or painting

LIMNAEID n type of snail

LIMNAEIDS > LIMNAEID

LIMNED > LIMN

LIMNER > LIMN

LIMNERS > LIMN

LIMNETIC adj of the open water of lakes down to the depth of light penetration

LIMNIC adj relating to lakes

LIMNING > LIMN

LIMNOLOGY n study of bodies of fresh water with reference to their plant and animal life, physical properties, geographical features, etc

LIMNS > LIMN

LIMO short for > LIMOUSINE

LIMONENE n liquid optically active terpene with a lemon-like odour

LIMONENES > LIMONENE

LIMONITE n common brown, black, or yellow amorphous secondary mineral

LIMONITES > LIMONITE

LIMONITIC > LIMONITE

LIMONIUM n sea plant with funnel-shaped flowers

LIMONIUMS > LIMONIUM

LIMOS > LIMO

LIMOSES > LIMOSIS

LIMOSIS n excessive hunger

LIMOUS adj muddy

LIMOUSINE n large luxurious car

LIMP vb walk with an uneven step ▷ n limping walk ▷ adj without firmness or stiffness

LIMPA n type of rye bread

LIMPAS > LIMPA

LIMPED > LIMP

LIMPER > LIMP

LIMPERS > LIMP

LIMPEST > LIMP

LIMPET n shellfish which sticks to rocks ▷ adj denoting weapons that are magnetically attached to their targets

LIMPETS > LIMPET

LIMPID adj clear or transparent

LIMPIDITY > LIMPID

LIMPIDLY > LIMPID

LIMPING > LIMP

LIMPINGLY > LIMP

LIMPINGS > LIMP

LIMPKIN n rail-like wading bird

LIMPKINS > LIMPKIN

LIMPLY > LIMP

LIMPNESS > LIMP

LIMPS > LIMP

LIMPSEY same as > LIMPSY

LIMPSIER > LIMPSY

LIMPSIEST > LIMPSY

LIMPSY adj limp

LIMULI > LIMULUS

LIMULOID n type of crab

LIMULOIDS > LIMULOID

LIMULUS n horseshoe crab

LIMULUSES > LIMULUS

LIMY adj of, like, or smeared with birdlime

LIN vb cease

LINABLE > LINE

LINAC n linear accelerator

LINACS > LINAC

LINAGE n number of lines in written or printed matter

LINAGES > LINAGE

LINALOL same as > LINALOOL

LINALOLS > LINALOL

LINALOOL n optically active colourless fragrant liquid

LINALOOLS > LINALOOL

LINCH n ledge

LINCHES > LINCH

LINCHET another word for > LINCH

LINCHETS > LINCHET

LINCHPIN n pin to hold a wheel on its axle

LINCHPINS > LINCHPIN

LINCRUSTA n type of wallpaper having a hard embossed surface

LINCTURE n medicine taken by licking

LINCTURES > LINCTURE

LINCTUS n cough medicine

LINCTUSES > LINCTUS

LIND variant of > LINDEN

LINDANE n white poisonous crystalline powder

LINDANES > LINDANE

LINDEN n large tree with heart-shaped leaves and fragrant yellowish flowers

LINDENS > LINDEN

LINDIED > LINDY

LINDIES > LINDY

LINDS > LIND

LINDWORM n wingless serpent-like dragon

LINDWORMS > LINDWORM

LINDY n lively dance ▷ vb perform the lindy

LINDYING > LINDY

LINE n long narrow mark ▷ vb mark with lines

LINEABLE > LINE

LINEAGE n descent from an ancestor

LINEAGES > LINEAGE

LINEAL adj in direct line of descent

LINEALITY > LINEAL

LINEALLY > LINEAL

LINEAMENT n facial feature

LINEAR adj of or in lines

LINEARISE same as > LINEARIZE

LINEARITY > LINEAR

LINEARIZE vb make linear

LINEARLY > LINEAR

LINEATE adj marked with lines

LINEATED same as > LINEATE

LINEATION n act of marking with lines

LINEBRED adj having an ancestor that is common to sire and dam

LINECUT n method of relief printing

LINECUTS > LINECUT

LINED > LINE

LINELESS > LINE

LINELIKE > LINE

LINEMAN same as > LINESMAN

LINEMATE n ice hockey player on the same line as another

LINEMATES > LINEMATE

LINEMEN > LINEMAN

LINEN n cloth or thread made from flax

LINENFOLD n form of decorative wood carving that resembles folded linen

LINENIER > LINENY

LINENIEST > LINENY

LINENS > LINEN

LINENY adj like linen

LINEOLATE adj marked with very fine parallel lines

LINER n large passenger ship

LINERLESS adj having no lining

LINERS > LINER

LINES > LINE

LINESCORE n horizontal chart showing scoring in a game

LINESMAN n (in some sports) an official who helps the referee or umpire

LINESMEN > LINESMAN

LINEUP n row or arrangement of people or things

LINEUPS > LINEUP

LINEY > LINE

LING n slender food fish

LINGA same as > LINGAM

LINGAM n (in Sanskrit) masculine gender

LINGAMS > LINGAM

LINGAS > LINGA

LINGBERRY same as > COWBERRY

LINGCOD n type of food fish

LINGCODS > LINGCOD

LINGEL *n* shoemaker's thread
LINGELS > LINGEL
LINGER *vb* delay or prolong departure
LINGERED > LINGER
LINGERER > LINGER
LINGERERS > LINGER
LINGERIE *n* women's underwear or nightwear
LINGERIES > LINGERIE
LINGERING > LINGER
LINGERS > LINGER
LINGIER > LINGY
LINGIEST > LINGY
LINGLE *same as* > LINGEL
LINGLES > LINGLE
LINGO *n* foreign or unfamiliar language or jargon
LINGOES > LINGO
LINGOS > LINGO
LINGOT *n* ingot
LINGOTS > LINGOT
LINGS > LING
LINGSTER *n* person able to communicate with aliens
LINGSTERS > LINGSTER
LINGUA *n* any tongue-like structure
LINGUAE > LINGUA
LINGUAL *adj* of the tongue ▷ *n* lingual consonant
LINGUALLY > LINGUAL
LINGUALS > LINGUAL
LINGUAS > LINGUA
LINGUICA *n* Portuguese sausage
LINGUICAS > LINGUICA
LINGUINE *n* kind of pasta in the shape of thin flat strands
LINGUINES > LINGUINE
LINGUINI *same as* > LINGUINE
LINGUINIS > LINGUINI
LINGUISA *same as* > LINGUICA
LINGUISAS > LINGUISA
LINGUIST *n* person skilled in foreign languages
LINGUISTS > LINGUIST
LINGULA *n* small tongue
LINGULAE > LINGULA
LINGULAR > LINGULA
LINGULAS > LINGULA
LINGULATE *adj* shaped like a tongue
LINGY *adj* heather-covered
LINHAY *n* farm building with an open front
LINHAYS > LINHAY
LINIER > LINE
LINIEST > LINE
LINIMENT *n* medicated liquid rubbed on the skin to relieve pain or stiffness

LINIMENTS > LINIMENT
LININ *n* network of viscous material in the nucleus of a cell
LINING *n* layer of cloth attached to the inside of a garment etc
LININGS > LINING
LININS > LININ
LINISH *vb* polish metal
LINISHED > LINISH
LINISHER > LINISH
LINISHERS > LINISH
LINISHES > LINISH
LINISHING > LINISH
LINK *n* any of the rings forming a chain ▷ *vb* connect with or as if with links
LINKABLE > LINK
LINKAGE *n* act of linking or the state of being linked
LINKAGES > LINKAGE
LINKBOY *n* (formerly) a boy who carried a torch for pedestrians in dark streets
LINKBOYS > LINKBOY
LINKED > LINK
LINKER *n* person or thing that links
LINKERS > LINKER
LINKIER > LINKY
LINKIEST > LINKY
LINKING > LINK
LINKMAN *same as* > LINKBOY
LINKMEN > LINKMAN
LINKROT *n* state of having expired hyperlinks on a website
LINKROTS > LINKROT
LINKS > LINK
LINKSLAND *n* land near sea used for golf
LINKSMAN *same as* > LINKBOY
LINKSMEN > LINKSMAN
LINKSPAN *n* hinged bridge on a quay, used to move vehicles on or off a vessel
LINKSPANS > LINKSPAN
LINKSTER *n* interpreter
LINKSTERS > LINKSTER
LINKUP *n* establishing of a union between objects, groups, organizations, etc
LINKUPS > LINKUP
LINKWORK *n* something made up of links
LINKWORKS > LINKWORK
LINKY *adj* (of countryside) consisting of links
LINN *n* waterfall or a pool at the foot of it
LINNED > LIN
LINNET *n* songbird of the finch family
LINNETS > LINNET
LINNEY *same as* > LINHAY
LINNEYS > LINNEY
LINNIES > LINNY
LINNING > LIN

LINNS > LINN
LINNY *same as* > LINHAY
LINO *same as* > LINOLEUM
LINOCUT *n* design cut in relief in lino mounted on a block of wood
LINOCUTS > LINOCUT
LINOLEATE *n* ester or salt of linoleic acid
LINOLEIC *adj* as in *linoleic acid* colourless oily essential fatty acid found in linseed
LINOLENIC *adj* as in *linolenic acid* colourless unsaturated essential fatty acid
LINOLEUM *n* type of floor covering
LINOLEUMS > LINOLEUM
LINOS > LINO
LINOTYPE *n* line of metal type produced by machine ▷ *vb* set as line of type
LINOTYPED > LINOTYPE
LINOTYPER > LINOTYPE
LINOTYPES > LINOTYPE
LINS > LIN
LINSANG *n* any of several forest-dwelling viverrine mammals
LINSANGS > LINSANG
LINSEED *n* seed of the flax plant
LINSEEDS > LINSEED
LINSEY *n* type of cloth
LINSEYS > LINSEY
LINSTOCK *n* long staff holding a lighted match, formerly used to fire a cannon
LINSTOCKS > LINSTOCK
LINT *n* shreds of fibre, etc ▷ *vb* shed or remove lint
LINTED *adj* having lint
LINTEL *n* horizontal beam at the top of a door or window
LINTELED *adj* (of a door or window) having a lintel
LINTELLED *adj* having a lintel
LINTELS > LINTEL
LINTER *n* machine for stripping the short fibres of ginned cotton seeds
LINTERS > LINTER
LINTIE *Scot word for* > LINNET
LINTIER > LINT
LINTIES > LINTIE
LINTIEST > LINT
LINTING *n* process of making lint
LINTINGS > LINTING
LINTLESS > LINT
LINTOL *same as* > LINTEL
LINTOLS > LINTOL
LINTS > LINT
LINTSEED *same as* > LINSEED

LINTSEEDS > LINTSEED
LINTSTOCK *same as* > LINSTOCK
LINTWHITE *n* linnet
LINTY > LINT
LINUM *n* type of plant of temperate regions
LINUMS > LINUM
LINURON *n* type of herbicide
LINURONS > LINURON
LINUX *n* nonproprietary computer operating system
LINUXES > LINUX
LINY > LINE
LION *n* large animal of the cat family
LIONCEL *n* (in heraldry) small lion
LIONCELLE *same as* > LIONCEL
LIONCELS > LIONCEL
LIONEL *same as* > LIONCEL
LIONELS > LIONEL
LIONESS *n* female lion
LIONESSES > LIONESS
LIONET *n* young lion
LIONETS > LIONET
LIONFISH *n* any of various scorpion fishes of the Pacific
LIONHEAD *n* small breed of rabbit with long fur around the face
LIONHEADS > LIONHEAD
LIONISE *same as* > LIONIZE
LIONISED > LIONISE
LIONISER > LIONISE
LIONISERS > LIONISE
LIONISES > LIONISE
LIONISING > LIONISE
LIONISM *n* the condition of being treated as a celebrity
LIONISMS > LIONISM
LIONIZE *vb* treat as a celebrity
LIONIZED > LIONIZE
LIONIZER > LIONIZE
LIONIZERS > LIONIZE
LIONIZES > LIONIZE
LIONIZING > LIONIZE
LIONLIER > LIONLY
LIONLIEST > LIONLY
LIONLIKE > LION
LIONLY *adj* like a lion
LIONS > LION
LIP *n* either of the fleshy edges of the mouth ▷ *vb* touch with the lips
LIPA *n* monetary unit of Croatia
LIPAEMIA *n* abnormally large amount of fat in the blood
LIPAEMIAS > LIPAEMIA
LIPARITE *n* type of igneous rock
LIPARITES > LIPARITE
LIPAS > LIPA
LIPASE *n* any of a group of enzymes that digest fat

LIPASES >LIPASE
LIPE n lurching or jerking movement
LIPECTOMY n surgical operation to remove fat
LIPEMIA same as >LIPAEMIA
LIPEMIAS >LIPEMIA
LIPES >LIPE
LIPGLOSS n cosmetic for the lips to give a sheen
LIPID n any of a group of organic compounds including fats, oils, waxes, and sterols
LIPIDE same as >LIPID
LIPIDES >LIPIDE
LIPIDIC >LIPID
LIPIDOSES >LIPIDOSIS
LIPIDOSIS n disorder in lipid metabolism
LIPIDS >LIPID
LIPIN n family of nuclear proteins
LIPINS >LIPIN
LIPLESS >LIP
LIPLIKE >LIP
LIPLINER n cosmetic used to outline the lips
LIPLINERS >LIPLINER
LIPO n liposuction
LIPOCYTE n fat-storing cell
LIPOCYTES >LIPOCYTE
LIPOGRAM n piece of writing in which all words containing a particular letter have been omitted
LIPOGRAMS >LIPOGRAM
LIPOIC adj as in lipoic acid sulphur-containing fatty acid
LIPOID n fatlike substance, such as wax
LIPOIDAL >LIPOID
LIPOIDS >LIPOID
LIPOLITIC same as >LIPOLYTIC
LIPOLYSES >LIPOLYSIS
LIPOLYSIS n hydrolysis of fats resulting in the production of carboxylic acids and glycerol
LIPOLYTIC adj fat-burning
LIPOMA n benign tumour composed of fatty tissue
LIPOMAS >LIPOMA
LIPOMATA >LIPOMA
LIPOPLAST n small particle in plant cytoplasm, esp that of seeds, in which fat is stored
LIPOS >LIPO
LIPOSOMAL >LIPOSOME
LIPOSOME n particle formed by lipids
LIPOSOMES >LIPOSOME
LIPOSUCK vb subject to liposuction

LIPOSUCKS >LIPOSUCK
LIPOTROPY n breaking down of fat in body
LIPPED >LIP
LIPPEN vb trust
LIPPENED >LIPPEN
LIPPENING >LIPPEN
LIPPENS >LIPPEN
LIPPER Scots word for >RIPPLE
LIPPERED >LIPPER
LIPPERING >LIPPER
LIPPERS >LIPPER
LIPPIE variant of >LIPPY
LIPPIER >LIPPY
LIPPIES >LIPPY
LIPPIEST >LIPPY
LIPPINESS >LIPPY
LIPPING >LIP
LIPPINGS >LIP
LIPPITUDE n state of having bleary eyes
LIPPY adj insolent or cheeky ▷ n lipstick
LIPREAD vb follow what someone says by watching their lips
LIPREADER >LIPREAD
LIPREADS >LIPREAD
LIPS >LIP
LIPSALVE n substance used to prevent or relieve chapped lips
LIPSALVES >LIPSALVE
LIPSTICK n cosmetic in stick form, for colouring the lips ▷ vb put lipstick on
LIPSTICKS >LIPSTICK
LIPURIA n presence of fat in the urine
LIPURIAS >LIPURIA
LIQUABLE adj that can be melted
LIQUATE vb separate one component by heating until the more fusible part melts
LIQUATED >LIQUATE
LIQUATES >LIQUATE
LIQUATING >LIQUATE
LIQUATION >LIQUATE
LIQUEFIED >LIQUEFY
LIQUEFIER >LIQUEFY
LIQUEFIES >LIQUEFY
LIQUEFY vb become liquid
LIQUESCE vb become liquid
LIQUESCED >LIQUESCE
LIQUESCES >LIQUESCE
LIQUEUR n flavoured and sweetened alcoholic spirit ▷ vb flavour with liqueur
LIQUEURED >LIQUEUR
LIQUEURS >LIQUEUR
LIQUID n substance in a physical state which can change shape but not size ▷ adj of or being a liquid
LIQUIDATE vb pay (a debt)
LIQUIDIER >LIQUIDY

LIQUIDISE same as >LIQUIDIZE
LIQUIDITY n state of being able to meet financial obligations
LIQUIDIZE vb make or become liquid
LIQUIDLY >LIQUID
LIQUIDS >LIQUID
LIQUIDUS n line on graph above which a substance is in liquid form
LIQUIDY adj having the nature of liquid
LIQUIFIED >LIQUIFY
LIQUIFIER n something that liquifies
LIQUIFIES >LIQUIFY
LIQUIFY same as >LIQUEFY
LIQUITAB n soluble plastic capsule containing liquid detergent or medicine
LIQUITABS >LIQUITAB
LIQUOR n alcoholic drink ▷ vb steep in warm water to form wort in brewing
LIQUORED >LIQUOR
LIQUORICE n black substance used in medicine and as a sweet
LIQUORING >LIQUOR
LIQUORISH same as >LICKERISH
LIQUORS >LIQUOR
LIRA n monetary unit of Turkey, Malta, and formerly of Italy
LIRAS >LIRA
LIRE >LIRA
LIRI >LIRA
LIRIOPE n grasslike plant
LIRIOPES >LIRIOPE
LIRIPIPE n tip of a graduate's hood
LIRIPIPES >LIRIPIPE
LIRIPOOP same as >LIRIPIPE
LIRIPOOPS >LIRIPOOP
LIRK vb wrinkle
LIRKED >LIRK
LIRKING >LIRK
LIRKS >LIRK
LIROT >LIRA
LIROTH >LIRA
LIS n fleur-de-lis
LISENTE >SENTE
LISK Yorkshire dialect for >GROIN
LISKS >LISK
LISLE n strong fine cotton thread or fabric
LISLES >LISLE
LISP n speech defect in which s and z are pronounced th ▷ vb speak or utter with a lisp
LISPED >LISP
LISPER >LISP
LISPERS >LISP
LISPING >LISP
LISPINGLY >LISP
LISPINGS >LISP

LISPOUND n unit of weight
LISPOUNDS >LISPOUND
LISPS >LISP
LISPUND same as >LISPOUND
LISPUNDS >LISPOUND
LISSES >LIS
LISSOM adj supple, agile
LISSOME same as >LISSOM
LISSOMELY >LISSOM
LISSOMLY >LISSOM
LIST n item-by-item record of names or things, usu written one below another ▷ vb make a list of
LISTABLE >LIST
LISTBOX n small box on a computer screen, showing a list of options
LISTBOXES >LISTBOX
LISTED >LIST
LISTEE n person on list
LISTEES >LISTEE
LISTEL another name for >FILLET
LISTELS >LISTEL
LISTEN vb concentrate on hearing something
LISTENED >LISTEN
LISTENER >LISTEN
LISTENERS >LISTEN
LISTENING >LISTEN
LISTENS >LISTEN
LISTER n plough that throws soil to the sides of a central furrow
LISTERIA n type of rodlike Gram-positive bacterium
LISTERIAL >LISTERIA
LISTERIAS >LISTERIA
LISTERS >LISTER
LISTETH >LIST
LISTFUL adj paying attention
LISTICLE n article which consists of a list
LISTICLES >LISTICLE
LISTING n list or an entry in a list
LISTINGS >LISTING
LISTLESS adj lacking interest or energy
LISTS pl n field of combat in a tournament
LISTSERV n email service for those with similar interests
LISTSERVS >LISTSERV
LIT n archaic word for dye or colouring
LITAI >LITAS
LITANIES >LITANY
LITANY n prayer with responses from the congregation
LITAS n monetary unit of Lithuania
LITCHI n Chinese tree with round edible fruits
LITCHIS >LITCHI**

LITE same as > LIGHT
LITED > LITE
LITENESS > LITE
LITER same as > LITRE
LITERACY n ability to read and write
LITERAL adj according to the explicit meaning of a word or text ▷ n misspelling in a text
LITERALLY adv in a literal manner
LITERALS > LITERAL
LITERARY adj of or knowledgeable about literature
LITERATE adj able to read and write ▷ n literate person
LITERATES > LITERATE
LITERATI pl n literary people
LITERATIM adv letter for letter
LITERATO > LITERATI
LITERATOR n professional writer
LITERATUS > LITERATI
LITEROSE adj affectedly literary
LITERS > LITER
LITES > LITE
LITEST > LITE
LITH n limb or joint
LITHARGE n lead monoxide
LITHARGES > LITHARGE
LITHATE n salt of uric acid
LITHATES > LITHATE
LITHE adj flexible or supple, pliant ▷ vb listen
LITHED > LITHE
LITHELY > LITHE
LITHEMIA n gout
LITHEMIAS > LITHEMIA
LITHEMIC > LITHEMIA
LITHENESS > LITHE
LITHER > LITHE
LITHERLY adj crafty; cunning
LITHES > LITHE
LITHESOME less common word for > LISSOM
LITHEST > LITHE
LITHIA n lithium present in mineral waters as lithium salts
LITHIAS > LITHIA
LITHIASES > LITHIASIS
LITHIASIS n formation of a calculus
LITHIC adj of stone
LITHIFIED > LITHIFY
LITHIFIES > LITHIFY
LITHIFY vb turn into rock
LITHING > LITHE
LITHISTID n type of sponge
LITHITE n part of cell with sensory element
LITHITES > LITHITE

LITHIUM n chemical element, the lightest known metal
LITHIUMS > LITHIUM
LITHO n lithography ▷ vb print using lithography
LITHOCYST n sac containing otoliths
LITHOED > LITHO
LITHOES > LITHO
LITHOID adj resembling rock
LITHOIDAL same as > LITHOID
LITHOING > LITHO
LITHOLOGY n physical characteristics of a rock
LITHOPONE n white pigment consisting of a mixture of zinc sulphide, zinc oxide, and barium sulphate
LITHOPS n fleshy-leaved plant
LITHOS > LITHO
LITHOSOL n type of azonal soil
LITHOSOLS > LITHOSOL
LITHOTOME n instrument used in lithotomy operation
LITHOTOMY n surgical removal of a calculus, esp one in the urinary bladder
LITHOTYPE n etched surface for printing a design
LITHS > LITH
LITIGABLE adj that may be the subject of litigation
LITIGANT n person involved in a lawsuit ▷ adj engaged in litigation
LITIGANTS > LITIGANT
LITIGATE vb bring or contest a law suit
LITIGATED > LITIGATE
LITIGATES > LITIGATE
LITIGATOR > LITIGATE
LITIGIOUS adj frequently going to law
LITING > LITE
LITMUS n soluble powder obtained from lichens
LITMUSES > LITMUS
LITORAL same as > LITTORAL
LITOTES n ironical understatement used for effect
LITOTIC > LITOTES
LITRE n unit of liquid measure
LITREAGE n volume in litres
LITREAGES > LITREAGE
LITRES > LITRE
LITS > LIT
LITTEN adj lighted
LITTER n untidy rubbish ▷ vb strew with litter

LITTERBAG n bag for putting rubbish in
LITTERBUG n person who tends to drop rubbish in public places
LITTERED > LITTER
LITTERER n one who litters
LITTERERS > LITTERER
LITTERIER > LITTERY
LITTERING > LITTER
LITTERS > LITTER
LITTERY adj covered in litter
LITTLE adj small ▷ adv not a lot ▷ n small amount, extent, or duration
LITTLER > LITTLE
LITTLES > LITTLE
LITTLEST > LITTLE
LITTLIE n young child
LITTLIES > LITTLIE
LITTLIN same as > LITTLING
LITTLING n child
LITTLINGS > LITTLING
LITTLINS > LITTLIN
LITTLISH adj rather small
LITTORAL adj of or by the seashore ▷ n coastal district
LITTORALS > LITTORAL
LITU > LITAS
LITURGIC > LITURGY
LITURGICS n study of liturgies
LITURGIES > LITURGY
LITURGISM > LITURGIST
LITURGIST n student or composer of liturgical forms
LITURGY n prescribed form of public worship
LITUUS n curved trumpet
LITUUSES > LITUUS
LIVABLE adj tolerable or pleasant to live (with)
LIVE vb be alive ▷ adj living, alive ▷ adv in the form of a live performance
LIVEABLE same as > LIVABLE
LIVEBLOG vb blog about (an event) as it happens
LIVEBLOGS > LIVEBLOG
LIVED > LIVE
LIVEDO n reddish discoloured patch on the skin
LIVEDOS > LIVEDO
LIVELIER > LIVELY
LIVELIEST > LIVELY
LIVELILY > LIVELY
LIVELOD n livelihood
LIVELODS > LIVELOD
LIVELONG adj long or seemingly long
LIVELONGS > LIVELONG
LIVELOOD n livelihood

LIVELOODS > LIVELOOD
LIVELY adj full of life or vigour
LIVEN vb make or become lively
LIVENED > LIVEN
LIVENER > LIVEN
LIVENERS > LIVEN
LIVENESS n state of being alive
LIVENING > LIVEN
LIVENS > LIVEN
LIVER n person who lives in a specified way
LIVERED adj having liver
LIVERIED adj wearing livery
LIVERIES > LIVERY
LIVERING n process of liquid becoming lumpy
LIVERINGS > LIVERING
LIVERISH adj having a disorder of the liver
LIVERLEAF n woodland plant
LIVERLESS > LIVER
LIVERS > LIVER
LIVERWORT n plant resembling seaweed or leafy moss
LIVERY n distinctive dress ▷ adj of or resembling liver
LIVERYMAN n member of a livery company
LIVERYMEN > LIVERYMAN
LIVES > LIFE
LIVEST > LIVE
LIVESTOCK n farm animals
LIVETRAP n box constructed to trap an animal without injuring it
LIVETRAPS > LIVETRAP
LIVEWARE n personnel working in a computer system
LIVEWARES > LIVEWARE
LIVEWELL n container of water on a fishing boat used to store live fish
LIVEWELLS > LIVEWELL
LIVEYER n (in Newfoundland) a full-time resident
LIVEYERE same as > LIVEYER
LIVEYERES > LIVEYERE
LIVEYERS > LIVEYER
LIVID adj angry or furious
LIVIDER > LIVID
LIVIDEST > LIVID
LIVIDITY n state of being livid
LIVIDLY > LIVID
LIVIDNESS > LIVID
LIVIER same as > LIVEYER
LIVIERS > LIVIER

LIVING adj possessing life, not dead or inanimate ▷ n means whereby one lives
LIVINGLY > LIVING
LIVINGS > LIVING
LIVOR another word for > LIVIDITY
LIVORS > LIVOR
LIVRAISON n one of the numbers of a book published in parts
LIVRE n former French unit of money of account
LIVRES > LIVRE
LIVYER same as > LIVEYER
LIVYERS > LIVYER
LIXIVIA > LIXIVIUM
LIXIVIAL > LIXIVIATE
LIXIVIATE less common word for > LEACH
LIXIVIOUS > LIXIVIUM
LIXIVIUM n alkaline solution obtained by leaching wood ash with water
LIXIVIUMS > LIXIVIUM
LIZARD n four-footed reptile with a long body and tail
LIZARDS > LIZARD
LIZZIE n as in tin lizzie old or decrepit car
LIZZIES > LIZZIE
LLAMA n woolly animal of the camel family
LLAMAS > LLAMA
LLANERO n native of llanos
LLANEROS > LLANERO
LLANO n extensive grassy treeless plain
LLANOS > LLANO
LO interj look!
LOACH n carplike fish
LOACHES > LOACH
LOAD n burden or weight ▷ vb put a load on or into
LOADABLE adj able to be loaded
LOADED adj containing a hidden trap
LOADEN vb load
LOADENED > LOADEN
LOADENING > LOADEN
LOADENS > LOADEN
LOADER n person who loads a gun or other firearm
LOADERS > LOADER
LOADING n load or burden
LOADINGS > LOADING
LOADS pl n lots or a lot
LOADSPACE n area in a motor vehicle where a load can be carried
LOADSTAR same as > LODESTAR
LOADSTARS > LOADSTAR
LOADSTONE same as > LODESTONE

LOAF n shaped mass of baked bread ▷ vb idle, loiter
LOAFED > LOAF
LOAFER n idler
LOAFERISH > LOAFER
LOAFERS > LOAFER
LOAFING > LOAF
LOAFINGS > LOAF
LOAFS > LOAF
LOAM n fertile soil ▷ vb cover, treat, or fill with loam
LOAMED > LOAM
LOAMIER > LOAM
LOAMIEST > LOAM
LOAMINESS > LOAM
LOAMING > LOAM
LOAMLESS > LOAM
LOAMS > LOAM
LOAMY > LOAM
LOAN n money lent at interest ▷ vb lend
LOANABLE > LOAN
LOANBACK n facility by which an individual can borrow from his or her pension fund ▷ vb make use of this facility
LOANBACKS > LOANBACK
LOANED > LOAN
LOANEE n sportsperson who is loaned out
LOANEES > LOANEE
LOANER > LOAN
LOANERS > LOAN
LOANING > LOAN
LOANINGS > LOANING
LOANS > LOAN
LOANSHIFT n adaptation of word from one language by another
LOANWORD n word adopted from one language into another
LOANWORDS > LOANWORD
LOAST > LOSE
LOATH adj unwilling or reluctant (to)
LOATHE vb hate
LOATHED > LOATHE
LOATHER > LOATHE
LOATHERS > LOATHE
LOATHES > LOATHE
LOATHEST > LOATH
LOATHFUL adj causing loathing
LOATHING n strong disgust
LOATHINGS > LOATHING
LOATHLIER > LOATHLY
LOATHLY adj loathsome
LOATHNESS > LOATH
LOATHSOME adj causing loathing
LOATHY obsolete form of > LOATHSOME
LOAVE vb form a loaf
LOAVED > LOAVE
LOAVES > LOAF
LOAVING > LOAVE
LOB n ball struck in a high arc ▷ vb strike in a high arc
LOBAR adj of or affecting a lobe

LOBATE adj with or like lobes
LOBATED same as > LOBATE
LOBATELY > LOBATE
LOBATION n division into lobes
LOBATIONS > LOBATION
LOBBED > LOB
LOBBER n one who lobs
LOBBERS > LOBBER
LOBBIED > LOBBY
LOBBIES > LOBBY
LOBBING > LOB
LOBBY n corridor into which rooms open ▷ vb try to influence (legislators) in the formulation of policy
LOBBYER > LOBBY
LOBBYERS > LOBBY
LOBBYGOW n errand boy
LOBBYGOWS > LOBBYGOW
LOBBYING > LOBBY
LOBBYINGS > LOBBY
LOBBYISM > LOBBYIST
LOBBYISMS > LOBBYIST
LOBBYIST n person who lobbies on behalf of a particular interest
LOBBYISTS > LOBBYIST
LOBE n rounded projection
LOBECTOMY n surgical removal of a lobe from any organ or gland in the body
LOBED > LOBE
LOBEFIN n type of fish
LOBEFINS > LOBEFIN
LOBELESS adj having no lobes
LOBELET n small lobe
LOBELETS > LOBELET
LOBELIA n garden plant
LOBELIAS > LOBELIA
LOBELIKE adj like a lobe
LOBELINE n crystalline alkaloid extracted from the seeds of the Indian tobacco plant
LOBELINES > LOBELINE
LOBES > LOBE
LOBI > LOBUS
LOBING n formation of lobes
LOBINGS > LOBING
LOBIPED adj with lobed toes
LOBLOLLY n southern US pine tree
LOBO n timber wolf
LOBOLA n (in African custom) price paid by a bridegroom's family to his bride's family
LOBOLAS > LOBOLA
LOBOLO same as > LOBOLA
LOBOLOS > LOBOLO
LOBOS > LOBO
LOBOSE another word for > LOBATE

LOBOTOMY n surgical incision into a lobe of the brain to treat certain disorders
LOBS > LOB
LOBSCOUSE n sailor's stew of meat, vegetables, and hardtack
LOBSTER n shellfish ▷ vb fish for lobsters
LOBSTERED > LOBSTER
LOBSTERER n person who catches lobsters
LOBSTERS > LOBSTER
LOBSTICK n tree used as landmark
LOBSTICKS > LOBSTICK
LOBTAIL vb (of a whale) hit a surface of water with the tail
LOBTAILED > LOBTAIL
LOBTAILS > LOBTAIL
LOBULAR > LOBULE
LOBULARLY > LOBULE
LOBULATE > LOBULE
LOBULATED > LOBULE
LOBULE n small lobe or a subdivision of a lobe
LOBULES > LOBULE
LOBULI > LOBULUS
LOBULOSE > LOBULE
LOBULUS n small lobe
LOBUS n lobe
LOBWORM same as > LUGWORM
LOBWORMS > LOBWORM
LOCA > LOCUS
LOCAL adj of a particular place ▷ n person from a particular place
LOCALE n scene of an event
LOCALES > LOCALE
LOCALISE same as > LOCALIZE
LOCALISED > LOCALISE
LOCALISER > LOCALISE
LOCALISES > LOCALISE
LOCALISM n pronunciation, phrase, etc, peculiar to a particular locality
LOCALISMS > LOCALISM
LOCALIST > LOCALISM
LOCALISTS > LOCALISM
LOCALITE n resident of an area
LOCALITES > LOCALITE
LOCALITY n neighbourhood or area
LOCALIZE vb restrict to a particular place
LOCALIZED > LOCALIZE
LOCALIZER > LOCALIZE
LOCALIZES > LOCALIZE
LOCALLY adv within a particular area or place
LOCALNESS > LOCAL

LOCALS > LOCAL
LOCATABLE > LOCATE
LOCATE vb discover the whereabouts of
LOCATED > LOCATE
LOCATER > LOCATE
LOCATERS > LOCATE
LOCATES > LOCATE
LOCATING > LOCATE
LOCATION n site or position
LOCATIONS > LOCATION
LOCATIVE adj (of a word or phrase) indicating place or direction ▷ n locative case
LOCATIVES > LOCATIVE
LOCATOR n part of index that shows where to find information
LOCATORS > LOCATOR
LOCAVORE n person who prefers locally produced food
LOCAVORES > LOCAVORE
LOCELLATE adj split into secondary cells
LOCH n lake
LOCHAN n small inland loch
LOCHANS > LOCHAN
LOCHE n freshwater fish of the cod family
LOCHES > LOCHE
LOCHIA n vaginal discharge following childbirth
LOCHIAL > LOCHIA
LOCHIAS > LOCHIA
LOCHS > LOCH
LOCI > LOCUS
LOCIE n type of logging engine
LOCIES > LOCIE
LOCIS > LOCUS
LOCK n appliance for fastening a door, case, etc ▷ vb fasten or become fastened securely
LOCKABLE > LOCK
LOCKAGE n system of locks in a canal
LOCKAGES > LOCKAGE
LOCKAWAY n investment intended to be held for a relatively long time
LOCKAWAYS > LOCKAWAY
LOCKBOX n system of collecting funds from companies by banks
LOCKBOXES > LOCKBOX
LOCKDOWN n device used to secure equipment, etc
LOCKDOWNS > LOCKDOWN
LOCKED > LOCK
LOCKER n small cupboard with a lock
LOCKERS > LOCKER
LOCKET n small hinged pendant for a portrait etc
LOCKETS > LOCKET
LOCKFAST adj securely fastened with a lock

LOCKFUL n sufficient to fill a canal lock
LOCKFULS > LOCKFUL
LOCKHOUSE n house of lock-keeper
LOCKING > LOCK
LOCKINGS > LOCK
LOCKJAW n tetanus
LOCKJAWS > LOCKJAW
LOCKLESS adj having no lock
LOCKMAKER n maker of locks
LOCKMAN n lock-keeper
LOCKMEN > LOCKMAN
LOCKNUT n nut screwed down on a primary nut to stop it from loosening
LOCKNUTS > LOCKNUT
LOCKOUT n closing of a workplace by an employer to force workers to accept terms
LOCKOUTS > LOCKOUT
LOCKPICK another word for > PICKLOCK
LOCKPICKS > LOCKPICK
LOCKRAM n type of linen cloth
LOCKRAMS > LOCKRAM
LOCKS > LOCK
LOCKSET n hardware used to lock door
LOCKSETS > LOCKSET
LOCKSMAN same as > LOCKMAN
LOCKSMEN > LOCKSMAN
LOCKSMITH n person who makes and mends locks
LOCKSTEP n method of marching in step as closely as possible
LOCKSTEPS > LOCKSTEP
LOCKUP n prison
LOCKUPS > LOCKUP
LOCO n locomotive ▷ vb poison with locoweed
LOCOED > LOCO
LOCOES > LOCO
LOCOFOCO n match
LOCOFOCOS > LOCOFOCO
LOCOING > LOCO
LOCOISM n disease of cattle, sheep, and horses caused by eating locoweed
LOCOISMS > LOCOISM
LOCOMAN n railwayman
LOCOMEN > LOCOMAN
LOCOMOTE vb move from one place to another
LOCOMOTED > LOCOMOTE
LOCOMOTES > LOCOMOTE
LOCOMOTOR adj of or relating to locomotion
LOCOPLANT another word for > LOCOWEED
LOCOS > LOCO
LOCOWEED n any of several perennial leguminous plants
LOCOWEEDS > LOCOWEED

LOCULAR adj divided into compartments by septa
LOCULATE same as > LOCULAR
LOCULATED same as > LOCULATE
LOCULE n any of the chambers of an ovary or anther
LOCULED adj having locules
LOCULES > LOCULE
LOCULI > LOCULUS
LOCULUS same as > LOCULE
LOCUM n temporary stand-in for a doctor, or clergyman or clergywoman
LOCUMS > LOCUM
LOCUPLETE adj well-stored
LOCUS n area or place where something happens
LOCUST n destructive insect ▷ vb ravage, as locusts
LOCUSTA n flower cluster unit in grasses
LOCUSTAE > LOCUSTA
LOCUSTAL > LOCUSTA
LOCUSTED > LOCUST
LOCUSTING > LOCUST
LOCUSTS > LOCUST
LOCUTION n manner or style of speech
LOCUTIONS > LOCUTION
LOCUTORY adj room intended for conversation
LOD n type of logarithm
LODE n vein of ore
LODEN n thick waterproof, woollen cloth
LODENS > LODEN
LODES > LODE
LODESMAN n pilot
LODESMEN > LODESMAN
LODESTAR n star used in navigation or astronomy as a point of reference
LODESTARS > LODESTAR
LODESTONE n magnetic iron ore
LODGE n gatekeeper's house ▷ vb live in another's house at a fixed charge
LODGEABLE > LODGE
LODGED > LODGE
LODGEMENT same as > LODGMENT
LODGEPOLE n type of pine tree
LODGER n tenant
LODGERS > LODGER
LODGES > LODGE
LODGING n temporary residence
LODGINGS pl n rented room or rooms in which to live, esp in another person's house
LODGMENT n act of lodging or the state of being lodged

LODGMENTS > LODGMENT
LODICULA n delicate scale in grass
LODICULAE > LODICULA
LODICULE n minute scale at the base of the ovary in grass flowers
LODICULES > LODICULE
LODS > LOD
LOERIE same as > LOURIE
LOERIES > LOERIE
LOESS n fine-grained soil
LOESSAL > LOESS
LOESSES > LOESS
LOESSIAL > LOESS
LOESSIC adj relating to or consisting of loess
LOFT n space between the top storey and roof of a building ▷ vb strike, throw, or kick (a ball) high into the air
LOFTED > LOFT
LOFTER n former type of golf club
LOFTERS > LOFTER
LOFTIER > LOFTY
LOFTIEST > LOFTY
LOFTILY > LOFTY
LOFTINESS > LOFTY
LOFTING > LOFT
LOFTLESS > LOFT
LOFTLIKE > LOFT
LOFTS > LOFT
LOFTSMAN n person who reproduces in actual size a draughtsman's design for a ship or an aircraft
LOFTSMEN > LOFTSMAN
LOFTY adj of great height
LOG n portion of a felled tree stripped of branches ▷ vb saw logs from a tree
LOGAN another name for > BOGAN
LOGANIA n type of Australian plant
LOGANIAS > LOGANIA
LOGANS > LOGAN
LOGAOEDIC adj of or relating to verse in which mixed metres are combined within a single line to give the effect of prose ▷ n line or verse of this kind
LOGARITHM n one of a series of arithmetical functions used to make certain calculations easier
LOGBOARD n board used for logging a ship's records
LOGBOARDS > LOGBOARD
LOGBOOK n book recording the details about a car or a ship's journeys
LOGBOOKS > LOGBOOK
LOGE n small enclosure or box in a theatre or opera house
LOGES > LOGE

LOGGAT n small piece of wood

LOGGATS > LOGGAT

LOGGED > LOG

LOGGER n tractor or crane for handling logs

LOGGERS > LOGGER

LOGGETS n old-fashioned game played with sticks

LOGGIA n covered gallery at the side of a building

LOGGIAS > LOGGIA

LOGGIE > LOGGIA

LOGGIER > LOGGY

LOGGIEST > LOGGY

LOGGING > LOG

LOGGINGS > LOG

LOGGISH > LOG

LOGGY adj sluggish

LOGIA > LOGION

LOGIC n philosophy of reasoning

LOGICAL adj of logic

LOGICALLY > LOGICAL

LOGICIAN n person who specializes in or is skilled at logic

LOGICIANS > LOGICIAN

LOGICISE same as > LOGICIZE

LOGICISED > LOGICISE

LOGICISES > LOGICISE

LOGICISM n philosophical theory that all of mathematics can be deduced from logic

LOGICISMS > LOGICISM

LOGICIST > LOGICISM

LOGICISTS > LOGICISM

LOGICIZE vb present reasons for or against

LOGICIZED > LOGICIZE

LOGICIZES > LOGICIZE

LOGICLESS > LOGIC

LOGICS > LOGIC

LOGIE n fireplace of a kiln

LOGIER > LOGY

LOGIES > LOGIE

LOGIEST > LOGY

LOGILY > LOGY

LOGIN n process by which a computer user logs on

LOGINESS > LOGY

LOGINS > LOGIN

LOGION n saying of Christ regarded as authentic

LOGIONS > LOGION

LOGISTIC n uninterpreted calculus or system of symbolic logic ▷ adj (of a curve) having a particular form of equation

LOGISTICS n detailed planning and organization of a large, esp military, operation

LOGJAM n blockage of logs in a river ▷ vb cause a logjam

LOGJAMMED > LOGJAM

LOGJAMS > LOGJAM

LOGJUICE n poor quality port wine

LOGJUICES > LOGJUICE

LOGLINE n synopsis of screenplay

LOGLINES > LOGLINE

LOGLOG n logarithm of a logarithm (in equations, etc)

LOGLOGS > LOGLOG

LOGNORMAL adj (maths) having a logarithm with normal distribution

LOGO same as > LOGOTYPE

LOGOED adj having a logo

LOGOFF n process by which a computer user logs out

LOGOFFS > LOGOFF

LOGOGRAM n single symbol representing an entire morpheme, word, or phrase

LOGOGRAMS > LOGOGRAM

LOGOGRAPH same as > LOGOGRAM

LOGOGRIPH n word puzzle, esp one based on recombination of the letters of a word

LOGOI > LOGOS

LOGOMACH n one who argues over words

LOGOMACHS > LOGOMACH

LOGOMACHY n argument about words or the meaning of words

LOGON variant of > LOGIN

LOGONS > LOGON

LOGOPEDIC adj of or relating to speech therapy

LOGOPHILE n one who loves words

LOGORRHEA n excessive or uncontrollable talkativeness

LOGOS n reason expressed in words and things, argument, or justification

LOGOTHETE n officer of Byzantine empire

LOGOTYPE n piece of type with several uncombined characters cast on it

LOGOTYPES > LOGOTYPE

LOGOTYPY > LOGOTYPE

LOGOUT variant of > LOGOFF

LOGOUTS > LOGOUT

LOGROLL vb procure the passage of (legislation) by trading votes

LOGROLLED > LOGROLL

LOGROLLER > LOGROLL

LOGROLLS > LOGROLL

LOGS > LOG

LOGWAY another name for > GANGWAY

LOGWAYS > LOGWAY

LOGWOOD n tree of the Caribbean and Central America

LOGWOODS > LOGWOOD

LOGY adj dull or listless

LOHAN another word for > ARHAT

LOHANS > LOHAN

LOIASES > LOIASIS

LOIASIS n disease caused by a tropical eye worm

LOIASISES > LOIASIS

LOID vb open (a lock) using a celluloid strip

LOIDED > LOID

LOIDING > LOID

LOIDS > LOID

LOIN n part of the body between the ribs and the hips

LOINCLOTH n piece of cloth covering the loins only

LOINS pl n hips and the inner surface of the legs

LOIPE n cross-country skiing track

LOIPEN > LOIPE

LOIR n large dormouse

LOIRS > LOIR

LOITER vb stand or wait aimlessly or idly

LOITERED > LOITER

LOITERER > LOITER

LOITERERS > LOITER

LOITERING > LOITER

LOITERS > LOITER

LOKE n track

LOKES > LOKE

LOKSHEN pl n noodles

LOLIGO n type of squid

LOLIGOS > LOLIGO

LOLIUM n type of grass

LOLIUMS > LOLIUM

LOLL vb lounge lazily ▷ n act or instance of lolling

LOLLED > LOLL

LOLLER > LOLL

LOLLERS > LOLL

LOLLIES > LOLLY

LOLLING > LOLL

LOLLINGLY > LOLL

LOLLIPOP n boiled sweet on a small wooden stick

LOLLIPOPS > LOLLIPOP

LOLLOP vb move clumsily

LOLLOPED > LOLLOP

LOLLOPIER > LOLLOPY

LOLLOPING > LOLLOP

LOLLOPS > LOLLOP

LOLLOPY adj moving with a lollop

LOLLS > LOLL

LOLLY n lollipop or ice lolly

LOLLYGAG same as > LALLYGAG

LOLLYGAGS > LALLYGAG

LOLLYPOP same as > LOLLIPOP

LOLLYPOPS > LOLLYPOP

LOLOG same as > LOGLOG

LOLOGS > LOLOG

LOLZ same as > LULZ

LOMA n lobe

LOMAS > LOMA

LOMATA > LOMA

LOME n fertile soil ▷ vb cover with lome

LOMED > LOME

LOMEIN n Chinese dish

LOMEINS > LOMEIN

LOMENT n pod of certain leguminous plants

LOMENTA > LOMENTUM

LOMENTS > LOMENT

LOMENTUM same as > LOMENT

LOMENTUMS > LOMENTUM

LOMES > LOME

LOMING > LOME

LOMPISH another word for > LUMPISH

LONE adj solitary

LONELIER > LONELY

LONELIEST > LONELY

LONELILY > LONELY

LONELY adj sad because alone

LONENESS > LONE

LONER n solitary person

LONERS > LONER

LONESOME adj lonely ▷ n own

LONESOMES > LONESOME

LONG adj having length ▷ adv for a certain time ▷ vb have a strong desire (for)

LONGA n long note

LONGAEVAL adj long-lived

LONGAN n sapindaceous tree of tropical and subtropical Asia

LONGANS > LONGAN

LONGAS > LONGA

LONGBOARD n type of surfboard

LONGBOAT n largest boat carried on a ship

LONGBOATS > LONGBOAT

LONGBOW n large powerful bow

LONGBOWS > LONGBOW

LONGCASE n as in longcase clock grandfather clock

LONGCLOTH n fine plain-weave cotton cloth made in long strips

LONGE n rope used in training a horse ▷ vb train using a longe

LONGED > LONG

LONGEING > LONGE

LONGER n line of barrels on a ship

LONGERON n main longitudinal structural member of an aircraft

LONGERONS > LONGERON

LONGERS > LONGER

LONGES > LONGE

LONGEST > LONG

LONGEVAL another word for > LONGAEVAL

LONGEVITY n long life

LONGEVOUS > LONGEVITY

LONGFORM adj (of a text) long in form

LONGHAIR n cat with long hair

LONGHAIRS > LONGHAIR

LONGHAND n ordinary writing, not shorthand or typing

LONGHANDS > LONGHAND

LONGHEAD n person with long head

LONGHEADS > LONGHEAD

LONGHORN n British breed of beef cattle with long curved horns

LONGHORNS > LONGHORN

LONGHOUSE n long communal dwelling of Native American peoples

LONGICORN n type of beetle with long antennae

LONGIES n long johns

LONGING n yearning ▷ adj having or showing desire

LONGINGLY > LONGING

LONGINGS > LONGING

LONGISH adj rather long

LONGITUDE n distance east or west from a standard meridian

LONGJUMP n jumping contest decided by length

LONGJUMPS > LONGJUMP

LONGLEAF n North American pine tree

LONGLINE n (tennis) straight stroke played down court

LONGLINER n person who fishes with a longline

LONGLINES > LONGLINE

LONGLIST n initial list from which a shortlist is selected ▷ vb include (eg a candidate) on a longlist

LONGLISTS > LONGLIST

LONGLY > LONG

LONGNECK n US, Canadian and Australian word for a 330-ml beer bottle with a long narrow neck

LONGNECKS > LONGNECK

LONGNESS > LONG

LONGS pl n full-length trousers

LONGSHIP n narrow open boat with oars and a square sail, used by the Vikings

LONGSHIPS > LONGSHIP

LONGSHORE adj situated on, relating to, or along the shore

LONGSOME adj slow; boring

LONGSPUR n any of various Arctic and North American buntings

LONGSPURS > LONGSPUR

LONGTIME adj of long standing

LONGUEUR n period of boredom or dullness

LONGUEURS > LONGUEUR

LONGWALL n long face in coal mine

LONGWALLS > LONGWALL

LONGWAYS adv lengthways

LONGWISE same as > LONGWAYS

LONGWORM n as in sea longworm kind of marine worm

LONGWORMS > LONGWORM

LONICERA n honeysuckle

LONICERAS > LONICERA

LOO n toilet ▷ vb Scots word meaning love

LOOBIER > LOOBY

LOOBIES > LOOBY

LOOBIEST > LOOBY

LOOBILY > LOOBY

LOOBY adj foolish ▷ n foolish or stupid person

LOOED > LOO

LOOEY n lieutenant

LOOEYS > LOOEY

LOOF n part of ship's side

LOOFA same as > LOOFAH

LOOFAH n sponge made from the dried pod of a gourd

LOOFAHS > LOOFAH

LOOFAS > LOOFA

LOOFFUL n handful

LOOFFULS > LOOFFUL

LOOFS > LOOF

LOOGIE n lump of spit and phlegm

LOOGIES > LOOGIE

LOOIE same as > LOOEY

LOOIES > LOOIE

LOOING > LOO

LOOK vb direct the eyes or attention (towards) ▷ n instance of looking

LOOKALIKE n person who is the double of another

LOOKDOWN n way paper appears when looked at under reflected light

LOOKDOWNS > LOOKDOWN

LOOKED > LOOK

LOOKER n person who looks

LOOKERS > LOOKER

LOOKIE interj look (over here)

LOOKING > LOOK

LOOKISM n discrimination because of appearance

LOOKISMS > LOOKISM

LOOKIST > LOOKISM

LOOKISTS > LOOKISM

LOOKIT interj look at this

LOOKOUT n act of watching for danger or for an opportunity ▷ vb be careful

LOOKOUTS > LOOKOUT

LOOKOVER n inspection, esp a brief one

LOOKOVERS > LOOKOVER

LOOKS > LOOK

LOOKSISM same as > LOOKISM

LOOKSISMS > LOOKSISM

LOOKUP n act of looking up information

LOOKUPS > LOOKUP

LOOKY same as > LOOKIE

LOOM n machine for weaving cloth ▷ vb appear dimly

LOOMED > LOOM

LOOMING > LOOM

LOOMS > LOOM

LOON n diving bird

LOONEY same as > LOONY

LOONEYS > LOONEY

LOONIE n Canadian dollar coin

LOONIER > LOONY

LOONIES > LOONY

LOONIEST > LOONY

LOONILY > LOONY

LOONINESS > LOONY

LOONING n cry of the loon

LOONINGS > LOONING

LOONS > LOON

LOONY adj very foolish ▷ n very foolish person

LOOP n round shape made by a curved line ▷ vb form with a loop

LOOPED > LOOP

LOOPER n person or thing that loops or makes loops

LOOPERS > LOOPER

LOOPHOLE n means of evading a rule without breaking it ▷ vb provide with loopholes

LOOPHOLED > LOOPHOLE

LOOPHOLES > LOOPHOLE

LOOPIER > LOOPY

LOOPIEST > LOOPY

LOOPILY > LOOPY

LOOPINESS > LOOPY

LOOPING > LOOP

LOOPINGS > LOOP

LOOPLIKE adj like a loop

LOOPS > LOOP

LOOPY adj curly or twisted

LOOR a Scots form of > LIEF

LOORD obsolete word for > LOUT

LOORDS > LOORD

LOOS > LOO

LOOSE adj not tight, fastened, fixed, or tense ▷ adv in a loose manner ▷ vb free

LOOSEBOX n enclosed stall with a door in which an animal can be kept

LOOSED > LOOSE

LOOSELY > LOOSE

LOOSEN vb make loose

LOOSENED > LOOSEN

LOOSENER > LOOSEN

LOOSENERS > LOOSEN

LOOSENESS > LOOSE

LOOSENING n act of loosening

LOOSENS > LOOSEN

LOOSER > LOOSE

LOOSES > LOOSE

LOOSEST > LOOSE

LOOSIE n informal word for loose forward

LOOSIES pl n cigarettes sold individually

LOOSING n celebration of one's 21st birthday

LOOSINGS > LOOSING

LOOT vb pillage ▷ n goods stolen during pillaging

LOOTED > LOOT

LOOTEN Scots past form of > LET

LOOTER > LOOT

LOOTERS > LOOT

LOOTING > LOOT

LOOTINGS > LOOT

LOOTS > LOOT

LOOVES > LOOF

LOP vb cut away ▷ n part(s) lopped off

LOPE vb run with long easy strides ▷ n loping stride

LOPED > LOPE

LOPER > LOPE

LOPERS > LOPE

LOPES > LOPE

LOPGRASS n smooth-bladed grass

LOPHODONT adj (of teeth) having elongated ridges

LOPING > LOPE

LOPINGLY adv in a loping manner

LOPOLITH n saucer- or lens-shaped body of intrusive igneous rock

LOPOLITHS > LOPOLITH

LOPPED > LOP

LOPPER n tool for lopping ▷ vb curdle

LOPPERED > LOPPER

LOPPERING > LOPPER

LOPPERS > LOPPER

LOPPET n long-distance cross-country ski race

LOPPETS > LOPPET

LOPPIER > LOPPY

LOPPIES > LOPPY

LOPPIEST > LOPPY

LOPPING > LOP

LOPPINGS > LOP

LOPPY adj floppy ▷ n ranch hand

LOPS > LOP

LOPSIDED adj greater in height, weight, or size on one side

LOPSTICK variant of > LOBSTICK

LOPSTICKS > LOPSTICK

LOQUACITY n tendency to talk a great deal

LOQUAT n ornamental evergreen rosaceous tree

LOQUATS > LOQUAT

LOQUITUR n stage direction meaning he or she speaks

LOR interj exclamation of surprise or dismay

LORAL adj of part of side of bird's head

LORAN n radio navigation system operating over long distances

LORANS > LORAN

LORATE adj like a strap

LORAZEPAM n type of tranquillizer

LORCHA n junk-rigged vessel

LORCHAS > LORCHA

LORD n person with power over others ▷ vb act in a superior way

LORDED > LORD

LORDING n gentleman

LORDINGS > LORDING

LORDKIN n little lord

LORDKINS > LORDKIN

LORDLESS > LORD

LORDLIER > LORDLY

LORDLIEST > LORDLY

LORDLIKE > LORD

LORDLING n young lord

LORDLINGS > LORDLING

LORDLY adj imperious, proud ▷ adv in the manner of a lord

LORDOMA same as > LORDOSIS

LORDOMAS > LORDOMA

LORDOSES > LORDOSIS

LORDOSIS n forward curvature of the lumbar spine

LORDOTIC > LORDOSIS

LORDS > LORD

LORDSHIP n position or authority of a lord

LORDSHIPS > LORDSHIP

LORDY interj exclamation of surprise or dismay

LORE n body of traditions

LOREAL adj concerning or relating to lore

LOREL another word for > LOSEL

LORELS > LOREL

LORES > LORE

LORETTE n concubine

LORETTES > LORETTE

LORGNETTE n pair of spectacles mounted on a long handle

LORGNON n monocle or pair of spectacles

LORGNONS > LORGNON

LORIC same as > LORICA

LORICA n hard outer covering of rotifers, ciliate protozoans, and similar organisms

LORICAE > LORICA

LORICAS > LORICA

LORICATE > LORICA

LORICATED > LORICA

LORICATES > LORICA

LORICS > LORIC

LORIES > LORY

LORIKEET n small brightly coloured Australian parrot

LORIKEETS > LORIKEET

LORIMER n (formerly) a person who made bits and spurs

LORIMERS > LORIMER

LORINER same as > LORIMER

LORINERS > LORINER

LORING n teaching

LORINGS > LORING

LORIOT n golden oriole (bird)

LORIOTS > LORIOT

LORIS n any of several prosimian primates

LORISES > LORIS

LORN adj forsaken or wretched

LORNER > LORN

LORNEST > LORN

LORNNESS > LORN

LORRELL obsolete word for > LOSEL

LORRELLS > LORRELL

LORRIES > LORRY

LORRY n large vehicle for transporting loads by road

LORY n small parrot of Australia and Indonesia

LOS n approval

LOSABLE > LOSE

LOSE vb part with

LOSED > LOSE

LOSEL n worthless person ▷ adj worthless

LOSELS > LOSEL

LOSEN same as > LOSE

LOSER n person or thing that loses

LOSERS > LOSER

LOSES > LOSE

LOSH interj lord

LOSING adj unprofitable; failing

LOSINGEST > LOSING

LOSINGLY > LOSE

LOSINGS pl n losses

LOSLYF n South African slang for a woman considered promiscuous

LOSLYFS > LOSLYF

LOSS n losing

LOSSES > LOSS

LOSSIER > LOSSY

LOSSIEST > LOSSY

LOSSLESS > LOSS

LOSSMAKER n organization, industry, or enterprise that consistently fails to make a profit

LOSSY adj designed to have a high attenuation

LOST adj missing

LOSTNESS > LOST

LOT pron great number ▷ n collection of people or things ▷ vb draw lots for

LOTA n globular water container

LOTAH same as > LOTA

LOTAHS > LOTAH

LOTAS > LOTA

LOTE another word for > LOTUS

LOTES > LOTE

LOTH same as > LOATH

LOTHARIO n rake, libertine, or seducer

LOTHARIOS > LOTHARIO

LOTHEFULL obsolete form of > LOATHFUL

LOTHER > LOTH

LOTHEST > LOTH

LOTHFULL obsolete form of > LOATHFUL

LOTHNESS > LOTH

LOTHSOME same as > LOATHSOME

LOTI n monetary unit of Lesotho

LOTIC adj of communities living in rapidly flowing water

LOTION n medical or cosmetic liquid for use on the skin

LOTIONS > LOTION

LOTO same as > LOTTO

LOTOS same as > LOTUS

LOTOSES > LOTOS

LOTS > LOT

LOTSA determiner lots of

LOTTA determiner lot of

LOTTE n type of fish

LOTTED > LOT

LOTTER n someone who works an allotment

LOTTERIES > LOTTERY

LOTTERS > LOTTER

LOTTERY n method of raising money by selling tickets that win prizes by chance

LOTTES > LOTTE

LOTTING > LOT

LOTTO n game of chance

LOTTOS > LOTTO

LOTUS n legendary plant whose fruit induces forgetfulness

LOTUSES > LOTUS

LOTUSLAND n idyllic place of contentment

LOU Scot word for > LOVE

LOUCHE adj shifty

LOUCHELY > LOUCHE

LOUCHER > LOUCHE

LOUCHEST > LOUCHE

LOUD adj noisy

LOUDEN vb make louder

LOUDENED > LOUDEN

LOUDENING > LOUDEN

LOUDENS > LOUDEN

LOUDER > LOUD

LOUDEST > LOUD

LOUDISH adj fairly loud

LOUDLIER > LOUD

LOUDLIEST > LOUD

LOUDLY > LOUD

LOUDMOUTH n person who talks too much, esp in a boastful or indiscreet way

LOUDNESS > LOUD

LOUED > LOU

LOUGH n loch

LOUGHS > LOUGH

LOUIE same as > LOOEY

LOUIES > LOUIE

LOUING > LOU

LOUIS n former French gold coin

LOUMA n market in developing countries

LOUMAS > LOUMA

LOUN same as > LOWN

LOUND same as > LOUN

LOUNDED > LOUND

LOUNDER vb beat severely

LOUNDERED > LOUNDER

LOUNDERS > LOUNDER

LOUNDING > LOUND

LOUNDS > LOUND

LOUNED > LOUN

LOUNGE n living room in a private house ▷ vb sit, lie, or stand in a relaxed manner

LOUNGED > LOUNGE

LOUNGER n extending chair

LOUNGERS > LOUNGER

LOUNGES > LOUNGE

LOUNGEY adj suggestive of a lounge bar or easy-listening music

LOUNGIER > LOUNGEY

LOUNGIEST > LOUNGEY

LOUNGING > LOUNGE

LOUNGINGS > LOUNGE

LOUNGY adj casual; relaxed

LOUNING > LOUN

LOUNS > LOUN

LOUP Scot word for > LEAP

LOUPE n magnifying glass used by jewellers, horologists, etc

LOUPED > LOUP

LOUPEN > LOUP

LOUPES > LOUPE

LOUPING > LOUP

LOUPIT > LOUP

LOUPS > LOUP

LOUR vb be overcast ▷ n menacing scowl

LOURE n slow, former French dance

LOURED > LOUR

LOURES > LOURE

LOURIE n type of African bird

LOURIER > LOURY

LOURIES > LOURIE

LOURIEST > LOURY

LOURING > LOUR

LOURINGLY > LOUR

LOURINGS > LOUR

LOURS > LOUR

LOURY adj sombre

LOUS > LOU

LOUSE n wingless parasitic insect ▷ vb ruin or spoil

LOUSED > LOUSE

LOUSER n mean nasty person

LOUSERS > LOUSER

LOUSES > LOUSE

LOUSEWORT n any of various N temperate scrophulariaceous plants

LOUSIER > LOUSY

LOUSIEST > LOUSY

LOUSILY > LOUSY

LOUSINESS > LOUSY

LOUSING n act or instance of removing lice

LOUSINGS > LOUSING

LOUSY adj mean or unpleasant

LOUT n crude person ▷ vb bow or stoop
LOUTED > LOUT
LOUTERIES > LOUTERY
LOUTERY n crude or boorish behaviour
LOUTING > LOUT
LOUTISH adj of a lout
LOUTISHLY > LOUTISH
LOUTS > LOUT
LOUVAR n large silvery whalelike scombroid fish
LOUVARS > LOUVAR
LOUVER same as > LOUVRE
LOUVERED same as > LOUVRED
LOUVERS > LOUVER
LOUVRE n one of a set of parallel slats slanted to admit air but not rain
LOUVRED adj having louvres
LOUVRES > LOUVRE
LOVABLE adj attracting or deserving affection
LOVABLY > LOVABLE
LOVAGE n European plant used for flavouring food
LOVAGES > LOVAGE
LOVAT n yellowish-or bluish-green mixture in tweeds
LOVATS > LOVAT
LOVE vb have a great affection for ▷ n great affection
LOVEABLE same as > LOVABLE
LOVEABLY > LOVABLE
LOVEBIRD n small parrot
LOVEBIRDS > LOVEBIRD
LOVEBITE n temporary red mark left on a person's skin by someone biting or sucking it
LOVEBITES > LOVEBITE
LOVEBUG n small US flying insect
LOVEBUGS > LOVEBUG
LOVED > LOVE
LOVEFEST n event when people talk about loving one another
LOVEFESTS > LOVEFEST
LOVELESS adj without love
LOVELIER > LOVELY
LOVELIES > LOVELY
LOVELIEST > LOVELY
LOVELIGHT n brightness of eyes of one in love
LOVELILY > LOVELY
LOVELOCK n long lock of hair worn on the forehead
LOVELOCKS > LOVELOCK
LOVELORN adj miserable because of unhappiness in love
LOVELY adj very attractive ▷ n attractive woman
LOVEMAKER n one involved in lovemaking

LOVER n person who loves something or someone
LOVERED adj having a lover
LOVERLESS > LOVER
LOVERLY adj like a lover
LOVERS > LOVER
LOVES > LOVE
LOVESEAT n armchair for two people
LOVESEATS > LOVESEAT
LOVESICK adj pining or languishing because of love
LOVESOME adj full of love
LOVEVINE n leafless parasitic vine
LOVEVINES > LOVEVINE
LOVEY adj loving; affectionate ▷ n affectionate person
LOVEYS > LOVEY
LOVIE n beloved person
LOVIER > LOVEY
LOVIES > LOVIE
LOVIEST > LOVEY
LOVING adj affectionate, tender ▷ n state of being in love
LOVINGLY > LOVING
LOVINGS > LOVING
LOW adj not high ▷ adv in a low position ▷ n low position ▷ vb moo
LOWAN n type of Australian bird
LOWANS > LOWAN
LOWBALL vb deliberately under-charge
LOWBALLED > LOWBALL
LOWBALLS > LOWBALL
LOWBORN adj of ignoble or common parentage
LOWBOY n table fitted with drawers
LOWBOYS > LOWBOY
LOWBRED same as > LOWBORN
LOWBROW adj with nonintellectual tastes and interests ▷ n person with nonintellectual tastes
LOWBROWED > LOWBROW
LOWBROWS > LOWBROW
LOWBUSH n type of blueberry bush
LOWBUSHES > LOWBUSH
LOWDOWN n inside info
LOWDOWNS > LOWDOWN
LOWE variant of > LOW
LOWED > LOW
LOWER adj below one or more others ▷ vb cause or allow to move down
LOWERABLE > LOWER
LOWERCASE n small letters ▷ adj non-capitalized
LOWERED > LOWER
LOWERIER > LOWERY
LOWERIEST > LOWERY
LOWERING > LOWER
LOWERINGS > LOWER
LOWERMOST adj lowest
LOWERS > LOWER

LOWERY adj sombre
LOWES > LOWE
LOWEST > LOW
LOWING > LOW
LOWINGS > LOW
LOWISH > LOW
LOWLAND n low-lying country ▷ adj of a lowland or lowlands
LOWLANDER > LOWLAND
LOWLANDS > LOWLAND
LOWLIER > LOWLY
LOWLIEST > LOWLY
LOWLIFE n member or members of the underworld
LOWLIFER > LOWLIFE
LOWLIFERS > LOWLIFE
LOWLIFES > LOWLIFE
LOWLIGHT n unenjoyable or unpleasant part of an event
LOWLIGHTS > LOWLIGHT
LOWLIHEAD n state of being humble
LOWLILY > LOWLY
LOWLINESS > LOWLY
LOWLIVES > LOWLIFE
LOWLY adj modest, humble ▷ adv in a low or lowly manner
LOWN vb calm
LOWND same as > LOWN
LOWNDED > LOWND
LOWNDING > LOWND
LOWNDS > LOWND
LOWNE same as > LOON
LOWNED > LOWN
LOWNES > LOWNE
LOWNESS > LOW
LOWNESSES > LOW
LOWNING > LOWN
LOWNS > LOWN
LOWP same as > LOUP
LOWPASS adj (of a filter) transmitting frequencies below a certain value
LOWPED > LOWP
LOWPING > LOWP
LOWPS > LOWP
LOWRIDER n car with body close to ground
LOWRIDERS > LOWRIDER
LOWRIE another name for > LORY
LOWRIES > LOWRY
LOWRY another name for > LORY
LOWS > LOW
LOWSE vb release or loose ▷ adj loose
LOWSED > LOWSE
LOWSENING same as > LOOSING
LOWSER > LOWSE
LOWSES > LOWSE
LOWSEST > LOWSE
LOWSING > LOWSE
LOWSIT > LOWSE
LOWT same as > LOUT
LOWTED > LOWT
LOWTING > LOWT
LOWTS > LOWT
LOWVELD n low ground in S Africa

LOWVELDS > LOWVELD
LOX vb load fuel tanks of spacecraft with liquid oxygen ▷ n kind of smoked salmon
LOXED > LOX
LOXES > LOX
LOXING > LOX
LOXODROME n line on globe crossing all meridians at same angle
LOXODROMY n technique of navigating using rhumb lines
LOXYGEN n liquid oxygen
LOXYGENS > LOXYGEN
LOY n narrow spade with a single footrest
LOYAL adj faithful
LOYALER > LOYAL
LOYALEST > LOYAL
LOYALISM n LOYALIST
LOYALISMS > LOYALIST
LOYALIST n patriotic supporter of the sovereign or government
LOYALISTS > LOYALIST
LOYALLER > LOYAL
LOYALLEST > LOYAL
LOYALLY > LOYAL
LOYALNESS > LOYAL
LOYALTIES > LOYALTY
LOYALTY n quality of being loyal
LOYS > LOY
LOZELL obsolete form of > LOSEL
LOZELLS > LOZELL
LOZEN n window pane
LOZENGE n medicated tablet
LOZENGED adj decorated with lozenges
LOZENGES > LOZENGE
LOZENGIER > LOZENGY
LOZENGY adj divided by diagonal lines to form a lattice
LOZENS > LOZEN
LUACH n Jewish calendar
LUAU n feast of Hawaiian food
LUAUS > LUAU
LUBBARD same as > LUBBER
LUBBARDS > LUBBARD
LUBBER n big, awkward, or stupid person
LUBBERLY adj big and awkward
LUBBERS > LUBBER
LUBE n lubricating oil ▷ vb lubricate with oil
LUBED > LUBE
LUBES > LUBE
LUBFISH n type of fish
LUBFISHES > LUBFISH
LUBING > LUBE
LUBRIC adj slippery
LUBRICAL same as > LUBRIC
LUBRICANT n lubricating substance, such as oil ▷ adj serving to lubricate
LUBRICATE vb oil or grease to lessen friction

LUBRICITY n smoothness or slipperiness
LUBRICOUS adj slippery
LUCARNE n type of dormer window
LUCARNES > LUCARNE
LUCE another name for > PIKE
LUCENCE > LUCENT
LUCENCES > LUCENT
LUCENCIES > LUCENT
LUCENCY > LUCENT
LUCENT adj brilliant
LUCENTLY > LUCENT
LUCERN same as > LUCERNE
LUCERNE n alfalfa
LUCERNES > LUCERNE
LUCERNS > LUCERN
LUCES > LUCE
LUCHOT > LUACH
LUCHOTH > LUACH
LUCID adj clear
LUCIDER > LUCID
LUCIDEST > LUCID
LUCIDITY > LUCID
LUCIDLY > LUCID
LUCIDNESS > LUCID
LUCIFER n friction match
LUCIFERIN n substance occurring in bioluminescent organisms, such as glow-worms and fireflies
LUCIFERS > LUCIFER
LUCIGEN n type of lamp
LUCIGENS > LUCIGEN
LUCITE n type of transparent acrylic-based plastic
LUCITES > LUCITE
LUCK n fortune, good or bad ▷ vb have good fortune
LUCKED > LUCK
LUCKEN adj shut
LUCKIE same as > LUCKY
LUCKIER > LUCKY
LUCKIES > LUCKY
LUCKIEST > LUCKY
LUCKILY > LUCKY
LUCKINESS > LUCKY
LUCKING > LUCK
LUCKLESS adj having bad luck
LUCKPENNY n coin kept for luck
LUCKS > LUCK
LUCKY adj having or bringing good luck ▷ n old woman
LUCRATIVE adj very profitable
LUCRE n money or wealth
LUCRES > LUCRE
LUCTATION n effort; struggle
LUCUBRATE vb write or study, esp at night
LUCULENT adj easily understood
LUCUMA n S American tree
LUCUMAS > LUCUMA
LUCUMO n Etruscan king
LUCUMONES > LUCUMO

LUCUMOS > LUCUMO
LUD n lord ▷ interj exclamation of dismay or surprise
LUDE n slang word for drug for relieving anxiety
LUDERICK n Australian fish, usu black or dark brown in colour
LUDERICKS > LUDERICK
LUDES > LUDE
LUDIC adj playful
LUDICALLY > LUDIC
LUDICROUS adj absurd or ridiculous
LUDO n game played with dice and counters on a board
LUDOS > LUDO
LUDS > LUD
LUDSHIP > LUD
LUDSHIPS > LUD
LUES n pestilence
LUETIC > LUES
LUETICS > LUES
LUFF vb sail (a ship) towards the wind ▷ n leading edge of a fore-and-aft sail
LUFFA same as > LOOFAH
LUFFAS > LUFFA
LUFFED > LUFF
LUFFING > LUFF
LUFFS > LUFF
LUG vb carry with great effort ▷ n projection serving as a handle
LUGE n racing toboggan ▷ vb ride on a luge
LUGED > LUGE
LUGEING > LUGE
LUGEINGS > LUGE
LUGER n pistol
LUGERS > LUGER
LUGES > LUGE
LUGGABLE n unwieldy portable computer
LUGGABLES > LUGGABLE
LUGGAGE n suitcases, bags, etc
LUGGAGES > LUGGAGE
LUGGED > LUG
LUGGER n small working boat with an oblong sail
LUGGERS > LUGGER
LUGGIE n wooden bowl
LUGGIES > LUGGIE
LUGGING > LUG
LUGHOLE informal word for > EAR
LUGHOLES > LUGHOLE
LUGING > LUGE
LUGINGS > LUGE
LUGS > LUG
LUGSAIL n four-sided sail
LUGSAILS > LUGSAIL
LUGWORM n large worm used as bait
LUGWORMS > LUGWORM
LUIT Scots past form of > LET
LUITEN same as > LUIT
LUKE variant of > LUKEWARM
LUKEWARM adj moderately warm, tepid

LULIBUB obsolete form of > LOLLIPOP
LULIBUBS > LULIBUB
LULL vb soothe (someone) by soft sounds or motions ▷ n brief time of quiet in a storm etc
LULLABIED > LULLABY
LULLABIES > LULLABY
LULLABY n quiet song ▷ vb quiet with a lullaby
LULLED > LULL
LULLER > LULL
LULLERS > LULL
LULLING > LULL
LULLINGLY adv in a lulling manner
LULLS > LULL
LULU n person or thing deemed to be outstanding
LULUS > LULU
LULZ pl n laughs at someone else's or one's own expense
LUM n chimney
LUMA n monetary unit of Armenia
LUMAS > LUMA
LUMBAGO n pain in the lower back
LUMBAGOS > LUMBAGO
LUMBANG n type of tree
LUMBANGS > LUMBANG
LUMBAR adj of the part of the body between the lowest ribs and the hipbones ▷ n old-fashioned kind of ship
LUMBARS > LUMBAR
LUMBER n unwanted disused household articles ▷ vb burden with something unpleasant
LUMBERED > LUMBER
LUMBERER > LUMBER
LUMBERERS > LUMBER
LUMBERING n business or trade of cutting, transporting, preparing, or selling timber ▷ adj awkward in movement
LUMBERLY adj heavy; clumsy
LUMBERMAN n person whose work involves felling trees
LUMBERMEN > LUMBERMAN
LUMBERS > LUMBER
LUMBI > LUMBUS
LUMBRICAL adj relating to any of the four wormlike muscles in the hand or foot
LUMBRICI > LUMBRICUS
LUMBRICUS n type of worm
LUMBUS n part of the lower back and sides between the pelvis and the ribs
LUMEN n derived SI unit of luminous flux
LUMENAL > LUMEN
LUMENS > LUMEN
LUMINA > LUMEN

LUMINAIRE n light fixture
LUMINAL > LUMEN
LUMINANCE n state or quality of radiating or reflecting light
LUMINANT n something used to give light
LUMINANTS > LUMINANT
LUMINARIA n type of candle
LUMINARY n famous person ▷ adj of, involving, or characterized by light or enlightenment
LUMINE vb illuminate
LUMINED > LUMINE
LUMINES > LUMINE
LUMINESCE vb exhibit luminescence
LUMINING > LUMINE
LUMINISM n US artistic movement
LUMINISMS > LUMINISM
LUMINIST > LUMINISM
LUMINISTS > LUMINISM
LUMINOUS adj reflecting or giving off light
LUMME interj exclamation of surprise or dismay
LUMMIER > LUMMY
LUMMIEST > LUMMY
LUMMOX n clumsy person
LUMMOXES > LUMMOX
LUMMY interj exclamation of surprise ▷ adj excellent
LUMP n shapeless mass ▷ vb consider as one group
LUMPED > LUMP
LUMPEN adj stupid or unthinking ▷ n member of underclass
LUMPENLY > LUMPEN
LUMPENS > LUMPEN
LUMPER n stevedore
LUMPERS > LUMPER
LUMPFISH n North Atlantic scorpaenoid fish
LUMPIA n type of Indonesian spring roll
LUMPIAS > LUMPIA
LUMPIER > LUMPY
LUMPIEST > LUMPY
LUMPILY > LUMPY
LUMPINESS > LUMPY
LUMPING > LUMP
LUMPINGLY > LUMP
LUMPISH adj stupid or clumsy
LUMPISHLY > LUMPISH
LUMPKIN n lout
LUMPKINS > LUMPKIN
LUMPS > LUMP
LUMPY adj full of lumps
LUMS > LUM
LUN n sheltered spot
LUNA n large American moth
LUNACIES > LUNACY
LUNACY n foolishness
LUNANAUT same as > LUNARNAUT
LUNANAUTS > LUNANAUT

LUNAR *adj* relating to the moon ▷ *n* lunar distance

LUNARIAN *n* inhabitant of the moon

LUNARIANS > LUNARIAN

LUNARIES > LUNARY

LUNARIST *n* one believing the moon influences weather

LUNARISTS > LUNARIST

LUNARNAUT *n* astronaut who travels to moon

LUNARS > LUNAR

LUNARY *n* moonwort herb

LUNAS > LUNA

LUNATE *adj* shaped like a crescent ▷ *n* crescent-shaped bone forming part of the wrist

LUNATED *variant of* > LUNATE

LUNATELY > LUNATE

LUNATES > LUNATE

LUNATIC *adj* foolish ▷ *n* foolish person

LUNATICAL *variant of* > LUNATIC

LUNATICS > LUNATIC

LUNATION *n* period of time taken by the moon to go around the earth

LUNATIONS > LUNATION

LUNCH *n* meal at midday ▷ *vb* eat lunch

LUNCHBOX *n* container for carrying a packed lunch

LUNCHED > LUNCH

LUNCHEON *n* formal lunch

LUNCHEONS > LUNCHEON

LUNCHER > LUNCH

LUNCHERS > LUNCH

LUNCHES > LUNCH

LUNCHING > LUNCH

LUNCHMEAT *n* mixture of meat and cereal

LUNCHPAIL *n* container for carrying a packed lunch

LUNCHROOM *n* room where lunch is served or people may eat lunches they bring

LUNCHTIME *n* time at which lunch is usually eaten

LUNE *same as* > LUNETTE

LUNES > LUNE

LUNET *n* small moon or satellite

LUNETS > LUNET

LUNETTE *n* anything that is shaped like a crescent

LUNETTES > LUNETTE

LUNG *n* organ that allows an animal or bird to breathe air

LUNGAN *same as* > LONGAN

LUNGANS > LUNGAN

LUNGE *n* sudden forward motion ▷ *vb* move with or make a lunge

LUNGED > LUNGE

LUNGEE *same as* > LUNGI

LUNGEES > LUNGEE

LUNGEING > LUNGE

LUNGER > LUNGE

LUNGERS > LUNGE

LUNGES > LUNGE

LUNGFISH *n* freshwater bony fish with an air-breathing lung

LUNGFUL > LUNG

LUNGFULS > LUNG

LUNGI *n* cotton cloth worn as a loincloth, sash, or turban

LUNGIE *n* guillemot

LUNGIES > LUNGIE

LUNGING > LUNGE

LUNGIS > LUNGI

LUNGLESS *adj* having no lungs

LUNGLIKE *adj* like a lung

LUNGS > LUNG

LUNGWORM *n* type of parasitic worm occurring in the lungs of mammals

LUNGWORMS > LUNGWORM

LUNGWORT *n* plant with spotted leaves

LUNGWORTS > LUNGWORT

LUNGYI *same as* > LUNGI

LUNGYIS > LUNGYI

LUNIER > LUNY

LUNIES > LUNY

LUNIEST > LUNY

LUNINESS > LUNY

LUNISOLAR *adj* resulting from or based on the combined gravitational attraction of the sun and moon

LUNITIDAL *adj* of or relating to tidal phenomena as produced by the moon

LUNK *n* awkward person

LUNKER *n* very large fish

LUNKERS > LUNKER

LUNKHEAD *n* stupid person

LUNKHEADS > LUNKHEAD

LUNKS > LUNK

LUNS > LUN

LUNT *vb* produce smoke

LUNTED > LUNT

LUNTING > LUNT

LUNTS > LUNT

LUNULA *n* white area at base of the fingernail

LUNULAE > LUNULA

LUNULAR *same as* > LUNULATE

LUNULATE *adj* having markings shaped like crescents

LUNULATED *same as* > LUNULATE

LUNULE *same as* > LUNULA

LUNULES > LUNULE

LUNY *same as* > LOONY

LUNYIE *same as* > LUNGIE

LUNYIES > LUNYIE

LUPANAR *n* brothel

LUPANARS > LUPANAR

LUPIN *n* garden plant

LUPINE *adj* like a wolf ▷ *n* lupin

LUPINES > LUPINE

LUPINS > LUPIN

LUPOID *adj* having lupus

LUPOUS *adj* relating to lupus

LUPPEN *Scots past form of* > LEAP

LUPULIN *n* resinous powder extracted from the hop plant

LUPULINE *adj* relating to lupulin

LUPULINIC *same as* > LUPULINE

LUPULINS > LUPULIN

LUPUS *n* ulcerous skin disease

LUPUSES > LUPUS

LUR *n* large bronze musical horn

LURCH *vb* tilt suddenly ▷ *n* lurching movement

LURCHED > LURCH

LURCHER *n* crossbred dog trained to hunt silently

LURCHERS > LURCHER

LURCHES > LURCH

LURCHING > LURCH

LURDAN *n* stupid or dull person ▷ *adj* dull or stupid

LURDANE *same as* > LURDAN

LURDANES > LURDANE

LURDANS > LURDAN

LURDEN *same as* > LURDAN

LURDENS > LURDEN

LURE *vb* tempt by promise of reward ▷ *n* person that lures

LURED > LURE

LURER > LURE

LURERS > LURE

LURES > LURE

LUREX *n* thin glittery thread

LUREXES > LUREX

LURGI *same as* > LURGY

LURGIES > LURGY

LURGIS > LURGI

LURGY *n* any undetermined illness

LURID *adj* sensational

LURIDER > LURID

LURIDEST > LURID

LURIDLY > LURID

LURIDNESS > LURID

LURING > LURE

LURINGLY > LURE

LURINGS > LURING

LURK *vb* lie hidden

LURKED > LURK

LURKER > LURK

LURKERS > LURK

LURKING *adj* lingering

LURKINGLY > LURKING

LURKINGS > LURKING

LURKS > LURK

LURRIES > LURRY

LURRY *n* confused jumble

LURS > LUR

LURVE *n* love

LURVES > LURVE

LUSCIOUS *adj* extremely pleasurable to taste or smell

LUSER *n* humorous term for computer user

LUSERS > LUSER

LUSH *adj* growing thickly ▷ *n* alcoholic ▷ *vb* drink to excess

LUSHED > LUSH

LUSHER *adj* more lush ▷ *n* drunkard

LUSHERS > LUSHER

LUSHES > LUSH

LUSHEST > LUSH

LUSHIER > LUSHY

LUSHIES > LUSHY

LUSHIEST > LUSHY

LUSHING > LUSH

LUSHLY > LUSH

LUSHNESS > LUSH

LUSHY *adj* slightly intoxicated ▷ *n* drunkard

LUSK *vb* lounge around

LUSKED > LUSK

LUSKING > LUSK

LUSKISH *adj* lazy

LUSKS > LUSK

LUST *n* strong desire ▷ *vb* have strong desire (for)

LUSTED > LUST

LUSTER *same as* > LUSTRE

LUSTERED > LUSTER

LUSTERING > LUSTER

LUSTERS > LUSTER

LUSTFUL *adj* driven by strong sexual desire

LUSTFULLY > LUSTFUL

LUSTICK *obsolete word for* > LUSTY

LUSTIER > LUSTY

LUSTIEST > LUSTY

LUSTIHEAD *n* vigour

LUSTIHOOD *n* vigour

LUSTILY > LUSTY

LUSTINESS > LUSTY

LUSTING > LUST

LUSTIQUE *obsolete word for* > LUSTY

LUSTLESS > LUST

LUSTRA > LUSTRUM

LUSTRAL *adj* of or relating to a ceremony of purification

LUSTRATE *vb* purify by means of religious rituals or ceremonies

LUSTRATED > LUSTRATE

LUSTRATES > LUSTRATE

LUSTRE *n* gloss, sheen ▷ *vb* make, be, or become lustrous

LUSTRED > LUSTRE

LUSTRES > LUSTRE

LUSTRINE *same as* > LUSTRING

LUSTRINES > LUSTRINE

LUSTRING *n* glossy silk cloth, formerly used for clothing, upholstery, etc

LUSTRINGS > LUSTRING

LUSTROUS > LUSTRE

LUSTRUM n period of five years

LUSTRUMS > LUSTRUM

LUSTS > LUST

LUSTY adj vigorous, healthy

LUSUS n freak, mutant

LUSUSES > LUSUS

LUTANIST same as > LUTENIST

LUTANISTS > LUTANIST

LUTE n musical instrument r ▷ vb seal with cement and clay

LUTEA adj yellow

LUTEAL adj relating to the development of the corpus luteum

LUTECIUM same as > LUTETIUM

LUTECIUMS > LUTECIUM

LUTED > LUTE

LUTEFISK n Scandinavian fish dish

LUTEFISKS > LUTEFISK

LUTEIN n xanthophyll pigment

LUTEINISE same as > LUTEINIZE

LUTEINIZE vb develop into part of corpus luteum

LUTEINS > LUTEIN

LUTELIKE adj like a lute

LUTENIST n person who plays the lute

LUTENISTS > LUTENIST

LUTEOLIN n yellow crystalline compound found in many plants

LUTEOLINS > LUTEOLIN

LUTEOLOUS > LUTEOLIN

LUTEOUS adj of a greenish-yellow colour

LUTER n lute player

LUTERS > LUTER

LUTES > LUTE

LUTESCENT adj yellowish in colour

LUTETIUM n silvery-white metallic element

LUTETIUMS > LUTETIUM

LUTEUM adj yellow

LUTFISK same as > LUTEFISK

LUTFISKS > LUTFISK

LUTHERN another name for > DORMER

LUTHERNS > LUTHERN

LUTHIER n lute-maker

LUTHIERS > LUTHIER

LUTING n cement and clay

LUTINGS > LUTING

LUTIST same as > LUTENIST

LUTISTS > LUTIST

LUTITE another name for > PELITE

LUTITES > LUTITE

LUTTEN > LOOT

LUTZ n skating jump

LUTZES > LUTZ

LUV n love ▷ vb love

LUVS > LUV

LUVVED > LUV

LUVVIE n person who is involved in acting or the theatre

LUVVIEDOM n theatrical world

LUVVIES > LUVVIE

LUVVING > LUV

LUVVY same as > LUVVIE

LUX n unit of illumination ▷ vb clean with a vacuum cleaner

LUXATE vb put (a shoulder, knee, etc) out of joint

LUXATED > LUXATE

LUXATES > LUXATE

LUXATING > LUXATE

LUXATION > LUXATE

LUXATIONS > LUXATE

LUXE adj luxurious

LUXED > LUX

LUXER > LUXE

LUXES > LUX

LUXEST > LUXE

LUXING > LUX

LUXMETER n device for measuring light

LUXMETERS > LUXMETER

LUXURIANT adj rich and abundant

LUXURIATE vb take self-indulgent pleasure (in)

LUXURIES > LUXURY

LUXURIOUS adj full of luxury, sumptuous

LUXURIST n person who loves luxurious things

LUXURISTS > LUXURIST

LUXURY n enjoyment of rich, very comfortable living ▷ adj of or providing luxury

LUZ n supposedly indestructible bone of the human body

LUZERN n alfalfa

LUZERNS > LUZERN

LUZZES > LUZ

LWEI n Angolan monetary unit

LWEIS > LWEI

LYAM n leash

LYAMS > LYAM

LYARD same as > LIARD

LYART same as > LIARD

LYASE n any enzyme that catalyses the separation of two parts of a molecule

LYASES > LYASE

LYCAENID n type of butterfly

LYCAENIDS > LYCAENID

LYCEA > LYCEUM

LYCEE n secondary school

LYCEES > LYCEE

LYCEUM n public building for concerts

LYCEUMS > LYCEUM

LYCH same as > LICH

LYCHEE same as > LITCHI

LYCHEES > LYCHEE

LYCHES > LYCH

LYCHGATE same as > LICHGATE

LYCHGATES > LYCHGATE

LYCHNIS n plant with red, pink, or white flowers

LYCHNISES > LYCHNIS

LYCOPENE n red pigment

LYCOPENES > LYCOPENE

LYCOPOD n type of moss

LYCOPODS > LYCOPOD

LYCOPSID n type of club moss

LYCOPSIDS > LYCOPSID

LYCRA n type of elastic fabric used for tight-fitting garments

LYCRAS > LYCRA

LYDDITE n explosive consisting chiefly of fused picric acid

LYDDITES > LYDDITE

LYE n caustic solution

LYES > LYE

LYFULL obsolete form of > LIFEFUL

LYING > LIE

LYINGLY > LIE

LYINGS > LIE

LYKEWAKE n watch held over a dead person, often with festivities

LYKEWAKES > LYKEWAKE

LYKEWALK variant of > LYKEWAKE

LYKEWALKS > LYKEWALK

LYM obsolete form of > LYAM

LYME n as in lyme grass type of perennial dune grass

LYMES > LYME

LYMITER same as > LIMITER

LYMITERS > LYMITER

LYMPH n colourless bodily fluid

LYMPHAD n ancient rowing boat

LYMPHADS > LYMPHAD

LYMPHATIC adj of, relating to, or containing lymph ▷ n lymphatic vessel

LYMPHOID adj of or resembling lymph, or relating to the lymphatic system

LYMPHOMA n any form of cancer of the lymph nodes

LYMPHOMAS > LYMPHOMA

LYMPHOUS adj resembling lymph

LYMPHS > LYMPH

LYMS > LYM

LYNAGE obsolete form of > LINEAGE

LYNAGES > LYNAGE

LYNCEAN adj of a lynx

LYNCH vb put to death without a trial

LYNCHED > LYNCH

LYNCHER > LYNCH

LYNCHERS > LYNCH

LYNCHES > LYNCH

LYNCHET n ridge formed by ploughing a hillside

LYNCHETS > LYNCHET

LYNCHING > LYNCH

LYNCHINGS > LYNCH

LYNCHPIN same as > LINCHPIN

LYNCHPINS > LINCHPIN

LYNE n flax

LYNES > LYNE

LYNX n animal of the cat family

LYNXES > LYNX

LYNXLIKE > LYNX

LYOLYSES > LYOLYSIS

LYOLYSIS n formation of an acid and a base from the interaction of a salt with a solvent

LYOMEROUS adj relating to Lyomeri fish

LYONNAISE adj (of food) cooked or garnished with onions, usually fried

LYOPHIL same as > LYOPHILIC

LYOPHILE same as > LYOPHILIC

LYOPHILED adj lyophilized

LYOPHILIC adj (of a colloid) having a dispersed phase with a high affinity for the continuous phase

LYOPHOBE same as > LYOPHOBIC

LYOPHOBIC adj (of a colloid) having a dispersed phase with little or no affinity for the continuous phase

LYRA n as in lyra viol lutelike musical instrument

LYRATE adj shaped like a lyre

LYRATED same as > LYRATE

LYRATELY > LYRATE

LYRE n ancient musical instrument

LYREBIRD n Australian bird, the male of which spreads its tail into the shape of a lyre

LYREBIRDS > LYREBIRD

LYRES > LYRE

LYRIC adj expressing emotion in songlike style ▷ n short poem in a songlike style

LYRICAL same as > LYRIC

LYRICALLY > LYRIC

LYRICISE same as > LYRICIZE

LYRICISED > LYRICISE

LYRICISES > LYRICISE

LYRICISM n quality or style of lyric poetry
LYRICISMS > LYRICISM
LYRICIST n person who writes the words of songs or musicals
LYRICISTS > LYRICIST
LYRICIZE vb write lyrics
LYRICIZED > LYRICIZE
LYRICIZES > LYRICIZE
LYRICON n wind synthesizer
LYRICONS > LYRICON
LYRICS > LYRIC
LYRIFORM adj lyre-shaped
LYRISM n art or technique of playing the lyre
LYRISMS > LYRISM
LYRIST same as > LYRICIST

LYRISTS > LYRIST
LYSATE n material formed by lysis
LYSATES > LYSATE
LYSE vb undergo lysis
LYSED > LYSE
LYSERGIC adj as in lysergic acid crystalline compound used in medical research
LYSERGIDE n LSD
LYSES > LYSIS
LYSIGENIC adj caused by breaking down of cells
LYSIMETER n instrument for determining solubility, esp the amount of water-soluble matter in soil
LYSIN n group of antibodies that dissolve cells
LYSINE n essential amino acid that occurs in proteins

LYSINES > LYSINE
LYSING > LYSE
LYSINS > LYSIN
LYSIS n destruction of cells by a lysin
LYSOGEN n lysis-inducing agent
LYSOGENIC > LYSOGEN
LYSOGENS > LYSOGEN
LYSOGENY > LYSOGEN
LYSOL n antiseptic solution
LYSOLS > LYSOL
LYSOSOMAL > LYSOSOME
LYSOSOME n any of numerous small particles that are present in the cytoplasm of most cells
LYSOSOMES > LYSOSOME
LYSOZYME n enzyme occurring in tears, certain body tissues, and egg white

LYSOZYMES > LYSOZYME
LYSSA less common word for > RABIES
LYSSAS > LYSSA
LYTE vb dismount
LYTED > LYTE
LYTES > LYTE
LYTHE n type of fish
LYTHES > LYTHE
LYTHRUM n genus of plants including loosestrife
LYTHRUMS > LYTHRUM
LYTIC adj relating to, causing, or resulting from lysis
LYTICALLY > LYTIC
LYTING > LYTE
LYTTA n mass of cartilage under the tongue in carnivores
LYTTAE > LYTTA
LYTTAS > LYTTA

Mm

MA *n* mother
MAA *vb* (of goats) bleat
MAAED > MAA
MAAING > MAA
MAAR *n* coneless volcanic crater
MAARE > MAAR
MAARS > MAAR
MAAS *n* thick soured milk
MAASES > MAAS
MAATJES *n* pickled herring
MABE *n* type of pearl
MABELA *n* ground sorghum
MABELAS > MABELA
MABES > MABE
MAC *n* macintosh
MACA *n* type of plant
MACABER *same as* > MACABRE
MACABRE *adj* strange and horrible, gruesome
MACABRELY > MACABRE
MACABRER > MACABRE
MACABREST > MACABRE
MACACO *n* type of lemur
MACACOS > MACACO
MACADAM *n* type of road surface
MACADAMED *adj* (of a road) paved with macadam
MACADAMIA *n* Australian tree with edible nuts
MACADAMS > MACADAM
MACAHUBA *n* South American palm tree
MACAHUBAS > MACAHUBA
MACALLUM *n* ice cream with raspberry sauce
MACALLUMS > MACALLUM
MACAQUE *n* monkey of Asia and Africa
MACAQUES > MACAQUE
MACARISE *vb* congratulate
MACARISED > MACARISE
MACARISES > MACARISE
MACARISM *n* blessing
MACARISMS > MACARISM
MACARIZE *same as* > MACARISE
MACARIZED > MACARIZE
MACARIZES > MACARIZE
MACARON *n* small meringue cake

MACARONI *n* pasta in short tube shapes
MACARONIC *adj* (of verse) characterized by a mixture of vernacular words jumbled together with Latin words or Latinized words or with words from one or more other foreign languages ▷ *n* macaronic verse
MACARONIS > MACARONI
MACARONS > MACARON
MACAROON *n* small biscuit or cake made with ground almonds
MACAROONS > MACAROON
MACAS > MACA
MACASSAR *n* oily preparation formerly put on the hair to make it smooth and shiny
MACASSARS > MACASSAR
MACAW *n* large tropical American parrot
MACAWS > MACAW
MACCABAW *same as* > MACCABOY
MACCABAWS > MACCABOY
MACCABOY *n* dark rose-scented snuff
MACCABOYS > MACCABOY
MACCARONI *same as* > MACARONI
MACCHIA *n* thicket in Italy
MACCHIATO *n* espresso coffee served with a dash of hot or cold milk
MACCHIE > MACCHIA
MACCOBOY *same as* > MACCABOY
MACCOBOYS > MACCABOY
MACE *n* club ▷ *vb* use a mace
MACED > MACE
MACEDOINE *n* hot or cold mixture of diced vegetables
MACER *n* macebearer, esp (in Scotland) an official who acts as usher in a court of law
MACERAL *n* any of the organic units that constitute coal
MACERALS > MACERAL
MACERATE *vb* soften by soaking

MACERATED > MACERATE
MACERATER > MACERATE
MACERATES > MACERATE
MACERATOR > MACERATE
MACERS > MACER
MACES > MACE
MACH *n* ratio of the speed of a body in a particular medium to the speed of sound in that medium
MACHACA *n* Mexican dish of shredded dried beef
MACHACAS > MACHACA
MACHAIR *n* (in the western Highlands of Scotland) a strip of sandy, grassy land
MACHAIRS > MACHAIR
MACHAN *n* (in India) a raised platform used in tiger hunting
MACHANS > MACHAN
MACHE *n* papier-mâché
MACHER *n* important or influential person
MACHERS > MACHER
MACHES > MACHE
MACHETE *n* broad heavy knife used for cutting or as a weapon
MACHETES > MACHETE
MACHI *n* as in *machi chips* in Indian English, fish and chips
MACHINATE *vb* contrive, plan, or devise (schemes, plots, etc)
MACHINE *n* apparatus designed to perform a task ▷ *vb* make or produce by machine
MACHINED > MACHINE
MACHINERY *n* machines or machine parts collectively
MACHINES > MACHINE
MACHINIMA *n* use of real-time 3-D graphics to generate computer animation
MACHINING > MACHINE
MACHINIST *n* person who operates a machine
MACHISMO *n* exaggerated or strong masculinity
MACHISMOS > MACHISMO
MACHMETER *n* instrument for measuring

the Mach number of an aircraft in flight
MACHO *adj* strongly masculine ▷ *n* strong masculinity
MACHOISM > MACHO
MACHOISMS > MACHO
MACHOS > MACHO
MACHREE *n* Irish form of address meaning my dear
MACHREES > MACHREE
MACHS > MACH
MACHZOR *n* Jewish prayer book
MACHZORIM > MACHZOR
MACHZORS > MACHZOR
MACING > MACE
MACINTOSH *n* waterproof raincoat
MACK *same as* > MAC
MACKEREL *n* edible sea fish
MACKERELS > MACKEREL
MACKINAW *n* thick short double-breasted plaid coat
MACKINAWS > MACKINAW
MACKLE *n* blurred impression ▷ *vb* mend hurriedly or in a makeshift way
MACKLED > MACKLE
MACKLES > MACKLE
MACKLING > MACKLE
MACKS > MACK
MACLE *n* crystal consisting of two parts
MACLED > MACLE
MACLES > MACLE
MACON *n* wine from the Mâcon area
MACONS > MACON
MACOYA *n* South American tree
MACOYAS > MACOYA
MACRAME *n* ornamental work of knotted cord
MACRAMES > MACRAME
MACRAMI *same as* > MACRAME
MACRAMIS > MACRAMI
MACRO *n* close-up lens
MACROBIAN *adj* long-lived
MACROCODE *n* computer instruction that triggers many other instructions
MACROCOPY *n* enlargement of printed material for easier reading
MACROCOSM *n* universe

MACROCYST n unusually large cyst

MACROCYTE n abnormally large red blood cell

MACRODOME n dome shape in crystal structure

MACRODONT adj having large teeth

MACROGLIA n one of the two types of non-nervous tissue (glia) found in the central nervous system: includes astrocytes

MACROLIDE n type of antibiotic drug

MACROLOGY n verbose but meaningless talk

MACROMERE n any of the large yolk-filled cells formed by unequal splitting of a fertilized ovum

MACROMOLE n large chemistry mole

MACRON n mark placed over a letter to represent a long vowel

MACRONS > MACRON

MACROPOD n member of kangaroo family

MACROPODS > MACROPOD

MACROPSIA n condition of seeing everything in the field of view as larger than it really is, which can occur in diseases of the retina or in some brain disorders

MACROS > MACRO

MACROTOUS adj having large ears

MACRURAL adj long-tailed

MACRURAN n type of decapod crustacean

MACRURANS > MACRURAN

MACRUROID adj long-tailed

MACRUROUS adj long-tailed

MACS > MAC

MACTATION n sacrificial killing

MACULA n small spot like a freckle

MACULAE > MACULA

MACULAR > MACULA

MACULAS > MACULA

MACULATE vb spot, stain, or pollute ▷ adj spotted or polluted

MACULATED > MACULATE

MACULATES > MACULATE

MACULE same as > MACKLE

MACULED > MACULE

MACULES > MACULE

MACULING > MACULE

MACULOSE adj having spots

MACUMBA n religious cult in Brazil

MACUMBAS > MACUMBA

MAD adj mentally deranged ▷ vb make mad

MADAFU n coconut milk

MADAFUS > MADAFU

MADAM n polite term of address for a woman ▷ vb call someone madam

MADAME n French title equivalent to Mrs

MADAMED > MADAM

MADAMES > MADAME

MADAMING > MADAM

MADAMS > MADAM

MADAROSES > MADAROSIS

MADAROSIS n abnormal loss of eyebrows or eyelashes

MADBRAIN adj slang word for rash or hotheaded ▷ n slang word for a rash person

MADBRAINS > MADBRAIN

MADCAP adj foolish or reckless ▷ n impulsive or reckless person

MADCAPS > MADCAP

MADDED > MAD

MADDEN vb infuriate or irritate

MADDENED > MADDEN

MADDENING adj irritating, annoying

MADDENS > MADDEN

MADDER n type of rose

MADDERS > MADDER

MADDEST > MAD

MADDING > MAD

MADDINGLY > MAD

MADDISH > MAD

MADDOCK same as > MATTOCK

MADDOCKS > MADDOCK

MADE > MAKE

MADEFIED > MADEFY

MADEFIES > MADEFY

MADEFY vb make moist

MADEFYING > MADEFY

MADEIRA n kind of rich sponge cake

MADEIRAS > MADEIRA

MADELEINE n small fancy sponge cake

MADERISE vb become reddish

MADERISED > MADERISE

MADERISES > MADERISE

MADERIZE same as > MADERISE

MADERIZED > MADERIZE

MADERIZES > MADERIZE

MADEUPPY adj artificial or contrived in an obvious way

MADGE n type of hammer

MADGES > MADGE

MADHOUSE n place filled with uproar or confusion

MADHOUSES > MADHOUSE

MADID adj wet

MADISON n type of cycle relay race

MADISONS > MADISON

MADLING n foolish person

MADLINGS > MADLING

MADLY adv with great speed and energy

MADMAN n reckless man

MADMEN > MADMAN

MADNESS n insanity

MADNESSES > MADNESS

MADONNA n picture or statue of the Virgin Mary

MADONNAS > MADONNA

MADOQUA n Ethiopian antelope

MADOQUAS > MADOQUA

MADRAS n medium-hot curry

MADRASA same as > MADRASAH

MADRASAH n educational institution, particularly for Islamic religious instruction

MADRASAHS > MADRASAH

MADRASAS > MADRASA

MADRASES > MADRAS

MADRASSA same as > MADRASAH

MADRASSAH same as > MADRASAH

MADRASSAS > MADRASSA

MADRE Spanish word for > MOTHER

MADREPORE n type of coral which often occurs in tropical seas and forms large coral reefs

MADRES > MADRE

MADRIGAL n 16th–17th-century part song for unaccompanied voices

MADRIGALS > MADRIGAL

MADRILENE n cold consommé flavoured with tomato juice

MADRONA n N American evergreen tree or shrub

MADRONAS > MADRONA

MADRONE same as > MADRONA

MADRONES > MADRONE

MADRONO same as > MADRONA

MADRONOS > MADRONO

MADS > MAD

MADTOM n species of catfish

MADTOMS > MADTOM

MADURO adj (of cigars) dark and strong ▷ n cigar of this type

MADUROS > MADURO

MADWOMAN n reckless woman

MADWOMEN > MADWOMAN

MADWORT n low-growing Eurasian plant with small blue flowers

MADWORTS > MADWORT

MADZOON same as > MATZOON

MADZOONS > MADZOON

MAE adj more

MAELID n mythical spirit of apple tree

MAELIDS > MAELID

MAELSTROM n great whirlpool

MAENAD n female disciple of Dionysus

MAENADES > MAENAD

MAENADIC > MAENAD

MAENADISM > MAENAD

MAENADS > MAENAD

MAERL n type of red coralline algae

MAERLS > MAERL

MAES > MAE

MAESTOSO adv be performed majestically ▷ n piece or passage directed to be played in this way

MAESTOSOS > MAESTOSO

MAESTRI > MAESTRO

MAESTRO n outstanding musician or conductor

MAESTROS > MAESTRO

MAFFIA same as > MAFIA

MAFFIAS > MAFFIA

MAFFICK vb celebrate extravagantly and publicly

MAFFICKED > MAFFICK

MAFFICKER > MAFFICK

MAFFICKS > MAFFICK

MAFFLED adj baffled

MAFFLIN n half-witted person

MAFFLING same as > MAFFLIN

MAFFLINGS > MAFFLING

MAFFLINS > MAFFLIN

MAFIA n international secret organization founded in Sicily

MAFIAS > MAFIA

MAFIC n minerals present in igneous rock

MAFICS > MAFIC

MAFIOSI > MAFIOSO

MAFIOSO n member of the Mafia

MAFIOSOS > MAFIOSO

MAFTED adj suffering under oppressive heat

MAFTIR n final section of the weekly Torah reading

MAFTIRS > MAFTIR

MAG vb talk ▷ n talk

MAGAININ n substance with antibacterial properties

MAGAININS > MAGAININ

MAGALOG same as > MAGALOGUE

MAGALOGS > MAGALOG

MAGALOGUE n combination of a magazine and a catalogue

MAGAZINE n periodical publication with articles by different writers

MAGAZINES > MAGAZINE

MAGDALEN n archaic term for a reformed prostitute

MAGDALENE same as > MAGDALEN

MAGDALENS > MAGDALEN

MAGE archaic word for
> MAGICIAN
MAGENTA adj deep
purplish-red ▷ n deep
purplish red
MAGENTAS > MAGENTA
MAGES > MAGE
MAGESHIP > MAGE
MAGESHIPS > MAGE
MAGG same as > MAG
MAGGED > MAG
MAGGIE n magpie
MAGGIES > MAGGIE
MAGGING > MAG
MAGGOT n larva of an
insect
MAGGOTIER > MAGGOTY
MAGGOTS > MAGGOT
MAGGOTY adj relating to,
resembling, or ridden with
maggots
MAGGS > MAGG
MAGI > MAGUS
MAGIAN > MAGUS
MAGIANISM > MAGUS
MAGIANS > MAGUS
MAGIC n supposed art of
invoking supernatural
powers to influence events
▷ vb transform or produce
by or as if by magic ▷ adj
of, using, or like magic
MAGICAL > MAGIC
MAGICALLY > MAGIC
MAGICIAN n conjuror
MAGICIANS
> MAGICIAN
MAGICKED > MAGIC
MAGICKING > MAGIC
MAGICS > MAGIC
MAGILP same as
> MEGILP
MAGILPS > MAGILP
MAGISM > MAGUS
MAGISMS > MAGUS
MAGISTER n person
entitled to teach in
medieval university
MAGISTERS
> MAGISTER
MAGISTERY n agency or
substance, such as the
philosopher's stone,
believed to transmute
other substances
MAGISTRAL adj of,
relating to, or
characteristic of a master
▷ n fortification in a
determining position
MAGLEV n type of
high-speed train
MAGLEVS > MAGLEV
MAGMA n molten rock
inside the earth's crust
MAGMAS > MAGMA
MAGMATA > MAGMA
MAGMATIC > MAGMA
MAGMATISM > MAGMA
MAGNALIUM n alloy of
magnesium and
aluminium
MAGNATE n influential or
wealthy person, esp in
industry
MAGNATES > MAGNATE
MAGNES n magnetic iron
ore

MAGNESES > MAGNES
MAGNESIA n white
tasteless substance used
as an antacid and a
laxative
MAGNESIAL
> MAGNESIA
MAGNESIAN
> MAGNESIA
MAGNESIAS
> MAGNESIA
MAGNESIC > MAGNESIA
MAGNESITE n white,
colourless, or lightly tinted
mineral
MAGNESIUM n
silvery-white metallic
element
MAGNET n piece of iron or
steel capable of attracting
iron and pointing north
when suspended
MAGNETAR n neutron star
with intense magnetic
field
MAGNETARS
> MAGNETAR
MAGNETIC adj having the
properties of a magnet
MAGNETICS n branch of
physics concerned with
magnetism
MAGNETISE same as
> MAGNETIZE
MAGNETISM n magnetic
property
MAGNETIST
> MAGNETISM
MAGNETITE n black
magnetizable mineral
that is an important
source of iron
MAGNETIZE vb make
into a magnet
MAGNETO n apparatus for
ignition in an
internal-combustion
engine
MAGNETON n unit of
magnetic moment
MAGNETONS
> MAGNETON
MAGNETOS > MAGNETO
MAGNETRON n electronic
valve used with a
magnetic field to generate
microwave oscillations,
used esp in radar
MAGNETS > MAGNET
MAGNIFIC adj
magnificent, grandiose, or
pompous
MAGNIFICO n magnate
MAGNIFIED > MAGNIFY
MAGNIFIER > MAGNIFY
MAGNIFIES > MAGNIFY
MAGNIFY vb increase in
apparent size, as with a
lens
MAGNITUDE n relative
importance or size
MAGNOLIA n shrub or
tree with showy white or
pink flowers
MAGNOLIAS
> MAGNOLIA
MAGNON n short for
Cro-Magnon
MAGNONS > MAGNON

MAGNOX n alloy used in
fuel elements of some
nuclear reactors
MAGNOXES > MAGNOX
MAGNUM n large wine
bottle holding about 1.5
litres
MAGNUMS > MAGNUM
MAGNUS adj as in magnus
hitch knot similar to a
clove hitch but having one
more turn
MAGOTS > MAGOT
MAGPIE n black-and-
white bird
MAGPIES > MAGPIE
MAGS > MAG
MAGSMAN n raconteur
MAGSMEN > MAGSMAN
MAGUEY n tropical
American agave plant
MAGUEYS > MAGUEY
MAGUS n Zoroastrian
priest of the ancient
Medes and Persians
MAGYAR adj of or relating
to a style of sleeve
MAHA n as in maha yoga
form of yoga
MAHANT n chief priest in a
Hindu temple
MAHANTS > MAHANT
MAHARAJA same as
> MAHARAJAH
MAHARAJAH n former
title of some Indian
princes
MAHARAJAS
> MAHARAJA
MAHARANEE same as
> MAHARANI
MAHARANI n wife of a
maharaja
MAHARANIS
> MAHARANI
MAHARISHI n Hindu
religious teacher or
mystic
MAHATMA n person
revered for holiness and
wisdom
MAHATMAS > MAHATMA
MAHEWU n (in South
Africa) fermented liquid
meal porridge
MAHEWUS > MAHEWU
MAHIMAHI n Pacific fish
MAHIMAHIS
> MAHIMAHI
MAHJONG n game of
Chinese origin, using tiles
MAHJONGG same as
> MAHJONG
MAHJONGGS
> MAHJONGG
MAHJONGS > MAHJONG
MAHLSTICK same as
> MAULSTICK
MAHMAL n litter used in
Muslim ceremony
MAHMALS > MAHMAL
MAHOE n New Zealand
tree
MAHOES > MAHOE

MAHOGANY n hard
reddish-brown wood of
several tropical trees ▷ adj
reddish-brown
MAHONIA n Asian and
American evergreen
shrub
MAHONIAS > MAHONIA
MAHOUT n (in India)
elephant driver or keeper
MAHOUTS > MAHOUT
MAHSEER n large
freshwater Indian fish
MAHSEERS > MAHSEER
MAHSIR same as
> MAHSEER
MAHSIRS > MAHSIR
MAHUA n Indian tree
MAHUANG n herbal
medicine from shrub
MAHUANGS > MAHUANG
MAHUAS > MAHUA
MAHWA same as > MAHUA
MAHWAS > MAHWA
MAHZOR same as
> MACHZOR
MAHZORIM > MAHZOR
MAHZORS > MAHZOR
MAIASAUR same as
> MAIASAURA
MAIASAURA n species of
dinosaur
MAIASAURS
> MAIASAURA
MAID n female servant
▷ vb work as maid
MAIDAN n (in Pakistan,
India, etc) open area
MAIDANS > MAIDAN
MAIDED > MAID
MAIDEN n young
unmarried woman ▷ adj
unmarried
MAIDENISH > MAIDEN
MAIDENLY adj modest
MAIDENS > MAIDEN
MAIDHOOD > MAID
MAIDHOODS > MAID
MAIDING > MAID
MAIDISH > MAID
MAIDISM n pellagra
MAIDISMS > MAIDISM
MAIDLESS > MAID
MAIDS > MAID
MAIEUTIC adj of or
relating to the Socratic
method of eliciting
knowledge by a series of
questions and answers
MAIEUTICS n Socratic
method
MAIGRE adj not
containing meat ▷ n
species of fish
MAIGRES > MAIGRE
MAIHEM same as
> MAYHEM
MAIHEMS > MAIHEM
MAIK n old halfpenny
MAIKO n apprentice
geisha
MAIKOS > MAIKO
MAIKS > MAIK
MAIL n letters and
packages transported and
delivered by the post office
▷ vb send by mail
MAILABLE > MAIL

MAILBAG n large bag for transporting or delivering mail

MAILBAGS > MAILBAG

MAILBOAT n boat that carries mail

MAILBOATS > MAILBOAT

MAILBOX n box into which letters and parcels are delivered

MAILBOXES > MAILBOX

MAILCAR same as > MAILCOACH

MAILCARS > MAILCAR

MAILCOACH n railway coach specially constructed for the transportation of mail

MAILE n halfpenny

MAILED > MAIL

MAILER n person who addresses or mails letters, etc

MAILERS > MAILER

MAILES > MAILE

MAILGRAM n telegram

MAILGRAMS > MAILGRAM

MAILING > MAIL

MAILINGS > MAILING

MAILL n Scots word meaning rent

MAILLESS > MAIL

MAILLOT n tights worn for ballet, gymnastics, etc

MAILLOTS > MAILLOT

MAILLS > MAILL

MAILMAN n postman

MAILMEN > MAILMAN

MAILMERGE n computer program for sending mass mailings

MAILPOUCH same as > MAILBAG

MAILROOM n room where mail to and from building is dealt with

MAILROOMS > MAILROOM

MAILS > MAIL

MAILSACK same as > MAILBAG

MAILSACKS > MAILSACK

MAILSHOT n posting of advertising material to many selected people at once

MAILSHOTS > MAILSHOT

MAILVAN n vehicle used to transport post

MAILVANS > MAILVAN

MAIM vb cripple or mutilate ▷ n injury or defect

MAIMED > MAIM

MAIMER > MAIM

MAIMERS > MAIM

MAIMING > MAIM

MAIMINGS > MAIM

MAIMS > MAIM

MAIN adj chief or principal ▷ n principal pipe or line carrying water, gas, or electricity ▷ vb lower sails

MAINBOOM n spar for mainsail

MAINBOOMS > MAINBOOM

MAINBRACE n brace attached to the mainyard

MAINDOOR n door from street into house

MAINDOORS > MAINDOOR

MAINED > MAIN

MAINER > MAIN

MAINEST > MAIN

MAINFRAME adj denoting a high-speed general-purpose computer ▷ n high-speed general-purpose computer, with a large store capacity

MAINING > MAIN

MAINLAND n stretch of land which forms the main part of a country

MAINLANDS > MAINLAND

MAINLINE n the trunk route between two points ▷ vb inject a drug into a vein ▷ adj having an important position

MAINLINED > MAINLINE

MAINLINER > MAINLINE

MAINLINES > MAINLINE

MAINLY adv for the most part, chiefly

MAINMAST n chief mast of a ship

MAINMASTS > MAINMAST

MAINOR n act of doing something

MAINORS > MAINOR

MAINOUR same as > MAINOR

MAINOURS > MAINOUR

MAINPRISE n former legal surety ▷ vb allow a prisoner to go free based on a guarantee that he or she will appear in court on the designated day

MAINS > MAIN

MAINSAIL n largest sail on a mainmast

MAINSAILS > MAINSAIL

MAINSHEET n line used to control the angle of the mainsail to the wind

MAINSTAGE n largest stage in a theatre complex

MAINSTAY n chief support

MAINSTAYS > MAINSTAY

MAINTAIN vb continue or keep in existence

MAINTAINS > MAINTAIN

MAINTOP n top or platform at the head of the mainmast

MAINTOPS > MAINTOP

MAINYARD n yard for a square mainsail

MAINYARDS > MAINYARD

MAIOLICA same as > MAJOLICA

MAIOLICAS > MAIOLICA

MAIR Scots form of > MORE

MAIRE n New Zealand tree

MAIREHAU n small aromatic shrub of New Zealand

MAIREHAUS > MAIREHAU

MAIRES > MAIRE

MAIRS > MAIR

MAISE n measure of herring

MAISES > MAISE

MAIST Scot word for > MOST

MAISTER Scots word for > MASTER

MAISTERED > MAISTER

MAISTERS > MAISTER

MAISTRIES > MAISTER

MAISTRING > MAISTER

MAISTRY > MAISTER

MAISTS > MAIST

MAIZE n type of corn with spikes of yellow grains

MAIZES > MAIZE

MAJAGUA same as > MAHOE

MAJAGUAS > MAJAGUA

MAJESTIC adj beautiful, dignified, and impressive

MAJESTIES > MAJESTY

MAJESTY n stateliness or grandeur

MAJLIS n (in Arab countries) an assembly

MAJLISES > MAJLIS

MAJOLICA n type of ornamented Italian pottery

MAJOLICAS > MAJOLICA

MAJOR adj greater in number, quality, or extent ▷ n middle-ranking army officer ▷ vb do one's principal study in (a particular subject)

MAJORAT n estate, the right to which is that of the first born child of a family

MAJORATS > MAJORAT

MAJORDOMO n chief steward or butler of a great household

MAJORED > MAJOR

MAJORETTE n one of a group of girls who practise formation marching and baton twirling

MAJORING > MAJOR

MAJORITY n greater number

MAJORLY adv very

MAJORS > MAJOR

MAJORSHIP > MAJOR

MAJUSCULE n large letter, either capital or uncial, used in printing or writing ▷ adj relating to, printed, or written in such letters

MAK Scot word for > MAKE

MAKABLE > MAKE

MAKAR same as > MAKER

MAKARS > MAKAR

MAKE vb create, construct, or establish ▷ n brand, type, or style

MAKEABLE n rough, unpolished stone

MAKEABLES > MAKEABLE

MAKEBATE n troublemaker

MAKEBATES > MAKEBATE

MAKEFAST n strong support to which a vessel is secured

MAKEFASTS > MAKEFAST

MAKELESS > MAKE

MAKEOVER vb transfer the title of (property, etc) ▷ n alterations to improve a person's appearance

MAKEOVERS > MAKEOVER

MAKER n person or company that makes something

MAKEREADY n process of preparing the forme and the cylinder or platen packing to achieve the correct impression all over the forme

MAKERS > MAKER

MAKES > MAKE

MAKESHIFT adj serving as a temporary substitute ▷ n something serving in this capacity

MAKEUP n cosmetics applied to the face

MAKEUPS > MAKEUP

MAKHANI n Indian dish made with butter or ghee ▷ adj denoting such a dish

MAKHANIS > MAKHANI

MAKI n in Japanese cuisine, rice and other ingredients wrapped in a short seaweed roll

MAKIMONO n Japanese scroll

MAKIMONOS > MAKIMONO

MAKING > MAKE

MAKINGS pl n potentials, qualities, or materials

MAKIS > MAKI

MAKO n powerful shark of the Atlantic and Pacific Oceans

MAKOS > MAKO

MAKS > MAK

MAKUTA plural of > LIKUTA

MAKUTU n Polynesian witchcraft ▷ vb cast a spell on

MAKUTUED > MAKUTU

MAKUTUING > MAKUTU

MAKUTUS > MAKUTU

MAL n illness

MALA n string of beads or knots, used in praying and meditating

MALACCA n stem of the rattan palm

MALACCAS > MALACCA

MALACHITE n green mineral

MALACIA n softening of an organ or tissue

MALACIAS > MALACIA

MALADIES > MALADY

MALADROIT adj clumsy or awkward

MALADY n disease or illness

MALAGUENA n Spanish dance similar to the fandango

MALAISE n something wrong which affects a section of society or area of activity

MALAISES > MALAISE

MALAM same as > MALLAM

MALAMS > MALAM

MALAMUTE n Alaskan sled dog of the spitz type, having a dense usually greyish coat

MALAMUTES
> MALAMUTE

MALANDER same as
> MALANDERS

MALANDERS pl n disease of horses characterized by an eczematous inflammation behind the knee

MALANGA same as
> COCOYAM

MALANGAS > MALANGA

MALAPERT adj saucy or impudent ▷ n saucy or impudent person

MALAPERTS
> MALAPERT

MALAPROP n word unintentionally confused with one of similar sound

MALAPROPS
> MALAPROP

MALAR n cheekbone ▷ adj of or relating to the cheek or cheekbone

MALARIA n infectious disease caused by mosquito bite

MALARIAL > MALARIA

MALARIAN > MALARIA

MALARIAS > MALARIA

MALARIOUS > MALARIA

MALARKEY n nonsense or rubbish

MALARKEYS
> MALARKEY

MALARKIES > MALARKY

MALARKY same as
> MALARKEY

MALAROMA n bad smell

MALAROMAS
> MALAROMA

MALARS > MALAR

MALAS > MALA

MALATE n any salt or ester of malic acid

MALATES > MALATE

MALATHION n yellow organophosphorus insecticide used as a dust or mist for the control of house flies and garden pests

MALAX vb soften

MALAXAGE > MALAX

MALAXAGES > MALAX

MALAXATE same as
> MALAX

MALAXATED
> MALAXATE

MALAXATES
> MALAXATE

MALAXATOR n machine for kneading or grinding

MALAXED > MALAX

MALAXES > MALAX

MALAXING > MALAX

MALE adj of the sex which can fertilize reproductive cells ▷ n male person or animal

MALEATE n any salt or ester of maleic acid

MALEATES > MALEATE

MALEDICT vb utter a curse against ▷ adj cursed or detestable

MALEDICTS
> MALEDICT

MALEFFECT n bad effect

MALEFIC adj causing evil

MALEFICE n wicked deed

MALEFICES
> MALEFICE

MALEIC adj as in maleic acid colourless soluble crystalline substance

MALEMIUT same as
> MALAMUTE

MALEMIUTS
> MALEMIUT

MALEMUTE same as
> MALAMUTE

MALEMUTES
> MALAMUTE

MALENESS > MALE

MALENGINE n wicked plan

MALES > MALE

MALFED adj having malfunctioned

MALFORMED adj deformed

MALGRADO prep in spite of

MALGRE same as
> MAUGRE

MALGRED > MALGRE

MALGRES > MALGRE

MALGRING > MALGRE

MALI n member of an Indian caste

MALIBU n as in malibu board lightweight surfboard

MALIC adj as in malic acid colourless crystalline compound occurring in apples

MALICE n desire to cause harm to others ▷ vb wish harm to

MALICED > MALICE

MALICES > MALICE

MALICHO n mischief

MALICHOS > MALICHO

MALICING > MALICE

MALICIOUS adj characterized by malice

MALIGN vb slander or defame ▷ adj evil in influence or effect

MALIGNANT adj seeking to harm others

MALIGNED > MALIGN

MALIGNER > MALIGN

MALIGNERS > MALIGN

MALIGNING > MALIGN

MALIGNITY n evil disposition

MALIGNLY > MALIGN

MALIGNS > MALIGN

MALIHINI n (in Hawaii) a foreigner or stranger

MALIHINIS
> MALIHINI

MALIK n person of authority in India

MALIKS > MALIK

MALINE n stiff net

MALINES > MALINE

MALINGER vb feign illness to avoid work

MALINGERS
> MALINGER

MALINGERY
> MALINGER

MALIS > MALI

MALISM n belief that evil dominates world

MALISMS > MALISM

MALISON archaic or poetic word for > CURSE

MALISONS > MALISON

MALIST > MALISM

MALKIN archaic or dialect name for a > CAT

MALKINS > MALKIN

MALL n street or shopping area closed to vehicles ▷ vb maul

MALLAM n (in W Africa) expert in the Koran

MALLAMS > MALLAM

MALLANDER same as
> MALANDERS

MALLARD n wild duck

MALLARDS > MALLARD

MALLCORE n type of rock music combining heavy metal and hip-hop

MALLCORES
> MALLCORE

MALLEABLE adj capable of being hammered or pressed into shape

MALLEABLY
> MALLEABLE

MALLEATE vb hammer

MALLEATED
> MALLEATE

MALLEATES
> MALLEATE

MALLECHO same as
> MALICHO

MALLECHOS
> MALLECHO

MALLED > MALL

MALLEE n low-growing eucalypt in dry regions

MALLEES > MALLEE

MALLEI > MALLEUS

MALLEMUCK n any of various sea birds, such as the albatross, fulmar, or shearwater

MALLENDER same as
> MALANDERS

MALLEOLAR
> MALLEOLUS

MALLEOLI
> MALLEOLUS

MALLEOLUS n either of two rounded bony projections of the tibia and fibula on the sides of each ankle joint

MALLET n (wooden) hammer

MALLETS > MALLET

MALLEUS n small bone in the middle ear

MALLEUSES > MALLEUS

MALLING > MALL

MALLINGS > MALL

MALLOW n plant with pink or purple flowers

MALLOWS > MALLOW

MALLS > MALL

MALM n soft greyish limestone that crumbles easily

MALMAG n Asian monkey

MALMAGS > MALMAG

MALMIER > MALMY

MALMIEST > MALMY

MALMS > MALM

MALMSEY n sweet Madeira wine

MALMSEYS > MALMSEY

MALMSTONE same as
> MALM

MALMY adj looking like malm

MALODOR same as
> MALODOUR

MALODORS > MALODOR

MALODOUR n unpleasant smell

MALODOURS
> MALODOUR

MALONATE n salt of malonic acid

MALONATES
> MALONATE

MALONIC adj as in malonic acid colourless crystalline compound

MALOTI plural of > LOTI

MALPIGHIA n type of tropical shrub

MALPOSED adj in abnormal position

MALS > MAL

MALSTICK same as
> MAULSTICK

MALSTICKS
> MALSTICK

MALT n grain, such as barley, dried in a kiln ▷ vb make into or make with malt

MALTALENT n evil intention

MALTASE n enzyme that hydrolyses maltose to glucose

MALTASES > MALTASE

MALTED n malted milk drink

MALTEDS > MALTED

MALTESE adj as in maltese cross cross-shaped part of a film projector

MALTHA n any of various naturally occurring mixtures of hydrocarbons

MALTHAS > MALTHA

MALTIER > MALTY
MALTIEST > MALTY
MALTINESS > MALTY
MALTING n building in which malt is made or stored
MALTINGS > MALTING
MALTIPOO n cross between a Maltese and a poodle
MALTIPOOS > MALTIPOO
MALTMAN same as > MALTSTER
MALTMEN > MALTMAN
MALTOL n food additive
MALTOLS > MALTOL
MALTOSE n sugar formed by the action of enzymes on starch
MALTOSES > MALTOSE
MALTREAT vb treat badly
MALTREATS > MALTREAT
MALTS > MALT
MALTSTER n person who makes or deals in malt
MALTSTERS > MALTSTER
MALTWORM n heavy drinker
MALTWORMS > MALTWORM
MALTY adj of, like, or containing malt
MALUS n financial penalty incurred by an investor
MALUSES > MALUS
MALVA n mallow plant
MALVAS > MALVA
MALVASIA n type of grape used to make malmsey
MALVASIAN > MALVASIA
MALVASIAS > MALVASIA
MALVESIE same as > MALMSEY
MALVESIES > MALVESIE
MALVOISIE n amber dessert wine made in France, similar to malmsey
MALWA n Ugandan drink brewed from millet
MALWARE n computer program designed to cause damage to a system
MALWARES > MALWARE
MALWAS > MALWA
MAM same as > MOTHER
MAMA n mother
MAMAGUY vb deceive or tease ⊳ n deception or flattery
MAMAGUYED > MAMAGUY
MAMAGUYS > MAMAGUY
MAMAKAU same as > MAMAKU
MAMAKAUS > MAMAKAU
MAMAKO same as > MAMAKU
MAMAKOS > MAMAKO
MAMAKU n tall edible New Zealand tree fern
MAMAKUS > MAMAKU

MAMALIGA same as > POLENTA
MAMALIGAS > MAMALIGA
MAMAS > MAMA
MAMASAN n (in Japan) woman in a position of authority
MAMASANS > MAMASAN
MAMATEEK n type of wigwam
MAMATEEKS > MAMATEEK
MAMBA n deadly S African snake
MAMBAS > MAMBA
MAMBO n Latin American dance resembling the rumba ⊳ vb perform this dance
MAMBOED > MAMBO
MAMBOES > MAMBO
MAMBOING > MAMBO
MAMBOS > MAMBO
MAMEE same as > MAMEY
MAMEES > MAMEE
MAMELON n small rounded hillock
MAMELONS > MAMELON
MAMELUCO n Brazilian of mixed European and South American descent
MAMELUCOS > MAMELUCO
MAMELUKE n member of a military class once ruling Egypt
MAMELUKES > MAMELUKE
MAMEY n tropical tree
MAMEYES > MAMEY
MAMEYS > MAMEY
MAMIE n tropical tree
MAMIES > MAMIE
MAMILLA n nipple or teat
MAMILLAE > MAMILLA
MAMILLAR adj of the breast
MAMILLARY > MAMILLA
MAMILLATE adj having nipples or nipple-like projections
MAMLUK same as > MAMELUKE
MAMLUKS > MAMLUK
MAMMA n buxom and voluptuous woman
MAMMAE > MAMMA
MAMMAL n animal of the type that suckles its young
MAMMALIAN > MAMMAL
MAMMALITY > MAMMAL
MAMMALOGY n branch of zoology concerned with the study of mammals
MAMMALS > MAMMAL
MAMMARIES > MAMMARY
MAMMARY adj of the breasts or milk-producing glands ⊳ n breast
MAMMAS > MAMMA
MAMMATE adj having breasts
MAMMATI > MAMMATUS
MAMMATUS n breast-shaped cloud
MAMMEE same as > MAMEY
MAMMEES > MAMMEE

MAMMER vb hesitate
MAMMERED > MAMMER
MAMMERING > MAMMER
MAMMERS > MAMMER
MAMMET same as > MAUMET
MAMMETRY n worship of idols
MAMMETS > MAMMET
MAMMEY same as > MAMEY
MAMMEYS > MAMMEY
MAMMIE same as > MAMMY
MAMMIES > MAMMY
MAMMIFER same as > MAMMAL
MAMMIFERS > MAMMIFER
MAMMIFORM adj in the form of a breast
MAMMILLA same as > MAMILLA
MAMMILLAE > MAMILLA
MAMMILLAR same as > MAMILLAR
MAMMITIS same as > MASTITIS
MAMMOCK n fragment ⊳ vb tear or shred
MAMMOCKED > MAMMOCK
MAMMOCKS > MAMMOCK
MAMMOGRAM n X-ray of a breast
MAMMON n wealth regarded as a source of evil
MAMMONISH > MAMMON
MAMMONISM > MAMMON
MAMMONIST > MAMMON
MAMMONITE > MAMMON
MAMMONS > MAMMON
MAMMOTH n extinct elephant-like mammal ⊳ adj colossal
MAMMOTHS > MAMMOTH
MAMMY same as > MOTHER
MAMPARA n foolish person, idiot
MAMPARAS > MAMPARA
MAMPOER n home-distilled brandy
MAMPOERS > MAMPOER
MAMS > MAM
MAMSELLE n mademoiselle
MAMSELLES > MAMSELLE
MAMZER n child of an incestuous or adulterous union
MAMZERIM > MAMZER
MAMZERS > MAMZER
MAN n adult male ⊳ vb supply with sufficient people for operation or defence
MANA n authority, influence
MANACLE vb handcuff or fetter ⊳ n metal ring or chain put round the wrists or ankles
MANACLED > MANACLE
MANACLES > MANACLE
MANACLING > MANACLE
MANAGE vb succeed in doing
MANAGED > MANAGE

MANAGER n person in charge of a business, institution, actor, sports team, etc
MANAGERS > MANAGER
MANAGES > MANAGE
MANAGING adj having administrative control or authority
MANAIA n figure in Māori carving
MANAIAS > MANAIA
MANAKIN same as > MANIKIN
MANAKINS > MANAKIN
MANANA n tomorrow ⊳ adv tomorrow
MANANAS > MANANA
MANAS > MANA
MANAT n standard monetary unit of Azerbaijan
MANATEE n large tropical plant-eating aquatic mammal
MANATEES > MANATEE
MANATI same as > MANATEE
MANATIS > MANATI
MANATOID > MANATEE
MANATS > MANAT
MANATU n large flowering deciduous New Zealand tree
MANATUS > MANATU
MANAWA in New Zealand, same as > MANGROVE
MANAWAS > MANAWA
MANBAG n small handbag with a shoulder strap, carried by men
MANBAGS > MANBAG
MANBAND n boy band whose members have reached maturity
MANBANDS > MANBAND
MANCALA n African and Asian board game
MANCALAS > MANCALA
MANCANDO adv musical direction meaning fading away
MANCHE n long sleeve
MANCHEGO n Spanish cheese
MANCHEGOS > MANCHEGO
MANCHES > MANCHE
MANCHET n type of bread
MANCHETS > MANCHET
MANCIPATE vb make legal transfer in ancient Rome
MANCIPLE n steward who buys provisions, esp in a college, Inn of Court, or monastery
MANCIPLES > MANCIPLE
MANCUS n former English coin
MANCUSES > MANCUS
MAND > MAN
MANDALA n circular design symbolizing the universe
MANDALAS > MANDALA
MANDALIC > MANDALA

m

MANDAMUS n order of a superior court

MANDARIN n high-ranking government official

MANDARINE same as > MANDARIN

MANDARINS > MANDARIN

MANDATARY same as > MANDATORY

MANDATE n official or authoritative command ▷ vb give authority to

MANDATED > MANDATE

MANDATES > MANDATE

MANDATING > MANDATE

MANDATOR > MANDATE

MANDATORS > MANDATE

MANDATORY adj compulsory ▷ n person or state holding a mandate

MANDI n (in India) a big market

MANDIBLE n lower jawbone or jawlike part

MANDIBLES > MANDIBLE

MANDILION same as > MANDYLION

MANDIOC same as > MANIOC

MANDIOCA same as > MANIOC

MANDIOCAS > MANDIOCA

MANDIOCCA same as > MANIOC

MANDIOCS > MANDIOC

MANDIR n Hindu or Jain temple

MANDIRA same as > MANDIR

MANDIRAS > MANDIRA

MANDIRS > MANDIR

MANDIS > MANDI

MANDOLA n early type of mandolin

MANDOLAS > MANDOLA

MANDOLIN n musical instrument with four pairs of strings

MANDOLINE same as > MANDOLIN

MANDOLINS > MANDOLIN

MANDOM n mankind

MANDOMS > MANDOM

MANDORA n ancestor of mandolin

MANDORAS > MANDORA

MANDORLA n area of light surrounding Christ in a painting

MANDORLAS > MANDORLA

MANDRAKE n plant with a forked root

MANDRAKES > MANDRAKE

MANDREL n shaft on which work is held in a lathe

MANDRELS > MANDREL

MANDRIL same as > MANDREL

MANDRILL n large blue-faced baboon

MANDRILLS > MANDRILL

MANDRILS > MANDRIL

MANDUCATE vb eat or chew

MANDYLION n loose garment formerly worn over armour

MANE n long hair on the neck of a horse, lion, etc

MANEB n powdered fungicide

MANEBS > MANEB

MANED > MANE

MANEGE n art of training horses and riders ▷ vb train horse

MANEGED > MANEGE

MANEGES > MANEGE

MANEGING > MANEGE

MANEH same as > MINA

MANEHS > MANEH

MANELESS > MANE

MANENT > MANET

MANES pl n spirits of the dead, often revered as minor deities

MANET vb theatre direction, remain on stage

MANEUVER same as > MANOEUVRE

MANEUVERS > MANEUVER

MANFUL adj determined and brave

MANFULLER > MANFUL

MANFULLY > MANFUL

MANG vb speak

MANGA n type of Japanese comic book

MANGABEY n large African monkey

MANGABEYS > MANGABEY

MANGABIES > MANGABY

MANGABY same as > MANGABEY

MANGAL n Turkish brazier

MANGALS > MANGAL

MANGANATE n salt of manganic acid

MANGANESE n brittle greyish-white metallic element

MANGANIC adj of or containing manganese in the trivalent state

MANGANIN n copper-based alloy

MANGANINS > MANGANIN

MANGANITE n blackish mineral

MANGANOUS adj of or containing manganese in the divalent state

MANGAS > MANGA

MANGE n skin disease of domestic animals

MANGEAO n small New Zealand tree with glossy leaves

MANGEAOS > MANGEAO

MANGED > MANG

MANGEL n Eurasian variety of the beet plant

MANGELS > MANGEL

MANGER n eating trough in a stable or barn

MANGERS > MANGER

MANGES > MANGE

MANGETOUT n variety of pea with an edible pod

MANGEY same as > MANGY

MANGIER > MANGY

MANGIEST > MANGY

MANGILY > MANGY

MANGINESS > MANGY

MANGING > MANG

MANGLE vb destroy by crushing and twisting ▷ n machine with rollers for squeezing water from washed clothes

MANGLED > MANGLE

MANGLER > MANGLE

MANGLERS > MANGLE

MANGLES > MANGLE

MANGLING > MANGLE

MANGO n tropical fruit with sweet juicy yellow flesh

MANGOES > MANGO

MANGOLD n type of root vegetable

MANGOLDS > MANGOLD

MANGONEL n war engine for hurling stones

MANGONELS > MANGONEL

MANGOS > MANGO

MANGOSTAN n Malaysian tree with thick leathery leaves and edible fruit

MANGOUSTE same as > MONGOOSE

MANGROVE n tropical tree with exposed roots, which grows beside water

MANGROVES > MANGROVE

MANGS > MANG

MANGULATE vb bend or twist out of shape

MANGY adj having mange

MANHANDLE vb treat roughly

MANHATTAN n mixed drink consisting of four parts whisky, one part vermouth, and a dash of bitters

MANHOLE n hole with a cover, through which a person can enter a drain or sewer

MANHOLES > MANHOLE

MANHOOD n state or quality of being a man or being manly

MANHOODS > MANHOOD

MANHUNT n organized search, usu by police, for a wanted man

MANHUNTER > MANHUNT

MANHUNTS > MANHUNT

MANI n place to pray

MANIA n extreme enthusiasm

MANIAC n person acting wildly

MANIACAL adj characteristic of mania

MANIACS > MANIAC

MANIAS > MANIA

MANIC adj extremely excited or energetic ▷ n person with mania

MANICALLY > MANIC

MANICOTTI pl n large tubular noodles, usually stuffed with ricotta cheese and baked in a tomato sauce

MANICS > MANIC

MANICURE n cosmetic care of the fingernails and hands ▷ vb care for (the fingernails and hands) in this way

MANICURED > MANICURE

MANICURES > MANICURE

MANIES > MANY

MANIFEST adj easily noticed, obvious ▷ vb show plainly ▷ n list of cargo or passengers for customs

MANIFESTO n declaration of policy as issued by a political party ▷ vb issued manifesto

MANIFESTS > MANIFEST

MANIFOLD adj numerous and varied ▷ n pipe with several outlets, esp in an internal-combustion engine ▷ vb duplicate (a page, book, etc)

MANIFOLDS > MANIFOLD

MANIFORM adj like hand

MANIHOC variation of > MANIOC

MANIHOCS > MANIHOC

MANIHOT n tropical American plant

MANIHOTS > MANIHOT

MANIKIN n little man or dwarf

MANIKINS > MANIKIN

MANILA n strong brown paper used for envelopes

MANILAS > MANILA

MANILLA n early currency in W Africa in the form of a small bracelet

MANILLAS > MANILLA

MANILLE n (in ombre and quadrille) the second best trump

MANILLES > MANILLE

MANIOC same as > CASSAVA

MANIOCA same as > MANIOC

MANIOCAS > MANIOCA

MANIOCS > MANIOC

MANIPLE n (in ancient Rome) a unit of 120 to 200 foot soldiers

MANIPLES > MANIPLE

MANIPLIES same as > MANYPLIES

MANIPULAR adj of or relating to an ancient Roman maniple

MANIS n pangolin

MANISES > MANIS

MANITO same as > MANITOU

MANITOS > MANITO
MANITOU n Native American deified spirit or force
MANITOUS > MANITOU
MANITU same as > MANITOU
MANITUS > MANITU
MANJACK n single individual
MANJACKS > MANJACK
MANKIER > MANKY
MANKIEST > MANKY
MANKIND n human beings collectively
MANKINDS > MANKIND
MANKINI n man's revealing swimming costume
MANKINIS > MANKINI
MANKY adj worthless, rotten, or in bad taste
MANLESS > MAN
MANLIER > MANLY
MANLIEST > MANLY
MANLIKE adj resembling or befitting a man
MANLIKELY > MANLIKE
MANLILY > MANLY
MANLINESS > MANLY
MANLY adj (possessing qualities) appropriate to a man
MANMADE adj made or produced by human beings
MANNA n miraculous food which sustained the Israelites in the wilderness
MANNAN n drug derived from mannose
MANNANS > MANNAN
MANNAS > MANNA
MANNED > MAN
MANNEQUIN n woman who models clothes at a fashion show
MANNER n way a thing happens or is done
MANNERED adj affected
MANNERISM n person's distinctive habit or trait
MANNERIST > MANNERISM
MANNERLY adj having good manners, polite ▷ adv with good manners
MANNERS pl n person's social conduct
MANNIKIN same as > MANIKIN
MANNIKINS > MANNIKIN
MANNING > MAN
MANNISH adj like a man
MANNISHLY > MANNISH
MANNITE same as > MANNITOL
MANNITES > MANNITE
MANNITIC > MANNITOL
MANNITOL n white crystalline water-soluble sweet-tasting substance
MANNITOLS > MANNITOL
MANNOSE n hexose sugar
MANNOSES > MANNOSE

MANO n stone for grinding grain
MANOAO n New Zealand shrub
MANOAOS > MANOAO
MANOES > MANO
MANOEUVER same as > MANOEUVRE
MANOEUVRE n skilful movement ▷ vb manipulate or contrive skilfully or cunningly
MANOMETER n instrument for comparing pressures
MANOMETRY > MANOMETER
MANOR n large country house and its lands
MANORIAL > MANOR
MANORS > MANOR
MANOS > MANO
MANOSCOPY n measurement of the densities of gases
MANPACK n load carried by one person
MANPACKS > MANPACK
MANPOWER n available number of workers
MANPOWERS > MANPOWER
MANQUE adj would-be ▷ n section on a roulette table
MANQUES > MANQUE
MANRED n homage
MANREDS > MANRED
MANRENT same as > MANRED
MANRENTS > MANRENT
MANRIDER n train carrying miners in coal mine
MANRIDERS > MANRIDER
MANRIDING adj carrying people rather than goods
MANROPE n rope railing
MANROPES > MANROPE
MANS > MAN
MANSARD n type of sloping roof
MANSARDED adj having mansard roof
MANSARDS > MANSARD
MANSCAPE vb groom a man's bodily hair for aesthetics
MANSCAPED > MANSCAPE
MANSCAPES > MANSCAPE
MANSE n house provided for a minister in some religious denominations
MANSES > MANSE
MANSHIFT n work done by one person in one shift
MANSHIFTS > MANSHIFT
MANSION n large house
MANSIONS > MANSION
MANSLAYER n person who kills a man
MANSONRY n mansions collectively
MANSPLAIN vb (of a man) explain something to a

woman in a condescending way
MANSPREAD vb (of a man) sit with the legs wide apart, denying others space
MANSUETE adj gentle
MANSWORN adj perjured ▷ n someone who perjures
MANSWORNS > MANSWORN
MANTA n type of large ray with very wide winglike pectoral fins
MANTAS > MANTA
MANTEAU n cloak or mantle
MANTEAUS > MANTEAU
MANTEAUX > MANTEAU
MANTEEL n cloak
MANTEELS > MANTEEL
MANTEL n structure round a fireplace ▷ vb construct a mantel
MANTELET n woman's short mantle, often lace-trimmed, worn in the mid-19th century
MANTELETS > MANTELET
MANTELS > MANTEL
MANTES > MANTIS
MANTIC adj of or relating to divination and prophecy
MANTICORA same as > MANTICORE
MANTICORE n mythical monster with body of lion and human head
MANTID same as > MANTIS
MANTIDS > MANTID
MANTIES > MANTY
MANTILLA n (in Spain) a lace scarf covering a woman's head and shoulders
MANTILLAS > MANTILLA
MANTIS n carnivorous insect like a grasshopper
MANTISES > MANTIS
MANTISSA n part of a common logarithm consisting of the decimal point and the figures following it
MANTISSAS > MANTISSA
MANTLE same as > MANTEL
MANTLED > MANTLE
MANTLES > MANTLE
MANTLET same as > MANTELET
MANTLETS > MANTLET
MANTLING n drapery or scrollwork around a shield
MANTLINGS > MANTLING
MANTO same as > MANTEAU
MANTOES > MANTO
MANTOS > MANTO
MANTRA n any sacred word or syllable used as an object of concentration
MANTRAM same as > MANTRA

MANTRAMS > MANTRAM
MANTRAP n snare for catching people, esp trespassers
MANTRAPS > MANTRAP
MANTRAS > MANTRA
MANTRIC > MANTRA
MANTUA n loose gown of the 17th and 18th centuries
MANTUAS > MANTUA
MANTY Scots variant of > MANTUA
MANTYHOSE n tights that are worn by men
MANUAL adj of or done with the hands ▷ n handbook
MANUALLY > MANUAL
MANUALS > MANUAL
MANUARY same as > MANUAL
MANUBRIA > MANUBRIUM
MANUBRIAL > MANUBRIUM
MANUBRIUM n any handle-shaped part, esp the upper part of the sternum
MANUCODE n bird of Paradise with blue-black plumage
MANUCODES > MANUCODE
MANUHIRI n visitor to a Māori marae
MANUHIRIS > MANUHIRI
MANUKA n New Zealand tree
MANUKAS > MANUKA
MANUL n Asian wildcat
MANULS > MANUL
MANUMATIC adj relating to a type of automatic car transmission
MANUMEA n pigeon of Samoa
MANUMEAS > MANUMEA
MANUMIT vb free from slavery
MANUMITS > MANUMIT
MANURANCE n cultivation of land
MANURE n animal excrement used as a fertilizer ▷ vb fertilize (land) with this
MANURED > MANURE
MANURER > MANURE
MANURERS > MANURE
MANURES > MANURE
MANURIAL > MANURE
MANURING > MANURE
MANURINGS > MANURE
MANUS n wrist and hand
MANWARD adv towards humankind
MANWARDS same as > MANWARD
MANWISE adv in a human way
MANY adj numerous ▷ n large number
MANYATA same as > MANYATTA
MANYATAS > MANYATTA
MANYATTA n settlement of Maasai people

MANYATTAS
> MANYATTA

MANYFOLD adj many in number

MANYPLIES n third component of the stomach of ruminants

MANZANITA n Californian plant

MANZELLO n instrument like saxophone

MANZELLOS
> MANZELLO

MAOMAO n fish of New Zealand seas

MAOMAOS > MAOMAO

MAORMOR same as
> MORMAOR

MAORMORS > MAORMOR

MAP n representation of the earth's surface or some part of it ▷ vb make a map of

MAPAU n small New Zealand tree

MAPAUS > MAPAU

MAPLE n tree with broad leaves, a variety of which yields sugar

MAPLELIKE > MAPLE

MAPLES > MAPLE

MAPLESS > MAP

MAPLIKE > MAP

MAPMAKER n person who draws maps

MAPMAKERS
> MAPMAKER

MAPMAKING
> MAPMAKER

MAPPABLE > MAP

MAPPED > MAP

MAPPEMOND n map of world

MAPPER > MAP

MAPPERIES > MAPPERY

MAPPERS > MAP

MAPPERY n making of maps

MAPPING > MAP

MAPPINGS > MAP

MAPPIST > MAP

MAPPISTS > MAP

MAPS > MAP

MAPSTICK same as
> MOPSTICK

MAPSTICKS
> MAPSTICK

MAPWISE adv like map

MAQUETTE n sculptor's small preliminary model or sketch

MAQUETTES > MAQUETTE

MAQUI n Chilean shrub

MAQUILA n US-owned factory in Mexico

MAQUILAS > MAQUILA

MAQUIS n French underground movement in World War II

MAQUISARD n member of French maquis

MAR vb spoil or impair ▷ n disfiguring mark

MARA n harelike S American rodent

MARABI n kind of music popular in S African townships in the 1930s

MARABIS > MARABI

MARABOU n large black-and-white African stork

MARABOUS > MARABOU

MARABOUT n Muslim holy man or hermit of North Africa

MARABOUTS > MARABOUT

MARABUNTA n any of several social wasps

MARACA n shaken percussion instrument

MARACAS > MARACA

MARAE n enclosed space in front of a Māori meeting house

MARAES > MARAE

MARAGING adj as in maraging steel strong low-carbon steel

MARAGINGS
> MARAGING

MARAH n bitterness

MARAHS > MARAH

MARAKA > MARKA

MARANATHA n member of Christian sect

MARANTA n tropical American plant

MARANTAS > MARANTA

MARARI n eel-like blennioid food fish

MARARIS > MARARI

MARAS > MARA

MARASCA n European cherry tree with red acid-tasting fruit

MARASCAS > MARASCA

MARASMIC > MARASMUS

MARASMOID
> MARASMUS

MARASMUS n emaciation

MARATHON n long-distance race of 26 miles 385 yards (42.195 kilometres) ▷ adj of or relating to a race on foot of 26 miles 385 yards (42.195 kilometres)

MARATHONS
> MARATHON

MARAUD vb wander or raid in search of plunder

MARAUDED > MARAUD

MARAUDER > MARAUD

MARAUDERS > MARAUD

MARAUDING adj wandering or raiding in search of plunder

MARAUDS > MARAUD

MARAVEDI n any of various Spanish coins of copper or gold

MARAVEDIS
> MARAVEDI

MARBELISE same as
> MARBELIZE

MARBELIZE same as
> MARBLEIZE

MARBLE n kind of limestone with a mottled appearance ▷ vb mottle with variegated streaks in imitation of marble

MARBLED > MARBLE

MARBLEISE same as
> MARBLEIZE

MARBLEIZE vb give a marble-like appearance to

MARBLER > MARBLE

MARBLERS > MARBLE

MARBLES n game in which marble balls are rolled at one another

MARBLIER > MARBLE

MARBLIEST > MARBLE

MARBLING n mottled effect or pattern resembling marble

MARBLINGS
> MARBLING

MARBLY > MARBLE

MARC n remains of grapes or other fruit that have been pressed for wine-making

MARCASITE n crystals of iron pyrites, used in jewellery

MARCATO adj (of notes) heavily accented ▷ adv with each note heavily accented ▷ n heavily accented note

MARCATOS > MARCATO

MARCEL n hairstyle characterized by repeated regular waves ▷ vb make such waves in (the hair)

MARCELLA n type of fabric

MARCELLAS
> MARCELLA

MARCELLED > MARCEL

MARCELLER > MARCEL

MARCELS > MARCEL

MARCH vb walk with a military step ▷ n action of marching

MARCHED > MARCH

MARCHEN n German story

MARCHER n person who marches

MARCHERS > MARCHER

MARCHES > MARCH

MARCHESA n (in Italy) the wife or widow of a marchese

MARCHESAS
> MARCHESA

MARCHESE n (in Italy) a nobleman ranking below a prince and above a count

MARCHESI > MARCHESE

MARCHING > MARCH

MARCHLAND n border land

MARCHLIKE adj like march in rhythm

MARCHMAN n person living on border

MARCHMEN > MARCHMAN

MARCHPANE same as
> MARZIPAN

MARCONI vb communicate by wireless

MARCONIED > MARCONI

MARCONIS > MARCONI

MARCS > MARC

MARD > MAR

MARDIED > MARDY

MARDIER > MARDY

MARDIES > MARDY

MARDIEST > MARDY

MARDY adj (of a child) spoilt ▷ vb behave in mardy way

MARDYING > MARDY

MARE n female horse or zebra

MAREMMA n marshy unhealthy region near the shore, esp in Italy

MAREMMAS > MAREMMA

MAREMME > MAREMMA

MARENGO adj browned in oil and cooked with tomatoes, mushrooms, garlic, wine, etc

MARERO n member of a C American organized criminal gang

MAREROS > MARERO

MARES > MARE

MARESCHAL same as
> MARSHAL

MARG short for
> MARGARINE

MARGARIC adj of or resembling pearl

MARGARIN n ester of margaric acid

MARGARINE n butter substitute made from animal or vegetable fats

MARGARINS
> MARGARIN

MARGARITA n mixed drink consisting of tequila and lemon juice

MARGARITE n pink pearly micaceous mineral

MARGATE n greyish fish of W Atlantic

MARGATES > MARGATE

MARGAY n feline mammal of Central and S America

MARGAYS > MARGAY

MARGE n margarine

MARGENT same as
> MARGIN

MARGENTED > MARGENT

MARGENTS > MARGENT

MARGES > MARGE

MARGIN n edge or border ▷ vb provide with a margin

MARGINAL adj insignificant, unimportant ▷ n marginal constituency

MARGINALS
> MARGINAL

MARGINATE vb provide with a margin or margins ▷ adj having a margin of a distinct colour or form

MARGINED > MARGIN

MARGINING > MARGIN

MARGINS > MARGIN

MARGOSA n Indian tree

MARGOSAS > MARGOSA

MARGRAVE n (formerly) a German nobleman ranking above a count

MARGRAVES
> MARGRAVE

MARGS > MARG

MARIA > MARE

MARIACHI n small ensemble of street musicians in Mexico

MARIACHIS
> MARIACHI

MARIALITE n silicate mineral

MARID n spirit in Muslim mythology

MARIDS > MARID

MARIES > MARY

MARIGOLD n plant with yellow or orange flowers

MARIGOLDS > MARIGOLD

MARIGRAM n graphic record of the tide levels at a particular coastal station

MARIGRAMS > MARIGRAM

MARIGRAPH n gauge for recording the levels of the tides

MARIHUANA same as > MARIJUANA

MARIJUANA n dried flowers and leaves of the cannabis plant

MARIMBA n Latin American percussion instrument

MARIMBAS > MARIMBA

MARIMBIST > MARIMBA

MARINA n harbour for yachts and other pleasure boats

MARINADE n seasoned liquid in which fish or meat is soaked before cooking

MARINADED > MARINADE

MARINADES > MARINADE

MARINARA n Italian pasta sauce

MARINARAS > MARINARA

MARINAS > MARINA

MARINATE vb soak in marinade

MARINATED > MARINATE

MARINATES > MARINATE

MARINE adj of the sea or shipping ▷ n (esp in Britain and the US) soldier trained for land and sea combat

MARINER n sailor

MARINERA n folk dance of Peru

MARINERAS > MARINERA

MARINERS > MARINER

MARINES > MARINE

MARINIERE adj served in white wine and onion sauce

MARIPOSA n plant of southwestern US and Mexico

MARIPOSAS > MARIPOSA

MARISCHAL Scots variant of > MARSHAL

MARISH n marsh

MARISHES > MARISH

MARITAGE n right of a lord to choose the spouses of his wards

MARITAGES > MARITAGE

MARITAL adj relating to marriage

MARITALLY > MARITAL

MARITIME adj relating to shipping

MARJORAM n aromatic herb used for seasoning food and in salads

MARJORAMS > MARJORAM

MARK n line, dot, scar, etc visible on a surface ▷ vb make a mark on

MARKA n unit of currency introduced as an interim currency in Bosnia-Herzegovina

MARKAS > MARKA

MARKDOWN n price reduction ▷ vb reduce in price

MARKDOWNS > MARKDOWN

MARKED adj noticeable

MARKEDLY > MARKED

MARKER n object used to show the position of something

MARKERS > MARKER

MARKET n assembly or place for buying and selling ▷ vb offer or produce for sale

MARKETED > MARKET

MARKETEER n person employed in marketing

MARKETER > MARKET

MARKETERS > MARKET

MARKETING n part of a business that controls the way that goods or services are sold

MARKETISE same as > MARKETIZE

MARKETIZE vb convert (a national economy) to a market economy

MARKETS > MARKET

MARKHOOR same as > MARKHOR

MARKHOORS > MARKHOOR

MARKHOR n large wild Himalayan goat

MARKHORS > MARKHOR

MARKING n arrangement of colours on an animal or plant

MARKINGS > MARKING

MARKKA n former standard monetary unit of Finland

MARKKAA > MARKKA

MARKKAS > MARKKA

MARKMAN n person owning land

MARKMEN > MARKMAN

MARKS > MARK

MARKSMAN n person skilled at shooting

MARKSMEN > MARKSMAN

MARKUP n percentage added to the cost of something to give the seller a profit

MARKUPS > MARKUP

MARL n soil formed of clay and lime, used as fertilizer ▷ vb fertilize (land) with marl

MARLE same as > MARVEL

MARLED > MARL

MARLES > MARLE

MARLIER > MARLY

MARLIEST > MARLY

MARLIN same as > MARLINE

MARLINE n light rope, usually tarred, made of two strands laid left-handed

MARLINES > MARLINE

MARLING same as > MARLINE

MARLINGS > MARLING

MARLINS > MARLIN

MARLITE n type of marl that contains clay and calcium carbonate

MARLITES > MARLITE

MARLITIC > MARLITE

MARLS > MARL

MARLSTONE same as > MARLITE

MARLY adj marl-like

MARM same as > MADAM

MARMALADE n jam made from citrus fruits ▷ adj (of cats) streaked orange or yellow and brown

MARMALISE vb beat soundly or defeat utterly

MARMALIZE same as > MARMALISE

MARMARISE same as > MARMARIZE

MARMARIZE vb turn to marble

MARMELISE same as > MARMELIZE

MARMELIZE vb beat soundly

MARMEM n as in marmem alloy type of alloy

MARMITE n large cooking pot

MARMITES > MARMITE

MARMOREAL adj of or like marble

MARMOREAN same as > MARMOREAL

MARMOSE n South American opossum

MARMOSES > MARMOSE

MARMOSET n small bushy-tailed monkey

MARMOSETS > MARMOSET

MARMOT n burrowing rodent

MARMOTS > MARMOT

MARMS > MARM

MAROCAIN n fabric of ribbed crepe

MAROCAINS > MAROCAIN

MARON n freshwater crustacean

MARONS > MARON

MAROON adj reddish-purple ▷ vb abandon ashore, esp on an island ▷ n exploding firework or flare used as a warning signal

MAROONED > MAROON

MAROONER > MAROON

MAROONERS > MAROON

MAROONING > MAROON

MAROONS > MAROON

MAROQUIN n morocco leather

MAROQUINS > MAROQUIN

MAROR n Jewish ceremonial dish of bitter herbs

MARORS > MAROR

MARPLOT n person who spoils a plot

MARPLOTS > MARPLOT

MARQUE n brand of product, esp of a car

MARQUEE n large tent used for a party or exhibition

MARQUEES > MARQUEE

MARQUES > MARQUE

MARQUESS n nobleman of the rank below a duke

MARQUETRY n ornamental inlaid work of wood

MARQUIS n (in some European countries) nobleman of the rank above a count

MARQUISE same as > MARQUEE

MARQUISES > MARQUISE

MARRA n (in N England) friend

MARRAM n as in marram grass any of several grasses that grow on sandy shores

MARRAMS > MARRAM

MARRANO n Spanish or Portuguese Jew of the late Middle Ages who was converted to Christianity

MARRANOS > MARRANO

MARRAS > MARRA

MARRED > MAR

MARRELS same as > MERILS

MARRER > MAR

MARRERS > MAR

MARRI n W Australian eucalyptus

MARRIAGE n state of being married

MARRIAGES > MARRIAGE

MARRIED > MARRY

MARRIEDS pl n married people

MARRIER > MARRY

MARRIERS > MARRY

MARRIES > MARRY

MARRING > MAR

MARRIS > MARRI

MARRON n large edible sweet chestnut

MARRONS > MARRON

MARROW n fatty substance inside bones ▷ vb be mate to

MARROWED > MARROW

MARROWFAT n variety of large pea

MARROWIER > MARROWY

MARROWING > MARROW

MARROWISH > MARROW

MARROWS > MARROW

MARROWSKY n spoonerism

MARROWY adj full of marrow

MARRUM same as >MARRAM

MARRUMS >MARRUM

MARRY vb take as a spouse ▷ interj exclamation of surprise or anger

MARRYING >MARRY

MARRYINGS >MARRY

MARS >MAR

MARSALA n dark sweet dessert wine made in Sicily

MARSALAS >MARSALA

MARSE same as >MASTER

MARSEILLE n strong cotton fabric with a raised pattern, used for bedspreads, etc

MARSES >MARSE

MARSH n low-lying wet land

MARSHAL n officer of the highest rank ▷ vb arrange in order

MARSHALCY >MARSHAL

MARSHALED >MARSHAL

MARSHALER >MARSHAL

MARSHALL n shortened form of Marshall Plan

MARSHALLS >MARSHALL

MARSHALS >MARSHAL

MARSHBUCK n antelope of the central African swamplands, with spreading hoofs adapted to boggy ground

MARSHED adj having a marsh

MARSHES >MARSH

MARSHIER >MARSHY

MARSHIEST >MARSHY

MARSHLAND n land consisting of marshes

MARSHLIKE >MARSH

MARSHWORT n type of creeping aquatic plant with small white flowers

MARSHY adj of, involving, or like a marsh

MARSPORT n spoilsport

MARSPORTS >MARSPORT

MARSQUAKE n Martian equivalent of earthquake

MARSUPIA >MARSUPIUM

MARSUPIAL n animal that carries its young in a pouch, such as a kangaroo ▷ adj of or like a marsupial

MARSUPIAN >MARSUPIAL

MARSUPIUM n external pouch in most female marsupials within which the newly born offspring are suckled and complete their development

MART n market ▷ vb sell or trade

MARTAGON n Eurasian lily plant cultivated for its mottled purplish-red flowers

MARTAGONS >MARTAGON

MARTED >MART

MARTEL n hammer-shaped weapon ▷ vb use such a weapon

MARTELLED >MARTEL

MARTELLO n small circular tower for coastal defence, formerly much used in Europe

MARTELLOS >MARTELLO

MARTELS >MARTEL

MARTEN n weasel-like animal

MARTENS >MARTEN

MARTEXT n preacher who makes many mistakes

MARTEXTS >MARTEXT

MARTIAL adj of war, warlike

MARTIALLY >MARTIAL

MARTIALS pl n as in court martials military courts that try people subject to military law

MARTIAN n inhabitant of Mars

MARTIANS >MARTIAN

MARTIN n bird with a slightly forked tail

MARTINET n person who maintains strict discipline

MARTINETS >MARTINET

MARTING >MART

MARTINGAL n strap of a horse's harness

MARTINI n cocktail of vermouth and gin

MARTINIS >MARTINI

MARTINS >MARTIN

MARTLET n footless bird often found in coats of arms

MARTLETS >MARTLET

MARTS >MART

MARTYR n person who dies or suffers for his or her beliefs ▷ vb make a martyr of

MARTYRDOM n sufferings or death of a martyr

MARTYRED >MARTYR

MARTYRIA >MARTYRIUM

MARTYRIES >MARTYRY

MARTYRING >MARTYR

MARTYRISE >MARTYR

MARTYRISH adj like a martyr

MARTYRIUM same as >MARTYRY

MARTYRIZE >MARTYR

MARTYRLY >MARTYR

MARTYRS >MARTYR

MARTYRY n shrine or chapel erected in honour of a martyr

MARVEL vb be filled with wonder ▷ n wonderful thing

MARVELED >MARVEL

MARVELER n (US) person who marvels

MARVELERS >MARVELER

MARVELING >MARVEL

MARVELLED >MARVEL

MARVELLER n person who marvels

MARVELOUS adj causing great wonder

MARVELS >MARVEL

MARVER vb roll molten glass on slab

MARVERED >MARVER

MARVERING >MARVER

MARVERS >MARVER

MARVIER >MARVY

MARVIEST >MARVY

MARVY shortened form of >MARVELOUS

MARXISANT adj sympathetic to Marxism

MARY n woman

MARYBUD n bud of marigold

MARYBUDS >MARYBUD

MARYJANE n woman's shoe with strap over the top

MARYJANES >MARYJANE

MARZIPAN n paste of ground almonds, sugar, and egg whites ▷ vb cover with marzipan

MARZIPANS >MARZIPAN

MAS >MA

MASA n Mexican maize dough

MASALA n mixture of spices ground into a paste ▷ adj spicy

MASALAS >MASALA

MASAS >MASA

MASCARA n cosmetic for darkening the eyelashes

MASCARAED adj wearing mascara

MASCARAS >MASCARA

MASCARON n in architecture, a face carved in stone or metal

MASCARONS n grotesque face used as decoration

MASCLE n charge consisting of a lozenge with a lozenge-shaped hole in the middle

MASCLED >MASCLE

MASCLES >MASCLE

MASCON n any of several lunar regions of high gravity

MASCONS >MASCON

MASCOT n person, animal, or thing supposed to bring good luck

MASCOTS >MASCOT

MASCULINE adj relating to males ▷ n short for masculine noun

MASCULIST n advocate of rights of men)

MASCULY >MASCLE

MASE vb function as maser

MASED >MASE

MASER n device for amplifying microwaves

MASERS >MASER

MASES >MASE

MASH n soft pulpy mass ▷ vb crush into a soft mass

MASHALLAH interj what Allah wishes

MASHED >MASH

MASHER >MASH

MASHERS >MASH

MASHES >MASH

MASHGIACH n person who ensures adherence to kosher rules

MASHGIAH same as >MASHGIACH

MASHGIHIM >MASHGIACH

MASHIACH n messiah

MASHIACHS >MASHIACH

MASHIE n former golf club, used for approach shots

MASHIER >MASHY

MASHIES >MASHIE

MASHIEST >MASHY

MASHING >MASH

MASHINGS >MASH

MASHLAM same as >MASLIN

MASHLAMS >MASHLAM

MASHLIM same as >MASLIN

MASHLIMS >MASHLIM

MASHLIN same as >MASLIN

MASHLINS >MASHLIN

MASHLOCH same as >MASLIN

MASHLOCHS >MASHLOCH

MASHLUM same as >MASLIN

MASHLUMS >MASHLUM

MASHMAN n brewery worker

MASHMEN >MASHMAN

MASHUA n South American plant

MASHUAS >MASHUA

MASHUP n piece of music in which a producer or DJ blends together two or more tracks

MASHUPS >MASHUP

MASHY adj like mash

MASING >MASE

MASJID same as >MOSQUE

MASJIDS >MASJID

MASK n covering for the face, as a disguise or protection ▷ vb cover with a mask

MASKABLE >MASK

MASKED adj disguised or covered by or as if by a mask

MASKEG n North American bog

MASKEGS >MASKEG

MASKER n person who wears a mask or takes part in a masque

MASKERS >MASKER

MASKING n act or practice of masking

MASKINGS >MASKING

MASKLIKE >MASK

MASKS >MASK

MASLIN n mixture of wheat, rye or other grain

MASLINS >MASLIN

MASOCHISM n gaining of pleasure from one's own pain or humiliation

MASOCHIST > MASOCHISM

MASON n person who works with stone ▷ vb construct or strengthen with masonry

MASONED > MASON

MASONIC adj of, characteristic of, or relating to Freemasons

MASONING > MASON

MASONITE n tradename for a kind of dark brown hardboard used for partitions, lining, etc

MASONITES > MASONITE

MASONRIED adj built of masonry

MASONRIES > MASONRY

MASONRY n stonework

MASONS > MASON

MASOOLAH n Indian boat used in surf

MASOOLAHS > MASOOLAH

MASOOLAS > MASOOLA

MASQUE n 16th–17th-century form of dramatic entertainment

MASQUER same as > MASKER

MASQUERS > MASQUER

MASQUES > MASQUE

MASS n coherent body of matter ▷ adj large-scale ▷ vb form into a mass

MASSA old fashioned variant of > MASTER

MASSACRE n indiscriminate killing of large numbers of people ▷ vb kill in large numbers

MASSACRED > MASSACRE

MASSACRER > MASSACRE

MASSACRES > MASSACRE

MASSAGE n rubbing and kneading of parts of the body to reduce pain or stiffness ▷ vb give a massage to

MASSAGED > MASSAGE

MASSAGER > MASSAGE

MASSAGERS > MASSAGE

MASSAGES > MASSAGE

MASSAGING > MASSAGE

MASSAGIST > MASSAGE

MASSAS > MASSA

MASSCULT n culture of masses

MASSCULTS > MASSCULT

MASSE n billiard stroke that makes the ball move in a curve around another ball

MASSED > MASS

MASSEDLY > MASS

MASSES pl n body of common people

MASSETER n muscle of the cheek used in moving the jaw, esp in chewing

MASSETERS > MASSETER

MASSEUR n person who gives massages

MASSEURS > MASSEUR

MASSEUSE n woman who gives massages, esp as a profession

MASSEUSES > MASSEUSE

MASSICOT n yellow earthy secondary mineral

MASSICOTS > MASSICOT

MASSIER > MASSY

MASSIEST > MASSY

MASSIF n connected group of mountains

MASSIFS > MASSIF

MASSINESS > MASSY

MASSING > MASS

MASSIVE adj large and heavy ▷ n group of friends or associates

MASSIVELY > MASSIVE

MASSIVES > MASSIVE

MASSLESS > MASS

MASSOOLA same as > MASOOLAH

MASSOOLAS > MASSOOLA

MASSTIGE n impression of exclusivity in mass-produced goods

MASSTIGES > MASSTIGE

MASSY literary word for > MASSIVE

MASSYMORE n underground prison

MAST n tall pole for supporting something, esp a ship's sails ▷ vb equip with a mast

MASTABA n mud-brick superstructure above tombs in ancient Egypt

MASTABAH same as > MASTABA

MASTABAHS > MASTABAH

MASTABAS > MASTABA

MASTED > MAST

MASTER n person in control, such as an owner of animals ▷ vb acquire knowledge of or skill in

MASTERATE n status of master

MASTERDOM > MASTER

MASTERED > MASTER

MASTERFUL adj domineering

MASTERIES > MASTERY

MASTERING > MASTER

MASTERLY adj showing great skill

MASTERS > MASTER

MASTERY n expertise

MASTFUL > MAST

MASTHEAD n head of a mast ▷ vb send (a sailor) to the masthead as a punishment

MASTHEADS > MASTHEAD

MASTHOUSE n place for storing masts

MASTIC n gum obtained from certain trees

MASTICATE vb chew

MASTICH same as > MASTIC

MASTICHE same as > MASTIC

MASTICHES > MASTICHE

MASTICHS > MASTICH

MASTICOT same as > MASSICOT

MASTICOTS > MASTICOT

MASTICS > MASTIC

MASTIER > MAST

MASTIEST > MAST

MASTIFF n large dog

MASTIFFS > MASTIFF

MASTING > MAST

MASTITIC > MASTITIS

MASTITIS n inflammation of a breast or udder

MASTIX n type of gum

MASTIXES > MASTIX

MASTLESS > MAST

MASTLIKE > MAST

MASTODON n extinct elephant-like mammal

MASTODONS > MASTODON

MASTODONT same as > MASTODON

MASTOID n projection of the bone behind the ear ▷ adj shaped like a nipple or breast

MASTOIDAL > MASTOID

MASTOIDS > MASTOID

MASTOPEXY n cosmetic surgery of breasts

MASTS > MAST

MASTY > MAST

MASU n Japanese salmon

MASULA same as > MASOOLAH

MASULAS > MASULA

MASURIUM n silver-grey metallic element

MASURIUMS > MASURIUM

MASUS > MASU

MAT n piece of fabric used as a floor covering or to protect a surface ▷ vb tangle or become tangled into a dense mass ▷ adj having a dull, lustreless, or roughened surface

MATACHIN n dancer with sword

MATACHINA n female matachin

MATACHINI > MATACHIN

MATACHINS > MATACHIN

MATADOR n bullfighter who kills the bull

MATADORA n female matador

MATADORAS > MATADORA

MATADORE n form of dominoes game

MATADORES > MATADORE

MATADORS > MATADOR

MATAGOURI n thorny bush of New Zealand that forms thickets in open country

MATAI n New Zealand tree, the wood of which is used for timber for building

MATAIS > MATAI

MATAMATA (in Malaysia) a former name for > POLICE

MATAMATAS > MATAMATA

MATAMBALA > TAMBALA

MATATA same as > FERNBIRD

MATATAS > MATATA

MATATU n type of shared taxi used in Kenya

MATATUS > MATATU

MATCH n contest in a game or sport ▷ vb be exactly like, equal to, or in harmony with

MATCHA n Japanese green tea

MATCHABLE > MATCH

MATCHAS > MATCHA

MATCHBOOK n number of cardboard matches attached in folder

MATCHBOX n small box for holding matches

MATCHED > MATCH

MATCHER > MATCH

MATCHERS > MATCH

MATCHES > MATCH

MATCHET same as > MACHETE

MATCHETS > MATCHET

MATCHING > MATCH

MATCHLESS adj unequalled

MATCHLOCK n obsolete type of gunlock igniting the powder by means of a slow match

MATCHMADE > MATCHMAKE

MATCHMAKE vb bring suitable people together for a romantic relationship

MATCHMARK n mark made on mating components of an engine, machine, etc, to ensure that the components are assembled in the correct relative positions ▷ vb stamp (an object) with matchmarks

MATCHPLAY adj of a golf scoring system relating to holes won and lost ▷ n (in golf) scoring system in which a point is earned for each hole won

MATCHUP n sports match

MATCHUPS > MATCHUP

MATCHWOOD n small splinters

MATE n friend ▷ vb pair (animals) or (of animals) be paired for reproduction

MATED > MATE

MATELASSE adj (in textiles) having a raised design, as quilting

MATELESS > MATE

MATELOT n sailor

MATELOTE n fish served with a sauce of wine, onions, seasonings, and fish stock

MATELOTES > MATELOTE

MATELOTS > MATELOT

MATELOTTE same as > MATELOTE

MATER n mother: often used facetiously

MATERIAL n substance of which a thing is made ▷ adj of matter or substance

MATERIALS pl n equipment necessary for a particular activity

MATERIEL n materials and equipment of an organization, esp of a military force

MATERIELS > MATERIEL

MATERNAL adj of a mother

MATERNITY n motherhood ▷ adj of or for pregnant women

MATERS > MATER

MATES > MATE

MATESHIP n comradeship of friends, usually male, viewed as an institution

MATESHIPS > MATESHIP

MATEY adj friendly or intimate ▷ n friend or fellow: usually used in direct address

MATEYNESS > MATEY

MATEYS > MATEY

MATFELLON n knapweed

MATFELON n knapweed

MATFELONS > MATFELON

MATGRASS n widespread European grass

MATH same as > MATHS

MATHESES > MATHESIS

MATHESIS n learning or wisdom

MATHS n science concerned with the study of numbers

MATICO n Peruvian shrub

MATICOS > MATICO

MATIER > MATEY

MATIES > MATEY

MATIEST > MATEY

MATILDA n bushman's swag

MATILDAS > MATILDA

MATILY > MATEY

MATIN adj of or relating to matins

MATINAL same as > MATIN

MATINEE n afternoon performance in a theatre or cinema

MATINEES > MATINEE

MATINESS > MATY

MATING > MATE

MATINGS > MATE

MATINS pl n early morning church service

MATIPO n New Zealand shrub

MATIPOS > MATIPO

MATJES same as > MAATJES

MATLESS > MAT

MATLO same as > MATELOT

MATLOS > MATLO

MATLOW same as > MATELOT

MATLOWS > MATLOW

MATOKE n (in Uganda) the flesh of bananas, boiled and mashed as a food

MATOKES > MATOKE

MATOOKE same as > MATOKE

MATOOKES > MATOOKE

MATRASS n long-necked glass flask

MATRASSES > MATRASS

MATRES > MATER

MATRIARCH n female head of a tribe or family

MATRIC n matriculation

MATRICE same as > MATRIX

MATRICES > MATRIX

MATRICIDE n crime of killing one's mother

MATRICS > MATRIC

MATRICULA n register

MATRILINY n attention to descent of kinship through the female line

MATRIMONY n marriage

MATRIX n substance or situation in which something originates, takes form, or is enclosed

MATRIXES > MATRIX

MATRON n staid or dignified married woman

MATRONAGE n state of being a matron

MATRONAL > MATRON

MATRONISE same as > MATRONIZE

MATRONIZE vb make matronly

MATRONLY adj (of a woman) middle-aged and plump

MATRONS > MATRON

MATROSS n gunner's assistant

MATROSSES > MATROSS

MATS > MAT

MATSAH same as > MATZO

MATSAHS > MATSAH

MATSURI n Japanese religious ceremony

MATSURIS > MATSURI

MATSUTAKE n Japanese mushroom

MATT adj dull, not shiny ▷ n dull surface

MATTAMORE n subterranean storehouse or dwelling

MATTE same as > MATT

MATTED > MAT

MATTEDLY > MAT

MATTER n substance of which something is made ▷ vb be of importance

MATTERED > MATTER

MATTERFUL > MATTER

MATTERIER > MATTERY

MATTERING > MATTER

MATTERS > MATTER

MATTERY adj containing pus

MATTES > MATTE

MATTIE n young herring

MATTIES > MATTIE

MATTIFIED > MATTIFY

MATTIFIES > MATTIFY

MATTIFY vb make (the skin of the face) less oily or shiny using cosmetics

MATTIN same as > MATIN

MATTING > MAT

MATTINGS > MAT

MATTINS same as > MATINS

MATTOCK n large pick with one of its blade ends flattened for loosening soil

MATTOCKS > MATTOCK

MATTOID n person displaying eccentric behaviour

MATTOIDS > MATTOID

MATTRASS same as > MATRASS

MATTRESS n large stuffed flat case, often with springs, used on or as a bed

MATTS > MATT

MATURABLE > MATURE

MATURATE vb mature or bring to maturity

MATURATED > MATURATE

MATURATES > MATURATE

MATURE adj fully developed or grown-up ▷ vb make or become mature

MATURED > MATURE

MATURELY > MATURE

MATURER > MATURE

MATURERS > MATURE

MATURES > MATURE

MATUREST > MATURE

MATURING > MATURE

MATURITY n state of being mature

MATUTINAL adj of, occurring in, or during the morning

MATUTINE same as > MATUTINAL

MATWEED n grass found on moors

MATWEEDS > MATWEED

MATY same as > MATEY

MATZA same as > MATZO

MATZAH same as > MATZO

MATZAHS > MATZAH

MATZAS > MATZA

MATZO n large very thin biscuit of unleavened bread

MATZOH same as > MATZO

MATZOHS > MATZOH

MATZOON n fermented milk product similar to yogurt

MATZOONS > MATZOON

MATZOS > MATZO

MATZOT > MATZO

MATZOTH > MATZOH

MAUBIES > MAUBY

MAUBY n Caribbean bittersweet drink

MAUD n shawl or rug of grey wool plaid

MAUDLIN adj foolishly or tearfully sentimental

MAUDLINLY > MAUDLIN

MAUDS > MAUD

MAUGER same as > MAUGRE

MAUGRE prep in spite of ▷ vb behave spitefully towards

MAUGRED > MAUGRE

MAUGRES > MAUGRE

MAUGRING > MAUGRE

MAUL vb handle roughly ▷ n loose scrum

MAULED > MAUL

MAULER > MAUL

MAULERS pl n hands

MAULGRE same as > MAUGRE

MAULGRED > MAULGRE

MAULGRES > MAULGRE

MAULGRING > MAULGRE

MAULING n act of mauling

MAULINGS > MAULING

MAULS > MAUL

MAULSTICK n long stick used by artists to steady the hand holding the brush

MAULVI n expert in Islamic law

MAULVIS > MAULVI

MAUMET n false god

MAUMETRY > MAUMET

MAUMETS > MAUMET

MAUN dialect word for > MUST

MAUND n unit of weight used in Asia ▷ vb beg

MAUNDED > MAUND

MAUNDER vb talk or act aimlessly or idly

MAUNDERED > MAUNDER

MAUNDERER > MAUNDER

MAUNDERS > MAUNDER

MAUNDIES > MAUNDY

MAUNDING > MAUND

MAUNDS > MAUND

MAUNDY n ceremonial washing of the feet of poor people

MAUNGIER > MAUNGY

MAUNGIEST > MAUNGY

MAUNGY adj (esp of a child) sulky, bad-tempered, or peevish

MAUNNA vb Scots term meaning must not

MAURI n soul

MAURIS > MAURI

MAUSIER > MAUSY

MAUSIEST > MAUSY

MAUSOLEA > MAUSOLEUM

MAUSOLEAN > MAUSOLEUM

MAUSOLEUM n stately tomb

MAUSY adj foggy; misty

MAUT same as > MAHOUT

MAUTHER n girl or young woman

MAUTHERS > MAUTHER

MAUTS > MAUT

MAUVAIS *adj* bad

MAUVAISE *feminine form of* > MAUVAIS

MAUVE *adj* pale purple ▷ *n* any of various pale purple colours

MAUVEIN *same as* > MAUVEINE

MAUVEINE *same as* > MAUVE

MAUVEINES > MAUVEINE

MAUVEINS > MAUVEIN

MAUVER > MAUVE

MAUVES > MAUVE

MAUVEST > MAUVE

MAUVIN *same as* > MAUVEINE

MAUVINE *same as* > MAUVEINE

MAUVINES > MAUVINE

MAUVINS > MAUVIN

MAUZIER > MAUZY

MAUZIEST > MAUZY

MAUZY *adj* foggy; misty

MAVEN *n* expert or connoisseur

MAVENS > MAVEN

MAVERICK *adj* independent and unorthodox ▷ *n* person of independent or unorthodox views ▷ *vb* take illegally

MAVERICKS > MAVERICK

MAVIE *n* type of thrush

MAVIES > MAVIE

MAVIN *same as* > MAVEN

MAVINS > MAVIN

MAVIS *n* song thrush

MAVISES > MAVIS

MAVOURNIN *n* Irish form of address meaning my darling

MAW *n* animal's mouth, throat, or stomach ▷ *vb* eat or bite

MAWBOUND *adj* (of cattle) constipated

MAWED > MAW

MAWGER *adj* (of persons or animals) thin or lean

MAWING > MAW

MAWK *n* maggot

MAWKIER > MAWK

MAWKIEST > MAWK

MAWKIN *n* slovenly woman

MAWKINS > MAWKIN

MAWKISH *adj* foolishly sentimental

MAWKISHLY > MAWKISH

MAWKS > MAWK

MAWKY > MAWK

MAWMET *same as* > MAUMET

MAWMETRY > MAWMET

MAWMETS > MAWMET

MAWN *n* measure of capacity

MAWNS > MAWN

MAWPUS *same as* > MOPUS

MAWPUSES > MAWPUS

MAWR *same as* > MAUTHER

MAWRS > MAWR

MAWS > MAW

MAWSEED *n* poppy seed

MAWSEEDS > MAWSEED

MAWTHER *same as* > MAUTHER

MAWTHERS > MAWTHER

MAX *vb* reach the full extent

MAXED > MAX

MAXES > MAX

MAXI *adj* (of a garment) very long ▷ *n* type of large racing yacht

MAXIBOAT *n* large racing yacht

MAXIBOATS > MAXIBOAT

MAXICOAT *n* long coat

MAXICOATS > MAXICOAT

MAXIDRESS *n* dress that reaches the ankle

MAXILLA *n* upper jawbone of a vertebrate

MAXILLAE > MAXILLA

MAXILLAR > MAXILLA

MAXILLARY > MAXILLA

MAXILLAS > MAXILLA

MAXILLULA *n* jaw in crustacean

MAXIM *n* general truth or principle

MAXIMA > MAXIMUM

MAXIMAL *adj* maximum ▷ *n* maximum

MAXIMALLY > MAXIMAL

MAXIMALS > MAXIMAL

MAXIMAND *n* something that is to be maximized

MAXIMANDS > MAXIMAND

MAXIMIN *n* highest of a set of minimum values

MAXIMINS > MAXIMIN

MAXIMISE *same as* > MAXIMIZE

MAXIMISED > MAXIMISE

MAXIMISER > MAXIMIZE

MAXIMISES > MAXIMISE

MAXIMIST > MAXIM

MAXIMISTS > MAXIM

MAXIMITE *n* type of explosive

MAXIMITES > MAXIMITE

MAXIMIZE *vb* increase to a maximum

MAXIMIZED > MAXIMIZE

MAXIMIZER > MAXIMIZE

MAXIMIZES > MAXIMIZE

MAXIMS > MAXIM

MAXIMUM *n* greatest possible (amount or number) ▷ *adj* of, being, or showing a maximum or maximums

MAXIMUMLY > MAXIMUM

MAXIMUMS > MAXIMUM

MAXIMUS *n* method rung on twelve bells

MAXIMUSES > MAXIMUS

MAXING > MAX

MAXIS > MAXI

MAXIXE *n* Brazilian dance in duple time

MAXIXES > MAXIXE

MAXWELL *n* cgs unit of magnetic flux

MAXWELLS > MAXWELL

MAY *vb* used as an auxiliary to express possibility, permission, opportunity, etc ▷ *vb* gather may (hawthorn)

MAYA *n* illusion, esp the material world of the senses regarded as illusory

MAYAN > MAYA

MAYAPPLE *n* American plant

MAYAPPLES > MAYAPPLE

MAYAS > MAYA

MAYBE *adv* perhaps, possibly ▷ *sentence substitute* possibly ▷ *n* possibility

MAYBES > MAYBE

MAYBIRD *n* American songbird

MAYBIRDS > MAYBIRD

MAYBUSH *n* flowering shrub

MAYBUSHES > MAYBUSH

MAYDAY *n* international radiotelephone distress signal

MAYDAYS > MAYDAY

MAYED > MAY

MAYEST *same as* > MAYST

MAYFISH *n* type of N American fish

MAYFISHES > MAYFISH

MAYFLIES > MAYFLY

MAYFLOWER *n* any of various plants that bloom in May

MAYFLY *n* short-lived aquatic insect

MAYHAP *archaic word for* > PERHAPS

MAYHAPPEN *same as* > MAYHAP

MAYHEM *n* violent destruction or confusion

MAYHEMS > MAYHEM

MAYING > MAY

MAYINGS > MAYING

MAYO *n* mayonnaise

MAYOR *n* head of a municipality

MAYORAL > MAYOR

MAYORALTY *n* (term of) office of a mayor

MAYORESS *n* female mayor

MAYORS > MAYOR

MAYORSHIP > MAYOR

MAYOS > MAYO

MAYPOLE *n* pole set up for dancing round on the first day of May to celebrate spring

MAYPOLES > MAYPOLE

MAYPOP *n* American wild flower

MAYPOPS > MAYPOP

MAYS > MAY

MAYST *singular form of the present tense of* > MAY

MAYSTER *same as* > MASTER

MAYSTERS > MAYSTER

MAYVIN *same as* > MAVEN

MAYVINS > MAYVIN

MAYWEED *n* widespread Eurasian weedy plant

MAYWEEDS > MAYWEED

MAZAEDIA > MAZAEDIUM

MAZAEDIUM *n* part of lichen

MAZARD *same as* > MAZER

MAZARDS > MAZARD

MAZARINE *n* blue colour

MAZARINES > MAZARINE

MAZE *n* complex network of paths or lines

MAZED > MAZE

MAZEDLY *adv* in a bewildered way

MAZEDNESS *n* bewilderment

MAZEFUL > MAZE

MAZELIKE > MAZE

MAZELTOV *interj* congratulations

MAZEMENT > MAZE

MAZEMENTS > MAZE

MAZER *n* large hardwood drinking bowl

MAZERS > MAZER

MAZES > MAZE

MAZEY *adj* dizzy

MAZHBI *n* low-caste Sikh

MAZHBIS > MAZHBI

MAZIER > MAZY

MAZIEST > MAZY

MAZILY > MAZY

MAZINESS > MAZY

MAZING > MAZE

MAZOURKA *same as* > MAZURKA

MAZOURKAS > MAZOURKA

MAZOUT *same as* > MAZUT

MAZOUTS > MAZOUT

MAZUMA *n* money

MAZUMAS > MAZUMA

MAZURKA *n* lively Polish dance

MAZURKAS > MAZURKA

MAZUT *n* residue left after distillation of petrol

MAZUTS > MAZUT

MAZY *adj* of or like a maze

MAZZARD *same as* > MAZARD

MAZZARDS > MAZZARD

MBAQANGA *n* style of Black popular music of urban South Africa

MBAQANGAS > MBAQANGA

MBIRA *n* African musical instrument

MBIRAS > MBIRA

ME *n* (in tonic sol-fa) third degree of any major scale ▷ *pron* refers to the speaker or writer

MEACOCK *n* timid person

MEACOCKS > MEACOCK

MEAD *n* alcoholic drink made from honey

MEADOW *n* piece of grassland

MEADOWIER > MEADOWY
MEADOWS > MEADOW
MEADOWY adj consisting of meadows
MEADS > MEAD
MEAGER same as > MEAGRE
MEAGERER > MEAGER
MEAGEREST > MEAGER
MEAGERLY > MEAGRE
MEAGRE adj scanty or insufficient ▷ n Mediterranean fish
MEAGRELY > MEAGRE
MEAGRER > MEAGRE
MEAGRES > MEAGRE
MEAGREST > MEAGRE
MEAL n occasion when food is served and eaten ▷ vb cover with meal
MEALED > MEAL
MEALER n person eating but not lodging at boarding house
MEALERS > MEALER
MEALIE n maize
MEALIER > MEALY
MEALIES > MEALIE
MEALIEST > MEALY
MEALINESS > MEALY
MEALING > MEAL
MEALLESS > MEAL
MEALS > MEAL
MEALTIME n time for meal
MEALTIMES > MEALTIME
MEALWORM n larva of various beetles which feeds on meal, flour, and similar stored foods
MEALWORMS > MEALWORM
MEALY adj resembling meal
MEALYBUG n plant-eating homopterous insect
MEALYBUGS > MEALYBUG
MEAN vb intend to convey or express ▷ adj miserly, ungenerous, or petty ▷ n middle point between two extremes
MEANDER vb follow a winding course ▷ n winding course
MEANDERED > MEANDER
MEANDERER > MEANDER
MEANDERS > MEANDER
MEANDRIAN > MEANDER
MEANDROUS > MEANDER
MEANE vb moan
MEANED > MEANE
MEANER > MEAN
MEANES > MEANE
MEANEST > MEAN
MEANIE n unkind or miserly person
MEANIES > MEANIE
MEANING n what something means
MEANINGLY > MEAN
MEANINGS > MEANING
MEANLY > MEAN
MEANNESS > MEAN
MEANS > MEAN

MEANT > MEAN
MEANTIME n intervening period ▷ adv meanwhile
MEANTIMES > MEANTIME
MEANWHILE adv during the intervening period
MEANY same as > MEANIE
MEARE same as > MERE
MEARES > MEARE
MEARING adj forming boundary
MEASE vb assuage
MEASED > MEASE
MEASES > MEASE
MEASING > MEASE
MEASLE vb infect with measles
MEASLED adj (of cattle, sheep, or pigs) infested with tapeworm larvae
MEASLES n infectious disease producing red spots
MEASLIER > MEASLY
MEASLIEST > MEASLY
MEASLING > MEASLE
MEASLY adj meagre
MEASURE n size or quantity ▷ vb determine the size or quantity of
MEASURED adj slow and steady
MEASURER > MEASURE
MEASURERS > MEASURE
MEASURES pl n rock strata that contain a particular type of deposit
MEASURING adj used to measure quantities, esp in cooking
MEAT n animal flesh as food
MEATAL > MEATUS
MEATAXE n meat cleaver
MEATAXES > MEATAXE
MEATBALL n minced beef, shaped into a ball before cooking
MEATBALLS > MEATBALL
MEATED adj fattened
MEATH same as > MEAD
MEATHE same as > MEAD
MEATHEAD n stupid person
MEATHEADS > MEATHEAD
MEATHES > MEATHE
MEATHOOK n hook on which to hang meat
MEATHOOKS > MEATHOOK
MEATHS > MEATH
MEATIER > MEATY
MEATIEST > MEATY
MEATILY > MEATY
MEATINESS > MEATY
MEATLESS > MEAT
MEATLOAF n chopped meat served in loaf-shaped mass
MEATMAN n meat seller
MEATMEN > MEATMAN
MEATS > MEAT
MEATSPACE n real physical world, as contrasted with the world of cyberspace

MEATUS n natural opening or channel
MEATUSES > MEATUS
MEATY adj (tasting) of or like meat
MEAWES same as > MEWS
MEAZEL same as > MESEL
MEAZELS > MEAZEL
MEBIBYTE n 2²⁰ bytes
MEBIBYTES > MEBIBYTE
MEBOS n South African dish of dried apricots
MEBOSES > MEBOS
MECCA n place that attracts many visitors
MECCAS > MECCA
MECH n mechanic
MECHANIC n person skilled in repairing or operating machinery
MECHANICS n scientific study of motion and force
MECHANISE same as > MECHANIZE
MECHANISM n way a machine works
MECHANIST same as > MECHANIC
MECHANIZE vb equip with machinery
MECHITZA n screen in synagogue separating men and women
MECHITZAS > MECHITZA
MECHITZOT > MECHITZA
MECHOUI n Canadian dish of meat roasted on a spit
MECHOUIS > MECHOUI
MECHS > MECH
MECK same as > MAIK
MECKS > MECK
MECLIZINE n drug used to treat motion sickness
MECONATE n salt of meconic acid
MECONATES > MECONATE
MECONIC adj derived from poppies
MECONIN n substance found in opium
MECONINS > MECONIN
MECONIUM n dark green mucoid material that forms the first faeces of a newborn infant
MECONIUMS > MECONIUM
MED n doctor
MEDACCA n Japanese freshwater fish
MEDACCAS > MEDACCA
MEDAILLON n small round thin piece of food
MEDAKA same as > MEDACCA
MEDAKAS > MEDAKA
MEDAL n piece of metal with an inscription etc, given as a reward or memento ▷ vb honour with a medal
MEDALED > MEDAL
MEDALET n small medal
MEDALETS > MEDALET

MEDALING > MEDAL
MEDALIST same as > MEDALLIST
MEDALISTS > MEDALIST
MEDALLED > MEDAL
MEDALLIC > MEDAL
MEDALLING > MEDAL
MEDALLION n disc-shaped ornament worn on a chain round the neck
MEDALLIST n winner of a medal
MEDALPLAY n (in golf) scoring system in which the score is based on the total number of strokes taken
MEDALS > MEDAL
MEDCINAL same as > MEDICINAL
MEDDLE vb interfere annoyingly
MEDDLED > MEDDLE
MEDDLER > MEDDLE
MEDDLERS > MEDDLE
MEDDLES > MEDDLE
MEDDLING > MEDDLE
MEDDLINGS > MEDDLE
MEDEVAC n evacuation of casualties ▷ vb transport (a wounded or sick person) to hospital
MEDEVACED > MEDEVAC
MEDEVACS > MEDEVAC
MEDFLIES > MEDFLY
MEDFLY n Mediterranean fruit fly
MEDIA n medium of cultivation, conveyance, or expression
MEDIACIES > MEDIACY
MEDIACY n quality or state of being mediate
MEDIAD adj situated near the median line or plane of an organism
MEDIAE > MEDIA
MEDIAEVAL adj of, relating to, or in the style of the Middle Ages ▷ n person living in medieval times
MEDIAL adj of or in the middle ▷ n speech sound between being fortis and lenis
MEDIALLY > MEDIAL
MEDIALS > MEDIAL
MEDIAN n middle (point or line) ▷ adj of, relating to, situated in, or directed towards the middle
MEDIANLY > MEDIAN
MEDIANS > MEDIAN
MEDIANT n third degree of a major or minor scale
MEDIANTS > MEDIANT
MEDIAS > MEDIA
MEDIATE vb intervene in a dispute to bring about agreement ▷ adj occurring as a result of or dependent upon mediation
MEDIATED > MEDIATE
MEDIATELY > MEDIATE

MEDIATES > MEDIATE
MEDIATING > MEDIATE
MEDIATION n act of mediating
MEDIATISE same as > MEDIATIZE
MEDIATIVE > MEDIATE
MEDIATIZE vb annex (a state) to another state, allowing the former ruler to retain their title and some authority
MEDIATOR > MEDIATE
MEDIATORS > MEDIATE
MEDIATORY > MEDIATE
MEDIATRIX n female mediator
MEDIC n doctor or medical student
MEDICABLE adj potentially able to be treated or cured medically
MEDICABLY > MEDICABLE
MEDICAID n US federal health insurance programme for persons on low income
MEDICAIDS > MEDICAID
MEDICAL adj of the science of medicine ▷ n medical examination
MEDICALLY > MEDICAL
MEDICALS > MEDICAL
MEDICANT n medicinal substance
MEDICANTS > MEDICANT
MEDICARE n US federal health insurance programme for older people
MEDICARES > MEDICARE
MEDICATE vb treat with a medicinal substance
MEDICATED adj (of a patient) having been treated with a medicine or drug
MEDICATES > MEDICATE
MEDICIDE n suicide assisted by doctor
MEDICIDES > MEDICIDE
MEDICINAL adj having therapeutic properties ▷ n medicinal substance
MEDICINE n substance used to treat disease ▷ vb treat with medicine
MEDICINED > MEDICINE
MEDICINER n physician
MEDICINES > MEDICINE
MEDICK n type of small leguminous plant with yellow or purple flowers
MEDICKS > MEDICK
MEDICO n doctor or medical student
MEDICOS > MEDICO
MEDICS > MEDIC
MEDIEVAL adj of the Middle Ages ▷ n person living in medieval times

MEDIEVALS > MEDIEVAL
MEDIGAP n private health insurance
MEDIGAPS > MEDIGAP
MEDII > MEDIUS
MEDINA n ancient quarter of North African city
MEDINAS > MEDINA
MEDIOCRE adj average in quality
MEDITATE vb reflect deeply, esp on spiritual matters
MEDITATED > MEDITATE
MEDITATES > MEDITATE
MEDITATOR > MEDITATE
MEDIUM adj midway between extremes, average ▷ n middle state, degree, or condition
MEDIUMS pl n medium-dated gilt-edged securities
MEDIUS n middle finger
MEDIUSES > MEDIUS
MEDIVAC variant spelling of > MEDEVAC
MEDIVACED > MEDIVAC
MEDIVACS > MEDIVAC
MEDLAR n apple-like fruit of a small tree
MEDLARS > MEDLAR
MEDLE same as > MEDDLE
MEDLED > MEDLE
MEDLES > MEDLE
MEDLEY n miscellaneous mixture ▷ adj of, being, or relating to a mixture or variety
MEDLEYS > MEDLEY
MEDLING > MEDLE
MEDRESA same as > MADRASAH
MEDRESAS > MEDRESA
MEDRESE same as > MADRASAH
MEDRESES > MEDRESE
MEDRESSEH same as > MADRASAH
MEDS > MED
MEDULLA n marrow, pith, or inner tissue
MEDULLAE > MEDULLA
MEDULLAR > MEDULLA
MEDULLARY > MEDULLA
MEDULLAS > MEDULLA
MEDULLATE adj having medulla
MEDUSA n jellyfish
MEDUSAE > MEDUSA
MEDUSAL > MEDUSA
MEDUSAN > MEDUSA
MEDUSANS > MEDUSA
MEDUSAS > MEDUSA
MEDUSOID same as > MEDUSA
MEDUSOIDS > MEDUSOID
MEE n Malaysian noodle dish
MEED n recompense
MEEDS > MEED
MEEK adj submissive or humble

MEEKEN vb make meek
MEEKENED > MEEKEN
MEEKENING > MEEKEN
MEEKENS > MEEKEN
MEEKER > MEEK
MEEKEST > MEEK
MEEKLY > MEEK
MEEKNESS > MEEK
MEEMIE n attack of hysteria
MEEMIES > MEEMIE
MEER same as > MERE
MEERCAT same as > MEERKAT
MEERCATS > MEERCAT
MEERED > MEER
MEERING > MEER
MEERKAT n S African mongoose
MEERKATS > MEERKAT
MEERS > MEER
MEES > MEE
MEET vb come together (with) ▷ n meeting, esp a sports meeting ▷ adj fit or suitable
MEETER > MEET
MEETERS > MEET
MEETEST > MEET
MEETING > MEET
MEETINGS > MEET
MEETLY > MEET
MEETNESS n properness
MEETS > MEET
MEFF dialect word for > TRAMP
MEFFS > MEFF
MEG short for > MEGABYTE
MEGA adj extremely good, great, or successful
MEGABAR n unit of million bars
MEGABARS > MEGABAR
MEGABIT n one million bits
MEGABITS > MEGABIT
MEGABUCK n million dollars
MEGABUCKS > MEGABUCK
MEGABYTE n 2^{20} or 1 048 576 bytes
MEGABYTES > MEGABYTE
MEGACITY n city with over 10 million inhabitants
MEGACURIE n unit of million curies
MEGACYCLE same as > MEGAHERTZ
MEGADEAL n very good deal
MEGADEALS > MEGADEAL
MEGADEATH n death of a million people, esp in a nuclear war or attack
MEGADOSE n very large dose, as of a medicine, vitamin, etc
MEGADOSES > MEGADOSE
MEGADYNE n unit of million dynes
MEGADYNES > MEGADYNE
MEGAFARAD n unit of million farads

MEGAFAUNA n component of the fauna of a region or period that comprises the larger terrestrial animals
MEGAFLOP n measure of a computer's processing speed
MEGAFLOPS > MEGAFLOP
MEGAFLORA n plants large enough to be seen by naked eye
MEGAFOG n amplified fog signal
MEGAFOGS > MEGAFOG
MEGAGAUSS n unit of million gauss
MEGAHERTZ n one million hertz
MEGAHIT n great success
MEGAHITS > MEGAHIT
MEGAJOULE n unit of million joules
MEGALITH n great stone, esp as part of a prehistoric monument
MEGALITHS > MEGALITH
MEGALITRE n one million litres
MEGALODON n an extinct giant shark of the Cenozoic era
MEGALOPIC adj having large eyes
MEGALOPS n crab in larval stage
MEGAMALL n very large shopping mall
MEGAMALLS > MEGAMALL
MEGAPHONE n cone-shaped instrument used to amplify the voice ▷ vb speak through megaphone
MEGAPHYLL n relatively large type of leaf produced by ferns and seed plants
MEGAPIXEL n one million pixels
MEGAPLEX n large cinema complex
MEGAPOD same as > MEGAPODE
MEGAPODE n bird of Australia, New Guinea, and adjacent islands
MEGAPODES > MEGAPODE
MEGAPODS > MEGAPOD
MEGAQUAKE n very large earthquake
MEGARA > MEGARON
MEGARAD n unit of million rads
MEGARADS > MEGARAD
MEGARON n tripartite rectangular room, found in Bronze Age Greece and Asia Minor
MEGARONS > MEGARON
MEGASCOPE n type of image projector
MEGASPORE n larger of the two types of spore produced by some spore-bearing plants,

which develops into the female gametophyte

MEGASS *another name for* > BAGASSE

MEGASSE *same as* > MEGASS

MEGASSES > MEGASS

MEGASTAR *n* very well-known personality in the entertainment business

MEGASTARS > MEGASTAR

MEGASTORE *n* very large store

MEGASTORM *n* very large storm

MEGATHERE *n* type of gigantic extinct American sloth common in late Cenozoic times

MEGATON *n* explosive power equal to that of one million tons of TNT

MEGATONIC > MEGATON

MEGATONS > MEGATON

MEGAVOLT *n* one million volts

MEGAVOLTS > MEGAVOLT

MEGAWATT *n* one million watts

MEGAWATTS > MEGAWATT

MEGILLA *same as* > MEGILLAH

MEGILLAH *n* scroll of the Book of Esther, read on the festival of Purim

MEGILLAHS > MEGILLAH

MEGILLAS > MEGILLA

MEGILLOTH > MEGILLAH

MEGILP *n* oil-painting medium of linseed oil mixed with mastic varnish or turpentine

MEGILPH *same as* > MEGILP

MEGILPHS > MEGILPH

MEGILPS > MEGILP

MEGOHM *n* one million ohms

MEGOHMS > MEGOHM

MEGRIM *n* caprice

MEGRIMS *n* period of low spirits

MEGS > MEG

MEH *interj* expression of indifference or boredom

MEHNDI *n* (esp in India) the practice of painting designs on the hands, feet, etc using henna

MEHNDIS > MEHNDI

MEIBOMIAN *adj* as in *meibomian gland* any of the small sebaceous glands in the eyelid, beneath the conjunctiva

MEIKLE *adj* Scots word meaning large

MEIN Scots word for > MOAN

MEINED > MEIN

MEINEY *same as* > MEINY

MEINEYS > MEINEY

MEINIE *same as* > MEINY

MEINIES > MEINY

MEINING > MEIN

MEINS > MEIN

MEINT *same as* > MING

MEINY *n* retinue or household

MEIOCYTE *n* cell that divides by meiosis to produce four haploid spores

MEIOCYTES > MEIOCYTE

MEIOFAUNA *n* component of the fauna of a sea or lake bed comprising small (but not microscopic) animals, such as tiny worms and crustaceans

MEIONITE *n* mineral containing silica

MEIONITES > MEIONITE

MEIOSES > MEIOSIS

MEIOSIS *n* type of cell division

MEIOSPORE *n* haploid spore

MEIOTIC > MEIOSIS

MEISHI *n* business card in Japan

MEISHIS > MEISHI

MEISTER *n* person who excels at a particular activity

MEISTERS > MEISTER

MEITH *n* landmark

MEITHS > MEITH

MEJLIS *same as* > MAJLIS

MEJLISES > MEJLIS

MEKKA *same as* > MECCA

MEKKAS > MEKKA

MEKOMETER *n* device for measuring distance

MEL *n* pure form of honey

MELA *n* Indian cultural or religious fair or festival

MELAENA *n* medical condition

MELAENAS > MELAENA

MELALEUCA *n* Australian shrub or tree with a white trunk and black branches

MELAMDIM > MELAMED

MELAMED *n* Hebrew teacher

MELAMINE *n* colourless crystalline compound used in making synthetic resins

MELAMINES > MELAMINE

MELAMPODE *n* poisonous plant

MELANGE *n* mixture

MELANGES > MELANGE

MELANIAN *n* freshwater mollusc

MELANIANS > MELANIAN

MELANIC *adj* relating to melanism or melanosis ▷ *n* darker form of creature

MELANICS > MELANIC

MELANIN *n* dark pigment found in the hair, skin, and eyes

MELANINS > MELANIN

MELANISE *same as* > MELANIZE

MELANISED > MELANISE

MELANISES > MELANISE

MELANISM *same as* > MELANOSIS

MELANISMS > MELANISM

MELANIST > MELANISM

MELANISTS > MELANISM

MELANITE *n* black variety of andradite garnet

MELANITES > MELANITE

MELANITIC > MELANITE

MELANIZE *vb* turn into melanin

MELANIZED > MELANIZE

MELANIZES > MELANIZE

MELANO *n* person with extremely dark skin

MELANOID *adj* resembling melanin ▷ *n* dark substance formed in skin

MELANOIDS > MELANOID

MELANOMA *n* tumour composed of dark-coloured cells, occurring in some skin cancers

MELANOMAS > MELANOMA

MELANOS > MELANO

MELANOSES > MELANOSIS

MELANOSIS *n* skin condition characterized by excessive deposits of melanin

MELANOTIC > MELANOSIS

MELANOUS *adj* having a dark complexion and black hair

MELANURIA *n* presence of melanin in urine

MELANURIC > MELANURIA

MELAPHYRE *n* type of weathered amygdaloidal basalt or andesite

MELAS > MELA

MELASTOME *n* tropical flowering plant

MELATONIN *n* hormone-like secretion of the pineal gland, causing skin colour changes in some animals and thought to be involved in reproductive function

MELBA *adj* relating to a type of dessert sauce or toast

MELD *vb* merge or blend ▷ *n* act of melding

MELDED > MELD

MELDER > MELD

MELDERS > MELD

MELDING > MELD

MELDS > MELD

MELEE *n* noisy confused fight or crowd

MELEES > MELEE

MELENA *n* excrement stained by blood

MELENAS > MELENA

MELIC *adj* (of poetry, esp ancient Greek lyric poems) intended to be sung ▷ *n* type of grass

MELICK *n* either of two pale green perennial grasses

MELICKS > MELICK

MELICS > MELIC

MELIK *same as* > MALIK

MELIKS > MELIK

MELILITE *n* mineral containing calcium

MELILITES > MELILITE

MELILOT *n* plant with small white or yellow fragrant flowers

MELILOTS > MELILOT

MELINITE *n* high explosive made from picric acid

MELINITES > MELINITE

MELIORATE *vb* improve

MELIORISM *n* notion that the world can be improved by human effort

MELIORIST > MELIORISM

MELIORITY *n* improved state

MELISMA *n* expressive vocal phrase or passage consisting of several notes sung to one syllable

MELISMAS > MELISMA

MELISMATA > MELISMA

MELITTIN *n* main toxic component in bee venom

MELITTINS > MELITTIN

MELL *vb* mix

MELLAY *same as* > MELEE

MELLAYS > MELLAY

MELLED > MELL

MELLIFIC *adj* forming or producing honey

MELLING > MELL

MELLITE *n* soft yellow mineral

MELLITES > MELLITE

MELLITIC > MELLITE

MELLOTRON *n* musical synthesizer

MELLOW *adj* soft, not harsh ▷ *vb* make or become mellow

MELLOWED > MELLOW

MELLOWER > MELLOW

MELLOWEST > MELLOW

MELLOWIER > MELLOWY

MELLOWING > MELLOW

MELLOWLY > MELLOW

MELLOWS > MELLOW

MELLOWY *adj* mellow

MELLS > MELL

MELOCOTON *n* variety of peach

MELODEON *n* small accordion

MELODEONS
> MELODEON
MELODIA same as
> MELODICA
MELODIAS > MELODIA
MELODIC adj of melody
MELODICA n type of flute
MELODICAS
> MELODICA
MELODICS n study of
melody
MELODIES > MELODY
MELODION same as
> MELODEON
MELODIONS
> MELODION
MELODIOUS adj pleasing
to the ear
MELODISE same as
> MELODIZE
MELODISED > MELODISE
MELODISER > MELODISE
MELODISES > MELODISE
MELODIST n composer of
melodies
MELODISTS
> MELODIST
MELODIZE vb provide
with a melody
MELODIZED
> MELODIZE
MELODIZER
> MELODIZE
MELODIZES
> MELODIZE
MELODRAMA n play full of
extravagant action and
emotion
MELODRAME same as
> MELODRAMA
MELODY n series of
musical notes which make
a tune
MELOID n type of
long-legged beetle
MELOIDS > MELOID
MELOMANIA n great
enthusiasm for music
MELOMANIC
> MELOMANIA
MELON n large round juicy
fruit with a hard rind
MELONGENE n aubergine
MELONIER > MELONY
MELONIEST > MELONY
MELONS > MELON
MELONY adj like a melon
MELOXICAM n
anti-inflammatory drug
used to treat
osteoarthritis
MELPHALAN n drug used
to treat leukaemia
MELS > MEL
MELT vb (cause to)
become liquid by heat ▷ n
act or process of melting
MELTABLE > MELT
MELTAGE n process or
result of melting or the
amount melted
MELTAGES > MELTAGE
MELTDOWN n (in a nuclear
reactor) melting of the fuel
rods, with the possible
release of radiation
MELTDOWNS
> MELTDOWN

MELTED > MELT
MELTEMI n northerly
wind in the northeast
Mediterranean
MELTEMIS > MELTEMI
MELTER > MELT
MELTERS > MELT
MELTIER > MELTY
MELTIEST > MELTY
MELTING > MELT
MELTINGLY > MELT
MELTINGS > MELT
MELTITH n meal
MELTITHS > MELTITH
MELTON n heavy smooth
woollen fabric with a short
nap, used esp for
overcoats
MELTONS > MELTON
MELTS > MELT
MELTWATER n melted
snow or ice
MELTY adj tending to melt
MELUNGEON n any of a
dark-skinned group of
people of the Appalachians
in E Tennessee, of mixed
Indian, White, and Black
ancestry
MEM n 13th letter in the
Hebrew alphabet,
transliterated as m
MEMBER n individual
making up a body or
society ▷ adj (of a country
or group) belonging to an
organization or alliance
MEMBERED adj having
members
MEMBERS > MEMBER
MEMBRAL adj of limbs
MEMBRANAL
> MEMBRANE
MEMBRANE n thin flexible
tissue in a plant or animal
body
MEMBRANED adj having
membrane
MEMBRANES
> MEMBRANE
MEME n idea or element of
social behaviour
MEMENTO n thing serving
to remind, souvenir
MEMENTOES > MEMENTO
MEMENTOS > MEMENTO
MEMES > MEME
MEMETIC adj of or
relating to a meme
MEMETICS n study of
genetic transmission of
culture
MEMO n memorandum
MEMOIR n biography or
historical account based
on personal knowledge
MEMOIRISM n writing of
memoirs
MEMOIRIST
> MEMOIRISM
MEMOIRS pl n collection
of reminiscences about a
period or series of events
MEMORABLE adj worth
remembering,
noteworthy
MEMORABLY
> MEMORABLE

MEMORANDA n plural of
memorandum: written
statement of
communications
MEMORIAL n something
serving to commemorate
a person or thing ▷ adj
serving as a memorial
MEMORIALS
> MEMORIAL
MEMORIES > MEMORY
MEMORISE same as
> MEMORIZE
MEMORISED
> MEMORISE
MEMORISER
> MEMORIZE
MEMORISES
> MEMORISE
MEMORITER adv from
memory
MEMORIZE vb commit to
memory
MEMORIZED
> MEMORIZE
MEMORIZER
> MEMORIZE
MEMORIZES
> MEMORIZE
MEMORY n ability to
remember
MEMOS > MEMO
MEMS > MEM
MEMSAHIB n (formerly, in
India) term of respect used
for a European married
woman
MEMSAHIBS
> MEMSAHIB
MEN > MAN
MENACE n threat ▷ vb
threaten, endanger
MENACED > MENACE
MENACER > MENACE
MENACERS > MENACE
MENACES > MENACE
MENACING > MENACE
MENAD same as > MAENAD
MENADIONE n yellow
crystalline compound
MENADS > MENAD
MENAGE old form of
> MANAGE
MENAGED > MENAGE
MENAGERIE n collection
of wild animals for
exhibition
MENAGES > MENAGE
MENAGING > MENAGE
MENARCHE n first
occurrence of
menstruation
MENARCHES > MENARCHE
MENAZON n type of
insecticide
MENAZONS > MENAZON
MEND vb repair or patch
▷ n mended area
MENDABLE > MEND
MENDACITY n (tendency
to) untruthfulness
MENDED > MEND
MENDER > MEND
MENDERS > MEND
MENDICANT adj begging
▷ n beggar
MENDICITY
> MENDICANT

MENDIGO n Spanish
beggar or vagrant
MENDIGOS > MENDIGO
MENDING n something to
be mended, esp clothes
MENDINGS > MENDING
MENDS > MEND
MENE Scots form of > MOAN
MENED > MENE
MENEER n S African title of
address
MENEERS > MENEER
MENES > MENE
MENFOLK pl n men
collectively, esp the men of
a particular family
MENFOLKS same as
> MENFOLK
MENG vb mix
MENGE same as > MENG
MENGED > MENG
MENGES > MENGE
MENGING > MENG
MENGS > MENG
MENHADEN n marine N
American fish, source of
fishmeal, fertilizer, and oil
MENHADENS
> MENHADEN
MENHIR n single upright
prehistoric stone
MENHIRS > MENHIR
MENIAL adj involving
boring work of low status
▷ n person with a menial
job
MENIALLY > MENIAL
MENIALS > MENIAL
MENILITE n liver opal
MENILITES
> MENILITE
MENING > MENE
MENINGEAL > MENINX
MENINGES > MENINX
MENINX n one of three
membranes that envelop
the brain and spinal cord
MENISCAL > MENISCUS
MENISCATE
> MENISCUS
MENISCI > MENISCUS
MENISCOID
> MENISCUS
MENISCUS n curved
surface of a liquid
MENO adv musical
instruction indicating 'less'
MENOLOGY n
ecclesiastical calendar of
the months
MENOMINEE n whitefish,
found in N America and
Siberia
MENOMINI same as
> MENOMINEE
MENOMINIS
> MENOMINI
MENOPAUSE n time when
a woman's menstrual
cycle ceases
MENOPOLIS n informal
word for an area with a
high proportion of single
men
MENOPOME n American
salamander
MENOPOMES
> MENOPOME

MENORAH n seven-branched candelabrum used as an emblem of Judaism

MENORAHS > MENORAH

MENORRHEA n normal menstrual flow

MENSA n faint constellation in the S hemisphere

MENSAE n star of the mensa constellation

MENSAL adj monthly

MENSAS > MENSA

MENSCH n decent person

MENSCHEN > MENSCH

MENSCHES > MENSCH

MENSCHIER > MENSCHY

MENSCHY adj decent

MENSE vb grace

MENSED > MENSE

MENSEFUL adj gracious

MENSELESS adj graceless

MENSES n menstruation

MENSH vb mention

MENSHED > MENSH

MENSHEN n Chinese door god

MENSHES > MENSH

MENSHING > MENSH

MENSING > MENSE

MENSTRUA > MENSTRUUM

MENSTRUAL adj of or relating to menstruation

MENSTRUUM n solvent, esp one used in the preparation of a drug

MENSUAL same as > MENSAL

MENSURAL adj of or involving measure

MENSWEAR n clothing for men

MENSWEARS > MENSWEAR

MENT same as > MING

MENTA > MENTUM

MENTAL adj of, in, or done by the mind

MENTALESE n picturing of concepts in mind without words

MENTALISM n doctrine that mind is the fundamental reality and that objects of knowledge exist only as aspects of the subject's consciousness

MENTALIST > MENTALISM

MENTALITY n way of thinking

MENTALLY > MENTAL

MENTATION n process or result of mental activity

MENTEE n person trained by mentor

MENTEES > MENTEE

MENTHENE n liquid obtained from menthol

MENTHENES > MENTHENE

MENTHOL n organic compound found in peppermint

MENTHOLS > MENTHOL

MENTICIDE n destruction of person's mental independence

MENTION vb refer to briefly ▷ n brief reference

MENTIONED > MENTION

MENTIONER > MENTION

MENTIONS > MENTION

MENTO n Jamaican song

MENTOR n adviser or guide ▷ vb act as a mentor to (someone)

MENTORED > MENTOR

MENTORIAL > MENTOR

MENTORING n (in business) the practice of assigning a junior member of staff to the care of a more experienced person who assists them in their career

MENTORS > MENTOR

MENTOS > MENTO

MENTUM n chin

MENU n list of dishes to be served, or from which to order

MENUDO n Mexican soup

MENUDOS > MENUDO

MENUISIER n joiner

MENUS > MENU

MENYIE same as > MEINIE

MENYIES > MENYIE

MEOU same as > MEOW

MEOUED > MEOU

MEOUING > MEOU

MEOUS > MEOU

MEOW vb (of a cat) to make a characteristic crying sound ▷ interj imitation of this sound

MEOWED > MEOW

MEOWING > MEOW

MEOWS > MEOW

MEPACRINE n drug formerly widely used to treat malaria

MEPHITIC adj poisonous

MEPHITIS n foul-smelling discharge

MEPHITISM n poisoning

MERANTI n wood from any of several Malaysian trees

MERANTIS > MERANTI

MERBROMIN n green iridescent crystalline compound

MERC n mercenary

MERCADO n market

MERCADOS > MERCADO

MERCAPTAN another name (not in technical usage) for > THIOL

MERCAPTO adj of a particular chemical group

MERCAT Scots word for > MARKET

MERCATS > MERCAT

MERCENARY adj influenced by greed ▷ n hired soldier

MERCER n dealer in textile fabrics and fine cloth

MERCERIES > MERCER

MERCERISE same as > MERCERIZE

MERCERIZE vb treat (cotton yarn) with an alkali to increase its strength and reception to dye and impart a lustrous silky appearance

MERCERS > MERCER

MERCERY > MERCER

MERCES > MERC

MERCH n merchandise

MERCHANT n person engaged in trade, wholesale trader ▷ adj of ships involved in commercial trade or their crews ▷ vb conduct trade in

MERCHANTS > MERCHANT

MERCHES > MERCH

MERCHET n type of fine paid by feudal tenant to his lord

MERCHETS > MERCHET

MERCHILD n mythical creature with upper body of child and lower body of fish

MERCIABLE adj merciful

MERCIES > MERCY

MERCIFIDE > MERCIFY

MERCIFIED > MERCIFY

MERCIFIES > MERCIFY

MERCIFUL adj compassionate

MERCIFY vb show mercy to

MERCILESS adj without mercy

MERCS > MERC

MERCURATE vb treat or mix with mercury

MERCURIAL adj lively, changeable ▷ n any salt of mercury for use as a medicine

MERCURIC adj of or containing mercury in the divalent state

MERCURIES > MERCURY

MERCURISE same as > MERCURATE

MERCURIZE same as > MERCURISE

MERCUROUS adj of or containing mercury in the monovalent state

MERCURY n silvery liquid metal

MERCY n compassionate treatment

MERDE French word for > EXCREMENT

MERDES > MERDE

MERE adj nothing more than ▷ n lake ▷ vb old form of survey

MERED adj forming a boundary

MEREL same as > MERIL

MERELL same as > MERIL

MERELLS same as > MERILS

MERELS > MEREL

MERELY adv only

MERENGUE n type of lively dance music

MERENGUES > MERENGUE

MEREOLOGY n formal study of the logical properties of the relation of part and whole

MERER > MERE

MERES > MERE

MERESMAN n man who decides on boundaries

MERESMEN > MERESMAN

MEREST > MERE

MERESTONE n stone marking boundary

MERFOLK n mermaids and mermen

MERFOLKS > MERFOLK

MERGANSER n large crested diving duck

MERGE vb combine or blend

MERGED > MERGE

MERGEE n business taken over by merger

MERGEES > MERGEE

MERGENCE > MERGE

MERGENCES > MERGE

MERGER n combination of business firms into one

MERGERS > MERGER

MERGES > MERGE

MERGING > MERGE

MERGINGS > MERGE

MERGUEZ n heavily spiced N African sausage

MERI n Māori war club

MERICARP n part of plant fruit

MERICARPS > MERICARP

MERIDIAN n imaginary circle of the earth passing through both poles ▷ adj along or relating to a meridian

MERIDIANS > MERIDIAN

MERIL n counter used in merils

MERILS n old board game

MERIMAKE n merrymaking

MERIMAKES > MERIMAKE

MERING > MERE

MERINGS > MERING

MERINGUE n baked mixture of egg whites and sugar

MERINGUES > MERINGUE

MERINO n breed of sheep with fine soft wool

MERINOS > MERINO

MERIS > MERI

MERISES > MERISIS

MERISIS n growth by division of cells

MERISM n duplication of biological parts

MERISMS > MERISM

MERISTEM n plant tissue responsible for growth

MERISTEMS > MERISTEM

MERISTIC adj of or relating to the number of organs or parts in an animal or plant body

MERIT n excellence or worth ▷ vb deserve

MERITED > MERIT

MERITING > MERIT

MERITLESS > MERIT

MERITS > MERIT

MERK *n* old Scots coin

MERKIN *n* artificial hairpiece for the pudendum

MERKINS > MERKIN

MERKS > MERK

MERL *same as >* MERLE

MERLE *adj* (of a dog, esp a collie) having a bluish-grey coat with speckles or streaks of black ▷ *n* dog with this coat

MERLES > MERLE

MERLIN *n* small falcon

MERLING *n* whiting

MERLINGS > MERLING

MERLINS > MERLIN

MERLON *n* solid upright section in a crenellated battlement

MERLONS > MERLON

MERLOT *n* type of black grape

MERLOTS > MERLOT

MERLS > MERL

MERMAID *n* imaginary sea creature with the upper part of a woman and the lower part of a fish

MERMAIDEN *same as >* MERMAID

MERMAIDS > MERMAID

MERMAN *n* male counterpart of the mermaid

MERMEN > MERMAN

MEROCRINE *adj* (of the secretion of glands) characterized by formation of the product without undergoing disintegration

MEROGONY *n* development of embryo from part of ovum

MEROISTIC *adj* producing yolk and ova

MEROME *same as >* MEROSOME

MEROMES > MEROME

MERONYM *n* part of something used to refer to the whole

MERONYMS > MERONYM

MERONYMY > MERONYM

MEROPIA *n* partial blindness

MEROPIAS > MEROPIA

MEROPIC > MEROPIA

MEROPIDAN *n* bird of bee-eater family

MEROSOME *n* segment in body of worm

MEROSOMES > MEROSOME

MEROZOITE *n* any of the cells formed by fission of a schizont during the life cycle of sporozoan protozoans, such as the malaria parasite

MERPEOPLE *same as >* MERFOLK

MERRIE *adj* (archaic) merry

MERRIER > MERRY

MERRIES > MERRY

MERRIEST > MERRY

MERRILY > MERRY

MERRIMENT *n* gaiety, fun, or mirth

MERRINESS > MERRY

MERRY *adj* cheerful or jolly ▷ *n* type of cherry

MERRYMAN *n* jester

MERRYMEN > MERRYMAN

MERSALYL *n* salt of sodium

MERSALYLS > MERSALYL

MERSE *n* low level ground by a river or shore

MERSES > MERSE

MERSION *n* dipping in water

MERSIONS > MERSION

MERYCISM *n* rumination

MERYCISMS > MERYCISM

MES > ME

MESA *n* flat-topped hill found in arid regions

MESAIL *n* visor

MESAILS > MESAIL

MESAL *same as >* MESIAL

MESALLY > MESAL

MESARAIC *adj* of mesentery

MESARCH *adj* having the first-formed xylem surrounded by that formed later

MESAS > MESA

MESCAL *n* spineless globe-shaped cactus

MESCALIN *same as >* MESCALINE

MESCALINE *n* hallucinogenic drug obtained from the tops of mescals

MESCALINS > MESCALIN

MESCALISM *n* addiction to mescal

MESCALS > MESCAL

MESCLUM *same as >* MESCLUN

MESCLUMS > MESCLUM

MESCLUN *n* type of green salad

MESCLUNS > MESCLUN

MESDAMES > MADAM

MESE *n* middle string on lyre

MESEEMED > MESEEMS

MESEEMETH *same as >* MESEEMS

MESEEMS *vb* it seems to me

MESEL *n* archaic word for a person with leprosy

MESELED *adj* archaic word meaning having leprosy

MESELS > MESEL

MESENTERA *n* plural of mesenteron, the midgut

MESENTERY *n* double layer of peritoneum that is attached to the back wall of the abdominal cavity and supports most of the small intestine

MESES > MESE

MESETA *n* plateau in Spain

MESETAS > MESETA

MESH *n* network or net ▷ *vb* (of gear teeth) engage ▷ *adj* made from mesh

MESHED > MESH

MESHES > MESH

MESHIER > MESH

MESHIEST > MESH

MESHING > MESH

MESHINGS > MESH

MESHUGA *n* crazy person

MESHUGAAS *n* madness

MESHUGAH *same as >* MESHUGA

MESHUGAS *adj* crazy

MESHUGGA *same as >* MESHUGA

MESHUGGAH *same as >* MESHUGA

MESHUGGE *same as >* MESHUGA

MESHWORK *n* network

MESHWORKS > MESHWORK

MESHY > MESH

MESIAD *adj* relating to or situated at the middle or centre

MESIAL *another word for >* MEDIAL

MESIALLY > MESIAL

MESIAN *same as >* MESIAL

MESIC > MESON

MESICALLY > MESON

MESMERIC *adj* holding (someone) as if spellbound

MESMERISE *same as >* MESMERIZE

MESMERISM *n* hypnotic state induced by the operator's imposition of their will on that of the patient

MESMERIST > MESMERISM

MESMERIZE *vb* hold spellbound

MESNALTY *n* lands of a mesne lord

MESNE *adj* (in law) intermediate or intervening

MESNES > MESNE

MESOBLAST *another name for >* MESODERM

MESOCARP *n* middle layer of the pericarp of a fruit, such as the flesh of a peach

MESOCARPS > MESOCARP

MESOCRANY *n* medium skull breadth

MESODERM *n* middle germ layer of an animal embryo

MESODERMS > MESODERM

MESOGLEA *n* gelatinous material found in jellyfish

MESOGLEAL > MESOGLEA

MESOGLEAS > MESOGLEA

MESOGLOEA *same as >* MESOGLEA

MESOLITE *n* type of mineral

MESOLITES > MESOLITE

MESOMERE *n* cell in fertilized ovum

MESOMERES > MESOMERE

MESOMORPH *n* person with a muscular body build: said to be correlated with somatotonia

MESON *n* elementary atomic particle

MESONIC > MESON

MESONS > MESON

MESOPAUSE *n* zone of minimum temperature between the mesosphere and the thermosphere

MESOPHILE *n* ideal growth temperature of 20-45 degrees

MESOPHYL *same as >* MESOPHYLL

MESOPHYLL *n* soft chlorophyll-containing tissue of a leaf between the upper and lower layers of epidermis: involved in photosynthesis

MESOPHYLS > MESOPHYL

MESOPHYTE *n* any plant that grows in surroundings receiving an average supply of water

MESOSAUR *n* extinct aquatic reptile

MESOSAURS > MESOSAUR

MESOSCALE *adj* of weather phenomena of medium duration

MESOSOME *n* part of bacterial cell

MESOSOMES > MESOSOME

MESOTRON *same as >* MESON

MESOTRONS > MESOTRON

MESOZOAN *n* type of parasite

MESOZOANS > MESOZOAN

MESOZOIC *adj* of, denoting, or relating to an era of geological time

MESPIL *n* type of N American tree

MESPILS > MESPIL

MESPRISE *same as >* MISPRISE

MESPRISES > MESPRISE

MESPRIZE *same as >* MISPRISE

MESPRIZES > MESPRIZE

MESQUIN *adj* mean

MESQUINE *same as >* MESQUIN

MESQUIT *same as >* MESQUITE

MESQUITE *n* small tree whose sugary pods are used as animal fodder

MESQUITES > MESQUITE

MESQUITS > MESQUIT
MESS n untidy or dirty confusion ▷ vb muddle or dirty
MESSAGE n communication sent ▷ vb send as a message
MESSAGED > MESSAGE
MESSAGES > MESSAGE
MESSAGING n sending and receiving of messages
MESSALINE n light lustrous twilled-silk fabric
MESSAN Scots word for > DOG
MESSANS > MESSAN
MESSED > MESS
MESSENGER n bearer of a message ▷ vb send by messenger
MESSES > MESS
MESSIAH n exceptional or hoped for liberator
MESSIAHS > MESSIAH
MESSIANIC adj of or relating to the Messiah, his awaited deliverance of the Jews, or the new age of peace expected to follow this
MESSIAS same as > MESSIAH
MESSIASES > MESSIAS
MESSIER > MESSY
MESSIEST > MESSY
MESSIEURS > MONSIEUR
MESSILY > MESSY
MESSINESS > MESSY
MESSING > MESS
MESSMAN n sailor working in ship's mess
MESSMATE n person with whom one shares meals in a mess, esp in the army
MESSMATES > MESSMATE
MESSMEN > MESSMAN
MESSUAGE n house together with outbuildings and adjacent land
MESSUAGES > MESSUAGE
MESSY adj dirty, confused, or untidy
MESTEE same as > MUSTEE
MESTEES > MESTEE
MESTER n master: used as a term of address for a man who is the head of a house
MESTERS > MESTER
MESTESO n Spanish music genre
MESTESOES > MESTESO
MESTESOS > MESTESO
MESTINO n person of mixed ancestry
MESTINOES > MESTINO
MESTINOS > MESTINO
MESTIZA > MESTIZO
MESTIZAS > MESTIZO
MESTIZO n person of mixed ancestry
MESTIZOES > MESTIZO
MESTIZOS > MESTIZO

MESTO adj sad
MESTOM same as > MESTOME
MESTOME n conducting tissue associated with parenchyma
MESTOMES > MESTOME
MESTOMS > MESTOM
MESTRANOL n synthetic oestrogen
MET n meteorology
META adj in a self-parodying style
METABASES > METABASIS
METABASIS n change
METABATIC > METABASIS
METABOLIC adj of or related to the sum total of the chemical processes that occurs in living organisms, resulting in growth, production of energy, elimination of waste material, etc
METABOLY n ability of some cells, esp protozoans, to alter their shape
METACARPI n skeleton of the hand between the wrist and the fingers
METADATA n data which accompanies digital data
METADATAS > METADATA
METAFILE n (in computing) file format that can hold other types of file
METAFILES > METAFILE
METAGE n official measuring of weight or contents
METAGENIC adj of or relating to metagenesis
METAGES > METAGE
METAIRIE n area of land on which farmer pays rent in kind
METAIRIES > METAIRIE
METAL n malleable element able to conduct heat and electricity ▷ adj made of metal ▷ vb fit or cover with metal
METALED > METAL
METALHEAD n fan of heavy metal music
METALING > METAL
METALISE same as > METALLIZE
METALISED > METALISE
METALISES > METALISE
METALIST same as > METALLIST
METALISTS > METALIST
METALIZE same as > METALLIZE
METALIZED > METALIZE
METALIZES > METALIZE

METALLED > METAL
METALLIC adj of or consisting of metal ▷ n something metallic
METALLICS > METALLIC
METALLIKE > METAL
METALLINE adj of, resembling, or relating to metals
METALLING > METAL
METALLISE same as > METALLIZE
METALLIST n person who works with metals
METALLIZE vb make metallic or to coat or treat with metal
METALLOID n nonmetallic element, such as arsenic or silicon, that has some of the properties of a metal ▷ adj of or being a metalloid
METALLY adj like metal
METALMARK n variety of butterfly
METALS > METAL
METALWARE n items made of metal
METALWORK n craft of making objects from metal
METAMALE n sterile male organism
METAMALES > METAMALE
METAMER n any of two or more isomeric compounds exhibiting metamerism
METAMERAL > METAMERE
METAMERE n body segment of invertebrates
METAMERES > METAMERE
METAMERIC adj divided into or consisting of metameres
METAMERS > METAMER
METAMICT adj of the amorphous state of a substance that has lost its crystalline structure
METANOIA n repentance
METANOIAS > METANOIA
METAPELET n foster mother
METAPHASE n second stage of mitosis during which the condensed chromosomes attach to the centre of the spindle
METAPHOR n type of figure of speech
METAPHORS > METAPHOR
METAPLASM n nonliving constituents, such as starch and pigment granules, of the cytoplasm of a cell
METAPLOT > METAPELET
METARCHON n nontoxic substance, such as a chemical to mask pheromones, that reduces the persistence of a pest

METASOMA n posterior part of an arachnid's abdomen (opisthosoma) that never carries appendages
METASOMAS > METASOMA
METATAG n element of HTML code used by search engines to index pages
METATAGS > METATAG
METATARSI pl n skeleton of human foot between toes and tarsus
METATE n stone for grinding grain on
METATES > METATE
METAVERSE n virtual universe, eg one of a computer or role-playing game
METAXYLEM n xylem tissue that consists of rigid thick-walled cells and occurs in parts of the plant that have finished growing
METAYAGE n farming in which rent is paid in kind
METAYAGES > METAYAGE
METAYER n farmer who pays rent in kind
METAYERS > METAYER
METAZOA > METAZOAN
METAZOAL > METAZOAN
METAZOAN n animal having a body composed of many cells ▷ adj of the metazoans
METAZOANS > METAZOAN
METAZOIC adj relating to the group of multicellular animals that includes all animals except sponges
METAZOON same as > METAZOAN
METCAST n weather forecast
METCASTS > METCAST
METE vb deal out as punishment ▷ n measure
METED > METE
METEOR n small fast-moving heavenly body
METEORIC adj of a meteor
METEORISM n distension of the abdomen
METEORIST n person who studies meteors
METEORITE n meteor that has fallen to earth
METEOROID n any of the small celestial bodies that are thought to orbit the sun. When they enter the earth's atmosphere, they become visible as meteors
METEOROUS > METEOR
METEORS > METEOR
METEPA n type of pesticide
METEPAS > METEPA
METER same as > METRE
METERAGE n act of measuring
METERAGES > METERAGE

METERED > METER
METERING > METER
METERS > METER
METES > METE
METESTICK n measuring rod
METESTRUS n period following oestrus
METEWAND same as **>** METESTICK
METEWANDS > METEWAND
METEYARD same as **>** METESTICK
METEYARDS > METEYARD
METFORMIN n drug used to treat diabetes
METH n methylated spirits
METHADON same as **>** METHADONE
METHADONE n drug similar to morphine
METHADONS > METHADON
METHANAL n colourless poisonous irritating gas
METHANALS > METHANAL
METHANE n colourless inflammable gas
METHANES > METHANE
METHANOIC adj as in methanoic acid systematic name for formic acid
METHANOL n colourless poisonous liquid used as a solvent and fuel
METHANOLS > METHANOL
METHANOYL n organic chemical compound
METHEGLIN n (esp formerly) spiced or medicated mead
METHINK same as **>** METHINKS
METHINKS vb it seems to me
METHO n methylated spirits
METHOD n way or manner
METHODIC same as **>** METHOD
METHODISE same as **>** METHODIZE
METHODISM n system and practices of the Methodist Church, developed by the English preacher John Wesley (1703–91) and his followers
METHODIST > METHODISM
METHODIZE vb organize according to a method
METHODS > METHOD
METHOS > METHO
METHOUGHT > METHINKS
METHOXIDE n saltlike compound in which the hydrogen atom in the hydroxyl group of methanol has been replaced by a metal atom
METHOXIES > METHOXY
METHOXY n steroid drug

METHOXYL n chemical compound of methyl and hydroxyl
METHOXYLS > METHOXYL
METHS n methylated spirits
METHYL n compound containing a saturated hydrocarbon group of atoms
METHYLAL n colourless volatile flammable liquid
METHYLALS > METHYLAL
METHYLASE n enzyme
METHYLATE vb mix with methanol
METHYLENE n divalent hydrocarbon group
METHYLIC > METHYL
METHYLS > METHYL
METHYSES > METHYSIS
METHYSIS n drunkenness
METHYSTIC adj intoxicating
METIC n (in ancient Greece) alien having some rights of citizenship
METICA n former proposed monetary unit of Mozambique
METICAIS > METICAL
METICAL n money unit in Mozambique
METICALS > METICAL
METICAS > METICA
METICS > METIC
METIER n profession or trade
METIERS > METIER
METIF n person of mixed ancestry
METIFS > METIF
METING > METE
METIS n person of mixed ancestry
METISSE > METIS
METISSES > METIS
METOL n organic substance used as a photographic developer
METOLS > METOL
METONYM n word used in a metonymy
METONYMIC > METONYMY
METONYMS > METONYM
METONYMY n figure of speech in which one thing is replaced by another associated with it
METOPAE > METOPE
METOPE n square space between two triglyphs in a Doric frieze
METOPES > METOPE
METOPIC adj of or relating to the forehead
METOPISM n congenital disfigurement of forehead
METOPISMS > METOPISM
METOPON n painkilling drug
METOPONS > METOPON
METOPRYL n type of anaesthetic

METOPRYLS > METOPRYL
METRALGIA n pain in the uterus
METRAZOL n drug used to improve blood circulation
METRAZOLS > METRAZOL
METRE n unit of length ▷ vb express in poetry
METRED > METRE
METRES > METRE
METRIC adj of the decimal system of weights and measures based on the metre
METRICAL adj of measurement
METRICATE vb convert a measuring system or instrument to metric units
METRICIAN n writer of metrical verse
METRICISE vb study metre of poetry
METRICISM > METRICISE
METRICIST same as **>** METRICIAN
METRICIZE same as **>** METRICISE
METRICS n art of using poetic metre
METRIFIED > METRIFY
METRIFIER > METRIFY
METRIFIES > METRIFY
METRIFY vb render into poetic metre
METRING > METRE
METRIST n person skilled in the use of poetic metre
METRISTS > METRIST
METRITIS n inflammation of the uterus
METRO n underground railway system, esp in Paris
METROLOGY n science of weights and measures
METRONOME n instrument which marks musical time by means of a ticking pendulum
METROPLEX n large urban area
METROS > METRO
METS > MET
METTLE n courage or spirit
METTLED adj spirited, courageous, or valiant
METTLES > METTLE
METUMP n band for carrying a load or burden
METUMPS > METUMP
MEU another name for **>** SPIGNEL
MEUNIERE adj cooked in butter with lemon juice and parsley
MEUS > MEU
MEUSE n gap through which an animal passed ▷ vb go through this gap
MEUSED > MEUSE
MEUSES > MEUSE
MEUSING > MEUSE

MEVE same as **>** MOVE
MEVED > MEVE
MEVES > MEVE
MEVING > MEVE
MEVROU n S African title of address
MEVROUS > MEVROU
MEW n cry of a cat ▷ vb utter this cry
MEWED > MEW
MEWING > MEW
MEWL vb (esp of a baby) to cry weakly ▷ n weak or whimpering cry
MEWLED > MEWL
MEWLER > MEWL
MEWLERS > MEWL
MEWLING > MEWL
MEWLS > MEWL
MEWS same as **>** MEUSE
MEWSED > MEWS
MEWSES > MEWS
MEWSING > MEWS
MEYNT > MING
MEZAIL same as **>** MESAIL
MEZAILS > MEZAIL
MEZCAL variant spelling of **>** MESCAL
MEZCALINE variant spelling of **>** MESCALINE
MEZCALS > MEZCAL
MEZE n type of hors d'oeuvre
MEZEREON same as **>** MEZEREUM
MEZEREONS > MEZEREON
MEZEREUM n dried bark of certain shrubs, formerly used to treat arthritis
MEZEREUMS > MEZEREUM
MEZES > MEZE
MEZQUIT same as **>** MESQUITE
MEZQUITE same as **>** MESQUITE
MEZQUITES > MEZQUITE
MEZQUITS > MEZQUIT
MEZUZA same as **>** MEZUZAH
MEZUZAH n piece of parchment inscribed with biblical passages
MEZUZAHS > MEZUZAH
MEZUZAS > MEZUZA
MEZUZOT > MEZUZAH
MEZUZOTH > MEZUZAH
MEZZ same as **>** MEZZANINE
MEZZALUNA n half-moon shaped kitchen chopper
MEZZANINE n intermediate storey, esp between the ground and first floor ▷ adj of or relating to an intermediate stage in a financial process
MEZZE same as **>** MEZE
MEZZES > MEZZE
MEZZO adv moderately ▷ n singer with voice between soprano and contralto
MEZZOS > MEZZO

m

MEZZOTINT n method of engraving by scraping the roughened surface of a metal plate ▷ vb engrave (a copper plate) in this fashion

MGANGA n witch doctor

MGANGAS > MGANGA

MHO former name for > SIEMENS

MHORR n African gazelle

MHORRS > MHORR

MHOS > MHO

MI n (in tonic sol-fa) the third degree of any major scale

MIAOU same as > MEOW

MIAOUED > MIAOU

MIAOUING > MIAOU

MIAOUS > MIAOU

MIAOW same as > MEOW

MIAOWED > MIAOW

MIAOWING > MIAOW

MIAOWS > MIAOW

MIASM same as > MIASMA

MIASMA n unwholesome or foreboding atmosphere

MIASMAL > MIASMA

MIASMAS > MIASMA

MIASMATA > MIASMA

MIASMATIC > MIASMA

MIASMIC > MIASMA

MIASMOUS > MIASMA

MIASMS > MIASM

MIAUL same as > MEOW

MIAULED > MIAUL

MIAULING > MIAUL

MIAULS > MIAUL

MIB n marble used in games

MIBS > MIB

MIBUNA n type of Japanese leafy vegetable

MIBUNAS > MIBUNA

MIC n microphone

MICA n glasslike mineral used as an electrical insulator

MICACEOUS > MICA

MICAS > MICA

MICATE vb add mica to

MICATED > MICATE

MICATES > MICATE

MICATING > MICATE

MICAWBER n person who idles and trusts to fortune

MICAWBERS > MICAWBER

MICE > MOUSE

MICELL same as > MICELLE

MICELLA same as > MICELLE

MICELLAE > MICELLA

MICELLAR > MICELLE

MICELLAS > MICELLA

MICELLE n charged aggregate of molecules of colloidal size in a solution

MICELLES > MICELLE

MICELLS > MICELL

MICH same as > MITCH

MICHAEL n as in take the michael teasing

MICHAELS > MICHAEL

MICHE same as > MICH

MICHED > MICH

MICHER > MICH

MICHERS > MICH

MICHES > MICH

MICHIGAN US name for > NEWMARKET

MICHIGANS > MICHIGAN

MICHING > MICH

MICHINGS > MICH

MICHT n Scots word for might

MICHTS > MICHT

MICKERIES > MICKERY

MICKERY n waterhole, esp in a dry riverbed

MICKEY n young bull ▷ vb drug a person's drink

MICKEYED > MICKEY

MICKEYING > MICKEY

MICKEYS > MICKEY

MICKIES > MICKY

MICKLE adj large or abundant ▷ adv much ▷ n great amount

MICKLER > MICKLE

MICKLES > MICKLE

MICKLEST > MICKLE

MICKY same as > MICKEY

MICO n marmoset

MICOS > MICO

MICRA > MICRON

MICRIFIED > MICRIFY

MICRIFIES > MICRIFY

MICRIFY vb make very small

MICRO n small computer

MICROBAR n millionth of a bar of pressure

MICROBARS > MICROBAR

MICROBE n minute organism, esp one causing disease

MICROBEAD n very small plastic particle

MICROBEAM n X-ray machine with narrow focussed beam

MICROBES > MICROBE

MICROBIAL > MICROBE

MICROBIAN > MICROBE

MICROBIC > MICROBE

MICROBLOG vb contribute to a blog which limits the length of individual postings

MICROBREW n beer made in small brewery

MICROBUS n small bus

MICROCAP adj (of investments) involving very small amounts of capital

MICROCAR n small car

MICROCARD n card containing microprint

MICROCARS > MICROCAR

MICROCHIP n small wafer of silicon containing electronic circuits ▷ vb implant (an animal) with a microchip tag for purposes of identification

MICROCODE n set of computer instructions

MICROCOPY n greatly reduced photographic copy of a printed page, drawing, etc, on microfilm or microfiche

MICROCOSM n miniature representation of something

MICROCYTE n unusually small red blood cell

MICRODONT adj having unusually small teeth

MICRODOT n photographic copy of a document reduced to pinhead size

MICRODOTS > MICRODOT

MICROFILM n miniaturized recording of books or documents on a roll of film ▷ vb photograph a page or document on microfilm

MICROFINE adj composed of tiny particles

MICROFORM n method of storing symbolic information by using photographic reduction techniques, such as microfilm, microfiche, etc

MICROGLIA n one of the two types of non-nervous tissue (glia) found in the central nervous system, having macrophage activity

MICROGRAM n photograph or drawing of an object as viewed through a microscope

MICROHM n millionth of an ohm

MICROHMS > MICROHM

MICROINCH n millionth of an inch

MICROJET n light jet-propelled aircraft

MICROJETS > MICROJET

MICROLITE n small private aircraft used in pleasure flying and racing

MICROLITH n small Mesolithic flint tool which was made from a blade and formed part of hafted tools

MICROLOAN n very small loan

MICROLOGY n study of microscopic things

MICROLUX n millionth of a lux

MICROMERE n any of the small cells formed by unequal splitting of a fertilized ovum

MICROMESH n very fine mesh

MICROMHO n millionth of a mho

MICROMHOS > MICROMHO

MICROMINI n very short skirt

MICROMOLE n millionth of a mole

MICROMORT n unit of risk

MICRON n unit of length equal to one millionth of a metre

MICRONISE same as > MICRONIZE

MICRONIZE vb break down to very small particles

MICRONS > MICRON

MICROPORE n very small pore

MICROPSIA n defect of vision in which objects appear to be smaller than they appear to a person with normal vision

MICROPUMP n small pump inserted in skin to automatically deliver medicine

MICROPYLE n small opening in the integuments of a plant ovule through which the male gametes pass

MICROS > MICRO

MICROSITE n website that is intended for a specific limited purpose and is often temporary

MICROSOME n any of the small particles consisting of ribosomes and fragments of attached endoplasmic reticulum that can be isolated from cells by centrifugal action

MICROTOME n instrument used for cutting thin sections, esp of biological material, for microscopical examination

MICROTOMY n cutting of sections with a microtome

MICROTONE n any musical interval smaller than a semitone

MICROTUBE n tiny tube

MICROVOLT n millionth of a volt

MICROWATT n millionth of a watt

MICROWAVE n electromagnetic wave with a wavelength of a few centimetres, used in radar and cooking ▷ vb cook in a microwave oven

MICROWIRE n very fine wire

MICRURGY n manipulation and examination of single cells under a microscope

MICS > MIC

MICTION n urination

MICTIONS > MICTION

MICTURATE vb urinate

MID adj intermediate, middle ▷ n middle ▷ prep amid

MIDAIR n some point above ground level, in the air

MIDAIRS > MIDAIR

MIDBAND adj using a range of frequencies between narrowband and broadband

MIDBRAIN n part of the brain that develops from the middle portion of the embryonic neural tube

MIDBRAINS > MIDBRAIN

MIDCALF n garment reaching to middle of the calf

MIDCALVES > MIDCALF

MIDCAP adj (of investments) involving medium-sized amounts of capital

MIDCOURSE adj in middle of course

MIDCULT n middlebrow culture

MIDCULTS > MIDCULT

MIDDAY n noon

MIDDAYS > MIDDAY

MIDDEN n rubbish heap

MIDDENS > MIDDEN

MIDDEST > MID

MIDDIE same as > MIDDY

MIDDIES > MIDDY

MIDDLE adj equidistant from two extremes ▷ n middle point or part ▷ vb place in the middle

MIDDLED > MIDDLE

MIDDLEMAN n trader who buys from the producer and sells to the consumer

MIDDLEMEN > MIDDLEMAN

MIDDLER n pupil in middle years at school

MIDDLERS > MIDDLER

MIDDLES > MIDDLE

MIDDLING adj mediocre ▷ adv moderately

MIDDLINGS pl n poorer or coarser part of flour or other products

MIDDORSAL adj in middle or back

MIDDY n middle-sized glass of beer

MIDFIELD n area between the two opposing defences

MIDFIELDS > MIDFIELD

MIDGE n small mosquito-like insect

MIDGES > MIDGE

MIDGET n very small thing ▷ adj much smaller than normal

MIDGETS > MIDGET

MIDGIE n informal word for a midge

MIDGIER > MIDGY

MIDGIES > MIDGIE

MIDGIEST > MIDGY

MIDGUT n middle part of the digestive tract

MIDGUTS > MIDGUT

MIDGY adj characterized by midges

MIDI adj (of a skirt, coat, etc) reaching to below the knee or midcalf ▷ n skirt, coat, etc reaching to below the knee or midcalf

MIDIBUS n medium-sized bus

MIDIBUSES > MIDIBUS

MIDINETTE n Parisian seamstress or salesgirl in a clothes shop

MIDIRON n golf club used for medium-length approach shots

MIDIRONS > MIDIRON

MIDIS > MIDI

MIDISKIRT n skirt of medium length

MIDLAND n middle part of a country

MIDLANDER n person living in the midlands

MIDLANDS > MIDLAND

MIDLEG n middle of leg

MIDLEGS > MIDLEG

MIDLIFE n middle age

MIDLIFER n middle-aged person

MIDLIFERS > MIDLIFER

MIDLINE n line at middle of something

MIDLINES > MIDLINE

MIDLIST n books in publisher's range that sell reasonably well

MIDLISTS > MIDLIST

MIDLIVES > MIDLIFE

MIDMONTH n middle of month

MIDMONTHS > MIDMONTH

MIDMOST adv in the middle or midst ▷ n the middle or midst

MIDMOSTS > MIDMOST

MIDNIGHT n twelve o'clock at night

MIDNIGHTS > MIDNIGHT

MIDNOON n noon

MIDNOONS > MIDNOON

MIDPAY adj paying more than an unskilled job but less than a high-income one

MIDPOINT n point on a line equally distant from either end

MIDPOINTS > MIDPOINT

MIDRANGE n part of loudspeaker

MIDRANGES > MIDRANGE

MIDRASH n homily on a Jewish scriptural passage

MIDRASHIC > MIDRASH

MIDRASHIM > MIDRASH

MIDRASHOT > MIDRASH

MIDRIB n main vein of a leaf

MIDRIBS > MIDRIB

MIDRIFF n middle part of the body

MIDRIFFS > MIDRIFF

MIDS > MID

MIDSEASON adj taking place in the middle of the season

MIDSHIP adj in, of, or relating to the middle of a vessel ▷ n middle of a vessel

MIDSHIPS same as > AMIDSHIPS

MIDSHORE adj between the inshore and the offshore

MIDSIZE adj medium-sized

MIDSIZED same as > MIDSIZE

MIDSOLE n layer between the inner and the outer sole of a shoe

MIDSOLES > MIDSOLE

MIDSPACE n area in middle of space

MIDSPACES > MIDSPACE

MIDST n middle

MIDSTORY n level of forest trees between smallest and tallest

MIDSTREAM n middle of a stream or river ▷ adj in or towards the middle of a stream or river

MIDSTS > MIDST

MIDSUMMER n middle of summer

MIDTERM n middle of a term in a school, university, etc

MIDTERMS > MIDTERM

MIDTHIGH n garment reaching to the middle of the thigh

MIDTHIGHS > MIDTHIGH

MIDTOWN n centre of a town

MIDTOWNS > MIDTOWN

MIDWATCH n naval watch period beginning at midnight

MIDWATER n middle part of a body of water

MIDWATERS > MIDWATER

MIDWAY adv halfway ▷ adj in or at the middle of the distance ▷ n place in a fair, carnival, etc, where sideshows are located

MIDWAYS > MIDWAY

MIDWEEK n middle of the week

MIDWEEKLY > MIDWEEK

MIDWEEKS > MIDWEEK

MIDWIFE n trained person who assists at childbirth ▷ vb act as midwife

MIDWIFED > MIDWIFE

MIDWIFERY n art or practice of a midwife

MIDWIFES > MIDWIFE

MIDWIFING > MIDWIFE

MIDWINTER n middle or depth of winter

MIDWIVE vb act as midwife

MIDWIVED > MIDWIVE

MIDWIVES > MIDWIFE

MIDWIVING > MIDWIVE

MIDYEAR n middle of the year

MIDYEARS > MIDYEAR

MIELIE same as > MEALIE

MIELIES > MIELIE

MIEN n person's bearing, demeanour, or appearance

MIENS > MIEN

MIEVE same as > MOVE

MIEVED > MIEVE

MIEVES > MIEVE

MIEVING > MIEVE

MIFF vb take offence or offend ▷ n petulant mood

MIFFED > MIFF

MIFFIER > MIFFY

MIFFIEST > MIFFY

MIFFILY > MIFFY

MIFFINESS > MIFFY

MIFFING > MIFF

MIFFS > MIFF

MIFFY adj easily upset

MIFTY same as > MIFFY

MIG n marble used in games

MIGAWD interj interjection used to express surprise

MIGG same as > MIG

MIGGLE n US word for playing marble

MIGGLES > MIGGLE

MIGGS > MIGG

MIGHT n physical strength

MIGHTEST > MAY

MIGHTFUL same as > MIGHTY

MIGHTIER > MIGHTY

MIGHTIEST > MIGHTY

MIGHTILY adv to a great extent, amount, or degree

MIGHTS > MIGHT

MIGHTST > MAY

MIGHTY adj powerful ▷ adv very

MIGMATITE n composite rock body containing two types of rock (esp igneous and metamorphic rock) that have interacted with each other but are nevertheless still distinguishable

MIGNON adj small and pretty ▷ n tender boneless cut of meat

MIGNONNE > MIGNON

MIGNONNES > MIGNON

MIGNONS > MIGNON

MIGRAINE n severe headache, often with nausea and visual disturbances

MIGRAINES > MIGRAINE

MIGRANT n person or animal that moves from one place to another ▷ adj moving from one place to another

MIGRANTS > MIGRANT

MIGRATE vb move from one place to settle in another

MIGRATED > MIGRATE

MIGRATES > MIGRATE

MIGRATING > MIGRATE

MIGRATION n act or an instance of migrating

MIGRATOR > MIGRATE

MIGRATORS > MIGRATE

MIGRATORY adj (of an animal) migrating every year

MIGS > MIG

MIHA n young fern frond which has not yet opened

MIHAS > MIHA

MIHI n Māori ceremonial greeting ▷ vb greet

MIHIED > MIHI

MIHIING > MIHI

MIHIS > MIHI

MIHRAB n niche in a mosque showing the direction of Mecca

MIHRABS > MIHRAB

MIJNHEER same as > MYNHEER

MIJNHEERS > MIJNHEER

MIKADO n Japanese emperor

MIKADOS > MIKADO

MIKE n microphone ▷ vb supply with a microphone

MIKED > MIKE

MIKES > MIKE

MIKING > MIKE

MIKRA > MIKRON

MIKRON same as > MICRON

MIKRONS > MIKRON

MIKVA n place for ritual bathing by Orthodox Jews

MIKVAH n pool used for ritual purification

MIKVAHS > MIKVAH

MIKVAS > MIKVA

MIKVEH same as > MIKVAH

MIKVEHS > MIKVEH

MIKVOS > MIKVEH

MIKVOT > MIKVEH

MIKVOTH > MIKVAH

MIL n unit of length equal to one thousandth of an inch

MILADI same as > MILADY

MILADIES > MILADY

MILADIS > MILADI

MILADY n (formerly) a continental title for an English gentlewoman

MILAGE same as > MILEAGE

MILAGES > MILAGE

MILCH adj (of a cow) giving milk

MILCHIG same as > MILCHIK

MILCHIK adj containing or used in the preparation of milk products

MILD adj not strongly flavoured ▷ n dark beer flavoured with fewer hops than bitter ▷ vb become gentle

MILDED > MILD

MILDEN vb make or become mild or milder

MILDENED > MILDEN

MILDENING > MILDEN

MILDENS > MILDEN

MILDER > MILD

MILDEST > MILD

MILDEW same as > MOULD

MILDEWED > MILDEW

MILDEWIER > MILDEWY

MILDEWING > MILDEW

MILDEWS > MILDEW

MILDEWY adj covered with mildew

MILDING > MILD

MILDISH adj rather mild

MILDLY > MILD

MILDNESS > MILD

MILDS > MILD

MILE n unit of length equal to 1760 yards or 1.609 kilometres

MILEAGE n distance travelled in miles

MILEAGES > MILEAGE

MILEPOST n signpost that shows the distance in miles to or from a place

MILEPOSTS > MILEPOST

MILER n athlete, horse, etc, that specializes in races of one mile

MILERS > MILER

MILES > MILE

MILESIAN adj Irish

MILESIMO n Spanish word meaning thousandth

MILESIMOS > MILESIMO

MILESTONE same as > MILEPOST

MILF n sexually attractive older woman

MILFOIL same as > YARROW

MILFOILS > MILFOIL

MILFS > MILF

MILIA > MILIUM

MILIARIA n acute itching eruption of the skin, caused by blockage of the sweat glands

MILIARIAL > MILIARIA

MILIARIAS > MILIARIA

MILIARY adj resembling or relating to millet seeds

MILIEU n environment or surroundings

MILIEUS > MILIEU

MILIEUX > MILIEU

MILING n activity of running one mile

MILINGS > MILING

MILITANCE n the condition or fact of being militant, esp in pursuing a political or social end

MILITANCY > MILITANT

MILITANT adj aggressive or vigorous in support of a cause ▷ n militant person

MILITANTS > MILITANT

MILITAR same as > MILITARY

MILITARIA pl n items of military interest, such as weapons, uniforms, medals, etc, esp from the past

MILITARY adj of or for soldiers, armies, or war ▷ n armed services

MILITATE vb have a strong influence or effect

MILITATED > MILITATE

MILITATES > MILITATE

MILITIA n military force of trained citizens

MILITIAS > MILITIA

MILIUM n pimple

MILK n white fluid produced by female mammals to feed their young ▷ vb draw milk from

MILKED > MILK

MILKEN adj of or like milk

MILKER n cow, goat, etc, that yields milk

MILKERS > MILKER

MILKFISH n type of large silvery tropical food and game fish

MILKIER > MILKY

MILKIEST > MILKY

MILKILY > MILKY

MILKINESS > MILKY

MILKING > MILK

MILKINGS > MILKING

MILKLESS > MILK

MILKLIKE > MILK

MILKMAID n (esp in former times) woman who milks cows

MILKMAIDS > MILKMAID

MILKMAN n man who delivers milk to people's houses

MILKMEN > MILKMAN

MILKO informal name for > MILKMAN

MILKOS > MILKO

MILKS > MILK

MILKSHAKE n drink of flavoured milk

MILKSHED n area where milk is produced

MILKSHEDS > MILKSHED

MILKSOP n feeble man

MILKSOPPY adj like a milksop

MILKSOPS > MILKSOP

MILKTOAST n meek, submissive, or timid person

MILKWEED n monarch butterfly

MILKWEEDS > MILKWEED

MILKWOOD n tree producing latex

MILKWOODS > MILKWOOD

MILKWORT n plant with small flowers

MILKWORTS > MILKWORT

MILKY adj of or like milk

MILL n factory ▷ vb grind, press, or process in or as if in a mill

MILLABLE > MILL

MILLAGE adj American tax rate calculated in thousandths per dollar

MILLAGES > MILLAGE

MILLBOARD n strong pasteboard, used esp in book covers

MILLCAKE n food for livestock

MILLCAKES > MILLCAKE

MILLDAM n dam built to raise the water level to turn a millwheel

MILLDAMS > MILLDAM

MILLE French word for > THOUSAND

MILLED adj crushed or ground in a mill

MILLENARY adj of or relating to a thousand or to a thousand years ▷ n adherent of millenarianism

MILLENNIA n plural of millennium: period or cycle of one thousand years

MILLEPED same as > MILLEPEDE

MILLEPEDE same as > MILLIPEDE

MILLEPEDS > MILLEPED

MILLEPORE n type of tropical colonial coral-like hydrozoan

MILLER n person who works in a mill

MILLERITE n yellow mineral consisting of nickel sulphide

MILLERS > MILLER

MILLES > MILLE

MILLET n type of cereal grass

MILLETS > MILLET

MILLHAND n person who works in a mill

MILLHANDS > MILLHAND

MILLHOUSE n house attached to mill

MILLIAMP n one thousandth of an ampere

MILLIAMPS > MILLIAMP

MILLIARD n one thousand millions

MILLIARDS > MILLIARD

MILLIARE n ancient Roman unit of distance

MILLIARES > MILLIARE

MILLIARY adj relating to or marking a distance equal to an ancient Roman mile of a thousand paces

MILLIBAR n unit of atmospheric pressure

MILLIBARS > MILLIBAR

MILLIE n insulting name for a young working-class woman

MILLIEME n Tunisian monetary unit worth one thousandth of a dinar

MILLIEMES > MILLIEME

MILLIER n metric weight of million grams

MILLIERS > MILLIER

MILLIES > MILLIE

MILLIGAL *n* unit of gravity
MILLIGALS > MILLIGAL
MILLIGRAM *n* thousandth part of a gram
MILLILUX *n* thousandth of lux
MILLIME *same as* > MILLIEME
MILLIMES > MILLIME
MILLIMHO *n* thousandth of mho
MILLIMHOS > MILLIMHO
MILLIMOLE *n* thousandth of mole
MILLINE *n* measurement of advertising space
MILLINER *n* maker or seller of women's hats
MILLINERS > MILLINER
MILLINERY *n* hats, trimmings, etc, sold by a milliner
MILLINES > MILLINE
MILLING *n* act or process of grinding, cutting, pressing, or crushing in a mill
MILLINGS > MILLING
MILLIOHM *n* thousandth of ohm
MILLIOHMS > MILLIOHM
MILLION *n* one thousand thousands
MILLIONS > MILLION
MILLIONTH *n* one of 1 000 000 approximately equal parts of something ▷ *adj* being the ordinal number of 1 000 000 in numbering or counting order, etc
MILLIPED *same as* > MILLIPEDE
MILLIPEDE *n* small animal with a jointed body and many pairs of legs
MILLIPEDS > MILLIPED
MILLIREM *n* unit of radiation
MILLIREMS > MILLIREM
MILLIVOLT *n* thousandth of volt
MILLIWATT *n* thousandth of watt
MILLOCRAT *n* member of a government of mill owners
MILLPOND *n* pool which provides water to turn a millwheel
MILLPONDS > MILLPOND
MILLRACE *n* current of water that turns a millwheel
MILLRACES > MILLRACE
MILLRIND *n* iron support fitted across an upper millstone
MILLRINDS > MILLRIND

MILLRUN *same as* > MILLRACE
MILLRUNS > MILLRUN
MILLS > MILL
MILLSCALE *n* scale on metal being heated
MILLSTONE *n* flat circular stone for grinding corn
MILLTAIL *n* channel carrying water away from mill
MILLTAILS > MILLTAIL
MILLWHEEL *n* waterwheel that drives a mill
MILLWORK *n* work done in a mill
MILLWORKS > MILLWORK
MILNEB *n* type of pesticide
MILNEBS > MILNEB
MILO *n* variety of sorghum with heads of yellow or pinkish seeds
MILOMETER *n* device that records the number of miles that a bicycle or motor vehicle has travelled
MILOR *same as* > MILORD
MILORD *n* (formerly) a continental title used for an English gentleman
MILORDS > MILORD
MILORS > MILOR
MILOS > MILO
MILPA *n* form of subsistence agriculture in Mexico
MILPAS > MILPA
MILREIS *n* former monetary unit of Portugal and Brazil
MILS > MIL
MILSEY *n* milk strainer
MILSEYS > MILSEY
MILT *n* reproductive fluid of male fish ▷ *vb* fertilize (the roe of a female fish) with milt
MILTED > MILT
MILTER *n* male fish that is mature and ready to breed
MILTERS > MILTER
MILTIER > MILTY
MILTIEST > MILTY
MILTING > MILT
MILTONIA *n* tropical American orchid
MILTONIAS > MILTONIA
MILTS > MILT
MILTY *adj* full of milt
MILTZ *same as* > MILT
MILTZES > MILTZ
MILVINE *adj* of kites and related birds
MIM *adj* prim, modest, or demure
MIMBAR *n* pulpit in mosque
MIMBARS > MIMBAR
MIME *n* acting without the use of words ▷ *vb* act in mime

MIMED > MIME
MIMEO *vb* mimeograph
MIMEOED > MIMEO
MIMEOING > MIMEO
MIMEOS > MIMEO
MIMER > MIME
MIMERS > MIME
MIMES > MIME
MIMESES > MIMESIS
MIMESIS *n* imitative representation of nature or human behaviour
MIMESISES > MIMESIS
MIMESTER > MIME
MIMESTERS > MIME
MIMETIC *adj* imitating or representing something
MIMETICAL > MIMETIC
MIMETITE *n* rare secondary mineral
MIMETITES > MIMETITE
MIMIC *vb* imitate (a person or manner), esp for satirical effect ▷ *n* person or animal that is good at mimicking ▷ *adj* of, relating to, or using mimicry
MIMICAL > MIMIC
MIMICKED > MIMIC
MIMICKER > MIMIC
MIMICKERS > MIMIC
MIMICKING > MIMIC
MIMICRIES > MIMICRY
MIMICRY *n* act or art of copying or imitating closely
MIMICS > MIMIC
MIMING > MIME
MIMIVIRUS *n* type of large virus
MIMMER > MIM
MIMMEST > MIM
MIMMICK *same as* > MINNICK
MIMMICKED > MIMMICK
MIMMICKS > MIMMICK
MIMOSA *n* shrub with fluffy yellow flowers and sensitive leaves
MIMOSAE > MIMOSA
MIMOSAS > MIMOSA
MIMSEY *same as* > MIMSY
MIMSIER > MIMSY
MIMSIEST > MIMSY
MIMSY *adj* prim, underwhelming, and ineffectual
MIMULUS *n* plants cultivated for their yellow or red flowers
MIMULUSES > MIMULUS
MINA *n* ancient unit of weight and money, used in Asia Minor
MINABLE > MINE
MINACIOUS *adj* threatening
MINACITY > MINACIOUS
MINAE > MINA
MINAR *n* tower
MINARET *n* tall slender tower of a mosque
MINARETED > MINARET
MINARETS > MINARET
MINARS > MINAR

MINAS > MINA
MINATORY *adj* threatening or menacing
MINBAR *same as* > MIMBAR
MINBARS > MINBAR
MINCE *vb* cut or grind into very small pieces ▷ *n* minced meat
MINCED > MINCE
MINCEMEAT *n* sweet mixture of dried fruit and spices
MINCER *n* machine for mincing meat
MINCERS > MINCER
MINCES > MINCE
MINCEUR *adj* (of food) low-fat
MINCIER > MINCY
MINCIEST > MINCY
MINCING *adj* affectedly elegant in manner
MINCINGLY > MINCING
MINCY *adj* excessively particular or fussy
MIND *n* thinking faculties ▷ *vb* take offence at
MINDED *adj* having an inclination as specified
MINDEDLY *adv* in the manner of a person with the kind of mind specified
MINDER *n* aide or bodyguard
MINDERS > MINDER
MINDFUCK *n* taboo term for deliberate infliction of psychological damage
MINDFUCKS > MINDFUCK
MINDFUL *adj* heedful
MINDFULLY > MINDFUL
MINDING > MIND
MINDINGS > MIND
MINDLESS *adj* stupid
MINDS > MIND
MINDSCAPE *n* extent of the imagination
MINDSET *n* ideas and attitudes with which a person approaches a situation
MINDSETS > MINDSET
MINDSHARE *n* level of awareness in the minds of consumers that a particular product commands
MINE *pron* belonging to me ▷ *n* deep hole for digging out coal, ores, etc ▷ *vb* dig for minerals
MINEABLE > MINE
MINED > MINE
MINEFIELD *n* area of land or water containing mines
MINELAYER *n* warship or aircraft for carrying and laying mines
MINEOLA *same as* > MINNEOLA
MINEOLAS > MINEOLA
MINER *n* person who works in a mine
MINERAL *n* naturally occurring inorganic

m

substance, such as metal ▷ *adj* of, containing, or like minerals

MINERALS >MINERAL

MINERS >MINER

MINES >MINE

MINESHAFT *n* vertical entrance into mine

MINESTONE *n* ore

MINETTE *n* type of rock

MINETTES >MINETTE

MINEVER *same as* >MINIVER

MINEVERS >MINEVER

MING *vb* mix

MINGE *n* vulgar word for female genitals

MINGED >MING

MINGER *n* insulting word for an unattractive person

MINGERS >MINGER

MINGES >MINGE

MINGIER >MINGY

MINGIEST >MINGY

MINGILY *adv* in a miserly manner

MINGINESS >MINGY

MINGING *adj* unattractive or unpleasant

MINGLE *vb* mix or blend

MINGLED >MINGLE

MINGLER >MINGLE

MINGLERS >MINGLE

MINGLES >MINGLE

MINGLING >MINGLE

MINGLINGS >MINGLE

MINGS >MING

MINGY *adj* miserly

MINI *same as* >MINIDRESS

MINIATE *vb* paint with minium

MINIATED >MINIATE

MINIATES >MINIATE

MINIATING >MINIATE

MINIATION >MINIATE

MINIATURE *n* small portrait, model, or copy ▷ *adj* small-scale ▷ *vb* reproduce in miniature

MINIBAR *n* selection of drinks and confectionery provided in a hotel room

MINIBARS >MINIBAR

MINIBIKE *n* light motorcycle

MINIBIKER >MINIBIKE

MINIBIKES >MINIBIKE

MINIBREAK *n* short holiday

MINIBUS *n* small bus

MINIBUSES >MINIBUS

MINICAB *n* ordinary car used as a taxi

MINICABS >MINICAB

MINICAM *n* portable television camera

MINICAMP *n* period spent together in isolation by sports team

MINICAMPS >MINICAMP

MINICAMS >MINICAM

MINICAR *n* small car

MINICARS >MINICAR

MINICOM *n* device allowing typed telephone messages to be sent and received

MINICOMS >MINICOM

MINIDISC *n* (esp formerly) small recordable compact disc

MINIDISCS >MINIDISC

MINIDISH *n* small parabolic aerial for reception or transmission to a communications satellite

MINIDISK *same as* >MINIDISC

MINIDISKS >MINIDISK

MINIDRESS *n* very short dress, at least four inches above the knee

MINIER >MINY

MINIEST >MINY

MINIFIED >MINIFY

MINIFIES >MINIFY

MINIFY *vb* minimize or lessen the size or importance of (something)

MINIFYING >MINIFY

MINIGOLF *n* putting game played via various obstacles

MINIGOLFS >MINIGOLF

MINIKIN *n* small, dainty, or affected person or thing ▷ *adj* dainty, prim, or affected

MINIKINS >MINIKIN

MINILAB *n* equipment for processing photographic film

MINILABS >MINILAB

MINIM *n* note half the length of a semibreve ▷ *adj* very small

MINIMA >MINIMUM

MINIMAL *adj* minimum ▷ *n* small surfboard

MINIMALLY >MINIMAL

MINIMALS >MINIMAL

MINIMART *n* convenience store

MINIMARTS >MINIMART

MINIMAX *n* lowest of a set of maximum values ▷ *vb* make maximum as low as possible

MINIMAXED >MINIMAX

MINIMAXES >MINIMAX

MINIMENT *same as* >MUNIMENT

MINIMENTS >MINIMENT

MINIMILL *n* small mill

MINIMILLS >MINIMILL

MINIMISE *same as* >MINIMIZE

MINIMISED >MINIMISE

MINIMISER >MINIMIZE

MINIMISES >MINIMISE

MINIMISM *n* desire to reduce to minimum

MINIMISMS >MINIMISM

MINIMIST >MINIMISM

MINIMISTS >MINIMISM

MINIMIZE *vb* reduce to a minimum

MINIMIZED >MINIMIZE

MINIMIZER >MINIMIZE

MINIMIZES >MINIMIZE

MINIMOTO *n* reduced-size replica motorcycle used for racing

MINIMOTOS >MINIMOTO

MINIMS >MINIM

MINIMUM *n* least possible (amount or number) ▷ *adj* of, being, or showing a minimum or minimums

MINIMUMS >MINIMUM

MINIMUS *adj* youngest: used after the surname of a schoolboy with elder brothers at the same school

MINIMUSES >MINIMUS

MINING *n* act, process, or industry of extracting coal or ores from the earth

MININGS >MINING

MINION *n* servile assistant ▷ *adj* dainty, pretty, or elegant

MINIONS >MINION

MINIPARK *n* small park

MINIPARKS >MINIPARK

MINIPILL *n* low-dose oral contraceptive containing a progestogen only

MINIPILLS >MINIPILL

MINIRUGBY *n* version of rugby with fewer players

MINIS >MINI

MINISCULE *same as* >MINUSCULE

MINISH *vb* diminish

MINISHED >MINISH

MINISHES >MINISH

MINISHING >MINISH

MINISKI *n* short ski

MINISKIRT *n* very short skirt

MINISKIS >MINISKI

MINISODE *n* episode of a television series shortened for broadcast on the internet

MINISODES >MINISODE

MINISTATE *n* small independent state

MINISTER *n* head of a government department ▷ *vb* attend to the needs of

MINISTERS >MINISTER

MINISTRY *n* profession or duties of a member of the clergy

MINITOWER *n* computer in small vertical cabinet

MINITRACK *n* satellite tracking system

MINIUM *n* bright red poisonous insoluble oxide of lead

MINIUMS >MINIUM

MINIVAN *n* small van, esp one with seats in the back for carrying passengers

MINIVANS >MINIVAN

MINIVER *n* white fur, used in ceremonial costumes

MINIVERS >MINIVER

MINIVET *n* brightly coloured tropical Asian cuckoo shrike

MINIVETS >MINIVET

MINK *n* stoat-like animal

MINKE *n* as in *minke whale* type of small whalebone whale or rorqual

MINKES >MINKE

MINKS >MINK

MINNEOLA *n* juicy citrus fruit that is a cross between a tangerine and a grapefruit

MINNEOLAS >MINNEOLA

MINNICK *vb* behave in fussy way

MINNICKED >MINNICK

MINNICKS >MINNICK

MINNIE *n* mother

MINNIES >MINNIE

MINNOCK *same as* >MINNICK

MINNOCKED >MINNOCK

MINNOCKS >MINNOCK

MINNOW *n* small freshwater fish

MINNOWS >MINNOW

MINNY *same as* >MINNIE

MINO *same as* >MYNAH

MINOR *adj* lesser ▷ *n* person regarded legally as a child ▷ *vb* take a minor

MINORCA *n* breed of light domestic fowl

MINORCAS >MINORCA

MINORED >MINOR

MINORING >MINOR

MINORITY *n* lesser number

MINORS >MINOR

MINORSHIP >MINOR

MINOS >MINO

MINOTAUR *n* as in *minotaur beetle* kind of dung-beetle

MINOXIDIL *n* drug used to counter baldness

MINSHUKU *n* guesthouse in Japan

MINSHUKUS >MINSHUKU

MINSTER *n* cathedral or large church

MINSTERS >MINSTER

MINSTREL *n* medieval singer or musician

MINSTRELS >MINSTREL

MINT *n* plant with aromatic leaves ▷ *vb* make (coins)

MINTAGE *n* process of minting

MINTAGES >MINTAGE

MINTED > MINT
MINTER > MINT
MINTERS > MINT
MINTIER > MINT
MINTIEST > MINT
MINTING > MINT
MINTLIKE adj like mint
MINTS > MINT
MINTY > MINT
MINUEND n number from which another number is to be subtracted
MINUENDS > MINUEND
MINUET n stately dance ▷ vb dance the minuet
MINUETED > MINUET
MINUETING > MINUET
MINUETS > MINUET
MINUS adj indicating subtraction ▷ n sign (-) denoting subtraction or a number less than zero ▷ prep reduced by the subtraction of
MINUSCULE adj very small ▷ n lower-case letter
MINUSES > MINUS
MINUTE n 60th part of an hour or degree ▷ vb record in the minutes ▷ adj very small
MINUTED > MINUTE
MINUTELY adv in great detail ▷ adj occurring every minute
MINUTEMAN n (in the War of American Independence) colonial militiaman who promised to be ready to fight at one minute's notice
MINUTEMEN > MINUTEMAN
MINUTER > MINUTE
MINUTES pl n official record of the proceedings of a meeting or conference
MINUTEST > MINUTE
MINUTIA singular noun of > MINUTIAE
MINUTIAE pl n trifling or precise details
MINUTIAL > MINUTIAE
MINUTING > MINUTE
MINUTIOSE > MINUTIAE
MINX n bold girl
MINXES > MINX
MINXISH > MINX
MINY adj of or like mines
MINYAN n number of persons required by Jewish law to be present for a religious service
MINYANIM > MINYAN
MINYANS > MINYAN
MIOCENE adj of, denoting, or formed in the fourth epoch of the Tertiary period
MIOMBO n (in E Africa) a dry wooded area with sparse deciduous growth
MIOMBOS > MIOMBO
MIOSES > MIOSIS
MIOSIS n excessive contraction of the pupil of the eye

MIOSISES > MIOSIS
MIOTIC > MIOSIS
MIOTICS > MIOSIS
MIPS n unit used to express the speed of a computer's central processing unit
MIQUELET n type of lock on old firearm
MIQUELETS > MIQUELET
MIR n peasant commune in prerevolutionary Russia
MIRABELLE n small sweet yellow-orange fruit that is a variety of greengage
MIRABILIA n wonders
MIRABILIS n tropical American plant
MIRABLE adj wonderful
MIRACIDIA n plural form of singular miracidium: flat ciliated larva of flukes that hatches from the egg and gives rise asexually to other larval forms
MIRACLE n wonderful supernatural event
MIRACLES > MIRACLE
MIRADOR n window, balcony, or turret
MIRADORS > MIRADOR
MIRAGE n optical illusion, esp one caused by hot air
MIRAGES > MIRAGE
MIRANDISE same as > MIRANDIZE
MIRANDIZE vb (in USA) inform arrested person of rights
MIRBANE n substance used in perfumes
MIRBANES > MIRBANE
MIRCHI Indian English word for > HOT
MIRE n swampy ground ▷ vb sink or be stuck in a mire
MIRED > MIRE
MIREPOIX n mixture of sautéed root vegetables
MIRES > MIRE
MIREX n type of insecticide
MIREXES > MIREX
MIRI > MIR
MIRID n variety of leaf bug
MIRIDS > MIRID
MIRIER > MIRE
MIRIEST > MIRE
MIRIFIC adj achieving wonderful things
MIRIFICAL same as > MIRIFIC
MIRIN n Japanese rice wine
MIRINESS > MIRE
MIRING > MIRE
MIRINS > MIRIN
MIRITI n South American palm
MIRITIS > MIRITI
MIRK same as > MURK
MIRKER > MIRK
MIRKEST > MIRK

MIRKIER > MIRK
MIRKIEST > MIRKY
MIRKILY > MIRK
MIRKINESS > MIRK
MIRKS > MIRK
MIRKY > MIRK
MIRLIER > MIRLY
MIRLIEST > MIRLY
MIRLIGOES n dizzy feeling
MIRLITON another name (chiefly US) for > CHAYOTE
MIRLITONS > MIRLITON
MIRLY same as > MARLY
MIRO n tall New Zealand tree
MIROMIRO n small New Zealand bird
MIROMIROS > MIROMIRO
MIROS > MIRO
MIRROR n coated glass surface for reflecting images ▷ vb reflect in or as if in a mirror
MIRRORED > MIRROR
MIRRORING n act of mirroring
MIRRORS > MIRROR
MIRS > MIR
MIRTH n laughter, merriment, or gaiety
MIRTHFUL > MIRTH
MIRTHLESS > MIRTH
MIRTHS > MIRTH
MIRV n missile with several warheads ▷ vb arm with mirvs
MIRVED > MIRV
MIRVING > MIRV
MIRVS > MIRV
MIRY > MIRE
MIRZA n title of respect placed before the surname of a distinguished man
MIRZAS > MIRZA
MIS > MI
MISACT vb act wrongly
MISACTED > MISACT
MISACTING > MISACT
MISACTS > MISACT
MISADAPT vb adapt badly
MISADAPTS > MISADAPT
MISADD vb add badly
MISADDED > MISADD
MISADDING > MISADD
MISADDS > MISADD
MISADJUST vb adjust wrongly
MISADVICE n bad advice
MISADVISE vb give bad advice to
MISAGENT n bad agent
MISAGENTS > MISAGENT
MISAIM vb aim badly
MISAIMED > MISAIM
MISAIMING > MISAIM
MISAIMS > MISAIM
MISALIGN vb align badly
MISALIGNS > MISALIGN
MISALLEGE vb allege wrongly

MISALLIED > MISALLY
MISALLIES > MISALLY
MISALLOT vb allot wrongly
MISALLOTS > MISALLOT
MISALLY vb form unsuitable alliance
MISALTER vb alter wrongly
MISALTERS > MISALTER
MISANDRY n hatred of men
MISAPPLY vb use something for a purpose for which it is not intended or is not suited
MISARRAY n disarray
MISARRAYS > MISARRAY
MISASSAY vb assay wrongly
MISASSAYS > MISASSAY
MISASSIGN vb assign wrongly
MISASSUME vb assume wrongly
MISATE > MISEAT
MISATONE vb atone wrongly
MISATONED > MISATONE
MISATONES > MISATONE
MISAUNTER n misadventure
MISAVER vb claim wrongly
MISAVERS > MISAVER
MISAVISED adj badly advised
MISAWARD vb award wrongly
MISAWARDS > MISAWARD
MISBECAME > MISBECOME
MISBECOME vb be unbecoming to or unsuitable for
MISBEGAN > MISBEGIN
MISBEGIN vb begin badly
MISBEGINS > MISBEGIN
MISBEGOT adj archaic word for illegitimate
MISBEGUN > MISBEGIN
MISBEHAVE vb behave badly
MISBELIEF n false or unorthodox belief
MISBESEEM vb be unsuitable for
MISBESTOW vb bestow wrongly
MISBIAS vb prejudice wrongly
MISBIASED > MISBIAS
MISBIASES > MISBIAS
MISBILL vb present inaccurate bill
MISBILLED > MISBILL
MISBILLS > MISBILL
MISBIND vb bind wrongly
MISBINDS > MISBIND
MISBIRTH n abortion

MISBIRTHS
>MISBIRTH
MISBORN adj born
prematurely
MISBOUND >MISBIND
MISBRAND vb put
misleading label on
MISBRANDS
>MISBRAND
MISBUILD vb build badly
MISBUILDS
>MISBUILD
MISBUILT >MISBUILD
MISBUTTON vb button
wrongly
MISCALL vb call by the
wrong name
MISCALLED >MISCALL
MISCALLER >MISCALL
MISCALLS >MISCALL
MISCARRY vb have a
miscarriage
MISCAST vb cast (a role
or actor) inappropriately
MISCASTS >MISCAST
MISCEGEN n person of
mixed ancestry
MISCEGENE same as
>MISCEGEN
MISCEGENS
>MISCEGEN
MISCEGINE same as
>MISCEGEN
MISCH adj as in misch
metal alloy of cerium and
other rare earth metals
MISCHANCE n unlucky
event
MISCHANCY adj unlucky
MISCHARGE vb charge
wrongly
MISCHIEF n annoying
but not malicious
behaviour
MISCHIEFS
>MISCHIEF
MISCHOICE n bad choice
MISCHOOSE vb make bad
choice
MISCHOSE
>MISCHOOSE
MISCHOSEN
>MISCHOOSE
MISCIBLE adj able to be
mixed
MISCITE vb cite wrongly
MISCITED >MISCITE
MISCITES >MISCITE
MISCITING >MISCITE
MISCLAIM vb claim
wrongly
MISCLAIMS
>MISCLAIM
MISCLASS vb class badly
MISCODE vb code
wrongly
MISCODED >MISCODE
MISCODES >MISCODE
MISCODING >MISCODE
MISCOIN vb coin wrongly
MISCOINED >MISCOIN
MISCOINS >MISCOIN
MISCOLOR same as
>MISCOLOUR
MISCOLORS
>MISCOLOR
MISCOLOUR vb give
wrong colour to

MISCOOK vb cook badly
MISCOOKED >MISCOOK
MISCOOKS >MISCOOK
MISCOPIED >MISCOPY
MISCOPIES >MISCOPY
MISCOPY vb copy badly
MISCOUNT vb count or
calculate incorrectly ▷ n
false count or calculation
MISCOUNTS
>MISCOUNT
MISCREANT n
wrongdoer ▷ adj evil or
villainous
MISCREATE vb create
(something) badly or
incorrectly ▷ adj badly or
unnaturally formed or
made
MISCREDIT vb disbelieve
MISCREED n false creed
MISCREEDS
>MISCREED
MISCUE n faulty stroke in
snooker, etc ▷ vb make a
miscue
MISCUED >MISCUE
MISCUEING >MISCUE
MISCUES >MISCUE
MISCUING >MISCUE
MISCUT vb cut wrongly
MISCUTS >MISCUT
MISDATE vb date (a
letter, event, etc) wrongly
MISDATED >MISDATE
MISDATES >MISDATE
MISDATING >MISDATE
MISDEAL vb deal out
cards incorrectly ▷ n
faulty deal
MISDEALER >MISDEAL
MISDEALS >MISDEAL
MISDEALT >MISDEAL
MISDEED n wrongful act
MISDEEDS >MISDEED
MISDEEM vb form bad
opinion of
MISDEEMED >MISDEEM
MISDEEMS >MISDEEM
MISDEFINE vb define
badly
MISDEMEAN rare word for
>MISBEHAVE
MISDEMPT >MISDEEM
MISDESERT n quality of
being undeserving
MISDIAL vb dial
telephone number
incorrectly
MISDIALED >MISDIAL
MISDIALS >MISDIAL
MISDID >MISDO
MISDIET n wrong diet
▷ vb diet or eat improperly
MISDIETED >MISDIET
MISDIETS >MISDIET
MISDIGHT adj done badly
▷ vb mismanage or treat
badly
MISDIGHTS
>MISDIGHT
MISDIRECT vb give
(someone) wrong
directions or instructions
MISDIVIDE vb divide
wrongly
MISDO vb do badly or
wrongly

MISDOER >MISDO
MISDOERS >MISDO
MISDOES >MISDO
MISDOING >MISDO
MISDOINGS >MISDO
MISDONE adj done badly
MISDONNE same as
>MISDONE
MISDOUBT archaic word
for >DOUBT
MISDOUBTS
>MISDOUBT
MISDRAW vb draw poorly
MISDRAWN >MISDRAW
MISDRAWS >MISDRAW
MISDREAD n fear of
approaching evil ▷ vb fear
or dread
MISDREADS
>MISDREAD
MISDREW >MISDRAW
MISDRIVE vb drive badly
MISDRIVEN
>MISDRIVE
MISDRIVES
>MISDRIVE
MISDROVE >MISDRIVE
MISE n issue in the
obsolete writ of right
MISEASE n unease
MISEASES >MISEASE
MISEAT vb eat unhealthy
food
MISEATEN >MISEAT
MISEATING >MISEAT
MISEATS >MISEAT
MISEDIT vb edit badly
MISEDITED >MISEDIT
MISEDITS >MISEDIT
MISEMPLOY vb employ
badly
MISENROL vb enrol
wrongly
MISENROLL same as
>MISENROL
MISENROLS
>MISENROL
MISENTER vb enter
wrongly
MISENTERS
>MISENTER
MISENTRY n wrong or
mistaken entry
MISER n person who
hoards money and hates
spending it
MISERABLE adj very
unhappy, wretched ▷ n
wretched person
MISERABLY
>MISERABLE
MISERE n call in solo
whist and other card
games declaring a hand
that will win no tricks
MISERERE n type of
psalm
MISERERES
>MISERERE
MISERES >MISERE
MISERIES >MISERY
MISERLIER >MISERLY
MISERLY adj of or
resembling a miser
MISERS >MISER
MISERY n great
unhappiness
MISES >MISE

MISESTEEM n lack of
respect
MISEVENT n mishap
MISEVENTS
>MISEVENT
MISFAITH n distrust
MISFAITHS
>MISFAITH
MISFALL vb happen as
piece of bad luck
MISFALLEN >MISFALL
MISFALLS >MISFALL
MISFALNE >MISFALL
MISFARE vb get on badly
MISFARED >MISFARE
MISFARES >MISFARE
MISFARING >MISFARE
MISFEASOR n someone
who carries out the
improper performance of
an act that is lawful in
itself
MISFED >MISFEED
MISFEED vb feed wrongly
MISFEEDS >MISFEED
MISFEIGN vb feign with
evil motive
MISFEIGNS
>MISFEIGN
MISFELL >MISFALL
MISFIELD vb fail to field
properly
MISFIELDS
>MISFIELD
MISFILE vb file (papers,
records, etc) wrongly
MISFILED >MISFILE
MISFILES >MISFILE
MISFILING >MISFILE
MISFIRE vb (of a firearm
or engine) fail to fire
correctly ▷ n act or an
instance of misfiring
MISFIRED >MISFIRE
MISFIRES >MISFIRE
MISFIRING >MISFIRE
MISFIT n person not
suited to his or her social
environment ▷ vb fail to fit
or be fitted
MISFITS >MISFIT
MISFITTED >MISFIT
MISFOCUS n wrong or
poor focus
MISFOLD vb fold wrongly
MISFOLDED >MISFOLD
MISFOLDS >MISFOLD
MISFORM vb form badly
MISFORMED >MISFORM
MISFORMS >MISFORM
MISFRAME vb frame
wrongly
MISFRAMED
>MISFRAME
MISFRAMES
>MISFRAME
MISGAGE vb gage
wrongly
MISGAGED >MISGAGE
MISGAGES >MISGAGE
MISGAGING >MISGAGE
MISGAUGE vb gauge
badly
MISGAUGED
>MISGAUGE
MISGAUGES
>MISGAUGE
MISGAVE >MISGIVE

MISGENDER vb refer to a person as the wrong gender
MISGIVE vb make or be apprehensive or suspicious
MISGIVEN > MISGIVE
MISGIVES > MISGIVE
MISGIVING n feeling of fear or doubt
MISGO vb go wrong way
MISGOES > MISGO
MISGOING > MISGO
MISGONE > MISGO
MISGOTTEN adj obtained dishonestly
MISGOVERN vb govern badly
MISGRADE vb grade wrongly
MISGRADED > MISGRADE
MISGRADES > MISGRADE
MISGRAFF adj badly done
MISGRAFT vb graft wrongly
MISGRAFTS > MISGRAFT
MISGREW > MISGROW
MISGROW vb grow in unsuitable way
MISGROWN > MISGROW
MISGROWS > MISGROW
MISGROWTH > MISGROW
MISGUESS vb guess wrongly
MISGUGGLE vb handle incompetently
MISGUIDE vb guide or direct wrongly or badly
MISGUIDED adj mistaken or unwise
MISGUIDER > MISGUIDE
MISGUIDES > MISGUIDE
MISHANDLE vb handle badly or inefficiently
MISHANTER n misfortune
MISHAP n minor accident ▷ vb happen as bad luck
MISHAPPED > MISHAP
MISHAPPEN vb happen as bad luck
MISHAPS > MISHAP
MISHAPT same as > MISSHAPEN
MISHEAR vb hear (what someone says) wrongly
MISHEARD > MISHEAR
MISHEARS > MISHEAR
MISHEGAAS same as > MESHUGAAS
MISHEGOSS same as > MESHUGAAS
MISHIT n faulty shot, kick, or stroke ▷ vb hit or kick a ball with a faulty stroke
MISHITS > MISHIT
MISHMASH n confused collection or mixture
MISHMEE n root of Asian plant
MISHMEES > MISHMEE

MISHMI n evergreen perennial plant
MISHMIS > MISHMI
MISHMOSH same as > MISHMASH
MISHUGAS same as > MESHUGAAS
MISINFER vb infer wrongly
MISINFERS > MISINFER
MISINFORM vb give incorrect information to
MISINTEND vb intend to harm
MISINTER vb bury wrongly
MISINTERS > MISINTER
MISJOIN vb join badly
MISJOINED > MISJOIN
MISJOINS > MISJOIN
MISJUDGE vb judge wrongly or unfairly
MISJUDGED > MISJUDGE
MISJUDGER > MISJUDGE
MISJUDGES > MISJUDGE
MISKAL n unit of weight in Iran
MISKALS > MISKAL
MISKEEP vb keep wrongly
MISKEEPS > MISKEEP
MISKEN vb be unaware of
MISKENNED > MISKEN
MISKENS > MISKEN
MISKENT > MISKEN
MISKEPT > MISKEEP
MISKEY vb key wrongly
MISKEYED > MISKEY
MISKEYING > MISKEY
MISKEYS > MISKEY
MISKICK vb fail to kick properly
MISKICKED > MISKICK
MISKICKS > MISKICK
MISKNEW > MISKNOW
MISKNOW vb have wrong idea about
MISKNOWN > MISKNOW
MISKNOWS > MISKNOW
MISLABEL vb label badly
MISLABELS > MISLABEL
MISLABOR vb labour wrongly
MISLABORS > MISLABOR
MISLABOUR vb labour wrongly
MISLAID > MISLAY
MISLAIN > MISLAY
MISLAY vb lose (something) temporarily
MISLAYER > MISLAY
MISLAYERS > MISLAY
MISLAYING > MISLAY
MISLAYS > MISLAY
MISLEAD vb give false or confusing information to
MISLEADER > MISLEAD
MISLEADS > MISLEAD
MISLEARED adj badly brought up
MISLEARN vb learn wrongly
MISLEARNS > MISLEARN

MISLEARNT > MISLEARN
MISLED > MISLEAD
MISLEEKE same as > MISLIKE
MISLEEKED > MISLEEKE
MISLEEKES > MISLEEKE
MISLETOE same as > MISTLETOE
MISLETOES > MISLETOE
MISLIE vb lie wrongly
MISLIES > MISLIE
MISLIGHT vb use light to lead astray
MISLIGHTS > MISLIGHT
MISLIKE vb dislike ▷ n dislike or aversion
MISLIKED > MISLIKE
MISLIKER > MISLIKE
MISLIKERS > MISLIKE
MISLIKES > MISLIKE
MISLIKING > MISLIKE
MISLIPPEN vb distrust
MISLIT > MISLIGHT
MISLIVE vb live wickedly
MISLIVED > MISLIVE
MISLIVES > MISLIVE
MISLIVING > MISLIVE
MISLOCATE vb put in wrong place
MISLODGE vb lodge wrongly
MISLODGED > MISLODGE
MISLODGES > MISLODGE
MISLUCK vb have bad luck
MISLUCKED > MISLUCK
MISLUCKS > MISLUCK
MISLYING > MISLIE
MISMADE > MISMAKE
MISMAKE vb make badly
MISMAKES > MISMAKE
MISMAKING > MISMAKE
MISMANAGE vb organize or run (something) badly
MISMARK vb mark wrongly
MISMARKED > MISMARK
MISMARKS > MISMARK
MISMARRY vb make unsuitable marriage
MISMATCH vb form an unsuitable partner, opponent, or set ▷ n unsuitable match
MISMATE vb mate wrongly
MISMATED > MISMATE
MISMATES > MISMATE
MISMATING n unintended breeding of domesticated animals
MISMEET vb fail to meet
MISMEETS > MISMEET
MISMET > MISMEET
MISMETRE vb fail to follow the metre of a poem
MISMETRED > MISMETRE
MISMETRES > MISMETRE
MISMOVE vb move badly

MISMOVED > MISMOVE
MISMOVES > MISMOVE
MISMOVING > MISMOVE
MISNAME vb name badly
MISNAMED > MISNAME
MISNAMES > MISNAME
MISNAMING > MISNAME
MISNOMER n incorrect or unsuitable name ▷ vb apply a misnomer to
MISNOMERS > MISNOMER
MISNUMBER vb number wrongly
MISO n thick brown salty paste made from soya beans
MISOCLERE adj hostile to clergy
MISOGAMIC > MISOGAMY
MISOGAMY n hatred of marriage
MISOGYNIC adj hating women
MISOGYNY n hatred of women
MISOLOGY n hatred of reasoning or reasoned argument
MISONEISM n hatred of anything new
MISONEIST > MISONEISM
MISORDER vb order badly
MISORDERS > MISORDER
MISORIENT vb orient incorrectly
MISOS > MISO
MISPAGE vb page wrongly
MISPAGED > MISPAGE
MISPAGES > MISPAGE
MISPAGING > MISPAGE
MISPAINT vb paint badly or wrongly
MISPAINTS > MISPAINT
MISPARSE vb parse wrongly
MISPARSED > MISPARSE
MISPARSES > MISPARSE
MISPART vb part wrongly
MISPARTED > MISPART
MISPARTS > MISPART
MISPATCH vb patch wrongly
MISPEN vb write wrongly
MISPENNED > MISPEN
MISPENS > MISPEN
MISPHRASE vb phrase badly
MISPICKEL n white or grey metallic mineral consisting of a sulphide of iron and arsenic that forms monoclinic crystals with an orthorhombic shape: an ore of arsenic
MISPLACE vb mislay
MISPLACED adj (of an emotion or action) directed towards a person or thing that does not deserve it

MISPLACES
>MISPLACE
MISPLAN vb plan badly or wrongly
MISPLANS >MISPLAN
MISPLANT vb plant badly or wrongly
MISPLANTS
>MISPLANT
MISPLAY vb play badly or wrongly in games or sports ▷ n wrong or unskilful play
MISPLAYED >MISPLAY
MISPLAYS >MISPLAY
MISPLEAD vb plead incorrectly
MISPLEADS
>MISPLEAD
MISPLEASE vb displease
MISPLED >MISPLEAD
MISPOINT vb punctuate badly
MISPOINTS
>MISPOINT
MISPOISE n lack of poise ▷ vb lack poise
MISPOISED
>MISPOISE
MISPOISES
>MISPOISE
MISPRAISE vb fail to praise properly
MISPRICE vb give the wrong price to
MISPRICED
>MISPRICE
MISPRICES
>MISPRICE
MISPRINT n printing error ▷ vb print a letter incorrectly
MISPRINTS
>MISPRINT
MISPRISE same as
>MISPRIZE
MISPRISED
>MISPRISE
MISPRISES
>MISPRISE
MISPRIZE vb fail to appreciate the value of
MISPRIZED
>MISPRIZE
MISPRIZER
>MISPRIZE
MISPRIZES
>MISPRIZE
MISPROUD adj undeservedly proud
MISQUOTE vb quote inaccurately
MISQUOTED
>MISQUOTE
MISQUOTER
>MISQUOTE
MISQUOTES
>MISQUOTE
MISRAISE vb raise wrongly or excessively
MISRAISED
>MISRAISE
MISRAISES
>MISRAISE
MISRATE vb rate wrongly
MISRATED >MISRATE
MISRATES >MISRATE
MISRATING >MISRATE

MISREAD vb misinterpret (a situation etc)
MISREADS >MISREAD
MISRECKON vb reckon wrongly
MISRECORD vb record wrongly
MISREFER vb refer wrongly
MISREFERS
>MISREFER
MISREGARD n lack of attention ▷ vb have no regard for; disregard
MISRELATE vb relate badly
MISRELIED >MISRELY
MISRELIES >MISRELY
MISRELY vb rely wrongly
MISRENDER vb render wrongly
MISREPORT vb report falsely or inaccurately ▷ n inaccurate or false report
MISRHYMED adj badly rhymed
MISROUTE vb send wrong way
MISROUTED
>MISROUTE
MISROUTES
>MISROUTE
MISRULE vb govern inefficiently or unjustly ▷ n inefficient or unjust government
MISRULED >MISRULE
MISRULES >MISRULE
MISRULING >MISRULE
MISS vb fail to notice, hear, hit, reach, find, or catch ▷ n fact or instance of missing
MISSA n Roman Catholic mass
MISSABLE >MISS
MISSAE >MISSA
MISSAID >MISSAY
MISSAL n book containing the prayers and rites of the Mass
MISSALS >MISSAL
MISSAW >MISSEE
MISSAY vb say wrongly
MISSAYING >MISSAY
MISSAYS >MISSAY
MISSEAT vb seat wrongly
MISSEATED >MISSEAT
MISSEATS >MISSEAT
MISSED >MISS
MISSEE vb see wrongly
MISSEEING >MISSEE
MISSEEM vb be unsuitable for
MISSEEMED >MISSEEM
MISSEEMS >MISSEEM
MISSEEN >MISSEE
MISSEES >MISSEE
MISSEL adj as in missel thrush large European thrush
MISSELL vb sell (a product, esp a financial one) misleadingly
MISSELLS >MISSELL
MISSELS >MISSEL
MISSEND vb send wrongly

MISSENDS >MISSEND
MISSENSE n type of genetic mutation ▷ vb give a wrong sense or meaning
MISSENSED
>MISSENSE
MISSENSES
>MISSENSE
MISSENT >MISSEND
MISSES >MISS
MISSET vb set wrongly
MISSETS >MISSET
MISSHAPE vb shape badly ▷ n something that is badly shaped
MISSHAPED >MISSHAPE
MISSHAPEN adj badly shaped, deformed
MISSHAPER
>MISSHAPE
MISSHAPES
>MISSHAPE
MISSHOD adj badly shod
MISSHOOD n state of being an unmarried woman
MISSHOODS
>MISSHOOD
MISSIER >MISSY
MISSIES >MISSY
MISSIEST >MISSY
MISSILE n rocket with an exploding warhead
MISSILEER n serviceman or servicewoman who is responsible for firing missiles
MISSILERY n missiles collectively
MISSILES >MISSILE
MISSILRY same as
>MISSILERY
MISSING adj lost or absent
MISSINGLY >MISSING
MISSION n specific task or duty ▷ vb direct a mission to or establish a mission in
MISSIONAL adj emphasizing preaching of gospel
MISSIONED >MISSION
MISSIONER n person heading a parochial mission in a Christian country
MISSIONS >MISSION
MISSIS same as
>MISSUS
MISSISES >MISSIS
MISSISH adj like a schoolgirl
MISSIVE n letter ▷ adj sent or intended to be sent
MISSIVES >MISSIVE
MISSOLD >MISSELL
MISSORT vb sort wrongly
MISSORTED >MISSORT
MISSORTS >MISSORT
MISSOUND vb sound wrongly
MISSOUNDS
>MISSOUND
MISSOUT n someone who has been overlooked

MISSOUTS >MISSOUT
MISSPACE vb space out wrongly
MISSPACED
>MISSPACE
MISSPACES
>MISSPACE
MISSPEAK vb speak wrongly
MISSPEAKS
>MISSPEAK
MISSPELL vb spell (a word) wrongly
MISSPELLS
>MISSPELL
MISSPELT >MISSPELL
MISSPEND vb waste or spend unwisely
MISSPENDS
>MISSPEND
MISSPENT >MISSPEND
MISSPOKE >MISSPEAK
MISSPOKEN
>MISSPEAK
MISSTAMP vb stamp badly
MISSTAMPS
>MISSTAMP
MISSTART vb start wrongly
MISSTARTS
>MISSTART
MISSTATE vb state incorrectly
MISSTATED
>MISSTATE
MISSTATES
>MISSTATE
MISSTEER vb steer badly
MISSTEERS
>MISSTEER
MISSTEP n false step ▷ vb take a false step
MISSTEPS >MISSTEP
MISSTOP vb stop wrongly
MISSTOPS >MISSTOP
MISSTRIKE vb fail to strike properly
MISSTRUCK
>MISSTRIKE
MISSTYLE vb call by the wrong name
MISSTYLED
>MISSTYLE
MISSTYLES
>MISSTYLE
MISSUIT vb be unsuitable for
MISSUITED >MISSUIT
MISSUITS >MISSUIT
MISSUS n one's wife or the wife of the person addressed or referred to
MISSUSES >MISSUS
MISSY n affectionate or disparaging form of address to a girl ▷ adj missish
MIST n thin fog ▷ vb cover or be covered with mist
MISTAKE n error or blunder ▷ vb misunderstand
MISTAKEN adj wrong in judgment or opinion
MISTAKER >MISTAKE
MISTAKERS >MISTAKE
MISTAKES >MISTAKE

MISTAKING > MISTAKE

MISTAL n cow shed

MISTALS > MISTAL

MISTAUGHT
> MISTEACH

MISTBOW same as
> FOGBOW

MISTBOWS > MISTBOW

MISTEACH vb teach badly

MISTED > MIST

MISTELL vb tell wrongly

MISTELLS > MISTELL

MISTEMPER vb make
disordered

MISTEND vb tend
wrongly

MISTENDED > MISTEND

MISTENDS > MISTEND

MISTER n informal form
of address for a man ▷ vb
call (someone) mister

MISTERED > MISTER

MISTERIES > MISTERY

MISTERING > MISTER

MISTERM vb term badly

MISTERMED > MISTERM

MISTERMS > MISTERM

MISTERS > MISTER

MISTERY same as
> MYSTERY

MISTEUK Scots variant of
> MISTOOK

MISTFUL > MIST

MISTHINK vb have poor
opinion of

MISTHINKS
> MISTHINK

MISTHREW > MISTHROW

MISTHROW vb fail to
throw properly

MISTHROWN
> MISTHROW

MISTHROWS
> MISTHROW

MISTICO n small
Mediterranean sailing ship

MISTICOS > MISTICO

MISTIER > MISTY

MISTIEST > MISTY

MISTIGRIS n joker or a
blank card used as a wild
card in a variety of draw
poker

MISTILY > MISTY

MISTIME vb do
(something) at the wrong
time

MISTIMED > MISTIME

MISTIMES > MISTIME

MISTIMING n act of
mistiming

MISTINESS > MISTY

MISTING n application of
a fake suntan by spray

MISTINGS > MISTING

MISTITLE vb name badly

MISTITLED
> MISTITLE

MISTITLES
> MISTITLE

MISTLE same as
> MIZZLE

MISTLED > MISTLE

MISTLES > MISTLE

MISTLETOE n evergreen
plant with white berries
growing as a parasite on
trees

MISTLING > MISTLE

MISTOLD > MISTELL

MISTOOK past tense of
> MISTAKE

MISTOUCH vb fail to
touch properly

MISTRACE vb trace
wrongly

MISTRACED
> MISTRACE

MISTRACES
> MISTRACE

MISTRAIN vb train
wrongly

MISTRAINS
> MISTRAIN

MISTRAL n strong dry
northerly wind of S France

MISTRALS > MISTRAL

MISTREAT vb treat (a
person or animal) badly

MISTREATS
> MISTREAT

MISTRESS n woman in a
position of authority,
ownership, or control ▷ vb
become a mistress

MISTRIAL n trial made
void because of some error

MISTRIALS
> MISTRIAL

MISTRUST vb have
doubts or suspicions
about ▷ n lack of trust

MISTRUSTS
> MISTRUST

MISTRUTH n something
untrue

MISTRUTHS
> MISTRUTH

MISTRYST vb fail to keep
an appointment with

MISTRYSTS
> MISTRYST

MISTS > MIST

MISTUNE vb fail to tune
properly

MISTUNED > MISTUNE

MISTUNES > MISTUNE

MISTUNING > MISTUNE

MISTUTOR vb instruct
badly

MISTUTORS
> MISTUTOR

MISTY adj full of mist

MISTYPE vb type badly

MISTYPED > MISTYPE

MISTYPES > MISTYPE

MISTYPING > MISTYPE

MISUNION n wrong or
bad union

MISUNIONS
> MISUNION

MISUSAGE > MISUSE

MISUSAGES > MISUSE

MISUSE n incorrect,
improper, or careless use
▷ vb use wrongly

MISUSED > MISUSE

MISUSER n abuse of
some right, privilege,
office, etc

MISUSERS > MISUSER

MISUSES > MISUSE

MISUSING > MISUSE

MISUST > MISUSE

MISVALUE vb value badly

MISVALUED > MISVALUE

MISVALUES
> MISVALUE

MISWEEN vb assess
wrongly

MISWEENED > MISWEEN

MISWEENS > MISWEEN

MISWEND vb become lost

MISWENDS > MISWEND

MISWENT > MISWEND

MISWORD vb word badly

MISWORDED > MISWORD

MISWORDS > MISWORD

MISWRIT > MISWRITE

MISWRITE vb write badly

MISWRITES
> MISWRITE

MISWROTE > MISWRITE

MISYOKE vb join wrongly

MISYOKED > MISYOKE

MISYOKES > MISYOKE

MISYOKING > MISYOKE

MITCH vb play truant from
school

MITCHED > MITCH

MITCHES > MITCH

MITCHING > MITCH

MITE n very small
spider-like animal

MITER same as > MITRE

MITERED > MITER

MITERER > MITER

MITERERS > MITER

MITERING > MITER

MITERS > MITER

MITERWORT same as
> MITREWORT

MITES > MITE

MITHER vb fuss over or
moan about something

MITHERED > MITHER

MITHERING > MITHER

MITHERS > MITHER

MITICIDAL
> MITICIDE

MITICIDE n any drug or
agent that destroys mites

MITICIDES
> MITICIDE

MITIER > MITY

MITIEST > MITY

MITIGABLE
> MITIGATE

MITIGANT adj acting to
mitigate ▷ n means of
easing, lessening, or
assuaging

MITIGANTS
> MITIGANT

MITIGATE vb make less
severe

MITIGATED
> MITIGATE

MITIGATES
> MITIGATE

MITIGATOR
> MITIGATE

MITIS n malleable iron

MITISES > MITIS

MITOGEN n any agent
that induces mitosis

MITOGENIC > MITOGEN

MITOGENS > MITOGEN

MITOMYCIN n kind of
antibiotic

MITOSES > MITOSIS

MITOSIS n type of cell
division

MITOTIC > MITOSIS

MITRAILLE n hail of
bullets

MITRAL adj of or like a
mitre

MITRE n bishop's pointed
headdress ▷ vb join with a
mitre joint

MITRED > MITRE

MITRES > MITRE

MITREWORT n Asian and
N American plant with
clusters of small white
flowers and capsules
resembling a bishop's
mitre

MITRIFORM adj shaped
like a mitre

MITRING > MITRE

MITSVAH same as
> MITZVAH

MITSVAHS > MITSVAH

MITSVOTH > MITSVAH

MITT same as > MITTEN

MITTEN n glove with one
section for the thumb and
one for the four fingers
together

MITTENED adj wearing
mittens

MITTENS > MITTEN

MITTIMUS n warrant of
commitment to prison

MITTS > MITT

MITUMBA n used clothes
imported for sale in
African countries

MITUMBAS > MITUMBA

MITY adj having mites

MITZVAH n
commandment or
precept, esp one found in
the Bible

MITZVAHS > MITZVAH

MITZVOTH > MITZVAH

MIURUS n type of rhythm
in poetry

MIURUSES > MIURUS

MIX vb combine or blend
into one mass ▷ n mixture

MIXABLE > MIX

MIXDOWN n (in sound
recording) the transfer
of a multitrack master
mix to two-track stereo
tape

MIXDOWNS > MIXDOWN

MIXED adj formed or
blended together by
mixing

MIXEDLY > MIXED

MIXEDNESS > MIXED

MIXEN n dunghill

MIXENS > MIXEN

MIXER n kitchen
appliance used for mixing
foods

MIXERS > MIXER

MIXES > MIX

MIXIBLE > MIX

MIXIER > MIXY

MIXIEST > MIXY

MIXING n act of mixing

MIXINGS > MIXING

MIXMASTER n disc jockey

MIXOLOGY n art of
mixing cocktails

MIXT > MIX

MIXTAPE n compilation of songs from various sources

MIXTAPES > MIXTAPE

MIXTE adj of a type of bicycle frame

MIXTION n amber-based mixture used in making gold leaf

MIXTIONS > MIXTION

MIXTURE n something mixed

MIXTURES > MIXTURE

MIXUP n something that is mixed up

MIXUPS > MIXUP

MIXY adj mixed

MIZ shortened form of > MISERY

MIZEN same as > MIZZEN

MIZENMAST n (on a yawl, ketch, or dandy) the after mast

MIZENS > MIZEN

MIZMAZE n maze

MIZMAZES > MIZMAZE

MIZUNA n Japanese variety of lettuce

MIZUNAS > MIZUNA

MIZZ same as > MIZ

MIZZEN n sail set on a mizzenmast ▷ adj of or relating to any kind of gear used with a mizzenmast

MIZZENS > MIZZEN

MIZZES > MIZ

MIZZLE vb decamp

MIZZLED > MIZZLE

MIZZLES > MIZZLE

MIZZLIER > MIZZLE

MIZZLIEST > MIZZLE

MIZZLING > MIZZLE

MIZZLINGS > MIZZLE

MIZZLY > MIZZLE

MIZZONITE n mineral containing sodium

MIZZY adj as in mizzy maze dialect expression meaning state of confusion

MM interj expression of enjoyment of taste or smell

MMM interj interjection expressing agreement or enjoyment

MNA same as > MINA

MNAS > MNA

MNEME n ability to retain memory

MNEMES > MNEME

MNEMIC > MNEME

MNEMON n unit of memory

MNEMONIC adj intended to help the memory ▷ n something, for instance a verse, intended to help the memory

MNEMONICS n art or practice of improving of or aiding the memory

MNEMONIST > MNEMONICS

MNEMONS > MNEMON

MO n moment

MOA n large extinct flightless New Zealand bird

MOAI n any of the gigantic carved stone figures found on Easter Island (Rapa Nui)

MOAN n low cry of pain ▷ vb make or utter with a moan

MOANED > MOAN

MOANER > MOAN

MOANERS > MOAN

MOANFUL > MOAN

MOANFULLY > MOAN

MOANING > MOAN

MOANINGLY > MOAN

MOANINGS > MOAN

MOANS > MOAN

MOAS > MOA

MOAT n deep wide ditch, esp round a castle ▷ vb surround with or as if with a moat

MOATED > MOAT

MOATING > MOAT

MOATLIKE > MOAT

MOATS > MOAT

MOB n disorderly crowd ▷ vb surround in a mob

MOBBED > MOB

MOBBER > MOB

MOBBERS > MOB

MOBBIE same as > MOBBY

MOBBIES > MOBBY

MOBBING > MOB

MOBBINGS > MOB

MOBBISH > MOB

MOBBISHLY > MOB

MOBBISM n behaviour as mob

MOBBISMS > MOBBISM

MOBBLE same as > MOBLE

MOBBLED > MOBBLE

MOBBLES > MOBBLE

MOBBLING > MOBBLE

MOBBY n (formerly) drink fermented from sweet potatoes or ginger

MOBCAP n woman's 18th-century cotton cap

MOBCAPS > MOBCAP

MOBCAST vb create and upload a podcast directly from a mobile phone

MOBCASTED > MOBCAST

MOBCASTS > MOBCAST

MOBE n mobile phone

MOBES > MOBE

MOBEY same as > MOBY

MOBEYS > MOBEY

MOBIE same as > MOBY

MOBIES > MOBY

MOBILE adj able to move ▷ n hanging structure designed to move in air currents

MOBILES > MOBILE

MOBILISE same as > MOBILIZE

MOBILISED > MOBILISE

MOBILISER > MOBILISE

MOBILISES > MOBILISE

MOBILITY n ability to move physically

MOBILIZE vb (of the armed services) prepare for active service

MOBILIZED > MOBILIZE

MOBILIZER > MOBILIZE

MOBILIZES > MOBILIZE

MOBISODE n episode of a TV show made for viewing on a mobile phone

MOBISODES > MOBISODE

MOBLE vb muffle

MOBLED > MOBLE

MOBLES > MOBLE

MOBLING > MOBLE

MOBLOG n blog recorded in the form of mobile phone calls, text messages, and photographs

MOBLOGGER > MOBLOG

MOBLOGS > MOBLOG

MOBOCRACY n rule or domination by a mob

MOBOCRAT > MOBOCRACY

MOBOCRATS > MOBOCRACY

MOBS > MOB

MOBSMAN n person in mob

MOBSMEN > MOBSMAN

MOBSTER n member of a criminal organization

MOBSTERS > MOBSTER

MOBY n mobile phone

MOC shortening of > MOCCASIN

MOCASSIN same as > MOCCASIN

MOCASSINS > MOCCASIN

MOCCASIN n soft leather shoe

MOCCASINS > MOCCASIN

MOCCIES pl n informal Australian word for moccasins

MOCH n spell of humid weather ▷ vb (of foods) become musty or spoiled

MOCHA n kind of strong dark coffee

MOCHAS > MOCHA

MOCHED > MOCH

MOCHELL same as > MUCH

MOCHELLS > MOCHELL

MOCHI n confection made with rice flour and sweetened bean paste

MOCHIE adj damp or humid

MOCHIER > MOCHIE

MOCHIEST > MOCHIE

MOCHILA n South American shoulder bag

MOCHILAS > MOCHILA

MOCHINESS > MOCHIE

MOCHING > MOCH

MOCHIS > MOCHI

MOCHS > MOCH

MOCHY same as > MOCHIE

MOCK vb make fun of ▷ adj sham or imitation ▷ n act of mocking

MOCKABLE > MOCK

MOCKADO n imitation velvet

MOCKADOES > MOCKADO

MOCKAGE same as > MOCKERY

MOCKAGES > MOCKAGE

MOCKED > MOCK

MOCKER vb dress up

MOCKERED > MOCKER

MOCKERIES > MOCKERY

MOCKERING > MOCKER

MOCKERNUT n type of smooth-barked hickory with fragrant foliage that turns bright yellow in autumn

MOCKERS > MOCKER

MOCKERY n derision

MOCKING > MOCK

MOCKINGLY > MOCK

MOCKINGS > MOCK

MOCKNEY n person who affects a cockney accent ▷ adj denoting an affected cockney accent or a person who has one

MOCKNEYS > MOCKNEY

MOCKS > MOCK

MOCKTAIL n cocktail without alcohol

MOCKTAILS > MOCKTAIL

MOCKUP n working full-scale model of a machine, apparatus, etc, for testing, research, etc

MOCKUPS > MOCKUP

MOCOCK n Native American birchbark container

MOCOCKS > MOCOCK

MOCS > MOC

MOCUCK same as > MOCOCK

MOCUCKS > MOCUCK

MOCUDDUM same as > MUQADDAM

MOCUDDUMS > MOCUDDUM

MOD n member of a group of fashionable young people, orig in the 1960s ▷ vb modify (a piece of software or hardware)

MODAFINIL n type of drug used as a stimulant

MODAL adj of or relating to mode or manner ▷ n modal word

MODALISM n type of Christian doctrine

MODALISMS > MODALISM

MODALIST > MODALISM

MODALISTS > MODALISM

MODALITY n condition of being modal

MODALLY > MODAL

MODALS > MODAL

MODDED > MOD

MODDER n person who modifies a piece of hardware or software

MODDERS > MODDER

MODDING n practice of modifying a car to alter its appearance or performance

MODDINGS > MODDING

MODE *n* method or manner

MODEL *n* (miniature) representation ▷ *adj* excellent or perfect ▷ *vb* make a model of

MODELED > MODEL

MODELER > MODEL

MODELERS > MODEL

MODELING *same as* **>** MODELLING

MODELINGS **>** MODELLING

MODELIST *same as* **>** MODELLIST

MODELISTS **>** MODELLIST

MODELLED > MODEL

MODELLER > MODEL

MODELLERS > MODEL

MODELLI > MODELLO

MODELLING *n* act or an instance of making a model

MODELLIST *n* person who makes models

MODELLO *n* artist's preliminary sketch or model

MODELLOS > MODELLO

MODELS > MODEL

MODEM *n* device for connecting two computers by a telephone line ▷ *vb* send or receive by modem

MODEMED > MODEM

MODEMING > MODEM

MODEMS > MODEM

MODENA *n* popular variety of domestic fancy pigeon

MODENAS > MODENA

MODER *n* intermediate layer in humus

MODERATE *adj* not extreme ▷ *n* person of moderate views ▷ *vb* make or become less violent or extreme

MODERATED **>** MODERATE

MODERATES **>** MODERATE

MODERATO *adv* at a moderate speed ▷ *n* moderato piece

MODERATOR *n* (Presbyterian Church) minister appointed to preside over a Church court, general assembly, etc

MODERATOS **>** MODERATO

MODERN *adj* of present or recent times ▷ *n* contemporary person

MODERNE *n* style of architecture and design of the late 1920s and 1930s ▷ *adj* of or relating to this style of architecture and design

MODERNER > MODERN

MODERNES > MODERNE

MODERNEST > MODERN

MODERNISE *same as* **>** MODERNIZE

MODERNISM *n* (support of) modern tendencies, thoughts, or styles

MODERNIST **>** MODERNISM

MODERNITY *n* quality or state of being modern

MODERNIZE *vb* bring up to date

MODERNLY > MODERN

MODERNS > MODERN

MODERS > MODER

MODES > MODE

MODEST *adj* not vain or boastful

MODESTER > MODEST

MODESTEST > MODEST

MODESTIES > MODESTY

MODESTLY > MODEST

MODESTY *n* quality or condition of being modest

MODGE *vb* do shoddily

MODGED > MODGE

MODGES > MODGE

MODGING > MODGE

MODI > MODUS

MODICA > MODICUM

MODICUM *n* small quantity

MODICUMS > MODICUM

MODIFIED > MODIFY

MODIFIER *n* word that qualifies the sense of another

MODIFIERS **>** MODIFIER

MODIFIES > MODIFY

MODIFY *vb* change slightly

MODIFYING > MODIFY

MODII > MODIUS

MODILLION *n* one of a set of ornamental brackets under a cornice, esp as used in the Corinthian order

MODIOLAR > MODIOLUS

MODIOLI > MODIOLUS

MODIOLUS *n* central bony pillar of the cochlea

MODISH *adj* in fashion

MODISHLY > MODISH

MODIST *n* follower of fashion

MODISTE *n* fashionable dressmaker or milliner

MODISTES > MODISTE

MODISTS > MODIST

MODIUS *n* ancient Roman quantity measure

MODIWORT *Scots variant of* **>** MOULDWARP

MODIWORTS **>** MODIWORT

MODS > MOD

MODULAR *adj* of, consisting of, or resembling a module or modulus ▷ *n* thing comprised of modules

MODULARLY > MODULAR

MODULARS > MODULAR

MODULATE *vb* vary in tone

MODULATED **>** MODULATE

MODULATES **>** MODULATE

MODULATOR **>** MODULATE

MODULE *n* self-contained unit, section, or component with a specific function

MODULES > MODULE

MODULI > MODULUS

MODULO *adv* with reference to modulus

MODULUS *n* coefficient expressing a specified property

MODUS *n* way of doing something

MOE *adv* more ▷ *n* wry face

MOELLON *n* rubble

MOELLONS > MOELLON

MOER *n* in South Africa, vulgar word for the womb ▷ *vb* in South Africa, attack (someone or something) violently

MOERED > MOER

MOERING > MOER

MOERS > MOER

MOES > MOE

MOFETTE *n* opening in a region of nearly extinct volcanic activity, through which gases pass

MOFETTES > MOFETTE

MOFFETTE *same as* **>** MOFETTE

MOFFETTES **>** MOFFETTE

MOFO *n* taboo term, a shortened form of motherfucker

MOFOS > MOFO

MOFUSSIL *n* provincial area in India

MOFUSSILS > MOFUSSIL

MOG *vb* go away

MOGGAN *n* stocking without foot

MOGGANS > MOGGAN

MOGGED > MOG

MOGGIE *same as* **>** MOGGY

MOGGIES > MOGGY

MOGGING > MOG

MOGGY *n* cat

MOGHUL *same as* **>** MOGUL

MOGHULS > MOGHUL

MOGS > MOG

MOGUL *n* important or powerful person

MOGULED *adj* having moguls

MOGULS > MOGUL

MOHAIR *n* fine hair of the Angora goat

MOHAIRS > MOHAIR

MOHALIM *same as* **>** MOHELIM

MOHAWK *n* half turn from either edge of either skate to the corresponding edge of the other skate

MOHAWKS > MOHAWK

MOHEL *n* man qualified to conduct circumcisions

MOHELIM > MOHEL

MOHELS > MOHEL

MOHICAN *n* punk hairstyle

MOHICANS > MOHICAN

MOHO *n* boundary between the earth's crust and mantle

MOHOS > MOHO

MOHR *same as* **>** MHORR

MOHRS > MOHR

MOHUA *n* small New Zealand bird

MOHUAS > MOHUA

MOHUR *n* former Indian gold coin worth 15 rupees

MOHURS > MOHUR

MOI *pron* (used facetiously) me

MOIDER *same as* **>** MOITHER

MOIDERED > MOIDER

MOIDERING > MOIDER

MOIDERS > MOIDER

MOIDORE *n* former Portuguese gold coin

MOIDORES > MOIDORE

MOIETIES > MOIETY

MOIETY *n* half

MOIL *vb* moisten or soil or become moist, soiled, etc ▷ *n* toil

MOILE *n* type of rice pudding made with almond milk

MOILED > MOIL

MOILER > MOIL

MOILERS > MOIL

MOILES > MOILE

MOILING > MOIL

MOILINGLY > MOIL

MOILS > MOIL

MOINEAU *n* small fortification

MOINEAUS > MOINEAU

MOIRA *n* fate

MOIRAI > MOIRA

MOIRE *adj* having a watered or wavelike pattern ▷ *n* any fabric that has such a pattern

MOIRES > MOIRE

MOISER *n* informer

MOISERS > MOISER

MOIST *adj* slightly wet ▷ *vb* moisten

MOISTED > MOIST

MOISTEN *vb* make or become moist

MOISTENED > MOISTEN

MOISTENER > MOISTEN

MOISTENS > MOISTEN

MOISTER > MOIST

MOISTEST > MOIST

MOISTFUL *adj* full of moisture

MOISTIFY *vb* moisten

MOISTING > MOIST

MOISTLY > MOIST

MOISTNESS > MOIST

MOISTS > MOIST

MOISTURE *n* liquid diffused as vapour or condensed in drops

MOISTURES **>** MOISTURE

MOIT *same as* **>** MOTE

MOITHER *vb* bother or bewilder

MOITHERED > MOITHER

MOITHERS > MOITHER

MOITS > MOIT

MOJAHEDIN *pl n* fundamentalist Muslim guerrillas

MOJARRA n tropical American sea fish

MOJARRAS > MOJARRA

MOJITO n rum-based cocktail

MOJITOS > MOJITO

MOJO n charm or magic spell

MOJOES > MOJO

MOJOS > MOJO

MOKADDAM same as > MUQADDAM

MOKADDAMS > MOKADDAM

MOKE n donkey

MOKES > MOKE

MOKI n edible sea fish of New Zealand

MOKIHI n Māori raft

MOKIHIS > MOKIHI

MOKIS > MOKI

MOKO n Māori tattoo or tattoo pattern

MOKOMOKO n type of skink found in New Zealand

MOKOMOKOS > MOKOMOKO

MOKOPUNA n grandchild or young person

MOKOPUNAS > MOKOPUNA

MOKORO n (in Botswana) the traditional dugout canoe of the people of the Okavango Delta

MOKOROS > MOKORO

MOKOS > MOKO

MOKSHA n freedom from the endless cycle of transmigration into a state of bliss

MOKSHAS > MOKSHA

MOL n the SI unit mole

MOLA another name for > SUNFISH

MOLAL adj of a solution containing one mole of solute per thousand grams of solvent

MOLALITY n measure of solvent concentration

MOLAR n large back tooth used for grinding ▷ adj of any of these teeth

MOLARITY n concentration

MOLARS > MOLAR

MOLAS > MOLA

MOLASSE n sediment from the erosion of mountain ranges

MOLASSES n dark syrup, a by-product of sugar refining

MOLD same as > MOULD

MOLDABLE > MOLD

MOLDAVITE n green tektite found in the Czech Republic, thought to be the product of an ancient meteorite impact in Germany

MOLDBOARD n curved blade of a plough

MOLDED > MOLD

MOLDER same as > MOULDER

MOLDERED > MOLDER

MOLDERING > MOLDER

MOLDERS > MOLDER

MOLDIER > MOLDY

MOLDIEST > MOLDY

MOLDINESS > MOLDY

MOLDING same as > MOULDING

MOLDINGS > MOLDING

MOLDS > MOLD

MOLDWARP same as > MOULDWARP

MOLDWARPS > MOLDWARP

MOLDY same as > MOULDY

MOLE n small dark raised spot on the skin ▷ vb as in mole out seek as if by burrowing

MOLECAST n molehill

MOLECASTS > MOLECAST

MOLECULAR adj of or relating to molecules

MOLECULE n simplest freely existing chemical unit, composed of two or more atoms

MOLECULES > MOLECULE

MOLED > MOLE

MOLEHILL n small mound of earth thrown up by a burrowing mole

MOLEHILLS > MOLEHILL

MOLEHUNT n hunt for a mole

MOLEHUNTS > MOLEHUNT

MOLELIKE adj like a mole

MOLES > MOLE

MOLESKIN n dark grey dense velvety pelt of a mole, used as a fur

MOLESKINS pl n clothing of moleskin

MOLEST vb disturb or annoy

MOLESTED > MOLEST

MOLESTER > MOLEST

MOLESTERS > MOLEST

MOLESTFUL adj molesting

MOLESTING > MOLEST

MOLESTS > MOLEST

MOLIES > MOLY

MOLIMEN n effort needed to perform bodily function

MOLIMENS > MOLIMEN

MOLINE adj (of a cross) having arms of equal length, forked and curved back at the ends ▷ n moline cross

MOLINES > MOLINE

MOLINET n stick for whipping chocolate

MOLINETS > MOLINET

MOLING > MOLE

MOLL n gangster's female accomplice

MOLLA same as > MOLLAH

MOLLAH same as > MULLAH

MOLLAHS > MOLLAH

MOLLAS > MOLLA

MOLLIE same as > MOLLY

MOLLIES > MOLLY

MOLLIFIED > MOLLIFY

MOLLIFIER > MOLLIFY

MOLLIFIES > MOLLIFY

MOLLIFY vb pacify or soothe

MOLLITIES n softness

MOLLS > MOLL

MOLLUSC n soft-bodied, usu hard-shelled, animal

MOLLUSCA n molluscs collectively

MOLLUSCAN > MOLLUSC

MOLLUSCS > MOLLUSC

MOLLUSCUM n viral skin infection

MOLLUSK same as > MOLLUSC

MOLLUSKAN > MOLLUSK

MOLLUSKS > MOLLUSK

MOLLY n American freshwater fish

MOLLYHAWK n juvenile of the southern black-backed gull

MOLLYMAWK informal name for > MALLEMUCK

MOLOCH n spiny Australian desert-living lizard

MOLOCHISE vb sacrifice to deity

MOLOCHIZE same as > MOLOCHISE

MOLOCHS > MOLOCH

MOLOSSI > MOLOSSUS

MOLOSSUS n division of metre in poetry

MOLS > MOL

MOLT same as > MOULT

MOLTED > MOLT

MOLTEN > MELT

MOLTENLY > MELT

MOLTER > MOLT

MOLTERS > MOLT

MOLTING > MOLT

MOLTO adv very

MOLTS > MOLT

MOLY n mythical magic herb

MOLYBDATE n salt or ester of a molybdic acid

MOLYBDIC adj of or containing molybdenum in the trivalent or hexavalent state

MOLYBDOUS adj of or containing molybdenum, esp in a low valence state

MOLYS > MOLY

MOM same as > MOTHER

MOME n fool

MOMENT n short space of time

MOMENTA > MOMENTUM

MOMENTANY same as > MOMENTARY

MOMENTARY adj lasting only a moment

MOMENTLY same as > MOMENT

MOMENTO same as > MEMENTO

MOMENTOES > MOMENTO

MOMENTOS > MOMENTO

MOMENTOUS adj of great significance

MOMENTS > MOMENT

MOMENTUM n impetus to go forward, develop, or get stronger

MOMENTUMS > MOMENTUM

MOMES > MOME

MOMI same as > MOM

MOMISM n excessive domination of a child by his or her mother

MOMISMS > MOMISM

MOMMA same as > MAMMA

MOMMAS > MOMMA

MOMMET same as > MAMMET

MOMMETS > MOMMET

MOMMIES > MOMMY

MOMMY same as > MOM

MOMOIR n memoir written by a woman about motherhood

MOMOIRS > MOMOIR

MOMS > MOM

MOMSER same as > MOMZER

MOMSERS > MOMSER

MOMUS n person who ridicules

MOMUSES > MOMUS

MOMZER same as > MAMZER

MOMZERIM > MOMZER

MOMZERS > MOMZER

MON dialect variant of > MAN

MONA n W African guenon monkey

MONACHAL less common word for > MONASTIC

MONACHISM > MONACHAL

MONACHIST > MONACHAL

MONACID same as > MONOACID

MONACIDIC same as > MONACID

MONACIDS > MONACID

MONACT n sponge spicule with a single ray

MONACTINE same as > MONACT

MONACTS > MONACT

MONAD n any fundamental singular metaphysical entity

MONADAL > MONAD

MONADES > MONAS

MONADIC adj being or relating to a monad

MONADICAL > MONAD

MONADISM n doctrine that monads are the ultimate units of reality

MONADISMS > MONADISM

MONADNOCK n residual hill that consists of hard rock in an otherwise eroded area

MONADS > MONAD

MONAL n S Asian pheasant

MONALS > MONAL

MONAMINE n type of amine

MONAMINES > MONAMINE

MONANDRY n custom of having only one male

partner over a period of time

MONARCH *n* sovereign ruler of a state

MONARCHAL >MONARCH

MONARCHIC >MONARCH

MONARCHS >MONARCH

MONARCHY *n* government by or a state ruled by a sovereign

MONARDA *n* mintlike N American plant

MONARDAS >MONARDA

MONAS *same as* >MONAD

MONASES >MONAS

MONASTERY *n* residence of a community of monks

MONASTIC *adj* of monks, nuns, or monasteries ▷ *n* person who is committed to this way of life, esp a monk

MONASTICS >MONASTIC

MONATOMIC *adj* consisting of single atoms

MONAUL *same as* >MONAL

MONAULS >MONAUL

MONAURAL *adj* relating to, having, or hearing with only one ear

MONAXIAL *another word for* >UNIAXIAL

MONAXON *n* type of sponge

MONAXONIC >MONAXON

MONAXONS >MONAXON

MONAZITE *n* yellow to reddish-brown mineral

MONAZITES >MONAZITE

MONDAIN *n* man who moves in fashionable society ▷ *adj* characteristic of fashionable society

MONDAINE *n* woman who moves in fashionable society ▷ *adj* characteristic of fashionable society

MONDAINES >MONDAINE

MONDAINS >MONDAIN

MONDE *n* French word meaning world or society

MONDES >MONDE

MONDIAL *adj* of or involving the whole world

MONDO *n* Buddhist questioning technique

MONDOS >MONDO

MONECIAN *same as* >MONECIOUS

MONECIOUS *adj* (of some flowering plants) having the male and female reproductive organs in separate flowers on the same plant

MONELLIN *n* sweet protein

MONELLINS >MONELLIN

MONEME *less common word for* >MORPHEME

MONEMES >MONEME

MONER *n* hypothetical simple organism

MONERA >MONER

MONERAN *n* type of bacterium

MONERANS >MONERAN

MONERGISM *n* Christian doctrine on spiritual regeneration

MONERON *same as* >MONER

MONETARY *adj* of money or currency

MONETH *same as* >MONTH

MONETHS >MONETH

MONETISE *same as* >MONETIZE

MONETISED >MONETISE

MONETISES >MONETISE

MONETIZE *vb* establish as the legal tender of a country

MONETIZED >MONETIZE

MONETIZES >MONETIZE

MONEY *n* medium of exchange, coins or banknotes

MONEYBAG *n* bag for money

MONEYBAGS *n* very rich person

MONEYBELT *n* belt with compartments for money

MONEYBOX *n* box for keeping money in

MONEYED *adj* rich

MONEYER *n* person who coins money

MONEYERS >MONEYER

MONEYLESS >MONEY

MONEYMAN *n* person supplying money

MONEYMEN >MONEY

MONEYS >MONEY

MONEYWORT *n* European and N American creeping plant with round leaves and yellow flowers

MONG *n* Australian shortening of mongrel

MONGCORN *same as* >MASLIN

MONGCORNS >MONGCORN

MONGEESE >MONGOOSE

MONGER *n* trader or dealer ▷ *vb* deal in

MONGERED >MONGER

MONGERIES >MONGER

MONGERING >MONGER

MONGERS >MONGER

MONGERY >MONGER

MONGO *same as* >MUNGO

MONGOE *same as* >MONGO

MONGOES >MONGOE

MONGOOSE *n* stoat-like mammal of Asia and Africa that kills snakes

MONGOOSES >MONGOOSE

MONGOS >MONGO

MONGREL *n* animal, esp a dog, of mixed breed ▷ *adj* of mixed breed or origin

MONGRELLY *adj* like a mongrel

MONGRELS >MONGREL

MONGS >MONG

MONGST *short for* >AMONGST

MONIAL *n* mullion

MONIALS >MONIAL

MONIC *adj* denoting a type of polynomial

MONICKER *same as* >MONIKER

MONICKERS >MONIKER

MONIE *Scots word for* >MANY

MONIED *same as* >MONEYED

MONIES >MONEY

MONIKER *n* person's name or nickname

MONIKERED *adj* having a moniker

MONIKERS >MONIKER

MONILIA *n* type of fungus

MONILIAE >MONILIA

MONILIAL *adj* denoting a thrush infection caused by a fungus

MONILIAS >MONILIA

MONIMENT *same as* >MONUMENT

MONIMENTS >MONIMENT

MONIPLIES *same as* >MANYPLIES

MONISH *same as* >ADMONISH

MONISHED >MONISH

MONISHES >MONISH

MONISHING >MONISH

MONISM *n* doctrine that reality consists of only one basic substance or element

MONISMS >MONISM

MONIST >MONISM

MONISTIC >MONISM

MONISTS >MONISM

MONITION *n* warning or caution

MONITIONS >MONITION

MONITIVE *adj* reproving

MONITOR *n* person or device that checks, controls, warns, or keeps a record of something ▷ *vb* watch and check on

MONITORED >MONITOR

MONITORS >MONITOR

MONITORY *adj* acting as or giving a warning ▷ *n* letter containing a monition

MONITRESS *n* female monitor

MONK *n* member of an all-male religious community

MONKERIES >MONKERY

MONKERY *n* derogatory word for monastic life or practices

MONKEY *n* long-tailed primate ▷ *vb* meddle or fool

MONKEYED >MONKEY

MONKEYING >MONKEY

MONKEYISH >MONKEY

MONKEYISM *n* practice of behaving like monkey

MONKEYPOD *n* Central American tree

MONKEYPOT *n* type of tropical tree

MONKEYPOX *n* rare viral disease found in Africa

MONKEYS >MONKEY

MONKFISH *n* type of fish

MONKHOOD *n* condition of being a monk

MONKHOODS >MONKHOOD

MONKISH *adj* of, relating to, or resembling a monk or monks

MONKISHLY >MONKISH

MONKS >MONK

MONKSHOOD *n* poisonous plant with hooded flowers

MONO *n* monophonic sound

MONOACID *adj* base which is capable of reacting with only one molecule of a monobasic acid

MONOACIDS >MONOACID

MONOAMINE *n* substance, such as adrenaline, noradrenaline, or serotonin, that contains a single amine group

MONOAO *n* New Zealand plant with rigid leaves

MONOAOS >MONOAO

MONOBASIC *adj* (of an acid, such as hydrogen chloride) having only one replaceable hydrogen atom per molecule

MONOBLOC *adj* made from a single piece of something

MONOBROW *n* appearance of a single eyebrow as a result of the eyebrows joining above a person's nose

MONOBROWS >MONOBROW

MONOCARP *n* plant that is monocarpic

MONOCARPS >MONOCARP

MONOCEROS *n* faint constellation on the celestial equator crossed by the Milky Way and lying close to Orion and Canis Major

MONOCHORD *n* instrument employed in acoustic analysis or investigation, consisting usually of one string stretched over a resonator of wood

MONOCLE *n* eyeglass for one eye only

MONOCLED >MONOCLE

MONOCLES >MONOCLE

MONOCLINE *n* fold in stratified rocks in which the strata are inclined in the same direction from the horizontal

MONOCOQUE *n* vehicle body moulded from a single piece of material with no separate load-bearing parts ▷ *adj* of or relating to the design characteristic of a monocoque

MONOCOT *n* type of flowering plant with a single embryonic seed leaf

MONOCOTS > MONOCOT

MONOCOTYL *same as* > MONOCOT

MONOCRACY *n* government by one person

MONOCRAT > MONOCRACY

MONOCRATS > MONOCRACY

MONOCROP *vb* plant the same crop in a field every year

MONOCROPS > MONOCROP

MONOCULAR *adj* having or for one eye only ▷ *n* device for use with one eye, such as a field glass

MONOCYCLE *another name for* > UNICYCLE

MONOCYTE *n* large phagocytic leucocyte with a spherical nucleus and clear cytoplasm

MONOCYTES > MONOCYTE

MONOCYTIC > MONOCYTE

MONODIC > MONODY

MONODICAL > MONODY

MONODIES > MONODY

MONODIST > MONODY

MONODISTS > MONODY

MONODONT *adj* (of certain animals, esp the male narwhal) having a single tooth throughout life

MONODRAMA *n* play or other dramatic piece for a single performer

MONODY *n* (in Greek tragedy) an ode sung by a single actor

MONOECIES > MONOECY

MONOECISM *n* being both male and female

MONOECY *same as* > MONOECISM

MONOESTER *n* type of ester

MONOFIL *n* synthetic thread or yarn composed of a single strand rather than twisted fibres

MONOFILS > MONOFIL

MONOFUEL *n* single type of fuel

MONOFUELS > MONOFUEL

MONOGAMIC > MONOGAMY

MONOGAMY *n* custom of being married to one person at a time

MONOGENIC *adj* of or relating to an inherited character difference that is controlled by a single gene

MONOGENY *n* the hypothetical descent of all organisms from a single cell or organism

MONOGERM *adj* containing single seed

MONOGLOT *n* person speaking only one language

MONOGLOTS > MONOGLOT

MONOGONY *n* asexual reproduction

MONOGRAM *n* design of combined letters, esp a person's initials ▷ *vb* decorate (clothing, stationery, etc) with a monogram

MONOGRAMS > MONOGRAM

MONOGRAPH *n* book or paper on a single subject ▷ *vb* write a monograph on

MONOGYNY *n* custom of having only one female partner over a period of time

MONOHULL *n* sailing vessel with a single hull

MONOHULLS > MONOHULL

MONOICOUS *adj* (of some flowering plants) having the male and female reproductive organs in separate flowers on the same plant

MONOKINE *n* type of protein

MONOKINES > MONOKINE

MONOKINI *n* bottom half of a bikini

MONOKINIS > MONOKINI

MONOLATER > MONOLATRY

MONOLATRY *n* exclusive worship of one god without excluding the existence of others

MONOLAYER *n* single layer of atoms or molecules adsorbed on a surface

MONOLINE *adj* as in *monoline insurer* insurer who pays the principal and interest on a bond in the event of a default

MONOLITH *n* large upright block of stone

MONOLITHS > MONOLITH

MONOLOG *same as* > MONOLOGUE

MONOLOGIC > MONOLOGUE

MONOLOGS > MONOLOG

MONOLOGUE *n* long speech by one person

MONOLOGY > MONOLOGUE

MONOMACHY *n* combat between two individuals

MONOMANIA *n* obsession with one thing

MONOMARK *n* series of letters or figures to identify goods, personal articles, etc

MONOMARKS > MONOMARK

MONOMER *n* compound whose molecules can join together to form a polymer

MONOMERIC > MONOMER

MONOMERS > MONOMER

MONOMETER *n* line of verse consisting of one metrical foot

MONOMIAL *n* expression consisting of a single term, such as $5ax$ ▷ *adj* consisting of a single algebraic term

MONOMIALS > MONOMIAL

MONOMODE *adj* denoting a type of optical fibre

MONONYM *n* person who is famous enough to be known only by one name

MONONYMS > MONONYM

MONOPHAGY *n* feeding on only one type of food

MONOPHASE *adj* having single alternating electric current ▷ *n* type of matter that contains only one phase or a clear-cut and unattached type of matter

MONOPHONY > MONO

MONOPHYLY *n* group of ancestor and all descendants

MONOPITCH *adj* (of a roof) having only one slope ▷ *n* a monotone

MONOPLANE *n* aeroplane with one pair of wings

MONOPLOID *less common word for* > HAPLOID

MONOPOD *same as* > MONOPODE

MONOPODE *n* tree stem which elongates from the tip and gives rise to lateral branches

MONOPODES > MONOPODE

MONOPODIA *pl n* main axes of growth in the pine tree and similar plants

MONOPODS > MONOPOD

MONOPODY *n* single-foot measure in poetry

MONOPOLE *n* magnetic pole considered in isolation

MONOPOLES > MONOPOLE

MONOPOLY *n* exclusive possession of or right to do something

MONOPRINT *n* single impression created from a design

MONOPSONY *n* situation in which the entire market demand for a product or service consists of only one buyer

MONOPTERA *n* plural of monopteron: circular

classical building, esp a temple, that has a single ring of columns surrounding it

MONOPTOTE *n* word with only one form

MONOPULSE *n* radar transmitting single pulse only

MONORAIL *n* single-rail railway

MONORAILS > MONORAIL

MONORCHID *adj* having one testicle ▷ *n* animal or person with one testicle

MONORHINE *adj* having single nostril ▷ *n* animal that has one nasal orifice

MONORHYME *n* poem in which all lines rhyme

MONOS > MONO

MONOSEMIC *adj* having only a single meaning

MONOSEMY *n* fact of having only a single meaning

MONOSES > MONOSIS

MONOSIES > MONOSY

MONOSIS *n* abnormal separation

MONOSKI *n* wide ski on which the skier stands with both feet ▷ *vb* ski on a monoski

MONOSKIED > MONOSKI

MONOSKIER > MONOSKI

MONOSKIS > MONOSKI

MONOSOME *n* unpaired chromosome, esp an X-chromosome in an otherwise diploid cell

MONOSOMES > MONOSOME

MONOSOMIC > MONOSOME

MONOSOMY *n* condition with a missing pair of chromosomes

MONOSTELE *n* type of plant tissue

MONOSTELY > MONOSTELE

MONOSTICH *n* poem of a single line

MONOSTOME *adj* having only one mouth, pore, or similar opening

MONOSTYLE *adj* having single shaft

MONOSY *same as* > MONOSIS

MONOTASK *vb* perform only one task at a time

MONOTASKS > MONOTASK

MONOTINT *n* black-and-white photograph or transparency

MONOTINTS > MONOTINT

MONOTONE *n* unvaried pitch in speech or sound ▷ *adj* unvarying ▷ *vb* speak in monotone

MONOTONED > MONOTONE

MONOTONES > MONOTONE

MONOTONIC *same as*
> MONOTONE

MONOTONY *n* wearisome routine, dullness

MONOTREME *n* type of primitive egg-laying toothless mammal of Australia and New Guinea

MONOTROCH *n* wheelbarrow

MONOTYPE *n* single print made from a metal or glass plate on which a picture has been painted

MONOTYPES
> MONOTYPE

MONOTYPIC *adj* (of a genus or species) consisting of only one type of animal or plant

MONOVULAR *adj* of a single ovum

MONOXIDE *n* oxide that contains one oxygen atom per molecule

MONOXIDES
> MONOXIDE

MONOXYLON *n* canoe made from one log

MONS > MON

MONSIEUR *n* French title of address equivalent to *sir* or *Mr*

MONSIGNOR *n* ecclesiastical title attached to certain offices or distinctions usually bestowed by the Pope

MONSOON *n* seasonal wind of SE Asia

MONSOONAL > MONSOON

MONSOONS > MONSOON

MONSTER *n* imaginary, usu frightening, beast ▷ *adj* huge ▷ *vb* criticize (a person or group) severely

MONSTERA *n* type of tropical climbing plant

MONSTERAS > MONSTERA

MONSTERED > MONSTER

MONSTERS > MONSTER

MONSTROUS *adj* unnatural or ugly

MONTADALE *n* breed of sheep

MONTAGE *n* (making of) a picture composed from pieces of others ▷ *vb* make as a montage

MONTAGED > MONTAGE

MONTAGES > MONTAGE

MONTAGING > MONTAGE

MONTAN *adj* as in *montan wax* hard wax obtained from lignite and peat

MONTANE *n* area of mountain dominated by vegetation ▷ *adj* of or inhabiting mountainous regions

MONTANES > MONTANE

MONTANT *n* vertical part in woodwork

MONTANTO *n* rising blow

MONTANTOS
> MONTANTO

MONTANTS > MONTANT

MONTARIA *n* Brazilian canoe

MONTARIAS
> MONTARIA

MONTE *n* gambling card game of Spanish origin

MONTEITH *n* large ornamental bowl

MONTEITHS
> MONTEITH

MONTEM *n* former money-raising practice at Eton school

MONTEMS > MONTEM

MONTERO *n* round cap with a flap at the back worn by hunters

MONTEROS > MONTERO

MONTES > MONTE

MONTH *n* one of the twelve divisions of the calendar year

MONTHLIES > MONTHLY

MONTHLING *n* month-old child

MONTHLONG *adj* lasting all month

MONTHLY *adj* happening or payable once a month ▷ *adv* once a month ▷ *n* monthly magazine

MONTHS > MONTH

MONTICLE *same as*
> MONTICULE

MONTICLES
> MONTICLE

MONTICULE *n* small hill or mound, such as a secondary volcanic cone

MONTIES > MONTY

MONTRE *n* pipes of organ

MONTRES > MONTRE

MONTURE *n* mount or frame

MONTURES > MONTURE

MONTY *n* complete form of something

MONUMENT *n* something, esp a building or statue, that commemorates something

MONUMENTS
> MONUMENT

MONURON *n* type of weedkiller

MONURONS > MONURON

MONY *Scot word for* > MANY

MONYPLIES *same as*
> MANYPLIES

MONZONITE *n* coarse-grained plutonic igneous rock consisting of equal amounts of plagioclase and orthoclase feldspar, with ferromagnesian minerals

MOO *n* long deep cry of a cow ▷ *vb* make this noise ▷ *interj* instance or imitation of this sound

MOOBIES *same as*
> MOOBS

MOOBS *pl n* overdeveloped breasts on a man

MOOCH *vb* loiter about aimlessly

MOOCHED > MOOCH

MOOCHER > MOOCH

MOOCHERS > MOOCH

MOOCHES > MOOCH

MOOCHING > MOOCH

MOOD *n* temporary (gloomy) state of mind

MOODIED > MOODY

MOODIER > MOODY

MOODIES > MOODY

MOODIEST > MOODY

MOODILY > MOODY

MOODINESS > MOODY

MOODS > MOOD

MOODY *adj* sullen or gloomy ▷ *vb* flatter

MOODYING > MOODY

MOOED > MOO

MOOI *adj* pleasing or nice

MOOING > MOO

MOOK *n* person regarded with contempt, esp a stupid person

MOOKS > MOOK

MOOKTAR *same as*
> MUKHTAR

MOOKTARS > MOOKTAR

MOOL *same as* > MOULD

MOOLA *same as* > MOOLAH

MOOLAH *slang word for*
> MONEY

MOOLAHS > MOOLAH

MOOLAS > MOOLA

MOOLED > MOOL

MOOLEY *same as* > MOOLY

MOOLEYS > MOOLEY

MOOLI *n* type of large white radish

MOOLIES > MOOLY

MOOLING > MOOL

MOOLIS > MOOLI

MOOLOO *n* person from the Waikato

MOOLOOS > MOOLOO

MOOLS > MOOL

MOOLVI *same as*
> MOOLVIE

MOOLVIE *n* (esp in India) Muslim learned man

MOOLVIES > MOOLVIE

MOOLVIS > MOOLVI

MOOLY *same as* > MULEY

MOON *n* natural satellite of the earth ▷ *vb* be idle in a listless or dreamy way

MOONBEAM *n* ray of moonlight

MOONBEAMS
> MOONBEAM

MOONBLIND *adj* (of horses) having a disorder which causes inflammation of the eyes and sometimes blindness

MOONBOOTS *pl n* thickly padded boots

MOONBOW *n* rainbow made by moonlight

MOONBOWS > MOONBOW

MOONCAKE *n* type of round Chinese cake

MOONCAKES
> MOONCAKE

MOONCALF *n* person who idles time away

MOONCHILD *n* someone who is born under the Cancer star sign

MOONCRAFT *n* lunar module

MOONDOG *n* bright spot in the sky caused by moonlight

MOONDOGS > MOONDOG

MOONDUST *n* dust on surface of moon

MOONDUSTS
> MOONDUST

MOONED *adj* decorated with a moon

MOONER *n* MOON

MOONERS > MOON

MOONEYE *n* N American large-eyed freshwater fish

MOONEYES > MOONEYE

MOONFACE *n* big round face ▷ *vb* have a moon face

MOONFACED
> MOONFACE

MOONFACES
> MOONFACE

MOONFISH *n* type of tropical fish

MOONG *n* as in *moong bean* kind of bean

MOONGATE *n* circular gateway in a wall

MOONGATES
> MOONGATE

MOONIER > MOONY

MOONIES > MOONY

MOONIEST > MOONY

MOONILY > MOONY

MOONINESS > MOONY

MOONING > MOON

MOONISH > MOON

MOONISHLY > MOON

MOONLESS > MOON

MOONLET *n* small moon

MOONLETS > MOONLET

MOONLIGHT *n* light from the moon ▷ *adj* illuminated by the moon ▷ *vb* work at a secondary job, esp illegally

MOONLIKE > MOON

MOONLIT *adj* illuminated by the moon

MOONPHASE *n* phase of moon

MOONPORT *n* place from which flights leave for moon

MOONPORTS
> MOONPORT

MOONQUAKE *n* light tremor of the moon, detected on the moon's surface

MOONRAKER *n* small square sail set above a skysail

MOONRISE *n* moment when the moon appears above the horizon

MOONRISES
> MOONRISE

MOONROCK *n* rock from moon

MOONROCKS
> MOONROCK

MOONROOF *same as*
> SUNROOF

MOONROOFS
> MOONROOF

MOONS > MOON

MOONSAIL *n* small sail high on a mast

MOONSAILS
> MOONSAIL

MOONSCAPE n surface of the moon or a picture or model of it

MOONSEED n type of climbing plant with red or black fruits

MOONSEEDS > MOONSEED

MOONSET n moment when the moon disappears below the horizon

MOONSETS > MOONSET

MOONSHEE same as > MUNSHI

MOONSHEES > MOONSHEE

MOONSHINE same as > MOONLIGHT

MOONSHINY adj lacking substance

MOONSHIP n lunar module

MOONSHIPS > MOONSHIP

MOONSHOT n launching of a spacecraft to the moon

MOONSHOTS > MOONSHOT

MOONSTONE n translucent semiprecious stone

MOONWALK n instance of walking on the moon

MOONWALKS > MOONWALK

MOONWARD adj towards moon

MOONWARDS adv towards the moon

MOONWORT n type of fern with crescent-shaped leaflets

MOONWORTS > MOONWORT

MOONY adj dreamy or listless ▷ n foolish person

MOOP same as > MOUP

MOOPED > MOOP

MOOPING > MOOP

MOOPS > MOOP

MOOR n tract of open uncultivated ground covered with grass and heather ▷ vb secure (a ship) with ropes etc

MOORAGE n place for mooring a vessel

MOORAGES > MOORAGE

MOORBURN n practice of burning off old growth on a heather moor

MOORBURNS > MOORBURN

MOORCOCK n male of the red grouse

MOORCOCKS > MOORCOCK

MOORED > MOOR

MOORFOWL n red grouse

MOORFOWLS > MOORFOWL

MOORHEN n small black water bird

MOORHENS > MOORHEN

MOORIER > MOOR

MOORIEST > MOOR

MOORILL n disease of cattle on moors

MOORILLS > MOORILL

MOORING n place for mooring a ship

MOORINGS pl n ropes and anchors used in mooring a vessel

MOORISH adj denoting a style of architecture in Spain

MOORLAND n area of moor

MOORLANDS > MOORLAND

MOORLOG n rotted wood below the surface of a moor

MOORLOGS > MOORLOG

MOORMAN n person living on a moor

MOORMEN > MOORMAN

MOORS > MOOR

MOORVA same as > MURVA

MOORVAS > MOORVA

MOORWORT n low-growing pink-flowered shrub that grows in peaty bogs

MOORWORTS > MOORWORT

MOORY > MOOR

MOOS > MOO

MOOSE n large N American deer

MOOSEBIRD n North American jay

MOOSEHAIR n hair of a moose

MOOSEHIDE n hide of a moose

MOOSEWOOD n North American tree

MOOSEYARD n place where moose spend winter

MOOT adj debatable ▷ vb bring up for discussion ▷ n (in Anglo-Saxon England) a local administrative assembly

MOOTABLE > MOOT

MOOTED > MOOT

MOOTER > MOOT

MOOTERS > MOOT

MOOTEST > MOOT

MOOTING > MOOT

MOOTINGS > MOOT

MOOTMAN n person taking part in a moot

MOOTMEN > MOOTMAN

MOOTNESS > MOOT

MOOTS > MOOT

MOOVE same as > MOVE

MOOVED > MOOVE

MOOVES > MOOVE

MOOVING > MOOVE

MOP n long stick with twists of cotton or a sponge on the end, used for cleaning ▷ vb clean or soak up with or as if with a mop

MOPANE same as > MOPANI

MOPANES > MOPANE

MOPANI n S African tree that is highly resistant to drought

MOPANIS > MOPANI

MOPBOARD n wooden border fixed round the base of an interior wall

MOPBOARDS > MOPBOARD

MOPE vb be gloomy and apathetic ▷ n gloomy person

MOPED n light motorized cycle

MOPEDS > MOPED

MOPEHAWK same as > MOPOKE

MOPEHAWKS > MOPEHAWK

MOPER > MOPE

MOPERIES > MOPERY

MOPERS > MOPE

MOPERY n gloominess

MOPES > MOPE

MOPEY same as > MOPY

MOPHEAD n person with shaggy hair

MOPHEADS > MOPHEAD

MOPIER > MOPE

MOPIEST > MOPE

MOPILY > MOPY

MOPINESS > MOPY

MOPING > MOPE

MOPINGLY > MOPE

MOPISH > MOPE

MOPISHLY > MOPE

MOPOKE n species of owl

MOPOKES > MOPOKE

MOPPED > MOP

MOPPER > MOP

MOPPERS > MOP

MOPPET same as > POPPET

MOPPETS > MOPPET

MOPPIER > MOPPY

MOPPIEST > MOPPY

MOPPING > MOP

MOPPY adj (of hair) thick, dishevelled

MOPS > MOP

MOPSIES > MOPSY

MOPSTICK n mop handle

MOPSTICKS > MOPSTICK

MOPSY n untidy or dowdy person

MOPUS n person who mopes

MOPUSES > MOPUS

MOPY > MOPE

MOQUETTE n thick velvety fabric used for carpets and upholstery

MOQUETTES > MOQUETTE

MOR n layer of acidic humus formed in cool moist areas

MORA n quantity of a short syllable in verse

MORACEOUS adj relating to a mostly tropical and subtropical family of trees and shrubs which includes the mulberry, fig, and breadfruit

MORAE > MORA

MORAINAL > MORAINE

MORAINE n accumulated mass of debris deposited by a glacier

MORAINES > MORAINE

MORAINIC > MORAINE

MORAL adj concerned with right and wrong conduct ▷ n lesson to be obtained from a story or event ▷ vb moralize

MORALE n degree of confidence or hope of a person or group

MORALES > MORALE

MORALISE same as > MORALIZE

MORALISED > MORALISE

MORALISER > MORALIZE

MORALISES > MORALISE

MORALISM n habit or practice of moralizing

MORALISMS > MORALISM

MORALIST n person with a strong sense of right and wrong

MORALISTS > MORALIST

MORALITY n good moral conduct

MORALIZE vb make moral pronouncements

MORALIZED > MORALIZE

MORALIZER > MORALIZE

MORALIZES > MORALIZE

MORALL same as > MURAL

MORALLED > MORALL

MORALLER > MORAL

MORALLERS > MORAL

MORALLING > MORALL

MORALLS > MORALL

MORALLY > MORAL

MORALS > MORAL

MORAS > MORA

MORASS n marsh

MORASSES > MORASS

MORASSIER > MORASSY

MORASSY adj swampy

MORAT n drink containing mulberry juice

MORATORIA pl n legally authorized postponements of the fulfilment of an obligation

MORATORY > MORATORIA

MORATS > MORAT

MORAY n large voracious eel

MORAYS > MORAY

MORBID adj unduly interested in death or unpleasant events

MORBIDER > MORBID

MORBIDEST > MORBID

MORBIDITY n state of being morbid

MORBIDLY > MORBID

MORBIFIC adj causing disease

MORBILLI same as > MEASLES

MORBUS n disease

MORBUSES > MORBUS

MORCEAU n fragment or morsel

MORCEAUX > MORCEAU

MORCHA *n* (in India) hostile demonstration

MORCHAS > MORCHA

MORDACITY *n* quality of sarcasm

MORDANCY > MORDANT

MORDANT *adj* sarcastic or scathing ▷ *n* substance used to fix dyes ▷ *vb* treat (a fabric, yarn, etc) with a mordant

MORDANTED > MORDANT

MORDANTLY > MORDANT

MORDANTS > MORDANT

MORDENT *n* melodic ornament in music

MORDENTS > MORDENT

MORE *adj* greater in amount or degree ▷ *adv* greater extent ▷ *pron* greater or additional amount or number

MOREEN *n* heavy, usually watered, fabric of wool or wool and cotton

MOREENS > MOREEN

MOREISH *adj* (of food) causing a desire for more

MOREL *n* edible mushroom with a pitted cap

MORELLE *n* nightshade

MORELLES > MORELLE

MORELLO *n* variety of small very dark sour cherry

MORELLOS > MORELLO

MORELS > MOREL

MORENDO *adv* (in music) dying away ▷ *n* gentle decrescendo at the end of a musical strain

MORENDOS > MORENDO

MORENESS > MORE

MOREOVER *adv* in addition to what has already been said

MOREPORK *same as* > MOPOKE

MOREPORKS > MOREPORK

MORES *pl n* customs and conventions embodying the fundamental values of a community

MORESQUE *adj* (esp of decoration and architecture) of Moorish style ▷ *n* Moorish design or decoration

MORESQUES > MORESQUE

MORGAN *n* American breed of small compact saddle horse

MORGANITE *n* pink variety of beryl, used as a gemstone

MORGANS > MORGAN

MORGAY *n* small dogfish

MORGAYS > MORGAY

MORGEN *n* South African unit of area

MORGENS > MORGEN

MORGUE *same as* > MORTUARY

MORGUES > MORGUE

MORIA *n* folly

MORIAS > MORIA

MORIBUND *adj* without force or vitality

MORICHE *same as* > MIRITI

MORICHES > MORICHE

MORION *n* 16th-century helmet with a brim and wide comb

MORIONS > MORION

MORISCO *n* morris dance

MORISCOES > MORISCO

MORISCOS > MORISCO

MORISH *same as* > MOREISH

MORKIN *n* animal dying in accident

MORKINS > MORKIN

MORLING *n* sheep killed by disease

MORLINGS > MORLING

MORMAOR *n* former high-ranking Scottish nobleman

MORMAORS > MORMAOR

MORN *n* morning

MORNAY *n* dish served with a cheese sauce

MORNAYS > MORNAY

MORNE *same as* > MOURN

MORNED > MORNE

MORNES > MORNE

MORNING *n* part of the day before noon

MORNINGS > MORNING

MORNS > MORN

MOROCCO *n* goatskin leather

MOROCCOS > MOROCCO

MORON *n* insulting term for a foolish or stupid person

MORONIC > MORON

MORONISM > MORON

MORONISMS > MORON

MORONITY > MORON

MORONS > MORON

MOROSE *adj* sullen or moody

MOROSELY > MOROSE

MOROSER > MOROSE

MOROSEST > MOROSE

MOROSITY > MOROSE

MORPH *n* phonological representation of a morpheme ▷ *vb* undergo or cause to undergo morphing

MORPHEAN *adj* of or relating to Morpheus, the god of sleep and dreams

MORPHED > MORPH

MORPHEME *n* speech element that cannot be subdivided

MORPHEMES > MORPHEME

MORPHEMIC > MORPHEME

MORPHETIC *same as* > MORPHEAN

MORPHEW *n* blemish on skin

MORPHEWS > MORPHEW

MORPHIA *same as* > MORPHINE

MORPHIAS > MORPHIA

MORPHIC *adj* as in *morphic resonance* idea that an event can lead to similar events in the future through a telepathic effect

MORPHIN *variant form of* > MORPHINE

MORPHINE *n* drug extracted from opium, used as an anaesthetic and sedative

MORPHINES > MORPHINE

MORPHING *n* one image changing to another by small gradual steps using computer animation

MORPHINGS > MORPHING

MORPHINIC > MORPHINE

MORPHINS > MORPHIN

MORPHO *n* type of butterfly

MORPHOGEN *n* chemical in body that influences growth

MORPHOS > MORPHO

MORPHOSES > MORPHOSIS

MORPHOSIS *n* development in an organism or its parts characterized by structural change

MORPHOTIC > MORPHOSIS

MORPHS > MORPH

MORRA *same as* > MORA

MORRAS > MORRA

MORRELL *n* tall SW Australian eucalyptus with pointed buds

MORRELLS > MORRELL

MORRHUA *n* cod

MORRHUAS > MORRHUA

MORRICE *same as* > MORRIS

MORRICES > MORRICE

MORRION *same as* > MORION

MORRIONS > MORRION

MORRIS *vb* perform morris dance

MORRISED > MORRIS

MORRISES > MORRIS

MORRISING > MORRIS

MORRO *n* rounded hill or promontory

MORROS > MORRO

MORROW *n* next day

MORROWS > MORROW

MORS > MOR

MORSAL *same as* > MORSEL

MORSALS > MORSAL

MORSE *n* clasp or fastening on a cope

MORSEL *n* small piece, esp of food ▷ *vb* divide into morsels

MORSELED > MORSEL

MORSELING > MORSEL

MORSELLED > MORSEL

MORSELS > MORSEL

MORSES > MORSE

MORSURE *n* bite

MORSURES > MORSURE

MORT *n* call blown on a hunting horn to signify the death of the animal hunted

MORTAL *adj* subject to death ▷ *n* human being

MORTALISE *same as* > MORTALIZE

MORTALITY *n* state of being mortal

MORTALIZE *vb* make mortal

MORTALLY > MORTAL

MORTALS > MORTAL

MORTAR *n* small cannon with a short range ▷ *vb* fire on with mortars

MORTARED > MORTAR

MORTARIER > MORTARY

MORTARING > MORTAR

MORTARMAN *n* person firing mortar

MORTARMEN > MORTAR

MORTARS > MORTAR

MORTARY *adj* of or like mortar

MORTBELL *n* bell rung for funeral

MORTBELLS > MORTBELL

MORTCLOTH *n* cloth spread over coffin

MORTGAGE *n* conditional pledging of property as security for the repayment of a loan ▷ *vb* pledge (property) as security thus ▷ *adj* of or relating to mortgage

MORTGAGED > MORTGAGE

MORTGAGEE *n* creditor in a mortgage

MORTGAGER *same as* > MORTGAGOR

MORTGAGES > MORTGAGE

MORTGAGOR *n* debtor in a mortgage

MORTICE *same as* > MORTISE

MORTICED > MORTICE

MORTICER > MORTICE

MORTICERS > MORTICE

MORTICES > MORTICE

MORTICIAN *n* undertaker

MORTICING > MORTICE

MORTIFIC *adj* causing death

MORTIFIED > MORTIFY

MORTIFIER > MORTIFY

MORTIFIES > MORTIFY

MORTIFY *vb* humiliate

MORTISE *n* slot cut into a piece of wood, stone, etc ▷ *vb* cut a slot in (a piece of wood, stone, etc)

MORTISED > MORTISE

MORTISER > MORTISE

MORTISERS > MORTISE

MORTISES > MORTISE

MORTISING > MORTISE

MORTLING *n* dead body

MORTLINGS > MORTLING

MORTMAIN *n* status of lands held inalienably by a church

MORTMAINS
> MORTMAIN

MORTS > MORT

MORTSAFE n cage placed over a grave to deter body snatchers

MORTSAFES
> MORTSAFE

MORTUARY n building where corpses are kept before burial or cremation ▷ adj of or relating to death or burial

MORULA n solid ball of cells resulting from the splitting of a fertilized ovum

MORULAE > MORULA

MORULAR > MORULA

MORULAS > MORULA

MORWONG n food fish of Australasian coastal waters

MORWONGS > MORWONG

MORYAH interj exclamation of annoyance, disbelief, etc

MOS > MO

MOSAIC n design or decoration using small pieces of coloured stone or glass

MOSAICISM n occurrence of different types of tissue side by side

MOSAICIST > MOSAIC

MOSAICKED adj arranged in mosaic form

MOSAICS > MOSAIC

MOSASAUR n type of extinct Cretaceous giant marine lizard, typically with paddle-like limbs

MOSASAURI
> MOSASAUR

MOSASAURS
> MOSASAUR

MOSCATO n type of sweet dessert wine

MOSCATOS > MOSCATO

MOSCHATE n odour like musk

MOSCHATEL n small N temperate plant with greenish-white musk-scented flowers

MOSCOVIUM n highly radioactive element

MOSE vb have glanders

MOSED > MOSE

MOSELLE n German white wine from the Moselle valley

MOSELLES > MOSELLE

MOSES > MOSE

MOSEY vb walk in a leisurely manner

MOSEYED > MOSEY

MOSEYING > MOSEY

MOSEYS > MOSEY

MOSH n dance performed to loud rock music ▷ vb dance in this manner

MOSHAV n cooperative settlement in Israel

MOSHAVIM > MOSHAV

MOSHED > MOSH

MOSHER > MOSH

MOSHERS > MOSH

MOSHES > MOSH

MOSHING > MOSH

MOSHINGS > MOSH

MOSING > MOSE

MOSK same as > MOSQUE

MOSKONFYT n South African grape syrup

MOSKS > MOSK

MOSLINGS pl n shavings from animal skin being prepared

MOSQUE n Muslim temple

MOSQUES > MOSQUE

MOSQUITO n blood-sucking flying insect

MOSQUITOS
> MOSQUITO

MOSS n small flowerless plant growing in masses on moist surfaces ▷ vb gather moss

MOSSBACK n old turtle, shellfish, etc, that has a growth of algae on its back

MOSSBACKS
> MOSSBACK

MOSSED > MOSS

MOSSER > MOSS

MOSSERS > MOSS

MOSSES > MOSS

MOSSGROWN adj covered in moss

MOSSIE n common sparrow

MOSSIER > MOSS

MOSSIES > MOSSIE

MOSSIEST > MOSS

MOSSINESS > MOSS

MOSSING > MOSS

MOSSLAND n land covered in peat

MOSSLANDS
> MOSSLAND

MOSSLIKE > MOSS

MOSSO adv to be performed with rapidity

MOSSPLANT n individual plant in moss

MOSSY > MOSS

MOST n greatest number or degree ▷ adj greatest in number or degree ▷ adv in the greatest degree

MOSTE > MOTE

MOSTEST > MOST

MOSTESTS > MOST

MOSTLY adv for the most part, generally

MOSTS > MOST

MOSTWHAT adv mostly

MOT n girl or young woman, esp one's girlfriend

MOTE n tiny speck ▷ vb may or might

MOTED adj containing motes

MOTEL n roadside hotel for motorists

MOTELIER n person running motel

MOTELIERS
> MOTELIER

MOTELS > MOTEL

MOTEN > MOTE

MOTES > MOTE

MOTET n short sacred choral song

MOTETS > MOTET

MOTETT same as > MOTET

MOTETTIST > MOTETT

MOTETTS > MOTETT

MOTEY adj containing motes ▷ n pigment made from earth

MOTEYS > MOTEY

MOTH n nocturnal insect like a butterfly

MOTHBALL n small ball of camphor or naphthalene used to repel moths from stored clothes ▷ vb store (something operational) for future use

MOTHBALLS > MOTHBALL

MOTHED adj damaged by moths

MOTHER n female parent ▷ adj native or inborn ▷ vb look after as a mother

MOTHERED > MOTHER

MOTHERESE n simplified and repetitive type of speech, with exaggerated intonation and rhythm, often used by adults when speaking to babies

MOTHERIER > MOTHERY

MOTHERING > MOTHER

MOTHERLY adj of or resembling a mother, esp in warmth, or protectiveness

MOTHERS > MOTHER

MOTHERY adj like mother of vinegar

MOTHIER > MOTHY

MOTHIEST > MOTHY

MOTHLIKE > MOTH

MOTHPROOF adj (esp of clothes) chemically treated so as to repel clothes moths ▷ vb make mothproof

MOTHS > MOTH

MOTHY adj ragged

MOTI n derogatory Indian English word for a fat woman or girl

MOTIER > MOTEY

MOTIEST > MOTEY

MOTIF n (recurring) theme or design

MOTIFIC adj causing motion

MOTIFS > MOTIF

MOTILE adj capable of independent movement ▷ n person whose mental imagery strongly reflects movement

MOTILES > MOTILE

MOTILITY > MOTILE

MOTION n process, action, or way of moving ▷ vb direct (someone) by gesture

MOTIONAL > MOTION

MOTIONED > MOTION

MOTIONER > MOTION

MOTIONERS > MOTION

MOTIONING > MOTION

MOTIONIST n person proposing many motions

MOTIONS > MOTION

MOTIS > MOTI

MOTIVATE vb give incentive to

MOTIVATED
> MOTIVATE

MOTIVATES
> MOTIVATE

MOTIVATOR
> MOTIVATE

MOTIVE n reason for a course of action ▷ adj causing motion ▷ vb motivate

MOTIVED > MOTIVE

MOTIVES > MOTIVE

MOTIVIC adj of musical motif

MOTIVING > MOTIVE

MOTIVITY n power of moving or of initiating motion

MOTLEY adj miscellaneous ▷ n costume of a jester

MOTLEYER > MOTLEY

MOTLEYEST > MOTLEY

MOTLEYS > MOTLEY

MOTLIER > MOTLEY

MOTLIEST > MOTLEY

MOTMOT n tropical American bird with a long tail and blue and brownish-green plumage

MOTMOTS > MOTMOT

MOTOCROSS n motorcycle race over a rough course

MOTOR n engine, esp of a vehicle ▷ vb travel by car ▷ adj of or relating to cars and other vehicles powered by engines

MOTORABLE adj (of a road) suitable for use by motor vehicles

MOTORAIL n transport of cars by train

MOTORAILS
> MOTORAIL

MOTORBIKE n motorcycle

MOTORBOAT n any boat powered by a motor

MOTORBUS n bus driven by an internal-combustion engine

MOTORCADE n procession of cars carrying important people

MOTORCAR n self-propelled electric railway car

MOTORCARS
> MOTORCAR

MOTORDOM n world of motor cars

MOTORDOMS
> MOTORDOM

MOTORED > MOTOR

MOTORHOME n large motor vehicle with living quarters behind the driver's compartment

MOTORIAL > MOTOR

MOTORIC n person trained in the muscular causes of vocal changes ▷ adj pertaining to motion

MOTORICS >MOTORIC
MOTORING >MOTOR
MOTORINGS >MOTOR
MOTORISE *same as*
>MOTORIZE
MOTORISED
>MOTORIZE
MOTORISES
>MOTORIZE
MOTORIST *n* driver of a car
MOTORISTS
>MOTORIST
MOTORIUM *n* area of nervous system involved in movement
MOTORIUMS >MOTORIUM
MOTORIZE *vb* equip with a motor
MOTORIZED
>MOTORIZE
MOTORIZES
>MOTORIZE
MOTORLESS >MOTOR
MOTORMAN *n* driver of an electric train
MOTORMEN >MOTORMAN
MOTORS >MOTOR
MOTORSHIP *n* ship with motor
MOTORWAY *n* main road for fast-moving traffic
MOTORWAYS
>MOTORWAY
MOTORY >MOTOR
MOTOSCAFI
>MOTOSCAFO
MOTOSCAFO *n* motorboat
MOTS >MOT
MOTSER *n* large sum of money, esp a gambling win
MOTSERS >MOTSER
MOTT *n* clump of trees
MOTTE *n* mound on which a castle was built
MOTTES >MOTTE
MOTTIER >MOTTY
MOTTIES >MOTTY
MOTTIEST >MOTTY
MOTTLE *vb* colour with streaks or blotches of different shades ▷ *n* mottled appearance, as of the surface of marble
MOTTLED >MOTTLE
MOTTLER *n* paintbrush for mottled effects
MOTTLERS >MOTTLER
MOTTLES >MOTTLE
MOTTLING >MOTTLE
MOTTLINGS >MOTTLE
MOTTO *n* saying expressing an ideal or rule of conduct
MOTTOED *adj* having motto
MOTTOES >MOTTO
MOTTOS >MOTTO
MOTTS >MOTT
MOTTY *n* target at which coins are aimed in pitch-and-toss ▷ *adj* containing motes
MOTU *n* derogatory Indian English word for a fat man or boy

MOTUCA *n* Brazilian fly
MOTUCAS >MOTUCA
MOTUS >MOTU
MOTZA *same as* >MOTSER
MOTZAS >MOTZA
MOU *Scots word for* >MOUTH
MOUCH *same as* >MOOCH
MOUCHARD *n* police informer
MOUCHARDS
>MOUCHARD
MOUCHED >MOUCH
MOUCHER >MOUCH
MOUCHERS >MOUCH
MOUCHES >MOUCH
MOUCHING >MOUCH
MOUCHOIR *n* handkerchief
MOUCHOIRS
>MOUCHOIR
MOUDIWART *same as*
>MOULDWARP
MOUDIWORT *same as*
>MOULDWARP
MOUE *n* disdainful or pouting look
MOUES >MOUE
MOUFFLON *same as*
>MOUFLON
MOUFFLONS
>MOUFFLON
MOUFLON *n* wild mountain sheep of Corsica and Sardinia
MOUFLONS >MOUFLON
MOUGHT >MAY
MOUILLE *adj* palatalized, as in the sounds represented by Spanish *ll* or *ñ*
MOUJIK *same as* >MUZHIK
MOUJIKS >MOUJIK
MOULAGE *n* mould making
MOULAGES >MOULAGE
MOULD *n* hollow container in which metal etc is cast ▷ *vb* shape
MOULDABLE >MOULD
MOULDED >MOULD
MOULDER *vb* decay into dust ▷ *n* person who moulds or makes moulds
MOULDERED >MOULDER
MOULDERS >MOULDER
MOULDIER >MOULDY
MOULDIEST >MOULDY
MOULDING *n* moulded ornamental edging
MOULDINGS
>MOULDING
MOULDS >MOULD
MOULDWARP *archaic or dialect name for a* >MOLE
MOULDY *adj* stale or musty
MOULIN *n* vertical shaft in a glacier
MOULINET *n* device for bending crossbow
MOULINETS
>MOULINET
MOULINS >MOULIN
MOULS *Scots word for*
>MOULD
MOULT *vb* shed feathers, hair, or skin to make way for new growth ▷ *n* process of moulting

MOULTED >MOULT
MOULTEN *adj* having moulted
MOULTER >MOULT
MOULTERS >MOULT
MOULTING >MOULT
MOULTINGS >MOULT
MOULTS >MOULT
MOUND *n* heap, esp of earth or stones ▷ *vb* gather into a mound
MOUNDBIRD *n* Australian bird laying eggs in mounds
MOUNDED >MOUND
MOUNDING >MOUND
MOUNDS >MOUND
MOUNSEER *same as*
>MONSIEUR
MOUNSEERS
>MOUNSEER
MOUNT *vb* climb or ascend ▷ *n* backing or support on which something is fixed
MOUNTABLE >MOUNT
MOUNTAIN *n* hill of great size ▷ *adj* of, found on, or for use on a mountain or mountains
MOUNTAINS
>MOUNTAIN
MOUNTAINY *adj* mountainous
MOUNTANT *n* adhesive for mounting pictures
MOUNTANTS
>MOUNTANT
MOUNTED *adj* riding horses
MOUNTER >MOUNT
MOUNTERS >MOUNT
MOUNTING *same as*
>MOUNT
MOUNTINGS
>MOUNTING
MOUNTS >MOUNT
MOUP *vb* nibble
MOUPED >MOUP
MOUPING >MOUP
MOUPS >MOUP
MOURN *vb* feel or express sorrow for (a dead person or lost thing)
MOURNED >MOURN
MOURNER *n* person attending a funeral
MOURNERS >MOURNER
MOURNFUL *adj* sad or dismal
MOURNING *n* grieving ▷ *adj* of or relating to mourning
MOURNINGS
>MOURNING
MOURNIVAL *n* card game
MOURNS >MOURN
MOURVEDRE *n* type of red wine grape
MOUS >MOU
MOUSAKA *same as*
>MOUSSAKA
MOUSAKAS >MOUSSAKA
MOUSE *n* small long-tailed rodent ▷ *vb* stalk and catch mice
MOUSEBIRD *another name for* >COLY
MOUSED >MOUSE
MOUSEKIN *n* little mouse

MOUSEKINS
>MOUSEKIN
MOUSELIKE >MOUSE
MOUSEMAT *n* piece of material on which a computer mouse is moved
MOUSEMATS
>MOUSEMAT
MOUSEOVER *n* on a web page, any item that changes or pops up when the pointer of a mouse moves over it
MOUSEPAD *n* pad for computer mouse
MOUSEPADS
>MOUSEPAD
MOUSER *n* cat used to catch mice
MOUSERIES >MOUSERY
MOUSERS >MOUSER
MOUSERY *n* place infested with mice
MOUSES >MOUSE
MOUSETAIL *n* N temperate plant with tail-like flower spikes
MOUSETRAP *n* spring-loaded trap for killing mice
MOUSEY *same as* >MOUSY
MOUSIE *n* little mouse
MOUSIER >MOUSY
MOUSIES >MOUSIE
MOUSIEST >MOUSY
MOUSILY >MOUSY
MOUSINESS >MOUSY
MOUSING *n* device for closing off a hook
MOUSINGS >MOUSING
MOUSLE *vb* handle roughly
MOUSLED >MOUSLE
MOUSLES >MOUSLE
MOUSLING >MOUSLE
MOUSME *n* Japanese girl or young woman
MOUSMEE *same as*
>MOUSME
MOUSMEES >MOUSMEE
MOUSMES >MOUSME
MOUSSAKA *n* dish made with meat, aubergines, and tomatoes, topped with cheese sauce
MOUSSAKAS
>MOUSSAKA
MOUSSE *n* dish of flavoured cream whipped and set ▷ *vb* apply mousse to
MOUSSED >MOUSSE
MOUSSES >MOUSSE
MOUSSEUX *n* type of sparkling wine
MOUSSING >MOUSSE
MOUST *same as* >MUST
MOUSTACHE *n* hair on the upper lip
MOUSTED >MOUST
MOUSTING >MOUST
MOUSTS >MOUST
MOUSY *adj* like a mouse, esp in hair colour
MOUTAN *n* variety of peony
MOUTANS >MOUTAN
MOUTER *same as*
>MULTURE

MOUTERED > MOUTER
MOUTERER > MOUTER
MOUTERERS > MOUTER
MOUTERING > MOUTER
MOUTERS > MOUTER
MOUTH n opening in the head for eating and issuing sounds ▷ vb form (words) with the lips without speaking
MOUTHABLE adj able to be recited
MOUTHED > MOUTH
MOUTHER > MOUTH
MOUTHERS > MOUTH
MOUTHFEEL n texture of a substance as it is perceived in the mouth
MOUTHFUL n amount of food or drink put into the mouth at any one time when eating or drinking
MOUTHFULS > MOUTHFUL
MOUTHIER > MOUTHY
MOUTHIEST > MOUTHY
MOUTHILY > MOUTHY
MOUTHING > MOUTH
MOUTHLESS > MOUTH
MOUTHLIKE > MOUTH
MOUTHPART n any of the paired appendages in arthropods that surround the mouth and are specialized for feeding
MOUTHS > MOUTH
MOUTHWASH n medicated liquid for gargling and cleansing the mouth
MOUTHY adj bombastic
MOUTON n sheepskin processed to resemble the fur of another animal
MOUTONNEE adj rounded by action of glacier
MOUTONS > MOUTON
MOVABLE adj able to be moved or rearranged ▷ n movable article, esp a piece of furniture
MOVABLES > MOVABLE
MOVABLY > MOVABLE
MOVANT n person who applies to a court of law
MOVANTS > MOVANT
MOVE vb change in place or position ▷ n moving
MOVEABLE same as
> MOVABLE
MOVEABLES
> MOVEABLE
MOVEABLY > MOVEABLE
MOVED > MOVE
MOVELESS adj immobile
MOVEMENT n action or process of moving
MOVEMENTS
> MOVEMENT
MOVER n person or animal that moves in a particular way
MOVERS > MOVER
MOVES > MOVE
MOVIE n cinema film
MOVIEDOM n world of cinema
MOVIEDOMS
> MOVIEDOM

MOVIEGOER n person who goes to cinema
MOVIELAND same as
> MOVIEDOM
MOVIEOKE n entertainment in which people act out scenes from movies
MOVIEOKES
> MOVIEOKE
MOVIEOLA same as
> MOVIOLA
MOVIEOLAS
> MOVIEOLA
MOVIES > MOVIE
MOVING adj arousing or touching the emotions
MOVINGLY > MOVING
MOVIOLA n viewing machine used in cutting and editing film
MOVIOLAS > MOVIOLA
MOW vb cut (grass or crops) ▷ n part of a barn where hay, straw, etc, is stored
MOWA same as > MAHUA
MOWAS > MOWA
MOWBURN vb heat up in mow
MOWBURNED > MOWBURN
MOWBURNS > MOWBURN
MOWBURNT adj (of hay, straw, etc) damaged by overheating in a mow
MOWDIE Scot word for
> MOLE
MOWDIES > MOWDIE
MOWED > MOW
MOWER > MOW
MOWERS > MOW
MOWING > MOW
MOWINGS > MOW
MOWN > MOW
MOWRA same as > MAHUA
MOWRAS > MOWRA
MOWS > MOW
MOXA n downy material obtained from various plants
MOXAS > MOXA
MOXIE n courage, nerve, or vigour
MOXIES > MOXIE
MOY n coin
MOYA n mud emitted from a volcano
MOYAS > MOYA
MOYGASHEL n type of Irish linen
MOYITIES > MOYITY
MOYITY same as
> MOIETY
MOYL same as > MOYLE
MOYLE vb toil
MOYLED > MOYLE
MOYLES > MOYLE
MOYLING > MOYLE
MOYLS > MOYL
MOYS > MOY
MOZ n hex
MOZE vb give nap to
MOZED > MOZE
MOZES > MOZ
MOZETTA same as
> MOZZETTA
MOZETTAS > MOZETTA
MOZETTE > MOZETTA
MOZING > MOZE

MOZO n porter in southwest USA
MOZOS > MOZO
MOZZ same as > MOZ
MOZZES > MOZZ
MOZZETTA n short hooded cape worn by the pope, cardinals, etc
MOZZETTAS
> MOZZETTA
MOZZETTE > MOZZETTA
MOZZIE same as
> MOSSIE
MOZZIES > MOZZIE
MOZZLE n luck ▷ vb hamper or impede (someone)
MOZZLED > MOZZLE
MOZZLES > MOZZLE
MOZZLING > MOZZLE
MPRET n former Albanian ruler
MPRETS > MPRET
MRIDAMGAM same as
> MRIDANG
MRIDANG n drum used in Indian music
MRIDANGA same as
> MRIDANG
MRIDANGAM same as
> MRIDANG
MRIDANGAS
> MRIDANGA
MRIDANGS > MRIDANG
MU n twelfth letter in the Greek alphabet
MUCATE n salt of mucic acid
MUCATES > MUCATE
MUCH adj large amount or degree of ▷ n large amount or degree ▷ adv great degree
MUCHACHA n (in Spain) young woman or female servant
MUCHACHAS
> MUCHACHA
MUCHACHO n (in Spain) young man or male servant
MUCHACHOS
> MUCHACHO
MUCHEL same as > MUCH
MUCHELL same as > MUCH
MUCHELLS > MUCHELL
MUCHELS > MUCHEL
MUCHES > MUCH
MUCHLY > MUCH
MUCHNESS n magnitude
MUCHO adv Spanish for very
MUCIC adj as in mucic acid colourless crystalline solid carboxylic acid
MUCID adj mouldy, musty, or slimy
MUCIDITY > MUCID
MUCIDNESS > MUCID
MUCIGEN n substance present in mucous cells that is converted into mucin
MUCIGENS > MUCIGEN
MUCILAGE n gum or glue
MUCILAGES
> MUCILAGE

MUCIN n any of a group of nitrogenous mucoproteins occurring in saliva, skin, tendon, etc
MUCINOGEN n substance forming mucin
MUCINOID adj of or like mucin
MUCINOUS > MUCIN
MUCINS > MUCIN
MUCK n dirt, filth
MUCKAMUCK n food ▷ vb consume food
MUCKED > MUCK
MUCKENDER n handkerchief
MUCKER n person who shifts broken rock or waste ▷ vb hoard
MUCKERED > MUCKER
MUCKERING > MUCKER
MUCKERISH > MUCKER
MUCKERS > MUCKER
MUCKHEAP n dunghill
MUCKHEAPS
> MUCKHEAP
MUCKIER > MUCKY
MUCKIEST > MUCKY
MUCKILY > MUCKY
MUCKINESS > MUCKY
MUCKING > MUCK
MUCKLE adj large
MUCKLER > MUCKLE
MUCKLES > MUCKLE
MUCKLEST > MUCKLE
MUCKLUCK same as
> MUKLUK
MUCKLUCKS > MUCKLUCK
MUCKRAKE n agricultural rake for spreading manure ▷ vb seek out and expose scandal, esp concerning public figures
MUCKRAKED
> MUCKRAKE
MUCKRAKER
> MUCKRAKE
MUCKRAKES
> MUCKRAKE
MUCKS > MUCK
MUCKSWEAT n profuse sweat
MUCKWORM n any larva or worm that lives in mud
MUCKWORMS
> MUCKWORM
MUCKY adj dirty or muddy
MUCKYMUCK n person who is or appears to be very important
MUCLUC same as
> MUKLUK
MUCLUCS > MUCLUC
MUCOID adj of the nature of or resembling mucin ▷ n substance like mucin
MUCOIDAL same as
> MUCOID
MUCOIDS > MUCOID
MUCOLYTIC adj breaking down mucus ▷ n agent that is able to break down mucus
MUCOR n type of fungus
MUCORS > MUCOR
MUCOSA n mucus-secreting membrane that lines body cavities

MUCOSAE >MUCOSA
MUCOSAL >MUCOSA
MUCOSAS >MUCOSA
MUCOSE same as
. >MUCOUS
MUCOSITY >MUCOUS
MUCOUS adj of,
resembling, or secreting
mucus
MUCRO n short pointed
projection from certain
parts or organs
MUCRONATE adj
terminating in a sharp
point
MUCRONES >MUCRO
MUCROS >MUCRO
MUCULENT adj like mucus
MUCUS n slimy secretion
of the mucous membranes
MUCUSES >MUCUS
MUD n wet soft earth ▷ vb
cover in mud
MUDBANK n sloping area
of mud beside a body of
water
MUDBANKS >MUDBANK
MUDBATH n medicinal
bath in heated mud
MUDBATHS >MUDBATH
MUDBUG n crayfish
MUDBUGS >MUDBUG
MUDCAP vb use explosive
charge in blasting
MUDCAPPED >MUDCAP
MUDCAPS >MUDCAP
MUDCAT n any of several
large North American
catfish
MUDCATS >MUDCAT
MUDDED >MUD
MUDDER n horse that runs
well in mud
MUDDERS >MUDDER
MUDDIED >MUDDY
MUDDIER >MUDDY
MUDDIES >MUDDY
MUDDIEST >MUDDY
MUDDILY >MUDDY
MUDDINESS >MUDDY
MUDDING >MUD
MUDDLE vb confuse ▷ n
state of confusion
MUDDLED >MUDDLE
MUDDLER n person who
muddles or muddles
through
MUDDLERS >MUDDLER
MUDDLES >MUDDLE
MUDDLIER >MUDDLE
MUDDLIEST >MUDDLE
MUDDLING >MUDDLE
MUDDLINGS >MUDDLE
MUDDLY >MUDDLE
MUDDY adj covered or filled
with mud ▷ vb make
muddy
MUDDYING >MUDDY
MUDEJAR n Spanish Moor
▷ adj of or relating to a
style of architecture
MUDEJARES >MUDEJAR
MUDEYE n larva of the
dragonfly
MUDEYES >MUDEYE
MUDFISH n fish that lives
at the muddy bottoms of
rivers, lakes, etc

MUDFISHES >MUDFISH
MUDFLAP n flap above
wheel to deflect mud
MUDFLAPS >MUDFLAP
MUDFLAT n tract of low
muddy land
MUDFLATS >MUDFLAT
MUDFLOW n flow of soil
mixed with water down a
steep unstable slope
MUDFLOWS >MUDFLOW
MUDGE vb speak vaguely
MUDGED >MUDGE
MUDGER >MUDGE
MUDGERS >MUDGE
MUDGES >MUDGE
MUDGING >MUDGE
MUDGUARD n cover over a
wheel to prevent mud or
water being thrown up by it
MUDGUARDS
>MUDGUARD
MUDHEN n water bird
living in muddy place
MUDHENS >MUDHEN
MUDHOLE n hole with
mud at bottom
MUDHOLES >MUDHOLE
MUDHOOK n anchor
MUDHOOKS >MUDHOOK
MUDHOPPER n type of
amphibious fish found on
mud flats and in mangrove
swamps
MUDIR n local governor
MUDIRIA n province of
mudir
MUDIRIAS >MUDIRIA
MUDIRIEH same as
>MUDIRIA
MUDIRIEHS
>MUDIRIEH
MUDIRS >MUDIR
MUDLARK n street urchin
▷ vb play in mud
MUDLARKED >MUDLARK
MUDLARKS >MUDLARK
MUDLOGGER n person
checking mud for traces of
oil
MUDPACK n cosmetic
paste applied to the face
MUDPACKS >MUDPACK
MUDPIE n small mass of
mud moulded into a pie
shape
MUDPIES >MUDPIE
MUDPUPPY n type of
salamander
MUDRA n hand movement
in Hindu religious dancing
MUDRAS >MUDRA
MUDROCK n type of
sedimentary rock
MUDROCKS >MUDROCK
MUDROOM n room where
muddy shoes may be left
MUDROOMS >MUDROOM
MUDS >MUD
MUDSCOW n boat for
travelling over mudflats
MUDSCOWS >MUDSCOW
MUDSILL n support for
building at or below
ground
MUDSILLS >MUDSILL
MUDSLIDE n landslide of
mud

MUDSLIDES
>MUDSLIDE
MUDSLING vb make
accusations against a rival
candidate
MUDSLINGS
>MUDSLING
MUDSLUNG >MUDSLING
MUDSTONE n dark grey
clay rock similar to shale
but with the lamination
less well developed
MUDSTONES
>MUDSTONE
MUDWORT n plant growing
in mud
MUDWORTS >MUDWORT
MUEDDIN same as
>MUEZZIN
MUEDDINS >MUEDDIN
MUENSTER n
whitish-yellow semihard
whole milk cheese, often
flavoured with caraway or
aniseed
MUENSTERS
>MUENSTER
MUESLI n mixture of
grain, nuts, and dried fruit
MUESLIS >MUESLI
MUEZZIN n official who
summons Muslims to
prayer
MUEZZINS >MUEZZIN
MUFF n tube-shaped
covering to keep the hands
warm ▷ vb bungle (an
action)
MUFFED >MUFF
MUFFETTEE n small muff
worn over the wrist
MUFFIN n light round flat
yeast cake
MUFFINEER n muffin
dish
MUFFING >MUFF
MUFFINS >MUFFIN
MUFFISH >MUFF
MUFFLE vb wrap up for
warmth or to deaden
sound ▷ n something that
muffles
MUFFLED >MUFFLE
MUFFLER n scarf
MUFFLERED adj with
muffler
MUFFLERS >MUFFLER
MUFFLES >MUFFLE
MUFFLING >MUFFLE
MUFFS >MUFF
MUFLON same as
>MOUFFLON
MUFLONS >MUFLON
MUFTI n civilian clothes
worn by a person who
usually wears a uniform
MUFTIS >MUFTI
MUG n large drinking cup
▷ vb attack in order to rob
MUGEARITE n crystalline
rock
MUGFUL same as >MUG
MUGFULS >MUGFUL
MUGG same as >MUG
MUGGA n Australian
eucalyptus tree
MUGGAR same as
>MUGGER

MUGGARS >MUGGAR
MUGGAS >MUGGA
MUGGED >MUG
MUGGEE n mugged
person
MUGGEES >MUGGEE
MUGGER n person who
commits robbery with
violence
MUGGERS >MUGGER
MUGGIER >MUGGY
MUGGIEST >MUGGY
MUGGILY >MUGGY
MUGGINESS >MUGGY
MUGGING >MUG
MUGGINGS >MUG
MUGGINS n stupid or
gullible person
MUGGINSES >MUGGINS
MUGGISH same as
>MUGGY
MUGGLE n person who
does not possess
supernatural powers
MUGGLES >MUGGLE
MUGGS >MUG
MUGGUR same as
>MUGGER
MUGGURS >MUGGUR
MUGGY adj (of weather)
damp and stifling
MUGHAL same as >MOGUL
MUGHALS >MUGHAL
MUGS >MUG
MUGSHOT n police
photograph of person's
face
MUGSHOTS >MUGSHOT
MUGWORT n N temperate
herbaceous plant with
aromatic leaves
MUGWORTS >MUGWORT
MUGWUMP n neutral or
independent person
MUGWUMPS >MUGWUMP
MUHLIES >MUHLY
MUHLY n American grass
MUID n former French
measure of capacity
MUIDS >MUID
MUIL same as >MULE
MUILS >MUIL
MUIR same as >MOOR
MUIRBURN same as
>MOORBURN
MUIRBURNS
>MUIRBURN
MUIRS >MUIR
MUIST same as >MUST
MUISTED >MUIST
MUISTING >MUIST
MUISTS >MUIST
MUJAHEDIN same as
>MUJAHEDDIN
MUJAHIDIN same as
>MUJAHEDDIN
MUJIK same as >MUZHIK
MUJIKS >MUJIK
MUKHTAR n lawyer in
India
MUKHTARS >MUKHTAR
MUKLUK n soft boot,
usually of sealskin
MUKLUKS >MUKLUK
MUKTUK n thin outer skin
of the beluga, used as food
MUKTUKS >MUKTUK

MULBERRY n tree whose leaves are used to feed silkworms ▷ adj dark purple

MULCH n mixture of wet straw, leaves, etc ▷ vb cover (land) with mulch

MULCHED > MULCH

MULCHES > MULCH

MULCHING > MULCH

MULCT vb cheat or defraud ▷ n fine or penalty

MULCTED > MULCT

MULCTING > MULCT

MULCTS > MULCT

MULE n offspring of a horse and a donkey ▷ vb strike coin with different die on each side

MULED > MULE

MULES vb surgically remove folds of skin from a sheep

MULESED > MULES

MULESES > MULES

MULESING > MULES

MULESINGS > MULESING

MULETA n small cape attached to a stick used by a matador

MULETAS > MULETA

MULETEER n mule driver

MULETEERS > MULETEER

MULEY adj (of cattle) having no horns ▷ n any hornless cow

MULEYS > MULEY

MULGA n Australian acacia shrub growing in desert regions

MULGAS > MULGA

MULIE n type of N American deer

MULIES > MULIE

MULING > MULE

MULISH adj obstinate

MULISHLY > MULISH

MULL vb think (over) or ponder ▷ n promontory or headland

MULLA same as > MULLAH

MULLAH n Muslim scholar, teacher, or religious leader

MULLAHED same as > MULLERED

MULLAHING same as > MULLERING

MULLAHISM n rule by mullahs

MULLAHS > MULLAH

MULLARKY same as > MALARKEY

MULLAS > MULLA

MULLED > MULL

MULLEIN n type of European plant

MULLEINS > MULLEIN

MULLEN same as > MULLEIN

MULLENS > MULLEN

MULLER n flat heavy implement used to grind material ▷ vb beat up or defeat thoroughly

MULLERED adj drunk

MULLERIAN adj relating to animal mimicry in which two or more harmful species resemble each other

MULLERING > MULLER

MULLERS > MULLER

MULLET n edible sea fish

MULLETS > MULLET

MULLEY same as > MULEY

MULLEYS > MULLEY

MULLIGAN n stew made from odds and ends of food

MULLIGANS > MULLIGAN

MULLING > MULL

MULLION n vertical dividing bar in a window ▷ vb furnish with mullions

MULLIONED > MULLION

MULLIONS > MULLION

MULLITE n colourless mineral

MULLITES > MULLITE

MULLOCK n waste material from a mine

MULLOCKS > MULLOCK

MULLOCKY adj like mullock

MULLOWAY n large Australian sea fish, valued for sport and food

MULLOWAYS > MULLOWAY

MULLS > MULL

MULMUL n muslin

MULMULL same as > MULMUL

MULMULLS > MULMULL

MULMULS > MULMUL

MULSE n drink containing honey

MULSES > MULSE

MULSH same as > MULCH

MULSHED > MULSH

MULSHES > MULSH

MULSHING > MULSH

MULTEITY n manifoldness

MULTIAGE adj involving different age groups

MULTIATOM adj involving many atoms

MULTIBAND adj involving more than one waveband

MULTIBANK adj involving more than one bank

MULTICAR adj involving several cars

MULTICAST n broadcast from one source simultaneously to several receivers on a network

MULTICELL adj involving many cells

MULTICIDE n mass murder

MULTICITY adj involving more than one city

MULTICOPY adj involving many copies ▷ n any of several or many copies (of a book, document, record, etc)

MULTICORE adj having multiple cores

MULTICULT adj multicultural

MULTIDAY adj involving more than one day

MULTIDISC adj involving more than one disc

MULTIDISK adj involving more than one disk

MULTIDRUG adj involving more than one drug

MULTIFID adj having or divided into many lobes or similar segments

MULTIFIL n fibre made up of many filaments

MULTIFILS > MULTIFIL

MULTIFOIL n ornamental design having a large number of foils

MULTIFOLD adj many times doubled

MULTIFORM adj having many shapes or forms

MULTIGENE n one of a group of closely related genes

MULTIGERM adj (of plants) having the ability to multiply germinate

MULTIGRID adj involving several grids

MULTIGYM n exercise apparatus incorporating a variety of weights, used for toning the muscles

MULTIGYMS > MULTIGYM

MULTIHUED adj having many colours

MULTIHULL n sailing vessel with two or more hulls

MULTIJET adj involving more than one jet

MULTILANE adj having several lanes

MULTILINE adj involving several lines ▷ n variety of crop with several lines, each having different genes to improve disease resistance

MULTILOBE adj having more than one lobe

MULTIMODE n device with several modes

MULTIPACK n form of packaging of foodstuffs, etc, that contains several units and is offered at a price below that of the equivalent number of units

MULTIPAGE adj involving many pages

MULTIPARA n woman who has given birth to more than one viable fetus or living child

MULTIPART adj involving many parts

MULTIPATH adj relating to television or radio signals that travel by more than one route from a transmitter and arrive at slightly different times, causing ghost images or audio distortion

MULTIPED adj having many feet ▷ n insect or animal having many feet

MULTIPEDE same as > MULTIPED

MULTIPEDS > MULTIPED

MULTIPION adj involving many pions

MULTIPLE adj having many parts ▷ n quantity which contains another an exact number of times

MULTIPLES > MULTIPLE

MULTIPLET n set of closely spaced lines in a spectrum, resulting from small differences between the energy levels of atoms or molecules

MULTIPLEX n purpose-built complex containing several cinemas and usu restaurants and bars ▷ adj having many elements, complex ▷ vb send (messages or signals) or (of messages or signals) be sent by multiplex

MULTIPLY vb increase in number or degree

MULTIPOLE adj involving more than one pole

MULTIPORT adj involving more than one port

MULTIRISK adj (of insurance) covering several risks

MULTIROLE adj having a number of roles, functions, etc

MULTIROOM adj having many rooms

MULTISITE adj involving more than one site

MULTISIZE adj involving more than size

MULTISTEP adj involving several steps

MULTITASK vb work at several different tasks simultaneously

MULTITIER adj having many tiers

MULTITON adj weighing several tons

MULTITONE adj involving more than one tone

MULTITOOL n device containing various tools attached to one handle

MULTITUDE n great number

MULTIUNIT adj involving more than one unit

MULTIUSE adj suitable for more than one use

MULTIUSER > MULTIUSE

MULTIWALL adj involving several layers

MULTIWAY adj having several paths or routes

MULTIYEAR adj involving more than one year

MULTUM n substance used in brewing

MULTUMS > MULTUM
MULTURE n fee formerly paid to a miller for grinding grain ▷ vb take multure
MULTURED > MULTURE
MULTURER > MULTURE
MULTURERS > MULTURE
MULTURES > MULTURE
MULTURING > MULTURE
MUM n mother ▷ vb act in a mummer's play
MUMBLE vb speak indistinctly, mutter ▷ n indistinct utterance
MUMBLED > MUMBLE
MUMBLER > MUMBLE
MUMBLERS > MUMBLE
MUMBLES > MUMBLE
MUMBLIER > MUMBLY
MUMBLIEST > MUMBLY
MUMBLING > MUMBLE
MUMBLINGS > MUMBLE
MUMBLY > MUMBLE
MUMCHANCE adj silent
MUMM same as > MUM
MUMMED > MUM
MUMMER n actor in a traditional English folk play ▷ vb perform as a mummer
MUMMERED > MUMMER
MUMMERIES > MUMMERY
MUMMERING n Christmas tradition of house-visiting in parts of Canada
MUMMERS > MUMMER
MUMMERY n performance by mummers
MUMMIA n mummified flesh used as medicine
MUMMIAS > MUMMIA
MUMMICHOG n small American fish
MUMMIED > MUMMY
MUMMIES > MUMMY
MUMMIFIED > MUMMIFY
MUMMIFIES > MUMMIFY
MUMMIFORM adj like a mummy ▷ n sarcophagus
MUMMIFY vb preserve a body as a mummy
MUMMING > MUM
MUMMINGS > MUM
MUMMOCK same as > MAMMOCK
MUMMOCKS > MUMMOCK
MUMMS > MUMM
MUMMY n body embalmed and wrapped for burial in ancient Egypt ▷ vb mummify
MUMMYING > MUMMY
MUMP vb be silent
MUMPED > MUMP
MUMPER > MUMP
MUMPERS > MUMP
MUMPING > MUMP
MUMPISH > MUMPS
MUMPISHLY > MUMPS
MUMPS n infectious disease with swelling in the glands of the neck
MUMPSIMUS n opinion held obstinately
MUMS > MUM
MUMSIER > MUMSY

MUMSIES > MUMSY
MUMSIEST > MUMSY
MUMSINESS n the state of being mumsy
MUMSY adj (of a woman) wearing clothes that are old-fashioned and unflattering ▷ n mother
MUMU n oven in Papua New Guinea
MUMUS > MUMU
MUN same as > MAUN
MUNCH vb chew noisily and steadily
MUNCHABLE > MUNCH
MUNCHED > MUNCH
MUNCHER > MUNCH
MUNCHERS > MUNCH
MUNCHES > MUNCH
MUNCHIE n small amount of food eaten between meals
MUNCHIER > MUNCHY
MUNCHIES pl n craving for food
MUNCHIEST > MUNCHY
MUNCHING > MUNCH
MUNCHKIN n undersized person or a child, esp an appealing one
MUNCHKINS > MUNCHKIN
MUNCHY adj suitable for snacking
MUNDANE adj everyday
MUNDANELY > MUNDANE
MUNDANER > MUNDANE
MUNDANEST > MUNDANE
MUNDANITY > MUNDANE
MUNDIC n iron pyrites
MUNDICS > MUNDIC
MUNDIFIED > MUNDIFY
MUNDIFIES > MUNDIFY
MUNDIFY vb cleanse
MUNDUNGO n tripe in Spain
MUNDUNGOS > MUNDUNGO
MUNDUNGUS n smelly tobacco
MUNG vb process (computer data)
MUNGA n army canteen
MUNGAS > MUNGA
MUNGCORN n maslin
MUNGCORNS > MUNGCORN
MUNGE vb modify a password into an unguessable state
MUNGED > MUNGE
MUNGES > MUNGE
MUNGING > MUNGE
MUNGO n cheap felted fabric made from waste wool
MUNGOES > MUNGO
MUNGOOSE same as > MONGOOSE
MUNGOOSES > MUNGOOSE
MUNGOS > MUNGO
MUNGS > MUNG
MUNI n municipal radio broadcast
MUNICIPAL adj relating to a city or town
MUNIFIED > MUNIFY

MUNIFIES > MUNIFY
MUNIFY vb fortify
MUNIFYING > MUNIFY
MUNIMENT n means of defence
MUNIMENTS pl n title deeds or similar documents
MUNIS > MUNI
MUNITE vb strengthen
MUNITED > MUNITE
MUNITES > MUNITE
MUNITING > MUNITE
MUNITION vb supply with munitions
MUNITIONS pl n military stores
MUNNION archaic word for > MULLION
MUNNIONS > MUNNION
MUNS > MUN
MUNSHI n secretary in India
MUNSHIS > MUNSHI
MUNSTER variant of > MUENSTER
MUNSTERS > MUNSTER
MUNTED adj destroyed or ruined
MUNTER n insulting word for an unattractive person
MUNTERS > MUNTER
MUNTIN n supporting or strengthening bar
MUNTINED adj having a muntin
MUNTING same as > MUNTIN
MUNTINGS > MUNTING
MUNTINS > MUNTIN
MUNTJAC n small Asian deer
MUNTJACS > MUNTJAC
MUNTJAK same as > MUNTJAC
MUNTJAKS > MUNTJAK
MUNTRIE n Australian shrub with green-red edible berries
MUNTRIES > MUNTRIE
MUON n elementary particle with a mass 207 times that of an electron
MUONIC > MUON
MUONIUM n form of hydrogen
MUONIUMS > MUONIUM
MUONS > MUON
MUPPET n stupid person
MUPPETS > MUPPET
MUQADDAM n person of authority in India
MUQADDAMS > MUQADDAM
MURA n group of people living together in Japanese countryside
MURAENA n moray eel
MURAENAS > MURAENA
MURAENID n eel of moray family
MURAENIDS > MURAENID
MURAGE n tax levied for the construction or maintenance of town walls
MURAGES > MURAGE

MURAL n painting on a wall ▷ adj of or relating to a wall
MURALED same as > MURALLED
MURALIST > MURAL
MURALISTS > MURAL
MURALLED adj decorated with mural
MURALS > MURAL
MURAS > MURA
MURDABAD interj down with
MURDER n unlawful intentional killing of a human being ▷ vb kill in this way
MURDERED > MURDER
MURDEREE n murder victim
MURDEREES > MURDEREE
MURDERER n person who murders someone
MURDERERS > MURDER
MURDERESS n female murderer
MURDERING > MURDER
MURDEROUS adj intending, capable of, or guilty of murder
MURDERS > MURDER
MURE archaic or literary word for > IMMURE
MURED > MURE
MUREIN n polymer found in cells
MUREINS > MUREIN
MURENA same as > MURAENA
MURENAS > MURAENA
MURES > MURE
MUREX n marine gastropod formerly used as a source of purple dye
MUREXES > MUREX
MURGEON vb grimace at
MURGEONED > MURGEON
MURGEONS > MURGEON
MURIATE obsolete name for a > CHLORIDE
MURIATED > MURIATE
MURIATES > MURIATE
MURIATIC adj as in muriatic acid former name for a strong acid used in many industrial processes
MURICATE adj having a surface roughened by numerous short points
MURICATED same as > MURICATE
MURICES > MUREX
MURID n animal of the mouse family
MURIDS > MURID
MURIFORM adj like mouse
MURINE n animal belonging to the family that includes rats and mice
MURINES > MURINE
MURING > MURE
MURK n thick darkness ▷ adj dark or gloomy ▷ vb murder (a person)
MURKED > MURK
MURKER > MURK

MURKEST > MURK
MURKIER > MURKY
MURKIEST > MURKY
MURKILY > MURKY
MURKINESS > MURKY
MURKING > MURK
MURKISH > MURK
MURKLY > MURK
MURKS > MURK
MURKSOME > MURK
MURKY *adj* dark or gloomy
MURL *vb* crumble
MURLAIN *n* type of basket
MURLAINS > MURLAIN
MURLAN *same as*
> MURLAIN
MURLANS > MURLAN
MURLED > MURL
MURLIER > MURL
MURLIEST > MURL
MURLIN *same as*
> MURLAIN
MURLING > MURL
MURLINS > MURLIN
MURLS > MURL
MURLY > MURL
MURMUR *vb* speak or say in a quiet indistinct way ▷ *n* continuous low indistinct sound
MURMURED > MURMUR
MURMURER > MURMUR
MURMURERS > MURMUR
MURMURING > MURMUR
MURMUROUS > MURMUR
MURMURS > MURMUR
MURPHIES > MURPHY
MURPHY *dialect or informal word for* > POTATO
MURR *n* former name for a cold
MURRA *same as*
> MURRHINE
MURRAGH *n* type of large caddis fly
MURRAGHS > MURRAGH
MURRAIN *n* cattle plague
MURRAINED > MURRAIN
MURRAINS > MURRAIN
MURRAM *n* type of gravel
MURRAMS > MURRAM
MURRAS > MURRA
MURRAY *n* large Australian freshwater fish
MURRAYS > MURRAY
MURRE *n* type of guillemot
MURREE *n* native Australian
MURREES > MURREE
MURRELET *n* type of small diving bird related to the auks
MURRELETS
> MURRELET
MURREN *same as*
> MURRAIN
MURRENS > MURREN
MURRES > MURRE
MURREY *adj* mulberry colour
MURREYS > MURREY
MURRHA *same as* > MURRA
MURRHAS > MURRHA
MURRHINE *adj* of or relating to an unknown substance used in ancient Rome to make vases,

cups, etc ▷ *n* substance so used
MURRHINES
> MURRHINE
MURRI *same as* > MURREE
MURRIES > MURRY
MURRIN *same as*
> MURRAIN
MURRINE *same as*
> MURRHINE
MURRINES > MURRINE
MURRINS > MURRIN
MURRION *same as*
> MURRAIN
MURRIONS > MURRION
MURRIS > MURRI
MURRS > MURR
MURRY *same as* > MORAY
MURSHID *n* Sufi master or guide
MURSHIDS > MURSHID
MURTHER *same as*
> MURDER
MURTHERED > MURTHER
MURTHERER > MURTHER
MURTHERS > MURTHER
MURTI *n* image of a deity, which itself is considered divine
MURTIS > MURTI
MURVA *n* type of hemp
MURVAS > MURVA
MUS > MU
MUSACEOUS *adj* of, relating to, a family of tropical flowering plants with large leaves and clusters of elongated berry fruits: includes the banana, edible plantain, and Manila hemp
MUSANG *n* catlike animal of Malaysia
MUSANGS > MUSANG
MUSAR *n* rabbinic literature concerned with ethics
MUSARS > MUSAR
MUSCA *n* small constellation in the S hemisphere
MUSCADEL *same as*
> MUSCATEL
MUSCADELS
> MUSCADEL
MUSCADET *n* white grape, used for making wine
MUSCADETS
> MUSCADET
MUSCADIN *n* Parisian dandy
MUSCADINE *n* woody climbing plant of the southeastern US
MUSCADINS
> MUSCADIN
MUSCAE > MUSCA
MUSCARINE *n* poisonous alkaloid occurring in certain mushrooms
MUSCAT *same as*
> MUSCATEL
MUSCATEL *n* rich sweet wine made from muscat grapes
MUSCATELS
> MUSCATEL

MUSCATS > MUSCAT
MUSCAVADO *same as*
> MUSCOVADO
MUSCID *n* type of fly
MUSCIDS > MUSCID
MUSCLE *n* tissue in the body which produces movement ▷ *vb* force one's way (in)
MUSCLED > MUSCLE
MUSCLEMAN *n* man with highly developed muscles
MUSCLEMEN
> MUSCLEMAN
MUSCLES > MUSCLE
MUSCLEY *adj* of a muscular build
MUSCLIER > MUSCLEY
MUSCLIEST > MUSCLEY
MUSCLING > MUSCLE
MUSCLINGS > MUSCLE
MUSCLY *same as*
> MUSCLEY
MUSCOID *adj* moss-like ▷ *n* moss-like plant
MUSCOIDS > MUSCOID
MUSCOLOGY *n* branch of botany
MUSCONE *same as*
> MUSKONE
MUSCONES > MUSCONE
MUSCOSE *adj* like moss
MUSCOVADO *n* raw sugar obtained from the juice of sugar cane by evaporating the molasses
MUSCOVITE *n* pale brown, or green, or colourless mineral of the mica group
MUSCOVY *adj* as in muscovy duck a kind of duck
MUSCULAR *adj* with well-developed muscles
MUSCULOUS *adj* muscular
MUSE *vb* ponder quietly ▷ *n* state of abstraction
MUSED > MUSE
MUSEFUL > MUSE
MUSEFULLY > MUSE
MUSEOLOGY *n* science of museum organization
MUSER > MUSE
MUSERS > MUSE
MUSES > MUSE
MUSET *same as* > MUSIT
MUSETS > MUSET
MUSETTE *n* type of bagpipe formerly popular in France
MUSETTES > MUSETTE
MUSEUM *n* building where objects are exhibited and preserved
MUSEUMS > MUSEUM
MUSH *n* soft pulpy mass ▷ *interj* order to dogs in a sled team to start up or go faster ▷ *vb* travel by or drive a dogsled
MUSHA *interj* Irish exclamation of surprise
MUSHED > MUSH
MUSHER > MUSH
MUSHERS > MUSH
MUSHES > MUSH
MUSHIE *n* mushroom

MUSHIER > MUSHY
MUSHIES > MUSHIE
MUSHIEST > MUSHY
MUSHILY > MUSHY
MUSHINESS > MUSHY
MUSHING *n* act of mushing
MUSHINGS > MUSHING
MUSHMOUTH *n* person speaking indistinctly
MUSHRAT *same as*
> MUSKRAT
MUSHRATS *same as*
> MUSHRAT
MUSHROOM *n* edible fungus with a stem and cap ▷ *vb* grow rapidly
MUSHROOMS
> MUSHROOM
MUSHROOMY *adj* like a mushroom
MUSHY *adj* soft and pulpy
MUSIC *n* art form using a melodious and harmonious combination of notes ▷ *vb* play music
MUSICAL *adj* of or like music ▷ *n* play or film with songs and dancing
MUSICALE *n* party or social evening with a musical programme
MUSICALES
> MUSICALE
MUSICALLY > MUSICAL
MUSICALS > MUSICAL
MUSICIAN *n* person who plays or composes music, esp as a profession
MUSICIANS
> MUSICIAN
MUSICK *same as* > MUSIC
MUSICKED > MUSIC
MUSICKER > MUSIC
MUSICKERS > MUSIC
MUSICKING > MUSIC
MUSICKS > MUSICK
MUSICLESS > MUSIC
MUSICS > MUSIC
MUSIMON *same as*
> MOUFFLON
MUSIMONS > MUSIMON
MUSING > MUSE
MUSINGLY > MUSE
MUSINGS > MUSE
MUSIT *n* gap in fence
MUSITS > MUSIT
MUSIVE *adj* mosaic
MUSJID *same as*
> MASJID
MUSJIDS > MUSJID
MUSK *n* scent obtained from a gland of the musk deer or produced synthetically ▷ *vb* perfume with musk
MUSKED > MUSK
MUSKEG *n* area of undrained boggy land
MUSKEGS > MUSKEG
MUSKET *n* long-barrelled gun
MUSKETEER *n* (formerly) a soldier armed with a musket
MUSKETOON *n* small musket

MUSKETRY n (use of) muskets

MUSKETS > MUSKET

MUSKIE n large North American freshwater game fish

MUSKIER > MUSKY

MUSKIES > MUSKIE

MUSKIEST > MUSKY

MUSKILY > MUSKY

MUSKINESS > MUSKY

MUSKING > MUSK

MUSKIT same as > MESQUITE

MUSKITS > MUSKIT

MUSKLE same as > MUSSEL

MUSKLES > MUSKLE

MUSKMELON n any of several varieties of melon, such as the cantaloupe and honeydew

MUSKONE n substance in musk

MUSKONES > MUSKONE

MUSKOX n large Canadian mammal

MUSKOXEN > MUSKOX

MUSKRAT n N American beaver-like rodent

MUSKRATS > MUSKRAT

MUSKROOT same as > MOSCHATEL

MUSKROOTS > MUSKROOT

MUSKS > MUSK

MUSKY adj smelling of musk

MUSLIN n fine cotton fabric

MUSLINED adj wearing muslin

MUSLINET n coarse muslin

MUSLINETS > MUSLINET

MUSLINS > MUSLIN

MUSMON same as > MUSIMON

MUSMONS > MUSMON

MUSO n musician who is concerned with technique rather than content or expression

MUSOS > MUSO

MUSPIKE n Canadian freshwater fish

MUSPIKES > MUSPIKE

MUSQUASH same as > MUSKRAT

MUSROL n part of bridle

MUSROLS > MUSROL

MUSS vb make untidy ▷ n state of disorder

MUSSE same as > MUSS

MUSSED > MUSS

MUSSEL n edible shellfish with a dark hinged shell

MUSSELLED adj poisoned through eating bad mussels

MUSSELS > MUSSEL

MUSSES > MUSS

MUSSIER > MUSSY

MUSSIEST > MUSSY

MUSSILY > MUSSY

MUSSINESS > MUSSY

MUSSING > MUSS

MUSSITATE vb mutter

MUSSY adj untidy or disordered

MUST vb used as an auxiliary to express obligation, certainty, or resolution ▷ n essential or necessary thing

MUSTACHE same as > MOUSTACHE

MUSTACHED > MUSTACHE

MUSTACHES > MUSTACHE

MUSTACHIO n moustache, esp a bushy or elaborate one

MUSTANG n wild horse of SW USA

MUSTANGS > MUSTANG

MUSTARD n paste made from the powdered seeds of a plant ▷ adj brownish-yellow

MUSTARDS > MUSTARD

MUSTARDY adj like mustard

MUSTED > MUST

MUSTEE n person of mixed ancestry

MUSTEES > MUSTEE

MUSTELID n member of weasel family

MUSTELIDS > MUSTELID

MUSTELINE n type of predatory mammal of the family which includes weasels, ferrets, polecats, badgers, and otters

MUSTER vb summon up ▷ n assembly of military personnel

MUSTERED > MUSTER

MUSTERER > MUSTER

MUSTERERS > MUSTER

MUSTERING > MUSTER

MUSTERS > MUSTER

MUSTH n state of frenzied excitement in the males of certain large mammals

MUSTHS > MUSTH

MUSTIER > MUSTY

MUSTIEST > MUSTY

MUSTILY > MUSTY

MUSTINESS > MUSTY

MUSTING > MUST

MUSTS > MUST

MUSTY adj smelling mouldy and stale

MUT another word for > EM

MUTABLE adj liable to change

MUTABLY > MUTABLE

MUTAGEN n any substance that can induce genetic mutation

MUTAGENIC > MUTAGEN

MUTAGENS > MUTAGEN

MUTANDA > MUTANDUM

MUTANDUM n something to be changed

MUTANT n mutated animal, plant, etc ▷ adj of or resulting from mutation

MUTANTS > MUTANT

MUTASE n type of enzyme

MUTASES > MUTASE

MUTATE vb (cause to) undergo mutation

MUTATED > MUTATE

MUTATES > MUTATE

MUTATING > MUTATE

MUTATION same as > MUTANT

MUTATIONS > MUTATION

MUTATIVE > MUTATE

MUTATOR n something that causes a mutation

MUTATORS > MUTATOR

MUTATORY adj subject to change

MUTCH n close-fitting linen cap ▷ vb cadge

MUTCHED > MUTCH

MUTCHES > MUTCH

MUTCHING > MUTCH

MUTCHKIN n Scottish unit of liquid measure equal to slightly less than one pint

MUTCHKINS > MUTCHKIN

MUTE adj silent ▷ vb reduce the volume or soften the tone of a musical instrument

MUTED adj (of sound or colour) softened

MUTEDLY > MUTED

MUTELY > MUTE

MUTENESS > MUTE

MUTER > MUTE

MUTES > MUTE

MUTEST > MUTE

MUTHA n taboo slang word derived from motherfucker

MUTHAS > MUTHA

MUTI n medicine, esp herbal medicine

MUTICATE same as > MUTICOUS

MUTICOUS adj lacking an awn, spine, or point

MUTILATE vb deprive of a limb or other part

MUTILATED > MUTILATE

MUTILATES > MUTILATE

MUTILATOR > MUTILATE

MUTINE vb mutiny

MUTINED > MUTINE

MUTINEER n person who mutinies

MUTINEERS > MUTINEER

MUTINES > MUTINE

MUTING > MUTE

MUTINIED > MUTINY

MUTINIES > MUTINY

MUTINING > MUTINE

MUTINOUS adj openly rebellious

MUTINY n rebellion against authority, esp by soldiers or sailors ▷ vb commit mutiny

MUTINYING > MUTINY

MUTIS > MUTI

MUTISM n state of being mute

MUTISMS > MUTISM

MUTON n part of gene

MUTONS > MUTON

MUTOSCOPE n early form of cine camera

MUTS > MUT

MUTT n mongrel dog

MUTTER vb utter or speak indistinctly ▷ n muttered sound or grumble

MUTTERED > MUTTER

MUTTERER > MUTTER

MUTTERERS > MUTTER

MUTTERING > MUTTER

MUTTERS > MUTTER

MUTTON n flesh of sheep, used as food

MUTTONIER > MUTTONY

MUTTONS > MUTTON

MUTTONY adj like mutton

MUTTS > MUTT

MUTUAL adj felt or expressed by each of two people about the other ▷ n mutual company

MUTUALISE same as > MUTUALIZE

MUTUALISM another name for > SYMBIOSIS

MUTUALIST > MUTUALISM

MUTUALITY > MUTUAL

MUTUALIZE vb make or become mutual

MUTUALLY > MUTUAL

MUTUALS > MUTUAL

MUTUCA same as > MOTUCA

MUTUCAS > MUTUCA

MUTUEL n system of betting

MUTUELS > MUTUEL

MUTULAR > MUTULE

MUTULE n flat block in a Doric cornice

MUTULES > MUTULE

MUTUUM n contract for loan of goods

MUTUUMS > MUTUUM

MUUMUU n loose brightly coloured dress worn by women in Hawaii

MUUMUUS > MUUMUU

MUX vb spoil

MUXED > MUX

MUXES > MUX

MUXING > MUX

MUZAK n piped background music

MUZAKIER > MUZAKY

MUZAKIEST > MUZAKY

MUZAKS > MUZAK

MUZAKY adj having a bland sound

MUZHIK n Russian peasant, esp under the tsars

MUZHIKS > MUZHIK

MUZJIK same as > MUZHIK

MUZJIKS > MUZJIK

MUZZ vb make (something) muzzy

MUZZED > MUZZ

MUZZES > MUZZ

MUZZIER > MUZZY

MUZZIEST > MUZZY

MUZZILY > MUZZY

MUZZINESS > MUZZY

MUZZING > MUZZ

MUZZLE n animal's mouth and nose ▷ vb prevent from being heard or noticed

MUZZLED > MUZZLE

MUZZLER > MUZZLE

MUZZLERS > MUZZLE

MUZZLES > MUZZLE

MUZZLING > MUZZLE

MUZZY adj confused or muddled

MVULE n tropical African tree

MVULES > MVULE

MWAH interj representation of the sound of a kiss

MWALIMU n teacher

MWALIMUS > MWALIMU

MY adj belonging to me ▷ interj exclamation of surprise or awe

MYAL > MYALISM

MYALGIA n pain in a muscle or a group of muscles

MYALGIAS > MYALGIA

MYALGIC > MYALGIA

MYALISM n kind of witchcraft

MYALISMS > MYALISM

MYALIST > MYALISM

MYALISTS > MYALISM

MYALL n Australian acacia with hard scented wood

MYALLS > MYALL

MYASES > MYASIS

MYASIS same as > MYIASIS

MYC n oncogene that aids the growth of tumorous cells

MYCELE n microscopic spike-like structure in mucus

MYCELES > MYCELE

MYCELIA > MYCELIUM

MYCELIAL > MYCELIUM

MYCELIAN > MYCELIUM

MYCELIUM n mass forming the body of a fungus

MYCELLA n blue-veined Danish cream cheese

MYCELLAS > MYCELLA

MYCELOID > MYCELIUM

MYCETES n fungus

MYCETOMA n chronic fungal infection

MYCETOMAS > MYCETOMA

MYCOBIONT n fungal constituent of a lichen

MYCOFLORA n all fungus growing in particular place

MYCOLOGIC > MYCOLOGY

MYCOLOGY n study of fungi

MYCOPHAGY n eating of mushrooms

MYCOPHILE n person who likes eating mushrooms

MYCORHIZA n association of a fungus

and a plant in which the fungus lives within or on the outside of the plant's roots forming a symbiotic or parasitic relationship

MYCOSES > MYCOSIS

MYCOSIS n any infection or disease caused by fungus

MYCOTIC > MYCOSIS

MYCOTOXIN n any of various toxic substances produced by fungi some of which may affect food and others of which are alleged to have been used in warfare

MYCOVIRUS n virus attacking fungi

MYCS > MYC

MYDRIASES > MYDRIASIS

MYDRIASIS n abnormal dilation of the pupil of the eye

MYDRIATIC adj relating to or causing mydriasis ▷ n mydriatic drug

MYELIN n white tissue forming an insulating sheath around certain nerve fibres

MYELINE same as > MYELIN

MYELINES > MYELINE

MYELINIC > MYELIN

MYELINS > MYELIN

MYELITES > MYELITIS

MYELITIS n inflammation of the spinal cord or of the bone marrow

MYELOCYTE n immature granulocyte, normally occurring in the bone marrow but detected in the blood in certain diseases

MYELOGRAM n X-ray of the spinal cord, after injection with a radio-opaque medium

MYELOID adj of or relating to the spinal cord or the bone marrow

MYELOMA n tumour of the bone marrow

MYELOMAS > MYELOMA

MYELOMATA > MYELOMA

MYELON n spinal cord

MYELONS > MYELON

MYGALE n large American spider

MYGALES > MYGALE

MYIASES > MYIASIS

MYIASIS n infestation of the body by the larvae of flies

MYIOPHILY same as > MYOPHILY

MYLAR n tradename for a kind of strong polyester film

MYLARS > MYLAR

MYLODON n prehistoric giant sloth

MYLODONS > MYLODON

MYLODONT same as > MYLODON

MYLODONTS > MYLODONT

MYLOHYOID n muscle in neck

MYLONITE n fine-grained metamorphic rock

MYLONITES > MYLONITE

MYLONITIC > MYLONITE

MYNA same as > MYNAH

MYNAH n tropical Asian starling which can mimic human speech

MYNAHS > MYNAH

MYNAS > MYNA

MYNHEER n Dutch title of address

MYNHEERS > MYNHEER

MYOBLAST n cell from which muscle develops

MYOBLASTS > MYOBLAST

MYOCARDIA pl n muscular tissues of the heart

MYOCLONIC > MYOCLONUS

MYOCLONUS n sudden involuntary muscle contraction

MYOFIBRIL n type of cell in muscle

MYOGEN n albumin found in muscle

MYOGENIC adj originating in or forming muscle tissue

MYOGENS > MYOGEN

MYOGLOBIN n protein that is the main oxygen-carrier of muscle

MYOGRAM n tracings of muscular contractions

MYOGRAMS > MYOGRAM

MYOGRAPH n instrument for recording tracings of muscular contractions

MYOGRAPHS > MYOGRAPH

MYOGRAPHY > MYOGRAPH

MYOID adj like muscle ▷ n section of a retinal cone or rod which is sensitive to changes in light intensity

MYOIDS > MYOID

MYOLOGIC > MYOLOGY

MYOLOGIES > MYOLOGY

MYOLOGIST > MYOLOGY

MYOLOGY n study of the structure and diseases of muscles

MYOMA n benign tumour composed of muscle tissue

MYOMANCY n divination through observing mice

MYOMANTIC > MYOMANCY

MYOMAS > MYOMA

MYOMATA > MYOMA

MYOMATOUS > MYOMA

MYOMERE n part of a vertebrate embryo

MYOMERES > MYOMERE

MYONEURAL adj involving muscle and nerve

MYOPATHIC > MYOPATHY

MYOPATHY n any disease affecting muscles or muscle tissue

MYOPE n a person with myopia

MYOPES > MYOPE

MYOPHILY n pollination of plants by flies

MYOPIA n short-sightedness

MYOPIAS > MYOPIA

MYOPIC n shortsighted person

MYOPICS > MYOPIC

MYOPIES > MYOPY

MYOPS same as > MYOPE

MYOPSES > MYOPS

MYOPY same as > MYOPIA

MYOSCOPE n electrical instrument for stimulating muscles

MYOSCOPES > MYOSCOPE

MYOSES > MYOSIS

MYOSIN n protein found in muscle

MYOSINS > MYOSIN

MYOSIS same as > MIOSIS

MYOSISES > MYOSIS

MYOSITIS n inflammation of muscle

MYOSOTE same as > MYOSOTIS

MYOSOTES > MYOSOTE

MYOSOTIS n type of hairy-leaved flowering plant, such as the forget-me-not

MYOSTATIN n protein that inhibits muscle tissue growth

MYOTIC > MIOSIS

MYOTICS > MIOSIS

MYOTOME n any segment of embryonic mesoderm that develops into skeletal muscle

MYOTOMES > MYOTOME

MYOTONIA n lack of muscle tone, frequently including muscle spasm or rigidity

MYOTONIAS > MYOTONIA

MYOTONIC > MYOTONIA

MYOTUBE n cylindrical cell in muscle

MYOTUBES > MYOTUBE

MYRBANE same as > MIRBANE

MYRBANES > MYRBANE

MYRIAD adj innumerable ▷ n large indefinite number

MYRIADS > MYRIAD

MYRIADTH > MYRIAD

MYRIADTHS > MYRIAD

MYRIAPOD n type of invertebrate with a long segmented body and many legs, such as a centipede

MYRIAPODS > MYRIAPOD

MYRICA n dried root bark of the wax myrtle
MYRICAS > MYRICA
MYRINGA n eardrum
MYRINGAS > MYRINGA
MYRIOPOD same as > MYRIAPOD
MYRIOPODS > MYRIOPOD
MYRIORAMA n picture made up of different parts
MYRISTIC adj of nutmeg plant family
MYRMECOID adj ant-like
MYRMIDON n follower or henchperson
MYRMIDONS > MYRMIDON
MYROBALAN n dried plumlike fruit of various tropical trees, used in dyeing, tanning, ink, and medicine
MYRRH n aromatic gum used in perfume, incense, and medicine
MYRRHIC > MYRRH
MYRRHIER > MYRRHY
MYRRHIEST > MYRRHY
MYRRHINE > MURRA
MYRRHOL n oil of myrrh
MYRRHOLS > MYRRHOL
MYRRHS > MYRRH
MYRRHY adj of or like myrrh
MYRTLE n flowering evergreen shrub
MYRTLES > MYRTLE
MYSELF pron reflexive form of I or me
MYSID n small shrimplike crustacean
MYSIDS > MYSID
MYSOST n Norwegian cheese
MYSOSTS > MYSOST

MYSPACE vb search for (someone) on the MySpace website
MYSPACED > MYSPACE
MYSPACES > MYSPACE
MYSPACING > MYSPACE
MYSTAGOG n person instructing others in religious mysteries
MYSTAGOGS > MYSTAGOG
MYSTAGOGY n instruction of those who are preparing for initiation into the mysteries
MYSTERIES > MYSTERY
MYSTERY n strange or inexplicable thing
MYSTIC n person who seeks spiritual knowledge ▷ adj mystical
MYSTICAL adj having a spiritual or religious significance beyond human understanding
MYSTICETE n species of whale
MYSTICISM n belief in or experience of a reality beyond normal human understanding or experience
MYSTICLY > MYSTIC
MYSTICS > MYSTIC
MYSTIFIED > MYSTIFY
MYSTIFIER > MYSTIFY
MYSTIFIES > MYSTIFY
MYSTIFY vb bewilder or puzzle
MYSTIQUE n aura of mystery or power
MYSTIQUES > MYSTIQUE
MYTH n tale with supernatural characters
MYTHI > MYTHUS
MYTHIC same as > MYTHICAL

MYTHICAL adj of or relating to myth
MYTHICISE same as > MYTHICIZE
MYTHICISM n theory that explains miracles as myths
MYTHICIST > MYTHICIZE
MYTHICIZE vb make into or treat as a myth
MYTHIER > MYTHY
MYTHIEST > MYTHY
MYTHISE same as > MYTHIZE
MYTHISED > MYTHISE
MYTHISES > MYTHISE
MYTHISING > MYTHISE
MYTHISM same as > MYTHICISM
MYTHISMS > MYTHISM
MYTHIST > MYTHISM
MYTHISTS > MYTHISM
MYTHIZE same as > MYTHICIZE
MYTHIZED > MYTHIZE
MYTHIZES > MYTHIZE
MYTHIZING > MYTHIZE
MYTHMAKER n person who creates myth
MYTHOI > MYTHOS
MYTHOLOGY n myths collectively
MYTHOMANE n obsession with lying, exaggerating, or relating incredible imaginary adventures as if they had really happened
MYTHOPEIC adj of myths
MYTHOPOET n poet writing on mythical theme
MYTHOS n beliefs of a specific group or society
MYTHS > MYTH
MYTHUS same as > MYTHOS

MYTHY adj of or like myth
MYTILOID adj like mussel
MYXAMEBA same as > MYXAMOEBA
MYXAMEBAE > MYXAMEBA
MYXAMEBAS > MYXAMEBA
MYXAMOEBA n cell produced by spore
MYXEDEMA same as > MYXOEDEMA
MYXEDEMAS > MYXEDEMA
MYXEDEMIC > MYXOEDEMA
MYXO n viral disease of rabbits
MYXOCYTE n cell in mucous tissue
MYXOCYTES > MYXOCYTE
MYXOEDEMA n disease caused by an underactive thyroid gland
MYXOID adj containing mucus
MYXOMA n tumour composed of mucous connective tissue
MYXOMAS > MYXOMA
MYXOMATA > MYXOMA
MYXOS > MYXO
MYXOVIRAL > MYXOVIRUS
MYXOVIRUS n any of a group of viruses that cause influenza, mumps, and certain other diseases
MZEE n old person ▷ adj advanced in years
MZEES > MZEE
MZUNGU n (in E Africa) White person
MZUNGUS > MZUNGU

Nn

NA *same as* > NAE
NAAM *same as* > NAM
NAAMS > NAAM
NAAN *n* slightly leavened flat Indian bread
NAANS > NAAN
NAARTJE *same as* > NAARTJIE
NAARTJES > NAARTJE
NAARTJIE *n* tangerine
NAARTJIES > NAARTJIE
NAB *vb* arrest (someone)
NABBED > NAB
NABBER *n* thief
NABBERS > NABBER
NABBING > NAB
NABE *n* Japanese hotpot
NABES > NABE
NABIS *n* Parisian art movement
NABK *n* edible berry
NABKS > NABK
NABLA *another name for* > DEL
NABLAS > NABLA
NABOB *n* rich, powerful, or important man
NABOBERY > NABOB
NABOBESS > NABOB
NABOBISH > NABOB
NABOBISM > NABOB
NABOBISMS > NABOB
NABOBS > NABOB
NABS > NAB
NACARAT *n* red-orange colour
NACARATS > NACARAT
NACELLE *n* streamlined enclosure on an aircraft
NACELLES > NACELLE
NACH *n* Indian dance
NACHAS *n* pleasure
NACHE *n* rump
NACHES > NACHE
NACHO *n* snack of a piece of tortilla with a topping
NACHOS > NACHO
NACHTMAAL *same as* > NAGMAAL
NACKET *n* light lunch, snack
NACKETS > NACKET
NACRE *n* mother of pearl
NACRED > NACRE
NACREOUS > NACRE
NACRES > NACRE
NACRITE *n* mineral
NACRITES > NACRITE
NACROUS > NACRE
NADA *n* nothing
NADAS > NADA

NADIR *n* point in the sky opposite the zenith
NADIRAL > NADIR
NADIRS > NADIR
NADORS *n* thirst brought on by excess of alcohol
NADS *pl n* vulgar word for testicles
NAE *Scot word for* > NO
NAEBODIES > NAEBODY
NAEBODY *Scots variant of* > NOBODY
NAES > NAE
NAETHING *Scots variant of* > NOTHING
NAETHINGS > NAETHING
NAEVE *n* birthmark
NAEVES > NAEVE
NAEVI > NAEVUS
NAEVOID > NAEVUS
NAEVUS *n* birthmark or mole
NAFF *adj* lacking quality or taste ▷ *vb* go away
NAFFED > NAFF
NAFFER > NAFF
NAFFEST > NAFF
NAFFING > NAFF
NAFFLY > NAFF
NAFFNESS > NAFF
NAFFS > NAFF
NAG *vb* scold or find fault constantly ▷ *n* person who nags
NAGA *n* cobra
NAGANA *n* disease of all domesticated animals of central and southern Africa
NAGANAS > NAGANA
NAGAPIE *n* bushbaby
NAGAPIES > NAGAPIE
NAGARI *n* scripts for writing several languages of India
NAGARIS > NAGARI
NAGAS > NAGA
NAGGED > NAG
NAGGER > NAG
NAGGERS > NAG
NAGGIER > NAG
NAGGIEST > NAG
NAGGING > NAG
NAGGINGLY > NAG
NAGGINGS > NAGGING
NAGGY > NAG
NAGMAAL *n* Communion
NAGMAALS > NAGMAAL
NAGOR *another name for* > REEDBUCK
NAGORS > NAGOR
NAGS > NAG

NAGWARE *n* software that is initially free and then requires payment
NAGWARES > NAGWARE
NAH *same as* > NO
NAHAL *n* agricultural settlement run by an Israeli military youth organization
NAHALS > NAHAL
NAIAD *n* nymph living in a lake or river
NAIADES > NAIAD
NAIADS > NAIAD
NAIANT *adj* swimming
NAIF *less common word for* > NAIVE
NAIFER > NAIF
NAIFEST > NAIF
NAIFLY > NAIF
NAIFNESS > NAIF
NAIFS > NAIF
NAIK *n* chief
NAIKS > NAIK
NAIL *n* pointed piece of metal used to join two objects together ▷ *vb* attach (something) with nails
NAILBITER *n* person who bites his or her nails
NAILBRUSH *n* small stiff-bristled brush for cleaning the fingernails
NAILED > NAIL
NAILER > NAIL
NAILERIES > NAILERY
NAILERS > NAIL
NAILERY *n* nail factory
NAILFILE *n* small metal file used to shape and smooth the nails
NAILFILES > NAILFILE
NAILFOLD *n* skin at base of fingernail
NAILFOLDS > NAILFOLD
NAILHEAD *n* decorative device, as on tooled leather, resembling the round head of a nail
NAILHEADS > NAILHEAD
NAILING > NAIL
NAILINGS > NAIL
NAILLESS > NAIL
NAILS > NAIL
NAILSET *n* punch for driving down the head of a nail
NAILSETS > NAILSET
NAIN *adj* own
NAINSELL *n* own self

NAINSELLS > NAINSELL
NAINSOOK *n* light soft plain-weave cotton fabric, used esp for babies' wear
NAINSOOKS > NAINSOOK
NAIRA *n* standard monetary unit of Nigeria, divided into 100 kobo
NAIRAS > NAIRA
NAIRU *n* Non-Accelerating Inflation Rate of Unemployment
NAIRUS > NAIRU
NAISSANCE *French for* > BIRTH
NAISSANT *adj* (of a beast) having only the forepart shown above a horizontal division of a shield
NAIVE *adj* innocent and gullible ▷ *n* person who is naive, esp in artistic style
NAIVELY > NAIVE
NAIVENESS > NAIVE
NAIVER > NAIVE
NAIVES > NAIVE
NAIVEST > NAIVE
NAIVETE *variant of* > NAIVETY
NAIVETES > NAIVETE
NAIVETIES > NAIVETY
NAIVETY *n* state or quality of being naive
NAIVIST > NAIVE
NAKED *adj* without clothes
NAKEDER > NAKED
NAKEDEST > NAKED
NAKEDLY > NAKED
NAKEDNESS > NAKED
NAKER *n* small kettledrum used in medieval music
NAKERS > NAKER
NAKFA *n* standard currency unit of Eritrea
NAKFAS > NAKFA
NALA *n* ravine
NALAS > NALA
NALED *n* type of insecticide
NALEDS > NALED
NALIDIXIC *adj* as in nalidixic acid type of acid
NALLA *n* ravine
NALLAH *same as* > NALLA
NALLAHS > NALLAH
NALLAS > NALLA
NALOXONE *n* substance that counteracts opiates
NALOXONES > NALOXONE

NAM n distraint
NAMABLE > NAME
NAMASKAR n salutation used in India
NAMASKARS > NAMASKAR
NAMASTE n Indian greeting
NAMASTES > NAMASTE
NAMAYCUSH n North American freshwater fish
NAME n word by which a person or thing is known ▷ vb give a name to
NAMEABLE > NAME
NAMECHECK vb mention (someone) by name ▷ n mention of someone's name, for example on a radio programme
NAMED > NAME
NAMELESS adj without a name
NAMELY adv that is to say
NAMEPLATE n small sign on or by a door giving the occupant's name and, sometimes, profession
NAMER > NAME
NAMERS > NAME
NAMES > NAME
NAMESAKE n person with the same name as another
NAMESAKES > NAMESAKE
NAMETAG n identification badge
NAMETAGS > NAMETAG
NAMETAPE n narrow cloth tape bearing the owner's name and attached to an article
NAMETAPES > NAMETAPE
NAMING > NAME
NAMINGS > NAME
NAMMA adj as in namma hole Australian word for a natural well in rock
NAMS > NAM
NAMU n black New Zealand sandfly
NAMUS > NAMU
NAN n grandmother
NANA same as > NAN
NANAS > NANA
NANDIN same as > NANDINA
NANDINA n type of shrub
NANDINAS > NANDINA
NANDINE n African palm civet
NANDINES > NANDINE
NANDINS > NANDIN
NANDOO same as > NANDU
NANDOOS > NANDOO
NANDU n type of ostrich
NANDUS > NANDU
NANE Scot word for > NONE
NANG adj excellent; cool
NANISM n dwarfism
NANISMS > NANISM
NANITE n microscopically small machine or robot
NANITES > NANITE
NANKEEN n hard-wearing buff-coloured cotton fabric

NANKEENS > NANKEEN
NANKIN same as > NANKEEN
NANKINS > NANKIN
NANNA same as > NAN
NANNAS > NANNA
NANNIE same as > NANNY
NANNIED > NANNY
NANNIES > NANNY
NANNY n woman whose job is looking after young children ▷ vb be too protective towards
NANNYGAI n edible sea fish of Australia which is red in colour and has large prominent eyes
NANNYGAIS > NANNYGAI
NANNYING n act of nannying
NANNYINGS > NANNYING
NANNYISH > NANNY
NANO n science concerned with materials on a molecular scale
NANOBE n microbe that is smaller than the smallest known bacterium
NANOBEE n artificial nanoparticle
NANOBEES > NANOBEE
NANOBES > NANOBE
NANOBOT n microscopically small robot
NANOBOTS > NANOBOT
NANODOT n microscopic cluster of atoms used to store data in a computer chip
NANODOTS > NANODOT
NANOGRAM n unit of measurement
NANOGRAMS > NANOGRAM
NANOGRASS n type of synthetic surface
NANOMETER same as > NANOMETRE
NANOMETRE n one thousand-millionth of a metre
NANOOK n polar bear
NANOOKS > NANOOK
NANOPORE n microscopically small pore in an electrically insulating membrane
NANOPORES > NANOPORE
NANOS > NANO
NANOSCALE adj on very small scale
NANOTECH n technology of very small objects
NANOTECHS > NANOTECH
NANOTESLA n unit of measurement
NANOTUBE n cylindrical molecule of carbon
NANOTUBES > NANOTUBE
NANOWATT n unit of measurement

NANOWATTS > NANOWATT
NANOWIRE n microscopically thin wire
NANOWIRES > NANOWIRE
NANOWORLD n world at a microscopic level, as dealt with by nanotechnology
NANS > NAN
NANUA same as > MOKI
NANUAS > NANUA
NAOI > NAOS
NAOS n ancient classical temple
NAOSES > NAOS
NAP n short sleep ▷ vb have a short sleep
NAPA n type of leather
NAPALM n highly inflammable jellied petrol, used in bombs ▷ vb attack (people or places) with napalm
NAPALMED > NAPALM
NAPALMING > NAPALM
NAPALMS > NAPALM
NAPAS > NAPA
NAPE n back of the neck ▷ vb attack with napalm
NAPED > NAPE
NAPERIES > NAPERY
NAPERY n household linen, esp table linen
NAPES > NAPE
NAPHTHA n liquid mixture used as a solvent and in petrol
NAPHTHAS > NAPHTHA
NAPHTHENE n any of a class of cycloalkanes found in petroleum
NAPHTHOL n white crystalline solid used in dyes
NAPHTHOLS > NAPHTHOL
NAPHTHOUS > NAPHTHA
NAPHTHYL n type of monovalent radical
NAPHTHYLS > NAPHTHYL
NAPHTOL same as > NAPHTHOL
NAPHTOLS > NAPHTOL
NAPIFORM adj shaped like a turnip
NAPING > NAPE
NAPKIN same as > NAPPY
NAPKINS > NAPKIN
NAPLESS adj threadbare
NAPOLEON n former French gold coin worth 20 francs
NAPOLEONS > NAPOLEON
NAPOO vb military slang meaning kill
NAPOOED > NAPOO
NAPOOING > NAPOO
NAPOOS > NAPOO
NAPPA n soft leather
NAPPAS > NAPPA
NAPPE n mass of rock that has been thrust from its original position by earth movements
NAPPED > NAP

NAPPER n person or thing that raises the nap on cloth
NAPPERS > NAPPER
NAPPES > NAPPE
NAPPIE same as > NAPPY
NAPPIER > NAPPY
NAPPIES > NAPPY
NAPPIEST > NAPPY
NAPPINESS > NAPPY
NAPPING > NAP
NAPPY n piece of absorbent material fastened round a baby's lower torso ▷ adj having a nap
NAPRON same as > APRON
NAPRONS > NAPRON
NAPROXEN n pain-killing drug
NAPROXENS > NAPROXEN
NAPS > NAP
NARAS same as > NARRAS
NARASES > NARAS
NARC n narcotics agent
NARCEEN same as > NARCEINE
NARCEENS > NARCEEN
NARCEIN same as > NARCEINE
NARCEINE n narcotic alkaloid that occurs in opium
NARCEINES > NARCEINE
NARCEINS > NARCEIN
NARCISM n exceptional admiration for oneself
NARCISMS > NARCISM
NARCISSI > NARCISSUS
NARCISSUS n yellow, orange, or white flower related to the daffodil
NARCIST n narcissist
NARCISTIC adj excessively admiring of oneself
NARCISTS > NARCIST
NARCO same as > NARC
NARCOMA n coma caused by intake of narcotic drugs
NARCOMAS > NARCOMA
NARCOMATA > NARCOMA
NARCOS > NARCO
NARCOSE same as > NARCOSIS
NARCOSES > NARCOSIS
NARCOSIS n effect of a narcotic
NARCOTIC adj of a drug which produces numbness and drowsiness ▷ n such a drug
NARCOTICS > NARCOTIC
NARCOTINE n type of drug
NARCOTISE same as > NARCOTIZE
NARCOTISM n addiction to narcotic drugs
NARCOTIST n person affected by narcotics
NARCOTIZE vb place under the influence of a narcotic drug

n

NARCS > NARC
NARD n any of several plants with aromatic roots ▷ vb anoint with nard oil
NARDED > NARD
NARDINE > NARD
NARDING > NARD
NARDOO n cloverlike fern which grows in swampy areas
NARDOOS > NARDOO
NARDS > NARD
NARE n nostril
NARES pl n nostrils
NARGHILE another name for > HOOKAH
NARGHILES > NARGHILE
NARGHILLY same as > NARGHILE
NARGHILY same as > NARGHILE
NARGILE same as > NARGHILE
NARGILEH same as > NARGHILE
NARGILEHS > NARGHILE
NARGILES > NARGILE
NARGILIES > NARGILE
NARGILY same as > NARGHILE
NARGUILEH n hookah
NARIAL adj of or relating to the nares
NARIC > NARES
NARICORN n bird's nostril
NARICORNS > NARICORN
NARINE same as > NARIAL
NARIS > NARES
NARK vb annoy ▷ n informer or spy
NARKED > NARK
NARKIER > NARKY
NARKIEST > NARKY
NARKING > NARK
NARKS > NARK
NARKY adj irritable or complaining
NARQUOIS adj malicious
NARRAS n type of shrub
NARRASES > NARRAS
NARRATE vb tell (a story)
NARRATED > NARRATE
NARRATER same as > NARRATOR
NARRATERS > NARRATER
NARRATES > NARRATE
NARRATING > NARRATE
NARRATION n narrating
NARRATIVE n account, story ▷ adj telling a story
NARRATOR n person who tells a story or gives an account of something
NARRATORS > NARRATOR
NARRATORY > NARRATIVE
NARRE adj nearer
NARROW adj small in breadth in comparison to length ▷ vb make or become narrow
NARROWED > NARROW

NARROWER > NARROW
NARROWEST > NARROW
NARROWING > NARROW
NARROWISH > NARROW
NARROWLY > NARROW
NARROWS pl n narrow part of a strait, river, or current
NARTHEX n portico at the west end of a basilica or church
NARTHEXES > NARTHEX
NARTJIE same as > NAARTJIE
NARTJIES > NARTJIE
NARWAL same as > NARWHAL
NARWALS > NARWAL
NARWHAL n Arctic whale with a long spiral tusk
NARWHALE same as > NARWHAL
NARWHALES > NARWHALE
NARWHALS > NARWHAL
NARY adv not
NAS vb has not
NASAL adj of the nose ▷ n nasal speech sound, such as English m, n, or ng
NASALISE same as > NASALIZE
NASALISED > NASALISE
NASALISES > NASALISE
NASALISM n nasal pronunciation
NASALISMS > NASALISM
NASALITY > NASAL
NASALIZE vb pronounce nasally
NASALIZED > NASALIZE
NASALIZES > NASALIZE
NASALLY > NASAL
NASALS > NASAL
NASARD n organ stop
NASARDS > NASARD
NASCENCE > NASCENT
NASCENCES > NASCENT
NASCENCY > NASCENT
NASCENT adj starting to grow or develop
NASEBERRY another name for > SAPODILLA
NASHGAB n chatter
NASHGABS > NASHGAB
NASHI n fruit of the Japanese pear
NASHIS > NASHI
NASIAL > NASION
NASION n craniometric point where the top of the nose meets the ridge of the forehead
NASIONS > NASION
NASSELLA n as in nassella tussock type of tussock grass
NASTALIK n type of script
NASTALIKS > NASTALIK
NASTIC adj (of movement of plants) independent of

the direction of the external stimulus
NASTIER > NASTY
NASTIES > NASTY
NASTIEST > NASTY
NASTILY > NASTY
NASTINESS > NASTY
NASTY adj unpleasant ▷ n something unpleasant
NASUTE n type of termite
NASUTES > NASUTE
NAT n supporter of nationalism
NATAL adj of or relating to birth
NATALITY n birth rate in a given place
NATANT adj (of aquatic plants) floating on the water
NATANTLY adv in a floating manner
NATATION n swimming
NATATIONS > NATATION
NATATORIA pl n indoor swimming pools
NATATORY adj of or relating to swimming
NATCH sentence substitute naturally ▷ n notch
NATCHES > NATCH
NATES pl n buttocks
NATHELESS prep notwithstanding
NATHEMO same as > NATHEMORE
NATHEMORE adv nevermore
NATHLESS same as > NATHELESS
NATIFORM adj resembling buttocks
NATION n country and its social and political structures
NATIONAL adj of or serving a nation as a whole ▷ n citizen of a nation
NATIONALS > NATIONAL
NATIONS > NATION
NATIS > NATES
NATIVE adj relating to a place where a person was born ▷ n person born in a place
NATIVELY > NATIVE
NATIVES > NATIVE
NATIVISM n policy of favouring the natives of a country over the immigrants
NATIVISMS > NATIVISM
NATIVIST > NATIVISM
NATIVISTS > NATIVISM
NATIVITY n birth or origin
NATRIUM obsolete name for > SODIUM
NATRIUMS > NATRIUM
NATROLITE n colourless, white, or yellow zeolite mineral

NATRON n whitish or yellow mineral
NATRONS > NATRON
NATS > NAT
NATTER vb talk idly or chatter ▷ n long idle chat
NATTERED > NATTER
NATTERER > NATTER
NATTERERS > NATTER
NATTERIER > NATTERY
NATTERING > NATTER
NATTERS > NATTER
NATTERY adj irritable
NATTIER > NATTY
NATTIEST > NATTY
NATTILY > NATTY
NATTINESS > NATTY
NATTY adj smart and spruce
NATURA n nature
NATURAE > NATURA
NATURAL adj normal or to be expected ▷ n person with an inborn talent or skill
NATURALLY > NATURAL
NATURALS > NATURAL
NATURE n whole system of the physical world not controlled by human beings
NATURED adj having a certain disposition
NATURES > NATURE
NATURING adj creative
NATURISM n nudism
NATURISMS > NATURISM
NATURIST > NATURISM
NATURISTS > NATURISM
NAUCH same as > NAUTCH
NAUCHES > NAUCH
NAUGAHYDE n type of vinyl-coated fabric
NAUGHT n nothing ▷ adv not at all
NAUGHTIER > NAUGHTY
NAUGHTIES > NAUGHTY
NAUGHTILY > NAUGHTY
NAUGHTS > NAUGHT
NAUGHTY adj disobedient or mischievous ▷ n act of sexual intercourse
NAUMACHIA n mock sea fight performed as an entertainment
NAUMACHY same as > NAUMACHIA
NAUNT n aunt
NAUNTS > NAUNT
NAUPLIAL adj of or like a nauplius, the larval form of certain crustaceans
NAUPLII > NAUPLIUS
NAUPLIOID > NAUPLIUS
NAUPLIUS n larva of many crustaceans
NAUSEA n feeling of being about to vomit
NAUSEANT n substance inducing nausea
NAUSEANTS > NAUSEANT
NAUSEAS > NAUSEA
NAUSEATE vb make (someone) feel sick

NAUSEATED
> NAUSEATE
NAUSEATES
> NAUSEATE
NAUSEOUS *adj* as if about to vomit
NAUTCH *n* intricate traditional Indian dance
NAUTCHES > NAUTCH
NAUTIC *same as* > NAUTICAL
NAUTICAL *adj* of the sea or ships
NAUTICS *n* science of navigation
NAUTILI > NAUTILUS
NAUTILOID *n* type of mollusc ▷ *adj* of this type of mollusc
NAUTILUS *n* shellfish with many tentacles
NAV *n* (short for) navigation
NAVAID *n* navigational aid
NAVAIDS > NAVAID
NAVAL *adj* of or relating to a navy or ships
NAVALISM *n* domination of naval interests
NAVALISMS
> NAVALISM
NAVALLY > NAVAL
NAVAR *n* system of air navigation
NAVARCH *n* admiral
NAVARCHS > NAVARCH
NAVARCHY *n* navarch's term of office
NAVARHO *n* aircraft navigation system
NAVARHOS > NAVARHO
NAVARIN *n* stew of mutton or lamb with root vegetables
NAVARINS > NAVARIN
NAVARS > NAVAR
NAVE *n* long central part of a church
NAVEL *n* hollow in the middle of the abdomen
NAVELS > NAVEL
NAVELWORT *another name for* > PENNYWORT
NAVES > NAVE
NAVETTE *n* gem cut
NAVETTES > NAVETTE
NAVEW *another name for* > TURNIP
NAVEWS > NAVEW
NAVICERT *n* certificate specifying the contents of a neutral ship's cargo
NAVICERTS
> NAVICERT
NAVICULA *n* incense holder
NAVICULAR *adj* shaped like a boat ▷ *n* small boat-shaped bone of the wrist or foot
NAVICULAS
> NAVICULA
NAVIES > NAVY
NAVIGABLE *adj* wide, deep, or safe enough to be sailed through
NAVIGABLY
> NAVIGABLE

NAVIGATE *vb* direct or plot the path or position of a ship, aircraft, or car
NAVIGATED
> NAVIGATE
NAVIGATES
> NAVIGATE
NAVIGATOR *n* person who is skilled in or performs navigation, esp on a ship or aircraft
NAVS > NAV
NAVVIED > NAVVY
NAVVIES > NAVVY
NAVVY *n* labourer employed on a road or a building site ▷ *vb* work as a navvy
NAVVYING > NAVVY
NAVY *n* warships with their crews and organization ▷ *adj* navy-blue
NAW *same as* > NO
NAWAB *n* (formerly) a Muslim ruler or landowner in India
NAWABS > NAWAB
NAY *interj* no ▷ *n* person who votes against a motion ▷ *adv* used for emphasis ▷ *sentence substitute* no
NAYS > NAY
NAYSAID > NAYSAY
NAYSAY *vb* say no
NAYSAYER > NAYSAY
NAYSAYERS
> NAYSAYER
NAYSAYING > NAYSAY
NAYSAYS > NAYSAY
NAYTHLES *same as* > NATHELESS
NAYWARD *n* as in *to the nayward* towards denial
NAYWARDS *same as* > NAYWARD
NAYWORD *n* proverb
NAYWORDS > NAYWORD
NAZE *n* flat marshy headland
NAZES > NAZE
NAZI *n* person who thinks or acts in a brutal or dictatorial way
NAZIFIED > NAZIFY
NAZIFIES > NAZIFY
NAZIFY *vb* make nazi in character
NAZIFYING > NAZIFY
NAZIR *n* Muslim official
NAZIRS > NAZIR
NAZIS > NAZI
NDUJA *n* spicy pork paste
NDUJAS > NDUJA
NE *conj* nor
NEAFE *same as* > NIEVE
NEAFES > NEAFE
NEAFFE *same as* > NIEVE
NEAFFES > NEAFFE
NEAL *same as* > ANNEAL
NEALED > NEAL
NEALING > NEAL
NEALS > NEAL
NEANIC *adj* of or relating to the early stages in a life cycle

NEAP *adj* of, relating to, or constituting a neap tide ▷ *vb* be grounded by a neap tide
NEAPED > NEAP
NEAPING > NEAP
NEAPS > NEAP
NEAR *adj* indicating a place or time not far away ▷ *vb* draw close (to) ▷ *prep* at or to a place or time not far away from ▷ *adv* at or to a place or time not far away ▷ *n* left side of a horse or vehicle
NEARBY *adj* not far away ▷ *adv* close at hand
NEARED > NEAR
NEARER > NEAR
NEAREST > NEAR
NEARING > NEAR
NEARISH *adj* quite near
NEARLIER > NEARLY
NEARLIEST > NEARLY
NEARLY *adv* almost
NEARNESS > NEAR
NEARS > NEAR
NEARSHORE *n* area of coastline water ▷ *adj* situated close to a shore ▷ *vb* get business services carried out in a neighbouring country
NEARSIDE *n* side of a vehicle that is nearer the kerb
NEARSIDES
> NEARSIDE
NEAT *adj* tidy and clean ▷ *n* domestic bovine animal
NEATEN *vb* make neat
NEATENED > NEATEN
NEATENING > NEATEN
NEATENS > NEATEN
NEATER > NEAT
NEATEST > NEAT
NEATH *short for* > BENEATH
NEATHERD *n* cowherd
NEATHERDS
> NEATHERD
NEATLY > NEAT
NEATNESS > NEAT
NEATNIK *n* very neat and tidy person
NEATNIKS > NEATNIK
NEATS > NEAT
NEB *n* beak of a bird or the nose of an animal ▷ *vb* look around nosily
NEBBED > NEB
NEBBICH *same as* > NEBBISH
NEBBICHS > NEBBICH
NEBBING > NEB
NEBBISH *n* timid person
NEBBISHE *same as* > NEBBISH
NEBBISHER *same as* > NEBBISH
NEBBISHES > NEBBISH
NEBBISHY *adj* timid
NEBBUK *n* type of shrub
NEBBUKS > NEBBUK
NEBECK *same as* > NEBBUK
NEBECKS > NEBECK

NEBEK *same as* > NEBBUK
NEBEKS > NEBEK
NEBEL *n* Hebrew musical instrument
NEBELS > NEBEL
NEBENKERN *n* component of insect sperm
NEBISH *same as* > NEBBISH
NEBISHES > NEBISH
NEBRIS *n* fawn-skin
NEBRISES > NEBRIS
NEBS > NEB
NEBULA *n* hazy cloud of particles and gases
NEBULAE > NEBULA
NEBULAR > NEBULA
NEBULAS > NEBULA
NEBULE *n* cloud
NEBULES > NEBULE
NEBULISE *same as* > NEBULIZE
NEBULISED
> NEBULISE
NEBULISER *same as* > NEBULIZER
NEBULISES
> NEBULISE
NEBULIUM *n* element
NEBULIUMS
> NEBULIUM
NEBULIZE *vb* turn (a liquid) into a fine spray
NEBULIZED
> NEBULIZE
NEBULIZER *n* device which turns a drug from a liquid into a fine spray which can be inhaled
NEBULIZES
> NEBULIZE
NEBULOSE *same as* > NEBULOUS
NEBULOUS *adj* vague and unclear
NEBULY *adj* wavy
NECESSARY *adj* needed to obtain the desired result
NECESSITY *n* circumstances that inevitably require a certain result
NECK *n* part of the body joining the head to the shoulders ▷ *vb* kiss and cuddle
NECKATEE *n* piece of ornamental cloth worn around the neck
NECKATEES
> NECKATEE
NECKBAND *n* band around the neck of a garment
NECKBANDS
> NECKBAND
NECKBEEF *n* cheap cattle flesh
NECKBEEFS
> NECKBEEF
NECKCLOTH *n* large ornamental usually white cravat worn formerly by men
NECKED > NECK
NECKER > NECK

NECKERS > NECK

NECKGEAR *n* any neck covering

NECKGEARS > NECKGEAR

NECKING *n* activity of kissing and embracing passionately

NECKINGS > NECKING

NECKLACE *n* decorative piece of jewellery worn around the neck ▷ *vb* kill (someone) by placing a burning tyre round his or her neck

NECKLACED > NECKLACE

NECKLACES > NECKLACE

NECKLESS > NECK

NECKLET *n* ornament worn round the neck

NECKLETS > NECKLET

NECKLIKE > NECK

NECKLINE *n* shape or position of the upper edge of a dress or top

NECKLINES > NECKLINE

NECKPIECE *n* piece of fur, cloth, etc, worn around the neck or neckline

NECKS > NECK

NECKSHOT *n* shot in the neck of an animal

NECKSHOTS > NECKSHOT

NECKTIE *same as* > TIE

NECKTIES > NECKTIE

NECKVERSE *n* verse read to prove clergy membership

NECKWEAR *n* articles of clothing, such as ties, scarves, etc, worn around the neck

NECKWEARS > NECKWEAR

NECKWEED *n* type of plant

NECKWEEDS > NECKWEED

NECROLOGY *n* list of people recently dead

NECROPHIL *n* person who is sexually attracted to dead bodies

NECROPOLI *pl n* burial sites or cemeteries

NECROPSY *n* postmortem examination ▷ *vb* carry out a necropsy

NECROSE *vb* cause or undergo necrosis

NECROSED > NECROSE

NECROSES > NECROSE

NECROSING > NECROSE

NECROSIS *n* death of cells in the body

NECROTIC > NECROSIS

NECROTISE *same as* > NECROTIZE

NECROTIZE *vb* undergo necrosis

NECROTOMY *n* dissection of a dead body

NECTAR *n* sweet liquid collected from flowers by bees

NECTAREAL *adj* of or like nectar

NECTAREAN *adj* of or like nectar

NECTARED *adj* filled with nectar

NECTARIAL > NECTARY

NECTARIED *adj* having nectaries

NECTARIES > NECTARY

NECTARINE *n* smooth-skinned peach

NECTAROUS > NECTAR

NECTARS > NECTAR

NECTARY *n* structure secreting nectar in a plant

NED *n* derogatory name for an adolescent hooligan

NEDDIER > NEDDY

NEDDIES > NEDDY

NEDDIEST > NEDDY

NEDDISH > NED

NEDDY *n* donkey ▷ *adj* of or relating to neds

NEDETTE *n* derogatory name for a female adolescent hooligan

NEDETTES > NEDETTE

NEDS > NED

NEE *prep* indicating the maiden name of a married woman ▷ *adj* indicating the maiden name of a married woman

NEED *vb* require or be in want of ▷ *n* condition of lacking something

NEEDED > NEED

NEEDER > NEED

NEEDERS > NEED

NEEDFIRE *n* beacon

NEEDFIRES > NEEDFIRE

NEEDFUL *adj* necessary or required

NEEDFULLY > NEEDFUL

NEEDFULS *n* must-haves

NEEDIER > NEEDY

NEEDIEST > NEEDY

NEEDILY > NEEDY

NEEDINESS *n* state of being needy

NEEDING > NEED

NEEDLE *n* thin pointed piece of metal with an eye through which thread is passed for sewing ▷ *vb* goad or provoke

NEEDLED > NEEDLE

NEEDLEFUL *n* length of thread cut for use in a needle

NEEDLER *n* needle maker

NEEDLERS > NEEDLER

NEEDLES > NEEDLE

NEEDLESS *adj* unnecessary

NEEDLIER > NEEDLY

NEEDLIEST > NEEDLE

NEEDLING > NEEDLE

NEEDLINGS > NEEDLE

NEEDLY *adj* like or full of needles

NEEDMENT *n* a necessity

NEEDMENTS > NEED

NEEDS *adv* necessarily ▷ *pl n* what is required

NEEDY *adj* poor, in need of financial support

NEELD *same as* > NEEDLE

NEELDS > NEELD

NEELE *same as* > NEEDLE

NEELES > NEELE

NEEM *n* type of large Indian tree

NEEMB *same as* > NEEM

NEEMBS > NEEMB

NEEMS > NEEM

NEEP *dialect name for* > TURNIP

NEEPS > NEEP

NEESBERRY *same as* > NASEBERRY

NEESE *same as* > NEEZE

NEESED > NEESE

NEESES > NEESE

NEESING > NEESE

NEEZE *vb* sneeze

NEEZED > NEEZE

NEEZES > NEEZE

NEEZING > NEEZE

NEF *n* church nave

NEFANDOUS *adj* unmentionable

NEFARIOUS *adj* wicked

NEFAST *adj* wicked

NEFS > NEF

NEG *n* photographic negative

NEGATE *vb* invalidate

NEGATED > NEGATE

NEGATER > NEGATE

NEGATERS > NEGATE

NEGATES > NEGATE

NEGATING > NEGATE

NEGATION *n* opposite or absence of something

NEGATIONS > NEGATION

NEGATIVE *adj* expressing a denial or refusal ▷ *n* negative word or statement

NEGATIVED > NEGATIVE

NEGATIVES > NEGATIVE

NEGATON *same as* > NEGATRON

NEGATONS > NEGATON

NEGATOR > NEGATE

NEGATORS > NEGATE

NEGATORY *adj* relating to the act of negation

NEGATRON *obsolete word for* > ELECTRON

NEGATRONS > NEGATRON

NEGLECT *vb* take no care of ▷ *n* neglecting or being neglected

NEGLECTED > NEGLECT

NEGLECTER > NEGLECT

NEGLECTOR > NEGLECT

NEGLECTS > NEGLECT

NEGLIGE *variant of* > NEGLIGEE

NEGLIGEE *n* woman's lightweight usu lace-trimmed dressing gown

NEGLIGEES > NEGLIGEE

NEGLIGENT *adj* habitually neglecting duties, responsibilities, etc

NEGLIGES > NEGLIGE

NEGOCIANT *n* wine merchant

NEGOTIANT *n* person, nation, organization, etc, involved in a negotiation

NEGOTIATE *vb* discuss in order to reach (an agreement)

NEGRITUDE *n* awareness and affirmation of Black African heritage

NEGRONI *n* type of cocktail

NEGRONIS > NEGRONI

NEGS > NEG

NEGUS *n* hot drink of port and lemon juice

NEGUSES > NEGUS

NEIF *same as* > NIEVE

NEIFS > NEIF

NEIGH *n* loud high-pitched sound made by a horse ▷ *vb* make this sound

NEIGHBOR *same as* > NEIGHBOUR

NEIGHBORS > NEIGHBOR

NEIGHBOUR *n* person who lives or is situated near another ▷ *vb* be or live close (to a person or thing)

NEIGHED > NEIGH

NEIGHING *n* act of neighing

NEIGHINGS > NEIGHING

NEIGHS > NEIGH

NEINEI *n* type of plant

NEINEIS > NEINEI

NEIST *Scots variant of* > NEXT

NEITHER *pron* not one nor the other ▷ *adj* not one nor the other (of two)

NEIVE *same as* > NIEVE

NEIVES > NEIVE

NEK *n* mountain pass

NEKS > NEK

NEKTON *n* free-swimming animals in the middle depths of a sea or lake

NEKTONIC > NEKTON

NEKTONS > NEKTON

NELIES *same as* > NELIS

NELIS *n* type of pear

NELLIE *n* type of albatross

NELLIES > NELLIE

NELLY *n* as in *not on your nelly* not under any circumstances

NELSON *n* type of wrestling hold

NELSONS > NELSON

NELUMBIUM *same as* > NELUMBO

NELUMBO *n* type of aquatic plant

NELUMBOS > NELUMBO

NEMA *n* filament

NEMAS > NEMA

NEMATIC *n* substance having a mesomorphic state

NEMATICS > NEMATIC

NEMATODE n slender cylindrical unsegmented worm
NEMATODES > NEMATODE
NEMATOID > NEMATODE
NEMERTEAN n type of ribbon-like marine worm ▷ adj of this worm
NEMERTIAN same as > NEMERTEAN
NEMERTINE same as > NEMERTEAN
NEMESES > NEMESIS
NEMESIA n type of southern African plant
NEMESIAS > NEMESIA
NEMESIS n retribution or vengeance
NEMN vb name
NEMNED > NEMN
NEMNING > NEMN
NEMNS > NEMN
NEMOPHILA n any of a genus of low-growing hairy annual plants
NEMORAL adj of a wood
NEMOROUS adj woody
NEMPT adj named
NENE n rare black-and-grey short-winged Hawaiian goose
NENES > NENE
NENNIGAI same as > NANNYGAI
NENNIGAIS > NENNIGAI
NENUPHAR n type of water lily
NENUPHARS > NENUPHAR
NEOBLAST n worm cell
NEOBLASTS > NEOBLAST
NEOCON n supporter of neoconservative politics
NEOCONS > NEOCON
NEOCORTEX n part of the brain
NEODYMIUM n silvery-white metallic element of lanthanide series
NEOGENE adj of, denoting, or formed during the Miocene and Pliocene epochs
NEOGOTHIC n style of architecture popular in Britain in the 18th and 19th centuries
NEOLITH n Neolithic stone implement
NEOLITHIC n historical period characterized by polished stone tools and weapons ▷ adj relating to this period
NEOLITHS > NEOLITH
NEOLOGIAN > NEOLOGY
NEOLOGIC > NEOLOGISM
NEOLOGIES > NEOLOGY
NEOLOGISE same as > NEOLOGIZE
NEOLOGISM n newly coined word or an established word used in a new sense

NEOLOGIST > NEOLOGISM
NEOLOGIZE vb invent or use neologisms
NEOLOGY same as > NEOLOGISM
NEOMORPH n genetic component
NEOMORPHS > NEOMORPH
NEOMYCIN n type of antibiotic obtained from a bacterium
NEOMYCINS > NEOMYCIN
NEON n element used in illuminated signs and lights ▷ adj of or illuminated by neon
NEONATAL adj relating to the first few weeks of a baby's life
NEONATE n newborn child
NEONATES > NEONATE
NEONED adj lit with neon
NEONOMIAN n Christian religious belief
NEONS > NEON
NEOPAGAN n advocate of the revival of paganism
NEOPAGANS > NEOPAGAN
NEOPHILE n person who welcomes new things
NEOPHILES > NEOPHILE
NEOPHILIA n tendency to like anything new
NEOPHOBE > NEOPHOBIA
NEOPHOBES > NEOPHOBIA
NEOPHOBIA n tendency to dislike anything new
NEOPHOBIC > NEOPHOBIA
NEOPHYTE n beginner or novice
NEOPHYTES > NEOPHYTE
NEOPHYTIC > NEOPHYTE
NEOPILINA n type of mollusc
NEOPLASIA n abnormal growth of tissue
NEOPLASM n any abnormal new growth of tissue
NEOPLASMS > NEOPLASM
NEOPLASTY n surgical formation of new tissue structures or repair of damaged structures
NEOPRENE n synthetic rubber used in waterproof products
NEOPRENES > NEOPRENE
NEOSOUL n soul music combined with other genres
NEOSOULS > NEOSOUL
NEOTEINIA n state of prolonged immaturity
NEOTENIC > NEOTENY
NEOTENIES > NEOTENY

NEOTENOUS > NEOTENY
NEOTENY n persistence of larval or fetal features in the adult form of an animal
NEOTERIC adj belonging to a new fashion or trend ▷ n new writer or philosopher
NEOTERICS > NEOTERIC
NEOTERISE same as > NEOTERIZE
NEOTERISM n the introduction of new things, especially words
NEOTERIST n one who introduces new words or phrases
NEOTERIZE vb introduce new things
NEOTOXIN n harmful agent
NEOTOXINS > NEOTOXIN
NEOTROPIC adj of tropical America
NEOTYPE n specimen selected to replace a type specimen that has been lost or destroyed
NEOTYPES > NEOTYPE
NEP n catmint
NEPENTHE n drug that ancient writers referred to as a means of forgetting grief or trouble
NEPENTHES > NEPENTHE
NEPER n unit expressing the ratio of two quantities
NEPERS > NEPER
NEPETA same as > CATMINT
NEPETAS > NEPETA
NEPHALISM n teetotalism
NEPHALIST n one who advocates or practices nephalism
NEPHELINE n whitish mineral
NEPHELITE same as > NEPHELINE
NEPHEW n son of one's sister or brother
NEPHEWS > NEPHEW
NEPHOGRAM n photograph of a cloud
NEPHOLOGY n study of clouds
NEPHRALGY n pain in a kidney
NEPHRIC adj renal
NEPHRIDIA pl n simple excretory organs of many invertebrates
NEPHRISM n chronic kidney disease
NEPHRISMS > NEPHRISM
NEPHRITE n tough fibrous amphibole mineral
NEPHRITES > NEPHRITE
NEPHRITIC adj of or relating to the kidneys
NEPHRITIS n inflammation of a kidney

NEPHROID adj kidney-shaped
NEPHRON n urine-secreting tubule in the kidney
NEPHRONS > NEPHRON
NEPHROSES > NEPHROSIS
NEPHROSIS n any noninflammatory degenerative kidney disease
NEPHROTIC > NEPHROSIS
NEPIONIC adj of or relating to the juvenile period in the life cycle of an organism
NEPIT n unit of information equal to 1.44 bits
NEPITS > NEPIT
NEPOTIC > NEPOTISM
NEPOTISM n favouritism in business shown to relatives and friends
NEPOTISMS > NEPOTISM
NEPOTIST > NEPOTISM
NEPOTISTS > NEPOTISM
NEPS > NEP
NEPTUNIUM n synthetic radioactive metallic element
NERAL n isomer of citral
NERALS > NERAL
NERD n boring person obsessed with a particular subject
NERDIC same as > GEEKSPEAK
NERDICS > NERDIC
NERDIER > NERDY
NERDIEST > NERDY
NERDINESS > NERD
NERDISH > NERD
NERDS > NERD
NERDY adj clumsy, socially inept
NEREID n sea nymph in Greek mythology
NEREIDES > NEREID
NEREIDS > NEREID
NEREIS n type of marine worm
NERINE n type of S African plant related to the amaryllis
NERINES > NERINE
NERITE n type of sea snail
NERITES > NERITE
NERITIC adj of or formed in shallow seas near a coastline
NERK n fool
NERKA n type of salmon
NERKAS > NERKA
NERKS > NERK
NEROL n scented liquid
NEROLI n brown oil used in perfumery
NEROLIS > NEROLI
NEROLS > NEROL
NERTS interj nuts
NERTZ same as > NERTS
NERVAL > NERVE

NERVATE *adj* (of leaves) with veins

NERVATION *less common word for* > VENATION

NERVATURE *same as* > NERVATION

NERVE *n* bundle of fibres that conducts impulses between the brain and body ▷ *vb* give courage to oneself

NERVED > NERVE

NERVELESS *adj* numb, without feeling

NERVELET *n* small nerve

NERVELETS > NERVELET

NERVER *n* someone or something which nerves

NERVERS > NERVER

NERVES > NERVE

NERVIER > NERVY

NERVIEST > NERVY

NERVILY > NERVY

NERVINE *adj* having a soothing effect upon the nerves ▷ *n* nervine drug or agent

NERVINES > NERVINE

NERVINESS > NERVY

NERVING > NERVE

NERVINGS > NERVE

NERVOSITY *n* nervousness

NERVOUS *adj* apprehensive or worried

NERVOUSLY > NERVOUS

NERVULAR *adj* relating to a nervule

NERVULE *n* small vein

NERVULES > NERVULE

NERVURE *n* stiff rod in an insect's wing

NERVURES > NERVURE

NERVY *adj* excitable or nervous

NESCIENCE *formal or literary word for* > IGNORANCE

NESCIENT > NESCIENCE

NESCIENTS > NESCIENCE

NESH *adj* sensitive to the cold

NESHER > NESH

NESHEST > NESH

NESHNESS > NESH

NESS *n* headland, cape

NESSES > NESS

NEST *n* place or structure in which birds or certain animals lay eggs or give birth to young ▷ *vb* make or inhabit a nest

NESTABLE > NEST

NESTED > NEST

NESTER > NEST

NESTERS > NEST

NESTFUL *n* the contents of a nest

NESTFULS > NESTFUL

NESTING > NEST

NESTINGS > NEST

NESTLE *vb* snuggle

NESTLED > NESTLE

NESTLER > NESTLE

NESTLERS > NESTLE

NESTLES > NESTLE

NESTLIKE > NEST

NESTLING *n* bird too young to leave the nest

NESTLINGS > NESTLING

NESTMATE *n* bird that shares a nest with another bird

NESTMATES > NESTMATE

NESTOR *n* wise old man

NESTORS > NESTOR

NESTS > NEST

NET *n* fabric of meshes of string, thread, or wire with many openings ▷ *vb* catch (a fish or animal) in a net ▷ *adj* left after all deductions

NETBALL *n* team game in which a ball has to be thrown through a high net

NETBALLER > NETBALL

NETBALLS > NETBALL

NETBOOK *n* type of small laptop computer

NETBOOKS > NETBOOK

NETE *n* lyre string

NETES > NETE

NETFUL *n* the contents of a net

NETFULS > NETFUL

NETHEAD *n* expert on the internet

NETHEADS > NETHEAD

NETHELESS *same as* > NATHELESS

NETHER *adj* lower

NETIZEN *n* person who regularly uses the internet

NETIZENS > NETIZEN

NETLESS *adj* without a net

NETLIKE *adj* resembling a net

NETMINDER *n* goalkeeper

NETOP *n* friend

NETOPS > NETOP

NETROOT *n* activist who promotes a cause via the internet

NETROOTS > NETROOT

NETS > NET

NETSPEAK *n* jargon, abbreviations, and emoticons typically used by frequent internet users

NETSPEAKS > NETSPEAK

NETSUKE *n* (in Japan) a carved ornamental toggle

NETSUKES > NETSUKE

NETSURF *vb* browse the internet for information

NETSURFED > NETSURF

NETSURFER *n* person who surfs the internet

NETSURFS > NETSURF

NETT *same as* > NET

NETTABLE *adj* that can be netted

NETTED > NET

NETTER *n* person that makes nets

NETTERS > NETTER

NETTIE *n* enthusiastic user of the internet

NETTIER > NETTY

NETTIES > NETTY

NETTIEST > NETTY

NETTING > NET

NETTINGS > NET

NETTLE *n* plant with stinging hairs on the leaves ▷ *vb* bother or irritate

NETTLED > NETTLE

NETTLER *n* one that nettles

NETTLERS > NETTLER

NETTLES > NETTLE

NETTLIER > NETTLY

NETTLIEST > NETTLE

NETTLING > NETTLE

NETTLY *adj* like a nettle

NETTS > NETT

NETTY *n* lavatory ▷ *adj* resembling a net

NETWORK *n* system of intersecting lines, roads, etc ▷ *vb* broadcast (a programme) over a network

NETWORKED > NETWORK

NETWORKER *n* person who forms business contacts through informal social meetings

NETWORKS > NETWORK

NEUK *Scot word for* > NOOK

NEUKS > NEUK

NEUM *same as* > NEUME

NEUMATIC *adj* relating to a neume

NEUME *n* notational symbol

NEUMES > NEUME

NEUMIC > NEUME

NEUMS > NEUM

NEURAL *adj* of a nerve or the nervous system

NEURALGIA *n* severe pain along a nerve

NEURALGIC > NEURALGIA

NEURALLY > NEURAL

NEURATION *n* arrangement of veins

NEURAXON *n* biological cell component

NEURAXONS > NEURAXON

NEURILITY *n* properties of the nerves

NEURINE *n* poisonous alkaloid

NEURINES > NEURINE

NEURISM *n* nerve force

NEURISMS > NEURISM

NEURITE *n* biological cell component

NEURITES > NEURITE

NEURITIC > NEURITIS

NEURITICS > NEURITIS

NEURITIS *n* inflammation of a nerve or nerves

NEUROCHIP *n* semiconductor chip designed for use in an electronic neural network

NEUROCOEL *n* cavity in brain

NEUROGLIA *another name for* > GLIA

NEUROGRAM *same as* > ENGRAM

NEUROID *adj* resembling a nerve ▷ *n* either of the halves of a neural arch

NEUROIDS > NEUROID

NEUROLOGY *n* scientific study of the nervous system

NEUROMA *n* any tumour composed of nerve tissue

NEUROMAS > NEUROMA

NEUROMAST *n* sensory cell in fish

NEUROMATA > NEUROMA

NEURON *same as* > NEURONE

NEURONAL > NEURONE

NEURONE *n* cell specialized to conduct nerve impulses

NEURONES > NEURONE

NEURONIC > NEURONE

NEURONS > NEURON

NEUROPATH *n* person predisposed to a disorder of the nervous system

NEUROPIL *n* dense network of neurons and glia in the central nervous system

NEUROPILS > NEUROPIL

NEUROSAL *adj* relating to neurosis

NEUROSES > NEUROSIS

NEUROSIS *n* disorder producing anxiety or obsessive behaviour

NEUROTIC *adj* emotionally unstable ▷ *n* neurotic person

NEUROTICS > NEUROTIC

NEUROTOMY *n* surgical cutting of a nerve, esp to relieve intractable pain

NEURULA *n* stage of embryonic development

NEURULAE > NEURULA

NEURULAR > NEURULA

NEURULAS > NEURULA

NEUSTIC *n* part of a sentence that differs with mood

NEUSTICS > NEUSTIC

NEUSTON *n* organisms that float on the surface of open water

NEUSTONIC > NEUSTON

NEUSTONS > NEUSTON

NEUTER *adj* belonging to a particular class of grammatical inflections in some languages ▷ *vb* castrate (an animal) ▷ *n* neuter gender

NEUTERED > NEUTER

NEUTERING *n* act of castrating or spaying an animal

NEUTERS > NEUTER

NEUTRAL *adj* taking neither side in a war or dispute ▷ *n* neutral person or nation

NEUTRALLY > NEUTRAL
NEUTRALS > NEUTRAL
NEUTRETTO *n* neutrino associated with the muon
NEUTRINO *n* elementary particle with no mass or electrical charge
NEUTRINOS > NEUTRINO
NEUTRON *n* electrically neutral elementary particle
NEUTRONIC > NEUTRON
NEUTRONS > NEUTRON
NEVE *n* mass of porous ice, formed from snow
NEVEL *vb* beat with the fists
NEVELLED > NEVEL
NEVELLING > NEVEL
NEVELS > NEVEL
NEVER *adv* at no time ▷ *sentence substitute* at no time ▷ *interj* surely not!
NEVERMIND *n* difference
NEVERMORE *adv* never again
NEVES > NEVE
NEVI > NEVUS
NEVOID > NAEVUS
NEVUS *same as* > NAEVUS
NEW *adj* not existing before ▷ *adv* recently ▷ *vb* make new
NEWB *n* newbie
NEWBIE *n* person new to a job, club, etc
NEWBIES > NEWBIE
NEWBORN *adj* recently or just born ▷ *n* newborn baby
NEWBORNS > NEWBORN
NEWBS > NEWB
NEWCOME *adj* recently arrived
NEWCOMER *n* recent arrival or participant
NEWCOMERS > NEWCOMER
NEWED > NEW
NEWEL *n* post at the top or bottom of a flight of stairs
NEWELL *n* new thing
NEWELLED > NEWELL
NEWELLS > NEWELL
NEWELS > NEWEL
NEWER > NEW
NEWEST > NEW
NEWFANGLE *adj* newly come into existence or fashion ▷ *n* newfangled thing
NEWFOUND *adj* newly or recently discovered
NEWIE *n* fresh idea or thing
NEWIES > NEWIE
NEWING > NEW
NEWISH *adj* fairly new
NEWISHLY > NEWISH
NEWLY *adv* recently
NEWLYWED *n* recently married person
NEWLYWEDS > NEWLYWED
NEWMARKET *n* double-breasted waisted coat with a full skirt

NEWMOWN *adj* freshly cut
NEWNESS > NEW
NEWNESSES > NEW
NEWS *n* important or interesting new happenings ▷ *vb* report
NEWSAGENT *n* shopkeeper who sells newspapers and magazines
NEWSBEAT *n* particular area of news reporting
NEWSBEATS > NEWSBEAT
NEWSBOY *n* boy who sells or delivers newspapers
NEWSBOYS > NEWSBOY
NEWSBREAK *n* newsflash
NEWSCAST *n* radio or television broadcast of the news
NEWSCASTS > NEWSCAST
NEWSCLIP *n* brief extract from news broadcast
NEWSCLIPS > NEWSCLIP
NEWSDESK *n* news gathering and reporting department
NEWSDESKS > NEWSDESK
NEWSED > NEWS
NEWSES > NEWS
NEWSFEED *n* service that provides news articles for distribution
NEWSFEEDS > NEWSFEED
NEWSFLASH *n* brief important news item, which interrupts a radio or television programme
NEWSGIRL *n* female newsreader or reporter
NEWSGIRLS > NEWSGIRL
NEWSGROUP *n* forum where subscribers exchange information about a specific subject by email
NEWSHAWK *n* newspaper reporter
NEWSHAWKS > NEWSHAWK
NEWSHOUND *same as* > NEWSHAWK
NEWSIE *same as* > NEWSY
NEWSIER > NEWSY
NEWSIES > NEWSY
NEWSIEST > NEWSY
NEWSINESS > NEWSY
NEWSING > NEWS
NEWSLESS > NEWS
NEWSMAKER *n* person whose activities are reported in news
NEWSMAN *n* male newsreader or reporter
NEWSMEN > NEWSMAN
NEWSPAPER *n* weekly or daily publication containing news ▷ *vb* do newspaper related work
NEWSPEAK *n* deliberately ambiguous and misleading language of politicians and officials

NEWSPEAKS > NEWSPEAK
NEWSPRINT *n* inexpensive paper used for newspapers
NEWSREEL *n* short film giving news
NEWSREELS > NEWSREEL
NEWSROOM *n* room where news is received and prepared for publication or broadcasting
NEWSROOMS > NEWSROOM
NEWSSHEET *n* sheet giving news and information
NEWSSTAND *n* portable stand from which newspapers are sold
NEWSTRADE *n* newspaper retail
NEWSWIRE *n* electronic means of delivering up-to-the-minute news
NEWSWIRES > NEWSWIRE
NEWSWOMAN *n* female newsreader or reporter
NEWSWOMEN > NEWSWOMAN
NEWSY *adj* full of news ▷ *n* newsagent
NEWT *n* small amphibious creature
NEWTON *n* unit of force
NEWTONS > NEWTON
NEWTS > NEWT
NEWWAVER *n* member of new wave
NEWWAVERS > NEWWAVER
NEXT *adv* immediately following ▷ *n* next person or thing
NEXTDOOR *adj* in or at the adjacent house or building
NEXTLY > NEXT
NEXTNESS > NEXT
NEXTS > NEXT
NEXUS *n* connection or link
NEXUSES > NEXUS
NGAI *n* clan or tribe
NGAIO *n* small New Zealand tree
NGAIOS > NGAIO
NGANA *same as* > NAGANA
NGANAS > NGANA
NGARARA *n* lizard found in New Zealand
NGARARAS > NGARARA
NGATI *n* (occurring as part of the tribe name) a tribe or clan
NGATIS > NGATI
NGOMA *n* type of drum
NGOMAS > NGOMA
NGULTRUM *n* standard monetary unit of Bhutan, divided into 100 chetrum
NGULTRUMS > NGULTRUM
NGWEE *n* Zambian monetary unit
NGWEES > NGWEE
NHANDU *n* type of spider

NHANDUS > NHANDU
NIACIN *n* vitamin of the B complex
NIACINS > NIACIN
NIAGARA *n* deluge or outpouring
NIAGARAS > NIAGARA
NIAISERIE *n* simplicity
NIALAMIDE *n* type of drug
NIB *n* writing point of a pen ▷ *vb* provide with a nib
NIBBED > NIB
NIBBING > NIB
NIBBLE *vb* take little bites (of) ▷ *n* little bite
NIBBLED > NIBBLE
NIBBLER *n* person, animal, or thing that nibbles
NIBBLERS > NIBBLER
NIBBLES > NIBBLE
NIBBLIES > NIBBLY
NIBBLING > NIBBLE
NIBBLINGS > NIBBLE
NIBBLY *n* small item of food
NIBLET *n* very small piece of food
NIBLETS > NIBLET
NIBLICK *n* former golf club giving a great deal of lift
NIBLICKS > NIBLICK
NIBLIKE > NIB
NIBS > NIB
NICAD *n* rechargeable dry-cell battery
NICADS > NICAD
NICCOLITE *n* copper-coloured mineral
NICE *adj* pleasant
NICEISH > NICE
NICELY > NICE
NICENESS > NICE
NICER > NICE
NICEST > NICE
NICETIES > NICETY
NICETY *n* subtle point
NICHE *n* hollow area in a wall ▷ *adj* of or aimed at a specialist group or market ▷ *vb* place (a statue) in a niche
NICHED > NICHE
NICHER *vb* snigger
NICHERED > NICHER
NICHERING > NICHER
NICHERS > NICHER
NICHES > NICHE
NICHING > NICHE
NICHROME *n* (tradename) alloy of nickel and chrome
NICHROMES > NICHROME
NICHT *Scot word for* > NIGHT
NICHTS > NICHT
NICISH > NICE
NICK *vb* make a small cut in ▷ *n* small cut
NICKAR *n* hard seed
NICKARS > NICKAR
NICKED > NICK
NICKEL *n* silvery-white metal often used in alloys ▷ *vb* plate with nickel

n

NICKELED > NICKEL
NICKELIC adj of or containing metallic nickel
NICKELINE another name for **>** NICCOLITE
NICKELING > NICKEL
NICKELISE same as **>** NICKELIZE
NICKELIZE vb treat with nickel
NICKELLED > NICKEL
NICKELOUS adj of or containing nickel, esp in the divalent state
NICKELS > NICKEL
NICKER n pound sterling **>** vb (of a horse) to neigh softly
NICKERED > NICKER
NICKERING > NICKER
NICKERNUT n nut of the bonduc tree
NICKERS > NICKER
NICKING > NICK
NICKLE same as **>** NICKEL
NICKLED > NICKLE
NICKLES > NICKLE
NICKLING > NICKLE
NICKNACK n cheap ornament or trinket
NICKNACKS > NICKNACK
NICKNAME n familiar name given to a person or place **>** vb call by a nickname
NICKNAMED > NICKNAME
NICKNAMER > NICKNAME
NICKNAMES > NICKNAME
NICKPOINT n break in the slope of a river caused by renewed erosion
NICKS > NICK
NICKSTICK n tally
NICKUM n mischievous person
NICKUMS > NICKUM
NICOISE adj prepared with tomatoes, black olives, garlic and anchovies
NICOL n device for producing plane-polarized light
NICOLS > NICOL
NICOMPOOP n stupid person
NICOTIAN n tobacco user
NICOTIANA n American and Australian plant such as tobacco, with white, yellow, or purple fragrant flowers
NICOTIANS > NICOTIAN
NICOTIN same as **>** NICOTINE
NICOTINE n poisonous substance found in tobacco
NICOTINED > NICOTINE
NICOTINES > NICOTINE

NICOTINIC > NICOTINE
NICOTINS same as **>** NICOTIN
NICTATE same as **>** NICTITATE
NICTATED > NICTATE
NICTATES > NICTATE
NICTATING > NICTATE
NICTATION n act of blinking
NICTITANT adj blinking
NICTITATE vb blink
NID same as **>** NIDE
NIDAL > NIDUS
NIDAMENTA pl n egg capsules
NIDATE vb undergo nidation
NIDATED > NIDATE
NIDATES > NIDATE
NIDATING > NIDATE
NIDATION n implantation
NIDATIONS > NIDATION
NIDDERING n coward **>** adj cowardly
NIDDICK n nape of the neck
NIDDICKS > NIDDICK
NIDE vb nest
NIDED > NIDE
NIDERING same as **>** NIDDERING
NIDERINGS > NIDDERING
NIDERLING same as **>** NIDDERING
NIDES > NIDE
NIDGET n type of hoe **>** vb assist a woman in labour
NIDGETED > NIDGET
NIDGETING > NIDGET
NIDGETS > NIDGET
NIDI > NIDUS
NIDIFIED > NIDIFY
NIDIFIES > NIDIFY
NIDIFY vb (of a bird) to make or build a nest
NIDIFYING > NIDIFY
NIDING n coward
NIDINGS > NIDING
NIDOR n cooking smell
NIDOROUS > NIDOR
NIDORS > NIDOR
NIDS > NID
NIDUS n nest in which insects or spiders deposit their eggs
NIDUSES > NIDUS
NIE archaic spelling of **>** NIGH
NIECE n daughter of one's sister or brother
NIECES > NIECE
NIED > NIE
NIEF same as **>** NIEVE
NIEFS > NIEF
NIELLATED > NIELLO
NIELLI > NIELLO
NIELLIST > NIELLO
NIELLISTS > NIELLO
NIELLO n black compound of sulphur and silver, lead, or copper **>** vb decorate or treat with niello

NIELLOED > NIELLO
NIELLOING > NIELLO
NIELLOS > NIELLO
NIENTE adv softly fading away
NIES > NIE
NIEVE n closed hand
NIEVEFUL n closed handful
NIEVEFULS > NIEVE
NIEVES > NIEVE
NIFE n earth's core
NIFES > NIFE
NIFF n stink **>** vb stink
NIFFED > NIFF
NIFFER vb barter
NIFFERED > NIFFER
NIFFERING > NIFFER
NIFFERS > NIFFER
NIFFIER > NIFF
NIFFIEST > NIFF
NIFFING > NIFF
NIFFNAFF vb trifle
NIFFNAFFS > NIFFNAFF
NIFFS > NIFF
NIFFY > NIFF
NIFTIER > NIFTY
NIFTIES > NIFTY
NIFTIEST > NIFTY
NIFTILY > NIFTY
NIFTINESS > NIFTY
NIFTY adj neat or smart **>** n nifty thing
NIGELLA n type of Mediterranean plant
NIGELLAS > NIGELLA
NIGGARD n stingy person **>** adj miserly **>** vb act in a niggardly way
NIGGARDED > NIGGARD
NIGGARDLY adj stingy **>** adv stingily
NIGGARDS > NIGGARD
NIGGLE vb worry slightly **>** n small worry or doubt
NIGGLED > NIGGLE
NIGGLER > NIGGLE
NIGGLERS > NIGGLE
NIGGLES > NIGGLE
NIGGLIER > NIGGLE
NIGGLIEST > NIGGLE
NIGGLING adj petty **>** n act or instance of niggling
NIGGLINGS > NIGGLING
NIGGLY > NIGGLE
NIGH prep near **>** adv nearly **>** adj near **>** vb approach
NIGHED > NIGH
NIGHER > NIGH
NIGHEST > NIGH
NIGHING > NIGH
NIGHLY > NIGH
NIGHNESS > NIGH
NIGHS > NIGH
NIGHT n time of darkness between sunset and sunrise **>** adj of, occurring, or working at night
NIGHTBIRD same as **>** NIGHTHAWK
NIGHTCAP n drink taken just before bedtime
NIGHTCAPS > NIGHTCAP

NIGHTCLUB n establishment for dancing, music, etc, open late at night **>** vb go to nightclubs
NIGHTED adj darkened
NIGHTFALL n approach of darkness
NIGHTFIRE n fire burned at night
NIGHTGEAR n nightclothes
NIGHTGLOW n faint light from the upper atmosphere in the night sky, esp in low latitudes
NIGHTGOWN n loose dress worn in bed by women
NIGHTHAWK n type of American nightjar
NIGHTIE n nightgown
NIGHTIES > NIGHTIE
NIGHTJAR n nocturnal bird with a harsh cry
NIGHTJARS > NIGHTJAR
NIGHTLESS > NIGHT
NIGHTLIFE n entertainment and social activities available at night in a town or city
NIGHTLIKE > NIGHT
NIGHTLONG adv throughout the night
NIGHTLY adv (happening) each night **>** adj happening each night
NIGHTMARE n very bad dream
NIGHTMARY adj characterized by nightmares
NIGHTS adv at night or on most nights
NIGHTSIDE n dark side
NIGHTSPOT n nightclub
NIGHTTIDE same as **>** NIGHTTIME
NIGHTTIME n time from sunset to sunrise
NIGHTWARD > NIGHT
NIGHTWEAR n apparel worn in bed or before retiring to bed
NIGHTY same as **>** NIGHTIE
NIGIRI n small oval block of cold rice, wasabi and fish
NIGIRIS > NIGIRI
NIGRICANT adj black
NIGRIFIED > NIGRIFY
NIGRIFIES > NIGRIFY
NIGRIFY vb blacken
NIGRITUDE n blackness
NIGROSIN same as **>** NIGROSINE
NIGROSINE n type of black pigment and dye used in inks and shoe polishes
NIGROSINS > NIGROSIN
NIHIL n nil
NIHILISM n rejection of all established authority and institutions

NIHILISMS
> NIHILISM
NIHILIST > NIHILISM
NIHILISTS
> NIHILISM
NIHILITY n state or condition of being nothing
NIHILS > NIHIL
NIHONGA n Japanese form of painting
NIHONGAS > NIHONGA
NIHONIUM n highly radioactive element
NIHONIUMS
> NIHONIUM
NIKAB same as > NIQAB
NIKABS > NIKAB
NIKAH n Islamic marriage contract
NIKAHS > NIKAH
NIKAU n palm tree native to New Zealand
NIKAUS > NIKAU
NIL n nothing, zero
NILGAI n large Indian antelope
NILGAIS > NILGAI
NILGAU same as
> NILGHAU
NILGAUS > NILGAU
NILGHAI same as
> NILGAI
NILGHAIS > NILGHAI
NILGHAU same as
> NILGAI
NILGHAUS > NILGHAU
NILL vb be unwilling
NILLED > NILL
NILLING > NILL
NILLS > NILL
NILPOTENT n quantity that equals zero when raised to a particular power
NILS > NIL
NIM n game involving removing one or more small items from several rows or piles ▷ vb steal
NIMB n halo
NIMBED > NIMB
NIMBI > NIMBUS
NIMBLE adj agile and quick
NIMBLER > NIMBLE
NIMBLESSE > NIMBLE
NIMBLEST > NIMBLE
NIMBLEWIT n alert, bright, and clever person
NIMBLY > NIMBLE
NIMBS > NIMB
NIMBUS n dark grey rain cloud
NIMBUSED > NIMBUS
NIMBUSES > NIMBUS
NIMBYISM n practice of objecting to something that will affect one or take place in one's locality
NIMBYISMS
> NIMBYISM
NIMBYNESS same as
> NIMBYISM
NIMIETIES > NIMIETY
NIMIETY rare word for
> EXCESS
NIMIOUS > NIMIETY
NIMMED > NIM

NIMMER > NIM
NIMMERS > NIM
NIMMING > NIM
NIMONIC adj as in nimonic alloy type of nickel-based alloy
NIMPS adj easy
NIMROD n hunter
NIMRODS > NIMROD
NIMS > NIM
NINCOM same as
> NICOMPOOP
NINCOMS > NINCOM
NINCUM same as
> NICOMPOOP
NINCUMS > NINCUM
NINE n one more than eight
NINEBARK n North American shrub
NINEBARKS
> NINEBARK
NINEFOLD adj having nine times as many or as much ▷ adv by nine times as much or as many
NINEHOLES n type of game
NINEPENCE n (former) coin worth nine pennies
NINEPENNY same as
> NINEPENCE
NINEPIN n skittle used in ninepins
NINEPINS n game of skittles
NINER n (US) student in the ninth grade
NINERS > NINER
NINES > NINE
NINESCORE n product of nine times twenty
NINETEEN n ten and nine
NINETEENS
> NINETEEN
NINETIES > NINETY
NINETIETH adj being the ordinal number of ninety in numbering order ▷ n one of 90 approximately equal parts of something
NINETY n ten times nine
NINHYDRIN n chemical reagent used for the detection and analysis of primary amines
NINJA n person skilled in ninjutsu
NINJAS > NINJA
NINJITSU same as
> NINJUTSU
NINJITSUS
> NINJUTSU
NINJUTSU n Japanese martial art
NINJUTSUS
> NINJUTSU
NINNIES > NINNY
NINNY n stupid person
NINNYISH > NINNY
NINON n fine strong silky fabric
NINONS > NINON
NINTH n number nine in a series ▷ adj coming after the eighth

NINTHLY adv in the ninth place or position
NINTHS > NINTH
NIOBATE n type of salt crystal
NIOBATES > NIOBATE
NIOBIC adj of or containing niobium in the pentavalent state
NIOBITE another name for
> COLUMBITE
NIOBITES > NIOBITE
NIOBIUM n white metallic element
NIOBIUMS > NIOBIUM
NIOBOUS adj of or containing niobium in the trivalent state
NIP vb hurry ▷ n pinch or light bite
NIPA n palm tree of S and SE Asia
NIPAS > NIPA
NIPCHEESE n ship's purser
NIPPED > NIP
NIPPER n small child ▷ vb secure with rope
NIPPERED > NIPPER
NIPPERING > NIPPER
NIPPERKIN n small quantity of alcohol
NIPPERS pl n instrument or tool for pinching or squeezing
NIPPIER > NIPPY
NIPPIEST > NIPPY
NIPPILY > NIPPY
NIPPINESS > NIPPY
NIPPING > NIP
NIPPINGLY > NIP
NIPPLE n projection in the centre of a breast ▷ vb provide with a nipple
NIPPLED > NIPPLE
NIPPLES > NIPPLE
NIPPLING > NIPPLE
NIPPY adj frosty or chilly
NIPS > NIP
NIPTER n type of religious ceremony
NIPTERS > NIPTER
NIQAAB same as > NIQAB
NIQAABS > NIQAAB
NIQAB n type of veil worn by some Muslim women
NIQABS > NIQAB
NIRAMIAI n sumo wrestling procedure
NIRAMIAIS
> NIRAMIAI
NIRL vb shrivel
NIRLED > NIRL
NIRLIE variant of
> NIRLY
NIRLIER > NIRLY
NIRLIEST > NIRLY
NIRLING > NIRL
NIRLIT > NIRL
NIRLS > NIRL
NIRLY adj shrivelled
NIRVANA n absolute spiritual enlightenment and bliss
NIRVANAS > NIRVANA
NIRVANIC > NIRVANA
NIS n friendly goblin

NISBERRY same as
> NASEBERRY
NISEI n native-born citizen of the US or Canada whose parents were Japanese
NISEIS > NISEI
NISGUL n smallest and weakest bird in a brood of chickens
NISGULS > NISGUL
NISH n nothing
NISHES > NISH
NISI adj (of a court order) coming into effect on a specified date
NISSE same as > NIS
NISSES > NISSE
NISUS n impulse towards or striving after a goal
NIT n egg or larva of a louse
NITE variant of > NIGHT
NITER same as > NITRE
NITERIE n nightclub
NITERIES > NITERIE
NITERS > NITER
NITERY > NITER
NITES > NITE
NITHER vb shiver
NITHERED > NITHER
NITHERING > NITHER
NITHERS > NITHER
NITHING n coward
NITHINGS > NITHING
NITID adj bright
NITINOL n metal alloy
NITINOLS > NITINOL
NITON less common name for > RADON
NITONS > NITON
NITPICK vb criticize unnecessarily
NITPICKED > NITPICK
NITPICKER > NITPICK
NITPICKS > NITPICK
NITPICKY > NITPICK
NITRAMINE another name for > TETRYL
NITRATE n compound of nitric acid, used as a fertilizer ▷ vb treat with nitric acid or a nitrate
NITRATED > NITRATE
NITRATES > NITRATE
NITRATINE n type of mineral
NITRATING > NITRATE
NITRATION > NITRATE
NITRATOR > NITRATE
NITRATORS > NITRATE
NITRE n potassium nitrate
NITREOUS adj as in nitreous silica another name for quartz glass
NITRES > NITRE
NITRIC adj of or containing nitrogen
NITRID same as
> NITRIDE
NITRIDE n compound of nitrogen ▷ vb make into a nitride
NITRIDED > NITRIDE
NITRIDES > NITRIDE
NITRIDING > NITRIDE
NITRIDS > NITRID

NITRIFIED > NITRIFY
NITRIFIER > NITRIFY
NITRIFIES > NITRIFY
NITRIFY vb treat or cause to react with nitrogen
NITRIL same as > NITRILE
NITRILE n any one of a particular class of organic compounds
NITRILES > NITRILE
NITRILS > NITRIL
NITRITE n salt or ester of nitrous acid
NITRITES > NITRITE
NITRO n nitroglycerine
NITROGEN n colourless odourless gas that forms four fifths of the air
NITROGENS > NITROGEN
NITROLIC adj pertaining to a group of acids
NITROS > NITRO
NITROSO adj of a particular monovalent group
NITROSYL another word for > NITROSO
NITROSYLS > NITROSYL
NITROUS adj derived from or containing nitrogen in a low valency state
NITROX n mixture of nitrogen and oxygen used in diving
NITROXES > NITROX
NITROXYL n type of chemical
NITROXYLS > NITROXYL
NITRY adj nitrous
NITRYL n chemical compound
NITRYLS > NITRYL
NITS > NIT
NITTIER > NITTY
NITTIEST > NITTY
NITTY adj infested with nits
NITWIT n stupid person
NITWITS > NITWIT
NITWITTED > NITWIT
NIVAL adj of or growing in or under snow
NIVATION n weathering of rock around a patch of snow by alternate freezing and thawing
NIVATIONS > NIVATION
NIVEOUS adj resembling snow, esp in colour
NIX sentence substitute be careful! watch out! ▷ n rejection or refusal ▷ vb veto, deny, reject, or forbid (plans, suggestions, etc)
NIXE n water sprite
NIXED > NIX
NIXER n spare-time job
NIXERS > NIXER
NIXES > NIX
NIXIE n female water sprite, usually unfriendly to humans

NIXIES > NIXIE
NIXING > NIX
NIXY same as > NIXIE
NIZAM n (formerly) a Turkish regular soldier
NIZAMATE n territory of the nizam
NIZAMATES > NIZAMATE
NIZAMS > NIZAM
NKOSI n term of address to a superior
NKOSIS > NKOSI
NO interj expresses denial, disagreement, or refusal ▷ adj not any, not a ▷ adv not at all ▷ n answer or vote of 'no'
NOAH n shark
NOAHS > NOAH
NOB n person of wealth or social distinction
NOBBIER > NOB
NOBBIEST > NOB
NOBBILY > NOB
NOBBINESS > NOB
NOBBLE vb attract the attention of
NOBBLED > NOBBLE
NOBBLER > NOBBLE
NOBBLERS > NOBBLE
NOBBLES > NOBBLE
NOBBLING > NOBBLE
NOBBUT adv nothing but
NOBBY > NOB
NOBELIUM n artificially produced radioactive element
NOBELIUMS > NOBELIUM
NOBILESSE same as > NOBLESSE
NOBILIARY adj of or relating to the nobility
NOBILITY n quality of being noble
NOBLE adj showing or having high moral qualities ▷ n member of the nobility
NOBLEMAN n man of noble rank
NOBLEMEN > NOBLEMAN
NOBLENESS > NOBLE
NOBLER > NOBLE
NOBLES > NOBLE
NOBLESSE n noble birth or condition
NOBLESSES > NOBLESSE
NOBLEST > NOBLE
NOBLY > NOBLE
NOBODIES > NOBODY
NOBODY pron no person ▷ n person of no importance
NOBS > NOB
NOCAKE n Indian meal made from dried corn
NOCAKES > NOCAKE
NOCEBO n harmless substance that causes harmful effects in patients who expect it to be harmful
NOCEBOS > NOCEBO
NOCENT n guilty person
NOCENTLY > NOCENT

NOCENTS > NOCENT
NOCHEL same as > NOTCHEL
NOCHELED same as > NOTCHELED
NOCHELING n refusal to pay another person's debts
NOCHELLED > NOCHEL
NOCHELS > NOCHEL
NOCK n notch on an arrow or a bow for the bowstring ▷ vb fit (an arrow) on a bowstring
NOCKED > NOCK
NOCKET same as > NACKET
NOCKETS > NOCKET
NOCKING > NOCK
NOCKS > NOCK
NOCTILIO n type of bat
NOCTILIOS > NOCTILIO
NOCTILUCA n type of bioluminescent unicellular marine organism
NOCTUA n type of moth
NOCTUARY n nightly journal
NOCTUAS > NOCTUA
NOCTUID n type of nocturnal moth ▷ adj of or relating to this type of moth
NOCTUIDS > NOCTUID
NOCTULE n any of several large Old World insectivorous bats
NOCTULES > NOCTULE
NOCTUOID adj of or like a noctuid ▷ n member of the family of moths Noctuidae
NOCTUOIDS > NOCTUOID
NOCTURIA n excessive urination during the night
NOCTURIAS > NOCTURIA
NOCTURN n any of the main sections of the office of matins
NOCTURNAL adj of the night ▷ n something active at night
NOCTURNE n short dreamy piece of music
NOCTURNES > NOCTURNE
NOCTURNS > NOCTURN
NOCUOUS adj harmful
NOCUOUSLY > NOCUOUS
NOD vb lower and raise (one's head) briefly in agreement or greeting ▷ n act of nodding
NODAL adj of or like a node
NODALISE same as > NODALIZE
NODALISED same as > NODALISE
NODALISES same as > NODALISE
NODALITY > NODAL
NODALIZE vb make something nodal
NODALIZED > NODALIZE

NODALIZES > NODALIZE
NODALLY > NODAL
NODATED adj knotted
NODATION n knottiness
NODATIONS > NODATION
NODDED > NOD
NODDER > NOD
NODDERS > NOD
NODDIER > NODDY
NODDIES > NODDY
NODDIEST > NODDY
NODDING > NOD
NODDINGLY > NOD
NODDINGS > NOD
NODDLE n head ▷ vb nod (the head), as through drowsiness
NODDLED > NODDLE
NODDLES > NODDLE
NODDLING > NODDLE
NODDY n tropical tern with a dark plumage ▷ adj very easy to use or understand
NODE n point on a plant stem from which leaves grow
NODES > NODE
NODI > NODUS
NODICAL adj of or relating to the nodes of a celestial body
NODOSE adj having nodes or knotlike swellings
NODOSITY > NODOSE
NODOUS same as > NODOSE
NODS > NOD
NODULAR > NODULE
NODULATED > NODULE
NODULE n small knot or lump
NODULED > NODULE
NODULES > NODULE
NODULOSE > NODULE
NODULOUS > NODULE
NODUS n problematic idea, situation, etc
NOEL n Christmas
NOELS > NOEL
NOES > NO
NOESES > NOESIS
NOESIS n exercise of reason
NOESISES > NOESIS
NOETIC adj of or relating to the mind
NOG same as > NOGGING
NOGAKU n Japanese style of drama
NOGG same as > NOG
NOGGED adj built with timber and brick
NOGGIN n head
NOGGING n short horizontal timber member
NOGGINGS > NOGGING
NOGGINS > NOGGIN
NOGGS > NOGG
NOGOODNIK n worthless person
NOGS > NOG
NOH n stylized classic drama of Japan

NOHOW adv under any conditions

NOHOWISH > NOHOW

NOIL n short or knotted fibres that are separated from the long fibres by combing

NOILIER > NOILY

NOILIES > NOILY

NOILIEST > NOILY

NOILS > NOIL

NOILY n dry white vermouth drink from France ▷ adj resembling a noil

NOINT vb anoint

NOINTED > NOINT

NOINTER n mischievous child

NOINTERS > NOINTER

NOINTING > NOINT

NOINTS > NOINT

NOIR adj (of a film) showing characteristics of a film noir, in plot or style ▷ n film noir

NOIRISH > NOIR

NOIRS > NOIR

NOISE n sound, usu a loud or disturbing one ▷ vb spread (news or gossip)

NOISED > NOISE

NOISEFUL > NOISE

NOISELESS adj making little or no sound

NOISENIK n rock musician who performs loud harsh music

NOISENIKS > NOISENIK

NOISES > NOISE

NOISETTE n hazelnut chocolate ▷ adj flavoured or made with hazelnuts

NOISETTES > NOISETTE

NOISIER > NOISY

NOISIEST > NOISY

NOISILY > NOISY

NOISINESS > NOISY

NOISING > NOISE

NOISOME adj (of smells) offensive

NOISOMELY > NOISOME

NOISY adj making a lot of noise

NOLE same as > NOLL

NOLES > NOLE

NOLITION n unwillingness

NOLITIONS > NOLITION

NOLL n head

NOLLS > NOLL

NOLO n as in nolo contendere plea indicating that the defendant does not wish to contest the case

NOLOS > NOLO

NOM n name

NOMA n gangrenous inflammation of the mouth

NOMAD n member of a tribe with no fixed dwelling place

NOMADE same as > NOMAD

NOMADES > NOMADE

NOMADIC adj relating to or characteristic of nomads

NOMADIES > NOMADY

NOMADISE same as > NOMADIZE

NOMADISED > NOMADISE

NOMADISES > NOMADISE

NOMADISM > NOMAD

NOMADISMS > NOMAD

NOMADIZE vb live as nomads

NOMADIZED > NOMADIZE

NOMADIZES > NOMADIZE

NOMADS > NOMAD

NOMADY n practice of living like nomads

NOMARCH n head of an ancient Egyptian nome

NOMARCHS > NOMARCH

NOMARCHY n any of the provinces of modern Greece

NOMAS > NOMA

NOMBLES variant spelling of > NUMBLES

NOMBRIL n point on a shield

NOMBRILS > NOMBRIL

NOME n any of the former provinces of modern Greece

NOMEN n ancient Roman's second name

NOMENS > NOMEN

NOMES > NOME

NOMIC adj normal or habitual

NOMINA > NOMEN

NOMINABLE adj that can be nominated

NOMINAL adj in name only ▷ n nominal element

NOMINALLY > NOMINAL

NOMINALS > NOMINAL

NOMINATE vb suggest as a candidate ▷ adj having a particular name

NOMINATED > NOMINATE

NOMINATES > NOMINATE

NOMINATOR > NOMINATE

NOMINEE n candidate

NOMINEES > NOMINEE

NOMISM n adherence to laws as a primary exercise of religion

NOMISMS > NOMISM

NOMISTIC > NOMISM

NOMOCRACY n government based on the rule of law rather than arbitrary will, terror, etc

NOMOGENY n law of life originating as a natural process

NOMOGRAM n arrangement of two linear or logarithmic scales

NOMOGRAMS > NOMOGRAM

NOMOGRAPH same as > NOMOGRAM

NOMOI > NOMOS

NOMOLOGIC > NOMOLOGY

NOMOLOGY n science of law and law-making

NOMOS n convention

NOMOTHETE n legislator

NOMS > NOM

NON adv not

NONA n sleeping sickness

NONACID adj not acid ▷ n nonacid substance

NONACIDIC adj not acidic

NONACIDS > NONACID

NONACTING adj not acting ▷ n acting of poor quality

NONACTION n not action

NONACTIVE adj not active

NONACTOR n person who is not an actor

NONACTORS > NONACTOR

NONADDICT n person who is not an addict

NONADULT n person who is not an adult

NONADULTS > NONADULT

NONAGE n state of being under full legal age

NONAGED > NONAGE

NONAGES > NONAGE

NONAGON n geometric figure with nine sides

NONAGONAL > NONAGON

NONAGONS > NONAGON

NONANE n type of chemical compound

NONANES > NONANE

NONANIMAL adj not animal

NONANOIC adj as in nonanoic acid colourless oily fatty acid with a rancid odour

NONANSWER n unsatisfactory reply ▷ vb decline to answer

NONARABLE adj not arable

NONARIES > NONARY

NONART n something that does not constitute art

NONARTIST n person who is not an artist

NONARTS > NONART

NONARY n set or group of nine

NONAS same as > NONES

NONATOMIC adj not atomic

NONAUTHOR n person who is not the author

NONAVIAN adj not relating to birds

NONBANK n business or institution that is not a bank but provides similar services

NONBANKS > NONBANK

NONBASIC adj not basic

NONBEING n philosophical problem relating to the question of existence

NONBEINGS > NONBEING

NONBELIEF n state of not believing

NONBINARY adj not binary

NONBITING adj not biting

NONBLACK n person who is not Black

NONBLACKS > NONBLACK

NONBODIES > NONBODY

NONBODY n nonphysical nature of a person

NONBONDED adj not bonded

NONBOOK n book with little substance

NONBOOKS > NONBOOK

NONBRAND adj not produced by a well-known company

NONBUYING adj not buying

NONCAKING adj not liable to cake

NONCAMPUS adj not on campus

NONCAREER adj not career-related

NONCASH adj other than cash

NONCASUAL adj not casual

NONCAUSAL adj not causal

NONCE n present time or occasion

NONCEREAL adj not cereal

NONCES > NONCE

NONCHURCH adj not related to the church ▷ vb take away the status of a church

NONCLASS n lack of class

NONCLING adj not liable to stick

NONCODING adj (of DNA) not containing instructions for making protein

NONCOITAL adj not involving sexual intercourse

NONCOKING adj not liable to coke

NONCOLA n soft drink other than cola

NONCOLAS > NONCOLA

NONCOLOR same as > NONCOLOUR

NONCOLORS > NONCOLOR

NONCOLOUR n colour such as black or white

NONCOM n person not involved in combat

NONCOMBAT adj not involved in combat

NONCOMS > NONCOM

NONCONCUR vb disagree

NONCORE adj not central or essential

NONCOUNT adj not capable of being counted

n

NONCOUNTY adj not controlled or run by a county

NONCREDIT adj relating to an educational course not providing a credit towards a degree

NONCRIME n incident that is not a crime

NONCRIMES > NONCRIME

NONCRISES > NONCRISIS

NONCRISIS n situation that is not a crisis

NONCYCLIC adj not cyclic

NONDAIRY adj not containing dairy products

NONDANCE n series of movements that do not constitute a dance

NONDANCER n person who is not a dancer

NONDANCES > NONDANCE

NONDEALER adj person who is not a dealer

NONDEGREE adj not leading to a degree

NONDEMAND adj not involving demand

NONDESERT adj not belonging to the desert

NONDOCTOR n person who is not a doctor

NONDOLLAR adj not involving the dollar

NONDRIP adj (of paint) specially formulated to minimize dripping during application

NONDRIVER n person who does not drive

NONDRUG adj not involving the use of drugs

NONDRYING adj not drying

NONE pron not any

NONEDIBLE n not edible

NONEGO n everything that is outside one's conscious self

NONEGOS > NONEGO

NONELECT n person not chosen

NONELECTS > NONELECT

NONELITE adj not elite

NONEMPTY adj not empty

NONENDING adj not ending

NONENERGY adj without energy

NONENTITY n insignificant person or thing

NONENTRY n failure to enter

NONEQUAL adj not equal ▷ n person who is not the equal of another person

NONEQUALS > NONEQUAL

NONEROTIC adj not erotic

NONES n (in the Roman calendar) the ninth day before the ides of each month

NONESUCH n matchless person or thing

NONET n piece of music composed for a group of nine instruments

NONETHNIC n not ethnic

NONETS > NONET

NONETTE same as > NONET

NONETTES > NONETTE

NONETTI > NONETTO

NONETTO same as > NONET

NONETTOS > NONETTO

NONEVENT n disappointing or insignificant occurrence

NONEVENTS > NONEVENT

NONEXEMPT adj not exempt

NONEXOTIC adj not exotic

NONEXPERT n person who is not an expert

NONEXTANT adj no longer in existence

NONFACT n event or thing not provable

NONFACTOR n something that is not a factor

NONFACTS > NONFACT

NONFADING adj colourfast

NONFAMILY n household that does not consist of a family

NONFAN n person who is not a fan

NONFANS > NONFAN

NONFARM adj not connected with a farm

NONFARMER n person who is not a farmer

NONFAT adj fat free

NONFATAL adj not resulting in or capable of causing death

NONFATTY adj not fatty

NONFEUDAL adj not feudal

NONFILIAL adj not involving parent-child relationship

NONFINAL adj not final

NONFINITE adj not finite

NONFISCAL adj not involving government funds

NONFLUID adj not fluid ▷ n something that is not a fluid

NONFLUIDS > NONFLUID

NONFLYING adj not capable of flying

NONFOCAL adj not focal

NONFOOD n item that is not food ▷ adj relating to items other than food

NONFOODS > NONFOOD

NONFORMAL adj not formal

NONFOSSIL adj not consisting of fossils

NONFROZEN adj not frozen

NONFUEL adj not relating to fuel ▷ n energy not used for generating heat, power, or electricity

NONFUELS > NONFUEL

NONFUNDED adj not receiving funding

NONG n stupid or incompetent person

NONGAME adj not pursued for competitive sport purposes

NONGAY n person who is not gay

NONGAYS > NONGAY

NONGHETTO adj not belonging to the ghetto

NONGLARE adj not causing glare ▷ n any of various nonglare materials

NONGLARES > NONGLARE

NONGLAZED adj not glazed

NONGLOSSY adj not glossy

NONGOLFER n person who is not a golfer

NONGRADED adj not graded

NONGREASY adj not greasy

NONGREEN adj not green

NONGROWTH n failure to grow ▷ adj characterized by a lack of growth

NONGS > NONG

NONGUEST n person who is not a guest

NONGUESTS > NONGUEST

NONGUILT n state of being innocent

NONGUILTS > NONGUILT

NONHARDY adj fragile

NONHEME adj of dietary iron, obtained from vegetable foods

NONHERO n person who is not a hero

NONHEROES > NONHERO

NONHEROIC adj not heroic

NONHOME adj not of the home

NONHUMAN n something not human

NONHUMANS > NONHUMAN

NONHUNTER n person or thing that does not hunt

NONI n tree of SE Asia and the Pacific islands

NONIDEAL adj not ideal

NONILLION n (in Britain, France, and Germany) the number represented as one followed by 54 zeros

NONIMAGE n person who is not a celebrity

NONIMAGES > NONIMAGE

NONIMMUNE adj not immune

NONIMPACT adj not involving impact ▷ n lack of impact

NONINERT adj not inert

NONINJURY adj not involving injury

NONINSECT n animal that is not an insect

NONIONIC adj not ionic

NONIRON adj not requiring ironing

NONIS > NONI

NONISSUE n matter of little importance

NONISSUES > NONISSUE

NONJOINER n person who does not join (an organisation, etc)

NONJURIES > NONJURY

NONJURING adj refusing the oath of allegiance

NONJUROR n person who refuses to take an oath, as of allegiance

NONJURORS > NONJUROR

NONJURY n trial without a jury

NONKIN n those who are not related to a person

NONKINS > NONKIN

NONKOSHER adj not kosher

NONLABOR same as > NONLABOUR

NONLABOUR adj not concerned with labour

NONLAWYER n person who is not a lawyer

NONLEADED adj not leaded

NONLEAFY adj not leafy

NONLEAGUE adj not belonging to a league

NONLEGAL adj not legal

NONLEGUME n not a pod of the pea or bean family

NONLETHAL adj not resulting in or capable of causing death

NONLEVEL adj not level

NONLIABLE adj not liable

NONLIFE n matter which is not living

NONLINEAL same as > NONLINEAR

NONLINEAR adj not of, in, along, or relating to a line

NONLIQUID n substance which is not liquid

NONLIVES > NONLIFE

NONLIVING adj not living

NONLOCAL adj not of, affecting, or confined to a limited area or part ▷ n person who is not local to an area

NONLOCALS > NONLOCAL

NONLOVING adj not loving

NONLOYAL adj not loyal

NONLYRIC adj without lyrics

NONMAJOR n student who is not majoring in a specified subject

NONMAJORS > NONMAJOR

NONMAN *n* being that is not a man

NONMANUAL *adj* not manual

NONMARKET *adj* not relating to markets

NONMATURE *adj* not mature

NONMEAT *n* substance that does not contain meat ▷ *adj* not containing meat

NONMEATS > NONMEAT

NONMEMBER *n* person who is not a member of a particular club or organization

NONMEN > NONMAN

NONMENTAL *adj* not mental

NONMETAL *n* chemical element that forms acidic oxides and is a poor conductor of heat and electricity

NONMETALS > NONMETAL

NONMETRIC *adj* not metric

NONMETRO *adj* not metropolitan

NONMOBILE *adj* not mobile

NONMODAL *adj* not modal

NONMODERN *adj* not modern

NONMONEY *adj* not involving money

NONMORAL *adj* not involving morality

NONMORTAL *adj* not fatal

NONMOTILE *adj* not capable of movement

NONMOVING *adj* not moving

NONMUSIC *n* (unpleasant) noise

NONMUSICS > NONMUSIC

NONMUTANT *n* person or thing that is not mutated

NONMUTUAL *adj* not mutual

NONNASAL *adj* not nasal

NONNATIVE *adj* not native ▷ *n* person who is not native to a place

NONNAVAL *adj* not belonging to the navy

NONNEURAL *adj* not neural

NONNEWS *adj* not concerned with news

NONNIES > NONNY

NONNOBLE *adj* not noble

NONNORMAL *adj* not normal

NONNOVEL *n* literary work that is not a novel

NONNOVELS > NONNOVEL

NONNY *n* meaningless word

NONOBESE *adj* not obese

NONOHMIC *adj* not having electrical resistance

NONOILY *adj* not oily

NONORAL *adj* not oral

NONORALLY > NONORAL

NONOWNER *n* person who is not an owner

NONOWNERS > NONOWNER

NONPAGAN *n* person who is not a pagan

NONPAGANS > NONPAGAN

NONPAID *adj* without payment

NONPAPAL *adj* not of the pope

NONPAR *adj* nonparticipating

NONPAREIL *n* person or thing that is unsurpassed ▷ *adj* having no match or equal

NONPARENT *n* person who is not a parent

NONPARITY *n* state of not being equal

NONPAROUS *adj* never having given birth

NONPARTY *adj* not connected with a political party

NONPAST *n* any grammatical tense that is not the past tense

NONPASTS > NONPAST

NONPAYING *adj* (of guests, customers, etc) not expected or requested to pay

NONPEAK *n* period of low demand

NONPEAKS > NONPEAK

NONPERSON *n* person regarded as nonexistent or unimportant

NONPLANAR *adj* not planar

NONPLAY *n* social behaviour that is not classed as play

NONPLAYER *n* person not playing

NONPLAYS > NONPLAY

NONPLIANT *adj* not pliant

NONPLUS *vb* put at a loss ▷ *n* state of utter perplexity prohibiting action or speech

NONPLUSED > NONPLUS

NONPLUSES > NONPLUS

NONPOETIC *adj* not poetic

NONPOINT *adj* without a specific site

NONPOLAR *adj* not polar

NONPOLICE *adj* not related to the police

NONPOOR *adj* not poor ▷ *n* person who is not poor

NONPOORS > NONPOOR

NONPOROUS *adj* not permeable to water, air, or other fluids

NONPOSTAL *adj* not postal

NONPRINT *adj* published in a format other than print on paper

NONPROFIT *n* organization that is not intended to make a profit

NONPROS *vb* enter a judgment of non prosequitur

NONPROVEN *adj* not tried and tested

NONPUBLIC *adj* not public

NONQUOTA *adj* not included in a quota

NONRACIAL *adj* not related to racial factors

NONRACISM *n* absence of racism

NONRANDOM *adj* not random

NONRATED *adj* not rated

NONREADER *n* person who does not or cannot read

NONRETURN *adj* denoting a mechanism that permits flow in a pipe in one direction only

NONRHOTIC *adj* denoting or speaking a dialect of English in which preconsonantal *r* s are not pronounced

NONRIGID *adj* not rigid

NONRIOTER *n* person who does not participate in a riot

NONRIVAL *n* person or thing not competing for success

NONRIVALS > NONRIVAL

NONROYAL *adj* not royal ▷ *n* person who is not a member of a royal family

NONROYALS > NONROYAL

NONRUBBER *adj* not containing rubber

NONRULING *adj* not ruling

NONRUN *adj* (of tights) not laddering

NONRUNNER *n* person who is not a runner

NONRURAL *adj* not rural

NONSACRED *adj* not sacred

NONSALINE *adj* not containing salt

NONSCHOOL *adj* not relating to school

NONSECRET *adj* not sacred

NONSECURE *adj* not secure

NONSELF *n* foreign molecule in the body

NONSELVES > NONSELF

NONSENSE *n* something that has or makes no sense ▷ *interj* exclamation of disagreement

NONSENSES > NONSENSE

NONSERIAL *adj* not serial

NONSEXIST *adj* not discriminating on the basis of gender, esp not against women

NONSEXUAL *adj* not sexual

NONSHRINK *adj* not likely to shrink

NONSIGNER *n* person who cannot use sign language

NONSKATER *n* person who does not skate

NONSKED *n* non-scheduled aeroplane

NONSKEDS > NONSKED

NONSKID *adj* designed to reduce skidding

NONSKIER *n* person who does not ski

NONSKIERS > NONSKIER

NONSLIP *adj* designed to prevent slipping

NONSMOKER *n* person who does not smoke

NONSOCIAL *adj* not social

NONSOLAR *adj* not related to the sun

NONSOLID *n* substance that is not a solid

NONSOLIDS > NONSOLID

NONSPEECH *adj* not involving speech ▷ *n* absence of speech

NONSTAPLE *adj* not staple

NONSTATE *adj* not relating to the state

NONSTATIC *adj* not static

NONSTEADY *adj* not steady

NONSTICK *adj* coated with a substance that food will not stick to when cooked

NONSTICKY *adj* not sticky

NONSTOP *adv* without a stop ▷ *adj* without a stop ▷ *n* nonstop flight

NONSTOPS > NONSTOP

NONSTORY *n* story of little substance or importance

NONSTYLE *n* style that cannot be identified

NONSTYLES > NONSTYLE

NONSUCH *same as* > NONESUCH

NONSUCHES > NONSUCH

NONSUGAR *n* substance that is not a sugar

NONSUGARS > NONSUGAR

NONSUIT *n* order of a judge dismissing a suit ▷ *vb* order the dismissal of the suit of (a person)

NONSUITED > NONSUIT

NONSUITS > NONSUIT

NONSYSTEM *adj* having no system

NONTALKER *n* person who does not talk

NONTARGET *adj* not being a target

NONTARIFF *adj* without tariff

NONTAX *n* tax that has little real effect

NONTAXES > NONTAX

NONTHEISM *n* belief there is no God

NONTHEIST n person who believes the existence or non-existence of God is irrelevant

NONTIDAL adj not having a tide

NONTITLE adj without title

NONTONAL adj not written in a key

NONTONIC adj not tonic

NONTOXIC n substance which is not poisonous ▷ adj not poisonous

NONTOXICS > NONTOXIC

NONTRAGIC adj not tragic

NONTRIBAL adj not tribal

NONTRUMP adj not of the trump suit

NONTRUTH same as > UNTRUTH

NONTRUTHS > NONTRUTH

NONUNION adj (of a company) not employing trade union members ▷ n failure of broken bones or bone fragments to heal

NONUNIONS > NONUNION

NONUNIQUE adj not unique

NONUPLE adj ninefold ▷ n ninefold number

NONUPLES > NONUPLE

NONUPLET n child born in a multiple birth of nine siblings

NONUPLETS > NONUPLET

NONURBAN adj rural

NONURGENT adj not urgent

NONUSABLE adj not usable

NONUSE n failure to use

NONUSER > NONUSE

NONUSERS > NONUSE

NONUSES > NONUSE

NONUSING > NONUSE

NONVACANT adj not vacant

NONVALID adj not valid

NONVECTOR n quantity without size and direction

NONVENOUS adj not venous

NONVERBAL adj not involving the use of language

NONVESTED adj not vested

NONVIABLE adj not viable

NONVIEWER n person who does not watch (television)

NONVIRAL adj not caused by a virus

NONVIRGIN n person who is not a virgin

NONVIRILE adj not virile

NONVISUAL adj not visual

NONVITAL adj not vital

NONVOCAL n music track without singing

NONVOCALS > NONVOCAL

NONVOTER n person who does not vote

NONVOTERS > NONVOTER

NONVOTING adj (of shares in a company) not entitling the owner to vote at company meetings

NONWAGE adj not part of wages

NONWAR n state of nonviolence

NONWARS > NONWAR

NONWHITE n person who is not White

NONWHITES > NONWHITE

NONWINGED adj without wings

NONWOODY adj not woody

NONWOOL adj not wool

NONWORD n series of letters not recognised as a word

NONWORDS > NONWORD

NONWORK adj not involving work ▷ n part of life which does not involve work

NONWORKER n person who does not work

NONWORKS > NONWORK

NONWOVEN n material made by a method other than weaving

NONWOVENS > NONWOVEN

NONWRITER n person who is not a writer

NONYL n type of chemical

NONYLS > NONYL

NONZERO adj not equal to zero

NOO n type of Japanese musical drama

NOOB same as > NEWBIE

NOOBS > NOOB

NOODGE vb annoy persistently

NOODGED > NOODGE

NOODGES > NOODGE

NOODGING > NOODGE

NOODLE n ribbon-like strip of pasta ▷ vb improvise aimlessly on a musical instrument

NOODLED > NOODLE

NOODLEDOM n state of being unintelligent

NOODLES > NOODLE

NOODLING n aimless musical improvisation

NOODLINGS > NOODLING

NOOGIE n act of inflicting pain by rubbing head hard

NOOGIES > NOOGIE

NOOIT interj South African exclamation of surprise

NOOK n corner or recess

NOOKIE same as > NOOKY

NOOKIER > NOOKY

NOOKIES > NOOKIE

NOOKIEST > NOOKY

NOOKLIKE > NOOK

NOOKS > NOOK

NOOKY n sexual intercourse ▷ adj resembling a nook

NOOLOGIES > NOOLOGY

NOOLOGY n study of intuition

NOOMETRY n mind measurement

NOON n twelve o'clock midday ▷ vb take a rest at noon

NOONDAY adj happening at noon ▷ n middle of the day

NOONDAYS > NOONDAY

NOONED > NOON

NOONER n event taking place in the middle of the day

NOONERS > NOONER

NOONING n midday break for rest or food

NOONINGS > NOONING

NOONS > NOON

NOONTIDE same as > NOONTIME

NOONTIDES > NOONTIDE

NOONTIME n middle of the day

NOONTIMES > NOONTIME

NOOP n point of the elbow

NOOPS > NOOP

NOOSE n loop in the end of a rope, tied with a slipknot ▷ vb catch in a noose

NOOSED > NOOSE

NOOSELIKE adj like a noose

NOOSER n person who uses a noose

NOOSERS > NOOSER

NOOSES > NOOSE

NOOSING > NOOSE

NOOSPHERE n sphere of human thought

NOOTROPIC adj acting on mind

NOPAL n type of cactus

NOPALES > NOPAL

NOPALITO n small cactus

NOPALITOS > NOPALITO

NOPALS > NOPAL

NOPE interj no

NOPLACE same as > NOWHERE

NOR prep and not

NORDIC adj of competitions in cross-country racing and ski-jumping

NORDICITY n quality of being Nordic

NORI n edible seaweed

NORIA n water wheel with buckets attached to its rim

NORIAS > NORIA

NORIMON n Japanese passenger vehicle

NORIMONS > NORIMON

NORIS > NORI

NORITE n variety of igneous rock

NORITES > NORITE

NORITIC > NORITE

NORK n vulgar word for a female breast

NORKS > NORK

NORLAND n north part of a country or the earth

NORLANDS > NORLAND

NORM n standard that is regarded as normal

NORMA n norm or standard

NORMAL adj usual, regular, or typical ▷ n usual or regular state, degree or form

NORMALCY > NORMAL

NORMALISE same as > NORMALIZE

NORMALITY > NORMAL

NORMALIZE vb make or become normal

NORMALLY adv as a rule

NORMALS > NORMAL

NORMAN n post used for winding on a ship

NORMANDE n type of cattle

NORMANDES > NORMANDE

NORMANS > NORMAN

NORMAS > NORMA

NORMATIVE adj of or setting a norm or standard

NORMCORE n deliberately normal style of dress

NORMCORES > NORMCORE

NORMED adj having been normalized

NORMLESS adj without a norm

NORMS > NORM

NOROVIRUS n virus that causes gastroenteritis

NORSEL vb fit with short lines for fastening hooks

NORSELLED > NORSEL

NORSELLER > NORSEL

NORSELS > NORSEL

NORTENA same as > NORTENO

NORTENAS > NORTENA

NORTENO n type of Mexican music

NORTENOS > NORTENO

NORTH n direction towards the North Pole, opposite south ▷ adj in the north ▷ adv in, to, or towards the north ▷ vb move north

NORTHEAST adv (in or to) direction between north and east ▷ n point of the compass or direction midway between north and east ▷ adj of or denoting the northeastern part of a specified country, area, etc

NORTHED > NORTH

NORTHER n wind or storm from the north ▷ vb move north

NORTHERED > NORTHER

NORTHERLY adj of or in the north ▷ adv towards

the north ▷ *n* wind from the north

NORTHERN *adj* situated in or towards the north ▷ *n* person from the north

NORTHERNS > NORTHERN

NORTHERS > NORTHER

NORTHING *n* movement or distance covered in a northerly direction

NORTHINGS > NORTHING

NORTHLAND *n* lands that are far to the north

NORTHMOST *adj* situated furthest north

NORTHS > NORTH

NORTHWARD *adv* towards the north

NORTHWEST *adv* (in or to) direction between north and west ▷ *n* point of the compass or direction midway between north and west ▷ *adj* of or denoting the northwestern part of a specified country, area, etc

NORWARD *same as* > NORTHWARD

NORWARDS *same as* > NORWARD

NOS > NO

NOSE *n* organ of smell, used also in breathing ▷ *vb* move forward slowly and carefully

NOSEAN *n* type of mineral

NOSEANS > NOSEAN

NOSEBAG *n* bag containing feed fastened round a horse's head

NOSEBAGS > NOSEBAG

NOSEBAND *n* part of a horse's bridle that goes around the nose

NOSEBANDS > NOSEBAND

NOSEBLEED *n* bleeding from the nose

NOSED > NOSE

NOSEDIVE *vb* (of an aircraft) plunge suddenly with the nose pointing downwards

NOSEDIVED > NOSEDIVE

NOSEDIVES > NOSEDIVE

NOSEDOVE > NOSEDIVE

NOSEGAY *n* small bunch of flowers

NOSEGAYS > NOSEGAY

NOSEGUARD *n* position in American football

NOSELESS > NOSE

NOSELIKE > NOSE

NOSELITE *same as* > NOSEAN

NOSELITES > NOSELITE

NOSEPIECE *same as* > NOSEBAND

NOSER *n* strong headwind

NOSERS > NOSER

NOSES > NOSE

NOSEWHEEL *n* wheel fitted under the nose of an aircraft

NOSEY *adj* prying or inquisitive ▷ *n* nosey person

NOSEYS > NOSEY

NOSH *n* food ▷ *vb* eat

NOSHED > NOSH

NOSHER > NOSH

NOSHERIE *same as* > NOSHERY

NOSHERIES > NOSHERIE

NOSHERS > NOSH

NOSHERY *n* restaurant or other place where food is served

NOSHES > NOSH

NOSHING > NOSH

NOSIER > NOSY

NOSIES > NOSY

NOSIEST > NOSY

NOSILY > NOSY

NOSINESS > NOSY

NOSING *n* edge of a step or stair tread

NOSINGS > NOSING

NOSODE *n* homeopathic remedy

NOSODES > NOSODE

NOSOLOGIC > NOSOLOGY

NOSOLOGY *n* branch of medicine concerned with the classification of diseases

NOSTALGIA *n* sentimental longing for the past

NOSTALGIC *adj* of or characterized by nostalgia ▷ *n* person who indulges in nostalgia

NOSTOC *n* type of bacterium occurring in moist places

NOSTOCS > NOSTOC

NOSTOI > NOSTOS

NOSTOLOGY *n* scientific study of ageing

NOSTOS *n* story of a return home

NOSTRIL *n* one of the two openings at the end of the nose

NOSTRILS > NOSTRIL

NOSTRO *adj* as in *nostro account* bank account conducted by a British bank with a foreign bank

NOSTRUM *n* quack medicine

NOSTRUMS > NOSTRUM

NOSY *adj* prying or inquisitive ▷ *n* inquisitive person

NOT *adv* expressing negation, refusal, or denial

NOTA > NOTUM

NOTABILIA *n* things worthy of notice

NOTABLE *adj* worthy of being noted, remarkable ▷ *n* person of distinction

NOTABLES > NOTABLE

NOTABLY *adv* particularly or especially

NOTAEUM *n* back of a bird's body

NOTAEUMS > NOTAEUM

NOTAIRE *n* (in France) notary

NOTAIRES > NOTAIRE

NOTAL > NOTUM

NOTANDA > NOTANDUM

NOTANDUM *n* notable fact

NOTAPHILY *n* study of paper money

NOTARIAL > NOTARY

NOTARIES > NOTARY

NOTARISE *same as* > NOTARISE

NOTARISED > NOTARISE

NOTARISES > NOTARISE

NOTARIZE *vb* attest to or authenticate (a document, contract, etc), as a notary

NOTARIZED > NOTARIZE

NOTARIZES > NOTARIZE

NOTARY *n* person authorized to witness legal documents

NOTATE *vb* write (esp music) in notation

NOTATED > NOTATE

NOTATES > NOTATE

NOTATING > NOTATE

NOTATION *n* representation of numbers or quantities in a system by a series of symbols

NOTATIONS > NOTATION

NOTATOR *n* person who notates

NOTATORS > NOTATOR

NOTCH *n* V-shaped cut ▷ *vb* make a notch in

NOTCHBACK *n* type of car

NOTCHED > NOTCH

NOTCHEL *vb* refuse to pay another person's debts

NOTCHELED > NOTCHEL

NOTCHELS > NOTCHEL

NOTCHER *n* person who cuts notches

NOTCHERS > NOTCHER

NOTCHES > NOTCH

NOTCHIER > NOTCHY

NOTCHIEST > NOTCHY

NOTCHING > NOTCH

NOTCHINGS > NOTCH

NOTCHY *adj* (of a motor vehicle gear mechanism) requiring careful gear-changing

NOTE *n* short letter ▷ *vb* notice, pay attention to

NOTEBANDI *n* (in India) demonetization

NOTEBOOK *n* book for writing in

NOTEBOOKS > NOTEBOOK

NOTECARD *n* greetings card with space to write note

NOTECARDS > NOTECARD

NOTECASE *same as* > WALLET

NOTECASES > NOTECASE

NOTED *adj* well-known

NOTEDLY > NOTED

NOTEDNESS > NOTED

NOTELESS > NOTE

NOTELET *n* small folded card with a design on the front

NOTELETS > NOTELET

NOTEPAD *n* number of sheets of paper fastened together

NOTEPADS > NOTEPAD

NOTEPAPER *n* paper used for writing letters

NOTER *n* person who takes notes

NOTERS > NOTER

NOTES > NOTE

NOTHER *same as* > OTHER

NOTHING *pron* not anything ▷ *adv* not at all ▷ *n* person or thing of no importance

NOTHINGS > NOTHING

NOTICE *n* observation or attention ▷ *vb* observe, become aware of

NOTICED > NOTICE

NOTICER *n* person who takes notice

NOTICERS > NOTICER

NOTICES > NOTICE

NOTICING > NOTICE

NOTIFIED > NOTIFY

NOTIFIER > NOTIFY

NOTIFIERS > NOTIFY

NOTIFIES > NOTIFY

NOTIFY *vb* inform

NOTIFYING > NOTIFY

NOTING > NOTE

NOTION *n* idea or opinion

NOTIONAL *adj* speculative, imaginary, or unreal

NOTIONIST *n* person whose opinions are merely notions

NOTIONS > NOTION

NOTITIA *n* register or list, esp of ecclesiastical districts

NOTITIAE > NOTITIA

NOTITIAS > NOTITIA

NOTOCHORD *n* fibrous longitudinal rod in all embryo and some adult chordate animals

NOTORIETY > NOTORIOUS

NOTORIOUS *adj* well known for something bad

NOTORNIS *n* rare flightless rail of New Zealand

NOTOUR *adj* notorious

NOTT *same as* > NOT

NOTTURNI > NOTTURNO

NOTTURNO *n* piece of music

NOTUM *n* cuticular plate on an insect

NOUGAT *n* chewy sweet containing nuts and fruit

NOUGATINE *n* type of brown nougat with a firm texture

NOUGATS > NOUGAT

NOUGHT *n* figure o

NOUGHTIES pl n decade from 2000 to 2009
NOUGHTS > NOUGHT
NOUL same as > NOLL
NOULD vb would not
NOULDE same as > NOULD
NOULE same as > NOLL
NOULES > NOULE
NOULS > NOUL
NOUMENA > NOUMENON
NOUMENAL > NOUMENON
NOUMENON n thing as it is in itself
NOUN n word that refers to a person, place, or thing
NOUNAL > NOUN
NOUNALLY > NOUN
NOUNIER > NOUNY
NOUNIEST > NOUNY
NOUNLESS > NOUN
NOUNS > NOUN
NOUNY adj like a noun
NOUP n steep headland
NOUPS > NOUP
NOURICE n nurse
NOURICES > NOURICE
NOURISH vb feed
NOURISHED > NOURISH
NOURISHER > NOURISH
NOURISHES > NOURISH
NOURITURE n nourishment
NOURSLE vb nurse
NOURSLED > NOURSLE
NOURSLES > NOURSLE
NOURSLING > NOURSLE
NOUS n common sense
NOUSELL vb foster
NOUSELLED > NOUSELL
NOUSELLS > NOUSELL
NOUSES > NOUS
NOUSLE vb nuzzle
NOUSLED > NOUSLE
NOUSLES > NOUSLE
NOUSLING > NOUSLE
NOUT same as > NOUGHT
NOUVEAU adj having recently become the thing specified
NOUVEAUX same as > NOUVEAU
NOUVELLE n long short story
NOUVELLES > NOUVELLE
NOVA n type of star
NOVAE > NOVA
NOVALIA n newly reclaimed land
NOVALIKE adj resembling a nova
NOVAS > NOVA
NOVATE vb substitute one thing in place of another
NOVATED adj as in novated lease Australian system of employer-aided car purchase
NOVATES > NOVATE
NOVATING > NOVATE
NOVATION n substitution of a new obligation for an old one by mutual agreement
NOVATIONS > NOVATION

NOVEL n long fictitious story in book form ▷ adj fresh, new, or original
NOVELDOM n realm of fiction
NOVELDOMS > NOVELDOM
NOVELESE n style of writing characteristic of poor novels
NOVELESES > NOVELESE
NOVELETTE n short novel, esp one regarded as trivial or sentimental
NOVELISE same as > NOVELIZE
NOVELISED > NOVELISE
NOVELISER n person who novelizes
NOVELISES > NOVELISE
NOVELISH adj resembling a novel
NOVELISM n innovation
NOVELISMS > NOVELISM
NOVELIST n writer of novels
NOVELISTS > NOVELIST
NOVELIZE vb convert (a true story, film, etc) into a novel
NOVELIZED > NOVELIZE
NOVELIZER n person who novelizes
NOVELIZES > NOVELIZE
NOVELLA n short novel
NOVELLAE > NOVELLA
NOVELLAS > NOVELLA
NOVELLE > NOVELLA
NOVELLY > NOVEL
NOVELS > NOVEL
NOVELTIES > NOVELTY
NOVELTY n newness
NOVEMBER n code word for the letter N
NOVEMBERS > NOVEMBER
NOVENA n set of prayers or services on nine consecutive days
NOVENAE > NOVENA
NOVENARY n set of nine
NOVENAS > NOVENA
NOVENNIAL adj recurring every ninth year
NOVERCAL adj stepmotherly
NOVERINT n writ
NOVERINTS > NOVERINT
NOVICE n beginner
NOVICES > NOVICE
NOVICHOK n powerful nerve agent developed in the former USSR
NOVICHOKS > NOVICHOK
NOVICIATE same as > NOVITIATE
NOVITIATE n period of being a novice
NOVITIES > NOVITY

NOVITY n novelty
NOVOCAINE n tradename of a painkilling substance used as a local anaesthetic
NOVODAMUS n type of charter
NOVUM n game played with dice
NOVUMS > NOVUM
NOW adv at or for the present time ▷ n the present time
NOWADAYS adv in these times
NOWAY adv in no manner
NOWAYS same as > NOWAY
NOWCAST n report on current weather conditions
NOWCASTS > NOWCAST
NOWED adj knotted
NOWHENCE adv from no place
NOWHERE adv not anywhere ▷ n nonexistent or insignificant place
NOWHERES > NOWHERE
NOWHITHER adv no place
NOWISE another word for > NOWAY
NOWL n crown of the head
NOWLS > NOWL
NOWN same as > OWN
NOWNESS > NOWN
NOWNESSES > NOWN
NOWS > NOW
NOWT n nothing
NOWTIER > NOWTY
NOWTIEST > NOWTY
NOWTS > NOWT
NOWTY adj bad-tempered
NOWY adj having a small projection at the centre (of a cross)
NOX n nitrogen oxide
NOXAL adj relating to damage done by something belonging to another
NOXES > NOX
NOXIOUS adj poisonous or harmful
NOXIOUSLY > NOXIOUS
NOY vb harass
NOYADE n execution by drowning
NOYADES > NOYADE
NOYANCE n nuisance
NOYANCES > NOYANCE
NOYAU n brandy-based liqueur
NOYAUS > NOYAU
NOYAUX > NOYAU
NOYED > NOY
NOYES archaic form of > NOISE
NOYESES > NOYES
NOYING > NOY
NOYOUS > NOY
NOYS > NOY
NOYSOME > NOY
NOZZER n new recruit (in the Navy)
NOZZERS > NOZZER
NOZZLE n projecting spout through which fluid is discharged

NOZZLES > NOZZLE
NTH adj of an unspecified number
NU n 13th letter in the Greek alphabet
NUANCE n subtle difference in colour, meaning, or tone ▷ vb give subtle differences to
NUANCED > NUANCE
NUANCES > NUANCE
NUANCING > NUANCE
NUB n point or gist (of a story etc) ▷ vb hang from the gallows
NUBBED > NUB
NUBBER n weakly hit ball in baseball
NUBBERS > NUBBER
NUBBIER > NUBBY
NUBBIEST > NUBBY
NUBBIN n something small or undeveloped, esp a fruit or ear of corn
NUBBINESS > NUBBY
NUBBING n act of hanging (a criminal)
NUBBINGS > NUBBING
NUBBINS > NUBBIN
NUBBLE n small lump ▷ vb dialect word for beat or pound using one's fists
NUBBLED > NUBBLE
NUBBLES > NUBBLE
NUBBLIER > NUBBLY
NUBBLIEST > NUBBLY
NUBBLING > NUBBLE
NUBBLY > NUBBLE
NUBBY adj having small lumps or protuberances
NUBECULA n small irregular galaxy near the S celestial pole
NUBECULAE > NUBECULA
NUBIA n fleecy scarf for the head, worn by women
NUBIAS > NUBIA
NUBIFORM adj cloudlike
NUBILE adj (of a girl or woman) mature enough for marriage
NUBILITY > NUBILE
NUBILOSE same as > NUBILOUS
NUBILOUS adj cloudy
NUBS > NUB
NUBUCK n type of leather with a velvety finish
NUBUCKS > NUBUCK
NUCELLAR > NUCELLUS
NUCELLI > NUCELLUS
NUCELLUS n central part of a plant ovule containing the embryo sac
NUCHA n back or nape of the neck
NUCHAE > NUCHA
NUCHAL n scale on a reptile's neck
NUCHALS > NUCHAL
NUCLEAL > NUCLEUS
NUCLEAR adj of nuclear weapons or energy
NUCLEASE n any of a group of enzymes that hydrolyse nucleic acids to simple nucleotides

NUCLEASES
> NUCLEASE

NUCLEATE adj having a nucleus ▷ vb form a nucleus

NUCLEATED
> NUCLEATE

NUCLEATES
> NUCLEATE

NUCLEATOR
> NUCLEATE

NUCLEI > NUCLEUS

NUCLEIC adj as in nucleic acid type of complex compound that is a vital constituent of living cells

NUCLEIDE same as
> NUCLIDE

NUCLEIDES
> NUCLEIDE

NUCLEIN n protein that occurs in the nuclei of living cells

NUCLEINIC > NUCLEIN

NUCLEINS > NUCLEIN

NUCLEOID n component of a bacterium

NUCLEOIDS
> NUCLEOID

NUCLEOLAR
> NUCLEOLUS

NUCLEOLE variant of
> NUCLEOLUS

NUCLEOLES
> NUCLEOLE

NUCLEOLI
> NUCLEOLUS

NUCLEOLUS n small rounded body within a resting nucleus that contains RNA and proteins

NUCLEON n proton or neutron

NUCLEONIC adj relating to the branch of physics concerned with the applications of nuclear energy

NUCLEONS > NUCLEON

NUCLEUS n centre, esp of an atom or cell

NUCLEUSES > NUCLEUS

NUCLIDE n species of atom characterized by its atomic number and its mass number

NUCLIDES > NUCLIDE

NUCLIDIC > NUCLIDE

NUCULE n small seed

NUCULES > NUCULE

NUDATION n act of removing a covering

NUDATIONS
> NUDATION

NUDDIES > NUDDY

NUDDY n as in in the nuddy in the nude

NUDE adj naked ▷ n naked figure in painting, sculpture, or photography

NUDELY > NUDE

NUDENESS > NUDE

NUDER > NUDE

NUDES > NUDE

NUDEST > NUDE

NUDGE vb push gently, esp with the elbow ▷ n gentle push or touch

NUDGED > NUDGE

NUDGER > NUDGE

NUDGERS > NUDGE

NUDGES > NUDGE

NUDGING > NUDGE

NUDICAUL adj (of plants) having stems without leaves

NUDIE n film, show, or magazine depicting nudity

NUDIES > NUDIE

NUDISM n practice of not wearing clothes

NUDISMS > NUDISM

NUDIST > NUDISM

NUDISTS > NUDISM

NUDITIES > NUDITY

NUDITY n state or fact of being nude

NUDNICK same as
> NUDNIK

NUDNICKS > NUDNICK

NUDNIK n boring person

NUDNIKS > NUDNIK

NUDZH same as > NUDGE

NUDZHED > NUDZH

NUDZHES > NUDZH

NUDZHING > NUDZH

NUFF slang form of
> ENOUGH

NUFFIN slang form of
> NOTHING

NUFFINS > NUFFIN

NUFFS > NUFF

NUG n lump of wood sawn from a log

NUGAE pl n jests

NUGATORY adj of little value

NUGGAR n sailing boat used to carry cargo on the Nile

NUGGARS > NUGGAR

NUGGET n small lump of gold in its natural state ▷ vb polish footwear

NUGGETED > NUGGET

NUGGETIER > NUGGETY

NUGGETING > NUGGET

NUGGETS > NUGGET

NUGGETTED > NUGGET

NUGGETY adj of or resembling a nugget

NUGS > NUG

NUISANCE n something or someone that causes annoyance or bother

NUISANCER n person or thing causing a nuisance

NUISANCES
> NUISANCE

NUKE vb attack with nuclear weapons ▷ n nuclear weapon

NUKED > NUKE

NUKES > NUKE

NUKING > NUKE

NULL adj without legal force ▷ vb make negative

NULLA same as > NULLAH

NULLAH n stream or drain

NULLAHS > NULLAH

NULLAS > NULLA

NULLED > NULL

NULLIFIED > NULLIFY

NULLIFIER > NULLIFY

NULLIFIES > NULLIFY

NULLIFY vb make ineffective

NULLING n knurling

NULLINGS > NULLING

NULLIPARA n woman who has never borne a child

NULLIPORE n any of several red seaweeds

NULLITIES > NULLITY

NULLITY n state of being null

NULLNESS > NULL

NULLS > NULL

NUMB adj without feeling, as through cold, shock, or fear ▷ vb make numb

NUMBAT n small Australian marsupial

NUMBATS > NUMBAT

NUMBED > NUMB

NUMBER n sum or quantity ▷ vb count

NUMBERED > NUMBER

NUMBERER n person who numbers

NUMBERERS
> NUMBERER

NUMBERING > NUMBER

NUMBERS > NUMBER

NUMBEST > NUMB

NUMBFISH n any of several electric ray fish

NUMBHEAD n insulting word for a stupid person

NUMBHEADS
> NUMBHEAD

NUMBING > NUMB

NUMBINGLY > NUMB

NUMBLES pl n animal organs, cooked for food

NUMBLY > NUMB

NUMBNESS > NUMB

NUMBNUT n insulting word for a stupid person

NUMBNUTS n insulting word for a stupid person

NUMBS > NUMB

NUMBSKULL n stupid person

NUMCHUCK same as
> NUNCHAKU

NUMCHUCKS
> NUMCHUCK

NUMDAH n coarse felt made esp in India

NUMDAHS > NUMDAH

NUMEN n deity or spirit presiding over a thing or place

NUMERABLE adj able to be numbered or counted

NUMERABLY
> NUMERABLE

NUMERACY n ability to use numbers, esp in arithmetical operations

NUMERAIRE n unit in which prices are measured

NUMERAL n word or symbol used to express a sum or quantity ▷ adj of, consisting of, or denoting a number

NUMERALLY > NUMERAL

NUMERALS > NUMERAL

NUMERARY adj of or relating to numbers

NUMERATE adj able to do basic arithmetic ▷ vb read (a numerical expression)

NUMERATED
> NUMERATE

NUMERATES
> NUMERATE

NUMERATOR n number above the line in a fraction

NUMERIC n number or numeral

NUMERICAL adj measured or expressed in numbers

NUMERICS > NUMERIC

NUMEROUS adj existing or happening in large numbers

NUMINA plural of
> NUMEN

NUMINOUS adj arousing religious or spiritual emotions ▷ n something that arouses religious or spiritual emotions

NUMMARY adj of or relating to coins

NUMMIER > NUMMY

NUMMIEST > NUMMY

NUMMULAR adj shaped like a coin

NUMMULARY
> NUMMULAR

NUMMULINE n coin-shaped fossil

NUMMULITE n type of large fossil protozoan

NUMMY adj delicious

NUMNAH same as
> NUMDAH

NUMNAHS > NUMNAH

NUMPKIN n stupid person

NUMPKINS > NUMPKIN

NUMPTIES > NUMPTY

NUMPTY n stupid person

NUMSKULL same as
> NUMBSKULL

NUMSKULLS
> NUMSKULL

NUN n female member of a religious order

NUNATAK n isolated mountain peak projecting through glacial ice

NUNATAKER > NUNATAK

NUNATAKS > NUNATAK

NUNCHAKU n throwing weapon used in martial arts

NUNCHAKUS
> NUNCHAKU

NUNCHEON n light snack

NUNCHEONS
> NUNCHEON

NUNCHUCK same as
> NUNCHUK

NUNCHUCKS
> NUNCHUCK

NUNCHUK n throwing weapon used in martial arts

NUNCHUKS > NUNCHUK

NUNCIO n pope's ambassador

NUNCIOS > NUNCIO

NUNCLE archaic or dialect word for > UNCLE

NUNCLES > NUNCLE

NUNCUPATE vb declare publicly

NUNDINAL n any of seven Roman letters indicating the days of the week

NUNDINALS > NUNDINAL

NUNDINE n market day

NUNDINES > NUNDINE

NUNHOOD n condition, practice, or character of a nun

NUNHOODS > NUNHOOD

NUNLIKE > NUN

NUNNATION n pronunciation of n at the end of words

NUNNERIES > NUNNERY

NUNNERY n convent

NUNNISH > NUN

NUNNY n as in nunny bag small sealskin haversack used in Canada

NUNS > NUN

NUNSHIP > NUN

NUNSHIPS > NUN

NUPTIAL adj relating to marriage

NUPTIALLY > NUPTIAL

NUPTIALS pl n wedding

NUR n wooden ball

NURAGHE n Sardinian round tower

NURAGHI > NURAGHE

NURAGHIC > NURAGHE

NURD same as > NERD

NURDIER > NURD

NURDIEST > NURD

NURDISH > NERD

NURDLE vb score runs in cricket by soft deflections

NURDLED > NURDLE

NURDLES > NURDLE

NURDLING > NURDLE

NURDS > NURD

NURDY > NURD

NURHAG n Sardinian round tower

NURHAGS > NURHAG

NURL variant of > KNURL

NURLED > NURL

NURLING > NURL

NURLS > NURL

NURR n wooden ball

NURRS > NURR

NURS > NUR

NURSE n person employed to look after sick people ▷ vb look after (a sick person)

NURSED > NURSE

NURSELIKE > NURSE

NURSELING same as > NURSLING

NURSEMAID n woman employed to look after children

NURSER n person who treats something carefully

NURSERIES > NURSERY

NURSERS > NURSER

NURSERY n room where children sleep or play

NURSES > NURSE

NURSING n practice or profession of caring for the sick and injured

NURSINGS > NURSING

NURSLE vb nuzzle

NURSLED > NURSLE

NURSLES > NURSLE

NURSLING n child or young animal that is being suckled, nursed, or fostered

NURSLINGS > NURSLING

NURTURAL > NURTURE

NURTURANT > NURTURE

NURTURE n act or process of promoting development ▷ vb promote or encourage development

NURTURED > NURTURE

NURTURER > NURTURE

NURTURERS > NURTURE

NURTURES > NURTURE

NURTURING > NURTURE

NUS > NU

NUT n fruit consisting of a hard shell and a kernel ▷ vb gather nuts

NUTANT adj having the apex hanging down

NUTARIAN n person whose diet is based around nuts

NUTARIANS > NUTARIAN

NUTATE vb nod

NUTATED > NUTATE

NUTATES > NUTATE

NUTATING > NUTATE

NUTATION n periodic variation in the precession of the earth's axis

NUTATIONS > NUTATION

NUTBAR n bar made from chopped nuts

NUTBARS > NUTBAR

NUTBROWN adj of a brownish colour, esp a reddish-brown

NUTBUTTER n ground nuts blended with butter

NUTCASE n slang word for a foolish or reckless person

NUTCASES > NUTCASE

NUTGALL n nut-shaped gall caused by gall wasps on the oak and other trees

NUTGALLS > NUTGALL

NUTGRASS n type of plant

NUTHATCH n small songbird

NUTHIN n nothing

NUTHOUSE n slang name for a psychiatric hospital

NUTHOUSES > NUTHOUSE

NUTJOB n slang word for a foolish or reckless person

NUTJOBBER n nuthatch

NUTJOBS > NUTJOB

NUTLET n portion of a fruit that fragments when mature

NUTLETS > NUTLET

NUTLIKE > NUT

NUTLOAF n savoury loaf made from nuts

NUTLOAVES > NUTLOAF

NUTMEAL n type of grain

NUTMEALS > NUTMEAL

NUTMEAT n kernel of a nut

NUTMEATS > NUTMEAT

NUTMEG n spice made from the seed of a tropical tree ▷ vb kick or hit the ball between the legs of (an opposing player)

NUTMEGGED > NUTMEG

NUTMEGGY adj of or similar to nutmeg

NUTMEGS > NUTMEG

NUTPECKER n nuthatch

NUTPICK n tool used to dig the meat from nuts

NUTPICKS > NUTPICK

NUTRIA n fur of the coypu

NUTRIAS > NUTRIA

NUTRIENT n substance that provides nourishment ▷ adj providing nourishment

NUTRIENTS > NUTRIENT

NUTRIMENT n food or nourishment required by all living things to grow and stay healthy

NUTRITION n process of taking in and absorbing nutrients

NUTRITIVE adj of nutrition ▷ n nutritious food

NUTS > NUT

NUTSEDGE same as > NUTGRASS

NUTSEDGES > NUTSEDGE

NUTSHELL n shell around the kernel of a nut

NUTSHELLS > NUTSHELL

NUTSIER > NUTSY

NUTSIEST > NUTSY

NUTSO n slang word for a foolish or reckless person

NUTSOS > NUTSO

NUTSY adj slang word for foolish or reckless

NUTTED > NUT

NUTTER n slang word for a foolish or reckless person

NUTTERIES > NUTTERY

NUTTERS > NUTTER

NUTTERY n place where nut trees grow

NUTTIER > NUTTY

NUTTIEST > NUTTY

NUTTILY > NUTTY

NUTTINESS > NUTTY

NUTTING n act of gathering nuts

NUTTINGS > NUTTING

NUTTY adj containing or resembling nuts

NUTWOOD n any of various nut-bearing trees, such as walnut

NUTWOODS > NUTWOOD

NUZZER n present given to a superior in India

NUZZERS > NUZZER

NUZZLE vb push or rub gently with the nose or snout

NUZZLED > NUZZLE

NUZZLER n person or thing that nuzzles

NUZZLERS > NUZZLER

NUZZLES > NUZZLE

NUZZLING > NUZZLE

NY same as > NIGH

NYAFF n small or contemptible person ▷ vb yelp like a small dog

NYAFFED > NYAFF

NYAFFING > NYAFF

NYAFFS > NYAFF

NYAH interj interjection used to express contempt

NYALA n spiral-horned southern African antelope

NYALAS > NYALA

NYANZA n (in E Africa) a lake

NYANZAS > NYANZA

NYAOPE n narcotic substance

NYAOPES > NYAOPE

NYAS n young hawk

NYASES > NYAS

NYBBLE n small byte

NYBBLES > NYBBLE

NYCTALOPE n person affected by nyctalopia

NYCTALOPS n person or thing with night-vision

NYE n flock of pheasants ▷ vb near

NYED > NYE

NYES > NYE

NYING > NYE

NYLGHAI same as > NILGAI

NYLGHAIS > NYLGHAI

NYLGHAU same as > NILGAI

NYLGHAUS > NYLGHAU

NYLON n synthetic material used for clothing etc

NYLONED adj wearing nylons

NYLONS pl n stockings made of nylon

NYM adj as in nym war dispute about publishing material online under a pseudonym

NYMPH n mythical spirit of nature, represented as a beautiful young woman ▷ vb fish with a particular type of fly on the hook

NYMPHA n either one of the labia minora

NYMPHAE > NYMPHA

NYMPHAEA n water lily

NYMPHAEAS > NYMPHAEA

NYMPHAEUM n shrine of the nymphs

NYMPHAL > NYMPH

NYMPHALID n butterfly of the family that includes the fritillaries and red admirals ▷ adj of this family of butterflies

NYMPHEAN > NYMPH

NYMPHED > NYMPH

NYMPHET n sexually precocious girl or young woman

NYMPHETIC > NYMPHET

NYMPHETS > NYMPHET
NYMPHETTE *same as* > NYMPHET
NYMPHIC > NYMPH
NYMPHICAL > NYMPH
NYMPHING > NYMPH
NYMPHISH > NYMPH

NYMPHLIER > NYMPHLY
NYMPHLIKE > NYMPH
NYMPHLY *adj* resembling a nymph
NYMPHO *n* nymphomaniac
NYMPHOS > NYMPHO
NYMPHS > NYMPH

NYS > NY
NYSSA *n* type of tree
NYSSAS > NYSSA
NYSTAGMIC > NYSTAGMUS
NYSTAGMUS *n* involuntary movement of the eye comprising a smooth drift followed by a flick back
NYSTATIN *n* type of antibiotic obtained from a bacterium
NYSTATINS > NYSTATIN

n

Oo

OAF _n_ stupid or clumsy person
OAFISH > OAF
OAFISHLY > OAF
OAFS > OAF
OAK _n_ deciduous forest tree
OAKED _adj_ relating to wine that is stored for a time in oak barrels prior to bottling
OAKEN _adj_ made of the wood of the oak
OAKENSHAW _n_ small forest of oaks
OAKER _same as_ > OCHRE
OAKERS > OAKER
OAKIER > OAKY
OAKIES > OAKY
OAKIEST > OAKY
OAKINESS _n_ quality of being oaky
OAKLEAF _n_ the leaf of the oak
OAKLEAVES > OAKLEAF
OAKLIKE > OAK
OAKLING _n_ young oak
OAKLINGS > OAKLING
OAKMOSS _n_ type of lichen
OAKMOSSES > OAKMOSS
OAKS > OAK
OAKUM _n_ fibre obtained by unravelling old rope
OAKUMS > OAKUM
OAKWOOD _n_ the wood of the oak
OAKWOODS > OAKWOOD
OAKY _adj_ hard like the wood of an oak ▷ _n_ ice cream
OANSHAGH _n_ foolish girl or woman
OANSHAGHS > OANSHAGH
OAR _n_ pole with a broad blade, used for rowing a boat ▷ _vb_ propel with oars
OARAGE _n_ use or number of oars
OARAGES > OARAGE
OARED _adj_ equipped with oars
OARFISH _n_ very long ribbonfish with long slender ventral fins
OARFISHES > OARFISH
OARIER > OARY
OARIEST > OARY
OARING > OAR
OARLESS > OAR
OARLIKE > OAR
OARLOCK _n_ swivelling device that holds an oar in place

OARLOCKS > OARLOCK
OARS > OAR
OARSMAN _n_ man who rows a boat
OARSMEN > OARSMAN
OARSWOMAN _n_ woman who rows a boat
OARSWOMEN > OARSWOMAN
OARWEED _n_ type of brown seaweed
OARWEEDS > OARWEED
OARY _adj_ of or like an oar
OASES > OASIS
OASIS _n_ fertile area in a desert
OAST _n_ oven for drying hops
OASTHOUSE _n_ building with kilns for drying hops
OASTS > OAST
OAT _n_ hard cereal grown as food
OATCAKE _n_ thin flat biscuit of oatmeal
OATCAKES > OATCAKE
OATEN _adj_ made of oats or oat straw
OATER _n_ film about the American Wild West
OATERS > OATER
OATH _n_ solemn promise, esp to be truthful in court
OATHABLE _adj_ able to take an oath
OATHS > OATH
OATIER > OATY
OATIEST > OATY
OATLIKE > OAT
OATMEAL _n_ coarse flour made from oats ▷ _adj_ pale brownish-cream
OATMEALS > OATMEAL
OATS > OAT
OATY _adj_ of, like, or containing oats
OAVES > OAF
OB _n_ expression of opposition
OBA _n_ (in W Africa) a Yoruba chief or ruler
OBANG _n_ former Japanese coin
OBANGS > OBANG
OBAS > OBA
OBBLIGATI > OBBLIGATO
OBBLIGATO _n_ essential part or accompaniment ▷ _adj_ not to be omitted in performance
OBCONIC _adj_ shaped like a cone and attached at the pointed end

OBCONICAL _same as_ > OBCONIC
OBCORDATE _adj_ heart-shaped and attached at the pointed end
OBDURACY > OBDURATE
OBDURATE _adj_ hardhearted or stubborn ▷ _vb_ make obdurate
OBDURATED > OBDURATE
OBDURATES > OBDURATE
OBDURE _vb_ make obdurate
OBDURED > OBDURE
OBDURES > OBDURE
OBDURING > OBDURE
OBE _n_ ancient Laconian village
OBEAH _vb_ cast spell on
OBEAHED > OBEAH
OBEAHING > OBEAH
OBEAHISM > OBEAH
OBEAHISMS > OBEAH
OBEAHS > OBEAH
OBECHE _n_ African tree
OBECHES > OBECHE
OBEDIENCE _n_ condition or quality of being obedient
OBEDIENT _adj_ obeying or willing to obey
OBEISANCE _n_ attitude of respect
OBEISANT > OBEISANCE
OBEISM _n_ belief in obeah
OBEISMS > OBEISM
OBELI > OBELUS
OBELIA _n_ type of jellyfish
OBELIAS > OBELIA
OBELION _n_ area of skull
OBELISCAL > OBELISK
OBELISE _same as_ > OBELIZE
OBELISED > OBELISE
OBELISES > OBELISE
OBELISING > OBELISE
OBELISK _n_ stone column tapering to a pyramid at the top
OBELISKS > OBELISK
OBELISM _n_ practice of marking passages in text
OBELISMS > OBELISM
OBELIZE _vb_ mark (a word or passage) with an obelus
OBELIZED > OBELIZE
OBELIZES > OBELIZE
OBELIZING > OBELIZE

OBELUS _n_ mark used to indicate spurious words or passages
OBENTO _n_ Japanese lunch box
OBENTOS > OBENTO
OBES > OBE
OBESE _adj_ very fat
OBESELY > OBESE
OBESENESS > OBESE
OBESER > OBESE
OBESEST > OBESE
OBESITIES > OBESITY
OBESITY > OBESE
OBESOGEN _n_ agent causing obesity
OBESOGENS > OBESOGEN
OBEY _vb_ carry out instructions or orders
OBEYABLE > OBEY
OBEYED > OBEY
OBEYER > OBEY
OBEYERS > OBEY
OBEYING > OBEY
OBEYS > OBEY
OBFUSCATE _vb_ make (something) confusing
OBI _n_ broad sash tied in a large flat bow at the back ▷ _vb_ bewitch
OBIA _same as_ > OBEAH
OBIAS > OBIA
OBIED > OBI
OBIING > OBI
OBIISM > OBI
OBIISMS > OBI
OBIIT _vb_ died
OBIS > OBI
OBIT _n_ memorial service
OBITAL _adj_ of obits
OBITER _adv_ by the way
OBITS > OBIT
OBITUAL _adj_ of obits
OBITUARY _n_ announcement of someone's death, esp in a newspaper
OBJECT _n_ physical thing ▷ _vb_ express disapproval
OBJECTED > OBJECT
OBJECTIFY _vb_ represent concretely
OBJECTING > OBJECT
OBJECTION _n_ expression or feeling of opposition or disapproval
OBJECTIVE _n_ aim or purpose ▷ _adj_ not biased
OBJECTOR > OBJECT
OBJECTORS > OBJECT
OBJECTS > OBJECT
OBJET _n_ object

OBJETS > OBJET

OBJURE vb put on oath

OBJURED > OBJURE

OBJURES > OBJURE

OBJURGATE vb scold or reprimand

OBJURING > OBJURE

OBLAST n administrative division of the constituent republics of Russia

OBLASTI > OBLAST

OBLASTS > OBLAST

OBLATE adj (of a sphere) flattened at the poles ▷ n person dedicated to a monastic or religious life

OBLATELY > OBLATE

OBLATES > OBLATE

OBLATION n religious offering

OBLATIONS > OBLATION

OBLATORY > OBLATION

OBLIGABLE > OBLIGATE

OBLIGANT n person promising to pay a sum

OBLIGANTS > OBLIGANT

OBLIGATE vb compel, constrain, or oblige morally or legally ▷ adj compelled, bound, or restricted

OBLIGATED > OBLIGATE

OBLIGATES > OBLIGATE

OBLIGATI > OBLIGATO

OBLIGATO same as > OBBLIGATO

OBLIGATOR > OBLIGATE

OBLIGATOS > OBLIGATO

OBLIGE vb compel (someone) morally or by law

OBLIGED > OBLIGE

OBLIGEE n person in whose favour an obligation, contract, or bond is created

OBLIGEES > OBLIGEE

OBLIGER > OBLIGE

OBLIGERS > OBLIGE

OBLIGES > OBLIGE

OBLIGING adj ready to help other people

OBLIGOR n person who binds themself by contract

OBLIGORS > OBLIGOR

OBLIQUE adj slanting ▷ n symbol (/) ▷ vb take or have an oblique direction

OBLIQUED > OBLIQUE

OBLIQUELY > OBLIQUE

OBLIQUER > OBLIQUE

OBLIQUES > OBLIQUE

OBLIQUEST > OBLIQUE

OBLIQUID adj oblique

OBLIQUING > OBLIQUE

OBLIQUITY n state or condition of being oblique

OBLIVION n state of being forgotten

OBLIVIONS > OBLIVION

OBLIVIOUS adj unaware

OBLONG adj having two long sides, two short sides, and four right angles ▷ n oblong figure

OBLONGLY > OBLONG

OBLONGS > OBLONG

OBLOQUIAL > OBLOQUY

OBLOQUIES > OBLOQUY

OBLOQUY n verbal abuse

OBNOXIOUS adj offensive

OBO n ship carrying oil and ore

OBOE n double-reeded woodwind instrument

OBOES > OBOE

OBOIST > OBOE

OBOISTS > OBOE

OBOL same as > OBOLUS

OBOLARY adj very poor

OBOLE n former weight unit in pharmacy

OBOLES > OBOLE

OBOLI > OBOLUS

OBOLS > OBOL

OBOLUS n Greek unit of weight

OBOS > OBO

OBOVATE adj shaped like the longitudinal section of an egg

OBOVATELY > OBOVATE

OBOVOID adj (of a fruit) egg-shaped with the narrower end at the base

OBREPTION n obtaining of something by giving false information

OBS > OB

OBSCENE adj indecent

OBSCENELY > OBSCENE

OBSCENER > OBSCENE

OBSCENEST > OBSCENE

OBSCENITY n state or quality of being obscene

OBSCURANT n opposer of reform and enlightenment ▷ adj of or relating to an obscurant

OBSCURE adj not well known ▷ vb make (something) obscure

OBSCURED > OBSCURE

OBSCURELY > OBSCURE

OBSCURER > OBSCURE

OBSCURERS > OBSCURE

OBSCURES > OBSCURE

OBSCUREST > OBSCURE

OBSCURING > OBSCURE

OBSCURITY n state or quality of being obscure

OBSECRATE rare word for > BESEECH

OBSEQUENT adj (of a river) flowing into a subsequent stream in the opposite direction to the original slope of the land

OBSEQUIAL > OBSEQUIES

OBSEQUIE same as > OBSEQUY

OBSEQUIES pl n funeral rites

OBSEQUY singular of > OBSEQUIES

OBSERVANT adj quick to notice things

OBSERVE vb see or notice

OBSERVED > OBSERVE

OBSERVER n person who observes, esp one who watches someone or something carefully

OBSERVERS > OBSERVER

OBSERVES > OBSERVE

OBSERVING > OBSERVE

OBSESS vb preoccupy (someone) compulsively

OBSESSED > OBSESS

OBSESSES > OBSESS

OBSESSING > OBSESS

OBSESSION n something that preoccupies a person to the exclusion of other things

OBSESSIVE adj motivated by a persistent overriding idea or impulse ▷ n person subject to obsession

OBSESSOR > OBSESS

OBSESSORS > OBSESS

OBSIDIAN n dark glassy volcanic rock

OBSIDIANS > OBSIDIAN

OBSIGN vb confirm

OBSIGNATE same as > OBSIGN

OBSIGNED > OBSIGN

OBSIGNING > OBSIGN

OBSIGNS > OBSIGN

OBSOLESCE vb become obsolete

OBSOLETE adj no longer in use ▷ vb make obsolete

OBSOLETED > OBSOLETE

OBSOLETES > OBSOLETE

OBSTACLE n something that makes progress difficult

OBSTACLES > OBSTACLE

OBSTETRIC adj of or relating to childbirth

OBSTINACY n state or quality of being obstinate

OBSTINATE adj s tubborn

OBSTRUCT vb block with an obstacle

OBSTRUCTS > OBSTRUCT

OBSTRUENT adj causing obstruction, esp of the intestinal tract ▷ n anything that causes obstruction

OBTAIN vb acquire intentionally

OBTAINED > OBTAIN

OBTAINER > OBTAIN

OBTAINERS > OBTAIN

OBTAINING > OBTAIN

OBTAINS > OBTAIN

OBTECT adj (of a pupa) encased in a hardened secretion

OBTECTED same as > OBTECT

OBTEMPER vb comply (with)

OBTEMPERS > OBTEMPER

OBTEND vb put forward

OBTENDED > OBTEND

OBTENDING > OBTEND

OBTENDS > OBTEND

OBTENTION n act of obtaining

OBTEST vb beg (someone) earnestly

OBTESTED > OBTEST

OBTESTING > OBTEST

OBTESTS > OBTEST

OBTRUDE vb push oneself or one's ideas on others

OBTRUDED > OBTRUDE

OBTRUDER > OBTRUDE

OBTRUDERS > OBTRUDE

OBTRUDES > OBTRUDE

OBTRUDING > OBTRUDE

OBTRUSION > OBTRUDE

OBTRUSIVE adj unpleasantly noticeable

OBTUND vb deaden or dull

OBTUNDED > OBTUND

OBTUNDENT > OBTUND

OBTUNDING > OBTUND

OBTUNDITY n semi-conscious state

OBTUNDS > OBTUND

OBTURATE vb stop up (an opening, esp the breech of a gun)

OBTURATED > OBTURATE

OBTURATES > OBTURATE

OBTURATOR > OBTURATE

OBTUSE adj not sharp or pointed

OBTUSELY > OBTUSE

OBTUSER > OBTUSE

OBTUSEST > OBTUSE

OBTUSITY > OBTUSE

OBUMBRATE vb overshadow

OBVENTION n incidental expense

OBVERSE n opposite way of looking at an idea ▷ adj facing or turned towards the observer

OBVERSELY > OBVERSE

OBVERSES > OBVERSE

OBVERSION > OBVERT

OBVERT vb deduce the obverse of (a proposition)

OBVERTED > OBVERT

OBVERTING > OBVERT

OBVERTS > OBVERT

OBVIABLE > OBVIATE

OBVIATE vb make unnecessary

OBVIATED > OBVIATE

OBVIATES > OBVIATE

OBVIATING > OBVIATE

OBVIATION > OBVIATE

OBVIATOR > OBVIATE

OBVIATORS > OBVIATE

OBVIOUS adj easy to see or understand, evident

OBVIOUSLY adv in a way that is easy to see or understand

OBVOLUTE adj (of leaves or petals in the bud) folded so that the margins overlap each other

OBVOLUTED same as
> OBVOLUTE
OBVOLVENT adj curving
around something
OBVS adv obviously
OCA n any of various South
American herbaceous
plants
OCARINA n small oval
wind instrument
OCARINAS > OCARINA
OCAS > OCA
OCCAM n computer
programming language
OCCAMIES > OCCAMY
OCCAMS > OCCAM
OCCAMY n type of alloy
OCCASION n time at
which a particular thing
happens ▷ vb cause
OCCASIONS pl n needs
OCCIDENT literary or
formal word for > WEST
OCCIDENTS > OCCIDENT
OCCIES > OCCY
OCCIPITA > OCCIPUT
OCCIPITAL adj of or
relating to the back of the
head or skull
OCCIPUT n back of the
head
OCCIPUTS > OCCIPUT
OCCLUDE vb obstruct
OCCLUDED > OCCLUDE
OCCLUDENT > OCCLUDE
OCCLUDER > OCCLUDE
OCCLUDERS > OCCLUDE
OCCLUDES > OCCLUDE
OCCLUDING > OCCLUDE
OCCLUSAL
> OCCLUSION
OCCLUSION n act or
process of occluding or the
state of being occluded
OCCLUSIVE adj of or
relating to the act of
occlusion ▷ n occlusive
speech sound
OCCLUSOR n muscle for
closing opening
OCCLUSORS
> OCCLUSOR
OCCULT adj relating to
the supernatural ▷ vb (of a
celestial body) to hide
(another celestial body)
from view
OCCULTED > OCCULT
OCCULTER n something
that obscures
OCCULTERS
> OCCULTER
OCCULTING > OCCULT
OCCULTISM n belief in
and the study and practice
of magic, astrology, etc
OCCULTIST
> OCCULTISM
OCCULTLY > OCCULT
OCCULTS > OCCULT
OCCUPANCE same as
> OCCUPANCY
OCCUPANCY n (length of)
a person's stay in a
specified place
OCCUPANT n person
occupying a specified
place

OCCUPANTS
> OCCUPANT
OCCUPATE same as
> OCCUPY
OCCUPATED
> OCCUPATE
OCCUPATES
> OCCUPATE
OCCUPIED > OCCUPY
OCCUPIER n person who
lives in a particular house,
whether as owner or
tenant
OCCUPIERS
> OCCUPIER
OCCUPIES > OCCUPY
OCCUPY vb live or work in
(a building)
OCCUPYING > OCCUPY
OCCUR vb happen
OCCURRED > OCCUR
OCCURRENT adj (of a
property) relating to some
observable feature of its
bearer
OCCURRING > OCCUR
OCCURS > OCCUR
OCCY n as in all over the
occy dialect expression
meaning in every
direction
OCEAN n vast area of sea
between continents
OCEANARIA pl n large
saltwater aquaria for
marine life
OCEANAUT n undersea
explorer
OCEANAUTS
> OCEANAUT
OCEANIC adj of or
relating to the ocean
OCEANID n ocean nymph
in Greek mythology
OCEANIDES > OCEANID
OCEANIDS > OCEANID
OCEANS > OCEAN
OCEANSIDE adj beside
the ocean
OCEANVIEW adj with a
view of the ocean
OCEANWARD adv towards
the ocean
OCELLAR > OCELLUS
OCELLATE > OCELLUS
OCELLATED > OCELLUS
OCELLI > OCELLUS
OCELLUS n simple eye of
insects and some other
invertebrates
OCELOID adj of or like an
ocelot
OCELOT n American wild
cat with a spotted coat
OCELOTS > OCELOT
OCH interj expression of
surprise, annoyance, or
disagreement
OCHE n (in darts) mark
behind which a player
must stand
OCHER same as > OCHRE
OCHERED > OCHER
OCHERIER > OCHERY
OCHERIEST > OCHERY
OCHERING > OCHER
OCHERISH adj (US)
resembling ochre

OCHEROID adj (US) of or
like ochre
OCHEROUS > OCHER
OCHERS > OCHER
OCHERY same as > OCHRY
OCHES > OCHE
OCHIDORE n type of crab
OCHIDORES > OCHIDORE
OCHLOCRAT n supporter
of rule by the mob
OCHONE interj expression
of sorrow or regret
OCHRE n brownish-yellow
earth ▷ adj moderate
yellow-orange to orange
▷ vb colour with ochre
OCHREA n cup-shaped
structure that sheathes
the stems of certain plants
OCHREAE > OCHREA
OCHREAS > OCHREA
OCHREATE same as
> OCREATE
OCHRED > OCHRE
OCHREOUS > OCHRE
OCHRES > OCHRE
OCHREY > OCHRE
OCHRIER > OCHRY
OCHRIEST > OCHRY
OCHRING > OCHRE
OCHROID > OCHRE
OCHROUS > OCHRE
OCHRY adj containing or
resembling ochre
OCICAT n breed of cat
with a spotted coat
OCICATS > OCICAT
OCKER n uncultivated or
boorish Australian
OCKERISM n Australian
boorishness
OCKERISMS
> OCKERISM
OCKERS > OCKER
OCKODOLS pl n one's feet
when wearing boots
OCOTILLO n cactus-like
tree
OCOTILLOS
> OCOTILLO
OCREA same as > OCHREA
OCREAE > OCREA
OCREAS > OCREA
OCREATE adj possessing
an ocrea
OCTA same as > OKTA
OCTACHORD n
eight-stringed musical
instrument
OCTAD n group or series of
eight
OCTADIC > OCTAD
OCTADS > OCTAD
OCTAGON n geometric
figure with eight sides
OCTAGONAL adj having
eight sides and eight
angles
OCTAGONS > OCTAGON
OCTAHEDRA pl n solid
eight-sided figures;
octahedrons
OCTAL n number system
with a base 8
OCTALS > OCTAL
OCTAMETER n verse line
consisting of eight
metrical feet

OCTAN n illness that
occurs weekly
OCTANE n hydrocarbon
found in petrol
OCTANES > OCTANE
OCTANGLE same as
> OCTAGON
OCTANGLES
> OCTANGLE
OCTANOL n alcohol
containing eight carbon
atoms
OCTANOLS > OCTANOL
OCTANS > OCTAN
OCTANT n any of the eight
parts into which the three
planes containing the
Cartesian coordinate axes
divide space
OCTANTAL > OCTANT
OCTANTS > OCTANT
OCTAPLA n book with
eight texts
OCTAPLAS > OCTAPLA
OCTAPLOID adj having
eight parts
OCTAPODIC
> OCTAPODY
OCTAPODY n line of verse
with eight metrical feet
OCTARCHY n government
by eight rulers
OCTAS > OCTA
OCTASTICH n verse of
eight lines
OCTASTYLE adj (of
building) having eight
columns
OCTAVAL > OCTAVE
OCTAVE n (interval
between the first and)
eighth note of a scale ▷ adj
consisting of eight parts
OCTAVES > OCTAVE
OCTAVO n book size in
which the sheets are
folded into eight leaves
OCTAVOS > OCTAVO
OCTENNIAL adj
occurring every eight
years
OCTET n group of eight
performers
OCTETS > OCTET
OCTETT same as > OCTET
OCTETTE same as
> OCTET
OCTETTES > OCTETTE
OCTETTS > OCTETT
OCTILLION n (in Britain
and Germany) the number
represented as one
followed by 48 zeros
OCTOFID adj divided into
eight
OCTOHEDRA same as
> OCTAHEDRA
OCTONARII pl n lines
with eight feet
OCTONARY adj relating to
or based on the number
eight ▷ n stanza of eight
lines
OCTOPI > OCTOPUS
OCTOPLOID same as
> OCTAPLOID
OCTOPOD n type of
mollusc ▷ adj of these
molluscs

OCTOPODAN > OCTOPOD
OCTOPODES > OCTOPOD
OCTOPODS > OCTOPOD
OCTOPOID *adj* of or like an octopus
OCTOPUS *n* sea creature with a soft body and eight tentacles
OCTOPUSES > OCTOPUS
OCTOPUSH *n* hockey-like game played underwater
OCTOSTYLE *same as* > OCTASTYLE
OCTOTHORP *n* type of symbol in printing
OCTROI *n* duty on various goods brought into certain European towns
OCTROIS > OCTROI
OCTUOR *n* octet
OCTUORS > OCTUOR
OCTUPLE *n* quantity or number eight times as great as another ▷ *adj* eight times as much or as many ▷ *vb* multiply by eight
OCTUPLED > OCTUPLE
OCTUPLES > OCTUPLE
OCTUPLET *n* one of eight offspring from one birth
OCTUPLETS > OCTUPLET
OCTUPLEX *n* something made up of eight parts
OCTUPLING > OCTUPLE
OCTUPLY *adv* by eight times
OCTYL *n* group of atoms
OCTYLS > OCTYL
OCULAR *adj* relating to the eyes or sight ▷ *n* lens in an optical instrument
OCULARIST *n* person who makes artificial eyes
OCULARLY > OCULAR
OCULARS > OCULAR
OCULATE *adj* possessing eyes
OCULATED *same as* > OCULATE
OCULI > OCULUS
OCULIST *n* ophthalmologist
OCULISTS > OCULIST
OCULUS *n* round window
OD *n* hypothetical force
ODA *n* room or chamber
ODAH *same as* > ODA
ODAHS > ODAH
ODAL *same as* > UDAL
ODALIQUE *same as* > ODALISQUE
ODALIQUES > ODALIQUE
ODALISK *same as* > ODALISQUE
ODALISKS > ODALISK
ODALISQUE *n* female slave in a harem
ODALLER > ODAL
ODALLERS > ODAL
ODALS > ODAL
ODAS > ODA
ODD *adj* unusual
ODDBALL *n* eccentric person ▷ *adj* strange or peculiar

ODDBALLS > ODDBALL
ODDER > ODD
ODDEST > ODD
ODDISH > ODD
ODDITIES > ODDITY
ODDITY *n* odd person or thing
ODDLY > ODD
ODDMENT *n* odd piece or thing
ODDMENTS > ODDMENT
ODDNESS > ODD
ODDNESSES > ODD
ODDS *pl n* probability of something happening
ODDSMAKER *n* person setting odds in betting
ODDSMAN *n* umpire
ODDSMEN > ODDSMAN
ODE *n* lyric poem, usu addressed to a particular subject
ODEA > ODEUM
ODEON *same as* > ODEUM
ODEONS > ODEON
ODES > ODE
ODEUM *n* ancient building for musical performances
ODEUMS > ODEUM
ODIC > OD
ODIFEROUS *adj* having odour
ODIOUS *adj* offensive
ODIOUSLY > ODIOUS
ODISM > OD
ODISMS > OD
ODIST > OD
ODISTS > OD
ODIUM *n* widespread dislike
ODIUMS > ODIUM
ODOGRAPH *same as* > ODOMETER
ODOGRAPHS > ODOGRAPH
ODOMETER *n* device that records the number of miles that a bicycle or motor vehicle has travelled
ODOMETERS > ODOMETER
ODOMETRY > ODOMETER
ODONATA *pl n* insects of an order that includes dragonflies
ODONATE *n* dragonfly or related insect
ODONATES > ODONATE
ODONATIST *n* dragonfly expert
ODONTALGY *n* toothache
ODONTIC *adj* of teeth
ODONTIST *n* dentist
ODONTISTS > ODONTIST
ODONTOID *adj* toothlike ▷ *n* bone in the spine
ODONTOIDS > ODONTOID
ODONTOMA *n* tumour near teeth
ODONTOMAS > ODONTOMA
ODOR *same as* > ODOUR
ODORANT *n* something with a strong smell
ODORANTS > ODORANT

ODORATE *adj* having a strong smell
ODORED *same as* > ODOURED
ODORFUL *same as* > ODOURFUL
ODORISE *same as* > ODORIZE
ODORISED > ODORISE
ODORISER *same as* > ODORIZER
ODORISERS > ODORISER
ODORISES > ODORISE
ODORISING > ODORISE
ODORIZE *vb* give an odour to
ODORIZED > ODORIZE
ODORIZER *n* something that odorizes
ODORIZERS > ODORIZER
ODORIZES > ODORIZE
ODORIZING > ODORIZE
ODORLESS > ODOR
ODOROUS *adj* having or emitting a characteristic smell
ODOROUSLY > ODOROUS
ODORS > ODOR
ODOUR *n* particular smell
ODOURED *adj* having an odour
ODOURFUL *adj* full of odour
ODOURLESS > ODOUR
ODOURS > ODOUR
ODS > OD
ODSO *n* cry of surprise
ODYL *same as* > OD
ODYLE *same as* > OD
ODYLES > ODYLE
ODYLISM > ODYL
ODYLISMS > ODYL
ODYLS > ODYL
ODYSSEAN *adj* of or like an odyssey
ODYSSEY *n* long eventful journey
ODYSSEYS > ODYSSEY
ODZOOKS *interj* cry of surprise
OE *n* grandchild
OECIST *n* colony founder
OECISTS > OECIST
OECOLOGIC *same as* > ECOLOGIC
OECOLOGY *less common spelling of* > ECOLOGY
OECUMENIC *variant of* > ECUMENIC
OEDEMA *n* abnormal swelling
OEDEMAS > OEDEMA
OEDEMATA > OEDEMA
OEDIPAL *adj* relating to a complex whereby a male child wants to replace his father
OEDIPALLY > OEDIPAL
OEDIPEAN *same as* > OEDIPAL
OEDOMETER *n* instrument for measuring the consolidation of a soil specimen under pressure
OEILLADE *n* suggestive glance

OEILLADES > OEILLADE
OENANTHIC *adj* smelling of or like wine
OENOLOGY *n* study of wine
OENOMANCY *n* divination by studying the colour of wine
OENOMANIA *n* craving for wine
OENOMEL *n* drink made of wine and honey
OENOMELS > OENOMEL
OENOMETER *n* device for measuring the strength of wine
OENOPHIL *same as* > OENOPHILE
OENOPHILE *n* lover or connoisseur of wines
OENOPHILS > OENOPHIL
OENOPHILY *n* love of wine
OENOTHERA *n* type of American plant with yellow flowers that open in the evening
OERLIKON *n* type of cannon
OERLIKONS > OERLIKON
OERSTED *n* cgs unit of magnetic field strength
OERSTEDS > OERSTED
OES > OE
OESOPHAGI *pl n* gullets
OESTRAL > OESTRUS
OESTRIN *obsolete term for* > OESTROGEN
OESTRINS > OESTRIN
OESTRIOL *n* weak oestrogenic hormone secreted by the mammalian ovary
OESTRIOLS > OESTRIOL
OESTROGEN *n* female hormone
OESTRONE *n* weak oestrogenic hormone secreted by the mammalian ovary
OESTRONES > OESTRONE
OESTROUS > OESTRUS
OESTRUAL *adj* relating to oestrus
OESTRUM *same as* > OESTRUS
OESTRUMS > OESTRUM
OESTRUS *n* regularly occurring period of fertility in female mammals
OESTRUSES > OESTRUS
OEUVRE *n* work of art, literature, music, etc
OEUVRES > OEUVRE
OF *prep* belonging to
OFF *prep* away from ▷ *adv* away ▷ *adj* not operating ▷ *n* side of the field to which the batsman's feet point ▷ *vb* take off
OFFA *prep* off
OFFAL *n* edible organs of an animal, such as liver or kidneys

OFFALS > OFFAL
OFFBEAT *adj* unusual or eccentric ▷ *n* any of the normally unaccented beats in a bar
OFFBEATS > OFFBEAT
OFFCAST *n* cast-off
OFFCASTS > OFFCAST
OFFCUT *n* piece remaining after the required parts have been cut out
OFFCUTS > OFFCUT
OFFED > OFF
OFFENCE *n* (cause of) hurt feelings or annoyance
OFFENCES > OFFENCE
OFFEND *vb* hurt the feelings of, insult
OFFENDED > OFFEND
OFFENDER > OFFEND
OFFENDERS > OFFEND
OFFENDING > OFFEND
OFFENDS > OFFEND
OFFENSE *same as* > OFFENCE
OFFENSES > OFFENSE
OFFENSIVE *adj* disagreeable ▷ *n* position or action of attack
OFFER *vb* present (something) for acceptance or rejection ▷ *n* something offered
OFFERABLE > OFFER
OFFERED > OFFER
OFFEREE *n* person to whom an offer is made
OFFEREES > OFFEREE
OFFERER > OFFER
OFFERERS > OFFER
OFFERING *n* thing offered
OFFERINGS > OFFERING
OFFEROR > OFFER
OFFERORS > OFFER
OFFERS > OFFER
OFFERTORY *n* offering of the bread and wine for Communion
OFFHAND *adj* casual, curt ▷ *adv* without preparation
OFFHANDED *adj* without care or consideration
OFFICE *n* room or building where people work at desks
OFFICER *n* person in authority in the armed services ▷ *vb* furnish with officers
OFFICERED > OFFICER
OFFICERS > OFFICER
OFFICES > OFFICE
OFFICIAL *adj* of a position of authority ▷ *n* person who holds a position of authority
OFFICIALS > OFFICIAL
OFFICIANT *n* person who presides and officiates at a religious ceremony
OFFICIARY *n* body of officials ▷ *adj* of, relating to, or derived from office

OFFICIATE *vb* act in an official role
OFFICINAL *adj* (of pharmaceutical products) available without prescription ▷ *n* officinal preparation or plant
OFFICIOUS *adj* interfering unnecessarily
OFFIE *n* off-licence
OFFIES > OFFIE
OFFING *n* area of the sea visible from the shore
OFFINGS > OFFING
OFFISH *adj* aloof or distant in manner
OFFISHLY > OFFISH
OFFKEY *adj* out of tune
OFFLINE *adj* disconnected from a computer or the internet
OFFLOAD *vb* pass responsibility to someone else
OFFLOADED > OFFLOAD
OFFLOADS > OFFLOAD
OFFPEAK *adj* relating to times outside periods of intensive use
OFFPRINT *n* separate reprint of an article that originally appeared in a larger publication ▷ *vb* reprint (an article taken from a larger publication) separately
OFFPRINTS > OFFPRINT
OFFPUT *n* act of putting off
OFFPUTS > OFFPUT
OFFRAMP *n* road allowing traffic to leave a motorway
OFFRAMPS > OFFRAMP
OFFS > OFF
OFFSADDLE *vb* unsaddle
OFFSCREEN *adj* unseen by film viewers
OFFSCUM *n* scum
OFFSCUMS > OFFSCUM
OFFSEASON *n* period of little trade in a business
OFFSET *vb* cancel out ▷ *n* printing method
OFFSETS > OFFSET
OFFSHOOT *n* something developed from something else
OFFSHOOTS > OFFSHOOT
OFFSHORE *adv* away from or at some distance from the shore ▷ *adj* sited or conducted at sea ▷ *n* company operating abroad where the tax system is more advantageous than at home ▷ *vb* transfer (work) to another country where wages are lower
OFFSHORED > OFFSHORE
OFFSHORES > OFFSHORE
OFFSIDE *adv* (positioned) illegally ahead of the ball ▷ *n* side of a vehicle nearest the centre of the road

OFFSIDER *n* partner or assistant
OFFSIDERS > OFFSIDER
OFFSIDES > OFFSIDE
OFFSPRING *n* child
OFFSTAGE *adv* out of the view of the audience ▷ *n* something that happens offstage
OFFSTAGES > OFFSTAGE
OFFTAKE *n* act of taking off
OFFTAKES > OFFTAKE
OFFTRACK *adj* not at a racetrack
OFFY *same as* > OFFIE
OFLAG *n* prisoner-of-war camp for officers in World War II
OFLAGS > OFLAG
OFT *adv* often
OFTEN *adv* frequently, much of the time
OFTENER > OFTEN
OFTENEST > OFTEN
OFTENNESS > OFTEN
OFTER > OFT
OFTEST > OFT
OFTTIMES *same as* > OFTEN
OGAM *same as* > OGHAM
OGAMIC > OGHAM
OGAMS > OGAM
OGANESSON *n* highly radioactive element
OGDOAD *n* group of eight
OGDOADS > OGDOAD
OGEE *n* moulding having a cross section in the form of a letter S
OGEED *adj* (of an arch or moulding) having an ogee
OGEES > OGEE
OGGIN *n* sea
OGGINS > OGGIN
OGHAM *n* ancient writing system used by the Celts
OGHAMIC > OGHAM
OGHAMIST > OGHAM
OGHAMISTS > OGHAM
OGHAMS > OGHAM
OGIVAL > OGIVE
OGIVE *n* diagonal rib or groin of a Gothic vault
OGIVES > OGIVE
OGLE *vb* stare or gape at ▷ *n* flirtatious look
OGLED > OGLE
OGLER > OGLE
OGLERS > OGLE
OGLES > OGLE
OGLING > OGLE
OGLINGS > OGLE
OGMIC > OGAM
OGRE *n* giant that eats human flesh
OGREISH > OGRE
OGREISHLY > OGRE
OGREISM > OGRE
OGREISMS > OGRE
OGRES > OGRE
OGRESS > OGRE
OGRESSES > OGRE
OGRISH > OGRE
OGRISHLY > OGRE

OGRISM > OGRE
OGRISMS > OGRE
OH *interj* exclamation of surprise, pain, etc ▷ *vb* say 'oh'
OHED > OH
OHIA *n* Hawaiian plant
OHIAS > OHIA
OHING > OH
OHM *n* unit of electrical resistance
OHMAGE *n* electrical resistance in ohms
OHMAGES > OHMAGE
OHMIC *adj* of or relating to a circuit element
OHMICALLY > OHMIC
OHMMETER *n* instrument for measuring electrical resistance
OHMMETERS > OHMMETER
OHMS > OHM
OHO *interj* exclamation expressing surprise, exultation, or derision
OHONE *same as* > OCHONE
OHS > OH
OI *interj* shout to attract attention ▷ *n* grey-faced petrel
OIDIA > OIDIUM
OIDIOID > OIDIUM
OIDIUM *n* type of fungal spore
OIK *n* insulting word for person regarded as inferior because ignorant or lower-class
OIKIST *same as* > OECIST
OIKISTS > OIKIST
OIKS > OIK
OIL *n* viscous liquid, insoluble in water and usu flammable ▷ *vb* lubricate (a machine) with oil
OILBIRD *n* type of nocturnal gregarious cave-dwelling bird
OILBIRDS > OILBIRD
OILCAMP *n* camp for oil workers
OILCAMPS > OILCAMP
OILCAN *n* container with a long nozzle for applying oil to machinery
OILCANS > OILCAN
OILCLOTH *n* waterproof material
OILCLOTHS > OILCLOTH
OILCUP *n* cup-shaped oil reservoir in a machine providing continuous lubrication for a bearing
OILCUPS > OILCUP
OILED > OIL
OILER *n* person, device, etc, that lubricates or supplies oil
OILERIES > OILERY
OILERS > OILER
OILERY *n* oil business
OILFIELD *n* area containing oil reserves
OILFIELDS > OILFIELD

OILFIRED *adj* using oil as fuel

OILGAS *n* gaseous mixture of hydrocarbons used as a fuel

OILGASES > OILGAS

OILHOLE *n* hole for oil

OILHOLES > OILHOLE

OILIER > OILY

OILIEST > OILY

OILILY > OILY

OILINESS > OILY

OILING > OIL

OILLET *same as* > EYELET

OILLETS > OILLET

OILMAN *n* person who owns or operates oil wells

OILMEN > OILMAN

OILNUT *n* nut from which oil is extracted

OILNUTS > OILNUT

OILPAN *n* sump

OILPANS > OILPAN

OILPAPER *n* oiled paper

OILPAPERS > OILPAPER

OILPROOF *adj* resistant to oil

OILS > OIL

OILSEED *n* seed from which oil is extracted

OILSEEDS > OILSEED

OILSKIN *n* (garment made from) waterproof material

OILSKINS > OILSKIN

OILSTONE *n* stone with a fine grain lubricated with oil and used for sharpening cutting tools

OILSTONES > OILSTONE

OILTIGHT *adj* not allowing oil through

OILWAY *n* channel for oil

OILWAYS > OILWAY

OILY *adj* soaked or covered with oil

OINK *n* grunt of a pig or an imitation of this ▷ *interj* imitation or representation of the grunt of a pig ▷ *vb* make noise of pig

OINKED > OINK

OINKING > OINK

OINKS > OINK

OINOLOGY *same as* > OENOLOGY

OINOMEL *same as* > OENOMEL

OINOMELS > OINOMEL

OINT *vb* anoint

OINTED > OINT

OINTING > OINT

OINTMENT *n* greasy substance used for healing skin or as a cosmetic

OINTMENTS > OINTMENT

OINTS > OINT

OIS > OI

OITICICA *n* South American tree

OITICICAS > OITICICA

OJIME *n* Japanese bead used to secure cords

OJIMES > OJIME

OK *interj* expression of approval

OKA *n* unit of weight used in Turkey

OKAPI *n* African animal related to the giraffe but with a shorter neck

OKAPIS > OKAPI

OKAS > OKA

OKAY *adj* satisfactory ▷ *vb* approve or endorse ▷ *n* approval or agreement ▷ *interj* expression of approval

OKAYED > OKAY

OKAYING > OKAY

OKAYS > OKAY

OKE *same as* > OKA

OKEH *variant of* > OKAY

OKEHS > OKEH

OKES > OKE

OKEYDOKE *variant of* > OKAY

OKEYDOKEY *variant of* > OKAY

OKIMONO *n* Japanese ornamental item

OKIMONOS > OKIMONO

OKRA *n* tropical plant with edible green pods

OKRAS > OKRA

OKTA *n* unit used in meteorology to measure cloud cover

OKTAS > OKTA

OLD *adj* having lived or existed for a long time ▷ *n* earlier or past time

OLDE *adj* old-world or quaint, used facetiously

OLDEN *adj* old ▷ *vb* grow old

OLDENED > OLDEN

OLDENING > OLDEN

OLDENS > OLDEN

OLDER > OLD

OLDEST > OLD

OLDIE *n* old but popular song or film

OLDIES > OLDIE

OLDISH > OLD

OLDNESS > OLD

OLDNESSES > OLD

OLDS > OLD

OLDSQUAW *n* type of long-tailed sea duck

OLDSQUAWS > OLDSQUAW

OLDSTER *n* older person

OLDSTERS > OLDSTER

OLDSTYLE *n* printing type style

OLDSTYLES > OLDSTYLE

OLDWIFE *n* any of various fishes, esp the menhaden or the alewife

OLDWIVES > OLDWIFE

OLDY *same as* > OLDIE

OLE *interj* exclamation of approval or encouragement customary at bullfights ▷ *n* cry of olé

OLEA > OLEUM

OLEACEOUS *adj* relating to a family of trees and shrubs, including the ash, jasmine, and olive

OLEANDER *n* Mediterranean flowering evergreen shrub

OLEANDERS > OLEANDER

OLEARIA *n* daisy bush

OLEARIAS > OLEARIA

OLEASTER *n* type of shrub with silver-white twigs and yellow flowers

OLEASTERS > OLEASTER

OLEATE *n* any salt or ester of oleic acid

OLEATES > OLEATE

OLECRANAL > OLECRANON

OLECRANON *n* bony projection of the ulna behind the elbow joint

OLEFIANT *adj* forming oil

OLEFIN *same as* > OLEFINE

OLEFINE *another name for* > ALKENE

OLEFINES > OLEFINE

OLEFINIC > OLEFINE

OLEFINS > OLEFIN

OLEIC *adj* as in *oleic acid* colourless oily liquid used in making soap

OLEIN *another name for* > TRIOLEIN

OLEINE *same as* > OLEIN

OLEINES > OLEINE

OLEINS > OLEIN

OLENT *adj* having smell

OLEO *n* as in *oleo oil* oil extracted from beef fat

OLEOGRAPH *n* chromolithograph printed in oil colours to imitate the appearance of an oil painting

OLEORESIN *n* semisolid mixture of a resin and essential oil

OLEOS > OLEO

OLES > OLE

OLESTRA *n* trademark term for an artificial fat

OLESTRAS > OLESTRA

OLEUM *n* type of sulphuric acid

OLEUMS > OLEUM

OLFACT *vb* smell something

OLFACTED > OLFACT

OLFACTING > OLFACT

OLFACTION *n* sense of smell

OLFACTIVE *adj* of sense of smell

OLFACTORY *adj* relating to the sense of smell ▷ *n* organ or nerve concerned with the sense of smell

OLFACTS > OLFACT

OLIBANUM *n* frankincense

OLIBANUMS > OLIBANUM

OLICOOK *n* doughnut

OLICOOKS > OLICOOK

OLID *adj* foul-smelling

OLIGAEMIA *n* reduction in the volume of the blood, as occurs after haemorrhage

OLIGAEMIC > OLIGAEMIA

OLIGARCH *n* member of an oligarchy

OLIGARCHS > OLIGARCH

OLIGARCHY *n* government by a small group of people

OLIGEMIA *same as* > OLIGAEMIA

OLIGEMIAS > OLIGAEMIA

OLIGEMIC > OLIGAEMIA

OLIGIST *n* type of iron ore

OLIGISTS > OLIGIST

OLIGOCENE *adj* belonging to geological time period

OLIGOGENE *n* type of gene

OLIGOMER *n* compound of relatively low molecular weight containing up to five monomer units

OLIGOMERS > OLIGOMER

OLIGOPOLY *n* market situation in which control over the supply of a commodity is held by a small number of producers

OLIGURIA *n* excretion of an abnormally small volume of urine

OLIGURIAS > OLIGURIA

OLIGURIC *adj* relating to oliguria

OLINGO *n* South American mammal

OLINGOS > OLINGO

OLINGUITO *n* type of small S American mammal

OLIO *n* dish of many different ingredients

OLIOS > OLIO

OLIPHANT *archaic variant of* > ELEPHANT

OLIPHANTS > OLIPHANT

OLITORIES > OLITORY

OLITORY *n* kitchen garden

OLIVARY *adj* shaped like an olive

OLIVE *n* small green or black fruit used as food or pressed for its oil ▷ *adj* greyish-green

OLIVENITE *n* green to black rare secondary mineral

OLIVER *n* as in *Bath oliver* type of unsweetened biscuit

OLIVERS > OLIVER

OLIVES > OLIVE

OLIVET *n* button shaped like olive

OLIVETS > OLIVET

OLIVEWOOD n the wood of the olive tree
OLIVINE n olive-green mineral of the olivine group
OLIVINES > OLIVINE
OLIVINIC adj containing olivine
OLLA n cooking pot
OLLAMH n old Irish term for a wise man
OLLAMHS > OLLAMH
OLLAS > OLLA
OLLAV same as > OLLAMH
OLLAVS > OLLAV
OLLER n waste ground
OLLERS > OLLER
OLLIE n type of skateboarding jump ▷ vb perform an ollie
OLLIED > OLLIE
OLLIEING > OLLIE
OLLIES > OLLIE
OLM n pale blind eel-like salamander
OLMS > OLM
OLOGIES > OLOGY
OLOGIST n scientist
OLOGISTS > OLOGIST
OLOGOAN vb complain loudly without reason
OLOGOANED > OLOGOAN
OLOGOANS > OLOGOAN
OLOGY n science or other branch of knowledge
OLOLIUQUI n medicinal plant used by the Aztecs
OLOROSO n golden-coloured sweet sherry
OLOROSOS > OLOROSO
OLPAE > OLPE
OLPE n ancient Greek jug
OLPES > OLPE
OLYCOOK same as > OLYKOEK
OLYCOOKS > OLYCOOK
OLYKOEK n American type of doughnut
OLYKOEKS > OLYKOEK
OLYMPIAD n staging of the modern Olympic Games
OLYMPIADS > OLYMPIAD
OLYMPICS pl n modern revival of the ancient Greek games, featuring sporting contests
OM n sacred syllable in Hinduism
OMA n grandmother
OMADHAUN n foolish man or boy
OMADHAUNS > OMADHAUN
OMAS > OMA
OMASA > OMASUM
OMASAL > OMASUM
OMASUM n compartment in the stomach of a ruminant animal
OMBER same as > OMBRE
OMBERS > OMBER
OMBRE n 18th-century card game
OMBRELLA old form of > UMBRELLA
OMBRELLAS > OMBRELLA

OMBRES > OMBRE
OMBROPHIL n plant flourishing in rainy conditions
OMBU n South American tree
OMBUDSMAN n official who investigates complaints against government organizations
OMBUDSMEN > OMBUDSMAN
OMBUS > OMBU
OMEGA n last letter in the Greek alphabet
OMEGAS > OMEGA
OMELET same as > OMELETTE
OMELETS > OMELET
OMELETTE n dish of eggs beaten and fried
OMELETTES > OMELETTE
OMEN n happening or object thought to foretell success or misfortune ▷ vb portend
OMENED > OMEN
OMENING > OMEN
OMENS > OMEN
OMENTA > OMENTUM
OMENTAL > OMENTUM
OMENTUM n double fold of the peritoneum
OMENTUMS > OMENTUM
OMER n ancient Hebrew unit of dry measure
OMERS > OMER
OMERTA n conspiracy of silence
OMERTAS > OMERTA
OMICRON n 15th letter in the Greek alphabet
OMICRONS > OMICRON
OMIGOD interj exclamation of surprise, pleasure, dismay, etc
OMIKRON same as > OMICRON
OMIKRONS > OMIKRON
OMINOUS adj worrying, seeming to foretell misfortune
OMINOUSLY > OMINOUS
OMISSIBLE > OMIT
OMISSION n something that has been left out or passed over
OMISSIONS > OMISSION
OMISSIVE > OMISSION
OMIT vb leave out
OMITS > OMIT
OMITTANCE n omission
OMITTED > OMIT
OMITTER > OMIT
OMITTERS > OMIT
OMITTING > OMIT
OMLAH n staff team in India
OMLAHS > OMLAH
OMMATEA > OMMATEUM
OMMATEUM n insect eye
OMMATIDIA pl n cone-shaped parts of the eyes of some arthropods
OMNEITIES > OMNEITY

OMNEITY n state of being all
OMNIANA n miscellaneous collection
OMNIANAS > OMNIANA
OMNIARCH n ruler of everything
OMNIARCHS > OMNIARCH
OMNIBUS n several books or TV or radio programmes made into one ▷ adj consisting of or dealing with several different things at once
OMNIBUSES > OMNIBUS
OMNIETIES > OMNIETY
OMNIETY same as > OMNEITY
OMNIFIC adj creating all things
OMNIFIED > OMNIFY
OMNIFIES > OMNIFY
OMNIFORM adj of all forms
OMNIFY vb make something universal
OMNIFYING > OMNIFY
OMNIMODE adj of all functions
OMNIRANGE n very-high-frequency ground radio navigational system
OMNIUM n total value
OMNIUMS > OMNIUM
OMNIVORA n group of omnivorous mammals
OMNIVORE n omnivorous animal
OMNIVORES > OMNIVORE
OMNIVORY n state of being omnivorous
OMOHYOID n muscle in shoulder
OMOHYOIDS > OMOHYOID
OMOPHAGIA n eating of raw food, esp meat
OMOPHAGIC > OMOPHAGIA
OMOPHAGY same as > OMOPHAGIA
OMOPHORIA pl n stole-like bands worn by some bishops
OMOPLATE n shoulder blade
OMOPLATES > OMOPLATE
OMOV n voting system in which each voter has one vote to cast
OMOVS > OMOV
OMPHACITE n type of mineral
OMPHALI > OMPHALOS
OMPHALIC > OMPHALOS
OMPHALOI > OMPHALOS
OMPHALOID adj like navel
OMPHALOS n (in the ancient world) a sacred conical object, esp a stone
OMRAH n Muslim noble
OMRAHS > OMRAH
OMS > OM

ON prep indicating position above, attachment, closeness, etc ▷ adv in operation ▷ adj operating ▷ n side of the field on which the batsman stands ▷ vb go on
ONAGER n wild ass of Persia
ONAGERS > ONAGER
ONAGRI > ONAGER
ONANISM n withdrawal in sexual intercourse before ejaculation
ONANISMS > ONANISM
ONANIST > ONANISM
ONANISTIC > ONANISM
ONANISTS > ONANISM
ONBEAT n first and third beats in a bar of four-four time
ONBEATS > ONBEAT
ONBOARD vb incorporate (a person) into a group
ONBOARDED > ONBOARD
ONBOARDS > ONBOARD
ONCE adv on one occasion ▷ n one occasion
ONCER n (formerly) a one-pound note
ONCERS > ONCER
ONCES > ONCE
ONCET dialect form of > ONCE
ONCIDIUM n American orchid
ONCIDIUMS > ONCIDIUM
ONCOGEN n substance causing tumours to form
ONCOGENE n gene that can cause cancer when abnormally activated
ONCOGENES > ONCOGENE
ONCOGENIC adj causing the formation of a tumour
ONCOGENS > ONCOGEN
ONCOLOGIC > ONCOLOGY
ONCOLOGY n branch of medicine concerned with the study, classification, and treatment of tumours
ONCOLYSES > ONCOLYSIS
ONCOLYSIS n destruction of tumours
ONCOLYTIC adj destroying tumours
ONCOME n act of coming on
ONCOMES > ONCOME
ONCOMETER n instrument for measuring body organs
ONCOMICE > ONCOMOUSE
ONCOMING adj approaching from the front ▷ n approach or onset
ONCOMINGS > ONCOMING
ONCOMOUSE n mouse bred for cancer treatment research
ONCOST same as > OVERHEADS

ONCOSTMAN *n* miner paid daily

ONCOSTMEN > ONCOSTMAN

ONCOSTS > ONCOST

ONCOTOMY *n* surgical cutting of a tumour

ONCOVIRUS *n* virus causing cancer

ONCUS *same as* > ONKUS

ONDATRA *same as* > MUSQUASH

ONDATRAS > ONDATRA

ONDINE *same as* > UNDINE

ONDINES > ONDINE

ONDING *Scots word for* > ONSET

ONDINGS > ONDING

ONDOGRAM *n* record made by ondograph

ONDOGRAMS > ONDOGRAM

ONDOGRAPH *n* instrument for producing a graphical recording of an alternating current

ONE *adj* single, lone ▷ *n* number or figure 1 ▷ *pron* any person

ONEFOLD *adj* simple

ONEIRIC *adj* of or relating to dreams

ONELY *same as* > ONLY

ONENESS *n* unity

ONENESSES > ONENESS

ONER *n* single continuous action

ONERIER > ONERY

ONERIEST > ONERY

ONEROUS *adj* (of a task) difficult to carry out

ONEROUSLY > ONEROUS

ONERS > ONER

ONERY *same as* > ORNERY

ONES > ONE

ONESELF *pron* reflexive form of *one*

ONESIE *n* one-piece garment combining a top with trousers

ONESIES > ONESIE

ONETIME *adj* at some time in the past

ONEYER *old form of* > ONE

ONEYERS > ONEYER

ONEYRE *same as* > ONEYER

ONEYRES > ONEYRE

ONFALL *n* attack or onset

ONFALLS > ONFALL

ONFLOW *n* flowing on

ONFLOWS > ONFLOW

ONGAONGA *n* New Zealand nettle with a severe or fatal sting

ONGAONGAS > ONGAONGA

ONGOING *adj* in progress, continuing

ONGOINGS *pl n* things that are happening

ONIE *variant spelling of* > ONY

ONION *n* strongly flavoured edible bulb ▷ *vb* add onion to

ONIONED > ONION

ONIONIER > ONION

ONIONIEST > ONION

ONIONING > ONION

ONIONS > ONION

ONIONSKIN *n* glazed translucent paper

ONIONY > ONION

ONIRIC *same as* > ONEIRIC

ONISCOID *adj* of or like woodlice

ONIUM *n* as in *onium compound* type of chemical salt

ONIUMS > ONIUM

ONKUS *adj* bad

ONLAY *n* artificial veneer for a tooth

ONLAYS > ONLAY

ONLIEST *same as* > ONLY

ONLINE *adj* connected to a computer or the internet

ONLINER *n* person who uses the internet regularly

ONLINERS > ONLINER

ONLOAD *vb* load files on to a computer

ONLOADED > ONLOAD

ONLOADING > ONLOAD

ONLOADS > ONLOAD

ONLOOKER *n* person who watches without taking part

ONLOOKERS > ONLOOKER

ONLOOKING > ONLOOKER

ONLY *adj* alone of its kind ▷ *adv* exclusively

ONNED > ON

ONNING > ON

ONO *n* Hawaiian fish

ONOMAST *n* person who studies proper names

ONOMASTIC *adj* of or relating to proper names

ONOMASTS > ONOMAST

ONOS > ONO

ONRUSH *n* forceful forward rush or flow

ONRUSHES > ONRUSH

ONRUSHING *adj* approaching quickly

ONS > ON

ONSCREEN *adj* appearing on screen

ONSET *n* beginning

ONSETS > ONSET

ONSETTER *n* attacker

ONSETTERS > ONSET

ONSETTING *n* attack

ONSHORE *adv* towards the land

ONSHORING *n* practice of employing white-collar workers from abroad

ONSIDE *adv* (of a player in various sports) in a legal position ▷ *adj* taking one's part or side ▷ *n* part of cricket field where a batsman stands

ONSIDES > ONSIDE

ONSLAUGHT *n* violent attack

ONST *same as* > ONCE

ONSTAGE *adj* visible by audience

ONSTEAD *Scots word for* > FARMSTEAD

ONSTEADS > ONSTEAD

ONSTREAM *adj* in operation

ONTIC *adj* having real existence

ONTICALLY > ONTIC

ONTO *prep* a position on

ONTOGENIC > ONTOGENY

ONTOGENY *n* entire sequence of events involved in the development of an individual organism

ONTOLOGIC > ONTOLOGY

ONTOLOGY *n* branch of philosophy concerned with existence

ONUS *n* responsibility or burden

ONUSES > ONUS

ONWARD *same as* > ONWARDS

ONWARDLY > ONWARD

ONWARDS *adv* at or towards a point or position ahead

ONY *Scots word for* > ANY

ONYCHA *n* part of mollusc

ONYCHAS > ONYCHA

ONYCHIA *n* inflammation of the nails or claws of animals

ONYCHIAS > ONYCHIA

ONYCHITE *n* type of stone

ONYCHITES > ONYCHITE

ONYCHITIS *n* inflammation of nails

ONYCHIUM *n* part of insect foot

ONYCHIUMS > ONYCHIUM

ONYMOUS *adj* (of a book) bearing its author's name

ONYX *n* type of quartz with coloured layers

ONYXES > ONYX

OO *Scots word for* > WOOL

OOBIT *n* hairy caterpillar

OOBITS > OOBIT

OOCYST *n* type of zygote

OOCYSTS > OOCYST

OOCYTE *n* immature female germ cell that gives rise to an ovum

OOCYTES > OOCYTE

OODLES *pl n* great quantities

OODLINS *same as* > OODLES

OOF *n* money

OOFIER > OOF

OOFIEST > OOF

OOFS > OOF

OOFTISH *n* money

OOFTISHES > OOFTISH

OOFY > OOF

OOGAMETE *n* female gamete

OOGAMETES > OOGAMETE

OOGAMIES > OOGAMY

OOGAMOUS > OOGAMY

OOGAMY *n* type of reproduction

OOGENESES > OOGENESIS

OOGENESIS *n* formation and maturation of ova from undifferentiated cells in the ovary

OOGENETIC > OOGENESIS

OOGENIES > OOGENY

OOGENY *same as* > OOGENESIS

OOGONIA > OOGONIUM

OOGONIAL > OOGONIUM

OOGONIUM *n* immature female germ cell forming oocytes by repeated divisions

OOGONIUMS > OOGONIUM

OOH *interj* exclamation of surprise, pleasure, pain, etc ▷ *vb* say ooh

OOHED > OOH

OOHING *n* act of exclaiming 'ooh'

OOHINGS > OOHING

OOHS > OOH

OOIDAL *adj* shaped like an egg

OOLACHAN *same as* > EULACHON

OOLACHANS > OOLACHAN

OOLAKAN *same as* > EULACHON

OOLAKANS > OOLAKAN

OOLICHAN *n* north Pacific candlefish

OOLICHANS > OOLICHAN

OOLITE *n* limestone made up of tiny grains of calcium carbonate

OOLITES > OOLITE

OOLITH *n* tiny spherical grain of sedimentary rock

OOLITHS > OOLITH

OOLITIC > OOLITE

OOLOGIC > OOLOGY

OOLOGICAL > OOLOGY

OOLOGIES > OOLOGY

OOLOGIST > OOLOGY

OOLOGISTS > OOLOGY

OOLOGY *n* study of birds' eggs

OOLONG *n* kind of dark tea

OOLONGS > OOLONG

OOM *n* title of respect used to refer to an elderly man

OOMIAC *same as* > UMIAK

OOMIACK *same as* > UMIAK

OOMIACKS > OOMIACK

OOMIACS > OOMIAC

OOMIAK *same as* > UMIAK

OOMIAKS > OOMIAK

OOMPAH *n* representation of the sound made by a deep brass instrument ▷ *vb* make the noise of a brass instrument

OOMPAHED > OOMPAH

OOMPAHING > OOMPAH

OOMPAHPAH *n* representation of the sound made by a deep brass instrument

OOMPAHS > OOMPAH

OOMPH n enthusiasm, vigour, or energy

OOMPHS > OOMPH

OOMS > OOM

OOMYCETE n organism formerly classified as fungi

OOMYCETES > OOMYCETE

OON Scots word for > OVEN

OONS > OON

OONT n camel

OONTS > OONT

OOP vb Scots word meaning to bind

OOPED > OOP

OOPHORON n ovary

OOPHORONS > OOPHORON

OOPHYTE n gametophyte in mosses, liverworts, and ferns

OOPHYTES > OOPHYTE

OOPHYTIC > OOPHYTE

OOPING > OOP

OOPS interj exclamation of surprise or apology

OOR Scots form of > OUR

OORALI n member of Indian people

OORALIS > OORALI

OORIAL n Himalayan sheep

OORIALS > OORIAL

OORIE adj Scots word meaning shabby

OORIER > OORIE

OORIEST > OORIE

OOS > OO

OOSE n dust

OOSES > OOSE

OOSIER > OOSE

OOSIEST > OOSE

OOSPERM n fertilized ovum

OOSPERMS > OOSPERM

OOSPHERE n large female gamete produced in the oogonia of algae and fungi

OOSPHERES > OOSPHERE

OOSPORE n thick-walled spore developed from a fertilized oosphere

OOSPORES > OOSPORE

OOSPORIC > OOSPORE

OOSPOROUS > OOSPORE

OOSY > OOSE

OOT Scots word for > OUT

OOTHECA n capsule containing eggs

OOTHECAE > OOTHECA

OOTHECAL > OOTHECA

OOTID n immature female gamete that develops into an ovum

OOTIDS > OOTID

OOTS > OOT

OOZE vb flow slowly ▷ n sluggish flow

OOZED > OOZE

OOZES > OOZE

OOZIER > OOZY

OOZIEST > OOZY

OOZILY > OOZY

OOZINESS > OOZY

OOZING > OOZE

OOZY adj moist or dripping

OP n operation

OPA n grandfather

OPACIFIED > OPACIFY

OPACIFIER > OPACIFY

OPACIFIES > OPACIFY

OPACIFY vb become or make opaque

OPACITIES > OPACITY

OPACITY n state or quality of being opaque

OPACOUS same as > OPAQUE

OPAH n large soft-finned deep-sea fish

OPAHS > OPAH

OPAL n iridescent precious stone

OPALED adj made like opal

OPALESCE vb exhibit a milky iridescence

OPALESCED > OPALESCE

OPALESCES > OPALESCE

OPALINE adj opalescent ▷ n opaque or semiopaque whitish glass

OPALINES > OPALINE

OPALISED same as > OPALIZED

OPALIZED adj made into opal

OPALS > OPAL

OPAQUE adj not able to be seen through, not transparent ▷ n opaque pigment used to block out particular areas on a negative ▷ vb make opaque

OPAQUED > OPAQUE

OPAQUELY > OPAQUE

OPAQUER > OPAQUE

OPAQUES > OPAQUE

OPAQUEST > OPAQUE

OPAQUING > OPAQUE

OPAS > OPA

OPCODE n computer code containing operating instructions

OPCODES > OPCODE

OPE archaic or poetic word for > OPEN

OPED > OPE

OPEN adj not closed ▷ vb (cause to) become open ▷ n competition which all may enter

OPENABLE > OPEN

OPENCAST adj as in opencast mining mining by excavating from the surface

OPENED > OPEN

OPENER n tool for opening cans and bottles

OPENERS > OPENER

OPENEST > OPEN

OPENING n beginning ▷ adj first

OPENINGS > OPENING

OPENLY > OPEN

OPENNESS > OPEN

OPENS > OPEN

OPENSIDE n in rugby, flanker who plays on the open side of the scrum

OPENSIDES > OPENSIDE

OPENWORK n ornamental work, as of metal or embroidery, having a pattern of openings or holes

OPENWORKS > OPENWORK

OPEPE n African tree

OPEPES > OPEPE

OPERA n drama in which the text is sung to an orchestral accompaniment

OPERABLE adj capable of being treated by a surgical operation

OPERABLY > OPERABLE

OPERAGOER n person who goes to operas

OPERAND n quantity, variable, or function upon which an operation is performed

OPERANDS > OPERAND

OPERANT adj producing effects ▷ n person or thing that operates

OPERANTLY > OPERANT

OPERANTS > OPERANT

OPERAS > OPERA

OPERATE vb (cause to) work

OPERATED > OPERATE

OPERATES > OPERATE

OPERATIC adj of or relating to opera

OPERATICS n performance of operas

OPERATING > OPERATE

OPERATION n method or procedure of working

OPERATISE same as > OPERATIZE

OPERATIVE adj working ▷ n worker with a special skill

OPERATIZE vb turn (a play, novel, etc) into an opera

OPERATOR n person who operates a machine or instrument

OPERATORS > OPERATOR

OPERCELE same as > OPERCULE

OPERCELES > OPERCELE

OPERCULA > OPERCULUM

OPERCULAR > OPERCULUM

OPERCULE n gill cover

OPERCULES > OPERCULE

OPERCULUM n covering flap or structure in animals or plants

OPERETTA n light-hearted comic opera

OPERETTAS > OPERETTA

OPERON n group of adjacent genes in bacteria

OPERONS > OPERON

OPEROSE adj laborious

OPEROSELY > OPEROSE

OPEROSITY > OPEROSE

OPES > OPE

OPGEFOK adj South African taboo slang for damaged or bungled

OPHIDIAN n reptile of the suborder which comprises the snakes

OPHIDIANS > OPHIDIAN

OPHIOLITE n type of mineral

OPHIOLOGY n branch of zoology that is concerned with the study of snakes

OPHITE n any of several greenish mottled rocks

OPHITES > OPHITE

OPHITIC adj having small elongated feldspar crystals enclosed

OPHIURA n sea creature like a starfish

OPHIURAN same as > OPHIURA

OPHIURANS > OPHIURA

OPHIURAS > OPHIURA

OPHIURID same as > OPHIURA

OPHIURIDS > OPHIURID

OPHIUROID adj of or like ophiura

OPIATE n narcotic drug containing opium ▷ adj containing or consisting of opium ▷ vb treat with an opiate

OPIATED > OPIATE

OPIATES > OPIATE

OPIATING > OPIATE

OPIFICER n craftsperson

OPIFICERS > OPIFICER

OPINABLE adj thinkable

OPINE vb express an opinion

OPINED > OPINE

OPINES > OPINE

OPING > OPE

OPINICUS n mythical monster

OPINING > OPINE

OPINION n personal belief or judgment

OPINIONED adj having strong opinions

OPINIONS > OPINION

OPIOID n substance that resembles morphine

OPIOIDS > OPIOID

OPIUM n addictive narcotic drug made from poppy seeds

OPIUMISM n addiction to opium

OPIUMISMS > OPIUMISM

OPIUMS > OPIUM

OPOBALSAM n soothing ointment

OPODELDOC n medical ointment

OPOPANAX n medical resin from plant

OPORICE n former medicine made from fruit
OPORICES > OPORICE
OPOSSUM n small marsupial of America or Australasia
OPOSSUMS > OPOSSUM
OPPIDAN adj of a town ▷ n person living in a town
OPPIDANS > OPPIDAN
OPPILANT > OPPILATE
OPPILATE vb block (the pores, bowels, etc)
OPPILATED > OPPILATE
OPPILATES > OPPILATE
OPPO n counterpart in another organization
OPPONENCY > OPPONENT
OPPONENS n muscle of the thumb
OPPONENT n person one is working against in a contest, battle, or argument ▷ adj opposite, as in position
OPPONENTS > OPPONENT
OPPORTUNE adj happening at a suitable time
OPPOS > OPPO
OPPOSABLE adj (of the thumb) capable of touching the tip of all the other fingers
OPPOSABLY > OPPOSABLE
OPPOSE vb work against
OPPOSED > OPPOSE
OPPOSER > OPPOSE
OPPOSERS > OPPOSE
OPPOSES > OPPOSE
OPPOSING > OPPOSE
OPPOSITE adj situated on the other side ▷ n person or thing that is opposite ▷ prep facing ▷ adv on the other side
OPPOSITES > OPPOSITE
OPPRESS vb control by cruelty or force
OPPRESSED > OPPRESS
OPPRESSES > OPPRESS
OPPRESSOR > OPPRESS
OPPUGN vb call into question
OPPUGNANT adj combative, antagonistic, or contrary
OPPUGNED > OPPUGN
OPPUGNER > OPPUGN
OPPUGNERS > OPPUGN
OPPUGNING > OPPUGN
OPPUGNS > OPPUGN
OPS > OP
OPSIMATH n person who learns late in life
OPSIMATHS > OPSIMATH
OPSIMATHY > OPSIMATH
OPSIN n type of protein
OPSINS > OPSIN

OPSOMANIA n extreme enthusiasm for a particular food
OPSONIC > OPSONIN
OPSONIFY same as > OPSONIZE
OPSONIN n constituent of blood serum
OPSONINS > OPSONIN
OPSONISE same as > OPSONIZE
OPSONISED > OPSONIZE
OPSONISES > OPSONIZE
OPSONIUM n relish eaten with bread
OPSONIUMS > OPSONIUM
OPSONIZE vb subject (bacteria) to the action of opsonins
OPSONIZED > OPSONIZE
OPSONIZES > OPSONIZE
OPT vb show a preference, choose
OPTANT n person who opts
OPTANTS > OPTANT
OPTATIVE adj indicating or expressing choice, preference, or wish ▷ n optative mood
OPTATIVES > OPTATIVE
OPTED > OPT
OPTER > OPT
OPTERS > OPT
OPTIC adj relating to the eyes or sight
OPTICAL adj of or involving light or optics
OPTICALLY > OPTICAL
OPTICIAN n person qualified to prescribe glasses
OPTICIANS > OPTICIAN
OPTICIST n optics expert
OPTICISTS > OPTICIST
OPTICS n science of sight and light
OPTIMA > OPTIMUM
OPTIMAL adj best or most favourable
OPTIMALLY > OPTIMAL
OPTIMATE n Roman aristocrat
OPTIMATES > OPTIMATE
OPTIME n mathematics student at Cambridge University
OPTIMES > OPTIME
OPTIMISE same as > OPTIMIZE
OPTIMISED > OPTIMISE
OPTIMISER > OPTIMISE
OPTIMISES > OPTIMISE
OPTIMISM n tendency to take the most hopeful view

OPTIMISMS > OPTIMISM
OPTIMIST > OPTIMISM
OPTIMISTS > OPTIMISM
OPTIMIZE vb make the most of
OPTIMIZED > OPTIMIZE
OPTIMIZER > OPTIMIZE
OPTIMIZES > OPTIMIZE
OPTIMUM n best possible conditions ▷ adj most favourable
OPTIMUMS > OPTIMUM
OPTING > OPT
OPTION n choice ▷ vb obtain an option on
OPTIONAL adj possible but not compulsory ▷ n optional thing
OPTIONALS > OPTIONAL
OPTIONED > OPTION
OPTIONEE n holder of a financial option
OPTIONEES > OPTIONEE
OPTIONING > OPTION
OPTIONS > OPTION
OPTOLOGY n science of sight
OPTOMETER n any of various instruments for measuring the refractive power of the eye
OPTOMETRY n science or practice of testing visual acuity and prescribing corrective lenses
OPTOPHONE n device for blind people that converts printed words into sounds
OPTRONIC adj relating to optronics
OPTRONICS n science of electronic and light signals
OPTS > OPT
OPULENCE > OPULENT
OPULENCES > OPULENT
OPULENCY > OPULENT
OPULENT adj having or indicating wealth
OPULENTLY > OPULENT
OPULUS n flowering shrub
OPULUSES > OPULUS
OPUNTIA n type of cactus
OPUNTIAS > OPUNTIA
OPUS n artistic creation, esp a musical work
OPUSCLE same as > OPUSCULE
OPUSCLES > OPUSCLE
OPUSCULA > OPUSCULUM
OPUSCULAR > OPUSCULE
OPUSCULE n small or insignificant artistic work
OPUSCULES > OPUSCULE
OPUSCULUM same as > OPUSCULE
OPUSES > OPUS

OQUASSA n American trout
OQUASSAS > OQUASSA
OR prep before ▷ adj of the metal gold ▷ n gold
ORA > OS
ORACH same as > ORACHE
ORACHE n type of plant
ORACHES > ORACHE
ORACIES > ORACY
ORACLE n shrine of an ancient god ▷ vb utter as an oracle
ORACLED > ORACLE
ORACLES > ORACLE
ORACLING > ORACLE
ORACULAR adj of or like an oracle
ORACULOUS adj of an oracle
ORACY n capacity to use speech
ORAD adv towards the mouth
ORAGIOUS adj stormy
ORAL adj spoken ▷ n spoken examination
ORALISM n oral method of communicating with deaf people
ORALISMS > ORALISM
ORALIST > ORALISM
ORALISTS > ORALISM
ORALITIES > ORALITY
ORALITY n state of being oral
ORALLY > ORAL
ORALS > ORAL
ORANG n orangutan
ORANGE n reddish-yellow citrus fruit ▷ adj reddish-yellow
ORANGEADE n orange-flavoured, usu fizzy drink
ORANGER > ORANGE
ORANGERIE archaic variant of > ORANGERY
ORANGERY n greenhouse for growing orange trees
ORANGES > ORANGE
ORANGEST > ORANGE
ORANGEY > ORANGE
ORANGIER > ORANGE
ORANGIEST > ORANGE
ORANGISH > ORANGE
ORANGS > ORANG
ORANGUTAN n large ape with shaggy reddish-brown hair
ORANGY > ORANGE
ORANT n artistic representation of worshipper
ORANTS > ORANT
ORARIA > ORARIUM
ORARIAN n person who lives on the coast
ORARIANS > ORARIAN
ORARION n garment worn by Greek clergyman
ORARIONS > ORARION
ORARIUM n handkerchief
ORATE vb make or give an oration
ORATED > ORATE
ORATES > ORATE
ORATING > ORATE

ORATION n formal speech
ORATIONS > ORATION
ORATOR n skilful public speaker
ORATORIAN n clergyman of a particular type of church
ORATORIES > ORATORY
ORATORIO n musical composition for choir and orchestra
ORATORIOS > ORATORIO
ORATORS > ORATOR
ORATORY n art of making speeches
ORATRESS n female orator
ORATRICES > ORATRIX
ORATRIX n female orator
ORATRIXES > ORATRIX
ORATURE n oral forms of literature
ORATURES > ORATURE
ORB n ceremonial decorated sphere ▷ vb make or become circular or spherical
ORBED > ORB
ORBICULAR adj circular or spherical
ORBIER > ORBY
ORBIEST > ORBY
ORBING > ORB
ORBIT n curved path ▷ vb move in an orbit around
ORBITA same as > ORBIT
ORBITAL adj of or denoting an orbit ▷ n region surrounding an atomic nucleus
ORBITALLY > ORBITAL
ORBITALS > ORBITAL
ORBITAS > ORBITA
ORBITED > ORBIT
ORBITER n spacecraft or satellite designed to orbit a planet without landing on it
ORBITERS > ORBITER
ORBITIES > ORBITY
ORBITING > ORBIT
ORBITS > ORBIT
ORBITY n bereavement
ORBLESS > ORB
ORBLIKE adj like an orb
ORBS > ORB
ORBY adj orb-shaped
ORC n any of various whales, such as the killer and grampus
ORCA n killer whale
ORCAS > ORCA
ORCEIN n brown crystalline material
ORCEINS > ORCEIN
ORCHARD n area where fruit trees are grown
ORCHARDS > ORCHARD
ORCHAT same as > ORCHARD
ORCHATS > ORCHAT
ORCHEL same as > ORCHIL
ORCHELLA same as > ORCHIL

ORCHELLAS > ORCHELLA
ORCHELS > ORCHEL
ORCHESES > ORCHESIS
ORCHESIS n art of dance
ORCHESTIC adj of dance
ORCHESTRA n large group of musicians, esp playing a variety of instruments
ORCHID n plant with flowers that have unusual lip-shaped petals
ORCHIDIST n orchid grower
ORCHIDS > ORCHID
ORCHIL n any of various lichens
ORCHILLA same as > ORCHIL
ORCHILLAS > ORCHILLA
ORCHILS > ORCHIL
ORCHIS n type of orchid
ORCHISES > ORCHIS
ORCHITIC > ORCHITIS
ORCHITIS n inflammation of one or both testicles
ORCIN same as > ORCINOL
ORCINE same as > ORCINOL
ORCINES > ORCINE
ORCINOL n colourless crystalline water-soluble solid
ORCINOLS > ORCINOL
ORCINS > ORCIN
ORCS > ORC
ORD n pointed weapon
ORDAIN vb make (someone) a member of the clergy
ORDAINED > ORDAIN
ORDAINER > ORDAIN
ORDAINERS > ORDAIN
ORDAINING > ORDAIN
ORDAINS > ORDAIN
ORDALIAN adj of an ordeal
ORDALIUM same as > ORDEAL
ORDALIUMS > ORDALIUM
ORDEAL n painful or difficult experience
ORDEALS > ORDEAL
ORDER n instruction to be carried out ▷ vb give an instruction to
ORDERABLE > ORDER
ORDERED > ORDER
ORDERER > ORDER
ORDERERS > ORDER
ORDERING > ORDER
ORDERINGS > ORDER
ORDERLESS > ORDER
ORDERLIES > ORDERLY
ORDERLY adj well-organized ▷ n hospital attendant ▷ adv according to custom or rule
ORDERS > ORDER
ORDINAIRE adj ordinary
ORDINAL adj denoting a certain position in a

sequence of numbers ▷ n book containing the forms of services for the ordination of ministers
ORDINALLY > ORDINAL
ORDINALS > ORDINAL
ORDINANCE n official rule or order
ORDINAND n candidate for ordination
ORDINANDS > ORDINAND
ORDINANT n person who ordains
ORDINANTS > ORDINANT
ORDINAR Scots word for > ORDINARY
ORDINARS > ORDINAR
ORDINARY adj usual or normal
ORDINATE n vertical coordinate of a point in a two-dimensional system of coordinates ▷ vb ordain
ORDINATED > ORDINATE
ORDINATES > ORDINATE
ORDINEE n person being ordained
ORDINEES > ORDINEE
ORDINES > ORDO
ORDNANCE n weapons and military supplies
ORDNANCES > ORDNANCE
ORDO n religious order
ORDOS > ORDO
ORDS > ORD
ORDURE n excrement
ORDURES > ORDURE
ORDUROUS > ORDURE
ORE n (rock containing) a mineral which yields metal
OREAD n mountain nymph
OREADES > OREAD
OREADS > OREAD
OREBODIES > OREBODY
OREBODY n mass of ore in a mine
ORECTIC adj of or relating to the desires
ORECTIVE > OREXIS
OREGANO n sweet-smelling herb used in cooking
OREGANOS > OREGANO
OREIDE same as > OROIDE
OREIDES > OREIDE
OREODONT n extinct prehistoric mammal
OREODONTS > OREODONT
OREOLOGY same as > OROLOGY
OREPEARCH same as > OVERPERCH
ORES > ORE
ORESTUNCK > OVERSTINK
OREWEED n seaweed
OREWEEDS > OREWEED
OREXIN n hormone that promotes wakefulness and stimulates the appetite

OREXINS > OREXIN
OREXIS n appetite
OREXISES > OREXIS
ORF n infectious disease of sheep
ORFE n small slender European fish
ORFES > ORFE
ORFRAY same as > ORPHREY
ORFRAYS > ORFRAY
ORFS > ORF
ORG n organization
ORGAN n part of an animal or plant that has a particular function
ORGANA > ORGANON
ORGANDIE n fine cotton fabric
ORGANDIES > ORGANDY
ORGANDY same as > ORGANDIE
ORGANELLE n structural and functional unit in a cell
ORGANIC adj of or produced from animals or plants ▷ n substance that is derived from animal or vegetable matter
ORGANICAL same as > ORGANIC
ORGANICS > ORGANIC
ORGANISE same as > ORGANIZE
ORGANISED same as > ORGANIZED
ORGANISER same as > ORGANIZER
ORGANISES > ORGANISE
ORGANISM n any living animal or plant
ORGANISMS > ORGANISM
ORGANIST n organ player
ORGANISTS > ORGANIST
ORGANITY same as > ORGANISM
ORGANIZE vb make arrangements for
ORGANIZED > ORGANIZE
ORGANIZER n person who organizes or is capable of organizing
ORGANIZES > ORGANIZE
ORGANON n system of logical or scientific rules
ORGANONS > ORGANON
ORGANOSOL n resin-based coating
ORGANOTIN adj of an organic compound used as a pesticide
ORGANS > ORGAN
ORGANUM same as > ORGANON
ORGANUMS > ORGANUM
ORGANZA n thin stiff fabric of silk, cotton, or synthetic fibre
ORGANZAS > ORGANZA
ORGANZINE n strong thread made of twisted strands of raw silk

ORGASM n most intense point of sexual pleasure ▷ vb experience orgasm
ORGASMED > ORGASM
ORGASMIC > ORGASM
ORGASMING > ORGASM
ORGASMS > ORGASM
ORGASTIC > ORGASM
ORGEAT n drink made with orange flower water
ORGEATS > ORGEAT
ORGIA same as > ORGY
ORGIAC > ORGY
ORGIAS > ORGIA
ORGIAST n person who indulges immoderately in an activity
ORGIASTIC > ORGY
ORGIASTS > ORGIAST
ORGIC > ORGY
ORGIES > ORGY
ORGILLOUS same as > ORGULOUS
ORGONE n substance claimed to be needed for mental health
ORGONES > ORGONE
ORGS > ORG
ORGUE n number of stakes lashed together
ORGUES > ORGUE
ORGULOUS adj proud
ORGY n act of immoderate indulgence
ORIBATID n type of mite
ORIBATIDS > ORIBATID
ORIBI n small African antelope
ORIBIS > ORIBI
ORICALCHE same as > ORICHALC
ORICHALC n type of alloy
ORICHALCS > ORICHALC
ORIEL n type of bay window
ORIELLED adj having an oriel
ORIELS > ORIEL
ORIENCIES > ORIENCY
ORIENCY n state of being iridescent
ORIENT vb position (oneself) according to one's surroundings ▷ n eastern sky or the dawn ▷ adj eastern
ORIENTAL adj eastern ▷ n slender breed of cat
ORIENTALS > ORIENTAL
ORIENTATE vb position (oneself) according to one's surroundings
ORIENTED > ORIENT
ORIENTEER vb take part in orienteering ▷ n person who takes part in orienteering
ORIENTER > ORIENT
ORIENTERS > ORIENT
ORIENTING > ORIENT
ORIENTS > ORIENT
ORIFEX same as > ORIFICE
ORIFEXES > ORIFEX

ORIFICE n opening or hole
ORIFICES > ORIFICE
ORIFICIAL > ORIFICE
ORIFLAMME n scarlet flag adopted as the national banner of France in the Middle Ages
ORIGAMI n Japanese decorative art of paper folding
ORIGAMIS > ORIGAMI
ORIGAN another name for > MARJORAM
ORIGANE same as > ORIGAN
ORIGANES > ORIGANE
ORIGANS > ORIGAN
ORIGANUM n type of aromatic plant
ORIGANUMS > ORIGANUM
ORIGIN n point from which something develops
ORIGINAL adj first or earliest ▷ n first version, from which others are copied
ORIGINALS > ORIGINAL
ORIGINARY adj native, indigenous
ORIGINATE vb come or bring into existence
ORIGINS > ORIGIN
ORIHOU n small New Zealand tree
ORIHOUS > ORIHOU
ORILLION n part of bastion
ORILLIONS > ORILLION
ORINASAL adj pronounced with simultaneous oral and nasal articulation ▷ n orinasal speech sound
ORINASALS > ORINASAL
ORIOLE n tropical or American songbird
ORIOLES > ORIOLE
ORISHA n any of the minor gods or spirits of traditional Yoruba religion
ORISHAS > ORISHA
ORISON another word for > PRAYER
ORISONS > ORISON
ORIXA same as > ORISHA
ORIXAS > ORIXA
ORLE n border around a shield
ORLEANS n type of fabric
ORLEANSES > ORLEANS
ORLES > ORLE
ORLISTAT n drug used for slimming
ORLISTATS > ORLISTAT
ORLON n crease-resistant acrylic fibre or fabric
ORLONS > ORLON
ORLOP n (in a vessel with four or more decks) the lowest deck
ORLOPS > ORLOP

ORMER n edible marine mollusc
ORMERS > ORMER
ORMOLU n gold-coloured alloy used for decoration
ORMOLUS > ORMOLU
ORNAMENT n decorative object ▷ vb decorate
ORNAMENTS > ORNAMENT
ORNATE adj highly decorated, elaborate
ORNATELY > ORNATE
ORNATER > ORNATE
ORNATEST > ORNATE
ORNERIER > ORNERY
ORNERIEST > ORNERY
ORNERY adj stubborn or vile-tempered
ORNIS less common word for > AVIFAUNA
ORNISES > ORNIS
ORNITHES > birds in Greek myth
ORNITHIC adj of or relating to birds or a bird fauna
ORNITHINE n type of amino acid
ORNITHOID adj like bird
OROGEN n part of earth subject to orogeny
OROGENIC > OROGENY
OROGENIES > OROGENY
OROGENS > OROGEN
OROGENY n formation of mountain ranges
OROGRAPHY n study or mapping of relief, esp of mountains
OROIDE n alloy containing copper, tin, and other metals
OROIDES > OROIDE
OROLOGIES > OROLOGY
OROLOGIST > OROLOGY
OROLOGY same as > OROGRAPHY
OROMETER n aneroid barometer with an altitude scale
OROMETERS > OROMETER
ORONASAL adj of or relating to the mouth and nose
OROPESA n float used in minesweeping
OROPESAS > OROPESA
OROTUND adj (of the voice) resonant and booming
OROTUNDLY adv in an orotund manner
ORPHAN n child whose parents are dead ▷ vb deprive of parents
ORPHANAGE n children's home for orphans
ORPHANED > ORPHAN
ORPHANING > ORPHAN
ORPHANISM n state of being an orphan
ORPHANS > ORPHAN
ORPHARION n large lute in use during the 16th and 17th centuries

ORPHIC adj mystical or occult
ORPHICAL same as > ORPHIC
ORPHISM n style of abstract art
ORPHISMS > ORPHISM
ORPHREY n richly embroidered band or border
ORPHREYED adj embroidered with gold
ORPHREYS > ORPHREY
ORPIMENT n yellow mineral
ORPIMENTS > ORPIMENT
ORPIN same as > ORPINE
ORPINE n type of plant
ORPINES > ORPINE
ORPINS > ORPIN
ORRA adj odd or unmatched
ORRAMAN n man who does odd jobs
ORRAMEN > ORRAMAN
ORRERIES > ORRERY
ORRERY n mechanical model of the solar system
ORRICE same as > ORRIS
ORRICES > ORRICE
ORRIS n kind of iris
ORRISES > ORRIS
ORRISROOT n rhizome of a type of iris, used as perfume
ORS > OR
ORSEILLE same as > ORCHIL
ORSEILLES > ORSEILLE
ORSELLIC > ORSEILLE
ORT n fragment
ORTANIQUE n hybrid between an orange and a tangerine
ORTHIAN adj having high pitch
ORTHICON n type of television camera tube
ORTHICONS > ORTHICON
ORTHO n type of photographic plate
ORTHOAXES > ORTHOAXIS
ORTHOAXIS n axis in a crystal
ORTHODOX adj conforming to established views
ORTHODOXY n orthodox belief or practice
ORTHOEPIC > ORTHOEPY
ORTHOEPY n study of correct or standard pronunciation
ORTHOPEDY n treatment of deformity
ORTHOPOD n surgeon
ORTHOPODS > ORTHOPOD
ORTHOPTER n type of aircraft propelled by flapping wings
ORTHOPTIC adj relating to normal binocular vision

o

ORTHOS > ORTHO
ORTHOSES > ORTHOSIS
ORTHOSIS n artificial or mechanical aid to support a weak part of the body
ORTHOTIC > ORTHOTICS
ORTHOTICS n use of artificial or mechanical aids to assist movement of weak joints or muscles
ORTHOTIST n person who is qualified to practise orthotics
ORTHOTONE adj (of a word) having an independent accent ▷ n independently accented word
ORTHROS n canonical hour in the Greek Church
ORTHROSES > ORTHROS
ORTOLAN n small European songbird eaten as a delicacy
ORTOLANS > ORTOLAN
ORTS pl n scraps or leavings
ORVAL n plant of sage family
ORVALS > ORVAL
ORYX n large African antelope
ORYXES > ORYX
ORZO n pasta in small grain shapes
ORZOS > ORZO
OS n mouth or mouthlike part or opening
OSAR > OS
OSCAR n cash
OSCARS > OSCAR
OSCHEAL adj of the scrotum
OSCILLATE vb swing back and forth
OSCINE n songbird ▷ adj of songbirds
OSCINES > OSCINE
OSCININE > OSCINE
OSCITANCE same as > OSCITANCY
OSCITANCY n state of being drowsy, lazy, or inattentive
OSCITANT > OSCITANCY
OSCITATE vb yawn
OSCITATED > OSCITATE
OSCITATES > OSCITATE
OSCULA > OSCULUM
OSCULANT adj possessing some of the characteristics of two different taxonomic groups
OSCULAR adj of or relating to an osculum
OSCULATE vb kiss
OSCULATED > OSCULATE
OSCULATES > OSCULATE
OSCULE n small mouth or opening
OSCULES > OSCULE

OSCULUM n mouthlike aperture
OSE same as > ESKER
OSES > OSE
OSETRA n type of caviar
OSETRAS > OSETRA
OSHAC n plant smelling of ammonia
OSHACS > OSHAC
OSIER n willow tree
OSIERED adj covered with osiers
OSIERIES > OSIERY
OSIERS > OSIER
OSIERY n work done with osiers
OSMATE n salt of osmic acid
OSMATES > OSMATE
OSMATIC adj relying on sense of smell
OSMETERIA pl n glands in some caterpillars that secrete foul-smelling substances to deter predators
OSMIATE same as > OSMATE
OSMIATES > OSMIATE
OSMIC adj of or containing osmium in a high valence state
OSMICALLY > OSMIC
OSMICS n science of smell
OSMIOUS same as > OSMOUS
OSMIUM n heaviest known metallic element
OSMIUMS > OSMIUM
OSMOL same as > OSMOLE
OSMOLAL > OSMOLE
OSMOLAR adj containing one osmole per litre
OSMOLE n unit of osmotic pressure
OSMOLES > OSMOLE
OSMOLS > OSMOL
OSMOMETER n instrument for measuring osmotic pressure
OSMOMETRY > OSMOMETER
OSMOSE vb undergo or cause to undergo osmosis
OSMOSED > OSMOSE
OSMOSES > OSMOSE
OSMOSING > OSMOSE
OSMOSIS n movement of a liquid through a membrane
OSMOTIC > OSMOSIS
OSMOUS adj of or containing osmium in a low valence state
OSMUND same as > OSMUNDA
OSMUNDA n type of fern
OSMUNDAS > OSMUNDA
OSMUNDINE n type of compost
OSMUNDS > OSMUND
OSNABURG n coarse plain-woven cotton used for sacks, furnishings, etc
OSNABURGS > OSNABURG
OSPREY n large fish-eating bird of prey

OSPREYS > OSPREY
OSSA > OS
OSSARIUM same as > OSSUARY
OSSARIUMS > OSSARIUM
OSSATURE n skeleton
OSSATURES > OSSATURE
OSSEIN n protein that forms the organic matrix of bone
OSSEINS > OSSEIN
OSSELET n growth on knee of horse
OSSELETS > OSSELET
OSSEOUS adj consisting of or like bone
OSSEOUSLY > OSSEOUS
OSSETER n sturgeon
OSSETERS > OSSETER
OSSETRA same as > OSSETRAS
OSSETRAS > OSSETRA
OSSIA n alternate version or passage ▷ conj or
OSSIAS > OSSIA
OSSICLE n small bone, esp one of those in the middle ear
OSSICLES > OSSICLE
OSSICULAR > OSSICLE
OSSIFIC adj making something turn to bone
OSSIFIED adj converted into bone
OSSIFIER > OSSIFY
OSSIFIERS > OSSIFY
OSSIFIES > OSSIFY
OSSIFRAGA n large sea bird
OSSIFRAGE n osprey
OSSIFY vb (cause to) become bone, harden
OSSIFYING > OSSIFY
OSSOBUCO n Italian dish of veal shank and vegetables stewed in wine
OSSOBUCOS > OSSOBUCO
OSSUARIES > OSSUARY
OSSUARY n any container for the burial of human bones, such as an urn or vault
OSTEAL adj of or relating to bone or to the skeleton
OSTEITIC > OSTEITIS
OSTEITIS n inflammation of a bone
OSTENSIVE adj directly showing or pointing out
OSTENSORY n (in the RC Church) receptacle for displaying the consecrated Host
OSTENT n appearance ▷ vb display boastfully
OSTENTED > OSTENT
OSTENTING > OSTENT
OSTENTS > OSTENT
OSTEOCYTE n bone cell
OSTEODERM n bony area in skin
OSTEOGEN n material from which bone forms
OSTEOGENS > OSTEOGEN

OSTEOGENY n forming of bone
OSTEOID adj of or resembling bone ▷ n bony deposit
OSTEOIDS > OSTEOID
OSTEOLOGY n study of the structure and function of bones
OSTEOMA n tumour composed of bone or bonelike tissue
OSTEOMAS > OSTEOMA
OSTEOMATA > OSTEOMA
OSTEOPATH n person who practises osteopathy
OSTEOSES > OSTEOSIS
OSTEOSIS n forming of bony tissue
OSTEOTOME n surgical instrument for cutting bone, usually a special chisel
OSTEOTOMY n surgical cutting or dividing of bone
OSTIA > OSTIUM
OSTIAL > OSTIUM
OSTIARIES > OSTIARY
OSTIARY another word for > PORTER
OSTIATE adj having ostium
OSTINATI > OSTINATO
OSTINATO n persistently repeated phrase or rhythm
OSTINATOS > OSTINATO
OSTIOLAR > OSTIOLE
OSTIOLATE > OSTIOLE
OSTIOLE n pore in the reproductive bodies of certain algae and fungi
OSTIOLES > OSTIOLE
OSTIUM n pore in sponges through which water enters the body
OSTLER n stableman at an inn
OSTLERESS n female ostler
OSTLERS > OSTLER
OSTMARK n currency of the former East Germany
OSTMARKS > OSTMARK
OSTOMATE n person with an ostomy
OSTOMATES > OSTOMATE
OSTOMIES > OSTOMY
OSTOMY n surgically made opening
OSTOSES > OSTOSIS
OSTOSIS n formation of bone
OSTOSISES > OSTOSIS
OSTRACA > OSTRACON
OSTRACEAN adj of oysters ▷ n type of bivalve
OSTRACISE same as > OSTRACIZE
OSTRACISM > OSTRACIZE
OSTRACIZE vb exclude (a person) from a group
OSTRACOD n type of minute crustacean
OSTRACODE adj of ostracods

OSTRACODS > OSTRACOD
OSTRACON n (in ancient Greece) a potsherd used for ostracizing
OSTRAKA > OSTRAKON
OSTRAKON same as > OSTRACON
OSTREGER n keeper of hawks
OSTREGERS > OSTREGER
OSTRICH n large African bird that runs fast but cannot fly
OSTRICHES > OSTRICH
OTAKU n Japanese computer geek
OTAKUS > OTAKU
OTALGIA technical name for > EARACHE
OTALGIAS > OTALGIA
OTALGIC > OTALGIA
OTALGIES > OTALGY
OTALGY same as > OTALGIA
OTARID adj of or like an otary, an eared seal
OTARIES > OTARY
OTARINE > OTARY
OTARY n seal with ears
OTHER vb regard (a person or people) as different from oneself or one's group
OTHERED > OTHER
OTHERING > OTHER
OTHERNESS n quality of being different or distinct in appearance, character, etc
OTHERS > OTHER
OTHERWISE adv differently, in another way ▷ adj of an unexpected nature ▷ pron something different in outcome
OTIC adj of or relating to the ear
OTIOSE adj not useful
OTIOSELY > OTIOSE
OTIOSITY > OTIOSE
OTITIC > OTITIS
OTITIDES > OTITIS
OTITIS n inflammation of the ear
OTITISES > OTITIS
OTOCYST n embryonic structure in vertebrates that develops into the inner ear
OTOCYSTIC > OTOCYST
OTOCYSTS > OTOCYST
OTOLITH n granule of calcium carbonate in the inner ear of vertebrates
OTOLITHIC > OTOLITH
OTOLITHS > OTOLITH
OTOLOGIC adj relating to otology
OTOLOGIES > OTOLOGY
OTOLOGIST > OTOLOGY
OTOLOGY n branch of medicine concerned with the ear
OTOPLASTY n cosmetic surgery on ears
OTORRHOEA n discharge from the ears

OTOSCOPE another name for > AURISCOPE
OTOSCOPES > OTOSCOPE
OTOSCOPIC > OTOSCOPY
OTOSCOPY n examination of ear using otoscope
OTOTOXIC adj toxic to the ear
OTTAR variant of > ATTAR
OTTARS > OTTAR
OTTAVA n interval of an octave
OTTAVAS > OTTAVA
OTTAVINO n piccolo
OTTAVINOS > OTTAVINO
OTTER n small brown freshwater mammal that eats fish ▷ vb fish using an otter board
OTTERED > OTTER
OTTERING > OTTER
OTTERS > OTTER
OTTO another name for > ATTAR
OTTOMAN n storage chest with a padded lid for use as a seat
OTTOMANS > OTTOMAN
OTTOS > OTTO
OTTRELITE n type of mineral
OU interj expressing concession ▷ n man, bloke, or chap
OUABAIN n poisonous white crystalline glycoside
OUABAINS > OUABAIN
OUAKARI n South American monkey
OUAKARIS > OUAKARI
OUBAAS n man in authority
OUBAASES > OUBAAS
OUBIT n hairy caterpillar
OUBITS > OUBIT
OUBLIETTE n dungeon entered only by a trapdoor
OUCH interj exclamation of sudden pain ▷ n brooch or clasp set with gems ▷ vb say ouch
OUCHED > OUCH
OUCHES > OUCH
OUCHING > OUCH
OUCHT Scots word for > ANYTHING
OUCHTS > OUCHT
OUD n Arabic stringed musical instrument
OUDS > OUD
OUENS > OU
OUGHLIED > OUGHLY
OUGHLIES > OUGHLY
OUGHLY variant of > UGLY
OUGHLYING > OUGHLY
OUGHT vb have an obligation ▷ n zero
OUGHTED > OUGHT
OUGHTING > OUGHT
OUGHTNESS n state of being right
OUGHTS > OUGHT
OUGIYA n standard monetary unit of Mauritania

OUGIYAS > OUGIYA
OUGLIE variant of > UGLY
OUGLIED > OUGLIE
OUGLIEING > OUGLIE
OUGLIES > OUGLIE
OUGUIYA n standard monetary unit of Mauritania
OUGUIYAS > OUGUIYA
OUIJA n tradename for a board through which spirits supposedly answer questions
OUIJAS > OUIJA
OUISTITI n marmoset
OUISTITIS > OUISTITI
OUK Scots word for > WEEK
OUKS > OUK
OULACHON same as > EULACHON
OULACHONS > OULACHON
OULAKAN same as > EULACHON
OULAKANS > OULAKAN
OULD Scots or Irish form of > OLD
OULDER > OULD
OULDEST > OULD
OULK Scots form of > WEEK
OULKS > OULK
OULONG same as > OOLONG
OULONGS > OULONG
OUMA n grandmother, often as a title with a surname
OUMAS > OUMA
OUNCE n unit of weight equal to one sixteenth of a pound
OUNCES > OUNCE
OUNDIER > OUNDY
OUNDIEST > OUNDY
OUNDY adj wavy
OUP same as > OOP
OUPA n grandfather, often as a title with a surname
OUPAS > OUPA
OUPED > OUP
OUPH same as > OAF
OUPHE same as > OAF
OUPHES > OUPHE
OUPHS > OUPH
OUPING > OUP
OUPS > OUP
OUR adj belonging to us ▷ determiner of, belonging to, or associated in some way with us
OURALI n plant from which curare comes
OURALIS > OURALI
OURANG same as > ORANG
OURANGS > OURANG
OURARI same as > OURALI
OURARIS > OURARI
OUREBI same as > ORIBI
OUREBIS > OUREBI
OURIE same as > OORIE
OURIER > OURIE
OURIEST > OURIE
OURN dialect form of > OUR
OUROBOROS n mythical serpent

OUROLOGY same as > UROLOGY
OUROSCOPY same as > UROSCOPY
OURS pron thing(s) belonging to us
OURSELF pron formal word for myself used by monarchs
OURSELVES pron reflexive form of we or us
OUS > OU
OUSEL same as > OUZEL
OUSELS > OUSEL
OUST vb force (someone) out, expel
OUSTED > OUST
OUSTER n act of forcing someone out of a position
OUSTERS > OUSTER
OUSTING > OUST
OUSTITI n device for opening locked door
OUSTITIS > OUSTITI
OUSTS > OUST
OUT adj denoting movement or distance away from ▷ vb put or throw out
OUTA prep informal contraction of out of
OUTACT vb surpass in acting
OUTACTED > OUTACT
OUTACTING > OUTACT
OUTACTS > OUTACT
OUTADD vb beat or surpass at adding
OUTADDED > OUTADD
OUTADDING > OUTADD
OUTADDS > OUTADD
OUTAGE n period of power failure
OUTAGES > OUTAGE
OUTARGUE vb defeat in argument
OUTARGUED > OUTARGUE
OUTARGUES > OUTARGUE
OUTASIGHT adj excellent or wonderful
OUTASITE adj amazing, excellent
OUTASK vb declare wedding banns
OUTASKED > OUTASK
OUTASKING > OUTASK
OUTASKS > OUTASK
OUTATE > OUTEAT
OUTBACK n remote bush country of Australia
OUTBACKER > OUTBACK
OUTBACKS > OUTBACK
OUTBAKE vb bake more or better than
OUTBAKED > OUTBAKE
OUTBAKES > OUTBAKE
OUTBAKING > OUTBAKE
OUTBAR vb keep out
OUTBARK vb bark more or louder than
OUTBARKED > OUTBARK
OUTBARKS > OUTBARK
OUTBARRED > OUTBAR
OUTBARS > OUTBAR
OUTBAWL vb bawl more or louder than

OUTBAWLED > OUTBAWL

OUTBAWLS > OUTBAWL

OUTBEAM vb beam more or brighter than

OUTBEAMED > OUTBEAM

OUTBEAMS > OUTBEAM

OUTBEG vb beg more or better than

OUTBEGGED > OUTBEG

OUTBEGS > OUTBEG

OUTBID vb offer a higher price than

OUTBIDDEN > OUTBID

OUTBIDDER > OUTBID

OUTBIDS > OUTBID

OUTBITCH vb bitch more or better than

OUTBLAZE vb blaze more or hotter than

OUTBLAZED > OUTBLAZE

OUTBLAZES > OUTBLAZE

OUTBLEAT vb bleat more or louder than

OUTBLEATS > OUTBLEAT

OUTBLESS vb bless more than

OUTBLOOM vb bloom more or better than

OUTBLOOMS > OUTBLOOM

OUTBLUFF vb surpass in bluffing

OUTBLUFFS > OUTBLUFF

OUTBLUSH vb blush more than

OUTBOARD adj (of a boat's engine) portable, with its own propeller ▷ adv away from the centre line of a vessel or aircraft ▷ n outboard motor

OUTBOARDS > OUTBOARD

OUTBOAST vb surpass in boasting

OUTBOASTS > OUTBOAST

OUTBOUGHT > OUTBUY

OUTBOUND adj going out

OUTBOUNDS n boundaries

OUTBOX vb surpass in boxing

OUTBOXED > OUTBOX

OUTBOXES > OUTBOX

OUTBOXING > OUTBOX

OUTBRAG vb brag more or better than

OUTBRAGS > OUTBRAG

OUTBRAVE vb surpass in bravery

OUTBRAVED > OUTBRAVE

OUTBRAVES > OUTBRAVE

OUTBRAWL vb defeat in a brawl

OUTBRAWLS > OUTBRAWL

OUTBRAZEN vb be more brazen than

OUTBREAK n sudden occurrence (of something unpleasant) ▷ vb break out

OUTBREAKS > OUTBREAK

OUTBRED > OUTBREED

OUTBREED vb produce offspring outside a particular family or tribe

OUTBREEDS > OUTBREED

OUTBRIBE vb bribe more than

OUTBRIBED > OUTBRIBE

OUTBRIBES > OUTBRIBE

OUTBROKE > OUTBREAK

OUTBROKEN > OUTBREAK

OUTBUILD vb exceed in building

OUTBUILDS > OUTBUILD

OUTBUILT > OUTBUILD

OUTBULGE vb bulge outwards

OUTBULGED > OUTBULGE

OUTBULGES > OUTBULGE

OUTBULK vb exceed in bulk

OUTBULKED > OUTBULK

OUTBULKS > OUTBULK

OUTBULLY vb exceed in bullying

OUTBURN vb burn longer or brighter than

OUTBURNED > OUTBURN

OUTBURNS > OUTBURN

OUTBURNT > OUTBURN

OUTBURST n sudden expression of emotion ▷ vb burst out

OUTBURSTS > OUTBURST

OUTBUY vb buy more than

OUTBUYING > OUTBUY

OUTBUYS > OUTBUY

OUTBY adv outside

OUTBYE same as > OUTBY

OUTCALL n visit to customer's home by professional ▷ vb bid higher than another player in a card game

OUTCALLED > OUTCALL

OUTCALLS > OUTCALL

OUTCAPER vb exceed in capering

OUTCAPERS > OUTCAPER

OUTCAST n person rejected by a particular group ▷ adj rejected, abandoned, or discarded

OUTCASTE n person who has been expelled from a caste ▷ vb cause (someone) to lose his or her caste

OUTCASTED > OUTCASTE

OUTCASTES > OUTCASTE

OUTCASTS > OUTCAST

OUTCATCH vb catch more than

OUTCAUGHT > OUTCATCH

OUTCAVIL vb exceed in cavilling

OUTCAVILS > OUTCAVIL

OUTCHARGE vb charge more than

OUTCHARM vb exceed in charming

OUTCHARMS > OUTCHARM

OUTCHEAT vb exceed in cheating

OUTCHEATS > OUTCHEAT

OUTCHID > OUTCHIDE

OUTCHIDE vb exceed in chiding

OUTCHIDED > OUTCHIDE

OUTCHIDES > OUTCHIDE

OUTCITIES > OUTCITY

OUTCITY n anywhere outside a city's confines

OUTCLASS vb surpass in quality

OUTCLIMB vb exceed in climbing

OUTCLIMBS > OUTCLIMB

OUTCLOMB > OUTCLIMB

OUTCOACH vb exceed in coaching

OUTCOME n result

OUTCOMES > OUTCOME

OUTCOOK vb cook more or better than

OUTCOOKED > OUTCOOK

OUTCOOKS > OUTCOOK

OUTCOUNT vb exceed in counting

OUTCOUNTS > OUTCOUNT

OUTCRAFTY vb be craftier than

OUTCRAWL vb crawl further or faster than

OUTCRAWLS > OUTCRAWL

OUTCRIED > OUTCRY

OUTCRIES > OUTCRY

OUTCROP n part of a rock formation that sticks out of the earth ▷ vb (of rock strata) to protrude through the surface of the earth

OUTCROPS > OUTCROP

OUTCROSS vb breed (animals or plants of the same breed but different strains) ▷ n animal or plant produced as a result of outcrossing

OUTCROW vb exceed in crowing

OUTCROWD vb have more crowd than

OUTCROWDS > OUTCROWD

OUTCROWED > OUTCROW

OUTCROWS > OUTCROW

OUTCRY n vehement or widespread protest ▷ vb cry louder or make more noise than (someone or something)

OUTCRYING > OUTCRY

OUTCURSE vb exceed in cursing

OUTCURSED > OUTCURSE

OUTCURSES > OUTCURSE

OUTCURVE n baseball thrown to curve away from batter

OUTCURVES > OUTCURVE

OUTDANCE vb surpass in dancing

OUTDANCED > OUTDANCE

OUTDANCES > OUTDANCE

OUTDARE vb be more brave than

OUTDARED > OUTDARE

OUTDARES > OUTDARE

OUTDARING > OUTDARE

OUTDATE vb make or become old-fashioned or obsolete

OUTDATED adj old-fashioned

OUTDATES > OUTDATE

OUTDATING > OUTDATE

OUTDAZZLE vb exceed in dazzling

OUTDEBATE vb exceed in debate

OUTDESIGN vb exceed in designing

OUTDID > OUTDO

OUTDO vb surpass in performance

OUTDODGE vb surpass in dodging

OUTDODGED > OUTDODGE

OUTDODGES > OUTDODGE

OUTDOER > OUTDO

OUTDOERS > OUTDO

OUTDOES > OUTDO

OUTDOING > OUTDO

OUTDONE > OUTDO

OUTDOOR adj taking place in the open air

OUTDOORS adv in(to) the open air ▷ n open air

OUTDOORSY adj taking part in activities relating to the outdoors

OUTDRAG vb beat in drag race

OUTDRAGS > OUTDRAG

OUTDRANK > OUTDRINK

OUTDRAW vb draw (a gun) faster than

OUTDRAWN > OUTDRAW

OUTDRAWS > OUTDRAW

OUTDREAM vb exceed in dreaming

OUTDREAMS > OUTDREAM

OUTDREAMT > OUTDREAM

OUTDRESS vb dress better than

OUTDREW > OUTDRAW

OUTDRINK vb drink more alcohol than

OUTDRINKS > OUTDRINK

OUTDRIVE vb exceed in driving

OUTDRIVEN
> OUTDRIVE
OUTDRIVES
> OUTDRIVE
OUTDROP *same as*
> OUTCROP
OUTDROPS > OUTDROP
OUTDROVE > OUTDRIVE
OUTDRUNK > OUTDRINK
OUTDUEL *vb* defeat in
duel
OUTDUELED > OUTDUEL
OUTDUELS > OUTDUEL
OUTDURE *vb* last longer
than
OUTDURED > OUTDURE
OUTDURES > OUTDURE
OUTDURING > OUTDURE
OUTDWELL *vb* live outside
something
OUTDWELLS
> OUTDWELL
OUTDWELT > OUTDWELL
OUTEARN *vb* earn more
than
OUTEARNED > OUTEARN
OUTEARNS > OUTEARN
OUTEAT *vb* eat more than
OUTEATEN > OUTEAT
OUTEATING > OUTEAT
OUTEATS > OUTEAT
OUTECHO *vb* echo more
than
OUTECHOED > OUTECHO
OUTECHOES > OUTECHO
OUTED > OUT
OUTEDGE *n* furthest limit
OUTEDGES > OUTEDGE
OUTER *adj* on the outside
▷ *n* white outermost ring
on a target
OUTERCOAT *same as*
> OVERCOAT
OUTERMOST *adj* furthest
out
OUTERS > OUTER
OUTERWEAR *n* clothes
worn on top of other
clothes
OUTFABLE *vb* exceed in
creating fables
OUTFABLED
> OUTFABLE
OUTFABLES
> OUTFABLE
OUTFACE *vb* subdue or
disconcert by staring
OUTFACED > OUTFACE
OUTFACES > OUTFACE
OUTFACING > OUTFACE
OUTFALL *n* mouth of a
river or drain
OUTFALLS > OUTFALL
OUTFAST *vb* fast longer
than
OUTFASTED > OUTFAST
OUTFASTS > OUTFAST
OUTFAWN *vb* exceed in
fawning
OUTFAWNED > OUTFAWN
OUTFAWNS > OUTFAWN
OUTFEAST *vb* exceed in
feasting
OUTFEASTS
> OUTFEAST
OUTFEEL *vb* exceed in
feeling
OUTFEELS > OUTFEEL

OUTFELT > OUTFEEL
OUTFENCE *vb* surpass at
fencing
OUTFENCED
> OUTFENCE
OUTFENCES
> OUTFENCE
OUTFIELD *n* area far
from the pitch
OUTFIELDS
> OUTFIELD
OUTFIGHT *vb* surpass in
fighting
OUTFIGHTS
> OUTFIGHT
OUTFIGURE *same as*
> OUTTHINK
OUTFIND *vb* exceed in
finding
OUTFINDS > OUTFIND
OUTFIRE *vb* exceed in
firing
OUTFIRED > OUTFIRE
OUTFIRES > OUTFIRE
OUTFIRING > OUTFIRE
OUTFISH *vb* catch more
fish than
OUTFISHED > OUTFISH
OUTFISHES > OUTFISH
OUTFIT *n* matching set of
clothes ▷ *vb* furnish or be
furnished with an outfit
OUTFITS > OUTFIT
OUTFITTED > OUTFIT
OUTFITTER *n* supplier of
clothes
OUTFLANK *vb* get round
the side of (an enemy
army)
OUTFLANKS
> OUTFLANK
OUTFLASH *vb* be flashier
than
OUTFLEW > OUTFLY
OUTFLIES > OUTFLY
OUTFLING *n* cutting
remark ▷ *vb* whip out
OUTFLINGS
> OUTFLING
OUTFLOAT *vb* surpass at
floating
OUTFLOATS
> OUTFLOAT
OUTFLOW *n* anything that
flows out, such as liquid or
money ▷ *vb* flow faster
than
OUTFLOWED > OUTFLOW
OUTFLOWN > OUTFLY
OUTFLOWS > OUTFLOW
OUTFLUNG > OUTFLING
OUTFLUSH *n* burst of
light
OUTFLY *vb* fly better or
faster than
OUTFLYING > OUTFLY
OUTFOOL *vb* be more
foolish than
OUTFOOLED > OUTFOOL
OUTFOOLS > OUTFOOL
OUTFOOT *vb* (of a boat) to
go faster than (another
boat)
OUTFOOTED > OUTFOOT
OUTFOOTS > OUTFOOT
OUTFOUGHT
> OUTFIGHT
OUTFOUND > OUTFIND

OUTFOX *vb* defeat or foil
by being more cunning
OUTFOXED > OUTFOX
OUTFOXES > OUTFOX
OUTFOXING > OUTFOX
OUTFROWN *vb* dominate
by frowning more than
OUTFROWNS
> OUTFROWN
OUTFUMBLE *vb* exceed in
fumbling
OUTGAIN *vb* gain more
than
OUTGAINED > OUTGAIN
OUTGAINS > OUTGAIN
OUTGALLOP *vb* gallop
faster than
OUTGAMBLE *vb* defeat at
gambling
OUTGAS *vb* undergo the
removal of adsorbed or
absorbed gas from
solids
OUTGASES > OUTGAS
OUTGASSED > OUTGAS
OUTGASSES > OUTGAS
OUTGATE *n* way out
OUTGATES > OUTGATE
OUTGAVE > OUTGIVE
OUTGAZE *vb* gaze beyond
OUTGAZED > OUTGAZE
OUTGAZES > OUTGAZE
OUTGAZING > OUTGAZE
OUTGIVE *vb* exceed in
giving
OUTGIVEN > OUTGIVE
OUTGIVES > OUTGIVE
OUTGIVING > OUTGIVE
OUTGLARE *vb* exceed in
glaring
OUTGLARED
> OUTGLARE
OUTGLARES
> OUTGLARE
OUTGLEAM *vb* gleam
more than
OUTGLEAMS
> OUTGLEAM
OUTGLOW *vb* glow more
than
OUTGLOWED > OUTGLOW
OUTGLOWS > OUTGLOW
OUTGNAW *vb* exceed in
gnawing
OUTGNAWED > OUTGNAW
OUTGNAWN > OUTGNAW
OUTGNAWS > OUTGNAW
OUTGO *vb* exceed or
outstrip ▷ *n* cost
OUTGOER > OUTGO
OUTGOERS > OUTGO
OUTGOES > OUTGO
OUTGOING *adj* leaving ▷ *n*
act of going out
OUTGOINGS *pl n*
expenses
OUTGONE > OUTGO
OUTGREW > OUTGROW
OUTGRIN *vb* exceed in
grinning
OUTGRINS > OUTGRIN
OUTGROSS *vb* earn more
than
OUTGROUP *n* group of
people outside one's own
group of people
OUTGROUPS
> OUTGROUP

OUTGROW *vb* become too
large or too old for
OUTGROWN > OUTGROW
OUTGROWS > OUTGROW
OUTGROWTH *n* natural
development
OUTGUARD *n* guard
furthest away from main
party
OUTGUARDS
> OUTGUARD
OUTGUESS *vb* surpass in
guessing
OUTGUIDE *n* folder in
filing system ▷ *vb* beat or
surpass at guiding
OUTGUIDED
> OUTGUIDE
OUTGUIDES
> OUTGUIDE
OUTGUN *vb* surpass in fire
power
OUTGUNNED > OUTGUN
OUTGUNS > OUTGUN
OUTGUSH *vb* gush out
OUTGUSHED > OUTGUSH
OUTGUSHES > OUTGUSH
OUTHANDLE *vb* handle
better than
OUTHARBOR *n* city or
town in Newfoundland
having a harbor
OUTHAUL *n* line or cable
for tightening the foot of a
sail
OUTHAULER *same as*
> OUTHAUL
OUTHAULS > OUTHAUL
OUTHEAR *vb* exceed in
hearing
OUTHEARD > OUTHEAR
OUTHEARS > OUTHEAR
OUTHER *same as* > OTHER
OUTHIRE *vb* hire out
OUTHIRED > OUTHIRE
OUTHIRES > OUTHIRE
OUTHIRING > OUTHIRE
OUTHIT *vb* hit something
further than (someone
else)
OUTHITS > OUTHIT
OUTHOMER *vb* score more
home runs than
OUTHOMERS
> OUTHOMER
OUTHOUSE *n* building
near a main building
OUTHOUSES
> OUTHOUSE
OUTHOWL *vb* exceed in
howling
OUTHOWLED > OUTHOWL
OUTHOWLS > OUTHOWL
OUTHUMOR *same as*
> OUTHUMOUR
OUTHUMORS
> OUTHUMOR
OUTHUMOUR *vb* exceed in
humouring
OUTHUNT *vb* exceed in
hunting
OUTHUNTED > OUTHUNT
OUTHUNTS > OUTHUNT
OUTHUSTLE *vb* be more
competitive than
OUTHYRE *same as*
> OUTHIRE
OUTHYRED > OUTHYRE

o

OUTHYRES > OUTHYRE
OUTHYRING > OUTHYRE
OUTING *n* leisure trip
OUTINGS > OUTING
OUTJEST *vb* exceed in jesting
OUTJESTED > OUTJEST
OUTJESTS > OUTJEST
OUTJET *n* projecting part
OUTJETS > OUTJET
OUTJINX *vb* exceed in jinxing
OUTJINXED > OUTJINX
OUTJINXES > OUTJINX
OUTJOCKEY *vb* outwit by deception
OUTJUGGLE *vb* surpass at juggling
OUTJUMP *vb* jump higher or farther than
OUTJUMPED > OUTJUMP
OUTJUMPS > OUTJUMP
OUTJUT *vb* jut out ▷ *n* projecting part
OUTJUTS > OUTJUT
OUTJUTTED > OUTJUT
OUTKEEP *vb* beat or surpass at keeping
OUTKEEPS > OUTKEEP
OUTKEPT > OUTKEEP
OUTKICK *vb* exceed in kicking
OUTKICKED > OUTKICK
OUTKICKS > OUTKICK
OUTKILL *vb* exceed in killing
OUTKILLED > OUTKILL
OUTKILLS > OUTKILL
OUTKISS *vb* exceed in kissing
OUTKISSED > OUTKISS
OUTKISSES > OUTKISS
OUTLAID > OUTLAY
OUTLAIN > OUTLAY
OUTLAND *adj* outlying or distant ▷ *n* outlying areas of a country or region
OUTLANDER *n* foreigner or stranger
OUTLANDS > OUTLAND
OUTLASH *n* sudden attack ▷ *vb* shed tears
OUTLASHED > OUTLASH
OUTLASHES > OUTLASH
OUTLAST *vb* last longer than
OUTLASTED > OUTLAST
OUTLASTS > OUTLAST
OUTLAUGH *vb* laugh longer or louder than
OUTLAUGHS
> OUTLAUGH
OUTLAUNCE *same as*
> OUTLAUNCH
OUTLAUNCH *vb* send out
OUTLAW *n* criminal deprived of legal protection, bandit ▷ *vb* make illegal
OUTLAWED > OUTLAW
OUTLAWING > OUTLAW
OUTLAWRY *n* act of outlawing or the state of being outlawed
OUTLAWS > OUTLAW
OUTLAY *n* expenditure ▷ *vb* spend (money)
OUTLAYING > OUTLAY

OUTLAYS > OUTLAY
OUTLEAD *vb* be better leader than
OUTLEADS > OUTLEAD
OUTLEAP *vb* leap higher or farther than
OUTLEAPED > OUTLEAP
OUTLEAPS > OUTLEAP
OUTLEAPT > OUTLEAP
OUTLEARN *vb* exceed in learning
OUTLEARNS
> OUTLEARN
OUTLEARNT
> OUTLEARN
OUTLED > OUTLEAD
OUTLER *n* farm animal kept out of doors
OUTLERS > OUTLER
OUTLET *n* means of expressing emotion
OUTLETS > OUTLET
OUTLIE *vb* lie outside a particular place
OUTLIED > OUTLIE
OUTLIER *n* outcrop of rocks that is entirely surrounded by older rocks
OUTLIERS > OUTLIER
OUTLIES > OUTLIE
OUTLINE *n* short general explanation ▷ *vb* summarize
OUTLINEAR > OUTLINE
OUTLINED > OUTLINE
OUTLINER > OUTLINE
OUTLINERS > OUTLINE
OUTLINES > OUTLINE
OUTLINING > OUTLINE
OUTLIVE *vb* live longer than
OUTLIVED > OUTLIVE
OUTLIVER > OUTLIVE
OUTLIVERS > OUTLIVE
OUTLIVES > OUTLIVE
OUTLIVING > OUTLIVE
OUTLOOK *n* attitude ▷ *vb* look out
OUTLOOKED > OUTLOOK
OUTLOOKS > OUTLOOK
OUTLOVE *vb* exceed in loving
OUTLOVED > OUTLOVE
OUTLOVES > OUTLOVE
OUTLOVING > OUTLOVE
OUTLUSTER *same as*
> OUTLUSTRE
OUTLUSTRE *vb* outshine
OUTLYING *adj* distant from the main area
OUTMAN *vb* surpass in manpower
OUTMANNED > OUTMAN
OUTMANS > OUTMAN
OUTMANTLE *vb* be better dressed than
OUTMARCH *vb* exceed in marching
OUTMASTER *vb* surpass
OUTMATCH *vb* surpass or outdo (someone)
OUTMODE *vb* make unfashionable
OUTMODED *adj* no longer fashionable or accepted
OUTMODES > OUTMODE

OUTMODING > OUTMODE
OUTMOST *another word for*
> OUTERMOST
OUTMOVE *vb* move faster or better than
OUTMOVED > OUTMOVE
OUTMOVES > OUTMOVE
OUTMOVING > OUTMOVE
OUTMUSCLE *vb* dominate by physical strength
OUTNAME *vb* be more notorious than
OUTNAMED > OUTNAME
OUTNAMES > OUTNAME
OUTNAMING > OUTNAME
OUTNESS *n* state or quality of being external
OUTNESSES > OUTNESS
OUTNIGHT *vb* refer to night more often than
OUTNIGHTS
> OUTNIGHT
OUTNUMBER *vb* exceed in number
OUTOFFICE *n* outbuilding
OUTPACE *vb* go faster than (someone)
OUTPACED > OUTPACE
OUTPACES > OUTPACE
OUTPACING > OUTPACE
OUTPAINT *vb* exceed in painting
OUTPAINTS
> OUTPAINT
OUTPART *n* remote region
OUTPARTS > OUTPART
OUTPASS *vb* exceed in passing
OUTPASSED > OUTPASS
OUTPASSES > OUTPASS
OUTPEEP *vb* peep out
OUTPEEPED > OUTPEEP
OUTPEEPS > OUTPEEP
OUTPEER *vb* surpass
OUTPEERED > OUTPEER
OUTPEERS > OUTPEER
OUTPEOPLE *vb* rid a country of its people
OUTPITCH *vb* exceed in pitching
OUTPITIED > OUTPITY
OUTPITIES > OUTPITY
OUTPITY *vb* exceed in pitying
OUTPLACE *vb* find job for ex-employee
OUTPLACED
> OUTPLACE
OUTPLACER
> OUTPLACE
OUTPLACES
> OUTPLACE
OUTPLAN *vb* exceed in planning
OUTPLANS > OUTPLAN
OUTPLAY *vb* perform better than one's opponent
OUTPLAYED > OUTPLAY
OUTPLAYS > OUTPLAY
OUTPLOD *vb* exceed in plodding
OUTPLODS > OUTPLOD
OUTPLOT *vb* exceed in plotting
OUTPLOTS > OUTPLOT

OUTPOINT *vb* score more points than
OUTPOINTS > OUTPOINT
OUTPOLL *vb* win more votes than
OUTPOLLED > OUTPOLL
OUTPOLLS > OUTPOLL
OUTPORT *n* isolated fishing village, esp in Newfoundland
OUTPORTER *n* inhabitant or native of a Newfoundland outport
OUTPORTS > OUTPORT
OUTPOST *n* outlying settlement
OUTPOSTS > OUTPOST
OUTPOUR *n* act of flowing or pouring out ▷ *vb* pour or cause to pour out freely or rapidly
OUTPOURED > OUTPOUR
OUTPOURER > OUTPOUR
OUTPOURS > OUTPOUR
OUTPOWER *vb* have more power than
OUTPOWERS
> OUTPOWER
OUTPRAY *vb* exceed in praying
OUTPRAYED > OUTPRAY
OUTPRAYS > OUTPRAY
OUTPREACH *vb* outdo in preaching
OUTPREEN *vb* exceed in preening
OUTPREENS
> OUTPREEN
OUTPRESS *vb* exceed in pressing
OUTPRICE *vb* sell at better price than
OUTPRICED
> OUTPRICE
OUTPRICES
> OUTPRICE
OUTPRIZE *vb* prize more highly than
OUTPRIZED
> OUTPRIZE
OUTPRIZES
> OUTPRIZE
OUTPSYCH *vb* defeat by psychological means
OUTPSYCHS
> OUTPSYCH
OUTPULL *vb* exceed in pulling
OUTPULLED > OUTPULL
OUTPULLS > OUTPULL
OUTPUNCH *vb* punch better than
OUTPUPIL *n* student sent to a different school to the one he or she would normally attend
OUTPUPILS
> OUTPUPIL
OUTPURSUE *vb* pursue farther than
OUTPUSH *vb* exceed in pushing
OUTPUSHED > OUTPUSH
OUTPUSHES > OUTPUSH
OUTPUT *n* amount produced ▷ *vb* produce (data) at the end of a process

OUTPUTS > OUTPUT

OUTPUTTED > OUTPUT

OUTQUOTE *vb* exceed in quoting

**OUTQUOTED
> OUTQUOTE**

**OUTQUOTES
> OUTQUOTE**

OUTRACE *vb* surpass in racing

OUTRACED > OUTRACE

OUTRACES > OUTRACE

OUTRACING > OUTRACE

OUTRAGE *n* great moral indignation ▷ *vb* offend morally

OUTRAGED > OUTRAGE

OUTRAGES > OUTRAGE

OUTRAGING > OUTRAGE

OUTRAISE *vb* raise more money than

**OUTRAISED
> OUTRAISE**

**OUTRAISES
> OUTRAISE**

OUTRAN > OUTRUN

OUTRANCE *n* furthest extreme

**OUTRANCES
> OUTRANCE**

OUTRANG > OUTRING

OUTRANGE *vb* have a greater range than

**OUTRANGED
> OUTRANGE**

**OUTRANGES
> OUTRANGE**

OUTRANK *vb* be of higher rank than (someone)

OUTRANKED > OUTRANK

OUTRANKS > OUTRANK

OUTRATE *vb* offer better rate than

OUTRATED > OUTRATE

OUTRATES > OUTRATE

OUTRATING > OUTRATE

OUTRAVE *vb* outdo in raving

OUTRAVED > OUTRAVE

OUTRAVES > OUTRAVE

OUTRAVING > OUTRAVE

OUTRE *adj* shockingly eccentric

OUTREACH *vb* surpass in reach ▷ *n* act or process of reaching out

OUTREAD *vb* outdo in reading

OUTREADS > OUTREAD

OUTREASON *vb* surpass in reasoning

OUTRECKON *vb* surpass in reckoning

OUTRED *vb* be redder than

OUTREDDED > OUTRED

OUTREDDEN *same as*
> OUTRED

OUTREDS > OUTRED

OUTREIGN *vb* reign for longer than

**OUTREIGNS
> OUTREIGN**

OUTRELIEF *n* aid given outdoors

OUTREMER *n* land overseas

**OUTREMERS
> OUTREMER**

OUTRIDDEN > OUTRIDE

OUTRIDE *vb* outdo by riding faster, farther, or better than ▷ *n* extra unstressed syllable within a metrical foot

OUTRIDER *n* motorcyclist acting as an escort

**OUTRIDERS
> OUTRIDER**

OUTRIDES > OUTRIDE

OUTRIDING *n* act or instance of riding faster, farther, or better than

OUTRIG *vb* supply with outfit

OUTRIGGED > OUTRIG

OUTRIGGER *n* stabilizing frame projecting from a boat

OUTRIGHT *adv* absolute(ly) ▷ *adj* complete

OUTRIGS > OUTRIG

OUTRING *vb* exceed in ringing

OUTRINGS > OUTRING

OUTRIVAL *vb* surpass

**OUTRIVALS
> OUTRIVAL**

OUTRO *n* instrumental passage that concludes a piece of music

OUTROAR *vb* roar louder than

OUTROARED > OUTROAR

OUTROARS > OUTROAR

OUTROCK *vb* outdo in rocking

OUTROCKED > OUTROCK

OUTROCKS > OUTROCK

OUTRODE > OUTRIDE

OUTROLL *vb* exceed in rolling

OUTROLLED > OUTROLL

OUTROLLS > OUTROLL

OUTROOP *n* auction

OUTROOPER > OUTROOP

OUTROOPS > OUTROOP

OUTROOT *vb* root out

OUTROOTED > OUTROOT

OUTROOTS > OUTROOT

OUTROPE *same as*
> OUTROOP

OUTROPER > OUTROPE

OUTROPERS > OUTROPE

OUTROPES > OUTROPE

OUTROS > OUTRO

OUTROW *vb* outdo in rowing

OUTROWED > OUTROW

OUTROWING > OUTROW

OUTROWS > OUTROW

OUTRUN *vb* run faster than

OUTRUNG > OUTRING

OUTRUNNER *n* attendant who runs in front of a carriage, etc

OUTRUNS > OUTRUN

OUTRUSH *n* flowing or rushing out ▷ *vb* rush out

OUTRUSHED > OUTRUSH

OUTRUSHES > OUTRUSH

OUTS > OUT

OUTSAID > OUTSAY

OUTSAIL *vb* sail better than

OUTSAILED > OUTSAIL

OUTSAILS > OUTSAIL

OUTSANG > OUTSING

OUTSAT > OUTSIT

OUTSAVOR *same as*
> OUTSAVOUR

**OUTSAVORS
> OUTSAVOR**

OUTSAVOUR *vb* exceed in savouring

OUTSAW > OUTSEE

OUTSAY *vb* say something out loud

OUTSAYING > OUTSAY

OUTSAYS > OUTSAY

OUTSCHEME *vb* outdo in scheming

OUTSCOLD *vb* outdo in scolding

**OUTSCOLDS
> OUTSCOLD**

OUTSCOOP *vb* outdo in achieving scoops

**OUTSCOOPS
> OUTSCOOP**

OUTSCORE *vb* score more than

**OUTSCORED
> OUTSCORE**

**OUTSCORES
> OUTSCORE**

OUTSCORN *vb* defy with scorn

**OUTSCORNS
> OUTSCORN**

OUTSCREAM *vb* scream louder than

OUTSEE *vb* exceed in seeing

OUTSEEING > OUTSEE

OUTSEEN > OUTSEE

OUTSEES > OUTSEE

OUTSELL *vb* be sold in greater quantities than

OUTSELLS > OUTSELL

OUTSERT *another word for*
> WRAPAROUND

OUTSERTS > OUTSERT

OUTSERVE *vb* serve better at tennis than

**OUTSERVED
> OUTSERVE**

**OUTSERVES
> OUTSERVE**

OUTSET *n* beginning

OUTSETS > OUTSET

OUTSHAME *vb* greatly shame

**OUTSHAMED
> OUTSHAME**

**OUTSHAMES
> OUTSHAME**

OUTSHINE *vb* surpass (someone) in excellence

**OUTSHINED
> OUTSHINE**

**OUTSHINES
> OUTSHINE**

OUTSHONE > OUTSHINE

OUTSHOOT *vb* surpass or excel in shooting ▷ *n* thing that projects or shoots out

**OUTSHOOTS
> OUTSHOOT**

OUTSHOT *n* projecting part

OUTSHOTS > OUTSHOT

OUTSHOUT *vb* shout louder than

**OUTSHOUTS
> OUTSHOUT**

OUTSIDE *adv* indicating movement to or position on the exterior or surface ▷ *adj* unlikely ▷ *n* external area or surface

OUTSIDER *n* person outside a specific group

**OUTSIDERS
> OUTSIDER**

OUTSIDES > OUTSIDE

OUTSIGHT *n* power of seeing

**OUTSIGHTS
> OUTSIGHT**

OUTSIN *vb* sin more than

OUTSING *vb* sing better or louder than

OUTSINGS > OUTSING

OUTSINNED > OUTSIN

OUTSINS > OUTSIN

OUTSIT *vb* sit longer than

OUTSITS > OUTSIT

OUTSIZE *adj* larger than normal ▷ *n* outsize garment

OUTSIZED *same as*
> OUTSIZE

OUTSIZES > OUTSIZE

OUTSKATE *vb* skate better than

**OUTSKATED
> OUTSKATE**

**OUTSKATES
> OUTSKATE**

OUTSKIRT *singular of*
> OUTSKIRTS

OUTSKIRTS *pl n* outer areas, esp of a town

OUTSLEEP *vb* sleep longer than

**OUTSLEEPS
> OUTSLEEP**

OUTSLEPT > OUTSLEEP

OUTSLICK *vb* outsmart

**OUTSLICKS
> OUTSLICK**

OUTSMART *vb* outwit

**OUTSMARTS
> OUTSMART**

OUTSMELL *vb* surpass in smelling

**OUTSMELLS
> OUTSMELL**

OUTSMELT > OUTSMELL

OUTSMILE *vb* outdo in smiling

**OUTSMILED
> OUTSMILE**

**OUTSMILES
> OUTSMILE**

OUTSMOKE *vb* smoke more than

**OUTSMOKED
> OUTSMOKE**

**OUTSMOKES
> OUTSMOKE**

OUTSNORE *vb* outdo in snoring

**OUTSNORED
> OUTSNORE**

**OUTSNORES
> OUTSNORE**

OUTSOAR *vb* fly higher than

O

OUTSOARED > OUTSOAR
OUTSOARS > OUTSOAR
OUTSOLD > OUTSELL
OUTSOLE *n* outermost sole of a shoe
OUTSOLES > OUTSOLE
OUTSOURCE *vb* subcontract (work) to another company
OUTSPAN *vb* relax
OUTSPANS > OUTSPAN
OUTSPEAK *vb* speak better or louder than
OUTSPEAKS
> OUTSPEAK
OUTSPED > OUTSPEED
OUTSPEED *vb* go faster than
OUTSPEEDS
> OUTSPEED
OUTSPELL *vb* exceed at spelling
OUTSPELLS
> OUTSPELL
OUTSPELT > OUTSPELL
OUTSPEND *vb* spend more than
OUTSPENDS
> OUTSPEND
OUTSPENT > OUTSPEND
OUTSPOKE > OUTSPEAK
OUTSPOKEN *adj* tending to say what one thinks
OUTSPORT *vb* sport in excess of
OUTSPORTS
> OUTSPORT
OUTSPRANG
> OUTSPRING
OUTSPREAD *adj* spread or stretched out as far as possible ▷ *vb* spread out or cause to spread out ▷ *n* spreading out
OUTSPRING *vb* spring out
OUTSPRINT *vb* run faster than (someone)
OUTSPRUNG
> OUTSPRING
OUTSTAND *vb* be outstanding or excel
OUTSTANDS
> OUTSTAND
OUTSTARE *vb* stare longer than
OUTSTARED
> OUTSTARE
OUTSTARES
> OUTSTARE
OUTSTART *vb* jump out ▷ *n* outset
OUTSTARTS
> OUTSTART
OUTSTATE *vb* surpass in stating
OUTSTATED
> OUTSTATE
OUTSTATES
> OUTSTATE
OUTSTAY *vb* overstay
OUTSTAYED
> OUTSTAY
OUTSTAYS > OUTSTAY
OUTSTEER *vb* steer better than
OUTSTEERS
> OUTSTEER

OUTSTEP *vb* step farther than
OUTSTEPS > OUTSTEP
OUTSTOOD > OUTSTAND
OUTSTRAIN *vb* strain too much
OUTSTRIDE *vb* surpass in striding
OUTSTRIKE *vb* exceed in striking
OUTSTRIP *vb* surpass
OUTSTRIPS
> OUTSTRIP
OUTSTRIVE *vb* strive harder than
OUTSTRODE
> OUTSTRIDE
OUTSTROKE *n* outward stroke
OUTSTROVE
> OUTSTRIVE
OUTSTRUCK
> OUTSTRIKE
OUTSTUDY *vb* outdo in studying
OUTSTUNT *vb* outdo in performing stunts
OUTSTUNTS
> OUTSTUNT
OUTSULK *vb* outdo in sulking
OUTSULKED > OUTSULK
OUTSULKS > OUTSULK
OUTSUM *vb* add up to more than
OUTSUMMED > OUTSUM
OUTSUMS > OUTSUM
OUTSUNG > OUTSING
OUTSWAM > OUTSWIM
OUTSWARE > OUTSWEAR
OUTSWEAR *vb* swear more than
OUTSWEARS
> OUTSWEAR
OUTSWEEP *n* outward movement of arms in swimming breaststroke
OUTSWEEPS
> OUTSWEEP
OUTSWELL *vb* exceed in swelling
OUTSWELLS
> OUTSWELL
OUTSWEPT *adj* curving outwards
OUTSWIM *vb* outdo in swimming
OUTSWIMS > OUTSWIM
OUTSWING *n* (in cricket) movement of a ball from leg to off through the air
OUTSWINGS
> OUTSWING
OUTSWORE > OUTSWEAR
OUTSWORN > OUTSWEAR
OUTSWUM > OUTSWIM
OUTSWUNG *adj* made to curve outwards
OUTTA *prep* informal contraction of out of
OUTTAKE *n* unreleased take from a recording session, film, or TV programme ▷ *vb* take out
OUTTAKEN > OUTTAKE
OUTTAKES > OUTTAKE
OUTTAKING > OUTTAKE

OUTTALK *vb* talk more, longer, or louder than (someone)
OUTTALKED > OUTTALK
OUTTALKS > OUTTALK
OUTTASK *vb* assign task to staff outside organization
OUTTASKED > OUTTASK
OUTTASKS > OUTTASK
OUTTELL *vb* make known
OUTTELLS > OUTTELL
OUTTHANK *vb* outdo in thanking
OUTTHANKS
> OUTTHANK
OUTTHIEVE *vb* surpass in stealing
OUTTHINK *vb* outdo in thinking
OUTTHINKS
> OUTTHINK
OUTTHREW > OUTTHROW
OUTTHROB *vb* outdo in throbbing
OUTTHROBS
> OUTTHROB
OUTTHROW *vb* throw better than
OUTTHROWN
> OUTTHROW
OUTTHROWS
> OUTTHROW
OUTTHRUST *vb* extend outwards
OUTTOLD > OUTTELL
OUTTONGUE *vb* speak louder than
OUTTOOK > OUTTAKE
OUTTOP *vb* rise higher than
OUTTOPPED > OUTTOP
OUTTOPS > OUTTOP
OUTTOWER *vb* tower over
OUTTOWERS
> OUTTOWER
OUTTRADE *vb* surpass in trading
OUTTRADED
> OUTTRADE
OUTTRADES
> OUTTRADE
OUTTRAVEL *vb* outdo in travelling
OUTTRICK *vb* outdo in trickery
OUTTRICKS
> OUTTRICK
OUTTROT *vb* exceed at trotting
OUTTROTS > OUTTROT
OUTTRUMP *vb* count for more than
OUTTRUMPS
> OUTTRUMP
OUTTURN *same as*
> OUTPUT
OUTTURNS > OUTTURN
OUTVALUE *vb* surpass in value
OUTVALUED
> OUTVALUE
OUTVALUES
> OUTVALUE
OUTVAUNT *vb* outdo in boasting
OUTVAUNTS
> OUTVAUNT

OUTVENOM *vb* surpass in venomousness
OUTVENOMS
> OUTVENOM
OUTVIE *vb* outdo in competition
OUTVIED > OUTVIE
OUTVIES > OUTVIE
OUTVOICE *vb* surpass in noise
OUTVOICED
> OUTVOICE
OUTVOICES
> OUTVOICE
OUTVOTE *vb* defeat by getting more votes than
OUTVOTED > OUTVOTE
OUTVOTER > OUTVOTE
OUTVOTERS > OUTVOTE
OUTVOTES > OUTVOTE
OUTVOTING > OUTVOTE
OUTVYING > OUTVIE
OUTWAIT *vb* wait longer than
OUTWAITED > OUTWAIT
OUTWAITS > OUTWAIT
OUTWALK *vb* walk farther or longer than
OUTWALKED > OUTWALK
OUTWALKS > OUTWALK
OUTWAR *vb* surpass or exceed in warfare
OUTWARD *same as*
> OUTWARDS
OUTWARDLY *adv* in outward appearance
OUTWARDS *adv* towards the outside
OUTWARRED > OUTWAR
OUTWARS > OUTWAR
OUTWASH *n* gravel carried and deposited by water from melting glaciers
OUTWASHES > OUTWASH
OUTWASTE *vb* outdo in wasting
OUTWASTED
> OUTWASTE
OUTWASTES
> OUTWASTE
OUTWATCH *vb* surpass in watching
OUTWEAR *vb* use up or destroy by wearing
OUTWEARS > OUTWEAR
OUTWEARY *vb* exhaust
OUTWEED *vb* root out
OUTWEEDED > OUTWEED
OUTWEEDS > OUTWEED
OUTWEEP *vb* outdo in weeping
OUTWEEPS > OUTWEEP
OUTWEIGH *vb* be more important, significant, or influential than
OUTWEIGHS > OUTWEIGH
OUTWELL *vb* pour out
OUTWELLED > OUTWELL
OUTWELLS > OUTWELL
OUTWENT > OUTGO
OUTWEPT > OUTWEEP
OUTWHIRL *vb* surpass at whirling
OUTWHIRLS
> OUTWHIRL
OUTWICK *vb* move one curling stone by striking with another

OUTWICKED > OUTWICK
OUTWICKS > OUTWICK
OUTWILE vb surpass in cunning
OUTWILED > OUTWILE
OUTWILES > OUTWILE
OUTWILING > OUTWILE
OUTWILL vb demonstrate stronger will than
OUTWILLED > OUTWILL
OUTWILLS > OUTWILL
OUTWIN vb get out of
OUTWIND vb unwind
OUTWINDED > OUTWIND
OUTWINDS > OUTWIND
OUTWING vb surpass in flying
OUTWINGED > OUTWING
OUTWINGS > OUTWING
OUTWINS > OUTWIN
OUTWISH vb surpass in wishing
OUTWISHED > OUTWISH
OUTWISHES > OUTWISH
OUTWIT vb get the better of (someone) by cunning
OUTWITH prep outside
OUTWITS > OUTWIT
OUTWITTED > OUTWIT
OUTWON > OUTWIN
OUTWORE > OUTWEAR
OUTWORK n defences which lie outside main defensive works ▷ vb work better, harder, etc, than
OUTWORKED > OUTWORK
OUTWORKER > OUTWORK
OUTWORKS > OUTWORK
OUTWORN adj no longer in use
OUTWORTH vb be more valuable than
OUTWORTHS > OUTWORTH
OUTWOUND > OUTWIND
OUTWREST vb extort
OUTWRESTS > OUTWREST
OUTWRIT > OUTWRITE
OUTWRITE vb outdo in writing
OUTWRITES > OUTWRITE
OUTWROTE > OUTWRITE
OUTYELL vb outdo in yelling
OUTYELLED > OUTYELL
OUTYELLS > OUTYELL
OUTYELP vb outdo in yelping
OUTYELPED > OUTYELP
OUTYELPS > OUTYELP
OUTYIELD vb yield more than
OUTYIELDS > OUTYIELD
OUVERT adj open
OUVERTE feminine form of > OUVERT
OUVRAGE n work
OUVRAGES > OUVRAGE
OUVRIER n worker
OUVRIERE feminine form of > OUVRIER
OUVRIERES > OUVRIERE
OUVRIERS > OUVRIER

OUZEL n type of bird
OUZELS > OUZEL
OUZO n strong aniseed-flavoured spirit from Greece
OUZOS > OUZO
OVA > OVUM
OVAL adj egg-shaped ▷ n anything that is oval in shape
OVALBUMIN n albumin in egg whites
OVALITIES > OVAL
OVALITY > OVAL
OVALLY > OVAL
OVALNESS > OVAL
OVALS > OVAL
OVARIAL > OVARY
OVARIAN > OVARY
OVARIES > OVARY
OVARIOLE n tube in insect ovary
OVARIOLES > OVARIOLE
OVARIOUS adj of eggs
OVARITIS n inflammation of an ovary
OVARY n female egg-producing organ
OVATE adj shaped like an egg ▷ vb give ovation
OVATED > OVATE
OVATELY > OVATE
OVATES > OVATE
OVATING > OVATE
OVATION n enthusiastic round of applause
OVATIONAL > OVATION
OVATIONS > OVATION
OVATOR > OVATE
OVATORS > OVATE
OVEL n mourner, esp during the first seven days after a death
OVELS > OVEL
OVEN n heated compartment or container for cooking ▷ vb cook in an oven
OVENABLE adj (of food) suitable for cooking in an oven
OVENBIRD n type of small brownish South American bird
OVENBIRDS > OVENBIRD
OVENED > OVEN
OVENING > OVEN
OVENLIKE > OVEN
OVENPROOF adj able to be used in an oven
OVENS > OVEN
OVENWARE n heat-resistant dishes in which food can be both cooked and served
OVENWARES > OVENWARE
OVENWOOD n pieces of wood for burning in an oven
OVENWOODS > OVENWOOD
OVER adv indicating position on the top of, amount greater than, etc ▷ adj finished ▷ n (in

cricket) series of six balls bowled from one end ▷ vb jump over
OVERABLE adj too able
OVERACT vb act in an exaggerated way
OVERACTED > OVERACT
OVERACTS > OVERACT
OVERACUTE adj too acute
OVERAGE adj beyond a specified age ▷ n amount beyond given limit
OVERAGED adj very old
OVERAGES > OVERAGE
OVERALERT adj abnormally alert
OVERALL adv in total ▷ n coat-shaped protective garment ▷ adj from one end to the other
OVERALLED adj wearing overalls
OVERALLS > OVERALL
OVERAPT adj tending excessively
OVERARCH vb form an arch over
OVERARM adv with the arm above the shoulder ▷ adj bowled, thrown, or performed with the arm raised above the shoulder ▷ vb throw (a ball) overarm
OVERARMED > OVERARM
OVERARMS > OVERARM
OVERATE > OVEREAT
OVERAWE vb affect (someone) with an overpowering sense of awe
OVERAWED > OVERAWE
OVERAWES > OVERAWE
OVERAWING > OVERAWE
OVERBAKE vb bake too long
OVERBAKED > OVERBAKE
OVERBAKES > OVERBAKE
OVERBANK n sediment deposited on the flood plain of a river
OVERBANKS > OVERBANK
OVERBEAR vb dominate or overcome
OVERBEARS > OVERBEAR
OVERBEAT vb beat too much
OVERBEATS > OVERBEAT
OVERBED adj fitting over bed
OVERBET vb bet too much
OVERBETS > OVERBET
OVERBID vb bid for more tricks than one can expect to win ▷ n bid higher than someone else's bid
OVERBIDS > OVERBID
OVERBIG adj too big
OVERBILL vb charge too much money
OVERBILLS > OVERBILL

OVERBITE n extension of the upper front teeth over the lower front teeth when the mouth is closed
OVERBITES > OVERBITE
OVERBLEW > OVERBLOW
OVERBLOW vb blow into (a wind instrument) with greater force than normal
OVERBLOWN adj excessive
OVERBLOWS > OVERBLOW
OVERBOARD adv from a boat into the water
OVERBOIL vb boil too much
OVERBOILS > OVERBOIL
OVERBOLD adj too bold
OVERBOOK vb accept too many bookings
OVERBOOKS > OVERBOOK
OVERBOOT n protective boot worn over an ordinary boot or shoe
OVERBOOTS > OVERBOOT
OVERBORE > OVERBEAR
OVERBORN > OVERBEAR
OVERBORNE > OVERBEAR
OVERBOUND vb jump over
OVERBRAKE vb brake too much
OVERBRED adj produced by too much selective breeding
OVERBREED vb produce by too much selective breeding
OVERBRIEF adj too brief
OVERBRIM vb overflow
OVERBRIMS > OVERBRIM
OVERBROAD adj not specific enough
OVERBROW vb hang over
OVERBROWS > OVERBROW
OVERBUILD vb build over or on top of
OVERBUILT > OVERBUILD
OVERBULK vb loom large over
OVERBULKS > OVERBULK
OVERBURN vb (formerly) copy information onto CD
OVERBURNS > OVERBURN
OVERBURNT > OVERBURN
OVERBUSY adj too busy ▷ vb make too busy
OVERBUY vb buy too much or too many
OVERBUYS > OVERBUY
OVERBY adv Scots expression meaning over the road or across the way
OVERCALL n bid higher than the preceding one ▷ vb bid higher than (an opponent)
OVERCALLS > OVERCALL

OVERCAME > OVERCOME

OVERCARRY vb carry too far or too many

OVERCAST adj (of the sky) covered by clouds ▷ vb make or become overclouded or gloomy ▷ n covering, as of clouds or mist

OVERCASTS > OVERCAST

OVERCATCH vb overtake

OVERCHEAP adj too cheap

OVERCHECK n thin leather strap attached to a horse's bit to keep its head up

OVERCHILL vb make too cold

OVERCIVIL adj too civil

OVERCLAD adj wearing too many clothes

OVERCLAIM vb claim too much

OVERCLASS n dominant group in society

OVERCLEAN adj too clean

OVERCLEAR adj too clear

OVERCLOCK vb modify a computer to run at greater speeds than originally intended

OVERCLOSE adj too close

OVERCLOUD vb make or become covered with clouds

OVERCLOY vb weary with excess

OVERCLOYS > OVERCLOY

OVERCLUB vb (in golf) use a club which causes the shot to go too far

OVERCLUBS > OVERCLUB

OVERCOACH vb coach too much

OVERCOAT n heavy coat

OVERCOATS > OVERCOAT

OVERCOLD adj too cold

OVERCOLOR vb colour too highly

OVERCOME vb gain control over after an effort

OVERCOMER > OVERCOME

OVERCOMES > OVERCOME

OVERCOOK vb spoil food by cooking it for too long

OVERCOOKS > OVERCOOK

OVERCOOL vb cool too much

OVERCOOLS > OVERCOOL

OVERCOUNT vb outnumber

OVERCOVER vb cover up

OVERCOY adj too modest

OVERCRAM vb fill too full

OVERCRAMS > OVERCRAM

OVERCRAW same as > OVERCROW

OVERCRAWS > OVERCRAW

OVERCROP vb exhaust (land) by excessive cultivation

OVERCROPS > OVERCROP

OVERCROW vb crow over

OVERCROWD vb fill with more people or things than is desirable

OVERCROWS > OVERCROW

OVERCURE vb take curing process too far

OVERCURED > OVERCURE

OVERCURES > OVERCURE

OVERCUT vb cut too much

OVERCUTS > OVERCUT

OVERDARE vb dare too much

OVERDARED > OVERDARE

OVERDARES > OVERDARE

OVERDATED adj outdated

OVERDEAR adj too dear

OVERDECK n upper deck

OVERDECKS > OVERDECK

OVERDID > OVERDO

OVERDIGHT adj covered up

OVERDO vb do to excess

OVERDOER > OVERDO

OVERDOERS > OVERDO

OVERDOES > OVERDO

OVERDOG n person or side in an advantageous position

OVERDOGS > OVERDOG

OVERDOING > OVERDO

OVERDONE > OVERDO

OVERDOSE n excessive dose of a drug ▷ vb take an overdose

OVERDOSED > OVERDOSE

OVERDOSES > OVERDOSE

OVERDRAFT n overdrawing

OVERDRANK > OVERDRINK

OVERDRAW vb withdraw more money than is in (one's bank account)

OVERDRAWN > OVERDRAW

OVERDRAWS > OVERDRAW

OVERDRESS vb dress (oneself or another) too elaborately or finely ▷ n dress that may be worn over a jumper, blouse, etc

OVERDREW > OVERDRAW

OVERDRIED > OVERDRY

OVERDRIES > OVERDRY

OVERDRINK vb drink too much alcohol

OVERDRIVE n very high gear in a motor vehicle

OVERDROVE > OVERDRIVE

OVERDRUNK > OVERDRINK

OVERDRY vb dry too much

OVERDUB vb add (new sounds) to an audio recording so that the old and the new sounds can be heard ▷ n sound or series of sounds added by this method

OVERDUBS > OVERDUB

OVERDUE adj still due after the time allowed

OVERDUST vb dust too much

OVERDUSTS > OVERDUST

OVERDYE vb dye (a fabric, yarn, etc) excessively

OVERDYED > OVERDYE

OVERDYER > OVERDYE

OVERDYERS > OVERDYE

OVERDYES > OVERDYE

OVEREAGER adj excessively eager or keen

OVEREASY adj too easy

OVEREAT vb eat more than is necessary or healthy

OVEREATEN > OVEREAT

OVEREATER > OVEREAT

OVEREATS > OVEREAT

OVERED > OVER

OVEREDIT vb edit too much

OVEREDITS > OVEREDIT

OVEREGG vb exaggerate absurdly

OVEREGGED > OVEREGG

OVEREGGS > OVEREGG

OVEREMOTE vb emote too much

OVEREQUIP vb equip, furnish with, or supply excessively

OVEREXERT vb exhaust or injure (oneself) by doing too much

OVEREYE vb survey

OVEREYED > OVEREYE

OVEREYES > OVEREYE

OVEREYING > OVEREYE

OVERFALL n turbulent stretch of water caused by marine currents over an underwater ridge ▷ vb fall over

OVERFALLS > OVERFALL

OVERFAR adv too far

OVERFAST adj too fast

OVERFAT adj too fat

OVERFAVOR vb favour too much

OVERFEAR vb fear too much

OVERFEARS > OVERFEAR

OVERFED > OVERFEED

OVERFEED vb give (a person, plant, or animal) more food than is necessary or healthy

OVERFEEDS > OVERFEED

OVERFELL > OVERFALL

OVERFILL vb put more into (something) than there is room for

OVERFILLS > OVERFILL

OVERFINE adj too fine

OVERFISH vb fish too much

OVERFIT adj too fit

OVERFLEW > OVERFLY

OVERFLIES > OVERFLY

OVERFLOOD vb flood excessively

OVERFLOW vb flow over ▷ n something that overflows

OVERFLOWN > OVERFLY

OVERFLOWS > OVERFLOW

OVERFLUSH adj too flush

OVERFLY vb fly over (a territory) or past (a point)

OVERFOCUS vb focus too much

OVERFOLD n fold in which one or both limbs have been inclined more than 90°

OVERFOLDS > OVERFOLD

OVERFOND adj excessively keen (on)

OVERFOUL adj too foul

OVERFRANK adj too frank

OVERFREE adj too forward

OVERFULL adj excessively full

OVERFUND vb supply with too much money

OVERFUNDS > OVERFUND

OVERFUSSY adj too fussy

OVERGALL vb make sore all over

OVERGALLS > OVERGALL

OVERGANG vb dominate

OVERGANGS > OVERGANG

OVERGAVE > OVERGIVE

OVERGEAR vb cause (a company) to have too high a proportion of loan stock

OVERGEARS > OVERGEAR

OVERGET vb overtake

OVERGETS > OVERGET

OVERGILD vb gild too much

OVERGILDS > OVERGILD

OVERGILT > OVERGILD

OVERGIRD vb gird too tightly

OVERGIRDS > OVERGIRD

OVERGIRT > OVERGIRD

OVERGIVE vb give up

OVERGIVEN > OVERGIVE

OVERGIVES > OVERGIVE

OVERGLAD adj too glad

OVERGLAZE adj (of decoration or colours) applied to porcelain above the glaze

OVERGLOOM vb make gloomy

OVERGO vb go beyond

OVERGOAD vb goad too much
OVERGOADS
> OVERGOAD
OVERGOES > OVERGO
OVERGOING > OVERGO
OVERGONE > OVERGO
OVERGORGE vb overeat
OVERGOT > OVERGET
OVERGRADE vb grade too highly
OVERGRAIN vb apply grainy texture to
OVERGRASS vb grow grass on top of
OVERGRAZE vb graze (land) too intensively
OVERGREAT adj too great
OVERGREEN vb cover with vegetation
OVERGREW > OVERGROW
OVERGROW vb grow over or across (an area, path, lawn, etc)
OVERGROWN
> OVERGROW
OVERGROWS
> OVERGROW
OVERHAILE vb pull over
OVERHAIR n outer coat of animal
OVERHAIRS
> OVERHAIR
OVERHALE same as
> OVERHAILE
OVERHALED
> OVERHALE
OVERHALES
> OVERHALE
OVERHAND adj thrown or performed with the hand raised above the shoulder ▷ adv with the hand above the shoulder ▷ vb sew with the thread passing over two edges in one direction
OVERHANDS
> OVERHAND
OVERHANG vb project beyond something ▷ n overhanging part
OVERHANGS
> OVERHANG
OVERHAPPY adj too happy
OVERHARD adj too hard
OVERHASTE n excessive haste
OVERHASTY
> OVERHASTE
OVERHATE vb hate too much
OVERHATED
> OVERHATE
OVERHATES
> OVERHATE
OVERHAUL vb examine and repair ▷ n examination and repair
OVERHAULS
> OVERHAUL
OVERHEAD adj above one's head ▷ adv over or above head height ▷ n stroke in racket games played from above head height

OVERHEADS pl n general cost of maintaining a business
OVERHEAP vb supply too much
OVERHEAPS
> OVERHEAP
OVERHEAR vb hear (a speaker or remark) unintentionally
OVERHEARD
> OVERHEAR
OVERHEARS
> OVERHEAR
OVERHEAT vb make or become excessively hot ▷ n condition of being overheated
OVERHEATS
> OVERHEAT
OVERHELD > OVERHOLD
OVERHENT vb overtake
OVERHENTS
> OVERHENT
OVERHIGH adj too high
OVERHIT vb hit too strongly
OVERHITS > OVERHIT
OVERHOLD vb value too highly
OVERHOLDS
> OVERHOLD
OVERHOLY adj too holy
OVERHONOR vb honour too highly
OVERHOPE vb hope too much
OVERHOPED
> OVERHOPE
OVERHOPES
> OVERHOPE
OVERHOT adj too hot
OVERHUNG > OVERHANG
OVERHUNT vb hunt too much
OVERHUNTS
> OVERHUNT
OVERHYPE vb hype too much
OVERHYPED
> OVERHYPE
OVERHYPES
> OVERHYPE
OVERIDLE adj too idle
OVERING > OVER
OVERINKED adj printed using too much ink
OVERISSUE vb issue (shares, banknotes, etc) in excess of demand or ability to pay ▷ n shares, banknotes, etc, thus issued
OVERJOY vb give great delight to
OVERJOYED adj extremely pleased
OVERJOYS > OVERJOY
OVERJUMP vb jump too far
OVERJUMPS
> OVERJUMP
OVERJUST adj too just
OVERKEEN adj too keen
OVERKEEP vb keep too long
OVERKEEPS
> OVERKEEP

OVERKEPT > OVERKEEP
OVERKEST same as
> OVERCAST
OVERKILL n treatment that is greater than required
OVERKILLS
> OVERKILL
OVERKIND adj too kind
OVERKING n supreme king
OVERKINGS
> OVERKING
OVERKNEE adj reaching to above knee
OVERLABOR vb spend too much work on
OVERLADE vb overburden
OVERLADED
> OVERLADE
OVERLADEN
> OVERLADE
OVERLADES
> OVERLADE
OVERLAID > OVERLAY
OVERLAIN > OVERLIE
OVERLAND adv by land ▷ vb drive (cattle or sheep) overland
OVERLANDS
> OVERLAND
OVERLAP vb share part of the same space or period of time (as) ▷ n area overlapping
OVERLAPS > OVERLAP
OVERLARD vb cover with lard
OVERLARDS
> OVERLARD
OVERLARGE adj excessively large
OVERLATE adj too late
OVERLAX adj too lax
OVERLAY vb cover with a thin layer ▷ n something that is laid over something else
OVERLAYS > OVERLAY
OVERLEAF adv on the back of the current page
OVERLEAP vb leap too far
OVERLEAPS
> OVERLEAP
OVERLEAPT
> OVERLEAP
OVERLEARN vb study too intensely
OVERLEND vb lend too much
OVERLENDS
> OVERLEND
OVERLENT > OVERLEND
OVERLET vb let to too many
OVERLETS > OVERLET
OVERLEWD adj too lewd
OVERLIE vb lie on or cover (something or someone)
OVERLIER > OVERLIE
OVERLIERS > OVERLIE
OVERLIES > OVERLIE
OVERLIGHT vb illuminate too brightly
OVERLIT > OVERLIGHT
OVERLIVE vb live longer than (another person)

OVERLIVED
> OVERLIVE
OVERLIVES
> OVERLIVE
OVERLOAD vb put too large a load on or in ▷ n excessive load
OVERLOADS
> OVERLOAD
OVERLOCK vb sew fabric with interlocking stitch
OVERLOCKS
> OVERLOCK
OVERLONG adj too or excessively long
OVERLOOK vb fail to notice ▷ n high place affording a view
OVERLOOKS
> OVERLOOK
OVERLORD n supreme lord or master
OVERLORDS
> OVERLORD
OVERLOUD adj too loud
OVERLOVE vb love too much
OVERLOVED
> OVERLOVE
OVERLOVES
> OVERLOVE
OVERLUSH adj too lush
OVERLUSTY adj too lusty
OVERLY adv excessively
OVERLYING > OVERLIE
OVERMAN vb provide with too many workers ▷ n man who oversees others
OVERMANS > OVERMAN
OVERMANY adj too many ▷ n excess of people
OVERMAST vb provide mast that is too big
OVERMASTS
> OVERMAST
OVERMATCH vb be more than a match for ▷ n person superior in ability
OVERMEEK adj too meek
OVERMELT vb melt too much
OVERMELTS
> OVERMELT
OVERMEN > OVERMAN
OVERMERRY adj very merry
OVERMILD adj too mild
OVERMILK vb milk too much
OVERMILKS
> OVERMILK
OVERMINE vb mine too much
OVERMINED
> OVERMINE
OVERMINES
> OVERMINE
OVERMIX vb mix too much
OVERMIXED > OVERMIX
OVERMIXES > OVERMIX
OVERMOUNT vb surmount
OVERMUCH adj too much ▷ n excessive amount
OVERNAME vb repeat (someone's) name
OVERNAMED
> OVERNAME

OVERNAMES
> OVERNAME
OVERNEAR adj too near
OVERNEAT adj too neat
OVERNET vb cover with net
OVERNETS > OVERNET
OVERNEW adj too new
OVERNICE adj too fastidious, precise, etc
OVERNIGHT adv (taking place) during one night ▷ adj done in, occurring in, or lasting the night ▷ vb stay the night
OVERPACK vb pack too much
OVERPACKS
> OVERPACK
OVERPAGE same as
> OVERLEAF
OVERPAID > OVERPAY
OVERPAINT vb apply too much paint
OVERPART vb give an actor too difficult a role
OVERPARTS
> OVERPART
OVERPASS vb pass over, through, or across
OVERPAST > OVERPASS
OVERPAY vb pay (someone) at too high a rate
OVERPAYS > OVERPAY
OVERPEDAL vb use piano pedal too much
OVERPEER vb look down over
OVERPEERS
> OVERPEER
OVERPERCH vb fly up to perch on
OVERPERT adj too insolent
OVERPITCH vb bowl (a cricket ball) so that it pitches too close to the stumps
OVERPLAID n plaid in double layer
OVERPLAN vb plan excessively
OVERPLANS
> OVERPLAN
OVERPLANT vb plant more than is necessary
OVERPLAST adj put above
OVERPLAY same as
> OVERACT
OVERPLAYS
> OVERPLAY
OVERPLIED > OVERPLY
OVERPLIES > OVERPLY
OVERPLOT vb plot onto existing graph or map
OVERPLOTS
> OVERPLOT
OVERPLUS n surplus or excess quantity
OVERPLY vb ply too much
OVERPOISE vb weigh more than
OVERPOST vb hurry over
OVERPOSTS
> OVERPOST

OVERPOWER vb subdue or overcome (someone)
OVERPRESS vb oppress
OVERPRICE vb put too high a price on
OVERPRINT vb print (additional matter) onto (something already printed) ▷ n additional matter printed onto something already printed
OVERPRIZE vb prize too highly
OVERPROOF adj containing more alcohol than standard spirit ▷ n spirit with a higher content of alcohol than standard spirit
OVERPROUD adj too proud
OVERPUMP vb pump too much
OVERPUMPS
> OVERPUMP
OVERQUICK adj too quick
OVERRACK vb strain too much
OVERRACKS
> OVERRACK
OVERRAKE vb rake over
OVERRAKED
> OVERRAKE
OVERRAKES
> OVERRAKE
OVERRAN > OVERRUN
OVERRANK adj too rank ▷ vb assign an unnecessarily high rank to
OVERRANKS
> OVERRANK
OVERRASH adj too rash
OVERRATE vb have too high an opinion of
OVERRATED
> OVERRATE
OVERRATES
> OVERRATE
OVERREACH vb defeat or thwart (oneself) by attempting to do or gain too much
OVERREACT vb react more strongly than is necessary
OVERREAD vb read over
OVERREADS
> OVERREAD
OVERRED vb paint over in red
OVERREDS > OVERRED
OVERREN same as
> OVERRUN
OVERRENS > OVERREN
OVERRICH adj (of food) excessively flavoursome or fatty
OVERRIDE vb overrule ▷ n device or system that can override an automatic control
OVERRIDER
> OVERRIDE
OVERRIDES
> OVERRIDE
OVERRIFE adj too rife
OVERRIGID adj too rigid
OVERRIPE adj (of a fruit or vegetable) so ripe that it has started to decay

OVERRIPEN vb become overripe
OVERROAST vb roast too long
OVERRODE > OVERRIDE
OVERRUDE adj very rude
OVERRUFF vb defeat trump card by playing higher trump
OVERRUFFS
> OVERRUFF
OVERRULE vb reverse the decision of (a person with less power)
OVERRULED
> OVERRULE
OVERRULER
> OVERRULE
OVERRULES
> OVERRULE
OVERRUN vb conquer rapidly ▷ n act or an instance of overrunning
OVERRUNS > OVERRUN
OVERS > OVER
OVERSAD adj too sad
OVERSAIL vb project beyond
OVERSAILS
> OVERSAIL
OVERSALE n selling of more than is available
OVERSALES
> OVERSALE
OVERSALT vb put too much salt in
OVERSALTS
> OVERSALT
OVERSAUCE vb put too much sauce on
OVERSAVE vb put too much money in savings
OVERSAVED
> OVERSAVE
OVERSAVES
> OVERSAVE
OVERSAW > OVERSEE
OVERSCALE adj at higher scale than standard
OVERSCORE vb cancel by drawing a line or lines over or through
OVERSEA same as
> OVERSEAS
OVERSEAS adj to, of, or from a distant country ▷ adv across the sea ▷ n foreign country or foreign countries collectively
OVERSEE vb watch over from a position of authority
OVERSEED vb plant too much seed in
OVERSEEDS
> OVERSEED
OVERSEEN > OVERSEE
OVERSEER n person who oversees others, esp workers
OVERSEERS
> OVERSEER
OVERSEES > OVERSEE
OVERSELL vb exaggerate the merits or abilities of
OVERSELLS
> OVERSELL
OVERSET vb disturb or upset

OVERSETS > OVERSET
OVERSEW vb sew (two edges) with stitches that pass over them both
OVERSEWED > OVERSEW
OVERSEWN > OVERSEW
OVERSEWS > OVERSEW
OVERSEXED adj more interested in sex than is thought decent
OVERSHADE vb appear more important than
OVERSHARE vb share too much about oneself
OVERSHARP adj too sharp
OVERSHINE vb shine down on
OVERSHIRT n shirt worn over lighter clothes
OVERSHOE n protective shoe worn over an ordinary shoe
OVERSHOES
> OVERSHOE
OVERSHONE
> OVERSHINE
OVERSHOOT vb go beyond (a mark or target) ▷ n act or instance of overshooting
OVERSHOT adj (of a water wheel) driven by a flow of water that passes over the wheel ▷ n type of fishing rod
OVERSHOTS
> OVERSHOT
OVERSICK adj too sick
OVERSIDE adv over the side (of a ship) ▷ n top side
OVERSIDES
> OVERSIDE
OVERSIGHT n mistake caused by not noticing something
OVERSIZE adj larger than the usual size ▷ n size larger than the usual or proper size
OVERSIZED same as
> OVERSIZE
OVERSIZES
> OVERSIZE
OVERSKATE vb (in ice hockey) skate beyond the puck
OVERSKIP vb skip over
OVERSKIPS
> OVERSKIP
OVERSKIRT n outer skirt, esp one that reveals a decorative underskirt
OVERSLEEP vb sleep beyond the intended time
OVERSLEPT
> OVERSLEEP
OVERSLIP vb slip past
OVERSLIPS
> OVERSLIP
OVERSLIPT
> OVERSLIP
OVERSLOW adj too slow
OVERSMAN n overseer
OVERSMEN > OVERSMAN
OVERSMOKE vb smoke something too much
OVERSOAK vb soak too much

OVERSOAKS
> OVERSOAK
OVERSOFT *adj* too soft
OVERSOLD > OVERSELL
OVERSOON *adv* too soon
OVERSOUL *n* universal divine essence
OVERSOULS
> OVERSOUL
OVERSOW *vb* sow again after first sowing
OVERSOWED > OVERSOW
OVERSOWN > OVERSOW
OVERSOWS > OVERSOW
OVERSPEND *vb* spend more than one can afford ▷ *n* amount by which someone or something is overspent
OVERSPENT
> OVERSPEND
OVERSPICE *vb* add too much spice to
OVERSPILL *n* rehousing of people from crowded cities in smaller towns ▷ *vb* overflow
OVERSPILT
> OVERSPILL
OVERSPIN *n* forward spinning motion
OVERSPINS
> OVERSPIN
OVERSTAFF *vb* provide an excessive number of staff for (a factory, hotel, etc)
OVERSTAIN *vb* stain too much
OVERSTAND *vb* remain longer than
OVERSTANK
> OVERSTINK
OVERSTARE *vb* outstare
OVERSTATE *vb* state too strongly
OVERSTAY *vb* stay beyond the limit or duration of
OVERSTAYS
> OVERSTAY
OVERSTEER *vb* (of a vehicle) to turn more sharply than is desirable or anticipated
OVERSTEP *vb* go beyond (a certain limit)
OVERSTEPS
> OVERSTEP
OVERSTINK *vb* exceed in stinking
OVERSTIR *vb* stir too much
OVERSTIRS
> OVERSTIR
OVERSTOCK *vb* hold or supply (a commodity) in excess of requirements
OVERSTOOD
> OVERSTAND
OVERSTORY *n* highest level of trees in a rainforest
OVERSTREW *vb* scatter over
OVERSTUDY *vb* study too much
OVERSTUFF *vb* force too much into

OVERSTUNK
> OVERSTINK
OVERSUDS *vb* produce too much lather
OVERSUP *vb* sup too much
OVERSUPS > OVERSUP
OVERSURE *adj* too sure
OVERSWAM > OVERSWIM
OVERSWAY *vb* overrule
OVERSWAYS
> OVERSWAY
OVERSWEAR *vb* swear again
OVERSWEET *adj* too sweet
OVERSWELL *vb* overflow
OVERSWIM *vb* swim across
OVERSWIMS
> OVERSWIM
OVERSWING *vb* swing too much or too far
OVERSWORE
> OVERSWEAR
OVERSWORN
> OVERSWEAR
OVERSWUM > OVERSWIM
OVERSWUNG
> OVERSWING
OVERT *adj* open, not hidden
OVERTAKE *vb* move past (a vehicle or person) travelling in the same direction
OVERTAKEN
> OVERTAKE
OVERTAKES
> OVERTAKE
OVERTALK *vb* talk over
OVERTALKS
> OVERTALK
OVERTAME *adj* too tame
OVERTART *adj* too bitter
OVERTASK *vb* impose too heavy a task upon
OVERTASKS
> OVERTASK
OVERTAX *vb* put too great a strain on
OVERTAXED > OVERTAX
OVERTAXES > OVERTAX
OVERTEACH *vb* teach too much
OVERTEEM *vb* be too full of something
OVERTEEMS
> OVERTEEM
OVERTHICK *adj* too thick
OVERTHIN *vb* make too thin
OVERTHINK *vb* give too much thought to
OVERTHINS
> OVERTHIN
OVERTHREW
> OVERTHROW
OVERTHROW *vb* defeat and replace ▷ *n* downfall, destruction
OVERTIGHT *adj* too tight
OVERTIME *adv* in addition to one's normal working hours ▷ *n* work at a regular job done in addition to regular working hours ▷ *vb*

exceed the required time for (a photographic exposure)
OVERTIMED
> OVERTIME
OVERTIMER
> OVERTIME
OVERTIMES
> OVERTIME
OVERTIMID *adj* too timid
OVERTIP *vb* give too much money as a tip
OVERTIPS > OVERTIP
OVERTIRE *vb* make too tired
OVERTIRED
> OVERTIRE
OVERTIRES
> OVERTIRE
OVERTLY > OVERT
OVERTNESS > OVERT
OVERTOIL *vb* work too hard
OVERTOILS
> OVERTOIL
OVERTONE *n* additional meaning
OVERTONES
> OVERTONE
OVERTOOK > OVERTAKE
OVERTOP *vb* exceed in height
OVERTOPS > OVERTOP
OVERTOWER *vb* tower above
OVERTRADE *vb* (of an enterprise) to trade in excess of working capital
OVERTRAIN *vb* train too much
OVERTREAT *vb* give too much medical treatment to
OVERTRICK *n* trick by which a player exceeds their contract
OVERTRIM *vb* trim too much
OVERTRIMS
> OVERTRIM
OVERTRIP *vb* tread lightly over
OVERTRIPS
> OVERTRIP
OVERTRUMP *vb* (in cards) play a trump higher than (one previously played to the trick)
OVERTRUST *vb* trust too much
OVERTURE *n* orchestral introduction ▷ *vb* make or present an overture to
OVERTURED
> OVERTURE
OVERTURES
> OVERTURE
OVERTURN *vb* turn upside down ▷ *n* act of overturning or the state of being overturned
OVERTURNS
> OVERTURN
OVERTYPE *vb* type over existing text
OVERTYPED
> OVERTYPE
OVERTYPES
> OVERTYPE

OVERURGE *vb* urge too strongly
OVERURGED
> OVERURGE
OVERURGES
> OVERURGE
OVERUSE *vb* use excessively ▷ *n* excessive use
OVERUSED > OVERUSE
OVERUSES > OVERUSE
OVERUSING > OVERUSE
OVERVALUE *vb* regard (someone or something) as much more important than is the case
OVERVEIL *vb* cover over
OVERVEILS
> OVERVEIL
OVERVIEW *n* general survey
OVERVIEWS
> OVERVIEW
OVERVIVID *adj* too vivid
OVERVOTE *vb* vote more times than is allowed
OVERVOTED
> OVERVOTE
OVERVOTES
> OVERVOTE
OVERWARM *vb* make too warm
OVERWARMS
> OVERWARM
OVERWARY *adj* excessively wary
OVERWASH *n* act of washing over something
OVERWATCH *vb* watch over
OVERWATER *vb* give too much water to
OVERWEAK *adj* too weak
OVERWEAR *vb* wear out
OVERWEARS
> OVERWEAR
OVERWEARY *vb* make too tired
OVERWEEN *vb* think too highly of
OVERWEENS
> OVERWEEN
OVERWEIGH *vb* exceed in weight
OVERWENT > OVERGO
OVERWET *vb* make too wet
OVERWETS > OVERWET
OVERWHELM *vb* overpower, esp emotionally
OVERWIDE *adj* too wide
OVERWILY *adj* too crafty
OVERWIND *vb* wind (a watch) beyond the proper limit
OVERWINDS > OVERWIND
OVERWING *vb* fly above
OVERWINGS
> OVERWING
OVERWISE *adj* too wise
OVERWORD *n* repeated word or phrase
OVERWORDS
> OVERWORD
OVERWORE > OVERWEAR
OVERWORK *vb* work too much ▷ *n* excessive work

OVERWORKS
> OVERWORK
OVERWORN > OVERWEAR
OVERWOUND
> OVERWIND
OVERWRAP vb cover with a wrapping
OVERWRAPS
> OVERWRAP
OVERWRAPT
> OVERWRAP
OVERWREST vb strain too much
OVERWRITE vb write (something) in an excessively ornate or prolix style
OVERWROTE
> OVERWRITE
OVERYEAR vb keep for later year
OVERYEARS
> OVERYEAR
OVERZEAL n excess of zeal
OVERZEALS
> OVERZEAL
OVIBOS n type of ox
OVIBOSES > OVIBOS
OVIBOVINE > OVIBOS
OVICIDAL > OVICIDE
OVICIDE n killing of sheep
OVICIDES > OVICIDE
OVIDUCAL > OVIDUCT
OVIDUCT n tube through which eggs are conveyed
OVIDUCTAL > OVIDUCT
OVIDUCTS > OVIDUCT
OVIFEROUS adj carrying or producing eggs or ova
OVIFORM adj shaped like an egg
OVIGEROUS same as
> OVIFEROUS
OVINE adj of or like a sheep ▷ n member of sheep family
OVINES > OVINE
OVIPARA n all oviparous animals
OVIPARITY
> OVIPAROUS
OVIPAROUS adj producing eggs that hatch outside the body of the mother
OVIPOSIT vb (of insects and fishes) to deposit eggs through an ovipositor
OVIPOSITS
> OVIPOSIT
OVIRAPTOR n egg-eating dinosaur
OVISAC n capsule or sac in which egg cells are produced
OVISACS > OVISAC
OVIST n person believing ovum contains all subsequent generations
OVISTS > OVIST
OVOID adj egg-shaped ▷ n something that is ovoid
OVOIDAL adj ovoid ▷ n something that is ovoid
OVOIDALS > OVOIDAL
OVOIDS > OVOID

OVOLI > OVOLO
OVOLO n type of convex moulding
OVOLOS > OVOLO
OVONIC adj using particular electronic storage batteries
OVONICS n science of ovonic equipment
OVOTESTES
> OVOTESTIS
OVOTESTIS n reproductive organ of snails
OVULAR > OVULE
OVULARY > OVULE
OVULATE vb produce or release an egg cell from an ovary
OVULATED > OVULATE
OVULATES > OVULATE
OVULATING > OVULATE
OVULATION > OVULATE
OVULATORY > OVULATE
OVULE n plant part that contains the egg cell
OVULES > OVULE
OVUM n unfertilized egg cell
OW interj exclamation of pain
OWCHE same as > OUCH
OWCHES > OWCHE
OWE vb be obliged to pay (a sum of money) to (a person)
OWED > OWE
OWELTIES > OWELTY
OWELTY n equality, esp in financial transactions
OWER Scots word for > OVER
OWERBY adv over there
OWERLOUP n Scots word meaning encroachment
OWERLOUPS
> OWERLOUP
OWES > OWE
OWIE n minor injury
OWIES > OWIE
OWING > OWE
OWL n night bird of prey ▷ vb act like an owl
OWLED > OWL
OWLER n smuggler
OWLERIES > OWLERY
OWLERS > OWLER
OWLERY n place where owls live
OWLET n young or nestling owl
OWLETS > OWLET
OWLIER > OWLY
OWLIEST > OWLY
OWLING > OWL
OWLISH adj like an owl
OWLISHLY > OWLISH
OWLLIKE > OWL
OWLS > OWL
OWLY same as > OWLISH
OWN adj used to emphasize possession ▷ pron thing(s) belonging to a particular person ▷ vb possess
OWNABLE adj able to be owned
OWNED > OWN
OWNER n person who owns

OWNERLESS > OWNER
OWNERS > OWNER
OWNERSHIP n state or fact of being an owner
OWNING > OWN
OWNS > OWN
OWNSOME n solitary state
OWNSOMES > OWNSOME
OWRE same as > OWER
OWRECAME > OWRECOME
OWRECOME n chorus of song ▷ vb overcome
OWRECOMES
> OWRECOME
OWRELAY Scots form of
> OVERLAY
OWRELAYS > OWRELAY
OWRES > OWRE
OWREWORD variant of
> OVERWORD
OWREWORDS
> OWREWORD
OWRIE same as > OORIE
OWRIER > OWRIE
OWRIEST > OWRIE
OWSE Scots form of > OX
OWSEN Scots word for
> OXEN
OWT dialect word for
> ANYTHING
OWTS > OWT
OX n castrated bull
OXACILLIN n antibiotic drug
OXALATE n salt or ester of oxalic acid ▷ vb treat with oxalate
OXALATED > OXALATE
OXALATES > OXALATE
OXALATING > OXALATE
OXALIC adj as in oxalic acid poisonous acid found in many plants
OXALIS n type of plant
OXALISES > OXALIS
OXAZEPAM n drug used to relieve anxiety
OXAZEPAMS
> OXAZEPAM
OXAZINE n type of chemical compound
OXAZINES > OXAZINE
OXAZOLE n type of liquid chemical compound
OXAZOLES > OXAZOLE
OXBLOOD n dark reddish-brown colour ▷ adj of this colour
OXBLOODS > OXBLOOD
OXBOW n piece of wood fitted around the neck of a harnessed ox
OXBOWS > OXBOW
OXCART n cart pulled by ox
OXCARTS > OXCART
OXEN > OX
OXER n high fence
OXERS > OXER
OXES > OX
OXEYE n daisy-like flower
OXEYES > OXEYE
OXFORD n type of stout laced shoe with a low heel
OXFORDS > OXFORD
OXGANG n old measure of farmland
OXGANGS > OXGANG

OXGATE same as
> OXGANG
OXGATES > OXGATE
OXHEAD n head of an ox
OXHEADS > OXHEAD
OXHEART n heart-shaped cherry
OXHEARTS > OXHEART
OXHERD n person who tends oxen
OXHERDS > OXHERD
OXHIDE n leather made from the hide of an ox
OXHIDES > OXHIDE
OXIC adj involving oxygen
OXID same as > OXIDE
OXIDABLE adj able to undergo oxidation
OXIDANT n substance that acts or is used as an oxidizing agent
OXIDANTS > OXIDANT
OXIDASE n enzyme that brings about oxidation
OXIDASES > OXIDASE
OXIDASIC > OXIDASE
OXIDATE another word for
> OXIDIZE
OXIDATED > OXIDATE
OXIDATES > OXIDATE
OXIDATING > OXIDATE
OXIDATION n oxidizing
OXIDATIVE
> OXIDATION
OXIDE n compound of oxygen and one other element
OXIDES > OXIDE
OXIDIC > OXIDE
OXIDISE same as
> OXIDIZE
OXIDISED > OXIDISE
OXIDISER same as
> OXIDIZER
OXIDISERS
> OXIDISER
OXIDISES > OXIDISE
OXIDISING > OXIDISE
OXIDIZE vb combine chemically with oxygen
OXIDIZED > OXIDIZE
OXIDIZER same as
> OXIDANT
OXIDIZERS
> OXIDIZER
OXIDIZES > OXIDIZE
OXIDIZING > OXIDIZE
OXIDS > OXID
OXIES > OXY
OXIM same as > OXIME
OXIME n type of chemical compound
OXIMES > OXIME
OXIMETER n instrument for measuring oxygen in blood
OXIMETERS > OXIMETER
OXIMETRY > OXIMETER
OXIMS > OXIM
OXLAND same as
> OXGANG
OXLANDS > OXLAND
OXLIKE > OX
OXLIP n type of woodland plant
OXLIPS > OXLIP
OXO n as in oxo acid acid that contains oxygen

OXONIUM *n* as in *oxonium compound* type of salt derived from an organic ether

OXONIUMS > OXONIUM

OXPECKER *n* type of African starling

OXPECKERS > OXPECKER

OXSLIP *same as* > OXLIP

OXSLIPS > OXSLIP

OXTAIL *n* tail of an ox, used in soups and stews

OXTAILS > OXTAIL

OXTER *n* armpit ▷ *vb* grip under arm

OXTERED > OXTER

OXTERING > OXTER

OXTERS > OXTER

OXTONGUE *n* type of plant

OXTONGUES > OXTONGUE

OXY > OX

OXYACID *n* any acid that contains oxygen

OXYACIDS > OXYACID

OXYANION *n* anion containing oxygen atoms

OXYANIONS > OXYANION

OXYCODONE *n* as in *oxycodone hydrochloride* opiate drug used as a painkiller

OXYGEN *n* gaseous element essential to life and combustion

OXYGENASE *n* enzyme

OXYGENATE *vb* add oxygen to

OXYGENIC > OXYGEN

OXYGENISE *variant of* > OXYGENIZE

OXYGENIZE *vb* add oxygen to

OXYGENOUS > OXYGEN

OXYGENS > OXYGEN

OXYMEL *n* mixture of vinegar and honey

OXYMELS > OXYMEL

OXYMORA > OXYMORON

OXYMORON *n* figure of speech that combines two apparently contradictory ideas

OXYMORONS > OXYMORON

OXYNTIC *adj* of or denoting stomach cells that secrete acid

OXYPHIL *n* type of cell found in glands

OXYPHILE *same as* > OXYPHIL

OXYPHILES > OXYPHILE

OXYPHILIC > OXYPHIL

OXYPHILS > OXYPHIL

OXYSALT *n* any salt of an oxyacid

OXYSALTS > OXYSALT

OXYSOME *n* group of molecules

OXYSOMES > OXYSOME

OXYTOCIC *adj* accelerating childbirth by stimulating uterine contractions ▷ *n* oxytocic drug or agent

OXYTOCICS > OXYTOCIC

OXYTOCIN *n* hormone that stimulates the ejection of milk in mammals

OXYTOCINS > OXYTOCIN

OXYTONE *adj* having an accent on the final syllable ▷ *n* oxytone word

OXYTONES > OXYTONE

OXYTONIC *adj* (of a word) having the stress or acute accent on the last syllable

OXYTROPE *n* type of flowering plant

OXYTROPES > OXYTROPE

OY *n* grandchild

OYE *same as* > OY

OYER *n* (in the 13th century) an assize

OYERS > OYER

OYES *same as* > OYEZ

OYESES > OYES

OYESSES > OYES

OYEZ *interj* shouted three times by a public crier calling for attention ▷ *n* such a cry

OYEZES > OYEZ

OYS > OY

OYSTER *n* edible shellfish ▷ *vb* dredge for, gather, or raise oysters

OYSTERED > OYSTER

OYSTERER *n* person fishing for oysters

OYSTERERS > OYSTERER

OYSTERING > OYSTER

OYSTERMAN *n* person who gathers, cultivates, or sells oysters

OYSTERMEN > OYSTERMAN

OYSTERS > OYSTER

OYSTRIGE *archaic variant of* > OSTRICH

OYSTRIGES > OYSTRIGE

OZAENA *n* inflammation of nasal mucous membrane

OZAENAS > OZAENA

OZALID *n* method of duplicating writing or illustrations

OZALIDS > OZALID

OZEKI *n* sumo wrestling champion

OZEKIS > OZEKI

OZOCERITE *n* brown or greyish wax

OZOKERITE *same as* > OZOCERITE

OZONATE *vb* add ozone to

OZONATED > OZONATE

OZONATES > OZONATE

OZONATING > OZONATE

OZONATION > OZONATE

OZONE *n* strong-smelling form of oxygen

OZONES > OZONE

OZONIC > OZONE

OZONIDE *n* type of unstable explosive compound

OZONIDES > OZONIDE

OZONISE *same as* > OZONIZE

OZONISED > OZONISE

OZONISER > OZONISE

OZONISERS > OZONISE

OZONISES > OZONISE

OZONISING > OZONISE

OZONIZE *vb* convert (oxygen) into ozone

OZONIZED > OZONIZE

OZONIZER > OZONIZE

OZONIZERS > OZONIZE

OZONIZES > OZONIZE

OZONIZING > OZONIZE

OZONOUS > OZONE

OZZIE *n* hospital

OZZIES > OZZIE

Pp

PA *n* (formerly) fortified Māori settlement

PAAL *n* stake driven into the ground

PAALS > PAAL

PAAN *n* leaf of the betel tree

PAANS > PAAN

PABLUM *same as* > PABULUM

PABLUMS > PABLUM

PABOUCHE *n* soft shoe

PABOUCHES > PABOUCHE

PABULAR > PABULUM

PABULOUS > PABULUM

PABULUM *n* food

PABULUMS > PABULUM

PAC *n* soft shoe

PACA *n* large burrowing rodent

PACABLE *adj* easily appeased

PACAS > PACA

PACATION *n* act of making peace

PACATIONS > PACATION

PACE *n* single step in walking ▷ *vb* walk up and down, esp in anxiety ▷ *prep* with due respect to: used to express polite disagreement

PACED > PACE

PACEMAKER *n* electronic device surgically implanted in a person with heart disease to regulate the heartbeat

PACEMAN *n* (in cricket) fast bowler

PACEMEN > PACEMAN

PACER *n* horse trained to move at a special gait, esp for racing

PACERS > PACER

PACES > PACE

PACEWAY *n* racecourse for trotting and pacing

PACEWAYS > PACEWAY

PACEY *adj* fast-moving, quick, lively

PACHA *same as* > PASHA

PACHADOM *n* rank of pacha

PACHADOMS > PACHADOM

PACHAK *n* fragrant roots of Asian plant

PACHAKS > PACHAK

PACHALIC *n* jurisdiction of pasha

PACHALICS > PACHALIC

PACHAS > PACHA

PACHINKO *n* Japanese game similar to pinball

PACHINKOS > PACHINKO

PACHISI *n* Indian game resembling backgammon

PACHISIS > PACHISI

PACHOULI *same as* > PATCHOULI

PACHOULIS > PACHOULI

PACHUCO *n* young Mexican living in the US

PACHUCOS > PACHUCO

PACHYDERM *n* thick-skinned animal such as an elephant

PACHYTENE *n* third stage of the prophase of meiosis during which the chromosomes become shorter and thicker and divide into chromatids

PACIER > PACY

PACIEST > PACY

PACIFIC *adj* tending to bring peace

PACIFICAE *pl n* medieval letters of introduction from the Church

PACIFICAL > PACIFIC

PACIFIED > PACIFY

PACIFIER *n* baby's dummy

PACIFIERS > PACIFIER

PACIFIES > PACIFY

PACIFISM *n* belief that violence is unjustifiable

PACIFISMS > PACIFISM

PACIFIST *n* person who refuses on principle to take part in war ▷ *adj* advocating, relating to, or characterized by pacifism

PACIFISTS > PACIFIST

PACIFY *vb* soothe, calm

PACIFYING > PACIFY

PACING *n* act of pacing

PACINGS > PACING

PACK *vb* put (clothes etc) together in a suitcase or bag ▷ *n* bag carried on a person's or animal's back

PACKABLE > PACK

PACKAGE *same as* > PACKET

PACKAGED > PACKAGE

PACKAGER *n* independent firm specializing in design and production

PACKAGERS > PACKAGER

PACKAGES > PACKAGE

PACKAGING *n* box or wrapping in which a product is offered for sale

PACKBOARD *n* frame for carrying goods

PACKCLOTH *n* cloth used for packing

PACKED *adj* completely filled

PACKER *n* person or company who packs goods

PACKERS > PACKER

PACKET *n* small container (and contents) ▷ *vb* wrap up in a packet or as a packet

PACKETED > PACKET

PACKETING > PACKET

PACKETISE *same as* > PACKETIZE

PACKETIZE *vb* form data into packets

PACKETS > PACKET

PACKFONG *n* Chinese alloy

PACKFONGS > PACKFONG

PACKFRAME *n* light metal frame with shoulder straps, used for carrying heavy or awkward loads

PACKHORSE *n* horse used for carrying goods

PACKING *n* material, such as paper or plastic, used to protect packed goods

PACKINGS > PACKING

PACKLY > PACK

PACKMAN *n* man carrying a pack

PACKMEN > PACKMAN

PACKMULE *n* mule used to carry burdens

PACKMULES > PACKMULE

PACKNESS > PACK

PACKS > PACK

PACKSACK *n* bag carried strapped on the back or shoulder

PACKSACKS > PACKSACK

PACKSHEET *n* cover for pack

PACKSTAFF *n* staff for supporting pack

PACKWAX *n* neck ligament

PACKWAXES > PACKWAX

PACKWAY *n* path for pack animals

PACKWAYS > PACKWAY

PACO *n* S American mammal

PACOS > PACO

PACS > PAC

PACT *n* formal agreement

PACTA > PACTUM

PACTION *vb* concur with

PACTIONAL > PACTION

PACTIONED > PACTION

PACTIONS > PACTION

PACTS > PACT

PACTUM *n* pact

PACY *same as* > PACEY

PACZKI *n* round filled doughnut

PACZKIS > PACZKI

PAD *n* piece of soft material used for protection, support, absorption of liquid, etc ▷ *vb* protect or fill with soft material

PADANG *n* (in Malaysia) playing field

PADANGS > PADANG

PADAUK *n* tropical African or Asian tree

PADAUKS > PADAUK

PADDED > PAD

PADDER *n* highwayman who robs on foot

PADDERS > PADDER

PADDIES > PADDY

PADDING > PAD

PADDINGS > PAD

PADDLE *n* short oar with a broad blade at one or each end ▷ *vb* move (a canoe etc) with a paddle

PADDLED > PADDLE

PADDLER > PADDLE

PADDLERS > PADDLE

PADDLES > PADDLE

PADDLING > PADDLE

PADDLINGS > PADDLE

PADDOCK *n* small field or enclosure for horses ▷ *vb* place (a horse) in a paddock

PADDOCKED > PADDOCK

PADDOCKS > PADDOCK

PADDY *n* fit of temper

PADDYWACK *vb* spank or smack

PADELLA *n* type of candle

PADELLAS > PADELLA

PADEMELON *n* small Australian wallaby

PADERERO same as > PATERERO

PADEREROS > PADERERO

PADI same as > PADDY

PADIS > PADI

PADISHAH n Iranian ruler

PADISHAHS > PADISHAH

PADKOS n snacks and provisions for a journey

PADLE another name for > LUMPFISH

PADLES > PADLE

PADLOCK n detachable lock with a hinged hoop ▷ vb fasten (something) with a padlock

PADLOCKED > PADLOCK

PADLOCKS > PADLOCK

PADMA n type of lotus

PADMAS > PADMA

PADNAG n ambling horse

PADNAGS > PADNAG

PADOUK same as > PADAUK

PADOUKS > PADOUK

PADRE n chaplain to the armed forces

PADRES > PADRE

PADRI > PADRE

PADRONA n female boss or employer

PADRONAS > PADRONA

PADRONE n owner or proprietor of an inn, esp in Italy

PADRONES > PADRONE

PADRONI > PADRONE

PADRONISM n system of work controlled by a padrone

PADS > PAD

PADSAW n small narrow saw used for cutting curves

PADSAWS > PADSAW

PADSHAH same as > PADISHAH

PADSHAHS > PADSHAH

PADUASOY n rich strong silk fabric used for hangings, vestments, etc

PADUASOYS > PADUASOY

PADYMELON same as > PADEMELON

PAEAN n song of triumph or thanksgiving

PAEANISM > PAEAN

PAEANISMS > PAEAN

PAEANS > PAEAN

PAEDERAST same as > PEDERAST

PAEDEUTIC adj of or relating to the study of teaching

PAEDIATRY n branch of medical science concerned with children and their diseases

PAEDO n paedophile

PAEDOLOGY n study of the character, growth, and development of children

PAEDOS > PAEDO

PAELLA n Spanish dish of rice, chicken, shellfish, and vegetables

PAELLAS > PAELLA

PAENULA n ancient Roman cloak

PAENULAE > PAENULA

PAENULAS > PAENULA

PAEON n metrical foot of four syllables

PAEONIC > PAEON

PAEONICS > PAEON

PAEONIES > PAEONY

PAEONS > PAEON

PAEONY same as > PEONY

PAESAN n fellow countryman

PAESANI > PAESANO

PAESANO n Italian-American man

PAESANOS > PAESANO

PAESANS > PAESAN

PAGAN adj not belonging to one of the world's main religions ▷ n pagan person

PAGANDOM > PAGAN

PAGANDOMS > PAGAN

PAGANISE same as > PAGANIZE

PAGANISED > PAGANIZE

PAGANISER > PAGANIZE

PAGANISES > PAGANISE

PAGANISH > PAGAN

PAGANISM > PAGAN

PAGANIST > PAGAN

PAGANISTS > PAGAN

PAGANIZE vb become pagan, render pagan, or convert to paganism

PAGANIZED > PAGANIZE

PAGANIZER > PAGANIZE

PAGANIZES > PAGANIZE

PAGANS > PAGAN

PAGE n (one side of) sheet of paper forming a book etc ▷ vb summon (someone) by bleeper or loudspeaker

PAGEANT n parade or display of people in costume

PAGEANTRY n spectacular display or ceremony

PAGEANTS > PAGEANT

PAGEBOY n type of hairstyle

PAGEBOYS > PAGEBOY

PAGED > PAGE

PAGEFUL n amount (of text, etc) that a page will hold

PAGEFULS > PAGEFUL

PAGEHOOD n state of being a page

PAGEHOODS > PAGEHOOD

PAGER n small electronic device, capable of receiving short messages

PAGERS > PAGER

PAGES > PAGE

PAGEVIEW n electronic page of information displayed at the request of a user

PAGEVIEWS > PAGEVIEW

PAGINAL adj page-for-page

PAGINATE vb number the pages of (a book, manuscript, etc) in sequence

PAGINATED > PAGINATE

PAGINATES > PAGINATE

PAGING > PAGE

PAGINGS > PAGE

PAGLE same as > PAIGLE

PAGLES > PAGLE

PAGOD same as > PAGODA

PAGODA n pyramid-shaped Asian temple or tower

PAGODAS > PAGODA

PAGODITE n type of soft mineral used for carving

PAGODITES > PAGODITE

PAGODS > PAGOD

PAGRI n type of turban

PAGRIS > PAGRI

PAGURIAN n type of decapod crustacean of the family which includes the hermit crabs

PAGURIANS > PAGURIAN

PAGURID same as > PAGURIAN

PAGURIDS > PAGURID

PAH same as > PA

PAHAUTEA same as > KAIKAWAKA

PAHAUTEAS > PAHAUTEA

PAHLAVI n former Iranian coin

PAHLAVIS > PAHLAVI

PAHOEHOE n hardened lava

PAHOEHOES > PAHOEHOE

PAHS > PAH

PAID > PAY

PAIDEUTIC same as > PAEDEUTIC

PAIDLE Scots variant of > PADDLE

PAIDLES > PAIDLE

PAIGLE n cowslip

PAIGLES > PAIGLE

PAIK vb thump or whack

PAIKED > PAIK

PAIKING > PAIK

PAIKS > PAIK

PAIL n bucket

PAILFUL same as > PAIL

PAILFULS > PAILFUL

PAILLARD n thin slice of meat

PAILLARDS > PAILLARD

PAILLASSE same as > PALLIASSE

PAILLETTE n sequin or spangle sewn onto a costume

PAILLON n thin leaf of metal

PAILLONS > PAILLON

PAILS > PAIL

PAILSFUL > PAILFUL

PAIN n physical or mental suffering ▷ vb cause (someone) mental or physical suffering

PAINCH Scots variant of > PAUNCH

PAINCHES > PAINCH

PAINED adj having or suggesting pain or distress

PAINFUL adj causing pain or distress

PAINFULLY > PAINFUL

PAINIM n heathen or pagan

PAINIMS > PAINIM

PAINING > PAIN

PAINLESS adj not causing pain or distress

PAINS pl n care or trouble

PAINT n coloured substance, spread on a surface with a brush or roller ▷ vb colour or coat with paint

PAINTABLE > PAINT

PAINTBALL n game in which teams of players simulate a military skirmish, shooting each other with paint pellets

PAINTBOX n box containing a tray of dry watercolour paints

PAINTED > PAINT

PAINTER n rope at the front of a boat, for tying it up

PAINTERLY adj having qualities peculiar to painting, esp the depiction of shapes by means of solid masses of colour, rather than by lines

PAINTERS > PAINTER

PAINTIER > PAINT

PAINTIEST > PAINT

PAINTING n picture produced by using paint

PAINTINGS > PAINTING

PAINTPOT n pot for holding paint

PAINTPOTS > PAINTPOT

PAINTRESS n female painter

PAINTS > PAINT

PAINTURE n art of painting

PAINTURES > PAINTURE

PAINTWORK n covering of paint on parts of a vehicle, building, etc

PAINTY > PAINT

PAIOCK obsolete word for > PEACOCK

PAIOCKE obsolete word for > PEACOCK

PAIOCKES > PAIOCKE

PAIOCKS > PAIOCK

PAIR n set of two things matched for use together ▷ vb group or be grouped in twos

PAIRE obsolete spelling of > PAIR

PAIRED > PAIR

PAIRER > PAIR

PAIRES > PAIRE

PAIREST > PAIR

PAIRIAL variant of > PRIAL

PAIRIALS > PAIRIAL

PAIRING > PAIR

PAIRINGS > PAIR

PAIRS > PAIR

PAIRWISE adv in pairs

PAIS n country

PAISA n monetary unit of Bangladesh, Bhutan, India, Nepal, and Pakistan

PAISAN n fellow countryman

PAISANA n female peasant

PAISANAS > PAISANA

PAISANO n friend

PAISANOS > PAISANO

PAISANS > PAISAN

PAISAS > PAISA

PAISE > PAISA

PAISLEY n pattern of small curving shapes with intricate detailing

PAISLEYS > PAISLEY

PAITRICK Scots word for > PARTRIDGE

PAITRICKS > PAITRICK

PAJAMA same as > PYJAMA

PAJAMAED adj wearing pajamas

PAJAMAS > PAJAMA

PAJOCK obsolete word for > PEACOCK

PAJOCKE obsolete word for > PEACOCK

PAJOCKES > PAJOCKE

PAJOCKS > PAJOCK

PAK n pack

PAKAHI n acid land that is unsuitable for cultivation

PAKAHIS > PAKAHI

PAKAPOO n Chinese lottery

PAKAPOOS > PAKAPOO

PAKEHA n person of European descent, as distinct from a Māori

PAKEHAS > PAKEHA

PAKFONG same as > PACKFONG

PAKFONGS > PAKFONG

PAKIHI n area of swampy infertile land

PAKIHIS > PAKIHI

PAKKA variant of > PUKKA

PAKOKO n small freshwater fish

PAKOKOS > PAKOKO

PAKORA n fried battered pieces of vegetable, chicken, etc

PAKORAS > PAKORA

PAKS > PAK

PAKTHONG n white alloy containing copper, zinc, and nickel

PAKTHONGS > PAKTHONG

PAKTONG same as > PAKTHONG

PAKTONGS > PAKTONG

PAL n friend ▷ vb associate as friends

PALABRA n word

PALABRAS > PALABRA

PALACE n residence of a king, bishop, etc

PALACED adj having palaces

PALACES > PALACE

PALACINKE n thin pancake of Central and Eastern Europe

PALADIN n knight who did battle for a monarch

PALADINS > PALADIN

PALAEOSOL n an ancient soil horizon

PALAESTRA n (in ancient Greece or Rome) public place devoted to the training of athletes

PALAFITTE n prehistoric dwelling

PALAGI n (in Samoa) European

PALAGIS > PALAGI

PALAIS n dance hall

PALAMA n webbing on bird's feet

PALAMAE > PALAMA

PALAMATE > PALAMA

PALAMINO same as > PALOMINO

PALAMINOS > PALOMINO

PALAMPORE same as > PALEMPORE

PALANKEEN same as > PALANQUIN

PALANQUIN n (formerly, in S Asia) covered litter carried on the shoulders

PALAPA n open-sided tropical building

PALAPAS > PALAPA

PALAS n East Indian tree

PALASES > PALAS

PALATABLE adj pleasant to taste

PALATABLY > PALATABLE

PALATAL adj of or relating to the palate ▷ n bony plate that forms the palate

PALATALLY > PALATAL

PALATALS > PALATAL

PALATE n roof of the mouth ▷ vb perceive by taste

PALATED > PALATE

PALATES > PALATE

PALATIAL adj like a palace, magnificent

PALATINE same as > PALATAL

PALATINES > PALATINE

PALATING > PALATE

PALAVER n time-wasting fuss ▷ vb (often used humorously) have a conference

PALAVERED > PALAVER

PALAVERER > PALAVER

PALAVERS > PALAVER

PALAY n type of rubber

PALAYS > PALAY

PALAZZI > PALAZZO

PALAZZO n Italian palace

PALAZZOS > PALAZZO

PALE adj light, whitish ▷ vb become pale ▷ n wooden or metal post used in fences

PALEA n bract in a grass spikelet

PALEAE > PALEA

PALEAL > PALEA

PALEATE adj having scales

PALEBUCK n small African antelope

PALEBUCKS > PALEBUCK

PALED > PALE

PALEFACE n White person, said to have been used by Native Americans

PALEFACES > PALEFACE

PALELY > PALE

PALEMPORE n bed covering

PALENESS > PALE

PALEOCENE adj belonging to geological time period

PALEOCON n extremely right-wing conservative

PALEOCONS > PALEOCON

PALEOGENE adj of early geological time period

PALEOLITH n Stone Age artefact

PALEOLOGY n study of prehistory

PALEOSOL n ancient soil horizon

PALEOSOLS > PALEOSOL

PALEOZOIC adj belonging to geological time period

PALER > PALE

PALES > PALE

PALEST > PALE

PALESTRA same as > PALAESTRA

PALESTRAE > PALESTRA

PALESTRAL > PALESTRA

PALESTRAS > PALESTRA

PALET n perpendicular band on escutcheon

PALETOT n loose outer garment

PALETOTS > PALETOT

PALETS > PALET

PALETTE n artist's flat board for mixing colours on

PALETTES > PALETTE

PALEWAYS same as > PALEWISE

PALEWISE adv by perpendicular lines

PALFREY n light saddle horse, esp ridden by women

PALFREYED > PALFREY

PALFREYS > PALFREY

PALI n cliff in Hawaii

PALIER > PALY

PALIEST > PALY

PALIFORM adj resembling coral

PALIKAR n Greek soldier

PALIKARS > PALIKAR

PALILALIA n speech disorder in which a word or phrase is rapidly repeated

PALILLOGY n repetition of word or phrase

PALIMONY n alimony awarded to a nonmarried partner after the break-up of a long-term relationship

PALING n wooden or metal post used in fences

PALINGS > PALING

PALINKA n type of apricot brandy

PALINKAS > PALINKA

PALINODE n poem in which the poet recants something he or she has said in a former poem

PALINODES > PALINODE

PALINODY > PALINODE

PALINOPIA n visual disorder in which the patient perceives a prolonged afterimage

PALIS > PALI

PALISADE n fence made of wooden posts driven into the ground ▷ vb enclose with a palisade

PALISADED > PALISADE

PALISADES > PALISADE

PALISADO same as > PALISADE

PALISH adj rather pale

PALKEE n (formerly, in S Asia) covered litter carried on the shoulders

PALKEES > PALKEE

PALKI same as > PALKEE

PALKIS > PALKI

PALL n cloth spread over a coffin ▷ vb become boring

PALLA n ancient Roman cloak

PALLADIA > PALLADIUM

PALLADIC adj of or containing palladium in the trivalent or tetravalent state

PALLADIUM n silvery-white element of the platinum metal group

PALLADOUS adj of or containing palladium in the divalent state

PALLAE > PALLA

PALLAH n S African antelope

PALLAHS > PALLAH

PALLASITE n meteorite composed of iron and olivine

PALLED > PALL**

PALLET same as
> PALETTE
PALLETED > PALLET
PALLETING > PALLET
PALLETISE same as
> PALLETIZE
PALLETIZE vb stack or
transport on a pallet or
pallets
PALLETS > PALLET
PALLETTE n armpit plate
of a suit of armour
PALLETTES
> PALLETTE
PALLIA > PALLIUM
PALLIAL adj relating to
cerebral cortex
PALLIARD n person who
begs
PALLIARDS
> PALLIARD
PALLIASSE n
straw-filled mattress
PALLIATE vb lessen the
severity of (something)
without curing it
PALLIATED
> PALLIATE
PALLIATES
> PALLIATE
PALLIATOR
> PALLIATE
PALLID adj pale, esp
because ill or weak
PALLIDER > PALLID
PALLIDEST > PALLID
PALLIDITY > PALLID
PALLIDLY > PALLID
PALLIED > PALLY
PALLIER > PALLY
PALLIES > PALLY
PALLIEST > PALLY
PALLING > PALL
PALLIUM n garment
worn by men in ancient
Greece or Rome
PALLIUMS > PALLIUM
PALLONE n Italian ball
game
PALLONES > PALLONE
PALLOR n paleness of
complexion
PALLORS > PALLOR
PALLS > PALL
PALLY adj on friendly
terms ▷ vb as in pally up
become friends with
PALLYING > PALLY
PALM n inner surface of
the hand ▷ vb conceal in
or about the hand, as in
sleight-of-hand tricks
PALMAR adj of or relating
to the palm of the hand
PALMARIAN adj
pre-eminent
PALMARY adj worthy of
praise
PALMATE adj shaped like
an open hand
PALMATED same as
> PALMATE
PALMATELY > PALMATE
PALMATION n state of
being palmate
PALMBALL n baseball
pitched from the palm and
thumb

PALMBALLS > PALMBALL
PALMED > PALM
PALMER n medieval
pilgrim
PALMERS > PALMER
PALMETTE n ornament
or design resembling the
palm leaf
PALMETTES
> PALMETTE
PALMETTO n small palm
tree with fan-shaped
leaves
PALMETTOS
> PALMETTO
PALMFUL n amount that
can be held in the palm of a
hand
PALMFULS > PALMFUL
PALMHOUSE n
greenhouse for palms, etc
PALMIE n palmtop
computer
PALMIER n type of French
pastry
PALMIERS > PALMIER
PALMIES > PALMIE
PALMIEST > PALMY
PALMIET n South African
rush
PALMIETS > PALMIET
PALMING > PALM
PALMIPED n web-footed
bird
PALMIPEDE same as
> PALMIPED
PALMIPEDS > PALMIPED
PALMIST > PALMISTRY
PALMISTER n person
telling fortunes by reading
palms
PALMISTRY n
fortune-telling from lines
on the palm of the hand
PALMISTS
> PALMISTRY
PALMITATE n any salt or
ester of palmitic acid
PALMITIC adj as in
palmitic acid white
crystalline solid that is a
saturated fatty acid
PALMITIN n colourless
glyceride of palmitic acid
PALMITINS
> PALMITIN
PALMLIKE > PALM
PALMPRINT n print of a
palm
PALMS > PALM
PALMTOP adj small
enough to be held in the
hand ▷ n computer small
enough to be held in the
hand
PALMTOPS > PALMTOP
PALMY adj successful,
prosperous and happy
PALMYRA n tall tropical
Asian palm
PALMYRAS > PALMYRA
PALOLO n polychaete
worm of the S Pacific
Ocean
PALOLOS > PALOLO
PALOMINO n
gold-coloured horse with
a white mane and tail

PALOMINOS
> PALOMINO
PALOOKA n stupid or
clumsy boxer or other
person
PALOOKAS > PALOOKA
PALOVERDE n thorny
American shrub
PALP n sensory
appendage in crustaceans
and insects ▷ vb feel
PALPABLE adj obvious
PALPABLY > PALPABLE
PALPAL > PALP
PALPATE vb examine (an
area of the body) by
touching ▷ adj of, relating
to, or possessing a palp or
palps
PALPATED > PALPATE
PALPATES > PALPATE
PALPATING > PALPATE
PALPATION > PALPATE
PALPATOR n type of
beetle
PALPATORS
> PALPATOR
PALPATORY > PALPATE
PALPEBRA n eyelid
PALPEBRAE
> PALPEBRA
PALPEBRAL adj of or
relating to the eyelid
PALPEBRAS
> PALPEBRA
PALPED > PALP
PALPI > PALPUS
PALPING > PALP
PALPITANT
> PALPITATE
PALPITATE vb (of the
heart) beat rapidly
PALPS > PALP
PALPUS same as > PALP
PALPUSES > PALPUS
PALS > PAL
PALSA n landform of
subarctic regions
PALSAS > PALSA
PALSGRAVE n German
count palatine
PALSHIP n state of being
pals
PALSHIPS > PALSHIP
PALSIED > PALSY
PALSIER > PALSY
PALSIES > PALSY
PALSIEST > PALSY
PALSTAFF variant of
> PALSTAVE
PALSTAFFS
> PALSTAFF
PALSTAVE n chisel made
to fit into a split wooden
handle
PALSTAVES
> PALSTAVE
PALSY n paralysis ▷ vb
paralyse ▷ adj friendly
PALSYING > PALSY
PALSYLIKE > PALSY
PALTER vb act or talk
insincerely
PALTERED > PALTER
PALTERER > PALTER
PALTERERS > PALTER
PALTERING > PALTER
PALTERS > PALTER

PALTRIER > PALTRY
PALTRIEST > PALTRY
PALTRILY > PALTRY
PALTRY adj insignificant
PALUDAL adj of, relating
to, or produced by
marshes
PALUDIC adj of malaria
PALUDINAL adj
inhabiting swamps
PALUDINE adj relating to
marsh
PALUDISM rare word for
> MALARIA
PALUDISMS
> PALUDISM
PALUDOSE adj growing
or living in marshes
PALUDOUS adj marshy
PALUSTRAL adj marshy
PALY adj vertically striped
PAM n knave of clubs
PAMPA n grassland area
PAMPAS pl n vast grassy
plains in S America
PAMPASES > PAMPAS
PAMPEAN > PAMPAS
PAMPEANS > PAMPAS
PAMPER vb treat
(someone) with great
indulgence, spoil
PAMPERED > PAMPER
PAMPERER > PAMPER
PAMPERERS > PAMPER
PAMPERING n act of
treating (someone) with
great indulgence
PAMPERO n dry cold wind
in South America
PAMPEROS > PAMPERO
PAMPERS > PAMPER
PAMPHLET n thin
paper-covered booklet
▷ vb produce pamphlets
PAMPHLETS
> PAMPHLET
PAMPHREY n cabbage
PAMPHREYS
> PAMPHREY
PAMPOEN n pumpkin
PAMPOENS > PAMPOEN
PAMPOOTIE n rawhide
slipper worn by men in the
Aran Islands
PAMS > PAM
PAN n wide long-handled
metal container used in
cooking ▷ vb sift gravel
from (a river) in a pan to
search for gold
PANACEA n remedy for all
diseases or problems
PANACEAN > PANACEA
PANACEAS > PANACEA
PANACHAEA variant of
> PANACEA
PANACHE n confident
elegant style
PANACHES > PANACHE
PANADA n mixture used as
a thickening in cookery
PANADAS > PANADA
PANAMA n hat made of
plaited leaves
PANAMAS > PANAMA
PANARIES > PANARY
PANARY n storehouse for
bread

p

PANATELA same as
> PANATELLA
PANATELAS
> PANATELLA
PANATELLA n long
slender cigar
PANAX n genus of
perennial herbs
PANAXES > PANAX
PANBROIL vb broil in a
pan
PANBROILS
> PANBROIL
PANCAKE n thin flat circle
of fried batter ▷ vb cause
(an aircraft) to make a
pancake landing
PANCAKED > PANCAKE
PANCAKES > PANCAKE
PANCAKING > PANCAKE
PANCE n pansy
PANCES > PANCE
PANCETTA n lightly
spiced cured bacon from
Italy
PANCETTAS
> PANCETTA
PANCHAX n brightly
coloured tropical Asian
cyprinodont fish
PANCHAXES > PANCHAX
PANCHAYAT n village
council in India
PANCHEON n shallow
bowl
PANCHEONS
> PANCHEON
PANCHION same as
> PANCHEON
PANCHIONS
> PANCHION
PANCOSMIC adj of every
cosmos
PANCRATIA n wrestling
and boxing contests
PANCRATIC
> PANCRATIA
PANCREAS n large gland
behind the stomach that
produces insulin and helps
digestion
PAND n valance
PANDA n large
black-and-white bearlike
mammal from China
PANDAN n type of palm of
S E Asia
PANDANI n tropical tree
PANDANIS > PANDANI
PANDANS > PANDAN
PANDANUS n Old World
tropical palmlike plant
PANDAR rare variant of
> PANDER
PANDARED > PANDAR
PANDARING > PANDAR
PANDARS > PANDAR
PANDAS > PANDA
PANDATION n warping
PANDECT n treatise
covering all aspects of a
particular subject
PANDECTS > PANDECT
PANDEMIA n epidemic
affecting everyone
PANDEMIAN adj sensual
PANDEMIAS
> PANDEMIA

PANDEMIC adj (of a
disease) occurring over a
wide area ▷ n pandemic
disease
PANDEMICS
> PANDEMIC
PANDER vb indulge (a
person his or her desires)
▷ n someone who
indulges a person in his or
her desires
PANDERED > PANDER
PANDERER n someone
who indulges a person in
his or her desires
PANDERERS
> PANDERER
PANDERESS n female
panderer
PANDERING n act or
instance of gratifying
someone's weaknesses or
desires
PANDERISM > PANDER
PANDERLY > PANDER
PANDEROUS > PANDER
PANDERS > PANDER
PANDIED > PANDY
PANDIES > PANDY
PANDIT same as
> PUNDIT
PANDITS > PANDIT
PANDOOR same as
> PANDOUR
PANDOORS > PANDOOR
PANDORA n handsome
red sea bream
PANDORAS > PANDORA
PANDORE another word for
> BANDORE
PANDORES > PANDORE
PANDOUR n one of an
18th-century force of
Croatian soldiers
PANDOURS > PANDOUR
PANDOWDY n deep-dish
pie made from fruit, esp
apples, with a cake
topping
PANDROP n hard
mint-flavoured sweet
PANDROPS > PANDROP
PANDS > PAND
PANDURA n ancient
stringed instrument
PANDURAS > PANDURA
PANDURATE adj (of plant
leaves) shaped like the
body of a fiddle
PANDY n (in schools)
stroke on the hand with a
strap as a punishment
▷ vb punish with such
strokes
PANDYING > PANDY
PANE n sheet of glass in a
window or door ▷ adj (of
fish, meat, etc) dipped or
rolled in breadcrumbs
before cooking
PANED > PANE
PANEER n soft white
cheese, used in Indian
cookery
PANEERS > PANEER
PANEGOISM n form of
scepticism
PANEGYRIC n formal
public commendation

PANEGYRY n formal
public commendation;
panegyric
PANEITIES > PANEITY
PANEITY n state of being
bread
PANEL n flat distinct
section of a larger surface,
for example in a door ▷ vb
cover or decorate with
panels ▷ adj of a group
acting as a panel
PANELED > PANEL
PANELESS > PANE
PANELING same as
> PANELLING
PANELINGS
> PANELING
PANELISED same as
> PANELIZED
PANELIST same as
> PANELLIST
PANELISTS
> PANELIST
PANELIZED adj made in
sections for quick
assembly
PANELLED > PANEL
PANELLING n panels
collectively, esp on a wall
PANELLIST n member of
a panel
PANELS > PANEL
PANES > PANE
PANETELA same as
> PANATELA
PANETELAS
> PANETELA
PANETELLA n long thin
cigar
PANETTONE n kind of
Italian spiced brioche
containing sultanas
PANETTONI
> PANETTONE
PANFISH n small food
fish ▷ vb fish for panfish
PANFISHED > PANFISH
PANFISHES > PANFISH
PANFORTE n hard spicy
cake
PANFORTES
> PANFORTE
PANFRIED > PANFRY
PANFRIES > PANFRY
PANFRY vb fry in a pan
PANFRYING > PANFRY
PANFUL n the contents of
a pan
PANFULS > PANFUL
PANG n sudden sharp
feeling of pain or sadness
▷ vb cause pain
PANGA n broad heavy
knife of E Africa, used as a
tool or weapon
PANGAMIC adj relating to
pangamy
PANGAMIES > PANGAMY
PANGAMY n unrestricted
mating
PANGAS > PANGA
PANGED > PANG
PANGEN same as
> PANGENE
PANGENE n hypothetical
particle of protoplasm
PANGENES > PANGENE

PANGENS > PANGEN
PANGING > PANG
PANGLESS adj without
pangs
PANGOLIN n mammal
with very long snout
PANGOLINS
> PANGOLIN
PANGRAM n sentence
incorporating all the
letters of the alphabet
PANGRAMS > PANGRAM
PANGS > PANG
PANHANDLE n (in the US)
narrow strip of land that
projects from one state
into another ▷ vb accost
and beg from (passers-by),
esp on the street
PANHUMAN adj relating to
all humanity
PANIC n sudden
overwhelming fear ▷ vb
feel or cause to feel panic
▷ adj of or resulting from
such terror
PANICALLY > PANIC
PANICK old word for
> PANIC
PANICKED > PANIC
PANICKIER > PANIC
PANICKING > PANIC
PANICKS > PANICK
PANICKY > PANIC
PANICLE n loose,
irregularly branched
cluster of flowers
PANICLED > PANICLE
PANICLES > PANICLE
PANICS > PANIC
PANICUM n type of
grass
PANICUMS > PANICUM
PANIER same as
> PANNIER
PANIERS > PANIER
PANIM n heathen or
pagan
PANIMS > PANIM
PANING > PANE
PANINI > PANINO
PANINIS > PANINI
PANINO n Italian
sandwich
PANISC n faun;
attendant of Pan
PANISCS > PANISC
PANISK same as
> PANISC
PANISKS > PANISK
PANISLAM n all of Islam
or the Muslim world
PANISLAMS
> PANISLAM
PANJANDRA pl n
pompous self-important
officials
PANKO n flaky
breadcrumbs used in
Japanese cookery
PANKOS > PANKO
PANLIKE adj resembling
a pan
PANLOGISM n
metaphysics of Leibniz
PANMICTIC
> PANMIXIA
PANMIXES > PANMIXIS

PANMIXIA n (in population genetics) random mating within an interbreeding population
PANMIXIAS > PANMIXIA
PANMIXIS same as > PANMIXIA
PANNAGE n pasturage for pigs, esp in a forest
PANNAGES > PANNAGE
PANNE n lightweight velvet fabric
PANNED > PAN
PANNELLED adj divided into panels
PANNER > PAN
PANNERS > PAN
PANNES > PANNE
PANNI > PANNUS
PANNICK old spelling of the noun > PANIC
PANNICKS > PANNICK
PANNICLE n thin layer of body tissue
PANNICLES > PANNICLE
PANNIER n bag fixed on the back of a cycle
PANNIERED > PANNIER
PANNIERS > PANNIER
PANNIKEL n skull
PANNIKELL same as > PANNIKEL
PANNIKELS > PANNIKEL
PANNIKIN n small metal cup or pan
PANNIKINS > PANNIKIN
PANNING > PAN
PANNINGS > PAN
PANNIST n person who plays a steel drum
PANNISTS > PANNIST
PANNOSE adj like felt
PANNUS n inflammatory fleshy lesion on the surface of the eye
PANNUSES > PANNUS
PANOCHA n coarse grade of sugar made in Mexico
PANOCHAS > PANOCHA
PANOCHE n type of dark sugar
PANOCHES > PANOCHE
PANOISTIC adj producing ova
PANOPLIED > PANOPLY
PANOPLIES > PANOPLY
PANOPLY n magnificent array
PANOPTIC adj taking in all parts, aspects, etc, in a single view
PANORAMA n wide unbroken view of a scene
PANORAMAS > PANORAMA
PANORAMIC > PANORAMA
PANPIPE n wind instrument
PANPIPES > PANPIPE
PANS > PAN
PANSEXUAL n person open to any sexual activity
PANSIED adj covered with pansies

PANSIES > PANSY
PANSOPHIC > PANSOPHY
PANSOPHY n universal knowledge
PANSPERMY n 19th-century evolutionary theory
PANSTICK n type of cosmetic in stick form
PANSTICKS > PANSTICK
PANSY n small garden flower
PANT vb breathe quickly and noisily during or after exertion ▷ n act of panting
PANTABLE n soft shoe
PANTABLES > PANTABLE
PANTAGAMY n marriage to everyone
PANTALEON n percussion instrument
PANTALET same as > PANTALETS
PANTALETS pl n long drawers, usually trimmed with ruffles, extending below the skirts
PANTALON n keyboard instrument
PANTALONE n Italian comic character
PANTALONS > PANTALON
PANTALOON n (in pantomime) absurd old man, the butt of the clown's tricks
PANTDRESS n dress with divided skirt
PANTED > PANT
PANTER n person who pants
PANTERS > PANTER
PANTHEISM n belief that God is present in everything
PANTHEIST > PANTHEISM
PANTHENOL n pantothenyl alcohol
PANTHEON n (in ancient Greece and Rome) temple built to honour all the gods
PANTHEONS > PANTHEON
PANTHER n leopard, esp a black one
PANTHERS > PANTHER
PANTIE same as > PANTY
PANTIES pl n women's underpants
PANTIHOSE same as > PANTYHOSE
PANTILE n roofing tile with an S-shaped cross section ▷ vb tile roof with pantiles
PANTILED > PANTILE
PANTILES > PANTILE
PANTILING > PANTILE
PANTINE n pasteboard puppet
PANTINES > PANTINE
PANTING > PANT
PANTINGLY > PANT

PANTINGS > PANT
PANTLEG n leg part of a pair of trousers
PANTLEGS > PANTLEG
PANTLER n pantry servant
PANTLERS > PANTLER
PANTO same as > PANTOMIME
PANTOFFLE same as > PANTOFLE
PANTOFLE n kind of slipper
PANTOFLES > PANTOFLE
PANTOMIME n play based on a fairy tale, performed at Christmas time
PANTON n type of horseshoe
PANTONS > PANTON
PANTOS > PANTO
PANTOUFLE same as > PANTOFLE
PANTOUM n verse form
PANTOUMS > PANTOUM
PANTRIES > PANTRY
PANTROPIC adj found throughout tropics
PANTRY n small room or cupboard for storing food
PANTRYMAN n pantry servant
PANTRYMEN > PANTRYMAN
PANTS pl n undergarment for the lower part of the body
PANTSUIT n woman's suit of a jacket or top and trousers
PANTSUITS > PANTSUIT
PANTUN n Malayan poetry
PANTUNS > PANTUN
PANTY n woman's undergarment
PANTYHOSE pl n women's tights
PANZER n German tank
PANZERS > PANZER
PANZOOTIC n disease that affects all the animals in a geographical area
PAOLI > PAOLO
PAOLO n former Italian coin
PAP n soft or semiliquid food ▷ vb (of the paparazzi) to follow and photograph (a famous person)
PAPA n father
PAPABLE adj suitable for papacy
PAPACIES > PAPACY
PAPACY n position or term of office of a pope
PAPADAM variant of > POPPADOM
PAPADAMS > PAPADAM
PAPADOM variant of > POPPADOM
PAPADOMS > PAPADOM
PAPADUM variant of > POPPADOM
PAPADUMS > PAPADUM

PAPAIN n enzyme in the unripe fruit of the papaya
PAPAINS > PAPAIN
PAPAL adj of the pope
PAPALISE same as > PAPALIZE
PAPALISED > PAPALISE
PAPALISES > PAPALISE
PAPALISM n papal system
PAPALISMS > PAPALISM
PAPALIST n supporter of a pope
PAPALISTS > PAPALIST
PAPALIZE vb make papal
PAPALIZED > PAPALIZE
PAPALIZES > PAPALIZE
PAPALLY > PAPAL
PAPARAZZI > PAPARAZZO
PAPARAZZO n photographer specializing in candid photographs of famous people
PAPAS > PAPA
PAPASAN n bowl-shaped chair
PAPASANS > PAPASAN
PAPAUMA n New Zealand word for broadleaf
PAPAUMAS > PAPAUMA
PAPAVER n genus of poppies
PAPAVERS > PAPAVER
PAPAW same as > PAPAYA
PAPAWS > PAPAW
PAPAYA n large sweet tropical fruit
PAPAYAN > PAPAYA
PAPAYAS > PAPAYA
PAPE n spiritual father
PAPER n material made in sheets from wood pulp or other fibres ▷ vb cover (walls) with wallpaper
PAPERBACK n book with covers made of flexible card ▷ adj of a paperback or publication of paperbacks ▷ vb publish in paperback
PAPERBARK n Australian tree of swampy regions, with spear-shaped leaves and papery bark
PAPERBOY n boy employed to deliver newspapers to people's homes
PAPERBOYS > PAPERBOY
PAPERCLIP n bent wire clip for holding sheets of paper together
PAPERED > PAPER
PAPERER > PAPER
PAPERERS > PAPER
PAPERGIRL n girl employed to deliver newspapers to people's homes
PAPERIER > PAPERY

P

PAPERIEST > PAPERY
PAPERING > PAPER
PAPERINGS > PAPER
PAPERLESS adj of, relating to, or denoting a means of communication, record keeping, etc, esp electronic, that does not use paper
PAPERS > PAPER
PAPERWARE n printed matter
PAPERWORK n clerical work, such as writing reports and letters
PAPERY adj like paper, esp in thinness, flimsiness, or dryness
PAPES > PAPE
PAPETERIE n box or case for papers and other writing materials
PAPHIAN n prostitute
PAPHIANS > PAPHIAN
PAPILIO n butterfly
PAPILIOS > PAPILIO
PAPILLA n small projection of tissue
PAPILLAE > PAPILLA
PAPILLAR > PAPILLA
PAPILLARY > PAPILLA
PAPILLATE > PAPILLA
PAPILLOMA n benign tumour derived from epithelial tissue and forming a rounded or lobulated mass
PAPILLON n breed of toy spaniel with large ears
PAPILLONS > PAPILLON
PAPILLOSE > PAPILLA
PAPILLOTE n paper frill around cutlets, etc
PAPILLOUS > PAPILLA
PAPILLULE n tubercle
PAPOOSE n Native American child
PAPOOSES > PAPOOSE
PAPPADAM same as > POPPADOM
PAPPADAMS > PAPPADAM
PAPPADOM same as > POPPADOM
PAPPADOMS > PAPPADOM
PAPPADUM n thin circle of dough fried in oil until crisp
PAPPADUMS > PAPPADUM
PAPPED > PAP
PAPPI > PAPPUS
PAPPIER > PAPPY
PAPPIES > PAPPY
PAPPIEST > PAPPY
PAPPING > PAP
PAPPOOSE same as > PAPOOSE
PAPPOOSES > PAPPOOSE
PAPPOSE > PAPPUS
PAPPOUS > PAPPUS
PAPPUS n ring of hairs surrounding the fruit in composite plants
PAPPUSES > PAPPUS

PAPPY adj resembling pap
PAPRICA same as > PAPRIKA
PAPRICAS > PAPRICA
PAPRIKA n mild powdered seasoning
PAPRIKAS same as > PAPRIKASH
PAPRIKASH n chicken dish from Hungary
PAPS > PAP
PAPULA same as > PAPULE
PAPULAE > PAPULA
PAPULAR > PAPULA
PAPULAS > PAPULA
PAPULE n small solid usually round elevation of the skin
PAPULES > PAPULE
PAPULOSE > PAPULE
PAPULOUS > PAPULE
PAPYRAL > PAPYRUS
PAPYRI > PAPYRUS
PAPYRIAN > PAPYRUS
PAPYRINE > PAPYRUS
PAPYRUS n tall water plant
PAPYRUSES > PAPYRUS
PAR n usual or average condition ▷ vb play (a golf hole) in par
PARA n paratrooper
PARABASES > PARABASIS
PARABASIS n (in classical Greek comedy) address from the chorus to the audience
PARABEMA n architectural feature
PARABEN n carcinogenic ester
PARABENS > PARABEN
PARABLAST n yolk of an egg, such as a hen's egg, that undergoes meroblastic splitting
PARABLE n story that illustrates a religious teaching ▷ vb write a parable
PARABLED > PARABLE
PARABLES > PARABLE
PARABLING > PARABLE
PARABOLA n regular curve resembling the course of an object thrown forward and up
PARABOLAE > PARABOLA
PARABOLAS > PARABOLA
PARABOLE n similitude
PARABOLES > PARABOLE
PARABOLIC adj of, relating to, or shaped like a parabola
PARABRAKE n parachute attached to the rear of a vehicle and opened to assist braking
PARACHOR n quantity constant over range of temperatures
PARACHORS > PARACHOR

PARACHUTE n large fabric canopy that slows the descent of a person or object from an aircraft ▷ vb land or drop by parachute
PARACLETE n mediator or advocate
PARACME n phase where fever lessens
PARACMES > PARACME
PARACRINE adj of signalling between biological cells
PARACUSES > PARACUSIS
PARACUSIS n hearing disorder
PARADE n procession or march ▷ vb display or flaunt
PARADED > PARADE
PARADER > PARADE
PARADERS > PARADE
PARADES > PARADE
PARADIGM n example or model
PARADIGMS > PARADIGM
PARADING > PARADE
PARADISAL adj of, relating to, or resembling paradise
PARADISE n heaven
PARADISES > PARADISE
PARADISIC > PARADISE
PARADOR n state-run hotel in Spain
PARADORES > PARADOR
PARADORS > PARADOR
PARADOS n bank behind a trench or other fortification
PARADOSES > PARADOS
PARADOX n person or thing made up of contradictory elements
PARADOXAL adj paradoxical
PARADOXER n proposer of paradox
PARADOXES > PARADOX
PARADOXY n state of being paradoxical
PARADROP n delivery of personnel or equipment from an aircraft by parachute
PARADROPS > PARADROP
PARAE n type of fish
PARAFFIN n liquid mixture distilled from petroleum and used as a fuel or solvent ▷ vb treat with paraffin or paraffin wax
PARAFFINE same as > PARAFFIN
PARAFFINS > PARAFFIN
PARAFFINY adj like paraffin
PARAFFLE n extravagant display
PARAFFLES > PARAFFLE

PARAFLE same as > PARAFFLE
PARAFLES > PARAFLE
PARAFOIL n airfoil used on a paraglider
PARAFOILS > PARAFOIL
PARAFORM n paraformaldehyde
PARAFORMS > PARAFORM
PARAGE n type of feudal land tenure
PARAGES > PARAGE
PARAGLIDE vb glide through the air on a special parachute
PARAGOGE n addition of a sound or a syllable to the end of a word
PARAGOGES > PARAGOGE
PARAGOGIC > PARAGOGE
PARAGOGUE same as > PARAGOGE
PARAGON n model of perfection ▷ vb equal or surpass
PARAGONED > PARAGON
PARAGONS > PARAGON
PARAGRAM n pun
PARAGRAMS > PARAGRAM
PARAGRAPH n section of a piece of writing starting on a new line ▷ vb put (a piece of writing) into paragraphs
PARAKEET n small long-tailed parrot
PARAKEETS > PARAKEET
PARAKELIA n succulent herb with purple flowers that thrives in inland Australia
PARAKITE n series of linked kites
PARAKITES > PARAKITE
PARALALIA n any of various speech disorders, esp the production of a sound different from that intended
PARALEGAL n person trained to assist lawyers but not qualified to practise law ▷ adj of or designating such a person
PARALEXIA n disorder of the ability to read in which words and syllables are meaninglessly transposed
PARALEXIC > PARALEXIA
PARALLAX n apparent change in an object's position due to a change in the observer's position
PARALLEL adj separated by an equal distance at every point ▷ n line separated from another by an equal distance at every point ▷ vb correspond to
PARALLELS > PARALLEL

PARALOGIA *n* self-deception

PARALOGUE *n* either of a pair of genes derived from the same ancestral gene

PARALOGY *n* anatomical similarity

PARALYSE *vb* affect with paralysis

PARALYSED > PARALYSE

PARALYSER > PARALYSE

PARALYSES > PARALYSIS

PARALYSIS *n* inability to move or feel, because of damage to the nervous system

PARALYTIC *adj* affected with paralysis ▷ *n* person who is paralysed

PARALYZE *same as* > PARALYSE

PARALYZED > PARALYZE

PARALYZER > PARALYZE

PARALYZES > PARALYZE

PARAMATTA *n* lightweight twill-weave fabric of wool with silk or cotton

PARAMECIA *n* freshwater protozoans

PARAMEDIC *n* person working in support of the medical profession ▷ *adj* of or designating such a person

PARAMENT *n* ecclesiastical vestment or decorative hanging

PARAMENTA > PARAMENT

PARAMENTS > PARAMENT

PARAMESE *n* note in ancient Greek music

PARAMESES > PARAMESE

PARAMETER *n* limiting factor, boundary

PARAMO *n* high plateau in the Andes

PARAMORPH *n* mineral that has undergone paramorphism

PARAMOS > PARAMO

PARAMOUNT *adj* of the greatest importance ▷ *n* supreme ruler

PARAMOUR *n* lover

PARAMOURS > PARAMOUR

PARAMYLUM *n* starch-like substance

PARANETE *n* note in ancient Greek music

PARANETES > PARANETE

PARANG *n* knife used by the Dyaks of Borneo

PARANGS > PARANG

PARANOEA *same as* > PARANOIA

PARANOEAS > PARANOEA

PARANOEIC *same as* > PARANOIAC

PARANOIA *n* disorder causing delusions of grandeur or persecution

PARANOIAC > PARANOIA

PARANOIAS > PARANOIA

PARANOIC > PARANOIA

PARANOICS > PARANOIA

PARANOID *adj* of, characterized by, or resembling paranoia ▷ *n* person who shows the behaviour patterns associated with paranoia

PARANOIDS > PARANOID

PARANYM *n* euphemism

PARANYMPH *n* bridesmaid or best man

PARANYMS > PARANYM

PARAPARA *n* small carnivorous New Zealand tree

PARAPARAS > PARAPARA

PARAPENTE *n* sport of jumping off high mountains wearing skis and a light parachute

PARAPET *n* low wall or railing along the edge of a balcony or roof ▷ *vb* provide with a parapet

PARAPETED > PARAPET

PARAPETS > PARAPET

PARAPH *n* flourish after a signature ▷ *vb* embellish signature

PARAPHED > PARAPH

PARAPHING > PARAPH

PARAPHS > PARAPH

PARAPODIA *n* paired unjointed lateral appendages of polychaete worms

PARAQUAT *n* yellow extremely poisonous soluble solid used in solution as a weedkiller

PARAQUATS > PARAQUAT

PARAQUET *n* long-tailed parrot

PARAQUETS > PARAQUET

PARAQUITO *n* parakeet

PARARHYME *n* type of rhyme

PARAS > PARA

PARASAIL *vb* glide through air on parachute towed by boat

PARASAILS > PARASAIL

PARASANG *n* Persian unit of distance equal to about 5.5 kilometres or 3.4 miles

PARASANGS > PARASANG

PARASCEVE *n* preparation

PARASHAH *n* section of the Torah read in the synagogue

PARASHAHS > PARASHAH

PARASHOT > PARASHAH

PARASHOTH > PARASHAH

PARASITE *n* animal or plant living in or on another

PARASITES > PARASITE

PARASITIC > PARASITE

PARASOL *n* umbrella-like sunshade

PARASOLED *adj* having a parasol

PARASOLS > PARASOL

PARATAXES > PARATAXIS

PARATAXIS *n* juxtaposition of clauses in a sentence without the use of a conjunction

PARATHA *n* (in Indian cookery) flat unleavened bread

PARATHAS > PARATHA

PARATHION *n* slightly water-soluble toxic oil, odourless and colourless when pure, used as an insecticide

PARATONIC *adj* (of a plant movement) occurring in response to an external stimulus

PARATROOP *n* paratrooper

PARAVAIL *adj* lowest

PARAVANE *n* device that cuts the anchors of moored mines

PARAVANES > PARAVANE

PARAVANT *adv* pre-eminently ▷ *n* pre-eminent person or thing

PARAVANTS > PARAVANT

PARAVAUNT *same as* > PARAVANT

PARAWING *n* paraglider

PARAWINGS > PARAWING

PARAXIAL *adj* (of a light ray) parallel to the axis of an optical system

PARAZOA > PARAZOAN

PARAZOAN *n* sea sponge

PARAZOANS > PARAZOAN

PARAZOON *n* parasitic animal

PARBAKE *vb* partially bake

PARBAKED > PARBAKE

PARBAKES > PARBAKE

PARBAKING > PARBAKE

PARBOIL *vb* boil until partly cooked

PARBOILED > PARBOIL

PARBOILS > PARBOIL

PARBREAK *vb* vomit

PARBREAKS > PARBREAK

PARBUCKLE *n* rope sling for lifting or lowering a heavy cylindrical object, such as a cask or tree trunk ▷ *vb* raise or lower (an object) with such a sling

PARCEL *n* something wrapped up, package ▷ *vb* wrap up

PARCELED > PARCEL

PARCELING > PARCEL

PARCELLED > PARCEL

PARCELS > PARCEL

PARCENARY *n* joint heirship

PARCENER *n* person who takes an equal share with another or others

PARCENERS > PARCENER

PARCH *vb* make very hot and dry

PARCHED > PARCH

PARCHEDLY > PARCH

PARCHEESI *n* modern board game derived from the ancient game of pachisi

PARCHES > PARCH

PARCHESI *same as* > PARCHEESI

PARCHESIS > PARCHESI

PARCHING > PARCH

PARCHISI *same as* > PARCHEESI

PARCHISIS > PARCHISI

PARCHMENT *n* thick smooth writing material made from animal skin

PARCIMONY *obsolete variant of* > PARSIMONY

PARCLOSE *n* screen or railing in a church separating off an altar, chapel, etc

PARCLOSES > PARCLOSE

PARD *n* leopard or panther

PARDAH *same as* > PURDAH

PARDAHS > PARDAH

PARDAL *variant spelling of* > PARDALE

PARDALE *n* leopard

PARDALES > PARDALE

PARDALIS *n* leopard

PARDALOTE *n* small Australian songbird

PARDALS > PARDAL

PARDED *adj* having spots

PARDEE *adv* certainly

PARDI *same as* > PARDEE

PARDIE *same as* > PARDEE

PARDINE *adj* spotted

PARDNER *n* friend or partner: used as a term of address

PARDNERS > PARDNER

PARDON *vb* forgive, excuse ▷ *n* forgiveness ▷ *interj* sorry ▷ *sentence substitute* sorry

PARDONED > PARDON

PARDONER *n* (before the Reformation) person licensed to sell ecclesiastical indulgences

PARDONERS > PARDONER

PARDONING > PARDON

PARDONS > PARDON

PARDS > PARD

PARDY *same as* **> PARDEE**

PARE *vb* cut off the skin or top layer of

PARECIOUS *adj* having the male and female reproductive organs at different levels on the same stem

PARECISM *n* state of having male and female organs close together

PARECISMS > PARECISM

PARED > PARE

PAREGORIC *n* medicine containing opium, benzoic acid, camphor or ammonia, and anise oil

PAREIRA *n* root of a South American climbing plant

PAREIRAS > PAREIRA

PARELLA *n* type of lichen

PARELLAS > PARELLA

PARELLE *same as* **> PARELLA**

PARELLES > PARELLE

PAREN *n* parenthesis

PARENESES > PARENESIS

PARENESIS *n* exhortation

PARENS > PAREN

PARENT *n* father or mother ⊳ *vb* raise offspring

PARENTAGE *n* ancestry or family

PARENTAL *adj* of or relating to a parent or parenthood

PARENTED > PARENT

PARENTING *n* activity of bringing up children

PARENTS > PARENT

PAREO *same as* **> PAREU**

PAREOS > PAREO

PARER > PARE

PARERA *n* New Zealand duck

PARERAS > PARERA

PARERGA > PARERGON

PARERGON *n* work that is not one's main employment

PARERS > PARE

PARES > PARE

PARESES > PARESIS

PARESIS *n* incomplete or slight paralysis of motor functions

PARETIC > PARESIS

PARETICS > PARESIS

PAREU *n* Polynesian skirt or loincloth

PAREUS > PAREU

PAREV *adj* containing neither meat nor milk products

PAREVE *same as* **> PAREV**

PARFAIT *n* dessert consisting of layers of ice cream, fruit, and sauce

PARFAITS > PARFAIT

PARFLECHE *n* sheet of rawhide that has been dried after soaking in lye

and water to remove the hair

PARFLESH *same as* **> PARFLECHE**

PARFOCAL *adj* with focal points in the same plane

PARGANA *n* Indian sub-district

PARGANAS > PARGANA

PARGASITE *n* dark green mineral

PARGE *vb* coat with plaster

PARGED > PARGE

PARGES > PARGE

PARGET *n* plaster, mortar, etc, used to line chimney flues or cover walls ⊳ *vb* cover or decorate with parget

PARGETED > PARGET

PARGETER *n* one who pargets

PARGETERS > PARGET

PARGETING *same as* **> PARGET**

PARGETS > PARGET

PARGETTED > PARGET

PARGETTER *n* plasterer

PARGING > PARGE

PARGINGS > PARGE

PARGO *n* sea bream

PARGOES > PARGO

PARGOS > PARGO

PARGYLINE *n* monoamine oxidase inhibitor

PARHELIA > PARHELION

PARHELIC > PARHELION

PARHELION *n* one of several bright spots on the parhelic circle or solar halo

PARHYPATE *n* note in ancient Greek music

PARIAH *n* social outcast

PARIAHS > PARIAH

PARIAL *n* pair royal of playing cards

PARIALS > PARIAL

PARIAN *n* type of marble or porcelain

PARIANS > PARIAN

PARIES *n* wall of an organ or bodily cavity

PARIETAL *adj* of the walls of a body cavity such as the skull ⊳ *n* parietal bone

PARIETALS > PARIETAL

PARIETES > PARIES

PARING *n* piece pared off

PARINGS > PARING

PARIS *n* type of herb

PARISCHAN *variant of* **> PAROCHIN**

PARISES > PARIS

PARISH *n* area that has its own church and a priest or pastor

PARISHAD *n* Indian assembly

PARISHADS > PARISHAD

PARISHEN *n* member of parish

PARISHENS > PARISHEN

PARISHES > PARISH

PARISON *n* unshaped mass of glass

PARISONS > PARISON

PARITIES > PARITY

PARITOR *n* official who summons witnesses

PARITORS > PARITOR

PARITY *n* equality or equivalence

PARK *n* area of open land for recreational use by the public ⊳ *vb* stop and leave (a vehicle) temporarily

PARKA *n* large waterproof jacket with a hood

PARKADE *n* building used as a car park

PARKADES > PARKADE

PARKAS > PARKA

PARKED > PARK

PARKEE *n* Inuit outer garment

PARKEES > PARKEE

PARKER > PARK

PARKERS > PARK

PARKETTE *n* small public car park

PARKETTES > PARKETTE

PARKI *variant of* **>** PARKA

PARKIE *n* park keeper

PARKIER > PARKY

PARKIES > PARKIE

PARKIEST > PARKY

PARKIN *n* moist spicy ginger cake

PARKING > PARK

PARKINGS > PARK

PARKINS > PARKIN

PARKIS > PARKI

PARKISH *adj* like a park

PARKLAND *n* grassland with scattered trees

PARKLANDS > PARKLAND

PARKLIKE > PARK

PARKLY *adj* having many parks or resembling a park

PARKOUR *n* sport of running in urban areas over obstacles

PARKOURS > PARKOUR

PARKS > PARK

PARKWARD *adv* towards a park

PARKWARDS *adv* towards a park

PARKWAY *n* wide road planted with trees, turf, etc

PARKWAYS > PARKWAY

PARKY *adj* (of the weather) chilly

PARLANCE *n* particular way of speaking, idiom

PARLANCES > PARLANCE

PARLANDO *adv* to be performed as though speaking

PARLANTE *same as* **> PARLANDO**

PARLAY *vb* stake (winnings from one bet)

on a subsequent wager ⊳ *n* bet in which winnings are parlayed

PARLAYED > PARLAY

PARLAYING > PARLAY

PARLAYS > PARLAY

PARLE *vb* speak

PARLED > PARLE

PARLEMENT *n* parliament

PARLES > PARLE

PARLEY *n* meeting between opponents to discuss terms ⊳ *vb* have a parley

PARLEYED > PARLEY

PARLEYER > PARLEY

PARLEYERS > PARLEY

PARLEYING > PARLEY

PARLEYS > PARLEY

PARLEYVOO *vb* speak French ⊳ *n* French language

PARLIES *pl n* small Scottish biscuits

PARLING > PARLE

PARLOR *same as* **> PARLOUR**

PARLORS > PARLOR

PARLOUR *n* living room for receiving visitors

PARLOURS > PARLOUR

PARLOUS *adj* dire ⊳ *adv* extremely

PARLOUSLY > PARLOUS

PARLY *n* short form of parliament

PARMA *n* breaded chicken dish

PARMAS > PARMA

PARMESAN *n* Italian hard cheese

PARMESANS > PARMESAN

PAROCHIAL *adj* narrow in outlook

PAROCHIN *n* old Scottish parish

PAROCHINE *same as* **> PAROCHIN**

PAROCHINS > PAROCHIN

PARODIC > PARODY

PARODICAL > PARODY

PARODIED > PARODY

PARODIES > PARODY

PARODIST > PARODY

PARODISTS > PARODY

PARODOI *n* path leading to Greek theatre

PARODOS *n* ode sung by Greek chorus

PARODY *n* exaggerated and amusing imitation of someone else's style ⊳ *vb* make a parody of

PARODYING > PARODY

PAROECISM *n* state of being paroecious

PAROEMIA *n* proverb

PAROEMIAC *adj* of proverbs

PAROEMIAL *adj* of proverbs

PAROEMIAS > PAROEMIA

PAROICOUS *same as* **> PARECIOUS**

PAROL n (formerly) pleadings in an action when presented by word of mouth ▷ adj (of a contract, lease, etc) not made under seal
PAROLABLE > PAROLE
PAROLE n early freeing of a prisoner on condition that he or she behaves well ▷ vb put on parole
PAROLED > PAROLE
PAROLEE > PAROLE
PAROLEES > PAROLE
PAROLES > PAROLE
PAROLING > PAROLE
PAROLS > PAROL
PARONYM n cognate word
PARONYMIC > PARONYM
PARONYMS > PARONYM
PARONYMY > PARONYM
PAROQUET n small long-tailed parrot
PAROQUETS > PARROQUET
PARORE n type of fish found around Australia and New Zealand
PARORES > PARORE
PAROSMIA n any disorder of the sense of smell
PAROSMIAS > PAROSMIA
PAROTIC adj situated near the ear
PAROTID adj relating to or situated near the parotid gland ▷ n parotid gland
PAROTIDES > PAROTID
PAROTIDS > PAROTID
PAROTIS n parotid gland
PAROTISES > PAROTIS
PAROTITIC > PAROTITIS
PAROTITIS n inflammation of the parotid gland
PAROTOID n poison gland on certain toads and salamanders ▷ adj resembling a parotid gland
PAROTOIDS > PAROTOID
PAROUS adj having given birth
PAROUSIA n Second Coming
PAROUSIAS > PAROUSIA
PAROXYSM n uncontrollable outburst of rage, delight, etc
PAROXYSMS > PAROXYSM
PARP vb make a honking sound
PARPANE n parapet on bridge
PARPANES > PARPANE
PARPED > PARP
PARPEN same as > PARPEND
PARPEND same as > PARPEN
PARPENDS > PARPEND
PARPENS > PARPEN

PARPENT n parapet on bridge
PARPENTS > PARPENT
PARPING > PARP
PARPOINT n parapet on bridge
PARPOINTS > PARPOINT
PARPS > PARP
PARQUET n floor covering made of wooden blocks ▷ vb cover with parquet
PARQUETED > PARQUET
PARQUETRY n pieces of wood arranged in a geometric pattern, used to cover floors
PARQUETS > PARQUET
PARR n salmon up to two years of age
PARRA n tourist or non-resident on a beach
PARRAKEET same as > PARAKEET
PARRAL same as > PARREL
PARRALS > PARRAL
PARRAS > PARRA
PARRED > PAR
PARREL n ring that holds the jaws of a boom to the mast
PARRELS > PARREL
PARRHESIA n boldness of speech
PARRICIDE n crime of killing either of one's parents
PARRIDGE Scottish variant of > PORRIDGE
PARRIDGES > PARRIDGE
PARRIED > PARRY
PARRIER > PARRY
PARRIERS > PARRY
PARRIES > PARRY
PARRING > PAR
PARRITCH Scottish variant of > PORRIDGE
PARROCK vb put (an animal) in a small field
PARROCKED > PARROCK
PARROCKS > PARROCK
PARROKET n small long-tailed parrot
PARROKETS > PARROKET
PARROQUET n small long-tailed parrot
PARROT n tropical bird with a short hooked beak ▷ vb repeat (someone else's words) without thinking
PARROTED > PARROT
PARROTER n person who repeats what is said
PARROTERS > PARROTER
PARROTIER > PARROTER
PARROTING > PARROT
PARROTRY > PARROT
PARROTS > PARROT
PARROTY adj like a parrot; chattering
PARRS > PARR
PARRY vb ward off (an attack) ▷ n parrying

PARRYING > PARRY
PARS > PAR
PARSABLE > PARSE
PARSE vb analyse (a sentence) in terms of grammar
PARSEC n unit of astronomical distance
PARSECS > PARSEC
PARSED > PARSE
PARSER n program that interprets input to a computer
PARSERS > PARSER
PARSES > PARSE
PARSIMONY n extreme caution in spending money
PARSING > PARSE
PARSINGS > PARSE
PARSLEY n herb used for seasoning and decorating food ▷ vb garnish with parsley
PARSLEYED > PARSLEY
PARSLEYS > PARSLEY
PARSLIED > PARSLEY
PARSNEP same as > PARSNIP
PARSNEPS > PARSNEP
PARSNIP n long tapering cream-coloured root vegetable
PARSNIPS > PARSNIP
PARSON n Anglican parish priest
PARSONAGE n parson's house
PARSONIC > PARSON
PARSONISH adj like a parson
PARSONS > PARSON
PART n one of the pieces that make up a whole ▷ vb divide or separate
PARTAKE vb take (food or drink)
PARTAKEN > PARTAKE
PARTAKER > PARTAKE
PARTAKERS > PARTAKE
PARTAKES > PARTAKE
PARTAKING > PARTAKE
PARTAN Scottish word for > CRAB
PARTANS > PARTAN
PARTED adj divided almost to the base
PARTER n thing that parts
PARTERRE n formally patterned flower garden
PARTERRES > PARTERRE
PARTERS > PARTER
PARTI n concept of architectural design
PARTIAL adj not complete ▷ n any of the component tones of a single musical sound ▷ vb remove (a factor) from a set of statistics
PARTIALLY > PARTIAL
PARTIALS > PARTIAL
PARTIBLE adj (esp of property or an inheritance) divisible
PARTICLE n extremely small piece or amount

PARTICLES > PARTICLE
PARTIED > PARTY
PARTIER n person who parties
PARTIERS > PARTIER
PARTIES > PARTY
PARTIEST > PARTY
PARTIM adv in part
PARTING same as > PART
PARTINGS > PARTING
PARTIS > PARTI
PARTISAN n strong supporter of a party or group ▷ adj prejudiced or one-sided
PARTISANS > PARTISAN
PARTITA n type of suite
PARTITAS > PARTITA
PARTITE adj composed of or divided into a specified number of parts
PARTITION n screen or thin wall that divides a room ▷ vb divide with a partition
PARTITIVE adj (of a noun) referring to part of something ▷ n partitive word
PARTITURA n music score for several parts
PARTIZAN same as > PARTISAN
PARTIZANS > PARTIZAN
PARTLET n woman's garment
PARTLETS > PARTLET
PARTLY adv not completely
PARTNER n either member of a couple in a relationship or activity ▷ vb be the partner of
PARTNERED > PARTNER
PARTNERS > PARTNER
PARTON n hypothetical elementary particle
PARTONS > PARTON
PARTOOK > PARTAKE
PARTRIDGE n game bird of the grouse family
PARTS pl n abilities or talents
PARTURE n departure
PARTURES > PARTURE
PARTWAY adv some of the way
PARTWORK n series of magazines issued at regular intervals
PARTWORKS > PARTWORK
PARTY n social gathering for pleasure ▷ vb celebrate, have fun ▷ adj divided into different colours
PARTYER n person who parties
PARTYERS > PARTYER
PARTYGOER n person who goes to party
PARTYING n act of partying
PARTYINGS > PARTYING

PARTYISM n devotion to a political party

PARTYISMS > PARTYISM

PARULIDES > PARULIS

PARULIS another name for > GUMBOIL

PARULISES > PARULIS

PARURA same as > PARURE

PARURAS > PARURA

PARURE n set of jewels or other ornaments

PARURES > PARURE

PARURESES > PARURES

PARURESIS n inability to urinate in the presence of others

PARURETIC n person unable to urinate in the presence of others

PARVE same as > PAREV

PARVENU n person newly risen to a position of power or wealth ▷ adj of or characteristic of a parvenu

PARVENUE n woman newly risen to a position of power or wealth ▷ adj of a parvenue

PARVENUES > PARVENUE

PARVENUS > PARVENU

PARVIS n court or portico in front of a building, esp a church

PARVISE same as > PARVIS

PARVISES > PARVISE

PARVO n disease of cattle and dogs

PARVOLIN n substance resulting from the putrefaction of flesh

PARVOLINE n liquid derived from coal tar

PARVOLINS > PARVOLIN

PARVOS > PARVO

PAS n dance step or movement, esp in ballet

PASCAL n unit of pressure

PASCALS > PASCAL

PASCHAL adj of the Passover or Easter ▷ n Passover or Easter

PASCHALS > PASCHAL

PASCUAL adj relating to pasture ▷ n plant that grows in pasture

PASCUALS > PASCUAL

PASE n movement of the cape or muleta by a matador

PASEAR vb go for a rambling walk

PASEARED > PASEAR

PASEARING > PASEAR

PASEARS > PASEAR

PASELA same as > BONSELA

PASELAS > PASELA

PASEO n bullfighters' procession

PASEOS > PASEO

PASES > PASE

PASH n infatuation ▷ vb throw or be thrown and break or be broken to bits

PASHA n high official of the Ottoman Empire

PASHADOM n territory of a pasha

PASHADOMS > PASHADOM

PASHALIC same as > PASHALIK

PASHALICS > PASHALIC

PASHALIK n province or jurisdiction of a pasha

PASHALIKS > PASHALIK

PASHAS > PASHA

PASHED > PASH

PASHES > PASH

PASHIM same as > PASHM

PASHIMS > PASHIM

PASHING > PASH

PASHKA n rich Russian dessert

PASHKAS > PASHKA

PASHM n underfur of various Tibetan animals, esp goats, used for cashmere shawls

PASHMINA n type of cashmere scarf or shawl made from the underfur of Tibetan goats

PASHMINAS > PASHMINA

PASHMS > PASHM

PASKA same as > PASKHA

PASKAS > PASKA

PASKHA n Russian dessert eaten at Easter

PASKHAS > PASKHA

PASODOBLE n fast modern ballroom dance

PASPALUM n type of grass with wide leaves

PASPALUMS > PASPALUM

PASPIES > PASPY

PASPY n piece of music in triple time

PASQUIL n abusive lampoon or satire ▷ vb ridicule with pasquil

PASQUILER n person who lampoons

PASQUILS > PASQUIL

PASS vb go by, past, or through ▷ n successful result in a test or examination

PASSABLE adj (just) acceptable

PASSABLY adv fairly

PASSADE n act of moving back and forth in the same place

PASSADES > PASSADE

PASSADO n forward thrust with sword

PASSADOES > PASSADO

PASSADOS > PASSADO

PASSAGE n channel or opening providing a way through ▷ vb move or cause to move at a passage

PASSAGED > PASSAGE

PASSAGER n as in passager hawk young hawk or falcon caught while on migration

PASSAGES > PASSAGE

PASSAGING > PASSAGE

PASSALONG adj (of plants) easily propagated and given to others

PASSAMENT vb sew border on garment

PASSANT adj (of a heraldic beast) walking

PASSATA n sauce made from sieved tomatoes

PASSATAS > PASSATA

PASSBAND n frequency band within which signals are transmitted by a filter

PASSBANDS > PASSBAND

PASSBOOK n record of a person's bank transactions

PASSBOOKS > PASSBOOK

PASSCODE n password composed of digits

PASSCODES > PASSCODE

PASSE adj out-of-date

PASSED > PASS

PASSEE adj out-of-date

PASSEL n group or quantity of no fixed number

PASSELS > PASSEL

PASSEMENT vb sew border on garment

PASSENGER n person travelling in a vehicle driven by someone else

PASSEPIED n lively minuet of Breton origin

PASSER n person or thing that passes

PASSERBY n person that is passing or going by, esp on foot

PASSERINE adj belonging to the order of perching birds ▷ n any bird of this order

PASSERS > PASSER

PASSERSBY > PASSERBY

PASSES > PASS

PASSIBLE adj susceptible to emotion or suffering

PASSIBLY > PASSIBLE

PASSIM adv everywhere, throughout

PASSING adj brief or transitory ▷ n death

PASSINGLY > PASSING

PASSINGS > PASSING

PASSION n intense love ▷ vb give passionate character to

PASSIONAL adj of, relating to, or due to passion or the passions ▷ n book recounting the sufferings of Christian martyrs or saints

PASSIONED > PASSION

PASSIONS > PASSION

PASSIVATE vb render (a metal) less susceptible to corrosion by coating the surface with a substance, such as an oxide

PASSIVE adj not playing an active part ▷ n passive form of a verb

PASSIVELY > PASSIVE

PASSIVES > PASSIVE

PASSIVISM n theory, belief, or practice of passive resistance

PASSIVIST > PASSIVISM

PASSIVITY > PASSIVE

PASSKEY n private key

PASSKEYS > PASSKEY

PASSLESS adj having no pass

PASSMAN n student who passes without honours

PASSMEN > PASSMAN

PASSMENT same as > PASSEMENT

PASSMENTS > PASSMENT

PASSOUT n (in ice hockey) pass by an attacking player from behind the opposition goal line

PASSOUTS > PASSOUT

PASSOVER n lamb eaten during Passover

PASSOVERS > PASSOVER

PASSPORT n official document of nationality granting permission to travel abroad ▷ vb (in the European Economic Area) award a firm the right to do business in every member state

PASSPORTS > PASSPORT

PASSUS n division or section of a poem, story, etc

PASSUSES > PASSUS

PASSWORD n secret word or phrase that ensures admission

PASSWORDS > PASSWORD

PAST adj of the time before the present ▷ n period of time before the present ▷ adv ago ▷ prep beyond

PASTA n type of food that is made from flour and water

PASTALIKE > PASTA

PASTANCE n activity that passes time

PASTANCES > PASTANCE

PASTAS > PASTA

PASTE n moist soft mixture, such as toothpaste ▷ vb fasten with paste

PASTED > PASTE

PASTEDOWN n portion of endpaper pasted to cover of book

PASTEL n coloured chalk crayon for drawing ▷ adj pale and delicate in colour

PASTELIKE adj like paste

PASTELIST > PASTEL

PASTELS > PASTEL

PASTER n person or thing that pastes

PASTERN n part of a horse's foot

PASTERNS > PASTERN

PASTERS > PASTER

PASTES > PASTE

PASTEUP n material pasted on a sheet of paper or board

PASTEUPS > PASTEUP

PASTICCI > PASTICCIO

PASTICCIO n art work borrowing various styles

PASTICHE n work of art that mixes styles or copies the style of another artist

PASTICHES > PASTICHE

PASTIE n decorative cover for nipple

PASTIER > PASTY

PASTIES > PASTY

PASTIEST > PASTY

PASTIL same as > PASTILLE

PASTILLE n small fruit-flavoured and sometimes medicated sweet

PASTILLES > PASTILLE

PASTILS > PASTIL

PASTILY > PASTY

PASTIME n activity that makes time pass pleasantly

PASTIMES > PASTIME

PASTINA n small pieces of pasta

PASTINAS > PASTINA

PASTINESS > PASTY

PASTING n heavy defeat

PASTINGS > PASTING

PASTIS n anise-flavoured alcoholic drink

PASTISES > PASTIS

PASTITSIO n Greek dish consisting of minced meat and macaroni topped with bechamel sauce

PASTITSO n Greek dish of baked pasta

PASTITSOS > PASTITSO

PASTLESS adj having no past

PASTNESS n quality of being past

PASTOR n member of the clergy in charge of a congregation ▷ vb act as a pastor

PASTORAL adj of or depicting country life ▷ n poem or picture portraying country life

PASTORALE n musical composition that suggests country life

PASTORALI > PASTORALE

PASTORALS > PASTORAL

PASTORATE n office or term of office of a pastor

PASTORED > PASTOR

PASTORING > PASTOR

PASTORIUM n residence of pastor

PASTORLY adj like a pastor

PASTORS > PASTOR

PASTRAMI n highly seasoned smoked beef

PASTRAMIS > PASTRAMI

PASTRIES > PASTRY

PASTROMI same as > PASTRAMI

PASTROMIS > PASTROMI

PASTRY n baking dough made of flour, fat, and water

PASTS > PAST

PASTURAGE n business of grazing cattle

PASTURAL adj of pasture

PASTURE n grassy land for farm animals to graze on ▷ vb cause (livestock) to graze

PASTURED > PASTURE

PASTURER n person who tends cattle

PASTURERS > PASTURER

PASTURES > PASTURE

PASTURING > PASTURE

PASTY adj (of a complexion) pale and unhealthy ▷ n round of pastry folded over a savoury filling

PAT vb tap lightly ▷ n gentle tap or stroke ▷ adj quick, ready, or glib

PATACA n monetary unit of Macao

PATACAS > PATACA

PATAGIA > PATAGIUM

PATAGIAL > PATAGIUM

PATAGIUM n web of skin acting as wings in bats

PATAKA n building on stilts, used for storing provisions

PATAKAS > PATAKA

PATAMAR n type of boat

PATAMARS > PATAMAR

PATBALL n game like squash but using hands

PATBALLS > PATBALL

PATCH n piece of material sewn on a garment ▷ vb mend with a patch

PATCHABLE > PATCH

PATCHED > PATCH

PATCHER > PATCH

PATCHERS > PATCH

PATCHERY n bungling work

PATCHES > PATCH

PATCHIER > PATCHY

PATCHIEST > PATCHY

PATCHILY > PATCHY

PATCHING > PATCH

PATCHINGS > PATCH

PATCHOCKE Spenserian word for > CLOWN

PATCHOULI n Asiatic tree, the leaves of which yield a heavy fragrant oil

PATCHOULY same as > PATCHOULI

PATCHWORK n needlework made of pieces of different materials sewn together

PATCHY adj of uneven quality or intensity

PATE n head

PATED > PATE

PATELLA n kneecap

PATELLAE > PATELLA

PATELLAR > PATELLA

PATELLAS > PATELLA

PATELLATE adj having the shape of a patella

PATEN n plate used for the bread at Communion

PATENCIES > PATENCY

PATENCY n condition of being obvious

PATENS > PATEN

PATENT n document giving the exclusive right to make or sell an invention ▷ adj open to public inspection ▷ vb obtain a patent for

PATENTED > PATENT

PATENTEE n person, group, company, etc, that has been granted a patent

PATENTEES > PATENTEE

PATENTING > PATENT

PATENTLY adv obviously

PATENTOR n person who or official body that grants a patent or patents

PATENTORS > PATENTOR

PATENTS > PATENT

PATER n father

PATERA n shallow ancient Roman bowl

PATERAE > PATERA

PATERCOVE n fraudulent priest

PATERERO n type of cannon

PATEREROS > PATERERO

PATERNAL adj fatherly

PATERNITY n fact or state of being a father

PATERS > PATER

PATES > PATE

PATH n surfaced walk or track ▷ vb make a path

PATHED > PATH

PATHETIC adj causing feelings of pity or sadness ▷ pl n pathetic sentiments ▷ n pathetic person

PATHETICS > PATHETIC

PATHIC n person who suffers ▷ adj of or relating to suffering

PATHICS > PATHIC

PATHING > PATH

PATHLESS > PATH

PATHNAME n description of where a file is found in a hierarchy of directories

PATHNAMES > PATHNAME

PATHOGEN n thing that causes disease

PATHOGENE same as > PATHOGEN

PATHOGENS > PATHOGEN

PATHOGENY n origin, development, and resultant effects of a disease

PATHOLOGY n scientific study of diseases

PATHOS n power of arousing pity or sadness

PATHOSES > PATHOS

PATHS > PATH

PATHWAY n path

PATHWAYS > PATHWAY

PATIBLE adj endurable

PATIENCE n quality of being patient

PATIENCES > PATIENCE

PATIENT adj enduring difficulties or delays calmly ▷ n person receiving medical treatment ▷ vb make calm

PATIENTED > PATIENT

PATIENTER > PATIENT

PATIENTLY > PATIENT

PATIENTS > PATIENT

PATIKI n New Zealand sand flounder or dab

PATIKIS > PATIKI

PATIN same as > PATEN

PATINA n fine layer on a surface

PATINAE > PATINA

PATINAED adj having a patina

PATINAS > PATINA

PATINATE vb coat with patina

PATINATED > PATINATE

PATINATES > PATINATE

PATINE vb cover with patina

PATINED > PATINE

PATINES > PATINE

PATINING > PATINE

PATINISE same as > PATINIZE

PATINISED > PATINISE

PATINISES > PATINISE

PATINIZE vb coat with patina

PATINIZED > PATINIZE

PATINIZES > PATINIZE

PATINS > PATIN

PATIO n paved area adjoining a house

PATIOS > PATIO

PATISSIER n pastry chef

PATKA n head covering worn by Sikh men

PATKAS > PATKA

PATLY adv fitly

PATNESS n appropriateness

PATNESSES > PATNESS

PATOIS n regional dialect, esp of French

PATONCE adj (of cross) with limbs which broaden from centre

PATOOT same as > PATOOTIE

PATOOTIE n person's bottom

PATOOTIES > PATOOTIE

PATOOTS > PATOOT

PATRIAL n (in Britain, formerly) person with a right to live in the United Kingdom

PATRIALS > PATRIAL

PATRIARCH n male head of a family or tribe

PATRIATE vb bring under the authority of an autonomous country

PATRIATED > PATRIATE

PATRIATES > PATRIATE

PATRICIAN n member of the nobility ▷ adj of noble birth

PATRICIDE n crime of killing one's father

PATRICK n former Irish coin

PATRICKS > PATRICK

PATRICO n fraudulent priest

PATRICOES > PATRICO

PATRICOS > PATRICO

PATRILINY n tracing of family descent through males

PATRIMONY n property inherited from ancestors

PATRIOT n person who loves his or her country

PATRIOTIC > PATRIOT

PATRIOTS > PATRIOT

PATRISTIC adj of or relating to the Fathers of the Church, their writings, or the study of these

PATROL n regular circuit by a guard ▷ vb go round on guard, or reconnoitring

PATROLLED > PATROL

PATROLLER > PATROL

PATROLMAN n man, esp a police officer, who patrols a certain area

PATROLMEN > PATROLMAN

PATROLOGY n study of the writings of the Fathers of the Church

PATROLS > PATROL

PATRON n person who gives financial support

PATRONAGE n support given by a patron

PATRONAL > PATRONESS

PATRONESS n woman who sponsors or aids artists, charities, etc

PATRONISE same as > PATRONIZE

PATRONIZE vb treat in a condescending way

PATRONLY adj like a patron

PATRONNE n woman who owns or manages a hotel, restaurant, or bar

PATRONNES > PATRONNE

PATRONS > PATRON

PATROON n Dutch land-holder in New Netherland and New York

PATROONS > PATROON

PATS > PAT

PATSIES > PATSY

PATSY n person who is easily cheated, victimized, etc

PATTAMAR n Indian courier

PATTAMARS > PATTAMAR

PATTE n band keeping belt in place

PATTED > PAT

PATTEE adj (of a cross) having triangular arms widening outwards

PATTEN n wooden clog or sandal ▷ vb wear pattens

PATTENED > PATTEN

PATTENING > PATTEN

PATTENS > PATTEN

PATTER vb make repeated soft tapping sounds ▷ n quick succession of taps

PATTERED > PATTER

PATTERER > PATTER

PATTERERS > PATTER

PATTERING > PATTER

PATTERN n arrangement of repeated parts or decorative designs ▷ vb model

PATTERNED > PATTERN

PATTERNS > PATTERN

PATTERS > PATTER

PATTES > PATTE

PATTEST > PAT

PATTIE same as > PATTY

PATTIES > PATTY

PATTING > PAT

PATTLE dialect for > PADDLE

PATTLES > PATTLE

PATTRESS n box for the space behind electrical sockets and switches

PATTY n small flattened cake of minced food

PATTYPAN n small round flattish squash

PATTYPANS > PATTYPAN

PATU n short Māori club, now used ceremonially

PATULENT adj spreading widely

PATULIN n toxic antibiotic

PATULINS > PATULIN

PATULOUS adj spreading widely or expanded

PATUS > PATU

PATUTUKI n blue cod

PATUTUKIS > PATUTUKI

PATY adj (of cross) having arms of equal length

PATZER n novice chess player

PATZERS > PATZER

PAUA n edible shellfish of New Zealand

PAUAS > PAUA

PAUCAL n grammatical number for words in contexts where a few of their referents are described ▷ adj relating to or inflected for this number

PAUCALS > PAUCAL

PAUCITIES > PAUCITY

PAUCITY n scarcity

PAUGHTIER > PAUGHTY

PAUGHTY Scots word for > HAUGHTY

PAUL same as > PAWL

PAULDRON n either of two metal plates worn with armour to protect the shoulders

PAULDRONS > PAULDRON

PAULIN n tarpaulin

PAULINS > PAULIN

PAULOWNIA n Japanese tree with large heart-shaped leaves and clusters of purplish or white flowers

PAULS > PAUL

PAUNCE n pansy

PAUNCES > PAUNCE

PAUNCH n protruding belly ▷ vb stab in the stomach

PAUNCHED > PAUNCH

PAUNCHES > PAUNCH

PAUNCHIER > PAUNCHY

PAUNCHING > PAUNCH

PAUNCHY adj having a protruding belly or abdomen

PAUPER n very poor person ▷ vb reduce to beggary

PAUPERDOM n state of being a pauper

PAUPERED > PAUPER

PAUPERESS n female pauper

PAUPERING > PAUPER

PAUPERISE same as > PAUPERIZE

PAUPERISM > PAUPER

PAUPERIZE vb make a pauper of

PAUPERS > PAUPER

PAUPIETTE n rolled stuffed fish or meat

PAURAQUE n type of long-tailed nocturnal bird

PAURAQUES > PAURAQUE

PAUROPOD n minute myriapod

PAUROPODS > PAUROPOD

PAUSAL > PAUSE

PAUSE vb stop for a time ▷ n stop or rest in speech or action

PAUSED > PAUSE

PAUSEFUL adj taking pauses

PAUSELESS adj without pauses

PAUSER > PAUSE

PAUSERS > PAUSE

PAUSES > PAUSE

PAUSING > PAUSE

PAUSINGLY adv with pauses

PAUSINGS > PAUSE

PAV short for > PAVLOVA

PAVAGE n tax towards paving streets

PAVAGES > PAVAGE

PAVAN same as > PAVANE

PAVANE n slow and stately dance

PAVANES > PAVANE

PAVANS > PAVAN

PAVE vb form (a surface) with stone or brick ▷ n paved surface, esp an uneven one

PAVED > PAVE

PAVEED adj (of jewels) set close together

PAVEMENT n paved path for pedestrians ▷ vb provide with pavement

PAVEMENTS > PAVEMENT

PAVEN same as > PAVANE

PAVENS > PAVEN

PAVER > PAVE

PAVERS > PAVE

PAVES > PAVE

PAVID adj fearful

PAVILION n building on a playing field etc ▷ vb place or set in or as if in a pavilion

PAVILIONS > PAVILION

PAVILLON n bell of wind instrument

PAVILLONS > PAVILLON

PAVIN same as > PAVANE

PAVING n paved surface ▷ adj of or for a paved surface or pavement

PAVINGS > PAVING

PAVINS > PAVIN

PAVIOR same as > PAVIOUR

PAVIORS > PAVIOR

PAVIOUR n person who lays paving

PAVIOURS > PAVIOUR

PAVIS n large square shield

PAVISE same as > PAVIS

PAVISER n soldier holding a pavis

PAVISERS > PAVISER

PAVISES > PAVISE

PAVISSE same as > PAVIS

PAVISSES > PAVISSE

PAVLOVA n meringue cake topped with whipped cream and fruit

PAVLOVAS > PAVLOVA

PAVONAZZO n white Italian marble

PAVONE n peacock

PAVONES > PAVONE

PAVONIAN same as
> PAVONINE
PAVONINE adj of or
resembling a peacock or
the colours, design, or
iridescence of a peacock's
tail
PAVS > PAV
PAW n animal's foot with
claws and pads ▷ vb
scrape with the paw or
hoof
PAWA old word for
> PEACOCK
PAWAS > PAWA
PAWAW vb recite N
American incantation
PAWAWED > PAWAW
PAWAWING > PAWAW
PAWAWS > PAWAW
PAWED > PAW
PAWER n person or animal
that paws
PAWERS > PAWER
PAWING > PAW
PAWK Scots word for
> TRICK
PAWKIER > PAWKY
PAWKIEST > PAWKY
PAWKILY > PAWKY
PAWKINESS > PAWKY
PAWKS > PAWK
PAWKY adj having or
characterized by a dry wit
PAWL n pivoted lever
shaped to engage with a
ratchet
PAWLS > PAWL
PAWN vb deposit (an
article) as security for
money borrowed ▷ n
chessman of the lowest
value
PAWNABLE > PAWN
PAWNAGE > PAWN
PAWNAGES > PAWN
PAWNCE old word for
> PANSY
PAWNCES > PAWNCE
PAWNED > PAWN
PAWNEE n one who
accepts goods in pawn
PAWNEES > PAWNEE
PAWNER n one who pawns
his or her possessions
PAWNERS > PAWNER
PAWNING > PAWN
PAWNOR same as
> PAWNER
PAWNORS > PAWNOR
PAWNS > PAWN
PAWNSHOP n premises of
a pawnbroker
PAWNSHOPS
> PAWNSHOP
PAWPAW same as > PAPAW
PAWPAWS > PAWPAW
PAWS > PAW
PAX n peace ▷ interj call
signalling a desire to end
hostilities
PAXES > PAX
PAXIUBA n tropical tree
PAXIUBAS > PAXIUBA
PAXWAX n strong
ligament in the neck of
many mammals
PAXWAXES > PAXWAX

PAY vb give money etc in
return for goods or
services ▷ n wages or
salary
PAYABLE adj due to be
paid ▷ n debt to be paid
PAYABLES > PAYABLE
PAYABLY > PAYABLE
PAYBACK n return on an
investment
PAYBACKS > PAYBACK
PAYCHECK n payment for
work done
PAYCHECKS
> PAYCHECK
PAYCHEQUE n payment
for work done
PAYDAY n day on which
wages or salaries are paid
PAYDAYS > PAYDAY
PAYDOWN n reduction of
debt through repayment
PAYDOWNS > PAYDOWN
PAYED > PAY
PAYEE n person to whom
money is paid or due
PAYEES > PAYEE
PAYER n person who pays
PAYERS > PAYER
PAYESS pl n uncut
sideburns worn by some
Jewish men
PAYFONE US spelling of
> PAYPHONE
PAYFONES > PAYFONE
PAYGRADE n military
rank
PAYGRADES
> PAYGRADE
PAYING > PAY
PAYINGS > PAY
PAYLIST n list of people
to be paid
PAYLISTS > PAYLIST
PAYLOAD n passengers or
cargo of an aircraft
PAYLOADS > PAYLOAD
PAYMASTER n official
responsible for the
payment of wages and
salaries
PAYMENT n act of paying
PAYMENTS > PAYMENT
PAYNIM n heathen or
pagan
PAYNIMRY n state of
being heathen
PAYNIMS > PAYNIM
PAYOFF n final
settlement, esp in
retribution
PAYOFFS > PAYOFF
PAYOLA n bribe to
promote a commercial
product
PAYOLAS > PAYOLA
PAYOR same as > PAYER
PAYORS > PAYOR
PAYOUT n sum of money
paid out
PAYOUTS > PAYOUT
PAYPHONE n
coin-operated telephone
PAYPHONES
> PAYPHONE
PAYROLL n list of
employees who receive
regular pay

PAYROLLS > PAYROLL
PAYS > PAY
PAYSAGE n landscape
PAYSAGES > PAYSAGE
PAYSAGIST n painter of
landscapes
PAYSD Spenserian form of
> POISED
PAYSLIP n note of
payment given to
employee
PAYSLIPS > PAYSLIP
PAYWALL n system that
denies access to a website
unless a payment is made
PAYWALLS > PAYWALL
PAZAZZ same as
> PIZZAZZ
PAZAZZES > PAZAZZ
PAZZAZZ same as
> PIZZAZZ
PAZZAZZES > PAZZAZZ
PE n 17th letter of the
Hebrew alphabet,
transliterated as p
PEA n climbing plant with
seeds growing in pods
PEABERRY n coffee berry
containing one seed
PEABRAIN n stupid
person
PEABRAINS
> PEABRAIN
PEACE n calm, quietness
PEACEABLE adj inclined
towards peace
PEACEABLY
> PEACEABLE
PEACED > PEACE
PEACEFUL adj not in a
state of war or
disagreement
PEACELESS adj without
peace
PEACENIK n activist who
opposes war
PEACENIKS
> PEACENIK
PEACES > PEACE
PEACETIME n period
without war
PEACH n soft juicy fruit
▷ adj pinkish-orange ▷ vb
inform against an
accomplice
PEACHBLOW n type of
glaze on porcelain
PEACHED > PEACH
PEACHER > PEACH
PEACHERS > PEACH
PEACHES > PEACH
PEACHICK n young
peafowl
PEACHICKS
> PEACHICK
PEACHIER > PEACHY
PEACHIEST > PEACHY
PEACHILY > PEACHY
PEACHING > PEACH
PEACHY adj of or like a
peach, esp in colour or
texture
PEACING > PEACE
PEACOAT n woollen
jacket
PEACOATS > PEACOAT
PEACOCK n large male
bird with a brilliantly

coloured fanlike tail ▷ vb
display (oneself) proudly
PEACOCKED > PEACOCK
PEACOCKS > PEACOCK
PEACOCKY > PEACOCK
PEACOD same as
> PEASCOD
PEACODS > PEACOD
PEAFOWL n peacock or
peahen
PEAFOWLS > PEAFOWL
PEAG n (formerly) money
used by Native Americans
PEAGE same as > PEAG
PEAGES > PEAGE
PEAGS > PEAG
PEAHEN > PEACOCK
PEAHENS > PEACOCK
PEAK n pointed top, esp of
a mountain ▷ vb form or
reach a peak ▷ adj of or at
the point of greatest
demand
PEAKED adj having a peak
PEAKIER > PEAK
PEAKIEST > PEAK
PEAKINESS n state of
being peaky
PEAKING n act of peaking
PEAKINGS > PEAKING
PEAKISH adj sickly
PEAKLESS adj without a
peak
PEAKLIKE > PEAK
PEAKS > PEAK
PEAKY > PEAK
PEAL n long loud echoing
sound, esp of bells or
thunder ▷ vb sound with a
peal or peals
PEALED > PEAL
PEALIKE > PEA
PEALING > PEAL
PEALS > PEAL
PEAN same as > PEEN
PEANED > PEAN
PEANING > PEAN
PEANS > PEAN
PEANUT n pea-shaped nut
that ripens underground
PEANUTS > PEANUT
PEANUTTY adj having the
taste of peanuts
PEAPOD n pod of the pea
plant
PEAPODS > PEAPOD
PEAR n sweet juicy fruit
with a narrow top and
rounded base
PEARCE old spelling of
> PIERCE
PEARCED > PEARCE
PEARCES > PEARCE
PEARCING > PEARCE
PEARE obsolete spelling of
> PEAR
PEARES > PEARE
PEARL same as > PURL
PEARLASH n granular
crystalline form of
potassium carbonate
PEARLED > PEARL
PEARLER n person who
dives for or trades in pearls
▷ adj excellent
PEARLERS > PEARLER
PEARLIER > PEARLY
PEARLIES > PEARLY

p

PEARLIEST > PEARLY

PEARLIN n type of lace used to trim clothes

PEARLING > PEARL

PEARLINGS > PEARL

PEARLINS n type of lace

PEARLISED same as > PEARLIZED

PEARLITE same as > PERLITE

PEARLITES > PEARLITE

PEARLITIC > PEARLITE

PEARLIZED adj having or given a pearly lustre

PEARLS > PEARL

PEARLWARE n goods made from pearl

PEARLWORT n plant with small white flowers that are spherical in bud

PEARLY adj resembling a pearl, esp in lustre ▷ n London costermonger who wears pearl buttons

PEARMAIN n any of several varieties of apple having a red skin

PEARMAINS > PEARMAIN

PEARS > PEAR

PEARST archaic variant of > PIERCED

PEART adj lively

PEARTER > PEART

PEARTEST > PEART

PEARTLY > PEART

PEARTNESS > PEART

PEARWOOD n wood from pear tree

PEARWOODS > PEARWOOD

PEAS > PEA

PEASANT n person working on the land

PEASANTRY n peasants collectively

PEASANTS > PEASANT

PEASANTY adj having qualities ascribed to traditional country life or people

PEASCOD n pod of a pea plant

PEASCODS > PEASCOD

PEASE n archaic or dialect word for pea ▷ vb appease

PEASECOD n pod of a pea plant

PEASECODS > PEASECOD

PEASED > PEASE

PEASEN obsolete plural of > PEASE

PEASES > PEASE

PEASING > PEASE

PEASON obsolete plural of > PEASE

PEASOUPER n thick fog

PEAT n decayed vegetable material found in bogs

PEATARIES > PEATARY

PEATARY n area covered with peat

PEATERIES > PEATERY

PEATERY same as > PEATARY

PEATIER > PEAT

PEATIEST > PEAT

PEATLAND n area of land consisting of peat bogs

PEATLANDS > PEATLAND

PEATMAN n person who collects peat

PEATMEN > PEATMAN

PEATS > PEAT

PEATSHIP n ship carrying peat

PEATSHIPS > PEATSHIP

PEATY > PEAT

PEAVEY n wooden lever used for handling logs

PEAVEYS > PEAVEY

PEAVIES > PEAVY

PEAVY same as > PEAVEY

PEAZE same as > PEASE

PEAZED > PEAZE

PEAZES > PEAZE

PEAZING > PEAZE

PEBA n type of armadillo

PEBAS > PEBA

PEBBLE n small roundish stone ▷ vb cover with pebbles

PEBBLED > PEBBLE

PEBBLES > PEBBLE

PEBBLIER > PEBBLE

PEBBLIEST > PEBBLE

PEBBLING n (in curling) act of spraying the rink with drops of hot water to slow down the stone

PEBBLINGS > PEBBLING

PEBBLY > PEBBLE

PEBIBYTE n two to the power of fifty bytes

PEBIBYTES > PEBIBYTE

PEBRINE n disease of silkworms

PEBRINES > PEBRINE

PEC n pectoral muscle

PECAN n edible nut of a N American tree

PECANS > PECAN

PECCABLE adj liable to sin

PECCANCY > PECCANT

PECCANT adj guilty of an offence

PECCANTLY > PECCANT

PECCARIES > PECCARY

PECCARY n piglike animal of American forests

PECCAVI n confession of guilt

PECCAVIS > PECCAVI

PECH Scottish word for > PANT

PECHAN Scots word for > STOMACH

PECHANS > PECHAN

PECHED > PECH

PECHING > PECH

PECHS > PECH

PECK vb strike or pick up with the beak ▷ n pecking movement

PECKE n quarter of bushel

PECKED > PECK

PECKER n short for woodpecker

PECKERS > PECKER

PECKES > PECKE

PECKIER > PECKY

PECKIEST > PECKY

PECKING > PECK

PECKINGS > PECK

PECKISH adj slightly hungry

PECKISHLY > PECKISH

PECKS > PECK

PECKY adj discoloured

PECORINI > PECORINO

PECORINO n Italian cheese made from ewes' milk

PECORINOS > PECORINO

PECS pl n pectoral muscles

PECTASE n enzyme occurring in certain ripening fruits

PECTASES > PECTASE

PECTATE n salt or ester of pectic acid

PECTATES > PECTATE

PECTEN n comblike structure in the eye of birds and reptiles

PECTENS > PECTEN

PECTIC > PECTIN

PECTIN n substance in fruit that makes jam set

PECTINAL adj resembling a comb ▷ n fish with bones or a spine resembling a comb

PECTINALS > PECTINAL

PECTINATE adj shaped like a comb

PECTINEAL adj relating to pubic bone

PECTINEI > PECTINEUS

PECTINES > PECTEN

PECTINEUS n muscle in the thigh

PECTINOUS > PECTIN

PECTINS > PECTIN

PECTISE same as > PECTIZE

PECTISED > PECTISE

PECTISES > PECTISE

PECTISING > PECTISE

PECTIZE vb change into a jelly

PECTIZED > PECTIZE

PECTIZES > PECTIZE

PECTIZING > PECTIZE

PECTOLITE n silicate of lime and soda

PECTORAL adj of the chest or thorax ▷ n pectoral muscle or fin

PECTORALS > PECTORAL

PECTOSE n insoluble carbohydrate found in unripe fruit

PECTOSES > PECTOSE

PECULATE vb embezzle (public money)

PECULATED > PECULATE

PECULATES > PECULATE

PECULATOR > PECULATE

PECULIA > PECULIUM

PECULIAR adj strange ▷ n special sort, esp an accented letter

PECULIARS > PECULIAR

PECULIUM n property that a father or master allowed his child or slave to hold as his own

PECUNIARY adj relating to, or consisting of, money

PECUNIOUS adj having lots of money

PED n pannier

PEDAGOG same as > PEDAGOGUE

PEDAGOGIC > PEDAGOGUE

PEDAGOGS > PEDAGOG

PEDAGOGUE n schoolteacher, esp a pedantic one

PEDAGOGY n principles, practice, or profession of teaching

PEDAL n foot-operated lever ▷ vb propel (a bicycle) by using its pedals ▷ adj of or relating to the foot or the feet

PEDALBOAT n boat that is propelled by operating the pedals

PEDALCAR n child's vehicle that is operated by pedals

PEDALCARS > PEDALCAR

PEDALED > PEDAL

PEDALER > PEDAL

PEDALERS > PEDAL

PEDALFER n type of zonal soil deficient in lime but containing deposits of aluminium and iron

PEDALFERS > PEDALFER

PEDALIER n pedal piano

PEDALIERS > PEDALIER

PEDALING > PEDAL

PEDALLED > PEDAL

PEDALLER n person who pedals

PEDALLERS > PEDALLER

PEDALLING > PEDAL

PEDALO n pedal-operated pleasure craft

PEDALOES > PEDALO

PEDALOS > PEDALO

PEDALS > PEDAL

PEDANT n person who is excessively concerned with details and rules

PEDANTIC adj of, relating to, or characterized by pedantry

PEDANTISE same as > PEDANTIZE

PEDANTISM > PEDANT

PEDANTIZE vb make pedantic comments

PEDANTRY n practice of being a pedant, esp in the minute observance of petty rules or details

PEDANTS > PEDANT

PEDATE adj (of a plant leaf) divided into several lobes arising at a common point

PEDATELY > PEDATE

PEDATIFID adj (of a plant leaf) pedately divided, with the divisions less deep than in a pedate leaf

PEDDER old form of > PEDLAR

PEDDERS > PEDDER

PEDDLE vb sell (goods) from door to door

PEDDLED > PEDDLE

PEDDLER same as > PEDLAR

PEDDLERS > PEDDLER

PEDDLERY n business of peddler

PEDDLES > PEDDLE

PEDDLING > PEDDLE

PEDDLINGS > PEDDLE

PEDERAST n man who has sexual relations with boys

PEDERASTS > PEDERAST

PEDERASTY n sexual relations between men and boys

PEDERERO n type of cannon

PEDEREROS > PEDERERO

PEDES > PES

PEDESES > PEDESIS

PEDESIS n random motion of small particles

PEDESTAL n base supporting a column, statue, etc

PEDESTALS > PEDESTAL

PEDETIC adj of feet

PEDI n pedicure

PEDIATRIC adj of or relating to the medical science of children and their diseases

PEDICAB n pedal-operated tricycle, available for hire

PEDICABS > PEDICAB

PEDICEL n stalk bearing a single flower of an inflorescence

PEDICELS > PEDICEL

PEDICLE n any small stalk

PEDICLED > PEDICLE

PEDICLES > PEDICLE

PEDICULAR adj relating to, infested with, or caused by lice

PEDICULI > PEDICULUS

PEDICULUS n wingless parasite

PEDICURE n medical or cosmetic treatment of the feet ▷ vb give a pedicure

PEDICURED > PEDICURE

PEDICURES > PEDICURE

PEDIFORM adj shaped like a foot

PEDIGREE n register of ancestors, esp of a purebred animal

PEDIGREED > PEDIGREE

PEDIGREES > PEDIGREE

PEDIMENT n triangular part over a door etc

PEDIMENTS > PEDIMENT

PEDIPALP n either member of the second pair of head appendages of arachnids

PEDIPALPI > PEDIPALP

PEDIPALPS > PEDIPALP

PEDIS > PEDI

PEDLAR n person who sells goods from door to door

PEDLARIES > PEDLARY

PEDLARS > PEDLAR

PEDLARY same as > PEDLERY

PEDLER same as > PEDLAR

PEDLERIES > PEDLERY

PEDLERS > PEDLER

PEDLERY n business of pedler

PEDOCAL n type of soil that is rich in lime

PEDOCALIC > PEDOCAL

PEDOCALS > PEDOCAL

PEDOGENIC adj relating to soil

PEDOLOGIC > PEDOLOGY

PEDOLOGY same as > PAEDOLOGY

PEDOMETER n instrument which measures the distance walked

PEDOPHILE n person who is sexually attracted to children

PEDORTHIC adj (of footwear) designed to alleviate foot problems

PEDRAIL n device replacing wheel on rough surfaces

PEDRAILS > PEDRAIL

PEDRERO n type of cannon

PEDREROES > PEDRERO

PEDREROS > PEDRERO

PEDRO n card game

PEDROS > PEDRO

PEDS > PED

PEDUNCLE same as > PEDICEL

PEDUNCLED > PEDUNCLE

PEDUNCLES > PEDUNCLE

PEDWAY n walkway for pedestrians only

PEDWAYS > PEDWAY

PEE vb urinate ▷ n urine

PEEBEEN n type of large evergreen

PEEBEENS > PEEBEEN

PEECE obsolete variant of > PIECE

PEECES > PEECE

PEED > PEE

PEEING > PEE

PEEK n peep or glance ▷ vb glance quickly or secretly

PEEKABO same as > PEEKABOO

PEEKABOO n game in which one person hides his or her face and suddenly reveals it ▷ adj made of fabric that is almost transparent

PEEKABOOS > PEEKABOO

PEEKABOS > PEEKABO

PEEKAPOO n cross between a Pekingese and a poodle

PEEKAPOOS > PEEKAPOO

PEEKED > PEEK

PEEKING > PEEK

PEEKS > PEEK

PEEL vb remove the skin or rind of (a vegetable or fruit) ▷ n rind or skin

PEELABLE > PEEL

PEELED > PEEL

PEELER n device for peeling vegetables, fruit, etc

PEELERS > PEELER

PEELING n strip that has been peeled off

PEELINGS > PEELING

PEELS > PEEL

PEEN n end of a hammer head opposite the striking face ▷ vb strike with the peen of a hammer

PEENED > PEEN

PEENGE vb complain

PEENGED > PEENGE

PEENGEING > PEENGE

PEENGES > PEENGE

PEENGING > PEENGE

PEENING n act of peening

PEENINGS > PEENING

PEENS > PEEN

PEEOY n homemade firework

PEEOYS > PEEOY

PEEP vb look slyly or quickly ▷ n peeping look

PEEPBO n game of peekaboo

PEEPBOS > PEEPBO

PEEPE old spelling of > PIP

PEEPED > PEEP

PEEPER n person who peeps

PEEPERS > PEEPER

PEEPES archaic spelling of > PEEPS

PEEPHOLE n small aperture for observation

PEEPHOLES > PEEPHOLE

PEEPING > PEEP

PEEPS > PEEP

PEEPSHOW n box containing a series of pictures that can be seen through a small hole

PEEPSHOWS > PEEPSHOW

PEEPTOE adj of a shoe in which the toe is not covered

PEEPUL n Indian moraceous tree

PEEPULS > PEEPUL

PEER n (in Britain) member of the nobility ▷ vb look closely and intently

PEERAGE n whole body of peers

PEERAGES > PEERAGE

PEERED > PEER

PEERESS n (in Britain) woman holding the rank of a peer

PEERESSES > PEERESS

PEERIE n spinning top ▷ adj small

PEERIER > PEERIE

PEERIES > PEERIE

PEERIEST > PEERIE

PEERING > PEER

PEERLESS adj unequalled, unsurpassed

PEERS > PEER

PEERY n child's spinning top

PEES > PEE

PEESWEEP n early spring storm

PEESWEEPS > PEESWEEP

PEETWEET n spotted sandpiper

PEETWEETS > PEETWEET

PEEVE vb irritate or annoy ▷ n something that irritates

PEEVED > PEEVE

PEEVER n hopscotch

PEEVERS > PEEVER

PEEVES > PEEVE

PEEVING > PEEVE

PEEVISH adj fretful or irritable

PEEVISHLY > PEEVISH

PEEWEE same as > PEWEE

PEEWEES > PEEWEE

PEEWIT same as > LAPWING

PEEWITS > PEEWIT

PEG n pin or clip for joining, fastening, marking, etc ▷ vb fasten with pegs

PEGASUS n winged horse

PEGASUSES > PEGASUS

PEGBOARD n board with holes into which pegs can be fitted

PEGBOARDS > PEGBOARD

PEGBOX n part of stringed instrument that holds tuning pegs

PEGBOXES > PEGBOX

PEGGED > PEG

PEGGIER > PEGGY

PEGGIES > PEGGY

PEGGIEST > PEGGY

PEGGING > PEG

PEGGINGS > PEG

p

PEGGY n type of small warbler ▷ adj resembling a peg

PEGH variant of > PECH

PEGHED > PEGH

PEGHING > PEGH

PEGHS > PEGH

PEGLEGGED adj having a wooden leg

PEGLESS > PEG

PEGLIKE > PEG

PEGMATITE n exceptionally coarse-grained intrusive igneous rock

PEGS > PEG

PEGTOP n type of spinning top

PEGTOPS > PEGTOP

PEH same as > PE

PEHS > PEH

PEIGNOIR n woman's light dressing gown

PEIGNOIRS > PEIGNOIR

PEIN same as > PEEN

PEINCT vb paint

PEINCTED > PEINCT

PEINCTING > PEINCT

PEINCTS > PEINCT

PEINED > PEIN

PEINING > PEIN

PEINS > PEIN

PEIRASTIC adj experimental

PEISE same as > PEIZE

PEISED > PEISE

PEISES > PEISE

PEISHWA n Indian leader

PEISHWAH same as > PEISHWA

PEISHWAHS > PEISHWAH

PEISHWAS > PEISHWA

PEISING > PEISE

PEIZE vb weight or poise

PEIZED > PEIZE

PEIZES > PEIZE

PEIZING > PEIZE

PEJORATE vb change for the worse

PEJORATED > PEJORATE

PEJORATES > PEJORATE

PEKAN n large North American marten

PEKANS > PEKAN

PEKE n Pekingese dog

PEKEPOO same as > PEEKAPOO

PEKEPOOS > PEKEPOO

PEKES > PEKE

PEKIN n silk fabric

PEKINS > PEKIN

PEKOE n high-quality tea

PEKOES > PEKOE

PEL n pixel

PELA n insect living on wax

PELAGE n coat of a mammal, consisting of hair, wool, fur, etc

PELAGES > PELAGE

PELAGIAL adj of the open sea ▷ n open body of water such as a lake or the sea

PELAGIALS > PELAGIAL

PELAGIAN adj of or inhabiting the open sea ▷ n pelagic creature

PELAGIANS > PELAGIAN

PELAGIC adj of or relating to the open sea ▷ n any pelagic creature

PELAGICS > PELAGIC

PELAS > PELA

PELAU n dish made with meat, rice, and pigeon peas

PELAUS > PELAU

PELE Spenserian variant of > PEAL

PELECYPOD another word for > BIVALVE

PELERINE n woman's narrow cape with long pointed ends in front

PELERINES > PELERINE

PELES > PELE

PELF n money or wealth

PELFS > PELF

PELHAM n horse's bit for a double bridle

PELHAMS > PELHAM

PELICAN n large water bird with a pouch beneath its bill

PELICANS > PELICAN

PELISSE n cloak or loose coat which is usually fur-trimmed

PELISSES > PELISSE

PELITE n any argillaceous rock such as shale

PELITES > PELITE

PELITIC > PELITE

PELL n hide of an animal ▷ vb hit violently

PELLACH same as > PELLACK

PELLACHS > PELLACH

PELLACK n porpoise

PELLACKS > PELLACK

PELLAGRA n disease caused by lack of vitamin B

PELLAGRAS > PELLAGRA

PELLAGRIN n person with pellagra

PELLED > PELL

PELLET n small ball of something ▷ vb strike with pellets

PELLETAL > PELLET

PELLETED > PELLET

PELLETIFY vb shape into pellets

PELLETING > PELLET

PELLETISE vb shape into pellets

PELLETIZE vb shape into pellets

PELLETS > PELLET

PELLICLE n thin skin or film

PELLICLES > PELLICLE

PELLING > PELL

PELLITORY n urticaceous plant

PELLMELL n disorder

PELLMELLS > PELLMELL

PELLOCK n porpoise

PELLOCKS > PELLOCK

PELLS > PELL

PELLUCID adj very clear

PELLUM n dust

PELLUMS > PELLUM

PELMA n sole of the foot

PELMANISM n memory card game

PELMAS > PELMA

PELMATIC > PELMA

PELMET n ornamental drapery or board, concealing a curtain rail

PELMETS > PELMET

PELOID n mud used therapeutically

PELOIDS > PELOID

PELOLOGY n study of therapeutic uses of mud

PELON adj hairless ▷ n hairless person or animal

PELONS > PELON

PELORIA n abnormal production of flowers in a plant

PELORIAN > PELORIA

PELORIAS > PELORIA

PELORIC > PELORIA

PELORIES > PELORY

PELORISED adj affected by peloria

PELORISM n floral mutation

PELORISMS > PELORISM

PELORIZED same as > PELORISED

PELORUS n sighting device

PELORUSES > PELORUS

PELORY n floral mutation

PELOTA n game where players propel a ball against a wall

PELOTAS > PELOTA

PELOTON n main field of riders in a bicycle road race

PELOTONS > PELOTON

PELS > PEL

PELT vb throw missiles at ▷ n skin of a fur-bearing animal

PELTA n small ancient shield

PELTAE > PELTA

PELTAS > PELTA

PELTAST n (in ancient Greece) lightly armed foot soldier

PELTASTS > PELTAST

PELTATE adj (of leaves) having the stalk attached to the centre of the lower surface

PELTATELY > PELTATE

PELTATION > PELTATE

PELTED > PELT

PELTER vb rain heavily

PELTERED > PELTER

PELTERING > PELT

PELTERS > PELTER

PELTING > PELT

PELTINGLY > PELT

PELTINGS > PELT

PELTLESS > PELT

PELTRIES > PELTRY

PELTRY n pelts of animals collectively

PELTS > PELT

PELVES > PELVIS

PELVIC adj of, near, or relating to the pelvis ▷ n pelvic bone

PELVICS > PELVIC

PELVIFORM adj shaped like pelvis

PELVIS n framework of bones at the base of the spine

PELVISES > PELVIS

PEMBINA n type of cranberry

PEMBINAS > PEMBINA

PEMBROKE n small table

PEMBROKES > PEMBROKE

PEMICAN same as > PEMMICAN

PEMICANS > PEMICAN

PEMMICAN n pressed cake of meat with fat and berries or dried fruits

PEMMICANS > PEMMICAN

PEMOLINE n mild stimulant

PEMOLINES > PEMOLINE

PEMPHIGI > PEMPHIGUS

PEMPHIGUS n any of a group of blistering skin diseases

PEMPHIX n type of crustacean

PEMPHIXES > PEMPHIX

PEN n instrument for writing in ink ▷ vb write or compose

PENAL adj of or used in punishment

PENALISE same as > PENALIZE

PENALISED > PENALISE

PENALISES > PENALISE

PENALITY > PENAL

PENALIZE vb impose a penalty on

PENALIZED > PENALIZE

PENALIZES > PENALIZE

PENALLY > PENAL

PENALTIES > PENALTY

PENALTY n punishment for a crime or offence

PENANCE n voluntary self-punishment ▷ vb impose a penance upon (a sinner)

PENANCED > PENANCE

PENANCES > PENANCE

PENANCING > PENANCE

PENANG variant of > PINANG

PENANGS > PENANG

PENATES pl n household gods

PENCE > PENNY

PENCEL n small pennon

PENCELS > PENCEL
PENCES > PENNY
PENCHANT n inclination or liking
PENCHANTS > PENCHANT
PENCIL n thin cylindrical instrument for writing or drawing ▷ vb draw, write, or mark with a pencil
PENCILED > PENCIL
PENCILER > PENCIL
PENCILERS > PENCIL
PENCILING > PENCIL
PENCILLED > PENCIL
PENCILLER > PENCIL
PENCILS > PENCIL
PENCRAFT n skill in writing
PENCRAFTS > PENCRAFT
PEND vb await judgment or settlement ▷ n archway or vaulted passage
PENDANT n ornament worn on a chain round the neck
PENDANTLY > PENDANT
PENDANTS > PENDANT
PENDED > PEND
PENDENCY > PENDENT
PENDENT adj hanging ▷ n pendant
PENDENTLY > PENDENT
PENDENTS > PENDENT
PENDICLE n something dependent on another
PENDICLER n person who rents a croft
PENDICLES > PENDICLE
PENDING prep while waiting for ▷ adj not yet decided or settled
PENDRAGON n supreme war chief or leader of the ancient Britons
PENDS > PEND
PENDU adj in informal Indian English, culturally backward
PENDULAR adj pendulous
PENDULATE vb swing as pendulum
PENDULE n type of climbing manoeuvre
PENDULES > PENDULE
PENDULINE adj building nests that hang down
PENDULOUS adj hanging, swinging
PENDULUM same as > PENDULE
PENDULUMS > PENDULUM
PENE variant of > PEEN
PENED > PENE
PENEPLAIN n relatively flat land surface produced by a long period of erosion
PENEPLANE same as > PENEPLAIN
PENES > PENIS
PENETRANT adj sharp ▷ n substance that lowers the surface tension of a liquid and thus causes it to penetrate or be absorbed more easily

PENETRATE vb find or force a way into or through
PENFOLD same as > PINFOLD
PENFOLDS > PENFOLD
PENFRIEND n person with whom one regularly exchanges letters
PENFUL n contents of pen
PENFULS > PENFUL
PENGO n former monetary unit of Hungary
PENGOS > PENGO
PENGUIN n flightless black-and-white sea bird
PENGUINRY n breeding place of penguins
PENGUINS > PENGUIN
PENHOLDER n container for pens
PENI old spelling of > PENNY
PENIAL > PENIS
PENICIL n small pad for wounds
PENICILLI n plural of penicillus, small pad for wounds
PENICILS > PENICIL
PENIE old spelling of > PENNY
PENIES > PENIE
PENILE adj of or relating to the penis
PENILL > PENILLION
PENILLION pl n Welsh art or practice of singing poetry in counterpoint to a traditional melody played on the harp
PENING > PENE
PENINSULA n strip of land nearly surrounded by water
PENIS n organ of copulation and urination in male mammals
PENISES > PENIS
PENISTONE n coarse woollen cloth
PENITENCE > PENITENT
PENITENCY > PENITENT
PENITENT adj feeling sorry for having done wrong ▷ n someone who is penitent
PENITENTS > PENITENT
PENK n small fish
PENKNIFE n small knife with a blade that folds into the handle
PENKNIVES > PENKNIFE
PENKS > PENK
PENLIGHT n small thin flashlight
PENLIGHTS > PENLIGHT
PENLIKE adj like a pen
PENLITE same as > PENLIGHT
PENLITES > PENLITE
PENMAN n person skilled in handwriting

PENMEN > PENMAN
PENNA n large feather
PENNAE > PENNA
PENNAL n first-year student of Protestant university
PENNALISM n menial choring at college
PENNALS > PENNAL
PENNAME n author's pseudonym
PENNAMES > PENNAME
PENNANT same as > PENDANT
PENNANTS > PENNANT
PENNATE adj having feathers, wings, or winglike structures
PENNATED same as > PENNATE
PENNATULA n sea pen
PENNE n pasta in the form of short tubes
PENNED > PEN
PENNEECH n card game
PENNEECHS > PENNEECH
PENNEECK same as > PENNEECH
PENNEECKS > PENNEECK
PENNER n person who writes
PENNERS > PENNER
PENNES > PENNE
PENNI n former Finnish monetary unit
PENNIA > PENNI
PENNIED adj having money
PENNIES > PENNY
PENNIFORM adj shaped like a feather
PENNILESS adj very poor
PENNILL n stanza in a Welsh poem
PENNINE n mineral found in the Pennine Alps
PENNINES > PENNINE
PENNING > PEN
PENNINITE n bluish-green variety of chlorite occurring in the form of thick crystals
PENNIS > PENNI
PENNON n triangular or tapering flag
PENNONCEL n small narrow flag
PENNONED adj equipped with a pennon
PENNONS > PENNON
PENNY n coin worth one hundredth of a pound
PENNYBOY n employee whose duties include menial tasks, such as running errands
PENNYBOYS > PENNYBOY
PENNYFEE n small payment
PENNYFEES > PENNYFEE
PENNYLAND n old Scottish division of land
PENNYWISE adj careful with small amounts of money

PENNYWORT n Eurasian rock plant with whitish-green tubular flowers and rounded leaves
PENOCHE n type of fudge
PENOCHES > PENOCHE
PENOLOGY n study of punishment and prison management
PENONCEL n small narrow flag
PENONCELS > PENONCEL
PENPOINT n tip of pen
PENPOINTS > PENPOINT
PENPUSHER n person whose work involves a lot of boring paperwork
PENS > PEN
PENSEE n thought put down on paper
PENSEES > PENSEE
PENSEL same as > PENCEL
PENSELS > PENSEL
PENSEROSO n pensive person
PENSIL same as > PENCEL
PENSILE adj designating or building a hanging nest
PENSILITY > PENSILE
PENSILS > PENSIL
PENSION n regular payment to people above a certain age, etc ▷ vb grant a pension to
PENSIONE n Italian boarding house
PENSIONED > PENSION
PENSIONER n person receiving a pension
PENSIONES > PENSIONE
PENSIONI > PENSIONE
PENSIONS > PENSION
PENSIVE adj deeply thoughtful, often with a tinge of sadness
PENSIVELY > PENSIVE
PENSTEMON n North American flowering plant with five stamens
PENSTER n writer
PENSTERS > PENSTER
PENSTOCK n conduit that supplies water to a hydroelectric power plant
PENSTOCKS > PENSTOCK
PENSUM n school exercise
PENSUMS > PENSUM
PENT n penthouse
PENTACLE same as > PENTAGRAM
PENTACLES > PENTACLE
PENTACT n sponge spicule with five rays
PENTACTS > PENTACT
PENTAD n group or series of five
PENTADIC > PENTAD
PENTADS > PENTAD
PENTAGON n geometric figure with five sides

P

PENTAGONS
> PENTAGON
PENTAGRAM n
five-pointed star
PENTALOGY n
combination of five closely
related symptoms
PENTALPHA n
five-pointed star
PENTAMERY n state of
consisting of five parts
PENTANE n alkane
hydrocarbon with three
isomers
PENTANES > PENTANE
PENTANGLE same as
> PENTAGRAM
PENTANOIC adj as in
pentanoic acid colourless
liquid carboxylic acid
PENTANOL n colourless
oily liquid
PENTANOLS
> PENTANOL
PENTAPODY n series or
measure of five feet
PENTARCH n member of
pentarchy
PENTARCHS
> PENTARCH
PENTARCHY n
government by five rulers
PENTATHLA n
pentathlons
PENTEL n type of pen
PENTELS > PENTEL
PENTENE n colourless
flammable liquid alkene
PENTENES > PENTENE
PENTHIA n child born
fifth
PENTHIAS > PENTHIA
PENTHOUSE n flat built
on the roof or top floor of a
building
PENTICE vb
accommodate in a
penthouse
PENTICED > PENTICE
PENTICES > PENTICE
PENTICING > PENTICE
PENTISE same as
> PENTICE
PENTISED > PENTISE
PENTISES > PENTISE
PENTISING > PENTISE
PENTITI > PENTITO
PENTITO n criminal who
offers information to the
police
PENTODE n electronic
valve having five
electrodes
PENTODES > PENTODE
PENTOMIC adj denoting
the subdivision of a military
division into five battle
groups
PENTOSAN n
polysaccharide occurring
in plants, humus, etc
PENTOSANE same as
> PENTOSAN
PENTOSANS
> PENTOSAN
PENTOSE n
monosaccharide
containing five atoms of
carbon per molecule

PENTOSES > PENTOSE
PENTOSIDE n compound
containing sugar
PENTOXIDE n oxide of an
element with five atoms of
oxygen per molecule
PENTROOF n lean-to
PENTROOFS
> PENTROOF
PENTS > PENT
PENTYL n one of a
particular chemical group
PENTYLENE n type of
chemical
PENTYLS > PENTYL
PENUCHE same as
> PANOCHA
PENUCHES > PENUCHE
PENUCHI same as
> PANOCHA
PENUCHIS > PENUCHI
PENUCHLE same as
> PINOCHLE
PENUCHLES
> PENUCHLE
PENUCKLE same as
> PENUCHLE
PENUCKLES
> PENUCKLE
PENULT n last syllable but
one in a word
PENULTIMA same as
> PENULT
PENULTS > PENULT
PENUMBRA n (in an
eclipse) partially
shadowed region which
surrounds the full shadow
PENUMBRAE
> PENUMBRA
PENUMBRAL
> PENUMBRA
PENUMBRAS
> PENUMBRA
PENURIES > PENURY
PENURIOUS adj
niggardly with money
PENURY n extreme
poverty
PENWIPER n something
for cleaning the ink from a
pen
PENWIPERS
> PENWIPER
PENWOMAN n female
writer
PENWOMEN > PENWOMAN
PEON n Spanish-American
farm labourer or unskilled
worker
PEONAGE n state of being
a peon
PEONAGES > PEONAGE
PEONES > PEON
PEONIES > PEONY
PEONISM same as
> PEONAGE
PEONISMS > PEONISM
PEONS > PEON
PEONY n garden plant
PEOPLE pl n persons
generally ▷ vb provide
with inhabitants
PEOPLED > PEOPLE
PEOPLER n settler
PEOPLERS > PEOPLER
PEOPLES > PEOPLE
PEOPLING > PEOPLE

PEP n high spirits, energy,
or enthusiasm ▷ vb liven
by imbuing with new
vigour
PEPERINO n type of
volcanic rock
PEPERINOS
> PEPERINO
PEPEROMIA n plant from
tropical and subtropical
America with slightly
fleshy ornamental leaves
PEPERONI same as
> PEPPERONI
PEPERONIS
> PEPPERONI
PEPFUL adj full of vitality
PEPINO n purple-striped
yellow fruit
PEPINOS > PEPINO
PEPITA n edible dried
seed of a squash
PEPITAS > PEPITA
PEPLA > PEPLUM
PEPLOS n part of a
woman's attire in ancient
Greece
PEPLOSES > PEPLOS
PEPLUM same as
> PEPLOS
PEPLUMED > PEPLUM
PEPLUMS > PEPLUM
PEPLUS same as
> PEPLOS
PEPLUSES > PEPLUS
PEPO n fruit such as the
melon, squash, cucumber,
or pumpkin
PEPONIDA variant of
> PEPO
PEPONIDAS > PEPO
PEPONIUM variant of
> PEPO
PEPONIUMS
> PEPONIUM
PEPOS > PEPO
PEPPED > PEP
PEPPER n sharp hot
condiment ▷ vb season
with pepper
PEPPERBOX n container
for pepper
PEPPERED > PEPPER
PEPPERER > PEPPER
PEPPERERS > PEPPER
PEPPERIER > PEPPERY
PEPPERING > PEPPER
PEPPERONI n dry
sausage of pork and beef
spiced with pepper
PEPPERS > PEPPER
PEPPERY adj tasting of
pepper
PEPPIER > PEPPY
PEPPIEST > PEPPY
PEPPILY > PEPPY
PEPPINESS > PEPPY
PEPPING > PEP
PEPPY adj full of vitality
PEPS > PEP
PEPSI n (trademark)
brand of soft drink
PEPSIN n enzyme
produced in the stomach
PEPSINATE vb treat (a
patient) with pepsin
PEPSINE same as
> PEPSIN

PEPSINES > PEPSINE
PEPSINS > PEPSIN
PEPSIS > PEPSI
PEPTALK n talk meant to
inspire ▷ vb give a peptalk
to
PEPTALKED > PEPTALK
PEPTALKS > PEPTALK
PEPTIC adj relating to
digestion or the digestive
juices ▷ n substance that
aids digestion
PEPTICITY > PEPTIC
PEPTICS > PEPTIC
PEPTID variant of
> PEPTIDE
PEPTIDASE n any of a
group of proteolytic
enzymes that hydrolyse
peptides to amino acids
PEPTIDE n organic
chemical compound
PEPTIDES > PEPTIDE
PEPTIDIC adj of
peptides
PEPTIDS > PEPTID
PEPTISE same as
> PEPTIZE
PEPTISED > PEPTISE
PEPTISER > PEPTISE
PEPTISERS > PEPTISE
PEPTISES > PEPTISE
PEPTISING > PEPTISE
PEPTIZE vb disperse into
a colloidal state
PEPTIZED > PEPTIZE
PEPTIZER > PEPTIZE
PEPTIZERS > PEPTIZE
PEPTIZES > PEPTIZE
PEPTIZING > PEPTIZE
PEPTONE n any of a group
of organic compounds
PEPTONES > PEPTONE
PEPTONIC > PEPTONE
PEPTONISE same as
> PEPTONIZE
PEPTONIZE vb hydrolyse
(a protein) to peptones by
enzymic action, esp by
pepsin or pancreatic
extract
PEQUISTE n in Canada,
member or supporter of
the Parti Québécois
PEQUISTES
> PEQUISTE
PER prep for each
PERACID n acid in which
the element forming the
acid radical exhibits its
highest valency
PERACIDS > PERACID
PERACUTE adj very acute
PERAEA > PERAEON
PERAEON same as
> PEREION
PERAEONS > PERAEON
PERAEOPOD same as
> PEREIOPOD
PERAI another name for
> PIRANHA
PERAIS > PERAI
PERBORATE n salt
derived, or apparently
derived, from perboric acid
PERBORIC adj as in
perboric acid, a
hypothetical acid

PERC n perchloride
PERCALE n close-textured woven cotton fabric
PERCALES > PERCALE
PERCALINE n fine light cotton fabric, used esp for linings
PERCASE adv perchance
PERCE obsolete word for > PIERCE
PERCEABLE adj pierceable
PERCEANT adj piercing
PERCED > PERCE
PERCEIVE vb become aware of (something) through the senses
PERCEIVED > PERCEIVE
PERCEIVER > PERCEIVE
PERCEIVES > PERCEIVE
PERCEN > PERCE
PERCENT n percentage or proportion
PERCENTAL > PERCENT
PERCENTS > PERCENT
PERCEPT n concept that depends on recognition of some external object or phenomenon
PERCEPTS > PERCEPT
PERCES > PERCE
PERCH n resting place for a bird ▷ vb alight, rest, or place on or as if on a perch
PERCHANCE adv perhaps
PERCHED > PERCH
PERCHER > PERCH
PERCHERON n compact heavy breed of carthorse
PERCHERS > PERCH
PERCHERY n barn in which hens are allowed to move without restriction
PERCHES > PERCH
PERCHING > PERCH
PERCHINGS > PERCH
PERCID n type of freshwater fish
PERCIDS > PERCID
PERCIFORM n perch-like fish ▷ adj of perch-like fish
PERCINE adj of perches ▷ n type of perch-like fish
PERCINES > PERCINE
PERCING > PERCE
PERCOCT adj well-cooked ▷ vb cook thoroughly
PERCOCTED > PERCOCT
PERCOCTS > PERCOCT
PERCOID n type of spiny-finned teleost fish
PERCOIDS > PERCOID
PERCOLATE vb pass or filter through small holes ▷ n product of percolation
PERCOLIN n pain-relieving drug
PERCOLINS > PERCOLIN
PERCS > PERC
PERCUSS vb strike sharply, rapidly, or suddenly

PERCUSSED > PERCUSS
PERCUSSES > PERCUSS
PERCUSSOR > PERCUSS
PERDENDO adj (of music) getting gradually quieter and slower
PERDIE adv certainly
PERDITION n spiritual ruin
PERDU adj (of a soldier) placed on hazardous sentry duty ▷ n soldier placed on hazardous sentry duty
PERDUE same as > PERDU
PERDUES > PERDUE
PERDURE vb last for long time
PERDURED > PERDURE
PERDURES > PERDURE
PERDURING > PERDURE
PERDUS > PERDU
PERDY adv certainly
PERE n addition to a French surname to specify the father
PEREA > PEREON
PEREGAL adj equal ▷ n equal
PEREGALS > PEREGAL
PEREGRIN variant spelling of > PEREGRINE
PEREGRINE adj coming from abroad
PEREGRINS > PEREGRIN
PEREIA > PEREION
PEREION n thorax of some crustaceans
PEREIONS > PEREION
PEREIOPOD n appendage of the pereion
PEREIRA n bark of a South American apocynaceous tree
PEREIRAS > PEREIRA
PERENNATE vb (of plants) live from one growing season to another
PERENNIAL adj lasting through many years ▷ n plant lasting more than two years
PERENNITY n state of being perennial
PERENTIE n large dark-coloured Australian monitor lizard
PERENTIES > PERENTY
PERENTY same as > PERENTIE
PEREON same as > PEREION
PEREONS > PEREON
PEREOPOD same as > PEREIOPOD
PEREOPODS > PEREOPOD
PERES > PERE
PERFAY interj by my faith
PERFECT adj having all the essential elements ▷ n perfect tense ▷ vb improve
PERFECTA n bet on the order of the first and second in a race

PERFECTAS > PERFECTA
PERFECTED > PERFECT
PERFECTER same as > PERFECTOR
PERFECTI n ascetic group of elite Cathars
PERFECTLY adv completely, utterly, or absolutely
PERFECTO n large cigar that is tapered from both ends
PERFECTOR n person who completes or makes something perfect
PERFECTOS > PERFECTO
PERFECTS > PERFECT
PERFERVID adj extremely ardent, enthusiastic, or zealous
PERFERVOR n zealous person
PERFET obsolete variant of > PERFECT
PERFIDIES > PERFIDY
PERFIDY n perfidious act
PERFIN former name for > SPIF
PERFING n practice of taking early retirement from the police force
PERFINGS > PERFING
PERFINS > PERFIN
PERFORANS adj perforating or penetrating
PERFORANT adj perforating
PERFORATE vb make holes in ▷ adj pierced by small holes
PERFORCE adv of necessity
PERFORM vb carry out (an action)
PERFORMED > PERFORM
PERFORMER > PERFORM
PERFORMS > PERFORM
PERFUME n liquid cosmetic worn for its pleasant smell ▷ vb give a pleasant smell to
PERFUMED > PERFUME
PERFUMER n person who makes or sells perfume
PERFUMERS > PERFUMER
PERFUMERY n perfumes in general
PERFUMES > PERFUME
PERFUMIER same as > PERFUMER
PERFUMING > PERFUME
PERFUMY adj like perfume
PERFUSATE n fluid flowing through tissue or organ
PERFUSE vb permeate through or over
PERFUSED > PERFUSE
PERFUSES > PERFUSE
PERFUSING > PERFUSE
PERFUSION > PERFUSE
PERFUSIVE > PERFUSE
PERGOLA n framework of trellis supporting climbing plants

PERGOLAS > PERGOLA
PERGUNNAH same as > PARGANA
PERHAPS adv possibly, maybe ▷ sentence substitute it may happen, be so, etc ▷ n something that might have happened
PERHAPSES > PERHAPS
PERI n (in Persian folklore) one of a race of beautiful supernatural beings
PERIAGUA n dugout canoe
PERIAGUAS > PERIAGUA
PERIAKTOI > PERIAKTOS
PERIAKTOS n ancient device for changing theatre scenery
PERIANTH n outer part of a flower
PERIANTHS > PERIANTH
PERIAPSES > PERIAPSIS
PERIAPSIS n closest point to a central body reached by a body in orbit
PERIAPT n charm or amulet
PERIAPTS > PERIAPT
PERIBLAST n tissue surrounding blastoderm in meroblastic eggs
PERIBLEM n layer of meristematic tissue in stems and roots that gives rise to the cortex
PERIBLEMS > PERIBLEM
PERIBOLI > PERIBOLOS
PERIBOLOI > PERIBOLOS
PERIBOLOS n enclosed court surrounding ancient temple
PERIBOLUS same as > PERIBOLOS
PERICARP n part of a fruit enclosing the seed that develops from the wall of the ovary
PERICARPS > PERICARP
PERICLASE n mineral consisting of magnesium oxide in the form of isometric crystals or grains
PERICLINE n white translucent variety of albite in the form of elongated crystals
PERICON n Argentinian dance
PERICONES > PERICON
PERICOPAE > PERICOPE
PERICOPAL > PERICOPE
PERICOPE n selection from a book, esp a passage from the Bible read at religious services
PERICOPES > PERICOPE

p

PERICOPIC
> PERICOPE
PERICYCLE n layer of plant tissue beneath the endodermis
PERIDERM n outer corky protective layer of woody stems and roots
PERIDERMS
> PERIDERM
PERIDIA > PERIDIUM
PERIDIAL > PERIDIUM
PERIDINIA n genus of flagellate organisms
PERIDIUM n distinct outer layer of the spore-bearing organ in many fungi
PERIDIUMS
> PERIDIUM
PERIDOT n pale green transparent gemstone
PERIDOTE same as
> PERIDOT
PERIDOTES
> PERIDOTE
PERIDOTIC > PERIDOT
PERIDOTS > PERIDOT
PERIDROME n space between the columns and inner room of a classical temple
PERIGEAL > PERIGEE
PERIGEAN > PERIGEE
PERIGEE n point in the orbit of the moon or a satellite that is nearest the earth
PERIGEES > PERIGEE
PERIGON n angle of 360°
PERIGONE n part enclosing the essential organs of a flower
PERIGONES
> PERIGONE
PERIGONIA n perigones
PERIGONS > PERIGON
PERIGYNY n condition of having the stamens and other floral parts at the same level as the carpels
PERIHELIA n points in the orbits of planets at which they are nearest the sun
PERIKARYA n parts of nerve cells that contain the nuclei
PERIL n great danger ▷ vb expose to danger
PERILED > PERIL
PERILING > PERIL
PERILLA n type of mint
PERILLAS > PERILLA
PERILLED > PERIL
PERILLING > PERIL
PERILOUS adj very hazardous and dangerous
PERILS > PERIL
PERILUNE n point in a lunar orbit when a spacecraft launched from the moon is nearest the moon
PERILUNES
> PERILUNE
PERILYMPH n fluid filling the space between the membranous and bony

labyrinths of the internal ear
PERIMETER n outer edge of an area
PERIMETRY
> PERIMETER
PERIMORPH n mineral that encloses another mineral of a different type
PERIMYSIA n sheaths of fibrous connective tissue surrounding the primary bundles of muscle fibres
PERINAEUM same as
> PERINEUM
PERINATAL adj of or in the weeks shortly before or after birth
PERINEA > PERINEUM
PERINEAL > PERINEUM
PERINEUM n region of the body between the anus and the genitals
PERINEUMS
> PERINEUM
PERIOD n particular portion of time ▷ adj (of furniture, dress, a play, etc) dating from or in the style of an earlier time ▷ vb divide into periods
PERIODATE n any salt or ester of a periodic acid
PERIODED > PERIOD
PERIODIC adj recurring at intervals
PERIODID n kind of iodide
PERIODIDE variant of
> PERIODID
PERIODIDS
> PERIODID
PERIODING > PERIOD
PERIODISE same as
> PERIODIZE
PERIODIZE vb divide (a portion of time) into periods
PERIODS > PERIOD
PERIOST n thick fibrous two-layered membrane covering the surface of bones
PERIOSTEA
> PERIOSTS
PERIOSTS > PERIOST
PERIOTIC adj of or relating to the structures situated around the internal ear ▷ n periotic bone
PERIOTICS
> PERIOTIC
PERIPATUS n wormlike arthropod with a segmented body and short unjointed limbs
PERIPETIA n abrupt turn of events or reversal of circumstances
PERIPETY n abrupt turn of events or reversal of circumstances
PERIPHERY n boundary or edge
PERIPLASM n region inside wall of biological cell

PERIPLAST n nutritive and supporting tissue in animal organ
PERIPLUS n circumnavigation
PERIPROCT n tough membrane surrounding anus in echinoderms
PERIPTER n type of ancient temple
PERIPTERS
> PERIPTER
PERIPTERY n region surrounding moving body
PERIQUE n strong highly flavoured tobacco
PERIQUES > PERIQUE
PERIS > PERI
PERISARC n outer chitinous layer secreted by colonial hydrozoan coelenterates
PERISARCS
> PERISARC
PERISCIAN adj person whose shadow moves round every point of compass during day
PERISCOPE n instrument used, esp in submarines, to give a view of objects on a different level
PERISH vb be destroyed or die
PERISHED adj (of a person, part of the body, etc) extremely cold
PERISHER n mischievous person
PERISHERS
> PERISHER
PERISHES > PERISH
PERISHING adj very cold
PERISPERM n nutritive tissue surrounding the embryo in certain seeds, and developing from the nucellus of the ovule
PERISTOME n fringe of pointed teeth surrounding the opening of a moss capsule
PERISTYLE n colonnade that surrounds a court or building
PERITI > PERITUS
PERITONEA n thin translucent serous sacs that line the walls of abdominal cavities and cover the viscera
PERITRACK another name for > TAXIWAY
PERITRICH n ciliate protozoan in which the cilia are restricted to a spiral around the mouth
PERITUS n Catholic theology consultant
PERIWIG same as
> PERUKE
PERIWIGS > PERIWIG
PERJINK adj prim or finicky
PERJURE vb render (oneself) guilty of perjury
PERJURED adj having sworn falsely

PERJURER > PERJURE
PERJURERS > PERJURE
PERJURES > PERJURE
PERJURIES > PERJURY
PERJURING > PERJURY
PERJUROUS > PERJURY
PERJURY n act or crime of lying while under oath in a court
PERK n incidental benefit gained from a job, such as a company car ▷ adj pert ▷ vb (of coffee) percolate
PERKED > PERK
PERKIER > PERKY
PERKIEST > PERKY
PERKILY > PERKY
PERKIN same as
> PARKIN
PERKINESS > PERKY
PERKING > PERK
PERKINS > PERKIN
PERKISH adj perky
PERKS > PERK
PERKY adj lively or cheerful
PERLEMOEN n edible sea creature with a shell lined with mother of pearl
PERLITE n variety of obsidian
PERLITES > PERLITE
PERLITIC > PERLITE
PERLOUS same as
> PERILOUS
PERM n long-lasting curly hairstyle ▷ vb give (hair) a perm
PERMABEAR n an investor who consistently acts in the expectation that the value of stocks and shares will fall
PERMABULL n an investor who consistently acts in the expectation that the value of stocks and shares will rise
PERMALINK n permanent internet hyperlink
PERMALLOY n any of various alloys containing iron and nickel
PERMANENT adj lasting forever
PERMATAN n permanent tan, esp artificial
PERMATANS
> PERMATAN
PERMEABLE adj able to be permeated, esp by liquid
PERMEABLY
> PERMEABLE
PERMEANCE n act of permeating
PERMEANT
> PERMEANCE
PERMEANTS
> PERMEANCE
PERMEASE n carrier protein
PERMEASES
> PERMEASE
PERMEATE vb pervade or pass through the whole of (something)

PERMEATED
> PERMEATE
PERMEATES
> PERMEATE
PERMEATOR
> PERMEATE
PERMED > PERM
PERMIAN *adj* of,
denoting, or formed in the
last period of the
Palaeozoic era
PERMIE *n* person, esp an
office worker, employed
by a firm on a permanent
basis
PERMIES > PERMIE
PERMING > PERM
PERMIT *vb* give
permission, allow ▷ *n*
document giving
permission to do
something
PERMITS > PERMIT
PERMITTED > PERMIT
PERMITTEE *n* person
given a permit
PERMITTER > PERMIT
PERMS > PERM
PERMUTATE *vb* alter the
sequence or arrangement
(of)
PERMUTE *vb* change the
sequence of
PERMUTED > PERMUTE
PERMUTES > PERMUTE
PERMUTING > PERMUTE
PERN *n* type of buzzard
▷ *vb* spin
PERNANCY *n* receiving of
rents
PERNED > PERN
PERNING > PERN
PERNIO *n* chilblain
PERNIONES > PERNIO
PERNOD *n* aniseed-
flavoured aperitif from
France
PERNODS > PERNOD
PERNS > PERN
PEROG *same as* > PIROG
PEROGEN > PEROG
PEROGI *n* type of Polish
dumpling
PEROGIE *same as*
> PEROGI
PEROGIES > PEROGI
PEROGIS > PEROGI
PEROGS > PEROG
PEROGY *same as*
> PEROGI
PERONE *n* fibula
PERONEAL *adj* of or
relating to the fibula or the
outer side of the leg
PERONEI > PERONEUS
PERONES > PERONE
PERONEUS *n* lateral
muscle of the leg
PERORAL *adj*
administered through
mouth
PERORALLY > PERORAL
PERORATE *vb* speak at
length, esp in a formal
manner
PERORATED
> PERORATE
PERORATES > PERORATE

PERORATOR
> PERORATE
PEROVSKIA *n* Russian
sage
PEROXID *variant of*
> PEROXIDE
PEROXIDE *n* hydrogen
peroxide used as a hair
bleach ▷ *adj* bleached
with or resembling
peroxide ▷ *vb* bleach (the
hair) with peroxide
PEROXIDED
> PEROXIDE
PEROXIDES
> PEROXIDE
PEROXIDIC
> PEROXIDE
PEROXIDS > PEROXID
PEROXO *n* type of acid
PEROXY *adj* containing
the peroxide group
PERP *n* someone who has
committed a crime
PERPEND *n* large stone
that passes through a wall
from one side to the other
▷ *vb* ponder
PERPENDED > PERPEND
PERPENDS > PERPEND
PERPENT *same as*
> PERPEND
PERPENTS > PERPENT
PERPETUAL *adj* lasting
forever ▷ *n* (of a crop
plant) continually
producing edible parts
PERPLEX *vb* puzzle,
bewilder
PERPLEXED > PERPLEX
PERPLEXER > PERPLEX
PERPLEXES > PERPLEX
PERPS > PERP
PERRADIAL *adj* situated
around radii of radiate
PERRADII
> PERRADIUS
PERRADIUS *n* primary
tentacle of a polyp
PERRIER *n* short mortar
PERRIERS > PERRIER
PERRIES > PERRY
PERRON *n* external flight
of steps
PERRONS > PERRON
PERRUQUE *old spelling of*
> PERUKE
PERRUQUES
> PERRUQUE
PERRY *n* alcoholic drink
made from fermented
pears
PERSALT *n* any salt of a
peracid
PERSALTS > PERSALT
PERSANT *adj* piercing
PERSAUNT *adj* piercing
PERSE *old variant of*
> PIERCE
PERSECUTE *vb* treat
cruelly because of
ethnicity, religion, etc
PERSEITY *n* quality of
having substance
independently of real
objects
PERSELINE *same as*
> PURSLANE

PERSES > PERSE
PERSEVERE *vb* keep
making an effort despite
difficulties
PERSICO *same as*
> PERSICOT
PERSICOS > PERSICO
PERSICOT *n* cordial
made from apricots
PERSICOTS
> PERSICOT
PERSIENNE *n* printed
calico
PERSIMMON *n* sweet red
tropical fruit
PERSING > PERSE
PERSIST *vb* continue to
be or happen, last
PERSISTED > PERSIST
PERSISTER > PERSIST
PERSISTS > PERSIST
PERSON *n* human being
PERSONA *n* someone's
personality as presented
to others
PERSONAE > PERSONA
PERSONAGE *n* important
person
PERSONAL *adj* individual
or private ▷ *n* item of
movable property
PERSONALS
> PERSONAL
PERSONAS > PERSONA
PERSONATE *vb* assume
the identity of (another
person) with intent to
deceive ▷ *adj* (of the
corollas of certain flowers)
having two lips in the form
of a face
PERSONIFY *vb* give
human characteristics to
PERSONISE *same as*
> PERSONIZE
PERSONIZE *vb* personify
PERSONNED *adj* manned
PERSONNEL *n* people
employed in an
organization
PERSONS > PERSON
PERSPEX *n* any of various
clear acrylic resins
PERSPEXES > PERSPEX
PERSPIRE *vb* sweat
PERSPIRED
> PERSPIRE
PERSPIRES
> PERSPIRE
PERSPIRY *adj* perspiring
PERST *adj* perished
PERSUADE *vb* make
(someone) do something
by argument, charm, etc
PERSUADED
> PERSUADE
PERSUADER
> PERSUADE
PERSUADES
> PERSUADE
PERSUE *obsolete form of*
> PURSUE
PERSUED > PERSUE
PERSUES > PERSUE
PERSUING > PERSUE
PERSWADE *obsolete form of*
> PERSUADE
PERSWADED > PERSWADE

PERSWADES
> PERSWADE
PERT *adj* saucy and
cheeky ▷ *n* pert person
PERTAIN *vb* belong or be
relevant (to)
PERTAINED > PERTAIN
PERTAINS > PERTAIN
PERTAKE *obsolete form of*
> PARTAKE
PERTAKEN > PERTAKE
PERTAKES > PERTAKE
PERTAKING > PERTAKE
PERTER > PERT
PERTEST > PERT
PERTHITE *n* type of
feldspar
PERTHITES
> PERTHITE
PERTHITIC
> PERTHITE
PERTINENT *adj* relevant
PERTLY > PERT
PERTNESS > PERT
PERTOOK > PERTAKE
PERTS > PERT
PERTURB *vb* disturb
greatly
PERTURBED > PERTURB
PERTURBER > PERTURB
PERTURBS > PERTURB
PERTUSATE *adj* pierced
at apex
PERTUSE *adj* having
holes
PERTUSED *adj* having
holes
PERTUSION *n* punched
hole
PERTUSSAL
> PERTUSSIS
PERTUSSES
> PERTUSSIS
PERTUSSIS *n* whooping
cough
PERUKE *n* wig for men
worn in the 17th and 18th
centuries
PERUKED *adj* wearing wig
PERUKES > PERUKE
PERUSABLE > PERUSE
PERUSAL > PERUSE
PERUSALS > PERUSE
PERUSE *vb* read in a
careful or leisurely manner
PERUSED > PERUSE
PERUSER > PERUSE
PERUSERS > PERUSE
PERUSES > PERUSE
PERUSING > PERUSE
PERV *n* pervert ▷ *vb* give a
person an erotic look
PERVADE *vb* spread right
through (something)
PERVADED > PERVADE
PERVADER > PERVADE
PERVADERS > PERVADE
PERVADES > PERVADE
PERVADING > PERVADE
PERVASION > PERVADE
PERVASIVE *adj*
pervading or tending to
pervade
PERVE *same as* > PERV
PERVED > PERV
PERVERSE *adj*
deliberately doing
something different from

P

what is thought normal or proper

PERVERSER > PERVERSE

PERVERT vb use or alter for a wrong purpose ▷ n person who practises sexual perversion

PERVERTED adj deviating greatly from what is regarded as normal or right

PERVERTER > PERVERT

PERVERTS > PERVERT

PERVES > PERV

PERVIATE vb perforate or burrow

PERVIATED > PERVIATE

PERVIATES > PERVIATE

PERVICACY n obstinacy

PERVIER > PERVY

PERVIEST > PERVY

PERVING > PERV

PERVIOUS adj able to be penetrated, permeable

PERVO n pervert

PERVOS > PERVO

PERVS > PERV

PERVY adj perverted

PES n animal part corresponding to the foot

PESADE n position in which the horse stands on the hind legs with the forelegs in the air

PESADES > PESADE

PESANT obsolete spelling of > PEASANT

PESANTE adv to be performed clumsily

PESANTS > PESANT

PESAUNT obsolete spelling of > PEASANT

PESAUNTS > PESAUNT

PESETA n former monetary unit of Spain

PESETAS > PESETA

PESEWA n Ghanaian monetary unit

PESEWAS > PESEWA

PESHMERGA n armed forces of Kurdish region of Iraq

PESHWA same as > PEISHWA

PESHWAS > PESHWA

PESKIER > PESKY

PESKIEST > PESKY

PESKILY > PESKY

PESKINESS > PESKY

PESKY adj troublesome

PESO n monetary unit of Argentina, Mexico, etc

PESOS > PESO

PESSARIES > PESSARY

PESSARY n appliance worn in the vagina

PESSIMA n lowest point

PESSIMAL adj (of animal's environment) least favourable for survival

PESSIMISM n tendency to expect the worst in all things

PESSIMIST > PESSIMISM

PESSIMUM same as > PESSIMAL

PEST n annoying person

PESTER vb annoy or nag continually

PESTERED > PESTER

PESTERER > PESTER

PESTERERS > PESTER

PESTERING > PESTER

PESTEROUS adj inclined to annoy

PESTERS > PESTER

PESTFUL adj causing annoyance

PESTHOLE n breeding ground for disease

PESTHOLES > PESTHOLE

PESTHOUSE n hospital for treating persons with infectious diseases

PESTICIDE n chemical for killing insect pests

PESTIER > PESTY

PESTIEST > PESTY

PESTILENT adj annoying, troublesome

PESTLE n club-shaped implement for grinding ▷ vb pound with or as if with a pestle

PESTLED > PESTLE

PESTLES > PESTLE

PESTLING > PESTLE

PESTO n sauce for pasta

PESTOLOGY n study of pests

PESTOS > PESTO

PESTS > PEST

PESTY adj persistently annoying

PET n animal kept for pleasure and companionship ▷ adj kept as a pet ▷ vb treat as a pet

PETABYTE n in computing, 10¹⁵ or 2⁵⁰ bytes

PETABYTES > PETABYTE

PETAFLOP n (in computing) unit of processing speed

PETAFLOPS > PETAFLOP

PETAHERTZ n very large unit of electrical frequency

PETAL n one of the brightly coloured outer parts of a flower

PETALED > PETAL

PETALINE > PETAL

PETALISM n ostracism in ancient Syracuse

PETALISMS > PETALISM

PETALLED > PETAL

PETALLIKE adj like a petal

PETALODIC > PETALODY

PETALODY n condition in which stamens or other flower parts assume the form and function of petals

PETALOID adj resembling a petal, esp in shape

PETALOUS adj bearing or having petals

PETALS > PETAL

PETAMETER same as > PETAMETRE

PETAMETRE n ten to the power of fifteen metres

PETANQUE n French game similar to bowls

PETANQUES > PETANQUE

PETAR obsolete variant of > PETARD

PETARA n clothes basket

PETARAS > PETARA

PETARD n device containing explosives

PETARDS > PETARD

PETARIES > PETARY

PETARS > PETAR

PETARY n weapon for hurling stones

PETASOS same as > PETASUS

PETASOSES > PETASOS

PETASUS n broad-brimmed hat worn by the ancient Greeks

PETASUSES > PETASUS

PETAURINE adj similar to a flying phalanger ▷ n a flying phalanger

PETAURIST n flying phalanger

PETCHARY n type of kingbird

PETCOCK n small valve

PETCOCKS > PETCOCK

PETECHIA n small discoloured spot on the skin

PETECHIAE > PETECHIA

PETECHIAL > PETECHIA

PETER vb fall (off) in volume, intensity, etc, and finally cease ▷ n act of petering

PETERED > PETER

PETERING > PETER

PETERMAN n burglar skilled in safe-breaking

PETERMEN > PETERMAN

PETERS > PETER

PETERSHAM n thick corded ribbon used to stiffen belts, button bands, etc

PETHER old variant of > PEDLAR

PETHERS > PETHER

PETHIDINE n white crystalline water-soluble drug used to relieve pain

PETILLANT adj (of wine) slightly effervescent

PETIOLAR > PETIOLE

PETIOLATE adj (of a plant or leaf) having a leafstalk

PETIOLE n stalk which attaches a leaf to a plant

PETIOLED > PETIOLE

PETIOLES > PETIOLE

PETIOLULE n stalk of any of the leaflets making up a compound leaf

PETIT adj of little or lesser importance

PETITE adj (of a woman) small and dainty ▷ n clothing size for small women

PETITES > PETITE

PETITIO n as in petitio principii, a form of fallacious reasoning

PETITION n formal request, esp one signed by many people and presented to parliament ▷ vb present a petition to

PETITIONS > PETITION

PETITIOS > PETITIO

PETITORY adj soliciting

PETNAP vb steal pet

PETNAPER > PETNAP

PETNAPERS > PETNAP

PETNAPING > PETNAP

PETNAPPED > PETNAP

PETNAPPER > PETNAP

PETNAPS > PETNAP

PETRALE n type of sole

PETRALES > PETRALE

PETRARIES > PETRARY

PETRARY n weapon for hurling stones

PETRE same as > SALTPETRE

PETREL n sea bird with a hooked bill and tubular nostrils

PETRELS > PETREL

PETRES > PETRE

PETRI n as in petri dish shallow glass dish used for cultures of bacteria

PETRICHOR n sweet smell caused by rain falling on parched earth

PETRIFIC adj petrifying

PETRIFIED > PETRIFY

PETRIFIER > PETRIFY

PETRIFIES > PETRIFY

PETRIFY vb frighten severely

PETROGENY n origin of rocks

PETROGRAM n prehistoric rock painting

PETROL n flammable liquid obtained from petroleum ▷ vb supply with petrol

PETROLAGE n addition of petrol (to a body of water) to get rid of mosquitoes

PETROLEUM n thick dark oil found underground

PETROLEUR n person using petrol to cause explosions

PETROLIC adj of, relating to, containing, or obtained from petroleum

PETROLLED > PETROL

PETROLOGY n study of the composition, origin, structure, and formation of rocks

PETROLS > PETROL

PETRONEL n obsolete cavalry firearm

PETRONELS
> PETRONEL
PETROSAL *adj* of the dense part of the temporal bone that surrounds the inner ear ▷ *n* petrosal bone
PETROSALS
> PETROSAL
PETROUS *adj* denoting the dense part of the temporal bone around the inner ear
PETS > PET
PETSAI *n* Chinese cabbage
PETSAIS > PETSAI
PETTABLE > PET
PETTED > PET
PETTEDLY > PET
PETTER > PET
PETTERS > PET
PETTI *n* petticoat
PETTICOAT *n* woman's skirt-shaped undergarment
PETTIER > PETTY
PETTIES > PETTI
PETTIEST > PETTY
PETTIFOG *vb* quibble or fuss over details
PETTIFOGS
> PETTIFOG
PETTILY > PETTY
PETTINESS > PETTY
PETTING > PET
PETTINGS > PET
PETTIS > PETTI
PETTISH *adj* peevish or fretful
PETTISHLY > PETTISH
PETTITOES *pl n* pig's trotters, esp when used as food
PETTLE *vb* pat animal
PETTLED > PETTLE
PETTLES > PETTLE
PETTLING > PETTLE
PETTO *n* breast of an animal
PETTY *adj* unimportant, trivial
PETULANCE
> PETULANT
PETULANCY
> PETULANT
PETULANT *adj* childishly irritable or peevish
PETUNIA *n* garden plant with funnel-shaped flowers
PETUNIAS > PETUNIA
PETUNTSE *n* fusible feldspathic mineral used in hard-paste porcelain
PETUNTSES
> PETUNTSE
PETUNTZE *same as*
> PETUNTSE
PETUNTZES
> PETUNTZE
PEW *n* fixed benchlike seat in a church
PEWEE *n* small N American flycatcher
PEWEES > PEWEE
PEWHOLDER *n* renter of pew

PEWIT *another name for*
> LAPWING
PEWITS > PEWIT
PEWS > PEW
PEWTER *n* greyish metal made of tin and lead
PEWTERER > PEWTER
PEWTERERS > PEWTER
PEWTERIER > PEWTERY
PEWTERS > PEWTER
PEWTERY *adj* of or like pewter
PEYOTE *another name for*
> MESCAL
PEYOTES > PEYOTE
PEYOTISM *n* ritual use of peyote
PEYOTISMS
> PEYOTISM
PEYOTIST *n* person who uses peyote
PEYOTISTS
> PEYOTIST
PEYOTL *same as*
> PEYOTE
PEYOTLS > PEYOTL
PEYSE *vb* weight or poise
PEYSED > PEYSE
PEYSES > PEYSE
PEYSING > PEYSE
PEYTRAL *same as*
> PEYTREL
PEYTRALS > PEYTRAL
PEYTREL *n* breastplate of horse's armour
PEYTRELS > PEYTREL
PEZANT *obsolete spelling of*
> PEASANT
PEZANTS > PEZANT
PEZIZOID *adj* having cup-like form
PFENNIG *n* former German monetary unit
PFENNIGE > PFENNIG
PFENNIGS > PFENNIG
PFENNING *old variant of*
> PFENNIG
PFENNINGS
> PFENNING
PFFT *interj* sound indicating sudden disappearance of something
PFUI *interj* phooey
PHABLET *n* type of handheld personal computer
PHABLETS > PHABLET
PHACELIA *n* plant grown for its large, deep blue bell flowers
PHACELIAS
> PHACELIA
PHACOID *adj* lentil- or lens-shaped
PHACOIDAL *same as*
> PHACOID
PHACOLITE *n* colourless variety of chabazite
PHACOLITH *n* lens-shaped igneous rock structure
PHAEIC *adj* (of animals) having dusky coloration
PHAEISM > PHAEIC
PHAEISMS > PHAEIC
PHAENOGAM *n* seed-bearing plant

PHAETON *n* light four-wheeled horse-drawn carriage
PHAETONS > PHAETON
PHAGE *n* parasitic virus that destroys its host
PHAGEDENA *n* rapidly spreading ulcer that destroys tissues as it increases in size
PHAGES > PHAGE
PHAGOCYTE *n* cell or protozoan that engulfs particles, such as microorganisms
PHAGOSOME *n* part of biological cell
PHALANGAL
> PHALANGE
PHALANGE *another name for* > PHALANX
PHALANGER *same as*
> POSSUM
PHALANGES > PHALANX
PHALANGID *n* type of arachnid
PHALANX *n* closely grouped mass of people
PHALANXES > PHALANX
PHALAROPE *n* aquatic shore bird of northern oceans and lakes
PHALLI > PHALLUS
PHALLIC *adj* of or resembling a penis
PHALLIN *n* poisonous substance from mushroom
PHALLINS > PHALLIN
PHALLISM *n* worship or veneration of the phallus
PHALLISMS
> PHALLISM
PHALLIST *n* worshipper or venerator of the phallus
PHALLISTS
> PHALLIST
PHALLOID *adj* resembling a penis
PHALLUS *n* penis
PHALLUSES > PHALLUS
PHANG *old variant spelling of* > FANG
PHANGED > PHANG
PHANGING > PHANG
PHANGS > PHANG
PHANSIGAR *n* Indian assassin
PHANTASIM *same as*
> PHANTASM
PHANTASM *n* unreal vision, illusion
PHANTASMA *same as*
> PHANTASM
PHANTASMS
> PHANTASM
PHANTAST *same as*
> FANTAST
PHANTASTS
> PHANTAST
PHANTASY *same as*
> FANTASY
PHANTOM *n* ghost ▷ *adj* deceptive or unreal
PHANTOMS > PHANTOM
PHANTOMY *adj* of phantoms

PHANTOSME *old spelling of* > PHANTASM
PHARAOH *n* ancient Egyptian king
PHARAOHS > PHARAOH
PHARAONIC *adj* of or relating to the Pharaohs
PHARE *n* beacon tower
PHARES > PHARE
PHARISAIC *n* righteously hypocritical
PHARISEE *n* self-righteous or hypocritical person
PHARISEES
> PHARISEE
PHARM *vb* redirect (a website user) to another, bogus website
PHARMA *n* pharmaceutical companies considered together as an industry
PHARMACY *n* preparation and dispensing of drugs and medicines
PHARMAS > PHARMA
PHARMED > PHARM
PHARMER *n* person who pharms
PHARMERS > PHARMER
PHARMING *n* rearing or growing genetically modified animals or plants in order to develop pharmaceuticals
PHARMINGS
> PHARMING
PHARMS > PHARM
PHAROS *n* lighthouse
PHAROSES > PHAROS
PHARYNGAL *adj* of, relating to, or situated in or near the pharynx
PHARYNGES > PHARYNX
PHARYNX *n* cavity forming the back part of the mouth
PHARYNXES > PHARYNX
PHASE *n* distinct or characteristic stage in a development or chain of events ▷ *vb* arrange or carry out in stages
PHASEAL > PHASE
PHASED > PHASE
PHASEDOWN *n* gradual reduction
PHASELESS > PHASE
PHASEOLIN *n* anti-fungal substance from kidney bean
PHASEOUT *n* gradual reduction
PHASEOUTS
> PHASEOUT
PHASER *n* type of science-fiction weapon
PHASERS > PHASER
PHASES > PHASE
PHASIC > PHASE
PHASING *n* effect achieved by varying the phase relationship of two similar audio signals
PHASINGS > PHASING
PHASIS *another word for* > PHASE

PHASMID n stick insect or leaf insect
PHASMIDS > PHASMID
PHASOR n rotating vector representing a quantity that varies sinusoidally
PHASORS > PHASOR
PHAT adj terrific
PHATIC adj (of speech) used to express sociability rather than specific meaning
PHATTER > PHAT
PHATTEST > PHAT
PHEASANT n game bird with bright plumage
PHEASANTS > PHEASANT
PHEAZAR old variant of > VIZIER
PHEAZARS > PHEAZAR
PHEER same as > FERE
PHEERE same as > FERE
PHEERES > PHEERE
PHEERS > PHEER
PHEESE vb worry
PHEESED > PHEESE
PHEESES > PHEESE
PHEESING > PHEESE
PHEEZE same as > PHEESE
PHEEZED > PHEEZE
PHEEZES > PHEEZE
PHEEZING > PHEEZE
PHELLEM technical name for > CORK
PHELLEMS > PHELLEM
PHELLOGEN n cork cambium
PHELLOID adj like cork
PHELONIA > PHELONION
PHELONION n vestment for an Orthodox priest
PHENACITE n colourless or white glassy mineral
PHENAKISM n deception
PHENAKITE same as > PHENACITE
PHENATE n ester or salt of phenol
PHENATES > PHENATE
PHENAZIN same as > PHENAZINE
PHENAZINE n yellow crystalline tricyclic compound
PHENAZINS > PHENAZIN
PHENE n genetically determined characteristic of organism
PHENES > PHENE
PHENETIC > PHENETICS
PHENETICS n system of classification based on similarities between organisms without regard to their evolutionary relationships
PHENETOL same as > PHENETOLE
PHENETOLE n colourless oily compound
PHENETOLS > PHENETOL
PHENGITE n type of alabaster

PHENGITES > PHENGITE
PHENIC adj of phenol
PHENIX same as > PHOENIX
PHENIXES > PHENIX
PHENOBARB n phenobarbital
PHENOCOPY n noninheritable change in an organism that is caused by environmental influence during development but resembles the effects of a genetic mutation
PHENOGAM same as > PHAENOGAM
PHENOGAMS > PHENOGAM
PHENOL n chemical used in disinfectants and antiseptics
PHENOLATE vb treat or disinfect with phenol
PHENOLIC adj of, containing, or derived from phenol ▷ n derivative of phenol
PHENOLICS > PHENOLIC
PHENOLOGY n study of recurring phenomena, such as animal migration, esp as influenced by climatic conditions
PHENOLS > PHENOL
PHENOM n person or thing of outstanding abilities
PHENOME n full complement of phenotypical traits of an organism, species, etc
PHENOMENA > phenomenons
PHENOMES > PHENOME
PHENOMS > PHENOM
PHENOTYPE n physical form of an organism as determined by the interaction of its genetic make-up and its environment
PHENOXIDE n any of a class of salts of phenol
PHENOXY modifier as in phenoxy resin any of a class of resins derived from polyhydroxy ethers
PHENYL n chemical substance
PHENYLENE n compound derived from benzene
PHENYLIC > PHENYL
PHENYLS > PHENYL
PHENYTOIN n anticonvulsant drug
PHEON n barbed iron head of dart
PHEONS > PHEON
PHERESES > PHERESIS
PHERESIS n specialized form of blood donation
PHEROMONE n chemical substance, secreted externally by certain animals, such as insects, affecting the behaviour or physiology of other

animals of the same species
PHESE same as > PHEESE
PHESED > PHESE
PHESES > PHESE
PHESING > PHESE
PHEW interj exclamation of relief, surprise, etc
PHI n 21st letter in the Greek alphabet
PHIAL n small bottle for medicine etc ▷ vb put in phial
PHIALLED > PHIAL
PHIALLING > PHIAL
PHIALS > PHIAL
PHILABEG same as > FILIBEG
PHILABEGS > PHILABEG
PHILAMOT variant of > FILEMOT
PHILAMOTS > PHILAMOT
PHILANDER vb (of a man) flirt or have many casual love affairs with women
PHILATELY n stamp collecting
PHILAVERY n collection of rare and obscure words
PHILHORSE n last horse in a team
PHILIBEG variant spelling of > FILIBEG
PHILIBEGS > PHILIBEG
PHILIPPIC n bitter or impassioned speech of denunciation, invective
PHILISTIA n domain of cultural philistine
PHILLABEG same as > FILIBEG
PHILLIBEG same as > FILIBEG
PHILOGYNY n fondness for women
PHILOLOGY n science of the structure and development of languages
PHILOMATH n lover of learning
PHILOMEL n nightingale
PHILOMELA same as > PHILOMEL
PHILOMELS > PHILOMEL
PHILOMOT n colour of dead leaf
PHILOMOTS > PHILOMOT
PHILOPENA n gift made as forfeit in game
PHILTER same as > PHILTRE
PHILTERED > PHILTER
PHILTERS > PHILTER
PHILTRA > PHILTRUM
PHILTRE n magic drink supposed to arouse love in the person who drinks it ▷ vb mix with love potion
PHILTRED > PHILTRE
PHILTRES > PHILTRE
PHILTRING > PHILTRE
PHILTRUM n indentation above the upper lip

PHIMOSES > PHIMOSIS
PHIMOSIS n abnormal tightness of the foreskin
PHIMOTIC > PHIMOSIS
PHINNOCK variant spelling of > FINNOCK
PHINNOCKS > PHINNOCK
PHIS > PHI
PHISH vb engage in phishing
PHISHED > PHISH
PHISHER n person who phishes
PHISHERS > PHISHER
PHISHES > PHISH
PHISHING n internet fraud to extract personal and financial details
PHISHINGS > PHISHING
PHISNOMY n physiognomy
PHIZ n face or a facial expression
PHIZES > PHIZ
PHIZOG same as > PHIZ
PHIZOGS > PHIZOG
PHIZZ n face
PHIZZES > PHIZ
PHLEBITIC > PHLEBITIS
PHLEBITIS n inflammation of a vein
PHLEGM n thick yellowish substance formed in the nose and throat during a cold
PHLEGMIER > PHLEGM
PHLEGMON n inflammatory mass that may progress to abscess
PHLEGMONS > PHLEGMON
PHLEGMS > PHLEGM
PHLEGMY > PHLEGM
PHLOEM n plant tissue that acts as a path for the distribution of food
PHLOEMS > PHLOEM
PHLOMIS n plant of Phlomis genus
PHLOMISES > PHLOMIS
PHLORIZIN n chemical found in root bark of fruit trees
PHLOX n flowering garden plant
PHLOXES > PHLOX
PHLYCTENA n small blister, vesicle, or pustule
PHO n Vietnamese noodle soup
PHOBIA n intense and unreasoning fear or dislike
PHOBIAS > PHOBIA
PHOBIC adj of, relating to, or arising from a phobia ▷ n person with a phobia
PHOBICS > PHOBIC
PHOBISM n phobia
PHOBISMS > PHOBISM
PHOBIST > PHOBISM
PHOBISTS > PHOBISM
PHOCA n genus of seals
PHOCAE > PHOCA
PHOCAS > PHOCA

PHOCINE *adj* of, relating to, or resembling a seal

PHOCOMELY *n* congenital deformity resulting from prenatal interference with the development of the fetal limbs, characterized esp by short stubby hands or feet attached close to the body

PHOEBE *n* greyish-brown North American flycatcher

PHOEBES > PHOEBE

PHOEBUS *n* sun

PHOEBUSES > PHOEBUS

PHOENIX *n* legendary bird said to set fire to itself and rise anew from its ashes

PHOENIXES > PHOENIX

PHOH *variant of >* FOH

PHOLADES > PHOLAS

PHOLAS *n* type of bivalve mollusc

PHON *n* unit of loudness

PHONAL *adj* relating to voice

PHONATE *vb* articulate speech sounds

PHONATED > PHONATE

PHONATES > PHONATE

PHONATHON *n* telephone-based fund-raising campaign

PHONATING > PHONATE

PHONATION > PHONATE

PHONATORY > PHONATE

PHONE *vb* telephone ▷ *n* single uncomplicated speech sound

PHONECAM *n* digital camera incorporated in a mobile phone

PHONECAMS > PHONECAM

PHONECARD *n* card used to operate certain public telephones

PHONED > PHONE

PHONEME *n* one of the set of speech sounds in a language

PHONEMES > PHONEME

PHONEMIC *adj* of or relating to the phoneme

PHONEMICS *n* classification and analysis of the phonemes of a language

PHONER *n* person making a telephone call

PHONERS > PHONER

PHONES > PHONE

PHONETIC *adj* of speech sounds

PHONETICS *n* science of speech sounds

PHONETISE *same as* **>** PHONETIZE

PHONETISM *n* phonetic writing

PHONETIST *n* person who advocates or uses a system of phonetic spelling

PHONETIZE *vb* represent by phonetic signs

PHONEY *adj* not genuine ▷ *n* phoney person or thing ▷ *vb* fake

PHONEYED > PHONEY

PHONEYING > PHONEY

PHONEYS > PHONEY

PHONIC > PHONICS

PHONICS *n* method of teaching people to read

PHONIED > PHONY

PHONIER > PHONY

PHONIES > PHONY

PHONIEST > PHONY

PHONILY > PHONY

PHONINESS > PHONY

PHONING > PHONE

PHONMETER *n* instrument measuring sound levels

PHONO *n* phonograph

PHONOGRAM *n* any written symbol standing for a sound, syllable, morpheme, or word

PHONOLITE *n* fine-grained volcanic igneous rock consisting of alkaline feldspars and nepheline

PHONOLOGY *n* study of the speech sounds in a language

PHONON *n* quantum of vibrational energy

PHONONS > PHONON

PHONOPORE *n* device for conveying sound

PHONOS > PHONO

PHONOTYPE *n* letter or symbol representing a sound

PHONOTYPY *n* transcription of speech into phonetic symbols

PHONS > PHON

PHONY *vb* fake

PHONYING > PHONY

PHOOEY *interj* exclamation of scorn or contempt

PHORATE *n* type of insecticide

PHORATES > PHORATE

PHORESIES > PHORESY

PHORESY *n* association in which one animal clings to another to ensure movement from place to place

PHORETIC *adj* relating to phoresy

PHORMINX *n* ancient Greek stringed instrument

PHORMIUM *n* New Zealand plant

PHORMIUMS
> PHORMIUM

PHORONID *n* small wormlike marine animal

PHORONIDS
> PHORONID

PHOS > PHO

PHOSGENE *n* poisonous gas used in warfare

PHOSGENES
> PHOSGENE

PHOSPHATE *n* compound of phosphorus

PHOSPHENE *n* sensation of light caused by pressure on the eyelid of a closed eye or by other mechanical or electrical interference with the visual system

PHOSPHID *same as* **>** PHOSPHIDE

PHOSPHIDE *n* any compound of phosphorus with another element, esp a more electropositive element

PHOSPHIDS
> PHOSPHID

PHOSPHIN *same as* **>** PHOSPHINE

PHOSPHINE *n* colourless flammable gas that is slightly soluble in water and has a strong fishy odour

PHOSPHINS
> PHOSPHIN

PHOSPHITE *n* any salt or ester of phosphorous acid

PHOSPHOR *n* synthetic fluorescent or phosphorescent substance

PHOSPHORE *same as* **>** PHOSPHOR

PHOSPHORI *n* plural of phosphorus

PHOSPHORS
> PHOSPHOR

PHOSSY *adj* as in *phossy jaw* gangrenous condition of the lower jawbone

PHOT *n* unit of illumination

PHOTIC *adj* of or concerned with light

PHOTICS *n* science of light

PHOTINIA *n* genus of garden plants

PHOTINIAS
> PHOTINIA

PHOTINO *n* hypothetical elementary particle

PHOTINOS > PHOTINO

PHOTISM *n* sensation of light or colour caused by stimulus of another sense

PHOTISMS > PHOTISM

PHOTO *n* photograph ▷ *vb* take a photograph of

PHOTOBLOG *n* blog in which the main content consists of photographs ▷ *vb* keep a photoblog

PHOTOBOMB *vb* intrude into the background of a photograph without the subject's knowledge

PHOTOCALL *n* occasion when people have their photograph taken together

PHOTOCARD *n* identity card containing a photograph of the bearer

PHOTOCELL *n* cell which produces a current or voltage when exposed to light or other electromagnetic radiation

PHOTOCOPY *n* photographic reproduction ▷ *vb* make a photocopy of

PHOTODISK *n* computer disk that contains photographs

PHOTOED > PHOTO

PHOTOFIT *n* combining of photographs of facial features into a composite picture of a face

PHOTOFITS
> PHOTOFIT

PHOTOG *n* photograph

PHOTOGEN *same as* **>** PHOTOGENE

PHOTOGENE *n* afterimage

PHOTOGENS
> PHOTOGEN

PHOTOGENY *n* photography

PHOTOGRAM *n* picture, usually abstract, produced on a photographic material without the use of a camera, as by placing an object on the material and exposing to light

PHOTOGS > PHOTOG

PHOTOING > PHOTO

PHOTOLYSE *vb* cause to undergo photolysis

PHOTOLYZE *same as* **>** PHOTOLYSE

PHOTOMAP *n* map constructed by adding grid lines, place names, etc, to aerial photographs ▷ *vb* map (an area) using aerial photography

PHOTOMAPS
> PHOTOMAP

PHOTOMASK *n* material on which etching pattern for integrated circuit is drawn

PHOTON *n* quantum of electromagnetic radiation energy

PHOTONIC > PHOTON

PHOTONICS *n* study and design of devices and systems, such as optical fibres, that depend on the transmission, modulation, or amplification of streams of photons

PHOTONS > PHOTON

PHOTOPHIL *n* light-seeking organism

PHOTOPIA *n* normal adaptation of the eye to light

PHOTOPIAS
> PHOTOPIA

PHOTOPIC > PHOTOPIA

PHOTOPLAY *n* play filmed as movie

PHOTOPSIA *n* appearance of flashes due to retinal irritation

PHOTOPSY *same as* **>** PHOTOPSIA

PHOTOS > PHOTO

PHOTOSCAN *n* photographic scan

PHOTOSET *vb* set (type matter) by photosetting

PHOTOSETS
> PHOTOSET

PHOTOSHOP *vb* edit or alter a picture digitally, usu with Adobe Photoshop

PHOTOSTAT *n* copy made by photocopying machine ▷ *vb* make a photostat copy (of)

PHOTOTAXY *n* movement of an entire organism in response to light

PHOTOTUBE *n* type of photocell in which radiation falling on a photocathode causes electrons to flow to an anode and thus produce an electric current

PHOTOTYPE *n* printing plate produced by photography ▷ *vb* reproduce (an illustration) using a phototype

PHOTOTYPY *n* process of producing phototypes

PHOTS > PHOT

PHPHT *interj* expressing irritation or reluctance

PHRASAL *adj* of, relating to, or composed of phrases

PHRASALLY > PHRASAL

PHRASE *n* group of words forming a unit of meaning, esp within a sentence ▷ *vb* express in words

PHRASED > PHRASE

PHRASEMAN *n* coiner of phrases

PHRASEMEN > PHRASEMAN

PHRASER > PHRASE

PHRASERS > PHRASE

PHRASES > PHRASE

PHRASIER > PHRASY

PHRASIEST > PHRASY

PHRASING *n* exact words used to say or write something

PHRASINGS > PHRASING

PHRASY *adj* containing phrases

PHRATRAL > PHRATRY

PHRATRIC > PHRATRY

PHRATRIES > PHRATRY

PHRATRY *n* group of people within a tribe who have a common ancestor

PHREAK *vb* hack into a telecommunications system

PHREAKED > PHREAK

PHREAKER > PHREAK

PHREAKERS > PHREAK

PHREAKING > PHREAK

PHREAKS > PHREAK

PHREATIC *adj* of or relating to ground water occurring below the water table

PHRENESES > PHRENESIS

PHRENESIS *n* state of frenzy

PHRENETIC *obsolete spelling of* > FRENETIC

PHRENIC *adj* of or relating to the diaphragm ▷ *n* (a nerve, blood vessel, etc) located in the diaphragm

PHRENICS > PHRENIC

PHRENISM *n* belief in non-physical life force

PHRENISMS > PHRENISM

PHRENITIC > PHRENITIS

PHRENITIS *n* state of frenzy

PHRENSIED > PHRENSY

PHRENSIES > PHRENSY

PHRENSY *obsolete spelling of* > FRENZY

PHRENTICK *obsolete spelling of* > PHRENETIC

PHRYGANA *another name for* > GARIGUE

PHRYGANAS > PHRYGANA

PHT *same as* > PHPHT

PHTHALATE *n* salt or ester of phthalic acid

PHTHALEIN *n* any of a class of organic compounds obtained by the reaction of phthalic anhydride with a phenol and used in dyes

PHTHALIC *adj* as in *phthalic anhydride* white crystalline substance used mainly in producing dyestuffs

PHTHALIN *n* colourless compound formed by reduction of phthalein

PHTHALINS > PHTHALIN

PHTHISES > PHTHISIS

PHTHISIC *adj* relating to or affected with phthisis ▷ *n* person with phthisis

PHTHISICS > PHTHISIC

PHTHISIS *n* any disease that causes wasting of the body, esp pulmonary tuberculosis

PHUT *vb* make muffled explosive sound

PHUTS > PHUT

PHUTTED > PHUT

PHUTTING > PHUT

PHWOAH *same as* > PHWOAR

PHWOAR *interj* expression of attraction

PHYCOCYAN *n* type of protein found in some algae

PHYCOLOGY *n* study of algae

PHYLA > PHYLUM

PHYLACTIC *adj* defending or protecting against disease

PHYLAE > PHYLE

PHYLAR > PHYLUM

PHYLARCH *n* chief of tribe

PHYLARCHS > PHYLARCH

PHYLARCHY > PHYLARCH

PHYLAXIS *n* protection against infection

PHYLE *n* tribe or clan of an ancient Greek people

PHYLESES > PHYLESIS

PHYLESIS *n* evolutionary events that modify taxon without causing speciation

PHYLETIC *adj* of or relating to the evolution of a species or group of organisms

PHYLETICS *n* study of the evolution of species

PHYLIC > PHYLE

PHYLLARY *n* bract subtending flower head of composite plant

PHYLLID *n* leaf of a liverwort or moss

PHYLLIDS > PHYLLID

PHYLLITE *n* compact lustrous metamorphic rock

PHYLLITES > PHYLLITE

PHYLLITIC > PHYLLITE

PHYLLO *variant of* > FILO

PHYLLODE *n* flattened leafstalk that resembles and functions as a leaf

PHYLLODES > PHYLLODE

PHYLLODIA > PHYLLODE

PHYLLODY *n* abnormal development of leaves from parts of flower

PHYLLOID *adj* resembling a leaf ▷ *n* leaf-like organ

PHYLLOIDS > PHYLLOID

PHYLLOME *n* leaf or a leaflike organ

PHYLLOMES > PHYLLOME

PHYLLOMIC > PHYLLOME

PHYLLOPOD *n* crustacean with leaf-like appendages

PHYLLOS > PHYLLO

PHYLOGENY *n* sequence of events involved in the evolution of a species, genus, etc

PHYLON *n* tribe

PHYLUM *n* major taxonomic division of animals and plants

PHYSALIA *n* Portuguese man-of-war

PHYSALIAS > PHYSALIA

PHYSALIS *n* strawberry tomato

PHYSED *n* physical education

PHYSEDS > PHYSED

PHYSES > PHYSIS

PHYSETER *n* machine for filtering

PHYSETERS > PHYSETER

PHYSIATRY *n* treatment of injury by physical means

PHYSIC *n* medicine or drug, esp a cathartic or purge ▷ *vb* treat (a patient) with medicine

PHYSICAL *adj* of the body, as contrasted with the mind or spirit

PHYSICALS *pl n* commodities that can be purchased and used, as opposed to those bought and sold in a futures market

PHYSICIAN *n* doctor of medicine

PHYSICISM *n* belief in the physical as opposed to the spiritual

PHYSICIST *n* person skilled in or studying physics

PHYSICKED > PHYSIC

PHYSICKY > PHYSIC

PHYSICS *n* science of the properties of matter and energy

PHYSIO *n* physiotherapist

PHYSIOS > PHYSIO

PHYSIQUE *n* person's bodily build and muscular development

PHYSIQUED *adj* having particular physique

PHYSIQUES > PHYSIQUE

PHYSIS *n* part of bone responsible for lengthening

PHYTANE *n* hydrocarbon found in fossilised plant remains

PHYTANES > PHYTANE

PHYTIN *n* substance from plants used as an energy supplement

PHYTINS > PHYTIN

PHYTOGENY *n* branch of botany that is concerned with the detailed description of plants

PHYTOID *adj* resembling plant

PHYTOL *n* alcohol used to synthesize some vitamins

PHYTOLITH *n* microscopic particle in plants

PHYTOLOGY *rare name for* > BOTANY

PHYTOLS > PHYTOL

PHYTON *n* unit of plant structure

PHYTONIC > PHYTON

PHYTONS > PHYTON

PHYTOSES > PHYTOSIS

PHYTOSIS *n* disease caused by vegetable parasite

PHYTOTOMY *n* dissection of plants

PHYTOTRON *n* building in which plants can be grown on a large scale, under controlled conditions

PI *n* sixteenth letter in the Greek alphabet ▷ *vb* spill and mix (set type) indiscriminately

PIA *n* innermost of the three membranes that cover the brain and the spinal cord

PIACEVOLE *adv* to be performed in playful manner

PIACULAR *adj* making expiation for a sacrilege

PIAFFE *n* passage done on the spot ▷ *vb* strut on the spot

PIAFFED > PIAFFE

PIAFFER > PIAFFE

PIAFFERS > PIAFFE

PIAFFES > PIAFFE

PIAFFING > PIAFFE

PIAL *adj* relating to pia mater

PIAN *n* contagious tropical skin disease

PIANETTE *n* small piano

PIANETTES
> PIANETTE

PIANI > PIANO

PIANIC *adj* of piano

PIANINO *n* small upright piano

PIANINOS > PIANINO

PIANISM *n* technique, skill, or artistry in playing the piano

PIANISMS > PIANISM

PIANIST *n* person who plays the piano

PIANISTE *variant of*
> PIANIST

PIANISTES
> PIANISTE

PIANISTIC > PIANISM

PIANISTS > PIANIST

PIANO *n* musical instrument with strings which are struck by hammers worked by a keyboard ▷ *adv* quietly

PIANOLA *n* type of player piano

PIANOLAS > PIANOLA

PIANOLESS *adj* without a piano

PIANOLIST *n* person who plays the Pianola

PIANOS > PIANO

PIANS > PIAN

PIARIST *n* member of a Roman religious order

PIARISTS > PIARIST

PIAS > PIA

PIASABA *same as*
> PIASSAVA

PIASABAS > PIASABA

PIASAVA *same as*
> PIASSAVA

PIASAVAS > PIASAVA

PIASSABA *same as*
> PIASSAVA

PIASSABAS
> PIASSABA

PIASSAVA *n* South American palm tree

PIASSAVAS
> PIASSAVA

PIASTER *same as*
> PIASTRE

PIASTERS > PIASTER

PIASTRE *n* fractional monetary unit of Egypt, Lebanon, Sudan, South Sudan, and Syria

PIASTRES > PIASTRE

PIAZZA *n* square or marketplace, esp in Italy

PIAZZAS > PIAZZA

PIAZZE > PIAZZA

PIAZZIAN > PIAZZA

PIBAL *n* method of measuring wind

PIBALS > PIBAL

PIBROCH *n* form of bagpipe music

PIBROCHS > PIBROCH

PIC *n* photograph or illustration

PICA *n* abnormal craving to ingest substances

PICACHO *n* pointed solitary mountain

PICACHOS > PICACHO

PICADILLO *n* Mexican dish

PICADOR *n* mounted bullfighter with a lance

PICADORES > PICADOR

PICADORS > PICADOR

PICAL *adj* relating to pica

PICAMAR *n* hydrocarbon extract of beechwood tar

PICAMARS > PICAMAR

PICANTE *adj* spicy

PICARA *n* female adventurer

PICARAS > PICARA

PICARIAN *n* tree-haunting bird

PICARIANS
> PICARIAN

PICARO *n* roguish adventurer

PICAROON *n* adventurer or rogue

PICAROONS
> PICAROON

PICAROS > PICARO

PICAS > PICA

PICAYUNE *adj* of small value or importance ▷ *n* any coin of little value, such as a five-cent piece

PICAYUNES
> PICAYUNE

PICCADILL *n* high stiff collar

PICCATA *adj* sautéed and served in a lemon sauce ▷ *n* dish of food sautéed and served in a lemon sauce

PICCATAS > PICCATA

PICCIES > PICCY

PICCOLO *n* small flute

PICCOLOS > PICCOLO

PICCY *n* picture or photograph

PICE *n* former Indian coin worth one sixty-fourth of a rupee

PICENE *n* type of hydrocarbon

PICENES > PICENE

PICEOUS *adj* of, relating to, or resembling pitch

PICHOLINE *n* variety of olive

PICHURIM *n* S American laurel tree

PICHURIMS
> PICHURIM

PICIFORM *adj* relating to certain tree-haunting birds

PICINE *adj* relating to woodpeckers

PICK *vb* choose ▷ *n* choice

PICKABACK *same as*
> PIGGYBACK

PICKABLE > PICK

PICKADIL *same as*
> PICCADILL

PICKADILL *same as*
> PICCADILL

PICKADILS
> PICKADIL

PICKAPACK *same as*
> PICKABACK

PICKAROON *same as*
> PICAROON

PICKAX *same as*
> PICKAXE

PICKAXE *n* large pick ▷ *vb* use a pickaxe on (earth, rocks, etc)

PICKAXED > PICKAXE

PICKAXES > PICKAXE

PICKAXING > PICKAXE

PICKBACK *vb* carry by piggyback

PICKBACKS
> PICKBACK

PICKED > PICK

PICKEER *vb* make raid for booty

PICKEERED > PICKEER

PICKEERER > PICKEER

PICKEERS > PICKEER

PICKER *n* person or thing that picks

PICKEREL *n* North American freshwater game fish

PICKERELS
> PICKEREL

PICKERIES > PICKERY

PICKERS > PICKER

PICKERY *n* petty theft

PICKET *n* person or group standing outside a workplace during a strike ▷ *vb* form a picket outside (a workplace)

PICKETED > PICKET

PICKETER > PICKET

PICKETERS > PICKET

PICKETING > PICKET

PICKETS > PICKET

PICKIER > PICKY

PICKIEST > PICKY

PICKILY > PICKY

PICKIN *n* small child

PICKINESS > PICKY

PICKING > PICK

PICKINGS *pl n* money easily acquired

PICKINS > PICKIN

PICKLE *n* food preserved in vinegar or salt water ▷ *vb* preserve in vinegar or salt water

PICKLED *adj* (of food) preserved

PICKLER > PICKLE

PICKLERS > PICKLE

PICKLES > PICKLE

PICKLING > PICKLE

PICKLOCK *n* person who picks locks, esp one who gains unlawful access to premises by this means

PICKLOCKS
> PICKLOCK

PICKMAW *n* type of gull

PICKMAWS > PICKMAW

PICKOFF *n* baseball play

PICKOFFS > PICKOFF

PICKPROOF *adj* (of a lock) unable to be picked

PICKS > PICK

PICKTHANK *n* flatterer

PICKUP *n* small truck with an open body and low sides

PICKUPS > PICKUP

PICKWICK *n* tool for raising the short wick of an oil lamp

PICKWICKS
> PICKWICK

PICKY *adj* fussy

PICLORAM *n* type of herbicide

PICLORAMS
> PICLORAM

PICNIC *n* informal meal out of doors ▷ *vb* have a picnic

PICNICKED > PICNIC

PICNICKER > PICNIC

PICNICKY *adj* like a picnic

PICNICS > PICNIC

PICOCURIE *n* unit of radioactivity

PICOFARAD *n* unit of capacitance

PICOGRAM *n* trillionth of gram

PICOGRAMS
> PICOGRAM

PICOLIN *variant of*
> PICOLINE

PICOLINE *n* liquid derivative of pyridine found in bone oil and coal tar

PICOLINES
> PICOLINE

PICOLINIC
> PICOLINE

PICOLINS > PICOLIN

PICOMETER *same as*
> PICOMETRE

PICOMETRE *n* trillionth fraction of metre

PICOMOLE *n* trillionth of a mole

PICOMOLES
> PICOMOLE

PICONG *n* any teasing or satirical banter

PICONGS > PICONG

PICOT *n* any of pattern of small loops, as on lace ▷ *vb* decorate material with small loops

PICOTE *adj* (of material) picoted

PICOTED > PICOT

PICOTEE *n* type of carnation

PICOTEES > PICOTEE

PICOTING > PICOT

PICOTITE *n* dark-brown mineral
PICOTITES > PICOTITE
PICOTS > PICOT
PICOWAVE *vb* treat food with gamma waves
PICOWAVED > PICOWAVE
PICOWAVES > PICOWAVE
PICQUET *vb* provide early warning of attack
PICQUETED > PICQUET
PICQUETS > PICQUET
PICRA *n* powder of aloes and canella
PICRAS > PICRA
PICRATE *n* any salt or ester of picric acid
PICRATED *adj* containing picrate
PICRATES > PICRATE
PICRIC *adj* as in *picric acid* toxic sparingly soluble crystalline yellow acid
PICRITE *n* coarse-grained ultrabasic igneous rock
PICRITES > PICRITE
PICRITIC > PICRITE
PICS > PIC
PICTARNIE *Scots word for* > TERN
PICTOGRAM *n* picture or symbol standing for a word or group of words, as in written Chinese
PICTORIAL *adj* of or in painting or pictures ▷ *n* newspaper etc with many pictures
PICTURAL *n* picture
PICTURALS > PICTURAL
PICTURE *n* drawing or painting ▷ *vb* visualize, imagine
PICTURED > PICTURE
PICTURES > PICTURE
PICTURING > PICTURE
PICTURISE *same as* > PICTURIZE
PICTURIZE *vb* adorn with pictures
PICUL *n* unit of weight, used in China, Japan, and SE Asia
PICULET *n* small tropical woodpecker with a short tail
PICULETS > PICULET
PICULS > PICUL
PIDDLE *vb* urinate
PIDDLED > PIDDLE
PIDDLER > PIDDLE
PIDDLERS > PIDDLE
PIDDLES > PIDDLE
PIDDLIER > PIDDLY
PIDDLIEST > PIDDLY
PIDDLING *adj* small or unimportant
PIDDLY *adj* trivial
PIDDOCK *n* marine bivalve that bores into rock, clay, or wood
PIDDOCKS > PIDDOCK
PIDGEON *variant of* > PIDGIN

PIDGEONS > PIDGEON
PIDGIN *n* language made up of elements of other languages
PIDGINISE *same as* > PIDGINIZE
PIDGINIZE *vb* create pidgin language
PIDGINS > PIDGIN
PIE *n* dish of meat, fruit, etc baked in pastry
PIEBALD *adj* (horse) with irregular black-and-white markings ▷ *n* black-and-white horse
PIEBALDS > PIEBALD
PIECE *n* separate bit or part
PIECED > PIECE
PIECELESS > PIECE
PIECEMEAL *adv* bit by bit ▷ *adj* fragmentary or unsystematic
PIECEN *vb* join broken threads
PIECENED > PIECEN
PIECENER > PIECEN
PIECENERS > PIECEN
PIECENING > PIECEN
PIECENS > PIECEN
PIECER *n* person who mends, repairs, or joins something
PIECERS > PIECER
PIECES > PIECE
PIECEWISE *adv* with respect to number of discrete pieces
PIECEWORK *n* work paid for according to the quantity produced
PIECING > PIECE
PIECINGS > PIECE
PIECRUST *n* pastry used for making pies
PIECRUSTS > PIECRUST
PIED > PI
PIEDFORT *n* coin thicker than normal
PIEDFORTS > PIEDFORT
PIEDISH *n* container for baking pies
PIEDISHES > PIEDISH
PIEDMONT *adj* (of glaciers, plains, etc) formed or situated at the foot of a mountain or mountain range ▷ *n* gentle slope leading from mountains to flat land
PIEDMONTS > PIEDMONT
PIEDNESS *n* state of being pied
PIEFORT *same as* > PIEDFORT
PIEFORTS > PIEFORT
PIEHOLE *n* person's mouth
PIEHOLES > PIEHOLE
PIEING *n* act of pushing a pie into a person's face
PIEINGS > PIEING
PIEMAN *n* seller of pies
PIEMEN > PIEMAN
PIEND *n* salient angle

PIENDS > PIEND
PIEPLANT *n* rhubarb
PIEPLANTS > PIEPLANT
PIEPOWDER *n* former court for dealing with certain disputes
PIER *n* platform on stilts sticking out into the sea
PIERAGE *n* accommodation for ships at piers
PIERAGES > PIERAGE
PIERCE *vb* make a hole in or through with a sharp instrument
PIERCED > PIERCE
PIERCER > PIERCE
PIERCERS > PIERCE
PIERCES > PIERCE
PIERCING *adj* (of a sound) shrill and high-pitched ▷ *n* art or practice of piercing body parts for the insertion of jewellery
PIERCINGS > PIERCING
PIERHEAD *n* end of a pier farthest from the shore
PIERHEADS > PIERHEAD
PIERID *n* type of butterfly
PIERIDINE *adj* relating to the family Pieridae of butterflies, that includes the whites, brimstones, and sulphurs
PIERIDS > PIERID
PIERIS *n* American or Asiatic shrub
PIERISES > PIERIS
PIEROG *same as* > PIROG
PIEROGEN > PIEROG
PIEROGI *n* Polish dumpling
PIEROGIES > PIEROGI
PIEROGS > PIEROG
PIERRETTE *n* female clown or masquerader with a whitened face
PIERROT *n* male clown or masquerader with a whitened face
PIERROTS > PIERROT
PIERS > PIER
PIERST *archaic spelling of* > PIERCED
PIERT *n* small plant with small greenish flowers
PIERTS > PIERT
PIES > PIE
PIET *n* magpie
PIETA *n* sculpture, painting, or drawing of the dead Christ, supported by the Virgin Mary
PIETAS > PIETA
PIETIES > PIETY
PIETISM *n* exaggerated piety
PIETISMS > PIETISM
PIETIST > PIETISM
PIETISTIC > PIETISM
PIETISTS > PIETISM
PIETS > PIET

PIETY *n* deep devotion to God and religion
PIEZO *adj* piezoelectric
PIFFERARI > PIFFERARO
PIFFERARO *n* player of piffero
PIFFERO *n* small rustic flute
PIFFEROS > PIFFERO
PIFFLE *n* nonsense ▷ *vb* talk or behave feebly
PIFFLED > PIFFLE
PIFFLER *n* talker of nonsense
PIFFLERS > PIFFLER
PIFFLES > PIFFLE
PIFFLING *adj* worthless
PIG *n* mammal with a long head and movable snout ▷ *vb* eat greedily
PIGBOAT *n* submarine
PIGBOATS > PIGBOAT
PIGEON *n* bird with a heavy body and short legs ▷ *vb* pigeonhole
PIGEONED > PIGEON
PIGEONING > PIGEON
PIGEONITE *n* brownish mineral
PIGEONRY *n* loft for keeping pigeons
PIGEONS > PIGEON
PIGFACE *n* creeping succulent plant
PIGFACES > PIGFACE
PIGFEED *n* food for pigs
PIGFEEDS > PIGFEED
PIGFISH *n* grunting fish of the North American Atlantic coast
PIGFISHES > PIGFISH
PIGGED > PIG
PIGGERIES > PIGGERY
PIGGERY *n* place for keeping and breeding pigs
PIGGIE *same as* > PIGGY
PIGGIER > PIGGY
PIGGIES > PIGGY
PIGGIEST > PIGGY
PIGGIN *n* small wooden bucket or tub
PIGGINESS > PIGGY
PIGGING > PIG
PIGGINGS > PIG
PIGGINS > PIGGIN
PIGGISH *adj* like a pig, esp in appetite or manners
PIGGISHLY > PIGGISH
PIGGY *n* child's word for a pig ▷ *adj* like a pig
PIGGYBACK *n* ride on someone's shoulders ▷ *adv* carried on someone's shoulders ▷ *adj* on the back and shoulders of another person ▷ *vb* give (a person) a piggyback on one's back and shoulders
PIGHEADED *adj* stupidly stubborn
PIGHT *vb* pierce
PIGHTED > PIGHT
PIGHTING > PIGHT
PIGHTLE *n* small enclosure
PIGHTLES > PIGHTLE
PIGHTS > PIGHT

PIGLET n young pig
PIGLETS > PIGLET
PIGLIKE > PIG
PIGLING n young pig
PIGLINGS > PIGLING
PIGMAEAN same as
> PYGMAEAN
PIGMAN n male pig farmer
PIGMEAN same as
> PYGMAEAN
PIGMEAT less common
name for > PORK
PIGMEATS > PIGMEAT
PIGMEN > PIGMAN
PIGMENT n colouring
matter, paint or dye ▷ vb
colour with pigment
PIGMENTAL > PIGMENT
PIGMENTED > PIGMENT
PIGMENTS > PIGMENT
PIGMIES > PIGMY
PIGMOID adj of pygmies
▷ n pygmy
PIGMOIDS > PIGMOID
PIGMY same as > PYGMY
PIGNERATE vb pledge or
pawn
PIGNOLI same as
> PIGNOLIA
PIGNOLIA n edible seed
of nut pine
PIGNOLIAS
> PIGNOLIA
PIGNOLIS > PIGNOLI
PIGNORA > PIGNUS
PIGNORATE same as
> PIGNERATE
PIGNUS n pawn or pledge
PIGNUT n bitter nut of
hickory trees
PIGNUTS > PIGNUT
PIGOUT n binge
PIGOUTS > PIGOUT
PIGPEN same as
> PIGSTY
PIGPENS > PIGPEN
PIGS > PIG
PIGSCONCE n foolish
person
PIGSKIN n skin of the
domestic pig ▷ adj made
of pigskin
PIGSKINS > PIGSKIN
PIGSNEY same as
> PIGSNY
PIGSNEYS > PIGSNEY
PIGSNIE same as
> PIGSNY
PIGSNIES > PIGSNIE
PIGSNY n archaic pet
name for a girl or woman
PIGSTICK vb (esp in
India) hunt and spear wild
boar, esp from horseback
PIGSTICKS
> PIGSTICK
PIGSTIES > PIGSTY
PIGSTUCK > PIGSTICK
PIGSTY n enclosure for
pigs
PIGSWILL n waste food
or other edible matter fed
to pigs
PIGSWILLS
> PIGSWILL
PIGTAIL n plait of hair
hanging from the back or
either side of the head

PIGTAILED > PIGTAIL
PIGTAILS > PIGTAIL·
PIGWASH n wet feed for
pigs
PIGWASHES > PIGWASH
PIGWEED n coarse North
American weed
PIGWEEDS > PIGWEED
PIHOIHOI n variety of
New Zealand pipit
PIHOIHOIS
> PIHOIHOI
PIING > PI
PIKA n burrowing
mammal
PIKAKE n type of Asian
vine
PIKAKES > PIKAKE
PIKAS > PIKA
PIKAU n pack, knapsack,
or rucksack
PIKAUS > PIKAU
PIKE n large predatory
freshwater fish ▷ vb stab
or pierce using a pike ▷ adj
(of the body position of a
diver) bent at the hips but
with the legs straight
PIKED > PIKE
PIKELET n small thick
pancake
PIKELETS > PIKELET
PIKELIKE adj like a pike
PIKEMAN n (formerly)
soldier armed with a pike
PIKEMEN > PIKEMAN
PIKEPERCH n pikelike
freshwater teleost fish
PIKER n shirker
PIKERS > PIKER
PIKES > PIKE
PIKESTAFF n wooden
handle of a pike
PIKI n bread made from
blue cornmeal
PIKING > PIKE
PIKINGS > PIKE
PIKIS > PIKI
PIKUL same as > PICUL
PIKULS > PIKUL
PILA n pillar-like
anatomical structure
PILAE > PILA
PILAF same as > PILAU
PILAFF same as > PILAU
PILAFFS > PILAFF
PILAFS > PILAF
PILAO same as > PILAU
PILAOS > PILAO
PILAR adj relating to hair
PILASTER n square
column, usu set in a wall
PILASTERS
> PILASTER
PILAU n Middle Eastern
dish
PILAUS > PILAU
PILAW same as > PILAU
PILAWS > PILAW
PILCH n outer garment,
originally one made of skin
PILCHARD n small edible
sea fish of the herring
family
PILCHARDS
> PILCHARD
PILCHER n scabbard for
sword

PILCHERS > PILCHER
PILCHES > PILCH
PILCORN n type of oat
PILCORNS > PILCORN
PILCROW n paragraph
mark
PILCROWS > PILCROW
PILE n number of things
lying on top of each other
▷ vb collect into a pile
PILEA n plant which
releases a cloud of pollen
when shaken
PILEAS > PILEA
PILEATE adj (of birds)
having a crest
PILEATED same as
> PILEATE
PILED > PILE
PILEI > PILEUS
PILELESS > PILE
PILEOUS adj hairy
PILER n placer of things
on pile
PILERS > PILER
PILES pl n swollen veins
in the rectum,
haemorrhoids
PILEUM n top of a bird's
head
PILEUP n multiple
collision of vehicles
PILEUPS > PILEUP
PILEUS n upper
cap-shaped part of a
mushroom
PILEWORK n
construction built from
heavy stakes or cylinders
PILEWORKS
> PILEWORK
PILEWORT n plant used
to treat piles
PILEWORTS
> PILEWORT
PILFER vb steal in small
quantities
PILFERAGE n act or
practice of stealing small
quantities or articles
PILFERED > PILFER
PILFERER > PILFER
PILFERERS > PILFER
PILFERIES > PILFERY
PILFERING > PILFER
PILFERS > PILFER
PILFERY n theft
PILGARLIC n bald head
or a man with a bald head
PILGRIM n person who
journeys to a holy place
▷ vb travel as a pilgrim
PILGRIMED > PILGRIM
PILGRIMER n one who
undertakes a pilgrimage
PILGRIMS > PILGRIM
PILI n Philippine tree
with edible seeds
resembling almonds
PILIER > PILY
PILIEST > PILY
PILIFORM adj
resembling a long hair
PILING n act of driving
piles
PILINGS > PILING
PILINUT n type of nut
found in the Philippines

PILINUTS > PILINUT
PILIS > PILI
PILL n small ball of
medicine swallowed
whole ▷ vb peel or skin
(something)
PILLAGE vb steal
property by violence in
war ▷ n violent seizure of
goods, esp in war
PILLAGED > PILLAGE
PILLAGER > PILLAGE
PILLAGERS > PILLAGE
PILLAGES > PILLAGE
PILLAGING n act of
pillaging
PILLAR n upright post,
usu supporting a roof ▷ vb
provide or support with
pillars
PILLARED > PILLAR
PILLARING > PILLAR
PILLARIST n recluse
who sat on high pillar
PILLARS > PILLAR
PILLAU same as > PILAU
PILLAUS > PILLAU
PILLBOX n small box for
pills
PILLBOXES > PILLBOX
PILLBUG n type of
woodlouse
PILLBUGS > PILLBUG
PILLED > PILL
PILLHEAD n person
addicted to pills
PILLHEADS
> PILLHEAD
PILLICOCK n penis
PILLIE n pilchard
PILLIES > PILLIE
PILLING > PILL
PILLINGS > PILL
PILLION n seat for a
passenger behind the rider
of a motorcycle ▷ adv on a
pillion ▷ vb ride pillion
PILLIONED > PILLION
PILLIONS > PILLION
PILLOCK n stupid or
annoying person
PILLOCKS > PILLOCK
PILLORIED > PILLORY
PILLORIES > PILLORY
PILLORISE same as
> PILLORIZE
PILLORIZE vb put in
pillory
PILLORY n frame in
which an offender was
locked and exposed to
public abuse ▷ vb ridicule
publicly
PILLOW n stuffed cloth
bag for supporting the
head in bed ▷ vb rest as if
on a pillow
PILLOWED > PILLOW
PILLOWIER > PILLOWY
PILLOWING > PILLOW
PILLOWS > PILLOW
PILLOWY adj like a
pillow
PILLS > PILL
PILLWORM n worm that
rolls up spirally
PILLWORMS
> PILLWORM

p

PILLWORT n small Eurasian water fern
PILLWORTS
> PILLWORT
PILOMOTOR adj causing movement of hairs
PILONIDAL adj of the crease above the buttocks
PILOSE adj covered with fine soft hairs
PILOSITY > PILOSE
PILOT n person qualified to fly an aircraft or spacecraft ▷ adj experimental and preliminary ▷ vb act as the pilot of
PILOTAGE n act of piloting an aircraft or ship
PILOTAGES
> PILOTAGE
PILOTED > PILOT
PILOTFISH n fish that accompanies sharks
PILOTING n navigational handling of a ship near land
PILOTINGS
> PILOTING
PILOTIS pl n posts raising a building up from the ground
PILOTLESS > PILOT
PILOTMAN n railway worker who directs trains through hazardous stretches of track
PILOTMEN > PILOTMAN
PILOTS > PILOT
PILOUS same as
> PILOSE
PILOW same as > PILAU
PILOWS > PILOW
PILSENER same as
> PILSNER
PILSENERS
> PILSENER
PILSNER n type of pale beer with a strong flavour of hops
PILSNERS > PILSNER
PILULA n pill
PILULAE > PILULA
PILULAR > PILULA
PILULAS > PILULA
PILULE n small pill
PILULES > PILULE
PILUM n ancient Roman javelin
PILUS > PILI
PILY adj like wool or pile
PIMA n type of cotton
PIMAS > PIMA
PIMENT n wine flavoured with spices
PIMENTO same as
> PIMIENTO
PIMENTON n smoked chilli powder
PIMENTONS
> PIMENTON
PIMENTOS > PIMENTO
PIMENTS > PIMENT
PIMIENTO n Spanish pepper with a red fruit used as a vegetable
PIMIENTOS
> PIMIENTO

PIMP n person who gets customers for a prostitute ▷ vb embellish
PIMPED > PIMP
PIMPERNEL n wild plant with small star-shaped flowers
PIMPING n embellishment
PIMPINGS > PIMPING
PIMPLE n small pus-filled spot on the skin
PIMPLED > PIMPLE
PIMPLES > PIMPLE
PIMPLIER > PIMPLE
PIMPLIEST > PIMPLE
PIMPLY > PIMPLE
PIMPS > PIMP
PIN n short thin piece of stiff wire with a point and head, for fastening things ▷ vb fasten with a pin
PINA n cone of silver amalgam
PINACEOUS adj relating to a family of conifers with needle-like leaves which includes the pine, spruce, fir, larch, and cedar
PINACOID n pair of opposite parallel faces of crystal
PINACOIDS > PINACOID
PINAFORE n apron
PINAFORED
> PINAFORE
PINAFORES
> PINAFORE
PINAKOID same as
> PINACOID
PINAKOIDS
> PINAKOID
PINANG n areca tree
PINANGS > PINANG
PINAS > PINA
PINASTER n Mediterranean pine tree
PINASTERS
> PINASTER
PINATA n papier-mâché party decoration filled with sweets
PINATAS > PINATA
PINBALL vb ricochet
PINBALLED > PINBALL
PINBALLS > PINBALL
PINBOARD n cork board for pinning notices, messages etc on
PINBOARDS
> PINBOARD
PINBONE n part of sirloin
PINBONES > PINBONE
PINCASE n case for holding pins
PINCASES > PINCASE
PINCER vb grip with pincers
PINCERED > PINCER
PINCERING > PINCER
PINCERS pl n tool consisting of two hinged arms, for gripping
PINCH vb squeeze between finger and thumb ▷ n act of pinching
PINCHBECK n alloy of zinc and copper, used as

imitation gold ▷ adj sham or cheap
PINCHBUG n type of crab
PINCHBUGS
> PINCHBUG
PINCHCOCK n clamp used to compress a flexible tube to control the flow of fluid through it
PINCHECK n small check woven into fabric
PINCHECKS
> PINCHECK
PINCHED > PINCH
PINCHER > PINCH
PINCHERS > PINCH
PINCHES > PINCH
PINCHFIST n mean person
PINCHGUT n miserly person
PINCHGUTS
> PINCHGUT
PINCHING > PINCH
PINCHINGS > PINCH
PINCURL n curl secured by a hairpin
PINCURLS > PINCURL
PINDAN n desert region of Western Australia
PINDANS > PINDAN
PINDAREE same as
> PINDARI
PINDAREES
> PINDAREE
PINDARI n former irregular Indian horseman
PINDARIS > PINDARI
PINDER n person who impounds
PINDERS > PINDER
PINDLING adj peevish or fractious
PINDOWN n wrestling manoeuvre
PINDOWNS > PINDOWN
PINE n evergreen coniferous tree ▷ vb feel great longing (for)
PINEAL adj resembling a pine cone ▷ n pineal gland
PINEALS > PINEAL
PINEAPPLE n large tropical fruit with juicy yellow flesh and a hard skin
PINECONE n seed-producing structure of a pine tree
PINECONES
> PINECONE
PINED > PINE
PINEDROPS n parasitic herb of pine trees
PINELAND n area covered with pine forest
PINELANDS
> PINELAND
PINELIKE > PINE
PINENE n isomeric terpene found in many essential oils
PINENES > PINENE
PINERIES > PINERY
PINERY n place, esp a hothouse, where pineapples are grown
PINES > PINE

PINESAP n red herb of N America
PINESAPS > PINESAP
PINETA > PINETUM
PINETUM n area of land where pine trees are grown
PINEWOOD n wood of pine trees
PINEWOODS
> PINEWOOD
PINEY > PINE
PINFALL another name for
> FALL
PINFALLS > PINFALL
PINFISH n small porgy of the Atlantic
PINFISHES > PINFISH
PINFOLD n pound for stray cattle ▷ vb gather or confine in or as if in a pinfold
PINFOLDED > PINFOLD
PINFOLDS > PINFOLD
PING n short high-pitched sound ▷ vb make such a noise
PINGED > PING
PINGER n device, esp a timer, that makes a pinging sound
PINGERS > PINGER
PINGING > PING
PINGLE vb enclose small area of ground
PINGLED > PINGLE
PINGLER > PINGLE
PINGLES > PINGLE
PINGLING > PINGLE
PINGO n mound of earth or gravel formed in Arctic regions
PINGOES > PINGO
PINGOS > PINGO
PINGPONG n Australian football
PINGPONGS
> PINGPONG
PINGRASS n weed with fernlike leaves
PINGS > PING
PINGUEFY vb become greasy or fat
PINGUID adj fatty, oily, or greasy
PINGUIN same as
> PENGUIN
PINGUINS > PINGUIN
PINHEAD n head of a pin
PINHEADED adj stupid or silly
PINHEADS > PINHEAD
PINHOLE n small hole made with or as if with a pin
PINHOLES > PINHOLE
PINHOOKER n trader of young thoroughbred horses
PINIER > PINY
PINIES > PINY
PINIEST > PINY
PINING > PINE
PINION n bird's wing ▷ vb immobilize (someone) by tying or holding his or her arms

PINIONED > PINION
PINIONING > PINION
PINIONS > PINION
PINITE n greyish-green or brown mineral
PINITES > PINITE
PINITOL n compound found in pinewood
PINITOLS > PINITOL
PINK n pale reddish colour ▷ adj of the colour pink ▷ vb (of an engine) make a metallic noise because not working properly
PINKED > PINK
PINKEN vb turn pink
PINKENED > PINKEN
PINKENING > PINKEN
PINKENS > PINKEN
PINKER n something that pinks
PINKERS > PINKER
PINKERTON n private detective
PINKEST > PINK
PINKEY n type of ship
PINKEYE n acute inflammation of the conjunctiva of the eye
PINKEYES > PINKEYE
PINKEYS > PINKEY
PINKIE n little finger
PINKIER > PINKY
PINKIES > PINKIE
PINKIEST > PINKIE
PINKINESS n quality of being pink
PINKING > PINK
PINKINGS > PINK
PINKISH > PINK
PINKLY > PINK
PINKNESS > PINK
PINKO n person regarded as mildly left-wing
PINKOES > PINKO
PINKOS > PINKO
PINKROOT n plant with red-and-yellow flowers and pink roots
PINKROOTS > PINKROOT
PINKS > PINK
PINKY adj of a pink colour
PINLESS adj without a pin
PINNA n external part of the ear
PINNACE n ship's boat
PINNACES > PINNACE
PINNACLE n highest point of fame or success ▷ vb set on or as if on a pinnacle
PINNACLED > PINNACLE
PINNACLES > PINNACLE
PINNAE > PINNA
PINNAL > PINNA
PINNAS > PINNA
PINNATE adj (of compound leaves) having leaflets growing opposite each other in pairs
PINNATED same as > PINNATE
PINNATELY > PINNATE
PINNATION > PINNATE

PINNED > PIN
PINNER n person or thing that pins
PINNERS > PINNER
PINNET n pinnacle
PINNETS > PINNET
PINNIE same as > PINNY
PINNIES > PINNIE
PINNING > PIN
PINNINGS > PIN
PINNIPED n aquatic placental mammal such as the seal, sea lion, walrus, etc
PINNIPEDE same as > PINNIPED
PINNIPEDS > PINNIPED
PINNOCK n small bird
PINNOCKS > PINNOCK
PINNOED adj held or bound by the arms
PINNULA same as > PINNULE
PINNULAE > PINNULA
PINNULAR > PINNULE
PINNULAS > PINNULA
PINNULATE > PINNULE
PINNULE n lobe of a leaflet of a pinnate compound leaf
PINNULES > PINNULE
PINNY informal or child's name for > PINAFORE
PINOCHLE n card game for two to four players similar to bezique
PINOCHLES > PINOCHLE
PINOCLE same as > PINOCHLE
PINOCLES > PINOCLE
PINOCYTIC adj of process of pinocytosis
PINOLE n flour made in the southwestern United States
PINOLES > PINOLE
PINON n low-growing pine
PINONES > PINON
PINONS > PINON
PINOT n any of several grape varieties
PINOTAGE n variety of red grape
PINOTAGES > PINOTAGE
PINOTS > PINOT
PINPOINT vb locate or identify exactly ▷ adj exact ▷ n insignificant or trifling thing
PINPOINTS > PINPOINT
PINPRICK n small irritation or annoyance ▷ vb puncture with or as if with a pin
PINPRICKS > PINPRICK
PINS > PIN
PINSCHER n breed of dog
PINSCHERS > PINSCHER
PINSETTER n device that sets pins in bowling alley

PINSPOT vb illuminate with a small spotlight
PINSPOTS > PINSPOT
PINSTRIPE n very narrow stripe in fabric
PINSWELL n small boil
PINSWELLS > PINSWELL
PINT n liquid measure, 1/8 gallon (.568 litre)
PINTA n pint of milk
PINTABLE n pinball machine
PINTABLES > PINTABLE
PINTADA same as > PINTADO
PINTADAS > PINTADA
PINTADERA n decorative stamp, usually made of clay, found in the Neolithic of the E Mediterranean and in many American cultures
PINTADO n species of seagoing petrel
PINTADOES > PINTADO
PINTADOS > PINTADO
PINTAIL n greyish-brown duck with a pointed tail
PINTAILED adj having tapered tail
PINTAILS > PINTAIL
PINTANO n tropical reef fish
PINTANOS > PINTANO
PINTAS > PINTA
PINTLE n pin or bolt forming the pivot of a hinge
PINTLES > PINTLE
PINTO adj marked with patches of white ▷ n pinto horse
PINTOES > PINTO
PINTOS > PINTO
PINTS > PINT
PINTSIZE same as > PINTSIZED
PINTSIZED adj very small
PINTUCK vb tuck with a narrow fold of fabric
PINTUCKED > PINTUCK
PINTUCKS > PINTUCK
PINUP n picture of a physically attractive person
PINUPS > PINUP
PINWALE n fabric with narrow ridges
PINWALES > PINWALE
PINWEED n herb with tiny flowers
PINWEEDS > PINWEED
PINWHEEL n cogwheel whose teeth are formed by small pins
PINWHEELS > PINWHEEL
PINWORK n (in needlepoint lace) fine raised stitches
PINWORKS > PINWORK
PINWORM n parasitic nematode worm
PINWORMS > PINWORM

PINWRENCH n wrench with a projection to fit a hole
PINXIT vb (he or she) painted (it)
PINY variant of > PEONY
PINYIN n system of romanized spelling for the Chinese language
PINYINS > PINYIN
PINYON n low-growing pine
PINYONS > PINYON
PIOLET n type of ice axe
PIOLETS > PIOLET
PION n type of subatomic particle
PIONED adj abounding in marsh marigolds
PIONEER n explorer or early settler of a new country ▷ vb be the pioneer or leader of
PIONEERED > PIONEER
PIONEERS > PIONEER
PIONER obsolete spelling of > PIONEER
PIONERS > PIONER
PIONEY same as > PEONY
PIONEYS > PIONEY
PIONIC > PION
PIONIES > PIONY
PIONING n work of pioneers
PIONINGS > PIONING
PIONS > PION
PIONY same as > PEONY
PIOPIO n New Zealand thrush, thought to be extinct
PIOPIOS > PIOPIO
PIOSITIES > PIOSITY
PIOSITY n grandiose display of piety
PIOTED adj pied
PIOUS adj deeply religious, devout
PIOUSLY > PIOUS
PIOUSNESS > PIOUS
PIOY variant of > PEEOY
PIOYE variant of > PEEOY
PIOYES > PIOYE
PIOYS > PIOY
PIP n small seed in a fruit ▷ vb chirp
PIPA n tongueless S American toad
PIPAGE n pipes collectively
PIPAGES > PIPAGE
PIPAL same as > PEEPUL
PIPALS > PIPAL
PIPAS > PIPA
PIPE n tube for conveying liquid or gas ▷ vb play on a pipe
PIPEAGE same as > PIPAGE
PIPEAGES > PIPEAGE
PIPECLAY n fine white clay used in tobacco pipes ▷ vb whiten with pipeclay
PIPECLAYS > PIPECLAY
PIPED > PIPE
PIPEFISH n fish with a long tubelike snout and an elongated body

p

PIPEFUL n as much tobacco, etc as will fill a pipe

PIPEFULS > PIPEFUL

PIPELESS > PIPE

PIPELIKE > PIPE

PIPELINE n long pipe for transporting oil, water, etc

PIPELINED > PIPELINE

PIPELINES > PIPELINE

PIPER n player on a pipe or bagpipes

PIPERIC > PIPERINE

PIPERINE n crystalline insoluble alkaloid that is the active ingredient of pepper

PIPERINES > PIPERINE

PIPERONAL n white fragrant aldehyde used in flavourings, perfumery, and suntan lotions

PIPERS > PIPER

PIPES > PIPE

PIPESTEM n hollow stem of pipe

PIPESTEMS > PIPESTEM

PIPESTONE n variety of consolidated red clay used by Native Americans to make tobacco pipes

PIPET same as > PIPETTE

PIPETS > PIPET

PIPETTE n slender glass tube used to transfer or measure fluids ▷ vb transfer or measure out (a liquid) using a pipette

PIPETTED > PIPETTE

PIPETTES > PIPETTE

PIPETTING > PIPETTE

PIPEWORK n stops and flues on pipe organ

PIPEWORKS > PIPEWORK

PIPEWORT n perennial plant with a twisted flower stalk and a greenish-grey scaly flower head

PIPEWORTS > PIPEWORT

PIPI n edible mollusc often used as bait

PIPIER > PIPE

PIPIEST > PIPE

PIPINESS n material's suitability for use as pipe

PIPING n system of pipes

PIPINGLY > PIPING

PIPINGS > PIPING

PIPIS > PIPI

PIPISTREL n species of bat

PIPIT n small brownish songbird

PIPITS > PIPIT

PIPKIN same as > PIGGIN

PIPKINS > PIPKIN

PIPLESS > PIP

PIPPED > PIP

PIPPIER > PIPPY

PIPPIEST > PIPPY

PIPPIN n type of eating apple

PIPPING > PIP

PIPPINS > PIPPIN

PIPPY adj containing many pips

PIPS > PIP

PIPSQUEAK n insignificant or contemptible person

PIPUL n Indian fig tree

PIPULS > PIPUL

PIPY > PIPE

PIQUANCE same as > PIQUANT

PIQUANCES > PIQUANT

PIQUANCY > PIQUANT

PIQUANT adj having a pleasant spicy taste

PIQUANTLY > PIQUANT

PIQUE n feeling of hurt pride, baffled curiosity, or resentment ▷ vb hurt the pride of

PIQUED > PIQUE

PIQUES > PIQUE

PIQUET n card game for two ▷ vb play game of piquet

PIQUETED > PIQUET

PIQUETING > PIQUET

PIQUETS > PIQUET

PIQUILLO n variety of sweet red pepper

PIQUILLOS > PIQUILLO

PIQUING > PIQUE

PIR n Sufi master

PIRACETAM n drug used to treat muscle spasm

PIRACIES > PIRACY

PIRACY n robbery on the seas

PIRAGUA same as > PIROGUE

PIRAGUAS > PIRAGUA

PIRAI n large S American fish

PIRAIS > PIRAI

PIRANA same as > PIRANHA

PIRANAS > PIRANA

PIRANHA n fierce fish of tropical America

PIRANHAS > PIRANHA

PIRARUCU n large S American food fish

PIRARUCUS > PIRARUCU

PIRATE n sea robber ▷ vb sell or reproduce (artistic work etc) illegally

PIRATED > PIRATE

PIRATES > PIRATE

PIRATIC > PIRATE

PIRATICAL > PIRATE

PIRATING n act of pirating

PIRATINGS > PIRATING

PIRAYA same as > PIRAI

PIRAYAS > PIRAYA

PIRIFORM adj shaped like pear

PIRL n ripple in water

PIRLICUE same as > PURLICUE

PIRLICUED > PIRLICUE

PIRLICUES > PIRLICUE

PIRLS > PIRL

PIRN n reel or bobbin

PIRNIE n stripy nightcap

PIRNIES > PIRNIE

PIRNIT adj striped

PIRNS > PIRN

PIROG n type of large Russian pie

PIROGEN n turnovers made from kneaded dough

PIROGHI > PIROG

PIROGI > PIROG

PIROGIES > PIROG

PIROGUE n any of various kinds of dugout canoes

PIROGUES > PIROGUE

PIROJKI same as > PIROSHKI

PIROPLASM n parasite of red blood cells

PIROQUE same as > PIROGUE

PIROQUES > PIROQUE

PIROSHKI same as > PIROZHKI

PIROUETTE n spinning turn balanced on the toes of one foot ▷ vb perform a pirouette

PIROZHKI > PIROZHOK

PIROZHOK n small triangular pastry filled with meat, vegetables, etc

PIRS > PIR

PIS > PI

PISCARIES > PISCARY

PISCARY n place where fishing takes place

PISCATOR n fisherman

PISCATORS > PISCATOR

PISCATORY adj of or relating to fish, fishing, or fishermen

PISCATRIX n female angler

PISCIFORM adj having form of fish

PISCINA n stone basin where water used at Mass is poured away

PISCINAE > PISCINA

PISCINAL > PISCINA

PISCINAS > PISCINA

PISCINE n pond or pool

PISCINES > PISCINE

PISCIVORE n eater of fish

PISCO n S American brandy

PISCOS > PISCO

PISE n rammed earth or clay used to make floors or walls

PISES > PISE

PISH interj exclamation of impatience or contempt ▷ vb make this exclamation at (someone or something)

PISHED > PISH

PISHEOG same as > PISHOGUE

PISHEOGS > PISHEOG

PISHER n Yiddish term for small boy

PISHERS > PISHER

PISHES > PISH

PISHING > PISH

PISHOGE same as > PISHOGUE

PISHOGES > PISHOGE

PISHOGUE n sorcery

PISHOGUES > PISHOGUE

PISIFORM adj resembling a pea ▷ n small pealike bone on the ulnar side of the carpus

PISIFORMS > PISIFORM

PISKIES > PISKY

PISKY n Cornish fairy

PISMIRE archaic or dialect word for > ANT

PISMIRES > PISMIRE

PISO n peso of the Philippines

PISOLITE n sedimentary rock

PISOLITES > PISOLITE

PISOLITH same as > PISOLITE

PISOLITHS > PISOLITH

PISOLITIC > PISOLITE

PISOS > PISO

PISS vb vulgar slang word for urinate ▷ n act of urinating

PISSANT n vulgar slang for an insignificant person

PISSANTS > PISSANT

PISSED adj slang word for drunk

PISSER n vulgar word meaning someone or something that pisses

PISSERS > PISSER

PISSES > PISS

PISSHEAD n vulgar slang for a drunkard

PISSHEADS > PISSHEAD

PISSHOLE n vulgar word for a hole made in soluble matter by urinating

PISSHOLES > PISSHOLE

PISSIER > PISSY

PISSIEST > PISSY

PISSING > PISS

PISSOIR n public urinal

PISSOIRS > PISSOIR

PISSY adj vulgar word meaning soiled with urine

PISTACHE n tree yielding pistachio nut

PISTACHES > PISTACHE

PISTACHIO n edible nut of a Mediterranean tree ▷ adj of a yellowish-green colour

PISTAREEN n Spanish coin, used in the US and the Caribbean until the 18th century

PISTE n ski slope

PISTED adj marked off into pistes

PISTES > PISTE

PISTIL n seed-bearing part of a flower

PISTILLAR adj relating to a pistil

PISTILS > PISTIL

PISTOL n short-barrelled handgun ▷ vb shoot with a pistol

PISTOLE n gold coin formerly used in Europe

PISTOLED > PISTOL

PISTOLEER n person, esp a soldier, who is armed with or fires a pistol

PISTOLERO n shooter of pistols

PISTOLES > PISTOLE

PISTOLET n small pistol

PISTOLETS > PISTOLET

PISTOLIER n shooter of pistols

PISTOLING > PISTOL

PISTOLLED > PISTOL

PISTOLS > PISTOL

PISTON n cylindrical part in an engine that slides to and fro in a cylinder

PISTONS > PISTON

PISTOU n French sauce

PISTOUS > PISTOU

PIT n deep hole in the ground ▷ vb mark with small dents or scars

PITA n any of several agave plants yielding a strong fibre

PITAHAYA n any giant cactus of Central America and the SW United States

PITAHAYAS > PITAHAYA

PITAPAT adv with quick light taps ▷ n such taps ▷ vb make quick light taps or beats

PITAPATS > PITAPAT

PITARA variant of > PETARA

PITARAH variant of > PETARA

PITARAHS > PITARAH

PITARAS > PITARA

PITAS > PITA

PITAYA same as > PITAHAYA

PITAYAS > PITAYA

PITCH vb throw, hurl ▷ n area marked out for playing sport

PITCHBEND n electronic device that enables a player to bend the pitch of a note being sounded on a synthesizer, usually with a pitch wheel, strip, or lever

PITCHED > PITCH

PITCHER n large jug with a narrow neck

PITCHERS > PITCHER

PITCHES > PITCH

PITCHFORK n large long-handled fork for lifting hay ▷ vb thrust abruptly or violently

PITCHIER > PITCHY

PITCHIEST > PITCHY

PITCHILY > PITCHY

PITCHING > PITCH

PITCHINGS > PITCH

PITCHMAN n itinerant pedlar of small merchandise who operates from a stand at a fair, etc

PITCHMEN > PITCHMAN

PITCHOUT n type of baseball pitch

PITCHOUTS > PITCHOUT

PITCHPINE n large N American pine tree

PITCHPIPE n small one-note pipe used for tuning instruments

PITCHPOLE vb turn end over end

PITCHY adj full of or covered with pitch

PITEOUS adj arousing pity

PITEOUSLY > PITEOUS

PITFALL n hidden difficulty or danger

PITFALLS > PITFALL

PITH n soft white lining of the rind of oranges etc ▷ vb destroy the brain and spinal cord of a laboratory animal

PITHBALL n type of conductor

PITHBALLS > PITHBALL

PITHEAD n top of a mine shaft and the buildings and hoisting gear around it

PITHEADS > PITHEAD

PITHECOID adj relating to apes ▷ n ape, esp an anthropoid ape

PITHED > PITH

PITHFUL > PITH

PITHIER > PITHY

PITHIEST > PITHY

PITHILY > PITHY

PITHINESS > PITHY

PITHING > PITH

PITHLESS > PITH

PITHLIKE > PITH

PITHOI > PITHOS

PITHOS n large ceramic container for oil or grain

PITHS > PITH

PITHY adj short and full of meaning

PITIABLE adj arousing or deserving pity or contempt

PITIABLY > PITIABLE

PITIED > PITY

PITIER > PITY

PITIERS > PITY

PITIES > PITY

PITIETH vb as in it pitieth me archaic inflection of 'pity'

PITIFUL adj arousing pity

PITIFULLY > PITIFUL

PITIKINS n as in ods pitikins mild oath

PITILESS adj feeling no pity or mercy

PITLIKE adj like a pit

PITMAN n coal miner ▷ n connecting rod (in a machine)

PITMANS > PITMAN

PITMEN > PITMAN

PITON n metal spike used in climbing to secure a rope

PITONS > PITON

PITOT n tube used to measure the pressure of a liquid stream

PITOTS > PITOT

PITPROP n support beam in mine shaft

PITPROPS > PITPROP

PITS > PIT

PITSAW n large saw formerly used for cutting logs into planks

PITSAWS > PITSAW

PITTA n small brightly coloured ground-dwelling tropical bird

PITTANCE n very small amount of money

PITTANCES > PITTANCE

PITTAS > PITTA

PITTED > PIT

PITTEN adj having been put

PITTER vb make pattering sound

PITTERED > PITTER

PITTERING > PITTER

PITTERS > PITTER

PITTING > PIT

PITTINGS > PIT

PITTITE n occupant of a theatre pit

PITTITES > PITTITE

PITUITA n thick nasal secretion

PITUITARY n gland at the base of the brain, that helps to control growth ▷ adj of or relating to the pituitary gland

PITUITAS > PITUITA

PITUITE n mucus

PITUITES > PITUITE

PITUITRIN n extract from pituitary gland

PITURI n Australian solanaceous shrub

PITURIS > PITURI

PITY n sympathy or sorrow for others' suffering ▷ vb feel pity for

PITYING > PITY

PITYINGLY > PITY

PITYROID adj resembling bran

PIU adv more (quickly, softly, etc)

PIUM n stinging insect

PIUMS > PIUM

PIUPIU n skirt worn by Māoris on ceremonial occasions

PIUPIUS > PIUPIU

PIVOT n central shaft on which something turns ▷ vb provide with or turn on a pivot

PIVOTABLE > PIVOT

PIVOTAL adj of crucial importance

PIVOTALLY > PIVOTAL

PIVOTED > PIVOT

PIVOTER > PIVOT

PIVOTERS > PIVOT

PIVOTING > PIVOT

PIVOTINGS > PIVOT

PIVOTMAN n person in rank around whom others wheel

PIVOTMEN > PIVOTMAN

PIVOTS > PIVOT

PIX less common spelling of > PYX

PIXEL n any of a number of very small picture elements

PIXELATE vb divide an image into pixels

PIXELATED > PIXELATE

PIXELATES > PIXELATE

PIXELLATE same as > PIXELATE

PIXELS > PIXEL

PIXES > PIX

PIXIE n (in folklore) fairy

PIXIEISH > PIXIE

PIXIES > PIXY

PIXILATE same as > PIXELATE

PIXILATED adj eccentric or whimsical

PIXILATES > PIXILATE

PIXILLATE same as > PIXELATE

PIXINESS > PIXIE

PIXY same as > PIXIE

PIXYISH > PIXY

PIZAZZ same as > PIZZAZZ

PIZAZZES > PIZAZZ

PIZAZZIER > PIZAZZY

PIZAZZY adj exciting and lively

PIZE vb strike (someone a blow)

PIZED > PIZE

PIZES > PIZE

PIZING > PIZE

PIZZA n flat disc of dough covered with a wide variety of savoury toppings and baked

PIZZAIOLA adj having a type of tomato sauce

PIZZALIKE > PIZZA

PIZZAS > PIZZA

PIZZAZ same as > PZAZZ

PIZZAZES > PIZZAZ

PIZZAZZ n attractive combination of energy and style

PIZZAZZES > PIZZAZZ

PIZZAZZY same as > PIZZAZZY

PIZZELLE n Italian sweet wafer

PIZZELLES > PIZZELLE

PIZZERIA n place where pizzas are made, sold, or eaten

PIZZERIAS > PIZZERIA

PIZZICATI
> PIZZICATO

PIZZICATO adj played by plucking the string of a violin etc with the finger ▷ adv (in music for the violin family) to be plucked with the finger ▷ n style or technique of playing a normally bowed stringed instrument in this manner

PIZZLE n archaic word for the penis of an animal

PIZZLES > PIZZLE

PLAAS n farm

PLAASES > PLAAS

PLACABLE adj easily placated or appeased

PLACABLY > PLACABLE

PLACARD n notice that is carried or displayed in public ▷ vb attach placards to

PLACARDED > PLACARD

PLACARDS > PLACARD

PLACATE vb make (someone) stop feeling angry or upset

PLACATED > PLACATE

PLACATER > PLACATE

PLACATERS > PLACATE

PLACATES > PLACATE

PLACATING > PLACATE

PLACATION > PLACATE

PLACATIVE same as
> PLACATORY

PLACATORY adj placating or intended to placate

PLACCAT variant of
> PLACKET

PLACCATE variant of
> PLACKET

PLACCATES
> PLACCATE

PLACCATS > PLACCAT

PLACE n particular part of an area or space ▷ vb put in a particular place

PLACEABLE > PLACE

PLACEBO n pill given to a patient instead of an active drug

PLACEBOES > PLACEBO

PLACEBOS > PLACEBO

PLACED > PLACE

PLACEKICK n (in football) kick in which the ball is placed in position before it is kicked ▷ vb take a placekick

PLACELESS adj not rooted in a specific place or community

PLACEMAN n person who holds a public office as a reward for political support

PLACEMAT n table mat for a person to put their plate on

PLACEMATS
> PLACEMAT

PLACEMEN > PLACEMAN

PLACEMENT n arrangement

PLACENTA n organ formed in the womb during pregnancy,

providing nutrients for the fetus

PLACENTAE
> PLACENTA

PLACENTAL adj (esp of animals) having a placenta

PLACENTAS
> PLACENTA

PLACER n surface sediment containing particles of gold or some other valuable mineral

PLACERS > PLACER

PLACES > PLACE

PLACET n vote or expression of assent

PLACETS > PLACET

PLACID adj not easily excited or upset, calm

PLACIDER > PLACID

PLACIDEST > PLACID

PLACIDITY > PLACID

PLACIDLY > PLACID

PLACING n method of issuing securities to the public using an intermediary

PLACINGS > PLACING

PLACIT n decree or dictum

PLACITA > PLACITUM

PLACITORY > PLACIT

PLACITS > PLACIT

PLACITUM n court or assembly in Middle Ages

PLACK n small former Scottish coin

PLACKET n opening at the waist of a dress or skirt

PLACKETS > PLACKET

PLACKLESS adj lacking money

PLACKS > PLACK

PLACODERM n extinct bony-plated fishlike vertebrate

PLACOID adj platelike or flattened ▷ n fish with placoid scales

PLACOIDS > PLACOID

PLAFOND n ceiling, esp one having ornamentation

PLAFONDS > PLAFOND

PLAGAL adj (of a cadence) progressing from the subdominant to the tonic chord

PLAGE n bright patch in the sun's chromosphere

PLAGES > PLAGE

PLAGIARY n person who plagiarizes or a piece of plagiarism

PLAGIUM n crime of kidnapping

PLAGIUMS > PLAGIUM

PLAGUE n fast-spreading fatal disease ▷ vb trouble or annoy continually

PLAGUED > PLAGUE

PLAGUER > PLAGUE

PLAGUERS > PLAGUE

PLAGUES > PLAGUE

PLAGUEY same as
> PLAGUY

PLAGUIER > PLAGUEY

PLAGUIEST > PLAGUEY

PLAGUILY > PLAGUY

PLAGUING > PLAGUE

PLAGUY adj disagreeable or vexing ▷ adv disagreeably or annoyingly

PLAICE n edible European flatfish

PLAICES > PLAICE

PLAID n long piece of tartan cloth worn as part of Highland dress ▷ vb weave cloth into plaid

PLAIDED > PLAID

PLAIDING > PLAID

PLAIDINGS > PLAID

PLAIDMAN n wearer of plaid

PLAIDMEN > PLAIDMAN

PLAIDS > PLAID

PLAIN adj easy to see or understand ▷ n large stretch of level country ▷ adv clearly or simply ▷ vb complain

PLAINANT n plaintiff

PLAINANTS
> PLAINANT

PLAINED > PLAIN

PLAINER > PLAIN

PLAINEST > PLAIN

PLAINFUL adj apt to complain

PLAINING > PLAIN

PLAININGS > PLAIN

PLAINISH > PLAIN

PLAINLY > PLAIN

PLAINNESS > PLAIN

PLAINS pl n extensive tracts of flat treeless countryside

PLAINSMAN n person who lives in a plains region, esp in the Great Plains of North America

PLAINSMEN
> PLAINSMAN

PLAINSONG n unaccompanied singing, esp in a medieval church

PLAINT n complaint or lamentation

PLAINTEXT n (in telecommunications) message set in a directly readable form rather than in coded groups

PLAINTFUL adj complaining

PLAINTIFF n person who sues in a court of law

PLAINTIVE adj sad, mournful

PLAINTS > PLAINT

PLAINWORK n weaving

PLAISTER n plaster

PLAISTERS
> PLAISTER

PLAIT n intertwined length of hair ▷ vb intertwine separate strands in a pattern

PLAITED > PLAIT

PLAITER > PLAIT

PLAITERS > PLAIT

PLAITING > PLAIT

PLAITINGS > PLAIT

PLAITS > PLAIT

PLAN n way thought out to do or achieve something ▷ vb arrange beforehand

PLANAR adj of or relating to a plane

PLANARIA n type of flatworm

PLANARIAN n type of flatworm

PLANARIAS > PLANARIA

PLANARITY > PLANAR

PLANATE adj having been flattened

PLANATION n erosion of a land surface until it is basically flat

PLANCH vb cover with planks

PLANCHE same as
> PLANCH

PLANCHED > PLANCH

PLANCHES > PLANCH

PLANCHET n piece of metal ready to be stamped as a coin, medal, etc

PLANCHETS
> PLANCHET

PLANCHING > PLANCH

PLANE n aeroplane ▷ adj perfectly flat or level ▷ vb glide or skim

PLANED > PLANE

PLANELOAD n amount or number carried by plane

PLANENESS > PLANE

PLANER n machine with a cutting tool that makes repeated horizontal strokes

PLANERS > PLANER

PLANES > PLANE

PLANESIDE n area next to aeroplane

PLANET n large body in space that revolves round the sun or another star

PLANETARY adj of or relating to a planet ▷ n train of planetary gears

PLANETIC > PLANET

PLANETOID same as
> ASTEROID

PLANETS > PLANET

PLANFORM n outline or silhouette of an object, esp an aircraft, as seen from above

PLANFORMS
> PLANFORM

PLANGENCY
> PLANGENT

PLANGENT adj (of sounds) mournful and resounding

PLANIGRAM n X-ray photograph of a plane section of something

PLANING > PLANE

PLANISH vb give a smooth surface to (a metal)

PLANISHED > PLANISH

PLANISHER > PLANISH

PLANISHES > PLANISH

PLANK n long flat piece of sawn timber ▷ vb cover or provide (an area) with planks

PLANKED > PLANK
PLANKING n number of planks
PLANKINGS > PLANKING
PLANKLIKE adj like a plank
PLANKS > PLANK
PLANKTER n organism in plankton
PLANKTERS > PLANKTER
PLANKTIC adj relating to plankton
PLANKTON n minute animals and plants floating in the surface water of a sea or lake
PLANKTONS > PLANKTON
PLANLESS adj having no plan
PLANNED > PLAN
PLANNER n person who makes plans
PLANNERS > PLANNER
PLANNING > PLAN
PLANNINGS > PLAN
PLANOGRAM n type of schematic plan for displaying merchandise in a shop
PLANOSOL n soil of humid or subhumid uplands
PLANOSOLS > PLANOSOL
PLANS > PLAN
PLANT n living organism that grows in the ground and has no power to move ▷ vb put in the ground to grow
PLANTA n sole of foot
PLANTABLE > PLANT
PLANTAE > PLANTA
PLANTAGE n plants
PLANTAGES > PLANTAGE
PLANTAIN n low-growing wild plant with broad leaves
PLANTAINS > PLANTAIN
PLANTAR adj of, relating to, or occurring on the sole of the foot
PLANTAS > PLANTA
PLANTED > PLANT
PLANTER n owner of a plantation
PLANTERS > PLANTER
PLANTING > PLANT
PLANTINGS > PLANT
PLANTLESS > PLANT
PLANTLET n small plant
PLANTLETS > PLANTLET
PLANTLIKE > PLANT
PLANTLING n young plant
PLANTS > PLANT
PLANTSMAN n experienced gardener who specializes in collecting rare or interesting plants
PLANTSMEN > PLANTSMAN

PLANTULE n embryo in act of germination
PLANTULES > PLANTULE
PLANULA n free-swimming larva of hydrozoan coelenterates
PLANULAE > PLANULA
PLANULAR > PLANULA
PLANULATE adj flat
PLANULOID adj of planula
PLANURIA n expulsion of urine from abnormal opening
PLANURIAS > PLANURIA
PLANURIES > PLANURY
PLANURY another name for > PLANURIA
PLANXTIES > PLANXTY
PLANXTY n Celtic melody for harp
PLAP same as > PLOP
PLAPPED > PLAP
PLAPPING > PLAP
PLAPS > PLAP
PLAQUE n inscribed commemorative stone or metal plate
PLAQUES > PLAQUE
PLAQUETTE n small plaque
PLASH same as > PLEACH
PLASHED > PLASH
PLASHER n type of farm tool
PLASHERS > PLASHER
PLASHES > PLASH
PLASHET n small pond
PLASHETS > PLASHET
PLASHIER > PLASHY
PLASHIEST > PLASHY
PLASHING > PLASH
PLASHINGS > PLASH
PLASHY adj wet or marshy
PLASM same as > PLASMA
PLASMA n clear liquid part of blood
PLASMAGEL another name for > ECTOPLASM
PLASMAS > PLASMA
PLASMASOL another name for > ENDOPLASM
PLASMATIC > PLASMA
PLASMIC > PLASMA
PLASMID n small circle of bacterial DNA
PLASMIDS > PLASMID
PLASMIN n proteolytic enzyme that causes fibrinolysis in blood clots
PLASMINS > PLASMIN
PLASMODIA n amoeboid masses of protoplasm, each containing many nuclei
PLASMOID n section of a plasma having a characteristic shape
PLASMOIDS > PLASMOID
PLASMON n sum total of plasmagenes in a cell
PLASMONS > PLASMON
PLASMS > PLASM
PLAST archaic past participle of > PLACE

PLASTE archaic past participle of > PLACE
PLASTER n mixture of lime, sand, etc for coating walls ▷ vb cover with plaster
PLASTERED adj drunk
PLASTERER > PLASTER
PLASTERS > PLASTER
PLASTERY adj like plaster
PLASTIC n synthetic material that can be moulded when soft but sets in a hard long-lasting shape ▷ adj made of plastic
PLASTICKY adj made of or resembling plastic
PLASTICLY > PLASTIC
PLASTICS > PLASTIC
PLASTID n small particle in the cells of plants and some animals
PLASTIDS > PLASTID
PLASTIQUE n easily moulded plastic explosive
PLASTISOL n suspension of resin particles convertible into solid plastic
PLASTRAL > PLASTRON
PLASTRON n bony plate forming the ventral part of the shell of a tortoise or turtle
PLASTRONS > PLASTRON
PLASTRUM variant of > PLASTRON
PLASTRUMS > PLASTRUM
PLAT n small area of ground
PLATAN n plane tree
PLATANE same as > PLATAN
PLATANES > PLATANE
PLATANNA n S African frog
PLATANNAS > PLATANNA
PLATANS > PLATAN
PLATBAND n border of flowers in garden
PLATBANDS > PLATBAND
PLATE n shallow dish for holding food ▷ vb cover with a thin coating of gold, silver, or other metal
PLATEASM n talking with mouth open too wide
PLATEASMS > PLATEASM
PLATEAU n area of level high land ▷ vb remain stable for a long period
PLATEAUED > PLATEAU
PLATEAUS > PLATEAU
PLATEAUX > PLATEAU
PLATED adj coated with a layer of metal
PLATEFUL same as > PLATE
PLATEFULS > PLATEFUL
PLATELESS adj having no plate

PLATELET n minute particle occurring in blood of vertebrates and involved in clotting of blood
PLATELETS > PLATELET
PLATELIKE > PLATE
PLATEMAN n one of crew of steam train
PLATEMARK another name for > HALLMARK
PLATEMEN > PLATEMAN
PLATEN n roller of a typewriter, against which the paper is held
PLATENS > PLATEN
PLATER n person or thing that plates
PLATERS > PLATER
PLATES > PLATE
PLATESFUL > PLATEFUL
PLATFORM n raised floor
PLATFORMS > PLATFORM
PLATIER > PLATY
PLATIES > PLATY
PLATIEST > PLATY
PLATINA n alloy of platinum and several other metals
PLATINAS > PLATINA
PLATING n coating of metal
PLATINGS > PLATING
PLATINIC adj of or containing platinum, esp in the tetravalent state
PLATINISE same as > PLATINIZE
PLATINIZE vb coat with platinum
PLATINOID adj containing or resembling platinum
PLATINOUS adj of or containing platinum, esp in the divalent state
PLATINUM n valuable silvery-white metal
PLATINUMS > PLATINUM
PLATITUDE n remark that is true but not interesting or original
PLATONIC adj (of a relationship) friendly or affectionate but not romantic ▷ n platonic friend
PLATONICS > PLATONIC
PLATONISM n philosophy of Plato
PLATOON n smaller unit within a company of soldiers ▷ vb organise into platoons
PLATOONED > PLATOON
PLATOONS > PLATOON
PLATS > PLAT
PLATT adj as in scale and platt denoting a straight staircase with landings, as opposed to a spiral staircase
PLATTED > PLAT
PLATTER n large dish

PLATTERS > PLATTER
PLATTING > PLAT
PLATTINGS > PLAT
PLATY *adj* of or designating rocks the constituents of which occur in flaky layers ▷ *n* brightly coloured freshwater fish
PLATYFISH *same as* > PLATY
PLATYPI > PLATYPUS
PLATYPUS *n* Australian egg-laying amphibious mammal
PLATYS > PLATY
PLATYSMA *n* muscle located on side of neck
PLATYSMAS > PLATYSMA
PLAUDIT *n* expression of enthusiastic approval
PLAUDITE *interj* give a round of applause!
PLAUDITS > PLAUDIT
PLAUSIBLE *adj* apparently true or reasonable
PLAUSIBLY > PLAUSIBLE
PLAUSIVE *adj* expressing praise or approval
PLAUSTRAL *adj* relating to wagons
PLAY *vb* occupy oneself in (a game or recreation) ▷ *n* story performed on stage or broadcast
PLAYA *n* (in the US) temporary lake in a desert basin
PLAYABLE > PLAY
PLAYACT *vb* pretend or make believe
PLAYACTED > PLAYACT
PLAYACTOR > PLAYACT
PLAYACTS > PLAYACT
PLAYAS > PLAYA
PLAYBACK *n* reproducing of a recording, esp formerly on magnetic tape ▷ *vb* listen to or watch (something recorded)
PLAYBACKS > PLAYBACK
PLAYBILL *n* poster or bill advertising a play
PLAYBILLS > PLAYBILL
PLAYBOOK *n* book containing a range of possible set plays
PLAYBOOKS > PLAYBOOK
PLAYBOY *n* rich man who lives only for pleasure
PLAYBOYS > PLAYBOY
PLAYBUS *n* mobile playground in a bus
PLAYBUSES > PLAYBUS
PLAYDATE *n* gathering of children at house for play
PLAYDATES > PLAYDATE
PLAYDAY *n* day given to play
PLAYDAYS > PLAYDAY
PLAYDOUGH *n* soft modelling material used by children

PLAYDOWN *same as* > PLAYOFF
PLAYDOWNS > PLAYDOWN
PLAYED > PLAY
PLAYER *n* person who plays a game or sport
PLAYERS > PLAYER
PLAYFIELD *n* field for sports
PLAYFUL *adj* lively
PLAYFULLY > PLAYFUL
PLAYGIRL *n* rich woman devoted to pleasure
PLAYGIRLS > PLAYGIRL
PLAYGOER *n* person who goes often to the theatre
PLAYGOERS > PLAYGOER
PLAYGOING > PLAYGOER
PLAYGROUP *n* playschool
PLAYHOUSE *n* theatre
PLAYING *n* act of playing
PLAYINGS > PLAYING
PLAYLAND *n* playground
PLAYLANDS > PLAYLAND
PLAYLESS > PLAY
PLAYLET *n* short play
PLAYLETS > PLAYLET
PLAYLIKE > PLAY
PLAYLIST *n* list of songs chosen for playing, such as on a radio station ▷ *vb* put (a song) on a playlist
PLAYLISTS > PLAYLIST
PLAYMAKER *n* player who creates scoring opportunities for his or her team-mates
PLAYMATE *n* companion in play
PLAYMATES > PLAYMATE
PLAYOFF *n* extra contest to decide the winner when two or more competitors are tied
PLAYOFFS > PLAYOFF
PLAYPEN *n* small portable enclosure in which a young child can safely be left to play
PLAYPENS > PLAYPEN
PLAYROOM *n* recreation room, esp for children
PLAYROOMS > PLAYROOM
PLAYS > PLAY
PLAYSET *n* outdoor equipment for children to play on
PLAYSETS > PLAYSET
PLAYSLIP *n* form used to select numbers in a lottery draw
PLAYSLIPS > PLAYSLIP
PLAYSOME *adj* playful
PLAYSUIT *n* woman's or child's outfit, usually comprising shorts and a top
PLAYSUITS > PLAYSUIT

PLAYTHING *n* toy
PLAYTIME *n* time for play or recreation, such as a school break
PLAYTIMES > PLAYTIME
PLAYWEAR *n* clothes suitable for playing in
PLAYWEARS > PLAYWEAR
PLAZA *n* open space or square
PLAZAS > PLAZA
PLEA *n* serious or urgent request, entreaty ▷ *vb* entreat
PLEACH *vb* interlace the stems or boughs of (a tree or hedge)
PLEACHED > PLEACH
PLEACHES > PLEACH
PLEACHING > PLEACH
PLEAD *vb* ask urgently or with deep feeling
PLEADABLE > PLEAD
PLEADED > PLEAD
PLEADER > PLEAD
PLEADERS > PLEAD
PLEADING > PLEAD
PLEADINGS > PLEAD
PLEADS > PLEAD
PLEAED > PLEA
PLEAING > PLEA
PLEAS > PLEA
PLEASABLE > PLEASE
PLEASANCE *n* secluded part of a garden laid out with trees, walks, etc
PLEASANT *adj* pleasing, enjoyable
PLEASE *vb* give pleasure or satisfaction to ▷ *adv* polite word of request
PLEASED > PLEASE
PLEASEDLY > PLEASE
PLEASEMAN *n* person who courts favour
PLEASEMEN > PLEASEMAN
PLEASER > PLEASE
PLEASERS > PLEASE
PLEASES > PLEASE
PLEASETH *obsolete inflection of* > PLEASE
PLEASING *adj* giving pleasure or satisfaction ▷ *n* act of giving pleasure
PLEASINGS > PLEASING
PLEASURE *n* feeling of happiness and satisfaction ▷ *vb* give pleasure to or take pleasure (in)
PLEASURED > PLEASURE
PLEASURER > PLEASURE
PLEASURES > PLEASURE
PLEAT *n* fold made by doubling material back on itself ▷ *vb* arrange (material) in pleats
PLEATED > PLEAT
PLEATER *n* attachment on a sewing machine that makes pleats
PLEATERS > PLEATER

PLEATHER *n* synthetic leather
PLEATHERS > PLEATHER
PLEATING *n* act of pleating
PLEATINGS > PLEATING
PLEATLESS > PLEAT
PLEATS > PLEAT
PLEB *n* common vulgar person
PLEBBIER > PLEBBY
PLEBBIEST > PLEBBY
PLEBBY *adj* common or vulgar
PLEBE *n* member of the lowest class at the US Naval Academy or Military Academy
PLEBEAN *old variant of* > PLEBEIAN
PLEBEIAN *adj* of the lower social classes ▷ *n* member of the lower social classes
PLEBEIANS > PLEBEIAN
PLEBES > PLEBE
PLEBIFIED > PLEBIFY
PLEBIFIES > PLEBIFY
PLEBIFY *vb* make plebeian
PLEBS *n* common people
PLECTRA > PLECTRUM
PLECTRE *variant of* > PLECTRUM
PLECTRES > PLECTRE
PLECTRON *same as* > PLECTRUM
PLECTRONS > PLECTRON
PLECTRUM *n* small implement for plucking the strings of a guitar etc
PLECTRUMS > PLECTRUM
PLED > PLEAD
PLEDGABLE > PLEDGE
PLEDGE *n* solemn promise ▷ *vb* promise solemnly
PLEDGED > PLEDGE
PLEDGEE *n* person to whom a pledge is given
PLEDGEES > PLEDGEE
PLEDGEOR *same as* > PLEDGOR
PLEDGEORS > PLEDGEOR
PLEDGER *same as* > PLEDGOR
PLEDGERS > PLEDGER
PLEDGES > PLEDGE
PLEDGET *n* small flattened pad of wool, cotton, etc
PLEDGETS > PLEDGET
PLEDGING > PLEDGE
PLEDGOR *n* person who gives or makes a pledge
PLEDGORS > PLEDGOR
PLEIAD *n* brilliant or talented group, esp one with seven members
PLEIADES > PLEIAD
PLEIADS > PLEIAD

PLEIOCENE variant spelling of > PLIOCENE

PLEIOMERY n state of having more than normal number

PLEIOTAXY n increase in whorls in flower

PLENA > PLENUM

PLENARIES > PLENARY

PLENARILY > PLENARY

PLENARTY n state of endowed church office when occupied

PLENARY adj (of a meeting) attended by all members ▷ n book read at the Eucharist

PLENCH n tool combining wrench and pliers

PLENCHES > PLENCH

PLENILUNE n full moon

PLENIPO n plenipotentiary diplomat

PLENIPOES > PLENIPO

PLENIPOS > PLENIPO

PLENISH vb fill, stock, or resupply

PLENISHED > PLENISH

PLENISHER > PLENISH

PLENISHES > PLENISH

PLENISM n philosophical theory

PLENISMS > PLENISM

PLENIST > PLENISM

PLENISTS > PLENISM

PLENITUDE n completeness, abundance

PLENTEOUS adj plentiful

PLENTIES > PLENTY

PLENTIFUL adj existing in large amounts or numbers

PLENTY n large amount or number ▷ adj very many ▷ adv more than adequately

PLENUM n enclosure containing gas at a high pressure

PLENUMS > PLENUM

PLEON n abdomen of crustacean

PLEONAL adj of the abdomen of a crustacean

PLEONASM n use of more words than necessary

PLEONASMS > PLEONASM

PLEONAST n person using more words than necessary

PLEONASTE n type of black mineral

PLEONASTS > PLEONAST

PLEONEXIA n greed

PLEONIC > PLEON

PLEONS > PLEON

PLEOPOD another name for > SWIMMERET

PLEOPODS > PLEOPOD

PLERION n filled-centre supernova remnant

PLERIONS > PLERION

PLEROMA n abundance

PLEROMAS > PLEROMA

PLEROME n central column in growing stem or root

PLEROMES > PLEROME

PLESH n small pool

PLESHES > PLESH

PLESSOR same as > PLEXOR

PLESSORS > PLESSOR

PLETHORA n excess

PLETHORAS > PLETHORA

PLETHORIC > PLETHORA

PLEUCH same as > PLEUGH

PLEUCHED > PLEUCH

PLEUCHING > PLEUCH

PLEUCHS > PLEUCH

PLEUGH Scottish word for > PLOUGH

PLEUGHED > PLEUGH

PLEUGHING > PLEUGH

PLEUGHS > PLEUGH

PLEURA n membrane covering the lungs

PLEURAE > PLEURA

PLEURAL > PLEURA

PLEURAS > PLEURA

PLEURISY n inflammation of the membrane covering the lungs

PLEURITIC > PLEURISY

PLEURITIS n pleurisy

PLEURON n part of the cuticle of arthropods

PLEURONIA n combined disorder of pleurisy and pneumonia

PLEUSTON n mass of small organisms, esp algae, floating at the surface of shallow pools

PLEUSTONS > PLEUSTON

PLEW n (formerly in Canada) beaver skin used as a standard unit of value in the fur trade

PLEWS > PLEW

PLEX n shortening of multiplex ▷ vb make a plexus

PLEXAL > PLEXUS

PLEXED > PLEX

PLEXES > PLEX

PLEXIFORM adj like or having the form of a network or plexus

PLEXING > PLEX

PLEXOR n small hammer with a rubber head

PLEXORS > PLEXOR

PLEXURE n act of weaving together

PLEXURES > PLEXURE

PLEXUS n complex network of nerves or blood vessels

PLEXUSES > PLEXUS

PLIABLE adj easily bent

PLIABLY > PLIABLE

PLIANCIES > PLIANT

PLIANCY > PLIANT

PLIANT adj pliable

PLIANTLY > PLIANT

PLICA n folding over of parts, such as a fold of skin, muscle, peritoneum, etc

PLICAE > PLICA

PLICAL > PLICA

PLICAS > PLICA

PLICATE adj having or arranged in parallel folds or ridges ▷ vb arrange into parallel folds

PLICATED > PLICATE

PLICATELY > PLICATE

PLICATES > PLICATE

PLICATING > PLICATE

PLICATION n act of folding or the condition of being folded or plicate

PLICATURE same as > PLICATION

PLIE n classic ballet practice posture with back erect and knees bent

PLIED > PLY

PLIER n person who plies a trade

PLIERS pl n tool with hinged arms and jaws for gripping

PLIES > PLY

PLIGHT vb pledge

PLIGHTED > PLIGHT

PLIGHTER > PLIGHT

PLIGHTERS > PLIGHT

PLIGHTFUL adj filled with distress

PLIGHTING > PLIGHT

PLIGHTS > PLIGHT

PLIM vb swell with water

PLIMMED > PLIM

PLIMMING > PLIM

PLIMS > PLIM

PLIMSOL same as > PLIMSOLL

PLIMSOLE same as > PLIMSOLL

PLIMSOLES > PLIMSOLE

PLIMSOLL n light rubber-soled canvas shoe worn for various sports

PLIMSOLLS > PLIMSOLL

PLIMSOLS > PLIMSOL

PLING n (in computer jargon) an exclamation mark ▷ vb beg from

PLINGED > PLING

PLINGING > PLING

PLINGS > PLING

PLINK n short sharp often metallic sound ▷ vb make such a noise

PLINKED > PLINK

PLINKER > PLINK

PLINKERS > PLINK

PLINKIER > PLINKY

PLINKIEST > PLINKY

PLINKING > PLINK

PLINKINGS > PLINK

PLINKS > PLINK

PLINKY adj (of a sound) short, sharp, and often metallic

PLINTH n slab forming the base of a statue, column, etc

PLINTHS > PLINTH

PLIOCENE adj of the Pliocene geological time period

PLIOFILM n transparent plastic material

PLIOFILMS > PLIOFILM

PLIOSAUR n type of dinosaur

PLIOSAURS > PLIOSAUR

PLIOTRON n type of vacuum tube

PLIOTRONS > PLIOTRON

PLISKIE n practical joke ▷ adj tricky or mischievous

PLISKIER > PLISKIE

PLISKIES > PLISKIE

PLISKIEST > PLISKIE

PLISKY same as > PLISKIE

PLISSE n fabric with a wrinkled finish, achieved by treatment involving caustic soda

PLISSES > PLISSE

PLOAT vb thrash

PLOATED > PLOAT

PLOATING > PLOAT

PLOATS > PLOAT

PLOD vb walk with slow heavy steps ▷ n act of plodding

PLODDED > PLOD

PLODDER n person who plods

PLODDERS > PLODDER

PLODDING > PLOD

PLODDINGS > PLOD

PLODGE vb wade in water, esp the sea ▷ n act of wading

PLODGED > PLODGE

PLODGES > PLODGE

PLODGING > PLODGE

PLODS > PLOD

PLOGGING n picking up litter while jogging

PLOGGINGS > PLOGGING

PLOIDIES > PLOIDY

PLOIDY n number of copies of set of chromosomes in cell

PLONG obsolete variant of > PLUNGE

PLONGD > PLONG

PLONGE same as > PLUNGE

PLONGED > PLONGE

PLONGES > PLONGE

PLONGING > PLONGE

PLONGS > PLONG

PLONK vb put (something) down heavily and carelessly ▷ n act of plonking ▷ interj exclamation imitative of this sound

PLONKED > PLONK

PLONKER n stupid person

PLONKERS > PLONKER

PLONKIER > PLONK

PLONKIEST > PLONK

PLONKING > PLONK

PLONKINGS > PLONK

PLONKO n alcoholic, esp one who drinks wine

PLONKOS > PLONKO

PLONKS > PLONK

P

PLONKY > PLONK
PLOOK same as > PLOUK
PLOOKIE same as
> PLOUKY
PLOOKIER > PLOOK
PLOOKIEST > PLOOK
PLOOKS > PLOOK
PLOOKY > PLOOK
PLOP n sound of an object
falling into water without
a splash ▷ vb make this
sound ▷ interj
exclamation imitative of
this sound
PLOPPED > PLOP
PLOPPING > PLOP
PLOPS > PLOP
PLOSION n sound of an
abrupt break or closure,
esp the audible release of a
stop
PLOSIONS > PLOSION
PLOSIVE adj pronounced
with a sudden release of
breath ▷ n plosive
consonant
PLOSIVES > PLOSIVE
PLOT n secret plan to do
something illegal or
wrong ▷ vb plan secretly,
conspire
PLOTFUL > PLOT
PLOTLESS > PLOT
PLOTLINE n literary or
dramatic plot
PLOTLINES
> PLOTLINE
PLOTS > PLOT
PLOTTAGE n land that
makes up plot
PLOTTAGES
> PLOTTAGE
PLOTTED > PLOT
PLOTTER same as
> PLOUTER
PLOTTERED > PLOTTER
PLOTTERS > PLOTTER
PLOTTIE n hot spiced
drink
PLOTTIER > PLOTTY
PLOTTIES > PLOTTIE
PLOTTIEST > PLOTTY
PLOTTING > PLOT
PLOTTINGS > PLOT
PLOTTY adj intricately
plotted
PLOTZ vb faint or collapse
PLOTZED > PLOTZ
PLOTZES > PLOTZ
PLOTZING > PLOTZ
PLOUGH n agricultural
tool for turning over soil
▷ vb turn over (earth) with
a plough
PLOUGHBOY n boy who
guides the animals
drawing a plough
PLOUGHED > PLOUGH
PLOUGHER > PLOUGH
PLOUGHERS > PLOUGH
PLOUGHING n act of
ploughing
PLOUGHMAN n man who
ploughs
PLOUGHMEN
> PLOUGHMAN
PLOUGHS > PLOUGH
PLOUK n pimple

PLOUKIE > PLOUK
PLOUKIER > PLOUK
PLOUKIEST > PLOUK
PLOUKS > PLOUK
PLOUKY > PLOUK
PLOUTER same as
> PLOWTER
PLOUTERED > PLOUTER
PLOUTERS > PLOUTER
PLOVER n shore bird with
a straight bill and long
pointed wings
PLOVERIER > PLOVERY
PLOVERS > PLOVER
PLOVERY adj
characterized by plovers
PLOW same as > PLOUGH
PLOWABLE > PLOW
PLOWBACK n
reinvestment of profits
PLOWBACKS
> PLOWBACK
PLOWBOY same as
> PLOUGHBOY
PLOWBOYS > PLOWBOY
PLOWED > PLOW
PLOWER > PLOW
PLOWERS > PLOW
PLOWHEAD n draught iron
of plow
PLOWHEADS
> PLOWHEAD
PLOWING > PLOUGHING
PLOWINGS > PLOWING
PLOWLAND n land plowed
PLOWLANDS
> PLOWLAND
PLOWMAN same as
> PLOUGHMAN
PLOWMEN > PLOWMAN
PLOWS > PLOW
PLOWSHARE n horizontal
pointed cutting blade of a
mouldboard plow
PLOWSTAFF n one of the
handles of a plow
PLOWTAIL n the end of a
plough where the handles
are
PLOWTAILS
> PLOWTAIL
PLOWTER vb work or play
in water or mud ▷ n act of
plowtering
PLOWTERED > PLOWTER
PLOWTERS > PLOWTER
PLOWWISE adv as in
ploughing
PLOY n manoeuvre
designed to gain an
advantage ▷ vb form a
column from a line of
troops
PLOYE n buckwheat
pancake
PLOYED > PLOY
PLOYES > PLOYE
PLOYING > PLOY
PLOYS > PLOY
PLU same as > PLEW
PLUCK vb pull or pick off
▷ n courage
PLUCKED > PLUCK
PLUCKER > PLUCK
PLUCKERS > PLUCK
PLUCKIER > PLUCKY
PLUCKIEST > PLUCKY
PLUCKILY > PLUCKY

PLUCKING > PLUCK
PLUCKS > PLUCK
PLUCKY adj brave
PLUE same as > PLEW
PLUES > PLUE
PLUFF vb expel in puffs
PLUFFED > PLUFF
PLUFFIER > PLUFF
PLUFFIEST > PLUFF
PLUFFING > PLUFF
PLUFFS > PLUFF
PLUFFY > PLUFF
PLUG n thing fitting into
and filling a hole ▷ vb
block or seal (a hole or gap)
with a plug
PLUGBOARD n device
with a large number of
sockets in which electrical
plugs can be inserted to
form many different
temporary circuits
PLUGGED > PLUG
PLUGGER > PLUG
PLUGGERS > PLUG
PLUGGING > PLUG
PLUGGINGS > PLUG
PLUGHOLE n hole at the
bottom of a bath or sink
which can be closed with
a plug
PLUGHOLES
> PLUGHOLE
PLUGLESS > PLUG
PLUGOLA n plugging of
products on television
PLUGOLAS > PLUGOLA
PLUGS > PLUG
PLUGUGLY n city tough;
ruffian
PLUM n oval stone dark red
fruit with a stone in the
middle ▷ adj dark
purplish-red
PLUMAGE n bird's feathers
PLUMAGED > PLUMAGE
PLUMAGES > PLUMAGE
PLUMATE adj of, relating
to, or possessing one or
more feathers or plumes
PLUMB vb understand
(something obscure)
▷ adv exactly ▷ n weight
suspended at the end of a
line
PLUMBABLE > PLUMB
PLUMBAGO n plant of
warm regions with
clusters of blue, white, or
red flowers
PLUMBAGOS
> PLUMBAGO
PLUMBATE n compound
formed from lead oxide
PLUMBATES
> PLUMBATE
PLUMBED > PLUMB
PLUMBEOUS adj made
of or relating to lead or
resembling lead in
colour
PLUMBER n person who
fits and repairs pipes and
fixtures for water and
drainage systems
PLUMBERS > PLUMBER
PLUMBERY same as
> PLUMBING

PLUMBIC adj of or
containing lead in the
tetravalent state
PLUMBING n pipes and
fixtures used in water and
drainage systems
PLUMBINGS
> PLUMBING
PLUMBISM n chronic lead
poisoning
PLUMBISMS
> PLUMBISM
PLUMBITE n substance
containing lead oxide
PLUMBITES
> PLUMBITE
PLUMBLESS adj
incapable of being
sounded
PLUMBNESS > PLUMB
PLUMBOUS adj of or
containing lead in the
divalent state
PLUMBS > PLUMB
PLUMBUM n obsolete
name for lead (the metal)
PLUMBUMS > PLUMBUM
PLUMCAKE n cake with
raisins in it
PLUMCAKES
> PLUMCAKE
PLUMCOT n hybrid of
apricot and plum
PLUMCOTS > PLUMCOT
PLUMDAMAS n prune
PLUME n feather, esp one
worn as an ornament ▷ vb
adorn or decorate with
feathers or plumes
PLUMED > PLUME
PLUMELESS > PLUME
PLUMELET n small plume
PLUMELETS
> PLUMELET
PLUMELIKE > PLUME
PLUMERIA n tropical tree
with candelabra-like
branches
PLUMERIAS
> PLUMERIA
PLUMERIES > PLUMERY
PLUMERY n plumes
collectively
PLUMES > PLUME
PLUMIER > PLUMY
PLUMIEST > PLUMY
PLUMING > PLUME
PLUMIPED n bird with
feathered feet
PLUMIPEDS
> PLUMIPED
PLUMIST n person who
makes plumes
PLUMISTS > PLUMIST
PLUMLIKE > PLUM
PLUMMER > PLUM
PLUMMEST > PLUM
PLUMMET vb plunge
downward ▷ n weight on
a plumb line or fishing line
PLUMMETED > PLUMMET
PLUMMETS > PLUMMET
PLUMMIER > PLUMMY
PLUMMIEST > PLUMMY
PLUMMY adj of, full of, or
like plums
PLUMOSE same as
> PLUMATE

PLUMOSELY > PLUMOSE
PLUMOSITY > PLUMOSE
PLUMOUS *adj* having plumes or feathers
PLUMP *adj* moderately or attractively fat ▷ *vb* sit or fall heavily and suddenly ▷ *n* heavy abrupt fall or the sound of this ▷ *adv* suddenly or heavily
PLUMPED > PLUMP
PLUMPEN *vb* make or become plump
PLUMPENED > PLUMPEN
PLUMPENS > PLUMPEN
PLUMPER *n* pad carried in the mouth by actors to round out the cheeks
PLUMPERS > PLUMPER
PLUMPEST > PLUMP
PLUMPIE *same as* > PLUMPY
PLUMPIER > PLUMPY
PLUMPIEST > PLUMPY
PLUMPING > PLUMP
PLUMPISH *adj* on the plump side
PLUMPLY > PLUMP
PLUMPNESS > PLUMP
PLUMPS > PLUMP
PLUMPY *adj* plump
PLUMS > PLUM
PLUMULA *n* down feather
PLUMULAE > PLUMULA
PLUMULAR > PLUMULE
PLUMULATE *adj* covered with soft fine feathers
PLUMULE *n* embryonic shoot of seed-bearing plants
PLUMULES > PLUMULE
PLUMULOSE *adj* having hairs branching out like feathers
PLUMY *adj* like a feather
PLUNDER *vb* take by force, esp in time of war ▷ *n* things plundered, spoils
PLUNDERED > PLUNDER
PLUNDERER > PLUNDER
PLUNDERS > PLUNDER
PLUNGE *vb* put or throw forcibly or suddenly (into) ▷ *n* plunging dive
PLUNGED > PLUNGE
PLUNGER *n* rubber suction cup used to clear blocked pipes
PLUNGERS > PLUNGER
PLUNGES > PLUNGE
PLUNGING > PLUNGE
PLUNGINGS > PLUNGE
PLUNK *vb* pluck the strings of (a banjo etc) to produce a twanging sound ▷ *n* act or sound of plunking ▷ *interj* exclamation imitative of the sound of something plunking ▷ *adv* exactly
PLUNKED > PLUNK
PLUNKER > PLUNK
PLUNKERS > PLUNK
PLUNKIER > PLUNKY
PLUNKIEST > PLUNKY
PLUNKING > PLUNK
PLUNKS > PLUNK

PLUNKY *adj* sounding like plucked banjo string
PLUOT *n* hybrid fruit of the plum and apricot
PLUOTS > PLUOT
PLURAL *adj* of or consisting of more than one ▷ *n* word indicating more than one
PLURALISE *same as* > PLURALIZE
PLURALISM *n* existence and toleration of a variety of peoples, opinions, etc in a society
PLURALIST > PLURALISM
PLURALITY *n* state of being plural
PLURALIZE *vb* make or become plural
PLURALLY > PLURAL
PLURALS > PLURAL
PLURIPARA *n* woman who has borne more than one child
PLURISIE *same as* > PLEURISY
PLURISIES > PLURISIE
PLURRY *euphemism for* > BLOODY
PLUS *vb* make or become greater in value
PLUSAGE *same as* > PLUSSAGE
PLUSAGES > PLUSAGE
PLUSED > PLUS
PLUSES > PLUS
PLUSH *n* fabric with long velvety pile ▷ *adj* luxurious
PLUSHED *adj* showily luxurious
PLUSHER > PLUSH
PLUSHES > PLUSH
PLUSHEST > PLUSH
PLUSHIER > PLUSHY
PLUSHIEST > PLUSHY
PLUSHILY > PLUSHY
PLUSHLY > PLUSH
PLUSHNESS > PLUSH
PLUSHY *same as* > PLUSH
PLUSING > PLUS
PLUSSAGE *n* amount over and above another amount
PLUSSAGES > PLUSSAGE
PLUSSED > PLUS
PLUSSES > PLUS
PLUSSING > PLUS
PLUTEAL > PLUTEUS
PLUTEI > PLUTEUS
PLUTEUS *n* larva of sea urchin
PLUTEUSES > PLUTEUS
PLUTO *vb* reduce in importance
PLUTOCRAT *n* person who is powerful because of being very rich
PLUTOED > PLUTO
PLUTOES > PLUTO
PLUTOID *n* dwarf planet whose orbit is beyond Neptune's
PLUTOIDS > PLUTOID
PLUTOING > PLUTO

PLUTOLOGY *n* study of wealth
PLUTON *n* any mass of igneous rock that has solidified below the surface of the earth
PLUTONIAN *adj* of or relating to the underworld
PLUTONIC *adj* formed from molten rock that has solidified below the earth's surface
PLUTONISM *n* theory that the earth's crust was formed by volcanoes
PLUTONIUM *n* radioactive metallic element used esp in nuclear reactors and weapons
PLUTONOMY *n* economics
PLUTONS > PLUTON
PLUTOS > PLUTO
PLUVIAL *n* period of high rainfall
PLUVIALS > PLUVIAL
PLUVIAN *n* crocodile bird
PLUVIANS > PLUVIAN
PLUVIOSE *same as* > PLUVIOUS
PLUVIOUS *adj* of or relating to rain
PLUVIUS *adj* as in *pluvius insurance* insurance against rain
PLY *vb* work at (a job or trade) ▷ *n* thickness of wool, fabric, etc
PLYER *n* person who plies trade
PLYERS > PLYER
PLYING > PLY
PLYINGLY > PLY
PLYWOOD *n* board made of thin layers of wood glued together
PLYWOODS > PLYWOOD
PNEUMA *n* person's vital spirit, soul, or creative energy
PNEUMAS > PNEUMA
PNEUMATIC *adj* worked by or inflated with wind or air
PNEUMONIA *n* inflammation of the lungs
PNEUMONIC *adj* of, relating to, or affecting the lungs
PO *n* chamberpot
POA *n* type of grass
POACEOUS *adj* relating to the plant family which comprises grasses
POACH *vb* catch (animals) illegally on someone else's land
POACHABLE > POACH
POACHED > POACH
POACHER *n* person who catches animals illegally on someone else's land
POACHERS > POACHER
POACHES > POACH
POACHIER > POACHY
POACHIEST > POACHY
POACHING > POACH
POACHINGS > POACH

POACHY *adj* (of land) wet and soft
POAKA *n* type of stilt (bird) native to New Zealand
POAKAS > POAKA
POAKE *n* waste matter from tanning of hides
POAKES > POAKE
POAS > POA
POBLANO *n* variety of chilli pepper
POBLANOS > POBLANO
POBOY *n* New Orleans sandwich
POBOYS > POBOY
POCHARD *n* European diving duck
POCHARDS > POCHARD
POCHAY *n* closed horse-drawn four-wheeled coach ▷ *vb* transport by pochay
POCHAYED > POCHAY
POCHAYING > POCHAY
POCHAYS > POCHAY
POCHETTE *n* envelope-shaped handbag
POCHETTES > POCHETTE
POCHOIR *n* print made from stencils
POCHOIRS > POCHOIR
POCK *n* pus-filled blister resulting from smallpox ▷ *vb* mark with scars
POCKARD *variant of* > POCHARD
POCKARDS > POCKARD
POCKED > POCK
POCKET *n* small bag sewn into clothing for carrying things ▷ *vb* put into one's pocket ▷ *adj* small
POCKETED > POCKET
POCKETER > POCKET
POCKETERS > POCKET
POCKETFUL *n* as much as a pocket will hold
POCKETING > POCKET
POCKETS > POCKET
POCKIER > POCK
POCKIES *pl n* woollen mittens
POCKIEST > POCK
POCKILY > POCK
POCKING > POCK
POCKMANKY *n* portmanteau
POCKMARK *n* pitted scar left on the skin after the healing of a smallpox or similar pustule ▷ *vb* scar or pit (a surface) with pockmarks
POCKMARKS > POCKMARK
POCKPIT *n* mark left on skin after a pock has gone
POCKPITS > POCKPIT
POCKS > POCK
POCKY > POCK
POCO *adv* little
POCOSEN *same as* > POCOSIN
POCOSENS > POCOSEN
POCOSIN *n* swamp in US upland coastal region
POCOSINS > POCOSIN

P

POCOSON same as > POCOSIN

POCOSONS > POCOSON

POD n long narrow seed case of peas, beans, etc ▷ vb remove the pod from

PODAGRA n gout of the foot or big toe

PODAGRAL > PODAGRA

PODAGRAS > PODAGRA

PODAGRIC > PODAGRA

PODAGROUS > PODAGRA

PODAL adj relating to feet

PODALIC adj relating to feet

PODARGUS n bird of SE Asia and Australia

PODCAST n audio file able to be downloaded and listened to on a computer or MP3 player ▷ vb make available in this format

PODCASTED > PODCAST

PODCASTER > PODCAST

PODCASTS > PODCAST

PODDED > POD

PODDIE n user of or enthusiast for the iPod, a portable digital music player

PODDIER > PODDY

PODDIES > PODDY

PODDIEST > PODDY

PODDING > POD

PODDLE vb move or travel in a leisurely manner

PODDLED > PODDLE

PODDLES > PODDLE

PODDLING > PODDLE

PODDY n handfed calf or lamb ▷ adj fat

PODESTA n (in modern Italy) subordinate magistrate in some towns

PODESTAS > PODESTA

PODEX n posterior

PODEXES > PODEX

PODGE n chubby person

PODGES > PODGE

PODGIER > PODGY

PODGIEST > PODGY

PODGILY > PODGY

PODGINESS > PODGY

PODGY adj chubby

PODIA > PODIUM

PODIAL > PODIUM

PODIATRIC > PODIATRY

PODIATRY another word for > CHIROPODY

PODITE n crustacean leg

PODITES > PODITE

PODITIC adj similar to the limb segment of an arthropod

PODIUM n small raised platform for a conductor or speaker ▷ vb finish in the top three places in a sporting competition

PODIUMED > PODIUM

PODIUMING > PODIUM

PODIUMS > PODIUM

PODLEY n young coalfish

PODLEYS > PODLEY

PODLIKE > POD

PODOCARP n stem supporting fruit

PODOCARPS > PODOCARP

PODOLOGY n study of feet

PODOMERE n segment of limb of arthropod

PODOMERES > PODOMERE

PODS > POD

PODSOL same as > PODZOL

PODSOLIC > PODZOL

PODSOLISE same as > PODZOLIZE

PODSOLIZE same as > PODZOLIZE

PODSOLS > PODSOL

PODUNK adj small or unimportant ▷ n small or unimportant thing

PODUNKS > PODUNK

PODZOL n type of soil characteristic of coniferous forest regions

PODZOLIC > PODZOL

PODZOLISE same as > PODZOLIZE

PODZOLIZE vb make into or form a podzol

PODZOLS > PODZOL

POECHORE n dry region

POECHORES > POECHORE

POEM n imaginative piece of writing in rhythmic lines

POEMATIC adj of poetry

POEMS > POEM

POENOLOGY same as > PENOLOGY

POEP n emission of gas from the anus ▷ vb break wind

POEPED > POEP

POEPING > POEP

POEPOL n South African slang for anus

POEPOLS > POEPOL

POEPS > POEP

POESIED > POESY

POESIES > POESY

POESY n poetry ▷ vb write poems

POESYING > POESY

POET n writer of poems

POETASTER n writer of inferior verse

POETASTRY > POETASTER

POETESS n female poet

POETESSES > POETESS

POETIC adj of or like poetry

POETICAL adj poetic n poet

POETICALS > POETICAL

POETICISE same as > POETICIZE

POETICISM > POETICISE

POETICIZE vb put into poetry or make poetic

POETICS n principles and forms of poetry or the study of these

POETICULE n inferior poet

POETISE same as > POETICIZE

POETISED > POETISE

POETISER > POETISE

POETISERS > POETISE

POETISES > POETISE

POETISING > POETISE

POETIZE same as > POETICIZE

POETIZED > POETIZE

POETIZER > POETIZE

POETIZERS > POETIZE

POETIZES > POETIZE

POETIZING > POETIZE

POETLESS > POET

POETLIKE > POET

POETRESSE old variant of > POETESS

POETRIES > POETRY

POETRY n poems

POETS > POET

POETSHIP n state of being poet

POETSHIPS > POETSHIP

POFFLE n small piece of land

POFFLES > POFFLE

POGEY n financial or other relief given to the unemployed by the government

POGEYS > POGEY

POGGE n European marine scorpaenoid fish

POGGES > POGGE

POGIES > POGY

POGO vb jump up and down on one spot

POGOED > POGO

POGOER > POGO

POGOERS > POGO

POGOES > POGO

POGOING > POGO

POGONIA n orchid with pink or white fragrant flowers

POGONIAS > POGONIA

POGONIP n icy winter fog

POGONIPS > POGONIP

POGOS > POGO

POGROM n organized persecution and massacre ▷ vb carry out a pogrom

POGROMED > POGROM

POGROMING > POGROM

POGROMIST > POGROM

POGROMS > POGROM

POGY same as > POGEY

POH interj exclamation expressing contempt or disgust ▷ vb reject contemptuously

POHED > POH

POHING > POH

POHIRI variant spelling of > POWHIRI

POHIRIS > POHIRI

POHS > POH

POI n ball of woven flax swung rhythmically by Māori women during poi dances

POIGNADO old variant of > PONIARD

POIGNANCE > POIGNANT

POIGNANCY > POIGNANT

POIGNANT adj sharply painful to the feelings

POILU n infantryman in the French Army

POILUS > POILU

POINADO old variant of > PONIARD

POINADOES > POINADO

POINCIANA n tropical leguminous tree with large orange or red flowers

POIND vb take (property of a debtor) in execution or by way of distress

POINDED > POIND

POINDER > POIND

POINDERS > POIND

POINDING > POIND

POINDINGS > POIND

POINDS > POIND

POINT n main idea in a discussion ▷ vb show the position of something by extending a finger towards it

POINTABLE > POINT

POINTE n tip of the toe

POINTED adj having a sharp end

POINTEDLY > POINTED

POINTEL n engraver's tool

POINTELLE n fabric design in form of chevrons

POINTELS > POINTEL

POINTER n helpful hint

POINTERS > POINTER

POINTES > POINTE

POINTIER > POINTY

POINTIEST > POINTY

POINTILLE n dotted lines and curves impressed on cover of book

POINTING n insertion of mortar between the joints in brickwork

POINTINGS > POINTING

POINTLESS adj meaningless, irrelevant

POINTLIKE adj like a point

POINTMAN n soldier who walks at the front of an infantry patrol in combat

POINTMEN > POINTMAN

POINTS > POINT

POINTSMAN n person who operates railway points

POINTSMEN > POINTSMAN

POINTY adj having a sharp point or points

POIS > POI

POISE n calm dignified manner ▷ vb be balanced or suspended

POISED adj absolutely ready

POISER n balancing organ of some insects

POISERS > POISER

POISES > POISE

POISHA n monetary unit of Bangladesh

POISHAS > POISHA

POISING > POISE

POISON n substance that kills or injures when

swallowed or absorbed ▷ *vb* give poison to
POISONED > POISON
POISONER > POISON
POISONERS > POISON
POISONING *n* the act of giving poison to someone
POISONOUS *adj* of or like a poison
POISONS > POISON
POISSON *n* fish
POISSONS > POISSON
POITIN *variant spelling of* > POTEEN
POITINS > POITIN
POITREL *n* breastplate of horse's armour
POITRELS > POITREL
POITRINE *n* woman's bosom
POITRINES > POITRINE
POKABLE > POKE
POKAL *n* tall drinking cup
POKALS > POKAL
POKE *vb* jab or prod with one's finger, a stick, etc ▷ *n* poking
POKEBERRY *same as* > POKEWEED
POKED > POKE
POKEFUL *n* contents of small bag
POKEFULS > POKEFUL
POKELOGAN *another name for* > BOGAN
POKER *n* metal rod for stirring a fire
POKERISH *adj* stiff like poker
POKEROOT *same as* > POKEWEED
POKEROOTS > POKEROOT
POKERS > POKER
POKERWORK *n* art of producing pictures or designs on wood by burning it with a heated metal point
POKES > POKE
POKEWEED *n* plant with a poisonous root used medicinally
POKEWEEDS > POKEWEED
POKEY *same as* > POKIE
POKEYS > POKEY
POKIE *n* poker machine
POKIER > POKY
POKIES > POKY
POKIEST > POKY
POKILY > POKY
POKINESS > POKY
POKING > POKE
POKY *adj* small and cramped
POL *n* political campaigner
POLACCA *same as* > POLACRE
POLACCAS > POLACCA
POLACRE *n* three-masted sailing vessel
POLACRES > POLACRE
POLAR *adj* of or near either of the earth's poles ▷ *n* type of line in geometry

POLARISE *same as* > POLARIZE
POLARISED > POLARIZE
POLARISER *same as* > POLARIZER
POLARISES > POLARISE
POLARITY *n* state of having two directly opposite tendencies or opinions
POLARIZE *vb* form or cause to form into groups with directly opposite views
POLARIZED > POLARIZE
POLARIZER *n* person or a device that causes polarization
POLARIZES > POLARIZE
POLARON *n* kind of electron
POLARONS > POLARON
POLARS > POLAR
POLDER *n* land reclaimed from the sea, esp in the Netherlands ▷ *vb* reclaim land from the sea
POLDERED > POLDER
POLDERING > POLDER
POLDERS > POLDER
POLE *n* long rounded piece of wood etc ▷ *vb* strike or push with a pole
POLEAX *same as* > POLEAXE
POLEAXE *vb* hit or stun with a heavy blow ▷ *n* axe formerly used in battle or used by a butcher
POLEAXED > POLEAXE
POLEAXES > POLEAXE
POLEAXING > POLEAXE
POLECAT *n* small animal of the weasel family
POLECATS > POLECAT
POLED > POLE
POLEIS > POLIS
POLELESS > POLE
POLEMARCH *n* (in ancient Greece) civilian official, originally a supreme general
POLEMIC *n* fierce attack on or defence of a particular opinion, belief, etc ▷ *adj* of or involving dispute or controversy
POLEMICAL *adj* related to polemics, debate
POLEMICS *n* art of dispute
POLEMISE *same as* > POLEMIZE
POLEMISED > POLEMISE
POLEMISES > POLEMISE
POLEMIST > POLEMIC
POLEMISTS > POLEMIC
POLEMIZE *vb* engage in controversy
POLEMIZED > POLEMIZE
POLEMIZES > POLEMIZE

POLENTA *n* thick porridge made in Italy, usually from maize
POLENTAS > POLENTA
POLER *n* person or thing that poles, esp a punter
POLERS > POLER
POLES > POLE
POLESTAR *n* guiding principle, rule, standard, etc
POLESTARS > POLESTAR
POLEWARD *adv* towards a pole
POLEY *adj* (of cattle) hornless or polled ▷ *n* animal with horns removed
POLEYN *n* piece of armour for protecting the knee
POLEYNS > POLEYN
POLEYS > POLEY
POLIANITE *n* manganese dioxide occurring as hard crystals
POLICE *n* organized force in a state which keeps law and order ▷ *vb* control or watch over with police or a similar body
POLICED > POLICE
POLICEMAN *n* male police officer
POLICEMEN > POLICEMAN
POLICER *n* computer device controlling use
POLICERS > POLICER
POLICES > POLICE
POLICIER *n* film featuring police investigating crimes
POLICIERS > POLICIER
POLICIES > POLICY
POLICING > POLICE
POLICINGS > POLICE
POLICY *n* plan of action adopted by a person, group, or state
POLIES > POLY
POLING > POLE
POLINGS > POLE
POLIO *n* acute viral disease
POLIOS > POLIO
POLIS *n* ancient Greek city-state
POLISES > POLIS
POLISH *vb* make smooth and shiny by rubbing ▷ *n* substance used for polishing
POLISHED *adj* accomplished
POLISHER > POLISH
POLISHERS > POLISH
POLISHES > POLISH
POLISHING > POLISH
POLITBURO *n* supreme policy-making authority in most communist countries
POLITE *adj* showing consideration for others in one's manners, speech, etc
POLITELY > POLITE

POLITER > POLITE
POLITESSE *n* formal or genteel politeness
POLITEST > POLITE
POLITIC *adj* wise and likely to prove advantageous
POLITICAL *adj* of the state, government, or public administration
POLITICK *vb* engage in politics
POLITICKS > POLITICK
POLITICLY > POLITIC
POLITICO *n* politician
POLITICOS > POLITICO
POLITICS *n* winning and using of power to govern society
POLITIES > POLITY
POLITIQUE *n* 16th-century French moderate
POLITY *n* politically organized state, church, or society
POLJE *n* large elliptical depression in karst regions
POLJES > POLJE
POLK *vb* dance a polka
POLKA *n* lively 19th-century dance ▷ *vb* dance a polka
POLKAED > POLKA
POLKAING > POLKA
POLKAS > POLKA
POLKED > POLK
POLKING > POLK
POLKS > POLK
POLL *n* questioning of a random sample of people to find out general opinion ▷ *vb* receive (votes)
POLLACK *n* food fish related to the cod, found in northern seas
POLLACKS > POLLACK
POLLAN *n* whitefish that occurs in lakes in Northern Ireland
POLLANS > POLLAN
POLLARD *n* animal that has shed its horns or has had them removed ▷ *vb* cut off the top of (a tree) to make it grow bushy
POLLARDED > POLLARD
POLLARDS > POLLARD
POLLAXE *same as* > POLEAXE
POLLAXED > POLLAXE
POLLAXES > POLLAXE
POLLAXING > POLLAXE
POLLED *adj* (of animals, esp cattle) having the horns cut off or being naturally hornless
POLLEE > POLL
POLLEES > POLL
POLLEN *n* fine dust produced by flowers to fertilize other flowers ▷ *vb* collect pollen
POLLENATE *same as* > POLLINATE
POLLENED > POLLEN

POLLENING > POLLEN
POLLENS > POLLEN
POLLENT adj strong
POLLER > POLL
POLLERS > POLL
POLLEX n first digit of the forelimb of amphibians, reptiles, birds, and mammals
POLLICAL > POLLEX
POLLICES > POLLEX
POLLICIE obsolete spelling of > POLICY
POLLICIES > POLLICIE
POLLICY obsolete spelling of > POLICY
POLLIES > POLLY
POLLINATE vb fertilize with pollen
POLLING n casting or registering of votes at an election
POLLINGS > POLLING
POLLINIA > POLLINIUM
POLLINIC > POLLEN
POLLINISE same as > POLLINIZE
POLLINIUM n mass of cohering pollen grains, produced by plants such as orchids and transported as a whole during pollination
POLLINIZE same as > POLLINATE
POLLIST n one advocating the use of polls
POLLISTS > POLLIST
POLLIWIG same as > POLLIWOG
POLLIWIGS > POLLIWOG
POLLIWOG n sailor who has not crossed the equator
POLLIWOGS > POLLIWOG
POLLMAN n one passing a degree without honours
POLLMEN > POLLMAN
POLLOCK same as > POLLACK
POLLOCKS > POLLOCK
POLLS > POLL
POLLSTER n person who conducts opinion polls
POLLSTERS > POLLSTER
POLLTAKER n person conducting poll
POLLUCITE n colourless rare mineral consisting of a hydrated caesium aluminium silicate
POLLUSION n comic Shakespearian character's version of 'allusion'
POLLUTANT n something that pollutes
POLLUTE vb contaminate with something poisonous or harmful
POLLUTED adj made unclean or impure
POLLUTER > POLLUTE
POLLUTERS > POLLUTE

POLLUTES > POLLUTE
POLLUTING > POLLUTE
POLLUTION n act of polluting or the state of being polluted
POLLUTIVE adj causing pollution
POLLY n politician
POLLYANNA n person who is constantly or excessively optimistic
POLLYWIG same as > POLLIWOG
POLLYWIGS > POLLIWOG
POLLYWOG same as > POLLIWOG
POLLYWOGS > POLLYWOG
POLO n game like hockey played by teams of players on horseback
POLOIDAL adj relating to a type of magnetic field
POLOIST n devotee of polo
POLOISTS > POLOIST
POLONAISE n old stately dance
POLONIE same as > POLONY
POLONIES > POLONY
POLONISE same as > POLONIZE
POLONISED > POLONISE
POLONISES > POLONISE
POLONISM > POLONISE
POLONISMS > POLONISE
POLONIUM n radioactive element that occurs in trace amounts in uranium ores
POLONIUMS > POLONIUM
POLONIZE vb make Polish
POLONIZED > POLONIZE
POLONIZES > POLONIZE
POLONY n bologna sausage
POLOS > POLO
POLS > POL
POLT n thump or blow ▷ vb strike
POLTED > POLT
POLTFEET > POLTFOOT
POLTFOOT adj having a club foot ▷ n club foot
POLTING > POLT
POLTROON n utter coward
POLTROONS > POLTROON
POLTS > POLT
POLVERINE n glassmakers' potash
POLY n polytechnic
POLYACID adj having two or more hydroxyl groups ▷ n compound made up of two or more hydroxyl groups

POLYACIDS > POLYACID
POLYACT adj (of a sea creature) having many tentacles or limb-like protrusions
POLYADIC adj (of a relation, operation, etc) having several argument places
POLYAMIDE n synthetic polymeric material
POLYAMINE n compound containing two or more amine groups
POLYAMORY n practice of openly having more than one romantic relationship at a time
POLYANDRY n practice of having more than one husband at the same time
POLYANTHA n type of flower
POLYANTHI n hybrid garden primroses
POLYARCH n member of polyarchy
POLYARCHY n political system in which power is dispersed
POLYAXIAL n joint in which movement occurs in more than one axis
POLYAXON n nerve cell with multiple branches
POLYAXONS > POLYAXON
POLYBAG vb put into a polythene bag
POLYBAGS > POLYBAG
POLYBASIC adj (of an acid) having two or more replaceable hydrogen atoms per molecule
POLYBRID n hybrid plant with more than two parental groups
POLYBRIDS > POLYBRID
POLYCARPY n condition of being able to produce flowers and fruit several times in successive years or seasons
POLYCHETE n variety of worm
POLYCONIC adj as in polyconic projection type of projection used in making maps of large areas
POLYCOT n plant that has or appears to have more than two cotyledons
POLYCOTS > POLYCOT
POLYDEMIC adj growing in or inhabiting more than two regions
POLYDRUG adj relating to using several drugs together
POLYENE n organic chemical compound
POLYENES > POLYENE
POLYENIC > POLYENE
POLYESTER n synthetic material used to make plastics and textile fibres

POLYGALA n herbaceous plant or small shrub
POLYGALAS > POLYGALA
POLYGAM n plant of the Polygamia class
POLYGAMIC > POLYGAMY
POLYGAMS > POLYGAM
POLYGAMY n practice of having more than one husband or wife at the same time
POLYGENE n any of a group of genes that each produce a small effect on a particular characteristic of the phenotype
POLYGENES > POLYGENE
POLYGENIC adj of, relating to, or controlled by polygenes
POLYGENY > POLYGENIC
POLYGLOT adj able to speak or write several languages ▷ n person who can speak many languages
POLYGLOTS > POLYGLOT
POLYGLOTT variant of > POLYGLOT
POLYGON n geometrical figure with three or more angles and sides
POLYGONAL > POLYGON
POLYGONS > POLYGON
POLYGONUM n plant with stems with knotlike joints and spikes of small white, green, or pink flowers
POLYGONY > POLYGON
POLYGRAPH n instrument for recording pulse rate and perspiration, used esp as a lie detector
POLYGYNE adj (of a colony of insects) having more than one egg-laying queen
POLYGYNY n practice of having more than one female partner at the same time
POLYHEDRA n solid figures, each consisting of four or more plane faces
POLYIMIDE n type of polymer
POLYLEMMA n debate forcing choice between contradictory positions
POLYMASTY n the presence of more than two breasts
POLYMATH n person of great and varied learning
POLYMATHS > POLYMATH
POLYMATHY > POLYMATH
POLYMER n chemical compound with large molecules made of simple molecules of the same kind

POLYMERIC adj of or being a polymer

POLYMERS > POLYMER

POLYMERY > POLYMER

POLYMORPH n species of animal or plant that exhibits polymorphism

POLYMYXIN n polypeptide antibiotic

POLYNIA same as > POLYNYA

POLYNIAS > POLYNIA

POLYNYA n stretch of open water surrounded by ice

POLYNYAS > POLYNYA

POLYNYI > POLYNYA

POLYOL n type of alcohol

POLYOLS > POLYOL

POLYOMA n type of tumour caused by virus

POLYOMAS > POLYOMA

POLYOMINO n polygon made from joining identical squares at their edges

POLYONYM n object with many names

POLYONYMS > POLYONYM

POLYONYMY > POLYONYM

POLYP n small simple sea creature with a hollow cylindrical body

POLYPARIA n polyparies

POLYPARY n common base and connecting tissue of a colony of coelenterate polyps, esp coral

POLYPE variant of > POLYP

POLYPED same as > POLYPOD

POLYPEDS > POLYPED

POLYPES > POLYPE

POLYPHAGY n insatiable appetite

POLYPHASE adj (of an electrical system, circuit, or device) having, generating, or using two or more alternating voltages of the same frequency, the phases of which are cyclically displaced by fractions of a period

POLYPHON n musical instrument resembling a lute

POLYPHONE n letter or character with more than one phonetic value

POLYPHONS > POLYPHON

POLYPHONY n polyphonic style of composition or a piece of music using it

POLYPI > POLYPUS

POLYPIDE n polyp forming part of a colonial animal

POLYPIDES > POLYPIDE

POLYPIDOM same as > POLYPARY

POLYPILL n pill containing a number of medicines that all treat the same condition

POLYPILLS > POLYPILL

POLYPINE adj of or relating to polyps

POLYPITE same as > POLYPIDE

POLYPITES > POLYPITE

POLYPLOID adj (of cells, organisms, etc) having more than twice the basic (haploid) number of chromosomes ▷ n individual or cell of this type

POLYPNEA n rapid breathing

POLYPNEAS > POLYPNEA

POLYPNEIC > POLYPNEA

POLYPOD adj (esp of insect larvae) having many legs or similar appendages ▷ n animal of this type

POLYPODS > POLYPOD

POLYPODY n fern with deeply divided leaves and round naked sori

POLYPOID > POLYP

POLYPORE n type of fungi

POLYPORES > POLYPORE

POLYPOSES > POLYPOSIS

POLYPOSIS n formation of many polyps

POLYPOUS > POLYP

POLYPS > POLYP

POLYPTYCH n altarpiece consisting of more than three panels, set with paintings or carvings, and usually hinged for folding

POLYPUS same as > POLYP

POLYPUSES > POLYPUS

POLYS > POLY

POLYSEME n word with many meanings

POLYSEMES > POLYSEME

POLYSEMIC > POLYSEME

POLYSEMY n existence of several meanings in a single word

POLYSOME n assemblage of ribosomes associated with a messenger RNA molecule

POLYSOMES > POLYSOME

POLYSOMIC adj of, relating to, or designating a basically diploid chromosome complement, in which some but not all the chromosomes are represented more than twice

POLYSOMY > POLYSOME

POLYSTYLE adj with many columns ▷ n

building with many columns

POLYTENE adj denoting a type of giant-size chromosome

POLYTENY > POLYTENE

POLYTHENE n light plastic used for bags etc

POLYTONAL adj using more than two different tones or keys simultaneously

POLYTYPE n crystal occurring in more than one form ▷ vb produce by use of a polytype

POLYTYPED > POLYTYPE

POLYTYPES > POLYTYPE

POLYTYPIC adj existing in, consisting of, or incorporating several different types or forms

POLYURIA n state of discharging abnormally large quantities of urine

POLYURIAS > POLYURIA

POLYURIC > POLYURIA

POLYVINYL n designating a plastic or resin formed by polymerization of a vinyl derivative

POLYWATER n liquid formerly supposed to be polymeric form of water

POLYZOA n small mosslike aquatic creatures

POLYZOAN another word for > BRYOZOAN

POLYZOANS > POLYZOAN

POLYZOARY n colony of bryozoan animals

POLYZOIC adj (of certain colonial animals) having many zooids or similar polyps

POLYZONAL adj having many zones

POLYZOOID adj resembling a polyzoon

POLYZOON n individual zooid within polyzoan

POM same as > POMMY

POMACE n apple pulp left after pressing for juice

POMACEOUS adj of, relating to, or bearing pomes, such as the apple, pear, and quince trees

POMACES > POMACE

POMADE n perfumed oil put on the hair to make it smooth and shiny ▷ vb put pomade on

POMADED > POMADE

POMADES > POMADE

POMADING > POMADE

POMANDER n mixture of sweet-smelling petals, herbs, etc

POMANDERS > POMANDER

POMATO n hybrid of tomato and potato

POMATOES > POMATO

POMATUM n pomade ▷ vb put pomatum on

POMATUMED > POMATUM

POMATUMS > POMATUM

POMBE n any alcoholic drink

POMBES > POMBE

POME n fleshy fruit of the apple and related plants

POMELIKE adj like a pome

POMELO n edible yellow fruit, like a grapefruit

POMELOS > POMELO

POMEROY n bullet used to down airships

POMEROYS > POMEROY

POMES > POME

POMFRET n small black rounded liquorice sweet

POMFRETS > POMFRET

POMMEE adj (of cross) having end of each arm ending in disk

POMMEL same as > PUMMEL

POMMELE adj having a pommel

POMMELED > POMMEL

POMMELING > POMMEL

POMMELLED > POMMEL

POMMELS > POMMEL

POMMETTY adj having a pommel

POMMIE same as > POMMY

POMMIES > POMMY

POMMY n word used by Australians and New Zealanders for a British person

POMO n postmodernist

POMOERIUM n space around town within city walls

POMOLOGY n branch of horticulture that is concerned with the study and cultivation of fruit

POMOS > POMO

POMP n stately display or ceremony

POMPADOUR n early 18th-century hairstyle for women, having the front hair arranged over a pad to give it greater height and bulk

POMPANO n deep-bodied carangid food fish

POMPANOS > POMPANO

POMPELO n large Asian citrus fruit

POMPELOS > POMPELO

POMPEY vb mollycoddle

POMPEYED > POMPEY

POMPEYING > POMPEY

POMPEYS > POMPEY

POMPHOLYX n type of eczema

POMPIER adj slavishly conventional ▷ n conventional or imitative artist

POMPIERS > POMPIER

POMPILID n spider-hunting wasp

POMPILIDS > POMPILID

POMPION n pumpkin
POMPIONS > POMPION
POMPOM n decorative ball of tufted wool, silk, etc
POMPOMS > POMPOM
POMPON same as > POMPOM
POMPONS > POMPOM
POMPOON variant of > POMPOM
POMPOONS > POMPOON
POMPOSITY n vain or ostentatious display of dignity or importance
POMPOSO adj (of music) to be played in a ceremonial manner
POMPOUS adj foolishly serious and grand, self-important
POMPOUSLY > POMPOUS
POMPS > POMP
POMROY variant of > POMEROY
POMROYS > POMROY
POMS > POM
POMWATER n kind of apple
POMWATERS > POMWATER
PONCE vb act stupidly or waste time
PONCEAU n scarlet red
PONCEAUS > PONCEAU
PONCEAUX > PONCEAU
PONCED > PONCE
PONCES > PONCE
PONCEY adj ostentatious or pretentious
PONCHO n loose circular cloak with a hole for the head
PONCHOED adj wearing poncho
PONCHOS > PONCHO
PONCIER > PONCEY
PONCIEST > PONCEY
PONCING > PONCE
PONCY same as > PONCEY
POND n small area of still water ▷ vb hold back (flowing water)
PONDAGE n water held in reservoir
PONDAGES > PONDAGE
PONDED > POND
PONDER vb think thoroughly or deeply (about)
PONDERAL adj relating to weight
PONDERATE vb consider
PONDERED > PONDER
PONDERER > PONDER
PONDERERS > PONDER
PONDERING > PONDER
PONDEROSA n N American pine tree
PONDEROUS adj serious and dull
PONDERS > PONDER
PONDING > POND
PONDOK n (in southern Africa) crudely made house or shack
PONDOKKIE same as > PONDOK
PONDOKS > PONDOK

PONDS > POND
PONDWEED n plant that grows in ponds
PONDWEEDS > PONDWEED
PONE n bread made of maize
PONENT adj westerly ▷ n the west
PONENTS > PONENT
PONES > PONE
PONEY same as > PONY
PONEYS > PONEY
PONG n strong unpleasant smell ▷ vb give off a strong unpleasant smell
PONGA n tall New Zealand tree fern
PONGAL n Indian dish of cooked rice
PONGALS > PONGAL
PONGAS > PONGA
PONGED > PONG
PONGEE n thin plain-weave silk fabric
PONGEES > PONGEE
PONGID n primate of the family which includes the gibbons and the great apes
PONGIDS > PONGID
PONGIER > PONG
PONGIEST > PONG
PONGING > PONG
PONGO n anthropoid ape, esp an orang-utan or (formerly) a gorilla
PONGOES > PONGO
PONGOS > PONGO
PONGS > PONG
PONGY > PONG
PONIARD n small slender dagger ▷ vb stab with a poniard
PONIARDED > PONIARD
PONIARDS > PONIARD
PONIED > PONY
PONIES > PONY
PONK n evil spirit ▷ vb stink
PONKED > PONK
PONKING > PONK
PONKS > PONK
PONS n bridge of connecting tissue
PONT n (in South Africa) river ferry
PONTAGE n tax paid for repairing bridge
PONTAGES > PONTAGE
PONTAL adj of or relating to the pons
PONTES > PONS
PONTIANAC same as > PONTIANAK
PONTIANAK n (in Malay folklore) female vampire
PONTIC adj of or relating to the pons
PONTIE same as > PONTY
PONTIES > PONTY
PONTIFEX n (in ancient Rome) any of the senior members of the Pontifical College
PONTIFF n Pope
PONTIFFS > PONTIFF
PONTIFIC > PONTIFF

PONTIFICE n structure of bridge
PONTIFIED > PONTIFY
PONTIFIES > PONTIFY
PONTIFY vb speak or behave in a pompous or dogmatic manner
PONTIL same as > PUNTY
PONTILE adj relating to pons ▷ n metal bar used in glass-making
PONTILES > PONTILE
PONTILS > PONTIL
PONTINE adj of or relating to bridges
PONTLEVIS n horse rearing repeatedly
PONTON variant of > PONTOON
PONTONEER same as > PONTONIER
PONTONIER n person in charge of or involved in building a pontoon bridge
PONTONS > PONTON
PONTOON n floating platform supporting a temporary bridge ▷ vb cross a river using pontoons
PONTOONED > PONTOON
PONTOONER > PONTOON
PONTOONS > PONTOON
PONTS > PONT
PONTY n rod used for shaping molten glass
PONY n small horse ▷ vb settle bill or debt
PONYING > PONY
PONYSKIN n leather from pony hide
PONYSKINS > PONYSKIN
PONYTAIL n long hair tied in one bunch at the back of the head
PONYTAILS > PONYTAIL
PONZU n type of Japanese dipping sauce
PONZUS > PONZU
POO vb defecate
POOBAH n influential person
POOBAHS > POOBAH
POOCH n slang word for dog ▷ vb bulge or protrude
POOCHED > POOCH
POOCHES > POOCH
POOCHING > POOCH
POOD n unit of weight, used in Russia
POODLE n dog with curly hair often clipped fancifully
POODLES > POODLE
POODS > POOD
POOED > POO
POOF interj expressing dismissal or a sudden happening
POOGYE n Hindu nose-flute
POOGYES > POOGYE
POOH interj exclamation of disdain, contempt, or disgust ▷ vb make such an exclamation

POOHED > POOH
POOHING > POOH
POOHS > POOH
POOING > POO
POOJA variant of > PUJA
POOJAH variant of > PUJA
POOJAHS > POOJAH
POOJAS > POOJA
POOK vb pluck
POOKA n malevolent Irish spirit
POOKAS > POOKA
POOKING > POOK
POOKIT > POOK
POOKS > POOK
POOL n small body of still water ▷ vb put in a common fund
POOLED > POOL
POOLER n person taking part in pool
POOLERS > POOLER
POOLHALL n room containing pool tables
POOLHALLS > POOLHALL
POOLING > POOL
POOLROOM n hall or establishment where pool, billiards, etc, are played
POOLROOMS > POOLROOM
POOLS pl n organized nationwide gambling pool
POOLSIDE n area surrounding swimming pool
POOLSIDES > POOLSIDE
POON n SE Asian tree
POONAC n coconut residue
POONACS > POONAC
POONCE vb act stupidly or waste time
POONCED > POONCE
POONCES > POONCE
POONCING > POONCE
POONS > POON
POONTANG n vulgar word for the female pudenda
POONTANGS > POONTANG
POOP n raised part at the back of a sailing ship ▷ vb (of a wave or sea) break over the stern of (a vessel)
POOPED > POOP
POOPER n as in party pooper person who spoils other people's enjoyment
POOPERS > POOPER
POOPIER > POOPY
POOPIEST > POOPY
POOPING > POOP
POOPS > POOP
POOPY adj stupid or ineffectual
POOR adj having little money and few possessions
POORBOX n box used for the collection of money for the poor
POORBOXES > POORBOX
POORER > POOR
POOREST > POOR

POORHOUSE n (formerly) publicly maintained institution offering accommodation to the poor

POORI n unleavened Indian bread

POORIS > POORI

POORISH > POOR

POORLIER > POORLY

POORLIEST > POORLY

POORLY adv in a poor manner ▷ adj not in good health

POORMOUTH vb complain about being poor

POORNESS > POOR

POORT n (in South Africa) steep narrow mountain pass

POORTITH same as > PUIRTITH

POORTITHS > POORTITH

POORTS > POORT

POORWILL n bird of N America

POORWILLS > POORWILL

POOS > POO

POOT vb break wind

POOTED > POOT

POOTER vb hurry away

POOTERED > POOTER

POOTERING > POOTER

POOTERS > POOT

POOTING > POOT

POOTLE vb travel or go in a relaxed or leisurely manner

POOTLED > POOTLE

POOTLES > POOTLE

POOTLING > POOTLE

POOTS > POOT

POP vb make or cause to make a small explosive sound ▷ n small explosive sound ▷ adj popular

POPADUM same as > POPPADOM

POPADUMS > POPADUM

POPCORN n grains of maize heated until they puff up and burst

POPCORNS > POPCORN

POPE n bishop of Rome as head of the Roman Catholic Church

POPEDOM n office or dignity of a pope

POPEDOMS > POPEDOM

POPEHOOD > POPE

POPEHOODS > POPE

POPELESS > POPE

POPELIKE > POPE

POPELING n deputy or supporter of pope

POPELINGS > POPELING

POPERA n pop music drawing on opera or classical music

POPERAS > POPERA

POPERIN n kind of pear

POPERINS > POPERIN

POPES > POPE

POPESEYE adj denoting a cut of steak

POPESHIP > POPE

POPESHIPS > POPE

POPETTE n young female fan or performer of pop music

POPETTES > POPETTE

POPEYED adj staring in astonishment

POPGUN n toy gun that fires a pellet or cork by means of compressed air

POPGUNS > POPGUN

POPINAC n type of thorny shrub

POPINAC same as > POPINAC

POPINACKS > POPINACK

POPINACS > POPINAC

POPINJAY n conceited, foppish, or overly talkative person

POPINJAYS > POPINJAY

POPJOY vb amuse oneself

POPJOYED > POPJOY

POPJOYING > POPJOY

POPJOYS > POPJOY

POPLAR n tall slender tree

POPLARS > POPLAR

POPLIN n ribbed cotton material

POPLINS > POPLIN

POPLITEAL adj of, relating to, or near the part of the leg behind the knee

POPLITEI > POPLITEUS

POPLITEUS n muscle in leg

POPLITIC same as > POPLITEAL

POPOUT n type of out in baseball

POPOUTS > POPOUT

POPOVER n individual Yorkshire pudding, often served with roast beef

POPOVERS > POPOVER

POPPA same as > PAPA

POPPADOM n thin round crisp Indian bread

POPPADOMS > POPPADOM

POPPADUM same as > POPPADOM

POPPADUMS > POPPADUM

POPPAS > POPPA

POPPED > POP

POPPER n press stud

POPPERING n method of fishing

POPPERS > POPPER

POPPET n term of affection for a small child or sweetheart

POPPETS > POPPET

POPPIED adj covered with poppies

POPPIER > POPPY

POPPIES > POPPY

POPPIEST > POPPY

POPPING > POP

POPPISH adj like pop music

POPPIT n bead used to form necklace

POPPITS > POPPIT

POPPLE vb (of boiling water or a choppy sea) to heave or toss

POPPLED > POPPLE

POPPLES > POPPLE

POPPLIER > POPPLY

POPPLIEST > POPPLY

POPPLING > POPPLE

POPPLY adj covered in small bumps

POPPY n plant with a large red flower ▷ adj reddish-orange

POPPYCOCK n nonsense

POPPYHEAD n hard dry seed-containing capsule of a poppy

POPPYSEED adj made with the seed of the poppy

POPRIN same as > POPERIN

POPS > POP

POPSICLE n tradename for a kind of ice lolly

POPSICLES > POPSICLE

POPSIE same as > POPSY

POPSIES > POPSY

POPSOCK n women's knee-length nylon stocking

POPSOCKS > POPSOCK

POPSTER n pop star

POPSTERS > POPSTER

POPSTREL n young, attractive female pop star

POPSTRELS > POPSTREL

POPSY n attractive young woman

POPTASTIC adj (of pop music) very good

POPULACE n ordinary people

POPULACES > POPULACE

POPULAR adj widely liked and admired ▷ n cheap newspapers with mass circulation

POPULARLY adv by the public as a whole

POPULARS > POPULAR

POPULATE vb live in, inhabit

POPULATED > POPULATE

POPULATES > POPULATE

POPULISM n political strategy based on an appeal to the prejudices of ordinary people

POPULISMS > POPULISM

POPULIST adj appealing to the interests or prejudices of ordinary people ▷ n person who appeals to the interests or prejudices of ordinary people

POPULISTS > POPULIST

POPULOUS adj densely populated

PORAE n large edible sea fish of New Zealand waters

PORAES > PORAE

PORAL adj relating to pores

PORANGI adj crazy

PORBEAGLE n kind of shark

PORCELAIN n fine china

PORCH n covered approach to the entrance of a building

PORCHED adj having a porch

PORCHES > PORCH

PORCHETTA n Italian boneless stuffed pork cut from a whole roast pig

PORCHLESS adj without a porch

PORCINE adj of or like a pig

PORCINI > PORCINO

PORCINIS > PORCINO

PORCINO n edible woodland fungus

PORCUPINE n animal covered with long pointed quills

PORCUPINY adj like a porcupine

PORE n tiny opening in the skin or in the surface of a plant ▷ vb make a close intent examination or study

PORED > PORE

PORER n person who pores

PORERS > PORER

PORES > PORE

PORGE vb cleanse (slaughtered animal) ceremonially

PORGED > PORGE

PORGES > PORGE

PORGIE same as > PORGY

PORGIES > PORGY

PORGING > PORGE

PORGY n any of various sparid fishes

PORIER > PORY

PORIEST > PORY

PORIFER n type of invertebrate

PORIFERAL > PORIFERAN

PORIFERAN n invertebrate of the phylum which comprises the sponges

PORIFERS > PORIFER

PORIN n protein through which molecules can pass

PORINA n moth the larva of which causes damage to grassland

PORINAS > PORINA

PORINESS > PORY

PORING > PORE

PORINS > PORIN

PORISM n type of mathematical proposition

PORISMS > PORISM

PORISTIC > PORISM

PORK vb eat ravenously ▷ n the flesh of pigs used as food

PORKED > PORK
PORKER n pig raised for food
PORKERS > PORKER
PORKIER > PORKY
PORKIES > PORKY
PORKIEST > PORKY
PORKINESS > PORKY
PORKING > PORK
PORKLING n pig
PORKLINGS
> PORKLING
PORKPIE n hat with a round flat crown and a brim that can be turned up or down
PORKPIES > PORKPIE
PORKS > PORK
PORKWOOD n wood of small American tree
PORKWOODS
> PORKWOOD
PORKY adj of or like pork ▷ n lie
PORLOCK vb interrupt or intrude at an awkward moment
PORLOCKED > PORLOCK
PORLOCKS > PORLOCK
PORN n pornography
PORNIER > PORNY
PORNIEST > PORNY
PORNO same as > PORN
PORNOMAG n pornographic magazine
PORNOMAGS
> PORNOMAG
PORNOS > PORNO
PORNS > PORN
PORNY adj pornographic
POROGAMIC
> POROGAMY
POROGAMY n fertilization of seed plants
POROMERIC adj (of a plastic) permeable to water vapour ▷ n substance having this characteristic, esp one based on polyurethane and used in place of leather in making shoe uppers
POROSCOPE n instrument for assessing porosity
POROSCOPY
> POROSCOPE
POROSE adj pierced with small pores
POROSES > POROSIS
POROSIS n porous condition of bones
POROSITY n state or condition of being porous
POROUS adj allowing liquid to pass through gradually
POROUSLY > POROUS
PORPESS n type of fish
PORPESSE same as > PORPOISE
PORPESSES > PORPESS
PORPHYRIA n hereditary disease of body metabolism, producing abdominal pain, mental confusion, etc

PORPHYRIC
> PORPHYRIA
PORPHYRIN n any of a group of pigments occurring widely in animal and plant tissues and having a heterocyclic structure formed from four pyrrole rings linked by four methylene groups
PORPHYRIO n aquatic bird
PORPHYRY n reddish rock with large crystals in it
PORPOISE n fishlike sea mammal ▷ vb (of an aeroplane) nose-dive during landing
PORPOISED
> PORPOISE
PORPOISES
> PORPOISE
PORPORATE adj wearing purple
PORRECT adj extended forwards ▷ vb stretch forward
PORRECTED > PORRECT
PORRECTS > PORRECT
PORRENGER same as > PORRINGER
PORRIDGE n breakfast food made of oatmeal cooked in water or milk
PORRIDGES
> PORRIDGE
PORRIDGY adj having the consistency of porridge
PORRIGO n disease of the scalp
PORRIGOS > PORRIGO
PORRINGER n small dish, often with a handle, used esp formerly for soup or porridge
PORT vb turn (a boat) towards its left side
PORTA n aperture in an organ
PORTABLE adj easily carried ▷ n article designed to be easily carried, such as a television or typewriter
PORTABLES
> PORTABLE
PORTABLY > PORTABLE
PORTAGE n (route for) transporting boats overland ▷ vb transport (boats) in this way
PORTAGED > PORTAGE
PORTAGES > PORTAGE
PORTAGING > PORTAGE
PORTAGUE n former Portuguese gold coin
PORTAGUES
> PORTAGUE
PORTAL n large imposing doorway or gate
PORTALED > PORTAL
PORTALS > PORTAL
PORTANCE n person's bearing
PORTANCES
> PORTANCE
PORTAPACK n the first combined videotape recorder and camera

PORTAPAK same as
> PORTAPACK
PORTAPAKS
> PORTAPAK
PORTAS > PORTA
PORTASES variant of
> PORTESSE
PORTATE adj diagonally athwart escutcheon
PORTATILE adj portable
PORTATIVE adj concerned with the act of carrying
PORTED > PORT
PORTEND vb be a sign of
PORTENDED > PORTEND
PORTENDS > PORTEND
PORTENT n sign of a future event
PORTENTS > PORTENT
PORTEOUS variant of
> PORTESSE
PORTER n person who carries luggage ▷ vb carry luggage
PORTERAGE n work of carrying supplies, goods, etc, done by porters
PORTERED > PORTER
PORTERESS n female porter
PORTERING > PORTER
PORTERLY adj like a porter
PORTERS > PORTER
PORTESS variant of
> PORTESSE
PORTESSE n prayer book
PORTESSES
> PORTESSE
PORTFIRE n slow-burning fuse formerly used in fireworks
PORTFIRES
> PORTFIRE
PORTFOLIO n (flat case for carrying) examples of an artist's work
PORTHOLE n small round window in a ship or aircraft
PORTHOLES
> PORTHOLE
PORTHORS same as
> PORTESSE
PORTHOS same as
> PORTESSE
PORTHOSES > PORTHOS
PORTHOUSE n company producing port
PORTICO n porch or covered walkway with columns supporting the roof
PORTICOED > PORTICO
PORTICOES > PORTICO
PORTICOS > PORTICO
PORTIER > PORTY
PORTIERE n curtain hung in a doorway
PORTIERED adj having a portiere, a curtain hanging across a doorway
PORTIERES
> PORTIERE
PORTIEST > PORTY
PORTIGUE same as
> PORTAGUE

PORTIGUES
> PORTIGUE
PORTING > PORT
PORTION n part or share ▷ vb divide (something) into shares
PORTIONED > PORTION
PORTIONER > PORTION
PORTIONS > PORTION
PORTLAND n type of rose
PORTLANDS
> PORTLAND
PORTLAST n gunwale of ship
PORTLASTS
> PORTLAST
PORTLESS > PORT
PORTLIER > PORTLY
PORTLIEST > PORTLY
PORTLY adj rather fat
PORTMAN n inhabitant of a port
PORTMEN > PORTMAN
PORTOISE same as
> PORTLAST
PORTOISES
> PORTOISE
PORTOLAN n book of sailing charts
PORTOLANI
> PORTOLANO
PORTOLANO variant of
> PORTOLAN
PORTOLANS
> PORTOLAN
PORTOUS variant of
> PORTESSE
PORTOUSES > PORTOUS
PORTRAIT n picture of a person ▷ adj (of a publication or an illustration in a publication) of greater height than width
PORTRAITS
> PORTRAIT
PORTRAY vb describe or represent by artistic means, as in writing or film
PORTRAYAL > PORTRAY
PORTRAYED > PORTRAY
PORTRAYER > PORTRAY
PORTRAYS > PORTRAY
PORTREEVE n Saxon magistrate
PORTRESS n female porter, esp a doorkeeper
PORTS > PORT
PORTSIDE adj beside port
PORTULACA n tropical American plant with yellow, pink, or purple showy flowers
PORTULAN same as
> PORTOLAN
PORTULANS
> PORTULAN
PORTY adj like port
PORWIGGLE n tadpole
PORY adj containing pores
POS > PO
POSABLE > POSE
POSADA n inn in a Spanish-speaking country
POSADAS > POSADA

POSAUNE n organ chorus reed

POSAUNES > POSAUNE

POSE vb place in or take up a particular position to be photographed or drawn ▷ n position while posing

POSEABLE adj able to be manipulated into poses

POSED > POSE

POSER n puzzling question

POSERISH same as > POSEY

POSERS > POSER

POSES > POSE

POSEUR n person who behaves in an affected way to impress others

POSEURS > POSEUR

POSEUSE n female poseur

POSEUSES > POSEUSE

POSEY adj (of a place) for, characteristic of, or full of posers

POSH adj smart, luxurious ▷ adv in a manner associated with the upper class ▷ vb make posh

POSHED > POSH

POSHER > POSH

POSHES > POSH

POSHEST > POSH

POSHING > POSH

POSHLY > POSH

POSHNESS > POSH

POSHO n corn meal

POSHOS > POSHO

POSHTEEN same as > POSTEEN

POSHTEENS > POSHTEEN

POSIDRIVE adj having a patent screwhead that allows greater torque

POSIER > POSY

POSIES > POSY

POSIEST > POSY

POSIGRADE adj producing positive thrust

POSING > POSE

POSINGLY > POSE

POSINGS > POSE

POSIT vb lay down as a basis for argument ▷ n fact, idea, etc, that is posited

POSITED > POSIT

POSITIF n (on older organs) manual controlling soft stops

POSITIFS > POSITIF

POSITING > POSIT

POSITION n place ▷ vb place

POSITIONS > POSITION

POSITIVE same as > PLUS

POSITIVER > POSITIVE

POSITIVES > POSITIVE

POSITON n part of chromosome

POSITONS > POSITON

POSITRON n particle with same mass as electron but positive charge

POSITRONS > POSITRON

POSITS > POSIT

POSNET n small basin or dish

POSNETS > POSNET

POSOLE n Central American stew

POSOLES > POSOLE

POSOLOGIC > POSOLOGY

POSOLOGY n branch of medicine concerned with appropriate doses of drugs

POSS vb wash (clothes) by agitating them with a long rod, pole, etc

POSSE n group of people organized to maintain law and order

POSSED > POSS

POSSER n short stick used for stirring clothes in a washtub

POSSERS > POSSER

POSSES > POSSE

POSSESS vb have as one's property

POSSESSED adj owning or having

POSSESSES > POSSESS

POSSESSOR > POSSESS

POSSET n drink of hot milk curdled with ale, beer, etc, flavoured with spices ▷ vb treat with a posset

POSSETED > POSSET

POSSETING > POSSET

POSSETS > POSSET

POSSIBLE adj able to exist, happen, or be done ▷ n person or thing that might be suitable or chosen

POSSIBLER > POSSIBLE

POSSIBLES > POSSIBLE

POSSIBLY adv perhaps, not necessarily

POSSIE n place

POSSIES > POSSIE

POSSING > POSS

POSSUM vb pretend to be dead, asleep, ignorant, etc

POSSUMED > POSSUM

POSSUMING > POSSUM

POSSUMS > POSSUM

POST n official system of delivering letters and parcels ▷ vb send by post

POSTAGE n charge for sending a letter or parcel by post

POSTAGES > POSTAGE

POSTAL adj of a Post Office or the mail-delivery service ▷ n postcard

POSTALLY > POSTAL

POSTALS > POSTAL

POSTANAL adj behind the anus

POSTAXIAL adj situated or occurring behind the axis of the body

POSTBAG n postperson's bag

POSTBAGS > POSTBAG

POSTBASE n morpheme used as a suffix on a root word

POSTBASES > POSTBASE

POSTBOX n box into which mail is put for collection by the postal service

POSTBOXES > POSTBOX

POSTBOY n man or boy who brings the post round to offices

POSTBOYS > POSTBOY

POSTBURN adj after injury from burns

POSTBUS n vehicle carrying the mail that also carries passengers

POSTBUSES > POSTBUS

POSTCARD n card for sending a message by post without an envelope

POSTCARDS > POSTCARD

POSTCAVA n inferior vena cava

POSTCAVAE > POSTCAVA

POSTCAVAL > POSTCAVA

POSTCAVAS > POSTCAVA

POSTCODE n system of letters and numbers used to aid the sorting of mail ▷ vb put a postcode on a letter

POSTCODED > POSTCODE

POSTCODES > POSTCODE

POSTCOUP adj after a coup

POSTCRASH adj after a crash

POSTDATE vb write a date on (a cheque) that is later than the actual date

POSTDATED > POSTDATE

POSTDATES > POSTDATE

POSTDIVE adj following a dive

POSTDOC n postdoctoral degree

POSTDOCS > POSTDOC

POSTDRUG adj of time after drug has been taken

POSTED > POST

POSTEEN n Afghan leather jacket

POSTEENS > POSTEEN

POSTER n large picture or notice stuck on a wall ▷ vb cover with posters

POSTERED > POSTER

POSTERING > POSTER

POSTERIOR n buttocks ▷ adj behind, at the back of

POSTERISE same as > POSTERIZE

POSTERITY n future generations, descendants

POSTERIZE vb humiliate (a sporting opponent) by performing a dramatic feat against them

POSTERN n small back door or gate ▷ adj situated at the rear or the side

POSTERNS > POSTERN

POSTERS > POSTER

POSTFACE n note added to the end of a text

POSTFACES > POSTFACE

POSTFACT adj relating to a culture in which appeals to the emotions prevail over facts

POSTFAULT adj after a fault

POSTFIRE adj of the period after a fire

POSTFIX vb add or append at the end of something

POSTFIXAL > POSTFIX

POSTFIXED > POSTFIX

POSTFIXES > POSTFIX

POSTFORM vb mould or shape (plastic) while it hot from reheating

POSTFORMS > POSTFORM

POSTGAME adj of period after sports match

POSTGRAD n graduate taking further degree

POSTGRADS > POSTGRAD

POSTHASTE adv with great speed ▷ n great haste

POSTHEAT n industrial heating process ▷ vb heat a material after welding to relieve stresses

POSTHEATS > POSTHEAT

POSTHOLE n hole dug in ground to hold fence post

POSTHOLES > POSTHOLE

POSTHORSE n horse kept at an inn or posthouse for use by postriders or for hire to travellers

POSTHOUSE n house or inn where horses were kept for postriders or for hire to travellers

POSTICAL adj (of the position of plant parts) behind another part

POSTICHE adj (of architectural ornament) inappropriately applied ▷ n imitation, counterfeit, or substitute

POSTICHES > POSTICHE

POSTICOUS same as > POSTICAL

POSTIE n postman or postwoman

POSTIES > POSTIE

POSTIL n commentary or marginal note, as in a Bible ▷ vb annotate (a biblical passage)

POSTILED > POSTIL

POSTILING > POSTIL
POSTILION n person riding one of a pair of horses drawing a carriage
POSTILLED > POSTIL
POSTILLER > POSTIL
POSTILS > POSTIL
POSTIN variant of > POSTEEN
POSTING n job to which someone is assigned
POSTINGS > POSTING
POSTINS > POSTIN
POSTIQUE variant of > POSTICHE
POSTIQUES > POSTIQUE
POSTLIKE adj like a post
POSTLUDE n final or concluding piece or movement
POSTLUDES > POSTLUDE
POSTMAN n man who collects and delivers post
POSTMARK n official mark stamped on letters showing place and date of posting ▷ vb put such a mark on (mail)
POSTMARKS > POSTMARK
POSTMEN > POSTMAN
POSTNASAL adj situated at the back of the nose
POSTNATAL adj occurring after childbirth
POSTNATI pl n those born in Scotland after its union with England
POSTOP n person recovering from surgery
POSTOPS > POSTOP
POSTORAL adj situated at the back of the mouth
POSTPAID adj with the postage prepaid
POSTPONE vb put off to a later time
POSTPONED > POSTPONE
POSTPONER > POSTPONE
POSTPONES > POSTPONE
POSTPOSE vb place (word or phrase) after other constituents in sentence
POSTPOSED > POSTPOSE
POSTPOSES > POSTPOSE
POSTPUNK adj (of pop music) belonging to a style that followed punk rock ▷ n musician of the musical trend after punk
POSTPUNKS > POSTPUNK
POSTRACE adj of the period after a race
POSTRIDER n (formerly) person who delivered post on horseback
POSTRIOT adj of the period after a riot
POSTS > POST

POSTSHOW adj of the period after a show
POSTSYNC vb add a sound recording to (and synchronize with) an existing video or film recording
POSTSYNCS > POSTSYNC
POSTTAX adj of the period after tax is paid
POSTTEEN n young adult
POSTTEENS > POSTTEEN
POSTTEST n test taken after a lesson
POSTTESTS > POSTTEST
POSTTRIAL adj of the period after a trial
POSTTRUTH adj relating to a culture in which appeals to the emotions prevail over facts
POSTULANT n candidate for admission to a religious order
POSTULATA pl n things postulated
POSTULATE vb assume to be true as the basis of an argument or theory ▷ n something postulated
POSTURAL > POSTURE
POSTURE n position or way in which someone stands, walks, etc ▷ vb behave in an exaggerated way to get attention
POSTURED > POSTURE
POSTURER > POSTURE
POSTURERS > POSTURE
POSTURES > POSTURE
POSTURING n act of posturing
POSTURISE same as > POSTURIZE
POSTURIST > POSTURE
POSTURIZE less common word for > POSTURE
POSTVIRAL adj as in postviral syndrome debilitating condition occurring as a sequel to viral illness
POSTWAR adj occurring or existing after a war
POSTWOMAN n woman who carries and delivers mail as a profession
POSTWOMEN > POSTWOMAN
POSY n small bunch of flowers
POT n round deep container ▷ vb plant in a pot
POTABLE adj drinkable ▷ n something fit to drink
POTABLES > POTABLE
POTAE n hat
POTAES > POTAE
POTAGE n thick soup
POTAGER n small kitchen garden
POTAGERS > POTAGER
POTAGES > POTAGE
POTALE n residue from a grain distillery, used as animal feed

POTALES > POTALE
POTAMIC adj of or relating to rivers
POTASH n white powdery substance obtained from ashes and used as fertilizer ▷ vb treat with potash
POTASHED > POTASH
POTASHES > POTASH
POTASHING > POTASH
POTASS abbreviated form of > POTASSIUM
POTASSA n potassium oxide
POTASSAS > POTASSA
POTASSES > POTASS
POTASSIC > POTASSIUM
POTASSIUM n silvery metallic element
POTATION n act of drinking
POTATIONS > POTATION
POTATO n roundish starchy vegetable that grows underground
POTATOBUG n Colorado beetle
POTATOES > POTATO
POTATORY adj of, relating to, or given to drinking
POTBELLY n bulging belly
POTBOIL vb boil in a pot
POTBOILED > POTBOIL
POTBOILER n inferior work of art produced quickly to make money
POTBOILS > POTBOIL
POTBOUND adj (of plant) unable to grow because pot is too small
POTBOY n (esp formerly) youth or man employed at a public house to serve beer, etc
POTBOYS > POTBOY
POTCH n inferior quality opal used in jewellery for mounting precious opals
POTCHE vb stab
POTCHED > POTCHE
POTCHER > POTCHE
POTCHERS > POTCHE
POTCHES > POTCH
POTCHING > POTCHE
POTE vb push
POTED > POTE
POTEEN n (in Ireland) illegally made alcoholic drink
POTEENS > POTEEN
POTENCE same as > POTENCY
POTENCES > POTENCE
POTENCIES > POTENCY
POTENCY n state or quality of being potent
POTENT adj having great power or influence ▷ n potentate or ruler
POTENTATE n ruler or monarch
POTENTIAL adj possible but not yet actual ▷ n ability or talent not yet fully used

POTENTISE same as > POTENTIZE
POTENTIZE vb make more potent
POTENTLY > POTENT
POTENTS > POTENT
POTES > POTE
POTFUL n amount held by a pot
POTFULS > POTFUL
POTGUN n pot-shaped mortar
POTGUNS > POTGUN
POTHEAD n habitual user of cannabis
POTHEADS > POTHEAD
POTHECARY n pharmacist
POTHEEN rare variant of > POTEEN
POTHEENS > POTHEEN
POTHER n fuss or commotion ▷ vb make or be troubled or upset
POTHERB n plant whose leaves, flowers, or stems are used in cooking
POTHERBS > POTHERB
POTHERED > POTHER
POTHERIER > POTHERY
POTHERING > POTHER
POTHERS > POTHER
POTHERY adj stuffy
POTHOLDER n piece of material used to protect hands while lifting pot from oven
POTHOLE n hole in the surface of a road
POTHOLED > POTHOLE
POTHOLER > POTHOLING
POTHOLERS > POTHOLING
POTHOLES > POTHOLE
POTHOLING n sport of exploring underground caves
POTHOOK n S-shaped hook for suspending a pot over a fire
POTHOOKS > POTHOOK
POTHOS n climbing plant
POTHOSES > POTHOS
POTHOUSE n (formerly) small tavern or pub
POTHOUSES > POTHOUSE
POTHUNTER n person who hunts for food or for profit without regard to the rules of sport
POTICARY obsolete spelling of > POTHECARY
POTICHE n tall vase or jar that narrows towards the neck
POTICHES > POTICHE
POTIN n bronze alloy with high tin content
POTING > POTE
POTINS > POTIN
POTION n dose of medicine or poison
POTIONS > POTION
POTJIE n three-legged iron pot used for cooking
POTJIES > POTJIE

POTLACH same as
> POTLATCH
POTLACHE same as
> POTLATCH
POTLACHES
> POTLACHE
POTLATCH n competitive ceremonial activity among certain Native American tribes
POTLIKE > POT
POTLINE n row of electrolytic cells for reducing metals
POTLINES > POTLINE
POTLUCK n whatever food happens to be available without special preparation
POTLUCKS > POTLUCK
POTMAN same as
> POTBOY
POTMEN > POTMAN
POTOMETER n apparatus that measures the rate of water uptake by a plant or plant part
POTOO n nocturnal tropical bird
POTOOS > POTOO
POTOROO n Australian leaping rodent
POTOROOS > POTOROO
POTPIE n meat and vegetable stew with a pie crust on top
POTPIES > POTPIE
POTPOURRI n fragrant mixture of dried flower petals
POTS > POT
POTSHARD same as
> POTSHERD
POTSHARDS
> POTSHARD
POTSHARE same as
> POTSHERD
POTSHARES
> POTSHARE
POTSHERD n broken fragment of pottery
POTSHERDS
> POTSHERD
POTSHOP n public house
POTSHOPS > POTSHOP
POTSHOT n shot taken without careful aim
POTSHOTS > POTSHOT
POTSIE same as > POTSY
POTSIES > POTSY
POTSTONE n impure massive variety of soapstone, formerly used for making cooking vessels
POTSTONES
> POTSTONE
POTSY n hopscotch
POTT old variant of > POT
POTTABLE adj (esp of a snooker ball) easily potted
POTTAGE n thick soup or stew
POTTAGES > POTTAGE
POTTED > POT
POTTEEN same as
> POTEEN
POTTEENS > POTTEEN

POTTER same as
> PUTTER
POTTERED > POTTER
POTTERER > POTTER
POTTERERS > POTTER
POTTERIES > POTTERY
POTTERING > POTTER
POTTERS > POTTER
POTTERY n articles made from baked clay
POTTIER > POTTY
POTTIES > POTTY
POTTIEST > POTTY
POTTINESS > POTTY
POTTING > POT
POTTINGAR same as
> POTTINGER
POTTINGER n apothecary
POTTLE n liquid measure equal to half a gallon
POTTLES > POTTLE
POTTO n short-tailed prosimian primate
POTTOS > POTTO
POTTS > POTT
POTTY adj silly or eccentric ⊳ n bowl used by a small child as a toilet
POTWALLER n man entitled to the franchise before 1832 by virtue of possession of his own fireplace
POTZER same as
> PATZER
POTZERS > POTZER
POUCH n small bag ⊳ vb place in or as if in a pouch
POUCHED > POUCH
POUCHES > POUCH
POUCHFUL n amount a pouch will hold
POUCHFULS
> POUCHFUL
POUCHIER > POUCH
POUCHIEST > POUCH
POUCHING > POUCH
POUCHLIKE adj like a pouch
POUCHY > POUCH
POUDER obsolete spelling of
> POWDER
POUDERS > POUDER
POUDRE old spelling of
> POWDER
POUDRES > POUDRE
POUF n large solid cushion used as a seat ⊳ vb pile up hair into rolled puffs
POUFED > POUF
POUFF same as > POUF
POUFFE same as > POUF
POUFFED > POUFFE
POUFFES > POUFFE
POUFFIER > POUFFY
POUFFIEST > POUFFY
POUFFING > POUFFE
POUFFS > POUFF
POUFFY adj (of hair) puffed out
POUFING > POUF
POUFS > POUF
POUK Scots variant of
> POKE
POUKE n mischievous spirit
POUKES > POUKE

POUKING > POUK
POUKIT > POUK
POUKS > POUK
POULAINE n tapering toe of shoe
POULAINES
> POULAINE
POULARD n hen that has been spayed for fattening
POULARDE same as
> POULARD
POULARDES
> POULARDE
POULARDS > POULARD
POULDER obsolete spelling of > POWDER
POULDERS > POULDER
POULDRE archaic spelling of > POWDER
POULDRES > POULDRE
POULDRON same as
> PAULDRON
POULDRONS
> POULDRON
POULE n fowl suitable for slow stewing
POULES > POULE
POULP n octopus
POULPE variant of
> POULP
POULPES > POULPE
POULPS > POULP
POULT n young of a gallinaceous bird
POULTER n poultry dealer
POULTERER same as
> POULTER
POULTERS > POULTER
POULTICE n moist dressing, often heated, applied to inflamed skin ⊳ vb apply poultice to
POULTICED
> POULTICE
POULTICES
> POULTICE
POULTRIES > POULTRY
POULTRY n domestic fowls
POULTS > POULT
POUNCE vb spring upon suddenly to attack or capture ⊳ n pouncing
POUNCED > POUNCE
POUNCER > POUNCE
POUNCERS > POUNCE
POUNCES > POUNCE
POUNCET n box with a perforated top used for perfume
POUNCETS > POUNCET
POUNCING old variant of
> PUNCHING
POUNCING > POUNCE
POUND n monetary unit of Britain and some other countries ⊳ vb hit heavily and repeatedly
POUNDAGE n charge of so much per pound of weight or sterling
POUNDAGES > POUNDAGE
POUNDAL n fps unit of force
POUNDALS > POUNDAL
POUNDCAKE n cake containing a pound of each ingredient

POUNDED > POUND
POUNDER > POUND
POUNDERS > POUND
POUNDING > POUND
POUNDINGS
> POUNDING
POUNDS > POUND
POUPE vb make sudden blowing sound
POUPED > POUPE
POUPES > POUPE
POUPING > POUPE
POUPT > POUPE
POUR vb flow or cause to flow out in a stream
POURABLE > POUR
POURBOIRE n tip or gratuity
POURED > POUR
POURER > POUR
POURERS > POUR
POURIE n jug
POURIES > POURIE
POURING > POUR
POURINGLY > POUR
POURINGS > POUR
POURPOINT n man's stuffed quilted doublet of a kind worn between the Middle Ages and the 17th century
POURS > POUR
POURSEW obsolete spelling of > PURSUE
POURSEWED > POURSEW
POURSEWS > POURSEW
POURSUE obsolete spelling of > PURSUE
POURSUED > POURSUE
POURSUES > POURSUE
POURSUING > POURSUE
POURSUIT same as
> PURSUIT
POURSUITS
> POURSUIT
POURTRAY obsolete spelling of > PORTRAY
POURTRAYD
> POURTRAY
POURTRAYS
> POURTRAY
POUSADA n traditional Portuguese hotel
POUSADAS > POUSADA
POUSOWDIE n Scottish stew made from sheep's head
POUSSE same as
> PEASE
POUSSES > POUSSE
POUSSETTE n figure in country dancing in which couples hold hands and move up or down the set to change positions ⊳ vb perform such a figure
POUSSIE old variant of
> PUSSY
POUSSIES > POUSSIE
POUSSIN n young chicken reared for eating
POUSSINS > POUSSIN
POUT vb thrust out one's lips, look sulky ⊳ n pouting look
POUTASSOU n another name for the blue whiting
POUTED > POUT

POUTER n pigeon that can puff out its crop
POUTERS > POUTER
POUTFUL adj tending to pout
POUTHER Scots variant of > POWDER
POUTHERED > POUTHER
POUTHERS > POUTHER
POUTIER > POUT
POUTIEST > POUT
POUTINE n dish of chipped potatoes topped with cheese and sauce
POUTINES > POUTINE
POUTING > POUT
POUTINGLY > POUT
POUTINGS > POUT
POUTS > POUT
POUTY > POUT
POVERTIES > POVERTY
POVERTY n state of being without enough food or money
POW interj exclamation to indicate that a collision or explosion has taken place ▷ n head or a head of hair
POWAN n type of freshwater whitefish occurring in some Scottish lakes
POWANS > POWAN
POWDER n substance in the form of tiny loose particles ▷ vb apply powder to
POWDERED > POWDER
POWDERER > POWDER
POWDERERS > POWDER
POWDERIER > POWDER
POWDERING n sprinkling of something on a surface
POWDERMAN n person who handles explosives in a demolition team
POWDERMEN > POWDERMAN
POWDERS > POWDER
POWDERY > POWDER
POWELLISE same as > POWELLIZE
POWELLITE n type of mineral
POWELLIZE vb treat wood with a sugar solution
POWER n ability to do or act ▷ vb give or provide power to
POWERBAND n range of speeds allowing efficient operation of an engine
POWERBOAT n fast powerful motorboat
POWERED > POWER
POWERFUL adj having great power or influence ▷ adv extremely
POWERING > POWER
POWERLESS adj without power or authority
POWERPLAY n behaviour intended to maximise person's power
POWERS > POWER
POWFAGGED adj exhausted

POWHIRI n Māori ceremony of welcome, esp to a marae
POWHIRIS > POWHIRI
POWIN n peacock
POWINS > POWIN
POWN variant of > POWIN
POWND obsolete spelling of > POUND
POWNDED > POWND
POWNDING > POWND
POWNDS > POWND
POWNEY old Scots spelling of > PONY
POWNEYS > POWNEY
POWNIE old Scots spelling of > PONY
POWNIES > POWNIE
POWNS > POWN
POWNY old Scots spelling of > PONY
POWRE obsolete spelling of > POWER
POWRED > POWRE
POWRES > POWRE
POWRING > POWRE
POWS > POW
POWSOWDY same as > POUSOWDIE
POWTER vb scrabble about
POWTERED > POWTER
POWTERING > POWTER
POWTERS > POWTER
POWWAW interj expression of disbelief or contempt
POWWOW n talk or conference ▷ vb hold a powwow
POWWOWED > POWWOW
POWWOWING > POWWOW
POWWOWS > POWWOW
POX n disease in which skin pustules form ▷ vb infect with pox
POXED > POX
POXES > POX
POXIER > POXY
POXIEST > POXY
POXING > POX
POXVIRUS n virus such as smallpox
POXY adj of poor quality; rotten
POYNANT old variant of > POIGNANT
POYNT obsolete spelling of > POINT
POYNTED > POYNT
POYNTING > POYNT
POYNTS > POYNT
POYOU n type of armadillo
POYOUS > POYOU
POYSE obsolete variant of > POISE
POYSED > POYSE
POYSES > POYSE
POYSING > POYSE
POYSON obsolete spelling of > POISON
POYSONED > POYSON
POYSONING > POYSON
POYSONS > POYSON
POZ adj positive
POZIDRIVE same as > POSIDRIVE
POZOLE same as > POSOLE

POZOLES > POZOLE
POZZ adj positive
POZZIES > POZZY
POZZOLAN same as > POZZOLANA
POZZOLANA n type of porous volcanic ash
POZZOLANS > POZZOLAN
POZZY same as > POSSIE
PRAAM same as > PRAM
PRAAMS > PRAAM
PRABBLE variant of > BRABBLE
PRABBLES > PRABBLE
PRACHARAK n (in India) person appointed to propagate a cause through personal contact, meetings, public lectures, etc
PRACTIC adj practical ▷ n practice ▷ vb put (a theory) into practice
PRACTICAL adj involving experience or actual use rather than theory ▷ n examination in which something has to be done or made
PRACTICE same as > PRACTISE
PRACTICED > PRACTICE
PRACTICER > PRACTICE
PRACTICES > PRACTICE
PRACTICK obsolete word for > PRACTICE
PRACTICKS > PRACTICK
PRACTICS > PRACTIC
PRACTICUM n course in which theory is put into practice
PRACTIQUE variant of > PRACTIC
PRACTISE vb do repeatedly so as to gain skill
PRACTISED > PRACTISE
PRACTISER > PRACTISE
PRACTISES > PRACTISE
PRACTIVE obsolete word for > ACTIVE
PRACTOLOL n type of drug
PRAD n horse
PRADHAN n (in India) chief or leader
PRADHANS > PRADHAN
PRADS > PRAD
PRAEAMBLE same as > PREAMBLE
PRAECIPE n written request addressed to court
PRAECIPES > PRAECIPE
PRAECOCES n division of birds whose young are able to run when first hatched
PRAEDIAL adj of or relating to land, farming, etc ▷ n slave attached to a farm

PRAEDIALS > PRAEDIAL
PRAEFECT same as > PREFECT
PRAEFECTS > PRAEFECT
PRAELECT same as > PRELECT
PRAELECTS > PRAELECT
PRAELUDIA n musical preludes
PRAENOMEN n ancient Roman's first or given name
PRAESES n Roman governor
PRAESIDIA n presidiums
PRAETOR n (in ancient Rome) senior magistrate ranking just below the consuls
PRAETORS > PRAETOR
PRAGMATIC adj concerned with practical consequences rather than theory
PRAHU same as > PROA
PRAHUS > PRAHU
PRAIRIE n large treeless area of grassland
PRAIRIED > PRAIRIE
PRAIRIES > PRAIRIE
PRAISE vb express approval of (someone or something) ▷ n something said or written to show approval
PRAISEACH n type of porridge
PRAISED > PRAISE
PRAISEFUL > PRAISE
PRAISER > PRAISE
PRAISERS > PRAISE
PRAISES > PRAISE
PRAISING > PRAISE
PRAISINGS > PRAISE
PRAJNA n wisdom or understanding
PRAJNAS > PRAJNA
PRALINE n sweet made of nuts and caramelized sugar
PRALINES > PRALINE
PRAM n four-wheeled carriage for a baby, pushed by hand
PRAMS > PRAM
PRANA n cosmic energy believed to come from the sun
PRANAS > PRANA
PRANAYAMA n breath control in yoga
PRANCE vb walk with exaggerated bouncing steps ▷ n act of prancing
PRANCED > PRANCE
PRANCER > PRANCE
PRANCERS > PRANCE
PRANCES > PRANCE
PRANCING > PRANCE
PRANCINGS > PRANCE
PRANCK obsolete variant of > PRANK
PRANCKE obsolete variant of > PRANK

PRANCKED > PRANCK
PRANCKES > PRANCKE
PRANCKING > PRANCK
PRANCKS > PRANCK
PRANDIAL *adj* of or relating to a meal
PRANG *n* crash in a car or aircraft ▷ *vb* crash or damage (an aircraft or car)
PRANGED > PRANG
PRANGING > PRANG
PRANGS > PRANG
PRANK *n* mischievous trick ▷ *vb* dress or decorate showily or gaudily
PRANKED > PRANK
PRANKFUL > PRANK
PRANKIER > PRANK
PRANKIEST > PRANK
PRANKING > PRANK
PRANKINGS > PRANK
PRANKISH > PRANK
PRANKLE *obsolete variant of* > PRANCE
PRANKLED > PRANKLE
PRANKLES > PRANKLE
PRANKLING > PRANKLE
PRANKS > PRANK
PRANKSOME > PRANK
PRANKSTER *n* practical joker
PRANKY > PRANK
PRAO *same as* > PROA
PRAOS > PRAO
PRASE *n* light green translucent variety of chalcedony
PRASES > PRASE
PRAT *n* stupid person
PRATE *vb* talk idly and at length ▷ *n* chatter
PRATED > PRATE
PRATER > PRATE
PRATERS > PRATE
PRATES > PRATE
PRATFALL *vb* fall upon one's buttocks
PRATFALLS > PRATFALL
PRATFELL > PRATFALL
PRATIE *n* potato
PRATIES > PRATIE
PRATING > PRATE
PRATINGLY > PRATE
PRATINGS > PRATE
PRATIQUE *n* formal permission given to a vessel to use a foreign port
PRATIQUES > PRATIQUE
PRATS > PRAT
PRATT *n* buttocks ▷ *vb* hit on the buttocks
PRATTED > PRATT
PRATTING > PRATT
PRATTLE *vb* chatter in a childish or foolish way ▷ *n* childish or foolish talk
PRATTLED > PRATTLE
PRATTLER > PRATTLE
PRATTLERS > PRATTLE
PRATTLES > PRATTLE
PRATTLING > PRATTLE
PRATTS > PRATT
PRATY *obsolete variant of* > PRETTY

PRAU *same as* > PROA
PRAUNCE *obsolete variant of* > PRANCE
PRAUNCED > PRAUNCE
PRAUNCES > PRAUNCE
PRAUNCING > PRAUNCE
PRAUS > PRAU
PRAVITIES > PRAVITY
PRAVITY *n* moral degeneracy
PRAWLE *n* Shakespearian spelling of 'brawl'
PRAWLES > PRAWLE
PRAWLIN *variant of* > PRALINE
PRAWLINS > PRAWLIN
PRAWN *n* edible shellfish like a large shrimp ▷ *vb* catch prawns
PRAWNED > PRAWN
PRAWNER > PRAWN
PRAWNERS > PRAWN
PRAWNING > PRAWN
PRAWNS > PRAWN
PRAXES > PRAXIS
PRAXIS *n* practice as opposed to theory
PRAXISES > PRAXIS
PRAY *vb* say prayers ▷ *adv* I beg you ▷ *interj* I beg you
PRAYED > PRAY
PRAYER *n* thanks or appeal addressed to one's God
PRAYERFUL *adj* inclined to or characterized by prayer
PRAYERS > PRAYER
PRAYING > PRAY
PRAYINGLY > PRAY
PRAYINGS > PRAY
PRAYS > PRAY
PRE *prep* before
PREABSORB *vb* absorb beforehand
PREACCUSE *vb* accuse beforehand
PREACE *obsolete variant of* > PRESS
PREACED > PREACE
PREACES > PREACE
PREACH *vb* give a talk on a religious theme as part of a church service
PREACHED > PREACH
PREACHER *n* person who preaches, esp in church
PREACHERS > PREACHER
PREACHES > PREACH
PREACHIER > PREACHY
PREACHIFY *vb* preach or moralize in a tedious manner
PREACHILY > PREACHY
PREACHING > PREACH
PREACHY *adj* inclined to or marked by preaching
PREACING > PREACE
PREACT *vb* act beforehand
PREACTED > PREACT
PREACTING > PREACT
PREACTS > PREACT
PREADAMIC *adj* of or relating to the belief that there were people on earth before Adam

PREADAPT *vb* adapt beforehand
PREADAPTS > PREADAPT
PREADJUST *vb* adjust beforehand
PREADMIT *vb* prepare patient prior to treatment
PREADMITS > PREADMIT
PREADOPT *vb* adopt in advance
PREADOPTS > PREADOPT
PREADULT *n* animal or person who has not reached adulthood
PREADULTS > PREADULT
PREAGED *adj* treated to appear older
PREALLOT *vb* allot beforehand
PREALLOTS > PREALLOT
PREALTER *vb* alter beforehand
PREALTERS > PREALTER
PREAMBLE *n* introductory part to something said or written ▷ *vb* write a preamble
PREAMBLED > PREAMBLE
PREAMBLES > PREAMBLE
PREAMP *n* electronic amplifier
PREAMPS > PREAMP
PREANAL *adj* situated in front of anus
PREAPPLY *vb* apply beforehand
PREARM *vb* arm beforehand
PREARMED > PREARM
PREARMING > PREARM
PREARMS > PREARM
PREASE *vb* crowd or press
PREASED > PREASE
PREASES > PREASE
PREASING > PREASE
PREASSE *obsolete spelling of* > PRESS
PREASSED > PREASSE
PREASSES > PREASSE
PREASSIGN *vb* assign beforehand
PREASSING > PREASSE
PREASSURE *vb* assure beforehand
PREATOMIC *adj* before the atomic age
PREATTUNE *vb* attune beforehand
PREAUDIT *n* examination of contracts before a transaction
PREAUDITS > PREAUDIT
PREAVER *vb* aver in advance
PREAVERS > PREAVER
PREAXIAL *adj* situated or occurring in front of the axis of the body
PREBADE > PREBID

PREBAKE *vb* bake before further cooking
PREBAKED > PREBAKE
PREBAKES > PREBAKE
PREBAKING > PREBAKE
PREBASAL *adj* in front of a base
PREBATTLE *adj* of the period before a battle
PREBEND *n* allowance paid to a canon or member of the cathedral chapter
PREBENDAL > PREBEND
PREBENDS > PREBEND
PREBID *vb* bid beforehand
PREBIDDEN > PREBID
PREBIDS > PREBID
PREBILL *vb* issue an invoice before the service has been provided
PREBILLED > PREBILL
PREBILLS > PREBILL
PREBIND *vb* bind a book in a hard-wearing binding
PREBINDS > PREBIND
PREBIOTIC *adj* of the period before the existence of life on earth
PREBIRTH *n* period of life before birth
PREBIRTHS > PREBIRTH
PREBLESS *vb* bless a couple before they marry
PREBOARD *vb* board an aircraft before other passengers
PREBOARDS > PREBOARD
PREBOIL *vb* boil beforehand
PREBOILED > PREBOIL
PREBOILS > PREBOIL
PREBOOK *vb* book well in advance
PREBOOKED > PREBOOK
PREBOOKS > PREBOOK
PREBOOM *adj* of the period before an economic boom
PREBORN *adj* unborn
PREBOUGHT > PREBUY
PREBOUND > PREBIND
PREBUDGET *adj* before budget
PREBUILD *vb* build beforehand
PREBUILDS > PREBUILD
PREBUILT > PREBUILD
PREBUTTAL *n* prepared response to an anticipated criticism
PREBUY *vb* buy in advance
PREBUYING > PREBUY
PREBUYS > PREBUY
PRECANCEL *vb* cancel (postage stamps) before placing them on mail ▷ *n* precancelled stamp
PRECANCER *n* condition that may develop into cancer
PRECARIAT *n* people without a long-term source of income

P

PRECAST adj cast in a particular form before being used ▷ vb cast (concrete) in a particular form before use

PRECASTS > PRECAST

PRECATIVE same as > PRECATORY

PRECATORY adj of, involving, or expressing entreaty

PRECAUDAL adj in front of the caudal fin

PRECAVA n superior vena cava

PRECAVAE > PRECAVA

PRECAVAL n type of vein

PRECAVALS > PRECAVAL

PRECEDE vb go or be before

PRECEDED > PRECEDE

PRECEDENT n previous case or occurrence regarded as an example to be followed ▷ adj preceding

PRECEDES > PRECEDE

PRECEDING adj going or coming before

PRECEESE Scots variant of > PRECISE

PRECENSOR vb censor (a film, play, book, etc) before its publication

PRECENT vb issue a command or law

PRECENTED > PRECENT

PRECENTOR n person who leads the singing in a church

PRECENTS > PRECENT

PRECEPIT old word for > PRECIPICE

PRECEPITS > PRECEPIT

PRECEPT n rule of behaviour

PRECEPTOR n instructor

PRECEPTS > PRECEPT

PRECES pl n prayers

PRECESS vb undergo or cause to undergo precession

PRECESSED > PRECESS

PRECESSES > PRECESS

PRECHARGE vb charge beforehand

PRECHECK vb check beforehand

PRECHECKS > PRECHECK

PRECHILL vb chill beforehand

PRECHILLS > PRECHILL

PRECHOOSE vb choose in advance

PRECHOSE > PRECHOOSE

PRECHOSEN > PRECHOOSE

PRECIEUSE n pretentious female

PRECIEUX n pretentious male

PRECINCT n area in a town closed to traffic

PRECINCTS pl n surrounding region

PRECIOUS adj of great value and importance ▷ adv very

PRECIP n precipitation

PRECIPE n type of legal document

PRECIPES > PRECIPE

PRECIPICE n very steep face of a cliff

PRECIPS > PRECIP

PRECIS n short written summary of a longer piece ▷ vb make a precis of

PRECISE adj exact, accurate in every detail

PRECISED > PRECIS

PRECISELY adv in a precise manner

PRECISER > PRECISE

PRECISES > PRECIS

PRECISEST > PRECISE

PRECISIAN n punctilious observer of rules or forms, esp in the field of religion

PRECISING > PRECIS

PRECISION n quality of being precise ▷ adj accurate

PRECISIVE adj limiting by cutting off all that is unnecessary

PRECITED adj cited previously

PRECLEAN vb clean beforehand

PRECLEANS > PRECLEAN

PRECLEAR vb approve in advance

PRECLEARS > PRECLEAR

PRECLUDE vb make impossible to happen

PRECLUDED > PRECLUDE

PRECLUDES > PRECLUDE

PRECOCIAL adj (of the young of some species of birds after hatching) covered with down, having open eyes, and capable of leaving the nest within a few days of hatching ▷ n precocial bird

PRECOCITY n early maturing or development

PRECODE vb code beforehand

PRECODED > PRECODE

PRECODES > PRECODE

PRECODING > PRECODE

PRECOITAL adj before sex

PRECONISE same as > PRECONIZE

PRECONIZE vb announce or commend publicly

PRECOOK vb cook (food) beforehand

PRECOOKED > PRECOOK

PRECOOKER n device for preparing food before cooking

PRECOOKS > PRECOOK

PRECOOL vb cool in advance

PRECOOLED > PRECOOL

PRECOOLS > PRECOOL

PRECOUP adj of the period before a coup

PRECRASH adj of the period before a crash

PRECREASE vb provide with a crease in advance

PRECRISIS adj occurring before a crisis

PRECURE vb cure in advance

PRECURED > PRECURE

PRECURES > PRECURE

PRECURING > PRECURE

PRECURRER > PRECURSE

PRECURSE n forerunning ▷ vb be a precursor of

PRECURSED > PRECURSE

PRECURSES > PRECURSE

PRECURSOR n something that precedes and is a signal of something else, forerunner

PRECUT vb cut in advance

PRECUTS > PRECUT

PRECYCLE vb preemptive approach to waste reduction involving minimal use of packaging

PRECYCLED > PRECYCLE

PRECYCLES > PRECYCLE

PREDACITY n predatory nature

PREDATE vb occur at an earlier date than

PREDATED > PREDATE

PREDATES > PREDATE

PREDATING > PREDATE

PREDATION n relationship between two species of animal in a community, in which one (the predator) hunts, kills, and eats the other (the prey)

PREDATISM n state of preying on other animals

PREDATIVE > PREDATE

PREDATOR n predatory animal

PREDATORS > PREDATOR

PREDATORY adj habitually hunting and killing other animals for food

PREDAWN n period before dawn

PREDAWNS > PREDAWN

PREDEATH n period immediately before death

PREDEATHS > PREDEATH

PREDEBATE adj before a debate

PREDEDUCT vb deduct beforehand

PREDEFINE vb define in advance

PREDELLA n series of small paintings or sculptures in a long narrow strip on an altarpiece

PREDELLAS > PREDELLA

PREDELLE > PREDELLA

PREDESIGN vb design beforehand

PREDEVOTE adj preordained ▷ vb devote or dedicate beforehand

PREDIAL same as > PRAEDIAL

PREDIALS > PREDIAL

PREDICANT same as > PREDIKANT

PREDICATE n part of a sentence in which something is said about the subject ▷ vb declare or assert ▷ adj of or relating to something that has been predicated

PREDICT vb tell about in advance, prophesy

PREDICTED > PREDICT

PREDICTER > PREDICT

PREDICTOR n person or thing that predicts

PREDICTS > PREDICT

PREDIED > PREDY

PREDIES > PREDY

PREDIGEST vb treat (food) artificially to aid subsequent digestion in the body

PREDIKANT n minister in the Dutch Reformed Church in South Africa

PREDILECT adj chosen or preferred

PREDINNER adj of the period before dinner

PREDIVE adj happening before a dive

PREDOOM vb pronounce (someone or something's) doom beforehand

PREDOOMED > PREDOOM

PREDOOMS > PREDOOM

PREDRAFT adj before a draft ▷ n preliminary draft prior to an official draft

PREDRAFTS > PREDRAFT

PREDRIED > PREDRY

PREDRIES > PREDRY

PREDRILL vb drill in advance

PREDRILLS > PREDRILL

PREDRY vb dry beforehand

PREDRYING > PREDRY

PREDUSK n period before dusk

PREDUSKS > PREDUSK

PREDY vb prepare for action

PREDYING > PREDY

PREE vb try or taste

PREED > PREE

PREEDIT vb edit beforehand

PREEDITED > PREEDIT

PREEDITS > PREEDIT
PREEING > PREE
PREELECT vb elect beforehand
PREELECTS > PREELECT
PREEMIE n premature infant
PREEMIES > PREEMIE
PREEMPT vb acquire in advance of or to the exclusion of others
PREEMPTED > PREEMPT
PREEMPTOR n one who preempts
PREEMPTS > PREEMPT
PREEN vb (of a bird) clean or trim (feathers) with the beak ▷ n pin, esp a decorative one
PREENACT vb enact beforehand
PREENACTS > PREENACT
PREENED > PREEN
PREENER > PREEN
PREENERS > PREEN
PREENING > PREEN
PREENS > PREEN
PREERECT vb erect beforehand
PREERECTS > PREERECT
PREES > PREE
PREEVE old form of > PROVE
PREEVED > PREEVE
PREEVES > PREEVE
PREEVING > PREEVE
PREEXCITE vb stimulate in preparation
PREEXEMPT vb exempt beforehand
PREEXILIC adj prior to the Babylonian exile of the Jews
PREEXIST vb exist beforehand
PREEXISTS > PREEXIST
PREEXPOSE vb expose beforehand
PREFAB n prefabricated house ▷ vb manufacture sections of (building) in factory
PREFABBED > PREFAB
PREFABS > PREFAB
PREFACE n introduction to a book ▷ vb serve as an introduction to (a book, speech, etc)
PREFACED > PREFACE
PREFACER > PREFACE
PREFACERS > PREFACE
PREFACES > PREFACE
PREFACIAL adj anterior to face
PREFACING > PREFACE
PREFADE vb fade beforehand
PREFADED > PREFADE
PREFADES > PREFADE
PREFADING > PREFADE
PREFARD vb old form of preferred
PREFATORY adj concerning a preface

PREFECT n senior pupil in a school, with limited power over others
PREFECTS > PREFECT
PREFER vb like better
PREFERRED > PREFER
PREFERRER > PREFER
PREFERS > PREFER
PREFEUDAL adj of the period before the feudal era
PREFIGHT adj of the period before a boxing match
PREFIGURE vb represent or suggest in advance
PREFILE vb file beforehand
PREFILED > PREFILE
PREFILES > PREFILE
PREFILING > PREFILE
PREFILLED adj having been filled beforehand
PREFIRE vb fire beforehand
PREFIRED > PREFIRE
PREFIRES > PREFIRE
PREFIRING > PREFIRE
PREFIX n letters put at the beginning of a word to make a new word ▷ vb put as an introduction or prefix (to)
PREFIXAL > PREFIX
PREFIXED > PREFIX
PREFIXES > PREFIX
PREFIXING > PREFIX
PREFIXION > PREFIX
PREFLAME adj of the period before combustion
PREFLIGHT adj of or relating to the period just prior to a plane taking off
PREFOCUS vb focus in advance
PREFORM vb form beforehand
PREFORMAT vb format in advance
PREFORMED > PREFORM
PREFORMS > PREFORM
PREFRANK vb frank in advance
PREFRANKS > PREFRANK
PREFREEZE vb freeze beforehand
PREFROZE > PREFREEZE
PREFROZEN > PREFREEZE
PREFUND vb pay for in advance
PREFUNDED > PREFUND
PREFUNDS > PREFUND
PREGAME vb consume alcoholic drinks before going to a social gathering
PREGAMED > PREGAME
PREGAMES > PREGAME
PREGAMING > PREGAME
PREGGERS informal word for > PREGNANT
PREGGIER > PREGGY
PREGGIEST > PREGGY
PREGGO adj slang word for pregnant

PREGGY informal word for > PREGNANT
PREGNABLE adj capable of being assailed or captured
PREGNANCE obsolete word for > PREGNANCY
PREGNANCY n state or condition of being pregnant
PREGNANT adj carrying a fetus in the womb
PREGROWTH n period before something begins to grow
PREGUIDE vb give guidance in advance
PREGUIDED > PREGUIDE
PREGUIDES > PREGUIDE
PREHAB n any programme of training designed to prevent sports injury
PREHABS > PREHAB
PREHALLUX n extra first toe
PREHANDLE vb handle beforehand
PREHARDEN vb harden beforehand
PREHEAT vb heat (an oven, grill, pan, etc) beforehand
PREHEATED > PREHEAT
PREHEATER > PREHEAT
PREHEATS > PREHEAT
PREHEND vb take hold of
PREHENDED > PREHEND
PREHENDS > PREHEND
PREHENSOR n part that grasps
PREHIRING adj relating to early hiring
PREHNITE n green mineral
PREHNITES > PREHNITE
PREHUMAN n hominid that predates human beings
PREHUMANS > PREHUMAN
PREIF old form of > PROOF
PREIFE old form of > PROOF
PREIFES > PREIFE
PREIFS > PREIF
PREIMPOSE vb impose beforehand
PREINFORM vb inform beforehand
PREINSERT vb insert beforehand
PREINVITE vb invite before others
PREJINK variant of > PERJINK
PREJUDGE vb judge beforehand without sufficient evidence
PREJUDGED > PREJUDGE
PREJUDGER > PREJUDGE
PREJUDGES > PREJUDGE

PREJUDICE n unreasonable or unfair dislike or preference ▷ vb cause (someone) to have a prejudice
PREJUDIZE old form of > PREJUDICE
PRELACIES > PRELACY
PRELACY n office or status of a prelate
PRELATE n bishop or other churchman of high rank
PRELATES > PRELATE
PRELATESS n female prelate
PRELATIAL > PRELATE
PRELATIC > PRELATE
PRELATIES > PRELATY
PRELATION n setting of one above another
PRELATISE same as > PRELATIZE
PRELATISH adj like a prelate
PRELATISM same as > PRELACY
PRELATIST > PRELATISM
PRELATIZE vb exercise prelatical power
PRELATURE same as > PRELACY
PRELATY n prelacy
PRELAUNCH adj of the period before a launch
PRELAW adj before taking up study of law
PRELECT vb lecture or discourse in public
PRELECTED > PRELECT
PRELECTOR > PRELECT
PRELECTS > PRELECT
PRELEGAL adj of the period before the start of a law course
PRELIFE n life lived before one's life on earth
PRELIM n event which precedes another
PRELIMIT vb limit beforehand
PRELIMITS > PRELIMIT
PRELIMS pl n pages of a book which come before the main text
PRELIVES > PRELIFE
PRELOAD vb load beforehand
PRELOADED > PRELOAD
PRELOADS > PRELOAD
PRELOCATE vb locate beforehand
PRELOVED adj previously owned or used
PRELUDE n introductory movement in music ▷ vb act as a prelude to (something)
PRELUDED > PRELUDE
PRELUDER > PRELUDE
PRELUDERS > PRELUDE
PRELUDES > PRELUDE
PRELUDI > PRELUDIO
PRELUDIAL > PRELUDE
PRELUDING > PRELUDE
PRELUDIO n musical prelude

p

PRELUDIOS
> PRELUDIO
PRELUNCH *adj* of the period before lunch
PRELUSION > PRELUDE
PRELUSIVE > PRELUDE
PRELUSORY > PRELUDE
PREM *n* informal word for a premature infant
PREMADE *adj* made in advance
PREMAKE *vb* make beforehand
PREMAKES > PREMAKE
PREMAKING > PREMAKE
PREMAN *n* hominid
PREMARKET *adj* of the period before a product is available
PREMATURE *adj* happening or done before the normal or expected time
PREMEAL *adj* of the period before a meal
PREMED *n* premedical student
PREMEDIC *same as* > PREMED
PREMEDICS > PREMEDIC
PREMEDS > PREMED
PREMEET *adj* happening before a meet
PREMEN > PREMAN
PREMERGER *adj* of the period prior to a merger
PREMIA > PREMIUM
PREMIE *same as* > PREEMIE
PREMIER *n* prime minister ▷ *adj* chief, leading
PREMIERE *n* first performance of a play, film, etc ▷ *vb* give, or (of a film, play, or opera) be, a premiere
PREMIERED > PREMIERE
PREMIERES > PREMIERE
PREMIERS > PREMIER
PREMIES > PREMIE
PREMISE *n* statement used as the basis of reasoning ▷ *vb* state or assume (a proposition) as a premise
PREMISED > PREMISE
PREMISES > PREMISE
PREMISING > PREMISE
PREMISS *same as* > PREMISE
PREMISSED > PREMISS
PREMISSES > PREMISS
PREMIUM *n* additional sum of money, as on a wage or charge
PREMIUMS > PREMIUM
PREMIX *vb* mix beforehand
PREMIXED > PREMIX
PREMIXES > PREMIX
PREMIXING > PREMIX
PREMIXT > PREMIX
PREMODERN *adj* of the period before a modern era

PREMODIFY *vb* modify in advance
PREMOLAR *n* tooth between the canine and first molar in adult humans ▷ *adj* situated before a molar tooth
PREMOLARS > PREMOLAR
PREMOLD *same as* > PREMOULD
PREMOLDED > PREMOLD
PREMOLDS > PREMOLD
PREMOLT *same as* > PREMOULT
PREMONISH *vb* admonish beforehand
PREMORAL *adj* not governed by sense of right and wrong
PREMORSE *adj* appearing as though the end had been bitten off
PREMOSAIC *adj* of the period before Moses
PREMOTION *n* previous motion
PREMOTOR *adj* relating to a part of the frontal lobe of the brain
PREMOULD *vb* mould in advance
PREMOULDS > PREMOULD
PREMOULT *adj* happening in the period before an animal moults
PREMOVE *vb* prompt to action
PREMOVED > PREMOVE
PREMOVES > PREMOVE
PREMOVING > PREMOVE
PREMS > PREM
PREMUNE *adj* having immunity to a disease as a result of latent infection
PREMY *variant of* > PREEMIE
PRENAME *n* forename
PRENAMES > PRENAME
PRENASAL *n* bone in the front of the nose
PRENASALS > PRENASAL
PRENATAL *adj* before birth, during pregnancy ▷ *n* prenatal examination
PRENATALS > PRENATAL
PRENEED *adj* arranged in advance of eventual requirements
PRENOMEN *less common spelling of* > PRAENOMEN
PRENOMENS > PRENOMEN
PRENOMINA > PRENOMEN
PRENOON *adj* of the period before noon
PRENOTIFY *vb* notify in advance
PRENOTION *n* preconception
PRENT *Scots variant of* > PRINT
PRENTED > PRENT
PRENTICE *vb* bind as an apprentice

PRENTICED > PRENTICE
PRENTICES > PRENTICE
PRENTING > PRENT
PRENTS > PRENT
PRENUBILE *adj* of the period from birth to puberty
PRENUMBER *vb* number in advance
PRENUP *n* prenuptial agreement
PRENUPS > PRENUP
PRENZIE *adj* Shakespearian word supposed by some to mean 'princely'
PREOBTAIN *vb* obtain in advance
PREOCCUPY *vb* fill the thoughts or attention of (someone) to the exclusion of other things
PREOCULAR *adj* relating to the scale in front of the eye of a reptile or fish ▷ *n* scale in front of the eye of a reptile or fish
PREON *n* (in particle physics) hypothetical subcomponent of a quark
PREONS > PREON
PREOP *n* patient being prepared for surgery
PREOPS > PREOP
PREOPTION *n* right of first choice
PREORAL *adj* situated in front of mouth
PREORDAIN *vb* ordain, decree, or appoint beforehand
PREORDER *vb* order in advance
PREORDERS > PREORDER
PREOWNED *adj* second-hand
PREP *vb* prepare
PREPACK *vb* pack in advance of sale
PREPACKED *adj* sold already wrapped
PREPACKS > PREPACK
PREPAID > PREPAY
PREPARE *vb* make or get ready
PREPARED > PREPARE
PREPARER > PREPARE
PREPARERS > PREPARE
PREPARES > PREPARE
PREPARING > PREPARE
PREPASTE *vb* paste in advance
PREPASTED > PREPASTE
PREPASTES > PREPASTE
PREPAVE *vb* pave beforehand
PREPAVED > PREPAVE
PREPAVES > PREPAVE
PREPAVING > PREPAVE
PREPAY *vb* pay for in advance
PREPAYING > PREPAY
PREPAYS > PREPAY

PREPENSE *adj* (usually in legal contexts) arranged in advance ▷ *vb* consider beforehand
PREPENSED > PREPENSE
PREPENSES > PREPENSE
PREPILL *adj* of the period before the contraceptive pill became available
PREPLACE *vb* place in advance
PREPLACED > PREPLACE
PREPLACES > PREPLACE
PREPLAN *vb* plan beforehand
PREPLANS > PREPLAN
PREPLANT *adj* planted in advance
PREPOLLEX *n* additional digit on thumb of some animals
PREPONE *vb* bring forward to an earlier time
PREPONED > PREPONE
PREPONES > PREPONE
PREPONING > PREPONE
PREPOSE *vb* place before
PREPOSED > PREPOSE
PREPOSES > PREPOSE
PREPOSING > PREPOSE
PREPOSTOR *n* prefect in certain public schools
PREPOTENT *adj* greater in power, force, or influence
PREPPED > PREP
PREPPIE *same as* > PREPPY
PREPPIER > PREPPY
PREPPIES > PREPPY
PREPPIEST > PREPPY
PREPPILY > PREPPY
PREPPING > PREP
PREPPY *adj* denoting a fashion style of neat, understated clothes ▷ *n* person exhibiting such style
PREPREG *n* material already impregnated with synthetic resin
PREPREGS > PREPREG
PREPRESS *adj* before printing
PREPRICE *vb* price in advance
PREPRICED > PREPRICE
PREPRICES > PREPRICE
PREPRINT *vb* print in advance
PREPRINTS > PREPRINT
PREPS > PREP
PREPUBES > PREPUBIS
PREPUBIS *n* animal hip bone
PREPUCE *n* foreskin
PREPUCES > PREPUCE
PREPUEBLO *adj* belonging to the period before the Pueblo Indians

PREPUNCH vb pierce with holes in advance

PREPUPA n insect in stage of life before pupa

PREPUPAE > PREPUPA

PREPUPAL adj of the period between the larval and pupal stages

PREPUPAS > PREPUPA

PREPUTIAL > PREPUCE

PREQUEL n film or book about an earlier stage of a story

PREQUELS > PREQUEL

PRERACE adj of the period before a race

PRERADIO adj before the invention of radio

PRERECORD vb record (music or a programme) in advance so that it can be played or broadcast later

PRERECTAL adj in front of the rectum

PREREFORM adj before reform

PRERENAL adj anterior to kidney

PRERETURN adj of the period before return

PREREVIEW vb make a preliminary review

PRERINSE vb treat before rinsing

PRERINSED
> PRERINSE

PRERINSES
> PRERINSE

PRERIOT adj of the period before a riot

PREROCK adj of the era before rock music

PRERUPT adj abrupt

PRESA n musical sign or symbol to indicate the entry of a part

PRESAGE vb be a sign or warning of ▷ n omen

PRESAGED > PRESAGE

PRESAGER > PRESAGE

PRESAGERS > PRESAGE

PRESAGES > PRESAGE

PRESAGING > PRESAGE

PRESALE n practice of arranging the sale of a product before it is available

PRESALES > PRESALE

PRESBYOPE n person with presbyopy

PRESBYOPY n diminishing ability of the eye to focus

PRESBYTE n person with presbyopy

PRESBYTER n (in some episcopal Churches) official with administrative and priestly duties

PRESBYTES
> PRESBYTE

PRESBYTIC
> PRESBYTE

PRESCHOOL adj of or for children below the age of five

PRESCIENT adj having knowledge of events before they take place

PRESCIND vb withdraw attention (from something)

PRESCINDS
> PRESCIND

PRESCIOUS adj prescient

PRESCORE vb record (the score of a film) before shooting

PRESCORED
> PRESCORE

PRESCORES
> PRESCORE

PRESCREEN vb screen in advance

PRESCRIBE vb recommend the use of (a medicine)

PRESCRIPT n something laid down or prescribed ▷ adj prescribed as a rule

PRESCUTA
> PRESCUTUM

PRESCUTUM n part of an insect's thorax

PRESE > PRESA

PRESEASON n period before the start of a sport season

PRESELECT vb select beforehand

PRESELL vb promote in advance of appearance

PRESELLS > PRESELL

PRESENCE n fact of being in a specified place

PRESENCES
> PRESENCE

PRESENILE adj occurring before the onset of old age

PRESENT adj being in a specified place ▷ n present time or tense ▷ vb introduce formally or publicly

PRESENTED > PRESENT

PRESENTEE n person who is presented, as at court

PRESENTER n person introducing a TV or radio show

PRESENTLY adv soon

PRESENTS pl n used in a deed or document to refer to itself

PRESERVE vb keep from being damaged, changed, or ended ▷ n area of interest restricted to a particular person or group

PRESERVED
> PRESERVE

PRESERVER
> PRESERVE

PRESERVES
> PRESERVE

PRESES variant of
> PRAESES

PRESET vb set a timer so that equipment starts to work at a specific time ▷ adj (of equipment) with the controls set in advance ▷ n control that is used to set initial conditions

PRESETS > PRESET

PRESETTLE vb settle beforehand

PRESHAPE vb shape beforehand

PRESHAPED
> PRESHAPE

PRESHAPES
> PRESHAPE

PRESHIP vb ship in advance

PRESHIPS > PRESHIP

PRESHOW vb show in advance

PRESHOWED > PRESHOW

PRESHOWN > PRESHOW

PRESHOWS > PRESHOW

PRESHRANK
> PRESHRINK

PRESHRINK vb subject to a shrinking process so that further shrinkage will not occur

PRESHRUNK
> PRESHRINK

PRESIDE vb be in charge, esp of a meeting

PRESIDED > PRESIDE

PRESIDENT n head of state in many countries

PRESIDER > PRESIDE

PRESIDERS > PRESIDE

PRESIDES > PRESIDE

PRESIDIA
> PRESIDIUM

PRESIDIAL adj presidential

PRESIDING > PRESIDE

PRESIDIO n military post or establishment, esp in countries formerly under Spanish control

PRESIDIOS
> PRESIDIO

PRESIDIUM n (in Communist countries) permanent administrative committee

PRESIFT vb sift beforehand

PRESIFTED > PRESIFT

PRESIFTS > PRESIFT

PRESIGNAL vb signal in advance

PRESLEEP adj of the period before sleep

PRESLICE vb slice in advance

PRESLICED
> PRESLICE

PRESLICES
> PRESLICE

PRESOAK vb soak beforehand

PRESOAKED > PRESOAK

PRESOAKS > PRESOAK

PRESOLD > PRESELL

PRESOLVE vb solve beforehand

PRESOLVED
> PRESOLVE

PRESOLVES
> PRESOLVE

PRESONG adj of the period before a song is sung

PRESORT vb sort in advance

PRESORTED > PRESORT

PRESORTS > PRESORT

PRESPLIT adj of the period prior to a split

PRESS vb apply force or weight to ▷ n printing machine

PRESSBACK adj (of an antique chair) with a pattern pressed into the back rail

PRESSED > PRESS

PRESSER > PRESS

PRESSERS > PRESS

PRESSES > PRESS

PRESSFAT n wine vat

PRESSFATS
> PRESSFAT

PRESSFUL > PRESS

PRESSFULS > PRESS

PRESSGANG n squad of sailors forcing others into navy

PRESSIE informal word for
> PRESENT

PRESSIES > PRESSIE

PRESSING adj urgent ▷ n large number of gramophone records produced at one time

PRESSINGS
> PRESSING

PRESSION n act of pressing

PRESSIONS
> PRESSION

PRESSMAN n man who works for the press

PRESSMARK n location mark on a book indicating a specific bookcase

PRESSMEN > PRESSMAN

PRESSOR n something that produces an increase in blood pressure

PRESSORS > PRESSOR

PRESSROOM n room in a printing establishment that houses the printing presses

PRESSRUN n number of books printed at one time

PRESSRUNS
> PRESSRUN

PRESSURE n force produced by pressing ▷ vb persuade forcefully

PRESSURED
> PRESSURE

PRESSURES
> PRESSURE

PRESSWORK n operation of a printing press

PRESSY same as
> PRESSIE

PREST adj prepared for action or use ▷ n loan of money ▷ vb give as a loan

PRESTAMP vb stamp in advance

PRESTAMPS
> PRESTAMP

PRESTED > PREST

PRESTER > PREST

PRESTERNA adj anterior to sternum

PRESTERS > PREST

PRESTIGE n high status or respect resulting from success or achievements

P

PRESTIGES
> PRESTIGE
PRESTING > PREST
PRESTO adv very quickly
▷ n passage to be played
very quickly
PRESTORE vb store in
advance
PRESTORED
> PRESTORE
PRESTORES
> PRESTORE
PRESTOS > PRESTO
PRESTRESS vb apply
tensile stress to (the steel
cables, wires, etc, of a
precast concrete part)
before the load is applied
PRESTRIKE adj of the
period before a strike
PRESTS > PREST
PRESUME vb suppose to
be the case
PRESUMED > PRESUME
PRESUMER > PRESUME
PRESUMERS > PRESUME
PRESUMES > PRESUME
PRESUMING > PRESUME
PRESUMMIT n meeting
held prior to a summit
PRESURVEY vb survey in
advance
PRETAPE vb (formerly)
tape in advance
PRETAPED > PRETAPE
PRETAPES > PRETAPE
PRETAPING > PRETAPE
PRETASTE vb taste in
advance
PRETASTED
> PRETASTE
PRETASTES
> PRETASTE
PRETAX adj before tax
PRETEEN n boy or girl
approaching his or her
teens
PRETEENS > PRETEEN
PRETELL vb predict
PRETELLS > PRETELL
PRETENCE n behaviour
intended to deceive,
pretending
PRETENCES
> PRETENCE
PRETEND vb claim
(something untrue) ▷ adj
fanciful
PRETENDED > PRETEND
PRETENDER n person
who makes a false or
disputed claim to a
position of power
PRETENDS > PRETEND
PRETENSE same as
> PRETENCE
PRETENSES
> PRETENSE
PRETERIST n person
interested in past
PRETERIT same as
> PRETERITE
PRETERITE n past tense
of verbs, such as jumped,
swam ▷ adj expressing
such a past tense
PRETERITS
> PRETERIT

PRETERM n premature
baby
PRETERMIT vb overlook
intentionally
PRETERMS > PRETERM
PRETEST vb test
(something) before
presenting it ▷ n act or
instance of pretesting
PRETESTED > PRETEST
PRETESTS > PRETEST
PRETEXT n false reason
given to hide the real one
▷ vb get personal
information under false
pretences
PRETEXTED > PRETEXT
PRETEXTS > PRETEXT
PRETOLD > PRETELL
PRETONIC adj relating to
the syllable before the one
bearing the primary stress
in a word
PRETOR same as
> PRAETOR
PRETORIAL > PRETOR
PRETORIAN n person
with the rank of praetor
PRETORS > PRETOR
PRETRAIN vb train in
advance
PRETRAINS
> PRETRAIN
PRETRAVEL adj of the
period before travel
PRETREAT vb treat in
advance
PRETREATS
> PRETREAT
PRETRIAL n hearing
prior to a trial
PRETRIALS
> PRETRIAL
PRETRIM vb trim in
advance
PRETRIMS > PRETRIM
PRETTIED > PRETTY
PRETTIER > PRETTY
PRETTIES > PRETTY
PRETTIEST > PRETTY
PRETTIFY vb make
pretty
PRETTILY > PRETTY
PRETTY adj pleasing to
look at ▷ adv fairly,
moderately ▷ vb pretty
PRETTYING > PRETTY
PRETTYISH adj quite
pretty
PRETTYISM n affectedly
pretty style
PRETYPE vb type in
advance
PRETYPED > PRETYPE
PRETYPES > PRETYPE
PRETYPING > PRETYPE
PRETZEL n brittle salted
biscuit ▷ vb bend or
twist
PRETZELS > PRETZEL
PREUNION n early form
of trade union
PREUNIONS
> PREUNION
PREUNITE vb unite in
advance
PREUNITED
> PREUNITE

PREUNITES
> PREUNITE
PREVAIL vb gain mastery
PREVAILED > PREVAIL
PREVAILER > PREVAIL
PREVAILS > PREVAIL
PREVALENT adj
widespread, common
PREVALUE vb value
beforehand
PREVALUED
> PREVALUE
PREVALUES
> PREVALUE
PREVE vb prove
PREVED > PREVE
PREVENE vb come before
PREVENED > PREVENE
PREVENES > PREVENE
PREVENING > PREVENE
PREVENT vb keep from
happening or doing
PREVENTED > PREVENT
PREVENTER n person or
thing that prevents
PREVENTS > PREVENT
PREVERB n particle
preceding root of verb
PREVERBAL > PREVERB
PREVERBS > PREVERB
PREVES > PREVE
PREVIABLE adj not yet
viable
PREVIEW n advance
showing of a film or
exhibition before it is
shown to the public ▷ vb
view in advance
PREVIEWED > PREVIEW
PREVIEWER > PREVIEW
PREVIEWS > PREVIEW
PREVING > PREVE
PREVIOUS adj coming or
happening before
PREVISE vb predict or
foresee
PREVISED > PREVISE
PREVISES > PREVISE
PREVISING > PREVISE
PREVISION n act or
power of foreseeing
PREVISIT vb visit
beforehand
PREVISITS
> PREVISIT
PREVISOR > PREVISE
PREVISORS > PREVISE
PREVUE same as
> PREVIEW
PREVUED > PREVUE
PREVUES > PREVUE
PREVUING > PREVUE
PREWAR adj relating to
the period before a war,
esp before World War I or II
PREWARM vb warm
beforehand
PREWARMED > PREWARM
PREWARMS > PREWARM
PREWARN vb warn in
advance
PREWARNED > PREWARN
PREWARNS > PREWARN
PREWASH vb give a
preliminary wash to
(clothes) ▷ n preliminary
wash
PREWASHED > PREWASH

PREWASHES > PREWASH
PREWEANED adj not yet
weaned
PREWEIGH vb weigh
beforehand
PREWEIGHS
> PREWEIGH
PREWIRE vb wire
beforehand
PREWIRED > PREWIRE
PREWIRES > PREWIRE
PREWIRING > PREWIRE
PREWORK vb work in
advance
PREWORKED > PREWORK
PREWORKS > PREWORK
PREWORN adj (of clothes)
second-hand
PREWRAP vb wrap in
advance
PREWRAPS > PREWRAP
PREWRITE vb write
beforehand
PREWRITES
> PREWRITE
PREWROTE > PREWRITE
PREWYN obsolete spelling of
> PRUNE
PREWYNS > PREWYN
PREX same as > PREXY
PREXES > PREX
PREXIE same as > PREXY
PREXIES > PREXY
PREXY n US college
president
PREY n animal hunted and
killed for food by another
animal ▷ vb hunt or seize
food by killing other
animals
PREYED > PREY
PREYER > PREY
PREYERS > PREY
PREYFUL adj rich in prey
PREYING > PREY
PREYS > PREY
PREZ n president
PREZES > PREZ
PREZZIE same as
> PRESSIE
PREZZIES > PREZZIE
PRIAL n pair royal of
cards
PRIALS > PRIAL
PRIAPEAN same as
> PRIAPIC
PRIAPI > PRIAPUS
PRIAPIC adj phallic
PRIAPISM n prolonged
painful erection of the
penis
PRIAPISMS
> PRIAPISM
PRIAPUS n
representation of the
penis
PRIAPUSES > PRIAPUS
PRIBBLE variant of
> PRABBLE
PRIBBLES > PRIBBLE
PRICE n amount of
money for which a thing is
bought or sold ▷ vb fix or
ask the price of
PRICEABLE > PRICE
PRICED > PRICE
PRICELESS adj very
valuable

PRICER > PRICE

PRICERS > PRICE

PRICES > PRICE

PRICEY adj expensive

PRICIER > PRICY

PRICIEST > PRICY

PRICILY > PRICEY

PRICINESS > PRICEY

PRICING > PRICE

PRICINGS > PRICE

PRICK vb pierce lightly with a sharp point ▷ n sudden sharp pain caused by pricking

PRICKED > PRICK

PRICKER n person or thing that pricks

PRICKERS > PRICKER

PRICKET n male deer in the second year of life

PRICKETS > PRICKET

PRICKIER > PRICKY

PRICKIEST > PRICKY

PRICKING > PRICK

PRICKINGS > PRICK

PRICKLE n thorn or spike on a plant ▷ vb have a tingling or pricking sensation

PRICKLED > PRICKLE

PRICKLES > PRICKLE

PRICKLIER > PRICKLY

PRICKLING > PRICKLE

PRICKLY adj having prickles

PRICKS > PRICK

PRICKWOOD n shrub with wood used for skewers

PRICKY adj covered with pricks

PRICY same as **>** PRICEY

PRIDE n feeling of pleasure and satisfaction when one has done well

PRIDED > PRIDE

PRIDEFUL > PRIDE

PRIDELESS > PRIDE

PRIDES > PRIDE

PRIDIAN adj relating to yesterday

PRIDING > PRIDE

PRIED > PRY

PRIEDIEU n piece of furniture for use when kneeling to pray

PRIEDIEUS > PRIEDIEU

PRIEDIEUX > PRIEDIEU

PRIEF obsolete variant of **>** PROOF

PRIEFE obsolete variant of **>** PROOF

PRIEFES > PRIEFE

PRIEFS > PRIEF

PRIER n person who pries

PRIERS > PRIER

PRIES > PRY

PRIEST n (in the Christian church) person who can administer the sacraments and preach ▷ vb make a priest

PRIESTED > PRIEST

PRIESTESS n female official who offers sacrifice on behalf of the people and performs various other religious ceremonies

PRIESTING > PRIEST

PRIESTLY adj of, relating to, characteristic of, or befitting a priest

PRIESTS > PRIEST

PRIEVE obsolete variant of **>** PROOF

PRIEVED > PRIEVE

PRIEVES > PRIEVE

PRIEVING > PRIEVE

PRIG n self-righteous person who acts as if superior to others

PRIGGED > PRIG

PRIGGER n thief

PRIGGERS > PRIGGER

PRIGGERY > PRIG

PRIGGING > PRIG

PRIGGINGS > PRIG

PRIGGISH > PRIG

PRIGGISM > PRIG

PRIGGISMS > PRIG

PRIGS > PRIG

PRILL vb convert (a material) into a granular free-flowing form ▷ n prilled material

PRILLED > PRILL

PRILLING > PRILL

PRILLS > PRILL

PRIM adj formal, proper, and rather prudish ▷ vb make prim

PRIMA same as **>** PRIMO

PRIMACIES > PRIMACY

PRIMACY n state of being first in rank, grade, etc

PRIMAEVAL same as **>** PRIMEVAL

PRIMAGE n tax added to customs duty

PRIMAGES > PRIMAGE

PRIMAL adj of basic causes or origins

PRIMALITY n state of being prime

PRIMALLY > PRIMAL

PRIMARIES > PRIMARY

PRIMARILY adv chiefly or mainly

PRIMARY adj chief, most important ▷ n person or thing that is first in position, time, or importance

PRIMAS > PRIMA

PRIMATAL n primate

PRIMATALS > PRIMATAL

PRIMATE n member of an order of mammals including monkeys and humans

PRIMATES > PRIMATE

PRIMATIAL > PRIMATE

PRIMATIC > PRIMATE

PRIMAVERA n springtime

PRIME adj main, most important ▷ n time when someone is most vigorous ▷ vb give (someone) information in advance

PRIMED > PRIME

PRIMELY > PRIME

PRIMENESS > PRIME

PRIMER n special paint applied to bare wood etc before the main paint

PRIMERO n 16th- and 17th-century card game

PRIMEROS > PRIMERO

PRIMERS > PRIMER

PRIMES > PRIME

PRIMETIME adj occurring during or designed for prime time

PRIMEUR n anything (esp fruit) produced early

PRIMEURS > PRIMEUR

PRIMEVAL adj of or like the earliest age of the world

PRIMI > PRIMO

PRIMINE n integument surrounding an ovule or the outer of two such integuments

PRIMINES > PRIMINE

PRIMING same as **>** PRIMER

PRIMINGS > PRIMING

PRIMIPARA n woman who has borne one child

PRIMITIAE pl n first fruits of the season

PRIMITIAL > PRIMITIAE

PRIMITIAS > PRIMITIAE

PRIMITIVE adj of an early simple stage of development ▷ n primitive person or thing

PRIMLY > PRIM

PRIMMED > PRIM

PRIMMER n elementary textbook

PRIMMERS > PRIMMER

PRIMMEST > PRIM

PRIMMING > PRIM

PRIMNESS > PRIM

PRIMO n upper or right-hand part in a piano duet

PRIMORDIA pl n organs or parts in the earliest stage of development

PRIMOS > PRIMO

PRIMP vb tidy (one's hair or clothes) fussily

PRIMPED > PRIMP

PRIMPING > PRIMP

PRIMPS > PRIMP

PRIMROSE n pale yellow spring flower ▷ adj pale yellow

PRIMROSED > PRIMROSE

PRIMROSES > PRIMROSE

PRIMROSY adj abounding in primroses

PRIMS > PRIM

PRIMSIE Scots variant of **>** PRIM

PRIMSIER > PRIMSIE

PRIMSIEST > PRIMSIE

PRIMULA n type of primrose with brightly coloured flowers

PRIMULAS > PRIMULA

PRIMULINE n type of dye

PRIMUS n presiding bishop in the Synod

PRIMUSES > PRIMUS

PRIMY adj prime

PRINCE n son of a king or queen ▷ vb act like a prince

PRINCED > PRINCE

PRINCEDOM n dignity, rank, or position of a prince

PRINCEKIN n young prince

PRINCELET n petty or minor prince

PRINCELY adj of or like a prince ▷ adv in a princely manner

PRINCES > PRINCE

PRINCESS n female member of a royal family, esp the daughter of the king or queen

PRINCESSE same as **>** PRINCESS

PRINCING > PRINCE

PRINCIPAL adj main, most important ▷ n head of a school or college

PRINCIPE n prince

PRINCIPI > PRINCIPE

PRINCIPIA n principles

PRINCIPLE n moral rule guiding behaviour

PRINCOCK same as **>** PRINCOX

PRINCOCKS > PRINCOCK

PRINCOX n pert youth

PRINCOXES > PRINCOX

PRINK vb dress (oneself) finely

PRINKED > PRINK

PRINKER > PRINK

PRINKERS > PRINK

PRINKING > PRINK

PRINKS > PRINK

PRINT vb reproduce (a newspaper, book, etc) in large quantities by mechanical or electronic means ▷ n printed words etc

PRINTABLE adj capable of being printed or of producing a print

PRINTED > PRINT

PRINTER n person or company engaged in printing

PRINTERS > PRINTER

PRINTERY n establishment in which printing is carried out

PRINTHEAD n component in a printer that forms a printed character

PRINTING n process of producing printed matter

PRINTINGS > PRINTING

PRINTLESS > PRINT

PRINTOUT n printed information produced by a computer output device

PRINTOUTS > PRINTOUT

PRINTS > PRINT

PRION n dovelike petrel with a serrated bill

PRIONS > PRION

PRIOR adj earlier ▷ n head monk in a priory

PRIORATE n office, status, or term of office of a prior

PRIORATES > PRIORATE

PRIORESS n deputy head nun in a convent

PRIORIES > PRIORY

PRIORITY n most important thing that must be dealt with first

PRIORLY > PRIOR

PRIORS > PRIOR

PRIORSHIP n office of prior

PRIORY n place where certain orders of monks or nuns live

PRISAGE n customs duty levied until 1809 upon wine imported into England

PRISAGES > PRISAGE

PRISE same as > PRY

PRISED > PRISE

PRISER > PRISE

PRISERE n primary sere or succession from bare ground to the community climax

PRISERES > PRISERE

PRISERS > PRISE

PRISES > PRISE

PRISING > PRISE

PRISM n transparent block used to disperse light into a spectrum

PRISMATIC adj of or shaped like a prism

PRISMOID n prism-like geometrical shape

PRISMOIDS > PRISMOID

PRISMS > PRISM

PRISMY > PRISM

PRISON n building where criminals and accused people are held ▷ vb imprison

PRISONED > PRISON

PRISONER n person held captive

PRISONERS > PRISONER

PRISONING > PRISON

PRISONOUS > PRISON

PRISONS > PRISON

PRISS n prissy person ▷ vb act prissily

PRISSED > PRISS

PRISSES > PRISS

PRISSIER > PRISSY

PRISSIES > PRISSY

PRISSIEST > PRISSY

PRISSILY > PRISSY

PRISSING > PRISS

PRISSY adj prim, correct, and easily shocked ▷ n prissy person

PRISTANE n colourless combustible liquid

PRISTANES > PRISTANE

PRISTINE adj clean, new, and unused

PRITHEE interj pray thee

PRIVACIES > PRIVACY

PRIVACY n condition of being private

PRIVADO n close friend

PRIVADOES > PRIVADO

PRIVADOS > PRIVADO

PRIVATE adj for the use of one person or group only ▷ n soldier of the lowest rank

PRIVATEER n privately owned armed vessel authorized by a government to take part in a war ▷ vb serve on a privateer

PRIVATELY > PRIVATE

PRIVATER > PRIVATE

PRIVATES > PRIVATE

PRIVATEST > PRIVATE

PRIVATION n loss or lack of the necessities of life

PRIVATISE same as > PRIVATIZE

PRIVATISM n lack of concern for public life

PRIVATIST > PRIVATISM

PRIVATIVE adj causing privation

PRIVATIZE vb sell (a publicly owned company) to individuals or a private company

PRIVET n bushy evergreen shrub used for hedges

PRIVETS > PRIVET

PRIVIER > PRIVY

PRIVIES > PRIVY

PRIVIEST > PRIVY

PRIVILEGE n advantage or favour that only some people have ▷ vb bestow a privilege or privileges upon

PRIVILY adv in a secret way

PRIVITIES > PRIVITY

PRIVITY n legally recognized relationship between two parties

PRIVY adj sharing knowledge of something secret ▷ n toilet, esp an outside one

PRIZABLE adj of worth

PRIZE n reward given for success in a competition etc ▷ adj winning or likely to win a prize ▷ vb value highly

PRIZED > PRIZE

PRIZEMAN n man who wins a prize

PRIZEMEN > PRIZEMAN

PRIZER n contender for prize

PRIZERS > PRIZER

PRIZES > PRIZE

PRIZING > PRIZE

PRO prep in favour of ▷ n professional ▷ adv in favour of a motion etc

PROA n canoe-like boat used in the South Pacific

PROACTION n action that initiates change as opposed to reaction to events

PROACTIVE adj tending to initiate change rather than reacting to events

PROAS > PROA

PROB n problem

PROBABLE adj likely to happen or be true ▷ n person who is likely to be chosen for a team, event, etc

PROBABLES > PROBABLE

PROBABLY adv in all likelihood ▷ sentence substitute I believe such a thing or situation may be the case

PROBALL adj believable

PROBAND n first patient to be investigated in a family study

PROBANDS > PROBAND

PROBANG n long flexible rod used to apply medication

PROBANGS > PROBANG

PROBATE n process of proving the validity of a will ▷ vb establish officially the authenticity and validity of (a will)

PROBATED > PROBATE

PROBATES > PROBATE

PROBATING > PROBATE

PROBATION n system of dealing with law-breakers, esp juvenile ones, by placing them under supervision

PROBATIVE adj serving to test or designed for testing

PROBATORY same as > PROBATIVE

PROBE vb search into or examine closely ▷ n surgical instrument used to examine a wound, cavity, etc

PROBEABLE > PROBE

PROBED > PROBE

PROBER > PROBE

PROBERS > PROBE

PROBES > PROBE

PROBING n act of making a thorough enquiry

PROBINGLY > PROBE

PROBINGS > PROBING

PROBIOTIC n bacterium that protects the body from harmful bacteria

PROBIT n statistical measurement

PROBITIES > PROBITY

PROBITS > PROBIT

PROBITY n honesty, integrity

PROBLEM n something difficult to deal with or solve ▷ adj of a literary work that deals with difficult moral questions

PROBLEMS > PROBLEM

PROBOSCIS n long trunk or snout

PROBS > PROB

PROCACITY n insolence

PROCAINE n colourless or white crystalline water-soluble substance

PROCAINES > PROCAINE

PROCAMBIA n plant part in stem and root

PROCARP n female reproductive organ in red algae

PROCARPS > PROCARP

PROCARYON same as > PROKARYON

PROCEDURE n way of doing something, esp the correct or usual one

PROCEED vb start or continue doing

PROCEEDED > PROCEED

PROCEEDER > PROCEED

PROCEEDS pl n money obtained from an event or activity

PROCERITY n tallness

PROCESS n series of actions or changes ▷ vb handle or prepare by a special method of manufacture

PROCESSED > PROCESS

PROCESSER same as > PROCESSOR

PROCESSES > PROCESS

PROCESSOR n person or thing that carries out a process

PROCHAIN variant of > PROCHEIN

PROCHEIN adj next or nearest

PROCHOICE adj in favour of women's right to abortion

PROCHURCH adj favourable to church

PROCIDENT adj relating to prolapsus

PROCINCT n state of preparedness

PROCINCTS > PROCINCT

PROCLAIM vb declare publicly

PROCLAIMS > PROCLAIM

PROCLISES > PROCLITIC

PROCLISIS > PROCLITIC

PROCLITIC adj denoting a monosyllabic word or form having no stress and pronounced as a prefix of the following word, as in English 't for it in 'twas ▷ n proclitic word or form

PROCLIVE adj prone

PROCONSUL n administrator or governor of a colony, occupied territory, or other dependency

PROCREANT > PROCREATE

PROCREATE vb produce offspring

PROCTAL adj relating to the rectum

PROCTITIS n inflammation of the rectum

PROCTODEA pl n parts of the anus

PROCTOR n university worker who enforces discipline ▷ vb invigilate (an examination)

PROCTORED > PROCTOR

PROCTORS > PROCTOR

PROCURACY n office of a procurator

PROCURAL > PROCURE

PROCURALS > PROCURE

PROCURE vb get, provide

PROCURED > PROCURE

PROCURER n person who provides something

PROCURERS
> PROCURER

PROCURES > PROCURE

PROCURESS n female procurer

PROCUREUR n law officer in Guernsey

PROCURING > PROCURE

PROCYONID n animal of the raccoon family

PROD vb poke with something pointed ▷ n prodding

PRODDED > PROD

PRODDER > PROD

PRODDERS > PROD

PRODDING n act of prodding

PRODDINGS
> PRODDING

PRODIGAL adj recklessly extravagant, wasteful ▷ n person who spends lavishly or squanders money

PRODIGALS
> PRODIGAL

PRODIGIES > PRODIGY

PRODIGY n person with some marvellous talent

PRODITOR n traitor

PRODITORS
> PRODITOR

PRODITORY
> PRODITOR

PRODNOSE vb make uninvited inquiries (about someone else's business, for example)

PRODNOSED
> PRODNOSE

PRODNOSES
> PRODNOSE

PRODROMA n symptom that signals the onset of a disease

PRODROMAL
> PRODROME

PRODROME n any symptom that signals the impending onset of a disease

PRODROMES
> PRODROME

PRODROMI > PRODROME

PRODROMIC
> PRODROME

PRODROMUS same as
> PRODROME

PRODRUG n compound that is metabolized in the body to produce an active drug

PRODRUGS > PRODRUG

PRODS > PROD

PRODUCE vb bring into existence ▷ n food grown for sale

PRODUCED > PRODUCE

PRODUCER n person with control over the making of a film, record, etc

PRODUCERS
> PRODUCER

PRODUCES > PRODUCE

PRODUCING > PRODUCE

PRODUCT n something produced

PRODUCTS > PRODUCT

PROEM n introduction or preface

PROEMBRYO n stage prior to embryo in plants

PROEMIAL > PROEM

PROEMS > PROEM

PROENZYME n inactive form of an enzyme

PROESTRUS n period in the estrous cycle that immediately precedes estrus

PROETTE n female golfing professional

PROETTES > PROETTE

PROF short for
> PROFESSOR

PROFACE interj much good may it do you

PROFAMILY adj in favour of family

PROFANE adj showing disrespect for religion or holy things ▷ vb treat (something sacred) irreverently, desecrate

PROFANED > PROFANE

PROFANELY > PROFANE

PROFANER > PROFANE

PROFANERS > PROFANE

PROFANES > PROFANE

PROFANING > PROFANE

PROFANITY n profane talk or behaviour, blasphemy

PROFESS vb state or claim (something as true), sometimes falsely

PROFESSED adj supposed

PROFESSES > PROFESS

PROFESSOR n teacher of the highest rank in a university

PROFFER vb offer ▷ n act of proffering

PROFFERED > PROFFER

PROFFERER > PROFFER

PROFFERS > PROFFER

PROFILE n outline, esp of the face, as seen from the side ▷ vb draw, write, or make a profile of

PROFILED > PROFILE

PROFILER n device that creates a profile

PROFILERS > PROFILER

PROFILES > PROFILE

PROFILING > PROFILE

PROFILIST > PROFILE

PROFIT n money gained ▷ vb gain or benefit

PROFITED > PROFIT

PROFITEER n person who makes excessive profits at the expense of the public ▷ vb make excessive profits

PROFITER > PROFIT

PROFITERS > PROFIT

PROFITING > PROFIT

PROFITS > PROFIT

PROFLUENT adj flowing smoothly or abundantly

PROFORMA n invoice issued before an order is placed

PROFORMAS
> PROFORMA

PROFOUND adj showing or needing great knowledge ▷ n great depth

PROFOUNDS
> PROFOUND

PROFS > PROF

PROFUSE adj plentiful

PROFUSELY > PROFUSE

PROFUSER > PROFUSE

PROFUSERS > PROFUSE

PROFUSION > PROFUSE

PROFUSIVE same as
> PROFUSE

PROG vb prowl about for or as if for food or plunder ▷ n food obtained by begging

PROGENIES > PROGENY

PROGENY n children

PROGERIA n premature old age in children

PROGERIAS
> PROGERIA

PROGESTIN n type of steroid hormone

PROGGED > PROG

PROGGER n fan of progressive rock

PROGGERS > PROGGER

PROGGING > PROG

PROGGINS n proctor

PROGNOSE vb predict course of disease

PROGNOSED
> PROGNOSE

PROGNOSES
> PROGNOSIS

PROGNOSIS n doctor's forecast about the progress of an illness

PROGRADE vb (of beach) advance towards sea

PROGRADED > PROGRADE

PROGRADES > PROGRADE

PROGRAM n sequence of coded instructions for a computer ▷ vb write a computer program

PROGRAMED > PROGRAM

PROGRAMER n US spelling of programmer

PROGRAMME n schedule or plan ▷ vb schedule as a programme

PROGRAMS > PROGRAM

PROGRESS n improvement, development ▷ vb become more advanced or skilful

PROGS > PROG

PROGUN adj in favour of public owning firearms

PROHIBIT vb forbid or prevent from happening

PROHIBITS
> PROHIBIT

PROIGN same as > PROIN

PROIGNED > PROIGN

PROIGNING > PROIGN

PROIGNS > PROIGN

PROIN vb trim or prune

PROINE same as
> PROIN

PROINED > PROIN

PROINES > PROINE

PROINING > PROIN

PROINS > PROIN

PROJECT n planned scheme to do or examine something over a period ▷ vb make a forecast based on known data

PROJECTED > PROJECT

PROJECTOR n apparatus for projecting photographic images, films, or slides on a screen

PROJECTS > PROJECT

PROJET n draft of a proposed treaty

PROJETS > PROJET

PROKARYON n nucleus of a prokaryote

PROKARYOT n any organism having cells in each of which the genetic material is in a single DNA chain, not enclosed in a nucleus

PROKE vb thrust or poke

PROKED > PROKE

PROKER > PROKE

PROKERS > PROKE

PROKES > PROKE

PROKING > PROKE

PROLABOR adj favouring the Labor party

PROLABOUR adj favouring an organized labour movement

PROLACTIN n gonadotrophic hormone secreted by the anterior lobe of the pituitary gland

PROLAMIN same as
> PROLAMINE

PROLAMINE n any of a group of simple plant proteins, including gliadin, hordein, and zein

PROLAMINS
> PROLAMIN

PROLAN n constituent of human pregnancy urine

PROLANS > PROLAN

PROLAPSE n slipping down of an internal organ of the body from its normal position ▷ vb (of an internal organ) slip from its normal position

PROLAPSED
> PROLAPSE

PROLAPSES
> PROLAPSE

PROLAPSUS same as
> PROLAPSE

p

PROLATE adj having a polar diameter which is longer than the equatorial diameter ▷ vb pronounce or utter

PROLATED > PROLATE

PROLATELY > PROLATE

PROLATES > PROLATE

PROLATING > PROLATE

PROLATION > PROLATE

PROLATIVE > PROLATE

PROLE old form of > PROWL

PROLED > PROLE

PROLEG n appendage on abdominal segment of a caterpillar

PROLEGS > PROLEG

PROLEPSES > PROLEPSIS

PROLEPSIS n rhetorical device by which objections are anticipated and answered in advance

PROLEPTIC > PROLEPSIS

PROLER n prowler

PROLERS > PROLER

PROLES > PROLE

PROLETARY n member of the proletariat

PROLICIDE n killing of one's child

PROLIFIC adj very productive

PROLINE n nonessential amino acid that occurs in protein

PROLINES > PROLINE

PROLING > PROLE

PROLIX adj (of speech or a piece of writing) overlong and boring

PROLIXITY > PROLIX

PROLIXLY > PROLIX

PROLL vb prowl or search

PROLLED > PROLL

PROLLER > PROLL

PROLLERS > PROLL

PROLLING > PROLL

PROLLS > PROLL

PROLLY adv probably

PROLOG same as > PROLOGUE

PROLOGED > PROLOG

PROLOGING > PROLOG

PROLOGISE same as > PROLOGIZE

PROLOGIST n prologue writer

PROLOGIZE vb write a prologue

PROLOGS > PROLOG

PROLOGUE n introduction to a play or book ▷ vb introduce or preface with or as if with a prologue

PROLOGUED > PROLOGUE

PROLOGUES > PROLOGUE

PROLONG vb make (something) last longer

PROLONGE n (formerly) rope used as part of the towing equipment of a gun carriage

PROLONGED > PROLONG

PROLONGER > PROLONG

PROLONGES > PROLONGE

PROLONGS > PROLONG

PROLUSION n preliminary written exercise

PROLUSORY > PROLUSION

PROM n formal dance held at a high school or college

PROMACHOS n defender or champion

PROMENADE n paved walkway along the seafront at a holiday resort ▷ vb take a leisurely walk

PROMETAL n type of cast iron

PROMETALS > PROMETAL

PROMETRIC adj in favour of the metric system

PROMINE n substance promoting cell growth

PROMINENT n feature that projects outwards ▷ adj very noticeable

PROMINES > PROMINE

PROMISE vb say that one will definitely do or not do something ▷ n undertaking to do or not to do something

PROMISED > PROMISE

PROMISEE n person to whom a promise is made

PROMISEES > PROMISEE

PROMISER > PROMISE

PROMISERS > PROMISE

PROMISES > PROMISE

PROMISING adj likely to succeed or turn out well

PROMISOR n person who makes a promise

PROMISORS > PROMISOR

PROMISSOR n (in law) person who makes a promise

PROMMER n spectator at promenade concert

PROMMERS > PROMMER

PROMO vb promote (something)

PROMODERN adj in favour of the modern

PROMOED > PROMO

PROMOING > PROMO

PROMOS > PROMO

PROMOTE vb help to make (something) happen or increase

PROMOTED > PROMOTE

PROMOTER n person who organizes or finances an event etc

PROMOTERS > PROMOTER

PROMOTES > PROMOTE

PROMOTING > PROMOTE

PROMOTION > PROMOTE

PROMOTIVE adj tending to promote

PROMOTOR variant of > PROMOTER

PROMOTORS > PROMOTOR

PROMPT vb cause (an action) ▷ adj done without delay ▷ adv exactly ▷ n anything that serves to remind

PROMPTED > PROMPT

PROMPTER n person offstage who prompts actors

PROMPTERS > PROMPTER

PROMPTEST > PROMPT

PROMPTING > PROMPT

PROMPTLY > PROMPT

PROMPTS > PROMPT

PROMPTURE n prompting

PROMS > PROM

PROMULGE vb bring to public knowledge

PROMULGED > PROMULGE

PROMULGES > PROMULGE

PROMUSCES > PROMUSCIS

PROMUSCIS n proboscis of certain insects

PRONAOI > PRONAOS

PRONAOS n inner area of the portico of a classical temple

PRONATE vb turn (a limb, hand, or foot) so that the palm or sole is directed downwards

PRONATED > PRONATE

PRONATES > PRONATE

PRONATING > PRONATE

PRONATION > PRONATE

PRONATOR n any muscle whose contractions produce or affect pronation

PRONATORS > PRONATOR

PRONE n sermon ▷ adj sloping downwards

PRONELY > PRONE

PRONENESS > PRONE

PRONEPHRA n parts of the kidneys of lower vertebrates

PRONER > PRONE

PRONES > PRONE

PRONEST > PRONE

PRONEUR n flatterer

PRONEURS > PRONEUR

PRONG n one spike of a fork or similar instrument ▷ vb prick or spear with or as if with a prong

PRONGBUCK n horned N American ruminant

PRONGED > PRONG

PRONGHORN n ruminant mammal inhabiting rocky deserts of North America and having small branched horns

PRONGING > PRONG

PRONGS > PRONG

PRONK vb jump straight up

PRONKED > PRONK

PRONKING > PRONK

PRONKINGS > PRONKING

PRONKS > PRONK

PRONOTA > PRONOTUM

PRONOTAL > PRONOTUM

PRONOTUM n notum of the prothorax of an insect

PRONOUN n word, such as she or it, used to replace a noun

PRONOUNCE vb form the sounds of (words or letters), esp clearly or in a particular way

PRONOUNS > PRONOUN

PRONTO adv at once

PRONUCLEI n plural of pronucleus, nucleus of a germ cell after meiosis

PRONUNCIO n papal ambassador

PROO interj (to a horse) stop!

PROOEMION n preface

PROOEMIUM n preface

PROOF n evidence that shows that something is true or has happened ▷ adj able to withstand ▷ vb take a proof from (type matter)

PROOFED > PROOF

PROOFER n reader of proofs

PROOFERS > PROOFER

PROOFING > PROOF

PROOFINGS > PROOF

PROOFLESS > PROOF

PROOFREAD vb read and correct (printer's proofs)

PROOFROOM n room for proofreading

PROOFS > PROOF

PROOTIC n bone in front of ear

PROOTICS > PROOTIC

PROP vb support (something) so that it stays upright or in place ▷ n pole, beam, etc used as a support

PROPAGATE vb spread (information and ideas)

PROPAGE vb propagate

PROPAGED > PROPAGE

PROPAGES > PROPAGE

PROPAGING > PROPAGE

PROPAGULA > PROPAGULE

PROPAGULE n plant part, such as a bud, that becomes detached from the rest of the plant and grows into a new plant

PROPALE vb publish (something)

PROPALED > PROPALE

PROPALES > PROPALE

PROPALING > PROPALE

PROPANE n flammable gas found in petroleum and used as a fuel

PROPANES > PROPANE

PROPANOIC adj as in propanoic acid colourless liquid carboxylic acid

PROPANOL n colourless alcohol

PROPANOLS
> PROPANOL
PROPANONE *n* systematic name of acetone
PROPEL *vb* cause to move forward
PROPELLED > PROPEL
PROPELLER *n* revolving shaft with blades for driving a ship or aircraft
PROPELLOR *same as*
> PROPELLER
PROPELS > PROPEL
PROPENAL *n* type of aldehyde used as a herbicide and tear gas
PROPENALS
> PROPENAL
PROPEND *vb* be inclined or disposed
PROPENDED > PROPEND
PROPENDS > PROPEND
PROPENE *n* colourless gaseous alkene obtained by cracking petroleum
PROPENES > PROPENE
PROPENOIC *adj* as in *propenoic acid* systematic name of acrylic acid
PROPENOL *n* liquid used to make allylic alcohol
PROPENOLS
> PROPENOL
PROPENSE *adj* inclining forward
PROPENYL *n* three-carbon radical
PROPENYLS
> PROPENYL
PROPER *adj* real or genuine ▷ *n* service or psalm regarded as appropriate to a specific day, season, etc
PROPERDIN *n* protein present in blood serum that, acting with complement, is involved in the destruction of alien cells, such as bacteria
PROPERER > PROPER
PROPEREST > PROPER
PROPERLY > PROPER
PROPERS > PROPER
PROPERTY *same as*
> PROPRIUM
PROPHAGE *n* type of virus in a bacterial cell
PROPHAGES
> PROPHAGE
PROPHASE *n* first stage of mitosis
PROPHASES
> PROPHASE
PROPHASIC
> PROPHASE
PROPHECY *n* prediction
PROPHESY *vb* foretell
PROPHET *n* person chosen by God to spread His word
PROPHETIC *adj* foretelling what will happen
PROPHETS > PROPHET
PROPHYLL *n* leaf-shaped plant structure
PROPHYLLS
> PROPHYLL

PROPINE *vb* drink a toast to
PROPINED > PROPINE
PROPINES > PROPINE
PROPINING > PROPINE
PROPIONIC *adj* as in *propionic acid* former name for propanoic acid
PROPJET *another name for*
> TURBOPROP
PROPJETS > PROPJET
PROPMAN *n* member of the stage crew in charge of the stage props
PROPMEN > PROPMAN
PROPODEON *n* part of an insect's thorax
PROPODEUM *variant of*
> PROPODEON
PROPOLIS *n* resinous aromatic substance collected by bees from trees
PROPONE *vb* propose or put forward, esp before a court
PROPONED > PROPONE
PROPONENT *n* person who argues in favour of something
PROPONES > PROPONE
PROPONING > PROPONE
PROPOSAL *n* act of proposing
PROPOSALS
> PROPOSAL
PROPOSE *vb* put forward for consideration
PROPOSED > PROPOSE
PROPOSER > PROPOSE
PROPOSERS > PROPOSE
PROPOSES > PROPOSE
PROPOSING > PROPOSE
PROPOSITA *n* woman from whom a line of descent is traced
PROPOSITI *n* people from whom lines of descent are traced
PROPOUND *vb* put forward for consideration
PROPOUNDS
> PROPOUND
PROPPANT *n* material used in the oil extraction process
PROPPANTS
> PROPPANT
PROPPED > PROP
PROPPING > PROP
PROPRETOR *n* (in ancient Rome) citizen, esp an ex-praetor, granted a praetor's imperium, to be exercised outside Rome
PROPRIA > PROPRIUM
PROPRIETY *n* quality of being appropriate or fitting
PROPRIUM *n* attribute that is not essential to a species but is common and peculiar to it
PROPS > PROP
PROPTOSES
> PROPTOSIS
PROPTOSIS *n* forward displacement of an organ or part, such as the eyeball

PROPULSOR *n* propeller
PROPYL *n* type of monovalent radical
PROPYLA > PROPYLON
PROPYLAEA *n* porticos, esp those that form the entrances to temples
PROPYLENE *n* gas found in petroleum and used to produce many organic compounds
PROPYLIC > PROPYL
PROPYLITE *n* altered andesite or similar rock containing calcite, chlorite, etc, produced by the action of hot water
PROPYLON *n* portico, esp one that forms the entrance to a temple
PROPYLONS > PROPYLON
PROPYLS > PROPYL
PROPYNE *n* type of gaseous methyl acetylene
PROPYNES > PROPYNE
PRORATE *vb* divide, assess, or distribute (something) proportionately
PRORATED > PRORATE
PRORATES > PRORATE
PRORATING > PRORATE
PRORATION > PRORATE
PRORE *n* forward part of ship
PRORECTOR *n* official in German academia
PROREFORM *adj* in favour of or supporting reform, esp within politics
PRORES > PRORE
PROROGATE *vb* discontinue legislative meetings
PROROGUE *vb* suspend (parliament) without dissolving it
PROROGUED
> PROROGUE
PROROGUES
> PROROGUE
PROS > PRO
PROSAIC *adj* lacking imagination, dull
PROSAICAL *same as*
> PROSAIC
PROSAISM *n* prosaic quality or style
PROSAISMS
> PROSAISM
PROSAIST > PROSAISM
PROSAISTS
> PROSAISM
PROSATEUR *n* writer of prose
PROSCENIA *pl n* arches or openings separating stages from auditoria together with the areas immediately in front of the arches
PROSCRIBE *vb* prohibit, outlaw
PROSCRIPT *n* proscription or prohibition
PROSE *n* ordinary speech or writing in contrast to poetry ▷ *vb* speak or write in a tedious style

PROSECCO *n* Italian sparkling white wine
PROSECCOS
> PROSECCO
PROSECT *vb* dissect a cadaver for a public demonstration
PROSECTED > PROSECT
PROSECTOR *n* person who prepares or dissects anatomical subjects for demonstration
PROSECTS > PROSECT
PROSECUTE *vb* bring a criminal charge against
PROSED > PROSE
PROSELIKE > PROSE
PROSELYTE *n* recent convert
PROSEMAN *n* writer of prose
PROSEMEN > PROSEMAN
PROSER *n* writer of prose
PROSERS > PROSER
PROSES > PROSE
PROSEUCHA *n* place of prayer
PROSEUCHE *n* prayer
PROSIER > PROSY
PROSIEST > PROSY
PROSIFIED > PROSIFY
PROSIFIES > PROSIFY
PROSIFY *vb* write prose
PROSILY > PROSY
PROSIMIAN *n* primate of the primitive suborder which includes lemurs, lorises, and tarsiers
PROSINESS > PROSY
PROSING > PROSE
PROSINGS > PROSE
PROSIT *interj* good health! cheers!
PROSO *n* millet
PROSOCIAL *adj* acting to the benefit of society
PROSODIAL *adj* of prosody
PROSODIAN *n* writer of prose
PROSODIC > PROSODY
PROSODIES > PROSODY
PROSODIST > PROSODY
PROSODY *n* study of poetic metre and techniques
PROSOMA *n* head and thorax of an arachnid
PROSOMAL > PROSOMA
PROSOMAS > PROSOMA
PROSOMATA > PROSOMA
PROSOPON *n* (in Christianity) manifestation of any of the persons of the Trinity
PROSOPONS
> PROSOPON
PROSOS > PROSO
PROSPECT *n* something anticipated ▷ *vb* explore, esp for gold
PROSPECTS
> PROSPECT
PROSPER *vb* be successful
PROSPERED > PROSPER
PROSPERS > PROSPER
PROSS *n* prostitute
PROSSES > PROSS

P

PROSSIE n prostitute
PROSSIES > PROSSIE
PROST same as > PROSIT
PROSTATE n gland in male mammals that surrounds the neck of the bladder ▷ adj of or relating to the prostate gland
PROSTATES > PROSTATE
PROSTATIC same as > PROSTATE
PROSTERNA n sternums or thoraces of insects
PROSTIE n prostitute
PROSTIES > PROSTIE
PROSTOMIA pl n lobes at the head ends of earthworms and other annelids
PROSTRATE adj lying face downwards ▷ vb lie face downwards
PROSTYLE adj (of a building) having a row of columns in front ▷ n prostyle building, portico, etc
PROSTYLES > PROSTYLE
PROSUMER n amateur user of electronic equipment suitable for professionals
PROSUMERS > PROSUMER
PROSY adj dull and long-winded
PROTAMIN same as > PROTAMINE
PROTAMINE n any of a group of basic simple proteins that occur in the sperm of some fish
PROTAMINS > PROTAMIN
PROTANDRY n condition (in hermaphrodite plants) of maturing the anthers before the stigma
PROTANOPE n person with type of colour blindness
PROTASES > PROTASIS
PROTASIS n antecedent of a conditional statement
PROTATIC > PROTASIS
PROTEA n African shrub with showy flowers
PROTEAN adj constantly changing ▷ n creature that can change shape
PROTEANS > PROTEAN
PROTEAS > PROTEA
PROTEASE n any enzyme involved in proteolysis
PROTEASES > PROTEASE
PROTECT vb defend from trouble, harm, or loss
PROTECTED > PROTECT
PROTECTER same as > PROTECTOR
PROTECTOR n person or thing that protects
PROTECTS > PROTECT
PROTEGE n person who is protected and helped by another

PROTEGEE n woman or girl who is protected and helped by another
PROTEGEES > PROTEGEE
PROTEGES > PROTEGE
PROTEI > PROTEUS
PROTEID n protein
PROTEIDE variant of > PROTEID
PROTEIDES > PROTEIDE
PROTEIDS > PROTEID
PROTEIN n any of a group of complex organic compounds that are essential for life
PROTEINIC > PROTEIN
PROTEINS > PROTEIN
PROTEND vb hold out or stretch
PROTENDED > PROTEND
PROTENDS > PROTEND
PROTENSE n extension
PROTENSES > PROTENSE
PROTEOME n full complement of proteins that occur within a cell, tissue, or organism
PROTEOMES > PROTEOME
PROTEOMIC > PROTEOME
PROTEOSE n compound formed during proteolysis
PROTEOSES > PROTEOSE
PROTEST n declaration or demonstration of objection ▷ vb object, disagree
PROTESTED > PROTEST
PROTESTER > PROTEST
PROTESTOR > PROTEST
PROTESTS > PROTEST
PROTEUS n aerobic bacterium
PROTEUSES > PROTEUS
PROTHALLI n small flat free-living gametophytes in ferns, club mosses etc
PROTHESES > PROTHESIS
PROTHESIS n process in the development of a language by which a phoneme or syllable is prefixed to a word to facilitate pronunciation
PROTHETIC > PROTHESIS
PROTHORAX n first segment of the thorax of an insect, which bears the first pair of walking legs
PROTHYL variant of > PROTYLE
PROTHYLS > PROTHYL
PROTIST n organism belonging to the protozoans, unicellular algae, and simple fungi
PROTISTAN > PROTIST
PROTISTIC > PROTIST
PROTISTS > PROTIST
PROTIUM n most common isotope of hydrogen

PROTIUMS > PROTIUM
PROTO adj as in proto team team of people trained to deal with underground rescues, etc
PROTOAVIS n bird-like fossil
PROTOCOL n rules of behaviour for formal occasions
PROTOCOLS > PROTOCOL
PROTODERM n outer primary meristem of a plant
PROTOGINE n type of granite
PROTOGYNY n (in hermaphrodite plants and animals) condition of producing female gametes before male ones
PROTON n positively charged particle in the nucleus of an atom
PROTONATE vb provide atom with proton
PROTONEMA n branched threadlike structure that grows from a moss spore and eventually develops into the moss plant
PROTONIC adj (of a solvent, such as water) able to donate hydrogen ions to solute molecules
PROTONS > PROTON
PROTOPOD n part of crustacean's leg
PROTOPODS > PROTOPOD
PROTORE n primary mineral deposit
PROTORES > PROTORE
PROTOSTAR n cloud of interstellar gas and dust that gradually collapses, forming a hot dense core, and evolves into a star once nuclear fusion can occur in the core
PROTOTYPE n original or model to be copied or developed
PROTOXID variant of > PROTOXIDE
PROTOXIDE n oxide of an element that contains the smallest amount of oxygen of any of its oxides
PROTOXIDS > PROTOXID
PROTOZOA > PROTOZOAN
PROTOZOAL > PROTOZOAN
PROTOZOAN n microscopic one-celled creature ▷ adj of or relating to protozoans
PROTOZOIC adj of or pertaining to the protozoa
PROTOZOON same as > PROTOZOAN
PROTRACT vb lengthen or extend (a situation etc)
PROTRACTS > PROTRACT

PROTRADE adj in favour of trade
PROTRUDE vb stick out, project
PROTRUDED > PROTRUDE
PROTRUDES > PROTRUDE
PROTURAN n any of an order of white wingless insects
PROTURANS > PROTURAN
PROTYL same as > PROTYLE
PROTYLE n hypothetical primitive substance
PROTYLES > PROTYLE
PROTYLS > PROTYL
PROUD adj feeling pleasure and satisfaction
PROUDER > PROUD
PROUDEST > PROUD
PROUDFUL adj full of pride
PROUDISH adj rather proud
PROUDLY > PROUD
PROUDNESS > PROUD
PROUL variant of > PROWL
PROULED > PROUL
PROULER Scots variant of > PROWLER
PROULERS > PROULER
PROULING > PROUL
PROULS > PROUL
PROUNION adj in favour of or supporting the constitutional union between two or more countries
PROUSTITE n red mineral consisting of silver arsenic sulphide in hexagonal crystalline form
PROVABLE > PROVE
PROVABLY > PROVE
PROVAND n food
PROVANDS > PROVAND
PROVANT adj supplied with provisions ▷ vb supply with provisions
PROVANTED > PROVANT
PROVANTS > PROVANT
PROVE vb establish the validity of
PROVEABLE adj able to be proved
PROVEABLY > PROVEABLE
PROVED > PROVE
PROVEDOR variant of > PROVEDORE
PROVEDORE n purveyor
PROVEDORS > PROVEDOR
PROVEN > PROVE
PROVEND same as > PROVAND
PROVENDER n fodder
PROVENDS > PROVEND
PROVENLY > PROVE
PROVER > PROVE
PROVERB n short saying that expresses a truth or gives a warning ▷ vb utter or describe (something) in the form of a proverb

PROVERBED > PROVERB

PROVERBS > PROVERB

PROVERS > PROVE

PROVES > PROVE

PROVIANT *variant of* > PROVAND

PROVIANTS > PROVIANT

PROVIDE *vb* make available

PROVIDED > PROVIDE

PROVIDENT *adj* thrifty

PROVIDER > PROVIDE

PROVIDERS > PROVIDE

PROVIDES > PROVIDE

PROVIDING > PROVIDE

PROVIDOR *variant of* > PROVEDORE

PROVIDORS > PROVIDOR

PROVINCE *n* area governed as a unit of a country or empire

PROVINCES > PROVINCE

PROVINE *vb* plant branch of vine in ground for propagation

PROVINED > PROVINE

PROVINES > PROVINE

PROVING > PROVE

PROVINGS > PROVE

PROVINING > PROVINE

PROVIRAL > PROVIRUS

PROVIRUS *n* inactive form of a virus in a host cell

PROVISION *n* act of supplying something ▷ *vb* supply with food

PROVISO *n* condition, stipulation

PROVISOES > PROVISO

PROVISOR *n* person who receives provision

PROVISORS > PROVISOR

PROVISORY *adj* containing a proviso

PROVISOS > PROVISO

PROVOCANT *n* provocateur; one who deliberately behaves controversially to provoke argument or other strong reactions

PROVOKE *vb* deliberately anger

PROVOKED > PROVOKE

PROVOKER > PROVOKE

PROVOKERS > PROVOKE

PROVOKES > PROVOKE

PROVOKING > PROVOKE

PROVOLONE *n* mellow, pale yellow, soft, and sometimes smoked cheese, made of cow's milk: usually moulded in the shape of a pear

PROVOST *n* head of certain university colleges in Britain

PROVOSTRY *n* office of provost

PROVOSTS > PROVOST

PROW *n* bow of a vessel ▷ *adj* gallant

PROWAR *adj* in favour of or supporting war

PROWER > PROW

PROWESS *n* superior skill or ability

PROWESSED *adj* brave or skilful

PROWESSES > PROWESS

PROWEST > PROW

PROWL *vb* move stealthily around a place as if in search of prey or plunder ▷ *n* prowling

PROWLED > PROWL

PROWLER > PROWL

PROWLERS > PROWL

PROWLING > PROWL

PROWLINGS > PROWL

PROWLS > PROWL

PROWS > PROW

PROXEMIC > PROXEMICS

PROXEMICS *n* study of spatial interrelationships in humans or in populations of animals of the same species

PROXIES > PROXY

PROXIMAL *same as* > PROXIMATE

PROXIMATE *adj* next or nearest in space or time

PROXIMITY *n* nearness in space or time

PROXIMO *adv* in or during the next or coming month

PROXY *n* person authorized to act on behalf of someone else

PROYN *obsolete spelling of* > PRUNE

PROYNE *obsolete spelling of* > PRUNE

PROYNED > PROYN

PROYNES > PROYNE

PROYNING > PROYN

PROYNS > PROYN

PROZYMITE *n* Christian using leavened bread for the Eucharist

PROZZIE *n* slang word for prostitute

PROZZIES > PROZZIE

PRUDE *n* person who is excessively modest, prim, or proper

PRUDENCE *n* caution in practical affairs

PRUDENCES > PRUDENCE

PRUDENT *adj* cautious, discreet, and sensible

PRUDENTLY > PRUDENT

PRUDERIES > PRUDE

PRUDERY > PRUDE

PRUDES > PRUDE

PRUDISH > PRUDE

PRUDISHLY > PRUDE

PRUH *variant of* > PROO

PRUINA *n* woolly white covering on some lichens

PRUINAS > PRUINA

PRUINE *obsolete spelling of* > PRUNE

PRUINES > PRUINE

PRUINOSE *adj* coated with a powdery or waxy bloom

PRUNABLE > PRUNE

PRUNE *n* dried plum ▷ *vb* cut off dead parts or excessive branches from (a tree or plant)

PRUNED > PRUNE

PRUNELLA *n* strong fabric, esp a twill-weave worsted, used for gowns and the uppers of some shoes

PRUNELLAS > PRUNELLA

PRUNELLE *same as* > PRUNELLA

PRUNELLES > PRUNELLE

PRUNELLO *same as* > PRUNELLA

PRUNELLOS > PRUNELLO

PRUNER > PRUNE

PRUNERS > PRUNE

PRUNES > PRUNE

PRUNEY *adj* resembling a prune

PRUNIER > PRUNEY

PRUNIEST > PRUNEY

PRUNING > PRUNE

PRUNINGS > PRUNE

PRUNT *n* glass ornamentation

PRUNTED > PRUNT

PRUNTS > PRUNT

PRUNUS *n* type of ornamental tree or shrub

PRUNUSES > PRUNUS

PRURIENCE > PRURIENT

PRURIENCY *n* sexual desire

PRURIENT *adj* excessively interested in sexual matters

PRURIGO *n* chronic inflammatory disease of the skin

PRURIGOS > PRURIGO

PRURITIC > PRURITUS

PRURITUS *n* any intense sensation of itching

PRUSIK *n* sliding knot used in climbing ▷ *vb* climb (up a rope) using prusiks

PRUSIKED > PRUSIK

PRUSIKING > PRUSIK

PRUSIKS > PRUSIK

PRUSSIAN *adj* as in *prussian blue* colour pigment, discovered in Berlin

PRUSSIATE *n* any cyanide, ferrocyanide, or ferricyanide

PRUSSIC *adj* as in *prussic acid* weakly acidic extremely poisonous aqueous solution of hydrogen cyanide

PRUTA *same as* > PRUTAH

PRUTAH *n* former Israeli coin

PRUTOT > PRUTAH

PRUTOTH > PRUTAH

PRY *vb* make an impertinent or uninvited inquiry into a private matter ▷ *n* act of prying

PRYER *same as* > PRIER

PRYERS > PRYER

PRYING > PRY

PRYINGLY > PRY

PRYINGS > PRY

PRYS *old variant of* > PRICE

PRYSE *old variant of* > PRICE

PRYSED > PRYSE

PRYSES > PRYSE

PRYSING > PRYSE

PRYTANEA > PRYTANEUM

PRYTANEUM *n* public hall of a city in ancient Greece

PRYTHEE *same as* > PRITHEE

PSALM *n* sacred song ▷ *vb* sing a psalm

PSALMBOOK *n* book of psalms

PSALMED > PSALM

PSALMIC > PSALM

PSALMING > PSALM

PSALMIST *n* writer of psalms

PSALMISTS > PSALMIST

PSALMODIC > PSALMODY

PSALMODY *n* singing of sacred music

PSALMS > PSALM

PSALTER *n* book containing a version of the Psalms

PSALTERIA *n* omasa

PSALTERS > PSALTER

PSALTERY *n* ancient instrument played by plucking strings

PSALTRESS *n* woman who sings psalms

PSALTRIES > PSALTRY

PSALTRY *same as* > PSALTERY

PSAMMITE *rare name for* > SANDSTONE

PSAMMITES > PSAMMITE

PSAMMITIC > PSAMMITE

PSAMMON *n* microscopic life forms living between grains of sand

PSAMMONS > PSAMMON

PSCHENT *n* ancient Egyptian crown

PSCHENTS > PSCHENT

PSELLISM *n* stammering

PSELLISMS > PSELLISM

PSEPHISM *n* proposition adopted by a majority vote

PSEPHISMS > PSEPHISM

PSEPHITE *n* any rock that consists of large fragments embedded in a finer matrix

PSEPHITES > PSEPHITE

PSEPHITIC > PSEPHITE

PSEUD *n* pretentious person

PSEUDAXES
> PSEUDAXIS

PSEUDAXIS *another name for* > SYMPODIUM

PSEUDERY *n* pretentious talk

PSEUDISH > PSEUD

PSEUDO *n* pretentious person

PSEUDONYM *n* fictitious name adopted esp by an author

PSEUDOPOD *n* temporary projection from the body of a single-celled animal

PSEUDOS > PSEUD

PSEUDS > PSEUD

PSHAW *n* exclamation of disgust, impatience, disbelief, etc ▷ *vb* make this exclamation

PSHAWED > PSHAW

PSHAWING > PSHAW

PSHAWS > PSHAW

PSI *n* 23rd letter of the Greek alphabet

PSILOCIN *n* hallucinogenic substance

PSILOCINS
> PSILOCIN

PSILOSES > PSILOSIS

PSILOSIS *n* disease of the small intestine

PSILOTIC > PSILOSIS

PSION *n* type of elementary particle

PSIONIC > PSIONICS

PSIONICS *n* study of the practical use of psychic powers

PSIONS > PSION

PSIS > PSI

PSOAE > PSOAS

PSOAI > PSOAS

PSOAS *n* either of two muscles of the loins that aid in flexing and rotating the thigh

PSOASES > PSOAS

PSOATIC > PSOAS

PSOCID *n* tiny wingless insect

PSOCIDS > PSOCID

PSORA *n* itching skin complaint

PSORALEA *n* type of tropical and subtropical plant with curly leaves and white or purple flowers

PSORALEAS
> PSORALEA

PSORALEN *n* treatment for some skin diseases

PSORALENS
> PSORALEN

PSORAS > PSORA

PSORIASES
> PSORIASIS

PSORIASIS *n* skin disease with reddish spots and patches covered with silvery scales

PSORIATIC
> PSORIASIS

PSORIC > PSORA

PSST *interj* sound made to attract someone's attention

PST *interj* sound made to attract someone's attention

PSYCH *vb* psychoanalyse

PSYCHE *same as* > PSYCH

PSYCHED > PSYCH

PSYCHES > PSYCH

PSYCHIC *adj* having mental powers which cannot be explained by natural laws ▷ *n* person with psychic powers

PSYCHICAL > PSYCHIC

PSYCHICS > PSYCHIC

PSYCHING > PSYCH

PSYCHISM *n* belief in a universal soul

PSYCHISMS
> PSYCHISM

PSYCHIST > PSYCHISM

PSYCHISTS
> PSYCHISM

PSYCHO *n* slang word for an extremely aggressive person

PSYCHOGAS *n* gas with a mind-altering effect

PSYCHOID *n* name for an animal's innate impetus to perform actions

PSYCHOIDS
> PSYCHOID

PSYCHOS > PSYCHO

PSYCHOSES
> PSYCHOSIS

PSYCHOSIS *n* severe disorder in which a person's contact with reality becomes distorted

PSYCHOTIC *adj* of, relating to, or characterized by psychosis ▷ *n* person with psychosis

PSYCHS > PSYCH

PSYLLA *same as* > PSYLLID

PSYLLAS > PSYLLA

PSYLLID *n* type of insect of the family which comprises the jumping plant lice

PSYLLIDS > PSYLLID

PSYLLIUM *n* grain, the husks of which are used as a laxative

PSYLLIUMS
> PSYLLIUM

PSYOP *n* psychological operation

PSYOPS > PSYOP

PSYWAR *n* psychological warfare

PSYWARS > PSYWAR

PTARMIC *n* material that causes sneezing

PTARMICS > PTARMIC

PTARMIGAN *n* bird of the grouse family which turns white in winter

PTERIA > PTERION

PTERIDINE *n* yellow crystalline base

PTERIN *n* compound such as folic acid

PTERINS > PTERIN

PTERION *n* point on the side of the skull where a number of bones meet

PTEROIC *adj* as in *pteroic acid* a kind of acid found in spinach

PTEROPOD *n* small marine gastropod mollusc

PTEROPODS > PTEROPOD

PTEROSAUR *n* extinct flying reptile

PTERYGIA
> PTERYGIUM

PTERYGIAL *adj* of or relating to a fin or wing

PTERYGIUM *n* abnormal tissue over corner of eye

PTERYGOID *n* either of two long bony plates extending downwards from each side of the sphenoid bone within the skull

PTERYLA *n* any of the tracts of skin that bear contour feathers

PTERYLAE > PTERYLA

PTILOSES > PTILOSIS

PTILOSIS *n* falling out of eye lashes

PTISAN *n* grape juice drained off without pressure

PTISANS > PTISAN

PTOMAIN *same as* > PTOMAINE

PTOMAINE *n* any of a group of poisonous alkaloids found in decaying matter

PTOMAINES
> PTOMAINE

PTOMAINIC
> PTOMAINE

PTOMAINS > PTOMAIN

PTOOEY *interj* imitation of the sound of spitting

PTOSES > PTOSIS

PTOSIS *n* prolapse or drooping of a part, esp the eyelid

PTOTIC > PTOSIS

PTUI *same as* > PTOOEY

PTYALIN *n* amylase secreted in the saliva of human beings and other animals

PTYALINS > PTYALIN

PTYALISE *same as* > PTYALIZE

PTYALISED
> PTYALISE

PTYALISES
> PTYALISE

PTYALISM *n* excessive secretion of saliva

PTYALISMS
> PTYALISM

PTYALIZE *vb* expel saliva from the mouth

PTYALIZED
> PTYALIZE

PTYALIZES
> PTYALIZE

PTYXES > PTYXIS

PTYXIS *n* folding of a leaf in a bud

PTYXISES > PTYXIS

PUB *n* building with a bar licensed to sell alcoholic drinks ▷ *vb* visit a pub or pubs

PUBBED > PUB

PUBBING > PUB

PUBBINGS > PUBBING

PUBCO *n* company operating a chain of pubs

PUBCOS > PUBCO

PUBE *n* vulgar word for a pubic hair

PUBERAL *adj* relating to puberty

PUBERTAL > PUBERTY

PUBERTIES > PUBERTY

PUBERTY *n* period at the beginning of adolescence

PUBES > PUBE

PUBESCENT *adj* reaching or having reached puberty

PUBIC *adj* of the lower abdomen

PUBIS *n* one of the three sections of the hipbone that forms part of the pelvis

PUBISES > PUBIS

PUBLIC *adj* of or concerning the people as a whole ▷ *n* community, people in general

PUBLICAN *n* person who owns or runs a pub

PUBLICANS
> PUBLICAN

PUBLICISE *same as* > PUBLICIZE

PUBLICIST *n* person, esp a press agent or journalist, who publicizes something

PUBLICITY *n* process or information used to arouse public attention

PUBLICIZE *vb* bring to public attention

PUBLICLY *adv* in a public manner

PUBLICS > PUBLIC

PUBLISH *vb* produce and issue (printed matter) for sale

PUBLISHED > PUBLISH

PUBLISHER *n* company or person that publishes books, periodicals, music, etc

PUBLISHES > PUBLISH

PUBS > PUB

PUCAN *n* traditional Connemara open sailing boat

PUCANS > PUCAN

PUCCOON *n* N American plant that yields a red dye

PUCCOONS > PUCCOON

PUCE *adj* purplish-brown ▷ *n* colour varying from deep red to dark purplish-brown

PUCELAGE *n* state of being a maid or girl

PUCELAGES > PUCELAGE

PUCELLE *n* maid or girl

PUCELLES > PUCELLE

PUCER > PUCE

PUCES > PUCE

PUCEST > PUCE

PUCK *n* mischievous or evil spirit ▷ *vb* strike (the ball) in hurling

PUCKA same as > PUKKA
PUCKED > PUCK
PUCKER vb gather into wrinkles ▷ n wrinkle or crease
PUCKERED > PUCKER
PUCKERER > PUCKER
PUCKERERS > PUCKER
PUCKERIER > PUCKERY
PUCKERIES > PUCKERY
PUCKERING > PUCKER
PUCKEROOD adj New Zealand informal word for exhausted
PUCKERS > PUCKER
PUCKERY adj tending to pucker ▷ n puckishness
PUCKFIST n puffball
PUCKFISTS
> PUCKFIST
PUCKING > PUCK
PUCKISH > PUCK
PUCKISHLY > PUCK
PUCKLE n early type of machine gun
PUCKLES > PUCKLE
PUCKOUT n (in hurling) free hit made by the goalkeeper
PUCKOUTS > PUCKOUT
PUCKS > PUCK
PUCKSTER n hockey player
PUCKSTERS
> PUCKSTER
PUD short for > PUDDING
PUDDEN dialect spelling of
> PUDDING
PUDDENING n rope fender on boat
PUDDENS > PUDDEN
PUDDER vb make bother or fuss
PUDDERED > PUDDER
PUDDERING > PUDDER
PUDDERS > PUDDER
PUDDIER > PUDDY
PUDDIES > PUDDY
PUDDIEST > PUDDY
PUDDING n dessert, esp a cooked one served hot
PUDDINGS > PUDDING
PUDDINGY adj having the consistency of a pudding
PUDDLE n small pool of water, esp of rain ▷ vb make (clay etc) into puddle
PUDDLED > PUDDLE
PUDDLER > PUDDLE
PUDDLERS > PUDDLE
PUDDLES > PUDDLE
PUDDLIER > PUDDLE
PUDDLIEST > PUDDLE
PUDDLING n process for converting pig iron into wrought iron
PUDDLINGS
> PUDDLING
PUDDLY > PUDDLE
PUDDOCK same as
> PADDOCK
PUDDOCKS > PUDDOCK
PUDDY n paw ▷ adj short and podgy
PUDENCIES > PUDENCY
PUDENCY n modesty, shame, or prudishness
PUDENDA > PUDENDUM

PUDENDAL > PUDENDUM
PUDENDOUS adj shameful
PUDENDUM n human external genital organs collectively, esp female
PUDENT adj lacking in ostentation; humble
PUDEUR n sense of shame or embarrassment
PUDEURS > PUDEUR
PUDGE same as > PODGE
PUDGES > PUDGE
PUDGIER > PUDGY
PUDGIEST > PUDGY
PUDGILY > PUDGY
PUDGINESS > PUDGY
PUDGY adj podgy
PUDIBUND adj prudish
PUDIC adj relating to the pudenda
PUDICITY n modesty
PUDOR n sense of shame
PUDORS > PUDOR
PUDS > PUD
PUDSEY variant of
> PUDSY
PUDSIER > PUDSY
PUDSIES > PUDSY
PUDSIEST > PUDSY
PUDSY adj plump ▷ n plump person
PUDU n diminutive Andean antelope
PUDUS > PUDU
PUEBLO n communal village of flat-roofed houses
PUEBLOS > PUEBLO
PUER vb steep hides in an alkaline substance from the dung of dogs
PUERED > PUER
PUERILE adj silly and childish
PUERILELY > PUERILE
PUERILISM n immature or childish behaviour by an adult
PUERILITY > PUERILE
PUERING > PUER
PUERPERA n woman who has recently given birth
PUERPERAE
> PUERPERA
PUERPERAL adj concerning the period following childbirth
PUERPERIA n periods of around six weeks following childbirths when uteruses return to their normal size and shape
PUERS > PUER
PUFF n (sound of) short blast of breath, wind, etc ▷ vb blow or breathe in short quick draughts
PUFFA adj type of quilted and padded jacket
PUFFBACK n type of small African bird
PUFFBACKS
> PUFFBACK
PUFFBALL n ball-shaped fungus

PUFFBALLS
> PUFFBALL
PUFFBIRD n brownish tropical American bird with a large head
PUFFBIRDS
> PUFFBIRD
PUFFED > PUFF
PUFFER n person or thing that puffs
PUFFERIES > PUFFERY
PUFFERS > PUFFER
PUFFERY n exaggerated praise, esp in publicity or advertising
PUFFIER > PUFFY
PUFFIEST > PUFFY
PUFFILY > PUFFY
PUFFIN n sea bird with a brightly coloured beak
PUFFINESS > PUFFY
PUFFING > PUFF
PUFFINGLY > PUFF
PUFFINGS > PUFF
PUFFINS > PUFFIN
PUFFS > PUFF
PUFFY adj short of breath
PUFTALOON n Australian fried scone
PUG n small snub-nosed dog ▷ vb mix or knead (clay) with water to form a malleable mass or paste
PUGAREE same as
> PUGGREE
PUGAREES > PUGAREE
PUGGAREE same as
> PUGGREE
PUGGAREES
> PUGGAREE
PUGGED > PUG
PUGGERIES > PUGGERY
PUGGERY same as
> PUGGREE
PUGGIE n Scottish word for fruit machine
PUGGIER > PUGGY
PUGGIES > PUGGIE
PUGGIEST > PUGGY
PUGGINESS > PUGGY
PUGGING > PUG
PUGGINGS > PUG
PUGGISH > PUG
PUGGLE vb stir up by poking
PUGGLED > PUGGLE
PUGGLES > PUGGLE
PUGGLING > PUGGLE
PUGGREE n scarf, usually pleated, around the crown of some hats, esp sun helmets
PUGGREES > PUGGREE
PUGGRIES > PUGGRY
PUGGRY same as
> PUGGREE
PUGGY adj sticky, claylike ▷ n term of endearment
PUGH interj exclamation of disgust
PUGIL n pinch or small handful
PUGILISM n art, practice, or profession of fighting with the fists
PUGILISMS
> PUGILISM
PUGILIST > PUGILISM

PUGILISTS
> PUGILISM
PUGILS > PUGIL
PUGMARK n trail of an animal
PUGMARKS > PUGMARK
PUGNACITY n readiness to fight
PUGREE same as
> PUGGREE
PUGREES > PUGREE
PUGS > PUG
PUH interj exclamation expressing contempt or disgust
PUHA n sow thistle
PUHAS > PUHA
PUIR Scottish word for
> POOR
PUIRER > PUIR
PUIREST > PUIR
PUIRTITH n poverty
PUIRTITHS
> PUIRTITH
PUISNE adj (esp of a subordinate judge) of lower rank ▷ n judge of lower rank
PUISNES > PUISNE
PUISNY adj younger or inferior
PUISSANCE n showjumping competition that tests a horse's ability to jump large obstacles
PUISSANT adj powerful
PUISSAUNT same as
> PUISSANT
PUJA n ritual in honour of the gods, performed either at home or in the mandir (temple)
PUJAH same as > PUJA
PUJAHS > PUJAH
PUJARI n Hindu priest
PUJARIS > PUJARI
PUJAS > PUJA
PUKA in New Zealand English, same as
> BROADLEAF
PUKAS > PUKA
PUKATEA n aromatic New Zealand tree
PUKATEAS > PUKATEA
PUKE vb vomit ▷ n act of vomiting
PUKED > PUKE
PUKEKO n brightly coloured New Zealand wading bird
PUKEKOS > PUKEKO
PUKER n person who vomits
PUKERS > PUKER
PUKES > PUKE
PUKEY adj of or like vomit
PUKIER > PUKEY
PUKIEST > PUKEY
PUKING > PUKE
PUKKA adj properly done, constructed, etc
PUKKAH adj genuine
PUKU n belly or stomach
PUKUS > PUKU
PUKY same as > PUKEY
PUL n Afghan monetary unit

P

PULA *n* standard monetary unit of Botswana

PULAO *same as* > PILAU

PULAOS > PULAO

PULAS > PULA

PULDRON *same as* > PAULDRON

PULDRONS > PULDRON

PULE *vb* whine or whimper

PULED > PULE

PULER > PULE

PULERS > PULE

PULES > PULE

PULI *n* Hungarian sheepdog

PULICENE *adj* flea-ridden

PULICIDE *n* flea-killing substance

PULICIDES > PULICIDE

PULIER > PULY

PULIEST > PULY

PULIK > PUL

PULING > PULE

PULINGLY > PULE

PULINGS > PULE

PULIS > PULI

PULK *same as* > PULKA

PULKA *n* reindeer-drawn sleigh

PULKAS > PULKA

PULKHA *same as* > PULKA

PULKHAS > PULKHA

PULKS > PULK

PULL *vb* exert force on (an object) to move it towards the source of the force ▷ *n* act of pulling

PULLBACK *n* act of pulling back

PULLBACKS > PULLBACK

PULLED > PULL

PULLER > PULL

PULLERS > PULL

PULLET *n* young hen

PULLETS > PULLET

PULLEY *n* device for lifting weights by a downward pull ▷ *vb* lift with a pulley

PULLEYED > PULLEY

PULLEYING > PULLEY

PULLEYS > PULLEY

PULLI > PULLUS

PULLIES > PULLY

PULLING > PULL

PULLMAN *n* luxurious railway coach, esp a sleeping car

PULLMANS > PULLMAN

PULLORUM *n* as in *pullorum disease* acute serious bacterial disease of very young birds

PULLOUT *n* removable section of a magazine, etc

PULLOUTS > PULLOUT

PULLOVER *n* sweater that is pulled on over the head

PULLOVERS > PULLOVER

PULLS > PULL

PULLULATE *vb* (of animals, etc) breed rapidly or abundantly

PULLUP *n* exercise in which the body is raised by the arms pulling on a horizontal bar

PULLUPS > PULLUP

PULLUS *n* technical term for a chick or young bird

PULLY *n* pullover

PULMO *n* lung

PULMONARY *adj* of the lungs

PULMONATE *adj* having lungs or lung-like organs ▷ *n* any pulmonate mollusc

PULMONES > PULMO

PULMONIC *adj* of or relating to the lungs ▷ *n* person with lung disease

PULMONICS > PULMONIC

PULMOTOR *n* apparatus for pumping oxygen into the lungs during artificial respiration

PULMOTORS > PULMOTOR

PULP *n* soft wet substance made from crushed or beaten matter ▷ *vb* reduce to pulp

PULPAL > PULP

PULPALLY > PULP

PULPBOARD *n* board made from wood pulp

PULPED > PULP

PULPER > PULP

PULPERS > PULP

PULPIER > PULPY

PULPIEST > PULPY

PULPIFIED > PULPIFY

PULPIFIES > PULPIFY

PULPIFY *vb* reduce to pulp

PULPILY > PULPY

PULPINESS > PULPY

PULPING *n* act of pulping

PULPINGS > PULPING

PULPIT *n* raised platform for a preacher

PULPITAL > PULPIT

PULPITED > PULPIT

PULPITEER *n* deliverer of sermon ▷ *vb* preach from a pulpit

PULPITER *n* preacher

PULPITERS > PULPITER

PULPITRY *n* art of delivering sermons

PULPITS > PULPIT

PULPITUM *n* stone screen dividing nave and choir

PULPITUMS > PULPITUM

PULPLESS > PULP

PULPMILL *n* mill making raw material for paper

PULPMILLS > PULPMILL

PULPOUS *adj* soft and yielding

PULPS > PULP

PULPSTONE *n* calcified mass in a tooth cavity

PULPWOOD *n* pine, spruce, or any other soft wood used to make paper

PULPWOODS > PULPWOOD

PULPY *adj* having a soft or soggy consistency

PULQUE *n* light alcoholic drink from Mexico

PULQUES > PULQUE

PULS > PUL

PULSANT *adj* vibrant

PULSAR *n* small dense star which emits regular bursts of radio waves

PULSARS > PULSAR

PULSATE *vb* throb, quiver

PULSATED > PULSATE

PULSATES > PULSATE

PULSATILE *adj* beating rhythmically

PULSATING > PULSATE

PULSATION *n* act of pulsating

PULSATIVE > PULSATE

PULSATOR *n* device that stimulates rhythmic motion of a body

PULSATORS > PULSATOR

PULSATORY *adj* of or relating to pulsation

PULSE *n* regular beating of blood through the arteries at each heartbeat ▷ *vb* beat, throb, or vibrate

PULSEBEAT *n* the pulse

PULSED > PULSE

PULSEJET *n* type of ramjet engine

PULSEJETS > PULSEJET

PULSELESS > PULSE

PULSER *n* thing that pulses

PULSERS > PULSER

PULSES > PULSE

PULSIDGE *archaic word for* > PULSE

PULSIDGES > PULSIDGE

PULSIFIC *adj* causing the pulse to increase

PULSING > PULSE

PULSION *n* act of driving forward

PULSIONS > PULSION

PULSOJET *same as* > PULSEJET

PULSOJETS > PULSOJET

PULTAN *n* native Indian regiment

PULTANS > PULTAN

PULTON *same as* > PULTAN

PULTONS > PULTON

PULTOON *same as* > PULTAN

PULTOONS > PULTOON

PULTRUDE *vb* produce reinforced plastic process by pultrusion

PULTRUDED > PULTRUDE

PULTRUDES > PULTRUDE

PULTUN *same as* > PULTAN

PULTUNS > PULTUN

PULTURE *n* food and drink claimed by foresters

PULTURES > PULTURE

PULU *n* substance used for stuffing cushions

PULUS > PULU

PULVER *vb* make into powder

PULVERED > PULVER

PULVERINE *n* ashes of the barilla plant

PULVERING > PULVER

PULVERISE *same as* > PULVERIZE

PULVERIZE *vb* reduce to fine pieces

PULVEROUS *adj* consisting of tiny particles

PULVERS > PULVER

PULVIL *vb* apply perfumed powder

PULVILIO *n* perfumed powder

PULVILIOS > PULVILIO

PULVILLAR *adj* like cushion

PULVILLE *same as* > PULVIL

PULVILLED > PULVIL

PULVILLES > PULVILLE

PULVILLI > PULVILLUS

PULVILLIO *same as* > PULVILIO

PULVILLUS *n* small pad between the claws at the end of an insect's leg

PULVILS > PULVIL

PULVINAR *n* part of the thalamus

PULVINARS > PULVINAR

PULVINATE *adj* (of a frieze) curved convexly

PULVINI > PULVINUS

PULVINULE *n* part of a leaf

PULVINUS *n* swelling at the base of a leafstalk

PULWAR *n* light Indian river boat

PULWARS > PULWAR

PULY *adj* whiny

PUMA *n* large American wild cat with a greyish-brown coat

PUMAS > PUMA

PUMELO *same as* > POMELO

PUMELOS > PUMELO

PUMICATE *vb* pound fruit with pumice to make juice

PUMICATED > PUMICATE

PUMICATES > PUMICATE

PUMICE *n* light porous stone used for scouring ▷ *vb* rub or polish with pumice

PUMICED > PUMICE

PUMICEOUS > PUMICE

PUMICER > PUMICE

PUMICERS > PUMICE

PUMICES > PUMICE

PUMICING > PUMICE

PUMICITE n fine-grained variety of pumice

PUMICITES > PUMICITE

PUMIE n small stone

PUMIES > PUMIE

PUMMEL vb strike repeatedly with or as if with the fists

PUMMELED > PUMMEL

PUMMELING > PUMMEL

PUMMELLED > PUMMEL

PUMMELO same as > POMELO

PUMMELOS > PUMMELO

PUMMELS > PUMMEL

PUMP n machine used to force a liquid or gas to move in a particular direction ▷ vb raise or drive with a pump

PUMPABLE adj capable of being pumped

PUMPED > PUMP

PUMPER > PUMP

PUMPERS > PUMP

PUMPHOOD n cover for the upper wheel of a chain pump

PUMPHOODS > PUMPHOOD

PUMPHOUSE n building where pumping equipment has been installed

PUMPING > PUMP

PUMPINGS > PUMPING

PUMPION archaic word for > PUMPKIN

PUMPIONS > PUMPION

PUMPJACK n pumping apparatus at an oil well

PUMPJACKS > PUMPJACK

PUMPKIN n large round fruit with an orange rind

PUMPKING n programmer with authority to change the master source code

PUMPKINGS > PUMPKING

PUMPKINS > PUMPKIN

PUMPLESS > PUMP

PUMPLIKE > PUMP

PUMPS > PUMP

PUMY adj large and round

PUN n use of words to exploit double meanings for humorous effect ▷ vb make puns

PUNA n high cold dry plateau, esp in the Andes

PUNAANI same as > PUNANI

PUNAANY same as > PUNANI

PUNALUA n marriage between the sisters of one family to the brothers of another

PUNALUAN > PUNALUA

PUNALUAS > PUNALUA

PUNANI n vulgar word for vagina

PUNANY same as > PUNANI

PUNAS > PUNA

PUNCE n kick ▷ vb kick

PUNCED > PUNCE

PUNCES > PUNCE

PUNCH vb strike at with a clenched fist ▷ n blow with a clenched fist

PUNCHBAG n stuffed bag punched for boxing training

PUNCHBAGS > PUNCHBAG

PUNCHBALL n stuffed or inflated ball supported by a flexible rod, that is punched for exercise, esp boxing training

PUNCHBOWL n large bowl for serving punch

PUNCHED > PUNCH

PUNCHEON n large cask of variable capacity, usually between 70 and 120 gallons

PUNCHEONS > PUNCHEON

PUNCHER > PUNCH

PUNCHERS > PUNCH

PUNCHES > PUNCH

PUNCHIER > PUNCHY

PUNCHIEST > PUNCHY

PUNCHILY > PUNCHY

PUNCHING > PUNCH

PUNCHLESS > PUNCH

PUNCHLINE n funny ending of a joke

PUNCHOUT n fist fight

PUNCHOUTS > PUNCHOUT

PUNCHY adj forceful

PUNCING > PUNCE

PUNCTA > PUNCTUM

PUNCTATE adj having or marked with minute spots, holes, or depressions

PUNCTATED same as > PUNCTATE

PUNCTATOR n marker of points

PUNCTILIO n strict attention to minute points of etiquette

PUNCTO n tip of a fencing sword

PUNCTOS > PUNCTO

PUNCTUAL adj arriving or taking place at the correct time

PUNCTUATE vb put punctuation marks in

PUNCTULE n very small opening

PUNCTULES > PUNCTULE

PUNCTUM n tip or small point

PUNCTUMS > PUNCTUM

PUNCTURE n small hole made by a sharp object, esp in a tyre ▷ vb pierce a hole in

PUNCTURED > PUNCTURE

PUNCTURER > PUNCTURE

PUNCTURES > PUNCTURE

PUNDIT n expert who speaks publicly on a subject

PUNDITIC adj of or relating to pundits

PUNDITRY n expressing of expert opinions

PUNDITS > PUNDIT

PUNDONOR n point of honour

PUNG n horse-drawn sleigh with a boxlike body on runners

PUNGA variant spelling of > PONGA

PUNGAS > PUNGA

PUNGENCE n pungency

PUNGENCES > PUNGENCE

PUNGENCY > PUNGENT

PUNGENT adj having a strong sharp bitter flavour

PUNGENTLY > PUNGENT

PUNGLE vb make payment

PUNGLED > PUNGLE

PUNGLES > PUNGLE

PUNGLING > PUNGLE

PUNGS > PUNG

PUNIER > PUNY

PUNIEST > PUNY

PUNILY > PUNY

PUNINESS > PUNY

PUNISH vb cause (someone) to suffer or undergo a penalty for some wrongdoing

PUNISHED > PUNISH

PUNISHER > PUNISH

PUNISHERS > PUNISH

PUNISHES > PUNISH

PUNISHING > PUNISH

PUNITION n punishment

PUNITIONS > PUNITION

PUNITIVE adj relating to punishment

PUNITORY same as > PUNITIVE

PUNJI n sharpened bamboo stick ▷ vb fortify with punjis

PUNJIED > PUNJI

PUNJIES > PUNJI

PUNJIING > PUNJI

PUNJIS > PUNJI

PUNK n style of rock music of the late 1970s ▷ adj relating to the punk movement

PUNKA n fan made of a palm leaf or leaves

PUNKAH same as > PUNKA

PUNKAHS > PUNKAH

PUNKAS > PUNKA

PUNKER > PUNK

PUNKERS > PUNK

PUNKEST > PUNK

PUNKETTE n female follower of punk music

PUNKETTES > PUNKETTE

PUNKEY n small winged insect

PUNKEYS > PUNKEY

PUNKIE same as > PUNKEY

PUNKIER > PUNKY

PUNKIES > PUNKIE

PUNKIEST > PUNKY

PUNKIN same as > PUMPKIN

PUNKINESS > PUNKY

PUNKINS > PUNKIN

PUNKISH > PUNK

PUNKS > PUNK

PUNKY adj of punk music

PUNNED > PUN

PUNNER > PUN

PUNNERS > PUN

PUNNET n small basket for fruit

PUNNETS > PUNNET

PUNNIER > PUNNY

PUNNIEST > PUNNY

PUNNING > PUN

PUNNINGLY > PUN

PUNNINGS > PUN

PUNNY adj of puns

PUNS > PUN

PUNSTER n person who is fond of making puns

PUNSTERS > PUNSTER

PUNT n open flat-bottomed boat propelled by a pole ▷ vb travel in a punt

PUNTED > PUNT

PUNTEE same as > PUNTY

PUNTEES > PUNTEE

PUNTER n informal word for a member of the public

PUNTERS > PUNTER

PUNTIES > PUNTY

PUNTING > PUNT

PUNTO n hit in fencing

PUNTOS > PUNTO

PUNTS > PUNT

PUNTSMAN n man in charge of a river punt

PUNTSMEN > PUNTSMAN

PUNTY n long iron rod used in the finishing process of glass-blowing

PUNY adj small and feeble

PUP n young of certain animals, such as dogs and seals ▷ vb (of dogs, seals, etc) to give birth to pups

PUPA n insect at the stage of development between a larva and an adult

PUPAE > PUPA

PUPAL > PUPA

PUPARIA > PUPARIUM

PUPARIAL > PUPARIUM

PUPARIUM n case enclosing the pupae of certain insects

PUPAS > PUPA

PUPATE vb (of an insect larva) to develop into a pupa

PUPATED > PUPATE

PUPATES > PUPATE

PUPATING > PUPATE

PUPATION > PUPATE

PUPATIONS > PUPATE

PUPFISH n type of small fish

PUPFISHES > PUPFISH

PUPIL n person who is taught by a teacher

PUPILAGE *same as*
> PUPILLAGE
PUPILAGES
> PUPILLAGE
PUPILAR > PUPIL
PUPILARY *same as*
> PUPILLARY
PUPILLAGE *n* condition
of being a pupil or duration
for which one is a pupil
PUPILLAR > PUPIL
PUPILLARY *adj* of or
relating to a pupil or a legal
ward
PUPILLATE *adj* with a
spot of a different colour in
the middle ▷ *vb* cry in the
manner of a peacock
PUPILS > PUPIL
PUPILSHIP *n* state of
being a pupil
PUPPED > PUP
PUPPET *n* small doll or
figure moved by strings or
by the operator's hand
PUPPETEER *n* person
who operates puppets
PUPPETRY *n* art of
making and manipulating
puppets and presenting
puppet shows
PUPPETS > PUPPET
PUPPIED > PUPPY
PUPPIES > PUPPY
PUPPING > PUP
PUPPODUM *same as*
> POPPADOM
PUPPODUMS
> PUPPODUM
PUPPY *n* young dog ▷ *vb*
have puppies
PUPPYDOM *n* state of
being a puppy
PUPPYDOMS
> PUPPYDOM
PUPPYHOOD > PUPPY
PUPPYING > PUPPY
PUPPYISH > PUPPY
PUPPYISM *n* impudence
PUPPYISMS
> PUPPYISM
PUPPYLIKE > PUPPY
PUPS > PUP
PUPU *n* Hawaiian dish
PUPUNHA *n* fruit of a type
of palm tree
PUPUNHAS > PUPUNHA
PUPUS > PUPU
PUR *same as* > PURR
PURANA *n* type of Sanskrit
sacred writing
PURANAS > PURANA
PURANIC > PURANA
PURBLIND *adj* partly or
nearly blind
PURCHASE *vb* obtain by
payment ▷ *n* thing that is
bought
PURCHASED
> PURCHASE
PURCHASER
> PURCHASE
PURCHASES
> PURCHASE
PURDA *same as* > PURDAH
PURDAH *n* Muslim and
Hindu custom of keeping
women in seclusion

PURDAHED > PURDAH
PURDAHS > PURDAH
PURDAS > PURDA
PURDONIUM *n* type of
coal scuttle having a
slanted cover that is raised
to open it, and an inner
removable metal
container for the coal
PURE *adj* unmixed,
untainted ▷ *vb* make pure
PUREBLOOD *n* purebred
animal
PUREBRED *adj* denoting a
pure strain obtained
through many
generations of controlled
breeding ▷ *n* purebred
animal
PUREBREDS
> PUREBRED
PURED > PURE
PUREE *n* smooth thick
pulp of cooked and sieved
fruit, vegetables, meat, or
fish ▷ *vb* make (cooked
foods) into a puree
PUREED > PUREE
PUREEING > PUREE
PUREES > PUREE
PURELY *adv* in a pure
manner
PURENESS > PURE
PURER > PURE
PURES > PURE
PUREST > PURE
PURFLE *n* ruffled or
curved ornamental band
▷ *vb* decorate with such a
band or bands
PURFLED > PURFLE
PURFLER > PURFLE
PURFLERS > PURFLE
PURFLES > PURFLE
PURFLING *same as*
> PURFLE
PURFLINGS
> PURFLING
PURFLY > PURFLE
PURGATION *n* act of
purging or state of being
purged
PURGATIVE *adj*
(medicine) designed to
cause defecation ▷ *n*
medicine for emptying the
bowels
PURGATORY *n* place or
state of temporary
suffering
PURGE *vb* rid (a thing or
place) of (unwanted
things or people) ▷ *n*
purging
PURGEABLE > PURGE
PURGED > PURGE
PURGER > PURGE
PURGERS > PURGE
PURGES > PURGE
PURGING > PURGE
PURGINGS > PURGE
PURI *n* unleavened flaky
Indian bread, that is
deep-fried in ghee and
served hot
PURIFIED > PURIFY
PURIFIER *n* device or
substance that frees
something of extraneous,

contaminating, or
debasing matter
PURIFIERS
> PURIFIER
PURIFIES > PURIFY
PURIFY *vb* make or
become pure
PURIFYING > PURIFY
PURIN *same as* > PURINE
PURINE *n* colourless
crystalline solid that can
be prepared from uric acid
PURINES > PURINE
PURING > PURE
PURINS > PURIN
PURIRI *n* forest tree of
New Zealand
PURIRIS > PURIRI
PURIS > PURI
PURISM *n* strict insistence
on the correct usage or
style
PURISMS > PURISM
PURIST > PURISM
PURISTIC > PURISM
PURISTS > PURISM
PURITAN *n* person who
follows strict moral or
religious principles ▷ *adj*
of or like a puritan
PURITANIC *adj* of or like
a puritan
PURITANS > PURITAN
PURITIES > PURITY
PURITY *n* state or quality
of being pure
PURL *n* stitch made by
knitting a plain stitch
backwards ▷ *vb* knit in
purl
PURLED > PURL
PURLER *n* headlong or
spectacular fall
PURLERS > PURLER
PURLICUE *vb* finish a pen
stroke with a flourish
PURLICUED
> PURLICUE
PURLICUES
> PURLICUE
PURLIEU *n* land on the
edge of a royal forest
PURLIEUS > PURLIEU
PURLIEUX > PURLIEU
PURLIN *n* horizontal
beam that supports the
rafters of a roof
PURLINE *same as*
> PURLIN
PURLINES > PURLINE
PURLING > PURL
PURLINGS > PURL
PURLINS > PURLIN
PURLOIN *vb* steal
PURLOINED > PURLOIN
PURLOINER > PURLOIN
PURLOINS > PURLOIN
PURLS > PURL
PUROMYCIN *n* type of
antibiotic
PURPIE *old Scots word for*
> PURSLANE
PURPIES > PURPIE
PURPLE *n* colour between
red and blue ▷ *adj* of a
colour between red and
blue ▷ *vb* make purple
PURPLED > PURPLE

PURPLER > PURPLE
PURPLES > PURPLE
PURPLEST > PURPLE
PURPLIER > PURPLE
PURPLIEST > PURPLE
PURPLING > PURPLE
PURPLISH > PURPLE
PURPLY > PURPLE
PURPORT *vb* claim (to be
or do something) ▷ *n*
apparent meaning,
significance
PURPORTED *adj* alleged
PURPORTS > PURPORT
PURPOSE *n* reason
something is done ▷ *vb*
intend to do (something)
PURPOSED > PURPOSE
PURPOSELY *adv*
intentionally
PURPOSES > PURPOSE
PURPOSING > PURPOSE
PURPOSIVE *adj* having or
showing a definite
intention
PURPURA *n* blood disease
causing purplish spots
PURPURAS > PURPURA
PURPURE *n* purple
PURPUREAL *adj* having a
purple colour
PURPURES > PURPURE
PURPURIC > PURPURA
PURPURIN *n* red
crystalline compound
used as a stain for
biological specimens
PURPURINS
> PURPURIN
PURPY *variant of*
> PURPIE
PURR *vb* (of cats) make
low vibrant sound, usu
when pleased ▷ *n* this
sound
PURRED > PURR
PURRING > PURR
PURRINGLY > PURR
PURRINGS > PURR
PURRS > PURR
PURS > PUR
PURSE *n* small bag for
money ▷ *vb* draw (one's
lips) together into a small
round shape
PURSED > PURSE
PURSEFUL *n* that which
can be contained in purse
PURSEFULS
> PURSEFUL
PURSELIKE > PURSE
PURSER *n* ship's officer
who keeps the accounts
PURSERS > PURSER
PURSES > PURSE
PURSEW *archaic spelling of*
> PURSUE
PURSEWED > PURSEW
PURSEWING > PURSEW
PURSEWS > PURSEW
PURSIER > PURSY
PURSIEST > PURSY
PURSILY > PURSY
PURSINESS > PURSY
PURSING > PURSE
PURSLAIN *same as*
> PURSLANE
PURSLAINS > PURSLAIN

PURSLANE *n* weedy plant used in salads
PURSLANES
> PURSLANE
PURSUABLE > PURSUE
PURSUAL *n* act of pursuit
PURSUALS > PURSUAL
PURSUANCE *n* carrying out of an action or plan
PURSUANT *adj* in agreement or conformity
PURSUE *vb* chase
PURSUED > PURSUE
PURSUER > PURSUE
PURSUERS > PURSUE
PURSUES > PURSUE
PURSUING > PURSUE
PURSUINGS > PURSUE
PURSUIT *n* pursuing
PURSUITS > PURSUIT
PURSY *adj* short-winded
PURTIER > PURTY
PURTIEST > PURTY
PURTRAID *variant of* > PURTRAYD
PURTRAYD *adj* archaic spelling of portrayed
PURTY *adj* pretty
PURULENCE
> PURULENT
PURULENCY
> PURULENT
PURULENT *adj* of or containing pus
PURVEY *vb* supply (provisions) ▷ *n* food and drink laid on at a wedding reception, etc
PURVEYED > PURVEY
PURVEYING > PURVEY
PURVEYOR *n* person, organization, etc, that supplies food and provisions
PURVEYORS
> PURVEYOR
PURVEYS > PURVEY
PURVIEW *n* scope or range of activity or outlook
PURVIEWS > PURVIEW
PUS *n* yellowish matter produced by infected tissue
PUSES > PUS
PUSH *vb* move or try to move by steady force ▷ *n* act of pushing
PUSHBACK *n* negative or unfavourable response
PUSHBACKS
> PUSHBACK
PUSHBALL *n* game in which two teams try to push a heavy ball towards opposite goals
PUSHBALLS
> PUSHBALL
PUSHBIKE *n* pedal-driven bicycle
PUSHBIKES
> PUSHBIKE
PUSHCART *n* handcart, typically having two wheels and a canvas roof, used esp by street vendors
PUSHCARTS
> PUSHCART

PUSHCHAIR *n* folding chair on wheels for a baby
PUSHDOWN *n* list in which the last item added is at the top
PUSHDOWNS
> PUSHDOWN
PUSHED *adj* short of
PUSHER *n* person who or thing that pushes
PUSHERS > PUSHER
PUSHES > PUSH
PUSHFUL > PUSH
PUSHFULLY > PUSH
PUSHIER > PUSHY
PUSHIEST > PUSHY
PUSHILY > PUSHY
PUSHINESS > PUSHY
PUSHING *prep* almost or nearly (a certain age, speed, etc) ▷ *adj* aggressively ambitious ▷ *adv* almost or nearly (a certain age, speed, etc)
PUSHINGLY > PUSHING
PUSHOVER *n* something easily achieved
PUSHOVERS
> PUSHOVER
PUSHPIN *n* pin with a small ball-shaped head
PUSHPINS > PUSHPIN
PUSHPIT *n* safety rail at the stern of a boat
PUSHPITS > PUSHPIT
PUSHROD *n* metal rod transmitting motion in an engine
PUSHRODS > PUSHROD
PUSHUP *n* exercise in which the body is raised and lowered to the floor by the arms
PUSHUPS > PUSHUP
PUSHY *adj* too assertive or ambitious
PUSLE *old spelling of* > PUZZLE
PUSLED > PUSLE
PUSLES > PUSLE
PUSLEY *same as* > PURSLANE
PUSLEYS > PUSLEY
PUSLIKE > PUS
PUSLING > PUSLE
PUSS *same as* > PUSSY
PUSSEL *n* maid or girl
PUSSELS > PUSSEL
PUSSER *n* naval purser
PUSSERS > PUSSER
PUSSES > PUSS
PUSSIER > PUSSY
PUSSIES > PUSSY
PUSSIEST > PUSSY
PUSSLEY *n* weedy trailing herb
PUSSLEYS > PUSSLEY
PUSSLIES > PUSSLY
PUSSLIKE > PUSS
PUSSLY *variant of* > PUSSLEY
PUSSY *n* cat ▷ *adj* containing or full of pus
PUSSYCAT *same as* > PUSSY
PUSSYCATS
> PUSSYCAT

PUSSYFOOT *vb* behave too cautiously ▷ *n* person who pussyfoots
PUSSYTOES *n* type of low-growing plant
PUSTULANT *adj* causing the formation of pustules ▷ *n* agent causing such formation
PUSTULAR > PUSTULE
PUSTULATE *vb* form into pustules ▷ *adj* covered with pustules
PUSTULE *n* pimple containing pus
PUSTULED > PUSTULE
PUSTULES > PUSTULE
PUSTULOUS > PUSTULE
PUT *vb* cause to be (in a position, state, or place) ▷ *n* throw in putting the shot
PUTAMEN *n* hard endocarp or stone of fruit
PUTAMENS > PUTAMEN
PUTAMINA > PUTAMEN
PUTATIVE *adj* reputed, supposed
PUTCHEON *n* trap for catching salmon
PUTCHEONS
> PUTCHEON
PUTCHER *n* trap for catching salmon
PUTCHERS > PUTCHER
PUTCHOCK *same as* > PACHAK
PUTCHOCKS
> PUTCHOCK
PUTCHUK *same as* > PACHAK
PUTCHUKS > PUTCHUK
PUTDOWN *n* snub or insult
PUTDOWNS > PUTDOWN
PUTEAL *n* enclosure around a well
PUTEALS > PUTEAL
PUTELI *n* (in India) type of boat
PUTELIS > PUTELI
PUTID *adj* having an unpleasant odour
PUTLOCK *same as* > PUTLOG
PUTLOCKS > PUTLOCK
PUTLOG *n* short horizontal beam that with others supports the floor planks of a scaffold
PUTLOGS > PUTLOG
PUTOFF *n* pretext or delay
PUTOFFS > PUTOFF
PUTOIS *n* brush to paint pottery
PUTON *n* hoax or piece of mockery
PUTONGHUA *n* Chinese language
PUTONS > PUTON
PUTOUT *n* baseball play in which the batter or runner is put out
PUTOUTS > PUTOUT
PUTREFIED > PUTREFY
PUTREFIER > PUTREFY
PUTREFIES > PUTREFY
PUTREFY *vb* rot and produce an offensive smell

PUTRID *adj* rotten and foul-smelling
PUTRIDER > PUTRID
PUTRIDEST > PUTRID
PUTRIDITY > PUTRID
PUTRIDLY > PUTRID
PUTS > PUT
PUTSCH *n* sudden violent attempt to remove a government from power
PUTSCHES > PUTSCH
PUTSCHIST *n* person taking part in putsch
PUTT *n* stroke on the putting green to roll the ball into or near the hole ▷ *vb* strike (the ball) in this way
PUTTED > PUTT
PUTTEE *n* strip of cloth worn wound around the leg
PUTTEES > PUTTEE
PUTTEN *old Scots past participle of* > PUT
PUTTER *n* golf club for putting ▷ *vb* busy oneself in a desultory though agreeable manner
PUTTERED > PUTTER
PUTTERER > PUTTER
PUTTERERS > PUTTER
PUTTERING > PUTTER
PUTTERS > PUTTER
PUTTI > PUTTO
PUTTIE *same as* > PUTTEE
PUTTIED > PUTTY
PUTTIER *n* glazier
PUTTIERS > PUTTIER
PUTTIES > PUTTY
PUTTING > PUT
PUTTINGS > PUT
PUTTO *n* representation of a small boy
PUTTOCK *n* type of bird of prey
PUTTOCKS > PUTTOCK
PUTTS > PUTT
PUTTY *n* stiff paste of whiting and linseed oil ▷ *vb* fill, fix, or coat with putty
PUTTYING > PUTTY
PUTTYLESS > PUTTY
PUTTYLIKE > PUTTY
PUTTYROOT *n* North American orchid
PUTURE *n* claim of foresters for food
PUTURES > PUTURE
PUTZ *n* despicable or stupid person ▷ *vb* waste time
PUTZED > PUTZ
PUTZES > PUTZ
PUTZING > PUTZ
PUY *n* small volcanic cone
PUYS > PUY
PUZEL *same as* > PUCELLE
PUZELS > PUZEL
PUZZEL *same as* > PUCELLE
PUZZELS > PUZZEL
PUZZLE *vb* perplex and confuse or be perplexed or confused ▷ *n* problem

P

that cannot be easily solved

PUZZLED > PUZZLE
PUZZLEDLY > PUZZLE
PUZZLEDOM > PUZZLE
PUZZLER n person or thing that puzzles
PUZZLERS > PUZZLER
PUZZLES > PUZZLE
PUZZLING > PUZZLE
PUZZOLANA same as
> POZZOLANA
PWN vb defeat (an opponent) in conclusive and humiliating fashion
PWNED > PWN
PWNING > PWN
PWNS > PWN
PYA n monetary unit of Myanmar worth one hundredth of a kyat
PYAEMIA n type of blood poisoning
PYAEMIAS > PYAEMIA
PYAEMIC > PYAEMIA
PYAS > PYA
PYAT n magpie ▷ adj pied
PYATS > PYAT
PYCNIC same as
> PYKNIC
PYCNIDIA
> PYCNIDIUM
PYCNIDIAL
> PYCNIDIUM
PYCNIDIUM n small flask-shaped structure containing spores that occurs in ascomycetes and certain other fungi
PYCNITE n variety of topaz
PYCNITES > PYCNITE
PYCNON old word for
> SEMITONE
PYCNONS > PYCNON
PYCNOSES > PYCNOSIS
PYCNOSIS n process of shrinking in a cell nucleus
PYCNOSOME n stocky body type
PYCNOTIC > PYCNOSIS
PYE same as > PIE
PYEBALD same as
> PIEBALD
PYEBALDS > PYEBALD
PYEING > PYE
PYELITIC > PYELITIS
PYELITIS n inflammation of the pelvis of the kidney
PYELOGRAM n film produced by pyelography
PYEMIA same as
> PYAEMIA
PYEMIAS > PYEMIA
PYEMIC > PYAEMIA
PYENGADU variant of
> PYINKADO
PYENGADUS
> PYENGADU
PYES > PYE
PYET same as > PYAT
PYETS > PYET
PYGAL n rear part
PYGALS > PYGAL
PYGARG n type of horned mammal
PYGARGS > PYGARG

PYGARGUS n white-tailed bird of prey
PYGIDIA > PYGIDIUM
PYGIDIAL > PYGIDIUM
PYGIDIUM n terminal division in certain invertebrates
PYGMAEAN > PYGMY
PYGMEAN > PYGMY
PYGMIES > PYGMY
PYGMOID adj of or like pygmies ▷ n pygmy
PYGMOIDS > PYGMOID
PYGMY n something that is a very small example of its type ▷ adj very small
PYGMYISH > PYGMY
PYGMYISM > PYGMY
PYGMYISMS > PYGMY
PYGOSTYLE n vertebral bone in birds
PYIC adj relating to pus
PYIN n constituent of pus
PYINKADO n leguminous tree native to India and Myanmar
PYINKADOS
> PYINKADO
PYINS > PYIN
PYJAMA same as
> PYJAMAS
PYJAMAED > PYJAMAS
PYJAMAS pl n loose-fitting trousers and top worn in bed
PYKNIC adj characterized by a broad squat fleshy physique ▷ n person with this physical type
PYKNICS > PYKNIC
PYKNOSES > PYKNOSIS
PYKNOSIS n thickening of a cell
PYKNOSOME n stocky body type
PYKNOTIC > PYKNOSIS
PYLON n steel tower-like structure supporting electrical cables
PYLONS > PYLON
PYLORI > PYLORUS
PYLORIC > PYLORUS
PYLORUS n small circular opening at the base of the stomach
PYLORUSES > PYLORUS
PYNE archaic variant of
> PINE
PYNED > PYNE
PYNES > PYNE
PYNING > PYNE
PYODERMA n any skin eruption characterized by pustules or the formation of pus
PYODERMAS
> PYODERMA
PYODERMIC
> PYODERMA
PYOGENIC adj of or relating to the formation of pus
PYOID adj resembling pus
PYONER old variant of
> PIONEER
PYONERS > PYONER
PYONINGS n old term for the work of pioneers

PYORRHEA same as
> PYORRHOEA
PYORRHEAL
> PYORRHOEA
PYORRHEAS
> PYORRHEA
PYORRHEIC
> PYORRHOEA
PYORRHOEA n disease of the gums and tooth sockets which causes bleeding of the gums and the formation of pus
PYOSES > PYOSIS
PYOSIS n formation of pus
PYOT same as > PYAT
PYOTS > PYOT
PYRACANTH n type of thorny shrub
PYRAL > PYRE
PYRALID n tropical moth
PYRALIDID same as
> PYRALID
PYRALIDS > PYRALID
PYRALIS same as
> PYRALID
PYRALISES > PYRALIS
PYRAMID n solid figure with a flat base and triangular sides sloping upwards to a point ▷ vb build up or be arranged in the form of a pyramid
PYRAMIDAL > PYRAMID
PYRAMIDED > PYRAMID
PYRAMIDES > PYRAMIS
PYRAMIDIA n plural of pyramidion, small pyramid on top of obelisk
PYRAMIDIC > PYRAMID
PYRAMIDON n type of pipe for an organ
PYRAMIDS > PYRAMID
PYRAMIS n pyramid-shaped structure
PYRAMISES > PYRAMIS
PYRAN n unsaturated heterocyclic organic compound
PYRANOID > PYRAN
PYRANOSE n structure in many sugars
PYRANOSES
> PYRANOSE
PYRANS > PYRAN
PYRAZOLE n crystalline soluble basic heterocyclic compound
PYRAZOLES
> PYRAZOLE
PYRE n pile of wood for burning a corpse on
PYRENE n solid polynuclear aromatic hydrocarbon extracted from coal tar
PYRENEITE n dark mineral found in the Pyrenees
PYRENES > PYRENE
PYRENOID n any of various small protein granules that occur in certain algae
PYRENOIDS
> PYRENOID
PYRES > PYRE

PYRETHRIN n oily water-insoluble compound used as an insecticide
PYRETHRUM n Eurasian chrysanthemum with white, pink, red, or purple flowers
PYRETIC adj of, relating to, or characterized by fever
PYREX n tradename for glass used in cookery and chemical apparatus
PYREXES > PYREX
PYREXIA technical name for > FEVER
PYREXIAL > PYREXIA
PYREXIAS > PYREXIA
PYREXIC > PYREXIA
PYRIC adj of or relating to burning
PYRIDIC > PYRIDINE
PYRIDINE n colourless hygroscopic liquid with a characteristic odour
PYRIDINES
> PYRIDINE
PYRIDOXAL n naturally occurring derivative of pyridoxine that is a precursor of a coenzyme involved in several enzymic reactions
PYRIDOXIN n derivative of pyridine
PYRIFORM adj (esp of organs of the body) pear-shaped
PYRITE n yellow mineral consisting of iron sulphide in cubic crystalline form
PYRITES same as
> PYRITE
PYRITIC > PYRITE
PYRITICAL > PYRITE
PYRITISE same as
> PYRITIZE
PYRITISED
> PYRITISE
PYRITISES
> PYRITISE
PYRITIZE vb convert into pyrites
PYRITIZED
> PYRITIZE
PYRITIZES
> PYRITIZE
PYRITOUS > PYRITE
PYRO n pyromaniac
PYROBORIC adj as in pyroboric acid, an acid obtained from boric acid
PYROCERAM n transparent ceramic material
PYROCLAST n piece of lava ejected from a volcano
PYROGEN n any of a group of substances that cause a rise in temperature in an animal body
PYROGENIC adj produced by or producing heat
PYROGENS > PYROGEN
PYROGIES > PYROGY
PYROGY same as
> PIEROGI

PYROHIES > PYROHY
PYROHY *same as* > PEROGI
PYROLA *n* evergreen perennial
PYROLAS > PYROLA
PYROLATER *n* worshipper of fire
PYROLATRY > PYROLATER
PYROLISE *same as* > PYROLIZE
PYROLISED > PYROLISE
PYROLISES > PYROLISE
PYROLIZE *vb* subject to pyrolysis
PYROLIZED > PYROLIZE
PYROLIZES > PYROLIZE
PYROLOGY *n* study of heat
PYROLYSE *vb* subject to pyrolysis
PYROLYSED > PYROLYSE
PYROLYSER > PYROLYSE
PYROLYSES > PYROLYSE
PYROLYSIS *n* application of heat to chemical compounds in order to cause decomposition
PYROLYTIC > PYROLYSIS
PYROLYZE *same as* > PYROLYSE
PYROLYZED > PYROLYZE
PYROLYZER > PYROLYSE

PYROLYZES > PYROLYZE
PYROMANCY *n* divination by fire or flames
PYROMANIA *n* uncontrollable urge to set things on fire
PYROMETER *n* instrument for measuring high temperatures
PYROMETRY > PYROMETER
PYRONE *n* type of heterocyclic compound
PYRONES > PYRONE
PYRONIN *n* red dye used as a biological stain
PYRONINE *same as* > PYRONIN
PYRONINES > PYRONINE
PYRONINS > PYRONIN
PYROPE *n* deep yellowish-red garnet used as a gemstone
PYROPES > PYROPE
PYROPHONE *n* musical instrument using hydrogen flames
PYROPUS *variant of* > PYROPE
PYROPUSES > PYROPUS
PYROS > PYRO
PYROSCOPE *n* instrument for measuring intensity of heat
PYROSES > PYROSIS
PYROSIS *technical name for* > HEARTBURN
PYROSISES > PYROSIS
PYROSOME *n* tube-shaped glowing marine creature

PYROSOMES > PYROSOME
PYROSTAT *n* device that activates an alarm or extinguisher in the event of a fire
PYROSTATS > PYROSTAT
PYROXENE *n* silicate mineral
PYROXENES > PYROXENE
PYROXENIC > PYROXENE
PYROXYLE *same as* > PYROXYLIN
PYROXYLES > PYROXYLE
PYROXYLIC > PYROXYLIN
PYROXYLIN *n* yellow substance obtained by nitrating cellulose with a mixture of nitric and sulphuric acids
PYRRHIC *n* metrical foot of two short or unstressed syllables ▷ *adj* of or relating to such a metrical foot
PYRRHICS > PYRRHIC
PYRRHOUS *adj* ruddy or reddish
PYRROL *same as* > PYRROLE
PYRROLE *n* colourless insoluble toxic liquid
PYRROLES > PYRROLE
PYRROLIC > PYRROLE
PYRROLS > PYRROL
PYRUVATE *n* ester or salt of pyruvic acid
PYRUVATES > PYRUVATE

PYRUVIC *adj* as in *pyruvic acid* colourless pleasant-smelling liquid
PYSANKA *n* hand-painted Ukrainian Easter egg
PYSANKY > PYSANKA
PYTHIUM *n* type of fungi
PYTHIUMS > PYTHIUM
PYTHON *n* large nonpoisonous snake that crushes its prey
PYTHONESS *n* woman, such as Apollo's priestess at Delphi, believed to be possessed by an oracular spirit
PYTHONIC > PYTHON
PYTHONS > PYTHON
PYURIA *n* any condition characterized by the presence of pus in the urine
PYURIAS > PYURIA
PYX *n* any receptacle for the Eucharistic Host ▷ *vb* put (something) in a pyx
PYXED > PYX
PYXES > PYX
PYXIDES > PYXIS
PYXIDIA > PYXIDIUM
PYXIDIUM *n* dry fruit of such plants as the plantain
PYXIE *n* creeping evergreen shrub of the eastern US
PYXIES > PYXIE
PYXING > PYX
PYXIS *same as* > PYXIDIUM
PZAZZ *same as* > PIZZAZZ
PZAZZES > PZAZZ

P

Qq

QABALA same as > KABBALAH

QABALAH same as > KABBALAH

QABALAHS > QABALAH

QABALAS > QABALAH

QABALISM > QABALAH

QABALISMS > QABALAH

QABALIST > QABALAH

QABALISTS > QABALAH

QADI variant spelling of > CADI

QADIS > QADI

QAID n chief

QAIDS > QAID

QAIMAQAM n Turkish officer or official

QAIMAQAMS > QAIMAQAM

QAJAQ n kayak

QAJAQS > QAJAQ

QALAMDAN n writing case

QALAMDANS > QALAMDAN

QAMUTIK n sledge with wooden runners

QAMUTIKS > QAMUTIK

QANAT n underground irrigation channel

QANATS > QANAT

QAPIK n monetary unit of Azerbaijan

QAPIKS > QAPIK

QASIDA n Arabic verse form

QASIDAS > QASIDA

QAT variant spelling of > KHAT

QATS > QAT

QAWWAL n qawwali singer

QAWWALI n Islamic religious song, esp in Asia

QAWWALIS > QAWWALI

QAWWALS > QAWWAL

QI n vital energy

QIBLA variant of > KIBLAH

QIBLAS > QIBLA

QIGONG n system of breathing and exercise

QIGONGS > QIGONG

QIN n Chinese stringed instrument related to the zither

QINDAR n Albanian monetary unit

QINDARKA > QINDAR

QINDARS > QINDAR

QINGHAOSU n Chinese herb

QINS > QIN

QINTAR same as > QINDAR

QINTARKA > QINTAR

QINTARS > QINTAR

QIS > QI

QIVIUT n soft muskox wool

QIVIUTS > QIVIUT

QOPH variant of > KOPH

QOPHS > QOPH

QORMA variant spelling of > KORMA

QORMAS > QORMA

QUA prep in the capacity of

QUAALUDE n methaqualone

QUAALUDES > QUAALUDE

QUACK vb (of a duck) utter a harsh guttural sound ▷ n unqualified person who claims medical knowledge

QUACKED > QUACK

QUACKER > QUACK

QUACKERS > QUACK

QUACKERY n activities or methods of a quack

QUACKIER > QUACK

QUACKIEST > QUACK

QUACKING > QUACK

QUACKISH > QUACK

QUACKISM same as > QUACKERY

QUACKISMS > QUACKISM

QUACKLE same as > QUACK

QUACKLED > QUACKLE

QUACKLES > QUACKLE

QUACKLING > QUACKLE

QUACKS > QUACK

QUACKY > QUACK

QUAD n quadrangle

QUADDED adj formed of multiple quads

QUADDING n birdwatching in a specified area

QUADDINGS > QUADDING

QUADPLAY same as > FOURPLAY

QUADPLAYS > QUADPLAY

QUADPLEX n apartment on four floors

QUADRANS n Roman coin

QUADRANT n quarter of a circle

QUADRANTS > QUADRANT

QUADRAT n area marked out for the study of plants

QUADRATE n cube or square, or a square or cubelike object ▷ vb make square or rectangular ▷ adj square or rectangular

QUADRATED > QUADRATE

QUADRATES > QUADRATE

QUADRATI > QUADRATUS

QUADRATIC n equation in which the variable is raised to the power of two, but nowhere raised to a higher power ▷ adj of the second power

QUADRATS > QUADRAT

QUADRATUS n type of muscle

QUADRELLA n four nominated horseraces in which the punter bets on selecting the four winners

QUADRIC adj having or characterized by an equation of the second degree ▷ n quadric curve or surface

QUADRICEP n muscle in thigh

QUADRICS > QUADRIC

QUADRIFID adj divided into four lobes or other parts

QUADRIGA n (in the classical world) a two-wheeled chariot drawn by four horses abreast

QUADRIGAE > QUADRIGA

QUADRIGAS > QUADRIGA

QUADRILLE n square dance for four couples

QUADRIVIA n higher divisions of the seven liberal arts

QUADRUMAN n nonhuman primate

QUADRUPED n any animal with four legs ▷ adj having four feet

QUADRUPLE vb multiply by four ▷ adj four times as much or as many ▷ n quantity or number four times as great as another

QUADRUPLY n reply to a triply

QUADS > QUAD

QUAERE n query or question ▷ interj ask or inquire ▷ vb ask

QUAERED > QUAERE

QUAEREING > QUAERE

QUAERES > QUAERE

QUAERITUR sentence substitute question is asked

QUAESITUM n object sought

QUAESTOR n any of several magistrates of ancient Rome, usually a financial administrator

QUAESTORS > QUAESTOR

QUAFF vb drink heartily or in one draught

QUAFFABLE > QUAFF

QUAFFED > QUAFF

QUAFFER > QUAFF

QUAFFERS > QUAFF

QUAFFING > QUAFF

QUAFFS > QUAFF

QUAG another word for > QUAGMIRE

QUAGGA n recently extinct zebra

QUAGGAS > QUAGGA

QUAGGIER > QUAGGY

QUAGGIEST > QUAGGY

QUAGGY adj resembling a marsh or quagmire

QUAGMIRE n soft wet area of land ▷ vb bog down

QUAGMIRED > QUAGMIRE

QUAGMIRES > QUAGMIRE

QUAGMIRY > QUAGMIRE

QUAGS > QUAG

QUAHAUG same as > QUAHOG

QUAHAUGS > QUAHAUG

QUAHOG n edible clam

QUAHOGS > QUAHOG

QUAI same as > QUAY

QUAICH n small shallow drinking cup

QUAICHES > QUAICH

QUAICHS > QUAICH

QUAIGH same as > QUAICH

QUAIGHS > QUAIGH

QUAIL n small game bird of the partridge family ▷ vb shrink back with fear

QUAILED > QUAIL

QUAILING > QUAIL

QUAILINGS > QUAIL

QUAILS > QUAIL

QUAINT adj attractively unusual, esp in an old-fashioned style

QUAINTER > QUAINT

QUAINTEST > QUAINT

QUAINTLY > QUAINT

QUAIR n book

q

QUAIRS > QUAIR

QUAIS > QUAI

QUAKE *vb* shake or tremble with or as if with fear ▷ *n* earthquake

QUAKED > QUAKE

QUAKER > QUAKE

QUAKERS > QUAKE

QUAKES > QUAKE

QUAKIER > QUAKY

QUAKIEST > QUAKY

QUAKILY > QUAKY

QUAKINESS > QUAKY

QUAKING > QUAKE

QUAKINGLY > QUAKE

QUAKINGS > QUAKE

QUAKY *adj* inclined to quake

QUALE *n* essential property or quality

QUALIA > QUALE

QUALIFIED > QUALIFY

QUALIFIER *n* person or thing that qualifies, esp a contestant in a competition who wins a preliminary heat or contest and so earns the right to take part in the next round

QUALIFIES > QUALIFY

QUALIFY *vb* provide or be provided with the abilities necessary

QUALITIED *adj* possessing qualities

QUALITIES > QUALITY

QUALITY *n* degree or standard of excellence ▷ *adj* excellent or superior

QUALM *n* pang of conscience

QUALMIER > QUALM

QUALMIEST > QUALM

QUALMING *adj* having a qualm ▷ *n* state of having a qualm

QUALMINGS > QUALMING

QUALMISH > QUALM

QUALMLESS > QUALM

QUALMS > QUALM

QUALMY > QUALM

QUAMASH another name for > CAMASS

QUAMASHES > QUAMASH

QUANDANG same as > QUANDONG

QUANDANGS > QUANDANG

QUANDARY *n* difficult situation or dilemma

QUANDONG *n* small Australian tree with edible fruit and nuts used in preserves

QUANDONGS > QUANDONG

QUANGO *n* partly independent official body set up by a government

QUANGOS > QUANGO

QUANNET *n* flat file with handle at one end

QUANNETS > QUANNET

QUANT *n* long pole for propelling a boat ▷ *vb* propel (a boat) with a quant

QUANTA > QUANTUM

QUANTAL *adj* of or relating to a quantum or an entity that is quantized

QUANTALLY > QUANTAL

QUANTED > QUANT

QUANTIC *n* mathematical function

QUANTICAL > QUANTIC

QUANTICS > QUANTIC

QUANTIFY *vb* discover or express the quantity of

QUANTILE *n* element of a division

QUANTILES > QUANTILE

QUANTING > QUANT

QUANTISE same as > QUANTIZE

QUANTISED > QUANTISE

QUANTISER > QUANTISE

QUANTISES > QUANTISE

QUANTITY *n* specified or definite amount or number

QUANTIZE *vb* restrict (a physical quantity) to one of a set of values characterized by quantum numbers

QUANTIZED > QUANTIZE

QUANTIZER > QUANTIZE

QUANTIZES > QUANTIZE

QUANTONG same as > QUANDONG

QUANTONGS > QUANTONG

QUANTS > QUANT

QUANTUM *n* desired or required amount ▷ *adj* of or designating a major breakthrough

QUANTUMS > QUANTUM

QUARE *adj* remarkable or strange

QUARENDEN *n* dark-red apple

QUARENDER same as > QUARENDEN

QUARER > QUARE

QUAREST > QUARE

QUARK *n* subatomic particle thought to be the fundamental unit of matter

QUARKS > QUARK

QUARREL *n* angry disagreement ▷ *vb* have a disagreement or dispute

QUARRELED > QUARREL

QUARRELER > QUARREL

QUARRELS > QUARREL

QUARRIAN *n* cockatiel of scrub and woodland regions of inland Australia

QUARRIANS > QUARRIAN

QUARRIED > QUARRY

QUARRIER another word for > QUARRYMAN

QUARRIERS > QUARRIER

QUARRIES > QUARRY

QUARRION same as > QUARRIAN

QUARRIONS > QUARRION

QUARRY *n* place where stone is dug from the surface of the earth ▷ *vb* extract (stone) from a quarry

QUARRYING > QUARRY

QUARRYMAN *n* man who works in or manages a quarry

QUARRYMEN > QUARRYMAN

QUART *n* unit of liquid measure equal to two pints (1.136 litres)

QUARTAN *adj* (esp of a malarial fever) occurring every third day ▷ *n* quartan malaria

QUARTANS > QUARTAN

QUARTE *n* fourth of eight basic positions from which a parry or attack can be made in fencing

QUARTER *n* one of four equal parts of something ▷ *vb* divide into four equal parts ▷ *adj* being or consisting of one of four equal parts

QUARTERED *adj* (of a shield) divided into four sections, each having contrasting arms or having two sets of arms, each repeated in diagonally opposite corners

QUARTERER > QUARTER

QUARTERLY *adj* occurring, due, or issued at intervals of three months ▷ *n* magazine issued every three months ▷ *adv* once every three months

QUARTERN *n* fourth part of certain weights or measures, such as a peck or a pound

QUARTERNS > QUARTERN

QUARTERS *pl n* accommodation, esp as provided for military personnel

QUARTES > QUARTE

QUARTET *n* group of four performers

QUARTETS > QUARTET

QUARTETT same as > QUARTET

QUARTETTE same as > QUARTET

QUARTETTI > QUARTETTO

QUARTETTO same as > QUARTET

QUARTETTS > QUARTETT

QUARTIC *n* biquadratic equation

QUARTICS > QUARTIC

QUARTIER *n* city district

QUARTIERS > QUARTIER

QUARTILE *n* one of three values of a variable dividing its distribution into four groups with equal frequencies ▷ *adj* of a quartile

QUARTILES > QUARTILE

QUARTO *n* book size in which the sheets are folded into four leaves

QUARTOS > QUARTO

QUARTS > QUART

QUARTZ *n* hard glossy mineral

QUARTZES > QUARTZ

QUARTZIER > QUARTZ

QUARTZITE *n* very hard metamorphic rock consisting of a mosaic of intergrown quartz crystals

QUARTZOSE > QUARTZ

QUARTZOUS > QUARTZ

QUARTZY > QUARTZ

QUASAR *n* extremely distant starlike object that emits powerful radio waves

QUASARS > QUASAR

QUASH *vb* annul or make void

QUASHED > QUASH

QUASHER > QUASH

QUASHERS > QUASH

QUASHES > QUASH

QUASHING > QUASH

QUASI *adv* as if

QUASS variant of > KVASS

QUASSES > QUASS

QUASSIA *n* tropical American tree

QUASSIAS > QUASSIA

QUASSIN *n* bitter crystalline substance

QUASSINS > QUASSIN

QUAT *n* spot ▷ *vb* beat down or squash

QUATCH *vb* move

QUATCHED > QUATCH

QUATCHES > QUATCH

QUATCHING > QUATCH

QUATE *n* fortune

QUATES > QUATE

QUATORZE *n* cards worth 14 points in piquet

QUATORZES > QUATORZE

QUATRAIN *n* stanza or poem of four lines

QUATRAINS > QUATRAIN

QUATRE *n* playing card with four pips

QUATRES > QUATRE

QUATS > QUAT

QUATTED > QUAT

QUATTING > QUAT

QUAVER *vb* (of a voice) quiver or tremble ▷ *n* note half the length of a crotchet

QUAVERED > QUAVER

QUAVERER > QUAVER

QUAVERERS > QUAVER

QUAVERIER > QUAVER

QUAVERING > QUAVER

QUAVERS > QUAVER

QUAVERY > QUAVER

q

QUAY n wharf built parallel to the shore

QUAYAGE n system of quays

QUAYAGES > QUAYAGE

QUAYD archaic past participle of > QUAIL

QUAYLIKE > QUAY

QUAYS > QUAY

QUAYSIDE n edge of a quay along the water

QUAYSIDES > QUAYSIDE

QUAZZIER > QUAZZY

QUAZZIEST > QUAZZY

QUAZZY adj unwell

QUBIT n quantum bit

QUBITS > QUBIT

QUBYTE n unit of eight qubits

QUBYTES > QUBYTE

QUEACH n thicket

QUEACHES > QUEACH

QUEACHIER > QUEACHY

QUEACHY adj unwell

QUEAN n Scots word for a young unmarried woman

QUEANS > QUEAN

QUEASIER > QUEASY

QUEASIEST > QUEASY

QUEASILY > QUEASY

QUEASY adj having the feeling that one is about to vomit

QUEAZIER > QUEAZY

QUEAZIEST > QUEAZY

QUEAZY same as > QUEASY

QUEBEC n code word for the letter Q

QUEBECS > QUEBEC

QUEBRACHO n anacardiaceous South American tree

QUEECHIER > QUEECHY

QUEECHY same as > QUEACHY

QUEEN n female sovereign who is the official ruler or head of state ▷ vb crown as queen

QUEENCAKE n small light cake containing currants

QUEENCUP n type of flowering plant

QUEENCUPS > QUEENCUP

QUEENDOM n territory, state, people, or community ruled over by a queen

QUEENDOMS > QUEENDOM

QUEENED > QUEEN

QUEENFISH n type of Californian marine fish

QUEENHOOD > QUEEN

QUEENIE n scallop

QUEENIER > QUEENY

QUEENIES > QUEENIE

QUEENIEST > QUEENY

QUEENING > QUEEN

QUEENINGS > QUEEN

QUEENITE n supporter of a queen

QUEENITES > QUEENITE

QUEENLESS > QUEEN

QUEENLET n queen of a small realm

QUEENLETS > QUEENLET

QUEENLIER > QUEENLY

QUEENLIKE adj like a queen

QUEENLY adj resembling or appropriate to a queen ▷ adv in a manner appropriate to a queen

QUEENS > QUEEN

QUEENSHIP > QUEEN

QUEENSIDE n half of a chessboard in which the queen starts

QUEENY adj resembling a queen

QUEER adj not normal or usual ▷ vb spoil or thwart

QUEERCORE n type of gay-oriented punk music

QUEERED > QUEER

QUEERER > QUEER

QUEEREST > QUEER

QUEERING > QUEER

QUEERISH > QUEER

QUEERITY > QUEER

QUEERLY > QUEER

QUEERNESS > QUEER

QUEERS > QUEER

QUEEST n wood pigeon

QUEESTS > QUEEST

QUEINT same as > QUAINT

QUELCH same as > SQUELCH

QUELCHED > QUELCH

QUELCHES > QUELCH

QUELCHING > QUELCH

QUELEA n East African weaver bird

QUELEAS > QUELEA

QUELL vb suppress

QUELLABLE > QUELL

QUELLED > QUELL

QUELLER > QUELL

QUELLERS > QUELL

QUELLING > QUELL

QUELLS > QUELL

QUEME vb please

QUEMED > QUEME

QUEMES > QUEME

QUEMING > QUEME

QUENA n Andean flute

QUENAS > QUENA

QUENCH vb satisfy (one's thirst)

QUENCHED > QUENCH

QUENCHER > QUENCH

QUENCHERS > QUENCH

QUENCHES > QUENCH

QUENCHING > QUENCH

QUENELLE n finely sieved mixture of cooked meat or fish shaped into various forms

QUENELLES > QUENELLE

QUEP interj expression of derision

QUERCETIC > QUERCETIN

QUERCETIN n yellow crystalline pigment found naturally in the rind and bark of many plants

QUERCETUM n group of oak trees

QUERCINE adj of or relating to oak trees

QUERCITIN same as > QUERCETIN

QUERIDA n sweetheart

QUERIDAS > QUERIDA

QUERIED > QUERY

QUERIER > QUERY

QUERIERS > QUERY

QUERIES > QUERY

QUERIMONY n complaint

QUERIST n person who makes inquiries or queries

QUERISTS > QUERIST

QUERN n stone hand mill for grinding corn

QUERNS > QUERN

QUERULOUS adj complaining or whining

QUERY n question, esp one raising doubt ▷ vb express uncertainty, doubt, or an objection

QUERYING > QUERY

QUERYINGS > QUERY

QUEST n long and difficult search ▷ vb go in search of

QUESTANT n one who quests

QUESTANTS > QUEST

QUESTED > QUEST

QUESTER > QUEST

QUESTERS > QUEST

QUESTING > QUEST

QUESTINGS > QUEST

QUESTION n form of words addressed to a person in order to obtain an answer ▷ vb put a question or questions to (a person)

QUESTIONS > QUESTION

QUESTOR same as > QUAESTOR

QUESTORS > QUESTOR

QUESTRIST n one who quests

QUESTS > QUEST

QUETCH vb move

QUETCHED > QUETCH

QUETCHES > QUETCH

QUETCHING > QUETCH

QUETHE vb say

QUETHES > QUETHE

QUETHING > QUETHE

QUETSCH n plum brandy

QUETSCHES > QUETSCH

QUETZAL n crested bird of Central and N South America

QUETZALES > QUETZAL

QUETZALS > QUETZAL

QUEUE n line of people or vehicles waiting for something ▷ vb form or remain in a line while waiting

QUEUED > QUEUE

QUEUEING > QUEUE

QUEUEINGS > QUEUE

QUEUER > QUEUE

QUEUERS > QUEUE

QUEUES > QUEUE

QUEUING > QUEUE

QUEUINGS > QUEUE

QUEY n young cow

QUEYN n girl or young woman

QUEYNIE same as > QUEYN

QUEYNIES > QUEYNIE

QUEYNS > QUEYN

QUEYS > QUEY

QUEZAL same as > QUETZAL

QUEZALES > QUEZAL

QUEZALS > QUEZAL

QUIBBLE vb make trivial objections ▷ n trivial objection

QUIBBLED > QUIBBLE

QUIBBLER > QUIBBLE

QUIBBLERS > QUIBBLE

QUIBBLES > QUIBBLE

QUIBBLING > QUIBBLE

QUIBLIN same as > QUIBBLE

QUIBLINS > QUIBLIN

QUICH vb move

QUICHE n savoury flan with an egg custard filling

QUICHED > QUICH

QUICHES > QUICHE

QUICHING > QUICH

QUICK adj speedy, fast ▷ n area of sensitive flesh under a nail ▷ adv in a rapid manner

QUICKBEAM n rowan tree

QUICKEN vb make or become faster ▷ n rowan tree

QUICKENED > QUICKEN

QUICKENER > QUICKEN

QUICKENS > QUICKEN

QUICKER > QUICK

QUICKEST > QUICK

QUICKFIRE adj designed for rapid continuous gunfire

QUICKIE n anything done or made hurriedly ▷ adj made or done rapidly

QUICKIES > QUICKIE

QUICKLIME n white solid used in the manufacture of glass and steel

QUICKLY > QUICK

QUICKNESS > QUICK

QUICKS > QUICK

QUICKSAND n deep mass of loose wet sand that sucks anything on top of it into it

QUICKSET adj (of plants or cuttings) planted so as to form a hedge ▷ n hedge composed of such plants

QUICKSETS > QUICKSET

QUICKSTEP n fast modern ballroom dance ▷ vb perform this dance

QUICKY same as > QUICKIE

QUID n pound (sterling)

QUIDAM n specified person

QUIDAMS > QUIDAM

QUIDDANY n quince jelly ▷ vb make into quince jelly

QUIDDIT same as > QUIDDITY

q

QUIDDITCH n imaginary game in which players fly on broomsticks
QUIDDITS > QUIDDIT
QUIDDITY n essential nature of something
QUIDDLE vb waste time
QUIDDLED > QUIDDLE
QUIDDLER > QUIDDLE
QUIDDLERS > QUIDDLE
QUIDDLES > QUIDDLE
QUIDDLING > QUIDDLE
QUIDNUNC n person eager to learn news and scandal
QUIDNUNCS > QUIDNUNC
QUIDS > QUID
QUIESCE vb quieten
QUIESCED > QUIESCE
QUIESCENT adj quiet, inactive, or dormant
QUIESCES > QUIESCE
QUIESCING > QUIESCE
QUIET adj with little noise ▷ n quietness ▷ vb make or become quiet
QUIETED > QUIET
QUIETEN vb make or become quiet
QUIETENED > QUIETEN
QUIETENER > QUIETEN
QUIETENS > QUIETEN
QUIETER > QUIET
QUIETERS > QUIET
QUIETEST > QUIET
QUIETING > QUIET
QUIETINGS > QUIET
QUIETISM n passivity and calmness of mind towards external events
QUIETISMS > QUIETISM
QUIETIST > QUIETISM
QUIETISTS > QUIETISM
QUIETIVE n sedative drug
QUIETIVES > QUIETIVE
QUIETLY > QUIET
QUIETNESS > QUIET
QUIETS > QUIET
QUIETSOME > QUIET
QUIETUDE n quietness, peace, or tranquillity
QUIETUDES > QUIETUDE
QUIETUS n release from life
QUIETUSES > QUIETUS
QUIFF n tuft of hair brushed up above the forehead
QUIFFED adj having a quiff
QUIFFS > QUIFF
QUIGHT vb quit
QUIGHTED > QUIGHT
QUIGHTING > QUIGHT
QUIGHTS > QUIGHT
QUILL n pen made from the feather of a bird's wing or tail ▷ vb wind (thread, yarn, etc) onto a spool or bobbin
QUILLAI another name for > SOAPBARK

QUILLAIA same as > QUILLAI
QUILLAIAS > QUILLAIA
QUILLAIS > QUILLAI
QUILLAJA same as > QUILLAI
QUILLAJAS > QUILLAJA
QUILLBACK n freshwater fish
QUILLED > QUILL
QUILLET n quibble or subtlety
QUILLETS > QUILLET
QUILLING n craftwork in which material is formed into small bands that form the basis of a design
QUILLINGS > QUILLING
QUILLMAN n clerk
QUILLMEN > QUILLMAN
QUILLON n either half of the extended crosspiece of a sword or dagger
QUILLONS > QUILLON
QUILLOW n quilt folded to make a pillow
QUILLOWS > QUILLOW
QUILLS > QUILL
QUILLWORK n embroidery using porcupine quills
QUILLWORT n aquatic tracheophyte plant with quill-like leaves
QUILT n padded covering for a bed ▷ vb stitch together two layers of (fabric) with padding between them
QUILTED > QUILT
QUILTER > QUILT
QUILTERS > QUILT
QUILTING n material used for making a quilt
QUILTINGS > QUILTING
QUILTS > QUILT
QUIM n vulgar word for the female genitals
QUIMS > QUIM
QUIN n short for quintuplet
QUINA n quinine
QUINARIES > QUINARY
QUINARY adj consisting of fives or by fives ▷ n set of five
QUINAS > QUINA
QUINATE adj arranged in or composed of five parts
QUINCE n acid-tasting pear-shaped fruit
QUINCES > QUINCE
QUINCHE vb move
QUINCHED > QUINCHE
QUINCHES > QUINCHE
QUINCHING > QUINCHE
QUINCUNX n five objects arranged in the shape of a rectangle with the fifth in the centre
QUINE variant of > QUEAN
QUINELA same as > QUINELLA
QUINELAS > QUINELA

QUINELLA n form of betting in which the punter bets on selecting the first and second place-winners in any order
QUINELLAS > QUINELLA
QUINES > QUINE
QUINIC adj as in quinic acid white crystalline soluble optically active carboxylic acid
QUINIDINE n crystalline alkaloid drug
QUINIE n girl or young woman
QUINIELA same as > QUINELLA
QUINIELAS > QUINIELA
QUINIES > QUINIE
QUININ same as > QUININE
QUININA same as > QUININE
QUININAS > QUININA
QUININE n bitter drug used as a tonic and formerly to treat malaria
QUININES > QUININE
QUININS > QUININ
QUINNAT n Pacific salmon
QUINNATS > QUINNAT
QUINO same as > KENO
QUINOA n type of grain high in nutrients
QUINOAS > QUINOA
QUINOID same as > QUINONOID
QUINOIDAL > QUINOID
QUINOIDS > QUINOID
QUINOL n white crystalline soluble phenol used as a photographic developer
QUINOLIN same as > QUINOLINE
QUINOLINE n oily colourless insoluble basic heterocyclic compound
QUINOLINS > QUINOLIN
QUINOLONE n any of a group of synthetic antibiotics
QUINOLS > QUINOL
QUINONE n yellow crystalline water-soluble unsaturated ketone
QUINONES > QUINONE
QUINONOID adj of, resembling, or derived from quinone
QUINOS > QUINO
QUINQUINA same as > QUININE
QUINS > QUIN
QUINSIED > QUINSY
QUINSIES > QUINSY
QUINSY n inflammation of the throat or tonsils
QUINT same as > QUIN
QUINTA n Portuguese vineyard where grapes for wine or port are grown
QUINTAIN n post or target set up for tilting

exercises for mounted knights or foot soldiers
QUINTAINS > QUINTAIN
QUINTAL n unit of weight
QUINTALS > QUINTAL
QUINTAN adj (of a fever) occurring every fourth day ▷ n quintan fever
QUINTANS > QUINTAN
QUINTAR n Albanian unit of currency
QUINTARS > QUINTAR
QUINTAS > QUINTA
QUINTE n fifth of eight basic positions from which a parry or attack can be made in fencing
QUINTES > QUINTE
QUINTET n group of five performers
QUINTETS > QUINTET
QUINTETT same as > QUINTET
QUINTETTE same as > QUINTET
QUINTETTI > QUINTETTO
QUINTETTO same as > QUINTET
QUINTETTS > QUINTETT
QUINTIC adj of or relating to the fifth degree ▷ n mathematical function
QUINTICS > QUINTIC
QUINTILE n aspect of 72° between two heavenly bodies
QUINTILES > QUINTILE
QUINTIN same as > QUINTAIN
QUINTINS > QUINTIN
QUINTS > QUINT
QUINTUPLE vb multiply by five ▷ adj five times as much or as many ▷ n quantity or number five times as great as another
QUINTUPLY n reply to a quadruply
QUINZE n card game where players aim to score 15
QUINZES > QUINZE
QUINZHEE n shelter made from hollowed-out snow
QUINZHEES > QUINZHEE
QUINZIE same as > QUINZHEE
QUINZIES > QUINZIE
QUIP n witty saying ▷ vb make a quip
QUIPO same as > QUIPU
QUIPOS > QUIPO
QUIPPED > QUIP
QUIPPER > QUIP
QUIPPERS > QUIP
QUIPPIER > QUIP
QUIPPIEST > QUIP
QUIPPING > QUIP
QUIPPISH > QUIP
QUIPPU same as > QUIPU
QUIPPUS > QUIPPU

q

QUIPPY > QUIP

QUIPS > QUIP

QUIPSTER n person inclined to make sarcastic or witty remarks

QUIPSTERS > QUIPSTER

QUIPU n device of the Incas used to record information using knotted cords

QUIPUS > QUIPU

QUIRE n set of 24 or 25 sheets of paper ▷ vb arrange in quires

QUIRED > QUIRE

QUIRES > QUIRE

QUIRING > QUIRE

QUIRISTER same as > CHORISTER

QUIRK n peculiarity of character ▷ vb quip

QUIRKED > QUIRK

QUIRKIER > QUIRK

QUIRKIEST > QUIRK

QUIRKILY > QUIRK

QUIRKING > QUIRK

QUIRKISH > QUIRK

QUIRKS > QUIRK

QUIRKY > QUIRK

QUIRT n whip with a leather thong at one end ▷ vb strike with a quirt

QUIRTED > QUIRT

QUIRTING > QUIRT

QUIRTS > QUIRT

QUISLING n traitor who aids an occupying enemy force

QUISLINGS > QUISLING

QUIST n wood pigeon

QUISTS > QUIST

QUIT vb stop (doing something) ▷ adj free (from)

QUITCH vb move

QUITCHED > QUITCH

QUITCHES > QUITCH

QUITCHING > QUITCH

QUITCLAIM n formal renunciation of any claim against a person or of a right to land ▷ vb renounce (a claim) formally

QUITE archaic form of > QUIT

QUITED > QUITE

QUITES > QUITE

QUITING > QUITE

QUITRENT n former rent payable by a freeholder to their lord that released them from performing services

QUITRENTS > QUITRENT

QUITS > QUIT

QUITTAL n repayment of an action with a similar action

QUITTALS > QUITTAL

QUITTANCE n release from debt or other obligation

QUITTED > QUIT

QUITTER n person who lacks perseverance

QUITTERS > QUITTER

QUITTING > QUIT

QUITTOR n infection of the cartilages on the side of a horse's foot

QUITTORS > QUITTOR

QUIVER vb shake with a tremulous movement ▷ n shaking or trembling

QUIVERED > QUIVER

QUIVERER > QUIVER

QUIVERERS > QUIVER

QUIVERFUL n amount that a quiver can hold

QUIVERIER > QUIVER

QUIVERING > QUIVER

QUIVERISH > QUIVER

QUIVERS > QUIVER

QUIVERY > QUIVER

QUIXOTE n impractical idealist

QUIXOTES > QUIXOTE

QUIXOTIC adj romantic and unrealistic

QUIXOTISM > QUIXOTIC

QUIXOTRY > QUIXOTE

QUIZ n entertainment in which the knowledge of the players is tested by a series of questions ▷ vb investigate by close questioning

QUIZZED > QUIZ

QUIZZER > QUIZ

QUIZZERS > QUIZ

QUIZZERY > QUIZ

QUIZZES > QUIZ

QUIZZICAL adj questioning and mocking

QUIZZIFY > QUIZ

QUIZZING > QUIZ

QUIZZINGS > QUIZ

QULLIQ n type of oil lamp used by Inuit people

QULLIQS > QULLIQ

QUOAD adv as far as

QUOD n jail ▷ vb say

QUODDED > QUOD

QUODDING > QUOD

QUODLIBET n light piece of music based on two or more popular tunes

QUODLIN n cooking apple

QUODLINS > QUODLIN

QUODS > QUOD

QUOHOG n edible clam

QUOHOGS > QUOHOG

QUOIF vb arrange (the hair)

QUOIFED > QUOIF

QUOIFING > QUOIF

QUOIFS > QUOIF

QUOIN n external corner of a building ▷ vb wedge

QUOINED > QUOIN

QUOINING > QUOIN

QUOININGS > QUOINING

QUOINS > QUOIN

QUOIST n wood pigeon

QUOISTS > QUOIST

QUOIT n large ring used in the game of quoits ▷ vb throw as a quoit

QUOITED > QUOIT

QUOITER > QUOIT

QUOITERS > QUOIT

QUOITING > QUOIT

QUOITS n game in which quoits are tossed at a stake in the ground

QUOKKA n small Australian wallaby

QUOKKAS > QUOKKA

QUOLL n Australian catlike carnivorous marsupial

QUOLLS > QUOLL

QUOMODO n manner

QUOMODOS > QUOMODO

QUONDAM adj of an earlier time

QUONK vb make an accidental noise while broadcasting

QUONKED > QUONK

QUONKING > QUONK

QUONKS > QUONK

QUOOKE archaic past participle of > QUAKE

QUOP vb pulsate or throb

QUOPPED > QUOP

QUOPPING > QUOP

QUOPS > QUOP

QUORATE adj having or being a quorum

QUORUM n minimum number of people required to be present at a meeting

QUORUMS > QUORUM

QUOTA n share that is due from, due to, or allocated to a group or person

QUOTABLE adj apt or suitable for quotation

QUOTABLY > QUOTABLE

QUOTAS > QUOTA

QUOTATION n written or spoken passage repeated exactly in a later work, speech, or conversation

QUOTATIVE n word indicating quotation ▷ adj introducing quoted words

QUOTE vb repeat (words) exactly ▷ n quotation ▷ interj expression used to indicate that the words that follow form a quotation

QUOTED > QUOTE

QUOTER > QUOTE

QUOTERS > QUOTE

QUOTES > QUOTE

QUOTH vb said

QUOTHA interj expression of mild sarcasm, used in picking up a word or phrase used by someone else

QUOTIDIAN adj daily ▷ n malarial fever characterized by attacks that recur daily

QUOTIENT n result of the division of one number or quantity by another

QUOTIENTS > QUOTIENT

QUOTING > QUOTE

QUOTITION n division by repeated subtraction

QUOTUM same as > QUOTA

QUOTUMS > QUOTUM

QURSH same as > QURUSH

QURSHES > QURSH

QURUSH n former Saudi Arabian currency unit

QURUSHES > QURUSH

QUYTE same as > QUIT

QUYTED > QUYTE

QUYTES > QUYTE

QUYTING > QUYTE

QWERTIES > QWERTY

QWERTY n standard English-language typewriter or computer keyboard

QWERTYS > QWERTY

q

Rr

RABANNA n Madagascan woven raffia
RABANNAS > RABANNA
RABASKA n large canoe
RABASKAS > RABASKA
RABAT vb rotate so that the plane rotated coincides with another
RABATINE n type of collar
RABATINES > RABATINE
RABATMENT > RABAT
RABATO n wired or starched collar
RABATOES > RABATO
RABATOS > RABATO
RABATS > RABAT
RABATTE same as > RABAT
RABATTED > RABAT
RABATTES > RABATTE
RABATTING > RABAT
RABBET n recess cut into a surface ▷ vb cut or form a rabbet in (timber)
RABBETED > RABBET
RABBETING > RABBET
RABBETS > RABBET
RABBI n Jewish spiritual leader
RABBIES > RABBI
RABBIN same as > RABBI
RABBINATE n position, function, or tenure of office of a rabbi
RABBINIC adj of or relating to rabbis
RABBINICS n study of rabbinic literature of the post-Talmudic period
RABBINISM n teachings and traditions of the rabbis of the Talmudic period
RABBINIST > RABBINISM
RABBINITE > RABBINISM
RABBINS > RABBIN
RABBIS > RABBI
RABBIT n small burrowing mammal with long ears ▷ vb talk too much
RABBITED > RABBIT
RABBITER n person who traps and sells rabbits
RABBITERS > RABBITER
RABBITIER > RABBITY
RABBITING n activity of hunting rabbits
RABBITO same as > RABBITOH

RABBITOH n (formerly) an itinerant seller of rabbits for eating
RABBITOHS > RABBITOH
RABBITOS > RABBITO
RABBITRY n place where tame rabbits are kept and bred
RABBITS > RABBIT
RABBITY adj like a rabbit
RABBLE n disorderly crowd of noisy people ▷ vb stir, mix, or skim (the molten charge) in a roasting furnace
RABBLED > RABBLE
RABBLER n device for stirring, mixing, or skimming a molten charge in a furnace
RABBLERS > RABBLER
RABBLES > RABBLE
RABBLING > RABBLE
RABBLINGS > RABBLE
RABBONI n very respectful Jewish title or form of address
RABBONIS > RABBONI
RABI n (in Pakistan, India, etc) a crop that is harvested at the end of winter
RABIC > RABIES
RABID adj fanatical
RABIDER > RABID
RABIDEST > RABID
RABIDITY > RABID
RABIDLY > RABID
RABIDNESS > RABID
RABIES n usu fatal viral disease transmitted by dogs and certain other animals
RABIETIC > RABIES
RABIS > RABI
RABONA n method of kicking a football
RABONAS > RABONA
RACA adj biblical word meaning worthless or empty-headed
RACAHOUT n acorn flour or drink made from it
RACAHOUTS > RACAHOUT
RACCAHOUT same as > RACAHOUT
RACCOON n small N American mammal with a long striped tail
RACCOONS > RACCOON
RACE n contest of speed ▷ vb compete with in a race

RACEABLE adj fit for racing
RACECARD n card providing information about a race meeting
RACECARDS > RACECARD
RACED > RACE
RACEGOER n one who attends a race meeting, esp a habitual frequenter of race meetings
RACEGOERS > RACEGOER
RACEGOING > RACEGOER
RACEHORSE n horse specially bred for racing
RACEMATE n racemic compound
RACEMATES > RACEMATE
RACEME n cluster of flowers along a central stem, as in the foxglove
RACEMED adj with or in racemes
RACEMES > RACEME
RACEMIC adj being a mixture of equal amounts of enantiomers
RACEMISE same as > RACEMIZE
RACEMISED > RACEMISE
RACEMISES > RACEMISE
RACEMISM > RACEMIC
RACEMISMS > RACEMIC
RACEMIZE vb change or cause to change into a racemic mixture
RACEMIZED > RACEMIZE
RACEMIZES > RACEMIZE
RACEMOID adj resembling a raceme
RACEMOSE adj being or resembling a raceme
RACEMOUS same as > RACEMOSE
RACEPATH same as > RACETRACK
RACEPATHS > RACEPATH
RACER n person, animal, or machine that races
RACERS > RACER
RACES > RACE
RACETRACK n track for racing
RACEWALK vb race by walking fast rather than running

RACEWALKS > RACEWALK
RACEWAY n racetrack, esp one for banger racing
RACEWAYS > RACEWAY
RACH n scent hound
RACHE same as > RACH
RACHES > RACH
RACHET same as > RATCHET
RACHETED > RACHET
RACHETING > RACHET
RACHETS > RACHET
RACHIAL > RACHIS
RACHIDES > RACHIS
RACHIDIAL > RACHIS
RACHIDIAN > RACHIS
RACHILLA n (in grasses) the short stem of a spikelet that bears the florets
RACHILLAE > RACHILLA
RACHILLAS > RACHILLA
RACHIS n main axis or stem of an inflorescence or compound leaf
RACHISES > RACHIS
RACHITIC > RACHITIS
RACHITIS another name for > RICKETS
RACIAL adj relating to the division of the human species into races
RACIALISE same as > RACIALIZE
RACIALISM same as > RACISM
RACIALIST > RACIALISM
RACIALIZE vb render racial in tone or content
RACIALLY > RACIAL
RACIATION n evolutionary development of races
RACIER > RACY
RACIEST > RACY
RACILY > RACY
RACINESS > RACY
RACING adj denoting or associated with horse races ▷ n practice of engaging in contests of speed
RACINGS > RACING
RACINO n combined racetrack and casino
RACINOS > RACINO
RACISM n discrimination against people of races other than one's own
RACISMS > RACISM

RACIST > RACISM

RACISTS > RACISM

RACK n framework for holding particular articles, such as coats or luggage ▷ vb cause great suffering to

RACKED > RACK

RACKER > RACK

RACKERS > RACK

RACKET n bat with strings stretched in an oval frame, used in tennis etc ▷ vb strike with a racket

RACKETED > RACKET

RACKETEER vb run an illegal enterprise for profit

RACKETER n someone making a racket

RACKETERS > RACKETER

RACKETIER > RACKETY

RACKETING > RACKET

RACKETRY n noise and commotion

RACKETS > RACKET

RACKETT n early double-reeded wind instrument

RACKETTS > RACKETT

RACKETY adj involving noise, commotion and excitement

RACKFUL > RACK

RACKFULS > RACK

RACKING > RACK

RACKINGLY > RACK

RACKINGS > RACK

RACKLE n (Scot) chain

RACKLES > RACKLE

RACKS > RACK

RACKWORK n mechanism with a rack and pinion

RACKWORKS > RACKWORK

RACLETTE n Swiss dish of melted cheese served on boiled potatoes

RACLETTES > RACLETTE

RACLOIR n scraper

RACLOIRS > RACLOIR

RACON n radar beacon

RACONS > RACON

RACONTEUR n skilled storyteller

RACOON same as > RACCOON

RACOONS > RACOON

RACQUET same as > RACKET

RACQUETED > RACQUET

RACQUETS > RACQUET

RACY adj slightly shocking

RAD n former unit of absorbed ionizing radiation dose ▷ vb fear ▷ adj slang term for great

RADAR n device for tracking distant objects

RADARS > RADAR

RADDED > RAD

RADDER > RAD

RADDEST > RAD

RADDING > RAD

RADDLE same as > RUDDLE

RADDLED adj (of a person) unkempt or run-down in appearance

RADDLEMAN same as > RUDDLEMAN

RADDLEMEN > RADDLEMAN

RADDLES > RADDLE

RADDLING > RADDLE

RADDOCKE same as > RUDDOCK

RADDOCKES > RADDOCKE

RADE (in Scots dialect) past tense of > RIDE

RADGE adj angry or uncontrollable ▷ n person acting in such a way

RADGER > RADGE

RADGES > RADGE

RADGEST > RADGE

RADIABLE adj able to be X-rayed

RADIAL adj spreading out from a common central point ▷ n radial-ply tyre

RADIALE n bone in the wrist

RADIALIA > RADIALE

RADIALISE same as > RADIALIZE

RADIALITY > RADIAL

RADIALIZE vb arrange in a pattern of radii

RADIALLY > RADIAL

RADIALS > RADIAL

RADIAN n unit for measuring angles, equal to 57.296°

RADIANCE n quality or state of being radiant

RADIANCES > RADIANCE

RADIANCY same as > RADIANCE

RADIANS > RADIAN

RADIANT adj looking happy ▷ n point or object that emits radiation

RADIANTLY > RADIANT

RADIANTS > RADIANT

RADIATA n type of pine tree

RADIATAS > RADIATA

RADIATE vb spread out from a centre ▷ adj having rays or a radial structure

RADIATED > RADIATE

RADIATELY > RADIATE

RADIATES > RADIATE

RADIATING > RADIATE

RADIATION n transmission of energy from one body to another

RADIATIVE adj emitting or causing the emission of radiation

RADIATOR n arrangement of pipes containing hot water or steam to heat a room

RADIATORS > RADIATOR

RADIATORY same as > RADIATIVE

RADICAL adj fundamental ▷ n person advocating fundamental (political) change

RADICALLY adv thoroughly

RADICALS > RADICAL

RADICAND n number from which a root is to be extracted

RADICANDS > RADICAND

RADICANT adj forming roots from the stem

RADICATE vb root or cause to take root

RADICATED > RADICATE

RADICATES > RADICATE

RADICCHIO n Italian variety of chicory, with purple leaves streaked with white that are eaten raw in salads

RADICEL n very small root

RADICELS > RADICEL

RADICES > RADIX

RADICLE n small or developing root

RADICLES > RADICLE

RADICULAR adj root-related

RADICULE same as > RADICLE

RADICULES > RADICULE

RADII > RADIUS

RADIO n use of electromagnetic waves for broadcasting, communication, etc ▷ vb transmit (a message) by radio ▷ adj of, relating to, or using radio

RADIOED > RADIO

RADIOES less common spelling of > RADIOS

RADIOGOLD n radioactive isotope of gold

RADIOGRAM n image produced on a specially sensitized photographic film or plate by radiation, usually by X-rays or gamma rays

RADIOING > RADIO

RADIOLOGY n science of using X-rays in medicine

RADIOMAN n radio operator

RADIOMEN > RADIOMAN

RADIONICS n dowsing technique using a pendulum to detect the energy fields that are emitted by all forms of matter

RADIOS > RADIO

RADIOTHON n lengthy radio programme to raise charity funds, etc

RADISH n small hot-flavoured root vegetable eaten raw in salads

RADISHES > RADISH

RADIUM n radioactive metallic element

RADIUMS > RADIUM

RADIUS n (length of) a straight line from the centre to the circumference of a circle ▷ vb give a round shape

RADIUSED > RADIUS

RADIUSES > RADIUS

RADIUSING > RADIUS

RADIX n any number that is the base of a number system or of a system of logarithms

RADIXES > RADIX

RADOME n protective housing for a radar antenna

RADOMES > RADOME

RADON n radioactive gaseous element

RADONS > RADON

RADS > RAD

RADULA n horny tooth-bearing strip on the tongue of molluscs

RADULAE > RADULA

RADULAR > RADULA

RADULAS > RADULA

RADULATE > RADULA

RADWASTE n radioactive waste

RADWASTES > RADWASTE

RAFALE n burst of artillery fire

RAFALES > RAFALE

RAFF n rubbish

RAFFIA n prepared palm fibre for weaving mats etc

RAFFIAS > RAFFIA

RAFFINATE n liquid left after a solute has been extracted by solvent extraction

RAFFINOSE n trisaccharide of fructose, glucose, and galactose

RAFFISH adj slightly disreputable

RAFFISHLY > RAFFISH

RAFFLE n lottery with goods as prizes ▷ vb offer as a prize in a raffle

RAFFLED > RAFFLE

RAFFLER > RAFFLE

RAFFLERS > RAFFLE

RAFFLES > RAFFLE

RAFFLESIA n any of various tropical parasitic leafless plants whose flowers smell of putrid meat

RAFFLING > RAFFLE

RAFFS > RAFF

RAFT n floating platform of logs, planks, etc ▷ vb convey on or travel by raft, or make a raft from

RAFTED > RAFT

RAFTER n one of the main beams of a roof ▷ vb fit with rafters

RAFTERED > RAFTER

RAFTERING > RAFTER

RAFTERS > RAFTER

RAFTING > RAFT

RAFTINGS > RAFT

RAFTMAN same as > RAFTSMAN

RAFTMEN > RAFTMAN

RAFTS > RAFT

RAFTSMAN n someone who does rafting

RAFTSMEN > RAFTSMAN

RAG n fragment of cloth ▷ vb tease ▷ adj of various charitable events at a British university

RAGA n pattern of melody and rhythm in Indian music

RAGAS > RAGA

RAGBAG n confused assortment, jumble

RAGBAGS > RAGBAG

RAGBOLT n bolt that has angled projections on it

RAGBOLTS > RAGBOLT

RAGDE archaic past form of > RAGE

RAGDOLL n breed of cat

RAGDOLLS > RAGDOLL

RAGE n violent anger or passion ▷ vb speak or act with fury

RAGED > RAGE

RAGEE same as > RAGI

RAGEES > RAGEE

RAGEFUL > RAGE

RAGER > RAGE

RAGERS > RAGE

RAGES > RAGE

RAGG same as > RAGSTONE

RAGGA n dance-oriented style of reggae

RAGGAS > RAGGA

RAGGED adj tattered

RAGGEDER > RAGGED

RAGGEDEST > RAGGED

RAGGEDIER > RAGGEDY

RAGGEDLY > RAGGED

RAGGEDY adj somewhat ragged

RAGGEE same as > RAGI

RAGGEES > RAGGEE

RAGGERIES > RAGGERY

RAGGERY n rags

RAGGIER > RAGGY

RAGGIES > RAGGY

RAGGIEST > RAGGY

RAGGING > RAG

RAGGINGS > RAGGING

RAGGLE n thin groove cut in stone or brickwork ▷ vb cut a raggle in

RAGGLED > RAGGLE

RAGGLES > RAGGLE

RAGGLING > RAGGLE

RAGGS > RAGG

RAGGY adj ragged ▷ n cereal grass cultivated in Africa and Asia for its edible grain

RAGI n cereal grass cultivated in Africa and Asia for its edible grain

RAGING > RAGE

RAGINGLY > RAGE

RAGINGS > RAGE

RAGINI n Indian musical form related to a raga

RAGINIS > RAGINI

RAGIS > RAGI

RAGLAN adj (of a sleeve) joined to a garment from the neck to the underarm ▷ n coat with sleeves that continue to the collar

RAGLANS > RAGLAN

RAGMAN n rag-and-bone man

RAGMANS > RAGMAN

RAGMEN > RAGMAN

RAGMENT n statute, roll, or list

RAGMENTS > RAGMENT

RAGOUT n richly seasoned stew of meat and vegetables ▷ vb make into a ragout

RAGOUTED > RAGOUT

RAGOUTING > RAGOUT

RAGOUTS > RAGOUT

RAGPICKER n rag-and-bone man

RAGS > RAG

RAGSTONE n hard sandstone or limestone, esp when used for building

RAGSTONES > RAGSTONE

RAGTAG n disparaging term for common people

RAGTAGS > RAGTAG

RAGTAIL adj ragged; shabby

RAGTIME n style of jazz piano music

RAGTIMER > RAGTIME

RAGTIMERS > RAGTIME

RAGTIMES > RAGTIME

RAGTOP n informal word for a car with a folding or removable roof

RAGTOPS > RAGTOP

RAGU n Italian meat and tomato sauce

RAGULED same as > RAGULY

RAGULY adj (in heraldry) having toothlike projections

RAGUS > RAGU

RAGWEED n any of several plants

RAGWEEDS > RAGWEED

RAGWHEEL n toothed wheel

RAGWHEELS > RAGWHEEL

RAGWORK n weaving or needlework using rags

RAGWORKS > RAGWORK

RAGWORM n type of worm that lives chiefly in burrows in sand or mud

RAGWORMS > RAGWORM

RAGWORT n plant with ragged leaves and yellow flowers

RAGWORTS > RAGWORT

RAH informal US word for > CHEER

RAHED > RAH

RAHING > RAH

RAHS > RAH

RAHUI n Māori prohibition

RAHUIS > RAHUI

RAI n type of Algerian popular music

RAIA same as > RAYAH

RAIAS > RAIA

RAID n sudden surprise attack or search ▷ vb make a raid on

RAIDED > RAID

RAIDER > RAID

RAIDERS > RAID

RAIDING > RAID

RAIDINGS > RAID

RAIDS > RAID

RAIK n wander ▷ vb wander

RAIKED > RAIK

RAIKING > RAIK

RAIKS > RAIK

RAIL n horizontal bar, esp as part of a fence or track ▷ vb complain bitterly or loudly

RAILAGE n cost of transporting goods by rail

RAILAGES > RAILAGE

RAILBED n ballast layer supporting the sleepers of a railway track

RAILBEDS > RAILBED

RAILBIRD n racing aficionado

RAILBIRDS > RAILBIRD

RAILBUS n bus-like vehicle for use on railway lines

RAILBUSES > RAILBUS

RAILCAR n passenger-carrying railway vehicle consisting of a single coach

RAILCARD n card entitling the holder to cheaper rail travel

RAILCARDS > RAILCARD

RAILCARS > RAILCAR

RAILE archaic spelling of > RAIL

RAILED > RAIL

RAILER > RAIL

RAILERS > RAIL

RAILES > RAILE

RAILHEAD n terminal of a railway

RAILHEADS > RAILHEAD

RAILING n fence made of rails supported by posts

RAILINGLY > RAIL

RAILINGS > RAILING

RAILLERY n teasing or joking

RAILLESS > RAIL

RAILLIES > RAILLY

RAILLY old word for > MOCK

RAILMAN n railway employee

RAILMEN > RAILMAN

RAILROAD same as > RAILWAY

RAILROADS > RAILROAD

RAILS > RAIL

RAILWAY n track of iron rails on which trains run

RAILWAYS > RAILWAY

RAILWOMAN n female railway employee

RAILWOMEN > RAILWOMAN

RAIMENT n clothing

RAIMENTS > RAIMENT

RAIN n water falling in drops from the clouds ▷ vb fall or pour down as rain

RAINBAND n dark band in the solar spectrum caused by water in the atmosphere

RAINBANDS > RAINBAND

RAINBIRD n bird whose call is believed to be a sign of impending rain

RAINBIRDS > RAINBIRD

RAINBOW n arch of colours in the sky

RAINBOWED adj resembling or involving a rainbow

RAINBOWS > RAINBOW

RAINBOWY adj resembling a rainbow

RAINCHECK n ticket stub allowing readmission to a game on a later date should bad weather prevent play

RAINCOAT n water-resistant overcoat

RAINCOATS > RAINCOAT

RAINDATE n US term for an alternative date in case of rain

RAINDATES > RAINDATE

RAINDROP n water droplet that falls from the sky when it is raining

RAINDROPS > RAINDROP

RAINE archaic spelling of > REIGN

RAINED > RAIN

RAINES > RAINE

RAINFALL n amount of rain

RAINFALLS > RAINFALL

RAINIER > RAINY

RAINIEST > RAINY

RAINILY > RAINY

RAININESS > RAINY

RAINING > RAIN

RAINLESS > RAIN

RAINMAKER n (among Native Americans) a professional practitioner of ritual incantations or other actions intended to cause rain to fall

RAINOUT n radioactive fallout or atmospheric pollution carried to the earth by rain

RAINOUTS > RAINOUT

RAINPROOF adj (of garments, materials, buildings, etc) impermeable to rainwater ▷ vb make rainproof

RAINS > RAIN

RAINSPOUT n waterspout

RAINSTICK n musical instrument consisting of a tube filled with sand or pebbles

RAINSTORM n storm with heavy rain

RAINSUIT n waterproof jacket and trousers

r

RAINSUITS
> RAINSUIT
RAINSWEPT adj (of a place) characterized by frequent heavy rain
RAINTIGHT same as
> RAINPROOF
RAINWASH n action of rain ▷ vb erode or wet as a result of rain
RAINWATER n water from rain
RAINWEAR n protective garments intended for use in wet weather
RAINWEARS
> RAINWEAR
RAINY adj characterized by a large rainfall
RAIRD same as > REIRD
RAIRDS > RAIRD
RAIS > RAI
RAISABLE > RAISE
RAISE vb lift up ▷ n increase in pay
RAISEABLE > RAISE
RAISED > RAISE
RAISER > RAISE
RAISERS > RAISE
RAISES > RAISE
RAISIN n dried grape
RAISING n rule that moves a constituent from an embedded clause into the main clause
RAISINGS > RAISING
RAISINIER
> RAISINY
RAISINS > RAISIN
RAISINY adj tasting of raisins
RAISONNE adj carefully thought out
RAIT same as > RET
RAITA n Indian dish of chopped cucumber, mint, etc in yogurt
RAITAS > RAITA
RAITED > RAIT
RAITING > RAIT
RAITS > RAIT
RAIYAT same as > RYOT
RAIYATS > RAIYAT
RAJ n (in India) government
RAJA same as > RAJAH
RAJAH n Indian ruler
RAJAHS > RAJAH
RAJAHSHIP > RAJAH
RAJAS > RAJA
RAJASHIP > RAJA
RAJASHIPS > RAJA
RAJES > RAJ
RAKE n tool used for smoothing earth or gathering leaves, hay, etc ▷ vb gather up or smooth with a rake
RAKED > RAKE
RAKEE same as > RAKI
RAKEES > RAKEE
RAKEHELL n dissolute man ▷ adj profligate
RAKEHELLS
> RAKEHELL
RAKEHELLY adj profligate
RAKELIKE adj like a rake

RAKEOFF n share of profits, esp one that is illegal or given as a bribe
RAKEOFFS > RAKEOFF
RAKER n person who rakes
RAKERIES > RAKERY
RAKERS > RAKER
RAKERY n rakish behaviour
RAKES > RAKE
RAKESHAME n old word for someone shamefully dissolute
RAKI n strong spirit distilled from grain
RAKIA n strong fruit-based alcoholic drink popular in the Balkans
RAKIAS > RAKIA
RAKIJA same as > RAKIA
RAKIJAS > RAKIJA
RAKING n (in rugby) offence of scraping an opponent with the studs
RAKINGS > RAKING
RAKIS > RAKI
RAKISH adj dashing or jaunty
RAKISHLY > RAKISH
RAKSHAS same as
> RAKSHASA
RAKSHASA n Hindu demon
RAKSHASAS
> RAKSHASA
RAKSHASES > RAKSHAS
RAKU n type of Japanese pottery
RAKUS > RAKU
RALE n abnormal coarse crackling sound heard on auscultation of the chest
RALES > RALE
RALLIED > RALLY
RALLIER > RALLY
RALLIERS > RALLY
RALLIES > RALLY
RALLIFORM adj of the rail family of birds
RALLINE adj relating to a family of birds that includes the rails, crakes, and coots
RALLY n large gathering of people for a meeting ▷ vb bring or come together after dispersal or for a common cause
RALLYE US variant of
> RALLY
RALLYES > RALLYE
RALLYING > RALLY
RALLYINGS > RALLY
RALLYIST > RALLY
RALLYISTS > RALLY
RALPH vb slang word meaning vomit
RALPHED > RALPH
RALPHING > RALPH
RALPHS > RALPH
RAM n male sheep ▷ vb strike against with force
RAMADA n outdoor eating area with roof but open sides
RAMADAS > RAMADA

RAMAKIN same as
> RAMEKIN
RAMAKINS > RAMAKIN
RAMAL adj relating to a branch or branches
RAMATE adj with branches
RAMBLA n dried-up riverbed
RAMBLAS > RAMBLA
RAMBLE vb walk without a definite route ▷ n walk, esp in the country
RAMBLED > RAMBLE
RAMBLER n person who rambles
RAMBLERS > RAMBLER
RAMBLES > RAMBLE
RAMBLING adj large and irregularly shaped ▷ n activity of going for long walks in the country
RAMBLINGS
> RAMBLING
RAMBUTAN n SE Asian tree that has bright red edible fruit
RAMBUTANS
> RAMBUTAN
RAMCAT n dialect word for a male cat
RAMCATS > RAMCAT
RAMEAL same as > RAMAL
RAMEE same as > RAMIE
RAMEES > RAMEE
RAMEKIN n small ovenproof dish for a single serving of food
RAMEKINS > RAMEKIN
RAMEN n Japanese dish consisting of a clear broth containing thin white noodles
RAMENS > RAMEN
RAMENTA > RAMENTUM
RAMENTUM n any of the thin brown scales that cover the stems and leaves of young ferns
RAMEOUS same as
> RAMAL
RAMEQUIN same as
> RAMEKIN
RAMEQUINS
> RAMEQUIN
RAMET n any of the individuals in a group of clones
RAMETS > RAMET
RAMI same as > RAMIE
RAMIE n woody Asian shrub with broad leaves
RAMIES > RAMIE
RAMIFIED > RAMIFY
RAMIFIES > RAMIFY
RAMIFORM adj having a branchlike shape
RAMIFY vb become complex
RAMIFYING > RAMIFY
RAMILIE same as
> RAMILLIE
RAMILIES > RAMILIE
RAMILLIE n wig with a plait at the back fashionable in the 18th century
RAMILLIES > RAMILLIE

RAMIN n swamp-growing tree found in Malaysia and Indonesia
RAMINS > RAMIN
RAMIS > RAMI
RAMJET n type of jet engine
RAMJETS > RAMJET
RAMMED > RAM
RAMMEL n discarded or waste matter
RAMMELS > RAMMEL
RAMMER > RAM
RAMMERS > RAM
RAMMIER > RAMMY
RAMMIES > RAMMY
RAMMIEST > RAMMY
RAMMING > RAM
RAMMISH adj like a ram, esp in being foul-smelling
RAMMISHLY > RAMMISH
RAMMLE n collection of items saved in case they become useful
RAMMLES > RAMMLE
RAMMY n Scots word for a noisy disturbance or free-for-all ▷ adj like a ram
RAMONA same as
> SAGEBRUSH
RAMONAS > RAMONA
RAMOSE adj having branches
RAMOSELY > RAMOSE
RAMOSITY > RAMOSE
RAMOUS same as > RAMOSE
RAMOUSLY > RAMOSE
RAMP n slope joining two level surfaces ▷ vb (esp of animals) to rush around in a wild excited manner
RAMPAGE vb dash about violently
RAMPAGED > RAMPAGE
RAMPAGER > RAMPAGE
RAMPAGERS > RAMPAGE
RAMPAGES > RAMPAGE
RAMPAGING > RAMPAGE
RAMPANCY > RAMPANT
RAMPANT adj growing or spreading uncontrollably
RAMPANTLY > RAMPANT
RAMPART n mound or wall for defence ▷ vb provide with a rampart
RAMPARTED > RAMPART
RAMPARTS > RAMPART
RAMPAUGE Scots variant of
> RAMPAGE
RAMPAUGED
> RAMPAUGE
RAMPAUGES
> RAMPAUGE
RAMPED > RAMP
RAMPER > RAMP
RAMPERS > RAMP
RAMPICK same as
> RAMPIKE
RAMPICKED > RAMPICK
RAMPICKS > RAMPICK
RAMPIKE n US or dialect word for a dead tree
RAMPIKES > RAMPIKE
RAMPING > RAMP
RAMPINGS > RAMP
RAMPION n European and Asian plant

RAMPIONS > RAMPION
RAMPIRE *archaic variant of* > RAMPART
RAMPIRED > RAMPIRE
RAMPIRES > RAMPIRE
RAMPOLE *same as* > RAMPIKE
RAMPOLES > RAMPOLE
RAMPS > RAMP
RAMPSMAN *n* mugger
RAMPSMEN > RAMPSMAN
RAMROD *n* long thin rod used for cleaning the barrel of a gun ▷ *adj* (of someone's posture) very straight and upright ▷ *vb* drive
RAMRODDED > RAMROD
RAMRODS > RAMROD
RAMS > RAM
RAMSHORN *n* any of various freshwater snails
RAMSHORNS > RAMSHORN
RAMSON *n* type of garlic
RAMSONS > RAMSON
RAMSTAM *adv* headlong ▷ *adj* headlong
RAMTIL *n* African plant grown in India esp for its oil
RAMTILLA *same as* > RAMTIL
RAMTILLAS > RAMTILLA
RAMTILS > RAMTIL
RAMULAR *adj* relating to a branch or branches
RAMULI > RAMULUS
RAMULOSE *adj* (of the parts or organs of animals and plants) having many small branches
RAMULOUS *same as* > RAMULOSE
RAMULUS *n* small branch
RAMUS *n* barb of a bird's feather
RAN > RUN
RANA *n* genus of frogs
RANARIAN *adj* of or relating to frogs
RANARIUM *n* place for keeping frogs
RANARIUMS > RANARIUM
RANAS > RANA
RANCE *Scots word for* > PROP
RANCED > RANCE
RANCEL *vb* (in Shetland and Orkney) carry out a search
RANCELLED > RANCEL
RANCELS > RANCEL
RANCES > RANCE
RANCH *n* large cattle farm in the American West ▷ *vb* run a ranch
RANCHED > RANCH
RANCHER *n* person who owns, manages, or works on a ranch
RANCHERA *n* type of Mexican country music
RANCHERAS > RANCHERA

RANCHERIA *n* Native American settlement or home of a rancher
RANCHERIE *n* (in British Columbia, Canada) a settlement of Native Americans, esp on a reserve
RANCHERO *another word for* > RANCHER
RANCHEROS > RANCHERO
RANCHERS > RANCHER
RANCHES > RANCH
RANCHETTE *n* small ranch
RANCHING > RANCH
RANCHINGS > RANCH
RANCHLAND *n* land occupied by a ranch
RANCHLESS > RANCH
RANCHLIKE > RANCH
RANCHMAN *n* man who owns, manages, or works on a ranch
RANCHMEN > RANCHMAN
RANCHO *n* hut or group of huts for housing ranch workers
RANCHOS > RANCHO
RANCID *adj* (of butter, bacon, etc) stale and having an offensive smell
RANCIDER > RANCID
RANCIDEST > RANCID
RANCIDITY > RANCID
RANCIDLY > RANCID
RANCING > RANCE
RANCOR *same as* > RANCOUR
RANCORED > RANCOR
RANCOROUS > RANCOUR
RANCORS > RANCOR
RANCOUR *n* deep bitter hate
RANCOURED > RANCOUR
RANCOURS > RANCOUR
RAND *n* leather strip on the heel of a shoe ▷ *vb* cut into rands
RANDAN *n* boat rowed by three people
RANDANS > RANDAN
RANDED > RAND
RANDEM *adv* with three horses harnessed together as a team ▷ *n* carriage or team of horses so driven
RANDEMS > RANDEM
RANDIE *same as* > RANDY
RANDIER > RANDY
RANDIES > RANDY
RANDIEST > RANDY
RANDILY > RANDY
RANDINESS > RANDY
RANDING > RAND
RANDLORD *n* mining magnate during the 19th-century gold boom in Johannesburg
RANDLORDS > RANDLORD
RANDOM *adj* made or done by chance or without a plan ▷ *n* (in mining) the course of a vein of ore
RANDOMISE *same as* > RANDOMIZE

RANDOMIZE *vb* set up (a selection process, sample, etc) in a deliberately random way in order to enhance the statistical validity of results
RANDOMLY > RANDOM
RANDOMS > RANDOM
RANDON *old variant of* > RANDOM
RANDONS > RANDON
RANDS > RAND
RANDY *adj* rude or reckless ▷ *n* rude or reckless person
RANEE *same as* > RANI
RANEES > RANEE
RANG *n* (Scot) rank
RANGA *n* Australian derogatory term for a person with red hair
RANGAS > RANGA
RANGATIRA *n* Māori chief
RANGE *n* limits of effectiveness or variation ▷ *vb* vary between one point and another
RANGED > RANGE
RANGELAND *n* land that naturally produces forage plants suitable for grazing but where rainfall is too low or erratic for growing crops
RANGER *n* official in charge of a nature reserve etc
RANGERS > RANGER
RANGES > RANGE
RANGI *n* sky
RANGIER > RANGY
RANGIEST > RANGY
RANGILY > RANGY
RANGINESS > RANGY
RANGING > RANGE
RANGINGS > RANGE
RANGIORA *n* evergreen New Zealand shrub or small tree
RANGIORAS > RANGIORA
RANGIS > RANGI
RANGOLI *n* traditional Indian ground decoration
RANGOLIS > RANGOLI
RANGS > RANG
RANGY *adj* having long slender limbs
RANI *n* wife or widow of a rajah
RANID *n* frog
RANIDS > RANID
RANIFORM *adj* froglike
RANINE *adj* relating to frogs
RANIS > RANI
RANK *n* relative place or position ▷ *vb* have a specific rank or position ▷ *adj* complete or absolute
RANKE *archaic variant of* > RANK
RANKED > RANK
RANKER *n* soldier in the ranks
RANKERS > RANKER
RANKES > RANKE
RANKEST > RANK

RANKING *adj* prominent ▷ *n* position on a scale
RANKINGS > RANKING
RANKISH *adj* old word meaning rather rank
RANKISM *n* discrimination against people on the grounds of rank
RANKISMS > RANKISM
RANKIST *n* person who discriminates on the grounds of rank
RANKISTS > RANKIST
RANKLE *vb* continue to cause resentment or bitterness
RANKLED > RANKLE
RANKLES > RANKLE
RANKLESS > RANK
RANKLING > RANKLE
RANKLY > RANK
RANKNESS > RANK
RANKS > RANK
RANKSHIFT *n* phenomenon in which a unit at one rank in the grammar has the function of a unit at a lower rank, as for example in the phrase *the house on the corner*, where the words *on the corner* shift down from the rank of group to the rank of word ▷ *vb* shift or be shifted from (one linguistic rank to another)
RANPIKE *same as* > RAMPIKE
RANPIKES > RANPIKE
RANSACK *vb* search thoroughly
RANSACKED > RANSACK
RANSACKER > RANSACK
RANSACKS > RANSACK
RANSEL *same as* > RANCEL
RANSELS > RANSEL
RANSHAKLE *Scots word for* > RANSACK
RANSOM *n* money demanded for the release of a kidnapped person ▷ *vb* pay money to obtain the release of a captive
RANSOMED > RANSOM
RANSOMER > RANSOM
RANSOMERS > RANSOM
RANSOMING > RANSOM
RANSOMS > RANSOM
RANT *vb* talk in a loud and excited way ▷ *n* loud excited speech
RANTED > RANT
RANTER > RANT
RANTERISM > RANT
RANTERS > RANT
RANTING > RANT
RANTINGLY > RANT
RANTINGS > RANT
RANTIPOLE *n* reckless person ▷ *vb* behave like a rantipole
RANTS > RANT
RANULA *n* saliva-filled cyst that develops under the tongue
RANULAR *adj* of a cyst under the tongue

RANULAS > RANULA

RANUNCULI pl n plants of the genus that includes the buttercup, crowfoot, spearwort, and lesser celandine

RANZEL same as > RANCEL

RANZELMAN n (in Shetland and Orkney) type of constable

RANZELMEN > RANZELMAN

RANZELS > RANZEL

RAOULIA n flowering plant of New Zealand

RAOULIAS > RAOULIA

RAP vb hit with a sharp quick blow ▷ n quick sharp blow

RAPACIOUS adj greedy or grasping

RAPACITY > RAPACIOUS

RAPE n plant with bright yellow flowers ▷ vb commit violent sexual crime

RAPED > RAPE

RAPER > RAPE

RAPERS > RAPER

RAPES > RAPE

RAPESEED n seed of the oilseed rape plant

RAPESEEDS > RAPESEED

RAPHAE > RAPHE

RAPHANIA n type of ergotism possibly resulting from consumption of radish seeds

RAPHANIAS > RAPHANIA

RAPHE n elongated ridge of conducting tissue along the side of certain seeds

RAPHES > RAPHE

RAPHIA same as > RAFFIA

RAPHIAS > RAPHIA

RAPHIDE n needle-shaped crystal that occurs in many plant cells

RAPHIDES > RAPHIDE

RAPHIS same as > RAPHIDE

RAPID adj quick, swift

RAPIDER > RAPID

RAPIDEST > RAPID

RAPIDITY > RAPID

RAPIDLY > RAPID

RAPIDNESS > RAPID

RAPIDS pl n part of a river with a fast, turbulent current

RAPIER n fine-bladed sword

RAPIERED adj carrying a rapier

RAPIERS > RAPIER

RAPINE n pillage or plundering

RAPINES > RAPINE

RAPING > RAPE

RAPINI n type of leafy vegetable

RAPINIS > RAPINI

RAPIST n person who commits rape

RAPISTS > RAPIST

RAPLOCH n Scots word for homespun woollen material ▷ adj Scots word meaning coarse or homemade

RAPLOCHS > RAPLOCH

RAPPAREE n Irish irregular soldier of the late 17th century

RAPPAREES > RAPPAREE

RAPPE n Arcadian dish of grated potatoes and pork or chicken

RAPPED > RAP

RAPPEE n moist English snuff of the 18th and 19th centuries

RAPPEES > RAPPEE

RAPPEL n (formerly) a drumbeat to call soldiers to arms ▷ vb abseil

RAPPELED > RAPPEL

RAPPELING > RAPPEL

RAPPELLED > RAPPEL

RAPPELS > RAPPEL

RAPPEN n Swiss coin equal to one hundredth of a franc

RAPPER n something used for rapping, such as a knocker on a door

RAPPERS > RAPPER

RAPPES > RAPPE

RAPPING > RAP

RAPPINGS > RAP

RAPPINI same as > RAPINI

RAPPORT n harmony or agreement

RAPPORTS > RAPPORT

RAPS > RAP

RAPT adj engrossed or spellbound

RAPTLY > RAPT

RAPTNESS > RAPT

RAPTOR n any bird of prey

RAPTORIAL adj (of the feet of birds) adapted for seizing prey

RAPTORS > RAPTOR

RAPTURE n ecstasy ▷ vb entrance

RAPTURED > RAPTURE

RAPTURES > RAPTURE

RAPTURING > RAPTURE

RAPTURISE same as > RAPTURIZE

RAPTURIST > RAPTURE

RAPTURIZE vb go into ecstasies

RAPTUROUS adj experiencing or manifesting ecstatic joy or delight

RARE adj uncommon ▷ vb rear

RAREBIT n as in Welsh rarebit dish made from melted cheese served on toast

RAREBITS > RAREBIT

RARED > RARE

RAREE n as in raree show street show or carnival

RAREFIED adj highly specialized, exalted

RAREFIER > RAREFY

RAREFIERS > RAREFY

RAREFIES > RAREFY

RAREFY vb make or become rarer or less dense

RAREFYING > RAREFY

RARELY adv seldom

RARENESS > RARE

RARER > RARE

RARERIPE adj ripening early ▷ n fruit or vegetable that ripens early

RARERIPES > RARERIPE

RARES > RARE

RAREST > RARE

RARIFIED same as > RAREFIED

RARIFIES > RARIFY

RARIFY same as > RAREFY

RARIFYING > RARIFY

RARING adj ready

RARITIES > RARITY

RARITY n something that is valuable because it is unusual

RARK vb as in rark up informal New Zealand expression meaning reprimand severely

RARKED > RARK

RARKING > RARK

RARKS > RARK

RAS n headland

RASBORA n often brightly coloured tropical fish

RASBORAS > RASBORA

RASCAILLE n rabble

RASCAL n rogue ▷ adj belonging to the mob or rabble

RASCALDOM > RASCAL

RASCALISM > RASCAL

RASCALITY n mischievous, disreputable, or dishonest character, behaviour, or action

RASCALLY adj dishonest or mean ▷ adv in a dishonest or mean fashion

RASCALS > RASCAL

RASCASSE n any of various fishes with venomous spines on the fins

RASCASSES > RASCASSE

RASCHEL n type of loosely knitted fabric

RASCHELS > RASCHEL

RASE same as > RAZE

RASED > RASE

RASER > RASE

RASERS > RASE

RASES > RASE

RASH adj hasty, reckless, or incautious ▷ n eruption of spots or patches on the skin ▷ vb (in old usage) cut

RASHED > RASH

RASHER n thin slice of bacon

RASHERS > RASHER

RASHES > RASH

RASHEST > RASH

RASHIE n protective shirt worn by surfers

RASHIES > RASHIE

RASHING > RASH

RASHLIKE > RASH

RASHLY > RASH

RASHNESS > RASH

RASING > RASE

RASMALAI n Indian dessert made from cheese, milk, and almonds

RASMALAIS > RASMALAI

RASORIAL adj (of birds such as domestic poultry) adapted for scratching the ground for food

RASP n harsh grating noise ▷ vb speak in a grating voice

RASPATORY n surgical instrument for abrading

RASPBERRY n red juicy edible berry

RASPED > RASP

RASPER > RASP

RASPERS > RASP

RASPIER > RASPY

RASPIEST > RASPY

RASPINESS > RASPY

RASPING adj (esp of a noise) harsh or grating

RASPINGLY > RASPING

RASPINGS pl n browned breadcrumbs for coating fish and other foods before frying, baking, etc

RASPISH > RASP

RASPS > RASP

RASPY same as > RASPING

RASSE n small S Asian civet

RASSES > RASSE

RASSLE dialect variant of > WRESTLE

RASSLED > RASSLE

RASSLER n wrestler

RASSLERS > RASSLER

RASSLES > RASSLE

RASSLING > RASSLE

RAST archaic past form of > RACE

RASTA adj rastafarian

RASTAFARI n Jamaican religious movement ▷ adj of or relating to the rastafari movement

RASTER n image consisting of rows of pixel information ▷ vb turn a digital image into a large picture

RASTERED > RASTER

RASTERING > RASTER

RASTERISE same as > RASTERIZE

RASTERIZE vb (in computing) convert into pixels for screen output

RASTERS > RASTER

RASTRUM n pen for drawing the five lines of a musical stave simultaneously

RASTRUMS > RASTRUM

RASURE n scraping

RASURES > RASURE
RAT n small rodent ⊳ vb inform (on)
RATA n New Zealand hardwood forest tree
RATABLE adj able to be rated or evaluated ⊳ n something that can be rated or evaluated
RATABLES pl n property that is liable to rates
RATABLY > RATABLE
RATAFEE same as > RATAFIA
RATAFEES > RATAFEE
RATAFIA n liqueur made from fruit
RATAFIAS > RATAFIA
RATAL n amount on which rates are assessed ⊳ adj of or relating to rates (local taxation)
RATALS > RATAL
RATAN same as > RATTAN
RATANIES > RATANY
RATANS > RATAN
RATANY n flowering desert shrub
RATAPLAN n drumming sound ⊳ vb drum
RATAPLANS > RATAPLAN
RATAS > RATA
RATATAT n sound of knocking on a door
RATATATS > RATATAT
RATBAG n insulting term for an eccentric or unreliable person
RATBAGS > RATBAG
RATBITE n as in ratbite fever acute infectious disease that can be caught from rats
RATCH same as > RATCHET
RATCHED > RATCH
RATCHES > RATCH
RATCHET n set of teeth on a bar or wheel allowing motion in one direction only ⊳ vb move using or as if using a ratchet system
RATCHETED > RATCHET
RATCHETS > RATCHET
RATCHING > RATCH
RATE n degree of speed or progress ⊳ vb consider or value
RATEABLE same as > RATABLE
RATEABLES > RATEABLE
RATEABLY > RATEABLE
RATED > RATE
RATEEN same as > RATINE
RATEENS > RATEEN
RATEL n large African and S Asian musteline mammal
RATELS > RATEL
RATEMETER n device for counting and averaging the number of events in a given time
RATEPAYER n person who pays local rates on a building

RATER > RATE
RATERS > RATE
RATES pl n (in some countries) a tax on property levied by a local authority
RATFINK n contemptible or undesirable person
RATFINKS > RATFINK
RATFISH n deep-sea fish with a whiplike tail
RATFISHES > RATFISH
RATH same as > RATHE
RATHA n (in India) a four-wheeled carriage drawn by horses or bullocks
RATHAS > RATHA
RATHE adj blossoming or ripening early in the season
RATHER adv to some extent ⊳ interj expression of strong affirmation, often in answer to a question
RATHEREST adv archaic word equivalent to soonest
RATHERIPE same as > RATHRIPE
RATHERISH adv (in informal English) quite or fairly
RATHEST adv dialect or archaic word meaning soonest
RATHOLE n rat's hiding place or burrow
RATHOLES > RATHOLE
RATHOUSE n Australian slang term for a psychiatric hospital
RATHOUSES > RATHOUSE
RATHRIPE adj dialect word meaning mature or ripe ahead of time ⊳ n variety of apple or other fruit that is quick to ripen
RATHRIPES > RATHRIPE
RATHS > RATH
RATICIDE n rat poison
RATICIDES > RATICIDE
RATIFIED > RATIFY
RATIFIER > RATIFY
RATIFIERS > RATIFY
RATIFIES > RATIFY
RATIFY vb give formal approval to
RATIFYING > RATIFY
RATINE n coarse loosely woven cloth
RATINES > RATINE
RATING n valuation or assessment
RATINGS > RATING
RATIO n relationship between two numbers or amounts expressed as a proportion
RATION n fixed allowance of food etc ⊳ vb limit to a certain amount per person
RATIONAL adj reasonable, sensible ⊳ n rational number

RATIONALE n reason for an action or decision
RATIONALS > RATIONAL
RATIONED > RATION
RATIONING n act of restricting the use or consumption of certain things
RATIONS pl n fixed daily allowance of food
RATIOS > RATIO
RATITE adj (of flightless birds) having a breastbone that lacks a keel ⊳ n bird that belongs to this group
RATITES > RATITE
RATLIKE > RAT
RATLIN same as > RATLINE
RATLINE n light line tied across the shrouds of a sailing vessel
RATLINES > RATLINE
RATLING n young rat
RATLINGS > RATLING
RATLINS > RATLIN
RATO n rocket-assisted take-off
RATOO same as > RATU
RATOON n new shoot that grows from near the root or crown of crop plants ⊳ vb propagate by such a growth
RATOONED > RATOON
RATOONER n plant that spreads by ratooning
RATOONERS > RATOONER
RATOONING > RATOON
RATOONS > RATOON
RATOOS > RATOO
RATOS > RATO
RATPACK n members of the press who pursue celebrities
RATPACKS > RATPACK
RATPROOF adj impenetrable by rats
RATS > RAT
RATSBANE n rat poison, esp arsenic oxide
RATSBANES > RATSBANE
RATTAIL n type of fish
RATTAILED adj having a tail like a rat
RATTAILS > RATTAIL
RATTAN n climbing palm with jointed stems used for canes
RATTANS > RATTAN
RATTED > RAT
RATTEEN same as > RATINE
RATTEENS > RATTEEN
RATTEN vb sabotage or steal tools in order to disrupt the work of
RATTENED > RATTEN
RATTENER > RATTEN
RATTENERS > RATTEN
RATTENING > RATTEN
RATTENS > RATTEN
RATTER n dog or cat that catches and kills rats
RATTERIES > RATTERY

RATTERS > RATTER
RATTERY n rats' dwelling area
RATTIER > RATTY
RATTIEST > RATTY
RATTILY > RATTY
RATTINESS > RATTY
RATTING > RAT
RATTINGS > RAT
RATTISH adj of, resembling, or infested with rats
RATTLE vb give out a succession of short sharp sounds ⊳ n short sharp sound
RATTLEBAG n rattle made out of a bag containing a variety of different things
RATTLEBOX n any of various tropical and subtropical leguminous plants which have inflated pods within which the seeds rattle
RATTLED > RATTLE
RATTLER n something that rattles
RATTLERS > RATTLER
RATTLES > RATTLE
RATTLIER > RATTLY
RATTLIEST > RATTLY
RATTLIN same as > RATLINE
RATTLINE same as > RATLINE
RATTLINES > RATTLINE
RATTLING adv exceptionally, very ⊳ n succession of short sharp sounds
RATTLINGS > RATTLING
RATTLINS > RATTLIN
RATTLY adj having a rattle
RATTON n dialect word for a little rat
RATTONS > RATTON
RATTOON same as > RATOON
RATTOONED > RATTOON
RATTOONS > RATTOON
RATTRAP n device for catching rats
RATTRAPS > RATTRAP
RATTY adj bad-tempered, irritable
RATU n title used by Fijian chiefs or nobles
RATUS > RATU
RAUCID adj raucous
RAUCITIES > RAUCOUS
RAUCITY > RAUCOUS
RAUCLE adj Scots word for rough or tough
RAUCLER > RAUCLE
RAUCLEST > RAUCLE
RAUCOUS adj hoarse or harsh
RAUCOUSLY > RAUCOUS
RAUGHT archaic past form of > REACH
RAUN n fish roe or spawn
RAUNCH n lack of polish or refinement ⊳ vb behave in a raunchy manner

r

RAUNCHED > RAUNCH
RAUNCHES > RAUNCH
RAUNCHIER > RAUNCHY
RAUNCHILY > RAUNCHY
RAUNCHING > RAUNCH
RAUNCHY adj earthy, sexy
RAUNGE archaic word for > RANGE
RAUNGED > RAUNGE
RAUNGES > RAUNGE
RAUNGING > RAUNGE
RAUNS > RAUN
RAUPATU n confiscation or seizure of land
RAUPATUS > RAUPATU
RAUPO n New Zealand bulrush
RAUPOS > RAUPO
RAURIKI n any of various plants with prickly leaves
RAURIKIS > RAURIKI
RAUWOLFIA n tropical tree or shrub
RAV n Hebrew word for rabbi
RAVAGE vb cause extensive damage to ▷ n destructive action
RAVAGED > RAVAGE
RAVAGER > RAVAGE
RAVAGERS > RAVAGE
RAVAGES > RAVAGE
RAVAGING > RAVAGE
RAVE vb talk wildly or with enthusiasm ▷ n enthusiastically good review
RAVED > RAVE
RAVEL vb tangle or become entangled ▷ n tangle or complication
RAVELED > RAVEL
RAVELER > RAVEL
RAVELERS > RAVEL
RAVELIN n outwork having two embankments at a salient angle
RAVELING > RAVEL
RAVELINGS > RAVEL
RAVELINS > RAVELIN
RAVELLED > RAVEL
RAVELLER > RAVEL
RAVELLERS > RAVEL
RAVELLIER > RAVELLY
RAVELLING > RAVEL
RAVELLY adj tangled
RAVELMENT n ravel or tangle
RAVELS > RAVEL
RAVEN n black bird like a large crow ▷ adj (of hair) shiny black ▷ vb seize or seek (plunder, prey, etc)
RAVENED > RAVEN
RAVENER > RAVEN
RAVENERS > RAVEN
RAVENEST > RAVEN
RAVENING adj (of animals) hungrily searching for prey
RAVENINGS pl n rapacious behaviour and activities
RAVENLIKE > RAVEN
RAVENOUS adj very hungry
RAVENS > RAVEN

RAVER n person who leads a wild or uninhibited social life
RAVERS > RAVER
RAVES > RAVE
RAVEY adj characteristic of a rave
RAVIER > RAVEY
RAVIEST > RAVEY
RAVIGOTE n rich white sauce with herbs and shallots
RAVIGOTES > RAVIGOTE
RAVIGOTTE n French salad sauce
RAVIN archaic spelling of > RAVEN
RAVINE n narrow steep-sided valley worn by a stream
RAVINED > RAVIN
RAVINES > RAVINE
RAVING adj delirious ▷ n frenzied, irrational, or wildly extravagant talk or utterances
RAVINGLY > RAVING
RAVINGS > RAVING
RAVINING > RAVIN
RAVINS > RAVIN
RAVIOLI n small squares of pasta with a savoury filling
RAVIOLIS > RAVIOLI
RAVISH vb enrapture
RAVISHED > RAVISH
RAVISHER > RAVISH
RAVISHERS > RAVISH
RAVISHES > RAVISH
RAVISHING adj lovely or entrancing
RAVS > RAV
RAW n as in in the raw without clothes ▷ adj uncooked
RAWARU n New Zealand name for blue cod
RAWARUS > RAWARU
RAWBONE archaic variant of > RAWBONED
RAWBONED adj having a lean bony physique
RAWER > RAW
RAWEST > RAW
RAWHEAD n bogeyman
RAWHEADS > RAWHEAD
RAWHIDE n untanned hide ▷ vb whip
RAWHIDED > RAWHIDE
RAWHIDES > RAWHIDE
RAWHIDING > RAWHIDE
RAWIN n monitoring of winds in the upper atmosphere using radar and a balloon
RAWING (in dialect) same as > ROWEN
RAWINGS > RAWING
RAWINS > RAWIN
RAWISH > RAW
RAWLY > RAW
RAWMAISH n Irish word for foolish or exaggerated talk
RAWN (in dialect) same as > ROWEN
RAWNESS > RAW

RAWNESSES > RAW
RAWNS > RAWN
RAWS > RAW
RAX vb stretch or extend ▷ n act of stretching or straining
RAXED > RAX
RAXES > RAX
RAXING > RAX
RAY n single line or narrow beam of light ▷ vb (of an object) to emit (light) in rays or (of light) to issue in the form of rays
RAYA same as > RAYAH
RAYAH n (formerly) a non-Muslim subject of the Ottoman Empire
RAYAHS > RAYAH
RAYAS > RAYA
RAYED > RAY
RAYGRASS same as > RYEGRASS
RAYING > RAY
RAYLE archaic spelling of > RAIL
RAYLED > RAYLE
RAYLES > RAYLE
RAYLESS adj dark
RAYLESSLY > RAYLESS
RAYLET n small ray
RAYLETS > RAYLET
RAYLIKE adj resembling a ray
RAYLING > RAYLE
RAYNE archaic spelling of > REIGN
RAYNES > RAYNE
RAYON n (fabric made of) a synthetic fibre
RAYONS > RAYON
RAYS > RAY
RAZE vb destroy (buildings or a town) completely
RAZED > RAZE
RAZEE n sailing ship that has had its upper deck or decks removed ▷ vb remove the upper deck or decks of (a sailing ship)
RAZEED > RAZEE
RAZEEING > RAZEE
RAZEES > RAZEE
RAZER > RAZE
RAZERS > RAZE
RAZES > RAZE
RAZING > RAZE
RAZMATAZ n noisy or showy fuss or activity
RAZOO n imaginary coin
RAZOOS > RAZOO
RAZOR n sharp instrument for shaving ▷ vb cut or shave with a razor
RAZORABLE adj able to be shaved
RAZORBACK n another name for the common rorqual
RAZORBILL n seabird of the North Atlantic with a stout sideways-flattened bill
RAZORCLAM n type of mollusc with a long, narrow shell
RAZORED > RAZOR

RAZORFISH n type of mollusc with a long, narrow shell
RAZORING > RAZOR
RAZORS > RAZOR
RAZURE same as > RASURE
RAZURES > RAZURE
RAZZ vb make fun of
RAZZBERRY US variant of > RASPBERRY
RAZZED > RAZZ
RAZZES > RAZZ
RAZZIA n raid for plunder or slaves
RAZZIAS > RAZZIA
RAZZING n act of making fun of someone
RAZZINGS > RAZZING
RAZZLE n as in on the razzle out enjoying oneself or celebrating
RAZZLES > RAZZLE
RE prep concerning ▷ n the second note of the musical scale
REABSORB vb absorb again
REABSORBS > REABSORB
REACCEDE vb accede again
REACCEDED > REACCEDE
REACCEDES > REACCEDE
REACCENT vb accent again
REACCENTS > REACCENT
REACCEPT vb accept again
REACCEPTS > REACCEPT
REACCLAIM vb acclaim again
REACCUSE vb accuse again
REACCUSED > REACCUSE
REACCUSES > REACCUSE
REACH vb arrive at ▷ n distance that one can reach
REACHABLE > REACH
REACHED > REACH
REACHER > REACH
REACHERS > REACH
REACHES > REACH
REACHING > REACH
REACHLESS adj unreachable or unattainable
REACQUIRE vb get or gain (something) again which one has owned
REACT vb act in response (to)
REACTANCE n resistance to the flow of an alternating current caused by the inductance or capacitance of the circuit
REACTANT n substance that participates in a chemical reaction

REACTANTS
> REACTANT
REACTED > REACT
REACTING > REACT
REACTION n physical or emotional response to a stimulus
REACTIONS
> REACTION
REACTIVE adj chemically active
REACTOR n apparatus in which a nuclear reaction is controlled to produce energy
REACTORS > REACTOR
REACTS > REACT
REACTUATE vb activate again
READ vb look at and understand or take in (written or printed matter) ▷ n matter suitable for reading
READABLE adj enjoyable to read
READABLY > READABLE
READAPT vb adapt again
READAPTED > READAPT
READAPTS > READAPT
READD vb add again
READDED > READD
READDICT vb cause to become addicted again
READDICTS
> READDICT
READDING > READD
READDRESS vb look at or discuss (an issue, situation, etc) from a new or different point of view
READDS > READD
READER n person who reads
READERLY adj pertaining to or suitable for a reader
READERS > READER
READIED > READY
READIER > READY
READIES pl n ready money
READIEST > READY
READILY adv promptly
READINESS n state of being ready or prepared
READING > READ
READINGS > READ
READJUST vb adapt to a new situation
READJUSTS > READJUST
README n document which accompanies computer files or software
READMES > README
READMIT vb let (a person, country, etc) back into a place or organization
READMITS > READMIT
READOPT vb adopt again
READOPTED > READOPT
READOPTS > READOPT
READORN vb adorn again
READORNED > READORN
READORNS > READORN
READOUT n act of retrieving information from a computer memory or storage device

READOUTS > READOUT
READS > READ
READVANCE vb advance again
READVISE vb advise again
READVISED
> READVISE
READVISES
> READVISE
READY adj prepared for use or action ▷ vb prepare
READYING > READY
READYMADE adj made for purchase and immediate use by any customer
REAEDIFY vb rebuild
REAEDIFYE same as
> REAEDIFY
REAFFIRM vb state again, confirm
REAFFIRMS
> REAFFIRM
REAFFIX vb affix again
REAFFIXED > REAFFIX
REAFFIXES > REAFFIX
REAGENCY > REAGENT
REAGENT n chemical substance that reacts with another
REAGENTS > REAGENT
REAGIN n type of antibody that is formed against an allergen
REAGINIC > REAGIN
REAGINS > REAGIN
REAIS > REAL
REAK same as > RECK
REAKED > REAK
REAKING > REAK
REAKS > REAK
REAL adj existing in fact ▷ n standard monetary unit of Brazil
REALER > REAL
REALES > REAL
REALEST > REAL
REALGAR n rare orange-red soft mineral
REALGARS > REALGAR
REALIA pl n real-life facts and material used in teaching
REALIGN vb change or put back to a new or former place or position
REALIGNED > REALIGN
REALIGNS > REALIGN
REALISE same as
> REALIZE
REALISED > REALISE
REALISER > REALISE
REALISERS > REALISE
REALISES > REALISE
REALISING > REALISE
REALISM n awareness or acceptance of things as they are
REALISMS > REALISM
REALIST n person who accepts events, etc as they are
REALISTIC adj seeing and accepting things as they really are, practical
REALISTS > REALIST
REALITIES > REALITY

REALITY n state of things as they are
REALIZE vb become aware of or grasp the significance of
REALIZED > REALIZE
REALIZER > REALIZE
REALIZERS > REALIZE
REALIZES > REALIZE
REALIZING > REALIZE
REALLIE old or dialect variant of > REALLY
REALLIED > REALLY
REALLIES > REALLY
REALLOT vb allot again
REALLOTS > REALLOT
REALLY adv very ▷ interj exclamation of dismay, doubt, or surprise ▷ vb (in archaic usage) rally
REALLYING > REALLY
REALM n kingdom
REALMLESS > REALM
REALMS > REALM
REALNESS > REAL
REALO n member of the German Green party with moderate views
REALOS > REALO
REALS > REAL
REALTER vb alter again
REALTERED > REALTER
REALTERS > REALTER
REALTIE n archaic word meaning sincerity
REALTIES > REALTY
REALTIME adj (of a data-processing system) constantly updating to reflect the latest changes in data
REALTONE n audio clip of an original recording, used as a mobile phone ringtone
REALTONES
> REALTONE
REALTOR n estate agent
REALTORS > REALTOR
REALTY n immovable property
REAM n twenty quires of paper, generally 500 sheets ▷ vb enlarge (a hole) by use of a reamer
REAME archaic variant of
> REALM
REAMED > REAM
REAMEND vb amend again
REAMENDED > REAMEND
REAMENDS > REAMEND
REAMER n tool used for smoothing the bores of holes accurately to size
REAMERS > REAMER
REAMES > REAME
REAMIER > REAMY
REAMIEST > REAMY
REAMING > REAM
REAMS > REAM
REAMY Scots for > CREAMY
REAN same as > REEN
REANALYSE vb analyse again
REANALYZE US spelling of
> REANALYSE
REANIMATE vb refresh or enliven (something) again

REANNEX vb annex again
REANNEXED > REANNEX
REANNEXES > REANNEX
REANOINT vb anoint again
REANOINTS
> REANOINT
REANS > REAN
REANSWER vb answer again
REANSWERS
> REANSWER
REAP vb cut and gather (a harvest)
REAPABLE > REAP
REAPED > REAP
REAPER n person who reaps or machine for reaping
REAPERS > REAPER
REAPHOOK n sickle
REAPHOOKS
> REAPHOOK
REAPING n act of reaping
REAPINGS > REAPING
REAPPAREL vb clothe again
REAPPEAR vb appear again
REAPPEARS
> REAPPEAR
REAPPLIED > REAPPLY
REAPPLIES > REAPPLY
REAPPLY vb put or spread (something) on again
REAPPOINT vb assign (a person, committee, etc) to a post or role again
REAPPROVE vb approve again
REAPS > REAP
REAR n back part ▷ vb care for and educate (children)
REARED > REAR
REARER > REAR
REARERS > REAR
REARGUARD n troops protecting the rear of an army
REARGUE vb argue again
REARGUED > REARGUE
REARGUES > REARGUE
REARGUING > REARGUE
REARHORSE n mantis
REARING n act of rearing
REARINGS > REARING
REARISE vb arise again
REARISEN > REARISE
REARISES > REARISE
REARISING > REARISE
REARLY old word for
> EARLY
REARM vb arm again
REARMED > REARM
REARMICE
> REARMOUSE
REARMING > REARM
REARMOST adj nearest the back
REARMOUSE same as
> REREMOUSE
REARMS > REARM
REAROSE > REARISE
REAROUSAL
> REAROUSE
REAROUSE vb arouse again

r

REAROUSED
> REAROUSE
REAROUSES
> REAROUSE
REARRANGE vb organize differently, alter
REARREST vb arrest again
REARRESTS
> REARREST
REARS > REAR
REARWARD adj in the rear ▷ adv towards the rear ▷ n position in the rear, esp the rear division of a military formation
REARWARDS same as > REARWARD
REASCEND vb ascend again
REASCENDS
> REASCEND
REASCENT n new ascent
REASCENTS
> REASCENT
REASON n cause or motive ▷ vb think logically in forming conclusions
REASONED adj well thought out or well presented
REASONER > REASON
REASONERS > REASON
REASONING n process of drawing conclusions from facts or evidence
REASONS > REASON
REASSAIL vb assail again
REASSAILS
> REASSAIL
REASSERT vb assert (rights, claims, etc) again
REASSERTS
> REASSERT
REASSESS vb reconsider the value or importance of
REASSIGN vb move (personnel, resources, etc) to a new post, department, location, etc
REASSIGNS
> REASSIGN
REASSORT vb assort again
REASSORTS
> REASSORT
REASSUME vb assume again
REASSUMED
> REASSUME
REASSUMES
> REASSUME
REASSURE vb restore confidence to
REASSURED
> REASSURE
REASSURER
> REASSURE
REASSURES
> REASSURE
REAST same as > REEST
REASTED > REAST
REASTIER > REASTY
REASTIEST > REASTY
REASTING > REAST
REASTS > REAST
REASTY adj (in dialect) rancid

REATA n lasso
REATAS > REATA
REATE n type of crowfoot
REATES > REATE
REATTACH vb attach again
REATTACK vb attack again
REATTACKS
> REATTACK
REATTAIN vb attain again
REATTAINS
> REATTAIN
REATTEMPT vb attempt again
REAVAIL vb avail again
REAVAILED > REAVAIL
REAVAILS > REAVAIL
REAVE vb carry off (property, prisoners, etc) by force
REAVED > REAVE
REAVER > REAVE
REAVERS > REAVE
REAVES > REAVE
REAVING > REAVE
REAVOW vb avow again
REAVOWED > REAVOW
REAVOWING > REAVOW
REAVOWS > REAVOW
REAWAKE vb awake again
REAWAKED > REAWAKE
REAWAKEN vb emerge or rouse from sleep
REAWAKENS
> REAWAKEN
REAWAKES > REAWAKE
REAWAKING > REAWAKE
REAWOKE > REAWAKE
REAWOKEN > REAWAKE
REB n Confederate soldier in the American Civil War
REBACK vb provide with a new back, backing, or lining
REBACKED > REBACK
REBACKING > REBACK
REBACKS > REBACK
REBADGE vb relaunch (a product) under a new name, brand, or logo
REBADGED > REBADGE
REBADGES > REBADGE
REBADGING > REBADGE
REBAIT vb bait again
REBAITED > REBAIT
REBAITING > REBAIT
REBAITS > REBAIT
REBALANCE vb balance again
REBAPTISE same as > REBAPTIZE
REBAPTISM n new baptism
REBAPTIZE vb baptize again
REBAR n rod providing reinforcement in concrete structures
REBARS > REBAR
REBASE vb set on a new foundation
REBASED > REBASE
REBASES > REBASE
REBASING > REBASE
REBATABLE > REBATE

REBATE n discount or refund ▷ vb cut a rabbet in
REBATED > REBATE
REBATER > REBATE
REBATERS > REBATE
REBATES > REBATE
REBATING > REBATE
REBATO same as > RABATO
REBATOES > REBATO
REBATOS > REBATO
REBBE n individual's chosen spiritual mentor
REBBES > REBBE
REBBETZIN n wife of a rabbi
REBEC n medieval stringed instrument resembling the violin
REBECK same as > REBEC
REBECKS > REBECK
REBECS > REBEC
REBEGAN > REBEGIN
REBEGIN vb begin again
REBEGINS > REBEGIN
REBEGUN > REBEGIN
REBEL vb revolt against the ruling power ▷ n person who rebels ▷ adj rebelling
REBELDOM > REBEL
REBELDOMS > REBEL
REBELLED > REBEL
REBELLER > REBEL
REBELLERS > REBEL
REBELLING > REBEL
REBELLION n organized open resistance to authority
REBELLOW vb reecho loudly
REBELLOWS
> REBELLOW
REBELS > REBEL
REBID vb bid again
REBIDDEN > REBID
REBIDDING > REBID
REBIDS > REBID
REBILL vb bill again
REBILLED > REBILL
REBILLING > REBILL
REBILLS > REBILL
REBIND vb bind again
REBINDING > REBIND
REBINDS > REBIND
REBIRTH n revival or renaissance
REBIRTHER n person who has undergone rebirthing therapy
REBIRTHS > REBIRTH
REBIT > REBITE
REBITE vb (in printing) to give another application of acid
REBITES > REBITE
REBITING > REBITE
REBITTEN > REBITE
REBLEND vb blend again
REBLENDED > REBLEND
REBLENDS > REBLEND
REBLENT same as > REBLEND
REBLOCHON n type of soft French cheese
REBLOOM vb bloom again
REBLOOMED > REBLOOM

REBLOOMER n flower that blooms more than once
REBLOOMS > REBLOOM
REBLOSSOM vb blossom again
REBOANT adj resounding or reverberating
REBOARD vb board again
REBOARDED > REBOARD
REBOARDS > REBOARD
REBOATION n repeated bellow
REBODIED > REBODY
REBODIES > REBODY
REBODY vb give a new body to
REBODYING > REBODY
REBOIL vb boil again
REBOILED > REBOIL
REBOILING > REBOIL
REBOILS > REBOIL
REBOOK vb book again
REBOOKED > REBOOK
REBOOKING > REBOOK
REBOOKS > REBOOK
REBOOT vb shut down and then restart (a computer system)
REBOOTED > REBOOT
REBOOTING > REBOOT
REBOOTS > REBOOT
REBOP same as > BEBOP
REBOPS > REBOP
REBORE n boring of a cylinder to restore its true shape ▷ vb carry out this process
REBORED > REBORE
REBORES > REBORE
REBORING > REBORE
REBORN adj active again after a period of inactivity
REBORROW vb borrow again
REBORROWS
> REBORROW
REBOTTLE vb bottle again
REBOTTLED
> REBOTTLE
REBOTTLES
> REBOTTLE
REBOUGHT > REBUY
REBOUND vb spring back ▷ n act of rebounding
REBOUNDED > REBOUND
REBOUNDER > REBOUND
REBOUNDS > REBOUND
REBOZO n long scarf covering the shoulders and head
REBOZOS > REBOZO
REBRACE vb brace again
REBRACED > REBRACE
REBRACES > REBRACE
REBRACING > REBRACE
REBRANCH vb branch again
REBRAND vb change or update the image of (an organization or product)
REBRANDED > REBRAND
REBRANDS > REBRAND
REBRED > REBREED
REBREED vb breed again
REBREEDS > REBREED

REBS > REB
REBUFF vb reject or snub ▷ n blunt refusal, snub
REBUFFED > REBUFF
REBUFFING > REBUFF
REBUFFS > REBUFF
REBUILD vb build (a building or town) again, after severe damage
REBUILDED archaic past form of > REBUILD
REBUILDS > REBUILD
REBUILT > REBUILD
REBUKABLE > REBUKE
REBUKE vb scold sternly ▷ n stern scolding
REBUKED > REBUKE
REBUKEFUL > REBUKE
REBUKER > REBUKE
REBUKERS > REBUKE
REBUKES > REBUKE
REBUKING > REBUKE
REBURIAL > REBURY
REBURIALS > REBURY
REBURIED > REBURY
REBURIES > REBURY
REBURY vb bury again
REBURYING > REBURY
REBUS n puzzle consisting of pictures and symbols representing words or syllables
REBUSES > REBUS
REBUT vb prove that (a claim) is untrue
REBUTMENT > REBUT
REBUTS > REBUT
REBUTTAL > REBUT
REBUTTALS > REBUT
REBUTTED > REBUT
REBUTTER n defendant's pleading in reply to a claimant's surrejoinder
REBUTTERS > REBUTTER
REBUTTING > REBUT
REBUTTON vb button again
REBUTTONS > REBUTTON
REBUY vb buy again
REBUYING > REBUY
REBUYS > REBUY
REC n short for recreation
RECAL same as > RECALL
RECALESCE vb glow again
RECALL vb recollect or remember ▷ n ability to remember
RECALLED > RECALL
RECALLER > RECALL
RECALLERS > RECALL
RECALLING > RECALL
RECALLS > RECALL
RECALMENT > RECAL
RECALS > RECAL
RECAMIER n shade of pink
RECAMIERS > RECAMIER
RECANE vb cane again
RECANED > RECANE
RECANES > RECANE
RECANING > RECANE
RECANT vb withdraw (a statement or belief) publicly
RECANTED > RECANT

RECANTER > RECANT
RECANTERS > RECANT
RECANTING > RECANT
RECANTS > RECANT
RECAP vb recapitulate ▷ n recapitulation
RECAPPED > RECAP
RECAPPING > RECAP
RECAPS > RECAP
RECAPTION n process of taking back one's property or persons under one's protection without causing a breach of the peace
RECAPTOR > RECAPTURE
RECAPTORS > RECAPTURE
RECAPTURE vb experience again ▷ n act of recapturing
RECARPET vb replace one carpet with another
RECARPETS > RECARPET
RECARRIED > RECARRY
RECARRIES > RECARRY
RECARRY vb carry again
RECAST vb organize or set out in a different way
RECASTING > RECAST
RECASTS > RECAST
RECATALOG vb catalogue again
RECATCH vb catch again
RECATCHES > RECATCH
RECAUGHT > RECATCH
RECAUTION vb caution again
RECCE vb reconnoitre ▷ n reconnaissance
RECCED > RECCE
RECCEED > RECCE
RECCEING > RECCE
RECCES > RECCE
RECCIED > RECCY
RECCIES > RECCY
RECCO same as > RECCE
RECCOS > RECCO
RECCY same as > RECCE
RECCYING > RECCY
RECEDE vb move to a more distant place
RECEDED > RECEDE
RECEDES > RECEDE
RECEDING > RECEDE
RECEIPT n written acknowledgment of money or goods received ▷ vb acknowledge payment of (a bill), as by marking it
RECEIPTED > RECEIPT
RECEIPTOR n person who receipts
RECEIPTS > RECEIPT
RECEIVAL n act of receiving or state of being received
RECEIVALS > RECEIVAL
RECEIVE vb take, accept, or get
RECEIVED adj generally accepted
RECEIVER n part of telephone that is held to the ear

RECEIVERS > RECEIVER
RECEIVES > RECEIVE
RECEIVING > RECEIVE
RECEMENT vb cement again
RECEMENTS > RECEMENT
RECENCIES > RECENT
RECENCY > RECENT
RECENSE vb revise
RECENSED > RECENSE
RECENSES > RECENSE
RECENSING > RECENSE
RECENSION n critical revision of a literary work
RECENSOR vb censor again
RECENSORS > RECENSOR
RECENT adj having happened lately
RECENTER > RECENT
RECENTEST > RECENT
RECENTLY > RECENT
RECENTRE vb centre again
RECENTRED > RECENTRE
RECENTRES > RECENTRE
RECEPT n idea or image formed in the mind by repeated experience
RECEPTION n area for receiving guests, clients, etc
RECEPTIVE adj willing to accept new ideas, suggestions, etc
RECEPTOR n sensory nerve ending that changes specific stimuli into nerve impulses
RECEPTORS > RECEPTOR
RECEPTS > RECEPT
RECERTIFY vb certify again
RECESS n niche or alcove ▷ vb place or set (something) in a recess
RECESSED > RECESS
RECESSES > RECESS
RECESSING > RECESS
RECESSION n period of economic difficulty when little is being bought or sold
RECESSIVE adj receding ▷ n recessive gene or character
RECHANGE vb change again
RECHANGED > RECHANGE
RECHANGES > RECHANGE
RECHANNEL vb channel again
RECHARGE vb cause (a battery etc) to take in and store electricity again
RECHARGED > RECHARGE
RECHARGER > RECHARGE
RECHARGES > RECHARGE

RECHART vb chart again
RECHARTED > RECHART
RECHARTER vb charter again
RECHARTS > RECHART
RECHATE same as > RECHEAT
RECHATES > RECHATE
RECHAUFFE n warmed-up leftover food
RECHEAT n (in a hunt) sounding of the horn to call back the hounds ▷ vb sound the horn to call back the hounds
RECHEATED > RECHEAT
RECHEATS > RECHEAT
RECHECK vb check again
RECHECKED > RECHECK
RECHECKS > RECHECK
RECHERCHE adj refined or elegant
RECHEW vb chew again
RECHEWED > RECHEW
RECHEWING > RECHEW
RECHEWS > RECHEW
RECHIE adj smoky
RECHIP vb put a new chip into (a stolen mobile phone) so it can be reused
RECHIPPED > RECHIP
RECHIPS > RECHIP
RECHLESSE archaic form of > RECKLESS
RECHOOSE vb choose again
RECHOOSES > RECHOOSE
RECHOSE > RECHOOSE
RECHOSEN > RECHOOSE
RECIPE n directions for cooking a dish
RECIPES > RECIPE
RECIPIENT n person who receives something
RECIRCLE vb circle again
RECIRCLED > RECIRCLE
RECIRCLES > RECIRCLE
RECISION n act of cancelling or rescinding
RECISIONS > RECISION
RECIT n narrative
RECITABLE > RECITE
RECITAL n musical performance by a soloist or soloists
RECITALS > RECITAL
RECITE vb repeat (a poem, story, etc) aloud to an audience
RECITED > RECITE
RECITER > RECITE
RECITERS > RECITE
RECITES > RECITE
RECITING > RECITE
RECITS > RECIT
RECK vb mind or care about (something)
RECKAN adj strained, tormented, or twisted ▷ n chain or hook for hanging a pot over a fire
RECKANS > RECKAN
RECKED > RECK
RECKING > RECK

RECKLESS *adj* heedless of danger
RECKLING *dialect word for* > RUNT
RECKLINGS > RECKLING
RECKON *vb* consider or think
RECKONED > RECKON
RECKONER *n* any of various devices or tables used to facilitate reckoning, esp a ready reckoner
RECKONERS > RECKONER
RECKONING *n* counting or calculating
RECKONS > RECKON
RECKS > RECK
RECLAD *vb* cover in a different substance
RECLADDED > RECLAD
RECLADS > RECLAD
RECLAIM *vb* regain possession of ▷ *n* act of reclaiming or state of being reclaimed
RECLAIMED > RECLAIM
RECLAIMER > RECLAIM
RECLAIMS > RECLAIM
RECLAME *n* public acclaim or attention
RECLAMES > RECLAME
RECLASP *vb* clasp again
RECLASPED > RECLASP
RECLASPS > RECLASP
RECLEAN *vb* clean again
RECLEANED > RECLEAN
RECLEANS > RECLEAN
RECLIMB *vb* climb again
RECLIMBED > RECLIMB
RECLIMBS > RECLIMB
RECLINATE *adj* (esp of a leaf or stem) naturally curved or bent backwards so that the upper part rests on the ground
RECLINE *vb* rest in a leaning position
RECLINED > RECLINE
RECLINER *n* armchair with adjustable back
RECLINERS > RECLINER
RECLINES > RECLINE
RECLINING > RECLINE
RECLOSE *vb* close again
RECLOSED > RECLOSE
RECLOSES > RECLOSE
RECLOSING > RECLOSE
RECLOTHE *vb* clothe again
RECLOTHED > RECLOTHE
RECLOTHES > RECLOTHE
RECLUSE *n* person who avoids other people ▷ *adj* solitary
RECLUSELY > RECLUSE
RECLUSES > RECLUSE
RECLUSION > RECLUSE
RECLUSIVE > RECLUSE
RECLUSORY *n* recluse's dwelling or cell
RECOAL *vb* supply or be supplied with fresh coal

RECOALED > RECOAL
RECOALING > RECOAL
RECOALS > RECOAL
RECOAT *vb* coat again
RECOATED > RECOAT
RECOATING > RECOAT
RECOATS > RECOAT
RECOCK *vb* cock again
RECOCKED > RECOCK
RECOCKING > RECOCK
RECOCKS > RECOCK
RECODE *vb* put into a new code
RECODED > RECODE
RECODES > RECODE
RECODIFY *vb* codify again
RECODING > RECODE
RECOGNISE *same as* > RECOGNIZE
RECOGNIZE *vb* identify as (a person or thing) already known
RECOIL *vb* jerk or spring back ▷ *n* backward jerk
RECOILED > RECOIL
RECOILER > RECOIL
RECOILERS > RECOIL
RECOILING > RECOIL
RECOILS > RECOIL
RECOIN *vb* coin again
RECOINAGE *n* new coinage
RECOINED > RECOIN
RECOINING > RECOIN
RECOINS > RECOIN
RECOLLECT *vb* call back to mind, remember
RECOLLET *n* member of a particular Franciscan order
RECOLLETS > RECOLLET
RECOLOR *same as* > RECOLOUR
RECOLORED > RECOLOR
RECOLORS > RECOLOR
RECOLOUR *vb* give a new colour to
RECOLOURS > RECOLOUR
RECOMB *vb* comb again
RECOMBED > RECOMB
RECOMBINE *vb* join together again
RECOMBING > RECOMB
RECOMBS > RECOMB
RECOMFORT *archaic word for* > COMFORT
RECOMMEND *vb* advise or counsel
RECOMMIT *vb* send (a bill) back to a committee for further consideration
RECOMMITS > RECOMMIT
RECOMPACT *vb* compact again
RECOMPILE *vb* compile again
RECOMPOSE *vb* restore to composure or calmness
RECOMPUTE *vb* compute again
RECON *vb* make a preliminary survey
RECONCILE *vb* harmonize (conflicting beliefs etc)

RECONDITE *adj* difficult to understand
RECONDUCT *vb* conduct again
RECONFER *vb* confer again
RECONFERS > RECONFER
RECONFINE *vb* confine again
RECONFIRM *vb* confirm (an arrangement, agreement, etc) again
RECONNECT *vb* link or be linked together again
RECONNED > RECON
RECONNING > RECON
RECONQUER *vb* conquer again
RECONS > RECON
RECONSIGN *vb* consign again
RECONSOLE *vb* console again
RECONSULT *vb* consult again
RECONTACT *vb* contact again
RECONTOUR *vb* contour again
RECONVENE *vb* gather together again after an interval
RECONVERT *vb* change (something) back to a previous state or form
RECONVEY *vb* convey again
RECONVEYS > RECONVEY
RECONVICT *vb* convict again
RECOOK *vb* cook again
RECOOKED > RECOOK
RECOOKING > RECOOK
RECOOKS > RECOOK
RECOPIED > RECOPY
RECOPIES > RECOPY
RECOPY *vb* copy again
RECOPYING > RECOPY
RECORD *n* document or other thing that preserves information ▷ *vb* put in writing
RECORDED > RECORD
RECORDER *n* person or machine that records, esp audio or video material
RECORDERS > RECORDER
RECORDING *n* something, esp music, that has been recorded
RECORDIST *n* person that records
RECORDS > RECORD
RECORK *vb* cork again
RECORKED > RECORK
RECORKING > RECORK
RECORKS > RECORK
RECOUNT *vb* tell in detail
RECOUNTAL > RECOUNT
RECOUNTED > RECOUNT
RECOUNTER *n* narrator of a story
RECOUNTS > RECOUNT
RECOUP *vb* regain or make good (a loss)

RECOUPE *vb* (in law) keep back or withhold
RECOUPED > RECOUP
RECOUPES > RECOUPE
RECOUPING > RECOUP
RECOUPLE *vb* couple again
RECOUPLED > RECOUPLE
RECOUPLES > RECOUPLE
RECOUPS > RECOUP
RECOURE *archaic variant of* > RECOVER
RECOURED > RECOURE
RECOURES > RECOURE
RECOURING > RECOURE
RECOURSE *archaic word for* > RETURN
RECOURSED > RECOURSE
RECOURSES > RECOURSE
RECOVER *vb* become healthy again
RECOVERED > RECOVER
RECOVEREE *n* (in law) person found against in a recovery case
RECOVERER > RECOVER
RECOVEROR *n* (in law) person successfully demanding a right in a recovery case
RECOVERS > RECOVER
RECOVERY *n* act of recovering from sickness, a shock, or a setback
RECOWER *archaic variant of* > RECOVER
RECOWERED > RECOWER
RECOWERS > RECOWER
RECOYLE *archaic spelling of* > RECOIL
RECOYLED > RECOYLE
RECOYLES > RECOYLE
RECOYLING > RECOYLE
RECRATE *vb* crate again
RECRATED > RECRATE
RECRATES > RECRATE
RECRATING > RECRATE
RECREANCE > RECREANT
RECREANCY > RECREANT
RECREANT *n* disloyal or cowardly person ▷ *adj* cowardly
RECREANTS > RECREANT
RECREATE *vb* amuse (oneself or someone else)
RECREATED > RECREATE
RECREATES > RECREATE
RECREATOR > RECREATE
RECREMENT *n* any substance, such as bile, that is secreted from a part of the body and later reabsorbed
RECROSS *vb* move or go across (something) again
RECROSSED > RECROSS
RECROSSES > RECROSS
RECROWN *vb* crown again

RECROWNED > RECROWN

RECROWNS > RECROWN

RECRUIT vb enlist (new soldiers, members, etc) ▷ n newly enlisted soldier

RECRUITAL n act of recruiting

RECRUITED > RECRUIT

RECRUITER > RECRUIT

RECRUITS > RECRUIT

RECS > REC

RECTA > RECTUM

RECTAL adj of the rectum

RECTALLY > RECTAL

RECTANGLE n oblong four-sided figure with four right angles

RECTI > RECTUS

RECTIFIED > RECTIFY

RECTIFIER n electronic device, such as a semiconductor diode or valve, that converts an alternating current to a direct current by suppression or inversion of alternate half cycles

RECTIFIES > RECTIFY

RECTIFY vb put right, correct

RECTION n (in grammar) the determination of the form of one word by another word

RECTIONS > RECTION

RECTITIC > RECTITIS

RECTITIS n inflammation of the rectum

RECTITUDE n moral correctness

RECTO n right-hand page of a book

RECTOCELE n protrusion or herniation of the rectum into the vagina

RECTOR n member of the clergy in charge of a parish

RECTORAL adj of or relating to God's rule or to a rector

RECTORATE > RECTOR

RECTORESS n female rector

RECTORIAL adj of or relating to a rector ▷ n election of a rector

RECTORIES > RECTORY

RECTORS > RECTOR

RECTORY n rector's house

RECTOS > RECTO

RECTRESS same as > RECTORESS

RECTRICES > RECTRIX

RECTRIX n any of the large stiff feathers of a bird's tail

RECTUM n final section of the large intestine

RECTUMS > RECTUM

RECTUS n straight muscle

RECUILE archaic variant of > RECOIL

RECUILED > RECUILE

RECUILES > RECUILE

RECUILING > RECUILE

RECULE archaic variant of > RECOIL

RECULED > RECULE

RECULES > RECULE

RECULING > RECULE

RECUMBENT adj lying down

RECUR vb happen again

RECURE vb archaic word for cure or recover

RECURED > RECURE

RECURES > RECURE

RECURING > RECURE

RECURRED > RECUR

RECURRENT adj happening or tending to happen again or repeatedly

RECURRING > RECUR

RECURS > RECUR

RECURSION n act or process of returning or running back

RECURSIVE > RECURSION

RECURVATE adj bent back

RECURVE vb curve or bend (something) back or down

RECURVED > RECURVE

RECURVES > RECURVE

RECURVING > RECURVE

RECUSAL n withdrawal of a judge from a case

RECUSALS > RECUSAL

RECUSANCE > RECUSANT

RECUSANCY > RECUSANT

RECUSANT n Roman Catholic who did not attend the services of the Church of England ▷ adj (formerly, of Catholics) refusing to attend services of the Church of England

RECUSANTS > RECUSANT

RECUSE vb (in law) object to or withdraw (a judge)

RECUSED > RECUSE

RECUSES > RECUSE

RECUSING > RECUSE

RECUT vb cut again

RECUTS > RECUT

RECUTTING > RECUT

RECYCLATE n recyclable material

RECYCLE vb reprocess (used materials) for further use ▷ n repetition of a fixed sequence of events

RECYCLED > RECYCLE

RECYCLER > RECYCLE

RECYCLERS > RECYCLE

RECYCLES > RECYCLE

RECYCLING n act of recycling

RECYCLIST > RECYCLE

RED adj of a colour varying from crimson to orange and seen in blood, fire, etc ▷ n red colour

REDACT vb compose or draft (an edict, proclamation, etc)

REDACTED > REDACT

REDACTING > REDACT

REDACTION > REDACT

REDACTOR > REDACT

REDACTORS > REDACT

REDACTS > REDACT

REDAMAGE vb damage again

REDAMAGED > REDAMAGE

REDAMAGES > REDAMAGE

REDAN n fortification of two parapets at a salient angle

REDANS > REDAN

REDARGUE vb archaic word for disprove or refute

REDARGUED > REDARGUE

REDARGUES > REDARGUE

REDATE vb change date of

REDATED > REDATE

REDATES > REDATE

REDATING > REDATE

REDBACK n small venomous Australian spider

REDBACKS > REDBACK

REDBAIT vb harass those with leftwing leanings

REDBAITED > REDBAIT

REDBAITER n person who harasses those with leftwing leanings

REDBAITS > REDBAIT

REDBAY n type of tree

REDBAYS > REDBAY

REDBELLY n any of various animals having red underparts

REDBIRD n type of bird, the male of which has bright red plumage

REDBIRDS > REDBIRD

REDBONE n type of American dog

REDBONES > REDBONE

REDBREAST n robin

REDBRICK n provincial British university of relatively recent foundation

REDBRICKS > REDBRICK

REDBUD n American tree with heart-shaped leaves

REDBUDS > REDBUD

REDBUG another name for > CHIGGER

REDBUGS > REDBUG

REDCAP n member of the military police

REDCAPS > REDCAP

REDCOAT n (formerly) a British soldier

REDCOATS > REDCOAT

REDD vb bring order to ▷ n act or an instance of redding

REDDED > REDD

REDDEN vb make or become red

REDDENDA > REDDENDUM

REDDENDO n Scottish legal clause specifying what duties are required in exchange for something

REDDENDOS > REDDENDO

REDDENDUM n legal clause specifying what shall be given in return for the granting of a lease

REDDENED > REDDEN

REDDENING > REDDEN

REDDENS > REDDEN

REDDER > REDD

REDDERS > REDD

REDDEST > RED

REDDIER > REDDY

REDDIEST > REDDY

REDDING > REDD

REDDINGS > REDD

REDDISH adj somewhat red

REDDISHLY > REDDISH

REDDLE same as > RUDDLE

REDDLED > REDDLE

REDDLEMAN same as > RUDDLEMAN

REDDLEMEN > REDDLEMAN

REDDLES > REDDLE

REDDLING > REDDLE

REDDS > REDD

REDDY adj reddish

REDE n advice or counsel ▷ vb advise

REDEAL vb deal again

REDEALING > REDEAL

REDEALS > REDEAL

REDEALT > REDEAL

REDEAR n variety of sunfish with a red flash above the gills

REDEARS > REDEAR

REDECIDE vb decide again

REDECIDED > REDECIDE

REDECIDES > REDECIDE

REDECRAFT n logic

REDED > REDE

REDEEM vb make up for

REDEEMED > REDEEM

REDEEMER > REDEEM

REDEEMERS > REDEEM

REDEEMING adj making up for faults or deficiencies

REDEEMS > REDEEM

REDEFEAT vb defeat again

REDEFEATS > REDEFEAT

REDEFECT vb defect back or again

REDEFECTS > REDEFECT

REDEFIED > REDEFY

REDEFIES > REDEFY

REDEFINE vb define (something) again or differently

REDEFINED > REDEFINE

REDEFINES > REDEFINE

REDEFY vb defy again

REDEFYING > REDEFY

REDELESS > REDE

REDELIVER vb deliver again

REDEMAND vb demand again

r

REDEMANDS
> REDEMAND

REDENIED > REDENY

REDENIES > REDENY

REDENY vb deny again

REDENYING > REDENY

REDEPLOY vb assign to a new position or task

REDEPLOYS
> REDEPLOY

REDEPOSIT vb deposit again

REDES > REDE

REDESCEND vb descend again

REDESIGN vb change the design of (something) ▷ n something that has been redesigned

REDESIGNS
> REDESIGN

REDEVELOP vb rebuild or renovate (an area or building)

REDEYE n inferior whiskey

REDEYES > REDEYE

REDFIN n any of various small fishes with reddish fins that are popular aquarium fishes

REDFINS > REDFIN

REDFISH n male salmon that has recently spawned

REDFISHES > REDFISH

REDFOOT n fatal disease of newborn lambs

REDFOOTS > REDFOOT

REDHANDED adj in the act of doing something criminal, wrong, or shameful

REDHEAD n person with reddish hair

REDHEADED > REDHEAD

REDHEADS > REDHEAD

REDHORSE n type of fish

REDHORSES
> REDHORSE

REDIA n parasitic larva of flukes

REDIAE > REDIA

REDIAL vb dial (a telephone number) again

REDIALED > REDIAL

REDIALING > REDIAL

REDIALLED > REDIAL

REDIALS > REDIAL

REDIAS > REDIA

REDICTATE vb dictate again

REDID > REDO

REDIGEST vb digest again

REDIGESTS
> REDIGEST

REDIGRESS vb digress again

REDING > REDE

REDINGOTE n woman's coat with a close-fitting top and a full skirt

REDIP vb dip again

REDIPPED > REDIP

REDIPPING > REDIP

REDIPS > REDIP

REDIPT archaic past form of > REDIP

REDIRECT vb send in a new direction or course

REDIRECTS > REDIRECT

REDISCUSS vb discuss again

REDISPLAY vb display again

REDISPOSE vb dispose again

REDISTIL vb distil again

REDISTILL US spelling of > REDISTIL

REDISTILS
> REDISTIL

REDIVIDE vb divide again

REDIVIDED
> REDIVIDE

REDIVIDES
> REDIVIDE

REDIVIVUS adj returned to life

REDIVORCE vb divorce again

REDLEG n bird with red legs

REDLEGS > REDLEG

REDLINE vb refuse a loan to (a person or country) because of the presumed risks involved

REDLINED > REDLINE

REDLINER > REDLINE

REDLINERS > REDLINE

REDLINES > REDLINE

REDLINING > REDLINE

REDLY > RED

REDNESS > RED

REDNESSES > RED

REDO vb do over again in order to improve ▷ n instance of redoing something

REDOCK vb dock again

REDOCKED > REDOCK

REDOCKING > REDOCK

REDOCKS > REDOCK

REDOES > REDO

REDOING > REDO

REDOLENCE
> REDOLENT

REDOLENCY
> REDOLENT

REDOLENT adj reminiscent (of)

REDON vb don again

REDONE > REDO

REDONNED > REDON

REDONNING > REDON

REDONS > REDON

REDOS > REDO

REDOUBLE vb increase, multiply, or intensify ▷ n act of redoubling

REDOUBLED
> REDOUBLE

REDOUBLER
> REDOUBLE

REDOUBLES
> REDOUBLE

REDOUBT n small fort defending a hilltop or pass ▷ vb fear

REDOUBTED > REDOUBT

REDOUBTS > REDOUBT

REDOUND vb cause advantage or disadvantage (to)

REDOUNDED > REDOUND

REDOUNDS > REDOUND

REDOUT n reddened vision caused by a rush of blood to the head

REDOUTS > REDOUT

REDOWA n Bohemian folk dance similar to the waltz

REDOWAS > REDOWA

REDOX n chemical reaction in which one substance is reduced and the other is oxidized

REDOXES > REDOX

REDPOLL n mostly grey-brown finch with a red crown and pink breast

REDPOLLS > REDPOLL

REDRAFT vb write a second copy of (a letter, proposal, essay, etc) ▷ n second draft

REDRAFTED > REDRAFT

REDRAFTS > REDRAFT

REDRAW vb draw or draw up (something) again or differently

REDRAWER > REDRAW

REDRAWERS > REDRAW

REDRAWING > REDRAW

REDRAWN > REDRAW

REDRAWS > REDRAW

REDREAM vb dream again

REDREAMED > REDREAM

REDREAMS > REDREAM

REDREAMT > REDREAM

REDRESS vb make amends for ▷ n compensation or amends

REDRESSAL n act of redressing

REDRESSED > REDRESS

REDRESSER > REDRESS

REDRESSES > REDRESS

REDRESSOR > REDRESS

REDREW > REDRAW

REDRIED > REDRY

REDRIES > REDRY

REDRILL vb drill again

REDRILLED > REDRILL

REDRILLS > REDRILL

REDRIVE vb drive again

REDRIVEN > REDRIVE

REDRIVES > REDRIVE

REDRIVING > REDRIVE

REDROOT n yellow-flowered bog plant whose roots yield a red dye

REDROOTS > REDROOT

REDROVE > REDRIVE

REDRY vb dry again

REDRYING > REDRY

REDS > RED

REDSEAR same as
> REDSHORT

REDSHANK n large Eurasian sandpiper with red legs

REDSHANKS
> REDSHANK

REDSHARE n red algae

REDSHIFT n shift in the lines of the spectrum of an astronomical object

REDSHIFTS
> REDSHIFT

REDSHIRE same as
> REDSHARE

REDSHIRT vb take a year out of a sports team

REDSHIRTS
> REDSHIRT

REDSHORT vb become brittle at red-hot temperatures

REDSTART n European bird of the thrush family

REDSTARTS
> REDSTART

REDSTREAK n variety of apple

REDTAIL n variety of bird with red colouring on its tail

REDTAILS > REDTAIL

REDTOP n sensationalist tabloid newspaper

REDTOPS > REDTOP

REDUB vb fix or repair

REDUBBED > REDUB

REDUBBING > REDUB

REDUBS > REDUB

REDUCE vb bring down, lower

REDUCED > REDUCE

REDUCER n chemical solution used to lessen the density of a negative or print

REDUCERS > REDUCER

REDUCES > REDUCE

REDUCIBLE > REDUCE

REDUCIBLY > REDUCE

REDUCING > REDUCE

REDUCTANT n reducing agent

REDUCTASE n any enzyme that catalyses a biochemical reduction reaction

REDUCTION n act of reducing

REDUCTIVE n relating to chemical reduction

REDUCTOR n apparatus in which substances can be reduced

REDUCTORS
> REDUCTOR

REDUIT n fortified part from which a garrison may fight on once an enemy has taken outworks

REDUITS > REDUIT

REDUNDANT adj (of a worker) no longer needed

REDUVIID n type of insect

REDUVIIDS
> REDUVIID

REDUX udj brought back or returned

REDWARE another name for
> KELP

REDWARES > REDWARE

REDWATER n tick-borne disease of cattle

REDWATERS
> REDWATER

REDWING n small European thrush

REDWINGS > REDWING

REDWOOD n giant Californian conifer with reddish bark

REDWOODS > REDWOOD

REDYE vb dye again
REDYED > REDYE
REDYEING > REDYE
REDYES > REDYE
REE n Scots word for walled enclosure
REEARN vb earn again
REEARNED > REEARN
REEARNING > REEARN
REEARNS > REEARN
REEBOK same as > RHEBOK
REEBOKS > REEBOK
REECH vb (in dialect) smoke
REECHED > REECH
REECHES > REECH
REECHIE same as > REECHY
REECHIER > REECHY
REECHIEST > REECHY
REECHING > REECH
REECHO vb echo again
REECHOED > REECHO
REECHOES > REECHO
REECHOING > REECHO
REECHY adj (in dialect) smoky
REED n tall grass that grows in swamps and shallow water
REEDBED n area of wetland with reeds growing in it
REEDBEDS > REEDBED
REEDBIRD n any of several birds that frequent reed beds, esp (in the US and Canada) the bobolink
REEDBIRDS > REEDBIRD
REEDBUCK n buff-coloured African antelope with inward-curving horns
REEDBUCKS > REEDBUCK
REEDE obsolete variant of > RED
REEDED > REED
REEDEN adj of or consisting of reeds
REEDER n thatcher
REEDERS > REEDER
REEDES > REEDE
REEDIER > REEDY
REEDIEST > REEDY
REEDIFIED > REEDIFY
REEDIFIES > REEDIFY
REEDIFY vb edify again or rebuild
REEDILY > REEDY
REEDINESS > REEDY
REEDING n set of small semicircular architectural mouldings
REEDINGS > REEDING
REEDIT vb edit again
REEDITED > REEDIT
REEDITING > REEDIT
REEDITION n new edition
REEDITS > REEDIT
REEDLIKE adj resembling a reed
REEDLING n tawny titlike Eurasian songbird common in reed beds

REEDLINGS > REEDLING
REEDMAN n musician who plays a wind instrument that has a reed
REEDMEN > REEDMAN
REEDS > REED
REEDSTOP n organ stop that controls a rank of reed pipes
REEDSTOPS > REEDSTOP
REEDUCATE vb educate again
REEDY adj harsh and thin in tone
REEF n ridge of rock or coral near the surface of the sea ▷ vb roll up part of a sail
REEFABLE > REEF
REEFED > REEF
REEFER n short thick jacket worn esp by sailors
REEFERS > REEFER
REEFIER > REEFY
REEFIEST > REEFY
REEFING > REEF
REEFINGS > REEF
REEFPOINT n short piece of rope for securing a sail
REEFS > REEF
REEFY adj with reefs
REEJECT vb eject again
REEJECTED > REEJECT
REEJECTS > REEJECT
REEK vb smell strongly ▷ n strong unpleasant smell
REEKED > REEK
REEKER > REEK
REEKERS > REEK
REEKIE same as > REEKY
REEKIER > REEKY
REEKIEST > REEKY
REEKING > REEK
REEKINGLY > REEK
REEKS > REEK
REEKY adj steamy or smoky
REEL n cylindrical object on which film, tape, thread, or wire is wound ▷ vb stagger, sway, or whirl
REELABLE > REEL
REELECT vb elect again
REELECTED > REELECT
REELECTS > REELECT
REELED > REEL
REELER > REEL
REELERS > REEL
REELEVATE vb elevate again
REELING > REEL
REELINGLY > REEL
REELINGS > REEL
REELMAN n (formerly) member of a beach life-saving team operating a winch
REELMEN > REELMAN
REELS > REEL
REEMBARK vb embark again
REEMBARKS > REEMBARK
REEMBODY vb embody again

REEMBRACE vb embrace again
REEMERGE vb emerge again
REEMERGED > REEMERGE
REEMERGES > REEMERGE
REEMIT vb emit again
REEMITS > REEMIT
REEMITTED > REEMIT
REEMPLOY vb employ again
REEMPLOYS > REEMPLOY
REEN n ditch, esp a drainage channel
REENACT vb enact again
REENACTED > REENACT
REENACTOR > REENACT
REENACTS > REENACT
REENDOW vb endow again
REENDOWED > REENDOW
REENDOWS > REENDOW
REENFORCE vb enforce again
REENGAGE vb engage again
REENGAGED > REENGAGE
REENGAGES > REENGAGE
REENGRAVE vb engrave again
REENJOY vb enjoy again
REENJOYED > REENJOY
REENJOYS > REENJOY
REENLARGE vb enlarge again
REENLIST vb enlist again
REENLISTS > REENLIST
REENROLL vb enrol again
REENROLLS > REENROLL
REENS > REEN
REENSLAVE vb enslave again
REENTER vb enter again
REENTERED > REENTER
REENTERS > REENTER
REENTRANT n reentering angle ▷ adj (of an angle) pointing inwards
REENTRIES > REENTRY
REENTRY n return of a spacecraft into the earth's atmosphere
REEQUIP vb equip again
REEQUIPS > REEQUIP
REERECT vb erect again
REERECTED > REERECT
REERECTS > REERECT
REES > REE
REEST vb (esp of horses) to be noisily uncooperative
REESTED > REEST
REESTIER > REESTY
REESTIEST > REESTY
REESTING > REEST
REESTS > REEST
REESTY same as > REASTY
REEVE n local representative of the king in a shire until the early 11th century ▷ vb pass (a

rope or cable) through an eye or other narrow opening
REEVED > REEVE
REEVES > REEVE
REEVESHIP n office of a reeve
REEVING > REEVE
REEVOKE vb evoke again
REEVOKED > REEVOKE
REEVOKES > REEVOKE
REEVOKING > REEVOKE
REEXAMINE vb examine again
REEXECUTE vb execute again
REEXHIBIT vb exhibit again
REEXPEL vb expel again
REEXPELS > REEXPEL
REEXPLAIN vb explain again
REEXPLORE vb explore again
REEXPORT vb export again
REEXPORTS > REEXPORT
REEXPOSE vb expose again
REEXPOSED > REEXPOSE
REEXPOSES > REEXPOSE
REEXPRESS vb express again
REF n referee in sport ▷ vb referee
REFACE vb repair or renew the facing of (a wall)
REFACED > REFACE
REFACES > REFACE
REFACING > REFACE
REFALL vb fall again
REFALLEN > REFALL
REFALLING > REFALL
REFALLS > REFALL
REFASHION vb give a new form to (something)
REFASTEN vb fasten again
REFASTENS > REFASTEN
REFECT vb archaic word for restore or refresh with food and drink
REFECTED > REFECT
REFECTING > REFECT
REFECTION n refreshment with food and drink
REFECTIVE > REFECT
REFECTORY n room for meals in a college etc
REFECTS > REFECT
REFEED > REFEED
REFEED vb feed again
REFEEDING n act or instance of feeding again
REFEEDS > REFEED
REFEEL vb feel again
REFEELING > REFEEL
REFEELS > REFEEL
REFEL vb refute
REFELL > REFALL
REFELLED > REFEL
REFELLING > REFEL

r

REFELS > REFEL
REFELT > REFEEL
REFENCE vb fence again
REFENCED > REFENCE
REFENCES > REFENCE
REFENCING > REFENCE
REFER vb allude (to)
REFERABLE > REFER
REFEREE n umpire in sports, esp soccer or boxing ▷ vb act as referee of
REFEREED > REFEREE
REFEREES > REFEREE
REFERENCE n act of referring
REFERENDA pl n polls to determine the view of the electorate on something; referendums
REFERENT n object or idea to which a word or phrase refers
REFERENTS > REFERENT
REFERRAL > REFER
REFERRALS > REFER
REFERRED > REFER
REFERRER > REFER
REFERRERS > REFER
REFERRING > REFER
REFERS > REFER
REFFED > REF
REFFING n act or instance of refereeing a sports match
REFFINGS > REFFING
REFI n refinancing of a debt
REFIGHT vb fight again ▷ n second or new fight
REFIGHTS > REFIGHT
REFIGURE vb figure again
REFIGURED > REFIGURE
REFIGURES > REFIGURE
REFILE vb file again
REFILED > REFILE
REFILES > REFILE
REFILING > REFILE
REFILL vb fill again ▷ n second or subsequent filling
REFILLED > REFILL
REFILLING > REFILL
REFILLS > REFILL
REFILM vb film again
REFILMED > REFILM
REFILMING > REFILM
REFILMS > REFILM
REFILTER vb filter again
REFILTERS > REFILTER
REFINABLE > REFINE
REFINANCE vb finance again
REFIND vb find again
REFINDING > REFIND
REFINDS > REFIND
REFINE vb purify
REFINED adj cultured or polite
REFINEDLY > REFINED
REFINER n person, device, or substance that removes impurities, etc

REFINERS > REFINER
REFINERY n place where sugar, oil, etc is refined
REFINES > REFINE
REFINING > REFINE
REFININGS > REFINE
REFINISH vb finish again
REFIRE vb fire again
REFIRED > REFIRE
REFIRES > REFIRE
REFIRING > REFIRE
REFIS > REFI
REFIT vb make ready for use again by repairing or reequipping ▷ n repair or reequipping for further use
REFITMENT > REFIT
REFITS > REFIT
REFITTED > REFIT
REFITTING > REFIT
REFIX vb fix again
REFIXED > REFIX
REFIXES > REFIX
REFIXING > REFIX
REFLAG vb flag again
REFLAGGED > REFLAG
REFLAGS > REFLAG
REFLATE vb inflate or be inflated again
REFLATED > REFLATE
REFLATES > REFLATE
REFLATING > REFLATE
REFLATION n increase in the supply of money and credit designed to encourage economic activity
REFLECT vb throw back, esp rays of light, heat, etc
REFLECTED > REFLECT
REFLECTER n archaic word for a critic
REFLECTOR n polished surface for reflecting light etc
REFLECTS > REFLECT
REFLET n iridescent glow or lustre, as on ceramic ware
REFLETS > REFLET
REFLEW > REFLY
REFLEX n involuntary response to a stimulus or situation ▷ adj (of a muscular action) involuntary ▷ vb bend, turn, or reflect backwards
REFLEXED > REFLEX
REFLEXES > REFLEX
REFLEXING > REFLEX
REFLEXION n act of reflecting or the state of being reflected
REFLEXIVE adj denoting a pronoun that refers back to the subject of a sentence or clause ▷ n reflexive pronoun or verb
REFLEXLY > REFLEX
REFLIES > REFLY
REFLOAT vb float again
REFLOATED > REFLOAT
REFLOATS > REFLOAT
REFLOOD vb flood again
REFLOODED > REFLOOD
REFLOODS > REFLOOD
REFLOW vb flow again

REFLOWED > REFLOW
REFLOWER vb flower again
REFLOWERS > REFLOWER
REFLOWING > REFLOW
REFLOWN > REFLY
REFLOWS > REFLOW
REFLUENCE > REFLUENT
REFLUENT adj flowing back
REFLUX vb boil in a vessel attached to a condenser, so that the vapour condenses and flows back in ▷ n act of refluxing
REFLUXED > REFLUX
REFLUXES > REFLUX
REFLUXING > REFLUX
REFLY vb fly again
REFLYING > REFLY
REFOCUS vb focus again or anew
REFOCUSED > REFOCUS
REFOCUSES > REFOCUS
REFOLD vb fold again
REFOLDED > REFOLD
REFOLDING > REFOLD
REFOLDS > REFOLD
REFOOT vb foot again
REFOOTED > REFOOT
REFOOTING > REFOOT
REFOOTS > REFOOT
REFOREST vb replant (an area that was formerly forested) with trees
REFORESTS > REFOREST
REFORGE vb forge again
REFORGED > REFORGE
REFORGES > REFORGE
REFORGING > REFORGE
REFORM n improvement ▷ vb improve
REFORMADE archaic variant of > REFORMADO
REFORMADO n formerly, an officer whose troops have been disbanded
REFORMAT vb format again
REFORMATE n gas formed in certain processes
REFORMATS > REFORMAT
REFORMED > REFORM
REFORMER > REFORM
REFORMERS > REFORM
REFORMING > REFORM
REFORMISM n doctrine or movement advocating reform, esp political or religious reform, rather than abolition
REFORMIST > REFORMISM
REFORMS > REFORM
REFORTIFY vb fortify again or further
REFOUGHT > REFIGHT
REFOUND vb found again
REFOUNDED > REFOUND
REFOUNDER > REFOUND
REFOUNDS > REFOUND
REFRACT vb change the course of (light etc)

passing from one medium to another
REFRACTED > REFRACT
REFRACTOR n object or material that refracts
REFRACTS > REFRACT
REFRAIN n frequently repeated part of a song ▷ vb abstain (from action)
REFRAINED > REFRAIN
REFRAINER > REFRAIN
REFRAINS > REFRAIN
REFRAME vb support or enclose (a picture, photograph, etc) in a new or different frame
REFRAMED > REFRAME
REFRAMES > REFRAME
REFRAMING > REFRAME
REFREEZE vb freeze or be frozen again after having defrosted
REFREEZES > REFREEZE
REFRESH vb revive or reinvigorate, as through food, drink, or rest
REFRESHED > REFRESH
REFRESHEN vb freshen again
REFRESHER n something that refreshes, such as a cold drink
REFRESHES > REFRESH
REFRIED > REFRY
REFRIES > REFRY
REFRINGE formerly used to mean > REFRACT
REFRINGED > REFRINGE
REFRINGES > REFRINGE
REFRONT vb put a new front on
REFRONTED > REFRONT
REFRONTS > REFRONT
REFROZE > REFREEZE
REFROZEN > REFREEZE
REFRY vb fry again
REFRYING > REFRY
REFS > REF
REFT > REAVE
REFUEL vb supply or be supplied with fresh fuel
REFUELED > REFUEL
REFUELING n act of refueling
REFUELLED > REFUEL
REFUELS > REFUEL
REFUGE n (source of) shelter or protection ▷ vb take refuge or give refuge to
REFUGED > REFUGE
REFUGEE n person who seeks refuge, esp in a foreign country
REFUGEES > REFUGEE
REFUGES > REFUGE
REFUGIA > REFUGIUM
REFUGING > REFUGE
REFUGIUM n region that has remained unaltered by a climatic change affecting surrounding regions
REFULGENT adj shining, radiant

REFUND vb pay back ▷ n return of money
REFUNDED > REFUND
REFUNDER > REFUND
REFUNDERS > REFUND
REFUNDING n act or instance of returning money spent
REFUNDS > REFUND
REFURB vb refurbish ▷ n (act or instance of) refurbishment
REFURBED > REFURB
REFURBING > REFURB
REFURBISH vb renovate and brighten up
REFURBS > REFURB
REFURNISH vb furnish again
REFUSABLE > REFUSE
REFUSAL n denial of anything demanded or offered
REFUSALS > REFUSAL
REFUSE vb decline, deny, or reject ▷ n rubbish or useless matter
REFUSED > REFUSE
REFUSENIK n person who refuses to obey a law or cooperate with the government because of strong beliefs
REFUSER > REFUSE
REFUSERS > REFUSE
REFUSES > REFUSE
REFUSING > REFUSE
REFUSION n new or further fusion
REFUSIONS > REFUSION
REFUSNIK same as > REFUSENIK
REFUSNIKS > REFUSNIK
REFUTABLE > REFUTE
REFUTABLY > REFUTE
REFUTAL n act or process of refuting
REFUTALS > REFUTAL
REFUTE vb disprove
REFUTED > REFUTE
REFUTER > REFUTE
REFUTERS > REFUTE
REFUTES > REFUTE
REFUTING > REFUTE
REG n large expanse of stony desert terrain
REGAIN vb get back or recover ▷ n process of getting something back, esp lost weight
REGAINED > REGAIN
REGAINER > REGAIN
REGAINERS > REGAIN
REGAINING > REGAIN
REGAINS > REGAIN
REGAL adj of or like a king or queen ▷ n portable organ equipped only with small reed pipes
REGALE vb entertain (someone) with stories etc ▷ n feast
REGALED > REGALE
REGALER > REGALE
REGALERS > REGALE
REGALES > REGALE

REGALIA pl n ceremonial emblems of royalty or high office
REGALIAN adj royal
REGALIAS > REGALIA
REGALING > REGALE
REGALISM n principle that the sovereign has supremacy in church affairs
REGALISMS > REGALISM
REGALIST > REGALISM
REGALISTS > REGALISM
REGALITY n state or condition of being royal
REGALLY > REGAL
REGALNESS > REGAL
REGALS > REGAL
REGAR same as > REGUR
REGARD vb consider ▷ n respect or esteem
REGARDANT adj (of a beast) shown looking backwards over its shoulder
REGARDED > REGARD
REGARDER > REGARD
REGARDERS > REGARD
REGARDFUL adj showing regard (for)
REGARDING prep on the subject of
REGARDS > REGARD
REGARS > REGAR
REGATHER vb gather again
REGATHERS > REGATHER
REGATTA n meeting for yacht or boat races
REGATTAS > REGATTA
REGAUGE vb gauge again
REGAUGED > REGAUGE
REGAUGES > REGAUGE
REGAUGING > REGAUGE
REGAVE > REGIVE
REGEAR vb readjust
REGEARED > REGEAR
REGEARING > REGEAR
REGEARS > REGEAR
REGELATE vb undergo or cause to undergo regelation, a type of refreezing
REGELATED > REGELATE
REGELATES > REGELATE
REGENCE old variant of > REGENCY
REGENCES > REGENCE
REGENCIES > REGENCY
REGENCY n status or period of office of a regent
REGENT n ruler of a kingdom during the absence, childhood, or illness of its monarch ▷ adj ruling as a regent
REGENTAL > REGENT
REGENTS > REGENT
REGES > REX
REGEST n archaic word for register ▷ vb register
REGESTED > REGEST

REGESTING > REGEST
REGESTS > REGEST
REGGAE n style of Jamaican popular music with a strong beat
REGGAES > REGGAE
REGGAETON n popular music genre from Puerto Rico
REGGO same as > REGO
REGGOS > REGGO
REGICIDAL > REGICIDE
REGICIDE n killing of a king
REGICIDES > REGICIDE
REGIE n government-directed management or government monopoly
REGIES > REGIE
REGIFT vb give (a previously received gift) to someone else
REGIFTED > REGIFT
REGIFTER n person who regifts something
REGIFTERS > REGIFTER
REGIFTING > REGIFT
REGIFTS > REGIFT
REGILD vb gild again
REGILDED > REGILD
REGILDING > REGILD
REGILDS > REGILD
REGILT archaic past form of > REGILD
REGIME n system of government
REGIMEN n prescribed system of diet etc
REGIMENS > REGIMEN
REGIMENT n organized body of troops as a unit of the army ▷ vb force discipline or order on, esp in a domineering manner
REGIMENTS > REGIMENT
REGIMES > REGIME
REGIMINAL adj regimen-related
REGINA n queen
REGINAE > REGINA
REGINAL adj queenly
REGINAS > REGINA
REGION n administrative division of a country
REGIONAL adj. of, characteristic of, or limited to a region ▷ n regional heat of a competition
REGIONALS > REGIONAL
REGIONARY same as > REGIONAL
REGIONS > REGION
REGISSEUR n official in a dance company with varying duties, usually including directing productions
REGISTER n (book containing) an official list or record of things ▷ vb enter in a register or set down in writing

REGISTERS > REGISTER
REGISTRAR n keeper of official records
REGISTRY n place where official records are kept
REGIUS adj as in regius professor Crown-appointed holder of a university chair
REGIVE vb give again or back
REGIVEN > REGIVE
REGIVES > REGIVE
REGIVING > REGIVE
REGLAZE vb glaze again
REGLAZED > REGLAZE
REGLAZES > REGLAZE
REGLAZING > REGLAZE
REGLET n flat narrow architectural moulding
REGLETS > REGLET
REGLORIFY vb glorify again
REGLOSS vb gloss again or give a new gloss to
REGLOSSED > REGLOSS
REGLOSSES > REGLOSS
REGLOW vb glow again
REGLOWED > REGLOW
REGLOWING > REGLOW
REGLOWS > REGLOW
REGLUE vb glue again
REGLUED > REGLUE
REGLUES > REGLUE
REGLUING > REGLUE
REGMA n type of fruit with cells that break open and break away when ripe
REGMAKER n drink taken to relieve the symptoms of a hangover
REGMAKERS > REGMAKER
REGMATA > REGMA
REGNA > REGNUM
REGNAL adj of a sovereign, reign, or kingdom
REGNANCY > REGNANT
REGNANT adj reigning
REGNUM n reign or rule
REGO n registration of a motor vehicle
REGOLITH n layer of loose material covering the bedrock of the earth and moon
REGOLITHS > REGOLITH
REGORGE vb vomit up
REGORGED > REGORGE
REGORGES > REGORGE
REGORGING > REGORGE
REGOS > REGO
REGOSOL n type of azonal soil
REGOSOLS > REGOSOL
REGRADE vb grade again
REGRADED > REGRADE
REGRADES > REGRADE
REGRADING > REGRADE
REGRAFT vb graft again
REGRAFTED > REGRAFT
REGRAFTS > REGRAFT
REGRANT vb grant again
REGRANTED > REGRANT
REGRANTS > REGRANT

r

REGRATE *vb* buy up (commodities) in advance so as to raise their price for resale

REGRATED > REGRATE

REGRATER > REGRATE

REGRATERS > REGRATE

REGRATES > REGRATE

REGRATING > REGRATE

REGRATOR > REGRATE

REGRATORS > REGRATE

REGREDE *vb* go back

REGREDED > REGREDE

REGREDES > REGREDE

REGREDING > REGREDE

REGREEN *vb* green again

REGREENED > REGREEN

REGREENS > REGREEN

REGREET *vb* greet again or return greetings of

REGREETED > REGREET

REGREETS > REGREET

REGRESS *vb* revert to a former worse condition ▷ *n* return to a former and worse condition

REGRESSED > REGRESS

REGRESSES > REGRESS

REGRESSOR > REGRESS

REGRET *vb* feel sorry about ▷ *n* feeling of repentance, guilt, or sorrow

REGRETFUL > REGRET

REGRETS > REGRET

REGRETTED > REGRET

REGRETTER > REGRET

REGREW > REGROW

REGRIND *vb* grind again

REGRINDS > REGRIND

REGROOM *vb* groom again

REGROOMED > REGROOM

REGROOMS > REGROOM

REGROOVE *vb* groove again

REGROOVED > REGROOVE

REGROOVES > REGROOVE

REGROUND > REGRIND

REGROUP *vb* reorganize (military forces) after an attack or a defeat

REGROUPED > REGROUP

REGROUPS > REGROUP

REGROW *vb* grow or be grown again after having been cut or having died or withered

REGROWING > REGROW

REGROWN > REGROW

REGROWS > REGROW

REGROWTH *n* growing back of hair, plants, etc

REGROWTHS > REGROWTH

REGS > REG

REGUERDON *vb* reward

REGULA *n* rule

REGULABLE *adj* able to be regulated

REGULAE > REGULA

REGULAR *adj* normal, customary, or usual ▷ *n* regular soldier

REGULARLY > REGULAR

REGULARS > REGULAR

REGULATE *vb* control, esp by rules

REGULATED > REGULATE

REGULATES > REGULATE

REGULATOR *n* device that automatically controls pressure, temperature, etc

REGULI > REGULUS

REGULINE > REGULUS

REGULISE *variant spelling of* > REGULIZE

REGULISED > REGULISE

REGULISES > REGULISE

REGULIZE *vb* turn into regulus

REGULIZED > REGULIZE

REGULIZES > REGULIZE

REGULO *n* any of a number of temperatures to which a gas oven may be set

REGULOS > REGULO

REGULUS *n* impure metal forming beneath the slag during the smelting of ores

REGULUSES > REGULUS

REGUR *n* black loamy Indian soil

REGURS > REGUR

REH *n* (in India) salty surface crust on the soil

REHAB *vb* help (a person) to readapt to society or a new job ▷ *n* treatment or help given to an addict, etc

REHABBED > REHAB

REHABBER > REHAB

REHABBERS > REHAB

REHABBING > REHAB

REHABS > REHAB

REHAMMER *vb* hammer again

REHAMMERS > REHAMMER

REHANDLE *vb* handle again

REHANDLED > REHANDLE

REHANDLES > REHANDLE

REHANG *vb* hang again

REHANGED > REHANG

REHANGING > REHANG

REHANGS > REHANG

REHARDEN *vb* harden again

REHARDENS > REHARDEN

REHASH *vb* rework or reuse ▷ *n* old ideas presented in a new form

REHASHED > REHASH

REHASHES > REHASH

REHASHING > REHASH

REHEAR *vb* hear again

REHEARD > REHEAR

REHEARING > REHEAR

REHEARS > REHEAR

REHEARSAL *n* preparatory practice session

REHEARSE *vb* practise (a play, concert, etc)

REHEARSED > REHEARSE

REHEARSER > REHEARSE

REHEARSES > REHEARSE

REHEAT *vb* heat or be heated again

REHEATED > REHEAT

REHEATER > REHEAT

REHEATERS > REHEAT

REHEATING > REHEAT

REHEATS > REHEAT

REHEEL *vb* put a new heel or new heels on

REHEELED > REHEEL

REHEELING > REHEEL

REHEELS > REHEEL

REHEM *vb* hem again

REHEMMED > REHEM

REHEMMING > REHEM

REHEMS > REHEM

REHINGE *vb* put a new hinge or new hinges on

REHINGED > REHINGE

REHINGES > REHINGE

REHINGING > REHINGE

REHIRE *vb* hire again

REHIRED > REHIRE

REHIRES > REHIRE

REHIRING > REHIRE

REHOBOAM *n* wine bottle holding the equivalent of six normal bottles (approximately 156 ounces)

REHOBOAMS > REHOBOAM

REHOME *vb* find a new home for (esp a pet)

REHOMED > REHOME

REHOMES > REHOME

REHOMING *n* act of rehoming

REHOMINGS > REHOMING

REHOUSE *vb* provide with a new (and better) home

REHOUSED > REHOUSE

REHOUSES > REHOUSE

REHOUSING > REHOUSE

REHS > REH

REHUNG > REHANG

REHYDRATE *vb* hydrate again

REI *n* name for a former Portuguese coin

REIF *n* Scots word meaning robbery or plunder

REIFTED > REIFY

REIFIER > REIFY

REIFIERS > REIFY

REIFIES > REIFY

REIFS > REIF

REIFY *vb* consider or make (an abstract idea or concept) real or concrete

REIFYING > REIFY

REIGN *n* period of a sovereign's rule ▷ *vb* rule (a country)

REIGNED > REIGN

REIGNING > REIGN

REIGNITE *vb* catch fire or cause to catch fire again

REIGNITED > REIGNITE

REIGNITES > REIGNITE

REIGNS > REIGN

REIK *Scots word for* > SMOKE

REIKI *n* form of therapy to encourage healing or restore wellbeing

REIKIS > REIKI

REIKS > REIK

REILLUME *vb* relight

REILLUMED > REILLUME

REILLUMES > REILLUME

REIMAGE *vb* image again

REIMAGED > REIMAGE

REIMAGES > REIMAGE

REIMAGINE *vb* imagine again

REIMAGING > REIMAGE

REIMBURSE *vb* refund, pay back

REIMMERSE *vb* immerse again

REIMPLANT *vb* implant again

REIMPORT *vb* import (goods manufactured from exported raw materials) ▷ *n* act of reimporting

REIMPORTS > REIMPORT

REIMPOSE *vb* establish previously imposed laws, controls, etc again

REIMPOSED > REIMPOSE

REIMPOSES > REIMPOSE

REIN *vb* check or manage with reins

REINCITE *vb* incite again

REINCITED > REINCITE

REINCITES > REINCITE

REINCUR *vb* incur again

REINCURS > REINCUR

REINDEER *n* deer of Arctic regions with large branched antlers

REINDEERS > REINDEER

REINDEX *vb* index again

REINDEXED > REINDEX

REINDEXES > REINDEX

REINDICT *vb* indict again

REINDICTS > REINDICT

REINDUCE *vb* induce again

REINDUCED > REINDUCE

REINDUCES > REINDUCE

REINDUCT *vb* induct again

REINDUCTS > REINDUCT

REINED > REIN

REINETTE *n* variety of apple

REINETTES
> REINETTE
REINFECT vb infect or contaminate again
REINFECTS
> REINFECT
REINFLAME vb inflame again
REINFLATE vb inflate again
REINFORCE vb give added emphasis to
REINFORM vb inform again
REINFORMS
> REINFORM
REINFUND vb archaic word for pour in again
REINFUNDS
> REINFUND
REINFUSE vb infuse again
REINFUSED
> REINFUSE
REINFUSES
> REINFUSE
REINHABIT vb inhabit again
REINING > REIN
REINJECT vb inject again
REINJECTS
> REINJECT
REINJURE vb injure again
REINJURED
> REINJURE
REINJURES
> REINJURE
REINJURY n further injury
REINK vb ink again
REINKED > REINK
REINKING > REINK
REINKS > REINK
REINLESS > REIN
REINS pl n narrow straps attached to a bit to guide a horse
REINSERT vb insert again
REINSERTS
> REINSERT
REINSMAN n driver in a trotting race
REINSMEN > REINSMAN
REINSPECT vb inspect again
REINSPIRE vb inspire again
REINSTAL same as
> REINSTALL
REINSTALL vb put in place and connect (machinery, equipment, etc) again
REINSTALS
> REINSTAL
REINSTATE vb restore to a former position
REINSURE vb insure again
REINSURED
> REINSURE
REINSURER
> REINSURE
REINSURES
> REINSURE

REINTER vb inter again
REINTERS > REINTER
REINVADE vb invade again
REINVADED
> REINVADE
REINVADES
> REINVADE
REINVENT vb replace (a product, etc) with an entirely new version
REINVENTS
> REINVENT
REINVEST vb put back profits from a previous investment into the same enterprise
REINVESTS
> REINVEST
REINVITE vb invite again
REINVITED
> REINVITE
REINVITES
> REINVITE
REINVOKE vb invoke again
REINVOKED
> REINVOKE
REINVOKES
> REINVOKE
REINVOLVE vb involve again
REIRD Scots word for
> DIN
REIRDS > REIRD
REIS n small branch
REISES > REIS
REISHI n type of mushroom with a shiny cap
REISHIS > REISHI
REISSUE n book, record, etc, that is released again after being unavailable ▷ vb release (a book, record, etc) again after a period of unavailability
REISSUED > REISSUE
REISSUER > REISSUE
REISSUERS > REISSUE
REISSUES > REISSUE
REISSUING > REISSUE
REIST same as > REEST
REISTAFEL same as
> RIJSTAFEL
REISTED > REIST
REISTING > REIST
REISTS > REIST
REITBOK same as
> REEDBUCK
REITBOKS > REITBOK
REITER n soldier in the German cavalry ▷ vb repeat something
REITERANT
> REITERATE
REITERATE vb repeat again and again
REITERED > REITER
REITERING > REITER
REITERS > REITER
REIVE vb go on a plundering raid
REIVED > REIVE
REIVER > REIVE
REIVERS > REIVE
REIVES > REIVE

REIVING n act of going on a plundering raid
REIVINGS > REIVING
REJACKET vb put a new jacket on
REJACKETS
> REJACKET
REJECT vb refuse to accept or believe ▷ n person or thing rejected as not up to standard
REJECTED > REJECT
REJECTEE n someone who has been rejected
REJECTEES
> REJECTEE
REJECTER > REJECT
REJECTERS > REJECT
REJECTING > REJECT
REJECTION > REJECT
REJECTIVE > REJECT
REJECTOR > REJECT
REJECTORS > REJECT
REJECTS > REJECT
REJIG vb reequip (a factory or plant) ▷ n act or process of rejigging
REJIGGED > REJIG
REJIGGER > REJIG
REJIGGERS > REJIG
REJIGGING > REJIG
REJIGS > REJIG
REJOICE vb feel or express great happiness
REJOICED > REJOICE
REJOICER > REJOICE
REJOICERS > REJOICE
REJOICES > REJOICE
REJOICING > REJOICE
REJOIN vb join again
REJOINDER n answer, retort
REJOINED > REJOIN
REJOINING > REJOIN
REJOINS > REJOIN
REJON n bullfighting lance
REJONEO n bullfighting activity in which a mounted bullfighter spears the bull with lances
REJONEOS > REJONEO
REJONES > REJON
REJOURN vb archaic word meaning postpone or adjourn
REJOURNED > REJOURN
REJOURNS > REJOURN
REJUDGE vb judge again
REJUDGED > REJUDGE
REJUDGES > REJUDGE
REJUDGING > REJUDGE
REJUGGLE vb juggle again
REJUGGLED
> REJUGGLE
REJUGGLES
> REJUGGLE
REJUSTIFY vb justify again
REKE same as > RECK
REKED > REKE
REKES > REKE
REKEY vb key again
REKEYED > REKEY
REKEYING > REKEY
REKEYS > REKEY

REKINDLE vb arouse former emotions or interests
REKINDLED
> REKINDLE
REKINDLES
> REKINDLE
REKING > REKE
REKNIT vb knit again
REKNITS > REKNIT
REKNITTED > REKNIT
REKNOT vb knot again
REKNOTS > REKNOT
REKNOTTED > REKNOT
RELABEL vb label again
RELABELED > RELABEL
RELABELS > RELABEL
RELACE vb lace again
RELACED > RELACE
RELACES > RELACE
RELACHE n break
RELACHES > RELACHE
RELACING > RELACE
RELACQUER vb apply a new coat of lacquer to
RELAID > RELAY
RELAND vb land again
RELANDED > RELAND
RELANDING > RELAND
RELANDS > RELAND
RELAPSE vb fall back into bad habits, illness, etc ▷ n return of bad habits, illness, etc
RELAPSED > RELAPSE
RELAPSER > RELAPSE
RELAPSERS > RELAPSE
RELAPSES > RELAPSE
RELAPSING > RELAPSE
RELATA > RELATUM
RELATABLE > RELATE
RELATE vb establish a relation between
RELATED adj linked by kinship or marriage
RELATEDLY > RELATED
RELATER > RELATE
RELATERS > RELATE
RELATES > RELATE
RELATING > RELATE
RELATION n connection between things
RELATIONS pl n social or political dealings between individuals or groups
RELATIVAL adj of or relating to a relative
RELATIVE adj true to a certain degree or extent ▷ n person connected by blood or marriage
RELATIVES
> RELATIVE
RELATOR n person who relates a story
RELATORS > RELATOR
RELATUM n one of the objects between which a relation is said to hold
RELAUNCH vb launch again ▷ n another launching, or something that is relaunched
RELAUNDER vb launder again
RELAX vb make or become looser, less tense, or less rigid

r

RELAXABLE > RELAX
RELAXANT n drug or agent that relaxes, esp one that relaxes tense muscles ▷ adj of, relating to, or tending to produce relaxation
RELAXANTS > RELAXANT
RELAXED > RELAX
RELAXEDLY > RELAX
RELAXER n person or thing that relaxes
RELAXERS > RELAXER
RELAXES > RELAX
RELAXIN n hormone secreted during pregnancy
RELAXING > RELAX
RELAXINS > RELAXIN
RELAY n fresh set of people or animals relieving others ▷ vb pass on (a message)
RELAYED > RELAY
RELAYING > RELAY
RELAYS > RELAY
RELEARN vb learn (something previously known) again
RELEARNED > RELEARN
RELEARNS > RELEARN
RELEARNT > RELEARN
RELEASE vb set free ▷ n setting free
RELEASED > RELEASE
RELEASEE n someone to whom an estate is released or someone released from captivity
RELEASEES > RELEASEE
RELEASER > RELEASE
RELEASERS > RELEASE
RELEASES > RELEASE
RELEASING > RELEASE
RELEASOR n someone releasing an estate to someone else
RELEASORS > RELEASOR
RELEGABLE adj able to be relegated
RELEGATE vb put in a less important position
RELEGATED > RELEGATE
RELEGATES > RELEGATE
RELEND vb lend again
RELENDING > RELEND
RELENDS > RELEND
RELENT vb give up a harsh intention, become less severe
RELENTED > RELENT
RELENTING > RELENT
RELENTS > RELENT
RELET vb let again
RELETS > RELET
RELETTER vb redo lettering of
RELETTERS > RELETTER
RELETTING > RELET
RELEVANCE > RELEVANT
RELEVANCY > RELEVANT

RELEVANT adj connected with the matter in hand
RELEVE n dance move in which heels are off the ground
RELEVES > RELEVE
RELIABLE adj able to be trusted, dependable ▷ n something or someone believed to be reliable
RELIABLES > RELIABLE
RELIABLY > RELIABLE
RELIANCE n dependence, confidence, or trust
RELIANCES > RELIANCE
RELIANT > RELIANCE
RELIANTLY > RELIANCE
RELIC n something that has survived from the past
RELICENSE vb license again
RELICS > RELIC
RELICT n relic
RELICTION n process by which sea water or fresh water recedes over time, changing the waterline and leaving land exposed
RELICTS > RELICT
RELIDE archaic past form of > RELY
RELIE archaic spelling of > RELY
RELIED > RELY
RELIEF n gladness at the end or removal of pain, distress, etc
RELIEFS > RELIEF
RELIER > RELY
RELIERS > RELY
RELIES > RELY
RELIEVE vb bring relief to
RELIEVED adj experiencing relief, esp from worry or anxiety
RELIEVER n person or thing that relieves
RELIEVERS > RELIEVER
RELIEVES > RELIEVE
RELIEVING > RELIEVE
RELIEVO same as > RELIEF
RELIEVOS > RELIEVO
RELIGHT vb ignite or cause to ignite again
RELIGHTED > RELIGHT
RELIGHTS > RELIGHT
RELIGIEUX n member of a monastic order or clerical body
RELIGION n system of belief in and worship of a supernatural power or god
RELIGIONS > RELIGION
RELIGIOSE adj affectedly or extremely pious
RELIGIOSO adj religious ▷ adv in a religious manner ▷ n musical piece meant to be played devotionally

RELIGIOUS adj of religion ▷ n monk or nun
RELINE vb line again or anew
RELINED > RELINE
RELINES > RELINE
RELINING > RELINE
RELINK vb link again
RELINKED > RELINK
RELINKING > RELINK
RELINKS > RELINK
RELIQUARY n case or shrine for holy relics
RELIQUE archaic spelling of > RELIC
RELIQUEFY vb liquefy again
RELIQUES > RELIQUE
RELIQUIAE pl n fossil remains of animals or plants
RELIQUIFY same as > RELIQUEFY
RELISH vb enjoy, like very much ▷ n liking or enjoyment
RELISHED > RELISH
RELISHES > RELISH
RELISHING > RELISH
RELIST vb list again
RELISTED > RELIST
RELISTEN vb listen again
RELISTENS > RELISTEN
RELISTING > RELIST
RELISTS > RELIST
RELIT > RELIGHT
RELIVABLE > RELIVE
RELIVE vb experience (a sensation etc) again, esp in the imagination
RELIVED > RELIVE
RELIVER vb deliver up again
RELIVERED > RELIVER
RELIVERS > RELIVER
RELIVES > RELIVE
RELIVING > RELIVE
RELLENO n Mexican dish of stuffed vegetable
RELLENOS > RELLENO
RELLIE n informal word for a relative
RELLIES > RELLIE
RELLISH (in music) variant of > RELISH
RELLISHED > RELLISH
RELLISHES > RELLISH
RELLO n informal Australian word for a relative
RELLOS > RELLO
RELOAD vb put fresh ammunition into (a firearm)
RELOADED > RELOAD
RELOADER > RELOAD
RELOADERS > RELOAD
RELOADING > RELOAD
RELOADS > RELOAD
RELOAN vb loan again
RELOANED > RELOAN
RELOANING > RELOAN
RELOANS > RELOAN
RELOCATE vb move to a new place to live or work

RELOCATED > RELOCATE
RELOCATEE n someone who is relocated
RELOCATES > RELOCATE
RELOCATOR n program designed to transfer files from one computer to another
RELOCK vb lock again
RELOCKED > RELOCK
RELOCKING > RELOCK
RELOCKS > RELOCK
RELOOK vb look again
RELOOKED > RELOOK
RELOOKING > RELOOK
RELOOKS > RELOOK
RELUCENT adj bright
RELUCT vb struggle or rebel
RELUCTANT adj unwilling or disinclined
RELUCTATE vb be or appear reluctant
RELUCTED > RELUCT
RELUCTING > RELUCT
RELUCTS > RELUCT
RELUME vb light or brighten again
RELUMED > RELUME
RELUMES > RELUME
RELUMINE same as > RELUME
RELUMINED > RELUMINE
RELUMINES > RELUMINE
RELUMING > RELUME
RELY vb depend (on)
RELYING > RELY
REM n dose of ionizing radiation
REMADE n object that has been reconstructed from original materials
REMADES > REMADE
REMAIL vb mail again
REMAILED > REMAIL
REMAILER n internet service that forwards emails anonymously
REMAILERS > REMAILER
REMAILING n act or instance of sending (an email) again
REMAILS > REMAIL
REMAIN vb continue
REMAINDER n part which is left ▷ vb offer (copies of a poorly selling book) at reduced prices
REMAINED > REMAIN
REMAINER n person who remains
REMAINERS > REMAINER
REMAINING > REMAIN
REMAINS pl n relics, esp of ancient buildings
REMAKE vb make again in a different way ▷ n new version of an old film
REMAKER > REMAKE
REMAKERS > REMAKE
REMAKES > REMAKE
REMAKING > REMAKE

REMAN *vb* man again or afresh

REMAND *vb* send back into custody or put on bail before trial

REMANDED > REMAND

REMANDING > REMAND

REMANDS > REMAND

REMANENCE *n* ability of a material to retain magnetization, equal to the magnetic flux density of the material after the removal of the magnetizing field

REMANENCY *archaic variant of* > REMANENCE

REMANENT *adj* remaining or left over ▷ *n* archaic word meaning remainder

REMANENTS > REMANENT

REMANET *n* something left over

REMANETS > REMANET

REMANIE *n* fragments and fossils of older origin found in a more recent deposit

REMANIES > REMANIE

REMANNED > REMAN

REMANNING > REMAN

REMANS > REMAN

REMAP *vb* map again

REMAPPED > REMAP

REMAPPING > REMAP

REMAPS > REMAP

REMARK *vb* make a casual comment (on) ▷ *n* observation or comment

REMARKED > REMARK

REMARKER > REMARK

REMARKERS > REMARK

REMARKET *vb* market again

REMARKETS > REMARKET

REMARKING > REMARK

REMARKS > REMARK

REMARQUE *n* printing mark in the margin of a plate

REMARQUED *adj* having had a remarque put on

REMARQUES > REMARQUE

REMARRIED > REMARRY

REMARRIES > REMARRY

REMARRY *vb* marry again

REMASTER *vb* make a new master audio recording from an earlier recording

REMASTERS > REMASTER

REMATCH *n* second or return game or contest between two players ▷ *vb* match (two contestants) again

REMATCHED > REMATCH

REMATCHES > REMATCH

REMATE *vb* mate (animals) again ▷ *n* finishing pass in bullfighting

REMATED > REMATE

REMATES > REMATE

REMATING > REMATE

REMBLAI *n* earth used for an embankment or rampart

REMBLAIS > REMBLAI

REMBLE *dialect word for* > REMOVE

REMBLED > REMBLE

REMBLES > REMBLE

REMBLING > REMBLE

REMEAD *archaic or dialect word for* > REMEDY

REMEADED > REMEAD

REMEADING > REMEAD

REMEADS > REMEAD

REMEASURE *vb* measure again

REMEDE *archaic or dialect word for* > REMEDY

REMEDED > REMEDE

REMEDES > REMEDE

REMEDIAL *adj* intended to correct or cure

REMEDIAT *archaic word for* > REMEDIAL

REMEDIATE *archaic word for* > REMEDIAL

REMEDIED > REMEDY

REMEDIES > REMEDY

REMEDING > REMEDE

REMEDY *n* means of curing pain or disease ▷ *vb* put right

REMEDYING > REMEDY

REMEET *vb* meet again

REMEETING > REMEET

REMEETS > REMEET

REMEID *archaic or dialect word for* > REMEDY

REMEIDED > REMEID

REMEIDING > REMEID

REMEIDS > REMEID

REMELT *vb* melt again

REMELTED > REMELT

REMELTING > REMELT

REMELTS > REMELT

REMEMBER *vb* retain in or recall to one's memory

REMEMBERS > REMEMBER

REMEN *n* ancient Egyptian measurement unit

REMEND *vb* mend again

REMENDED > REMEND

REMENDING > REMEND

REMENDS > REMEND

REMENS > REMEN

REMERCIED > REMERCY

REMERCIES > REMERCY

REMERCY *vb* archaic word for thank

REMERGE *vb* merge again

REMERGED > REMERGE

REMERGES > REMERGE

REMERGING > REMERGE

REMET > REMEET

REMEX *n* any of the large flight feathers of a bird's wing

REMIGATE *vb* row

REMIGATED > REMIGATE

REMIGATES > REMIGATE

REMIGES > REMEX

REMIGIAL > REMEX

REMIGRATE *vb* migrate again

REMIND *vb* cause to remember

REMINDED > REMIND

REMINDER *n* something that recalls the past

REMINDERS > REMINDER

REMINDFUL *adj* serving to remind

REMINDING > REMIND

REMINDS > REMIND

REMINISCE *vb* talk or write of past times, experiences, etc

REMINT *vb* mint again

REMINTED > REMINT

REMINTING > REMINT

REMINTS > REMINT

REMISE *vb* give up or relinquish (a right, claim, etc) ▷ *n* second thrust made on the same lunge after the first has missed

REMISED > REMISE

REMISES > REMISE

REMISING > REMISE

REMISS *adj* negligent or careless

REMISSION *n* reduction in the length of a prison term

REMISSIVE > REMISSION

REMISSLY > REMISS

REMISSORY *adj* liable to or intended to gain remission

REMIT *vb* send (money) for goods, services, etc, esp by post ▷ *n* area of competence or authority

REMITMENT *n* archaic word for remittance or remission

REMITS > REMIT

REMITTAL > REMIT

REMITTALS > REMIT

REMITTED > REMIT

REMITTEE *n* recipient of a remittance

REMITTEES > REMITTEE

REMITTENT *adj* (of a disease) periodically less severe

REMITTER *n* person who remits

REMITTERS > REMITTER

REMITTING > REMIT

REMITTOR *same as* > REMITTER

REMITTORS > REMITTOR

REMIX *vb* change the relative prominence of each performer's part of (a recording) ▷ *n* remixed version of a recording

REMIXED > REMIX

REMIXER *n* person who remixes a recording

REMIXERS > REMIXER

REMIXES > REMIX

REMIXING > REMIX

REMIXT *informal past form of* > REMIX

REMIXTURE > REMIX

REMNANT *n* small piece, esp of fabric, left over ▷ *adj* remaining

REMNANTAL *adj* existing as remnant

REMNANTS > REMNANT

REMODEL *vb* give a different shape or form to ▷ *n* something that has been remodelled

REMODELED > REMODEL

REMODELER *n* person who remodels

REMODELS > REMODEL

REMODIFY *vb* modify again

REMOISTEN *vb* moisten again

REMOLADE *same as* > REMOULADE

REMOLADES > REMOLADE

REMOLD *US spelling of* > REMOULD

REMOLDED > REMOLD

REMOLDING > REMOLD

REMOLDS > REMOLD

REMONTANT *adj* (esp of cultivated roses) flowering more than once in a single season ▷ *n* rose having such a growth

REMONTOIR *n* any of various devices used in watches, clocks, etc, to compensate for errors arising from the changes in the force driving the escapement

REMORA *n* spiny-finned fish

REMORAS > REMORA

REMORID > REMORA

REMORSE *n* feeling of sorrow and regret for something one did

REMORSES > REMORSE

REMOTE *adj* far away, distant ▷ *n* (in informal usage) remote control

REMOTELY > REMOTE

REMOTER > REMOTE

REMOTES > REMOTE

REMOTEST > REMOTE

REMOTION *n* removal

REMOTIONS > REMOTION

REMOUD *Spenserian variant of* > REMOVED

REMOULADE *n* mayonnaise sauce flavoured with herbs, mustard, and capers, served with salads, cold meat, etc

REMOULD *vb* change completely ▷ *n* renovated tyre

REMOULDED > REMOULD

REMOULDS > REMOULD

REMOUNT *vb* get on (a horse, bicycle, etc) again ▷ *n* fresh horse

REMOUNTED > REMOUNT

REMOUNTS > REMOUNT

REMOVABLE > REMOVE

REMOVABLY > REMOVE

r

REMOVAL n act of removing, esp changing residence

REMOVALS > REMOVAL

REMOVE vb take away or off ▷ n degree of difference

REMOVED adj very different or distant

REMOVEDLY adv at a distance

REMOVER > REMOVE

REMOVERS > REMOVE

REMOVES > REMOVE

REMOVING > REMOVE

REMS > REM

REMUAGE n process of turning wine bottles to let the sediment out

REMUAGES > REMUAGE

REMUDA n stock of horses enabling riders to change mounts

REMUDAS > REMUDA

REMUEUR n person carrying out remuage

REMUEURS > REMUEUR

REMURMUR vb murmur again or murmur in reply

REMURMURS > REMURMUR

REN archaic variant of > RUN

RENAGUE same as > RENEGE

RENAGUED > RENAGUE

RENAGUES > RENAGUE

RENAGUING > RENAGUE

RENAIL vb nail again

RENAILED > RENAIL

RENAILING > RENAIL

RENAILS > RENAIL

RENAL adj of the kidneys

RENAME vb change the name of (someone or something)

RENAMED > RENAME

RENAMES > RENAME

RENAMING > RENAME

RENASCENT adj becoming active or vigorous again

RENATURE vb return to natural state

RENATURED > RENATURE

RENATURES > RENATURE

RENAY vb archaic word meaning renounce

RENAYED > RENAY

RENAYING > RENAY

RENAYS > RENAY

RENCONTRE n unexpected meeting ▷ vb meet, esp under negative circumstances

REND vb tear or wrench apart

RENDANG n spicy Indonesian meat dish

RENDANGS > RENDANG

RENDED > REND

RENDER vb cause to become ▷ n first thin coat of plaster applied to a surface

RENDERED > RENDER

RENDERER > RENDER

RENDERERS > RENDER

RENDERING n act or instance of performing a play, piece of music, etc

RENDERS > RENDER

RENDIBLE > REND

RENDING > REND

RENDITION n performance ▷ vb subject someone to an extrajudicial trial

RENDS > REND

RENDZINA n dark soil found in grassy or formerly grassy areas of moderate rainfall

RENDZINAS > RENDZINA

RENEAGUE same as > RENEGE

RENEAGUED > RENEAGUE

RENEAGUES > RENEAGUE

RENEGADE n person who deserts a cause ▷ vb become a renegade

RENEGADED > RENEGADE

RENEGADES > RENEGADE

RENEGADO archaic word for > RENEGADE

RENEGADOS > RENEGADO

RENEGATE old variant of > RENEGADE

RENEGATES > RENEGATE

RENEGE vb go back (on a promise etc)

RENEGED > RENEGE

RENEGER > RENEGE

RENEGERS > RENEGE

RENEGES > RENEGE

RENEGING > RENEGE

RENEGUE same as > RENEGE

RENEGUED > RENEGUE

RENEGUER > RENEGUE

RENEGUERS > RENEGUE

RENEGUES > RENEGUE

RENEGUING > RENEGUE

RENEST vb nest again or form a new nest

RENESTED > RENEST

RENESTING > RENEST

RENESTS > RENEST

RENEW vb begin again

RENEWABLE > RENEW

RENEWABLY > RENEW

RENEWAL n act of renewing or state of being renewed

RENEWALS > RENEWAL

RENEWED > RENEW

RENEWEDLY > RENEW

RENEWER > RENEW

RENEWERS > RENEW

RENEWING > RENEW

RENEWINGS > RENEW

RENEWS > RENEW

RENEY same as > RENAY

RENEYED > RENEY

RENEYING > RENEY

RENEYS > RENEY

RENFIERST adj archaic word for turned fierce

RENFORCE vb archaic word for reinforce

RENFORCED > RENFORCE

RENFORCES > RENFORCE

RENFORST > RENFORCE

RENGA n type of collaborative poetry found in Japan

RENGAS > RENGA

RENIED > RENY

RENIES > RENY

RENIFORM adj having the shape or profile of a kidney

RENIG same as > RENEGE

RENIGGED > RENIG

RENIGGING > RENIG

RENIGS > RENIG

RENIN n enzyme secreted by the kidneys

RENINS > RENIN

RENITENCE > RENITENT

RENITENCY > RENITENT

RENITENT adj reluctant

RENK adj unpleasant

RENKER > RENK

RENKEST > RENK

RENMINBI same as > YUAN

RENMINBIS > RENMINBI

RENNASE same as > RENNIN

RENNASES > RENNASE

RENNE archaic variant of > RUN

RENNED > REN

RENNES > RENNE

RENNET n substance for curdling milk to make cheese

RENNETS > RENNET

RENNIN n enzyme that occurs in gastric juice

RENNING > REN

RENNINGS > REN

RENNINS > RENNIN

RENO n renovated house

RENOGRAM n X-ray kidney image

RENOGRAMS > RENOGRAM

RENOS > RENO

RENOTIFY vb notify again

RENOUNCE vb give up (a belief, habit, etc) voluntarily ▷ n failure to follow suit in a card game

RENOUNCED > RENOUNCE

RENOUNCER > RENOUNCE

RENOUNCES > RENOUNCE

RENOVATE vb restore to good condition

RENOVATED > RENOVATE

RENOVATES > RENOVATE

RENOVATOR > RENOVATE

RENOWN n widespread good reputation ▷ vb make famous

RENOWNED adj famous

RENOWNER n renown giver

RENOWNERS > RENOWNER

RENOWNING > RENOWN

RENOWNS > RENOWN

RENS > REN

RENT n payment made by a tenant to a landlord or owner of a property ▷ vb grant the right to use one's property for payment

RENTABLE > REND

RENTAL n sum payable as rent ▷ adj of or relating to rent

RENTALLER n (in Scots law) tenant with very favourable terms

RENTALS > RENTAL

RENTE n annual income from capital investment

RENTED > RENT

RENTER n person who lets his or her property in return for rent

RENTERS > RENTER

RENTES > RENTE

RENTIER n person who lives off unearned income such as rents or interest

RENTIERS > RENTIER

RENTING > RENT

RENTINGS > RENT

RENTS > RENT

RENUMBER vb number again or afresh

RENUMBERS > RENUMBER

RENVERSE vb archaic word meaning overturn

RENVERSED > RENVERSE

RENVERSES > RENVERSE

RENVERST > RENVERSE

RENVOI n referring of a dispute to a jurisdiction other than that in which it arose

RENVOIS > RENVOI

RENVOY old variant of > RENVOI

RENVOYS > RENVOY

RENY same as > RENAY

RENYING > RENY

REO n New Zealand language

REOBJECT vb object again

REOBJECTS > REOBJECT

REOBSERVE vb observe again

REOBTAIN vb obtain again

REOBTAINS > REOBTAIN

REOCCUPY vb occupy (a building, area, etc) again

REOCCUR vb happen, take place, or come about again

REOCCURS > REOCCUR

REOFFEND vb commit another offence

REOFFENDS
> REOFFEND
REOFFER vb offer again
REOFFERED > REOFFER
REOFFERS > REOFFER
REOIL vb oil again
REOILED > REOIL
REOILING > REOIL
REOILS > REOIL
REOPEN vb open again after a period of being closed or suspended
REOPENED > REOPEN
REOPENER n clause in a legal document allowing for an issue to be revisited at a subsequent date
REOPENERS
> REOPENER
REOPENING n act of reopening
REOPENS > REOPEN
REOPERATE vb operate again
REOPPOSE vb oppose again
REOPPOSED
> REOPPOSE
REOPPOSES
> REOPPOSE
REORDAIN vb ordain again
REORDAINS
> REORDAIN
REORDER vb change the order of
REORDERED > REORDER
REORDERS > REORDER
REORG vb reorganize
REORGED > REORG
REORGING > REORG
REORGS > REORG
REORIENT vb adjust or align (something) in a new or different way
REORIENTS
> REORIENT
REOS > REO
REOUTFIT vb outfit again
REOUTFITS
> REOUTFIT
REOVIRUS n type of virus
REOXIDISE same as
> REOXIDIZE
REOXIDIZE vb oxidize again
REP n sales representative ▷ vb work as a representative
REPACIFY vb pacify again
REPACK vb place or arrange (articles) again or in a container) again or in a different way
REPACKAGE vb wrap or put (something) in a package again
REPACKED > REPACK
REPACKING > REPACK
REPACKS > REPACK
REPAID > REPAY
REPAINT vb apply a new or fresh coat of paint
REPAINTED > REPAINT
REPAINTS > REPAINT

REPAIR vb restore to good condition, mend ▷ n act of repairing
REPAIRED > REPAIR
REPAIRER > REPAIR
REPAIRERS > REPAIR
REPAIRING > REPAIR
REPAIRMAN n man whose job it is to repair machines, appliances, etc
REPAIRMEN
> REPAIRMAN
REPAIRS > REPAIR
REPAND adj having a wavy margin
REPANDLY > REPAND
REPANEL vb panel again or anew
REPANELED > REPANEL
REPANELS > REPANEL
REPAPER vb paper again or afresh
REPAPERED > REPAPER
REPAPERS > REPAPER
REPARABLE adj able to be repaired or remedied
REPARABLY
> REPARABLE
REPARK vb park again
REPARKED > REPARK
REPARKING > REPARK
REPARKS > REPARK
REPARTEE n interchange of witty retorts ▷ vb retort
REPARTEED
> REPARTEE
REPARTEES
> REPARTEE
REPASS vb pass again
REPASSAGE n passage back or return
REPASSED > REPASS
REPASSES > REPASS
REPASSING > REPASS
REPAST n meal ▷ vb feed (on)
REPASTED > REPAST
REPASTING > REPAST
REPASTS > REPAST
REPASTURE old word for
> FOOD
REPATCH vb patch again
REPATCHED > REPATCH
REPATCHES > REPATCH
REPATTERN vb pattern again
REPAVE vb pave again
REPAVED > REPAVE
REPAVES > REPAVE
REPAVING > REPAVE
REPAY vb pay back, refund
REPAYABLE > REPAY
REPAYING > REPAY
REPAYMENT > REPAY
REPAYS > REPAY
REPEAL vb cancel (a law) officially ▷ n act of repealing
REPEALED > REPEAL
REPEALER > REPEAL
REPEALERS > REPEAL
REPEALING > REPEAL
REPEALS > REPEAL
REPEAT vb say or do again ▷ n act or instance of repeating

REPEATED adj done, made, or said again and again
REPEATER n firearm that may be discharged many times without reloading
REPEATERS
> REPEATER
REPEATING > REPEAT
REPEATS > REPEAT
REPECHAGE n extra heat or test providing second chance to previous losers or failing candidates
REPEG vb peg again
REPEGGED > REPEG
REPEGGING > REPEG
REPEGS > REPEG
REPEL vb be disgusting to
REPELLANT same as
> REPELLENT
REPELLED > REPEL
REPELLENT adj distasteful ▷ n something that repels, esp a chemical to repel insects
REPELLER > REPEL
REPELLERS > REPEL
REPELLING > REPEL
REPELS > REPEL
REPENT vb feel regret for (a deed or omission) ▷ adj lying or creeping along the ground
REPENTANT adj reproaching oneself for one's past actions or sins
REPENTED > REPENT
REPENTER > REPENT
REPENTERS > REPENT
REPENTING > REPENT
REPENTS > REPENT
REPEOPLE vb people again
REPEOPLED
> REPEOPLE
REPEOPLES
> REPEOPLE
REPERCUSS vb have repercussions
REPEREPE n New Zealand word for the elephant fish
REPEREPES
> REPEREPE
REPERK vb perk again
REPERKED > REPERK
REPERKING > REPERK
REPERKS > REPERK
REPERTORY n repertoire
REPERUSAL n fresh perusal
REPERUSE vb peruse again
REPERUSED
> REPERUSE
REPERUSES
> REPERUSE
REPETEND n digit or series of digits in a recurring decimal that repeats itself
REPETENDS
> REPETEND
REPHRASE vb express in different words
REPHRASED
> REPHRASE

REPHRASES
> REPHRASE
REPIGMENT vb pigment again
REPIN vb pin again
REPINE vb fret or complain
REPINED > REPINE
REPINER > REPINE
REPINERS > REPINE
REPINES > REPINE
REPINING > REPINE
REPININGS > REPINE
REPINNED > REPIN
REPINNING > REPIN
REPINS > REPIN
REPIQUE n score of 30 in the card-game piquet ▷ vb score a repique against (someone)
REPIQUED > REPIQUE
REPIQUES > REPIQUE
REPIQUING > REPIQUE
REPLA > REPLUM
REPLACE vb substitute for
REPLACED > REPLACE
REPLACER > REPLACE
REPLACERS > REPLACE
REPLACES > REPLACE
REPLACING > REPLACE
REPLAN vb plan again
REPLANNED > REPLAN
REPLANS > REPLAN
REPLANT vb plant again
REPLANTED > REPLANT
REPLANTS > REPLANT
REPLASTER vb plaster again
REPLATE vb plate again
REPLATED > REPLATE
REPLATES > REPLATE
REPLATING > REPLATE
REPLAY n immediate reshowing on TV of an incident in sport ▷ vb play (a match, recording, etc) again
REPLAYED > REPLAY
REPLAYING > REPLAY
REPLAYS > REPLAY
REPLEAD vb plead again
REPLEADED > REPLEAD
REPLEADER n right to plead again
REPLEADS > REPLEAD
REPLED > REPLEAD
REPLEDGE vb pledge again
REPLEDGED
> REPLEDGE
REPLEDGES
> REPLEDGE
REPLENISH vb fill up again, resupply
REPLETE adj filled or gorged ▷ vb fill again
REPLETED > REPLETE
REPLETELY > REPLETE
REPLETES > REPLETE
REPLETING > REPLETE
REPLETION n state or condition of being replete
REPLEVIED > REPLEVY
REPLEVIES > REPLEVY
REPLEVIN n recovery of goods unlawfully taken

REPLEVINS
> REPLEVIN
REPLEVY vb recover possession of (goods) by replevin
REPLICA n exact copy
REPLICANT n (in science fiction) android indistinguishable from a human being
REPLICAS > REPLICA
REPLICASE n type of enzyme
REPLICATE vb make or be a copy of ▷ adj folded back on itself
REPLICON n region of a DNA molecule that is replicated from a single origin
REPLICONS
> REPLICON
REPLIED > REPLY
REPLIER > REPLY
REPLIERS > REPLY
REPLIES > REPLY
REPLOT vb plot again
REPLOTS > REPLOT
REPLOTTED > REPLOT
REPLOUGH vb plough again
REPLOUGHS
> REPLOUGH
REPLOW vb plow again
REPLOWED > REPLOW
REPLOWING > REPLOW
REPLOWS > REPLOW
REPLUM n internal separating wall in some fruits
REPLUMB vb plumb again
REPLUMBED > REPLUMB
REPLUMBS > REPLUMB
REPLUNGE vb plunge again
REPLUNGED
> REPLUNGE
REPLUNGES
> REPLUNGE
REPLY vb answer or respond ▷ n answer or response
REPLYING > REPLY
REPO n act of repossessing
REPOINT vb repair the joints of (brickwork, masonry, etc) with mortar or cement
REPOINTED > REPOINT
REPOINTS > REPOINT
REPOLISH vb polish again
REPOLL vb poll again
REPOLLED > REPOLL
REPOLLING > REPOLL
REPOLLS > REPOLL
REPOMAN n man employed to repossess goods in cases of non-payment
REPOMEN > REPOMAN
REPONE vb restore (someone) to his or her former status, office, etc
REPONED > REPONE
REPONES > REPONE
REPONING > REPONE

REPORT vb give an account of ▷ n account or statement
REPORTAGE n act or process of reporting news or other events of general interest
REPORTED > REPORT
REPORTER n person who gathers news for a newspaper, TV, etc
REPORTERS
> REPORTER
REPORTING > REPORT
REPORTS > REPORT
REPOS > REPO
REPOSAL n repose
REPOSALL archaic spelling of > REPOSAL
REPOSALLS
> REPOSALL
REPOSALS > REPOSAL
REPOSE n peace ▷ vb lie or lay at rest
REPOSED > REPOSE
REPOSEDLY > REPOSE
REPOSEFUL > REPOSE
REPOSER > REPOSE
REPOSERS > REPOSE
REPOSES > REPOSE
REPOSING > REPOSE
REPOSIT vb put away, deposit, or store up
REPOSITED > REPOSIT
REPOSITOR n any instrument used for correcting the position of displaced organs or bones
REPOSITS > REPOSIT
REPOSSESS vb (of a lender) take back property from a customer who is behind with payments
REPOST vb post again
REPOSTED > REPOST
REPOSTING > REPOST
REPOSTS > REPOST
REPOSURE old word for > REPOSE
REPOSURES
> REPOSURE
REPOT vb put (a house plant) into a new usually larger pot
REPOTS > REPOT
REPOTTED > REPOT
REPOTTING > REPOT
REPOUR vb pour back or again
REPOURED > REPOUR
REPOURING > REPOUR
REPOURS > REPOUR
REPOUSSE adj raised in relief ▷ n design or surface made in this way
REPOUSSES
> REPOUSSE
REPOWER vb put new engine in
REPOWERED > REPOWER
REPOWERS > REPOWER
REPP same as > REP
REPPED > REP
REPPING > REP
REPPINGS > REP
REPPS > REPP
REPREEVE archaic spelling of > REPRIEVE

REPREEVED
> REPREEVE
REPREEVES
> REPREEVE
REPREHEND vb find fault with
REPRESENT vb act as a delegate or substitute for
REPRESS vb keep (feelings) in check
REPRESSED adj (of a person) repressing feelings, instincts, desires, etc
REPRESSER > REPRESS
REPRESSES > REPRESS
REPRESSOR n protein synthesized under the control of a repressor gene, which has the capacity to bind to the operator gene and thereby shut off the expression of the structural genes of an operon
REPRICE vb price again
REPRICED > REPRICE
REPRICES > REPRICE
REPRICING > REPRICE
REPRIEFE n (in archaic usage) reproof
REPRIEFES
> REPRIEFE
REPRIEVAL old word for
> REPRIEVE
REPRIEVE vb postpone the execution of (a condemned person) ▷ n (document granting) postponement or cancellation of a punishment
REPRIEVED
> REPRIEVE
REPRIEVER
> REPRIEVE
REPRIEVES
> REPRIEVE
REPRIMAND vb blame (someone) officially for a fault ▷ n official blame
REPRIME vb prime again
REPRIMED > REPRIME
REPRIMES > REPRIME
REPRIMING > REPRIME
REPRINT vb print further copies of (a book) ▷ n reprinted copy
REPRINTED > REPRINT
REPRINTER > REPRINT
REPRINTS > REPRINT
REPRISAL n retaliation
REPRISALS
> REPRISAL
REPRISE n repeating of an earlier theme ▷ vb repeat an earlier theme
REPRISED > REPRISE
REPRISES > REPRISE
REPRISING > REPRISE
REPRIVE archaic spelling of > REPRIEVE
REPRIVED > REPRIVE
REPRIVES > REPRIVE
REPRIVING > REPRIVE
REPRIZE archaic spelling of > REPRISE
REPRIZED > REPRIZE

REPRIZES > REPRIZE
REPRIZING > REPRIZE
REPRO n imitation or facsimile of a work of art; reproduction
REPROACH vb blame, rebuke
REPROBACY
> REPROBATE
REPROBATE n depraved or disreputable (person) ▷ adj morally unprincipled ▷ vb disapprove of
REPROBE vb probe again
REPROBED > REPROBE
REPROBES > REPROBE
REPROBING > REPROBE
REPROCESS vb treat or prepare (something) by a special method again
REPRODUCE vb produce a copy of
REPROGRAM vb program again
REPROOF n severe blaming of someone for a fault ▷ vb treat (a coat, jacket, etc) so as to renew its texture, etc
REPROOFED > REPROOF
REPROOFS > REPROOF
REPROS > REPRO
REPROVAL same as
> REPROOF
REPROVALS
> REPROVAL
REPROVE vb speak severely to (someone) about a fault
REPROVED > REPROVE
REPROVER > REPROVE
REPROVERS > REPROVE
REPROVES > REPROVE
REPROVING > REPROVE
REPRYVE archaic spelling of > REPRIEVE
REPRYVED > REPRYVE
REPRYVES > REPRYVE
REPRYVING > REPRYVE
REPS > REP
REPTANT adj creeping, crawling, or lying along the ground
REPTATION n creeping action
REPTILE n cold-blooded egg-laying vertebrate with horny scales or plates ▷ adj creeping, crawling, or squirming
REPTILES > REPTILE
REPTILIA
> REPTILIUM
REPTILIAN adj of, relating to, resembling, or characteristic of reptiles
REPTILIUM n place where live reptiles are kept for show
REPTILOID n reptile or organism resembling a reptile
REPUBLIC n government in which the people possess the supreme power
REPUBLICS
> REPUBLIC

REPUBLISH vb publish again

REPUDIATE vb reject the authority or validity of

REPUGN vb oppose or conflict (with)

REPUGNANT adj offensive or distasteful

REPUGNED > REPUGN

REPUGNING > REPUGN

REPUGNS > REPUGN

REPULP vb pulp again

REPULPED > REPULP

REPULPING > REPULP

REPULPS > REPULP

REPULSE vb be disgusting to ▷ n act of driving back

REPULSED > REPULSE

REPULSER > REPULSE

REPULSERS > REPULSE

REPULSES > REPULSE

REPULSING > REPULSE

REPULSION n distaste or aversion

REPULSIVE adj loathsome, disgusting

REPUMP vb pump again

REPUMPED > REPUMP

REPUMPING > REPUMP

REPUMPS > REPUMP

REPUNIT n any number that consists entirely of the same repeated digits

REPUNITS > REPUNIT

REPURE vb archaic word meaning make pure again

REPURED > REPURE

REPURES > REPURE

REPURIFY vb purify again

REPURING > REPURE

REPURPOSE vb find new purpose for

REPURSUE vb pursue again

REPURSUED > REPURSUE

REPURSUES > REPURSUE

REPUTABLE adj of good reputation, respectable

REPUTABLY > REPUTABLE

REPUTE n reputation ▷ vb consider (a person or thing) to be as specified

REPUTED adj supposed

REPUTEDLY adv according to general belief or supposition

REPUTES > REPUTE

REPUTING > REPUTE

REPUTINGS > REPUTE

REQUALIFY vb qualify again

REQUERE archaic variant of > REQUIRE

REQUERED > REQUERE

REQUERES > REQUERE

REQUERING > REQUERE

REQUEST vb ask ▷ n asking

REQUESTED > REQUEST

REQUESTER > REQUEST

REQUESTOR > REQUEST

REQUESTS > REQUEST

REQUICKEN vb quicken again

REQUIEM n Mass celebrated for the dead

REQUIEMS > REQUIEM

REQUIGHT archaic spelling of > REQUITE

REQUIGHTS > REQUIGHT

REQUIN vb type of shark

REQUINS > REQUIN

REQUINTO n type of small guitar

REQUINTOS > REQUINTO

REQUIRE vb want or need

REQUIRED > REQUIRE

REQUIRER > REQUIRE

REQUIRERS > REQUIRE

REQUIRES > REQUIRE

REQUIRING > REQUIRE

REQUISITE adj necessary, essential ▷ n essential thing

REQUIT vb quit again

REQUITAL n act or an instance of requiting

REQUITALS > REQUITAL

REQUITE vb return to someone (the same treatment or feeling as received)

REQUITED > REQUITE

REQUITER > REQUITE

REQUITERS > REQUITE

REQUITES > REQUITE

REQUITING > REQUITE

REQUITS > REQUIT

REQUITTED > REQUIT

REQUOTE vb quote again

REQUOTED > REQUOTE

REQUOTES > REQUOTE

REQUOTING > REQUOTE

REQUOYLE archaic spelling of > RECOIL

REQUOYLED > REQUOYLE

REQUOYLES > REQUOYLE

RERACK vb rack again

RERACKED > RERACK

RERACKING > RERACK

RERACKS > RERACK

RERADIATE vb radiate again

RERAIL vb put back on a railway line

RERAILED > RERAIL

RERAILING n replacement of existing rails on a railway line

RERAILS > RERAIL

RERAISE vb raise again

RERAISED > RERAISE

RERAISES > RERAISE

RERAISING > RERAISE

RERAN > RERUN

REREAD vb read (something) again

REREADING > REREAD

REREADS > REREAD

REREBRACE n armour worn on the upper arm

RERECORD vb record again

RERECORDS > RERECORD

REREDOS n ornamental screen behind an altar

REREDOSES > REREDOS

REREDOSSE same as > REREDOS

RERELEASE vb release again

REREMAI n New Zealand word for the basking shark

REREMAIS > REREMAI

REREMICE > REREMOUSE

REREMIND vb remind again

REREMINDS > REREMIND

REREMOUSE n archaic or dialect word for 'bat' (the animal)

RERENT vb rent again

RERENTED > RERENT

RERENTING > RERENT

RERENTS > RERENT

REREPEAT vb repeat again

REREPEATS > REREPEAT

REREVIEW vb review again

REREVIEWS > REREVIEW

REREVISE vb revise again

REREVISED > REREVISE

REREVISES > REREVISE

REREWARD archaic spelling of > REARWARD

REREWARDS archaic spelling of > REARWARDS

RERIG vb rig again

RERIGGED > RERIG

RERIGGING > RERIG

RERIGS > RERIG

RERISE vb rise again

RERISEN > RERISE

RERISES > RERISE

RERISING > RERISE

REROLL vb roll again

REROLLED > REROLL

REROLLER > REROLL

REROLLERS > REROLL

REROLLING > REROLL

REROLLS > REROLL

REROOF vb put a new roof or roofs on

REROOFED > REROOF

REROOFING > REROOF

REROOFS > REROOF

REROSE > RERISE

REROUTE vb send or direct by a different route

REROUTED > REROUTE

REROUTES > REROUTE

REROUTING > REROUTE

RERUN n film or programme that is broadcast again, repeat ▷ vb put on (a film or programme) again

RERUNNING > RERUN

RERUNS > RERUN

RES informal word for > RESIDENCE

RESADDLE vb saddle again

RESADDLED > RESADDLE

RESADDLES > RESADDLE

RESAID > RESAY

RESAIL vb sail again

RESAILED > RESAIL

RESAILING > RESAIL

RESAILS > RESAIL

RESALABLE > RESALE

RESALE n selling of something purchased earlier

RESALES > RESALE

RESALGAR archaic variant of > REALGAR

RESALGARS > RESALGAR

RESALUTE vb salute back or again

RESALUTED > RESALUTE

RESALUTES > RESALUTE

RESAMPLE vb (in graphics or digital photography) change the size or resolution of

RESAMPLED > RESAMPLE

RESAMPLES > RESAMPLE

RESAT > RESIT

RESAW vb saw again

RESAWED > RESAW

RESAWING > RESAW

RESAWN > RESAW

RESAWS > RESAW

RESAY vb say again or in response

RESAYING > RESAY

RESAYS > RESAY

RESCALE vb resize

RESCALED > RESCALE

RESCALES > RESCALE

RESCALING > RESCALE

RESCHOOL vb retrain

RESCHOOLS > RESCHOOL

RESCIND vb annul or repeal

RESCINDED > RESCIND

RESCINDER > RESCIND

RESCINDS > RESCIND

RESCORE vb score afresh

RESCORED > RESCORE

RESCORES > RESCORE

RESCORING > RESCORE

RESCREEN vb screen again

RESCREENS > RESCREEN

RESCRIPT n ordinance taking the form of a reply by the Roman emperor to a point of law

RESCRIPTS > RESCRIPT

RESCUABLE > RESCUE

RESCUE vb deliver from danger or trouble, save ▷ n act of rescuing

RESCUED > RESCUE

RESCUEE n person who is rescued

RESCUEES > RESCUEE

RESCUER > RESCUE

RESCUERS > RESCUE

RESCUES > RESCUE

RESCUING > RESCUE

r

RESCULPT vb sculpt again

RESCULPTS > RESCULPT

RESEAL vb close or secure tightly again

RESEALED > RESEAL

RESEALING > RESEAL

RESEALS > RESEAL

RESEARCH n systematic investigation to discover facts or collect information ▷ vb carry out investigations

RESEASON vb season again

RESEASONS > RESEASON

RESEAT vb show (a person) to a new seat

RESEATED > RESEAT

RESEATING > RESEAT

RESEATS > RESEAT

RESEAU n mesh background to a lace or other pattern

RESEAUS > RESEAU

RESEAUX > RESEAU

RESECT vb cut out part of (a bone, an organ, or other structure or part)

RESECTED > RESECT

RESECTING > RESECT

RESECTION n excision of part of a bone, organ, or other part

RESECTS > RESECT

RESECURE vb secure again

RESECURED > RESECURE

RESECURES > RESECURE

RESEDA n plant that has small spikes of grey-green flowers ▷ adj of a greyish-green colour

RESEDAS > RESEDA

RESEE vb see again

RESEED vb form seed and reproduce naturally, forming a constant plant population

RESEEDED > RESEED

RESEEDING > RESEED

RESEEDS > RESEED

RESEEING > RESEE

RESEEK vb seek again

RESEEKING > RESEEK

RESEEKS > RESEEK

RESEEN > RESEE

RESEES > RESEE

RESEIZE vb seize again

RESEIZED > RESEIZE

RESEIZES > RESEIZE

RESEIZING > RESEIZE

RESEIZURE > RESEIZE

RESELECT vb choose (someone or something) again

RESELECTS > RESELECT

RESELL vb sell (something) one has previously bought

RESELLER > RESELL

RESELLERS > RESELL

RESELLING > RESELL

RESELLS > RESELL

RESEMBLE vb be or look like

RESEMBLED > RESEMBLE

RESEMBLER > RESEMBLE

RESEMBLES > RESEMBLE

RESEND vb send again

RESENDING > RESEND

RESENDS > RESEND

RESENT vb feel bitter about

RESENTED > RESENT

RESENTER > RESENT

RESENTERS > RESENT

RESENTFUL adj feeling or characterized by resentment

RESENTING > RESENT

RESENTIVE archaic word for > RESENTFUL

RESENTS > RESENT

RESERPINE n insoluble alkaloid used medicinally to lower blood pressure and as a sedative

RESERVE vb set aside, keep for future use ▷ n something, esp money or troops, kept for emergencies

RESERVED adj not showing one's feelings, lacking friendliness

RESERVER > RESERVE

RESERVERS > RESERVE

RESERVES > RESERVE

RESERVICE vb service again

RESERVING > RESERVE

RESERVIST n member of a military reserve

RESERVOIR n natural or artificial lake storing water for community supplies

RESES > RES

RESET vb set again (a broken bone, matter in type, a gemstone, etc) ▷ n act or an instance of setting again

RESETS > RESET

RESETTED same as > RESET

RESETTER > RESET

RESETTERS > RESET

RESETTING > RESET

RESETTLE vb settle to live in a different place

RESETTLED > RESETTLE

RESETTLES > RESETTLE

RESEW vb sew again

RESEWED > RESEW

RESEWING > RESEW

RESEWN > RESEW

RESEWS > RESEW

RESH n 20th letter of the Hebrew alphabet

RESHAPE vb shape (something) again or differently

RESHAPED > RESHAPE

RESHAPER > RESHAPE

RESHAPERS > RESHAPE

RESHAPES > RESHAPE

RESHAPING n act of reshaping

RESHARPEN vb sharpen again

RESHAVE vb shave again

RESHAVED > RESHAVE

RESHAVEN > RESHAVE

RESHAVES > RESHAVE

RESHAVING > RESHAVE

RESHES > RESH

RESHINE vb shine again

RESHINED > RESHINE

RESHINES > RESHINE

RESHINGLE vb put new shingles on

RESHINING > RESHINE

RESHIP vb ship again

RESHIPPED > RESHIP

RESHIPPER > RESHIP

RESHIPS > RESHIP

RESHOD > RESHOE

RESHOE vb put a new shoe or shoes on

RESHOED > RESHOE

RESHOEING > RESHOE

RESHOES > RESHOE

RESHONE > RESHINE

RESHOOT vb shoot again

RESHOOTS > RESHOOT

RESHOT > RESHOOT

RESHOW vb show again

RESHOWED > RESHOW

RESHOWER vb have another shower

RESHOWERS > RESHOWER

RESHOWING n act or instance of showing (a film, etc) again

RESHOWN > RESHOW

RESHOWS > RESHOW

RESHUFFLE n reorganization ▷ vb reorganize

RESIANCE archaic word for > RESIDENCE

RESIANCES > RESIANCE

RESIANT archaic word for > RESIDENT

RESIANTS > RESIANT

RESID n residual oil left over from the petroleum distillation process

RESIDE vb dwell permanently

RESIDED > RESIDE

RESIDENCE n home or house

RESIDENCY n regular series of concerts by a band or singer at one venue

RESIDENT n person who lives in a place ▷ adj living in a place

RESIDENTS > RESIDENT

RESIDER > RESIDE

RESIDERS > RESIDE

RESIDES > RESIDE

RESIDING > RESIDE

RESIDS > RESID

RESIDUA > RESIDUUM

RESIDUAL adj of or being a remainder ▷ n

something left over as a residue

RESIDUALS > RESIDUAL

RESIDUARY adj of, relating to, or constituting a residue

RESIDUE n what is left, remainder

RESIDUES > RESIDUE

RESIDUOUS adj residual

RESIDUUM n residue

RESIDUUMS > RESIDUUM

RESIFT vb sift again

RESIFTED > RESIFT

RESIFTING > RESIFT

RESIFTS > RESIFT

RESIGHT vb sight again

RESIGHTED > RESIGHT

RESIGHTS > RESIGHT

RESIGN vb give up office, a job, etc

RESIGNED adj content to endure

RESIGNER > RESIGN

RESIGNERS > RESIGN

RESIGNING > RESIGN

RESIGNS > RESIGN

RESILE vb spring or shrink back

RESILED > RESILE

RESILES > RESILE

RESILIENT adj (of a person) recovering quickly from a shock etc

RESILIN n substance found in insect bodies

RESILING > RESILE

RESILINS > RESILIN

RESILVER vb silver again

RESILVERS > RESILVER

RESIN n sticky substance from plants, esp pines ▷ vb treat or coat with resin

RESINATA n type of wine

RESINATAS > RESINATA

RESINATE vb impregnate with resin

RESINATED > RESINATE

RESINATES > RESINATE

RESINED > RESIN

RESINER n applier or collector of resin

RESINERS > RESINER

RESINIER > RESINY

RESINIEST > RESINY

RESINIFY vb become or cause to be resinous

RESINING > RESIN

RESINISE variant spelling of > RESINIZE

RESINISED > RESINISE

RESINISES > RESINISE

RESINIZE vb apply resin to

RESINIZED > RESINIZE

RESINIZES > RESINIZE

RESINLIKE > RESIN

RESINOID *adj* resembling, characteristic of, or containing resin ▷ *n* any resinoid substance, esp a synthetic compound
RESINOIDS > RESINOID
RESINOSES > RESINOSIS
RESINOSIS *n* excessive resin loss in diseased or damaged conifers
RESINOUS > RESIN
RESINS > RESIN
RESINY *adj* resembling, containing or covered with resin
RESIST *vb* withstand or oppose ▷ *n* substance used to protect something
RESISTANT *adj* characterized by or showing resistance ▷ *n* person or thing that resists
RESISTED > RESIST
RESISTENT *same as* > RESISTANT
RESISTER > RESIST
RESISTERS > RESIST
RESISTING > RESIST
RESISTIVE *adj* exhibiting electrical resistance
RESISTOR *n* component of an electrical circuit producing resistance
RESISTORS > RESISTOR
RESISTS > RESIST
RESIT *vb* take (an exam) again ▷ *n* exam that has to be taken again
RESITE *vb* move to a different site
RESITED > RESITE
RESITES > RESITE
RESITING > RESITE
RESITS > RESIT
RESITTING > RESIT
RESITUATE *vb* situate elsewhere
RESIZABLE *adj* capable of being resized
RESIZE *vb* change size of
RESIZED > RESIZE
RESIZES > RESIZE
RESIZING > RESIZE
RESKETCH *vb* sketch again
RESKEW *archaic spelling of* > RESCUE
RESKEWED > RESKEW
RESKEWING > RESKEW
RESKEWS > RESKEW
RESKILL *vb* train (workers) to acquire new skills
RESKILLED > RESKILL
RESKILLS > RESKILL
RESKIN *vb* replace the outermost layer of an aircraft
RESKINNED > RESKIN
RESKINS > RESKIN
RESKUE *archaic spelling of* > RESCUE
RESKUED > RESKUE

RESKUES > RESKUE
RESKUING > RESKUE
RESLATE *vb* slate again
RESLATED > RESLATE
RESLATES > RESLATE
RESLATING > RESLATE
RESMELT *vb* smelt again
RESMELTED > RESMELT
RESMELTS > RESMELT
RESMOOTH *vb* smooth again
RESMOOTHS > RESMOOTH
RESNATRON *n* tetrode used to generate high power at high frequencies
RESOAK *vb* soak again
RESOAKED > RESOAK
RESOAKING > RESOAK
RESOAKS > RESOAK
RESOD *vb* returf
RESODDED > RESOD
RESODDING > RESOD
RESODS > RESOD
RESOFTEN *vb* soften again
RESOFTENS > RESOFTEN
RESOJET *n* type of jet engine
RESOJETS > RESOJET
RESOLD > RESELL
RESOLDER *vb* solder again
RESOLDERS > RESOLDER
RESOLE *vb* put a new sole or new soles on
RESOLED > RESOLE
RESOLES > RESOLE
RESOLING > RESOLE
RESOLUBLE *adj* able to be resolved
RESOLUTE *adj* firm in purpose ▷ *n* someone resolute
RESOLUTER > RESOLUTE
RESOLUTES > RESOLUTE
RESOLVE *vb* decide with an effort of will ▷ *n* absolute determination
RESOLVED *adj* determined
RESOLVENT *adj* serving to dissolve or separate something into its elements ▷ *n* something that resolves
RESOLVER > RESOLVE
RESOLVERS > RESOLVE
RESOLVES > RESOLVE
RESOLVING > RESOLVE
RESONANCE *n* echoing, esp with a deep sound
RESONANT *adj* resounding or reechoing ▷ *n* type of unobstructed speech sound
RESONANTS > RESONANT
RESONATE *vb* resound or cause to resound
RESONATED > RESONATE
RESONATES > RESONATE

RESONATOR *n* any body or system that displays resonance, esp a tuned electrical circuit or a conducting cavity in which microwaves are generated by a resonant current
RESORB *vb* absorb again
RESORBED > RESORB
RESORBENT > RESORB
RESORBING > RESORB
RESORBS > RESORB
RESORCIN *n* substance used principally in dyeing
RESORCINS > RESORCIN
RESORT *vb* have recourse (to) for help etc ▷ *n* place for holidays
RESORTED > RESORT
RESORTER > RESORT
RESORTERS > RESORT
RESORTING > RESORT
RESORTS > RESORT
RESOUGHT > RESEEK
RESOUND *vb* echo or ring with sound
RESOUNDED > RESOUND
RESOUNDS > RESOUND
RESOURCE *n* thing resorted to for support ▷ *vb* provide funding or other resources for
RESOURCED > RESOURCE
RESOURCES > RESOURCE
RESOW *vb* sow again
RESOWED > RESOW
RESOWING > RESOW
RESOWN > RESOW
RESOWS > RESOW
RESPACE *vb* change the spacing of
RESPACED > RESPACE
RESPACES > RESPACE
RESPACING > RESPACE
RESPADE *vb* dig over
RESPADED > RESPADE
RESPADES > RESPADE
RESPADING > RESPADE
RESPEAK *vb* speak further
RESPEAKS > RESPEAK
RESPECIFY *vb* specify again
RESPECT *n* consideration ▷ *vb* treat with esteem
RESPECTED > RESPECT
RESPECTER *n* person who respects someone or something
RESPECTS > RESPECT
RESPELL *vb* spell again
RESPELLED > RESPELL
RESPELLS > RESPELL
RESPELT > RESPELL
RESPIRE *vb* breathe
RESPIRED > RESPIRE
RESPIRES > RESPIRE
RESPIRING > RESPIRE
RESPITE *n* pause, interval of rest ▷ *vb* grant a respite to
RESPITED > RESPITE
RESPITES > RESPITE
RESPITING > RESPITE

RESPLEND *vb* be resplendent
RESPLENDS > RESPLEND
RESPLICE *vb* splice again
RESPLICED > RESPLICE
RESPLICES > RESPLICE
RESPLIT *vb* split again
RESPLITS > RESPLIT
RESPOKE > RESPEAK
RESPOKEN > RESPEAK
RESPOND *vb* answer ▷ *n* pilaster or an engaged column that supports an arch or a lintel
RESPONDED > RESPOND
RESPONDER > RESPOND
RESPONDS > RESPOND
RESPONSA *n* that part of rabbinic literature concerned with written rulings in answer to questions
RESPONSE *n* answer
RESPONSER *n* radio or radar receiver used to receive and display signals from a transponder
RESPONSES > RESPONSE
RESPONSOR *same as* > RESPONSER
RESPONSUM *n* written answer from a rabbinic authority to a question submitted
RESPOOL *vb* rewind onto spool
RESPOOLED > RESPOOL
RESPOOLS > RESPOOL
RESPOT *vb* (in billiards) replace (a ball) on one of the spots
RESPOTS > RESPOT
RESPOTTED > RESPOT
RESPRANG > RESPRING
RESPRAY *n* new coat of paint applied to a car, van, etc ▷ *vb* spray (a car, wheels, etc) with a new coat of paint
RESPRAYED > RESPRAY
RESPRAYS > RESPRAY
RESPREAD *vb* spread again
RESPREADS > RESPREAD
RESPRING *vb* put new springs in
RESPRINGS > RESPRING
RESPROUT *vb* sprout again
RESPROUTS > RESPROUT
RESPRUNG > RESPRING
RESSALDAR *n* Indian cavalry commander in mixed Anglo-Indian army
REST *n* freedom from exertion etc ▷ *vb* take a rest
RESTABLE *vb* put in stable again or elsewhere
RESTABLED > RESTABLE

RESTABLES
> RESTABLE
RESTACK vb stack again
RESTACKED > RESTACK
RESTACKS > RESTACK
RESTAFF vb staff again
RESTAFFED > RESTAFF
RESTAFFS > RESTAFF
RESTAGE vb produce or perform a new production of (a play)
RESTAGED > RESTAGE
RESTAGES > RESTAGE
RESTAGING > RESTAGE
RESTAMP vb stamp again
RESTAMPED > RESTAMP
RESTAMPS > RESTAMP
RESTART vb commence (something) or set (something) in motion again ▷ n act or an instance of starting again
RESTARTED > RESTART
RESTARTER > RESTART
RESTARTS > RESTART
RESTATE vb state or affirm (something) again or in a different way
RESTATED > RESTATE
RESTATES > RESTATE
RESTATING > RESTATE
RESTATION vb station elsewhere
RESTED > REST
RESTEM vb stem again
RESTEMMED > RESTEM
RESTEMS > RESTEM
RESTER > REST
RESTERS > REST
RESTFUL adj relaxing or soothing
RESTFULLY > RESTFUL
RESTIER > RESTY
RESTIEST > RESTY
RESTIFF same as
> RESTIVE
RESTIFORM adj (esp of bundles of nerve fibres) shaped like a cord or rope
RESTING > REST
RESTINGS > REST
RESTITCH vb stitch again
RESTITUTE vb restore
RESTIVE adj restless or impatient
RESTIVELY > RESTIVE
RESTLESS adj bored or dissatisfied
RESTO n restored antique, vintage car, etc
RESTOCK vb replenish stores or supplies
RESTOCKED > RESTOCK
RESTOCKS > RESTOCK
RESTOKE vb stoke again
RESTOKED > RESTOKE
RESTOKES > RESTOKE
RESTOKING > RESTOKE
RESTORAL n restoration
RESTORALS
> RESTORAL
RESTORE vb return (a building, painting, etc) to its original condition
RESTORED > RESTORE
RESTORER > RESTORE

RESTORERS > RESTORE
RESTORES > RESTORE
RESTORING > RESTORE
RESTOS > RESTO
RESTRAIN vb hold (someone) back from action
RESTRAINS
> RESTRAIN
RESTRAINT n something that restrains
RESTRESS vb stress again or differently
RESTRETCH vb stretch again
RESTRICT vb confine to certain limits
RESTRICTS
> RESTRICT
RESTRIKE vb strike again
RESTRIKES
> RESTRIKE
RESTRING vb string again or anew
RESTRINGE vb restrict
RESTRINGS
> RESTRING
RESTRIVE vb strive again
RESTRIVEN
> RESTRIVE
RESTRIVES
> RESTRIVE
RESTROOM n room in a public building having lavatories and washing facilities
RESTROOMS
> RESTROOM
RESTROVE > RESTRIVE
RESTRUCK > RESTRIKE
RESTRUNG > RESTRING
RESTS > REST
RESTUDIED > RESTUDY
RESTUDIES > RESTUDY
RESTUDY vb study again
RESTUFF vb put new stuffing in
RESTUFFED > RESTUFF
RESTUFFS > RESTUFF
RESTUMP vb provide with new stumps
RESTUMPED > RESTUMP
RESTUMPS > RESTUMP
RESTY adj restive
RESTYLE vb style again
RESTYLED > RESTYLE
RESTYLES > RESTYLE
RESTYLING > RESTYLE
RESUBJECT vb subject again
RESUBMIT vb submit again
RESUBMITS
> RESUBMIT
RESULT n outcome or consequence ▷ vb be the outcome or consequence (of)
RESULTANT adj arising as a result ▷ n sum of two or more vectors, such as the force resulting from two or more forces acting on a single point
RESULTED > RESULT
RESULTFUL > RESULT
RESULTING > RESULT

RESULTS > RESULT
RESUMABLE > RESUME
RESUME vb begin again ▷ n summary
RESUMED > RESUME
RESUMER > RESUME
RESUMERS > RESUME
RESUMES > RESUME
RESUMING > RESUME
RESUMMON vb summon again
RESUMMONS
> RESUMMON
RESUPINE adj lying on the back
RESUPPLY vb provide (with something) again
RESURFACE vb arise or occur again
RESURGE vb rise again from or as if from the dead
RESURGED > RESURGE
RESURGENT adj rising again, as to new life, vigour, etc
RESURGES > RESURGE
RESURGING > RESURGE
RESURRECT vb restore to life
RESURVEY vb survey again
RESURVEYS
> RESURVEY
RESUS n (short for) resuscitation room
RESUSES > RESUS
RESUSPEND vb put back into suspension
RESUSSES > RESUS
RESWALLOW vb swallow again
RET vb moisten or soak (flax, hemp, jute, etc) to facilitate separation of fibres
RETABLE n ornamental screenlike structure above and behind an altar
RETABLES > RETABLE
RETABLO n shelf for panels behind an altar
RETABLOS > RETABLO
RETACK vb tack again
RETACKED > RETACK
RETACKING > RETACK
RETACKLE vb tackle again
RETACKLED
> RETACKLE
RETACKLES
> RETACKLE
RETACKS > RETACK
RETAG vb tag again
RETAGGED > RETAG
RETAGGING > RETAG
RETAGS > RETAG
RETAIL n selling of goods individually or in small amounts to the public ▷ adj of or engaged in such selling ▷ adv by retail ▷ vb sell or be sold retail
RETAILED > RETAIL
RETAILER > RETAIL
RETAILERS > RETAIL
RETAILING > RETAIL
RETAILOR vb tailor afresh

RETAILORS
> RETAILOR
RETAILS > RETAIL
RETAIN vb keep in one's possession
RETAINED > RETAIN
RETAINER n fee to retain someone's services
RETAINERS
> RETAINER
RETAINING > RETAIN
RETAINS > RETAIN
RETAKE vb recapture ▷ n act of rephotographing a scene
RETAKEN > RETAKE
RETAKER > RETAKE
RETAKERS > RETAKE
RETAKES > RETAKE
RETAKING > RETAKE
RETAKINGS > RETAKE
RETALIATE vb repay an injury or wrong in kind
RETALLIED > RETALLY
RETALLIES > RETALLY
RETALLY vb count up again
RETAMA n type of shrub
RETAMAS > RETAMA
RETAPE vb tape again
RETAPED > RETAPE
RETAPES > RETAPE
RETAPING > RETAPE
RETARD vb delay or slow (progress or development)
RETARDANT n substance that reduces the rate of a chemical reaction ▷ adj having a slowing effect
RETARDED > RETARD
RETARDER n substance that slows down chemical change
RETARDERS
> RETARDER
RETARDING > RETARD
RETARDS > RETARD
RETARGET vb target afresh or differently
RETARGETS
> RETARGET
RETASTE vb taste again
RETASTED > RETASTE
RETASTES > RETASTE
RETASTING > RETASTE
RETAUGHT > RETEACH
RETAX vb tax again
RETAXED > RETAX
RETAXES > RETAX
RETAXING > RETAX
RETCH vb try to vomit ▷ n involuntary spasm of the stomach
RETCHED > RETCH
RETCHES > RETCH
RETCHING n act of retching
RETCHINGS
> RETCHING
RETCHLESS archaic variant of > RECKLESS
RETE n any network of nerves or blood vessels
RETEACH vb teach again
RETEACHES > RETEACH
RETEAM vb team up again
RETEAMED > RETEAM

RETEAMING > RETEAM
RETEAMS > RETEAM
RETEAR vb tear again
RETEARING > RETEAR
RETEARS > RETEAR
RETELL vb relate (a story, etc) again or differently
RETELLER > RETELL
RETELLERS > RETELL
RETELLING > RETELL
RETELLS > RETELL
RETEM n type of shrub
RETEMPER vb temper again
RETEMPERS > RETEMPER
RETEMS > RETEM
RETENE n yellow crystalline hydrocarbon found in tar oils
RETENES > RETENE
RETENTION n retaining
RETENTIVE adj capable of retaining or remembering
RETEST vb test (something) again or differently
RETESTED > RETEST
RETESTIFY vb testify again
RETESTING > RETEST
RETESTS > RETEST
RETEXTURE vb restore natural texture to
RETHINK vb consider again, esp with a view to changing one's tactics ▷ n act or an instance of thinking again
RETHINKER > RETHINK
RETHINKS > RETHINK
RETHOUGHT > RETHINK
RETHREAD vb thread again
RETHREADS > RETHREAD
RETIA > RETE
RETIAL > RETE
RETIARII > RETIARIUS
RETIARIUS n (in ancient Rome) a gladiator armed with a net and trident
RETIARY adj of, relating to, or resembling a net or web
RETICELLA n form of lace
RETICENCE > RETICENT
RETICENCY > RETICENT
RETICENT adj uncommunicative, reserved
RETICLE n network of fine lines, wires, etc, used in optical instruments
RETICLES > RETICLE
RETICULA > RETICULUM
RETICULAR adj in the form of a network or having a network of parts
RETICULE same as > RETICLE

RETICULES > RETICULE
RETICULUM n any fine network, esp one in the body composed of cells, fibres, etc
RETIE vb tie again
RETIED > RETIE
RETIEING > RETIE
RETIES > RETIE
RETIFORM adj netlike
RETIGHTEN vb tighten again
RETILE vb put new tiles in or on
RETILED > RETILE
RETILES > RETILE
RETILING > RETILE
RETIME vb time again or alter time of
RETIMED > RETIME
RETIMES > RETIME
RETIMING > RETIME
RETINA n light-sensitive membrane at the back of the eye
RETINAE > RETINA
RETINAL adj of or relating to the retina ▷ n aldehyde form of the polyene retinol
RETINALS > RETINAL
RETINAS > RETINA
RETINE n chemical found in body cells that slows cell growth and division
RETINENE n aldehyde form of the polyene retinol
RETINENES > RETINENE
RETINES > RETINE
RETINITE n any of various resins of fossil origin, esp one derived from lignite
RETINITES > RETINITE
RETINITIS n inflammation of the retina
RETINOIC adj containing or derived from retinoid
RETINOID adj resinlike ▷ n derivative of vitamin A
RETINOIDS > RETINOID
RETINOL n another name for vitamin A and rosin oil
RETINOLS > RETINOL
RETINT vb tint again or change tint of
RETINTED > RETINT
RETINTING > RETINT
RETINTS > RETINT
RETINUE n band of attendants
RETINUED > RETINUE
RETINUES > RETINUE
RETINULA n part of the compound eye in certain arthropods
RETINULAE > RETINULA
RETINULAR > RETINULA
RETINULAS > RETINULA
RETIRACY n (in US English) retirement

RETIRAL n act of retiring from office, one's work, etc
RETIRALS > RETIRAL
RETIRANT n (in US English) retired person
RETIRANTS > RETIRANT
RETIRE vb (cause to) give up office or work, esp through age
RETIRED adj having retired from work etc
RETIREDLY > RETIRED
RETIREE n person who has retired from work
RETIREES > RETIREE
RETIRER > RETIRE
RETIRERS > RETIRE
RETIRES > RETIRE
RETIRING adj shy
RETITLE vb give a new title to
RETITLED > RETITLE
RETITLES > RETITLE
RETITLING > RETITLE
RETOLD > RETELL
RETOOK > RETAKE
RETOOL vb replace, reequip, or rearrange the tools in (a factory, etc)
RETOOLED > RETOOL
RETOOLING > RETOOL
RETOOLS > RETOOL
RETORE > RETEAR
RETORN > RETEAR
RETORSION n retaliatory action taken by a state whose citizens have been mistreated by a foreign power by treating the subjects of that power similarly
RETORT vb reply quickly, wittily, or angrily ▷ n quick, witty, or angry reply
RETORTED > RETORT
RETORTER > RETORT
RETORTERS > RETORT
RETORTING > RETORT
RETORTION n act of retorting
RETORTIVE > RETORT
RETORTS > RETORT
RETOTAL vb add up again
RETOTALED > RETOTAL
RETOTALS > RETOTAL
RETOUCH vb restore or improve by new touches, esp of paint ▷ n art or practice of retouching
RETOUCHED > RETOUCH
RETOUCHER > RETOUCH
RETOUCHES > RETOUCH
RETOUR vb (in Scottish law) to return as heir
RETOURED > RETOUR
RETOURING > RETOUR
RETOURS > RETOUR
RETOX vb embark on a binge of something unhealthy after a period of abstinence
RETOXED > RETOX
RETOXES > RETOX
RETOXING > RETOX
RETRACE vb go back over (a route etc) again
RETRACED > RETRACE

RETRACER > RETRACE
RETRACERS > RETRACE
RETRACES > RETRACE
RETRACING > RETRACE
RETRACK vb track again
RETRACKED > RETRACK
RETRACKS > RETRACK
RETRACT vb withdraw (a statement etc)
RETRACTED > RETRACT
RETRACTOR n any of various muscles that retract an organ or part
RETRACTS > RETRACT
RETRAICT archaic form of > RETREAT
RETRAICTS > RETRAICT
RETRAIN vb train to do a new or different job
RETRAINED > RETRAIN
RETRAINEE > RETRAIN
RETRAINS > RETRAIN
RETRAIT archaic form of > RETREAT
RETRAITE archaic form of > RETREAT
RETRAITES > RETRAITE
RETRAITS > RETRAIT
RETRAITT n archaic word meaning portrait
RETRAITTS > RETRAITT
RETRAL adj at, near, or towards the back
RETRALLY > RETRAL
RETRATE archaic form of > RETREAT
RETRATED > RETRATE
RETRATES > RETRATE
RETRATING > RETRATE
RETREAD n remould ▷ vb remould
RETREADED > RETREAD
RETREADS > RETREAD
RETREAT vb move back from a position, withdraw ▷ n act of or military signal for retiring or withdrawal
RETREATED > RETREAT
RETREATER > RETREAT
RETREATS > RETREAT
RETREE n imperfectly made paper
RETREES > RETREE
RETRENCH vb reduce expenditure, cut back
RETRIAL n second trial of a case or defendant in a court of law
RETRIALS > RETRIAL
RETRIBUTE vb give back
RETRIED > RETRY
RETRIES > RETRY
RETRIEVAL n act or process of retrieving
RETRIEVE vb fetch back again ▷ n chance of being retrieved
RETRIEVED > RETRIEVE
RETRIEVER n dog trained to retrieve shot game
RETRIEVES > RETRIEVE
RETRIM vb trim again

RETRIMMED > RETRIM

RETRIMS > RETRIM

RETRO *adj* associated with or revived from the past ▷ *n* a retro style of art

RETROACT *vb* act in opposition

RETROACTS > RETROACT

RETROCEDE *vb* give back

RETROD > RETREAD

RETRODDEN > RETREAD

RETRODICT *vb* make surmises about the past using information from the present

RETROFIRE *n* act of firing a retrorocket

RETROFIT *vb* equip (a piece of equipment) with new parts after manufacture

RETROFITS > RETROFIT

RETROFLEX *adj* bent or curved backwards ▷ *vb* bend or turn backwards

RETROJECT *vb* throw backwards

RETRONYM *n* word coined for existing thing to distinguish it from new thing

RETRONYMS > RETRONYM

RETROPACK *n* system of retrorockets on a spacecraft

RETRORSE *adj* (esp of plant parts) pointing backwards or in a direction opposite to normal

RETROS > RETRO

RETROUSSE *adj* (of a nose) turned upwards

RETROVERT *vb* turn back

RETRY *vb* try again (a case already determined)

RETRYING > RETRY

RETS > RET

RETSINA *n* Greek wine flavoured with resin

RETSINAS > RETSINA

RETTED > RET

RETTERIES > RETTERY

RETTERY *n* flax-retting place

RETTING > RET

RETUND *vb* weaken or blunt

RETUNDED > RETUND

RETUNDING > RETUND

RETUNDS > RETUND

RETUNE *vb* tune (a musical instrument) differently or again

RETUNED > RETUNE

RETUNES > RETUNE

RETUNING > RETUNE

RETURF *vb* turf again

RETURFED > RETURF

RETURFING > RETURF

RETURFS > RETURF

RETURN *vb* go or come back ▷ *n* returning ▷ *adj* of or being a return

RETURNED > RETURN

RETURNEE *n* person who returns to his or her native country, esp after war service

RETURNEES > RETURNEE

RETURNER *n* person or thing that returns

RETURNERS > RETURNER

RETURNIK *n* someone returning to the former Soviet Union

RETURNIKS > RETURNIK

RETURNING > RETURN

RETURNS > RETURN

RETUSE *adj* having a rounded apex and a central depression

RETWEET *vb* post (another user's post) on the Twitter website for one's own followers

RETWEETED > RETWEET

RETWEETS > RETWEET

RETWIST *vb* twist again

RETWISTED > RETWIST

RETWISTS > RETWIST

RETYING > RETIE

RETYPE *vb* type again

RETYPED > RETYPE

RETYPES > RETYPE

RETYPING > RETYPE

REUNIFIED > REUNIFY

REUNIFIES > REUNIFY

REUNIFY *vb* bring together again something previously divided

REUNION *n* meeting of people who have been apart

REUNIONS > REUNION

REUNITE *vb* bring or come together again after a separation

REUNITED > REUNITE

REUNITER > REUNITE

REUNITERS > REUNITE

REUNITES > REUNITE

REUNITING > REUNITE

REUPTAKE *vb* absorb again ▷ *n* act of reabsorbing

REUPTAKEN > REUPTAKE

REUPTAKES > REUPTAKE

REUPTOOK > REUPTAKE

REURGE *vb* urge again

REURGED > REURGE

REURGES > REURGE

REURGING > REURGE

REUSABLE *adj* able to be used more than once

REUSABLES *pl n* products which can be used more than once

REUSE *vb* use again ▷ *n* act of using something again

REUSED > REUSE

REUSES > REUSE

REUSING > REUSE

REUTILISE *same as* > REUTILIZE

REUTILIZE *vb* utilize again

REUTTER *vb* utter again

REUTTERED > REUTTER

REUTTERS > REUTTER

REV *n* revolution (of an engine) ▷ *vb* increase the speed of revolution of (an engine)

REVALENTA *n* lentil flour

REVALUATE *same as* > REVALUE

REVALUE *vb* adjust the exchange value of (a currency) upwards

REVALUED > REVALUE

REVALUES > REVALUE

REVALUING > REVALUE

REVAMP *vb* renovate or restore ▷ *n* something that has been renovated or revamped

REVAMPED > REVAMP

REVAMPER > REVAMP

REVAMPERS > REVAMP

REVAMPING > REVAMP

REVAMPS > REVAMP

REVANCHE *n* revenge

REVANCHES > REVANCHE

REVARNISH *vb* varnish again

REVEAL *vb* make known ▷ *n* vertical side of an opening in a wall

REVEALED > REVEAL

REVEALER > REVEAL

REVEALERS > REVEAL

REVEALING *adj* disclosing information that one did not know

REVEALS > REVEAL

REVEHENT *adj* (in anatomy) carrying back

REVEILLE *n* morning bugle call to waken soldiers

REVEILLES > REVEILLE

REVEL *vb* take pleasure (in) ▷ *n* occasion of noisy merrymaking

REVELATOR *n* revealer

REVELED > REVEL

REVELER > REVEL

REVELERS > REVEL

REVELING > REVEL

REVELLED > REVEL

REVELLER > REVEL

REVELLERS > REVEL

REVELLING > REVEL

REVELMENT > REVEL

REVELRIES > REVELRY

REVELROUS > REVELRY

REVELRY *n* festivity

REVELS > REVEL

REVENANT *n* something, esp a ghost, that returns

REVENANTS > REVENANT

REVENGE *n* retaliation for wrong done ▷ *vb* make retaliation for

REVENGED > REVENGE

REVENGER > REVENGE

REVENGERS > REVENGE

REVENGES > REVENGE

REVENGING > REVENGE

REVENGIVE > REVENGE

REVENUAL > REVENUE

REVENUE *n* income, esp of a state

REVENUED > REVENUE

REVENUER *n* revenue officer or cutter

REVENUERS > REVENUER

REVENUES > REVENUE

REVERABLE > REVERE

REVERB *n* electronic device that creates artificial acoustics ▷ *vb* reverberate

REVERBED > REVERB

REVERBING > REVERB

REVERBS > REVERB

REVERE *vb* be in awe of and respect greatly

REVERED > REVERE

REVERENCE *n* awe mingled with respect

REVEREND *adj* worthy of reverence ▷ *n* member of the clergy

REVERENDS > REVEREND

REVERENT *adj* showing reverence

REVERER > REVERE

REVERERS > REVERE

REVERES > REVERE

REVERIE *n* absent-minded daydream

REVERIES > REVERIE

REVERIFY *vb* verify again

REVERING > REVERE

REVERIST *n* someone given to reveries

REVERISTS > REVERIST

REVERS *n* turned back part of a garment, such as a lapel

REVERSAL *n* act or an instance of reversing

REVERSALS > REVERSAL

REVERSE *vb* turn upside down or the other way round ▷ *n* opposite ▷ *adj* opposite or contrary

REVERSED > REVERSE

REVERSELY > REVERSE

REVERSER > REVERSE

REVERSERS > REVERSE

REVERSES > REVERSE

REVERSI *n* game played on a draughtboard

REVERSING > REVERSE

REVERSION *n* return to a former state, practice, or belief

REVERSIS *n* type of card game

REVERSO *another name for* > VERSO

REVERSOS > REVERSO

REVERT *vb* return to a former state

REVERTANT *n* mutant that has reverted to an earlier form ▷ *adj* having mutated to an earlier form

REVERTED > REVERT

REVERTER > REVERT

REVERTERS > REVERT

REVERTING > REVERT

REVERTIVE > REVERT

REVERTS > REVERT

REVERY *same as* **> REVERIE**

REVEST *vb* restore (former power, authority, status, etc, to a person)

REVESTED > REVEST

REVESTING > REVEST

REVESTRY *same as* **> VESTRY**

REVESTS > REVEST

REVET *vb* face (a wall or embankment) with stones

REVETMENT *n* facing of stones, sandbags, etc, to protect a wall, embankment, or earthworks

REVETS > REVET

REVETTED > REVET

REVETTING > REVET

REVEUR *n* daydreamer

REVEURS > REVEUR

REVEUSE *n* female daydreamer

REVEUSES > REVEUSE

REVIBRATE *vb* vibrate again

REVICTUAL *vb* victual again

REVIE *vb* archaic cards term meaning challenge by placing a larger stake

REVIED > REVIE

REVIES > REVIE

REVIEW *n* critical assessment of a book, concert, etc ▷ *vb* hold or write a review of

REVIEWAL *same as* **> REVIEW**

REVIEWALS **> REVIEWAL**

REVIEWED > REVIEW

REVIEWER > REVIEW

REVIEWERS > REVIEW

REVIEWING > REVIEW

REVIEWS > REVIEW

REVILE *vb* be abusively scornful of

REVILED > REVILE

REVILER > REVILE

REVILERS > REVILE

REVILES > REVILE

REVILING > REVILE

REVILINGS > REVILE

REVIOLATE *vb* violate again

REVISABLE > REVISE

REVISAL > REVISE

REVISALS > REVISE

REVISE *vb* change or alter ▷ *n* act, process, or result of revising

REVISED > REVISE

REVISER > REVISE

REVISERS > REVISE

REVISES > REVISE

REVISING > REVISE

REVISION *n* act of revising

REVISIONS **> REVISION**

REVISIT *vb* visit again

REVISITED > REVISIT

REVISITS > REVISIT

REVISOR > REVISE

REVISORS > REVISE

REVISORY *adj* of or having the power of revision

REVIVABLE > REVIVE

REVIVABLY > REVIVE

REVIVAL *n* reviving or renewal

REVIVALS > REVIVAL

REVIVE *vb* bring or come back to life, vigour, use, etc

REVIVED > REVIVE

REVIVER > REVIVE

REVIVERS > REVIVE

REVIVES > REVIVE

REVIVIFY *vb* give new life to

REVIVING > REVIVE

REVIVINGS > REVIVE

REVIVOR *n* means of reviving a lawsuit that has been suspended

REVIVORS > REVIVOR

REVOCABLE *adj* capable of being revoked

REVOCABLY **> REVOCABLE**

REVOICE *vb* utter again

REVOICED > REVOICE

REVOICES > REVOICE

REVOICING > REVOICE

REVOKABLE *same as* **> REVOCABLE**

REVOKABLY **> REVOCABLE**

REVOKE *vb* cancel (a will, agreement, etc) ▷ *n* act of revoking

REVOKED > REVOKE

REVOKER > REVOKE

REVOKERS > REVOKE

REVOKES > REVOKE

REVOKING > REVOKE

REVOLT *n* uprising against authority ▷ *vb* rise in rebellion

REVOLTED > REVOLT

REVOLTER > REVOLT

REVOLTERS > REVOLT

REVOLTING *adj* disgusting, horrible

REVOLTS > REVOLT

REVOLUTE *adj* (esp of the margins of a leaf) rolled backwards and downwards

REVOLVE *vb* turn round, rotate ▷ *n* circular section of a stage that can be rotated

REVOLVED > REVOLVE

REVOLVER *n* repeating pistol

REVOLVERS **> REVOLVER**

REVOLVES > REVOLVE

REVOLVING *adj* denoting or relating to an engine, such as a radial aero engine, in which the cylinders revolve about a fixed shaft

REVOTE *vb* decide or grant again by a new vote

REVOTED > REVOTE

REVOTES > REVOTE

REVOTING > REVOTE

REVS > REV

REVUE *n* theatrical entertainment with topical sketches and songs

REVUES > REVUE

REVUIST > REVUE

REVUISTS > REVUE

REVULSED *adj* filled with disgust

REVULSION *n* strong disgust

REVULSIVE *adj* of or causing revulsion ▷ *n* counterirritant

REVVED > REV

REVVING > REV

REVYING > REVIE

REW *archaic spelling of* **> RUE**

REWAKE *vb* awaken again

REWAKED > REWAKE

REWAKEN *vb* awaken again

REWAKENED > REWAKEN

REWAKENS > REWAKEN

REWAKES > REWAKE

REWAKING > REWAKE

REWAN *archaic past form of* **> REWIN**

REWARD *n* something given in return for a service ▷ *vb* pay or give something to (someone) for a service, information, etc

REWARDED > REWARD

REWARDER > REWARD

REWARDERS > REWARD

REWARDFUL > REWARD

REWARDING *adj* giving personal satisfaction, worthwhile

REWARDS > REWARD

REWAREWA *n* New Zealand tree

REWAREWAS **> REWAREWA**

REWARM *vb* warm again

REWARMED > REWARM

REWARMING > REWARM

REWARMS > REWARM

REWASH *vb* wash again

REWASHED > REWASH

REWASHES > REWASH

REWASHING > REWASH

REWATER *vb* water again

REWATERED > REWATER

REWATERS > REWATER

REWAX *vb* wax again

REWAXED > REWAX

REWAXES > REWAX

REWAXING > REWAX

REWEAR *vb* wear again

REWEARING > REWEAR

REWEARS > REWEAR

REWEAVE *vb* weave again

REWEAVED > REWEAVE

REWEAVES > REWEAVE

REWEAVING > REWEAVE

REWED *vb* wed again

REWEDDED > REWED

REWEDDING > REWED

REWEDS > REWED

REWEIGH *vb* weigh again

REWEIGHED > REWEIGH

REWEIGHS > REWEIGH

REWELD *vb* weld again

REWELDED > REWELD

REWELDING > REWELD

REWELDS > REWELD

REWET *vb* wet again

REWETS > REWET

REWETTED > REWET

REWETTING > REWET

REWIDEN *vb* widen again

REWIDENED > REWIDEN

REWIDENS > REWIDEN

REWILD *vb* return areas of land to a wild state

REWILDED > REWILD

REWILDING *n* process of returning land to a wild state

REWILDS > REWILD

REWIN *vb* win again

REWIND *vb* wind again

REWINDED > REWIND

REWINDER > REWIND

REWINDERS > REWIND

REWINDING *n* act of rewinding

REWINDS > REWIND

REWINNING > REWIN

REWINS > REWIN

REWIRABLE > REWIRE

REWIRE *vb* provide (a house, engine, etc) with new wiring

REWIRED > REWIRE

REWIRES > REWIRE

REWIRING *n* act of rewiring

REWIRINGS **> REWIRING**

REWOKE > REWAKE

REWOKEN > REWAKE

REWON > REWIN

REWORD *vb* alter the wording of

REWORDED > REWORD

REWORDING > REWORD

REWORDS > REWORD

REWORE > REWEAR

REWORK *vb* improve or bring up to date

REWORKED > REWORK

REWORKING > REWORK

REWORKS > REWORK

REWORN > REWEAR

REWOUND > REWIND

REWOVE > REWEAVE

REWOVEN > REWEAVE

REWRAP *vb* wrap again

REWRAPPED > REWRAP

REWRAPS > REWRAP

REWRAPT > REWRAP

REWRITE *vb* write again in a different way ▷ *n* something rewritten

REWRITER > REWRITE

REWRITERS > REWRITE

REWRITES > REWRITE

REWRITING > REWRITE

REWRITTEN > REWRITE

REWROTE > REWRITE

REWROUGHT > REWORK

REWS > REW

REWTH *archaic variant of* **> RUTH**

REWTHS > REWTH

REX *n* king

REXES > REX

REXINE *n* tradename for a form of artificial leather

REXINES > REXINE

REYNARD *n* fox

r

REYNARDS > REYNARD
REZ *n* informal word for an instance of reserving; reservation
REZERO *vb* reset to zero
REZEROED > REZERO
REZEROES > REZERO
REZEROING > REZERO
REZEROS > REZERO
REZES > REZ
REZONE *vb* zone again
REZONED > REZONE
REZONES > REZONE
REZONING *n* act of changing the land use classification of an area
REZONINGS > REZONING
REZZES > REZ
RHABDOID *adj* rod-shaped ▷ *n* rod-shaped structure found in cells of some plants and animals
RHABDOIDS > RHABDOID
RHABDOM *n* rodlike structure found in the eye of insects
RHABDOMAL > RHABDOM
RHABDOME *same as* > RHABDOM
RHABDOMES > RHABDOME
RHABDOMS > RHABDOM
RHABDUS *n* sponge spicule
RHABDUSES > RHABDUS
RHACHIAL > RACHIS
RHACHIDES > RHACHIS
RHACHILLA *same as* > RACHILLA
RHACHIS *same as* > RACHIS
RHACHISES > RHACHIS
RHACHITIS *same as* > RACHITIS
RHAGADES *pl n* cracks found in the skin
RHAMNOSE *n* type of plant sugar
RHAMNOSES > RHAMNOSE
RHAMNUS *n* buckthorn
RHAMNUSES > RHAMNUS
RHAMPHOID *adj* beaklike
RHANJA *n* Indian English word for a male lover
RHANJAS > RHANJA
RHAPHAE *same as* > RAPHE
RHAPHES > RHAPHE
RHAPHIDE *same as* > RAPHIDE
RHAPHIDES > RHAPHIDE
RHAPHIS *same as* > RAPHIDE
RHAPONTIC *n* rhubarb
RHAPSODE *n* (in ancient Greece) professional reciter of poetry
RHAPSODES > RHAPSODE
RHAPSODIC *adj* of or like a rhapsody
RHAPSODY *n* freely structured emotional piece of music

RHATANIES > RHATANY
RHATANY *n* S American leguminous shrub
RHEA *n* S American three-toed ostrich
RHEAS > RHEA
RHEBOK *n* woolly brownish-grey southern African antelope
RHEBOKS > RHEBOK
RHEMATIC *adj* of or relating to word formation
RHEME *n* constituent of a sentence that adds most new information
RHEMES > RHEME
RHENIUM *n* silvery-white metallic element with a high melting point
RHENIUMS > RHENIUM
RHEOBASE *n* minimum nerve impulse required to elicit a response from a tissue
RHEOBASES > RHEOBASE
RHEOBASIC > RHEOBASE
RHEOCHORD *n* wire inserted into an electrical circuit to vary or regulate the current
RHEOCORD *same as* > RHEOCHORD
RHEOCORDS > RHEOCORD
RHEOLOGIC > RHEOLOGY
RHEOLOGY *n* branch of physics concerned with the flow and change of shape of matter
RHEOMETER *n* instrument for measuring the velocity of the blood flow
RHEOMETRY > RHEOMETER
RHEOPHIL *adj* liking flowing water
RHEOPHILE *n* something that likes flowing water
RHEOSCOPE *n* device that detects an electric current
RHEOSTAT *n* instrument for varying the resistance of an electrical circuit
RHEOSTATS > RHEOSTAT
RHEOTAXES > RHEOTAXIS
RHEOTAXIS *n* movement of an organism towards or away from a current of water
RHEOTOME *n* interrupter
RHEOTOMES > RHEOTOME
RHEOTROPE *n* electric-current-reversing device
RHESUS *n* macaque monkey
RHESUSES > RHESUS
RHETOR *n* teacher of rhetoric
RHETORIC *n* art of effective speaking or writing

RHETORICS > RHETORIC
RHETORISE *same as* > RHETORIZE
RHETORIZE *vb* make use of rhetoric
RHETORS > RHETOR
RHEUM *n* watery discharge from the eyes or nose
RHEUMATIC *adj* affected by rheumatism ▷ *n* person affected by rheumatism
RHEUMATIZ *n* dialect word meaning rheumatism, any painful disorder of joints, muscles, or connective tissue
RHEUMED *adj* rheumy
RHEUMIC *adj* of or relating to rheum
RHEUMIER > RHEUMY
RHEUMIEST > RHEUMY
RHEUMS > RHEUM
RHEUMY *adj* of the nature of rheum
RHEXES > RHEXIS
RHEXIS *n* rupture
RHEXISES > RHEXIS
RHIES > RHY
RHIGOLENE *n* volatile liquid obtained from petroleum and used as a local anaesthetic
RHIME *old spelling of* > RHYME
RHIMES > RHIME
RHINAL *adj* of or relating to the nose
RHINE *n* dialect word for a ditch
RHINES > RHINE
RHINITIC > RHINITIS
RHINITIS *n* inflammation of the mucous membrane that lines the nose
RHINO *n* rhinoceros
RHINOCERI > rhinoceroses
RHINOLITH *n* calculus formed in the nose
RHINOLOGY *n* branch of medical science concerned with the nose and its diseases
RHINOS > RHINO
RHIPIDATE *adj* shaped like a fan
RHIPIDION *n* fan found in Greek Orthodox churches
RHIPIDIUM *n* on a plant, a fan-shaped arrangement of flowers
RHIZIC *adj* of or relating to the root of an equation
RHIZINE *same as* > RHIZOID
RHIZINES > RHIZINE
RHIZOBIA > RHIZOBIUM
RHIZOBIAL > RHIZOBIUM
RHIZOBIUM *n* type of rod-shaped bacterium typically occurring in the root nodules of leguminous plants

RHIZOCARP *n* plant that fruits underground or whose root remains intact while the leaves die off annually
RHIZOCAUL *n* rootlike stem
RHIZOID *n* hairlike structure in mosses, ferns, and related plants
RHIZOIDAL > RHIZOID
RHIZOIDS > RHIZOID
RHIZOMA *same as* > RHIZOME
RHIZOMATA > RHIZOMA
RHIZOME *n* thick underground stem producing new plants
RHIZOMES > RHIZOME
RHIZOMIC > RHIZOME
RHIZOPI > RHIZOPUS
RHIZOPOD *n* type of protozoan of the phylum which includes the amoebas
RHIZOPODS > RHIZOPOD
RHIZOPUS *n* type of fungus
RHIZOTOMY *n* surgical incision into the roots of spinal nerves, esp for the relief of pain
RHO *n* 17th letter in the Greek alphabet
RHODAMIN *same as* > RHODAMINE
RHODAMINE *n* any one of a group of synthetic red or pink basic dyestuffs used for wool and silk. They are made from phthalic anhydride and aminophenols
RHODAMINS > RHODAMIN
RHODANATE *n* a salt of thiocyanic acid
RHODANIC *adj* of or relating to thiocyanic acid
RHODANISE *same as* > RHODANIZE
RHODANIZE *vb* plate with rhodium
RHODIC *adj* of or containing rhodium, esp in the tetravalent state
RHODIE *same as* > RHODY
RHODIES > RHODY
RHODINAL *n* substance with a lemon-like smell found esp in citronella and certain eucalyptus oils
RHODINALS > RHODINAL
RHODIUM *n* hard metallic element
RHODIUMS > RHODIUM
RHODOLITE *n* pale violet or red variety of garnet, used as a gemstone
RHODONITE *n* brownish translucent mineral
RHODOPSIN *n* red pigment in the rods of the retina in vertebrates
RHODORA *n* type of shrub
RHODORAS > RHODORA

RHODOUS adj of or containing rhodium (but proportionally more than a rhodic compound)
RHODY n rhododendron
RHOEADINE n alkaloid found in the poppy
RHOMB same as > RHOMBUS
RHOMBI > RHOMBUS
RHOMBIC adj relating to or having the shape of a rhombus
RHOMBICAL same as > RHOMBIC
RHOMBOI > RHOMBOS
RHOMBOID n parallelogram with adjacent sides of unequal length ▷ adj having such a shape
RHOMBOIDS > RHOMBOID
RHOMBOS n wooden slat attached to a thong that makes a roaring sound when the thong is whirled
RHOMBS > RHOMB
RHOMBUS n diamond-shaped figure
RHOMBUSES > RHOMBUS
RHONCHAL > RHONCHUS
RHONCHI > RHONCHUS
RHONCHIAL > RHONCHUS
RHONCHUS n respiratory sound resembling snoring
RHONCUS n respiratory sound resembling snoring
RHONCUSES > RHONCUS
RHONE same as > RONE
RHONES > RHONE
RHOPALIC adj (of verse) with each word having one more syllable than the word before
RHOPALISM > RHOPALIC
RHOS > RHO
RHOTACISE same as > RHOTACIZE
RHOTACISM n excessive use or idiosyncratic pronunciation of r
RHOTACIST > RHOTACISM
RHOTACIZE vb pronounce r excessively or idiosyncratically
RHOTIC adj denoting or speaking a dialect of English in which postvocalic rs are pronounced
RHOTICITY > RHOTIC
RHUBARB n garden plant with fleshy stalks ▷ interj noise made by actors to simulate conversation ▷ vb simulate conversation in this way
RHUBARBED > RHUBARB
RHUBARBS > RHUBARB
RHUBARBY adj tasting of rhubarb
RHUMB n imaginary line on the surface of a sphere that intersects all meridians at the same angle

RHUMBA same as > RUMBA
RHUMBAED > RHUMBA
RHUMBAING > RHUMBA
RHUMBAS > RHUMBA
RHUMBS > RHUMB
RHUS n genus of shrubs and small trees
RHUSES > RHUS
RHY archaic spelling of > RYE
RHYME n sameness of the final sounds at the ends of lines of verse, or in words ▷ vb make a rhyme
RHYMED > RHYME
RHYMELESS > RHYME
RHYMER same as > RHYMESTER
RHYMERS > RHYMER
RHYMES > RHYME
RHYMESTER n mediocre poet
RHYMING > RHYME
RHYMIST > RHYME
RHYMISTS > RHYME
RHYNE same as > RHINE
RHYNES > RHYNE
RHYOLITE n fine-grained igneous rock
RHYOLITES > RHYOLITE
RHYOLITIC > RHYOLITE
RHYTA > RHYTON
RHYTHM n any regular movement or beat
RHYTHMAL adj rhythmic
RHYTHMED > RHYTHM
RHYTHMI > RHYTHMUS
RHYTHMIC adj of, relating to, or characterized by rhythm, as in movement or sound
RHYTHMICS n study of rhythmic movement
RHYTHMISE same as > RHYTHMIZE
RHYTHMIST n person who has a good sense of rhythm
RHYTHMIZE vb make rhythmic
RHYTHMS > RHYTHM
RHYTHMUS n rhythm
RHYTIDOME n bark
RHYTINA n type of sea cow
RHYTINAS > RHYTINA
RHYTON n (in ancient Greece) horn-shaped drinking vessel
RHYTONS > RHYTON
RIA n long narrow inlet of the seacoast
RIAD n traditional Moroccan house with an interior garden
RIADS > RIAD
RIAL n standard monetary unit of Iran
RIALS > RIAL
RIALTO n market or exchange
RIALTOS > RIALTO
RIANCIES > RIANCY
RIANCY > RIANT
RIANT adj laughing
RIANTLY > RIANT

RIAS > RIA
RIATA same as > REATA
RIATAS > RIATA
RIB n one of the curved bones forming the framework of the upper part of the body ▷ vb provide or mark with ribs
RIBA n (in Islam) interest or usury
RIBALD adj humorously or mockingly rude ▷ n ribald person
RIBALDER > RIBALD
RIBALDEST > RIBALD
RIBALDLY > RIBALD
RIBALDRY n ribald language or behaviour
RIBALDS > RIBALD
RIBAND n ribbon awarded for some achievement
RIBANDS > RIBAND
RIBAS > RIBA
RIBATTUTA n (in music) type of trill
RIBAUD archaic variant of > RIBALD
RIBAUDRED archaic variant of > RIBALD
RIBAUDRY archaic variant of > RIBALDRY
RIBAUDS > RIBAUD
RIBAVIRIN n type of antiviral drug
RIBBAND same as > RIBAND
RIBBANDS > RIBBAND
RIBBED > RIB
RIBBER n someone who ribs
RIBBERS > RIBBER
RIBBIE n baseball run batted in
RIBBIER > RIBBY
RIBBIES > RIBBIE
RIBBIEST > RIBBY
RIBBING > RIB
RIBBINGS > RIB
RIBBIT n sound a frog makes
RIBBITS > RIBBIT
RIBBON n narrow band of fabric used for trimming, tying, etc ▷ vb adorn with a ribbon or ribbons
RIBBONED > RIBBON
RIBBONIER > RIBBONY
RIBBONING > RIBBON
RIBBONRY n ribbons or ribbon work
RIBBONS > RIBBON
RIBBONY adj resembling ribbons
RIBBY adj with noticeable ribs
RIBCAGE n bony structure of ribs enclosing the lungs
RIBCAGES > RIBCAGE
RIBES n genus of shrubs that includes currants
RIBEYE n beefsteak cut from the outer side of the rib section
RIBEYES > RIBEYE
RIBGRASS same as > RIBWORT

RIBIBE n rebeck
RIBIBES > RIBIBE
RIBIBLE same as > RIBIBE
RIBIBLES > RIBIBLE
RIBIER n variety of grape
RIBIERS > RIBIER
RIBLESS > RIB
RIBLET n small rib
RIBLETS > RIBLET
RIBLIKE > RIB
RIBOSE n pentose sugar that occurs in RNA and riboflavin
RIBOSES > RIBOSE
RIBOSOMAL > RIBOSOME
RIBOSOME n any of numerous minute particles in the cytoplasm of cells
RIBOSOMES > RIBOSOME
RIBOZYMAL > RIBOZYME
RIBOZYME n RNA molecule capable of catalysing a chemical reaction
RIBOZYMES > RIBOZYME
RIBS > RIB
RIBSTON n variety of apple
RIBSTONE same as > RIBSTON
RIBSTONES > RIBSTONE
RIBSTONS > RIBSTON
RIBULOSE n type of sugar
RIBULOSES > RIBULOSE
RIBWORK n work or structure involving ribs
RIBWORKS > RIBWORK
RIBWORT n Eurasian plant with lancelike ribbed leaves
RIBWORTS > RIBWORT
RICE n cereal plant grown on wet ground in warm countries ▷ vb sieve (vegetables) to a coarse mashed consistency
RICEBIRD n any of various birds frequenting rice fields, esp the Java sparrow
RICEBIRDS > RICEBIRD
RICED > RICE
RICEFIELD n field used for growing rice
RICEGRASS n type of grass
RICER n kitchen utensil through which soft foods are pressed to form a coarse mash
RICERCAR same as > RICERCARE
RICERCARE n elaborate polyphonic composition making extensive use of contrapuntal imitation and usually very slow in tempo

r

RICERCARI
> RICERCARE

RICERCARS
> RICERCARE

RICERCATA same as
> RICERCARE

RICERS > RICER

RICES > RICE

RICEY adj resembling or
containing rice

RICH adj owning a lot of
money or property,
wealthy ▷ vb (in archaic
usage) enrich

RICHED > RICH

RICHEN vb enrich

RICHENED > RICHEN

RICHENING > RICHEN

RICHENS > RICHEN

RICHER > RICH

RICHES pl n wealth

RICHESSE n wealth or
richness

RICHESSES
> RICHESSE

RICHEST > RICH

RICHING > RICH

RICHLY adv elaborately

RICHNESS n state or
quality of being rich

RICHT Scots variant of
> RIGHT

RICHTED > RICHT

RICHTER > RICHT

RICHTEST > RICHT

RICHTING > RICHT

RICHTS > RICHT

RICHWEED n type of plant

RICHWEEDS
> RICHWEED

RICIER > RICY

RICIEST > RICY

RICIN n highly toxic
protein, a lectin, derived
from castor-oil seeds

RICING > RICE

RICINS > RICIN

RICINUS n genus of
plants

RICINUSES > RICINUS

RICK n stack of hay etc
▷ vb wrench or sprain (a
joint)

RICKED > RICK

RICKER n young kauri
tree of New Zealand

RICKERS > RICKER

RICKET n mistake

RICKETIER > RICKETY

RICKETILY > RICKETY

RICKETS n disease of
children marked by
softening of the bones,
bow legs, etc

RICKETTY same as
> RICKETY

RICKETY adj shaky or
unstable

RICKEY n cocktail
consisting of gin or vodka,
lime juice, and soda water,
served iced

RICKEYS > RICKEY

RICKING > RICK

RICKLE n unsteady or
shaky structure

RICKLES > RICKLE

RICKLIER > RICKLY

RICKLIEST > RICKLY

RICKLY adj archaic word
for run-down or rickety

RICKRACK n zigzag braid
used for trimming

RICKRACKS
> RICKRACK

RICKS > RICK

RICKSHA same as
> RICKSHAW

RICKSHAS > RICKSHA

RICKSHAW n light
two-wheeled vehicle
pulled by one or two
people

RICKSHAWS
> RICKSHAW

RICKSTAND n platform
on which to put a rick

RICKSTICK n tool used
when making hayricks

RICKYARD n place where
hayricks are put

RICKYARDS
> RICKYARD

RICOCHET vb (of a bullet)
rebound from a solid
surface ▷ n such a
rebound

RICOCHETS
> RICOCHET

RICOTTA n soft white
unsalted Italian cheese
made from sheep's milk

RICOTTAS > RICOTTA

RICRAC same as
> RICKRACK

RICRACS > RICRAC

RICTAL > RICTUS

RICTUS n gape or cleft of
an open mouth or beak

RICTUSES > RICTUS

RICY same as > RICEY

RID vb clear or relieve (of)

RIDABLE > RIDE

RIDDANCE n act of
getting rid of something
undesirable or unpleasant

RIDDANCES
> RIDDANCE

RIDDED > RID

RIDDEN > RIDE

RIDDER > RID

RIDDERS > RID

RIDDING > RID

RIDDLE n question made
puzzling to test one's
ingenuity ▷ vb speak in
riddles

RIDDLED > RIDDLE

RIDDLER > RIDDLE

RIDDLERS > RIDDLE

RIDDLES > RIDDLE

RIDDLING > RIDDLE

RIDDLINGS > RIDDLE

RIDE vb sit on and control
or propel (a horse, bicycle,
etc) ▷ n journey on a horse
etc

RIDEABLE > RIDE

RIDENT adj laughing,
smiling, or happy

RIDER n person who rides

RIDERED > RIDER

RIDERLESS > RIDER

RIDERS > RIDER

RIDERSHIP > RIDER

RIDES > RIDE

RIDGE n long narrow hill
▷ vb form into a ridge or
ridges

RIDGEBACK n as in
Rhodesian ridgeback breed
of dog characterized by a
ridge of hair growing
along the back in the
opposite direction to the
rest of the coat

RIDGED > RIDGE

RIDGEL same as
> RIDGELING

RIDGELIKE > RIDGE

RIDGELINE n ridge

RIDGELING n domestic
male animal with one
testicle

RIDGELS > RIDGEL

RIDGEPOLE n timber
along the ridge of a roof, to
which the rafters are
attached

RIDGER n plough used to
form furrows and ridges

RIDGERS > RIDGER

RIDGES > RIDGE

RIDGETOP n summit of
ridge

RIDGETOPS > RIDGETOP

RIDGETREE another name
for > RIDGEPOLE

RIDGEWAY n road or
track along a ridge, esp
one of great antiquity

RIDGEWAYS
> RIDGEWAY

RIDGIER > RIDGE

RIDGIEST > RIDGE

RIDGIL same as
> RIDGELING

RIDGILS > RIDGIL

RIDGING > RIDGE

RIDGINGS > RIDGE

RIDGLING same as
> RIDGELING

RIDGLINGS
> RIDGLING

RIDGY > RIDGE

RIDIC adj ridiculous

RIDICULE n treatment
of a person or thing as
ridiculous ▷ vb laugh at,
make fun of

RIDICULED
> RIDICULE

RIDICULER
> RIDICULE

RIDICULES
> RIDICULE

RIDING > RIDE

RIDINGS > RIDE

RIDLEY n marine turtle

RIDLEYS > RIDLEY

RIDOTTO n
entertainment with music
and dancing, often in
masquerade

RIDOTTOS > RIDOTTO

RIDS > RID

RIEL n standard
monetary unit of
Cambodia

RIELS > RIEL

RIEM n strip of hide

RIEMPIE n leather thong
or lace used mainly to
make chair seats

RIEMPIES > RIEMPIE

RIEMS > RIEM

RIESLING n type of
white wine

RIESLINGS
> RIESLING

RIEVE vb archaic word for
rob or plunder

RIEVED > RIEVE

RIEVER n archaic word
for robber or plunderer

RIEVERS > RIEVER

RIEVES > RIEVE

RIEVING > RIEVE

RIF vb lay off

RIFAMPIN n drug used in
the treatment of
tuberculosis, meningitis,
and leprosy

RIFAMPINS
> RIFAMPIN

RIFAMYCIN n antibiotic

RIFE adj widespread or
common

RIFELY > RIFE

RIFENESS > RIFE

RIFER > RIFE

RIFEST > RIFE

RIFF n short repeated
melodic figure ▷ vb play or
perform riffs in jazz or rock
music

RIFFAGE n (in jazz or rock
music) act or an instance
of playing a short series of
chords

RIFFAGES > RIFFAGE

RIFFED > RIFF

RIFFING > RIFF

RIFFLE vb flick through
(pages etc) quickly ▷ n
rapid in a stream

RIFFLED > RIFFLE

RIFFLER n file with a
curved face for filing
concave surfaces

RIFFLERS > RIFFLER

RIFFLES > RIFFLE

RIFFLING > RIFFLE

RIFFOLA n use of an
abundance of dominant
riffs

RIFFOLAS > RIFFOLA

RIFFRAFF n rabble,
disreputable people

RIFFRAFFS
> RIFFRAFF

RIFFS > RIFF

RIFLE n firearm with a
long barrel ▷ vb cut spiral
grooves inside the barrel of
a gun

RIFLEBIRD n any of
various birds of paradise

RIFLED > RIFLE

RIFLEMAN n person
skilled in the use of a rifle,
esp a soldier

RIFLEMEN > RIFLEMAN

RIFLER > RIFLE

RIFLERIES > RIFLERY

RIFLERS > RIFLE

RIFLERY n rifle shots

RIFLES > RIFLE

RIFLING n cutting of
spiral grooves on the
inside of a firearm's barrel

RIFLINGS > RIFLING

RIFLIP n genetic difference between two individuals

RIFLIPS > RIFLIP

RIFS > RIF

RIFT n break in friendly relations ▷ vb burst or cause to burst open

RIFTE archaic word for > RIFT

RIFTED > RIFT

RIFTIER > RIFT

RIFTIEST > RIFT

RIFTING > RIFT

RIFTLESS > RIFT

RIFTS > RIFT

RIFTY > RIFT

RIG vb arrange in a dishonest way ▷ n apparatus for drilling for oil and gas

RIGADOON n old Provençal dance in lively duple time

RIGADOONS > RIGADOON

RIGATONI n macaroni in the form of short ridged often slightly curved pieces

RIGATONIS > RIGATONI

RIGAUDON same as > RIGADOON

RIGAUDONS > RIGADOON

RIGG n type of fish

RIGGALD same as > RIDGELING

RIGGALDS > RIGGALD

RIGGED > RIG

RIGGER n person who rigs vessels, etc

RIGGERS > RIGGER

RIGGING > RIG

RIGGINGS > RIG

RIGGISH adj dialect word meaning wanton

RIGGS > RIGG

RIGHT adj just ▷ adv correctly ▷ n claim, title, etc allowed or due ▷ vb bring or come back to a normal or correct state

RIGHTABLE adj capable of being righted

RIGHTABLY > RIGHTABLE

RIGHTED > RIGHT

RIGHTEN vb set right

RIGHTENED > RIGHTEN

RIGHTENS > RIGHTEN

RIGHTEOUS adj upright, godly, or virtuous

RIGHTER > RIGHT

RIGHTERS > RIGHT

RIGHTEST > RIGHT

RIGHTFUL adj in accordance with what is right

RIGHTIER > RIGHTY

RIGHTIES > RIGHTY

RIGHTIEST > RIGHTY

RIGHTING > RIGHT

RIGHTINGS > RIGHT

RIGHTISH adj somewhat right, esp politically

RIGHTISM > RIGHTIST

RIGHTISMS > RIGHTIST

RIGHTIST adj on the political right ▷ n supporter of the political right

RIGHTISTS > RIGHTIST

RIGHTLESS > RIGHT

RIGHTLY adv in accordance with the true facts or justice

RIGHTMOST > RIGHT

RIGHTNESS n state or quality of being right

RIGHTO interj expression of agreement or compliance

RIGHTS > RIGHT

RIGHTSIZE vb restructure (an organization) to cut costs and improve effectiveness without ruthlessly downsizing

RIGHTWARD adj situated on or directed towards the right ▷ adv towards or on the right

RIGHTY n right-handed person ▷ adj right-handed

RIGID adj inflexible or strict ▷ adv completely or excessively ▷ n strict and unbending person

RIGIDER > RIGID

RIGIDEST > RIGID

RIGIDIFY vb make or become rigid

RIGIDISE same as > RIGIDIZE

RIGIDISED > RIGIDISE

RIGIDISES > RIGIDISE

RIGIDITY > RIGID

RIGIDIZE vb make or become rigid

RIGIDIZED > RIGIDIZE

RIGIDIZES > RIGIDIZE

RIGIDLY > RIGID

RIGIDNESS > RIGID

RIGIDS > RIGID

RIGLIN same as > RIDGELING

RIGLING same as > RIDGELING

RIGLINGS > RIGLING

RIGLINS > RIGLIN

RIGMAROLE n long complicated procedure

RIGOL n (in dialect) ditch or gutter

RIGOLL same as > RIGOL

RIGOLLS > RIGOLL

RIGOLS > RIGOL

RIGOR same as > RIGOUR

RIGORISM n strictness in judgment or conduct

RIGORISMS > RIGORISM

RIGORIST > RIGORISM

RIGORISTS > RIGORIST

RIGOROUS adj harsh, severe, or stern

RIGORS > RIGOR

RIGOUR n harshness, severity, or strictness

RIGOURS > RIGOUR

RIGOUT n person's clothing

RIGOUTS > RIGOUT

RIGS > RIG

RIGSDALER n any of various former Scandinavian or Dutch small silver coins

RIGWIDDIE n part of a carthorse's harness to which the shafts of the cart attach

RIGWOODIE same as > RIGWIDDIE

RIJSTAFEL n assortment of Indonesian rice dishes

RIKISHA same as > RICKSHAW

RIKISHAS > RIKISHA

RIKISHI n sumo wrestler

RIKSHAW same as > RICKSHAW

RIKSHAWS > RIKSHAW

RILE vb anger or annoy

RILED > RILE

RILES > RILE

RILEY adj cross or irritable

RILIER > RILEY

RILIEST > RILEY

RILIEVI > RILIEVO

RILIEVO same as > RELIEF

RILING > RILE

RILL n small stream ▷ vb trickle

RILLE same as > RILL

RILLED > RILL

RILLES > RILLE

RILLET n little rill

RILLETS > RILLET

RILLETTES pl n potted meat

RILLING > RILL

RILLMARK n mark left by the trickle of a rill

RILLMARKS > RILLMARK

RILLS > RILL

RIM n edge or border ▷ vb put a rim on (a pot, cup, wheel, etc)

RIMA n long narrow opening

RIMAE > RIMA

RIMAYE n crevasse at the head of a glacier

RIMAYES > RIMAYE

RIME same as > RHYME

RIMED > RIME

RIMELESS > RHYME

RIMER same as > RHYMER

RIMERS > RIMER

RIMES > RIME

RIMESTER same as > RHYMESTER

RIMESTERS > RIMESTER

RIMFIRE adj (of a cartridge) having the primer in the rim of the base ▷ n cartridge of this type

RIMFIRES > RIMFIRE

RIMIER > RIMY

RIMIEST > RIMY

RIMINESS > RIMY

RIMING > RIME

RIMLAND n area situated on the outer edges of a region

RIMLANDS > RIMLAND

RIMLESS > RIM

RIMMED > RIM

RIMMER n tool for shaping the edge of something

RIMMERS > RIMMER

RIMMING > RIM

RIMMINGS > RIM

RIMOSE adj (esp of plant parts) having the surface marked by a network of intersecting cracks

RIMOSELY > RIMOSE

RIMOSITY > RIMOSE

RIMOUS same as > RIMOSE

RIMPLE vb crease or wrinkle

RIMPLED > RIMPLE

RIMPLES > RIMPLE

RIMPLING > RIMPLE

RIMROCK n rock forming the boundaries of a sandy or gravelly alluvial deposit

RIMROCKS > RIMROCK

RIMS > RIM

RIMSHOT n deliberate simultaneous striking of skin and rim of drum

RIMSHOTS > RIMSHOT

RIMU n New Zealand tree

RIMUS > RIMU

RIMY adj coated with rime

RIN Scots variant of > RUN

RIND n tough outer coating of fruits, cheese, or bacon ▷ vb take the bark off

RINDED > RIND

RINDIER > RINDY

RINDIEST > RINDY

RINDING > RIND

RINDLESS > RIND

RINDS > RIND

RINDY adj with a rind or rindlike skin

RINE archaic variant of > RIND

RINES > RINE

RING vb give out a clear resonant sound, as a bell ▷ n instance of ringing

RINGBARK vb cut away a circular strip of bark from a tree or branch

RINGBARKS > RINGBARK

RINGBIT n type of bit worn by a horse

RINGBITS > RINGBIT

RINGBOLT n bolt with a ring fitted through an eye attached to the bolt head

RINGBOLTS > RINGBOLT

RINGBONE n abnormal bony growth affecting the

pastern of a horse, often causing lameness

RINGBONES
> RINGBONE

RINGDOVE n large Eurasian pigeon with white patches on the wings and neck

RINGDOVES
> RINGDOVE

RINGED > RING

RINGENT adj (of the corolla of plants) consisting of two gaping lips

RINGER n person or thing apparently identical to another

RINGERS > RINGER

RINGETTE n team sport played on ice, using straight sticks to control a rubber ring

RINGETTES
> RINGETTE

RINGGIT n standard monetary unit of Malaysia

RINGGITS > RINGGIT

RINGHALS n variety of cobra

RINGING > RING

RINGINGLY > RING

RINGINGS > RING

RINGLESS > RING

RINGLET n curly lock of hair

RINGLETED > RINGLET

RINGLETS > RINGLET

RINGLETY adj resembling a ringlet

RINGLIKE > RING

RINGMAN n (in dialect) ring finger

RINGMEN > RINGMAN

RINGNECK n any bird that has ringlike markings round its neck

RINGNECKS
> RINGNECK

RINGS > RING

RINGSIDE n row of seats nearest a boxing or circus ring ▷ adj providing a close uninterrupted view

RINGSIDER n someone with a ringside seat or position

RINGSIDES
> RINGSIDE

RINGSTAND n stand for laboratory equipment

RINGSTER n member of a ring controlling a market in antiques, art treasures, etc

RINGSTERS
> RINGSTER

RINGTAIL n possum with a curling tail used to grip branches while climbing

RINGTAILS
> RINGTAIL

RINGTAW n game in which the aim is to knock marbles out of a ring

RINGTAWS > RINGTAW

RINGTONE n musical tune played by a mobile

phone when a call is received

RINGTONES
> RINGTONE

RINGTOSS n game in which participants try to throw hoops onto an upright stick

RINGWAY n bypass

RINGWAYS > RINGWAY

RINGWISE adj used to being in the ring and able to respond appropriately

RINGWOMB n complication at lambing resulting from failure of the cervix to open

RINGWOMBS
> RINGWOMB

RINGWORK n circular earthwork

RINGWORKS
> RINGWORK

RINGWORM n fungal skin disease in circular patches

RINGWORMS
> RINGWORM

RINK n sheet of ice for skating or curling ▷ vb skate on a rink

RINKED > RINK

RINKHALS n S African cobra that can spit venom

RINKING > RINK

RINKS > RINK

RINKSIDE n area at the side of a rink

RINKSIDES
> RINKSIDE

RINNING > RIN

RINS > RIN

RINSABLE > RINSE

RINSE vb remove soap from (washed clothes, hair, etc) by applying clean water ▷ n act of rinsing

RINSEABLE > RINSE

RINSED > RINSE

RINSER > RINSE

RINSERS > RINSE

RINSES > RINSE

RINSIBLE > RINSE

RINSING > RINSE

RINSINGS > RINSE

RIOJA n red or white Spanish wine with a vanilla bouquet and flavour

RIOJAS > RIOJA

RIOT n disorderly unruly disturbance ▷ vb take part in a riot

RIOTED > RIOT

RIOTER > RIOT

RIOTERS > RIOT

RIOTING > RIOT

RIOTINGS > RIOT

RIOTISE n archaic word for riotous behaviour and excess

RIOTISES > RIOTISE

RIOTIZE same as
> RIOTISE

RIOTIZES > RIOTIZE

RIOTOUS adj unrestrained

RIOTOUSLY > RIOTOUS

RIOTRIES > RIOTRY

RIOTRY n riotous behaviour

RIOTS > RIOT

RIP vb tear violently ▷ n split or tear

RIPARIAL > RIPARIAN

RIPARIALS
> RIPARIAL

RIPARIAN adj of or on the banks of a river ▷ n person who owns land on a riverbank

RIPARIANS
> RIPARIAN

RIPCORD n cord pulled to open a parachute

RIPCORDS > RIPCORD

RIPE adj ready to be reaped, eaten, etc ▷ vb ripen

RIPECK same as
> RYEPECK

RIPECKS > RIPECK

RIPED > RIPE

RIPELY > RIPE

RIPEN vb grow ripe

RIPENED > RIPEN

RIPENER > RIPEN

RIPENERS > RIPEN

RIPENESS > RIPE

RIPENING > RIPEN

RIPENS > RIPEN

RIPER adj more ripe ▷ n old Scots word meaning plunderer

RIPERS > RIPER

RIPES > RIPE

RIPEST > RIPE

RIPIENI > RIPIENO

RIPIENIST n orchestral member who is there to swell the sound rather than play solo

RIPIENO n (in baroque concertos and concerti grossi) the full orchestra

RIPIENOS > RIPIENO

RIPING > RIPE

RIPOFF n grossly overpriced article

RIPOFFS > RIPOFF

RIPOST same as
> RIPOSTE

RIPOSTE n verbal retort ▷ vb make a riposte

RIPOSTED > RIPOSTE

RIPOSTES > RIPOSTE

RIPOSTING > RIPOSTE

RIPOSTS > RIPOST

RIPP n old Scots word for a handful of grain

RIPPABLE > RIP

RIPPED > RIP

RIPPER n person who rips

RIPPERS > RIPPER

RIPPIER n archaic word for fish seller

RIPPIERS > RIPPIER

RIPPING > RIP

RIPPINGLY > RIP

RIPPINGS > RIPPING

RIPPLE n slight wave or ruffling of a surface ▷ vb flow or form into little waves (on)

RIPPLED > RIPPLE

RIPPLER > RIPPLE

RIPPLERS > RIPPLE

RIPPLES > RIPPLE

RIPPLET n tiny ripple

RIPPLETS > RIPPLET

RIPPLIER > RIPPLE

RIPPLIEST > RIPPLE

RIPPLING > RIPPLE

RIPPLINGS > RIPPLE

RIPPLY > RIPPLE

RIPPS > RIPP

RIPRAP vb deposit broken stones in or on

RIPRAPPED > RIPRAP

RIPRAPS > RIPRAP

RIPS > RIP

RIPSAW n handsaw for cutting along the grain of timber ▷ vb saw with a ripsaw

RIPSAWED > RIPSAW

RIPSAWING > RIPSAW

RIPSAWN > RIPSAW

RIPSAWS > RIPSAW

RIPSTOP n tear-resistant cloth

RIPSTOPS > RIPSTOP

RIPT archaic past form of
> RIP

RIPTIDE n stretch of turbulent water in the sea

RIPTIDES > RIPTIDE

RIRORIRO n small New Zealand bush bird

RIRORIROS
> RIRORIRO

RISALDAR n Indian cavalry officer

RISALDARS
> RISALDAR

RISE vb get up from a lying, sitting, or kneeling position ▷ n act of rising

RISEN > RISE

RISER n person who rises, esp from bed

RISERS > RISER

RISES > RISE

RISHI n Indian seer or sage

RISHIS > RISHI

RISIBLE adj causing laughter, ridiculous

RISIBLES pl n sense of humour

RISIBLY > RISIBLE

RISING > RISE

RISINGS > RISE

RISK n chance of disaster or loss ▷ vb act in spite of the possibility of (injury or loss)

RISKED > RISK

RISKER > RISK

RISKERS > RISK

RISKFUL > RISK

RISKIER > RISKY

RISKIEST > RISKY

RISKILY > RISKY

RISKINESS > RISKY

RISKING > RISK

RISKLESS > RISK

RISKS > RISK

RISKY adj full of risk, dangerous

RISOLUTO adj musical term meaning firm and decisive ▷ adv firmly and decisively

RISORII > RISORIUS
RISORIUS n facial muscle responsible for smiling
RISOTTO n dish of rice cooked in stock with vegetables, meat, etc
RISOTTOS > RISOTTO
RISP vb Scots word meaning rasp
RISPED > RISP
RISPETTI > RISPETTO
RISPETTO n kind of folk song
RISPING > RISP
RISPINGS > RISP
RISPS > RISP
RISQUE same as > RISK
RISQUES > RISQUE
RISSOLE n cake of minced meat, coated with breadcrumbs and fried
RISSOLES > RISSOLE
RISTRA n string of dried chilli peppers
RISTRAS > RISTRA
RISTRETTO n strong espresso coffee
RISUS n involuntary grinning expression
RISUSES > RISUS
RIT vb Scots word for cut or slit
RITARD n (in music) a slowing down
RITARDS > RITARD
RITE n formal practice or custom, esp religious
RITELESS > RITE
RITENUTO adv held back momentarily ▷ n (in music) a slowing down
RITENUTOS > RITENUTO
RITES > RITE
RITONAVIR n drug used to treat HIV
RITORNEL n (in music) orchestral passage
RITORNELL same as > RITORNEL
RITORNELS > RITORNEL
RITS > RIT
RITT same as > RIT
RITTED > RIT
RITTER n knight or horseman/horsewoman
RITTERS > RITTER
RITTING > RIT
RITTS > RITT
RITUAL n prescribed order of rites ▷ adj concerning rites
RITUALISE same as > RITUALIZE
RITUALISM n exaggerated emphasis on the importance of rites and ceremonies
RITUALIST > RITUALISM
RITUALIZE vb engage in ritualism or devise rituals
RITUALLY > RITUAL
RITUALS > RITUAL
RITUXIMAB n drug used to treat non-Hodgkin's lymphoma

RITZ n ostentatious display
RITZES > RITZ
RITZIER > RITZY
RITZIEST > RITZY
RITZILY > RITZY
RITZINESS > RITZY
RITZY adj luxurious or elegant
RIVA n rock cleft
RIVAGE n bank, shore, or coast
RIVAGES > RIVAGE
RIVAL n person or thing that competes with another ▷ adj in the position of a rival ▷ vb (try to) equal
RIVALED > RIVAL
RIVALLESS n female rival
RIVALING > RIVAL
RIVALISE same as > RIVALIZE
RIVALISED > RIVALISE
RIVALISES > RIVALISE
RIVALITY > RIVAL
RIVALIZE vb become a rival
RIVALIZED > RIVALIZE
RIVALIZES > RIVALIZE
RIVALLED > RIVAL
RIVALLESS > RIVAL
RIVALLING > RIVAL
RIVALRIES > RIVALRY
RIVALROUS > RIVALRY
RIVALRY n keen competition
RIVALS > RIVAL
RIVALSHIP > RIVAL
RIVAS > RIVA
RIVE vb split asunder
RIVED > RIVE
RIVEL vb archaic word meaning wrinkle
RIVELLED > RIVEL
RIVELLING > RIVEL
RIVELS > RIVEL
RIVEN > RIVE
RIVER n large natural stream of water
RIVERAIN same as > RIPARIAN
RIVERAINS > RIVERAIN
RIVERBANK n bank of a river
RIVERBED n bed of a river
RIVERBEDS > RIVERBED
RIVERBOAT n boat, especially a barge, designed for use on rivers
RIVERED adj with a river or rivers
RIVERET n archaic word for rivulet or stream
RIVERETS > RIVERET
RIVERHEAD n source of river
RIVERIER > RIVERY
RIVERIEST > RIVERY
RIVERINE same as > RIPARIAN
RIVERLESS > RIVER

RIVERLIKE adj resembling a river
RIVERMAN n boatman or man earning his living working on a river
RIVERMEN > RIVERMAN
RIVERS > RIVER
RIVERSIDE n area beside a river
RIVERWALK n paved walkway along the side of a river
RIVERWARD adj towards the river ▷ adv towards the river
RIVERWAY n river serving as a waterway
RIVERWAYS > RIVERWAY
RIVERWEED n type of plant found growing near rivers
RIVERY adj riverlike
RIVES > RIVE
RIVET n bolt for fastening metal plates ▷ vb fasten with rivets
RIVETED > RIVET
RIVETER > RIVET
RIVETERS > RIVET
RIVETING > RIVET
RIVETINGS > RIVET
RIVETS > RIVET
RIVETTED > RIVET
RIVETTING > RIVET
RIVIERA n coastline resembling the Mediterranean Riviera
RIVIERAS > RIVIERA
RIVIERE n necklace of diamonds which gradually increase in size
RIVIERES > RIVIERE
RIVING > RIVE
RIVLIN n Scots word for rawhide shoe
RIVLINS > RIVLIN
RIVO interj (in the past) an informal toast
RIVULET n small stream
RIVULETS > RIVULET
RIVULOSE adj having meandering lines
RIVULUS n type of small tropical American fish
RIVULUSES > RIVULUS
RIYAL n standard monetary unit of Qatar, divided into 100 dirhams
RIYALS > RIYAL
RIZ (in some dialects) past form of > RISE
RIZA n partial icon cover made from precious metal
RIZARD n redcurrant
RIZARDS > RIZARD
RIZAS > RIZA
RIZZAR n Scots word for redcurrant ▷ vb Scots word for sun-dry
RIZZARED > RIZZAR
RIZZARING > RIZZAR
RIZZARS > RIZZAR
RIZZART n Scots word for redcurrant
RIZZARTS > RIZZART
RIZZER same as > RIZZAR

RIZZERED > RIZZER
RIZZERING > RIZZER
RIZZERS > RIZZER
RIZZOR vb dry
RIZZORED > RIZZOR
RIZZORING > RIZZOR
RIZZORS > RIZZOR
ROACH n Eurasian freshwater fish ▷ vb clip (mane) short so that it stands upright
ROACHED adj arched convexly, as the back of certain breeds of dog, such as the whippet
ROACHES > ROACH
ROACHING > ROACH
ROAD n way prepared for passengers, vehicles, etc
ROADBED n material used to make a road
ROADBEDS > ROADBED
ROADBLOCK n barricade across a road to stop traffic for inspection etc
ROADCRAFT n skills and knowledge of a road user
ROADEO n competition testing driving skills
ROADEOS > ROADEO
ROADHOG n selfish or aggressive driver
ROADHOGS > ROADHOG
ROADHOUSE n pub or restaurant on a country road
ROADIE n person who transports and sets up equipment for a band
ROADIES > ROADIE
ROADING n road building
ROADINGS > ROADING
ROADKILL n remains of an animal or animals killed on the road by motor vehicles
ROADKILLS > ROADKILL
ROADLESS > ROAD
ROADMAN n someone involved in road repair or construction
ROADMEN > ROADMAN
ROADS > ROAD
ROADSHOW n radio show broadcast live from a place being visited by a touring disc jockey
ROADSHOWS > ROADSHOW
ROADSIDE n side of a road ▷ adj situated beside a road
ROADSIDES > ROADSIDE
ROADSMAN same as > ROADMAN
ROADSMEN > ROADSMAN
ROADSTEAD same as > ROAD
ROADSTER n open car with only two seats
ROADSTERS > ROADSTER
ROADWAY n part of a road used by vehicles
ROADWAYS > ROADWAY

r

ROADWORK n sports training by running along roads

ROADWORKS pl n repairs to a road, esp blocking part of the road

ROAM vb wander about ▷ n act of roaming

ROAMED > ROAM

ROAMER > ROAM

ROAMERS > ROAM

ROAMING > ROAM

ROAMINGS > ROAM

ROAMS > ROAM

ROAN adj (of a horse) having a brown or black coat sprinkled with white hairs ▷ n roan horse

ROANPIPE n Scots word for a drainpipe leading down from a gutter

ROANPIPES > ROANPIPE

ROANS > ROAN

ROAR vb make or utter a loud deep hoarse sound like that of a lion ▷ n such a sound

ROARED > ROAR

ROARER > ROAR

ROARERS > ROAR

ROARIE Scots word for > NOISY

ROARIER > ROARY

ROARIEST > ROARY

ROARING > ROAR

ROARINGLY > ROARING

ROARINGS > ROAR

ROARMING adj severe

ROARS > ROAR

ROARY adj sounding like a roar or tending to roar

ROAST vb cook by dry heat, as in an oven ▷ n roasted joint of meat ▷ adj roasted

ROASTED > ROAST

ROASTER n person or thing that roasts

ROASTERS > ROASTER

ROASTIE n roast potato

ROASTIES > ROASTIE

ROASTING adj extremely hot ▷ n severe criticism or scolding

ROASTINGS > ROASTING

ROASTS > ROAST

ROATE archaic form of > ROTE

ROATED > ROATE

ROATES > ROATE

ROATING > ROATE

ROB vb steal from

ROBALO n tropical fish

ROBALOS > ROBALO

ROBAND n piece of marline used for fastening a sail to a spar

ROBANDS > ROBAND

ROBATA n grill used for Japanese cooking

ROBATAS > ROBATA

ROBBED > ROB

ROBBER > ROB

ROBBERIES > ROBBERY

ROBBERS > ROB

ROBBERY n stealing of property from a person by using or threatening to use force

ROBBIN same as > ROBAND

ROBBING > ROB

ROBBINS > ROBBIN

ROBE n long loose outer garment ▷ vb put a robe on

ROBED > ROBE

ROBELIKE adj like a robe

ROBES > ROBE

ROBIN n small brown bird with a red breast

ROBING > ROBE

ROBINGS > ROBE

ROBINIA n type of leguminous tree

ROBINIAS > ROBINIA

ROBINS > ROBIN

ROBLE n oak tree

ROBLES > ROBLE

ROBOCALL n automated telephone call that delivers a message to a large number of people

ROBOCALLS > ROBOCALL

ROBORANT adj tending to fortify or increase strength ▷ n drug or agent that increases strength

ROBORANTS > ROBORANT

ROBOT n automated machine, esp one performing functions in a human manner

ROBOTIC > ROBOT

ROBOTICS n science of designing and using robots

ROBOTISE same as > ROBOTIZE

ROBOTISED > ROBOTISE

ROBOTISES > ROBOTISE

ROBOTISM > ROBOT

ROBOTISMS > ROBOT

ROBOTIZE vb automate

ROBOTIZED > ROBOTIZE

ROBOTIZES > ROBOTIZE

ROBOTRIES > ROBOT

ROBOTRY > ROBOT

ROBOTS > ROBOT

ROBS > ROB

ROBURITE n flameless explosive

ROBURITES > ROBURITE

ROBUST adj very strong and healthy

ROBUSTA n species of coffee tree

ROBUSTAS > ROBUSTA

ROBUSTER > ROBUST

ROBUSTEST > ROBUST

ROBUSTLY > ROBUST

ROC n monstrous bird of Arabian mythology

ROCAILLE n decorative rock or shell work

ROCAILLES > ROCAILLE

ROCAMBOLE n variety of sand leek whose garlic-like bulb is used for seasoning

ROCH same as > ROTCH

ROCHES > ROCH

ROCHET n white surplice with tight sleeves, worn by Church dignitaries

ROCHETS > ROCHET

ROCK n hard mineral substance that makes up part of the earth's crust, stone ▷ vb (cause to) sway to and fro ▷ adj of or relating to rock music

ROCKABIES > ROCKABY

ROCKABLE > ROCK

ROCKABY same as > ROCKABYE

ROCKABYE n lullaby or rocking motion used with a baby during lullabies

ROCKABYES > ROCKABYE

ROCKAWAY n four-wheeled horse-drawn carriage, usually with two seats and a hard top

ROCKAWAYS > ROCKAWAY

ROCKBOUND adj hemmed in or encircled by rocks

ROCKBURST n sudden rupture of rock in a mine

ROCKCRESS n any plant of the annual or perennial genus Arabis

ROCKED > ROCK

ROCKER n rocking chair

ROCKERIES > ROCKERY

ROCKERS > ROCKER

ROCKERY n garden featuring rocks

ROCKET n self-propelling device powered by the burning of explosive contents ▷ vb move fast, esp upwards

ROCKETED > ROCKET

ROCKETEER n engineer or scientist concerned with the design, operation, or launching of rockets

ROCKETER n bird that launches itself into the air like a rocket when flushed

ROCKETERS > ROCKETER

ROCKETING > ROCKET

ROCKETRY n science and technology of the design and operation of rockets

ROCKETS > ROCKET

ROCKFALL n instance of rocks breaking away and falling from an outcrop

ROCKFALLS > ROCKFALL

ROCKFISH n any of various fishes that live among rocks

ROCKHOUND n person interested in rocks and minerals

ROCKIER n archaic or dialect word for rock pigeon

ROCKIERS > ROCKIER

ROCKIEST > ROCKY

ROCKILY > ROCKY

ROCKINESS > ROCKY

ROCKING > ROCK

ROCKINGLY > ROCKING

ROCKINGS > ROCK

ROCKLAY same as > ROKELAY

ROCKLAYS > ROCKLAY

ROCKLESS > ROCK

ROCKLIKE > ROCK

ROCKLING n any of various small sea fishes having an elongated body and barbels around the mouth

ROCKLINGS > ROCKLING

ROCKOON n rocket fired from a balloon at high altitude

ROCKOONS > ROCKOON

ROCKROSE n any of various shrubs or herbaceous plants cultivated for their roselike flowers

ROCKROSES > ROCKROSE

ROCKS > ROCK

ROCKSHAFT n shaft that rotates backwards and forwards rather than continuously, esp one used in the valve gear of a steam engine

ROCKSLIDE n fall of rocks down a hillside

ROCKWATER n water that comes out of rock

ROCKWEED n any of various seaweeds that grow on rocks exposed at low tide

ROCKWEEDS > ROCKWEED

ROCKWOOL n mineral wool used for insulation

ROCKWOOLS > ROCKWOOL

ROCKWORK n structure made of rock

ROCKWORKS > ROCKWORK

ROCKY adj having many rocks

ROCOCO adj (of furniture, architecture, etc) having much elaborate decoration ▷ n style of architecture and decoration characterized by elaborate ornamentation

ROCOCOS > ROCOCO

ROCQUET n another name for the salad plant rocket

ROCQUETS > ROCQUET

ROCS > ROC

ROD n slender straight bar, stick ▷ vb clear with a rod

RODDED > ROD

RODDING > ROD

RODDINGS > ROD

RODE vb (of the male woodcock) to perform a display flight

RODED > RODE

RODENT n animal with teeth specialized for gnawing

RODENTIAL adj relating to rodents

RODENTS > RODENT

RODEO n display of skill by cowboys, such as bareback riding ▷ vb take part in a rodeo

RODEOED > RODEO

RODEOING > RODEO

RODEOS > RODEO

RODES > RODE

RODEWAY archaic spelling of > ROADWAY

RODEWAYS > RODEWAY

RODFISHER n angler

RODGERSIA n flowering plant

RODING > RODE

RODINGS > RODE

RODLESS > ROD

RODLIKE > ROD

RODMAN n someone who uses or fishes with a rod

RODMEN > RODMAN

RODNEY n type of small fishing boat used in Canada

RODNEYS > RODNEY

RODS > ROD

RODSMAN same as > RODMAN

RODSMEN > RODSMAN

RODSTER n angler

RODSTERS > RODSTER

ROE n mass of eggs in a fish, sometimes eaten as food

ROEBUCK n male of the roe deer

ROEBUCKS > ROEBUCK

ROED adj with roe inside

ROEMER n drinking glass, typically having an ovoid bowl on a short stem

ROEMERS > ROEMER

ROENTGEN n unit measuring a radiation dose

ROENTGENS > ROENTGEN

ROES > ROE

ROESTI same as > ROSTI

ROESTIS > ROESTI

ROESTONE same as > OOLITE

ROESTONES > ROESTONE

ROGALLO n flexible fabric delta wing

ROGALLOS > ROGALLO

ROGATION n solemn supplication, esp in a form of ceremony prescribed by the Church

ROGATIONS > ROGATION

ROGATORY adj (esp in legal contexts) seeking or authorized to seek information

ROGER interj (used in signalling) message received ▷ vb acknowledge a received message

ROGERED > ROGER

ROGERING > ROGER

ROGERINGS > ROGER

ROGERS > ROGER

ROGNON n isolated rock outcrop on a glacier

ROGNONS > ROGNON

ROGUE n dishonest or unprincipled person ▷ adj (of a wild beast) living apart from the herd ▷ vb rid (a field or crop) of inferior or unwanted plants

ROGUED > ROGUE

ROGUEING > ROGUE

ROGUER n rogue

ROGUERIES > ROGUERY

ROGUERS > ROGUER

ROGUERY n dishonest or immoral behaviour

ROGUES > ROGUE

ROGUESHIP n condition of being a rogue

ROGUIER > ROGUY

ROGUIEST > ROGUY

ROGUING > ROGUE

ROGUISH adj dishonest or unprincipled

ROGUISHLY > ROGUISH

ROGUY adj roguish

ROHE n territory of a Māori tribal group

ROHES > ROHE

ROID n short form of steroid

ROIDS > ROID

ROIL vb make (a liquid) cloudy or turbid by stirring up dregs or sediment

ROILED > ROIL

ROILIER > ROILY

ROILIEST > ROILY

ROILING > ROIL

ROILS > ROIL

ROILY adj cloudy or muddy

ROIN same as > ROYNE

ROINED > ROIN

ROINING > ROIN

ROINISH same as > ROYNISH

ROINS > ROIN

ROIST archaic variant of > ROISTER

ROISTED > ROIST

ROISTER vb make merry noisily or boisterously

ROISTERED > ROISTER

ROISTERER > ROISTER

ROISTERS > ROISTER

ROISTING > ROIST

ROISTS > ROIST

ROJAK n (in Malaysia) a salad dish served in chilli sauce

ROJAKS > ROJAK

ROJI n Japanese tea garden or its path of stones

ROJIS > ROJI

ROK same as > ROC

ROKE vb (in dialect) steam or smoke

ROKED > ROKE

ROKELAY n type of cloak

ROKELAYS > ROKELAY

ROKER n variety of ray

ROKERS > ROKER

ROKES > ROKE

ROKIER > ROKY

ROKIEST > ROKY

ROKING > ROKE

ROKKAKU n hexagonal Japanese kite

ROKS > ROK

ROKY adj (in dialect) steamy or smoky

ROLAG n roll of carded wool ready for spinning

ROLAGS > ROLAG

ROLAMITE n type of bearing using two rollers and a moving flexible band

ROLAMITES > ROLAMITE

ROLE n task or function

ROLES > ROLE

ROLF vb massage following a particular technique

ROLFED > ROLF

ROLFER > ROLF

ROLFERS > ROLF

ROLFING > ROLF

ROLFINGS > ROLF

ROLFS > ROLF

ROLL vb move by turning over and over ▷ n act of rolling over or from side to side

ROLLABLE > ROLL

ROLLAWAY n mounted on rollers so as to be easily moved, esp to be stored away after use

ROLLAWAYS > ROLLAWAY

ROLLBACK n reduction to a previous price

ROLLBACKS > ROLLBACK

ROLLBAR n bar that reinforces the frame of a car

ROLLBARS > ROLLBAR

ROLLED > ROLL

ROLLER n rotating cylinder

ROLLERS > ROLLER

ROLLICK vb behave in a boisterous manner ▷ n boisterous or carefree escapade

ROLLICKED > ROLLICK

ROLLICKS > ROLLICK

ROLLICKY adj rollicking

ROLLIE n hand-rolled cigarette

ROLLIES > ROLLIE

ROLLING > ROLL

ROLLINGS > ROLL

ROLLMOP n herring fillet rolled round onion slices and pickled

ROLLMOPS > ROLLMOP

ROLLNECK adj (of a garment) having a high neck that is worn rolled over ▷ n rollneck sweater or other garment

ROLLNECKS > ROLLNECK

ROLLOCK same as > ROWLOCK

ROLLOCKS > ROLLOCK

ROLLOUT n presentation to the public of a new aircraft, product, etc; launch

ROLLOUTS > ROLLOUT

ROLLOVER n instance of a prize continuing in force for an additional period

ROLLOVERS > ROLLOVER

ROLLS > ROLL

ROLLTOP n as in rolltop desk desk having a slatted wooden panel that can be pulled down over the writing surface

ROLLUP n something rolled into a tube shape

ROLLUPS > ROLLUP

ROLLWAY n incline down which logs are rolled

ROLLWAYS > ROLLWAY

ROM n member of a European nomadic people

ROMA n member of a European nomadic people

ROMAGE archaic variant of > RUMMAGE

ROMAGES > ROMAGE

ROMAIKA n Greek dance

ROMAIKAS > ROMAIKA

ROMAINE n cos (lettuce)

ROMAINES > ROMAINE

ROMAJI n Roman alphabet as used to write Japanese

ROMAJIS > ROMAJI

ROMAL same as > RUMAL

ROMALS > ROMAL

ROMAN adj in or relating to the vertical style of printing type used for most printed matter ▷ n roman type

ROMANCE n love affair ▷ vb exaggerate or fantasize

ROMANCED > ROMANCE

ROMANCER > ROMANCE

ROMANCERS > ROMANCE

ROMANCES > ROMANCE

ROMANCING > ROMANCE

ROMANESCO n type of green cauliflower

ROMANISE same as > ROMANIZE

ROMANISED > ROMANISE

ROMANISES > ROMANISE

ROMANIZE vb impart a Roman Catholic character to (a ceremony, practice, etc)

ROMANIZED > ROMANIZE

ROMANIZES > ROMANIZE

ROMANO n hard light-coloured sharp-tasting cheese

ROMANOS > ROMANO

ROMANS > ROMAN

ROMANTIC adj of or dealing with love ▷ n romantic person or artist

r

ROMANTICS
> ROMANTIC

ROMANZA n short instrumental piece of song-like character

ROMANZAS > ROMANZA

ROMAUNT n verse romance

ROMAUNTS > ROMAUNT

ROMCOM n comedy based around the romantic relationships of the characters

ROMCOMS > ROMCOM

ROMELDALE n type of sheep

ROMEO n male sweetheart

ROMEOS > ROMEO

ROMNEYA n bushy type of poppy

ROMNEYAS > ROMNEYA

ROMP vb play wildly and joyfully ▷ n boisterous activity

ROMPED > ROMP

ROMPER n playful or boisterous child

ROMPERS pl n child's overalls

ROMPING > ROMP

ROMPINGLY > ROMP

ROMPISH adj inclined to romp

ROMPISHLY > ROMP

ROMPS > ROMP

ROMS > ROM

RONCADOR n any of several types of fish

RONCADORS
> RONCADOR

RONDACHE n round shield

RONDACHES
> RONDACHE

RONDAVEL n circular building, often thatched

RONDAVELS
> RONDAVEL

RONDE n round dance

RONDEAU n poem with the opening words of the first line used as a refrain

RONDEAUX > RONDEAU

RONDEL n rondeau with a two-line refrain appearing twice or three times

RONDELET n brief rondeau, having five or seven lines and a refrain taken from the first line

RONDELETS
> RONDELET

RONDELLE n type of bead

RONDELLES
> RONDELLE

RONDELS > RONDEL

RONDES > RONDE

RONDINO n short rondo

RONDINOS > RONDINO

RONDO n piece of music with a leading theme continually returned to

RONDOS > RONDO

RONDURE n circle or curve

RONDURES > RONDURE

RONE n Scots word for a gutter carrying rainwater from a roof

RONEO vb duplicate (a document) from a stencil ▷ n document reproduced by this process

RONEOED > RONEO

RONEOING > RONEO

RONEOS > RONEO

RONEPIPE same as
> RONE

RONEPIPES > RONEPIPE

RONES > RONE

RONG archaic past participle of > RING

RONGGENG n Malay traditional dance

RONGGENGS
> RONGGENG

RONIN n lordless samurai, esp one whose feudal lord had been deprived of his territory

RONINS > RONIN

RONION same as
> RUNNION

RONIONS > RONION

RONNE archaic form of
> RUN

RONNEL n type of pesticide

RONNELS > RONNEL

RONNIE n Dublin slang word for moustache

RONNIES > RONNIE

RONNING > RONNE

RONT archaic variant of
> RUNT

RONTE archaic variant of
> RUNT

RONTES > RONTE

RONTGEN variant spelling of > ROENTGEN

RONTGENS > RONTGEN

RONTS > RONT

RONYON same as
> RUNNION

RONYONS > RONYON

RONZ n rest of New Zealand (in relation to Auckland)

RONZER n New Zealander not from Auckland

RONZERS > RONZER

ROO n kangaroo

ROOD n crucifix

ROODS > ROOD

ROOF n outside upper covering of a building, car, etc ▷ vb put a roof on

ROOFED > ROOF

ROOFER > ROOF

ROOFERS > ROOF

ROOFIE n tablet of sedative drug

ROOFIER > ROOFY

ROOFIES > ROOFIE

ROOFIEST > ROOFY

ROOFING n material used to build a roof

ROOFINGS > ROOFING

ROOFLESS > ROOF

ROOFLIKE > ROOF

ROOFLINE n uppermost edge of a roof

ROOFLINES
> ROOFLINE

ROOFS > ROOF

ROOFSCAPE n view of the rooftops of a town, city, etc

ROOFTOP n outside part of the roof of a building

ROOFTOPS > ROOFTOP

ROOFTREE same as
> RIDGEPOLE

ROOFTREES
> ROOFTREE

ROOFY adj with roofs

ROOIBOS n tea prepared from the dried leaves of an African plant

ROOIBOSES > ROOIBOS

ROOIKAT n South African lynx

ROOIKATS > ROOIKAT

ROOINEK n South African derogatory or jocular name for an English person

ROOINEKS > ROOINEK

ROOK n Eurasian bird of the crow family ▷ vb swindle

ROOKED > ROOK

ROOKERIES > ROOKERY

ROOKERY n colony of rooks, penguins, or seals

ROOKIE n new recruit

ROOKIER > ROOKY

ROOKIES > ROOKIE

ROOKIEST > ROOKY

ROOKING > ROOK

ROOKISH > ROOK

ROOKS > ROOK

ROOKY adj abounding in rooks

ROOM n enclosed area in a building ▷ vb occupy or share a room

ROOMED > ROOM

ROOMER > ROOM

ROOMERS > ROOM

ROOMETTE n self-contained compartment in a railway sleeping carriage

ROOMETTES
> ROOMETTE

ROOMFUL n number or quantity sufficient to fill a room

ROOMFULS > ROOMFUL

ROOMIE n roommate

ROOMIER > ROOMY

ROOMIES > ROOMIE

ROOMIEST > ROOMY

ROOMILY > ROOMY

ROOMINESS > ROOMY

ROOMING > ROOM

ROOMMATE n person with whom one shares a room or apartment

ROOMMATES
> ROOMMATE

ROOMS > ROOM

ROOMSFUL > ROOMFUL

ROOMSOME adj archaic word meaning roomy

ROOMY adj spacious

ROON n Scots word for shred or strip

ROONS > ROON

ROOP same as > ROUP

ROOPED > ROOP

ROOPIER > ROOPY

ROOPIEST > ROOPY

ROOPING > ROOP

ROOPIT same as > ROOPY

ROOPS > ROOP

ROOPY adj (in dialect) hoarse

ROORBACH same as
> ROORBACK

ROORBACHS
> ROORBACH

ROORBACK n false or distorted report or account, used to obtain political advantage

ROORBACKS
> ROORBACK

ROOS > ROO

ROOSA n type of grass

ROOSAS > ROOSA

ROOSE vb flatter

ROOSED > ROOSE

ROOSER > ROOSE

ROOSERS > ROOSE

ROOSES > ROOSE

ROOSING > ROOSE

ROOST n perch for fowls ▷ vb perch

ROOSTED > ROOST

ROOSTER n domestic cock

ROOSTERS > ROOSTER

ROOSTING > ROOST

ROOSTS > ROOST

ROOT n part of a plant that grows down into the earth obtaining nourishment ▷ vb establish a root and start to grow

ROOTAGE n root system

ROOTAGES > ROOTAGE

ROOTBALL n mass of the roots of a plant

ROOTBALLS
> ROOTBALL

ROOTBOUND adj (of a pot plant) having outgrown its pot, so that the roots are cramped and tangled

ROOTCAP n layer of cells at root tip

ROOTCAPS > ROOTCAP

ROOTED > ROOT

ROOTEDLY > ROOT

ROOTER > ROOT

ROOTERS > ROOT

ROOTHOLD > ROOT

ROOTHOLDS > ROOT

ROOTIER > ROOTY

ROOTIES > ROOTY

ROOTIEST > ROOTY

ROOTINESS > ROOT

ROOTING > ROOT

ROOTINGS > ROOT

ROOTKIT n set of programs used to gain unauthorized access to a computer system

ROOTKITS > ROOTKIT

ROOTLE vb search unsystematically

ROOTLED > ROOTLE

ROOTLES > ROOTLE

ROOTLESS adj having no sense of belonging

ROOTLET n small root or branch of a root

ROOTLETS > ROOTLET

ROOTLIKE > ROOT

ROOTLING > ROOTLE

ROOTS adj (of popular music) going back to the origins of a style

ROOTSIER > ROOTS
ROOTSIEST > ROOTS
ROOTSTALK *same as* > RHIZOME
ROOTSTOCK *same as* > RHIZOME
ROOTSY > ROOTS
ROOTWORM *n* beetle larva feeding on roots
ROOTWORMS > ROOTWORM
ROOTY *adj* rootlike ▷ *n* (in military slang) bread
ROPABLE *adj* capable of being roped
ROPE *n* thick cord ▷ *vb* bind or fasten with rope
ROPEABLE *same as* > ROPABLE
ROPED > ROPE
ROPELIKE > ROPE
ROPER *n* someone who makes ropes
ROPERIES > ROPERY
ROPERS > ROPER
ROPERY *n* place where ropes are made
ROPES > ROPE
ROPEWALK *n* long narrow usually covered path or shed where ropes are made
ROPEWALKS > ROPEWALK
ROPEWAY *n* type of aerial lift
ROPEWAYS > ROPEWAY
ROPEWORK *n* making, mending, or tying ropes
ROPEWORKS > ROPEWORK
ROPEY *adj* inferior or inadequate
ROPIER > ROPY
ROPIEST > ROPY
ROPILY > ROPEY
ROPINESS > ROPEY
ROPING > ROPE
ROPINGS > ROPE
ROPY *same as* > ROPEY
ROQUE *n* game developed from croquet
ROQUEFORT *n* type of French blue cheese
ROQUES > ROQUE
ROQUET *vb* drive one's ball against (another person's ball) in croquet ▷ *n* act of roqueting
ROQUETED > ROQUET
ROQUETING > ROQUET
ROQUETS > ROQUET
ROQUETTE *n* another name for the salad plant rocket
ROQUETTES > ROQUETTE
RORAL *archaic word for* > DEWY
RORE *archaic spelling of* > ROAR
RORES > RORE
RORIC *same as* > RORAL
RORID *same as* > RORAL
RORIE *same as* > ROARY
RORIER > RORY
RORIEST > RORY
RORQUAL *n* toothless whale with a dorsal fin

RORQUALS > RORQUAL
RORT *n* dishonest scheme ▷ *vb* take unfair advantage of something
RORTED > RORT
RORTER *n* small-scale confidence trickster
RORTERS > RORTER
RORTIER > RORT
RORTIEST > RORT
RORTING > RORT
RORTINGS > RORTING
RORTS > RORT
RORTY > RORT
RORY *adj* dewy
ROSACE *another name for* > ROSETTE
ROSACEA *n* chronic inflammatory disease affecting the skin of the face
ROSACEAS > ROSACEA
ROSACEOUS *adj* of or belonging to a family of plants typically having five-petalled flowers, which includes the rose, strawberry, and many fruit trees
ROSACES > ROSACE
ROSAKER *archaic word for* > REALGAR
ROSAKERS > ROSAKER
ROSALIA *n* melody which is repeated but at a higher pitch each time
ROSALIAS > ROSALIA
ROSANILIN *n* reddish-brown crystalline insoluble derivative of aniline used as a red dye
ROSARIA > ROSARIUM
ROSARIAN *n* person who cultivates roses, esp professionally
ROSARIANS > ROSARIAN
ROSARIES > ROSARY
ROSARIUM *n* rose garden
ROSARIUMS > ROSARIUM
ROSARY *n* series of prayers
ROSBIF *n* term used in France for an English person
ROSBIFS > ROSBIF
ROSCID *adj* dewy
ROSCOE *slang word for* > GUN
ROSCOES > ROSCOE
ROSE *n* flowering plant ▷ *vb* cause to redden
ROSEAL *adj* rosy or roselike
ROSEATE *adj* rose-coloured
ROSEATELY > ROSEATE
ROSEBAY *n* perennial plant with spikes of deep pink flowers
ROSEBAYS > ROSEBAY
ROSEBED *n* part of a garden where roses grow
ROSEBEDS > ROSEBED
ROSEBOWL *n* bowl for displaying roses or other flowers

ROSEBOWLS > ROSEBOWL
ROSEBUD *n* rose which has not yet fully opened
ROSEBUDS > ROSEBUD
ROSEBUSH *n* flowering shrub
ROSED > ROSE
ROSEFINCH *n* any of various finches with pink patches
ROSEFISH *n* red food fish of North Atlantic coastal waters
ROSEHIP *n* berry-like fruit of a rose plant
ROSEHIPS > ROSEHIP
ROSELESS > RISE
ROSELIKE > RISE
ROSELLA *n* type of Australian parrot
ROSELLAS > ROSELLA
ROSELLE *n* Indian flowering plant
ROSELLES > ROSELLE
ROSEMARY *n* fragrant flowering shrub
ROSEOLA *n* feverish condition of young children caused by a virus
ROSEOLAR > ROSEOLA
ROSEOLAS > ROSEOLA
ROSERIES > ROSERY
ROSEROOT *n* Eurasian mountain plant
ROSEROOTS > ROSEROOT
ROSERY *n* bed or garden of roses
ROSES > ROSE
ROSESLUG *n* one of various types of pest that feed on roses
ROSESLUGS > ROSESLUG
ROSET *n* Scots word meaning rosin ▷ *vb* rub rosin on
ROSETED > ROSET
ROSETING > ROSET
ROSETS > ROSET
ROSETTE *n* rose-shaped ornament
ROSETTED > ROSET
ROSETTES > ROSETTE
ROSETTING *n* abnormal leaf formation in a plant due to disease
ROSETTY > ROSET
ROSETY > ROSET
ROSEWATER *n* scented water used as a perfume and in cooking, made by the distillation of rose petals or by impregnation with oil of roses
ROSEWOOD *n* fragrant wood used to make furniture
ROSEWOODS > ROSEWOOD
ROSHAMBO *n* the game of rock-paper-scissors
ROSHAMBOS > ROSHAMBO
ROSHI *n* teacher of Zen Buddhism
ROSHIS > ROSHI

ROSIED > ROSY
ROSIER *archaic word for* > ROSEBUSH
ROSIERE *archaic word for* > ROSEBUSH
ROSIERES > ROSIERE
ROSIERS > ROSIER
ROSIES > ROSY
ROSIEST > ROSY
ROSILY > ROSY
ROSIN *n* resin used for treating the bows of violins etc ▷ *vb* apply rosin to
ROSINATE *n* chemical compound
ROSINATES > ROSINATE
ROSINED > ROSIN
ROSINER *n* strong alcoholic drink
ROSINERS > ROSINER
ROSINESS > ROSY
ROSING > ROSE
ROSINIER > ROSINY
ROSINIEST > ROSINY
ROSINING > ROSIN
ROSINOL *n* yellowish fluorescent oily liquid obtained from certain resins
ROSINOLS > ROSINOL
ROSINOUS *adj* rosiny
ROSINS > ROSIN
ROSINWEED *n* N American plant with resinous juice, sticky foliage, and a strong smell
ROSINY *adj* resembling rosin
ROSIT *same as* > ROSET
ROSITED > ROSIT
ROSITING > ROSIT
ROSITS > ROSIT
ROSMARINE *archaic form of* > ROSEMARY
ROSOGLIO *same as* > ROSOLIO
ROSOGLIOS > ROSOGLIO
ROSOLIO *n* type of cordial
ROSOLIOS > ROSOLIO
ROSSER *n* bark-removing machine
ROSSERS > ROSSER
ROST *archaic spelling of* > ROAST
ROSTED > ROST
ROSTELLA > ROSTELLUM
ROSTELLAR > ROSTELLUM
ROSTELLUM *n* small beaklike process, such as the hooked projection from the top of the head in tapeworms or the outgrowth from the stigma of an orchid
ROSTER *n* list of people and their turns of duty ▷ *vb* place on a roster
ROSTERED > ROSTER
ROSTERING > ROSTER
ROSTERS > ROSTER
ROSTI *n* Swiss dish of fried grated potato
ROSTING > ROST

ROSTIS > ROSTI
ROSTRA > ROSTRUM
ROSTRAL adj of or like a beak or snout
ROSTRALLY > ROSTRAL
ROSTRATE adj having a beak or beaklike process
ROSTRATED same as > ROSTRATE
ROSTRUM n platform or stage
ROSTRUMS > ROSTRUM
ROSTS > ROST
ROSULA n rosette
ROSULAS > ROSULA
ROSULATE adj in the form of a rose
ROSY adj pink-coloured ▷ vb redden or make pink
ROSYING > ROSY
ROT vb decompose or decay ▷ n decay
ROTA n list of people who take it in turn to do a particular task
ROTACHUTE n device like a parachute, with rotor blades instead of a canopy
ROTAL adj of or relating to wheels or rotation
ROTAMETER n device for measuring the flow of a liquid
ROTAN another name for > RATTAN
ROTANS > ROTAN
ROTAPLANE n aircraft that derives its lift from freely revolving rotor blades
ROTARIES > ROTARY
ROTARY adj revolving ▷ n traffic roundabout
ROTAS > ROTA
ROTATABLE > ROTATE
ROTATE vb (cause to) move round a centre or on a pivot
ROTATED > ROTATE
ROTATES > ROTATE
ROTATING adj revolving around a central axis, line, or point
ROTATION n act of rotating
ROTATIONS > ROTATION
ROTATIVE same as > ROTATORY
ROTATOR n person, device, part, or muscle that rotates or causes rotation
ROTATORES > ROTATOR
ROTATORS > ROTATOR
ROTATORY adj of, relating to, possessing, or causing rotation
ROTAVATE same as > ROTOVATE
ROTAVATED > ROTAVATE
ROTAVATES > ROTAVATE
ROTAVATOR n type of machine with rotating blades that will break up soil

ROTAVIRAL adj of or caused by a rotavirus
ROTAVIRUS n any member of a genus of viruses that cause worldwide endemic infections
ROTCH n little auk
ROTCHE same as > ROTCH
ROTCHES > ROTCH
ROTCHIE same as > ROTCH
ROTCHIES > ROTCHIE
ROTE n mechanical repetition ▷ vb learn by rote
ROTED > ROTE
ROTELY adv by rote
ROTENONE n white odourless crystalline substance
ROTENONES > ROTENONE
ROTES > ROTE
ROTGRASS n type of grass blamed for sheeprot
ROTGUT n alcoholic drink of inferior quality
ROTGUTS > ROTGUT
ROTHER dialect word for > OX
ROTHERS > ROTHER
ROTI n (in India and the Caribbean) a type of unleavened bread
ROTIFER n minute aquatic multicellular invertebrate
ROTIFERAL > ROTIFER
ROTIFERAN > ROTIFER
ROTIFERS > ROTIFER
ROTIFORM adj in the shape of a wheel
ROTING > ROTE
ROTINI n type of small spiral-shaped pasta
ROTINIS > ROTINI
ROTIS > ROTI
ROTL n unit of weight used in Muslim countries
ROTLS > ROTL
ROTO n printing process using a cylinder etched with many small recesses in a rotary press
ROTOGRAPH n photograph which is printed white on black ▷ vb create such a photograph
ROTOLI > ROTOLO
ROTOLO n (in Italian cuisine) a roll
ROTOLOS > ROTOLO
ROTON n quantum of vortex motion
ROTONS > ROTON
ROTOR n revolving portion of a dynamo, motor, or turbine
ROTORS > ROTOR
ROTOS > ROTO
ROTOSCOPE n projection device used for creating animated images out of live-action ones ▷ vb create animated images using a rotoscope

ROTOTILL vb break up soil using a machine with revolving blades
ROTOTILLS > ROTOTILL
ROTOVATE vb break up (the surface of the earth, or an area of ground) using a rotavator
ROTOVATED > ROTOVATE
ROTOVATES > ROTOVATE
ROTOVATOR same as > ROTAVATOR
ROTPROOF adj proof against rot
ROTS > ROT
ROTTAN n (in dialect) a rat
ROTTANS > ROTTAN
ROTTE n ancient stringed instrument
ROTTED > ROT
ROTTEN adj decaying ▷ n (in dialect) a rat
ROTTENER > ROTTEN
ROTTENEST > ROTTEN
ROTTENLY > ROTTEN
ROTTENS > ROTTEN
ROTTER n despicable person
ROTTERS > ROTTER
ROTTES > ROTTE
ROTTING > ROT
ROTULA n kneecap
ROTULAE > ROTULA
ROTULAS > ROTULA
ROTUND adj round and plump ▷ vb make round
ROTUNDA n circular building or room, esp with a dome
ROTUNDAS > ROTUNDA
ROTUNDATE adj rounded
ROTUNDED > ROTUND
ROTUNDER > ROTUND
ROTUNDEST > ROTUND
ROTUNDING > ROTUND
ROTUNDITY > ROTUND
ROTUNDLY > ROTUND
ROTUNDS > ROTUND
ROTURIER n freeholder or ordinary person
ROTURIERS > ROTURIER
ROUBLE n monetary unit of Russia, Belarus, and Tajikistan
ROUBLES > ROUBLE
ROUCHE same as > RUCHE
ROUCHED adj trimmed with a rouche
ROUCHES > ROUCHE
ROUCHING n lace trimming
ROUCHINGS > ROUCHING
ROUCOU another name for > ANNATTO
ROUCOUS > ROUCOU
ROUE n man given to immoral living
ROUEN n breed of duck
ROUENS > ROUEN
ROUES > ROUE
ROUGE n red cosmetic used to colour the cheeks ▷ vb apply rouge to

ROUGED > ROUGE
ROUGES > ROUGE
ROUGH adj uneven or irregular ▷ vb make rough ▷ n rough state or area
ROUGHAGE n indigestible constituents of food which aid digestion
ROUGHAGES > ROUGHAGE
ROUGHBACK n rough-skinned flatfish
ROUGHCAST n mixture of plaster and small stones for outside walls ▷ vb coat with this ▷ adj covered with or denoting roughcast
ROUGHDRY vb dry (clothes or linen) without smoothing
ROUGHED > ROUGH
ROUGHEN vb make or become rough
ROUGHENED > ROUGHEN
ROUGHENS > ROUGHEN
ROUGHER n person that does the rough preparatory work on something ▷ adj more rough
ROUGHERS > ROUGHER
ROUGHEST > ROUGHER
ROUGHHEW vb cut or hew (timber, stone, etc) roughly without finishing the surface
ROUGHHEWN > ROUGHHEW
ROUGHHEWS > ROUGHHEW
ROUGHIE n small food fish found in Australian waters
ROUGHIES > ROUGHIE
ROUGHING n (in ice hockey) excessive use of force
ROUGHINGS > ROUGHING
ROUGHISH adj somewhat rough
ROUGHLEG n any of several kinds of large hawk with feathered legs
ROUGHLEGS > ROUGHLEG
ROUGHLY adv without being exact or fully authenticated
ROUGHNECK n violent person
ROUGHNESS > ROUGH
ROUGHOUT n unfinished roughly shaped artefact
ROUGHOUTS > ROUGHOUT
ROUGHS > ROUGH
ROUGHSHOD adj (of a horse) shod with rough-bottomed shoes to prevent sliding
ROUGHT archaic past form of > REACH
ROUGHY spelling variant of > ROUGHIE
ROUGING > ROUGE
ROUILLE n kind of sauce
ROUILLES > ROUILLE

ROUL archaic form of > ROLL

ROULADE n slice of meat rolled and cooked

ROULADES > ROULADE

ROULE archaic form of > ROLL

ROULEAU n roll of paper containing coins

ROULEAUS > ROULEAU

ROULEAUX > ROULEAU

ROULES > ROULE

ROULETTE n gambling game played with a revolving wheel and a ball ▷ vb use a toothed wheel on (something), as in engraving, making stationery, etc

ROULETTED > ROULETTE

ROULETTES > ROULETTE

ROULS > ROUL

ROUM archaic spelling of > ROOM

ROUMING n portion of common pastureland

ROUMINGS > ROUMING

ROUMS > ROUM

ROUNCE n handle that is turned to move paper and plates on a printing press

ROUNCES > ROUNCE

ROUNCEVAL n giant or monster

ROUNCIES > ROUNCY

ROUNCY archaic word for > HORSE

ROUND adj spherical, cylindrical, circular, or curved ▷ prep indicating an encircling movement, presence on all sides, etc ▷ vb move round ▷ n round shape

ROUNDARCH adj with rounded arches

ROUNDBALL n form of basketball

ROUNDED adj round or curved

ROUNDEDLY > ROUNDED

ROUNDEL same as > ROUNDELAY

ROUNDELAY n simple song with a refrain

ROUNDELS > ROUNDEL

ROUNDER n run round all four bases after one hit in rounders

ROUNDERS n bat-and-ball team game

ROUNDEST > ROUND

ROUNDHAND n style of handwriting with large rounded curves

ROUNDHEEL n derogatory term for a woman considered immodest

ROUNDING n process in which a number with a fraction is approximated as the closest number up or down

ROUNDINGS > ROUNDING

ROUNDISH adj somewhat round

ROUNDLE same as > ROUNDEL

ROUNDLES > ROUNDLE

ROUNDLET n small circle

ROUNDLETS > ROUNDLET

ROUNDLY adv thoroughly

ROUNDNESS > ROUND

ROUNDS > ROUND

ROUNDSMAN n person who makes rounds, as for inspection or to deliver goods

ROUNDSMEN > ROUNDSMAN

ROUNDTRIP n US term for return trip

ROUNDUP n act of gathering together

ROUNDUPS > ROUNDUP

ROUNDURE n archaic word meaning roundness

ROUNDURES > ROUNDURE

ROUNDWOOD n small pieces of timber (about 5–15 centimetres in diameter)

ROUNDWORM n worm that is a common intestinal parasite of human beings

ROUP n any of various chronic respiratory diseases of birds, esp poultry ▷ vb sell by auction

ROUPED > ROUP

ROUPET adj Scots word meaning hoarse or croaky

ROUPIER > ROUP

ROUPIEST > ROUP

ROUPILY > ROUP

ROUPING > ROUP

ROUPIT same as > ROUPET

ROUPS > ROUP

ROUPY > ROUP

ROUSABLE adj capable of being roused

ROUSANT adj (in heraldry) rising

ROUSE vb provoke or excite

ROUSED > ROUSE

ROUSEMENT n stirring up

ROUSER n person or thing that rouses people

ROUSERS > ROUSER

ROUSES > ROUSE

ROUSING adj lively, vigorous

ROUSINGLY > ROUSING

ROUSSEAU n pemmican fried in its own fat

ROUSSEAUS > ROUSSEAU

ROUSSETTE n dogfish

ROUST vb rout or stir, as out of bed

ROUSTED > ROUST

ROUSTER n unskilled labourer on an oil rig

ROUSTERS > ROUSTER

ROUSTING > ROUST

ROUSTS > ROUST

ROUT n overwhelming defeat ▷ vb defeat and put to flight

ROUTE n roads taken to reach a destination ▷ vb send by a particular route

ROUTED > ROUTE

ROUTEING > ROUTE

ROUTEMAN n (in US English) delivery man or salesman doing a particular round

ROUTEMEN > ROUTEMAN

ROUTER n device that allows data to be moved between points on a network

ROUTERS > ROUTER

ROUTES > ROUTE

ROUTEWAY n track, road, or waterway, etc, used as a route to somewhere

ROUTEWAYS > ROUTEWAY

ROUTH n abundance ▷ adj abundant

ROUTHIE adj abundant, plentiful, or well filled

ROUTHIER > ROUTHIE

ROUTHIEST > ROUTHIE

ROUTHS > ROUTH

ROUTINE n usual or regular method of procedure ▷ adj ordinary or regular

ROUTINEER n someone who believes in routine

ROUTINELY > ROUTINE

ROUTINES > ROUTINE

ROUTING > ROUT

ROUTINGS > ROUT

ROUTINISE same as > ROUTINIZE

ROUTINISM > ROUTINE

ROUTINIST > ROUTINE

ROUTINIZE vb make routine

ROUTOUS > ROUT

ROUTOUSLY > ROUT

ROUTS > ROUT

ROUX n fat and flour cooked together as a basis for sauces

ROVE vb wander about

ROVED > ROVE

ROVEN > ROVE

ROVER n wanderer, traveller

ROVERS > ROVER

ROVES > ROVE

ROVING > ROVE

ROVINGLY > ROVE

ROVINGS > ROVE

ROW n straight line of people or things ▷ vb propel (a boat) by oars

ROWABLE > ROW

ROWAN n tree producing bright red berries; mountain ash

ROWANS > ROWAN

ROWBOAT n small boat propelled by one or more pairs of oars

ROWBOATS > ROWBOAT

ROWDEDOW same as > ROWDYDOW

ROWDEDOWS > ROWDEDOW

ROWDIER > ROWDY

ROWDIES > ROWDY

ROWDIEST > ROWDY

ROWDILY > ROWDY

ROWDINESS > ROWDY

ROWDY adj disorderly, noisy, and rough ▷ n person like this

ROWDYDOW n hullabaloo ▷ vb make noise

ROWDYDOWS > ROWDYDOW

ROWDYISH > ROWDY

ROWDYISM n rowdy behaviour or tendencies or a habitual pattern of rowdy behaviour

ROWDYISMS > ROWDYISM

ROWED > ROW

ROWEL n small spiked wheel on a spur ▷ vb goad (a horse) using a rowel

ROWELED > ROWEL

ROWELING > ROWEL

ROWELLED > ROWEL

ROWELLING > ROWEL

ROWELS > ROWEL

ROWEN another word for > AFTERMATH

ROWENS > ROWEN

ROWER > ROW

ROWERS > ROW

ROWIE n Scottish bread roll made with butter and fat

ROWIES > ROWIE

ROWING > ROW

ROWINGS > ROW

ROWLOCK n device on a boat that holds an oar in place

ROWLOCKS > ROWLOCK

ROWME archaic variant of > ROOM

ROWMES > ROWME

ROWND archaic variant of > ROUND

ROWNDED > ROWND

ROWNDELL archaic variant of > ROUNDEL

ROWNDELLS > ROWNDELL

ROWNDING > ROWND

ROWNDS > ROWND

ROWOVER n act of winning a rowing race unopposed

ROWOVERS > ROWOVER

ROWS > ROW

ROWT archaic variant of > ROUT

ROWTED > ROWT

ROWTH same as > ROUTH

ROWTHS > ROWTH

ROWTING > ROWT

ROWTS > ROWT

ROYAL adj of, befitting, or supported by a king or queen ▷ n member of a royal family

ROYALET n minor king

ROYALETS > ROYALET

ROYALISE same as > ROYALIZE

ROYALISED > ROYALISE

ROYALISES > ROYALISE

ROYALISM > ROYALIST

ROYALISMS
> ROYALIST
ROYALIST n supporter of monarchy ▷ adj of or relating to royalists
ROYALISTS
> ROYALIST
ROYALIZE vb make royal
ROYALIZED
> ROYALIZE
ROYALIZES
> ROYALIZE
ROYALLER > ROYAL
ROYALLEST > ROYAL
ROYALLY > ROYAL
ROYALMAST n highest part of mast
ROYALS > ROYAL
ROYALTIES > ROYALTY
ROYALTY n royal people
ROYNE archaic word for > GNAW
ROYNED > ROYNE
ROYNES > ROYNE
ROYNING > ROYNE
ROYNISH archaic word for > MANGY
ROYST same as > ROIST
ROYSTED > ROYST
ROYSTER same as > ROISTER
ROYSTERED > ROYSTER
ROYSTERER > ROYSTER
ROYSTERS > ROYSTER
ROYSTING > ROYST
ROYSTS > ROYST
ROZELLE same as > ROSELLE
ROZELLES > ROZELLE
ROZET same as > ROSET
ROZETED > ROZET
ROZETING > ROZET
ROZETS > ROZET
ROZIT same as > ROSET
ROZITED > ROZIT
ROZITING > ROZIT
ROZITS > ROZIT
ROZZER n slang word for a police officer
ROZZERS > ROZZER
RUANA n woollen wrap resembling a poncho
RUANAS > RUANA
RUB vb apply pressure with a circular or backwards-and-forwards movement ▷ n act of rubbing
RUBABOO n soup or stew made by boiling pemmican
RUBABOOS > RUBABOO
RUBACE same as > RUBASSE
RUBACES > RUBACE
RUBAI n verse form of Persian origin consisting of four-line stanzas
RUBAIS > RUBAI
RUBAIYAT n (in Persian poetry) a verse form consisting of four-line stanzas
RUBASSE n type of quartz containing red haematite
RUBASSES > RUBASSE
RUBATI > RUBATO

RUBATO n expressive flexibility of tempo ▷ adv with a flexible tempo
RUBATOS > RUBATO
RUBBABOO same as > RUBABOO
RUBBABOOS > RUBABOO
RUBBED > RUB
RUBBER n strong waterproof elastic material ▷ adj made of or producing rubber ▷ vb provide with rubber coating
RUBBERED > RUBBER
RUBBERIER > RUBBERY
RUBBERING > RUBBER
RUBBERISE same as > RUBBERIZE
RUBBERIZE vb coat or treat with rubber
RUBBERS > RUBBER
RUBBERY adj having the texture of or resembling rubber, esp in flexibility or toughness
RUBBET old Scots past form of > ROB
RUBBIDIES > RUBBIDY
RUBBIDY same as > RUBBITY
RUBBIES > RUBBY
RUBBING > RUB
RUBBINGS > RUB
RUBBISH n waste matter ▷ vb criticize
RUBBISHED > RUBBISH
RUBBISHES > RUBBISH
RUBBISHLY adj like rubbish
RUBBISHY adj worthless, of poor quality, or useless
RUBBIT old Scots past form of > ROB
RUBBITIES > RUBBITY
RUBBITY n pub
RUBBLE n fragments of broken stone, brick, etc ▷ vb turn into rubble
RUBBLED > RUBBLE
RUBBLES > RUBBLE
RUBBLIER > RUBBLE
RUBBLIEST > RUBBLE
RUBBLING > RUBBLE
RUBBLY > RUBBLE
RUBBOARD n board for scrubbing clothes on
RUBBOARDS > RUBBOARD
RUBBY n slang word for rubbing alcohol
RUBBYDUB n person who drinks cheap alcohol mixtures
RUBBYDUBS > RUBBYDUB
RUBDOWN n act of drying or cleaning vigorously
RUBDOWNS > RUBDOWN
RUBE n unsophisticated countryman
RUBEFIED > RUBEFY
RUBEFIES > RUBEFY
RUBEFY vb make red
RUBEFYING > RUBEFY
RUBEL n currency unit of Belarus

RUBELLA n mild contagious viral disease
RUBELLAN n red-coloured mineral
RUBELLANS > RUBELLAN
RUBELLAS > RUBELLA
RUBELLITE n red transparent variety of tourmaline, used as a gemstone
RUBELS > RUBEL
RUBEOLA technical name for > MEASLES
RUBEOLAR > RUBEOLA
RUBEOLAS > RUBEOLA
RUBES > RUBE
RUBESCENT adj reddening
RUBICELLE n variety of spinel that is orange or yellow in colour
RUBICON n point of no return ▷ vb (in bezique) to beat before the loser has managed to gain as many as 1000 points
RUBICONED > RUBICON
RUBICONS > RUBICON
RUBICUND adj ruddy
RUBIDIC > RUBIDIUM
RUBIDIUM n soft highly reactive radioactive element
RUBIDIUMS > RUBIDIUM
RUBIED > RUBY
RUBIER > RUBY
RUBIES > RUBY
RUBIEST > RUBY
RUBIFIED > RUBIFY
RUBIFIES > RUBIFY
RUBIFY same as > RUBEFY
RUBIFYING > RUBIFY
RUBIGO old Scots word for > PENIS
RUBIGOS > RUBIGO
RUBIN archaic word for > RUBY
RUBINE archaic word for > RUBY
RUBINEOUS same as > RUBIOUS
RUBINES > RUBINE
RUBINS > RUBIN
RUBIOUS adj of the colour ruby
RUBLE same as > ROUBLE
RUBLES > RUBLE
RUBLI > RUBLE
RUBOFF n resulting effect on something else; consequences
RUBOFFS > RUBOFF
RUBOUT n killing or elimination
RUBOUTS > RUBOUT
RUBRIC n set of rules for behaviour ▷ adj written, printed, or marked in red
RUBRICAL > RUBRIC
RUBRICATE vb print (a book or manuscript) with red titles, headings, etc
RUBRICIAN n authority on liturgical rubrics
RUBRICS > RUBRIC

RUBS > RUB
RUBSTONE n stone used for sharpening or smoothing, esp a whetstone
RUBSTONES > RUBSTONE
RUBUS n fruit-bearing genus of shrubs
RUBUSES > RUBUS
RUBY n red precious gemstone ▷ adj deep red ▷ vb redden
RUBYING > RUBY
RUBYLIKE > RUBY
RUC same as > ROC
RUCHE n pleat or frill of lace etc as a decoration ▷ vb put a ruche on
RUCHED > RUCHE
RUCHES > RUCHE
RUCHING n material used for a ruche
RUCHINGS > RUCHING
RUCK n rough crowd of common people ▷ vb wrinkle or crease
RUCKED > RUCK
RUCKING > RUCK
RUCKLE another word for > RUCK
RUCKLED > RUCKLE
RUCKLES > RUCKLE
RUCKLING > RUCKLE
RUCKMAN n person who plays in a ruck
RUCKMEN > RUCKMAN
RUCKS > RUCK
RUCKSACK n large pack carried on the back
RUCKSACKS > RUCKSACK
RUCKSEAT n seat fixed to or forming part of a rucksack
RUCKSEATS > RUCKSEAT
RUCKUS n uproar
RUCKUSES > RUCKUS
RUCOLA n another name for the salad plant rocket
RUCOLAS > RUCOLA
RUCS > RUC
RUCTATION n archaic word meaning eructation or belch
RUCTION n uproar
RUCTIONS > RUCTION
RUCTIOUS adj tending or likely to cause ructions
RUD n red or redness ▷ vb redden
RUDACEOUS adj (of conglomerate, breccia, and similar rocks) composed of coarse-grained material
RUDAS n Scots word for a coarse, rude old woman
RUDASES > RUDAS
RUDBECKIA n N American plant cultivated for its showy flowers
RUDD n European freshwater fish
RUDDED > RUD
RUDDER n device for steering a boat or aircraft

RUDDERS > RUDDER
RUDDIED > RUDDY
RUDDIER > RUDDY
RUDDIES > RUDDY
RUDDIEST > RUDDY
RUDDILY > RUDDY
RUDDINESS > RUDDY
RUDDING > RUD
RUDDLE *n* red ochre, used esp to mark sheep ▷ *vb* mark (sheep) with ruddle
RUDDLED > RUDDLE
RUDDLEMAN *n* ruddle dealer
RUDDLEMEN > RUDDLEMAN
RUDDLES > RUDDLE
RUDDLING > RUDDLE
RUDDOCK *dialect name for the* > ROBIN
RUDDOCKS > RUDDOCK
RUDDS > RUDD
RUDDY *adj* of a fresh healthy red colour ▷ *adv* bloody ▷ *vb* redden
RUDDYING > RUDDY
RUDE *adj* insulting or impolite ▷ *n* archaic spelling of rood (crucifix)
RUDELY > RUDE
RUDENESS > RUDE
RUDER > RUDE
RUDERAL *n* plant that grows on waste ground ▷ *adj* growing in waste places
RUDERALS > RUDERAL
RUDERIES > RUDE
RUDERY > RUDE
RUDES > RUDE
RUDESBIES > RUDESBY
RUDESBY *n* archaic word for rude person
RUDEST > RUDE
RUDI *same as* > RUDIE
RUDIE *n* member of a youth movement originating in the 1960s
RUDIES > RUDIE
RUDIMENT *n* first principle or elementary stage of a subject
RUDIMENTS > RUDIMENT
RUDIS > RUDI
RUDISH *adj* somewhat rude
RUDIST *n* cone-shaped extinct mollusc
RUDISTID *same as* > RUDIST
RUDISTIDS > RUDISTID
RUDISTS > RUDIST
RUDS > RUD
RUDY *same as* > RUDIE
RUE *vb* feel regret for ▷ *n* plant with evergreen bitter leaves
RUED > RUE
RUEDA *n* type of Cuban round dance
RUEDAS > RUEDA
RUEFUL *adj* regretful or sorry
RUEFULLY > RUEFUL
RUEING > RUE
RUEINGS > RUE

RUELLE *n* area between bed and wall
RUELLES > RUELLE
RUELLIA *n* genus of plants
RUELLIAS > RUELLIA
RUER > RUE
RUERS > RUE
RUES > RUE
RUFESCENT *adj* tinged with red or becoming red
RUFF *n* circular pleated, gathered, or fluted collar ▷ *vb* trump
RUFFE *n* European freshwater fish
RUFFED > RUFF
RUFFES > RUFFE
RUFFIAN *n* violent lawless person ▷ *vb* act like a ruffian
RUFFIANED > RUFFIAN
RUFFIANLY > RUFFIAN
RUFFIANS > RUFFIAN
RUFFIN *archaic name for* > RUFFE
RUFFING > RUFF
RUFFINS > RUFFIN
RUFFLE *vb* disturb the calm of ▷ *n* frill or pleat
RUFFLED > RUFFLE
RUFFLER *n* person or thing that ruffles
RUFFLERS > RUFFLER
RUFFLES > RUFFLE
RUFFLIER > RUFFLY
RUFFLIEST > RUFFLY
RUFFLIKE > RUFF
RUFFLING > RUFFLE
RUFFLINGS > RUFFLE
RUFFLY *adj* ruffled
RUFFS > RUFF
RUFIYAA *n* standard monetary unit of the Maldives
RUFIYAAS > RUFIYAA
RUFOUS *n* reddish-brown colour
RUFOUSES > RUFOUS
RUG *n* small carpet ▷ *vb* (in dialect) tug
RUGA *n* fold, wrinkle, or crease
RUGAE > RUGA
RUGAL *adj* (in anatomy) with ridges or folds
RUGALACH *same as* > RUGELACH
RUGATE *same as* > RUGOSE
RUGBIES > RUGBY
RUGBY *n* form of football played with an oval ball which may be handled by the players
RUGELACH *n* fruit and nut pastry shaped like a croissant
RUGELACHS > RUGELACH
RUGGED *adj* rocky or steep
RUGGEDER > RUGGED
RUGGEDEST > RUGGED
RUGGEDISE *same as* > RUGGEDIZE
RUGGEDIZE *vb* make durable, as for military use
RUGGEDLY > RUGGED

RUGGELACH *same as* > RUGELACH
RUGGER *same as* > RUGBY
RUGGERS > RUGGER
RUGGIER > RUGGY
RUGGIEST > RUGGY
RUGGING > RUG
RUGGINGS > RUG
RUGGY *adj* (in dialect) rough or rugged
RUGLIKE > RUG
RUGOLA *n* another name for the salad plant rocket
RUGOLAS > RUGOLA
RUGOSA *n* any of various shrubs descended from a particular type of wild rose
RUGOSAS > RUGOSA
RUGOSE *adj* wrinkled
RUGOSELY > RUGOSE
RUGOSITY > RUGOSE
RUGOUS *same as* > RUGOSE
RUGRAT *n* informal word for a young child
RUGRATS > RUGRAT
RUGS > RUG
RUGULOSE *adj* with little wrinkles
RUIN *vb* destroy or spoil completely ▷ *n* destruction or decay
RUINABLE > RUIN
RUINATE *vb* archaic word for bring or come to ruin
RUINATED > RUINATE
RUINATES > RUINATE
RUINATING > RUINATE
RUINATION *n* act of ruining
RUINED > RUIN
RUINER > RUIN
RUINERS > RUIN
RUING > RUE
RUINGS > RUE
RUINING > RUIN
RUININGS > RUIN
RUINOUS *adj* causing ruin
RUINOUSLY > RUINOUS
RUINS > RUIN
RUKH *same as* > ROC
RUKHS > RUKH
RULABLE > RULE
RULE *n* statement of what is allowed, for example in a game or procedure ▷ *vb* govern
RULED > RULE
RULELESS > RULE
RULER *n* person who governs ▷ *vb* punish by hitting with a ruler
RULERED > RULER
RULERING > RULER
RULERS > RULER
RULERSHIP > RULER
RULES > RULE
RULESSE *adj* archaic word meaning ruleless or without rules
RULIER > RULY
RULIEST > RULY
RULING *n* formal decision ▷ *adj* controlling or exercising authority
RULINGS > RULING
RULLION *n* Scots word for rawhide shoe

RULLIONS > RULLION
RULLOCK *same as* > ROWLOCK
RULLOCKS > RULLOCK
RULY *adj* orderly
RUM *n* alcoholic drink distilled from sugar cane ▷ *adj* odd, strange
RUMAKI *n* savoury of chicken liver and sliced water chestnut wrapped in bacon
RUMAKIS > RUMAKI
RUMAL *n* handkerchief or type of cloth
RUMALS > RUMAL
RUMBA *n* lively ballroom dance of Cuban origin ▷ *vb* dance the rumba
RUMBAED > RUMBA
RUMBAING > RUMBA
RUMBAS > RUMBA
RUMBELOW *n* nonsense word used in the refrain of certain sea shanties
RUMBELOWS > RUMBELOW
RUMBLE *vb* make a low continuous noise ▷ *n* deep resonant sound
RUMBLED > RUMBLE
RUMBLER > RUMBLE
RUMBLERS > RUMBLE
RUMBLES > RUMBLE
RUMBLIER > RUMBLY
RUMBLIEST > RUMBLY
RUMBLING > RUMBLE
RUMBLINGS > RUMBLE
RUMBLY *adj* rumbling or liable to rumble
RUMBO *n* rum-based cocktail
RUMBOS > RUMBO
RUMDUM *n* alcoholic
RUMDUMS > RUMDUM
RUME *archaic form of* > RHEUM
RUMEN *n* first compartment of the stomach of ruminants
RUMENS > RUMEN
RUMES > RUME
RUMINA > RUMEN
RUMINAL > RUMEN
RUMINANT *n* cud-chewing (animal, such as a cow, sheep, or deer) ▷ *adj* of ruminants
RUMINANTS > RUMINANT
RUMINATE *vb* chew the cud
RUMINATED > RUMINATE
RUMINATES > RUMINATE
RUMINATOR > RUMINATE
RUMKIN *n* archaic term for a drinking vessel
RUMKINS > RUMKIN
RUMLY > RUM
RUMMAGE *vb* search untidily and at length ▷ *n* untidy search through a collection of things
RUMMAGED > RUMMAGE
RUMMAGER > RUMMAGE

r

RUMMAGERS > RUMMAGE
RUMMAGES > RUMMAGE
RUMMAGING > RUMMAGE
RUMMER n drinking glass
RUMMERS > RUMMER
RUMMEST > RUM
RUMMIER > RUMMY
RUMMIES > RUMMY
RUMMIEST > RUMMY
RUMMILY > RUMMY
RUMMINESS > RUMMY
RUMMISH adj rather
strange, peculiar, or odd
▷ vb roar or protest
RUMMISHED > RUMMISH
RUMMISHES > RUMMISH
RUMMY n card game in
which players try to collect
sets or sequences ▷ adj of
or like rum in taste or smell
RUMNESS > RUM
RUMNESSES > RUM
RUMOR same as > RUMOUR
RUMORED > RUMOR
RUMORER n person given
to spreading rumours
RUMORERS > RUMORER
RUMORING > RUMOR
RUMOROUS adj involving
or containing rumours
RUMORS > RUMOR
RUMOUR n unproved
statement ▷ vb pass
around or circulate in the
form of a rumour
RUMOURED > RUMOUR
RUMOURER n someone
given to spreading
rumours
RUMOURERS > RUMOURER
RUMOURING > RUMOUR
RUMOURS > RUMOUR
RUMP n buttocks ▷ vb turn
back on
RUMPED > RUMP
RUMPIER > RUMPY
RUMPIES > RUMPY
RUMPIEST > RUMPY
RUMPING > RUMP
RUMPLE vb make untidy,
crumpled, or dishevelled
▷ n wrinkle, fold, or crease
RUMPLED > RUMPLE
RUMPLES > RUMPLE
RUMPLESS > RUMP
RUMPLIER > RUMPLE
RUMPLIEST > RUMPLE
RUMPLING > RUMPLE
RUMPLY > RUMPLE
RUMPO n slang word for
sexual intercourse
RUMPOS > RUMPO
RUMPOT n alcoholic
RUMPOTS > RUMPOT
RUMPS > RUMP
RUMPUS n noisy
commotion
RUMPUSES > RUMPUS
RUMPY n tailless Manx cat
▷ adj with a large or
noticeable rump
RUMRUNNER n alcohol
smuggler
RUMS > RUM
RUN vb move with a more
rapid gait than walking
▷ n act or spell of running

RUNABOUT n small car
used for short journeys
▷ vb move busily from
place to place
RUNABOUTS
> RUNABOUT
RUNAGATE n vagabond,
fugitive, or renegade
RUNAGATES
> RUNAGATE
RUNANGA n Māori
assembly or council
RUNANGAS > RUNANGA
RUNAROUND n deceitful
or evasive treatment of a
person
RUNAWAY n person or
animal that runs away
RUNAWAYS > RUNAWAY
RUNBACK n (in tennis) the
areas behind the baselines
of the court
RUNBACKS > RUNBACK
RUNCH n another name
for white charlock
RUNCHES > RUNCH
RUNCIBLE adj as in
runcible spoon forklike
utensil with two prongs
and one sharp curved
prong
RUNCINATE adj (of a leaf)
having a saw-toothed
margin with the teeth or
lobes pointing backwards
RUND same as > ROON
RUNDALE n system of
land tenure in Ireland
RUNDALES > RUNDALE
RUNDLE n rung of a ladder
RUNDLED adj rounded
RUNDLES > RUNDLE
RUNDLET n liquid
measure, generally about
15 gallons
RUNDLETS > RUNDLET
RUNDOWN adj tired;
exhausted ▷ n brief
review, résumé, or
summary
RUNDOWNS > RUNDOWN
RUNDS > RUND
RUNE n any character of
the earliest Germanic
alphabet
RUNECRAFT n
understanding of and skill
working with runes
RUNED adj with runes on
RUNELIKE adj
resembling a rune or runes
RUNES > RUNE
RUNFLAT adj having a
safety feature that
prevents tyres becoming
dangerous when flat
RUNFLATS > RUNFLAT
RUNG n crosspiece on
ladder
RUNGED adj having rungs
RUNGLESS > RUNG
RUNGS > RUNG
RUNIC > RUNE
RUNKLE vb (in dialect)
crease or wrinkle
RUNKLED > RUNKLE
RUNKLES > RUNKLE
RUNKLING > RUNKLE

RUNLESS > RUN
RUNLET n cask for wine,
beer, etc
RUNLETS > RUNLET
RUNNABLE > RUN
RUNNEL n small brook
RUNNELS > RUNNEL
RUNNER n competitor in a
race
RUNNERS > RUNNER
RUNNET dialect word for
> RENNET
RUNNETS > RUNNET
RUNNIER > RUNNY
RUNNIEST > RUNNY
RUNNINESS > RUNNY
RUNNING > RUN
RUNNINGLY > RUN
RUNNINGS > RUN
RUNNION n archaic
pejorative term for a
woman
RUNNIONS > RUNNION
RUNNY adj tending to flow
RUNOFF n extra race to
decide the winner after a
tie
RUNOFFS > RUNOFF
RUNOUT n dismissal of a
batsman by running them
out
RUNOUTS > RUNOUT
RUNOVER n incident in
which someone is run over
by a vehicle
RUNOVERS > RUNOVER
RUNPROOF adj (of
stockings or tights)
designed to be especially
resistant to being ripped
RUNRIG same as
> RUNDALE
RUNRIGS > RUNRIG
RUNROUND same as
> RUNAROUND
RUNROUNDS
> RUNROUND
RUNS > RUN
RUNT n smallest animal in
a litter
RUNTED adj stunted
RUNTIER > RUNT
RUNTIEST > RUNT
RUNTINESS > RUNT
RUNTISH > RUNT
RUNTISHLY > RUNT
RUNTS > RUNT
RUNTY > RUNT
RUNWAY n hard level
roadway where aircraft
take off and land
RUNWAYS > RUNWAY
RUPEE n monetary unit of
India and Pakistan
RUPEES > RUPEE
RUPIA n type of skin
eruption
RUPIAH n standard
monetary unit of
Indonesia
RUPIAHS > RUPIAH
RUPIAS > RUPIA
RUPTURE n breaking,
breach ▷ vb break, burst,
or sever
RUPTURED > RUPTURE
RUPTURES > RUPTURE
RUPTURING > RUPTURE

RURAL adj in or of the
countryside ▷ n country
dweller
RURALISE same as
> RURALIZE
RURALISED > RURALISE
RURALISES > RURALISE
RURALISM > RURAL
RURALISMS > RURAL
RURALIST > RURAL
RURALISTS > RURAL
RURALITE > RURAL
RURALITES > RURAL
RURALITY > RURAL
RURALIZE vb make rural
in character, appearance,
etc
RURALIZED > RURALIZE
RURALIZES > RURALIZE
RURALLY > RURAL
RURALNESS > RURAL
RURALS > RURAL
RURBAN adj part country,
part urban
RURP n very small piton
RURPS > RURP
RURU another name for
> MOPOKE
RURUS > RURU
RUSA n type of deer with a
mane
RUSALKA n water nymph
or spirit
RUSALKAS > RUSALKA
RUSAS > RUSA
RUSCUS n type of shrub
RUSCUSES > RUSCUS
RUSE n stratagem or trick
RUSES > RUSE
RUSH vb move or do very
quickly ▷ n sudden quick
or violent movement ▷ adj
done with speed, hasty
RUSHED > RUSH
RUSHEE n someone
interested in gaining
fraternity or sorority
membership
RUSHEES > RUSHEE
RUSHEN adj made of
rushes
RUSHER > RUSH
RUSHERS > RUSH
RUSHES pl n (in
film-making) the initial
prints of a scene or scenes
before editing
RUSHIER > RUSHY
RUSHIEST > RUSHY
RUSHINESS > RUSHY
RUSHING > RUSH
RUSHINGS > RUSH
RUSHLIGHT n narrow
candle, formerly in use,
made of the pith of various
types of rush dipped in
tallow
RUSHLIKE > RUSH
RUSHY adj full of rushes
RUSINE adj of or relating
to rusa deer
RUSK n hard brown crisp
biscuit, used esp for
feeding babies
RUSKS > RUSK
RUSMA n Turkish
depilatory
RUSMAS > RUSMA

RUSSE adj as in charlotte russe cold dessert made from cream, etc, surrounded by sponge fingers

RUSSEL n type of woollen fabric

RUSSELS > RUSSEL

RUSSET adj reddish-brown ▷ n apple with rough reddish-brown skin ▷ vb become russet-coloured

RUSSETED > RUSSET

RUSSETIER > RUSSETY

RUSSETING > RUSSET

RUSSETS > RUSSET

RUSSETY adj of a russet colour

RUSSIA n Russia leather

RUSSIAS > RUSSIA

RUSSIFIED > RUSSIFY

RUSSIFIES > RUSSIFY

RUSSIFY vb cause to become Russian in character

RUSSULA n type of fungus, typically of toadstool shape

RUSSULAE > RUSSULA

RUSSULAS > RUSSULA

RUST n reddish-brown coating formed on iron etc that has been exposed to moisture ▷ adj reddish-brown ▷ vb become coated with rust

RUSTABLE adj liable to rust

RUSTED > RUST

RUSTIC adj of or resembling country people ▷ n person from the country

RUSTICAL n rustic

RUSTICALS > RUSTICAL

RUSTICANA pl n objects, such as agricultural implements, garden furniture, etc, made in imitation of rustic styles

RUSTICATE vb banish temporarily from university as a punishment

RUSTICIAL made-up variant of **>** RUSTIC

RUSTICISE same as **>** RUSTICIZE

RUSTICISM > RUSTIC

RUSTICITY > RUSTIC

RUSTICIZE vb make rustic

RUSTICLY > RUSTIC

RUSTICS > RUSTIC

RUSTIER > RUSTY

RUSTIEST > RUSTY

RUSTILY > RUSTY

RUSTINESS > RUSTY

RUSTING > RUST

RUSTINGS > RUST

RUSTLE n low whispering sound ▷ vb steal (cattle)

RUSTLED > RUSTLE

RUSTLER n cattle thief

RUSTLERS > RUSTLER

RUSTLES > RUSTLE

RUSTLESS > RUST

RUSTLING > RUSTLE

RUSTLINGS > RUSTLE

RUSTPROOF adj treated against rusting

RUSTRE n (in heraldry) lozenge with a round hole in the middle showing the background colour

RUSTRED > RUSTRE

RUSTRES > RUSTRE

RUSTS > RUST

RUSTY adj coated with rust

RUT n furrow made by wheels ▷ vb make ruts in

RUTABAGA n plant with a bulbous edible root

RUTABAGAS > RUTABAGA

RUTACEOUS adj relating to a family of tropical and temperate flowering plants which includes rue and citrus trees

RUTH n pity

RUTHENIC adj of or containing ruthenium, esp in a high valency state

RUTHENIUM n rare hard brittle white element

RUTHER adv rather

RUTHFUL adj full of or causing sorrow or pity

RUTHFULLY > RUTHFUL

RUTHLESS adj pitiless, merciless

RUTHS > RUTH

RUTILANT adj of a reddish colour or glow

RUTILATED adj (of minerals, esp quartz) containing needles of rutile

RUTILE n black, yellowish, or reddish-brown mineral

RUTILES > RUTILE

RUTIN n bioflavonoid found in various plants including rue

RUTINS > RUTIN

RUTS > RUT

RUTTED > RUT

RUTTER n (in history) type of cavalry soldier

RUTTERS > RUTTER

RUTTIER > RUTTY

RUTTIEST > RUTTY

RUTTILY > RUTTY

RUTTINESS > RUTTY

RUTTING > RUT

RUTTINGS > RUT

RUTTISH adj (of an animal) in a condition of rut

RUTTISHLY > RUTTISH

RUTTY adj full of ruts or holes

RYA n type of rug originating in Scandinavia

RYAL n one of several old coins

RYALS > RYAL

RYAS > RYA

RYBAT n polished stone piece forming the side of a window or door

RYBATS > RYBAT

RYBAUDRYE archaic variant of **>** RIBALDRY

RYE n kind of grain used for fodder and bread

RYEBREAD n bread made from rye flour

RYEBREADS > RYEBREAD

RYEFLOUR n flour made from rye

RYEFLOURS > RYEFLOUR

RYEGRASS n type of grass, widely cultivated as a forage crop

RYEPECK n punt-mooring pole

RYEPECKS > RYEPECK

RYES > RYE

RYFE archaic variant of **>** RIFE

RYKE Scots variant of **>** REACH

RYKED > RYKE

RYKES > RYKE

RYKING > RYKE

RYMME same as **>** RIM

RYMMED > RYMME

RYMMES > RYMME

RYMMING > RYMME

RYND n (in milling) crossbar piece forming part of the support structure of the upper millstone

RYNDS > RYND

RYOKAN n traditional Japanese inn

RYOKANS > RYOKAN

RYOT n (in India) a peasant or tenant farmer

RYOTS > RYOT

RYOTWARI n (in India) system of land tenure in which land taxes are paid to the state

RYOTWARIS > RYOTWARI

RYPE n ptarmigan

RYPECK same as **>** RYEPECK

RYPECKS > RYPECK

RYPER > RYPE

RYU n school of Japanese martial arts

RYUS > RYU

r

Ss

SAAG n (in Indian cookery) spinach

SAAGS > SAAG

SAB n person engaged in direct action to prevent a targeted action taking place ▷ vb take part in such action

SABADILLA n tropical American liliaceous plant

SABAL n variety of palm tree

SABALS > SABAL

SABATON n foot covering in suit of armour

SABATONS > SABATON

SABAYON n dessert or sweet sauce made with egg yolks, sugar, and wine

SABAYONS > SABAYON

SABBAT n midnight meeting of witches

SABBATH n period of rest

SABBATHS > SABBATH

SABBATIC n period of leave granted to university staff

SABBATICS
> SABBATIC

SABBATINE adj of Saturday

SABBATISE same as
> SABBATIZE

SABBATISM n sabbath observance

SABBATIZE vb observe as sabbath

SABBATS > SABBAT

SABBED > SAB

SABBING > SAB

SABBINGS > SABBING

SABE n very informal word meaning sense or savvy ▷ vb very informal word meaning know or savvy

SABED > SABE

SABEING > SABE

SABELLA n marine worm

SABELLAS > SABELLA

SABER same as > SABRE

SABERED > SABER

SABERING > SABER

SABERLIKE > SABER

SABERS > SABER

SABES > SABE

SABHA n set of Muslim prayer beads

SABHAS > SABHA

SABICU n type of Caribbean tree

SABICUS > SABICU

SABIN n unit of acoustic absorption

SABINE variant of
> SAVIN

SABINES > SABINE

SABINS > SABIN

SABIR n member of ancient Turkic people

SABIRS > SABIR

SABKHA n flat coastal plain with a salt crust, common in Arabia

SABKHAH n sabkha

SABKHAHS > SABKHAH

SABKHAS > SABKHA

SABKHAT n sabkha

SABKHATS > SABKHAT

SABLE n dark fur from a small weasel-like Arctic animal ▷ adj black

SABLED > SABLE

SABLEFISH n North American fish

SABLER > SABLE

SABLES > SABLE

SABLEST > SABLE

SABLING > SABLE

SABOT n wooden shoe traditionally worn by peasants in France

SABOTAGE n intentional damage done to machinery, systems, etc ▷ vb damage intentionally

SABOTAGED
> SABOTAGE

SABOTAGES
> SABOTAGE

SABOTED adj wearing sabots

SABOTEUR n person who commits sabotage

SABOTEURS
> SABOTEUR

SABOTIER n wearer of wooden clogs

SABOTIERS
> SABOTIER

SABOTS > SABOT

SABRA n native-born Israeli Jew

SABRAS > SABRA

SABRE n curved cavalry sword ▷ vb injure or kill with a sabre

SABRED > SABRE

SABRELIKE
> SABERLIKE

SABRES > SABRE

SABREUR n person wielding sabre

SABREURS > SABREUR

SABREWING n large type of hummingbird with long curved wings

SABRING > SABRE

SABS > SAB

SABULINE same as
> SABULOUS

SABULOSE same as
> SABULOUS

SABULOUS adj like sand in texture

SABURRA n granular deposit

SABURRAL > SABURRA

SABURRAS > SABURRA

SAC n pouchlike structure in an animal or plant

SACATON n coarse grass of the southwestern US and Mexico

SACATONS > SACATON

SACBUT n medieval trombone

SACBUTS > SACBUT

SACCADE n movement of the eye when it makes a sudden change of fixation, as in reading

SACCADES > SACCADE

SACCADIC > SACCADE

SACCATE adj in the form of a sac

SACCHARIC adj as in saccharic acid white soluble solid acid

SACCHARIN n artificial sweetener

SACCHARUM n cane sugar

SACCIFORM adj like a sac

SACCOI > SACCOS

SACCOS n bishop's garment in the Orthodox Church

SACCOSES > SACCOS

SACCULAR adj of or resembling a sac

SACCULATE adj of, relating to, or possessing a saccule, saccules, or a sacculus

SACCULE n small sac

SACCULES > SACCULE

SACCULI > SACCULUS

SACCULUS same as
> SACCULE

SACELLA > SACELLUM

SACELLUM n tomb within a church

SACHEM same as
> SAGAMORE

SACHEMDOM > SACHEM

SACHEMIC > SACHEM

SACHEMS > SACHEM

SACHET n small envelope or bag containing a single portion

SACHETED adj contained in a sachet

SACHETS > SACHET

SACK n large bag made of coarse material ▷ vb dismiss

SACKABLE adj of an offence that is sufficiently serious to warrant dismissal from a job

SACKAGE n act of sacking a place ▷ vb sack or plunder

SACKAGED > SACKAGE

SACKAGES > SACKAGE

SACKAGING > SACKAGE

SACKBUT n medieval form of trombone

SACKBUTS > SACKBUT

SACKCLOTH n coarse fabric used for sacks, formerly worn as a penance

SACKED > SACK

SACKER > SACK

SACKERS > SACK

SACKFUL > SACK

SACKFULS > SACKFUL

SACKING n rough woven material used for sacks

SACKINGS > SACKING

SACKLESS adj old word meaning innocent

SACKLIKE > SACK

SACKLOAD n amount of something that a sack contains

SACKLOADS
> SACKLOAD

SACKS > SACK

SACKSFUL > SACKFUL

SACLESS adj old word meaning unchallengeable

SACLIKE > SAC

SACQUE same as > SACK

SACQUES > SACQUE

SACRA > SACRUM

SACRAL adj of or associated with sacred rites ▷ n sacral vertebra

SACRALGIA n pain in sacrum

SACRALISE same as
> SACRALIZE

SACRALITY n sacredness

SACRALIZE vb make sacred

SACRALS > SACRAL

SACRAMENT n ceremony of the Christian Church, esp Communion

SACRARIA
> SACRARIUM

SACRARIAL
> SACRARIUM

SACRARIUM n sanctuary of a church
SACRED adj holy
SACREDER > SACRED
SACREDEST > SACRED
SACREDLY > SACRED
SACRIFICE n giving something up ▷ vb offer as a sacrifice
SACRIFIDE vb old form of sacrifice
SACRIFIED > SACRIFY
SACRIFIES > SACRIFY
SACRIFY vb old form of sacrifice
SACRILEGE n misuse or desecration of something sacred
SACRING n act or ritual of consecration
SACRINGS > SACRING
SACRIST same as > SACRISTAN
SACRISTAN n person in charge of the contents of a church
SACRISTS > SACRIST
SACRISTY n room in a church where sacred objects are kept
SACRUM n wedge-shaped bone at the base of the spine
SACRUMS > SACRUM
SACS > SAC
SAD adj sorrowful, unhappy ▷ vb New Zealand word meaning express sadness or displeasure strongly
SADDED > SAD
SADDEN vb make (someone) sad
SADDENED > SADDEN
SADDENING > SADDEN
SADDENS > SADDEN
SADDER > SAD
SADDEST > SAD
SADDHU same as > SADHU
SADDHUS > SADDHU
SADDIE same as > SADDO
SADDIES > SADDIE
SADDING > SAD
SADDISH > SAD
SADDLE n rider's seat on a horse or bicycle ▷ vb put a saddle on (a horse)
SADDLEBAG n pouch or small bag attached to the saddle of a horse, bicycle, or motorcycle
SADDLEBOW n pommel of a saddle
SADDLED > SADDLE
SADDLER n maker or seller of saddles
SADDLERS > SADDLER
SADDLERY n saddles and harness for horses collectively
SADDLES > SADDLE
SADDLING > SADDLE
SADDO vb make sad ▷ n socially inadequate or pathetic person
SADDOES > SADDO
SADDOS > SADDO

SADE same as > SADHE
SADES > SADE
SADHANA n one of a number of spiritual practices which lead to perfection
SADHANAS > SADHANA
SADHE n 18th letter in the Hebrew alphabet
SADHES > SADHE
SADHU n Hindu wandering holy man
SADHUS > SADHU
SADI variant of > SADHE
SADIRON n heavy iron pointed at both ends, for pressing clothes
SADIRONS > SADIRON
SADIS > SADI
SADISM n gaining of pleasure from inflicting suffering
SADISMS > SADISM
SADIST > SADISM
SADISTIC > SADISM
SADISTS > SADISM
SADLY > SAD
SADNESS > SAD
SADNESSES > SAD
SADO variant of > CHADO
SADOS > SADO
SADS > SAD
SADZA n southern African porridge
SADZAS > SADZA
SAE Scot word for > SO
SAECULA > SAECULUM
SAECULUM n age in astronomy
SAECULUMS > SAECULUM
SAETER n upland pasture in Norway
SAETERS > SAETER
SAFARI n expedition to hunt or observe wild animals, esp in Africa ▷ vb go on safari
SAFARIED > SAFARI
SAFARIING > SAFARI
SAFARIS > SAFARI
SAFARIST n person on safari
SAFARISTS > SAFARIST
SAFE adj secure, protected ▷ n strong lockable container ▷ vb make safe
SAFED > SAFE
SAFEGUARD vb protect ▷ n protection
SAFELIGHT n light that can be used in a room in which photographic material is handled, transmitting only those colours to which a particular type of film, plate, or paper is relatively insensitive
SAFELY > SAFE
SAFENESS > SAFE
SAFER > SAFE
SAFES > SAFE
SAFEST > SAFE
SAFETIED > SAFETY
SAFETIES > SAFETY

SAFETY n state of being safe ▷ vb make safe
SAFETYING > SAFETY
SAFETYMAN n defensive player in American football
SAFETYMEN > SAFETYMAN
SAFFIAN n leather tanned with sumach and usually dyed a bright colour
SAFFIANS > SAFFIAN
SAFFLOWER n thistle-like plant with flowers used for dye and oil
SAFFRON n orange-coloured flavouring obtained from a crocus ▷ adj orange
SAFFRONED adj containing saffron
SAFFRONS > SAFFRON
SAFFRONY adj like saffron
SAFING > SAFE
SAFRANIN same as > SAFRANINE
SAFRANINE n any of a class of azine dyes, used for textiles and biological stains
SAFRANINS > SAFRANIN
SAFROL n oily liquid obtained from sassafras
SAFROLE n colourless or yellowish oily water-insoluble liquid
SAFROLES > SAFROLE
SAFROLS > SAFROL
SAFRONAL n oily liquid derived from saffron
SAFRONALS > SAFRONAL
SAFT Scot word for > SOFT
SAFTER > SAFT
SAFTEST > SAFT
SAG vb sink in the middle ▷ n droop
SAGA n legend of Norse heroes
SAGACIOUS adj wise
SAGACITY n foresight, discernment, or keen perception
SAGAMAN n person reciting Norse sagas
SAGAMEN > SAGAMAN
SAGAMORE n (among some Native Americans) a chief or eminent man
SAGAMORES > SAGAMORE
SAGANASH n Algonquian term for an Englishman
SAGAPENUM n resin formerly used as drug
SAGAS > SAGA
SAGATHIES > SAGATHY
SAGATHY n type of light fabric
SAGBUT n medieval trombone
SAGBUTS > SAGBUT
SAGE n very wise person ▷ adj wise
SAGEBRUSH n aromatic plant of West N America

SAGEHOOD n state of being wise
SAGEHOODS > SAGEHOOD
SAGELY > SAGE
SAGENE n fishing net
SAGENES > SAGENE
SAGENESS > SAGE
SAGENITE n mineral found in crystal form
SAGENITES > SAGENITE
SAGENITIC > SAGENITE
SAGER > SAGE
SAGES > SAGE
SAGEST > SAGE
SAGGAR n box in which fragile ceramic wares are placed for protection ▷ vb put in a saggar
SAGGARD n saggar
SAGGARDS > SAGGARD
SAGGARED > SAGGAR
SAGGARING > SAGGAR
SAGGARS > SAGGAR
SAGGED > SAG
SAGGER same as > SAGGAR
SAGGERED > SAGGER
SAGGERING > SAGGER
SAGGERS > SAGGER
SAGGIER > SAGGY
SAGGIEST > SAGGY
SAGGING > SAG
SAGGINGS > SAG
SAGGY adj tending to sag
SAGIER > SAGY
SAGIEST > SAGY
SAGINATE vb fatten livestock
SAGINATED > SAGINATE
SAGINATES > SAGINATE
SAGITTA n sine of an arc
SAGITTAL adj resembling an arrow
SAGITTARY n centaur
SAGITTAS > SAGITTA
SAGITTATE adj (esp of leaves) shaped like the head of an arrow
SAGO n starchy cereal from the powdered pith of the sago palm tree
SAGOIN n South American monkey
SAGOINS > SAGOIN
SAGOS > SAGO
SAGOUIN n South American monkey
SAGOUINS > SAGOUIN
SAGRADA adj as in cascara sagrada dried bark of the cascara buckthorn
SAGS > SAG
SAGUARO n giant cactus of desert regions
SAGUAROS > SAGUARO
SAGUIN n South American monkey
SAGUINS > SAGUIN
SAGUM n Roman soldier's cloak
SAGY adj like or containing sage
SAHEB same as > SAHIB

S

SAHEBS > SAHEB
SAHIB n Indian term of address placed after a man's name as a mark of respect
SAHIBA n respectful Indian term of address for woman
SAHIBAH n sahiba
SAHIBAHS > SAHIBAH
SAHIBAS > SAHIBA
SAHIBS > SAHIB
SAHIWAL n breed of cattle in India
SAHIWALS > SAHIWAL
SAHUARO same as > SAGUARO
SAHUAROS > SAHUARO
SAI n South American monkey
SAIBLING n freshwater fish
SAIBLINGS > SAIBLING
SAIC n boat of eastern Mediterranean
SAICE same as > SYCE
SAICES > SAICE
SAICK n boat of eastern Mediterranean
SAICKS > SAICK
SAICS > SAIC
SAID same as > SAYYID
SAIDEST > SAY
SAIDS > SAID
SAIDST > SAY
SAIGA n either of two antelopes of the plains of central Asia
SAIGAS > SAIGA
SAIKEI n Japanese ornamental miniature landscape
SAIKEIS > SAIKEI
SAIKLESS old Scots word for > INNOCENT
SAIL n sheet of fabric stretched to catch the wind for propelling a sailing boat ▷ vb travel by water
SAILABLE > SAIL
SAILBOARD n board with a mast and single sail, used for windsurfing
SAILBOAT n boat propelled chiefly by sail
SAILBOATS > SAILBOAT
SAILCLOTH n fabric for making sails
SAILED > SAIL
SAILER n vessel, esp one equipped with sails, with specified sailing characteristics
SAILERS > SAILER
SAILFISH n large tropical game fish, with a long sail-like fin on its back
SAILING n practice, art, or technique of sailing a vessel
SAILINGS > SAILING
SAILLESS > SAIL
SAILMAKER n person who makes sails

SAILOR n member of a ship's crew
SAILORING n activity of working as sailor
SAILORLY adj like a sailor
SAILORS > SAILOR
SAILPAST n sailing of ships past a particular place
SAILPASTS > SAILPAST
SAILPLANE n high-performance glider
SAILROOM n space on ship for storing sails
SAILROOMS > SAILROOM
SAILS > SAIL
SAIM Scots word for > LARD
SAIMIN n Hawaiian dish of noodles
SAIMINS > SAIMIN
SAIMIRI n South American monkey
SAIMIRIS > SAIMIRI
SAIMS > SAIM
SAIN vb make the sign of the cross over so as to bless or protect from evil or sin
SAINE vb old form of say
SAINED > SAIN
SAINFOIN n Eurasian plant with pink flowers, widely grown as feed for grazing farm animals
SAINFOINS > SAINFOIN
SAINING > SAIN
SAINS > SAIN
SAINT n person venerated after death as specially holy ▷ vb canonize
SAINTDOM > SAINT
SAINTDOMS > SAINT
SAINTED adj formally recognized by a Christian Church as a saint
SAINTESS n female saint
SAINTFOIN n sainfoin
SAINTHOOD n state or character of being a saint
SAINTING > SAINT
SAINTISH > SAINT
SAINTISM n quality of being saint
SAINTISMS > SAINTISM
SAINTLESS > SAINT
SAINTLIER > SAINTLY
SAINTLIKE > SAINT
SAINTLILY > SAINTLY
SAINTLING n little saint
SAINTLY adj behaving in a very good, patient, or holy way
SAINTS > SAINT
SAINTSHIP > SAINT
SAIQUE n boat in eastern Mediterranean
SAIQUES > SAIQUE
SAIR Scot word for > SORE
SAIRED > SAIR
SAIRER > SAIR
SAIREST > SAIR
SAIRING > SAIR
SAIRS > SAIR

SAIS > SAI
SAIST > SAY
SAITH form of the present tense (indicative mood) of > SAY
SAITHE n dark-coloured food fish found in northern seas
SAITHES > SAITHE
SAITHS > SAITH
SAIYID n Muslim descended from Muhammad's grandson
SAIYIDS > SAIYID
SAJOU n South American monkey
SAJOUS > SAJOU
SAKE n benefit
SAKER n large falcon of E Europe and central Asia
SAKERET n male saker
SAKERETS > SAKERET
SAKERS > SAKER
SAKES > SAKE
SAKI n small arboreal monkey
SAKIA n water wheel in Middle East
SAKIAS > SAKIA
SAKIEH same as > SAKIA
SAKIEHS > SAKIEH
SAKIS > SAKI
SAKIYEH same as > SAKIA
SAKIYEHS > SAKIYEH
SAKKOI > SAKKOS
SAKKOS n bishop's garment in Orthodox Church
SAKKOSES > SAKKOS
SAKSAUL n Asian tree
SAKSAULS > SAKSAUL
SAKTI n wife of a Hindu god
SAKTIS > SAKTI
SAL pharmacological term for > SALT
SALAAM n low bow of greeting among Muslims ▷ vb make a salaam
SALAAMED > SALAAM
SALAAMING > SALAAM
SALAAMS > SALAAM
SALABLE same as > SALEABLE
SALABLY > SALEABLY
SALACIOUS adj excessively concerned with sexual matters
SALACITY n excessive interest in sexual matters
SALAD n dish of raw vegetables, eaten as a meal or part of a meal
SALADANG n variety of ox
SALADANGS > SALADANG
SALADE same as > SALLET
SALADES > SALADE
SALADING n ingredients for salad
SALADINGS > SALADING
SALADS > SALAD
SALAL n North American shrub
SALALS > SALAL

SALAMI n highly spiced sausage
SALAMIS > SALAMI
SALAMON n word used in old oaths
SALAMONS > SALAMON
SALANGANE n Asian swift
SALARIAT n salary-earning class
SALARIATS > SALARIAT
SALARIED adj earning or providing a salary
SALARIES > SALARY
SALARY n fixed regular payment, usu monthly, to an employee ▷ vb pay a salary to
SALARYING > SALARY
SALARYMAN n (in Japan) an office worker
SALARYMEN > SALARYMAN
SALAT n obligatory series of Islamic prayers facing towards Mecca
SALATS > SALAT
SALBAND n coating of mineral
SALBANDS > SALBAND
SALCHOW n type of figure-skating jump
SALCHOWS > SALCHOW
SALE n exchange of goods for money
SALEABLE adj fit or likely to be sold
SALEABLY > SALEABLE
SALEP n dried ground starchy tubers of various orchids
SALEPS > SALEP
SALERATUS n sodium bicarbonate when used in baking powder
SALERING n enclosed area for livestock at market
SALERINGS > SALERING
SALEROOM n place where goods are sold by auction
SALEROOMS > SALEROOM
SALES > SALE
SALESGIRL n person who sells goods
SALESLADY n person who sells goods
SALESMAN n man who sells goods
SALESMEN > SALESMAN
SALESROOM n room in which merchandise or sale is displayed
SALET same as > SALLET
SALETS > SALET
SALEWD > SALUE
SALEYARD n area with pens for holding animals before auction
SALEYARDS > SALEYARD
SALFERN n plant of borage family
SALFERNS > SALFERN
SALIAUNCE n old word meaning onslaught

SALIC adj (of rocks and minerals) having a high content of silica and alumina

SALICES > SALIX

SALICET n soft-toned organ stop

SALICETA > SALICETUM

SALICETS > SALICET

SALICETUM n plantation of willows

SALICIN n colourless or white crystalline water-soluble glucoside

SALICINE same as > SALICIN

SALICINES > SALICINE

SALICINS > SALICIN

SALICYLIC adj as in salicylic acid white crystalline substance with a sweet taste and a bitter aftertaste

SALIENCE > SALIENT

SALIENCES > SALIENT

SALIENCY n quality of being prominent

SALIENT adj prominent, noticeable ▷ n projecting part of a front line

SALIENTLY > SALIENT

SALIENTS > SALIENT

SALIFIED > SALIFY

SALIFIES > SALIFY

SALIFY vb treat, mix with, or cause to combine with a salt

SALIFYING > SALIFY

SALIGOT n water chestnut

SALIGOTS > SALIGOT

SALIMETER n hydrometer for measuring salt in a solution

SALIMETRY > SALIMETER

SALINA n salt marsh, lake, or spring

SALINAS > SALINA

SALINE adj containing salt ▷ n solution of sodium chloride and water

SALINES > SALINE

SALINISE same as > SALINIZE

SALINISED > SALINISE

SALINISES > SALINISE

SALINITY > SALINE

SALINIZE vb treat with salt

SALINIZED > SALINIZE

SALINIZES > SALINIZE

SALIVA n liquid that forms in the mouth, spittle

SALIVAL > SALIVA

SALIVARY > SALIVA

SALIVAS > SALIVA

SALIVATE vb produce saliva

SALIVATED > SALIVATE

SALIVATES > SALIVATE

SALIVATOR > SALIVATE

SALIX n plant or tree of willow family

SALL archaic form of > SHALL

SALLAD old spelling of > SALAD

SALLADS > SALLAD

SALLAL n North American shrub

SALLALS > SALLAL

SALLE n hall

SALLEE n SE Australian eucalyptus

SALLEES > SALLEE

SALLES > SALLE

SALLET n light round helmet

SALLETS > SALLET

SALLIED > SALLY

SALLIER > SALLY

SALLIERS > SALLY

SALLIES > SALLY

SALLOW adj of an unhealthy pale or yellowish colour ▷ vb make sallow ▷ n any of several small willow trees

SALLOWED > SALLOW

SALLOWER > SALLOW

SALLOWEST > SALLOW

SALLOWIER > SALLOWY

SALLOWING > SALLOW

SALLOWISH > SALLOW

SALLOWLY > SALLOW

SALLOWS > SALLOW

SALLOWY adj full of sallows

SALLY n violent excursion ▷ vb set or rush out

SALLYING > SALLY

SALLYPORT n opening in a fortified place from which troops may make a sally

SALMI n ragout of game stewed in a rich brown sauce

SALMIS same as > SALMI

SALMON n large fish with orange-pink flesh valued as food ▷ adj orange-pink

SALMONET n young salmon

SALMONETS > SALMONET

SALMONID n type of soft-finned fish of the family which includes the salmon

SALMONIDS > SALMONID

SALMONIER > SALMONY

SALMONOID adj belonging to the order of soft-finned teleost fishes that includes the salmon, whitefish, grayling, and char ▷ n any of these fish

SALMONS > SALMON

SALMONY adj of or like a salmon

SALOL n white sparingly soluble crystalline compound

SALOLS > SALOL

SALOMETER n instrument for measuring salt in solution

SALON n commercial premises of a hairdresser, beautician, etc

SALONS > SALON

SALOON n closed car with four or more seats

SALOONS > SALOON

SALOOP n infusion of aromatic herbs or other plant parts formerly used as a tonic or cure

SALOOPS > SALOOP

SALOP variant of > SALOOP

SALOPIAN > SALOOP

SALOPS > SALOP

SALP n minute animal floating in sea

SALPA n any of various minute floating animals of warm oceans

SALPAE > SALPA

SALPAS > SALPA

SALPIAN n minute animal floating in sea

SALPIANS > SALPIAN

SALPICON n mixture of chopped fish, meat, or vegetables in a sauce

SALPICONS > SALPICON

SALPID n minute animal floating in sea

SALPIDS > SALPID

SALPIFORM > SALPA

SALPINGES > SALPINX

SALPINX n Fallopian tube or Eustachian tube

SALPINXES > SALPINX

SALPS > SALP

SALS > SAL

SALSA n lively Puerto Rican dance ▷ vb dance the salsa

SALSAED > SALSA

SALSAING > SALSA

SALSAS > SALSA

SALSE n volcano expelling mud

SALSES > SALSE

SALSIFIES > SALSIFY

SALSIFY n Mediterranean plant with a long white edible root

SALSILLA n tropical American vine

SALSILLAS > SALSILLA

SALT n white crystalline substance used to season food ▷ vb season or preserve with salt

SALTANDO n staccato piece of violin playing

SALTANDOS > SALTANDO

SALTANT adj (of an organism) differing from others of its species because of a saltation ▷ n saltant organism

SALTANTS > SALTANT

SALTATE vb go through saltation

SALTATED > SALTATE

SALTATES > SALTATE

SALTATING > SALTATE

SALTATION n abrupt variation in the appearance of an organism, usu caused by genetic mutation

SALTATO n staccato piece of violin playing

SALTATORY adj specialized for jumping

SALTATOS > SALTATO

SALTBOX n box for salt with a sloping lid

SALTBOXES > SALTBOX

SALTBUSH n shrub that grows in alkaline desert regions

SALTCAT n salty medicine for pigeons

SALTCATS > SALTCAT

SALTCHUCK n any body of salt water

SALTED adj seasoned, preserved, or treated with salt

SALTER n person who deals in or manufactures salt

SALTERIES > SALTERY

SALTERN n place where salt is obtained from pools of evaporated sea water

SALTERNS > SALTERN

SALTERS > SALTER

SALTERY n factory where fish is salted for storage

SALTEST > SALT

SALTFISH n salted cod

SALTIE n saltwater crocodile

SALTIER same as > SALTIRE

SALTIERS > SALTIER

SALTIES > SALTIE

SALTIEST > SALTY

SALTILY > SALTY

SALTINE n salty biscuit

SALTINES > SALTINE

SALTINESS > SALTY

SALTING n area of low ground regularly inundated with salt water

SALTINGS > SALTING

SALTIRE n diagonal cross on a shield

SALTIRES > SALTIRE

SALTISH > SALT

SALTISHLY > SALT

SALTLESS > SALT

SALTLIKE > SALT

SALTLY > SALT

SALTNESS > SALT

SALTO n daring jump ▷ vb perform a daring jump

SALTOED > SALTO

SALTOING > SALTO

SALTOS > SALTO

SALTPAN n shallow basin containing salt from an evaporated salt lake

SALTPANS > SALTPAN

SALTPETER same as > SALTPETRE

SALTPETRE n compound used in gunpowder and as a preservative

SALTS > SALT

SALTUS n break in the continuity of a sequence

SALTUSES > SALTUS

SALTWATER n sea water ▷ adj living in the sea

SALTWORK n place where salt is refined

SALTWORKS n place, building, or factory where salt is produced

SALTWORT n any of several chenopodiaceous plants

SALTWORTS > SALTWORT

SALTY adj of, tasting of, or containing salt

SALUBRITY n quality of being favourable to health or wholesome

SALUE vb old word meaning salute

SALUED > SALUE

SALUES > SALUE

SALUING > SALUE

SALUKI n type of tall hound with a smooth coat

SALUKIS > SALUKI

SALURETIC n drug that increases secretion of salt in urine

SALUT interj cheers!

SALUTARY adj producing a beneficial result

SALUTE n motion of the arm as a formal military sign of respect ▷ vb greet with a salute

SALUTED > SALUTE

SALUTER > SALUTE

SALUTERS > SALUTE

SALUTES > SALUTE

SALUTING > SALUTE

SALVABLE adj capable of or suitable for being saved or salvaged

SALVABLY > SALVABLE

SALVAGE n saving of a ship or other property from destruction ▷ vb save from destruction or waste

SALVAGED > SALVAGE

SALVAGEE n rope on sailing ship

SALVAGEES > SALVAGEE

SALVAGER > SALVAGE

SALVAGERS > SALVAGE

SALVAGES > SALVAGE

SALVAGING > SALVAGE

SALVARSAN n old medicine containing arsenic

SALVATION n fact or state of being saved from harm or the consequences of sin

SALVATORY n place for storing something safely

SALVE n healing or soothing ointment ▷ vb soothe or appease

SALVED > SALVE

SALVER same as > SALVOR

SALVERS > SALVER

SALVES > SALVE

SALVETE n Latin greeting

SALVETES > SALVETE

SALVIA n plant with blue or red flowers

SALVIAS > SALVIA

SALVIFIC adj acting to salve

SALVING > SALVE

SALVINGS > SALVE

SALVO n simultaneous discharge of guns etc ▷ vb attack with a salvo

SALVOED > SALVO

SALVOES > SALVO

SALVOING > SALVO

SALVOR n person instrumental in salvaging a vessel or its cargo

SALVORS > SALVOR

SALVOS > SALVO

SALWAR n pair of loose-fitting trousers narrowing around the ankles

SALWARS > SALWAR

SAM vb collect

SAMA n Japanese title of respect

SAMAAN n South American tree

SAMAANS > SAMAAN

SAMADHI n state of deep meditative contemplation

SAMADHIS > SAMADHI

SAMAN n South American tree

SAMANS > SAMAN

SAMARA n dry indehiscent one-seeded fruit

SAMARAS > SAMARA

SAMARITAN n kindly person who helps another in distress

SAMARIUM n silvery metallic element

SAMARIUMS > SAMARIUM

SAMAS > SAMA

SAMBA n lively Brazilian dance ▷ vb perform such a dance

SAMBAED > SAMBA

SAMBAING > SAMBA

SAMBAL n Malaysian dish

SAMBALS > SAMBAL

SAMBAR n S Asian deer with three-tined antlers

SAMBARS > SAMBAR

SAMBAS > SAMBA

SAMBHAR n Indian dish

SAMBHARS > SAMBHAR

SAMBHUR n Asian deer

SAMBHURS > SAMBHUR

SAMBO n type of wrestling based on judo

SAMBOES > SAMBO

SAMBOS > SAMBO

SAMBUCA n Italian liqueur

SAMBUCAS > SAMBUCA

SAMBUKE n ancient Greek stringed instrument

SAMBUKES > SAMBUKE

SAMBUR same as > SAMBAR

SAMBURS > SAMBUR

SAME adj identical, not different, unchanged ▷ n something identical

SAMECH n letter in Hebrew alphabet

SAMECHS > SAMECH

SAMEK variant of > SAMEKH

SAMEKH n 15th letter in the Hebrew alphabet

SAMEKHS > SAMEKH

SAMEKS > SAMEK

SAMEL adj of brick, not sufficiently fired

SAMELY adj the same

SAMEN old Scots form of > SAME

SAMENESS n state or quality of being the same

SAMES > SAME

SAMEY adj monotonous

SAMEYNESS n quality of being samey

SAMFOO n style of casual dress worn by Chinese women

SAMFOOS > SAMFOO

SAMFU same as > SAMFOO

SAMFUS > SAMFU

SAMIEL same as > SIMOOM

SAMIELS > SAMIEL

SAMIER > SAMEY

SAMIEST > SAMEY

SAMISEN n Japanese plucked stringed instrument with a long neck

SAMISENS > SAMISEN

SAMITE n heavy fabric of silk used in the Middle Ages

SAMITES > SAMITE

SAMITHI same as > SAMITI

SAMITHIS > SAMITHI

SAMITI n (in India) an association, esp one formed to organize political activity

SAMITIS > SAMITI

SAMIZDAT n system of secret printing and distribution of banned literature in the former USSR

SAMIZDATS > SAMIZDAT

SAMLET n young salmon

SAMLETS > SAMLET

SAMLOR n motor vehicle in Thailand

SAMLORS > SAMLOR

SAMMED > SAM

SAMMIE n sandwich

SAMMIES > SAMMY

SAMMING > SAM

SAMMY n (in South Africa) an Indian fruit and vegetable vendor

SAMNITIS n poisonous plant mentioned by Spenser

SAMOSA n (in Indian cookery) a small fried triangular piece of meat or vegetable pasty

SAMOSAS > SAMOSA

SAMOVAR n Russian tea urn

SAMOVARS > SAMOVAR

SAMOYED n Siberian breed of dog with a tightly curled tail

SAMOYEDS > SAMOYED

SAMP n crushed maize used for porridge

SAMPAN n small boat with oars used in China

SAMPANS > SAMPAN

SAMPHIRE n plant found on rocks by the seashore

SAMPHIRES > SAMPHIRE

SAMPI n old Greek number character

SAMPIRE n samphire

SAMPIRES > SAMPIRE

SAMPIS > SAMPI

SAMPLE n part taken as representative of a whole ▷ vb take and test a sample of

SAMPLED > SAMPLE

SAMPLER n piece of embroidery showing the embroiderer's skill

SAMPLERS > SAMPLER

SAMPLERY n making of samplers

SAMPLES > SAMPLE

SAMPLING n process of selecting a random sample

SAMPLINGS > SAMPLING

SAMPS > SAMP

SAMS > SAM

SAMSARA n endless cycle of birth, death, and rebirth

SAMSARAS > SAMSARA

SAMSARIC adj relating to the eternal cycle of birth, suffering, death and rebirth in Indian religions

SAMSHOO same as > SAMSHU

SAMSHOOS > SAMSHOO

SAMSHU n alcoholic drink made from fermented rice

SAMSHUS > SAMSHU

SAMSKARA n Hindu purification ceremony

SAMSKARAS > SAMSKARA

SAMURAI n member of an ancient Japanese warrior caste

SAMURAIS > SAMURAI

SAN n sanatorium

SANATIVE less common word for > CURATIVE

SANATORIA pl n institutions for the care of chronically ill people

SANATORY adj healing

SANBENITO n yellow garment bearing a red cross, worn by penitent heretics in the Inquisition

SANCAI n glaze in Chinese pottery

SANCAIS > SANCAI

SANCHO n African stringed instrument

SANCHOS > SANCHO

SANCTA > SANCTUM

SANCTIFY vb make holy

SANCTION n permission, authorization ▷ vb allow, authorize

SANCTIONS > SANCTION

SANCTITY n sacredness, inviolability

SANCTUARY n holy place

SANCTUM n sacred place

SANCTUMS > SANCTUM

SAND n substance consisting of small grains of rock, esp on a beach or in a desert ▷ vb smooth with sandpaper

SANDABLE > SAND

SANDAL n light shoe consisting of a sole attached by straps ▷ vb put sandals on

SANDALED > SANDAL

SANDALING > SANDAL

SANDALLED > SANDAL

SANDALS > SANDAL

SANDARAC n either of two coniferous trees having hard fragrant dark wood

SANDARACH same as > SANDARAC

SANDARACS > SANDARAC

SANDBAG n bag filled with sand, used as protection against flood water ▷ vb protect with sandbags

SANDBAGS > SANDBAG

SANDBANK n bank of sand below the surface of a river or sea

SANDBANKS > SANDBANK

SANDBAR n ridge of sand in a river or sea, often exposed at low tide

SANDBARS > SANDBAR

SANDBLAST n jet of sand blown from a nozzle under pressure ▷ vb clean or decorate (a surface) with a sandblast

SANDBOX n container on a locomotive from which sand is released onto the rails

SANDBOXES > SANDBOX

SANDBOY n as in happy as a sandboy very happy or high-spirited

SANDBOYS > SANDBOY

SANDBUR n variety of wild grass

SANDBURR n variety of wild grass

SANDBURRS > SANDBURR

SANDBURS > SANDBUR

SANDCRACK n crack in horse's hoof

SANDDAB n type of small Pacific flatfish

SANDDABS > SANDDAB

SANDED > SAND

SANDEK n man who holds a baby being circumcised

SANDEKS > SANDEK

SANDER n power tool for smoothing surfaces

SANDERS > SANDER

SANDERSES > SANDER

SANDFISH n burrowing Pacific fish

SANDFLIES > SANDFLY

SANDFLY n any of various small mothlike flies

SANDGLASS less common word for > HOURGLASS

SANDHEAP n heap of sand

SANDHEAPS > SANDHEAP

SANDHI n modification of a word under the influence of an adjacent word

SANDHILL n hill of sand

SANDHILLS > SANDHILL

SANDHIS > SANDHI

SANDHOG n person who works in underground or underwater construction projects

SANDHOGS > SANDHOG

SANDIER > SANDY

SANDIEST > SANDY

SANDINESS > SANDY

SANDING > SAND

SANDINGS > SAND

SANDIVER n scum forming on molten glass

SANDIVERS > SANDIVER

SANDLESS > SAND

SANDLIKE > SAND

SANDLING n sand eel

SANDLINGS > SANDLING

SANDLOT n area of vacant ground used for children's games

SANDLOTS > SANDLOT

SANDMAN n (in folklore) a magical person supposed to put children to sleep

SANDMEN > SANDMAN

SANDPAPER n paper coated with sand for smoothing a surface ▷ vb smooth with sandpaper

SANDPEEP n small sandpiper

SANDPEEPS > SANDPEEP

SANDPILE n pile of sand

SANDPILES > SANDPILE

SANDPIPER n shore bird with a long bill and slender legs

SANDPIT n shallow pit or container holding sand for children to play in

SANDPITS > SANDPIT

SANDPUMP n pump for wet sand

SANDPUMPS > SANDPUMP

SANDS > SAND

SANDSHOE n light canvas shoe with a rubber sole

SANDSHOES > SANDSHOE

SANDSOAP n gritty general-purpose soap

SANDSOAPS > SANDSOAP

SANDSPIT n small point of land created by sand dunes

SANDSPITS > SANDSPIT

SANDSPOUT n sand sucked into air by whirlwind

SANDSPUR n American wild grass

SANDSPURS > SANDSPUR

SANDSTONE n rock composed of sand

SANDSTORM n desert wind that whips up clouds of sand

SANDWICH n two slices of bread with a layer of food between ▷ vb insert between two other things

SANDWORM n any of various polychaete worms that live in burrows on sandy shores, esp the lugworm

SANDWORMS > SANDWORM

SANDWORT n any of numerous caryophyllaceous plants

SANDWORTS > SANDWORT

SANDY adj covered with sand

SANDYISH adj somewhat sandy or covered with sand

SANE adj of sound mind ▷ vb heal

SANED > SANE

SANELY > SANE

SANENESS > SANE

SANER > SANE

SANES > SANE

SANEST > SANE

SANG Scots word for > SONG

SANGA n Ethiopian ox

SANGAR n breastwork of stone or sods

SANGAREE n spiced drink similar to sangria

SANGAREES > SANGAREE

SANGARS > SANGAR

SANGAS > SANGA

SANGEET n Indian pre-wedding celebration

SANGEETS > SANGEET

SANGER n sandwich

SANGERS > SANGER

SANGFROID n composure or self-possession

SANGH n Indian union or association

SANGHA n Buddhist monastic order or community

SANGHAS > SANGHA

SANGHAT n local Sikh community or congregation

SANGHATS > SANGHAT

SANGHS > SANGH

SANGLIER n wild boar

SANGLIERS > SANGLIER

SANGO same as > SANGER

SANGOMA n witch doctor or herbalist

SANGOMAS > SANGOMA

SANGOS > SANGO

SANGRAIL n legendary cup used by Christ at the Last Supper

SANGRAILS > SANGRAIL

SANGREAL same as > SANGRAIL

SANGREALS > SANGREAL

SANGRIA n Spanish drink of red wine and fruit

SANGRIAS > SANGRIA

SANGS > SANG

SANGUIFY vb turn into blood

SANGUINE adj cheerful, optimistic ▷ n red pencil containing ferric oxide, used in drawing

SANGUINED > SANGUINE

SANGUINES > SANGUINE

SANICLE n type of plant with clusters of small white flowers

SANICLES > SANICLE

SANIDINE n alkali feldspar that is found in lavas

SANIDINES > SANIDINE

SANIES n thin greenish foul-smelling discharge from a wound, etc

SANIFIED > SANIFY

SANIFIES > SANIFY

SANIFY vb make healthy

SANIFYING > SANIFY

SANING > SANE

SANIOUS > SANIES

SANITARIA variant of > SANATORIA

SANITARY adj promoting health by getting rid of dirt and germs

SANITATE vb make sanitary

SANITATED > SANITATE

SANITATES > SANITATE

SANITIES > SANITY

SANITISE same as > SANITIZE

SANITISED > SANITISE

SANITISER > SANITISE

SANITISES > SANITISE

SANITIZE vb omit unpleasant details to make (news) more acceptable

SANITIZED > SANITIZE

SANITIZER > SANITIZE

SANITIZES > SANITIZE

SANITORIA variant of > SANATORIA

S

SANITY n state of having a normal healthy mind
SANJAK n (in the Turkish Empire) a subdivision of a vilayet
SANJAKS > SANJAK
SANK > SINK
SANKO n African stringed instrument
SANKOS > SANKO
SANNIE Scots word for > SANDSHOE
SANNIES > SANNIE
SANNOP n Native American married man
SANNOPS > SANNOP
SANNUP n Native American married man
SANNUPS > SANNUP
SANNYASI n Brahman who having attained the last stage of life as a beggar will not be reborn
SANNYASIN same as > SANNYASI
SANNYASIS > SANNYASI
SANPAN n sampan
SANPANS > SANPAN
SANPRO n sanitary-protection products collectively
SANPROS > SANPRO
SANS archaic word for > WITHOUT
SANSA n African musical instrument
SANSAR n name of a wind that blows in Iran
SANSARS > SANSAR
SANSAS > SANSA
SANSEI n American whose parents were Japanese immigrants
SANSEIS > SANSEI
SANSERIF n style of printer's typeface
SANSERIFS > SANSERIF
SANT n devout person in India
SANTAL n sandalwood
SANTALIC adj of sandalwood
SANTALIN n substance giving sandalwood its colour
SANTALINS > SANTALIN
SANTALOL n liquid from sandalwood used in perfume
SANTALOLS > SANTALOL
SANTALS > SANTAL
SANTERA n priestess of santeria
SANTERAS > SANTERA
SANTERIA n Caribbean religious cult
SANTERIAS > SANTERIA
SANTERO n priest of santeria
SANTEROS > SANTERO
SANTIM n former money unit in Latvia
SANTIMI > SANTIM

SANTIMS > SANTIM
SANTIMU > SANTIM
SANTIR n Middle Eastern stringed instrument
SANTIRS > SANTIR
SANTO n saint or representation of one
SANTOKU n type of Japanese knife
SANTOKUS > SANTOKU
SANTOL n fruit from Southeast Asia
SANTOLINA n any plant of an evergreen Mediterranean genus grown for its silvery-grey felted foliage
SANTOLS > SANTOL
SANTON n French figurine
SANTONICA n Asian wormwood plant
SANTONIN n soluble substance extracted from santonica
SANTONINS > SANTONIN
SANTONS > SANTON
SANTOOR same as > SANTIR
SANTOORS > SANTOOR
SANTOS > SANTO
SANTOUR n Middle Eastern stringed instrument
SANTOURS > SANTOUR
SANTS > SANT
SANTUR n Middle Eastern stringed instrument
SANTURS > SANTUR
SANYASI same as > SANNYASI
SANYASIS > SANYASI
SAOLA n small, very rare bovine mammal of Vietnam and Laos
SAOLAS > SAOLA
SAOUARI n tropical American tree
SAOUARIS > SAOUARI
SAP n moisture that circulates in plants ▷ vb undermine
SAPAJOU n capuchin monkey
SAPAJOUS > SAPAJOU
SAPAN n tropical tree
SAPANS > SAPAN
SAPANWOOD n small S Asian tree
SAPEGO n skin disease
SAPEGOES > SAPEGO
SAPELE n type of W African tree
SAPELES > SAPELE
SAPFUL adj full of sap
SAPHEAD n idiot or fool
SAPHEADED > SAPHEAD
SAPHEADS > SAPHEAD
SAPHENA n either of two large superficial veins of the legs
SAPHENAE > SAPHENA
SAPHENAS > SAPHENA
SAPHENOUS > SAPHENA
SAPID adj having a pleasant taste
SAPIDER > SAPID
SAPIDEST > SAPID

SAPIDITY > SAPID
SAPIDLESS adj lacking flavour
SAPIDNESS > SAPID
SAPIENCE > SAPIENT
SAPIENCES > SAPIENT
SAPIENCY > SAPIENT
SAPIENS adj relating to or like modern human beings
SAPIENT adj wise, shrewd ▷ n wise person
SAPIENTLY > SAPIENT
SAPIENTS > SAPIENT
SAPLESS > SAP
SAPLING n young tree
SAPLINGS > SAPLING
SAPODILLA n large tropical American evergreen tree
SAPOGENIN n substance derived from saponin
SAPONARIA same as > SOAPWORT
SAPONATED adj treated or combined with soap
SAPONIFY vb convert (a fat) into a soap by treatment with alkali
SAPONIN n any of a group of plant glycosides
SAPONINE n saponin
SAPONINES > SAPONINE
SAPONINS > SAPONIN
SAPONITE n type of clay mineral
SAPONITES > SAPONITE
SAPOR n quality in a substance that is perceived by the sense of taste
SAPORIFIC > SAPOR
SAPOROUS > SAPOR
SAPORS > SAPOR
SAPOTA same as > SAPODILLA
SAPOTAS > SAPOTA
SAPOTE n Central American tree
SAPOTES > SAPOTE
SAPOUR variant of > SAPOR
SAPOURS > SAPOUR
SAPPAN n tropical tree
SAPPANS > SAPPAN
SAPPED > SAP
SAPPER n soldier in an engineering unit
SAPPERS > SAPPER
SAPPHIC adj lesbian ▷ n verse written in a particular form
SAPPHICS > SAPPHIC
SAPPHIRE n blue precious stone ▷ adj deep blue
SAPPHIRED adj blue-coloured
SAPPHIRES > SAPPHIRE
SAPPHISM n lesbianism
SAPPHISMS > SAPPHISM
SAPPHIST n lesbian
SAPPHISTS > SAPPHIST

SAPPIER > SAPPY
SAPPIEST > SAPPY
SAPPILY > SAPPY
SAPPINESS > SAPPY
SAPPING n act of sapping
SAPPINGS > SAPPING
SAPPLE vb Scots word meaning wash in water
SAPPLED > SAPPLE
SAPPLES > SAPPLE
SAPPLING > SAPPLE
SAPPY adj (of plants) full of sap
SAPRAEMIA n blood poisoning caused by toxins of putrefactive bacteria
SAPRAEMIC > SAPRAEMIA
SAPREMIA American spelling of > SAPRAEMIA
SAPREMIAS > SAPREMIA
SAPREMIC > SAPREMIA
SAPROBE n organism that lives on decaying organisms
SAPROBES > SAPROBE
SAPROBIAL > SAPROBE
SAPROBIC > SAPROBE
SAPROBITY n state of being a saprobe
SAPROLITE n deposit of earth, etc, formed by decomposition of rocks that has remained in its original site
SAPROPEL n decomposed remains of aquatic organisms at the bottoms of lakes and oceans
SAPROPELS > SAPROPEL
SAPROZOIC adj (of animals or plants) feeding on dead organic matter
SAPS > SAP
SAPSAGO n hard greenish Swiss cheese
SAPSAGOS > SAPSAGO
SAPSUCKER n either of two North American woodpeckers
SAPUCAIA n Brazilian tree
SAPUCAIAS > SAPUCAIA
SAPWOOD n soft wood, just beneath the bark in tree trunks, that consists of living tissue
SAPWOODS > SAPWOOD
SAR n marine fish ▷ vb Scots word meaning savour
SARABAND same as > SARABANDE
SARABANDE n slow stately Spanish dance
SARABANDS > SARABAND
SARAFAN n Russian woman's cloak
SARAFANS > SARAFAN
SARAN n any one of a class of thermoplastic resins

SARANGI n stringed instrument of India played with a bow

SARANGIS > SARANGI

SARANS > SARAN

SARAPE n serape

SARAPES > SARAPE

SARBACANE n type of blowpipe

SARCASM n (use of) bitter or wounding ironic language

SARCASMS > SARCASM

SARCASTIC adj full of or showing sarcasm

SARCENET n fine soft silk fabric formerly from Italy and used for clothing, ribbons, etc

SARCENETS > SARCENET

SARCINA n type of bacterium

SARCINAE > SARCINA

SARCINAS > SARCINA

SARCOCARP n fleshy mesocarp of such fruits as the peach or plum

SARCODE n material making up living cell

SARCODES > SARCODE

SARCODIC > SARCODE

SARCOID adj of, relating to, or resembling flesh ▷ n tumour resembling a sarcoma

SARCOIDS > SARCOID

SARCOLOGY n study of flesh

SARCOMA n malignant tumour beginning in connective tissue

SARCOMAS > SARCOMA

SARCOMATA > SARCOMA

SARCOMERE n any of the units that together comprise skeletal muscle

SARCONET n type of silk

SARCONETS > SARCONET

SARCOPTIC adj relating to mange

SARCOSOME n energy-producing tissue in muscle

SARCOUS adj (of tissue) muscular or fleshy

SARD n orange, red, or brown variety of chalcedony

SARDANA n Catalan dance

SARDANAS > SARDANA

SARDAR n title used before the name of Sikh men

SARDARS > SARDAR

SARDEL n small fish

SARDELLE n small fish

SARDELLES > SARDELLE

SARDELS > SARDEL

SARDINE n small fish of the herring family ▷ vb cram together

SARDINED > SARDINE

SARDINES > SARDINE

SARDINING > SARDINE

SARDIUS same as > SARD

SARDIUSES > SARDIUS

SARDONIAN adj sardonic ▷ n person who flatters with harmful intent

SARDONIC adj mocking or scornful

SARDONYX n brown-and-white gemstone

SARDS > SARD

SARED > SAR

SAREE same as > SARI

SAREES > SAREE

SARGASSA > SARGASSUM

SARGASSO same as > SARGASSUM

SARGASSOS > SARGASSO

SARGASSUM n type of floating seaweed

SARGE n sergeant

SARGES > SARGE

SARGO same as > SARGUS

SARGOS variant of > SARGUS

SARGOSES > SARGOS

SARGUS n species of sea fish

SARGUSES > SARGUS

SARI n long piece of cloth draped around the body and over one shoulder

SARIN n chemical used in warfare as a lethal nerve gas producing asphyxia

SARING > SAR

SARINS > SARIN

SARIS > SARI

SARK n shirt or (formerly) chemise

SARKIER > SARKY

SARKIEST > SARKY

SARKILY > SARKY

SARKINESS n quality of being sarcastic

SARKING n flat planking supporting the roof cladding of a building

SARKINGS > SARKING

SARKS > SARK

SARKY adj sarcastic

SARMENT n thin twig

SARMENTA > SARMENTUM

SARMENTS > SARMENT

SARMENTUM n runner on plant

SARMIE n sandwich

SARMIES > SARMIE

SARNEY n sandwich

SARNEYS > SARNEY

SARNIE n sandwich

SARNIES > SARNIE

SAROD n Indian stringed musical instrument

SARODE n Indian stringed instrument

SARODES > SARODE

SARODIST n sarod player

SARODISTS > SARODIST

SARODS > SAROD

SARONG n long piece of cloth tucked around the waist or under the armpits

SARONGS > SARONG

SARONIC > SAROS

SAROS n cycle in which eclipses of the sun and moon occur in the same sequence

SAROSES > SAROS

SARPANCH n head of a panchayat

SARRASIN n buckwheat

SARRASINS > SARRASIN

SARRAZIN same as > SARRASIN

SARRAZINS > SARRAZIN

SARS > SAR

SARSAR same as > SANSAR

SARSARS > SARSAR

SARSDEN n sarsen

SARSDENS > SARSDEN

SARSEN n boulder of silicified sandstone

SARSENET same as > SARCENET

SARSENETS > SARSENET

SARSENS > SARSEN

SARSNET n type of silk

SARSNETS > SARSNET

SARTOR humorous or literary word for > TAILOR

SARTORIAL adj of clothes or tailoring

SARTORIAN adj of tailoring

SARTORII > SARTORIUS

SARTORIUS n long ribbon-shaped muscle that aids in flexing the knee

SARTORS > SARTOR

SARUS n Indian bird of crane family

SARUSES > SARUS

SASANQUA n type of camellia

SASANQUAS > SASANQUA

SASARARA n scolding

SASARARAS > SASARARA

SASER n device for amplifying ultrasound

SASERS > SASER

SASH n decorative strip of cloth worn round the waist or over one shoulder ▷ vb furnish with a sash, sashes, or sash windows

SASHAY vb move or walk in a casual or a showy manner

SASHAYED > SASHAY

SASHAYING > SASHAY

SASHAYS > SASHAY

SASHED > SASH

SASHES > SASH

SASHIMI n Japanese dish of thin fillets of raw fish

SASHIMIS > SASHIMI

SASHING > SASH

SASHLESS > SASH

SASIN another name for > BLACKBUCK

SASINE n granting of legal possession of feudal property

SASINES > SASINE

SASINS > SASIN

SASKATOON n species of serviceberry of W Canada

SASQUATCH n (in Canadian folklore) hairy beast or manlike monster said to leave huge footprints

SASS n insolent or impudent talk or behaviour ▷ vb talk or answer back in such a way

SASSABIES > SASSABY

SASSABY n African antelope of grasslands and semideserts

SASSAFRAS n American tree with aromatic bark used medicinally

SASSARARA n scolding

SASSE n old word meaning canal lock

SASSED > SASS

SASSES > SASS

SASSIER > SASSY

SASSIES > SASSY

SASSIEST > SASSY

SASSILY > SASSY

SASSINESS > SASSY

SASSING > SASS

SASSOLIN n boric acid

SASSOLINS > SASSOLIN

SASSOLITE n boric acid

SASSWOOD same as > SASSY

SASSWOODS > SASSWOOD

SASSY adj insolent, impertinent ▷ n W African leguminous tree with poisonous bark

SASSYWOOD n trial by ordeal in Liberia

SASTRA same as > SHASTRA

SASTRAS > SASTRA

SASTRUGA n ridge on a snow-covered plain

SASTRUGI > SASTRUGA

SAT > SIT

SATAI same as > SATAY

SATAIS > SATAI

SATANG n monetary unit of Thailand worth one hundredth of a baht

SATANGS > SATANG

SATANIC adj of Satan

SATANICAL same as > SATANIC

SATANISM n worship of the devil

SATANISMS > SATANISM

SATANIST > SATANISM

SATANISTS > SATANISM

SATANITY n quality of being satanic

SATARA n type of cloth

SATARAS > SATARA

SATAY n Indonesian and Malaysian dish

SATAYS > SATAY

SATCHEL n bag, usu with a shoulder strap, for carrying books

SATCHELED adj carrying a satchel

SATCHELS > SATCHEL

SATCOM n satellite communications

SATCOMS > SATCOM

SATE vb satisfy (a desire or appetite) fully

SATED > SATE

SATEDNESS > SATE

SATEEN n glossy linen or cotton fabric, woven in such a way that it resembles satin

SATEENS > SATEEN

SATELESS adj old word meaning insatiable

SATELLES n species of bacteria

SATELLITE n device sent into orbit in space ▷ adj of or used in the transmission of television signals from a satellite to the home ▷ vb transmit by communications satellite

SATEM adj denoting or belonging to a particular group of Indo-European languages

SATES > SATE

SATI n Indian widow suicide

SATIABLE adj capable of being satiated

SATIABLY > SATIABLE

SATIATE vb provide with more than enough, so as to disgust

SATIATED > SATIATE

SATIATES > SATIATE

SATIATING > SATIATE

SATIATION > SATIATE

SATIETIES > SATIETY

SATIETY n feeling of having had too much

SATIN n silky fabric with a glossy surface on one side ▷ adj like satin in texture ▷ vb cover with satin

SATINED > SATIN

SATINET n thin or imitation satin

SATINETS > SATINET

SATINETTA n thin satin

SATINETTE same as > SATINET

SATING > SATE

SATINIER > SATINY

SATINIEST > SATINY

SATINING > SATIN

SATINPOD n honesty (the plant)

SATINPODS > SATINPOD

SATINS > SATIN

SATINWOOD n tropical tree yielding hard wood

SATINY adj like satin

SATIRE n use of ridicule to expose vice or folly

SATIRES > SATIRE

SATIRIC same as > SATIRICAL

SATIRICAL adj of, relating to, or containing satire

SATIRISE same as > SATIRIZE

SATIRISED > SATIRISE

SATIRISER > SATIRISE

SATIRISES > SATIRISE

SATIRIST n writer of satire

SATIRISTS > SATIRIST

SATIRIZE vb ridicule by means of satire

SATIRIZED > SATIRIZE

SATIRIZER > SATIRIZE

SATIRIZES > SATIRIZE

SATIS > SATI

SATISFICE vb act in such a way as to satisfy the minimum requirements for achieving a particular result

SATISFIED > SATISFY

SATISFIER > SATISFY

SATISFIES > SATISFY

SATISFY vb please, content

SATIVE adj old word meaning cultivated

SATNAV n satellite navigation system

SATNAVS > SATNAV

SATORI n state of sudden indescribable intuitive enlightenment

SATORIS > SATORI

SATRAP n (in ancient Persia) a provincial governor or subordinate ruler

SATRAPAL > SATRAP

SATRAPIES > SATRAPY

SATRAPS > SATRAP

SATRAPY n province, office, or period of rule of a satrap

SATSANG n sacred gathering in Hinduism

SATSANGS > SATSANG

SATSUMA n kind of small orange

SATSUMAS > SATSUMA

SATURABLE adj capable of being saturated

SATURANT n substance that causes a solution, etc, to be saturated ▷ adj (of a substance) causing saturation

SATURANTS > SATURANT

SATURATE vb soak thoroughly

SATURATED adj (of a solution or solvent) containing the maximum amount of solute that can normally be dissolved at a given temperature and pressure

SATURATER > SATURATE

SATURATES > SATURATE

SATURATOR > SATURATE

SATURNIC adj poisoned by lead

SATURNIID n type of mainly tropical moth, usu with large brightly coloured wings

SATURNINE adj gloomy in temperament or appearance

SATURNISM n lead poisoning

SATURNIST n old word meaning glum person

SATYR n woodland god, part man, part goat

SATYRA n female satyr

SATYRAL n mythical beast in heraldry

SATYRALS > SATYRAL

SATYRAS > SATYRA

SATYRE n as in sea satyre sea creature mentioned in Spenser's poetry

SATYRES > SATYRE

SATYRESS n female satyr

SATYRIC > SATYR

SATYRICAL > SATYR

SATYRID n butterfly with typically brown or dark wings with paler markings

SATYRIDS > SATYRID

SATYRISK n small satyr

SATYRISKS > SATYRISK

SATYRLIKE > SATYR

SATYRS > SATYR

SAU archaic past tense of > SEE

SAUBA n South American ant

SAUBAS > SAUBA

SAUCE n liquid added to food to enhance flavour ▷ vb prepare (food) with sauce

SAUCEBOAT n gravy boat

SAUCEBOX n saucy person

SAUCED > SAUCE

SAUCELESS > SAUCE

SAUCEPAN n cooking pot with a long handle

SAUCEPANS > SAUCEPAN

SAUCEPOT n cooking pot with lid

SAUCEPOTS > SAUCEPOT

SAUCER n small round dish put under a cup

SAUCERFUL > SAUCER

SAUCERS > SAUCER

SAUCES > SAUCE

SAUCH n sallow or willow

SAUCHS > SAUCH

SAUCIER n chef who makes sauces

SAUCIERS > SAUCIER

SAUCIEST > SAUCY

SAUCILY > SAUCY

SAUCINESS > SAUCY

SAUCING > SAUCE

SAUCISSE n type of explosive fuse

SAUCISSES > SAUCISSE

SAUCISSON n type of explosive fuse

SAUCY adj impudent

SAUFGARD old form of > SAFEGUARD

SAUFGARDS > SAUFGARD

SAUGER n small North American pikeperch

SAUGERS > SAUGER

SAUGH same as > SAUCH

SAUGHS > SAUGH

SAUGHY adj Scots word meaning made of willow

SAUL Scots word for > SOUL

SAULGE n old word for sage plant

SAULGES > SAULGE

SAULIE n Scots word meaning professional mourner

SAULIES > SAULIE

SAULS > SAUL

SAULT n waterfall in Canada

SAULTS > SAULT

SAUNA n Finnish-style steam bath ▷ vb have a sauna

SAUNAED > SAUNA

SAUNAING > SAUNA

SAUNAS > SAUNA

SAUNT Scots form of > SAINT

SAUNTED > SAUNT

SAUNTER vb walk in a leisurely manner, stroll ▷ n leisurely walk

SAUNTERED > SAUNTER

SAUNTERER > SAUNTER

SAUNTERS > SAUNTER

SAUNTING > SAUNT

SAUNTS > SAUNT

SAUREL n type of mackerel

SAURELS > SAUREL

SAURIAN n lizard

SAURIANS > SAURIAN

SAURIES > SAURY

SAUROID adj like a lizard ▷ n type of fish

SAUROIDS > SAUROID

SAUROPOD n type of herbivorous dinosaur including the brontosaurus and the diplodocus

SAUROPODS > SAUROPOD

SAURY n type of fish of tropical and temperate seas

SAUSAGE n minced meat in an edible tube-shaped skin

SAUSAGES > SAUSAGE

SAUT Scot word for > SALT

SAUTE vb fry quickly in a little fat ▷ n dish of sautéed food ▷ adj sautéed until lightly brown

SAUTED > SAUT

SAUTEED > SAUTE

SAUTEEING > SAUTE

SAUTEING > SAUTE

SAUTERNE n sauternes

SAUTERNES n sweet white French wine

SAUTES > SAUTE

SAUTING > SAUT
SAUTOIR *n* long necklace or pendant
SAUTOIRE *variant of* **> SAUTOIR**
SAUTOIRES > SAUTOIRE
SAUTOIRS > SAUTOIR
SAUTS > SAUT
SAV *short for* **> SAVELOY**
SAVABLE > SAVE
SAVAGE *adj* wild, untamed ▷ *n* uncivilized person ▷ *vb* attack ferociously
SAVAGED > SAVAGE
SAVAGEDOM > SAVAGE
SAVAGELY > SAVAGE
SAVAGER > SAVAGE
SAVAGERY *n* viciousness and cruelty
SAVAGES > SAVAGE
SAVAGEST > SAVAGE
SAVAGING > SAVAGE
SAVAGISM > SAVAGE
SAVAGISMS > SAVAGE
SAVANNA *n* open grasslands of tropical Africa
SAVANNAH *same as* **> SAVANNA**
SAVANNAHS > SAVANNAH
SAVANNAS > SAVANNA
SAVANT *n* learned person
SAVANTE > SAVANT
SAVANTES > SAVANT
SAVANTS > SAVANT
SAVARIN *n* type of cake
SAVARINS > SAVARIN
SAVASANA *n* type of pose in yoga
SAVASANAS **> SAVASANA**
SAVATE *n* form of boxing in which blows may be delivered with the feet
SAVATES > SAVATE
SAVE *vb* rescue or preserve from harm, protect ▷ *n* act of preventing a goal ▷ *prep* except
SAVEABLE > SAVE
SAVED > SAVE
SAVEGARD *vb* old word meaning protect
SAVEGARDS **> SAVEGARD**
SAVELOY *n* spicy smoked sausage
SAVELOYS > SAVELOY
SAVER > SAVE
SAVERS > SAVE
SAVES > SAVE
SAVEY *vb* understand
SAVEYED > SAVEY
SAVEYING > SAVEY
SAVEYS > SAVEY
SAVIN *n* small spreading juniper bush of Europe, N Asia, and North America
SAVINE *same as* **> SAVIN**
SAVINES > SAVINE
SAVING *n* economy ▷ *prep* except ▷ *adj* tending to save or preserve
SAVINGLY > SAVING

SAVINGS > SAVING
SAVINS > SAVIN
SAVIOR *same as* **> SAVIOUR**
SAVIORS > SAVIOR
SAVIOUR *n* person who rescues another
SAVIOURS > SAVIOUR
SAVOR *same as* **> SAVOUR**
SAVORED > SAVOR
SAVORER > SAVOR
SAVORERS > SAVOR
SAVORIER > SAVORY
SAVORIES > SAVORY
SAVORIEST > SAVORY
SAVORILY > SAVORY
SAVORING > SAVOR
SAVORLESS > SAVOUR
SAVOROUS > SAVOUR
SAVORS > SAVOR
SAVORY *same as* **> SAVOURY**
SAVOUR *vb* enjoy, relish ▷ *n* characteristic taste or odour
SAVOURED > SAVOUR
SAVOURER > SAVOUR
SAVOURERS > SAVOUR
SAVOURIER > SAVOURY
SAVOURIES > SAVOURY
SAVOURILY > SAVOURY
SAVOURING > SAVOUR
SAVOURLY *adv* old word meaning refreshingly
SAVOURS > SAVOUR
SAVOURY *adj* salty or spicy ▷ *n* savoury dish served before or after a meal
SAVOY *n* variety of cabbage
SAVOYARD *n* person keenly interested in the operettas of Gilbert and Sullivan
SAVOYARDS **> SAVOYARD**
SAVOYS > SAVOY
SAVS > SAV
SAVVEY *vb* understand
SAVVEYED > SAVVEY
SAVVEYING > SAVVEY
SAVVEYS > SAVVEY
SAVVIED > SAVVY
SAVVIER > SAVVY
SAVVIES > SAVVY
SAVVIEST > SAVVY
SAVVILY > SAVVY
SAVVINESS > SAVVY
SAVVY *vb* understand ▷ *n* understanding, intelligence ▷ *adj* shrewd
SAVVYING > SAVVY
SAW *n* hand tool for cutting wood and metal ▷ *vb* cut with a saw
SAWAH *n* paddy field
SAWAHS > SAWAH
SAWBILL *n* type of hummingbird
SAWBILLS > SAWBILL
SAWBLADE *n* blade of a saw
SAWBLADES **> SAWBLADE**
SAWBONES *n* surgeon or doctor

SAWBUCK *n* structure for supporting wood that is being sawn
SAWBUCKS > SAWBUCK
SAWDER *n* flattery ▷ *vb* flatter
SAWDERED > SAWDER
SAWDERING > SAWDER
SAWDERS > SAWDER
SAWDUST *n* fine wood fragments formed by sawing ▷ *vb* cover with sawdust
SAWDUSTED > SAWDUST
SAWDUSTS > SAWDUST
SAWDUSTY *adj* covered in sawdust
SAWED > SAW
SAWER > SAW
SAWERS > SAW
SAWFISH *n* fish with a long toothed snout
SAWFISHES > SAWFISH
SAWFLIES > SAWFLY
SAWFLY *n* any of various hymenopterous insects, the females of which have a sawlike ovipositor
SAWGRASS *n* type of sedge with serrated leaves
SAWHORSE *n* structure for supporting wood that is being sawn
SAWHORSES **> SAWHORSE**
SAWING > SAW
SAWINGS > SAW
SAWLIKE > SAW
SAWLOG *n* log suitable for sawing
SAWLOGS > SAWLOG
SAWMILL *n* mill where timber is sawn into planks
SAWMILLER *n* person who operates a sawmill
SAWMILLS > SAWMILL
SAWN *past participle of* **> SAW**
SAWNEY *n* derogatory word for a fool
SAWNEYS > SAWNEY
SAWPIT *n* pit above which a log is sawn into planks
SAWPITS > SAWPIT
SAWS > SAW
SAWSHARK *n* shark with long sawlike snout
SAWSHARKS **> SAWSHARK**
SAWTEETH > SAWTOOTH
SAWTIMBER *n* wood for sawing
SAWTOOTH *n* one of the teeth of a saw
SAWYER *n* person who saws timber for a living
SAWYERS > SAWYER
SAX *same as* **> SAXOPHONE**
SAXATILE *adj* living among rocks
SAXAUL *n* Asian tree
SAXAULS > SAXAUL
SAXE *adj* as in *saxe blue* light greyish-blue colour
SAXES > SAX
SAXHORN *n* valved brass instrument used chiefly in brass and military bands

SAXHORNS > SAXHORN
SAXICOLE *variant of* **> SAXATILE**
SAXIFRAGE *n* alpine rock plant with small flowers
SAXIST *n* saxophone player
SAXISTS > SAXIST
SAXITOXIN *n* poison extracted from mollusc
SAXMAN *n* saxophone player
SAXMEN > SAXMAN
SAXONIES > SAXONY
SAXONITE *n* igneous rock
SAXONITES **> SAXONITE**
SAXONY *n* fine three-ply yarn
SAXOPHONE *n* brass wind instrument with keys and a curved body
SAXTUBA *n* bass saxhorn
SAXTUBAS > SAXTUBA
SAY *vb* speak or utter ▷ *n* right or chance to speak
SAYABLE *n* anything that can be said
SAYABLES > SAYABLE
SAYED *same as* **> SAYYID**
SAYEDS > SAYED
SAYER > SAY
SAYERS > SAY
SAYEST > SAY
SAYID *same as* **> SAYYID**
SAYIDS > SAYID
SAYING > SAY
SAYINGS > SAY
SAYNE > SAY
SAYON *n* type of tunic
SAYONARA *n* Japanese farewell
SAYONARAS **> SAYONARA**
SAYONS > SAYON
SAYS > SAY
SAYST > SAY
SAYYID *n* Muslim descended from Muhammad's grandson
SAYYIDS > SAYYID
SAZ *n* Middle Eastern stringed instrument
SAZERAC *n* mixed drink of whisky, Pernod, syrup, bitters, and lemon
SAZERACS > SAZERAC
SAZES > SAZ
SAZHEN *n* Russian measure of length
SAZHENS > SAZHEN
SAZZES > SAZ
SBIRRI > SBIRRO
SBIRRO *n* Italian police officer
SCAB *n* crust formed over a wound ▷ *vb* become covered with a scab
SCABBARD *n* sheath for a sword or dagger
SCABBARDS **> SCABBARD**
SCABBED > SCAB
SCABBIER > SCABBY
SCABBIEST > SCABBY
SCABBILY > SCABBY
SCABBING > SCAB

S

SCABBLE vb shape (stone) roughly
SCABBLED > SCABBLE
SCABBLES > SCABBLE
SCABBLING > SCABBLE
SCABBY adj covered with scabs
SCABIES n itchy skin disease
SCABIETIC > SCABIES
SCABIOSA n flowering plant
SCABIOSAS > SCABIOSA
SCABIOUS n plant with showy blue, red, or whitish dome-shaped flower heads ▷ adj having or covered with scabs
SCABLAND n barren rocky land
SCABLANDS pl n type of terrain consisting of bare rock surfaces, with little or no soil cover and scanty vegetation
SCABLIKE > SCAB
SCABRID adj having a rough or scaly surface
SCABROUS adj rough and scaly
SCABS > SCAB
SCAD n any of various carangid fishes
SCADS pl n large amount or number
SCAFF n Scots word meaning food ▷ vb ask for (food) in a mean or rude manner
SCAFFED > SCAFF
SCAFFIE n Scots word meaning street cleaner
SCAFFIER > SCAFFY
SCAFFIES > SCAFFIE
SCAFFIEST > SCAFFY
SCAFFING > SCAFF
SCAFFOLD n temporary platform for builders or other tradespeople ▷ vb provide with a scaffold
SCAFFOLDS > SCAFFOLD
SCAFFS > SCAFF
SCAFFY adj having little value, cheap
SCAG n tear in a garment or piece of cloth ▷ vb make a tear in (cloth)
SCAGGED > SCAG
SCAGGING > SCAG
SCAGLIA n type of limestone
SCAGLIAS > SCAGLIA
SCAGLIOLA n type of imitation marble made of glued gypsum
SCAGS > SCAG
SCAIL vb Scots word meaning disperse
SCAILED > SCAIL
SCAILING > SCAIL
SCAILS > SCAIL
SCAITH vb old word meaning injure
SCAITHED > SCAITH
SCAITHING > SCAITH
SCAITHS > SCAITH

SCALA n passage inside the cochlea
SCALABLE adj capable of being scaled or climbed
SCALABLY > SCALABLE
SCALADE short for > ESCALADE
SCALADES > SCALADE
SCALADO same as > SCALADE
SCALADOS > SCALADO
SCALAE > SCALA
SCALAGE n percentage deducted from the price of goods liable to shrink or leak
SCALAGES > SCALAGE
SCALAR adj having magnitude but no direction ▷ n quantity that has magnitude but not direction
SCALARE another name for > ANGELFISH
SCALARES > SCALARE
SCALARS > SCALAR
SCALATION n way scales are arranged
SCALAWAG same as > SCALLYWAG
SCALAWAGS > SCALAWAG
SCALD vb burn with hot liquid ▷ n (in ancient Scandinavia) a bard or minstrel
SCALDED > SCALD
SCALDER > SCALD
SCALDERS > SCALDER
SCALDFISH n small European flatfish
SCALDHEAD n diseased scalp
SCALDIC > SCALD
SCALDING n instance of burning with hot liquid
SCALDINGS > SCALDING
SCALDINI > SCALDINO
SCALDINO n Italian brazier
SCALDS > SCALD
SCALDSHIP n (in ancient Scandinavia) position of bard
SCALE n one of the thin overlapping plates covering fishes and reptiles ▷ vb remove scales from
SCALEABLE same as > SCALABLE
SCALEABLY same as > SCALABLY
SCALED > SCALE
SCALELESS > SCALE
SCALELIKE > SCALE
SCALENE n triangle with three unequal sides
SCALENES > SCALENE
SCALENI > SCALENUS
SCALENUS n any one of the three muscles situated on each side of the neck
SCALEPAN n part of scales holding weighed object

SCALEPANS > SCALEPAN
SCALER n person or thing that scales
SCALERS > SCALER
SCALES > SCALE
SCALETAIL n type of squirrel
SCALEUP n increase
SCALEUPS > SCALEUP
SCALEWORK n artistic representation of scales
SCALIER > SCALY
SCALIEST > SCALY
SCALINESS > SCALY
SCALING > SCALE
SCALINGS > SCALE
SCALL n disease of the scalp characterized by itching and scab formation
SCALLAWAG same as > SCALLYWAG
SCALLED > SCALL
SCALLIES > SCALLY
SCALLION same as > SHALLOT
SCALLIONS > SCALLION
SCALLOP n edible shellfish with two fan-shaped shells ▷ vb decorate (an edge) with scallops
SCALLOPED > SCALLOP
SCALLOPER > SCALLOP
SCALLOPS > SCALLOP
SCALLS > SCALL
SCALLY n rascal
SCALLYWAG n scamp, rascal
SCALOGRAM n scale for measuring opinion
SCALP n skin and hair on top of the head ▷ vb cut off the scalp of
SCALPED > SCALP
SCALPEL n small surgical knife
SCALPELS > SCALPEL
SCALPER > SCALP
SCALPERS > SCALP
SCALPING n process in which the top portion of a metal ingot is machined away before use
SCALPINGS > SCALPING
SCALPINS n small stones
SCALPLESS > SCALP
SCALPRUM n large scalpel
SCALPRUMS > SCALPRUM
SCALPS > SCALP
SCALY adj resembling or covered in scales
SCAM n dishonest scheme ▷ vb swindle (someone) by means of a trick
SCAMBLE vb scramble
SCAMBLED > SCAMBLE
SCAMBLER > SCAMBLE
SCAMBLERS > SCAMBLE
SCAMBLES > SCAMBLE
SCAMBLING > SCAMBLE
SCAMEL n Shakespearian word of uncertain meaning

SCAMELS > SCAMEL
SCAMMED > SCAM
SCAMMER n person who perpetrates a scam
SCAMMERS > SCAMMER
SCAMMING > SCAM
SCAMMONY n twining Asian convolvulus plant
SCAMP n mischievous child ▷ vb perform without care
SCAMPED > SCAMP
SCAMPER vb run about hurriedly or in play ▷ n scampering
SCAMPERED > SCAMP
SCAMPERER > SCAMPER
SCAMPERS > SCAMPER
SCAMPI pl n large prawns
SCAMPIES > SCAMPI
SCAMPING > SCAMP
SCAMPINGS > SCAMP
SCAMPIS > SCAMPI
SCAMPISH > SCAMP
SCAMPS > SCAMP
SCAMS > SCAM
SCAMSTER same as > SCAMMER
SCAMSTERS > SCAMSTER
SCAMTO n argot of urban Black people in South Africa
SCAMTOS > SCAMTO
SCAN vb scrutinize carefully ▷ n scanning
SCAND > SCAN
SCANDAL n disgraceful action or event ▷ vb disgrace
SCANDALED > SCANDAL
SCANDALS > SCANDAL
SCANDENT adj (of plants) having a climbing habit
SCANDIA n scandium oxide
SCANDIAS > SCANDIA
SCANDIC adj of or containing scandium
SCANDIUM n rare silvery-white metallic element
SCANDIUMS > SCANDIUM
SCANNABLE > SCAN
SCANNED > SCAN
SCANNER n electronic device used for scanning
SCANNERS > SCANNER
SCANNING > SCAN
SCANNINGS > SCAN
SCANS > SCAN
SCANSION n metrical scanning of verse
SCANSIONS > SCANSION
SCANT adj barely sufficient, meagre ▷ vb limit in size or quantity ▷ adv scarcely
SCANTED > SCANT
SCANTER > SCANT
SCANTEST > SCANT
SCANTIER > SCANTY
SCANTIES pl n women's underwear
SCANTIEST > SCANTY
SCANTILY > SCANTY

S

SCANTING > SCANT
SCANTITY *n* quality of being scant
SCANTLE *vb* stint
SCANTLED > SCANTLE
SCANTLES > SCANTLE
SCANTLING *n* piece of sawn timber, such as a rafter, that has a small cross section
SCANTLY > SCANT
SCANTNESS > SCANT
SCANTS > SCANT
SCANTY *adj* barely sufficient or not sufficient
SCAPA *variant of* > SCARPER
SCAPAED > SCAPA
SCAPAING > SCAPA
SCAPAS > SCAPA
SCAPE *n* leafless stalk in plants ▷ *vb* archaic word for escape
SCAPED > SCAPE
SCAPEGOAT *n* person made to bear the blame for others ▷ *vb* make a scapegoat of
SCAPELESS *adj* allowing no escape
SCAPEMENT *n* escapement
SCAPES > SCAPE
SCAPHOID *obsolete word for* > NAVICULAR
SCAPHOIDS > SCAPHOID
SCAPHOPOD *n* type of marine mollusc of the class which includes tusk (or tooth) shells
SCAPI > SCAPUS
SCAPING > SCAPE
SCAPOLITE *n* any of a group of colourless, white, grey, or violet fluorescent minerals
SCAPOSE > SCAPE
SCAPPLE *vb* shape roughly
SCAPPLED > SCAPPLE
SCAPPLES > SCAPPLE
SCAPPLING > SCAPPLE
SCAPULA *n* shoulder blade
SCAPULAE > SCAPULA
SCAPULAR *adj* of the scapula ▷ *n* loose sleeveless garment worn by monks over their habits
SCAPULARS > SCAPULAR
SCAPULARY *same as* > SCAPULAR
SCAPULAS > SCAPULA
SCAPUS *n* flower stalk
SCAR *n* mark left by a healed wound ▷ *vb* mark or become marked with a scar
SCARAB *n* sacred beetle of ancient Egypt
SCARABAEI *pl n* scarabs
SCARABEE *n* old word for scarab beetle
SCARABEES > SCARABEE

SCARABOID *adj* resembling a scarab beetle ▷ *n* beetle that resembles a scarab
SCARABS > SCARAB
SCARCE *adj* insufficient to meet demand
SCARCELY *adv* hardly at all
SCARCER > SCARCE
SCARCEST > SCARCE
SCARCITY *n* inadequate supply
SCARE *vb* frighten or be frightened ▷ *n* fright, sudden panic ▷ *adj* causing (needless) fear or alarm
SCARECROW *n* figure dressed in old clothes, set up to scare birds away from crops
SCARED > SCARE
SCAREDER > SCARE
SCAREDEST > SCARE
SCAREDIES > SCAREDY
SCAREDY *n* someone who is easily frightened
SCAREHEAD *n* newspaper headline intended to shock
SCARER > SCARE
SCARERS > SCARE
SCARES > SCARE
SCAREWARE *n* type of malware which tricks the user into downloading it
SCAREY *adj* frightening
SCARF *n* piece of material worn round the neck, head, or shoulders ▷ *vb* join
SCARFED > SCARF
SCARFER > SCARF
SCARFERS > SCARF
SCARFING > SCARF
SCARFINGS > SCARF
SCARFISH *n* type of fish
SCARFPIN *n* decorative pin securing a scarf
SCARFPINS > SCARFPIN
SCARFS > SCARF
SCARFSKIN *n* outermost layer of the skin
SCARFWISE *adv* like a scarf
SCARIER > SCARY
SCARIEST > SCARY
SCARIFIED > SCARIFY
SCARIFIER > SCARIFY
SCARIFIES > SCARIFY
SCARIFY *vb* scratch or cut slightly all over
SCARILY > SCARY
SCARINESS > SCARY
SCARING > SCARE
SCARIOSE *same as* > SCARIOUS
SCARIOUS *adj* (of plant parts) membranous, dry, and brownish in colour
SCARLESS > SCAR
SCARLET *n* brilliant red ▷ *adj* bright red ▷ *vb* make scarlet
SCARLETED > SCARLET
SCARLETS > SCARLET

SCARMOGE *n* old form of skirmish
SCARMOGES > SCARMOGE
SCARP *n* steep slope ▷ *vb* wear or cut so as to form a steep slope
SCARPA *vb* run away
SCARPAED > SCARPA
SCARPAING > SCARPA
SCARPAS > SCARPA
SCARPED > SCARP
SCARPER *vb* run away ▷ *n* hasty departure
SCARPERED > SCARPER
SCARPERS > SCARPER
SCARPETTI > SCARPETTO
SCARPETTO *n* type of shoe
SCARPH *vb* join with scarf joint
SCARPHED > SCARPH
SCARPHING > SCARPH
SCARPHS > SCARPH
SCARPINES *n* device for torturing feet
SCARPING > SCARP
SCARPINGS > SCARP
SCARPS > SCARP
SCARRE *n* Shakespearian word of unknown meaning
SCARRED > SCAR
SCARRES > SCARRE
SCARRIER > SCAR
SCARRIEST > SCAR
SCARRING > SCAR
SCARRINGS > SCAR
SCARRY > SCAR
SCARS > SCAR
SCART *vb* scratch or scrape ▷ *n* scratch or scrape
SCARTED > SCART
SCARTH *Scots word for* > CORMORANT
SCARTHS > SCARTH
SCARTING > SCART
SCARTS > SCART
SCARVED *adj* wearing a scarf
SCARVES > SCARF
SCARY *adj* frightening
SCAT *vb* go away ▷ *n* jazz singing using improvised vocal sounds instead of words
SCATBACK *n* American football player
SCATBACKS > SCATBACK
SCATCH *same as* > STILT
SCATCHES > SCATCH
SCATH *vb* old word meaning injure
SCATHE *vb* attack with severe criticism ▷ *n* harm
SCATHED > SCATHE
SCATHEFUL *adj* old word meaning harmful
SCATHES > SCATHE
SCATHING *adj* harshly critical
SCATHS > SCATH
SCATOLE *n* substance found in coal
SCATOLES > SCATOLE

SCATOLOGY *n* scientific study of excrement
SCATS > SCAT
SCATT *n* old word meaning tax ▷ *vb* tax
SCATTED > SCAT
SCATTER *vb* throw about in various directions ▷ *n* scattering
SCATTERED > SCATTER
SCATTERER > SCATTER
SCATTERS > SCATTER
SCATTERY *adj* dispersed
SCATTIER > SCATTY
SCATTIEST > SCATTY
SCATTILY > SCATTY
SCATTING > SCAT
SCATTINGS > SCAT
SCATTS > SCATT
SCATTY *adj* empty-headed
SCAUD *Scot word for* > SCALD
SCAUDED > SCAUD
SCAUDING > SCAUD
SCAUDS > SCAUD
SCAUP *variant of* > SCALP
SCAUPED > SCAUP
SCAUPER *same as* > SCORPER
SCAUPERS > SCAUPER
SCAUPING > SCAUP
SCAUPS > SCAUP
SCAUR *same as* > SCAR
SCAURED > SCAUR
SCAURIES > SCAURY
SCAURING > SCAUR
SCAURS > SCAUR
SCAURY *n* young seagull
SCAVAGE *n* old word meaning toll ▷ *vb* scavenge
SCAVAGED > SCAVAGE
SCAVAGER > SCAVAGE
SCAVAGERS > SCAVAGE
SCAVAGES > SCAVAGE
SCAVAGING > SCAVAGE
SCAVENGE *vb* search for (anything usable) among discarded material
SCAVENGED > SCAVENGE
SCAVENGER *n* person who scavenges
SCAVENGES > SCAVENGE
SCAW *n* headland
SCAWS > SCAW
SCAWTITE *n* mineral containing calcium
SCAWTITES > SCAWTITE
SCAZON *n* metre in poetry
SCAZONS > SCAZON
SCAZONTES > SCAZON
SCAZONTIC > SCAZON
SCEAT *n* Anglo-Saxon coin
SCEATS > SCEAT
SCEATT *same as* > SCEAT
SCEATTAS > SCEAT
SCEATTS > SCEAT
SCEDULE *old spelling of* > SCHEDULE
SCEDULED > SCEDULE
SCEDULES > SCEDULE
SCEDULING > SCEDULE

SCELERAT *n* villain
SCELERATE *n* villain
SCELERATS
> SCELERAT
SCENA *n* scene in an opera, usually longer than a single aria
SCENARIES > SCENARY
SCENARIO *n* summary of the plot of a play or film
SCENARIOS
> SCENARIO
SCENARISE *same as*
> SCENARIZE
SCENARIST
> SCENARIO
SCENARIZE *vb* create scenario
SCENARY *n* scenery
SCENAS > SCENA
SCEND *vb* (of a vessel) to surge upwards in a heavy sea ▷ *n* upward heaving of a vessel pitching
SCENDED > SCEND
SCENDING > SCEND
SCENDS > SCEND
SCENE *n* place of action of a real or imaginary event ▷ *vb* set in a scene
SCENED > SCENE
SCENEMAN *n* person shifting stage scenery
SCENEMEN > SCENEMAN
SCENERIES > SCENERY
SCENERY *n* natural features of a landscape
SCENES > SCENE
SCENESTER *n* person who tries to fit into a particular cultural scene
SCENIC *adj* picturesque ▷ *n* something scenic
SCENICAL > SCENE
SCENICS > SCENIC
SCENING > SCENE
SCENT *n* pleasant smell ▷ *vb* detect by smell
SCENTED > SCENT
SCENTFUL *adj* old word meaning having scent
SCENTING > SCENT
SCENTINGS > SCENT
SCENTLESS > SCENT
SCENTS > SCENT
SCEPSIS *n* doubt
SCEPSISES > SCEPSIS
SCEPTER *same as*
> SCEPTRE
SCEPTERED > SCEPTER
SCEPTERS > SCEPTER
SCEPTIC *n* person who habitually doubts generally accepted beliefs ▷ *adj* of or relating to sceptics
SCEPTICAL *adj* not convinced that something is true
SCEPTICS > SCEPTIC
SCEPTRAL *adj* royal
SCEPTRE *n* ornamental rod symbolizing royal power ▷ *vb* invest with authority
SCEPTRED > SCEPTRE
SCEPTRES > SCEPTRE
SCEPTRING > SCEPTRE

SCEPTRY *adj* having sceptre
SCERNE *vb* old word meaning discern
SCERNED > SCERNE
SCERNES > SCERNE
SCERNING > SCERNE
SCHANSE > SCHANTZE
SCHANSES > SCHANSE
SCHANTZE *n* stones heaped to shelter soldier in battle
SCHANTZES > SCHANTZE
SCHANZE *same as*
> SCHANTZE
SCHANZES > SCHANZE
SCHAPPE *n* yarn or fabric made from waste silk
SCHAPPED > SCHAPPE
SCHAPPES > SCHAPPE
SCHAPSKA *n* cap worn by lancer
SCHAPSKAS
> SCHAPSKA
SCHATCHEN *same as*
> SHADCHAN
SCHAV *n* Polish soup
SCHAVS > SCHAV
SCHECHITA *n* slaughter of animals according to Jewish law
SCHEDULAR
> SCHEDULE
SCHEDULE *n* plan of procedure for a project ▷ *vb* plan to occur at a certain time
SCHEDULED *adj* arranged or planned according to a programme, timetable, etc
SCHEDULER
> SCHEDULE
SCHEDULES
> SCHEDULE
SCHEELITE *n* white, brownish, or greenish mineral
SCHELLIES > SCHELLY
SCHELLUM *n* Scots word meaning rascal
SCHELLUMS
> SCHELLUM
SCHELLY *n* freshwater whitefish of the English Lake District
SCHELM *n* South African word meaning rascal
SCHELMS > SCHELM
SCHEMA *n* overall plan or diagram
SCHEMAS > SCHEMA
SCHEMATA > SCHEMA
SCHEMATIC *adj* presented as a plan or diagram ▷ *n* schematic diagram, esp of an electrical circuit
SCHEME *n* systematic plan ▷ *vb* plan in an underhand manner
SCHEMED > SCHEME
SCHEMER > SCHEME
SCHEMERS > SCHEME
SCHEMES > SCHEME
SCHEMIE *n* insulting Scots word for a resident of a housing scheme

SCHEMIES > SCHEMIE
SCHEMING *adj* given to making plots ▷ *n* intrigues
SCHEMINGS
> SCHEMING
SCHERZI > SCHERZO
SCHERZO *n* brisk lively piece of music
SCHERZOS > SCHERZO
SCHIAVONE *n* type of sword
SCHIEDAM *n* type of gin produced in the Netherlands
SCHIEDAMS
> SCHIEDAM
SCHILLER *n* unusual iridescent or metallic lustre in some minerals
SCHILLERS
> SCHILLER
SCHILLING *n* former monetary unit of Austria
SCHIMMEL *n* roan horse
SCHIMMELS
> SCHIMMEL
SCHISM *n* (group resulting from) division in an organization
SCHISMA *n* short musical interval of half a comma
SCHISMAS > SCHISMA
SCHISMS > SCHISM
SCHIST *n* crystalline rock which splits into layers
SCHISTOSE > SCHIST
SCHISTOUS > SCHIST
SCHISTS > SCHIST
SCHIZOID *adj* relating to a disorder characterized by self-absorption ▷ *n* person with schizoid personality disorder
SCHIZOIDS
> SCHIZOID
SCHIZONT *n* cell formed from a trophozoite during the life cycle of sporozoan protozoans
SCHIZONTS
> SCHIZONT
SCHIZOPOD *n* any of various shrimplike crustaceans
SCHLAGER *n* German duelling sword
SCHLAGERS
> SCHLAGER
SCHLEMIEL *n* awkward or unlucky person whose endeavours usually fail
SCHLEMIHL *same as*
> SCHLEMIEL
SCHLEP *vb* drag or lug (oneself or an object) with difficulty ▷ *n* arduous journey or procedure
SCHLEPP *vb* schlep
SCHLEPPED > SCHLEP
SCHLEPPER *n* incompetent person
SCHLEPPS > SCHLEPP
SCHLEPPY *same as*
> SHLEPPY
SCHLEPS > SCHLEP
SCHLICH *n* finely crushed ore
SCHLICHS > SCHLICH

SCHLIERE *n* (in physics or geology) streak of different density or composition from surroundings
SCHLIEREN
> SCHLIERE
SCHLIERIC
> SCHLIERE
SCHLOCK *n* goods of cheap or inferior quality ▷ *adj* cheap, inferior, or trashy
SCHLOCKER *n* thing of poor quality
SCHLOCKEY *adj* of inferior quality ▷ *n* something of inferior quality
SCHLOCKS > SCHLOCK
SCHLOCKY *adj* of poor quality
SCHLONG *vulgar slang word for* > PENIS
SCHLONGS > SCHLONG
SCHLOSS *n* German castle
SCHLOSSES > SCHLOSS
SCHLUB *n* coarse or contemptible person
SCHLUBS > SCHLUB
SCHLUMP *vb* move in lazy way
SCHLUMPED > SCHLUMP
SCHLUMPS > SCHLUMP
SCHLUMPY > SCHLUMP
SCHMALTZ *n* excessive sentimentality
SCHMALTZY *adj* excessively sentimental
SCHMALZ *same as*
> SCHMALTZ
SCHMALZES > SCHMALZ
SCHMALZY *adj* schmaltzy
SCHMATTE *same as*
> SCHMUTTER
SCHMATTES
> SCHMATTE
SCHMEAR *n* situation, matter, or affair ▷ *vb* spread or smear
SCHMEARED > SCHMEAR
SCHMEARS > SCHMEAR
SCHMECK *n* taste ▷ *vb* taste good
SCHMECKED > SCHMECK
SCHMECKER *n* heroin user
SCHMECKS > SCHMECK
SCHMEER *same as*
> SCHMEAR
SCHMEERED > SCHMEER
SCHMEERS > SCHMEER
SCHMELZ *n* ornamental glass
SCHMELZE *variant of*
> SCHMELZ
SCHMELZES > SCHMELZ
SCHMICK *adj* (in Australia) excellent, elegant, or stylish
SCHMICKER > SCHMICK
SCHMO *n* dull, stupid, or boring person
SCHMOCK *n* stupid person
SCHMOCKS > SCHMOCK
SCHMOE *same as* > SCHMO
SCHMOES > SCHMOE

SCHMOOS variant of
> SCHMOOSE
SCHMOOSE vb chat
SCHMOOSED
> SCHMOOSE
SCHMOOSES
> SCHMOOSE
SCHMOOZ n chat
SCHMOOZE vb chat or
gossip ▷ n trivial
conversation
SCHMOOZED
> SCHMOOZE
SCHMOOZER
> SCHMOOZE
SCHMOOZES
> SCHMOOZE
SCHMOOZY > SCHMOOZE
SCHMOS > SCHMO
SCHMUCK n stupid or
contemptible person ▷ vb
act as a schmuck
SCHMUCKED > SCHMUCK
SCHMUCKS > SCHMUCK
SCHMUCKY adj foolish
SCHMUTTER n cloth or
clothing
SCHMUTZ n dirt; grime
SCHMUTZES > SCHMUTZ
SCHNAPPER same as
> SNAPPER
SCHNAPPS n strong
alcoholic spirit
SCHNAPS same as
> SCHNAPPS
SCHNAPSES > SCHNAPS
SCHNAUZER n
wire-haired breed of dog
of the terrier type,
originally from Germany
SCHNECKE
> SCHNECKEN
SCHNECKEN pl n sweet
spiral-shaped bread roll
flavoured with cinnamon
and nuts
SCHNEID n succession of
losses
SCHNEIDS > SCHNEID
SCHNELL adj German
word meaning quick
SCHNITZEL n thin slice
of meat, esp veal
SCHNOODLE n cross
between a schnauzer and
a poodle
SCHNOOK n stupid or
gullible person
SCHNOOKS > SCHNOOK
SCHNORKEL less common
variant of > SNORKEL
SCHNORR vb beg
SCHNORRED > SCHNORR
SCHNORRER n person
who lives off the charity of
others
SCHNORRS > SCHNORR
SCHNOZ n nose
SCHNOZES > SCHNOZ
SCHNOZZ n nose
SCHNOZZES > SCHNOZZ
SCHNOZZLE slang word for
> NOSE
SCHOLAR n learned
person
SCHOLARCH n head of
school
SCHOLARLY > SCHOLAR

SCHOLARS > SCHOLAR
SCHOLIA > SCHOLIUM
SCHOLIAST n medieval
annotator, esp of classical
texts
SCHOLION n scholarly
annotation
SCHOLIUM n
commentary or
annotation, esp on a
classical text
SCHOLIUMS
> SCHOLIUM
SCHOOL n place where
children are taught or
instruction is given in a
subject ▷ vb educate or
train
SCHOOLBAG n school
pupil's bag
SCHOOLBOY n child
attending school
SCHOOLDAY n day for
going to school
SCHOOLE n old form of
shoal
SCHOOLED > SCHOOL
SCHOOLER n pupil at a
school of a specified kind
SCHOOLERS
> SCHOOLER
SCHOOLERY n old word
meaning something
taught
SCHOOLES > SCHOOLE
SCHOOLIE n
schoolteacher or a
high-school student
SCHOOLIES
> SCHOOLIE
SCHOOLING n education
SCHOOLKID n child who
goes to school
SCHOOLMAN n scholar
versed in the learning of
the Schoolmen
SCHOOLMEN
> SCHOOLMAN
SCHOOLS > SCHOOL
SCHOONER n sailing ship
rigged fore-and-aft
SCHOONERS
> SCHOONER
SCHORL n type of black
tourmaline
SCHORLS > SCHORL
SCHOUT n council officer
in Netherlands
SCHOUTS > SCHOUT
SCHRIK variant of
> SKRIK
SCHRIKS > SCHRIK
SCHROD n young cod
SCHRODS > SCHROD
SCHTICK same as
> SHTICK
SCHTICKS > SCHTICK
SCHTIK n schtick
SCHTIKS > SCHTIK
SCHTOOK n trouble
SCHTOOKS > SCHTOOK
SCHTOOM adj silent
SCHTUCK n trouble
SCHTUCKS > SCHTUCK
SCHTUM adj silent
SCHTUP same as > SHTUP
SCHTUPPED > SCHTUP
SCHTUPS > SCHTUP

SCHUIT n Dutch boat
with flat bottom
SCHUITS > SCHUIT
SCHUL same as > SHUL
SCHULN > SCHUL
SCHULS > SCHUL
SCHUSS n straight
high-speed downhill
run ▷ vb perform a
schuss
SCHUSSED > SCHUSS
SCHUSSER > SCHUSS
SCHUSSERS > SCHUSS
SCHUSSES > SCHUSS
SCHUSSING > SCHUSS
SCHUYT n Dutch boat
with flat bottom
SCHUYTS > SCHUYT
SCHVITZ same as
> SHVITZ
SCHVITZED > SCHVITZ
SCHVITZES > SCHVITZ
SCHWA n vowel
representing the sound in
unstressed syllables
SCHWAG n promotional
material given away for
free
SCHWAGS > SCHWAG
SCHWAS > SCHWA
SCIAENID adj of or
relating to a family of
mainly tropical and
subtropical marine
percoid fishes ▷ n any of
these fish
SCIAENIDS
> SCIAENID
SCIAENOID same as
> SCIAENID
SCIAMACHY n fight with
an imaginary enemy
SCIARID n small fly
SCIARIDS > SCIARID
SCIATIC adj of the hip
▷ n sciatic part of the body
SCIATICA n severe pain
in the large nerve in the
back of the leg
SCIATICAL
> SCIATICA
SCIATICAS
> SCIATICA
SCIATICS > SCIATIC
SCIENCE n systematic
study and knowledge of
natural or physical
phenomena
SCIENCED adj old word
meaning learned
SCIENCES > SCIENCE
SCIENT adj old word
meaning scientific
SCIENTER adv
knowingly
SCIENTIAL adj of or
relating to science
SCIENTISE same as
> SCIENTIZE
SCIENTISM n
application of, or belief in,
the scientific method
SCIENTIST n person
who studies or practises a
science
SCIENTIZE vb treat
scientifically
SCILICET adv namely

SCILLA n plant with
small bell-shaped flowers
SCILLAS > SCILLA
SCIMETAR n scimitar
SCIMETARS
> SCIMETAR
SCIMITAR n curved
sword
SCIMITARS
> SCIMITAR
SCIMITER n scimitar
SCIMITERS
> SCIMITER
SCINCOID adj of, relating
to, or resembling a skink
▷ n any animal, esp a
lizard, resembling a skink
SCINCOIDS
> SCINCOID
SCINTILLA n very small
amount
SCIOLISM n practice of
opinionating on subjects
of which one has only
superficial knowledge
SCIOLISMS
> SCIOLISM
SCIOLIST > SCIOLISM
SCIOLISTS
> SCIOLISM
SCIOLOUS > SCIOLISM
SCIOLTO adv musical
direction meaning freely
SCIOMACHY same as
> SCIAMACHY
SCIOMANCY n divination
with the help of ghosts
SCION n descendant or
heir
SCIONS > SCION
SCIOPHYTE n any plant
that grows best in the
shade
SCIOSOPHY n
unscientific system of
knowledge
SCIROC > SCIROCCO
SCIROCCO n hot
Mediterranean wind
SCIROCCOS
> SCIROCCO
SCIROCS > SCIROC
SCIRRHI > SCIRRHUS
SCIRRHOID
> SCIRRHUS
SCIRRHOUS adj of or
resembling a scirrhus
SCIRRHUS n hard
cancerous growth
composed of fibrous
tissues
SCISSEL n waste metal
left over from sheet metal
after discs have been
punched out of it
SCISSELS > SCISSEL
SCISSIL n scissel
SCISSILE adj capable of
being cut or divided
SCISSILS > SCISSIL
SCISSION n act or an
instance of cutting,
splitting, or dividing
SCISSIONS
> SCISSION
SCISSOR vb cut (an
object) with scissors
SCISSORED > SCISSOR

S

SCISSORER > SCISSOR

SCISSORS pl n cutting instrument with two crossed pivoted blades

SCISSURE n longitudinal cleft

SCISSURES > SCISSURE

SCIURID n squirrel or related rodent

SCIURIDS > SCIURID

SCIURINE adj relating to a family of rodents that includes squirrels, marmots, and chipmunks ▷ n any sciurine animal

SCIURINES > SCIURINE

SCIUROID adj (of an animal) resembling a squirrel

SCLAFF vb cause (the club) to hit (the ground behind the ball) when making a stroke ▷ n sclaffing stroke or shot

SCLAFFED > SCLAFF

SCLAFFER > SCLAFF

SCLAFFERS > SCLAFF

SCLAFFING > SCLAFF

SCLAFFS > SCLAFF

SCLATE vb (Scots) slate ▷ n (Scots) slate

SCLATED > SCLATE

SCLATES > SCLATE

SCLATING > SCLATE

SCLAUNDER n old form of slander

SCLAVE n old form of slave

SCLAVES > SCLAVE

SCLERA n tough white substance that forms the outer covering of the eyeball

SCLERAE > SCLERA

SCLERAL > SCLERA

SCLERAS > SCLERA

SCLERE n supporting anatomical structure

SCLEREID n type of biological cell

SCLEREIDE n type of biological cell

SCLEREIDS > SCLEREID

SCLEREMA n condition in which body tissues harden

SCLEREMAS > SCLEREMA

SCLERES > SCLERE

SCLERITE n any of the hard chitinous plates that make up the exoskeleton of an arthropod

SCLERITES > SCLERITE

SCLERITIC > SCLERITE

SCLERITIS n inflammation of the sclera

SCLEROID adj (of organisms and their parts) hard or hardened

SCLEROMA n any small area of abnormally hard tissue, esp in a mucous membrane

SCLEROMAS > SCLEROMA

SCLEROSAL > SCLEROSIS

SCLEROSE vb affect with sclerosis

SCLEROSED adj hardened

SCLEROSES > SCLEROSIS

SCLEROSIS n abnormal hardening of body tissues

SCLEROTAL n bony area in sclerotic

SCLEROTIA pl n masses of hyphae formed in certain fungi

SCLEROTIC same as > SCLERA

SCLEROTIN n protein in the cuticle of insects that becomes hard and dark

SCLEROUS adj hard

SCLIFF n Scots word for small piece

SCLIFFS > SCLIFF

SCLIM vb Scots word meaning climb

SCLIMMED > SCLIM

SCLIMMING > SCLIM

SCLIMS > SCLIM

SCODIER > SCODY

SCODIEST > SCODY

SCODY adj unkempt

SCOFF vb express derision ▷ n mocking expression

SCOFFED > SCOFF

SCOFFER > SCOFF

SCOFFERS > SCOFF

SCOFFING > SCOFF

SCOFFINGS > SCOFF

SCOFFLAW n person who habitually flouts or violates the law

SCOFFLAWS > SCOFFLAW

SCOFFS > SCOFF

SCOG vb shelter

SCOGGED > SCOG

SCOGGING > SCOG

SCOGS > SCOG

SCOINSON n part of door or window frame

SCOINSONS > SCOINSON

SCOLD vb find fault with, reprimand ▷ n person who scolds

SCOLDABLE > SCOLD

SCOLDED > SCOLD

SCOLDER > SCOLD

SCOLDERS > SCOLD

SCOLDING > SCOLD

SCOLDINGS > SCOLD

SCOLDS > SCOLD

SCOLECES > SCOLEX

SCOLECID n variety of worm

SCOLECIDS > SCOLECID

SCOLECITE n white zeolite mineral

SCOLECOID adj like scolex

SCOLEX n headlike part of a tapeworm

SCOLIA > SCOLION

SCOLICES > SCOLEX

SCOLIOMA n condition with abnormal curvature of spine

SCOLIOMAS > SCOLIOMA

SCOLION n ancient Greek drinking song

SCOLIOSES > SCOLIOSIS

SCOLIOSIS n abnormal lateral curvature of the spine

SCOLIOTIC > SCOLIOSIS

SCOLLOP variant of > SCALLOP

SCOLLOPED > SCOLLOP

SCOLLOPS > SCOLLOP

SCOLYTID n type of beetle

SCOLYTIDS > SCOLYTID

SCOLYTOID n type of beetle

SCOMBRID n fish of mackerel family

SCOMBRIDS > SCOMBRID

SCOMBROID adj relating to a suborder of marine spiny-finned fishes ▷ n any fish belonging to this suborder

SCOMFISH vb Scots word meaning stifle

SCONCE n bracket on a wall for holding candles or lights ▷ vb challenge (a fellow student) to drink a large quantity of beer

SCONCED > SCONCE

SCONCES > SCONCE

SCONCHEON n part of door or window frame

SCONCING > SCONCE

SCONE n small plain cake baked in an oven or on a griddle

SCONES > SCONE

SCONTION n part of door or window frame

SCONTIONS > SCONTION

SCOOBIES > SCOOBY

SCOOBY n slang for a clue, notion

SCOOCH vb compress one's body into smaller space

SCOOCHED > SCOOCH

SCOOCHES > SCOOCH

SCOOCHING > SCOOCH

SCOOG vb shelter

SCOOGED > SCOOG

SCOOGING > SCOOG

SCOOGS > SCOOG

SCOOP n shovel-like tool for ladling or hollowing out ▷ vb take up or hollow out with or as if with a scoop

SCOOPABLE > SCOOP

SCOOPED > SCOOP

SCOOPER > SCOOP

SCOOPERS > SCOOP

SCOOPFUL > SCOOP

SCOOPFULS > SCOOP

SCOOPING > SCOOP

SCOOPINGS > SCOOP

SCOOPS > SCOOP

SCOOPSFUL > SCOOP

SCOOSH vb squirt ▷ n squirt or rush of liquid

SCOOSHED > SCOOSH

SCOOSHES > SCOOSH

SCOOSHING > SCOOSH

SCOOT vb leave or move quickly ▷ n act of scooting

SCOOTCH same as > SCOOCH

SCOOTCHED > SCOOTCH

SCOOTCHES > SCOOTCH

SCOOTED > SCOOT

SCOOTER n child's vehicle propelled by pushing on the ground with one foot ▷ vb go on a scooter

SCOOTERED > SCOOTER

SCOOTERS > SCOOTER

SCOOTING > SCOOT

SCOOTS > SCOOT

SCOP n (in Anglo-Saxon England) a bard or minstrel

SCOPA n tuft of hairs on the abdomen or hind legs of a bee

SCOPAE > SCOPA

SCOPAS > SCOPA

SCOPATE adj having tuft-type hairs

SCOPE n opportunity for using abilities ▷ vb look at or examine carefully

SCOPED > SCOPE

SCOPELID n deep-sea fish

SCOPELIDS > SCOPELID

SCOPELOID n deep-sea fish

SCOPES > SCOPE

SCOPING > SCOPE

SCOPOLINE n soluble crystalline alkaloid

SCOPS > SCOP

SCOPULA n small tuft of dense hairs on the legs and chelicerae of some spiders

SCOPULAE > SCOPULA

SCOPULAS > SCOPULA

SCOPULATE > SCOPULA

SCORBUTIC adj of or having scurvy

SCORCH vb burn on the surface ▷ n slight burn

SCORCHED > SCORCH

SCORCHER n very hot day

SCORCHERS > SCORCHER

SCORCHES > SCORCH

SCORCHING > SCORCH

SCORDATO adj musical term meaning out of tune

SCORE n points gained in a game or competition ▷ vb gain (points) in a game

SCORECARD n card on which scores are recorded in games such as golf

SCORED > SCORE

SCORELESS adj without anyone scoring

SCORELINE n final score in game

SCOREPAD n pad for recording score in game
SCOREPADS > SCOREPAD
SCORER > SCORE
SCORERS > SCORE
SCORES > SCORE
SCORIA n mass of solidified lava containing many cavities
SCORIAC > SCORIA
SCORIAE > SCORIA
SCORIFIED > SCORIFY
SCORIFIER > SCORIFY
SCORIFIES > SCORIFY
SCORIFY vb remove (impurities) from metals by forming scoria
SCORING n act or practice of scoring
SCORINGS > SCORING
SCORIOUS > SCORIA
SCORN n open contempt ▷ vb despise
SCORNED > SCORN
SCORNER > SCORN
SCORNERS > SCORN
SCORNFUL > SCORN
SCORNING > SCORN
SCORNINGS > SCORN
SCORNS > SCORN
SCORODITE n mineral containing iron and aluminium
SCORPER n kind of fine chisel with a square or curved tip
SCORPERS > SCORPER
SCORPIOID adj of, relating to, or resembling scorpions
SCORPION n small lobster-shaped animal with a sting at the end of a jointed tail
SCORPIONS > SCORPION
SCORRENDO adj musical term meaning gliding
SCORSE vb exchange
SCORSED > SCORSE
SCORSER > SCORSE
SCORSERS > SCORSE
SCORSES > SCORSE
SCORSING > SCORSE
SCOT n payment or tax
SCOTCH vb put an end to ▷ n gash
SCOTCHED > SCOTCH
SCOTCHES > SCOTCH
SCOTCHING > SCOTCH
SCOTER n type of sea duck
SCOTERS > SCOTER
SCOTIA n deep concave moulding
SCOTIAS > SCOTIA
SCOTOMA n blind spot
SCOTOMAS > SCOTOMA
SCOTOMATA > SCOTOMA
SCOTOMIA n dizziness
SCOTOMIAS > SCOTOMIA
SCOTOMIES > SCOTOMY
SCOTOMY n dizziness
SCOTOPHIL adj liking darkness

SCOTOPIA n ability of the eye to adjust for night vision
SCOTOPIAS > SCOTOPIA
SCOTOPIC > SCOTOPIA
SCOTS > SCOT
SCOTTIE n type of small sturdy terrier
SCOTTIES > SCOTTIE
SCOUG vb shelter
SCOUGED > SCOUG
SCOUGING > SCOUG
SCOUGS > SCOUG
SCOUNDREL n cheat or deceiver
SCOUP vb Scots word meaning jump
SCOUPED > SCOUP
SCOUPING > SCOUP
SCOUPS > SCOUP
SCOUR vb clean or polish by rubbing with something rough ▷ n scouring
SCOURED > SCOUR
SCOURER > SCOUR
SCOURERS > SCOUR
SCOURGE n person or thing causing severe suffering ▷ vb cause severe suffering to
SCOURGED > SCOURGE
SCOURGER > SCOURGE
SCOURGERS > SCOURGE
SCOURGES > SCOURGE
SCOURGING n act of scourging
SCOURIE n young seagull
SCOURIES > SCOURIE
SCOURING > SCOUR
SCOURINGS pl n residue left after cleaning grain
SCOURS > SCOUR
SCOURSE vb exchange
SCOURSED > SCOURSE
SCOURSES > SCOURSE
SCOURSING > SCOURSE
SCOUSE n stew made from left-over meat
SCOUSER n inhabitant of Liverpool
SCOUSERS > SCOUSER
SCOUSES > SCOUSE
SCOUT n person sent out to reconnoitre ▷ vb act as a scout
SCOUTED > SCOUT
SCOUTER > SCOUT
SCOUTERS > SCOUT
SCOUTH n Scots word meaning plenty of scope
SCOUTHER vb Scots word meaning scorch
SCOUTHERS > SCOUTHER
SCOUTHERY > SCOUTHER
SCOUTHS > SCOUTH
SCOUTING > SCOUT
SCOUTINGS > SCOUT
SCOUTS > SCOUT
SCOW n unpowered barge used for carrying freight ▷ vb transport by scow
SCOWDER vb Scots word meaning scorch
SCOWDERED > SCOWDER

SCOWDERS > SCOWDER
SCOWED > SCOW
SCOWING > SCOW
SCOWL vb have an angry or sullen expression
SCOWLED > SCOWL
SCOWLER n person who scowls
SCOWLERS > SCOWLER
SCOWLING > SCOWL
SCOWLS > SCOWL
SCOWP vb Scots word meaning jump
SCOWPED > SCOWP
SCOWPING > SCOWP
SCOWPS > SCOWP
SCOWRER n old word meaning hooligan
SCOWRERS > SCOWRER
SCOWRIE n young seagull
SCOWRIES > SCOWRIE
SCOWS > SCOW
SCOWTH n Scots word meaning plenty of scope
SCOWTHER vb Scots word meaning scorch
SCOWTHERS > SCOWTHER
SCOWTHS > SCOWTH
SCOZZA n rowdy person, esp one who drinks a lot of alcohol
SCOZZAS > SCOZZA
SCRAB vb scratch
SCRABBED > SCRAB
SCRABBING > SCRAB
SCRABBLE vb scrape at with the hands, feet, or claws ▷ n board game in which words are formed by letter tiles
SCRABBLED > SCRABBLE
SCRABBLER > SCRABBLE
SCRABBLES > SCRABBLE
SCRABBLY adj covered with stunted trees
SCRABS > SCRAB
SCRAE Scots word for > SCREE
SCRAES > SCRAE
SCRAG n thin end of a neck of mutton ▷ vb wring the neck of
SCRAGGED > SCRAG
SCRAGGIER > SCRAGGY
SCRAGGILY > SCRAGGY
SCRAGGING > SCRAG
SCRAGGLY adj untidy or irregular
SCRAGGY adj thin, bony
SCRAGS > SCRAG
SCRAICH vb Scots word meaning scream
SCRAICHED > SCRAICH
SCRAICHS > SCRAICH
SCRAIGH same as > SCRAICH
SCRAIGHED > SCRAIGH
SCRAIGHS > SCRAIGH
SCRAM vb go away quickly ▷ n emergency shutdown of a nuclear reactor
SCRAMB vb scratch with nails or claws
SCRAMBED > SCRAMB

SCRAMBING > SCRAMB
SCRAMBLE vb climb or crawl hastily or awkwardly ▷ n scrambling
SCRAMBLED > SCRAMBLE
SCRAMBLER n electronic device that makes transmitted speech unintelligible
SCRAMBLES > SCRAMBLE
SCRAMBS > SCRAMB
SCRAMJET n type of jet engine
SCRAMJETS > SCRAMJET
SCRAMMED > SCRAM
SCRAMMING > SCRAM
SCRAMS > SCRAM
SCRAN n food
SCRANCH vb crunch
SCRANCHED > SCRANCH
SCRANCHES > SCRANCH
SCRANNEL adj thin ▷ n thin person or thing
SCRANNELS > SCRANNEL
SCRANNIER > SCRANNY
SCRANNY adj scrawny
SCRANS > SCRAN
SCRAP n small piece ▷ vb discard as useless
SCRAPABLE > SCRAPE
SCRAPBOOK n book with blank pages in which newspaper cuttings or pictures are stuck ▷ vb keep (cuttings etc) in a scrapbook
SCRAPE vb rub with something rough or sharp ▷ n act or sound of scraping
SCRAPED > SCRAPE
SCRAPEGUT n old word for fiddle player
SCRAPER > SCRAPE
SCRAPERS > SCRAPE
SCRAPES > SCRAPE
SCRAPHEAP n pile of discarded material
SCRAPIE n disease of sheep and goats
SCRAPIES > SCRAPIE
SCRAPING n act of scraping
SCRAPINGS > SCRAPING
SCRAPPAGE n act of scrapping
SCRAPPED > SCRAP
SCRAPPER n person who scraps
SCRAPPERS > SCRAPPER
SCRAPPIER > SCRAPPY
SCRAPPILY > SCRAPPY
SCRAPPING n act of scrapping
SCRAPPLE n scraps of pork cooked with cornmeal and formed into a loaf
SCRAPPLES > SCRAPPLE
SCRAPPY adj fragmentary, disjointed

SCRAPS > SCRAP

SCRAPYARD *n* place for scrap metal

SCRAT *vb* scratch

SCRATCH *vb* mark or cut with anything rough or sharp ▷ *n* wound, mark, or sound made by scratching ▷ *adj* put together at short notice

SCRATCHED > SCRATCH

SCRATCHER *n* person, animal, or thing that scratches

SCRATCHES *n* disease of horses characterized by dermatitis in the region of the fetlock

SCRATCHIE *n* scratchcard

SCRATCHY > SCRATCH

SCRATS > SCRAT

SCRATTED > SCRAT

SCRATTING > SCRAT

SCRATTLE *vb* dialect word meaning scratch

SCRATTLED > SCRATTLE

SCRATTLES > SCRATTLE

SCRAUCH *vb* squawk

SCRAUCHED > SCRAUCH

SCRAUCHS > SCRAUCH

SCRAUGH *vb* squawk

SCRAUGHED > SCRAUGH

SCRAUGHS > SCRAUGH

SCRAVEL *vb* move quickly

SCRAVELED > SCRAVEL

SCRAVELS > SCRAVEL

SCRAW *n* sod from the surface of a peat bog or from a field

SCRAWB *same as* **>** SCROB

SCRAWBED > SCRAWB

SCRAWBING > SCRAWB

SCRAWBS > SCRAWB

SCRAWL *vb* write carelessly or hastily ▷ *n* scribbled writing

SCRAWLED > SCRAWL

SCRAWLER > SCRAWL

SCRAWLERS > SCRAWL

SCRAWLIER > SCRAWL

SCRAWLING > SCRAWL

SCRAWLS > SCRAWL

SCRAWLY > SCRAWL

SCRAWM *vb* dialect word meaning scratch

SCRAWMED > SCRAWM

SCRAWMING > SCRAWM

SCRAWMS > SCRAWM

SCRAWNIER > SCRAWNY

SCRAWNILY > SCRAWNY

SCRAWNY *adj* thin and bony

SCRAWP *vb* scratch (the skin) to relieve itching

SCRAWPED > SCRAWP

SCRAWPING > SCRAWP

SCRAWPS > SCRAWP

SCRAWS > SCRAW

SCRAY *n* tern

SCRAYE *n* tern

SCRAYES > SCRAYE

SCRAYS > SCRAY

SCREAK *vb* screech or creak ▷ *n* screech or creak

SCREAKED > SCREAK

SCREAKIER > SCREAK

SCREAKING *n* screeching or creaking

SCREAKS > SCREAK

SCREAKY > SCREAK

SCREAM *vb* utter a piercing cry, esp of fear or pain ▷ *n* shrill piercing cry

SCREAMED > SCREAM

SCREAMER *n* person or thing that screams

SCREAMERS > SCREAMER

SCREAMING *n* act or instance of screaming

SCREAMO *n* type of emo music featuring screaming vocals

SCREAMOS > SCREAMO

SCREAMS > SCREAM

SCREE *n* slope of loose shifting stones

SCREECH *n* shrill cry ▷ *vb* utter a shrill cry

SCREECHED > SCREECH

SCREECHER > SCREECH

SCREECHES > SCREECH

SCREECHY *adj* loud and shrill

SCREED *n* long tedious piece of writing ▷ *vb* rip

SCREEDED > SCREED

SCREEDER > SCREED

SCREEDERS > SCREED

SCREEDING > SCREED

SCREEDS > SCREED

SCREEN *n* surface of a television set, VDU, etc ▷ *vb* shelter or conceal with or as if with a screen

SCREENED > SCREEN

SCREENER > SCREEN

SCREENERS > SCREEN

SCREENFUL > SCREEN

SCREENIE *n* informal Australian word for screensaver

SCREENIES > SCREENIE

SCREENING > SCREEN

SCREENS > SCREEN

SCREES > SCREE

SCREET *vb* shed tears ▷ *n* act or sound of crying

SCREETED > SCREET

SCREETING > SCREET

SCREETS > SCREET

SCREEVE *vb* write

SCREEVED > SCREEVE

SCREEVER > SCREEVE

SCREEVERS > SCREEVE

SCREEVES > SCREEVE

SCREEVING > SCREEVE

SCREICH *same as* **>** SCREIGH

SCREICHED > SCREICH

SCREICHS > SCREICH

SCREIGH *Scot word for* **>** SCREECH

SCREIGHED > SCREIGH

SCREIGHS > SCREIGH

SCREW *n* metal pin with a spiral ridge along its length ▷ *vb* turn (a screw)

SCREWABLE > SCREW

SCREWBALL *n* odd or eccentric person ▷ *adj* crazy or eccentric

SCREWBEAN *n* variety of mesquite

SCREWED *adj* fastened by a screw or screws

SCREWER > SCREW

SCREWERS > SCREW

SCREWHEAD *n* head of a screw

SCREWIER > SCREWY

SCREWIEST > SCREWY

SCREWING > SCREW

SCREWINGS > SCREW

SCREWLIKE > SCREW

SCREWS > SCREW

SCREWTOP *n* lid with a threaded rim that is turned to close it securely

SCREWTOPS > SCREWTOP

SCREWUP *n* something done badly

SCREWUPS > SCREWUP

SCREWWORM *n* larva of a fly that develops beneath the skin of living mammals often causing illness or death

SCREWY *adj* odd or eccentric

SCRIBABLE > SCRIBE

SCRIBAL > SCRIBE

SCRIBBLE *vb* write hastily or illegibly ▷ *n* something scribbled

SCRIBBLED > SCRIBBLE

SCRIBBLER *n* often derogatory term for a writer of poetry, novels, journalism, etc

SCRIBBLES > SCRIBBLE

SCRIBBLY > SCRIBBLE

SCRIBE *n* person who copies documents ▷ *vb* score a line with a pointed instrument

SCRIBED > SCRIBE

SCRIBER *n* pointed steel tool used to score materials as a guide to cutting, etc

SCRIBERS > SCRIBER

SCRIBES > SCRIBE

SCRIBING > SCRIBE

SCRIBINGS > SCRIBE

SCRIBISM > SCRIBE

SCRIBISMS > SCRIBE

SCRIECH *vb* Scots word meaning screech

SCRIECHED > SCRIECH

SCRIECHS > SCRIECH

SCRIED > SCRY

SCRIENE *n* old form of screen

SCRIENES > SCRIENE

SCRIES > SCRY

SCRIEVE *vb* Scots word meaning write

SCRIEVED > SCRIEVE

SCRIEVES > SCRIEVE

SCRIEVING > SCRIEVE

SCRIGGLE *vb* wriggle

SCRIGGLED > SCRIGGLE

SCRIGGLES > SCRIGGLE

SCRIGGLY > SCRIGGLE

SCRIKE *vb* old word meaning shriek

SCRIKED > SCRIKE

SCRIKES > SCRIKE

SCRIKING > SCRIKE

SCRIM *n* open-weave muslin or hessian fabric

SCRIMMAGE *n* rough or disorderly struggle ▷ *vb* engage in a scrimmage

SCRIMP *vb* be very economical

SCRIMPED > SCRIMP

SCRIMPER > SCRIMP

SCRIMPERS > SCRIMP

SCRIMPIER > SCRIMP

SCRIMPILY > SCRIMP

SCRIMPING *n* act of scrimping

SCRIMPIT *adj* Scots word meaning ungenerous

SCRIMPLY *adv* sparingly

SCRIMPS > SCRIMP

SCRIMPY > SCRIMP

SCRIMS > SCRIM

SCRIMSHAW *n* art of decorating or carving shells, etc, done by sailors as a leisure activity ▷ *vb* produce scrimshaw (from)

SCRIMURE *old word for* **>** FENCER

SCRIMURES > SCRIMURE

SCRINE *n* old form of shrine

SCRINES > SCRINE

SCRIP *n* certificate representing a claim to stocks or shares

SCRIPPAGE *n* contents of scrip

SCRIPS > SCRIP

SCRIPT *n* text of a film, play, or TV programme ▷ *vb* write a script for

SCRIPTED > SCRIPT

SCRIPTER *n* person who writes scripts for films, play, or television dramas

SCRIPTERS > SCRIPTER

SCRIPTING > SCRIPT

SCRIPTORY *adj* of writing

SCRIPTS > SCRIPT

SCRIPTURE *n* sacred writings of a religion

SCRITCH *vb* screech

SCRITCHED > SCRITCH

SCRITCHES > SCRITCH

SCRIVE *Scots word for* **>** WRITE

SCRIVED > SCRIVE

SCRIVENER *n* person who writes out deeds, letters, etc

SCRIVES > SCRIVE

SCRIVING > SCRIVE

SCROB *vb* scrape with claws

SCROBBED > SCROB

SCROBBING > SCROB

SCROBBLE *vb* record a person's music preferences in order to recommend similar music

SCROBBLED
> SCROBBLE
SCROBBLES
> SCROBBLE
SCROBE *n* groove
SCROBES > SCROBE
SCROBS > SCROB
SCROD *n* young cod or haddock
SCRODDLED *adj* made of scraps of pottery
SCRODS > SCROD
SCROFULA *n* tuberculosis of the lymphatic glands
SCROFULAS
> SCROFULA
SCROG *n* Scots word meaning small tree
SCROGGIE *adj* having scrogs upon it
SCROGGIER
> SCROGGIE
SCROGGIN *n* mixture of nuts and dried fruits
SCROGGINS
> SCROGGIN
SCROGGY *variant of*
> SCROGGIE
SCROGS > SCROG
SCROLL *n* roll of parchment or paper ▷ *vb* move (text) up or down on a VDU screen
SCROLLED > SCROLL
SCROLLER *n* person or thing that scrolls
SCROLLERS
> SCROLLER
SCROLLING > SCROLL
SCROLLS > SCROLL
SCROME *vb* crawl or climb
SCROMED > SCROME
SCROMES > SCROME
SCROMING > SCROME
SCROOCH *vb* scratch (the skin) to relieve itching
SCROOCHED > SCROOCH
SCROOCHES > SCROOCH
SCROOGE *variant of*
> SCROUGE
SCROOGED > SCROOGE
SCROOGES > SCROOGE
SCROOGING > SCROOGE
SCROOP *vb* emit a grating or creaking sound ▷ *n* such a sound
SCROOPED > SCROOP
SCROOPING > SCROOP
SCROOPS > SCROOP
SCROOTCH *vb* hunch up
SCRORP *n* deep scratch or weal
SCRORPS > SCRORP
SCROTA > SCROTUM
SCROTAL > SCROTUM
SCROTE *n* slang derogatory word meaning a worthless fellow
SCROTES > SCROTE
SCROTUM *n* pouch of skin containing the testicles
SCROTUMS > SCROTUM
SCROUGE *vb* crowd or press
SCROUGED > SCROUGE
SCROUGER *n* American word meaning whopper

SCROUGERS
> SCROUGER
SCROUGES > SCROUGE
SCROUGING > SCROUGE
SCROUNGE *vb* get by cadging or begging
SCROUNGED
> SCROUNGE
SCROUNGER
> SCROUNGE
SCROUNGES
> SCROUNGE
SCROUNGY *adj* shabby
SCROW *n* scroll
SCROWDGE *vb* squeeze
SCROWDGED
> SCROWDGE
SCROWDGES
> SCROWDGE
SCROWL *vb* old form of scroll
SCROWLE *vb* old form of scroll
SCROWLED > SCROWL
SCROWLES > SCROWLE
SCROWLING > SCROWL
SCROWLS > SCROWL
SCROWS > SCROW
SCROYLE *n* old word meaning wretch
SCROYLES > SCROYLE
SCRUB *vb* clean by rubbing, often with a hard brush and water ▷ *n* instance of scrubbing ▷ *adj* stunted or inferior
SCRUBBED > SCRUB
SCRUBBER *n* person or thing that scrubs
SCRUBBERS
> SCRUBBER
SCRUBBIER > SCRUBBY
SCRUBBILY > SCRUBBY
SCRUBBING > SCRUB
SCRUBBY *adj* covered with scrub
SCRUBLAND *n* area of scrub vegetation
SCRUBS > SCRUB
SCRUFF *same as* > SCUM
SCRUFFED > SCRUFF
SCRUFFIER > SCRUFFY
SCRUFFILY > SCRUFFY
SCRUFFING > SCRUFF
SCRUFFS > SCRUFF
SCRUFFY *adj* unkempt or shabby
SCRUM *n* restarting of play in rugby ▷ *vb* form a scrum
SCRUMDOWN *n* forming of scrum in rugby
SCRUMMAGE *same as*
> SCRUM
SCRUMMED > SCRUM
SCRUMMIE *n* informal word for a scrum half
SCRUMMIER > SCRUMMY
SCRUMMIES
> SCRUMMIE
SCRUMMING > SCRUM
SCRUMMY *adj* delicious
SCRUMP *vb* steal (apples) from an orchard or garden
SCRUMPED > SCRUMP
SCRUMPIES > SCRUMPY
SCRUMPING > SCRUMP
SCRUMPLE *vb* crumple or crush

SCRUMPLED
> SCRUMPLE
SCRUMPLES
> SCRUMPLE
SCRUMPOX *n* skin infection spread among players in scrum
SCRUMPS > SCRUMP
SCRUMPY *n* rough dry cider
SCRUMS > SCRUM
SCRUNCH *vb* crumple or crunch or be crumpled or crunched ▷ *n* act or sound of scrunching
SCRUNCHED > SCRUNCH
SCRUNCHES > SCRUNCH
SCRUNCHIE *n* loop of elastic covered loosely with fabric, used to hold the hair in a ponytail
SCRUNCHIN *n* piece of deep-fried pork fat
SCRUNCHY *adj* crunchy
SCRUNT *n* Scots word meaning stunted thing
SCRUNTIER > SCRUNT
SCRUNTS > SCRUNT
SCRUNTY > SCRUNT
SCRUPLE *n* doubt produced by one's conscience or morals ▷ *vb* have doubts on moral grounds
SCRUPLED > SCRUPLE
SCRUPLER > SCRUPLE
SCRUPLERS > SCRUPLE
SCRUPLES > SCRUPLE
SCRUPLING > SCRUPLE
SCRUTABLE *adj* open to or able to be understood by scrutiny
SCRUTATOR *n* person who examines or scrutinizes
SCRUTINY *n* close examination
SCRUTO *n* trapdoor on stage
SCRUTOIRE *n* writing desk
SCRUTOS > SCRUTO
SCRUZE *vb* old word meaning squeeze
SCRUZED > SCRUZE
SCRUZES > SCRUZE
SCRUZING > SCRUZE
SCRY *vb* divine, esp by crystal gazing
SCRYDE > SCRY
SCRYER > SCRY
SCRYERS > SCRY
SCRYING > SCRY
SCRYINGS > SCRY
SCRYNE *n* old form of shrine
SCRYNES > SCRYNE
SCUBA *n* apparatus used in diving ▷ *vb* dive using scuba equipment
SCUBAED > SCUBA
SCUBAING > SCUBA
SCUBAS > SCUBA
SCUCHIN *n* old form of scutcheon
SCUCHINS > SCUCHIN
SCUD *vb* move along swiftly ▷ *n* act of scudding

SCUDDALER *n* Scots word meaning leader of festivities
SCUDDED > SCUD
SCUDDER > SCUD
SCUDDERS > SCUD
SCUDDING > SCUD
SCUDDLE *vb* scuttle
SCUDDLED > SCUDDLE
SCUDDLES > SCUDDLE
SCUDDLING > SCUDDLE
SCUDI > SCUDO
SCUDLER *n* Scots word meaning leader of festivities
SCUDLERS > SCUDLER
SCUDO *n* any of several former Italian coins
SCUDS > SCUD
SCUFF *vb* drag (the feet) while walking ▷ *n* mark caused by scuffing
SCUFFED > SCUFF
SCUFFER *n* type of sandal
SCUFFERS > SCUFFER
SCUFFING > SCUFF
SCUFFLE *vb* fight in a disorderly manner ▷ *n* disorderly struggle
SCUFFLED > SCUFFLE
SCUFFLER > SCUFFLE
SCUFFLERS > SCUFFLE
SCUFFLES > SCUFFLE
SCUFFLING *n* act of scuffling
SCUFFS > SCUFF
SCUFT *n* dialect word meaning nape of neck
SCUFTS > SCUFT
SCUG *vb* shelter
SCUGGED > SCUG
SCUGGING > SCUG
SCUGS > SCUG
SCUL *n* old form of school
SCULCH *n* rubbish
SCULCHES > SCULCH
SCULK *vb* old form of skulk
SCULKED > SCULK
SCULKER > SCULK
SCULKERS > SCULK
SCULKING > SCULK
SCULKS > SCULK
SCULL *n* small oar ▷ *vb* row (a boat) using sculls
SCULLE *n* old form of school
SCULLED > SCULL
SCULLER > SCULL
SCULLERS > SCULL
SCULLERY *n* small room where washing-up and other kitchen work is done
SCULLES > SCULLE
SCULLING > SCULL
SCULLINGS > SCULL
SCULLION *n* servant employed to do the hard work in a kitchen
SCULLIONS
> SCULLION
SCULLS > SCULL
SCULP *variant of*
> SCULPTURE
SCULPED > SCULP
SCULPIN *n* type of fish of the family which includes

S

bullheads and sea scorpions

SCULPING > SCULP

SCULPINS > SCULPIN

SCULPS > SCULP

SCULPSIT vb (he or she) sculptured it: used formerly on sculptures next to a sculptor's name

SCULPT same as > SCULPTURE

SCULPTED > SCULPT

SCULPTING n act or practice of sculpting

SCULPTOR n person who makes sculptures

SCULPTORS > SCULPTOR

SCULPTS > SCULPT

SCULPTURE n art of making figures or designs in wood, stone, etc ▷ vb represent in sculpture

SCULS > SCUL

SCULTCH same as > SCULCH

SCULTCHES > SCULTCH

SCUM n impure or waste matter on the surface of a liquid ▷ vb remove scum from

SCUMBAG n offensive or despicable person

SCUMBAGS > SCUMBAG

SCUMBALL n contemptible person

SCUMBALLS > SCUMBALL

SCUMBER vb old word meaning defecate

SCUMBERED > SCUMBER

SCUMBERS > SCUMBER

SCUMBLE vb soften or blend (an outline or colour) with a thin upper coat of opaque colour ▷ n upper layer of colour applied in this way

SCUMBLED > SCUMBLE

SCUMBLES > SCUMBLE

SCUMBLING > SCUMBLE

SCUMFISH vb Scots word meaning disgust

SCUMLESS > SCUM

SCUMLIKE > SCUM

SCUMMED > SCUM

SCUMMER > SCUM

SCUMMERS > SCUM

SCUMMIER > SCUMMY

SCUMMIEST > SCUMMY

SCUMMILY > SCUMMY

SCUMMING > SCUM

SCUMMINGS > SCUM

SCUMMY adj of, resembling, consisting of, or covered with scum

SCUMS > SCUM

SCUNCHEON n inner part of a door jamb or window frame

SCUNDERED adj Irish dialect word for embarrassed

SCUNGE vb borrow ▷ n dirty or worthless person

SCUNGED > SCUNGE

SCUNGES > SCUNGE

SCUNGIER > SCUNGY

SCUNGIEST > SCUNGY

SCUNGILE same as > SCUNGILLE

SCUNGILI same as > SCUNGILLI

SCUNGILLE n meat of a conch, eaten as a delicacy

SCUNGILLI n seafood dish of conch

SCUNGING > SCUNGE

SCUNGY adj sordid or dirty

SCUNNER vb Scot word meaning to feel aversion ▷ n strong aversion

SCUNNERED adj annoyed, discontented, or bored

SCUNNERS > SCUNNER

SCUP n common sparid fish of American coastal regions of the Atlantic

SCUPPAUG n sea fish

SCUPPAUGS > SCUPPAUG

SCUPPER vb defeat or ruin ▷ n drain in the side of a ship

SCUPPERED > SCUPPER

SCUPPERS > SCUPPER

SCUPS > SCUP

SCUR n small unattached growth of horn at the site of a normal horn in cattle

SCURF n flaky skin on the scalp

SCURFIER > SCURF

SCURFIEST > SCURF

SCURFS > SCURF

SCURFY > SCURF

SCURRED > SCUR

SCURRIED > SCURRY

SCURRIER n old word meaning scout

SCURRIERS > SCURRIER

SCURRIES > SCURRY

SCURRIL adj old word meaning vulgar

SCURRILE adj old word meaning vulgar

SCURRING > SCUR

SCURRIOUR n old word meaning scout

SCURRY vb move hastily ▷ n act or sound of scurrying

SCURRYING > SCURRY

SCURS > SCUR

SCURVIER > SCURVY

SCURVIES > SCURVY

SCURVIEST > SCURVY

SCURVILY > SCURVY

SCURVY n disease caused by lack of vitamin C ▷ adj mean and despicable

SCUSE shortened form of > EXCUSE

SCUSED > SCUSE

SCUSES > SCUSE

SCUSING > SCUSE

SCUT n short tail of the hare, rabbit, or deer

SCUTA > SCUTUM

SCUTAGE n payment to a lord from his vassal in lieu of military service

SCUTAGES > SCUTAGE

SCUTAL > SCUTE

SCUTATE adj (of animals) having or covered with large bony or horny plates

SCUTATION > SCUTATE

SCUTCH vb separate the fibres from the woody part of (flax) by pounding ▷ n tool used for this

SCUTCHED > SCUTCH

SCUTCHEON same as > SHIELD

SCUTCHER same as > SCUTCH

SCUTCHERS > SCUTCHER

SCUTCHES > SCUTCH

SCUTCHING > SCUTCH

SCUTE n horny or chitinous plate that makes up part of the exoskeleton in armadillos, etc

SCUTELLA > SCUTELLUM

SCUTELLAR > SCUTELLUM

SCUTELLUM n last of three plates into which the notum of an insect's thorax is divided

SCUTES > SCUTE

SCUTIFORM adj (esp of plant parts) shaped like a shield

SCUTIGER n species of centipede

SCUTIGERS > SCUTIGER

SCUTS > SCUT

SCUTTER informal word for > SCURRY

SCUTTERED > SCUTTER

SCUTTERS > SCUTTER

SCUTTLE n fireside container for coal ▷ vb run with short quick steps

SCUTTLED > SCUTTLE

SCUTTLER > SCUTTLE

SCUTTLERS > SCUTTLE

SCUTTLES > SCUTTLE

SCUTTLING n act of scuttling

SCUTUM n middle of three plates into which the notum of an insect's thorax is divided

SCUTWORK n menial or dull work

SCUTWORKS > SCUTWORK

SCUZZ n dirt

SCUZZBAG n disagreeable or disgusting person

SCUZZBAGS > SCUZZBAG

SCUZZBALL n despicable person

SCUZZES > SCUZZ

SCUZZIER > SCUZZY

SCUZZIEST > SCUZZY

SCUZZY adj unkempt, dirty, or squalid

SCYBALA > SCYBALUM

SCYBALOUS > SCYBALUM

SCYBALUM n hard faeces in stomach

SCYE n Scots word meaning sleeve-hole

SCYES > SCYE

SCYPHATE adj shaped like cup

SCYPHI > SCYPHUS

SCYPHUS n ancient Greek two-handled drinking cup

SCYTALE n coded message in ancient Sparta

SCYTALES > SCYTALE

SCYTHE n long-handled tool with a curved blade for cutting grass ▷ vb cut with a scythe

SCYTHED > SCYTHE

SCYTHEMAN n scythe user

SCYTHEMEN > SCYTHEMAN

SCYTHER > SCYTHE

SCYTHERS > SCYTHE

SCYTHES > SCYTHE

SCYTHING > SCYTHE

SDAINE vb old form of disdain

SDAINED > SDAINE

SDAINES > SDAINE

SDAINING > SDAINE

SDAYN vb old form of disdain

SDAYNED > SDAYN

SDAYNING > SDAYN

SDAYNS > SDAYN

SDEIGN vb old form of disdain

SDEIGNE vb old form of disdain

SDEIGNED > SDEIGN

SDEIGNES > SDEIGNE

SDEIGNING > SDEIGN

SDEIGNS > SDEIGN

SDEIN vb old form of disdain

SDEINED > SDEIN

SDEINING > SDEIN

SDEINS > SDEIN

SEA n mass of salt water covering three quarters of the earth's surface

SEABAG n canvas bag for holding a sailor's belongings

SEABAGS > SEABAG

SEABANK n sea shore

SEABANKS > SEABANK

SEABEACH n beach at seaside

SEABED n bottom of sea

SEABEDS > SEABED

SEABIRD n bird that lives on the sea

SEABIRDS > SEABIRD

SEABLITE n prostrate annual plant of the goosefoot family

SEABLITES > SEABLITE

SEABOARD n coast

SEABOARDS > SEABOARD

SEABOOT n sailor's waterproof boot

SEABOOTS > SEABOOT

SEABORNE adj carried on or by the sea

SEABOTTLE n type of seaweed

SEABREAM n type of food fish of European seas
SEABREAMS > SEABREAM
SEACOAST n land bordering on the sea
SEACOASTS > SEACOAST
SEACOCK n valve in the hull of a vessel below the water line
SEACOCKS > SEACOCK
SEACRAFT n skill of a sailor
SEACRAFTS > SEACRAFT
SEACUNNY n steersman on an Indian ship
SEADOG another word for > FOGBOW
SEADOGS > SEADOG
SEADROME n aerodrome floating on sea
SEADROMES > SEADROME
SEAFARER n traveller who goes by sea
SEAFARERS > SEAFARER
SEAFARING adj working or travelling by sea ▷ n act of travelling by sea
SEAFLOOR n bottom of the sea
SEAFLOORS > SEAFLOOR
SEAFOAM n foam formed on the sea
SEAFOAMS > SEAFOAM
SEAFOLK n people who sail the sea
SEAFOLKS > SEAFOLK
SEAFOOD n edible saltwater fish or shellfish
SEAFOODS > SEAFOOD
SEAFOWL n seabird
SEAFOWLS > SEAFOWL
SEAFRONT n built-up area facing the sea
SEAFRONTS > SEAFRONT
SEAGIRT adj surrounded by the sea
SEAGOING adj built for travelling on the sea
SEAGRASS n grass which grows by or in the sea
SEAGULL n gull
SEAGULLS > SEAGULL
SEAHAWK n skua
SEAHAWKS > SEAHAWK
SEAHOG n porpoise
SEAHOGS > SEAHOG
SEAHORSE n marine fish with a horselike head that swims upright
SEAHORSES > SEAHORSE
SEAHOUND n dogfish
SEAHOUNDS > SEAHOUND
SEAKALE n European coastal plant
SEAKALES > SEAKALE
SEAKINDLY adj (of a ship) easy to sail
SEAL n piece of wax, etc attached to a document as

a mark of authentication ▷ vb close with or as if with a seal
SEALABLE > SEAL
SEALANT n any substance used for sealing
SEALANTS > SEALANT
SEALCH Scots word for > SEAL
SEALCHS > SEALCH
SEALED adj (of a road) having a hard surface
SEALER n person or thing that seals
SEALERIES > SEALERY
SEALERS > SEALER
SEALERY n occupation of hunting seals
SEALGH Scots word for > SEAL
SEALGHS > SEALGH
SEALIFT vb transport by ship
SEALIFTED > SEALIFT
SEALIFTS > SEALIFT
SEALINE n company running regular sailings
SEALINES > SEALINE
SEALING > SEAL
SEALINGS > SEAL
SEALLIKE adj resembling a seal
SEALPOINT n popular variety of Siamese cat
SEALS > SEAL
SEALSKIN n skin or prepared fur of a seal, used to make coats
SEALSKINS > SEALSKIN
SEALWAX n sealing wax
SEALWAXES > SEALWAX
SEALYHAM n type of short-legged terrier
SEALYHAMS > SEALYHAM
SEAM n line where two edges are joined, as by stitching ▷ vb mark with furrows or wrinkles
SEAMAID n mermaid
SEAMAIDS > SEAMAID
SEAMAN n sailor
SEAMANLY adj like or appropriate to a seaman
SEAMARK n conspicuous object on a shore used as a guide
SEAMARKS > SEAMARK
SEAME n old word meaning grease
SEAMED > SEAM
SEAMEN > SEAMAN
SEAMER n bowler who makes the ball bounce on its seam
SEAMERS > SEAMER
SEAMES > SEAME
SEAMFREE adj having no seam
SEAMIER > SEAMY
SEAMIEST > SEAMY
SEAMINESS > SEAMY
SEAMING > SEAM
SEAMINGS > SEAMING
SEAMLESS adj (of a garment) without seams
SEAMLIKE > SEAM

SEAMOUNT n submarine mountain rising more than 1000 metres above the surrounding ocean floor
SEAMOUNTS > SEAMOUNT
SEAMS > SEAM
SEAMSET n tool for flattening seams in metal
SEAMSETS > SEAMSET
SEAMSTER n person who sews
SEAMSTERS > SEAMSTER
SEAMY adj sordid
SEAN vb fish with seine net
SEANCE n meeting at which spiritualists attempt to communicate with the dead
SEANCES > SEANCE
SEANED > SEAN
SEANING > SEAN
SEANNACHY n Highland genealogist, chronicler, or bard
SEANS > SEAN
SEAPIECE n artwork depicting sea
SEAPIECES > SEAPIECE
SEAPLANE n aircraft designed to take off from and land on water
SEAPLANES > SEAPLANE
SEAPORT n town or city with a harbour for boats and ships
SEAPORTS > SEAPORT
SEAQUAKE n agitation and disturbance of the sea caused by an earthquake at the sea bed
SEAQUAKES > SEAQUAKE
SEAQUARIA pl n areas of salt water where sea animals are kept
SEAR vb scorch, burn the surface of ▷ n mark caused by searing ▷ adj dried up
SEARAT n pirate
SEARATS > SEARAT
SEARCE vb sift
SEARCED > SEARCE
SEARCES > SEARCE
SEARCH vb examine closely in order to find something ▷ n instance of searching
SEARCHED > SEARCH
SEARCHER > SEARCH
SEARCHERS > SEARCH
SEARCHES > SEARCH
SEARCHING n act of searching
SEARCING > SEARCE
SEARE adj old word meaning dry and withered
SEARED > SEAR
SEARER > SEAR
SEAREST > SEAR
SEARING > SEAR
SEARINGLY > SEAR

SEARINGS > SEAR
SEARNESS > SEAR
SEAROBIN n type of American gurnard
SEAROBINS > SEAROBIN
SEARS > SEAR
SEAS > SEA
SEASCAPE n picture of a scene at sea
SEASCAPES > SEASCAPE
SEASCOUT n member of seagoing scouts
SEASCOUTS > SEASCOUT
SEASE vb old form of seize
SEASED > SEASE
SEASES > SEASE
SEASHELL n empty shell of a mollusc
SEASHELLS > SEASHELL
SEASHORE n land bordering on the sea
SEASHORES > SEASHORE
SEASICK adj suffering from nausea caused by the motion of a ship
SEASICKER > SEASICK
SEASIDE n area, esp a holiday resort, on the coast
SEASIDES > SEASIDE
SEASING > SEASE
SEASON n one of four divisions of the year ▷ vb flavour with salt, herbs, etc
SEASONAL adj depending on or varying with the seasons ▷ n seasonal thing
SEASONALS > SEASONAL
SEASONED > SEASON
SEASONER > SEASON
SEASONERS > SEASON
SEASONING n salt, herbs, etc added to food to enhance flavour
SEASONS > SEASON
SEASPEAK n language used by sailors
SEASPEAKS > SEASPEAK
SEASTRAND n seashore
SEASURE n old form of seizure
SEASURES > SEASURE
SEAT n thing designed or used for sitting on ▷ vb cause to sit
SEATBACK n back of seat
SEATBACKS > SEATBACK
SEATBELT n safety belt in vehicle
SEATBELTS > SEATBELT
SEATED > SEAT
SEATER n person or thing that seats
SEATERS > SEATER
SEATING n supply or arrangement of seats ▷ adj of or relating to the provision of places to sit

S

SEATINGS > SEATING

SEATLESS > SEAT

SEATMATE *n* person sitting in next seat

SEATMATES > SEATMATE

SEATRAIN *n* ship that can carry a train

SEATRAINS > SEATRAIN

SEATROUT *n* trout living in the sea

SEATROUTS > SEATROUT

SEATS > SEAT

SEATWORK *n* school work done at pupils' desks

SEATWORKS > SEATWORK

SEAWALL *n* wall built to prevent encroachment or erosion by the sea

SEAWALLED *adj* having a seawall

SEAWALLS > SEAWALL

SEAWAN *n* shell beads used by certain Native Americans as money

SEAWANS > SEAWAN

SEAWANT *n* Native American name for silver coins

SEAWANTS > SEAWANT

SEAWARD *same as* > SEAWARDS

SEAWARDLY > SEAWARD

SEAWARDS *adv* towards the sea

SEAWARE *n* any of numerous large coarse seaweeds

SEAWARES > SEAWARE

SEAWATER *n* water from sea

SEAWATERS > SEAWATER

SEAWAY *n* waterway giving access to an inland port

SEAWAYS > SEAWAY

SEAWEED *n* plant growing in the sea

SEAWEEDS > SEAWEED

SEAWEEDY *adj* full of seaweed

SEAWIFE *n* variety of sea fish

SEAWIVES > SEAWIFE

SEAWOMAN *n* sailor

SEAWOMEN > SEAWOMAN

SEAWORM *n* marine worm

SEAWORMS > SEAWORM

SEAWORTHY *adj* (of a ship) in fit condition for a sea voyage

SEAZE *vb* old form of seize

SEAZED > SEAZE

SEAZES > SEAZE

SEAZING > SEAZE

SEBACEOUS *adj* of, like, or secreting fat or oil

SEBACIC *adj* derived from sebacic acid, a white crystalline acid

SEBASIC *same as* > SEBACIC

SEBATE *n* salt of sebacic acid

SEBATES > SEBATE

SEBESTEN *n* Asian tree

SEBESTENS > SEBESTEN

SEBIFIC *adj* producing fat

SEBORRHEA *n* skin disease in which excessive oil is secreted

SEBUM *n* oily substance secreted by the sebaceous glands

SEBUMS > SEBUM

SEBUNDIES > SEBUNDY

SEBUNDY *n* irregular soldier in India

SEC *same as* > SECANT

SECALOSE *n* type of sugar

SECALOSES > SECALOSE

SECANT *n* the ratio of the length of the hypotenuse to the length of the adjacent side

SECANTLY > SECANT

SECANTS > SECANT

SECATEUR *n* secateurs

SECATEURS *pl n* small pruning shears

SECCO *n* wall painting done on dried plaster with tempera

SECCOS > SECCO

SECEDE *vb* withdraw formally from a political alliance or federation

SECEDED > SECEDE

SECEDER > SECEDE

SECEDERS > SECEDE

SECEDES > SECEDE

SECEDING > SECEDE

SECERN *vb* (of a gland or follicle) to secrete

SECERNED > SECERN

SECERNENT > SECERN

SECERNING > SECERN

SECERNS > SECERN

SECESH *n* secessionist in US Civil War

SECESHER *n* secessionist in US Civil War

SECESHERS > SECESHER

SECESHES > SECESH

SECESSION *n* act of seceding

SECH *n* hyperbolic secant

SECHS > SECH

SECKEL *variant of* > SECKLE

SECKELS > SECKEL

SECKLE *n* type of pear

SECKLES > SECKLE

SECLUDE *vb* keep (a person) from contact with others

SECLUDED *adj* private, sheltered

SECLUDES > SECLUDE

SECLUDING > SECLUDE

SECLUSION *n* state of being secluded

SECLUSIVE *adj* tending to seclude

SECO *adj* (of wine) dry

SECODONT *n* animal with cutting back teeth

SECODONTS > SECODONT

SECONAL *n* tradename for secobarbital

SECONALS > SECONAL

SECOND *adj* coming directly after the first ▷ *n* person or thing coming second ▷ *vb* express formal support for (a motion proposed in a meeting)

SECONDARY *adj* of less importance ▷ *n* person or thing that is secondary

SECONDE *n* second of eight positions from which a parry or attack can be made in fencing

SECONDED > SECOND

SECONDEE *n* person who is seconded

SECONDEES > SECONDEE

SECONDER > SECOND

SECONDERS > SECOND

SECONDES > SECONDE

SECONDI > SECONDO

SECONDING *n* act of seconding

SECONDLY *adv* in the second place or position

SECONDO *n* left-hand part in a piano duet

SECONDS > SECOND

SECPAR *n* distance unit in astronomy

SECPARS > SECPAR

SECRECIES > SECRECY

SECRECY *n* state of being secret

SECRET *adj* kept from the knowledge of others ▷ *n* something kept secret

SECRETA *n* secretions

SECRETAGE *n* use of mercury in treating furs

SECRETARY *n* person who deals with correspondence and general clerical work

SECRETE *vb* (of an organ, gland, etc) produce and release (a substance)

SECRETED > SECRETE

SECRETER > SECRET

SECRETES > SECRETE

SECRETEST > SECRET

SECRETIN *n* peptic hormone secreted by the mucosae of the duodenum and jejunum

SECRETING > SECRETE

SECRETINS > SECRETIN

SECRETION *n* substance that is released from a cell, organ, or gland

SECRETIVE *adj* inclined to keep things secret

SECRETLY > SECRET

SECRETOR > SECRETE

SECRETORS > SECRETE

SECRETORY *adj* of, relating to, or producing a secretion

SECRETS > SECRET

SECS > SEC

SECT *n* subdivision of a religious or political group

SECTARIAL > SECT

SECTARIAN *adj* of a sect ▷ *n* member of a sect

SECTARIES > SECTARY

SECTARY *n* member of a sect

SECTATOR *n* member of sect

SECTATORS > SECTATOR

SECTILE *adj* able to be cut smoothly

SECTILITY > SECTILE

SECTION *n* part cut off ▷ *vb* cut or divide into sections

SECTIONAL *adj* concerned with a particular area or group within a country or community

SECTIONED > SECTION

SECTIONS > SECTION

SECTOR *n* part or subdivision ▷ *vb* divide into sectors

SECTORAL > SECTOR

SECTORED > SECTOR

SECTORIAL *adj* of or relating to a sector

SECTORING > SECTOR

SECTORISE *same as* > SECTORIZE

SECTORIZE *vb* split into sectors

SECTORS > SECTOR

SECTS > SECT

SECULA > SECULUM

SECULAR *adj* worldly, as opposed to sacred ▷ *n* member of the secular clergy

SECULARLY > SECULAR

SECULARS > SECULAR

SECULUM *n* age in astronomy

SECULUMS > SECULUM

SECUND *adj* having or designating parts arranged on or turned to one side of the axis

SECUNDINE *n* one of the two integuments surrounding the ovule of a plant

SECUNDLY > SECUND

SECUNDUM *adj* according to

SECURABLE > SECURE

SECURANCE > SECURE

SECURE *adj* free from danger ▷ *vb* obtain

SECURED > SECURE

SECURELY > SECURE

SECURER > SECURE

SECURERS > SECURE

SECURES > SECURE

SECUREST > SECURE

SECURING > SECURE

SECURITAN *n* person believing they are secure

SECURITY *n* precautions against theft, espionage, or other danger

SED *old spelling of* > SAID

SEDAN *same as* > SALOON

SEDANS > SEDAN
SEDARIM > SEDER
SEDATE adj calm and dignified ▷ vb give a sedative drug to
SEDATED > SEDATE
SEDATELY > SEDATE
SEDATER > SEDATE
SEDATES > SEDATE
SEDATEST > SEDATE
SEDATING > SEDATE
SEDATION n state of calm, esp when brought about by sedatives
SEDATIONS > SEDATION
SEDATIVE adj having a soothing or calming effect ▷ n sedative drug
SEDATIVES > SEDATIVE
SEDENT adj seated
SEDENTARY adj done sitting down, involving little exercise
SEDER n Jewish ceremonial meal held on the first night or first two nights of Passover
SEDERS > SEDER
SEDERUNT n sitting of an ecclesiastical assembly, court, etc
SEDERUNTS > SEDERUNT
SEDES Latin word for > SEAT
SEDGE n coarse grasslike plant growing on wet ground
SEDGED adj having sedge
SEDGELAND n land covered with sedge
SEDGES > SEDGE
SEDGIER > SEDGE
SEDGIEST > SEDGE
SEDGY > SEDGE
SEDILE n seat for clergy in church
SEDILIA n group of three seats where the celebrant and ministers sit during High Mass
SEDILIUM n seat for clergy in church
SEDIMENT n matter which settles to the bottom of a liquid
SEDIMENTS > SEDIMENT
SEDITION n speech or action encouraging rebellion against the government
SEDITIONS > SEDITION
SEDITIOUS adj of, like, or causing sedition
SEDUCE vb win over or attract
SEDUCED > SEDUCE
SEDUCER n person who entices, allures, or seduces
SEDUCERS > SEDUCER
SEDUCES > SEDUCE
SEDUCIBLE > SEDUCE
SEDUCING > SEDUCE
SEDUCINGS > SEDUCE

SEDUCIVE adj seductive
SEDUCTION n act of seducing or the state of being seduced
SEDUCTIVE adj attractive, enticing
SEDUCTOR n person who seduces
SEDUCTORS > SEDUCTOR
SEDULITY > SEDULOUS
SEDULOUS adj diligent or persevering
SEDUM n rock plant
SEDUMS > SEDUM
SEE vb perceive with the eyes or mind ▷ n diocese of a bishop
SEEABLE > SEE
SEECATCH n male seal in Aleutians
SEED n mature fertilized grain of a plant ▷ vb sow with seed
SEEDBED n area of soil prepared for the growing of seedlings before they are transplanted
SEEDBEDS > SEEDBED
SEEDBOX n part of plant that contains seeds
SEEDBOXES > SEEDBED
SEEDCAKE n sweet cake flavoured with caraway seeds and lemon rind or essence
SEEDCAKES > SEEDCAKE
SEEDCASE n part of a fruit enclosing the seeds
SEEDCASES > SEEDCASE
SEEDEATER n bird feeding on seeds
SEEDED > SEED
SEEDER n person or thing that seeds
SEEDERS > SEEDER
SEEDHEAD n seed-containing part of a plant
SEEDHEADS > SEEDHEAD
SEEDIER > SEEDY
SEEDIEST > SEEDY
SEEDILY > SEEDY
SEEDINESS > SEEDY
SEEDING > SEED
SEEDINGS > SEED
SEEDLESS > SEED
SEEDLIKE > SEED
SEEDLING n young plant raised from a seed
SEEDLINGS > SEEDLING
SEEDLIP n basket holding seeds to be sown
SEEDLIPS > SEEDLIP
SEEDMAN n seller of seeds
SEEDMEN > SEEDMAN
SEEDNESS n old word meaning sowing of seeds
SEEDPOD n carpel enclosing the seeds of a flowering plant
SEEDPODS > SEEDPOD
SEEDS > SEED
SEEDSMAN n seller of seeds

SEEDSMEN > SEEDSMAN
SEEDSTOCK n livestock used for breeding
SEEDTIME n season when seeds are sown
SEEDTIMES > SEEDTIME
SEEDY adj shabby
SEEING > SEE
SEEINGS > SEE
SEEK vb try to find or obtain
SEEKER > SEEK
SEEKERS > SEEK
SEEKING > SEEK
SEEKS > SEEK
SEEL vb sew up the eyelids of (a hawk or falcon) so as to render it tame
SEELD adj old word meaning rare
SEELED > SEEL
SEELIE pl n good benevolent fairies
SEELIER > SEELY
SEELIEST > SEELY
SEELING > SEEL
SEELINGS > SEEL
SEELS > SEEL
SEELY adj old word meaning happy
SEEM vb appear to be
SEEMED > SEEM
SEEMER > SEEM
SEEMERS > SEEM
SEEMING adj apparent but not real ▷ n outward or false appearance
SEEMINGLY adv in appearance but not necessarily in actuality
SEEMINGS > SEEMING
SEEMLESS adj old word meaning unseemly
SEEMLIER > SEEMLY
SEEMLIEST > SEEMLY
SEEMLIHED n old word meaning seemliness
SEEMLY adj proper or fitting ▷ adv properly or decorously
SEEMLYHED n old word meaning seemliness
SEEMS > SEEM
SEEN > SEE
SEEP vb trickle through slowly, ooze ▷ n small spring or place where water, oil, etc, has oozed through the ground
SEEPAGE n act or process of seeping
SEEPAGES > SEEPAGE
SEEPED > SEEP
SEEPIER > SEEPY
SEEPIEST > SEEPY
SEEPING > SEEP
SEEPS > SEEP
SEEPY adj tending to seep
SEER n person who sees
SEERESS > SEER
SEERESSES > SEER
SEERS > SEER
SEES > SEE
SEESAW n plank balanced in the middle so that two people seated on either

end ride up and down alternately ▷ vb move up and down
SEESAWED > SEESAW
SEESAWING > SEESAW
SEESAWS > SEESAW
SEETHE vb be very agitated ▷ n act or state of seething
SEETHED > SEETHE
SEETHER > SEETHE
SEETHERS > SEETHE
SEETHES > SEETHE
SEETHING adj boiling or foaming as if boiling
SEETHINGS > SEETHING
SEEWING n suing
SEEWINGS > SEEWING
SEFER n scrolls of the Law
SEG n metal stud on shoe sole
SEGAR n cigar
SEGARS > SEGAR
SEGETAL adj (of weeds) growing amongst crops
SEGGAR n box in which pottery is baked
SEGGARS > SEGGAR
SEGHOL n pronunciation mark in Hebrew
SEGHOLATE n vowel sound in Hebrew
SEGHOLS > SEGHOL
SEGMENT n one of several sections into which something may be divided ▷ vb divide into segments
SEGMENTAL adj of, like, or having the form of a segment
SEGMENTED > SEGMENT
SEGMENTS > SEGMENT
SEGNI > SEGNO
SEGNO n sign at the beginning or end of a section directed to be repeated
SEGNOS > SEGNO
SEGO n American variety of lily
SEGOL variant of > SEGHOL
SEGOLATE variant of > SEGHOLATE
SEGOLATES > SEGOLATE
SEGOLS > SEGOL
SEGOS > SEGO
SEGREANT adj having raised wings in heraldry
SEGREGANT n organism different because of segregation
SEGREGATE vb set apart
SEGS > SEG
SEGUE vb proceed from one section or piece of music to another without a break ▷ n practice or an instance of playing music in this way
SEGUED > SEGUE
SEGUEING > SEGUE
SEGUES > SEGUE
SEGUGIO n Italian breed of dog
SEGUGIOS > SEGUGIO

S

SEHRI n meal eaten before sunrise by Muslims fasting during Ramadan
SEHRIS > SEHRI
SEI n type of rorqual
SEICENTO n 17th century with reference to Italian art and literature
SEICENTOS > SEICENTO
SEICHE n periodic oscillation of the surface of an enclosed or partially enclosed body of water
SEICHES > SEICHE
SEIDEL n vessel for drinking beer
SEIDELS > SEIDEL
SEIF n long ridge of blown sand in a desert
SEIFS > SEIF
SEIGNEUR n feudal lord
SEIGNEURS > SEIGNEUR
SEIGNEURY n estate of a seigneur
SEIGNIOR n (in England) the lord of a seigniory
SEIGNIORS > SEIGNIOR
SEIGNIORY n (in England) the fee or manor of a seignior
SEIGNORAL adj relating to the quality of being a lord
SEIGNORY n lordship
SEIK Scot word for > SICK
SEIKER > SEIK
SEIKEST > SEIK
SEIL vb dialect word meaning strain
SEILED > SEIL
SEILING > SEIL
SEILS > SEIL
SEINE n large fishing net that hangs vertically from floats ▷ vb catch (fish) using this net
SEINED > SEINE
SEINER > SEINE
SEINERS > SEINE
SEINES > SEINE
SEINING > SEINE
SEININGS > SEINE
SEIR n fish of Indian seas
SEIRS > SEIR
SEIS > SEI
SEISABLE > SEISE
SEISE vb put into legal possession of (property, etc)
SEISED > SEISE
SEISER > SEISE
SEISERS > SEISE
SEISES > SEISE
SEISIN n feudal possession of an estate in land
SEISING > SEISE
SEISINGS > SEISE
SEISINS > SEISIN
SEISM n earthquake
SEISMAL adj of earthquakes
SEISMIC adj relating to earthquakes

SEISMICAL same as > SEISMIC
SEISMISM n occurrence of earthquakes
SEISMISMS > SEISMISM
SEISMS > SEISM
SEISOR n person who takes seisin
SEISORS > SEISOR
SEISURE n act of seisin
SEISURES > SEISURE
SEITAN same as > SEITEN
SEITANS > SEITAN
SEITEN n gluten from wheat
SEITENS > SEITEN
SEITIES > SEITY
SEITY n selfhood
SEIZA n traditional Japanese kneeling position
SEIZABLE > SEIZE
SEIZAS > SEIZA
SEIZE vb take hold of forcibly or quickly
SEIZED > SEIZE
SEIZER > SEIZE
SEIZERS > SEIZE
SEIZES > SEIZE
SEIZIN same as > SEISIN
SEIZING n binding used for holding together two ropes, two spars, etc
SEIZINGS > SEIZING
SEIZINS > SEIZIN
SEIZOR n person who takes seisin
SEIZORS > SEIZOR
SEIZURE n sudden violent attack of an illness
SEIZURES > SEIZURE
SEJANT adj (of a beast) shown seated
SEJEANT same as > SEJANT
SEKOS n holy place
SEKOSES > SEKOS
SEKT n German sparkling wine
SEKTS > SEKT
SEL Scot word for > SELF
SELACHIAN adj relating to a large subclass of cartilaginous fishes including the sharks, rays, dogfish, and skates ▷ n any fish belonging to this subclass
SELADANG n Malaysian tapir
SELADANGS > SELADANG
SELAH n Hebrew word of unknown meaning occurring in the Old Testament psalms
SELAHS > SELAH
SELAMLIK n men's quarters in Turkish house
SELAMLIKS > SELAMLIK
SELCOUTH adj old word meaning strange
SELD adj old word meaning rare

SELDOM adv not often, rarely
SELDOMLY > SELDOM
SELDSEEN adj old word meaning seldom seen
SELDSHOWN adj old word meaning seldom shown
SELE n old word meaning happiness
SELECT vb pick out or choose ▷ adj chosen in preference to others
SELECTA n disc jockey
SELECTAS > SELECTA
SELECTED > SELECT
SELECTEE n person who is selected, esp for military service
SELECTEES > SELECTEE
SELECTING > SELECT
SELECTION n selecting
SELECTIVE adj chosen or choosing carefully
SELECTLY > SELECT
SELECTMAN n any of the members of the local boards of most New England towns
SELECTMEN > SELECTMAN
SELECTOR n person or thing that selects
SELECTORS > SELECTOR
SELECTS > SELECT
SELENATE n any salt or ester formed by replacing one or both of the hydrogens of selenic acid with metal ions or organic groups
SELENATES > SELENATE
SELENIAN adj of the moon
SELENIC adj of or containing selenium, esp in the hexavalent state
SELENIDE n compound containing selenium
SELENIDES > SELENIDE
SELENIOUS adj of or containing selenium in the divalent or tetravalent state
SELENITE n colourless glassy variety of gypsum
SELENITES > SELENITE
SELENITIC > SELENITE
SELENIUM n nonmetallic element with photoelectric properties
SELENIUMS > SELENIUM
SELENOSES > SELENOSIS
SELENOSIS n poisoned condition caused by selenium
SELENOUS same as > SELENIOUS
SELES > SELE
SELF n distinct individuality or identity of a person or thing ▷ pron

myself, yourself, himself, or herself ▷ vb reproduce by oneself
SELFDOM n selfhood
SELFDOMS > SELFDOM
SELFED > SELF
SELFHEAL n low-growing European herbaceous plant
SELFHEALS > SELFHEAL
SELFHOOD n state of having a distinct identity
SELFHOODS > SELFHOOD
SELFIE n photograph taken by pointing a camera at oneself
SELFIES > SELFIE
SELFING > SELF
SELFINGS > SELF
SELFISH adj caring too much about oneself and not enough about others
SELFISHLY > SELFISH
SELFISM n emphasis on self
SELFISMS > SELFISM
SELFIST > SELFISM
SELFISTS > SELFISM
SELFLESS adj unselfish
SELFNESS n egotism
SELFS > SELF
SELFSAME adj very same
SELFWARD adj toward self
SELFWARDS adv towards self
SELICTAR n Turkish sword-bearer
SELICTARS > SELICTAR
SELKIE same as > SILKIE
SELKIES > SELKIE
SELL vb exchange (something) for money ▷ n manner of selling
SELLA n area of bone in body
SELLABLE > SELL
SELLAE > SELLA
SELLAS > SELLA
SELLE n old word meaning seat
SELLER n person who sells
SELLERS > SELLER
SELLES > SELLE
SELLING n providing goods or services to customers in exchange for money
SELLINGS > SELLING
SELLOFF n act of selling cheaply
SELLOFFS > SELLOFF
SELLOTAPE n tradename for a type of transparent adhesive tape
SELLOUT n performance of a show etc for which all the tickets are sold
SELLOUTS > SELLOUT
SELLS > SELL
SELS > SEL
SELSYN same as > SYNCHRO**

SELSYNS > SELSYN
SELTZER n natural effervescent water containing minerals
SELTZERS > SELTZER
SELVA n dense equatorial forest
SELVAGE n edge of cloth, woven so as to prevent unravelling ▷ vb edge or border
SELVAGED > SELVAGE
SELVAGEE n rope used as strap
SELVAGEES > SELVAGEE
SELVAGES > SELVAGE
SELVAGING > SELVAGE
SELVAS > SELVA
SELVEDGE same as > SELVAGE
SELVEDGED > SELVEDGE
SELVEDGES > SELVEDGE
SELVES > SELF
SEMAINIER n chest of drawers
SEMANTEME same as > SEMEME
SEMANTIC adj relating to the meaning of words
SEMANTICS n study of linguistic meaning
SEMANTIDE n type of molecule
SEMANTRA > SEMANTRON
SEMANTRON n bar struck instead of bell in Orthodox church
SEMAPHORE n system of signalling by holding two flags in different positions to represent letters of the alphabet ▷ vb signal (information) by semaphore
SEMATIC adj acting as a warning, esp to potential predators
SEMBLABLE adj resembling or similar ▷ n something that resembles another thing
SEMBLABLY > SEMBLABLE
SEMBLANCE n outward or superficial appearance
SEMBLANT n semblance
SEMBLANTS > SEMBLANT
SEMBLE vb seem
SEMBLED > SEMBLE
SEMBLES > SEMBLE
SEMBLING > SEMBLE
SEME adj dotted (with)
SEMEE variant of > SEME
SEMEED adj seme
SEMEIA > SEMEION
SEMEION n unit of metre in ancient poetry
SEMEIOTIC same as > SEMIOTIC
SEMEME n meaning of a morpheme
SEMEMES > SEMEME
SEMEMIC > SEMEME

SEMEN n sperm-carrying fluid produced by male animals
SEMENS > SEMEN
SEMES > SEME
SEMESTER vb organize the academic year into two divisions
SEMESTERS > SEMESTER
SEMESTRAL > SEMESTER
SEMI n semidetached house
SEMIANGLE n half angle
SEMIARID adj denoting land that lies on the edges of a desert but has a slightly higher rainfall
SEMIBALD adj partly bald
SEMIBOLD adj denoting a weight of typeface between medium and bold face ▷ n semibold type
SEMIBOLDS > SEMIBOLD
SEMIBREVE n musical note four beats long
SEMIBULL n papal bull issued before coronation
SEMIBULLS > SEMIBULL
SEMICOLON n punctuation mark (;)
SEMICOMA n condition similar to a coma
SEMICOMAS > SEMICOMA
SEMICURED adj partly cured
SEMIDEAF adj partly deaf
SEMIDEIFY vb treat almost as a god
SEMIDOME n half-dome, esp one used to cover a semicircular apse
SEMIDOMED adj having semidome
SEMIDOMES > SEMIDOME
SEMIDRIER > SEMIDRY
SEMIDRY adj partly dry
SEMIDWARF adj smaller than standard variety
SEMIE n historical name for a student in second year at a Scottish university
SEMIERECT adj partly erect
SEMIES > SEMIE
SEMIFINAL n match or round before the final
SEMIFIT adj not fully fit
SEMIFLUID adj having properties between those of a liquid and those of a solid ▷ n substance that has such properties because of high viscosity
SEMIGALA adj characterized by quite a lot of celebration and fun ▷ n occasion that is festive but not to the degree of a gala
SEMIGALAS > SEMIGALA

SEMIGLOBE n half globe
SEMIGLOSS adj (of paint) giving finish between matt and gloss
SEMIGROUP n type of set in mathematics
SEMIHARD adj partly hard
SEMIHIGH adj moderately high
SEMIHOBO n person looking almost like hobo
SEMIHOBOS > SEMIHOBO
SEMILLON n grape used to make wine
SEMILLONS > SEMILLON
SEMILOG adj semilogarithmic
SEMILUNAR adj shaped like a crescent or half-moon
SEMILUNE n half-moon shape
SEMILUNES > SEMILUNE
SEMIMAT adj semimatt
SEMIMATT adj with surface midway between matt and gloss
SEMIMATTE adj semimatt
SEMIMETAL n metal not fully malleable
SEMIMICRO adj using microwaves
SEMIMILD adj somewhat mild
SEMIMOIST adj slightly wet
SEMINA > SEMEN
SEMINAL adj original and influential
SEMINALLY > SEMINAL
SEMINAR n meeting of a group of students for discussion
SEMINARS > SEMINAR
SEMINARY n college for priests
SEMINATE vb sow
SEMINATED > SEMINATE
SEMINATES > SEMINATE
SEMINOMA n malignant tumour of the testicle
SEMINOMAD n person living partly nomadic life
SEMINOMAS > SEMINOMA
SEMINUDE adj partly nude
SEMIOLOGY same as > SEMIOTICS
SEMIOPEN adj half-open
SEMIOSES > SEMIOSIS
SEMIOSIS n action involving establishing a relationship between signs
SEMIOTIC adj relating to signs and symbols, esp spoken or written signs
SEMIOTICS n study of human communications, esp signs and symbols

SEMIOVAL adj shaped like half of an oval
SEMIPED n measure in poetic metre
SEMIPEDS > SEMIPED
SEMIPIOUS adj quite pious
SEMIPLUME n type of bird feather
SEMIPOLAR adj as in semipolar bond type of chemical bond
SEMIPRO n semiprofessional
SEMIPROS > SEMIPRO
SEMIRAW adj not fully cooked or processed
SEMIRIGID adj (of an airship) maintaining shape by means of a main supporting keel and internal gas pressure
SEMIROUND adj with one flat side and one round side ▷ n something semiround
SEMIRURAL adj partly rural
SEMIS n ancient Roman coin
SEMISES > SEMIS
SEMISOFT adj partly soft
SEMISOLID adj having a viscosity and rigidity intermediate between that of a solid and a liquid ▷ n substance in this state
SEMISOLUS n advertisement that appears on the same page as another advertisement but not adjacent to it
SEMISTIFF adj partly stiff
SEMISWEET adj partly sweet
SEMITAR old spelling of > SCIMITAR
SEMITARS > SEMITAR
SEMITAUR old spelling of > SCIMITAR
SEMITAURS > SEMITAUR
SEMITIST n student of Semitic languages and culture
SEMITISTS > SEMITIST
SEMITONAL > SEMITONE
SEMITONE n smallest interval between two notes in Western music
SEMITONES > SEMITONE
SEMITONIC > SEMITONE
SEMITRUCK n articulated lorry
SEMIURBAN adj suburban
SEMIVOCAL adj of or relating to a semivowel
SEMIVOWEL n vowel-like sound that acts like a consonant, such as the sound w in well
SEMIWATER adj as in semiwater gas a mixed gas of steam and air

SEMIWILD adj not fully domesticated
SEMIWORKS adj equipped to manufacture but not in great numbers
SEMMIT n Scots word meaning a vest
SEMMITS > SEMMIT
SEMOLINA n hard grains of wheat left after the milling of flour, used to make puddings and pasta
SEMOLINAS > SEMOLINA
SEMPER adv Latin word meaning always
SEMPLE adj Scots word meaning simple
SEMPLER > SEMPLE
SEMPLEST > SEMPLE
SEMPLICE adv performed in a simple manner
SEMPRE adv (preceding a tempo or dynamic marking) always
SEMPSTER n person who sews
SEMPSTERS > SEMPSTER
SEMSEM n sesame
SEMSEMS > SEMSEM
SEMUNCIA n ancient Roman coin
SEMUNCIAE > SEMUNCIA
SEMUNCIAL > SEMUNCIA
SEMUNCIAS > SEMUNCIA
SEN n monetary unit of Brunei, Cambodia, Indonesia, and Malaysia
SENA n (in India) the army
SENARIES > SENARY
SENARII > SENARIUS
SENARIUS n type of poem
SENARY adj of or relating to the number six
SENAS > SENA
SENATE n main governing body at some universities
SENATES > SENATE
SENATOR n member of a senate
SENATORS > SENATOR
SEND vb cause (a person or thing) to go to or be taken or transmitted to a place
SENDABLE > SEND
SENDAL n fine silk fabric used for ceremonial clothing, etc
SENDALS > SENDAL
SENDED vb old word meaning sent
SENDER > SEND
SENDERS > SEND
SENDING > SEND
SENDINGS > SEND
SENDOFF n demonstration of good wishes at a person's departure ▷ vb dispatch (something, such as a letter)
SENDOFFS > SENDOFF

SENDS > SEND
SENDUP n parody or imitation
SENDUPS > SENDUP
SENE n money unit in Samoa
SENECA variant of > SENEGA
SENECAS > SENECA
SENECIO n type of plant of the genus which includes groundsels and ragworts
SENECIOS > SENECIO
SENEGA n milkwort plant of the eastern US
SENEGAS > SENEGA
SENES > SENE
SENESCE vb grow old
SENESCED > SENESCE
SENESCENT adj growing old
SENESCES > SENESCE
SENESCHAL n steward of the household of a medieval prince or nobleman
SENESCING > SENESCE
SENGI n African shrew
SENGIS > SENGI
SENGREEN n house leek
SENGREENS > SENGREEN
SENHOR n Portuguese term of address for man
SENHORA n Portuguese term of address for woman
SENHORAS > SENHORA
SENHORES > SENHOR
SENHORITA n Portuguese term of address for a young woman
SENHORS > SENHOR
SENILE adj mentally or physically weak because of old age ▷ n senile person
SENILELY > SENILE
SENILES > SENILE
SENILITY > SENILE
SENIOR adj superior in rank or standing ▷ n senior person
SENIORITY n state of being senior
SENIORS > SENIOR
SENITI n money unit in Tonga
SENITIS > SENITI
SENNA n tropical plant
SENNACHIE n Gaelic storyteller
SENNAS > SENNA
SENNET n fanfare: used as a stage direction in Elizabethan drama
SENNETS > SENNET
SENNIGHT archaic word for > WEEK
SENNIGHTS > SENNIGHT
SENNIT n flat braided cordage used on ships
SENNITS > SENNIT
SENOPIA n short-sightedness in old age
SENOPIAS > SENOPIA

SENOR n Spanish term of address equivalent to sir or Mr
SENORA n Spanish term of address equivalent to madam or Mrs
SENORAS > SENORA
SENORES > SENOR
SENORITA n Spanish term of address equivalent to madam or Miss
SENORITAS > SENORITA
SENORS > SENOR
SENRYU n Japanese short poem
SENS > SEN
SENSA > SENSUM
SENSATE adj perceived by the senses ▷ vb make sensate
SENSATED > SENSATE
SENSATELY > SENSATE
SENSATES > SENSATE
SENSATING > SENSATE
SENSATION n ability to feel things physically
SENSE n any of the faculties of perception or feeling ▷ vb perceive
SENSED > SENSE
SENSEFUL adj full of sense
SENSEI n martial arts teacher
SENSEIS > SENSEI
SENSELESS adj foolish
SENSES > SENSE
SENSI same as > SENSEI
SENSIBLE adj having or showing good sense ▷ n sensible thing or person
SENSIBLER > SENSIBLE
SENSIBLES > SENSIBLE
SENSIBLY > SENSIBLE
SENSILE adj capable of feeling
SENSILLA > SENSILLUM
SENSILLAE > SENSILLUM
SENSILLUM n sense organ in insects
SENSING > SENSE
SENSINGS > SENSE
SENSIS > SENSI
SENSISM n theory that ideas spring from senses
SENSISMS > SENSISM
SENSIST > SENSISM
SENSISTS > SENSISM
SENSITISE same as > SENSITIZE
SENSITIVE adj easily hurt or offended
SENSITIZE vb make sensitive
SENSOR n device that detects or measures the presence of something, such as radiation
SENSORIA > SENSORIUM
SENSORIAL same as > SENSORY
SENSORILY > SENSORY

SENSORIUM n area of the brain considered responsible for receiving and integrating sensations from the outside world
SENSORS > SENSOR
SENSORY adj of the senses or sensation
SENSUAL adj giving pleasure to the body and senses rather than the mind
SENSUALLY > SENSUAL
SENSUM n sensation detached from the information it conveys
SENSUOUS adj pleasing to the senses
SENT n former monetary unit of Estonia ▷ vb old spelling of scent
SENTE n money unit in Lesotho
SENTED > SENT
SENTENCE n sequence of words capable of standing alone as a statement, question, or command ▷ vb pass sentence on (a convicted person)
SENTENCED > SENTENCE
SENTENCER > SENTENCE
SENTENCES > SENTENCE
SENTENTIA n opinion
SENTI > SENT
SENTIENCE n state or quality of being sentient
SENTIENCY same as > SENTIENCE
SENTIENT adj capable of feeling ▷ n sentient person or thing
SENTIENTS > SENTIENT
SENTIMENT n thought, opinion, or attitude
SENTIMO n money unit in Philippines
SENTIMOS > SENTIMO
SENTINEL n sentry ▷ vb guard as a sentinel
SENTINELS > SENTINEL
SENTING > SENT
SENTRIES > SENTRY
SENTRY n soldier on watch
SENTS > SENT
SENVIES > SENVY
SENVY n mustard
SENZA prep without
SEPAD vb suppose
SEPADDED > SEPAD
SEPADDING > SEPAD
SEPADS > SEPAD
SEPAL n leaflike division of the calyx of a flower
SEPALED > SEPAL
SEPALINE same as > SEPALOID
SEPALLED > SEPAL
SEPALODY n changing of a flower part into a sepal

SEPALOID *adj* (esp of petals) resembling a sepal in structure and function

SEPALOUS *adj* with sepals

SEPALS > SEPAL

SEPARABLE *adj* able to be separated

SEPARABLY > SEPARABLE

SEPARATA > SEPARATUM

SEPARATE *vb* act as a barrier between ▷ *adj* not the same, different ▷ *n* item of clothing that only covers half the body

SEPARATED > SEPARATE

SEPARATES > SEPARATE

SEPARATOR *n* person or thing that separates

SEPARATUM *n* separate printing of article from magazine

SEPHEN *n* stingray

SEPHENS > SEPHEN

SEPIA *n* reddish-brown pigment ▷ *adj* dark reddish-brown

SEPIAS > SEPIA

SEPIC *adj* of sepia

SEPIMENT *n* hedge

SEPIMENTS > SEPIMENT

SEPIOLITE *n* meerschaum

SEPIOST *n* cuttlefish bone

SEPIOSTS > SEPIOST

SEPIUM *n* cuttlefish bone

SEPIUMS > SEPIUM

SEPMAG *adj* designating a film, etc for which the sound is recorded on separate magnetic material

SEPOY *n* (formerly) Indian soldier in the service of the British

SEPOYS > SEPOY

SEPPUKU *n* Japanese ritual suicide

SEPPUKUS > SEPPUKU

SEPS *n* species of lizard

SEPSES > SEPSIS

SEPSIS *n* poisoning caused by pus-forming bacteria

SEPT *n* clan, esp in Ireland or Scotland

SEPTA > SEPTUM

SEPTAGE *n* waste removed from septic tank

SEPTAGES > SEPTAGE

SEPTAL *adj* of or relating to a septum

SEPTARIA > SEPTARIUM

SEPTARIAN > SEPTARIUM

SEPTARIUM *n* mass of mineral substance having cracks filled with another mineral

SEPTATE *adj* divided by septa

SEPTATION *n* division by partitions

SEPTEMFID *adj* divided into seven

SEPTEMVIR *n* member of government of seven people

SEPTENARY *adj* of or relating to the number seven ▷ *n* number seven

SEPTENNIA *pl n* cycles of seven years

SEPTET *n* group of seven performers

SEPTETS > SEPTET

SEPTETTE *same as* > SEPTET

SEPTETTES > SEPTETTE

SEPTIC *adj* (of a wound) infected ▷ *n* infected wound

SEPTICAL > SEPTIC

SEPTICITY > SEPTIC

SEPTICS > SEPTIC

SEPTIFORM *adj* acting as partition

SEPTIMAL *adj* of number seven

SEPTIME *n* seventh of eight basic positions from which a parry can be made in fencing

SEPTIMES > SEPTIME

SEPTIMOLE *n* group of seven musical notes

SEPTLEVA *n* gambling term from old card game

SEPTLEVAS > SEPTLEVA

SEPTORIA *n* any of various parasitic fungi

SEPTORIAS > SEPTORIA

SEPTS > SEPT

SEPTUM *n* dividing partition between two cavities in the body

SEPTUMS > SEPTUM

SEPTUOR *n* group of seven musicians

SEPTUORS > SEPTUOR

SEPTUPLE *vb* multiply by seven ▷ *adj* seven times as much or as many ▷ *n* quantity or number seven times as great as another

SEPTUPLED > SEPTUPLE

SEPTUPLES > SEPTUPLE

SEPTUPLET *n* group of seven notes played in a time value of six, eight, etc

SEPULCHER *same as* > SEPULCHRE

SEPULCHRE *n* tomb or burial vault ▷ *vb* bury in a sepulchre

SEPULTURE *n* act of placing in a sepulchre

SEQUACITY *n* quality of being pliant or controllable

SEQUEL *n* novel, play, or film that continues the story of an earlier one

SEQUELA *n* disease related to or arising from a pre-existing disease

SEQUELAE > SEQUELA

SEQUELISE *same as* > SEQUELIZE

SEQUELIZE *vb* create sequel to

SEQUELS > SEQUEL

SEQUENCE *n* arrangement of two or more things in successive order ▷ *vb* arrange in a sequence

SEQUENCED > SEQUENCE

SEQUENCER *n* electronic device that determines the order in which a number of operations occur

SEQUENCES > SEQUENCE

SEQUENCY *n* number of changes in a mathematical list

SEQUENT *adj* following in order or succession ▷ *n* something that follows

SEQUENTLY > SEQUENT

SEQUENTS > SEQUENT

SEQUESTER *vb* seclude

SEQUESTRA *pl n* detached pieces of necrotic bone that often migrate to wounds

SEQUIN *n* small ornamental metal disc on a garment ▷ *vb* apply sequins

SEQUINED > SEQUIN

SEQUINING > SEQUIN

SEQUINNED > SEQUIN

SEQUINS > SEQUIN

SEQUITUR *n* conclusion that follows from the premises

SEQUITURS > SEQUITUR

SEQUOIA *n* giant Californian coniferous tree

SEQUOIAS > SEQUOIA

SER *n* unit of weight used in India

SERA > SERUM

SERAC *n* pinnacle of ice among crevasses on a glacier, usually on a steep slope

SERACS > SERAC

SERAFILE *n* line of soldiers

SERAFILES > SERAFILE

SERAFIN *n* old silver coin of Goa

SERAFINS > SERAFIN

SERAGLIO *n* sultan's palace

SERAGLIOS > SERAGLIO

SERAI *n* caravanserai or inn

SERAIL *same as* > SERAGLIO

SERAILS > SERAIL

SERAIS > SERAI

SERAL > SERE

SERANG *n* captain of a crew of sailors in SE Asia

SERANGS > SERANG

SERAPE *n* blanket-like shawl often of brightly-coloured wool

SERAPES > SERAPE

SERAPH *n* member of the highest order of angels

SERAPHIC *adj* of or resembling a seraph

SERAPHIM > SERAPH

SERAPHIMS > SERAPH

SERAPHIN *n* angel

SERAPHINE *n* old keyboard instrument

SERAPHINS > SERAPHIN

SERAPHS > SERAPH

SERASKIER *n* Turkish military leader

SERDAB *n* secret chamber in an ancient Egyptian tomb

SERDABS > SERDAB

SERE *adj* dried up or withered ▷ *n* series of changes occurring in the ecological succession of a particular community ▷ *vb* sear

SERED > SERE

SEREIN *n* fine rain falling from a clear sky after sunset

SEREINS > SEREIN

SERENADE *n* music played or sung to a person by an admirer ▷ *vb* sing or play a serenade to (someone)

SERENADED > SERENADE

SERENADER > SERENADE

SERENADES > SERENADE

SERENATA *n* 18th-century cantata, often dramatic in form

SERENATAS > SERENATA

SERENATE *n* old form of serenade ▷ *vb* make serene

SERENATED > SERENATE

SERENATES > SERENATE

SERENE *adj* calm, peaceful ▷ *vb* make serene

SERENED > SERENE

SERENELY > SERENE

SERENER > SERENE

SERENES > SERENE

SERENEST > SERENE

SERENING > SERENE

SERENITY *n* state or quality of being serene

SERER > SERE

SERES > SERE

SEREST > SERE

SERF *n* medieval farm labourer who could not leave the land they worked on

SERFAGE > SERF

SERFAGES > SERF

SERFDOM > SERF

SERFDOMS > SERF

SERFHOOD > SERF

S

SERFHOODS > SERF

SERFISH > SERF

SERFLIKE > SERF

SERFS > SERF

SERFSHIP > SERF

SERFSHIPS > SERF

SERGE n strong woollen fabric

SERGEANCY > SERGEANT

SERGEANT n noncommissioned officer in the army

SERGEANTS > SERGEANT

SERGEANTY n form of feudal tenure

SERGED adj with sewn seam

SERGER n sewing machine attachment for finishing seams

SERGERS > SERGER

SERGES > SERGE

SERGING n type of sewing

SERGINGS > SERGING

SERIAL n story or play produced in successive instalments ▷ adj of or forming a series

SERIALISE same as > SERIALIZE

SERIALISM n musical technique using a sequence of notes in a definite order

SERIALIST n writer of serials

SERIALITY > SERIAL

SERIALIZE vb publish or present as a serial

SERIALLY > SERIAL

SERIALS > SERIAL

SERIATE adj forming a series ▷ vb form into a series

SERIATED > SERIATE

SERIATELY > SERIATE

SERIATES > SERIATE

SERIATIM adv in a series

SERIATING > SERIATE

SERIATION > SERIATE

SERIC adj of silk

SERICEOUS adj covered with a layer of small silky hairs

SERICIN n gelatinous protein found on the fibres of raw silk

SERICINS > SERICIN

SERICITE n type of mica

SERICITES > SERICITE

SERICITIC > SERICITE

SERICON n solution used in alchemy

SERICONS > SERICON

SERIEMA n either of two cranelike South American birds

SERIEMAS > SERIEMA

SERIES n group or succession of related things, usu arranged in order

SERIF n small line at the extremities of a main stroke in a type character

SERIFED adj having serifs

SERIFFED adj having serifs

SERIFS > SERIF

SERIGRAPH n colour print made by an adaptation of the silk-screen process

SERIN n any of various small yellow-and-brown finches

SERINE n sweet-tasting amino acid

SERINES > SERINE

SERINETTE n barrel organ

SERING > SERE

SERINGA n any of several trees that yield rubber

SERINGAS > SERINGA

SERINS > SERIN

SERIOUS adj giving cause for concern

SERIOUSLY adv in a serious manner or to a serious degree

SERIPH same as > SERIF

SERIPHS > SERIPH

SERJEANCY n rank of sergeant

SERJEANT same as > SERGEANT

SERJEANTS > SERJEANT

SERJEANTY n type of feudal tenure

SERK Scots word for > SHIRT

SERKALI n government in Africa

SERKALIS > SERKALI

SERKS > SERK

SERMON n speech on a religious or moral subject ▷ vb deliver a sermon

SERMONED > SERMON

SERMONEER n preacher

SERMONER variant of > SERMONEER

SERMONERS > SERMONER

SERMONET n short sermon

SERMONETS > SERMONET

SERMONIC > SERMON

SERMONING n preaching a sermon

SERMONISE same as > SERMONIZE

SERMONIZE vb make a long moralizing speech

SERMONS > SERMON

SEROGROUP n group of bacteria with a common antigen

SEROLOGIC > SEROLOGY

SEROLOGY n science concerned with serums

SEROMA n abnormal pocket of clear fluid in the body

SEROMAS > SEROMA

SERON n crate

SERONS > SERON

SEROON n crate

SEROONS > SEROON

SEROPUS n liquid consisting of serum and pus

SEROPUSES > SEROPUS

SEROSA n one of the thin membranes surrounding the embryo in an insect's egg

SEROSAE > SEROSA

SEROSAL > SEROSA

SEROSAS > SEROSA

SEROSITY > SEROUS

SEROTINAL same as > SEROTINE

SEROTINE adj produced, flowering, or developing late in the season ▷ n either of two insectivorous bats

SEROTINES > SEROTINE

SEROTINY n state of being serotinous

SEROTONIN n compound that occurs in the brain, intestines, and blood platelets and acts as a neurotransmitter

SEROTYPE n category into which material is placed based on its serological activity ▷ vb class according to serotype

SEROTYPED > SEROTYPE

SEROTYPES > SEROTYPE

SEROTYPIC adj relating to a serotype

SEROUS adj of, containing, or like serum

SEROVAR n subdivision of species

SEROVARS > SEROVAR

SEROW n either of two antelopes of mountainous regions of S and SE Asia

SEROWS > SEROW

SERPENT n snake

SERPENTRY n serpents

SERPENTS > SERPENT

SERPIGO n any progressive skin eruption

SERPIGOES > SERPIGO

SERPIGOS > SERPIGO

SERPULA n type of marine mollusc

SERPULAE > SERPULA

SERPULAS > SERPULA

SERPULID n marine polychaete worm

SERPULIDS > SERPULID

SERPULITE n variety of fossil

SERR vb press close together

SERRA n sawlike part or organ

SERRAE > SERRA

SERRAN n species of fish

SERRANID n type of marine fish of the family which includes the sea bass and sea perch

SERRANIDS > SERRANID

SERRANO n type of Spanish ham

SERRANOID same as > SERRANID

SERRANOS > SERRANO

SERRANS > SERRAN

SERRAS > SERRA

SERRATE adj (of leaves) having a margin of forward pointing teeth ▷ vb make serrate

SERRATED adj having a notched or sawlike edge

SERRATES > SERRATE

SERRATI > SERRATUS

SERRATING > SERRATE

SERRATION n state or condition of being serrated

SERRATURE same as > SERRATION

SERRATUS n muscle in thorax

SERRE vb press close together

SERRED > SERRE

SERREFILE n file of soldiers

SERRES > SERRE

SERRICORN n beetle with serrate antennae ▷ adj (of a beetle) with serrate antennae

SERRIED adj in close formation

SERRIEDLY > SERRIED

SERRIES > SERRY

SERRIFORM adj resembling a notched or sawlike edge

SERRING > SERRE

SERRS > SERR

SERRULATE adj (esp of leaves) minutely serrate

SERRY vb close together

SERRYING > SERRY

SERS > SER

SERUEWE vb old word meaning survey

SERUEWED > SERUEWE

SERUEWES > SERUEWE

SERUEWING > SERUEWE

SERUM n watery fluid left after blood has clotted

SERUMAL > SERUM

SERUMS > SERUM

SERVABLE > SERVE

SERVAL n feline African mammal

SERVALS > SERVAL

SERVANT n person employed to do household work for another ▷ vb work as a servant

SERVANTED > SERVANT

SERVANTRY n servants

SERVANTS > SERVANT

SERVE vb work for (a person, community, or cause) ▷ n act of serving the ball

SERVEABLE > SERVE

SERVED > SERVE

SERVER n player who serves in racket games

SERVERIES > SERVERY

SERVERS > SERVER
SERVERY *n* room from which food is served
SERVES > SERVE
SERVEWARE *n* articles by or on which food is served
SERVEWE *vb* old word meaning survey
SERVEWED > SERVEWE
SERVEWES > SERVEWE
SERVEWING > SERVEWE
SERVICE *n* serving ▷ *adj* serving the public rather than producing goods ▷ *vb* provide a service or services to
SERVICED > SERVICE
SERVICER > SERVICE
SERVICERS > SERVICE
SERVICES > SERVICE
SERVICING *n* act of servicing
SERVIENT *adj* subordinate
SERVIETTE *n* table napkin
SERVILE *adj* too eager to obey people, fawning ▷ *n* servile person
SERVILELY > SERVILE
SERVILES > SERVILE
SERVILISM *n* condition of being servile
SERVILITY > SERVILE
SERVING *n* portion of food
SERVINGS > SERVING
SERVITOR *n* servant or attendant
SERVITORS > SERVITOR
SERVITUDE *n* bondage or slavery
SERVLET *n* small program that runs on a web server
SERVLETS > SERVLET
SERVO *n* servomechanism ▷ *adj* of a servomechanism
SERVOS > SERVO
SERVQUAL *n* provision of high-quality products backed by a high level of customer service
SERVQUALS > SERVQUAL
SESAME *n* plant cultivated for its seeds and oil
SESAMES > SESAME
SESAMOID *adj* of or relating to various small bones formed in tendons ▷ *n* sesamoid bone
SESAMOIDS > SESAMOID
SESE *interj* exclamation found in Shakespeare
SESELI *n* garden plant
SESELIS > SESELI
SESEY *interj* exclamation found in Shakespeare
SESH *short for* > SESSION
SESHES > SESH
SESS *n* old word meaning tax ▷ *vb* assess or impose (a tax)

SESSA *interj* exclamation found in Shakespeare
SESSED > SESS
SESSES > SESS
SESSILE *adj* (of flowers or leaves) having no stalk
SESSILITY > SESSILE
SESSING > SESS
SESSION *n* period spent in an activity
SESSIONAL > SESSION
SESSIONS > SESSION
SESSPOOL *n* cesspool
SESSPOOLS > SESSPOOL
SESTERCE *n* silver or, later, bronze coin of ancient Rome worth a quarter of a denarius
SESTERCES > SESTERCE
SESTERTIA *pl n* ancient Roman money accounts
SESTERTII *pl n* sesterces
SESTET *n* last six lines of a sonnet
SESTETS > SESTET
SESTETT *n* group of six
SESTETTE *n* group of six
SESTETTES > SESTETTE
SESTETTO *n* composition for six musicians
SESTETTOS > SESTETTO
SESTETTS > SESTETT
SESTINA *n* elaborate verse form of Italian origin
SESTINAS > SESTINA
SESTINE *n* poem of six lines
SESTINES > SESTINE
SESTON *n* type of plankton
SESTONS > SESTON
SET *vb* put in a specified position or state ▷ *n* setting or being set ▷ *adj* fixed or established beforehand
SETA *n* bristle or bristle-like appendage
SETACEOUS > SETA
SETAE > SETA
SETAL > SETA
SETBACK *n* anything that delays progress
SETBACKS > SETBACK
SETENANT *n* pair of postage stamps of different values joined together
SETENANTS > SETENANT
SETIFORM *adj* shaped like a seta
SETLINE *n* any of various types of fishing line
SETLINES > SETLINE
SETNESS > SET
SETNESSES > SET
SETOFF *n* counterbalance
SETOFFS > SETOFF
SETON *n* surgical thread inserted below the skin
SETONS > SETON

SETOSE *adj* covered with setae
SETOUS > SETA
SETOUT *n* beginning or outset
SETOUTS > SETOUT
SETS > SET
SETSCREW *n* screw that fits into the boss or hub of a wheel
SETSCREWS > SETSCREW
SETT *n* badger's burrow
SETTEE *n* couch
SETTEES > SETTEE
SETTER *n* long-haired gun dog ▷ *vb* treat with a piece of setterwort
SETTERED > SETTER
SETTERING > SETTER
SETTERS > SETTER
SETTING > SET
SETTINGS > SET
SETTLE *vb* arrange or put in order ▷ *n* long wooden bench with high back and arms
SETTLED > SETTLE
SETTLER *n* colonist
SETTLERS > SETTLER
SETTLES > SETTLE
SETTLING > SETTLE
SETTLINGS *pl n* any matter or substance that has settled at the bottom of a liquid
SETTLOR *n* person who settles property on someone
SETTLORS > SETTLOR
SETTS > SETT
SETUALE *n* valerian
SETUALES > SETUALE
SETULE *n* small bristle
SETULES > SETULE
SETULOSE > SETULE
SETULOUS > SETULE
SETUP *n* way in which anything is organized or arranged
SETUPS > SETUP
SETWALL *n* valerian
SETWALLS > SETWALL
SEV *n* Indian snack of deep-fried noodles
SEVEN *n* one more than six
SEVENFOLD *adj* having seven times as many or as much ▷ *adv* by seven times as many or as much
SEVENISH *adj* about seven
SEVENS *n* Rugby Union match or series of matches played with seven players on each side
SEVENTEEN *n* ten and seven
SEVENTH *n* number seven in a series ▷ *adj* coming after the sixth and before the eighth
SEVENTHLY *adv* in the seventh place or position
SEVENTHS > SEVENTH
SEVENTIES > SEVENTY

SEVENTY *n* ten times seven
SEVER *vb* cut through or off
SEVERABLE *adj* able to be severed
SEVERAL *adj* some, a few ▷ *n* individual person
SEVERALLY *adv* separately
SEVERALS > SEVERAL
SEVERALTY *n* state of being several or separate
SEVERANCE *n* act of severing or state of being severed
SEVERE *adj* strict or harsh
SEVERED > SEVER
SEVERELY > SEVERE
SEVERER > SEVERE
SEVEREST > SEVERE
SEVERIES > SEVERY
SEVERING > SEVER
SEVERITY > SEVERE
SEVERS > SEVER
SEVERY *n* part of vaulted ceiling
SEVICHE *n* Mexican fish dish
SEVICHES > SEVICHE
SEVRUGA *n* species of sturgeon
SEVRUGAS > SEVRUGA
SEVS > SEV
SEW *vb* join with thread repeatedly passed through with a needle
SEWABLE > SEW
SEWAGE *n* waste matter carried away in sewers
SEWAGES > SEWAGE
SEWAN *same as* > SEAWAN
SEWANS > SEWAN
SEWAR *n* Asian dagger
SEWARS > SEWAR
SEWED > SEW
SEWEL *n* scarecrow
SEWELLEL *n* mountain beaver
SEWELLELS > SEWELLEL
SEWELS > SEWEL
SEWEN *same as* > SEWIN
SEWENS > SEWEN
SEWER *n* drain to remove waste water and sewage ▷ *vb* provide with sewers
SEWERAGE *n* system of sewers
SEWERAGES > SEWERAGE
SEWERED > SEWER
SEWERING > SEWER
SEWERINGS > SEWER
SEWERLESS > SEWER
SEWERLIKE > SEWER
SEWERS > SEWER
SEWIN *n* sea trout
SEWING > SEW
SEWINGS > SEW
SEWINS > SEWIN
SEWN > SEW
SEWS > SEW
SEX *n* state of being biologically male or female ▷ *vb* find out the sex of

S

SEXAHOLIC n person who is addicted to sex

SEXCAPADE n sexual escapade

SEXED > SEX

SEXENNIAL adj occurring once every six years or over a period of six years ▷ n sixth anniversary

SEXER n person who determines the sex of chickens

SEXERCISE n sexual activity, regarded as a way of keeping fit

SEXERS > SEXER

SEXES > SEX

SEXFID adj split into six

SEXFOIL n flower with six petals or leaves

SEXFOILS > SEXFOIL

SEXIER > SEXY

SEXIEST > SEXY

SEXILY > SEXY

SEXINESS > SEXY

SEXING > SEX

SEXINGS > SEXING

SEXISM n discrimination on the basis of a person's gender

SEXISMS > SEXISM

SEXIST > SEXISM

SEXISTS > SEXISM

SEXLESS adj neither male nor female

SEXLESSLY > SEXLESS

SEXLINKED adj (of a gene) found on a sex chromosome

SEXOLOGIC > SEXOLOGY

SEXOLOGY n study of sexual behaviour in human beings

SEXPERT n person who professes a knowledge of sexual matters

SEXPERTS > SEXPERT

SEXPOT n person considered as sexually very attractive

SEXPOTS > SEXPOT

SEXT n sexually explicit text message ▷ vb send a sexually explicit text message

SEXTAIN same as > SESTINA

SEXTAINS > SEXTAIN

SEXTAN adj (of a fever) marked by paroxysms that recur after an interval of five days

SEXTANS n ancient Roman coin

SEXTANSES > SEXTANS

SEXTANT n navigator's instrument for measuring angles

SEXTANTAL > SEXTANT

SEXTANTS > SEXTANT

SEXTARII > SEXTARIUS

SEXTARIUS n ancient Roman quantity measure

SEXTED > SEXT

SEXTET n group of six performers

SEXTETS > SEXTET

SEXTETT n sextet

SEXTETTE same as > SEXTET

SEXTETTES > SEXTETTE

SEXTETTS > SEXTETT

SEXTILE n value of a variable dividing its distribution into six groups with equal frequencies

SEXTILES > SEXTILE

SEXTING n practice of sending sexually explicit text messages

SEXTINGS > SEXTING

SEXTO same as > SIXMO

SEXTOLET n group of six musical notes

SEXTOLETS > SEXTOLET

SEXTON n official in charge of a church and churchyard

SEXTONESS n female sexton

SEXTONS > SEXTON

SEXTOS > SEXTO

SEXTS > SEXT

SEXTUOR n sextet

SEXTUORS > SEXTUOR

SEXTUPLE vb multiply by six ▷ adj six times as much or as many ▷ n quantity or number six times as great as another

SEXTUPLED > SEXTUPLE

SEXTUPLES > SEXTUPLE

SEXTUPLET n one of six children born at one birth

SEXTUPLY > SEXTUPLE

SEXUAL adj of or characterized by sex

SEXUALISE same as > SEXUALIZE

SEXUALISM n emphasizing of sexuality

SEXUALIST > SEXUALISM

SEXUALITY n state of being sexual

SEXUALIZE vb make or become sexual

SEXUALLY > SEXUAL

SEXVALENT adj with valency of six

SEXY adj exciting or attractive

SEY n Scots word meaning part of a cow carcase

SEYEN n old form of scion

SEYENS > SEYEN

SEYS > SEY

SEYSURE n old form of seizure

SEYSURES > SEYSURE

SEZ vb informal spelling of 'says'

SFERICS same as > SPHERICS

SFORZANDI > SFORZANDO

SFORZANDO adv to be played with strong initial attack ▷ n symbol written above a note, indicating this

SFORZATI > SFORZATO

SFORZATO same as > SFORZANDO

SFORZATOS > SFORZATO

SFUMATO n gradual transition between areas of different colour in painting

SFUMATOS > SFUMATO

SGRAFFITI > SGRAFFITO

SGRAFFITO n technique in mural or ceramic decoration in which the top layer of glaze is incised with a design to reveal parts of the ground

SH interj hush

SHA interj be quiet

SHABASH interj (in Indian English) bravo or well done

SHABBATOT pl n Jewish sabbaths

SHABBIER > SHABBY

SHABBIEST > SHABBY

SHABBILY > SHABBY

SHABBLE n Scots word meaning old sword

SHABBLES > SHABBLE

SHABBY adj worn or dilapidated in appearance

SHABRACK n saddlecloth of a cavalry horse

SHABRACKS > SHABRACK

SHACK n rough hut ▷ vb evade (work or responsibility)

SHACKED > SHACK

SHACKIER > SHACKY

SHACKIEST > SHACKY

SHACKING > SHACK

SHACKLE n metal ring for securing a person's wrists or ankles ▷ vb fasten with shackles

SHACKLED > SHACKLE

SHACKLER > SHACKLE

SHACKLERS > SHACKLE

SHACKLES > SHACKLE

SHACKLING > SHACKLE

SHACKO same as > SHAKO

SHACKOES > SHACKO

SHACKOS > SHACKO

SHACKS > SHACK

SHACKTOWN n collection of huts or other temporary housing

SHACKY adj resembling a shack; dilapidated

SHAD n herring-like fish

SHADBERRY n edible purplish berry of the shadbush

SHADBLOW n type of shrub

SHADBLOWS > SHADBLOW

SHADBUSH n type of N American tree or shrub

SHADCHAN n Jewish marriage broker

SHADCHANS > SHADCHAN

SHADDOCK another name for > POMELO

SHADDOCKS > SHADDOCK

SHADDUP interj shut up

SHADE n relative darkness ▷ vb screen from light

SHADED > SHADE

SHADELESS > SHADE

SHADER > SHADE

SHADERS > SHADE

SHADES pl n gathering darkness at nightfall

SHADFLIES > SHADFLY

SHADFLY American name for > MAYFLY

SHADIER > SHADY

SHADIEST > SHADY

SHADILY > SHADY

SHADINESS > SHADY

SHADING n graded areas of tone indicating light and dark in a painting or drawing

SHADINGS > SHADING

SHADKHAN same as > SHADCHAN

SHADKHANS > SHADKHAN

SHADOOF n mechanism for raising water

SHADOOFS > SHADOOF

SHADOW n dark shape cast on a surface when something stands between a light and the surface ▷ vb cast a shadow over

SHADOWBOX vb practise boxing against an imaginary opponent

SHADOWED > SHADOW

SHADOWER > SHADOW

SHADOWERS > SHADOW

SHADOWIER > SHADOWY

SHADOWILY > SHADOWY

SHADOWING > SHADOW

SHADOWS > SHADOW

SHADOWY adj (of a place) full of shadows

SHADRACH n lump of iron that has not been melted in the furnace

SHADRACHS > SHADRACH

SHADS > SHAD

SHADUF same as > SHADOOF

SHADUFS > SHADUF

SHADY adj situated in or giving shade

SHAFT n long narrow straight handle of a tool or weapon ▷ vb treat badly

SHAFTED > SHAFT

SHAFTER > SHAFT

SHAFTERS > SHAFT

SHAFTING n assembly of rotating shafts for transmitting power

SHAFTINGS > SHAFTING

SHAFTLESS > SHAFT

SHAFTS > SHAFT

SHAG n cormorant ▷ adj (of a carpet) having a long pile ▷ vb make shaggy

SHAGBARK n North American hickory tree
SHAGBARKS > SHAGBARK
SHAGGABLE adj vulgar word meaning sexually attractive
SHAGGED adj shaggy
SHAGGER n vulgar word for a person who has sexual intercourse
SHAGGERS > SHAGGER
SHAGGIER > SHAGGY
SHAGGIEST > SHAGGY
SHAGGILY > SHAGGY
SHAGGING > SHAG
SHAGGY adj covered with rough hair or wool
SHAGPILE adj (of carpet) having long fibres
SHAGREEN n sharkskin
SHAGREENS > SHAGREEN
SHAGROON n nineteenth-century Australian settler in Canterbury
SHAGROONS > SHAGROON
SHAGS > SHAG
SHAH n formerly, ruler of Iran
SHAHADA n Islamic declaration of faith
SHAHADAH same as > SHAHADA
SHAHADAHS > SHAHADAH
SHAHADAS > SHAHADA
SHAHDOM > SHAH
SHAHDOMS > SHAH
SHAHEED same as > SHAHID
SHAHEEDS > SHAHEED
SHAHID n Muslim martyr
SHAHIDS > SHAHID
SHAHS > SHAH
SHAHTOOSH n soft wool that comes from the protected Tibetan antelope
SHAIKH n sheikh
SHAIKHS > SHAIKH
SHAIRD n Scots word meaning shred
SHAIRDS > SHAIRD
SHAIRN Scots word for > DUNG
SHAIRNS > SHAIRN
SHAITAN n (in Muslim countries) an evil spirit
SHAITANS > SHAITAN
SHAKABLE > SHAKE
SHAKE vb move quickly up and down or back and forth ▷ n act of shaking
SHAKEABLE > SHAKE
SHAKED vb old form of shook
SHAKEDOWN n act of extortion
SHAKEN > SHAKE
SHAKEOUT n process of reducing the number of people in a workforce
SHAKEOUTS > SHAKEOUT

SHAKER n container in which drinks are mixed or from which powder is shaken
SHAKERS > SHAKER
SHAKES > SHAKE
SHAKEUP n radical reorganization
SHAKEUPS > SHAKEUP
SHAKIER > SHAKY
SHAKIEST > SHAKY
SHAKILY > SHAKY
SHAKINESS > SHAKY
SHAKING > SHAKE
SHAKINGS > SHAKE
SHAKO n tall cylindrical peaked military hat with a plume
SHAKOES > SHAKO
SHAKOS > SHAKO
SHAKT vb old form of shook
SHAKUDO n Japanese alloy of copper and gold
SHAKUDOS > SHAKUDO
SHAKY adj unsteady
SHALE n flaky sedimentary rock
SHALED > SHALE
SHALELIKE > SHALE
SHALES > SHALE
SHALEY > SHALE
SHALIER > SHALE
SHALIEST > SHALE
SHALING > SHALE
SHALL vb used as an auxiliary to make the future tense
SHALLI n type of fabric
SHALLIS > SHALLI
SHALLON n American shrub
SHALLONS > SHALLON
SHALLOON n light twill-weave woollen fabric used chiefly for coat linings, etc
SHALLOONS > SHALLOON
SHALLOP n light boat used for rowing in shallow water
SHALLOPS > SHALLOP
SHALLOT n kind of small onion
SHALLOTS > SHALLOT
SHALLOW adj not deep ▷ n shallow place in a body of water ▷ vb make or become shallow
SHALLOWED > SHALLOW
SHALLOWER > SHALLOW
SHALLOWLY > SHALLOW
SHALLOWS > SHALLOW
SHALM n old woodwind instrument
SHALMS > SHALM
SHALOM n Jewish greeting meaning 'peace be with you'
SHALOMS > SHALOM
SHALOT n shallot
SHALOTS > SHALOT
SHALT singular form of the present tense (indicative mood) of > SHALL
SHALWAR n pair of loose-fitting trousers

narrowing around the ankles
SHALWARS > SHALWAR
SHALY > SHALE
SHAM n thing or person that is not genuine ▷ adj not genuine ▷ vb fake, feign
SHAMA n Indian songbird
SHAMABLE > SHAME
SHAMABLY > SHAME
SHAMAL n hot northwesterly wind
SHAMALS > SHAMAL
SHAMAN n priest of shamanism
SHAMANIC > SHAMAN
SHAMANISM n religion of northern Asia, based on a belief in good and evil spirits
SHAMANIST > SHAMANISM
SHAMANS > SHAMAN
SHAMAS > SHAMA
SHAMATEUR n sportsperson who is officially an amateur but accepts payment
SHAMBA n (in E Africa) any field used for growing crops
SHAMBAS > SHAMBA
SHAMBLE vb walk in a shuffling awkward way ▷ n awkward or shuffling walk
SHAMBLED > SHAMBLE
SHAMBLES n disorderly event or place
SHAMBLIER > SHAMBLE
SHAMBLING > SHAMBLE
SHAMBLY > SHAMBLE
SHAMBOLIC adj completely disorganized
SHAME n painful emotion caused by awareness of having done something foolish ▷ vb cause to feel shame
SHAMEABLE > SHAME
SHAMEABLY > SHAME
SHAMED > SHAME
SHAMEFAST adj old form of shamefaced
SHAMEFUL adj causing or deserving shame
SHAMELESS adj with no sense of shame
SHAMER n cause of shame
SHAMERS > SHAMER
SHAMES > SHAME
SHAMIANA n tent in India
SHAMIANAH n tent in India
SHAMIANAS > SHAMIANA
SHAMINA n wool blend of pashm and shahtoosh
SHAMINAS > SHAMINA
SHAMING n act or attempt to embarrass someone
SHAMINGS > SHAMING
SHAMISEN n Japanese stringed instrument
SHAMISENS > SHAMISEN

SHAMMAS same as > SHAMMES
SHAMMASH same as > SHAMMES
SHAMMASIM > SHAMMES
SHAMMED > SHAM
SHAMMER > SHAM
SHAMMERS > SHAM
SHAMMES n official acting as the beadle, sexton, and caretaker of a synagogue
SHAMMIED > SHAMMY
SHAMMIES > SHAMMY
SHAMMING > SHAM
SHAMMOS same as > SHAMMES
SHAMMOSIM > SHAMMES
SHAMMY n piece of chamois leather ▷ vb rub with a shammy
SHAMMYING > SHAMMY
SHAMOIS n chamois ▷ vb clean with shamois
SHAMOISED > SHAMOIS
SHAMOISES > SHAMOIS
SHAMOS same as > SHAMMES
SHAMOSIM > SHAMMES
SHAMOY n chamois ▷ vb rub with a shamoy
SHAMOYED > SHAMOY
SHAMOYING > SHAMOY
SHAMOYS > SHAMOY
SHAMPOO n liquid soap for washing hair, carpets, or upholstery ▷ vb wash with shampoo
SHAMPOOED > SHAMPOO
SHAMPOOER > SHAMPOO
SHAMPOOS > SHAMPOO
SHAMROCK n clover leaf, esp as the Irish emblem
SHAMROCKS > SHAMROCK
SHAMS > SHAM
SHAMUS n police or private detective
SHAMUSES > SHAMUS
SHAN variant of > SHAND
SHANACHIE n Gaelic storyteller
SHAND n old word meaning fake coin
SHANDIES > SHANDY
SHANDRIES > SHANDRY
SHANDRY n light horse-drawn cart
SHANDS > SHAND
SHANDY n drink made of beer and lemonade
SHANGHAI vb force or trick (someone) into doing something ▷ n catapult
SHANGHAIS > SHANGHAI
SHANK n lower leg ▷ vb (of fruits, roots, etc) to show disease symptoms
SHANKBONE n bone in lower leg
SHANKED > SHANK
SHANKING > SHANK
SHANKS > SHANK
SHANNIES > SHANNY
SHANNY n European blenny of rocky coastal waters
SHANS > SHAN

SHANTEY same as
> SHANTY
SHANTEYS > SHANTEY
SHANTI n peace
SHANTIES > SHANTY
SHANTIH same as
> SHANTI
SHANTIHS > SHANTIH
SHANTIS > SHANTI
SHANTUNG n soft Chinese silk with a knobbly surface
SHANTUNGS > SHANTUNG
SHANTY n shack or crude dwelling
SHANTYMAN n man living in a shanty
SHANTYMEN
> SHANTYMAN
SHAPABLE > SHAPE
SHAPE n outward form of an object ▷ vb form or mould
SHAPEABLE > SHAPE
SHAPED > SHAPE
SHAPELESS adj (of a person or object) lacking a pleasing shape
SHAPELIER > SHAPELY
SHAPELY adj having an attractive shape
SHAPEN vb shape
SHAPENED > SHAPEN
SHAPENING > SHAPEN
SHAPENS > SHAPEN
SHAPER > SHAPE
SHAPERS > SHAPE
SHAPES > SHAPE
SHAPEUP n system of hiring dockers for a day's work
SHAPEUPS > SHAPEUP
SHAPEWEAR n underwear that shapes body
SHAPING > SHAPE
SHAPINGS > SHAPE
SHAPS n leather over-trousers worn by cowboys
SHARABLE > SHARE
SHARD n broken piece of pottery or glass
SHARDED adj old word meaning hidden under dung
SHARDS > SHARD
SHARE n part of something that belongs to or is contributed by a person ▷ vb give or take a share of (something)
SHAREABLE adj that can be shared
SHARECROP vb cultivate (farmland) as a sharecropper
SHARED > SHARE
SHAREMAN n member of fishing-boat crew who shares profits
SHAREMEN > SHAREMAN
SHARER > SHARE
SHARERS > SHARE
SHARES > SHARE
SHARESMAN n member of fishing-boat crew who shares profits
SHARESMEN
> SHARESMAN

SHAREWARE n software available to all users without the need for a licence
SHARIA n body of doctrines that regulate the lives of Muslims
SHARIAH same as
> SHARIA
SHARIAHS > SHARIAH
SHARIAS > SHARIA
SHARIAT n Islamic religious law
SHARIATS > SHARIAT
SHARIF same as
> SHERIF
SHARIFIAN > SHARIF
SHARIFS > SHARIF
SHARING > SHARE
SHARINGS > SHARE
SHARK n large usu predatory sea fish ▷ vb obtain (something) by cheating or deception
SHARKED > SHARK
SHARKER n shark hunter
SHARKERS > SHARKER
SHARKING > SHARK
SHARKINGS > SHARK
SHARKISH adj resembling or behaving like a shark
SHARKLIKE > SHARK
SHARKS > SHARK
SHARKSKIN n stiff glossy fabric
SHARN Scots word for
> DUNG
SHARNIER > SHARNY
SHARNIES > SHARNY
SHARNIEST > SHARN
SHARNS > SHARN
SHARNY n (Scot) person who cleans a cow-house ▷ adj (Scot) covered in dung
SHARON n as in sharon fruit persimmon
SHARP adj having a keen cutting edge or fine point ▷ adv promptly ▷ n symbol raising a note one semitone above natural pitch ▷ vb make sharp
SHARPED > SHARP
SHARPEN vb make or become sharp or sharper
SHARPENED > SHARPEN
SHARPENER > SHARPEN
SHARPENS > SHARPEN
SHARPER n person who cheats
SHARPERS > SHARPER
SHARPEST > SHARP
SHARPIE n member of a teenage group having short hair and distinctive clothes
SHARPIES > SHARPIE
SHARPING > SHARP
SHARPINGS > SHARP
SHARPISH adj fairly sharp ▷ adv promptly
SHARPLY > SHARP
SHARPNESS > SHARP
SHARPS > SHARP
SHARPTAIL n type of grouse

SHARPY n swindler
SHASH vb old form of sash
SHASHED > SHASH
SHASHES > SHASH
SHASHING > SHASH
SHASHLICK same as
> SHASHLIK
SHASHLIK n type of kebab
SHASHLIKS
> SHASHLIK
SHASLIK n type of kebab
SHASLIKS > SHASLIK
SHASTA n plant of the daisy family
SHASTAS > SHASTA
SHASTER same as
> SHASTRA
SHASTERS > SHASTER
SHASTRA n any of the sacred writings of Hinduism
SHASTRAS > SHASTRA
SHAT past tense and past participle of > SHIT
SHATOOSH same as
> SHAHTOOSH
SHATTER vb break into pieces ▷ n fragment
SHATTERED adj completely exhausted
SHATTERER > SHATTER
SHATTERS > SHATTER
SHATTERY adj liable to shatter
SHAUCHLE vb Scots word meaning shuffle
SHAUCHLED
> SHAUCHLE
SHAUCHLES
> SHAUCHLE
SHAUCHLY > SHAUCHLE
SHAUGH n old word meaning small wood
SHAUGHS > SHAUGH
SHAUL vb old form of shawl
SHAULED > SHAUL
SHAULING > SHAUL
SHAULS > SHAUL
SHAVABLE > SHAVE
SHAVASANA n type of yoga posture
SHAVE vb remove (hair) from (the face, head, or body) with a razor or shaver ▷ n act of shaving
SHAVEABLE > SHAVE
SHAVED > SHAVE
SHAVELING n archaic term for a young fellow
SHAVEN adj closely shaved or tonsured
SHAVER n electric razor
SHAVERS > SHAVER
SHAVES > SHAVE
SHAVETAIL n American slang for second lieutenant
SHAVIE n Scots word meaning trick
SHAVIES > SHAVIE
SHAVING > SHAVE
SHAVINGS > SHAVE
SHAW n small wood ▷ vb show
SHAWARMA n strips of lamb, usu served in a pitta

SHAWARMAS
> SHAWARMA
SHAWED > SHAW
SHAWING > SHAW
SHAWL n piece of cloth worn over a woman's shoulders or wrapped around a baby ▷ vb cover with a shawl
SHAWLED > SHAWL
SHAWLEY same as
> SHAWLIE
SHAWLEYS > SHAWLEY
SHAWLIE n insulting term for a working-class woman who wears a shawl
SHAWLIES > SHAWLIE
SHAWLING > SHAWL
SHAWLINGS > SHAWL
SHAWLLESS > SHAWL
SHAWLS > SHAWL
SHAWM n medieval form of the oboe with a conical bore and flaring bell
SHAWMS > SHAWM
SHAWN variant of > SHAWM
SHAWS > SHAW
SHAY dialect word for
> CHAISE
SHAYA n Indian plant
SHAYAS > SHAYA
SHAYKH same as
> SHEIKH
SHAYKHS > SHAYKH
SHAYS > SHAY
SHAZAM interj magic slogan
SHCHI n Russian cabbage soup
SHCHIS > SHCHI
SHE pron female person or animal previously mentioned ▷ n female person or animal
SHEA n tropical African tree
SHEADING n any of the six subdivisions of the Isle of Man
SHEADINGS
> SHEADING
SHEAF n bundle of papers ▷ vb tie into a sheaf
SHEAFED > SHEAF
SHEAFIER > SHEAF
SHEAFIEST > SHEAF
SHEAFING > SHEAF
SHEAFLIKE > SHEAF
SHEAFS > SHEAF
SHEAFY > SHEAF
SHEAL vb old word meaning shell
SHEALED > SHEAL
SHEALING > SHEAL
SHEALINGS > SHEAL
SHEALS > SHEAL
SHEAR vb clip hair or wool from ▷ n breakage caused through strain or twisting
SHEARED > SHEAR
SHEARER > SHEAR
SHEARERS > SHEAR
SHEARING > SHEAR
SHEARINGS > SHEAR
SHEARLEG n one spar of shearlegs

SHEARLEGS same as
> SHEERLEGS
SHEARLING n young
sheep after its first
shearing
SHEARMAN n person who
trims cloth
SHEARMEN > SHEARMAN
SHEARS > SHEAR
SHEAS > SHEA
SHEATFISH n European
catfish
SHEATH n close-fitting
cover, esp for a knife or
sword
SHEATHE vb put into a
sheath
SHEATHED > SHEATHE
SHEATHER > SHEATHE
SHEATHERS > SHEATHE
SHEATHES > SHEATHE
SHEATHIER > SHEATHE
SHEATHING n any
material used as an outer
layer
SHEATHS > SHEATH
SHEATHY > SHEATHE
SHEAVE vb gather or bind
into sheaves ▷ n wheel
with a grooved rim
SHEAVED > SHEAVE
SHEAVES > SHEAF
SHEAVING > SHEAVE
SHEBANG n situation,
matter, or affair
SHEBANGS > SHEBANG
SHEBEAN same as
> SHEBEEN
SHEBEANS > SHEBEAN
SHEBEEN n place where
alcohol is sold illegally
▷ vb run a shebeen
SHEBEENED > SHEBEEN
SHEBEENER > SHEBEEN
SHEBEENS > SHEBEEN
SHECHITA n Jewish
method of killing animals
for food
SHECHITAH same as
> SHECHITA
SHECHITAS
> SHECHITA
SHED n building used for
storage or shelter or as a
workshop ▷ vb get rid of
SHEDABLE > SHED
SHEDDABLE > SHED
SHEDDED > SHED
SHEDDER n person or
thing that sheds
SHEDDERS > SHEDDER
SHEDDING > SHED
SHEDDINGS > SHED
SHEDFUL n quantity or
amount contained in a
shed
SHEDFULS > SHEDFUL
SHEDHAND n labourer
working in a shearing
shed
SHEDHANDS
> SHEDHAND
SHEDLIKE > SHED
SHEDLOAD n very large
amount or number
SHEDLOADS
> SHEDLOAD
SHEDS > SHED

SHEEL vb old word
meaning shell
SHEELED > SHEEL
SHEELING > SHEEL
SHEELS > SHEEL
SHEEN n glistening
brightness on the surface
of something ▷ adj
shining and beautiful ▷ vb
give a sheen to
SHEENED > SHEEN
SHEENFUL > SHEEN
SHEENIER > SHEEN
SHEENIEST > SHEEN
SHEENING > SHEEN
SHEENS > SHEEN
SHEENY > SHEEN
SHEEP n ruminant animal
bred for wool and meat
SHEEPCOT n sheepcote
SHEEPCOTE another word
for > SHEEPFOLD
SHEEPCOTS
> SHEEPCOT
SHEEPDOG n dog used for
herding sheep
SHEEPDOGS
> SHEEPDOG
SHEEPFOLD n pen or
enclosure for sheep
SHEEPHEAD n species of
fish
SHEEPIER > SHEEP
SHEEPIEST > SHEEP
SHEEPISH adj
embarrassed because of
feeling foolish
SHEEPLE n group of
people who follow the
majority in matters of
opinion, taste, etc
SHEEPLES > SHEEPLE
SHEEPLIKE > SHEEP
SHEEPMAN n person who
keeps sheep
SHEEPMEN > SHEEPMAN
SHEEPO n person
employed to bring sheep
to the catching pen in a
shearing shed
SHEEPOS > SHEEPO
SHEEPSKIN n skin of a
sheep with the fleece still
on, used for clothing or
rugs
SHEEPWALK n tract of
land for grazing sheep
SHEEPY > SHEEP
SHEER adj absolute,
complete ▷ adv steeply
▷ vb change course
suddenly ▷ n any
transparent fabric used for
making garments
SHEERED > SHEER
SHEERER > SHEER
SHEEREST > SHEER
SHEERING > SHEER
SHEERLEG n one spar of
sheerlegs
SHEERLEGS n device for
lifting heavy weights
SHEERLY > SHEER
SHEERNESS > SHEER
SHEERS > SHEER
SHEESH interj
exclamation of surprise or
annoyance

SHEESHA n water-pipe
for smoking tobacco
SHEESHAS > SHEESHA
SHEET n large piece of
cloth used as an inner bed
cover ▷ vb provide with,
cover, or wrap in a sheet
SHEETED > SHEET
SHEETER > SHEET
SHEETERS > SHEET
SHEETFED adj printing
on separate sheets of
paper
SHEETIER > SHEET
SHEETIEST > SHEET
SHEETING n material
from which sheets are
made
SHEETINGS
> SHEETING
SHEETLESS > SHEET
SHEETLIKE > SHEET
SHEETROCK n brand
name for plasterboard
SHEETS > SHEET
SHEETY > SHEET
SHEEVE n part of mine
winding gear
SHEEVES > SHEEVE
SHEHITA n slaughter of
animals according to
Jewish religious law
SHEHITAH same as
> SHEHITA
SHEHITAHS
> SHEHITAH
SHEHITAS > SHEHITA
SHEHNAI n Indian wind
instrument
SHEHNAIS > SHEHNAI
SHEIK same as > SHEIKH
SHEIKDOM same as
> SHEIKHDOM
SHEIKDOMS
> SHEIKDOM
SHEIKH n Arab chief
SHEIKHA n chief wife of a
sheikh
SHEIKHAS > SHEIKHA
SHEIKHDOM n territory
ruled by a sheikh
SHEIKHS > SHEIKH
SHEIKS > SHEIK
SHEILA n girl or woman
SHEILAS > SHEILA
SHEILING n hut used by
shepherds
SHEILINGS
> SHEILING
SHEITAN n Muslim
demon
SHEITANS > SHEITAN
SHEITEL n traditional
wig worn by Orthodox
Jewish women
SHEITELS > SHEITEL
SHEKALIM > SHEKEL
SHEKEL n monetary unit
of Israel
SHEKELIM > SHEKEL
SHEKELS > SHEKEL
SHELDDUCK n species of
large duck
SHELDRAKE same as
> SHELDUCK
SHELDUCK n large
brightly coloured wild
duck of Europe and Asia

SHELDUCKS
> SHELDUCK
SHELF n board fixed
horizontally for holding
things ▷ vb put on a shelf
SHELFED > SHELF
SHELFFUL > SHELF
SHELFFULS > SHELF
SHELFIER > SHELF
SHELFIEST > SHELF
SHELFING > SHELF
SHELFLIKE > SHELF
SHELFROOM n space on
shelf
SHELFS > SHELF
SHELFY > SHELF
SHELL n hard outer
covering of an egg, nut, or
certain animals ▷ vb take
the shell from
SHELLAC n resin used in
varnishes ▷ vb coat with
shellac
SHELLACK vb shellac
SHELLACKS > SHELLAC
SHELLACS > SHELLAC
SHELLBACK n sailor who
has crossed the equator
SHELLBARK same as
> SHAGBARK
SHELLDUCK n shelduck
SHELLED > SHELL
SHELLER > SHELL
SHELLERS > SHELL
SHELLFIRE n firing of
artillery shells
SHELLFISH n sea-living
animal, esp one that can
be eaten, with a shell
SHELLFUL > SHELL
SHELLFULS > SHELL
SHELLIER > SHELL
SHELLIEST > SHELL
SHELLING > SHELL
SHELLINGS > SHELL
SHELLS > SHELL
SHELLWORK n decoration
with shells
SHELLY > SHELL
SHELTA n secret
language used by some
travelling people in Britain
and Ireland
SHELTAS > SHELTA
SHELTER n structure
providing protection from
danger or the weather
▷ vb give shelter to
SHELTERED adj
protected from wind and
rain
SHELTERER > SHELTER
SHELTERS > SHELTER
SHELTERY adj giving
shelter
SHELTIE n small dog
similar to a collie
SHELTIES > SHELTY
SHELTY same as
> SHELTIE
SHELVE vb put aside or
postpone
SHELVED > SHELVE
SHELVER > SHELVE
SHELVERS > SHELVE
SHELVES > SHELF
SHELVIER > SHELVY
SHELVIEST > SHELVY

S

SHELVING n (material for) shelves
SHELVINGS > SHELVING
SHELVY adj having shelves
SHEMOZZLE n noisy confusion or dispute
SHEN n (in Chinese thought) spiritual element of the psyche
SHENAI same as > SHEHNAI
SHENAIS > SHENAI
SHEND vb put to shame
SHENDING > SHEND
SHENDS > SHEND
SHENT > SHEND
SHEOL n hell
SHEOLS > SHEOL
SHEPHERD n person who tends sheep ▷ vb guide or watch over (people)
SHEPHERDS > SHEPHERD
SHEQALIM n plural of sheqel
SHEQEL same as > SHEKEL
SHEQELS > SHEQEL
SHERANG n person in charge
SHERANGS > SHERANG
SHERBERT same as > SHERBET
SHERBERTS > SHERBET
SHERBET n fruit-flavoured fizzy powder
SHERBETS > SHERBET
SHERD same as > SHARD
SHERDS > SHERD
SHERE old spelling of > SHEER
SHEREEF same as > SHERIF
SHEREEFS > SHEREEF
SHERIA same as > SHARIA
SHERIAS > SHERIA
SHERIAT n Muslim religious law
SHERIATS > SHERIAT
SHERIF n descendant of Muhammad through his daughter Fatima
SHERIFF n (in the US) chief law enforcement officer of a county
SHERIFFS > SHERIFF
SHERIFIAN > SHERIF
SHERIFS > SHERIF
SHERLOCK n detective ▷ vb investigate (something)
SHERLOCKS > SHERLOCK
SHERO n woman considered a hero
SHEROES > SHERO
SHEROOT n cheroot
SHEROOTS > SHEROOT
SHERPA n official who assists at a summit meeting
SHERPAS > SHERPA
SHERRIED adj flavoured with sherry
SHERRIES > SHERRY

SHERRIS n old form of sherry
SHERRISES > SHERRIS
SHERRY n pale or dark brown fortified wine
SHERWANI n long coat closed up to the neck, worn by men in India
SHERWANIS > SHERWANI
SHES > SHE
SHET vb old form of shut
SHETLAND n type of wool spun in the Shetland islands
SHETLANDS > SHETLAND
SHETS > SHET
SHETTING > SHET
SHEUCH n ditch or trough ▷ vb dig
SHEUCHED > SHEUCH
SHEUCHING > SHEUCH
SHEUCHS > SHEUCH
SHEUGH same as > SHEUCH
SHEUGHED > SHEUGH
SHEUGHING > SHEUGH
SHEUGHS > SHEUGH
SHEVA n mark in Hebrew writing
SHEVAS > SHEVA
SHEW archaic spelling of > SHOW
SHEWBREAD n loaves of bread placed every Sabbath on the table beside the altar of incense in the tabernacle of ancient Israel
SHEWED > SHEW
SHEWEL n old word meaning scarecrow
SHEWELS > SHEWEL
SHEWER > SHEW
SHEWERS > SHEW
SHEWING > SHEW
SHEWN > SHEW
SHEWS > SHEW
SHH interj sound made to ask for silence
SHHH interj used to request quietness
SHIAI n judo contest
SHIAIS > SHIAI
SHIATSU n type of massage
SHIATSUS > SHIATSU
SHIATZU n shiatsu
SHIATZUS > SHIATZU
SHIBAH n Jewish period of mourning
SHIBAHS > SHIBAH
SHIBUICHI n Japanese alloy of copper and silver
SHICKER n alcoholic drink
SHICKERED adj drunk
SHICKERS > SHICKER
SHIDDER n old word meaning a female animal
SHIDDERS > SHIDDER
SHIDDUCH n arranged marriage
SHIED > SHY
SHIEL vb sheal
SHIELD n piece of armour carried on the arm to

protect the body from blows or missiles ▷ vb protect
SHIELDED > SHIELD
SHIELDER > SHIELD
SHIELDERS > SHIELD
SHIELDING > SHIELD
SHIELDS > SHIELD
SHIELED > SHIEL
SHIELING n rough hut or shelter used by people keeping cattle on high or remote ground
SHIELINGS > SHIELING
SHIELS > SHIEL
SHIER n horse that shies habitually
SHIERS > SHIER
SHIES > SHY
SHIEST > SHY
SHIFT vb move ▷ n shifting
SHIFTABLE > SHIFT
SHIFTED > SHIFT
SHIFTER > SHIFT
SHIFTERS > SHIFT
SHIFTIER > SHIFTY
SHIFTIEST > SHIFTY
SHIFTILY > SHIFTY
SHIFTING > SHIFT
SHIFTINGS > SHIFT
SHIFTLESS adj lacking in ambition or initiative
SHIFTS > SHIFT
SHIFTWORK n system of employment where an individual's normal hours of work are outside the period of normal day working
SHIFTY adj evasive or untrustworthy
SHIGELLA n type of rod-shaped Gram-negative bacterium
SHIGELLAE > SHIGELLA
SHIGELLAS > SHIGELLA
SHIITAKE n kind of mushroom widely used in East Asian cookery
SHIITAKES > SHIITAKE
SHIKAR n hunting, esp big-game hunting ▷ vb hunt (game, esp big game)
SHIKARA n (in Kashmir) light, flat-bottomed boat
SHIKARAS > SHIKARA
SHIKAREE same as > SHIKARI
SHIKAREES > SHIKAREE
SHIKARI n (in India) a hunter
SHIKARIS > SHIKARI
SHIKARRED > SHIKAR
SHIKARS > SHIKAR
SHIKKER n Yiddish term for drunk person
SHIKKERED same as > SHICKERED
SHIKKERS > SHIKKER
SHIKRA n small Asian sparrowhawk
SHIKRAS > SHIKRA

SHILINGI n money unit in Tanzania
SHILINGIS > SHILINGI
SHILL n confidence trickster's assistant ▷ vb act as a shill
SHILLABER n keen customer
SHILLALA n short Irish club or cudgel
SHILLALAH same as > SHILLALA
SHILLALAS > SHILLALA
SHILLED > SHILL
SHILLELAH same as > SHILLALA
SHILLING n former British coin
SHILLINGS > SHILLING
SHILLS > SHILL
SHILPIT adj puny
SHILY > SHY
SHIM n thin strip of material placed between two close surfaces to fill a gap ▷ vb fit or fill up with a shim
SHIMAAL n hot Middle Eastern wind
SHIMAALS > SHIMAAL
SHIMMED > SHIM
SHIMMER n faint unsteady light ▷ vb shine with a faint unsteady light
SHIMMERED > SHIMMER
SHIMMERS > SHIMMER
SHIMMERY adj shining with a glistening or tremulous light
SHIMMEY n chemise
SHIMMEYS > SHIMMEY
SHIMMIED > SHIMMY
SHIMMIES > SHIMMY
SHIMMING > SHIM
SHIMMY n American ragtime dance ▷ vb dance the shimmy
SHIMMYING > SHIMMY
SHIMOZZLE n predicament
SHIMS > SHIM
SHIN n front of the lower leg ▷ vb climb by using the hands or arms and legs
SHINBONE n tibia
SHINBONES > SHINBONE
SHINDIES > SHINDY
SHINDIG n noisy party
SHINDIGS > SHINDIG
SHINDY n quarrel or commotion
SHINDYS > SHINDY
SHINE vb give out or reflect light; cause to gleam ▷ n brightness or lustre
SHINED > SHINE
SHINELESS > SHINE
SHINER n black eye
SHINERS > SHINER
SHINES > SHINE
SHINESS > SHY
SHINESSES > SHY

SHINGLE *n* wooden roof tile ▷ *vb* cover (a roof) with shingles
SHINGLED > SHINGLE
SHINGLER > SHINGLE
SHINGLERS > SHINGLE
SHINGLES *n* disease causing a rash of small blisters along a nerve
SHINGLIER > SHINGLE
SHINGLING > SHINGLE
SHINGLY > SHINGLE
SHINGUARD *n* rigid piece of plastic to protect footballer's shin
SHINIER > SHINY
SHINIES > SHINY
SHINIEST > SHINY
SHINILY > SHINY
SHININESS > SHINY
SHINING > SHINE
SHININGLY > SHINE
SHINJU *n* (formerly, in Japan) a ritual double suicide of lovers
SHINJUS > SHINJU
SHINKIN *n* worthless person
SHINKINS > SHINKIN
SHINLEAF *n* wintergreen
SHINLEAFS > SHINLEAF
SHINNE *n* old form of chin
SHINNED > SHIN
SHINNERY *n* American oak tree
SHINNES > SHINNE
SHINNEY *vb* climb with hands and legs
SHINNEYED > SHINNEY
SHINNEYS > SHINNEY
SHINNIED > SHINNY
SHINNIES > SHINNY
SHINNING > SHIN
SHINNY *same as* > SHINTY
SHINNYING > SHINNY
SHINOLA *n* tradename of a kind of boot polish
SHINOLAS > SHINOLA
SHINS > SHIN
SHINTIED > SHINTY
SHINTIES > SHINTY
SHINTY *n* game like hockey ▷ *vb* play shinty
SHINTYING > SHINTY
SHINY *adj* bright and polished
SHIP *n* large seagoing vessel ▷ *vb* send or transport by carrier, esp a ship
SHIPBOARD *adj* taking place or used aboard a ship
SHIPBORNE *adj* carried on ship
SHIPFUL *n* amount carried by ship
SHIPFULS > SHIPFUL
SHIPLAP *n* method of constructing ship hull
SHIPLAPS > SHIPLAP
SHIPLESS > SHIP
SHIPLOAD *n* quantity carried by a ship
SHIPLOADS > SHIPLOAD

SHIPMAN *n* master or captain of a ship
SHIPMATE *n* sailor serving on the same ship as another
SHIPMATES > SHIPMATE
SHIPMEN > SHIPMAN
SHIPMENT *n* act of shipping cargo
SHIPMENTS > SHIPMENT
SHIPOWNER *n* person who owns or has shares in a ship or ships
SHIPPABLE > SHIP
SHIPPED > SHIP
SHIPPEN *n* dialect word for cattle shed
SHIPPENS > SHIPPEN
SHIPPER *n* person or company that ships
SHIPPERS > SHIPPER
SHIPPIE *n* prostitute who solicits at a port
SHIPPIES > SHIPPIE
SHIPPING > SHIP
SHIPPINGS > SHIP
SHIPPO *n* Japanese enamel work
SHIPPON *n* dialect word for cattle shed
SHIPPONS > SHIPPON
SHIPPOS > SHIPPO
SHIPPOUND *n* Baltic weight measure
SHIPS > SHIP
SHIPSHAPE *adj* orderly or neat ▷ *adv* in a neat and orderly manner
SHIPSIDE *n* part of wharf next to ship
SHIPSIDES > SHIPSIDE
SHIPTIME *n* arrival time of a supply ship
SHIPTIMES > SHIPTIME
SHIPWAY *n* structure on which a vessel is built, then launched
SHIPWAYS > SHIPWAY
SHIPWORM *n* type of wormlike marine bivalve mollusc
SHIPWORMS > SHIPWORM
SHIPWRECK *n* destruction of a ship through storm or collision ▷ *vb* cause to undergo shipwreck
SHIPYARD *n* place where ships are built
SHIPYARDS > SHIPYARD
SHIR *n* gathering in material
SHIRALEE *n* swag
SHIRALEES > SHIRALEE
SHIRAZ *n* variety of black grape used for wine
SHIRAZES > SHIRAZ
SHIRE *n* county ▷ *vb* refresh or rest
SHIRED > SHIRE
SHIREMAN *n* sheriff

SHIREMEN > SHIREMAN
SHIRES > SHIRE
SHIRETOWN *n* chief town of a shire
SHIRING > SHIRE
SHIRK *vb* avoid (duty or work) ▷ *n* person who shirks
SHIRKED > SHIRK
SHIRKER > SHIRK
SHIRKERS > SHIRK
SHIRKING > SHIRK
SHIRKS > SHIRK
SHIRR *vb* gather (fabric) into parallel rows to decorate a dress, etc ▷ *n* series of gathered rows decorating a dress, etc
SHIRRA *old Scots word for* > SHERIFF
SHIRRALEE *n* swagman's bundle of possessions
SHIRRAS > SHIRRA
SHIRRED > SHIRR
SHIRRING > SHIRR
SHIRRINGS > SHIRR
SHIRRS > SHIRR
SHIRS > SHIR
SHIRT *n* garment for the upper part of the body ▷ *vb* put a shirt on
SHIRTBAND *n* neckband on shirt
SHIRTED > SHIRT
SHIRTIER > SHIRTY
SHIRTIEST > SHIRTY
SHIRTILY > SHIRTY
SHIRTING *n* fabric used in making men's shirts
SHIRTINGS > SHIRTING
SHIRTLESS > SHIRT
SHIRTLIKE *adj* like a shirt
SHIRTS > SHIRT
SHIRTTAIL *n* part of a shirt that extends below the waist
SHIRTY *adj* bad-tempered or annoyed
SHISH *adj* as in *shish kebab* dish of meat and vegetables grilled on skewers
SHISHA *n* water-pipe for smoking tobacco
SHISHAS > SHISHA
SHISO *n* Asian plant with aromatic leaves
SHISOS > SHISO
SHIST *n* schist
SHISTS > SHIST
SHIT *vb* vulgar word for defecate ▷ *n* excrement
SHITAKE *same as* > SHIITAKE
SHITAKES > SHITAKE
SHITBAG *n* vulgar word for a contemptible person
SHITBAGS > SHITBAG
SHITCAN *vb* vulgar word meaning discard
SHITCANS > SHITCAN
SHITE *same as* > SHIT
SHITED > SHITE
SHITES > SHITE

SHITFACE *n* vulgar word for a despicable person
SHITFACED *adj* vulgar word for drunk
SHITFACES > SHITFACE
SHITHEAD *n* vulgar word for a fool
SHITHEADS > SHITHEAD
SHITHEEL *n* vulgar word for a contemptible person
SHITHEELS > SHITHEEL
SHITHOLE *n* vulgar word for a dirty place
SHITHOLES > SHITHOLE
SHITHOUSE *n* vulgar word for a lavatory
SHITING > SHITE
SHITLESS *adj* vulgar word for very frightened
SHITLIST *n* vulgar word for a list of hated things
SHITLISTS > SHITLIST
SHITLOAD *n* vulgar word for a lot
SHITLOADS > SHITLOAD
SHITS > SHIT
SHITSTORM *n* vulgar word for a very difficult situation
SHITTAH *n* tree mentioned in the Old Testament
SHITTAHS > SHITTAH
SHITTED > SHIT
SHITTER *n* vulgar word for a toilet
SHITTERS > SHITTER
SHITTIER > SHIT
SHITTIEST > SHIT
SHITTILY > SHIT
SHITTIM > SHITTAH
SHITTIMS > SHITTAH
SHITTING > SHIT
SHITTY > SHIT
SHITWORK *n* vulgar word for work considered to be menial
SHITWORKS > SHITWORK
SHITZU *n* breed of small dog with long, silky fur
SHITZUS > SHITZU
SHIUR *n* lesson in which a passage of the Talmud is studied
SHIURIM > SHIUR
SHIV *variant spelling of* > CHIV
SHIVA *variant of* > SHIVAH
SHIVAH *n* Jewish period of formal mourning
SHIVAHS > SHIVAH
SHIVAREE *n* discordant mock serenade to newlyweds, made with pans, kettles, etc
SHIVAREED > SHIVAREE
SHIVAREES > SHIVAREE
SHIVAS > SHIVA

S

SHIVE n flat cork or bung for wide-mouthed bottles

SHIVER vb tremble, as from cold or fear ▷ n shivering

SHIVERED > SHIVER

SHIVERER > SHIVER

SHIVERERS > SHIVER

SHIVERIER > SHIVERY

SHIVERING > SHIVER

SHIVERS > SHIVER

SHIVERY adj inclined to shiver or tremble

SHIVES > SHIVE

SHIVITI n Jewish decorative plaque with religious message

SHIVITIS > SHIVITI

SHIVOO n Australian word meaning rowdy party

SHIVOOS > SHIVOO

SHIVS > SHIV

SHIVVED > SHIV

SHIVVING > SHIV

SHIZZLE n form of US rap slang

SHIZZLES > SHIZZLE

SHLEMIEHL Yiddish word for > FOOL

SHLEMIEL same as > SCHLEMIEL

SHLEMIELS > SHLEMIEL

SHLEP vb schlep

SHLEPP vb schlep

SHLEPPED > SHLEP

SHLEPPER > SHLEP

SHLEPPERS > SHLEP

SHLEPPIER > SHLEPPY

SHLEPPING > SHLEP

SHLEPPS > SHLEPP

SHLEPPY adj dingy, shabby, or rundown

SHLEPS > SHLEP

SHLIMAZEL n unlucky person

SHLOCK n something of poor quality

SHLOCKIER > SHLOCK

SHLOCKS > SHLOCK

SHLOCKY > SHLOCK

SHLONG same as > SCHLONG

SHLONGS > SHLONG

SHLOSHIM n period of thirty days' deep mourning following a death

SHLOSHIMS > SHLOSHIM

SHLUB same as > SCHLUB

SHLUBS > SHLUB

SHLUMP vb move in lazy way

SHLUMPED > SHLUMP

SHLUMPIER > SHLUMPY

SHLUMPING > SHLUMP

SHLUMPS > SHLUMP

SHLUMPY > SHLUMP

SHMALTZ n schmaltz

SHMALTZES > SHMALTZ

SHMALTZY > SHMALTZ

SHMATTE n rag

SHMATTES > SHMATTE

SHMEAR same as > SCHMEAR

SHMEARED > SHMEAR

SHMEARING > SHMEAR

SHMEARS > SHMEAR

SHMEER same as > SCHMEAR

SHMEERED > SHMEER

SHMEERING > SHMEER

SHMEERS > SHMEER

SHMEK n smell

SHMEKS > SHMEK

SHMO same as > SCHMO

SHMOCK n despicable person

SHMOCKS > SHMOCK

SHMOE same as > SCHMOE

SHMOES > SHMO

SHMOOSE variant of > SCHMOOZE

SHMOOSED > SHMOOSE

SHMOOSES > SHMOOSE

SHMOOSING > SHMOOSE

SHMOOZE variant of > SCHMOOZE

SHMOOZED > SHMOOZE

SHMOOZER same as > SCHMOOZER

SHMOOZERS > SHMOOZER

SHMOOZES > SHMOOZE

SHMOOZIER > SHMOOZY

SHMOOZING > SHMOOZE

SHMOOZY adj talking casually, gossipy

SHMUCK n despicable person

SHMUCKIER > SHMUCKY

SHMUCKS > SHMUCK

SHMUCKY same as > SCHMUCKY

SHNAPPS same as > SCHNAPPS

SHNAPS n schnaps

SHNOOK n stupid person

SHNOOKS > SHNOOK

SHNORRER same as > SCHNORRER

SHNORRERS > SCHNORRER

SHO adj sure, as pronounced in southern US

SHOAL n large number of fish swimming together ▷ vb make or become shallow ▷ adj (of the draught of a vessel) drawing little water

SHOALED > SHOAL

SHOALER > SHOAL

SHOALEST > SHOAL

SHOALIER > SHOALY

SHOALIEST > SHOALY

SHOALING > SHOAL

SHOALINGS > SHOAL

SHOALNESS > SHOAL

SHOALS > SHOAL

SHOALWISE adv in a large group or in large groups

SHOALY adj shallow

SHOAT n piglet that has recently been weaned

SHOATS > SHOAT

SHOCHET n (in Judaism) a person licensed to slaughter animals and birds

SHOCHETIM > SHOCHET

SHOCHETS > SHOCHET

SHOCHU n type of Japanese alcoholic spirit

SHOCHUS > SHOCHU

SHOCK vb horrify, disgust, or astonish ▷ n sudden violent emotional disturbance ▷ adj bushy

SHOCKABLE > SHOCK

SHOCKED > SHOCK

SHOCKER n person or thing that shocks or horrifies

SHOCKERS > SHOCKER

SHOCKING adj causing horror, disgust, or astonishment

SHOCKS > SHOCK

SHOD > SHOE

SHODDEN vb old form of shod

SHODDIER > SHODDY

SHODDIES > SHODDY

SHODDIEST > SHODDY

SHODDILY > SHODDY

SHODDY adj made or done badly ▷ n yarn or fabric made from wool waste or clippings

SHODER n skins used in making gold leaf

SHODERS > SHODER

SHOE n outer covering for the foot, ending below the ankle ▷ vb fit with a shoe or shoes

SHOEBILL n large wading bird of tropical E African swamps

SHOEBILLS > SHOEBILL

SHOEBLACK n (esp formerly) a person who shines boots and shoes

SHOEBOX n cardboard box for shoes

SHOEBOXES > SHOEBOX

SHOEBRUSH n brush for cleaning shoes

SHOED > SHOE

SHOEHORN n smooth curved implement inserted at the heel of a shoe to ease the foot into it ▷ vb cram (people or things) into a very small space

SHOEHORNS > SHOEHORN

SHOEING > SHOE

SHOEINGS > SHOE

SHOELACE n cord for fastening shoes

SHOELACES > SHOELACE

SHOELESS > SHOE

SHOEMAKER n person who makes or repairs shoes or boots

SHOEPAC n waterproof boot

SHOEPACK n waterproof boot

SHOEPACKS > SHOEPACK

SHOEPACS > SHOEPAC

SHOER n person who shoes horses

SHOERS > SHOER

SHOES > SHOE

SHOESHINE n act or an instance of polishing a pair of shoes

SHOETREE n piece of metal, wood, or plastic inserted in a shoe to keep its shape

SHOETREES > SHOETREE

SHOFAR n ram's horn sounded in Jewish synagogue

SHOFARS > SHOFAR

SHOFROTH > SHOFAR

SHOG vb shake

SHOGGED > SHOG

SHOGGING > SHOG

SHOGGLE vb shake

SHOGGLED > SHOGGLE

SHOGGLES > SHOGGLE

SHOGGLIER > SHOGGLE

SHOGGLING > SHOGGLE

SHOGGLY > SHOGGLE

SHOGI n Japanese chess

SHOGIS > SHOGI

SHOGS > SHOG

SHOGUN n Japanese chief military commander

SHOGUNAL > SHOGUN

SHOGUNATE n office or rule of a shogun

SHOGUNS > SHOGUN

SHOJI n Japanese rice-paper screen in a sliding wooden frame

SHOJIS > SHOJI

SHOJO n genre of Japanese comics intended for girls

SHOLA n Indian plant

SHOLAS > SHOLA

SHOLOM n Hebrew greeting

SHOLOMS > SHOLOM

SHONE > SHINE

SHONEEN n Irishman who imitates English ways

SHONEENS > SHONEEN

SHONKIER > SHONKY

SHONKIEST > SHONKY

SHONKY adj unreliable or unsound

SHOO interj go away! ▷ vb drive away as by saying 'shoo'

SHOOED > SHOO

SHOOFLIES > SHOOFLY

SHOOFLY n as in shoofly pie US dessert similar to treacle tart

SHOOGIE vb Scots word meaning swing

SHOOGIED > SHOOGIE

SHOOGIES > SHOOGIE

SHOOGLE vb shake, sway, or rock back and forth ▷ n rocking motion

SHOOGLED > SHOOGLE

SHOOGLES > SHOOGLE

SHOOGLIER > SHOOGLE

SHOOGLING > SHOOGLE

SHOOGLY > SHOOGLE

SHOOING > SHOO

SHOOK n set of parts ready for assembly

SHOOKS > SHOOK

SHOOL dialect word for > SHOVEL

SHOOLE *dialect word for*
> SHOVEL
SHOOLED > SHOOL
SHOOLES > SHOOLE
SHOOLING > SHOOL
SHOOLS > SHOOL
SHOON *plural of* > SHOE
SHOORA *same as* > SHURA
SHOORAS > SHOORA
SHOOS > SHOO
SHOOSH *vb* make a
rushing sound when
moving
SHOOSHED > SHOOSH
SHOOSHES > SHOOSH
SHOOSHING > SHOOSH
SHOOT *vb* hit, wound, or
kill with a missile fired
from a weapon ▷ *n* new
branch or sprout of a plant
SHOOTABLE > SHOOT
SHOOTDOWN *n* act of
shooting down aircraft
SHOOTER *n* person or
thing that shoots
SHOOTERS > SHOOTER
SHOOTIE *n* type of shoe
that covers the ankle
SHOOTIES > SHOOTIE
SHOOTING > SHOOT
SHOOTINGS > SHOOT
SHOOTIST *n* person who
shoots
SHOOTISTS
> SHOOTIST
SHOOTOUT *n* conclusive
gunfight
SHOOTOUTS
> SHOOTOUT
SHOOTS > SHOOT
SHOP *n* place for sale of
goods and services ▷ *vb*
visit a shop or shops to buy
goods
SHOPBOARD *n* shop
counter
SHOPBOT *n* price-
comparison website
SHOPBOTS > SHOPBOT
SHOPBOY *n* boy working
in shop
SHOPBOYS > SHOPBOY
SHOPE *n* old form of shape
SHOPFRONT *n* area of
shop facing street
SHOPFUL *n* amount
stored in shop
SHOPFULS > SHOPFUL
SHOPGIRL *n* young
woman working in a shop
SHOPGIRLS
> SHOPGIRL
SHOPHAR *same as*
> SHOFAR
SHOPHARS > SHOPHAR
SHOPHOUSE *n* (in SE Asia)
shop that is also the
owner's residence
SHOPHROTH > SHOPHAR
SHOPLESS *adj* (of an
area) having no shops
SHOPLIFT *vb* steal from
shop
SHOPLIFTS
> SHOPLIFT
SHOPMAN *n* man working
in shop
SHOPMEN > SHOPMAN

SHOPPE *old-fashioned
spelling of* > SHOP
SHOPPED > SHOP
SHOPPER *n* person who
buys goods in a shop
SHOPPERS > SHOPPER
SHOPPES > SHOPPE
SHOPPIER > SHOPPY
SHOPPIES > SHOPPY
SHOPPIEST > SHOPPY
SHOPPING > SHOP
SHOPPINGS > SHOP
SHOPPY *adj* of a shop
▷ *n* shop assistant
SHOPS > SHOP
SHOPTALK *n*
conversation about one's
work, carried on outside
working hours
SHOPTALKS
> SHOPTALK
SHOPWOMAN *n* woman
working in a shop
SHOPWOMEN
> SHOPWOMAN
SHOPWORN *adj* worn or
faded from being
displayed in a shop
SHORAN *n* short-range
radar system
SHORANS > SHORAN
SHORE *n* edge of a sea
or lake ▷ *vb* prop or
support
SHOREBIRD *n* bird that
lives close to the water
SHORED > SHORE
SHOREFAST *adj* (of ice)
attached to the shore
SHORELESS *adj* without
a shore suitable for
landing
SHORELINE *n* edge of a
sea, lake, or wide river
SHOREMAN *n* person who
lives on the shore
SHOREMEN > SHOREMAN
SHORER > SHORE
SHORERS > SHORE
SHORES > SHORE
SHORESIDE *n* area at the
shore
SHORESMAN *n* fishing
industry worker on the
shore
SHORESMEN
> SHORESMAN
SHOREWARD *adj* near or
facing the shore ▷ *adv*
towards the shore
SHOREWEED *n* tufty
aquatic perennial plant
SHORING > SHORE
SHORINGS > SHORE
SHORL *n* black mineral
SHORLS > SHORL
SHORN *past participle of*
> SHEAR
SHORT *adj* not long ▷ *adv*
abruptly ▷ *n* drink of
spirits ▷ *vb* short-circuit
SHORTAGE *n* deficiency
SHORTAGES
> SHORTAGE
SHORTARM *adj* (of a
punch) with the arm bent
SHORTARSE *n* short
person

SHORTCAKE *n* shortbread
SHORTCUT *n* route that is
shorter than the usual one
SHORTCUTS
> SHORTCUT
SHORTED > SHORT
SHORTEN *vb* make or
become shorter
SHORTENED > SHORTEN
SHORTENER > SHORTEN
SHORTENS > SHORTEN
SHORTER > SHORT
SHORTEST > SHORT
SHORTFALL *n* deficit
SHORTGOWN *n* old Scots
word meaning woman's
jacket
SHORTHAIR *n* cat with
short fur
SHORTHAND *n* system of
rapid writing using
symbols to represent
words
SHORTHEAD *n* species of
fish
SHORTHOLD *n* as in
shorthold tenancy letting of
a dwelling for between
one and five years at a fair
rent
SHORTHORN *n* member of
a breed of cattle with
short horns
SHORTIA *n* American
flowering plant
SHORTIAS > SHORTIA
SHORTIE *n* person or
thing that is extremely
short
SHORTIES > SHORTIE
SHORTING > SHORT
SHORTISH > SHORT
SHORTLIST *n* list of
suitable applicants for a
job, etc
SHORTLY *adv* soon
SHORTNESS > SHORT
SHORTS *pl n* trousers
reaching the top of the
thigh or partway to the
knee
SHORTSTOP *n* fielding
position to the left of
second base viewed from
home plate
SHORTWAVE *n* radio wave
with a wavelength in the
range 10–100 metres
SHORTY *same as*
> SHORTIE
SHOT *vb* load with shot
SHOTCRETE *n* type of
concrete sprayed from a
hose
SHOTE *same as* > SHOAT
SHOTES > SHOTE
SHOTFIRER *n* person
detonating a blasting
charge
SHOTGUN *n* gun for firing
a charge of shot at short
range ▷ *adj* involving
coercion or duress ▷ *vb*
shoot or threaten with or
as if with a shotgun
SHOTGUNS > SHOTGUN
SHOTHOLE *n* drilled hole
into which explosive is put
for blasting

SHOTHOLES
> SHOTHOLE
SHOTMAKER *n* sport
player making good shots
SHOTPROOF *adj* able to
withstand shot
SHOTS > SHOT
SHOTT *n* shallow
temporary salt lake or
marsh in the North African
desert
SHOTTE *n* old form of
shoat
SHOTTED > SHOT
SHOTTEN *adj* (of fish, such
herring) having recently
spawned
SHOTTES > SHOTTE
SHOTTING > SHOT
SHOTTLE *n* small drawer
SHOTTLES > SHOTTLE
SHOTTS > SHOTT
SHOUGH *n* old word ·
meaning lapdog
SHOUGHS > SHOUGH
SHOULD > SHALL
SHOULDER *n* part of the
body to which an arm,
foreleg, or wing is
attached ▷ *vb* bear (a
burden or responsibility)
SHOULDERS
> SHOULDER
SHOULDEST *same as*
> SHOULDST
SHOULDST *form of the past
tense of* > SHALL
SHOUSE *n* toilet ▷ *adj*
unwell or in poor spirits
SHOUSES > SHOUSE
SHOUT *n* loud cry ▷ *vb* cry
out loudly
SHOUTED > SHOUT
SHOUTER > SHOUT
SHOUTERS > SHOUT
SHOUTHER *Scots form of*
> SHOULDER
SHOUTHERS
> SHOUTHER
SHOUTIER > SHOUTY
SHOUTIEST > SHOUTY
SHOUTING > SHOUT
SHOUTINGS > SHOUT
SHOUTLINE *n* line in
advertisement made
prominent to catch
attention
SHOUTOUT *n* public
greeting, esp one
broadcast via television or
radio
SHOUTOUTS
> SHOUTOUT
SHOUTS > SHOUT
SHOUTY *adj* characterized
by or involving shouting
SHOVE *vb* push roughly
▷ *n* rough push
SHOVED > SHOVE
SHOVEL *n* tool for lifting
or moving loose material
▷ *vb* lift or move as with a
shovel
SHOVELED > SHOVEL
SHOVELER *n* type of duck
SHOVELERS
> SHOVELER
SHOVELFUL > SHOVEL

S

SHOVELING > SHOVEL
SHOVELLED > SHOVEL
SHOVELLER > SHOVEL
SHOVELS > SHOVEL
SHOVER > SHOVE
SHOVERS > SHOVE
SHOVES > SHOVE
SHOVING n act of pushing hard
SHOVINGS > SHOVING
SHOW vb make, be, or become noticeable or visible ▷ n public exhibition
SHOWABLE > SHOW
SHOWBIZ n entertainment industry including theatre, films, and TV
SHOWBIZZY adj characteristic of showbiz
SHOWBOAT n paddle-wheel river steamer with a theatre and a repertory company ▷ vb perform or behave in a showy and flamboyant way
SHOWBOATS > SHOWBOAT
SHOWBOX n box containing showman's material
SHOWBOXES > SHOWBOX
SHOWBREAD same as > SHEWBREAD
SHOWCASE n situation in which something is displayed to best advantage ▷ vb exhibit or display ▷ adj displayed or meriting display as in a showcase
SHOWCASED > SHOWCASE
SHOWCASES > SHOWCASE
SHOWD vb rock or sway to and fro ▷ n rocking motion
SHOWDED > SHOWD
SHOWDING > SHOWD
SHOWDOWN n confrontation that settles a dispute
SHOWDOWNS > SHOWDOWN
SHOWDS > SHOWD
SHOWED > SHOW
SHOWER n kind of bath in which a person stands while being sprayed with water ▷ vb wash in a shower
SHOWERED > SHOWER
SHOWERER > SHOWER
SHOWERERS > SHOWER
SHOWERFUL > SHOWER
SHOWERIER > SHOWER
SHOWERING > SHOWER
SHOWERS > SHOWER
SHOWERY > SHOWER
SHOWGHE n old word meaning lapdog
SHOWGHES > SHOWGHE
SHOWGIRL n young woman who appears in shows, esp as a singer or dancer

SHOWGIRLS > SHOWGIRL
SHOWGOER n member of the audience of a play, film, or show
SHOWGOERS > SHOWGOER
SHOWIER > SHOWY
SHOWIEST > SHOWY
SHOWILY > SHOWY
SHOWINESS > SHOWY
SHOWING > SHOW
SHOWINGS > SHOW
SHOWJUMP vb take part in a showjumping competition
SHOWJUMPS > SHOWJUMP
SHOWMAN n man skilled at presenting anything spectacularly
SHOWMANCE n romance between two stars that lasts only for the run of the show they are in
SHOWMANLY adj like a showman
SHOWMEN > SHOWMAN
SHOWN > SHOW
SHOWOFF n person who makes a vain display of himself or herself
SHOWOFFS > SHOWOFF
SHOWPIECE n excellent specimen shown for display or as an example
SHOWPLACE n place visited for its beauty or interest
SHOWRING n area where animals are displayed for sale or competition
SHOWRINGS > SHOWRING
SHOWROOM n room in which goods for sale are on display
SHOWROOMS > SHOWROOM
SHOWS > SHOW
SHOWTIME n time when show begins
SHOWTIMES > SHOWTIME
SHOWY adj gaudy
SHOWYARD n yard where cattle are displayed
SHOWYARDS > SHOWYARD
SHOYU n Japanese variety of soy sauce
SHOYUS > SHOYU
SHRADDHA n Hindu offering to an ancestor
SHRADDHAS > SHRADDHA
SHRANK > SHRINK
SHRAPNEL n artillery shell filled with pellets which scatter on explosion
SHRAPNELS > SHRAPNEL
SHRED n long narrow strip torn from something ▷ vb tear to shreds
SHREDDED > SHRED
SHREDDER > SHRED
SHREDDERS > SHRED

SHREDDIER > SHRED
SHREDDING > SHRED
SHREDDY > SHRED
SHREDLESS > SHRED
SHREDS > SHRED
SHREEK old spelling of > SHRIEK
SHREEKED > SHREEK
SHREEKING > SHREEK
SHREEKS > SHREEK
SHREIK old spelling of > SHRIEK
SHREIKED > SHREIK
SHREIKING > SHREIK
SHREIKS > SHREIK
SHREW n small mouselike animal ▷ vb curse or damn
SHREWD adj clever and perceptive
SHREWDER > SHREWD
SHREWDEST > SHREWD
SHREWDIE n shrewd person
SHREWDIES > SHREWDIE
SHREWDLY > SHREWD
SHREWED > SHREW
SHREWING > SHREW
SHREWISH adj bad-tempered and nagging
SHREWLIKE > SHREW
SHREWMICE pl n shrews
SHREWS > SHREW
SHRI n Indian title of respect
SHRIECH old spelling of > SHRIEK
SHRIECHED > SHRIECH
SHRIECHES > SHRIECH
SHRIEK n shrill cry ▷ vb utter (with) a shriek
SHRIEKED > SHRIEK
SHRIEKER > SHRIEK
SHRIEKERS > SHRIEK
SHRIEKIER > SHRIEK
SHRIEKING > SHRIEK
SHRIEKS > SHRIEK
SHRIEKY > SHRIEK
SHRIEVAL adj of or relating to a sheriff
SHRIEVE archaic word for > SHERIFF
SHRIEVED > SHRIEVE
SHRIEVES > SHRIEVE
SHRIEVING > SHRIEVE
SHRIFT n act or an instance of shriving or being shriven
SHRIFTS > SHRIFT
SHRIGHT n old word meaning shriek
SHRIGHTS > SHRIGHT
SHRIKE n songbird with a heavy hooked bill ▷ vb archaic word for shriek
SHRIKED > SHRIKE
SHRIKES > SHRIKE
SHRIKING > SHRIKE
SHRILL adj (of a sound) sharp and high-pitched ▷ vb utter shrilly
SHRILLED > SHRILL
SHRILLER > SHRILL
SHRILLEST > SHRILL
SHRILLIER > SHRILL
SHRILLING > SHRILL

SHRILLS > SHRILL
SHRILLY > SHRILL
SHRIMP n small edible shellfish ▷ vb fish for shrimps
SHRIMPED > SHRIMP
SHRIMPER > SHRIMP
SHRIMPERS > SHRIMP
SHRIMPIER > SHRIMP
SHRIMPING > SHRIMP
SHRIMPS > SHRIMP
SHRIMPY > SHRIMP
SHRINAL > SHRINE
SHRINE n place of worship associated with a sacred person or object ▷ vb enshrine
SHRINED > SHRINE
SHRINES > SHRINE
SHRINING > SHRINE
SHRINK vb become or make smaller ▷ n psychiatrist
SHRINKAGE n decrease in size, value, or weight
SHRINKER > SHRINK
SHRINKERS > SHRINK
SHRINKING > SHRINK
SHRINKS > SHRINK
SHRIS > SHRI
SHRITCH vb old word meaning shriek
SHRITCHED > SHRITCH
SHRITCHES > SHRITCH
SHRIVE vb hear the confession of (a penitent)
SHRIVED > SHRIVE
SHRIVEL vb shrink and wither
SHRIVELED > SHRIVEL
SHRIVELS > SHRIVEL
SHRIVEN > SHRIVE
SHRIVER > SHRIVE
SHRIVERS > SHRIVE
SHRIVES > SHRIVE
SHRIVING > SHRIVE
SHRIVINGS > SHRIVE
SHROFF n (in China and Japan) expert employed to identify counterfeit money ▷ vb test (money) and separate out the counterfeit and base
SHROFFAGE > SHROFF
SHROFFED > SHROFF
SHROFFING > SHROFF
SHROFFS > SHROFF
SHROOM n slang for magic mushroom ▷ vb take magic mushrooms
SHROOMED > SHROOM
SHROOMER > SHROOM
SHROOMERS > SHROOM
SHROOMING > SHROOM
SHROOMS > SHROOM
SHROUD n piece of cloth used to wrap a dead body ▷ vb conceal
SHROUDED > SHROUD
SHROUDIER > SHROUD
SHROUDING > SHROUD
SHROUDS > SHROUD
SHROUDY > SHROUD
SHROVE vb dialect word meaning to observe Shrove-tide
SHROVED > SHROVE

SHROVES > SHROVE
SHROVING > SHROVE
SHROW vb old form of shrew
SHROWD adj old form of shrewd
SHROWED > SHROW
SHROWING > SHROW
SHROWS > SHROW
SHRUB n woody plant smaller than a tree ▷ vb plant shrubs
SHRUBBED > SHRUB
SHRUBBERY n area planted with shrubs
SHRUBBIER > SHRUBBY
SHRUBBING > SHRUB
SHRUBBY adj consisting of, planted with, or abounding in shrubs
SHRUBLAND n land covered by shrubs
SHRUBLESS > SHRUB
SHRUBLIKE > SHRUB
SHRUBS > SHRUB
SHRUG vb raise and then drop (the shoulders) as a sign of indifference or doubt ▷ n shrugging
SHRUGGED > SHRUG
SHRUGGING > SHRUG
SHRUGS > SHRUG
SHRUNK > SHRINK
SHRUNKEN adj reduced in size
SHTCHI n Russian cabbage soup
SHTCHIS > SHTCHI
SHTETEL same as
> SHTETL
SHTETELS > SHTETEL
SHTETL n Jewish community in Eastern Europe
SHTETLACH > SHTETL
SHTETLS > SHTETL
SHTICK n comedian's routine
SHTICKIER > SHTICK
SHTICKS > SHTICK
SHTICKY > SHTICK
SHTIK n shtick
SHTIKS > SHTIK
SHTOOK n trouble
SHTOOKS > SHTOOK
SHTOOM adj silent
SHTOOMER > SHTOOM
SHTOOMEST > SHTOOM
SHTREIMEL n broad-brimmed hat worn by some Hasidic Jews
SHTUCK n trouble
SHTUCKS > SHTUCK
SHTUM adj silent
SHTUMM adj silent
SHTUMMER > SHTUMM
SHTUMMEST > SHTUMM
SHTUP vb vulgar slang word meaning to have sex (with)
SHTUPPED > SHTUP
SHTUPPING > SHTUP
SHTUPS > SHTUP
SHUBUNKIN n type of goldfish
SHUCK n outer covering of something ▷ vb remove the shucks from

SHUCKED > SHUCK
SHUCKER > SHUCK
SHUCKERS > SHUCK
SHUCKING > SHUCK
SHUCKINGS > SHUCK
SHUCKS pl n something of little value ▷ interj exclamation of disappointment, annoyance, etc
SHUDDER vb shake or tremble violently, esp with horror ▷ n instance of shaking or trembling
SHUDDERED > SHUDDER
SHUDDERS > SHUDDER
SHUDDERY adj shuddering
SHUFFLE vb walk without lifting the feet ▷ n act of shuffling
SHUFFLED > SHUFFLE
SHUFFLER > SHUFFLE
SHUFFLERS > SHUFFLE
SHUFFLES > SHUFFLE
SHUFFLING > SHUFFLE
SHUFTI same as
> SHUFTY
SHUFTIES > SHUFTY
SHUFTIS > SHUFTI
SHUFTY n look
SHUGGIES > SHUGGY
SHUGGY n swing, as at a fairground
SHUL Yiddish word for
> SYNAGOGUE
SHULE vb saunter
SHULED > SHULE
SHULES > SHULE
SHULING > SHULE
SHULN > SHUL
SHULS > SHUL
SHUMAI pl n (in Japan) small stuffed dumplings
SHUN vb avoid
SHUNLESS adj old word meaning not to be shunned
SHUNNABLE > SHUN
SHUNNED > SHUN
SHUNNER > SHUN
SHUNNERS > SHUN
SHUNNING > SHUN
SHUNPIKE vb take side road to avoid toll at turnpike
SHUNPIKED
> SHUNPIKE
SHUNPIKER
> SHUNPIKE
SHUNPIKES
> SHUNPIKE
SHUNS > SHUN
SHUNT vb move (objects or people) to a different position ▷ n shunting
SHUNTED > SHUNT
SHUNTER n small railway locomotive used for manoeuvring coaches
SHUNTERS > SHUNTER
SHUNTING > SHUNT
SHUNTINGS > SHUNT
SHUNTS > SHUNT
SHURA n consultative council or assembly
SHURAS > SHURA

SHURIKEN n Japanese weapon with blades or points, thrown by hand
SHURIKENS
> SHURIKEN
SHUSH interj be quiet! ▷ vb quiet by saying 'shush'
SHUSHED > SHUSH
SHUSHER > SHUSH
SHUSHERS > SHUSH
SHUSHES > SHUSH
SHUSHING > SHUSH
SHUT vb bring together or fold, close
SHUTDOWN n closing of a factory, shop, or other business ▷ vb discontinue operations permanently
SHUTDOWNS
> SHUTDOWN
SHUTE variant of **>** CHUTE
SHUTED > SHUTE
SHUTES > SHUTE
SHUTEYE n sleep
SHUTEYES > SHUTEYE
SHUTING > SHUTE
SHUTOFF n device that shuts something off
SHUTOFFS > SHUTOFF
SHUTOUT n game in which the opposing team does not score
SHUTOUTS > SHUTOUT
SHUTS > SHUT
SHUTTER n hinged doorlike cover for closing off a window ▷ vb close or equip with a shutter
SHUTTERED > SHUTTER
SHUTTERS > SHUTTER
SHUTTING > SHUT
SHUTTLE n bobbin-like device used in weaving ▷ vb move by or as if by a shuttle
SHUTTLED > SHUTTLE
SHUTTLER > SHUTTLE
SHUTTLERS > SHUTTLE
SHUTTLES > SHUTTLE
SHUTTLING > SHUTTLE
SHVITZ vb sweat
SHVITZED > SHVITZ
SHVITZES > SHVITZ
SHVITZING > SHVITZ
SHWA same as **>** SCHWA
SHWANPAN same as
> SWANPAN
SHWANPANS
> SHWANPAN
SHWAS > SHWA
SHWESHWE n African cotton print fabric
SHWESHWES
> SHWESHWE
SHY adj not at ease in company ▷ vb start back in fear ▷ n throw
SHYER > SHY
SHYERS > SHY
SHYEST > SHY
SHYING > SHY
SHYISH > SHY
SHYLOCK vb lend money at an exorbitant rate of interest
SHYLOCKED > SHYLOCK
SHYLOCKS > SHYLOCK
SHYLY > SHY

SHYNESS > SHY
SHYNESSES > SHY
SHYPOO n liquor of poor quality
SHYPOOS > SHYPOO
SHYSTER n person who uses discreditable or unethical methods
SHYSTERS > SHYSTER
SI same as **>** TE
SIAL n silicon-rich and aluminium-rich rocks of the earth's continental upper crust
SIALIC > SIAL
SIALID n species of fly
SIALIDAN > SIALID
SIALIDANS > SIALID
SIALIDS > SIALID
SIALOGRAM n X-ray of salivary gland
SIALOID adj resembling saliva
SIALOLITH n hard deposit formed in salivary gland
SIALON n type of ceramic
SIALONS > SIALON
SIALS > SIAL
SIAMANG n large black gibbon
SIAMANGS > SIAMANG
SIAMESE variant of
> SIAMEZE
SIAMESED > SIAMESE
SIAMESES > SIAMESE
SIAMESING > SIAMESE
SIAMEZE vb join together
SIAMEZED > SIAMEZE
SIAMEZES > SIAMEZE
SIAMEZING > SIAMEZE
SIB n blood relative
SIBB n sib
SIBBS > SIBB
SIBILANCE
> SIBILANT
SIBILANCY
> SIBILANT
SIBILANT adj hissing ▷ n consonant pronounced with a hissing sound
SIBILANTS
> SIBILANT
SIBILATE vb pronounce or utter (words or speech) with a hissing sound
SIBILATED
> SIBILATE
SIBILATES
> SIBILATE
SIBILATOR
> SIBILATE
SIBILOUS > SIBILANT
SIBLING n brother or sister
SIBLINGS > SIBLING
SIBS > SIB
SIBSHIP n group of children of the same parents
SIBSHIPS > SIBSHIP
SIBYL n (in ancient Greece and Rome) prophetess
SIBYLIC > SIBYL
SIBYLLIC > SIBYL
SIBYLLINE > SIBYL
SIBYLS > SIBYL**

S

SIC *adv* thus ▷ *vb* attack
SICARIO *n* hired gunman, esp in Latin America
SICARIOS > SICARIO
SICCAN *adj* Scots word meaning such
SICCAR *adj* sure
SICCATIVE *n* substance added to a liquid to promote drying
SICCED > SIC
SICCING > SIC
SICCITIES > SICCITY
SICCITY *n* dryness
SICE *same as* > SYCE
SICES > SICE
SICH *adj* old form of such
SICHT *Scot word for* > SIGHT
SICHTED > SICHT
SICHTING > SICHT
SICHTS > SICHT
SICILIANA *n* Sicilian dance
SICILIANE > SICILIANA
SICILIANO *n* old dance in six-beat or twelve-beat time
SICK *adj* vomiting or likely to vomit ▷ *n* vomit ▷ *vb* vomit
SICKBAY *n* room for the treatment of sick people
SICKBAYS > SICKBAY
SICKBED *n* bed where sick person lies
SICKBEDS > SICKBED
SICKED > SICK
SICKEE *n* person off work through illness
SICKEES > SICKEE
SICKEN *vb* make nauseated or disgusted
SICKENED > SICKEN
SICKENER *n* something that induces sickness or nausea
SICKENERS > SICKENER
SICKENING *adj* causing horror or disgust
SICKENS > SICKEN
SICKER > SICK
SICKERLY *adv* Scots word meaning surely
SICKEST > SICK
SICKIE *n* day of sick leave from work
SICKIES > SICKIE
SICKING > SICK
SICKISH > SICK
SICKISHLY > SICK
SICKLE *n* tool with a curved blade for cutting grass or grain ▷ *vb* cut with a sickle
SICKLED > SICKLE
SICKLEMAN *n* person reaping with sickle
SICKLEMEN > SICKLEMAN
SICKLEMIA *n* form of anaemia
SICKLEMIC > SICKLEMIA
SICKLES > SICKLE

SICKLIED > SICKLY
SICKLIER > SICKLY
SICKLIES > SICKLY
SICKLIEST > SICKLY
SICKLILY > SICKLY
SICKLING > SICKLE
SICKLY *adj* unhealthy, weak ▷ *adv* suggesting sickness ▷ *vb* make sickly
SICKLYING > SICKLY
SICKNESS *n* particular illness or disease
SICKNURSE *n* person nursing sick person ▷ *vb* act as a sicknurse
SICKO *n* person who is perverted ▷ *adj* perverted or in bad taste
SICKOS > SICKO
SICKOUT *n* industrial action in which all workers report sick simultaneously
SICKOUTS > SICKOUT
SICKROOM *n* room to which a person who is ill is confined
SICKROOMS > SICKROOM
SICKS > SICK
SICKY *n* day off work due to illness
SICLIKE *adj* Scots word meaning suchlike
SICS > SIC
SIDA *n* Australian hemp plant
SIDALCEA *n* type of perennial N American plant
SIDALCEAS > SIDALCEA
SIDAS > SIDA
SIDDHA *n* (in Hinduism) person who has achieved perfection
SIDDHAS > SIDDHA
SIDDHI *n* (in Hinduism) power attained with perfection
SIDDHIS > SIDDHI
SIDDHUISM *n* (in Indian English) any contrived metaphor or simile
SIDDUR *n* Jewish prayer book
SIDDURIM > SIDDUR
SIDDURS > SIDDUR
SIDE *n* line or surface that borders anything ▷ *adj* at or on the side
SIDEARM *n* weapon worn on belt ▷ *vb* provide with a sidearm
SIDEARMED > SIDEARM
SIDEARMER *n* person who pitches a ball with the arm parallel to the ground
SIDEARMS > SIDEARM
SIDEBAND *n* frequency band either above or below the carrier frequency
SIDEBANDS > SIDEBAND
SIDEBAR *n* small newspaper article beside larger one
SIDEBARS > SIDEBAR

SIDEBOARD *n* piece of furniture for holding plates, cutlery, etc in a dining room
SIDEBONE *n* damage to the cartilage in a horse's hoof
SIDEBONES *n* part of horse's hoof
SIDEBURN *n* strip of whiskers down one side of the face
SIDEBURNS > SIDEBURN
SIDECAR *n* small passenger car on the side of a motorcycle
SIDECARS > SIDECAR
SIDECHAIR *n* chair without arms
SIDECHECK *n* part of horse's harness
SIDED > SIDE
SIDEDLY *adv* pertaining to given number of sides
SIDEDNESS > SIDE
SIDEDRESS *vb* place fertilizer in the soil near the roots of a plant
SIDEHILL *n* side of hill
SIDEHILLS > SIDEHILL
SIDEKICK *n* close friend or associate
SIDEKICKS > SIDEKICK
SIDELESS *adj* without sides
SIDELIGHT *n* either of two small lights on the front of a vehicle
SIDELINE *n* subsidiary interest or source of income ▷ *vb* prevent (a player) from taking part in a game
SIDELINED > SIDELINE
SIDELINER > SIDELINE
SIDELINES *pl n* area immediately outside the playing area, where substitute players sit
SIDELING *adj* to one side ▷ *adv* sideways ▷ *n* slope, esp on the side of a road
SIDELINGS > SIDELING
SIDELOCK *n* long lock of hair on side of head
SIDELOCKS > SIDELOCK
SIDELONG *adj* sideways ▷ *adv* obliquely
SIDEMAN *n* member of a dance band or a jazz group other than the leader
SIDEMEAT *n* meat from the side of a pig
SIDEMEATS > SIDEMEAT
SIDEMEN > SIDEMAN
SIDENOTE *n* note written in margin
SIDENOTES > SIDENOTE
SIDEPATH *n* minor path

SIDEPATHS > SIDEPATH
SIDEPIECE *n* part forming side of something
SIDER *n* one who sides with another
SIDERAL *adj* from the stars
SIDERATE *vb* strike violently
SIDERATED > SIDERATE
SIDERATES > SIDERATE
SIDEREAL *adj* of or determined with reference to the stars
SIDERITE *n* pale yellow to brownish-black mineral
SIDERITES > SIDERITE
SIDERITIC > SIDERITE
SIDEROAD *n* (esp in Ontario) a road going at right angles to concession roads
SIDEROADS > SIDEROAD
SIDEROSES > SIDEROSIS
SIDEROSIS *n* lung disease caused by breathing in fine particles of iron or other metallic dust
SIDEROTIC > SIDEROSIS
SIDERS > SIDER
SIDES > SIDE
SIDESHOOT *n* minor shoot growing on plant
SIDESHOW *n* entertainment offered along with the main show
SIDESHOWS > SIDESHOW
SIDESLIP *same as* > SLIP
SIDESLIPS > SIDESLIP
SIDESMAN *n* man elected to help the parish church warden
SIDESMEN > SIDESMAN
SIDESPIN *n* horizontal spin put on ball
SIDESPINS > SIDESPIN
SIDESPLIT *n* house with a higher storey at the side
SIDESTEP *vb* dodge (an issue) ▷ *n* movement to one side, such as in dancing or boxing
SIDESTEPS > SIDESTEP
SIDESWIPE *n* unexpected criticism of someone or something while discussing another subject ▷ *vb* make a sideswipe
SIDETABLE *n* small table at the side of a room
SIDETRACK *vb* divert from the main topic ▷ *n* railway siding

SIDEWALK n paved path for pedestrians, at the side of a road

SIDEWALKS > SIDEWALK

SIDEWALL n either of the sides of a pneumatic tyre between the tread and the rim

SIDEWALLS > SIDEWALL

SIDEWARD adj directed or moving towards one side ▷ adv towards one side

SIDEWARDS adv towards one side

SIDEWAY variant of > SIDEWAYS

SIDEWAYS adv or from the side ▷ adj moving or directed to or from one side

SIDEWHEEL n one of the paddle wheels of a sidewheeler

SIDEWISE adv sideways

SIDH pl n fairy people

SIDHA n (in Hinduism) person who has achieved perfection

SIDHAS > SIDHA

SIDHE pl n inhabitants of fairyland

SIDHUISM n contrived metaphor or simile

SIDHUISMS > SIDHUISM

SIDING n short stretch of railway track on which trains are shunted from the main line

SIDINGS > SIDING

SIDLE vb walk in a furtive manner ▷ n sideways movement

SIDLED > SIDLE

SIDLER > SIDLE

SIDLERS > SIDLE

SIDLES > SIDLE

SIDLING > SIDLE

SIDLINGLY > SIDLE

SIECLE n century, period, or era

SIECLES > SIECLE

SIEGE n surrounding and blockading of a place ▷ vb lay siege to

SIEGED > SIEGE

SIEGER n person who besieges

SIEGERS > SIEGER

SIEGES > SIEGE

SIEGING > SIEGE

SIELD adj (archaic) provided with a ceiling

SIEMENS n SI unit of electrical conductance

SIEMENSES > SIEMENS

SIEN n old word meaning scion

SIENITE n type of igneous rock

SIENITES > SIENITE

SIENNA n reddish- or yellowish-brown pigment made from natural earth

SIENNAS > SIENNA

SIENS > SIEN

SIENT n old word meaning scion

SIENTS > SIENT

SIEROZEM n type of soil

SIEROZEMS > SIEROZEM

SIERRA n range of mountains in Spain or America with jagged peaks

SIERRAN > SIERRA

SIERRAS > SIERRA

SIES interj in South Africa, an exclamation of disgust

SIESTA n afternoon nap, taken in hot countries

SIESTAS > SIESTA

SIETH n old form of scythe

SIETHS > SIETH

SIEUR n French word meaning lord

SIEURS > SIEUR

SIEVE n utensil with mesh through which a substance is sifted or strained ▷ vb sift or strain through a sieve

SIEVED > SIEVE

SIEVELIKE > SIEVE

SIEVERT n derived SI unit of dose equivalent, equal to 1 joule per kilogram

SIEVERTS > SIEVERT

SIEVES > SIEVE

SIEVING > SIEVE

SIF adj South African slang for disgusting

SIFAKA n either of two large rare arboreal lemuroid primates

SIFAKAS > SIFAKA

SIFFLE vb whistle

SIFFLED > SIFFLE

SIFFLES > SIFFLE

SIFFLEUR n male professional whistler

SIFFLEURS > SIFFLEUR

SIFFLEUSE n female professional whistler

SIFFLING > SIFFLE

SIFREI > SEFER

SIFT vb remove the coarser particles from a substance with a sieve

SIFTED > SIFT

SIFTER > SIFT

SIFTERS > SIFT

SIFTING > SIFT

SIFTINGLY > SIFT

SIFTINGS pl n material or particles separated out by or as if by a sieve

SIFTS > SIFT

SIG n short for signature

SIGANID n tropical fish

SIGANIDS > SIGANID

SIGH n long audible breath expressing sadness, tiredness, relief, or longing ▷ vb utter a sigh

SIGHED > SIGH

SIGHER > SIGH

SIGHERS > SIGH

SIGHFUL > SIGH

SIGHING n act of sighing

SIGHINGLY > SIGH

SIGHINGS > SIGHING

SIGHLESS > SIGH

SIGHLIKE > SIGH

SIGHS > SIGH

SIGHT n ability to see ▷ vb catch sight of

SIGHTABLE > SIGHT

SIGHTED adj not blind

SIGHTER n any of six practice shots allowed to each competitor in a tournament

SIGHTERS > SIGHTER

SIGHTING > SIGHT

SIGHTINGS > SIGHT

SIGHTLESS adj blind

SIGHTLIER > SIGHTLY

SIGHTLINE n uninterrupted line of vision

SIGHTLY adj pleasing or attractive to see

SIGHTS > SIGHT

SIGHTSAW > SIGHTSEE

SIGHTSEE vb visit the famous or interesting sights of (a place)

SIGHTSEEN > SIGHTSEE

SIGHTSEER > SIGHTSEE

SIGHTSEES > SIGHTSEE

SIGHTSMAN n tourist guide

SIGHTSMEN > SIGHTSMAN

SIGIL n seal or signet

SIGILLARY > SIGIL

SIGILLATE adj closed with seal

SIGILS > SIGIL

SIGISBEI > SIGISBEO

SIGISBEO n male escort for a married woman

SIGLA n list of symbols used in a book

SIGLAS > SIGLA

SIGLOI > SIGLOS

SIGLOS n silver coin of ancient Persia

SIGLUM n symbol used in book

SIGMA n 18th letter in the Greek alphabet

SIGMAS > SIGMA

SIGMATE adj shaped like the Greek letter sigma or the Roman S ▷ n sigmate thing ▷ vb add a sigma

SIGMATED > SIGMATE

SIGMATES > SIGMATE

SIGMATIC > SIGMATE

SIGMATING > SIGMATE

SIGMATION > SIGMATE

SIGMATISM n repetition of letter s

SIGMATRON n machine for generating X-rays

SIGMOID adj shaped like the letter S ▷ n S-shaped bend in the final portion of the large intestine

SIGMOIDAL variant of > SIGMOID

SIGMOIDS > SIGMOID

SIGN n indication of something not immediately or outwardly observable ▷ vb write (one's name) on (a document or letter) to show its authenticity

SIGNA pl n symbols

SIGNABLE > SIGN

SIGNAGE n signs collectively

SIGNAGES > SIGNAGE

SIGNAL n sign or gesture to convey information ▷ adj very important ▷ vb convey (information) by signal

SIGNALED > SIGNAL

SIGNALER > SIGNAL

SIGNALERS > SIGNAL

SIGNALING > SIGNAL

SIGNALISE same as > SIGNALIZE

SIGNALIZE vb make noteworthy or conspicuous

SIGNALLED > SIGNAL

SIGNALLER > SIGNAL

SIGNALLY adv conspicuously or especially

SIGNALMAN n railwayman in charge of signals and points

SIGNALMEN > SIGNALMAN

SIGNALS > SIGNAL

SIGNARIES > SIGNARY

SIGNARY n set of symbols

SIGNATORY n one of the parties who sign a document ▷ adj having signed a document or treaty

SIGNATURE n person's name written by himself or herself in signing something

SIGNBOARD n board carrying a sign or notice, often to advertise a business or product

SIGNED > SIGN

SIGNEE n person signing document

SIGNEES > SIGNEE

SIGNER n person who signs something

SIGNERS > SIGNER

SIGNET n small seal used to authenticate documents ▷ vb stamp or authenticate with a signet

SIGNETED > SIGNET

SIGNETING > SIGNET

SIGNETS > SIGNET

SIGNEUR old spelling of > SENIOR

SIGNEURIE n old word meaning seniority

SIGNIEUR n old word meaning lord

SIGNIEURS > SIGNIEUR

SIGNIFICS n study of meaning

SIGNIFIED > SIGNIFY

SIGNIFIER > SIGNIFY

SIGNIFIES > SIGNIFY

S

SIGNIFY *vb* indicate or suggest

SIGNING *n* system of communication using hand and arm movements

SIGNINGS > SIGNING

SIGNIOR *same as* > SIGNOR

SIGNIORI > SIGNOR

SIGNIORS > SIGNOR

SIGNIORY *n* old word meaning lordship

SIGNLESS > SIGN

SIGNOR *n* Italian term of address equivalent to *sir* or *Mr*

SIGNORA *n* Italian term of address equivalent to *madam* or *Mrs*

SIGNORAS > SIGNORA

SIGNORE *n* Italian man: a title of respect equivalent to *sir*

SIGNORES > SIGNORE

SIGNORI > SIGNORE

SIGNORIA *n* government of Italian city

SIGNORIAL > SIGNORIA

SIGNORIAS > SIGNORIA

SIGNORIES > SIGNORY

SIGNORINA *n* Italian term of address equivalent to *madam* or *Miss*

SIGNORINE > SIGNORINA

SIGNORINI > SIGNORINO

SIGNORINO *n* young gentleman

SIGNORS > SIGNOR

SIGNORY *same as* > SEIGNIORY

SIGNPOST *n* post bearing a sign that shows the way ▷ *vb* mark with signposts

SIGNPOSTS > SIGNPOST

SIGNS > SIGN

SIGS > SIG

SIJO *n* Korean poem

SIJOS > SIJO

SIK *adj* excellent

SIKA *n* Japanese forest-dwelling deer

SIKAS > SIKA

SIKE *n* small stream

SIKER *adj* old spelling of sicker

SIKES > SIKE

SIKORSKY *n* type of helicopter

SIKSIK *n* Arctic ground squirrel

SIKSIKS > SIKSIK

SILAGE *n* fodder crop harvested while green and partially fermented in a silo ▷ *vb* make silage

SILAGED > SILAGE

SILAGEING > SILAGE

SILAGES > SILAGE

SILAGING > SILAGE

SILANE *n* gas containing silicon

SILANES > SILANE

SILASTIC *n* tradename for a type of flexible silicone rubber

SILASTICS > SILASTIC

SILD *n* any of various small young herrings

SILDS > SILD

SILE *vb* pour with rain

SILED > SILE

SILEN *n* god of woodland

SILENCE *n* absence of noise or speech ▷ *vb* make silent

SILENCED *adj* (of a member of the clergy) forbidden to preach or perform clerical functions

SILENCER *n* device to reduce the noise of an engine exhaust or gun

SILENCERS > SILENCER

SILENCES > SILENCE

SILENCING > SILENCE

SILENE *n* type of plant with mostly red or pink flowers, often grown as a garden plant

SILENES > SILENE

SILENI > SILENUS

SILENS > SILEN

SILENT *adj* tending to speak very little ▷ *n* silent film

SILENTER > SILENT

SILENTEST > SILENT

SILENTLY > SILENT

SILENTS > SILENT

SILENUS *n* woodland deity

SILER *n* strainer

SILERS > SILER

SILES > SILE

SILESIA *n* twill-weave fabric of cotton or other fibre

SILESIAS > SILESIA

SILEX *n* type of heat-resistant glass made from fused quartz

SILEXES > SILEX

SILICA *n* hard glossy mineral found as quartz and in sandstone

SILICAS > SILICA

SILICATE *n* compound of silicon, oxygen, and a metal

SILICATED > SILICATE

SILICATES > SILICATE

SILICEOUS *adj* of, relating to, or containing abundant silica

SILICIC *adj* of, concerned with, or containing silicon or an acid obtained from silicon

SILICIDE *n* any one of a class of binary compounds formed between silicon and certain metals

SILICIDES > SILICIDE

SILICIFY *vb* convert or be converted into silica

SILICIOUS *same as* > SILICEOUS

SILICIUM *rare name for* > SILICON

SILICIUMS > SILICIUM

SILICLE *same as* > SILICULA

SILICLES > SILICLE

SILICON *n* brittle nonmetallic element ▷ *adj* denoting an area that contains much high-technology industry

SILICONE *n* tough synthetic substance made from silicon and used in lubricants

SILICONES > SILICONE

SILICONS > SILICON

SILICOSES > SILICOSIS

SILICOSIS *n* lung disease caused by inhaling silica dust

SILICOTIC *n* person with silicosis

SILICULA *n* short broad siliqua occurring in cruciferous plants

SILICULAE > SILICULA

SILICULAS > SILICULA

SILICULE *same as* > SILICULA

SILICULES > SILICULE

SILING > SILE

SILIQUA *n* long dry dehiscent fruit of cruciferous plants such as the wallflower

SILIQUAE > SILIQUA

SILIQUAS > SILIQUA

SILIQUE *same as* > SILIQUA

SILIQUES > SILIQUE

SILIQUOSE > SILIQUA

SILIQUOUS > SILIQUA

SILK *n* fibre made by the larva of a certain moth ▷ *vb* (of maize) develop long hairlike styles

SILKALENE *same as* > SILKALINE

SILKALINE *n* fine smooth cotton fabric used for linings, etc

SILKED > SILK

SILKEN *adj* made of silk ▷ *vb* make like silk

SILKENED > SILKEN

SILKENING > SILKEN

SILKENS > SILKEN

SILKIE *n* Scots word for a seal

SILKIER > SILKY

SILKIES > SILKIE

SILKIEST > SILKY

SILKILY > SILKY

SILKINESS > SILKY

SILKING > SILK

SILKLIKE > SILK

SILKOLINE *n* material like silk

SILKS > SILK

SILKTAIL *n* waxwing

SILKTAILS > SILKTAIL

SILKWEED *another name for* > MILKWEED

SILKWEEDS > SILKWEED

SILKWORM *n* caterpillar that spins a cocoon of silk

SILKWORMS > SILKWORM

SILKY *adj* of or like silk

SILL *n* ledge at the bottom of a window or door

SILLABUB *same as* > SYLLABUB

SILLABUBS > SILLABUB

SILLADAR *n* Indian irregular cavalryman

SILLADARS > SILLADAR

SILLER *n* silver ▷ *adj* silver

SILLERS > SILLER

SILLIBUB *n* syllabub

SILLIBUBS > SILLIBUB

SILLIER > SILLY

SILLIES > SILLY

SILLIEST > SILLY

SILLILY > SILLY

SILLINESS > SILLY

SILLOCK *n* young coalfish

SILLOCKS > SILLOCK

SILLS > SILL

SILLY *adj* foolish ▷ *n* foolish person

SILO *n* pit or airtight tower for storing silage or grains ▷ *vb* put in a silo

SILOED > SILO

SILOING > SILO

SILOS > SILO

SILOXANE *n* any of a class of compounds containing alternate silicon and oxygen atoms

SILOXANES > SILOXANE

SILPHIA > SILPHIUM

SILPHIUM *n* American flowering wild plant

SILPHIUMS > SILPHIUM

SILT *n* mud deposited by moving water ▷ *vb* fill or be choked with silt

SILTATION > SILT

SILTED > SILT

SILTIER > SILT

SILTIEST > SILT

SILTING > SILT

SILTS > SILT

SILTSTONE *n* variety of fine sandstone formed from consolidated silt

SILTY > SILT

SILURIAN *adj* formed in the third period of the Palaeozoic

SILURID *n* type of freshwater fish of the family which includes catfish

SILURIDS > SILURID

SILURIST n member of ancient Silurian tribe
SILURISTS > SILURIST
SILUROID n freshwater fish
SILUROIDS > SILUROID
SILVA same as > SYLVA
SILVAE > SILVA
SILVAN same as > SYLVAN
SILVANS > SILVAN
SILVAS > SILVA
SILVATIC adj wild, not domestic
SILVER n white precious metal ▷ adj made of or of the colour of silver ▷ vb coat with silver
SILVERED > SILVER
SILVERER > SILVER
SILVERERS > SILVER
SILVEREYE n greenish-coloured songbird of Africa, Australia, New Zealand, and Asia
SILVERIER > SILVERY
SILVERING > SILVER
SILVERISE same as > SILVERIZE
SILVERIZE vb coat with silver
SILVERLY adv like silver
SILVERN adj silver
SILVERS > SILVER
SILVERTIP n mature grizzly bear
SILVERY adj like silver
SILVEX n type of weedkiller
SILVEXES > SILVEX
SILVICAL adj of trees
SILVICS n study of trees
SILYMARIN n antioxidant found in milk thistle
SIM n computer game that simulates an activity
SIMA n silicon-rich and magnesium-rich rocks of the earth's oceanic crust
SIMAR variant spelling of > CYMAR
SIMAROUBA n tropical American tree with divided leaves and fleshy fruits
SIMARRE n woman's loose gown
SIMARRES > SIMARRE
SIMARS > SIMAR
SIMARUBA same as > SIMAROUBA
SIMARUBAS > SIMARUBA
SIMAS > SIMA
SIMATIC > SIMA
SIMAZINE n organic weedkiller
SIMAZINES > SIMAZINE
SIMBA E African word for > LION
SIMBAS > SIMBA
SIMCHA n Jewish celebration or festival

SIMCHAS > SIMCHA
SIMI n East African sword
SIMIAL adj of apes
SIMIAN n monkey or ape ▷ adj of or resembling a monkey or ape
SIMIANS > SIMIAN
SIMILAR adj alike but not identical
SIMILARLY > SIMILAR
SIMILE n figure of speech comparing one thing to another, using 'as' or 'like'
SIMILES > SIMILE
SIMILISE same as > SIMILIZE
SIMILISED > SIMILISE
SIMILISES > SIMILISE
SIMILIZE vb use similes
SIMILIZED > SIMILIZE
SIMILIZES > SIMILIZE
SIMILOR n alloy used in cheap jewellery
SIMILORS > SIMILOR
SIMIOID adj of apes
SIMIOUS adj of apes
SIMIS > SIMI
SIMITAR same as > SCIMITAR
SIMITARS > SIMITAR
SIMKIN word used in India for > CHAMPAGNE
SIMKINS > SIMKIN
SIMLIN n American variety of squash plant
SIMLINS > SIMLIN
SIMMER vb cook gently at just below boiling point ▷ n state of simmering
SIMMERED > SIMMER
SIMMERING > SIMMER
SIMMERS > SIMMER
SIMNEL n fruit cake with marzipan eaten at Easter
SIMNELS > SIMNEL
SIMOLEON n American slang for dollar
SIMOLEONS > SIMOLEON
SIMONIAC n person who is guilty of practising simony
SIMONIACS > SIMONIAC
SIMONIES > SIMONY
SIMONIOUS > SIMONY
SIMONISE same as > SIMONIZE
SIMONISED > SIMONISE
SIMONISES > SIMONISE
SIMONIST > SIMONY
SIMONISTS > SIMONY
SIMONIZE vb polish with wax
SIMONIZED > SIMONIZE
SIMONIZES > SIMONIZE
SIMONY n practice of buying or selling Church benefits

SIMOOM n hot suffocating sand-laden desert wind
SIMOOMS > SIMOOM
SIMOON same as > SIMOOM
SIMOONS > SIMOON
SIMORG n bird in Persian myth
SIMORGS > SIMORG
SIMP short for > SIMPLETON
SIMPAI n Indonesian monkey
SIMPAIS > SIMPAI
SIMPATICO adj pleasant or congenial
SIMPER vb smile in a silly or affected way ▷ n simpering smile
SIMPERED > SIMPER
SIMPERER > SIMPER
SIMPERERS > SIMPER
SIMPERING > SIMPER
SIMPERS > SIMPER
SIMPKIN word used in India for > CHAMPAGNE
SIMPKINS > SIMPKIN
SIMPLE adj easy to understand or do ▷ vb archaic word meaning to look for medicinal herbs
SIMPLED > SIMPLE
SIMPLER > SIMPLE
SIMPLERS > SIMPLE
SIMPLES > SIMPLE
SIMPLESSE n old word meaning simplicity
SIMPLEST > SIMPLE
SIMPLETON n unintelligent person
SIMPLEX adj permitting the transmission of signals in only one direction in a radio circuit ▷ n simple not a compound word
SIMPLEXES > SIMPLEX
SIMPLICES > SIMPLEX
SIMPLICIA n species of moth
SIMPLIFY vb make less complicated
SIMPLING > SIMPLE
SIMPLINGS > SIMPLE
SIMPLISM n quality of being extremely naive
SIMPLISMS > SIMPLISM
SIMPLIST n old word meaning expert in herbal medicine
SIMPLISTE adj simplistic ▷ n person who tends to oversimplify
SIMPLISTS > SIMPLIST
SIMPLY adv in a simple manner
SIMPS > SIMP
SIMS > SIM
SIMUL adj simultaneous ▷ n simultaneous broadcast
SIMULACRA pl n representations of things
SIMULACRE n resemblance
SIMULANT adj simulating ▷ n simulant thing

SIMULANTS > SIMULANT
SIMULAR n person or thing that simulates or imitates ▷ adj fake
SIMULARS > SIMULAR
SIMULATE vb make a pretence of ▷ adj assumed or simulated
SIMULATED adj being an imitation of the genuine article, usually made from cheaper material
SIMULATES > SIMULATE
SIMULATOR n device that simulates specific conditions for the purposes of research or training
SIMULCAST vb broadcast (a programme) simultaneously on radio and television ▷ n programme broadcast in this way
SIMULIUM n tropical fly
SIMULIUMS > SIMULIUM
SIMULS > SIMUL
SIMURG same as > SIMURGH
SIMURGH n bird in Persian myth
SIMURGHS > SIMURGH
SIMURGS > SIMURG
SIN n offence or transgression ▷ vb commit a sin
SINAPISM n mixture of black mustard seeds and an adhesive, applied to the skin
SINAPISMS > SINAPISM
SINCE prep during the period of time after ▷ adv from that time
SINCERE adj without pretence or deceit
SINCERELY > SINCERE
SINCERER > SINCERE
SINCEREST > SINCERE
SINCERITY > SINCERE
SINCIPITA > SINCIPUT
SINCIPUT n forward upper part of the skull
SINCIPUTS > SINCIPUT
SIND variant of > SYNE
SINDED > SIND
SINDING > SIND
SINDINGS > SIND
SINDON n type of cloth
SINDONS > SINDON
SINDS > SIND
SINE same as > SYNE
SINECURE n paid job with minimal duties
SINECURES > SINECURE
SINED > SINE
SINES > SINE
SINEW n tough fibrous tissue joining muscle to bone ▷ vb make strong
SINEWED adj having sinews

SINEWIER > SINEWY
SINEWIEST > SINEWY
SINEWING > SINEW
SINEWLESS > SINEW
SINEWS > SINEW
SINEWY adj lean and muscular
SINFONIA n symphony orchestra
SINFONIAS > SINFONIA
SINFONIE > SINFONIA
SINFUL adj guilty of sin
SINFULLY > SINFUL
SING vb make musical sounds with the voice ▷ n act or performance of singing
SINGABLE > SING
SINGALONG n act of singing along with a performer
SINGE vb burn the surface of ▷ n superficial burn
SINGED > SINGE
SINGEING > SINGE
SINGER n person who sings, esp professionally
SINGERS > SINGER
SINGES > SINGE
SINGING > SING
SINGINGLY > SING
SINGINGS > SING
SINGLE adj one only ▷ n single thing ▷ vb pick out from others
SINGLED > SINGLE
SINGLEDOM n state of being unmarried or not involved in a long-term relationship
SINGLES > SINGLE
SINGLET n sleeveless vest
SINGLETON n only card of a particular suit held by a player
SINGLETS > SINGLET
SINGLING > SINGLE
SINGLINGS > SINGLE
SINGLY adv one at a time
SINGS > SING
SINGSONG n informal singing session ▷ adj (of the voice) repeatedly rising and falling in pitch
SINGSONGS > SINGSONG
SINGSONGY adj having a singsong rhythm
SINGSPIEL n type of German comic opera with spoken dialogue
SINGULAR adj (of a word or form) denoting one person or thing ▷ n singular form of a word
SINGULARS > SINGULAR
SINGULARY adj (of an operator) monadic
SINGULT n old word meaning sob
SINGULTS > SINGULT
SINGULTUS technical name for > HICCUP
SINH n hyperbolic sine
SINHS > SINH

SINICAL > SINE
SINICISE same as > SINICIZE
SINICISED > SINICISE
SINICISES > SINICISE
SINICIZE vb make Chinese
SINICIZED > SINICIZE
SINICIZES > SINICIZE
SINING > SINE
SINISTER adj threatening or suggesting evil or harm
SINISTRAL adj of, relating to, or located on the left side, esp the left side of the body
SINK vb submerge (in liquid) ▷ n fixed basin with a water supply and drainage pipe
SINKABLE > SINK
SINKAGE n act of sinking or degree to which something sinks or has sunk
SINKAGES > SINKAGE
SINKER n weight for a fishing line
SINKERS > SINKER
SINKFUL n amount that can be held in a sink
SINKFULS > SINKFUL
SINKHOLE n depression in the ground surface where a stream disappears underground
SINKHOLES > SINKHOLE
SINKIER > SINKY
SINKIEST > SINKY
SINKING > SINK
SINKINGS > SINK
SINKS > SINK
SINKY adj giving underfoot
SINLESS adj free from sin or guilt
SINLESSLY > SINLESS
SINNED > SIN
SINNER n person that sins ▷ vb behave like a sinner
SINNERED > SINNER
SINNERING > SINNER
SINNERS > SINNER
SINNET n braided rope
SINNETS > SINNET
SINNING > SIN
SINNINGIA n tropical flowering plant
SINOLOGUE n person who studies Chinese culture, etc
SINOLOGY n study of Chinese culture, etc
SINOPIA n pigment made from iron ore
SINOPIAS > SINOPIA
SINOPIE > SINOPIA
SINOPIS n pigment made from iron ore
SINOPISES > SINOPIS
SINOPITE n iron ore

SINOPITES > SINOPITE
SINS > SIN
SINSYNE adv Scots word meaning since
SINTER n whitish porous incrustation deposited from hot springs ▷ vb form large particles from (powders) by heating or pressure
SINTERED > SINTER
SINTERIER > SINTERY
SINTERING > SINTER
SINTERS > SINTER
SINTERY adj consisting of sinter
SINUATE vb wind
SINUATED same as > SINUATE
SINUATELY > SINUATE
SINUATES > SINUATE
SINUATING > SINUATE
SINUATION same as > SINUOSITY
SINUITIS variant of > SINUSITIS
SINUOSE adj sinuous
SINUOSITY n quality of being sinuous
SINUOUS adj full of turns or curves
SINUOUSLY > SINUOUS
SINUS n hollow space in a bone, esp an air passage opening into the nose
SINUSES > SINUS
SINUSITIS n inflammation of a sinus membrane
SINUSLIKE > SINUS
SINUSOID n blood vessel in certain organs ▷ adj resembling a sinus
SINUSOIDS > SINUSOID
SIP vb drink in small mouthfuls ▷ n amount sipped
SIPE vb soak
SIPED > SIPE
SIPES > SIPE
SIPHON n bent tube which uses air pressure to draw liquid from a container ▷ vb draw off thus
SIPHONAGE > SIPHON
SIPHONAL adj like a siphon
SIPHONATE adj having a syphon
SIPHONED > SIPHON
SIPHONET n sucking tube on an aphid
SIPHONETS > SIPHONET
SIPHONIC same as > SIPHONAL
SIPHONING > SIPHON
SIPHONS > SIPHON
SIPHUNCLE n tube inside shellfish
SIPING > SIPE
SIPPABLE adj able to be sipped
SIPPED > SIP
SIPPER > SIP

SIPPERS > SIP
SIPPET n small piece of toast eaten with soup or gravy
SIPPETS > SIPPET
SIPPING > SIP
SIPPLE vb sip
SIPPLED > SIPPLE
SIPPLES > SIPPLE
SIPPLING > SIPPLE
SIPPY adj as in sippy cup infant's drinking cup with a tight-fitting lid and perforated spout
SIPS > SIP
SIR n polite term of address for a man ▷ vb call someone 'sir'
SIRCAR n government in India
SIRCARS > SIRCAR
SIRDAR same as > SARDAR
SIRDARS > SIRDAR
SIRE n male parent of a horse or other domestic animal ▷ vb father
SIRED > SIRE
SIREE emphasized form of > SIR
SIREES > SIREE
SIREN n device making a loud wailing noise as a warning
SIRENIAN n animal such as the dugong and manatee
SIRENIANS > SIRENIAN
SIRENIC > SIREN
SIRENISE variant of > SIRENIZE
SIRENISED > SIRENISE
SIRENISES > SIRENISE
SIRENIZE vb bewitch
SIRENIZED > SIRENIZE
SIRENIZES > SIRENIZE
SIRENS > SIREN
SIRES > SIRE
SIRGANG n Asian bird
SIRGANGS > SIRGANG
SIRI n betel
SIRIASES > SIRIASIS
SIRIASIS n sunstroke
SIRIH n betel
SIRIHS > SIRIH
SIRING > SIRE
SIRINGS > SIRING
SIRIS > SIRI
SIRKAR n government in India
SIRKARS > SIRKAR
SIRLOIN n prime cut of loin of beef
SIRLOINS > SIRLOIN
SIRNAME vb old form of surname
SIRNAMED > SIRNAME
SIRNAMES > SIRNAME
SIRNAMING > SIRNAME
SIROC n sirocco
SIROCCO n hot wind blowing from N Africa into S Europe

SIROCCOS > SIROCCO
SIROCS > SIROC
SIRONISE *same as*
> SIRONIZE
SIRONISED
> SIRONISE
SIRONISES
> SIRONISE
SIRONIZE *vb* treat (a woollen fabric) chemically to prevent it wrinkling after being washed
SIRONIZED
> SIRONIZE
SIRONIZES
> SIRONIZE
SIROSET *adj* of the chemical treatment of woollen fabrics to give a permanent-press effect
SIRRA *disrespectful form of*
> SIR
SIRRAH *n* contemptuous term used in addressing a man or boy
SIRRAHS > SIRRAH
SIRRAS > SIRRA
SIRRED > SIR
SIRREE *n* form of 'sir' used for emphasis
SIRREES > SIRREE
SIRRING > SIR
SIRS > SIR
SIRTUIN *n* protein that regulates cell metabolism and ageing
SIRTUINS > SIRTUIN
SIRUP *same as* **>** SYRUP
SIRUPED > SIRUP
SIRUPIER > SIRUP
SIRUPIEST > SIRUP
SIRUPING > SIRUP
SIRUPS > SIRUP
SIRUPY > SIRUP
SIRVENTE *n* verse form employed by the troubadours of Provence to satirize political themes
SIRVENTES
> SIRVENTE
SIS *n* sister
SISAL *n* (fibre of) plant used in making ropes
SISALS > SISAL
SISERARY *n* scolding
SISES > SIS
SISKIN *n* yellow-and-black finch
SISKINS > SISKIN
SISS *shortening of*
> SISTER
SISSES > SISS
SISSIER > SISSY
SISSIES > SISSY
SISSIEST > SISSY
SISSIFIED > SISSY
SISSINESS > SISSY
SISSOO *n* Indian tree
SISSOOS > SISSOO
SISSY *n* derogatory word for a weak or cowardly (person) ▷ *adj* weak or cowardly
SISSYISH > SISSY
SISSYNESS > SISSY
SIST *vb* Scottish law term meaning stop

SISTA *n* informal term for an African-American woman
SISTAS > SISTA
SISTED > SIST
SISTER *n* girl or woman with the same parents as another person ▷ *adj* closely related, similar ▷ *vb* be or be like a sister
SISTERED > SISTER
SISTERING > SISTER
SISTERLY *adj* of or like a sister
SISTERS > SISTER
SISTING > SIST
SISTRA > SISTRUM
SISTROID *adj* contained between the convex sides of two intersecting curves
SISTRUM *n* musical instrument of ancient Egypt consisting of a metal rattle
SISTRUMS > SISTRUM
SISTS > SIST
SIT *vb* rest one's body upright on the buttocks
SITAR *n* Indian stringed musical instrument
SITARIST > SITAR
SITARISTS > SITAR
SITARS > SITAR
SITATUNGA *another name for* **>** MARSHBUCK
SITCOM *n* situation comedy
SITCOMS > SITCOM
SITE *n* place where something is, was, or is intended to be located ▷ *vb* provide with a site
SITED > SITE
SITELLA *n* a type of small generally black-and-white bird
SITELLAS > SITELLA
SITES > SITE
SITFAST *n* sore on a horse's back caused by rubbing of the saddle
SITFASTS > SITFAST
SITH *archaic word for*
> SINCE
SITHE *vb* old form of scythe
SITHED > SITHE
SITHEE *interj* look here! listen!
SITHEN *adv* old word meaning since
SITHENCE *adv* old word meaning since
SITHENS *adv* old word meaning since
SITHES > SITHE
SITHING > SITHE
SITING > act of siting
SITINGS > SITING
SITIOLOGY *n* study of diet and nutrition
SITKA *modifier* as in *sitka spruce* tall North American spruce tree
SITKAMER *n* sitting room
SITKAMERS
> SITKAMER

SITOLOGY *n* scientific study of food, diet, and nutrition
SITREP *n* military situation report
SITREPS > SITREP
SITS > SIT
SITTAR *n* sitar
SITTARS > SITTAR
SITTELLA *variant spelling of* **>** SITELLA
SITTELLAS
> SITTELLA
SITTEN *adj* dialect word for in the saddle
SITTER *n* baby-sitter
SITTERS > SITTER
SITTINE *adj* of nuthatch bird family ▷ *n* type of nuthatch
SITTINES > SITTINE
SITTING > SIT
SITTINGS > SIT
SITUATE *vb* place ▷ *adj* (now used esp in legal contexts) situated
SITUATED > SITUATE
SITUATES > SITUATE
SITUATING > SITUATE
SITUATION *n* state of affairs
SITULA *n* bucket-shaped container
SITULAE > SITULA
SITUP *n* exercise in which the body is brought into a sitting position
SITUPS > SITUP
SITUS *n* position or location
SITUSES > SITUS
SITUTUNGA *n* African antelope
SITZ *n* as in *sitz bath* bath in which the buttocks and hips are immersed in hot water
SITZKRIEG *n* period during a war in which both sides change positions very slowly or not at all
SITZMARK *n* depression in the snow where a skier has fallen
SITZMARKS
> SITZMARK
SIVER *same as* **>** SYVER
SIVERS > SIVER
SIWASH *vb* (in the Pacific Northwest) to camp out with only natural shelter
SIWASHED > SIWASH
SIWASHES > SIWASH
SIWASHING > SIWASH
SIX *n* one more than five
SIXAIN *n* stanza or poem of six lines
SIXAINE *n* six-line stanza of poetry
SIXAINES > SIXAINE
SIXAINS > SIXAIN
SIXER *same as* **>** SIX
SIXERS > SIXER
SIXES > SIX
SIXFOLD *adj* having six times as many or as much ▷ *adv* by six times as many or as much

SIXISH *adj* around six years of age
SIXMO *n* book size resulting from folding a sheet of paper into six leaves
SIXMOS > SIXMO
SIXPENCE *n* former British and Australian coin worth six pennies
SIXPENCES
> SIXPENCE
SIXPENNY *adj* (of a nail) two inches in length
SIXSCORE *n* hundred and twenty
SIXSCORES > SIXSCORE
SIXTE *n* sixth of eight basic positions from which a parry or attack can be made in fencing
SIXTEEN *n* six and ten
SIXTEENER *n* poem verse with sixteen syllables
SIXTEENMO *n* book size resulting from folding a sheet of paper into 16 leaves or 32 pages
SIXTEENS > SIXTEEN
SIXTEENTH *adj* coming after the fifteenth in numbering order ▷ *n* one of 16 equal or nearly equal parts of something
SIXTES > SIXTE
SIXTH *n* number six in a series ▷ *adj* coming after the fifth and before the seventh in numbering order
SIXTHLY *adv* in the sixth place or position
SIXTHS > SIXTH
SIXTIES > SIXTY
SIXTIETH *adj* being the ordinal number of *sixty* in numbering order ▷ *n* one of 60 approximately equal parts of something
SIXTIETHS
> SIXTIETH
SIXTY *n* six times ten
SIXTYFOLD *adj* multiplied sixty times
SIXTYISH > SIXTY
SIZABLE *adj* quite large
SIZABLY > SIZABLE
SIZAR *n* undergraduate receiving a maintenance grant from the college
SIZARS > SIZAR
SIZARSHIP > SIZAR
SIZE *n* dimensions, bigness ▷ *vb* arrange according to size
SIZEABLE *same as*
> SIZABLE
SIZEABLY > SIZABLE
SIZED *adj* of a specified size
SIZEISM *n* discrimination on the basis of a person's size
SIZEISMS > SIZEISM
SIZEIST > SIZEISM
SIZEISTS > SIZEISM
SIZEL *n* scrap metal clippings

S

SIZELS > SIZEL
SIZER > SIZE
SIZERS > SIZE
SIZES > SIZE
SIZIER > SIZE
SIZIEST > SIZE
SIZINESS > SIZE
SIZING > SIZE
SIZINGS > SIZE
SIZISM *n* discrimination against people because of weight
SIZISMS > SIZISM
SIZIST > SIZISM
SIZISTS > SIZISM
SIZY > SIZE
SIZZLE *vb* make a hissing sound like frying fat ▷ *n* hissing sound
SIZZLED > SIZZLE
SIZZLER *n* something that sizzles
SIZZLERS > SIZZLER
SIZZLES > SIZZLE
SIZZLING *adj* extremely hot
SIZZLINGS
> SIZZLING
SJAMBOK *n* whip or riding crop made of hide ▷ *vb* beat with a sjambok
SJAMBOKED > SJAMBOK
SJAMBOKS > SJAMBOK
SJOE *interj* South African exclamation of surprise, admiration, exhaustion, etc
SKA *n* type of Jamaican pop music of the 1960s
SKAG *same as* > SCAG
SKAGS > SKAG
SKAIL *vb* Scots word meaning disperse
SKAILED > SKAIL
SKAILING > SKAIL
SKAILS > SKAIL
SKAITH *vb* Scots word meaning injure
SKAITHED > SKAITH
SKAITHING > SKAITH
SKAITHS > SKAITH
SKALD *n* (in ancient Scandinavia) a bard or minstrel
SKALDIC > SKALD
SKALDS > SKALD
SKALDSHIP *n* (in ancient Scandinavia) position of bard
SKANGER *n* insulting Irish word for a young working-class person who wears casual sports clothes
SKANGERS > SKANGER
SKANK *n* fast dance to reggae music ▷ *vb* perform this dance
SKANKED > SKANK
SKANKER > SKANK
SKANKERS > SKANK
SKANKIER > SKANKY
SKANKIEST > SKANKY
SKANKING > SKANK
SKANKINGS > SKANK
SKANKS > SKANK
SKANKY *adj* dirty or unattractive

SKART *Scots word for* > CORMORANT
SKARTH *Scots word for* > CORMORANT
SKARTHS > SKARTH
SKARTS > SKART
SKAS > SKA
SKAT *n* three-handed card game using 32 cards
SKATE *n* boot with a steel blade or sets of wheels attached to the sole ▷ *vb* glide on or as if on skates
SKATED > SKATE
SKATEPARK *n* place for skateboarding
SKATEPUNK *n* member of a skateboarding subculture
SKATER *n* person who skates
SKATERS > SKATER
SKATES > SKATE
SKATING > SKATE
SKATINGS > SKATE
SKATOL *n* skatole
SKATOLE *n* white or brownish crystalline solid
SKATOLES > SKATOLE
SKATOLS > SKATOL
SKATS > SKAT
SKATT *n* dialect word meaning throw
SKATTS > SKATT
SKAW *variant of* > SCAW
SKAWS > SKAW
SKEAN *n* kind of double-edged dagger
SKEANE *same as* > SKEIN
SKEANES > SKEANE
SKEANS > SKEAN
SKEAR *dialect form of* > SCARE
SKEARED > SKEAR
SKEARIER > SKEARY
SKEARIEST > SKEARY
SKEARING > SKEAR
SKEARS > SKEAR
SKEARY *dialect form of* > SCARY
SKED *vb* short for schedule
SKEDADDLE *vb* run off ▷ *n* hasty retreat
SKEDDED > SKED
SKEDDING > SKED
SKEDS > SKED
SKEE *variant spelling of* > SKI
SKEECHAN *n* old Scots type of beer
SKEECHANS
> SKEECHAN
SKEED > SKEE
SKEEF *adj* South African slang for at an oblique angle
SKEEING > SKEE
SKEELIER > SKEELY
SKEELIEST > SKEELY
SKEELY *adj* Scots word meaning skilful
SKEEN *n* type of ibex
SKEENS > SKEEN
SKEER *dialect form of* > SCARE
SKEERED > SKEER
SKEERIER > SKEERY

SKEERIEST > SKEERY
SKEERING > SKEER
SKEERS > SKEER
SKEERY *dialect form of* > SCARY
SKEES > SKEE
SKEESICKS *American word meaning* > ROGUE
SKEET *n* form of clay-pigeon shooting
SKEETER *informal word for* > MOSQUITO
SKEETERS > SKEETER
SKEETS > SKEET
SKEEVIER > SKEEVY
SKEEVIEST > SKEEVY
SKEEVY *adj* repulsive
SKEG *n* reinforcing brace between the after end of a keel and the rudderpost
SKEGG *n* skeg
SKEGGER *n* young salmon
SKEGGERS > SKEGGER
SKEGGS > SKEGG
SKEGS > SKEG
SKEIGH *adj* Scots word meaning shy
SKEIGHER > SKEIGH
SKEIGHEST > SKEIGH
SKEIN *n* yarn wound in a loose coil ▷ *vb* wind into a skein
SKEINED > SKEIN
SKEINING > SKEIN
SKEINS > SKEIN
SKELDER *vb* beg
SKELDERED > SKELDER
SKELDERS > SKELDER
SKELETAL > SKELETON
SKELETON *n* framework of bones inside a person's or animal's body ▷ *adj* reduced to a minimum
SKELETONS
> SKELETON
SKELF *n* splinter of wood, esp when embedded accidentally in the skin
SKELFS > SKELF
SKELL *n* homeless person
SKELLIE *adj* skelly
SKELLIED > SKELLY
SKELLIER > SKELLY
SKELLIES > SKELLY
SKELLIEST > SKELLY
SKELLOCH *n* Scots word meaning scream
SKELLOCHS
> SKELLOCH
SKELLS > SKELL
SKELLUM *n* rogue
SKELLUMS > SKELLUM
SKELLY *n* whitefish of certain lakes in the Lake District ▷ *vb* look sideways or squint ▷ *adj* cross-eyed
SKELLYING > SKELLY
SKELM *n* villain or crook
SKELMS > SKELM
SKELP *vb* slap ▷ *n* slap
SKELPED > SKELP
SKELPING > SKELP
SKELPINGS > SKELP
SKELPIT *vb* Scots word meaning skelped
SKELPS > SKELP

SKELTER *vb* scurry
SKELTERED > SKELTER
SKELTERS > SKELTER
SKELUM *n* Scots word meaning rascal
SKELUMS > SKELUM
SKEN *vb* squint or stare
SKENE *n* Scots word meaning dagger
SKENES > SKENE
SKENNED > SKEN
SKENNING > SKEN
SKENS > SKEN
SKEO *n* Scots dialect word meaning hut
SKEOES > SKEO
SKEOS > SKEO
SKEP *n* beehive, esp one constructed of straw ▷ *vb* gather into a hive
SKEPFUL *n* amount skep will hold
SKEPFULS > SKEPFUL
SKEPPED > SKEP
SKEPPING > SKEP
SKEPS > SKEP
SKEPSIS *n* doubt
SKEPSISES > SKEPSIS
SKEPTIC *same as* > SCEPTIC
SKEPTICAL > SKEPTIC
SKEPTICS > SKEPTIC
SKER *vb* scour
SKERRED > SKER
SKERRICK *n* small fragment or amount
SKERRICKS
> SKERRICK
SKERRIES > SKERRY
SKERRING > SKER
SKERRY *n* rocky island or reef
SKERS > SKER
SKET *vb* splash (water)
SKETCH *n* rough drawing ▷ *vb* make a sketch (of)
SKETCHED > SKETCH
SKETCHER > SKETCH
SKETCHERS > SKETCH
SKETCHES > SKETCH
SKETCHIER > SKETCHY
SKETCHILY > SKETCHY
SKETCHING > SKETCH
SKETCHPAD *n* pad of paper for sketching
SKETCHY *adj* incomplete or inadequate
SKETS > SKET
SKETTED > SKET
SKETTING > SKET
SKEW *vb* make slanting or crooked ▷ *adj* slanting or crooked ▷ *n* slanting position
SKEWBACK *n* sloping surface on both sides of a segmental arch that takes the thrust
SKEWBACKS
> SKEWBACK
SKEWBALD *adj* (horse) marked with patches of white and another colour ▷ *n* horse with this marking
SKEWBALDS
> SKEWBALD
SKEWED > SKEW

SKEWER *n* pin to hold meat together during cooking ▷ *vb* fasten with a skewer

SKEWERED > SKEWER

SKEWERING > SKEWER

SKEWERS > SKEWER

SKEWEST > SKEW

SKEWING > SKEW

SKEWNESS *n* quality or condition of being skew

SKEWS > SKEW

SKEWWHIFF *adj* crooked or slanting

SKI *n* one of a pair of long runners fastened to boots for gliding over snow or water ▷ *vb* travel on skis

SKIABLE > SKI

SKIAGRAM *n* picture made from shadows

SKIAGRAMS > SKIAGRAM

SKIAGRAPH *n* skiagram

SKIAMACHY *same as* > SCIAMACHY

SKIASCOPE *n* medical instrument for examining the eye to detect errors of refraction

SKIASCOPY *n* retinoscopy

SKIATRON *n* type of cathode ray tube

SKIATRONS > SKIATRON

SKIBOB *n* vehicle made of two short skis for gliding down snow slopes

SKIBOBBED > SKIBOB

SKIBOBBER > SKIBOB

SKIBOBS > SKIBOB

SKID *vb* (of a moving vehicle) slide sideways uncontrollably ▷ *n* skidding

SKIDDED > SKID

SKIDDER > SKID

SKIDDERS > SKID

SKIDDIER > SKID

SKIDDIEST > SKID

SKIDDING *n* act of skidding

SKIDDINGS > SKIDDING

SKIDDOO *vb* go away quickly

SKIDDOOED > SKIDDOO

SKIDDOOS > SKIDDOO

SKIDDY > SKID

SKIDLID *n* crash helmet

SKIDLIDS > SKIDLID

SKIDMARK *n* mark left by a skid

SKIDMARKS > SKIDMARK

SKIDOO *n* snowmobile ▷ *vb* travel on a skidoo

SKIDOOED > SKIDOO

SKIDOOER *n* person who rides a skidoo

SKIDOOERS > SKIDOOER

SKIDOOING *n* act or instance of riding a snowmobile

SKIDOOS > SKIDOO

SKIDPAD *n* area of road used to test skidding

SKIDPADS > SKIDPAD

SKIDPAN *n* area made slippery so that vehicle drivers can practise controlling skids

SKIDPANS > SKIDPAN

SKIDPROOF *adj* (of a road surface, tyre, etc) preventing or resistant to skidding

SKIDS > SKID

SKIDWAY *n* platform on which logs ready for sawing are piled

SKIDWAYS > SKIDWAY

SKIED > SKY

SKIER > SKI

SKIERS > SKI

SKIES > SKY

SKIEY *adj* of the sky

SKIEYER > SKIEY

SKIEYEST > SKIEY

SKIFF *n* small boat ▷ *vb* travel in a skiff

SKIFFED > SKIFF

SKIFFING > SKIFF

SKIFFLE *n* style of popular music of the 1950s ▷ *vb* play this style of music

SKIFFLED > SKIFFLE

SKIFFLES > SKIFFLE

SKIFFLESS > SKIFF

SKIFFLING > SKIFFLE

SKIFFS > SKIFF

SKIING > SKI

SKIINGS > SKI

SKIJORER > SKIJORING

SKIJORERS > SKIJORING

SKIJORING *n* sport in which a skier is pulled over snow or ice, usually by a horse

SKIJUMPER *n* one who engages in the sport of skijumping

SKIKJORER *n* one who engages in the sport of skijoring

SKILFUL *adj* having or showing skill

SKILFULL *less common spelling of* > SKILFUL

SKILFULLY > SKILFUL

SKILL *n* special ability or expertise

SKILLED *adj* possessing or demonstrating skill, or special training

SKILLESS > SKILL

SKILLET *n* small frying pan or shallow cooking pot

SKILLETS > SKILLET

SKILLFUL *same as* > SKILFUL

SKILLIER > SKILLY

SKILLIES > SKILLY

SKILLIEST > SKILLY

SKILLING *n* former Scandinavian coin of low denomination

SKILLINGS > SKILLING

SKILLION *n* part of a building having a lower, esp sloping, roof

SKILLIONS > SKILLION

SKILLS > SKILL

SKILLY *n* thin soup or gruel ▷ *adj* skilled

SKIM *vb* remove floating matter from the surface of (a liquid) ▷ *n* act or process of skimming

SKIMBOARD *n* type of surfboard, shorter than standard and rounded at both ends ▷ *vb* surf on a skimboard

SKIMMED > SKIM

SKIMMER *n* person or thing that skims

SKIMMERS > SKIMMER

SKIMMIA *n* shrub of S and SE Asia

SKIMMIAS > SKIMMIA

SKIMMING > SKIM

SKIMMINGS *pl n* material that is skimmed off a liquid

SKIMOBILE *n* motor vehicle with skis for travelling on snow

SKIMP *vb* not invest enough time, money, material, etc

SKIMPED > SKIMP

SKIMPIER > SKIMPY

SKIMPIEST > SKIMPY

SKIMPILY > SKIMPY

SKIMPING > SKIMP

SKIMPS > SKIMP

SKIMPY *adj* scanty or insufficient

SKIMS > SKIM

SKIN *n* outer covering of the body ▷ *vb* remove the skin of

SKINCARE *n* use of cosmetics in taking care of skin

SKINCARES > SKINCARE

SKINFLICK *n* film containing much nudity and sex

SKINFLINT *n* miser

SKINFOOD *n* cosmetic cream for the skin

SKINFOODS > SKINFOOD

SKINFUL *n* sufficient alcoholic drink to make one drunk

SKINFULS > SKINFUL

SKINHEAD *n* youth with very short hair

SKINHEADS > SKTNHEAD

SKINK *n* type of lizard with reduced limbs and smooth scales ▷ *vb* serve a drink

SKINKED > SKINK

SKINKER > SKINK

SKINKERS > SKINK

SKINKING > SKINK

SKINKS > SKINK

SKINLESS > SKIN

SKINLIKE > SKIN

SKINNED > SKIN

SKINNER *n* person who prepares or deals in animal skins

SKINNERS > SKINNER

SKINNIER > SKINNY

SKINNIES > SKINNY

SKINNIEST > SKINNY

SKINNING > SKIN

SKINNY *adj* thin ▷ *n* information

SKINS > SKIN

SKINSUIT *n* skintight one-piece garment worn by cyclists to reduce friction

SKINSUITS > SKINSUIT

SKINT *adj* having no money

SKINTER > SKINT

SKINTEST > SKINT

SKINTIGHT *adj* fitting tightly over the body ▷ *n* tight-fitting garment

SKIO *n* Scots dialect word meaning hut

SKIOES > SKIO

SKIORER *n* one who engages in the sport of skioring

SKIORERS > SKIORER

SKIORING *n* sport of being towed on skis by horse

SKIORINGS > SKIORING

SKIOS > SKIO

SKIP *vb* leap lightly from one foot to the other ▷ *n* skipping

SKIPJACK *n* important food fish of tropical seas

SKIPJACKS > SKIPJACK

SKIPLANE *n* aircraft fitted with skis to enable it to land on and take off from snow

SKIPLANES > SKIPLANE

SKIPPABLE > SKIP

SKIPPED > SKIP

SKIPPER *vb* captain ▷ *n* captain of a ship or aircraft

SKIPPERED > SKIPPER

SKIPPERS > SKIPPER

SKIPPET *n* small round box for preserving a document or seal

SKIPPETS > SKIPPET

SKIPPIER > SKIPPY

SKIPPIEST > SKIPPY

SKIPPING > SKIP

SKIPPINGS > SKIP

SKIPPY *adj* in high spirits

SKIPS > SKIP

SKIRL *n* sound of bagpipes ▷ *vb* (of bagpipes) to give out a shrill sound

SKIRLED > SKIRL

SKIRLING > SKIRL

SKIRLINGS > SKIRL

SKIRLS > SKIRL

SKIRMISH *n* brief or minor fight or argument ▷ *vb* take part in a skirmish

S

SKIRR vb move, run, or fly rapidly ▷ n whirring or grating sound, as of the wings of birds in flight
SKIRRED > SKIRR
SKIRRET n umbelliferous Old World plant
SKIRRETS > SKIRRET
SKIRRING > SKIRR
SKIRRS > SKIRR
SKIRT n woman's garment hanging from the waist ▷ vb border
SKIRTED > SKIRT
SKIRTER n person who skirts fleeces
SKIRTERS > SKIRTER
SKIRTING n border fixed round the base of an interior wall to protect it from kicks, dirt, etc
SKIRTINGS pl n ragged edges trimmed from the fleece of a sheep
SKIRTLESS > SKIRT
SKIRTLIKE > SKIRT
SKIRTS > SKIRT
SKIS > SKI
SKIT n brief satirical sketch
SKITCH vb (of a dog) to attack
SKITCHED > SKITCH
SKITCHES > SKITCH
SKITCHING > SKITCH
SKITE vb boast ▷ vb boast
SKITED > SKITE
SKITES > SKITE
SKITING > SKITE
SKITS > SKIT
SKITTER vb move or run rapidly or lightly
SKITTERED > SKITTER
SKITTERS > SKITTER
SKITTERY adj moving lightly and rapidly
SKITTISH adj playful or lively
SKITTLE n bottle-shaped object used as a target in some games ▷ vb play skittles
SKITTLED > SKITTLE
SKITTLES > SKITTLE
SKITTLING > SKITTLE
SKIVE vb evade work or responsibility
SKIVED > SKIVE
SKIVER n tanned outer layer split from a skin ▷ vb cut leather
SKIVERED > SKIVER
SKIVERING > SKIVER
SKIVERS > SKIVER
SKIVES > SKIVE
SKIVIE adj old Scots word meaning disarranged
SKIVIER > SKIVIE
SKIVIEST > SKIVIE
SKIVING > SKIVE
SKIVINGS > SKIVE
SKIVVIED > SKIVVY
SKIVVIES > SKIVVY
SKIVVY n female servant who does menial work ▷ vb work as a skivvy

SKIVVYING > SKIVVY
SKIVY > SKIVE
SKIWEAR n clothes for skiing in
SKIWEARS > SKIWEAR
SKLATE Scots word for > SLATE
SKLATED > SKLATE
SKLATES > SKLATE
SKLATING > SKLATE
SKLENT Scots word for > SLANT
SKLENTED > SKLENT
SKLENTING > SKLENT
SKLENTS > SKLENT
SKLIFF n Scots word meaning little piece ▷ vb shuffle (the feet)
SKLIFFED > SKLIFF
SKLIFFING > SKLIFF
SKLIFFS > SKLIFF
SKLIM vb Scots word meaning climb
SKLIMMED > SKLIM
SKLIMMING > SKLIM
SKLIMS > SKLIM
SKOAL same as > SKOL
SKOALED > SKOAL
SKOALING > SKOAL
SKOALS > SKOAL
SKODIER > SKODY
SKODIEST > SKODY
SKODY adj dirty, unkempt
SKOFF vb eat greedily
SKOFFED > SKOFF
SKOFFING > SKOFF
SKOFFS > SKOFF
SKOG same as > SCOG
SKOGGED > SKOG
SKOGGING > SKOG
SKOGS > SKOG
SKOKIAAN n (in South Africa) a potent alcoholic beverage
SKOKIAANS > SKOKIAAN
SKOL sentence substitute good health! (a drinking toast) ▷ vb down (an alcoholic drink) in one go
SKOLED > SKOL
SKOLIA > SKOLION
SKOLING > SKOL
SKOLION n ancient Greek drinking song
SKOLLED > SKOL
SKOLLIE same as > SKOLLY
SKOLLIES > SKOLLY
SKOLLING > SKOL
SKOLLY n hooligan, usually one of a gang
SKOLS > SKOL
SKOOKUM adj strong or brave ▷ n strong or brave person
SKOOKUMS > SKOOKUM
SKOOL childish spelling of > SCHOOL
SKOOLS > SKOOL
SKOOSH vb Scots word meaning squirt
SKOOSHED > SKOOSH
SKOOSHES > SKOOSH
SKOOSHING > SKOOSH
SKORDALIA n Greek potato and garlic dip

SKORT n pair of shorts with a front panel which gives the appearance of a skirt
SKORTS > SKORT
SKOSH n little bit
SKOSHES > SKOSH
SKRAN n food
SKRANS > SKRAN
SKREEGH same as > SKREIGH
SKREEGHED > SKREEGH
SKREEGHS > SKREEGH
SKREEN n screen
SKREENS > SKREEN
SKREIGH vb Scots word meaning screech
SKREIGHED > SKREIGH
SKREIGHS > SKREIGH
SKRIECH same as > SKREIGH
SKRIECHED > SKRIECH
SKRIECHS > SKRIECH
SKRIED > SKRY
SKRIEGH same as > SKREIGH
SKRIEGHED > SKRIEGH
SKRIEGHS > SKRIEGH
SKRIES > SKRY
SKRIK n South African word meaning fright
SKRIKE vb cry
SKRIKED > SKRIKE
SKRIKES > SKRIKE
SKRIKING > SKRIKE
SKRIKS > SKRIK
SKRIMMAGE vb scrimmage
SKRIMP vb steal apples
SKRIMPED > SKRIMP
SKRIMPING > SKRIMP
SKRIMPS > SKRIMP
SKRONK n type of dissonant, grating popular music
SKRONKS > SKRONK
SKRUMP vb steal apples
SKRUMPED > SKRUMP
SKRUMPING > SKRUMP
SKRUMPS > SKRUMP
SKRY vb try to tell future
SKRYER > SKRY
SKRYERS > SKRY
SKRYING > SKRY
SKUA n large predatory gull
SKUAS > SKUA
SKUDLER n Scots word meaning leader of festivities
SKUDLERS > SKUDLER
SKUG vb shelter
SKUGGED > SKUG
SKUGGING > SKUG
SKUGS > SKUG
SKULK vb move stealthily ▷ n person who skulks
SKULKED > SKULK
SKULKER > SKULK
SKULKERS > SKULK
SKULKING > SKULK
SKULKINGS > SKULK
SKULKS > SKULK
SKULL n bony framework of the head ▷ vb strike on the head
SKULLCAP n close-fitting brimless cap

SKULLCAPS > SKULLCAP
SKULLED > SKULL
SKULLING > SKULL
SKULLS > SKULL
SKULPIN n North American fish
SKULPINS > SKULPIN
SKUMMER same as > SCUMBER
SKUMMERED > SKUMMER
SKUMMERS > SKUMMER
SKUNK n small mammal which emits a foul-smelling fluid when attacked ▷ vb defeat overwhelmingly in a game
SKUNKBIRD n North American songbird
SKUNKED > SKUNK
SKUNKIER > SKUNK
SKUNKIEST > SKUNK
SKUNKING > SKUNK
SKUNKS > SKUNK
SKUNKWEED n low-growing fetid swamp plant of N America
SKUNKY > SKUNK
SKURRIED > SKURRY
SKURRIES > SKURRY
SKURRY vb scurry
SKURRYING > SKURRY
SKUTTLE vb scuttle
SKUTTLED > SKUTTLE
SKUTTLES > SKUTTLE
SKUTTLING > SKUTTLE
SKY n upper atmosphere as seen from the earth ▷ vb hit high in the air
SKYBOARD n small board used for skysurfing
SKYBOARDS > SKYBOARD
SKYBORN adj born in heaven
SKYBORNE adj flying through sky
SKYBOX n luxurious suite high up in the stand of a sports stadium
SKYBOXES > SKYBOX
SKYBRIDGE n covered, elevated bridge connecting two buildings
SKYCAP n luggage porter at American airport
SKYCAPS > SKYCAP
SKYCLAD adj naked
SKYDIVE vb take part in skydiving
SKYDIVED > SKYDIVE
SKYDIVER > SKYDIVE
SKYDIVERS > SKYDIVE
SKYDIVES > SKYDIVE
SKYDIVING n sport of jumping from an aircraft and performing manoeuvres before opening one's parachute
SKYDOVE > SKYDIVE
SKYED > SKY
SKYER n cricket ball hit up into air
SKYERS > SKYER
SKYEY adj of the sky
SKYEYER > SKYEY
SKYEYEST > SKYEY

SKYF n South African slang for a cigarette or substance for smoking ▷ vb smoke a cigarette
SKYFED > SKYF
SKYFING > SKYF
SKYFS > SKYF
SKYGLOW n glow in the night sky caused by urban lights
SKYGLOWS > SKYGLOW
SKYHOME n Australian word for a sub-penthouse flat in a tall building
SKYHOMES > SKYHOME
SKYHOOK n hook hung from a helicopter
SKYHOOKS > SKYHOOK
SKYIER > SKYEY
SKYIEST > SKYEY
SKYING > SKY
SKYISH > SKY
SKYJACK vb hijack (an aircraft)
SKYJACKED > SKYJACK
SKYJACKER > SKYJACK
SKYJACKS > SKYJACK
SKYLAB n orbiting space station
SKYLABS > SKYLAB
SKYLARK n lark that sings while soaring at a great height ▷ vb play or frolic
SKYLARKED > SKYLARK
SKYLARKER > SKYLARK
SKYLARKS > SKYLARK
SKYLESS adj having no sky
SKYLIGHT n window in a roof or ceiling
SKYLIGHTS > SKYLIGHT
SKYLIKE > SKY
SKYLINE n outline of buildings, trees, etc against the sky
SKYLINES > SKYLINE
SKYLIT adj having skylight
SKYMAN n paratrooper
SKYMEN > SKYMAN
SKYPHOI > SKYPHOS
SKYPHOS n ancient Greek drinking cup
SKYR n Scandinavian cheese
SKYRE vb Scots word meaning shine
SKYRED > SKYRE
SKYRES > SKYRE
SKYRING > SKYRE
SKYRMION n (in theoretical physics) mathematical model used to model baryons
SKYRMIONS > SKYRMION
SKYROCKET vb rise very quickly
SKYRS > SKYR
SKYSAIL n square sail set above the royal on a square-rigger
SKYSAILS > SKYSAIL
SKYSCAPE n painting, drawing, photograph, etc, representing or depicting the sky

SKYSCAPES > SKYSCAPE
SKYSURF vb perform freefall aerobatics
SKYSURFED > SKYSURF
SKYSURFER n someone who performs stunts with a small board attached to his or her feet while in free fall
SKYSURFS > SKYSURF
SKYTE vb Scots word meaning slide
SKYTED > SKYTE
SKYTES > SKYTE
SKYTING > SKYTE
SKYWALK n tightrope walk at great height
SKYWALKS > SKYWALK
SKYWARD adj towards the sky ▷ adv towards the sky
SKYWARDS same as > SKYWARD
SKYWATCH vb watch the sky in search of celestial bodies or aircraft
SKYWAY n air route
SKYWAYS > SKYWAY
SKYWRITE vb write message in sky with smoke from aircraft
SKYWRITER > SKYWRITE
SKYWRITES > SKYWRITE
SKYWROTE > SKYWRITE
SLAB n broad flat piece ▷ vb cut or make into a slab or slabs
SLABBED > SLAB
SLABBER vb dribble from the mouth
SLABBERED > SLABBER
SLABBERER > SLABBER
SLABBERS > SLABBER
SLABBERY > SLABBER
SLABBIER > SLABBY
SLABBIES > SLABBY
SLABBIEST > SLAB
SLABBING n act of slabbing
SLABBINGS > SLABBING
SLABBY n person who works with slabs of timber
SLABLIKE > SLAB
SLABS > SLAB
SLABSTONE n flagstone
SLACK same as > SLAKE
SLACKED > SLACK
SLACKEN vb make or become slack
SLACKENED > SLACKEN
SLACKENER > SLACKEN
SLACKENS > SLACKEN
SLACKER n person who evades work or duty
SLACKERS > SLACKER
SLACKEST > SLACK
SLACKING > SLACK
SLACKLY > SLACK
SLACKNESS > SLACK
SLACKS pl n casual trousers
SLADANG n Malayan tapir
SLADANGS > SLADANG
SLADE n little valley
SLADES > SLADE

SLAE Scots word for > SLOE
SLAES > SLAE
SLAG n waste left after metal is smelted ▷ vb criticize
SLAGGED > SLAG
SLAGGIER > SLAG
SLAGGIEST > SLAG
SLAGGING > SLAG
SLAGGINGS > SLAG
SLAGGY > SLAG
SLAGHEAP n heap of slag waste
SLAGHEAPS > SLAGHEAP
SLAGS > SLAG
SLAHAL same as > LAHAL
SLAHALS > SLAHAL
SLAID vb (Scot) sledge
SLAIDS > SLAID
SLAIN > SLAY
SLAINTE interj cheers!
SLAIRG Scots word for > SPREAD
SLAIRGED > SLAIRG
SLAIRGING > SLAIRG
SLAIRGS > SLAIRG
SLAISTER vb cover with a sloppy mess ▷ n sloppy mess
SLAISTERS > SLAISTER
SLAISTERY > SLAISTER
SLAKABLE > SLAKE
SLAKE vb satisfy (thirst or desire)
SLAKEABLE > SLAKE
SLAKED > SLAKE
SLAKELESS adj impossible to slake
SLAKER > SLAKE
SLAKERS > SLAKE
SLAKES > SLAKE
SLAKING > SLAKE
SLALOM n skiing or canoeing race over a winding course ▷ vb take part in a slalom
SLALOMED > SLALOM
SLALOMER > SLALOM
SLALOMERS > SLALOM
SLALOMING > SLALOM
SLALOMIST > SLALOM
SLALOMS > SLALOM
SLAM vb shut, put down, or hit violently and noisily ▷ n act or sound of slamming
SLAMDANCE vb dance aggressively, bumping into others
SLAMMAKIN n woman's loose dress
SLAMMED > SLAM
SLAMMER n prison
SLAMMERS > SLAMMER
SLAMMING > SLAM
SLAMMINGS > SLAM
SLAMS > SLAM
SLANDER n false and malicious statement about a person ▷ vb utter slander about
SLANDERED > SLANDER
SLANDERER > SLANDER
SLANDERS > SLANDER

SLANE n spade for cutting turf
SLANES > SLANE
SLANG n very informal language ▷ vb use insulting language to (someone)
SLANGED > SLANG
SLANGER n street vendor
SLANGERS > SLANGER
SLANGIER > SLANG
SLANGIEST > SLANG
SLANGILY > SLANG
SLANGING > SLANG
SLANGINGS > SLANG
SLANGISH > SLANG
SLANGS > SLANG
SLANGUAGE n language using slang
SLANGULAR adj of or using slang
SLANGY > SLANG
SLANK dialect word for > LANK
SLANT vb lean at an angle, slope ▷ n slope
SLANTED > SLANT
SLANTER same as > SLINTER
SLANTERS > SLANTER
SLANTIER > SLANTY
SLANTIEST > SLANTY
SLANTING > SLANT
SLANTLY > SLANT
SLANTS > SLANT
SLANTWAYS same as > SLANTWISE
SLANTWISE adj in a slanting or oblique direction
SLANTY adj slanting
SLAP n blow with the open hand or a flat object ▷ vb strike with the open hand or a flat object
SLAPDASH adj careless and hasty ▷ adv carelessly or hastily ▷ n slapdash activity or work ▷ vb do in a hurried and careless manner
SLAPHAPPY adj cheerfully irresponsible or careless
SLAPHEAD n derogatory term for a bald person
SLAPHEADS > SLAPHEAD
SLAPJACK n simple card game
SLAPJACKS > SLAPJACK
SLAPPED > SLAP
SLAPPER > SLAP
SLAPPERS > SLAP
SLAPPING > SLAP
SLAPPINGS > SLAPPING
SLAPS > SLAP
SLAPSHOT n hard, fast, often wild, shot executed with a powerful downward swing
SLAPSHOTS > SLAPSHOT
SLAPSTICK n boisterous knockabout comedy
SLART vb spill (something)

S

SLARTED > SLART

SLARTING > SLART

SLARTS > SLART

SLASH vb cut with a sweeping stroke ▷ n sweeping stroke

SLASHED > SLASH

SLASHER n machine used for cutting scrub or undergrowth in the bush

SLASHERS > SLASHER

SLASHES > SLASH

SLASHFEST n film or computer game that features bloody killings involving blades

SLASHING adj aggressively critical ▷ n act of slashing

SLASHINGS > SLASHING

SLAT n narrow strip of wood or metal ▷ vb provide with slats

SLATCH n slack part of rope

SLATCHES > SLATCH

SLATE n rock which splits easily into thin layers ▷ vb cover with slates ▷ adj dark grey

SLATED > SLATE

SLATELIKE > SLATE

SLATER n person trained in laying roof slates

SLATERS > SLATER

SLATES > SLATE

SLATEY adj slightly mad

SLATHER vb spread quickly or lavishly

SLATHERED > SLATHER

SLATHERS > SLATHER

SLATIER > SLATY

SLATIEST > SLATY

SLATINESS > SLATY

SLATING n act or process of laying slates

SLATINGS > SLATING

SLATS > SLAT

SLATTED > SLAT

SLATTER vb be slovenly

SLATTERED > SLATTER

SLATTERN n derogatory term for a slovenly woman

SLATTERNS > SLATTERN

SLATTERS > SLATTER

SLATTERY adj slovenly

SLATTING > SLAT

SLATTINGS > SLAT

SLATY adj consisting of or resembling slate

SLAUGHTER vb kill (animals) for food ▷ n slaughtering

SLAVE n person legally owned by another and forced to work for them ▷ vb work like a slave

SLAVED > SLAVE

SLAVER n person or ship engaged in the slave trade ▷ vb dribble saliva from the mouth

SLAVERED > SLAVER

SLAVERER > SLAVER

SLAVERERS > SLAVER

SLAVERIES > SLAVERY

SLAVERING > SLAVER

SLAVERS > SLAVER

SLAVERY n state or condition of being a slave

SLAVES > SLAVE

SLAVEY n female general servant

SLAVEYS > SLAVEY

SLAVING > SLAVE

SLAVISH adj of or like a slave

SLAVISHLY > SLAVISH

SLAVOCRAT n US slaveholder before the Civil War

SLAVOPHIL n person who admires the Slavs or their cultures

SLAW short for > COLESLAW

SLAWS > SLAW

SLAY vb kill

SLAYABLE > SLAY

SLAYED > SLAY

SLAYER > SLAY

SLAYERS > SLAY

SLAYING n act of slaying

SLAYINGS > SLAYING

SLAYS > SLAY

SLEAVE n tangled thread ▷ vb disentangle (twisted thread, etc)

SLEAVED > SLEAVE

SLEAVES > SLEAVE

SLEAVING > SLEAVE

SLEAZE n behaviour considered dishonest or disreputable ▷ vb behave in a sleazy manner

SLEAZEBAG n sleazy person

SLEAZED > SLEAZE

SLEAZES > SLEAZE

SLEAZIER > SLEAZY

SLEAZIEST > SLEAZY

SLEAZILY > SLEAZY

SLEAZING > SLEAZE

SLEAZO n sleazy person

SLEAZOID n sleazy person

SLEAZOIDS > SLEAZOID

SLEAZOS > SLEAZO

SLEAZY adj run-down or sordid

SLEB n celebrity

SLEBS > SLEB

SLED same as > SLEDGE

SLEDDED > SLED

SLEDDER > SLED

SLEDDERS > SLED

SLEDDING > SLED

SLEDDINGS > SLED

SLEDED > SLED

SLEDGE n carriage on runners for sliding on snow ▷ vb travel by sledge

SLEDGED > SLEDGE

SLEDGER > SLEDGE

SLEDGERS > SLEDGE

SLEDGES > SLEDGE

SLEDGING > SLEDGE

SLEDGINGS > SLEDGE

SLEDS > SLED

SLEE Scots word for > SLY

SLEECH n slippery mud

SLEECHES > SLEECH

SLEECHIER > SLEECH

SLEECHY > SLEECH

SLEEK adj glossy, smooth, and shiny ▷ vb make smooth and glossy, as by grooming, etc

SLEEKED > SLEEK

SLEEKEN vb make sleek

SLEEKENED > SLEEKEN

SLEEKENS > SLEEKEN

SLEEKER > SLEEK

SLEEKERS > SLEEK

SLEEKEST > SLEEK

SLEEKIER > SLEEK

SLEEKIEST > SLEEK

SLEEKING > SLEEK

SLEEKINGS > SLEEK

SLEEKIT adj smooth

SLEEKLY > SLEEK

SLEEKNESS > SLEEK

SLEEKS > SLEEK

SLEEKY > SLEEK

SLEEP n state of rest characterized by unconsciousness ▷ vb be in or as if in a state of sleep

SLEEPAWAY adj describing a type of camp for teenagers

SLEEPER n railway car fitted for sleeping in

SLEEPERS > SLEEPER

SLEEPERY Scots word for > SLEEPY

SLEEPIER > SLEEPY

SLEEPIEST > SLEEPY

SLEEPILY > SLEEPY

SLEEPING > SLEEP

SLEEPINGS > SLEEP

SLEEPLESS adj (of a night) one during which one does not sleep

SLEEPLIKE > SLEEP

SLEEPOUT n small building for sleeping in

SLEEPOUTS > SLEEPOUT

SLEEPOVER n occasion when a person stays overnight at a friend's house

SLEEPRY Scots word for > SLEEPY

SLEEPS > SLEEP

SLEEPSUIT n baby's sleeping garment

SLEEPWALK vb walk while asleep

SLEEPWEAR n clothes for sleeping in

SLEEPY adj needing sleep

SLEER > SLEE

SLEEST > SLEE

SLEET n rain and snow or hail falling together ▷ vb fall as sleet

SLEETED > SLEET

SLEETIER > SLEET

SLEETIEST > SLEET

SLEETING > SLEET

SLEETS > SLEET

SLEETY > SLEET

SLEEVE n part of a garment which covers the arm

SLEEVED > SLEEVE

SLEEVEEN n sly obsequious smooth-tongued person

SLEEVEENS > SLEEVEEN

SLEEVELET n protective covering for forearm

SLEEVER n old beer measure

SLEEVERS > SLEEVER

SLEEVES > SLEEVE

SLEEVING n tubular flexible insulation into which bare wire can be inserted

SLEEVINGS > SLEEVING

SLEEZIER > SLEEZY

SLEEZIEST > SLEEZY

SLEEZY adj sleazy

SLEIDED adj old word meaning separated

SLEIGH same as > SLEDGE

SLEIGHED > SLEIGH

SLEIGHER > SLEIGH

SLEIGHERS > SLEIGH

SLEIGHING > SLEIGH

SLEIGHS > SLEIGH

SLEIGHT n skill or cunning

SLEIGHTS > SLEIGHT

SLENDER adj slim

SLENDERER > SLENDER

SLENDERLY > SLENDER

SLENTER same as > SLINTER

SLENTERS > SLENTER

SLEPT > SLEEP

SLEUTH n detective ▷ vb track or follow

SLEUTHED > SLEUTH

SLEUTHING > SLEUTH

SLEUTHS > SLEUTH

SLEW vb twist sideways, esp awkwardly

SLEWED > SLEW

SLEWING > SLEW

SLEWS > SLEW

SLEY n weaver's tool for separating threads

SLEYS > SLEY

SLICE n thin flat piece cut from something ▷ vb cut into slices

SLICEABLE > SLICE

SLICED > SLICE

SLICER > SLICE

SLICERS > SLICE

SLICES > SLICE

SLICING > SLICE

SLICINGS > SLICE

SLICK adj persuasive and glib ▷ n patch of oil on water ▷ vb make smooth or sleek

SLICKED > SLICK

SLICKEN vb make smooth

SLICKENED > SLICKEN

SLICKENER > SLICKEN

SLICKENS > SLICKEN

SLICKER n sly or untrustworthy person

SLICKERED adj wearing a waterproof jacket

SLICKERS > SLICKER

SLICKEST > SLICK

SLICKING > SLICK

SLICKINGS > SLICK

SLICKLY > SLICK
SLICKNESS > SLICK
SLICKROCK n weathered and smooth sandstone or other rock
SLICKS > SLICK
SLICKSTER n dishonest person
SLID > SLIDE
SLIDABLE > SLIDE
SLIDDEN > SLIDE
SLIDDER vb slip
SLIDDERED > SLIDDER
SLIDDERS > SLIDDER
SLIDDERY adj slippery
SLIDE vb slip smoothly along (a surface) ▷ n act of sliding
SLIDED > SLIDE
SLIDER > SLIDE
SLIDERS > SLIDE
SLIDES > SLIDE
SLIDESHOW n display in the form of a series of images
SLIDEWAY n sloping channel down which things are slid
SLIDEWAYS > SLIDEWAY
SLIDING > SLIDE
SLIDINGLY > SLIDE
SLIDINGS > SLIDE
SLIER > SLY
SLIEST > SLY
SLIEVE n Irish mountain
SLIEVES > SLIEVE
SLIGHT adj small in quantity or extent ▷ n snub ▷ vb insult (someone) by behaving rudely
SLIGHTED > SLIGHT
SLIGHTER > SLIGHT
SLIGHTERS > SLIGHT
SLIGHTEST > SLIGHT
SLIGHTING adj characteristic of a slight
SLIGHTISH > SLIGHT
SLIGHTLY adv in small measure or degree
SLIGHTS > SLIGHT
SLILY > SLY
SLIM adj not heavy or stout, thin ▷ vb make or become slim by diet and exercise
SLIMDOWN n instance of an organization cutting staff
SLIMDOWNS > SLIMDOWN
SLIME n unpleasant thick slippery substance ▷ vb cover with slime
SLIMEBAG n odious and contemptible person
SLIMEBAGS > SLIMEBAG
SLIMEBALL n odious and contemptible person
SLIMED > SLIME
SLIMES > SLIME
SLIMIER > SLIMY
SLIMIEST > SLIMY
SLIMILY > SLIMY
SLIMINESS > SLIMY
SLIMING > SLIME

SLIMLINE adj slim
SLIMLY > SLIM
SLIMMED > SLIM
SLIMMER > SLIM
SLIMMERS > SLIM
SLIMMEST > SLIM
SLIMMING > SLIM
SLIMMINGS > SLIM
SLIMMISH > SLIM
SLIMNESS > SLIM
SLIMPSIER > SLIMPSY
SLIMPSY adj thin and flimsy
SLIMS > SLIM
SLIMSIER > SLIMSY
SLIMSIEST > SLIMSY
SLIMSY adj frail
SLIMY adj of, like, or covered with slime
SLING n bandage hung from the neck to support an injured hand or arm ▷ vb throw
SLINGBACK n shoe with a strap that goes around the back of the heel
SLINGER > SLING
SLINGERS > SLING
SLINGIER > SLINGY
SLINGIEST > SLINGY
SLINGING > SLING
SLINGS > SLING
SLINGSHOT n Y-shaped implement with a loop of elastic fastened to the ends of the two prongs, used for shooting small stones, etc
SLINGY adj resembling the act of using a sling
SLINK vb move furtively or guiltily ▷ n animal, esp a calf, born prematurely
SLINKED > SLINK
SLINKER > SLINK
SLINKERS > SLINK
SLINKIER > SLINKY
SLINKIEST > SLINKY
SLINKILY > SLINKY
SLINKING > SLINK
SLINKS > SLINK
SLINKSKIN n skin of premature calf
SLINKWEED n plant believed to make cow give birth prematurely
SLINKY adj (of clothes) figure-hugging
SLINTER n dodge, trick, or stratagem
SLINTERS > SLINTER
SLIOTAR n ball used in hurling
SLIOTARS > SLIOTAR
SLIP vb lose balance by sliding ▷ n slipping
SLIPCASE n protective case for a book
SLIPCASED adj having a slipcase
SLIPCASES > SLIPCASE
SLIPCOVER n fitted but easily removable cloth cover for a chair, sofa, etc
SLIPDRESS n silky sleeveless dress

SLIPE n wool removed from the pelt of a slaughtered sheep ▷ vb remove skin
SLIPED > SLIPE
SLIPES > SLIPE
SLIPFORM n mould used in building
SLIPFORMS > SLIPFORM
SLIPING > SLIPE
SLIPKNOT n knot tied so that it will slip along the rope round which it is made
SLIPKNOTS > SLIPKNOT
SLIPLESS > SLIP
SLIPNOOSE n noose made with a slipknot, so that it tightens when pulled
SLIPOUT n instance of slipping out
SLIPOUTS > SLIPOUT
SLIPOVER adj of or denoting a garment that can be put on easily over the head ▷ n such a garment, esp a sleeveless pullover
SLIPOVERS > SLIPOVER
SLIPPAGE n act or an instance of slipping
SLIPPAGES > SLIPPAGE
SLIPPED > SLIP
SLIPPER n light shoe for indoor wear ▷ vb hit or beat with a slipper
SLIPPERED > SLIPPER
SLIPPERS > SLIPPER
SLIPPERY adj so smooth or wet as to cause slipping or be difficult to hold
SLIPPIER > SLIPPY
SLIPPIEST > SLIPPY
SLIPPILY > SLIPPY
SLIPPING > SLIP
SLIPPY adj slippery
SLIPRAIL n rail in a fence that can be slipped out of place to make an opening
SLIPRAILS > SLIPRAIL
SLIPS > SLIP
SLIPSHEET n sheet of paper that is interleaved between freshly printed sheets
SLIPSHOD adj (of an action) careless
SLIPSLOP n weak or unappetizing food or drink
SLIPSLOPS > SLIPSLOP
SLIPSOLE n separate sole on shoe
SLIPSOLES > SLIPSOLE
SLIPT vb old form of slipped
SLIPUP n mistake or mishap
SLIPUPS > SLIPUP
SLIPWARE n pottery that has been decorated with clay

SLIPWARES > SLIPWARE
SLIPWAY n launching slope on which ships are built or repaired
SLIPWAYS > SLIPWAY
SLISH n old word meaning cut
SLISHES > SLISH
SLIT n long narrow cut or opening ▷ vb make a long straight cut in
SLITHER vb slide unsteadily ▷ n slithering movement
SLITHERED > SLITHER
SLITHERS > SLITHER
SLITHERY adj moving with a slithering motion
SLITLESS > SLIT
SLITLIKE > SLIT
SLITS > SLIT
SLITTED > SLIT
SLITTER > SLIT
SLITTERS > SLIT
SLITTIER > SLIT
SLITTIEST > SLIT
SLITTING > SLIT
SLITTY > SLIT
SLIVE vb slip
SLIVED > SLIVE
SLIVEN > SLIVE
SLIVER n small thin piece ▷ vb cut into slivers
SLIVERED > SLIVER
SLIVERER > SLIVER
SLIVERERS > SLIVER
SLIVERING > SLIVER
SLIVERS > SLIVER
SLIVES > SLIVE
SLIVING > SLIVE
SLIVOVIC n plum brandy
SLIVOVICA n plum brandy
SLIVOVITZ n plum brandy from E Europe
SLIVOWITZ n plum brandy
SLOAN n severe telling-off
SLOANS > SLOAN
SLOB n lazy and untidy person ▷ vb behave like a slob
SLOBBED > SLOB
SLOBBER vb dribble or drool ▷ n liquid or saliva spilt from the mouth
SLOBBERED > SLOBBER
SLOBBERER > SLOBBER
SLOBBERS > SLOBBER
SLOBBERY > SLOBBER
SLOBBIER > SLOB
SLOBBIEST > SLOB
SLOBBING > SLOB
SLOBBISH > SLOB
SLOBBY > SLOB
SLOBLAND n muddy ground
SLOBLANDS > SLOBLAND
SLOBS > SLOB
SLOCKEN vb Scots word meaning slake
SLOCKENED > SLOCKEN
SLOCKENS > SLOCKEN
SLOE n sour blue-black fruit

S

SLOEBUSH n bush on which sloes grow
SLOES > SLOE
SLOETHORN n sloe plant
SLOETREE n sloe plant
SLOETREES
> SLOETREE
SLOG vb work hard and steadily ▷ n long and exhausting work or walk
SLOGAN n catchword or phrase used in politics or advertising
SLOGANED adj having a slogan
SLOGANEER n person who coins or employs slogans frequently ▷ vb coin or employ slogans so as to sway opinion
SLOGANISE same as > SLOGANIZE
SLOGANIZE vb use slogans
SLOGANS > SLOGAN
SLOGGED > SLOG
SLOGGER > SLOG
SLOGGERS > SLOG
SLOGGING > SLOG
SLOGS > SLOG
SLOID n Swedish woodwork
SLOIDS > SLOID
SLOJD same as > SLOID
SLOJDS > SLOJD
SLOKEN vb Scots word meaning slake
SLOKENED > SLOKEN
SLOKENING > SLOKEN
SLOKENS > SLOKEN
SLOMMOCK vb walk assertively with a hip-rolling gait
SLOMMOCKS
> SLOMMOCK
SLOMO n slow-motion sequence in a film
SLOMOS > SLOMO
SLOOM vb slumber
SLOOMED > SLOOM
SLOOMIER > SLOOM
SLOOMIEST > SLOOM
SLOOMING > SLOOM
SLOOMS > SLOOM
SLOOMY > SLOOM
SLOOP n small single-masted ship
SLOOPS > SLOOP
SLOOSH vb wash with water
SLOOSHED > SLOOSH
SLOOSHES > SLOOSH
SLOOSHING > SLOOSH
SLOOT n ditch for irrigation or drainage
SLOOTS > SLOOT
SLOP vb splash or spill ▷ n spilt liquid
SLOPE vb slant ▷ n sloping surface
SLOPED > SLOPE
SLOPER > SLOPE
SLOPERS > SLOPE
SLOPES > SLOPE
SLOPESIDE n side of a slope
SLOPEWISE > SLOPE
SLOPIER > SLOPE

SLOPIEST > SLOPE
SLOPING > SLOPE
SLOPINGLY > SLOPE
SLOPPED > SLOP
SLOPPIER > SLOPPY
SLOPPIEST > SLOPPY
SLOPPILY > SLOPPY
SLOPPING > SLOP
SLOPPY adj careless or untidy
SLOPS > SLOP
SLOPWORK n manufacture of cheap shoddy clothing or the clothes so produced
SLOPWORKS
> SLOPWORK
SLOPY > SLOPE
SLORM vb wipe carelessly
SLORMED > SLORM
SLORMING > SLORM
SLORMS > SLORM
SLOSH vb pour carelessly ▷ n splashing sound
SLOSHED > SLOSH
SLOSHES > SLOSH
SLOSHIER > SLOSH
SLOSHIEST > SLOSH
SLOSHING > SLOSH
SLOSHINGS > SLOSH
SLOSHY > SLOSH
SLOT n narrow opening for inserting something ▷ vb make a slot or slots in
SLOTBACK n American football player
SLOTBACKS
> SLOTBACK
SLOTH n slow-moving animal of tropical America ▷ vb be lazy
SLOTHED > SLOTH
SLOTHFUL adj lazy or idle
SLOTHING > SLOTH
SLOTHS > SLOTH
SLOTS > SLOT
SLOTTED > SLOT
SLOTTER > SLOT
SLOTTERS > SLOT
SLOTTING > SLOT
SLOUCH vb sit, stand, or move with a drooping posture ▷ n drooping posture
SLOUCHED > SLOUCH
SLOUCHER > SLOUCH
SLOUCHERS > SLOUCH
SLOUCHES > SLOUCH
SLOUCHIER > SLOUCHY
SLOUCHILY > SLOUCHY
SLOUCHING > SLOUCH
SLOUCHY adj slouching
SLOUGH n bog ▷ vb (of a snake) shed (its skin)
SLOUGHED > SLOUGH
SLOUGHI n N African breed of dog resembling a greyhound
SLOUGHIER > SLOUGH
SLOUGHING > SLOUGH
SLOUGHIS > SLOUGHI
SLOUGHS > SLOUGH
SLOUGHY > SLOUGH
SLOVE > SLIVE
SLOVEN n habitually dirty or untidy person

SLOVENLY adj dirty or untidy ▷ adv in a slovenly manner
SLOVENRY n quality of being slovenly
SLOVENS > SLOVEN
SLOW adj taking a longer time than is usual or expected ▷ adv slowly ▷ vb reduce the speed (of)
SLOWBACK n lazy person
SLOWBACKS
> SLOWBACK
SLOWCOACH n person who moves or works slowly
SLOWDOWN n any slackening of pace
SLOWDOWNS
> SLOWDOWN
SLOWED > SLOW
SLOWER > SLOW
SLOWEST > SLOW
SLOWING > SLOW
SLOWINGS > SLOW
SLOWISH > SLOW
SLOWLY > SLOW
SLOWNESS > SLOW
SLOWPOKE same as > SLOWCOACH
SLOWPOKES
> SLOWPOKE
SLOWS > SLOW
SLOWWORM n small legless lizard
SLOWWORMS
> SLOWWORM
SLOYD n Swedish woodwork
SLOYDS > SLOYD
SLUB n lump in yarn or fabric ▷ vb draw out and twist (a sliver of fibre) before spinning ▷ adj (of material) having an irregular appearance
SLUBB same as > SLUB
SLUBBED > SLUB
SLUBBER vb smear
SLUBBERED > SLUBBER
SLUBBERS > SLUBBER
SLUBBEST > SLUB
SLUBBIER > SLUB
SLUBBIEST > SLUB
SLUBBING > SLUB
SLUBBINGS > SLUB
SLUBBS > SLUBB
SLUBBY > SLUB
SLUBS > SLUB
SLUDGE n thick mud ▷ vb convert into sludge
SLUDGED > SLUDGE
SLUDGES > SLUDGE
SLUDGIER > SLUDGY
SLUDGIEST > SLUDGY
SLUDGING > SLUDGE
SLUDGY adj consisting of, containing, or like sludge
SLUE same as > SLEW
SLUED > SLUE
SLUEING > SLUE
SLUES > SLUE
SLUFF same as > SLOUGH
SLUFFED > SLUFF
SLUFFING > SLUFF
SLUFFS > SLUFF
SLUG n land snail with no shell ▷ vb hit hard

SLUGABED n person who remains in bed through laziness
SLUGABEDS
> SLUGABED
SLUGFEST n fist fight
SLUGFESTS
> SLUGFEST
SLUGGABED same as > SLUGABED
SLUGGARD n lazy person ▷ adj lazy
SLUGGARDS
> SLUGGARD
SLUGGED > SLUG
SLUGGER n (esp in boxing, baseball, etc) a person who strikes hard
SLUGGERS > SLUGGER
SLUGGING > SLUG
SLUGGISH adj slow-moving, lacking energy
SLUGHORN same as > SLOGAN
SLUGHORNE same as > SLOGAN
SLUGHORNS
> SLUGHORN
SLUGLIKE adj like a slug
SLUGS > SLUG
SLUICE n channel that carries a rapid current of water ▷ vb drain water by means of a sluice
SLUICED > SLUICE
SLUICES > SLUICE
SLUICEWAY same as > SLUICE
SLUICIER > SLUICE
SLUICIEST > SLUICE
SLUICING > SLUICE
SLUICY > SLUICE
SLUING > SLUE
SLUIT n water channel in South Africa
SLUITS > SLUIT
SLUM n squalid overcrowded house or area ▷ vb experience poorer places or conditions than usual
SLUMBER n sleep ▷ vb sleep
SLUMBERED > SLUMBER
SLUMBERER > SLUMBER
SLUMBERS > SLUMBER
SLUMBERY adj sleepy
SLUMBROUS adj sleepy
SLUMBRY same as > SLUMBERY
SLUMGUM n material left after wax is extracted from honeycomb
SLUMGUMS > SLUMGUM
SLUMISM n existence of slums
SLUMISMS > SLUMISM
SLUMLORD n absentee landlord of slum property, esp one who profiteers
SLUMLORDS
> SLUMLORD
SLUMMED > SLUM
SLUMMER > SLUM
SLUMMERS > SLUM
SLUMMIER > SLUM
SLUMMIEST > SLUM

SLUMMING > SLUM
SLUMMINGS > SLUM
SLUMMOCK *vb* move slowly and heavily
SLUMMOCKS > SLUMMOCK
SLUMMY > SLUM
SLUMP *vb* (of prices or demand) decline suddenly ▷ *n* sudden decline in prices or demand
SLUMPED > SLUMP
SLUMPIER > SLUMPY
SLUMPIEST > SLUMPY
SLUMPING > SLUMP
SLUMPS > SLUMP
SLUMPY *adj* boggy
SLUMS > SLUM
SLUNG > SLING
SLUNGSHOT *n* weight attached to the end of a cord and used as a weapon
SLUNK > SLINK
SLUR *vb* pronounce or utter (words) indistinctly ▷ *n* slurring of words
SLURB *n* suburban slum
SLURBAN > SLURB
SLURBS > SLURB
SLURP *vb* eat or drink noisily ▷ *n* slurping sound
SLURPED > SLURP
SLURPER > SLURP
SLURPERS > SLURP
SLURPIER > SLURPY
SLURPIEST > SLURPY
SLURPING > SLURP
SLURPS > SLURP
SLURPY *adj* making a slurping noise
SLURRED > SLUR
SLURRIED > SLURRY
SLURRIES > SLURRY
SLURRING > SLUR
SLURRY *n* muddy liquid mixture ▷ *vb* spread slurry
SLURRYING > SLURRY
SLURS > SLUR
SLURVE *n* pitch in baseball combining elements of the slider and the curveball
SLURVES > SLURVE
SLUSE *same as* > SLUICE
SLUSES > SLUSE
SLUSH *n* watery muddy substance ▷ *vb* make one's way through or as if through slush
SLUSHED > SLUSH
SLUSHES > SLUSH
SLUSHIER > SLUSHY
SLUSHIES > SLUSHY
SLUSHIEST > SLUSHY
SLUSHILY > SLUSHY
SLUSHING > SLUSH
SLUSHY *adj* of, resembling, or consisting of slush ▷ *n* unskilled kitchen assistant
SLUT *n* derogatory term for a woman considered immoral
SLUTCH *n* mud
SLUTCHES > SLUTCH
SLUTCHIER > SLUTCH
SLUTCHY > SLUTCH

SLUTS > SLUT
SLUTTERY *n* state of being slutty
SLUTTIER > SLUT
SLUTTIEST > SLUT
SLUTTILY > SLUTTY
SLUTTISH > SLUT
SLUTTY > SLUT
SLY *adj* crafty
SLYBOOTS *pl n* person who is sly
SLYER > SLY
SLYEST > SLY
SLYISH > SLY
SLYLY > SLY
SLYNESS > SLY
SLYNESSES > SLY
SLYPE *n* covered passageway in a church
SLYPES > SLYPE
SMA *Scots word for* > SMALL
SMAAK *vb* South African slang for like or love
SMAAKED > SMAAK
SMAAKING > SMAAK
SMAAKS > SMAAK
SMACK *vb* slap sharply ▷ *n* sharp slap ▷ *adv* squarely or directly
SMACKDOWN *n* severe beating or defeat
SMACKED > SMACK
SMACKER *n* loud kiss
SMACKEROO *n* loud kiss
SMACKERS > SMACKER
SMACKHEAD *n* person who is addicted to heroin
SMACKING *adj* brisk
SMACKINGS > SMACKING
SMACKS > SMACK
SMAIK *n* Scots word meaning rascal
SMAIKS > SMAIK
SMALL *adj* not large in size, number, or amount ▷ *n* narrow part of the lower back ▷ *adv* into small pieces ▷ *vb* make small
SMALLAGE *n* wild celery
SMALLAGES > SMALLAGE
SMALLBOY *n* steward's assistant or deputy steward in European households in W Africa
SMALLBOYS > SMALLBOY
SMALLED > SMALL
SMALLER > SMALL
SMALLEST > SMALL
SMALLING > SMALL
SMALLISH > SMALL
SMALLNESS > SMALL
SMALLPOX *n* contagious disease with blisters that leave scars
SMALLS > SMALL
SMALLSAT *n* small communications satellite
SMALLSATS > SMALLSAT
SMALLTIME *adj* unimportant
SMALM *same as* > SMARM
SMALMED > SMALM
SMALMIER > SMALMY

SMALMIEST > SMALMY
SMALMILY > SMALMY
SMALMING > SMALM
SMALMS > SMALM
SMALMY *same as* > SMARMY
SMALT *n* type of silica glass coloured deep blue with cobalt oxide
SMALTI > SMALTO
SMALTINE *n* mineral containing cobalt
SMALTINES > SMALTINE
SMALTITE *n* silver-white to greyish mineral
SMALTITES > SMALTITE
SMALTO *n* coloured glass, etc, used in mosaics
SMALTOS > SMALTO
SMALTS > SMALT
SMARAGD *n* any green gemstone, such as the emerald
SMARAGDE *same as* > SMARAGD
SMARAGDES > SMARAGD
SMARAGDS > SMARAGD
SMARM *vb* bring (oneself) into favour (with) ▷ *n* obsequious flattery
SMARMED > SMARM
SMARMIER > SMARMY
SMARMIEST > SMARMY
SMARMILY > SMARMY
SMARMING > SMARM
SMARMS > SMARM
SMARMY *adj* unpleasantly suave or flattering
SMART *adj* well-kept and neat ▷ *vb* feel or cause stinging pain ▷ *n* stinging pain ▷ *adv* in a smart manner
SMARTARSE *n* derogatory term for a clever person, esp one who parades their knowledge
SMARTASS *same as* > SMARTARSE
SMARTED > SMART
SMARTEN *vb* make or become smart
SMARTENED > SMARTEN
SMARTENS > SMARTEN
SMARTER > SMART
SMARTEST > SMART
SMARTIE *same as* > SMARTY
SMARTIES > SMARTY
SMARTING > SMART
SMARTISH > SMART
SMARTLY > SMART
SMARTNESS > SMART
SMARTS *pl n* know-how, intelligence, or wits
SMARTWEED *n* grass with acrid smell
SMARTY *n* would-be clever person
SMASH *vb* break violently and noisily ▷ *n* act or sound of smashing ▷ *adv* with a smash
SMASHABLE > SMASH

SMASHED > SMASH
SMASHER *n* attractive person or thing
SMASHEROO *n* excellent person or thing
SMASHERS > SMASHER
SMASHES > SMASH
SMASHING *adj* excellent
SMASHINGS > SMASHING
SMASHUP *n* bad collision of cars
SMASHUPS > SMASHUP
SMATCH *less common word for* > SMACK
SMATCHED > SMATCH
SMATCHES > SMATCH
SMATCHING > SMATCH
SMATTER *n* smattering ▷ *vb* prattle
SMATTERED > SMATTER
SMATTERER > SMATTER
SMATTERS > SMATTER
SMAZE *n* smoky haze, less damp than fog
SMAZES > SMAZE
SMEAR *vb* spread with a greasy or sticky substance ▷ *n* dirty mark or smudge
SMEARCASE *n* American type of cottage cheese
SMEARED > SMEAR
SMEARER > SMEAR
SMEARERS > SMEAR
SMEARIER > SMEARY
SMEARIEST > SMEARY
SMEARILY > SMEARY
SMEARING > SMEAR
SMEARS > SMEAR
SMEARY *adj* smeared, dirty
SMEATH *n* duck
SMEATHS > SMEATH
SMECTIC *adj* (of a substance) existing in state in which the molecules are oriented in layers
SMECTITE *n* type of clay mineral
SMECTITES > SMECTITE
SMECTITIC > SMECTITE
SMEDDUM *n* any fine powder
SMEDDUMS > SMEDDUM
SMEE *n* duck
SMEECH *Southwest English dialect form of* > SMOKE
SMEECHED > SMEECH
SMEECHES > SMEECH
SMEECHING > SMEECH
SMEEK *vb* smoke
SMEEKED > SMEEK
SMEEKING > SMEEK
SMEEKS > SMEEK
SMEES > SMEE
SMEETH *n* duck ▷ *vb* make smooth
SMEETHED > SMEETH
SMEETHING > SMEETH
SMEETHS > SMEETH
SMEGMA *n* whitish sebaceous secretion that accumulates beneath the prepuce
SMEGMAS > SMEGMA

S

SMEIK same as > SMEKE
SMEIKED > SMEIK
SMEIKING same as
> SMEKING
SMEIKS > SMEIK
SMEKE n smoke ▷ vb smoke
SMEKED > SMEKE
SMEKES > SMEKE
SMEKING > SMEKE
SMELL vb perceive (a scent or odour) by means of the nose ▷ n ability to perceive odours by the nose
SMELLABLE adj capable of being smelled
SMELLED > SMELL
SMELLER > SMELL
SMELLERS > SMELL
SMELLIER > SMELLY
SMELLIES pl n pleasant-smelling products such as perfumes, body lotions, bath salts, etc
SMELLIEST > SMELLY
SMELLING > SMELL
SMELLINGS > SMELL
SMELLS > SMELL
SMELLY adj having a nasty smell
SMELT vb extract metal from an ore
SMELTED > SMELT
SMELTER n industrial plant where smelting is carried out
SMELTERS > SMELTER
SMELTERY variant of
> SMELTER
SMELTING > SMELT
SMELTINGS > SMELL
SMELTS > SMELT
SMERK same as > SMIRK
SMERKED > SMERK
SMERKING > SMERK
SMERKS > SMERK
SMEUSE n way through hedge
SMEUSES > SMEUSE
SMEW n duck of N Europe and Asia
SMEWS > SMEW
SMICKER vb smirk
SMICKERED > SMICKER
SMICKERS > SMICKER
SMICKET n smock
SMICKETS > SMICKET
SMICKLY adv amorously
SMIDDIED > SMIDDY
SMIDDIES > SMIDDY
SMIDDY Scots word for
> SMITHY
SMIDDYING > SMIDDY
SMIDGE n very small amount or part
SMIDGEN n very small amount or part
SMIDGENS > SMIDGEN
SMIDGEON same as
> SMIDGEN
SMIDGEONS
> SMIDGEON
SMIDGES > SMIDGE
SMIDGIN same as
> SMIDGEN
SMIDGINS > SMIDGIN

SMIERCASE same as
> SMEARCASE
SMIGHT same as > SMITE
SMIGHTING > SMIGHT
SMIGHTS > SMIGHT
SMILAX n type of climbing shrub
SMILAXES > SMILAX
SMILE n turning up of the corners of the mouth to show pleasure or friendliness ▷ vb give a smile
SMILED > SMILE
SMILEFUL adj full of smiles
SMILELESS > SMILE
SMILER > SMILE
SMILERS > SMILE
SMILES > SMILE
SMILET n little smile
SMILETS > SMILET
SMILEY n symbol depicting a smile or other facial expression ▷ adj cheerful
SMILEYS > SMILEY
SMILIER > SMILEY
SMILIES > SMILEY
SMILIEST > SMILEY
SMILING > SMILE
SMILINGLY > SMILE
SMILINGS > SMILE
SMILODON n extinct sabre-toothed tiger
SMILODONS
> SMILODON
SMIR n drizzly rain ▷ vb drizzle lightly
SMIRCH n stain ▷ vb disgrace
SMIRCHED > SMIRCH
SMIRCHER > SMIRCH
SMIRCHERS > SMIRCH
SMIRCHES > SMIRCH
SMIRCHING > SMIRCH
SMIRK n smug smile ▷ vb give a smirk
SMIRKED > SMIRK
SMIRKER > SMIRK
SMIRKERS > SMIRK
SMIRKIER > SMIRK
SMIRKIEST > SMIRK
SMIRKILY > SMIRK
SMIRKING > SMIRK
SMIRKS > SMIRK
SMIRKY > SMIRK
SMIRR same as > SMIR
SMIRRED > SMIRR
SMIRRIER > SMIRR
SMIRRIEST > SMIRR
SMIRRING > SMIRR
SMIRRS > SMIRR
SMIRRY > SMIRR
SMIRS > SMIR
SMIRTING n flirting amongst those smoking outside a non-smoking office, pub, etc
SMIRTINGS
> SMIRTING
SMISHING n phishing via text messages
SMISHINGS
> SMISHING
SMIT > SMITE
SMITE vb strike hard

SMITER > SMITE
SMITERS > SMITE
SMITES > SMITE
SMITH n worker in metal ▷ vb work in metal
SMITHED > SMITH
SMITHERS pl n little shattered pieces
SMITHERY n trade or craft of a blacksmith
SMITHIED > SMITHY
SMITHIES > SMITHY
SMITHING n act of working as a smith
SMITHINGS
> SMITHING
SMITHS > SMITH
SMITHY n blacksmith's workshop ▷ vb work as a smith
SMITHYING > SMITHY
SMITING > SMITE
SMITS > SMIT
SMITTED > SMIT
SMITTEN > SMITE
SMITTING > SMIT
SMITTLE adj infectious
SMOCK n loose overall ▷ vb gather (material) by sewing in a honeycomb pattern
SMOCKED > SMOCK
SMOCKING n ornamental needlework used to gather material
SMOCKINGS
> SMOCKING
SMOCKLIKE > SMOCK
SMOCKS > SMOCK
SMOG n mixture of smoke and fog
SMOGGIER > SMOG
SMOGGIEST > SMOG
SMOGGY > SMOG
SMOGLESS > SMOG
SMOGS > SMOG
SMOILE same as > SMILE
SMOILED > SMOILE
SMOILES > SMOILE
SMOILING > SMOILE
SMOKABLE > SMOKE
SMOKE n cloudy mass that rises from something burning ▷ vb give off smoke or treat with smoke
SMOKEABLE > SMOKE
SMOKEBOX n part of a steam engine or boiler
SMOKEBUSH n plant with purple leaves and small flowers that turn grey-white
SMOKED > SMOKE
SMOKEHO same as
> SMOKO
SMOKEHOOD n hood worn to keep out smoke
SMOKEHOS > SMOKEHO
SMOKEJACK n device formerly used for turning a roasting spit, operated by the movement of ascending gases in a chimney
SMOKELESS adj having or producing little or no smoke
SMOKELIKE > SMOKE

SMOKEPOT n device for producing smoke
SMOKEPOTS
> SMOKEPOT
SMOKER n person who habitually smokes tobacco
SMOKERS > SMOKER
SMOKES > SMOKE
SMOKEY > SMOKY
SMOKEYS > SMOKEY
SMOKIE n smoked haddock
SMOKIER > SMOKY
SMOKIES > SMOKY
SMOKIEST > SMOKY
SMOKILY > SMOKY
SMOKINESS > SMOKY
SMOKING > SMOKE
SMOKINGS > SMOKING
SMOKO n short break from work for tea or a cigarette
SMOKOS > SMOKO
SMOKY adj filled with or giving off smoke, sometimes excessively ▷ n haddock that has been smoked
SMOLDER same as
> SMOULDER
SMOLDERED > SMOLDER
SMOLDERS > SMOLDER
SMOLT n young salmon at the stage when it migrates to the sea
SMOLTS > SMOLT
SMOOCH vb kiss and cuddle ▷ n smooching
SMOOCHED > SMOOCH
SMOOCHER > SMOOCH
SMOOCHERS > SMOOCH
SMOOCHES > SMOOCH
SMOOCHIER > SMOOCHY
SMOOCHING > SMOOCH
SMOOCHY adj romantic
SMOODGE same as
> SMOOCH
SMOODGED > SMOODGE
SMOODGES > SMOODGE
SMOODGING > SMOODGE
SMOOGE same as
> SMOOCH
SMOOGED > SMOOGE
SMOOGES > SMOOGE
SMOOGING > SMOOGE
SMOOR vb Scots word meaning put out fire
SMOORED > SMOOR
SMOORING > SMOOR
SMOORS > SMOOR
SMOOSH vb paint to give softened look
SMOOSHED > SMOOSH
SMOOSHES > SMOOSH
SMOOSHING > SMOOSH
SMOOT vb work as printer
SMOOTED > SMOOT
SMOOTH adj even in surface, texture, or consistency ▷ vb make smooth ▷ adv in a smooth manner ▷ n smooth part of something
SMOOTHE same as
> SMOOTH
SMOOTHED > SMOOTH
SMOOTHEN vb make or become smooth

SMOOTHENS
> SMOOTHEN
SMOOTHER > SMOOTH
SMOOTHERS > SMOOTH
SMOOTHES > SMOOTH
SMOOTHEST > SMOOTH
SMOOTHIE *n* smooth thick drink made with fruit and milk and sometimes ice cream
SMOOTHIES > SMOOTHY
SMOOTHING > SMOOTH
SMOOTHISH > SMOOTH
SMOOTHLY > SMOOTH
SMOOTHS > SMOOTH
SMOOTHY *same as*
> SMOOTHIE
SMOOTING > SMOOT
SMOOTS > SMOOT
SMORBROD *n* Danish hors d'oeuvre
SMORBRODS
> SMORBROD
SMORE *same as* > SMOOR
SMORED > SMORE
SMORES > SMORE
SMORG *n* short for smorgasbord
SMORGS > SMORG
SMORING > SMORE
SMORZANDO *adv* musical instruction meaning fading away gradually
SMORZATO *same as*
> SMORZANDO
SMOTE > SMITE
SMOTHER *vb* suffocate or stifle ▷ *n* anything, such as a cloud of smoke, that stifles
SMOTHERED > SMOTHER
SMOTHERER > SMOTHER
SMOTHERS > SMOTHER
SMOTHERY *adj* tending to smother
SMOUCH *vb* kiss
SMOUCHED > SMOUCH
SMOUCHES > SMOUCH
SMOUCHING > SMOUCH
SMOULDER *vb* burn slowly with smoke but no flame ▷ *n* dense smoke, as from a smouldering fire
SMOULDERS
> SMOULDER
SMOULDRY *adj* smouldering
SMOUSE *vb* South African word meaning peddle
SMOUSED > SMOUSE
SMOUSER > SMOUSE
SMOUSERS > SMOUSE
SMOUSES > SMOUSE
SMOUSING > SMOUSE
SMOUT *n* child or undersized person ▷ *vb* creep or sneak
SMOUTED > SMOUT
SMOUTING > SMOUT
SMOUTS > SMOUT
SMOWT *same as* > SMOUT
SMOWTS > SMOWT
SMOYLE *same as* > SMILE
SMOYLED > SMOYLE
SMOYLES > SMOYLE
SMOYLING > SMOYLE
SMRITI *n* class of Hindu sacred literature

SMRITIS > SMRITI
SMUDGE *vb* make or become smeared or soiled ▷ *n* dirty mark
SMUDGED > SMUDGE
SMUDGEDLY > SMUDGE
SMUDGER > SMUDGE
SMUDGERS > SMUDGE
SMUDGES > SMUDGE
SMUDGIER > SMUDGY
SMUDGIEST > SMUDGY
SMUDGILY > SMUDGE
SMUDGING > SMUDGE
SMUDGINGS > SMUDGE
SMUDGY *adj* smeared, blurred, or soiled, or likely to become so
SMUG *adj* self-satisfied ▷ *vb* make neat
SMUGGED > SMUG
SMUGGER > SMUG
SMUGGERY *n* condition or an instance of being smug
SMUGGEST > SMUG
SMUGGING > SMUG
SMUGGLE *vb* import or export (goods) secretly and illegally
SMUGGLED > SMUGGLE
SMUGGLER > SMUGGLE
SMUGGLERS > SMUGGLE
SMUGGLES > SMUGGLE
SMUGGLING > SMUGGLE
SMUGLY > SMUG
SMUGNESS > SMUG
SMUGS > SMUG
SMUR *same as* > SMIR
SMURFING *n* intentionally overwhelming a computer network with messages
SMURFINGS
> SMURFING
SMURRED > SMUR
SMURRIER > SMUR
SMURRIEST > SMUR
SMURRING > SMUR
SMURRY > SMUR
SMURS > SMUR
SMUSH *vb* crush
SMUSHED > SMUSH
SMUSHES > SMUSH
SMUSHING > SMUSH
SMUT *n* small dark smudge or stain ▷ *vb* mark or become marked or smudged
SMUTCH *vb* smudge ▷ *n* mark
SMUTCHED > SMUTCH
SMUTCHES > SMUTCH
SMUTCHIER > SMUTCH
SMUTCHING > SMUTCH
SMUTCHY > SMUTCH
SMUTS > SMUT
SMUTTED > SMUT
SMUTTIER > SMUT
SMUTTIEST > SMUT
SMUTTILY > SMUT
SMUTTING > SMUT
SMUTTY > SMUT
SMYTRIE *n* Scots word meaning collection
SMYTRIES > SMYTRIE
SNAB *same as* > SNOB
SNABBLE *same as*
> SNAFFLE

SNABBLED > SNABBLE
SNABBLES > SNABBLE
SNABBLING > SNABBLE
SNABS > SNAB
SNACK *n* light quick meal ▷ *vb* eat a snack
SNACKED > SNACK
SNACKER > SNACK
SNACKERS > SNACK
SNACKETTE *n* snack bar
SNACKIER > SNACKY
SNACKIEST > SNACKY
SNACKING > SNACK
SNACKS > SNACK
SNACKY *adj* of the nature of a snack
SNAFFLE *n* jointed bit for a horse ▷ *vb* steal
SNAFFLED > SNAFFLE
SNAFFLES > SNAFFLE
SNAFFLING > SNAFFLE
SNAFU *n* confusion or chaos regarded as the normal state ▷ *adj* confused or muddled up, as usual ▷ *vb* throw into chaos
SNAFUED > SNAFU
SNAFUING > SNAFU
SNAFUS > SNAFU
SNAG *n* difficulty or disadvantage ▷ *vb* catch or tear on a point
SNAGGED > SNAG
SNAGGER *n* type of fishing hook
SNAGGERS > SNAGGER
SNAGGIER > SNAGGY
SNAGGIEST > SNAGGY
SNAGGING > SNAG
SNAGGLE *n* tangled mass
SNAGGLES > SNAGGLE
SNAGGY *adj* having sharp protuberances
SNAGLIKE > SNAG
SNAGS > SNAG
SNAIL *n* slow-moving mollusc with a spiral shell ▷ *vb* move slowly
SNAILED > SNAIL
SNAILERY *n* place where snails are bred
SNAILFISH *n* sea snail
SNAILIER > SNAIL
SNAILIEST > SNAIL
SNAILING > SNAIL
SNAILLIKE *adj* resembling a snail
SNAILS > SNAIL
SNAILY > SNAIL
SNAKE *n* long thin scaly limbless reptile ▷ *vb* move in a winding course like a snake
SNAKEBIRD *n* darter bird
SNAKEBIT *adj* bitten by snake
SNAKEBITE *n* bite of a snake
SNAKED > SNAKE
SNAKEFISH *n* fish resembling snake
SNAKEHEAD *n* Chinese criminal involved in the illegal transport of Chinese citizens to other parts of the world
SNAKELIKE > SNAKE

SNAKEPIT *n* pit filled with snakes
SNAKEPITS
> SNAKEPIT
SNAKEROOT *n* any of various North American plants
SNAKES > SNAKE
SNAKESKIN *n* skin of a snake, esp when made into a leather valued for handbags, shoes, etc
SNAKEWEED *same as*
> SNAKEROOT
SNAKEWISE *adv* in snakelike way
SNAKEWOOD *n* South American tree
SNAKEY *same as* > SNAKY
SNAKIER > SNAKY
SNAKIEST > SNAKY
SNAKILY > SNAKY
SNAKINESS > SNAKY
SNAKING > SNAKE
SNAKISH > SNAKE
SNAKY *adj* twisted or winding
SNAP *vb* break suddenly ▷ *n* act or sound of snapping ▷ *adj* made on the spur of the moment ▷ *adv* with a snap
SNAPBACK *n* sudden rebound or change in direction
SNAPBACKS
> SNAPBACK
SNAPHANCE *n* flintlock gun
SNAPLESS > SNAP
SNAPLINK *n* metal link used in mountaineering
SNAPLINKS
> SNAPLINK
SNAPPABLE > SNAP
SNAPPED > SNAP
SNAPPER *n* food fish of Australia and New Zealand ▷ *vb* stumble
SNAPPERED > SNAPPER
SNAPPERS > SNAPPER
SNAPPIER > SNAPPY
SNAPPIEST > SNAPPY
SNAPPILY > SNAPPY
SNAPPING > SNAP
SNAPPINGS > SNAP
SNAPPISH *same as*
> SNAPPY
SNAPPY *adj* irritable
SNAPS > SNAP
SNAPSHOT *n* informal photograph
SNAPSHOTS
> SNAPSHOT
SNAPTIN *n* container for food
SNAPTINS > SNAPTIN
SNAPWEED *n* impatiens
SNAPWEEDS
> SNAPWEED
SNAR *same as* > SNARL
SNARE *n* trap with a noose ▷ *vb* catch in or as if in a snare
SNARED > SNARE
SNARELESS > SNARE
SNARER > SNARE
SNARERS > SNARE

S

SNARES > SNARE
SNARF *vb* eat or drink greedily
SNARFED > SNARF
SNARFING > SNARF
SNARFLE *vb* (of an animal) grunt and snort while rooting for food
SNARFLED > SNARFLE
SNARFLES > SNARFLE
SNARFLING > SNARFLE
SNARFS > SNARF
SNARIER > SNARE
SNARIEST > SNARE
SNARING > SNARE
SNARINGS > SNARE
SNARK *n* imaginary creature in Lewis Carroll's poetry
SNARKIER > SNARKY
SNARKIEST > SNARKY
SNARKILY > SNARKY
SNARKS > SNARK
SNARKY *adj* unpleasant and scornful
SNARL *vb* (of an animal) growl with bared teeth ▷ *n* act or sound of snarling
SNARLED > SNARL
SNARLER > SNARL
SNARLERS > SNARL
SNARLIER > SNARL
SNARLIEST > SNARL
SNARLING > SNARL
SNARLINGS > SNARL
SNARLS > SNARL
SNARLY > SNARL
SNARRED > SNAR
SNARRING > SNAR
SNARS > SNAR
SNARY > SNARE
SNASH *vb* Scots word meaning speak cheekily
SNASHED > SNASH
SNASHES > SNASH
SNASHING > SNASH
SNASTE *n* candle wick
SNASTES > SNASTE
SNATCH *vb* seize or try to seize suddenly ▷ *n* snatching
SNATCHED > SNATCH
SNATCHER > SNATCH
SNATCHERS > SNATCH
SNATCHES > SNATCH
SNATCHIER > SNATCHY
SNATCHILY > SNATCHY
SNATCHING > SNATCH
SNATCHY *adj* disconnected or spasmodic
SNATH *n* handle of a scythe
SNATHE *same as* **>** SNATH
SNATHES > SNATHE
SNATHS > SNATH
SNAW *Scots variant of* **>** SNOW
SNAWED > SNAW
SNAWING > SNAW
SNAWS > SNAW
SNAZZIER > SNAZZY
SNAZZIEST > SNAZZY
SNAZZILY > SNAZZY
SNAZZY *adj* stylish and flashy
SNEAD *n* scythe handle

SNEADS > SNEAD
SNEAK *vb* move furtively ▷ *n* cowardly or underhand person ▷ *adj* without warning
SNEAKBOX *n* small camouflaged boat, used for wildfowl hunting
SNEAKED > SNEAK
SNEAKER *n* canvas shoe with rubber sole
SNEAKERED *adj* wearing sneakers
SNEAKERS > SNEAKER
SNEAKEUP *n* sneaky person
SNEAKEUPS **>** SNEAKEUP
SNEAKIER > SNEAK
SNEAKIEST > SNEAK
SNEAKILY > SNEAK
SNEAKING *adj* slight but persistent
SNEAKISH *adj* typical of a sneak
SNEAKS > SNEAK
SNEAKSBY *n* sneak
SNEAKY > SNEAK
SNEAP *vb* nip
SNEAPED > SNEAP
SNEAPING > SNEAP
SNEAPS > SNEAP
SNEATH *same as* **>** SNATH
SNEATHS > SNEATH
SNEB *same as* **>** SNIB
SNEBBE *same as* **>** SNUB
SNEBBED > SNEB
SNEBBES > SNEBBE
SNEBBING > SNEB
SNEBS > SNEB
SNECK *n* small squared stone used in a rubble wall to fill spaces between stones ▷ *vb* fasten (a latch)
SNECKED > SNECK
SNECKING > SNECK
SNECKS > SNECK
SNED *vb* prune or trim
SNEDDED > SNED
SNEDDING > SNED
SNEDS > SNED
SNEE *vb* cut
SNEED > SNEE
SNEEING > SNEE
SNEER *n* contemptuous expression or remark ▷ *vb* show contempt by a sneer
SNEERED > SNEER
SNEERER > SNEER
SNEERERS > SNEER
SNEERFUL > SNEER
SNEERIER > SNEERY
SNEERIEST > SNEERY
SNEERING > SNEER
SNEERINGS > SNEER
SNEERS > SNEER
SNEERY *adj* contemptuous or scornful
SNEES > SNEE
SNEESH *n* Scots word meaning pinch of snuff ▷ *vb* take snuff
SNEESHAN *n* Scots word meaning pinch of snuff
SNEESHANS **>** SNEESHAN

SNEESHED > SNEESH
SNEESHES > SNEESH
SNEESHIN *same as* **>** SNEESHAN
SNEESHING *same as* **>** SNEESHAN
SNEESHINS **>** SNEESHIN
SNEEZE *vb* expel air from the nose suddenly, involuntarily, and noisily ▷ *n* act or sound of sneezing
SNEEZED > SNEEZE
SNEEZER > SNEEZE
SNEEZERS > SNEEZE
SNEEZES > SNEEZE
SNEEZIER > SNEEZE
SNEEZIEST > SNEEZE
SNEEZING > SNEEZE
SNEEZINGS > SNEEZE
SNEEZY > SNEEZE
SNELL *adj* biting ▷ *vb* attach hook to fishing line
SNELLED > SNELL
SNELLER > SNELL
SNELLEST > SNELL
SNELLING > SNELL
SNELLS > SNELL
SNELLY > SNELL
SNIB *n* catch of a door or window ▷ *vb* bolt or fasten (a door)
SNIBBED > SNIB
SNIBBING > SNIB
SNIBS > SNIB
SNICK *n* small cut or notch ▷ *vb* make a small cut or notch in (something)
SNICKED > SNICK
SNICKER *same as* **>** SNIGGER
SNICKERED > SNICKER
SNICKERER > SNICKER
SNICKERS > SNICKER
SNICKERY *adj* tending to snicker
SNICKET *n* passageway between walls or fences
SNICKETS > SNICKET
SNICKING > SNICK
SNICKS > SNICK
SNIDE *adj* critical in an unfair and nasty way ▷ *n* sham jewellery ▷ *vb* fill or load
SNIDED > SNIDE
SNIDELY > SNIDE
SNIDENESS > SNIDE
SNIDER > SNIDE
SNIDES > SNIDE
SNIDEST > SNIDE
SNIDEY *same as* **>** SNIDE
SNIDIER > SNIDEY
SNIDIEST > SNIDEY
SNIDING > SNIDE
SNIES > SNY
SNIFF *vb* inhale through the nose in short audible breaths ▷ *n* act or sound of sniffing
SNIFFABLE > SNIFF
SNIFFED > SNIFF
SNIFFER *n* device for detecting hidden substances such as drugs
SNIFFERS > SNIFFER

SNIFFIER > SNIFFY
SNIFFIEST > SNIFFY
SNIFFILY > SNIFFY
SNIFFING > SNIFF
SNIFFINGS > SNIFF
SNIFFISH *adj* disdainful
SNIFFLE *vb* sniff repeatedly, as when suffering from a cold ▷ *n* slight cold
SNIFFLED > SNIFFLE
SNIFFLER > SNIFFLE
SNIFFLERS > SNIFFLE
SNIFFLES > SNIFFLE
SNIFFLIER > SNIFFLE
SNIFFLING > SNIFFLE
SNIFFLY > SNIFFLE
SNIFFS > SNIFF
SNIFFY *adj* contemptuous or scornful
SNIFT *same as* **>** SNIFF
SNIFTED > SNIFT
SNIFTER *n* small quantity of alcoholic drink ▷ *vb* sniff
SNIFTERED > SNIFTER
SNIFTERS > SNIFTER
SNIFTIER > SNIFTY
SNIFTIEST > SNIFTY
SNIFTING > SNIFT
SNIFTS > SNIFT
SNIFTY *adj* slang word meaning excellent
SNIG *vb* drag (a felled log) by a chain or cable
SNIGGED > SNIG
SNIGGER *n* sly laugh ▷ *vb* laugh slyly
SNIGGERED > SNIGGER
SNIGGERER > SNIGGER
SNIGGERS > SNIGGER
SNIGGING > SNIG
SNIGGLE *vb* fish for eels by dangling or thrusting a baited hook into cavities ▷ *n* baited hook used for sniggling eels
SNIGGLED > SNIGGLE
SNIGGLER > SNIGGLE
SNIGGLERS > SNIGGLE
SNIGGLES > SNIGGLE
SNIGGLING > SNIGGLE
SNIGLET *n* invented word
SNIGLETS > SNIGLET
SNIGS > SNIG
SNIP *vb* cut in small quick strokes with scissors or shears ▷ *n* bargain ▷ *interj* representation of the sound of scissors or shears closing
SNIPE *n* wading bird with a long straight bill ▷ *vb* shoot at (a person) from cover
SNIPED > SNIPE
SNIPEFISH *n* type of fish of tropical and temperate seas, with a long snout and a single dorsal fin
SNIPELIKE > SNIPE
SNIPER *n* person who shoots at someone from cover
SNIPERS > SNIPER
SNIPES > SNIPE
SNIPIER > SNIPY

SNIPIEST > SNIPY
SNIPING > SNIPE
SNIPINGS > SNIPE
SNIPPED > SNIP
SNIPPER > SNIP
SNIPPERS > SNIP
SNIPPET *n* small piece
SNIPPETS > SNIPPET
SNIPPETY > SNIPPET
SNIPPIER > SNIPPY
SNIPPIEST > SNIPPY
SNIPPILY > SNIPPY
SNIPPING > SNIP
SNIPPINGS > SNIP
SNIPPY *adj* scrappy
SNIPS > SNIP
SNIPY *adj* like a snipe
SNIRT *n* Scots word
meaning suppressed
laugh ▷ *vb* to snigger
SNIRTED > SNIRT
SNIRTING > SNIRT
SNIRTLE *vb* Scots word
meaning snicker
SNIRTLED > SNIRTLE
SNIRTLES > SNIRTLE
SNIRTLING > SNIRTLE
SNIRTS > SNIRT
SNIT *n* fit of temper
SNITCH *vb* act as an
informer ▷ *n* informer
SNITCHED > SNITCH
SNITCHER > SNITCH
SNITCHERS > SNITCH
SNITCHES > SNITCH
SNITCHIER > SNITCHY
SNITCHING > SNITCH
SNITCHY *adj*
bad-tempered or irritable
SNITS > SNIT
SNITTIER > SNITTY
SNITTIEST > SNITTY
SNITTY *adj* cross or
irritable
SNIVEL *vb* cry in a
whining way ▷ *n* act of
snivelling
SNIVELED > SNIVEL
SNIVELER > SNIVEL
SNIVELERS > SNIVEL
SNIVELIER > SNIVELY
SNIVELING *n* act or
instance of crying in a
whining way
SNIVELLED > SNIVEL
SNIVELLER > SNIVEL
SNIVELLY *adj* tending to
snivel
SNIVELS > SNIVEL
SNIVELY *adj* tending to
snivel
SNOB *n* person who judges
others by social rank
SNOBBERY > SNOB
SNOBBIER > SNOB
SNOBBIEST > SNOB
SNOBBILY > SNOB
SNOBBISH > SNOB
SNOBBISM > SNOB
SNOBBISMS > SNOB
SNOBBY > SNOB
SNOBLING *n* little snob
SNOBLINGS > SNOBLING
SNOBS > SNOB
SNOCOACH *n* bus-like
vehicle for travelling on
snow

SNOD *adj* Scots word
meaning tidy ▷ *vb* make
tidy
SNODDED > SNOD
SNODDER > SNOD
SNODDEST > SNOD
SNODDING > SNOD
SNODDIT > SNOD
SNODS > SNOD
SNOEK *n* edible marine
fish
SNOEKS > SNOEK
SNOEP *adj* mean or
tight-fisted
SNOG *vb* kiss and cuddle
▷ *n* act of kissing and
cuddling
SNOGGED > SNOG
SNOGGER *n* person who
snogs
SNOGGERS > SNOGGER
SNOGGING > SNOG
SNOGS > SNOG
SNOKE *same as* > SNOOK
SNOKED > SNOKE
SNOKES > SNOKE
SNOKING > SNOKE
SNOOD *n* pouch loosely
holding the hair at the
back ▷ *vb* hold (the hair) in
a snood
SNOODED > SNOOD
SNOODING > SNOOD
SNOODS > SNOOD
SNOOK *n* any of several
large game fishes ▷ *vb* lurk
SNOOKED > SNOOK
SNOOKER *n* game played
on a billiard table ▷ *vb*
leave (a snooker
opponent) unable to hit
the target ball
SNOOKERED > SNOOKER
SNOOKERS > SNOOKER
SNOOKING > SNOOK
SNOOKS > SNOOK
SNOOL *vb* Scots word
meaning dominate
SNOOLED > SNOOL
SNOOLING > SNOOL
SNOOLS > SNOOL
SNOOP *vb* pry ▷ *n*
snooping
SNOOPED > SNOOP
SNOOPER *n* person who
snoops
SNOOPERS > SNOOPER
SNOOPIER > SNOOP
SNOOPIEST > SNOOP
SNOOPILY > SNOOP
SNOOPING > SNOOP
SNOOPS > SNOOP
SNOOPY > SNOOP
SNOOSE *n* snuff
SNOOSES > SNOOSE
SNOOT *n* nose ▷ *vb* look
contemptuously at
SNOOTED > SNOOT
SNOOTFUL *n* enough
alcohol to make someone
drunk
SNOOTFULS
> SNOOTFUL
SNOOTIER > SNOOTY
SNOOTIEST > SNOOTY
SNOOTILY > SNOOTY
SNOOTING > SNOOT

SNOOTS > SNOOT
SNOOTY *adj* haughty
SNOOZE *vb* take a brief
light sleep ▷ *n* brief light
sleep
SNOOZED > SNOOZE
SNOOZER > SNOOZE
SNOOZERS > SNOOZE
SNOOZES > SNOOZE
SNOOZIER > SNOOZE
SNOOZIEST > SNOOZE
SNOOZING > SNOOZE
SNOOZLE *vb* cuddle and
sleep
SNOOZLED > SNOOZLE
SNOOZLES > SNOOZLE
SNOOZLING > SNOOZLE
SNOOZY > SNOOZE
SNORE *vb* make snoring
sounds while sleeping ▷ *n*
sound of snoring
SNORED > SNORE
SNORER > SNORE
SNORERS > SNORE
SNORES > SNORE
SNORING > SNORE
SNORINGS > SNORE
SNORKEL *n* tube allowing
a swimmer to breathe ▷ *vb*
swim using a snorkel
SNORKELED > SNORKEL
SNORKELER > SNORKEL
SNORKELS > SNORKEL
SNORT *vb* exhale noisily
through the nostrils ▷ *n*
act or sound of snorting
SNORTED > SNORT
SNORTER *n* person or
animal that snorts
SNORTERS > SNORTER
SNORTIER > SNORT
SNORTIEST > SNORT
SNORTING > SNORT
SNORTINGS > SNORT
SNORTS > SNORT
SNORTY > SNORT
SNOT *n* mucus from the
nose ▷ *vb* blow one's nose
SNOTRAG *n* handkerchief
SNOTRAGS > SNOTRAG
SNOTS > SNOT
SNOTTED > SNOT
SNOTTER *vb* breathe
through obstructed
nostrils
SNOTTERED > SNOTTER
SNOTTERS > SNOTTER
SNOTTERY *n* snot
SNOTTIE *n* midshipman
SNOTTIER > SNOTTY
SNOTTIES > SNOTTY
SNOTTIEST > SNOTTY
SNOTTILY > SNOTTY
SNOTTING > SNOT
SNOTTY *adj* covered with
mucus from the nose
SNOUT *n* animal's
projecting nose and jaws
▷ *vb* have or give a snout
SNOUTED > SNOUT
SNOUTIER > SNOUT
SNOUTIEST > SNOUT
SNOUTING > SNOUT
SNOUTISH > SNOUT
SNOUTLESS > SNOUT
SNOUTLIKE > SNOUT
SNOUTS > SNOUT

SNOUTY > SNOUT
SNOW *n* frozen vapour
falling from the sky in
flakes ▷ *vb* fall as or like
snow
SNOWBALL *n* snow
pressed into a ball for
throwing ▷ *vb* increase
rapidly
SNOWBALLS
> SNOWBALL
SNOWBANK *n* bank of
snow
SNOWBANKS
> SNOWBANK
SNOWBELL *n* Asian shrub
SNOWBELLS
> SNOWBELL
SNOWBELT *n* northern
states of USA
SNOWBELTS
> SNOWBELT
SNOWBERRY *n* shrub
grown for its white
berries
SNOWBIRD *n* bird of Arctic
regions
SNOWBIRDS
> SNOWBIRD
SNOWBLINK *n* whitish
glare in the sky reflected
from snow
SNOWBOARD *n* board on
which a person stands to
slide across the snow
SNOWBOOT *n* boot for
walking in snow
SNOWBOOTS
> SNOWBOOT
SNOWBOUND *adj* shut in
by snow
SNOWBRUSH *n* brush for
clearing snow
SNOWBUSH *n* North
American plant
SNOWCAP *n* cap of snow
on top of a mountain
SNOWCAPS > SNOWCAP
SNOWCAT *n* tracked
vehicle for travelling over
snow
SNOWCATS > SNOWCAT
SNOWCLONE *n* reusable
verbal formula
SNOWCOACH *n* bus
equipped to travel on
snow
SNOWDOME *n* leisure
centre with facilities for
skiing, skating, etc
SNOWDOMES
> SNOWDOME
SNOWDRIFT *n* bank of
deep snow
SNOWDROP *n* small white
bell-shaped spring flower
SNOWDROPS
> SNOWDROP
SNOWED > SNOW
SNOWFALL *n* fall of snow
SNOWFALLS
> SNOWFALL
SNOWFIELD *n* large area
of permanent snow
SNOWFLAKE *n* single
crystal of snow
SNOWFLEA *n* wingless
insect that lives on or in
snow

SNOWFLEAS
> SNOWFLEA
SNOWFLECK n snow bunting
SNOWFLICK same as
> SNOWFLECK
SNOWGLOBE n transparent sphere filled with water and white particles which resemble snow falling when shaken
SNOWIER > SNOWY
SNOWIEST > SNOWY
SNOWILY > SNOWY
SNOWINESS > SNOWY
SNOWING > SNOW
SNOWISH adj like snow
SNOWK same as > SNOOK
SNOWKED > SNOWK
SNOWKING > SNOWK
SNOWKS > SNOWK
SNOWLAND n area where snow lies
SNOWLANDS
> SNOWLAND
SNOWLESS > SNOW
SNOWLIKE > SNOW
SNOWLINE n limit of permanent snow
SNOWLINES
> SNOWLINE
SNOWMAKER n machine making artificial snow
SNOWMAN n figure shaped out of snow
SNOWMELT n melting of snow in spring
SNOWMELTS
> SNOWMELT
SNOWMEN > SNOWMAN
SNOWMOLD same as
> SNOWMOULD
SNOWMOLDS
> SNOWMOULD
SNOWMOULD n fungus growing on grass under snow
SNOWPACK n body of hard-packed snow
SNOWPACKS
> SNOWPACK
SNOWPLOW n implement or vehicle for clearing snow away
SNOWPLOWS
> SNOWPLOW
SNOWS > SNOW
SNOWSCAPE n snow-covered landscape
SNOWSHED n shelter built over an exposed section of railway track
SNOWSHEDS
> SNOWSHED
SNOWSHOE n racket-shaped frame with a network of thongs stretched across it for walking on snow ▷ vb walk using snowshoes
SNOWSHOED
> SNOWSHOE
SNOWSHOER
> SNOWSHOE
SNOWSHOES
> SNOWSHOE
SNOWSLIDE n snow avalanche

SNOWSLIP n small snow avalanche
SNOWSLIPS
> SNOWSLIP
SNOWSNAKE n Native American game in which a wooden rod is slid over snow
SNOWSTORM n storm with heavy snow
SNOWSUIT n one-piece winter outer garment for child
SNOWSUITS
> SNOWSUIT
SNOWY adj covered with or abounding in snow
SNUB vb insult deliberately ▷ n deliberate insult ▷ adj (of a nose) short and blunt
SNUBBE n stub
SNUBBED > SNUB
SNUBBER > SNUB
SNUBBERS > SNUB
SNUBBES > SNUBBE
SNUBBEST > SNUB
SNUBBIER > SNUB
SNUBBIEST > SNUB
SNUBBING > SNUB
SNUBBINGS > SNUB
SNUBBISH > SNUB
SNUBBY > SNUB
SNUBFIN adj as in snubfin dolphin Australian dolphin with a small dorsal fin
SNUBNESS > SNUB
SNUBS > SNUB
SNUCK past tense and past participle of > SNEAK
SNUDGE vb be miserly
SNUDGED > SNUDGE
SNUDGES > SNUDGE
SNUDGING > SNUDGE
SNUFF n powdered tobacco for sniffing up the nostrils ▷ vb extinguish (a candle)
SNUFFBOX n small container for holding snuff
SNUFFED > SNUFF
SNUFFER > SNUFF
SNUFFERS > SNUFF
SNUFFIER > SNUFFY
SNUFFIEST > SNUFFY
SNUFFILY > SNUFFY
SNUFFING > SNUFF
SNUFFINGS > SNUFF
SNUFFLE vb breathe noisily or with difficulty ▷ n act or the sound of snuffling
SNUFFLED > SNUFFLE
SNUFFLER > SNUFFLE
SNUFFLERS > SNUFFLE
SNUFFLES same as
> SNIFFLES
SNUFFLIER > SNUFFLE
SNUFFLING > SNUFFLE
SNUFFLY > SNUFFLE
SNUFFS > SNUFF
SNUFFY adj of, relating to, or resembling snuff
SNUG adj warm and comfortable ▷ n small peg that stops a bolt from turning ▷ vb make or become comfortable and warm

SNUGGED > SNUG
SNUGGER > SNUG
SNUGGERIE n small bar in pub
SNUGGEST > SNUG
SNUGGIES pl n specially warm underwear
SNUGGING > SNUG
SNUGGLE vb nestle into a person or thing for warmth or from affection ▷ n act of snuggling
SNUGGLED > SNUGGLE
SNUGGLES > SNUGGLE
SNUGGLIER > SNUGGLY
SNUGGLING > SNUGGLE
SNUGGLY adj comfortably warm and suitable for snuggling
SNUGLY > SNUG
SNUGNESS > SNUG
SNUGS > SNUG
SNUSH vb take snuff
SNUSHED > SNUSH
SNUSHES > SNUSH
SNUSHING > SNUSH
SNUZZLE vb root in ground
SNUZZLED > SNUZZLE
SNUZZLES > SNUZZLE
SNUZZLING > SNUZZLE
SNY same as > SNYE
SNYE n side channel of a river
SNYES > SNYE
SO adv such an extent ▷ interj exclamation of surprise, triumph, or realization ▷ n the fifth note of the musical scale
SOAK vb make wet ▷ n soaking
SOAKAGE n process or a period in which a permeable substance is soaked in a liquid
SOAKAGES > SOAKAGE
SOAKAWAY n pit filled with rubble, etc, into which rain or waste water drains
SOAKAWAYS
> SOAKAWAY
SOAKED > SOAK
SOAKEN > SOAK
SOAKER > SOAK
SOAKERS > SOAK
SOAKING > SOAK
SOAKINGLY > SOAK
SOAKINGS > SOAK
SOAKS > SOAK
SOAP n compound of alkali and fat, used with water as a cleaning agent ▷ vb apply soap to
SOAPBARK n W South American rosaceous tree
SOAPBARKS
> SOAPBARK
SOAPBERRY n any of various chiefly tropical American sapindaceous trees
SOAPBOX n crate used as a platform for speech-making ▷ vb

deliver a speech from a soapbox
SOAPBOXED > SOAPBOX
SOAPBOXES > SOAPBOX
SOAPDISH n dish for holding soap
SOAPED > SOAP
SOAPER n soap opera
SOAPERS > SOAPER
SOAPFISH n tropical fish with toxic mucus
SOAPIE n soap opera
SOAPIER > SOAPY
SOAPIES > SOAPIE
SOAPIEST > SOAPY
SOAPILY > SOAPY
SOAPINESS > SOAPY
SOAPING > SOAP
SOAPLAND n Japanese massage parlour and brothel
SOAPLANDS
> SOAPLAND
SOAPLESS > SOAP
SOAPLIKE > SOAP
SOAPROOT n plant with roots used as soap substitute
SOAPROOTS
> SOAPROOT
SOAPS > SOAP
SOAPSTONE n soft mineral used for making table tops and ornaments
SOAPSUDS pl n foam or lather produced when soap is mixed with water
SOAPSUDSY adj like soapsuds
SOAPWORT n Eurasian plant with clusters of fragrant pink or white flowers
SOAPWORTS
> SOAPWORT
SOAPY adj covered with soap
SOAR vb rise or fly upwards ▷ n act of soaring
SOARAWAY adj exceedingly successful
SOARE n young hawk
SOARED > SOAR
SOARER > SOAR
SOARERS > SOAR
SOARES > SOARE
SOARING > SOAR
SOARINGLY > SOAR
SOARINGS > SOAR
SOARS > SOAR
SOAVE n dry white Italian wine
SOAVES > SOAVE
SOB vb weep with convulsive gasps ▷ n act or sound of sobbing
SOBA n (in Japanese cookery) noodles made from buckwheat flour
SOBAS > SOBA
SOBBED > SOB
SOBBER > SOB
SOBBERS > SOB
SOBBING > SOB
SOBBINGLY > SOB
SOBBINGS > SOB
SOBEIT conj provided that

SOBER adj not drunk ▷ vb make or become sober
SOBERED > SOBER
SOBERER > SOBER
SOBEREST > SOBER
SOBERING > SOBER
SOBERISE same as > SOBERIZE
SOBERISED > SOBERISE
SOBERISES > SOBERISE
SOBERIZE vb make sober
SOBERIZED > SOBERIZE
SOBERIZES > SOBERIZE
SOBERLY > SOBER
SOBERNESS > SOBER
SOBERS > SOBER
SOBFUL adj tearful
SOBOLE n creeping underground stem that produces roots and buds
SOBOLES > SOBOLE
SOBRIETY n state of being sober
SOBRIQUET n nickname
SOBS > SOB
SOC n feudal right to hold court
SOCA n mixture of soul and calypso music
SOCAGE n tenure of land by certain services
SOCAGER > SOCAGE
SOCAGERS > SOCAGE
SOCAGES > SOCAGE
SOCAS > SOCA
SOCCAGE same as > SOCAGE
SOCCAGES > SOCCAGE
SOCCER n football played by two teams of eleven kicking a spherical ball
SOCCERS > SOCCER
SOCES > SOC
SOCIABLE adj friendly or companionable ▷ n type of open carriage with two seats facing each other
SOCIABLES > SOCIABLE
SOCIABLY > SOCIABLE
SOCIAL adj living in a community ▷ n informal gathering
SOCIALISE same as > SOCIALIZE
SOCIALISM n political system which advocates public ownership of industries, resources, and transport
SOCIALIST n supporter or advocate of socialism ▷ adj of or relating to socialism
SOCIALITE n member of fashionable society
SOCIALITY n tendency of groups and persons to develop social links and live in communities
SOCIALIZE vb meet others socially
SOCIALLY > SOCIAL

SOCIALS > SOCIAL
SOCIATE n associate
SOCIATES > SOCIATE
SOCIATION n plant community
SOCIATIVE adj of association
SOCIETAL adj of or relating to society, esp human society or social relations
SOCIETIES > SOCIETY
SOCIETY n human beings considered as a group
SOCIOGRAM n chart showing social relationships
SOCIOLECT n language spoken by particular social class
SOCIOLOGY n study of human societies
SOCIOPATH n person with a personality disorder characterized by a tendency to commit antisocial acts without any feelings of guilt
SOCK n knitted covering for the foot ▷ vb hit hard
SOCKED > SOCK
SOCKET n hole or recess into which something fits ▷ vb furnish with or place into a socket
SOCKETED > SOCKET
SOCKETING > SOCKET
SOCKETS > SOCKET
SOCKETTE n sock not covering ankle
SOCKETTES > SOCKETTE
SOCKEYE n Pacific salmon with red flesh
SOCKEYES > SOCKEYE
SOCKING > SOCK
SOCKLESS > SOCK
SOCKMAN same as > SOCMAN
SOCKMEN > SOCKMAN
SOCKO adj excellent
SOCKS > SOCK
SOCLE another name for > PLINTH
SOCLES > SOCLE
SOCMAN n tenant holding land by socage
SOCMEN > SOCMAN
SOCS > SOC
SOD n (piece of) turf ▷ vb cover with sods
SODA n compound of sodium
SODAIC adj containing soda
SODAIN same as > SUDDEN
SODAINE same as > SUDDEN
SODALESS > SODA
SODALIST n member of sodality
SODALISTS > SODALIST
SODALITE n blue, grey, yellow, or colourless mineral

SODALITES > SODALITE
SODALITY n religious or charitable society
SODAMIDE n white crystalline compound used as a dehydrating agent
SODAMIDES > SODAMIDE
SODAS > SODA
SODBUSTER n farmer who grows crops
SODDED > SOD
SODDEN adj soaked ▷ vb make or become sodden
SODDENED > SODDEN
SODDENING > SODDEN
SODDENLY > SODDEN
SODDENS > SODDEN
SODDIE n house made of sod
SODDIER > SODDY
SODDIES > SODDY
SODDIEST > SODDY
SODDING > SOD
SODDY adj covered with turf
SODGER dialect variant of > SOLDIER
SODGERED > SODGER
SODGERING > SODGER
SODGERS > SODGER
SODIC adj containing sodium
SODICITY > SODIC
SODIUM n silvery-white metallic element
SODIUMS > SODIUM
SODOM n person who performs sodomy
SODOMIES > SODOMY
SODOMISE same as > SODOMIZE
SODOMISED > SODOMISE
SODOMISES > SODOMISE
SODOMIST > SODOMY
SODOMISTS > SODOMY
SODOMITE n person who practises sodomy
SODOMITES > SODOMITE
SODOMITIC > SODOMY
SODOMIZE vb be the active partner in anal intercourse
SODOMIZED > SODOMIZE
SODOMIZES > SODOMIZE
SODOMS > SODOM
SODOMY n anal intercourse
SODS > SOD
SOEVER adv in any way at all
SOFA n couch
SOFABED n sofa that converts into a bed
SOFABEDS > SOFABED
SOFAR n system for determining a position at sea
SOFARS > SOFAR
SOFAS > SOFA
SOFFIONI pl n holes in volcano that emit steam

SOFFIT n underside of a part of a building or a structural component
SOFFITS > SOFFIT
SOFT adj easy to shape or cut ▷ adv softly ▷ vb soften
SOFTA n Muslim student of divinity and jurisprudence
SOFTAS > SOFTA
SOFTBACK n paperback
SOFTBACKS > SOFTBACK
SOFTBALL n game similar to baseball, played using a larger softer ball
SOFTBALLS > SOFTBALL
SOFTBOUND adj having paperback binding
SOFTCORE adj describing pornography that is not explicit
SOFTCOVER n book with paper covers
SOFTED > SOFT
SOFTEN vb make or become soft or softer
SOFTENED > SOFTEN
SOFTENER n substance added to another substance to increase its softness
SOFTENERS > SOFTENER
SOFTENING > SOFTEN
SOFTENS > SOFTEN
SOFTER > SOFT
SOFTEST > SOFT
SOFTGOODS n clothing and soft furniture
SOFTHEAD n insulting word for a stupid person
SOFTHEADS > SOFTHEAD
SOFTIE n person who is easily upset
SOFTIES > SOFTY
SOFTING > SOFT
SOFTISH > SOFT
SOFTLING n weakling
SOFTLINGS > SOFTLING
SOFTLY > SOFT
SOFTNESS n quality or an instance of being soft
SOFTPASTE adj as in softpaste porcelain a type of porcelain
SOFTS > SOFT
SOFTSCAPE n vegetation featuring in a landscape
SOFTSHELL n crab or turtle with a soft shell
SOFTWARE n computer programs
SOFTWARES > SOFTWARE
SOFTWOOD n wood of a coniferous tree
SOFTWOODS > SOFTWOOD
SOFTY same as > SOFTIE
SOG vb soak
SOGER same as > SODGER
SOGERS > SOGER
SOGGED > SOG

SOGGIER > SOGGY
SOGGIEST > SOGGY
SOGGILY > SOGGY
SOGGINESS > SOGGY
SOGGING > SOG
SOGGINGS > SOG
SOGGY *adj* soaked
SOGS > SOG
SOH *n* (in tonic sol-fa) fifth degree of any major scale
SOHO *interj* exclamation announcing the sighting of a hare
SOHS > SOH
SOHUR *same as >* SUHUR
SOHURS > SOHUR
SOIGNE *adj* well-groomed, elegant
SOIGNEE *variant of >* SOIGNE
SOIL *n* top layer of earth ▷ *vb* make or become dirty
SOILAGE *n* green fodder
SOILAGES > SOILAGE
SOILBORNE *adj* carried in soil
SOILED > SOIL
SOILIER > SOIL
SOILIEST > SOIL
SOILINESS > SOIL
SOILING > SOIL
SOILINGS > SOIL
SOILLESS > SOIL
SOILS > SOIL
SOILURE *n* act of soiling or the state of being soiled
SOILURES > SOILURE
SOILY > SOIL
SOIREE *n* evening party or gathering
SOIREES > SOIREE
SOJA *same as >* SOYA
SOJAS > SOJA
SOJOURN *n* temporary stay ▷ *vb* stay temporarily
SOJOURNED > SOJOURN
SOJOURNER > SOJOURN
SOJOURNS > SOJOURN
SOJU *n* type of Korean vodka
SOJUS > SOJU
SOKAH *same as >* SOCA
SOKAHS > SOKAH
SOKAIYA *n* Japanese extortionist
SOKE *n* right to hold a local court
SOKEMAN *same as >* SOCMAN
SOKEMANRY *n* feudal tenure by socage
SOKEMEN > SOKEMAN
SOKEN *n* feudal district
SOKENS > SOKEN
SOKES > SOKE
SOKOL *n* Czech gymnastic association
SOKOLS > SOKOL
SOL *n* liquid colloidal solution
SOLA *n* Indian plant
SOLACE *vb* comfort in distress ▷ *n* comfort in misery or disappointment
SOLACED > SOLACE
SOLACER > SOLACE
SOLACERS > SOLACE

SOLACES > SOLACE
SOLACING > SOLACE
SOLACIOUS *adj* providing solace
SOLAH *n* Indian plant
SOLAHS > SOLAH
SOLAN *archaic name for >* GANNET
SOLAND *n* solan goose
SOLANDER *n* box for specimens, maps, etc, in the form of a book with a lid
SOLANDERS > SOLANDER
SOLANDS > SOLAND
SOLANIN *same as >* SOLANINE
SOLANINE *n* poisonous alkaloid found in various solanaceous plants
SOLANINES > SOLANINE
SOLANINS > SOLANIN
SOLANO *n* hot wind in Spain
SOLANOS > SOLANO
SOLANS > SOLAN
SOLANUM *n* any plant of the genus that includes the potato
SOLANUMS > SOLANUM
SOLAR *adj* of the sun ▷ *n* upper room
SOLARIA > SOLARIUM
SOLARISE *same as >* SOLARIZE
SOLARISED > SOLARISE
SOLARISES > SOLARISE
SOLARISM *n* explanation of myths in terms of the movements and influence of the sun
SOLARISMS > SOLARISM
SOLARIST > SOLARISM
SOLARISTS > SOLARISM
SOLARIUM *n* place with beds and ultraviolet lights used for acquiring an artificial suntan
SOLARIUMS > SOLARIUM
SOLARIZE *vb* treat by exposure to the sun's rays
SOLARIZED > SOLARIZE
SOLARIZES > SOLARIZE
SOLARS > SOLAR
SOLAS > SOLA
SOLATE *vb* change from gel to liquid
SOLATED > SOLATE
SOLATES > SOLATE
SOLATIA > SOLATIUM
SOLATING > SOLATE
SOLATION *n* liquefaction of a gel
SOLATIONS > SOLATION
SOLATIUM *n* compensation awarded for injury to the feelings

SOLD *n* obsolete word for salary
SOLDADO *n* soldier
SOLDADOES > SOLDADO
SOLDADOS > SOLDADO
SOLDAN *archaic word for >* SULTAN
SOLDANS > SOLDAN
SOLDE *n* wages
SOLDER *n* soft alloy used to join two metal surfaces ▷ *vb* join with solder
SOLDERED > SOLDER
SOLDERER > SOLDER
SOLDERERS > SOLDER
SOLDERING > SOLDER
SOLDERS > SOLDER
SOLDES > SOLDE
SOLDI > SOLDO
SOLDIER *n* member of an army ▷ *vb* serve in an army
SOLDIERED > SOLDIER
SOLDIERLY *adj* of or befitting a good soldier
SOLDIERS > SOLDIER
SOLDIERY *n* soldiers collectively
SOLDO *n* former Italian copper coin
SOLDS > SOLD
SOLE *adj* one and only ▷ *n* underside of the foot ▷ *vb* provide (a shoe) with a sole
SOLECISE *variant of >* SOLECIZE
SOLECISED > SOLECISE
SOLECISES > SOLECISE
SOLECISM *n* minor grammatical mistake
SOLECISMS > SOLECISM
SOLECIST > SOLECISM
SOLECISTS > SOLECISM
SOLECIZE *vb* commit a solecism
SOLECIZED > SOLECIZE
SOLECIZES > SOLECIZE
SOLED > SOLE
SOLEI > SOLEUS
SOLEIN *same as >* SULLEN
SOLELESS > SOLE
SOLELY *adv* only, completely
SOLEMN *adj* serious, deeply sincere
SOLEMNER > SOLEMN
SOLEMNESS > SOLEMN
SOLEMNEST > SOLEMN
SOLEMNIFY *vb* make serious or grave
SOLEMNISE *same as >* SOLEMNIZE
SOLEMNITY *n* state or quality of being solemn
SOLEMNIZE *vb* celebrate or perform (a ceremony)
SOLEMNLY > SOLEMN
SOLENESS > SOLE
SOLENETTE *n* small European sole

SOLENODON *n* either of two rare shrewlike nocturnal mammals of the Caribbean
SOLENOID *n* coil of wire magnetized by passing a current through it
SOLENOIDS > SOLENOID
SOLEPLATE *n* joist forming the lowest member of a timber frame
SOLEPRINT *n* print of sole of foot
SOLER *same as >* SOLE
SOLERA *n* system for ageing sherry and other fortified wines
SOLERAS > SOLERA
SOLERET *n* armour for foot
SOLERETS > SOLERET
SOLERS > SOLER
SOLES > SOLE
SOLEUS *n* muscle in calf of leg
SOLEUSES > SOLEUS
SOLFATARA *n* volcanic vent emitting only sulphurous gases and water vapour or sometimes hot mud
SOLFEGE *variant of >* SOLFEGGIO
SOLFEGES > SOLFEGE
SOLFEGGI > SOLFEGGIO
SOLFEGGIO *n* voice exercise in which runs, scales, etc, are sung to the same syllable or syllables
SOLFERINO *n* moderate purplish-red colour
SOLGEL *adj* changing between sol and gel
SOLI *adv* to be performed by or with soloists
SOLICIT *vb* request
SOLICITED > SOLICIT
SOLICITOR *n* lawyer who advises clients and prepares documents and cases
SOLICITS > SOLICIT
SOLICITY *n* act of making a request
SOLID *adj* (of a substance) keeping its shape ▷ *n* three-dimensional shape
SOLIDAGO *n* chiefly American plant of the genus which includes the goldenrods
SOLIDAGOS > SOLIDAGO
SOLIDARE *n* old coin
SOLIDARES > SOLIDARE
SOLIDARY *adj* marked by unity of interests, responsibilities, etc
SOLIDATE *vb* consolidate
SOLIDATED > SOLIDATE
SOLIDATES > SOLIDATE
SOLIDER > SOLID
SOLIDEST > SOLID

S

SOLIDI > SOLIDUS
SOLIDIFY vb make or become solid or firm
SOLIDISH > SOLID
SOLIDISM n belief that diseases spring from damage to solid parts of body
SOLIDISMS > SOLIDISM
SOLIDIST > SOLIDISM
SOLIDISTS > SOLIDISM
SOLIDITY > SOLID
SOLIDLY > SOLID
SOLIDNESS > SOLID
SOLIDS > SOLID
SOLIDUM n part of pedestal
SOLIDUMS > SOLIDUM
SOLIDUS same as > SLASH
SOLILOQUY n speech made by a person while alone, esp in a play
SOLING > SOLE
SOLION n amplifier used in chemistry
SOLIONS > SOLION
SOLIPED n animal whose hooves are not cloven
SOLIPEDS > SOLIPED
SOLIPSISM n doctrine that the self is the only thing known to exist
SOLIPSIST > SOLIPSISM
SOLIQUID n semi-solid, semi-liquid solution
SOLIQUIDS > SOLIQUID
SOLITAIRE n game for one person played with pegs set in a board
SOLITARY adj alone, single ▷ n hermit
SOLITO adv musical instruction meaning play in usual manner
SOLITON n type of isolated particle-like wave
SOLITONS > SOLITON
SOLITUDE n state of being alone
SOLITUDES > SOLITUDE
SOLIVE n type of joist
SOLIVES > SOLIVE
SOLLAR n archaic word meaning attic ▷ vb put in a sollar
SOLLARED > SOLLAR
SOLLARING > SOLLAR
SOLLARS > SOLLAR
SOLLER same as > SOLLAR
SOLLERET n protective covering for the foot consisting of riveted plates of armour
SOLLERETS > SOLLERET
SOLLERS > SOLLER
SOLLICKER n something very large
SOLO n music for one performer ▷ adj done alone ▷ adv by oneself,

alone ▷ vb undertake a venture alone
SOLOED > SOLO
SOLOES > SOLO
SOLOING > SOLO
SOLOIST n person who performs a solo
SOLOISTIC > SOLOIST
SOLOISTS > SOLOIST
SOLON n US congressperson
SOLONCHAK n type of intrazonal soil of arid regions with a greyish surface crust
SOLONETS same as > SOLONETZ
SOLONETZ n type of intrazonal soil with a high saline content characterized by leaching
SOLONS > SOLON
SOLOS > SOLO
SOLPUGID n venomous arachnid
SOLPUGIDS > SOLPUGID
SOLS > SOL
SOLSTICE n either the shortest (in winter) or longest (in summer) day of the year
SOLSTICES > SOLSTICE
SOLUBLE adj able to be dissolved ▷ n soluble substance
SOLUBLES > SOLUBLE
SOLUBLY > SOLUBLE
SOLUM n upper layers of the soil profile
SOLUMS > SOLUM
SOLUNAR adj relating to sun and moon
SOLUS n advert printed or published separately from others
SOLUSES > SOLUS
SOLUTAL adj relating to a solute
SOLUTE n substance in a solution that is dissolved ▷ adj loose or unattached
SOLUTES > SOLUTE
SOLUTION n answer to a problem
SOLUTIONS > SOLUTION
SOLUTIVE adj dissolving ▷ n solvent or laxative
SOLUTIVES > SOLUTIVE
SOLVABLE adj capable of being solved
SOLVATE vb undergo, cause to undergo, or partake in solvation
SOLVATED > SOLVATE
SOLVATES > SOLVATE
SOLVATING > SOLVATE
SOLVATION n type of chemical process
SOLVE vb find the answer to (a problem)
SOLVED > SOLVE
SOLVENCY n ability to pay all debts
SOLVENT adj having enough money to pay

one's debts ▷ n liquid capable of dissolving other substances
SOLVENTLY > SOLVENT
SOLVENTS > SOLVENT
SOLVER > SOLVE
SOLVERS > SOLVE
SOLVES > SOLVE
SOLVING > SOLVE
SOM n currency of Kyrgyzstan and Uzbekistan
SOMA n body of an organism as distinct from the germ cells
SOMAN n compound developed as a nerve gas
SOMANS > SOMAN
SOMAS > SOMA
SOMASCOPE n instrument for inspecting internal organs
SOMATA > SOMA
SOMATIC adj of the body, as distinct from the mind
SOMATISM n materialism
SOMATISMS > SOMATISM
SOMATIST > SOMATISM
SOMATISTS > SOMATISM
SOMBER adj (in the US) sombre ▷ vb (in the US) make sombre
SOMBERED > SOMBER
SOMBERER > SOMBER
SOMBEREST > SOMBER
SOMBERING > SOMBER
SOMBERLY > SOMBER
SOMBERS > SOMBER
SOMBRE adj dark, gloomy ▷ vb make sombre
SOMBRED > SOMBRE
SOMBRELY > SOMBRE
SOMBRER > SOMBRE
SOMBRERO n wide-brimmed Mexican hat
SOMBREROS > SOMBRERO
SOMBRES > SOMBRE
SOMBREST > SOMBRE
SOMBRING > SOMBRE
SOMBROUS > SOMBRE
SOME pron certain unknown or unspecified people or things ▷ adv approximately
SOMEBODY pron some person ▷ n important person
SOMEDAY adv at some unspecified time in the future
SOMEDEAL adv to some extent ▷ n some part of something
SOMEDEALS > SOMEDEAL
SOMEDELE same as > SOMEDEAL
SOMEGATE adv Scots word meaning somehow
SOMEHOW adv in some unspecified way
SOMEONE pron somebody ▷ n significant or important person

SOMEONES > SOMEONE
SOMEPLACE adv in, at, or to some unspecified place or region
SOMERSET n somersault
SOMERSETS > SOMERSET
SOMETHING pron unknown or unspecified thing or amount ▷ n impressive or important person or thing
SOMETIME adv at some unspecified time ▷ adj former
SOMETIMES adv from time to time, now and then
SOMEWAY adv in some unspecified manner
SOMEWAYS same as > SOMEWAY
SOMEWHAT adv some extent, rather ▷ n vague amount
SOMEWHATS > SOMEWHAT
SOMEWHEN adv at some time
SOMEWHERE adv in, to, or at some unspecified or unknown place
SOMEWHILE adv sometimes
SOMEWHY adv for some reason
SOMEWISE adv in some way or to some degree
SOMITAL > SOMITE
SOMITE n segment of mesoderm in vertebrate embryos
SOMITES > SOMITE
SOMITIC > SOMITE
SOMMELIER n wine steward in a restaurant or hotel
SOMNIAL adj of dreams
SOMNIATE vb dream
SOMNIATED > SOMNIATE
SOMNIATES > SOMNIATE
SOMNIFIC adj inducing sleep
SOMNOLENT adj drowsy
SOMONI n monetary unit of Tajikistan
SOMONIS > SOMONI
SOMS > SOM
SOMY > SOM
SON n male offspring
SONANCE > SONANT
SONANCES > SONANT
SONANCIES > SONANT
SONANCY > SONANT
SONANT n voiced sound able to form a syllable or syllable nucleus ▷ adj denoting a voiced sound like this
SONANTAL > SONANT
SONANTIC > SONANT
SONANTS > SONANT
SONAR n device for detecting underwater objects by the reflection of sound waves

S

SONARMAN n sonar operator
SONARMEN > SONARMAN
SONARS > SONAR
SONATA n piece of music in several movements for one instrument
SONATAS > SONATA
SONATINA n short sonata
SONATINAS > SONATINA
SONATINE same as > SONATINA
SONCE n Scots word meaning good luck
SONCES > SONCE
SONDAGE n deep trial trench for inspecting stratigraphy
SONDAGES > SONDAGE
SONDE n rocket, balloon, or probe used for observing in the upper atmosphere
SONDELI n Indian shrew
SONDELIS > SONDELI
SONDER n yacht category
SONDERS > SONDER
SONDES > SONDE
SONE n subjective unit of loudness
SONERI n Indian cloth of gold
SONERIS > SONERI
SONES > SONE
SONG n music for the voice
SONGBIRD n any bird with a musical call
SONGBIRDS > SONGBIRD
SONGBOOK n book of songs
SONGBOOKS > SONGBOOK
SONGCRAFT n art of songwriting
SONGFEST n event with many songs
SONGFESTS > SONGFEST
SONGFUL adj tuneful
SONGFULLY > SONGFUL
SONGKOK n (in Malaysia and Indonesia) a kind of oval brimless hat, resembling a skull
SONGKOKS > SONGKOK
SONGLESS > SONG
SONGLIKE > SONG
SONGMAN n singer
SONGMEN > SONGMAN
SONGOLOLO n kind of millipede
SONGS > SONG
SONGSHEET n piece of paper with the words to a song on it
SONGSMITH n person who writes songs
SONGSTER n singer
SONGSTERS > SONGSTER
SONHOOD > SON
SONHOODS > SON
SONIC adj of or producing sound
SONICALLY > SONIC

SONICATE vb subject to sound waves
SONICATED > SONICATE
SONICATES > SONICATE
SONICATOR > SONICATE
SONICS n study of mechanical vibrations in matter
SONLESS > SON
SONLIER > SONLY
SONLIEST > SONLY
SONLIKE > SON
SONLY adj like a son
SONNE same as > SON
SONNES > SONNE
SONNET n fourteen-line poem ▷ vb compose sonnets
SONNETARY > SONNET
SONNETED > SONNET
SONNETEER n writer of sonnets
SONNETING > SONNET
SONNETISE same as > SONNETIZE
SONNETIZE vb write sonnets
SONNETS > SONNET
SONNETTED > SONNET
SONNIES > SONNY
SONNY n term of address to a boy
SONOBUOY n buoy equipped to detect underwater noises and transmit them by radio
SONOBUOYS > SONOBUOY
SONOGRAM n three-dimensional representation of a sound signal
SONOGRAMS > SONOGRAM
SONOGRAPH n device for scanning sound
SONOMETER same as > MONOCHORD
SONORANT n type of frictionless continuant or nasal
SONORANTS > SONORANT
SONORITY > SONOROUS
SONOROUS adj (of sound) deep or resonant
SONOVOX n device used to alter sound of human voice in music recordings
SONOVOXES > SONOVOX
SONS > SON
SONSE same as > SONCE
SONSES > SONSE
SONSHIP > SON
SONSHIPS > SON
SONSIE same as > SONSY
SONSIER > SONSY
SONSIEST > SONSY
SONSY adj plump
SONTAG n type of knitted women's cape
SONTAGS > SONTAG
SONTIES n Shakespearian oath

SOOCHONG same as > SOUCHONG
SOOCHONGS > SOOCHONG
SOOEY interj call used to summon pigs
SOOGEE vb clean a ship using a special solution
SOOGEED > SOOGEE
SOOGEEING > SOOGEE
SOOGEES > SOOGEE
SOOGIE same as > SOOGEE
SOOGIED > SOOGIE
SOOGIEING > SOOGIE
SOOGIES > SOOGIE
SOOJEY same as > SOOGEE
SOOJEYS > SOOJEY
SOOK n baby ▷ vb suck
SOOKED > SOOK
SOOKIER > SOOKY
SOOKIEST > SOOKY
SOOKING > SOOK
SOOKS > SOOK
SOOKY adj tending to complain peevishly
SOOL vb incite (a dog) to attack
SOOLE same as > SOOL
SOOLED > SOOL
SOOLER n person who incites a dog to attack
SOOLERS > SOOLER
SOOLES > SOOLE
SOOLING > SOOL
SOOLS > SOOL
SOOM Scots word for > SWIM
SOOMED > SOOM
SOOMING > SOOM
SOOMS > SOOM
SOON adv in a short time
SOONER adv rather ▷ n idler or shirker
SOONERS > SOONER
SOONEST adv as soon as possible
SOONISH adj somewhat soon
SOOP Scots word for > SWEEP
SOOPED > SOOP
SOOPING > SOOP
SOOPINGS > SOOP
SOOPS > SOOP
SOOPSTAKE adv sweeping up all stakes
SOOT n black powder formed by the incomplete burning of an organic substance ▷ vb cover with soot
SOOTE n sweet
SOOTED > SOOT
SOOTERKIN n mythical black afterbirth of Dutch women that was believed to result from their warming themselves on stoves
SOOTES > SOOT
SOOTFLAKE n speck of soot
SOOTH n truth or reality ▷ adj true or real
SOOTHE vb make calm
SOOTHED > SOOTHE
SOOTHER vb flatter

SOOTHERED > SOOTHE
SOOTHERS > SOOTHER
SOOTHES > SOOTHE
SOOTHEST > SOOTH
SOOTHFAST adj truthful
SOOTHFUL adj truthful
SOOTHING adj having a calming, assuaging, or relieving effect
SOOTHINGS > SOOTHING
SOOTHLICH adv truly
SOOTHLY > SOOTH
SOOTHS > SOOTH
SOOTHSAID > SOOTHSAY
SOOTHSAY vb predict the future
SOOTHSAYS > SOOTHSAY
SOOTIER > SOOTY
SOOTIEST > SOOTY
SOOTILY > SOOTY
SOOTINESS > SOOTY
SOOTING n state of becoming covered with soot
SOOTINGS > SOOTING
SOOTLESS > SOOT
SOOTS > SOOT
SOOTY adj covered with soot
SOP n concession to pacify someone ▷ vb mop up or absorb (liquid)
SOPAPILLA n Mexican deep-fried pastry
SOPH shortened form of > SOPHOMORE
SOPHERIC > SOPHERIM
SOPHERIM n Jewish scribes
SOPHIES > SOPHY
SOPHISM n argument that seems reasonable but is actually false and misleading
SOPHISMS > SOPHISM
SOPHIST n person who uses clever but invalid arguments
SOPHISTER n (esp formerly) a second-year undergraduate at certain British universities
SOPHISTIC adj of or relating to sophists or sophistry
SOPHISTRY n clever but invalid argument
SOPHISTS > SOPHIST
SOPHOMORE n student in second year at college
SOPHS > SOPH
SOPHY n title of the Persian monarchs
SOPITE vb lull to sleep
SOPITED > SOPITE
SOPITES > SOPITE
SOPITING > SOPITE
SOPOR n abnormally deep sleep
SOPORIFIC adj causing sleep ▷ n drug that causes sleep
SOPOROSE adj sleepy
SOPOROUS same as > SOPOROUS

SOPORS > SOPOR
SOPPED > SOP
SOPPIER > SOPPY
SOPPIEST > SOPPY
SOPPILY > SOPPY
SOPPINESS > SOPPY
SOPPING > SOP
SOPPINGS > SOP
SOPPY *adj* over-sentimental
SOPRA *adv* musical instruction meaning above
SOPRANI > SOPRANO
SOPRANINI
> SOPRANINO
SOPRANINO *n* instrument with the highest possible pitch in a family of instruments
SOPRANIST *n* soprano
SOPRANO *n* singer with the highest female or boy's voice ▷ *adj* of a musical instrument that is the highest or second highest pitched in its family
SOPRANOS > SOPRANO
SOPS > SOP
SORA *n* North American rail with a yellow bill
SORAGE *n* first year in hawk's life
SORAGES > SORAGE
SORAL > SORUS
SORAS > SORA
SORB *n* any of various related trees, esp the mountain ash ▷ *vb* absorb or adsorb
SORBABLE > SORB
SORBARIA *n* Asian shrub
SORBARIAS
> SORBARIA
SORBATE *n* salt of sorbic acid
SORBATES > SORBATE
SORBED > SORB
SORBENT > SORB
SORBENTS > SORB
SORBET *same as*
> SHERBET
SORBETS > SORBET
SORBIC > SORB
SORBING > SORB
SORBITAN *n* any of a group of compounds derived from sorbitol
SORBITANS
> SORBITAN
SORBITE *n* mineral found in steel
SORBITES > SORBITE
SORBITIC > SORBITE
SORBITISE *same as*
> SORBITIZE
SORBITIZE *vb* turn metal into form containing sorbite
SORBITOL *n* white water-soluble crystalline alcohol with a sweet taste
SORBITOLS
> SORBITOL
SORBO *n* as in *sorbo rubber* spongy form of rubber
SORBOSE *n* sugar derived from the berries of the mountain ash

SORBOSES > SORBOSE
SORBS > SORB
SORBUS *n* rowan or related tree
SORBUSES > SORBUS
SORCERER *n* magician
SORCERERS
> SORCERER
SORCERESS *n* female sorcerer
SORCERIES > SORCERY
SORCEROUS > SORCERY
SORCERY *n* witchcraft or magic
SORD *n* flock of mallard ducks ▷ *vb* ascend in flight
SORDA *n* deaf woman
SORDED > SORD
SORDES *pl n* dark incrustations on the lips and teeth of patients with prolonged fever
SORDID *adj* dirty, squalid
SORDIDER > SORDID
SORDIDEST > SORDID
SORDIDLY > SORDID
SORDINE *same as*
> SORDINO
SORDINES > SORDINE
SORDING > SORD
SORDINI > SORDINO
SORDINO *n* mute for a stringed or brass musical instrument
SORDO *n* deaf man
SORDOR *n* sordidness
SORDORS > SORDOR
SORDS > SORD
SORE *adj* painful ▷ *n* painful area on the body ▷ *adv* greatly ▷ *vb* make sore
SORED > SORE
SOREDIA > SOREDIUM
SOREDIAL > SOREDIUM
SOREDIATE
> SOREDIUM
SOREDIUM *n* organ of vegetative reproduction in lichens
SOREE *same as* **>** SORA
SOREES > SOREE
SOREHEAD *n* peevish or disgruntled person
SOREHEADS
> SOREHEAD
SOREHON *n* old Irish feudal right
SOREHONS > SOREHON
SOREL *variant of*
> SORREL
SORELL *same as*
> SORREL
SORELLS > SORELL
SORELS > SORREL
SORELY *adv* greatly
SORENESS > SORE
SORER > SORE
SORES > SORE
SOREST > SORE
SOREX *n* shrew or related animal
SOREXES > SOREX
SORGHO *same as* **>** SORGO
SORGHOS > SORGHO
SORGHUM *n* kind of grass cultivated for grain
SORGHUMS > SORGHUM

SORGO *n* any of several varieties of sorghum that have watery sweet juice
SORGOS > SORGO
SORI > SORUS
SORICINE *adj* of or resembling a shrew
SORICOID *same as*
> SORICINE
SORING > SORE
SORINGS > SORE
SORITES *n* type of syllogism in which only the final conclusion is stated
SORITIC > SORITES
SORITICAL > SORITES
SORN *vb* obtain food, etc, from another person by presuming on his or her generosity
SORNED > SORN
SORNER > SORN
SORNERS > SORN
SORNING > SORN
SORNINGS > SORN
SORNS > SORN
SOROBAN *n* Japanese abacus
SOROBANS > SOROBAN
SOROCHE *n* altitude sickness
SOROCHES > SOROCHE
SORORAL *adj* of sister
SORORALLY > SORORAL
SORORATE *n* custom in some societies of a widower marrying his deceased wife's younger sister
SORORATES
> SORORATE
SORORIAL *same as*
> SORORAL
SORORISE *same as*
> SORORIZE
SORORISED
> SORORISE
SORORISES
> SORORISE
SORORITY *n* society for female students
SORORIZE *vb* socialize in sisterly way
SORORIZED
> SORORIZE
SORORIZES
> SORORIZE
SOROSES > SOROSIS
SOROSIS *n* fleshy multiple fruit
SOROSISES > SOROSIS
SORPTION *n* process in which one substance takes up or holds another
SORPTIONS
> SORPTION
SORPTIVE > SORPTION
SORRA *Irish word for*
> SORROW
SORRAS > SORRA
SORREL *n* bitter-tasting plant
SORRELS > SORREL
SORRIER > SORRY
SORRIEST > SORRY
SORRILY > SORRY
SORRINESS > SORRY

SORROW *n* grief or sadness ▷ *vb* grieve
SORROWED > SORROW
SORROWER > SORROW
SORROWERS > SORROW
SORROWFUL > SORROW
SORROWING > SORROW
SORROWS > SORROW
SORRY *adj* feeling pity or regret ▷ *interj* exclamation expressing apology or asking someone to repeat what he or she has said
SORRYISH > SORRY
SORT *n* group all sharing certain qualities or characteristics ▷ *vb* arrange according to kind
SORTA *adv* phonetic representation of 'sort of'
SORTABLE > SORT
SORTABLY > SORT
SORTAL *n* type of logical or linguistic concept
SORTALS > SORTAL
SORTANCE *n* suitableness
SORTANCES
> SORTANCE
SORTATION *n* act of sorting
SORTED *interj* exclamation of satisfaction, approval, etc ▷ *adj* having been corrected or made ready
SORTER > SORT
SORTERS > SORT
SORTES *pl n* divination by opening book at random
SORTIE *n* relatively short return trip ▷ *vb* make a sortie
SORTIED > SORTIE
SORTIEING > SORTIE
SORTIES > SORTIE
SORTILEGE *n* act or practice of divination by drawing lots
SORTILEGY *same as*
> SORTILEGE
SORTING > SORT
SORTINGS > SORT
SORTITION *n* act of casting lots
SORTMENT *n* assortment
SORTMENTS
> SORTMENT
SORTS > SORT
SORUS *n* cluster of sporangia on the undersurface of certain fern leaves
SOS > SO
SOSATIE *n* skewer of curried meat pieces
SOSATIES > SOSATIE
SOSS *vb* make dirty or muddy
SOSSED > SOSS
SOSSES > SOSS
SOSSING > SOSS
SOSSINGS > SOSS
SOSTENUTI
> SOSTENUTO
SOSTENUTO *adv* to be performed in a smooth sustained manner

SOT n habitual drunkard ▷ adv indeed: used to contradict a negative statement ▷ vb be a drunkard

SOTERIAL adj of salvation

SOTH archaic variant of > SOOTH

SOTHS > SOTH

SOTOL n American plant related to agave

SOTOLS > SOTOL

SOTS > SOT

SOTTED > SOT

SOTTEDLY > SOT

SOTTING > SOT

SOTTINGS > SOT

SOTTISH > SOT

SOTTISHLY > SOT

SOTTISIER n collection of jokes

SOU n former French coin

SOUARI n tree of tropical America

SOUARIS > SOUARI

SOUBISE n purée of onions mixed into a thick white sauce and served over eggs, fish, etc

SOUBISES > SOUBISE

SOUBRETTE n minor female role in comedy

SOUCAR n Indian banker

SOUCARS > SOUCAR

SOUCE same as > SOUSE

SOUCED > SOUCE

SOUCES > SOUCE

SOUCHONG n black tea with large leaves

SOUCHONGS > SOUCHONG

SOUCING > SOUCE

SOUCT > SOUCE

SOUDAN obsolete variant of > SULTAN

SOUDANS > SOUDAN

SOUFFLE n light fluffy dish made with beaten egg whites ▷ adj made light and puffy

SOUFFLED > SOUFFLE

SOUFFLEED > SOUFFLE

SOUFFLES > SOUFFLE

SOUGH vb (of the wind) make a sighing sound ▷ n soft continuous murmuring sound

SOUGHED > SOUGH

SOUGHING > SOUGH

SOUGHS > SOUGH

SOUGHT > SEEK

SOUK same as > SOOK

SOUKED > SOUK

SOUKING > SOUK

SOUKOUS n style of African popular music

SOUKOUSES > SOUKOUS

SOUKS > SOUK

SOUL n spiritual and immortal part of a human being

SOULDAN same as > SOLDAN

SOULDANS > SOULDAN

SOULDIER same as > SOLDIER

SOULDIERS > SOULDIER

SOULED adj having soul

SOULFUL adj full of emotion

SOULFULLY > SOULFUL

SOULLESS adj lacking human qualities, mechanical

SOULLIKE adj resembling a soul

SOULMATE n person with whom one has most affinity

SOULMATES > SOULMATE

SOULS > SOUL

SOULSTER n soul music singer

SOULSTERS > SOULSTER

SOUM vb decide how many animals can graze particular pasture

SOUMED > SOUM

SOUMING > SOUM

SOUMINGS > SOUM

SOUMS > SOUM

SOUND n something heard, noise ▷ vb make or cause to make a sound ▷ adj in good condition ▷ adv soundly

SOUNDABLE > SOUND

SOUNDBAR n long, slender speaker

SOUNDBARS > SOUNDBAR

SOUNDBITE n short pithy sentence or phrase extracted from a longer speech

SOUNDBOX n resonating chamber of the hollow body of a violin, guitar, etc

SOUNDCARD n component giving computer sound effects

SOUNDED > SOUND

SOUNDER n device formerly used to convert electric signals into sounds

SOUNDERS > SOUNDER

SOUNDEST > SOUND

SOUNDING adj resounding

SOUNDINGS > SOUNDING

SOUNDLESS adj extremely still or silent

SOUNDLY > SOUND

SOUNDMAN n sound recorder in television crew

SOUNDMEN > SOUNDMAN

SOUNDNESS > SOUND

SOUNDPOST n small post on guitars, violins, etc, that joins the front surface to the back and allows the whole body of the instrument to vibrate

SOUNDS > SOUND

SOUP n liquid food made from meat, vegetables, etc ▷ vb give soup to

SOUPCON n small amount

SOUPCONS > SOUPCON

SOUPED > SOUP

SOUPER n person dispensing soup

SOUPERS > SOUPER

SOUPFIN n Pacific requiem shark valued for its fins

SOUPFINS > SOUPFIN

SOUPIER > SOUPY

SOUPIEST > SOUPY

SOUPILY adv in a soupy manner

SOUPINESS n quality of being soupy

SOUPING > SOUP

SOUPLE same as > SUPPLE

SOUPLED > SOUPLE

SOUPLES > SOUPLE

SOUPLESS > SOUP

SOUPLIKE > SOUP

SOUPLING > SOUPLE

SOUPS > SOUP

SOUPSPOON n spoon for eating soup

SOUPY adj having the appearance or consistency of soup

SOUR adj sharp-tasting ▷ vb make or become sour

SOURBALL n tart-flavoured boiled sweet

SOURBALLS > SOURBALL

SOURCE n origin or starting point ▷ vb establish a supplier of (a product, etc)

SOURCED > SOURCE

SOURCEFUL adj offering useful things

SOURCES > SOURCE

SOURCING > SOURCE

SOURCINGS > SOURCE

SOURDINE n soft stop on an organ or harmonium

SOURDINES > SOURDINE

SOURDOUGH adj (of bread) made with fermented dough used as a leaven ▷ n (in Western US, Canada, and Alaska) an old-time prospector or pioneer

SOURED > SOUR

SOURER > SOUR

SOUREST > SOUR

SOURGUM n tree of eastern N America

SOURGUMS > SOURGUM

SOURING > SOUR

SOURINGS > SOUR

SOURISH > SOUR

SOURISHLY > SOUR

SOURLY > SOUR

SOURNESS > SOUR

SOUROCK n Scots word for sorrel plant

SOUROCKS > SOUROCK

SOURPUSS n person who is always gloomy, pessimistic, or bitter

SOURS > SOUR

SOURSE same as > SOURCE

SOURSES > SOURSE

SOURSOP n small tropical American tree

SOURSOPS > SOURSOP

SOURVELD n grazing field with long coarse grass

SOURVELDS > SOURVELD

SOURWOOD n sorrel tree

SOURWOODS > SOURWOOD

SOUS > SOU

SOUSE vb plunge (something) into liquid ▷ n liquid used in pickling

SOUSED > SOUSE

SOUSER n person who frequently gets drunk

SOUSERS > SOUSER

SOUSES > SOUSE

SOUSING > SOUSE

SOUSINGS > SOUSE

SOUSLIK same as > SUSLIK

SOUSLIKS > SOUSLIK

SOUT same as > SOOT

SOUTACHE n narrow braid used as a decorative trimming

SOUTACHES > SOUTACHE

SOUTANE n Roman Catholic priest's cassock

SOUTANES > SOUTANE

SOUTAR same as > SOUTER

SOUTARS > SOUTAR

SOUTENEUR n pimp

SOUTER n shoemaker or cobbler

SOUTERLY > SOUTER

SOUTERS > SOUTER

SOUTH n direction towards the South Pole, opposite north ▷ adj in the south ▷ adv in, to, or towards the south ▷ vb turn south

SOUTHEAST adv (in or to) direction between south and east ▷ n point of the compass or the direction midway between south and east ▷ adj of or denoting the southeastern part of a specified country, area, etc

SOUTHED > SOUTH

SOUTHER n strong wind or storm from the south ▷ vb turn south

SOUTHERED > SOUTHER

SOUTHERLY adj of or in the south ▷ adv towards the south ▷ n wind from the south

SOUTHERN adj situated in or towards the south ▷ n southerner

SOUTHERNS > SOUTHERN

SOUTHERS > SOUTHER

SOUTHING n movement, deviation, or distance covered in a southerly direction

SOUTHINGS > SOUTHING

SOUTHLAND n southern part of country

SOUTHMOST adj situated or occurring farthest south

SOUTHPAW n left-handed person, esp a boxer ▷ adj left-handed
SOUTHPAWS > SOUTHPAW
SOUTHRON n southerner
SOUTHRONS > SOUTHRON
SOUTHS > SOUTH
SOUTHSAID > SOUTHSAY
SOUTHSAY same as > SOOTHSAY
SOUTHSAYS > SOUTHSAY
SOUTHWARD adv towards the south
SOUTHWEST adv (in or to) direction between south and west ▷ n point of the compass or the direction midway between west and south ▷ adj of or denoting the southwestern part of a specified country, area, etc
SOUTIE same as > SOUTPIEL
SOUTIES > SOUTIE
SOUTPIEL n South African derogatory slang for an English-speaking South African
SOUTPIELS > SOUTPIEL
SOUTS > SOUT
SOUVENIR n keepsake, memento ▷ vb steal or keep (something, esp a small article) for one's own use
SOUVENIRS > SOUVENIR
SOUVLAKI same as > SOUVLAKIA
SOUVLAKIA n Greek dish of kebabs, esp made with lamb
SOUVLAKIS > SOUVLAKI
SOV shortening of > SOVEREIGN
SOVENANCE n memory
SOVEREIGN n king or queen ▷ adj (of a state) independent
SOVIET n formerly, elected council in the USSR ▷ adj of the former USSR
SOVIETIC > SOVIET
SOVIETISE same as > SOVIETIZE
SOVIETISM n principle or practice of government through soviets
SOVIETIST > SOVIETISM
SOVIETIZE vb bring (a country, person, etc) under Soviet control or influence
SOVIETS > SOVIET
SOVKHOZ n large mechanized farm in former USSR
SOVKHOZES > SOVKHOZ
SOVKHOZY > SOVKHOZ

SOVRAN literary word for > SOVEREIGN
SOVRANLY > SOVRAN
SOVRANS > SOVRAN
SOVRANTY > SOVRAN
SOVS > SOV
SOW vb scatter or plant (seed) in or on (the ground) ▷ n female adult pig
SOWABLE > SOW
SOWANS same as > SOWENS
SOWAR n Indian cavalryman
SOWARREE n Indian mounted escort
SOWARREES > SOWARREE
SOWARRIES > SOWARRY
SOWARRY same as > SOWARREE
SOWARS > SOWAR
SOWBACK another name for > HOGBACK
SOWBACKS > SOWBACK
SOWBELLY n salt pork from pig's belly
SOWBREAD n S European primulaceous plant
SOWBREADS > SOWBREAD
SOWBUG n (in N America) woodlouse
SOWBUGS > SOWBUG
SOWCAR same as > SOUCAR
SOWCARS > SOWCAR
SOWCE same as > SOUSE
SOWCED > SOWCE
SOWCES > SOWCE
SOWCING > SOWCE
SOWDER same as > SAWDER
SOWDERS > SOWDER
SOWED > SOW
SOWENS n pudding made from oatmeal husks steeped and boiled
SOWER > SOW
SOWERS > SOW
SOWF same as > SOWTH
SOWFED > SOWF
SOWFF same as > SOWTH
SOWFFED > SOWFF
SOWFFING > SOWFF
SOWFFS > SOWFF
SOWFING > SOWF
SOWFS > SOWF
SOWING > SOW
SOWINGS > SOW
SOWL same as > SOLE
SOWLE same as > SOLE
SOWLED > SOWL
SOWLES > SOWLE
SOWLING > SOWL
SOWLS > SOWL
SOWM same as > SOUM
SOWMED > SOWM
SOWMING > SOWM
SOWMS > SOWM
SOWN > SOW
SOWND vb wield
SOWNDED > SOWND
SOWNDING > SOWND
SOWNDS > SOWND
SOWNE same as > SOUND

SOWNES > SOWNE
SOWP n spoonful ▷ vb soak
SOWPED > SOWP
SOWPING > SOWP
SOWPS > SOWP
SOWS > SOW
SOWSE same as > SOUSE
SOWSED > SOWSE
SOWSES > SOWSE
SOWSING > SOWSE
SOWSSE same as > SOUSE
SOWSSED > SOWSSE
SOWSSES > SOWSSE
SOWSSING > SOWSSE
SOWTER same as > SOUTER
SOWTERS > SOWTER
SOWTH vb Scots word meaning whistle
SOWTHED > SOWTH
SOWTHING > SOWTH
SOWTHS > SOWTH
SOX pl n informal spelling of 'socks'
SOY n soya bean
SOYA n plant whose edible bean is used for food and as a source of oil
SOYAS > SOYA
SOYBEAN n soya bean
SOYBEANS > SOYBEAN
SOYBURGER n burger made with soya bean
SOYLE n body ▷ vb elucidate
SOYLED > SOYLE
SOYLES > SOYLE
SOYLING > SOYLE
SOYMEAL n foodstuff made from soybeans
SOYMEALS > SOYMEAL
SOYMILK n milk substitute made from soya
SOYMILKS > SOYMILK
SOYS > SOY
SOYUZ n Russian spacecraft
SOYUZES > SOYUZ
SOZ interj (slang) sorry
SOZIN n form of protein
SOZINE same as > SOZIN
SOZINES > SOZINE
SOZINS > SOZIN
SOZZLE vb make wet
SOZZLED adj drunk
SOZZLES > SOZZLE
SOZZLIER > SOZZLY
SOZZLIEST > SOZZLY
SOZZLING > SOZZLE
SOZZLY adj wet
SPA n resort with a mineral-water spring ▷ vb visit a spa
SPACE n unlimited expanse in which all objects exist and move ▷ vb place at intervals
SPACEBAND n device on a linecaster for evening up the spaces between words
SPACED > SPACE
SPACELAB n laboratory in space where scientific experiments are performed
SPACELABS > SPACELAB

SPACELESS adj having no limits in space
SPACEMAN n man who travels in space
SPACEMEN > SPACEMAN
SPACEPORT n base equipped to launch, maintain, and test spacecraft
SPACER n piece of material used to create or maintain a space between two things
SPACERS > SPACER
SPACES > SPACE
SPACESHIP n (in science fiction) a spacecraft used for travel between planets and galaxies
SPACESUIT n sealed pressurized suit worn by an astronaut
SPACETIME n four-dimensional continuum having three spatial coordinates and one time coordinate
SPACEWALK n instance of floating and manoeuvring in space, outside but attached by a lifeline to a spacecraft ▷ vb float and manoeuvre in space while outside but attached to a spacecraft
SPACEWARD adv into space
SPACEY adj vague and dreamy
SPACIAL same as > SPATIAL
SPACIALLY > SPACIAL
SPACIER > SPACEY
SPACIEST > SPACEY
SPACINESS > SPACEY
SPACING n arrangement of letters, words, etc, on a page in order to achieve legibility
SPACINGS > SPACING
SPACIOUS adj having a large capacity or area
SPACKLE vb fill holes in plaster
SPACKLED > SPACKLE
SPACKLES > SPACKLE
SPACKLING > SPACKLE
SPACY same as > SPACEY
SPADASSIN n swordsman
SPADE n tool for digging
SPADED > SPADE
SPADEFEET > SPADEFOOT
SPADEFISH n type of spiny-finned food fish
SPADEFOOT n type of toad
SPADEFUL n amount spade will hold
SPADEFULS > SPADEFUL
SPADELIKE > SPADE
SPADEMAN n man who works with spade
SPADEMEN > SPADEMAN
SPADER > SPADE
SPADERS > SPADE
SPADES > SPADE

S

SPADESMAN same as
> SPADEMAN
SPADESMEN
> SPADEMAN
SPADEWORK n hard
preparatory work
SPADGER n sparrow
SPADGERS > SPADGER
SPADICES > SPADIX
SPADILLE n (in ombre
and quadrille) the ace of
spades
SPADILLES
> SPADILLE
SPADILLIO same as
> SPADILLE
SPADILLO same as
> SPADILLE
SPADILLOS
> SPADILLO
SPADING > SPADE
SPADIX n spike of small
flowers on a fleshy stem
SPADIXES > SPADIX
SPADO n neutered animal
SPADOES > SPADO
SPADONES > SPADO
SPADOS > SPADO
SPADROON n type of
sword
SPADROONS
> SPADROON
SPAE vb foretell (the
future)
SPAED > SPAE
SPAEING > SPAE
SPAEINGS > SPAE
SPAEMAN n man who can
supposedly foretell the
future
SPAEMEN > SPAEMAN
SPAER > SPAE
SPAERS > SPAE
SPAES > SPAE
SPAETZLE n German
noodle dish
SPAETZLES
> SPAETZLE
SPAEWIFE n woman
who can supposedly
foretell the future
SPAEWIVES
> SPAEWIFE
SPAG vb (of a cat) to scratch
(a person) with the claws
SPAGERIC same as
> SPAGYRIC
SPAGGED > SPAG
SPAGGING > SPAG
SPAGHETTI n pasta in
the form of long strings
SPAGIRIC same as
> SPAGYRIC
SPAGIRIST n an
alchemist
SPAGS > SPAG
SPAGYRIC adj of or
relating to alchemy ▷ n
alchemist
SPAGYRICS
> SPAGYRIC
SPAGYRIST
> SPAGYRIC
SPAHEE same as > SPAHI
SPAHEES > SPAHEE
SPAHI n (formerly) an
irregular cavalryman in
the Turkish armed forces

SPAHIS > SPAHI
SPAIL Scots word for
> SPALL
SPAILS > SPAIL
SPAIN variant of
> SPANE
SPAINED > SPAIN
SPAING > SPA
SPAINGS > SPA
SPAINING > SPAIN
SPAINS > SPAIN
SPAIRGE Scots word for
> SPARGE
SPAIRGED > SPAIRGE
SPAIRGES > SPAIRGE
SPAIRGING > SPAIRGE
SPAIT same as > SPATE
SPAITS > SPAIT
SPAKE past tense of
> SPEAK
SPALD same as > SPAULD
SPALDEEN n ball used in
street game
SPALDEENS
> SPALDEEN
SPALDS > SPALD
SPALE Scots word for
> SPALL
SPALES > SPALE
SPALL n splinter or chip of
ore, rock, or stone ▷ vb
split or cause to split into
such fragments
SPALLABLE > SPALL
SPALLE same as
> SPAULD
SPALLED > SPALL
SPALLER > SPALL
SPALLERS > SPALL
SPALLES > SPALLE
SPALLING > SPALL
SPALLINGS > SPALL
SPALLS > SPALL
SPALPEEN n itinerant
seasonal labourer
SPALPEENS
> SPALPEEN
SPALT vb split
SPALTED > SPALT
SPALTING > SPALT
SPALTS > SPALT
SPAM vb send unsolicited
email simultaneously to a
number of newsgroups on
the internet ▷ n
unsolicited electronic mail
or text messages sent in
this way
SPAMBOT n computer
program that sends spam
SPAMBOTS > SPAMBOT
SPAMMED > SPAM
SPAMMER > SPAM
SPAMMERS > SPAM
SPAMMIE n love bite
SPAMMIER > SPAMMY
SPAMMIES > SPAMMIE
SPAMMIEST > SPAMMY
SPAMMING > SPAM
SPAMMINGS > SPAM
SPAMMY adj bland
SPAMS > SPAM
SPAN n space between
two points ▷ vb stretch or
extend across
SPANAEMIA n lack of red
corpuscles in blood

SPANAEMIC
> SPANAEMIA
SPANCEL n length of rope
for hobbling an animal
▷ vb hobble (an animal)
with a loose rope
SPANCELED > SPANCEL
SPANCELS > SPANCEL
SPANDEX n type of
synthetic stretch fabric
made from polyurethane
fibre
SPANDEXED adj wearing
spandex
SPANDEXES > SPANDEX
SPANDREL n triangular
surface bounded by the
outer curve of an arch and
the adjacent wall
SPANDRELS
> SPANDREL
SPANDRIL same as
> SPANDREL
SPANDRILS
> SPANDRIL
SPANE vb Scots word
meaning wean
SPANED > SPANE
SPANES > SPANE
SPANG adv exactly, firmly,
or straight ▷ vb dash
SPANGED > SPANG
SPANGHEW vb throw in air
SPANGHEWS
> SPANGHEW
SPANGING > SPANG
SPANGLE n small shiny
metallic ornament ▷ vb
decorate with spangles
SPANGLED > SPANGLE
SPANGLER > SPANGLE
SPANGLERS > SPANGLE
SPANGLES > SPANGLE
SPANGLET n little
spangle
SPANGLETS > SPANGLET
SPANGLIER > SPANGLE
SPANGLING > SPANGLE
SPANGLY > SPANGLE
SPANGS > SPANG
SPANIEL n dog with long
ears and silky hair
SPANIELS > SPANIEL
SPANING > SPANE
SPANK vb slap with the
open hand, on the
buttocks or legs ▷ n such a
slap
SPANKED > SPANK
SPANKER n fore-and-aft
sail or a mast that is
aftermost in a sailing
vessel
SPANKERS > SPANKER
SPANKING adj
outstandingly fine or
smart ▷ n series of spanks,
usually as a punishment
for children
SPANKINGS
> SPANKING
SPANKS > SPANK
SPANLESS adj impossible
to span
SPANNED > SPAN
SPANNER n tool for
gripping and turning a nut
or bolt

SPANNERS > SPANNER
SPANNING > SPAN
SPANS > SPAN
SPANSPEK n cantaloupe
melon
SPANSPEKS
> SPANSPEK
SPANSULE n
modified-release capsule
of a drug
SPANSULES
> SPANSULE
SPANWORM n larva of a
type of moth
SPANWORMS
> SPANWORM
SPAR n pole used as a
ship's mast, boom, or yard
▷ vb box or fight using
light blows for practice
SPARABLE n small nail
with no head, used for
fixing the soles and heels
of shoes
SPARABLES
> SPARABLE
SPARAXIS n type of plant
with dainty spikes of
star-shaped purple, red, or
orange flowers
SPARD > SPARE
SPARE adj extra ▷ n
duplicate kept in case of
damage or loss ▷ vb
refrain from punishing or
harming
SPAREABLE > SPARE
SPARED > SPARE
SPARELESS adj
merciless
SPARELY > SPARE
SPARENESS > SPARE
SPARER > SPARE
SPARERIB n cut of pork
ribs with most of the meat
trimmed off
SPARERIBS
> SPARERIB
SPARERS > SPARE
SPARES > SPARE
SPAREST > SPARE
SPARGE vb sprinkle or
scatter (something)
SPARGED > SPARGE
SPARGER > SPARGE
SPARGERS > SPARGE
SPARGES > SPARGE
SPARGING > SPARGE
SPARID n type of marine
percoid fish ▷ adj of or
belonging to this family of
fish
SPARIDS > SPARID
SPARING adj economical
SPARINGLY > SPARING
SPARK n fiery particle
thrown out from a fire or
caused by friction ▷ vb
give off sparks
SPARKE n weapon
SPARKED > SPARK
SPARKER > SPARK
SPARKERS > SPARK
SPARKES > SPARKE
SPARKIE n electrician
SPARKIER > SPARKY
SPARKIES > SPARKIE
SPARKIEST > SPARKY

SPARKILY > SPARKY
SPARKING > SPARK
SPARKISH > SPARK
SPARKLE vb glitter with many points of light ▷ n sparkling points of light
SPARKLED > SPARKLE
SPARKLER n hand-held firework that emits sparks
SPARKLERS > SPARKLER
SPARKLES > SPARKLE
SPARKLESS > SPARK
SPARKLET n little spark
SPARKLETS > SPARKLET
SPARKLIER > SPARKLY
SPARKLIES > SPARKLY
SPARKLING adj (of wine or mineral water) slightly fizzy
SPARKLY adj sparkling ▷ n sparkling thing
SPARKPLUG n device in an engine that ignites the fuel
SPARKS n electrician
SPARKY adj lively
SPARLIKE > SPAR
SPARLING n European smelt
SPARLINGS > SPARLING
SPAROID same as > SPARID
SPAROIDS > SPAROID
SPARRE same as > SPAR
SPARRED > SPAR
SPARRER > SPAR
SPARRERS > SPAR
SPARRES > SPARRE
SPARRIER > SPARRY
SPARRIEST > SPARRY
SPARRING > SPAR
SPARRINGS > SPAR
SPARROW n small brownish bird
SPARROWS > SPARROW
SPARRY adj (of minerals) containing, relating to, or resembling spar
SPARS > SPAR
SPARSE adj thinly scattered
SPARSEDLY > SPARSE
SPARSELY > SPARSE
SPARSER > SPARSE
SPARSEST > SPARSE
SPARSITY > SPARSE
SPART n esparto
SPARTAN adj strict and austere ▷ n disciplined or brave person
SPARTANS > SPARTAN
SPARTEINE n viscous oily alkaloid extracted from the broom plant and lupin seeds
SPARTERIE n things made from esparto
SPARTH n type of battle-axe
SPARTHE same as > SPARTH
SPARTHES > SPARTHE
SPARTHS > SPARTH
SPARTICLE n hypothetical elementary

particle thought to have been produced in the Big Bang
SPARTINA n grass growing in salt marshes
SPARTINAS > SPARTINA
SPARTS > SPART
SPAS > SPA
SPASM n involuntary muscular contraction ▷ vb go into spasm
SPASMATIC > SPASM
SPASMED > SPASM
SPASMIC > SPASM
SPASMING > SPASM
SPASMODIC adj occurring in spasms
SPASMS > SPASM
SPASTIC adj affected by spasms
SPAT vb have a quarrel
SPATE n large number of things happening within a period of time
SPATES > SPATE
SPATFALL n mass of larvae on sea bed
SPATFALLS > SPATFALL
SPATHAL > SPATHE
SPATHE n large sheathlike leaf enclosing a flower cluster
SPATHED > SPATHE
SPATHES > SPATHE
SPATHIC adj (of minerals) resembling spar
SPATHOSE same as > SPATHIC
SPATIAL adj of or in space
SPATIALLY > SPATIAL
SPATLESE n type of German wine, usu white
SPATLESEN > SPATLESE
SPATLESES > SPATLESE
SPATS > SPAT
SPATTEE n type of gaiter
SPATTEES > SPATTEE
SPATTER vb scatter or be scattered in drops over (something) ▷ n spattering sound
SPATTERED > SPATTER
SPATTERS > SPATTER
SPATTING > SPAT
SPATULA n utensil with a broad flat blade for spreading or stirring
SPATULAR > SPATULA
SPATULAS > SPATULA
SPATULATE adj shaped like a spatula
SPATULE n spatula
SPATULES > SPATULE
SPATZLE same as > SPAETZLE
SPATZLES > SPATZLE
SPAUL same as > SPAULD
SPAULD n shoulder
SPAULDS > SPAULD
SPAULS > SPAUL
SPAVIE Scots variant of > SPAVIN

SPAVIES > SPAVIE
SPAVIET adj Scots word meaning spavined
SPAVIN n enlargement of the hock of a horse by a bony growth
SPAVINED adj affected with spavin
SPAVINS > SPAVIN
SPAW same as > SPA
SPAWL vb spit
SPAWLED > SPAWL
SPAWLING > SPAWL
SPAWLS > SPAWL
SPAWN n jelly-like mass of eggs of fish, frogs, or molluscs ▷ vb (of fish, frogs, or molluscs) lay eggs
SPAWNED > SPAWN
SPAWNER > SPAWN
SPAWNERS > SPAWN
SPAWNIER > SPAWNY
SPAWNIEST > SPAWNY
SPAWNING > SPAWN
SPAWNINGS > SPAWN
SPAWNS > SPAWN
SPAWNY adj like spawn
SPAWS > SPAW
SPAY vb remove the ovaries from (a female animal)
SPAYAD n male deer
SPAYADS > SPAYAD
SPAYD same as > SPAYAD
SPAYDS > SPAYD
SPAYED > SPAY
SPAYING > SPAY
SPAYS > SPAY
SPAZA adj as in spaza shop South African slang for a small shop in a township
SPEAK vb say words, talk
SPEAKABLE > SPEAK
SPEAKEASY n place where alcoholic drink was sold illegally during Prohibition
SPEAKER n person who speaks, esp at a formal occasion
SPEAKERS > SPEAKER
SPEAKING > SPEAK
SPEAKINGS > SPEAK
SPEAKOUT n firm or brave statement of one's beliefs
SPEAKOUTS > SPEAKOUT
SPEAKS > SPEAK
SPEAL same as > SPULE
SPEALS > SPEAL
SPEAN same as > SPANE
SPEANED > SPEAN
SPEANING > SPEAN
SPEANS > SPEAN
SPEAR n weapon consisting of a long shaft with a sharp point ▷ vb pierce with or as if with a spear
SPEARED > SPEAR
SPEARER > SPEAR
SPEARERS > SPEAR
SPEARFISH another name for > MARLIN
SPEARGUN n device for shooting spears underwater

SPEARGUNS > SPEARGUN
SPEARHEAD vb lead (an attack or campaign) ▷ n leading force in an attack or campaign
SPEARIER > SPEAR
SPEARIEST > SPEAR
SPEARING n act of spearing
SPEARINGS > SPEARING
SPEARLIKE > SPEAR
SPEARMAN n soldier armed with a spear
SPEARMEN > SPEARMAN
SPEARMINT n type of mint
SPEARS > SPEAR
SPEARWORT n any of several Eurasian ranunculaceous plants
SPEARY > SPEAR
SPEAT same as > SPATE
SPEATS > SPEAT
SPEC vb set specifications
SPECCED > SPEC
SPECCIER > SPECCY
SPECCIES > SPECCY
SPECCIEST > SPECCY
SPECCING > SPEC
SPECCY n person wearing spectacles ▷ adj wearing spectacles
SPECIAL adj distinguished from others of its kind ▷ n product, programme, etc which is only available at a certain time ▷ vb advertise and sell (an item) at a reduced price
SPECIALER > SPECIAL
SPECIALLY > SPECIAL
SPECIALS > SPECIAL
SPECIALTY n special interest or skill
SPECIATE vb form or develop into a new biological species
SPECIATED > SPECIATE
SPECIATES > SPECIATE
SPECIE n coins as distinct from paper money
SPECIES n group of plants or animals that are related closely enough to interbreed naturally
SPECIFIC adj particular, definite ▷ n drug used to treat a particular disease
SPECIFICS > SPECIFIC
SPECIFIED > SPECIFY
SPECIFIER > SPECIFY
SPECIFIES > SPECIFY
SPECIFY vb refer to or state specifically
SPECIMEN n individual or part typifying a whole
SPECIMENS > SPECIMEN
SPECIOUS adj apparently true, but actually false
SPECK n small spot or particle ▷ vb mark with specks or spots

S

SPECKED > SPECK
SPECKIER > SPECKY
SPECKIES > SPECKY
SPECKIEST > SPECKY
SPECKING > SPECK
SPECKLE n small spot ⊳ vb mark with speckles
SPECKLED > SPECKLE
SPECKLES > SPECKLE
SPECKLESS > SPECK
SPECKLING > SPECKLE
SPECKS > SPECK
SPECKY same as > SPECCY
SPECS pl n spectacles
SPECT vb expect
SPECTACLE n strange, interesting, or ridiculous sight
SPECTATED vb watch
SPECTATED > SPECTATE
SPECTATES > SPECTATE
SPECTATOR n person viewing anything, onlooker
SPECTED > SPECT
SPECTER same as > SPECTRE
SPECTERS > SPECTER
SPECTING > SPECT
SPECTRA > SPECTRUM
SPECTRAL adj of or like a spectre
SPECTRE n ghost
SPECTRES > SPECTRE
SPECTRIN n any one of a class of fibrous proteins found in the membranes of red blood cells
SPECTRINS > SPECTRIN
SPECTRUM n range of different colours, radio waves, etc in order of their wavelengths
SPECTRUMS > SPECTRUM
SPECTS > SPECT
SPECULA > SPECULUM
SPECULAR adj of, relating to, or having the properties of a mirror
SPECULATE vb guess, conjecture
SPECULUM n medical instrument for examining body cavities
SPECULUMS > SPECULUM
SPED > SPEED
SPEECH n act, power, or manner of speaking ⊳ vb make a speech
SPEECHED > SPEECH
SPEECHES > SPEECH
SPEECHFUL > SPEECH
SPEECHIFY vb make speeches, esp boringly
SPEECHING > SPEECH
SPEED n swiftness ⊳ vb go quickly
SPEEDBALL n mixture of heroin with amphetamine or cocaine
SPEEDBOAT n light fast motorboat

SPEEDED > SPEED
SPEEDER > SPEED
SPEEDERS > SPEED
SPEEDFUL > SPEED
SPEEDIER > SPEEDY
SPEEDIEST > SPEEDY
SPEEDILY > SPEEDY
SPEEDING > SPEED
SPEEDINGS > SPEED
SPEEDLESS > SPEED
SPEEDO n speedometer
SPEEDOS > SPEEDO
SPEEDREAD vb read very quickly
SPEEDS > SPEED
SPEEDSTER n fast car, esp a sports model
SPEEDUP n acceleration
SPEEDUPS > SPEEDUP
SPEEDWALK n an endless conveyor belt or moving walkway used to transport standing persons from place to place
SPEEDWAY n track for motorcycle racing
SPEEDWAYS > SPEEDWAY
SPEEDWELL n plant with small blue flowers
SPEEDY adj prompt
SPEEL n splinter of wood ⊳ vb Scots word meaning climb
SPEELED > SPEEL
SPEELER > SPEEL
SPEELERS > SPEEL
SPEELING > SPEEL
SPEELS > SPEEL
SPEER same as > SPEIR
SPEERED > SPEER
SPEERING > SPEER
SPEERINGS > SPEER
SPEERS > SPEER
SPEIL dialect word for > CLIMB
SPEILED > SPEIL
SPEILING > SPEIL
SPEILS > SPEIL
SPEIR vb ask
SPEIRED > SPEIR
SPEIRING > SPEIR
SPEIRINGS > SPEIR
SPEIRS > SPEIR
SPEISE same as > SPEISS
SPEISES > SPEISE
SPEISS n compounds formed when ores containing arsenic or antimony are smelted
SPEISSES > SPEISS
SPEK n bacon, fat, or fatty pork used for larding venison or other game
SPEKBOOM n South African shrub
SPEKBOOMS > SPEKBOOM
SPEKS > SPEK
SPELAEAN adj of, found in, or inhabiting caves
SPELD vb Scots word meaning spread
SPELDED > SPELD
SPELDER same as > SPELD

SPELDERED > SPELDER
SPELDERS > SPELDER
SPELDIN n fish split and dried
SPELDING same as > SPELDIN
SPELDINGS > SPELDING
SPELDINS > SPELDIN
SPELDRIN same as > SPELDIN
SPELDRING same as > SPELDIN
SPELDRINS > SPELDRIN
SPELDS > SPELD
SPELEAN same as > SPELAEAN
SPELK n splinter of wood
SPELKS > SPELK
SPELL vb give in correct order the letters that form (a word) ⊳ n formula of words supposed to have magic power
SPELLABLE > SPELL
SPELLBIND vb cause to be spellbound
SPELLDOWN n spelling competition
SPELLED > SPELL
SPELLER n person who spells words in the manner specified
SPELLERS > SPELLER
SPELLFUL adj magical
SPELLICAN same as > SPILLIKIN
SPELLING > SPELL
SPELLINGS > SPELL
SPELLS > SPELL
SPELT n wheat variety
SPELTER n impure zinc, usually containing about 3 per cent of lead and other impurities
SPELTERS > SPELTER
SPELTS > SPELT
SPELTZ n wheat variety
SPELTZES > SPELTZ
SPELUNK vb explore caves
SPELUNKED > SPELUNK
SPELUNKER n person whose hobby is the exploration and study of caves
SPELUNKS > SPELUNK
SPENCE n larder or pantry
SPENCER n short fitted coat or jacket
SPENCERS > SPENCER
SPENCES > SPENCE
SPEND vb pay out (money)
SPENDABLE > SPEND
SPENDALL n spendthrift
SPENDALLS > SPENDALL
SPENDER n person who spends money in a manner specified
SPENDERS > SPENDER
SPENDIER > SPENDY
SPENDIEST > SPENDY
SPENDING > SPEND
SPENDINGS > SPEND
SPENDS > SPEND
SPENDY adj expensive

SPENSE same as > SPENCE
SPENSES > SPENSE
SPENT > SPEND
SPEOS n (esp in ancient Egypt) a temple or tomb cut into a rock face
SPEOSES > SPEOS
SPERLING same as > SPARLING
SPERLINGS > SPARLING
SPERM n male reproductive cell
SPERMARIA pl n spermaries
SPERMARY n any organ in which sperm are produced
SPERMATIA pl n male reproductive cells in red algae and some fungi
SPERMATIC adj of or relating to spermatozoa
SPERMATID n any of four immature male gametes that are formed from a spermatocyte
SPERMIC same as > SPERMATIC
SPERMINE n colourless basic water-soluble amine
SPERMINES > SPERMINE
SPERMOUS same as > SPERMATIC
SPERMS > SPERM
SPERRE vb bolt
SPERRED > SPERRE
SPERRES > SPERRE
SPERRING > SPERRE
SPERSE vb disperse
SPERSED > SPERSE
SPERSES > SPERSE
SPERSING > SPERSE
SPERST > SPERSE
SPERTHE same as > SPARTH
SPERTHES > SPERTHE
SPET same as > SPIT
SPETCH n piece of animal skin
SPETCHED > SPETCH
SPETCHES > SPETCH
SPETCHING > SPETCH
SPETS > SPET
SPETSNAZ n Soviet intelligence force
SPETTING > SPET
SPETZNAZ same as > SPETSNAZ
SPEUG n Scots word for sparrow
SPEUGS > SPEUG
SPEW vb vomit ⊳ n something ejected from the mouth
SPEWED > SPEW
SPEWER > SPEW
SPEWERS > SPEW
SPEWIER > SPEWY
SPEWIEST > SPEWY
SPEWINESS > SPEWY
SPEWING > SPEW
SPEWS > SPEW
SPEWY adj marshy
SPHACELUS n death of living tissue

SPHAER same as > SPHERE
SPHAERE same as > SPHERE
SPHAERES > SPHAERE
SPHAERITE n aluminium phosphate
SPHAERS > SPHAER
SPHAGNOUS > SPHAGNUM
SPHAGNUM n moss found in bogs
SPHAGNUMS > SPHAGNUM
SPHAIREE n game resembling tennis played with wooden bats and a perforated plastic ball
SPHAIREES > SPHAIREE
SPHEAR same as > SPHERE
SPHEARE same as > SPHERE
SPHEARES > SPHEARE
SPHEARS > SPHEAR
SPHENDONE n ancient Greek headband
SPHENE n brown, yellow, green, or grey lustrous mineral
SPHENES > SPHENE
SPHENIC adj having the shape of a wedge
SPHENODON technical name for the > TUATARA
SPHENOID adj wedge-shaped ▷ n wedge-shaped thing
SPHENOIDS > SPHENOID
SPHERAL adj of or shaped like a sphere
SPHERE n perfectly round solid object ▷ vb surround or encircle
SPHERED > SPHERE
SPHERES > SPHERE
SPHERIC same as > SPHERICAL
SPHERICAL adj shaped like a sphere
SPHERICS n geometry and trigonometry of figures on the surface of a sphere
SPHERIER > SPHERY
SPHERIEST > SPHERY
SPHERING > SPHERE
SPHEROID n solid figure that is almost but not exactly a sphere
SPHEROIDS > SPHEROID
SPHERULAR > SPHERULE
SPHERULE n very small sphere or globule
SPHERULES > SPHERULE
SPHERY adj resembling a sphere
SPHINCTER n ring of muscle which controls the opening and closing of a hollow organ
SPHINGES > SPHINX
SPHINGID n hawk moth

SPHINGIDS > SPHINGID
SPHINX n huge statue built by the ancient Egyptians
SPHINXES > SPHINX
SPHYGMIC adj of or relating to the pulse
SPHYGMOID adj resembling the pulse
SPHYGMUS n person's pulse
SPHYNX n breed of cat
SPHYNXES > SPHYNX
SPIAL n observation
SPIALS > SPIAL
SPICA n spiral bandage formed by a series of overlapping figure-of-eight turns
SPICAE > SPICA
SPICAS > SPICA
SPICATE adj having, arranged in, or relating to spikes
SPICATED same as > SPICATE
SPICCATO n style of playing a stringed instrument in which the bow bounces lightly off the strings
SPICCATOS > SPICCATO
SPICE n aromatic substance used as flavouring ▷ vb flavour with spices
SPICEBUSH n North American lauraceous shrub
SPICED > SPICE
SPICELESS > SPICE
SPICER > SPICE
SPICERIES > SPICERY
SPICERS > SPICE
SPICERY n spices collectively
SPICES > SPICE
SPICEY same as > SPICY
SPICIER > SPICY
SPICIEST > SPICY
SPICILEGE n anthology
SPICILY > SPICY
SPICINESS > SPICY
SPICING > SPICE
SPICK adj neat and clean
SPICKER > SPICK
SPICKEST > SPICK
SPICKNEL same as > SPIGNEL
SPICKNELS > SPICKNEL
SPICULA same as > SPICULUM
SPICULAE > SPICULA
SPICULAR > SPICULUM
SPICULATE > SPICULE
SPICULE n small slender pointed structure or crystal
SPICULES > SPICULE
SPICULUM same as > SPICULE
SPICY adj flavoured with spices
SPIDE n insulting Irish word for a young

working-class man who dresses in casual sports clothes
SPIDER n small eight-legged creature which spins a web to catch insects for food ▷ vb follow internet links to gather information
SPIDERED > SPIDER
SPIDERIER > SPIDERY
SPIDERING > SPIDER
SPIDERISH > SPIDER
SPIDERMAN n person who erects the steel structure of a building
SPIDERMEN > SPIDERMAN
SPIDERS > SPIDER
SPIDERWEB n spider's web
SPIDERY adj thin and angular like a spider's legs
SPIDES > SPIDE
SPIE same as > SPY
SPIED > SPY
SPIEGEL n manganese-rich pig iron
SPIEGELS > SPIEGEL
SPIEL n speech made to persuade someone to do something ▷ vb deliver a prepared spiel
SPIELED > SPIEL
SPIELER > SPIEL
SPIELERS > SPIEL
SPIELING > SPIEL
SPIELS > SPIEL
SPIER variant of > SPEIR
SPIERED > SPIER
SPIERING > SPIER
SPIERS > SPIER
SPIES > SPY
SPIF n postage stamp perforated with the initials of a firm to avoid theft by employees
SPIFF vb make smart
SPIFFED > SPIFF
SPIFFIED > SPIFFY
SPIFFIER > SPIFFY
SPIFFIES > SPIFFY
SPIFFIEST > SPIFFY
SPIFFILY > SPIFFY
SPIFFING adj excellent
SPIFFS > SPIFF
SPIFFY adj smart ▷ n smart thing or person ▷ vb smarten
SPIFFYING > SPIFFY
SPIFS > SPIF
SPIGHT same as > SPITE
SPIGHTED > SPIGHT
SPIGHTING > SPIGHT
SPIGHTS > SPIGHT
SPIGNEL n European umbelliferous plant
SPIGNELS > SPIGNEL
SPIGOT n stopper for, or tap fitted to, a cask
SPIGOTS > SPIGOT
SPIKE n sharp point ▷ vb put spikes on
SPIKED > SPIKE
SPIKEFISH n large sea fish
SPIKELET n unit of a grass inflorescence

SPIKELETS > SPIKELET
SPIKELIKE > SPIKE
SPIKENARD n fragrant Indian plant with rose-purple flowers
SPIKER > SPIKE
SPIKERIES > SPIKERY
SPIKERS > SPIKE
SPIKERY n High-Church Anglicanism
SPIKES > SPIKE
SPIKEY same as > SPIKY
SPIKIER > SPIKY
SPIKIEST > SPIKY
SPIKILY > SPIKY
SPIKINESS > SPIKY
SPIKING > SPIKE
SPIKY adj resembling a spike
SPILE n heavy timber stake or pile ▷ vb provide or support with a spile
SPILED > SPILE
SPILES > SPILE
SPILIKIN same as > SPILLIKIN
SPILIKINS > SPILIKIN
SPILING > SPILE
SPILINGS > SPILE
SPILITE n type of igneous rock
SPILITES > SPILITE
SPILITIC > SPILITE
SPILL vb pour from or as if from a container ▷ n fall
SPILLABLE > SPILL
SPILLAGE n instance or the process of spilling
SPILLAGES > SPILLAGE
SPILLED > SPILL
SPILLER > SPILL
SPILLERS > SPILL
SPILLIKIN n thin strip of wood, cardboard, or plastic used in spillikins
SPILLING > SPILL
SPILLINGS > SPILL
SPILLOVER n act of spilling over
SPILLS > SPILL
SPILLWAY n channel that carries away surplus water, as from a dam
SPILLWAYS > SPILLWAY
SPILOSITE n form of slate
SPILT > SPILL
SPILTH n something spilled
SPILTHS > SPILTH
SPIM n spam sent and received via an instant-messaging system
SPIMMER n person who sends spam via an instant-messaging system
SPIMMERS > SPIMMER
SPIMMING n the sending of spam via an instant-messaging system
SPIMMINGS > SPIMMING
SPIMS > SPIM

S

SPIN vb revolve or cause to revolve rapidly ▷ n revolving motion

SPINA n spine

SPINACENE n type of vaccine

SPINACH n dark green leafy vegetable

SPINACHES > SPINACH

SPINACHY adj tasting of spinach

SPINAE > SPINA

SPINAGE same as > SPINACH

SPINAGES > SPINAGE

SPINAL adj of the spine ▷ n anaesthetic administered in the spine

SPINALLY > SPINAL

SPINALS > SPINAL

SPINAR n fast-spinning star

SPINARAMA n evasive move in ice hockey

SPINARS > SPINAR

SPINAS > SPINA

SPINATE adj having a spine

SPINDLE n rotating rod that acts as an axle ▷ vb form into a spindle or equip with spindles

SPINDLED > SPINDLE

SPINDLER > SPINDLE

SPINDLERS > SPINDLE

SPINDLES > SPINDLE

SPINDLIER > SPINDLY

SPINDLING adj long and slender, esp disproportionately so ▷ n spindling person or thing

SPINDLY adj long, slender, and frail

SPINDRIFT n spray blown up from the sea

SPINE n backbone

SPINED > SPINE

SPINEL n any of a group of hard glassy minerals of variable colour

SPINELESS adj lacking courage

SPINELIKE > SPINE

SPINELLE same as > SPINEL

SPINELLES > SPINELLE

SPINELS > SPINEL

SPINES > SPINE

SPINET n small harpsichord

SPINETS > SPINET

SPINETTE same as > SPINET

SPINETTES > SPINETTE

SPINIER > SPINY

SPINIEST > SPINY

SPINIFEX n coarse spiny Australian grass

SPINIFORM adj like a thorn

SPININESS > SPINY

SPINK n finch ▷ vb (of a finch) chirp

SPINKED > SPINK

SPINKING > SPINK

SPINKS > SPINK

SPINLESS > SPIN

SPINNAKER n large sail on a racing yacht

SPINNER n bowler who makes the ball change direction when it bounces

SPINNERET n organ through which silk threads come out of a spider

SPINNERS > SPINNER

SPINNERY n spinning mill

SPINNET same as > SPINET

SPINNETS > SPINNET

SPINNEY n small wood

SPINNEYS > SPINNEY

SPINNIER > SPINNY

SPINNIES > SPINNY

SPINNIEST > SPINNY

SPINNING > SPIN

SPINNINGS > SPIN

SPINNY adj crazy

SPINODE another name for > CUSP

SPINODES > SPINODE

SPINOFF n development derived incidentally from an existing enterprise

SPINOFFS > SPINOFF

SPINONE n as in Italian spinone wiry-coated gun dog

SPINONI > SPINONE

SPINOR n type of mathematical object

SPINORS > SPINOR

SPINOSE adj (esp of plants) bearing many spines

SPINOSELY > SPINOSE

SPINOSITY > SPINOSE

SPINOUS adj resembling a spine or thorn

SPINOUT n spinning skid that causes a car to run off the road

SPINOUTS > SPINOUT

SPINS > SPIN

SPINSTER n unmarried woman

SPINSTERS > SPINSTER

SPINTEXT n preacher

SPINTEXTS > SPINTEXT

SPINTO n lyrical singing voice

SPINTOS > SPINTO

SPINULA n small spine

SPINULAE > SPINULA

SPINULATE adj like a spine

SPINULE n very small spine, thorn, or prickle

SPINULES > SPINULE

SPINULOSE > SPINULE

SPINULOUS > SPINULE

SPINY adj covered with spines

SPIRACLE n small blowhole for breathing through, such as that of a whale

SPIRACLES > SPIRACLE

SPIRACULA pl n spiracles

SPIRAEA n plant with small white or pink flowers

SPIRAEAS > SPIRAEA

SPIRAL n continuous curve formed by a point winding about a central axis ▷ vb move in a spiral ▷ adj having the form of a spiral

SPIRALED > SPIRAL

SPIRALING > SPIRAL

SPIRALISM n ascent in spiral structure

SPIRALIST > SPIRALISM

SPIRALITY > SPIRAL

SPIRALLED > SPIRAL

SPIRALLY > SPIRAL

SPIRALS > SPIRAL

SPIRANT n fricative consonant

SPIRANTS > SPIRANT

SPIRASTER n part of living sponge

SPIRATED adj twisted in spiral

SPIRATION n breathing

SPIRE n pointed part of a steeple ▷ vb assume the shape of a spire

SPIREA same as > SPIRAEA

SPIREAS > SPIREA

SPIRED > SPIRE

SPIRELESS > SPIRE

SPIRELET another name for > FLECHE

SPIRELETS > SPIRELET

SPIREM same as > SPIREME

SPIREME n tangled mass of chromatin threads

SPIREMES > SPIREME

SPIREMS > SPIREM

SPIRES > SPIRE

SPIREWISE > SPIRE

SPIRIC n type of curve

SPIRICS > SPIRIC

SPIRIER > SPIRE

SPIRIEST > SPIRE

SPIRILLA > SPIRILLUM

SPIRILLAR > SPIRILLUM

SPIRILLUM n any bacterium having a curved or spirally twisted rodlike body

SPIRING > SPIRE

SPIRIT n nonphysical aspect of a person concerned with profound thoughts ▷ vb carry away mysteriously

SPIRITED adj lively

SPIRITFUL > SPIRIT

SPIRITING > SPIRIT

SPIRITISM n belief that the spirits of the dead can communicate with the living

SPIRITIST > SPIRITISM

SPIRITOSO adv to be played in a spirited or animated manner

SPIRITOUS adj high-spirited

SPIRITS > SPIRIT

SPIRITUAL adj relating to the spirit ▷ n type of religious song originating among enslaved Black people in America

SPIRITUEL adj having a refined and lively mind or wit

SPIRITUS n spirit

SPIRITY adj spirited

SPIRLING same as > SPARLING

SPIRLINGS > SPIRLING

SPIROGRAM n record made by spirograph

SPIROGYRA n green freshwater plant that floats on the surface of ponds and ditches

SPIROID adj resembling a spiral or displaying a spiral form

SPIRT same as > SPURT

SPIRTED > SPIRT

SPIRTING > SPIRT

SPIRTLE same as > SPURTLE

SPIRTLES > SPIRTLE

SPIRTS > SPIRT

SPIRULA n tropical cephalopod mollusc

SPIRULAE > SPIRULA

SPIRULAS > SPIRULA

SPIRULINA n type of cyanobacterium processed as a source of nutrients

SPIRY > SPIRE

SPIT vb eject (saliva or food) from the mouth ▷ n saliva

SPITAL n obsolete word for hospital

SPITALS > SPITAL

SPITBALL n small missile made from chewed paper ▷ vb make suggestions

SPITBALLS > SPITBALL

SPITCHER adj doomed ▷ vb be doomed

SPITCHERS > SPITCHER

SPITE n deliberate nastiness ▷ vb annoy or hurt from spite

SPITED > SPITE

SPITEFUL adj full of or motivated by spite

SPITES > SPITE

SPITFIRE n person with a fiery temper

SPITFIRES > SPITFIRE

SPITTING > SPITE

SPITS > SPIT

SPITTED > SPIT

SPITTEN > SPIT

SPITTER > SPIT

SPITTERS > SPIT

SPITTIER > SPITTY

SPITTIEST > SPITTY

SPITTING > SPIT

SPITTINGS > SPIT
SPITTLE n fluid produced in the mouth, saliva
SPITTLES > SPITTLE
SPITTLIER > SPITTLY
SPITTLY adj covered with spittle
SPITTOON n bowl to spit into
SPITTOONS > SPITTOON
SPITTY adj covered with saliva
SPITZ n stockily built dog with a tightly curled tail
SPITZES > SPITZ
SPIV n smartly dressed man who makes a living by shady dealings
SPIVS > SPIV
SPIVVERY n behaviour of spivs
SPIVVIER > SPIV
SPIVVIEST > SPIV
SPIVVISH adj characteristic of a spiv
SPIVVY > SPIV
SPLAKE n type of hybrid trout bred by Canadian zoologists
SPLAKES > SPLAKE
SPLASH vb scatter liquid on (something) ▷ n splashing sound
SPLASHED > SPLASH
SPLASHER n anything used for protection against splashes
SPLASHERS > SPLASHER
SPLASHES > SPLASH
SPLASHIER > SPLASHY
SPLASHILY > SPLASHY
SPLASHING > SPLASH
SPLASHY adj having irregular marks
SPLAT n wet slapping sound ▷ vb make wet slapping sound
SPLATCH vb splash
SPLATCHED > SPLATCH
SPLATCHES > SPLATCH
SPLATS > SPLAT
SPLATTED > SPLAT
SPLATTER n splash ▷ vb splash (something or someone) with small blobs
SPLATTERS > SPLATTER
SPLATTING > SPLAT
SPLAY vb spread out, with ends spreading in different directions ▷ adj spread out ▷ n surface of a wall that forms an oblique angle to the main flat surfaces
SPLAYED > SPLAY
SPLAYFEET > SPLAYFOOT
SPLAYFOOT n foot of which the toes are spread out
SPLAYING > SPLAY
SPLAYS > SPLAY

SPLEEN n abdominal organ which filters bacteria from the blood
SPLEENFUL adj bad-tempered or irritable
SPLEENIER > SPLEEN
SPLEENISH > SPLEEN
SPLEENS > SPLEEN
SPLEENY > SPLEEN
SPLENDENT adj shining brightly
SPLENDID adj excellent
SPLENDOR same as > SPLENDOUR
SPLENDORS > SPLENDOR
SPLENDOUR n state or quality of being splendid
SPLENETIC adj spiteful or irritable ▷ n spiteful or irritable person
SPLENIA > SPLENIUM
SPLENIAL > SPLENIUS
SPLENIC adj of, relating to, or in the spleen
SPLENII > SPLENIUS
SPLENITIS n inflammation of the spleen
SPLENIUM n structure in brain
SPLENIUMS > SPLENIUM
SPLENIUS n either of two flat muscles situated at the back of the neck
SPLENT same as > SPLINT
SPLENTS > SPLENT
SPLEUCHAN n pouch for tobacco
SPLICE vb join by interweaving or overlapping ends
SPLICED > SPLICE
SPLICER > SPLICE
SPLICERS > SPLICE
SPLICES > SPLICE
SPLICING > SPLICE
SPLICINGS > SPLICING
SPLIFF n cannabis, used as a drug
SPLIFFS > SPLIFF
SPLINE n type of narrow key around a shaft that fits into a corresponding groove ▷ vb provide (a shaft, part, etc) with splines
SPLINED > SPLINE
SPLINES > SPLINE
SPLINING > SPLINE
SPLINT n rigid support for a broken bone ▷ vb apply a splint to (a broken arm, etc)
SPLINTED > SPLINT
SPLINTER n thin sharp piece broken off, esp from wood ▷ vb break into fragments
SPLINTERS > SPLINTER
SPLINTERY adj liable to produce or break into splinters
SPLINTING > SPLINT

SPLINTS > SPLINT
SPLISH vb splash
SPLISHED > SPLISH
SPLISHES > SPLISH
SPLISHING > SPLISH
SPLIT vb break into separate pieces ▷ n splitting
SPLITS > SPLIT
SPLITTED > SPLIT
SPLITTER > SPLIT
SPLITTERS > SPLIT
SPLITTING n Freudian psychological defence mechanism
SPLITTISM n advocation of separatism from a larger body
SPLITTIST n person who advocates separatism from a larger body
SPLODGE n large uneven spot or stain ▷ vb mark (something) with a splodge or splodges
SPLODGED > SPLODGE
SPLODGES > SPLODGE
SPLODGIER > SPLODGE
SPLODGILY > SPLODGE
SPLODGING > SPLODGE
SPLODGY > SPLODGE
SPLOG n spam blog
SPLOGS > SPLOG
SPLOOSH vb splash or cause to splash about uncontrollably ▷ n instance or sound of splooshing
SPLOOSHED > SPLOOSH
SPLOOSHES > SPLOOSH
SPLORE n revel
SPLORES > SPLORE
SPLOSH vb scatter (liquid) vigorously about in blobs ▷ n instance or sound of sploshing
SPLOSHED > SPLOSH
SPLOSHES > SPLOSH
SPLOSHING > SPLOSH
SPLOTCH vb splash, daub
SPLOTCHED > SPLOTCH
SPLOTCHES > SPLOTCH
SPLOTCHY > SPLOTCH
SPLURGE vb spend money extravagantly ▷ n bout of extravagance
SPLURGED > SPLURGE
SPLURGER > SPLURGE
SPLURGERS > SPLURGE
SPLURGES > SPLURGE
SPLURGIER > SPLURGE
SPLURGING > SPLURGE
SPLURGY > SPLURGE
SPLURT vb gush out
SPLURTED > SPLURT
SPLURTING > SPLURT
SPLURTS > SPLURT
SPLUTTER vb utter with spitting or choking sounds ▷ n spluttering
SPLUTTERS > SPLUTTER
SPLUTTERY adj spluttering
SPOD adj boring, unattractive, or overly studious

SPODDIER > SPOD
SPODDIEST > SPOD
SPODDY > SPOD
SPODE n type of English china or porcelain
SPODES > SPODE
SPODIUM n black powder
SPODIUMS > SPODIUM
SPODOGRAM n ash from plant used in studying it
SPODOSOL n ashy soil
SPODOSOLS > SPODOSOL
SPODS > SPOD
SPODUMENE n greyish-white, green, or lilac pyroxene mineral
SPOFFISH adj officious
SPOFFY same as > SPOFFISH
SPOIL vb damage
SPOILABLE > SPOIL
SPOILAGE n amount of material that has been spoilt
SPOILAGES > SPOILAGE
SPOILED > SPOIL
SPOILER n device on an aircraft or car to increase drag
SPOILERS > SPOILER
SPOILFIVE n card game for two or more players with five cards each
SPOILFUL adj taking spoils
SPOILING > SPOIL
SPOILS > SPOIL
SPOILSMAN n person who shares in the spoils of office or advocates the spoils system
SPOILSMEN > SPOILSMAN
SPOILT > SPOIL
SPOKE n radial member of a wheel ▷ vb equip with spokes
SPOKED > SPOKE
SPOKEN > SPEAK
SPOKES > SPOKE
SPOKESMAN n person chosen to speak on behalf of a group
SPOKESMEN > SPOKESMAN
SPOKEWISE > SPEAK
SPOKING > SPOKE
SPOLIATE less common word for > DESPOIL
SPOLIATED > SPOLIATE
SPOLIATES > SPOLIATE
SPOLIATOR > SPOLIATE
SPONDAIC adj of, relating to, or consisting of spondees ▷ n spondaic line
SPONDAICS > SPONDAIC
SPONDEE n metrical foot of two long syllables
SPONDEES > SPONDEE
SPONDULIX n money
SPONDYL n vertebra

SPONDYLS > SPONDYL
SPONGE n sea animal with a porous absorbent skeleton ▷ vb wipe with a sponge
SPONGEBAG n small bag for holding toiletries when travelling
SPONGED > SPONGE
SPONGEING same as > SPONGING
SPONGEOUS adj spongy
SPONGER n person who sponges on others
SPONGERS > SPONGER
SPONGES > SPONGE
SPONGIER > SPONGY
SPONGIEST > SPONGY
SPONGILY > SPONGY
SPONGIN n fibrous horny protein in sponges
SPONGING > SPONGE
SPONGINS > SPONGIN
SPONGIOSE > SPONGE
SPONGIOUS > SPONGE
SPONGOID > SPONGE
SPONGY adj of or resembling a sponge
SPONSAL n marriage
SPONSALIA n marriage ceremony
SPONSIBLE adj responsible
SPONSING same as > SPONSON
SPONSINGS > SPONSING
SPONSION n act or process of becoming surety
SPONSIONS > SPONSION
SPONSON n outboard support for a gun enabling it to fire fore and aft
SPONSONS > SPONSON
SPONSOR n person who promotes something ▷ vb act as a sponsor for
SPONSORED > SPONSOR
SPONSORS > SPONSOR
SPONTOON n infantry weapon used in the 18th and 19th centuries
SPONTOONS > SPONTOON
SPOOF n mildly satirical parody ▷ vb fool (a person) with a trick or deception
SPOOFED > SPOOF
SPOOFER > SPOOF
SPOOFERS > SPOOF
SPOOFERY > SPOOF
SPOOFIER > SPOOFY
SPOOFIEST > SPOOFY
SPOOFING > SPOOF
SPOOFINGS > SPOOF
SPOOFS > SPOOF
SPOOFY > SPOOF
SPOOK n ghost ▷ vb frighten
SPOOKED > SPOOK
SPOOKERY n spooky events
SPOOKIER > SPOOKY
SPOOKIEST > SPOOKY
SPOOKILY > SPOOKY
SPOOKING > SPOOK

SPOOKISH > SPOOK
SPOOKS > SPOOK
SPOOKY adj ghostly or eerie
SPOOL n cylinder round which something can be wound ▷ vb wind or be wound onto a spool or reel
SPOOLED > SPOOL
SPOOLER > SPOOL
SPOOLERS > SPOOL
SPOOLING > SPOOL
SPOOLINGS > SPOOL
SPOOLS > SPOOL
SPOOM vb sail fast before wind
SPOOMED > SPOOM
SPOOMING > SPOOM
SPOOMS > SPOOM
SPOON n shallow bowl attached to a handle for eating, stirring, or serving food ▷ vb lift with a spoon
SPOONBAIT n type of lure used in angling
SPOONBILL n wading bird of warm regions with a long flat bill
SPOONED > SPOON
SPOONER n person who engages in spooning
SPOONERS > SPOONER
SPOONEY same as > SPOONY
SPOONEYS > SPOONEY
SPOONFED adj having been given someone else's opinions
SPOONFUL n amount that a spoon is able to hold
SPOONFULS > SPOONFUL
SPOONHOOK n type of fishing lure
SPOONIER > SPOONY
SPOONIES > SPOONY
SPOONIEST > SPOONY
SPOONILY > SPOONY
SPOONING > SPOON
SPOONLIKE adj like a spoon
SPOONS > SPOON
SPOONSFUL > SPOONFUL
SPOONWAYS adv like spoons
SPOONWISE same as > SPOONWAYS
SPOONWORM n type of small marine worm with a spoonlike proboscis
SPOONY adj foolishly or stupidly in love ▷ n fool or silly person, esp one in love
SPOOR n trail of an animal ▷ vb track (an animal) by following its trail
SPOORED > SPOOR
SPOORER > SPOOR
SPOORERS > SPOOR
SPOORING > SPOOR
SPOORS > SPOOR
SPOOT n razor shell
SPOOTS > SPOOT
SPORADIC adj intermittent, scattered
SPORAL > SPORE

SPORANGIA pl n organs in fungi in which asexual spores are produced
SPORE n minute reproductive body of some plants ▷ vb produce, carry, or release spores
SPORED > SPORE
SPORELIKE adj like a spore
SPORES > SPORE
SPORICIDE n substance killing spores
SPORIDESM n group of spores
SPORIDIA > SPORIDIUM
SPORIDIAL > SPORIDIUM
SPORIDIUM n type of spore
SPORING > SPORE
SPORK n spoon-shaped piece of cutlery with tines like a fork
SPORKS > SPORK
SPOROCARP n specialized leaf branch in certain aquatic ferns that encloses the sori
SPOROCYST n thick-walled rounded structure produced by sporozoan protozoans
SPOROCYTE n diploid cell that divides by meiosis to produce four haploid spores
SPOROGENY n process of spore formation in plants and animals
SPOROGONY n process in sporozoans by which sporozoites are formed
SPOROID adj of or like a spore
SPOROPHYL n leaf in ferns that bears the sporangia
SPOROZOA n class of microscopic creature
SPOROZOAL > SPOROZOA
SPOROZOAN n type of parasitic protozoan
SPOROZOIC > SPOROZOA
SPOROZOON same as > SPOROZOAN
SPORRAN n pouch worn in front of a kilt
SPORRANS > SPORRAN
SPORT n activity for pleasure, competition, or exercise ▷ vb wear proudly
SPORTABLE adj playful
SPORTANCE n playing
SPORTBIKE n type of high-performance motorcycle
SPORTCOAT n sports jacket
SPORTED > SPORT
SPORTER > SPORT
SPORTERS > SPORT
SPORTFUL > SPORT
SPORTIER > SPORTY
SPORTIES > SPORTY
SPORTIEST > SPORTY

SPORTIF adj sporty ▷ n sporty person
SPORTIFS > SPORTIF
SPORTILY > SPORTY
SPORTING adj of sport
SPORTIVE adj playful
SPORTLESS > SPORT
SPORTS adj of or used in sports ▷ n meeting held at a school or college for competitions in athletic events
SPORTSMAN n man who engages in sports
SPORTSMEN > SPORTSMAN
SPORTY adj (of a person) interested in sport ▷ n young person who takes an interest in sport and fitness
SPORULAR > SPORULE
SPORULATE vb produce spores, esp by multiple fission
SPORULE n spore, esp a very small spore
SPORULES > SPORULE
SPOSH n slush
SPOSHES > SPOSH
SPOSHIER > SPOSH
SPOSHIEST > SPOSH
SPOSHY > SPOSH
SPOT n small mark on a surface ▷ vb notice
SPOTLESS adj absolutely clean
SPOTLIGHT n powerful light illuminating a small area ▷ vb draw attention to
SPOTLIT > SPOTLIGHT
SPOTS > SPOT
SPOTTABLE > SPOT
SPOTTED > SPOT
SPOTTER n person who notes numbers or types of trains or planes
SPOTTERS > SPOTTER
SPOTTIE n young deer of up to three months of age
SPOTTIER > SPOTTY
SPOTTIES > SPOTTIE
SPOTTIEST > SPOTTY
SPOTTILY > SPOTTY
SPOTTING > SPOT
SPOTTINGS > SPOT
SPOTTY adj with spots
SPOUSAGE n marriage
SPOUSAGES > SPOUSAGE
SPOUSAL n marriage ceremony ▷ adj of or relating to marriage
SPOUSALLY > SPOUSAL
SPOUSALS > SPOUSAL
SPOUSE n person to whom one is married ▷ vb marry
SPOUSED > SPOUSE
SPOUSES > SPOUSE
SPOUSING > SPOUSE
SPOUT vb pour out in a stream or jet ▷ n projecting tube or lip for pouring liquids
SPOUTED > SPOUT
SPOUTER > SPOUT

SPOUTERS > SPOUT
SPOUTIER > SPOUT
SPOUTIEST > SPOUT
SPOUTING n rainwater downpipe on the outside of a building
SPOUTINGS > SPOUTING
SPOUTLESS > SPOUT
SPOUTS > SPOUT
SPOUTY > SPOUT
SPRACK adj vigorous
SPRACKLE vb clamber
SPRACKLED > SPRACKLE
SPRACKLES > SPRACKLE
SPRAD > SPREAD
SPRADDLE n disease of fowl preventing them from standing
SPRADDLED adj affected by spraddle
SPRADDLES > SPRADDLE
SPRAG n device used to prevent a vehicle from running backwards on an incline ▷ vb use sprag to prevent vehicle from moving
SPRAGGED > SPRAG
SPRAGGING > SPRAG
SPRAGS > SPRAG
SPRAID vb chapped
SPRAIN vb injure (a joint) by a sudden twist ▷ n such an injury
SPRAINED > SPRAIN
SPRAINING > SPRAIN
SPRAINS > SPRAIN
SPRAINT n piece of otter's dung
SPRAINTS > SPRAINT
SPRANG n branch
SPRANGLE vb sprawl
SPRANGLED > SPRANGLE
SPRANGLES > SPRANGLE
SPRANGS > SPRANG
SPRAT n small sea fish
SPRATS > SPRAT
SPRATTLE vb scramble
SPRATTLED > SPRATTLE
SPRATTLES > SPRATTLE
SPRAUCHLE same as > SPRACKLE
SPRAUNCY adj smart
SPRAWL vb lie or sit with the limbs spread out ▷ n part of a city that has spread untidily over a large area
SPRAWLED > SPRAWL
SPRAWLER > SPRAWL
SPRAWLERS > SPRAWL
SPRAWLIER > SPRAWL
SPRAWLING > SPRAWL
SPRAWLS > SPRAWL
SPRAWLY > SPRAWL
SPRAY n (device for producing) fine drops of liquid ▷ vb scatter in fine drops
SPRAYED > SPRAY

SPRAYER > SPRAY
SPRAYERS > SPRAY
SPRAYEY > SPRAY
SPRAYIER > SPRAY
SPRAYIEST > SPRAY
SPRAYING > SPRAY
SPRAYINGS > SPRAY
SPRAYS > SPRAY
SPREAD vb open out or be displayed to the fullest extent ▷ n spreading ▷ adj extended or stretched out, esp to the fullest extent
SPREADER n machine or device used for scattering bulk materials over a relatively wide area
SPREADERS > SPREADER
SPREADING > SPREAD
SPREADS > SPREAD
SPREAGH n cattle raid
SPREAGHS > SPREAGH
SPREATHE vb chap
SPREATHED adj sore
SPREATHES > SPREATHE
SPREAZE same as > SPREATHE
SPREAZED same as > SPREATHED
SPREAZES > SPREAZE
SPREAZING > SPREAZE
SPRECHERY n theft of cattle
SPRECKLED adj speckled
SPRED same as > SPREAD
SPREDD same as > SPREAD
SPREDDE same as > SPREAD
SPREDDEN > SPREDDE
SPREDDES > SPREDDE
SPREDDING > SPREDDE
SPREDDS > SPREDD
SPREDS > SPRED
SPREE n session of overindulgence, usu in drinking or spending money ▷ vb go on a spree
SPREED > SPREE
SPREEING > SPREE
SPREES > SPREE
SPREETHE same as > SPREATHE
SPREETHED > SPREETHE
SPREETHES > SPREETHE
SPREEZE same as > SPREATHE
SPREEZED > SPREEZE
SPREEZES > SPREEZE
SPREEZING > SPREEZE
SPREKELIA n bulbous plant grown for its striking crimson or white pendent flowers
SPRENT adj sprinkled ▷ vb leap forward in an agile manner
SPRENTED > SPRENT
SPRENTING > SPRENT
SPRENTS > SPRENT
SPREW same as > SPRUE
SPREWS > SPREW
SPRIER > SPRY
SPRIEST > SPRY

SPRIG n twig or shoot ▷ vb fasten or secure with sprigs
SPRIGGED > SPRIG
SPRIGGER > SPRIG
SPRIGGERS > SPRIG
SPRIGGIER > SPRIG
SPRIGGING > SPRIG
SPRIGGY > SPRIG
SPRIGHT same as > SPRITE
SPRIGHTED > SPRIGHT
SPRIGHTLY adj lively and brisk ▷ adv in a lively manner
SPRIGHTS > SPRIGHT
SPRIGS > SPRIG
SPRIGTAIL n species of duck
SPRING vb move suddenly upwards or forwards in a single motion, jump ▷ n season between winter and summer
SPRINGAL n young man
SPRINGALD same as > SPRINGAL
SPRINGALS > SPRINGAL
SPRINGBOK n S African antelope
SPRINGE n type of snare for catching small wild animals or birds ▷ vb set such a snare
SPRINGED > SPRINGE
SPRINGER n small spaniel
SPRINGERS > SPRINGER
SPRINGES > SPRINGE
SPRINGIER > SPRINGY
SPRINGILY > SPRINGY
SPRINGING > SPRING
SPRINGLE same as > SPRINGE
SPRINGLES > SPRINGE
SPRINGLET n small spring
SPRINGS > SPRING
SPRINGY adj elastic
SPRINKLE vb scatter (liquid or powder) in tiny drops or particles over (something) ▷ n act or an instance of sprinkling or a quantity that is sprinkled
SPRINKLED > SPRINKLE
SPRINKLER n device with small holes that is attached to a garden hose or watering can and used to spray water
SPRINKLES > SPRINKLE
SPRINT n short race run at top speed ▷ vb run a short distance at top speed
SPRINTED > SPRINT
SPRINTER > SPRINT
SPRINTERS > SPRINT
SPRINTING > SPRINT
SPRINTS > SPRINT
SPRIT n small spar set diagonally across a sail to extend it

SPRITE n elf
SPRITEFUL adj lively
SPRITELY same as > SPRIGHTLY
SPRITES > SPRITE
SPRITS > SPRIT
SPRITSAIL n sail extended by a sprit
SPRITZ vb spray liquid
SPRITZED > SPRITZ
SPRITZER n tall drink of wine and soda water
SPRITZERS > SPRITZER
SPRITZES > SPRITZ
SPRITZIER > SPRITZY
SPRITZIG adj (of wine) sparkling ▷ n sparkling wine
SPRITZIGS > SPRITZIG
SPRITZING > SPRITZ
SPRITZY adj fizzy
SPROCKET n wheel with teeth on the rim, that drives or is driven by a chain
SPROCKETS > SPROCKET
SPROD n young salmon
SPRODS > SPROD
SPROG n child
SPROGLET n small child
SPROGLETS > SPROGLET
SPROGS > SPROG
SPRONG > SPRING
SPROUT vb put forth shoots ▷ n shoot
SPROUTED > SPROUT
SPROUTING > SPROUT
SPROUTS > SPROUT
SPRUCE n kind of fir ▷ adj neat and smart
SPRUCED > SPRUCE
SPRUCELY > SPRUCE
SPRUCER > SPRUCE
SPRUCES > SPRUCE
SPRUCEST > SPRUCE
SPRUCIER > SPRUCE
SPRUCIEST > SPRUCE
SPRUCING > SPRUCE
SPRUCY > SPRUCE
SPRUE n vertical channel in a mould
SPRUES > SPRUE
SPRUG n sparrow
SPRUGS > SPRUG
SPRUIK vb old word meaning speak in public
SPRUIKED > SPRUIK
SPRUIKER > SPRUIK
SPRUIKERS > SPRUIK
SPRUIKING > SPRUIK
SPRUIKS > SPRUIK
SPRUIT n small tributary stream or watercourse
SPRUITS > SPRUIT
SPRUNG > SPRING
SPRUSH Scots form of > SPRUCE
SPRUSHED > SPRUSH
SPRUSHES > SPRUSH
SPRUSHING > SPRUSH
SPRY adj active or nimble
SPRYER > SPRY
SPRYEST > SPRY

S

SPRYLY > SPRY

SPRYNESS > SPRY

SPUD n potato ▷ vb remove (bark) or eradicate (weeds) with a spud

SPUDDED > SPUD

SPUDDER same as > SPUD

SPUDDERS > SPUDDER

SPUDDIER > SPUDDY

SPUDDIEST > SPUDDY

SPUDDING > SPUD

SPUDDINGS > SPUD

SPUDDLE n feeble movement

SPUDDLES > SPUDDLE

SPUDDY adj short and fat

SPUDGEL n bucket on a long handle

SPUDGELS > SPUDGEL

SPUDS > SPUD

SPUE same as > SPEW

SPUED > SPUE

SPUEING > SPUE

SPUER > SPUE

SPUERS > SPUE

SPUES > SPUE

SPUG same as > SPUGGY

SPUGGIES > SPUGGY

SPUGGY n house sparrow

SPUGS > SPUG

SPUILZIE vb plunder

SPUILZIED > SPUILZIE

SPUILZIES > SPUILZIE

SPUING > SPUE

SPULE Scots word for > SHOULDER

SPULES > SPULE

SPULYE same as > SPUILZIE

SPULYED > SPULYE

SPULYEING > SPULYE

SPULYES > SPULYE

SPULYIE same as > SPUILZIE

SPULYIED > SPULYIE

SPULYIES > SPULYIE

SPULZIE same as > SPUILZIE

SPULZIED > SPULZIE

SPULZIES > SPULZIE

SPUMANTE n Italian sparkling wine

SPUMANTES > SPUMANTE

SPUME vb froth ▷ n foam or froth on the sea

SPUMED > SPUME

SPUMES > SPUME

SPUMIER > SPUMY

SPUMIEST > SPUMY

SPUMING > SPUME

SPUMONE n creamy Italian ice cream

SPUMONES > SPUMONE

SPUMONI same as > SPUMONE

SPUMONIS > SPUMONI

SPUMOUS > SPUME

SPUMY > SPUME

SPUN > SPIN

SPUNGE same as > SPONGE

SPUNGES > SPUNGE

SPUNK n courage, spirit ▷ vb catch fire

SPUNKED > SPUNK

SPUNKIE n will-o'-the-wisp

SPUNKIER > SPUNK

SPUNKIES > SPUNKIE

SPUNKIEST > SPUNK

SPUNKILY > SPUNK

SPUNKING > SPUNK

SPUNKS > SPUNK

SPUNKY > SPUNK

SPUNYARN n small stuff made from rope yarns twisted together

SPUNYARNS > SPUNYARN

SPUR n stimulus or incentive ▷ vb urge on, incite

SPURDOG n the dogfish

SPURDOGS > SPURDOG

SPURGALL vb prod with spur

SPURGALLS > SPURGALL

SPURGE n plant with milky sap

SPURGES > SPURGE

SPURIAE n type of bird feathers

SPURIOUS adj not genuine

SPURLESS > SPUR

SPURLIKE adj like a spur

SPURLING same as > SPARLING

SPURLINGS > SPURLING

SPURN vb reject with scorn ▷ n instance of spurning

SPURNED > SPURN

SPURNER > SPURN

SPURNERS > SPURN

SPURNES > SPURNE

SPURNING > SPURN

SPURNINGS > SPURN

SPURNS > SPURN

SPURRED > SPUR

SPURRER > SPUR

SPURRERS > SPUR

SPURREY n any of several low-growing European plants

SPURREYS > SPURREY

SPURRIER n maker of spurs

SPURRIERS > SPURRIER

SPURRIES > SPURRY

SPURRIEST > SPURRY

SPURRING > SPUR

SPURRINGS > SPUR

SPURRY n spurrey ▷ adj resembling a spur

SPURS > SPUR

SPURT vb gush or cause to gush out in a jet ▷ n short sudden burst of activity or speed

SPURTED > SPURT

SPURTER > SPURT

SPURTERS > SPURT

SPURTING > SPURT

SPURTLE n wooden spoon for stirring porridge

SPURTLES > SPURTLE

SPURTS > SPURT

SPURWAY n path used by riders

SPURWAYS > SPURWAY

SPUTA > SPUTUM

SPUTNIK n early Soviet artificial satellite

SPUTNIKS > SPUTNIK

SPUTTER n splutter ▷ vb splutter

SPUTTERED > SPUTTER

SPUTTERER > SPUTTER

SPUTTERS > SPUTTER

SPUTTERY adj sputtering

SPUTUM n mass of spittle ejected from the mouth

SPUTUMS > SPUTUM

SPY n person employed to obtain secret information ▷ vb act as a spy

SPYAL n spy

SPYALS > SPYAL

SPYCAM n camera used for covert surveillance

SPYCAMS > SPYCAM

SPYGLASS n small telescope

SPYHOLE n small hole in a door, etc through which one may watch secretly

SPYHOLES > SPYHOLE

SPYING > SPY

SPYINGS > SPY

SPYMASTER n person who controls spy network

SPYPLANE n military aeroplane used to spy on enemy

SPYPLANES > SPYPLANE

SPYRE same as > SPIRE

SPYRES > SPYRE

SPYWARE n software used to gain information about a computer user

SPYWARES > SPYWARE

SQUAB n young bird yet to leave the nest ▷ adj (of birds) recently hatched and still unfledged ▷ vb fall

SQUABASH vb crush

SQUABBED > SQUAB

SQUABBER > SQUAB

SQUABBEST > SQUAB

SQUABBIER > SQUAB

SQUABBING > SQUAB

SQUABBISH > SQUAB

SQUABBLE n petty or noisy quarrel ▷ vb quarrel over a small matter

SQUABBLED > SQUABBLE

SQUABBLER > SQUABBLE

SQUABBLES > SQUABBLE

SQUABBY > SQUAB

SQUABS > SQUAB

SQUACCO n S European heron

SQUACCOS > SQUACCO

SQUAD n small group of people working or training together ▷ vb set up squads

SQUADDED > SQUAD

SQUADDIE n private soldier

SQUADDIES > SQUADDY

SQUADDING > SQUAD

SQUADDY same as > SQUADDIE

SQUADOOSH n (US slang) nothing

SQUADRON n division of an air force, fleet, or cavalry regiment ▷ vb assign to squadrons

SQUADRONE n former Scottish political party

SQUADRONS > SQUADRON

SQUADS > SQUAD

SQUAIL vb throw sticks at

SQUAILED > SQUAIL

SQUAILER > SQUAIL

SQUAILERS > SQUAIL

SQUAILING > SQUAIL

SQUAILS > SQUAIL

SQUALENE n terpene first found in the liver of sharks

SQUALENES > SQUALENE

SQUALID adj dirty and unpleasant

SQUALIDER > SQUALID

SQUALIDLY > SQUALID

SQUALL n sudden strong wind ▷ vb cry noisily, yell

SQUALLED > SQUALL

SQUALLER > SQUALL

SQUALLERS > SQUALL

SQUALLIER > SQUALL

SQUALLING > SQUALL

SQUALLISH > SQUALL

SQUALLS > SQUALL

SQUALLY > SQUALL

SQUALOID adj of or like a shark

SQUALOR n disgusting dirt and filth

SQUALORS > SQUALOR

SQUAMA n scale or scalelike structure

SQUAMAE > SQUAMA

SQUAMATE > SQUAMA

SQUAMATES > SQUAMA

SQUAME same as > SQUAMA

SQUAMELLA n small scale

SQUAMES > SQUAME

SQUAMOSAL n thin platelike paired bone in the skull of vertebrates ▷ adj of or relating to this bone

SQUAMOSE same as > SQUAMOUS

SQUAMOUS adj (of epithelium) consisting of one or more layers of flat platelike cells

SQUAMULA same as > SQUAMELLA

SQUAMULAS > SQUAMULA

SQUAMULE same as > SQUAMELLA

SQUAMULES > SQUAMULE

SQUANDER vb waste (money or resources) ▷ n extravagance or dissipation

SQUANDERS
> SQUANDER
SQUARE n geometric figure with four equal sides and four right angles ▷ adj square in shape ▷ vb multiply (a number) by itself ▷ adv directly
SQUARED > SQUARE
SQUARELY adv in a direct way
SQUARER > SQUARE
SQUARERS > SQUARE
SQUARES > SQUARE
SQUAREST > SQUARE
SQUARIAL n type of square dish for receiving satellite television
SQUARIALS > SQUARIAL
SQUARING > SQUARE
SQUARINGS > SQUARE
SQUARISH > SQUARE
SQUARK n hypothetical boson partner of a quark
SQUARKS > SQUARK
SQUARROSE adj having a rough surface
SQUARSON n member of the clergy who is also a landowner
SQUARSONS > SQUARSON
SQUASH vb crush flat ▷ n sweet fruit drink diluted with water
SQUASHED > SQUASH
SQUASHER > SQUASH
SQUASHERS > SQUASH
SQUASHES > SQUASH
SQUASHIER > SQUASHY
SQUASHILY > SQUASHY
SQUASHING > SQUASH
SQUASHY adj soft and easily squashed
SQUAT vb crouch with the knees bent and the weight on the feet ▷ n place where squatters live ▷ adj short and broad
SQUATLY > SQUAT
SQUATNESS > SQUAT
SQUATS > SQUAT
SQUATTED > SQUAT
SQUATTER n illegal occupier of unused premises ▷ vb splash along
SQUATTERS > SQUATTER
SQUATTEST > SQUAT
SQUATTIER > SQUATTY
SQUATTILY > SQUATTY
SQUATTING n act of squatting
SQUATTLE vb squat
SQUATTLED > SQUATTLE
SQUATTLES > SQUATTLE
SQUATTY adj short and broad
SQUAWBUSH n American shrub
SQUAWFISH n North American minnow
SQUAWK n loud harsh cry ▷ vb utter a squawk

SQUAWKED > SQUAWK
SQUAWKER > SQUAWK
SQUAWKERS > SQUAWK
SQUAWKIER > SQUAWK
SQUAWKING > SQUAWK
SQUAWKS > SQUAWK
SQUAWKY > SQUAWK
SQUAWROOT n North American parasitic plant
SQUEAK n short shrill cry or sound ▷ vb make or utter a squeak
SQUEAKED > SQUEAK
SQUEAKER > SQUEAK
SQUEAKERS > SQUEAK
SQUEAKERY > SQUEAK
SQUEAKIER > SQUEAK
SQUEAKILY > SQUEAK
SQUEAKING > SQUEAK
SQUEAKS > SQUEAK
SQUEAKY > SQUEAK
SQUEAL n long shrill cry or sound ▷ vb make or utter a squeal
SQUEALED > SQUEAL
SQUEALER > SQUEAL
SQUEALERS > SQUEAL
SQUEALING > SQUEAL
SQUEALS > SQUEAL
SQUEAMISH adj easily sickened or shocked
SQUEEGEE n tool with a rubber blade for clearing water from a surface ▷ vb remove (water or other liquid) from (something) by use of a squeegee
SQUEEGEED > SQUEEGEE
SQUEEGEES > SQUEEGEE
SQUEEZE vb grip or press firmly ▷ n squeezing
SQUEEZED > SQUEEZE
SQUEEZER > SQUEEZE
SQUEEZERS > SQUEEZE
SQUEEZES > SQUEEZE
SQUEEZIER > SQUEEZE
SQUEEZING > SQUEEZE
SQUEEZY > SQUEEZE
SQUEG vb oscillate
SQUEGGED > SQUEG
SQUEGGER > SQUEG
SQUEGGERS > SQUEG
SQUEGGING > SQUEG
SQUEGS > SQUEG
SQUELCH vb make a wet sucking sound, as by walking through mud ▷ n squelching sound
SQUELCHED > SQUELCH
SQUELCHER > SQUELCH
SQUELCHES > SQUELCH
SQUELCHY > SQUELCH
SQUIB n small firework that hisses before exploding
SQUIBBED > SQUIB
SQUIBBER n (in baseball) ground ball that becomes a base hit
SQUIBBERS > SQUIBBER
SQUIBBING > SQUIB
SQUIBS > SQUIB
SQUID n sea creature with tentacles ▷ vb (of a parachute) to assume an elongated shape

SQUIDDED > SQUID
SQUIDDING > SQUID
SQUIDGE vb squash
SQUIDGED > SQUIDGE
SQUIDGES > SQUIDGE
SQUIDGIER > SQUIDGY
SQUIDGING > SQUIDGE
SQUIDGY adj soft, moist, and squashy
SQUIDLIKE adj like a squid
SQUIDS > SQUID
SQUIER same as > SQUIRE
SQUIERS > SQUIER
SQUIFF same as > SQUIFFY
SQUIFFED same as > SQUIFFY
SQUIFFER n concertina
SQUIFFERS > SQUIFFER
SQUIFFIER > SQUIFFY
SQUIFFY adj slightly drunk
SQUIGGLE n wavy line ▷ vb wriggle
SQUIGGLED > SQUIGGLE
SQUIGGLER > SQUIGGLE
SQUIGGLES > SQUIGGLE
SQUIGGLY > SQUIGGLE
SQUILGEE same as > SQUEEGEE
SQUILGEED > SQUILGEE
SQUILGEES > SQUILGEE
SQUILL n Mediterranean plant of the lily family
SQUILLA n type of mantis shrimp
SQUILLAE > SQUILLA
SQUILLAS > SQUILLA
SQUILLION n extremely large but unspecified number, quantity, or amount
SQUILLS > SQUILL
SQUINANCY same as > QUINSY
SQUINCH n small arch across an internal corner of a tower ▷ vb squeeze
SQUINCHED > SQUINCH
SQUINCHES > SQUINCH
SQUINIED > SQUINY
SQUINIES > SQUINY
SQUINNIED > SQUINNY
SQUINNIER > SQUINNY
SQUINNIES > SQUINNY
SQUINNY vb squint ▷ adj squint
SQUINT vb have eyes which face in different directions ▷ n squinting condition of the eye ▷ adj crooked
SQUINTED > SQUINT
SQUINTER > SQUINT
SQUINTERS > SQUINT
SQUINTEST > SQUINT
SQUINTIER > SQUINT
SQUINTING > SQUINT
SQUINTS > SQUINT
SQUINTY > SQUINT

SQUINY same as > SQUINNY
SQUINYING > SQUINY
SQUIRAGE n body of squires
SQUIRAGES > SQUIRAGE
SQUIRALTY same as > SQUIRAGE
SQUIRARCH n person who believes in government by squires
SQUIRE n country gentleman, usu the main landowner in a community ▷ vb (of a man) escort (a woman)
SQUIREAGE same as > SQUIRAGE
SQUIRED > SQUIRE
SQUIREDOM > SQUIRE
SQUIREEN n petty squire
SQUIREENS > SQUIREEN
SQUIRELY > SQUIRE
SQUIRES > SQUIRE
SQUIRESS n wife of squire
SQUIRING > SQUIRE
SQUIRISH > SQUIRE
SQUIRL n decorative flourish in handwriting
SQUIRLS > SQUIRL
SQUIRM vb wriggle, writhe ▷ n wriggling movement
SQUIRMED > SQUIRM
SQUIRMER > SQUIRM
SQUIRMERS > SQUIRM
SQUIRMIER > SQUIRMY
SQUIRMING > SQUIRM
SQUIRMS > SQUIRM
SQUIRMY adj moving with a wriggling motion
SQUIRR same as > SKIRR
SQUIRRED > SQUIRR
SQUIRREL n small bushy-tailed tree-living animal ▷ vb store for future use
SQUIRRELS > SQUIRREL
SQUIRRELY adj like a squirrel
SQUIRRING > SQUIRR
SQUIRRS > SQUIRR
SQUIRT vb force (a liquid) or (of a liquid) be forced out of a narrow opening ▷ n jet of liquid
SQUIRTED > SQUIRT
SQUIRTER > SQUIRT
SQUIRTERS > SQUIRT
SQUIRTING > SQUIRT
SQUIRTS > SQUIRT
SQUISH n soft squelching sound ▷ vb crush (something) with a soft squelching sound
SQUISHED > SQUISH
SQUISHES > SQUISH
SQUISHIER > SQUISHY
SQUISHING > SQUISH
SQUISHY adj soft and yielding to the touch
SQUIT n insignificant person
SQUITCH n couch grass
SQUITCHES > SQUITCH

S

SQUITS > SQUIT

SQUITTERS pl n slang word for diarrhoea

SQUIZ n look or glance, esp an inquisitive one

SQUIZZES > SQUIZ

SQUOOSH vb squash

SQUOOSHED > SQUOOSH

SQUOOSHES > SQUOOSH

SQUOOSHY > SQUOOSH

SQUUSH same as > SQUOOSH

SQUUSHED > SQUUSH

SQUUSHES > SQUUSH

SQUUSHING > SQUUSH

SRADDHA n Hindu offering to ancestor

SRADDHAS > SRADDHA

SRADHA same as > SRADDHA

SRADHAS > SRADHA

SRI n title of respect used when addressing a Hindu

SRIRACHA n type of spicy sauce

SRIRACHAS > SRIRACHA

SRIS > SRI

ST interj exclamation to attract attention

STAB vb pierce with something pointed ▷ n instance of stabbing

STABBED > STAB

STABBER > STAB

STABBERS > STAB

STABBING > STAB

STABBINGS > STAB

STABILATE n preserved collection of tiny animals

STABILE n stationary abstract construction, usually of wire, metal, wood, etc ▷ adj fixed

STABILES > STABILE

STABILISE same as > STABILIZE

STABILITY n quality of being stable

STABILIZE vb make or become stable

STABLE n building in which horses are kept ▷ vb put or keep (a horse) in a stable ▷ adj firmly fixed or established

STABLEBOY n boy or man who works in a stable

STABLED > STABLE

STABLEMAN same as > STABLEBOY

STABLEMEN > STABLEMAN

STABLER n stable owner

STABLERS > STABLER

STABLES > STABLE

STABLEST > STABLE

STABLING n stable buildings or accommodation

STABLINGS > STABLING

STABLISH archaic variant of > ESTABLISH

STABLY > STABLE

STABS > STAB

STACATION n holiday spent at home, rather than travelling

STACCATI > STACCATO

STACCATO adv with the notes sharply separated ▷ adj consisting of short abrupt sounds ▷ n staccato note

STACCATOS > STACCATO

STACHYS n type of plant of the genus which includes lamb's ears and betony

STACHYSES > STACHYS

STACK n ordered pile ▷ vb pile in a stack

STACKABLE > STACK

STACKED > STACK

STACKER > STACK

STACKERS > STACK

STACKET n fence of wooden posts

STACKETS > STACKET

STACKING n arrangement of aircraft traffic in busy flight lanes

STACKINGS > STACKING

STACKLESS > STACK

STACKROOM n area of library where books are not on open shelves

STACKS > STACK

STACKUP n number of aircraft waiting to land

STACKUPS > STACKUP

STACKYARD n place where livestock are kept

STACTE n one of several sweet-smelling spices used in incense

STACTES > STACTE

STADDA n type of saw

STADDAS > STADDA

STADDLE n type of support or prop

STADDLES > STADDLE

STADE same as > STADIUM

STADES > STADE

STADIA n instrument used in surveying

STADIAL n stage in development of glacier

STADIALS > STADIAL

STADIAS > STADIA

STADIUM n sports arena with tiered seats for spectators

STADIUMS > STADIUM

STAFF n people employed in an organization ▷ vb supply with personnel

STAFFAGE n ornamentation in work of art

STAFFAGES > STAFFAGE

STAFFED > STAFF

STAFFER n member of staff, esp, in journalism, of editorial staff

STAFFERS > STAFFER

STAFFING n act of hiring employees

STAFFINGS > STAFFING

STAFFMAN n person who holds the levelling staff

when a survey is being made

STAFFMEN > STAFFMAN

STAFFROOM n common room for teachers

STAFFS > STAFF

STAG n adult male deer ▷ adv without a female escort ▷ vb apply for (shares) with the intention of selling them for quick profit

STAGE n step or period of development ▷ vb put (a play) on stage

STAGEABLE > STAGE

STAGED > STAGE

STAGEFUL n amount that can appear on stage

STAGEFULS > STAGEFUL

STAGEHAND n person who moves props and scenery on a stage

STAGEHEAD n part of a fishing stage which extends into the water

STAGELIKE > STAGE

STAGER n person of experience

STAGERIES > STAGERY

STAGERS > STAGER

STAGERY n theatrical effects or techniques

STAGES > STAGE

STAGETTE n young unmarried professional woman

STAGETTES > STAGETTE

STAGEY same as > STAGY

STAGGARD n male red deer in the fourth year of life

STAGGARDS > STAGGARD

STAGGART same as > STAGGARD

STAGGARTS > STAGGART

STAGGED > STAG

STAGGER vb walk unsteadily ▷ n staggering

STAGGERED > STAGGER

STAGGERER > STAGGER

STAGGERS n disease of horses and other domestic animals that causes staggering

STAGGERY adj tending to stagger

STAGGIE n little stag

STAGGIER > STAG

STAGGIES > STAGGIE

STAGGIEST > STAG

STAGGING > STAG

STAGGY > STAG

STAGHORN n type of fern with fronds that resemble antlers

STAGHORNS > STAGHORN

STAGHOUND n breed of hound similar in appearance to the foxhound but larger

STAGIER > STAGY

STAGIEST > STAGY

STAGILY > STAGY

STAGINESS > STAGY

STAGING n temporary support used in building

STAGINGS > STAGING

STAGNANCE > STAGNANT

STAGNANCY > STAGNANT

STAGNANT adj (of water or air) stale from not moving

STAGNATE vb be stagnant

STAGNATED > STAGNATE

STAGNATES > STAGNATE

STAGS > STAG

STAGY adj too theatrical or dramatic

STAID adj sedate, serious, and rather dull

STAIDER > STAID

STAIDEST > STAID

STAIDLY > STAID

STAIDNESS > STAID

STAIG Scots variant of > STAG

STAIGS > STAIG

STAIN vb discolour, mark ▷ n discoloration or mark

STAINABLE > STAIN

STAINED > STAIN

STAINER > STAIN

STAINERS > STAIN

STAINING > STAIN

STAININGS > STAIN

STAINLESS adj resistant to discoloration, esp discoloration resulting from corrosion ▷ n stainless steel

STAINS > STAIN

STAIR n one step in a flight of stairs

STAIRCASE n flight of stairs with a handrail or banisters ▷ vb buy different houses in the same building

STAIRED adj having stairs

STAIRFOOT n place at foot of stairs

STAIRHEAD n top of a flight of stairs

STAIRLESS > STAIR

STAIRLIFT n wall-mounted lifting device to carry person up stairs

STAIRLIKE > STAIR

STAIRS pl n flight of steps between floors, usu indoors

STAIRSTEP n one of the steps in a staircase

STAIRWAY n staircase

STAIRWAYS > STAIRWAY

STAIRWELL n vertical shaft in a building that contains a staircase

STAIRWISE adv by steps

STAIRWORK n unseen plotting

STATTH *same as*
> STAITHE
STAITHE *n* wharf
STAITHES > STAITHE
STAITHS > STAITH
STAKE *n* pointed stick or post driven into the ground as a support or marker ▷ *vb* support or mark out with stakes
STAKED > STAKE
STAKEOUT *n* police surveillance of an area or house ▷ *vb* keep an area or house under surveillance
STAKEOUTS
> STAKEOUT
STAKER *n* person who marks off an area with stakes
STAKERS > STAKER
STAKES > STAKE
STAKING > STAKE
STALACTIC *adj* relating to the masses of calcium carbonate hanging from the roofs of limestone caves
STALAG *n* German prisoner-of-war camp
STALAGMA *n* stalagmite
STALAGMAS
> STALAGMA
STALAGS > STALAG
STALE *adj* not fresh ▷ *vb* make or become stale ▷ *n* urine of horses or cattle
STALED > STALE
STALELY > STALE
STALEMATE *n* (in chess) position in which any of a player's moves would put their king in check, resulting in a draw ▷ *vb* subject to a stalemate
STALENESS > STALE
STALER > STALE
STALES > STALE
STALEST > STALE
STALING > STALE
STALK *n* plant's stem ▷ *vb* follow or approach stealthily
STALKED > STALK
STALKER > STALK
STALKERS > STALK
STALKIER > STALKY
STALKIEST > STALKY
STALKILY > STALKY
STALKING > STALK
STALKINGS > STALK
STALKLESS > STALK
STALKLIKE > STALK
STALKO *n* idle gentleman
STALKOES > STALKO
STALKOS > STALKO
STALKS > STALK
STALKY *adj* like a stalk
STALL *n* small stand for the display and sale of goods ▷ *vb* (of a motor vehicle or engine) stop accidentally
STALLAGE *n* rent paid for market stall
STALLAGES
> STALLAGE
STALLED > STALL

STALLING > STALL
STALLINGS > STALL
STALLION *n* uncastrated male horse
STALLIONS
> STALLION
STALLMAN *n* keeper of a stall
STALLMEN > STALLMAN
STALLS > STALL
STALWART *adj* strong and sturdy ▷ *n* stalwart person
STALWARTS
> STALWART
STALWORTH *n* stalwart person
STAMEN *n* pollen-producing part of a flower
STAMENED *adj* having stamen
STAMENS > STAMEN
STAMINA *n* enduring energy and strength
STAMINAL > STAMINA
STAMINAS > STAMINA
STAMINATE *adj* (of plants) having stamens, esp having stamens but no carpels
STAMINEAL *adj* having a stamen
STAMINODE *n* stamen that produces no pollen
STAMINODY *n* development of any of various plant organs into stamens
STAMINOID *adj* like a stamen
STAMMEL *n* coarse woollen cloth in former use for undergarments
STAMMELS > STAMMEL
STAMMER *vb* speak or say with involuntary pauses or repetition of syllables ▷ *n* tendency to stammer
STAMMERED > STAMMER
STAMMERER > STAMMER
STAMMERS > STAMMER
STAMNOI > STAMNOS
STAMNOS *n* ancient Greek jar
STAMP *n* piece of gummed paper stuck to an envelope or parcel ▷ *vb* bring (one's foot) down forcefully
STAMPED > STAMP
STAMPEDE *n* sudden rush of frightened animals or of a crowd ▷ *vb* (cause to) take part in a stampede
STAMPEDED
> STAMPEDE
STAMPEDER
> STAMPEDE
STAMPEDES
> STAMPEDE
STAMPEDO *same as*
> STAMPEDE
STAMPEDOS
> STAMPEDO
STAMPER > STAMP
STAMPERS > STAMP
STAMPING > STAMP
STAMPINGS > STAMP
STAMPLESS > STAMP

STAMPS > STAMP
STANCE *n* attitude
STANCES > STANCE
STANCH *vb* stem the flow of (a liquid, esp blood) ▷ *adj* loyal and dependable
STANCHED > STANCH
STANCHEL *same as*
> STANCHION
STANCHELS
> STANCHEL
STANCHER > STANCH
STANCHERS > STANCH
STANCHES > STANCH
STANCHEST > STANCH
STANCHING > STANCH
STANCHION *n* upright bar used as a support ▷ *vb* provide or support with a stanchion or stanchions
STANCHLY > STANCH
STANCK *adj* faint
STAND *vb* be in, rise to, or place in an upright position ▷ *n* stall for the sale of goods
STANDARD *n* level of quality ▷ *adj* usual, regular, or average
STANDARDS
> STANDARD
STANDAWAY *adj* erect
STANDBY *n* person or thing that is ready for use
STANDBYS > STANDBY
STANDDOWN *n* return to normal after alert
STANDEE *n* person who stands
STANDEES > STANDEE
STANDEN > STAND
STANDER > STAND
STANDERS > STAND
STANDFAST *n* reliable person or thing
STANDGALE *same as*
> STANIEL
STANDING > STAND
STANDINGS > STAND
STANDISH *n* stand, usually of metal, for pens, ink bottles, etc
STANDOFF *n* act or an instance of standing off or apart ▷ *vb* stay at a distance
STANDOFFS
> STANDOFF
STANDOUT *n* distinctive or outstanding person or thing
STANDOUTS
> STANDOUT
STANDOVER *n* threatening or intimidating act
STANDPAT *n* (in poker) refusal to change one's card
STANDPIPE *n* tap attached to a water main to provide a public water supply
STANDS > STAND
STANDUP *n* comedian who performs solo
STANDUPS > STANDUP

STANE *Scot word for*
> STONE
STANED > STANE
STANES > STANE
STANG *vb* sting
STANGED > STANG
STANGING > STANG
STANGS > STANG
STANHOPE *n* light one-seater carriage with two or four wheels
STANHOPES
> STANHOPE
STANIEL *n* kestrel
STANIELS > STANIEL
STANINE *n* scale of nine levels
STANINES > STANINE
STANING > STANE
STANK *vb* dam
STANKED > STANK
STANKING > STANK
STANKS > STANK
STANNARY *n* place or region where tin is mined or worked
STANNATE *n* salt of stannic acid
STANNATES
> STANNATE
STANNATOR *n* member of old Cornish parliament
STANNEL *same as*
> STANIEL
STANNELS > STANNEL
STANNIC *adj* of or containing tin, esp in the tetravalent state
STANNITE *n* grey metallic mineral
STANNITES
> STANNITE
STANNOUS *adj* of or containing tin, esp in the divalent state
STANNUM *n* tin (the metal)
STANNUMS > STANNUM
STANOL *n* drug taken to prevent heart disease
STANOLS > STANOL
STANYEL *same as*
> STANIEL
STANYELS > STANYEL
STANZA *n* verse of a poem
STANZAED > STANZA
STANZAIC > STANZA
STANZAS > STANZA
STANZE *same as*
> STANZA
STANZES > STANZE
STANZO *same as*
> STANZA
STANZOES > STANZO
STANZOS > STANZO
STAP *same as* > STOP
STAPEDES > STAPES
STAPEDIAL > STAPES
STAPEDII
> STAPEDIUS
STAPEDIUS *n* muscle in the stapes
STAPELIA *n* fleshy cactus-like leafless African plant
STAPELIAS
> STAPELIA

S

STAPES *n* stirrup-shaped bone in the middle ear of mammals

STAPH *n* staphylococcus

STAPHS > STAPH

STAPLE *n* U-shaped piece of metal used to fasten papers ▷ *vb* fasten with staples ▷ *adj* of prime importance

STAPLED > STAPLE

STAPLER *n* small device for fastening papers together

STAPLERS > STAPLER

STAPLES > STAPLE

STAPLING *n* as in *stomach stapling* surgical treatment for obesity

STAPLINGS > STAPLING

STAPPED > STAP

STAPPING > STAP

STAPPLE *same as* > STOPPLE

STAPPLES > STAPPLE

STAPS > STAP

STAR *n* hot gaseous mass in space, visible in the night sky as a point of light ▷ *vb* feature or be featured as a star ▷ *adj* leading, famous

STARAGEN *n* tarragon

STARAGENS > STARAGEN

STARBOARD *n* right-hand side of a ship, when facing forward ▷ *adj* of or on this side ▷ *vb* turn or be turned towards the starboard

STARBURST *n* pattern of rays or lines radiating from a light source

STARCH *n* carbohydrate forming the main food element in bread, potatoes, etc ▷ *vb* stiffen (fabric) with starch ▷ *adj* (of a person) formal

STARCHED > STARCH

STARCHER > STARCH

STARCHERS > STARCH

STARCHES > STARCH

STARCHIER > STARCHY

STARCHILY > STARCHY

STARCHING > STARCH

STARCHY *adj* containing starch

STARDOM *n* status of a star in the entertainment or sports world

STARDOMS > STARDOM

STARDRIFT *n* regular movement of stars

STARDUST *n* dusty material found between the stars

STARDUSTS > STARDUST

STARE *vb* look or gaze fixedly (at) ▷ *n* fixed gaze

STARED > STARE

STARER > STARE

STARERS > STARE

STARES > STARE

STARETS *n* Russian holy man

STARETSES > STARETS

STARETZ *same as* > STARETS

STARETZES > STARETZ

STARFISH *n* star-shaped sea creature

STARFRUIT *n* tree with edible yellow fruit which is star-shaped on cross section

STARGAZE *vb* observe the stars

STARGAZED > STARGAZE

STARGAZER > STARGAZE

STARGAZES > STARGAZE

STARGAZEY *adj* as in *stargazey pie* Cornish fish pie

STARING > STARE

STARINGLY > STARE

STARINGS > STARE

STARK *adj* harsh, unpleasant, and plain ▷ *adv* completely ▷ *vb* stiffen

STARKED > STARK

STARKEN *vb* become or make stark

STARKENED > STARKEN

STARKENS > STARKEN

STARKER > STARK

STARKERS *adj* completely naked

STARKEST > STARK

STARKING > STARK

STARKLY > STARK

STARKNESS > STARK

STARKS > STARK

STARLESS > STAR

STARLET *n* young actress presented as a future star

STARLETS > STARLET

STARLIGHT *n* light that comes from the stars ▷ *adj* of or like starlight

STARLIKE > STAR

STARLING *n* songbird with glossy black speckled feathers

STARLINGS > STARLING

STARLIT *same as* > STARLIGHT

STARN *same as* > STERN

STARNED > STARN

STARNIE *n* Scots word for little star

STARNIES > STARNIE

STARNING > STARN

STARNOSE *n* American mole with starlike nose

STARNOSES > STARNOSE

STARNS > STARN

STAROSTA *n* headman of Russian village

STAROSTAS > STAROSTA

STAROSTY *n* estate of Polish nobleman

STARR *n* (in Judaism) release from a debt

STARRED > STAR

STARRIER > STARRY

STARRIEST > STARRY

STARRILY > STARRY

STARRING > STAR

STARRINGS > STARE

STARRS > STARR

STARRY *adj* full of or like stars

STARS > STAR

STARSHINE *n* starlight

STARSHIP *n* spacecraft in science fiction

STARSHIPS > STARSHIP

STARSPOT *n* dark patch on surface of star

STARSPOTS > STARSPOT

STARSTONE *n* precious stone reflecting light in starlike pattern

START *vb* take the first step, begin ▷ *n* first part of something

STARTED > START

STARTER *n* first course of a meal

STARTERS > STARTER

STARTFUL *adj* tending to start

STARTING > START

STARTINGS > START

STARTISH *same as* > STARTFUL

STARTLE *vb* slightly surprise or frighten

STARTLED > STARTLE

STARTLER > STARTLE

STARTLERS > STARTLE

STARTLES > STARTLE

STARTLIER > STARTLY

STARTLING *adj* causing surprise or fear

STARTLISH *adj* easily startled

STARTLY *adj* (of a horse) prone to starting

STARTS > START

STARTSY > STARETS

STARTUP *n* business enterprise that has been launched recently

STARTUPS > STARTUP

STARVE *vb* die or suffer or cause to die or suffer from hunger

STARVED > STARVE

STARVER > STARVE

STARVERS > STARVE

STARVES > STARVE

STARVING > STARVE

STARVINGS > STARVE

STARWORT *n* plant with star-shaped flowers

STARWORTS > STARWORT

STASES > STASIS

STASH *vb* store in a secret place ▷ *n* secret store

STASHED > STASH

STASHES > STASH

STASHIE *same as* > STUSHIE

STASHIES > STASHIE

STASHING > STASH

STASIDION *n* stall in Greek church

STASIMA > STASIMON

STASIMON *n* ode sung in Greek tragedy

STASIS *n* stagnation in the normal flow of bodily fluids

STAT *n* statistic

STATABLE > STATE

STATAL *adj* of a federal state

STATANT *adj* (of an animal) in profile with all four feet on the ground

STATE *n* condition of a person or thing ▷ *adj* of or concerning the State ▷ *vb* express in words

STATEABLE > STATE

STATED *adj* (esp of a sum) determined by agreement

STATEDLY > STATED

STATEHOOD > STATE

STATELESS *adj* not belonging to any country

STATELET *n* small state

STATELETS > STATELET

STATELIER > STATELY

STATELILY > STATELY

STATELY *adj* dignified or grand ▷ *adv* in a stately manner

STATEMENT *n* something stated ▷ *vb* assess (a pupil) with regard to his or her special educational needs

STATER *n* any of various usually silver coins of ancient Greece

STATEROOM *n* private cabin on a ship

STATERS > STATER

STATES > STATE

STATESIDE *adv* of, in, to, or towards the US

STATESMAN *n* experienced and respected political leader

STATESMEN > STATESMAN

STATEWIDE *adj* throughout a state

STATIC *adj* stationary or inactive ▷ *n* crackling sound or speckled picture caused by interference in radio or TV reception

STATICAL > STATIC

STATICE *n* plant name formerly used for both thrift and sea lavender

STATICES > STATICE

STATICKY *adj* characterized by static

STATICS *n* study of the forces producing a state of equilibrium

STATIM *adv* right away

STATIN *n* type of drug that lowers the levels of low-density lipoproteins in the blood

STATING > STATE

STATINS > STATIN

STATION *n* place where trains stop for passengers ▷ *vb* assign (someone) to a particular place

STATIONAL > STATION

STATIONED > STATION

STATIONER *n* dealer in stationery

STATIONS > STATION

STATISM n theory or practice of concentrating economic and political power in the state

STATISMS > STATISM

STATIST n advocate of statism ▷ adj of, characteristic of, advocating, or relating to statism

STATISTIC n numerical fact collected and classified systematically

STATISTS > STATIST

STATIVE adj denoting a verb describing a state rather than an activity, act, or event ▷ n stative verb

STATIVES > STATIVE

STATOCYST n organ of balance in some invertebrates

STATOLITH n any of the granules of calcium carbonate occurring in a statocyst

STATOR n stationary part of a rotary machine or device

STATORS > STATOR

STATS > STAT

STATTO n person preoccupied with the facts and figures of a subject

STATTOS > STATTO

STATUA same as > STATUE

STATUARY n statues collectively ▷ adj of, relating to, or suitable for statues

STATUAS > STATUA

STATUE n large sculpture of a human or animal figure

STATUED adj decorated with or portrayed in a statue or statues

STATUES > STATUE

STATUETTE n small statue

STATURE n person's height

STATURED adj having stature

STATURES > STATURE

STATUS n social position

STATUSES > STATUS

STATUSIER > STATUSY

STATUSY adj conferring or having status

STATUTE n written law

STATUTES > STATUTE

STATUTORY adj required or authorized by law

STAUMREL n stupid person

STAUMRELS > STAUMREL

STAUN Scot word for > STAND

STAUNCH same as > STANCH

STAUNCHED > STAUNCH

STAUNCHER > STAUNCH

STAUNCHES > STAUNCH

STAUNCHLY > STAUNCH

STAUNING > STAUN

STAUNS > STAUN

STAVE same as > STAFF

STAVED > STAVE

STAVES > STAVE

STAVING > STAVE

STAVUDINE n drug used to treat HIV

STAW Scots form of > STALL

STAWED > STAW

STAWING > STAW

STAWS > STAW

STAY vb remain in a place or condition ▷ n period of staying in a place

STAYAWAY n strike in South Africa

STAYAWAYS > STAYAWAY

STAYED > STAY

STAYER n person or thing that stays

STAYERS > STAYER

STAYING > STAY

STAYLESS adj with no stays or support

STAYMAKER n corset maker

STAYNE same as > STAIN

STAYNED > STAYNE

STAYNES > STAYNE

STAYNING > STAYNE

STAYRE same as > STAIR

STAYRES > STAYRE

STAYS pl n old-fashioned corsets with bones in them

STAYSAIL n sail fastened on a stay

STAYSAILS > STAYSAIL

STEAD n place or function that should be taken by another ▷ vb help or benefit

STEADED > STEAD

STEADFAST adj firm, determined

STEADIED > STEADY

STEADIER > STEADY

STEADIERS > STEADY

STEADIES > STEADY

STEADIEST > STEADY

STEADILY > STEADY

STEADING n farmstead

STEADINGS > STEADING

STEADS > STEAD

STEADY adj not shaky or wavering ▷ vb make steady ▷ adv in a steady manner

STEADYING > STEADY

STEAK n thick slice of meat, esp beef

STEAKETTE n thin minced beef patty

STEAKS > STEAK

STEAL vb take unlawfully or without permission

STEALABLE > STEAL

STEALAGE n theft

STEALAGES > STEALAGE

STEALE n handle

STEALED > STEAL

STEALER n person who steals something

STEALERS > STEALER

STEALES > STEALE

STEALING > STEAL

STEALINGS > STEAL

STEALS > STEAL

STEALT > STEAL

STEALTH n moving carefully and quietly ▷ adj (of technology) able to render an aircraft almost invisible to radar ▷ vb approach undetected

STEALTHED > STEALTH

STEALTHS > STEALTH

STEALTHY adj characterized by great caution, secrecy, etc

STEAM n vapour into which water changes when boiled ▷ vb give off steam

STEAMBOAT n boat powered by a steam engine

STEAMED > STEAM

STEAMER n steam-propelled ship ▷ vb travel by steamer

STEAMERED > STEAMER

STEAMERS > STEAMER

STEAMIE n public wash house

STEAMIER > STEAMY

STEAMIES > STEAMIE

STEAMIEST > STEAMY

STEAMILY > STEAMY

STEAMING adj very hot ▷ n robbery by a large gang of youths

STEAMINGS > STEAMING

STEAMPUNK n subgenre of science fiction set in Victorian times

STEAMROLL vb crush (opposition) by overpowering force

STEAMS > STEAM

STEAMSHIP n ship powered by steam engines

STEAMY adj full of steam

STEAN n earthenware vessel

STEANE same as > STEEN

STEANED > STEANE

STEANES > STEANE

STEANING > STEANE

STEANINGS > STEANE

STEANS > STEAN

STEAPSIN n pancreatic lipase

STEAPSINS > STEAPSIN

STEAR same as > STEER

STEARAGE same as > STEERAGE

STEARAGES > STEERAGE

STEARATE n any salt or ester of stearic acid

STEARATES > STEARATE

STEARD > STEAR

STEARE same as > STEER

STEARED > STEARE

STEARES > STEARE

STEARIC adj of or relating to suet or fat

STEARIN n colourless crystalline ester of glycerol and stearic acid

STEARINE same as > STEARIN

STEARINES > STEARINE

STEARING > STEAR

STEARINS > STEARIN

STEARS > STEAR

STEARSMAN same as > STEERSMAN

STEARSMEN > STEARSMAN

STEATITE same as > SOAPSTONE

STEATITES > STEATITE

STEATITIC > STEATITE

STEATOMA n tumour of sebaceous gland

STEATOMAS > STEATOMA

STEATOSES > STEATOSIS

STEATOSIS n abnormal accumulation of fat

STED same as > STEAD

STEDD same as > STEAD

STEDDE same as > STEAD

STEDDED > STED

STEDDES > STEDDE

STEDDIED > STEDDY

STEDDIES > STEDDY

STEDDING > STED

STEDDS > STEDD

STEDDY same as > STEADY

STEDDYING > STEDDY

STEDE same as > STEAD

STEDED > STEDE

STEDES > STEDE

STEDFAST same as > STEADFAST

STEDING > STEDE

STEDS > STED

STEED same as > STEAD

STEEDED > STEED

STEEDIED > STEEDY

STEEDIES > STEEDY

STEEDING > STEED

STEEDLIKE > STEED

STEEDS > STEED

STEEDY same as > STEADY

STEEDYING > STEEDY

STEEK vb Scots word meaning shut

STEEKED > STEEK

STEEKING > STEEK

STEEKIT > STEEK

STEEKS > STEEK

STEEL n hard malleable alloy of iron and carbon ▷ vb prepare (oneself) for something unpleasant

STEELBOW n material lent to tenant by landlord

STEELBOWS > STEELBOW

STEELD > STEEL

STEELED > STEEL

STEELHEAD n silvery North Pacific variety of the rainbow trout

STEELIE n steel ball bearing used as marble

S

STEELIER > STEEL
STEELIES > STEELIE
STEELIEST > STEELIE
STEELING > STEEL
STEELINGS > STEEL
STEELMAN n man working in the steel industry
STEELMEN > STEELMAN
STEELS pl n shares and bonds of steel companies
STEELWARE n things made of steel
STEELWORK n frame, foundation, building, or article made of steel
STEELY > STEEL
STEELYARD n portable balance consisting of a pivoted bar with two unequal arms
STEEM variant of > ESTEEM
STEEMED > STEEM
STEEMING > STEEM
STEEMS > STEEM
STEEN vb line with stone
STEENBOK n small antelope of central and southern Africa
STEENBOKS > STEENBOK
STEENBRAS n variety of sea bream
STEENBUCK same as > STEENBOK
STEENED > STEEN
STEENING > STEEN
STEENINGS > STEEN
STEENKIRK n type of cravat
STEENS > STEEN
STEEP adj sloping sharply ▷ vb soak or be soaked in liquid ▷ n instance or the process of steeping
STEEPED > STEEP
STEEPEN vb become steep or steeper
STEEPENED > STEEPEN
STEEPENS > STEEPEN
STEEPER > STEEP
STEEPERS > STEEP
STEEPEST > STEEP
STEEPEUP adj very steep
STEEPIER > STEEPY
STEEPIEST > STEEPY
STEEPING > STEEP
STEEPISH > STEEP
STEEPLE same as > SPIRE
STEEPLED > STEEPLE
STEEPLES > STEEPLE
STEEPLING adj going up on a steep trajectory
STEEPLY > STEEP
STEEPNESS > STEEP
STEEPS > STEEP
STEEPUP adj very steep
STEEPY same as > STEEP
STEER vb direct the course of (a vehicle or ship) ▷ n castrated male ox
STEERABLE > STEER
STEERAGE n cheapest accommodation on a passenger ship

STEERAGES > STEERAGE
STEERED > STEER
STEERER > STEER
STEERERS > STEER
STEERIER > STEERY
STEERIES > STEERY
STEERIEST > STEERY
STEERING > STEER
STEERINGS > STEER
STEERLING n young steer
STEERS > STEER
STEERSMAN n person who steers a vessel
STEERSMEN > STEERSMAN
STEERY n commotion ▷ adj busy or bustling
STEEVE n spar having a pulley block at one end ▷ vb stow (cargo) securely in the hold of a ship
STEEVED > STEEVE
STEEVELY > STEEVE
STEEVER > STEEVE
STEEVES > STEEVE
STEEVEST > STEEVE
STEEVING > STEEVE
STEEVINGS > STEEVE
STEGNOSES > STEGNOSIS
STEGNOSIS n constriction of bodily pores
STEGNOTIC n medicine that stops bleeding
STEGODON n mammal of Pliocene to Pleistocene times, similar to the mastodon
STEGODONS > STEGODON
STEGODONT same as > STEGODON
STEGOMYIA former name for > AEDES
STEGOSAUR n quadrupedal herbivorous dinosaur
STEIL same as > STEAL
STEILS > STEIL
STEIN same as > STEEN
STEINBOCK another name for > IBEX
STEINBOK same as > STEENBOK
STEINBOKS > STEINBOK
STEINED > STEIN
STEINING > STEIN
STEININGS > STEIN
STEINKIRK same as > STEENKIRK
STEINS > STEIN
STELA same as > STELE
STELAE > STELA
STELAI > STELA
STELAR > STELE
STELE n upright stone slab or column decorated with figures or inscriptions
STELENE > STELE
STELES > STELE
STELIC > STELE
STELL n shelter for cattle or sheep built on moorland or hillsides ▷ vb position or place

STELLA n star or something star-shaped
STELLAR adj of stars
STELLAS > STELLA
STELLATE adj resembling a star in shape
STELLATED same as > STELLATE
STELLED > STELL
STELLERID n starfish
STELLIFY vb change or be changed into a star
STELLING > STELL
STELLIO n as in stellio lizard type of lizard
STELLION n Mediterranean lizard
STELLIONS > STELLION
STELLITE n alloy containing cobalt, chromium, carbon, tungsten, and molybdenum
STELLITES > STELLITE
STELLS > STELL
STELLULAR adj displaying or abounding in small stars
STEM vb stop (the flow of something) ▷ n main axis of a plant, which bears the leaves, axillary buds, and flowers
STEMBOK same as > STEENBOK
STEMBOKS > STEMBOK
STEMBUCK same as > STEENBOK
STEMBUCKS > STEMBUCK
STEME same as > STEAM
STEMED > STEME
STEMES > STEME
STEMHEAD n head of the stem of a vessel
STEMHEADS > STEMHEAD
STEMING > STEME
STEMLESS > STEM
STEMLET n little stem
STEMLETS > STEMLET
STEMLIKE > STEM
STEMMA n family tree
STEMMAS > STEMMA
STEMMATA > STEMMA
STEMMATIC > STEMMA
STEMME archaic variant of > STEM
STEMMED > STEM
STEMMER > STEM
STEMMERS > STEM
STEMMERY n tobacco factory
STEMMES > STEMME
STEMMIER > STEMMY
STEMMIEST > STEMMY
STEMMING > STEM
STEMMINGS > STEM
STEMMY adj (of wine) young and raw
STEMPEL n timber support
STEMPELS > STEMPEL
STEMPLE same as > STEMPEL
STEMPLES > STEMPLE

STEMS > STEM
STEMSON n curved timber at the bow of a wooden vessel
STEMSONS > STEMSON
STEMWARE n collective term for glasses, goblets, etc with stems
STEMWARES > STEMWARE
STEN vb stride
STENCH n foul smell ▷ vb cause to smell
STENCHED > STENCH
STENCHES > STENCH
STENCHFUL > STENCH
STENCHIER > STENCH
STENCHING > STENCH
STENCHY > STENCH
STENCIL n thin sheet through which ink passes to form a pattern on the surface below ▷ vb make (a pattern) with a stencil
STENCILED > STENCIL
STENCILER > STENCIL
STENCILS > STENCIL
STEND vb Scots word meaning bound
STENDED > STEND
STENDING > STEND
STENDS > STEND
STENGAH same as > STINGER
STENGAHS > STENGAH
STENLOCK n fish of northern seas
STENLOCKS > STENLOCK
STENNED > STEN
STENNING > STEN
STENO n stenographer
STENOBATH n stenobathic organism
STENOKIES > STENOKY
STENOKOUS adj able to live in narrow range of environments
STENOKY n survival dependent on conditions remaining within a narrow range of variables
STENOPAIC adj having a narrow opening
STENOS > STENO
STENOSED adj abnormally contracted
STENOSES > STENOSIS
STENOSING adj causing or characterized by stenosis
STENOSIS n abnormal narrowing of a bodily canal or passage
STENOTIC > STENOSIS
STENOTYPE n machine with a keyboard for recording speeches in a phonetic shorthand
STENOTYPY n form of shorthand in which alphabetic combinations are used to represent groups of sounds or short common words
STENS > STEN
STENT n surgical implant used to keep an artery open ▷ vb assess

STENTED > STENT
STENTING > STENT
STENTOR *n* person with an unusually loud voice
STENTORS > STENTOR
STENTOUR *n* tax assessor
STENTOURS > STENTOUR
STENTS > STENT
STEP *vb* move and set down the foot, as when walking ▷ *n* stepping
STEPBAIRN *Scots word for* > STEPCHILD
STEPCHILD *n* stepson or stepdaughter
STEPDAD *n* stepfather
STEPDADS > STEPDAD
STEPDAME *n* old word for a stepmother
STEPDAMES > STEPDAME
STEPHANE *n* ancient Greek headdress
STEPHANES > STEPHANE
STEPLESS *adj* without steps
STEPLIKE > STEP
STEPMOM *n* stepmother
STEPMOMS > STEPMOM
STEPNEY *n* spare wheel
STEPNEYS > STEPNEY
STEPOVER *n* (in football) instance of raising the foot over the ball as a feint
STEPOVERS > STEPOVER
STEPPE *n* extensive grassy plain usually without trees
STEPPED > STEP
STEPPER *n* person who or animal that steps, esp a horse or a dancer
STEPPERS > STEPPER
STEPPES > STEPPE
STEPPING > STEP
STEPS > STEP
STEPSON *n* son of one's spouse by an earlier relationship
STEPSONS > STEPSON
STEPSTOOL *n* stool able to be used as step
STEPT > STEP
STEPWISE *adj* arranged in the manner of or resembling steps ▷ *adv* with the form or appearance of steps
STERADIAN *n* SI unit of solid angle
STERANE *n* any of a class of hydrocarbons found in crude oils
STERANES > STERANE
STERCORAL *adj* relating to excrement
STERCULIA *n* dietary fibre used as a food stabilizer and denture adhesive
STERE *n* unit used to measure volumes of stacked timber
STEREO *n* stereophonic record player ▷ *adj* feeding

two loudspeakers through separate channels ▷ *vb* make stereophonic
STEREOED > STEREO
STEREOING > STEREO
STEREOME *n* tissue of a plant that provides mechanical support
STEREOMES > STEREOME
STEREOS > STEREO
STERES > STERE
STERIC *adj* of or caused by the spatial arrangement of atoms in a molecule
STERICAL *same as* > STERIC
STERIGMA *n* minute stalk bearing a spore or chain of spores in certain fungi
STERIGMAS > STERIGMA
STERILANT *n* any substance or agent used in sterilization
STERILE *adj* free from germs
STERILELY > STERILE
STERILISE *same as* > STERILIZE
STERILITY > STERILE
STERILIZE *vb* make sterile
STERLET *n* small sturgeon of N Asia and E Europe
STERLETS > STERLET
STERLING *n* British money system ▷ *adj* genuine and reliable
STERLINGS > STERLING
STERN *adj* severe, strict ▷ *n* rear part of a ship ▷ *vb* row boat backward
STERNA > STERNUM
STERNAGE *n* sterns
STERNAGES > STERNAGE
STERNAL > STERNUM
STERNEBRA *n* part of breastbone
STERNED > STERN
STERNER > STERN
STERNEST > STERN
STERNFAST *n* rope for securing boat at stern
STERNING > STERN
STERNITE *n* part of an arthropod
STERNITES > STERNITE
STERNITIC > STERNITE
STERNLY > STERN
STERNMOST *adj* farthest to the stern
STERNNESS > STERN
STERNPORT *n* opening in stern of ship
STERNPOST *n* main upright timber or structure at the stern of a vessel
STERNS > STERN
STERNSON *n* timber bolted to the sternpost

and keelson at the stern of a wooden vessel
STERNSONS > STERNSON
STERNUM *n* long flat bone to which most of the ribs are attached
STERNUMS > STERNUM
STERNWARD *adv* towards the stern
STERNWAY *n* movement of a vessel sternforemost
STERNWAYS > STERNWAY
STEROID *n* organic compound containing a carbon ring system
STEROIDAL > STEROID
STEROIDS > STEROID
STEROL *n* natural insoluble alcohol such as cholesterol and ergosterol
STEROLS > STEROL
STERTOR *n* laborious or noisy breathing
STERTORS > STERTOR
STERVE *same as* > STARVE
STERVED > STERVE
STERVES > STERVE
STERVING > STERVE
STET *interj* instruction to ignore an alteration previously made ▷ *vb* indicate to a printer that deleted matter is to be kept ▷ *n* mark indicating that deleted matter is to be kept
STETS > STET
STETSON *n* cowboy hat
STETSONS > STETSON
STETTED > STET
STETTING > STET
STEVEDORE *n* person who loads and unloads ships ▷ *vb* load or unload (a ship, ship's cargo, etc)
STEVEN *n* voice
STEVENS > STEVEN
STEVIA *n* any of a genus of plant with sweet leaves
STEVIAS > STEVIA
STEW *n* food cooked slowly in a closed pot ▷ *vb* cook slowly in a closed pot
STEWABLE > STEW
STEWARD *n* person who looks after passengers on a ship or aircraft ▷ *vb* act as a steward (of)
STEWARDED > STEWARD
STEWARDRY *n* office of steward
STEWARDS > STEWARD
STEWARTRY *variant of* > STEWARDRY
STEWBUM *n* drunkard
STEWBUMS > STEWBUM
STEWED *adj* (of food) cooked by stewing
STEWER > STEW
STEWERS > STEW
STEWIER > STEW
STEWIEST > STEW
STEWING > STEW
STEWINGS > STEW

STEWPAN *n* pan used for making stew
STEWPANS > STEWPAN
STEWPOND *n* fishpond
STEWPONDS > STEWPOND
STEWPOT *n* pot used for making stew
STEWPOTS > STEWPOT
STEWS > STEW
STEWY > STEW
STEY *adj* (Scots) steep ▷ *n* ladder
STEYER > STEY
STEYEST > STEY
STEYS > STEY
STHENIA *n* abnormal strength
STHENIAS > STHENIA
STHENIC *adj* abounding in energy or bodily strength
STIBBLE *Scots form of* > STUBBLE
STIBBLER *n* horse allowed to eat stubble
STIBBLERS > STIBBLE
STIBBLES > STIBBLE
STIBIAL > STIBIUM
STIBINE *n* colourless slightly soluble poisonous gas
STIBINES > STIBINE
STIBIUM *obsolete name for* > ANTIMONY
STIBIUMS > STIBIUM
STIBNITE *n* soft greyish mineral
STIBNITES > STIBNITE
STICCADO *n* type of xylophone
STICCADOS > STICCADO
STICCATO *same as* > STICCADO
STICCATOS > STICCADO
STICH *n* line of poetry
STICHARIA *pl n* priest's robes of the Greek Church
STICHERA > STICHERON
STICHERON *n* short hymn in the Greek Church
STICHIC > STICH
STICHIDIA *pl n* seaweed branches
STICHOI > STICHOS
STICHOS *n* line of poem
STICHS > STICH
STICK *n* long thin piece of wood ▷ *vb* push (a pointed object) into (something)
STICKABLE > STICK
STICKBALL *n* form of baseball played in the street
STICKED > STICK
STICKER *n* adhesive label or sign ▷ *vb* put stickers on
STICKERED > STICKER
STICKERS > STICKER
STICKFUL > STICK
STICKFULS > STICK
STICKIE *n* notepaper with an adhesive strip
STICKIED > STICKY

STICKIER > STICKY
STICKIES > STICKIE
STICKIEST > STICKY
STICKILY > STICKY
STICKING > STICK
STICKINGS > STICK
STICKIT *Scots form of* > STUCK
STICKJAW *n* stodgy food
STICKJAWS > STICKJAW
STICKLE *vb* dispute stubbornly, esp about minor points
STICKLED > STICKLE
STICKLER *n* person who insists on something
STICKLERS > STICKLER
STICKLES > STICKLE
STICKLIKE > STICK
STICKLING *n* act of making insistent demands
STICKMAN *n* human figure drawn in thin strokes
STICKMEN > STICKMAN
STICKOUT *n* conspicuous person or thing
STICKOUTS > STICKOUT
STICKPIN *n* tiepin
STICKPINS > STICKPIN
STICKS > STICK
STICKSEED *n* type of Eurasian and North American plant
STICKUM *n* adhesive
STICKUMS > STICKUM
STICKUP *n* robbery at gun-point
STICKUPS > STICKUP
STICKWEED *n* any of several plants that have clinging fruits or seeds, esp the ragweed
STICKWORK *n* use of stick in hockey
STICKY *adj* covered with an adhesive substance ▷ *vb* make sticky ▷ *n* inquisitive look or stare
STICKYING > STICKY
STICTION *n* frictional force to be overcome to set one object in motion when it is in contact with another
STICTIONS > STICTION
STIDDIE *same as* > STITHY
STIDDIED > STIDDIE
STIDDIES > STIDDIE
STIE *same as* > STY
STIED > STY
STIES > STY
STIEVE *same as* > STEEVE
STIEVELY > STIEVE
STIEVER > STIEVE
STIEVEST > STIEVE
STIFF *adj* not easily bent or moved ▷ *n* loser or failure ▷ *adv* completely or utterly ▷ *vb* fail completely

STIFFED > STIFF
STIFFEN *vb* make or become stiff
STIFFENED > STIFFEN
STIFFENER > STIFFEN
STIFFENS > STIFFEN
STIFFER > STIFF
STIFFEST > STIFF
STIFFIE *n* vulgar word for an erection of the penis
STIFFIES > STIFFIE
STIFFING > STIFF
STIFFISH > STIFF
STIFFLY > STIFF
STIFFNESS > STIFF
STIFFS > STIFF
STIFFWARE *n* computer software that is hard to modify
STIFFY *n* vulgar word for an erection of the penis
STIFLE *vb* suppress ▷ *n* joint in the hind leg of a horse, dog, etc
STIFLED > STIFLE
STIFLER > STIFLE
STIFLERS > STIFLE
STIFLES > STIFLE
STIFLING *adj* uncomfortably hot and stuffy
STIFLINGS > STIFLING
STIGMA *n* mark of social disgrace
STIGMAL *adj* of part of insect wing
STIGMAS > STIGMA
STIGMATA > STIGMA
STIGMATIC *adj* relating to or having a stigma or stigmata ▷ *n* person marked with the stigmata
STIGME *n* dot in Greek punctuation
STIGMES > STIGME
STILB *n* unit of luminance
STILBENE *n* colourless or slightly yellow crystalline hydrocarbon used in the manufacture of dyes
STILBENES > STILBENE
STILBITE *n* white or yellow zeolite mineral
STILBITES > STILBITE
STILBS > STILB
STILE *same as* > STYLE
STILED > STILE
STILES > STILE
STILET *same as* > STYLET
STILETS > STILET
STILETTO *n* small narrow dagger ▷ *vb* stab with a stiletto
STILETTOS > STILETTO
STILING > STILE
STILL *adv* now or in the future as before ▷ *adj* motionless ▷ *n* calmness; apparatus for distillation ▷ *vb* make still

STILLAGE *n* frame or stand for keeping things off the ground, such as casks in a brewery
STILLAGES > STILLAGE
STILLBORN *adj* born dead ▷ *n* stillborn fetus or baby
STILLED > STILL
STILLER > STILL
STILLERS > STILL
STILLEST > STILL
STILLIER > STILLY
STILLIEST > STILLY
STILLING > STILL
STILLINGS > STILL
STILLION *n* stand for cask
STILLIONS > STILLION
STILLMAN *n* someone involved in the operation of a still
STILLMEN > STILLMAN
STILLNESS > STILL
STILLROOM *n* room in which distilling is carried out
STILLS > STILL
STILLSON *n* type of wrench
STILLSONS > STILLSON
STILLY *adv* quietly or calmly ▷ *adj* still, quiet, or calm
STILT *n* either of a pair of long poles with footrests for walking raised from the ground ▷ *vb* raise or place on or as if on stilts
STILTBIRD *n* long-legged wading bird
STILTED *adj* stiff and formal in manner
STILTEDLY > STILTED
STILTER > STILT
STILTERS > STILT
STILTIER > STILT
STILTIEST > STILT
STILTING > STILT
STILTINGS > STILT
STILTISH > STILT
STILTLIKE *adj* like a stilt
STILTS > STILT
STILTY > STILT
STIM *n* very small amount
STIME *same as* > STYME
STIMED > STIME
STIMES > STIME
STIMIE *same as* > STYMIE
STIMIED > STIMIE
STIMIES > STIMIE
STIMING > STIME
STIMS > STIM
STIMULANT *n* something, such as a drug, that acts as a stimulus ▷ *adj* stimulating
STIMULATE *vb* act as a stimulus (on)
STIMULI > STIMULUS
STIMULUS *n* something that rouses a person or thing to activity

STIMY *same as* > STYMIE
STIMYING > STIMY
STING *vb* (of certain animals or plants) wound by injecting with poison ▷ *n* wound or pain caused by or as if by stinging
STINGAREE *popular name for* > STINGRAY
STINGBULL *n* spiny fish
STINGE *n* stingy or miserly person
STINGED > STING
STINGER *n* person, plant, animal, etc, that stings or hurts
STINGERS > STINGER
STINGES > STINGE
STINGFISH *same as* > STINGBULL
STINGIER > STINGY
STINGIES > STINGY
STINGIEST > STINGY
STINGILY > STINGY
STINGING > STING
STINGINGS > STING
STINGLESS > STING
STINGO *n* strong alcohol
STINGOS > STINGO
STINGRAY *n* flatfish capable of inflicting painful wounds
STINGRAYS > STINGRAY
STINGS > STING
STINGY *adj* mean or miserly ▷ *n* stinging nettle
STINK *n* strong unpleasant smell ▷ *vb* give off a strong unpleasant smell
STINKARD *n* smelly person
STINKARDS > STINKARD
STINKBIRD *same as* > HOATZIN
STINKBUG *n* type of insect that releases an unpleasant odour
STINKBUGS > STINKBUG
STINKER *n* difficult or unpleasant person or thing
STINKEROO *n* bad or contemptible person or thing
STINKERS > STINKER
STINKHORN *n* type of fungus with an offensive odour
STINKIER > STINKY
STINKIEST > STINKY
STINKING > STINK
STINKO *adj* drunk
STINKPOT *n* thing that stinks
STINKPOTS > STINKPOT
STINKS > STINK
STINKWEED *n* plant that has a disagreeable smell when bruised
STINKWOOD *n* any of various trees having offensive-smelling wood

STINKY *adj* having a foul smell
STINT *vb* be miserly with (something) ▷ *n* allotted amount of work
STINTED > STINT
STINTEDLY > STINT
STINTER > STINT
STINTERS > STINT
STINTIER > STINT
STINTIEST > STINT
STINTING > STINT
STINTINGS > STINT
STINTLESS > STINT
STINTS > STINT
STINTY > STINT
STIPA *n* variety of grass
STIPAS > STIPA
STIPE *n* stalk in plants that bears reproductive structures
STIPED *same as* > STIPITATE
STIPEL *n* small paired leaflike structure at the base of certain leaflets
STIPELS > STIPEL
STIPEND *n* regular allowance or salary
STIPENDS > STIPEND
STIPES *n* second maxillary segment in insects and crustaceans
STIPIFORM > STIPES
STIPITATE *adj* possessing or borne on the end of a stipe
STIPITES > STIPES
STIPPLE *vb* paint, draw, or engrave using dots ▷ *n* technique of stippling
STIPPLED > STIPPLE
STIPPLER > STIPPLE
STIPPLERS > STIPPLE
STIPPLES > STIPPLE
STIPPLING > STIPPLE
STIPULAR > STIPULE
STIPULARY > STIPULE
STIPULATE *vb* specify as a condition of an agreement ▷ *adj* (of a plant) having stipules
STIPULE *n* small paired usually leaflike outgrowth occurring at the base of a leaf or its stalk
STIPULED > STIPULE
STIPULES > STIPULE
STIR *vb* mix up (a liquid) by moving a spoon etc around in it ▷ *n* stirring
STIRABOUT *n* kind of porridge originally made in Ireland
STIRE *same as* > STEER
STIRED > STIRE
STIRES > STIRE
STIRING > STIRE
STIRK *n* heifer of 6 to 12 months old
STIRKS > STIRK
STIRLESS > STIR
STIRP *same as* > STIRPS
STIRPES > STIRPS
STIRPS *n* line of descendants from an ancestor
STIRRA *same as* > SIRRA

STIRRABLE > STIR
STIRRAH *same as* > SIRRAH
STIRRAHS > STIRRAH
STIRRAS > STIRRA
STIRRE *same as* > STEER
STIRRED > STIR
STIRRER *n* person who deliberately causes trouble
STIRRERS > STIRRER
STIRRES > STIRRE
STIRRING > STIR
STIRRINGS > STIR
STIRRUP *n* metal loop attached to a saddle for supporting a rider's foot
STIRRUPS > STIRRUP
STIRS > STIR
STISHIE *same as* > STUSHIE
STISHIES > STISHIE
STITCH *n* link made by drawing thread through material with a needle ▷ *vb* sew
STITCHED > STITCH
STITCHER > STITCH
STITCHERS > STITCH
STITCHERY *n* needlework, esp modern embroidery
STITCHES > STITCH
STITCHING > STITCH
STITHIED > STITHY
STITHIES > STITHY
STITHY *n* forge or anvil ▷ *vb* forge on an anvil
STITHYING > STITHY
STIVE *vb* stifle
STIVED > STIVE
STIVER *n* former Dutch coin
STIVERS > STIVER
STIVES > STIVE
STIVIER > STIVY
STIVIEST > STIVY
STIVING > STIVE
STIVY *adj* stuffy
STOA *n* covered walk that has a colonnade on one or both sides
STOAE > STOA
STOAI > STOA
STOAS > STOA
STOAT *n* small mammal of the weasel family
STOATS > STOAT
STOB *same as* > STAB
STOBBED > STOB
STOBBING > STOB
STOBIE *adj* as in *stobie pole* steel and concrete pole for supporting electricity wires
STOBS > STOB
STOCCADO *n* fencing thrust
STOCCADOS > STOCCADO
STOCCATA *same as* > STOCCADO
STOCCATAS > STOCCATA
STOCIOUS *same as* > STOTIOUS
STOCK *n* total amount of goods available for sale in

a shop ▷ *adj* kept in stock, standard ▷ *vb* keep for sale or future use
STOCKADE *n* enclosure or barrier made of stakes ▷ *vb* surround with a stockade
STOCKADED > STOCKADE
STOCKADES > STOCKADE
STOCKAGE *n* livestock put to graze on crops
STOCKAGES > STOCKAGE
STOCKCAR *n* car that has been strengthened for a form of racing in which the cars often collide
STOCKCARS > STOCKCAR
STOCKED > STOCK
STOCKER > STOCK
STOCKERS > STOCK
STOCKFISH *n* fish, such as cod or haddock, cured by splitting and drying in the air
STOCKHORN *n* type of obsolete woodwind instrument made from an animal horn
STOCKIER > STOCKY
STOCKIEST > STOCKY
STOCKILY > STOCKY
STOCKINET *n* machine-knitted elastic fabric
STOCKING *n* close-fitting covering for the foot and leg
STOCKINGS > STOCKING
STOCKISH *adj* stupid or dull
STOCKIST *n* dealer who stocks a particular product
STOCKISTS > STOCKIST
STOCKLESS > STOCK
STOCKLIST *n* list of items in stock
STOCKLOCK *n* lock that is enclosed in a wooden case
STOCKMAN *n* man engaged in the rearing or care of farm livestock, esp cattle
STOCKMEN > STOCKMAN
STOCKPILE *vb* store a large quantity of (something) for future use ▷ *n* accumulated store
STOCKPOT *n* pot in which stock for soup is made
STOCKPOTS > STOCKPOT
STOCKROOM *n* room in which a stock of goods is kept in a shop or factory
STOCKS *pl n* instrument of punishment in which an offender was locked
STOCKTAKE *vb* take stock
STOCKTOOK > STOCKTAKE
STOCKWORK *n* group of veins in mine

STOCKY *adj* (of a person) broad and sturdy
STOCKYARD *n* yard where farm animals are sold
STODGE *n* heavy starchy food ▷ *vb* stuff (oneself or another) with food
STODGED > STODGE
STODGER *n* dull person
STODGERS > STODGER
STODGES > STODGE
STODGIER > STODGY
STODGIEST > STODGY
STODGILY > STODGY
STODGING > STODGE
STODGY *adj* (of food) heavy and starchy
STOEP *n* verandah
STOEPS > STOEP
STOGEY *same as* > STOGY
STOGEYS > STOGEY
STOGIE *same as* > STOGY
STOGIES > STOGY
STOGY *n* any long cylindrical inexpensive cigar
STOIC *n* person who suffers hardship without showing his or her feelings ▷ *adj* suffering hardship without showing one's feelings
STOICAL *adj* suffering great difficulties without showing one's feelings
STOICALLY > STOICAL
STOICISM *n* indifference to pleasure and pain
STOICISMS > STOICISM
STOICS > STOIC
STOIT *vb* bounce
STOITED > STOIT
STOITER *vb* stagger
STOITERED > STOITER
STOITERS > STOITER
STOITING > STOIT
STOITS > STOIT
STOKE *vb* feed and tend (a fire or furnace)
STOKED *adj* very pleased
STOKEHOLD *n* hold for a ship's boilers
STOKEHOLE *n* hole in a furnace through which it is stoked
STOKER *n* person employed to tend a furnace on a ship or train powered by steam
STOKERS > STOKER
STOKES *n* cgs unit of kinematic viscosity
STOKESIA *n* American flowering plant
STOKESIAS > STOKESIA
STOKING > STOKE
STOKVEL *n* (in S Africa) informal savings pool or syndicate
STOKVELS > STOKVEL
STOLE *n* long scarf or shawl
STOLED *adj* wearing a stole
STOLEN > STEAL

S

STOLES > STOLE
STOLID adj showing little emotion or interest
STOLIDER > STOLID
STOLIDEST > STOLID
STOLIDITY > STOLID
STOLIDLY > STOLID
STOLLEN n rich sweet bread containing nuts, raisins, etc
STOLLENS > STOLLEN
STOLN > STEAL
STOLON n long horizontal stem that grows along the surface of the soil
STOLONATE adj having a stolon
STOLONIC > STOLON
STOLONS > STOLON
STOLPORT n airport for short take-off aircraft
STOLPORTS > STOLPORT
STOMA n pore in a plant leaf that controls the passage of gases
STOMACH n organ in the body which digests food ▷ vb put up with
STOMACHAL n stomach medication
STOMACHED > STOMACH
STOMACHER n decorative V-shaped panel of stiff material worn over the chest and stomach
STOMACHIC adj stimulating gastric activity ▷ n stomachic medicine
STOMACHS > STOMACH
STOMACHY adj having a large belly
STOMACK n as in have a stomack (in E Africa) be pregnant
STOMACKS > STOMACK
STOMAL > STOMA
STOMAS > STOMA
STOMATA > STOMA
STOMATAL adj of, relating to, or possessing stomata or a stoma
STOMATE n opening on leaf through which water evaporates
STOMATES > STOMATE
STOMATIC adj of or relating to a mouth or mouthlike part
STOMATOUS same as > STOMATAL
STOMIA > STOMIUM
STOMIUM n part of the sporangium of ferns that ruptures to release the spores
STOMIUMS > STOMIUM
STOMODAEA > STOMODEUM
STOMODEA > STOMODEUM
STOMODEAL > STOMODEUM
STOMODEUM n oral cavity of a vertebrate embryo
STOMP vb tread heavily ▷ n rhythmic stamping jazz dance

STOMPED > STOMP
STOMPER n song with a strong beat
STOMPERS > STOMPER
STOMPIE n cigarette butt
STOMPIER > STOMPY
STOMPIES > STOMPIE
STOMPIEST > STOMPY
STOMPING > STOMP
STOMPS > STOMP
STOMPY adj (of music) encouraging stomping of the feet
STONABLE > STONE
STOND same as > STAND
STONDS > STOND
STONE n material of which rocks are made ▷ vb throw stones at
STONEABLE > STONE
STONEBOAT n type of sleigh used for moving rocks from fields
STONECAST n short distance
STONECHAT n songbird that has black feathers and a reddish-brown breast
STONECROP n type of plant with fleshy leaves and red, yellow, or white flowers
STONECUT n (print made from) a carved block of stone
STONECUTS > STONECUT
STONED > STONE
STONEFISH n venomous tropical marine scorpaenid fish
STONEFLY n type of insect whose larvae are aquatic
STONEHAND n type of compositor
STONELESS > STONE
STONELIKE > STONE
STONEN adj of stone
STONER n device for removing stones from fruit
STONERAG n type of lichen
STONERAGS > STONERAG
STONERAW same as > STONERAG
STONERAWS > STONERAW
STONERN same as > STONEN
STONERS > STONER
STONES > STONE
STONESHOT n stone's throw
STONEWALL vb obstruct or hinder discussion
STONEWARE n hard kind of pottery fired at a very high temperature ▷ adj made of stoneware
STONEWASH vb wash with stones to give worn appearance
STONEWORK n part of a building made of stone

STONEWORT n any of various green algae which grow in brackish or fresh water
STONEY same as > STONY
STONG > STING
STONIED > STONY
STONIER > STONY
STONIES > STONY
STONIEST > STONY
STONILY > STONY
STONINESS > STONY
STONING > STONE
STONINGS > STONE
STONISH same as > ASTONISH
STONISHED > STONISH
STONISHES > STONISH
STONK vb bombard (soldiers, buildings, etc) with artillery ▷ n concentrated bombardment
STONKED > STONK
STONKER vb destroy
STONKERED adj completely exhausted or beaten
STONKERS > STONKER
STONKING > STONK
STONKS > STONK
STONN same as > STUN
STONNE same as > STUN
STONNED > STONNE
STONNES > STONNE
STONNING > STONN
STONNS > STONN
STONY adj of or like stone ▷ vb astonish
STONYING > STONY
STOOD > STAND
STOODEN > STAND
STOOGE n actor who feeds lines to a comedian ▷ vb act as a stooge
STOOGED > STOOGE
STOOGES > STOOGE
STOOGING > STOOGE
STOOK n number of sheaves set upright in a field to dry ▷ vb set up (sheaves) in stooks
STOOKED > STOOK
STOOKER > STOOK
STOOKERS > STOOK
STOOKIE n stucco
STOOKIES > STOOKIE
STOOKING n act of stooking
STOOKINGS > STOOKING
STOOKS > STOOK
STOOL n chair without arms or back ▷ vb (of a plant) send up shoots from the base of the stem
STOOLBALL n game resembling cricket
STOOLED > STOOL
STOOLIE n police informer
STOOLIES > STOOLIE
STOOLING > STOOL
STOOLS > STOOL
STOOLY n (US) informant for the police
STOOP vb bend forward and downward

STOOPBALL n American street game
STOOPE same as > STOUP
STOOPED > STOOP
STOOPER > STOOP
STOOPERS > STOOP
STOOPES > STOOPE
STOOPING > STOOP
STOOPS > STOOP
STOOR same as > STOUR
STOORS > STOOR
STOOSHIE same as > STUSHIE
STOOSHIES > STOOSHIE
STOOZE vb borrow money cheaply and invest it to make a profit
STOOZED > STOOZE
STOOZER n person who stoozes
STOOZERS > STOOZER
STOOZES > STOOZE
STOOZING > STOOZE
STOOZINGS > STOOZING
STOP vb cease or cause to cease from doing (something) ▷ n stopping or being stopped
STOPBAND n band of frequencies stopped by a filter
STOPBANDS > STOPBAND
STOPBANK n embankment to prevent flooding
STOPBANKS > STOPBANK
STOPCOCK n valve to control or stop the flow of fluid in a pipe
STOPCOCKS > STOPCOCK
STOPE n steplike excavation made in a mine to extract ore ▷ vb mine (ore, etc) by cutting stopes
STOPED > STOPE
STOPER n drill used in mining
STOPERS > STOPER
STOPES > STOPE
STOPGAP n temporary substitute
STOPGAPS > STOPGAP
STOPING n process by which country rock is broken up and engulfed by magma
STOPINGS > STOPING
STOPLESS > STOP
STOPLIGHT n red light on a traffic signal indicating that vehicles coming towards it should stop
STOPOFF n break in a journey
STOPOFFS > STOPOFF
STOPOVER n short break in a journey ▷ vb make a stopover
STOPOVERS > STOPOVER
STOPPABLE > STOP

STOPPAGE n act of stopping something or the state of being stopped
STOPPAGES > STOPPAGE
STOPPED > STOP
STOPPER n plug for closing a bottle etc ▷ vb close or fit with a stopper
STOPPERED > STOPPER
STOPPERS > STOPPER
STOPPING > STOP
STOPPINGS > STOP
STOPPLE same as > STOPPER
STOPPLED > STOPPLE
STOPPLES > STOPPLE
STOPPLING > STOPPLE
STOPS > STOP
STOPT > STOP
STOPWATCH n watch which can be stopped instantly for exact timing of a sporting event
STOPWORD n common word not used in computer search engines
STOPWORDS > STOPWORD
STORABLE > STORE
STORABLES > STORE
STORAGE n storing
STORAGES > STORAGE
STORAX n type of tree or shrub with white flowers
STORAXES > STORAX
STORE vb collect and keep (things) for future use ▷ n shop
STORECARD n charge card specific to one chain of shops
STORED > STORE
STOREMAN n man looking after storeroom
STOREMEN > STOREMAN
STORER > STORE
STOREROOM n room in which things are stored
STORERS > STORE
STORES pl n supply of food and essentials for a journey
STORESHIP n ship carrying naval stores
STOREWIDE adj throughout stores
STOREY n floor or level of a building
STOREYED adj having a storey or storeys
STOREYS > STOREY
STORGE n affection
STORGES > STORGE
STORIATED adj decorated with flowers or animals
STORIED > STORY
STORIES > STORY
STORIETTE n short story
STORING > STORE
STORK n large wading bird
STORKS > STORK
STORM n violent weather with wind, rain, or snow ▷ vb attack or capture (a place) suddenly
STORMBIRD n petrel

STORMCOCK n mistle thrush
STORMED > STORM
STORMER n outstanding example of its kind
STORMERS > STORMER
STORMFUL > STORM
STORMIER > STORMY
STORMIEST > STORMY
STORMILY > STORMY
STORMING adj characterized by or displaying dynamism, speed, and energy
STORMINGS > STORM
STORMLESS > STORM
STORMLIKE > STORM
STORMS > STORM
STORMY adj characterized by storms
STORNELLI > STORNELLO
STORNELLO n type of Italian poem
STORY n narration of a chain of events ▷ vb decorate with scenes from history
STORYBOOK n book containing stories for children ▷ adj better or happier than in real life
STORYETTE n short story
STORYING > STORY
STORYINGS > STORY
STORYLESS adj without a story
STORYLINE n plot of a book, film, play, etc
STORYTIME n time set aside for reading stories aloud
STOSS adj (of the side of a hill) facing the onward flow of a glacier ▷ n hillside facing glacier flow
STOSSES > STOSS
STOT n bullock ▷ vb bounce or cause to bounce
STOTIN n former monetary unit of Slovenia
STOTINKA n monetary unit of Bulgaria, worth one hundredth of a lev
STOTINKAS > STOTINKA
STOTINKI > STOTINKA
STOTINOV > STOTIN
STOTINS > STOTIN
STOTIOUS adj drunk
STOTS > STOT
STOTT same as > STOT
STOTTED > STOT
STOTTER same as > STOT
STOTTERED > STOTTER
STOTTERS > STOTTER
STOTTIE n wedge of bread cut from a flat round loaf
STOTTIES > STOTTIE
STOTTING > STOT
STOTTS > STOTT
STOTTY same as > STOTTIE
STOUN same as > STUN
STOUND n short while ▷ vb ache
STOUNDED > STOUND

STOUNDING > STOUND
STOUNDS > STOUND
STOUNING > STOUN
STOUNS > STOUN
STOUP n small basin for holy water
STOUPS > STOUP
STOUR n turmoil or conflict
STOURE same as > STOUR
STOURES > STOURE
STOURIE same as > STOURY
STOURIER > STOURY
STOURIEST > STOURY
STOURS > STOUR
STOURY adj dusty
STOUSH vb hit or punch (someone) ▷ n fighting or violence
STOUSHED > STOUSH
STOUSHES > STOUSH
STOUSHIE same as > STUSHIE
STOUSHIES > STOUSHIE
STOUSHING > STOUSH
STOUT adj fat ▷ n strong dark beer
STOUTEN vb make or become stout
STOUTENED > STOUTEN
STOUTENS > STOUTEN
STOUTER > STOUT
STOUTEST > STOUT
STOUTH n Scots word meaning theft
STOUTHS > STOUTH
STOUTISH > STOUT
STOUTLY > STOUT
STOUTNESS > STOUT
STOUTS > STOUT
STOVAINE n anaesthetic drug
STOVAINES > STOVAINE
STOVE n apparatus for cooking or heating ▷ vb process (ceramics, metalwork, etc) by heating in a stove
STOVED > STOVE
STOVEPIPE n pipe that takes fumes and smoke away from a stove
STOVER n fodder
STOVERS > STOVER
STOVES > STOVE
STOVETOP US word for > HOB
STOVETOPS > STOVETOP
STOVEWOOD n wood cut for use in a stove
STOVIES pl n potatoes stewed with onions
STOVING > STOVE
STOVINGS > STOVE
STOW vb pack or store
STOWABLE > STOW
STOWAGE n space or charge for stowing goods
STOWAGES > STOWAGE
STOWAWAY n person who hides on a ship or aircraft in order to travel free ▷ vb travel in such a way

STOWAWAYS > STOWAWAY
STOWDOWN n packing of ship's hold
STOWDOWNS > STOWDOWN
STOWED > STOW
STOWER > STOW
STOWERS > STOW
STOWING > STOW
STOWINGS > STOW
STOWLINS adv stealthily
STOWN > STEAL
STOWND same as > STOUND
STOWNDED > STOWND
STOWNDING > STOWND
STOWNDS > STOWND
STOWNLINS same as > STOWLINS
STOWP same as > STOUP
STOWPS > STOWP
STOWRE same as > STOUR
STOWRES > STOWRE
STOWS > STOW
STRABISM n abnormal alignment of one or both eyes
STRABISMS > STRABISM
STRACK vb archaic past tense form of strike
STRAD n violin made by Stradivarius
STRADDLE vb have one leg or part on each side of (something) ▷ n act or position of straddling
STRADDLED > STRADDLE
STRADDLER > STRADDLE
STRADDLES > STRADDLE
STRADIOT n Venetian cavalryman
STRADIOTS > STRADIOT
STRADS > STRAD
STRAE Scots form of > STRAW
STRAES > STRAE
STRAFE vb attack (an enemy) with machine guns from the air ▷ n act or instance of strafing
STRAFED > STRAFE
STRAFER > STRAFE
STRAFERS > STRAFE
STRAFES > STRAFE
STRAFF same as > STRAFE
STRAFFED > STRAFF
STRAFFING > STRAFF
STRAFFS > STRAFF
STRAFING n act of strafing
STRAFINGS > STRAFING
STRAG n straggler
STRAGGLE vb go or spread in a rambling or irregular way
STRAGGLED > STRAGGLE
STRAGGLER > STRAGGLE

STRAGGLES
> STRAGGLE
STRAGGLY > STRAGGLE
STRAGS > STRAG
STRAICHT Scots word for
> STRAIGHT
STRAIGHT adj not curved
or crooked ▷ adv in a
straight line ▷ n straight
part, esp of a racetrack
▷ vb tighten
STRAIGHTS
> STRAIGHT
STRAIK Scots word for
> STROKE
STRAIKED > STRAIK
STRAIKING > STRAIK
STRAIKS > STRAIK
STRAIN vb subject to
mental tension ▷ n
tension or tiredness
STRAINED adj not
natural, forced
STRAINER n sieve
STRAINERS
> STRAINER
STRAINING > STRAIN
STRAINS > STRAIN
STRAINT n pressure
STRAINTS > STRAINT
STRAIT n narrow
channel connecting two
areas of sea ▷ adj (of
spaces, etc) affording little
room ▷ vb tighten
STRAITED > STRAIT
STRAITEN vb embarrass
or distress, esp financially
STRAITENS
> STRAITEN
STRAITER > STRAIT
STRAITEST > STRAIT
STRAITING > STRAIT
STRAITLY > STRAIT
STRAITS > STRAIT
STRAK vb archaic past
tense form of strike
STRAKE n curved metal
plate forming part of the
metal rim on a wooden
wheel
STRAKED adj having a
strake
STRAKES > STRAKE
STRAMACON same as
> STRAMAZON
STRAMASH n uproar ▷ vb
destroy
STRAMAZON n downward
fencing stroke
STRAMMEL same as
> STRUMMEL
STRAMMELS
> STRAMMEL
STRAMONY n former
asthma medicine made
from the dried leaves and
flowers of the thorn apple
STRAMP Scots variant of
> TRAMP
STRAMPED > STRAMP
STRAMPING > STRAMP
STRAMPS > STRAMP
STRAND vb run aground
▷ n shore
STRANDED > STRAND
STRANDER > STRAND
STRANDERS > STRAND

STRANDING > STRAND
STRANDS > STRAND
STRANG dialect variant of
> STRONG
STRANGE adj odd or
unusual ▷ n odd or
unfamiliar person or thing
STRANGELY > STRANGE
STRANGER n person who
is not known or is new to a
place or experience
STRANGERS
> STRANGER
STRANGES > STRANGE
STRANGEST > STRANGE
STRANGLE vb kill by
squeezing the throat
STRANGLED
> STRANGLE
STRANGLER n person or
thing that strangles
STRANGLES n acute
bacterial disease of horses
STRANGURY n painful
excretion of urine caused
by muscular spasms of the
urinary tract
STRAP n strip of flexible
material for lifting or
holding in place ▷ vb
fasten with a strap or
straps
STRAPHANG vb travel
standing on public
transport
STRAPHUNG
> STRAPHANG
STRAPLESS adj (of
women's clothes) without
straps over the shoulders
STRAPLIKE adj like a
strap
STRAPLINE n
subheading in a
newspaper or magazine
article or in any
advertisement
STRAPPADO n system of
torture in which a person
was hoisted by a rope tied
to the wrists ▷ vb subject
to strappado
STRAPPED > STRAP
STRAPPER n strapping
person
STRAPPERS
> STRAPPER
STRAPPIER > STRAPPY
STRAPPING > STRAP
STRAPPY adj having
straps
STRAPS > STRAP
STRAPWORT n plant with
leaves like straps
STRASS another word for
> PASTE
STRASSES > STRASS
STRATA > STRATUM
STRATAGEM n clever
plan, trick
STRATAL > STRATUM
STRATAS > STRATUM
STRATEGIC adj
advantageous
STRATEGY n overall plan
STRATH n flat river valley
STRATHS > STRATH
STRATI > STRATUS

STRATIFY vb form or be
formed in layers or strata
STRATONIC adj of army
STRATOSE adj formed in
strata
STRATOUS adj of stratus
STRATUM n layer, esp of
rock
STRATUMS > STRATUM
STRATUS n grey layer
cloud
STRATUSES > STRATUS
STRAUCHT Scots word for
> STRETCH
STRAUCHTS
> STRAUCHT
STRAUGHT same as
> STRAUCHT
STRAUGHTS
> STRAUGHT
STRAUNGE same as
> STRANGE
STRAVAGE same as
> STRAVAIG
STRAVAGED
> STRAVAGE
STRAVAGES
> STRAVAGE
STRAVAIG vb wander
aimlessly
STRAVAIGS
> STRAVAIG
STRAW n dried stalks of
grain ▷ vb spread around
STRAWED > STRAW
STRAWEN adj of straw
STRAWHAT adj of summer
dramatic performance
STRAWIER > STRAWY
STRAWIEST > STRAWY
STRAWING > STRAW
STRAWLESS > STRAW
STRAWLIKE > STRAW
STRAWN > STREW
STRAWS > STRAW
STRAWWORM n aquatic
larva of a caddis fly
STRAWY adj containing
straw, or like straw in
colour or texture
STRAY vb wander ▷ adj
having strayed ▷ n stray
animal
STRAYED > STRAY
STRAYER > STRAY
STRAYERS > STRAY
STRAYING > STRAY
STRAYINGS > STRAY
STRAYLING n stray
STRAYS > STRAY
STRAYVE vb wander
aimlessly
STRAYVED > STRAYVE
STRAYVES > STRAYVE
STRAYVING > STRAYVE
STREAK n long band of
contrasting colour or
substance ▷ vb mark with
streaks
STREAKED > STREAK
STREAKER > STREAK
STREAKERS > STREAK
STREAKIER > STREAKY
STREAKILY > STREAKY
STREAKING > STREAK
STREAKS > STREAK
STREAKY adj marked
with streaks

STREAM n small river ▷ vb
flow steadily
STREAMBED n bottom of
stream
STREAMED > STREAM
STREAMER n strip of
coloured paper that
unrolls when tossed
STREAMERS
> STREAMER
STREAMIER > STREAMY
STREAMING > STREAM
STREAMLET > STREAM
STREAMS > STREAM
STREAMY adj (of an area,
land, etc) having many
streams
STREEK Scots word for
> STRETCH
STREEKED > STREEK
STREEKER > STREEK
STREEKERS > STREEK
STREEKING > STREEK
STREEKS > STREEK
STREEL vb trail
STREELED > STREEL
STREELING > STREEL
STREELS > STREEL
STREET n public road,
usu lined with buildings
▷ vb lay out a street or
streets
STREETAGE n toll
charged for using a street
STREETBOY n boy living
on the street
STREETCAR n tram
STREETED > STREET
STREETFUL n amount of
people or things a street
can hold
STREETIER > STREETY
STREETING > STREET
STREETS > STREET
STREETY adj of streets
STREIGHT same as
> STRAIT
STREIGHTS
> STREIGHT
STREIGNE same as
> STRAIN
STREIGNED
> STREIGNE
STREIGNES
> STREIGNE
STRELITZ n former
Russian soldier
STRELITZI
> STRELITZ
STRENE same as
> STRAIN
STRENES > STRENE
STRENGTH n quality of
being strong
STRENGTHS
> STRENGTH
STRENUITY
> STRENUOUS
STRENUOUS adj requiring
great energy or effort
STREP n streptococcus
STREPENT adj noisy
STREPS > STREP
STRESS n tension or
strain ▷ vb emphasize
STRESSED > STRESS
STRESSES > STRESS
STRESSFUL > STRESS

S

STRESSIER > STRESSY
STRESSING > STRESS
STRESSOR *n* event, experience, etc, that causes stress
STRESSORS > STRESSOR
STRESSY *adj* characterized by stress
STRETCH *vb* extend or be extended ▷ *n* stretching
STRETCHED > STRETCH
STRETCHER *n* frame covered with canvas on which an injured person is carried ▷ *vb* transport (a sick or injured person) on a stretcher
STRETCHES > STRETCH
STRETCHY *adj* characterized by elasticity
STRETTA *same as* **> STRETTO**
STRETTAS > STRETTA
STRETTE > STRETTA
STRETTI > STRETTO
STRETTO *n* (in a fugue) the close overlapping of two parts or voices
STRETTOS > STRETTO
STREUSEL *n* crumbly topping for rich pastries
STREUSELS > STREUSEL
STREW *vb* scatter (things) over a surface
STREWAGE > STREW
STREWAGES > STREW
STREWED > STREW
STREWER > STREW
STREWERS > STREW
STREWING > STREW
STREWINGS > STREW
STREWMENT *n* strewing
STREWN > STREW
STREWS > STREW
STREWTH *interj* expression of surprise or alarm
STRIA *n* scratch or groove on the surface of a rock crystal
STRIAE > STRIA
STRIATA > STRIATUM
STRIATAL *adj* relating to the corpus striatum in the brain
STRIATE *adj* marked with striae ▷ *vb* mark with striae
STRIATED *adj* having a pattern of scratches or grooves
STRIATES > STRIATE
STRIATING > STRIATE
STRIATION *same as* **> STRIA**
STRIATUM *n* part of brain
STRIATUMS > STRIATUM
STRIATURE *n* way something is striated
STRICH *n* screech owl
STRICHES > STRICH
STRICK *n* any bast fibres preparatory to being made into slivers**

STRICKEN *adj* seriously affected by disease, grief, pain, etc
STRICKLE *n* board used for sweeping off excess material in a container ▷ *vb* level, form, or sharpen with a strickle
STRICKLED > STRICKLE
STRICKLES > STRICKLE
STRICKS > STRICK
STRICT *adj* stern or severe
STRICTER > STRICT
STRICTEST > STRICT
STRICTION *n* act of restricting
STRICTISH > STRICT
STRICTLY > STRICT
STRICTURE *n* severe criticism
STRIDDEN > STRIDE
STRIDDLE *same as* **> STRADDLE**
STRIDDLED > STRIDDLE
STRIDDLES > STRIDDLE
STRIDE *vb* walk with long steps ▷ *n* long step
STRIDENCE > STRIDENT
STRIDENCY > STRIDENT
STRIDENT *adj* loud and harsh
STRIDER > STRIDE
STRIDERS > STRIDE
STRIDES > STRIDE
STRIDING > STRIDE
STRIDLING *adv* astride
STRIDOR *n* high-pitched whistling sound made during respiration
STRIDORS > STRIDOR
STRIFE *n* conflict, quarrelling
STRIFEFUL > STRIFE
STRIFES > STRIFE
STRIFT *n* struggle
STRIFTS > STRIFT
STRIG *vb* remove stalk from
STRIGA *same as* **> STRIA**
STRIGAE > STRIGA
STRIGATE *adj* streaked
STRIGGED > STRIG
STRIGGING > STRIG
STRIGIL *n* curved blade used to scrape the body after bathing
STRIGILS > STRIGIL
STRIGINE *adj* of or like owl
STRIGOSE *adj* bearing stiff hairs or bristles
STRIGS > STRIG
STRIKABLE *adj* capable of being struck
STRIKE *vb* cease work as a protest ▷ *n* stoppage of work as a protest
STRIKEOUT *n* dismissal in baseball due to three successive failures to hit the ball

STRIKER *n* striking worker
STRIKERS > STRIKER
STRIKES > STRIKE
STRIKING > STRIKE
STRIKINGS > STRIKE
STRIM *vb* cut (grass) using an electric trimmer
STRIMMED > STRIM
STRIMMING > STRIM
STRIMS > STRIM
STRINE *n* informal name for Australian English
STRINES > STRINE
STRING *n* thin cord used for tying ▷ *vb* provide with a string or strings
STRINGED *adj* (of a musical instrument) having strings that are plucked or played with a bow
STRINGENT *adj* strictly controlled or enforced
STRINGER *n* journalist retained by a newspaper to cover a particular town or area
STRINGERS > STRINGER
STRINGIER > STRINGY
STRINGILY > STRINGY
STRINGING > STRING
STRINGS > STRING
STRINGY *adj* like string
STRINKLE *Scots variant of* **> SPRINKLE**
STRINKLED > STRINKLE
STRINKLES > STRINKLE
STRIP *vb* take (the covering or clothes) off ▷ *n* act of stripping
STRIPE *n* long narrow band of contrasting colour or substance ▷ *vb* mark (something) with stripes
STRIPED *adj* marked or decorated with stripes
STRIPER *n* officer who has a stripe or stripes on his or her uniform
STRIPERS > STRIPER
STRIPES > STRIPE
STRIPEY *same as* **> STRIPY**
STRIPIER > STRIPY
STRIPIEST > STRIPY
STRIPING > STRIPE
STRIPINGS > STRIPE
STRIPLING *n* youth
STRIPPED > STRIP
STRIPPER *n* device or substance for removing paint etc
STRIPPERS > STRIPPER
STRIPPING > STRIP
STRIPS > STRIP
STRIPT > STRIP
STRIPY *adj* marked by or with stripes
STRIVE *vb* make a great effort
STRIVED > STRIVE
STRIVEN > STRIVE
STRIVER > STRIVE

STRIVERS > STRIVE
STRIVES > STRIVE
STRIVING > STRIVE
STRIVINGS > STRIVE
STROAM *vb* wander
STROAMED > STROAM
STROAMING > STROAM
STROAMS > STROAM
STROBE *n* high intensity flashing beam of light ▷ *vb* give the appearance of slow motion by using a strobe
STROBED > STROBE
STROBES > STROBE
STROBIC *adj* spinning or appearing to spin
STROBIL *n* scaly multiple fruit
STROBILA *n* body of a tapeworm, consisting of a string of similar segments
STROBILAE > STROBILA
STROBILAR > STROBILA
STROBILE *same as* **> STROBILUS**
STROBILES > STROBILE
STROBILI > STROBILUS
STROBILS > STROBIL
STROBILUS *technical name for* **> CONE**
STROBING > STROBE
STROBINGS > STROBE
STRODDLE *same as* **> STRADDLE**
STRODDLED > STRODDLE
STRODDLES > STRODDLE
STRODE > STRIDE
STRODLE *same as* **> STRADDLE**
STRODLED > STRODLE
STRODLES > STRODLE
STRODLING > STRODLE
STROKABLE *adj* appearing pleasant to stroke
STROKE *vb* touch or caress lightly with the hand ▷ *n* light touch or caress with the hand
STROKED > STROKE
STROKEN > STRIKE
STROKER > STROKE
STROKERS > STROKE
STROKES > STROKE
STROKING > STROKE
STROKINGS > STROKE
STROLL *vb* walk in a leisurely manner ▷ *n* leisurely walk
STROLLED > STROLL
STROLLER *n* chair-shaped carriage for a baby
STROLLERS > STROLLER
STROLLING > STROLL
STROLLS > STROLL
STROMA *n* gel-like matrix of chloroplasts and certain cells
STROMAL > STROMA

S

STROMATA > STROMA
STROMATIC > STROMA
STROMB n shellfish like a whelk
STROMBS > STROMB
STROMBUS same as > STROMB
STROND same as > STRAND
STRONDS > STROND
STRONG adj having physical power
STRONGARM adj involving physical force
STRONGBOX n box in which valuables are locked for safety
STRONGER > STRONG
STRONGEST > STRONG
STRONGISH > STRONG
STRONGLY > STRONG
STRONGMAN n performer, esp one in a circus, who performs feats of strength
STRONGMEN > STRONGMAN
STRONGYL same as > STRONGYLE
STRONGYLE n type of parasitic worm chiefly occurring in the intestines of horses
STRONGYLS > STRONGYL
STRONTIA > STRONTIUM
STRONTIAN n type of white mineral
STRONTIAS > STRONTIA
STRONTIC > STRONTIUM
STRONTIUM n silvery-white metallic element
STROOK > STRIKE
STROOKE n stroke
STROOKEN same as > STRICKEN
STROOKES > STROOKE
STROP n leather strap for sharpening razors ▷ vb sharpen (a razor, etc) on a strop
STROPHE n movement made by chorus during a choral ode
STROPHES > STROPHE
STROPHIC adj of, relating to, or employing a strophe or strophes
STROPHOID n type of curve on graph
STROPHULI pl n skin inflammations seen primarily on small children
STROPPED > STROP
STROPPER > STROP
STROPPERS > STROP
STROPPIER > STROPPY
STROPPILY > STROPPY
STROPPING > STROP
STROPPY adj angry or awkward
STROPS > STROP
STROSSERS same as > TROUSERS

STROUD n coarse woollen fabric
STROUDING n woolly material for making strouds
STROUDS > STROUD
STROUP Scots word for > SPOUT
STROUPACH n cup of tea
STROUPAN same as > STROUPACH
STROUPANS > STROUPAN
STROUPS > STROUP
STROUT vb bulge
STROUTED > STROUT
STROUTING > STROUT
STROUTS > STROUT
STROVE > STRIVE
STROW archaic variant of > STREW
STROWED > STROW
STROWER > STROW
STROWERS > STROW
STROWING > STROW
STROWINGS > STROW
STROWN > STROW
STROWS > STROW
STROY archaic variant of > DESTROY
STROYED > STROY
STROYER > STROY
STROYERS > STROY
STROYING > STROY
STROYS > STROY
STRUCK > STRIKE
STRUCKEN same as > STRICKEN
STRUCTURE n complex construction ▷ vb give a structure to
STRUDEL n thin sheet of filled dough rolled up and baked
STRUDELS > STRUDEL
STRUGGLE vb work, strive, or make one's way with difficulty ▷ n striving
STRUGGLED > STRUGGLE
STRUGGLER > STRUGGLE
STRUGGLES > STRUGGLE
STRUM vb play (a guitar, etc) by sweeping the thumb across the strings
STRUMA n abnormal enlargement of the thyroid gland
STRUMAE > STRUMA
STRUMAS > STRUMA
STRUMATIC > STRUMA
STRUMITIS n inflammation of thyroid gland
STRUMMED > STRUM
STRUMMEL n straw
STRUMMELS > STRUMMEL
STRUMMER > STRUM
STRUMMERS > STRUM
STRUMMING > STRUM
STRUMOSE > STRUMA
STRUMOUS > STRUMA
STRUMPET n prostitute ▷ vb turn into a strumpet
STRUMPETS > STRUMPET

STRUMS > STRUM
STRUNG > STRING
STRUNT Scots word for > STRUT
STRUNTED > STRUNT
STRUNTING > STRUNT
STRUNTS > STRUNT
STRUT vb walk pompously, swagger ▷ n bar supporting a structure
STRUTS > STRUT
STRUTTED > STRUT
STRUTTER > STRUT
STRUTTERS > STRUT
STRUTTING > STRUT
STRYCHNIA n strychnine
STRYCHNIC adj of, relating to, or derived from strychnine
STUB n short piece left after use ▷ vb strike (the toe) painfully against an object
STUBBED > STUB
STUBBIE same as > STUBBY
STUBBIER > STUBBY
STUBBIES > STUBBY
STUBBIEST > STUBBY
STUBBILY > STUBBY
STUBBING > STUB
STUBBLE n short stalks of grain left in a field after reaping
STUBBLED adj having the stubs of stalks left after a crop has been cut and harvested
STUBBLES > STUBBLE
STUBBLIER > STUBBLE
STUBBLY > STUBBLE
STUBBORN adj refusing to agree or give in ▷ vb make stubborn
STUBBORNS > STUBBORN
STUBBY adj short and broad ▷ n small bottle of beer
STUBS > STUB
STUCCO n plaster used for coating or decorating walls ▷ vb apply stucco to (a building)
STUCCOED > STUCCO
STUCCOER > STUCCO
STUCCOERS > STUCCO
STUCCOES > STUCCO
STUCCOING > STUCCO
STUCCOS > STUCCO
STUCK n thrust
STUCKS > STUCK
STUD n small piece of metal attached to a surface for decoration ▷ vb set with studs
STUDBOOK n written record of the pedigree of a purebred stock, esp of racehorses
STUDBOOKS > STUDBOOK
STUDDED > STUD
STUDDEN > STAND
STUDDIE Scots word for > ANVIL
STUDDIES > STUDDIE
STUDDING > STUD

STUDDINGS > STUD
STUDDLE n post
STUDDLES > STUDDLE
STUDE vb past tense and past participle of staun (Scots form of stand)
STUDENT n person who studies a subject, esp at university
STUDENTRY n body of students
STUDENTS > STUDENT
STUDENTY adj denoting the characteristics believed typical of a student
STUDFARM n farm where horses are bred
STUDFARMS > STUDFARM
STUDFISH n American minnow
STUDHORSE another word for > STALLION
STUDIED adj carefully practised
STUDIEDLY > STUDIED
STUDIER > STUDY
STUDIERS > STUDY
STUDIES > STUDY
STUDIO n workroom of an artist or photographer
STUDIOS > STUDIO
STUDIOUS adj fond of study
STUDLIER > STUDLY
STUDLIEST > STUDLY
STUDLIKE adj like a stud
STUDLY adj strong and virile
STUDS > STUD
STUDWORK n work decorated with studs
STUDWORKS > STUDWORK
STUDY vb be engaged in learning (a subject) ▷ n act or process of studying
STUDYING > STUDY
STUFF n substance or material ▷ vb pack, cram, or fill completely
STUFFED > STUFF
STUFFER > STUFF
STUFFERS > STUFF
STUFFIER > STUFFY
STUFFIEST > STUFFY
STUFFILY > STUFFY
STUFFING n seasoned mixture with which food is stuffed
STUFFINGS > STUFFING
STUFFLESS > STUFF
STUFFS > STUFF
STUFFY adj lacking fresh air
STUGGIER > STUGGY
STUGGIEST > STUGGY
STUGGY adj stout
STUIVER same as > STIVER
STUIVERS > STUIVER
STUKKEND adj South African slang for broken or wrecked
STULL n timber prop or platform in a stope

STULLS > STULL
STULM *n* shaft
STULMS > STULM
STULTIFY *vb* dull (the mind) by boring routine
STUM *n* partly fermented wine added to fermented wine as a preservative ▷ *vb* preserve (wine) by adding stum
STUMBLE *vb* trip and nearly fall ▷ *n* stumbling
STUMBLED > STUMBLE
STUMBLER > STUMBLE
STUMBLERS > STUMBLE
STUMBLES > STUMBLE
STUMBLIER > STUMBLY
STUMBLING > STUMBLE
STUMBLY *adj* tending to stumble
STUMER *n* forgery or cheat
STUMERS > STUMER
STUMM *same as* > SHTOOM
STUMMED > STUM
STUMMEL *n* bowl of a smoker's pipe
STUMMELS > STUMMEL
STUMMING > STUM
STUMP *n* base of a tree left when the main trunk has been cut away ▷ *vb* baffle
STUMPAGE *n* standing timber or its value
STUMPAGES > STUMPAGE
STUMPED > STUMP
STUMPER > STUMP
STUMPERS > STUMP
STUMPIER > STUMPY
STUMPIES > STUMPY
STUMPIEST > STUMPY
STUMPILY > STUMPY
STUMPING > STUMP
STUMPINGS > STUMPING
STUMPS > STUMP
STUMPWORK *n* type of embroidery featuring raised figures, padded with cotton wool or hair
STUMPY *adj* short and thick ▷ *n* stumpy thing
STUMS > STUM
STUN *vb* shock or overwhelm ▷ *n* state or effect of being stunned
STUNG > STING
STUNK > STINK
STUNKARD *adj* sulky
STUNNED > STUN
STUNNER *n* beautiful person or thing
STUNNERS > STUNNER
STUNNING > STUN
STUNNINGS > STUN
STUNS > STUN
STUNSAIL *n* type of light auxiliary sail
STUNSAILS > STUNSAIL
STUNT *vb* prevent or impede the growth of ▷ *n* acrobatic or dangerous action
STUNTED > STUNT
STUNTING > STUNT

STUNTMAN *n* man who performs dangerous acts in a film, etc in place of an actor
STUNTMEN > STUNTMAN
STUNTS > STUNT
STUPA *n* domed edifice housing Buddhist or Jain relics
STUPAS > STUPA
STUPE *n* hot damp cloth applied to the body to relieve pain ▷ *vb* treat with a stupe
STUPED > STUPE
STUPEFIED > STUPEFY
STUPEFIER > STUPEFY
STUPEFIES > STUPEFY
STUPEFY *vb* make insensitive or lethargic
STUPENT *adj* astonished
STUPES > STUPE
STUPID *adj* lacking intelligence ▷ *n* stupid person
STUPIDER > STUPID
STUPIDEST > STUPID
STUPIDITY *n* quality or state of being stupid
STUPIDLY > STUPID
STUPIDS > STUPID
STUPING > STUPE
STUPOR *n* dazed or unconscious state
STUPOROUS > STUPOR
STUPORS > STUPOR
STUPRATE *vb* ravish
STUPRATED > STUPRATE
STUPRATES > STUPRATE
STURDIED > STURDY
STURDIER > STURDY
STURDIES > STURDY
STURDIEST > STURDY
STURDILY > STURDY
STURDY *adj* healthy and robust ▷ *n* disease of sheep
STURE *same as* > STOOR
STURGEON *n* fish from which caviar is obtained
STURGEONS > STURGEON
STURMER *n* type of eating apple with pale green skin
STURMERS > STURMER
STURNINE > STURNUS
STURNOID > STURNUS
STURNUS *n* bird of starling family
STURNUSES > STURNUS
STURT *vb* bother
STURTED > STURT
STURTING > STURT
STURTS > STURT
STUSHIE *n* commotion, rumpus, or row
STUSHIES > STUSHIE
STUTTER *vb* speak with repetition of initial consonants ▷ *n* tendency to stutter
STUTTERED > STUTTER
STUTTERER > STUTTER
STUTTERS > STUTTER
STY *vb* climb
STYE *n* inflammation at the base of an eyelash

STYED > STYE
STYES > STYE
STYGIAN *adj* dark, gloomy, or hellish
STYING > STY
STYLAR > STYLUS
STYLATE *adj* having style
STYLE *n* shape or design ▷ *vb* shape or design
STYLEBOOK *n* book containing rules of punctuation, etc, for the use of writers, editors, and printers
STYLED > STYLE
STYLEE *same as* > STYLE
STYLEES > STYLEE
STYLELESS > STYLE
STYLER > STYLE
STYLERS > STYLE
STYLES > STYLE
STYLET *n* wire to stiffen a flexible cannula or catheter
STYLETS > STYLET
STYLI > STYLUS
STYLIE *adj* fashion-conscious
STYLIER > STYLIE
STYLIEST > STYLIE
STYLIFORM *adj* shaped like a stylus or bristle
STYLING > STYLE
STYLINGS > STYLE
STYLISE *same as* > STYLIZE
STYLISED > STYLISE
STYLISER > STYLISE
STYLISERS > STYLISE
STYLISES > STYLISE
STYLISH *adj* smart, elegant, and fashionable
STYLISHLY > STYLISH
STYLISING > STYLISE
STYLIST *n* hairdresser
STYLISTIC *adj* of literary or artistic style
STYLISTS > STYLIST
STYLITE *n* one of a class of recluses who in ancient times lived on the top of high pillars
STYLITES > STYLITE
STYLITIC > STYLITE
STYLITISM > STYLITE
STYLIZE *vb* cause to conform to an established stylistic form
STYLIZED > STYLIZE
STYLIZER > STYLIZE
STYLIZERS > STYLIZE
STYLIZES > STYLIZE
STYLIZING > STYLIZE
STYLO *n* type of fountain pen
STYLOBATE *n* continuous horizontal course of masonry that supports a colonnade
STYLOID *adj* resembling a stylus ▷ *n* spiny growth
STYLOIDS > STYLOID
STYLOLITE *n* any of the small striated columnar or irregular structures within the strata of some limestones
STYLOPES > STYLOPS

STYLOPID *n* type of parasitic insect
STYLOPIDS > STYLOPID
STYLOPISE *same as* > STYLOPIZE
STYLOPIZE *vb* (of a stylops) to parasitize (a host)
STYLOPS *n* type of insect that lives as a parasite in other insects
STYLOS > STYLO
STYLUS *n* needle-like device on a record player
STYLUSES > STYLUS
STYME *vb* peer
STYMED > STYME
STYMES > STYME
STYMIE *vb* hinder or thwart
STYMIED > STYMY
STYMIEING > STYMIE
STYMIES > STYMY
STYMING > STYME
STYMY *same as* > STYMIE
STYMYING > STYMY
STYPSIS *n* action, application, or use of a styptic
STYPSISES > STYPSIS
STYPTIC *adj* (drug) used to stop bleeding ▷ *n* styptic drug
STYPTICAL > STYPTIC
STYPTICS > STYPTIC
STYRAX *n* type of tropical or subtropical tree
STYRAXES > STYRAX
STYRE *same as* > STIR
STYRED > STYRE
STYRENE *n* colourless flammable liquid
STYRENES > STYRENE
STYRES > STYRE
STYRING > STYRE
STYROFOAM *n* tradename for a light expanded polystyrene plastic
STYTE *vb* bounce
STYTED > STYTE
STYTES > STYTE
STYTING > STYTE
SUABILITY > SUABLE
SUABLE *adj* liable to be sued in a court
SUABLY > SUABLE
SUASIBLE > SUASION
SUASION *n* persuasion
SUASIONS > SUASION
SUASIVE > SUASION
SUASIVELY > SUASION
SUASORY > SUASION
SUAVE *adj* smooth and sophisticated in manner
SUAVELY > SUAVE
SUAVENESS > SUAVE
SUAVER > SUAVE
SUAVEST > SUAVE
SUAVITIES > SUAVE
SUAVITY > SUAVE
SUB *n* subeditor ▷ *vb* act as a substitute
SUBA *n* shepherd's cloak
SUBABBOT *n* abbot who is subordinate to another abbot

SUBABBOTS
> SUBABBOT
SUBACID adj (esp of some fruits) moderately acid or sour
SUBACIDLY > SUBACID
SUBACRID adj slightly acrid
SUBACT vb subdue
SUBACTED > SUBACT
SUBACTING > SUBACT
SUBACTION > SUBACT
SUBACTS > SUBACT
SUBACUTE adj intermediate between acute and chronic
SUBADAR n chief native officer of a company of Indian soldiers in the British service
SUBADARS > SUBADAR
SUBADULT n animal not quite at adult stage
SUBADULTS
> SUBADULT
SUBAERIAL adj in open air
SUBAGENCY n agency employed by larger agency
SUBAGENT n agent who is subordinate to another agent
SUBAGENTS
> SUBAGENT
SUBAH same as
> SUBADAR
SUBAHDAR same as
> SUBADAR
SUBAHDARS
> SUBAHDAR
SUBAHDARY n office of subahdar
SUBAHS > SUBAH
SUBAHSHIP > SUBAH
SUBALAR adj below a wing
SUBALPINE adj situated in or relating to the regions at the foot of mountains
SUBALTERN n British army officer below the rank of captain ▷ adj of inferior position or rank
SUBAPICAL adj below an apex
SUBAQUA adj of or relating to underwater sport
SUBARCTIC adj of or relating to latitudes immediately south of the Arctic Circle
SUBAREA n area within a larger area
SUBAREAS > SUBAREA
SUBARID adj receiving slightly more rainfall than arid regions
SUBAS > SUBA
SUBASTRAL adj terrestrial
SUBATOM n part of an atom
SUBATOMIC adj of or being one of the particles which make up an atom
SUBATOMS > SUBATOM

SUBAUDIO adj (of sound) low frequency
SUBAURAL adj below the ear
SUBAXIAL adj below an axis of the body
SUBBASAL > SUBBASE
SUBBASE same as
> SUBBASS
SUBBASES > SUBBASE
SUBBASIN n geographical basin within larger basin
SUBBASINS
> SUBBASIN
SUBBASS another name for
> BOURDON
SUBBASSES > SUBBASS
SUBBED > SUB
SUBBIE n subcontractor
SUBBIES > SUBBIE
SUBBING > SUB
SUBBINGS > SUB
SUBBLOCK n part of mathematical matrix
SUBBLOCKS
> SUBBLOCK
SUBBRANCH n branch within another branch
SUBBREED n breed within a larger breed
SUBBREEDS
> SUBBREED
SUBBUREAU n bureau subordinate to the main bureau
SUBBY same as
> SUBBIE
SUBCANTOR n deputy to a cantor
SUBCASTE n subdivision of a caste
SUBCASTES
> SUBCASTE
SUBCAUDAL adj below a tail
SUBCAUSE n factor less important than a cause
SUBCAUSES
> SUBCAUSE
SUBCAVITY n cavity within a larger cavity
SUBCELL n cell within a larger cell
SUBCELLAR n cellar below another cellar
SUBCELLS > SUBCELL
SUBCENTER n secondary center
SUBCENTRE same as
> SUBCENTER
SUBCHASER n anti-submarine warship
SUBCHIEF n chief below the main chief
SUBCHIEFS
> SUBCHIEF
SUBCHORD n part of a curve
SUBCHORDS
> SUBCHORD
SUBCLAIM n claim that is part of a larger claim
SUBCLAIMS
> SUBCLAIM
SUBCLAN n clan within a larger clan
SUBCLANS > SUBCLAN

SUBCLASS n principal subdivision of a class ▷ vb assign to a subclass
SUBCLAUSE n subordinate section of a larger clause in a document
SUBCLERK n clerk who is subordinate to another clerk
SUBCLERKS
> SUBCLERK
SUBCLIMAX n community in which development has been arrested before climax has been attained
SUBCODE n computer tag identifying data
SUBCODES > SUBCODE
SUBCOLONY n colony established by existing colony
SUBCONSUL n assistant to a consul
SUBCOOL vb make colder
SUBCOOLED > SUBCOOL
SUBCOOLS > SUBCOOL
SUBCORTEX n matter of the brain situated beneath the cerebral cortex
SUBCOSTA n vein in insect wing
SUBCOSTAE
> SUBCOSTA
SUBCOSTAL adj below the rib
SUBCOUNTY n division of a county
SUBCRUST n secondary crust below main crust
SUBCRUSTS
> SUBCRUST
SUBCULT n cult within larger cult
SUBCULTS > SUBCULT
SUBCUTES > SUBCUTIS
SUBCUTIS n layer of tissue beneath outer skin
SUBDEACON n cleric who assists at High Mass
SUBDEALER n dealer who buys from other dealer
SUBDEAN n deputy of dean
SUBDEANS > SUBDEAN
SUBDEB n young woman who is not yet a debutante
SUBDEBS > SUBDEB
SUBDEPOT n depot within a larger depot
SUBDEPOTS
> SUBDEPOT
SUBDEPUTY n assistant to a deputy
SUBDERMAL adj below the skin
SUBDEW same as
> SUBDUE
SUBDEWED > SUBDEW
SUBDEWING > SUBDEW
SUBDEWS > SUBDEW
SUBDIVIDE vb divide (a part of something) into smaller parts
SUBDOLOUS adj clever
SUBDORSAL adj situated close to the back

SUBDUABLE > SUBDUE
SUBDUABLY > SUBDUE
SUBDUAL > SUBDUE
SUBDUALS > SUBDUE
SUBDUCE vb withdraw
SUBDUCED > SUBDUCE
SUBDUCES > SUBDUCE
SUBDUCING > SUBDUCE
SUBDUCT vb draw or turn (the eye, etc) downwards
SUBDUCTED > SUBDUCT
SUBDUCTS > SUBDUCT
SUBDUE vb overcome
SUBDUED adj cowed, passive, or shy
SUBDUEDLY > SUBDUED
SUBDUER > SUBDUE
SUBDUERS > SUBDUE
SUBDUES > SUBDUE
SUBDUING > SUBDUE
SUBDUPLE adj in proportion of one to two
SUBDURAL adj between the dura mater and the arachnoid
SUBDWARF n star smaller than a dwarf star
SUBDWARFS
> SUBDWARF
SUBECHO n echo resonating more quietly than another echo
SUBECHOES > SUBECHO
SUBEDAR same as
> SUBADAR
SUBEDARS > SUBEDAR
SUBEDIT vb edit and correct (written or printed material)
SUBEDITED > SUBEDIT
SUBEDITOR n person who checks and edits text for a newspaper or magazine
SUBEDITS > SUBEDIT
SUBENTIRE adj slightly indented
SUBENTRY n entry within another entry
SUBEPOCH n epoch within another epoch
SUBEPOCHS
> SUBEPOCH
SUBEQUAL adj not quite equal
SUBER n cork
SUBERATE n salt of suberic acid
SUBERATES
> SUBERATE
SUBERECT adj not quite erect
SUBEREOUS same as
> SUBEROSE
SUBERIC same as
> SUBEROSE
SUBERIN n fatty or waxy substance that is present in the walls of cork cells
SUBERINS > SUBERIN
SUBERISE same as
> SUBERIZE
SUBERISED
> SUBERISE
SUBERISES
> SUBERISE
SUBERIZE vb impregnate (cell walls)

with suberin during the formation of corky tissue

SUBERIZED
> SUBERIZE

SUBERIZES
> SUBERIZE

SUBEROSE *adj* relating to, resembling, or consisting of cork

SUBEROUS *same as*
> SUBEROSE

SUBERS > SUBER

SUBFAMILY *n* taxonomic group that is a subdivision of a family

SUBFEU *vb* grant feu or land rights to a vassal

SUBFEUED > SUBFEU

SUBFEUING > SUBFEU

SUBFEUS > SUBFEU

SUBFIELD *n* subdivision of a field

SUBFIELDS
> SUBFIELD

SUBFILE *n* file within another file

SUBFILES > SUBFILE

SUBFIX *n* suffix

SUBFIXES > SUBFIX

SUBFLOOR *n* rough floor that forms a base for a finished floor

SUBFLOORS
> SUBFLOOR

SUBFLUID *adj* viscous

SUBFOLDER *n* subdivision of a folder

SUBFOSSIL *n* something partly fossilized

SUBFRAME *n* frame on which car body is built

SUBFRAMES
> SUBFRAME

SUBFUSC *adj* devoid of brightness or appeal ▷ *n* (at Oxford University) formal academic dress

SUBFUSCS > SUBFUSC

SUBFUSK *same as*
> SUBFUSC

SUBFUSKS > SUBFUSK

SUBGENERA
> SUBGENUS

SUBGENRE *n* genre within a larger genre

SUBGENRES
> SUBGENRE

SUBGENUS *n* taxonomic group that is a subdivision of a genus but of higher rank than a species

SUBGOAL *n* secondary goal

SUBGOALS > SUBGOAL

SUBGRADE *n* ground beneath a roadway or pavement

SUBGRADES
> SUBGRADE

SUBGRAPH *n* graph sharing vertices of other graph

SUBGRAPHS
> SUBGRAPH

SUBGROUP *n* small group that is part of a larger group

SUBGROUPS
> SUBGROUP

SUBGUM *n* Chinese dish

SUBGUMS > SUBGUM

SUBHA *n* string of beads used in praying and meditating

SUBHAS > SUBHA

SUBHEAD *n* heading of a subsection in a printed work

SUBHEADS > SUBHEAD

SUBHEDRAL *adj* with some characteristics of crystal

SUBHUMAN *adj* less than human

SUBHUMANS
> SUBHUMAN

SUBHUMID *adj* not wet enough for trees to grow

SUBIDEA *n* secondary idea

SUBIDEAS > SUBIDEA

SUBIMAGO *n* first winged stage of the mayfly

SUBIMAGOS
> SUBIMAGO

SUBINCISE *vb* perform subincision

SUBINDEX *same as*
> SUBSCRIPT

SUBINFEUD *vb* to grant feu or land rights to a vassal

SUBITEM *n* item that is less important than another item

SUBITEMS > SUBITEM

SUBITISE *same as*
> SUBITIZE

SUBITISED
> SUBITISE

SUBITISES
> SUBITISE

SUBITIZE *vb* perceive the number of (a group of items) at a glance and without counting

SUBITIZED > SUBITIZE

SUBITIZES
> SUBITIZE

SUBITO *adv* (preceding or following a dynamic marking, etc) suddenly

SUBJACENT *adj* forming a foundation

SUBJECT *n* person or thing being dealt with or studied ▷ *adj* being under the rule of a monarch or government ▷ *vb* cause to undergo

SUBJECTED > SUBJECT

SUBJECTS > SUBJECT

SUBJOIN *vb* add or attach at the end of something spoken, written, etc

SUBJOINED > SUBJOIN

SUBJOINS > SUBJOIN

SUBJUGATE *vb* bring (a group of people) under one's control

SUBLATE *vb* deny

SUBLATED > SUBLATE

SUBLATES > SUBLATE

SUBLATING > SUBLATE

SUBLATION > SUBLATE

SUBLEASE *n* lease of property made by a person

who is a lessee of that property ▷ *vb* grant a sublease of (property)

SUBLEASED
> SUBLEASE

SUBLEASES
> SUBLEASE

SUBLESSEE
> SUBLEASE

SUBLESSOR
> SUBLEASE

SUBLET *vb* rent out (property rented from someone else) ▷ *n* sublease

SUBLETHAL *adj* not strong enough to kill

SUBLETS > SUBLET

SUBLETTER > SUBLET

SUBLEVEL *n* subdivision of a level

SUBLEVELS
> SUBLEVEL

SUBLIMATE *vb* direct the energy of (a strong desire) into socially acceptable activities ▷ *n* material obtained when a substance is sublimed ▷ *adj* exalted or purified

SUBLIME *adj* of high moral, intellectual, or spiritual value ▷ *vb* change from a solid to a vapour without first melting

SUBLIMED > SUBLIME

SUBLIMELY > SUBLIME

SUBLIMER > SUBLIME

SUBLIMERS > SUBLIME

SUBLIMES > SUBLIME

SUBLIMEST > SUBLIME

SUBLIMING > SUBLIME

SUBLIMISE *same as*
> SUBLIMIZE

SUBLIMIT *n* limit on a subcategory

SUBLIMITS > SUBLIMIT

SUBLIMITY > SUBLIME

SUBLIMIZE *vb* make sublime

SUBLINE *n* secondary headline

SUBLINEAR *adj* beneath a line

SUBLINES > SUBLINE

SUBLOT *n* subdivision of a lot

SUBLOTS > SUBLOT

SUBLUNAR *same as*
> SUBLUNARY

SUBLUNARY *adj* situated between the moon and the earth

SUBLUNATE *adj* almost crescent-shaped

SUBLUXATE *vb* partially dislocate

SUBMAN *n* primitive form of human

SUBMARINE *n* vessel which can operate below the surface of the sea ▷ *adj* below the surface of the sea ▷ *vb* slide beneath seatbelt in car crash

SUBMARKET *n* specialized market within larger market

SUBMATRIX *n* part of matrix

SUBMEN > SUBMAN

SUBMENTA
> SUBMENTUM

SUBMENTAL *adj* situated beneath the chin

SUBMENTUM *n* base of insect lip

SUBMENU *n* further list of options within computer menu

SUBMENUS > SUBMENU

SUBMERGE *vb* put or go below the surface of water or other liquid

SUBMERGED *adj* (of plants or plant parts) growing beneath the surface of the water

SUBMERGES
> SUBMERGE

SUBMERSE *same as*
> SUBMERGE

SUBMERSED *same as*
> SUBMERGED

SUBMERSES
> SUBMERSE

SUBMICRON *n* object only visible through a powerful microscope

SUBMISS *adj* old word meaning docile or submissive

SUBMISSLY *adv* old word meaning submissively

SUBMIT *vb* surrender

SUBMITS > SUBMIT

SUBMITTAL > SUBMIT

SUBMITTED > SUBMIT

SUBMITTER > SUBMIT

SUBMUCOSA *n* connective tissue beneath a mucous membrane

SUBMUCOUS
> SUBMUCOSA

SUBNASAL *adj* beneath nose

SUBNET *n* part of network

SUBNETS > SUBNET

SUBNEURAL *adj* beneath a nerve centre

SUBNICHE *n* subdivision of a niche

SUBNICHES
> SUBNICHE

SUBNIVEAL *adj* beneath the snow

SUBNIVEAN *same as*
> SUBNIVEAL

SUBNODAL *adj* below the level of a node

SUBNORMAL *adj* less than normal ▷ *n* in geometry, part of the x-axis of a curve

SUBNUCLEI *pl n* plural of subnucleus, secondary nucleus

SUBOCEAN *adj* beneath the ocean

SUBOCTAVE *n* octave below another

SUBOCULAR *adj* below the eye

SUBOFFICE *n* office that is subordinate to another office

SUBOPTIC *adj* below the eye

S

SUBORAL *adj* not quite oral

SUBORDER *n* taxonomic group that is a subdivision of an order

SUBORDERS
> SUBORDER

SUBORN *vb* bribe or incite (a person) to commit a wrongful act

SUBORNED > SUBORN

SUBORNER > SUBORN

SUBORNERS > SUBORN

SUBORNING > SUBORN

SUBORNS > SUBORN

SUBOSCINE *adj* belonging to a subfamily of birds

SUBOVAL *adj* not quite oval

SUBOVATE *adj* almost egg-shaped

SUBOXIDE *n* oxide of an element containing less oxygen than the common oxide formed by the element

SUBOXIDES
> SUBOXIDE

SUBPANEL *n* panel that is part of larger panel

SUBPANELS
> SUBPANEL

SUBPAR *adj* not up to standard

SUBPART *n* part within another part

SUBPARTS > SUBPART

SUBPENA *same as*
> SUBPOENA

SUBPENAED > SUBPENA

SUBPENAS > SUBPENA

SUBPERIOD *n* subdivision of a time period

SUBPHASE *n* subdivision of a phase

SUBPHASES
> SUBPHASE

SUBPHYLA
> SUBPHYLUM

SUBPHYLAR
> SUBPHYLUM

SUBPHYLUM *n* taxonomic group that is a subdivision of a phylum

SUBPLOT *n* secondary plot in a novel, play, or film

SUBPLOTS > SUBPLOT

SUBPOENA *n* writ requiring a person to appear before a law court ▷ *vb* summon (someone) with a subpoena

SUBPOENAS
> SUBPOENA

SUBPOLAR *adj* of the areas south of the Arctic and north of the Antarctic

SUBPOTENT *adj* not at full strength

SUBPRIME *n* loan made to a borrower with a poor credit rating

SUBPRIMES
> SUBPRIME

SUBPRIOR *n* monk junior to a prior

SUBPRIORS
> SUBPRIOR

SUBPUBIC *adj* beneath the pubic bone

SUBRACE *n* subdivision of a race

SUBRACES > SUBRACE

SUBREGION *n* subdivision of a region, esp a zoogeographical or ecological region

SUBRENT *n* rent paid to renter who rents to another ▷ *vb* rent out (a property that is already rented)

SUBRENTED > SUBRENT

SUBRENTS > SUBRENT

SUBRING *n* mathematical ring that is a subset of another ring

SUBRINGS > SUBRING

SUBROGATE *vb* put (one person or thing) in the place of another in respect of a right or claim

SUBRULE *n* rule within another rule

SUBRULES > SUBRULE

SUBS > SUB

SUBSACRAL *adj* below the sacrum

SUBSALE *n* sale carried out within the process of a larger sale

SUBSALES > SUBSALE

SUBSAMPLE *vb* take further sample from existing sample

SUBSCALE *n* scale within a scale

SUBSCALES
> SUBSCALE

SUBSCHEMA *n* part of computer database used by an individual

SUBSCRIBE *vb* pay (a subscription)

SUBSCRIPT *adj* (character) printed below the line ▷ *n* subscript character

SUBSEA *adj* undersea

SUBSECIVE *adj* left over

SUBSECT *n* sect within a larger sect

SUBSECTOR *n* subdivision of sector

SUBSECTS > SUBSECT

SUBSELLIA *pl n* ledges underneath the hinged seats in a church

SUBSENSE *n* definition that is a division of a wider definition

SUBSENSES
> SUBSENSE

SUBSERE *n* secondary sere arising when the progress of a sere has been interrupted

SUBSERES > SUBSERE

SUBSERIES *n* series within a larger series

SUBSERVE *vb* be helpful or useful to

SUBSERVED
> SUBSERVE

SUBSERVES > SUBSERVE

SUBSET *n* mathematical set contained within a larger set

SUBSETS > SUBSET

SUBSHAFT *n* secondary shaft in a mine

SUBSHAFTS
> SUBSHAFT

SUBSHELL *n* part of a shell of an atom

SUBSHELLS
> SUBSHELL

SUBSHRUB *n* small bushy plant that is woody except for the tips of the branches

SUBSHRUBS
> SUBSHRUB

SUBSIDE *vb* become less intense

SUBSIDED > SUBSIDE

SUBSIDER > SUBSIDE

SUBSIDERS > SUBSIDE

SUBSIDES > SUBSIDE

SUBSIDIES > SUBSIDY

SUBSIDING > SUBSIDE

SUBSIDISE *same as*
> SUBSIDIZE

SUBSIDIZE *vb* help financially

SUBSIDY *n* financial aid

SUBSIST *vb* manage to live

SUBSISTED > SUBSIST

SUBSISTER > SUBSIST

SUBSISTS > SUBSIST

SUBSITE *n* location within a website

SUBSITES > SUBSITE

SUBSIZAR *n* type of undergraduate at Cambridge

SUBSIZARS
> SUBSIZAR

SUBSKILL *n* element of a wider skill

SUBSKILLS
> SUBSKILL

SUBSOCIAL *adj* lacking a complex or definite social structure

SUBSOIL *n* earth just below the surface soil ▷ *vb* plough (land) to a depth below the normal ploughing level

SUBSOILED > SUBSOIL

SUBSOILER > SUBSOIL

SUBSOILS > SUBSOIL

SUBSOLAR *adj* (of a point on the earth) directly below the sun

SUBSONG *n* subdued form of birdsong modified from the full territorial song

SUBSONGS > SUBSONG

SUBSONIC *adj* moving at a speed less than that of sound

SUBSPACE *n* part of a mathematical matrix

SUBSPACES
> SUBSPACE

SUBSTAGE *n* part of a microscope below the stage

SUBSTAGES
> SUBSTAGE

SUBSTANCE *n* physical composition of something

SUBSTATE *n* subdivision of state

SUBSTATES
> SUBSTATE

SUBSTORM *n* disturbance in the magnetic field of a planet

SUBSTORMS
> SUBSTORM

SUBSTRACT *same as*
> SUBTRACT

SUBSTRATA *pl n* layers lying underneath other layers

SUBSTRATE *n* substance upon which an enzyme acts

SUBSTRUCT *vb* build as a foundation

SUBSTYLAR
> SUBSTYLE

SUBSTYLE *n* line on a dial

SUBSTYLES
> SUBSTYLE

SUBSULTUS *n* abnormal twitching

SUBSUME *vb* include (an idea, case, etc) under a larger classification or group

SUBSUMED > SUBSUME

SUBSUMES > SUBSUME

SUBSUMING > SUBSUME

SUBSYSTEM *n* system operating within a larger system

SUBTACK *Scots word for*
> SUBLEASE

SUBTACKS > SUBTACK

SUBTALAR *adj* beneath the ankle-bone

SUBTASK *n* task that is part of a larger task

SUBTASKS > SUBTASK

SUBTAXA > SUBTAXON

SUBTAXON *n* supplementary piece of identifying information in plant or animal scientific name

SUBTAXONS
> SUBTAXON

SUBTEEN *n* young person who has not yet become a teenager

SUBTEENS > SUBTEEN

SUBTENANT *n* person who rents property from a tenant

SUBTEND *vb* be opposite (an angle or side)

SUBTENDED > SUBTEND

SUBTENDS > SUBTEND

SUBTENSE *n* line that subtends

SUBTENSES
> SUBTENSE

SUBTENURE *n* tenancy given by another tenant

SUBTEST *n* test that is part of a larger test

SUBTESTS > SUBTEST

SUBTEXT *n* underlying theme in a piece of writing

SUBTEXTS > SUBTEXT

SUBTHEME *n* secondary theme

SUBTHEMES
> SUBTHEME
SUBTIDAL adj below the level of low tide
SUBTIL same as
> SUBTLE
SUBTILE rare spelling of
> SUBTLE
SUBTILELY > SUBTILE
SUBTILER > SUBTILE
SUBTILEST > SUBTILE
SUBTILIN n antibiotic drug
SUBTILINS
> SUBTILIN
SUBTILISE same as
> SUBTILIZE
SUBTILITY > SUBTILE
SUBTILIZE vb bring to a purer state
SUBTILTY > SUBTILE
SUBTITLE n secondary title of a book ▷ vb provide with a subtitle or subtitles
SUBTITLED
> SUBTITLE
SUBTITLES
> SUBTITLE
SUBTLE adj not immediately obvious
SUBTLER > SUBTLE
SUBTLEST > SUBTLE
SUBTLETY n fine distinction
SUBTLY > SUBTLE
SUBTONE n subdivision of a tone
SUBTONES > SUBTONE
SUBTONIC n seventh degree of a major or minor scale
SUBTONICS
> SUBTONIC
SUBTOPIA n suburban development that encroaches on rural areas
SUBTOPIAN
> SUBTOPIA
SUBTOPIAS
> SUBTOPIA
SUBTOPIC n topic within a larger topic
SUBTOPICS
> SUBTOPIC
SUBTORRID same as
> SUBTROPIC
SUBTOTAL n total made up by a column of figures, forming part of the total made up by a larger group ▷ vb work out a subtotal for (a group)
SUBTOTALS
> SUBTOTAL
SUBTRACT vb take (one number or quantity) from another
SUBTRACTS
> SUBTRACT
SUBTRADE n (in N America) specialist hired by a building contractor
SUBTRADES
> SUBTRADE
SUBTREND n minor trend
SUBTRENDS
> SUBTREND
SUBTRIBE n tribe within a larger tribe

SUBTRIBES
> SUBTRIBE
SUBTRIST adj slightly sad
SUBTROPIC adj relating to the region lying between the tropics and the temperate lands
SUBTRUDE vb intrude stealthily
SUBTRUDED
> SUBTRUDE
SUBTRUDES
> SUBTRUDE
SUBTUNIC adj below membrane ▷ n garment worn under a tunic
SUBTUNICS
> SUBTUNIC
SUBTWEET vb post a negative tweet about someone without naming them
SUBTWEETS
> SUBTWEET
SUBTYPE n secondary or subordinate type or genre
SUBTYPES > SUBTYPE
SUBUCULA n ancient Roman man's undergarment
SUBUCULAS
> SUBUCULA
SUBULATE adj (esp of plant parts) tapering to a point
SUBUNIT n distinct part or component of something larger
SUBUNITS > SUBUNIT
SUBURB n residential area on the outskirts of a city
SUBURBAN adj mildly derogatory term for inhabiting a suburb ▷ n mildly derogatory term for a person who lives in a suburb
SUBURBANS
> SUBURBAN
SUBURBED > SUBURB
SUBURBIA n suburbs and their inhabitants
SUBURBIAS
> SUBURBIA
SUBURBS > SUBURB
SUBURSINE adj of a bear subspecies
SUBVASSAL n vassal of a vassal
SUBVENE vb happen in such a way as to be of assistance
SUBVENED > SUBVENE
SUBVENES > SUBVENE
SUBVENING > SUBVENE
SUBVERSAL > SUBVERT
SUBVERSE same as
> SUBVERT
SUBVERSED
> SUBVERSE
SUBVERSES
> SUBVERSE
SUBVERST > SUBVERSE
SUBVERT vb overthrow the authority of
SUBVERTED > SUBVERT
SUBVERTER > SUBVERT
SUBVERTS > SUBVERT

SUBVICAR n assistant to a vicar
SUBVICARS
> SUBVICAR
SUBVIRAL adj of, caused by, or denoting a part of the structure of a virus
SUBVIRUS n organism smaller than a virus
SUBVISUAL adj not visible to the naked eye
SUBVOCAL adj formed in mind without being spoken aloud
SUBWARDEN n assistant to a warden
SUBWAY n passage under a road or railway ▷ vb travel by subway
SUBWAYED > SUBWAY
SUBWAYING > SUBWAY
SUBWAYS > SUBWAY
SUBWOOFER n loudspeaker for very low tones
SUBWORLD n underworld
SUBWORLDS > SUBWORLD
SUBWRITER n person carrying out writing tasks for other writer
SUBZERO adj lower than zero
SUBZONAL > SUBZONE
SUBZONE n subdivision of a zone
SUBZONES > SUBZONE
SUCCADE n piece of candied fruit
SUCCADES > SUCCADE
SUCCAH same as
> SUKKAH
SUCCAHS > SUCCAH
SUCCEDENT adj following ▷ n successor
SUCCEED vb accomplish an aim
SUCCEEDED > SUCCEED
SUCCEEDER > SUCCEED
SUCCEEDS > SUCCEED
SUCCENTOR n deputy of the precentor of a cathedral that has retained its statutes from pre-Reformation days
SUCCES French word for
> SUCCESS
SUCCESS n achievement of something attempted
SUCCESSES > SUCCESS
SUCCESSOR n person who succeeds someone in a position
SUCCI > SUCCUS
SUCCINATE n any salt or ester of succinic acid
SUCCINCT adj brief and clear
SUCCINIC adj of, relating to, or obtained from amber
SUCCINITE n type of amber
SUCCINYL n constituent of succinic acid
SUCCINYLS
> SUCCINYL
SUCCISE adj ending abruptly, as if cut off

SUCCOR same as
> SUCCOUR
SUCCORED > SUCCOR
SUCCORER > SUCCOR
SUCCORERS > SUCCOR
SUCCORIES > SUCCORY
SUCCORING > SUCCORY
SUCCORS > SUCCOR
SUCCORY another name for
> CHICORY
SUCCOS same as
> SUCCOTH
SUCCOSE > SUCCUS
SUCCOT same as
> SUKKOTH
SUCCOTASH n mixture of cooked sweet corn kernels and lima beans, served as a vegetable
SUCCOTH variant of
> SUKKOTH
SUCCOUR n help in distress ▷ vb give aid to (someone in time of difficulty)
SUCCOURED > SUCCOUR
SUCCOURER > SUCCOUR
SUCCOURS > SUCCOUR
SUCCOUS > SUCCUS
SUCCUBA same as
> SUCCUBUS
SUCCUBAE > SUCCUBA
SUCCUBAS > SUCCUBA
SUCCUBI > SUCCUBUS
SUCCUBINE
> SUCCUBUS
SUCCUBOUS adj having the leaves arranged so that the upper margin of each leaf is covered by the lower margin of the next leaf along
SUCCUBUS n female demon believed to have sex with sleeping men
SUCCULENT adj juicy and delicious ▷ n succulent plant
SUCCUMB vb give way (to something overpowering)
SUCCUMBED > SUCCUMB
SUCCUMBER > SUCCUMB
SUCCUMBS > SUCCUMB
SUCCURSAL adj (esp of a religious establishment) subsidiary ▷ n subsidiary establishment
SUCCUS n fluid
SUCCUSS vb shake (a patient) to detect the sound of fluid in a cavity
SUCCUSSED > SUCCUSS
SUCCUSSES > SUCCUSS
SUCH adj of the kind specified ▷ pron such things
SUCHLIKE pron such or similar things ▷ n such or similar things ▷ adj of such a kind
SUCHLIKES
> SUCHLIKE
SUCHNESS > SUCH
SUCHWISE > SUCH
SUCK vb draw (liquid or air) into the mouth ▷ n sucking
SUCKED > SUCK

S

SUCKEN Scots word for
> DISTRICT
SUCKENER n tenant
SUCKENERS
> SUCKENER
SUCKENS > SUCKEN
SUCKER n person who is
easily deceived or
swindled ▷ vb strip off the
suckers from (a plant)
SUCKERED > SUCKER
SUCKERING > SUCKER
SUCKERS > SUCKER
SUCKET same as
> SUCCADE
SUCKETS > SUCKET
SUCKFISH n type of
spiny-finned marine fish
SUCKHOLE n sycophant
▷ vb behave in a
sycophantic manner
SUCKHOLED
> SUCKHOLE
SUCKHOLES
> SUCKHOLE
SUCKIER > SUCKY
SUCKIEST > SUCKY
SUCKINESS n state of
inferiority
SUCKING adj not yet
weaned
SUCKINGS > SUCKING
SUCKLE vb feed at the
breast
SUCKLED > SUCKLE
SUCKLER > SUCKLE
SUCKLERS > SUCKLE
SUCKLES > SUCKLE
SUCKLESS > SUCK
SUCKLING n unweaned
baby or young animal
SUCKLINGS
> SUCKLING
SUCKS interj expression of
disappointment
SUCKY adj despicable
SUCRALOSE n artificial
sweetener
SUCRASE another name for
> INVERTASE
SUCRASES > SUCRASE
SUCRE n former standard
monetary unit of Ecuador
SUCRES > SUCRE
SUCRIER n small
container for sugar at
table
SUCRIERS > SUCRIER
SUCROSE same as
> SUGAR
SUCROSES > SUCROSE
SUCTION n sucking ▷ vb
subject to suction
SUCTIONAL > SUCTION
SUCTIONED > SUCTION
SUCTIONS > SUCTION
SUCTORIAL adj
specialized for sucking or
adhering
SUCTORIAN n
microscopic creature
SUCURUJU n anaconda
SUCURUJUS
> SUCURUJU
SUD singular of > SUDS
SUDAMEN n small cavity in
the skin
SUDAMENS > SUDAMEN

SUDAMINA > SUDAMEN
SUDAMINAL > SUDAMEN
SUDARIA > SUDARIUM
SUDARIES > SUDARY
SUDARIUM n room in a
Roman bathhouse where
sweating is induced by
heat
SUDARY same as
> SUDARIUM
SUDATE vb sweat
SUDATED > SUDATE
SUDATES > SUDATE
SUDATING > SUDATE
SUDATION > SUDATE
SUDATIONS > SUDATE
SUDATORIA same as
> SUDARIA
SUDATORY > SUDATE
SUDD n floating masses of
reeds and weeds on the
White Nile
SUDDEN adj done or
occurring quickly and
unexpectedly
SUDDENLY adv quickly
and without warning
SUDDENS > SUDDEN
SUDDENTY n suddenness
SUDDER n supreme court
in India
SUDDERS > SUDDER
SUDDS > SUDD
SUDOKU n type of puzzle
in which numbers must be
arranged in a grid
according to certain rules
SUDOKUS > SUDOKU
SUDOR technical name for
> SWEAT
SUDORAL > SUDOR
SUDORIFIC adj (drug)
causing sweating ▷ n drug
that causes sweating
SUDOROUS > SUDOR
SUDORS > SUDOR
SUDS pl n froth of soap and
water, lather ▷ vb wash in
suds
SUDSED > SUDS
SUDSER n soap opera
SUDSERS > SUDSER
SUDSES > SUDS
SUDSIER > SUDS
SUDSIEST > SUDS
SUDSING > SUDS
SUDSLESS > SUDS
SUDSY > SUDS
SUE vb start legal
proceedings against
SUEABLE > SUE
SUED > SUE
SUEDE n leather with a
velvety finish on one side
▷ vb give a suede finish to
SUEDED > SUEDE
SUEDELIKE adj like
suede
SUEDES > SUEDE
SUEDETTE n imitation
suede fabric
SUEDETTES
> SUEDETTE
SUEDING > SUEDE
SUENT adj smooth
SUER > SUE
SUERS > SUE
SUES > SUE

SUET n hard fat obtained
from sheep and cattle
SUETE n southeasterly
wind in Cape Breton
Island
SUETES > SUETE
SUETIER > SUET
SUETIEST > SUET
SUETS > SUET
SUETTIER > SUET
SUETTIEST > SUET
SUETTY > SUET
SUETY > SUET
SUFFARI same as
> SAFARI
SUFFARIS > SUFFARI
SUFFECT adj additional
▷ n additional consul in
ancient Rome
SUFFECTS > SUFFECT
SUFFER vb undergo or be
subjected to
SUFFERED > SUFFER
SUFFERER > SUFFER
SUFFERERS > SUFFER
SUFFERING n pain,
misery, or loss experienced
by a person who suffers
SUFFERS > SUFFER
SUFFETE n official in
ancient Carthage
SUFFETES > SUFFETE
SUFFICE vb be enough
for a purpose
SUFFICED > SUFFICE
SUFFICER > SUFFICE
SUFFICERS > SUFFICE
SUFFICES > SUFFICE
SUFFICING > SUFFICE
SUFFIX n letters added to
the end of a word to form
another word ▷ vb add
(letters) to the end of a
word to form another
word
SUFFIXAL > SUFFIX
SUFFIXED > SUFFIX
SUFFIXES > SUFFIX
SUFFIXING > SUFFIX
SUFFIXION > SUFFIX
SUFFLATE archaic word
for > INFLATE
SUFFLATED
> SUFFLATE
SUFFLATES
> SUFFLATE
SUFFOCATE vb kill or be
killed by deprivation of
oxygen
SUFFRAGAN n bishop
appointed to assist an
archbishop ▷ adj (of any
bishop of a diocese)
subordinate to and
assisting the superior
archbishop
SUFFRAGE n right to vote
in public elections
SUFFRAGES
> SUFFRAGE
SUFFUSE vb spread
through or over
(something)
SUFFUSED > SUFFUSE
SUFFUSES > SUFFUSE
SUFFUSING > SUFFUSE
SUFFUSION > SUFFUSE
SUFFUSIVE > SUFFUSE

SUG vb sell a product while
pretending to conduct
market research
SUGAN n straw rope
SUGANS > SUGAN
SUGAR n carbohydrate
used to sweeten food and
drinks ▷ vb sweeten or
cover with sugar
SUGARALLY n liquorice
SUGARBUSH n area
covered in sugar maple
trees
SUGARCANE n coarse
grass that yields sugar
SUGARCOAT vb cover
with sugar
SUGARED adj made
sweeter or more appealing
with or as with sugar
SUGARER > SUGAR
SUGARERS > SUGAR
SUGARIER > SUGARY
SUGARIEST > SUGARY
SUGARING n method of
removing unwanted body
hair
SUGARINGS
> SUGARING
SUGARLESS > SUGAR
SUGARLIKE > SUGAR
SUGARLOAF n large
conical mass of unrefined
sugar
SUGARPLUM n
crystallized plum
SUGARS > SUGAR
SUGARY adj of, like, or
containing sugar
SUGGED > SUG
SUGGEST vb put forward
(an idea) for consideration
SUGGESTED > SUGGEST
SUGGESTER > SUGGEST
SUGGESTS > SUGGEST
SUGGING n practice of
selling products under the
pretence of conducting
market research
SUGGINGS > SUGGING
SUGH same as > SOUGH
SUGHED > SUGH
SUGHING > SUGH
SUGHS > SUGH
SUGO n Italian pasta sauce
SUGOS > SUGO
SUGS > SUG
SUHUR n meal eaten
before sunrise by Muslims
fasting during Ramadan
SUHURS > SUHUR
SUI adj of itself
SUICIDAL adj tending
towards suicide
SUICIDE n killing oneself
intentionally ▷ vb die by
suicide
SUICIDED > SUICIDE
SUICIDES > SUICIDE
SUICIDING > SUICIDE
SUID n pig or related
animal
SUIDIAN > SUID
SUIDIANS > SUID
SUIDS > SUID
SUILLINE adj of or like a
pig
SUING > SUE

SUINGS > SUE
SUINT *n* water-soluble substance found in the fleece of sheep
SUINTS > SUINT
SUIPLAP *n* South African slang for a drunkard
SUIPLAPS > SUIPLAP
SUIT *n* set of clothes designed to be worn together ▷ *vb* be appropriate for
SUITABLE *adj* appropriate or proper
SUITABLY > SUITABLE
SUITCASE *n* portable travelling case for clothing
SUITCASES > SUITCASE
SUITE *n* set of connected rooms in a hotel
SUITED > SUIT
SUITER *n* piece of luggage for carrying suits and dresses
SUITERS > SUITER
SUITES > SUITE
SUITING *n* fabric used for suits
SUITINGS > SUITING
SUITLIKE > SUIT
SUITOR *n* person who is courting someone ▷ *vb* act as a suitor
SUITORED > SUITOR
SUITORING > SUITOR
SUITORS > SUITOR
SUITRESS *n* female suitor
SUITS > SUIT
SUIVANTE *n* lady's maid
SUIVANTES > SUIVANTE
SUIVEZ *vb* musical direction meaning follow
SUJEE *same as* > SOOGEE
SUJEES > SUJEE
SUK *same as* > SUQ
SUKH *same as* > SUQ
SUKHS > SUKH
SUKIYAKI *n* Japanese dish consisting of sliced meat and vegetables
SUKIYAKIS > SUKIYAKI
SUKKAH *n* structure in which orthodox Jews eat and sleep during Sukkoth
SUKKAHS > SUKKAH
SUKKOS *same as* > SUKKOTH
SUKKOT *same as* > SUKKOTH
SUKKOTH *n* eight-day Jewish harvest festival
SUKS > SUK
SUKUK *n* financial certificate conforming to Islam lending principles
SUKUKS > SUKUK
SULCAL > SULCUS
SULCALISE *same as* > SULCALIZE
SULCALISE *vb* furrow
SULCATE *adj* marked with longitudinal parallel grooves

SULCATED *same as* > SULCATE
SULCATION > SULCATE
SULCI > SULCUS
SULCUS *n* linear groove, furrow, or slight depression
SULDAN *same as* > SULTAN
SULDANS > SULDAN
SULFA *same as* > SULPHA
SULFAS > SULFA
SULFATASE *n* type of enzyme
SULFATE *same as* > SULPHATE
SULFATED > SULFATE
SULFATES > SULFATE
SULFATIC *adj* relating to sulphate
SULFATING > SULFATE
SULFATION > SULFATE
SULFID *same as* > SULPHIDE
SULFIDE *same as* > SULPHIDE
SULFIDES > SULFIDE
SULFIDS > SULFID
SULFINYL *same as* > SULPHINYL
SULFINYLS > SULFINYL
SULFITE *same as* > SULPHITE
SULFITES > SULFITE
SULFITIC > SULFITE
SULFO *same as* > SULPHONIC
SULFONATE *n* salt or ester of sulphonic acid
SULFONE *same as* > SULPHONE
SULFONES > SULFONE
SULFONIC > SULFONE
SULFONIUM *n* one of a type of salts
SULFONYL *same as* > SULPHURYL
SULFONYLS > SULFONYL
SULFOXIDE *n* compound containing sulphur
SULFUR *variant of* > SULPHUR
SULFURATE *vb* treat with sulphur
SULFURED > SULFUR
SULFURET *same as* > SULPHURET
SULFURETS > SULFURET
SULFURIC > SULFUR
SULFURIER > SULFURY
SULFURING > SULFUR
SULFURISE *variant of* > SULFURIZE
SULFURIZE *vb* combine or treat with sulphur
SULFUROUS *adj* resembling sulphur
SULFURS > SULFUR
SULFURY *adj* containing sulfur
SULFURYL *same as* > SULPHURYL
SULFURYLS > SULFURYL

SULK *vb* be silent and sullen because of resentment or bad temper ▷ *n* resentful or sullen mood
SULKED > SULK
SULKER *same as* > SULK
SULKERS > SULKER
SULKIER > SULKY
SULKIES > SULKY
SULKIEST > SULKY
SULKILY > SULKY
SULKINESS > SULKY
SULKING > SULK
SULKS > SULK
SULKY *adj* moody or silent because of anger or resentment ▷ *n* light two-wheeled vehicle for one person
SULLAGE *n* filth or waste, esp sewage
SULLAGES > SULLAGE
SULLEN *adj* unwilling to talk or be sociable ▷ *n* sullen mood
SULLENER > SULLEN
SULLENEST > SULLEN
SULLENLY > SULLEN
SULLENS > SULLEN
SULLIABLE > SULLY
SULLIED > SULLY
SULLIES > SULLY
SULLY *vb* ruin (someone's reputation) ▷ *n* stain
SULLYING > SULLY
SULPH *n* amphetamine sulphate
SULPHA *n* any of a group of sulphonamides that prevent the growth of bacteria
SULPHAS > SULPHA
SULPHATE *n* salt or ester of sulphuric acid ▷ *vb* treat with a sulphate or convert into a sulphate
SULPHATED > SULPHATE
SULPHATES > SULPHATE
SULPHATIC > SULPHATE
SULPHID *same as* > SULPHIDE
SULPHIDE *n* compound of sulphur with another element
SULPHIDES > SULPHIDE
SULPHIDS > SULPHID
SULPHINYL *another term for* > THIONYL
SULPHITE *n* salt or ester of sulphurous acid
SULPHITES > SULPHITE
SULPHITIC > SULPHITE
SULPHONE *n* type of organic compound
SULPHONES > SULPHONE
SULPHONIC *adj* as in sulphonic acid type of strong organic acid
SULPHONYL *same as* > SULPHURYL

SULPHS > SULPH
SULPHUR *n* pale yellow nonmetallic element ▷ *vb* treat with sulphur
SULPHURED > SULPHUR
SULPHURET *vb* treat or combine with sulphur
SULPHURIC > SULPHUR
SULPHURS > SULPHUR
SULPHURY *adj* containing sulphur
SULPHURYL *n* particular chemical divalent group
SULTAN *n* sovereign of a Muslim country
SULTANA *n* kind of raisin
SULTANAS > SULTANA
SULTANATE *n* territory of a sultan
SULTANESS *same as* > SULTANA
SULTANIC > SULTAN
SULTANS > SULTAN
SULTRIER > SULTRY
SULTRIEST > SULTRY
SULTRILY > SULTRY
SULTRY *adj* (of weather or climate) hot and humid
SULU *n* type of sarong worn in Fiji
SULUS > SULU
SUM *n* result of addition, total ▷ *vb* add or form a total of (something)
SUMAC *same as* > SUMACH
SUMACH *n* type of temperate or subtropical shrub or small tree
SUMACHS > SUMACH
SUMACS > SUMAC
SUMATRA *n* violent storm blowing from the direction of Sumatra
SUMATRAS > SUMATRA
SUMBITCH *n* son of a bitch
SUMI *n* type of black ink used in Japan
SUMIS > SUMI
SUMLESS *adj* uncountable
SUMMA *n* compendium of theology, philosophy, or canon law
SUMMABLE > SUM
SUMMAE > SUMMA
SUMMAND *n* number or quantity forming part of a sum
SUMMANDS > SUMMAND
SUMMAR *Scots variant of* > SUMMER
SUMMARIES > SUMMARY
SUMMARILY > SUMMARY
SUMMARISE *same as* > SUMMARIZE
SUMMARIST > SUMMARIZE
SUMMARIZE *vb* make or be a summary of (something)
SUMMARY *n* brief account giving the main points of something ▷ *adj* done quickly, without formalities
SUMMAS > SUMMA

S

SUMMAT pron something ▷ n impressive or important person or thing
SUMMATE vb add up
SUMMATED > SUMMATE
SUMMATES > SUMMATE
SUMMATING > SUMMATE
SUMMATION n summary
SUMMATIVE > SUMMATION
SUMMATS > SUMMAT
SUMMED > SUM
SUMMER n warmest season of the year ▷ vb spend the summer (at a place)
SUMMERED > SUMMER
SUMMERIER > SUMMER
SUMMERING > SUMMER
SUMMERLY adj like summer
SUMMERS > SUMMER
SUMMERSET n somersault
SUMMERY > SUMMER
SUMMING > SUM
SUMMINGS > SUM
SUMMIST n writer of summae
SUMMISTS > SUMMIST
SUMMIT n top of a mountain or hill ▷ vb reach summit
SUMMITAL > SUMMIT
SUMMITED > SUMMIT
SUMMITER n person who participates in a summit conference
SUMMITING > SUMMIT
SUMMITRY n practice of conducting international negotiations by summit conferences
SUMMITS > SUMMIT
SUMMON vb order (someone) to come
SUMMONED > SUMMON
SUMMONER > SUMMON
SUMMONERS > SUMMON
SUMMONING > SUMMON
SUMMONS n command summoning someone ▷ vb order (someone) to appear in court
SUMMONSED > SUMMONS
SUMMONSES > SUMMONS
SUMO n Japanese style of wrestling
SUMOIST > SUMO
SUMOISTS > SUMO
SUMOS > SUMO
SUMOTORI n sumo wrestler
SUMOTORIS > SUMOTORI
SUMP n container in an internal-combustion engine into which oil can drain
SUMPH n stupid person
SUMPHISH > SUMPH
SUMPHS > SUMPH
SUMPIT n Malay blowpipe
SUMPITAN same as > SUMPIT
SUMPITANS > SUMPITAN

SUMPITS > SUMPIT
SUMPS > SUMP
SUMPSIMUS n correct form of expression
SUMPTER n packhorse, mule, or other beast of burden
SUMPTERS > SUMPTER
SUMPTUARY adj controlling expenditure or extravagant use of resources
SUMPTUOUS adj lavish, magnificent
SUMPWEED n American weed
SUMPWEEDS > SUMPWEED
SUMS > SUM
SUMY pl n the monetary units of Uzbekistan
SUN n star around which the earth and other planets revolve ▷ vb expose (oneself) to the sun's rays
SUNBACK adj (of dress) cut low at back
SUNBAKE vb sunbathe, esp in order to become tanned ▷ n period of sunbaking
SUNBAKED adj (esp of roads, etc) dried or cracked by the sun's heat
SUNBAKES > SUNBAKE
SUNBAKING > SUNBAKE
SUNBATH n exposure of the body to the sun to get a suntan
SUNBATHE vb lie in the sunshine in order to get a suntan
SUNBATHED > SUNBATHE
SUNBATHER > SUNBATHE
SUNBATHES > SUNBATHE
SUNBATHS > SUNBATH
SUNBEAM n ray of sun
SUNBEAMED > SUNBEAM
SUNBEAMS > SUNBEAM
SUNBEAMY adj full of sunbeams
SUNBEAT adj exposed to sun
SUNBEATEN same as > SUNBEAT
SUNBED n machine for giving an artificial tan
SUNBEDS > SUNBED
SUNBELT n southern states of the US
SUNBELTS > SUNBELT
SUNBERRY n red fruit like the blackberry
SUNBIRD n type of small songbird with a bright plumage in the males
SUNBIRDS > SUNBIRD
SUNBLIND n blind that shades a room from the sun's glare
SUNBLINDS > SUNBLIND
SUNBLOCK n cream applied to the skin to protect it from the sun's rays

SUNBLOCKS > SUNBLOCK
SUNBONNET n hat that shades the face and neck from the sun
SUNBOW n bow of colours produced when sunlight shines through spray
SUNBOWS > SUNBOW
SUNBRIGHT adj bright as the sun
SUNBURN n painful reddening of the skin caused by overexposure to the sun ▷ vb become sunburnt
SUNBURNED > SUNBURN
SUNBURNS > SUNBURN
SUNBURNT > SUNBURN
SUNBURST n burst of sunshine, as through a break in the clouds
SUNBURSTS > SUNBURST
SUNCARE n use of products in protecting skin from the sun
SUNCARES > SUNCARE
SUNCHOKE n Jerusalem artichoke
SUNCHOKES > SUNCHOKE
SUNDAE n ice cream topped with fruit etc
SUNDAES > SUNDAE
SUNDARI n Indian tree
SUNDARIS > SUNDARI
SUNDECK n upper open deck on a passenger ship
SUNDECKS > SUNDECK
SUNDER vb break apart
SUNDERED > SUNDER
SUNDERER > SUNDER
SUNDERERS > SUNDER
SUNDERING > SUNDER
SUNDERS > SUNDER
SUNDEW n type of bog plant with leaves covered in sticky hairs
SUNDEWS > SUNDEW
SUNDIAL n device showing the time by means of a pointer that casts a shadow
SUNDIALS > SUNDIAL
SUNDOG n small rainbow or halo near the horizon
SUNDOGS > SUNDOG
SUNDOWN same as > SUNSET
SUNDOWNED > SUNDOWN
SUNDOWNER n tramp, esp one who seeks food and lodging at sundown when it is too late to work
SUNDOWNS > SUNDOWN
SUNDRA same as > SUNDARI
SUNDRAS > SUNDRA
SUNDRESS n strapped dress worn in hot weather
SUNDRI same as > SUNDARI
SUNDRIES > SUNDRY
SUNDRILY > SUNDRY
SUNDRIS > SUNDRI
SUNDROPS pl n any of various American primroses

SUNDRY adj several, various
SUNFAST adj not fading in sunlight
SUNFISH n large sea fish with a rounded body
SUNFISHES > SUNFISH
SUNFLOWER n tall plant with large golden flowers
SUNG > SING
SUNGAR same as > SANGAR
SUNGARS > SUNGAR
SUNGAZER n person who practises sungazing
SUNGAZERS > SUNGAZER
SUNGAZING n staring directly at the sun
SUNGLASS n convex lens used to focus the sun's rays and thus produce heat or ignition
SUNGLOW n pinkish glow often seen in the sky before sunrise or after sunset
SUNGLOWS > SUNGLOW
SUNGREBE another name for > FINFOOT
SUNGREBES > SUNGREBE
SUNHAT n hat that shades the face and neck from the sun
SUNHATS > SUNHAT
SUNI n S African dwarf antelope
SUNIS > SUNI
SUNK n bank or pad
SUNKEN adj unhealthily hollow
SUNKER n rock (partially) submerged in shallow water
SUNKERS > SUNKER
SUNKET n something good to eat
SUNKETS > SUNKET
SUNKIE n little stool
SUNKIES > SUNKIE
SUNKS > SUNK
SUNLAMP n lamp that generates ultraviolet rays
SUNLAMPS > SUNLAMP
SUNLAND n sunny area
SUNLANDS > SUNLAND
SUNLESS adj without sun or sunshine
SUNLESSLY > SUNLESS
SUNLIGHT n light that comes from the sun
SUNLIGHTS > SUNLIGHT
SUNLIKE > SUN
SUNLIT > SUNLIGHT
SUNN n tropical leguminous plant
SUNNA n body of traditional Islamic law
SUNNAH same as > SUNNA
SUNNAHS > SUNNAH
SUNNAS > SUNNA
SUNNED > SUN
SUNNIER > SUNNY
SUNNIES pl n pair of sunglasses
SUNNIEST > SUNNY

SUNNILY > SUNNY
SUNNINESS > SUNNY
SUNNING > SUN
SUNNS > SUNN
SUNNY *adj* full of or exposed to sunlight
SUNPORCH *n* porch for sunbathing on
SUNPROOF > SUN
SUNRAY *n* ray of light from the sun
SUNRAYS > SUNRAY
SUNRISE *n* daily appearance of the sun above the horizon
SUNRISES > SUNRISE
SUNRISING *same as* > SUNRISE
SUNROOF *n* panel in the roof of a car that opens to let in air
SUNROOFS > SUNROOF
SUNROOM *n* room or glass-enclosed porch designed to display beautiful views
SUNROOMS > SUNROOM
SUNS > SUN
SUNSCALD *n* sun damage on tomato plants
SUNSCALDS > SUNSCALD
SUNSCREEN *n* cream or lotion applied to exposed skin to protect it from the ultraviolet rays of the sun
SUNSEEKER *n* person looking for sunny weather
SUNSET *vb* phase out
SUNSETS > SUNSET
SUNSETTED > SUNSET
SUNSHADE *n* anything used to shade people from the sun, such as a parasol or awning
SUNSHADES > SUNSHADE
SUNSHINE *n* light and warmth from the sun
SUNSHINES > SUNSHINE
SUNSHINY *adj* sunny
SUNSPECS *pl n* sunglasses
SUNSPOT *n* dark patch appearing temporarily on the sun's surface
SUNSPOTS > SUNSPOT
SUNSTAR *n* type of starfish with up to 13 arms
SUNSTARS > SUNSTAR
SUNSTONE *n* type of translucent feldspar with reddish-gold speckles
SUNSTONES > SUNSTONE
SUNSTROKE *n* illness caused by prolonged exposure to intensely hot sunlight
SUNSTRUCK *adj* suffering from sunstroke
SUNSUIT *n* child's outfit consisting of a brief top and shorts or a short skirt
SUNSUITS > SUNSUIT
SUNTAN *n* browning of the skin caused by exposure to the sun

SUNTANNED > SUNTAN
SUNTANS > SUNTAN
SUNTRAP *n* very sunny sheltered place
SUNTRAPS > SUNTRAP
SUNUP *same as* > SUNRISE
SUNUPS > SUNUP
SUNWARD *same as* > SUNWARDS
SUNWARDS *adv* towards the sun
SUNWISE *adv* moving in the same direction as the sun
SUP *same as* > SUPINE
SUPAWN *same as* > SUPPAWN
SUPAWNS > SUPAWN
SUPE *n* superintendent
SUPER *adj* excellent ▷ *n* superannuation ▷ *interj* enthusiastic expression of approval or assent ▷ *vb* work as superintendent
SUPERABLE *adj* able to be surmounted or overcome
SUPERABLY > SUPERABLE
SUPERADD *vb* add (something) to something that has already been added
SUPERADDS > SUPERADD
SUPERATE *vb* overcome
SUPERATED > SUPERATE
SUPERATES > SUPERATE
SUPERATOM *n* cluster of atoms behaving like a single atom
SUPERB *adj* excellent, impressive, or splendid
SUPERBAD *adj* exceptionally bad
SUPERBANK *n* bank that owns other banks
SUPERBER > SUPERB
SUPERBEST > SUPERB
SUPERBIKE *n* high-performance motorcycle
SUPERBITY > SUPERB
SUPERBLY > SUPERB
SUPERBOLD *adj* exceptionally bold
SUPERBOMB *n* large bomb
SUPERBRAT *n* exceptionally unpleasant child
SUPERBUG *n* bacterium resistant to antibiotics
SUPERBUGS > SUPERBUG
SUPERCAR *n* very expensive fast or powerful car with a centrally located engine
SUPERCARS > SUPERCAR
SUPERCEDE *former variant of* > SUPERSEDE
SUPERCELL *n* unusually large storm cell

SUPERCHIC *adj* highly chic
SUPERCITY *n* very large city
SUPERCLUB *n* large and important club
SUPERCOIL *vb* form a complex coil
SUPERCOLD *adj* very cold
SUPERCOOL *vb* cool or be cooled to a temperature below that at which freezing or crystallization should occur
SUPERCOP *n* high-ranking police officer
SUPERCOPS > SUPERCOP
SUPERCOW *n* dairy cow that produces a very high milk yield
SUPERCOWS > SUPERCOW
SUPERCUTE *adj* very cute
SUPERED > SUPER
SUPEREGO *n* that part of the unconscious mind that governs ideas about what is right and wrong
SUPEREGOS > SUPEREGO
SUPERETTE *n* small store or dairy laid out along the lines of a supermarket
SUPERFAN *n* very devoted fan
SUPERFANS > SUPERFAN
SUPERFARM *n* very large farm
SUPERFAST *adj* very fast
SUPERFINE *adj* of exceptional fineness or quality
SUPERFIRM *adj* very firm
SUPERFIT *adj* highly fit
SUPERFIX *n* linguistic feature distinguishing the meaning of one word from another
SUPERFLUX *n* superfluity
SUPERFLY *adj* pretentiously flamboyant
SUPERFOOD *n* food thought to be beneficial to health
SUPERFUND *n* large fund
SUPERFUSE *vb* pour or be poured so as to cover something
SUPERGENE *n* cluster of genes
SUPERGLUE *n* extremely strong and quick-drying glue ▷ *vb* fix with superglue
SUPERGOOD *adj* very good
SUPERGUN *n* large powerful gun
SUPERGUNS > SUPERGUN
SUPERHARD *adj* extremely hard
SUPERHEAT *vb* heat (a vapour, esp steam) to a temperature above its saturation point for a given pressure

SUPERHERO *n* any of various comic-strip characters with superhuman abilities or magical powers
SUPERHET *n* type of radio receiver
SUPERHETS > SUPERHET
SUPERHIGH *adj* extremely high
SUPERHIT *n* very popular hit
SUPERHITS > SUPERHIT
SUPERHIVE *n* upper part of beehive
SUPERHOT *adj* very hot
SUPERHYPE *n* exaggerated hype
SUPERING > SUPER
SUPERIOR *adj* greater in quality, quantity, or merit ▷ *n* person of greater rank or status
SUPERIORS > SUPERIOR
SUPERJET *n* supersonic aircraft
SUPERJETS > SUPERJET
SUPERJOCK *n* very athletic person
SUPERLAIN > SUPERLIE
SUPERLAY > SUPERLIE
SUPERLIE *vb* lie above
SUPERLIES > SUPERLIE
SUPERLOAD *n* variable weight on a structure
SUPERLONG *adj* very long
SUPERLOO *n* automated public toilet
SUPERLOOS > SUPERLOO
SUPERMALE *former name for* > METAMALE
SUPERMAN *n* man with great physical or mental powers
SUPERMART *n* large self-service store selling food and household supplies
SUPERMAX *n* jail or other facility having the very highest levels of security
SUPERMEN > SUPERMAN
SUPERMIND *n* very powerful brain
SUPERMINI *n* small car, usually a hatchback, that is economical to run but has a high level of performance
SUPERMOM *n* very capable and busy mother
SUPERMOMS > SUPERMOM
SUPERMOON *n* occasion when the perigee coincides with a full moon
SUPERMOTO *n* form of motorcycle racing over part-tarmac and part-dirt circuits
SUPERNAL *adj* of or from the world of the divine

S

SUPERNATE n liquid lying above a sediment ▷ vb float on (a surface)

SUPERNOVA n star that explodes and briefly becomes exceptionally bright

SUPERPIMP n pimp controlling many prostitutes

SUPERPLUS n surplus

SUPERPORT n large port

SUPERPOSE vb transpose (the coordinates of one geometric figure) to coincide with those of another

SUPERPRO n person regarded as a real professional

SUPERPROS > SUPERPRO

SUPERRACE n race believed superior to others

SUPERREAL adj surreal

SUPERRICH adj exceptionally wealthy

SUPERROAD n very large road

SUPERS > SUPER

SUPERSAFE adj very safe

SUPERSALE n large sale

SUPERSALT n acid salt

SUPERSAUR n very large dinosaur

SUPERSEDE vb replace, supplant

SUPERSELL vb sell in very large numbers

SUPERSET n set containing all the members of another set plus other members

SUPERSETS > SUPERSET

SUPERSEX n in genetics, type of sterile organism

SUPERSHOW n very impressive show

SUPERSIZE vb make larger

SUPERSOFT adj very soft

SUPERSOLD > SUPERSELL

SUPERSPY n highly accomplished spy

SUPERSTAR n very famous entertainer or sportsperson

SUPERSTUD n highly virile man

SUPERTAX n extra tax on incomes above a certain level

SUPERTHIN adj very thin

SUPERTRAM n type of tram with greater capacity and speed than conventional trams

SUPERUSER n type of administration-level account in a computing system

SUPERVENE vb occur as an unexpected development

SUPERVISE vb watch over to direct or check

SUPERWAIF n very young and very thin supermodel

SUPERWAVE n large wave

SUPERWEED n hybrid plant that contains genes for herbicide resistance

SUPERWIDE n very wide lens

SUPERWIFE n highly accomplished wife

SUPES > SUPE

SUPINATE vb turn (the hand and forearm) so that the palm faces up or forwards

SUPINATED > SUPINATE

SUPINATES > SUPINATE

SUPINATOR n muscle of the forearm that can produce the motion of supination

SUPINE adj lying flat on one's back ▷ n noun form derived from a verb in Latin

SUPINELY > SUPINE

SUPINES > SUPINE

SUPLEX n type of wrestling hold

SUPLEXES > SUPLEX

SUPPAWN n kind of porridge

SUPPAWNS > SUPPAWN

SUPPEAGO same as > SERPIGO

SUPPED > SUP

SUPPER n light evening meal ▷ vb eat supper

SUPPERED > SUPPER

SUPPERING > SUPPER

SUPPERS > SUPPER

SUPPING > SUP

SUPPLANT vb take the place of, oust

SUPPLANTS > SUPPLANT

SUPPLE adj (of a person) moving and bending easily and gracefully ▷ vb make or become supple

SUPPLED > SUPPLE

SUPPLELY same as > SUPPLY

SUPPLER > SUPPLE

SUPPLES > SUPPLE

SUPPLEST > SUPPLE

SUPPLIAL n instance of supplying

SUPPLIALS > SUPPLIAL

SUPPLIANT n person who requests humbly

SUPPLICAT n university petition

SUPPLIED > SUPPLY

SUPPLIER > SUPPLY

SUPPLIERS > SUPPLY

SUPPLIES > SUPPLY

SUPPLING > SUPPLE

SUPPLY vb provide with something required ▷ n supplying ▷ adj acting as a temporary substitute ▷ adv in a supple manner

SUPPLYING > SUPPLY

SUPPORT vb bear the weight of ▷ n supporting

SUPPORTED > SUPPORT

SUPPORTER n person who supports a team, principle, etc

SUPPORTS > SUPPORT

SUPPOSAL n supposition

SUPPOSALS > SUPPOSAL

SUPPOSE vb presume to be true

SUPPOSED adj presumed to be true without proof, doubtful

SUPPOSER > SUPPOSE

SUPPOSERS > SUPPOSE

SUPPOSES > SUPPOSE

SUPPOSING > SUPPOSE

SUPPRESS vb put an end to

SUPPURATE vb (of a wound etc) produce pus

SUPRA adv above, esp referring to earlier parts of a book etc

SUPREMA > SUPREMUM

SUPREMACY n supreme power

SUPREME adj highest in authority, rank, or degree ▷ n rich sauce made with a base of veal or chicken stock

SUPREMELY > SUPREME

SUPREMER > SUPREME

SUPREMES > SUPREME

SUPREMEST > SUPREME

SUPREMITY n supremeness

SUPREMO n person in overall authority

SUPREMOS > SUPREMO

SUPREMUM n (in maths) smallest quantity greater than or equal to each of a set or subset

SUPREMUMS > SUPREMUM

SUPS > SUP

SUQ n open-air marketplace

SUQS > SUQ

SUR prep above

SURA n any of the 114 chapters of the Koran

SURAH n twill-weave fabric of silk or rayon, used for dresses, blouses, etc

SURAHS > SURAH

SURAL adj of or relating to the calf of the leg

SURAMIN n drug used in treating sleeping sickness

SURAMINS > SURAMIN

SURANCE same as > ASSURANCE

SURANCES > SURANCE

SURAS > SURA

SURAT n cotton fabric from Surat in India

SURATS > SURAT

SURBAHAR n Indian string instrument

SURBAHARS > SURBAHAR

SURBASE n uppermost part, such as a moulding,

of a pedestal, base, or skirting

SURBASED adj having a surbase

SURBASES > SURBASE

SURBATE vb make feet sore through walking

SURBATED > SURBATE

SURBATES > SURBATE

SURBATING > SURBATE

SURBED vb put something on its edge

SURBEDDED > SURBED

SURBEDS > SURBED

SURBET > SURBATE

SURCEASE n cessation or intermission ▷ vb desist from (some action)

SURCEASED > SURCEASE

SURCEASES > SURCEASE

SURCHARGE n additional charge ▷ vb charge (someone) an additional sum or tax

SURCINGLE n girth for a horse which goes around the body, used esp with a racing saddle ▷ vb put a surcingle on or over (a horse)

SURCOAT n tunic worn by a knight over their armour

SURCOATS > SURCOAT

SURCULI > SURCULUS

SURCULOSE adj (of a plant) bearing suckers

SURCULUS n sucker on plant

SURD n number that cannot be expressed in whole numbers ▷ adj of or relating to a surd

SURDITIES > SURDITY

SURDITY n deafness

SURDS > SURD

SURE adj free from uncertainty or doubt ▷ interj certainly ▷ vb archaic form of sewer

SURED > SURE

SUREFIRE adj certain to succeed

SURELY adv it must be true that

SURENESS > SURE

SURER > SURE

SURES > SURE

SUREST > SURE

SURETIED > SURETY

SURETIES > SURETY

SURETY n person who takes responsibility for the fulfilment of another's obligation ▷ vb be surety for

SURETYING > SURETY

SURF n foam caused by waves breaking on the shore ▷ vb take part in surfing

SURFABLE > SURF

SURFACE n outside or top of an object ▷ vb become apparent

SURFACED > SURFACE

SURFACER > SURFACE

SURFACERS > SURFACE
SURFACES > SURFACE
SURFACING > SURFACE
SURFBIRD n American shore bird
SURFBIRDS > SURFBIRD
SURFBOARD n long smooth board used in surfing
SURFBOAT n boat with a high bow and stern and flotation chambers
SURFBOATS > SURFBOAT
SURFED > SURF
SURFEIT n excessive amount ▷ vb supply or feed excessively
SURFEITED > SURFEIT
SURFEITER > SURFEIT
SURFEITS > SURFEIT
SURFER > SURFING
SURFERS > SURFING
SURFFISH n fish of American coastal seas
SURFICIAL adj superficial
SURFIE n young person whose main interest is in surfing
SURFIER > SURF
SURFIES > SURFIE
SURFIEST > SURF
SURFING n sport of riding on a board on the crest of a wave
SURFINGS > SURFING
SURFLIKE > SURF
SURFMAN n sailor skilled in sailing through surf
SURFMEN > SURFMAN
SURFPERCH n type of marine fish of North American Pacific coastal waters
SURFRIDE vb ride on surf
SURFRIDER > SURFRIDE
SURFRIDES > SURFRIDE
SURFRODE > SURFRIDE
SURFS > SURF
SURFSIDE adj next to the sea
SURFY > SURF
SURGE n sudden powerful increase ▷ vb increase suddenly
SURGED > SURGE
SURGEFUL > SURGE
SURGELESS > SURGE
SURGENT > SURGE
SURGEON n doctor who specializes in surgery
SURGEONCY n office, duties, or position of a surgeon, esp in the army or navy
SURGEONS > SURGEON
SURGER > SURGE
SURGERIES > SURGERY
SURGERS > SURGE
SURGERY n treatment in which the patient's body is cut open in order to treat the affected part
SURGES > SURGE

SURGICAL adj involving or used in surgery
SURGIER > SURGE
SURGIEST > SURGE
SURGING > SURGE
SURGINGS > SURGE
SURGY > SURGE
SURICATE n type of meerkat
SURICATES > SURICATE
SURIMI n blended seafood product made from precooked fish
SURIMIS > SURIMI
SURING > SURE
SURLIER > SURLY
SURLIEST > SURLY
SURLILY > SURLY
SURLINESS > SURLY
SURLOIN same as > SIRLOIN
SURLOINS > SURLOIN
SURLY adj ill-tempered and rude
SURMASTER n deputy headmaster
SURMISAL > SURMISE
SURMISALS > SURMISE
SURMISE n guess, conjecture ▷ vb guess (something) from incomplete or uncertain evidence
SURMISED > SURMISE
SURMISER > SURMISE
SURMISERS > SURMISE
SURMISES > SURMISE
SURMISING > SURMISE
SURMOUNT vb overcome (a problem)
SURMOUNTS > SURMOUNT
SURMULLET n red mullet
SURNAME n family name ▷ vb furnish with or call by a surname
SURNAMED > SURNAME
SURNAMER > SURNAME
SURNAMERS > SURNAME
SURNAMES > SURNAME
SURNAMING > SURNAME
SURPASS vb be greater than or superior to
SURPASSED > SURPASS
SURPASSER > SURPASS
SURPASSES > SURPASS
SURPLICE n loose white robe worn by members of the clergy and choristers
SURPLICED > SURPLICE
SURPLICES > SURPLICE
SURPLUS n amount left over in excess of what is required ▷ adj extra ▷ vb be left over in excess of what is required
SURPLUSED > SURPLUS
SURPLUSES > SURPLUS
SURPRINT vb print (additional matter) over something already printed ▷ n marks, printed matter, etc, that have been surprinted
SURPRINTS > SURPRINT

SURPRISAL > SURPRISE
SURPRISE n unexpected event ▷ vb cause to feel amazement or wonder
SURPRISED > SURPRISE
SURPRISER > SURPRISE
SURPRISES > SURPRISE
SURPRIZE same as > SURPRISE
SURPRIZED > SURPRIZE
SURPRIZES > SURPRIZE
SURQUEDY n arrogance
SURQUEDY same as > SURQUEDRY
SURRA n tropical febrile disease of animals
SURRAS > SURRA
SURREAL adj bizarre ▷ n atmosphere or qualities evoked by surrealism
SURREALLY > SURREAL
SURREALS > SURREAL
SURREBUT vb give evidence to support the surrebutter
SURREBUTS > SURREBUT
SURREINED adj (of horse) ridden too much
SURREJOIN vb reply to legal rejoinder
SURRENDER vb give oneself up ▷ n surrendering
SURRENDRY same as > SURRENDER
SURREY n light horse-drawn carriage
SURREYS > SURREY
SURROGACY > SURROGATE
SURROGATE n substitute ▷ adj acting as a substitute ▷ vb put in another's position as a deputy, substitute, etc
SURROUND vb be, come, or place all around (a person or thing) ▷ n border or edging
SURROUNDS > SURROUND
SURROYAL n high point on stag's horns
SURROYALS > SURROYAL
SURTAX n extra tax on incomes above a certain level ▷ vb assess for liability to surtax
SURTAXED > SURTAX
SURTAXES > SURTAX
SURTAXING > SURTAX
SURTITLE n printed translation of the libretto of an opera in a language foreign to the audience
SURTITLES pl n brief translations of the text of an opera or play projected above the stage
SURTOUT n man's overcoat resembling a frock coat

SURTOUTS > SURTOUT
SURUCUCU n South American snake
SURUCUCUS > SURUCUCU
SURVEIL same as > SURVEILLE
SURVEILED > SURVEIL
SURVEILLE vb observe closely
SURVEILS > SURVEIL
SURVEY vb view or consider in a general way ▷ n surveying
SURVEYAL > SURVEY
SURVEYALS > SURVEY
SURVEYED > SURVEY
SURVEYING n practice of measuring altitudes, angles, and distances on the land surface so that they can be accurately plotted on a map
SURVEYOR n person whose occupation is to survey land or buildings
SURVEYORS > SURVEYOR
SURVEYS > SURVEY
SURVIEW vb survey
SURVIEWED > SURVIEW
SURVIEWS > SURVIEW
SURVIVAL n condition of having survived ▷ adj of, relating to, or assisting the act of surviving
SURVIVALS > SURVIVAL
SURVIVE vb continue to live or exist after (a difficult experience)
SURVIVED > SURVIVE
SURVIVER same as > SURVIVOR
SURVIVERS > SURVIVOR
SURVIVES > SURVIVE
SURVIVING > SURVIVE
SURVIVOR n person or thing that survives
SURVIVORS > SURVIVOR
SUS same as > SUSS
SUSCEPTOR n sponsor
SUSCITATE vb excite
SUSED > SUS
SUSES > SUS
SUSHI n Japanese dish of small cakes of cold rice with a topping of raw fish
SUSHIS > SUSHI
SUSING > SUS
SUSLIK n central Eurasian ground squirrel
SUSLIKS > SUSLIK
SUSPECT vb believe (someone) to be guilty without having any proof ▷ adj not to be trusted ▷ n person who is suspected
SUSPECTED > SUSPECT
SUSPECTER > SUSPECT
SUSPECTS > SUSPECT
SUSPENCE same as > SUSPENSE
SUSPEND vb hang from a high place
SUSPENDED > SUSPEND

S

SUSPENDER n elastic strap for holding up women's stockings
SUSPENDS > SUSPEND
SUSPENS same as > SUSPENSE
SUSPENSE n state of uncertainty while awaiting news, an event, etc
SUSPENSER n film that creates a feeling of suspense
SUSPENSES > SUSPENSE
SUSPENSOR n ligament or muscle that holds a part in position
SUSPICION n feeling of not trusting a person or thing
SUSPIRE vb sigh or utter with a sigh
SUSPIRED > SUSPIRE
SUSPIRES > SUSPIRE
SUSPIRING > SUSPIRE
SUSS vb attempt to work out (a situation, etc), using one's intuition ▷ n sharpness of mind
SUSSED > SUSS
SUSSES > SUSS
SUSSING > SUSS
SUSTAIN vb maintain or prolong ▷ n prolongation of a note, by playing technique or electronics
SUSTAINED > SUSTAIN
SUSTAINER n rocket engine that maintains the velocity of a space vehicle after the booster has been jettisoned
SUSTAINS > SUSTAIN
SUSTINENT adj sustaining
SUSU n (in the Caribbean) savings fund shared by friends
SUSURRANT > SUSURRATE
SUSURRATE vb make a soft rustling sound
SUSURROUS adj full of murmuring sounds
SUSURRUS > SUSURRATE
SUSUS > SUSU
SUTILE adj involving sewing
SUTLER n merchant who accompanied an army in order to sell provisions
SUTLERIES > SUTLER
SUTLERS > SUTLER
SUTLERY > SUTLER
SUTOR n cobbler
SUTORIAL > SUTOR
SUTORIAN > SUTOR
SUTORS > SUTOR
SUTRA n Sanskrit sayings or collections of sayings
SUTRAS > SUTRA
SUTTA n Buddhist scripture
SUTTAS > SUTTA
SUTTEE n custom whereby a widow burnt

herself on her husband's funeral pyre
SUTTEEISM > SUTTEE
SUTTEES > SUTTEE
SUTTLE vb work as a sutler
SUTTLED > SUTTLE
SUTTLES > SUTTLE
SUTTLETIE same as > SUBTLETY
SUTTLING > SUTTLE
SUTTLY > SUBTLE
SUTURAL > SUTURE
SUTURALLY > SUTURE
SUTURE n stitch joining the edges of a wound ▷ vb join (the edges of a wound, etc) by means of sutures
SUTURED > SUTURE
SUTURES > SUTURE
SUTURING > SUTURE
SUZERAIN n state or sovereign with limited authority over another self-governing state
SUZERAINS > SUZERAIN
SVARAJ same as > SWARAJ
SVARAJES > SVARAJ
SVASTIKA same as > SWASTIKA
SVASTIKAS > SVASTIKA
SVEDBERG n unit used in physics
SVEDBERGS > SVEDBERG
SVELTE adj attractively or gracefully slim
SVELTELY > SVELTE
SVELTER > SVELTE
SVELTEST > SVELTE
SWAB n small piece of cotton wool used to apply medication, clean a wound, etc ▷ vb clean (a wound) with a swab
SWABBED > SWAB
SWABBER n person who uses a swab
SWABBERS > SWABBER
SWABBIE same as > SWABBY
SWABBIES > SWABBY
SWABBING > SWAB
SWABBY n seaman
SWABS > SWAB
SWACHH adj (in Indian English) clean
SWACK adj flexible ▷ vb strike
SWACKED > SWACK
SWACKING > SWACK
SWACKS > SWACK
SWAD n loutish person
SWADDIE same as > SWADDY
SWADDIES > SWADDY
SWADDLE vb wrap (a baby) in swaddling clothes ▷ n swaddling clothes
SWADDLED > SWADDLE
SWADDLER > SWADDLE
SWADDLERS > SWADDLE
SWADDLES > SWADDLE
SWADDLING > SWADDLE
SWADDY n private soldier

SWADS > SWAD
SWAG n stolen property ▷ vb sway from side to side
SWAGE n shaped tool or die used in forming cold metal by hammering ▷ vb form (metal) with a swage
SWAGED > SWAGE
SWAGER > SWAGE
SWAGERS > SWAGE
SWAGES > SWAGE
SWAGGED > SWAG
SWAGGER vb walk or behave arrogantly ▷ n arrogant walk or manner ▷ adj elegantly fashionable
SWAGGERED > SWAGGER
SWAGGERER > SWAGGER
SWAGGERS > SWAGGER
SWAGGIE same as > SWAGGER
SWAGGIES > SWAGGIE
SWAGGING > SWAG
SWAGING > SWAGE
SWAGMAN n tramp who carries their belongings in a bundle on their back
SWAGMEN > SWAGMAN
SWAGS > SWAG
SWAGSHOP n shop selling cheap goods
SWAGSHOPS > SWAGSHOP
SWAGSMAN same as > SWAGMAN
SWAGSMEN > SWAGSMAN
SWAIL same as > SWALE
SWAILS > SWAIL
SWAIN n suitor
SWAINING n acting as suitor
SWAININGS > SWAINING
SWAINISH > SWAIN
SWAINS > SWAIN
SWALE n moist depression in a tract of land ▷ vb sway
SWALED > SWALE
SWALES > SWALE
SWALIER > SWALE
SWALIEST > SWALE
SWALING > SWALE
SWALINGS > SWALE
SWALLET n hole where water goes underground
SWALLETS > SWALLET
SWALLIES > SWALLY
SWALLOW vb cause to pass down one's throat ▷ n swallowing
SWALLOWED > SWALLOW
SWALLOWER > SWALLOW
SWALLOWS > SWALLOW
SWALLY n alcoholic drink
SWALY > SWALE
SWAM > SWIM
SWAMI n Hindu religious teacher
SWAMIES > SWAMI
SWAMIS > SWAMI
SWAMP n watery area of land, bog ▷ vb cause (a boat) to fill with water and sink
SWAMPED > SWAMP
SWAMPER n person who lives or works in a swampy region

SWAMPERS > SWAMPER
SWAMPIER > SWAMP
SWAMPIEST > SWAMP
SWAMPING > SWAMP
SWAMPISH > SWAMP
SWAMPLAND n permanently waterlogged area
SWAMPLESS > SWAMP
SWAMPS > SWAMP
SWAMPY > SWAMP
SWAMY same as > SWAMI
SWAN n large usu white water bird with a long graceful neck ▷ vb wander about idly
SWANG > SWING
SWANHERD n person who herds swans
SWANHERDS > SWANHERD
SWANK vb show off or boast ▷ n showing off or boasting
SWANKED > SWANK
SWANKER > SWANK
SWANKERS > SWANK
SWANKEST > SWANK
SWANKEY same as > SWANKY
SWANKEYS > SWANKEY
SWANKIE same as > SWANKY
SWANKIER > SWANKY
SWANKIES > SWANKY
SWANKIEST > SWANKY
SWANKILY > SWANKY
SWANKING > SWANK
SWANKPOT same as > SWANK
SWANKPOTS > SWANKPOT
SWANKS > SWANK
SWANKY adj expensive and showy, stylish ▷ n lively person
SWANLIKE > SWAN
SWANNED > SWAN
SWANNERY n place where swans are kept and bred
SWANNIE n (in New Zealand) type of heavy woollen shirt
SWANNIER > SWANNY
SWANNIES > SWANNIE
SWANNIEST > SWANNY
SWANNING > SWAN
SWANNINGS > SWAN
SWANNY adj swanlike
SWANPAN n Chinese abacus
SWANPANS > SWANPAN
SWANS > SWAN
SWANSDOWN n fine soft feathers of a swan
SWANSKIN n skin of a swan with the feathers attached
SWANSKINS > SWANSKIN
SWANSONG n beautiful song fabled to be sung by a swan before it dies
SWANSONGS > SWANSONG
SWAP vb exchange (something) for something else ▷ n exchange

SWAPFILE *n* computer file which provides space for transferred programs
SWAPFILES
> SWAPFILE
SWAPPABLE *adj* capable of being swapped
SWAPPED > SWAP
SWAPPER > SWAP
SWAPPERS > SWAP
SWAPPING > SWAP
SWAPPINGS > SWAP
SWAPS > SWAP
SWAPT > SWAP
SWAPTION *another name for* > SWAP
SWAPTIONS
> SWAPTION
SWARAJ *n* (in British India) self-government
SWARAJES > SWARAJ
SWARAJISM > SWARAJ
SWARAJIST > SWARAJ
SWARD *n* stretch of short grass ▷ *vb* cover or become covered with grass
SWARDED > SWARD
SWARDIER > SWARDY
SWARDIEST > SWARDY
SWARDING > SWARD
SWARDS > SWARD
SWARDY *adj* covered with sward
SWARE > SWEAR
SWARF *n* material removed by cutting tools in the machining of metals, stone, etc ▷ *vb* faint
SWARFED > SWARF
SWARFING > SWARF
SWARFS > SWARF
SWARM *n* large group of bees or other insects ▷ *vb* move in a swarm
SWARMED > SWARM
SWARMER > SWARM
SWARMERS > SWARM
SWARMING > SWARM
SWARMINGS > SWARM
SWARMS > SWARM
SWART *adj* swarthy
SWARTH *same as* > SWART
SWARTHIER > SWARTHY
SWARTHILY > SWARTHY
SWARTHS > SWARTH
SWARTHY *adj* dark-complexioned
SWARTIER > SWARTY
SWARTIEST > SWARTY
SWARTNESS > SWART
SWARTY *adj* swarthy
SWARVE *same as* > SWARF
SWARVED > SWARF
SWARVES > SWARF
SWARVING > SWARF
SWASH *n* rush of water up a beach following each break of the waves ▷ *vb* wash or move with noisy splashing
SWASHED > SWASH
SWASHER *n* braggart
SWASHERS > SWASHER
SWASHES > SWASH
SWASHIER > SWASHY

SWASHIEST > SWASHY
SWASHING > SWASH
SWASHINGS > SWASH
SWASHWORK *n* type of work done on a lathe
SWASHY *adj* slushy
SWASTICA *same as* > SWASTIKA
SWASTICAS > SWASTICA
SWASTIKA *n* primitive religious symbol in the shape of a Greek cross
SWASTIKAS
> SWASTIKA
SWAT *vb* strike or hit sharply ▷ *n* swatter
SWATCH *n* sample of cloth
SWATCHES > SWATCH
SWATH *n* width of one sweep of a scythe or of the blade of a mowing machine
SWATHABLE > SWATHE
SWATHE *vb* bandage or wrap completely ▷ *n* bandage or wrapping
SWATHED > SWATHE
SWATHER > SWATHE
SWATHERS > SWATHE
SWATHES > SWATHE
SWATHIER > SWATH
SWATHIEST > SWATH
SWATHING *n* act of enveloping (with a garment, bandage, etc)
SWATHINGS
> SWATHING
SWATHS > SWATH
SWATHY > SWATH
SWATS > SWAT
SWATTED > SWAT
SWATTER *n* device for killing insects ▷ *vb* splash
SWATTERED > SWATTER
SWATTERS > SWATTER
SWATTIER *same as* > SWOTTIER
SWATTIEST *same as* > SWOTTIEST
SWATTING > SWAT
SWATTINGS > SWAT
SWATTY *same as* > SWOTTY
SWAY *vb* swing to and fro or from side to side ▷ *n* power or influence
SWAYABLE > SWAY
SWAYBACK *n* abnormal sagging in the spine of older horses
SWAYBACKS
> SWAYBACK
SWAYED > SWAY
SWAYER > SWAY
SWAYERS > SWAY
SWAYFUL > SWAY
SWAYING > SWAY
SWAYINGS > SWAY
SWAYL *same as* > SWEAL
SWAYLED > SWAYL
SWAYLING > SWAYL
SWAYLINGS > SWAYL
SWAYLS > SWAYL
SWAYS > SWAY
SWAZZLE *n* small metal instrument used to produce a shrill voice
SWAZZLES > SWAZZLE

SWEAL *vb* scorch
SWEALED > SWEAL
SWEALING > SWEAL
SWEALINGS > SWEAL
SWEALS > SWEAL
SWEAR *vb* use obscene or blasphemous language
SWEARD *same as* > SWORD
SWEARDS > SWEARD
SWEARER > SWEAR
SWEARERS > SWEAR
SWEARIER > SWEARY
SWEARIEST > SWEARY
SWEARING > SWEAR
SWEARINGS > SWEAR
SWEARS > SWEAR
SWEARWORD *n* word considered obscene or blasphemous
SWEARY *adj* using swear-words
SWEAT *n* salty liquid given off through the pores of the skin ▷ *vb* have sweat coming through the pores
SWEATBAND *n* strip of cloth tied around the forehead or wrist to absorb sweat
SWEATBOX *n* device for causing tobacco leaves, fruit, or hides to sweat
SWEATED *adj* made by exploited labour
SWEATER *n* (woollen) garment for the upper part of the body
SWEATERED *adj* wearing a sweater
SWEATERS > SWEATER
SWEATIER > SWEATY
SWEATIEST > SWEATY
SWEATILY > SWEATY
SWEATING > SWEAT
SWEATINGS > SWEAT
SWEATLESS > SWEAT
SWEATS > SWEAT
SWEATSHOP *n* place where employees work long hours in poor conditions for low pay
SWEATSUIT *n* knitted suit worn by athletes for training
SWEATY *adj* covered with sweat
SWEDE *n* kind of turnip
SWEDES > SWEDE
SWEDGER *n* Scots dialect word for sweet
SWEDGERS > SWEDGER
SWEE *vb* sway
SWEED > SWEE
SWEEING > SWEE
SWEEL *same as* > SWEAL
SWEELED > SWEEL
SWEELING > SWEEL
SWEELS > SWEEL
SWEENEY *n* police flying squad
SWEENEYS > SWEENEY
SWEENIES > SWEENY
SWEENY *n* wasting of the shoulder muscles of a horse
SWEEP *vb* remove dirt from (a floor) with a broom ▷ *n* sweeping

SWEEPBACK *n* rearward inclination of a component or surface
SWEEPER *n* device used to sweep carpets
SWEEPERS > SWEEPER
SWEEPIER > SWEEP
SWEEPIEST > SWEEP
SWEEPING > SWEEP
SWEEPINGS *pl n* debris, litter, or refuse
SWEEPS > SWEEP
SWEEPY > SWEEP
SWEER *variant of* > SWEIR
SWEERED > SWEER
SWEERING > SWEER
SWEERS > SWEER
SWEERT *variant of* > SWEER
SWEES > SWEE
SWEET *adj* tasting of or like sugar ▷ *n* shaped piece of food consisting mainly of sugar ▷ *vb* sweeten
SWEETCORN *n* variety of maize, the kernels of which are eaten when young
SWEETED > SWEET
SWEETEN *vb* make (food or drink) sweet or sweeter
SWEETENED > SWEETEN
SWEETENER *n* sweetening agent that does not contain sugar
SWEETENS > SWEETEN
SWEETER > SWEET
SWEETEST > SWEET
SWEETFISH *n* small Japanese fish
SWEETIE *n* lovable person
SWEETIES > SWEETIE
SWEETING *n* variety of sweet apple
SWEETINGS
> SWEETING
SWEETISH > SWEET
SWEETLIP *n* type of Australian fish with big lips
SWEETLIPS
> SWEETLIP
SWEETLY > SWEET
SWEETMAN *n* (in the Caribbean) a man kept by a woman
SWEETMEAL *adj* (of biscuits) sweet and wholemeal
SWEETMEAT *n* sweet delicacy such as a small cake
SWEETMEN > SWEETMAN
SWEETNESS > SWEET
SWEETS > SWEET
SWEETSHOP *n* shop selling confectionery
SWEETSOP *n* small tropical American tree
SWEETSOPS
> SWEETSOP
SWEETVELD *n* grazing field with high-quality grass
SWEETWOOD *n* tropical tree

S

SWEETY same as
> SWEETIE
SWEIR vb swear ▷ adj lazy
SWEIRED > SWEIR
SWEIRER > SWEIR
SWEIREST > SWEIR
SWEIRING > SWEIR
SWEIRNESS > SWEIR
SWEIRS > SWEIR
SWEIRT variant of
> SWEIR
SWELCHIE n whirlpool in
Orkney
SWELCHIES
> SWELCHIE
SWELL vb expand or
increase ▷ n swelling or
being swollen ▷ adj
excellent or fine
SWELLDOM n fashionable
society
SWELLDOMS
> SWELLDOM
SWELLED > SWELL
SWELLER > SWELL
SWELLERS > SWELL
SWELLEST > SWELL
SWELLFISH popular name
for > PUFFER
SWELLHEAD n conceited
person
SWELLING > SWELL
SWELLINGS > SWELL
SWELLISH > SWELL
SWELLS > SWELL
SWELT vb die
SWELTED > SWELT
SWELTER vb feel
uncomfortably hot ▷ n
hot and uncomfortable
condition
SWELTERED > SWELTER
SWELTERS > SWELTER
SWELTING > SWELT
SWELTRIER > SWELTRY
SWELTRY adj sultry
SWELTS > SWELT
SWEPT > SWEEP
SWEPTBACK adj (of an
aircraft wing) having the
leading edge inclined
backwards towards the
rear
SWEPTWING adj (of an
aircraft) having wings
swept backwards
SWERF same as > SWARF
SWERFED > SWERF
SWERFING > SWERF
SWERFS > SWERF
SWERVABLE > SWERVE
SWERVE vb turn aside
from a course sharply
or suddenly ▷ n
swerving
SWERVED > SWERVE
SWERVER > SWERVE
SWERVERS > SWERVE
SWERVES > SWERVE
SWERVING > SWERVE
SWERVINGS > SWERVE
SWEVEN n vision or dream
SWEVENS > SWEVEN
SWEY same as > SWEE
SWEYED > SWEY
SWEYING > SWEY
SWEYS > SWEY

SWIDDEN n area of land
where slash-and-burn
techniques have been
used
SWIDDENS > SWIDDEN
SWIES > SWY
SWIFT adj moving or able
to move quickly ▷ n
fast-flying bird with
pointed wings ▷ adv
swiftly or quickly ▷ vb
make tight
SWIFTED > SWIFT
SWIFTER n line run
around the ends of
capstan bars
SWIFTERS > SWIFTER
SWIFTEST > SWIFT
SWIFTIE n trick, ruse, or
deception
SWIFTIES > SWIFTY
SWIFTING > SWIFT
SWIFTLET n type of
small Asian swift
SWIFTLETS
> SWIFTLET
SWIFTLY > SWIFT
SWIFTNESS > SWIFT
SWIFTS > SWIFT
SWIFTY same as
> SWIFTIE
SWIG n large mouthful of
drink ▷ vb drink in large
mouthfuls
SWIGGED > SWIG
SWIGGER > SWIG
SWIGGERS > SWIG
SWIGGING > SWIG
SWIGS > SWIG
SWILE n seal (the marine
animal)
SWILER n (in
Newfoundland) a seal
hunter
SWILERS > SWILER
SWILES > SWILE
SWILING n practice of
hunting seals
SWILINGS > SWILING
SWILL vb drink greedily
▷ n sloppy mixture
containing waste food,
fed to pigs
SWILLED > SWILL
SWILLER > SWILL
SWILLERS > SWILL
SWILLING > SWILL
SWILLINGS > SWILL
SWILLS > SWILL
SWIM vb move along in
water by movements of
the limbs ▷ n act or period
of swimming
SWIMMABLE > SWIM
SWIMMER > SWIM
SWIMMERET n any of the
small paired appendages
on the abdomen of
crustaceans
SWIMMERS pl n
swimming costume
SWIMMIER > SWIMMY
SWIMMIEST > SWIMMY
SWIMMILY > SWIMMY
SWIMMING > SWIM
SWIMMINGS > SWIM
SWIMMY adj dizzy
SWIMS > SWIM

SWIMSUIT n woman's
swimming garment that
leaves the arms and legs
bare
SWIMSUITS
> SWIMSUIT
SWIMWEAR n swimming
costumes
SWIMWEARS > SWIMWEAR
SWINDGE same as
> SWINGE
SWINDGED > SWINDGE
SWINDGES > SWINDGE
SWINDGING > SWINDGE
SWINDLE vb cheat
(someone) out of money
▷ n instance of swindling
SWINDLED > SWINDLE
SWINDLER > SWINDLE
SWINDLERS > SWINDLE
SWINDLES > SWINDLE
SWINDLING > SWINDLE
SWINE n contemptible
person
SWINEHERD n person
who looks after pigs
SWINEHOOD > SWINE
SWINELIKE > SWINE
SWINEPOX n acute
infectious viral disease
of pigs
SWINERIES > SWINERY
SWINERY n pig farm
SWINES > SWINE
SWING vb move to and fro,
sway ▷ n swinging
SWINGARM n main part of
the rear suspension on a
motorcycle
SWINGARMS
> SWINGARM
SWINGBEAT n type of
modern dance music that
combines soul, rhythm
and blues, and hip-hop
SWINGBIN n rubbish bin
with a lid that swings shut
after being opened
SWINGBINS
> SWINGBIN
SWINGBOAT n piece of
fairground equipment
consisting of a
boat-shaped carriage for
swinging in
SWINGBY n act of
spacecraft passing close
to planet
SWINGBYS > SWINGBY
SWINGE vb beat, flog, or
punish
SWINGED > SWINGE
SWINGEING > SWINGE
SWINGER n person
regarded as being modern
and lively
SWINGERS > SWINGER
SWINGES > SWINGE
SWINGIER > SWINGY
SWINGIEST > SWINGY
SWINGING adj lively and
modern
SWINGINGS > SWING
SWINGISM n former
resistance to use of
agricultural machines
SWINGISMS
> SWINGISM

SWINGLE n flat-bladed
wooden instrument used
for beating and scraping
flax ▷ vb use a swingle on
SWINGLED > SWINGLE
SWINGLES > SWINGLE
SWINGLING > SWINGLE
SWINGMAN n musician
specializing in swing
music
SWINGMEN > SWINGMAN
SWINGS > SWING
SWINGTAIL n as in
swingtail cargo aircraft kind
of cargo aircraft
SWINGTREE n crossbar in
a horse's harness
SWINGY adj lively and
modern
SWINISH > SWINE
SWINISHLY > SWINE
SWINK vb toil or drudge
▷ n toil or drudgery
SWINKED > SWINK
SWINKER > SWINK
SWINKERS > SWINK
SWINKING > SWINK
SWINKS > SWINK
SWINNEY variant of
> SWEENY
SWINNEYS > SWINNEY
SWIPE vb strike (at) with a
sweeping blow ▷ n hard
blow
SWIPED > SWIPE
SWIPER > SWIPE
SWIPERS > SWIPE
SWIPES pl n beer, esp
when poor or weak
SWIPEY adj drunk
SWIPIER > SWIPEY
SWIPIEST > SWIPEY
SWIPING > SWIPE
SWIPLE same as
> SWIPPLE
SWIPLES > SWIPLE
SWIPPLE n part of a flail
that strikes the grain
SWIPPLES > SWIPPLE
SWIRE n neck
SWIRES > SWIRE
SWIRL vb turn with a
whirling motion ▷ n
whirling motion
SWIRLED > SWIRL
SWIRLIER > SWIRL
SWIRLIEST > SWIRL
SWIRLING > SWIRL
SWIRLS > SWIRL
SWIRLY > SWIRL
SWISH vb move with a
whistling or hissing sound
▷ n whistling or hissing
sound ▷ adj fashionable,
smart
SWISHED > SWISH
SWISHER > SWISH
SWISHERS > SWISH
SWISHES > SWISH
SWISHEST > SWISH
SWISHIER > SWISHY
SWISHIEST > SWISHY
SWISHING > SWISH
SWISHINGS > SWISH
SWISHY adj moving with
a swishing sound
SWISS n type of muslin

S

SWISSES > SWISS
SWISSING n method of treating cloth
SWISSINGS > SWISSING
SWITCH n device for opening and closing an electric circuit ▷ vb change abruptly
SWITCHED > SWITCH
SWITCHEL n type of beer
SWITCHELS > SWITCHEL
SWITCHER > SWITCH
SWITCHERS > SWITCH
SWITCHES > SWITCH
SWITCHIER > SWITCH
SWITCHING > SWITCH
SWITCHMAN n person who operates railway points
SWITCHMEN > SWITCHMAN
SWITCHY > SWITCH
SWITH adv swiftly
SWITHE same as > SWITH
SWITHER vb hesitate or be indecisive ▷ n state of hesitation or uncertainty
SWITHERED > SWITHER
SWITHERS > SWITHER
SWITHLY > SWITH
SWITS same as > SWITCH
SWITSES > SWITS
SWIVE vb have sexual intercourse with (a person)
SWIVED > SWIVE
SWIVEL vb turn on a central point ▷ n coupling device that allows an attached object to turn freely
SWIVELED > SWIVEL
SWIVELING > SWIVEL
SWIVELLED > SWIVEL
SWIVELS > SWIVEL
SWIVES > SWIVE
SWIVET n nervous state
SWIVETS > SWIVET
SWIVING > SWIVE
SWIZ n swindle or disappointment
SWIZZ same as > SWIZ
SWIZZED > SWIZZ
SWIZZES > SWIZZ
SWIZZING > SWIZZ
SWIZZLE vb cheat or con ▷ n act of cheating or conning
SWIZZLED > SWIZZLE
SWIZZLER > SWIZZLE
SWIZZLERS > SWIZZLE
SWIZZLES > SWIZZLE
SWIZZLING > SWIZZLE
SWOB less common word for > SWAB
SWOBBED > SWOB
SWOBBER > SWOB
SWOBBERS > SWOB
SWOBBING > SWOB
SWOBS > SWOB
SWOFFER > SWOFFING
SWOFFERS > SWOFFING
SWOFFING n sport of saltwater fly-fishing
SWOFFINGS > SWOFFING

SWOLE adj muscular from weight training
SWOLER > SWOLE
SWOLEST > SWOLE
SWOLLEN > SWELL
SWOLLENLY > SWELL
SWOLN > SWELL
SWOON n faint ▷ vb faint because of shock or strong emotion
SWOONED > SWOON
SWOONER > SWOON
SWOONERS > SWOON
SWOONIER > SWOONY
SWOONIEST > SWOONY
SWOONING > SWOON
SWOONINGS > SWOON
SWOONS > SWOON
SWOONY adj romantic
SWOOP vb sweep down or pounce on suddenly ▷ n swooping
SWOOPED > SWOOP
SWOOPER > SWOOP
SWOOPERS > SWOOP
SWOOPIER > SWOOP
SWOOPIEST > SWOOP
SWOOPING > SWOOP
SWOOPS > SWOOP
SWOOPY > SWOOP
SWOOSH vb make a swirling or rustling sound when moving or pouring out ▷ n swirling or rustling sound or movement
SWOOSHED > SWOOSH
SWOOSHES > SWOOSH
SWOOSHING > SWOOSH
SWOP same as > SWAP
SWOPPABLE same as > SWAPPABLE
SWOPPED > SWOP
SWOPPER > SWOP
SWOPPERS > SWOP
SWOPPING > SWOP
SWOPPINGS > SWOP
SWOPS > SWOP
SWOPT > SWOP
SWORD n weapon with a long sharp blade ▷ vb bear a sword
SWORDBILL n South American hummingbird
SWORDED > SWORD
SWORDER n fighter with sword
SWORDERS > SWORDER
SWORDFERN n type of fern with long thin fronds
SWORDFISH n large fish with a very long upper jaw
SWORDING > SWORD
SWORDLESS > SWORD
SWORDLIKE > SWORD
SWORDMAN same as > SWORDSMAN
SWORDMEN > SWORDMAN
SWORDPLAY n action or art of fighting with a sword
SWORDS > SWORD
SWORDSMAN n man skilled in the use of a sword
SWORDSMEN > SWORDSMAN

SWORDTAIL n type of small freshwater fish of Central America
SWORE > SWEAR
SWORN > SWEAR
SWOT vb study (a subject) intensively ▷ n person who studies hard
SWOTS > SWOT
SWOTTED > SWOT
SWOTTER same as > SWOT
SWOTTERS > SWOTTER
SWOTTIER > SWOTTY
SWOTTIEST > SWOTTY
SWOTTING > SWOT
SWOTTINGS > SWOT
SWOTTY adj given to studying hard, esp to the exclusion of other activities
SWOUN same as > SWOON
SWOUND same as > SWOON
SWOUNDED > SWOUND
SWOUNDING > SWOUND
SWOUNDS less common spelling of > ZOUNDS
SWOUNE same as > SWOON
SWOUNED > SWOUNE
SWOUNES > SWOUNE
SWOUNING > SWOUNE
SWOUNS > SWOUN
SWOWND same as > SWOON
SWOWNDS > SWOWND
SWOWNE same as > SWOON
SWOWNES > SWOWNE
SWOZZLE same as > SWAZZLE
SWOZZLES > SWOZZLE
SWUM > SWIM
SWUNG > SWING
SWY n Australian gambling game involving two coins
SYBARITE n lover of luxury ▷ adj luxurious
SYBARITES > SYBARITE
SYBARITIC > SYBARITE
SYBBE same as > SIB
SYBBES > SYBBE
SYBIL same as > SIBYL
SYBILS > SYBIL
SYBO n spring onion
SYBOE same as > SYBO
SYBOES > SYBOE
SYBOTIC adj of a swineherd
SYBOTISM > SYBOTIC
SYBOTISMS > SYBOTIC
SYBOW same as > SYBO
SYBOWS > SYBOW
SYCAMINE n mulberry tree mentioned in the Bible, thought to be the black mulberry
SYCAMINES > SYCAMINE
SYCAMORE n tree with five-pointed leaves and two-winged fruits
SYCAMORES > SYCAMORE
SYCE n (formerly, in India) a servant employed to look after horses, etc
SYCEE n silver ingots formerly used as a medium of exchange in China

SYCEES > SYCEE
SYCES > SYCE
SYCOMORE same as > SYCAMORE
SYCOMORES > SYCOMORE
SYCON n type of sponge
SYCONIA > SYCONIUM
SYCONIUM n fleshy fruit of the fig
SYCONOID adj of or like a sycon
SYCONS > SYCON
SYCOPHANT n person who uses flattery to win favour from people with power or influence
SYCOSES > SYCOSIS
SYCOSIS n chronic inflammation of the hair follicles
SYE vb strain
SYED > SYE
SYEING > SYE
SYEN same as > SCION
SYENITE n light-coloured coarse-grained plutonic igneous rock
SYENITES > SYENITE
SYENITIC > SYENITE
SYENS > SYEN
SYES > SYE
SYKE same as > SIKE
SYKER adv surely
SYKES > SYKE
SYLI n Finnish unit of volume
SYLIS > SYLI
SYLLABARY n table or list of syllables
SYLLABI > SYLLABUS
SYLLABIC adj of or relating to syllables ▷ n syllabic consonant
SYLLABICS > SYLLABIC
SYLLABIFY vb divide (a word) into syllables
SYLLABISE same as > SYLLABIZE
SYLLABISM n use of a writing system consisting of characters for syllables
SYLLABIZE vb divide into syllables
SYLLABLE n part of a word pronounced as a unit
SYLLABLED > SYLLABLE
SYLLABLES > SYLLABLE
SYLLABUB n dessert of beaten cream, sugar, and wine
SYLLABUBS > SYLLABUB
SYLLABUS n list of subjects for a course of study
SYLLEPSES > SYLLEPSIS
SYLLEPSIS n (in grammar or rhetoric) the use of a single sentence construction in which a verb, adjective, etc is made to cover two syntactical functions

SYLLEPTIC
> SYLLEPSIS
SYLLOGE n collection or summary
SYLLOGES > SYLLOGE
SYLLOGISE same as
> SYLLOGIZE
SYLLOGISM n form of logical reasoning consisting of two premises and a conclusion
SYLLOGIST
> SYLLOGISM
SYLLOGIZE vb reason or infer by using syllogisms
SYLPH n slender, graceful girl or woman
SYLPHIC > SYLPH
SYLPHID n little sylph
SYLPHIDE same as
> SYLPHID
SYLPHIDES
> SYLPHIDE
SYLPHIDS > SYLPHID
SYLPHIER > SYLPH
SYLPHIEST > SYLPH
SYLPHINE > SYLPH
SYLPHISH > SYLPH
SYLPHLIKE > SYLPH
SYLPHS > SYLPH
SYLPHY > SYLPH
SYLVA n trees growing in a particular region
SYLVAE > SYLVA
SYLVAN adj relating to woods and trees ▷ n inhabitant of the woods, esp a spirit
SYLVANER n German variety of grape
SYLVANERS
> SYLVANER
SYLVANITE n silver-white mineral
SYLVANS > SYLVAN
SYLVAS > SYLVA
SYLVATIC adj growing, living, or occurring in a wood or beneath a tree
SYLVIA n songbird
SYLVIAS > SYLVIA
SYLVIINE > SYLVIA
SYLVIN same as
> SYLVITE
SYLVINE same as
> SYLVITE
SYLVINES > SYLVINE
SYLVINITE n rock containing sylvine
SYLVINS > SYLVIN
SYLVITE n soluble colourless, white, or coloured mineral
SYLVITES > SYLVITE
SYMAR same as > CYMAR
SYMARS > SYMAR
SYMBION same as
> SYMBIONT
SYMBIONS > SYMBION
SYMBIONT n organism living in a state of symbiosis
SYMBIONTS
> SYMBIONT
SYMBIOSES
> SYMBIOSIS
SYMBIOSIS n close association of two species

living together to their mutual benefit
SYMBIOT same as
> SYMBIONT
SYMBIOTE same as
> SYMBIONT
SYMBIOTES
> SYMBIOTE
SYMBIOTIC
> SYMBIOSIS
SYMBIOTS > SYMBIOT
SYMBOL n sign or thing that stands for something else ▷ vb be a symbol
SYMBOLE same as
> CYMBAL
SYMBOLED > SYMBOL
SYMBOLES > SYMBOLE
SYMBOLIC adj of or relating to a symbol or symbols
SYMBOLICS n study of beliefs
SYMBOLING > SYMBOL
SYMBOLISE same as
> SYMBOLIZE
SYMBOLISM n representation of something by symbols
SYMBOLIST n person who uses or can interpret symbols ▷ adj of, relating to, or characterizing symbolism or symbolists
SYMBOLIZE vb be a symbol of
SYMBOLLED > SYMBOL
SYMBOLOGY n use, study, or interpretation of symbols
SYMBOLS > SYMBOL
SYMITAR same as
> SCIMITAR
SYMITARE same as
> SCIMITAR
SYMITARES
> SYMITARE
SYMITARS > SYMITAR
SYMMETRAL
> SYMMETRY
SYMMETRIC adj (of a disease) affecting both sides of the body
SYMMETRY n state of having two halves that are mirror images of each other
SYMPATHIN n substance released at certain sympathetic nerve endings
SYMPATHY n compassion for someone's pain or distress
SYMPATICO adj nice
SYMPATRIC adj (of biological speciation or species) existing in the same geographical areas
SYMPATRY n existing of organisms together without interbreeding
SYMPETALY n quality of having petals that are united
SYMPHILE n insect that lives in the nests of social insects and is fed and reared by the inmates

SYMPHILES
> SYMPHILE
SYMPHILY n presence of different kinds of animal in ants' nests
SYMPHONIC
> SYMPHONY
SYMPHONY n composition for orchestra, with several movements
SYMPHYSES
> SYMPHYSIS
SYMPHYSIS n growing together of parts or structures
SYMPHYTIC
> SYMPHYSIS
SYMPLAST n continuous system of protoplasts, linked by plasmodesmata and bounded by the cell wall
SYMPLASTS
> SYMPLAST
SYMPLOCE n word repetition in successive clauses
SYMPLOCES
> SYMPLOCE
SYMPODIA
> SYMPODIUM
SYMPODIAL
> SYMPODIUM
SYMPODIUM n main axis of growth in the grapevine and similar plants
SYMPOSIA
> SYMPOSIUM
SYMPOSIAC adj of, suitable for, or occurring at a symposium
SYMPOSIAL
> SYMPOSIUM
SYMPOSIUM n conference for discussion of a particular topic
SYMPTOM n sign indicating the presence of an illness
SYMPTOMS > SYMPTOM
SYMPTOSES
> SYMPTOSIS
SYMPTOSIS n wasting condition
SYMPTOTIC
> SYMPTOSIS
SYN Scots word for > SINCE
SYNAGOG same as
> SYNAGOGUE
SYNAGOGAL
> SYNAGOGUE
SYNAGOGS > SYNAGOG
SYNAGOGUE n Jewish place of worship and religious instruction
SYNALEPHA n elision of vowels in speech
SYNANDRIA pl n peculiar bunchings of stamens
SYNANGIA
> SYNANGIUM
SYNANGIUM n junction between arteries
SYNANON n type of therapy given to drug addicts
SYNANONS > SYNANON
SYNANTHIC
> SYNANTHY

SYNANTHY n abnormal joining between flowers
SYNAPHEA n continuity in metre of verses of poem
SYNAPHEAS
> SYNAPHEA
SYNAPHEIA same as
> SYNAPHEA
SYNAPSE n gap where nerve impulses pass between two nerve cells ▷ vb create a synapse
SYNAPSED > SYNAPSE
SYNAPSES > SYNAPSIS
SYNAPSID n prehistoric mammal-like reptile
SYNAPSIDS
> SYNAPSID
SYNAPSING > SYNAPSE
SYNAPSIS n association in pairs of homologous chromosomes at the start of meiosis
SYNAPTASE n type of enzyme
SYNAPTE n litany in Greek Orthodox Church
SYNAPTES > SYNAPTE
SYNAPTIC adj of or relating to a synapse
SYNARCHY n joint rule
SYNASTRY n coincidence of astrological influences
SYNAXARIA pl n readings in the Greek Orthodox Church
SYNAXES > SYNAXIS
SYNAXIS n early Christian meeting
SYNBIOTIC n synthesis of prebiotic bacteria and one or more probiotics, used in food products
SYNC n synchronization ▷ vb synchronize
SYNCARP n fleshy multiple fruit
SYNCARPS > SYNCARP
SYNCARPY n quality of consisting of united carpels
SYNCED > SYNC
SYNCH same as > SYNC
SYNCHED > SYNCH
SYNCHING > SYNCH
SYNCHRO n type of electrical device
SYNCHRONY n state of being synchronous
SYNCHROS > SYNCHRO
SYNCHS > SYNCH
SYNCHYSES
> SYNCHYSIS
SYNCHYSIS n muddled meaning
SYNCING > SYNC
SYNCLINAL
> SYNCLINE
SYNCLINE n downward slope of stratified rock
SYNCLINES
> SYNCLINE
SYNCOM n communications satellite in stationary orbit
SYNCOMS > SYNCOM
SYNCOPAL > SYNCOPE

S

SYNCOPATE *vb* stress the weak beats in (a rhythm) instead of the strong ones
SYNCOPE *n* omission of one or more sounds or letters from the middle of a word
SYNCOPES > SYNCOPE
SYNCOPIC > SYNCOPE
SYNCOPTIC > SYNCOPE
SYNCRETIC *adj* of the tendency of languages to reduce their use of inflection
SYNCS > SYNC
SYNCYTIA > SYNCYTIUM
SYNCYTIAL **>** SYNCYTIUM
SYNCYTIUM *n* mass of cytoplasm containing many nuclei and enclosed in a cell membrane
SYND *same as* **>** SYNE
SYNDACTYL *adj* (of certain animals) having two or more digits growing fused together ▷ *n* animal with this arrangement of digits
SYNDED > SYND
SYNDESES > SYNDESIS
SYNDESIS *n* use of syndetic constructions
SYNDET *n* synthetic detergent
SYNDETIC *adj* denoting a grammatical construction in which two clauses are connected by a conjunction
SYNDETON *n* syndetic construction
SYNDETONS **>** SYNDETON
SYNDETS > SYNDET
SYNDIC *n* business or legal agent of some institutions
SYNDICAL *adj* relating to the theory that syndicates of workers should seize the means of production
SYNDICATE *n* group of people or firms undertaking a joint business project ▷ *vb* publish (material) in several newspapers
SYNDICS > SYNDIC
SYNDING > SYND
SYNDINGS > SYND
SYNDROME *n* combination of symptoms indicating a particular disease
SYNDROMES **>** SYNDROME
SYNDROMIC **>** SYNDROME
SYNDS > SYND
SYNE *vb* rinse ▷ *n* rinse ▷ *adv* since
SYNECHIA *n* abnormality of the eye
SYNECHIAS **>** SYNECHIA
SYNECIOUS *adj* having male and female organs together on a branch

SYNECTIC **>** SYNECTICS
SYNECTICS *n* method of identifying and solving problems that depends on creative thinking
SYNED > SYNE
SYNEDRIA **>** SYNEDRION
SYNEDRIAL **>** SYNEDRION
SYNEDRION *n* assembly of judges
SYNEDRIUM *same as* **>** SYNEDRION
SYNERESES **>** SYNERESIS
SYNERESIS *n* process in which a gel contracts on standing and exudes liquid
SYNERGIA *same as* **>** SYNERGY
SYNERGIAS **>** SYNERGIA
SYNERGIC > SYNERGY
SYNERGID *n* type of cell in embryo
SYNERGIDS **>** SYNERGID
SYNERGIES > SYNERGY
SYNERGISE *same as* **>** SYNERGIZE
SYNERGISM *same as* **>** SYNERGY
SYNERGIST *n* drug, muscle, etc, that increases the action of another ▷ *adj* of or relating to synergism
SYNERGIZE *vb* act in synergy
SYNERGY *n* collective effect that is greater than the sum of individual effects
SYNES > SYNE
SYNESES > SYNESIS
SYNESIS *n* grammatical construction in which the form of a word is conditioned by the meaning
SYNESISES > SYNESIS
SYNFUEL *n* synthetic fuel
SYNFUELS > SYNFUEL
SYNGAMIC > SYNGAMY
SYNGAMIES > SYNGAMY
SYNGAMOUS > SYNGAMY
SYNGAMY *n* reproduction involving the fusion of male and female gametes
SYNGAS *n* mixture of carbon monoxide and hydrogen
SYNGASES > SYNGAS
SYNGASSES > SYNGAS
SYNGENEIC *adj* with identical genes
SYNGENIC *same as* **>** SYNGENEIC
SYNGRAPH *n* document signed by several parties
SYNGRAPHS **>** SYNGRAPH
SYNING > SYNE
SYNIZESES **>** SYNIZESIS
SYNIZESIS *n* contraction of two vowels originally belonging to

separate syllables into a single syllable
SYNKARYA **>** SYNKARYON
SYNKARYON *n* nucleus of a fertilized egg
SYNOD *n* church council
SYNODAL *adj* of or relating to a synod ▷ *n* money paid to a bishop by less senior members of the clergy at a synod
SYNODALS > SYNODAL
SYNODIC *adj* involving conjunction of the same star, planet, or satellite
SYNODICAL > SYNOD
SYNODS > SYNOD
SYNODSMAN *n* layman at synod
SYNODSMEN **>** SYNODSMAN
SYNOECETE *same as* **>** SYNOEKETE
SYNOECISE *same as* **>** SYNOECIZE
SYNOECISM *n* union
SYNOECIZE *vb* unite
SYNOEKETE *n* insect that lives in the nests of social insects without receiving any attentions from the inmates
SYNOICOUS *variant of* **>** SYNECIOUS
SYNONYM *n* word with the same meaning as another
SYNONYME *same as* **>** SYNONYM
SYNONYMES **>** SYNONYME
SYNONYMIC > SYNONYM
SYNONYMS > SYNONYM
SYNONYMY *n* study of synonyms
SYNOPSES > SYNOPSIS
SYNOPSIS *n* summary or outline
SYNOPSISE *same as* **>** SYNOPSIZE
SYNOPSIZE *vb* make a synopsis of
SYNOPTIC *adj* of or relating to a synopsis ▷ *n* any of the three synoptic Gospels
SYNOPTICS **>** SYNOPTIC
SYNOPTIST **>** SYNOPTIC
SYNOVIA *n* clear thick fluid that lubricates the body joints
SYNOVIAL *adj* of or relating to the synovia
SYNOVIAS > SYNOVIA
SYNOVITIC **>** SYNOVITIS
SYNOVITIS *n* inflammation of the membrane surrounding a joint
SYNROC *n* titanium-ceramic substance that can incorporate nuclear waste in its crystals
SYNROCS > SYNROC
SYNTACTIC *adj* relating to or determined by syntax

SYNTAGM *same as* **>** SYNTAGMA
SYNTAGMA *n* syntactic unit or a word or phrase forming a syntactic unit
SYNTAGMAS **>** SYNTAGMA
SYNTAGMIC **>** SYNTAGMA
SYNTAGMS > SYNTAGM
SYNTAN *n* synthetic tanning substance
SYNTANS > SYNTAN
SYNTAX *n* way in which words are arranged to form phrases and sentences
SYNTAXES > SYNTAX
SYNTECTIC **>** SYNTEXIS
SYNTENIC > SYNTENY
SYNTENIES > SYNTENY
SYNTENY *n* presence of two or more genes on the same chromosome
SYNTEXIS *n* liquefaction
SYNTH *n* type of electrophonic musical instrument operated by a keyboard and pedals
SYNTHASE *n* enzyme that catalyses a synthesis process
SYNTHASES **>** SYNTHASE
SYNTHESES **>** SYNTHESIS
SYNTHESIS *n* combination of objects or ideas into a whole
SYNTHETIC *adj* (of a substance) made artificially ▷ *n* synthetic substance or material
SYNTHON *n* molecule used in synthesis
SYNTHONS > SYNTHON
SYNTHPOP *n* pop music using synthesizers
SYNTHPOPS **>** SYNTHPOP
SYNTHRONI *pl n* combined thrones for bishops and their subordinates
SYNTHS > SYNTH
SYNTONE *n* person who is syntonic
SYNTONES > SYNTONE
SYNTONIC *adj* emotionally in harmony with one's environment
SYNTONIES > SYNTONY
SYNTONIN *n* substance in muscle
SYNTONINS **>** SYNTONIN
SYNTONISE *same as* **>** SYNTONIZE
SYNTONIZE *vb* make frequencies match
SYNTONOUS *same as* **>** SYNTONIC
SYNTONY *n* matching of frequencies
SYNTYPE *n* original specimen by which a new species is described
SYNTYPES > SYNTYPE

S

SYNURA *n* variety of microbe

SYNURAE > SYNURA

SYPE *same as* > SIPE

SYPED > SYPE

SYPES > SYPE

SYPH *shortening of* > SYPHILIS

SYPHER *vb* lap (a chamfered edge) in order to form a flush surface

SYPHERED > SYPHER

SYPHERING > SYPHER

SYPHERS > SYPHER

SYPHILIS *n* serious sexually transmitted disease

SYPHILISE *same as* > SYPHILIZE

SYPHILIZE *vb* infect with syphilis

SYPHILOID > SYPHILIS

SYPHILOMA *n* tumour or gumma caused by infection with syphilis

SYPHON *same as* > SIPHON

SYPHONAGE *n* action of a syphon

SYPHONAL *same as* > SIPHONAL

SYPHONED > SYPHON

SYPHONIC *same as* > SIPHONIC

SYPHONING > SYPHON

SYPHONS > SYPHON

SYPHS > SYPH

SYPING > SYPE

SYRAH *n* type of French red wine

SYRAHS > SYRAH

SYREN *same as* > SIREN

SYRENS > SYREN

SYRETTE *n* small disposable syringe

SYRETTES > SYRETTE

SYRINGA *n* mock orange or lilac

SYRINGAS > SYRINGA

SYRINGE *n* device for withdrawing or injecting fluids ▷ *vb* wash out or inject with a syringe

SYRINGEAL > SYRINX

SYRINGED > SYRINGE

SYRINGES > SYRINX

SYRINGING > SYRINGE

SYRINX *n* vocal organ of a bird

SYRINXES > SYRINX

SYRPHIAN *same as* > SYRPHID

SYRPHIANS > SYRPHIAN

SYRPHID *n* type of fly

SYRPHIDS > SYRPHID

SYRTES > SYRTIS

SYRTIS *n* area of quicksand

SYRUP *n* solution of sugar in water ▷ *vb* bring to the consistency of syrup

SYRUPED > SYRUP

SYRUPIER > SYRUPY

SYRUPIEST > SYRUPY

SYRUPING > SYRUP

SYRUPLIKE > SYRUP

SYRUPS > SYRUP

SYRUPY *adj* thick and sweet

SYSADMIN *n* computer system administrator

SYSADMINS > SYSADMIN

SYSOP *n* person who runs a system or network

SYSOPS > SYSOP

SYSSITIA *n* ancient Spartan communal meal

SYSSITIAS > SYSSITIA

SYSTALTIC *adj* (esp of the action of the heart) characterized by alternate contractions and dilations

SYSTEM *n* method or set of methods

SYSTEMED *adj* having system

SYSTEMIC *adj* affecting the entire animal or body ▷ *n* systemic pesticide, fungicide, etc

SYSTEMICS > SYSTEMIC

SYSTEMISE *same as* > SYSTEMIZE

SYSTEMIZE *vb* give a system to

SYSTEMS > SYSTEM

SYSTOLE *n* regular contraction of the heart as it pumps blood

SYSTOLES > SYSTOLE

SYSTOLIC > SYSTOLE

SYSTYLE *n* building with different types of columns

SYSTYLES > SYSTYLE

SYTHE *same as* > SITH

SYTHES > SYTHE

SYVER *n* street drain or the grating over it

SYVERS > SYVER

SYZYGAL > SYZYGY

SYZYGETIC > SYZYGY

SYZYGIAL > SYZYGY

SYZYGIES > SYZYGY

SYZYGY *n* position of a celestial body when sun, earth, and the body are in line

Tt

TA *interj* thank you ▷ *n* thank you

TAAL *n* language: usually, by implication, Afrikaans

TAALS > TAAL

TAATA *n* (in E Africa) father

TAATAS > TAATA

TAB *n* small flap or projecting label ▷ *vb* supply with a tab

TABANID *n* stout-bodied fly

TABANIDS > TABANID

TABARD *n* short sleeveless tunic decorated with a coat of arms, worn in medieval times

TABARDED *adj* wearing a tabard

TABARDS > TABARD

TABARET *n* hard-wearing fabric of silk or similar cloth with stripes of satin or moire

TABARETS > TABARET

TABASHEER *n* dried bamboo sap, used medicinally

TABASHIR *same as* > TABASHEER

TABASHIRS > TABASHIR

TABBED > TAB

TABBIED > TABBY

TABBIER > TABBY

TABBIES > TABBY

TABBIEST > TABBY

TABBINET *same as* > TABINET

TABBINETS > TABBINET

TABBING *n* act of supplying with tabs

TABBINGS > TABBING

TABBIS *n* silken cloth

TABBISES > TABBIS

TABBOULEH *n* kind of Middle Eastern salad made with cracked wheat, mint, parsley, and usually cucumber

TABBOULI *same as* > TABBOULEH

TABBOULIS > TABBOULI

TABBY *vb* make (a material) appear wavy ▷ *n* female domestic cat ▷ *adj* brindled

TABBYHOOD *n* spinsterhood

TABBYING > TABBY

TABEFIED > TABEFY

TABEFIES > TABEFY

TABEFY *vb* emaciate or become emaciated

TABEFYING > TABEFY

TABELLION *n* scribe or notary authorized by the Roman Empire

TABER *old variant of* > TABOR

TABERD *same as* > TABARD

TABERDAR *n* holder of a scholarship at Queen's College, Oxford

TABERDARS > TABERDAR

TABERDS > TABERD

TABERED > TABER

TABERING > TABER

TABERS > TABER

TABES *n* wasting of a bodily organ or part

TABESCENT *adj* progressively emaciating

TABETIC > TABES

TABETICS > TABES

TABI *n* thick-soled Japanese sock, worn with sandals

TABID *adj* emaciated

TABINET *n* type of tabbied fabric

TABINETS > TABINET

TABIS > TABI

TABLA *n* one of a pair of Indian drums played with the hands

TABLAS > TABLA

TABLATURE *n* any of a number of forms of musical notation, esp for playing the lute, consisting of letters and signs indicating rhythm and fingering

TABLE *n* piece of furniture with a flat top supported by legs ▷ *vb* submit (a motion) for discussion by a meeting

TABLEAU *n* silent motionless group arranged to represent some scene

TABLEAUS > TABLEAU

TABLEAUX > TABLEAU

TABLED > TABLE

TABLEFUL > TABLE

TABLEFULS > TABLE

TABLELAND *n* high plateau

TABLELESS > TABLE

TABLEMAT *n* small mat used for protecting the surface of a table from hot dishes

TABLEMATE *n* someone with whom one shares a table

TABLEMATS > TABLEMAT

TABLES > TABLE

TABLESFUL > TABLE

TABLESIDE *adj* (of cooking) performed beside the table of a diner

TABLET *n* medicinal pill ▷ *vb* make (something) into a tablet

TABLETED > TABLET

TABLETING > TABLET

TABLETOP *n* upper surface of a table

TABLETOPS > TABLETOP

TABLETS > TABLET

TABLETTED > TABLET

TABLEWARE *n* articles such as dishes, plates, knives, forks, etc, used at meals

TABLEWISE *adv* in the form of a table

TABLIER *n* (formerly) part of a dress resembling an apron

TABLIERS > TABLIER

TABLING > TABLE

TABLINGS > TABLE

TABLOID *n* small-sized newspaper with many photographs

TABLOIDS > TABLOID

TABLOIDY *adj* characteristic of a tabloid newspaper; trashy

TABOGGAN *same as* > TOBOGGAN

TABOGGANS > TABOGGAN

TABOO *n* prohibition resulting from religious or social conventions ▷ *adj* forbidden by a taboo ▷ *vb* place under a taboo

TABOOED > TABOO

TABOOING > TABOO

TABOOLEY *variant of* > TABBOULEH

TABOOLEYS > TABOOLEY

TABOOS > TABOO

TABOR *n* small drum ▷ *vb* play the tabor

TABORED > TABOR

TABORER > TABOR

TABORERS > TABOR

TABORET *n* low stool, originally in the shape of a drum

TABORETS > TABORET

TABORIN *same as* > TABORET

TABORINE *same as* > TABOURIN

TABORINES > TABORINE

TABORING > TABOR

TABORINS > TABORIN

TABORS > TABOR

TABOULEH *variant of* > TABBOULEH

TABOULEHS > TABOULEH

TABOULI *same as* > TABBOULEH

TABOULIS > TABOULI

TABOUR *same as* > TABOR

TABOURED > TABOUR

TABOURER > TABOUR

TABOURERS > TABOUR

TABOURET *same as* > TABORET

TABOURETS > TABOURET

TABOURIN *same as* > TABORET

TABOURING > TABOUR

TABOURINS > TABOURIN

TABOURS > TABOUR

TABRERE *same as* > TABOR

TABRERES > TABRERE

TABRET *n* smaller version of a tabor

TABRETS > TABRET

TABS > TAB

TABU *same as* > TABOO

TABUED > TABU

TABUING > TABU

TABULA *n* tablet for writing on

TABULABLE > TABULATE

TABULAE > TABULA

TABULAR *adj* arranged in a table

TABULARLY > TABULAR

TABULATE *vb* arrange (information) in a table ▷ *adj* having a flat surface

TABULATED > TABULATE

TABULATES > TABULATE

TABULATOR *n* key on a typewriter or word processor that sets stops so that data can be arranged and presented in columns

TABULI *variant of* > TABBOULEH

TABULIS > TABULI

TABUN *n* organic compound used as a lethal nerve gas

TABUNS > TABUN

TABUS > TABU

TACAHOUT *n* abnormal outgrowth on the tamarisk plant

TACAHOUTS > TACAHOUT

TACAMAHAC *n* any of several strong-smelling resinous gums obtained from certain trees, used in making ointments, incense, etc

TACAN *n* electronic ultrahigh-frequency navigation system for aircraft

TACANS > TACAN

TACE *same as* > TASSET

TACES > TACE

TACET *adv* (in a musical direction) indicating that an instrument or singer does not take part

TACH *n* device for measuring speed

TACHE *n* buckle, clasp, or hook

TACHES > TACHE

TACHINA *n* as in *tachina* fly bristly fly

TACHINID *n* type of fly

TACHINIDS > TACHINID

TACHISM *same as* > TACHISME

TACHISME *n* type of action painting evolved in France

TACHISMES > TACHISME

TACHISMS > TACHISM

TACHIST > TACHISM

TACHISTE > TACHISME

TACHISTES > TACHISME

TACHISTS > TACHIST

TACHO *same as* > TACHOGRAM

TACHOGRAM *n* graphical record of readings

TACHOS > TACHO

TACHS > TACH

TACHYLITE *same as* > TACHYLYTE

TACHYLYTE *n* black basaltic glass often found on the edges of intrusions of basalt

TACHYON *n* hypothetical elementary particle

TACHYONIC > TACHYON

TACHYONS > TACHYON

TACHYPNEA *n* abnormally rapid breathing

TACIT *adj* implied but not spoken

TACITLY > TACIT

TACITNESS > TACIT

TACITURN *adj* habitually uncommunicative

TACK *n* short nail with a large head ▷ *vb* fasten with tacks

TACKBOARD *n* noticeboard

TACKED > TACK

TACKER > TACK

TACKERS > TACK

TACKET *n* nail, esp a hobnail

TACKETIER > TACKETY

TACKETS > TACKET

TACKETY *adj* studded with tackets

TACKEY *same as* > TACKY

TACKIER > TACKY

TACKIES *pl n* S African word for plimsolls

TACKIEST > TACKY

TACKIFIED > TACKIFY

TACKIFIER > TACKIFY

TACKIFIES > TACKIFY

TACKIFY *vb* give (eg rubber) a sticky feel

TACKILY > TACKY

TACKINESS > TACKY

TACKING > TACK

TACKINGS > TACK

TACKLE *vb* deal with (a task) ▷ *n* act of tackling an opposing player

TACKLED > TACKLE

TACKLER > TACKLE

TACKLERS > TACKLE

TACKLES > TACKLE

TACKLESS > TACK

TACKLING > TACKLE

TACKLINGS > TACKLE

TACKS > TACK

TACKSMAN *n* leaseholder, esp a tenant in the Highlands who sublets

TACKSMEN > TACKSMAN

TACKY *adj* slightly sticky

TACMAHACK *same as* > TACAMAHAC

TACNODE *n* point at which two branches of a curve have a common tangent

TACNODES > TACNODE

TACO *n* tortilla fried until crisp, served with a filling

TACONITE *n* fine-grained sedimentary rock

TACONITES > TACONITE

TACOS > TACO

TACRINE *n* drug used to treat Alzheimer's disease

TACRINES > TACRINE

TACT *n* skill in avoiding giving offence

TACTFUL > TACT

TACTFULLY > TACT

TACTIC *n* method or plan to achieve an end

TACTICAL *adj* of or employing tactics

TACTICIAN > TACTICS

TACTICITY *n* quality of regularity in the arrangement of repeated units within a polymer chain

TACTICS *n* art of directing military forces in battle

TACTILE *adj* of or having the sense of touch

TACTILELY > TACTILE

TACTILIST *n* artist whose work strives to appeal to the sense of touch

TACTILITY > TACTILE

TACTION *n* act of touching

TACTIONS > TACTION

TACTISM *another word for* > TAXIS

TACTISMS > TACTISM

TACTLESS > TACT

TACTS > TACT

TACTUAL *adj* caused by touch

TACTUALLY > TACTUAL

TAD *n* small bit or piece

TADALAFIL *n* drug used to treat erectile dysfunction

TADDIE *short for* > TADPOLE

TADDIES > TADDIE

TADPOLE *n* limbless tailed larva of a frog or toad

TADPOLES > TADPOLE

TADS > TAD

TAE *Scots form of* > TOE

TAED > TAE

TAEDIUM *archaic spelling of* > TEDIUM

TAEDIUMS > TAEDIUM

TAEING > TAE

TAEKWONDO *n* Korean martial art

TAEL *n* unit of weight, used in East Asia

TAELS > TAEL

TAENIA *n* (in ancient Greece) a narrow fillet or headband for the hair

TAENIAE > TAENIA

TAENIAS > TAENIA

TAENIASES > TAENIASIS

TAENIASIS *n* infestation with tapeworms

TAENIATE *adj* ribbon-like

TAENIOID *adj* ribbon-like

TAENITE *n* nickel-iron alloy found in meteorites

TAENITES > TAENITE

TAES > TAE

TAFFAREL *same as* > TAFFRAIL

TAFFARELS > TAFFAREL

TAFFEREL *same as* > TAFFRAIL

TAFFERELS > TAFFEREL

TAFFETA *n* shiny silk or rayon fabric

TAFFETAS *same as* > TAFFETA

TAFFETIER > TAFFETY

TAFFETY *adj* made of taffeta

TAFFIA *same as* > TAFIA

TAFFIAS > TAFFIA

TAFFIES > TAFFY

TAFFRAIL *n* rail at the back of a ship or boat

TAFFRAILS > TAFFRAIL

TAFFY *same as* > TOFFEE

TAFIA *n* type of rum, esp from Guyana or the Caribbean

TAFIAS > TAFIA

TAG *n* label bearing information ▷ *vb* attach a tag to

TAGALONG *n* one who trails behind, esp uninvited; a hanger-on

TAGALONGS > TAGALONG

TAGAREEN *n* junk shop

TAGAREENS > TAGAREEN

TAGBOARD *n* sturdy form of cardboard

TAGBOARDS > TAGBOARD

TAGETES *n* any of a genus of plants with yellow or orange flowers

TAGGANT *n* microscopic material added to substance to identify it

TAGGANTS > TAGGANT

TAGGED > TAG

TAGGEE *n* one who has been made to wear a tag

TAGGEES > TAGGEE

TAGGER *n* one who marks with a tag

TAGGERS > TAGGER

TAGGIER > TAGGY

TAGGIEST > TAGGY

TAGGING > TAG

TAGGINGS > TAG

TAGGY *adj* (of wool, hair, etc) matted

TAGHAIRM *n* form of divination once practised in the Highlands of Scotland

TAGHAIRMS > TAGHAIRM

TAGINE *n* large, heavy N African cooking pot

TAGINES > TAGINE

TAGLESS *adj* having no tag

TAGLIKE *adj* resembling a tag

TAGLINE *n* funny line of a joke

TAGLINES > TAGLINE

TAGLIONI *n* type of coat

TAGLIONIS > TAGLIONI

TAGMA *n* distinct region of the body of an arthropod

TAGMATA > TAGMA

TAGMEME *n* class of speech elements all of which may fulfil the same grammatical role

TAGMEMES > TAGMEME

TAGMEMIC > TAGMEME

TAGMEMICS > TAGMEME

TAGRAG *same as* > RAGTAG

TAGRAGS > TAGRAG

TAGS > TAG

TAGUAN *n* nocturnal flying squirrel

TAGUANS > TAGUAN

TAHA *n* type of South African bird
TAHAS > TAHA
TAHINA *same as* > TAHINI
TAHINAS > TAHINA
TAHINI *n* paste made from ground sesame seeds
TAHINIS > TAHINI
TAHR *n* goatlike mammal of mountainous regions of S and SW Asia
TAHRS > TAHR
TAHSIL *n* administrative division of a zila in certain states in India
TAHSILDAR *n* officer in charge of the collection of revenues, etc, in a tahsil
TAHSILS > TAHSIL
TAI *n* type of sea bream
TAIAHA *n* carved weapon in the form of a staff, now used in Māori ceremonial oratory
TAIAHAS > TAIAHA
TAIGA *n* belt of coniferous forest
TAIGAS > TAIGA
TAIGLACH *same as* > TEIGLACH
TAIGLE *vb* entangle or impede
TAIGLED > TAIGLE
TAIGLES > TAIGLE
TAIGLING > TAIGLE
TAIHOA *vb* in New Zealand English, wait
TAIHOAED > TAIHOA
TAIHOAING > TAIHOA
TAIHOAS > TAIHOA
TAIKO *n* large Japanese drum
TAIKONAUT *n* astronaut from the People's Republic of China
TAIKOS > TAIKO
TAIL *n* rear part of an animal's body, usu forming a flexible appendage ▷ *adj* at the rear ▷ *vb* follow (someone) secretly
TAILARD *n* one having a tail
TAILARDS > TAILARD
TAILBACK *n* queue of traffic stretching back from an obstruction
TAILBACKS > TAILBACK
TAILBOARD *n* removable or hinged rear board on a truck etc
TAILBONE *nontechnical name for* > COCCYX
TAILBONES > TAILBONE
TAILCOAT *n* man's black coat with a tapering tail
TAILCOATS > TAILCOAT
TAILED > TAIL
TAILENDER *n* (in cricket) the batter last in the batting order
TAILER *n* one that tails
TAILERON *n* aileron located on the tailplane of an aircraft

TAILERONS > TAILERON
TAILERS > TAILER
TAILFAN *n* fanned structure at the hind end of a lobster
TAILFANS > TAILFAN
TAILFIN *n* decorative projection at the back of a car
TAILFINS > TAILFIN
TAILFLIES > TAILFLY
TAILFLY *n* in angling, the lowest fly on a wet-fly cast
TAILGATE *n* door at the rear of a hatchback vehicle ▷ *vb* drive very close behind (a vehicle)
TAILGATED > TAILGATE
TAILGATER > TAILGATE
TAILGATES > TAILGATE
TAILHOOK *n* hook on an aircraft that catches a braking cable
TAILHOOKS > TAILHOOK
TAILING *n* part of a beam, rafter, projecting brick or stone, etc, embedded in a wall
TAILINGS *pl n* waste left over after milling processes
TAILLAMP *n* rear light
TAILLAMPS > TAILLAMP
TAILLE *n* (in France before 1789) a tax levied by a king or overlord on his subjects
TAILLES > TAILLE
TAILLESS > TAIL
TAILLEUR *n* woman's suit
TAILLEURS > TAILLEUR
TAILLIE *n* (in Scots law) the limitation of an estate or interest to a person and their heirs
TAILLIES > TAILLIE
TAILLIGHT *same as* > TAILLAMP
TAILLIKE *adj* resembling a tail
TAILOR *n* person who makes men's clothes ▷ *vb* cut or style (a garment) to specific requirements
TAILORED > TAILOR
TAILORESS *n* female tailor
TAILORING > TAILOR
TAILORS > TAILOR
TAILPIECE *n* piece added at the end of something, for example a report
TAILPIPE *vb* attach an object, esp a tin can, to the tail of an animal
TAILPIPED > TAILPIPE
TAILPIPES > TAILPIPE

TAILPLANE *n* small stabilizing wing at the rear of an aircraft
TAILRACE *n* channel that carries water away from a water wheel, turbine, etc
TAILRACES > TAILRACE
TAILS *adv* with the side of a coin that does not have a portrait of a head on it uppermost
TAILSKID *n* runner under the tail of an aircraft
TAILSKIDS > TAILSKID
TAILSLIDE *n* backwards descent of an aeroplane after stalling while in an upward trajectory
TAILSPIN *n* uncontrolled spinning dive of an aircraft ▷ *vb* go into a tailspin
TAILSPINS > TAILSPIN
TAILSPUN > TAILSPIN
TAILSTOCK *n* casting that slides on the bed of a lathe in alignment with the headstock and is locked in position to support the free end of a workpiece
TAILWATER *n* water flowing in a tailrace
TAILWHEEL *n* wheel fitted to the rear of a vehicle, esp the landing wheel under the tail of an aircraft
TAILWIND *n* wind coming from the rear
TAILWINDS > TAILWIND
TAILYE *same as* > TAILLIE
TAILYES > TAILYE
TAILZIE *same as* > TAILLIE
TAILZIES > TAILZIE
TAIN *n* tinfoil used in backing mirrors
TAINS > TAIN
TAINT *vb* spoil with a small amount of decay or other bad quality ▷ *n* something that taints
TAINTED > TAINT
TAINTING > TAINT
TAINTLESS > TAINT
TAINTS > TAINT
TAINTURE *n* contamination; staining
TAINTURES > TAINTURE
TAIPAN *n* large poisonous Australian snake
TAIPANS > TAIPAN
TAIRA *same as* > TAYRA
TAIRAS > TAIRA
TAIS > TAI
TAISCH *n* (in Scotland) apparition of a person whose death is imminent
TAISCHES > TAISCH
TAISH *same as* > TAISCH

TAISHES > TAISH
TAIT *same as* > TATE
TAITS > TAIT
TAIVER *same as* > TAVER
TAIVERED > TAIVER
TAIVERING > TAIVER
TAIVERS > TAIVER
TAIVERT *adj* Scots word meaning confused or bewildered
TAJ *n* tall conical cap worn as a mark of distinction by Muslims
TAJES > TAJ
TAJINE *same as* > TAGINE
TAJINES > TAJINE
TAK *Scots variant spelling of* > TAKE
TAKA *n* standard monetary unit of Bangladesh, divided into 100 paise
TAKABLE > TAKE
TAKAHE *n* very rare flightless New Zealand bird
TAKAHES > TAKAHE
TAKAMAKA *same as* > TACAMAHAC
TAKAMAKAS > TAKAMAKA
TAKAS > TAKA
TAKE *vb* remove from a place ▷ *n* one of a series of recordings from which the best will be used
TAKEABLE > TAKE
TAKEAWAY *adj* (of food) sold for consumption away from the premises ▷ *n* shop or restaurant selling meals for eating elsewhere
TAKEAWAYS > TAKEAWAY
TAKEDOWN *n* disassembly
TAKEDOWNS > TAKEDOWN
TAKEN > TAKE
TAKEOFF *n* act or process of making an aircraft airborne
TAKEOFFS > TAKEOFF
TAKEOUT *n* shop or restaurant that sells such food
TAKEOUTS > TAKEOUT
TAKEOVER *n* act of taking control of a company by buying a large number of its shares
TAKEOVERS > TAKEOVER
TAKER *n* person who agrees to take something that is offered
TAKERS > TAKER
TAKES > TAKE
TAKEUP *n* claiming or acceptance of something that is due or available
TAKEUPS > TAKEUP
TAKHI *n* type of wild Mongolian horse
TAKHIS > TAKHI
TAKI *same as* > TAKHI
TAKIER > TAKY

TAKIEST > TAKY
TAKIN *n* bovid mammal of mountainous regions of S Asia
TAKING > TAKE
TAKINGLY > TAKE
TAKINGS > TAKE
TAKINS > TAKIN
TAKIS > TAKI
TAKKIES > TAKKY
TAKKY *n* S African word for plimsoll
TAKS > TAK
TAKY *adj* appealing
TALA *n* standard monetary unit of Samoa, divided into 100 sene
TALAK *same as* > TALAQ
TALAKS > TALAK
TALANT *old variant of* > TALON
TALANTS > TALANT
TALAPOIN *n* smallest of the guenon monkeys
TALAPOINS > TALAPOIN
TALAQ *n* Muslim form of divorce
TALAQS > TALAQ
TALAR *n* ankle-length robe
TALARIA *pl n* winged sandals, such as those worn by Hermes
TALARS > TALAR
TALAS > TALA
TALAUNT *old variant of* > TALON
TALAUNTS > TALAUNT
TALAYOT *n* ancient Balearic stone tower
TALAYOTS > TALAYOT
TALBOT *n* ancient breed of large hound
TALBOTS > TALBOT
TALBOTYPE *n* early type of photographic process (invented by W H Fox Talbot) or a photograph produced using it
TALC *n* talcum powder ▷ *vb* apply talc to ▷ *adj* of, or relating to, talc
TALCED > TALC
TALCIER > TALCY
TALCIEST > TALCY
TALCING > TALC
TALCKED > TALC
TALCKIER > TALCKY
TALCKIEST > TALCKY
TALCKING > TALC
TALCKY *same as* > TALCY
TALCOSE > TALC
TALCOUS > TALC
TALCS > TALC
TALCUM *n* white, grey, brown, or pale green mineral ▷ *vb* apply talcum to
TALCUMED > TALCUM
TALCUMING > TALCUM
TALCUMS > TALCUM
TALCY *adj* like, containing, or covered in talc
TALE *n* story
TALEA *n* rhythmic pattern in certain mediaeval choral compositions

TALEAE > TALEA
TALEFUL *adj* having many tales
TALEGALLA *n* brush turkey of New Guinea and Australia
TALEGGIO *n* Italian cheese
TALEGGIOS > TALEGGIO
TALENT *n* natural ability
TALENTED > TALENT
TALENTS > TALENT
TALER *same as* > THALER
TALERS > TALER
TALES *n* group of persons summoned to fill vacancies on a jury panel
TALESMAN > TALES
TALESMEN > TALES
TALEYSIM > TALLITH
TALI > TALUS
TALIGRADE *adj* (of mammals) walking on the outer side of the foot
TALION *n* principle of making punishment correspond to the crime
TALIONIC *adj* of or relating to talion
TALIONS > TALION
TALIPAT *same as* > TALIPOT
TALIPATS > TALIPAT
TALIPED *adj* having a club foot ▷ *n* club-footed person
TALIPEDS > TALIPED
TALIPES *n* congenital deformity of the foot by which it is twisted in any of various positions
TALIPOT *n* palm tree of East India
TALIPOTS > TALIPOT
TALISMAN *n* object believed to have magic power
TALISMANS > TALISMAN
TALK *vb* express ideas or feelings by means of speech ▷ *n* speech or lecture
TALKABLE > TALK
TALKATHON *n* epic bout of discussion or speechifying
TALKATIVE *adj* fond of talking
TALKBACK *n* broadcast in which telephone comments or questions from the public are transmitted live
TALKBACKS > TALKBACK
TALKBOX *n* voice box
TALKBOXES > TALKBOX
TALKED > TALK
TALKER > TALK
TALKERS > TALK
TALKFEST *n* lengthy discussion
TALKFESTS > TALKFEST
TALKIE *n* early film with a soundtrack

TALKIER > TALKY
TALKIES > TALKIE
TALKIEST > TALKY
TALKINESS *n* quality or condition of being talky
TALKING *n* speech; the act of speaking
TALKINGS > TALKING
TALKS > TALK
TALKTIME *n* length of time a mobile phone can be used before its battery runs out
TALKTIMES > TALKTIME
TALKY *adj* containing too much dialogue or inconsequential talk
TALL *adj* higher than average
TALLAGE *n* tax levied on Crown lands and royal towns ▷ *vb* levy a tax (upon)
TALLAGED > TALLAGE
TALLAGES > TALLAGE
TALLAGING > TALLAGE
TALLAISIM > TALLITH
TALLAT *same as* > TALLET
TALLATS > TALLAT
TALLBOY *n* high chest of drawers
TALLBOYS > TALLBOY
TALLENT *n* archaic word meaning abundance
TALLENTS > TALLENT
TALLER > TALL
TALLEST > TALL
TALLET *n* loft
TALLETS > TALLET
TALLGRASS *n* long grass in North American prairie
TALLIABLE *adj* taxable
TALLIATE *vb* levy a tax
TALLIATED > TALLIATE
TALLIATES > TALLIATE
TALLIED > TALLY
TALLIER > TALLY
TALLIERS > TALLY
TALLIES > TALLY
TALLIS *variant of* > TALLITH
TALLISES > TALLIS
TALLISH *adj* quite tall
TALLISIM > TALLIS
TALLIT *variant of* > TALLITH
TALLITES > TALLIT
TALLITH *n* shawl worn by Jewish males in religious services
TALLITHES > TALLITH
TALLITHIM > TALLITH
TALLITHS > TALLITH
TALLITIM > TALLIT
TALLITOT > TALLIT
TALLITOTH > TALLITH
TALLITS > TALLIT
TALLNESS > TALL
TALLOL *n* oily liquid used for making soaps, lubricants, etc
TALLOLS > TALLOL
TALLOT *same as* > TALLET

TALLOTS > TALLOT
TALLOW *n* hard animal fat used to make candles ▷ *vb* cover or smear with tallow
TALLOWED > TALLOW
TALLOWIER > TALLOWY
TALLOWING > TALLOW
TALLOWISH > TALLOW
TALLOWS > TALLOW
TALLOWY *adj* like tallow
TALLS > TALL
TALLY *vb* (of two things) correspond ▷ *n* record of a debt or score
TALLYHO *n* cry to encourage hounds when the quarry is sighted ▷ *vb* make the cry of tallyho
TALLYHOED > TALLYHO
TALLYHOES > TALLYHO
TALLYHOS > TALLYHO
TALLYING > TALLY
TALLYMAN *n* male scorekeeper or recorder
TALLYMEN > TALLYMAN
TALLYSHOP *n* shop that allows customers to pay in instalments
TALMA *n* short cloak
TALMAS > TALMA
TALMUD *n* primary source of Jewish religious law, consisting of the Mishnah and the Gemara
TALMUDIC > TALMUD
TALMUDISM > TALMUD
TALMUDS > TALMUD
TALON *n* bird's hooked claw
TALONED > TALON
TALONS > TALON
TALOOKA *same as* > TALUK
TALOOKAS > TALOOKA
TALPA *n* sebaceous cyst
TALPAE > TALPA
TALPAS > TALPA
TALUK *n* subdivision of a district
TALUKA *same as* > TALUK
TALUKAS > TALUKA
TALUKDAR *n* person in charge of a taluk
TALUKDARS > TALUKDAR
TALUKS > TALUK
TALUS *n* bone of the ankle that articulates with the leg bones to form the ankle joint
TALUSES > TALUS
TALWEG *same as* > THALWEG
TALWEGS > TALWEG
TAM *n* type of hat
TAMABLE > TAME
TAMAL *same as* > TAMALE
TAMALE *n* Mexican dish of minced meat wrapped in maize husks and steamed
TAMALES > TAMALE
TAMALS > TAMAL
TAMANDU *same as* > TAMANDUA
TAMANDUA *n* small arboreal edentate mammal

TAMANDUAS
> TAMANDUA
TAMANDUS > TAMANDU
TAMANOIR *n* anteater
TAMANOIRS
> TAMANOIR
TAMANU *n* poon tree
TAMANUS > TAMANU
TAMARA *n* powder consisting of cloves, cinnamon, fennel, coriander, etc
TAMARACK *n* North American larch
TAMARACKS
> TAMARACK
TAMARAO *same as*
> TAMARAU
TAMARAOS > TAMARAO
TAMARAS > TAMARA
TAMARAU *n* small rare member of a cattle tribe in the Philippines
TAMARAUS > TAMARAU
TAMARI *n* Japanese variety of soy sauce
TAMARILLO *n* shrub with a red oval edible fruit
TAMARIN *n* small monkey of South and Central America
TAMARIND *n* tropical tree
TAMARINDS
> TAMARIND
TAMARINS > TAMARIN
TAMARIS > TAMARI
TAMARISK *n* evergreen shrub with slender branches and feathery flower clusters
TAMARISKS
> TAMARISK
TAMASHA *n* (in India) a show
TAMASHAS > TAMASHA
TAMBAC *same as*
> TOMBAC
TAMBACS > TAMBAC
TAMBAK *same as*
> TOMBAC
TAMBAKS > TAMBAK
TAMBALA *n* unit of Malawian currency
TAMBALAS > TAMBALA
TAMBER *same as*
> TIMBRE
TAMBERS > TAMBER
TAMBOUR *n* embroidery frame consisting of two hoops ▷ *vb* embroider (fabric or a design) on a tambour
TAMBOURA *n* stringed instrument used in Indian music
TAMBOURAS
> TAMBOURA
TAMBOURED > TAMBOUR
TAMBOURER *n* one who embroiders on a tambour
TAMBOURIN *n* 18th-century Provençal folk dance
TAMBOURS > TAMBOUR
TAMBUR *n* old Turkish stringed instrument
TAMBURA *n* Middle-Eastern stringed

instrument with a long neck
TAMBURAS > TAMBURA
TAMBURIN *n* Spenserian form of 'tambourine'
TAMBURINS > TAMBURIN
TAMBURS > TAMBUR
TAME *adj* (of animals) brought under human control ▷ *vb* make tame
TAMEABLE > TAME
TAMED > TAME
TAMEIN *n* Burmese skirt
TAMEINS > TAMEIN
TAMELESS > TAME
TAMELY > TAME
TAMENESS > TAME
TAMER > TAME
TAMERS > TAME
TAMES > TAME
TAMEST > TAME
TAMIN *n* thin woollen fabric
TAMINE *same as* > TAMIN
TAMINES > TAMINE
TAMING *n* act of making (something) tame
TAMINGS > TAMING
TAMINS > TAMIN
TAMIS *same as* > TAMMY
TAMISE *n* type of thin cloth
TAMISES > TAMIS
TAMMAR *n* small scrub wallaby
TAMMARS > TAMMAR
TAMMIE *n* short for tam-o'-shanter, a traditional Scottish hat
TAMMIED > TAMMY
TAMMIES > TAMMIE
TAMMY *n* glazed woollen or mixed fabric ▷ *vb* strain (sauce, soup, etc) through a tammy
TAMMYING > TAMMY
TAMOXIFEN *n* drug that antagonizes the action of oestrogen
TAMP *vb* pack down by repeated taps
TAMPALA *n* Asian plant, eaten as food
TAMPALAS > TAMPALA
TAMPAN *n* biting mite
TAMPANS > TAMPAN
TAMPED > TAMP
TAMPER *vb* interfere ▷ *n* person or thing that tamps
TAMPERED > TAMPER
TAMPERER > TAMPER
TAMPERERS > TAMPER
TAMPERING > TAMPER
TAMPERS > TAMPER
TAMPING *adj* very angry ▷ *n* act or instance of tamping
TAMPINGS > TAMPING
TAMPION *n* plug placed in a gun's muzzle to keep out moisture and dust
TAMPIONS > TAMPION
TAMPON *n* plug of cotton wool inserted into a wound or body cavity to absorb blood ▷ *vb* use a tampon

TAMPONADE > TAMPON
TAMPONAGE > TAMPON
TAMPONED > TAMPON
TAMPONING > TAMPON
TAMPONS > TAMPON
TAMPS > TAMP
TAMS > TAM
TAMWORTH *n* any of a hardy rare breed of long-bodied reddish pigs
TAMWORTHS
> TAMWORTH
TAN *n* brown coloration of the skin from exposure to sunlight ▷ *vb* (of skin) go brown from exposure to sunlight ▷ *adj* yellowish-brown
TANA *n* small Madagascan lemur
TANADAR *n* commanding officer of an Indian police station
TANADARS > TANADAR
TANAGER *n* American songbird with a short thick bill
TANAGERS > TANAGER
TANAGRA *n* type of tanager
TANAGRAS > TANAGRA
TANAGRINE *adj* of or relating to the tanager
TANAISTE *n* deputy prime minister of the Republic of Ireland
TANAISTES
> TANAISTE
TANALISED *adj* having been treated with the trademarked timber preservative Tanalith
TANALIZED *same as*
> TANALISED
TANAS > TANA
TANBARK *n* bark of certain trees, esp the oak and hemlock, used as a source of tannin
TANBARKS > TANBARK
TANDEM *n* bicycle for two riders, one behind the other
TANDEMS > TANDEM
TANDOOR *n* type of Indian clay oven
TANDOORI *adj* (of food) cooked in an Indian clay oven ▷ *n* Indian method of cooking meat or vegetables on a spit in a clay oven
TANDOORIS
> TANDOORI
TANDOORS > TANDOOR
TANE *old Scottish variant of*
> TAKEN
TANG *n* strong taste or smell ▷ *vb* cause to ring
TANGA *n* triangular loincloth worn by indigenous peoples in tropical America
TANGAS > TANGA
TANGED > TANG
TANGELO *n* hybrid produced by crossing a tangerine tree with a grapefruit tree

TANGELOS > TANGELO
TANGENCE *n* touching
TANGENCES
> TANGENCE
TANGENCY > TANGENT
TANGENT *n* line that touches a curve without intersecting it
TANGENTAL > TANGENT
TANGENTS > TANGENT
TANGERINE *n* small orange-like fruit of an Asian citrus tree ▷ *adj* reddish-orange
TANGHIN *n* poison formerly used in Madagascar to determine the guilt of crime suspects
TANGHININ *n* active ingredient in tanghin
TANGHINS > TANGHIN
TANGI *n* Māori funeral ceremony
TANGIBLE *adj* able to be touched ▷ *n* tangible thing or asset
TANGIBLES
> TANGIBLE
TANGIBLY > TANGIBLE
TANGIE *n* water spirit of Orkney, appearing as a figure draped in seaweed, or as a seahorse
TANGIER > TANGY
TANGIES > TANGIE
TANGIEST > TANGY
TANGINESS > TANGY
TANGING > TANG
TANGIS > TANGI
TANGLE *n* confused mass or situation ▷ *vb* twist together in a tangle
TANGLED > TANGLE
TANGLER > TANGLE
TANGLERS > TANGLE
TANGLES > TANGLE
TANGLIER > TANGLE
TANGLIEST > TANGLE
TANGLING *n* act or condition of tangling
TANGLINGS
> TANGLING
TANGLY > TANGLE
TANGO *n* S American dance ▷ *vb* dance a tango
TANGOED > TANGO
TANGOES > TANGO
TANGOING > TANGO
TANGOIST > TANGO
TANGOISTS > TANGO
TANGOLIKE > TANGO
TANGOS > TANGO
TANGRAM *n* type of Chinese puzzle
TANGRAMS > TANGRAM
TANGS > TANG
TANGUN *n* small and sturdy Tibetan pony
TANGUNS > TANGUN
TANGY *adj* having a pungent, fresh, or briny flavour or aroma
TANH *n* hyperbolic tangent
TANHS > TANH
TANIST *n* heir apparent of a Celtic chieftain
TANISTRY > TANIST

TANISTS > TANIST
TANIWHA n mythical Māori monster that lives in water
TANIWHAS > TANIWHA
TANK n container for liquids or gases ▷ vb put or keep in a tank
TANKA n Japanese verse form consisting of five lines
TANKAGE n capacity or contents of a tank or tanks
TANKAGES > TANKAGE
TANKARD n large beer-mug, often with a hinged lid
TANKARDS > TANKARD
TANKAS > TANKA
TANKED > TANK
TANKER n ship or truck for carrying liquid in bulk ▷ vb transport by means of a tanker
TANKERED > TANKER
TANKERING > TANKER
TANKERS > TANKER
TANKFUL n quantity contained in a tank
TANKFULS > TANKFUL
TANKIA n type of boat used in Canton
TANKIAS > TANKIA
TANKIES > TANKY
TANKING n heavy defeat
TANKINGS > TANKING
TANKINI n swimming costume consisting of a camisole top and bikini briefs
TANKINIS > TANKINI
TANKLESS > TANK
TANKLIKE > TANK
TANKS > TANK
TANKSHIP same as > TANKER
TANKSHIPS > TANKSHIP
TANKY n die-hard communist
TANLING n suntanned person
TANLINGS > TANLING
TANNA n Indian police station or army base
TANNABLE > TAN
TANNAGE n act or process of tanning
TANNAGES > TANNAGE
TANNAH same as > TANNA
TANNAHS > TANNAH
TANNAS > TANNA
TANNATE n any salt or ester of tannic acid
TANNATES > TANNATE
TANNED > TAN
TANNER > TAN
TANNERIES > TANNERY
TANNERS > TAN
TANNERY n place where hides are tanned
TANNEST > TAN
TANNIC adj of, containing, or produced from tannin or tannic acid
TANNIE n in S Africa, title of respect used to refer to an elderly woman

TANNIES > TANNIE
TANNIN n vegetable substance used in tanning
TANNING > TAN
TANNINGS > TAN
TANNINS > TANNIN
TANNISH > TAN
TANNOY n sound-amplifying apparatus used as a public-address system ▷ vb announce (something) using a Tannoy system
TANNOYED > TANNOY
TANNOYING > TANNOY
TANNOYS > TANNOY
TANOREXIC n person obsessed with maintaining a tan
TANREC same as > TENREC
TANRECS > TANREC
TANS > TAN
TANSIES > TANSY
TANSY n yellow-flowered plant
TANTALATE n any of various salts of tantalic acid formed when the pentoxide of tantalum dissolves in an alkali
TANTALIC adj of or containing tantalum, esp in the pentavalent state
TANTALISE same as > TANTALIZE
TANTALISM > TANTALISE
TANTALITE n heavy brownish mineral consisting of a tantalum oxide of iron and manganese in orthorhombic crystalline form
TANTALIZE vb torment by showing but withholding something desired
TANTALOUS adj of or containing tantalum in the trivalent state
TANTALUM n hard greyish-white metallic element
TANTALUMS > TANTALUM
TANTALUS n case in which bottles of drink are locked with their contents tantalizingly visible
TANTARA n blast, as on a trumpet or horn
TANTARARA same as > TANTARA
TANTARAS > TANTARA
TANTI adj old word for worthwhile
TANTIES > TANTY
TANTIVIES > TANTIVY
TANTIVY adv at full speed ▷ n hunting cry, esp at full gallop
TANTO adv too much ▷ n type of Japanese sword
TANTONIES > TANTONY
TANTONY n runt
TANTOS > TANTO

TANTRA n sacred books of Tantrism
TANTRAS > TANTRA
TANTRIC > TANTRA
TANTRISM n teaching of tantra
TANTRISMS > TANTRISM
TANTRIST n person who practises or teaches tantrism
TANTRISTS > TANTRIST
TANTRUM n childish outburst of temper
TANTRUMS > TANTRUM
TANTY n tantrum
TANUKI n animal similar to a raccoon, found in Japan
TANUKIS > TANUKI
TANYARD n part of a tannery
TANYARDS > TANYARD
TANZANITE n blue gemstone
TAO n (in Confucian philosophy) the correct course of action
TAONGA n New Zealand word meaning treasure
TAONGAS > TAONGA
TAOS > TAO
TAP vb knock lightly and usu repeatedly ▷ n light knock
TAPA n inner bark of the paper mulberry
TAPACOLO n small bird of Chile and Argentina
TAPACOLOS > TAPACOLO
TAPACULO same as > TAPACOLO
TAPACULOS > TAPACOLO
TAPADERA n leather covering for the stirrup on an American saddle
TAPADERAS > TAPADERA
TAPADERO same as > TAPADERA
TAPADEROS > TAPADERO
TAPALO n Latin American scarf, often patterned and brightly coloured
TAPALOS > TAPALO
TAPAS pl n (in Spanish cookery) light snacks or appetizers
TAPE n narrow long strip of material ▷ vb (formerly) record on magnetic tape
TAPEABLE > TAPE
TAPED > TAPE
TAPELESS > TAPE
TAPELIKE > TAPE
TAPELINE n tape used for measuring and fitting garments
TAPELINES > TAPELINE
TAPEN adj made of tape
TAPENADE n savoury paste made from capers, olives, and anchovies,

with olive oil and lemon juice
TAPENADES > TAPENADE
TAPER > TAPE
TAPERED > TAPE
TAPERER > TAPE
TAPERERS > TAPE
TAPERING > TAPE
TAPERINGS > TAPE
TAPERNESS n state or quality of being tapered
TAPERS > TAPE
TAPERWISE adv in the manner of a taper
TAPES > TAPE
TAPESTRY n fabric decorated with coloured woven designs ▷ vb portray in tapestry
TAPET n example of tapestry ▷ vb decorate with tapestries
TAPETA > TAPETUM
TAPETAL > TAPETUM
TAPETED > TAPET
TAPETI n forest rabbit of Brazil
TAPETING > TAPET
TAPETIS > TAPETI
TAPETS > TAPET
TAPETUM n layer of nutritive cells that surrounds developing spore cells
TAPETUMS > TAPETUM
TAPEWORM n long flat parasitic worm living in the intestines of vertebrates
TAPEWORMS > TAPEWORM
TAPHOLE n hole in a furnace for running off molten metal or slag
TAPHOLES > TAPHOLE
TAPHONOMY n study of the processes affecting an organism after death that result in its fossilization
TAPHOUSE n inn or bar
TAPHOUSES > TAPHOUSE
TAPING n act of taping
TAPINGS > TAPING
TAPIOCA n beadlike starch made from cassava root
TAPIOCAS > TAPIOCA
TAPIR n piglike mammal of tropical America and SE Asia, with a long snout
TAPIROID > TAPIR
TAPIROIDS > TAPIROID
TAPIRS > TAPIR
TAPIS n tapestry or carpeting
TAPISES > TAPIS
TAPIST n person who records printed matter in an audio format
TAPISTS > TAPIST
TAPLASH n dregs of beer
TAPLASHES > TAPLASH
TAPLESS adj without a tap
TAPPA same as > TAPA

TAPPABLE > TAP
TAPPAS > TAPPA
TAPPED > TAP
TAPPER n person who taps
TAPPERS > TAPPER
TAPPET n short steel rod in an engine, transferring motion from one part to another
TAPPETS > TAPPET
TAPPICE vb hide
TAPPICED > TAPPICE
TAPPICES > TAPPICE
TAPPICING > TAPPICE
TAPPING > TAP
TAPPINGS > TAP
TAPPIT adj crested; topped
TAPROOM n public bar in a hotel or pub
TAPROOMS > TAPROOM
TAPROOT n main root of a plant, growing straight down
TAPROOTED > TAPROOT
TAPROOTS > TAPROOT
TAPS > TAP
TAPSMAN n old word for a barman
TAPSMEN > TAPSMAN
TAPSTER n bartender
TAPSTERS > TAPSTER
TAPSTRESS n female bartender
TAPSTRIES > TAPSTRY
TAPSTRY adj relating to tapestry ▷ n taproom in a public house
TAPU adj sacred ▷ n Māori religious or superstitious restriction on something ▷ vb put a tapu on something
TAPUED > TAPU
TAPUING > TAPU
TAPUS > TAPU
TAQUERIA n restaurant specializing in tacos
TAQUERIAS > TAQUERIA
TAR n thick black liquid distilled from coal etc ▷ vb coat with tar
TARA same as > TARO
TARABISH n type of card game
TARAIRE n type of New Zealand tree
TARAIRES > TARAIRE
TARAKIHI n common edible sea fish of New Zealand waters
TARAKIHIS > TARAKIHI
TARAMA n cod roe
TARAMAS > TARAMA
TARAMEA n variety of New Zealand speargrass
TARAMEAS > TARAMEA
TARAND n northern animal of legend, now supposed to have been the reindeer
TARANDS > TARAND
TARANTARA same as > TANTARA

TARANTAS same as > TARANTASS
TARANTASS n large horse-drawn four-wheeled Russian carriage without springs
TARANTISM n nervous disorder marked by uncontrollable bodily movement, widespread in S Italy during the 15th to 17th centuries: popularly thought to be caused by the bite of a tarantula
TARANTIST > TARANTISM
TARANTULA n large hairy spider with a poisonous bite
TARAS > TARA
TARAXACUM n perennial plant with dense heads of small yellow flowers and seeds with a feathery attachment
TARBOGGIN same as > TOBOGGAN
TARBOOSH n brimless cap formerly worn by Muslim men
TARBOUCHE same as > TARBOOSH
TARBOUSH same as > TARBOOSH
TARBOY n boy who applies tar to the skin of sheep cut during shearing
TARBOYS > TARBOY
TARBUSH same as > TARBOOSH
TARBUSHES > TARBUSH
TARCEL same as > TERCEL
TARCELS > TARCEL
TARDIED > TARDY
TARDIER > TARDY
TARDIES > TARDY
TARDIEST > TARDY
TARDILY > TARDY
TARDINESS > TARDY
TARDIVE adj tending to develop late
TARDO adj (of music) slow; to be played slowly
TARDY adj slow or late ▷ vb delay or impede (something or someone)
TARDYING > TARDY
TARDYON n particle travelling more slowly than the speed of light
TARDYONS > TARDYON
TARE n weight of the wrapping or container of goods ▷ vb weigh (a package, etc) in order to calculate the amount of tare
TARED > TARE
TARES > TARE
TARGA n as in targa top denotes removable hard roof on a car
TARGAS > TARGA
TARGE vb interrogate
TARGED > TARGE
TARGES > TARGE
TARGET n object or person a missile is aimed at ▷ vb aim or direct

TARGETED > TARGET
TARGETEER n soldier armed with a small round shield
TARGETING n act of targeting
TARGETS > TARGET
TARGING > TARGE
TARIFF n tax levied on imports ▷ vb impose punishment for a criminal offence
TARIFFED > TARIFF
TARIFFING > TARIFF
TARIFFS > TARIFF
TARING > TARE
TARINGS > TARE
TARLATAN n open-weave cotton fabric, used for stiffening garments
TARLATANS > TARLATAN
TARLETAN same as > TARLATAN
TARLETANS > TARLETAN
TARMAC same as > MACADAM
TARMACKED > TARMAC
TARMACS > TARMAC
TARN n small mountain lake
TARNAL adj damned ▷ adv extremely
TARNALLY > TARNAL
TARNATION euphemism for > DAMNATION
TARNISH vb make or become stained or less bright ▷ n discoloration or blemish
TARNISHED > TARNISH
TARNISHER > TARNISH
TARNISHES > TARNISH
TARNS > TARN
TARO n plant with a large edible rootstock
TAROC old variant of > TAROT
TAROCS > TAROC
TAROK old variant of > TAROT
TAROKS > TAROK
TAROS > TARO
TAROT n special pack of cards used mainly in fortune-telling ▷ adj relating to tarot cards
TAROTS > TAROT
TARP informal word for > TARPAULIN
TARPAN n European wild horse common in prehistoric times
TARPANS > TARPAN
TARPAPER n paper coated or impregnated with tar
TARPAPERS > TARPAPER
TARPAULIN n (sheet of) heavy waterproof fabric
TARPON n large silvery clupeoid game fish found in warm Atlantic waters
TARPONS > TARPON
TARPS > TARP

TARRAGON n aromatic herb
TARRAGONS > TARRAGON
TARRAS same as > TRASS
TARRASES > TARRAS
TARRE vb old word meaning to provoke or goad
TARRED > TAR
TARRES > TARRE
TARRIANCE archaic word for > DELAY
TARRIED > TARRY
TARRIER > TARRY
TARRIERS > TARRY
TARRIES > TARRY
TARRIEST > TARRY
TARRINESS > TAR
TARRING > TAR
TARRINGS > TAR
TARROCK n seabird
TARROCKS > TARROCK
TARROW vb exhibit reluctance
TARROWED > TARROW
TARROWING > TARROW
TARROWS > TARROW
TARRY vb linger or delay ▷ adj covered in or resembling tar
TARRYING > TARRY
TARS > TAR
TARSAL adj of the tarsus or tarsi ▷ n tarsal bone
TARSALGIA n pain in the tarsus
TARSALS > TARSAL
TARSEAL n bitumen surface of a road
TARSEALS > TARSEAL
TARSEL same as > TERCEL
TARSELS > TARSEL
TARSI > TARSUS
TARSIA another term for > INTARSIA
TARSIAS > TARSIA
TARSIER n small nocturnal primate
TARSIERS > TARSIER
TARSIOID adj resembling a tarsier ▷ n type of fossil
TARSIOIDS > TARSIOID
TARSIPED n generic term for a number of marsupials
TARSIPEDS > TARSIPED
TARSUS n bones of the heel and ankle collectively
TART n pie or flan with a sweet filling ▷ adj sharp or bitter ▷ vb (of food, drink, etc) become tart (sour)
TARTAN n design of straight lines crossing at right angles
TARTANA n small Mediterranean sailing boat
TARTANAS > TARTANA
TARTANE same as > TARTANA
TARTANED > TARTAN
TARTANES > TARTANE

t

TARTANRY n excessive use of Scottish imagery to produce a distorted sentimental view of Scotland

TARTANS > TARTAN

TARTAR n hard deposit on the teeth

TARTARE n mayonnaise sauce mixed with hard-boiled egg yolks, herbs, etc

TARTARES > TARTARE

TARTARIC adj of or derived from tartar or tartaric acid

TARTARISE same as > TARTARIZE

TARTARIZE vb impregnate or treat with tartar or tartar emetic

TARTARLY adj resembling a tartar

TARTAROUS adj consisting of, containing, or resembling tartar

TARTARS > TARTAR

TARTED > TART

TARTER > TART

TARTEST > TART

TARTIER > TARTY

TARTIEST > TARTY

TARTILY > TARTY

TARTINE n slice of bread with butter or jam spread on it

TARTINES > TARTINE

TARTINESS > TARTY

TARTING > TART

TARTISH > TART

TARTISHLY > TART

TARTLET n individual pastry case with a filling of fruit or other sweet or savoury mixture

TARTLETS > TARTLET

TARTLY > TART

TARTNESS > TART

TARTRATE n any salt or ester of tartaric acid

TARTRATED adj being in the form of a tartrate

TARTRATES > TARTRATE

TARTS > TART

TARTUFE same as > TARTUFFE

TARTUFES > TARTUFE

TARTUFFE n person who hypocritically pretends to be deeply pious

TARTUFFES > TARTUFFE

TARTUFI > TARTUFO

TARTUFO n Italian mousse-like chocolate dessert

TARTUFOS > TARTUFO

TARTY adj provocative in a cheap and bawdy way

TARWEED n resinous Californian plant

TARWEEDS > TARWEED

TARWHINE n bream of E Australia, silver in colour with gold streaks

TARWHINES > TARWHINE

TARZAN n man with great physical strength

TARZANS > TARZAN

TAS > TA

TASAR same as > TUSSORE

TASARS > TASAR

TASBIH n form of Islamic prayer

TASBIHS > TASBIH

TASE vb stun with a taser gun

TASED > TASE

TASER vb use a taser stun gun on (someone)

TASERED > TASER

TASERING > TASER

TASERS > TASER

TASES > TASE

TASH vb stain or besmirch

TASHED > TASH

TASHES > TASH

TASHING > TASH

TASIMETER n device for measuring small temperature changes. It depends on the changes of pressure resulting from expanding or contracting solids

TASIMETRY > TASIMETER

TASING > TASE

TASK n piece of work to be done ▷ vb give someone a task to do

TASKBAR n area of computer screen showing what programs are running

TASKBARS > TASKBAR

TASKED > TASK

TASKER > TASK

TASKERS > TASK

TASKING > TASK

TASKINGS > TASK

TASKLESS > TASK

TASKS > TASK

TASKWORK n hard or unpleasant work

TASKWORKS > TASKWORK

TASLET same as > TASSET

TASLETS > TASLET

TASS n cup, goblet, or glass

TASSA n type of Indian kettledrum

TASSAS > TASSA

TASSE same as > TASSET

TASSEL n decorative fringed knot of threads ▷ vb adorn with a tassel or tassels

TASSELED > TASSEL

TASSELIER > TASSELY

TASSELING > TASSEL

TASSELL same as > TASSEL

TASSELLED > TASSEL

TASSELLS > TASSELL

TASSELLY adj adorned with tassels

TASSELS > TASSEL

TASSELY adj decorated with tassels

TASSES > TASSE

TASSET n piece of armour to protect the thigh

TASSETS > TASSET

TASSIE same as > TASS

TASSIES > TASSIE

TASSO n spicy cured pork cut into strips

TASSOS > TASSO

TASSWAGE vb archaic contraction of 'to assuage'

TASTABLE > TASTE

TASTE n sense by which the flavour of a substance is distinguished ▷ vb distinguish the taste of (a substance)

TASTEABLE > TASTE

TASTED > TASTE

TASTEFUL adj having or showing good taste

TASTELESS adj bland or insipid

TASTER n person employed to test the quality of food or drink by tasting it

TASTERS > TASTER

TASTES > TASTE

TASTEVIN n small shallow cup for wine tasting

TASTEVINS > TASTEVIN

TASTIER > TASTY

TASTIEST > TASTY

TASTILY > TASTY

TASTINESS > TASTY

TASTING > TASTE

TASTINGS > TASTE

TASTY adj pleasantly flavoured

TAT n tatty or tasteless articles ▷ vb make (something) by tatting

TATAHASH n stew containing potatoes and cheap cuts of meat

TATAMI n thick rectangular mat of woven straw

TATAMIS > TATAMI

TATAR n brutal person

TATARS > TATAR

TATE n small tuft of fibre

TATER n potato

TATERS > TATER

TATES > TATE

TATH vb (of cattle) to defecate

TATHATA n (in Buddhism) ultimate nature of things

TATHATAS > TATHATA

TATHED > TATH

TATHING > TATH

TATHS > TATH

TATIE same as > TATTIE

TATIES > TATIE

TATLER old variant of > TATTLER

TATLERS > TATLER

TATOU n armadillo

TATOUAY n large armadillo of South America

TATOUAYS > TATOUAY

TATOUS > TATOU

TATS > TAT

TATSOI n variety of Chinese cabbage

TATSOIS > TATSOI

TATT same as > TAT

TATTED > TAT

TATTER vb make or become torn

TATTERED > TATTER

TATTERIER > TATTERY

TATTERING > TATTER

TATTERS > TATTER

TATTERY adj ragged

TATTIE Scot or dialect word for > POTATO

TATTIER > TATTY

TATTIES > TATTIE

TATTIEST > TATTY

TATTILY > TATTY

TATTINESS > TATTY

TATTING > TAT

TATTINGS > TAT

TATTLE n gossip or chatter ▷ vb gossip or chatter

TATTLED > TATTLE

TATTLER n person who tattles

TATTLERS > TATTLER

TATTLES > TATTLE

TATTLING > TATTLE

TATTLINGS > TATTLE

TATTOO n pattern made on the body by pricking the skin and staining it with indelible inks ▷ vb make such a pattern on the skin

TATTOOED > TATTOO

TATTOOER > TATTOO

TATTOOERS > TATTOO

TATTOOING > TATTOO

TATTOOIST > TATTOO

TATTOOS > TATTOO

TATTOW old variant of > TATTOO

TATTOWED > TATTOW

TATTOWING > TATTOW

TATTOWS > TATTOW

TATTS > TATT

TATTY adj worn out, shabby, tawdry, or unkempt

TATU old variant of > TATTOO

TATUED > TATU

TATUING > TATU

TATUS > TATU

TAU n 19th letter in the Greek alphabet

TAUBE n type of obsolete German aeroplane

TAUBES > TAUBE

TAUGHT > TEACH

TAUHINU New Zealand name for > POPLAR

TAUHINUS > TAUHINU

TAUHOU same as > SILVEREYE

TAUHOUS > TAUHOU

TAUIWI n Māori term for the non-Māori people of New Zealand

TAUIWIS > TAUIWI

TAULD vb old Scots variant of told

TAUNT vb tease with jeers ▷ n jeering remark ▷ adj (of the mast or masts of a sailing vessel) unusually tall

TAUNTED > TAUNT
TAUNTER > TAUNT
TAUNTERS > TAUNT
TAUNTING > TAUNT
TAUNTINGS > TAUNT
TAUNTS > TAUNT
TAUON n negatively charged elementary particle
TAUONS > TAUON
TAUPATA n New Zealand shrub or tree
TAUPATAS > TAUPATA
TAUPE adj brownish-grey ▷ n brownish-grey colour
TAUPES > TAUPE
TAUPIE same as **> TAWPIE**
TAUPIES > TAUPIE
TAUREAN adj born under or characteristic of Taurus
TAURIC same as **> TAUREAN**
TAURIFORM adj in the form of a bull
TAURINE adj of, relating to, or resembling a bull ▷ n substance obtained from the bile of animals
TAURINES > TAURINE
TAUS > TAU
TAUT adj drawn tight ▷ vb Scots word meaning to tangle
TAUTAUG same as **> TAUTOG**
TAUTAUGS > TAUTAUG
TAUTED > TAUT
TAUTEN vb make or become taut
TAUTENED > TAUTEN
TAUTENING > TAUTEN
TAUTENS > TAUTEN
TAUTER > TAUT
TAUTEST > TAUT
TAUTING > TAUT
TAUTIT adj Scots word meaning tangled
TAUTLY > TAUT
TAUTNESS > TAUT
TAUTOG n large dark-coloured wrasse, used as a food fish
TAUTOGS > TAUTOG
TAUTOLOGY n use of words which merely repeat something already stated
TAUTOMER n either of the two forms of a chemical compound that exhibits tautomerism
TAUTOMERS > TAUTOMER
TAUTONYM n taxonomic name in which the generic and specific components are the same
TAUTONYMS > TAUTONYM
TAUTONYMY > TAUTONYM
TAUTS > TAUT
TAV n 23rd and last letter in the Hebrew alphabet

TAVA n thick Indian frying pan
TAVAH variant of **> TAVA**
TAVAHS > TAVAH
TAVAS > TAVA
TAVER vb wander about
TAVERED > TAVER
TAVERING > TAVER
TAVERN n pub
TAVERNA n Greek restaurant
TAVERNAS > TAVERNA
TAVERNER n keeper of a tavern
TAVERNERS > TAVERNER
TAVERNS > TAVERN
TAVERS > TAVER
TAVERT adj bewildered or confused
TAVS > TAV
TAW vb convert skins into leather
TAWA n tall timber tree from New Zealand
TAWAI n New Zealand beech
TAWAIS > TAWAI
TAWAS > TAWA
TAWDRIER > TAWDRY
TAWDRIES > TAWDRY
TAWDRIEST > TAWDRY
TAWDRILY > TAWDRY
TAWDRY adj cheap, showy, and of poor quality ▷ n gaudy finery of poor quality
TAWED > TAW
TAWER > TAW
TAWERIES > TAWERY
TAWERS > TAW
TAWERY n place where tawing is carried out
TAWHAI same as **> TAWAI**
TAWHAIS > TAWHAI
TAWHIRI n small New Zealand tree with wavy green glossy leaves
TAWHIRIS > TAWHIRI
TAWIE adj easily persuaded or managed
TAWIER > TAWIE
TAWIEST > TAWIE
TAWING > TAW
TAWINGS > TAW
TAWNEY same as **> TAWNY**
TAWNEYS > TAWNEY
TAWNIER > TAWNY
TAWNIES > TAWNY
TAWNIEST > TAWNY
TAWNILY > TAWNY
TAWNINESS > TAWNY
TAWNY adj yellowish-brown ▷ n light brown to brownish-orange colour
TAWPIE n Scottish word for a foolish young woman
TAWPIES > TAWPIE
TAWS same as **> TAWSE**
TAWSE n leather strap with one end cut into thongs ▷ vb punish (someone) with or as if with a tawse
TAWSED > TAWSE
TAWSES > TAWSE
TAWSING > TAWSE

TAWT same as **> TAUT**
TAWTED > TAWT
TAWTIE > TAWT
TAWTIER > TAWT
TAWTIEST > TAWT
TAWTING > TAWT
TAWTS > TAWT
TAX n compulsory payment levied by a government on income, property, etc to raise revenue ▷ vb levy a tax on
TAXA > TAXON
TAXABLE adj capable of being taxed ▷ n person, income, property, etc, that is subject to tax
TAXABLES > TAXABLE
TAXABLY > TAXABLE
TAXACEOUS adj relating to a family of coniferous trees that includes the yews
TAXAMETER old variant of **> TAXIMETER**
TAXATION n levying of taxes
TAXATIONS > TAXATION
TAXATIVE > TAXATION
TAXED > TAX
TAXEME n any element of speech that may differentiate meaning
TAXEMES > TAXEME
TAXEMIC > TAXEME
TAXER > TAX
TAXERS > TAX
TAXES > TAX
TAXI n car with a driver that may be hired ▷ vb (of an aircraft) run along the ground
TAXIARCH n (in ancient Greece) soldier in charge of troops
TAXIARCHS > TAXIARCH
TAXICAB same as **> TAXI**
TAXICABS > TAXICAB
TAXIDERMY n art of stuffing and mounting animal skins to give them a lifelike appearance
TAXIED > TAXI
TAXIES > TAXI
TAXIING > TAXI
TAXIMAN n taxi driver
TAXIMEN > TAXIMAN
TAXIMETER n meter fitted to a taxi to register the fare, based on the length of the journey
TAXING adj demanding, onerous
TAXINGLY > TAXING
TAXINGS > TAX
TAXIPLANE n aircraft that is available for hire
TAXIS n movement of a cell or organism in response to an external stimulus
TAXISES > TAXIS
TAXITE n type of volcanic rock
TAXITES > TAXITE
TAXITIC > TAXITE

TAXIWAY n marked path along which aircraft taxi to or from a runway, parking area, etc
TAXIWAYS > TAXIWAY
TAXLESS > TAX
TAXMAN n collector of taxes
TAXMEN > TAXMAN
TAXOL n trademarked anti-cancer drug
TAXOLS > TAXOL
TAXON n any taxonomic group or rank
TAXONOMER > TAXONOMY
TAXONOMIC > TAXONOMY
TAXONOMY n classification of plants and animals into groups
TAXONS > TAXON
TAXOR > TAX
TAXORS > TAX
TAXPAID adj having had the applicable tax paid already
TAXPAYER n person or organization that pays taxes
TAXPAYERS > TAXPAYER
TAXPAYING > TAXPAYER
TAXUS n genus of conifers
TAXWISE adv regarding tax
TAXYING > TAXI
TAY Irish dialect word for **> TEA**
TAYASSUID n peccary
TAYBERRY n hybrid shrub produced by crossing a blackberry, raspberry, and loganberry
TAYRA n large arboreal mammal of Central and South America
TAYRAS > TAYRA
TAYS > TAY
TAZZA n cup with a shallow bowl and a circular foot
TAZZAS > TAZZA
TAZZE > TAZZA
TCHICK vb make a clicking noise with the tongue
TCHICKED > TCHICK
TCHICKING > TCHICK
TCHICKS > TCHICK
TCHOTCHKE n trinket
TE n (in tonic sol-fa) seventh degree of any major scale
TEA n drink made from infusing the dried leaves of an Asian bush in boiling water ▷ vb take tea
TEABAG n porous bag of tea leaves for infusion
TEABAGS > TEABAG
TEABERRY n berry of the wintergreen
TEABOARD n tea tray
TEABOARDS > TEABOARD

t

TEABOWL n small bowl used (instead of a teacup) for serving tea

TEABOWLS > TEABOWL

TEABOX n box for storing tea

TEABOXES > TEABOX

TEABREAD n loaf-shaped cake with dried fruit which has been steeped in tea before baking

TEABREADS > TEABREAD

TEACAKE n flat bun, usually eaten toasted and buttered

TEACAKES > TEACAKE

TEACART n trolley from which tea is served

TEACARTS > TEACART

TEACH vb tell or show (someone) how to do something

TEACHABLE > TEACH

TEACHABLY > TEACH

TEACHER n person who teaches, esp in a school

TEACHERLY adj like a teacher

TEACHERS > TEACHER

TEACHES > TEACH

TEACHIE old form of > TETCHY

TEACHING > TEACH

TEACHINGS > TEACH

TEACHLESS adj unable to be taught

TEACUP n cup out of which tea may be drunk

TEACUPFUL n amount a teacup will hold, about four fluid ounces

TEACUPS > TEACUP

TEAD old word for > TORCH

TEADE same as > TEAD

TEADES > TEADE

TEADS > TEAD

TEAED > TEA

TEAGLE vb raise or hoist using a tackle

TEAGLED > TEAGLE

TEAGLES > TEAGLE

TEAGLING > TEAGLE

TEAHOUSE n restaurant, esp in Japan or China, where tea and light refreshments are served

TEAHOUSES > TEAHOUSE

TEAING > TEA

TEAK n very hard wood of a tropical tree

TEAKETTLE n kettle for boiling water to make tea

TEAKS > TEAK

TEAKWOOD another word for > TEAK

TEAKWOODS > TEAKWOOD

TEAL n kind of small duck

TEALIGHT n small candle

TEALIGHTS > TEALIGHT

TEALIKE adj resembling tea

TEALS > TEAL

TEAM n group of people forming one side in a game

▷ vb make or cause to make a team

TEAMAKER n person or thing that makes tea

TEAMAKERS > TEAMAKER

TEAMED > TEAM

TEAMER > TEAM

TEAMERS > TEAM

TEAMING > TEAM

TEAMINGS > TEAM

TEAMMATE n fellow member of a team

TEAMMATES > TEAMMATE

TEAMS > TEAM

TEAMSTER n (in N America) truck driver

TEAMSTERS > TEAMSTER

TEAMWISE adv in respect of a team; in the manner of a team

TEAMWORK n cooperative work by a team

TEAMWORKS > TEAMWORK

TEAPOT n container for making and serving tea

TEAPOTS > TEAPOT

TEAPOY n small table or stand with a tripod base

TEAPOYS > TEAPOY

TEAR n drop of fluid appearing in and falling from the eye ▷ vb rip a hole in

TEARABLE > TEAR

TEARAWAY n wild or unruly person

TEARAWAYS > TEARAWAY

TEARDOWN n demolition; disassembly

TEARDOWNS > TEARDOWN

TEARDROP same as > TEAR

TEARDROPS > TEARDROP

TEARED > TEAR

TEARER > TEAR

TEARERS > TEAR

TEARFUL adj weeping or about to weep

TEARFULLY > TEARFUL

TEARGAS n gas or vapour that makes the eyes smart and water ▷ vb deploy teargas against

TEARGASES > TEARGAS

TEARIER > TEARY

TEARIEST > TEARY

TEARILY > TEARY

TEARINESS > TEARY

TEARING > TEAR

TEARLESS > TEAR

TEARLIKE adj like a tear

TEAROOM same as > TEASHOP

TEAROOMS > TEAROOM

TEARS > TEAR

TEARSHEET n page in a newspaper or periodical that is cut or perforated so that it can be easily torn out

TEARSTAIN n stain or streak left by tears

TEARSTRIP n part of packaging torn to open it

TEARY adj characterized by, covered with, or secreting tears

TEAS > TEA

TEASABLE > TEASE

TEASE vb make fun of (someone) in a provoking or playful way ▷ n person who teases

TEASED > TEASE

TEASEL n plant with prickly leaves and flowers ▷ vb tease (a fabric)

TEASELED > TEASEL

TEASELER > TEASEL

TEASELERS > TEASEL

TEASELING > TEASEL

TEASELLED > TEASEL

TEASELLER > TEASEL

TEASELS > TEASEL

TEASER n annoying or difficult problem

TEASERS > TEASER

TEASES > TEASE

TEASHOP n restaurant where tea and light refreshments are served

TEASHOPS > TEASHOP

TEASING > TEASE

TEASINGLY > TEASE

TEASINGS > TEASE

TEASPOON n small spoon for stirring tea

TEASPOONS > TEASPOON

TEAT n nipple of a breast or udder

TEATASTER n person assessing teas by tasting them

TEATED > TEAT

TEATIME n late afternoon

TEATIMES > TEATIME

TEATS > TEAT

TEAWARE n implements for brewing and serving tea

TEAWARES > TEAWARE

TEAZE old variant of > TEASE

TEAZED > TEAZE

TEAZEL same as > TEASEL

TEAZELED > TEAZEL

TEAZELING > TEAZEL

TEAZELLED > TEAZEL

TEAZELS > TEAZEL

TEAZES > TEAZE

TEAZING > TEAZE

TEAZLE same as > TEASEL

TEAZLED > TEAZLE

TEAZLES > TEAZLE

TEAZLING > TEAZLE

TEBBAD n sandstorm

TEBBADS > TEBBAD

TEBIBYTE n 2^{40} bytes

TEBIBYTES > TEBIBYTE

TEC short for > DETECTIVE

TECH n technical college

TECHED adj slightly mad

TECHIE n person who is skilled in the use of technology ▷ adj relating to or skilled in the use of technology

TECHIER > TECHY

TECHIES > TECHIE

TECHIEST > TECHY

TECHILY > TECHY

TECHINESS > TECHY

TECHNIC another word for > TECHNIQUE

TECHNICAL adj of or specializing in industrial, practical, or mechanical arts and applied sciences ▷ n small armed military truck

TECHNICS n study or theory of industry and industrial arts

TECHNIKON n technical college

TECHNIQUE n method or skill used for a particular task

TECHNO n type of electronic dance music with a very fast beat

TECHNOID n technician

TECHNOIDS > TECHNOID

TECHNOPOP n pop music sharing certain features with techno

TECHNOS > TECHNO

TECHS > TECH

TECHY same as > TECHIE

TECKEL n dachshund

TECKELS > TECKEL

TECS > TEC

TECTA > TECTUM

TECTAL > TECTUM

TECTIFORM adj in the form of a roof

TECTITE same as > TEKTITE

TECTITES > TECTITE

TECTONIC adj denoting or relating to construction or building

TECTONICS n study of the earth's crust and the forces affecting it

TECTONISM > TECTONIC

TECTORIAL adj as in tectorial membrane membrane in the inner ear that covers the organ of Corti

TECTRICES > TECTRIX

TECTRIX n small feather on a bird's wing or tail

TECTUM n any roof-like structure in the body

TECTUMS > TECTUM

TED vb shake out (hay), so as to dry it

TEDDED > TED

TEDDER n machine equipped with a series of small rotating forks for tedding hay

TEDDERED > TEDDER

TEDDERING > TEDDER

TEDDERS > TEDDER

TEDDIE *same as* > TEDDY
TEDDIES > TEDDY
TEDDING > TED
TEDDY *n* teddy bear
TEDIER > TEDY
TEDIEST > TEDY
TEDIOSITY > TEDIOUS
TEDIOUS *adj* causing fatigue or boredom
TEDIOUSLY > TEDIOUS
TEDISOME *old Scottish variant of* > TEDIOUS
TEDIUM *n* monotony
TEDIUMS > TEDIUM
TEDS > TED
TEDY *same as* > TEDIOUS
TEE *n* small peg from which a golf ball can be played at the start of each hole ▷ *vb* position (the ball) ready for striking, on or as if on a tee
TEED > TEE
TEEING > TEE
TEEK *adj* in Indian English, well
TEEL *same as* > SESAME
TEELS > TEEL
TEEM *vb* be full of
TEEMED > TEEM
TEEMER > TEEM
TEEMERS > TEEM
TEEMFUL > TEEM
TEEMING > TEEM
TEEMINGLY > TEEM
TEEMLESS > TEEM
TEEMS > TEEM
TEEN *n* teenager ▷ *vb* set alight
TEENAGE *adj* (of a person) aged between 13 and 19 ▷ *n* this period of time
TEENAGED *adj* (of a person) aged between 13 and 19
TEENAGER *n* person aged between 13 and 19
TEENAGERS > TEENAGER
TEENAGES > TEENAGE
TEEND *same as* > TIND
TEENDED > TEEND
TEENDING > TEEND
TEENDOM *n* state of being a teenager
TEENDOMS > TEENDOM
TEENDS > TEEND
TEENE *n* affliction or woe
TEENED > TEEN
TEENER > TEEN
TEENERS > TEEN
TEENES > TEENE
TEENFUL *adj* troublesome or harmful
TEENIER > TEENY
TEENIEST > TEENY
TEENING > TEEN
TEENS > TEEN
TEENSIER > TEENSY
TEENSIEST > TEENSY
TEENSY *same as* > TEENY
TEENTIER > TEENTY
TEENTIEST > TEENTY
TEENTSIER > TEENTSY
TEENTSY *same as* > TEENY
TEENTY *same as* > TEENY

TEENY *adj* extremely small
TEENYBOP *adj* of or relating to a teenager who avidly follows fashions in pop music and clothes
TEEPEE *same as* > TEPEE
TEEPEES > TEEPEE
TEER *vb* smear; daub
TEERED > TEER
TEERING > TEER
TEERS > TEER
TEES > TEE
TEETER *vb* wobble or move unsteadily
TEETERED > TEETER
TEETERING > TEETER
TEETERS > TEETER
TEETH > TOOTH
TEETHE *vb* (of a baby) grow his or her first teeth
TEETHED > TEETHE
TEETHER *n* object for an infant to bite on during teething
TEETHERS > TEETHER
TEETHES > TEETHE
TEETHING > TEETHE
TEETHINGS > TEETHING
TEETHLESS > TEETH
TEETOTAL *adj* drinking no alcohol ▷ *vb* advocate total abstinence from alcohol
TEETOTALS > TEETOTAL
TEETOTUM *n* spinning top bearing letters of the alphabet on its four sides
TEETOTUMS > TEETOTUM
TEEVEE *n* television
TEEVEES > TEEVEE
TEF *n* annual grass, of NE Africa, grown for its grain
TEFF *same as* > TEF
TEFFS > TEFF
TEFILLAH *n* either of the pair of blackened square cases worn by Jewish men during weekday morning prayers
TEFILLIN > TEFILLAH
TEFLON *n* substance used in nonstick cooking vessels
TEFLONS > TEFLON
TEFS > TEF
TEG *n* two-year-old sheep
TEGG *same as* > TEG
TEGGS > TEGG
TEGMEN *n* either of the leathery forewings of the cockroach and related insects
TEGMENTA > TEGMENTUM
TEGMENTAL > TEGMENTUM
TEGMENTUM *n* hard protective leaf surrounding a plant bud
TEGMINA > TEGMEN
TEGMINAL > TEGMEN
TEGS > TEG
TEGU *n* large South American lizard

TEGUA *n* type of moccasin
TEGUAS > TEGUA
TEGUEXIN *same as* > TEGU
TEGUEXINS > TEGUEXIN
TEGULA *n* one of a pair of coverings of the forewings of certain insects
TEGULAE > TEGULA
TEGULAR *adj* of, relating to, or resembling a tile or tiles
TEGULARLY > TEGULAR
TEGULATED *adj* overlapping in the manner of roof tiles
TEGUMEN *same as* > TEGMEN
TEGUMENT *n* protective layer around an ovule
TEGUMENTS > TEGUMENT
TEGUMINA > TEGUMEN
TEGUS > TEGU
TEHR *same as* > TAHR
TEHRS > TEHR
TEHSIL *n* administrative region in some S Asian countries
TEHSILDAR *n* person who administrates a tehsil
TEHSILS > TEHSIL
TEIGLACH *pl n* morsels of dough boiled in honey, eaten as a dessert
TEIID *n* member of the Teiidae family of lizards
TEIIDS > TEIID
TEIL *n* lime tree
TEILS > TEIL
TEIN *n* monetary unit of Kazakhstan
TEIND *Scot and northern English word for* > TITHE
TEINDED > TEIND
TEINDING > TEIND
TEINDS > TEIND
TEINS > TEIN
TEKKIE *variant of* > TECHIE
TEKKIES > TEKKIE
TEKNONYMY *n* practice of naming a child after his or her parent
TEKTITE *n* small dark glassy object found in several areas around the world
TEKTITES > TEKTITE
TEKTITIC > TEKTITE
TEL *same as* > TELL
TELA *n* any delicate tissue or weblike structure
TELAE > TELA
TELAMON *n* column in the form of a male figure
TELAMONES > TELAMON
TELAMONS > TELAMON
TELARY *adj* capable of spinning a web
TELCO *n* telecommunications company
TELCOS > TELCO
TELD *same as* > TAULD
TELE *same as* > TELLY

TELECAST *vb* broadcast by television ▷ *n* television broadcast
TELECASTS > TELECAST
TELECHIR *n* robot arm controlled by a human operator
TELECHIRS > TELECHIR
TELECINE *n* apparatus for producing a television signal from cinematograph film
TELECINES > TELECINE
TELECOM *n* telecommunications
TELECOMM *n* telecommunication
TELECOMMS > TELECOMM
TELECOMS *same as* > TELECOM
TELECON *n* (short for) teleconference
TELECONS > TELECON
TELECOPY *n* message or document sent by fax
TELEDU *n* badger of SE Asia and Indonesia
TELEDUS > TELEDU
TELEFAX *another word for* > FAX
TELEFAXED > TELEFAX
TELEFAXES > TELEFAX
TELEFILM *n* film made for TV
TELEFILMS > TELEFILM
TELEGA *n* rough four-wheeled cart used in Russia
TELEGAS > TELEGA
TELEGENIC *adj* having or showing a pleasant television image
TELEGONIC > TELEGONY
TELEGONY *n* supposed influence of a previous sire on offspring borne by a female to other sires
TELEGRAM *n* formerly, a message sent by telegraph ▷ *vb* send a telegram
TELEGRAMS > TELEGRAM
TELEGRAPH *n* formerly, a system for sending messages over a distance along a cable ▷ *vb* communicate by telegraph
TELEMAN *n* noncommissioned officer in the US navy
TELEMARK *n* turn in which one ski is placed far forward of the other and turned gradually inwards ▷ *vb* perform a telemark turn
TELEMARKS > TELEMARK
TELEMATIC *adj* of, or relating to, the branch of science concerned with the use of technological

devices to transmit information over long distances

TELEMEN > TELEMAN

TELEMETER n any device for recording or measuring a distant event and transmitting the data to a receiver or observer ▷ vb obtain and transmit (data) from a distant source, esp from a spacecraft

TELEMETRY n use of electronic devices to record or measure a distant event and transmit the data to a receiver

TELEOLOGY n belief that all things have a predetermined purpose

TELEONOMY n condition of having a fundamental purpose

TELEOSAUR n type of crocodile from the Jurassic period

TELEOST n bony fish with rayed fins and a swim bladder ▷ adj of, relating to, or belonging to this type of fish

TELEOSTS > TELEOST

TELEPATH n person who is telepathic ▷ vb practise telepathy

TELEPATHS > TELEPATH

TELEPATHY n direct communication between minds

TELEPHEME n any message sent by telephone

TELEPHONE n device for transmitting sound over a distance along wires ▷ vb call or talk to (a person) by telephone ▷ adj of or using a telephone

TELEPHONY n system of telecommunications for the transmission of speech or other sounds

TELEPHOTO n short for telephoto lens: a compound camera lens that produces a magnified image of distant objects

TELEPIC n feature-length film made for television

TELEPICS > TELEPIC

TELEPLAY n play written for television

TELEPLAYS > TELEPLAY

TELEPOINT n system providing a place where a cordless telephone can be connected to a telephone network

TELEPORT vb (in science fiction) to transport (a person or object) across a distance instantaneously

TELEPORTS > TELEPORT

TELEPRINT vb print (a message) with a teleprinter

TELERAN n electronic navigational aid

TELERANS > TELERAN

TELERGIC > TELERGY

TELERGIES > TELERGY

TELERGY n name for the form of energy supposedly transferred during telepathy

TELEROBOT n remote-controlled robot

TELES > TELE

TELESALE > TELESALES

TELESALES n selling of a product or service by telephone

TELESCOPE n optical instrument for magnifying distant objects ▷ vb shorten

TELESCOPY n branch of astronomy concerned with the use and design of telescopes

TELESEME n old-fashioned electric signalling system

TELESEMES > TELESEME

TELESES > TELESIS

TELESHOP vb buy goods by telephone or internet

TELESHOPS > TELESHOP

TELESIS n purposeful use of natural and social processes to obtain specific social goals

TELESM n talisman

TELESMS > TELESM

TELESTIC adj relating to a hierophant

TELESTICH n short poem in which the last letters of each successive line form a word

TELESTICS n ancient pseudoscientific art of animating statues, idols, etc

TELETEX n international means of communicating text between a variety of terminals

TELETEXES > TELETEX

TELETEXT n system which shows information and news on television screens

TELETEXTS > TELETEXT

TELETHON n lengthy television programme to raise charity funds, etc

TELETHONS > TELETHON

TELETRON n system for showing enlarged televisual images, eg in sports stadiums

TELETRONS > TELETRON

TELETYPE vb send typed message by telegraph

TELETYPED > TELETYPE

TELETYPES > TELETYPE

TELEVIEW vb watch television

TELEVIEWS > TELEVIEW

TELEVISE vb broadcast on television

TELEVISED > TELEVISE

TELEVISER > TELEVISE

TELEVISES > TELEVISE

TELEVISOR n apparatus through which one transmits or receives televisual images

TELEWORK vb work from home, communicating by computer, telephone etc

TELEWORKS > TELEWORK

TELEX n (formerly) international communication service using teleprinters ▷ vb (formerly) transmit by telex

TELEXED > TELEX

TELEXES > TELEX

TELEXING > TELEX

TELFER n overhead transport system

TELFERAGE n overhead transport system in which an electrically driven truck runs along a single rail or cable, the load being suspended in a separate car beneath

TELFERED > TELFER

TELFERIC > TELFER

TELFERING > TELFER

TELFERS > TELFER

TELFORD n road built using a method favoured by Thomas Telford

TELFORDS > TELFORD

TELIA > TELIUM

TELIAL > TELIUM

TELIC adj directed or moving towards some goal

TELICALLY > TELIC

TELICITY n quality of being telic

TELIUM n spore-producing body of some rust fungi in which the teliospores are formed

TELL vb make known in words ▷ n large mound resulting from the accumulation of rubbish

TELLABLE > TELL

TELLAR same as > TILLER

TELLARED > TELLAR

TELLARING > TELLAR

TELLARS > TELLAR

TELLEN same as > TELLIN

TELLENS > TELLEN

TELLER n narrator ▷ vb (of a plant) to produce tillers

TELLERED > TELLER

TELLERING > TELLER

TELLERS > TELLER

TELLIES > TELLY

TELLIN n slim marine bivalve molluscs that live in intertidal sand

TELLING > TELL

TELLINGLY > TELL

TELLINGS > TELL

TELLINOID > TELLIN

TELLINS > TELLIN

TELLS > TELL

TELLTALE n person who reveals secrets ▷ adj revealing

TELLTALES > TELLTALE

TELLURAL adj of or relating to the earth

TELLURATE n any salt or ester of telluric acid

TELLURIAN same as > TELLURION

TELLURIC adj of, relating to, or originating on or in the earth or soil

TELLURIDE n any compound of tellurium

TELLURION n instrument that shows how day and night and the seasons result from the tilt of the earth, its rotation on its axis, and its revolution around the sun

TELLURISE same as > TELLURIZE

TELLURITE n any salt or ester of tellurous acid

TELLURIUM n brittle silvery-white nonmetallic element

TELLURIZE vb mix or combine with tellurium

TELLUROUS adj of or containing tellurium, esp in a low valence state

TELLUS n earth

TELLUSES > TELLUS

TELLY n television

TELLYS > TELLY

TELNET n system allowing remote access to other computers on the same network ▷ vb use a telnet system

TELNETED > TELNET

TELNETING > TELNET

TELNETS > TELNET

TELNETTED > TELNET

TELOGEN n phase of hair growth

TELOGENS > TELOGEN

TELOI > TELOS

TELOME n fundamental unit of a plant's structure

TELOMERE n either of the ends of a chromosome

TELOMERES > TELOMERE

TELOMES > TELOME

TELOMIC > TELOME

TELOPHASE n final stage of mitosis, a type of cell division

TELOS n objective; ultimate purpose

TELOTAXES > TELOTAXIS

TELOTAXIS n movement of an organism

in response to one particular stimulus, overriding any response to other stimuli present

TELPHER *same as* > TELFERAGE
TELPHERED > TELPHER
TELPHERIC > TELPHER
TELPHERS > TELPHER
TELS > TEL
TELSON *n* segment of the body of crustaceans and arachnids
TELSONIC > TELSON
TELSONS > TELSON
TELT *same as* > TAULD
TEMAZEPAM *n* sedative in the form of a gel-like capsule
TEMBLOR *n* earthquake or earth tremor
TEMBLORES > TEMBLOR
TEMBLORS > TEMBLOR
TEME *old variant of* > TEAM
TEMED > TEME
TEMENE > TEMENOS
TEMENOS *n* sacred area, esp one surrounding a temple
TEMERITY *n* boldness or audacity
TEMEROUS > TEMERITY
TEMES > TEME
TEMP *vb* work for an employer on a temporary basis
TEMPED > TEMP
TEMPEH *n* fermented soya beans
TEMPEHS > TEMPEH
TEMPER *n* outburst of anger ▷ *vb* make less extreme
TEMPERA *n* painting medium for powdered pigments
TEMPERAS > TEMPERA
TEMPERATE *adj* (of climate) not extreme ▷ *vb* temper
TEMPERED *adj* having the frequency differences between notes adjusted in accordance with the system of equal temperament
TEMPERER > TEMPER
TEMPERERS > TEMPER
TEMPERING > TEMPER
TEMPERS > TEMPER
TEMPEST *n* violent storm ▷ *vb* agitate or disturb violently
TEMPESTED > TEMPEST
TEMPESTS > TEMPEST
TEMPI > TEMPO
TEMPING *n* act of working temporarily for an employer
TEMPINGS > TEMPING
TEMPLAR *n* lawyer who has chambers in the Inner or Middle Temple in London
TEMPLARS > TEMPLAR
TEMPLATE *n* pattern used to cut out shapes accurately

TEMPLATES > TEMPLATE
TEMPLE *n* building for worship
TEMPLED > TEMPLE
TEMPLES > TEMPLE
TEMPLET *same as* > TEMPLATE
TEMPLETS > TEMPLET
TEMPO *n* rate or pace
TEMPORAL *adj* of time ▷ *n* any body part relating to or near the temple or temples
TEMPORALS > TEMPORAL
TEMPORARY *adj* lasting only for a short time ▷ *n* person, esp a secretary or other office worker, employed on a temporary basis
TEMPORE *adv* in the time of
TEMPORISE *same as* > TEMPORIZE
TEMPORIZE *vb* gain time by negotiation or evasiveness
TEMPOS > TEMPO
TEMPS > TEMP
TEMPT *vb* entice (a person) to do something wrong
TEMPTABLE > TEMPT
TEMPTED > TEMPT
TEMPTER > TEMPT
TEMPTERS > TEMPT
TEMPTING *adj* attractive or inviting
TEMPTINGS > TEMPTING
TEMPTRESS *n* woman who sets out to allure someone
TEMPTS > TEMPT
TEMPURA *n* Japanese dish of seafood or vegetables dipped in batter and deep-fried
TEMPURAS > TEMPURA
TEMS *same as* > TEMSE
TEMSE *vb* sieve
TEMSED > TEMSE
TEMSES > TEMSE
TEMSING > TEMSE
TEMULENCE *n* drunkenness
TEMULENCY *same as* > TEMULENCE
TEMULENT > TEMULENCE
TEN *n* one more than nine
TENABLE *adj* able to be upheld or maintained
TENABLY > TENABLE
TENACE *n* holding of two nonconsecutive high cards of a suit, such as the ace and queen
TENACES > TENACE
TENACIOUS *adj* holding fast
TENACITY > TENACIOUS
TENACULA > TENACULUM

TENACULUM *n* surgical or dissecting instrument for grasping and holding parts, consisting of a slender hook mounted in a handle
TENAIL *same as* > TENAILLE
TENAILLE *n* low outwork in the main ditch between two bastions
TENAILLES > TENAILLE
TENAILLON *n* outwork shoring up a ravelin
TENAILS > TENAIL
TENANCIES > TENANCY
TENANCY *n* temporary possession of property owned by somebody else
TENANT *n* person who rents land or a building ▷ *vb* hold (land or property) as a tenant
TENANTED > TENANT
TENANTING > TENANT
TENANTRY *n* tenants collectively
TENANTS > TENANT
TENCH *n* freshwater game fish of the carp family
TENCHES > TENCH
TEND *vb* be inclined
TENDANCE *n* care and attention
TENDANCES > TENDANCE
TENDED > TEND
TENDENCE *same as* > TENDENCY
TENDENCES > TENDENCE
TENDENCY *n* inclination to act in a certain way
TENDENZ *same as* > TENDENCY
TENDENZEN > TENDENZ
TENDER *adj* not tough ▷ *vb* offer ▷ *n* such an offer
TENDERED > TENDER
TENDERER > TENDER
TENDERERS > TENDER
TENDEREST > TENDER
TENDERING > TENDER
TENDERISE *same as* > TENDERIZE
TENDERIZE *vb* soften (meat) by pounding or treatment with a special substance
TENDERLY > TENDER
TENDERS > TENDER
TENDING > TEND
TENDINOUS *adj* of, relating to, possessing, or resembling tendons
TENDON *n* strong tissue attaching a muscle to a bone
TENDONS > TENDON
TENDRE *n* care
TENDRES > TENDRE
TENDRESSE *n* feeling of love; tenderness
TENDRIL *n* slender stem by which a climbing plant clings
TENDRILED > TENDRIL

TENDRILLY *adj* of or similar to a tendril
TENDRILS > TENDRIL
TENDRON *n* shoot
TENDRONS > TENDRON
TENDS > TEND
TENDU *n* position in ballet
TENDUS > TENDU
TENE *same as* > TEEN
TENEBRAE *n* darkness
TENEBRIO *n* type of small mealworm
TENEBRIOS > TENEBRIO
TENEBRISM *n* school, style, or method of painting, adopted chiefly by 17th-century Spanish and Neapolitan painters, esp Caravaggio, characterized by large areas of dark colours, usually relieved with a shaft of light
TENEBRIST > TENEBRISM
TENEBRITY *n* darkness; gloominess
TENEBROSE *same as* > TENEBROUS
TENEBROUS *adj* gloomy, shadowy, or dark
TENEMENT *n* (esp in Scotland or the US) building divided into several flats
TENEMENTS > TENEMENT
TENENDA > TENENDUM
TENENDUM *n* part of a deed that specifies the terms of tenure
TENENDUMS > TENENDUM
TENES > TENE
TENESI *n* monetary unit of Turkmenistan
TENESMIC > TENESMUS
TENESMUS *n* bowel disorder
TENET *n* doctrine or belief
TENETS > TENET
TENFOLD *n* one tenth
TENFOLDS > TENFOLD
TENGE *n* standard monetary unit of Kazakhstan
TENGES > TENGE
TENIA *same as* > TAENIA
TENIACIDE *n* substance, esp a drug, that kills tapeworms
TENIAE > TENIA
TENIAFUGE *same as* > TENIACIDE
TENIAS > TENIA
TENIASES > TENIASIS
TENIASIS *same as* > TAENIASIS
TENIOID > TENIA
TENNE *n* tawny colour
TENNER *n* ten-pound note
TENNERS > TENNER
TENNES > TENNE
TENNESI *same as* > TENESI
TENNIES > TENNY

t

TENNIS n game in which players use rackets to hit a ball back and forth over a net

TENNISES > TENNIS

TENNIST n tennis player

TENNISTS > TENNIST

TENNO n formal title of the Japanese emperor

TENNOS > TENNO

TENNY same as > TENNE

TENON n projecting end on a piece of wood fitting into a slot in another ▷ vb form a tenon on (a piece of wood)

TENONED > TENON

TENONER > TENON

TENONERS > TENON

TENONING > TENON

TENONS > TENON

TENOR n (singer with) the second highest male voice ▷ adj (of a voice or instrument) between alto and baritone

TENORINI > TENORINO

TENORINO n high tenor

TENORIST n musician playing any tenor instrument

TENORISTS > TENORIST

TENORITE n black mineral found in copper deposits

TENORITES > TENORITE

TENORLESS > TENOR

TENORMAN n person who plays tenor saxophone

TENORMEN > TENORMAN

TENOROON n tenor bassoon

TENOROONS > TENOROON

TENORS > TENOR

TENOTOMY n surgical division of a tendon

TENOUR old variant of > TENOR

TENOURS > TENOUR

TENPENCE n sum of money equivalent to ten pennies

TENPENCES > TENPENCE

TENPENNY adj (of a nail) three inches in length

TENPIN n one of the pins used in tenpin bowling

TENPINNER n player of tenpin bowling

TENPINS > TENPIN

TENREC n small mammal resembling hedgehogs or shrews

TENRECS > TENREC

TENS > TEN

TENSE adj emotionally strained ▷ vb make or become tense ▷ n form of a verb showing the time of action

TENSED > TENSE

TENSELESS > TENSE

TENSELY > TENSE

TENSENESS > TENSE

TENSER > TENSE

TENSES > TENSE

TENSEST > TENSE

TENSIBLE adj capable of being stretched

TENSIBLY > TENSIBLE

TENSILE adj of tension

TENSILELY > TENSILE

TENSILITY > TENSILE

TENSING > TENSE

TENSION n hostility or suspense ▷ vb tighten

TENSIONAL > TENSION

TENSIONED > TENSION

TENSIONER > TENSION

TENSIONS > TENSION

TENSITIES > TENSITY

TENSITY rare word for > TENSION

TENSIVE adj of or causing tension or strain

TENSON n type of French lyric poem

TENSONS > TENSON

TENSOR n any muscle that can cause a part to become firm or tense

TENSORIAL > TENSOR

TENSORS > TENSOR

TENT n portable canvas shelter ▷ vb camp in a tent

TENTACLE n flexible organ of many invertebrates, used for grasping, feeding, etc

TENTACLED > TENTACLE

TENTACLES > TENTACLE

TENTACULA > TENTACLE

TENTAGE n tents collectively

TENTAGES > TENTAGE

TENTATION n method of achieving the correct adjustment of a mechanical device by a series of trials

TENTATIVE adj provisional or experimental ▷ n investigative attempt

TENTED > TENT

TENTER > TENT

TENTERED > TENT

TENTERING > TENT

TENTERS > TENT

TENTFUL n number of people or objects that can fit in a tent

TENTFULS > TENTFUL

TENTH n number ten in a series ▷ adj coming after the ninth in numbering or counting order, position, time, etc

TENTHLY adv in the tenth place or position

TENTHS > TENTH

TENTIE adj wary

TENTIER > TENTIE

TENTIEST > TENTIE

TENTIGO n morbid preoccupation with sex

TENTIGOS > TENTIGO

TENTING > TENT

TENTINGS > TENT

TENTLESS > TENT

TENTLIKE > TENT

TENTMAKER n maker of tents

TENTORIA > TENTORIUM

TENTORIAL > TENTORIUM

TENTORIUM n tough membrane covering the upper part of the cerebellum

TENTPOLE n film whose high earnings offset the cost of less profitable ones

TENTPOLES > TENTPOLE

TENTS > TENT

TENTWISE adv in the manner of a tent

TENTY same as > TENTIE

TENUE n deportment

TENUES > TENUIS

TENUIOUS same as > TENUOUS

TENUIS n (in the grammar of classical Greek) any of the voiceless stops

TENUITIES > TENUOUS

TENUITY > TENUOUS

TENUOUS adj slight or flimsy

TENUOUSLY > TENUOUS

TENURABLE > TENURE

TENURE n (period of) the holding of an office or position ▷ vb assign a tenured position to

TENURED adj having tenure of office

TENURES > TENURE

TENURIAL > TENURE

TENURING > TENURE

TENUTI > TENUTO

TENUTO adv (of a note) to be held for or beyond its full time value ▷ n note sustained thus

TENUTOS > TENUTO

TENZON same as > TENSON

TENZONS > TENZON

TEOCALLI n any of various truncated pyramids built by the Aztecs as bases for their temples

TEOCALLIS > TEOCALLI

TEOPAN n enclosure surrounding a teocalli

TEOPANS > TEOPAN

TEOSINTE n tall Central American annual grass

TEOSINTES > TEOSINTE

TEPA n type of tree native to South America

TEPACHE n type of Mexican soft drink

TEPACHES > TEPACHE

TEPAL n subdivisions of a perianth

TEPALS > TEPAL

TEPAS > TEPA

TEPEE n cone-shaped tent, formerly used by Native Americans

TEPEES > TEPEE

TEPEFIED > TEPEFY

TEPEFIES > TEPEFY

TEPEFY vb make or become tepid

TEPEFYING > TEPEFY

TEPHIGRAM n chart depicting variations in atmospheric conditions relative to altitude

TEPHILLAH same as > TEFILLAH

TEPHILLIN > TEPHILLAH

TEPHRA n solid matter ejected during a volcanic eruption

TEPHRAS > TEPHRA

TEPHRITE n variety of basalt

TEPHRITES > TEPHRITE

TEPHRITIC > TEPHRITE

TEPHROITE n manganese silicate

TEPID adj slightly warm

TEPIDARIA pl n in Ancient Rome, the warm rooms of the baths

TEPIDER > TEPID

TEPIDEST > TEPID

TEPIDITY > TEPID

TEPIDLY > TEPID

TEPIDNESS > TEPID

TEPOY same as > TEAPOY

TEPOYS > TEPOY

TEQUILA n Mexican alcoholic drink

TEQUILAS > TEQUILA

TEQUILLA same as > TEQUILA

TEQUILLAS > TEQUILLA

TERABYTE n large unit of computer memory

TERABYTES > TERABYTE

TERAFLOP n large unit of computer processing speed

TERAFLOPS > TERAFLOP

TERAGLIN n edible marine fish of Australia which has fine scales and is blue in colour

TERAGLINS > TERAGLIN

TERAHERTZ n large unit of electrical frequency

TERAI n felt hat with a wide brim worn in subtropical regions

TERAIS > TERAI

TERAKIHI same as > TARAKIHI

TERAKIHIS > TARAKIHI

TERAMETER n 10^{12} metres

TERAOHM n unit of resistance

TERAOHMS > TERAOHM

TERAPH n household god or image venerated by ancient Semitic peoples

TERAPHIM > TERAPH

TERAPHIMS > TERAPH

TERAS n monstrosity; teratism

TERATA > TERAS

TERATISM n malformed animal or human, esp in the fetal stage

TERATISMS > TERATISM

TERATOGEN n any substance, organism, or process that causes malformations in a fetus

TERATOID adj resembling a monster

TERATOMA n tumour or group of tumours composed of tissue foreign to the site of growth

TERATOMAS > TERATOMA

TERAWATT n unit of power equal to one million megawatts

TERAWATTS > TERAWATT

TERBIA n amorphous white insoluble powder

TERBIAS > TERBIA

TERBIC > TERBIUM

TERBIUM n rare metallic element

TERBIUMS > TERBIUM

TERCE n third of the seven canonical hours of the divine office

TERCEL n male falcon or hawk, esp as used in falconry

TERCELET same as > TERCEL

TERCELETS > TERCELET

TERCELS > TERCEL

TERCES > TERCE

TERCET n group of three lines of verse that rhyme together

TERCETS > TERCET

TERCIO n regiment of Spanish or Italian infantry

TERCIOS > TERCIO

TEREBENE n mixture of hydrocarbons prepared from oil of turpentine and sulphuric acid

TEREBENES > TEREBENE

TEREBIC adj as in terebic acid white crystalline carboxylic acid produced by the action of nitric acid on turpentine

TEREBINTH n small anacardiaceous tree with winged leafstalks and clusters of small flowers, and yielding a turpentine

TEREBRA n ancient Roman device used for boring holes in defensive walls

TEREBRAE > TEREBRA

TEREBRANT n type of hymenopterous insect

TEREBRAS > TEREBRA

TEREBRATE adj (of animals, esp insects) having a boring or penetrating organ, such as a sting ▷ vb bore

TEREDINES > TEREDO

TEREDO n marine mollusc that bores into and destroys submerged timber

TEREDOS > TEREDO

TEREFA same as > TREF

TEREFAH same as > TREF

TEREK n type of sandpiper

TEREKS > TEREK

TERES n shoulder muscle

TERESES > TERES

TERETE adj (esp of plant parts) smooth and usually cylindrical and tapering

TERETES > TERES

TERF old variant of > TURF

TERFE old variant of > TURF

TERFES > TERFE

TERFS > TERF

TERGA > TERGUM

TERGAL > TERGUM

TERGITE n constituent part of a tergum

TERGITES > TERGITE

TERGUM n cuticular plate covering the dorsal surface of a body segment of an arthropod

TERIYAKI adj basted with soy sauce and rice wine and broiled over an open fire ▷ n dish prepared in this way

TERIYAKIS > TERIYAKI

TERM n word or expression ▷ vb name or designate

TERMAGANT n unpleasant and bad-tempered woman

TERMED > TERM

TERMER same as > TERMOR

TERMERS > TERMER

TERMINAL adj (of an illness) ending in death ▷ n place where people or vehicles begin or end a journey

TERMINALS > TERMINAL

TERMINATE vb bring or come to an end

TERMINER n person or thing that limits or determines

TERMINERS > TERMINER

TERMING > TERM

TERMINI > TERMINUS

TERMINISM n philosophical theory

TERMINIST > TERMINISM

TERMINUS n railway or bus station at the end of a line

TERMITARY n termite nest

TERMITE n white antlike insect that destroys timber

TERMITES > TERMITE

TERMITIC > TERMITE

TERMLESS adj without limit or boundary

TERMLIES > TERMLY

TERMLY n publication issued once a term

TERMOR n person who holds an estate for a term of years or until he or she dies

TERMORS > TERMOR

TERMS > TERM

TERMTIME n time during a term, esp a school or university term

TERMTIMES > TERMTIME

TERN n gull-like sea bird with a forked tail and pointed wings

TERNAL > TERN

TERNARIES > TERNARY

TERNARY adj consisting of three parts ▷ n group of three

TERNATE adj (esp of a leaf) consisting of three leaflets or other parts

TERNATELY > TERNATE

TERNE n alloy of lead containing tin and antimony ▷ vb coat with this alloy

TERNED > TERNE

TERNES > TERNE

TERNING > TERNE

TERNION n group of three

TERNIONS > TERNION

TERNS > TERN

TERPENE n unsaturated hydrocarbon found in the essential oils of many plants

TERPENES > TERPENE

TERPENIC > TERPENE

TERPENOID > TERPENE

TERPINE n type of expectorant

TERPINEOL n terpene alcohol with an odour of lilac, present in several essential oils

TERPINES > TERPINE

TERPINOL same as > TERPINEOL

TERPINOLS > TERPINOL

TERRA n (in legal contexts) earth or land

TERRACE n row of houses built as one block ▷ vb form into or provide with a terrace

TERRACED > TERRACE

TERRACES > TERRACE

TERRACING n series of terraces, esp one dividing a slope into a steplike system of flat narrow fields

TERRAE > TERRA

TERRAFORM vb engage in planetary engineering to enhance the capacity of an extraterrestrial planetary environment to sustain life

TERRAIN same as > TERRANE

TERRAINS > TERRAIN

TERRAMARA n neolithic Italian pile-dwelling

TERRAMARE > TERRAMARA

TERRANE n series of rock formations

TERRANES > TERRANE

TERRAPIN n small turtle-like reptile

TERRAPINS > TERRAPIN

TERRARIA > TERRARIUM

TERRARIUM n enclosed container for small plants or animals

TERRAS same as > TRASS

TERRASES > TERRAS

TERRASSE n paved area alongside a café

TERRASSES > TERRASSE

TERRAZZO n floor of marble chips set in mortar and polished

TERRAZZOS > TERRAZZO

TERREEN old variant of > TUREEN

TERREENS > TERREEN

TERRELLA n magnetic globe designed to simulate and demonstrate the earth's magnetic fields

TERRELLAS > TERRELLA

TERRENE adj of or relating to the earth ▷ n land

TERRENELY > TERRENE

TERRENES > TERRENE

TERRET n ring on a harness saddle through which the reins are passed

TERRETS > TERRET

TERRIBLE adj very serious ▷ n something terrible

TERRIBLES > TERRIBLE

TERRIBLY adv in a terrible manner

TERRICOLE n plant or animal living on land

TERRIER n any of various breeds of small active dog

TERRIERS > TERRIER

TERRIES > TERRY

TERRIFIC adj great or intense

TERRIFIED > TERRIFY

TERRIFIER > TERRIFY

TERRIFIES > TERRIFY

TERRIFY vb fill with fear

TERRINE n earthenware dish with a lid

TERRINES > TERRINE

TERRIT same as > TERRET

t

TERRITORY n district

TERRITS > TERRIT

TERROIR n combination of factors that gives a wine its distinctive character

TERROIRS > TERROIR

TERROR n great fear

TERRORFUL > TERROR

TERRORISE same as > TERRORIZE

TERRORISM n use of violence and intimidation to achieve political ends

TERRORIST n person who employs terror or terrorism, esp as a political weapon

TERRORIZE vb force or oppress by fear or violence

TERRORS > TERROR

TERRY n fabric with small loops covering both sides

TERSE adj neat and concise

TERSELY > TERSE

TERSENESS > TERSE

TERSER > TERSE

TERSEST > TERSE

TERSION n action of rubbing off or wiping

TERSIONS > TERSION

TERTIA same as > TERCIO

TERTIAL same as > TERTIARY

TERTIALS > TERTIAL

TERTIAN adj (of a fever or the symptoms of a disease) occurring every other day ▷ n tertian fever or symptoms

TERTIANS > TERTIAN

TERTIARY adj third in degree, order, etc ▷ n any of the tertiary feathers

TERTIAS > TERTIA

TERTIUM adj as in tertium quid unknown or indefinite thing related in some way to two known or definite things, but distinct from both

TERTIUS n third (in a group)

TERTIUSES > TERTIUS

TERTS n card game using 32 cards

TERVALENT same as > TRIVALENT

TERYLENE n tradename for a synthetic polyester fibre based on terephthalic acid

TERYLENES > TERYLENE

TERZETTA n tercet

TERZETTAS > TERZETTA

TERZETTI > TERZETTO

TERZETTO n trio, esp a vocal one

TERZETTOS > TERZETTO

TES > TE

TESLA n derived SI unit of magnetic flux density

TESLAS > TESLA

TESSELATE vb cover with small tiles

TESSELLA n little tessera

TESSELLAE > TESSELLA

TESSELLAR adj of or relating to tessellae

TESSERA n small square tile used in mosaics

TESSERACT n cube inside another cube

TESSERAE > TESSERA

TESSERAL > TESSERA

TESSITURA n general pitch level of a piece of vocal music

TESSITURE > TESSITURA

TEST vb try out to ascertain the worth, capability, or endurance of ▷ n critical examination

TESTA n hard outer layer of a seed

TESTABLE > TEST

TESTACEAN n microscopic animal with hard shell

TESTACIES > TESTATE

TESTACY > TESTATE

TESTAE > TESTA

TESTAMENT n proof or tribute

TESTAMUR n certificate proving an examination has been passed

TESTAMURS > TESTAMUR

TESTATA > TESTATUM

TESTATE adj having left a valid will ▷ n person who dies and leaves a legally valid will

TESTATES > TESTATE

TESTATION > TESTATOR

TESTATOR n maker of a will

TESTATORS > TESTATOR

TESTATRIX n woman who makes a will

TESTATUM n part of a purchase deed

TESTATUMS > TESTATUM

TESTCROSS vb subject to a testcross, a genetic test for ascertaining whether an individual is homozygous or heterozygous

TESTE n witness

TESTED > TEST

TESTEE n person subjected to a test

TESTEES > TESTEE

TESTER n person or thing that tests or is used for testing

TESTERN vb give (someone) a teston

TESTERNED > TESTERN

TESTERNS > TESTERN

TESTERS > TESTER

TESTES > TESTIS

TESTICLE n either of the two male reproductive glands

TESTICLES > TESTICLE

TESTIER > TESTY

TESTIEST > TESTY

TESTIFIED > TESTIFY

TESTIFIER > TESTIFY

TESTIFIES > TESTIFY

TESTIFY vb give evidence under oath

TESTILY > TESTY

TESTIMONY n declaration of truth or fact ▷ vb testify

TESTINESS > TESTY

TESTING > TEST

TESTINGS > TEST

TESTIS same as > TESTICLE

TESTON n French silver coin of the 16th century

TESTONS > TESTON

TESTOON same as > TESTON

TESTOONS > TESTOON

TESTRIL same as > TESTRILL

TESTRILL n sixpence

TESTRILLS > TESTRILL

TESTRILS > TESTRIL

TESTS > TEST

TESTUDO n protective cover used by the ancient Roman army

TESTUDOS > TESTUDO

TESTY adj irritable or touchy

TET same as > TETH

TETANAL > TETANUS

TETANIC adj of, relating to, or producing tetanus ▷ n tetanic drug or agent

TETANICAL > TETANUS

TETANICS > TETANIC

TETANIES > TETANY

TETANISE same as > TETANIZE

TETANISED > TETANISE

TETANISES > TETANISE

TETANIZE vb induce tetanus in (a muscle)

TETANIZED > TETANIZE

TETANIZES > TETANIZE

TETANOID > TETANUS

TETANUS n acute infectious disease producing muscular spasms and convulsions

TETANUSES > TETANUS

TETANY n abnormal increase in the excitability of nerves and muscles

TETCHED same as > TECHED

TETCHIER > TETCHY

TETCHIEST > TETCHY

TETCHILY > TETCHY

TETCHY adj cross and irritable

TETE n elaborate hairstyle

TETES > TETE

TETH n ninth letter of the Hebrew alphabet

TETHER n rope or chain for tying an animal to a spot ▷ vb tie up with rope

TETHERED > TETHER

TETHERING > TETHER

TETHERS > TETHER

TETHS > TETH

TETOTUM same as > TEETOTUM

TETOTUMS > TETOTUM

TETRA n brightly coloured tropical freshwater fish

TETRACID adj (of a base) capable of reacting with four molecules of a monobasic acid ▷ n tetracid base

TETRACIDS > TETRACID

TETRACT n sponge spicule with four rays

TETRACTS > TETRACT

TETRAD n group or series of four

TETRADIC > TETRAD

TETRADITE n person who believes that the number four has supernatural significance

TETRADS > TETRAD

TETRAGON n figure with four angles and four sides

TETRAGONS > TETRAGON

TETRAGRAM n any word of four letters

TETRALOGY n series of four related works

TETRAMER n four-molecule polymer

TETRAMERS > TETRAMER

TETRAPLA n book containing versions of the same text in four languages

TETRAPLAS > TETRAPLA

TETRAPOD n any vertebrate that has four limbs

TETRAPODS > TETRAPOD

TETRAPODY n metrical unit consisting of four feet

TETRARCH n ruler of one fourth of a country

TETRARCHS > TETRARCH

TETRARCHY > TETRARCH

TETRAS > TETRA

TETRAXON n four-pointed spicule

TETRAXONS > TETRAXON

TETRI n currency unit of Georgia

TETRIS > TETRI

TETRODE n electronic valve having four electrodes

TETRODES > TETRODE

TETRONAL n sedative drug

TETRONALS > TETRONAL

TETROSE n type of sugar
TETROSES > TETROSE
TETROXID same as > TETROXIDE
TETROXIDE n any oxide that contains four oxygen atoms per molecule
TETROXIDS > TETROXID
TETRYL n yellow crystalline explosive solid used in detonators
TETRYLS > TETRYL
TETS > TET
TETTER n blister or pimple ▷ vb cause a tetter to erupt (on)
TETTERED > TETTER
TETTERING > TETTER
TETTEROUS > TETTER
TETTERS > TETTER
TETTIX n cicada
TETTIXES > TETTIX
TEUCH Scots variant of > TOUGH
TEUCHAT Scots variant of > TEWIT
TEUCHATS > TEUCHAT
TEUCHER > TEUCH
TEUCHEST > TEUCH
TEUCHTER n in Scotland, derogatory word used by Lowlanders for a Highlander
TEUCHTERS > TEUCHTER
TEUGH same as > TEUCH
TEUGHER > TEUGH
TEUGHEST > TEUGH
TEUGHLY > TEUGH
TEUTONISE same as > TEUTONIZE
TEUTONIZE vb make or become Germanic
TEVATRON n machine used in nuclear research
TEVATRONS > TEVATRON
TEW vb work hard
TEWART same as > TUART
TEWARTS > TEWART
TEWED > TEW
TEWEL n horse's rectum
TEWELS > TEWEL
TEWHIT same as > TEWIT
TEWHITS > TEWHIT
TEWING > TEW
TEWIT n lapwing
TEWITS > TEWIT
TEWS > TEW
TEX n unit of weight used to measure yarn density
TEXAS n structure on the upper deck of a paddle-steamer
TEXASES > TEXAS
TEXES > TEX
TEXT n main body of a book as distinct from illustrations etc ▷ vb send a text message to (someone)
TEXTBOOK n standard book on a particular subject ▷ adj perfect
TEXTBOOKS > TEXTBOOK

TEXTED > TEXT
TEXTER n person who communicates by text messaging
TEXTERS > TEXTER
TEXTILE n fabric or cloth, esp woven ▷ adj of (the making of) fabrics
TEXTILES > TEXTILE
TEXTING > TEXT
TEXTINGS > TEXTING
TEXTISM n word typically used in a text message
TEXTISMS > TEXTISM
TEXTLESS > TEXT
TEXTONYM n one of two or more words that can be created by pressing the same combination of numbers on a mobile phone
TEXTONYMS > TEXTONYM
TEXTORIAL adj of or relating to weaving or weavers
TEXTPHONE n phone designed to translate speech into text and vice versa
TEXTS > TEXT
TEXTSPEAK n jargon and abbreviations typically used by frequent senders of text messages
TEXTUAL adj of, based on, or relating to, a text or texts
TEXTUALLY > TEXTUAL
TEXTUARY adj of, relating to, or contained in a text ▷ n textual critic
TEXTURAL > TEXTURE
TEXTURE n structure, feel, or consistency ▷ vb give a distinctive texture to (something)
TEXTURED > TEXTURE
TEXTURES > TEXTURE
TEXTURING n process of giving a rough or grainy texture to
TEXTURISE same as > TEXTURIZE
TEXTURIZE vb texture
TEXTUROUS adj having texture
THACK Scots word for > THATCH
THACKED > THACK
THACKING > THACK
THACKS > THACK
THAE Scots word for > THOSE
THAGI same as > THUGGEE
THAGIS > THAGI
THAIM Scots variant of > THEM
THAIRM n catgut
THAIRMS > THAIRM
THALAMI > THALAMUS
THALAMIC > THALAMUS
THALAMUS n mass of grey matter at the base of the brain
THALASSIC adj of or relating to the sea

THALE n as in thale cress cruciferous wall plant
THALER n former German, Austrian, or Swiss silver coin
THALERS > THALER
THALI n Indian meal consisting of several small dishes
THALIAN adj of or relating to comedy
THALIS > THALI
THALLI > THALLUS
THALLIC adj of or containing thallium
THALLINE n type of chemical used in medicine
THALLINES > THALLINE
THALLIOUS > THALLIUM
THALLIUM n highly toxic metallic element
THALLIUMS > THALLIUM
THALLOID > THALLUS
THALLOUS adj of or containing thallium, esp in the monovalent state
THALLUS n undifferentiated vegetative body of algae, fungi, and lichens
THALLUSES > THALLUS
THALWEG n longitudinal outline of a riverbed from source to mouth
THALWEGS > THALWEG
THAN prep used to introduce the second element of a comparison ▷ n old variant of 'then' (that time)
THANA same as > TANA
THANADAR same as > TANADAR
THANADARS > THANADAR
THANAGE n state of being a thane
THANAGES > THANAGE
THANAH same as > TANA
THANAHS > THANAH
THANAS > THANA
THANATISM n belief that the soul ceases to exist when the body dies
THANATIST > THANATISM
THANATOID adj like death
THANATOS n Greek personification of death
THANE n Anglo-Saxon or medieval Scottish nobleman
THANEDOM > THANE
THANEDOMS > THANE
THANEHOOD > THANE
THANES > THANE
THANESHIP > THANE
THANG n thing
THANGKA n (in Tibetan Buddhism) a religious painting on a scroll
THANGKAS > THANGKA
THANGS > THANG

THANK vb express gratitude to
THANKED > THANK
THANKEE interj thank you
THANKER > THANK
THANKERS > THANK
THANKFUL adj grateful
THANKING > THANK
THANKINGS > THANK
THANKIT adj as in be thankit thank God
THANKLESS adj unrewarding or unappreciated
THANKS pl n words of gratitude ▷ interj polite expression of gratitude
THANKYOU n conventional expression of gratitude
THANKYOUS > THANKYOU
THANNA same as > TANA
THANNAH same as > TANA
THANNAHS > THANNAH
THANNAS > THANNA
THANS > THAN
THANX interj informal spelling of 'thanks'
THAR same as > TAHR
THARM n stomach
THARMS > THARM
THARS > THAR
THAT pron used to refer to something already mentioned or familiar, or further away
THATAWAY adv that way
THATCH n roofing material of reeds or straw ▷ vb roof (a house) with reeds or straw
THATCHED > THATCH
THATCHER > THATCH
THATCHERS > THATCH
THATCHES > THATCH
THATCHIER > THATCH
THATCHING > THATCH
THATCHT old variant of > THATCHED
THATCHY > THATCH
THATNESS n state or quality of being 'that'
THAUMATIN n type of natural sweetener
THAW vb make or become unfrozen ▷ n thawing
THAWED > THAW
THAWER > THAW
THAWERS > THAW
THAWIER > THAWY
THAWIEST > THAWY
THAWING > THAW
THAWINGS > THAW
THAWLESS > THAW
THAWS > THAW
THAWY adj tending to thaw
THE determiner definite article, used before a noun
THEACEOUS adj relating to a family of evergreen trees and shrubs of tropical and warm regions
THEANDRIC adj both divine and human
THEANINE n amino acid found in tea leaves

THEANINES
> THEANINE
THEARCHIC
> THEARCHY
THEARCHY n rule or government by God or gods
THEATER same as > THEATRE
THEATERS > THEATER
THEATRAL adj of or relating to the theatre
THEATRE n place where plays etc are performed
THEATRES > THEATRE
THEATRIC adj of or relating to the theatre
THEATRICS n art of staging plays
THEAVE n young ewe
THEAVES > THEAVE
THEBAINE n poisonous white crystalline alkaloid, found in opium but without opioid actions
THEBAINES > THEBAINE
THEBE n monetary unit of Botswana
THEBES > THEBE
THECA n enclosing organ, cell, or spore case
THECAE > THECA
THECAL > THECA
THECATE > THECA
THECODONT adj (of mammals and certain reptiles) having teeth that grow in sockets ▷ n extinct reptile
THEE pron refers to the person addressed ▷ vb use the word 'thee'
THEED > THEE
THEEING > THEE
THEEK Scots variant of > THATCH
THEEKED > THEEK
THEEKING > THEEK
THEEKS > THEEK
THEELIN trade name for > ESTRONE
THEELINS > THEELIN
THEELOL n estriol
THEELOLS > THEELOL
THEES > THEE
THEFT n act or an instance of stealing
THEFTLESS > THEFT
THEFTS > THEFT
THEFTUOUS adj tending to commit theft
THEGITHER Scots variant of > TOGETHER
THEGN same as > THANE
THEGNLIER > THEGNLY
THEGNLY adj like a thegn
THEGNS > THEGN
THEIC n person who drinks excessive amounts of tea
THEICS > THEIC
THEIN old variant of > THANE
THEINE another name for > CAFFEINE
THEINES > THEINE
THEINS > THEIN

THEIR determiner of, belonging to, or associated in some way with them
THEIRS pron something belonging to them
THEIRSELF pron dialect form of themselves: reflexive form of they or them
THEISM n belief in a God or gods
THEISMS > THEISM
THEIST > THEISM
THEISTIC > THEISM
THEISTS > THEISM
THELEMENT n old contraction of 'the element'
THELF n old contraction of 'the elf'
THELITIS n inflammation of the nipple
THELVES > THELF
THELYTOKY n type of reproduction resulting in female offspring only
THEM pron refers to people or things other than the speaker or those addressed
THEMA n theme
THEMATA > THEMA
THEMATIC adj of, relating to, or consisting of a theme or themes ▷ n thematic vowel
THEMATICS > THEMATIC
THEMATISE same as > THEMATIZE
THEMATIZE vb make thematic
THEME n main idea or subject being discussed ▷ vb design, decorate, arrange, etc, in accordance with a theme
THEMED > THEME
THEMELESS > THEME
THEMES > THEME
THEMING > THEME
THEMSELF pron reflexive form of one, whoever, anybody
THEN adv at that time ▷ pron that time ▷ adj existing or functioning at that time ▷ n that time
THENABOUT adv around then
THENAGE old variant of > THANAGE
THENAGES > THENAGE
THENAL adj of or relating to the thenar
THENAR n palm of the hand ▷ adj of or relating to the palm or the region at the base of the thumb
THENARS > THENAR
THENCE adv from that place or time
THENS > THEN
THEOCON n person who believes that religion should play a greater role in politics

THEOCONS > THEOCON
THEOCRACY n government by a god or priests
THEOCRASY n mingling into one of deities or divine attributes previously regarded as distinct
THEOCRAT > THEOCRACY
THEOCRATS > THEOCRACY
THEODICY n branch of theology concerned with defending the attributes of God
THEOGONIC > THEOGONY
THEOGONY n origin and descent of the gods
THEOLOG same as > THEOLOGUE
THEOLOGER n theologian
THEOLOGIC > THEOLOGY
THEOLOGS > THEOLOG
THEOLOGUE n theologian
THEOLOGY n study of religions and religious beliefs
THEOMACHY n battle among the gods or against them
THEOMANCY n divination or prophecy by an oracle
THEOMANIA n religious madness, esp when it takes the form of believing oneself to be a god
THEONOMY n state of being governed by God
THEOPATHY n religious emotion engendered by the contemplation of or meditation upon God
THEOPHAGY n sacramental eating of a god
THEOPHANY n manifestation of a deity to human beings in a form that, though visible, is not necessarily material
THEORBIST > THEORBO
THEORBO n obsolete form of the lute, having two necks
THEORBOS > THEORBO
THEOREM n proposition that can be proved by reasoning
THEOREMIC > THEOREM
THEOREMS > THEOREM
THEORETIC adj of, or based on, a theory
THEORIC n theory; conjecture
THEORICS > THEORIC
THEORIES > THEORY
THEORIQUE same as > THEORIC
THEORISE same as > THEORIZE
THEORISED > THEORISE
THEORISER > THEORISE
THEORISES > THEORISE

THEORIST n originator of a theory
THEORISTS > THEORIST
THEORIZE vb form theories, speculate
THEORIZED > THEORIZE
THEORIZER > THEORIZE
THEORIZES > THEORIZE
THEORY n set of ideas to explain something
THEOSOPH n proponent of theosophy
THEOSOPHS > THEOSOPH
THEOSOPHY n religious or philosophical system claiming to be based on intuitive insight into the divine nature
THEOTOKOI > THEOTOKOS
THEOTOKOS n mother of God
THEOW n slave in Anglo-Saxon Britain
THEOWS > THEOW
THERALITE n type of igneous rock
THERAPIES > THERAPY
THERAPISE same as > THERAPIZE
THERAPIST n person skilled in a particular type of therapy
THERAPIZE vb subject to therapy
THERAPSID n extinct reptile considered to be the ancestors of mammals
THERAPY n curing treatment
THERBLIG n basic unit of work in an industrial process
THERBLIGS > THERBLIG
THERE adv in or to that place ▷ n that place
THEREAT adv at that point or time
THEREAWAY adv in that direction
THEREBY adv by that means
THEREFOR adv for this, that, or it
THEREFORE adv consequently, that being so
THEREFROM adv from that or there
THEREIN adv in or into that place or thing
THEREINTO adv into that place, circumstance, etc
THEREMIN n musical instrument played by moving the hands through electromagnetic fields
THEREMINS > THEREMIN
THERENESS n quality of having existence
THEREOF adv of or concerning that or it

THEREON *archaic word for* > THEREUPON

THEREOUT *another word for* > THEREFROM

THERES > THERE

THERETO *adv* to that or it

THEREUNTO *adv* to that

THEREUPON *adv* immediately after that

THEREWITH *adv* with or in addition to that

THERIAC *n* ointment or potion used as an antidote to a poison

THERIACA *same as* > THERIAC

THERIACAL > THERIAC

THERIACAS > THERIACA

THERIACS > THERIAC

THERIAN *n* animal of the class Theria, a subclass of mammals

THERIANS > THERIAN

THERM *n* unit of measurement of heat

THERMAE *pl n* public baths or hot springs, esp in ancient Greece or Rome

THERMAL *adj* of heat ⊳ *n* rising current of warm air

THERMALLY > THERMAL

THERMALS > THERMAL

THERME *old variant of* > THERM

THERMEL *n* type of thermometer using thermoelectric current

THERMELS > THERMEL

THERMES > THERME

THERMETTE *n* device, used outdoors, for boiling water rapidly

THERMIC *same as* > THERMAL

THERMICAL *same as* > THERMAL

THERMIDOR *adj* as in *lobster thermidor* dish of cooked lobster

THERMION *n* electron or ion emitted by a body at high temperature

THERMIONS > THERMION

THERMIT *variant of* > THERMITE

THERMITE *adj* as in *thermite process* process for reducing metallic oxides

THERMITES > THERMITE

THERMITS > THERMIT

THERMOS *n* trademark for a stoppered vacuum flask

THERMOSES > THERMOS

THERMOSET *n* material (esp a synthetic plastic or resin) that hardens permanently after one application of heat and pressure

THERMOTIC *adj* of or because of heat

THERMS > THERM

THEROID *adj* of, relating to, or resembling a beast

THEROLOGY *n* study of mammals

THEROPOD *n* bipedal carnivorous saurischian dinosaur with strong hind legs and grasping hands

THEROPODS > THEROPOD

THESAURAL > THESAURUS

THESAURI > THESAURUS

THESAURUS *n* book containing lists of synonyms and related words

THESE *determiner* form of this used before a plural noun

THESES > THESIS

THESIS *n* written work submitted for a degree

THESP *short for* > THESPIAN

THESPIAN *adj* of or relating to drama and the theatre ⊳ *n* actor or actress

THESPIANS > THESPIAN

THESPS > THESP

THETA *n* eighth letter of the Greek alphabet

THETAS > THETA

THETCH *old variant spelling of* > THATCH

THETCHED > THETCH

THETCHES > THETCH

THETCHING > THETCH

THETE *n* member of the lowest order of freeman in ancient Athens

THETES > THETE

THETHER *old variant of* > THITHER

THETIC *adj* (in classical prosody) of, bearing, or relating to a metrical stress

THETICAL *another word for* > THETIC

THETRI *n* currency unit of Georgia

THETRIS > THETRI

THEURGIC > THEURGY

THEURGIES > THEURGY

THEURGIST > THEURGY

THEURGY *n* intervention of a divine or supernatural agency in the affairs of human beings

THEW *n* muscle, esp if strong or well-developed

THEWED *adj* strong; muscular

THEWES > THEW

THEWIER > THEW

THEWIEST > THEW

THEWLESS > THEW

THEWS > THEW

THEWY > THEW

THEY *pron* people or things other than the speaker or people addressed

THIAMIN *same as* > THIAMINE

THIAMINE *n* vitamin found in the outer coat of rice and other grains

THIAMINES > THIAMINE

THIAMINS > THIAMIN

THIASUS *n* people gathered to sing and dance in honour of a god

THIASUSES > THIASUS

THIAZIDE *n* diuretic drug

THIAZIDES > THIAZIDE

THIAZIN *same as* > THIAZINE

THIAZINE *n* organic compound containing a ring system composed of four carbon atoms, a sulphur atom, and a nitrogen atom

THIAZINES > THIAZINE

THIAZINS > THIAZIN

THIAZOL *same as* > THIAZOLE

THIAZOLE *n* colourless liquid with a pungent smell

THIAZOLES > THIAZOLE

THIAZOLS > THIAZOL

THIBET *n* coloured woollen cloth

THIBETS > THIBET

THIBLE *n* stick for stirring porridge

THIBLES > THIBLE

THICK *adj* of great or specified extent from one side to the other ⊳ *vb* thicken

THICKED > THICK

THICKEN *vb* make or become thick or thicker

THICKENED > THICKEN

THICKENER > THICKEN

THICKENS > THICKEN

THICKER > THICK

THICKEST > THICK

THICKET *n* dense growth of small trees

THICKETED *adj* covered in thicket

THICKETS > THICKET

THICKETY *adj* covered in thickets

THICKHEAD *n* insulting word for a stupid person

THICKIE *same as* > THICKO

THICKIES > THICKY

THICKING > THICK

THICKISH > THICK

THICKLEAF *n* succulent plant with sessile or short-stalked fleshy leaves

THICKLY > THICK

THICKNESS *n* state of being thick

THICKO *n* insulting word for a stupid person

THICKOES > THICKO

THICKOS > THICKO

THICKS > THICK

THICKSET *adj* stocky in build ⊳ *n* thicket

THICKSETS > THICKSET

THICKSKIN *n* insensitive person

THICKY *same as* > THICKO

THIEF *n* person who steals

THIEFLIKE *adj* like a thief

THIEVE *vb* steal

THIEVED > THIEVE

THIEVERY > THIEVE

THIEVES > THIEVE

THIEVING *adj* given to stealing other people's possessions

THIEVINGS > THIEVING

THIEVISH > THIEF

THIG *vb* beg

THIGGED > THIG

THIGGER > THIG

THIGGERS > THIG

THIGGING > THIG

THIGGINGS > THIG

THIGGIT *Scots inflection of* > THIG

THIGH *n* upper part of the human leg

THIGHBONE *same as* > FEMUR

THIGHED *adj* having thighs

THIGHS > THIGH

THIGS > THIG

THILK *pron* that same

THILL *another word for* > SHAFT

THILLER *n* horse that goes between the thills of a cart

THILLERS > THILLER

THILLS > THILL

THIMBLE *n* cap protecting the end of the finger when sewing ⊳ *vb* use a thimble

THIMBLED > THIMBLE

THIMBLES > THIMBLE

THIMBLING > THIMBLE

THIN *adj* not thick ⊳ *vb* make or become thin ⊳ *adv* in order to produce something thin

THINCLAD *n* track-and-field athlete

THINCLADS > THINCLAD

THINDOWN *n* reduction in the amount of particles of very high energy penetrating the earth's atmosphere

THINDOWNS > THINDOWN

THINE *adj* of or associated with you (thou) ⊳ *pron* something belonging to you (thou)

THING *n* material object

THINGAMY *n* person or thing whose name is temporarily forgotten

THINGHOOD *n* existence; state or condition of being a thing

THINGIER > THINGY

THINGIES > THINGY

THINGIEST > THINGY

t

THINGNESS n state of being a thing

THINGO n thing the name of which is temporarily forgotten

THINGOS > THINGO

THINGS > THING

THINGUMMY n person or thing whose name is temporarily forgotten

THINGY adj existing in reality; actual ▷ n person or thing whose name is temporarily forgotten

THINK vb consider, judge, or believe

THINKABLE adj able to be conceived or considered

THINKABLY > THINKABLE

THINKER n > THINK

THINKERS > THINK

THINKING > THINK

THINKINGS > THINK

THINKS > THINK

THINLY > THIN

THINNED > THIN

THINNER > THIN

THINNERS > THIN

THINNESS > THIN

THINNEST > THIN

THINNING > THIN

THINNINGS > THIN

THINNISH > THIN

THINS > THIN

THIO adj of, or relating to, sulphur

THIOFURAN another name for > THIOPHEN

THIOL n any of a class of sulphur-containing organic compounds

THIOLIC > THIOL

THIOLS > THIOL

THIONATE n any salt or ester of thionic acid

THIONATES > THIONATE

THIONIC adj of, relating to, or containing sulphur

THIONIN same as > THIONINE

THIONINE n crystalline derivative of thiazine used as a violet dye to stain microscope specimens

THIONINES > THIONINE

THIONINS > THIONIN

THIONYL n the divalent group SO

THIONYLS > THIONYL

THIOPHEN n colourless liquid heterocyclic compound found in the benzene fraction of coal tar

THIOPHENE same as > THIOPHEN

THIOPHENS > THIOPHEN

THIOPHIL adj having an attraction to sulphur

THIOTEPA n drug used in chemotherapy

THIOTEPAS > THIOTEPA

THIOUREA n white water-soluble crystalline substance with a bitter taste

THIOUREAS > THIOUREA

THIR Scots word for > THESE

THIRAM n antifungal agent

THIRAMS > THIRAM

THIRD adj of number three in a series ▷ n one of three equal parts ▷ vb divide (something) by three

THIRDED > THIRD

THIRDHAND adv from the second of two intermediaries

THIRDING > THIRD

THIRDINGS > THIRD

THIRDLY adv in the third place or position

THIRDS > THIRD

THIRDSMAN n intermediary

THIRDSMEN > THIRDSMAN

THIRL vb bore or drill

THIRLAGE n obligation imposed upon tenants requiring them to have their grain ground at a specified mill

THIRLAGES > THIRLAGE

THIRLED > THIRL

THIRLING > THIRL

THIRLS > THIRL

THIRST n desire to drink ▷ vb feel thirst

THIRSTED > THIRST

THIRSTER > THIRST

THIRSTERS > THIRSTER

THIRSTFUL > THIRST

THIRSTIER > THIRSTY

THIRSTILY > THIRSTY

THIRSTING > THIRST

THIRSTS > THIRST

THIRSTY adj feeling a desire to drink

THIRTEEN n three and ten

THIRTEENS > THIRTEEN

THIRTIES > THIRTY

THIRTIETH adj being the ordinal number of thirty in counting order, position, time, etc: often written 30th ▷ n one of 30 approximately equal parts of something

THIRTY n three times ten

THIRTYISH adj around thirty years of age

THIS pron used to refer to a thing or person nearby, just mentioned, or about to be mentioned ▷ adj used to refer to the present time

THISAWAY adv this way

THISNESS n state or quality of being this

THISTLE n prickly plant with dense flower heads

THISTLES > THISTLE

THISTLIER > THISTLE

THISTLY > THISTLE

THITHER adv or towards that place

THITHERTO adv until that time

THIVEL same as > THIBLE

THIVELS > THIVEL

THLIPSES > THLIPSIS

THLIPSIS n compression, esp of part of the body

THO short for > THOUGH

THOFT n bench (in a boat) upon which a rower sits

THOFTS > THOFT

THOLE n wooden pin set in the side of a rowing boat to serve as a fulcrum for rowing ▷ vb bear or put up with

THOLED > THOLE

THOLEIITE n type of volcanic rock

THOLEPIN same as > THOLE

THOLEPINS > THOLEPIN

THOLES > THOLE

THOLI > THOLUS

THOLING > THOLE

THOLOBATE n structure supporting a dome

THOLOI > THOLOS

THOLOS n beehive-shaped tomb associated with Mycenaean Greece

THOLUS n domed tomb

THON Scot word for > YON

THONDER Scot word for > YONDER

THONG n thin strip of leather etc ▷ vb decorate with a thong or thongs

THONGED adj fastened with a thong

THONGIER > THONGY

THONGIEST > THONGY

THONGING > THONG

THONGS > THONG

THONGY adj resembling a thong

THORACAL another word for > THORACIC

THORACES > THORAX

THORACIC adj of, near, or relating to the thorax

THORAX n part of the body between the neck and the abdomen

THORAXES > THORAX

THORIA n insoluble white powder

THORIAS > THORIA

THORIC > THORIUM

THORITE n yellow, brownish, or black radioactive mineral

THORITES > THORITE

THORIUM n radioactive metallic element

THORIUMS > THORIUM

THORN n prickle on a plant ▷ vb jag or prick (something) as if with a thorn

THORNBACK n European ray with a row of spines along the back and tail

THORNBILL n S American hummingbird

THORNBIRD n small S American bird

THORNBUSH n tree, shrub, or bush with thorns

THORNED > THORN

THORNIER > THORNY

THORNIEST > THORNY

THORNILY > THORNY

THORNING > THORN

THORNLESS > THORN

THORNLIKE > THORN

THORNS > THORN

THORNSET adj set with thorns

THORNTAIL n tropical hummingbird

THORNTREE n tree with thorns

THORNY adj covered with thorns

THORO (nonstandard) variant spelling of > THOROUGH

THORON n radioisotope of radon that is a decay product of thorium

THORONS > THORON

THOROUGH adj complete ▷ n passage

THOROUGHS > THOROUGH

THORP n small village

THORPE same as > THORP

THORPES > THORPE

THORPS > THORP

THOSE determiner form of that used before a plural noun

THOTHER pron old contraction of the other

THOU pron used when talking to one person ▷ n one thousandth of an inch ▷ vb use the word thou

THOUED > THOU

THOUGH adv nevertheless

THOUGHT n concept or opinion

THOUGHTED adj with thoughts

THOUGHTEN adj convinced

THOUGHTS > THOUGHT

THOUING > THOU

THOUS > THOU

THOUSAND n ten hundred ▷ adj amounting to a thousand ▷ determiner amounting to a thousand

THOUSANDS > THOUSAND

THOWEL old variant of > THOLE

THOWELS > THOWEL

THOWL old variant of > THOLE

THOWLESS adj lacking in vigour

THOWLS > THOWL

THRAE same as > FRAE

THRAIPING n thrashing

THRALDOM same as > THRALL

THRALDOMS
> THRALDOM
THRALL n state of being in the power of another person ▷ vb enslave or dominate
THRALLDOM same as > THRALL
THRALLED > THRALL
THRALLING > THRALL
THRALLS > THRALL
THRANG n throng ▷ vb throng ▷ adj crowded
THRANGED > THRANG
THRANGING > THRANG
THRANGS > THRANG
THRAPPLE n throat or windpipe ▷ vb throttle
THRAPPLED
> THRAPPLE
THRAPPLES
> THRAPPLE
THRASH vb beat, esp with a stick or whip ▷ n party
THRASHED > THRASH
THRASHER same as > THRESHER
THRASHERS
> THRASHER
THRASHES > THRASH
THRASHIER > THRASHY
THRASHING n severe beating
THRASHY adj relating to thrash punk
THRASONIC adj bragging or boastful
THRAVE n twenty-four sheaves of corn
THRAVES > THRAVE
THRAW vb twist (something); make something thrawn
THRAWARD adj contrary or stubborn
THRAWART same as > THRAWARD
THRAWED > THRAW
THRAWING > THRAW
THRAWN adj crooked or twisted
THRAWNLY > THRAWN
THRAWS > THRAW
THREAD n fine strand or yarn ▷ vb pass thread through
THREADED > THREAD
THREADEN adj made of thread
THREADER > THREAD
THREADERS > THREAD
THREADFIN n spiny-finned tropical marine fish
THREADIER > THREADY
THREADING > THREAD
THREADS slang word for > CLOTHES
THREADY adj of, relating to, or resembling a thread or threads
THREAP vb scold
THREAPED > THREAP
THREAPER > THREAP
THREAPERS > THREAP
THREAPING > THREAP
THREAPIT variant past participle of > THREAP

THREAPS > THREAP
THREAT n declaration of intent to harm
THREATED > THREAT
THREATEN vb make or be a threat to
THREATENS
> THREATEN
THREATFUL > THREAT
THREATING > THREAT
THREATS > THREAT
THREAVE same as > THRAVE
THREAVES > THREAVE
THREE n one more than two
THREEFOLD adv (having) three times as many or as much ▷ adj having three times as many or as much
THREENESS n state or quality of being three
THREEP same as > THREAP
THREEPEAT n third consecutive win of a particular sporting championship ▷ vb win a sporting championship for the third consecutive time
THREEPED > THREEP
THREEPER > THREAP
THREEPERS > THREAP
THREEPING > THREEP
THREEPIT variant past participle of > THREEP
THREEPS > THREEP
THREEQUEL n third instalment in a series of films, books, plays, etc
THREES > THREE
THREESOME n group of three
THRENE n dirge; threnody
THRENES > THRENE
THRENETIC > THRENE
THRENODE same as > THRENODY
THRENODES
> THRENODE
THRENODIC
> THRENODY
THRENODY n lament for the dead
THRENOS n threnody; lamentation
THRENOSES > THRENOS
THREONINE n essential amino acid that occurs in certain proteins
THRESH vb beat (wheat etc) to separate the grain from the husks and straw ▷ n act of threshing
THRESHED > THRESH
THRESHEL n flail
THRESHELS
> THRESHEL
THRESHER n large shark of tropical and temperate seas
THRESHERS
> THRESHER
THRESHES > THRESH
THRESHING > THRESH
THRESHOLD n bar forming the bottom of a doorway

THRETTIES > THRETTY
THRETTY nonstandard variant of > THIRTY
THREW > THROW
THRICE adv three times
THRID old variant of > THREAD
THRIDACE n sedative made from lettuce juice
THRIDACES
> THRIDACE
THRIDDED > THRID
THRIDDING > THRID
THRIDS > THRID
THRIFT n wisdom and caution with money
THRIFTIER > THRIFTY
THRIFTILY > THRIFTY
THRIFTS > THRIFT
THRIFTY adj not wasteful with money
THRILL n sudden feeling of excitement ▷ vb (cause to) feel a thrill
THRILLANT another word for > THRILLING
THRILLED > THRILL
THRILLER n book, film, etc with an atmosphere of mystery or suspense
THRILLERS
> THRILLER
THRILLIER > THRILLY
THRILLING adj very exciting or stimulating
THRILLS > THRILL
THRILLY adj causing thrills
THRIMSA same as > THRYMSA
THRIMSAS > THRIMSA
THRIP same as > THRIPS
THRIPS n small slender-bodied insect with piercing mouthparts that feeds on plant sap
THRIPSES > THRIPS
THRISSEL Scots variant of > THISTLE
THRISSELS
> THRISSEL
THRIST old variant of > THIRST
THRISTED > THRIST
THRISTING > THRIST
THRISTLE Scots variant of > THISTLE
THRISTLES
> THRISTLE
THRISTS > THRIST
THRISTY > THRIST
THRIVE vb flourish or prosper
THRIVED > THRIVE
THRIVEN > THRIVE
THRIVER > THRIVE
THRIVERS > THRIVE
THRIVES > THRIVE
THRIVING > THRIVE
THRIVINGS > THRIVE
THRO same as > THROUGH
THROAT n passage from the mouth and nose to the stomach and lungs ▷ vb vocalize in the throat
THROATED > THROAT
THROATIER > THROATY
THROATILY > THROATY

THROATING > THROAT
THROATS > THROAT
THROATY adj (of the voice) hoarse
THROB vb pulsate repeatedly ▷ n throbbing
THROBBED > THROB
THROBBER > THROB
THROBBERS > THROB
THROBBING > THROB
THROBLESS > THROB
THROBS > THROB
THROE n pang or pain ▷ vb endure throes
THROED > THROE
THROEING > THROE
THROES pl n violent pangs or pains
THROMBI > THROMBUS
THROMBIN n enzyme that acts on fibrinogen in blood, causing it to clot
THROMBINS > THROMBIN
THROMBOSE vb become or affect with a thrombus
THROMBUS n clot of coagulated blood that remains at the site of its formation
THRONE n ceremonial seat of a monarch or bishop ▷ vb place or be placed on a throne
THRONED > THRONE
THRONES > THRONE
THRONG vb crowd ▷ n great number of people or things crowded together ▷ adj busy
THRONGED > THRONG
THRONGFUL > THRONG
THRONGING > THRONG
THRONGS > THRONG
THRONING > THRONE
THRONNER n person who is good at doing odd jobs
THRONNERS
> THRONNER
THROPPLE vb strangle or choke
THROPPLED
> THROPPLE
THROPPLES
> THROPPLE
THROSTLE n song thrush
THROSTLES
> THROSTLE
THROTTLE n device controlling the amount of fuel entering an engine ▷ vb control the flow of fluid in an engine by using the throttle
THROTTLED
> THROTTLE
THROTTLER
> THROTTLE
THROTTLES
> THROTTLE
THROUGH prep from end to end or side to side of ▷ adj finished
THROUGHLY adv thoroughly
THROVE > THRIVE
THROW vb hurl through the air ▷ n instance of throwing

t

THROWABLE adj capable of being thrown
THROWAWAY adj done or said casually ▷ n handbill or advertisement distributed in a public place
THROWBACK n person or thing that reverts to an earlier type
THROWDOWN n challenge to a physical or artistic competition
THROWE old variant of > THROE
THROWER > THROW
THROWERS > THROW
THROWES > THROWE
THROWING > THROW
THROWINGS > THROW
THROWN > THROW
THROWOVER n material placed over an object for decoration or protection
THROWS > THROW
THROWSTER n person who twists silk or other fibres into yarn
THRU same as > THROUGH
THRUM vb strum rhythmically but without expression ▷ n in textiles, unwoven ends of warp thread
THRUMMED > THRUM
THRUMMER > THRUM
THRUMMERS > THRUM
THRUMMIER > THRUMMY
THRUMMING > THRUM
THRUMMY adj made of thrums
THRUMS > THRUM
THRUPENNY n twelve-sided British coin of nickel-brass, valued at three old pence, obsolete since 1971
THRUPUT n quantity of raw material or information processed in a given period
THRUPUTS > THRUPUT
THRUSH n brown songbird
THRUSHES > THRUSH
THRUST vb push forcefully ▷ n forceful stab
THRUSTED > THRUST
THRUSTER n person or thing that thrusts
THRUSTERS > THRUSTER
THRUSTFUL > THRUST
THRUSTING > THRUST
THRUSTOR variant of > THRUSTER
THRUSTORS > THRUSTOR
THRUSTS > THRUST
THRUTCH n narrow, fast-moving stream ▷ vb thrust
THRUTCHED > THRUTCH
THRUTCHES > THRUTCH
THRUWAY n thoroughfare
THRUWAYS > THRUWAY
THRYMSA n gold coin used in Anglo-Saxon England

THRYMSAS > THRYMSA
THUD n dull heavy sound ▷ vb make such a sound
THUDDED > THUD
THUDDING n act of thudding
THUDDINGS > THUDDING
THUDS > THUD
THUG n violent person, esp a criminal
THUGGEE n (formerly) the methods of thugs in India
THUGGEES > THUGGEE
THUGGERY > THUG
THUGGISH > THUG
THUGGISM > THUG
THUGGISMS > THUG
THUGGO n tough and violent person
THUGGOS > THUGGO
THUGS > THUG
THUJA n coniferous tree of North America and East Asia
THUJAS > THUJA
THULIA n oxide of thulium
THULIAS > THULIA
THULITE n rose-coloured zoisite sometimes incorporated into jewellery
THULITES > THULITE
THULIUM n malleable ductile silvery-grey element
THULIUMS > THULIUM
THUMB n short thick finger set apart from the others ▷ vb touch or handle with the thumb
THUMBED > THUMB
THUMBHOLE n hole for putting the thumb into
THUMBIER > THUMBY
THUMBIEST > THUMBY
THUMBING > THUMB
THUMBKIN n thumbscrew
THUMBKINS n thumbscrew
THUMBLESS > THUMB
THUMBLIKE > THUMB
THUMBLING n extremely small person
THUMBNAIL n nail of the thumb ▷ adj concise and brief
THUMBNUT n nut with projections enabling it to be turned by the thumb and forefinger
THUMBNUTS > THUMBNUT
THUMBPOT n tiny flowerpot
THUMBPOTS > THUMBPOT
THUMBS > THUMB
THUMBTACK n short tack with a broad smooth head for fastening papers to a drawing board, etc
THUMBY adj clumsy; uncoordinated
THUMP n (sound of) a dull heavy blow ▷ vb strike heavily

THUMPED > THUMP
THUMPER > THUMP
THUMPERS > THUMP
THUMPING adj huge or excessive
THUMPS > THUMP
THUNDER n loud noise accompanying lightning ▷ vb rumble with thunder
THUNDERED > THUNDER
THUNDERER > THUNDER
THUNDERS > THUNDER
THUNDERY > THUNDER
THUNDROUS > THUNDER
THUNK another word for > THUD
THUNKED > THUNK
THUNKING > THUNK
THUNKS > THUNK
THURIBLE same as > CENSER
THURIBLES > THURIBLE
THURIFER n person appointed to carry the censer at religious ceremonies
THURIFERS > THURIFER
THURIFIED > THURIFY
THURIFIES > THURIFY
THURIFY vb burn incense near or before an altar, shrine, etc
THURL same as > THIRL
THURLS > THURL
THUS adv in this manner ▷ n aromatic gum resin
THUSES > THUS
THUSLY adv in such a way; thus
THUSNESS n state or quality of being thus
THUSWISE adj in this way; thus
THUYA same as > THUJA
THUYAS > THUYA
THWACK n whack ▷ vb beat with something flat ▷ interj exclamation imitative of this sound
THWACKED > THWACK
THWACKER > THWACK
THWACKERS > THWACK
THWACKING > THWACK
THWACKS > THWACK
THWAITE n piece of land cleared from forest or reclaimed from wasteland
THWAITES > THWAITE
THWART vb foil or frustrate ▷ n seat across a boat ▷ adj passing or being situated across ▷ adv across
THWARTED > THWART
THWARTER > THWART
THWARTERS > THWART
THWARTING > THWART
THWARTLY > THWART
THWARTS > THWART
THY adj of or associated with you (thou) ▷ determiner belonging to or associated in some way with you (thou)
THYINE adj of relating to the sandarac tree

THYLACINE n extinct doglike Tasmanian marsupial
THYLAKOID n small membranous sac within a chloroplast
THYLOSE old variant of > TYLOSIS
THYLOSES > THYLOSIS
THYLOSIS same as > TYLOSIS
THYME n aromatic herb
THYMES > THYME
THYMEY > THYME
THYMI > THYMUS
THYMIC adj of or relating to the thymus
THYMIDINE n crystalline nucleoside of thymine, found in DNA
THYMIER > THYME
THYMIEST > THYME
THYMINE n white crystalline pyrimidine base found in DNA
THYMINES > THYMINE
THYMOCYTE n lymphocyte found in the thymus
THYMOL n substance obtained from thyme
THYMOLS > THYMOL
THYMOMA n type of tumour
THYMOMAS > THYMOMA
THYMOMATA > THYMOMA
THYMOSIN n hormone secreted by the thymus
THYMOSINS > THYMOSIN
THYMUS n small gland at the base of the neck
THYMUSES > THYMUS
THYMY > THYME
THYRATRON n gas-filled tube that has three electrodes and can be switched between an 'off' state and an 'on' state
THYREOID same as > THYROID
THYREOIDS > THYROID
THYRISTOR n any of a group of semiconductor devices, such as the silicon-controlled rectifier, that can be switched between two states
THYROID n gland in the neck controlling body growth ▷ adj of or relating to the thyroid gland
THYROIDAL > THYROID
THYROIDS > THYROID
THYROXIN same as > THYROXINE
THYROXINE n principal hormone produced by the thyroid gland
THYROXINS > THYROXIN
THYRSE n type of inflorescence, occurring in the lilac and grape
THYRSES > THYRSE
THYRSI > THYRSUS
THYRSOID > THYRSE

THYRSUS same as > THYRSE

THYSELF pron reflexive form of thou

TI same as > TE

TIAN n traditional French vegetable stew or earthenware dish it is cooked in

TIANS > TIAN

TIAR same as > TIARA

TIARA n semicircular jewelled headdress

TIARAED > TIARA

TIARAS > TIARA

TIARS > TIAR

TIBIA n inner bone of the lower leg

TIBIAE > TIBIA

TIBIAL > TIBIA

TIBIALES > TIBIALIS

TIBIALIS n muscle in the calf of the leg

TIBIAS > TIBIA

TIC n spasmodic muscular twitch ▷ vb move in a spasmodic twitch

TICAL n former standard monetary unit of Thailand

TICALS > TICAL

TICCA adj acquired for temporary use in exchange for payment

TICCED > TIC

TICCING > TIC

TICE vb tempt or allure; entice

TICED > TICE

TICES > TICE

TICH same as > TITCH

TICHES > TICH

TICHIER > TICHY

TICHIEST > TICHY

TICHY same as > TITCHY

TICING > TICE

TICK n mark used to check off or indicate the correctness of something ▷ vb mark with a tick

TICKED > TICK

TICKEN same as > TICKING

TICKENS > TICKEN

TICKER n heart

TICKERS > TICKER

TICKET n card or paper entitling the holder to admission, travel, etc ▷ vb attach or issue a ticket to

TICKETED > TICKET

TICKETING > TICKET

TICKETS pl n death or ruin

TICKEY n former South African threepenny piece

TICKEYS > TICKEY

TICKIES > TICKY

TICKING n strong material for mattress covers

TICKINGS > TICKING

TICKLACE n (in Newfoundland) a kittiwake

TICKLACES > TICKLACE

TICKLE vb touch or stroke (a person) to produce laughter ▷ n tickling

TICKLEASS n informal name for a kittiwake

TICKLED > TICKLE

TICKLER n difficult or delicate problem

TICKLERS > TICKLER

TICKLES > TICKLE

TICKLIER > TICKLE

TICKLIEST > TICKLE

TICKLING > TICKLE

TICKLINGS > TICKLE

TICKLISH adj sensitive to tickling

TICKLY > TICKLE

TICKS > TICK

TICKSEED another name for > COREOPSIS

TICKSEEDS > TICKSEED

TICKTACK n sound made by a clock ▷ vb make a ticking sound

TICKTACKS > TICKTACK

TICKTOCK n ticking sound made by a clock ▷ vb make a ticking sound

TICKTOCKS > TICKTOCK

TICKY same as > TICKEY

TICS > TIC

TICTAC same as > TICKTACK

TICTACKED > TICTAC

TICTACS > TICTAC

TICTOC same as > TICKTOCK

TICTOCKED > TICTOC

TICTOCS > TICTOC

TID n mood or humour

TIDAL adj (of a river, lake, or sea) having tides

TIDALLY > TIDAL

TIDBIT same as > TITBIT

TIDBITS > TIDBIT

TIDDIER > TIDDY

TIDDIES > TIDDY

TIDDIEST > TIDDY

TIDDLE vb busy oneself with inconsequential tasks

TIDDLED > TIDDLE

TIDDLER n very small fish

TIDDLERS > TIDDLER

TIDDLES > TIDDLE

TIDDLEY same as > TIDDLY

TIDDLEYS > TIDDLEY

TIDDLIER > TIDDLY

TIDDLIES > TIDDLY

TIDDLIEST > TIDDLY

TIDDLING > TIDDLE

TIDDLY adj tiny ▷ n alcoholic beverage

TIDDY n four of trumps in the card game gleek

TIDE n rise and fall of the sea caused by the gravitational pull of the sun and moon ▷ vb carry or be carried with or as if with the tide

TIDED > TIDE

TIDELAND n land between high-water and low-water marks

TIDELANDS > TIDELAND

TIDELESS > TIDE

TIDELIKE > TIDE

TIDELINE n high-water mark left by the retreating tide

TIDELINES > TIDELINE

TIDEMARK n mark left by the highest or lowest point of a tide

TIDEMARKS > TIDEMARK

TIDEMILL n watermill powered by the force of the tide

TIDEMILLS > TIDEMILL

TIDERIP same as > RIPTIDE

TIDERIPS > TIDERIP

TIDES > TIDE

TIDESMAN n customs official at a port

TIDESMEN > TIDESMAN

TIDEWATER n water that advances and recedes with the tide

TIDEWAVE n undulation of the earth's water levels as the tide moves around it

TIDEWAVES > TIDEWAVE

TIDEWAY n strong tidal current or its channel, esp the tidal part of a river

TIDEWAYS > TIDEWAY

TIDIED > TIDY

TIDIER > TIDY

TIDIERS > TIDY

TIDIES > TIDY

TIDIEST > TIDY

TIDILY > TIDY

TIDINESS > TIDY

TIDING > TIDE

TIDINGS pl n news

TIDIVATE same as > TITIVATE

TIDIVATED > TITIVATE

TIDIVATES > TITIVATE

TIDS > TID

TIDY adj neat and orderly ▷ vb put in order ▷ n small container for odds and ends

TIDYING > TIDY

TIDYTIPS n herb with flowers resembling those of the daisy

TIE vb fasten or be fastened with string, rope, etc ▷ n long narrow piece of material worn knotted round the neck

TIEBACK n length of cord, ribbon, or other fabric used for tying a curtain to one side

TIEBACKS > TIEBACK

TIEBREAK n deciding game in drawn match

TIEBREAKS > TIEBREAK

TIECLASP n clip, often ornamental, which holds a tie in place against a shirt

TIECLASPS > TIECLASP

TIED > TIE

TIEING same as > TIE

TIELESS > TIE

TIEPIN n ornamental pin used to pin the two ends of a tie to a shirt

TIEPINS > TIEPIN

TIER n one of a set of rows placed one above and behind the other ▷ vb be or arrange in tiers

TIERCE same as > TERCE

TIERCED adj (of a shield) divided into three sections of similar size but different colour

TIERCEL same as > TERCEL

TIERCELET another name for > TERCEL

TIERCELS > TIERCEL

TIERCERON n (in Gothic architecture) a type of rib on a vault

TIERCES > TIERCE

TIERCET same as > TERCET

TIERCETS > TIERCET

TIERED > TIER

TIERING > TIER

TIERS > TIER

TIES > TIE

TIETAC n fastener for holding a tie in place

TIETACK same as > TIETAC

TIETACKS > TIETACK

TIETACS > TIETAC

TIFF n petty quarrel ▷ vb have or be in a tiff

TIFFANIES > TIFFANY

TIFFANY n sheer fine gauzy fabric

TIFFED > TIFF

TIFFIN n (in India) a light meal, esp at midday ▷ vb take tiffin

TIFFINED > TIFFIN

TIFFING > TIFF

TIFFINGS > TIFF

TIFFINING > TIFFIN

TIFFINS > TIFFIN

TIFFS > TIFF

TIFO n organized fan display during a football match

TIFOS > TIFO

TIFOSI > TIFOSO

TIFOSO n (in sport) a fanatical fan

TIFOSOS > TIFOSO

TIFT Scots variant of > TIFF

TIFTED > TIFT

TIFTING > TIFT

TIFTS > TIFT

TIG n child's game

TIGE n trunk of an architectural column

TIGER n large yellow-and-black striped Asian cat

TIGEREYE n golden brown silicified variety of crocidolite, used as an ornamental stone

TIGEREYES > TIGEREYE

TIGERIER > TIGERY

TIGERIEST > TIGERY

TIGERISH > TIGER

TIGERISM n arrogant and showy manner

TIGERISMS > TIGERISM

TIGERLIER > TIGERLY

TIGERLIKE adj resembling a tiger

TIGERLY adj of or like a tiger

TIGERS > TIGER

TIGERWOOD n striped wood used in cabinetmaking

TIGERY adj like a tiger

TIGES > TIGE

TIGGED > TIG

TIGGER vb damage beyond repair by tinkering

TIGGERED > TIGGER

TIGGERING > TIGGER

TIGGERS > TIGGER

TIGGING > TIG

TIGHT adj stretched or drawn taut ▷ adv in a close, firm, or secure way

TIGHTASS n slang word for an excessively self-controlled person

TIGHTEN vb make or become tight or tighter

TIGHTENED > TIGHTEN

TIGHTENER > TIGHTEN

TIGHTENS > TIGHTEN

TIGHTER > TIGHT

TIGHTEST > TIGHT

TIGHTISH > TIGHT

TIGHTKNIT adj closely integrated

TIGHTLY > TIGHT

TIGHTNESS > TIGHT

TIGHTROPE n rope stretched taut on which acrobats perform

TIGHTS pl n one-piece clinging garment covering the body from the waist to the feet

TIGHTWAD n stingy person

TIGHTWADS > TIGHTWAD

TIGHTWIRE n wire tightrope

TIGLIC adj as in tiglic acid syrupy liquid or crystalline colourless unsaturated carboxylic acid

TIGLON same as > TIGON

TIGLONS > TIGLON

TIGNON n type of cloth headdress

TIGNONS > TIGNON

TIGON n hybrid offspring of a male tiger and a female lion

TIGONS > TIGON

TIGRESS n female tiger

TIGRESSES > TIGRESS

TIGRIDIA n type of tropical American plant

TIGRIDIAS > TIGRIDIA

TIGRINE adj of, characteristic of, or resembling a tiger

TIGRISH > TIGER

TIGRISHLY > TIGER

TIGROID adj resembling a tiger

TIGS > TIG

TIK n South African slang term for crystal meth

TIKA same as > TIKKA

TIKANGA n Māori ways or customs

TIKANGAS > TIKANGA

TIKAS > TIKA

TIKE same as > TYKE

TIKES > TIKE

TIKI n small carving of a grotesque person worn as a pendant ▷ vb take a scenic tour around an area

TIKIED > TIKI

TIKIING > TIKI

TIKINAGAN n Native American device allowing an infant to be carried on someone's back

TIKIS > TIKI

TIKKA adj marinated in spices and dry-roasted ▷ n coloured spot or mark worn by Hindus

TIKKAS > TIKKA

TIKOLOSHE same as > TOKOLOSHE

TIKS > TIK

TIKTAALIK n extinct species thought to be a missing link between water and land animals

TIL another name for > SESAME

TILAK n coloured spot or mark worn by Hindus

TILAKS > TILAK

TILAPIA n type of fish

TILAPIAS > TILAPIA

TILBURIES > TILBURY

TILBURY n light two-wheeled horse-drawn open carriage

TILDE n mark used in Spanish to indicate pronunciation

TILDES > TILDE

TILE n flat piece of ceramic, plastic, etc used to cover a roof, floor, or wall ▷ vb cover with tiles

TILED > TILE

TILEFISH n large brightly coloured deep-sea percoid food fish

TILELIKE adj like a tile

TILER > TILE

TILERIES > TILERY

TILERS > TILE

TILERY n place where tiles are produced

TILES > TILE

TILING n tiles collectively

TILINGS > TILING

TILL prep until ▷ vb cultivate (land) ▷ n drawer for money, usu in a cash register

TILLABLE > TILL

TILLAGE n act, process, or art of tilling

TILLAGES > TILLAGE

TILLED > TILL

TILLER n on boats, a handle fixed to the top of a rudderpost to serve as a lever in steering ▷ vb use a tiller

TILLERED > TILLER

TILLERING n (of a plant) the production of shoots

TILLERMAN n one working a tiller

TILLERMEN > TILLERMAN

TILLERS > TILLER

TILLICUM n (in the Pacific Northwest) a friend

TILLICUMS > TILLICUM

TILLIER > TILL

TILLIEST > TILL

TILLING > TILL

TILLINGS > TILL

TILLITE n rock formed from hardened till

TILLITES > TILLITE

TILLS > TILL

TILLY > TILL

TILS > TIL

TILT vb slant at an angle ▷ n slope

TILTABLE > TILT

TILTED > TILT

TILTER > TILT

TILTERS > TILT

TILTH n (condition of) land that has been tilled

TILTHS > TILTH

TILTING > TILT

TILTINGS > TILT

TILTMETER n instrument for measuring the tilt of the earth's surface

TILTROTOR n aircraft with rotors that can be tilted

TILTS > TILT

TILTYARD n (formerly) an enclosed area for jousting

TILTYARDS > TILTYARD

TIMARAU same as > TAMARAU

TIMARAUS > TIMARAU

TIMARIOT n one holding a fief in feudal Turkey

TIMARIOTS > TIMARIOT

TIMBAL n type of kettledrum

TIMBALE n mixture of meat, fish, etc, in a rich sauce

TIMBALES > TIMBALE

TIMBALS > TIMBAL

TIMBER n wood as a building material ▷ adj made out of timber ▷ vb provide with timbers

▷ interj lumberjack's shouted warning when a tree is about to fall

TIMBERED adj made of or containing timber or timbers

TIMBERIER > TIMBERY

TIMBERING n timbers collectively

TIMBERMAN n any of various longicorn beetles that have destructive wood-eating larvae

TIMBERMEN > TIMBERMAN

TIMBERS > TIMBER

TIMBERY adj like timber

TIMBO n Amazonian vine from which a useful insecticide can be derived

TIMBOS > TIMBO

TIMBRAL adj relating to timbre

TIMBRE n distinctive quality of sound of a voice or instrument

TIMBREL n tambourine

TIMBRELS > TIMBREL

TIMBRES > TIMBRE

TIME n past, present, and future as a continuous whole ▷ vb note the time taken by

TIMEBOMB n bomb containing a timing mechanism that determines the time it will detonate

TIMEBOMBS > TIMEBOMB

TIMECARD n card used with a time clock

TIMECARDS > TIMECARD

TIMED > TIME

TIMEFRAME n period of time within which certain events are scheduled to occur

TIMELESS adj unaffected by time

TIMELIER > TIMELY

TIMELIEST > TIMELY

TIMELINE n graphic representation showing the passage of time as a line

TIMELINES > TIMELINE

TIMELY adj at the appropriate time ▷ adv at the right or an appropriate time

TIMENOGUY n taut rope on a ship

TIMEOUS adj in good time

TIMEOUSLY > TIMEOUS

TIMEOUT n in sport, interruption in play during which players rest, etc

TIMEOUTS > TIMEOUT

TIMEPASS n way of passing the time ▷ vb pass the time

TIMEPIECE n watch or clock

TIMER n device for measuring time

TIMERS > TIMER

TIMES > TIME

TIMESAVER *n* something that saves time

TIMESCALE *n* period of time within which events occur or are due to occur

TIMESHARE *n* time-shared property

TIMESHIFT *vb* enable the viewing of a programme later than its original broadcast

TIMESTAMP *vb* (of a computer) add a record of the date and time of an event to (data)

TIMETABLE *n* plan showing the times when something takes place, the departure and arrival times of trains or buses, etc ▷ *vb* set a time when a particular thing should be done

TIMEWORK *n* work paid for by the length of time taken, esp by the hour or the day

TIMEWORKS > TIMEWORK

TIMEWORN *adj* showing the adverse effects of overlong use or of old age

TIMID *adj* easily frightened

TIMIDER > TIMID

TIMIDEST > TIMID

TIMIDITY > TIMID

TIMIDLY > TIMID

TIMIDNESS > TIMID

TIMING *n* ability to judge when to do or say something so as to make the best effect

TIMINGS > TIMING

TIMIST *n* one concerned with time

TIMISTS > TIMIST

TIMOCRACY *n* political unit or system in which possession of property serves as the first requirement for participation in government

TIMOLOL *n* relaxant medicine used (for example) to reduce blood pressure

TIMOLOLS > TIMOLOL

TIMON *n* apparatus by which a vessel is steered

TIMONEER *n* helmsman; tillerman

TIMONEERS > TIMONEER

TIMONS > TIMON

TIMOROUS *adj* timid

TIMORSOME *adj* timorous; timid

TIMOTHIES > TIMOTHY

TIMOTHY *n* perennial grass of temperate regions

TIMOUS *same as* > TIMEOUS

TIMOUSLY > TIMOUS

TIMPANA *n* traditional Maltese baked pasta and pastry dish

TIMPANAS > TIMPANA

TIMPANI *pl n* set of kettledrums

TIMPANIST > TIMPANI

TIMPANO *n* kettledrum

TIMPANUM *same as* > TYMPANUM

TIMPANUMS > TIMPANUM

TIMPS *same as* > TIMPANI

TIN *n* soft metallic element ▷ *vb* put (food) into tins

TINA *n* slang word for crystal meth

TINAJA *n* large jar for cooling water

TINAJAS > TINAJA

TINAMOU *n* type of bird of Central and S America

TINAMOUS > TINAMOU

TINAS > TINA

TINCAL *another name for* > BORAX

TINCALS > TINCAL

TINCHEL *n* in Scotland, a circle of deer hunters who gradually close in on their quarry

TINCHELS > TINCHEL

TINCT *vb* tint ▷ *adj* tinted or coloured

TINCTED > TINCT

TINCTING > TINCT

TINCTS > TINCT

TINCTURE *n* medicinal extract in a solution of alcohol ▷ *vb* give a tint or colour to

TINCTURED > TINCTURE

TINCTURES > TINCTURE

TIND *vb* set alight

TINDAL *n* petty officer

TINDALS > TINDAL

TINDED > TIND

TINDER *n* dry easily burning material used to start a fire

TINDERBOX *n* formerly, small box for tinder, esp one fitted with a flint and steel

TINDERIER > TINDERY

TINDERS > TINDER

TINDERY *adj* like tinder

TINDING > TIND

TINDS > TIND

TINE *n* prong of a fork or antler ▷ *vb* lose

TINEA *n* any fungal skin disease, esp ringworm

TINEAL > TINEA

TINEAS > TINEA

TINED > TINE

TINEID *n* type of moth of the family which includes the clothes moths

TINEIDS > TINEID

TINES > TINE

TINFOIL *n* paper-thin sheet of metal, used for wrapping foodstuffs

TINFOILS > TINFOIL

TINFUL *n* contents of a tin or the amount a tin will hold

TINFULS > TINFUL

TING *same as* > THING

TINGE *n* slight tint ▷ *vb* give a slight tint or trace to

TINGED > TINGE

TINGEING > TINGE

TINGES > TINGE

TINGING > TINGE

TINGLE *n* prickling or stinging sensation ▷ *vb* feel a mild prickling or stinging sensation, as from cold or excitement

TINGLED > TINGLE

TINGLER > TINGLE

TINGLERS > TINGLE

TINGLES > TINGLE

TINGLIER > TINGLY

TINGLIEST > TINGLY

TINGLING > TINGLE

TINGLINGS > TINGLE

TINGLISH *adj* exciting

TINGLY > TINGLE

TINGS > TING

TINGUAÍTE *n* type of igneous rock

TINHORN *n* cheap pretentious person ▷ *adj* cheap and showy

TINHORNS > TINHORN

TINIER > TINY

TINIES *pl n* small children

TINIEST > TINY

TINILY > TINY

TININESS > TINY

TINING > TINE

TINK *vb* make short sound like a bell

TINKED > TINK

TINKER *n* (formerly) travelling mender of pots and pans ▷ *vb* fiddle with (an engine etc) in an attempt to repair it

TINKERED > TINKER

TINKERER > TINKER

TINKERERS > TINKER

TINKERING > TINKER

TINKERMAN *n* football coach who continually changes the team line-up or formation between games

TINKERMEN > TINKERMAN

TINKERS > TINKER

TINKERTOY *n* children's construction set

TINKING > TINK

TINKLE *vb* ring with a high tinny sound like a small bell ▷ *n* this sound or action

TINKLED > TINKLE

TINKLER *same as* > TINKER

TINKLERS > TINKLER

TINKLES > TINKLE

TINKLIER > TINKLE

TINKLIEST > TINKLE

TINKLING > TINKLE

TINKLINGS > TINKLE

TINKLY > TINKLE

TINKS > TINK

TINLIKE > TIN

TINMAN *n* one who works with tin or tin plate

TINMEN > TINMAN

TINNED > TIN

TINNER *n* tin miner

TINNERS > TINNER

TINNIE *same as* > TINNY

TINNIER > TINNY

TINNIES > TINNY

TINNIEST > TINNY

TINNILY > TINNY

TINNINESS > TINNY

TINNING > TIN

TINNINGS > TIN

TINNITUS *n* ringing or hissing sensation in one or both ears

TINNY *adj* (of sound) thin and metallic ▷ *n* can of beer

TINPLATE *n* thin steel sheet coated with tin ▷ *vb* coat (a metal or object) with a layer of tin

TINPLATED > TINPLATE

TINPLATES > TINPLATE

TINPOT *adj* worthless or unimportant ▷ *n* pot made of tin

TINPOTS > TINPOT

TINS > TIN

TINSEL *n* decorative metallic strips or threads ▷ *adj* made of or decorated with tinsel ▷ *vb* decorate with or as if with tinsel

TINSELED > TINSEL

TINSELIER > TINSELY

TINSELING > TINSEL

TINSELLED > TINSEL

TINSELLY *adj* adorned with tinsel

TINSELRY *n* tinsel-like material

TINSELS > TINSEL

TINSELY *adj* (US) like tinsel

TINSEY *old variant of* > TINSEL

TINSEYS > TINSEY

TINSMITH *n* person who works with tin or tin plate

TINSMITHS > TINSMITH

TINSNIPS *pl n* metal cutters

TINSTONE *n* black or brown stone

TINSTONES > TINSTONE

TINT *n* (pale) shade of a colour ▷ *vb* give a tint to

TINTACK *n* tin-plated tack

TINTACKS > TINTACK

TINTED > TINT

TINTER > TINT

TINTERS > TINT

TINTIER > TINTY

TINTIEST > TINTY

TINTINESS > TINTY

TINTING > TINT

TINTINGS > TINT

TINTLESS > TINT

TINTOOKIE *n* in informal Australian English, fawning or servile person

TINTS > TINT

t

TINTY adj having many tints

TINTYPE another name for > FERROTYPE

TINTYPES > TINTYPE

TINWARE n objects made of tin plate

TINWARES > TINWARE

TINWORK n objects made of tin

TINWORKS n place where tin is mined, smelted, or rolled

TINY adj very small

TIP n narrow or pointed end of anything ▷ vb put a tip on

TIPCART n cart that can be tipped to empty out its contents

TIPCARTS > TIPCART

TIPCAT n game in which a piece of wood is tipped in the air with a stick

TIPCATS > TIPCAT

TIPI variant spelling of > TEPEE

TIPIS > TIPI

TIPLESS > TIP

TIPOFF n warning or hint, esp given confidentially

TIPOFFS > TIPOFF

TIPPED > TIP

TIPPEE n person who receives a tip, esp regarding share prices

TIPPEES > TIPPEE

TIPPER n person who gives or leaves a tip

TIPPERS > TIPPER

TIPPET n fur cape for the shoulders

TIPPETS > TIPPET

TIPPIER > TIPPY

TIPPIEST > TIPPY

TIPPING > TIP

TIPPINGS > TIP

TIPPLE vb drink alcohol habitually, esp in small quantities ▷ n alcoholic drink

TIPPLED > TIPPLE

TIPPLER > TIPPLE

TIPPLERS > TIPPLE

TIPPLES > TIPPLE

TIPPLING > TIPPLE

TIPPY adj extremely fashionable or stylish

TIPPYTOE same as > TIPTOE

TIPPYTOED > TIPPYTOE

TIPPYTOES > TIPPYTOE

TIPS > TIP

TIPSHEET n list of advice or instructions

TIPSHEETS > TIPSHEET

TIPSIER > TIPSY

TIPSIEST > TIPSY

TIPSIFIED > TIPSIFY

TIPSIFIES > TIPSIFY

TIPSIFY vb make tipsy

TIPSILY > TIPSY

TIPSINESS > TIPSY

TIPSTAFF n court official

TIPSTAFFS > TIPSTAFF

TIPSTAVES > TIPSTAFF

TIPSTER n person who sells tips about races

TIPSTERS > TIPSTER

TIPSTOCK n detachable section of a gunstock, usually gripped by the left hand of the user

TIPSTOCKS > TIPSTOCK

TIPSY adj slightly drunk

TIPT > TIP

TIPTOE vb walk quietly with the heels off the ground

TIPTOED > TIPTOE

TIPTOEING > TIPTOE

TIPTOES > TIPTOE

TIPTOP adj of the highest quality or condition ▷ n . best in quality

TIPTOPS > TIPTOP

TIPTRONIC n type of gearbox that has both automatic and manual options

TIPULA n crane fly

TIPULAS > TIPULA

TIPUNA n ancestor

TIPUNAS > TIPUNA

TIRADE n long angry speech

TIRADES > TIRADE

TIRAGE n drawing of wine from a barrel prior to bottling

TIRAGES > TIRAGE

TIRAMISU n Italian coffee-flavoured dessert

TIRAMISUS > TIRAMISU

TIRASSE n mechanism in an organ connecting two pedals

TIRASSES > TIRASSE

TIRE vb reduce the energy of, as by exertion

TIRED adj exhausted

TIREDER > TIRED

TIREDEST > TIRED

TIREDLY > TIRED

TIREDNESS > TIRED

TIRELESS adj energetic and determined

TIRELING n fatigued person or animal

TIRELINGS > TIRELING

TIREMAKER same as > TYREMAKER

TIRES > TIRE

TIRESOME adj boring and irritating

TIREWOMAN n an obsolete term for lady's maid

TIREWOMEN > TIREWOMAN

TIRING > TIRE

TIRINGS > TIRE

TIRITI n another name for the Treaty of Waitangi

TIRITIS > TIRITI

TIRL vb turn

TIRLED > TIRL

TIRLING > TIRL

TIRLS > TIRL

TIRO same as > TYRO

TIROES > TIRO

TIRONIC variant of > TYRONIC

TIROS > TIRO

TIRR vb strip or denude

TIRRED > TIRR

TIRRING > TIRR

TIRRIT n panic; scare

TIRRITS > TIRRIT

TIRRIVEE n Scots word for an outburst of bad temper

TIRRIVEES > TIRRIVEE

TIRRIVIE same as > TIRRIVEE

TIRRIVIES > TIRRIVIE

TIRRS > TIRR

TIS > TI

TISANE n infusion of dried or fresh leaves or flowers

TISANES > TISANE

TISICK n splutter; cough

TISICKS > TISICK

TISSUAL adj relating to tissue

TISSUE n substance of an animal body or plant ▷ vb weave into tissue

TISSUED > TISSUE

TISSUES > TISSUE

TISSUEY adj like tissue

TISSUIER > TISSUEY

TISSUIEST > TISSUEY

TISSUING > TISSUE

TISSULAR adj relating to tissue

TISWAS n state of anxiety or excitement

TISWASES > TISWAS

TIT n any of various small songbirds ▷ vb jerk or tug

TITAN n person who is huge, strong, or very important

TITANATE n any salt or ester of titanic acid

TITANATES > TITANATE

TITANESS n woman who is huge, strong, or very important

TITANIA n titanium dioxide

TITANIAS > TITANIA

TITANIC adj huge or very important

TITANIS n large predatory flightless prehistoric bird

TITANISES > TITANIS

TITANISM n titanic power

TITANISMS > TITANISM

TITANITE another name for > SPHENE

TITANITES > TITANITE

TITANIUM n strong light metallic element used to make alloys

TITANIUMS > TITANIUM

TITANOUS adj of or containing titanium, esp in the trivalent state

TITANS > TITAN

TITBIT n tasty piece of food

TITBITS > TITBIT

TITCH n small person

TITCHES > TITCH

TITCHIE same as > TITCHY

TITCHIER > TITCHY

TITCHIEST > TITCHY

TITCHY adj very small

TITE adj immediate

TITELY adv immediately

TITER same as > TITRE

TITERS > TITER

TITFER n hat

TITFERS > TITFER

TITHABLE adj (until 1936) liable to pay tithes

TITHE n esp formerly, one tenth of one's income or produce paid to the church as a tax ▷ vb charge or pay a tithe

TITHED > TITHE

TITHER > TITHE

TITHERS > TITHE

TITHES > TITHE

TITHING > TITHE

TITHINGS > TITHING

TITHONIA n Central American herb with flowers resembling sunflowers

TITHONIAS > TITHONIA

TITI n small omnivorous monkey

TITIAN n reddish gold colour

TITIANS > TITIAN

TITILLATE vb excite or stimulate pleasurably

TITIS > TITI

TITIVATE vb smarten up

TITIVATED > TITIVATE

TITIVATES > TITIVATE

TITIVATOR > TITIVATE

TITLARK another name for > PIPIT

TITLARKS > TITLARK

TITLE n name of a book, film, etc ▷ vb give a title to

TITLED adj aristocratic

TITLELESS > TITLE

TITLER n one who writes titles

TITLERS > TITLER

TITLES > TITLE

TITLIKE adj like a tit

TITLING > TITLE

TITLINGS > TITLE

TITLIST n titleholder

TITLISTS > TITLIST

TITMAN n (of pigs) the runt of a litter

TITMEN > TITMAN

TITMICE > TITMOUSE

TITMOSE old spelling of > TITMOUSE

TITMOUSE n any small active songbird

TITOKI n New Zealand evergreen tree with a spreading crown and glossy green leaves

TITOKIS > TITOKI

TITRABLE > TITRATE

TITRANT n solution in a titration that is added to a measured quantity of another solution

TITRANTS > TITRANT

TITRATE vb measure the volume or concentration of (a solution) by titration

TITRATED > TITRATE

TITRATES > TITRATE

TITRATING > TITRATE

TITRATION n operation in which a measured amount of one solution is added to a known quantity of another solution until the reaction between the two is complete

TITRATOR n device used to perform titration

TITRATORS > TITRATOR

TITRE n concentration of a solution as determined by titration

TITRES > TITRE

TITS > TIT

TITTED > TIT

TITTER vb laugh in a suppressed way ▷ n suppressed laugh

TITTERED > TITTER

TITTERER > TITTER

TITTERERS > TITTER

TITTERING > TITTER

TITTERS > TITTER

TITTIE n dialect word for a sister or young woman

TITTIES > TITTIE

TITTING > TIT

TITTISH adj testy

TITTIVATE same as > TITIVATE

TITTLE n very small amount ▷ vb chatter; tattle

TITTLEBAT n child's name for the stickleback fish

TITTLED > TITTLE

TITTLES > TITTLE

TITTLING > TITTLE

TITTUP vb prance or frolic ▷ n caper

TITTUPED > TITTUP

TITTUPIER > TITTUPY

TITTUPING > TITTUP

TITTUPPED > TITTUP

TITTUPPY same as > TITTUPY

TITTUPS > TITTUP

TITTUPY adj sprightly; lively

TITTY same as > TITTIE

TITUBANCY n act of staggering

TITUBANT adj staggering

TITUBATE vb stagger

TITUBATED > TITUBATE

TITUBATES > TITUBATE

TITULAR adj in name only ▷ n bearer of a title

TITULARLY > TITULAR

TITULARS > TITULAR

TITULARY same as > TITULAR

TITULE same as > TITLE

TITULED > TITULE

TITULES > TITULE

TITULI > TITULUS

TITULING > TITULE

TITULUS n sign attached to the top of the cross during crucifixion

TITUP same as > TITTUP

TITUPED > TITTUP

TITUPIER > TITUPY

TITUPIEST > TITUPY

TITUPING > TITUP

TITUPPED > TITUP

TITUPPING > TITUP

TITUPS > TITUP

TITUPY same as > TITTUPY

TIVY same as > TANTIVY

TIX pl n tickets

TIYIN n monetary unit of Uzbekistan and Kyrgyzstan

TIYINS > TIYIN

TIYN same as > TIYIN

TIYNS > TIYN

TIZ n state of confusion

TIZES > TIZ

TIZWAS same as > TISWAS

TIZWASES > TIZWAS

TIZZ same as > TIZZY

TIZZES > TIZZ

TIZZIES > TIZZY

TIZZY n confused or agitated state

TJANTING n pen-like tool used in batik for applying molten wax to fabric

TJANTINGS > TJANTING

TMESES > TMESIS

TMESIS n interpolation of a word between the parts of a compound word

TO prep indicating movement towards, equality or comparison, etc ▷ adv a closed position

TOAD n animal like a large frog

TOADEATER rare word for > TOADY

TOADFISH n spiny-finned fish with a wide mouth

TOADFLAX n plant with narrow leaves and yellow-orange flowers

TOADGRASS another name for > TOADRUSH

TOADIED > TOADY

TOADIES > TOADY

TOADISH > TOAD

TOADLESS adj having no toads

TOADLET n small toad

TOADLETS > TOADLET

TOADLIKE > TOAD

TOADRUSH n annual rush growing in damp lowlands

TOADS > TOAD

TOADSTONE n amygdaloidal basalt occurring in the limestone regions of Derbyshire

TOADSTOOL n poisonous fungus like a mushroom

TOADY n ingratiating person ▷ vb be ingratiating

TOADYING n act of toadying

TOADYINGS > TOADYING

TOADYISH > TOADY

TOADYISM > TOADY

TOADYISMS > TOADY

TOAST n sliced bread browned by heat ▷ vb brown (bread) by heat

TOASTED > TOAST

TOASTER > TOAST

TOASTERS > TOAST

TOASTIE same as > TOASTY

TOASTIER > TOASTY

TOASTIES > TOASTY

TOASTIEST > TOASTY

TOASTING > TOAST

TOASTINGS > TOAST

TOASTS > TOAST

TOASTY n toasted sandwich ▷ adj tasting or smelling like toast

TOAZE variant spelling of > TOZE

TOAZED > TOAZE

TOAZES > TOAZE

TOAZING > TOAZE

TOBACCO n plant with large leaves dried for smoking

TOBACCOES > TOBACCO

TOBACCOS > TOBACCO

TOBIES > TOBY

TOBOGGAN n narrow sledge for sliding over snow ▷ vb ride a toboggan

TOBOGGANS > TOBOGGAN

TOBOGGIN variant spelling of > TOBOGGAN

TOBOGGINS > TOBOGGIN

TOBY n water stopcock at the boundary of a street and house section

TOC n in communications code, signal for letter t

TOCCATA n rapid piece of music for a keyboard instrument

TOCCATAS > TOCCATA

TOCCATE > TOCCATA

TOCCATINA n short toccata

TOCHER n dowry ▷ vb give a dowry to

TOCHERED > TOCHER

TOCHERING > TOCHER

TOCHERS > TOCHER

TOCK n sound made by a clock ▷ vb (of a clock) make such a sound

TOCKED > TOCK

TOCKIER > TOCKY

TOCKIEST > TOCKY

TOCKING > TOCK

TOCKLEY n slang word for a penis

TOCKLEYS > TOCKLEY

TOCKS > TOCK

TOCKY adj muddy

TOCO n punishment

TOCOLOGY n branch of medicine concerned with childbirth

TOCOS > TOCO

TOCS > TOC

TOCSIN n warning signal

TOCSINS > TOCSIN

TOD n unit of weight, used for wool, etc ▷ vb produce a tod

TODAY n this day ▷ adv on this day

TODAYS > TODAY

TODDE same as > TOD

TODDED > TOD

TODDES > TODDE

TODDIES > TODDY

TODDING > TOD

TODDLE vb walk with short unsteady steps ▷ n act or an instance of toddling

TODDLED > TODDLE

TODDLER n child beginning to walk

TODDLERS > TODDLER

TODDLES > TODDLE

TODDLING > TODDLE

TODDY n sweetened drink of spirits and hot water

TODGER n slang word for a penis

TODGERS > TODGER

TODIES > TODY

TODS > TOD

TODY n small bird of the Caribbean

TOE n digit of the foot ▷ vb touch or kick with the toe

TOEA n monetary unit of Papua New Guinea

TOEAS > TOEA

TOEBIE n South African slang for sandwich

TOEBIES > TOEBIE

TOECAP n strengthened covering for the toe of a shoe

TOECAPS > TOECAP

TOECLIP n clip on a bicycle pedal for the toes

TOECLIPS > TOECLIP

TOED > TOE

TOEHOLD n small space on a mountain for supporting the toe of the foot in climbing

TOEHOLDS > TOEHOLD

TOEIER > TOEY

TOEIEST > TOEY

TOEING > TOE

TOELESS adj not having toes

TOELIKE > TOE

TOENAIL n thin hard clear plate covering part of the upper surface of the end of each toe ▷ vb join (beams) by driving nails obliquely

TOENAILED > TOENAIL

TOENAILS > TOENAIL

TOEPIECE *n* part of a shoe that covers the toes

TOEPIECES > TOEPIECE

TOEPLATE *n* metal reinforcement of the part of the sole of a shoe or boot underneath the toes

TOEPLATES > TOEPLATE

TOERAG *n* contemptible person

TOERAGGER *same as* **> TOERAG**

TOERAGS > TOERAG

TOES > TOE

TOESHOE *n* ballet pump with padded toes

TOESHOES > TOESHOE

TOETOE *same as* **> TOITOI**

TOETOES > TOETOE

TOEY *adj* (of a person) nervous or anxious

TOFF *n* well-dressed or upper-class person

TOFFEE *n* chewy sweet made of boiled sugar

TOFFEES > TOFFEE

TOFFIER > TOFFY

TOFFIES > TOFFY

TOFFIEST > TOFFY

TOFFISH *adj* belonging to or characteristic of the upper class

TOFFS *adj* like a toff

TOFFY *same as* **> TOFFEE**

TOFORE *prep* before

TOFT *n* homestead

TOFTS > TOFT

TOFU *n* soft food made from soya-bean curd

TOFUS > TOFU

TOFUTTI *n* tradename for nondairy, soya-based food products

TOFUTTIS > TOFUTTI

TOG *n* unit for measuring the insulating power of duvets ▷ *vb* dress oneself

TOGA *n* garment worn by citizens of ancient Rome ▷ *vb* wear a toga

TOGAE > TOGA

TOGAED > TOGA

TOGAS > TOGA

TOGATE *adj* clad in a toga

TOGATED *same as* **> TOGATE**

TOGAVIRUS *n* one of family of viruses

TOGE *old variant of* **> TOGA**

TOGED > TOGE

TOGES > TOGE

TOGETHER *adv* in company ▷ *adj* organized

TOGGED > TOG

TOGGER *vb* play football ▷ *n* football player

TOGGERED > TOGGER

TOGGERIES > TOGGERY

TOGGERING > TOGGER

TOGGERS > TOGGER

TOGGERY *n* clothes

TOGGING > TOG

TOGGLE *n* small bar-shaped button inserted through a loop for fastening ▷ *vb* supply or fasten with a toggle or toggles

TOGGLED > TOGGLE

TOGGLER > TOGGLE

TOGGLERS > TOGGLE

TOGGLES > TOGGLE

TOGGLING > TOGGLE

TOGROG *n* unit of currency in Mongolia

TOGROGS > TOGROG

TOGS > TOG

TOGUE *n* large North American freshwater game fish

TOGUES > TOGUE

TOHEROA *n* large edible mollusc of New Zealand

TOHEROAS > TOHEROA

TOHO *n* (to a hunting dog) an instruction to stop

TOHOS > TOHO

TOHUNGA *n* Māori priest

TOHUNGAS > TOHUNGA

TOIL *n* hard work ▷ *vb* work hard

TOILE *n* transparent linen or cotton fabric

TOILED > TOIL

TOILER > TOIL

TOILERS > TOIL

TOILES > TOILE

TOILET *n* bowl connected to a drain for receiving and disposing of urine and faeces ▷ *vb* go to the toilet

TOILETED > TOILET

TOILETING *n* act of using a toilet

TOILETRY *n* object or cosmetic used to clean or groom oneself

TOILETS > TOILET

TOILETTE *same as* **> TOILET**

TOILETTES **> TOILETTE**

TOILFUL *same as* **> TOILSOME**

TOILFULLY > TOILFUL

TOILINET *n* type of fabric with a woollen weft and a cotton or silk warp

TOILINETS **> TOILINET**

TOILING > TOIL

TOILINGS > TOIL

TOILLESS > TOIL

TOILS > TOIL

TOILSOME *adj* requiring hard work

TOILWORN *adj* fatigued, wearied by work

TOING *n* as in *toing and froing* state of going back and forth

TOINGS > TOING

TOISE *n* obsolete French unit of length roughly equal to 2 metres

TOISEACH *n* ancient Celtic nobleman

TOISEACHS **> TOISEACH**

TOISECH *same as* **> TOISEACH**

TOISECHS > TOISECH

TOISES > TOISE

TOISON *n* fleece

TOISONS > TOISON

TOIT *vb* walk or move in an unsteady manner, as from old age

TOITED > TOIT

TOITING > TOIT

TOITOI *n* tall grasses with feathery fronds

TOITOIS > TOITOI

TOITS > TOIT

TOKAMAK *n* reactor used in thermonuclear experiments

TOKAMAKS > TOKAMAK

TOKAY *n* small gecko of S and SE Asia, having a retractile claw at the tip of each digit

TOKAYS > TOKAY

TOKE *n* draw on a cannabis cigarette ▷ *vb* take a draw on a cannabis cigarette

TOKED > TOKE

TOKEN *n* sign or symbol ▷ *adj* nominal or slight ▷ *vb* act as a symbol

TOKENED > TOKEN

TOKENING > TOKEN

TOKENISM *n* policy of making only a token effort, esp to comply with a law

TOKENISMS **> TOKENISM**

TOKENS > TOKEN

TOKER > TOKE

TOKERS > TOKE

TOKES > TOKE

TOKING > TOKE

TOKO *same as* **> TOCO**

TOKOLOGY *same as* **> TOCOLOGY**

TOKOLOSHE *n* (in African folklore) malevolent mythical animal of short stature

TOKOLOSHI *variant of* **> TOKOLOSHE**

TOKOMAK *variant spelling of* **> TOKAMAK**

TOKOMAKS > TOKOMAK

TOKONOMA *n* recess off a living room in a Japanese house

TOKONOMAS **> TOKONOMA**

TOKOS > TOKO

TOKOTOKO *n* ceremonial carved Māori walking stick

TOKOTOKOS **> TOKOTOKO**

TOKTOKKIE *n* large South African beetle

TOLA *n* unit of weight, used in India

TOLAN *n* white crystalline derivative of acetylene

TOLANE *same as* **> TOLAN**

TOLANES > TOLANE

TOLANS > TOLAN

TOLAR *n* former monetary unit of Slovenia

TOLARJEV > TOLAR

TOLARJI > TOLAR

TOLARS > TOLAR

TOLAS > TOLA

TOLBOOTH *same as* **> TOLLBOOTH**

TOLBOOTHS **> TOLBOOTH**

TOLD > TELL

TOLE *same as* **> TOLL**

TOLED > TOLE

TOLEDO *n* type of sword originally made in Toledo

TOLEDOS > TOLEDO

TOLERABLE *adj* bearable

TOLERABLY **> TOLERABLE**

TOLERANCE *n* acceptance of other people's rights to their own opinions or actions

TOLERANT *adj* able to tolerate the beliefs, actions, opinions, etc, of others

TOLERATE *vb* allow to exist or happen

TOLERATED **> TOLERATE**

TOLERATES **> TOLERATE**

TOLERATOR **> TOLERATE**

TOLES > TOLE

TOLEWARE *n* enamelled or lacquered metalware, usually gilded

TOLEWARES **> TOLEWARE**

TOLIDIN *same as* **> TOLIDINE**

TOLIDINE *n* compound used in dyeing and chemical analysis

TOLIDINES **> TOLIDINE**

TOLIDINS > TOLIDIN

TOLING > TOLE

TOLINGS > TOLE

TOLL *vb* ring (a bell) slowly and regularly ▷ *n* instance of tolling

TOLLABLE > TOLL

TOLLAGE *same as* **> TOLL**

TOLLAGES > TOLLAGE

TOLLBAR *n* bar blocking passage of a thoroughfare, raised on payment of a toll

TOLLBARS > TOLLBAR

TOLLBOOTH *n* booth or kiosk at which a toll is collected

TOLLDISH *n* dish used to measure out the portion of grain given to a miller as payment for their work

TOLLED > TOLL

TOLLER > TOLL

TOLLERS > TOLLER

TOLLEY *n* large shooting marble used in a game of marbles

TOLLEYS > TOLLEY

TOLLGATE *n* gate across a toll road or bridge at which travellers must pay

TOLLGATED **> TOLLGATE**

TOLLGATES
> TOLLGATE
TOLLHOUSE n small house at a tollgate occupied by a toll collector
TOLLIE same as > TOLLY
TOLLIES > TOLLY
TOLLING > TOLL
TOLLINGS > TOLL
TOLLMAN n man who collects tolls
TOLLMEN > TOLLMAN
TOLLS > TOLL
TOLLWAY n road on which users must pay tolls to travel
TOLLWAYS > TOLLWAY
TOLLY n castrated calf
TOLSEL n tolbooth
TOLSELS > TOLSEL
TOLSEY n tolbooth
TOLSEYS > TOLSEY
TOLT n type of obsolete English writ
TOLTER vb struggle or move with difficulty, as in mud
TOLTERED > TOLTER
TOLTERING > TOLTER
TOLTERS > TOLTER
TOLTS > TOLT
TOLU n sweet-smelling balsam obtained from a South American tree
TOLUATE n any salt or ester of any of the three isomeric forms of toluic acid
TOLUATES > TOLUATE
TOLUENE n colourless volatile flammable liquid obtained from petroleum and coal tar
TOLUENES > TOLUENE
TOLUIC adj as in toluic acid white crystalline derivative of toluene
TOLUID n white crystalline derivative of glycocoll
TOLUIDE variant of > TOLUID
TOLUIDES > TOLUIDE
TOLUIDIDE n chemical deriving from toluene
TOLUIDIN n type of dye
TOLUIDINE n compound used in dye production
TOLUIDINS
> TOLUIDIN
TOLUIDS > TOLUID
TOLUOL another name for
> TOLUENE
TOLUOLE another name for
> TOLUENE
TOLUOLES > TOLUOLE
TOLUOLS > TOLUOL
TOLUS > TOLU
TOLUYL n any of three groups derived from a toluic acid
TOLUYLS > TOLUYL
TOLYL n type of monovalent radical
TOLYLS > TOLYL
TOLZEY n tolbooth
TOLZEYS > TOLZEY

TOM n male cat ▷ adj (of an animal) male ▷ vb prostitute oneself
TOMAHAWK n fighting axe of the Native Americans
TOMAHAWKS
> TOMAHAWK
TOMALLEY n fat from a lobster, eaten as a delicacy
TOMALLEYS
> TOMALLEY
TOMAN n gold coin formerly issued in Persia
TOMANS > TOMAN
TOMATILLO n Mexican plant bearing edible berries of the same name
TOMATO n red fruit used in salads and as a vegetable
TOMATOES > TOMATO
TOMATOEY adj tasting of tomato
TOMATOIER
> TOMATOEY
TOMB n grave ▷ vb place in a tomb
TOMBAC n any of various brittle alloys containing copper and zinc
TOMBACK variant spelling of > TOMBAC
TOMBACKS > TOMBACK
TOMBACS > TOMBAC
TOMBAK same as
> TOMBAC
TOMBAKS > TOMBAK
TOMBAL adj like or relating to a tomb
TOMBED > TOMB
TOMBIC adj of or relating to tombs
TOMBING > TOMB
TOMBLESS > TOMB
TOMBLIKE > TOMB
TOMBOC n weapon
TOMBOCS > TOMBOC
TOMBOLA n lottery with tickets drawn from a revolving drum
TOMBOLAS > TOMBOLA
TOMBOLO n narrow bar linking a small island with another island or the mainland
TOMBOLOS > TOMBOLO
TOMBOY n girl who acts or dresses in a traditionally boyish way
TOMBOYISH > TOMBOY
TOMBOYS > TOMBOY
TOMBS > TOMB
TOMBSTONE n gravestone
TOMCAT n male cat ▷ vb (of a man) to be promiscuous
TOMCATS > TOMCAT
TOMCATTED > TOMCAT
TOMCOD n small fish resembling the cod
TOMCODS > TOMCOD
TOME n large heavy book
TOMENTA > TOMENTUM
TOMENTOSE
> TOMENTUM
TOMENTOUS
> TOMENTUM

TOMENTUM n feltlike covering of downy hairs on leaves and other plant parts
TOMES > TOME
TOMFOOL n fool ▷ vb act the fool
TOMFOOLED > TOMFOOL
TOMFOOLS > TOMFOOL
TOMIA > TOMIUM
TOMIAL > TOMIUM
TOMIUM n sharp edge of a bird's beak
TOMMED > TOM
TOMMIED > TOMMY
TOMMIES > TOMMY
TOMMING > TOM
TOMMY n private in the British Army ▷ vb (formerly) to exploit workers by paying them in goods rather than in money
TOMMYCOD n type of cod
TOMMYCODS
> TOMMYCOD
TOMMYING > TOMMY
TOMMYROT n utter nonsense
TOMMYROTS
> TOMMYROT
TOMO n shaft formed by the action of water on limestone or volcanic rock
TOMOGRAM n X-ray photograph of a selected plane section of a solid object
TOMOGRAMS
> TOMOGRAM
TOMOGRAPH n device for making tomograms
TOMORROW n the day after today ▷ adv on the day after today
TOMORROWS
> TOMORROW
TOMOS > TOMO
TOMPION same as
> TAMPION
TOMPIONS > TOMPION
TOMPON same as
> TAMPON
TOMPONED > TOMPON
TOMPONING > TOMPON
TOMPONS > TOMPON
TOMPOT adj as in tompot blenny variety of blenny with tentacles over its eyes
TOMS > TOM
TOMTIT n small European bird that eats insects and seeds
TOMTITS > TOMTIT
TON n unit of weight
TONAL adj written in a key
TONALITE n igneous rock found in the Italian Alps
TONALITES
> TONALITE
TONALITIC adj relating to or consisting of tonalite
TONALITY n presence of a musical key in a composition
TONALLY > TONAL

TONANT adj very loud
TONDI > TONDO
TONDINI > TONDINO
TONDINO n small tondo
TONDINOS > TONDINO
TONDO n circular easel painting or relief carving
TONDOS > TONDO
TONE n sound with reference to its pitch, volume, etc ▷ vb harmonize (with)
TONEARM same as
> PICKUP
TONEARMS > TONEARM
TONED > TONE
TONELESS adj having no tone
TONEME n phoneme that is distinguished from another phoneme only by its tone
TONEMES > TONEME
TONEMIC > TONEME
TONEPAD n keypad used to transmit information
TONEPADS > TONEPAD
TONER n cosmetic applied to the skin to reduce oiliness
TONERS > TONER
TONES > TONE
TONETIC adj (of a language) distinguishing words by tone as well as by other sounds
TONETICS pl n area of linguistics concentrating on the use of tone to distinguish words semantically
TONETTE n small musical instrument resembling a recorder
TONETTES > TONETTE
TONEY variant spelling of
> TONY
TONG vb gather or seize with tongs ▷ n (formerly) a Chinese secret society
TONGA n light two-wheeled vehicle used in rural areas of India
TONGAS > TONGA
TONGED > TONG
TONGER n one who uses tongs to gather oysters
TONGERS > TONGER
TONGING > TONG
TONGMAN another word for
> TONGER
TONGMEN > TONGMAN
TONGS pl n large pincers for grasping and lifting
TONGSTER n tong member
TONGSTERS
> TONGSTER
TONGUE n muscular organ in the mouth, used in speaking and tasting ▷ vb use the tongue
TONGUED > TONGUE
TONGUELET n small tongue
TONGUES > TONGUE
TONGUING > TONGUE
TONGUINGS > TONGUE

TONIC n medicine to improve body tone ▷ adj invigorating
TONICALLY > TONIC
TONICITY n state, condition, or quality of being tonic
TONICS > TONIC
TONIER > TONY
TONIES > TONY
TONIEST > TONY
TONIFIED > TONIFY
TONIFIES > TONIFY
TONIFY vb give tone to
TONIFYING > TONIFY
TONIGHT n the night or evening of this day ▷ adv in or during the night or evening of this day
TONIGHTS > TONIGHT
TONING > TONE
TONINGS > TONE
TONISH adj stylish or fashionable
TONISHLY > TONISH
TONITE n explosive used in quarrying
TONITES > TONITE
TONK vb strike with a heavy blow
TONKA n as in tonka bean tall leguminous tree of tropical America
TONKED > TONK
TONKER > TONK
TONKERS > TONK
TONKING > TONK
TONKS > TONK
TONLET n skirt of a suit of armour, consisting of overlapping metal bands
TONLETS > TONLET
TONNAG n type of (usually tartan) shawl
TONNAGE n weight capacity of a ship
TONNAGES > TONNAGE
TONNAGS > TONNAG
TONNE same as > TON
TONNEAU n detachable cover to protect the rear part of an open car
TONNEAUS > TONNEAU
TONNEAUX > TONNEAU
TONNELL old spelling of > TUNNEL
TONNELLS > TONNELL
TONNER n something that weighs one ton
TONNERS > TONNER
TONNES > TONNE
TONNISH adj stylish or fashionable
TONNISHLY > TONNISH
TONOMETER n instrument for measuring the pitch of a sound, esp one consisting of a set of tuning forks
TONOMETRY > TONOMETER
TONOPLAST n membrane enclosing a vacuole in a plant cell
TONS > TON
TONSIL n small gland in the throat
TONSILAR > TONSIL

TONSILLAR > TONSIL
TONSILS > TONSIL
TONSOR n barber
TONSORIAL adj of a barber or their trade
TONSORS > TONSOR
TONSURE n shaving of all or the top of the head as a religious or monastic practice ▷ vb shave the head of
TONSURED > TONSURE
TONSURES > TONSURE
TONSURING > TONSURE
TONTINE n type of annuity scheme
TONTINER n subscriber to a tontine
TONTINERS > TONTINER
TONTINES > TONTINE
TONUS n normal tension of a muscle at rest
TONUSES > TONUS
TONY adj stylish or distinctive ▷ n stylish or distinctive person
TOO adv also, as well
TOOART variant spelling of > TUART
TOOARTS > TOOART
TOODLE vb tootle
TOODLED > TOODLE
TOODLES > TOODLE
TOODLING > TOODLE
TOOK > TAKE
TOOL n implement used by hand ▷ vb work on with a tool
TOOLBAG n bag for storing or carrying tools
TOOLBAGS > TOOLBAG
TOOLBAR n row or column of selectable buttons displayed on a computer screen
TOOLBARS > TOOLBAR
TOOLBOX n box for storing or carrying tools
TOOLBOXES > TOOLBOX
TOOLCASE n case for tools
TOOLCASES > TOOLCASE
TOOLCHEST n chest for tools
TOOLED > TOOL
TOOLER > TOOL
TOOLERS > TOOL
TOOLHEAD n adjustable attachment for a machine tool that holds the tool in position
TOOLHEADS > TOOLHEAD
TOOLHOUSE another word for > TOOLSHED
TOOLIE n adult who gatecrashes social events for school leavers
TOOLIES > TOOLIE
TOOLING n any decorative work done with a tool
TOOLINGS > TOOLING
TOOLKIT n set of tools designed to be used together or for a particular purpose

TOOLKITS > TOOLKIT
TOOLLESS adj having no tools
TOOLMAKER n person who makes tools
TOOLMAN n person who works with tools
TOOLMEN > TOOLMAN
TOOLPUSH n worker who directs the drilling on an oil rig
TOOLROOM n room, as in a machine shop, where tools are made or stored
TOOLROOMS > TOOLROOM
TOOLS > TOOL
TOOLSET n set of tools associated with a computer application
TOOLSETS > TOOLSET
TOOLSHED n small shed used for storing tools
TOOLSHEDS > TOOLSHED
TOOLTIP n temporary window containing information about a tool on a computer application
TOOLTIPS > TOOLTIP
TOOM vb empty (something) ▷ adj empty
TOOMED > TOOM
TOOMER > TOOM
TOOMEST > TOOM
TOOMING > TOOM
TOOMS > TOOM
TOON n large tree of East Asia and Australia
TOONIE n Canadian two-dollar coin
TOONIES > TOONIE
TOONS > TOON
TOORIE n tassel or bobble on a bonnet
TOORIES > TOORIE
TOOSHIE adj angry
TOOSHIER > TOOSHIE
TOOSHIEST > TOOSHIE
TOOT n short hooting sound ▷ vb (cause to) make such a sound
TOOTED > TOOT
TOOTER > TOOT
TOOTERS > TOOT
TOOTH n bonelike projection in the jaws of most vertebrates for biting and chewing
TOOTHACHE n pain in or near a tooth
TOOTHCOMB n comb with fine teeth set closely together
TOOTHED adj having a tooth or teeth
TOOTHFISH n as in Patagonian toothfish Chilean sea bass
TOOTHFUL n little (esp alcoholic) drink
TOOTHFULS > TOOTHFUL
TOOTHIER > TOOTHY
TOOTHIEST > TOOTHY
TOOTHILY > TOOTHY
TOOTHING > TOOTH
TOOTHINGS > TOOTH

TOOTHLESS > TOOTH
TOOTHLIKE > TOOTH
TOOTHPICK n small stick for removing scraps of food from between the teeth
TOOTHS > TOOTH
TOOTHSOME adj delicious or appetizing in appearance, flavour, or smell
TOOTHWASH n tooth-cleaning liquid
TOOTHWORT n parasitic plant
TOOTHY adj having or showing numerous, large, or prominent teeth
TOOTING > TOOT
TOOTLE vb hoot softly or repeatedly ▷ n soft hoot or series of hoots
TOOTLED > TOOTLE
TOOTLER > TOOTLE
TOOTLERS > TOOTLE
TOOTLES > TOOTLE
TOOTLING > TOOTLE
TOOTS Scots version of > TUT
TOOTSED > TOOTS
TOOTSES > TOOTS
TOOTSIE same as > TOOTSY
TOOTSIES > TOOTSY
TOOTSING > TOOTS
TOOTSY n (in US English) darling or sweetheart
TOP n highest point or part ▷ adj at or of the top ▷ vb form a top on
TOPALGIA n pain restricted to a particular spot: a neurotic or hysterical symptom
TOPALGIAS > TOPALGIA
TOPARCH n ruler of a small state or realm
TOPARCHS > TOPARCH
TOPARCHY > TOPARCH
TOPAZ n semiprecious stone in various colours
TOPAZES > TOPAZ
TOPAZINE adj like topaz
TOPCOAT n overcoat
TOPCOATS > TOPCOAT
TOPCROSS n class of hybrid
TOPE vb drink alcohol regularly ▷ n small European shark
TOPECTOMY n (formerly) the surgical removal of part of the cerebral cortex to relieve certain psychiatric disorders
TOPED > TOPE
TOPEE n lightweight hat worn in tropical countries
TOPEES > TOPEE
TOPEK same as > TUPIK
TOPEKS > TOPEK
TOPER > TOPE
TOPERS > TOPE
TOPES > TOPE
TOPFLIGHT adj superior or excellent quality; outstanding

TOPFUL *variant spelling of* > TOPFULL

TOPFULL *adj* full to the top

TOPH *n* variety of sandstone

TOPHE *variant spelling of* > TOPH

TOPHES > TOPHE

TOPHI > TOPHUS

TOPHS > TOPH

TOPHUS *n* deposit of sodium urate in the helix of the ear or surrounding a joint

TOPI *same as* > TOPEE

TOPIARIAN > TOPIARY

TOPIARIES > TOPIARY

TOPIARIST > TOPIARY

TOPIARY *n* art of trimming trees and bushes into decorative shapes ▷ *adj* of or relating to topiary

TOPIC *n* subject of a conversation, book, etc

TOPICAL *adj* relating to current events ▷ *n* type of anaesthetic

TOPICALLY > TOPICAL

TOPICALS > TOPICAL

TOPICS > TOPIC

TOPING > TOPE

TOPIS > TOPI

TOPKICK *n* (formerly) sergeant

TOPKICKS > TOPKICK

TOPKNOT *n* crest, tuft, decorative bow, etc, on the top of the head

TOPKNOTS > TOPKNOT

TOPLESS *adj* having no top

TOPLINE *vb* headline; be the main focus of a newspaper story

TOPLINED > TOPLINE

TOPLINER > TOPLINE

TOPLINERS > TOPLINE

TOPLINES > TOPLINE

TOPLINING > TOPLINE

TOPLOFTY *adj* haughty or pretentious

TOPMAKER *n* wool dealer

TOPMAKERS > TOPMAKER

TOPMAKING > TOPMAKER

TOPMAN *n* sailor positioned in the rigging of the topsail

TOPMAST *n* mast next above a lower mast on a sailing vessel

TOPMASTS > TOPMAST

TOPMEN > TOPMAN

TOPMINNOW *n* small American freshwater cyprinodont fish

TOPMOST *adj* highest or best

TOPNOTCH *adj* excellent

TOPO *n* picture of a mountain with details of climbing routes superimposed on it

TOPOGRAPH *n* type of X-ray photograph

TOPOI > TOPOS

TOPOLOGIC > TOPOLOGY

TOPOLOGY *n* geometry of the properties of a shape which are unaffected by continuous distortion

TOPOMETRY *n* measurement of the surface features of a region

TOPONYM *n* name of a place

TOPONYMAL > TOPONYMY

TOPONYMIC > TOPONYMY

TOPONYMS > TOPONYM

TOPONYMY *n* study of place names

TOPOS *n* basic theme or concept

TOPOTYPE *n* specimen plant or animal taken from an area regarded as the typical habitat

TOPOTYPES > TOPOTYPE

TOPPED > TOP

TOPPER *n* top hat

TOPPERS > TOPPER

TOPPIER > TOPPY

TOPPIEST > TOPPY

TOPPING > TOP

TOPPINGLY > TOP

TOPPINGS > TOP

TOPPLE *vb* (cause to) fall over

TOPPLED > TOPPLE

TOPPLES > TOPPLE

TOPPLING > TOPPLE

TOPPY *adj* (of audio reproduction) having too many high-frequency sounds

TOPRAIL *n* top rail on something such as a piece of furniture

TOPRAILS > TOPRAIL

TOPS > TOP

TOPSAIL *n* square sail carried on a yard set on a topmast

TOPSAILS > TOPSAIL

TOPSCORE *vb* score the highest in a sports match or competition

TOPSCORED > TOPSCORE

TOPSCORES > TOPSCORE

TOPSIDE *n* lean cut of beef from the thigh

TOPSIDER *n* person in charge

TOPSIDERS > TOPSIDER

TOPSIDES > TOPSIDE

TOPSMAN *n* chief drover

TOPSMEN > TOPSMAN

TOPSOIL *n* surface layer of soil ▷ *vb* spread topsoil on (land)

TOPSOILED > TOPSOIL

TOPSOILS > TOPSOIL

TOPSPIN *n* spin imparted to make a ball bounce or travel exceptionally far, high, or quickly

TOPSPINS > TOPSPIN

TOPSTITCH *vb* stitch a line along the outside of a garment

TOPSTONE *n* stone forming the top of something

TOPSTONES > TOPSTONE

TOPWATER *adj* floating on the top of the water

TOPWORK *vb* graft shoots or twigs onto the main branches of (a tree)

TOPWORKED > TOPWORK

TOPWORKS > TOPWORK

TOQUE *same as* > TUQUE

TOQUES > TOQUE

TOQUET *same as* > TOQUE

TOQUETS > TOQUET

TOQUILLA *another name for* > JIPIJAPA

TOQUILLAS > TOQUILLA

TOR *n* high rocky hill

TORA *variant spelling of* > TORAH

TORAH *n* whole body of traditional Jewish teaching

TORAHS > TORAH

TORAN *n* (in Indian architecture) an archway

TORANA *same as* > TORAN

TORANAS > TORANA

TORANS > TORAN

TORAS > TORA

TORBANITE *n* type of oil shale

TORC *same as* > TORQUE

TORCH *n* small portable battery-powered lamp ▷ *vb* deliberately set (a building) on fire

TORCHABLE > TORCH

TORCHED > TORCH

TORCHER > TORCH

TORCHERE *n* tall narrow stand for holding a candelabrum

TORCHERES > TORCHERE

TORCHERS > TORCH

TORCHES > TORCH

TORCHIER *n* standing lamp with a bowl for casting light upwards

TORCHIERE *same as* > TORCHIER

TORCHIERS > TORCHIER

TORCHIEST > TORCHY

TORCHING > TORCH

TORCHINGS > TORCH

TORCHLIKE > TORCH

TORCHLIT *adj* lit by torches

TORCHON *n* coarse linen or cotton lace with a simple openwork pattern

TORCHONS > TORCHON

TORCHWOOD *n* rutaceous tree or shrub of Florida and the Caribbean, with hard resinous wood used for torches

TORCHY *adj* sentimental; maudlin; characteristic of a torch song

TORCS > TORC

TORCULAR *n* tourniquet

TORCULARS > TORCULAR

TORDION *n* old triple-time dance for two people

TORDIONS > TORDION

TORE *same as* > TORUS

TOREADOR *n* bullfighter

TOREADORS > TOREADOR

TORERO *n* bullfighter, esp one on foot

TOREROS > TORERO

TORES > TORE

TOREUTIC > TOREUTICS

TOREUTICS *n* art of making detailed ornamental reliefs, esp in metal, by embossing and chasing

TORGOCH *n* type of char

TORGOCHS > TORGOCH

TORI > TORUS

TORIC *adj* of, relating to, or having the form of a torus

TORICS > TORIC

TORIES > TORY

TORII *n* gateway, esp one at the entrance to a Japanese Shinto temple

TORMENT *vb* cause (someone) great suffering ▷ *n* great suffering

TORMENTA > TORMENTUM

TORMENTED > TORMENT

TORMENTER *same as* > TORMENTOR

TORMENTIL *n* creeping plant with yellow four-petalled flowers

TORMENTOR *n* person or thing that torments

TORMENTS > TORMENT

TORMENTUM *n* type of Roman catapult

TORMINA *pl n* severe stomach pains

TORMINAL > TORMINA

TORMINOUS > TORMINA

TORN > TEAR

TORNADE *same as* > TORNADO

TORNADES > TORNADE

TORNADIC > TORNADO

TORNADO *n* violent whirlwind

TORNADOES > TORNADO

TORNADOS > TORNADO

TORNILLO *n* shrub found in Mexico and some southwestern states of the US

TORNILLOS > TORNILLO

TORO *n* bull

TOROID *n* surface generated by rotating a closed plane curve about a coplanar line that does not intersect it

TOROIDAL > TOROID

TOROIDS > TOROID

TOROS > TORO

t

TOROSE adj (of a cylindrical part) having irregular swellings

TOROSITY > TOROSE

TOROT > TORAH

TOROTH > TORAH

TOROUS same as > TOROSE

TORPEDO n self-propelled underwater missile ▷ vb attack or destroy with or as if with torpedoes

TORPEDOED > TORPEDO

TORPEDOER > TORPEDO

TORPEDOES > TORPEDO

TORPEDOS > TORPEDO

TORPEFIED > TORPEFY

TORPEFIES > TORPEFY

TORPEFY vb make torpid

TORPID adj sluggish and inactive

TORPIDITY > TORPID

TORPIDLY > TORPID

TORPIDS pl n series of boat races held at Oxford University

TORPITUDE another word for > TORPOR

TORPOR n torpid state

TORPORS > TORPOR

TORQUATE > TORQUES

TORQUATED > TORQUES

TORQUE n force causing rotation ▷ vb apply torque to (something)

TORQUED > TORQUE

TORQUER > TORQUE

TORQUERS > TORQUE

TORQUES n distinctive band of hair, feathers, skin, or colour around the neck of an animal

TORQUESES > TORQUES

TORQUEY adj providing torque

TORQUIER > TORQUEY

TORQUIEST > TORQUEY

TORQUING > TORQUE

TORR n unit of pressure

TORREFIED > TORREFY

TORREFIES > TORREFY

TORREFY vb dry (ores, etc) by subjection to intense heat

TORRENT n rushing stream ▷ adj like or relating to a torrent

TORRENTS > TORRENT

TORRET same as > TERRET

TORRETS > TORRET

TORRID adj very hot and dry

TORRIDER > TORRID

TORRIDEST > TORRID

TORRIDITY > TORRID

TORRIDLY > TORRID

TORRIFIED > TORRIFY

TORRIFIES > TORRIFY

TORRIFY same as > TORREFY

TORRS > TORR

TORS > TOR

TORSADE n ornamental twist or twisted cord, as on hats

TORSADES > TORSADE

TORSE same as > TORSO

TORSEL n wooden beam along the top of a wall

TORSELS > TORSEL

TORSES > TORSE

TORSI > TORSO

TORSION n twisting of a part by equal forces being applied at both ends but in opposite directions

TORSIONAL > TORSION

TORSIONS > TORSION

TORSIVE adj twisted

TORSK n fish with a single long dorsal fin

TORSKS > TORSK

TORSO n trunk of the human body

TORSOS > TORSO

TORT n civil wrong or injury for which damages may be claimed

TORTA n (in mining) a flat circular pile of silver ore

TORTAS > TORTA

TORTE n rich cake, originating in Austria

TORTELLI pl n type of stuffed pasta

TORTELLIS > TORTELLI

TORTEN > TORTE

TORTES > TORTE

TORTIE n tortoiseshell cat

TORTIES > TORTIE

TORTILE adj twisted or coiled

TORTILITY > TORTILE

TORTILLA n thin Mexican pancake

TORTILLAS > TORTILLA

TORTILLON another word for > STUMP

TORTIOUS adj having the nature of or involving a tort

TORTIVE adj twisted

TORTOISE n slow-moving land reptile with a dome-shaped shell

TORTOISES > TORTOISE

TORTONI n rich ice cream often flavoured with sherry

TORTONIS > TORTONI

TORTRICES > TORTRIX

TORTRICID n type of small moth of the family which includes the codling moth

TORTRIX n type of moth

TORTRIXES > TORTRIX

TORTS > TORT

TORTUOUS adj winding or twisting

TORTURE vb cause (someone) severe pain or mental anguish ▷ n severe physical or mental pain

TORTURED > TORTURE

TORTURER > TORTURE

TORTURERS > TORTURE

TORTURES > TORTURE

TORTURING > TORTURE

TORTUROUS > TORTURE

TORULA n any of various species of fungal microorganisms

TORULAE > TORULA

TORULAS > TORULA

TORULI > TORULUS

TORULIN n vitamin found in yeast

TORULINS > TORULIN

TORULOSE adj (of something cylindrical) alternately swollen and pinched along its length

TORULOSES > TORULOSIS

TORULOSIS n infection by one of the torula

TORULUS n socket in an insect's head in which its antenna is attached

TORUS n large convex moulding approximately semicircular in cross section

TORUSES > TORUS

TORY n conservative or reactionary person ▷ adj conservative or reactionary

TOSA n large reddish dog, originally bred for fighting

TOSAS > TOSA

TOSE same as > TOZE

TOSED > TOSE

TOSES > TOSE

TOSH n nonsense ▷ vb tidy or trim

TOSHACH n military leader of a clan

TOSHACHS > TOSHACH

TOSHED > TOSH

TOSHER > TOSH

TOSHERS > TOSH

TOSHES > TOSH

TOSHIER > TOSHY

TOSHIEST > TOSHY

TOSHING > TOSH

TOSHY adj neat; trim

TOSING > TOSE

TOSS vb throw lightly ▷ n instance of tossing

TOSSED > TOSS

TOSSEN old past participle of > TOSS

TOSSER n slang for a stupid or despicable person

TOSSERS > TOSSER

TOSSES > TOSS

TOSSIER > TOSSY

TOSSIEST > TOSSY

TOSSILY > TOSSY

TOSSING > TOSS

TOSSINGS > TOSS

TOSSPOT n habitual drinker

TOSSPOTS > TOSSPOT

TOSSUP n instance of tossing up a coin

TOSSUPS > TOSSUP

TOSSY adj impudent

TOST old past participle of > TOSS

TOSTADA n crispy deep-fried tortilla topped with meat, cheese, and refried beans

TOSTADAS > TOSTADA

TOSTADO same as > TOSTADA

TOSTADOS > TOSTADO

TOSTONE n Mexican dish of fried plantains

TOSTONES > TOSTONE

TOT n small child ▷ vb total

TOTABLE > TOTE

TOTAL n whole, esp a sum of parts ▷ adj complete ▷ vb amount to

TOTALED > TOTAL

TOTALING > TOTAL

TOTALISE same as > TOTALIZE

TOTALISED > TOTALISE

TOTALISER > TOTALISE

TOTALISES > TOTALISE

TOTALISM n practice of a one-party state that regulates every area of life

TOTALISMS > TOTALISM

TOTALIST > TOTALISM

TOTALISTS > TOTALISM

TOTALITY n whole amount

TOTALIZE vb combine or make into a total

TOTALIZED > TOTALIZE

TOTALIZER > TOTALIZE

TOTALIZES > TOTALIZE

TOTALLED > TOTAL

TOTALLING > TOTAL

TOTALLY > TOTAL

TOTALS > TOTAL

TOTANUS another name for > REDSHANK

TOTANUSES > TOTANUS

TOTAQUINE n mixture of quinine and other alkaloids derived from cinchona bark, used as a substitute for quinine in treating malaria

TOTARA n tall coniferous forest tree of New Zealand

TOTARAS > TOTARA

TOTE vb carry (a gun etc) ▷ n act of or an instance of toting

TOTEABLE > TOTE

TOTED > TOTE

TOTEM n tribal badge or emblem

TOTEMIC > TOTEM

TOTEMISM n belief in kinship of groups or individuals having a common totem

TOTEMISMS > TOTEMISM

TOTEMIST > TOTEMISM

TOTEMISTS > TOTEMISM

TOTEMITE > TOTEMISM

TOTEMITES > TOTEMITE

TOTEMS > TOTEM

TOTER > TOTE

TOTERS > TOTE
TOTES > TOTE
TOTHER *n* other ▷ *adj* the other
TOTHERS > TOTHER
TOTIENT *n* quantity of numbers less than, and sharing no common factors with, a number
TOTIENTS > TOTIENT
TOTING > TOTE
TOTITIVE *n* number less than, and having no common factors with, a given number
TOTITIVES > TOTITIVE
TOTS > TOT
TOTTED > TOT
TOTTER *vb* move unsteadily ▷ *n* act or an instance of tottering
TOTTERED > TOTTER
TOTTERER > TOTTER
TOTTERERS > TOTTER
TOTTERIER > TOTTERY
TOTTERING > TOTTER
TOTTERS > TOTTER
TOTTERY *adj* tending to totter
TOTTIE *adj* very small
TOTTIER > TOTTY
TOTTIES > TOTTY
TOTTIEST > TOTTY
TOTTING > TOT
TOTTINGS > TOT
TOTTRING *adj* Shakespearian word meaning ragged
TOTTY *n* small child ▷ *adj* very small
TOUCAN *n* tropical American bird with a large bill
TOUCANET *n* type of small toucan
TOUCANETS > TOUCANET
TOUCANS > TOUCAN
TOUCH *vb* come into contact with ▷ *n* sense by which an object's qualities are perceived when they come into contact with part of the body ▷ *adj* of a non-contact version of a particular sport
TOUCHABLE > TOUCH
TOUCHABLY *adv* in a touchable manner
TOUCHBACK *n* play in which the ball is put down by a player behind their own goal line when the ball has been put across the goal line by an opponent
TOUCHDOWN *n* moment at which a landing aircraft or spacecraft comes into contact with the landing surface ▷ *vb* (of an aircraft or spacecraft) to land
TOUCHE *interj* acknowledgment of a remark or witty reply
TOUCHED *adj* emotionally moved
TOUCHER > TOUCH
TOUCHERS > TOUCH

TOUCHES > TOUCH
TOUCHHOLE *n* hole in the breech of early cannon and firearms through which the charge was ignited
TOUCHIER > TOUCHY
TOUCHIEST > TOUCHY
TOUCHILY > TOUCHY
TOUCHING *adj* emotionally moving ▷ *prep* relating to or concerning ▷ *n* instance of touching
TOUCHINGS > TOUCHING
TOUCHLESS > TOUCH
TOUCHLINE *n* sideline of the pitch in some games
TOUCHMARK *n* maker's mark stamped on pewter objects
TOUCHPAD *n* part of laptop computer functioning like a mouse
TOUCHPADS > TOUCHPAD
TOUCHTONE *adj* relating to a telephone dialling system in which each of the buttons pressed generates a tone of a different pitch
TOUCHUP *n* renovation or retouching, as of a painting
TOUCHUPS > TOUCHUP
TOUCHWOOD *n* something, esp dry wood, used as tinder
TOUCHY *adj* easily offended
TOUGH *adj* strong or resilient ▷ *n* rough violent person ▷ *vb* stand firm, hold out
TOUGHED > TOUGH
TOUGHEN *vb* make or become tough or tougher
TOUGHENED > TOUGHEN
TOUGHENER > TOUGHEN
TOUGHENS > TOUGHEN
TOUGHER > TOUGH
TOUGHEST > TOUGH
TOUGHIE *n* person who is tough
TOUGHIES > TOUGHIE
TOUGHING > TOUGH
TOUGHISH > TOUGH
TOUGHLY > TOUGH
TOUGHNESS *n* quality or an instance of being tough
TOUGHS > TOUGH
TOUGHY *same as* > TOUGHIE
TOUK *same as* > TUCK
TOUKED > TOUK
TOUKING > TOUK
TOUKS > TOUK
TOULADI *same as* > TULADI
TOULADIS > TOULADI
TOUN *n* Scots word for a town
TOUNS > TOUN
TOUPEE *n* small wig
TOUPEED *adj* wearing a toupee
TOUPEES > TOUPEE

TOUPET *same as* > TOUPEE
TOUPETS > TOUPET
TOUPIE *n* round boneless smoked ham
TOUPIES > TOUPIE
TOUR *n* journey visiting places of interest along the way ▷ *vb* make a tour (of)
TOURACO *n* brightly coloured crested arboreal African bird
TOURACOS > TOURACO
TOURED > TOUR
TOURER *n* large open car with a folding top
TOURERS > TOURER
TOURIE *same as* > TOORIE
TOURIES > TOURIE
TOURING > TOUR
TOURINGS > TOUR
TOURISM *n* tourist travel as an industry
TOURISMS > TOURISM
TOURIST *n* person travelling for pleasure ▷ *adj* of or relating to tourists or tourism
TOURISTA *variant of* > TOURIST
TOURISTAS > TOURISTA
TOURISTED *adj* busy with tourists
TOURISTIC > TOURIST
TOURISTS > TOURIST
TOURISTY *adj* informal term for full of tourists or tourist attractions
TOURNEDOS *n* thick round steak of beef
TOURNEY *n* knightly tournament ▷ *vb* engage in a tourney
TOURNEYED > TOURNEY
TOURNEYER > TOURNEY
TOURNEYS > TOURNEY
TOURNURE *n* outline or contour
TOURNURES > TOURNURE
TOURS > TOUR
TOURTIERE *n* type of meat pie
TOUSE *vb* tangle, ruffle, or disarrange; treat roughly
TOUSED > TOUSE
TOUSER > TOUSE
TOUSERS > TOUSE
TOUSES > TOUSE
TOUSIER > TOUSY
TOUSIEST > TOUSY
TOUSING > TOUSE
TOUSINGS > TOUSE
TOUSLE *vb* make (hair or clothes) ruffled and untidy ▷ *n* disorderly, tangled, or rumpled state
TOUSLED > TOUSLE
TOUSLES > TOUSLE
TOUSLING > TOUSLE
TOUSTIE *adj* irritable; testy
TOUSTIER > TOUSTIE
TOUSTIEST > TOUSTIE

TOUSY *adj* tousled
TOUT *vb* seek business in a persistent manner ▷ *n* person who sells tickets for a popular event at inflated prices
TOUTED > TOUT
TOUTER > TOUT
TOUTERS > TOUT
TOUTIE *adj* childishly irritable or sullen
TOUTIER > TOUTIE
TOUTIEST > TOUTIE
TOUTING > TOUT
TOUTON *n* deep-fried round of bread dough
TOUTONS > TOUTON
TOUTS > TOUT
TOUZE *variant spelling of* > TOUSE
TOUZED > TOUZE
TOUZES > TOUZE
TOUZIER > TOUZY
TOUZIEST > TOUZY
TOUZING > TOUZE
TOUZLE *rare spelling of* > TOUSLE
TOUZLED > TOUZLE
TOUZLES > TOUZLE
TOUZLING > TOUZLE
TOUZY *variant spelling of* > TOUSY
TOVARICH *same as* > TOVARISCH
TOVARISCH *n* comrade: a term of address
TOVARISH *same as* > TOVARISCH
TOW *vb* drag, esp by means of a rope ▷ *n* instance of towing
TOWABLE > TOW
TOWAGE *n* charge made for towing
TOWAGES > TOWAGE
TOWARD *same as* > TOWARDS
TOWARDLY *adj* compliant
TOWARDS *prep* in the direction of
TOWAWAY *n* vehicle which has been towed away
TOWAWAYS > TOWAWAY
TOWBAR *n* metal bar on a car for towing vehicles
TOWBARS > TOWBAR
TOWBOAT *n* another word for tug (the boat)
TOWBOATS > TOWBOAT
TOWED > TOW
TOWEL *n* cloth for drying things ▷ *vb* dry or wipe with a towel
TOWELED > TOWEL
TOWELETTE *n* paper towel
TOWELING *same as* > TOWELLING
TOWELINGS > TOWELLING
TOWELLED > TOWEL
TOWELLING *n* material used for making towels
TOWELS > TOWEL
TOWER *n* tall structure, often forming part of a larger building ▷ *vb* rise like a tower

t

TOWERED adj having a tower or towers

TOWERIER > TOWERY

TOWERIEST > TOWERY

TOWERING adj very tall or impressive

TOWERLESS adj not having a tower

TOWERLIKE adj like a tower

TOWERS > TOWER

TOWERY adj with towers

TOWHEAD n person with blond or yellowish hair

TOWHEADED adj having a blonde or yellowish hair

TOWHEADS > TOWHEAD

TOWHEE n N American brownish-coloured sparrow

TOWHEES > TOWHEE

TOWIE n truck used for towing

TOWIER > TOW

TOWIES > TOWIE

TOWIEST > TOW

TOWING > TOW

TOWINGS > TOW

TOWKAY n sir

TOWKAYS > TOWKAY

TOWLINE same as > TOWROPE

TOWLINES > TOWLINE

TOWMON same as > TOWMOND

TOWMOND n old word for year

TOWMONDS > TOWMOND

TOWMONS > TOWMON

TOWMONT same as > TOWMOND

TOWMONTS > TOWMONT

TOWN n group of buildings larger than a village

TOWNEE same as > TOWNIE

TOWNEES > TOWNEE

TOWNFOLK same as > TOWNSFOLK

TOWNHALL adj of a variety of the Asian plant moschatel

TOWNHOME another word for > TOWNHOUSE

TOWNHOMES > TOWNHOME

TOWNHOUSE n terraced house in an urban area, esp a fashionable one, often having the main living room on the first floor with an integral garage on the ground floor

TOWNIE n resident of a town

TOWNIER > TOWNY

TOWNIES > TOWNY

TOWNIEST > TOWNY

TOWNISH > TOWN

TOWNLAND n division of land of various sizes

TOWNLANDS > TOWNLAND

TOWNLESS > TOWN

TOWNLET n small town

TOWNLETS > TOWNLET

TOWNLIER > TOWNLY

TOWNLIEST > TOWNLY

TOWNLING n person who lives in a town

TOWNLINGS > TOWNLING

TOWNLY adj characteristic of a town

TOWNS > TOWN

TOWNSCAPE n view of an urban scene

TOWNSFOLK n people of a town

TOWNSHIP n small town

TOWNSHIPS > TOWNSHIP

TOWNSITE n site of a town

TOWNSITES > TOWNSITE

TOWNSKIP n old term for a mischievous and roguish child who frequents city streets

TOWNSKIPS > TOWNSKIP

TOWNSMAN n inhabitant of a town

TOWNSMEN > TOWNSMAN

TOWNWARD adv in the direction of a town

TOWNWEAR n clothes suitable for wearing while pursuing activities usually associated with towns

TOWNWEARS > TOWNWEAR

TOWNY adj characteristic of a town

TOWPATH n path beside a canal or river

TOWPATHS > TOWPATH

TOWPLANE n aeroplane that tows gliders

TOWPLANES > TOWPLANE

TOWROPE n rope or cable used for towing a vehicle or vessel

TOWROPES > TOWROPE

TOWS > TOW

TOWSACK n sack made from tow

TOWSACKS > TOWSACK

TOWSE same as > TOUSE

TOWSED > TOWSE

TOWSER > TOWSE

TOWSERS > TOWSE

TOWSES > TOWSE

TOWSIER > TOWSY

TOWSIEST > TOWSY

TOWSING > TOWSE

TOWSY same as > TOUSY

TOWT vb sulk

TOWTED > TOWT

TOWTING > TOWT

TOWTS > TOWT

TOWY > TOW

TOWZE same as > TOUSE

TOWZED > TOWZE

TOWZES > TOWZE

TOWZIER > TOWZY

TOWZIEST > TOWZY

TOWZING > TOWZE

TOWZY same as > TOUSY

TOXAEMIA n blood poisoning

TOXAEMIAS > TOXAEMIA

TOXAEMIC > TOXAEMIA

TOXAPHENE n amber waxy solid with a pleasant pine odour, consisting of chlorinated terpenes, esp chlorinated camphene: used as an insecticide

TOXEMIA same as > TOXAEMIA

TOXEMIAS > TOXEMIA

TOXEMIC > TOXAEMIA

TOXIC adj poisonous ▷ n toxic substance

TOXICAL adj toxic

TOXICALLY > TOXIC

TOXICANT n toxic substance ▷ adj poisonous

TOXICANTS > TOXICANT

TOXICITY n degree of strength of a poison

TOXICOSES > TOXICOSIS

TOXICOSIS n any disease or condition caused by poisoning

TOXICS > TOXIC

TOXIGENIC adj producing poison

TOXIN n poison of bacterial origin

TOXINE nonstandard variant spelling of > TOXIN

TOXINES > TOXINE

TOXINS > TOXIN

TOXOCARA n parasitic worm infesting the intestines of cats and dogs

TOXOCARAL adj relating to toxocara

TOXOCARAS > TOXOCARA

TOXOID n toxin that has been treated to reduce its toxicity

TOXOIDS > TOXOID

TOXOPHILY n archery

TOY n something designed to be played with ▷ adj designed to be played with ▷ vb play, fiddle, or flirt

TOYBOX n box for toys

TOYBOXES > TOYBOX

TOYCHEST n chest for toys

TOYCHESTS > TOYCHEST

TOYED > TOY

TOYER > TOY

TOYERS > TOY

TOYETIC adj (of a film or television franchise) able to generate revenue via spin-off toys

TOYING > TOY

TOYINGS > TOY

TOYISH adj resembling a toy

TOYISHLY > TOYISH

TOYLAND n toy industry

TOYLANDS > TOYLAND

TOYLESOME old spelling of > TOILSOME

TOYLESS > TOY

TOYLIKE > TOY

TOYLSOM old spelling of > TOILSOME

TOYMAN n man who sells toys

TOYMEN > TOYMAN

TOYO n Japanese straw-like material made out of rice paper and used to make hats

TOYON n shrub related to the rose

TOYONS > TOYON

TOYOS > TOYO

TOYS > TOY

TOYSHOP n shop selling toys

TOYSHOPS > TOYSHOP

TOYSOME adj playful

TOYTOWN adj having an unreal and picturesque appearance ▷ n place with an unreal and picturesque appearance

TOYTOWNS > TOYTOWN

TOYWOMAN n woman who sells toys

TOYWOMEN > TOYWOMAN

TOZE vb tease out; (of wool, etc) card

TOZED > TOZE

TOZES > TOZE

TOZIE n type of shawl

TOZIES > TOZIE

TOZING > TOZE

TRABEATE same as > TRABEATED

TRABEATED adj constructed with horizontal beams as opposed to arches

TRABECULA n any of various rod-shaped structures that divide organs into separate chambers

TRABS pl n training shoes

TRACE vb locate or work out (the cause of something) ▷ n track left by something

TRACEABLE > TRACE

TRACEABLY > TRACE

TRACED > TRACE

TRACELESS > TRACE

TRACER n projectile which leaves a visible trail

TRACERIED > TRACERY

TRACERIES > TRACERY

TRACERS > TRACER

TRACERY n pattern of interlacing lines

TRACES > TRACE

TRACEUR n parkour participant

TRACEURS > TRACEUR

TRACHEA n windpipe

TRACHEAE > TRACHEA

TRACHEAL > TRACHEA

TRACHEARY adj using tracheae to breathe

TRACHEAS > TRACHEA

TRACHEATE > TRACHEA

TRACHEID n element of xylem tissue

TRACHEIDE same as > TRACHEID

TRACHEIDS > TRACHEID

TRACHEOLE n small trachea found in some insects

TRACHINUS n weever fish

TRACHITIS n another spelling of tracheitis (inflammation of the trachea)

TRACHLE vb Scots word meaning make (hair, clothing, etc) untidy

TRACHLED > TRACHLE

TRACHLES > TRACHLE

TRACHLING > TRACHLE

TRACHOMA n chronic contagious disease of the eye

TRACHOMAS > TRACHOMA

TRACHYTE n light-coloured fine-grained volcanic rock

TRACHYTES > TRACHYTE

TRACHYTIC adj (of the texture of certain igneous rocks) characterized by a parallel arrangement of crystals

TRACING n traced copy

TRACINGS > TRACING

TRACK n rough road or path ▷ vb follow the trail or path of

TRACKABLE > TRACK

TRACKAGE n collective term for railway tracks

TRACKAGES > TRACKAGE

TRACKBALL n device consisting of a small ball, mounted in a cup, which can be rotated to move the cursor around the screen

TRACKBED n foundation on which railway tracks are laid

TRACKBEDS > TRACKBED

TRACKED > TRACK

TRACKER > TRACK

TRACKERS > TRACK

TRACKIE adj resembling or forming part of a tracksuit

TRACKIES pl n loose-fitting trousers with elasticated cuffs

TRACKING n act or process of following something or someone

TRACKINGS > TRACKING

TRACKLESS adj having or leaving no trace or trail

TRACKMAN n labourer who lays and maintains railway track

TRACKMEN > TRACKMAN

TRACKPAD same as > TOUCHPAD

TRACKPADS > TRACKPAD

TRACKROAD another word for > TOWPATH

TRACKS > TRACK

TRACKSIDE n area alongside a track

TRACKSUIT n warm loose-fitting suit worn by athletes etc, esp during training

TRACKWAY n path or track

TRACKWAYS > TRACKWAY

TRACT n wide area ▷ vb track

TRACTABLE adj easy to manage or control

TRACTABLY > TRACTABLE

TRACTATE n short tract

TRACTATES > TRACTATE

TRACTATOR n person who writes tracts

TRACTED > TRACT

TRACTILE adj capable of being drawn out

TRACTING > TRACT

TRACTION n pulling, esp by engine power

TRACTIONS > TRACTION

TRACTIVE > TRACTION

TRACTOR n motor vehicle with large rear wheels for pulling farm machinery

TRACTORS > TRACTOR

TRACTRIX n (in geometry) type of curve

TRACTS > TRACT

TRACTUS n anthem sung in some RC masses

TRACTUSES > TRACTUS

TRAD n traditional jazz, as revived in the 1950s

TRADABLE > TRADE

TRADE n buying, selling, or exchange of goods ▷ vb buy and sell ▷ adj intended for or available only to people in industry or business

TRADEABLE > TRADE

TRADED > TRADE

TRADEFUL adj (of shops, for example) full of trade

TRADELESS > TRADE

TRADEMARK n (legally registered) name or symbol used by a firm to distinguish its goods ▷ vb label with a trademark

TRADENAME n name used by a trade to refer to a commodity, service, etc

TRADEOFF n exchange, esp as a compromise

TRADEOFFS > TRADEOFF

TRADER n person who engages in trade

TRADERS > TRADER

TRADES > TRADE

TRADESMAN n skilled worker

TRADESMEN > TRADESMAN

TRADIE n tradesperson

TRADIES > TRADIE

TRADING > TRADE

TRADINGS > TRADE

TRADITION n handing down of customs and beliefs through generations

TRADITIVE adj traditional

TRADITOR n Christian who betrayed fellow Christians at the time of the Roman persecutions

TRADITORS > TRADITOR

TRADS > TRAD

TRADUCE vb slander

TRADUCED > TRADUCE

TRADUCER > TRADUCE

TRADUCERS > TRADUCE

TRADUCES > TRADUCE

TRADUCIAN > TRADUCE

TRADUCING > TRADUCE

TRAFFIC n vehicles coming and going on a road ▷ vb trade

TRAFFICKY adj (of a street, area, town, etc) busy with motor vehicles

TRAFFICS > TRAFFIC

TRAGAL > TRAGUS

TRAGEDIAN n person who acts in or writes tragedies

TRAGEDIES > TRAGEDY

TRAGEDY n shocking or sad event

TRAGELAPH n mythical animal: a cross between a goat and a stag

TRAGI > TRAGUS

TRAGIC adj of or like a tragedy ▷ n tragedian

TRAGICAL same as > TRAGIC

TRAGICS > TRAGIC

TRAGOPAN n pheasant of S and SE Asia

TRAGOPANS > TRAGOPAN

TRAGULE n mouse deer

TRAGULES > TRAGULE

TRAGULINE adj like or characteristic of a tragule

TRAGUS n fleshy projection that partially covers the entrance to the external ear

TRAHISON n treason

TRAHISONS > TRAHISON

TRAIK vb Scots word for trudge

TRAIKED > TRAIK

TRAIKING > TRAIK

TRAIKIT > TRAIK

TRAIKS > TRAIK

TRAIL n path, track, or road ▷ vb drag along the ground

TRAILABLE adj capable of being trailed

TRAILED > TRAIL

TRAILER n vehicle designed to be towed by another vehicle ▷ vb use a trailer to advertise (something)

TRAILERED > TRAILER

TRAILERS > TRAILER

TRAILHEAD n place where a trail begins

TRAILING adj (of a plant) having a long stem which spreads over the ground or hangs loosely

TRAILLESS adj without trail

TRAILS > TRAIL

TRAILSIDE adj beside a trail

TRAIN vb instruct in a skill ▷ n line of railway coaches or wagons drawn by an engine

TRAINABLE > TRAIN

TRAINBAND n company of English militia from the 16th to the 18th century

TRAINED > TRAIN

TRAINEE n person being trained ▷ adj (of a person) undergoing training

TRAINEES > TRAINEE

TRAINER n person who trains an athlete or sportsperson

TRAINERS pl n shoes in the style of those used for sports training

TRAINFUL n quantity of people or cargo that would be capable of filling a train

TRAINFULS > TRAINFUL

TRAINING n process of bringing a person to an agreed standard of proficiency by instruction

TRAININGS > TRAINING

TRAINLESS > TRAIN

TRAINLOAD n quantity of people or cargo sufficient to fill a train

TRAINMAN n man who works on a train

TRAINMEN > TRAINMAN

TRAINS > TRAIN

TRAINWAY n railway track; channel in a built-up area through which a train passes

TRAINWAYS > TRAINWAY

TRAIPSE vb walk wearily ▷ n long or tiring walk

TRAIPSED > TRAIPSE

TRAIPSES > TRAIPSE

TRAIPSING > TRAIPSE

TRAIT n characteristic feature

TRAITOR n person guilty of treason or treachery

TRAITORLY adj of or characteristic of a traitor

TRAITORS > TRAITOR

TRAITRESS > TRAITOR

TRAITS > TRAIT

TRAJECT vb transport or transmit

TRAJECTED > TRAJECT

TRAJECTS > TRAJECT

TRAM n electric public transport vehicle ▷ vb adjust (a mechanism) to a fine degree

TRAMCAR same as > TRAM

TRAMCARS > TRAMCAR

t

TRAMEL *vb* hinder or restrain

TRAMELED > TRAMEL

TRAMELING > TRAMEL

TRAMELL *old variant of* > TRAMMEL

TRAMELLED > TRAMEL

TRAMELLS > TRAMELL

TRAMELS > TRAMEL

TRAMLESS > TRAM

TRAMLINE *n* tracks on which a tram runs

TRAMLINED *adj* having tramlines

TRAMLINES > TRAMLINE

TRAMMED > TRAM

TRAMMEL *n* hindrance to free action or movement ▷ *vb* hinder or restrain

TRAMMELED > TRAMMEL

TRAMMELER > TRAMMEL

TRAMMELS > TRAMMEL

TRAMMIE *n* conductor or driver of a tram

TRAMMIES > TRAMMIE

TRAMMING > TRAM

TRAMP *vb* travel on foot, hike ▷ *n* homeless person who travels on foot

TRAMPED > TRAMP

TRAMPER *n* person who tramps

TRAMPERS > TRAMPER

TRAMPET *variant spelling of* > TRAMPETTE

TRAMPETS > TRAMPET

TRAMPETTE *n* small trampoline

TRAMPIER > TRAMPY

TRAMPIEST > TRAMPY

TRAMPING > TRAMP

TRAMPINGS > TRAMP

TRAMPISH > TRAMP

TRAMPLE *vb* tread on and crush ▷ *n* action or sound of trampling

TRAMPLED > TRAMPLE

TRAMPLER > TRAMPLE

TRAMPLERS > TRAMPLE

TRAMPLES > TRAMPLE

TRAMPLING > TRAMPLE

TRAMPOLIN *n* variant of trampoline: a tough canvass sheet suspended by springs from a frame, used by acrobats, gymnasts, etc

TRAMPS > TRAMP

TRAMPY *adj* like or characteristic of a tramp

TRAMROAD *same as* > TRAMWAY

TRAMROADS > TRAMROAD

TRAMS > TRAM

TRAMWAY *same as* > TRAMLINE

TRAMWAYS > TRAMWAY

TRANCE *n* unconscious or dazed state ▷ *vb* put into or as into a trance

TRANCED > TRANCE

TRANCEDLY > TRANCE

TRANCES > TRANCE

TRANCEY *adj* (of music) characteristic of the trance sub-genre

TRANCHE *n* portion of something large

TRANCHES > TRANCHE

TRANCHET *n* Stone Age cutting tool

TRANCHETS > TRANCHET

TRANCIER > TRANCEY

TRANCIEST > TRANCEY

TRANCING > TRANCE

TRANECT *n* ferry

TRANECTS > TRANECT

TRANGAM *n* bauble or trinket

TRANGAMS > TRANGAM

TRANGLE *n* (in heraldry) a small fesse

TRANGLES > TRANGLE

TRANK *n* tranquillizer ▷ *vb* administer a tranquillizer

TRANKED > TRANK

TRANKING > TRANK

TRANKS > TRANK

TRANKUM *same as* > TRANGAM

TRANKUMS > TRANKUM

TRANNIE *n* transistor radio

TRANNIES > TRANNIE

TRANNY *same as* > TRANNIE

TRANQ *same as* > TRANK

TRANQS > TRANQ

TRANQUIL *adj* calm and quiet

TRANS *n* short form of translation

TRANSACT *vb* conduct or negotiate (a business deal)

TRANSACTS > TRANSACT

TRANSAXLE *n* combined axle and gearbox

TRANSCEND *vb* rise above

TRANSCODE *vb* convert (digital computer data) from one format to another

TRANSDUCE *vb* change one form of energy to another

TRANSE *n* way through; passage

TRANSECT *n* sample strip of land used to monitor plant distribution and animal populations ▷ *vb* cut or divide crossways

TRANSECTS > TRANSECT

TRANSENNA *n* screen around a shrine

TRANSEPT *n* either of the two shorter wings of a cross-shaped church

TRANSEPTS > TRANSEPT

TRANSES > TRANSE

TRANSEUNT *adj* (of a mental act) causing effects outside the mind

TRANSFARD *old past participle of* > TRANSFER

TRANSFECT *vb* transfer genetic material isolated from a cell or virus into another cell

TRANSFER *vb* move or send from one person or place to another ▷ *n* instance of transferring

TRANSFERS > TRANSFER

TRANSFIX *vb* astound or stun

TRANSFIXT > TRANSFIX

TRANSFORM *vb* change the shape or character of ▷ *n* result of a mathematical transformation

TRANSFUSE *vb* give a transfusion to

TRANSGENE *n* gene that is transferred from an organism of one species to an organism of another species by genetic engineering

TRANSHIP *same as* > TRANSSHIP

TRANSHIPS > TRANSHIP

TRANSHUME *vb* (of livestock) move to suitable grazing grounds according to the season

TRANSIENT *same as* > TRANSEUNT

TRANSIRE *n* document allowing goods to pass through customs

TRANSIRES > TRANSIRE

TRANSIT *n* passage or conveyance of goods or people ▷ *vb* make a transit

TRANSITED > TRANSIT

TRANSITS > TRANSIT

TRANSLATE *vb* turn from one language into another

TRANSMAN *n* transgender man

TRANSMEN > TRANSMAN

TRANSMEW *old variant of* > TRANSMUTE

TRANSMEWS > TRANSMEW

TRANSMIT *vb* pass (something) from one person or place to another

TRANSMITS > TRANSMIT

TRANSMOVE *vb* change the form, character, or substance of

TRANSMUTE *vb* change the form or nature of

TRANSOM *n* horizontal bar across a window

TRANSOMED > TRANSOM

TRANSOMS > TRANSOM

TRANSONIC *adj* of or relating to conditions when travelling at or near the speed of sound

TRANSPIRE *vb* become known

TRANSPORT *vb* convey from one place to another ▷ *n* business or system of transporting

TRANSPOSE *vb* interchange two things ▷ *n* matrix resulting from

interchanging the rows and columns of a given matrix

TRANSSHIP *vb* transfer or be transferred from one ship or vehicle to another

TRANSUDE *vb* (of a fluid) ooze or pass through interstices, pores, or small holes

TRANSUDED > TRANSUDE

TRANSUDES > TRANSUDE

TRANSUME *vb* make an official transcription of

TRANSUMED > TRANSUME

TRANSUMES > TRANSUME

TRANSUMPT *n* official transcription

TRANSVEST *vb* wear clothes traditionally associated with the opposite sex

TRANT *vb* travel from place to place selling goods

TRANTED > TRANT

TRANTER > TRANT

TRANTERS > TRANT

TRANTING > TRANT

TRANTS > TRANT

TRAP *n* device for catching animals ▷ *vb* catch

TRAPAN *same as* > TREPAN

TRAPANNED > TRAPAN

TRAPANNER > TRAPAN

TRAPANS > TRAPAN

TRAPBALL *n* obsolete ball game

TRAPBALLS > TRAPBALL

TRAPDOOR *n* door in a floor or roof

TRAPDOORS > TRAPDOOR

TRAPE *same as* > TRAIPSE

TRAPED > TRAPE

TRAPES *same as* > TRAIPSE

TRAPESED > TRAPES

TRAPESES > TRAPES

TRAPESING > TRAPES

TRAPEZE *n* horizontal bar suspended from two ropes, used by circus acrobats ▷ *vb* swing on a trapeze

TRAPEZED > TRAPEZE

TRAPEZES > TRAPEZE

TRAPEZIA > TRAPEZIUM

TRAPEZIAL > TRAPEZIUM

TRAPEZII > TRAPEZIUS

TRAPEZING > TRAPEZE

TRAPEZIST *n* trapeze artist

TRAPEZIUM *n* quadrilateral figure

TRAPEZIUS *n* either of two flat triangular muscles, one covering each side of the back and shoulders, that rotate the shoulder blades

TRAPEZOID *n* quadrilateral figure

TRAPFALL *n* trapdoor that opens under the feet

TRAPFALLS > TRAPFALL

TRAPING > TRAPE

TRAPLIKE > TRAP

TRAPLINE *n* line of traps

TRAPLINES > TRAPLINE

TRAPNEST *n* nest that holds the eggs of a single hen

TRAPNESTS > TRAPNEST

TRAPPEAN *adj* of, relating to, or consisting of igneous rock, esp a basalt

TRAPPED > TRAP

TRAPPER *n* person who traps animals for their fur

TRAPPERS > TRAPPER

TRAPPIER > TRAPPY

TRAPPIEST > TRAPPY

TRAPPING > TRAP

TRAPPINGS *pl n* accessories that symbolize an office or position

TRAPPOSE *adj* of or relating to traprock

TRAPPOUS *same as* > TRAPPOSE

TRAPPY *adj* having many traps

TRAPROCK *n* igneous rock, esp a basalt

TRAPROCKS > TRAPROCK

TRAPS > TRAP

TRAPSE *vb* traipse

TRAPSED > TRAPSE

TRAPSES > TRAPSE

TRAPSING > TRAPSE

TRAPT *old past participle of* > TRAP

TRAPUNTO *n* type of quilting that is only partly padded in a design

TRAPUNTOS > TRAPUNTO

TRASH *n* anything worthless ▷ *vb* attack or destroy maliciously

TRASHCAN *n* dustbin

TRASHCANS > TRASHCAN

TRASHED > TRASH

TRASHER > TRASH

TRASHERS > TRASH

TRASHERY > TRASH

TRASHES > TRASH

TRASHIER > TRASHY

TRASHIEST > TRASHY

TRASHILY > TRASHY

TRASHING > TRASH

TRASHMAN *n* (in US English) binman

TRASHMEN > TRASHMAN

TRASHTRIE *n* trash

TRASHY *adj* cheap, worthless, or badly made

TRASS *n* variety of the volcanic rock tuff

TRASSES > TRASS

TRAT *n* type of fishing line holding a series of baited hooks

TRATS > TRAT

TRATT *short for* > TRATTORIA

TRATTORIA *n* Italian restaurant

TRATTORIE > TRATTORIA

TRATTS > TRATT

TRAUCHLE *vb* Scots word meaning walk or work slowly and wearily

TRAUCHLED *adj* Scots word meaning exhausted

TRAUCHLES > TRAUCHLE

TRAUMA *n* emotional shock

TRAUMAS > TRAUMA

TRAUMATA > TRAUMA

TRAUMATIC > TRAUMA

TRAVAIL *n* labour or toil ▷ *vb* suffer or labour painfully

TRAVAILED > TRAVAIL

TRAVAILS > TRAVAIL

TRAVE *n* stout wooden cage in which difficult horses are shod

TRAVEL *vb* go from one place to another, through an area, or for a specified distance ▷ *n* act of travelling, esp as a tourist

TRAVELED *same as* > TRAVELLED

TRAVELER *same as* > TRAVELLER

TRAVELERS > TRAVELER

TRAVELING > TRAVEL

TRAVELLED *adj* having experienced or undergone much travelling

TRAVELLER *n* person who makes a journey or travels a lot

TRAVELOG *n* film, lecture, or brochure on travel

TRAVELOGS > TRAVELOG

TRAVELS > TRAVEL

TRAVERSAL > TRAVERSE

TRAVERSE *vb* pass or go over

TRAVERSED > TRAVERSE

TRAVERSER > TRAVERSE

TRAVERSES > TRAVERSE

TRAVERTIN *n* porous rock

TRAVES > TRAVE

TRAVESTY *n* grotesque imitation or mockery ▷ *vb* make or be a travesty of

TRAVIS *same as* > TREVISS

TRAVISES > TRAVIS

TRAVOIS *n* sledge used for dragging logs

TRAVOISE *same as* > TRAVOIS

TRAVOISES > TRAVOISE

TRAWL *n* net dragged at deep levels behind a fishing boat ▷ *vb* fish with such a net

TRAWLED > TRAWL

TRAWLER *n* trawling boat

TRAWLERS > TRAWLER

TRAWLEY *same as* > TROLLEY

TRAWLEYS > TRAWLEY

TRAWLING > TRAWL

TRAWLINGS > TRAWL

TRAWLNET *n* large net used by trawlers

TRAWLNETS > TRAWLNET

TRAWLS > TRAWL

TRAY *n* flat board, usu with a rim, for carrying things

TRAYBAKE *n* flat cake which is baked in a tray and cut into small squares

TRAYBAKES > TRAYBAKE

TRAYBIT *n* threepenny bit

TRAYBITS > TRAYBIT

TRAYCLOTH *n* cloth for covering a tray

TRAYF *adj* not prepared according to Jewish law

TRAYFUL *n* as many or as much as will fit on a tray

TRAYFULS > TRAYFUL

TRAYNE *old spelling of* > TRAIN

TRAYNED > TRAYNE

TRAYNES > TRAYNE

TRAYNING > TRAYNE

TRAYS > TRAY

TRAZODONE *n* drug used to treat depression

TREACHER *n* traitor; treacherous person

TREACHERS > TREACHER

TREACHERY *n* wilful betrayal

TREACHOUR *same as* > TREACHER

TREACLE *n* thick dark syrup produced when sugar is refined ▷ *vb* add treacle to

TREACLED > TREACLE

TREACLES > TREACLE

TREACLIER > TREACLE

TREACLING > TREACLE

TREACLY > TREACLE

TREAD *vb* set one's foot on ▷ *n* way of walking or dancing

TREADED > TREAD

TREADER > TREAD

TREADERS > TREAD

TREADING > TREAD

TREADINGS > TREAD

TREADLE *n* lever worked by the foot to turn a wheel ▷ *vb* work (a machine) with a treadle

TREADLED > TREADLE

TREADLER > TREADLE

TREADLERS > TREADLE

TREADLES > TREADLE

TREADLESS *adj* (of a tyre) having no tread

TREADLING > TREADLE

TREADMILL *n* cylinder turned by treading on steps projecting from it

TREADS > TREAD

TREAGUE *n* agreement to stop fighting

TREAGUES > TREAGUE

TREASON *n* betrayal of one's sovereign or country

TREASONS > TREASON

TREASURE *n* collection of wealth, esp gold or jewels ▷ *vb* prize or cherish

TREASURED > TREASURE

TREASURER *n* official in charge of funds

TREASURES > TREASURE

TREASURY *n* storage place for treasure

TREAT *vb* deal with or regard in a certain manner ▷ *n* pleasure, entertainment, etc given or paid for by someone else

TREATABLE > TREAT

TREATED > TREAT

TREATER > TREAT

TREATERS > TREAT

TREATIES > TREATY

TREATING > TREAT

TREATINGS > TREAT

TREATISE *n* formal piece of writing on a particular subject

TREATISES > TREATISE

TREATMENT *n* medical care

TREATS > TREAT

TREATY *n* signed contract between states

TREBBIANO *n* grape used to make wine

TREBLE *adj* triple ▷ *n* (singer with or part for) a soprano voice ▷ *vb* increase three times

TREBLED > TREBLE

TREBLES > TREBLE

TREBLIER > TREBLY

TREBLIEST > TREBLY

TREBLING *n* act of trebling

TREBLINGS > TREBLING

TREBLY *adj* (of music) tinny

TREBUCHET *n* large medieval siege engine for hurling missiles consisting of a sling on a pivoted wooden arm set in motion by the fall of a weight

TREBUCKET *same as* > TREBUCHET

TRECENTO *n* 14th century, esp with reference to Italian art and literature

TRECENTOS > TRECENTO

TRECK *same as* > TREK

TRECKED > TRECK

TRECKING > TRECK

TRECKS > TRECK

TREDDLE variant spelling of > TREADLE

TREDDLED > TREDDLE

TREDDLES > TREDDLE

TREDDLING > TREDDLE

TREDILLE same as > TREDRILLE

TREDILLES > TREDRILLE

TREDRILLE n card game for three players

TREE n large perennial plant with a woody trunk ▷ vb drive or force up a tree

TREED > TREE

TREEHOUSE n house built in tree

TREEING > TREE

TREELAWN n narrow band of grass between a road and a pavement, usually planted with trees

TREELAWNS > TREELAWN

TREELESS > TREE

TREELIKE > TREE

TREELINE n line marking the altitude above which trees will not grow

TREELINES > TREELINE

TREEN adj made of wood ▷ n art of making treenware

TREENAIL n dowel used for pinning planks or timbers together

TREENAILS > TREENAIL

TREENS > TREEN

TREENWARE n dishes and other household utensils made of wood, as by pioneers in North America

TREES > TREE

TREESHIP n state of being a tree

TREESHIPS > TREESHIP

TREETOP n top of a tree

TREETOPS > TREETOP

TREEWARE n reading materials that are printed on paper as opposed to a digital format

TREEWARES > TREEWARE

TREEWAX n any wax secreted by a tree

TREEWAXES > TREEWAX

TREF adj in Judaism, ritually unfit to be eaten

TREFA same as > TREF

TREFAH same as > TREF

TREFOIL n plant with a three-lobed leaf

TREFOILED > TREFOIL

TREFOILS > TREFOIL

TREGETOUR n juggler

TREGGINGS pl n thick close-fitting leggings

TREHALA n edible sugary substance from the cocoon of an Asian weevil

TREHALAS > TREHALA

TREHALOSE n white crystalline disaccharide

that occurs in yeast and certain fungi

TREIF same as > TREF

TREIFA same as > TREF

TREILLAGE n latticework

TREILLE another word for > TRELLIS

TREILLES > TREILLE

TREK n long difficult journey, esp on foot ▷ vb make such a journey

TREKKED > TREK

TREKKER > TREK

TREKKERS > TREK

TREKKING n as in pony trekking the act of riding ponies cross-country

TREKKINGS > TREKKING

TREKS > TREK

TRELLIS n framework of horizontal and vertical strips of wood ▷ vb interweave (strips of wood, etc) to make a trellis

TRELLISED > TRELLIS

TRELLISES > TRELLIS

TREM n lever for producing a tremolo on a guitar

TREMA n mark placed over vowel to indicate it is to be pronounced separately

TREMAS > TREMA

TREMATIC adj relating to the gills

TREMATODE n parasitic flatworm

TREMATOID > TREMATODE

TREMBLANT adj (of jewels) set in such a way that they shake when the wearer moves

TREMBLE vb shake or quiver ▷ n instance of trembling

TREMBLED > TREMBLE

TREMBLER n device that vibrates to make or break an electrical circuit

TREMBLERS > TREMBLER

TREMBLES n disease of cattle and sheep

TREMBLIER > TREMBLE

TREMBLING > TREMBLE

TREMBLOR n earth tremor

TREMBLORS > TREMBLOR

TREMBLY > TREMBLE

TREMIE n metal hopper and pipe used to distribute freshly mixed concrete underwater

TREMIES > TREMIE

TREMOLANT another word for > TREMOLO

TREMOLITE n white or pale green mineral of the amphibole group consisting of calcium magnesium silicate

TREMOLO n quivering effect in singing or playing

TREMOLOS > TREMOLO

TREMOR n involuntary shaking ▷ vb tremble

TREMORED > TREMOR

TREMORING > TREMOR

TREMOROUS > TREMOR

TREMORS > TREMOR

TREMS > TREM

TREMULANT n device on an organ that produces a tremolo effect

TREMULATE vb produce a tremulous sound

TREMULOUS adj trembling, as from fear or excitement

TRENAIL same as > TREENAIL

TRENAILS > TRENAIL

TRENCH n long narrow ditch, esp one used as a shelter in war ▷ adj of or involving military trenches ▷ vb make a trench in (a place)

TRENCHAND old variant of > TRENCHANT

TRENCHANT adj incisive

TRENCHARD same as > TRENCHER

TRENCHED > TRENCH

TRENCHER n wooden plate for serving food

TRENCHERS > TRENCHER

TRENCHES > TRENCH

TRENCHING > TRENCH

TREND n general tendency or direction ▷ vb take a certain trend

TRENDED > TREND

TRENDIER > TRENDY

TRENDIES > TRENDY

TRENDIEST > TRENDY

TRENDIFY vb render fashionable

TRENDILY > TRENDY

TRENDING > TREND

TRENDOID n follower of trends

TRENDOIDS > TRENDOID

TRENDS > TREND

TRENDY n consciously fashionable person ▷ adj consciously fashionable

TRENDYISM > TRENDY

TRENISE n one of the figures in a quadrille

TRENISES > TRENISE

TRENTAL n mass said in remembrance of a person 30 days after his or her death

TRENTALS > TRENTAL

TREPAN same as > TREPHINE

TREPANG n any of various large sea cucumbers

TREPANGS > TREPANG

TREPANNED > TREPAN

TREPANNER > TREPAN

TREPANS > TREPAN

TREPHINE n surgical instrument for removing circular sections of bone ▷ vb remove a circular section of bone from

TREPHINED > TREPHINE

TREPHINER > TREPHINE

TREPHINES > TREPHINE

TREPID adj trembling

TREPIDANT adj trembling

TREPONEMA n anaerobic spirochaete bacterium that causes syphilis

TREPONEME same as > TREPONEMA

TRES adj very

TRESPASS vb go onto another's property without permission ▷ n act of trespassing

TRESS n lock of hair, esp a long lock of woman's hair ▷ vb arrange in tresses

TRESSED adj having a tress or tresses

TRESSEL variant spelling of > TRESTLE

TRESSELS > TRESSEL

TRESSES > TRESS

TRESSIER > TRESS

TRESSIEST > TRESS

TRESSING > TRESS

TRESSOUR same as > TRESSURE

TRESSOURS > TRESSOUR

TRESSURE n narrow inner border on a shield, usually decorated with fleurs-de-lys

TRESSURED > TRESSURE

TRESSURES > TRESSURE

TRESSY > TRESS

TREST old variant of > TRESTLE

TRESTLE n board fixed on pairs of spreading legs, used as a support

TRESTLES > TRESTLE

TRESTS > TREST

TRET n (formerly) allowance granted for waste due to transportation

TRETINOIN n retinoid drug used to treat certain skin conditions

TRETS > TRET

TREVALLY n any of various food and game fishes

TREVALLYS > TREVALLY

TREVET same as > TRIVET

TREVETS > TREVET

TREVIS variant spelling of > TREVISS

TREVISES > TREVIS

TREVISS n partition in a stable for keeping animals apart

TREVISSES > TREVISS

TREW old variant spelling of > TRUE

TREWS pl n close-fitting tartan trousers

TREWSMAN n Highlander
TREWSMEN > TREWSMAN
TREY n any card or dice throw with three spots
TREYBIT same as > TRAYBIT
TREYBITS > TREYBIT
TREYF adj not prepared according to Jewish law
TREYFA same as > TREYF
TREYS > TREY
TREZ same as > TREY
TREZES > TREZ
TRIABLE adj liable to be tried judicially
TRIAC n device for regulating the amount of electric current reaching a circuit
TRIACID adj (of a base) capable of reacting with three molecules of a monobasic acid
TRIACIDS > TRIACID
TRIACS > TRIAC
TRIACT adj having three rays ▷ n sponge spicule with three rays
TRIACTINE same as > TRIACT
TRIACTOR n type of bet
TRIACTORS > TRIACTOR
TRIACTS > TRIACT
TRIAD n group of three
TRIADIC adj characteristic of a triad n something that has the characteristics of a triad
TRIADICS > TRIADIC
TRIADISM > TRIAD
TRIADISMS > TRIAD
TRIADIST > TRIAD
TRIADISTS > TRIAD
TRIADS > TRIAD
TRIAGE n sorting emergency patients into categories of priority ▷ vb sort (patients) into categories of priority
TRIAGED > TRIAGE
TRIAGES > TRIAGE
TRIAGING > TRIAGE
TRIAL n investigation of a case before a judge ▷ vb test or try out
TRIALED > TRIAL
TRIALING > TRIAL
TRIALISM n belief that humans consist of body, soul, and spirit
TRIALISMS > TRIALISM
TRIALIST same as > TRIALLIST
TRIALISTS > TRIALLIST
TRIALITY > TRIALISM
TRIALLED > TRIAL
TRIALLING > TRIAL
TRIALLIST n person who takes part in a competition
TRIALOGUE n dialogue between three people
TRIALS > TRIAL
TRIALWARE n computer software that can be used without charge for a limited evaluation period

TRIANGLE n geometric figure with three sides
TRIANGLED > TRIANGLE
TRIANGLES > TRIANGLE
TRIAPSAL adj (of a church) having three apses
TRIARCH n one of three rulers of a triarchy
TRIARCHS > TRIARCH
TRIARCHY n government by three people
TRIASSIC adj of, denoting, or formed in the first period of the Mesozoic era
TRIATHLON n athletic contest in which each athlete competes in three different events: swimming, cycling, and running
TRIATIC n rope between a ship's mastheads
TRIATICS > TRIATIC
TRIATOMIC adj (of a molecule) having three atoms
TRIAXIAL adj having three axes ▷ n sponge spicule with three axes
TRIAXIALS > TRIAXIAL
TRIAXON another name for > TRIAXIAL
TRIAXONS > TRIAXON
TRIAZIN same as > TRIAZINE
TRIAZINE n any of three azines that contain three nitrogen atoms in their molecules
TRIAZINES > TRIAZINE
TRIAZINS > TRIAZIN
TRIAZOLE n heterocyclic compound
TRIAZOLES > TRIAZOLE
TRIAZOLIC > TRIAZOLE
TRIBADE n lesbian, esp one who practises tribadism
TRIBADES > TRIBADE
TRIBADIC > TRIBADE
TRIBADIES > TRIBADY
TRIBADISM n lesbian sexual activity
TRIBADY another word for > TRIBADISM
TRIBAL adj of or denoting a tribe or tribes ▷ n member of a tribal community
TRIBALISM n loyalty to a tribe
TRIBALIST > TRIBALISM
TRIBALLY > TRIBAL
TRIBALS > TRIBAL
TRIBASIC adj (of an acid) containing three replaceable hydrogen atoms in the molecule
TRIBBLE n frame for drying paper
TRIBBLES > TRIBBLE

TRIBE n group of clans or families believed to have a common ancestor
TRIBELESS > TRIBE
TRIBES > TRIBE
TRIBESMAN n man who is a member of a tribe
TRIBESMEN > TRIBESMAN
TRIBLET n spindle or mandrel used in making rings, tubes, etc
TRIBLETS > TRIBLET
TRIBOLOGY n study of friction, lubrication, and wear between moving surfaces
TRIBRACH n metrical foot of three short syllables
TRIBRACHS > TRIBRACH
TRIBULATE vb trouble
TRIBUNAL n board appointed to inquire into a specific matter
TRIBUNALS > TRIBUNAL
TRIBUNARY > TRIBUNE
TRIBUNATE n office or rank of a tribune
TRIBUNE n people's representative, esp in ancient Rome
TRIBUNES > TRIBUNE
TRIBUTARY n stream or river flowing into a larger one ▷ adj (of a stream or river) flowing into a larger one
TRIBUTE n sign of respect or admiration
TRIBUTER n miner
TRIBUTERS > TRIBUTER
TRIBUTES > TRIBUTE
TRICAR n car with three wheels
TRICARS > TRICAR
TRICE n moment ▷ vb haul up or secure
TRICED > TRICE
TRICEP same as > TRICEPS
TRICEPS n muscle at the back of the upper arm
TRICEPSES > TRICEPS
TRICERION n candlestick with three arms
TRICES > TRICE
TRICHINA n parasitic nematode worm
TRICHINAE > TRICHINA
TRICHINAL > TRICHINA
TRICHINAS > TRICHINA
TRICHITE n any of various needle-shaped crystals that occur in some glassy volcanic rocks
TRICHITES > TRICHITE
TRICHITIC > TRICHITE
TRICHOID adj resembling a hair

TRICHOME n any hairlike outgrowth from the surface of a plant
TRICHOMES > TRICHOME
TRICHOMIC > TRICHOME
TRICHORD n musical instrument with three strings
TRICHORDS > TRICHORD
TRICHOSES > TRICHOSIS
TRICHOSIS n any abnormal condition or disease of the hair
TRICHROIC n state of having three colours
TRICHROME adj three-coloured
TRICING > TRICE
TRICITIES > TRICITY
TRICITY n area that comprises three adjoining cities
TRICK n deceitful or cunning action or plan ▷ vb cheat or deceive
TRICKED > TRICK
TRICKER > TRICK
TRICKERS > TRICK
TRICKERY n practice or an instance of using tricks
TRICKIE Scots form of > TRICKY
TRICKIER > TRICKY
TRICKIEST > TRICKY
TRICKILY > TRICKY
TRICKING > TRICK
TRICKINGS > TRICK
TRICKISH same as > TRICKY
TRICKLE vb (cause to) flow in a thin stream or drops ▷ n gradual flow
TRICKLED > TRICKLE
TRICKLES > TRICKLE
TRICKLESS > TRICK
TRICKLET n tiny trickle
TRICKLETS > TRICKLET
TRICKLIER > TRICKLE
TRICKLING > TRICKLE
TRICKLY > TRICKLE
TRICKS > TRICK
TRICKSIER > TRICKSY
TRICKSILY > TRICKSY
TRICKSOME adj full of tricks
TRICKSTER n person who deceives or plays tricks
TRICKSY adj playing tricks habitually
TRICKY adj difficult, needing careful handling
TRICLAD n type of worm having a tripartite intestine
TRICLADS > TRICLAD
TRICLINIA n plural of triclinium: in Ancient Rome, reclining couch
TRICLINIC adj relating to or belonging to the crystal system characterized by three

t

unequal axes, no pair of which are perpendicular

TRICLOSAN n drug used to treat skin infections

TRICOLOR same as > TRICOLOUR

TRICOLORS > TRICOLOR

TRICOLOUR n three-coloured striped flag ▷ adj having or involving three colours

TRICORN n cocked hat with opposing brims turned back and caught in three places ▷ adj having three horns or corners

TRICORNE same as > TRICORN

TRICORNES > TRICORNE

TRICORNS > TRICORN

TRICOT n thin rayon or nylon fabric knitted or resembling knitting, used for dresses, etc

TRICOTINE n twill-weave woollen fabric resembling gabardine

TRICOTS > TRICOT

TRICROTIC adj (of the pulse) having a tracing characterized by three elevations with each beat

TRICTRAC n game similar to backgammon

TRICTRACS > TRICTRAC

TRICUSPID adj having three points, cusps, or segments ▷ n tooth having three cusps

TRICYCLE n three-wheeled cycle ▷ vb ride a tricycle

TRICYCLED > TRICYCLE

TRICYCLER > TRICYCLE

TRICYCLES > TRICYCLE

TRICYCLIC adj (of a chemical compound) containing three rings in the molecular structure ▷ n antidepressant drug having a tricyclic molecular structure

TRIDACNA n giant clam

TRIDACNAS > TRIDACNA

TRIDACTYL adj having three digits on one hand or foot

TRIDARN n sideboard with three levels

TRIDARNS > TRIDARN

TRIDE old spelling of the past tense of > TRY

TRIDENT n three-pronged spear ▷ adj having three prongs

TRIDENTAL adj having three prongs, teeth, etc

TRIDENTED adj having three prongs

TRIDENTS > TRIDENT

TRIDUAN adj three days long

TRIDUUM n period of three days for prayer before a feast

TRIDUUMS > TRIDUUM

TRIDYMITE n form of silica

TRIE old spelling of > TRY

TRIECIOUS adj (of a plant) having male, female, and hermaphroditic flowers

TRIED > TRY

TRIELLA n bet on the winners of three nominated horse races

TRIELLAS > TRIELLA

TRIENE n chemical compound containing three double bonds

TRIENES > TRIENE

TRIENNIA > TRIENNIUM

TRIENNIAL adj happening every three years ▷ n event occurring every three years

TRIENNIUM n period or cycle of three years

TRIENS n Byzantine gold coin worth one third of a solidus

TRIENTES > TRIENS

TRIER n person or thing that tries

TRIERARCH n citizen responsible for fitting out a state trireme, esp in Athens

TRIERS > TRIER

TRIES > TRY

TRIETERIC adj occurring once every two years

TRIETHYL adj consisting of three groups of ethyls

TRIFACIAL adj relating to the trigeminal nerve

TRIFECTA n form of betting in which the better selects the first three place-winners in a horse race in the correct order

TRIFECTAS > TRIFECTA

TRIFF adj terrific; very good indeed

TRIFFER > TRIFF

TRIFFEST > TRIFF

TRIFFIC adj terrific; very good indeed

TRIFFID n fictional plant that could kill humans

TRIFFIDS > TRIFFID

TRIFFIDY adj resembling a triffid

TRIFID adj divided or split into three parts or lobes

TRIFLE n insignificant thing or amount ▷ vb deal (with) as if worthless

TRIFLED > TRIFLE

TRIFLER > TRIFLE

TRIFLERS > TRIFLE

TRIFLES > TRIFLE

TRIFLING adj insignificant

TRIFLINGS > TRIFLE

TRIFOCAL adj having three focuses

TRIFOCALS pl n glasses that have trifocal lenses

TRIFOLD less common word for > TRIPLE

TRIFOLIA > TRIFOLIUM

TRIFOLIES > TRIFOLY

TRIFOLIUM n leguminous plant with leaves divided into three leaflets and dense heads of small white, yellow, red, or purple flowers

TRIFOLY same as > TREFOIL

TRIFORIA > TRIFORIUM

TRIFORIAL > TRIFORIUM

TRIFORIUM n arcade above the arches of the nave, choir, or transept of a church

TRIFORM adj having three parts

TRIFORMED same as > TRIFORM

TRIG adj neat or spruce ▷ vb make or become spruce

TRIGAMIES > TRIGAMY

TRIGAMIST > TRIGAMY

TRIGAMOUS > TRIGAMY

TRIGAMY n condition of having three spouses

TRIGEMINI pl n facial nerves

TRIGGED > TRIG

TRIGGER n small lever releasing a catch on a gun or machine ▷ vb set (an action or process) in motion

TRIGGERED > TRIGGER

TRIGGERS > TRIGGER

TRIGGEST > TRIG

TRIGGING > TRIG

TRIGLOT n person who can speak three languages

TRIGLOTS > TRIGLOT

TRIGLY > TRIG

TRIGLYPH n stone block in a Doric frieze, having three vertical channels

TRIGLYPHS > TRIGLYPH

TRIGNESS > TRIG

TRIGO n wheat field

TRIGON n (in classical Greece or Rome) a triangular harp or lyre

TRIGONAL adj triangular

TRIGONIC > TRIGON

TRIGONOUS adj (of stems, seeds, and similar parts) having a triangular cross section

TRIGONS > TRIGON

TRIGOS > TRIGO

TRIGRAM n three-letter inscription

TRIGRAMS > TRIGRAM

TRIGRAPH n combination of three letters used to represent a single speech sound

TRIGRAPHS > TRIGRAPH

TRIGS > TRIG

TRIGYNIAN adj relating to the Trigynia order of plants

TRIGYNOUS adj (of a plant) having three pistils

TRIHEDRA > TRIHEDRON

TRIHEDRAL adj having or formed by three plane faces meeting at a point ▷ n figure formed by the intersection of three lines in different planes

TRIHEDRON n figure determined by the intersection of three planes

TRIHYBRID n hybrid that differs from its parents in three genetic traits

TRIHYDRIC adj (of an alcohol or similar compound) containing three hydroxyl groups

TRIJET n jet with three engines

TRIJETS > TRIJET

TRIJUGATE adj in three pairs

TRIJUGOUS same as > TRIJUGATE

TRIKE n tricycle

TRIKES > TRIKE

TRILBIED adj wearing a trilby

TRILBIES > TRILBY

TRILBY n soft felt hat

TRILBYS > TRILBY

TRILD old past tense of > TRILL

TRILEMMA n quandary posed by three alternative courses of action

TRILEMMAS > TRILEMMA

TRILINEAR adj consisting of, bounded by, or relating to three lines

TRILITH same as > TRILITHON

TRILITHIC > TRILITHON

TRILITHON n structure consisting of two upright stones with a third placed across the top, such as those of Stonehenge

TRILITHS > TRILITH

TRILL n rapid alternation between two notes ▷ vb play or sing a trill

TRILLED > TRILL

TRILLER > TRILL

TRILLERS > TRILL

TRILLING > TRILL

TRILLINGS > TRILL

TRILLION n one million million ▷ adj amounting to a trillion

TRILLIONS > TRILLION

TRILLIUM n plant of Asia and North America

TRILLIUMS > TRILLIUM

TRILLO n (in music) a trill

TRILLOES > TRILLO

TRILLS > TRILL

TRILOBAL > TRILOBE

TRILOBATE adj (esp of a leaf) consisting of or having three lobes or parts

TRILOBE n three-lobed thing

TRILOBED adj having three lobes

TRILOBES > TRILOBE

TRILOBITE n small prehistoric sea animal

TRILOGIES > TRILOGY

TRILOGY n series of three related books, plays, etc

TRIM adj neat and smart ▷ vb cut or prune into good shape ▷ n decoration

TRIMARAN n three-hulled boat

TRIMARANS > TRIMARAN

TRIMER n polymer or a molecule of a polymer consisting of three identical monomers

TRIMERIC > TRIMER

TRIMERISM > TRIMER

TRIMEROUS adj (of plants) having parts arranged in groups of three

TRIMERS > TRIMER

TRIMESTER n period of three months

TRIMETER n verse line consisting of three metrical feet ▷ adj designating such a line

TRIMETERS > TRIMETER

TRIMETHYL adj having three methyl groups

TRIMETRIC adj of, relating to, or consisting of a trimeter or trimeters

TRIMIX n gas mixture of nitrogen, helium and oxygen used by deep-sea divers

TRIMIXES > TRIMIX

TRIMLY > TRIM

TRIMMED > TRIM

TRIMMER > TRIM

TRIMMERS > TRIM

TRIMMEST > TRIM

TRIMMING > TRIM

TRIMMINGS > TRIM

TRIMNESS > TRIM

TRIMORPH n substance, esp a mineral, that exists in three distinct forms

TRIMORPHS > TRIMORPH

TRIMOTOR n vehicle with three motors

TRIMOTORS > TRIMOTOR

TRIMPHONE n type of phone designed in the 1960s

TRIMPOT n small instrument for adjusting resistance or voltage

TRIMPOTS > TRIMPOT

TRIMS > TRIM

TRIMTAB n small control surface to enable the pilot to balance an aircraft

TRIMTABS > TRIMTAB

TRIN n triplet

TRINAL > TRINE

TRINARY adj made up of three parts

TRINDLE vb move heavily on (or as if on) wheels

TRINDLED > TRINDLE

TRINDLES > TRINDLE

TRINDLING > TRINDLE

TRINE n aspect of 120° between two planets, an orb of 8° being allowed ▷ adj of or relating to a trine ▷ vb put in a trine aspect

TRINED > TRINE

TRINES > TRINE

TRINGLE n slim rod

TRINGLES > TRINGLE

TRINING > TRINE

TRINITIES > TRINITY

TRINITRIN n pale yellow viscous explosive liquid substance made from glycerol and nitric and sulphuric acids

TRINITY n group of three

TRINKET n small or worthless ornament or piece of jewellery ▷ vb ornament with trinkets

TRINKETED > TRINKET

TRINKETER > TRINKET

TRINKETRY > TRINKET

TRINKETS > TRINKET

TRINKUM n trinket or bauble

TRINKUMS > TRINKUM

TRINODAL adj having three nodes

TRINOMIAL adj consisting of or relating to three terms ▷ n polynomial consisting of three terms

TRINS > TRIN

TRIO n group of three

TRIODE n electronic valve having three electrodes, a cathode, an anode, and a grid

TRIODES > TRIODE

TRIOL n any of a class of alcohols that have three hydroxyl groups per molecule

TRIOLEIN n naturally occurring glyceride of oleic acid, found in fats and oils

TRIOLEINS > TRIOLEIN

TRIOLET n verse form of eight lines

TRIOLETS > TRIOLET

TRIOLS > TRIOL

TRIONES pl n seven stars of the constellation Ursa Major

TRIONYM another name for > TRINOMIAL

TRIONYMAL > TRIONYM

TRIONYMS > TRIONYM

TRIOR old form of > TRIER

TRIORS > TRIOR

TRIOS > TRIO

TRIOSE n simple monosaccharide produced by the oxidation of glycerol

TRIOSES > TRIOSE

TRIOXID same as > TRIOXIDE

TRIOXIDE n any oxide that contains three oxygen atoms per molecule

TRIOXIDES > TRIOXIDE

TRIOXIDS > TRIOXID

TRIOXYGEN technical name for > OXYGEN

TRIP n journey to a place and back, esp for pleasure ▷ vb (cause to) stumble

TRIPACK n pack of three

TRIPACKS > TRIPACK

TRIPART adj composed of three parts

TRIPE n stomach of a cow used as food

TRIPEDAL adj having three feet

TRIPERIES > TRIPERY

TRIPERY n place where tripe is prepared

TRIPES > TRIPE

TRIPEY > TRIPE

TRIPHASE adj having three phases

TRIPHONE n group of three phonemes

TRIPHONES > TRIPHONE

TRIPIER > TRIPE

TRIPIEST > TRIPE

TRIPITAKA n three collections of books making up the Buddhist canon of scriptures

TRIPLANE n aeroplane having three wings arranged one above the other

TRIPLANES > TRIPLANE

TRIPLE adj having three parts ▷ vb increase three times ▷ n something that is, or contains, three times as much as normal

TRIPLED > TRIPLE

TRIPLES > TRIPLE

TRIPLET n one of three babies born at one birth

TRIPLETS > TRIPLET

TRIPLEX n building divided into three separate dwellings ▷ vb separate into three parts

TRIPLEXED > TRIPLEX

TRIPLEXES > TRIPLEX

TRIPLIED > TRIPLY

TRIPLIES > TRIPLY

TRIPLING > TRIPLE

TRIPLINGS > TRIPLE

TRIPLITE n brownish-red phosphate

TRIPLITES > TRIPLITE

TRIPLOID adj having or relating to three times the haploid number of chromosomes ▷ n triploid organism

TRIPLOIDS > TRIPLOID

TRIPLOIDY n triploid state

TRIPLY vb give a reply to a duply

TRIPLYING > TRIPLY

TRIPMAN n man working on a trip

TRIPMEN > TRIPMAN

TRIPMETER n vehicle instrument displaying the distance travelled on a trip

TRIPOD n three-legged stand, stool, etc

TRIPODAL > TRIPOD

TRIPODIC > TRIPOD

TRIPODIES > TRIPODY

TRIPODS > TRIPOD

TRIPODY n metrical unit consisting of three feet

TRIPOLI n lightweight porous siliceous rock

TRIPOLIS > TRIPOLI

TRIPOS n final examinations for an honours degree at Cambridge University

TRIPOSES > TRIPOS

TRIPPANT adj (in heraldry) in the process of tripping

TRIPPED > TRIP

TRIPPER n tourist

TRIPPERS > TRIPPER

TRIPPERY adj like a tripper

TRIPPET n any mechanism that strikes or is struck at regular intervals, as by a cam

TRIPPETS > TRIPPET

TRIPPIER > TRIPPY

TRIPPIEST > TRIPPY

TRIPPING > TRIP

TRIPPINGS > TRIP

TRIPPLE vb canter

TRIPPLED > TRIPPLE

TRIPPLER > TRIPPLE

TRIPPLERS > TRIPPLE

TRIPPLES > TRIPPLE

TRIPPLING > TRIPPLE

TRIPPY adj suggestive of or resembling the effect produced by a hallucinogenic drug

TRIPS > TRIP

TRIPSES > TRIPSIS

TRIPSIS n act of kneading the body to promote circulation, suppleness, etc

TRIPTAN n drug used to treat migraine

TRIPTANE n colourless highly flammable liquid

TRIPTANES > TRIPTANE

TRIPTANS > TRIPTAN

TRIPTOTE n word that has only three cases

TRIPTOTES > TRIPTOTE

TRIPTYCA variant of > TRIPTYCH

TRIPTYCAS
> TRIPTYCA

TRIPTYCH n painting or carving on three hinged panels, often forming an altarpiece

TRIPTYCHS
> TRIPTYCH

TRIPTYQUE n customs permit for the temporary importation of a motor vehicle

TRIPUDIA
> TRIPUDIUM

TRIPUDIUM n ancient religious dance

TRIPWIRE n wire that activates a trap, mine, etc when tripped over

TRIPWIRES
> TRIPWIRE

TRIPY > TRIPE

TRIQUETRA n ornament in the shape of three intersecting ellipses roughly forming a triangle

TRIRADIAL adj having or consisting of three rays or radiating branches

TRIREME n ancient Greek warship with three rows of oars on each side

TRIREMES > TRIREME

TRISAGION n old hymn

TRISCELE variant spelling of > TRISKELE

TRISCELES
> TRISCELE

TRISECT vb divide into three parts, esp three equal parts

TRISECTED > TRISECT

TRISECTOR > TRISECT

TRISECTS > TRISECT

TRISEME n metrical foot of a length equal to three short syllables

TRISEMES > TRISEME

TRISEMIC > TRISEME

TRISERIAL adj arranged in three rows or series

TRISHAW another name for > RICKSHAW

TRISHAWS > TRISHAW

TRISKELE n three-limbed symbol

TRISKELES
> TRISKELE

TRISKELIA n plural of singular triskelion: three-limbed symbol

TRISMIC > TRISMUS

TRISMUS n state of being unable to open the mouth

TRISMUSES > TRISMUS

TRISODIUM adj containing three sodium atoms

TRISOME n chromosome occurring three times (rather than twice) in a cell

TRISOMES > TRISOME

TRISOMIC > TRISOMY

TRISOMICS n study of trisomy

TRISOMIES > TRISOMY

TRISOMY n condition of having one chromosome represented three times

TRIST variant spelling of > TRISTE

TRISTATE adj (of a digital computer chip) having high, low, and floating output states

TRISTE adj sad

TRISTESSE n sadness

TRISTEZA n disease affecting citrus trees

TRISTEZAS
> TRISTEZA

TRISTFUL same as > TRISTE

TRISTICH n poem, stanza, or strophe that consists of three lines

TRISTICHS
> TRISTICH

TRISUL n trident symbol of Siva

TRISULA same as > TRISUL

TRISULAS > TRISULA

TRISULS > TRISUL

TRITANOPE n person who cannot distinguish the colour blue

TRITE adj (of a remark or idea) commonplace and unoriginal ▷ n (on a lyre) the third string from the highest in pitch

TRITELY > TRITE

TRITENESS > TRITE

TRITER > TRITE

TRITES > TRITE

TRITEST > TRITE

TRITHEISM n belief in three gods, esp in the Trinity as consisting of three distinct gods

TRITHEIST
> TRITHEISM

TRITHING n tripartition

TRITHINGS
> TRITHING

TRITIATE vb replace normal hydrogen atoms in (a compound) by those of tritium

TRITIATED
> TRITIATE

TRITIATES
> TRITIATE

TRITICAL adj trite; hackneyed

TRITICALE n fertile hybrid cereal

TRITICISM n something trite

TRITICUM n type of cereal grass of the genus which includes the wheats

TRITICUMS
> TRITICUM

TRITIDE n tritium compound

TRITIDES > TRITIDE

TRITIUM n radioactive isotope of hydrogen

TRITIUMS > TRITIUM

TRITOMA another name for > KNIPHOFIA

TRITOMAS > TRITOMA

TRITON n any of various chiefly tropical marine gastropod molluscs

TRITONE n musical interval consisting of three whole tones

TRITONES > TRITONE

TRITONIA n type of plant with typically scarlet or orange flowers

TRITONIAS
> TRITONIA

TRITONS > TRITON

TRITURATE vb grind or rub into a fine powder or pulp ▷ n powder or pulp resulting from this grinding

TRIUMPH n (happiness caused by) victory or success ▷ vb be victorious or successful

TRIUMPHAL adj celebrating a triumph

TRIUMPHED > TRIUMPH

TRIUMPHER > TRIUMPH

TRIUMPHS > TRIUMPH

TRIUMVIR n (esp in ancient Rome) a member of a triumvirate

TRIUMVIRI
> TRIUMVIR

TRIUMVIRS
> TRIUMVIR

TRIUMVIRY n triumvirate

TRIUNE adj constituting three things in one ▷ n group of three

TRIUNES > TRIUNE

TRIUNITY > TRIUNE

TRIVALENT adj having a valency of three

TRIVALVE n animal having three valves

TRIVALVED adj having three valves

TRIVALVES
> TRIVALVE

TRIVET n metal stand for a pot or kettle

TRIVETS > TRIVET

TRIVIA pl n trivial things or details

TRIVIAL adj of little importance

TRIVIALLY > TRIVIAL

TRIVIUM n (in medieval learning) the lower division of the seven liberal arts

TRIVIUMS > TRIVIUM

TRIWEEKLY adv every three weeks ▷ n triweekly publication

TRIZONAL > TRIZONE

TRIZONE n area comprising three zones

TRIZONES > TRIZONE

TROAD same as > TROD

TROADE same as > TROD

TROADES > TROADE

TROADS > TROAD

TROAK old form of > TRUCK

TROAKED > TROAK

TROAKING > TROAK

TROAKS > TROAK

TROAT vb (of a rutting buck) to call or bellow

TROATED > TROAT

TROATING > TROAT

TROATS > TROAT

TROCAR n surgical instrument for removing fluid from bodily cavities

TROCARS > TROCAR

TROCHAIC adj of, relating to, or consisting of trochees ▷ n verse composed of trochees

TROCHAICS
> TROCHAIC

TROCHAL adj shaped like a wheel

TROCHAR old variant spelling of > TROCAR

TROCHARS > TROCHAR

TROCHE another name for > LOZENGE

TROCHEE n metrical foot of one long and one short syllable

TROCHEES > TROCHEE

TROCHES > TROCHE

TROCHI > TROCHUS

TROCHIL same as > TROCHILUS

TROCHILI
> TROCHILUS

TROCHILIC adj relating to the movement of a hummingbird's wings

TROCHILS > TROCHIL

TROCHILUS n any of several Old World warblers

TROCHISCI n plural of trochiscus, a kind of lozenge

TROCHISK another word for > TROCHE

TROCHISKS
> TROCHISK

TROCHITE n joint of a crinoid

TROCHITES
> TROCHITE

TROCHLEA n any bony or cartilaginous part with a grooved surface

TROCHLEAE
> TROCHLEA

TROCHLEAR n as in trochlear nerve either one of the fourth pair of cranial nerves, which supply the superior oblique muscle of the eye

TROCHLEAS
> TROCHLEA

TROCHOID n curve described by a fixed point on the radius or extended radius of a circle as the circle rolls along a straight line ▷ adj rotating about a central axis

TROCHOIDS
> TROCHOID

TROCHUS n hoop (used in exercise)

TROCHUSES > TROCHUS

TROCK same as > TRUCK

TROCKED > TROCK

TROCKEN adj dry (used of wine)

TROCKING > TROCK

TROCKS > TROCK

TROD vb past participle of tread ▷ n path

TRODDEN > TREAD

TRODE same as > TROD

TRODES > TRODE

TRODS > TROD

TROELIE same as > TROOLIE

TROELIES > TROELIE

TROELY same as > TROOLIE

TROFFER n fixture for holding and reflecting light from a fluorescent tube

TROFFERS > TROFFER

TROG vb walk, esp aimlessly or heavily

TROGGED > TROG

TROGGING > TROG

TROGGS n Scots word meaning fidelity, loyalty

TROGON n bird of tropical and subtropical America, Africa, and Asia

TROGONS > TROGON

TROGS > TROG

TROIKA n Russian vehicle drawn by three horses abreast

TROIKAS > TROIKA

TROILISM n sexual activity involving three people

TROILISMS > TROILISM

TROILIST > TROILISM

TROILISTS > TROILISM

TROILITE n iron sulphide present in most meteorites

TROILITES > TROILITE

TROILUS n type of large butterfly

TROILUSES > TROILUS

TROIS Scots form of > TROY

TROJAN n bug inserted into a computer program

TROJANS > TROJAN

TROKE same as > TRUCK

TROKED > TROKE

TROKES > TROKE

TROKING > TROKE

TROLAND n unit of light intensity in the eye

TROLANDS > TROLAND

TROLL n giant or dwarf in Scandinavian folklore ▷ vb fish by dragging a lure through the water

TROLLED > TROLL

TROLLER > TROLL

TROLLERS > TROLL

TROLLEY n small wheeled table for food and drink ▷ vb transport on a trolley

TROLLEYED > TROLLEY

TROLLEYS > TROLLEY

TROLLIED > TROLLEY

TROLLIES > TROLLEY

TROLLING > TROLL

TROLLINGS > TROLL

TROLLISH adj like a troll

TROLLIUS n plant with globe-shaped flowers

TROLLOP n derogatory term for a woman considered slovenly ▷ vb behave like a trollop

TROLLOPED > TROLLOP

TROLLOPEE n loose dress or gown

TROLLOPS > TROLLOP

TROLLOPY adj like a trollop

TROLLS > TROLL

TROLLY same as > TROLLEY

TROLLYING > TROLLY

TROMBONE n brass musical instrument with a sliding tube

TROMBONES > TROMBONE

TROMINO n shape made from three squares, each joined to the next along one full side

TROMINOES > TROMINO

TROMINOS > TROMINO

TROMMEL n revolving cylindrical sieve used to screen crushed ore

TROMMELS > TROMMEL

TROMP vb trample

TROMPE n apparatus for supplying the blast of air in a forge

TROMPED > TROMP

TROMPES > TROMPE

TROMPING > TROMP

TROMPS > TROMP

TRON n public weighing machine

TRONA n greyish mineral that occurs in salt deposits

TRONAS > TRONA

TRONC n pool into which waiters, waitresses, hotel workers, etc pay their tips

TRONCS > TRONC

TRONE same as > TRON

TRONES > TRONE

TRONK n jail

TRONKS > TRONK

TRONS > TRON

TROOLIE n large palm leaf

TROOLIES > TROOLIE

TROOP n large group ▷ vb move in a crowd

TROOPED > TROOP

TROOPER n cavalry soldier

TROOPERS > TROOPER

TROOPIAL same as > TROUPIAL

TROOPIALS > TROOPIAL

TROOPING > TROOP

TROOPS > TROOP

TROOPSHIP n ship used to transport military personnel

TROOSTITE n reddish or greyish mineral that is a variety of willemite in which some of the zinc is replaced by manganese

TROOZ same as > TREWS

TROP adv too, too much

TROPAEOLA n plural of singular tropaeolum (a garden plant)

TROPARIA > TROPARION

TROPARION n short hymn

TROPE n figure of speech ▷ vb use tropes

TROPED > TROPE

TROPEOLIN n type of dye

TROPES > TROPE

TROPHESY n disorder of the nerves relating to nutrition

TROPHI pl n collective term for the mandibles and other parts of an insect's mouth

TROPHIC adj of or relating to nutrition

TROPHIED > TROPHY

TROPHIES > TROPHY

TROPHY n cup, shield, etc given as a prize ▷ adj regarded as a highly desirable symbol of wealth or success ▷ vb award a trophy to (someone)

TROPHYING > TROPHY

TROPIC n either of two lines of latitude at 23½°N or 23½°S

TROPICAL adj of or in the tropics ▷ n tropical thing or place

TROPICALS > TROPICAL

TROPICS > TROPIC

TROPIN n adrenal androgen

TROPINE n white crystalline poisonous alkaloid

TROPINES > TROPINE

TROPING > TROPE

TROPINS > TROPIN

TROPISM n tendency of a plant or animal to turn in response to an external stimulus

TROPISMS > TROPISM

TROPIST > TROPISM

TROPISTIC > TROPISM

TROPISTS > TROPISM

TROPOLOGY n use of figurative language in speech or writing

TROPONIN n muscle-tissue protein involved in the controlling of muscle contraction

TROPONINS > TROPONIN

TROPPO adv too much ▷ adj mentally affected by a tropical climate

TROSSERS old form of > TROUSERS

TROT vb (of a horse) move at a medium pace, lifting the feet in diagonal pairs ▷ n act of trotting

TROTH n pledge of devotion, esp a betrothal ▷ vb promise to marry (someone)

TROTHED > TROTH

TROTHFUL > TROTH

TROTHING > TROTH

TROTHLESS > TROTH

TROTHS > TROTH

TROTLINE n line suspended across a stream to which shorter hooked and baited lines are attached

TROTLINES > TROTLINE

TROTS > TROT

TROTTED > TROT

TROTTER n pig's foot

TROTTERS > TROTTER

TROTTING > TROT

TROTTINGS > TROT

TROTTOIR n pavement

TROTTOIRS > TROTTOIR

TROTYL n yellow solid used chiefly as a high explosive

TROTYLS > TROTYL

TROU pl n trousers

TROUBLE n (cause of) distress or anxiety ▷ vb (cause to) worry

TROUBLED > TROUBLE

TROUBLER > TROUBLE

TROUBLERS > TROUBLE

TROUBLES > TROUBLE

TROUBLING > TROUBLE

TROUBLOUS adj unsettled or agitated

TROUCH n rubbish

TROUCHES > TROUCH

TROUGH n long open container, esp for animals' food or water ▷ vb eat, consume, or take greedily

TROUGHED > TROUGH

TROUGHING n as in troughing and peaking reaching the lowest and highest levels in a range

TROUGHS > TROUGH

TROULE old variant of > TROLL

TROULED > TROULE

TROULES > TROULE

TROULING > TROULE

TROUNCE vb defeat utterly

TROUNCED > TROUNCE

TROUNCER > TROUNCE

TROUNCERS > TROUNCE

TROUNCES > TROUNCE

TROUNCING > TROUNCE

TROUPE n company of performers ▷ vb (esp of actors) to move or travel in a group

TROUPED > TROUPE

TROUPER n member of a troupe

TROUPERS > TROUPER

TROUPES > TROUPE

TROUPIAL n any of various American orioles

TROUPIALS > TROUPIAL

TROUPING > TROUPE

TROUSE pl n close-fitting breeches worn in Ireland

TROUSER vb take (something, esp money), often surreptitiously or unlawfully

TROUSERED > TROUSERS

t

TROUSERS *pl n*
two-legged outer
garment with legs
reaching usu to the ankles

TROUSES > TROUSE

TROUSSEAU *n* bride's
collection of clothing etc
for her marriage

TROUT *n* game fish related
to the salmon ▷ *vb* fish for
trout

TROUTER > TROUT

TROUTERS > TROUT

TROUTFUL *adj* (of a body
of water) full of trout

TROUTIER > TROUT

TROUTIEST > TROUT

TROUTING > TROUT

TROUTINGS > TROUT

TROUTLESS > TROUT

TROUTLET *n* small trout

TROUTLETS
> TROUTLET

TROUTLIKE *adj* like a
trout

TROUTLING *n* small trout

TROUTS > TROUT

TROUTY > TROUT

TROUVERE *n* poet of N
France during the 12th and
13th centuries

TROUVERES
> TROUVERE

TROUVEUR *same as*
> TROUVERE

TROUVEURS
> TROUVEUR

TROVE *n* as in
treasure-trove valuable
articles found hidden in
the earth

TROVER *n* act of assuming
proprietary rights over
goods or property
belonging to another

TROVERS > TROVER

TROVES > TROVE

TROW *vb* think, believe, or
trust

TROWED > TROW

TROWEL *n* hand tool with
a wide blade ▷ *vb* use a
trowel on (plaster, soil, etc)

TROWELED > TROWEL

TROWELER > TROWEL

TROWELERS > TROWEL

TROWELING > TROWEL

TROWELLED > TROWEL

TROWELLER > TROWEL

TROWELS > TROWEL

TROWING > TROW

TROWS > TROW

TROWSERS *old spelling of*
> TROUSERS

TROWTH *variant spelling of*
> TROTH

TROWTHS > TROWTH

TROY *n* system of weights
used for precious metals
and gemstones

TROYS > TROY

TRUANCIES > TRUANT

TRUANCY > TRUANT

TRUANT *n* pupil who stays
away from school without
permission ▷ *adj* being or
relating to a truant ▷ *vb*
play truant

TRUANTED > TRUANT

TRUANTING *n* act of
playing truant

TRUANTLY > TRUANT

TRUANTRY > TRUANT

TRUANTS > TRUANT

TRUCAGE *n* art forgery

TRUCAGES > TRUCAGE

TRUCE *n* temporary
agreement to stop
fighting ▷ *vb* make a truce

TRUCED > TRUCE

TRUCELESS > TRUCE

TRUCES > TRUCE

TRUCHMAN *n* interpreter;
translator

TRUCHMANS
> TRUCHMAN

TRUCHMEN > TRUCHMAN

TRUCIAL > TRUCE

TRUCING > TRUCE

TRUCK *n* railway goods
wagon ▷ *vb* exchange
(goods); barter

TRUCKABLE > TRUCK

TRUCKAGE *n* conveyance
of cargo by truck

TRUCKAGES
> TRUCKAGE

TRUCKED > TRUCK

TRUCKER *n* truck driver

TRUCKERS > TRUCKER

TRUCKFUL *n* amount of
something that can be
conveyed in a truck

TRUCKFULS
> TRUCKFUL

TRUCKIE *n* truck driver

TRUCKIES > TRUCKIE

TRUCKING *n*
transportation of goods
by lorry

TRUCKINGS
> TRUCKING

TRUCKLE *vb* yield weakly
or give in ▷ *n* small wheel

TRUCKLED > TRUCKLE

TRUCKLER > TRUCKLE

TRUCKLERS > TRUCKLE

TRUCKLES > TRUCKLE

TRUCKLINE *n*
organisation that conveys
freight by truck

TRUCKLING > TRUCKLE

TRUCKLOAD *n* amount
carried by a truck

TRUCKMAN *n* truck driver

TRUCKMEN > TRUCKMAN

TRUCKS > TRUCK

TRUCKSTOP *n* place
providing fuel, oil, and
often service facilities for
truck drivers

TRUCULENT *adj*
aggressively defiant

TRUDGE *vb* walk heavily
or wearily ▷ *n* long tiring
walk

TRUDGED > TRUDGE

TRUDGEN *n* type of
swimming stroke

TRUDGENS > TRUDGEN

TRUDGEON *nonstandard
variant of* > TRUDGEN

TRUDGEONS
> TRUDGEON

TRUDGER > TRUDGE

TRUDGERS > TRUDGE

TRUDGES > TRUDGE

TRUDGING > TRUDGE

TRUDGINGS > TRUDGE

TRUE *adj* in accordance
with facts

TRUEBLUE *n* staunch
royalist or Conservative

TRUEBLUES
> TRUEBLUE

TRUEBORN *adj* being such
by birth

TRUEBRED *adj*
thoroughbred

TRUED > TRUE

TRUEING > TRUE

TRUELOVE *n* person that
one loves

TRUELOVES
> TRUELOVE

TRUEMAN *n* honest
person

TRUEMEN > TRUEMAN

TRUENESS > TRUE

TRUEPENNY *n* truthful
person

TRUER > TRUE

TRUES > TRUE

TRUEST > TRUE

TRUFFE *rare word for*
> TRUFFLE

TRUFFES > TRUFFE

TRUFFLE *n* edible
underground fungus ▷ *vb*
hunt for truffles

TRUFFLED > TRUFFLE

TRUFFLES > TRUFFLE

TRUFFLING > TRUFFLE

TRUG *n* long shallow
basket used by gardeners

TRUGO *n* game similar to
croquet

TRUGOS > TRUGO

TRUGS > TRUG

TRUING > TRUE

TRUISM *n* self-evident
truth

TRUISMS > TRUISM

TRUISTIC > TRUISM

TRULL *n* prostitute

TRULLS > TRULL

TRULY *adv* in a true
manner

TRUMEAU *n* section of a
wall or pillar between two
openings

TRUMEAUX > TRUMEAU

TRUMP *adj* (in card games)
of the suit outranking the
others ▷ *vb* play a trump
card on (another card)

TRUMPED > TRUMP

TRUMPERY *n* something
useless or worthless ▷ *adj*
useless or worthless

TRUMPET *n* valved brass
instrument with a flared
tube ▷ *vb* proclaim
loudly

TRUMPETED > TRUMPET

TRUMPETER *n* person
who plays the trumpet,
esp one whose duty it is to
play fanfares, signals, etc

TRUMPETS > TRUMPET

TRUMPING > TRUMP

TRUMPINGS > TRUMP

TRUMPLESS > TRUMP

TRUMPS > TRUMP

TRUNCAL *adj* of or
relating to the trunk

TRUNCATE *vb* cut short
▷ *adj* cut short

TRUNCATED *adj* (of a
cone, pyramid, prism, etc)
having an apex or end
removed by a plane
intersection that is usually
nonparallel to the base

TRUNCATES
> TRUNCATE

TRUNCHEON *n* club
formerly carried by a police
officer ▷ *vb* beat with a
truncheon

TRUNDLE *vb* move heavily
on wheels ▷ *n* act or an
instance of trundling

TRUNDLED > TRUNDLE

TRUNDLER *n* golf or
shopping trolley

TRUNDLERS
> TRUNDLER

TRUNDLES > TRUNDLE

TRUNDLING > TRUNDLE

TRUNK *n* main stem of a
tree ▷ *vb* lop or truncate

TRUNKED > TRUNK

TRUNKFISH *n* tropical
fish, having the body
encased in bony plates
with openings for the fins,
eyes, mouth, etc

TRUNKFUL > TRUNK

TRUNKFULS > TRUNK

TRUNKING *n* cables that
take a common route
through an exchange
building linking ranks of
selectors

TRUNKINGS
> TRUNKING

TRUNKLESS > TRUNK

TRUNKLIKE *adj* like a
trunk

TRUNKS *pl n* shorts worn
by a man for swimming

TRUNKWORK *n*
clandestine action of
visiting someone in a
trunk

TRUNNEL *same as*
> TREENAIL

TRUNNELS > TRUNNEL

TRUNNION *n* one of a pair
of coaxial projections
attached to opposite sides
of a cannon

TRUNNIONS
> TRUNNION

TRUQUAGE *variant of*
> TRUCAGE

TRUQUAGES
> TRUQUAGE

TRUQUEUR *n* art forger

TRUQUEURS
> TRUQUEUR

TRUSS *vb* tie or bind up
▷ *n* device for holding a
hernia, etc in place

TRUSSED > TRUSS

TRUSSER > TRUSS

TRUSSERS > TRUSS

TRUSSES > TRUSS

TRUSSING *n* system of
trusses, esp for
strengthening or
reinforcing a structure

TRUSSINGS > TRUSSING

TRUST *vb* believe in and rely on ▷ *n* confidence in the truth, reliability, etc of a person or thing ▷ *adj* of or relating to a trust or trusts

TRUSTABLE > TRUST

TRUSTED > TRUST

TRUSTEE *n* person holding property on another's behalf ▷ *vb* act as a trustee

TRUSTEED > TRUSTEE

TRUSTEES > TRUSTEE

TRUSTER > TRUST

TRUSTERS > TRUST

TRUSTFUL *adj* inclined to trust others

TRUSTIER > TRUSTY

TRUSTIES > TRUSTY

TRUSTIEST > TRUSTY

TRUSTILY > TRUSTY

TRUSTING *same as* > TRUSTFUL

TRUSTLESS *adj* untrustworthy

TRUSTOR *n* person who sets up a trust

TRUSTORS > TRUSTOR

TRUSTS > TRUST

TRUSTY *adj* faithful or reliable ▷ *n* trustworthy convict to whom special privileges are granted

TRUTH *n* state of being true

TRUTHER *n* person who does not believe official accounts of the 9/11 attacks on the US

TRUTHERS > TRUTHER

TRUTHFUL *adj* honest

TRUTHIER > TRUTHY

TRUTHIEST > TRUTHY

TRUTHLESS > TRUTH

TRUTHLIKE *n* truthful

TRUTHS > TRUTH

TRUTHY *adj* truthful

TRY *vb* make an effort or attempt ▷ *n* attempt or effort

TRYE *adj* very good; select

TRYER *variant of* > TRIER

TRYERS > TRYER

TRYING > TRY

TRYINGLY > TRY

TRYINGS > TRY

TRYKE *variant spelling of* > TRIKE

TRYKES > TRYKE

TRYMA *n* drupe produced by the walnut and similar plants

TRYMATA > TRYMA

TRYOUT *n* trial or test, as of an athlete or actor

TRYOUTS > TRYOUT

TRYP *n* parasitic protozoan

TRYPAN *modifier* as in *trypan blue* dye used for staining cells in biological research

TRYPS > TRYP

TRYPSIN *n* enzyme occurring in pancreatic juice

TRYPSINS > TRYPSIN

TRYPTIC > TRYPSIN

TRYSAIL *n* small fore-and-aft sail on a sailing vessel

TRYSAILS > TRYSAIL

TRYST *n* arrangement to meet ▷ *vb* meet at or arrange a tryst

TRYSTE *variant spelling of* > TRYST

TRYSTED > TRYST

TRYSTER > TRYST

TRYSTERS > TRYST

TRYSTES > TRYSTE

TRYSTING > TRYST

TRYSTS > TRYST

TRYWORKS *n* furnace for rendering blubber

TSADDIK *variant of* > ZADDIK

TSADDIKIM > TSADDIK

TSADDIKS > TSADDIK

TSADDIQ *variant of* > ZADDIK

TSADDIQIM > TSADDIQ

TSADDIQS > TSADDIQ

TSADE *variant spelling of* > SADHE

TSADES > TSADE

TSADI *variant of* > SADHE

TSADIK *same as* > ZADDIK

TSADIKS > TSADIK

TSADIS > TSADI

TSAMBA *n* Tibetan dish made from roasted barley and tea

TSAMBAS > TSAMBA

TSANTSA *n* shrunken head of an enemy kept as a trophy

TSANTSAS > TSANTSA

TSAR *n* Russian emperor

TSARDOM > TSAR

TSARDOMS > TSARDOM

TSAREVICH *n* son of a tsar

TSAREVNA *n* daughter of a tsar

TSAREVNAS > TSAREVNA

TSARINA *n* wife of a tsar

TSARINAS > TSARINA

TSARISM *n* system of government by a tsar

TSARISMS > TSARISM

TSARIST *n* supporter of a tsar

TSARISTS > TSARIST

TSARITSA *n* wife of a tsar

TSARITSAS > TSARITSA

TSARITZA *variant spelling of* > TSARITSA

TSARITZAS > TSARITZA

TSARS > TSAR

TSATSKE *variant of* > TCHOTCHKE

TSATSKES > TSATSKE

TSESSEBE *South African variant of* > SASSABY

TSESSEBES > TSESSEBE

TSETSE *n* any of various bloodsucking African flies

TSETSES > TSETSE

TSIGANE *variant of* > TZIGANE

TSIGANES > TSIGANE

TSIMMES *variant spelling of* > TZIMMES

TSITSITH *n* tassels or fringes of thread attached to the four corners of the tallith

TSK *vb* utter the sound 'tsk', usu in disapproval

TSKED > TSK

TSKING > TSK

TSKS > TSK

TSKTSK *same as* > TSK

TSKTSKED > TSKTSK

TSKTSKING > TSKTSK

TSKTSKS > TSKTSK

TSOORIS *variant of* > TSURIS

TSORES *variant of* > TSURIS

TSORIS *variant of* > TSURIS

TSORRISS *variant of* > TSURIS

TSOTSI *n* (in South Africa) an urban thug or gang member

TSOTSIS > TSOTSI

TSOURIS *variant of* > TSURIS

TSOURISES > TSOURIS

TSUBA *n* sword guard of a Japanese sword

TSUBAS > TSUBA

TSUBO *n* unit of area

TSUBOS > TSUBO

TSUNAMI *n* tidal wave, usu caused by an earthquake under the sea

TSUNAMIC > TSUNAMI

TSUNAMIS > TSUNAMI

TSURIS *n* grief or strife

TSURISES > TSURIS

TSUTSUMU *n* Japanese art of wrapping gifts

TSUTSUMUS > TSUTSUMU

TUAN *n* lord

TUANS > TUAN

TUART *n* eucalyptus tree of Australia

TUARTS > TUART

TUATARA *n* large lizard-like New Zealand reptile

TUATARAS > TUATARA

TUATERA *variant spelling of* > TUATARA

TUATERAS > TUATERA

TUATH *n* territory of an ancient Irish tribe

TUATHS > TUATH

TUATUA *n* edible marine bivalve of New Zealand waters

TUATUAS > TUATUA

TUB *n* open, usu round container ▷ *vb* wash (oneself or another) in a tub

TUBA *n* valved low-pitched brass instrument

TUBAE > TUBA

TUBAGE *n* insertion of a tube

TUBAGES > TUBAGE

TUBAIST > TUBA

TUBAISTS > TUBA

TUBAL *adj* of or relating to a tube

TUBAR *another word for* > TUBULAR

TUBAS > TUBA

TUBATE *less common word for* > TUBULAR

TUBBABLE > TUB

TUBBED > TUB

TUBBER > TUB

TUBBERS > TUB

TUBBIER > TUBBY

TUBBIEST > TUBBY

TUBBINESS > TUBBY

TUBBING > TUB

TUBBINGS > TUB

TUBBISH *adj* fat

TUBBY *adj* (of a person) short and fat

TUBE *n* hollow cylinder

TUBECTOMY *n* excision of the Fallopian tubes

TUBED > TUBE

TUBEFUL *n* quantity (of something) that a tube can hold

TUBEFULS > TUBEFUL

TUBELESS *adj* without a tube

TUBELIKE *adj* resembling a tube

TUBENOSE *n* seabird with tubular nostrils on its beak

TUBENOSES > TUBENOSE

TUBER *n* fleshy underground root of a plant such as a potato

TUBERCLE *n* small rounded swelling

TUBERCLED *adj* having tubercles

TUBERCLES > TUBERCLE

TUBERCULA *pl n* plural of tuberculum (another name for 'tubercle')

TUBERCULE *variant of* > TUBERCLE

TUBEROID *adj* resembling a tuber ▷ *n* fleshy root resembling a tuber

TUBEROIDS > TUBEROID

TUBEROSE *same as* > TUBEROUS

TUBEROSES > TUBEROSE

TUBEROUS *adj* (of plants) forming, bearing, or resembling a tuber or tubers

TUBERS > TUBER

TUBES > TUBE

TUBEWELL *n* type of water well

TUBEWELLS > TUBEWELL

TUBEWORK *n* collective term for tubes or tubing

TUBEWORKS > TUBEWORK

TUBEWORM *n* undersea worm

TUBEWORMS
> TUBEWORM
TUBFAST n period of fasting and sweating in a tub, intended as a cure for disease
TUBFASTS > TUBFAST
TUBFISH another name for > GURNARD
TUBFISHES > TUBFISH
TUBFUL n amount a tub will hold
TUBFULS > TUBFUL
TUBICOLAR adj tube-dwelling
TUBICOLE n tube-dwelling creature
TUBICOLES
> TUBICOLE
TUBIFEX n type of small reddish freshwater worm
TUBIFEXES > TUBIFEX
TUBIFICID n type of threadlike annelid worm
TUBIFORM same as > TUBULAR
TUBING n length of tube
TUBINGS > TUBING
TUBIST > TUBA
TUBISTS > TUBA
TUBLIKE > TUB
TUBS > TUB
TUBULAR adj of or shaped like a tube ▷ n type of tyre
TUBULARLY > TUBULAR
TUBULARS > TUBULAR
TUBULATE vb form or shape into a tube
TUBULATED
> TUBULATE
TUBULATES
> TUBULATE
TUBULATOR
> TUBULATE
TUBULE n any small tubular structure
TUBULES > TUBULE
TUBULIN n protein forming the basis of microtubules
TUBULINS > TUBULIN
TUBULOSE adj tube-shaped; consisting of tubes
TUBULOUS adj tube-shaped
TUBULURE n tube leading into a retort or other receptacle
TUBULURES
> TUBULURE
TUCHIS n buttocks
TUCHISES > TUCHIS
TUCHUN n (formerly) a Chinese military governor or warlord
TUCHUNS > TUCHUN
TUCHUS same as
> TUCHIS
TUCHUSES > TUCHUS
TUCK vb push or fold into a small space ▷ n stitched fold
TUCKAHOE n type of edible root
TUCKAHOES
> TUCKAHOE

TUCKAMORE n Newfoundland spruce tree bent by winds
TUCKBOX n box used for carrying food to school
TUCKBOXES > TUCKBOX
TUCKED > TUCK
TUCKER n food ▷ vb weary or tire completely
TUCKERBAG n in Australia, bag or box used for carrying food
TUCKERBOX same as > TUCKERBAG
TUCKERED > TUCKER
TUCKERING > TUCKER
TUCKERS > TUCKER
TUCKET n flourish on a trumpet
TUCKETS > TUCKET
TUCKING n act of tucking
TUCKINGS > TUCKING
TUCKS > TUCK
TUCKSHOP n shop, esp one in or near a school, where food such as cakes and sweets are sold
TUCKSHOPS
> TUCKSHOP
TUCOTUCO n colonial burrowing South American rodent
TUCOTUCOS
> TUCOTUCO
TUCUTUCO variant spelling of > TUCOTUCO
TUCUTUCOS
> TUCUTUCO
TUCUTUCU same as
> TUCOTUCO
TUCUTUCUS
> TUCUTUCU
TUFA n porous rock formed as a deposit from springs
TUFACEOUS > TUFA
TUFAS > TUFA
TUFF n porous rock formed from volcanic dust or ash
TUFFE old form of > TUFT
TUFFES > TUFFE
TUFFET n small mound or seat
TUFFETS > TUFFET
TUFFS > TUFF
TUFOLI n type of tubular pasta
TUFOLIS > TUFOLI
TUFT n bunch of feathers, grass, hair, etc held or growing together at the base ▷ vb provide or decorate with a tuft or tufts
TUFTED adj having a tuft or tufts
TUFTER > TUFT
TUFTERS > TUFT
TUFTIER > TUFT
TUFTIEST > TUFT
TUFTILY > TUFT
TUFTING > TUFT
TUFTINGS > TUFT
TUFTS > TUFT
TUFTY > TUFT
TUG vb pull hard ▷ n hard pull

TUGBOAT n boat used for towing barges, ships, etc
TUGBOATS > TUGBOAT
TUGGED > TUG
TUGGER > TUG
TUGGERS > TUG
TUGGING > TUG
TUGGINGLY > TUG
TUGGINGS > TUG
TUGHRA n Turkish Sultan's official emblem
TUGHRAS > TUGHRA
TUGHRIK same as
> TUGRIK
TUGHRIKS > TUGHRIK
TUGLESS > TUG
TUGRA variant of
> TUGHRA
TUGRAS > TUGRA
TUGRIK n standard monetary unit of Mongolia
TUGRIKS > TUGRIK
TUGS > TUG
TUI n New Zealand honeyeater that mimics human speech and the songs of other birds
TUILE n type of almond-flavoured dessert biscuit
TUILES > TUILE
TUILLE n (in a suit of armour) hanging plate protecting the thighs
TUILLES > TUILLE
TUILLETTE n little tuille
TUILYIE vb fight
TUILYIED > TUILYIE
TUILYIES > TUILYIE
TUILZIE variant form of
> TUILYIE
TUILZIED > TUILZIE
TUILZIES > TUILZIE
TUINA n form of massage originating in China
TUINAS > TUINA
TUIS > TUI
TUISM n practice of putting the interests of another before one's own
TUISMS > TUISM
TUITION n instruction, esp received individually or in a small group
TUITIONAL > TUITION
TUITIONS > TUITION
TUKTOO same as
> TUKTU
TUKTOOS > TUKTOO
TUKTU (in Canada) another name for > CARIBOU
TUKTUS > TUKTU
TULADI n large trout found in Canada and the northern US
TULADIS > TULADI
TULAREMIA n infectious disease of rodents
TULAREMIC
> TULAREMIA
TULBAN old form of
> TURBAN
TULBANS > TULBAN
TULCHAN n skin of a calf placed next to a cow to induce it to give milk
TULCHANS > TULCHAN

TULE n type of bulrush found in California
TULES > TULE
TULIP n plant with bright cup-shaped flowers
TULIPANT n turban
TULIPANTS
> TULIPANT
TULIPLIKE > TULIP
TULIPS > TULIP
TULIPWOOD n light soft wood of the tulip tree, used in making furniture and veneer
TULLE n fine net fabric of silk etc
TULLES > TULLE
TULLIBEE n cisco of the Great Lakes of Canada
TULLIBEES
> TULLIBEE
TULPA n being or object created through willpower and visualization techniques
TULPAS > TULPA
TULSI n type of basil
TULSIS > TULSI
TULWAR n Indian sabre
TULWARS > TULWAR
TUM informal or childish word for > STOMACH
TUMBLE vb (cause to) fall, esp awkwardly or violently ▷ n fall
TUMBLEBUG n type of beetle
TUMBLED > TUMBLE
TUMBLER n stemless drinking glass
TUMBLERS > TUMBLER
TUMBLES > TUMBLE
TUMBLESET n somersault
TUMBLING > TUMBLE
TUMBLINGS
> TUMBLING
TUMBREL n farm cart for carrying manure
TUMBRELS > TUMBREL
TUMBRIL same as
> TUMBREL
TUMBRILS > TUMBRIL
TUMEFIED > TUMEFY
TUMEFIES > TUMEFY
TUMEFY vb make or become tumid
TUMEFYING > TUMEFY
TUMESCE vb swell
TUMESCED > TUMESCE
TUMESCENT adj swollen or becoming swollen
TUMESCES > TUMESCE
TUMESCING > TUMESCE
TUMID adj (of an organ or part of the body) enlarged or swollen
TUMIDITY > TUMID
TUMIDLY > TUMID
TUMIDNESS > TUMID
TUMMIES > TUMMY
TUMMLER n entertainer employed to encourage audience participation
TUMMLERS > TUMMLER
TUMMY n stomach
TUMOR same as > TUMOUR
TUMORAL > TUMOUR

TUMORLIKE > TUMOUR
TUMOROUS > TUMOUR
TUMORS > TUMOR
TUMOUR n abnormal growth in or on the body
TUMOURS > TUMOUR
TUMP n small mound or clump ▷ vb make a tump around
TUMPED > TUMP
TUMPHIES > TUMPHY
TUMPHY n dolt; fool
TUMPIER > TUMP
TUMPIEST > TUMP
TUMPING > TUMP
TUMPLINE n band strung across the forehead or chest and attached to a pack in order to support it
TUMPLINES > TUMPLINE
TUMPS > TUMP
TUMPY > TUMP
TUMS > TUM
TUMSHIE n turnip
TUMSHIES > TUMSHIE
TUMULAR adj of, relating to, or like a mound
TUMULARY same as > TUMULAR
TUMULI > TUMULUS
TUMULOSE adj abounding in small hills or mounds
TUMULOUS same as > TUMULOSE
TUMULT n uproar or commotion ▷ vb stir up a commotion
TUMULTED > TUMULT
TUMULTING > TUMULT
TUMULTS > TUMULT
TUMULUS n burial mound
TUMULUSES > TUMULUS
TUN n large beer cask ▷ vb put into or keep in tuns
TUNA n large marine food fish
TUNABLE adj able to be tuned
TUNABLY > TUNABLE
TUNAS > TUNA
TUNBELLY n large round belly
TUND vb beat; strike
TUNDED > TUND
TUNDING > TUND
TUNDISH n type of funnel
TUNDISHES > TUNDISH
TUNDRA n vast treeless Arctic region with permanently frozen subsoil
TUNDRAS > TUNDRA
TUNDS > TUND
TUNDUN n wooden instrument used by Aboriginal Australians in religious rites
TUNDUNS > TUNDUN
TUNE n (pleasing) sequence of musical notes ▷ vb adjust (a musical instrument) so that it is in tune
TUNEABLE same as > TUNABLE
TUNEABLY > TUNEABLE
TUNEAGE n music

TUNEAGES > TUNEAGE
TUNED > TUNE
TUNEFUL adj having a pleasant tune
TUNEFULLY > TUNEFUL
TUNELESS adj having no melody or tune
TUNER n part of a radio or television receiver for selecting channels
TUNERS > TUNER
TUNES > TUNE
TUNESMITH n composer of light or popular music and songs
TUNEUP n adjustments made to an engine to improve its performance
TUNEUPS > TUNEUP
TUNG n fast-drying oil obtained from the seeds of a central Asian tree
TUNGS > TUNG
TUNGSTATE n salt of tungstic acid
TUNGSTEN n greyish-white metal
TUNGSTENS > TUNGSTEN
TUNGSTIC adj of or containing tungsten, esp in a high valence state
TUNGSTITE n yellow earthy rare secondary mineral that consists of tungsten oxide and occurs with tungsten ores
TUNGSTOUS adj of or containing tungsten in a low valence state
TUNIC n close-fitting jacket forming part of some uniforms
TUNICA n tissue forming a layer or covering of an organ or part
TUNICAE > TUNICA
TUNICATE n minute primitive marine chordate animal ▷ adj of, relating to this animal ▷ vb wear a tunic
TUNICATED > TUNICATE
TUNICATES > TUNICATE
TUNICIN n cellulose-like substance found in tunicates
TUNICINS > TUNICIN
TUNICKED adj wearing a tunic
TUNICLE n vestment worn at High Mass and other religious ceremonies
TUNICLES > TUNICLE
TUNICS > TUNIC
TUNIER > TUNY
TUNIEST > TUNY
TUNING n set of pitches to which the open strings of a guitar, violin, etc are tuned
TUNINGS > TUNING
TUNKET n hell
TUNKETS > TUNKET
TUNNAGE same as > TONNAGE

TUNNAGES > TUNNAGE
TUNNED > TUN
TUNNEL n underground passage ▷ vb make a tunnel (through)
TUNNELED > TUNNEL
TUNNELER > TUNNEL
TUNNELERS > TUNNEL
TUNNELING > TUNNEL
TUNNELLED > TUNNEL
TUNNELLER > TUNNEL
TUNNELS > TUNNEL
TUNNIES > TUNNY
TUNNING > TUN
TUNNINGS > TUN
TUNNY same as > TUNA
TUNS > TUN
TUNY adj having an easily discernible melody
TUP n male sheep ▷ vb cause (a ram) to mate with a ewe
TUPEK same as > TUPIK
TUPEKS > TUPEK
TUPELO n large tree of deep swamps and rivers of the southern US
TUPELOS > TUPELO
TUPIK n tent of seal or caribou skin used for shelter by Inuit people in summer
TUPIKS > TUPIK
TUPLE n row of values in a relational database
TUPLES > TUPLE
TUPPED > TUP
TUPPENCE same as > TWOPENCE
TUPPENCES > TUPPENCE
TUPPENNY same as > TWOPENNY
TUPPING n act of sheep mating
TUPPINGS > TUPPING
TUPS > TUP
TUPTOWING n study of Greek grammar
TUPUNA same as > TIPUNA
TUPUNAS > TUPUNA
TUQUE n knitted cap with a long tapering end
TUQUES > TUQUE
TURACIN n red pigment found in touraco feathers
TURACINS > TURACIN
TURACO same as > TOURACO
TURACOS > TURACO
TURACOU variant of > TOURACO
TURACOUS > TURACOU
TURBAN n Muslim, Hindu, or Sikh man's head covering
TURBAND old variant of > TURBAN
TURBANDS > TURBAND
TURBANED > TURBAN
TURBANNED > TURBAN
TURBANS > TURBAN
TURBANT old variant of > TURBAN
TURBANTS > TURBANT
TURBARIES > TURBARY

TURBARY n land where peat or turf is cut or has been cut
TURBETH variant of > TURPETH
TURBETHS > TURBETH
TURBID adj muddy, not clear
TURBIDITE n sediment deposited by a turbidity current
TURBIDITY > TURBID
TURBIDLY > TURBID
TURBINAL same as > TURBINATE
TURBINALS > TURBINAL
TURBINATE adj of or relating to any of the thin scroll-shaped bones situated on the walls of the nasal passages ▷ n turbinate bone
TURBINE n machine or generator driven by gas, water, etc turning blades
TURBINED adj having a turbine
TURBINES > TURBINE
TURBIT n crested breed of domestic pigeon
TURBITH variant of > TURPETH
TURBITHS > TURBITH
TURBITS > TURBIT
TURBO n compressor in an engine
TURBOCAR n car driven by a gas turbine
TURBOCARS > TURBOCAR
TURBOFAN n engine in which a fan driven by a turbine forces air rearwards to increase thrust
TURBOFANS > TURBOFAN
TURBOJET n gas turbine in which the exhaust gases provide the propulsive thrust to drive an aircraft
TURBOJETS > TURBOJET
TURBOND old variant of > TURBAN
TURBONDS > TURBOND
TURBOPROP n gas turbine for driving an aircraft propeller
TURBOS > TURBO
TURBOT n large European edible flatfish
TURBOTS > TURBOT
TURBULENT adj involving a lot of sudden changes and conflicting elements
TURCOPOLE n lightly armed and highly mobile class of Crusader
TURD n slang word for a piece of excrement
TURDINE adj of, relating to, or characteristic of thrushes
TURDION variant of > TORDION
TURDIONS > TURDION

TURDOID *same as*
> TURDINE
TURDS > TURD
TURDUCKEN *n* turkey stuffed with duck stuffed with chicken
TUREEN *n* serving dish for soup
TUREENS > TUREEN
TURF *n* short thick even grass ▷ *vb* cover with turf
TURFED > TURF
TURFEN *adj* made of turf
TURFGRASS *n* grass grown for lawns
TURFIER > TURFY
TURFIEST > TURFY
TURFINESS > TURFY
TURFING > TURF
TURFINGS > TURF
TURFITE *same as*
> TURFMAN
TURFITES > TURFITE
TURFLESS > TURF
TURFLIKE > TURF
TURFMAN *n* person devoted to horse racing
TURFMEN > TURFMAN
TURFS > TURF
TURFSKI *n* a ski down a grassy hill on skis modified with integral wheels
TURFSKIS > TURFSKI
TURFY *adj* of, covered with, or resembling turf
TURGENCY > TURGENT
TURGENT *obsolete word for*
> TURGID
TURGENTLY > TURGENT
TURGID *adj* (of language) pompous
TURGIDER > TURGID
TURGIDEST > TURGID
TURGIDITY > TURGID
TURGIDLY > TURGID
TURGITE *n* red or black mineral consisting of hydrated ferric oxide
TURGITES > TURGITE
TURGOR *n* normal rigid state of a cell
TURGORS > TURGOR
TURION *n* perennating bud produced by many aquatic plants
TURIONS > TURION
TURISTA *n* traveller's diarrhoea
TURISTAS > TURISTA
TURK *n* as in *young turk* person who agitates for radical reform
TURKEY *n* large bird bred for food
TURKEYS > TURKEY
TURKIES *old form of*
> TURQUOISE
TURKIESES > TURKIES
TURKIS *old form of*
> TURQUOISE
TURKISES > TURKIS
TURKOIS *old form of*
> TURQUOISE
TURKOISES > TURKOIS
TURKS > TURK
TURLOUGH *n* seasonal lake or pond
TURLOUGHS > TURLOUGH

TURM *n* troop of horsemen
TURME *variant of* > TURM
TURMERIC *n* yellow spice obtained from the root of an Asian plant
TURMERICS
> TURMERIC
TURMES > TURME
TURMOIL *n* agitation or confusion ▷ *vb* make or become turbulent
TURMOILED > TURMOIL
TURMOILS > TURMOIL
TURMS > TURM
TURN *vb* change the position or direction (of) ▷ *n* turning
TURNABLE > TURN
TURNABOUT *n* act of turning so as to face a different direction
TURNAGAIN *n* revolution
TURNBACK *n* one who turns back (from a challenge, for example)
TURNBACKS
> TURNBACK
TURNCOAT *n* person who deserts one party or cause to join another
TURNCOATS
> TURNCOAT
TURNCOCK *n* (formerly) official employed to turn on the water for the mains supply
TURNCOCKS
> TURNCOCK
TURNDOWN *adj* capable of being or designed to be folded or doubled down ▷ *n* instance of turning down
TURNDOWNS
> TURNDOWN
TURNDUN *another name for*
> TUNDUN
TURNDUNS > TURNDUN
TURNED > TURN
TURNER *n* person or thing that turns
TURNERIES > TURNERY
TURNERS > TURNER
TURNERY *n* objects made on a lathe
TURNHALL *n* building in which gymnastics is taught and practised
TURNHALLS
> TURNHALL
TURNING *n* road or path leading off a main route
TURNINGS > TURNING
TURNIP *n* root vegetable with orange or white flesh ▷ *vb* sow (a field) with turnips
TURNIPED > TURNIP
TURNIPIER > TURNIPY
TURNIPING > TURNIP
TURNIPS > TURNIP
TURNIPY *adj* like a turnip
TURNKEY *n* jailer ▷ *adj* denoting a project in which a single contractor has responsibility for the complete job
TURNKEYS > TURNKEY

TURNOFF *n* road or other way branching off from the main
TURNOFFS > TURNOFF
TURNON *n* something sexually exciting
TURNONS > TURNON
TURNOUT *n* number of people appearing at a gathering
TURNOUTS > TURNOUT
TURNOVER *n* total sales made by a business over a certain period
TURNOVERS
> TURNOVER
TURNPIKE *n* road where a toll is collected at barriers
TURNPIKES
> TURNPIKE
TURNROUND *n* act or process in which a ship, aircraft, etc unloads passengers and freight and reloads for the next trip
TURNS > TURN
TURNSKIN *n* old name for a werewolf
TURNSKINS
> TURNSKIN
TURNSOLE *n* any of various plants having flowers that are said to turn towards the sun
TURNSOLES
> TURNSOLE
TURNSPIT *n* servant whose job was to turn the spit on which meat was roasting
TURNSPITS
> TURNSPIT
TURNSTILE *n* revolving gate for admitting one person at a time
TURNSTONE *n* shore bird
TURNT *adj* slang word for intoxicated
TURNTABLE *n* revolving platform
TURNUP *n* the turned-up fold at the bottom of some trouser legs
TURNUPS > TURNUP
TUROPHILE *n* person who loves cheese
TURPETH *n* convolvulaceous plant of India, having roots with purgative properties
TURPETHS > TURPETH
TURPITUDE *n* wickedness
TURPS *n* colourless, flammable liquid
TURQUOIS *variant of*
> TURQUOISE
TURQUOISE *adj* blue-green ▷ *n* blue-green precious stone
TURR *n* Newfoundland name for the guillemot
TURRET *n* small tower
TURRETED *adj* having or resembling a turret or turrets
TURRETS > TURRET

TURRIBANT *old variant of*
> TURBAN
TURRICAL *adj* of, relating to, or resembling a turret
TURRS > TURR
TURTLE *n* sea tortoise ▷ *vb* catch turtles
TURTLED > TURTLE
TURTLER > TURTLE
TURTLERS > TURTLE
TURTLES > TURTLE
TURTLING *n* act of catching turtles
TURTLINGS
> TURTLING
TURVES > TURF
TUSCHE *n* substance used in lithography for drawing the design
TUSCHES > TUSCHE
TUSH *interj* exclamation of disapproval or contempt ▷ *n* small tusk ▷ *vb* utter the interjection 'tush'
TUSHED > TUSH
TUSHERIES > TUSHERY
TUSHERY *n* use of affectedly archaic language in novels, etc
TUSHES > TUSH
TUSHIE *n* pair of buttocks
TUSHIES > TUSHIE
TUSHING > TUSH
TUSHKAR *variant of*
> TUSKAR
TUSHKARS > TUSHKAR
TUSHKER *variant of*
> TUSKAR
TUSHKERS > TUSHKER
TUSHY *variant of*
> TUSHIE
TUSK *n* long pointed tooth of an elephant, walrus, etc ▷ *vb* stab, tear, or gore with the tusks
TUSKAR *n* peat-cutting spade
TUSKARS > TUSKAR
TUSKED > TUSK
TUSKER *n* any animal with prominent tusks, esp a wild boar or elephant
TUSKERS > TUSKER
TUSKIER > TUSK
TUSKIEST > TUSK
TUSKING > TUSK
TUSKINGS > TUSK
TUSKLESS > TUSK
TUSKLIKE > TUSK
TUSKS > TUSK
TUSKY > TUSK
TUSSAC *modifier* as in *tussac grass* kind of grass
TUSSAH *same as*
> TUSSORE
TUSSAHS > TUSSAH
TUSSAL > TUSSIS
TUSSAR *variant of*
> TUSSORE
TUSSARS > TUSSAR
TUSSEH *variant of*
> TUSSORE
TUSSEHS > TUSSEH
TUSSER *same as*
> TUSSORE
TUSSERS > TUSSER
TUSSES > TUSSIS

TUSSIS *technical name for a* > COUGH
TUSSISES > TUSSIS
TUSSIVE > TUSSIS
TUSSLE *vb* fight or scuffle ▷ *n* energetic fight, struggle, or argument
TUSSLED > TUSSLE
TUSSLES > TUSSLE
TUSSLING > TUSSLE
TUSSOCK *n* tuft of grass
TUSSOCKED *adj* having tussocks
TUSSOCKS > TUSSOCK
TUSSOCKY *adj* covered with tussocks
TUSSOR *variant of* > TUSSORE
TUSSORE *n* strong coarse brownish Indian silk
TUSSORES > TUSSORE
TUSSORS > TUSSOR
TUSSUCK *variant of* > TUSSOCK
TUSSUCKS > TUSSUCK
TUSSUR *variant of* > TUSSORE
TUSSURS > TUSSUR
TUT *interj* exclamation of mild disapproval, or surprise ▷ *vb* express disapproval by the exclamation of 'tut-tut' ▷ *n* payment system based on measurable work done
TUTANIA *n* alloy of low melting point used mostly for decorative purposes
TUTANIAS > TUTANIA
TUTEE *n* one who is tutored, esp in a university
TUTEES > TUTEE
TUTELAGE *n* instruction or guidance, esp by a tutor
TUTELAGES > TUTELAGE
TUTELAR *same as* > TUTELARY
TUTELARS > TUTELAR
TUTELARY *adj* having the role of guardian or protector ▷ *n* tutelary person, deity, or saint
TUTENAG *n* zinc alloy
TUTENAGS > TUTENAG
TUTIORISM *n* (in Roman Catholic moral theology) the doctrine that in cases of moral doubt it is best to follow the safer course or that in agreement with the law
TUTIORIST > TUTIORISM
TUTMAN *n* one who does tutwork
TUTMEN > TUTMAN
TUTOR *n* person teaching individuals or small groups ▷ *vb* act as a tutor to
TUTORAGE > TUTOR
TUTORAGES > TUTOR
TUTORED > TUTOR
TUTORESS *n* female tutor
TUTORIAL *n* period of instruction with a tutor ▷ *adj* of or relating to a tutor

TUTORIALS > TUTORIAL
TUTORING > TUTOR
TUTORINGS > TUTOR
TUTORISE *variant spelling of* > TUTORIZE
TUTORISED > TUTORISE
TUTORISES > TUTORISE
TUTORISM > TUTOR
TUTORISMS > TUTOR
TUTORIZE *vb* tutor
TUTORIZED > TUTOR
TUTORIZES > TUTORIZE
TUTORS > TUTOR
TUTORSHIP > TUTOR
TUTOYED *adj* addressed in a familiar way
TUTOYER *vb* speak to someone on familiar terms
TUTOYERED > TUTOYER
TUTOYERS > TUTOYER
TUTRESS *same as* > TUTORESS
TUTRESSES > TUTRESS
TUTRICES > TUTRIX
TUTRIX *n* female tutor; tutoress
TUTRIXES > TUTRIX
TUTS *Scots version of* > TUT
TUTSAN *n* woodland shrub of Europe and W Asia
TUTSANS > TUTSAN
TUTSED > TUTS
TUTSES > TUTS
TUTSING > TUTS
TUTTED > TUT
TUTTI *adv* to be performed by the whole orchestra or choir ▷ *n* piece of tutti music
TUTTIES > TUTTY
TUTTING > TUT
TUTTINGS > TUT
TUTTIS > TUTTI
TUTTY *n* finely powdered impure zinc oxide
TUTU *n* short stiff skirt worn by ballerinas
TUTUED *adj* wearing tutu
TUTUS > TUTU
TUTWORK *n* work paid using a tut system
TUTWORKER > TUTWORK
TUTWORKS > TUTWORK
TUX *short for* > TUXEDO
TUXEDO *n* dinner jacket
TUXEDOED *adj* wearing a tuxedo
TUXEDOES > TUXEDO
TUXEDOS > TUXEDO
TUXES > TUX
TUYER *variant of* > TUYERE
TUYERE *n* water-cooled nozzle through which air is blown into a cupola, blast furnace, or forge
TUYERES > TUYERE
TUYERS > TUYER
TUZZ *n* tuft or clump of hair
TUZZES > TUZZ

TWA *Scots word for* > TWO
TWADDLE *n* silly or pretentious talk or writing ▷ *vb* talk or write in a silly or pretentious way
TWADDLED > TWADDLE
TWADDLER > TWADDLE
TWADDLERS > TWADDLE
TWADDLES > TWADDLE
TWADDLIER > TWADDLE
TWADDLING > TWADDLE
TWADDLY > TWADDLE
TWAE *same as* > TWA
TWAES > TWAE
TWAFALD *Scots variant of* > TWOFOLD
TWAIN *n* two
TWAINS > TWAIN
TWAITE *n* herring-like food fish
TWAITES > TWAITE
TWAL *n* Scots word meaning twelve
TWALPENNY *n* old Scots shilling
TWALS > TWAL
TWANG *n* sharp ringing sound ▷ *vb* (cause to) make a twang
TWANGED > TWANG
TWANGER > TWANG
TWANGERS > TWANG
TWANGIER > TWANG
TWANGIEST > TWANG
TWANGING > TWANG
TWANGINGS > TWANG
TWANGLE *vb* make a continuous loose twanging sound
TWANGLED > TWANGLE
TWANGLER > TWANGLE
TWANGLERS > TWANGLE
TWANGLES > TWANGLE
TWANGLING > TWANGLE
TWANGS > TWANG
TWANGY > TWANG
TWANK *vb* make a sharply curtailed twang
TWANKAY *n* variety of Chinese green tea
TWANKAYS > TWANKAY
TWANKED > TWANK
TWANKIES > TWANKY
TWANKING > TWANK
TWANKS > TWANK
TWANKY *same as* > TWANKAY
TWAS > TWA
TWASOME *same as* > TWOSOME
TWASOMES > TWASOME
TWAT *vb* hit or strike violently
TWATS > TWAT
TWATTED > TWAT
TWATTING > TWAT
TWATTLE *rare word for* > TWADDLE
TWATTLED > TWATTLE
TWATTLER > TWATTLE
TWATTLERS > TWATTLE
TWATTLES > TWATTLE
TWATTLING > TWATTLE
TWAY *old variant of* > TWAIN
TWAYBLADE *n* type of orchid

TWAYS > TWAY
TWEAK *vb* pinch or twist sharply ▷ *n* instance of tweaking
TWEAKED > TWEAK
TWEAKER *n* engineer's small screwdriver
TWEAKERS > TWEAKER
TWEAKIER > TWEAK
TWEAKIEST > TWEAK
TWEAKING > TWEAK
TWEAKINGS > TWEAK
TWEAKS > TWEAK
TWEAKY > TWEAK
TWEE *adj* too sentimental, sweet, or pretty
TWEED *n* thick woollen cloth
TWEEDIER > TWEEDY
TWEEDIEST > TWEEDY
TWEEDILY *adv* in a manner characteristic of upper-class people who live in the country
TWEEDLE *vb* improvise aimlessly on a musical instrument
TWEEDLED > TWEEDLE
TWEEDLER > TWEEDLE
TWEEDLERS > TWEEDLE
TWEEDLES > TWEEDLE
TWEEDLING > TWEEDLE
TWEEDS > TWEED
TWEEDY *adj* of or made of tweed
TWEEL *variant of* > TWILL
TWEELED > TWEEL
TWEELING > TWEEL
TWEELS > TWEEL
TWEELY > TWEE
TWEEN *same as* > BETWEEN
TWEENAGE *adj* (of a child) between about eight and fourteen years old
TWEENAGER *n* child of approximately eight to fourteen years of age
TWEENER *same as* > TWEENAGER
TWEENERS > TWEENER
TWEENESS > TWEE
TWEENIE *same as* > TWEENY
TWEENIES > TWEENY
TWEENS > TWEEN
TWEENY *n* maid who assists both cook and housemaid
TWEEP *n* person who uses Twitter
TWEEPLE *pl n* people who communicate via the Twitter website
TWEEPS > TWEEP
TWEER *variant of* > TWIRE
TWEERED > TWEER
TWEERING > TWEER
TWEERS > TWEER
TWEEST > TWEE
TWEET *vb* chirp ▷ *interj* imitation of the thin chirping sound made by small birds
TWEETABLE *adj* (of a message) short enough to be posted on Twitter
TWEETED > TWEET

TWEETER n loudspeaker reproducing high-frequency sounds
TWEETERS > TWEETER
TWEETING > TWEET
TWEETS > TWEET
TWEETUP n online meeting of individuals arranged on the social networking website Twitter
TWEETUPS > TWEETUP
TWEEZE vb take hold of or pluck (hair, small objects, etc) with or as if with tweezers
TWEEZED > TWEEZE
TWEEZER same as > TWEEZERS
TWEEZERS pl n small pincer-like tool
TWEEZES > TWEEZE
TWEEZING > TWEEZE
TWELFTH n number twelve in a series ▷ adj of or being number twelve in a series
TWELFTHLY adv in the twelfth place or position
TWELFTHS > TWELFTH
TWELVE n two more than ten
TWELVEMO another word for > DUODECIMO
TWELVEMOS > TWELVEMO
TWELVES > TWELVE
TWENTIES > TWENTY
TWENTIETH adj coming after the nineteenth in numbering or counting order, position, time, etc ▷ n one of 20 approximately equal parts of something
TWENTY n two times ten
TWENTYISH adj around 20
TWERK vb dance provocatively by moving the hips rapidly back and forth
TWERKED > TWERK
TWERKING n type of dance involving rapid hip movement
TWERKINGS > TWERKING
TWERKS > TWERK
TWERP n silly person
TWERPIER > TWERP
TWERPIEST > TWERP
TWERPS > TWERP
TWERPY > TWERP
TWIBIL same as > TWIBILL
TWIBILL n mattock with a blade shaped like an adze at one end and like an axe at the other
TWIBILLS > TWIBILL
TWIBILS > TWIBIL
TWICE adv two times
TWICER n someone who does something twice
TWICERS > TWICER
TWICHILD n old word for a person in his or her dotage

TWIDDLE vb fiddle or twirl in an idle way ▷ n act or instance of twiddling
TWIDDLED > TWIDDLE
TWIDDLER > TWIDDLE
TWIDDLERS > TWIDDLE
TWIDDLES > TWIDDLE
TWIDDLIER > TWIDDLE
TWIDDLING > TWIDDLE
TWIDDLY > TWIDDLE
TWIER variant of > TUYERE
TWIERS > TWIER
TWIFOLD variant of > TWOFOLD
TWIFORKED adj having two forks; bifurcate
TWIFORMED adj having two forms
TWIG n small branch or shoot ▷ vb realize or understand
TWIGGED > TWIG
TWIGGEN adj made of twigs
TWIGGER > TWIG
TWIGGERS > TWIG
TWIGGIER > TWIGGY
TWIGGIEST > TWIGGY
TWIGGING > TWIG
TWIGGY adj of or relating to a twig or twigs
TWIGHT old variant of > TWIT
TWIGHTED > TWIGHT
TWIGHTING > TWIGHT
TWIGHTS > TWIGHT
TWIGLESS > TWIG
TWIGLET n small twig
TWIGLETS > TWIGLET
TWIGLIKE > TWIG
TWIGLOO n temporary shelter made from twigs, branches, leaves, etc
TWIGLOOS > TWIGLOO
TWIGS > TWIG
TWIGSOME adj covered with twigs; twiggy
TWILIGHT n soft dim light just after sunset ▷ adj of or relating to the period towards the end of the day
TWILIGHTS > TWILIGHT
TWILIT > TWILIGHT
TWILL n fabric woven to produce parallel ridges ▷ adj of a weave in which the weft yarns are worked around two or more warp yarns ▷ vb weave in this fashion
TWILLED > TWILL
TWILLIES > TWILLY
TWILLING > TWILL
TWILLINGS > TWILL
TWILLS > TWILL
TWILLY n machine having revolving spikes for opening and cleaning raw textile fibres
TWILT variant of > QUILT
TWILTED > TWILT
TWILTING > TWILT
TWILTS > TWILT
TWIN n one of a pair, esp of two children born at one birth ▷ vb pair or be paired

TWINBERRY n creeping wooden plant
TWINBORN adj born as a twin
TWINE n string or cord ▷ vb twist or coil round
TWINED > TWINE
TWINER > TWINE
TWINERS > TWINE
TWINES > TWINE
TWINGE n sudden sharp pain or emotional pang ▷ vb have or cause to have a twinge
TWINGED > TWINGE
TWINGEING > TWINGE
TWINGES > TWINGE
TWINGING > TWINGE
TWINIER > TWINE
TWINIEST > TWINE
TWINIGHT adj (of a baseball double-header) held in the late afternoon and evening
TWINING > TWINE
TWININGLY > TWINE
TWININGS > TWINE
TWINJET n jet aircraft with two engines
TWINJETS > TWINJET
TWINK n white correction fluid for deleting written text ▷ vb twinkle
TWINKED > TWINK
TWINKIE n stupid person
TWINKIES > TWINKIE
TWINKING > TWINK
TWINKLE vb shine brightly but intermittently ▷ n flickering brightness
TWINKLED > TWINKLE
TWINKLER > TWINKLE
TWINKLERS > TWINKLE
TWINKLES > TWINKLE
TWINKLIER > TWINKLY
TWINKLING n very short time
TWINKLY adj sparkling
TWINKS > TWINK
TWINKY n stupid person
TWINLING old name for > TWIN
TWINLINGS > TWINLING
TWINNED > TWIN
TWINNING > TWIN
TWINNINGS > TWIN
TWINS > TWIN
TWINSET n matching jumper and cardigan
TWINSETS > TWINSET
TWINSHIP n condition of being a twin or twins
TWINSHIPS > TWIN
TWINTER n animal that is two years old
TWINTERS > TWINTER
TWINY > TWINE
TWIRE vb look intently at with (or as if with) difficulty
TWIRED > TWIRE
TWIRES > TWIRE
TWIRING > TWIRE
TWIRL vb turn or spin around quickly ▷ n whirl or twist
TWIRLED > TWIRL

TWIRLER > TWIRL
TWIRLERS > TWIRL
TWIRLIER > TWIRL
TWIRLIEST > TWIRL
TWIRLING > TWIRL
TWIRLS > TWIRL
TWIRLY > TWIRL
TWIRP same as > TWERP
TWIRPIER > TWIRP
TWIRPIEST > TWIRP
TWIRPS > TWIRP
TWIRPY > TWIRP
TWISCAR variant of > TUSKAR
TWISCARS > TWISCAR
TWIST vb turn out of the natural position ▷ n twisting
TWISTABLE > TWIST
TWISTED > TWIST
TWISTER n swindler
TWISTERS > TWISTER
TWISTIER > TWIST
TWISTIEST > TWIST
TWISTING > TWIST
TWISTINGS > TWIST
TWISTOR n variable corresponding to the coordinates of a point in space and time
TWISTORS > TWISTOR
TWISTS > TWIST
TWISTY > TWIST
TWIT vb poke fun at (someone) ▷ n foolish person
TWITCH vb move spasmodically ▷ n nervous muscular spasm
TWITCHED > TWITCH
TWITCHER n bird-watcher who tries to spot as many rare varieties as possible
TWITCHERS > TWITCHER
TWITCHES > TWITCH
TWITCHIER > TWITCHY
TWITCHILY > TWITCHY
TWITCHING > TWITCH
TWITCHY adj nervous, worried, and ill-at-ease
TWITE n N European finch with a brown streaked plumage
TWITES > TWITE
TWITS > TWIT
TWITTED > TWIT
TWITTEN n narrow alleyway
TWITTENS > TWITTEN
TWITTER vb (of birds) utter chirping sounds ▷ n act or sound of twittering
TWITTERED > TWITTER
TWITTERER > TWITTER
TWITTERS > TWITTER
TWITTERY adj making a chirping sound
TWITTING > TWIT
TWITTINGS > TWIT
TWITTISH adj silly; foolish
TWIXT same as > BETWIXT
TWIZZLE vb spin around
TWIZZLED > TWIZZLE

TWIZZLES > TWIZZLE
TWIZZLING > TWIZZLE
TWO n one more than one
TWOCCER > TWOCCING
TWOCCERS > TWOCCING
TWOCCING n act of breaking into a motor vehicle and driving it away
TWOCCINGS > TWOCCING
TWOCKER > TWOCCING
TWOCKERS > TWOCCING
TWOCKING same as > TWOCCING
TWOCKINGS > TWOCKING
TWOER n (in a game) something that scores two
TWOERS > TWOER
TWOFER n single ticket allowing the buyer entrance to two events
TWOFERS > TWOFER
TWOFOLD adj having twice as many or as much ▷ adv by twice as many or as much ▷ n folding piece of theatrical scenery
TWOFOLDS > TWOFOLD
TWONESS n state or condition of being two
TWONESSES > TWONESS
TWONIE same as > TOONIE
TWONIES > TWONIE
TWOONIE variant of > TOONIE
TWOONIES > TWOONIE
TWOPENCE n sum of two pennies
TWOPENCES > TWOPENCE
TWOPENNY adj cheap or tawdry
TWOS > TWO
TWOSEATER n vehicle providing seats for two people
TWOSOME n group of two people
TWOSOMES > TWOSOME
TWOSTROKE adj relating to or designating an internal-combustion engine whose piston makes two strokes for every explosion
TWP adj Welsh dialect word meaning stupid
TWYER same as > TUYERE
TWYERE variant of > TUYERE
TWYERES > TWYERE
TWYERS > TWYER
TWYFOLD adj twofold
TYCHISM n theory that chance is an objective reality at work in the universe
TYCHISMS > TYCHISM
TYCOON n powerful wealthy businessperson; shogun
TYCOONATE n office or rule of a tycoon
TYCOONERY > TYCOON
TYCOONS > TYCOON

TYDE old variant of the past participle of > TIE
TYE n trough used in mining to separate valuable material from dross ▷ vb (in mining) isolate valuable material from dross using a tye
TYED > TYE
TYEE n large northern Pacific salmon
TYEES > TYEE
TYEING > TYE
TYER > TYE
TYERS > TYE
TYES > TYE
TYG n mug with two handles
TYGS > TYG
TYIN variant of > TYIYN
TYING > TIE
TYIYN n money unit of Kyrgyzstan
TYIYNS > TYIYN
TYKE n dog
TYKES > TYKE
TYKISH > TYKE
TYLECTOMY n excision of a breast tumour
TYLER variant of > TILER
TYLERS > TYLER
TYLOPOD n mammal with padded feet, such as a camel or llama
TYLOPODS > TYLOPOD
TYLOSES > TYLOSIS
TYLOSIN n broad spectrum antibiotic
TYLOSINS > TYLOSIN
TYLOSIS n bladder-like outgrowth from certain cells in woody tissue
TYLOTE n knobbed sponge spicule
TYLOTES > TYLOTE
TYMBAL same as > TIMBAL
TYMBALS > TYMBAL
TYMP n blast furnace outlet through which molten metal flows
TYMPAN same as > TYMPANUM
TYMPANA > TYMPANUM
TYMPANAL adj relating to the tympanum
TYMPANI same as > TIMPANI
TYMPANIC adj of, relating to, or having a tympanum ▷ n part of the temporal bone in the mammalian skull that surrounds the auditory canal
TYMPANICS > TYMPANIC
TYMPANIES > TYMPANY
TYMPANIST > TIMPANI
TYMPANO > TYMPANI
TYMPANS > TYMPAN
TYMPANUM n cavity of the middle ear
TYMPANUMS > TYMPANUM
TYMPANY n distention of the abdomen
TYMPS > TYMP
TYND variant of > TIND

TYNDE variant of > TIND
TYNE variant of > TINE
TYNED > TYNE
TYNES > TYNE
TYNING > TYNE
TYPABLE > TYPE
TYPAL rare word for > TYPICAL
TYPE n class or category ▷ vb print with a typewriter or word processor
TYPEABLE > TYPE
TYPEBAR n one of the bars in a typewriter that carry the type and are operated by keys
TYPEBARS > TYPEBAR
TYPECASE n compartmental tray for storing printer's type
TYPECASES > TYPECASE
TYPECAST vb continually cast (an actor or actress) in similar roles
TYPECASTS > TYPECAST
TYPED > TYPE
TYPEFACE n style of the type
TYPEFACES > TYPEFACE
TYPES > TYPE
TYPESET vb set (text for printing) in type
TYPESETS > TYPESET
TYPESTYLE another word for > TYPEFACE
TYPEWRITE vb write by means of a typewriter
TYPEWROTE > TYPEWRITE
TYPEY variant of > TYPY
TYPHLITIC > TYPHLITIS
TYPHLITIS n inflammation of the caecum
TYPHOID adj of or relating to typhoid fever ▷ n typhoid fever
TYPHOIDAL > TYPHOID
TYPHOIDIN n culture of dead typhoid bacillus for injection into the skin to test for typhoid fever
TYPHOIDS > TYPHOID
TYPHON n whirlwind
TYPHONIAN > TYPHON
TYPHONIC > TYPHOON
TYPHONS > TYPHON
TYPHOON n violent tropical storm
TYPHOONS > TYPHOON
TYPHOSE adj relating to typhoid
TYPHOUS > TYPHUS
TYPHUS n infectious feverish disease
TYPHUSES > TYPHUS
TYPIC same as > TYPICAL
TYPICAL adj true to type, characteristic
TYPICALLY > TYPICAL
TYPIER > TYPY
TYPIEST > TYPY

TYPIFIED > TYPIFY
TYPIFIER > TYPIFY
TYPIFIERS > TYPIFY
TYPIFIES > TYPIFY
TYPIFY vb be typical of
TYPIFYING > TYPIFY
TYPING n work or activity of using a typewriter or word processor
TYPINGS > TYPING
TYPIST n person who types with a typewriter or word processor
TYPISTS > TYPIST
TYPO n typographical error
TYPOGRAPH n person skilled in the art of composing type and printing from it
TYPOLOGIC > TYPOLOGY
TYPOLOGY n study of types
TYPOMANIA n obsession with typology
TYPOS > TYPO
TYPP n unit of thickness of yarn
TYPPS > TYPP
TYPTO vb learn Greek conjugations
TYPTOED > TYPTO
TYPTOING > TYPTO
TYPTOS > TYPTO
TYPY adj (of an animal) typifying the breed
TYRAMINE n colourless crystalline amine derived from phenol
TYRAMINES > TYRAMINE
TYRAN vb act as a tyrant
TYRANED > TYRAN
TYRANING > TYRAN
TYRANNE variant of > TYRAN
TYRANNED > TYRANNE
TYRANNES > TYRANNE
TYRANNESS n female tyrant
TYRANNIC > TYRANNY
TYRANNIES > TYRANNY
TYRANNING > TYRANNE
TYRANNIS n tyrannical government
TYRANNISE same as > TYRANNIZE
TYRANNIZE vb exert power (over) oppressively or cruelly
TYRANNOUS > TYRANNY
TYRANNY n tyrannical rule
TYRANS > TYRAN
TYRANT n oppressive or cruel ruler ▷ vb act the tyrant
TYRANTED > TYRANT
TYRANTING > TYRANT
TYRANTS > TYRANT
TYRE n rubber ring, usu inflated, over the rim of a vehicle's wheel to grip the road ▷ vb fit a tyre or tyres to (a wheel, vehicle, etc)
TYRED > TYRE
TYRELESS > TYRE

t

TYREMAKER n one who makes tyres

TYRES > TYRE

TYRING > TYRE

TYRO n novice or beginner

TYROCIDIN n antibiotic

TYROES > TYRO

TYRONES > TYRO

TYRONIC > TYRO

TYROPITA n Greek cheese pie

TYROPITAS > TYROPITA

TYROPITTA n Greek cheese pie

TYROS > TYRO

TYROSINE n aromatic nonessential amino acid

TYROSINES > TYROSINE

TYSTIE n black guillemot

TYSTIES > TYSTIE

TYTE variant spelling of > TITE

TYTHE variant of > TITHE

TYTHED > TYTHE

TYTHES > TYTHE

TYTHING > TYTHE

TZADDI same as > SADHE

TZADDIK variant of > ZADDIK

TZADDIKIM > TZADDIK

TZADDIKS > TZADDIK

TZADDIQ variant of > ZADDIK

TZADDIQIM > TZADDIQ

TZADDIQS > TZADDIQ

TZADDIS > TZADDI

TZADIK same as > ZADDIK

TZADIKS > TZADIK

TZAR same as > TSAR

TZARDOM > TZAR

TZARDOMS > TZARDOM

TZAREVNA variant of > TSAREVNA

TZAREVNAS > TZAREVNA

TZARINA variant of > TSARINA

TZARINAS > TZARINA

TZARISM variant of > TSARISM

TZARISMS > TZARISM

TZARIST variant of > TSARIST

TZARISTS > TZARIST

TZARITZA variant of > TSARITSA

TZARITZAS > TZARITZA

TZARS > TZAR

TZATZIKI n Greek dip made from yogurt, chopped cucumber, and mint

TZATZIKIS > TZATZIKI

TZEDAKAH n charitable donations as a Jewish moral obligation

TZEDAKAHS > TZEDAKAH

TZETSE variant of > TSETSE

TZETSES > TZETSE

TZETZE variant of > TSETSE

TZETZES > TZETZE

TZIGANE n Romany dance

TZIGANES > TZIGANE

TZIGANIES > TZIGANY

TZIGANY variant of > TZIGANE

TZIMMES n traditional Jewish stew

TZITZIS variant of > TSITSITH

TZITZIT variant of > TSITSITH

TZITZITH variant of > TSITSITH

TZURIS variant of > TSURIS

TZURISES > TZURIS

Uu

UAKARI *n* type of monkey
UAKARIS > UAKARI
UBEROUS *adj* abundant
UBERTIES > UBERTY
UBERTY *n* abundance
UBIETIES > UBIETY
UBIETY *n* condition of being in a particular place
UBIQUE *adv* everywhere
UBIQUITIN *n* type of polypeptide
UBIQUITY *n* state of apparently being everywhere at once; omnipresence
UBUNTU *n* quality of compassion and humanity
UBUNTUS > UBUNTU
UCKERS *n* type of naval game
UDAL *n* form of freehold possession of land used in Orkney and Shetland
UDALLER *n* person possessing a udal
UDALLERS > UDALLER
UDALS > UDAL
UDDER *n* large baglike milk-producing gland of cows, sheep, or goats
UDDERED > UDDER
UDDERFUL *n* capacity of an udder
UDDERFULS > UDDERFUL
UDDERLESS > UDDER
UDDERS > UDDER
UDO *n* stout perennial plant of Japan and China
UDOMETER *n* archaic term for an instrument for measuring rainfall or snowfall
UDOMETERS > UDOMETER
UDOMETRIC > UDOMETER
UDOMETRY > UDOMETER
UDON *n* (in Japanese cookery) large noodles made of wheat flour
UDONS > UDON
UDOS > UDO
UDS *interj* God's or God save
UEY *n* u-turn
UEYS > UEY
UFO *n* flying saucer
UFOLOGIES > UFOLOGY
UFOLOGIST > UFOLOGY
UFOLOGY *n* study of UFOs
UFOS > UFO
UG *vb* hate

UGALI *n* type of stiff porridge
UGALIS > UGALI
UGGED > UG
UGGING > UG
UGH *interj* exclamation of disgust ▷ *n* sound made to indicate disgust
UGHS > UGH
UGLIED > UGLY
UGLIER > UGLY
UGLIES > UGLY
UGLIEST > UGLY
UGLIFIED > UGLIFY
UGLIFIER > UGLIFY
UGLIFIERS > UGLIFY
UGLIFIES > UGLIFY
UGLIFY *vb* make or become ugly or more ugly
UGLIFYING > UGLIFY
UGLILY > UGLY
UGLINESS > UGLY
UGLY *adj* of unpleasant appearance ▷ *vb* make ugly
UGLYING > UGLY
UGS > UG
UGSOME *adj* loathsome
UH *interj* used to express hesitation
UHLAN *n* member of a body of lancers first employed in the Polish army
UHLANS > UHLAN
UHURU *n* national independence
UHURUS > UHURU
UILLEAN *adj* as in *uillean pipes* bagpipes developed in Ireland
UILLEANN *same as* > UILLEAN
UINTAHITE *same as* > UINTAITE
UINTAITE *n* variety of asphalt
UINTAITES > UINTAITE
UITLANDER *n* S African word for a foreigner
UJAMAA *n* communally organized village in Tanzania
UJAMAAS > UJAMAA
UKASE *n* (in imperial Russia) a decree from the tsar
UKASES > UKASE
UKE *short form of* > UKULELE
UKELELE *same as* > UKULELE
UKELELES > UKELELE

UKES > UKE
UKULELE *n* small guitar with four strings
UKULELES > UKULELE
ULAMA *n* body of Muslim scholars or religious leaders
ULAMAS > ULAMA
ULAN *same as* > UHLAN
ULANS > ULAN
ULCER *n* open sore on the surface of the skin or mucous membrane. ▷ *vb* make or become ulcerous
ULCERATE *vb* make or become ulcerous
ULCERATED > ULCERATE
ULCERATES > ULCERATE
ULCERED > ULCER
ULCERING > ULCER
ULCEROUS *adj* of, like, or characterized by ulcers
ULCERS > ULCER
ULE *n* rubber tree
ULEMA *same as* > ULAMA
ULEMAS > ULEMA
ULES > ULE
ULEX *n* variety of shrub
ULEXES > ULEX
ULEXITE *n* type of mineral
ULEXITES > ULEXITE
ULICES > ULEX
ULICON *same as* > EULACHON
ULICONS > ULICON
ULIGINOSE *same as* > ULIGINOUS
ULIGINOUS *adj* marshy
ULIKON *same as* > EULACHON
ULIKONS > ULIKON
ULITIS *n* gingivitis
ULITISES > ULITIS
ULLAGE *n* volume by which a liquid container falls short of being full ▷ *vb* create ullage in
ULLAGED > ULLAGE
ULLAGES > ULLAGE
ULLAGING > ULLAGE
ULLING *n* process of filling
ULLINGS > ULLING
ULMACEOUS *adj* relating to the family of deciduous trees and shrubs which includes the elms
ULMIN *n* substance found in decaying vegetation
ULMINS > ULMIN

ULNA *n* inner and longer of the two bones of the human forearm
ULNAD *adv* towards the ulna
ULNAE > ULNA
ULNAR > ULNA
ULNARE *n* bone in the wrist
ULNARIA > ULNARE
ULNAS > ULNA
ULOSES > ULOSIS
ULOSIS *n* formation of a scar
ULOTRICHY *n* state of having woolly or curly hair
ULPAN *n* Israeli study centre
ULPANIM > ULPAN
ULSTER *n* man's heavy double-breasted overcoat
ULSTERED *adj* wearing an ulster
ULSTERS > ULSTER
ULTERIOR *adj* (of an aim, reason, etc) concealed or hidden
ULTIMA *n* final syllable of a word
ULTIMACY > ULTIMATE
ULTIMAS > ULTIMA
ULTIMATA > ULTIMATUM
ULTIMATE *adj* final in a series or process ▷ *n* most significant, highest, furthest, or greatest thing ▷ *vb* end
ULTIMATED > ULTIMATE
ULTIMATES > ULTIMATE
ULTIMATUM *n* final warning stating that action will be taken unless certain conditions are met
ULTIMO *adv* in or during the previous month
ULTION *n* vengeance
ULTIONS > ULTION
ULTISOL *n* reddish-yellow acid soil
ULTISOLS > ULTISOL
ULTRA *n* person who has extreme or immoderate beliefs or opinions ▷ *adj* extreme or immoderate, esp in beliefs or opinions
ULTRACHIC *adj* extremely chic
ULTRACOLD *adj* extremely cold
ULTRACOOL *adj* extremely cool

u

ULTRADRY adj extremely dry

ULTRAFAST adj extremely fast

ULTRAFINE adj extremely fine

ULTRAHEAT vb sterilize through extreme heat treatment

ULTRAHIGH adj as in *ultrahigh frequency* radio-frequency band or radio frequency lying between 3000 and 300 megahertz

ULTRAHIP adj extremely trendy

ULTRAHOT adj extremely hot

ULTRAISM n extreme philosophy, belief, or action

ULTRAISMS > ULTRAISM

ULTRAIST > ULTRAISM

ULTRAISTS > ULTRAISM

ULTRALEFT n extreme political Left ▷ adj of the extreme political Left or extremely radical

ULTRALOW adj extremely low

ULTRAPOSH adj extremely posh

ULTRAPURE adj extremely pure

ULTRARARE adj extremely rare

ULTRARED obsolete word for > INFRARED

ULTRAREDS > ULTRARED

ULTRARICH adj extremely rich

ULTRAS > ULTRA

ULTRASAFE adj extremely safe

ULTRASLOW adj extremely slow

ULTRASOFT adj extremely soft

ULTRATHIN adj extremely thin

ULTRATINY adj extremely small

ULTRAWIDE adj extremely wide

ULU n type of knife

ULULANT > ULULATE

ULULATE vb howl or wail

ULULATED > ULULATE

ULULATES > ULULATE

ULULATING > ULULATE

ULULATION > ULULATE

ULUS > ULU

ULVA n genus of seaweed

ULVAS > ULVA

ULYIE Scots variant of > OIL

ULYIES > ULYIE

ULZIE Scots variant of > OIL

ULZIES > ULZIE

UM interj representation of a common sound made when hesitating in speech ▷ vb hesitate while speaking

UMAMI n savoury flavour

UMAMIS > UMAMI

UMANGITE n type of mineral

UMANGITES > UMANGITE

UMBEL n umbrella-like flower cluster

UMBELED same as > UMBELLED

UMBELLAR > UMBEL

UMBELLATE > UMBEL

UMBELLED adj having umbels

UMBELLET same as > UMBELLULE

UMBELLETS > UMBELLET

UMBELLULE n any of the small secondary umbels that make up a compound umbel

UMBELS > UMBEL

UMBELULE n secondary umbel

UMBELULES > UMBELULE

UMBER adj dark brown to reddish-brown ▷ n type of dark brown earth containing ferric oxide (rust) ▷ vb stain with umber

UMBERED > UMBER

UMBERIER > UMBERY

UMBERIEST > UMBERY

UMBERING > UMBER

UMBERS > UMBER

UMBERY adj like umber

UMBILICAL adj of the navel

UMBILICI > UMBILICUS

UMBILICUS n navel

UMBLE adj as in *umble pie* (formerly) a pie made from the heart, entrails, etc of a deer

UMBLES another term for > NUMBLES

UMBO n small hump projecting from the centre of the cap in certain mushrooms

UMBONAL > UMBO

UMBONATE > UMBO

UMBONES > UMBO

UMBONIC > UMBO

UMBOS > UMBO

UMBRA n shadow, esp the shadow cast by the moon onto the earth during a solar eclipse

UMBRACULA pl n umbrella-like structures

UMBRAE > UMBRA

UMBRAGE n displeasure or resentment ▷ vb shade

UMBRAGED > UMBRAGE

UMBRAGES > UMBRAGE

UMBRAGING > UMBRAGE

UMBRAL > UMBRA

UMBRAS > UMBRA

UMBRATED adj shown in a faint manner

UMBRATIC > UMBRA

UMBRATILE adj shadowy ▷ n person who spends

their time in the shade or shadows

UMBRE same as > UMBRETTE

UMBREL n umbrella

UMBRELLA n portable device used for protection against rain ▷ adj containing many different organizations

UMBRELLAS > UMBRELLA

UMBRELLO same as > UMBRELLA

UMBRELLOS > UMBRELLO

UMBRELS > UMBREL

UMBRERE n helmet visor

UMBRERES > UMBRERE

UMBRES > UMBRE

UMBRETTE n African wading bird

UMBRETTES > UMBRETTE

UMBRIERE same as > UMBRERE

UMBRIERES > UMBRIERE

UMBRIL same as > UMBRERE

UMBRILS > UMBRIL

UMBROSE same as > UMBROUS

UMBROUS adj shady

UME n sour Japanese fruit

UMEBOSHI n dried and pickled ume

UMEBOSHIS > UMEBOSHI

UMES > UME

UMFAZI n African married woman

UMFAZIS > UMFAZI

UMIAC variant of > UMIAK

UMIACK variant of > UMIAK

UMIACKS > UMIACK

UMIACS > UMIAC

UMIAK n Inuit boat made of skins

UMIAKS > UMIAK

UMIAQ same as > UMIAK

UMIAQS > UMIAQ

UMLAUT n mark (¨) placed over a vowel, esp in German, to indicate a change in its sound ▷ vb modify by umlaut

UMLAUTED > UMLAUT

UMLAUTING > UMLAUT

UMLAUTS > UMLAUT

UMM same as > UM

UMMA n Muslim community

UMMAH same as > UMMA

UMMAHS > UMMAH

UMMAS > UMMA

UMMED > UM

UMMING > UM

UMP short for > UMPIRE

UMPED > UMP

UMPH same as > HUMPH

UMPHS > UMPH

UMPIE informal word for > UMPIRE

UMPIES > UMPY

UMPING > UMP

UMPIRAGE > UMPIRE

UMPIRAGES > UMPIRE

UMPIRE n official who rules on the playing of a game ▷ vb act as umpire in (a game)

UMPIRED > UMPIRE

UMPIRES > UMPIRE

UMPIRING > UMPIRE

UMPS > UMP

UMPTEEN adj very many

UMPTEENTH n latest in a tediously long series

UMPTIER > UMPTY

UMPTIEST > UMPTY

UMPTIETH same as > UMPTEENTH

UMPTY adj very many

UMPY same as > UMPIE

UMQUHILE adv formerly

UMRA n pilgrimage to Mecca that can be made at any time of the year

UMRAH same as > UMRA

UMRAHS > UMRAH

UMRAS > UMRA

UMS > UM

UMTEENTH same as > UMPTEENTH

UMU n type of oven

UMUS > UMU

UMWELT n environmental factors that affect the behaviour of an animal or individual

UMWELTS > UMWELT

UMWHILE same as > UMQUHILE

UN pron spelling of 'one' intended to reflect a dialectal or informal pronunciation

UNABASHED adj not ashamed or embarrassed

UNABATED adv without any reduction in force ▷ adj not losing any original force or violence

UNABATING adj not growing less in strength

UNABETTED adj without assistance

UNABIDING adj not lasting

UNABJURED adj not denied

UNABLE adj lacking the necessary power, ability, or authority (to do something)

UNABORTED adj not aborted

UNABRADED adj not eroded

UNABUSED adj not abused

UNABUSIVE adj not abusive

UNACCRUED adj not accrued

UNACCUSED adj not charged with wrongdoing

UNACERBIC adj not acerbic

UNACHING adj not aching

UNACIDIC adj not acidic

UNACTABLE adj unable to be acted

UNACTED adj not acted or performed
UNACTIVE adj inactive ▷ vb make (a person) inactive
UNACTIVED > UNACTIVE
UNACTIVES > UNACTIVE
UNADAPTED adj not adapted
UNADDED adj not added
UNADEPT adj not adept ▷ n person who is not adept
UNADEPTLY > UNADEPT
UNADEPTS > UNADEPT
UNADMIRED adj not admired
UNADOPTED adj (of a road) not maintained by a local authority
UNADORED adj not adored
UNADORNED adj not decorated
UNADULT adj not mature
UNADVISED adj rash or unwise
UNAFRAID adj not frightened or nervous
UNAGED adj not old
UNAGEING adj not ageing
UNAGILE adj not agile
UNAGING same as > UNAGEING
UNAGREED adj not agreed
UNAI same as > UNAU
UNAIDABLE adj unable to be helped
UNAIDED adv without any help or assistance ▷ adj not having received any help
UNAIDEDLY > UNAIDED
UNAIMED adj not aimed or specifically targeted
UNAIRED adj not aired
UNAIS > UNAI
UNAKIN adj not related
UNAKING Shakespearean form of > UNACHING
UNAKITE n type of mineral
UNAKITES > UNAKITE
UNALARMED adj not alarmed
UNALERTED adj not alerted
UNALIGNED adj not aligned
UNALIKE adj not similar
UNALIST n priest holding only one benefice
UNALISTS > UNALIST
UNALIVE adj unaware
UNALLAYED adj not allayed
UNALLEGED adj not alleged
UNALLIED adj not allied
UNALLOWED adj not allowed
UNALLOYED adj not spoiled by being mixed with anything else
UNALTERED adj not altered

UNAMASSED adj not amassed
UNAMAZED adj not greatly surprised
UNAMENDED adj not amended
UNAMERCED adj not amerced
UNAMIABLE adj not amiable
UNAMUSED adj not entertained, diverted, or laughing
UNAMUSING adj not entertaining
UNANCHOR vb remove anchor
UNANCHORS > UNANCHOR
UNANELED adj not having received extreme unction
UNANIMITY > UNANIMOUS
UNANIMOUS adj in complete agreement
UNANNEXED adj not annexed
UNANNOYED adj not annoyed
UNANXIOUS adj not anxious
UNAPPAREL vb undress
UNAPPLIED adj not applied
UNAPT adj not suitable or qualified
UNAPTLY > UNAPT
UNAPTNESS > UNAPT
UNARCHED adj not arched
UNARGUED adj not debated
UNARISEN adj not having risen
UNARM less common word for > DISARM
UNARMED adj without weapons
UNARMING > UNARM
UNARMORED adj without armour
UNARMS > UNARM
UNAROUSED adj not aroused
UNARRAYED adj not arrayed
UNARTFUL adj not artful
UNARY adj consisting of, or affecting, a single element or component
UNASHAMED adj not embarrassed, esp when doing something some people might find offensive
UNASKED adv without being asked to do something ▷ adj (of a question) not asked, although sometimes implied
UNASSAYED adj untried
UNASSUMED adj not assumed
UNASSURED adj insecure
UNATONED adj not atoned for
UNATTIRED adj unclothed

UNATTUNED adj unaccustomed
UNAU n two-toed sloth
UNAUDITED adj not having been audited
UNAUS > UNAU
UNAVENGED adj not avenged
UNAVERAGE adj not average
UNAVERTED adj not averted
UNAVOIDED adj not avoided
UNAVOWED adj not openly admitted
UNAWAKE adj not awake
UNAWAKED adj not aroused
UNAWARDED adj not awarded
UNAWARE adj not aware or conscious ▷ adv by surprise
UNAWARELY > UNAWARE
UNAWARES adv by surprise
UNAWED adj not awed
UNAWESOME adj not awesome
UNAXED adj not axed
UNBACKED adj (of a book, chair, etc) not having a back
UNBAFFLED adj not baffled
UNBAG vb take out of a bag
UNBAGGED > UNBAG
UNBAGGING > UNBAG
UNBAGS > UNBAG
UNBAITED adj not baited
UNBAKED adj not having been baked
UNBALANCE vb upset the equilibrium or balance of ▷ n imbalance or instability
UNBALE vb remove from bale
UNBALED > UNBALE
UNBALES > UNBALE
UNBALING > UNBALE
UNBAN vb stop banning or permit again
UNBANDAGE vb remove bandage from
UNBANDED adj not fastened with a band
UNBANKED adj not having been banked
UNBANNED > UNBAN.
UNBANNING n act of permitting again
UNBANS > UNBAN
UNBAPTISE same as > UNBAPTIZE
UNBAPTIZE vb remove the effect of baptism
UNBAR vb take away a bar or bars from
UNBARBED adj without barbs
UNBARE vb expose
UNBARED > UNBARE
UNBARES > UNBARE
UNBARING > UNBARE
UNBARK vb strip bark from

UNBARKED > UNBARK
UNBARKING > UNBARK
UNBARKS > UNBARK
UNBARRED > UNBAR
UNBARRING > UNBAR
UNBARS > UNBAR
UNBASED adj not having a base
UNBASHFUL adj not shy
UNBASTED adj not basted
UNBATED adj (of a sword, lance, etc) not covered with a protective button
UNBATHED adj unwashed
UNBE vb make non-existent
UNBEAR vb release (horse) from the bearing rein
UNBEARDED adj not having a beard
UNBEARED > UNBEAR
UNBEARING > UNBEAR
UNBEARS > UNBEAR
UNBEATEN adj having suffered no defeat
UNBED vb remove from bed
UNBEDDED > UNBED
UNBEDDING > UNBED
UNBEDS > UNBED
UNBEEN > UNBE
UNBEGET vb deprive of existence
UNBEGETS > UNBEGET
UNBEGGED adj not obtained by begging
UNBEGOT adj unbegotten
UNBEGUILE vb undeceive
UNBEGUN adj not commenced
UNBEING n non-existence
UNBEINGS > UNBEING
UNBEKNOWN adv without the knowledge (of a person) ▷ adj not known (to)
UNBELIEF n disbelief or rejection of belief
UNBELIEFS > UNBELIEF
UNBELIEVE vb disbelieve
UNBELOVED adj unhappy in love
UNBELT vb unbuckle the belt of (a garment)
UNBELTED > UNBELT
UNBELTING > UNBELT
UNBELTS > UNBELT
UNBEMUSED adj not bemused
UNBEND vb become less strict or more informal in one's attitudes or behaviour
UNBENDED > UNBEND
UNBENDING adj rigid or inflexible
UNBENDS > UNBEND
UNBENIGN adj not benign
UNBENT adj not bent or bowed
UNBEREFT adj not bereft
UNBERUFEN adj not called for
UNBESEEM vb be unbefitting to

u

UNBESEEMS
> UNBESEEM

UNBESPEAK vb annul

UNBESPOKE adj not bespoken

UNBIAS vb free from prejudice

UNBIASED adj not having or showing prejudice or favouritism

UNBIASES > UNBIAS

UNBIASING n act or process of making unbiased

UNBIASSED same as > UNBIASED

UNBIASSES > UNBIAS

UNBID same as > UNBIDDEN

UNBIDDEN adj not ordered or asked

UNBIGOTED adj not bigoted

UNBILLED adj not having been billed

UNBIND vb set free from bonds or chains

UNBINDING > UNBIND

UNBINDS > UNBIND

UNBISHOP vb remove from the position of bishop

UNBISHOPS
> UNBISHOP

UNBITT vb remove (cable) from the bitts

UNBITTED > UNBITT

UNBITTEN adj not having been bitten

UNBITTER adj not bitter

UNBITTING > UNBITT

UNBITTS > UNBITT

UNBLAMED adj not blamed

UNBLENDED adj not blended

UNBLENT same as > UNBLENDED

UNBLESS vb deprive of a blessing

UNBLESSED adj deprived of blessing

UNBLESSES > UNBLESS

UNBLEST same as > UNBLESSED

UNBLIND vb rid of blindness

UNBLINDED > UNBLIND

UNBLINDS > UNBLIND

UNBLOCK vb remove a blockage from

UNBLOCKED > UNBLOCK

UNBLOCKS > UNBLOCK

UNBLOODED adj not bloodied

UNBLOODY adj not covered with blood

UNBLOTTED adj not blotted

UNBLOWED same as > UNBLOWN

UNBLOWN adj (of a flower) still in the bud

UNBLUNTED adj not blunted

UNBLURRED adj not blurred

UNBOARDED adj not boarded

UNBOBBED adj not bobbed

UNBODIED adj having no body

UNBODING adj having no presentiment

UNBOILED adj not boiled

UNBOLT vb unfasten a bolt of (a door)

UNBOLTED adj (of grain, meal, or flour) not sifted

UNBOLTING > UNBOLT

UNBOLTS > UNBOLT

UNBONDED adj not bonded

UNBONE vb remove bone from

UNBONED adj (of meat, fish, etc) not having had the bones removed

UNBONES > UNBONE

UNBONING > UNBONE

UNBONNET vb remove the bonnet from

UNBONNETS
> UNBONNET

UNBOOKED adj not reserved

UNBOOKISH adj not studious

UNBOOT vb remove boots from

UNBOOTED > UNBOOT

UNBOOTING > UNBOOT

UNBOOTS > UNBOOT

UNBORE adj unborn

UNBORN adj not yet born

UNBORNE adj not borne

UNBOSOM vb relieve (oneself) of (secrets or feelings) by telling someone

UNBOSOMED > UNBOSOM

UNBOSOMER > UNBOSOM

UNBOSOMS > UNBOSOM

UNBOTTLE vb allow out of bottle

UNBOTTLED
> UNBOTTLE

UNBOTTLES
> UNBOTTLE

UNBOUGHT adj not purchased

UNBOUNCY adj not bouncy

UNBOUND adj (of a book) not bound within a cover

UNBOUNDED adj having no boundaries or limits

UNBOWED adj not giving in or submitting

UNBOWING adj not bowing

UNBOX vb empty a box

UNBOXED > UNBOX

UNBOXES > UNBOX

UNBOXING > UNBOX

UNBRACE vb remove tension or strain from

UNBRACED > UNBRACE

UNBRACES > UNBRACE

UNBRACING > UNBRACE

UNBRAID vb remove braids from

UNBRAIDED > UNBRAID

UNBRAIDS > UNBRAID

UNBRAKE vb stop reducing speed by releasing brake

UNBRAKED > UNBRAKE

UNBRAKES > UNBRAKE

UNBRAKING > UNBRAKE

UNBRANDED adj not having a brand name

UNBRASTE archaic past form of > UNBRACE

UNBRED adj not taught or instructed

UNBREECH vb remove breech from

UNBRIDGED adj not spanned by a bridge

UNBRIDLE vb remove the bridle from (a horse)

UNBRIDLED adj (of feelings or behaviour) not controlled in any way

UNBRIDLES
> UNBRIDLE

UNBRIEFED adj not instructed

UNBRIGHT adj not bright

UNBRIZZED same as > UNBRUISED

UNBROILED adj not broiled

UNBROKE same as > UNBROKEN

UNBROKEN adj complete or whole

UNBROWNED adj not browned

UNBRUISED adj not bruised

UNBRUSED same as > UNBRUISED

UNBRUSHED adj not brushed

UNBUCKLE vb undo the buckle or buckles of

UNBUCKLED
> UNBUCKLE

UNBUCKLES
> UNBUCKLE

UNBUDDED adj not having buds

UNBUDGING adj not moving

UNBUILD vb destroy

UNBUILDS > UNBUILD

UNBUILT > UNBUILD

UNBULKIER > UNBULKY

UNBULKY adj not bulky

UNBUNDLE vb separate (hardware from software) for sales purposes

UNBUNDLED
> UNBUNDLE

UNBUNDLER
> UNBUNDLE

UNBUNDLES
> UNBUNDLE

UNBURDEN vb relieve (one's mind or oneself) of a worry by confiding in someone

UNBURDENS
> UNBURDEN

UNBURIED > UNBURY

UNBURIES > UNBURY

UNBURNED same as > UNBURNT

UNBURNT adj not burnt

UNBURROW vb remove from a burrow

UNBURROWS
> UNBURROW

UNBURTHEN same as > UNBURDEN

UNBURY vb unearth

UNBURYING > UNBURY

UNBUSIED > UNBUSY

UNBUSIER > UNBUSY

UNBUSIES > UNBUSY

UNBUSIEST > UNBUSY

UNBUSTED adj unbroken

UNBUSY adj not busy ▷ vb make less busy

UNBUSYING > UNBUSY

UNBUTTON vb undo by unfastening the buttons of (a garment)

UNBUTTONS
> UNBUTTON

UNCAGE vb release from a cage

UNCAGED adj at liberty

UNCAGES > UNCAGE

UNCAGING > UNCAGE

UNCAKE vb remove compacted matter from

UNCAKED > UNCAKE

UNCAKES > UNCAKE

UNCAKING > UNCAKE

UNCALLED adj not called

UNCANDID adj not frank

UNCANDLED adj not illuminated by candle

UNCANDOR n lack of candor

UNCANDORS
> UNCANDOR

UNCANDOUR n lack of candour

UNCANNED adj not canned

UNCANNIER > UNCANNY

UNCANNILY > UNCANNY

UNCANNY adj weird or mysterious

UNCANONIC adj unclerical

UNCAP vb remove a cap or top from (a container)

UNCAPABLE same as > INCAPABLE

UNCAPE vb remove the cape from

UNCAPED > UNCAPE

UNCAPES > UNCAPE

UNCAPING > UNCAPE

UNCAPPED > UNCAP

UNCAPPING > UNCAP

UNCAPS > UNCAP

UNCARDED adj not carded

UNCARED adj as in uncared for not cared (for)

UNCAREFUL adj careless

UNCARING adj thoughtless

UNCART vb remove from a cart

UNCARTED > UNCART

UNCARTING > UNCART

UNCARTS > UNCART

UNCARVED adj not carved

UNCASE vb display

UNCASED > UNCASE

UNCASES > UNCASE

UNCASHED adj not cashed

UNCASING > UNCASE

UNCASKED adj removed from a cask

UNCAST *adj* not cast ▷ *vb* undo the process of casting

UNCASTED > UNCAST

UNCASTING > UNCAST

UNCASTS > UNCAST

UNCATCHY *adj* not catchy

UNCATE *same as* > UNCINATE

UNCATERED *adj* not catered

UNCAUGHT *adj* not caught

UNCAUSED *adj* not brought into existence by any cause

UNCE *same as* > OUNCE

UNCEASING *adj* continuing without a break

UNCEDED *adj* not ceded

UNCERTAIN *adj* not able to be accurately known or predicted

UNCES > UNCE

UNCESSANT *same as* > INCESSANT

UNCHAIN *vb* remove a chain or chains from

UNCHAINED > UNCHAIN

UNCHAINS > UNCHAIN

UNCHAIR *vb* unseat from chair

UNCHAIRED > UNCHAIR

UNCHAIRS > UNCHAIR

UNCHANCY *adj* unlucky, ill-omened, or dangerous

UNCHANGED *adj* remaining the same

UNCHARGE *vb* unload

UNCHARGED *adj* (of land or other property) not subject to a charge

UNCHARGES > UNCHARGE

UNCHARIER > UNCHARY

UNCHARITY *n* lack of charity

UNCHARM *vb* disenchant

UNCHARMED > UNCHARM

UNCHARMS > UNCHARM

UNCHARNEL *vb* exhume

UNCHARRED *adj* not charred

UNCHARTED *adj* (of an area of sea or land) not having had a map made of it, esp because it is unexplored

UNCHARY *adj* not cautious

UNCHASTE *adj* not chaste

UNCHASTER > UNCHASTE

UNCHECK *vb* remove check mark from

UNCHECKED *adj* not prevented from continuing or growing ▷ *adv* without being stopped or hindered

UNCHECKS > UNCHECK

UNCHEERED *adj* miserable

UNCHEWED *adj* not chewed

UNCHIC *adj* not chic

UNCHICLY > UNCHIC

UNCHILD *vb* deprive of children

UNCHILDED > UNCHILD

UNCHILDS > UNCHILD

UNCHILLED *adj* not chilled

UNCHOKE *vb* unblock

UNCHOKED > UNCHOKE

UNCHOKES > UNCHOKE

UNCHOKING > UNCHOKE

UNCHOSEN *adj* not chosen

UNCHRISOM *adj* unchristened

UNCHURCH *vb* excommunicate

UNCI > UNCUS

UNCIA *n* twelfth part

UNCIAE > UNCIA

UNCIAL *adj* of a writing style used in manuscripts of the third to ninth centuries ▷ *n* uncial letter or manuscript

UNCIALLY > UNCIAL

UNCIALS > UNCIAL

UNCIFORM *adj* having the shape of a hook ▷ *n* any hook-shaped structure or part, esp a small bone of the wrist

UNCIFORMS > UNCIFORM

UNCINAL *same as* > UNCINATE

UNCINARIA *same as* > HOOKWORM

UNCINATE *adj* shaped like a hook

UNCINATED > UNCINATE

UNCINI > UNCINUS

UNCINUS *n* small hooked structure

UNCIPHER *vb* decode

UNCIPHERS > UNCIPHER

UNCITED *adj* not quoted

UNCIVIL *adj* impolite, rude or bad-mannered

UNCIVILLY > UNCIVIL

UNCLAD *adj* having no clothes on

UNCLAIMED *adj* not having been claimed

UNCLAMP *vb* remove clamp from

UNCLAMPED > UNCLAMP

UNCLAMPS > UNCLAMP

UNCLARITY *adj* lack of clarity

UNCLASP *vb* unfasten the clasp of (something)

UNCLASPED > UNCLASP

UNCLASPS > UNCLASP

UNCLASSED *adj* not divided into classes

UNCLASSY *adj* not classy

UNCLAWED *adj* not clawed

UNCLE *n* brother of one's father or mother ▷ *vb* refer to as uncle

UNCLEAN *adj* lacking moral, spiritual, or physical cleanliness

UNCLEANED *adj* not cleaned

UNCLEANER > UNCLEAN

UNCLEANLY *adv* in an unclean manner ▷ *adj* characterized by an absence of cleanliness

UNCLEAR *adj* confusing or hard to understand

UNCLEARED *adj* not cleared

UNCLEARER > UNCLEAR

UNCLEARLY > UNCLEAR

UNCLED > UNCLE

UNCLEFT *adj* not cleft

UNCLENCH *vb* relax from a clenched position

UNCLES > UNCLE

UNCLESHIP *n* position of an uncle

UNCLEW *vb* undo

UNCLEWED > UNCLEW

UNCLEWING > UNCLEW

UNCLEWS > UNCLEW

UNCLICHED *adj* not cliched

UNCLIMBED *adj* not climbed

UNCLINCH *same as* > UNCLENCH

UNCLING > UNCLE

UNCLIP *vb* remove clip from

UNCLIPPED > UNCLIP

UNCLIPS > UNCLIP

UNCLIPT *archaic past form of* > UNCLIP

UNCLOAK *vb* remove cloak from

UNCLOAKED > UNCLOAK

UNCLOAKS > UNCLOAK

UNCLOG *vb* remove an obstruction from (a drain, etc)

UNCLOGGED > UNCLOG

UNCLOGS > UNCLOG

UNCLONED *adj* not cloned

UNCLOSE *vb* open or cause to open

UNCLOSED > UNCLOSE

UNCLOSES > UNCLOSE

UNCLOSING > UNCLOSE

UNCLOTHE *vb* take off garments from

UNCLOTHED > UNCLOTHE

UNCLOTHES > UNCLOTHE

UNCLOUD *vb* clear clouds from

UNCLOUDED > UNCLOUD

UNCLOUDS > UNCLOUD

UNCLOUDY *adj* not cloudy

UNCLOVEN *adj* not cleaved

UNCLOYED *adj* not cloyed

UNCLOYING *adj* not cloying

UNCLUTCH *vb* open from tight grip

UNCLUTTER *vb* tidy and straighten up

UNCO *adj* Scots word meaning unfamiliar or strange ▷ *n* remarkable person or thing

UNCOATED *adj* not covered with a layer

UNCOATING *n* process whereby a virus exposes its genome in order to replicate

UNCOBBLED *adj* not cobbled

UNCOCK *vb* remove from a cocked position

UNCOCKED > UNCOCK

UNCOCKING > UNCOCK

UNCOCKS > UNCOCK

UNCODED *adj* not coded

UNCOER > UNCO

UNCOERCED *adj* unforced

UNCOES > UNCO

UNCOEST > UNCO

UNCOFFIN *vb* take out of a coffin

UNCOFFINS > UNCOFFIN

UNCOIL *vb* unwind or untwist

UNCOILED > UNCOIL

UNCOILING > UNCOIL

UNCOILS > UNCOIL

UNCOINED *adj* (of a metal) not made into coin

UNCOLORED *adj* not coloured

UNCOLT *vb* divest of a horse

UNCOLTED > UNCOLT

UNCOLTING > UNCOLT

UNCOLTS > UNCOLT

UNCOMBED *adj* not combed

UNCOMBINE *vb* break apart

UNCOMELY *adj* not attractive

UNCOMFIER > UNCOMFY

UNCOMFY *adj* not comfortable

UNCOMIC *adj* not comical

UNCOMMON *adj* not happening or encountered often

UNCONCERN *n* apathy or indifference

UNCONFINE *vb* remove restrictions from

UNCONFORM *adj* dissimilar

UNCONFUSE *vb* remove confusion from

UNCONGEAL *vb* become liquid again

UNCOOKED *adj* raw

UNCOOL *adj* unsophisticated

UNCOOLED *adj* not cooled

UNCOPE *vb* unmuzzle

UNCOPED > UNCOPE

UNCOPES > UNCOPE

UNCOPING > UNCOPE

UNCORD *vb* release from cords

UNCORDED > UNCORD

UNCORDIAL *adj* unfriendly

UNCORDING > UNCORD

UNCORDS > UNCORD

UNCORK *vb* remove the cork from (a bottle)

UNCORKED > UNCORK

UNCORKING > UNCORK

UNCORKS > UNCORK

UNCORRUPT *adj* not corrupt

UNCOS > UNCO

u

UNCOSTLY adj inexpensive

UNCOUNTED adj unable to be counted

UNCOUPLE vb disconnect or become disconnected

UNCOUPLED
> UNCOUPLE

UNCOUPLER
> UNCOUPLE

UNCOUPLES
> UNCOUPLE

UNCOURTLY adj not courtly

UNCOUTH adj lacking in good manners, refinement, or grace

UNCOUTHER > UNCOUTH

UNCOUTHLY > UNCOUTH

UNCOVER vb reveal or disclose

UNCOVERED adj not covered

UNCOVERS > UNCOVER

UNCOWL vb remove hood from

UNCOWLED > UNCOWL

UNCOWLING > UNCOWL

UNCOWLS > UNCOWL

UNCOY adj not modest

UNCOYNED same as
> UNCOINED

UNCRACKED adj not cracked

UNCRATE vb remove from a crate

UNCRATED > UNCRATE

UNCRATES > UNCRATE

UNCRATING > UNCRATE

UNCRAZIER > UNCRAZY

UNCRAZY adj not crazy

UNCREASED adj not creased

UNCREATE vb unmake

UNCREATED
> UNCREATE

UNCREATES
> UNCREATE

UNCREWED adj not crewed

UNCROPPED adj not cropped

UNCROSS vb cease to cross

UNCROSSED > UNCROSS

UNCROSSES > UNCROSS

UNCROWDED adj (of a confined space, area, etc) not containing too many people or things

UNCROWN vb take the crown from

UNCROWNED adj having the powers, but not the title, of royalty

UNCROWNS > UNCROWN

UNCRUDDED adj uncurdled

UNCRUMPLE vb remove creases from

UNCRUSHED adj not crushed

UNCTION n act of anointing with oil in a sacramental ceremony

UNCTIONS > UNCTION

UNCTUOUS adj pretending to be kind and concerned

UNCUFF vb remove handcuffs from

UNCUFFED > UNCUFF

UNCUFFING > UNCUFF

UNCUFFS > UNCUFF

UNCULLED adj not culled

UNCURABLE same as
> INCURABLE

UNCURABLY
> UNCURABLE

UNCURB vb remove curbs from (a horse)

UNCURBED > UNCURB

UNCURBING > UNCURB

UNCURBS > UNCURB

UNCURDLED adj not curdled

UNCURED adj not cured

UNCURIOUS adj not curious

UNCURL vb move or cause to move out of a curled or rolled up position

UNCURLED > UNCURL

UNCURLING > UNCURL

UNCURLS > UNCURL

UNCURRENT adj not current

UNCURSE vb remove curse from

UNCURSED > UNCURSE

UNCURSES > UNCURSE

UNCURSING > UNCURSE

UNCURTAIN vb reveal

UNCURVED adj not curved

UNCUS n hooked part or process, as in the human cerebrum

UNCUT adj not shortened or censored

UNCUTE adj not cute

UNCYNICAL adj not cynical

UNDAM vb free from a dam

UNDAMAGED adj not spoilt or damaged

UNDAMMED > UNDAM

UNDAMMING > UNDAM

UNDAMNED adj not damned

UNDAMPED adj (of an oscillating system) having unrestricted motion

UNDAMS > UNDAM

UNDARING adj not daring

UNDASHED adj not dashed

UNDATABLE adj not able to be dated

UNDATE vb remove date from

UNDATED adj (of a manuscript, letter, etc) not having an identifying date

UNDATES > UNDATE

UNDATING > UNDATE

UNDAUNTED adj not put off, discouraged, or beaten

UNDAWNING adj not dawning

UNDAZZLE vb recover from a daze

UNDAZZLED
> UNDAZZLE

UNDAZZLES
> UNDAZZLE

UNDE same as > UNDEE

UNDEAD adj alive

UNDEAF vb restore hearing to

UNDEAFED > UNDEAF

UNDEAFING > UNDEAF

UNDEAFS > UNDEAF

UNDEALT adj not dealt (with)

UNDEAR adj not dear

UNDEBASED adj not debased

UNDEBATED adj not debated

UNDECAGON n polygon having eleven sides

UNDECAYED adj not rotten

UNDECEIVE vb reveal the truth to (someone previously misled or deceived)

UNDECENT same as
> INDECENT

UNDECIDED adj not having made up one's mind

UNDECIMAL adj based on the number 11

UNDECK vb remove decorations from

UNDECKED > UNDECK

UNDECKING > UNDECK

UNDECKS > UNDECK

UNDEE adj wavy

UNDEEDED adj not transferred by deed

UNDEFACED adj not spoilt

UNDEFIDE same as
> UNDEFIED

UNDEFIED adj not challenged

UNDEFILED adj not defiled

UNDEFINED adj not defined or made clear

UNDEIFIED > UNDEIFY

UNDEIFIES > UNDEIFY

UNDEIFY vb strip of the status of a deity

UNDELAYED adj not delayed

UNDELETE vb restore (a deleted computer file or text)

UNDELETED adj not deleted, or restored after being deleted

UNDELETES > UNDELETE

UNDELIGHT n absence of delight

UNDELUDED adj not deluded

UNDENIED adj not denied

UNDENTED adj not dented

UNDER adv indicating movement to or position beneath the underside or base ▷ prep less than

UNDERACT vb play (a role) without adequate emphasis

UNDERACTS
> UNDERACT

UNDERAGE adj below the required or standard age ▷ n shortfall

UNDERAGED adj not old enough

UNDERAGES > UNDERAGE

UNDERARM adj denoting a style of throwing in which the hand is swung below shoulder level ▷ adv in an underarm style ▷ n armpit

UNDERARMS
> UNDERARM

UNDERATE > UNDEREAT

UNDERBAKE vb bake insufficiently

UNDERBEAR vb endure

UNDERBID vb submit a bid lower than that of (others)

UNDERBIDS
> UNDERBID

UNDERBIT
> UNDERBITE

UNDERBITE vb use insufficient acid in etching

UNDERBODY n underpart of a body, as of an animal or motor vehicle

UNDERBORE
> UNDERBEAR

UNDERBOSS n person who is second in command

UNDERBRED adj of impure stock

UNDERBRIM n part of a hat under the brim

UNDERBUD vb produce fewer buds than expected

UNDERBUDS
> UNDERBUD

UNDERBUSH n undergrowth or underbrush

UNDERBUY vb buy (stock in trade) in amounts lower than required

UNDERBUYS
> UNDERBUY

UNDERCARD n event supporting a main event

UNDERCART n aircraft undercarriage

UNDERCAST vb cast beneath

UNDERCLAD adj not wearing enough clothes

UNDERCLAY n grey or whitish clay rock containing fossilized plant roots and occurring beneath coal seams. When used as a refractory, it is known as fireclay

UNDERCLUB vb use a golf club that will not hit the ball as far as required

UNDERCOAT n coat of paint applied before the final coat ▷ vb apply an undercoat to a surface

UNDERCOOK vb cook for too short a time or at too low a temperature

UNDERCOOL vb cool insufficiently

UNDERCUT vb charge less than (a competitor) to obtain trade ▷ n act or an instance of cutting underneath

UNDERCUTS
> UNDERCUT
UNDERDAKS *pl n*
underpants
UNDERDECK *n* lower deck
of a vessel
UNDERDID > UNDERDO
UNDERDO *vb* do
(something) inadequately
UNDERDOER > UNDERDO
UNDERDOES > UNDERDO
UNDERDOG *n* person or
team in a weak or
underprivileged position
UNDERDOGS
> UNDERDOG
UNDERDONE *adj* not
cooked enough
UNDERDOSE *vb* give
insufficient dose
UNDERDRAW *vb* sketch
the subject before
painting it on the same
surface
UNDERDREW
> UNDERDRAW
UNDEREAT *vb* not eat
enough
UNDEREATS
> UNDEREAT
UNDERFED
> UNDERFEED
UNDERFEED *vb* give
too little food to ▷ *n*
apparatus by which fuel,
etc is supplied from
below
UNDERFELT *n* thick felt
laid under a carpet to
increase insulation
UNDERFIRE *vb* bake
insufficiently
UNDERFISH *vb* catch
fewer fish than the
permitted maximum
amount
UNDERFLOW *n*
undercurrent
UNDERFONG *vb* receive
UNDERFOOT *adv* under
the feet
UNDERFUND *vb* provide
insufficient funding
UNDERFUR *n* layer of
dense soft fur occurring
beneath the outer coarser
fur in certain mammals
UNDERFURS
> UNDERFUR
UNDERGIRD *vb*
strengthen or reinforce by
passing a rope, cable, or
chain around the
underside of (an object,
load, etc)
UNDERGIRT
> UNDERGIRD
UNDERGO *vb* experience,
endure, or sustain
UNDERGOD *n* subordinate
god
UNDERGODS
> UNDERGOD
UNDERGOER > UNDERGO
UNDERGOES > UNDERGO
UNDERGONE > UNDERGO
UNDERGOWN *n* gown
worn under another
article of clothing

UNDERGRAD *n* person
studying for a first degree;
undergraduate
UNDERHAIR *n* lower layer
of animal's hair
UNDERHAND *vb* throw
with the arm kept below
the level of the shoulder
UNDERHEAT *vb* heat
insufficiently
UNDERHUNG *adj* (of the
lower jaw) projecting
beyond the upper jaw
UNDERIVED *adj* not
derived
UNDERJAW *n* lower jaw
UNDERJAWS
> UNDERJAW
UNDERKEEP *vb* suppress
UNDERKEPT
> UNDERKEEP
UNDERKILL *n* less force
than is needed to defeat
enemy
UNDERKING *n* ruler
subordinate to a king
UNDERLAID *adj* laid
underneath
UNDERLAIN
> UNDERLIE
UNDERLAP *vb* project
under the edge of
UNDERLAPS
> UNDERLAP
UNDERLAY *n* felt or
rubber laid beneath a
carpet to increase
insulation and resilience
▷ *vb* place (something)
under or beneath
UNDERLAYS
> UNDERLAY
UNDERLEAF *n* (in
liverworts) any of the
leaves forming a row on
the underside of the stem:
usually smaller than the
two rows of lateral leaves
and sometimes absent
UNDERLET *vb* let for a
price lower than expected
or justified
UNDERLETS
> UNDERLET
UNDERLIE *vb* lie or be
placed under
UNDERLIER
> UNDERLIE
UNDERLIES
> UNDERLIE
UNDERLINE *vb* draw a
line under ▷ *n* line
underneath, esp under
written matter
UNDERLING *n*
subordinate
UNDERLIP *n* lower lip
UNDERLIPS
> UNDERLIP
UNDERLIT *adj* lit from
beneath
UNDERLOAD *vb* load
incompletely
UNDERMAN *vb* supply
with insufficient staff ▷ *n*
subordinate man
UNDERMANS
> UNDERMAN
UNDERMEN > UNDERMAN

UNDERMINE *vb* weaken
gradually
UNDERMOST *adj* being
the furthest under ▷ *adv*
in the lowest place
UNDERN *n* time between
sunrise and noon
UNDERNOTE *n* undertone
UNDERNS > UNDERN
UNDERPAD *n* layer of
soft foam laid under
carpeting
UNDERPADS
> UNDERPAD
UNDERPAID *adj* not paid
as much as the job
deserves
UNDERPART *n* lower part
or underside of something
such as an animal
UNDERPASS *n* section of
a road that passes under
another road or a railway
line
UNDERPAY *vb* pay
someone insufficiently
UNDERPAYS
> UNDERPAY
UNDERPEEP *vb* peep
under
UNDERPIN *vb* give
strength or support to
UNDERPINS
> UNDERPIN
UNDERPLAY *vb* achieve
(an effect) by deliberate
lack of emphasis
UNDERPLOT *n* subsidiary
plot in a literary or
dramatic work
UNDERPROP *vb* prop up
from beneath
UNDERRAN > UNDERRUN
UNDERRATE *vb*
underestimate
UNDERRIPE *adj* not quite
ripe
UNDERRUN *vb* run
beneath
UNDERRUNS
> UNDERRUN
UNDERSAID
> UNDERSAY
UNDERSAY *vb* say by way
of response
UNDERSAYS
> UNDERSAY
UNDERSEA *adv* below the
surface of the sea
UNDERSEAL *n* coating of
tar etc applied to the
underside of a motor
vehicle to prevent
corrosion ▷ *vb* apply such
a coating to a motor
vehicle
UNDERSEAS *same as*
> UNDERSEA
UNDERSELF *n*
subconscious or person
within
UNDERSELL *vb* sell at a
price lower than that of
another seller
UNDERSET *n* ocean
undercurrent ▷ *vb*
support from underneath
UNDERSETS
> UNDERSET

UNDERSHOT *adj* (of the
lower jaw) projecting
beyond the upper jaw
UNDERSIDE *n* bottom or
lower surface
UNDERSIGN *vb* sign the
bottom (of a document)
UNDERSIZE *adj* smaller
than normal
UNDERSKY *n* lower sky
UNDERSOIL *another word*
for > SUBSOIL
UNDERSOLD
> UNDERSELL
UNDERSONG *n*
accompanying secondary
melody
UNDERSOW *vb* sow a
later-growing crop on
already-seeded land
UNDERSOWN
> UNDERSOW
UNDERSOWS
> UNDERSOW
UNDERSPIN *n* backspin
UNDERTAKE *vb* agree or
commit oneself to
(something) or to do
(something)
UNDERTANE
Shakespearean past
participle of > UNDERTAKE
UNDERTAX *vb* tax
insufficiently
UNDERTIME *n* time spent
by an employee at work in
non-work-related
activities like socializing,
surfing the internet,
making personal
telephone calls, etc
UNDERTINT *n* slight,
subdued, or delicate tint
UNDERTONE *n* quiet tone
of voice
UNDERTOOK *past tense of*
> UNDERTAKE
UNDERTOW *n* strong
undercurrent flowing in a
different direction from
the surface current
UNDERTOWS
> UNDERTOW
UNDERUSE *vb* use less
than normal
UNDERUSED
> UNDERUSE
UNDERUSES
> UNDERUSE
UNDERVEST *another name*
for > VEST
UNDERVOTE *n* vote cast
but invalid
UNDERWAY *adj* in progress
▷ *adv* in progress
UNDERWEAR *n* clothing
worn under the outer
garments and next to
the skin
UNDERWENT *past tense of*
> UNDERGO
UNDERWING *n* hind wing
of an insect, esp when
covered by the forewing
UNDERWIRE *vb* support
with wire underneath
UNDERWIT *n* halfwit
UNDERWITS
> UNDERWIT

UNDERWOOD n small trees, bushes, ferns, etc growing beneath taller trees in a wood or forest
UNDERWOOL n lower layer of an animal's coat
UNDERWORK vb do less work than expected
UNDESERT n lack of worth
UNDESERTS > UNDESERT
UNDESERVE vb fail to deserve
UNDESIRED adj not desired
UNDEVOUT adj not devout
UNDID > UNDO
UNDIES pl n underwear, esp women's
UNDIGHT vb remove
UNDIGHTS > UNDIGHT
UNDIGNIFY vb divest of dignity
UNDILUTED adj (of a liquid) not having any water added to it
UNDIMMED adj (of eyes, light, etc) still bright or shining
UNDINE n female water spirit
UNDINES > UNDINE
UNDINISM n obsession with water
UNDINISMS > UNDINISM
UNDINTED adj not dinted
UNDIPPED adj not dipped
UNDIVIDED adj total and whole-hearted
UNDIVINE adj not divine
UNDO vb open, unwrap ▷ n instance of undoing something
UNDOABLE adj impossible
UNDOCILE adj not docile
UNDOCK vb take out of a dock
UNDOCKED > UNDOCK
UNDOCKING > UNDOCK
UNDOCKS > UNDOCK
UNDOER > UNDO
UNDOERS > UNDO
UNDOES > UNDO
UNDOING n cause of someone's downfall
UNDOINGS > UNDOING
UNDONE adj not done or completed
UNDOOMED adj not doomed
UNDOS > UNDO
UNDOTTED adj not dotted
UNDOUBLE vb stretch out
UNDOUBLED > UNDOUBLE
UNDOUBLES > UNDOUBLE
UNDOUBTED adj certain or indisputable
UNDOWERED adj not dowered
UNDRAINED adj not drained
UNDRAPE vb remove drapery from
UNDRAPED > UNDRAPE

UNDRAPES > UNDRAPE
UNDRAPING > UNDRAPE
UNDRAW vb open (curtains)
UNDRAWING > UNDRAW
UNDRAWN > UNDRAW
UNDRAWS > UNDRAW
UNDREADED adj not feared
UNDREAMED adj not thought of or imagined
UNDREAMT same as > UNDREAMED
UNDRESS vb take off clothes from (oneself or another) ▷ n partial or complete nakedness ▷ adj characterized by or requiring informal or normal working dress or uniform
UNDRESSED adj partially or completely naked
UNDRESSES > UNDRESS
UNDREST same as > UNDRESSED
UNDREW > UNDRAW
UNDRIED adj not dried
UNDRILLED adj not drilled
UNDRIVEN adj not driven
UNDROSSY adj pure
UNDROWNED adj not drowned
UNDRUNK adj not drunk
UNDUBBED adj (of a film, etc) not dubbed
UNDUE adj greater than is reasonable; excessive
UNDUG adj not having been dug
UNDULANCE > UNDULANT
UNDULANCY > UNDULANT
UNDULANT adj resembling waves
UNDULAR > UNDULATE
UNDULATE vb move in waves ▷ adj having a wavy or rippled appearance, margin, or form
UNDULATED > UNDULATE
UNDULATES > UNDULATE
UNDULATOR > UNDULATE
UNDULLED adj not dulled
UNDULOSE same as > UNDULOUS
UNDULOUS adj undulate
UNDULY adv excessively
UNDUTEOUS same as > UNDUTIFUL
UNDUTIFUL adj not dutiful
UNDY same as > UNDEE
UNDYED adj not dyed
UNDYING adj never ending, eternal
UNDYINGLY > UNDYING
UNDYNAMIC adj not dynamic
UNEAGER adj nonchalant
UNEAGERLY > UNEAGER
UNEARED adj not ploughed

UNEARNED adj not deserved
UNEARTH vb reveal or discover by searching
UNEARTHED > UNEARTH
UNEARTHLY adj ghostly or eerie
UNEARTHS > UNEARTH
UNEASE > UNEASY
UNEASES > UNEASY
UNEASIER > UNEASY
UNEASIEST > UNEASY
UNEASILY > UNEASY
UNEASY adj (of a person) anxious or apprehensive
UNEATABLE adj (of food) so rotten or unattractive as to be unfit to eat
UNEATEN adj (of food) not having been consumed
UNEATH adv not easily
UNEATHES > UNEATH
UNEDGE vb take the edge off
UNEDGED > UNEDGE
UNEDGES > UNEDGE
UNEDGING > UNEDGE
UNEDIBLE variant of > INEDIBLE
UNEDITED adj not edited
UNEFFACED adj not destroyed
UNELATED adj not elated
UNELECTED adj not elected
UNEMPTIED adj not emptied
UNENDED adj without end
UNENDING adj not showing any signs of ever stopping
UNENDOWED adj not endowed
UNENGAGED adj not engaged
UNENJOYED adj not enjoyed
UNENSURED adj not ensured
UNENTERED adj not having been entered previously
UNENVIED adj not envied
UNENVIOUS adj not envious
UNENVYING adj not envying
UNEQUABLE adj unstable
UNEQUAL adj not equal in quantity, size, rank, value, etc ▷ n person who is not equal
UNEQUALED adj (in US English) not equalled
UNEQUALLY > UNEQUAL
UNEQUALS > UNEQUAL
UNERASED adj not rubbed out
UNEROTIC adj not erotic
UNERRING adj never mistaken, consistently accurate
UNERUPTED adj (of a volcano) not having erupted
UNESPIED adj unnoticed
UNESSAYED adj untried

UNESSENCE vb deprive of being
UNETH same as > UNEATH
UNETHICAL adj morally wrong
UNEVADED adj not evaded
UNEVEN adj not level or flat
UNEVENER > UNEVEN
UNEVENEST > UNEVEN
UNEVENLY > UNEVEN
UNEVOLVED adj not evolved
UNEXALTED adj not exalted
UNEXCITED adj not aroused to pleasure, interest, agitation, etc
UNEXCUSED adj not excused
UNEXOTIC adj not exotic
UNEXPERT same as > INEXPERT
UNEXPIRED adj not having expired
UNEXPOSED adj not having been exhibited or brought to public notice
UNEXTINCT adj not extinct
UNEXTREME adj not extreme
UNEYED adj unseen
UNFABLED adj not fictitious
UNFACETED adj not faceted
UNFACT n event or thing not provable
UNFACTS > UNFACT
UNFADABLE adj incapable of fading
UNFADED adj not faded
UNFADING adj not fading
UNFAILING adj continuous or reliable
UNFAIR adj not right, fair, or just ▷ vb disfigure
UNFAIRED > UNFAIR
UNFAIRER > UNFAIR
UNFAIREST > UNFAIR
UNFAIRING > UNFAIR
UNFAIRLY > UNFAIR
UNFAIRS > UNFAIR
UNFAITH n lack of faith
UNFAITHS > UNFAITH
UNFAKED adj not faked
UNFALLEN adj not fallen
UNFAMED adj not famous
UNFAMOUS adj not famous
UNFANCIED > UNFANCY
UNFANCIER > UNFANCY
UNFANCY vb consider (a sportsperson or team) unlikely to win or succeed ▷ adj not fancy
UNFANNED adj not fanned
UNFASTEN vb undo, untie, or open or become undone, untied, or opened
UNFASTENS > UNFASTEN
UNFAULTY adj not faulty
UNFAVORED adj (in US English) not favoured

UNFAZABLE *adj* not capable of being fazed
UNFAZED *adj* not disconcerted
UNFEARED *adj* unafraid
UNFEARFUL *adj* not scared
UNFEARING *adj* having no fear
UNFED *adj* not fed
UNFEED *adj* unpaid
UNFEELING *adj* without sympathy
UNFEIGNED *adj* not feigned
UNFELLED *adj* not cut down
UNFELT *adj* not felt
UNFELTED *adj* not felted
UNFENCE *vb* remove a fence from
UNFENCED *adj* not enclosed by a fence
UNFENCES > UNFENCE
UNFENCING > UNFENCE
UNFERTILE *same as* > INFERTILE
UNFETTER *vb* release from fetters, bonds, etc
UNFETTERS > UNFETTER
UNFEUDAL *adj* not feudal
UNFEUED *adj* not feued
UNFIGURED *adj* not numbered
UNFILDE *archaic form of* > UNFILED
UNFILED *adj* not filed
UNFILIAL *adj* not filial
UNFILLED *adj* (of a container, receptacle, etc) not having become or been made full
UNFILMED *adj* not filmed
UNFINE *adj* not fine
UNFIRED *adj* not fired
UNFIRM *adj* soft or unsteady
UNFISHED *adj* not used for fishing
UNFIT *adj* unqualified or unsuitable ▷ *vb* make unfit
UNFITLY *adv* in an unfit way
UNFITNESS > UNFIT
UNFITS > UNFIT
UNFITTED *adj* unsuitable
UNFITTER > UNFIT
UNFITTEST > UNFIT
UNFITTING *adj* not fitting
UNFIX *vb* unfasten, detach, or loosen
UNFIXED *adj* not fixed
UNFIXES > UNFIX
UNFIXING > UNFIX
UNFIXITY *n* instability
UNFIXT *variant of* > UNFIXED
UNFLAPPED *adj* not agitated or excited
UNFLASHY *adj* not flashy
UNFLAWED *adj* perfect
UNFLEDGED *adj* (of a young bird) not having developed adult feathers

UNFLESH *vb* remove flesh from
UNFLESHED > UNFLESH
UNFLESHES > UNFLESH
UNFLESHLY *adj* immaterial
UNFLEXED *adj* unbent
UNFLOORED *adj* without flooring
UNFLUSH *vb* lose the colour caused by flushing
UNFLUSHED > UNFLUSH
UNFLUSHES > UNFLUSH
UNFLUTED *adj* not fluted
UNFLYABLE *adj* unable to be flown
UNFOCUSED *adj* blurry
UNFOILED *adj* not thwarted
UNFOLD *vb* open or spread out from a folded state
UNFOLDED > UNFOLD
UNFOLDER > UNFOLD
UNFOLDERS > UNFOLD
UNFOLDING > UNFOLD
UNFOLDS > UNFOLD
UNFOLLOW *vb* stop following a person on a social networking site
UNFOLLOWS > UNFOLLOW
UNFOND *adj* not fond
UNFONDLY *adv* in an unfond manner
UNFOOL *vb* undeceive
UNFOOLED > UNFOOL
UNFOOLING > UNFOOL
UNFOOLS > UNFOOL
UNFOOTED *adj* untrodden
UNFORBID *adj* archaic word meaning unforbidden
UNFORCED *adj* not forced or having been forced
UNFORGED *adj* genuine
UNFORGOT *adj* archaic word meaning unforgotten
UNFORKED *adj* not forked
UNFORM *vb* make formless
UNFORMAL *same as* > INFORMAL
UNFORMED *adj* in an early stage of development
UNFORMING > UNFORM
UNFORMS > UNFORM
UNFORTUNE *n* misfortune
UNFOUGHT *adj* not fought
UNFOUND *adj* not found
UNFOUNDED *adj* not based on facts or evidence
UNFRAMED *adj* not framed
UNFRANKED *adj* not franked
UNFRAUGHT *adj* not fraught
UNFREE *vb* remove freedom from
UNFREED > UNFREE
UNFREEDOM *n* lack of freedom
UNFREEING > UNFREE
UNFREEMAN *n* person who is not a freeman
UNFREEMEN > UNFREEMAN

UNFREES > UNFREE
UNFREEZE *vb* thaw or cause to thaw
UNFREEZES > UNFREEZE
UNFRETTED *adj* not worried
UNFRIEND *vb* remove someone from one's list of friends on a social networking site
UNFRIENDS > UNFRIEND
UNFROCK *vb* deprive (a priest in holy orders) of his or her priesthood
UNFROCKED > UNFROCK
UNFROCKS > UNFROCK
UNFROZE > UNFREEZE
UNFROZEN > UNFREEZE
UNFUELLED *adj* not fuelled
UNFUMED *adj* not fumigated
UNFUNDED *adj* not funded
UNFUNNIER > UNFUNNY
UNFUNNILY *adv* in an unfunny manner
UNFUNNY *adj* not funny
UNFURL *vb* unroll or unfold
UNFURLED > UNFURL
UNFURLING > UNFURL
UNFURLS > UNFURL
UNFURNISH *vb* clear
UNFURRED *adj* not adorned with fur
UNFUSED *adj* not fused
UNFUSSED *adj* not fussed
UNFUSSIER > UNFUSSY
UNFUSSILY > UNFUSSY
UNFUSSY *adj* not characterized by overelaborate detail
UNGAG *vb* restore freedom of speech to
UNGAGGED > UNGAG
UNGAGGING > UNGAG
UNGAGS > UNGAG
UNGAIN *adj* inconvenient
UNGAINFUL > UNGAIN
UNGAINLY *adj* lacking grace when moving ▷ *adv* clumsily
UNGALLANT *adj* not gallant
UNGALLED *adj* not annoyed
UNGARBED *adj* undressed
UNGARBLED *adj* clear
UNGATED *adj* without a gate
UNGAUGED *adj* not measured
UNGAZED *adj* as in *ungazed at/ungazed upon* not gazed (at or upon)
UNGAZING *adj* not gazing
UNGEAR *vb* disengage
UNGEARED > UNGEAR
UNGEARING > UNGEAR
UNGEARS > UNGEAR
UNGELDED *adj* not gelded
UNGENIAL *adj* unfriendly
UNGENTEEL *adj* impolite
UNGENTLE *adj* not gentle

UNGENTLER > UNGENTLE
UNGENTLY > UNGENTLE
UNGENUINE *adj* false
UNGERMANE *adj* inappropriate
UNGET *vb* get rid of
UNGETS > UNGET
UNGETTING > UNGET
UNGHOSTED *adj* not ghostwritten
UNGHOSTLY *adj* not ghostly
UNGIFTED *adj* not talented
UNGILD *vb* remove gilding from
UNGILDED > UNGILD
UNGILDING > UNGILD
UNGILDS > UNGILD
UNGILT > UNGILD
UNGIRD *vb* remove belt from
UNGIRDED > UNGIRD
UNGIRDING > UNGIRD
UNGIRDS > UNGIRD
UNGIRT *adj* not belted
UNGIRTH *vb* release from a girth
UNGIRTHED > UNGIRTH
UNGIRTHS > UNGIRTH
UNGIVING *adj* inflexible
UNGLAD *adj* not glad
UNGLAZED *adj* not glazed
UNGLITZY *adj* not glitzy
UNGLOSSED *adj* not glossed
UNGLOVE *vb* remove a glove or gloves
UNGLOVED > UNGLOVE
UNGLOVES > UNGLOVE
UNGLOVING > UNGLOVE
UNGLUE *vb* remove adhesive from
UNGLUED > UNGLUE
UNGLUES > UNGLUE
UNGLUING > UNGLUE
UNGOD *vb* remove status of being a god from
UNGODDED > UNGOD
UNGODDING > UNGOD
UNGODLIER > UNGODLY
UNGODLIKE *adj* not godlike
UNGODLILY > UNGODLY
UNGODLY *adj* unreasonable or outrageous
UNGODS > UNGOD
UNGORD *same as* > UNGORED
UNGORED *adj* not gored
UNGORGED *same as* > UNGORED
UNGOT *same as* > UNGOTTEN
UNGOTTEN *adj* not obtained or won
UNGOWN *vb* remove a gown from
UNGOWNED > UNGOWN
UNGOWNING > UNGOWN
UNGOWNS > UNGOWN
UNGRACED *adj* not graced
UNGRADED *adj* not graded
UNGRASSED *adj* not covered with grass

u

UNGRAVELY *adv* Shakespearian word meaning not in a serious or solemn manner
UNGRAZED *adj* not grazed
UNGREASED *adj* not greased
UNGREEDY *adj* not greedy
UNGREEN *adj* not environmentally friendly
UNGREENER > UNGREEN
UNGROOMED *adj* not groomed
UNGROUND *adj* not crushed
UNGROUP *vb* separate from a group
UNGROUPED *adj* not placed in a group
UNGROUPS > UNGROUP
UNGROWN *adj* not fully developed
UNGRUDGED *adj* not grudged
UNGUAL *adj* of, relating to, or affecting the fingernails or toenails
UNGUARD *vb* expose (to attack)
UNGUARDED *adj* not protected
UNGUARDS > UNGUARD
UNGUENT *n* ointment
UNGUENTA > UNGUENTUM
UNGUENTS > UNGUENT
UNGUENTUM *same as* > UNGUENT
UNGUES > UNGUIS
UNGUESSED *adj* unexpected
UNGUIDED *adj* not having a flight path controlled internally or externally
UNGUIFORM *adj* shaped like a nail or claw
UNGUILTY *adj* innocent
UNGUINOUS *adj* fatty
UNGUIS *n* nail, claw, or hoof, or the part of the digit giving rise to it
UNGULA *n* truncated cone, cylinder, etc
UNGULAE > UNGULA
UNGULAR > UNGULA
UNGULATE *n* hoofed mammal
UNGULATES > UNGULATE
UNGULED *adj* hoofed
UNGUM *vb* remove adhesive from
UNGUMMED > UNGUM
UNGUMMING > UNGUM
UNGUMS > UNGUM
UNGYVE *vb* release from shackles
UNGYVED > UNGYVE
UNGYVES > UNGYVE
UNGYVING > UNGYVE
UNHABLE *same as* > UNABLE
UNHACKED *adj* not hacked
UNHAILED *adj* not hailed
UNHAIR *vb* remove the hair from (a hide)
UNHAIRED > UNHAIR

UNHAIRER > UNHAIR
UNHAIRERS > UNHAIR
UNHAIRING > UNHAIR
UNHAIRS > UNHAIR
UNHALLOW *vb* desecrate
UNHALLOWS > UNHALLOW
UNHALSED *adj* not hailed
UNHALVED *adj* not divided in half
UNHAND *vb* release from one's grasp
UNHANDED > UNHAND
UNHANDIER > UNHANDY
UNHANDILY > UNHANDY
UNHANDING > UNHAND
UNHANDLED *adj* not handled
UNHANDS > UNHAND
UNHANDY *adj* not skilful with one's hands
UNHANG *vb* take down from hanging position
UNHANGED *adj* not executed by hanging
UNHANGING > UNHANG
UNHANGS > UNHANG
UNHAPPEN *vb* become as though never having happened
UNHAPPENS > UNHAPPEN
UNHAPPIED > UNHAPPY
UNHAPPIER > UNHAPPY
UNHAPPIES > UNHAPPY
UNHAPPILY > UNHAPPY
UNHAPPY *adj* sad, miserable ▷ *vb* make unhappy
UNHARBOUR *vb* force out of shelter
UNHARDIER > UNHARDY
UNHARDY *adj* fragile
UNHARMED *adj* not hurt or damaged in any way
UNHARMFUL *adj* not harmful
UNHARMING *adj* not capable of harming
UNHARNESS *vb* remove the harness from (a horse, etc)
UNHARRIED *adj* not harried
UNHASP *vb* unfasten
UNHASPED > UNHASP
UNHASPING > UNHASP
UNHASPS > UNHASP
UNHASTIER > UNHASTY
UNHASTING *adj* not rushing
UNHASTY *adj* not speedy
UNHAT *vb* doff one's hat
UNHATCHED *adj* (of an egg) not having broken to release the fully developed young
UNHATS > UNHAT
UNHATTED > UNHAT
UNHATTING > UNHAT
UNHAUNTED *adj* not haunted
UNHEAD *vb* remove the head from
UNHEADED *adj* not having a heading
UNHEADING > UNHEAD
UNHEADS > UNHEAD

UNHEAL *vb* expose
UNHEALED *adj* not having healed physically, mentally, or emotionally
UNHEALING *adj* not healing
UNHEALS > UNHEAL
UNHEALTH *n* illness
UNHEALTHS > UNHEALTH
UNHEALTHY *adj* likely to cause poor health
UNHEARD *adj* not listened to
UNHEARSE *vb* remove from a hearse
UNHEARSED > UNHEARSE
UNHEARSES > UNHEARSE
UNHEART *vb* discourage
UNHEARTED > UNHEART
UNHEARTS > UNHEART
UNHEATED *adj* not having been warmed up
UNHEDGED *adj* unprotected
UNHEEDED *adj* noticed but ignored
UNHEEDFUL *adj* not heedful
UNHEEDIER > UNHEEDY
UNHEEDILY *adv* carelessly
UNHEEDING *adj* not heeding
UNHEEDY *adj* not heedful
UNHELE *same as* > UNHEAL
UNHELED > UNHELE
UNHELES > UNHELE
UNHELING > UNHELE
UNHELM *vb* remove the helmet (of oneself or another)
UNHELMED > UNHELM
UNHELMING > UNHELM
UNHELMS > UNHELM
UNHELPED *adj* without help
UNHELPFUL *adj* doing nothing to improve a situation
UNHEMMED *adj* not hemmed
UNHEPPEN *adj* awkward
UNHEROIC *adj* not heroic
UNHERST *archaic past form of* > UNHEARSE
UNHEWN *adj* not hewn
UNHIDDEN *adj* not hidden
UNHINGE *vb* derange or unbalance (a person or his or her mind)
UNHINGED > UNHINGE
UNHINGES > UNHINGE
UNHINGING > UNHINGE
UNHIP *adj* not at all fashionable or up to date
UNHIPPER > UNHIP
UNHIPPEST > UNHIP
UNHIRABLE *adj* not fit to be hired
UNHIRED *adj* not hired
UNHITCH *vb* unfasten or detach
UNHITCHED > UNHITCH

UNHITCHES > UNHITCH
UNHIVE *vb* remove from a hive
UNHIVED > UNHIVE
UNHIVES > UNHIVE
UNHIVING > UNHIVE
UNHOARD *vb* remove from a hoard
UNHOARDED > UNHOARD
UNHOARDS > UNHOARD
UNHOLIER > UNHOLY
UNHOLIEST > UNHOLY
UNHOLILY > UNHOLY
UNHOLPEN *same as* > UNHELPED
UNHOLSTER *vb* remove (a gun) from a holster
UNHOLY *adj* immoral or wicked
UNHOMELY *adj* not homely
UNHONEST *same as* > DISHONEST
UNHONORED *adj* not honoured
UNHOOD *vb* remove a hood from
UNHOODED > UNHOOD
UNHOODING > UNHOOD
UNHOODS > UNHOOD
UNHOOK *vb* unfasten the hooks of (a garment)
UNHOOKED > UNHOOK
UNHOOKING > UNHOOK
UNHOOKS > UNHOOK
UNHOOP *vb* remove a hoop from
UNHOOPED > UNHOOP
UNHOOPING > UNHOOP
UNHOOPS > UNHOOP
UNHOPED *adj* not anticipated
UNHOPEFUL *adj* not hopeful
UNHORSE *vb* knock or throw from a horse
UNHORSED > UNHORSE
UNHORSES > UNHORSE
UNHORSING > UNHORSE
UNHOSTILE *adj* not hostile
UNHOUSE *vb* remove from a house
UNHOUSED > UNHOUSE
UNHOUSES > UNHOUSE
UNHOUSING > UNHOUSE
UNHUMAN *adj* inhuman or not human
UNHUMANLY > UNHUMAN
UNHUMBLED *adj* not humbled
UNHUNG > UNHANG
UNHUNTED *adj* not hunted
UNHURRIED *adj* done at a leisurely pace, without any rush or anxiety
UNHURT *adj* not injured in an accident, attack, etc
UNHURTFUL *adj* not hurtful
UNHUSK *vb* remove the husk from
UNHUSKED > UNHUSK
UNHUSKING > UNHUSK
UNHUSKS > UNHUSK
UNI *n* (in informal English) university

UNIALGAL adj containing only one species of alga

UNIAXIAL adj (esp of plants) having an unbranched main axis

UNIBODIES > UNIBODY

UNIBODY adj of a vehicle in which the frame and body are one unit ▷ n vehicle in which the frame and body are one unit

UNIBROW n informal word for eyebrows that meet above the nose

UNIBROWS > UNIBROW

UNICA > UNICUM

UNICED adj not iced

UNICITIES > UNICITY

UNICITY n oneness

UNICOLOR same as > UNICOLOUR

UNICOLOUR adj of one colour

UNICOM n designated radio frequency at some airports

UNICOMS > UNICOM

UNICORN n imaginary horselike creature with one horn growing from its forehead

UNICORNS > UNICORN

UNICUM n unique example or specimen

UNICYCLE n one-wheeled vehicle driven by pedals, used in a circus ▷ vb ride a unicycle

UNICYCLED > UNICYCLE

UNICYCLES > UNICYCLE

UNIDEAED adj not having ideas

UNIDEAL adj not ideal

UNIFACE n type of tool

UNIFACES > UNIFACE

UNIFIABLE > UNIFY

UNIFIC adj unifying

UNIFIED > UNIFY

UNIFIER > UNIFY

UNIFIERS > UNIFY

UNIFIES > UNIFY

UNIFILAR adj composed of, having, or using only one wire, thread, filament, etc

UNIFORM n special set of clothes for the members of an organization ▷ adj regular and even throughout, unvarying ▷ vb fit out (a body of soldiers, etc) with uniforms

UNIFORMED > UNIFORM

UNIFORMER > UNIFORM

UNIFORMLY > UNIFORM

UNIFORMS > UNIFORM

UNIFY vb make or become one

UNIFYING > UNIFY

UNIFYINGS > UNIFY

UNIGNITED adj not ignited

UNIJUGATE adj (of a compound leaf) having only one pair of leaflets

UNILINEAL same as > UNILINEAR

UNILINEAR adj developing in a progressive sequence

UNILLUMED adj not illuminated

UNILOBAR adj having one lobe

UNILOBED same as > UNILOBAR

UNIMBUED adj not imbued

UNIMODAL adj having or involving one mode

UNIMPEDED adj not stopped or disrupted by anything

UNIMPOSED adj not imposed

UNINCITED adj unprovoked

UNINDEXED adj not indexed

UNINJURED adj not having sustained any injury

UNINSTAL same as > UNINSTALL

UNINSTALL vb remove from a computer system

UNINSTALS > UNINSTAL

UNINSURED adj not covered by insurance

UNINURED adj unaccustomed

UNINVITED adj not having been asked ▷ adv without having been asked

UNINVOKED adj not invoked

UNION n act of uniting or being united ▷ adj of a trade union

UNIONISE same as > UNIONIZE

UNIONISED > UNIONISE

UNIONISER > UNIONISE

UNIONISES > UNIONISE

UNIONISM n principles of trade unions

UNIONISMS > UNIONISM

UNIONIST n member or supporter of a union ▷ adj of or relating to a union or unionism

UNIONISTS > UNIONIST

UNIONIZE vb organize (workers) into a trade union

UNIONIZED > UNIONIZE

UNIONIZER > UNIONIZE

UNIONIZES > UNIONIZE

UNIONS > UNION

UNIPAROUS adj (of certain animals) producing a single offspring at each birth

UNIPED n person or thing with one foot

UNIPEDS > UNIPED

UNIPLANAR adj situated in one plane

UNIPOD n one-legged support, as for a camera

UNIPODS > UNIPOD

UNIPOLAR adj of, concerned with, or having a single magnetic or electric pole

UNIPOTENT adj able to form only one type of cell

UNIQUE adj being the only one of a particular type ▷ n person or thing that is unique

UNIQUELY > UNIQUE

UNIQUER > UNIQUE

UNIQUES > UNIQUE

UNIQUEST > UNIQUE

UNIRAMOSE same as > UNIRAMOUS

UNIRAMOUS adj (esp of the appendages of crustaceans) consisting of a single branch

UNIRONED adj not ironed

UNIRONIC adj not ironic

UNIS > UNI

UNISERIAL adj in or relating to a single series

UNISEX adj not associated with a specific gender ▷ n style not associated with a specific gender

UNISEXES > UNISEX

UNISEXUAL adj of one sex only

UNISIZE adj in one size only

UNISON n complete agreement

UNISONAL > UNISON

UNISONANT > UNISON

UNISONOUS > UNISON

UNISONS > UNISON

UNISSUED adj not issued

UNIT n single undivided entity or whole

UNITAGE > UNIT

UNITAGES > UNIT

UNITAL > UNIT

UNITARD n all-in-one skintight suit

UNITARDS > UNITARD

UNITARIAN n supporter of unity or centralization ▷ adj of or relating to unity or centralization

UNITARILY > UNITARY

UNITARITY n quality of being unitary

UNITARY adj consisting of a single undivided whole

UNITE vb make or become an integrated whole ▷ n English gold coin minted in the Stuart period

UNITED adj produced by two or more people or things in combination

UNITEDLY > UNITED

UNITER > UNITE

UNITERS > UNITE

UNITES > UNITE

UNITIES > UNITY

UNITING > UNITE

UNITINGS > UNITE

UNITION n joining

UNITIONS > UNITION

UNITISE same as > UNITIZE

UNITISED > UNITISE

UNITISER same as > UNITIZER

UNITISERS > UNITISER

UNITISES > UNITISE

UNITISING > UNITISE

UNITIVE adj tending to unite or capable of uniting

UNITIVELY > UNITIVE

UNITIZE vb convert (an investment trust) into a unit trust

UNITIZED > UNITIZE

UNITIZER n person or thing that arranges units into batches

UNITIZERS > UNITIZER

UNITIZES > UNITIZE

UNITIZING > UNITIZE

UNITRUST n type of income-producing trust fund

UNITRUSTS > UNITRUST

UNITS > UNIT

UNITY n state of being one

UNIVALENT adj (of a chromosome during meiosis) not paired with its homologue

UNIVALVE adj relating to a mollusc shell that consists of a single piece (valve) ▷ n gastropod mollusc or its shell

UNIVALVED > UNIVALVE

UNIVALVES > UNIVALVE

UNIVERSAL adj of or typical of the whole of mankind or of nature ▷ n something which exists or is true in all places and all situations

UNIVERSE n whole of all existing matter, energy, and space

UNIVERSES > UNIVERSE

UNIVOCAL adj unambiguous or unmistakable ▷ n word or term that has only one meaning

UNIVOCALS > UNIVOCAL

UNJADED adj not jaded

UNJAM vb remove blockage from

UNJAMMED > UNJAM

UNJAMMING > UNJAM

UNJAMS > UNJAM

UNJEALOUS adj not jealous

UNJOINED adj not joined

UNJOINT vb disjoint

UNJOINTED > UNJOINT

u

UNJOINTS > UNJOINT
UNJOYFUL adj not joyful
UNJOYOUS adj not joyous
UNJUDGED adj not judged
UNJUST adj not fair or just
UNJUSTER > UNJUST
UNJUSTEST > UNJUST
UNJUSTLY > UNJUST
UNKED adj alien
UNKEELED adj without a keel
UNKEMPT adj (of the hair) not combed
UNKEMPTLY > UNKEMPT
UNKEND same as > UNKENNED
UNKENNED adj unknown
UNKENNEL vb release from a kennel
UNKENNELS > UNKENNEL
UNKENT same as > UNKENNED
UNKEPT adj not kept
UNKET same as > UNKED
UNKID same as > UNKED
UNKIND adj unsympathetic or cruel
UNKINDER > UNKIND
UNKINDEST > UNKIND
UNKINDLED adj not kindled
UNKINDLY > UNKIND
UNKING vb strip of sovereignty
UNKINGED > UNKING
UNKINGING > UNKING
UNKINGLY adj not kingly
UNKINGS > UNKING
UNKINK vb straighten out
UNKINKED > UNKINK
UNKINKING > UNKINK
UNKINKS > UNKINK
UNKISS vb cancel (a previous action) with a kiss
UNKISSED adj not kissed
UNKISSES > UNKISS
UNKISSING > UNKISS
UNKNELLED adj not tolled
UNKNIGHT vb strip of knighthood
UNKNIGHTS > UNKNIGHT
UNKNIT vb make or become undone, untied, or unravelled
UNKNITS > UNKNIT
UNKNITTED > UNKNIT
UNKNOT vb disentangle or undo a knot or knots in
UNKNOTS > UNKNOT
UNKNOTTED > UNKNOT
UNKNOWING adj unaware or ignorant
UNKNOWN adj not known ▷ n unknown person, quantity, or thing
UNKNOWNS > UNKNOWN
UNKOSHER adj not conforming to Jewish religious law
UNLABELED adj not labelled
UNLABORED adj not laboured

UNLACE vb loosen or undo the lacing of (shoes, garments, etc)
UNLACED adj not laced
UNLACES > UNLACE
UNLACING > UNLACE
UNLADE less common word for > UNLOAD
UNLADED > UNLADE
UNLADEN adj not laden
UNLADES > UNLADE
UNLADING > UNLADE
UNLADINGS > UNLADE
UNLAID > UNLAY
UNLASH vb untie or unfasten
UNLASHED > UNLASH
UNLASHES > UNLASH
UNLASHING > UNLASH
UNLAST archaic variant of > UNLACED
UNLASTE archaic variant of > UNLACED
UNLATCH vb open or unfasten by the lifting or release of a latch
UNLATCHED > UNLATCH
UNLATCHES > UNLATCH
UNLAW vb penalize
UNLAWED > UNLAW
UNLAWFUL adj not permitted by law
UNLAWING > UNLAW
UNLAWS > UNLAW
UNLAY vb untwist (a rope or cable) to separate its strands
UNLAYING > UNLAY
UNLAYS > UNLAY
UNLEAD vb strip off lead
UNLEADED adj (of petrol) containing less tetraethyl lead ▷ n petrol containing a reduced amount of tetraethyl lead
UNLEADEDS > UNLEADED
UNLEADING > UNLEAD
UNLEADS > UNLEAD
UNLEAL adj treacherous
UNLEARN vb try to forget something learnt or to discard accumulated knowledge
UNLEARNED same as > UNLEARNT
UNLEARNS > UNLEARN
UNLEARNT adj denoting knowledge or skills innately present rather than learnt
UNLEASED adj not leased
UNLEASH vb set loose or cause (something bad)
UNLEASHED > UNLEASH
UNLEASHES > UNLEASH
UNLED adj not led
UNLESS conj except under the circumstances that ▷ prep except
UNLET adj not rented
UNLETHAL adj not deadly
UNLETTED adj unimpeded
UNLEVEL adj not level ▷ vb make unbalanced
UNLEVELED > UNLEVEL
UNLEVELS > UNLEVEL

UNLEVIED adj not levied
UNLICH Spenserian form of > UNLIKE
UNLICKED adj not licked
UNLID vb remove lid from
UNLIDDED > UNLID
UNLIDDING > UNLID
UNLIDS > UNLID
UNLIGHTED adj not lit
UNLIKABLE adj not likable
UNLIKE adj dissimilar or different ▷ prep not like or typical of ▷ n person or thing that is unlike another
UNLIKED adj not liked
UNLIKELY adj improbable
UNLIKES > UNLIKE
UNLIMBER vb disengage (a gun) from its limber
UNLIMBERS > UNLIMBER
UNLIME vb detach
UNLIMED > UNLIME
UNLIMES > UNLIME
UNLIMING > UNLIME
UNLIMITED adj apparently endless
UNLINE vb remove the lining from
UNLINEAL adj not lineal
UNLINED adj not having any lining
UNLINES > UNLINE
UNLINING > UNLINE
UNLINK vb undo the link or links between
UNLINKED > UNLINK
UNLINKING > UNLINK
UNLINKS > UNLINK
UNLISTED adj not entered on a list
UNLIT adj (of a fire, cigarette, etc) not lit and therefore not burning
UNLIVABLE adj not fit for living in
UNLIVE vb live so as to nullify, undo, or live down (past events or times)
UNLIVED > UNLIVE
UNLIVELY adj lifeless
UNLIVES > UNLIVE
UNLIVING > UNLIVE
UNLOAD vb remove (cargo) from (a ship, truck, or plane)
UNLOADED > UNLOAD
UNLOADER > UNLOAD
UNLOADERS > UNLOAD
UNLOADING > UNLOAD
UNLOADS > UNLOAD
UNLOBED adj without lobes
UNLOCATED adj not located
UNLOCK vb unfasten (a lock or door)
UNLOCKED adj not locked
UNLOCKING > UNLOCK
UNLOCKS > UNLOCK
UNLOGICAL same as > ILLOGICAL
UNLOOKED adj not looked (at)

UNLOOSE vb set free or release
UNLOOSED > UNLOOSE
UNLOOSEN same as > UNLOOSE
UNLOOSENS > UNLOOSEN
UNLOOSES > UNLOOSE
UNLOOSING > UNLOOSE
UNLOPPED adj not chopped off
UNLORD vb remove from position of being lord
UNLORDED > UNLORD
UNLORDING > UNLORD
UNLORDLY adv not in a lordlike manner
UNLORDS > UNLORD
UNLOSABLE adj unable to be lost
UNLOST adj not lost
UNLOVABLE adj too unpleasant or unattractive to be loved
UNLOVE vb stop loving
UNLOVED adj not loved by anyone
UNLOVELY adj unpleasant in appearance or character
UNLOVES > UNLOVE
UNLOVING adj not feeling or showing love and affection
UNLUCKIER > UNLUCKY
UNLUCKILY > UNLUCKY
UNLUCKY adj having bad luck, unfortunate
UNLYRICAL adj not lyrical
UNMACHO adj not macho
UNMADE adj (of a bed) with the bedclothes not smoothed and tidied
UNMAILED adj not sent by post
UNMAIMED adj not injured
UNMAKABLE adj unable to be made
UNMAKE vb undo or destroy
UNMAKER > UNMAKE
UNMAKERS > UNMAKE
UNMAKES > UNMAKE
UNMAKING > UNMAKE
UNMAKINGS > UNMAKE
UNMAN vb cause to lose courage or nerve
UNMANACLE vb release from manacles
UNMANAGED adj not managed
UNMANFUL adj unmanly
UNMANLIER > UNMANLY
UNMANLIKE adj not worthy of a man
UNMANLY adj not masculine
UNMANNED adj having no personnel or crew
UNMANNING > UNMAN
UNMANNISH adj not mannish
UNMANS > UNMAN
UNMANTLE vb remove mantle from
UNMANTLED > UNMANTLE

UNMANTLES
> UNMANTLE
UNMANURED adj not treated with manure
UNMAPPED adj not charted
UNMARD same as
> UNMARRED
UNMARKED adj having no signs of damage or injury
UNMARRED adj not marred
UNMARRIED adj not married
UNMARRIES > UNMARRY
UNMARRY vb divorce
UNMASK vb remove the mask or disguise from
UNMASKED > UNMASK
UNMASKER > UNMASK
UNMASKERS > UNMASK
UNMASKING > UNMASK
UNMASKS > UNMASK
UNMATCHED adj not equalled or surpassed
UNMATED adj not mated
UNMATTED adj not matted
UNMATURED adj not matured
UNMEANING adj having no meaning
UNMEANT adj unintentional
UNMEEK adj not submissive
UNMEET adj not meet
UNMEETLY > UNMEET
UNMELLOW adj not mellow
UNMELTED adj not melted
UNMENDED adj not mended
UNMERITED adj not merited or deserved
UNMERRIER > UNMERRY
UNMERRY adj not merry
UNMESH vb release from mesh
UNMESHED > UNMESH
UNMESHES > UNMESH
UNMESHING > UNMESH
UNMET adj unfulfilled
UNMETED adj unmeasured
UNMETERED adj not metered
UNMEW vb release from confinement
UNMEWED > UNMEW
UNMEWING > UNMEW
UNMEWS > UNMEW
UNMILKED adj not milked
UNMILLED adj not milled
UNMINDED adj disregarded
UNMINDFUL adj careless, heedless, or forgetful
UNMINED adj not mined
UNMINGLE vb separate
UNMINGLED
> UNMINGLE
UNMINGLES
> UNMINGLE
UNMIRIER > UNMIRY
UNMIRIEST > UNMIRY
UNMIRY adj not swampy

UNMISSED adj unnoticed
UNMITER same as
> UNMITRE
UNMITERED > UNMITER
UNMITERS > UNMITER
UNMITRE vb divest of a mitre
UNMITRED > UNMITRE
UNMITRES > UNMITRE
UNMITRING > UNMITRE
UNMIX vb separate
UNMIXABLE adj incapable of being mixed
UNMIXED > UNMIX
UNMIXEDLY > UNMIXED
UNMIXES > UNMIX
UNMIXING > UNMIX
UNMIXT same as > UNMIX
UNMOANED adj unmourned
UNMODISH adj passé
UNMOLD same as
> UNMOLDED
UNMOLDED > UNMOLD
UNMOLDING > UNMOLD
UNMOLDS > UNMOLD
UNMOLTEN adj not molten
UNMONEYED adj poor
UNMONIED same as
> UNMONEYED
UNMOOR vb weigh the anchor or drop the mooring of (a vessel)
UNMOORED > UNMOOR
UNMOORING > UNMOOR
UNMOORS > UNMOOR
UNMORAL adj outside morality
UNMORALLY > UNMORAL
UNMORTISE vb release from a mortise
UNMOTIVED adj without motive
UNMOULD vb change the shape of
UNMOULDED > UNMOULD
UNMOULDS > UNMOULD
UNMOUNT vb dismount
UNMOUNTED > UNMOUNT
UNMOUNTS > UNMOUNT
UNMOURNED adj not mourned
UNMOVABLE adj not movable
UNMOVABLY
> UNMOVABLE
UNMOVED adj not affected by emotion, indifferent
UNMOVEDLY > UNMOVED
UNMOVING adj still and motionless
UNMOWN adj not mown
UNMUFFLE vb remove a muffle or muffles from
UNMUFFLED
> UNMUFFLE
UNMUFFLES
> UNMUFFLE
UNMUSICAL adj (of a person) unable to appreciate or play music
UNMUZZLE vb take the muzzle off (a dog, etc)
UNMUZZLED
> UNMUZZLE
UNMUZZLES
> UNMUZZLE

UNNAIL vb unfasten by removing nails
UNNAILED > UNNAIL
UNNAILING > UNNAIL
UNNAILS > UNNAIL
UNNAMABLE adj that cannot or must not be named
UNNAMED adj not mentioned by name
UNNANELD same as
> UNANELED
UNNATIVE adj not native ▷ vb no longer be a native of a place
UNNATIVED
> UNNATIVE
UNNATIVES
> UNNATIVE
UNNATURAL adj strange and frightening because not usual
UNNEATH adj archaic word for underneath
UNNEEDED adj not needed
UNNEEDFUL adj not needful
UNNERVE vb cause to lose courage, confidence, or self-control
UNNERVED > UNNERVE
UNNERVES > UNNERVE
UNNERVING > UNNERVE
UNNEST vb remove from a nest
UNNESTED > UNNEST
UNNESTING > UNNEST
UNNESTS > UNNEST
UNNETHES same as
> UNNEATH
UNNETTED adj not having or not enclosed in a net
UNNOBLE vb strip of nobility
UNNOBLED > UNNOBLE
UNNOBLES > UNNOBLE
UNNOBLING > UNNOBLE
UNNOISIER > UNNOISY
UNNOISY adj quiet
UNNOTED adj not noted
UNNOTICED adj without being seen or noticed
UNNUANCED adj without nuances
UNOAKED adj (of wine) not matured in an oak barrel
UNOBEYED adj not obeyed
UNOBVIOUS adj unapparent
UNOFFERED adj not offered
UNOFTEN adv infrequently
UNOILED adj not lubricated with oil
UNOPEN adj not open
UNOPENED adj closed, barred, or sealed
UNOPPOSED adj not opposed
UNORDER vb cancel an order
UNORDERED adj not ordered
UNORDERLY adj not orderly or disorderly

UNORDERS > UNORDER
UNORNATE same as
> INORNATE
UNOWED same as
> UNOWNED
UNOWNED adj not owned
UNPACED adj without the aid of a pacemaker
UNPACK vb remove the contents of (a suitcase, trunk, etc)
UNPACKED > UNPACK
UNPACKER > UNPACK
UNPACKERS > UNPACK
UNPACKING > UNPACK
UNPACKS > UNPACK
UNPADDED adj not padded
UNPAGED adj (of a book) having no page numbers
UNPAID adj without a salary or wage
UNPAINED adj not suffering pain
UNPAINFUL adj painless
UNPAINT vb remove paint from
UNPAINTED > UNPAINT
UNPAINTS > UNPAINT
UNPAIRED adj not paired up
UNPALSIED adj not affected with palsy
UNPANEL vb unsaddle
UNPANELS > UNPANEL
UNPANGED adj without pain or sadness
UNPANNEL same as
> UNPANEL
UNPANNELS
> UNPANNEL
UNPAPER vb remove paper from
UNPAPERED > UNPAPER
UNPAPERS > UNPAPER
UNPARED adj not pared
UNPARTED adj not parted
UNPARTIAL same as
> IMPARTIAL
UNPATCHED adj not patched
UNPATHED adj not having a path
UNPAVED adj not covered in paving
UNPAY vb undo
UNPAYABLE adj incapable of being paid
UNPAYING > UNPAY
UNPAYS > UNPAY
UNPEELED adj not peeled
UNPEERED adj unparalleled
UNPEG vb remove a peg or pegs from, esp to unfasten
UNPEGGED > UNPEG
UNPEGGING > UNPEG
UNPEGS > UNPEG
UNPEN vb release from a pen
UNPENNED > UNPEN
UNPENNIED adj not having pennies
UNPENNING > UNPEN
UNPENS > UNPEN
UNPENT archaic past form of > UNPEN

u

UNPEOPLE vb empty of people

UNPEOPLED > UNPEOPLE

UNPEOPLES > UNPEOPLE

UNPERCH vb remove from a perch

UNPERCHED > UNPERCH

UNPERCHES > UNPERCH

UNPERFECT same as > IMPERFECT

UNPERPLEX vb remove confusion from

UNPERSON n person whose existence is officially denied or ignored

UNPERSONS > UNPERSON

UNPERVERT vb free (someone) from perversion

UNPICK vb undo (the stitches) of (a piece of sewing)

UNPICKED adj (of knitting, sewing, etc) having been unravelled or picked out

UNPICKING > UNPICK

UNPICKS > UNPICK

UNPIERCED adj not pierced

UNPILE vb remove from a pile

UNPILED > UNPILE

UNPILES > UNPILE

UNPILING > UNPILE

UNPILOTED adj unguided

UNPIN vb remove a pin or pins from

UNPINKED adj not decorated with a perforated pattern

UNPINKT same as > UNPINKED

UNPINNED > UNPIN

UNPINNING > UNPIN

UNPINS > UNPIN

UNPITIED adj not pitied

UNPITIFUL adj pitiless

UNPITTED adj not having had pits removed

UNPITYING adj not pitying

UNPLACE same as > DISPLACE

UNPLACED adj not given or put in a particular place

UNPLACES > UNPLACE

UNPLACING > UNPLACE

UNPLAGUED adj not plagued

UNPLAINED adj unmourned

UNPLAIT vb remove plaits from

UNPLAITED > UNPLAIT

UNPLAITS > UNPLAIT

UNPLANKED adj not planked

UNPLANNED adj not intentional or deliberate

UNPLANTED adj not planted

UNPLAYED adj not played

UNPLEASED adj not pleased or displeased

UNPLEATED adj not pleated

UNPLEDGED adj not pledged

UNPLIABLE adj not easily bent

UNPLIABLY > UNPLIABLE

UNPLIANT adj not pliant

UNPLOWED adj not ploughed

UNPLUCKED adj not plucked

UNPLUG vb disconnect (a piece of electrical equipment)

UNPLUGGED adj using acoustic rather than electric instruments

UNPLUGS > UNPLUG

UNPLUMB vb remove lead from

UNPLUMBED adj not measured

UNPLUMBS > UNPLUMB

UNPLUME vb remove feathers from

UNPLUMED > UNPLUME

UNPLUMES > UNPLUME

UNPLUMING > UNPLUME

UNPOETIC adj not poetic

UNPOINTED adj not pointed

UNPOISED adj not poised

UNPOISON vb extract poison from

UNPOISONS > UNPOISON

UNPOLICED adj without police control

UNPOLISH vb remove polish from

UNPOLITE same as > IMPOLITE

UNPOLITIC another word for > IMPOLITIC

UNPOLLED adj not included in an opinion poll

UNPOPE vb strip of popedom

UNPOPED > UNPOPE

UNPOPES > UNPOPE

UNPOPING > UNPOPE

UNPOPULAR adj generally disliked or disapproved of

UNPOSED adj not posed

UNPOSTED adj not sent by post

UNPOTABLE adj undrinkable

UNPOTTED adj not planted in a pot

UNPOURED adj not poured

UNPOWERED adj not powered

UNPRAISE vb withhold praise from

UNPRAISED > UNPRAISE

UNPRAISES > UNPRAISE

UNPRAY vb withdraw (a prayer)

UNPRAYED > UNPRAY

UNPRAYING > UNPRAY

UNPRAYS > UNPRAY

UNPREACH vb retract (a sermon)

UNPRECISE same as > IMPRECISE

UNPREDICT vb retract (a previous prediction)

UNPREPARE vb make unprepared

UNPRESSED adj not pressed

UNPRETTY adj unattractive

UNPRICED adj having no fixed or marked price

UNPRIEST vb strip of priesthood

UNPRIESTS > UNPRIEST

UNPRIMED adj not primed

UNPRINTED adj not printed

UNPRISON vb release from prison

UNPRISONS > UNPRISON

UNPRIZED adj not treasured

UNPROBED adj not examined

UNPROP vb remove support from

UNPROPER same as > IMPROPER

UNPROPPED > UNPROP

UNPROPS > UNPROP

UNPROVED adj not having been established as true, valid, or possible

UNPROVEN adj not established as true by evidence or demonstration

UNPROVIDE vb fail to supply requirements for

UNPROVOKE vb remove provocation from

UNPRUNED adj not pruned

UNPUCKER vb remove wrinkles from

UNPUCKERS > UNPUCKER

UNPULLED adj not pulled

UNPURE same as > IMPURE

UNPURELY > UNPURE

UNPURGED adj not purged

UNPURSE vb relax (lips) from pursed position

UNPURSED > UNPURSE

UNPURSES > UNPURSE

UNPURSING > UNPURSE

UNPURSUED adj not followed

UNPUZZLE vb figure out

UNPUZZLED > UNPUZZLE

UNPUZZLES > UNPUZZLE

UNQUAKING adj not quaking

UNQUALIFY vb disqualify

UNQUEEN vb depose from the position of queen

UNQUEENED > UNQUEEN

UNQUEENLY adv not in a queenlike manner

UNQUEENS > UNQUEEN

UNQUELLED adj not quelled

UNQUIET adj anxious or uneasy ▷ n state of unrest ▷ vb disquiet

UNQUIETED > UNQUIET

UNQUIETER > UNQUIET

UNQUIETLY > UNQUIET

UNQUIETS > UNQUIET

UNQUOTE interj expression used to indicate the end of a quotation ▷ vb close (a quotation), esp in printing

UNQUOTED > UNQUOTE

UNQUOTES > UNQUOTE

UNQUOTING > UNQUOTE

UNRACED adj not raced

UNRACKED adj not stretched

UNRAISED adj not raised

UNRAKE vb unearth through raking

UNRAKED adj not raked

UNRAKES > UNRAKE

UNRAKING > UNRAKE

UNRANKED adj not ranked

UNRATED adj not rated

UNRAVAGED adj not ravaged

UNRAVEL vb reduce (something knitted or woven) to separate strands

UNRAVELED > UNRAVEL

UNRAVELS > UNRAVEL

UNRAZED adj not razed

UNRAZORED adj unshaven

UNREACHED adj not reached

UNREAD adj (of a book or article) not yet read

UNREADIER > UNREADY

UNREADILY > UNREADY

UNREADY adj not ready or prepared

UNREAL adj (as if) existing only in the imagination

UNREALISE same as > UNREALIZE

UNREALISM n abstractionism

UNREALITY n quality or state of being unreal, fanciful, or impractical

UNREALIZE vb make unreal

UNREALLY > UNREAL

UNREAPED adj not reaped

UNREASON n irrationality or madness ▷ vb deprive of reason

UNREASONS > UNREASON

UNREAVE vb unwind

UNREAVED > UNREAVE

UNREAVES > UNREAVE

UNREAVING > UNREAVE

UNREBATED adj not refunded

UNREBUKED adj not rebuked

UNRECKED adj disregarded

UNRED same as > UNREAD

UNREDREST adj not redressed

UNREDUCED adj not reduced

UNREDY same as > UNREADY

UNREEL vb unwind from a reel

UNREELED > UNREEL

UNREELER n machine that unwinds something from a reel

UNREELERS > UNREELER

UNREELING > UNREEL

UNREELS > UNREEL

UNREEVE vb withdraw (a rope) from a block, thimble, etc

UNREEVED > UNREEVE

UNREEVES > UNREEVE

UNREEVING > UNREEVE

UNREFINED adj (of substances such as petroleum, ores, and sugar) not processed into a pure or usable form

UNREFUTED adj not refuted

UNREIN vb free from reins

UNREINED > UNREIN

UNREINING > UNREIN

UNREINS > UNREIN

UNRELATED adj not connected with each other

UNRELAXED adj not relaxed

UNREMOVED adj not removed

UNRENEWED adj not renewed

UNRENT adj not torn

UNRENTED adj not rented

UNREPAID adj not repaid

UNREPAIR less common word for > DISREPAIR

UNREPAIRS > UNREPAIR

UNRESERVE n candour

UNREST n rebellious state of discontent

UNRESTED adj not rested

UNRESTFUL adj restless

UNRESTING adj not resting

UNRESTS > UNREST

UNRETIRE vb resume work after retiring

UNRETIRED > UNRETIRE

UNRETIRES > UNRETIRE

UNREVISED adj not revised

UNREVOKED adj not revoked

UNRHYMED adj not rhymed

UNRIBBED adj not ribbed

UNRID adj unridden

UNRIDABLE adj not capable of being ridden

UNRIDDEN adj not or never ridden

UNRIDDLE vb solve or puzzle out

UNRIDDLED > UNRIDDLE

UNRIDDLER > UNRIDDLE

UNRIDDLES > UNRIDDLE

UNRIDGED adj not ridged

UNRIFLED adj (of a firearm or its bore) not rifled

UNRIG vb strip (a vessel) of standing and running rigging

UNRIGGED > UNRIG

UNRIGGING > UNRIG

UNRIGHT n wrong ▷ adj not right or fair ▷ vb make wrong

UNRIGHTED > UNRIGHT

UNRIGHTS > UNRIGHT

UNRIGS > UNRIG

UNRIMED same as > UNRHYMED

UNRINGED adj not having or wearing a ring

UNRINSED adj not rinsed

UNRIP vb rip open

UNRIPE adj not fully matured

UNRIPELY > UNRIPE

UNRIPENED same as > UNRIPE

UNRIPER > UNRIPE

UNRIPEST > UNRIPE

UNRIPPED > UNRIP

UNRIPPING > UNRIP

UNRIPS > UNRIP

UNRISEN adj not risen

UNRIVALED adj (in US English) matchless or unrivalled

UNRIVEN adj not torn apart

UNRIVET vb remove rivets from

UNRIVETED > UNRIVET

UNRIVETS > UNRIVET

UNROASTED adj not roasted

UNROBE same as > DISROBE

UNROBED > UNROBE

UNROBES > UNROBE

UNROBING > UNROBE

UNROLL vb open out or unwind (something rolled or coiled)

UNROLLED > UNROLL

UNROLLING > UNROLL

UNROLLS > UNROLL

UNROOF vb remove the roof from

UNROOFED > UNROOF

UNROOFING > UNROOF

UNROOFS > UNROOF

UNROOST vb remove from a perch

UNROOSTED > UNROOST

UNROOSTS > UNROOST

UNROOT less common word for > UPROOT

UNROOTED > UNROOT

UNROOTING > UNROOT

UNROOTS > UNROOT

UNROPE vb release from a rope

UNROPED > UNROPE

UNROPES > UNROPE

UNROPING > UNROPE

UNROSINED adj not coated with rosin

UNROTTED adj not rotted

UNROTTEN adj not rotten

UNROUGED adj not coloured with rouge

UNROUGH adj not rough

UNROUND vb release (lips) from a rounded position

UNROUNDED adj articulated with the lips spread

UNROUNDS > UNROUND

UNROUSED adj not roused

UNROVE > UNREEVE

UNROVEN > UNREEVE

UNROYAL adj not royal

UNROYALLY > UNROYAL

UNRUBBED adj not rubbed

UNRUDE adj not rude

UNRUFFE same as > UNROUGH

UNRUFFLE vb calm

UNRUFFLED adj calm and unperturbed

UNRUFFLES > UNRUFFLE

UNRULE n lack of authority

UNRULED adj not ruled

UNRULES > UNRULE

UNRULIER > UNRULY

UNRULIEST > UNRULY

UNRULY adj difficult to control or organize

UNRUMPLED adj neat

UNRUSHED adj unhurried

UNRUSTED adj not rusted

UNS > UN

UNSADDLE vb remove the saddle from (a horse)

UNSADDLED > UNSADDLE

UNSADDLES > UNSADDLE

UNSAFE adj dangerous

UNSAFELY > UNSAFE

UNSAFER > UNSAFE

UNSAFEST > UNSAFE

UNSAFETY n lack of safety

UNSAID adj not said or expressed

UNSAILED adj not sailed

UNSAINED adj not blessed

UNSAINT vb remove status of being a saint from

UNSAINTED > UNSAINT

UNSAINTLY adj not saintly

UNSAINTS > UNSAINT

UNSALABLE adj not capable of being sold

UNSALABLY > UNSALABLE

UNSALTED adj not seasoned, preserved, or treated with salt

UNSALUTED adj not saluted

UNSAMPLED adj not sampled

UNSAPPED adj not undermined

UNSASHED adj not furnished with a sash

UNSATABLE adj not able to be sated; insatiable

UNSATED adj not sated

UNSATIATE adj insatiable

UNSATING adj not satisfying

UNSAVED adj not saved

UNSAVORY same as > UNSAVOURY

UNSAVOURY adj distasteful or objectionable

UNSAW > UNSEE

UNSAWED same as > UNSAWN

UNSAWN adj not cut with a saw

UNSAY vb retract or withdraw (something said or written)

UNSAYABLE adj that cannot be said

UNSAYING > UNSAY

UNSAYS > UNSAY

UNSCALE same as > DESCALE

UNSCALED > UNSCALE

UNSCALES > UNSCALE

UNSCALING > UNSCALE

UNSCANNED adj not scanned

UNSCARIER > UNSCARY

UNSCARRED adj not scarred

UNSCARY adj not scary

UNSCATHED adj not harmed or injured

UNSCENTED adj not filled or impregnated with odour or fragrance

UNSCOURED adj not scoured

UNSCREW vb loosen (a screw or lid) by turning it

UNSCREWED > UNSCREW

UNSCREWS > UNSCREW

UNSCYTHED adj not cut with a scythe

UNSEAL vb remove or break the seal of

UNSEALED > UNSEAL

UNSEALING > UNSEAL

UNSEALS > UNSEAL

UNSEAM vb open or undo the seam of

UNSEAMED > UNSEAM

UNSEAMING > UNSEAM

UNSEAMS > UNSEAM

UNSEARED adj not seared

UNSEASON vb affect unfavourably

UNSEASONS > UNSEASON

UNSEAT vb throw or displace from a seat or saddle

UNSEATED > UNSEAT

UNSEATING > UNSEAT

UNSEATS > UNSEAT

UNSECRET adj not secret ▷ vb inform or make aware

UNSECRETS > UNSECRET

UNSECULAR adj not secular

UNSECURED adj (of a loan, etc) secured only against general assets and not against a specific asset
UNSEDUCED adj not seduced
UNSEE vb undo the act of seeing something
UNSEEABLE adj not able to be seen
UNSEEDED adj not given a top player's ranking in a tournament
UNSEEING adj not noticing or looking at anything
UNSEEL vb undo seeing
UNSEELED > UNSEEL
UNSEELIE pl n evil malevolent fairies ▷ adj of or belonging to the unseelie
UNSEELING > UNSEEL
UNSEELS > UNSEEL
UNSEEMING adj unseemly
UNSEEMLY adj not according to expected standards of behaviour ▷ adv in an unseemly manner
UNSEEN adj hidden or invisible ▷ adv without being seen ▷ n passage given to students for translation without them having seen it in advance
UNSEENS > UNSEEN
UNSEES > UNSEE
UNSEIZED adj not seized
UNSELDOM adv frequently
UNSELF vb remove self-centredness from ▷ n lack of self
UNSELFED > UNSELF
UNSELFING > UNSELF
UNSELFISH adj concerned about other people's wishes and needs rather than one's own
UNSELFS > UNSELF
UNSELL vb speak unfavourably and off-puttingly of (something or someone)
UNSELLING > UNSELL
UNSELLS > UNSELL
UNSELVES > UNSELF
UNSENSE vb remove sense from
UNSENSED > UNSENSE
UNSENSES > UNSENSE
UNSENSING > UNSENSE
UNSENT adj not sent
UNSERIOUS adj not serious
UNSERVED adj not served
UNSET adj not yet solidified or firm ▷ vb displace
UNSETS > UNSET
UNSETTING > UNSET
UNSETTLE vb change or become changed from a fixed or settled condition
UNSETTLED adj lacking order or stability
UNSETTLES > UNSETTLE

UNSEVERED adj not severed
UNSEW vb undo stitching of
UNSEWED > UNSEW
UNSEWING > UNSEW
UNSEWN > UNSEW
UNSEWS > UNSEW
UNSEX vb deprive (a person) of the attributes of his or her sex
UNSEXED > UNSEX
UNSEXES > UNSEX
UNSEXIER > UNSEXY
UNSEXIEST > UNSEXY
UNSEXILY adv in an unsexy manner
UNSEXING > UNSEX
UNSEXIST adj not sexist
UNSEXUAL adj not sexual
UNSEXY adj not exciting or attractive
UNSHACKLE vb release from shackles
UNSHADED adj not shaded
UNSHADOW vb remove shadow from
UNSHADOWS > UNSHADOW
UNSHAKED same as > UNSHAKEN
UNSHAKEN adj (of faith or feelings) not having been weakened
UNSHALE vb expose
UNSHALED > UNSHALE
UNSHALES > UNSHALE
UNSHALING > UNSHALE
UNSHAMED same as > UNASHAMED
UNSHAPE vb make shapeless
UNSHAPED > UNSHAPE
UNSHAPELY adj not shapely
UNSHAPEN adj having no definite shape
UNSHAPES > UNSHAPE
UNSHAPING > UNSHAPE
UNSHARED adj not shared
UNSHARP adj not sharp
UNSHAVED adj not shaved
UNSHAVEN adj having a stubbled chin
UNSHEATHE vb pull (a weapon) from a sheath
UNSHED adj not shed
UNSHELL vb remove from a shell
UNSHELLED > UNSHELL
UNSHELLS > UNSHELL
UNSHENT adj undamaged
UNSHEWN adj unshown
UNSHIFT vb release the shift key on a keyboard
UNSHIFTED > UNSHIFT
UNSHIFTS > UNSHIFT
UNSHIP vb be or cause to be unloaded, discharged, or disembarked from a ship
UNSHIPPED > UNSHIP
UNSHIPS > UNSHIP
UNSHIRTED adj not wearing a shirt
UNSHOCKED adj not shocked

UNSHOD adj not wearing shoes
UNSHOE vb remove shoes from
UNSHOED same as > UNSHOD
UNSHOEING > UNSHOE
UNSHOES > UNSHOE
UNSHOOT Shakespearean variant of > UNSHOUT
UNSHOOTED > UNSHOOT
UNSHOOTS > UNSHOOT
UNSHORN adj not cut
UNSHOT adj not shot ▷ vb remove shot from
UNSHOTS > UNSHOT
UNSHOTTED > UNSHOT
UNSHOUT vb revoke (an earlier statement) by shouting a contrary one
UNSHOUTED > UNSHOUT
UNSHOUTS > UNSHOUT
UNSHOWIER > UNSHOWY
UNSHOWN adj not shown
UNSHOWY adj not showy
UNSHRIVED same as > UNSHRIVEN
UNSHRIVEN adj not shriven
UNSHROUD vb uncover
UNSHROUDS > UNSHROUD
UNSHRUBD adj old word meaning not having shrubs
UNSHRUNK adj not shrunk
UNSHUNNED adj not shunned
UNSHUT vb open
UNSHUTS > UNSHUT
UNSHUTTER vb remove shutters from
UNSICKER adj old Scottish word meaning unsettled
UNSICKLED adj not cut with a sickle
UNSIFTED adj not strained
UNSIGHING adj not lamenting
UNSIGHT vb obstruct vision of
UNSIGHTED adj not sighted
UNSIGHTLY adj unpleasant to look at
UNSIGHTS > UNSIGHT
UNSIGNED adj (of a letter etc) anonymous
UNSILENT adj not silent
UNSIMILAR adj not similar
UNSINEW vb weaken
UNSINEWED > UNSINEW
UNSINEWS > UNSINEW
UNSINFUL adj without sin
UNSISTING adj Shakespearean term, possibly meaning insisting
UNSIZABLE adj of inadequate size
UNSIZED adj not made or sorted according to size
UNSKILFUL adj lacking dexterity or proficiency

UNSKILLED adj not having or requiring any special skill or training
UNSKIMMED adj not skimmed
UNSKINNED adj not skinned
UNSLAIN adj not killed
UNSLAKED adj not slaked
UNSLICED adj not sliced
UNSLICK adj not slick
UNSLING vb remove or release from a slung position
UNSLINGS > UNSLING
UNSLUICE vb let flow
UNSLUICED > UNSLUICE
UNSLUICES > UNSLUICE
UNSLUNG > UNSLING
UNSMART adj not smart
UNSMILING adj not wearing or assuming a smile
UNSMITTEN adj not smitten
UNSMOKED adj not smoked
UNSMOOTH vb roughen
UNSMOOTHS > UNSMOOTH
UNSMOTE same as > UNSMITTEN
UNSNAG vb remove snags from
UNSNAGGED > UNSNAG
UNSNAGS > UNSNAG
UNSNAP vb unfasten (the snap or catch) of (something)
UNSNAPPED > UNSNAP
UNSNAPS > UNSNAP
UNSNARL vb free from a snarl or tangle
UNSNARLED > UNSNARL
UNSNARLS > UNSNARL
UNSNECK vb unlatch
UNSNECKED > UNSNECK
UNSNECKS > UNSNECK
UNSNUFFED adj not snuffed
UNSOAKED adj not soaked
UNSOAPED adj not rubbed with soap
UNSOBER adj not sober ▷ vb make unrefined in manners
UNSOBERED > UNSOBER
UNSOBERLY > UNSOBER
UNSOBERS > UNSOBER
UNSOCIAL adj avoiding the company of other people
UNSOCKET vb remove from a socket
UNSOCKETS > UNSOCKET
UNSOD same as > UNSODDEN
UNSODDEN adj not soaked
UNSOFT adj hard
UNSOILED adj not soiled
UNSOLACED adj not comforted
UNSOLD adj not sold

UNSOLDER vb remove soldering from
UNSOLDERS > UNSOLDER
UNSOLEMN adj unceremonious
UNSOLID adj not solid
UNSOLIDLY > UNSOLID
UNSOLVED adj not having been solved or explained
UNSONCY same as > UNSONSY
UNSONSIE same as > UNSONSY
UNSONSIER > UNSONSY
UNSONSY adj unfortunate
UNSOOTE adj not sweet
UNSOOTHED adj not soothed
UNSORTED adj not sorted
UNSOUGHT adj not sought after
UNSOUL vb cause to be soulless
UNSOULED > UNSOUL
UNSOULING > UNSOUL
UNSOULS > UNSOUL
UNSOUND adj unhealthy or unstable
UNSOUNDED adj not sounded
UNSOUNDER > UNSOUND
UNSOUNDLY > UNSOUND
UNSOURCED adj without a source
UNSOURED adj not soured
UNSOWED same as > UNSOWN
UNSOWN adj not sown
UNSPAR vb open
UNSPARED adj not spared
UNSPARING adj very generous
UNSPARRED > UNSPAR
UNSPARS > UNSPAR
UNSPEAK obsolete word for > UNSAY
UNSPEAKS > UNSPEAK
UNSPED adj not achieved
UNSPELL vb release from a spell
UNSPELLED > UNSPELL
UNSPELLS > UNSPELL
UNSPENT adj not spent
UNSPHERE vb remove from its, one's, etc sphere or place
UNSPHERED > UNSPHERE
UNSPHERES > UNSPHERE
UNSPIDE same as > UNSPIED
UNSPIED adj unnoticed
UNSPILLED same as > UNSPILT
UNSPILT adj not spilt
UNSPLIT adj not split
UNSPOILED adj not damaged or harmed
UNSPOILT same as > UNSPOILED
UNSPOKE > UNSPEAK
UNSPOKEN adj not openly expressed
UNSPOOL vb unwind from spool
UNSPOOLED > UNSPOOL

UNSPOOLS > UNSPOOL
UNSPOTTED adj without spots or stains
UNSPRAYED adj not sprayed
UNSPRUNG adj without springs
UNSPUN adj not spun
UNSQUARED adj not made into a square shape
UNSTABLE adj lacking stability or firmness
UNSTABLER > UNSTABLE
UNSTABLY > UNSTABLE
UNSTACK vb remove from a stack
UNSTACKED > UNSTACK
UNSTACKS > UNSTACK
UNSTAGED adj not staged
UNSTAID adj not staid
UNSTAINED adj not stained
UNSTALKED adj without a stalk
UNSTAMPED adj not stamped
UNSTARCH vb remove starch from
UNSTARRED adj not marked with a star
UNSTARRY adj not resembling or characteristic of a star from the entertainment world
UNSTATE vb deprive of state
UNSTATED adj not having been articulated or uttered
UNSTATES > UNSTATE
UNSTATING > UNSTATE
UNSTAYED adj unhindered
UNSTAYING adj nonstop
UNSTEADY adj not securely fixed ▷ vb make unsteady
UNSTEEL vb make (the heart, feelings, etc) more gentle or compassionate
UNSTEELED > UNSTEEL
UNSTEELS > UNSTEEL
UNSTEMMED adj without a stem
UNSTEP vb remove (a mast) from its step
UNSTEPPED > UNSTEP
UNSTEPS > UNSTEP
UNSTERILE adj not free from living, esp pathogenic, microorganisms
UNSTICK vb free or loosen (something stuck)
UNSTICKS > UNSTICK
UNSTIFFEN vb remove the stiffness from
UNSTIFLED adj not suppressed
UNSTILLED adj not reduced
UNSTINTED adj not stinted
UNSTIRRED adj not stirred

UNSTITCH vb remove stitching from
UNSTOCK vb remove stock from
UNSTOCKED adj without stock
UNSTOCKS > UNSTOCK
UNSTONED adj not stoned
UNSTOP vb remove the stop or stopper from
UNSTOPPED adj not obstructed or stopped up
UNSTOPPER vb unplug
UNSTOPS > UNSTOP
UNSTOW vb remove from storage
UNSTOWED > UNSTOW
UNSTOWING > UNSTOW
UNSTOWS > UNSTOW
UNSTRAP vb undo the straps fastening (something) in position
UNSTRAPS > UNSTRAP
UNSTRESS n weak syllable ▷ vb become less stressed
UNSTRING vb remove the strings of
UNSTRINGS > UNSTRING
UNSTRIP vb strip
UNSTRIPED adj (esp of smooth muscle) not having stripes
UNSTRIPS > UNSTRIP
UNSTRUCK adj not struck
UNSTRUNG adj emotionally distressed
UNSTUCK adj freed from being stuck, glued, fastened, etc
UNSTUDIED adj natural or spontaneous
UNSTUFFED adj not stuffed
UNSTUFFY adj well-ventilated
UNSTUFT same as > UNSTUFFED
UNSTUNG adj not stung
UNSTYLISH adj unfashionable
UNSUBDUED adj not subdued
UNSUBJECT adj not subject ▷ vb remove from subjugation
UNSUBTLE adj not subtle
UNSUBTLER > UNSUBTLE
UNSUBTLY > UNSUBTLE
UNSUCCESS n failure
UNSUCKED adj not sucked
UNSUIT vb make unsuitable
UNSUITED adj not appropriate for a particular task or situation
UNSUITING > UNSUIT
UNSUITS > UNSUIT
UNSULLIED adj (of a reputation, etc) not stained or tarnished
UNSUMMED adj not calculated
UNSUNG adj not acclaimed or honoured
UNSUNK adj not sunken

UNSUNNED adj not subjected to sunlight
UNSUNNIER > UNSUNNY
UNSUNNY adj not sunny
UNSUPPLE adj rigid
UNSURE adj lacking assurance or self-confidence
UNSURED adj not assured
UNSURELY > UNSURE
UNSURER > UNSURE
UNSUREST > UNSURE
UNSUSPECT adj not open to suspicion
UNSWADDLE same as > UNSWATHE
UNSWATHE vb unwrap
UNSWATHED > UNSWATHE
UNSWATHES > UNSWATHE
UNSWAYED adj not swayed
UNSWEAR vb retract or revoke (a sworn oath)
UNSWEARS > UNSWEAR
UNSWEET adj not sweet
UNSWEPT adj not swept
UNSWOLLEN adj not swollen
UNSWORE > UNSWEAR
UNSWORN > UNSWEAR
UNTACK vb remove saddle and harness, etc from
UNTACKED > UNTACK
UNTACKING > UNTACK
UNTACKLE vb remove tackle from
UNTACKLED > UNTACKLE
UNTACKLES > UNTACKLE
UNTACKS > UNTACK
UNTACTFUL adj not tactful
UNTAGGED adj without a label
UNTAILED adj tailless
UNTAINTED adj not tarnished, contaminated, or polluted
UNTAKEN adj not taken
UNTAMABLE adj (of an animal or person) not capable of being tamed, subdued, or made obedient
UNTAMABLY > UNTAMABLE
UNTAME vb undo the taming of
UNTAMED adj not brought under human control
UNTAMES > UNTAME
UNTAMING > UNTAME
UNTANGLE vb free from tangles or confusion
UNTANGLED > UNTANGLE
UNTANGLES > UNTANGLE
UNTANNED adj not tanned
UNTAPPED adj not yet used
UNTARRED adj not coated with tar
UNTASTED adj not tasted

u

UNTAUGHT adj without training or education

UNTAX vb stop taxing

UNTAXABLE adj not taxable

UNTAXED adj not subject to taxation

UNTAXES > UNTAX

UNTAXING > UNTAX

UNTEACH vb cause to disbelieve (teaching)

UNTEACHES > UNTEACH

UNTEAM vb disband a team

UNTEAMED > UNTEAM

UNTEAMING > UNTEAM

UNTEAMS > UNTEAM

UNTEMPER vb soften

UNTEMPERS > UNTEMPER

UNTEMPTED adj not tempted

UNTENABLE adj (of a theory, idea, etc) incapable of being defended

UNTENABLY > UNTENABLE

UNTENANT vb remove (a tenant)

UNTENANTS > UNTENANT

UNTENDED adj not cared for or attended to

UNTENDER adj not tender

UNTENT vb remove from a tent

UNTENTED > UNTENT

UNTENTIER > UNTENTY

UNTENTING > UNTENT

UNTENTS > UNTENT

UNTENTY adj inattentive

UNTENURED adj not having tenure

UNTESTED adj not having been tested or examined

UNTETHER vb untie

UNTETHERS > UNTETHER

UNTHANKED adj not thanked

UNTHATCH vb remove the thatch from

UNTHAW same as > THAW

UNTHAWED adj not thawed

UNTHAWING > UNTHAW

UNTHAWS > UNTHAW

UNTHINK vb reverse one's opinion about

UNTHINKS > UNTHINK

UNTHOUGHT > UNTHINK

UNTHREAD vb draw out the thread or threads from (a needle, etc)

UNTHREADS > UNTHREAD

UNTHRIFT n unthrifty person

UNTHRIFTS > UNTHRIFT

UNTHRIFTY adj careless with money

UNTHRONE less common word for > DETHRONE

UNTHRONED > UNTHRONE

UNTHRONES > UNTHRONE

UNTIDIED > UNTIDY

UNTIDIER > UNTIDY

UNTIDIES > UNTIDY

UNTIDIEST > UNTIDY

UNTIDILY > UNTIDY

UNTIDY adj messy and disordered ▷ vb make untidy

UNTIDYING > UNTIDY

UNTIE vb open or free (something that is tied)

UNTIED > UNTIE

UNTIEING > UNTIE

UNTIES > UNTIE

UNTIL prep in or throughout the period before

UNTILE vb strip tiles from

UNTILED > UNTILE

UNTILES > UNTILE

UNTILING > UNTILE

UNTILLED adj not tilled

UNTILTED adj not tilted

UNTIMED adj not timed

UNTIMELY adj occurring before the expected or normal time ▷ adv prematurely or inopportunely

UNTIMEOUS same as > UNTIMELY

UNTIN vb remove tin from

UNTINGED adj not tinged

UNTINNED > UNTIN

UNTINNING > UNTIN

UNTINS > UNTIN

UNTIPPED adj not tipped

UNTIRABLE adj not able to be fatigued

UNTIRED adj not tired

UNTIRING adj continuing without declining in strength

UNTITLED adj without a title

UNTO prep to

UNTOILING adj not labouring

UNTOLD adj incapable of description

UNTOMB vb exhume

UNTOMBED > UNTOMB

UNTOMBING > UNTOMB

UNTOMBS > UNTOMB

UNTONED adj not toned

UNTOOLED adj not tooled

UNTOOTHED adj not toothed

UNTORN adj not torn

UNTOUCHED adj not changed, moved, or affected

UNTOWARD adj causing misfortune or annoyance

UNTRACE vb remove traces from

UNTRACED adj not traced

UNTRACES > UNTRACE

UNTRACING > UNTRACE

UNTRACK vb remove from a track

UNTRACKED adj not tracked

UNTRACKS > UNTRACK

UNTRADED adj not traded

UNTRAINED adj without formal or adequate training or education

UNTRAPPED adj not trapped

UNTREAD vb retrace (a course, path, etc)

UNTREADED > UNTREAD

UNTREADS > UNTREAD

UNTREATED adj (of an illness, etc) not having been dealt with

UNTRENDY adj not trendy

UNTRESSED adj not tressed or braided

UNTRIDE same as > UNTRIED

UNTRIED adj not yet used, done, or tested

UNTRIM vb deprive of elegance or adornment

UNTRIMMED > UNTRIM

UNTRIMS > UNTRIM

UNTROD > UNTREAD

UNTRODDEN > UNTREAD

UNTRUE adj incorrect or false

UNTRUER > UNTRUE

UNTRUEST > UNTRUE

UNTRUISM n something that is false

UNTRUISMS > UNTRUISM

UNTRULY > UNTRUE

UNTRUSS vb release from or as if from a truss

UNTRUSSED > UNTRUSS

UNTRUSSER n person who untrusses

UNTRUSSES > UNTRUSS

UNTRUST n mistrust

UNTRUSTED adj not trusted

UNTRUSTS > UNTRUST

UNTRUSTY adj not trusty

UNTRUTH n statement that is not true, lie

UNTRUTHS > UNTRUTH

UNTUCK vb become or cause to become loose or not tucked in

UNTUCKED > UNTUCK

UNTUCKING > UNTUCK

UNTUCKS > UNTUCK

UNTUFTED adj not having tufts

UNTUMBLED adj not tumbled

UNTUNABLE adj not tuneful

UNTUNABLY > UNTUNABLE

UNTUNE vb make out of tune

UNTUNED > UNTUNE

UNTUNEFUL adj not tuneful

UNTUNES > UNTUNE

UNTUNING > UNTUNE

UNTURBID adj clear

UNTURF vb remove turf from

UNTURFED > UNTURF

UNTURFING > UNTURF

UNTURFS > UNTURF

UNTURN vb turn in a reverse direction

UNTURNED adj not turned

UNTURNING > UNTURN

UNTURNS > UNTURN

UNTUTORED adj without formal education

UNTWILLED adj not twilled

UNTWINE vb untwist, unravel, and separate

UNTWINED > UNTWINE

UNTWINES > UNTWINE

UNTWINING > UNTWINE

UNTWIST vb twist apart and loosen

UNTWISTED > UNTWIST

UNTWISTS > UNTWIST

UNTYING > UNTIE

UNTYINGS > UNTIE

UNTYPABLE adj incapable of being typed

UNTYPICAL adj not representative or characteristic of a particular type, person, etc

UNUNBIUM n chemical element

UNUNBIUMS > UNUNBIUM

UNUNITED adj separated

UNUNUNIUM n chemical element

UNURGED adj not urged

UNUSABLE adj not in good enough condition to be used

UNUSABLY > UNUSABLE

UNUSED adj not being or never having been used

UNUSEFUL adj useless

UNUSHERED adj not escorted

UNUSUAL adj uncommon or extraordinary

UNUSUALLY > UNUSUAL

UNUTTERED adj not uttered

UNVAIL same as > UNVEIL

UNVAILE same as > UNVEIL

UNVAILED > UNVAIL

UNVAILES > UNVAIL

UNVAILING > UNVAIL

UNVAILS > UNVAIL

UNVALUED adj not appreciated or valued

UNVARIED adj not varied

UNVARYING adj always staying the same

UNVEIL vb ceremonially remove the cover from (a new picture, plaque, etc)

UNVEILED > UNVEIL

UNVEILER n person who removes a veil

UNVEILERS > UNVEILER

UNVEILING n ceremony involving the removal of a veil covering a statue

UNVEILS > UNVEIL

UNVEINED adj without veins

UNVENTED adj not vented

UNVERSED adj not versed

UNVESTED adj not vested

UNVETTED adj not thoroughly examined

UNVEXED *adj* not annoyed
UNVEXT *same as* > UNVEXED
UNVIABLE *adj* not capable of succeeding, esp financially
UNVIEWED *adj* not viewed
UNVIRTUE *n* state of having no virtue
UNVIRTUES > UNVIRTUE
UNVISITED *adj* not visited
UNVISOR *vb* remove a visor from
UNVISORED > UNVISOR
UNVISORS > UNVISOR
UNVITAL *adj* not vital
UNVIZARD *same as* > UNVISOR
UNVIZARDS > UNVIZARD
UNVOCAL *adj* not vocal
UNVOICE *vb* pronounce without vibration of the vocal cords
UNVOICED *adj* not expressed or spoken
UNVOICES > UNVOICE
UNVOICING > UNVOICE
UNVULGAR *adj* not vulgar
UNWAGED *adj* (of a person) not having a paid job
UNWAISTED *adj* not waisted
UNWAKED *same as* > UNWAKENED
UNWAKENED *adj* not roused from sleep
UNWALLED *adj* not surrounded by walls
UNWANING *adj* not waning
UNWANTED *adj* not wanted or welcome
UNWARDED *adj* not warded
UNWARE *same as* > UNAWARE
UNWARELY > UNWARE
UNWARES *same as* > UNAWARES
UNWARIE *same as* > UNWARY
UNWARIER > UNWARY
UNWARIEST > UNWARY
UNWARILY > UNWARY
UNWARLIKE *adj* not warlike
UNWARMED *adj* not warmed
UNWARNED *adj* not warned
UNWARPED *adj* not warped
UNWARY *adj* not careful or cautious and therefore likely to be harmed
UNWASHED *n* ordinary people collectively
UNWASHEDS > UNWASHED
UNWASHEN *same as* > UNWASHED
UNWASTED *adj* not wasted

UNWASTING *adj* not wasting
UNWATCHED *adj* (of an automatic device, such as a beacon) not manned
UNWATER *vb* dry out
UNWATERED > UNWATER
UNWATERS > UNWATER
UNWATERY *adj* not watery
UNWAXED *adj* not treated with wax
UNWAYED *adj* having no routes
UNWEAL *n* ill or sorrow
UNWEALS > UNWEAL
UNWEANED *adj* not weaned
UNWEAPON *vb* disarm
UNWEAPONS > UNWEAPON
UNWEARIED *adj* not abating or tiring
UNWEARIER > UNWEARY
UNWEARIES > UNWEARY
UNWEARY *adj* not weary ▷ *vb* refresh or energize
UNWEAVE *vb* undo or unravel
UNWEAVES > UNWEAVE
UNWEAVING > UNWEAVE
UNWEBBED *adj* not webbed
UNWED *adj* not wed
UNWEDDED *adj* not wedded
UNWEEDED *adj* not weeded
UNWEENED *adj* unknown
UNWEETING *same as* > UNWITTING
UNWEIGHED *adj* (of quantities purchased, etc) not measured for weight
UNWEIGHT *vb* remove weight from
UNWEIGHTS > UNWEIGHT
UNWELCOME *adj* unpleasant and unwanted
UNWELDED *adj* not welded
UNWELDY *same as* > UNWIELDY
UNWELL *adj* not healthy, ill
UNWEPT *adj* not wept for or lamented
UNWET *adj* not wet
UNWETTED *same as* > UNWET
UNWHIPPED *adj* not whipped
UNWHIPT *same as* > UNWHIPPED
UNWHITE *adj* not white
UNWIELDILY *same as* > UNWIELDY
UNWIELDY *adj* too heavy, large, or awkward to be easily handled
UNWIFELY *adj* not like a wife
UNWIGGED *adj* without a wig
UNWILFUL *adj* complaisant
UNWILL *vb* will the reversal of (something that has already occurred)

UNWILLED *adj* not intentional
UNWILLING *adj* reluctant
UNWILLS > UNWILL
UNWIND *vb* relax after a busy or tense time
UNWINDER > UNWIND
UNWINDERS > UNWIND
UNWINDING > UNWIND
UNWINDS > UNWIND
UNWINGED *adj* without wings
UNWINKING *adj* vigilant
UNWIPED *adj* not wiped
UNWIRE *vb* remove wiring from
UNWIRED > UNWIRE
UNWIRES > UNWIRE
UNWIRING > UNWIRE
UNWISDOM *n* imprudence
UNWISDOMS > UNWISDOM
UNWISE *adj* foolish
UNWISELY > UNWISE
UNWISER > UNWISE
UNWISEST > UNWISE
UNWISH *vb* retract or revoke (a wish)
UNWISHED *adj* not desired
UNWISHES > UNWISH
UNWISHFUL *adj* not wishful
UNWISHING > UNWISH
UNWIST *adj* unknown
UNWIT *vb* divest of wit
UNWITCH *vb* release from witchcraft
UNWITCHED > UNWITCH
UNWITCHES > UNWITCH
UNWITS > UNWIT
UNWITTED > UNWIT
UNWITTIER > UNWITTY
UNWITTILY > UNWITTY
UNWITTING *adj* not intentional
UNWITTY *adj* not clever and amusing
UNWIVE *vb* remove a wife from
UNWIVED > UNWIVE
UNWIVES > UNWIVE
UNWIVING > UNWIVE
UNWOMAN *vb* remove womanly qualities from
UNWOMANED > UNWOMAN
UNWOMANLY *adj* not womanly
UNWOMANS > UNWOMAN
UNWON *adj* not won
UNWONT *adj* unaccustomed
UNWONTED *adj* out of the ordinary
UNWOODED *adj* not wooded
UNWOOED *adj* not wooed
UNWORDED *adj* not expressed in words
UNWORK *vb* destroy (work previously done)
UNWORKED *adj* not worked
UNWORKING > UNWORK
UNWORKS > UNWORK
UNWORLDLY *adj* not concerned with material values or pursuits

UNWORMED *adj* not rid of worms
UNWORN *adj* not having deteriorated through use or age
UNWORRIED *adj* not bothered or perturbed
UNWORTH *n* lack of value
UNWORTHS > UNWORTH
UNWORTHY *adj* not deserving or worthy
UNWOUND *past tense and past participle of* > UNWIND
UNWOUNDED *adj* not wounded
UNWOVE > UNWEAVE
UNWOVEN > UNWEAVE
UNWRAP *vb* remove the wrapping from (something)
UNWRAPPED > UNWRAP
UNWRAPS > UNWRAP
UNWREAKED *adj* unavenged
UNWREATHE *vb* untwist from a wreathed shape
UNWRINKLE *vb* remove wrinkles from
UNWRITE *vb* cancel (what has been written)
UNWRITES > UNWRITE
UNWRITING > UNWRITE
UNWRITTEN *adj* not printed or in writing
UNWROTE > UNWRITE
UNWROUGHT *adj* not worked
UNWRUNG *adj* not twisted
UNYEANED *adj* not having given birth
UNYIELDED *adj* not yielded
UNYOKE *vb* release (an animal, etc) from a yoke
UNYOKED > UNYOKE
UNYOKES > UNYOKE
UNYOKING > UNYOKE
UNYOUNG *adj* not young
UNZEALOUS *adj* unenthusiastic
UNZIP *vb* unfasten the zip of (a garment)
UNZIPPED > UNZIP
UNZIPPING > UNZIP
UNZIPS > UNZIP
UNZONED *adj* not divided into zones
UP *adv* indicating movement to or position at a higher place ▷ *adj* of a high or higher position ▷ *vb* increase or raise
UPADAISY *same as* > UPSADAISY
UPAITHRIC *adj* without a roof
UPALONG *n* location away from a place
UPALONGS > UPALONG
UPAS *n* large Javan tree with whitish bark and poisonous milky sap
UPASES > UPAS
UPBEAR *vb* sustain
UPBEARER > UPBEAR
UPBEARERS > UPBEAR
UPBEARING > UPBEAR
UPBEARS > UPBEAR

UPBEAT *adj* cheerful and optimistic ▷ *n* unaccented beat
UPBEATS > UPBEAT
UPBIND *vb* bind up
UPBINDING > UPBIND
UPBINDS > UPBIND
UPBLEW > UPBLOW
UPBLOW *vb* inflate
UPBLOWING > UPBLOW
UPBLOWN > UPBLOW
UPBLOWS > UPBLOW
UPBOIL *vb* boil up
UPBOILED > UPBOIL
UPBOILING > UPBOIL
UPBOILS > UPBOIL
UPBORE > UPBEAR
UPBORNE *adj* held up
UPBOUND *adj* travelling upwards
UPBOUNDEN *same as* > UPBOUND
UPBOW *n* stroke of the bow from its tip to its nut on a stringed instrument
UPBOWS > UPBOW
UPBRAID *vb* scold or reproach
UPBRAIDED > UPBRAID
UPBRAIDER > UPBRAID
UPBRAIDS > UPBRAID
UPBRAST *same as* > UPBURST
UPBRAY *vb* shame
UPBRAYED > UPBRAY
UPBRAYING > UPBRAY
UPBRAYS > UPBRAY
UPBREAK *vb* escape upwards
UPBREAKS > UPBREAK
UPBRING *vb* rear
UPBRINGS > UPBRING
UPBROKE > UPBREAK
UPBROKEN > UPBREAK
UPBROUGHT > UPBRING
UPBUILD *vb* build up
UPBUILDER > UPBUILD
UPBUILDS > UPBUILD
UPBUILT > UPBUILD
UPBURNING *adj* burning upwards
UPBURST *vb* burst upwards
UPBURSTS > UPBURST
UPBY *same as* > UPBYE
UPBYE *adv* yonder
UPCAST *n* material cast or thrown up ▷ *adj* directed or thrown upwards ▷ *vb* throw or cast up
UPCASTING > UPCAST
UPCASTS > UPCAST
UPCATCH *vb* catch up
UPCATCHES > UPCATCH
UPCAUGHT > UPCATCH
UPCHEER *vb* cheer up
UPCHEERED > UPCHEER
UPCHEERS > UPCHEER
UPCHUCK *vb* vomit
UPCHUCKED > UPCHUCK
UPCHUCKS > UPCHUCK
UPCLIMB *vb* ascend
UPCLIMBED > UPCLIMB
UPCLIMBS > UPCLIMB
UPCLOSE *vb* close up
UPCLOSED > UPCLOSE
UPCLOSES > UPCLOSE

UPCLOSING > UPCLOSE
UPCOAST *adv* up the coast
UPCOIL *vb* make into a coil
UPCOILED > UPCOIL
UPCOILING > UPCOIL
UPCOILS > UPCOIL
UPCOME *vb* come up
UPCOMES > UPCOME
UPCOMING *adj* coming soon
UPCOUNTRY *adj* of or from the interior of a country ▷ *adv* towards or in the interior of a country ▷ *n* interior part of a region or country
UPCOURT *adv* (in basketball) away from one's own basket
UPCURL *vb* curl up
UPCURLED > UPCURL
UPCURLING > UPCURL
UPCURLS > UPCURL
UPCURVE *vb* curve upwards
UPCURVED > UPCURVE
UPCURVES > UPCURVE
UPCURVING > UPCURVE
UPCYCLE *vb* recycle a disposable product into an object of greater value
UPCYCLED > UPCYCLE
UPCYCLES > UPCYCLE
UPCYCLING > UPCYCLE
UPDART *vb* dart upwards
UPDARTED > UPDART
UPDARTING > UPDART
UPDARTS > UPDART
UPDATABLE *adj* capable of being updated
UPDATE *vb* bring up to date ▷ *n* act of updating or something that is updated
UPDATED > UPDATE
UPDATER > UPDATE
UPDATERS > UPDATE
UPDATES > UPDATE
UPDATING > UPDATE
UPDIVE *vb* leap upwards
UPDIVED > UPDIVE
UPDIVES > UPDIVE
UPDIVING > UPDIVE
UPDO *n* type of hairstyle
UPDOMING *n* expansion of a rock upwards into a dome shape
UPDOMINGS > UPDOMING
UPDOS > UPDO
UPDOVE > UPDIVE
UPDRAFT *n* upward air current
UPDRAFTS > UPDRAFT
UPDRAG *vb* drag up
UPDRAGGED > UPDRAG
UPDRAGS > UPDRAG
UPDRAUGHT *n* upward movement of air or other gas
UPDRAW *vb* draw up
UPDRAWING > UPDRAW
UPDRAWN > UPDRAW
UPDRAWS > UPDRAW
UPDREW > UPDRAW

UPDRIED > UPDRY
UPDRIES > UPDRY
UPDRY *vb* dry up
UPDRYING > UPDRY
UPEND *vb* turn or set (something) on its end
UPENDED > UPEND
UPENDING > UPEND
UPENDS > UPEND
UPFIELD *adj* in sport, away from the defending team's goal
UPFILL *vb* fill up
UPFILLED > UPFILL
UPFILLING > UPFILL
UPFILLS > UPFILL
UPFLING *vb* throw upwards
UPFLINGS > UPFLING
UPFLOW *vb* flow upwards
UPFLOWED > UPFLOW
UPFLOWING > UPFLOW
UPFLOWS > UPFLOW
UPFLUNG > UPFLING
UPFOLD *vb* fold up
UPFOLDED > UPFOLD
UPFOLDING > UPFOLD
UPFOLDS > UPFOLD
UPFOLLOW *vb* follow
UPFOLLOWS > UPFOLLOW
UPFRONT *adj* open and frank ▷ *adv* (of money) paid out at the beginning of a business arrangement
UPFURL *vb* roll up
UPFURLED > UPFURL
UPFURLING > UPFURL
UPFURLS > UPFURL
UPGANG *n* climb
UPGANGS > UPGANG
UPGATHER *vb* draw together
UPGATHERS > UPGATHER
UPGAZE *vb* gaze upwards
UPGAZED > UPGAZE
UPGAZES > UPGAZE
UPGAZING > UPGAZE
UPGIRD *vb* support or hold up
UPGIRDED > UPGIRD
UPGIRDING > UPGIRD
UPGIRDS > UPGIRD
UPGIRT *same as* > UPGIRD
UPGIRTED > UPGIRT
UPGIRTING > UPGIRT
UPGIRTS > UPGIRT
UPGO *vb* ascend
UPGOES > UPGO
UPGOING > UPGO
UPGOINGS > UPGO
UPGONE > UPGO
UPGRADE *vb* promote (a person or job) to a higher rank
UPGRADED > UPGRADE
UPGRADER > UPGRADE
UPGRADERS > UPGRADE
UPGRADES > UPGRADE
UPGRADING > UPGRADE
UPGREW > UPGROW
UPGROW *vb* grow up
UPGROWING > UPGROW
UPGROWN > UPGROW
UPGROWS > UPGROW

UPGROWTH *n* process of developing or growing upwards
UPGROWTHS > UPGROWTH
UPGUSH *vb* flow upwards
UPGUSHED > UPGUSH
UPGUSHES > UPGUSH
UPGUSHING > UPGUSH
UPHAND *adj* lifted by hand
UPHANG *vb* hang up
UPHANGING > UPHANG
UPHANGS > UPHANG
UPHAUD *Scots variant of* > UPHOLD
UPHAUDING > UPHAUD
UPHAUDS > UPHAUD
UPHEAP *vb* heap or pile up
UPHEAPED > UPHEAP
UPHEAPING > UPHEAP
UPHEAPS > UPHEAP
UPHEAVAL *n* strong, sudden, or violent disturbance
UPHEAVALS > UPHEAVAL
UPHEAVE *vb* heave or rise upwards
UPHEAVED > UPHEAVE
UPHEAVER > UPHEAVE
UPHEAVERS > UPHEAVE
UPHEAVES > UPHEAVE
UPHEAVING > UPHEAVE
UPHELD > UPHOLD
UPHILD *archaic past form of* > UPHOLD
UPHILL *adj* sloping or leading upwards ▷ *adv* up a slope ▷ *n* difficulty
UPHILLS > UPHILL
UPHOARD *vb* hoard up
UPHOARDED > UPHOARD
UPHOARDS > UPHOARD
UPHOIST *vb* raise
UPHOISTED > UPHOIST
UPHOISTS > UPHOIST
UPHOLD *vb* maintain or defend against opposition
UPHOLDER > UPHOLD
UPHOLDERS > UPHOLD
UPHOLDING > UPHOLD
UPHOLDS > UPHOLD
UPHOLSTER *vb* fit (a chair or sofa) with padding, springs, and covering
UPHOORD *vb* heap up
UPHOORDED > UPHOORD
UPHOORDS > UPHOORD
UPHOVE > UPHEAVE
UPHROE *variant spelling of* > EUPHROE
UPHROES > UPHROE
UPHUDDEN > UPHAUD
UPHUNG > UPHANG
UPHURL *vb* throw upwards
UPHURLED > UPHURL
UPHURLING > UPHURL
UPHURLS > UPHURL
UPJET *vb* stream upwards
UPJETS > UPJET
UPJETTED > UPJET
UPJETTING > UPJET
UPKEEP *n* act, process, or cost of keeping something in good repair
UPKEEPS > UPKEEP

UPKNIT vb bind
UPKNITS > UPKNIT
UPKNITTED > UPKNIT
UPLAID > UPLAY
UPLAND adj of or in an area of high or relatively high ground ▷ n area of high or relatively high ground
UPLANDER n person hailing from the uplands
UPLANDERS > UPLANDER
UPLANDISH > UPLAND
UPLANDS > UPLAND
UPLAY vb stash
UPLAYING > UPLAY
UPLAYS > UPLAY
UPLEAD vb lead upwards
UPLEADING > UPLEAD
UPLEADS > UPLEAD
UPLEAN vb lean on something
UPLEANED > UPLEAN
UPLEANING > UPLEAN
UPLEANS > UPLEAN
UPLEANT > UPLEAN
UPLEAP vb jump upwards
UPLEAPED > UPLEAP
UPLEAPING > UPLEAP
UPLEAPS > UPLEAP
UPLEAPT > UPLEAP
UPLED > UPLEAD
UPLIFT vb raise or lift up ▷ n act or process of improving moral, social, or cultural conditions
UPLIFTED > UPLIFT
UPLIFTER > UPLIFT
UPLIFTERS > UPLIFT
UPLIFTING adj acting to raise moral, spiritual, cultural, etc levels
UPLIFTS > UPLIFT
UPLIGHT n lamp or wall light designed or positioned to cast its light upwards ▷ vb light in an upward direction
UPLIGHTED > UPLIGHT
UPLIGHTER n lamp or wall light designed or positioned to cast its light upwards
UPLIGHTS > UPLIGHT
UPLINK n transmitter that sends signals up to a communications satellite ▷ vb send (data) to a communications satellite
UPLINKED > UPLINK
UPLINKING > UPLINK
UPLINKS > UPLINK
UPLIT > UPLIGHT
UPLOAD vb transfer (data or a program) into the memory of another computer
UPLOADED > UPLOAD
UPLOADING > UPLOAD
UPLOADS > UPLOAD
UPLOCK vb lock up
UPLOCKED > UPLOCK
UPLOCKING > UPLOCK
UPLOCKS > UPLOCK
UPLOOK vb look up
UPLOOKED > UPLOOK
UPLOOKING > UPLOOK

UPLOOKS > UPLOOK
UPLYING adj raised
UPMADE > UPMAKE
UPMAKE vb make up
UPMAKER > UPMAKE
UPMAKERS > UPMAKE
UPMAKES > UPMAKE
UPMAKING > UPMAKE
UPMAKINGS > UPMAKE
UPMANSHIP n one-upmanship
UPMARKET adj expensive and of superior quality ▷ vb make something upmarket
UPMARKETS > UPMARKET
UPMOST another word for > UPPERMOST
UPO prep upon
UPON prep on
UPPED > UP
UPPER adj higher or highest in physical position, wealth, rank, or status ▷ n part of a shoe above the sole
UPPERCASE adj capitalized ▷ vb capitalize or print in capitals
UPPERCUT n short swinging upward punch delivered to the chin ▷ vb hit (an opponent) with an uppercut
UPPERCUTS > UPPERCUT
UPPERMOST adj highest in position, power, or importance ▷ adv in or into the highest place or position
UPPERPART n highest part
UPPERS > UPPER
UPPILE vb pile up
UPPILED > UPPILE
UPPILES > UPPILE
UPPILING > UPPILE
UPPING > UP
UPPINGS > UP
UPPISH adj snobbish, arrogant, or presumptuous
UPPISHLY > UPPISH
UPPITIER > UPPITY
UPPITIEST > UPPITY
UPPITY adj snobbish, arrogant, or presumptuous
UPPROP vb support
UPPROPPED > UPPROP
UPPROPS > UPPROP
UPRAISE vb lift up
UPRAISED > UPRAISE
UPRAISER > UPRAISE
UPRAISERS > UPRAISE
UPRAISES > UPRAISE
UPRAISING > UPRAISE
UPRAN > UPRUN
UPRATE vb raise the value, rate, or size of, upgrade
UPRATED > UPRATE
UPRATES > UPRATE
UPRATING > UPRATE
UPREACH vb reach up
UPREACHED > UPREACH

UPREACHES > UPREACH
UPREAR vb lift up
UPREARED > UPREAR
UPREARING > UPREAR
UPREARS > UPREAR
UPREST n uprising
UPRESTS > UPREST
UPRIGHT adj vertical or erect ▷ adv vertically or in an erect position ▷ n vertical support, such as a post ▷ vb make upright
UPRIGHTED > UPRIGHT
UPRIGHTLY > UPRIGHT
UPRIGHTS > UPRIGHT
UPRISAL > UPRISE
UPRISALS > UPRISE
UPRISE vb rise up
UPRISEN > UPRISE
UPRISER > UPRISE
UPRISERS > UPRISE
UPRISES > UPRISE
UPRISING n rebellion or revolt
UPRISINGS > UPRISING
UPRIST same as > UPREST
UPRISTS > UPRIST
UPRIVER adv towards or near the source of a river ▷ n area located upstream
UPRIVERS > UPRIVER
UPROAR n disturbance characterized by loud noise and confusion ▷ vb cause an uproar
UPROARED > UPROAR
UPROARING > UPROAR
UPROARS > UPROAR
UPROLL vb roll up
UPROLLED > UPROLL
UPROLLING > UPROLL
UPROLLS > UPROLL
UPROOT vb pull up by or as if by the roots
UPROOTAL > UPROOT
UPROOTALS > UPROOT
UPROOTED > UPROOT
UPROOTER > UPROOT
UPROOTERS > UPROOT
UPROOTING > UPROOT
UPROOTS > UPROOT
UPROSE > UPRISE
UPROUSE vb rouse or stir up
UPROUSED > UPROUSE
UPROUSES > UPROUSE
UPROUSING > UPROUSE
UPRUN vb run up
UPRUNNING > UPRUN
UPRUNS > UPRUN
UPRUSH n upward rush, as of consciousness ▷ vb rush upwards
UPRUSHED > UPRUSH
UPRUSHES > UPRUSH
UPRUSHING > UPRUSH
UPRYST same as > UPREST
UPS > UP
UPSADAISY interj expression of reassurance often uttered when someone stumbles or is lifted up

UPSCALE adj of or for the upper end of an economic or social scale ▷ vb upgrade
UPSCALED > UPSCALE
UPSCALES > UPSCALE
UPSCALING > UPSCALE
UPSEE n drunken revel
UPSEES > UPSEE
UPSELL vb persuade a customer to buy a more expensive or additional item
UPSELLING > UPSELL
UPSELLS > UPSELL
UPSEND vb send up
UPSENDING > UPSEND
UPSENDS > UPSEND
UPSENT > UPSEND
UPSET adj emotionally or physically disturbed or distressed ▷ vb tip over ▷ n unexpected defeat or reversal
UPSETS > UPSET
UPSETTER > UPSET
UPSETTERS > UPSET
UPSETTING > UPSET
UPSEY same as > UPSEE
UPSEYS > UPSEY
UPSHIFT vb move up (a gear)
UPSHIFTED > UPSHIFT
UPSHIFTS > UPSHIFT
UPSHOOT vb shoot upwards
UPSHOOTS > UPSHOOT
UPSHOT n final result or conclusion
UPSHOTS > UPSHOT
UPSIDE n upper surface or part
UPSIDES > UPSIDE
UPSIES > UPSY
UPSILON n 20th letter in the Greek alphabet
UPSILONS > UPSILON
UPSITTING n sitting up of a woman after childbirth
UPSIZE vb increase in size
UPSIZED > UPSIZE
UPSIZES > UPSIZE
UPSIZING > UPSIZE
UPSKILL vb improve the aptitude for work of (a person)
UPSKILLED > UPSKILL
UPSKILLS > UPSKILL
UPSKIRT n photo of a woman's exposed underwear taken without her consent
UPSKIRTS > UPSKIRT
UPSLOPE adv up a slope ▷ n upward slope
UPSLOPES > UPSLOPE
UPSOAR vb soar up
UPSOARED > UPSOAR
UPSOARING > UPSOAR
UPSOARS > UPSOAR
UPSOLD > UPSELL
UPSPAKE > UPSPEAK
UPSPEAK vb speak with rising intonation
UPSPEAKS > UPSPEAK

u

UPSPEAR vb grow upwards in a spear-like manner
UPSPEARED > UPSPEAR
UPSPEARS > UPSPEAR
UPSPOKE > UPSPEAK
UPSPOKEN > UPSPEAK
UPSPRANG > UPSPRING
UPSPRING vb spring up or come into existence ▷ n leap forwards or upwards
UPSPRINGS > UPSPRING
UPSPRUNG > UPSPRING
UPSTAGE adj at the back half of the stage ▷ vb draw attention to oneself from (someone else) ▷ adv on, at, or to the rear of the stage ▷ n back half of the stage
UPSTAGED > UPSTAGE
UPSTAGER > UPSTAGE
UPSTAGERS > UPSTAGE
UPSTAGES > UPSTAGE
UPSTAGING > UPSTAGE
UPSTAIR same as > UPSTAIRS
UPSTAIRS adv to or on an upper floor of a building ▷ n upper floor ▷ adj situated on an upper floor
UPSTAND vb rise
UPSTANDS > UPSTAND
UPSTARE vb stare upwards
UPSTARED > UPSTARE
UPSTARES > UPSTARE
UPSTARING > UPSTARE
UPSTART n person who has risen suddenly to a position of power and behaves arrogantly ▷ vb start up, as in surprise, etc
UPSTARTED > UPSTART
UPSTARTS > UPSTART
UPSTATE adv towards, in, from, or relating to the outlying or northern sections of a state ▷ n outlying, esp northern, sections of a state
UPSTATER > UPSTATE
UPSTATERS > UPSTATE
UPSTATES > UPSTATE
UPSTAY vb support
UPSTAYED > UPSTAY
UPSTAYING > UPSTAY
UPSTAYS > UPSTAY
UPSTEP n type of vocal intonation
UPSTEPPED > UPSTEP
UPSTEPS > UPSTEP
UPSTIR vb stir up ▷ n commotion
UPSTIRRED > UPSTIR
UPSTIRS > UPSTIR
UPSTOOD > UPSTAND
UPSTREAM adj in or towards the higher part of a stream ▷ vb stream upwards
UPSTREAMS > UPSTREAM
UPSTROKE n upward stroke or movement, as of a pen or brush

UPSTROKES > UPSTROKE
UPSURGE n rapid rise or swell ▷ vb surge up
UPSURGED > UPSURGE
UPSURGES > UPSURGE
UPSURGING > UPSURGE
UPSWARM vb rise or send upwards in a swarm
UPSWARMED > UPSWARM
UPSWARMS > UPSWARM
UPSWAY vb swing in the air
UPSWAYED > UPSWAY
UPSWAYING > UPSWAY
UPSWAYS > UPSWAY
UPSWEEP n curve or sweep upwards ▷ vb sweep, curve, or brush or be swept, curved, or brushed upwards
UPSWEEPS > UPSWEEP
UPSWELL vb swell up or cause to swell up
UPSWELLED > UPSWELL
UPSWELLS > UPSWELL
UPSWEPT > UPSWEEP
UPSWING n recovery period in a trade cycle ▷ vb swing or move up
UPSWINGS > UPSWING
UPSWOLLEN > UPSWELL
UPSWUNG > UPSWING
UPSY same as > UPSEE
UPTA same as > UPTER
UPTAK same as > UPTAKE
UPTAKE n numbers taking up something such as an offer or the act of taking it up ▷ vb take up
UPTAKEN > UPTAKE
UPTAKES > UPTAKE
UPTAKING > UPTAKE
UPTAKS > UPTAK
UPTALK n style of speech in which every sentence ends with a rising tone ▷ vb talk in this manner
UPTALKED > UPTALK
UPTALKING > UPTALK
UPTALKS > UPTALK
UPTEAR vb tear up
UPTEARING > UPTEAR
UPTEARS > UPTEAR
UPTEMPO adj fast ▷ n uptempo piece
UPTEMPOS > UPTEMPO
UPTER adj of poor quality
UPTHREW > UPTHROW
UPTHROW n upward movement of rocks on one side of a fault plane relative to rocks on the other side ▷ vb throw upwards
UPTHROWN > UPTHROW
UPTHROWS > UPTHROW
UPTHRUST n upward push
UPTHRUSTS > UPTHRUST
UPTHUNDER vb make a noise like thunder
UPTICK n rise or increase
UPTICKS > UPTICK
UPTIE vb tie up
UPTIED > UPTIE
UPTIES > UPTIE

UPTIGHT adj nervously tense, irritable, or angry
UPTIGHTER > UPTIGHT
UPTILT vb tilt up
UPTILTED > UPTILT
UPTILTING > UPTILT
UPTILTS > UPTILT
UPTIME n time during which a machine, such as a computer, actually operates
UPTIMES > UPTIME
UPTITLING n practice of conferring grandiose job titles to employees performing relatively menial jobs
UPTOOK > UPTAKE
UPTORE > UPTEAR
UPTORN > UPTEAR
UPTOSS vb throw upwards
UPTOSSED > UPTOSS
UPTOSSES > UPTOSS
UPTOSSING > UPTOSS
UPTOWN adv towards or in a part of a town that is away from the centre ▷ n such a part of town, esp a residential part
UPTOWNER > UPTOWN
UPTOWNERS > UPTOWN
UPTOWNS > UPTOWN
UPTRAIN vb train up
UPTRAINED > UPTRAIN
UPTRAINS > UPTRAIN
UPTREND n upward trend
UPTRENDS > UPTREND
UPTRILLED adj trilled high
UPTURN n upward trend or improvement ▷ vb turn or cause to turn over or upside down
UPTURNED > UPTURN
UPTURNING > UPTURN
UPTURNS > UPTURN
UPTYING > UPTIE
UPVALUE vb raise the value of
UPVALUED > UPVALUE
UPVALUES > UPVALUE
UPVALUING > UPVALUE
UPVOTE vb publicly approve of a social media post
UPVOTED > UPVOTE
UPVOTES > UPVOTE
UPVOTING > UPVOTE
UPWAFT vb waft upwards
UPWAFTED > UPWAFT
UPWAFTING > UPWAFT
UPWAFTS > UPWAFT
UPWARD same as > UPWARDS
UPWARDLY > UPWARD
UPWARDS adv from a lower to a higher place, level, condition, etc
UPWELL vb well up
UPWELLED > UPWELL
UPWELLING > UPWELL
UPWELLS > UPWELL
UPWENT > UPGO
UPWHIRL vb spin upwards
UPWHIRLED > UPWHIRL
UPWHIRLS > UPWHIRL

UPWIND adv into or against the wind ▷ adj going against the wind ▷ vb wind up
UPWINDING > UPWIND
UPWINDS > UPWIND
UPWOUND > UPWIND
UPWRAP vb wrap up
UPWRAPS > UPWRAP
UPWROUGHT adj wrought up
UR interj hesitant utterance used to fill gaps in talking
URACHI > URACHUS
URACHUS n cord of tissue connected to the bladder
URACHUSES > URACHUS
URACIL n pyrimidine present in all living cells
URACILS > URACIL
URAEI > URAEUS
URAEMIA n accumulation of waste products in the blood
URAEMIAS > URAEMIA
URAEMIC > URAEMIA
URAEUS n sacred serpent of ancient Egypt
URAEUSES > URAEUS
URALI n type of plant
URALIS > URALI
URALITE n mineral that replaces pyroxene in some rocks
URALITES > URALITE
URALITIC > URALITE
URALITISE same as > URALITIZE
URALITIZE vb turn into uralite
URANIA n uranium dioxide
URANIAN adj heavenly
URANIAS > URANIA
URANIC adj of or containing uranium, esp in a high valence state
URANIDE n any element having an atomic number greater than that of protactinium
URANIDES > URANIDE
URANIN n type of alkaline substance
URANINITE n blackish heavy radioactive mineral consisting of uranium oxide in cubic crystalline form together with radium, lead, helium, etc: occurs in coarse granite
URANINS > URANIN
URANISCI > URANISCUS
URANISCUS n palate
URANISM n old word for homosexuality
URANISMS > URANISM
URANITE n any of various minerals containing uranium, esp torbernite or autunite
URANITES > URANITE
URANITIC > URANITE
URANIUM n radioactive silvery-white metallic element

URANIUMS > URANIUM

URANOLOGY *n* study of the universe and planets

URANOUS *adj* of or containing uranium, esp in a low valence state

URANYL *n* type of divalent ion

URANYLIC > URANYL

URANYLS > URANYL

URAO *n* type of mineral

URAOS > URAO

URARE *same as* > URALI

URARES > URARE

URARI *same as* > URALI

URARIS > URARI

URASE *same as* > UREASE

URASES > URASE

URATE *n* any salt or ester of uric acid

URATES > URATE

URATIC > URATE

URB *n* urban area

URBAN *adj* of or living in a city or town

URBANE *adj* characterized by courtesy, elegance, and sophistication

URBANELY > URBANE

URBANER > URBANE

URBANEST > URBANE

URBANISE *same as* > URBANIZE

URBANISED > URBANISE

URBANISES > URBANISE

URBANISM *n* character of city life

URBANISMS > URBANISM

URBANIST *n* person who studies towns and cities

URBANISTS > URBANIST

URBANITE *n* resident of an urban community

URBANITES > URBANITE

URBANITY *n* quality of being urbane

URBANIZE *vb* make (a rural area) more industrialized and urban

URBANIZED > URBANIZE

URBANIZES > URBANIZE

URBEX *n* short for urban exploration, the hobby of exploring derelict urban structures

URBEXES > URBEX

URBIA *n* urban area

URBIAS > URBIA

URBS > URB

URCEOLATE *adj* shaped like an urn or pitcher

URCEOLI > URCEOLUS

URCEOLUS *n* organ of a plant

URCHIN *n* mischievous child

URCHINS > URCHIN

URD *n* type of plant with edible seeds

URDE *adj* (in heraldry) having points

URDEE *same as* > URDE

URDS > URD

URDY *n* heraldic line pattern

URE *same as* > AUROCHS

UREA *n* white soluble crystalline compound found in urine

UREAL > UREA

UREAS > UREA

UREASE *n* enzyme that converts urea to ammonium carbonate

UREASES > UREASE

UREDIA > UREDIUM

UREDIAL > UREDIUM

UREDINE > UREDO

UREDINES > UREDO

UREDINIA > UREDINIUM

UREDINIAL > UREDINIUM

UREDINIUM *same as* > UREDIUM

UREDINOUS > UREDO

UREDIUM *n* spore-producing body of some rust fungi in which uredospores are formed

UREDO *less common name for* > URTICARIA

UREDOS > UREDO

UREDOSORI *pl n* spore-producing bodies of some rust fungi in which uredospores are formed; uredia

UREIC > UREA

UREIDE *n* any of a class of organic compounds derived from urea

UREIDES > UREIDE

UREMIA *same as* > URAEMIA

UREMIAS > UREMIA

UREMIC > UREMIA

URENA *n* plant genus

URENAS > URENA

URENT *adj* burning

UREOTELIC *adj* excreting urea

URES > URE

URESES > URESIS

URESIS *n* urination

URETER *n* tube that conveys urine from the kidney to the bladder

URETERAL > URETER

URETERIC > URETER

URETERS > URETER

URETHAN *same as* > URETHANE

URETHANE *n* short for the synthetic material polyurethane ▷ *vb* treat with urethane

URETHANED > URETHANE

URETHANES > URETHANE

URETHANS > URETHAN

URETHRA *n* canal that carries urine from the bladder out of the body

URETHRAE > URETHRA

URETHRAL > URETHRA

URETHRAS > URETHRA

URETIC *adj* of or relating to urine

URGE *n* strong impulse, inner drive, or yearning ▷ *vb* plead with or press (a person to do something)

URGED > URGE

URGENCE > URGENT

URGENCES > URGENT

URGENCIES > URGENT

URGENCY > URGENT

URGENT *adj* requiring speedy action or attention

URGENTLY > URGENT

URGER > URGE

URGERS > URGE

URGES > URGE

URGING > URGE

URGINGLY > URGE

URGINGS > URGE

URIAL *n* type of sheep

URIALS > URIAL

URIC *adj* of or derived from urine

URICASE *n* type of enzyme

URICASES > URICASE

URIDINE *n* nucleoside present in all living cells in a combined form, esp in RNA

URIDINES > URIDINE

URIDYLIC *adj* as in *uridylic acid* nucleotide consisting of uracil, ribose, and a phosphate group

URINAL *n* sanitary fitting used by men for urination

URINALS > URINAL

URINANT *adj* having the head downwards

URINARIES > URINARY

URINARY *adj* of urine or the organs that secrete and pass urine ▷ *n* reservoir for urine

URINATE *vb* discharge urine

URINATED > URINATE

URINATES > URINATE

URINATING > URINATE

URINATION > URINATE

URINATIVE > URINATE

URINATOR > URINATE

URINATORS > URINATE

URINE *n* pale yellow fluid passed as waste from the body ▷ *vb* urinate

URINED > URINE

URINEMIA *same as* > UREMIA

URINEMIAS > URINEMIA

URINEMIC > URINEMIA

URINES > URINE

URINING > URINE

URINOLOGY *same as* > UROLOGY

URINOSE *same as* > URINOUS

URINOUS *adj* of, resembling, or containing urine

URITE *n* part of the abdomen

URITES > URITE

URMAN *n* forest

URMANS > URMAN

URN *n* vase used as a container for the ashes of the dead ▷ *vb* put in an urn

URNAL > URN

URNED > URN

URNFIELD *n* cemetery full of individual cremation urns ▷ *adj* characterized by cremation in urns

URNFIELDS > URNFIELD

URNFUL *n* capacity of an urn

URNFULS > URNFUL

URNING *n* old word for a homosexual man

URNINGS > URNING

URNLIKE > URN

URNS > URN

UROBILIN *n* brownish pigment found in faeces and sometimes in urine

UROBILINS > UROBILIN

UROBORIC *adj* of or like a uroboros

UROBOROS *same as* > OUROBOROS

UROCHORD *n* notochord of a larval tunicate, typically confined to the tail region

UROCHORDS > UROCHORD

UROCHROME *n* yellowish pigment that colours urine

URODELAN > URODELE

URODELANS > URODELAN

URODELE *n* amphibian of the order which includes the salamanders and newts

URODELES > URODELE

URODELOUS > URODELE

UROGENOUS *adj* producing or derived from urine

UROGRAM *n* X-ray of the urinary tract

UROGRAMS > UROGRAM

UROGRAPHY *n* branch of radiology concerned with X-ray examination of the kidney and associated structures

UROKINASE *n* biochemical catalyst

UROLAGNIA *n* sexual arousal involving urination

UROLITH *n* calculus in the urinary tract

UROLITHIC > UROLITH

UROLITHS > UROLITH

UROLOGIC > UROLOGY

UROLOGIES > UROLOGY

UROLOGIST > UROLOGY

UROLOGY *n* branch of medicine concerned with the urinary system and its diseases

UROMERE *n* part of the abdomen

UROMERES > UROMERE

UROPOD *n* paired appendage that forms part of the tailfan in lobsters

UROPODAL > UROPOD

UROPODOUS > UROPOD

u

UROPODS > UROPOD
UROPYGIA
> UROPYGIUM
UROPYGIAL
> UROPYGIUM
UROPYGIUM n hindmost part of a bird's body, from which the tail feathers grow
UROSCOPIC
> UROSCOPY
UROSCOPY n examination of urine
UROSES > UROSIS
UROSIS n urinary disease
UROSOME n abdomen of arthropods
UROSOMES > UROSOME
UROSTEGE n part of a serpent's tail
UROSTEGES
> UROSTEGE
UROSTOMY n type of urinary surgery
UROSTYLE n bony rod forming the last segment of the vertebral column of frogs and toads
UROSTYLES
> UROSTYLE
URP dialect word for
> VOMIT
URPED > URP
URPING > URP
URPS > URP
URSA n she-bear
URSAE > URSA
URSID n meteor
URSIDS > URSID
URSIFORM adj bear-shaped or bearlike in form
URSINE adj of or like a bear
URSON n type of porcupine
URSONS > URSON
URTEXT n earliest form of a text
URTEXTE same as
> URTEXTS
URTEXTS > URTEXT
URTICA n type of nettle
URTICANT n something that causes itchiness and irritation
URTICANTS
> URTICANT
URTICARIA n skin condition characterized by the formation of itchy red or whitish raised patches, usually caused by an allergy
URTICAS > URTICA
URTICATE adj characterized by the presence of weals ▷ vb sting
URTICATED
> URTICATE
URTICATES
> URTICATE
URUBU n type of bird
URUBUS > URUBU
URUS another name for the
> AUROCHS
URUSES > URUS

URUSHIOL n poisonous pale yellow liquid occurring in poison ivy and the lacquer tree
URUSHIOLS
> URUSHIOL
URVA n Indian mongoose
URVAS > URVA
US pron refers to the speaker or writer and another person or other people
USABILITY > USABLE
USABLE adj able to be used
USABLY > USABLE
USAGE n regular or constant use
USAGER n person who has the use of something in trust
USAGERS > USAGER
USAGES > USAGE
USANCE n period of time permitted for the redemption of foreign bills of exchange
USANCES > USANCE
USAUNCE same as
> USANCE
USAUNCES > USAUNCE
USE vb put into service or action ▷ n using or being used
USEABLE same as
> USABLE
USEABLY > USABLE
USED adj second-hand
USEFUL adj able to be used advantageously or for several different purposes ▷ n odd-jobman or general factotum
USEFULLY > USEFUL
USEFULS > USEFUL
USELESS adj having no practical use
USELESSLY > USELESS
USER n continued exercise, use, or enjoyment of a right, esp in property
USERNAME n name given by computer user to gain access
USERNAMES
> USERNAME
USERS > USER
USES > USE
USHER n official who shows people to their seats, as in a church ▷ vb conduct or escort
USHERED > USHER
USHERESS n female usher
USHERETTE n female assistant in a cinema who shows people to their seats
USHERING > USHER
USHERINGS > USHER
USHERS > USHER
USHERSHIP > USHER
USING > USE
USNEA n type of lichen
USNEAS > USNEA
USQUABAE n whisky

USQUABAES
> USQUABAE
USQUE n whisky
USQUEBAE same as
> USQUABAE
USQUEBAES
> USQUEBAE
USQUES > USQUE
USTION n burning
USTIONS > USTION
USTULATE adj charred ▷ vb give a charred appearance to
USTULATED
> USTULATE
USTULATES
> USTULATE
USUAL adj of the most normal, frequent, or regular type ▷ n ordinary or commonplace events
USUALLY adv most often, in most cases
USUALNESS > USUAL
USUALS > USUAL
USUCAPION n method of acquiring property
USUCAPT > USUCAPION
USUCAPTED
> USUCAPION
USUCAPTS
> USUCAPION
USUFRUCT n right to use and derive profit from a piece of property belonging to another
USUFRUCTS
> USUFRUCT
USURE vb be involved in usury
USURED > USURE
USURER n person who lends funds at an exorbitant rate of interest
USURERS > USURER
USURES > USURE
USURESS n female usurer
USURESSES > USURESS
USURIES > USURY
USURING > USURE
USURIOUS > USURY
USUROUS > USURY
USURP vb seize (a position or power) without authority
USURPED > USURP
USURPEDLY > USURP
USURPER > USURP
USURPERS > USURP
USURPING > USURP
USURPINGS > USURP
USURPS > USURP
USURY n practice of lending money at an extremely high rate of interest
USWARD adv towards us
USWARDS same as
> USWARD
UT n syllable used in the fixed system of solmization for the note C
UTA n side-blotched lizard
UTAS n eighth day of a festival
UTASES > UTAS
UTE n small truck with low sides

UTENSIL n tool or container for practical use
UTENSILS > UTENSIL
UTERI > UTERUS
UTERINE adj of or affecting the womb
UTERITIS n inflammation of the womb
UTEROTOMY n surgery on the uterus
UTERUS n womb
UTERUSES > UTERUS
UTES > UTE
UTILE n W African tree
UTILES > UTILE
UTILIDOR n above-ground insulated casing for pipes in permafrost regions
UTILIDORS
> UTILIDOR
UTILISE same as
> UTILIZE
UTILISED > UTILISE
UTILISER > UTILISE
UTILISERS > UTILISE
UTILISES > UTILISE
UTILISING > UTILISE
UTILITIES > UTILITY
UTILITY n usefulness ▷ adj designed for use rather than beauty
UTILIZE vb make practical use of
UTILIZED > UTILIZE
UTILIZER > UTILIZE
UTILIZERS > UTILIZE
UTILIZES > UTILIZE
UTILIZING > UTILIZE
UTIS n uproar
UTISES > UTIS
UTMOST n the greatest possible degree or amount ▷ adj of the greatest possible degree or amount
UTMOSTS > UTMOST
UTOPIA n real or imaginary society, place, state, etc considered to be perfect or ideal
UTOPIAN adj of or relating to a perfect or ideal existence ▷ n idealistic social reformer
UTOPIANS > UTOPIAN
UTOPIAS > UTOPIA
UTOPIAST > UTOPIA
UTOPIASTS > UTOPIA
UTOPISM > UTOPIA
UTOPISMS > UTOPIA
UTOPIST > UTOPIA
UTOPISTIC > UTOPIA
UTOPISTS > UTOPIA
UTRICLE n larger of the two parts of the membranous labyrinth of the internal ear
UTRICLES > UTRICLE
UTRICULAR > UTRICLE
UTRICULI
> UTRICULUS
UTRICULUS same as
> UTRICLE
UTS > UT
UTTER vb express (something) in sounds or words ▷ adj total or absolute

UTTERABLE > UTTER
UTTERANCE *n* something uttered
UTTERED > UTTER
UTTERER > UTTER
UTTERERS > UTTER
UTTEREST > UTTER
UTTERING > UTTER
UTTERINGS > UTTER
UTTERLESS > UTTER
UTTERLY *adv* extremely
UTTERMOST *same as* > UTMOST
UTTERNESS > UTTER
UTTERS > UTTER

UTU *n* reward
UTUS > UTU
UVA *n* grape or fruit resembling this
UVAE > UVA
UVAROVITE *n* emerald-green garnet found in chromium deposits: consists of calcium chromium silicate
UVAS > UVA
UVEA *n* part of the eyeball consisting of the iris, ciliary body, and choroid
UVEAL > UVEA

UVEAS > UVEA
UVEITIC > UVEITIS
UVEITIS *n* inflammation of the uvea
UVEITISES > UVEITIS
UVEOUS > UVEA
UVULA *n* small fleshy part of the soft palate that hangs in the back of the throat
UVULAE > UVULA
UVULAR *adj* of or relating to the uvula ▷ *n* uvular consonant
UVULARLY > UVULAR

UVULARS > UVULAR
UVULAS > UVULA
UVULITIS *n* inflammation of the uvula
UXORIAL *adj* of or relating to a wife
UXORIALLY > UXORIAL
UXORICIDE *n* act of killing one's wife
UXORIOUS *adj* excessively fond of or dependent on one's wife

u

Vv

VAC *vb* clean with a vacuum cleaner
VACANCE *n* vacant period
VACANCES > VACANCE
VACANCIES > VACANCY
VACANCY *n* unfilled job
VACANT *adj* (of a toilet, room, etc) unoccupied
VACANTLY > VACANT
VACATABLE > VACATE
VACATE *vb* cause (something) to be empty by leaving
VACATED > VACATE
VACATES > VACATE
VACATING > VACATE
VACATION *n* time when universities and law courts are closed ▷ *vb* take a vacation
VACATIONS > VACATION
VACATUR *n* annulment
VACATURS > VACATUR
VACCINA *same as* > VACCINIA
VACCINAL *adj* of or relating to vaccine or vaccination
VACCINAS > VACCINA
VACCINATE *vb* inject with a vaccine
VACCINE *n* substance designed to make a person immune to a disease
VACCINEE *n* person who has been vaccinated
VACCINEES > VACCINEE
VACCINES > VACCINE
VACCINIA *technical name for* > COWPOX
VACCINIAL > VACCINIA
VACCINIAS > VACCINIA
VACCINIUM *n* shrub genus
VACHERIN *n* soft cheese made from cows' milk
VACHERINS > VACHERIN
VACILLANT *adj* indecisive
VACILLATE *vb* keep changing one's mind or opinions
VACKED > VAC
VACKING > VAC
VACS > VAC
VACUA > VACUUM
VACUATE *vb* empty
VACUATED > VACUATE

VACUATES > VACUATE
VACUATING > VACUATE
VACUATION > VACUATE
VACUIST *n* person believing in the existence of vacuums in nature
VACUISTS > VACUIST
VACUITIES > VACUITY
VACUITY *n* absence of intelligent thought or ideas
VACUOLAR > VACUOLE
VACUOLATE > VACUOLE
VACUOLE *n* fluid-filled cavity in the cytoplasm of a cell
VACUOLES > VACUOLE
VACUOUS *adj* not expressing intelligent thought
VACUOUSLY > VACUOUS
VACUUM *n* empty space from which all or most air or gas has been removed ▷ *vb* clean with a vacuum cleaner
VACUUMED > VACUUM
VACUUMING > VACUUM
VACUUMS > VACUUM
VADE *vb* fade
VADED > VADE
VADES > VADE
VADING > VADE
VADOSE *adj* of or derived from water occurring above the water table
VAE *same as* > VOE
VAES > VAE
VAG *n* informal Australian word for a vagrant ▷ *vb* arrest someone for vagrancy
VAGABOND *n* person with no fixed home, esp a beggar
VAGABONDS > VAGABOND
VAGAL *adj* of, relating to, or affecting the vagus nerve
VAGALLY > VAGAL
VAGARIES > VAGARY
VAGARIOUS *adj* characterized or caused by vagaries
VAGARISH > VAGARY
VAGARY *n* unpredictable change
VAGGED > VAG
VAGGING > VAG
VAGI > VAGUS
VAGILE *adj* able to move freely
VAGILITY > VAGILE

VAGINA *n* (in female mammals) passage from the womb to the external genitals
VAGINAE > VAGINA
VAGINAL > VAGINA
VAGINALLY > VAGINA
VAGINANT *adj* (of a leaf) sheathing its stem with its base
VAGINAS > VAGINA
VAGINATE *adj* (esp of plant parts) having a sheath
VAGINATED > VAGINATE
VAGINITIS *n* inflammation of the vagina
VAGINOSES > VAGINOSIS
VAGINOSIS *n* bacterial vaginal infection
VAGINULA *n* little sheath
VAGINULAE > VAGINULA
VAGINULE *same as* > VAGINULA
VAGINULES > VAGINULE
VAGITUS *n* newborn baby's cry
VAGITUSES > VAGITUS
VAGOTOMY *n* surgical division of the vagus nerve
VAGOTONIA *n* pathological overactivity of the vagus nerve
VAGOTONIC > VAGOTONIA
VAGRANCY *n* state or condition of being a vagrant
VAGRANT *n* person with no settled home ▷ *adj* wandering
VAGRANTLY > VAGRANT
VAGRANTS > VAGRANT
VAGROM *same as* > VAGRANT
VAGS > VAG
VAGUE *adj* not clearly explained ▷ *vb* wander
VAGUED > VAGUE
VAGUELY > VAGUE
VAGUENESS > VAGUE
VAGUER > VAGUE
VAGUES > VAGUE
VAGUEST > VAGUE
VAGUING > VAGUE
VAGUISH *adj* rather vague
VAGUS *n* tenth cranial nerve, which supplies the heart, lungs, and viscera

VAHANA *n* vehicle
VAHANAS > VAHANA
VAHINE *n* Polynesian woman
VAHINES > VAHINE
VAIL *vb* lower (something, such as a weapon), esp as a sign of deference or submission
VAILED > VAIL
VAILING > VAIL
VAILS > VAIL
VAIN *adj* excessively proud, esp of one's appearance
VAINER > VAIN
VAINESSE *n* vainness
VAINESSES > VAINESSE
VAINEST > VAIN
VAINGLORY *n* boastfulness or vanity
VAINLY > VAIN
VAINNESS > VAIN
VAIR *n* fur used to trim robes in the Middle Ages
VAIRE *adj* of Russian squirrel fur
VAIRIER > VAIR
VAIRIEST > VAIR
VAIRS > VAIR
VAIRY > VAIR
VAIVODE *n* Slavic governor
VAIVODES > VAIVODE
VAJAZZLE *vb* decorate the female genitals with jewellery
VAJAZZLED > VAJAZZLE
VAJAZZLES > VAJAZZLE
VAKAS *n* Armenian priestly collar
VAKASES > VAKAS
VAKASS *n* Armenian priestly collar
VAKASSES > VAKASS
VAKEEL *n* (in India) ambassador
VAKEELS > VAKEEL
VAKIL *same as* > VAKEEL
VAKILS > VAKIL
VALANCE *n* piece of drapery round the edge of a bed ▷ *vb* provide with a valance
VALANCED > VALANCE
VALANCES > VALANCE
VALANCING > VALANCE
VALE *n* valley ▷ *sentence substitute* farewell
VALENCE *same as* > VALENCY

V

VALENCES > VALENCE
VALENCIA n type of fabric
VALENCIAS
> VALENCIA
VALENCIES > VALENCY
VALENCY n power of an atom to make molecular bonds
VALENTINE n (person to whom one sends) a romantic card on Saint Valentine's Day, 14th February
VALERATE n salt of valeric acid
VALERATES
> VALERATE
VALERIAN n herb used as a sedative
VALERIANS
> VALERIAN
VALERIC adj of, relating to, or derived from valerian
VALES > VALE
VALET n man's personal male servant ▷ vb act as a valet (for)
VALETA n old-time dance in triple time
VALETAS > VALETA
VALETE n farewell
VALETED > VALET
VALETES > VALETE
VALETING > VALET
VALETINGS > VALET
VALETS > VALET
VALGOID > VALGUS
VALGOUS same as
> VALGUS
VALGUS adj denoting a deformity of a limb ▷ n abnormal position of a limb
VALGUSES > VALGUS
VALI n Turkish civil governor
VALIANCE > VALIANT
VALIANCES > VALIANT
VALIANCY > VALIANT
VALIANT adj brave or courageous ▷ n brave person
VALIANTLY > VALIANT
VALIANTS > VALIANT
VALID adj soundly reasoned
VALIDATE vb make valid
VALIDATED
> VALIDATE
VALIDATES
> VALIDATE
VALIDATOR n person who validates
VALIDER > VALID
VALIDEST > VALID
VALIDITY > VALID
VALIDLY > VALID
VALIDNESS > VALID
VALINE n essential amino acid
VALINES > VALINE
VALIS > VALI
VALISE n small suitcase
VALISES > VALISE
VALIUM n as in valium picnic refers to a day on the

New York Stock Exchange when business is slow
VALIUMS > VALIUM
VALKYR variant of
> VALKYRIE
VALKYRIE n Norse maiden who collects dead warriors to take to Valhalla
VALKYRIES > VALKYRIE
VALKYRS > VALKYR
VALLAR adj pertaining to a rampart ▷ n gold Roman crown awarded to the first soldier who broke into the enemy's camp
VALLARIES > VALLARY
VALLARS > VALLAR
VALLARY same as
> VALLAR
VALLATE adj surrounded with a wall
VALLATION n act or process of building fortifications
VALLECULA n any of various natural depressions or crevices
VALLEY n low area between hills, often with a river running through it
VALLEYED adj having a valley
VALLEYS > VALLEY
VALLHUND n Swedish breed of dog
VALLHUNDS
> VALLHUND
VALLONIA same as
> VALONIA
VALLONIAS
> VALLONIA
VALLUM n Roman rampart or earthwork
VALLUMS > VALLUM
VALONEA same as
> VALONIA
VALONEAS > VALONEA
VALONIA n acorn cups and unripe acorns of a particular oak
VALONIAS > VALONIA
VALOR same as > VALOUR
VALORISE same as
> VALORIZE
VALORISED
> VALORISE
VALORISES
> VALORISE
VALORIZE vb fix and maintain an artificial price for (a commodity) by governmental action
VALORIZED
> VALORIZE
VALORIZES
> VALORIZE
VALOROUS > VALOUR
VALORS > VALOR
VALOUR n bravery; brave person
VALOURS > VALOUR
VALPROATE n medicament derived from valproic acid
VALPROIC adj as in valproic acid synthetic crystalline compound, used as an anticonvulsive

VALSE another word for
> WALTZ
VALSED > VALSE
VALSES > VALSE
VALSING > VALSE
VALUABLE adj having great worth ▷ n valuable article of personal property, esp jewellery
VALUABLES
> VALUABLE
VALUABLY > VALUABLE
VALUATE vb value or evaluate
VALUATED > VALUATE
VALUATES > VALUATE
VALUATING > VALUATE
VALUATION n assessment of worth
VALUATOR n person who estimates the value of objects, paintings, etc
VALUATORS
> VALUATOR
VALUE n importance, usefulness ▷ vb assess the worth or desirability of
VALUED > VALUE
VALUELESS adj having or possessing no value
VALUER > VALUE
VALUERS > VALUE
VALUES > VALUE
VALUING > VALUE
VALUTA n value of one currency in terms of its exchange rate with another
VALUTAS > VALUTA
VALVAL same as
> VALVULAR
VALVAR same as
> VALVULAR
VALVASSOR same as
> VAVASOR
VALVATE adj furnished with a valve or valves
VALVE n device to control the movement of fluid through a pipe ▷ vb provide with a valve
VALVED > VALVE
VALVELESS > VALVE
VALVELET same as
> VALVULE
VALVELETS
> VALVELET
VALVELIKE > VALVE
VALVES > VALVE
VALVING > VALVE
VALVULA same as
> VALVULE
VALVULAE > VALVULA
VALVULAR adj of or having valves
VALVULE n small valve or a part resembling one
VALVULES > VALVULE
VAMBRACE n piece of armour used to protect the arm
VAMBRACED
> VAMBRACE
VAMBRACES
> VAMBRACE
VAMOOSE vb leave a place hurriedly
VAMOOSED > VAMOOSE

VAMOOSES > VAMOOSE
VAMOOSING > VAMOOSE
VAMOSE same as
> VAMOOSE
VAMOSED > VAMOSE
VAMOSES > VAMOSE
VAMOSING > VAMOSE
VAMP n attractive woman who exploits men ▷ vb exploit (a man) in the fashion of a vamp
VAMPED > VAMP
VAMPER > VAMP
VAMPERS > VAMP
VAMPIER > VAMP
VAMPIEST > VAMP
VAMPING > VAMP
VAMPINGS > VAMP
VAMPIRE n (in folklore) corpse that rises at night to drink the blood of the living ▷ vb assail
VAMPIRED > VAMPIRE
VAMPIRES > VAMPIRE
VAMPIRIC > VAMPIRE
VAMPIRING > VAMPIRE
VAMPIRISE same as
> VAMPIRIZE
VAMPIRISH > VAMPIRE
VAMPIRISM n belief in the existence of vampires
VAMPIRIZE vb suck blood from
VAMPISH > VAMP
VAMPISHLY > VAMP
VAMPLATE n piece of metal mounted on a lance to protect the hand
VAMPLATES > VAMPLATE
VAMPS > VAMP
VAMPY > VAMP
VAN n motor vehicle for transporting goods ▷ vb send in a van
VANADATE n any salt or ester of a vanadic acid
VANADATES
> VANADATE
VANADIATE same as
> VANADATE
VANADIC adj of or containing vanadium, esp in a trivalent or pentavalent state
VANADIUM n metallic element, used in steel
VANADIUMS
> VANADIUM
VANADOUS adj of or containing vanadium
VANASPATI n hydrogenated vegetable fat commonly used in India as a substitute for butter
VANDA n type of orchid
VANDAL n person who deliberately damages property
VANDALIC > VANDAL
VANDALISE same as
> VANDALIZE
VANDALISH > VANDAL
VANDALISM n wanton or deliberate destruction caused by a vandal or an instance of such destruction

V

VANDALIZE *vb* cause damage to (personal or public property) deliberately

VANDALS > VANDAL

VANDAS > VANDA

VANDYKE *n* short pointed beard ▷ *vb* cut with deep zigzag indentations

VANDYKED > VANDYKE

VANDYKES > VANDYKE

VANDYKING > VANDYKE

VANE *n* flat blade on a rotary device such as a weathercock or propeller

VANED > VANE

VANELESS > VANE

VANES > VANE

VANESSA *n* type of butterfly

VANESSAS > VANESSA

VANESSID *n* type of butterfly ▷ *adj* relating to this butterfly

VANESSIDS > VANESSID

VANG *n* type of rope or tackle on a sailing ship

VANGS > VANG

VANGUARD *n* unit of soldiers leading an army

VANGUARDS > VANGUARD

VANILLA *n* seed pod of a tropical climbing orchid, used for flavouring ▷ *adj* flavoured with vanilla

VANILLAS > VANILLA

VANILLIC *adj* of, resembling, containing, or derived from vanilla or vanillin

VANILLIN *n* white crystalline aldehyde found in vanilla

VANILLINS > VANILLIN

VANISH *vb* disappear suddenly or mysteriously ▷ *n* second and weaker of the two vowels in a falling diphthong

VANISHED > VANISH

VANISHER > VANISH

VANISHERS > VANISH

VANISHES > VANISH

VANISHING > VANISH

VANITAS *n* type of Dutch painting

VANITASES > VANITAS

VANITIED *adj* with vanity units or mirrors

VANITIES > VANITY

VANITORY *n* vanity unit

VANITY *n* (display of) excessive pride

VANLIKE *adj* like a van

VANLOAD *n* amount van will carry

VANLOADS > VANLOAD

VANMAN *n* man in control of a van

VANMEN > VANMAN

VANNED > VAN

VANNER *n* horse used to pull delivery vehicles

VANNERS > VANNER

VANNING > VAN

VANNINGS > VAN

VANPOOL *n* van-sharing group

VANPOOLS > VANPOOL

VANQUISH *vb* defeat (someone) utterly

VANS > VAN

VANT *archaic word for* > VANGUARD

VANTAGE *n* state, position, or opportunity offering advantage ▷ *vb* benefit

VANTAGED > VANTAGE

VANTAGES > VANTAGE

VANTAGING > VANTAGE

VANTBRACE *n* armour for the arm

VANTBRASS > VAMBRACE

VANTS > VANT

VANWARD *adv* in or towards the front

VAPE *vb* inhale nicotine vapour (from an electronic cigarette)

VAPED > VAPE

VAPER *n* one who inhales nicotine vapour from an electronic cigarette

VAPERS > VAPER

VAPES > VAPE

VAPID *adj* lacking character, dull

VAPIDER > VAPID

VAPIDEST > VAPID

VAPIDITY > VAPID

VAPIDLY > VAPID

VAPIDNESS > VAPID

VAPING *n* the practice of inhaling nicotine vapour (from an electronic cigarette)

VAPINGS > VAPING

VAPOR *same as* > VAPOUR

VAPORABLE > VAPOR

VAPORED > VAPOR

VAPORER > VAPOR

VAPORERS > VAPOR

VAPORETTI > VAPORETTO

VAPORETTO *n* steam-powered passenger boat, as used on the canals in Venice

VAPORIER > VAPORY

VAPORIEST > VAPORY

VAPORIFIC *adj* producing, causing, or tending to produce vapour

VAPORING > VAPOR

VAPORINGS > VAPOR

VAPORISE *same as* > VAPORIZE

VAPORISED > VAPORISE

VAPORISER *same as* > VAPORIZER

VAPORISES > VAPORISE

VAPORISH > VAPOR

VAPORIZE *vb* change into a vapour

VAPORIZED > VAPORIZE

VAPORIZER *n* substance that vaporizes or a device that causes vaporization

VAPORIZES > VAPORIZE

VAPORLESS > VAPOR

VAPORLIKE > VAPOR

VAPOROUS *same as* > VAPORIFIC

VAPORS > VAPOR

VAPORWARE *n* new software that has not yet been produced

VAPORY *same as* > VAPOURY

VAPOUR *n* moisture suspended in air as steam or mist ▷ *vb* evaporate

VAPOURED > VAPOUR

VAPOURER > VAPOUR

VAPOURERS > VAPOUR

VAPOURIER > VAPOURY

VAPOURING > VAPOUR

VAPOURISH > VAPOUR

VAPOUROUS *adj* like vapour

VAPOURS > VAPOUR

VAPOURY *adj* full of vapours

VAPULATE *vb* strike

VAPULATED > VAPULATE

VAPULATES > VAPULATE

VAQUERO *n* cattle-hand

VAQUEROS > VAQUERO

VAR *n* unit of reactive power of an alternating current

VARA *n* unit of length used in Spain, Portugal, and South America

VARACTOR *n* semiconductor diode that acts as a voltage-dependent capacitor

VARACTORS > VARACTOR

VARAN *n* type of lizard

VARANS > VARAN

VARAS > VARA

VARDIES > VARDY

VARDY *n* verdict

VARE *n* rod

VAREC *n* ash obtained from kelp

VARECH *same as* > VAREC

VARECHS > VARECH

VARECS > VAREC

VARENYKY *pl n* Ukrainian stuffed dumplings

VARES > VARE

VAREUSE *n* type of coat

VAREUSES > VAREUSE

VARGUENO *n* type of Spanish cabinet

VARGUENOS > VARGUENO

VARIA *n* collection or miscellany, esp of literary works

VARIABLE *adj* not always the same, changeable ▷ *n* something that is subject to variation

VARIABLES > VARIABLE

VARIABLY > VARIABLE

VARIANCE *n* act of varying

VARIANCES > VARIANCE

VARIANT *adj* differing from a standard or type ▷ *n* something that differs from a standard or type

VARIANTS > VARIANT

VARIAS > VARIA

VARIATE *n* random variable or a numerical value taken by it ▷ *vb* vary

VARIATED > VARIATE

VARIATES > VARIATE

VARIATING > VARIATE

VARIATION *n* something presented in a slightly different form

VARIATIVE > VARIATE

VARICEAL *adj* relating to a varix

VARICELLA *n* chickenpox

VARICES > VARIX

VARICOID *same as* > CIRSOID

VARICOSE *adj* of or resulting from varicose veins

VARICOSED *same as* > VARICOSE

VARICOSES > VARICOSIS

VARICOSIS *n* any condition characterized by distension of the veins

VARIED > VARY

VARIEDLY > VARY

VARIEGATE *vb* alter the appearance of, esp by adding different colours

VARIER *n* person who varies

VARIERS > VARIER

VARIES > VARY

VARIETAL *adj* of or forming a variety, esp a biological variety ▷ *n* wine labelled with the name of the grape from which it is pressed

VARIETALS > VARIETAL

VARIETIES > VARIETY

VARIETY *n* state of being diverse or various

VARIFOCAL *adj* gradated to permit any length of vision between near and distant ▷ *n* lens of this type

VARIFORM *adj* varying in form or shape

VARIOLA *n* smallpox

VARIOLAR > VARIOLA

VARIOLAS > VARIOLA

VARIOLATE *vb* inoculate with the smallpox virus ▷ *adj* marked or pitted with or as if with the scars of smallpox

VARIOLE *n* any of the rounded masses that make up the rock variolite

VARIOLES > VARIOLE

VARIOLITE *n* type of basic igneous rock

VARIOLOID *adj* resembling smallpox ▷ *n* mild form of smallpox occurring in persons with partial immunity

VARIOLOUS adj relating to or resembling smallpox

VARIORUM adj containing notes by various scholars or critics or various versions of the text ▷ n edition or text of this kind

VARIORUMS > VARIORUM

VARIOUS adj of several kinds

VARIOUSLY > VARIOUS

VARISCITE n green secondary mineral

VARISIZED adj of different sizes

VARISTOR n type of semiconductor device

VARISTORS > VARISTOR

VARITYPE vb produce (copy) on a Varityper ▷ n copy produced on a Varityper

VARITYPED > VARITYPE

VARITYPES > VARITYPE

VARIX n tortuous dilated vein

VARLET n menial servant

VARLETESS n female varlet

VARLETRY n varlets collectively

VARLETS > VARLET

VARLETTO same as > VARLET

VARLETTOS > VARLETTO

VARMENT same as > VARMINT

VARMENTS > VARMENT

VARMINT n irritating or obnoxious person or animal

VARMINTS > VARMINT

VARNA n any of the four Hindu castes

VARNAS > VARNA

VARNISH n solution of oil and resin, put on a surface to make it hard and glossy ▷ vb apply varnish to

VARNISHED > VARNISH

VARNISHER > VARNISH

VARNISHES > VARNISH

VARNISHY adj like varnish

VAROOM same as > VROOM

VAROOMED same as > VAROOM

VAROOMING same as > VAROOM

VAROOMS same as > VAROOM

VARROA n small parasite

VARROAS > VARROA

VARS > VAR

VARSAL adj universal

VARSITIES > VARSITY

VARSITY n university

VARTABED n position in the Armenian church

VARTABEDS > VARTABED

VARUS adj denoting a deformity of a limb ▷ n

abnormal position of a limb

VARUSES > VARUS

VARVE n typically thin band of sediment deposited annually in glacial lakes

VARVED adj having layers of sedimentary deposit

VARVEL n piece of falconry equipment

VARVELLED adj having varvels

VARVELS > VARVEL

VARVES > VARVE

VARY vb change

VARYING > VARY

VARYINGLY > VARY

VARYINGS > VARY

VAS n vessel or tube that carries a fluid

VASA > VAS

VASAL > VAS

VASCULA > VASCULUM

VASCULAR adj relating to vessels

VASCULUM n metal box used by botanists in the field for carrying botanical specimens

VASCULUMS > VASCULUM

VASE n ornamental jar, esp for flowers

VASECTOMY n removal of part of the vas deferens

VASEFUL n contents of a vase

VASEFULS > VASEFUL

VASELIKE > VASE

VASELINE n translucent gelatinous substance obtained from petroleum ▷ vb apply vaseline to

VASELINED > VASELINE

VASELINES > VASELINE

VASES > VASE

VASIFORM > VAS

VASOMOTOR adj (of a drug, agent, nerve, etc) affecting the diameter of blood vessels

VASOSPASM n sudden contraction of a blood vessel

VASOTOCIN n chemical found in birds, reptiles, and some amphibians

VASOTOMY n surgery on the vas deferens

VASOVAGAL adj relating to blood vessels and the vagus nerve

VASSAIL archaic variant of > VASSAL

VASSAILS > VASSAIL

VASSAL n man given land by a lord in return for military service ▷ adj of or relating to a vassal ▷ vb vassalize

VASSALAGE n condition of being a vassal or the obligations to which a vassal was liable

VASSALESS > VASSAL

VASSALISE same as > VASSALIZE

VASSALIZE vb make a vassal of

VASSALLED > VASSAL

VASSALRY n vassalage

VASSALS > VASSAL

VAST adj extremely large ▷ n immense or boundless space

VASTER > VAST

VASTEST > VAST

VASTIDITY n vastness

VASTIER > VASTY

VASTIEST > VASTY

VASTITIES > VAST

VASTITUDE n condition or quality of being vast

VASTITY > VAST

VASTLY > VAST

VASTNESS > VAST

VASTS > VAST

VASTY archaic or poetic word for > VAST

VAT n large container for liquids ▷ vb place, store, or treat in a vat

VATABLE adj subject to VAT

VATFUL n amount enough to fill a vat

VATFULS > VATFUL

VATIC adj of or characteristic of a prophet

VATICAL same as > VATIC

VATICIDE n murder of a prophet

VATICIDES > VATICIDE

VATICINAL adj foretelling or prophesying

VATMAN n Customs and Excise employee

VATMEN > VATMAN

VATS > VAT

VATTED > VAT

VATTER n person who works with vats; blender

VATTERS > VATTER

VATTING > VAT

VATU n standard monetary unit of Vanuatu

VATUS > VATU

VAU same as > VAV

VAUCH vb move fast

VAUCHED > VAUCH

VAUCHES > VAUCH

VAUCHING > VAUCH

VAUDOO same as > VOODOO

VAUDOOS > VAUDOO

VAUDOUX same as > VOODOO

VAULT n secure room for storing valuables ▷ vb jump over (something) by resting one's hand(s) on it

VAULTAGE n group of vaults

VAULTAGES > VAULTAGE

VAULTED > VAULT

VAULTER > VAULT

VAULTERS > VAULT

VAULTIER > VAULTY

VAULTIEST > VAULTY

VAULTING n arrangement of ceiling vaults in a building ▷ adj excessively confident

VAULTINGS > VAULTING

VAULTLIKE > VAULT

VAULTS > VAULT

VAULTY adj arched

VAUNCE same as > ADVANCE

VAUNCED > VAUNCE

VAUNCES > VAUNCE

VAUNCING > VAUNCE

VAUNT vb describe or display (success or possessions) boastfully ▷ n boast

VAUNTAGE archaic variant of > VANTAGE

VAUNTAGES > VAUNTAGE

VAUNTED > VAUNT

VAUNTER > VAUNT

VAUNTERS > VAUNT

VAUNTERY n bravado

VAUNTFUL > VAUNT

VAUNTIE same as > VAUNTY

VAUNTIER > VAUNTY

VAUNTIEST > VAUNT

VAUNTING > VAUNT

VAUNTINGS > VAUNT

VAUNTS > VAUNT

VAUNTY adj proud

VAURIEN n rascal

VAURIENS > VAURIEN

VAUS > VAU

VAUT same as > VAULT

VAUTE same as > VAULT

VAUTED > VAUTE

VAUTES > VAUTE

VAUTING > VAUTE

VAUTS > VAUT

VAV n sixth letter of the Hebrew alphabet

VAVASOR n (in feudal society) vassal who also has their own vassals

VAVASORS > VAVASOR

VAVASORY n lands held by a vavasor

VAVASOUR same as > VAVASOR

VAVASOURS > VAVASOUR

VAVASSOR same as > VAVASOR

VAVASSORS > VAVASSOR

VAVS > VAV

VAW same as > VAV

VAWARD n vanguard

VAWARDS > VAWARD

VAWNTIE > VAUNT

VAWNTIER > VAWNTIE

VAWNTIEST > VAWNTIE

VAWS > VAW

VAWTE same as > VAULT

VAWTED > VAWTE

VAWTES > VAWTE

VAWTING > VAWTE

VAX n vaccination

VAXES > VAX

VEAL n calf meat ▷ vb rear (calves) for use as veal

VEALE Spenserian word for > VEIL

VEALED > VEAL

VEALER n young bovine animal of up to 14 months old grown for veal

V

VEALERS > VEALER

VEALES > VEALE

VEALIER > VEAL

VEALIEST > VEAL

VEALING > VEAL

VEALS > VEAL

VEALY > VEAL

VECTOR n quantity that has size and direction, such as force ▷ vb direct or guide (a pilot) by directions transmitted by radio

VECTORED > VECTOR

VECTORIAL > VECTOR

VECTORING > VECTOR

VECTORISE same as > VECTORIZE

VECTORIZE vb convert from a bitmap representation to a vector representation

VECTORS > VECTOR

VEDALIA n Australian ladybird which is a pest of citrus fruits

VEDALIAS > VEDALIA

VEDETTE n small patrol vessel

VEDETTES > VEDETTE

VEDUTA n painting of a town or city

VEDUTAS > VEDUTA

VEDUTE > VEDUTA

VEDUTISTA n artist who creates vedutas

VEDUTISTE > VEDUTISTA

VEDUTISTI > VEDUTISTA

VEE n letter 'v'

VEEJAY n video jockey

VEEJAYS > VEEJAY

VEENA same as > VINA

VEENAS > VEENA

VEEP n vice president

VEEPEE n vice president

VEEPEES > VEEPEE

VEEPS > VEEP

VEER vb change direction suddenly ▷ n change of course or direction

VEERED > VEER

VEERIES > VEERY

VEERING > VEER

VEERINGLY > VEER

VEERINGS > VEER

VEERS > VEER

VEERY n tawny brown North American thrush

VEES > VEE

VEG n vegetable or vegetables ▷ vb relax

VEGA n tobacco plantation

VEGAN n person who eats no meat, fish, eggs, or dairy products ▷ adj suitable for a vegan

VEGANIC adj farmed without the use of animal products or byproducts

VEGANISM > VEGAN

VEGANISMS > VEGAN

VEGANS > VEGAN

VEGAS > VEGA

VEGELATE n type of chocolate

VEGELATES > VEGELATE

VEGEMITE n informal Australian word for a child

VEGEMITES > VEGEMITE

VEGES > VEG

VEGETABLE n edible plant ▷ adj of or like plants or vegetables

VEGETABLY adj full of vegetables

VEGETAL adj of or relating to plant life ▷ n vegetable

VEGETALLY > VEGETAL

VEGETALS > VEGETAL

VEGETANT adj causing growth

VEGETATE vb live a dull boring life with no mental stimulation

VEGETATED > VEGETATE

VEGETATES > VEGETATE

VEGETE adj lively

VEGETIST n vegetable cultivator or enthusiast

VEGETISTS > VEGETIST

VEGETIVE adj dull or passive ▷ n vegetable

VEGETIVES > VEGETIVE

VEGGED > VEG

VEGGES > VEG

VEGGIE n vegetable ▷ adj vegetarian

VEGGIER > VEGGIE

VEGGIES > VEGGIE

VEGGIEST > VEGGIE

VEGGING > VEG

VEGIE n vegetable ▷ adj vegetarian

VEGIER > VEGIE

VEGIES > VEGIE

VEGIEST > VEGIE

VEGO adj vegetarian ▷ n vegetarian

VEGOS > VEGO

VEHEMENCE > VEHEMENT

VEHEMENCY > VEHEMENT

VEHEMENT adj expressing strong feelings

VEHICLE n machine for carrying people or objects

VEHICLES > VEHICLE

VEHICULAR > VEHICLE

VEHM n type of medieval German court

VEHME > VEHM

VEHMIC > VEHM

VEHMIQUE > VEHM

VEIL n piece of thin cloth covering the head or face ▷ vb cover with or as if with a veil

VEILED adj disguised

VEILEDLY > VEILED

VEILER > VEIL

VEILERS > VEIL

VEILIER > VEIL

VEILIEST > VEIL

VEILING n veil or the fabric used for veils

VEILINGS > VEILING

VEILLESS > VEIL

VEILLEUSE n small night-light

VEILLIKE > VEIL

VEILS > VEIL

VEILY > VEIL

VEIN n tube that takes blood to the heart ▷ vb diffuse over or cause to diffuse over in streaked patterns

VEINAL > VEIN

VEINED > VEIN

VEINER n wood-carving tool

VEINERS > VEINER

VEINIER > VEIN

VEINIEST > VEIN

VEINING n pattern or network of veins or streaks

VEININGS > VEINING

VEINLESS > VEIN

VEINLET n any small vein or venule

VEINLETS > VEINLET

VEINLIKE > VEIN

VEINOUS > VEIN

VEINS > VEIN

VEINSTONE another word for > GANGUE

VEINSTUFF another word for > GANGUE

VEINULE less common spelling of > VENULE

VEINULES > VEINULE

VEINULET same as > VEINLET

VEINULETS > VEINULET

VEINY > VEIN

VELA > VELUM

VELAMEN n thick layer of dead cells that covers the aerial roots of certain orchids

VELAMINA > VELAMEN

VELAR adj of, relating to, or attached to a velum ▷ n velar sound

VELARIA > VELARIUM

VELARIC > VELAR

VELARISE same as > VELARIZE

VELARISED > VELARISE

VELARISES > VELARISE

VELARIUM n awning used to protect the audience in ancient Roman theatres and amphitheatres

VELARIZE vb supplement the pronunciation of (a speech sound) with articulation at the soft palate

VELARIZED > VELARIZE

VELARIZES > VELARIZE

VELARS > VELAR

VELATE adj having or covered with velum

VELATED same as > VELATE

VELATURA n overglaze

VELATURAS > VELATURA

VELCRO n tradename for a fastening of two strips of nylon fabric pressed together

VELCROS > VELCRO

VELD n high grassland in southern Africa

VELDS > VELD

VELDSKOEN n leather ankle boot

VELDT same as > VELD

VELDTS > VELDT

VELE same as > VEIL

VELES > VELE

VELETA same as > VALETA

VELETAS > VELETA

VELIGER n free-swimming larva of many molluscs

VELIGERS > VELIGER

VELITES pl n light-armed troops in ancient Rome, drawn from the poorer classes

VELL n salted calf's stomach, used in cheese making

VELLEITY n weakest level of desire or volition

VELLENAGE n (in Medieval Europe) status of being a villein

VELLET n velvet

VELLETS > VELLET

VELLICATE vb twitch, pluck, or pinch

VELLON n silver and copper alloy used in old Spanish coins

VELLONS > VELLON

VELLS > VELL

VELLUM n fine calfskin parchment ▷ adj made of or resembling vellum

VELLUMS > VELLUM

VELLUS n as in vellus hair short fine unpigmented hair covering the human body

VELOCE adv to be played rapidly

VELOCITY n speed of movement in a given direction

VELODROME n arena with a banked track for cycle racing

VELOUR n fabric similar to velvet

VELOURS same as > VELOUR

VELOUTE n rich white sauce or soup made from stock, egg yolks, and cream

VELOUTES > VELOUTE

VELOUTINE n type of velvety fabric

VELSKOEN n leather ankle boot

VELSKOENS > VELSKOEN

VELUM n any of various membranous structures

VELURE n velvet or a similar fabric ▷ vb cover with velure

VELURED > VELURE
VELURES > VELURE
VELURING > VELURE
VELVERET n type of velvet-like fabric
VELVERETS
    > VELVERET
VELVET n fabric with a thick soft pile ▷ vb cover with velvet
VELVETED > VELVET
VELVETEEN n cotton velvet
VELVETIER > VELVET
VELVETING > VELVET
VELVETS > VELVET
VELVETY > VELVET
VENA n vein in the body
VENAE > VENA
VENAL adj easily bribed
VENALITY > VENAL
VENALLY > VENAL
VENATIC adj of, relating to, or used in hunting
VENATICAL same as
    > VENATIC
VENATION n arrangement of the veins in a leaf or in the wing of an insect
VENATIONS
    > VENATION
VENATOR n hunter
VENATORS > VENATOR
VEND vb sell
VENDABLE > VEND
VENDABLES > VEND
VENDACE n either of two small whitefish occurring in lakes in Scotland and NW England
VENDACES > VENDACE
VENDAGE n vintage
VENDAGES > VENDAGE
VENDANGE same as
    > VENDAGE
VENDANGES
    > VENDANGE
VENDED > VEND
VENDEE n person to whom something, esp real property, is sold
VENDEES > VENDEE
VENDER same as
    > VENDOR
VENDERS > VENDER
VENDETTA n long-lasting quarrel between people in which they attempt to harm each other
VENDETTAS
    > VENDETTA
VENDEUSE n female salesperson
VENDEUSES > VENDEUSE
VENDIBLE adj saleable or marketable ▷ n saleable object
VENDIBLES
    > VENDIBLE
VENDIBLY > VENDIBLE
VENDING > VEND
VENDINGS > VEND
VENDIS same as
    > VENDACE
VENDISES > VENDIS
VENDISS same as
    > VENDACE

VENDISSES > VENDIS
VENDITION > VEND
VENDOR n person who sells goods such as newspapers or hamburgers from a stall or cart
VENDORS > VENDOR
VENDS > VEND
VENDUE n public sale
VENDUES > VENDUE
VENEER n thin layer of wood etc covering a cheaper material ▷ vb cover (a surface) with a veneer
VENEERED > VENEER
VENEERER > VENEER
VENEERERS > VENEER
VENEERING n material used as veneer or a veneered surface
VENEERS > VENEER
VENEFIC adj having poisonous effects
VENEFICAL same as
    > VENEFIC
VENENATE vb poison
VENENATED
    > VENENATE
VENENATES
    > VENENATE
VENENE n medicine from snake venom
VENENES > VENENE
VENENOSE adj poisonous
VENERABLE adj worthy of deep respect
VENERABLY
    > VENERABLE
VENERATE vb hold (a person) in deep respect
VENERATED
    > VENERATE
VENERATES
    > VENERATE
VENERATOR
    > VENERATE
VENEREAL adj of or involving the genitals
VENEREAN n sex addict
VENEREANS
    > VENEREAN
VENEREOUS adj libidinous
VENERER n hunter
VENERERS > VENERER
VENERIES > VENERY
VENERY n pursuit of sexual gratification
VENETIAN n Venetian blind
VENETIANS
    > VENETIAN
VENEWE same as **>** VENUE
VENEWES > VENEWE
VENEY n thrust
VENEYS > VENEY
VENGE vb avenge
VENGEABLE > VENGE
VENGEABLY > VENGE
VENGEANCE n revenge
VENGED > VENGE
VENGEFUL adj wanting revenge
VENGEMENT > VENGE
VENGER > VENGE
VENGERS > VENGE

VENGES > VENGE
VENGING > VENGE
VENIAL adj (of a sin or fault) easily forgiven
VENIALITY > VENIAL
VENIALLY > VENIAL
VENIDIUM n genus of flowering plants
VENIDIUMS
    > VENIDIUM
VENIN n any of the poisonous constituents of animal venoms
VENINE same as **>** VENIN
VENINES > VENINE
VENINS > VENIN
VENIRE n list from which jurors are selected
VENIREMAN n person summoned for jury service
VENIREMEN
    > VENIREMAN
VENIRES > VENIRE
VENISON n deer meat
VENISONS > VENISON
VENITE n musical setting for the 95th psalm
VENITES > VENITE
VENNEL n lane
VENNELS > VENNEL
VENOGRAM n X-ray of a vein
VENOGRAMS
    > VENOGRAM
VENOLOGY n study of veins
VENOM n malice or spite ▷ vb poison
VENOMED > VENOM
VENOMER > VENOM
VENOMERS > VENOM
VENOMING > VENOM
VENOMLESS > VENOM
VENOMOUS > VENOM
VENOMS > VENOM
VENOSE adj having veins
VENOSITY n excessive quantity of blood in the venous system or in an organ or part
VENOUS adj of veins
VENOUSLY > VENOUS
VENT n outlet releasing fumes or fluid ▷ vb express (an emotion) freely
VENTAGE n small opening
VENTAGES > VENTAGE
VENTAIL n (in medieval armour) a covering for the lower part of the face
VENTAILE same as
    > VENTAIL
VENTAILES
    > VENTAILE
VENTAILS > VENTAIL
VENTANA n window
VENTANAS > VENTANA
VENTAYLE same as
    > VENTAIL
VENTAYLES
    > VENTAYLE
VENTED > VENT
VENTER > VENT
VENTERS > VENT
VENTIDUCT n air pipe
VENTIFACT n pebble that has been shaped by wind-blown sand

VENTIGE same as
    > VENTAGE
VENTIGES > VENTIGE
VENTIL n valve on a musical instrument
VENTILATE vb let fresh air into
VENTILS > VENTIL
VENTING > VENT
VENTINGS > VENT
VENTLESS > VENT
VENTOSE adj full of wind ▷ n apparatus sometimes used to assist the delivery of a baby
VENTOSES > VENTOSE
VENTOSITY n flatulence
VENTOUSE n ventose
VENTOUSES
    > VENTOUSE
VENTRAL adj relating to the front of the body ▷ n ventral fin
VENTRALLY > VENTRAL
VENTRALS > VENTRAL
VENTRE same as
    > VENTURE
VENTRED > VENTRE
VENTRES > VENTRE
VENTRICLE n cavity in an organ such as the heart
VENTRING > VENTRE
VENTRINGS > VENTRE
VENTROUS > VENTRE
VENTS > VENT
VENTURE n risky undertaking, esp in business ▷ vb do something risky
VENTURED > VENTURE
VENTURER > VENTURE
VENTURERS > VENTURE
VENTURES > VENTURE
VENTURI n tube used to control the flow of fluid
VENTURING > VENTURE
VENTURIS > VENTURI
VENTUROUS adj adventurous
VENUE n place where an organized gathering is held
VENUES > VENUE
VENULAR > VENULE
VENULE n any of the small branches of a vein
VENULES > VENULE
VENULOSE > VENULE
VENULOUS > VENULE
VENUS n type of marine bivalve mollusc
VENUSES > VENUS
VENVILLE n type of parish tenure
VENVILLES
    > VENVILLE
VERA adj as in aloe vera plant substance used in skin and hair preparations
VERACIOUS adj habitually truthful
VERACITY n truthfulness
VERANDA n porch or portico along the outside of a building
VERANDAED > VERANDA
VERANDAH same as
    > VERANDA

V

VERANDAHS
> VERANDAH
VERANDAS > VERANDA
VERAPAMIL n
calcium-channel blocker
used in the treatment of
some types of irregular
heart rhythm
VERATRIA same as
> VERATRINE
VERATRIAS
> VERATRIA
VERATRIN same as
> VERATRINE
VERATRINE n white
poisonous mixture
obtained from the seeds
of sabadilla
VERATRINS
> VERATRIN
VERATRUM n genus of
herbs
VERATRUMS
> VERATRUM
VERB n word that
expresses the idea of
action, happening, or
being
VERBAL adj spoken ▷ n
abuse or invective ▷ vb
implicate (someone) in a
crime by quoting an
alleged admission of guilt
in court
VERBALISE same as
> VERBALIZE
VERBALISM n
exaggerated emphasis on
the importance of words
VERBALIST n person
who deals with words
alone, rather than facts,
ideas, feeling, etc
VERBALITY > VERBAL
VERBALIZE vb express
(something) in words
VERBALLED > VERBAL
VERBALLY > VERBAL
VERBALS > VERBAL
VERBARIAN n inventor
of words
VERBASCUM same as
> MULLEIN
VERBATIM adj word for
word ▷ adv using exactly
the same words
VERBENA n plant with
sweet-smelling flowers
VERBENAS > VERBENA
VERBERATE vb lash
VERBIAGE n excessive
use of words
VERBIAGES
> VERBIAGE
VERBICIDE n person
who destroys a word
VERBID n any nonfinite
form of a verb or any
nonverbal word derived
from a verb
VERBIDS > VERBID
VERBIFIED > VERBIFY
VERBIFIES > VERBIFY
VERBIFY another word for
> VERBALIZE
VERBILE n person who
is best stimulated by
words
VERBILES > VERBILE

VERBING n use of nouns
as verbs
VERBINGS > VERBING
VERBLESS > VERB
VERBOSE adj speaking at
tedious length
VERBOSELY > VERBOSE
VERBOSER > VERBOSE
VERBOSEST > VERBOSE
VERBOSITY > VERBOSE
VERBOTEN adj forbidden
VERBS > VERB
VERD n as in verd antique
dark green mottled
impure variety of
serpentine marble
VERDANCY > VERDANT
VERDANT adj covered in
green vegetation
VERDANTLY > VERDANT
VERDELHO n type of
grape
VERDELHOS
> VERDELHO
VERDERER n officer
responsible for the
maintenance of law and
order in the royal forests
VERDERERS
> VERDERER
VERDEROR same as
> VERDERER
VERDERORS
> VERDEROR
VERDET n type of
verdigris
VERDETS > VERDET
VERDICT n decision of a
jury
VERDICTS > VERDICT
VERDIGRIS n green film
on copper, brass, or bronze
VERDIN n small W North
American tit having grey
plumage with a yellow
head
VERDINS > VERDIN
VERDIT same as
> VERDICT
VERDITE n type of rock
used in jewellery
VERDITER n blue-green
pigment made from
copper
VERDITERS
> VERDITER
VERDITES > VERDITE
VERDITS > VERDIT
VERDOY n floral or leafy
shield decoration
VERDOYS > VERDOY
VERDURE n flourishing
green vegetation
VERDURED > VERDURE
VERDURES > VERDURE
VERDUROUS > VERDURE
VERECUND adj shy or
modest
VERGE n grass border
along a road ▷ vb move in
a specified direction
VERGED > VERGE
VERGENCE n inward or
outward turning
movement of the eyes in
convergence or divergence
VERGENCES
> VERGENCE

VERGENCY adj inclination
VERGER n church
caretaker
VERGERS > VERGER
VERGES > VERGE
VERGING > VERGE
VERGLAS n thin film of ice
on rock
VERGLASES > VERGLAS
VERIDIC same as
> VERIDICAL
VERIDICAL adj truthful
VERIER > VERY
VERIEST > VERY
VERIFIED > VERIFY
VERIFIER > VERIFY
VERIFIERS > VERIFY
VERIFIES > VERIFY
VERIFY vb check the
truth or accuracy of
VERIFYING > VERIFY
VERILY adv in truth
VERISM n extreme
naturalism in art or
literature
VERISMO n school of
composition that
originated in Italian opera
VERISMOS > VERISMO
VERISMS > VERISM
VERIST > VERISM
VERISTIC > VERISM
VERISTS > VERISM
VERITABLE adj rightly
called, without
exaggeration
VERITABLY
> VERITABLE
VERITAS n truth
VERITATES > VERITAS
VERITE adj involving a
high degree of realism or
naturalism ▷ n this kind of
realism in film
VERITES > VERITE
VERITIES > VERITY
VERITY n true statement
or principle
VERJUICE n acid juice of
unripe grapes, apples, or
crab apples ▷ vb make
sour
VERJUICED
> VERJUICE
VERJUICES
> VERJUICE
VERJUS n acid juice of
unripe grapes, apples, or
crab apples
VERJUSES > VERJUS
VERKLEMPT adj
emotional
VERKRAMP adj bigoted or
illiberal
VERLAN n variety of
French slang in which the
syllables are inverted
VERLANS > VERLAN
VERLIG adj enlightened
VERLIGTE n (during
apartheid) a White
political liberal
VERLIGTES
> VERLIGTE
VERMAL > VERMIS
VERMEIL n gilded silver,
bronze, or other metal,
used esp in the 19th

century ▷ vb decorate
with vermeil ▷ adj
vermilion
VERMEILED > VERMEIL
VERMEILLE variant of
> VERMEIL
VERMEILS > VERMEIL
VERMELL same as
> VERMEIL
VERMELLS > VERMELL
VERMES > VERMIS
VERMIAN > VERMIS
VERMICIDE n any
substance used to kill
worms
VERMICULE n small
worm
VERMIFORM adj shaped
like a worm
VERMIFUGE n any drug
or agent able to destroy or
expel intestinal worms
VERMIL same as
> VERMEIL
VERMILIES > VERMILY
VERMILION adj
orange-red ▷ n mercuric
sulphide, used as an
orange-red pigment
VERMILLED > VERMIL
VERMILS > VERMIL
VERMILY > VERMEIL
VERMIN n small animals
collectively that are
troublesome to humans or
domestic animals
VERMINATE vb breed
vermin
VERMINED adj plagued
with vermin
VERMINIER > VERMINY
VERMINOUS adj relating
to, infested with, or
suggestive of vermin
VERMINS > VERMIN
VERMINY adj full of
vermin
VERMIS n middle lobe
connecting the two halves
of the cerebellum
VERMOULU adj
worm-eaten
VERMOUTH n wine
flavoured with herbs
VERMOUTHS
> VERMOUTH
VERMUTH same as
> VERMOUTH
VERMUTHS > VERMUTH
VERNACLE same as
> VERNICLE
VERNACLES
> VERNACLE
VERNAL adj occurring in
spring
VERNALISE same as
> VERNALIZE
VERNALITY > VERNAL
VERNALIZE vb subject
(ungerminated or
germinating seeds) to low
temperatures
VERNALLY > VERNAL
VERNANT > VERNAL
VERNATION n way in
which leaves are arranged
in the bud
VERNICLE n veronica

VERNICLES
> VERNICLE
VERNIER n movable scale on a measuring instrument for taking readings in fractions
VERNIERS > VERNIER
VERNIX n white substance covering the skin of a foetus
VERNIXES > VERNIX
VERONAL n long-acting barbiturate used medicinally
VERONALS > VERONAL
VERONICA n plant with small blue, pink, or white flowers
VERONICAS
> VERONICA
VERONIQUE adj (of a dish) garnished with seedless white grapes
VERQUERE n type of backgammon game
VERQUERES
> VERQUERE
VERQUIRE variant of
> VERQUERE
VERQUIRES
> VERQUIRE
VERRA Scot word for
> VERY
VERREL n ferrule
VERRELS > VERREL
VERREY same as > VAIR
VERRINE n starter, dessert, or other dish served in a glass
VERRINES > VERRINE
VERRUCA n wart, usu on the foot
VERRUCAE > VERRUCA
VERRUCAS > VERRUCA
VERRUCOSE adj covered with warts
VERRUCOUS same as
> VERRUCOSE
VERRUGA same as
> VERRUCA
VERRUGAS > VERRUGA
VERRY same as > VAIR
VERS n verse
VERSAL n embellished letter
VERSALS > VERSAL
VERSANT n side or slope of a mountain or mountain range
VERSANTS > VERSANT
VERSATILE adj having many skills or uses
VERSE n group of lines forming part of a song or poem ▷ vb write in verse
VERSED adj thoroughly knowledgeable (about)
VERSELET n small verse
VERSELETS
> VERSELET
VERSEMAN n man who writes verse
VERSEMEN > VERSEMAN
VERSER n versifier
VERSERS > VERSER
VERSES > VERSE
VERSET n short, often sacred, verse

VERSETS > VERSET
VERSICLE n short verse
VERSICLES
> VERSICLE
VERSIFIED > VERSIFY
VERSIFIER > VERSIFY
VERSIFIES > VERSIFY
VERSIFORM adj changing in form
VERSIFY vb write in verse
VERSIN same as
> VERSINE
VERSINE n trigonometric function
VERSINES > VERSINE
VERSING > VERSE
VERSINGS > VERSE
VERSINS > VERSIN
VERSION n form of something, with some differences from other forms ▷ vb keep track of the changes made to a computer file at different stages
VERSIONAL > VERSION
VERSIONED > VERSION
VERSIONER n translator
VERSIONS > VERSION
VERSO n left-hand page of a book
VERSOS > VERSO
VERST n unit of length used in Russia
VERSTE same as > VERST
VERSTES > VERSTE
VERSTS > VERST
VERSUS prep in opposition to or in contrast with
VERSUTE adj cunning
VERT n right to cut green wood in a forest ▷ vb turn
VERTEBRA n one of the bones that form the spine
VERTEBRAE
> VERTEBRA
VERTEBRAL
> VERTEBRA
VERTEBRAS
> VERTEBRA
VERTED > VERT
VERTEX n point on a geometric figure where the sides form an angle
VERTEXES > VERTEX
VERTICAL adj straight up and down ▷ n vertical direction
VERTICALS
> VERTICAL
VERTICES > VERTEX
VERTICIL n circular arrangement of parts about an axis, esp leaves around a stem
VERTICILS
> VERTICIL
VERTICITY n ability to turn
VERTIGO n dizziness, usu when looking down from a high place
VERTIGOES > VERTIGO
VERTIGOS > VERTIGO
VERTING > VERT

VERTIPORT n type of airport
VERTISOL n type of clayey soil
VERTISOLS
> VERTISOL
VERTS > VERT
VERTU same as > VIRTU
VERTUE same as
> VIRTU
VERTUES > VERTUE
VERTUOUS > VERTU
VERTUS > VERTU
VERVAIN n plant with spikes of blue, purple, or white flowers
VERVAINS > VERVAIN
VERVE n enthusiasm or liveliness
VERVEL same as
> VARVEL
VERVELLED > VERVEL
VERVELS > VERVEL
VERVEN same as
> VERVAIN
VERVENS > VERVEN
VERVES > VERVE
VERVET n variety of South African guenon monkey
VERVETS > VERVET
VERY adv more than usually, extremely ▷ adj absolute, exact
VESICA n bladder
VESICAE > VESICA
VESICAL adj of or relating to a vesica, esp the urinary bladder
VESICANT n any substance that causes blisters ▷ adj acting as a vesicant
VESICANTS
> VESICANT
VESICAS > VESICA
VESICATE vb blister
VESICATED
> VESICATE
VESICATES
> VESICATE
VESICLE n sac or small cavity
VESICLES > VESICLE
VESICULA n vesicle
VESICULAE
> VESICULA
VESICULAR > VESICLE
VESPA n type of wasp
VESPAS > VESPA
VESPER n evening prayer, service, or hymn
VESPERAL n liturgical book containing the prayers, psalms, and hymns used at vespers
VESPERALS
> VESPERAL
VESPERS pl n service of evening prayer
VESPIARY n nest or colony of social wasps or hornets
VESPID n insect of the family that includes the common wasp and hornet ▷ adj of or belonging to this family
VESPIDS > VESPID

VESPINE adj of, relating to, or resembling a wasp or wasps
VESPOID adj like a wasp
VESSAIL archaic variant of
> VESSEL
VESSAILS > VESSAIL
VESSEL n container or ship ▷ adj contained in a vessel
VESSELED > VESSEL
VESSELS > VESSEL
VEST n undergarment worn on the top half of the body ▷ vb give (authority) to (someone)
VESTA n short friction match, usually of wood
VESTAL adj pure, chaste ▷ n chaste woman
VESTALLY > VESTAL
VESTALS > VESTAL
VESTAS > VESTA
VESTED adj having an existing right to the immediate or future possession of property
VESTEE n person having a vested interest in something
VESTEES > VESTEE
VESTIARY n room for storing clothes or dressing in, such as a vestry ▷ adj of or relating to clothes
VESTIBULA
> VESTIBULE
VESTIBULE n small entrance hall
VESTIGE n small amount or trace
VESTIGES > VESTIGE
VESTIGIA
> VESTIGIUM
VESTIGIAL adj remaining after a larger or more important thing has gone
VESTIGIUM n trace
VESTMENT same as
> VESTMENT
VESTING > VEST
VESTINGS > VEST
VESTITURE n investiture
VESTLESS > VEST
VESTLIKE > VEST
VESTMENT n garment or robe, esp one denoting office, authority, or rank
VESTMENTS > VESTMENT
VESTRAL > VESTRY
VESTRIES > VESTRY
VESTRY n room in a church used as an office by the priest or minister
VESTRYMAN n member of a church vestry
VESTRYMEN
> VESTRYMAN
VESTS > VEST
VESTURAL > VESTURE
VESTURE n garment or something that seems like a garment ▷ vb clothe
VESTURED > VESTURE
VESTURER n person in charge of church vestments

V

VESTURERS
> VESTURER
VESTURES > VESTURE
VESTURING > VESTURE
VESUVIAN n match for lighting cigars
VESUVIANS
> VESUVIAN
VET vb check the suitability of ▷ n military veteran
VETCH n climbing plant with a beanlike fruit used as fodder
VETCHES > VETCH
VETCHIER > VETCHY
VETCHIEST > VETCHY
VETCHLING n type of climbing plant
VETCHY adj consisting of vetches
VETERAN n person with long experience in a particular activity ▷ adj long-serving
VETERANS > VETERAN
VETIVER n tall hairless grass of tropical and subtropical Asia
VETIVERS > VETIVER
VETIVERT n oil from the vetiver
VETIVERTS
> VETIVERT
VETKOEK n South African cake
VETKOEKS > VETKOEK
VETO n official power to cancel a proposal ▷ vb enforce a veto against
VETOED > VETO
VETOER > VETO
VETOERS > VETO
VETOES > VETO
VETOING > VETO
VETOLESS > VETO
VETS > VET
VETTED > VET
VETTER > VET
VETTERS > VET
VETTING n act of checking the suitability of someone or something
VETTINGS > VETTING
VETTURA n Italian mode of transport
VETTURAS > VETTURA
VETTURINI
> VETTURINO
VETTURINO n person who drives a vettura
VEX vb frustrate, annoy
VEXATION n something annoying
VEXATIONS
> VEXATION
VEXATIOUS adj vexing
VEXATORY > VEX
VEXED adj annoyed and puzzled
VEXEDLY > VEXED
VEXEDNESS > VEXED
VEXER > VEX
VEXERS > VEX
VEXES > VEX
VEXIL same as
> VEXILLUM
VEXILLA > VEXILLUM

VEXILLAR > VEXILLUM
VEXILLARY
> VEXILLUM
VEXILLATE
> VEXILLUM
VEXILLUM n vane of a feather
VEXILS > VEXIL
VEXING > VEX
VEXINGLY > VEX
VEXINGS > VEX
VEXT same as > VEXED
VEZIR same as > VIZIER
VEZIRS > VEZIR
VIA prep by way of ▷ n road
VIABILITY > VIABLE
VIABLE adj able to be put into practice
VIABLY > VIABLE
VIADUCT n bridge over a valley
VIADUCTS > VIADUCT
VIAE > VIA
VIAL n small bottle for liquids ▷ vb put into a vial
VIALED > VIAL
VIALFUL > VIAL
VIALFULS > VIAL
VIALING > VIAL
VIALLED > VIAL
VIALLING > VIAL
VIALS > VIAL
VIAMETER n device to measure distance travelled
VIAMETERS
> VIAMETER
VIAND n type of food, esp a delicacy
VIANDS > VIAND
VIAS > VIA
VIATIC same as
> VIATICAL
VIATICA > VIATICUM
VIATICAL adj of a road or a journey ▷ n purchase of a terminal patient's life assurance policy so that he or she may make use of the proceeds
VIATICALS
> VIATICAL
VIATICUM n Holy Communion given to a person who is dying or in danger of death
VIATICUMS
> VIATICUM
VIATOR n traveller
VIATORES > VIATOR
VIATORIAL adj pertaining to travelling
VIATORS > VIATOR
VIBE n feeling or flavour of the kind specified
VIBES pl n vibrations
VIBEX n mark under the skin
VIBEY adj lively and vibrant
VIBICES > VIBEX
VIBIER > VIBEY
VIBIEST > VIBEY
VIBIST n person who plays a vibraphone in a jazz band or group
VIBISTS > VIBIST

VIBRACULA pl n bristle-like polyps in certain bryozoans
VIBRAHARP n type of percussion instrument
VIBRANCE n vibrancy
VIBRANCES > VIBRANCE
VIBRANCY > VIBRANT
VIBRANT adj vigorous in appearance, energetic ▷ n trilled or rolled speech sound
VIBRANTLY > VIBRANT
VIBRANTS > VIBRANT
VIBRATE vb move back and forth rapidly
VIBRATED > VIBRATE
VIBRATES > VIBRATE
VIBRATING > VIBRATE
VIBRATION n instance of vibrating
VIBRATIVE > VIBRATE
VIBRATO n rapid fluctuation in the pitch of a note
VIBRATOR n device that produces vibratory motion
VIBRATORS
> VIBRATOR
VIBRATORY > VIBRATE
VIBRATOS > VIBRATO
VIBRIO n curved or spiral rodlike bacterium
VIBRIOID > VIBRIO
VIBRION same as
> VIBRIO
VIBRIONIC > VIBRIO
VIBRIONS > VIBRION
VIBRIOS > VIBRIO
VIBRIOSES
> VIBRIOSIS
VIBRIOSIS n bacterial disease
VIBRISSA n any of the bristle-like sensitive hairs on the face of many mammals
VIBRISSAE
> VIBRISSA
VIBRISSAL
> VIBRISSA
VIBRONIC adj of, concerned with, or involving both electronic and vibrational energy levels of a molecule
VIBS pl n type of climbing shoes
VIBURNUM n subtropical shrub with white flowers and berry-like fruits
VIBURNUMS
> VIBURNUM
VICAR n member of the clergy in charge of a parish
VICARAGE n vicar's house
VICARAGES
> VICARAGE
VICARATE same as
> VICARIATE
VICARATES
> VICARATE
VICARESS n rank of nun
VICARIAL adj of or relating to a vicar, vicars, or a vicariate

VICARIANT n any of several closely related species, etc, each of which exists in a separate geographical area
VICARIATE n office, rank, or authority of a vicar
VICARIES > VICARY
VICARIOUS adj felt indirectly by imagining what another person experiences
VICARLIER > VICARLY
VICARLY adj like a vicar
VICARS > VICAR
VICARSHIP same as
> VICARIATE
VICARY n office of a vicar
VICE n immoral or evil habit or action ▷ adj serving in place of ▷ vb grip (something) with or as if with a vice ▷ prep instead of
VICED > VICE
VICEGERAL adj of or relating to a person who deputizes for another
VICELESS > VICE
VICELIKE > VICE
VICENARY adj relating to or consisting of 20
VICENNIAL adj occurring every 20 years
VICEREGAL adj of a viceroy
VICEREINE n wife of a viceroy
VICEROY n governor of a colony who represented the monarch
VICEROYS > VICEROY
VICES > VICE
VICESIMAL same as
> VIGESIMAL
VICHIES > VICHY
VICHY n French mineral water
VICIATE same as
> VITIATE
VICIATED > VICIATE
VICIATES > VICIATE
VICIATING > VICIATE
VICINAGE n residents of a particular neighbourhood
VICINAGES
> VICINAGE
VICINAL adj neighbouring
VICING > VICE
VICINITY n surrounding area
VICIOSITY same as
> VITIOSITY
VICIOUS adj cruel and violent
VICIOUSLY > VICIOUS
VICOMTE n French nobleman
VICOMTES > VICOMTE
VICTIM n person or thing harmed or killed
VICTIMISE same as
> VICTIMIZE
VICTIMIZE vb punish unfairly

VICTIMS > VICTIM
VICTOR *n* person who has defeated an opponent, esp in war or in sport
VICTORESS *same as* **>** VICTRESS
VICTORIA *n* large sweet plum, red and yellow in colour
VICTORIAS > VICTORIA
VICTORIES > VICTORY
VICTORINE *n* woman's article of clothing
VICTORS > VICTOR
VICTORY *n* winning of a battle or contest
VICTRESS *n* female victor
VICTRIX *same as* **>** VICTRESS
VICTRIXES > VICTRIX
VICTROLA *n* gramophone
VICTROLAS > VICTROLA
VICTUAL *vb* supply with or obtain victuals
VICTUALED > VICTUAL
VICTUALER > VICTUAL
VICTUALS *pl n* food and drink
VICUGNA *same as* **>** VICUNA
VICUGNAS > VICUGNA
VICUNA *n* S American animal like the llama
VICUNAS > VICUNA
VID *same as* **>** VIDEO
VIDALIA *n* type of sweet onion
VIDALIAS > VIDALIA
VIDAME *n* French nobleman
VIDAMES > VIDAME
VIDE *interj* look
VIDELICET *adv* namely: used to specify items
VIDENDA > VIDENDUM
VIDENDUM *n* that which is to be seen
VIDEO *vb* record (a TV programme or event) on video ▷ *adj* relating to or used in producing television images ▷ *n* recording and showing of films and events
VIDEOCAM *n* camera for recording video footage
VIDEOCAMS > VIDEOCAM
VIDEODISC *variant of* **>** VIDEODISK
VIDEODISK *n* (formerly) disk on which information is stored in digital form
VIDEOED > VIDEO
VIDEOFIT *n* computer-generated picture of a person sought by the police
VIDEOFITS > VIDEOFIT
VIDEOGRAM *n* audiovisual recording
VIDEOING > VIDEO
VIDEOLAND *n* world of television and televised images

VIDEOS > VIDEO
VIDEOTAPE *vb* (formerly) record (a TV programme) on video tape
VIDEOTEX *n* information system that displays data from a distant computer on a screen
VIDEOTEXT *n* means of representing on a TV screen information that is held in a computer
VIDETTE *same as* **>** VEDETTE
VIDETTES > VIDETTE
VIDICON *n* small television camera tube used in closed-circuit television
VIDICONS > VIDICON
VIDIMUS *n* inspection
VIDIMUSES > VIDIMUS
VIDIOT *n* person who watches a lot of low-quality television
VIDIOTS > VIDIOT
VIDS > VID
VIDSCREEN *n* video screen
VIDUAGE *n* widows collectively
VIDUAGES > VIDUAGE
VIDUAL *adj* widowed
VIDUITIES > VIDUITY
VIDUITY *n* widowhood
VIDUOUS *adj* empty
VIE *vb* compete (with someone)
VIED > VIE
VIELLE *n* stringed musical instrument
VIELLES > VIELLE
VIENNA *n* as in *vienna loaf*, *vienna steak* associated with Vienna
VIER > VIE
VIERS > VIE
VIES > VIE
VIEW *n* opinion or belief ▷ *vb* think of (something) in a particular way
VIEWABLE > VIEW
VIEWBOOK *n* promotional booklet for a college or university
VIEWBOOKS **>** VIEWBOOK
VIEWDATA *n* interactive form of videotext
VIEWDATAS **>** VIEWDATA
VIEWED > VIEW
VIEWER *n* person who watches television
VIEWERS > VIEWER
VIEWIER > VIEWY
VIEWIEST > VIEWY
VIEWINESS > VIEWY
VIEWING *n* act of watching television
VIEWINGS > VIEWING
VIEWLESS *adj* (of windows, etc) not affording a view
VIEWLY *adj* pleasant on the eye
VIEWPHONE *n* videophone

VIEWPOINT *n* person's attitude towards something
VIEWPORT *n* viewable area on a computer display
VIEWPORTS **>** VIEWPORT
VIEWS > VIEW
VIEWSHED *n* natural environment visible from a specific point
VIEWSHEDS **>** VIEWSHED
VIEWY *adj* having fanciful opinions or ideas
VIFDA *same as* **>** VIVDA
VIFDAS > VIFDA
VIFF *vb* (of an aircraft) change direction abruptly
VIFFED > VIFF
VIFFING > VIFF
VIFFS > VIFF
VIG *n* interest on a loan that is paid to a moneylender
VIGA *n* rafter
VIGAS > VIGA
VIGESIMAL *adj* relating to or based on the number 20
VIGIA *n* navigational hazard whose existence has not been confirmed
VIGIAS > VIGIA
VIGIL *n* night-time period of staying awake to look after a sick person, pray, etc
VIGILANCE *n* careful attention
VIGILANT *adj* watchful in case of danger
VIGILANTE *n* person who takes it upon himself or herself to enforce the law
VIGILS > VIGIL
VIGNERON *n* person who grows grapes for winemaking
VIGNERONS **>** VIGNERON
VIGNETTE *n* small illustration placed at the beginning or end of a chapter or book ▷ *vb* portray in a vignette
VIGNETTED **>** VIGNETTE
VIGNETTER *n* device used in printing vignettes
VIGNETTES **>** VIGNETTE
VIGOR *same as* **>** VIGOUR
VIGORISH *n* type of commission
VIGORO *n* women's game similar to cricket
VIGOROS > VIGORO
VIGOROSO *adv* in music, emphatically
VIGOROUS *adj* having physical or mental energy
VIGORS > VIGOR
VIGOUR *n* physical or mental energy
VIGOURS > VIGOUR
VIGS > VIG

VIHARA *n* type of Buddhist temple
VIHARAS > VIHARA
VIHUELA *n* obsolete plucked stringed instrument of Spain
VIHUELAS > VIHUELA
VIKING *n* Dane, Norwegian, or Swede who raided by sea between the 8th and 11th centuries
VIKINGISM > VIKING
VIKINGS > VIKING
VILAYET *n* major administrative division of Turkey
VILAYETS > VILAYET
VILD *same as* **>** VILE
VILDE *same as* **>** VILE
VILDLY > VILD
VILDNESS > VILD
VILE *adj* very wicked
VILELY > VILE
VILENESS > VILE
VILER > VILE
VILEST > VILE
VILIACO *n* coward
VILIACOES > VILIACO
VILIACOS > VILIACO
VILIAGO *same as* **>** VILIACO
VILIAGOES > VILIAGO
VILIAGOS > VILIAGO
VILIFIED > VILIFY
VILIFIER > VILIFY
VILIFIERS > VILIFY
VILIFIES > VILIFY
VILIFY *vb* attack the character of
VILIFYING > VILIFY
VILIPEND *vb* treat or regard with contempt
VILIPENDS **>** VILIPEND
VILL *n* township
VILLA *n* large house with gardens
VILLADOM > VILLA
VILLADOMS > VILLA
VILLAE > VILLA
VILLAGE *n* small group of houses in a country area
VILLAGER *n* inhabitant of a village
VILLAGERS **>** VILLAGER
VILLAGERY *n* villages
VILLAGES > VILLAGE
VILLAGEY *adj* of or like a village
VILLAGIER **>** VILLAGEY
VILLAGIO *same as* **>** VILIACO
VILLAGIOS **>** VILLAGIO
VILLAGREE *variant of* **>** VILLAGERY
VILLAIN *n* wicked person
VILLAINS > VILLAIN
VILLAINY *n* evil or vicious behaviour
VILLAN *same as* **>** VILLEIN
VILLANAGE > VILLAN
VILLANIES > VILLANY

V

VILLANOUS > VILLAIN
VILLANS > VILLAN
VILLANY same as > VILLAINY
VILLAR > VILL
VILLAS > VILLA
VILLATIC adj of or relating to a villa, village, or farm
VILLEIN n peasant bound in service to their lord
VILLEINS > VILLEIN
VILLENAGE n villein's status
VILLI > VILLUS
VILLIACO n coward
VILLIACOS > VILLIACO
VILLIAGO same as > VILIACO
VILLIAGOS > VILLIAGO
VILLIFORM adj having the form of a villus or a series of villi
VILLOSE same as > VILLOUS
VILLOSITY n state of being villous
VILLOUS adj (of plant parts) covered with long hairs
VILLOUSLY > VILLOUS
VILLS > VILL
VILLUS n one of the finger-like projections in the small intestine of many vertebrates
VIM n force, energy
VIMANA n Indian mythological chariot of the gods
VIMANAS > VIMANA
VIMEN n long flexible shoot that occurs in certain plants
VIMINA > VIMEN
VIMINAL > VIMEN
VIMINEOUS adj having, producing, or resembling long flexible shoots
VIMS > VIM
VIN n French wine
VINA n stringed musical instrument related to the sitar
VINACEOUS adj of, relating to, or containing wine
VINAL n type of manmade fibre
VINALS > VINAL
VINAS > VINA
VINASSE n residue left in a still after distilling spirits, esp brandy
VINASSES > VINASSE
VINCA n type of trailing plant with blue flowers
VINCAS > VINCA
VINCIBLE adj capable of being defeated or overcome
VINCIBLY > VINCIBLE
VINCULA > VINCULUM
VINCULAR adj of or like a vinculum

VINCULUM n horizontal line drawn above a group of mathematical terms
VINCULUMS > VINCULUM
VINDALOO n type of very hot Indian curry
VINDALOOS > VINDALOO
VINDEMIAL adj relating to a grape harvest
VINDICATE vb clear (someone) of guilt
VINE n climbing plant, esp one producing grapes ▷ vb form like a vine
VINEAL adj relating to wines
VINED > VINE
VINEGAR n acid liquid made from wine, beer, or cider ▷ vb apply vinegar to
VINEGARED > VINEGAR
VINEGARS > VINEGAR
VINEGARY adj containing vinegar
VINELESS > VINE
VINELIKE > VINE
VINER n vinedresser
VINERIES > VINERY
VINERS > VINER
VINERY n hothouse for growing grapes
VINES > VINE
VINEW vb become mouldy
VINEWED > VINEW
VINEWING > VINEW
VINEWS > VINEW
VINEYARD n plantation of grape vines
VINEYARDS > VINEYARD
VINIC adj of, relating to, or contained in wine
VINIER > VINE
VINIEST > VINE
VINIFERA n species of vine
VINIFERAS > VINIFERA
VINIFIED > VINIFY
VINIFIES > VINIFY
VINIFY vb convert into wine
VINIFYING > VINIFY
VINING > VINE
VINO n wine
VINOLENT adj drunken
VINOLOGY n scientific study of vines
VINOS > VINO
VINOSITY n distinctive and essential quality and flavour of wine
VINOUS adj of or characteristic of wine
VINOUSLY > VINOUS
VINS > VIN
VINT vb sell (wine)
VINTAGE n wine from a particular harvest of grapes ▷ adj best and most typical ▷ vb gather (grapes) or make (wine)
VINTAGED > VINTAGE
VINTAGER n grape harvester

VINTAGERS > VINTAGER
VINTAGES > VINTAGE
VINTAGING > VINTAGE
VINTED > VINT
VINTING > VINT
VINTNER n dealer in wine
VINTNERS > VINTNER
VINTRIES > VINTRY
VINTRY n place where wine is sold
VINTS > VINT
VINY > VINE
VINYL n type of plastic, used in mock leather and records ▷ adj of or containing a particular group of atoms
VINYLIC > VINYL
VINYLS > VINYL
VIOL n early stringed instrument preceding the violin
VIOLA n stringed instrument lower in pitch than a violin
VIOLABLE > VIOLATE
VIOLABLY > VIOLATE
VIOLAS > VIOLA
VIOLATE vb break (a law or agreement) ▷ adj violated or dishonoured
VIOLATED > VIOLATE
VIOLATER > VIOLATE
VIOLATERS > VIOLATE
VIOLATES > VIOLATE
VIOLATING > VIOLATE
VIOLATION > VIOLATE
VIOLATIVE > VIOLATE
VIOLATOR > VIOLATE
VIOLATORS > VIOLATE
VIOLD archaic or poetic past form of > VIAL
VIOLENCE n use of physical force, usu intended to cause injury or destruction
VIOLENCES > VIOLENCE
VIOLENT adj using physical force with the intention of causing injury ▷ vb coerce
VIOLENTED > VIOLENT
VIOLENTLY > VIOLENT
VIOLENTS > VIOLENT
VIOLER n person who plays the viol
VIOLERS > VIOLER
VIOLET n plant with bluish-purple flowers ▷ adj bluish-purple
VIOLETS > VIOLET
VIOLIN n small four-stringed musical instrument played with a bow
VIOLINIST n person who plays the violin
VIOLINS > VIOLIN
VIOLIST n person who plays the viola
VIOLISTS > VIOLIST
VIOLONE n double-bass member of the viol family
VIOLONES > VIOLONE
VIOLS > VIOL

VIOMYCIN n type of antibiotic
VIOMYCINS > VIOMYCIN
VIOSTEROL n type of vitamin
VIPASSANA n type of meditative practice in Buddhism
VIPER n poisonous snake
VIPERFISH n predatory deep-sea fish
VIPERINE same as > VIPEROUS
VIPERISH same as > VIPEROUS
VIPERLIKE adj like a viper
VIPEROUS adj of, relating to, or resembling a viper
VIPERS > VIPER
VIRAEMIA n condition in which virus particles circulate and reproduce in the bloodstream
VIRAEMIAS > VIRAEMIA
VIRAEMIC > VIRAEMIA
VIRAGO n aggressive woman
VIRAGOES > VIRAGO
VIRAGOISH > VIRAGO
VIRAGOS > VIRAGO
VIRAL adj of or caused by a virus ▷ n video, image, etc that spreads quickly on the internet
VIRALITY n the state of being viral
VIRALLY > VIRAL
VIRALS > VIRAL
VIRANDA same as > VERANDA
VIRANDAS > VIRANDA
VIRANDO same as > VERANDA
VIRANDOS > VIRANDO
VIRE vb turn
VIRED > VIRE
VIRELAI same as > VIRELAY
VIRELAIS > VIRELAI
VIRELAY n old French verse form
VIRELAYS > VIRELAY
VIREMENT n administrative transfer of funds from one part of a budget to another
VIREMENTS > VIREMENT
VIREMIA same as > VIRAEMIA
VIREMIAS > VIREMIA
VIREMIC > VIREMIA
VIRENT adj green
VIREO n American songbird
VIREONINE > VIREO
VIREOS > VIREO
VIRES > VIRE
VIRESCENT adj greenish or becoming green
VIRETOT n as in on the viretot in a rush
VIRETOTS > VIRETOT
VIRGA n wisps of rain or snow that evaporate before reaching the earth

VIRGAE > VIRGA
VIRGAS > VIRGA
VIRGATE adj long, straight, and thin ▷ n obsolete measure of land area
VIRGATES > VIRGATE
VIRGE n rod
VIRGER n rod-bearer
VIRGERS > VIRGER
VIRGES > VIRGE
VIRGIN n person who has not had sexual intercourse ▷ adj chaste ▷ vb behave like a virgin
VIRGINAL adj like a virgin ▷ n early keyboard instrument like a small harpsichord
VIRGINALS > VIRGINAL
VIRGINED > VIRGIN
VIRGINIA n type of flue-cured tobacco grown originally in Virginia
VIRGINIAS > VIRGINIA
VIRGINING > VIRGIN
VIRGINITY n condition or fact of being a virgin
VIRGINIUM former name for > FRANCIUM
VIRGINLY > VIRGIN
VIRGINS > VIRGIN
VIRGULATE adj rod-shaped or rodlike
VIRGULE another name for > SLASH
VIRGULES > VIRGULE
VIRICIDAL > VIRICIDE
VIRICIDE n substance that destroys viruses
VIRICIDES > VIRICIDE
VIRID adj verdant
VIRIDIAN n green pigment consisting of a hydrated form of chromic oxide
VIRIDIANS > VIRIDIAN
VIRIDITE n greenish mineral
VIRIDITES > VIRIDITE
VIRIDITY n quality or state of being green
VIRILE adj having traditional male characteristics
VIRILELY > VIRILE
VIRILISE same as > VIRILIZE
VIRILISED > VIRILISE
VIRILISES > VIRILISE
VIRILISM n development in a woman of male secondary sex characteristics
VIRILISMS > VIRILISM
VIRILITY > VIRILE
VIRILIZE vb cause male characteristics to appear in a female

VIRILIZED > VIRILIZE
VIRILIZES > VIRILIZE
VIRILOCAL adj living in or near a husband's home or community after marriage
VIRING > VIRE
VIRINO n entity postulated to be the causative agent of BSE
VIRINOS > VIRINO
VIRION n virus in infective form, consisting of an RNA particle within a protein covering
VIRIONS > VIRION
VIRL same as > FERRULE
VIRLS > VIRL
VIROGENE n type of viral gene
VIROGENES > VIROGENE
VIROID n any of various infective RNA particles
VIROIDS > VIROID
VIROLOGIC > VIROLOGY
VIROLOGY n study of viruses
VIROSE adj poisonous
VIROSES > VIROSIS
VIROSIS n viral disease
VIROUS same as > VIROSE
VIRTU n taste or love for curios or works of fine art
VIRTUAL adj having the effect but not the form of
VIRTUALLY adv practically, almost
VIRTUE n moral goodness
VIRTUES > VIRTUE
VIRTUOSA n female virtuoso
VIRTUOSAS > VIRTUOSA
VIRTUOSE > VIRTUOSA
VIRTUOSI > VIRTUOSO
VIRTUOSIC > VIRTUOSO
VIRTUOSO n person with impressive esp musical skill ▷ adj showing exceptional skill or brilliance
VIRTUOSOS > VIRTUOSO
VIRTUOUS adj morally good
VIRTUS > VIRTU
VIRUCIDAL > VIRUCIDE
VIRUCIDE same as > VIRICIDE
VIRUCIDES > VIRUCIDE
VIRULENCE n quality of being virulent
VIRULENCY same as > VIRULENCE
VIRULENT adj extremely bitter or hostile
VIRUS n microorganism that causes disease in humans, animals, and plants

VIRUSES > VIRUS
VIRUSLIKE > VIRUS
VIRUSOID n small plant virus
VIRUSOIDS > VIRUSOID
VIS n power, force, or strength
VISA n permission to enter a country, shown by a stamp on the passport ▷ vb enter a visa into (a passport)
VISAED > VISA
VISAGE n face
VISAGED > VISAGE
VISAGES > VISAGE
VISAGIST same as > VISAGISTE
VISAGISTE n person who designs and applies face make-up
VISAGISTS > VISAGIST
VISAING > VISA
VISARD same as > VIZARD
VISARDS > VISARD
VISAS > VISA
VISCACHA n South American rodent
VISCACHAS > VISCACHA
VISCARIA n type of perennial plant
VISCARIAS > VISCARIA
VISCERA pl n large abdominal organs
VISCERAL adj instinctive
VISCERATE vb disembowel
VISCID adj sticky
VISCIDITY > VISCID
VISCIDLY > VISCID
VISCIN n sticky substance found on plants
VISCINS > VISCIN
VISCOID adj (of a fluid) somewhat viscous
VISCOIDAL same as > VISCOID
VISCOSE same as > VISCOUS
VISCOSES > VISCOSE
VISCOSITY n state of being viscous
VISCOUNT n British nobleman ranking between an earl and a baron
VISCOUNTS > VISCOUNT
VISCOUNTY > VISCOUNT
VISCOUS adj thick and sticky
VISCOUSLY > VISCOUS
VISCUM n shrub genus
VISCUMS > VISCUM
VISCUS n internal organ
VISE n (in US English) vice ▷ vb (in US English) hold in a vice ▷ vb award a visa to
VISED > VISE
VISEED > VISE
VISEING > VISE
VISELIKE > VICE

VISES > VISE
VISHING n telephone scam used to gain access to credit card numbers or bank details
VISHINGS > VISHING
VISIBLE adj able to be seen ▷ n visible item of trade
VISIBLES > VISIBLE
VISIBLY > VISIBLE
VISIE same as > VIZY
VISIED > VISIE
VISIEING > VISIE
VISIER > VISIE
VISIERS > VISIE
VISIES > VISIE
VISILE n person best stimulated by vision
VISILES > VISILE
VISING > VISE
VISION n ability to see ▷ vb see or show in or as if in a vision
VISIONAL adj of, relating to, or seen in a vision, apparition, etc
VISIONARY adj showing foresight ▷ n visionary person
VISIONED > VISION
VISIONER n visionary
VISIONERS > VISIONER
VISIONING > VISION
VISIONIST n type of visionary
VISIONS > VISION
VISIT vb go or come to see ▷ n instance of visiting
VISITABLE > VISIT
VISITANT n ghost or apparition ▷ adj paying a visit
VISITANTS > VISITANT
VISITATOR n official visitor
VISITE n type of cape
VISITED > VISIT
VISITEE n person who is visited
VISITEES > VISITEE
VISITER variant of > VISITOR
VISITERS > VISITER
VISITES > VISITE
VISITING > VISIT
VISITINGS > VISIT
VISITOR n person who visits a person or place
VISITORS > VISITOR
VISITRESS n female visitor
VISITS > VISIT
VISIVE adj visual
VISNE n neighbourhood
VISNES > VISNE
VISNOMIE same as > VISNOMY
VISNOMIES > VISNOMY
VISNOMY n method of judging character from facial features
VISON n type of mink
VISONS > VISON
VISOR n transparent part of a helmet that pulls

down over the face ▷ *vb* cover, provide, or protect with a visor

VISORED > VISOR

VISORING > VISOR

VISORLESS > VISOR

VISORS > VISOR

VISTA *n* (beautiful) extensive view ▷ *vb* make into vistas

VISTAED > VISTA

VISTAING > VISTA

VISTAL > VISTA

VISTALESS > VISTA

VISTAS > VISTA

VISTO *same as* > VISTA

VISTOS > VISTO

VISUAL *adj* done by or used in seeing ▷ *n* sketch to show the proposed layout of an advertisement

VISUALISE *same as* > VISUALIZE

VISUALIST *n* visualiser

VISUALITY > VISUAL

VISUALIZE *vb* form a mental image of

VISUALLY > VISUAL

VISUALS > VISUAL

VITA *n* curriculum vitae

VITACEOUS *adj* of a family of flowering plants that includes the grapevine

VITAE > VITA

VITAL *adj* essential or highly important

VITALISE *same as* > VITALIZE

VITALISED > VITALISE

VITALISER > VITALISE

VITALISES > VITALISE

VITALISM *n* philosophical doctrine that the phenomena of life cannot be explained in purely mechanical terms

VITALISMS > VITALISM

VITALIST > VITALISM

VITALISTS > VITALISM

VITALITY *n* physical or mental energy

VITALIZE *vb* fill with life or vitality

VITALIZED > VITALIZE

VITALIZER > VITALIZE

VITALIZES > VITALIZE

VITALLY > VITAL

VITALNESS > VITAL

VITALS *pl n* bodily organs that are necessary to maintain life

VITAMER *n* type of chemical

VITAMERS > VITAMER

VITAMIN *n* one of a group of substances that are essential in the diet

VITAMINE *same as* > VITAMIN

VITAMINES > VITAMINE

VITAMINIC > VITAMIN

VITAMINS > VITAMIN

VITAS > VITA

VITASCOPE *n* early type of film projector

VITATIVE *adj* fond of life

VITE *adv* musical direction

VITELLARY *n* location within an egg where the yolk is formed

VITELLI > VITELLUS

VITELLIN *n* phosphoprotein that is the major protein in egg yolk

VITELLINE *adj* of or relating to the yolk of an egg

VITELLINS > VITELLIN

VITELLUS *n* yolk of an egg

VITESSE *n* speed

VITESSES > VITESSE

VITEX *n* type of herb

VITEXES > VITEX

VITIABLE > VITIATE

VITIATE *vb* spoil the effectiveness of

VITIATED > VITIATE

VITIATES > VITIATE

VITIATING > VITIATE

VITIATION > VITIATE

VITIATOR > VITIATE

VITIATORS > VITIATE

VITICETA > VITICETUM

VITICETUM *n* place where vines are cultivated

VITICIDE *n* vine killer

VITICIDES > VITICIDE

VITILIGO *n* area of skin that is white from albinism or loss of melanin pigmentation

VITILIGOS > VITILIGO

VITIOSITY *n* viciousness

VITIOUS *adj* mistaken

VITRAGE *n* light fabric

VITRAGES > VITRAGE

VITRAIL *n* stained glass

VITRAIN *n* type of coal

VITRAINS > VITRAIN

VITRAUX > VITRAIL

VITREOUS *adj* like or made from glass

VITREUM *n* vitreous body

VITREUMS > VITREUM

VITRIC *adj* of, relating to, resembling, or having the nature of glass

VITRICS *pl n* glass products

VITRIFIED > VITRIFY

VITRIFIES > VITRIFY

VITRIFORM *adj* having the form or appearance of glass

VITRIFY *vb* change or be changed into glass or a glassy substance

VITRINE *n* glass display case or cabinet for works of art, curios, etc

VITRINES > VITRINE

VITRIOL *n* language expressing bitterness and hatred ▷ *vb* injure with or as if with vitriol (sulphuric acid)

VITRIOLED > VITRIOL

VITRIOLIC *adj* (of language) severely bitter or harsh

VITRIOLS > VITRIOL

VITRO *n* as in *in vitro* (of processes) made to occur in an artificial environment

VITTA *n* tubelike cavity containing oil that occurs in the fruits of certain plants

VITTAE > VITTA

VITTATE > VITTA

VITTLE *obsolete or dialect spelling of* > VICTUAL

VITTLED > VITTLE

VITTLES *obsolete or dialect spelling of* > VICTUALS

VITTLING > VITTLE

VITULAR *same as* > VITULINE

VITULINE *adj* of or resembling a calf or veal

VIVA *interj* long live (a person or thing) ▷ *n* examination in the form of an interview ▷ *vb* examine (a candidate) in a spoken interview

VIVACE *adv* in a lively manner ▷ *n* piece of music to be performed in this way

VIVACES > VIVACE

VIVACIOUS *adj* full of energy and enthusiasm

VIVACITY *n* quality of being vivacious

VIVAED > VIVA

VIVAING > VIVA

VIVAMENTE *adv* in a lively manner

VIVANDIER *n* sutler

VIVARIA > VIVARIUM

VIVARIES > VIVARY

VIVARIUM *n* place where animals are kept in natural conditions

VIVARIUMS > VIVARIUM

VIVARY *same as* > VIVARIUM

VIVAS > VIVA

VIVAT *interj* long live ▷ *n* expression of acclamation

VIVATS > VIVAT

VIVDA *n* method of drying meat

VIVDAS > VIVDA

VIVE *interj* long live

VIVELY *adv* in a lively manner

VIVENCIES > VIVENCY

VIVENCY *n* physical or mental energy

VIVER *n* fish pond

VIVERRA *n* civet genus

VIVERRAS > VIVERRA

VIVERRID > VIVERRINE

VIVERRIDS > VIVERRINE

VIVERRINE *n* type of mammal of Eurasia and Africa ▷ *adj* of this family of mammals

VIVERS > VIVER

VIVES *n* disease found in horses

VIVIANITE *n* type of mineral

VIVID *adj* very bright

VIVIDER > VIVID

VIVIDEST > VIVID

VIVIDITY > VIVID

VIVIDLY > VIVID

VIVIDNESS > VIVID

VIVIFIC *adj* giving life

VIVIFIED > VIVIFY

VIVIFIER > VIVIFY

VIVIFIERS > VIVIFY

VIVIFIES > VIVIFY

VIVIFY *vb* animate, inspire

VIVIFYING > VIVIFY

VIVIPARA *pl n* animals that produce offspring that develop as embryos within the female parent

VIVIPARY *n* act of giving birth producing offspring that have developed as embryos

VIVISECT *vb* practise vivisection

VIVISECTS > VIVISECT

VIVO *adv* with life and vigour

VIVRES *pl n* provisions

VIXEN *n* female fox

VIXENISH > VIXEN

VIXENLY > VIXEN

VIXENS > VIXEN

VIZAMENT *n* consultation

VIZAMENTS > VIZAMENT

VIZARD *n* means of disguise ▷ *vb* conceal by means of a disguise

VIZARDED > VIZARD

VIZARDING > VIZARD

VIZARDS > VIZARD

VIZCACHA *same as* > VISCACHA

VIZCACHAS > VIZCACHA

VIZIED > VIZY

VIZIER *n* high official in certain Muslim countries

VIZIERATE *n* position, rank, or authority of a vizier

VIZIERIAL > VIZIER

VIZIERS > VIZIER

VIZIES > VIZY

VIZIR *same as* > VIZIER

VIZIRATE > VIZIR

VIZIRATES > VIZIR

VIZIRIAL > VIZIR

VIZIRS > VIZIR

VIZIRSHIP > VIZIR

VIZOR *same as* > VISOR

VIZORED > VIZOR

VIZORING > VIZOR

VIZORLESS > VIZOR

VIZORS > VIZOR

VIZSLA *n* breed of Hungarian hunting dog

VIZSLAS > VIZSLA

VIZY *vb* look

VIZYING > VIZY

VIZZIE *same as >* VIZY

VIZZIED > VIZZIE

VIZZIEING > VIZZIE

VIZZIES > VIZZIE

VLEI *n* area of low marshy ground

VLEIS > VLEI

VLIES > VLY

VLOG *n* video blog ▷ *vb* make and upload a vlog

VLOGGED > VLOG

VLOGGER *n* person who keeps a video blog

VLOGGERS > VLOGGER

VLOGGING *n* action of keeping a video blog

VLOGGINGS
> VLOGGING

VLOGS > VLOG

VLY *same as >* VLEI

VOAR *n* spring

VOARS > VOAR

VOCAB *n* vocabulary

VOCABLE *n* word regarded as a sequence of letters or sounds ▷ *adj* capable of being uttered

VOCABLES > VOCABLE

VOCABLY > VOCABLE

VOCABS > VOCAB

VOCABULAR > VOCABLE

VOCAL *adj* relating to the voice ▷ *n* piece of jazz or pop music that is sung

VOCALESE *n* style of jazz singing

VOCALESES
> VOCALESE

VOCALIC *adj* of, relating to, or containing a vowel or vowels

VOCALICS *n* non-verbal aspects of voice

VOCALION *n* type of musical instrument

VOCALIONS
> VOCALION

VOCALISE *same as*
> VOCALIZE

VOCALISED
> VOCALISE

VOCALISER
> VOCALISE

VOCALISES
> VOCALISE

VOCALISM *n* exercise of the voice, as in singing or speaking

VOCALISMS
> VOCALISM

VOCALIST *n* singer

VOCALISTS
> VOCALIST

VOCALITY > VOCAL

VOCALIZE *vb* express with the voice

VOCALIZED
> VOCALIZE

VOCALIZER > VOCALIZE

VOCALIZES
> VOCALIZE

VOCALLY > VOCAL

VOCALNESS > VOCAL

VOCALS > VOCAL

VOCATION *n* profession or trade

VOCATIONS
> VOCATION

VOCATIVE *n* (in some languages) case of nouns used when addressing a person ▷ *adj* relating to, used in, or characterized by calling

VOCATIVES
> VOCATIVE

VOCES > VOX

VOCODER *n* type of synthesizer that uses the human voice as an oscillator

VOCODERED *adj* synthesized by a vocoder

VOCODERS > VOCODER

VOCULAR > VOCULE

VOCULE *n* faint noise made when articulating certain sounds

VOCULES > VOCULE

VODCAST *vb* podcast with video

VODCASTED > VODCAST

VODCASTER > VODCAST

VODCASTS > VODCAST

VODDIES > VODDY

VODDY *n* informal word for vodka

VODKA *n* (Russian) spirit distilled from potatoes or grain

VODKAS > VODKA

VODOU *variant of*
> VOODOO

VODOUN *same as >* VODUN

VODOUNS > VODOUN

VODOUS > VODOU

VODUN *n* voodoo

VODUNS > VODUN

VOE *n* (in Orkney and Shetland) a small bay or narrow creek

VOEMA *n* vigour or energy

VOEMAS > VOEMA

VOERTSAK *variant of*
> VOETSEK

VOERTSEK *variant of*
> VOETSEK

VOES > VOE

VOETSAK *same as*
> VOETSEK

VOETSEK *interj* S African offensive expression of rejection

VOG *n* air pollution caused by volcanic dust

VOGIE *adj* conceited

VOGIER > VOGIE

VOGIEST > VOGIE

VOGS > VOG

VOGUE *n* popular style ▷ *adj* popular or fashionable ▷ *vb* bring into vogue

VOGUED > VOGUE

VOGUEING *n* dance style of the late 1980s

VOGUEINGS > VOGUEING

VOGUER > VOGUE

VOGUERS > VOGUE

VOGUES > VOGUE

VOGUEY > VOGUE

VOGUIER > VOGUE

VOGUIEST > VOGUE

VOGUING *same as*
> VOGUEING

VOGUINGS > VOGUING

VOGUISH > VOGUE

VOGUISHLY > VOGUE

VOICE *n* (quality of) sound made when speaking or singing ▷ *vb* express verbally

VOICED *adj* articulated with accompanying vibration of the vocal cords

VOICEFUL > VOICE

VOICELESS *adj* without a voice

VOICEMAIL *n* facility of leaving recorded message by telephone

VOICEOVER *n* spoken commentary by unseen narrator on film

VOICER > VOICE

VOICERS > VOICE

VOICES > VOICE

VOICING > VOICE

VOICINGS > VOICE

VOID *adj* not legally binding ▷ *n* feeling of deprivation ▷ *vb* make invalid

VOIDABLE *adj* capable of being voided

VOIDANCE *n* annulment, as of a contract

VOIDANCES
> VOIDANCE

VOIDED *adj* (of a design) with a hole in the centre of the same shape as the design

VOIDEE *n* light meal eaten before bed

VOIDEES > VOIDEE

VOIDER > VOID

VOIDERS > VOID

VOIDING > VOID

VOIDINGS > VOID

VOIDNESS > VOID

VOIDS > VOID

VOILA *interj* word used to express satisfaction

VOILE *n* light semitransparent fabric

VOILES > VOILE

VOIP *n* voice over internet protocol

VOIPS > VOIP

VOISINAGE *n* district or neighbourhood

VOITURE *n* type of vehicle

VOITURES > VOITURE

VOITURIER *n* driver of a voiture

VOIVODE *n* Slavic governor

VOIVODES > VOIVODE

VOL *n* heraldic wings

VOLA *n* palm of hand or sole of foot

VOLABLE *adj* quick-witted

VOLAE > VOLA

VOLAGE *adj* changeable

VOLANT *adj* in a flying position

VOLANTE *n* Spanish horse carriage

VOLANTES > VOLANTE

VOLAR *adj* of or relating to the palm of the hand or the sole of the foot

VOLARIES > VOLARY

VOLARY *n* large bird enclosure

VOLATIC *adj* flying ▷ *n* creature with wings

VOLATICS > VOLATIC

VOLATILE *adj* liable to sudden change, esp in behaviour ▷ *n* volatile substance

VOLATILES
> VOLATILE

VOLCANIAN *same as*
> VOLCANIC

VOLCANIC *adj* of or relating to volcanoes

VOLCANICS *pl n* types of rock formed from magma from volcanoes

VOLCANISE *same as*
> VOLCANIZE

VOLCANISM *n* processes that result in the formation of volcanoes

VOLCANIST *n* person who studies volcanoes

VOLCANIZE *vb* subject to the effects of or change by volcanic heat

VOLCANO *n* mountain with a vent through which lava is ejected

VOLCANOES > VOLCANO

VOLCANOS > VOLCANO

VOLE *n* small rodent ▷ *vb* win by taking all the tricks in a deal

VOLED > VOLE

VOLELIKE *adj* like a vole

VOLENS *adj* as in *nolens volens* whether willing or unwilling

VOLERIES > VOLERY

VOLERY *same as*
> VOLARY

VOLES > VOLE

VOLET *n* type of veil

VOLETS > VOLET

VOLING > VOLE

VOLITANT *adj* flying or moving about rapidly

VOLITATE *vb* flutter

VOLITATED
> VOLITATE

VOLITATES
> VOLITATE

VOLITIENT
> VOLITION

VOLITION *n* ability to decide things for oneself

VOLITIONS
> VOLITION

VOLITIVE *adj* of, relating to, or emanating from the will ▷ *n* (in some languages) a verb form or mood used to express a wish or desire

VOLITIVES
> VOLITIVE

VOLK n people or nation, esp the nation of Afrikaners

VOLKS > VOLK

VOLKSLIED n German folk song

VOLKSRAAD n Boer assembly in South Africa in the 19th century

VOLLEY n simultaneous discharge of ammunition ▷ vb discharge (ammunition) in a volley

VOLLEYED > VOLLEY

VOLLEYER > VOLLEY

VOLLEYERS > VOLLEY

VOLLEYING > VOLLEY

VOLLEYS > VOLLEY

VOLOST n (in the former Soviet Union) a rural soviet

VOLOSTS > VOLOST

VOLPINO n Italian breed of dog

VOLPINOS > VOLPINO

VOLPLANE vb glide in an aeroplane

VOLPLANED
> VOLPLANE

VOLPLANES
> VOLPLANE

VOLS > VOL

VOLT n unit of electric potential ▷ vb (in fencing) make a quick movement to avoid a thrust

VOLTA n quick-moving Italian dance

VOLTAGE n electric potential difference expressed in volts

VOLTAGES > VOLTAGE

VOLTAIC adj producing an electric current

VOLTAISM another name for > GALVANISM

VOLTAISMS
> VOLTAISM

VOLTE same as > VOLT

VOLTED > VOLT

VOLTES > VOLTE

VOLTI n musical direction meaning turn the page

VOLTIGEUR n French infantry member

VOLTING > VOLT

VOLTINISM n number of annual broods of an animal

VOLTIS > VOLTI

VOLTMETER n instrument for measuring voltage

VOLTS > VOLT

VOLUBIL same as > VOLUBLE

VOLUBLE adj talking easily and at length

VOLUBLY > VOLUBLE

VOLUCRINE adj relating to birds

VOLUME n size of the space occupied by something ▷ vb billow or surge in volume

VOLUMED > VOLUME

VOLUMES > VOLUME

VOLUMETER n any instrument for measuring the volume of a solid, liquid, or gas

VOLUMETRY n act of measuring by volume

VOLUMINAL > VOLUME

VOLUMING > VOLUME

VOLUMISE same as > VOLUMISE

VOLUMISED
> VOLUMISE

VOLUMISER same as > VOLUMIZER

VOLUMISES
> VOLUMISE

VOLUMIST n author

VOLUMISTS
> VOLUMIST

VOLUMIZE vb create volume in something

VOLUMIZED
> VOLUMIZE

VOLUMIZER n product used to give extra body to hair

VOLUMIZES
> VOLUMIZE

VOLUNTARY adj done by choice ▷ n organ solo in a church service

VOLUNTEER n person who offers voluntarily to do something ▷ vb offer one's services

VOLUSPA n Icelandic mythological poem

VOLUSPAS > VOLUSPA

VOLUTE n spiral or twisting turn, form, or object ▷ adj having the form of a volute

VOLUTED > VOLUTE

VOLUTES > VOLUTE

VOLUTIN n granular substance found in cells

VOLUTINS > VOLUTIN

VOLUTION n rolling, revolving, or spiral form or motion

VOLUTIONS
> VOLUTION

VOLUTOID > VOLUTE

VOLVA n cup-shaped structure that sheathes the base of the stalk of certain mushrooms

VOLVAE > VOLVA

VOLVAS > VOLVA

VOLVATE > VOLVA

VOLVE vb turn over

VOLVED > VOLVE

VOLVES > VOLVE

VOLVING > VOLVE

VOLVOX n freshwater protozoan

VOLVOXES > VOLVOX

VOLVULI > VOLVULUS

VOLVULUS n abnormal twisting of the intestines causing obstruction

VOM vb vomit

VOMER n thin flat bone separating the nasal passages in mammals

VOMERINE > VOMER

VOMERS > VOMER

VOMICA n pus-containing cavity

VOMICAE > VOMICA

VOMICAS > VOMICA

VOMIT vb eject (the contents of the stomach) through the mouth ▷ n matter vomited

VOMITED > VOMIT

VOMITER > VOMIT

VOMITERS > VOMIT

VOMITIER > VOMITY

VOMITIEST > VOMITY

VOMITING > VOMIT

VOMITINGS > VOMIT

VOMITIVE same as > VOMITORY

VOMITIVES
> VOMITIVE

VOMITO n form of yellow fever

VOMITORIA n entrances in an amphitheatre

VOMITORY adj causing vomiting ▷ n vomitory agent

VOMITOS > VOMITO

VOMITOUS adj arousing feelings of disgust

VOMITS > VOMIT

VOMITUS n matter that has been vomited

VOMITUSES > VOMITUS

VOMITY adj resembling or smelling of vomit

VOMMED > VOM

VOMMING > VOM

VOMS > VOM

VONGOLE pl n (in Italian cookery) clams

VOODOO n religion involving ancestor worship and witchcraft ▷ adj of or relating to voodoo ▷ vb affect by or as if by the power of voodoo

VOODOOED > VOODOO

VOODOOING > VOODOO

VOODOOISM same as > VOODOO

VOODOOIST > VOODOO

VOODOOS > VOODOO

VOORKAMER n (in South Africa) front room of a house

VOORSKOT n (in South Africa) advance payment made to a farmer for crops

VOORSKOTS
> VOORSKOT

VOR vb (in dialect) warn

VORACIOUS adj craving great quantities of food

VORACITY
> VORACIOUS

VORAGO n chasm

VORAGOES > VORAGO

VORAGOS > VORAGO

VORANT adj devouring

VORLAGE n skiing position

VORLAGES > VORLAGE

VORPAL adj sharp

VORRED > VOR

VORRING > VOR

VORS > VOR

VORTEX n whirlpool

VORTEXES > VORTEX

VORTICAL > VORTEX

VORTICES > VORTEX

VORTICISM n art movement in 20th-century England

VORTICIST
> VORTICISM

VORTICITY n rotational spin in a fluid

VORTICOSE adj rotating quickly

VOSTRO adj as in vostro account bank account held by a foreign bank with a British bank

VOTABLE > VOTE

VOTARESS n female votary

VOTARIES > VOTARY

VOTARIST variant of > VOTARY

VOTARISTS
> VOTARIST

VOTARY n person dedicated to a religion or to a cause ▷ adj ardently devoted to a deity

VOTE n choice made by a participant in a shared decision ▷ vb make a choice by a vote

VOTEABLE > VOTE

VOTED > VOTE

VOTEEN n devotee

VOTEENS > VOTEEN

VOTELESS > VOTE

VOTER n person who can or does vote

VOTERS > VOTER

VOTES > VOTE

VOTING > VOTE

VOTINGS > VOTE

VOTIVE adj done or given to fulfil a vow ▷ n votive offering

VOTIVELY > VOTIVE

VOTIVES > VOTIVE

VOTRESS > VOTARESS

VOTRESSES > VOTRESS

VOUCH vb give personal assurance ▷ n act of vouching

VOUCHED > VOUCH

VOUCHEE n person summoned to court to defend a title

VOUCHEES > VOUCHEE

VOUCHER n ticket used instead of money to buy specified goods ▷ vb summon someone to court as a vouchee

VOUCHERED > VOUCHER

VOUCHERS > VOUCHER

VOUCHES > VOUCH

VOUCHING > VOUCH

VOUCHSAFE vb give, entrust

VOUDON variant of > VOODOO

VOUDONS > VOUDON

VOUDOU same as > VOODOO

VOUDOUED > VOUDOU

VOUDOUING > VOUDOU

VOUDOUN variant of > VOODOO

VOUDOUNS > VOUDOUN

VOUDOUS > VOUDOU
VOUGE n form of pike used by foot soldiers in the 14th century and later
VOUGES > VOUGE
VOULGE n type of medieval weapon
VOULGES > VOULGE
VOULU adj deliberate
VOUSSOIR n wedge-shaped stone or brick that is used with others to construct an arch
VOUSSOIRS > VOUSSOIR
VOUTSAFE same as > VOUCHSAFE
VOUTSAFED > VOUTSAFE
VOUTSAFES > VOUTSAFE
VOUVRAY n dry white French wine
VOUVRAYS > VOUVRAY
VOW n solemn and binding promise ▷ vb promise solemnly
VOWED > VOW
VOWEL n speech sound made without obstructing the flow of breath ▷ vb say as a vowel
VOWELED adj having vowels
VOWELISE same as > VOWELIZE
VOWELISED > VOWELISE
VOWELISES > VOWELISE
VOWELIZE vb mark the vowel points in (a Hebrew word or text)
VOWELIZED > VOWELIZE
VOWELIZES > VOWELIZE
VOWELLED > VOWEL
VOWELLESS > VOWEL
VOWELLIER > VOWELLY
VOWELLING > VOWEL
VOWELLY adj marked by vowels
VOWELS > VOWEL
VOWER > VOW
VOWERS > VOW
VOWESS n nun
VOWESSES > VOWESS
VOWING > VOW

VOWLESS > VOW
VOWS > VOW
VOX n voice or sound
VOXEL n any of a number of very small elements in a 3D image
VOXELS > VOXEL
VOYAGE n long journey by sea or in space ▷ vb make a voyage
VOYAGED > VOYAGE
VOYAGER > VOYAGE
VOYAGERS > VOYAGE
VOYAGES > VOYAGE
VOYAGEUR n French canoeman who transported furs from trading posts in N America
VOYAGEURS > VOYAGEUR
VOYAGING n act of voyaging
VOYAGINGS > VOYAGING
VOYEUR n person abnormally interested in other people's distress
VOYEURISM > VOYEUR
VOYEURS > VOYEUR
VOZHD n Russian leader
VOZHDS > VOZHD
VRAIC n type of seaweed
VRAICKER n person who gathers vraic
VRAICKERS > VRAICKER
VRAICKING n act of gathering vraic
VRAICS > VRAIC
VRIL n life force
VRILS > VRIL
VROOM interj exclamation imitative of a car engine revving up ▷ vb move noisily and at high speed
VROOMED > VROOM
VROOMING > VROOM
VROOMS > VROOM
VROT adj South African slang for rotten
VROU n South African word for a woman or wife
VROUS > VROU
VROUW n Afrikaner woman
VROUWS > VROUW
VROW same as > VROUW
VROWS > VROW
VRYSTATER n (in S Africa) inhabitant of the

Free State, esp one who is White
VUG n small cavity in a rock or vein, usually lined with crystals
VUGG same as > VUG
VUGGIER > VUG
VUGGIEST > VUG
VUGGS > VUGG
VUGGY > VUG
VUGH same as > VUG
VUGHIER > VUGH
VUGHIEST > VUGH
VUGHS > VUGH
VUGHY > VUGH
VUGS > VUG
VUGULAR adj relating to vugs
VULCAN n blacksmith
VULCANIAN adj of or relating to a volcanic eruption
VULCANIC same as > VOLCANIC
VULCANISE same as > VULCANIZE
VULCANISM same as > VOLCANISM
VULCANIST same as > VOLCANIST
VULCANITE n vulcanized rubber
VULCANIZE vb strengthen (rubber) by treating it with sulphur
VULCANS > VULCAN
VULGAR adj showing lack of good taste, decency, or refinement ▷ n common and ignorant person
VULGARER > VULGAR
VULGAREST > VULGAR
VULGARIAN n vulgar (rich) person
VULGARISE same as > VULGARIZE
VULGARISM n coarse word or phrase
VULGARITY n condition of being vulgar
VULGARIZE vb make vulgar or too common
VULGARLY > VULGAR
VULGARS > VULGAR
VULGATE n commonly recognized text or version
VULGATES > VULGATE
VULGO adv generally
VULGUS n the common people

VULGUSES > VULGUS
VULN vb wound
VULNED > VULN
VULNERARY adj of, relating to, or used to heal a wound ▷ n vulnerary drug or agent
VULNERATE vb wound
VULNING > VULN
VULNS > VULN
VULPICIDE n person who kills foxes
VULPINE adj of or like a fox
VULPINISM > VULPINE
VULPINITE n type of granular anhydrite
VULSELLA n forceps
VULSELLAE > VULSELLA
VULSELLUM variant of > VULSELLA
VULTURE n large bird that feeds on the flesh of dead animals
VULTURES > VULTURE
VULTURINE adj of, relating to, or resembling a vulture
VULTURISH > VULTURE
VULTURISM n greed
VULTURN n type of turkey
VULTURNS > VULTURN
VULTUROUS same as > VULTURINE
VULVA n female external genitals
VULVAE > VULVA
VULVAL > VULVA
VULVAR > VULVA
VULVAS > VULVA
VULVATE > VULVA
VULVIFORM > VULVA
VULVITIS n inflammation of the vulva
VUM vb swear
VUMMED > VUM
VUMMING > VUM
VUMS > VUM
VUTTIER > VUTTY
VUTTIEST > VUTTY
VUTTY adj dirty
VUVUZELA n South African instrument blown by football fans
VUVUZELAS > VUVUZELA
VYING > VIE
VYINGLY > VIE
VYINGS > VIE

Ww

WAAC n (formerly) member of the Women's Auxiliary Army Corp

WAACS > WAAC

WAAH interj interjection used to express wailing

WAB n skin web between the digits of certain animals

WABAIN same as **>** OUABAIN

WABAINS > WABAIN

WABBIT adj Scots word meaning weary

WABBLE same as **>** WOBBLE

WABBLED > WABBLE

WABBLER > WABBLE

WABBLERS > WABBLE

WABBLES > WABBLE

WABBLIER > WABBLE

WABBLIEST > WABBLE

WABBLING > WABBLE

WABBLY > WABBLE

WABOOM another word for **>** WAGENBOOM

WABOOMS > WABOOM

WABS > WAB

WABSTER Scots form of **>** WEBSTER

WABSTERS > WABSTER

WACK n friend ▷ adj bad or inferior

WACKE n any of various soft earthy rocks that resemble or are derived from basaltic rocks

WACKED adj exhausted

WACKER same as **>** WACK

WACKERS > WACKER

WACKES > WACKE

WACKEST > WACK

WACKIER > WACKY

WACKIEST > WACKY

WACKILY > WACKY

WACKINESS > WACKY

WACKO n odd or eccentric person

WACKOES > WACKO

WACKOS > WACKO

WACKS > WACK

WACKY adj eccentric or funny

WACONDA n supernatural force in Sioux belief

WACONDAS > WACONDA

WAD n black earthy ore of manganese ▷ n small mass of soft material ▷ vb form (something) into a wad

WADABLE > WADE

WADD same as **>** WAD

WADDED > WAD

WADDER > WAD

WADDERS > WAD

WADDIE same as **>** WADDY

WADDIED > WADDY

WADDIES > WADDY

WADDING > WAD

WADDINGS > WAD

WADDLE vb walk with short swaying steps ▷ n swaying walk

WADDLED > WADDLE

WADDLER > WADDLE

WADDLERS > WADDLE

WADDLES > WADDLE

WADDLIER > WADDLE

WADDLIEST > WADDLE

WADDLING > WADDLE

WADDLY > WADDLE

WADDS > WADD

WADDY n heavy wooden club used by Aboriginal Australians ▷ vb hit with a waddy

WADDYING > WADDY

WADE vb walk with difficulty through water or mud ▷ n act or an instance of wading

WADEABLE > WADE

WADED > WADE

WADER n long-legged water bird

WADERS pl n long waterproof boots which completely cover the legs

WADES > WADE

WADGE n large or roughly cut portion

WADGES > WADGE

WADI n (in N Africa and Arabia) river which is dry except in the wet season

WADIES > WADY

WADING > WADE

WADINGS > WADE

WADIS > WADI

WADMAAL same as **>** WADMAL

WADMAALS > WADMAAL

WADMAL n coarse thick woollen fabric, formerly woven for outer garments

WADMALS > WADMAL

WADMEL same as **>** WADMAL

WADMELS > WADMEL

WADMOL same as **>** WADMAL

WADMOLL same as **>** WADMAL

WADMOLLS > WADMOLL

WADMOLS > WADMOL

WADS > WAD

WADSET vb pledge or mortgage

WADSETS > WADSET

WADSETT same as **>** WADSET

WADSETTED > WADSET

WADSETTER > WADSET

WADSETTS > WADSETT

WADT same as **>** WAD

WADTS > WADT

WADY same as **>** WADI

WAE old form of **>** WOE

WAEFUL old form of **>** WOEFUL

WAENESS n sorrow

WAENESSES > WAENESS

WAES > WAE

WAESOME adj sorrowful

WAESUCK interj Scots word meaning alas

WAESUCKS interj alas

WAFER n thin crisp biscuit ▷ vb seal, fasten, or attach with a wafer

WAFERED > WAFER

WAFERIER > WAFERY

WAFERIEST > WAFERY

WAFERING > WAFER

WAFERS > WAFER

WAFERY adj like wafer; thin

WAFF n gust or puff of air ▷ vb flutter or cause to flutter

WAFFED > WAFF

WAFFIE n person regarded as having little worth to society

WAFFIES > WAFFIE

WAFFING > WAFF

WAFFLE vb speak or write in a vague wordy way ▷ n vague wordy talk or writing

WAFFLED > WAFFLE

WAFFLER > WAFFLE

WAFFLERS > WAFFLE

WAFFLES > WAFFLE

WAFFLIER > WAFFLE

WAFFLIEST > WAFFLE

WAFFLING > WAFFLE

WAFFLINGS > WAFFLE

WAFFLY > WAFFLE

WAFFS > WAFF

WAFT vb drift or carry gently through the air ▷ n something wafted

WAFTAGE > WAFT

WAFTAGES > WAFT

WAFTED > WAFT

WAFTER n device that causes a draught

WAFTERS > WAFTER

WAFTING > WAFT

WAFTINGS > WAFT

WAFTS > WAFT

WAFTURE n act of wafting or waving

WAFTURES > WAFTURE

WAG vb move rapidly from side to side ▷ n wagging movement

WAGE n payment for work done, esp when paid weekly ▷ vb engage in (an activity)

WAGED > WAGE

WAGELESS > WAGE

WAGENBOOM n S African tree

WAGER vb bet on the outcome of something ▷ n bet on the outcome of an event or activity

WAGERED > WAGER

WAGERER > WAGER

WAGERERS > WAGER

WAGERING n act of wagering

WAGERINGS > WAGERING

WAGERS > WAGER

WAGES > WAGE

WAGGA n blanket or bed covering made out of sacks stitched together

WAGGAS > WAGGA

WAGGED > WAG

WAGGER > WAG

WAGGERIES > WAGGERY

WAGGERS > WAG

WAGGERY n quality of being humorous

WAGGING > WAG

WAGGISH adj jocular or humorous

WAGGISHLY > WAGGISH

WAGGLE vb move with a rapid shaking or wobbling motion ▷ n rapid shaking or wobbling motion

WAGGLED > WAGGLE

WAGGLER n float only the bottom of which is attached to the fishing line

WAGGLERS > WAGGLER

WAGGLES > WAGGLE

WAGGLIER > WAGGLE

WAGGLIEST > WAGGLE

WAGGLING > WAGGLE

WAGGLY > WAGGLE

WAGGON same as **>** WAGON

WAGGONED > WAGGON

WAGGONER same as **>** WAGONER

WAGGONERS > WAGGONER

WAGGONING > WAGGON
WAGGONS > WAGGON
WAGHALTER n person likely to be hanged
WAGING > WAGE
WAGMOIRE obsolete word for > QUAGMIRE
WAGMOIRES > WAGMOIRE
WAGON n four-wheeled vehicle for heavy loads ▷ vb transport by wagon
WAGONAGE n money paid for transport by wagon
WAGONAGES > WAGONAGE
WAGONED > WAGON
WAGONER n person who drives a wagon
WAGONERS > WAGONER
WAGONETTE n light four-wheeled horse-drawn vehicle with two lengthwise seats facing each other behind a crosswise driver's seat
WAGONFUL > WAGON
WAGONFULS > WAGON
WAGONING > WAGON
WAGONLESS > WAGON
WAGONLOAD n load that is or can be carried by a wagon
WAGONS > WAGON
WAGS > WAG
WAGSOME another word for > WAGGISH
WAGTAIL n small long-tailed bird
WAGTAILS > WAGTAIL
WAGYU n Japanese breed of beef cattle
WAGYUS > WAGYU
WAHCONDA n (in Native American culture) supreme being
WAHCONDAS > WAHCONDA
WAHINE n Māori woman, esp a wife
WAHINES > WAHINE
WAHOO n food and game fish of tropical seas
WAHOOS > WAHOO
WAI n in New Zealand, water
WAIATA n Māori song
WAIATAS > WAIATA
WAID > WEIGH
WAIDE > WEIGH
WAIF n young person who is, or seems, homeless or neglected ▷ vb treat as a waif
WAIFED > WAIF
WAIFING > WAIF
WAIFISH > WAIF
WAIFLIKE > WAIF
WAIFS > WAIF
WAIFT n piece of lost property found by someone other than the owner
WAIFTS > WAIFT
WAIL vb cry out in pain or misery ▷ n mournful cry
WAILED > WAIL
WAILER > WAIL

WAILERS > WAIL
WAILFUL > WAIL
WAILFULLY > WAIL
WAILING > WAIL
WAILINGLY > WAIL
WAILINGS > WAIL
WAILS > WAIL
WAILSOME > WAIL
WAIN vb transport ▷ n farm wagon
WAINAGE n carriages etc for transportation of goods
WAINAGES > WAINAGE
WAINED > WAIN
WAINING > WAIN
WAINS > WAIN
WAINSCOT n wooden lining of the lower part of the walls of a room ▷ vb line (a wall of a room) with a wainscot
WAINSCOTS > WAINSCOT
WAIR vb spend
WAIRED > WAIR
WAIRING > WAIR
WAIRS > WAIR
WAIRSH variant spelling of > WERSH
WAIRSHER > WAIRSH
WAIRSHEST > WAIRSH
WAIRUA n in New Zealand, spirit or soul
WAIRUAS > WAIRUA
WAIS > WAI
WAIST n part of the trunk between the ribs and the hips
WAISTBAND n band of material sewn onto the waist of a garment to strengthen it
WAISTBELT n belt
WAISTCOAT n sleeveless garment which buttons up the front, usu worn over a shirt and under a jacket
WAISTED adj having a waist or waistlike part
WAISTER n sailor performing menial duties
WAISTERS > WAISTER
WAISTING n act of wasting
WAISTINGS > WAISTING
WAISTLESS > WAIST
WAISTLINE n (size of) the waist of a person or garment
WAISTS > WAIST
WAIT vb remain inactive in expectation (of something) ▷ n act or period of waiting
WAITE old form of > WAIT
WAITED > WAIT
WAITER n person who serves in a restaurant etc ▷ vb serve at table
WAITERAGE n service
WAITERED > WAITER
WAITERING n act of serving at table
WAITERS > WAITER
WAITES > WAITE

WAITING > WAIT
WAITINGLY > WAIT
WAITINGS > WAIT
WAITLIST n waiting list
WAITLISTS > WAITLIST
WAITRESS n woman who serves people with food and drink in a restaurant ▷ vb work as a waitress
WAITRON n waiter or waitress
WAITRONS > WAITRON
WAITS > WAIT
WAITSTAFF n waiters and waitresses collectively
WAIVE vb refrain from enforcing (a law, right, etc)
WAIVED > WAIVE
WAIVER n act or instance of voluntarily giving up a claim, right, etc
WAIVERS > WAIVER
WAIVES > WAIVE
WAIVING > WAIVE
WAIVODE same as > VOIVODE
WAIVODES > WAIVODE
WAIWODE same as > VOIVODE
WAIWODES > WAIWODE
WAKA n Māori canoe
WAKAME n edible seaweed
WAKAMES > WAKAME
WAKANDA n supernatural quality in Native American belief system
WAKANDAS > WAKANDA
WAKANE n type of seaweed
WAKANES > WAKANE
WAKAS > WAKA
WAKE vb rouse from sleep or inactivity ▷ n vigil beside a body the night before the funeral
WAKEBOARD n short surfboard for a rider towed behind a motorboat ▷ vb ride a wakeboard
WAKED > WAKE
WAKEFUL adj unable to sleep
WAKEFULLY > WAKEFUL
WAKELESS adj (of sleep) deep or unbroken
WAKEMAN n watchman
WAKEMEN > WAKEMAN
WAKEN vb wake
WAKENED > WAKEN
WAKENER > WAKEN
WAKENERS > WAKEN
WAKENING > WAKEN
WAKENINGS > WAKEN
WAKENS > WAKEN
WAKER > WAKE
WAKERIFE adj watchful
WAKERS > WAKE
WAKES > WAKE
WAKF same as > WAQF
WAKFS > WAKF
WAKIKI n Melanesian shell currency
WAKIKIS > WAKIKI
WAKING > WAKE
WAKINGS > WAKE
WALD Scots form of > WELD

WALDFLUTE n organ flute stop
WALDGRAVE n (in medieval Germany) an officer with jurisdiction over a royal forest
WALDHORN n organ reed stop
WALDHORNS > WALDHORN
WALDO n gadget for manipulating objects by remote control
WALDOES > WALDO
WALDOS > WALDO
WALDRAPP n type of ibis
WALDRAPPS > WALDRAPP
WALDS > WALD
WALE same as > WEAL
WALED > WALE
WALER > WALE
WALERS > WALE
WALES > WALE
WALI same as > VALI
WALIE adj robust or strong
WALIER > WALY
WALIES > WALY
WALIEST > WALY
WALING > WALE
WALIS > WALI
WALISE same as > VALISE
WALISES > WALISE
WALK vb move on foot with at least one foot always on the ground ▷ n short journey on foot, usu for pleasure
WALKABLE > WALK
WALKABOUT n informal walk among the public by royalty etc
WALKATHON n long walk done, esp for charity
WALKAWAY n easily achieved victory
WALKAWAYS > WALKAWAY
WALKED > WALK
WALKER n person who walks
WALKERS > WALKER
WALKIES pl n as in go walkies a walk
WALKING adj (of a person) considered to possess the qualities of something inanimate as specified ▷ n act of walking
WALKINGS > WALKING
WALKMILL same as > WAULKMILL
WALKMILLS > WALKMILL
WALKOUT n strike
WALKOUTS > WALKOUT
WALKOVER n easy victory
WALKOVERS > WALKOVER
WALKS > WALK
WALKUP n building with stairs to upper floors
WALKUPS > WALKUP
WALKWAY n path designed for use by pedestrians
WALKWAYS > WALKWAY

W

WALKYRIE *variant of* > VALKYRIE

WALKYRIES > VALKYRIE

WALL *n* structure of brick, stone, etc used to enclose, divide, or support ▷ *vb* enclose or seal with a wall or walls

WALLA *same as* > WALLAH

WALLABA *n* type of S American tree

WALLABAS > WALLABA

WALLABIES > WALLABY

WALLABY *n* marsupial like a small kangaroo

WALLAH *n* person involved with or in charge of a specified thing

WALLAHS > WALLAH

WALLAROO *n* large stocky Australian kangaroo of rocky regions

WALLAROOS > WALLAROO

WALLAS > WALLA

WALLBOARD *n* thin board made of materials such as compressed wood fibres, used to cover walls, partitions, etc

WALLCHART *n* chart on wall

WALLED > WALL

WALLER > WALL

WALLERS > WALL

WALLET *n* small folding case for paper money, documents, etc

WALLETS > WALLET

WALLEY *n* type of jump in figure skating

WALLEYE *n* fish with large staring eyes

WALLEYED > WALLEYE

WALLEYES > WALLEYE

WALLEYS > WALLEY

WALLFISH *n* snail

WALLIE *same as* > WALLY

WALLIER > WALLY

WALLIES > WALLY

WALLIEST > WALLY

WALLING > WALL

WALLINGS > WALL

WALLOP *vb* hit hard ▷ *n* hard blow

WALLOPED > WALLOP

WALLOPER *n* person or thing that wallops

WALLOPERS > WALLOPER

WALLOPING *n* thrashing ▷ *adj* large or great

WALLOPS > WALLOP

WALLOW *vb* revel in an emotion ▷ *n* act or instance of wallowing

WALLOWED > WALLOW

WALLOWER > WALLOW

WALLOWERS > WALLOW

WALLOWING > WALLOW

WALLOWS > WALLOW

WALLPAPER *n* decorative paper to cover interior walls ▷ *vb* cover (walls) with wallpaper

WALLS > WALL

WALLSEND *n* type of coal

WALLSENDS > WALLSEND

WALLWORT *n* type of plant

WALLWORTS > WALLWORT

WALLY *n* stupid person ▷ *adj* fine, pleasing, or splendid

WALLYBALL *n* ball game played on court

WALLYDRAG *n* worthless person or animal

WALNUT *n* edible nut with a wrinkled shell ▷ *adj* made from the wood of a walnut tree

WALNUTS > WALNUT

WALRUS *n* large sea mammal with long tusks

WALRUSES > WALRUS

WALTIER > WALTY

WALTIEST > WALTY

WALTY *adj* (of a ship) likely to roll over

WALTZ *n* ballroom dance ▷ *vb* dance a waltz

WALTZED > WALTZ

WALTZER *n* person who waltzes

WALTZERS > WALTZER

WALTZES > WALTZ

WALTZING > WALTZ

WALTZINGS > WALTZ

WALTZLIKE > WALTZ

WALY *same as* > WALLY

WAMBENGER *another name for* > TUAN

WAMBLE *vb* move unsteadily ▷ *n* unsteady movement

WAMBLED > WAMBLE

WAMBLES > WAMBLE

WAMBLIER > WAMBLE

WAMBLIEST > WAMBLE

WAMBLING > WAMBLE

WAMBLINGS > WAMBLE

WAMBLY > WAMBLE

WAME *n* belly, abdomen, or womb

WAMED > WAME

WAMEFOU *Scots variant of* > WAMEFUL

WAMEFOUS > WAMEFOU

WAMEFUL *n* bellyful

WAMEFULS > WAMEFUL

WAMES > WAME

WAMMUL *n* dog

WAMMULS > WAMMUL

WAMMUS *same as* > WAMUS

WAMMUSES > WAMMUS

WAMPEE *n* type of Asian fruit tree

WAMPEES > WAMPEE

WAMPISH *vb* wave

WAMPISHED > WAMPISH

WAMPISHES > WAMPISH

WAMPUM *n* shells woven together, formerly used by Native Americans as money

WAMPUMS > WAMPUM

WAMPUS *same as* > WAMUS

WAMPUSES > WAMPUS

WAMUS *n* type of cardigan or jacket

WAMUSES > WAMUS

WAN *adj* pale and sickly looking ▷ *vb* make or become wan

WANCHANCY *adj* infelicitous

WAND *n* thin rod, esp one used in performing magic tricks

WANDER *vb* move about without a definite destination or aim ▷ *n* act or instance of wandering

WANDERED > WANDER

WANDERER > WANDER

WANDERERS > WANDER

WANDERING > WANDER

WANDEROO *n* macaque of India and Sri Lanka

WANDEROOS > WANDEROO

WANDERS > WANDER

WANDLE *adj* supple ▷ *vb* walk haltingly

WANDLED > WANDLE

WANDLES > WANDLE

WANDLIKE > WAND

WANDLING > WANDLE

WANDOO *n* eucalyptus tree of W Australia, having white bark and durable wood

WANDOOS > WANDOO

WANDS > WAND

WANE *vb* decrease gradually in size or strength

WANED > WANE

WANES > WANE

WANEY > WANE

WANG *n* cheekbone

WANGAN *same as* > WANIGAN

WANGANS > WANGAN

WANGLE *vb* get by devious methods ▷ *n* act or an instance of wangling

WANGLED > WANGLE

WANGLER > WANGLE

WANGLERS > WANGLE

WANGLES > WANGLE

WANGLING > WANGLE

WANGLINGS > WANGLE

WANGS > WANG

WANGUN *same as* > WANIGAN

WANGUNS > WANGUN

WANHOPE *n* delusion

WANHOPES > WANHOPE

WANIER > WANY

WANIEST > WANY

WANIGAN *n* provisions for camp

WANIGANS > WANIGAN

WANING > WANE

WANINGS > WANE

WANION *n* vehemence

WANIONS > WANION

WANK *vb* vulgar slang word for masturbate ▷ *n* instance of masturbating ▷ *adj* bad, useless, or worthless

WANKED > WANK

WANKER *n* vulgar slang word for a worthless person

WANKERS > WANKER

WANKIER > WANKY

WANKIEST > WANKY

WANKING > WANK

WANKLE *adj* unstable

WANKS > WANK

WANKSTA *n* slang word for a person who acts like a gangster but is not involved in crime

WANKSTAS > WANKSTA

WANKY *adj* slang word for pretentious

WANLE *same as* > WANDLE

WANLY > WAN

WANNA *vb* spelling of 'want to' intended to reflect a dialectal or informal pronunciation

WANNABE *adj* wanting to be, or be like, a particular person or thing ▷ *n* person who wants to be, or be like, a particular person or thing

WANNABEE *same as* > WANNABE

WANNABEES > WANNABEE

WANNABES > WANNABE

WANNED > WAN

WANNEL *same as* > WANDLE

WANNER > WAN

WANNESS > WAN

WANNESSES > WAN

WANNEST > WAN

WANNIGAN *same as* > WANIGAN

WANNIGANS > WANNIGAN

WANNING > WAN

WANNION *same as* > WANION

WANNIONS > WANNION

WANNISH *adj* rather wan

WANS > WAN

WANT *vb* need or long for ▷ *n* act or instance of wanting

WANTAGE *n* shortage

WANTAGES > WANTAGE

WANTAWAY *n* footballer who wants to transfer to another club

WANTAWAYS > WANTAWAY

WANTED > WANT

WANTER > WANT

WANTERS > WANT

WANTHILL *n* molehill

WANTHILLS > WANTHILL

WANTIES > WANTY

WANTING *adj* lacking ▷ *prep* without

WANTON *adj* without motive, provocation, or justification ▷ *n* playful or capricious person ▷ *vb* squander or waste

WANTONED > WANTON

WANTONER > WANTON

WANTONERS > WANTON

WANTONEST > WANTON

WANTONING > WANTON

WANTONISE *same as* > WANTONIZE

WANTONIZE *vb* behave wantonly

WANTONLY > WANTON

WANTONS > WANTON

WANTS > WANT

WANTY n belt
WANWORDY adj without merit
WANWORTH n inexpensive purchase
WANWORTHS > WANWORTH
WANY > WANE
WANZE vb wane
WANZED > WANZE
WANZES > WANZE
WANZING > WANZE
WAP vb strike
WAPENSHAW n showing of weapons
WAPENTAKE n subdivision of certain shires or counties, esp in the Midlands and North of England
WAPINSHAW same as > WAPENSHAW
WAPITI n large N American deer
WAPITIS > WAPITI
WAPPED > WAP
WAPPEND adj tired
WAPPER vb blink
WAPPERED > WAPPER
WAPPERING > WAPPER
WAPPERS > WAPPER
WAPPING > WAP
WAPS > WAP
WAQF n endowment in Muslim law
WAQFS > WAQF
WAR n fighting between nations ▷ adj of, like, or caused by war ▷ vb conduct a war
WARAGI n Ugandan alcoholic drink made from bananas
WARAGIS > WARAGI
WARATAH n Australian shrub with crimson flowers
WARATAHS > WARATAH
WARB n dirty or insignificant person
WARBIER > WARB
WARBIEST > WARB
WARBIRD n vintage military aeroplane
WARBIRDS > WARBIRD
WARBLE vb sing in a trilling voice ▷ n act or an instance of warbling
WARBLED > WARBLE
WARBLER n any of various small songbirds
WARBLERS > WARBLER
WARBLES > WARBLE
WARBLIER > WARBLY
WARBLIEST > WARBLY
WARBLING > WARBLE
WARBLINGS > WARBLE
WARBLY adj said in a quavering manner
WARBONNET n headband with trailing feathers worn by certain Native American warriors
WARBOT n any robot or unmanned vehicle or device designed for and used in warfare
WARBOTS > WARBOT

WARBS > WARB
WARBY > WARB
WARCRAFT n skill in warfare
WARCRAFTS > WARCRAFT
WARD n room in a hospital for patients needing a similar kind of care ▷ vb guard or protect
WARDCORN n payment of corn
WARDCORNS > WARDCORN
WARDED > WARD
WARDEN n person in charge of a building and its occupants ▷ vb act as a warden
WARDENED > WARDEN
WARDENING > WARDEN
WARDENRY > WARDEN
WARDENS > WARDEN
WARDER vb guard ▷ n prison officer
WARDERED > WARDER
WARDERING > WARDER
WARDERS > WARDER
WARDIAN n as in wardian case type of glass container for housing delicate plants
WARDING > WARD
WARDINGS > WARD
WARDLESS > WARD
WARDMOTE n assembly of the citizens or liverymen of an area
WARDMOTES > WARDMOTE
WARDOG n veteran warrior
WARDOGS > WARDOG
WARDRESS n female officer in charge of prisoners in a jail
WARDROBE n cupboard for hanging clothes in
WARDROBED > WARDROBE
WARDROBER n person in charge of someone's wardrobe
WARDROBES > WARDROBE
WARDROOM n officers' quarters on a warship
WARDROOMS > WARDROOM
WARDROP obsolete form of > WARDROBE
WARDROPS > WARDROP
WARDS > WARD
WARDSHIP n state of being a ward
WARDSHIPS > WARDSHIP
WARE n articles of a specified type or material ▷ vb spend or squander
WARED > WARE
WAREHOU n any of several edible saltwater New Zealand fish
WAREHOUS > WAREHOU
WAREHOUSE n building for storing goods prior to sale or distribution ▷ vb store or place in a

warehouse, esp a bonded warehouse
WARELESS adj careless
WAREROOM n storeroom
WAREROOMS > WAREROOM
WARES pl n goods for sale
WAREZ pl n illegally copied computer software
WARFARE vb engage in war ▷ n fighting or hostilities
WARFARED > WARFARE
WARFARER > WARFARE
WARFARERS > WARFARE
WARFARES > WARFARE
WARFARIN n crystalline compound, used as a medical anticoagulant
WARFARING > WARFARE
WARFARINS > WARFARIN
WARGAME vb engage in simulated military conflicts
WARGAMED > WARGAME
WARGAMER n person who takes part in wargames
WARGAMERS > WARGAMER
WARGAMES > WARGAME
WARGAMING n activity of playing war games
WARHABLE adj able to fight in war
WARHEAD n explosive front part of a missile
WARHEADS > WARHEAD
WARHORSE n (formerly) a horse used in battle
WARHORSES > WARHORSE
WARIBASHI n pair of disposable chopsticks
WARIER > WARY
WARIEST > WARY
WARILY > WARY
WARIMENT n caution
WARIMENTS > WARIMENT
WARINESS > WARY
WARING > WARE
WARISON n (esp formerly) a bugle note used as an order to a military force to attack
WARISONS > WARISON
WARK Scots form of > WORK
WARKED > WARK
WARKING > WARK
WARKS > WARK
WARLESS > WAR
WARLIKE adj of or relating to war
WARLING n one who is not liked
WARLINGS > WARLING
WARLOCK n man who practises black magic
WARLOCKRY n witchcraft
WARLOCKS > WARLOCK
WARLORD n military leader of a nation or part of a nation
WARLORDS > WARLORD
WARM adj moderately hot ▷ vb make or become warm ▷ n warm place or area

WARMAKER n one who wages war
WARMAKERS > WARMAKER
WARMAN n one experienced in warfare
WARMBLOOD n type of horse
WARMED > WARM
WARMEN > WARMAN
WARMER > WARM
WARMERS > WARM
WARMEST > WARM
WARMING > WARM
WARMINGS > WARM
WARMISH > WARM
WARMIST n person who believes global warming results from human activity
WARMISTS > WARMIST
WARMLY > WARM
WARMNESS > WARM
WARMONGER n person who encourages war
WARMOUTH n type of fish
WARMOUTHS > WARMOUTH
WARMS > WARM
WARMTH n mild heat
WARMTHS > WARMTH
WARMUP n preparatory exercise routine
WARMUPS > WARMUP
WARN vb make aware of possible danger or harm
WARNED > WARN
WARNER > WARN
WARNERS > WARN
WARNING n something that warns ▷ adj giving or serving as a warning
WARNINGLY > WARNING
WARNINGS > WARNING
WARNS > WARN
WARP vb twist out of shape ▷ n state of being warped
WARPAGE > WARP
WARPAGES > WARP
WARPAINT n paint used to decorate the face and body before battle
WARPAINTS > WARPAINT
WARPATH n route taken by Native Americans on a warlike expedition
WARPATHS > WARPATH
WARPED > WARP
WARPER > WARP
WARPERS > WARP
WARPING > WARP
WARPINGS > WARP
WARPLANE n any aircraft designed for and used in warfare
WARPLANES > WARPLANE
WARPOWER n ability to wage war
WARPOWERS > WARPOWER
WARPS > WARP
WARPWISE adv (weaving) in the direction of the warp
WARRAGAL same as > WARRIGAL

W

WARRAGALS
> WARRAGAL
WARRAGLE same as
> WARRIGAL
WARRAGLES
> WARRAGLE
WARRAGUL same as
> WARRIGAL
WARRAGULS
> WARRAGUL
WARRAN same as
> WARRANT
WARRAND same as
> WARRANT
WARRANDED > WARRAND
WARRANDS > WARRAND
WARRANED > WARRAN
WARRANING > WARRAN
WARRANS > WARRAN
WARRANT n (document
giving) official
authorization ▷ vb make
necessary
WARRANTED > WARRANT
WARRANTEE n person to
whom a warranty is given
WARRANTER > WARRANT
WARRANTOR n person or
company that provides a
warranty
WARRANTS > WARRANT
WARRANTY n (document
giving) a guarantee
WARRAY vb wage war on
WARRAYED > WARRAY
WARRAYING > WARRAY
WARRAYS > WARRAY
WARRE same as > WAR
WARRED > WAR
WARREN n series of
burrows in which rabbits
live
WARRENER n gamekeeper
or keeper of a warren
WARRENERS
> WARRENER
WARRENS > WARREN
WARREY same as
> WARRAY
WARREYED > WARREY
WARREYING > WARREY
WARREYS > WARREY
WARRIGAL n dingo ▷ adj
wild
WARRIGALS
> WARRIGAL
WARRING > WAR
WARRIOR n person who
fights in a war
WARRIORS > WARRIOR
WARRISON same as
> WARISON
WARRISONS
> WARRISON
WARS > WAR
WARSAW n type of grouper
fish
WARSAWS > WARSAW
WARSHIP n ship designed
and equipped for naval
combat
WARSHIPS > WARSHIP
WARSLE dialect word for
> WRESTLE
WARSLED > WARSLE
WARSLER > WARSLE
WARSLERS > WARSLE
WARSLES > WARSLE

WARSLING > WARSLE
WARST obsolete form of
> WORST
WARSTLE dialect form of
> WRESTLE
WARSTLED > WARSTLE
WARSTLER > WARSTLE
WARSTLERS > WARSTLE
WARSTLES > WARSTLE
WARSTLING > WARSTLE
WART n small hard growth
on the skin
WARTED > WART
WARTHOG n wild African
pig with wartlike lumps on
the face
WARTHOGS > WARTHOG
WARTIER > WART
WARTIEST > WART
WARTIME n time of war
▷ adj of or in a time of war
WARTIMES > WARTIME
WARTLESS > WART
WARTLIKE > WART
WARTS > WART
WARTWEED n type of plant
WARTWEEDS
> WARTWEED
WARTWORT another word
for > WARTWEED
WARTWORTS
> WARTWORT
WARTY > WART
WARWOLF n Roman
engine of war
WARWOLVES > WARWOLF
WARWORK n work
contributing to war effort
WARWORKS > WARWORK
WARWORN adj worn down
by war
WARY adj watchful or
cautious
WARZONE n area where a
war is taking place or there
is some other violent
conflict
WARZONES > WARZONE
WAS vb form of the past
tense of be
WASABI n Japanese
cruciferous plant
cultivated for its thick
green pungent root
WASABIS > WASABI
WASE n pad to relieve
pressure of load carried on
head
WASES > WASE
WASH vb clean (oneself,
clothes, etc) with water
and usu soap ▷ n act or
process of washing
WASHABLE n thing that
can be washed ▷ adj (esp
of fabrics or clothes)
capable of being washed
without deteriorating
WASHABLES
> WASHABLE
WASHAWAY another word
for > WASHOUT
WASHAWAYS
> WASHAWAY
WASHBAG n small bag for
carrying toiletries when
travelling
WASHBAGS > WASHBAG

WASHBALL n ball of soap
WASHBALLS
> WASHBALL
WASHBASIN n basin for
washing the face and
hands
WASHBOARD n board
having a surface on which
clothes can be scrubbed
WASHBOWL same as
> WASHBASIN
WASHBOWLS
> WASHBOWL
WASHCLOTH n small
piece of cloth used to wash
the face and hands
WASHDAY n day on which
clothes and linen are
washed, often the same
day each week
WASHDAYS > WASHDAY
WASHDOWN n the act of
washing (oneself or
something) down
WASHDOWNS
> WASHDOWN
WASHED > WASH
WASHEN > WASH
WASHER n ring put under
a nut or bolt or in a tap as a
seal ▷ vb fit with a washer
WASHERED > WASHER
WASHERIES > WASHERY
WASHERING > WASHER
WASHERMAN n man who
washes clothes for a living
WASHERMEN
> WASHERMAN
WASHERS > WASHER
WASHERY n plant where
liquid is used to remove
dirt from a mineral
WASHES > WASH
WASHFAST adj not fading
when washed
WASHHAND n as in
washhand basin, washhand
stand for the washing of
hands
WASHHOUSE n (formerly)
building in which laundry
was done
WASHIER > WASHY
WASHIEST > WASHY
WASHILY > WASHY
WASHIN n increase in the
angle of attack of an
aircraft wing towards the
wing tip
WASHINESS > WASHY
WASHING n clothes to be
washed
WASHINGS > WASHING
WASHINS > WASHIN
WASHLAND n frequently
flooded plain
WASHLANDS
> WASHLAND
WASHOUT n complete
failure
WASHOUTS > WASHOUT
WASHPOT n pot for
washing things in
WASHPOTS > WASHPOT
WASHRAG same as
> WASHCLOTH
WASHRAGS > WASHRAG
WASHROOM n toilet

WASHROOMS > WASHROOM
WASHSTAND n piece of
furniture designed to hold
a basin for washing the
face and hands in
WASHTUB n tub or large
container used for
washing anything, esp
clothes
WASHTUBS > WASHTUB
WASHUP n outcome of a
process
WASHUPS > WASHUP
WASHWIPE n windscreen
spray-cleaning
mechanism
WASHWIPES
> WASHWIPE
WASHWOMAN n woman
who washes clothes for a
living
WASHWOMEN
> WASHWOMAN
WASHY adj overdiluted or
weak
WASM n obsolete belief; an
out-of-fashion 'ism'
WASMS > WASM
WASP n stinging insect
with a slender
black-and-yellow striped
body
WASPIE n tight-waisted
corset
WASPIER > WASP
WASPIES > WASPIE
WASPIEST > WASP
WASPILY > WASP
WASPINESS > WASP
WASPISH adj
bad-tempered
WASPISHLY > WASPISH
WASPLIKE > WASP
WASPNEST n nest of
wasps
WASPNESTS
> WASPNEST
WASPS > WASP
WASPY > WASP
WASSAIL n formerly,
festivity when much
drinking took place ▷ vb
drink health of (a person)
at a wassail
WASSAILED > WASSAIL
WASSAILER > WASSAIL
WASSAILRY > WASSAIL
WASSAILS > WASSAIL
WASSERMAN n
man-shaped sea monster
WASSERMEN
> WASSERMAN
WASSUP sentence substitute
what is happening?
WAST singular form of the
past tense of > BE
WASTABLE > WASTE
WASTAGE n loss by wear
or waste
WASTAGES > WASTAGE
WASTE vb use pointlessly
or thoughtlessly ▷ n act of
wasting or state of being
wasted ▷ adj rejected as
worthless or surplus to
requirements
WASTEBIN n bin for
rubbish

WASTEBINS
> WASTEBIN

WASTED > WASTE

WASTEFUL *adj* extravagant

WASTEL *n* fine bread or cake

WASTELAND *n* barren or desolate area of land

WASTELOT *n* piece of waste ground in a city

WASTELOTS
> WASTELOT

WASTELS > WASTEL

WASTENESS > WASTE

WASTER *vb* waste ▷ *n* layabout

WASTERED > WASTER

WASTERFUL *Scots variant of* > WASTEFUL

WASTERIE *same as* > WASTERY

WASTERIES
> WASTERIE

WASTERING > WASTER

WASTERS > WASTER

WASTERY *n* extravagance

WASTES > WASTE

WASTEWAY *n* open ditch

WASTEWAYS
> WASTEWAY

WASTEWEIR *another name for* > SPILLWAY

WASTFULL *obsolete form of* > WASTEFUL

WASTING *adj* reducing the vitality and strength of the body

WASTINGLY > WASTING

WASTINGS > WASTE

WASTNESS *same as* > WASTENESS

WASTREL *n* lazy or worthless person

WASTRELS > WASTREL

WASTRIE *same as* > WASTERY

WASTRIES > WASTRIE

WASTRIFE *n* wastefulness

WASTRIFES
> WASTRIFE

WASTRY *n* wastefulness

WASTS > WAST

WAT *adj* wet

WATAP *n* stringy thread made by Native Americans from the roots of conifers

WATAPE *same as* > WATAP

WATAPES > WATAPE

WATAPS > WATAP

WATCH *vb* look at closely ▷ *n* portable timepiece for the wrist or pocket

WATCHA *interj* greeting meaning 'what are you?'

WATCHABLE *adj* interesting, enjoyable, or entertaining

WATCHBAND *n* watch strap

WATCHBOX *n* sentry's box

WATCHCASE *n* protective case for a watch, generally of metal such as gold, silver, brass, or gunmetal

WATCHCRY *n* slogan used to rally support

WATCHDOG *n* dog kept to guard property

WATCHDOGS
> WATCHDOG

WATCHED > WATCH

WATCHER *n* person who watches

WATCHERS > WATCHER

WATCHES > WATCH

WATCHET *n* shade of blue

WATCHETS > WATCHET

WATCHEYE *n* eye with a light-coloured iris

WATCHEYES
> WATCHEYE

WATCHFUL *adj* vigilant or alert

WATCHING > WATCH

WATCHLIST *n* list of things to be monitored

WATCHMAN *n* man employed to guard a building or property

WATCHMEN > WATCHMAN

WATCHOUT *n* lookout

WATCHOUTS
> WATCHOUT

WATCHWORD *n* word or phrase that sums up the attitude of a particular group

WATE > WIT

WATER *n* clear colourless tasteless liquid that falls as rain and forms rivers etc ▷ *vb* put water on or into

WATERAGE *n* transportation of cargo by means of ships, or the charges for such transportation

WATERAGES
> WATERAGE

WATERBED *n* watertight mattress filled with water

WATERBEDS
> WATERBED

WATERBIRD *n* any aquatic bird

WATERBUCK *n* any of various antelopes of the swampy areas of Africa

WATERBUS *n* boat offering a regular transport service

WATERDOG *n* dog trained to hunt in water

WATERDOGS
-> WATERDOG

WATERED > WATER

WATERER > WATER

WATERERS > WATER

WATERFALL *n* place where the waters of a river drop vertically

WATERFOWL *n* bird that swims on water, such as a duck or swan

WATERGATE *n* gate opening onto a stretch of water

WATERHEAD *n* source of river

WATERHEN *another name for* > GALLINULE

WATERHENS
> WATERHEN

WATERHOLE *n* hole in which water collects

WATERIER > WATERY

WATERIEST > WATERY

WATERILY > WATERY

WATERING > WATER

WATERINGS > WATER

WATERISH > WATER

WATERJET *n* jet of water

WATERJETS
> WATERJET

WATERLEAF *n* carved column design

WATERLESS > WATER

WATERLILY *n* any of various aquatic plants having large leaves and showy flowers that float on the surface of the water

WATERLINE *n* level to which a ship's hull will be immersed when afloat

WATERLOG *vb* flood with water

WATERLOGS
> WATERLOG

WATERLOO *n* total defeat

WATERLOOS
> WATERLOO

WATERMAN *n* skilled boatman

WATERMARK *n* faint translucent design in a sheet of paper ▷ *vb* mark (paper) with a watermark

WATERMEN > WATERMAN

WATERMILL *n* mill driven by water

WATERPOX *n* chickenpox

WATERS > WATER

WATERSHED *n* important period or factor serving as a dividing line

WATERSIDE *n* area of land beside a river or lake

WATERSKI *vb* ski on water towed behind motorboat

WATERSKIS
> WATERSKI

WATERWAY *n* river, canal, or other navigable channel used as a means of travel or transport

WATERWAYS
> WATERWAY

WATERWEED *n* any of various weedy aquatic plants

WATERWORK *n* machinery, etc for storing, purifying, and distributing water

WATERWORN *adj* worn smooth by the action or passage of water

WATERY *adj* of, like, or containing water

WATERZOOI *n* type of Flemish stew

WATS > WAT

WATT *n* unit of power

WATTAGE *n* electrical power expressed in watts

WATTAGES > WATTAGE

WATTAPE *same as* > WATTAP

WATTAPES > WATTAPE

WATTER > WAT

WATTEST > WAT

WATTHOUR *n* unit of energy equal to the power of one watt operating for an hour

WATTHOURS > WATTHOUR

WATTLE *n* branches woven over sticks to make a fence ▷ *adj* made of, formed by, or covered with wattle ▷ *vb* construct from wattle

WATTLED > WATTLE

WATTLES > WATTLE

WATTLESS > WATT

WATTLING > WATTLE

WATTLINGS > WATTLE

WATTMETER *n* meter for measuring electric power in watts

WATTS > WATT

WAUCHT *same as* > WAUGHT

WAUCHTED > WAUCHT

WAUCHTING > WAUCHT

WAUCHTS > WAUCHT

WAUFF *same as* > WAFF

WAUFFED > WAUFF

WAUFFING > WAUFF

WAUFFS > WAUFF

WAUGH *vb* bark

WAUGHED > WAUGH

WAUGHING > WAUGH

WAUGHS > WAUGH

WAUGHT *vb* drink in large amounts

WAUGHTED > WAUGHT

WAUGHTING > WAUGHT

WAUGHTS > WAUGHT

WAUK *vb* full (cloth)

WAUKED > WAUK

WAUKER > WAUK

WAUKERS > WAUK

WAUKING > WAUK

WAUKMILL *same as* > WAULKMILL

WAUKMILLS
> WAUKMILL

WAUKRIFE *variant of* > WAKERIFE

WAUKS > WAUK

WAUL *vb* cry or wail plaintively like a cat

WAULED > WAUL

WAULING > WAUL

WAULINGS > WAUL

WAULK *same as* > WAUK

WAULKED > WAULK

WAULKER > WAULK

WAULKERS > WAULK

WAULKING > WAULK

WAULKMILL *n* cloth-fulling mill

WAULKS > WAULK

WAULS > WAUL

WAUR *obsolete form of* > WAR

WAURED > WAUR

WAURING > WAUR

WAURS > WAUR

WAURST > WAUR

WAVE *vb* move the hand to and fro as a greeting or signal ▷ *n* moving ridge on water

WAVEBAND *n* range of wavelengths or frequencies used for a particular type of radio transmission

W

WAVEBANDS
> WAVEBAND

WAVED > WAVE

WAVEFORM n shape of the graph of a wave or oscillation obtained by plotting the value of some changing quantity against time

WAVEFORMS > WAVEFORM

WAVEFRONT n surface associated with a propagating wave and passing through all points in the wave that have the same phase

WAVEGUIDE n solid rod of dielectric or a hollow metal tube, usually of rectangular cross section, used as a path to guide microwaves

WAVELESS > WAVE

WAVELET n small wave

WAVELETS > WAVELET

WAVELIKE > WAVE

WAVELLITE n greyish-white, yellow, or brown mineral

WAVEMETER n instrument for measuring the frequency or wavelength of radio waves

WAVEOFF n signal or instruction to an aircraft not to land

WAVEOFFS > WAVEOFF

WAVER vb hesitate or be irresolute ▷ n act or an instance of wavering

WAVERED > WAVER

WAVERER > WAVER

WAVERERS > WAVER

WAVERIER > WAVERY

WAVERIEST > WAVERY

WAVERING > WAVER

WAVERINGS > WAVER

WAVEROUS same as > WAVERY

WAVERS > WAVER

WAVERY adj lacking firmness

WAVES > WAVE

WAVESHAPE another word for > WAVEFORM

WAVESON n goods floating on waves after shipwreck

WAVESONS > WAVESON

WAVETABLE n table of recorded sound waves used in certain types of synthesizers

WAVEY n snow goose or other wild goose

WAVEYS > WAVEY

WAVICLE n origin of wave

WAVICLES > WAVICLE

WAVIER > WAVY

WAVIES > WAVY

WAVIEST > WAVY

WAVILY > WAVY

WAVINESS > WAVY

WAVING > WAVE

WAVINGS > WAVE

WAVY adj having curves ▷ n snow goose or other wild goose

WAW another name for > VAV

WAWA n speech ▷ vb speak

WAWAED > WAWA

WAWAING > WAWA

WAWAS > WAWA

WAWE same as > WAW

WAWES > WAWE

WAWL same as > WAUL

WAWLED > WAWL

WAWLING > WAWL

WAWLINGS > WAWL

WAWLS > WAWL

WAWS > WAW

WAX n solid fatty or oily substance used for sealing, making candles, etc ▷ vb coat or polish with wax

WAXABLE > WAX

WAXBERRY n waxy fruit of the wax myrtle or the snowberry

WAXBILL n any of various chiefly African finchlike weaverbirds

WAXBILLS > WAXBILL

WAXCLOTH another name for > OILCLOTH

WAXCLOTHS > WAXCLOTH

WAXED > WAX

WAXEN adj made of or like wax

WAXER > WAX

WAXERS > WAX

WAXES > WAX

WAXEYE n small New Zealand bird

WAXEYES > WAXEYE

WAXFLOWER n any of various plants with waxy flowers

WAXIER > WAXY

WAXIEST > WAXY

WAXILY > WAXY

WAXINESS > WAXY

WAXING > WAX

WAXINGS > WAX

WAXLIKE > WAX

WAXPLANT n climbing shrub of E Asia and Australia

WAXPLANTS
> WAXPLANT

WAXWEED n type of wild flower

WAXWEEDS > WAXWEED

WAXWING n type of songbird

WAXWINGS > WAXWING

WAXWORK n lifelike wax model of a (famous) person

WAXWORKER > WAXWORK

WAXWORKS > WAXWORK

WAXWORM n wax moth larva

WAXWORMS > WAXWORM

WAXY adj resembling wax in colour, appearance, or texture

WAY n manner or method ▷ vb travel

WAYANG n type of Indonesian performance with dancers or puppets

WAYANGS > WAYANG

WAYBACK n area in the rear of a vehicle

WAYBACKS > WAYBACK

WAYBILL n document stating the nature, origin, and destination of goods being transported

WAYBILLS > WAYBILL

WAYBOARD n thin geological seam separating larger strata

WAYBOARDS
> WAYBOARD

WAYBREAD n plantain

WAYBREADS
> WAYBREAD

WAYED > WAY

WAYFARE vb travel

WAYFARED > WAYFARE

WAYFARER n traveller

WAYFARERS
> WAYFARER

WAYFARES > WAYFARE

WAYFARING > WAYFARE

WAYGOING n leaving

WAYGOINGS
> WAYGOING

WAYGONE adj travel-weary

WAYGOOSE same as > WAYZGOOSE

WAYGOOSES
> WAYGOOSE

WAYING > WAY

WAYLAID > WAYLAY

WAYLAY vb lie in wait for and accost or attack

WAYLAYER > WAYLAY

WAYLAYERS > WAYLAY

WAYLAYING > WAYLAY

WAYLAYS > WAYLAY

WAYLEAVE n access to property granted by a landowner for payment

WAYLEAVES
> WAYLEAVE

WAYLEGGO interj away here! let go!

WAYLESS > WAY

WAYMARK n symbol or signpost marking the route of a footpath ▷ vb mark out with waymarks

WAYMARKED > WAYMARK

WAYMARKS > WAYMARK

WAYMENT vb express grief

WAYMENTED > WAYMENT

WAYMENTS > WAYMENT

WAYPOINT n stopping point on route

WAYPOINTS
> WAYPOINT

WAYPOST n signpost

WAYPOSTS > WAYPOST

WAYS > WAY

WAYSIDE n side of a road

WAYSIDES > WAYSIDE

WAYWARD adj erratic, selfish, or stubborn

WAYWARDLY > WAYWARD

WAYWISER n device for measuring distance

WAYWISERS
> WAYWISER

WAYWODE n Slavic governor

WAYWODES > WAYWODE

WAYWORN adj worn or tired by travel

WAYZGOOSE n works outing made annually by a printing house

WAZ same as > WAZZ

WAZIR another word for > VIZIER

WAZIRS > WAZIR

WAZOO n slang word for person's bottom

WAZOOS > WAZOO

WAZZ vb urinate ▷ n act of urinating

WAZZED > WAZZ

WAZZES > WAZZ

WAZZING > WAZZ

WAZZOCK n foolish or annoying person

WAZZOCKS > WAZZOCK

WE pron speaker or writer and one or more others

WEAK adj lacking strength

WEAKEN vb make or become weak

WEAKENED > WEAKEN

WEAKENER > WEAKEN

WEAKENERS > WEAKEN

WEAKENING n act of weakening

WEAKENS > WEAKEN

WEAKER > WEAK

WEAKEST > WEAK

WEAKFISH n any of several sea trouts

WEAKISH > WEAK

WEAKISHLY > WEAK

WEAKLIER > WEAKLY

WEAKLIEST > WEAKLY

WEAKLING n feeble person or animal

WEAKLINGS
> WEAKLING

WEAKLY adv feebly ▷ adj weak or sickly

WEAKNESS n deficiency or failing

WEAKON n subatomic particle

WEAKONS > WEAKON

WEAKSIDE n (in basketball) side of court away from ball

WEAKSIDES
> WEAKSIDE

WEAL n raised mark left on the skin by a blow

WEALD n open or forested country

WEALDS > WEALD

WEALS > WEAL

WEALSMAN n statesman

WEALSMEN > WEALSMAN

WEALTH n state of being rich

WEALTHIER > WEALTHY

WEALTHILY > WEALTHY

WEALTHS > WEALTH

WEALTHY adj possessing wealth

WEAMB same as > WAME

WEAMBS > WEAMB

WEAN vb accustom (a baby or young mammal) to food other than mother's milk

WEANED > WEAN

WEANEL n recently weaned child or animal

WEANELS > WEANEL

WEANER n person or thing that weans
WEANERS > WEANER
WEANING > WEAN
WEANINGS > WEAN
WEANLING n child or young animal recently weaned
WEANLINGS > WEANLING
WEANS > WEAN
WEAPON vb arm ▷ n object used in fighting
WEAPONED > WEAPON
WEAPONEER n person associated with the use or maintenance of weapons, esp nuclear weapons ▷ vb supply with weapons
WEAPONING > WEAPON
WEAPONISE same as > WEAPONIZE
WEAPONIZE vb adapt (a chemical, bacillus, etc) in such a way that it can be used as a weapon
WEAPONRY n weapons collectively
WEAPONS > WEAPON
WEAR vb have on the body as clothing or ornament ▷ n clothes suitable for a particular time or purpose
WEARABLE adj suitable for wear or able to be worn ▷ n any garment that can be worn
WEARABLES > WEARABLE
WEARED > WEAR
WEARER > WEAR
WEARERS > WEAR
WEARIED > WEARY
WEARIER > WEARY
WEARIES > WEARY
WEARIEST > WEARY
WEARIFUL same as > WEARISOME
WEARILESS adj not wearied or able to be wearied
WEARILY > WEARY
WEARINESS > WEARY
WEARING adj tiring ▷ n act of wearing
WEARINGLY > WEARING
WEARINGS > WEAR
WEARISH adj withered
WEARISOME adj tedious
WEARPROOF adj resistant to damage from normal wear or usage
WEARS > WEAR
WEARY adj tired or exhausted ▷ vb make or become weary
WEARYING > WEARY
WEASAND former name for the > TRACHEA
WEASANDS > WEASAND
WEASEL n small carnivorous mammal with a long body and short legs ▷ vb use ambiguous language to avoid speaking directly or honestly
WEASELED > WEASEL

WEASELER > WEASEL
WEASELERS > WEASEL
WEASELIER > WEASELY
WEASELING > WEASEL
WEASELLED > WEASEL
WEASELLER > WEASEL
WEASELLY adj devious, cunning
WEASELS > WEASEL
WEASELY adj devious, cunning
WEASON Scots form of > WEASAND
WEASONS > WEASON
WEATHER n day-to-day atmospheric conditions of a place ▷ vb (cause to) be affected by the weather
WEATHERED adj affected by exposure to the action of the weather
WEATHERER > WEATHER
WEATHERLY adj (of a sailing vessel) making very little leeway when close-hauled, even in a stiff breeze
WEATHERS > WEATHER
WEAVE vb make (fabric) by interlacing (yarn) on a loom
WEAVED > WEAVE
WEAVER n person who weaves, esp as a means of livelihood
WEAVERS > WEAVER
WEAVES > WEAVE
WEAVING > WEAVE
WEAVINGS > WEAVE
WEAZAND same as > WEASAND
WEAZANDS > WEAZAND
WEAZEN same as > WIZEN
WEAZENED > WEAZEN
WEAZENING > WEAZEN
WEAZENS > WEAZEN
WEB n net spun by a spider ▷ vb cover with or as if with a web
WEBAPP n application program that is accessed on the internet
WEBAPPS > WEBAPP
WEBBED > WEB
WEBBIE n person who is well versed in the use of the World Wide Web
WEBBIER > WEBBY
WEBBIES > WEBBIE
WEBBIEST > WEBBY
WEBBING n anything that forms a web
WEBBINGS > WEBBING
WEBBY adj of, relating to, resembling, or consisting of a web
WEBCAM n camera that transmits images over the internet
WEBCAMS > WEBCAM
WEBCAST n broadcast of an event over the internet ▷ vb make such a broadcast
WEBCASTED > WEBCAST
WEBCASTER > WEBCAST
WEBCASTS > WEBCAST

WEBCHAT vb exchange messages via the internet
WEBCHATS > WEBCHAT
WEBER n SI unit of magnetic flux
WEBERS > WEBER
WEBFED adj (of printing press) printing from rolls of paper
WEBFEET > WEBFOOT
WEBFOOT n foot having the toes connected by folds of skin
WEBFOOTED > WEBFOOT
WEBHEAD n person who uses the internet a lot
WEBHEADS > WEBHEAD
WEBIFIED > WEBIFY
WEBIFIES > WEBIFY
WEBIFY vb convert (information) for display on the internet
WEBIFYING > WEBIFY
WEBINAR n interactive seminar conducted over the World Wide Web
WEBINARS > WEBINAR
WEBISODE n episode (of a television series) intended for online viewing
WEBISODES > WEBISODE
WEBLESS > WEB
WEBLIKE > WEB
WEBLISH n shorthand form of English that is used in text messaging, chatrooms, etc
WEBLISHES > WEBLISH
WEBLOG n person's online journal
WEBLOGGER > WEBLOG
WEBLOGS > WEBLOG
WEBMAIL n system of electronic mail accessed via the internet
WEBMAILS > WEBMAIL
WEBMASTER n person responsible for the administration of a website on the World Wide Web
WEBPAGE n page on a website
WEBPAGES > WEBPAGE
WEBRING n group of websites organized in a circular structure
WEBRINGS > WEBRING
WEBS > WEB
WEBSITE n group of connected pages on the World Wide Web
WEBSITES > WEBSITE
WEBSPACE n storage space on a web server
WEBSPACES > WEBSPACE
WEBSTER archaic word for > WEAVER
WEBSTERS > WEBSTER
WEBWHEEL n wheel containing a plate or web instead of spokes
WEBWHEELS > WEBWHEEL
WEBWORK n work done using the World Wide Web

WEBWORKS > WEBWORK
WEBWORM n type of caterpillar
WEBWORMS > WEBWORM
WEBZINE n magazine published on the internet
WEBZINES > WEBZINE
WECHT n agricultural tool ▷ vb winnow (corn)
WECHTED > WECHT
WECHTING > WECHT
WECHTS > WECHT
WED vb marry
WEDDED > WED
WEDDER dialect form of > WEATHER
WEDDERED > WEDDER
WEDDERING > WEDDER
WEDDERS > WEDDER
WEDDING > WED
WEDDINGS > WEDDING
WEDEL variant of > WEDELN
WEDELED > WEDEL
WEDELING > WEDEL
WEDELN n succession of high-speed turns performed in skiing ▷ vb perform a wedeln
WEDELNED > WEDELN
WEDELNING > WEDELN
WEDELNS > WEDELN
WEDELS > WEDEL
WEDGE n piece of material thick at one end and thin at the other ▷ vb fasten or split with a wedge
WEDGED > WEDGE
WEDGELIKE > WEDGE
WEDGES > WEDGE
WEDGEWISE adv in manner of a wedge
WEDGIE n wedge-heeled shoe
WEDGIER > WEDGE
WEDGIES > WEDGIE
WEDGIEST > WEDGE
WEDGING > WEDGE
WEDGINGS > WEDGE
WEDGY > WEDGE
WEDLOCK n marriage
WEDLOCKS > WEDLOCK
WEDS > WED
WEE adj small or short ▷ n instance of urinating ▷ vb urinate
WEED n plant growing where undesired ▷ vb clear of weeds
WEEDBED n body of water having lots of weeds
WEEDBEDS > WEEDBED
WEEDED > WEED
WEEDER > WEED
WEEDERIES > WEEDERY
WEEDERS > WEED
WEEDERY n weed-ridden area
WEEDHEAD n habitual user of marijuana
WEEDHEADS > WEEDHEAD
WEEDICIDE n weedkiller
WEEDIER > WEEDY
WEEDIEST > WEEDY
WEEDILY > WEEDY
WEEDINESS > WEEDY

W

WEEDING > WEED
WEEDINGS > WEED
WEEDLESS > WEED
WEEDLIKE > WEED
WEEDLINE n edge of a weedbed
WEEDLINES > WEEDLINE
WEEDS pl n widow's mourning clothes
WEEDY adj (of a person) thin and weak
WEEING > WEE
WEEJUNS pl n moccasin-style shoes for casual wear
WEEK n period of seven days, esp one beginning on a Sunday ▷ adv seven days before or after a specified day
WEEKDAY n any day of the week except Saturday or Sunday
WEEKDAYS > WEEKDAY
WEEKE same as > WICK
WEEKEND n Saturday and Sunday ▷ vb spend or pass a weekend
WEEKENDED > WEEKEND
WEEKENDER n person spending a weekend holiday in a place, esp habitually
WEEKENDS adv at the weekend, esp regularly or during every weekend
WEEKES > WEEKE
WEEKLIES > WEEKLY
WEEKLONG adj lasting a week
WEEKLY adv happening, done, etc once a week ▷ n newspaper or magazine published once a week ▷ adj happening once a week or every week
WEEKNIGHT n evening or night of a weekday
WEEKS > WEEK
WEEL Scot word for > WELL
WEELS > WEEL
WEEM n underground home
WEEMS > WEEM
WEEN vb think or imagine (something)
WEENED > WEEN
WEENIE adj very small ▷ n wiener
WEENIER > WEENY
WEENIES > WEENIE
WEENIEST > WEENY
WEENING > WEEN
WEENS > WEEN
WEENSIER > WEENSY
WEENSIEST > WEENSY
WEENSY same as > WEENY
WEENY adj very small
WEEP vb shed tears ▷ n spell of weeping
WEEPER n person who weeps, esp a hired mourner
WEEPERS > WEEPER
WEEPHOLE n small drain hole in wall
WEEPHOLES > WEEPHOLE

WEEPIE same as > WEEPY
WEEPIER > WEEPY
WEEPIES > WEEPY
WEEPIEST > WEEPY
WEEPILY > WEEPY
WEEPINESS > WEEPY
WEEPING adj (of plants) having slender hanging branches
WEEPINGLY > WEEPING
WEEPINGS > WEEPING
WEEPS > WEEP
WEEPY adj liable to cry ▷ n sentimental film or book
WEER > WEE
WEES > WEE
WEEST > WEE
WEET dialect form of > WET
WEETE same as > WIT
WEETED > WEETE
WEETEN same as > WIT
WEETER > WEET
WEETEST > WEET
WEETING > WEET
WEETINGLY > WEET
WEETLESS obsolete variant of > WITLESS
WEETS > WEET
WEEVER n type of small fish
WEEVERS > WEEVER
WEEVIL n small beetle that eats grain etc
WEEVILED same as > WEEVILLED
WEEVILIER > WEEVILY
WEEVILLED adj weevil-ridden
WEEVILLY adj full of weevils
WEEVILS > WEEVIL
WEEVILY adj full of weevils
WEEWEE vb urinate
WEEWEED > WEEWEE
WEEWEEING > WEEWEE
WEEWEES > WEEWEE
WEFT n cross threads in weaving ▷ vb form weft
WEFTAGE n texture
WEFTAGES > WEFTAGE
WEFTE n forsaken child
WEFTED > WEFT
WEFTES > WEFTE
WEFTING > WEFT
WEFTS > WEFT
WEFTWISE adv in the direction of the weft
WEID n sudden illness
WEIDS > WEID
WEIGELA n type of shrub
WEIGELAS > WEIGELA
WEIGELIA same as > WEIGELA
WEIGELIAS > WEIGELIA
WEIGH vb have a specified weight
WEIGHABLE > WEIGH
WEIGHAGE n duty paid for weighing goods
WEIGHAGES > WEIGHAGE
WEIGHED > WEIGH
WEIGHER > WEIGH
WEIGHERS > WEIGH
WEIGHING > WEIGH

WEIGHINGS > WEIGH
WEIGHMAN n person responsible for weighing goods
WEIGHMEN > WEIGHMAN
WEIGHS > WEIGH
WEIGHT n heaviness of an object ▷ vb add weight to
WEIGHTAGE same as > WEIGHTING
WEIGHTED > WEIGHT
WEIGHTER > WEIGHT
WEIGHTERS > WEIGHT
WEIGHTIER > WEIGHTY
WEIGHTILY > WEIGHTY
WEIGHTING n extra allowance paid in special circumstances
WEIGHTS > WEIGHT
WEIGHTY adj important or serious
WEIL n whirlpool
WEILS > WEIL
WEINER same as > WIENER
WEINERS > WEINER
WEIR vb ward off ▷ n river dam
WEIRD adj strange or bizarre ▷ vb warn beforehand
WEIRDED > WEIRD
WEIRDER > WEIRD
WEIRDEST > WEIRD
WEIRDIE same as > WEIRDO
WEIRDIES > WEIRDIE
WEIRDING > WEIRD
WEIRDLY > WEIRD
WEIRDNESS > WEIRD
WEIRDO n peculiar person
WEIRDOES > WEIRDO
WEIRDOS > WEIRDO
WEIRDS > WEIRD
WEIRDY n weird person
WEIRED > WEIR
WEIRING > WEIR
WEIRS > WEIR
WEISE same as > WISE
WEISED > WEISE
WEISES > WEISE
WEISING > WEISE
WEIZE same as > WISE
WEIZED > WEIZE
WEIZES > WEIZE
WEIZING > WEIZE
WEKA n flightless New Zealand rail
WEKAS > WEKA
WELAWAY same as > WELLAWAY
WELCH same as > WELSH
WELCHED > WELCH
WELCHER > WELCH
WELCHERS > WELCH
WELCHES > WELCH
WELCHING > WELCH
WELCOME vb greet with pleasure ▷ n kindly greeting ▷ adj received gladly
WELCOMED > WELCOME
WELCOMELY > WELCOME
WELCOMER > WELCOME
WELCOMERS > WELCOME
WELCOMES > WELCOME
WELCOMING > WELCOME

WELD vb join (pieces of metal or plastic) by softening with heat ▷ n welded joint
WELDABLE > WELD
WELDED > WELD
WELDER > WELD
WELDERS > WELD
WELDING > WELD
WELDINGS > WELD
WELDLESS > WELD
WELDMENT n unit composed of welded pieces
WELDMENTS > WELDMENT
WELDMESH n type of fencing consisting of wire mesh reinforced by welding
WELDOR > WELD
WELDORS > WELDOR
WELDS > WELD
WELFARE n wellbeing
WELFARES > WELFARE
WELFARISM n policies or attitudes associated with a welfare state
WELFARIST > WELFARISM
WELFARITE n (US) person who is on welfare
WELK vb wither; dry up
WELKE obsolete form of > WELK
WELKED > WELK
WELKES > WELKE
WELKIN n sky, heavens, or upper air
WELKING > WELK
WELKINS > WELKIN
WELKS > WELK
WELKT adj twisted
WELL adv satisfactorily ▷ adj in good health ▷ interj exclamation of surprise, interrogation, etc ▷ n hole sunk into the earth to reach water, oil, or gas ▷ vb flow upwards or outwards
WELLADAY interj alas
WELLADAYS interj alas
WELLANEAR interj alas
WELLAWAY interj alas
WELLAWAYS interj alas
WELLBEING n state of being well, happy, or prosperous
WELLBORN adj having been born into a wealthy family
WELLCURB n stone surround at top of well
WELLCURBS > WELLCURB
WELLDOER n moral person
WELLDOERS > WELLDOER
WELLED > WELL
WELLHEAD n source of a well or stream
WELLHEADS > WELLHEAD
WELLHOLE n well shaft
WELLHOLES > WELLHOLE

WELLHOUSE n housing for well
WELLIE n wellington boot
WELLIES > WELLY
WELLING > WELL
WELLINGS > WELL
WELLNESS n state of being in good physical and mental health
WELLS > WELL
WELLSITE n site of well
WELLSITES > WELLSITE
WELLY n energy or commitment
WELS n type of catfish
WELSH vb fail to pay a debt or fulfil an obligation
WELSHED > WELSH
WELSHER > WELSH
WELSHERS > WELSH
WELSHES > WELSH
WELSHING > WELSH
WELT same as > WEAL
WELTED > WELT
WELTER n jumbled mass ▷ vb roll about, writhe, or wallow
WELTERED > WELTER
WELTERING > WELTER
WELTERS > WELTER
WELTING > WELT
WELTINGS > WELT
WELTS > WELT
WEM same as > WAME
WEMB same as > WAME
WEMBS > WEMB
WEMS > WEM
WEN n cyst on the scalp
WENA pron South African word for you
WENCH n old word for a female servant ▷ vb frequent the company of prostitutes
WENCHED > WENCH
WENCHER > WENCH
WENCHERS > WENCH
WENCHES > WENCH
WENCHING > WENCH
WEND vb go or travel
WENDED > WEND
WENDIGO n evil spirit or cannibal
WENDIGOES > WENDIGO
WENDIGOS > WENDIGO
WENDING > WEND
WENDS > WEND
WENGE n type of tree found in central and West Africa
WENGES > WENGE
WENNIER > WEN
WENNIEST > WEN
WENNISH > WEN
WENNY > WEN
WENS > WEN
WENT n path
WENTS > WENT
WEPT > WEEP
WERE vb form of the past tense of be
WEREGILD same as > WERGILD
WEREGILDS > WEREGILD

WEREWOLF n (in folklore) person who can turn into a wolf
WERGELD same as > WERGILD
WERGELDS > WERGELD
WERGELT same as > WERGILD
WERGELTS > WERGELT
WERGILD n price set on a person's life, to be paid as compensation by their slayer
WERGILDS > WERGILD
WERNERITE another name for > SCAPOLITE
WERO n challenge made by an armed Māori warrior to a visitor to a marae
WEROS > WERO
WERRIS Australian slang word for > URINATION
WERRISES > WERRIS
WERSH adj tasteless
WERSHER > WERSH
WERSHEST > WERSH
WERT singular form of the past tense of > BE
WERWOLF same as > WEREWOLF
WERWOLVES > WERWOLF
WESAND same as > WEASAND
WESANDS > WESAND
WESKIT informal word for > WAISTCOAT
WESKITS > WESKIT
WESSAND same as > WEASAND
WESSANDS > WESSAND
WEST n part of the horizon where the sun sets ▷ adj in the west ▷ adv in, to, or towards the west ▷ vb move in westerly direction
WESTABOUT adv in, to, or towards the west
WESTBOUND adj going towards the west
WESTED > WEST
WESTER vb move or appear to move towards the west ▷ n strong wind or storm from the west
WESTERED > WESTER
WESTERING > WESTER
WESTERLY adj of or in the west ▷ adv towards the west ▷ n wind blowing from the west
WESTERN adj of or in the west ▷ n film or story about cowboys in the western US
WESTERNER n person from the west of a country or area
WESTERNS > WESTERN
WESTERS > WESTER
WESTIE n insulting word for a young working-class person from the western suburbs of Sydney
WESTIES > WESTIE
WESTING n movement, deviation, or distance covered in a westerly direction
WESTINGS > WESTING

WESTLIN Scots word for > WESTERN
WESTLINS adv to or in west
WESTMOST adj most western
WESTS > WEST
WESTWARD adv towards the west ▷ n westward part or direction ▷ adj moving, facing, or situated in the west
WESTWARDS same as > WESTWARD
WET adj covered or soaked with water or another liquid ▷ n moisture or rain ▷ vb make wet
WETA n type of wingless insect
WETAS > WETA
WETHER n male sheep
WETHERS > WETHER
WETLAND n area of marshy land
WETLANDS > WETLAND
WETLY > WET
WETNESS n the state of being wet
WETNESSES > WET
WETPROOF adj waterproof
WETS > WET
WETSUIT n body suit for diving
WETSUITS > WETSUIT
WETTABLE > WET
WETTED > WET
WETTER > WET
WETTERS > WET
WETTEST > WET
WETTIE n wetsuit
WETTIES > WETTIE
WETTING > WET
WETTINGS > WET
WETTISH > WET
WETWARE n the brain, as opposed to computers
WETWARES > WETWARE
WEX obsolete form of > WAX
WEXE obsolete form of > WAX
WEXED > WEX
WEXES > WEX
WEXING > WEX
WEY n measurement of weight
WEYARD obsolete form of > WEIRD
WEYS > WEY
WEYWARD obsolete form of > WEIRD
WEZAND obsolete form of > WEASAND
WEZANDS > WEZAND
WHA Scot word for > WHO
WHACK vb strike with a resounding blow ▷ n such a blow
WHACKED > WHACK
WHACKER > WHACK
WHACKERS > WHACK
WHACKIER > WHACKY
WHACKIEST > WHACKY
WHACKING adj huge ▷ n severe beating ▷ adv extremely
WHACKINGS > WHACKING

WHACKO n odd or eccentric person
WHACKOES > WHACKO
WHACKOS > WHACKO
WHACKS > WHACK
WHACKY variant spelling of > WACKY
WHAE same as > WHA
WHAISLE Scots form of > WHEEZE
WHAISLED > WHAISLE
WHAISLES > WHAISLE
WHAISLING > WHAISLE
WHAIZLE same as > WHAISLE
WHAIZLED > WHAIZLE
WHAIZLES > WHAIZLE
WHAIZLING > WHAIZLE
WHAKAIRO n art of carving
WHAKAIROS > WHAKAIRO
WHAKAPAPA n New Zealand word meaning genealogy
WHALE n large fish-shaped sea mammal ▷ vb hunt for whales
WHALEBACK n something shaped like the back of a whale
WHALEBOAT n narrow boat from 20 to 30 feet long having a sharp prow and stern, formerly used in whaling
WHALEBONE n horny substance hanging from the upper jaw of toothless whales
WHALED > WHALE
WHALELIKE > WHALE
WHALEMAN n person employed in whaling
WHALEMEN > WHALEMAN
WHALER n ship or person involved in whaling
WHALERIES > WHALERY
WHALERS > WHALER
WHALERY n whaling
WHALES > WHALE
WHALING n hunting of whales for food and oil ▷ adv extremely
WHALINGS > WHALING
WHALLY adj (of eyes) with light-coloured irises
WHAM interj expression indicating suddenness or forcefulness ▷ n forceful blow or impact ▷ vb strike or cause to strike with great force
WHAMMED > WHAM
WHAMMIES > WHAMMY
WHAMMING > WHAM
WHAMMO n sound of a sudden collision
WHAMMOS > WHAMMO
WHAMMY n devastating setback
WHAMO same as > WHAMMO
WHAMPLE n strike
WHAMPLES > WHAMPLE
WHAMS > WHAM
WHANAU n (in Māori societies) a family, esp an extended family

WHANAUS > WHANAU

WHANG vb strike or be struck so as to cause a resounding noise ▷ n resounding noise produced by a heavy blow

WHANGAM n imaginary creature

WHANGAMS > WHANGAM

WHANGED > WHANG

WHANGEE n tall woody grass grown for its stems, which are used for bamboo canes

WHANGEES > WHANGEE

WHANGING > WHANG

WHANGS > WHANG

WHAP same as > WHOP

WHAPPED > WHAP

WHAPPER same as > WHOPPER

WHAPPERS > WHAPPER

WHAPPING > WHAP

WHAPS > WHAP

WHARE n Māori hut or dwelling place

WHARENUI n (in New Zealand) meeting house

WHARENUIS > WHARENUI

WHAREPUNI n (in a Māori community) a tall carved building used as a guesthouse

WHARES > WHARE

WHARF n platform at a harbour for loading and unloading ships ▷ vb put (goods, etc) on a wharf

WHARFAGE n accommodation for ships at wharves

WHARFAGES > WHARFAGE

WHARFED > WHARF

WHARFIE n person employed to load and unload ships

WHARFIES > WHARFIE

WHARFING > WHARF

WHARFINGS > WHARF

WHARFS > WHARF

WHARVE n wooden disc or wheel on a shaft serving as a flywheel or pulley

WHARVES > WHARVE

WHAT pron which thing ▷ interj exclamation of anger, surprise, etc ▷ adv in which way, how much ▷ n part; portion

WHATA n building on stilts or a raised platform for storing provisions

WHATAS > WHATA

WHATCHA interj greeting meaning 'what are you?'

WHATEN adj what; what kind of

WHATEVER pron everything or anything that ▷ determiner intensive form of what

WHATEVS interj whatever

WHATNA another word for > WHATEN

WHATNESS n what something is

WHATNOT n similar unspecified thing

WHATNOTS > WHATNOT

WHATS > WHAT

WHATSIS US form of > WHATSIT

WHATSISES > WHATSIS

WHATSIT n person or thing the name of which is temporarily forgotten

WHATSITS > WHATSIT

WHATSO adj of whatever kind

WHATTEN same as > WHATEN

WHAUP n curlew

WHAUPS > WHAUP

WHAUR Scot word for > WHERE

WHAURS > WHAUR

WHEAL same as > WEAL

WHEALS > WHEAL

WHEAR obsolete variant of > WHERE

WHEARE obsolete variant of > WHERE

WHEAT n grain used in making flour, bread, and pasta

WHEATEAR n small songbird

WHEATEARS > WHEATEAR

WHEATEN n type of dog ▷ adj made of the grain or flour of wheat

WHEATENS > WHEATEN

WHEATGERM n vitamin-rich embryo of the wheat kernel

WHEATIER > WHEATY

WHEATIEST > WHEATY

WHEATLAND n region where wheat is grown

WHEATLESS > WHEAT

WHEATLIKE adj like wheat

WHEATMEAL n brown, but not wholemeal, flour

WHEATS > WHEAT

WHEATWORM n parasitic nematode worm that forms galls in the seeds of wheat

WHEATY adj having a wheat-like taste

WHEE interj exclamation of joy, thrill, etc

WHEECH vb Scots word meaning move quickly

WHEECHED > WHEECH

WHEECHING > WHEECH

WHEECHS > WHEECH

WHEEDLE vb coax or cajole

WHEEDLED > WHEEDLE

WHEEDLER > WHEEDLE

WHEEDLERS > WHEEDLE

WHEEDLES > WHEEDLE

WHEEDLING > WHEEDLE

WHEEL n disc that revolves on an axle ▷ vb push or pull (something with wheels)

WHEELBASE n distance between a vehicle's front and back axles

WHEELED adj having or equipped with a wheel or wheels

WHEELER n horse or other draught animal nearest the wheel

WHEELERS > WHEELER

WHEELIE n manoeuvre on a bike in which the front wheel is raised off the ground

WHEELIER > WHEELY

WHEELIES > WHEELIE

WHEELIEST > WHEELY

WHEELING > WHEEL

WHEELINGS > WHEEL

WHEELLESS adj having no wheels

WHEELMAN n helmsman

WHEELMEN > WHEELMAN

WHEELS > WHEEL

WHEELSMAN same as > WHEELMAN

WHEELSMEN > WHEELSMAN

WHEELSPIN n rotation of a wheel when it is not achieving any grip on a surface

WHEELWORK n arrangement of wheels in a machine, esp a train of gears

WHEELY adj resembling a wheel

WHEEN n few

WHEENGE Scots form of > WHINGE

WHEENGED > WHEENGE

WHEENGES > WHEENGE

WHEENGING > WHEENGE

WHEENS > WHEEN

WHEEP vb fly quickly and lightly

WHEEPED > WHEEP

WHEEPING > WHEEP

WHEEPLE vb whistle weakly

WHEEPLED > WHEEPLE

WHEEPLES > WHEEPLE

WHEEPLING > WHEEPLE

WHEEPS > WHEEP

WHEESH vb Scots word meaning silence (a person, noise, etc)

WHEESHED > WHEESH

WHEESHES > WHEESH

WHEESHING > WHEESH

WHEESHT same as > WHEESH

WHEESHTED > WHEESHT

WHEESHTS > WHEESHT

WHEEZE vb breathe with a hoarse whistling noise ▷ n wheezing sound

WHEEZED > WHEEZE

WHEEZER > WHEEZE

WHEEZERS > WHEEZE

WHEEZES > WHEEZE

WHEEZIER > WHEEZE

WHEEZIEST > WHEEZE

WHEEZILY > WHEEZE

WHEEZING > WHEEZE

WHEEZINGS > WHEEZE

WHEEZLE vb make hoarse breathing sound

WHEEZLED > WHEEZLE

WHEEZLES > WHEEZLE

WHEEZLING > WHEEZLE

WHEEZY > WHEEZE

WHEFT same as > WAFT

WHEFTS > WHEFT

WHELK n edible snail-like shellfish

WHELKED adj having or covered with whelks

WHELKIER > WHELK

WHELKIEST > WHELK

WHELKS > WHELK

WHELKY > WHELK

WHELM vb engulf entirely with or as if with water

WHELMED > WHELM

WHELMING > WHELM

WHELMS > WHELM

WHELP n pup or cub ▷ vb (of an animal) give birth

WHELPED > WHELP

WHELPING > WHELP

WHELPLESS > WHELP

WHELPS > WHELP

WHEMMLE vb overturn

WHEMMLED > WHEMMLE

WHEMMLES > WHEMMLE

WHEMMLING > WHEMMLE

WHEN adv at what time? ▷ pron at which time ▷ n question of when

WHENAS conj while; inasmuch as

WHENCE n point of origin ▷ adv from what place or source ▷ pron from what place, cause, or origin

WHENCES > WHENCE

WHENCEVER adv out of whatsoever place, cause or origin

WHENEVER adv at whatever time

WHENS > WHEN

WHENUA n land

WHENUAS > WHENUA

WHENWE n White immigrant to South Africa from Zimbabwe

WHENWES > WHENWE

WHERE adv in, at, or to what place? ▷ pron in, at, or to which place ▷ n question as to the position, direction, or destination of something

WHEREAS n testimonial introduced by whereas

WHEREASES > WHEREAS

WHEREAT adv at or to which place

WHEREBY pron by which ▷ adv how? by what means?

WHEREFOR adv for which ▷ n explanation or reason

WHEREFORE adv why ▷ n explanation or reason

WHEREFORS > WHEREFOR

WHEREFROM adv from what or where? whence? ▷ pron from which place

WHEREIN adv in what place or respect? ▷ pron in which place or thing

WHEREINTO adv into what place? ▷ pron into which place

WHERENESS *n* state of having a place
WHEREOF *adv* of what or which person or thing ▷ *pron* of which person or thing
WHEREON *adv* on what thing or place? ▷ *pron* on which thing, place, etc
WHEREOUT *adv* out of which
WHERES > WHERE
WHERESO *adv* in or to an unspecified place
WHERETO *adv* towards what (place, end, etc)? ▷ *pron* to which
WHEREUNTO *same as* > WHERETO
WHEREUPON *adv* upon what?
WHEREVER *adv* at whatever place ▷ *pron* at, in, or to every place or point which
WHEREWITH *pron* with or by which ▷ *adv* with what?
WHERRET *vb* strike (someone) a blow ▷ *n* blow, esp a slap on the face
WHERRETED > WHERRET
WHERRETS > WHERRET
WHERRIED > WHERRY
WHERRIES > WHERRY
WHERRIT *vb* worry or cause to worry
WHERRITED > WHERRIT
WHERRITS > WHERRIT
WHERRY *n* any of certain kinds of half-decked commercial boats ▷ *vb* travel in a wherry
WHERRYING > WHERRY
WHERRYMAN > WHERRY
WHERRYMEN > WHERRY
WHERVE *same as* > WHARVE
WHERVES > WHERVE
WHET *vb* sharpen (a tool) ▷ *n* act of whetting
WHETHER *conj* used to introduce any indirect question
WHETS > WHET
WHETSTONE *n* stone for sharpening tools
WHETTED > WHET
WHETTER > WHET
WHETTERS > WHET
WHETTING > WHET
WHEUGH *same as* > WHEW
WHEUGHED > WHEUGH
WHEUGHING > WHEUGH
WHEUGHS > WHEUGH
WHEW *interj* exclamation expressing relief, delight, etc ▷ *vb* express relief
WHEWED > WHEW
WHEWING > WHEW
WHEWS > WHEW
WHEY *n* watery liquid that separates from the curd when milk is clotted
WHEYEY > WHEY
WHEYFACE *n* pale bloodless face
WHEYFACED > WHEYFACE

WHEYFACES > WHEYFACE
WHEYIER > WHEY
WHEYIEST > WHEY
WHEYISH > WHEY
WHEYLIKE > WHEY
WHEYS > WHEY
WHICH *pron* used to request or refer to a choice from different possibilities ▷ *adj* used with a noun in requesting that a particular thing is further identified or distinguished
WHICHEVER *pron* any out of several ▷ *determiner* any (one, two, etc, out of several)
WHICKER *vb* (of a horse) to whinny or neigh
WHICKERED > WHICKER
WHICKERS > WHICKER
WHID *vb* move quickly
WHIDAH *same as* > WHYDAH
WHIDAHS > WHIDAH
WHIDDED > WHID
WHIDDER *vb* move with force
WHIDDERED > WHIDDER
WHIDDERS > WHIDDER
WHIDDING > WHID
WHIDS > WHID
WHIFF *n* puff of air or odour ▷ *vb* come, convey, or go in whiffs
WHIFFED > WHIFF
WHIFFER > WHIFF
WHIFFERS > WHIFF
WHIFFET *n* insignificant person
WHIFFETS > WHIFFET
WHIFFIER > WHIFFY
WHIFFIEST > WHIFFY
WHIFFING > WHIFF
WHIFFINGS > WHIFF
WHIFFLE *vb* think or behave in an erratic or unpredictable way
WHIFFLED > WHIFFLE
WHIFFLER *n* person who whiffles
WHIFFLERS > WHIFFLER
WHIFFLERY *n* frivolity
WHIFFLES > WHIFFLE
WHIFFLING > WHIFFLE
WHIFFS > WHIFF
WHIFFY *adj* smelly
WHIFT *n* brief emission of air
WHIFTS > WHIFT
WHIG *vb* go quickly
WHIGGED > WHIG
WHIGGING > WHIG
WHIGS > WHIG
WHILE *n* period of time ▷ *vb* pass time idly and pleasantly
WHILED > WHILE
WHILERE *adv* a while ago
WHILES *adv* at times
WHILEVER *conj* as long as
WHILING > WHILE
WHILK *archaic and dialect word for* > WHICH
WHILLIED > WHILLY
WHILLIES > WHILLY

WHILLY *vb* influence by flattery
WHILLYING > WHILLY
WHILLYWHA *variant of* > WHILLY
WHILOM *adv* formerly ▷ *adj* one-time
WHILST *same as* > WHILE
WHIM *n* sudden fancy ▷ *vb* have a whim
WHIMBERRY *n* whortleberry
WHIMBREL *n* small European curlew with a striped head
WHIMBRELS > WHIMBREL
WHIMMED > WHIM
WHIMMIER > WHIMMY
WHIMMIEST > WHIMMY
WHIMMING > WHIM
WHIMMY *adj* having whims
WHIMPER *vb* cry in a soft whining way ▷ *n* soft plaintive whine
WHIMPERED > WHIMPER
WHIMPERER > WHIMPER
WHIMPERS > WHIMPER
WHIMPLE *same as* > WIMPLE
WHIMPLED > WHIMPLE
WHIMPLES > WHIMPLE
WHIMPLING > WHIMPLE
WHIMS > WHIM
WHIMSEY *same as* > WHIMSY
WHIMSEYS > WHIMSEY
WHIMSICAL *adj* unusual, playful, and fanciful
WHIMSIED > WHIMSY
WHIMSIER > WHIMSY
WHIMSIES > WHIMSY
WHIMSIEST > WHIMSY
WHIMSILY > WHIMSY
WHIMSY *n* capricious idea ▷ *adj* quaint, comical, or unusual
WHIN *n* gorse
WHINBERRY *same as* > WHIMBERRY
WHINCHAT *n* type of songbird
WHINCHATS > WHINCHAT
WHINE *n* high-pitched plaintive cry ▷ *vb* make such a sound
WHINED > WHINE
WHINER > WHINE
WHINERS > WHINE
WHINES > WHINE
WHINEY *same as* > WHINY
WHINGDING *same as* > WINGDING
WHINGE *vb* complain ▷ *n* complaint
WHINGED > WHINGE
WHINGEING > WHINGE
WHINGER > WHINGE
WHINGERS > WHINGE
WHINGES > WHINGE
WHINGIER > WHINGY
WHINGIEST > WHINGY
WHINGING > WHINGE
WHINGY *adj* complaining peevishly, whining
WHINIARD *same as* > WHINYARD

WHINIARDS > WHINIARD
WHINIER > WHINY
WHINIEST > WHINY
WHININESS > WHINY
WHINING > WHINE
WHININGLY > WHINE
WHININGS > WHINE
WHINNIED > WHINNY
WHINNIER > WHINNY
WHINNIES > WHINNY
WHINNIEST > WHINNY
WHINNY *vb* neigh softly ▷ *n* soft neigh ▷ *adj* covered in whin
WHINNYING > WHINNY
WHINS > WHIN
WHINSTONE *n* any dark hard fine-grained rock, such as basalt
WHINY *adj* high-pitched and plaintive
WHINYARD *n* sword
WHINYARDS > WHINYARD
WHIO *n* New Zealand mountain duck with blue plumage
WHIOS > WHIO
WHIP *n* cord attached to a handle, used for beating animals or people ▷ *vb* strike with a whip, strap, or cane
WHIPBIRD *n* any of several birds having a whistle ending in a whipcrack note
WHIPBIRDS > WHIPBIRD
WHIPCAT *n* tailor
WHIPCATS > WHIPCAT
WHIPCORD *n* strong worsted or cotton fabric with a diagonally ribbed surface
WHIPCORDS > WHIPCORD
WHIPCORDY *adj* whipcord-like
WHIPCRACK *n* sound made by a whip
WHIPJACK *n* beggar imitating a sailor
WHIPJACKS > WHIPJACK
WHIPLASH *n* quick lash of a whip
WHIPLESS *adj* without a whip
WHIPLIKE > WHIP
WHIPPED > WHIP
WHIPPER > WHIP
WHIPPERS > WHIP
WHIPPET *n* racing dog like a small greyhound
WHIPPETS > WHIPPET
WHIPPIER > WHIPPY
WHIPPIEST > WHIPPY
WHIPPING > WHIP
WHIPPINGS > WHIP
WHIPPIT *n* small canister of nitrous oxide
WHIPPITS > WHIPPIT
WHIPPY *adj* springy
WHIPRAY *n* stingray
WHIPRAYS > WHIPRAY
WHIPS > WHIP

W

WHIPSAW n any saw with a flexible blade, such as a bandsaw ▷ vb saw with a whipsaw

WHIPSAWED > WHIPSAW

WHIPSAWN > WHIPSAW

WHIPSAWS > WHIPSAW

WHIPSNAKE n thin snake like leather whip

WHIPSTAFF n ship's steering bar

WHIPSTALL n stall in which an aircraft goes into a nearly vertical climb, pauses, slips backwards momentarily, and drops suddenly with its nose down

WHIPSTER n insignificant but pretentious or cheeky person, esp a young one

WHIPSTERS > WHIPSTER

WHIPSTOCK n handle of a whip

WHIPT old past tense of > WHIP

WHIPTAIL n type of lizard

WHIPTAILS > WHIPTAIL

WHIPWORM n parasitic worm living in the intestines of mammals

WHIPWORMS > WHIPWORM

WHIR n prolonged soft swish or buzz ▷ vb make or cause to make a whir

WHIRL vb spin or revolve ▷ n whirling movement

WHIRLBAT n medieval weapon

WHIRLBATS > WHIRLBAT

WHIRLED > WHIRL

WHIRLER > WHIRL

WHIRLERS > WHIRL

WHIRLIER > WHIRLY

WHIRLIES pl n illness induced by excessive use of alcohol

WHIRLIEST > WHIRLY

WHIRLIGIG same as > WINDMILL

WHIRLING > WHIRL

WHIRLINGS > WHIRL

WHIRLPOOL n strong circular current of water

WHIRLS > WHIRL

WHIRLWIND n column of air whirling violently upwards in a spiral ▷ adj much quicker than normal

WHIRLY adj characterized by whirling

WHIRR same as > WHIR

WHIRRA interj exclamation of sorrow or deep concern

WHIRRED > WHIR

WHIRRET vb strike with sharp blow

WHIRRETED > WHIRRET

WHIRRETS > WHIRRET

WHIRRIED > WHIRRY

WHIRRIER > WHIRRY

WHIRRIES > WHIRRY

WHIRRIEST > WHIRRY

WHIRRING > WHIR

WHIRRINGS > WHIR

WHIRRS > WHIRR

WHIRRY vb move quickly ▷ adj characteristic of a whir

WHIRRYING > WHIRRY

WHIRS > WHIR

WHIRTLE same as > WORTLE

WHIRTLES > WHIRTLE

WHISHED > WHISH

WHISHES > WHISH

WHISHING > WHISH

WHISHT interj hush!, be quiet! ▷ adj silent or still ▷ vb make or become silent

WHISHTED > WHISHT

WHISHTING > WHISHT

WHISHTS > WHISHT

WHISK vb move or remove quickly ▷ n quick movement

WHISKED > WHISK

WHISKER n any of the long stiff hairs on the face of a cat or other mammal

WHISKERED adj having whiskers

WHISKERS > WHISKER

WHISKERY adj having whiskers

WHISKET same as > WISKET

WHISKETS > WHISKET

WHISKEY n Irish or American whisky

WHISKEYS > WHISKEY

WHISKIES > WHISKY

WHISKING > WHISK

WHISKS > WHISK

WHISKY n spirit distilled from fermented cereals

WHISPER vb speak softly, without vibration of the vocal cords ▷ n soft voice

WHISPERED > WHISPER

WHISPERER n person or thing that whispers

WHISPERS > WHISPER

WHISPERY adj like a whisper

WHISS vb hiss

WHISSED > WHISS

WHISSES > WHISS

WHISSING > WHISS

WHIST same as > WHISHT

WHISTED > WHIST

WHISTING > WHIST

WHISTLE vb produce a shrill sound ▷ n whistling sound

WHISTLED > WHISTLE

WHISTLER n person or thing that whistles

WHISTLERS > WHISTLER

WHISTLES > WHISTLE

WHISTLING > WHISTLE

WHISTS > WHIST

WHIT n smallest particle

WHITE adj of the colour of snow ▷ n colour of snow

WHITEBAIT n small edible fish

WHITEBASS n type of fish

WHITEBEAM n type of tree

WHITECAP n wave with a white broken crest

WHITECAPS > WHITECAP

WHITECOAT n person who wears a white coat

WHITECOMB n fungal disease infecting the combs of certain fowls

WHITED adj as in whited sepulchre hypocrite

WHITEDAMP n mixture of poisonous gases, mainly carbon monoxide, occurring in coal mines

WHITEFACE n white stage make-up

WHITEFISH n type of fish

WHITEFLY n tiny whitish insect that is harmful to greenhouse plants

WHITEHEAD n type of pimple with a white head

WHITELIST n list of email contacts from whom messages are regarded as acceptable by the user ▷ vb put (an email contact) on a whitelist

WHITELY > WHITE

WHITEN vb make or become white or whiter

WHITENED > WHITEN

WHITENER n substance that makes something white or whiter

WHITENERS > WHITENER

WHITENESS > WHITE

WHITENING > WHITEN

WHITENS > WHITEN

WHITEOUT n atmospheric condition in which blizzards or low clouds make it very difficult to see

WHITEOUTS > WHITEOUT

WHITEPOT n custard or milk pudding

WHITEPOTS > WHITEPOT

WHITER > WHITE

WHITES pl n white clothes, as worn for playing cricket

WHITEST > WHITE

WHITETAIL n type of deer

WHITEWALL n pneumatic tyre having white sidewalls

WHITEWARE n white ceramics

WHITEWASH n substance for whitening walls ▷ vb cover with whitewash

WHITEWING n type of bird

WHITEWOOD n light-coloured wood often prepared for staining

WHITEY same as > WHITY

WHITHER same as > WUTHER

WHITHERED > WHITHER

WHITHERS > WHITHER

WHITIER > WHITY

WHITIEST > WHITY

WHITING n edible sea fish

WHITINGS > WHITING

WHITISH > WHITE

WHITLING n type of trout

WHITLINGS > WHITLING

WHITLOW n inflamed sore on a finger or toe, esp round a nail

WHITLOWS > WHITLOW

WHITRACK n weasel or stoat

WHITRACKS > WHITRACK

WHITRET same as > WHITTRET

WHITRETS > WHITRET

WHITRICK n dialect word for a male weasel

WHITRICKS > WHITRICK

WHITS > WHIT

WHITSTER n person who whitens clothes

WHITSTERS > WHITSTER

WHITTAW same as > WHITTAWER

WHITTAWER n person who treats leather

WHITTAWS > WHITTAW

WHITTER variant spelling of > WITTER

WHITTERED > WHITTER

WHITTERS > WHITTER

WHITTLE vb cut or carve (wood) with a knife ▷ n knife, esp a large one

WHITTLED > WHITTLE

WHITTLER > WHITTLE

WHITTLERS > WHITTLE

WHITTLES > WHITTLE

WHITTLING > WHITTLE

WHITTRET n male weasel

WHITTRETS > WHITTRET

WHITY adj of a white colour

WHIZ same as > WHIZZ

WHIZBANG n small-calibre shell

WHIZBANGS > WHIZBANG

WHIZZ vb make a loud buzzing sound ▷ n loud buzzing sound

WHIZZBANG same as > WHIZBANG

WHIZZED > WHIZZ

WHIZZER > WHIZZ

WHIZZERS > WHIZZ

WHIZZES > WHIZZ

WHIZZIER > WHIZZY

WHIZZIEST > WHIZZY

WHIZZING > WHIZZ

WHIZZINGS > WHIZZ

WHIZZO same as > WHIZZY

WHIZZY adj using sophisticated technology

WHO pron which person

WHOA interj command used to stop or slow down

WHODUNIT same as > WHODUNNIT

WHODUNITS > WHODUNIT

WHODUNNIT n detective story, play, or film

WHOEVER pron any person who

WHOLE adj containing all the elements or parts ▷ n complete thing or system

WHOLEFOOD n food that has been processed as little as possible ▷ adj of or relating to wholefood

WHOLEMEAL adj (of flour) made from the whole wheat grain

WHOLENESS > WHOLE

WHOLES > WHOLE

WHOLESALE adv dealing by selling goods in large quantities to retailers ▷ n business of selling goods in large quantities and at lower prices to retailers for resale

WHOLESOME adj physically or morally beneficial

WHOLISM same as > HOLISM

WHOLISMS > WHOLISM

WHOLIST same as > HOLIST

WHOLISTIC same as > HOLISTIC

WHOLISTS > WHOLIST

WHOLLY adv completely or totally

WHOLPHIN n whale-dolphin hybrid

WHOLPHINS > WHOLPHIN

WHOM pron objective form of who

WHOMBLE same as > WHEMMLE

WHOMBLED > WHOMBLE

WHOMBLES > WHOMBLE

WHOMBLING > WHOMBLE

WHOMEVER pron objective form of whoever

WHOMMLE same as > WHEMMLE

WHOMMLED > WHOMMLE

WHOMMLES > WHOMMLE

WHOMMLING > WHOMMLE

WHOMP vb strike; thump

WHOMPED > WHOMP

WHOMPING > WHOMP

WHOMPS > WHOMP

WHOMSO pron whom; whomever

WHOOBUB same as > HUBBUB

WHOOBUBS > WHOOBUB

WHOOF same as > WOOF

WHOOFED > WHOOF

WHOOFING > WHOOF

WHOOFS > WHOOF

WHOOMP n sudden loud sound

WHOOMPH same as > WHOOMP

WHOOMPHS > WHOOMPH

WHOOMPS > WHOOMP

WHOONGA n narcotic smoked as a recreational drug in S Africa

WHOONGAS > WHOONGA

WHOOP n shout or cry to express excitement ▷ vb emit a whoop

WHOOPED > WHOOP

WHOOPEE n cry of joy

WHOOPEES > WHOOPEE

WHOOPER n type of swan

WHOOPERS > WHOOPER

WHOOPIE same as > WHOOPEE

WHOOPIES > WHOOPIE

WHOOPING > WHOOP

WHOOPINGS > WHOOPING

WHOOPLA n commotion; fuss

WHOOPLAS > WHOOPLA

WHOOPS interj exclamation of surprise or of apology

WHOOPSIE n animal excrement

WHOOPSIES > WHOOPSIE

WHOOSH n hissing or rushing sound ▷ vb make or move with a hissing or rushing sound

WHOOSHED > WHOOSH

WHOOSHES > WHOOSH

WHOOSHING > WHOOSH

WHOOSIS n thingamajig

WHOOSISES > WHOOSIS

WHOOT obsolete variant of > HOOT

WHOOTED > WHOOT

WHOOTING > WHOOT

WHOOTS > WHOOT

WHOP vb strike, beat, or thrash

WHOPPED > WHOP

WHOPPER n anything unusually large

WHOPPERS > WHOPPER

WHOPPING n beating as punishment ▷ adj unusually large ▷ adv extremely

WHOPPINGS > WHOPPING

WHOPS > WHOP

WHORE n old-fashioned word for a prostitute ▷ vb be or act as a prostitute

WHORED > WHORE

WHOREDOM n old-fashioned word for a state of being a prostitute

WHOREDOMS > WHOREDOM

WHORES > WHORE

WHORESON n archaic derogatory word for a person whose parents are not married ▷ adj vile or hateful

WHORESONS > WHORESON

WHORING n act of whoring

WHORINGS > WHORING

WHORISH > WHORE

WHORISHLY > WHORE

WHORL n ring of leaves or petals ▷ vb form a whorl or whorls

WHORLBAT same as > WHIRLBAT

WHORLBATS > WHORLBAT

WHORLED > WHORL

WHORLING > WHORL

WHORLS > WHORL

WHORT n small shrub bearing blackish edible sweet berries

WHORTLE n whortleberry

WHORTLES > WHORTLE

WHORTS > WHORT

WHOSE pron of whom or of which ▷ determiner of whom or of which

WHOSESO adj possessive form of whoso

WHOSEVER pron belonging to whoever

WHOSIS n thingamajig

WHOSISES > WHOSIS

WHOSIT n object or person whose name is not known

WHOSITS > WHOSIT

WHOSO archaic word for > WHOEVER

WHOSOEVER same as > WHOEVER

WHOT obsolete variant of > HOT

WHOW interj wow ▷ vb to wow

WHOWED > WHOW

WHOWING > WHOW

WHOWS > WHOW

WHUMMLE same as > WHEMMLE

WHUMMLED > WHUMMLE

WHUMMLES > WHUMMLE

WHUMMLING > WHUMMLE

WHUMP vb make a dull thud ▷ n dull thud

WHUMPED > WHUMP

WHUMPING > WHUMP

WHUMPS > WHUMP

WHUNSTANE Scots variant of > WHINSTONE

WHUP vb defeat totally

WHUPPED > WHUP

WHUPPING > WHUP

WHUPPINGS > WHUPPING

WHUPS > WHUP

WHY adv for what reason ▷ pron because of which ▷ n reason, purpose, or cause of something

WHYDA same as > WHYDAH

WHYDAH n type of black African bird

WHYDAHS > WHYDAH

WHYDAS > WHYDA

WHYDUNIT same as > WHYDUNNIT

WHYDUNITS > WHYDUNIT

WHYDUNNIT n novel, film, etc concerned with the motives of the criminal rather than his or her identity

WHYEVER adv for whatever reason

WHYS > WHY

WIBBLE vb wobble

WIBBLED > WIBBLE

WIBBLES > WIBBLE

WIBBLING > WIBBLE

WICCA n cult or practice of witchcraft

WICCAN n practitioner of wicca

WICCANS > WICCAN

WICCAS > WICCA

WICE Scots form of > WISE

WICH n variant of wych

WICHES > WICH

WICK n cord through a lamp or candle which carries fuel to the flame ▷ adj lively or active ▷ vb (of a material) draw in (water, fuel, etc)

WICKAPE same as > WICOPY

WICKAPES > WICKAPE

WICKED adj morally bad ▷ n wicked person

WICKEDER > WICKED

WICKEDEST > WICKED

WICKEDLY > WICKED

WICKEDS > WICKED

WICKEN same as > QUICKEN

WICKENS > WICKEN

WICKER adj made of woven cane ▷ n slender flexible twig or shoot, esp of willow

WICKERED > WICKER

WICKERS > WICKER

WICKET n set of three cricket stumps and two bails

WICKETS > WICKET

WICKIES > WICKY

WICKING > WICK

WICKINGS > WICK

WICKIUP n crude shelter made of brushwood, mats, or grass and having an oval frame

WICKIUPS > WICKIUP

WICKLESS > WICK

WICKS > WICK

WICKTHING n creeping animal, such as a woodlouse

WICKY same as > QUICKEN

WICKYUP same as > WICKIUP

WICKYUPS > WICKYUP

WICOPIES > WICOPY

WICOPY n any of various North American trees, shrubs, or herbaceous plants

WIDDER same as > WIDOW

WIDDERS > WIDDER

WIDDIE same as > WIDDY

WIDDIES > WIDDY

WIDDLE vb urinate ▷ n urine

WIDDLED > WIDDLE

WIDDLES > WIDDLE

WIDDLING > WIDDLE

WIDDY vb rope made of twigs

WIDE adj large from side to side ▷ adv the full extent

W

▷ *n* (in cricket) a ball outside a batsman's reach

WIDEAWAKE *n* hat with a low crown and a very wide brim

WIDEBAND *n* wide bandwidth transmission medium ▷ *adj* capable of transmitting on a wide bandwidth

WIDEBANDS > WIDEBAND

WIDEBODY *n* aircraft with a wide fuselage

WIDELY > WIDE

WIDEN *vb* make or become wider

WIDENED > WIDEN

WIDENER > WIDEN

WIDENERS > WIDEN

WIDENESS > WIDE

WIDENING *n* act of widening

WIDENINGS > WIDENING

WIDENS > WIDEN

WIDEOUT *n* (in American football) player who catches passes from the quarterback

WIDEOUTS > WIDEOUT

WIDER > WIDE

WIDES > WIDE

WIDEST > WIDE

WIDGEON *same as* > WIGEON

WIDGEONS > WIDGEON

WIDGET *n* any small device, the name of which is unknown or forgotten

WIDGETS > WIDGET

WIDGIE *n* Australian word for a female hooligan

WIDGIES > WIDGIE

WIDISH > WIDE

WIDOW *n* woman whose spouse is dead and who has not remarried ▷ *vb* cause to become a widow

WIDOWBIRD *n* whydah

WIDOWED > WIDOW

WIDOWER *n* man whose spouse is dead and who has not remarried

WIDOWERED > WIDOWER

WIDOWERS > WIDOWER

WIDOWHOOD > WIDOW

WIDOWING > WIDOW

WIDOWMAN *n* widower

WIDOWMEN > WIDOWMAN

WIDOWS > WIDOW

WIDTH *n* distance from side to side

WIDTHS > WIDTH

WIDTHWAY *adj* across the width

WIDTHWAYS *same as* > WIDTHWISE

WIDTHWISE *adv* in the direction of the width

WIEL *same as* > WEEL

WIELD *vb* hold and use (a weapon)

WIELDABLE > WIELD

WIELDED > WIELD

WIELDER > WIELD

WIELDERS > WIELD

WIELDIER > WIELDY

WIELDIEST > WIELDY

WIELDING > WIELD

WIELDLESS *adj* unwieldy

WIELDS > WIELD

WIELDY *adj* easily handled, used, or managed

WIELS > WIEL

WIENER *n* kind of smoked beef or pork sausage, similar to a frankfurter

WIENERS > WIENER

WIENIE *same as* > WIENER

WIENIES > WIENIE

WIFE *n* woman to whom one is married ▷ *vb* marry

WIFED > WIFE

WIFEDOM *n* state of being a wife

WIFEDOMS > WIFEDOM

WIFEHOOD > WIFE

WIFEHOODS > WIFE

WIFELESS > WIFE

WIFELIER > WIFE

WIFELIEST > WIFE

WIFELIKE > WIFE

WIFELY > WIFE

WIFES > WIFE

WIFEY *n* wife

WIFEYS > WIFEY

WIFIE *n* woman

WIFIES > WIFIE

WIFING > WIFE

WIFTIER > WIFTY

WIFTIEST > WIFTY

WIFTY *adj* scatterbrained

WIG *n* artificial head of hair ▷ *vb* furnish with a wig

WIGAN *n* stiff fabric

WIGANS > WIGAN

WIGEON *n* duck found in marshland

WIGEONS > WIGEON

WIGGED > WIG

WIGGERIES > WIGGERY

WIGGERY *n* wigs

WIGGIER > WIGGY

WIGGIEST > WIGGY

WIGGING > WIG

WIGGINGS > WIG

WIGGLE *vb* move jerkily from side to side ▷ *n* wiggling movement

WIGGLED > WIGGLE

WIGGLER > WIGGLE

WIGGLERS > WIGGLE

WIGGLES > WIGGLE

WIGGLIER > WIGGLE

WIGGLIEST > WIGGLE

WIGGLING > WIGGLE

WIGGLY > WIGGLE

WIGGY *adj* eccentric

WIGHT *vb* blame ▷ *n* human being ▷ *adj* strong and brave

WIGHTED > WIGHT

WIGHTING > WIGHT

WIGHTLY *adv* swiftly

WIGHTS > WIGHT

WIGLESS > WIG

WIGLET *n* small wig

WIGLETS > WIGLET

WIGLIKE > WIG

WIGMAKER *n* person who makes wigs

WIGMAKERS > WIGMAKER

WIGS > WIG

WIGWAG *vb* move (something) back and forth ▷ *n* system of communication by flag semaphore

WIGWAGGED > WIGWAG

WIGWAGGER > WIGWAG

WIGWAGS > WIGWAG

WIGWAM *n* Native American's tent

WIGWAMS > WIGWAM

WIKI *n* website consisting mainly of user-generated content

WIKIALITY *n* version of facts which is agreed to be true, but which may not actually be true

WIKIS > WIKI

WIKIUP *same as* > WICKIUP

WIKIUPS > WIKIUP

WILCO *interj* expression indicating that the message just received will be complied with

WILD *same as* > WIELD

WILDCARD *n* person given entry to a competition without qualifying

WILDCARDS > WILDCARD

WILDCAT *n* European wild animal like a large domestic cat ▷ *adj* risky and financially unsound ▷ *vb* drill for petroleum or natural gas in an area having no known reserves

WILDCATS > WILDCAT

WILDED > WILD

WILDER *vb* lead or be led astray

WILDERED > WILDER

WILDERING > WILDER

WILDERS > WILDER

WILDEST > WILD

WILDFIRE *n* highly flammable material, such as Greek fire, formerly used in warfare

WILDFIRES > WILDFIRE

WILDFOWL *n* wild bird that is hunted for sport or food

WILDFOWLS > WILDFOWL

WILDGRAVE *same as* > WALDGRAVE

WILDING *n* uncultivated plant

WILDINGS > WILDING

WILDISH > WILD

WILDLAND *n* land which has not been cultivated

WILDLANDS > WILDLAND

WILDLIFE *n* wild animals and plants collectively

WILDLIFES > WILDLIFE

WILDLING *same as* > WILDING

WILDLINGS > WILDLING

WILDLY > WILD

WILDMAN *n* man who lives in the wild

WILDMEN > WILDMAN

WILDNESS > WILD

WILDS > WILD

WILDWOOD *n* wood or forest growing in a natural uncultivated state

WILDWOODS > WILDWOOD

WILE *n* trickery, cunning, or craftiness ▷ *vb* lure, beguile, or entice

WILED > WILE

WILEFUL *adj* deceitful

WILES > WILE

WILFUL *adj* headstrong or obstinate

WILFULLY > WILFUL

WILGA *n* small drought-resistant tree of Australia

WILGAS > WILGA

WILI *n* spirit

WILIER > WILY

WILIEST > WILY

WILILY > WILY

WILINESS > WILY

WILING > WILE

WILIS > WILI

WILJA *same as* > WILTJA

WILJAS > WILJA

WILL *vb* used as an auxiliary to form the future tense or to indicate intention, ability, or expectation ▷ *n* strong determination

WILLABLE *adj* able to be wished or determined by the will

WILLED *adj* having a will as specified

WILLEMITE *n* secondary mineral consisting of zinc silicate

WILLER > WILL

WILLERS > WILL

WILLEST > WILL

WILLET *n* large American shore bird

WILLETS > WILLET

WILLEY *same as* > WILLY

WILLEYED > WILLEY

WILLEYING > WILLEY

WILLEYS > WILLEY

WILLFUL *same as* > WILFUL

WILLFULLY > WILLFUL

WILLIAM *n* as in *sweet william* flowering plant

WILLIAMS > WILLIAM

WILLIE *n* informal word for a penis

WILLIED > WILLY

WILLIES > WILLY

WILLING *adj* ready or inclined (to do something)

WILLINGER > WILLING

WILLINGLY > WILLING

WILLIWAU *same as* > WILLIWAW

WILLIWAUS > WILLIWAU

WILLIWAW *n* sudden strong gust of cold wind blowing offshore from a mountainous coast

WILLIWAWS
> WILLIWAW
WILLOW n tree with thin flexible branches ▷ vb open and clean (fibres) with rotating spikes
WILLOWED > WILLOW
WILLOWER n willow
WILLOWERS
> WILLOWER
WILLOWIER > WILLOWY
WILLOWING > WILLOW
WILLOWISH > WILLOW
WILLOWS > WILLOW
WILLOWY adj slender and graceful
WILLPOWER n ability to control oneself and one's actions
WILLS > WILL
WILLY vb clean in a willowing-machine
WILLYARD adj timid
WILLYART same as
> WILLYARD
WILLYING > WILLY
WILLYWAW same as
> WILLIWAW
WILLYWAWS
> WILLYWAW
WILT vb (cause to) become limp or lose strength ▷ n act of wilting or state of becoming wilted
WILTED > WILT
WILTING > WILT
WILTJA n Aboriginal Australian shelter
WILTJAS > WILTJA
WILTS > WILT
WILY adj crafty or sly
WIMBLE n any of a number of hand tools used for boring holes ▷ vb bore (a hole) with or as if with a wimble
WIMBLED > WIMBLE
WIMBLES > WIMBLE
WIMBLING > WIMBLE
WIMBREL same as
> WHIMBREL
WIMBRELS > WIMBREL
WIMMIN pl n intentional non-standard spelling of 'women'
WIMP n feeble ineffectual person ▷ vb as in wimp out fail to complete something through fear
WIMPED > WIMP
WIMPIER > WIMP
WIMPIEST > WIMP
WIMPINESS > WIMP
WIMPING > WIMP
WIMPISH > WIMP
WIMPISHLY > WIMP
WIMPLE n garment framing the face, worn by medieval women and now by nuns ▷ vb ripple or cause to ripple or undulate
WIMPLED > WIMPLE
WIMPLES > WIMPLE
WIMPLING > WIMPLE
WIMPS > WIMP
WIMPY > WIMP

WIN vb come first in (a competition, fight, etc) ▷ vb dry (grain, hay, etc) by exposure to sun and air ▷ n victory, esp in a game
WINCE vb draw back, as if in pain ▷ n wincing
WINCED > WINCE
WINCER > WINCE
WINCERS > WINCE
WINCES > WINCE
WINCEY n plain- or twill-weave cloth
WINCEYS > WINCEY
WINCH n machine for lifting or hauling using a cable or chain wound round a drum ▷ vb lift or haul using a winch
WINCHED > WINCH
WINCHER > WINCH
WINCHERS > WINCH
WINCHES > WINCH
WINCHING > WINCH
WINCHMAN n man who operates a winch
WINCHMEN > WINCHMAN
WINCING > WINCE
WINCINGLY adv while wincing or in a wincing manner
WINCINGS > WINCE
WINCOPIPE n type of plant
WIND n current of air ▷ vb render short of breath
WINDABLE n able to be wound
WINDAC same as > WINDAS
WINDACS > WINDAC
WINDAGE n deflection of a projectile as a result of the effect of the wind
WINDAGES > WINDAGE
WINDAS n windlass
WINDASES > WINDAS
WINDBAG n person who talks much but uninterestingly
WINDBAGS > WINDBAG
WINDBELL n light bell made to be sounded by wind
WINDBELLS
> WINDBELL
WINDBILL n bill of exchange cosigned by a guarantor
WINDBILLS
> WINDBILL
WINDBLAST n strong gust of wind
WINDBLOW n uprooting of trees by wind
WINDBLOWN adj blown about by the wind
WINDBLOWS
> WINDBLOW
WINDBORNE adj (of plant seeds, etc) borne on the wind
WINDBOUND adj (of a sailing vessel) prevented from sailing by an unfavourable wind
WINDBREAK n fence or line of trees providing shelter from the wind

WINDBURN n irritation and redness of the skin caused by exposure to wind
WINDBURNS
> WINDBURN
WINDBURNT
> WINDBURN
WINDCHILL n chilling effect of wind and low temperature
WINDED > WIND
WINDER n person or device that winds, as an engine for hoisting the cages in a mine shaft
WINDERS > WINDER
WINDFALL n unexpected good luck
WINDFALLS
> WINDFALL
WINDFLAW n squall
WINDFLAWS
> WINDFLAW
WINDGALL n soft swelling in the area of the fetlock joint of a horse
WINDGALLS
> WINDGALL
WINDGUN n air gun
WINDGUNS > WINDGUN
WINDHOVER dialect name for > KESTREL
WINDIER > WINDY
WINDIEST > WINDY
WINDIGO same as
> WENDIGO
WINDIGOES > WINDIGO
WINDIGOS > WINDIGO
WINDILY > WINDY
WINDINESS > WINDY
WINDING > WIND
WINDINGLY > WINDING
WINDINGS > WIND
WINDLASS n winch worked by a crank ▷ vb raise or haul (a weight, etc) by means of a windlass
WINDLE vb wind something round continuously
WINDLED > WINDLE
WINDLES > WINDLE
WINDLESS > WIND
WINDLING > WINDLE
WINDLINGS > WINDLE
WINDLOAD n force on a structure from wind
WINDLOADS
> WINDLOAD
WINDMILL n machine for grinding or pumping driven by sails turned by the wind ▷ vb move or cause to move like the arms of a windmill
WINDMILLS
> WINDMILL
WINDOCK same as
> WINNOCK
WINDOCKS > WINDOCK
WINDORE n window
WINDORES > WINDORE
WINDOW n opening in a wall to let in light or air ▷ vb furnish with windows
WINDOWED > WINDOW

WINDOWIER > WINDOWY
WINDOWING > WINDOW
WINDOWS > WINDOW
WINDOWY adj having many windows
WINDPACK n snow that has been compacted by the wind
WINDPACKS
> WINDPACK
WINDPIPE n tube linking the throat and the lungs
WINDPIPES
> WINDPIPE
WINDPROOF adj not penetrable by wind ▷ vb make windproof
WINDRING adj winding
WINDROW n long low ridge or line of hay or a similar crop ▷ vb put (hay or a similar crop) into windrows
WINDROWED > WINDROW
WINDROWER > WINDROW
WINDROWS > WINDROW
WINDS > WIND
WINDSAIL n sail rigged as an air scoop over a hatch or companionway
WINDSAILS
> WINDSAIL
WINDSES pl n ventilation shafts within mines
WINDSHAKE n crack between the annual rings in wood
WINDSHIP n ship propelled by wind
WINDSHIPS
> WINDSHIP
WINDSLAB n crust formed on soft snow by the wind
WINDSLABS
> WINDSLAB
WINDSOCK n cloth cone on a mast at an airfield to indicate wind direction
WINDSOCKS
> WINDSOCK
WINDSTORM n storm consisting of violent winds
WINDSURF vb sail standing on a board equipped with a mast, sail, and boom
WINDSURFS
> WINDSURF
WINDSWEPT adj exposed to the wind
WINDTHROW n uprooting of trees by wind
WINDTIGHT adj impenetrable by wind
WINDUP n prank or hoax
WINDUPS > WINDUP
WINDWARD n direction from which the wind is blowing ▷ adj of or in the direction from which the wind blows ▷ adv towards the wind
WINDWARDS adv in the direction of the wind
WINDWAY n part of wind instrument
WINDWAYS > WINDWAY

W

WINDY *adj* denoting a time or conditions in which there is a strong wind

WINE *n* alcoholic drink made from fermented grapes ▷ *adj* of a dark purplish-red colour ▷ *vb* give wine to

WINEBERRY another name for > MAKO

WINED > WINE

WINEGLASS *n* glass for wine, usually with a small bowl on a stem with a flared base

WINELESS > WINE

WINEMAKER *n* maker of wine

WINEPRESS *n* any equipment used for squeezing the juice from grapes in order to make wine

WINERIES > WINERY

WINERY *n* place where wine is made

WINES > WINE

WINESAP *n* variety of apple

WINESAPS > WINESAP

WINESHOP *n* shop where wine is sold

WINESHOPS > WINESHOP

WINESKIN *n* skin of a sheep or goat sewn up and used as a holder for wine

WINESKINS > WINESKIN

WINESOP *n* old word for an alcoholic

WINESOPS > WINESOP

WINEY *adj* having the taste or qualities of wine

WING *n* one of the limbs or organs of a bird, insect, or bat that are used for flying ▷ *vb* fly

WINGBACK *n* position in some team sports

WINGBACKS > WINGBACK

WINGBEAT *n* complete cycle of moving the wing by a bird in flight

WINGBEATS > WINGBEAT

WINGBOW *n* distinctive band of colour marking the wing of a bird

WINGBOWS > WINGBOW

WINGCHAIR *n* chair with wings on each side

WINGDING *n* noisy lively party or festivity

WINGDINGS > WINGDING

WINGE same as > WHINGE

WINGED *adj* furnished with wings

WINGEDLY > WINGED

WINGEING > WINGE

WINGER *n* player positioned on a wing

WINGERS > WINGER

WINGES > WINGE

WINGIER > WINGY

WINGIEST > WINGY

WINGING > WING

WINGLESS *adj* having no wings or vestigial wings

WINGLET *n* small wing

WINGLETS > WINGLET

WINGLIKE > WING

WINGMAN *n* player in the wing position in Australian Rules

WINGMEN > WINGMAN

WINGNUT *n* nut with projections for gripping with the thumb and finger

WINGNUTS > WINGNUT

WINGOVER *n* manoeuvre for reversing the direction of flight of an aircraft

WINGOVERS > WINGOVER

WINGS > WING

WINGSPAN *n* distance between the wing tips of an aircraft, bird, or insect

WINGSPANS > WINGSPAN

WINGSUIT *n* type of skydiving suit

WINGSUITS > WINGSUIT

WINGTIP *n* outermost edge of a wing

WINGTIPS > WINGTIP

WINGY *adj* having wings

WINIER > WINY

WINIEST > WINY

WINING > WINE

WINISH > WINE

WINK *vb* close and open (an eye) quickly as a signal ▷ *n* winking

WINKED > WINK

WINKER *n* person or thing that winks

WINKERS > WINKER

WINKING > WINK

WINKINGLY > WINK

WINKINGS > WINK

WINKLE *n* shellfish with a spiral shell ▷ *vb* extract or prise out

WINKLED > WINKLE

WINKLER *n* one who forces a person or thing out

WINKLERS > WINKLER

WINKLES > WINKLE

WINKLING > WINKLE

WINKS > WINK

WINLESS *adj* not having won anything

WINN *n* penny

WINNA *vb* will not

WINNABLE > WIN

WINNARD *n* heron

WINNARDS > WINNARD

WINNED > WIN

WINNER *n* person or thing that wins

WINNERS > WINNER

WINNING *adj* (of a person) charming, attractive, etc

WINNINGLY > WINNING

WINNINGS *pl n* money or prizes won

WINNLE *n* machine for winding thread or yarn

WINNLES > WINNLE

WINNOCK *n* window

WINNOCKS > WINNOCK

WINNOW *vb* separate (chaff) from (grain) ▷ *n* device for winnowing

WINNOWED > WINNOW

WINNOWER > WINNOW

WINNOWERS > WINNOW

WINNOWING > WINNOW

WINNOWS > WINNOW

WINNS > WINN

WINO *n* destitute person who habitually drinks cheap wine

WINOES > WINO

WINOS > WINO

WINS > WIN

WINSEY same as > WINCEY

WINSEYS > WINSEY

WINSOME *adj* charming or winning

WINSOMELY > WINSOME

WINSOMER > WINSOME

WINSOMEST > WINSOME

WINTER *n* coldest season ▷ *vb* spend the winter

WINTERED > WINTER

WINTERER > WINTER

WINTERERS > WINTER

WINTERFED *vb* past tense of 'winterfeed' (to feed (livestock) in winter when the grazing is not rich enough)

WINTERIER > WINTERY

WINTERING > WINTER

WINTERISE same as > WINTERIZE

WINTERISH > WINTER

WINTERIZE *vb* prepare (a house, car, etc) to withstand winter conditions

WINTERLY *adj* like winter

WINTERS > WINTER

WINTERY same as > WINTRY

WINTLE *vb* reel; stagger

WINTLED > WINTLE

WINTLES > WINTLE

WINTLING > WINTLE

WINTRIER > WINTRY

WINTRIEST > WINTRY

WINTRILY > WINTRY

WINTRY *adj* of or like winter

WINY same as > WINEY

WINZE *n* steeply inclined shaft, as for ventilation between levels

WINZES > WINZE

WIPE *vb* clean or dry by rubbing ▷ *n* act of wiping

WIPEABLE *adj* able to be wiped

WIPED > WIPE

WIPEOUT *n* instance of wiping out

WIPEOUTS > WIPEOUT

WIPER *n* any piece of cloth, such as a handkerchief, towel, etc, used for wiping

WIPERS > WIPER

WIPES > WIPE

WIPING > WIPE

WIPINGS > WIPE

WIPPEN *n* part of the hammer action in a piano

WIPPENS > WIPPEN

WIRABLE *adj* that can be wired

WIRE *n* thin flexible strand of metal ▷ *vb* fasten with wire

WIRED *adj* excited or nervous

WIREDRAW *vb* convert (metal) into wire by drawing through successively smaller dies

WIREDRAWN > WIREDRAW

WIREDRAWS > WIREDRAW

WIREDREW > WIREDRAW

WIREFRAME *n* visual representation of the structure of a web page

WIREGRASS *n* fine variety of grass

WIREHAIR *n* type of terrier

WIREHAIRS > WIREHAIR

WIRELESS *adj* (of a computer network) connected by radio rather than by cables or fibre optics ▷ *n* old-fashioned name for radio ▷ *vb* send by wireless

WIRELIKE > WIRE

WIRELINE *n* telegraph or telephone line

WIRELINES > WIRELINE

WIREMAN *n* person who installs and maintains electric wiring, cables, etc

WIREMEN > WIREMAN

WIREPHOTO *n* facsimile of a photograph transmitted electronically via a telephone system

WIRER *n* person who sets or uses wires to snare rabbits and similar animals

WIRERS > WIRER

WIRES > WIRE

WIRETAP *vb* obtain information secretly via telegraph or telephone

WIRETAPS > WIRETAP

WIREWAY *n* tube for electric wires

WIREWAYS > WIREWAY

WIREWORK *n* functional or decorative work made of wire

WIREWORKS *n* factory where wire or articles of wire are made

WIREWORM *n* destructive wormlike beetle larva

WIREWORMS > WIREWORM

WIREWOVE *adj* woven out of wire

WIRIER > WIRY

WIRIEST > WIRY

WIRILDA *n* SE Australian acacia tree with edible seeds

WIRILDAS > WIRILDA

WIRILY > WIRY

WIRINESS > WIRY

WIRING n system of wires ▷ adj used in wiring

WIRINGS > WIRING

WIRRA interj exclamation of sorrow or deep concern

WIRRAH n Australian saltwater fish with bright blue spots

WIRRAHS > WIRRAH

WIRRICOW same as > WORRICOW

WIRRICOWS > WIRRICOW

WIRY adj lean and tough

WIS vb know or suppose (something)

WISARD obsolete spelling of > WIZARD

WISARDS > WISARD

WISDOM n good sense and judgment

WISDOMS > WISDOM

WISE vb guide ▷ adj having wisdom ▷ n manner

WISEACRE n person who wishes to seem wise

WISEACRES > WISEACRE

WISEASS n person who thinks he or she is being witty or clever

WISEASSES > WISEASS

WISECRACK n clever, sometimes unkind, remark ▷ vb make a wisecrack

WISED > WISE

WISEGUY n person who wants to seem clever

WISEGUYS > WISEGUY

WISELIER > WISE

WISELIEST > WISE

WISELING n one who claims to be wise

WISELINGS > WISELING

WISELY > WISE

WISENESS > WISE

WISENT n European bison

WISENTS > WISENT

WISER > WISE

WISES > WISE

WISEST > WISE

WISEWOMAN n witch

WISEWOMEN > WISEWOMAN

WISH vb want or desire ▷ n expression of a desire

WISHA interj expression of surprise

WISHBONE n V-shaped bone above the breastbone of a fowl

WISHBONES > WISHBONE

WISHED > WISH

WISHER > WISH

WISHERS > WISH

WISHES > WISH

WISHFUL adj too optimistic

WISHFULLY > WISHFUL

WISHING > WISH

WISHINGS > WISH

WISHLESS > WISH

WISHT variant of > WHISHT

WISING > WISE

WISKET n basket

WISKETS > WISKET

WISP n light delicate streak ▷ vb move or act like a wisp

WISPED > WISP

WISPIER > WISPY

WISPIEST > WISPY

WISPILY > WISPY

WISPINESS > WISPY

WISPING > WISP

WISPISH > WISP

WISPLIKE > WISP

WISPS > WISP

WISPY adj thin, fine, or delicate

WISS vb urinate

WISSED > WIS

WISSES > WIS

WISSING > WIS

WIST vb know

WISTARIA same as > WISTERIA

WISTARIAS > WISTARIA

WISTED > WIST

WISTERIA n climbing shrub with blue or purple flowers

WISTERIAS > WISTERIA

WISTFUL adj sadly longing

WISTFULLY > WISTFUL

WISTING > WIST

WISTITI n marmoset

WISTITIS > WISTITI

WISTLY adv intently

WISTS > WIST

WIT vb be aware of; know ▷ n ability to use words or ideas in a clever and amusing way

WITAN n Anglo-Saxon assembly that met to counsel the king

WITANS > WITAN

WITBLITS n illegally distilled strong alcoholic drink

WITCH n person, usu female, who practises (black) magic ▷ vb cause or change by or as if by witchcraft

WITCHED > WITCH

WITCHEN n rowan tree

WITCHENS > WITCHEN

WITCHERY n practice of witchcraft

WITCHES > WITCH

WITCHETTY n edible larva of certain Australian moths and beetles

WITCHHOOD > WITCH

WITCHIER > WITCHY

WITCHIEST > WITCHY

WITCHING adj relating to or appropriate for witchcraft ▷ n witchcraft

WITCHINGS > WITCHING

WITCHKNOT n knot in hair

WITCHLIKE > WITCH

WITCHWEED n type of plant that is a serious pest of grain crops in parts of Africa and Asia

WITCHY adj like a witch

WITE vb blame

WITED > WITE

WITELESS adj witless

WITES > WITE

WITGAT n type of S African tree

WITGATS > WITGAT

WITH prep indicating presence alongside, possession, means of performance, characteristic manner, etc ▷ n division between flues in chimney

WITHAL adv as well

WITHDRAW vb take or move out or away

WITHDRAWN adj unsociable

WITHDRAWS > WITHDRAW

WITHDREW > WITHDRAW

WITHE n strong flexible twig suitable for binding things together ▷ vb bind with withes

WITHED > WITHE

WITHER vb wilt or dry up

WITHERED > WITHER

WITHERER > WITHER

WITHERERS > WITHER

WITHERING > WITHER

WITHERITE n white, grey, or yellowish mineral

WITHEROD n American shrub

WITHERODS > WITHEROD

WITHERS pl n ridge between a horse's shoulder blades

WITHES > WITHE

WITHHAULT > WITHHOLD

WITHHELD > WITHHOLD

WITHHOLD vb refrain from giving

WITHHOLDS > WITHHOLD

WITHIER > WITHY

WITHIES > WITHY

WITHIEST > WITHY

WITHIN adv in or inside ▷ prep in or inside ▷ n something that is within

WITHING > WITHE

WITHINS > WITHIN

WITHOUT prep not accompanied by, using, or having ▷ adv outside ▷ n person who is without

WITHOUTEN obsolete form of > WITHOUT

WITHOUTS > WITHOUT

WITHS > WITH

WITHSTAND vb oppose or resist successfully

WITHSTOOD > WITHSTAND

WITHWIND n bindweed

WITHWINDS > WITHWIND

WITHY n willow tree, esp an osier ▷ adj (of people) tough and agile

WITHYWIND same as > WITHWIND

WITING > WITE

WITLESS adj foolish

WITLESSLY > WITLESS

WITLING n person who thinks themself witty

WITLINGS > WITLING

WITLOOF n chicory

WITLOOFS > WITLOOF

WITNESS n person who has seen something happen ▷ vb see at first hand

WITNESSED > WITNESS

WITNESSER > WITNESS

WITNESSES > WITNESS

WITNEY n type of blanket; heavy cloth

WITNEYS > WITNEY

WITS > WIT

WITTED adj having wit

WITTER vb chatter pointlessly or at unnecessary length ▷ n pointless chat

WITTERED > WITTER

WITTERING > WITTER

WITTERS > WITTER

WITTICISM n witty remark

WITTIER > WITTY

WITTIEST > WITTY

WITTILY > WITTY

WITTINESS > WITTY

WITTING adj deliberate ▷ n act of becoming aware

WITTINGLY > WITTING

WITTINGS > WITTING

WITTOL n man who tolerates his wife's unfaithfulness

WITTOLLY > WITTOL

WITTOLS > WITTOL

WITTY adj clever and amusing

WITWALL n golden oriole

WITWALLS > WITWALL

WITWANTON vb be disrespectfully witty

WIVE vb marry (a woman)

WIVED > WIVE

WIVEHOOD obsolete variant of > WIFEHOOD

WIVEHOODS > WIVEHOOD

WIVER another word for > WIVERN

WIVERN same as > WYVERN

WIVERNS > WIVERN

WIVERS > WIVER

WIVES > WIFE

WIVING > WIVE

WIZ shortened form of > WIZARD

WIZARD n magician ▷ adj superb

WIZARDER > WIZARD

WIZARDEST > WIZARD

WIZARDLY adj like a wizard

WIZARDRY n magic or sorcery

WIZARDS > WIZARD

WIZEN vb make or become shrivelled ▷ n archaic word for 'weasand' (the gullet) ▷ adj wizened

WIZENED adj shrivelled or wrinkled
WIZENER > WIZEN
WIZENEST > WIZEN
WIZENING > WIZEN
WIZENS > WIZEN
WIZES > WIZ
WIZIER same as > VIZIER
WIZIERS > WIZIER
WIZZEN same as > WIZEN
WIZZENS > WIZZEN
WIZZES > WIZ
WO archaic spelling of > WOE
WOAD n blue dye obtained from a plant
WOADED adj coloured blue with woad
WOADS > WOAD
WOADWAX same as > WOADWAXEN
WOADWAXEN n small Eurasian leguminous shrub
WOADWAXES > WOADWAX
WOAH same as > WHOA
WOALD same as > WELD
WOALDS > WOALD
WOBBEGONG n Australian shark with brown-and-white skin
WOBBLE vb move unsteadily ▷ n wobbling movement or sound
WOBBLED > WOBBLE
WOBBLER > WOBBLE
WOBBLERS > WOBBLE
WOBBLES > WOBBLE
WOBBLIER > WOBBLY
WOBBLIES > WOBBLY
WOBBLIEST > WOBBLY
WOBBLING > WOBBLE
WOBBLINGS > WOBBLE
WOBBLY adj unsteady ▷ n temper tantrum
WOBEGONE same as > WOEBEGONE
WOCK same as > WOK
WOCKS > WOCK
WODGE n thick lump or chunk
WODGES > WODGE
WOE n grief
WOEBEGONE adj looking miserable
WOEFUL adj extremely sad
WOEFULLER > WOEFUL
WOEFULLY > WOEFUL
WOENESS > WOE
WOENESSES > WOE
WOES > WOE
WOESOME adj woeful
WOF n fool
WOFS > WOF
WOFUL same as > WOEFUL
WOFULLER > WOFUL
WOFULLEST > WOFUL
WOFULLY > WOFUL
WOFULNESS > WOFUL
WOGGLE n ring of leather through which a Scout neckerchief is threaded
WOGGLES > WOGGLE
WOIWODE same as > VOIVODE
WOIWODES > WOIWODE

WOJUS adj (Irish) of a poor quality
WOK n bowl-shaped Chinese cooking pan, used for stir-frying
WOKE adj alert to social and political injustice
WOKEN > WAKE
WOKER > WOKE
WOKEST > WOKE
WOKKA modifier as in wokka board piece of fibreboard used as a musical instrument
WOKS > WOK
WOLD same as > WELD
WOLDS > WOLD
WOLF n wild predatory canine mammal ▷ vb eat ravenously
WOLFBERRY n type of shrub
WOLFED > WOLF
WOLFER same as > WOLVER
WOLFERS > WOLFER
WOLFFISH n type of large northern deep-sea fish with large sharp teeth
WOLFHOUND n very large breed of dog
WOLFING > WOLF
WOLFINGS > WOLF
WOLFISH > WOLF
WOLFISHLY > WOLF
WOLFKIN n young wolf
WOLFKINS > WOLFKIN
WOLFLIKE > WOLF
WOLFLING n young wolf
WOLFLINGS > WOLFLING
WOLFRAM another name for > TUNGSTEN
WOLFRAMS > WOLFRAM
WOLFS > WOLF
WOLFSBANE n type of poisonous plant with yellow hoodlike flowers
WOLFSKIN n skin of wolf used for clothing, etc
WOLFSKINS > WOLFSKIN
WOLLIES > WOLLY
WOLLY n pickled cucumber or olive
WOLVE vb hunt for wolves
WOLVED > WOLVE
WOLVER n person who hunts wolves
WOLVERENE same as > WOLVERINE
WOLVERINE n carnivorous mammal of Arctic regions
WOLVERS > WOLVER
WOLVES > WOLF
WOLVING > WOLVE
WOLVINGS > WOLVE
WOLVISH same as > WOLFISH
WOLVISHLY > WOLVISH
WOMAN n adult human female ▷ vb provide with a woman or women
WOMANED > WOMAN
WOMANHOOD n state of being a woman

WOMANING > WOMAN
WOMANISE same as > WOMANIZE
WOMANISED > WOMANISE
WOMANISER > WOMANISE
WOMANISES > WOMANISE
WOMANISH adj effeminate
WOMANISM n feminism among Black women
WOMANISMS > WOMANISM
WOMANIST > WOMANISM
WOMANISTS > WOMANISM
WOMANIZE vb indulge in many casual affairs with women
WOMANIZED > WOMANIZE
WOMANIZER > WOMANIZE
WOMANIZES > WOMANIZE
WOMANKIND n all women considered as a group
WOMANLESS > WOMAN
WOMANLIER > WOMANLY
WOMANLIKE adj like a woman
WOMANLY adj having qualities traditionally associated with a woman
WOMANNED > WOMAN
WOMANNESS > WOMAN
WOMANNING > WOMAN
WOMANS > WOMAN
WOMB vb enclose ▷ n hollow organ in female mammals where babies develop
WOMBAT n small heavily built burrowing Australian marsupial
WOMBATS > WOMBAT
WOMBED > WOMB
WOMBIER > WOMBY
WOMBIEST > WOMBY
WOMBING > WOMB
WOMBLIKE > WOMB
WOMBS > WOMB
WOMBY adj hollow; spacious
WOMEN > WOMAN
WOMENFOLK pl n women collectively
WOMENKIND same as > WOMANKIND
WOMERA same as > WOOMERA
WOMERAS > WOMERA
WOMMERA same as > WOOMERA
WOMMERAS > WOMMERA
WOMMIT n foolish person
WOMMITS > WOMMIT
WOMYN n intentional non-standard spelling of 'women'
WON n standard monetary unit of North Korea ▷ vb live or dwell
WONDER vb be curious about ▷ n wonderful thing ▷ adj spectacularly successful

WONDERED > WONDER
WONDERER > WONDER
WONDERERS > WONDER
WONDERFUL adj very fine
WONDERING > WONDER
WONDERKID n informal word for an exceptionally successful young person
WONDEROUS obsolete variant of > WONDROUS
WONDERS > WONDER
WONDRED adj splendid
WONDROUS adj wonderful
WONGA n money
WONGAS > WONGA
WONGI vb talk informally
WONGIED > WONGI
WONGIING > WONGI
WONGIS > WONGI
WONING > WON
WONINGS > WON
WONK n person who is obsessively interested in a specified subject
WONKERIES > WONKERY
WONKERY n activities of a wonk
WONKIER > WONKY
WONKIEST > WONKY
WONKILY adv in a wonky manner
WONKINESS n state of being wonky
WONKISH adj like a wonk
WONKS > WONK
WONKY adj shaky or unsteady
WONNED > WON
WONNER > WON
WONNERS > WON
WONNING > WON
WONNINGS > WON
WONS > WON
WONT adj accustomed ▷ n custom ▷ vb become or cause to become accustomed
WONTED adj accustomed or habituated (to doing something)
WONTEDLY > WONTED
WONTING > WONT
WONTLESS > WONT
WONTON n dumpling filled with spiced minced pork
WONTONS > WONTON
WONTS > WONT
WOO vb seek the love or affection of
WOOABLE adj able to be wooed
WOOBUT same as > WOUBIT
WOOBUTS > WOOBUT
WOOD n substance trees are made of, used in carpentry and as fuel ▷ adj made of or using wood ▷ vb (of land) plant with trees
WOODBIN n box for firewood
WOODBIND same as > WOODBINE
WOODBINDS > WOODBIND
WOODBINE n honeysuckle

WOODBINES
> WOODBINE
WOODBINS > WOODBIN
WOODBLOCK *n* hollow block of wood used as a percussion instrument
WOODBORER *n* type of beetle whose larvae bore into and damage wood
WOODBOX *n* box for firewood
WOODBOXES > WOODBOX
WOODCHAT *n* European and N African songbird
WOODCHATS
> WOODCHAT
WOODCHIP *n* textured wallpaper
WOODCHIPS
> WOODCHIP
WOODCHOP *n* wood-chopping competition
WOODCHOPS
> WOODCHOP
WOODCHUCK *n* N American marmot with coarse reddish-brown fur
WOODCOCK *n* game bird
WOODCOCKS
> WOODCOCK
WOODCRAFT *n* ability and experience in matters concerned with living in a wood or forest
WOODCUT *n* (print made from) an engraved block of wood
WOODCUTS > WOODCUT
WOODED *adj* covered with trees
WOODEN *adj* made of wood ▷ *vb* fell or kill (a person or animal)
WOODENED > WOODEN
WOODENER > WOODEN
WOODENEST > WOODEN
WOODENING > WOODEN
WOODENLY > WOODEN
WOODENS > WOODEN
WOODENTOP *n* dull, foolish, or unintelligent person
WOODFERN *n* type of evergreen fern
WOODFERNS
> WOODFERN
WOODFREE *adj* (of paper) made from pulp that has been treated to remove impurities
WOODGRAIN *n* grain in wood
WOODHEN *another name for* > WEKA
WOODHENS > WOODHEN
WOODHOLE *n* store area for wood
WOODHOLES
> WOODHOLE
WOODHORSE *n* frame for holding wood being sawn
WOODHOUSE *n* shed for firewood
WOODIE *n* gallows rope
WOODIER > WOODY
WOODIES > WOODIE
WOODIEST > WOODY

WOODINESS > WOODY
WOODING > WOOD
WOODLAND *n* forest ▷ *adj* living in woods
WOODLANDS
> WOODLAND
WOODLARK *n* type of Old World lark
WOODLARKS
> WOODLARK
WOODLESS > WOOD
WOODLICE
> WOODLOUSE
WOODLORE *n* woodcraft skills
WOODLORES
> WOODLORE
WOODLOT *n* area restricted to the growing of trees
WOODLOTS > WOODLOT
WOODLOUSE *n* small insect-like creature with many legs
WOODMAN *same as* > WOODSMAN
WOODMEAL *n* sawdust powder
WOODMEALS
> WOODMEAL
WOODMEN > WOODMAN
WOODMICE
> WOODMOUSE
WOODMOUSE *n* field mouse
WOODNESS > WOOD
WOODNOTE *n* natural musical note or song, like that of a wild bird
WOODNOTES
> WOODNOTE
WOODPILE *n* heap of firewood
WOODPILES
> WOODPILE
WOODPRINT *another name for* > WOODCUT
WOODRAT *n* pack-rat
WOODRATS > WOODRAT
WOODREEVE *n* steward responsible for wood
WOODROOF *same as* > WOODRUFF
WOODROOFS
> WOODROOF
WOODRUFF *n* plant with small sweet-smelling white flowers and sweet-smelling leaves
WOODRUFFS
> WOODRUFF
WOODRUSH *n* plant with grasslike leaves and small brown flowers
WOODS *pl n* closely packed trees forming a forest or wood
WOODSCREW *n* metal screw that tapers to a point so that it can be driven into wood by a screwdriver
WOODSHED *n* small outbuilding where firewood, garden tools, etc are stored
WOODSHEDS
> WOODSHED
WOODSHOCK *n* type of bird

WOODSIA *n* type of small fern with tufted rhizomes and wiry fronds
WOODSIAS > WOODSIA
WOODSIER > WOODSY
WOODSIEST > WOODSY
WOODSKIN *n* canoe made of bark
WOODSKINS
> WOODSKIN
WOODSMAN *n* person who lives in a wood or who is skilled at woodwork or carving
WOODSMEN > WOODSMAN
WOODSMOKE *n* smoke produced by burning wood
WOODSPITE *n* green woodpecker
WOODSTONE *n* type of stone resembling wood
WOODSTOVE *n* wood-burning stove
WOODSY *adj* of, reminiscent of, or connected with woods
WOODTONE *n* colour matching that of wood
WOODTONES
> WOODTONE
WOODWALE *n* green woodpecker
WOODWALES
> WOODWALE
WOODWARD *n* person in charge of a forest or wood
WOODWARDS
> WOODWARD
WOODWASP *n* large wasplike insect
WOODWASPS
> WOODWASP
WOODWAX *same as* > WOADWAXEN
WOODWAXEN *same as* > WOADWAXEN
WOODWAXES > WOODWAX
WOODWIND *n* type of wind instrument made of wood ▷ *adj* of or denoting a type of wind instrument, such as the oboe
WOODWINDS
> WOODWIND
WOODWORK *n* parts of a room or building made of wood
WOODWORKS
> WOODWORK
WOODWORM *n* insect larva that bores into wood
WOODWORMS
> WOODWORM
WOODWOSE *n* hairy wildman of the woods
WOODWOSES
> WOODWOSE
WOODY *adj* (of a plant) having a very hard stem
WOODYARD *n* place where timber is cut and stored
WOODYARDS
> WOODYARD
WOOED > WOO
WOOER > WOO
WOOERS > WOO
WOOF *vb* (of dogs) bark
WOOFED > WOOF

WOOFER *n* loudspeaker reproducing low-frequency sounds
WOOFERS > WOOFER
WOOFIER > WOOFY
WOOFIEST > WOOFY
WOOFING > WOOF
WOOFS > WOOF
WOOFY *adj* with close, dense texture
WOOHOO *interj* expression of joy, approval, etc
WOOING > WOO
WOOINGLY > WOO
WOOINGS > WOO
WOOL *n* soft hair of sheep, goats, etc
WOOLD *vb* wind (rope)
WOOLDED > WOOLD
WOOLDER *n* stick for winding rope
WOOLDERS > WOOLDER
WOOLDING > WOOLD
WOOLDINGS > WOOLD
WOOLDS > WOOLD
WOOLED *same as* > WOOLLED
WOOLEN *same as* > WOOLLEN
WOOLENS > WOOLEN
WOOLER *same as* > WOOLDER
WOOLERS > WOOLER
WOOLFAT *same as* > LANOLIN
WOOLFATS > WOOLFAT
WOOLFELL *n* skin of a sheep or similar animal with the fleece still attached
WOOLFELLS
> WOOLFELL
WOOLHAT *n* hat made of wool
WOOLHATS > WOOLHAT
WOOLIE *n* wool garment
WOOLIER > WOOLY
WOOLIES > WOOLY
WOOLIEST > WOOLY
WOOLILY > WOOLY
WOOLINESS > WOOLY
WOOLLED *adj* (of animals) having wool
WOOLLEN *adj* relating to or consisting partly or wholly of wool ▷ *n* garment or piece of cloth made of wool
WOOLLENS > WOOLLEN
WOOLLIER > WOOLLY
WOOLLIES > WOOLLY
WOOLLIEST > WOOLLY
WOOLLIKE > WOOL
WOOLLILY > WOOLLY
WOOLLY *adj* of or like wool ▷ *n* knitted woollen garment
WOOLMAN *n* wool trader
WOOLMEN > WOOLMAN
WOOLPACK *n* cloth or canvas wrapping used to pack a bale of wool
WOOLPACKS
> WOOLPACK
WOOLS > WOOL
WOOLSACK *n* sack containing or intended to contain wool

W

WOOLSACKS
> WOOLSACK

WOOLSEY n cotton and wool blend

WOOLSEYS > WOOLSEY

WOOLSHED n large building in which sheep shearing takes place

WOOLSHEDS
> WOOLSHED

WOOLSKIN n sheepskin with wool still on

WOOLSKINS
> WOOLSKIN

WOOLWARD adv with woollen side touching the skin

WOOLWORK n embroidery with wool

WOOLWORKS
> WOOLWORK

WOOLY same as > WOOLLY

WOOMERA n notched stick used by Aboriginal Australians to aid the propulsion of a spear

WOOMERANG same as
> WOOMERA

WOOMERAS > WOOMERA

WOON same as > WON

WOONED > WOON

WOONERF n (in the Netherlands) road primarily for cyclists and pedestrians

WOONERFS > WOONERF

WOONING > WOON

WOONS > WOON

WOOPIE n well-off older person

WOOPIES > WOOPIE

WOOPS vb (esp of small child) vomit

WOOPSED > WOOPS

WOOPSES > WOOPS

WOOPSING > WOOPS

WOOPY n well-off older person

WOORALI less common name for > CURARE

WOORALIS > WOORALI

WOORARA same as
> WOURALI

WOORARAS > WOORARA

WOORARI same as
> WOURALI

WOORARIS > WOORARI

WOOS > WOO

WOOSE same as > WUSS

WOOSEL same as > OUZEL

WOOSELL same as
> OUZEL

WOOSELLS > WOOSELL

WOOSELS > WOOSEL

WOOSES > WOOSE

WOOSH same as > WHOOSH

WOOSHED > WOOSH

WOOSHES > WOOSH

WOOSHING > WOOSH

WOOT interj (esp used by players in online games) shout of joy, victory, etc

WOOTZ n Middle-Eastern steel

WOOTZES > WOOTZ

WOOZIER > WOOZY

WOOZIEST > WOOZY

WOOZILY > WOOZY

WOOZINESS > WOOZY

WOOZY adj weak, dizzy, and confused

WOP vb strike, beat, or thrash

WOPPED > WOP

WOPPING > WOP

WOPS > WOP

WORCESTER n type of woollen fabric

WORD n smallest single meaningful unit of speech or writing ▷ vb express in words

WORDAGE n words considered collectively, esp a quantity of words

WORDAGES > WORDAGE

WORDBOOK n book containing words, usually with their meanings

WORDBOOKS
> WORDBOOK

WORDBOUND adj unable to find words to express something

WORDBREAK n point at which a word is divided when it runs over from one line of print to the next

WORDCOUNT n count of words in a document

WORDED > WORD

WORDGAME n any game involving the formation, discovery, or alteration of a word or words

WORDGAMES > WORDGAME

WORDIE n person who loves words

WORDIER > WORDY

WORDIES > WORDIE

WORDIEST > WORDY

WORDILY > WORDY

WORDINESS > WORDY

WORDING n choice and arrangement of words

WORDINGS > WORDING

WORDISH adj talkative

WORDLESS adj inarticulate or silent

WORDLORE n knowledge about words

WORDLORES
> WORDLORE

WORDPLAY n verbal wit based on the meanings and ambiguities of words

WORDPLAYS
> WORDPLAY

WORDS > WORD

WORDSMITH n person skilled in using words

WORDWRAP n word-processing function that shifts a word at the end of a line to a new line to keep within preset margins

WORDWRAPS
> WORDWRAP

WORDY adj using too many words

WORE > WEAR

WORK n physical or mental effort directed to making or doing something ▷ adj of or for work ▷ vb (cause to) do work

WORKABLE adj able to operate efficiently

WORKABLY > WORKABLE

WORKADAY n working day
▷ adj ordinary

WORKADAYS
> WORKADAY

WORKBAG n container for implements, tools, or materials

WORKBAGS > WORKBAG

WORKBENCH n heavy table at which a craftsman or mechanic works

WORKBOAT n boat used for tasks

WORKBOATS
> WORKBOAT

WORKBOOK n exercise book or textbook used for study, esp a textbook with spaces for answers

WORKBOOKS
> WORKBOOK

WORKBOOT n type of sturdy leather boot

WORKBOOTS
> WORKBOOT

WORKBOX same as
> WORKBAG

WORKBOXES > WORKBOX

WORKDAY another word for
> WORKADAY

WORKDAYS > WORKDAY

WORKED adj made or decorated with evidence of workmanship

WORKER n person who works in a specified way

WORKERIST n supporter of working-class politics

WORKERS > WORKER

WORKFARE n scheme in which unemployed people are required to do community work or job training in return for payments

WORKFARES
> WORKFARE

WORKFLOW n rate of progress of work

WORKFLOWS
> WORKFLOW

WORKFOLK pl n working people, esp labourers on a farm

WORKFOLKS same as
> WORKFOLK

WORKFORCE n total number of workers

WORKFUL adj hardworking

WORKGIRL n young female manual worker

WORKGIRLS
> WORKGIRL

WORKGROUP n collection of networked computers

WORKHORSE n person or thing that does a lot of dull or routine work

WORKHOUR n time set aside for work

WORKHOURS
> WORKHOUR

WORKHOUSE n (in England, formerly) institution where the poor

were given food and lodgings in return for work

WORKING n operation or mode of operation of something ▷ adj relating to or concerned with a person or thing that works

WORKINGS > WORKING

WORKLESS > WORK

WORKLOAD n amount of work to be done, esp in a specified period

WORKLOADS
> WORKLOAD

WORKMAN n manual worker

WORKMANLY adj efficient but not particularly original

WORKMATE n person who works with another person

WORKMATES
> WORKMATE

WORKMEN > WORKMAN

WORKOUT n session of physical exercise for training or fitness

WORKOUTS > WORKOUT

WORKPIECE n piece of metal or other material that is in the process of being worked on or made or has actually been cut or shaped by a hand tool or machine

WORKPLACE n place, such as a factory or office, where people work

WORKPRINT n unfinished print of a cinema film

WORKROOM n room in which work, usually manual labour, is done

WORKROOMS
> WORKROOM

WORKS > WORK

WORKSAFE adj (of an internet link) suitable for viewing in the workplace

WORKSHEET n sheet of paper containing exercises to be completed by a student

WORKSHOP n room or building for a manufacturing process
▷ vb perform (a play) with no costumes, set, or musical accompaniment

WORKSHOPS
> WORKSHOP

WORKSHY adj not inclined to work

WORKSITE n area where work is done

WORKSITES
> WORKSITE

WORKSOME adj hardworking

WORKSONG n song sung while doing physical work

WORKSONGS
> WORKSONG

WORKSPACE n area set aside for work

WORKTABLE n table at which writing, sewing, or other work may be done

WORKTOP n surface used for food preparation
WORKTOPS > WORKTOP
WORKUP n medical examination
WORKUPS > WORKUP
WORKWEAR n clothes, such as overalls, as worn for work in a factory, shop, etc
WORKWEARS > WORKWEAR
WORKWEEK n number of hours or days in a week actually or officially allocated to work
WORKWEEKS > WORKWEEK
WORKWOMAN n female manual worker
WORKWOMEN > WORKWOMAN
WORLD n planet earth ▷ adj of the whole world
WORLDBEAT n genre blending folk and popular music
WORLDED adj incorporating worlds
WORLDER n person who belongs to a specified class or domain
WORLDERS > WORLDER
WORLDIE n world-class performance, achievement, person, etc
WORLDIES > WORLDIE
WORLDLIER > WORLDLY
WORLDLING n person who is primarily concerned with worldly matters or material things
WORLDLY adj not spiritual ▷ adv in a worldly manner
WORLDS > WORLD
WORLDVIEW n comprehensive view of human life and the universe
WORLDWIDE adj applying or extending throughout the world
WORM n small limbless invertebrate animal ▷ vb rid of worms
WORMCAST n coil of earth excreted by a burrowing worm
WORMCASTS > WORMCAST
WORMED > WORM
WORMER > WORM
WORMERIES > WORMERY
WORMERS > WORM
WORMERY n piece of apparatus in which worms are kept for study
WORMFLIES > WORMFLY
WORMFLY n type of lure dressed on a double hook
WORMGEAR n gear with screw thread
WORMGEARS > WORMGEAR
WORMHOLE n hole made by a worm in timber, plants, or fruit
WORMHOLED > WORMHOLE

WORMHOLES > WORMHOLE
WORMIER > WORMY
WORMIEST > WORMY
WORMIL n burrowing larva of type of fly
WORMILS > WORMIL
WORMINESS > WORMY
WORMING > WORM
WORMISH > WORM
WORMLIKE > WORM
WORMROOT n plant used to cure worms
WORMROOTS > WORMROOT
WORMS n disease caused by parasitic worms living in the intestines
WORMSEED n any of various plants used to treat worm infestation
WORMSEEDS > WORMSEED
WORMWHEEL n wheel of a wormgear
WORMWOOD n bitter plant
WORMWOODS > WORMWOOD
WORMY adj infested with or eaten by worms
WORN > WEAR
WORNNESS n quality or condition of being worn
WORRAL n type of lizard
WORRALS > WORRAL
WORREL same as > WORRAL
WORRELS > WORREL
WORRICOW n frightening creature
WORRICOWS > WORRICOW
WORRIED > WORRY
WORRIEDLY > WORRY
WORRIER > WORRY
WORRIERS > WORRY
WORRIES > WORRY
WORRIMENT n anxiety or the trouble that causes it
WORRISOME adj causing worry
WORRIT vb tease or worry
WORRITED > WORRIT
WORRITING > WORRIT
WORRITS > WORRIT
WORRY vb (cause to) be anxious or uneasy ▷ n (cause of) anxiety or concern
WORRYCOW same as > WORRICOW
WORRYCOWS > WORRYCOW
WORRYGUTS n person who tends to worry, esp about insignificant matters
WORRYING > WORRY
WORRYINGS > WORRY
WORRYWART same as > WORRYGUTS
WORSE vb defeat
WORSED > WORSE
WORSEN vb make or grow worse
WORSENED > WORSEN
WORSENESS n state or condition of being worse

WORSENING n act of worsening
WORSENS > WORSEN
WORSER archaic or nonstandard word for > WORSE
WORSES > WORSE
WORSET n worsted fabric
WORSETS > WORSET
WORSHIP vb show religious devotion to ▷ n act or instance of worshipping
WORSHIPED > WORSHIP
WORSHIPER n worshipper
WORSHIPS > WORSHIP
WORSING > WORSE
WORST n worst thing ▷ vb defeat
WORSTED n type of woollen yarn or fabric
WORSTEDS > WORSTED
WORSTING > WORST
WORSTS > WORST
WORT n any of various plants formerly used to cure diseases
WORTH prep having a value of ▷ n value or price ▷ vb happen or betide
WORTHED > WORTH
WORTHFUL adj worthy
WORTHIED > WORTHY
WORTHIER > WORTHY
WORTHIES > WORTHY
WORTHIEST > WORTHY
WORTHILY > WORTHY
WORTHING > WORTH
WORTHLESS adj without value or usefulness
WORTHS > WORTH
WORTHY adj deserving admiration or respect ▷ n notable person ▷ vb make worthy
WORTHYING > WORTHY
WORTLE n plate with holes for drawing wire through
WORTLES > WORTLE
WORTS > WORT
WOS > WO
WOSBIRD n archaic word for an illegitimate child
WOSBIRDS > WOSBIRD
WOST form of the second person singular of > WIT
WOT form of the present tense of > WIT
WOTCHA same as > WOTCHER
WOTCHER sentence substitute slang term of greeting
WOTS > WOT
WOTTED > WOT
WOTTEST > WOT
WOTTETH > WOT
WOTTING > WOT
WOUBIT n type of caterpillar
WOUBITS > WOUBIT
WOULD > WILL
WOULDEST same as > WOULDST
WOULDS same as > WOULDST

WOULDST singular form of the past tense of > WILL
WOUND vb injure ▷ n injury
WOUNDABLE > WOUND
WOUNDED adj suffering from wounds
WOUNDEDLY > WOUNDED
WOUNDER > WOUND
WOUNDERS > WOUND
WOUNDIER > WOUNDY
WOUNDIEST > WOUNDY
WOUNDILY > WOUNDY
WOUNDING > WOUND
WOUNDINGS > WOUND
WOUNDLESS > WOUND
WOUNDS > WOUND
WOUNDWORT n type of plant formerly used for dressing wounds
WOUNDY adj extreme
WOURALI n plant from which curare is obtained
WOURALIS > WOURALI
WOVE > WEAVE
WOVEN n article made from woven cloth
WOVENS > WOVEN
WOW interj exclamation of astonishment ▷ n astonishing person or thing ▷ vb be a great success with
WOWED > WOW
WOWEE stronger form of > WOW
WOWF adj mad
WOWFER > WOWF
WOWFEST > WOWF
WOWING > WOW
WOWS > WOW
WOWSER n puritanical person
WOWSERS > WOWSER
WOX > WAX
WOXEN > WAX
WRACK n seaweed ▷ vb strain or shake (something) violently
WRACKED > WRACK
WRACKFUL adj ruinous
WRACKING > WRACK
WRACKS > WRACK
WRAITH n ghost
WRAITHS > WRAITH
WRANG Scot word for > WRONG
WRANGED > WRANG
WRANGING > WRANG
WRANGLE vb argue noisily ▷ n noisy argument
WRANGLED > WRANGLE
WRANGLER n one who wrangles
WRANGLERS > WRANGLER
WRANGLES > WRANGLE
WRANGLING > WRANGLE
WRANGS > WRANG
WRAP vb fold (something) round (a person or thing) so as to cover ▷ n garment wrapped round the shoulders
WRAPOVER adj (of a garment) worn wrapped round the body and fastened so that the open edges overlap ▷ n such a garment

WRAPOVERS > WRAPOVER

WRAPPAGE n material for wrapping

WRAPPAGES > WRAPPAGE

WRAPPED > WRAP

WRAPPER vb cover with wrapping ▷ n cover for a product

WRAPPERED > WRAPPER

WRAPPERS > WRAPPER

WRAPPING > WRAP

WRAPPINGS > WRAP

WRAPROUND same as > WRAPOVER

WRAPS > WRAP

WRAPT same as > RAPT

WRASSE n colourful sea fish

WRASSES > WRASSE

WRASSLE same as > WRESTLE

WRASSLED > WRASSLE

WRASSLES > WRASSLE

WRASSLING > WRASSLE

WRAST same as > WREST

WRASTED > WRAST

WRASTING > WRAST

WRASTLE same as > WRESTLE

WRASTLED > WRASTLE

WRASTLES > WRASTLE

WRASTLING > WRASTLE

WRASTS > WRAST

WRATE > WRITE

WRATH n intense anger ▷ adj incensed ▷ vb make angry

WRATHED > WRATH

WRATHFUL adj full of wrath

WRATHIER > WRATHY

WRATHIEST > WRATHY

WRATHILY > WRATHY

WRATHING > WRATH

WRATHLESS > WRATH

WRATHS > WRATH

WRATHY same as > WRATHFUL

WRAWL vb howl

WRAWLED > WRAWL

WRAWLING > WRAWL

WRAWLS > WRAWL

WRAXLE vb wrestle

WRAXLED > WRAXLE

WRAXLES > WRAXLE

WRAXLING > WRAXLE

WRAXLINGS > WRAXLE

WREAK vb inflict (vengeance, etc) or cause (chaos, etc)

WREAKED > WREAK

WREAKER > WREAK

WREAKERS > WREAK

WREAKFUL adj seeking revenge

WREAKING > WREAK

WREAKLESS adj unrevengeful

WREAKS > WREAK

WREATH n twisted ring or band of flowers or leaves used as a memorial or tribute

WREATHE vb form into or take the form of a wreath by twisting together

WREATHED > WREATHE

WREATHEN adj twisted into a wreath

WREATHER > WREATHE

WREATHERS > WREATHE

WREATHES > WREATHE

WREATHIER > WREATHY

WREATHING > WREATHE

WREATHS > WREATH

WREATHY adj twisted into wreath

WRECK vb destroy ▷ n remains of something that has been destroyed or badly damaged

WRECKAGE n wrecked remains

WRECKAGES > WRECKAGE

WRECKED > WRECK

WRECKER n formerly, person who lured ships onto the rocks in order to plunder them

WRECKERS > WRECKER

WRECKFISH n large sea perch

WRECKFUL adj causing wreckage

WRECKING > WRECK

WRECKINGS > WRECK

WRECKS > WRECK

WREN n small brown songbird

WRENCH vb twist or pull violently ▷ n violent twist or pull

WRENCHED > WRENCH

WRENCHER > WRENCH

WRENCHERS > WRENCH

WRENCHES > WRENCH

WRENCHING > WRENCH

WRENS > WREN

WRENTIT n type of long-tailed North American bird

WRENTITS > WRENTIT

WREST vb twist violently ▷ n act or an instance of wresting

WRESTED > WREST

WRESTER > WREST

WRESTERS > WREST

WRESTING > WREST

WRESTLE vb fight by grappling with an opponent ▷ n act of wrestling

WRESTLED > WRESTLE

WRESTLER > WRESTLE

WRESTLERS > WRESTLE

WRESTLES > WRESTLE

WRESTLING n sport in which each contestant tries to overcome the other either by throwing or pinning him or her to the ground or by forcing a submission

WRESTS > WREST

WRETCH n despicable person

WRETCHED adj miserable or unhappy

WRETCHES > WRETCH

WRETHE same as > WREATHE

WRETHED > WRETHE

WRETHES > WRETHE

WRETHING > WRETHE

WRICK variant spelling (chiefly Brit) of > RICK

WRICKED > WRICK

WRICKING > WRICK

WRICKS > WRICK

WRIED > WRY

WRIER > WRY

WRIES > WRY

WRIEST > WRY

WRIGGLE vb move with a twisting action ▷ n wriggling movement

WRIGGLED > WRIGGLE

WRIGGLER > WRIGGLE

WRIGGLERS > WRIGGLE

WRIGGLES > WRIGGLE

WRIGGLIER > WRIGGLE

WRIGGLING > WRIGGLE

WRIGGLY > WRIGGLE

WRIGHT n maker

WRIGHTS > WRIGHT

WRING vb twist, esp to squeeze liquid out of

WRINGED > WRING

WRINGER same as > MANGLE

WRINGERS > WRINGER

WRINGING > WRING

WRINGS > WRING

WRINKLE n slight crease, esp one in the skin due to age ▷ vb make or become slightly creased

WRINKLED > WRINKLE

WRINKLES > WRINKLE

WRINKLIE n derogatory word for an old person

WRINKLIER > WRINKLE

WRINKLIES pl n derogatory word for old people

WRINKLING > WRINKLE

WRINKLY > WRINKLE

WRIST n joint between the hand and the arm ▷ vb hit an object with a twist of the wrist

WRISTBAND n band around the wrist, esp one attached to a watch or forming part of a long sleeve

WRISTED > WRIST

WRISTER n type of shot in hockey

WRISTERS > WRISTER

WRISTIER > WRISTY

WRISTIEST > WRISTY

WRISTING > WRIST

WRISTLET n band or bracelet worn around the wrist

WRISTLETS > WRISTLET

WRISTLOCK n wrestling hold in which a wrestler seizes their opponent's wrist and exerts pressure against the joints of their hand, arm, or shoulder

WRISTS > WRIST

WRISTY adj characterized by considerable movement of the wrist

WRIT n written legal command

WRITABLE > WRITE

WRITATIVE adj inclined to write a lot

WRITE vb mark paper etc with symbols or words

WRITEABLE > WRITE

WRITEDOWN n reduction in the estimated value of an asset

WRITEOFF n uncollectible debt that is cancelled

WRITEOFFS > WRITEOFF

WRITER n author

WRITERESS n female writer

WRITERLY adj of or characteristic of a writer

WRITERS > WRITER

WRITES > WRITE

WRITHE vb twist or squirm in or as if in pain ▷ n act or an instance of writhing

WRITHED > WRITHE

WRITHEN adj twisted

WRITHER > WRITHE

WRITHERS > WRITHE

WRITHES > WRITHE

WRITHING > WRITHE

WRITHINGS > WRITHE

WRITHLED adj wrinkled

WRITING > WRITE

WRITINGS > WRITE

WRITS > WRIT

WRITTEN > WRITE

WRIZLED adj wrinkled

WROATH n unforeseen trouble

WROATHS > WROATH

WROKE > WREAK

WROKEN > WREAK

WRONG adj incorrect or mistaken ▷ adv in a wrong manner ▷ n something immoral or unjust ▷ vb treat unjustly

WRONGDOER n person who acts immorally or illegally

WRONGED > WRONG

WRONGER > WRONG

WRONGERS > WRONG

WRONGEST > WRONG

WRONGFUL adj unjust or illegal

WRONGING > WRONG

WRONGLY > WRONG

WRONGNESS > WRONG

WRONGOUS adj unfair

WRONGS > WRONG

WROOT obsolete form of > ROOT

WROOTED > WROOT

WROOTING > WROOT

WROOTS > WROOT

WROTE > WRITE

WROTH adj angry

WROTHFUL same as > WRATHFUL

WROUGHT adj (of metals) shaped by hammering or beating

WRUNG > WRING

WRY adj drily humorous ▷ vb twist or contort

WRYBILL *n* New Zealand plover whose bill is bent to one side
WRYBILLS > WRYBILL
WRYER > WRY
WRYEST > WRY
WRYING > WRY
WRYLY > WRY
WRYNECK *n* woodpecker that has a habit of twisting its neck round
WRYNECKS > WRYNECK
WRYNESS > WRY
WRYNESSES > WRY
WRYTHEN *adj* twisted
WUD *Scots form of* > WOOD
WUDDED > WUD
WUDDIES > WUDDY
WUDDING > WUD
WUDDY *n* loop at the end of a rope
WUDJULA *n* Australian word for a non-Aboriginal person
WUDJULAS > WUDJULA
WUDS > WUD
WUDU *n* Muslim practice of ritual washing before daily prayer
WUDUS > WUDU

WUKKAS *pl n* as in *no wukkas* Australian slang expression for 'no problem'
WULFENITE *n* yellow, orange, red, or grey lustrous secondary mineral
WULL *obsolete form of* > WILL
WULLED > WULL
WULLING > WULL
WULLS > WULL
WUNNER *same as* > ONER
WUNNERS > WUNNER
WURLEY *n* Aboriginal Australian hut
WURLEYS > WURLEY
WURLIE *same as* > WURLEY
WURLIES > WURLIE
WURST *n* large sausage, esp of a type made in Germany, Austria, etc
WURSTS > WURST
WURTZITE *n* zinc sulphide
WURTZITES > WURTZITE
WURZEL *n* root
WURZELS > WURZEL
WUS *n* Welsh dialect term of address

WUSES > WUS
WUSHU *n* Chinese martial arts
WUSHUS > WUSHU
WUSS *n* feeble person
WUSSES > WUSS
WUSSIER > WUSSY
WUSSIES > WUSSY
WUSSIEST > WUSSY
WUSSY *adj* feeble ▷ *n* feeble person
WUTHER *vb* (of wind) blow and roar
WUTHERED > WUTHER
WUTHERING *adj* (of a wind) blowing strongly with a roaring sound
WUTHERS > WUTHER
WUXIA *n* Chinese fiction concerning the adventures of sword-wielding heroes
WUXIAS > WUXIA
WUZ *vb* nonstandard spelling of was
WUZZLE *vb* mix up
WUZZLED > WUZZLE
WUZZLES > WUZZLE
WUZZLING > WUZZLE
WYANDOTTE *n* heavy

American breed of domestic fowl
WYCH *n* type of tree having flexible branches
WYCHES > WYCH
WYE *n* Y-shaped pipe
WYES > WYE
WYLE *vb* entice
WYLED > WYLE
WYLES > WYLE
WYLIECOAT *n* petticoat
WYLING > WYLE
WYN *n* rune equivalent to English 'w'
WYND *n* narrow lane or alley
WYNDS > WYND
WYNN *same as* > WYN
WYNNS > WYNN
WYNS > WYN
WYSIWYG *adj* denoting a computer screen display showing exactly what will print out
WYTE *vb* blame
WYTED > WYTE
WYTES > WYTE
WYTING > WYTE
WYVERN *n* heraldic beast
WYVERNS > WYVERN

W

Xx

XANTHAM *n* acacia gum

XANTHAMS > XANTHAM

XANTHAN *same as* > XANTHAM

XANTHANS > XANTHAN

XANTHATE *n* any salt or ester of xanthic acid

XANTHATES > XANTHATE

XANTHEIN *n* soluble part of the yellow pigment that is found in the cell sap of some flowers

XANTHEINS > XANTHEIN

XANTHENE *n* yellowish crystalline heterocyclic compound used as a fungicide

XANTHENES > XANTHENE

XANTHIC *adj* of, containing, or derived from xanthic acid

XANTHIN *n* any of a group of yellow or orange carotene derivatives

XANTHINE *n* crystalline compound found in urine, blood, certain plants, and certain animal tissues

XANTHINES > XANTHINE

XANTHINS > XANTHIN

XANTHISM *n* condition of skin, fur, or feathers in which yellow coloration predominates

XANTHISMS > XANTHISM

XANTHOMA *n* presence in the skin of fatty yellow or brownish plaques or nodules

XANTHOMAS > XANTHOMA

XANTHONE *n* crystalline compound

XANTHONES > XANTHONE

XANTHOUS *adj* yellow-coloured

XANTHOXYL *n* South American plant

XEBEC *n* small three-masted Mediterranean vessel

XEBECS > XEBEC

XED *adj* having a cross against

XENIA *n* influence of pollen upon the form of the fruit developing after pollination

XENIAL > XENIA

XENIAS > XENIA

XENIC *adj* denoting the presence of bacteria

XENIUM *n* diplomatic gift

XENOBLAST *n* type of mineral deposit

XENOCRYST *n* crystal included within an igneous rock as the magma cooled but not formed from it

XENOGAMY *n* fertilization by the fusion of male and female gametes from different individuals of the same species

XENOGENIC *adj* relating to the supposed production of offspring completely unlike either parent

XENOGENY *n* offspring unlike either parent

XENOGRAFT *n* tissue graft obtained from a donor of a different species from the recipient

XENOLITH *n* fragment of rock differing in origin, structure, etc from the igneous rock enclosing it

XENOLITHS > XENOLITH

XENOMANIA *n* passion for foreign things

XENOMENIA *n* menstruation from unusual orifices

XENON *n* colourless odourless gas

XENONS > XENON

XENOPHILE *n* person who likes foreigners or things foreign

XENOPHOBE *n* person who hates or fears foreigners or strangers

XENOPHOBY *n* hatred or fear of foreigners or strangers

XENOPHYA *pl n* parts of shell or skeleton formed by foreign bodies

XENOPUS *n* African frog

XENOPUSES > XENOPUS

XENOTIME *n* yellow-brown mineral

XENOTIMES > XENOTIME

XENURINE *adj* relating to a type of armadillo ▷ *n* type of armadillo

XENURINES > XENURINE

XERAFIN *n* Indian coin

XERAFINS > XERAFIN

XERANSES > XERANSIS

XERANSIS *n* gradual loss of tissue moisture

XERANTIC > XERANSIS

XERAPHIN *same as* > XERAFIN

XERAPHINS > XERAPHIN

XERARCH *adj* (of a sere) having its origin in a dry habitat

XERASIA *n* dryness of the hair

XERASIAS > XERASIA

XERIC *adj* of, relating to, or growing in dry conditions

XERICALLY > XERIC

XERISCAPE *n* landscape designed to conserve water ▷ *vb* landscape (an area) so that it needs little water

XEROCHASY *n* release of seeds or pollen on drying

XERODERMA *n* condition characterized by abnormal dryness of the skin

XEROMA *n* excessive dryness of the cornea

XEROMAS > XEROMA

XEROMATA > XEROMA

XEROMORPH *n* plant adapted for living in dry surroundings

XEROPHAGY *n* fasting by eating only dry food

XEROPHILE *n* plant or animal adapted for living in dry surroundings

XEROPHILY > XEROPHILE

XEROPHYTE *n* plant adapted for living in dry surroundings

XEROSERE *n* sere that originates in dry surroundings

XEROSERES > XEROSERE

XEROSES > XEROSIS

XEROSIS *n* abnormal dryness of bodily tissues

XEROSTOMA *n* abnormal lack of saliva; dryness of the mouth

XEROTES *same as* > XEROSIS

XEROTIC > XEROSIS

XEROX *n* trade name for a machine employing a xerographic copying process ▷ *vb* produce a copy (of a document, etc) using such a machine

XEROXED > XEROX

XEROXES > XEROX

XEROXING > XEROX

XERUS *n* ground squirrel

XERUSES > XERUS

XI *n* 14th letter in the Greek alphabet

XIPHOID *adj* shaped like a sword ▷ *n* part of the sternum

XIPHOIDAL > XIPHOID

XIPHOIDS > XIPHOID

XIPHOPAGI *n* twins conjoined at the lower sternum

XIS > XI

XOANA > XOANON

XOANON *n* primitive image of a god supposed to have fallen from heaven

XRAY *n* code word for the letter X

XRAYS > XRAY

XU *n* Vietnamese currency unit

XYLAN *n* yellow polysaccharide consisting of xylose units

XYLANS > XYLAN

XYLEM *n* plant tissue that conducts water and minerals from the roots to all other parts

XYLEMS > XYLEM

XYLENE *n* type of hydrocarbon

XYLENES > XYLENE

XYLENOL *n* synthetic resin made from xylene

XYLENOLS > XYLENOL

XYLIC > XYLEM

XYLIDIN *same as* > XYLIDINE

XYLIDINE *n* mixture of six isomeric amines derived from xylene and used in dyes

XYLIDINES > XYLIDINE

XYLIDINS > XYLIDIN

XYLITOL *n* crystalline alcohol used as a sweetener

XYLITOLS > XYLITOL

XYLOCARP *n* fruit, such as a coconut, having a hard woody pericarp

XYLOCARPS > XYLOCARP

XYLOGEN *same as* > XYLEM

XYLOGENS > XYLOGEN

XYLOGRAPH *n* engraving in wood ▷ *vb* print (a design, illustration, etc) from a wood engraving

XYLOID *adj* of, relating to, or resembling wood

XYLOIDIN *n* type of explosive

XYLOIDINE *same as* **>** XYLOIDIN

XYLOIDINS > XYLOIDIN

XYLOL *another name (not in technical usage) for* **>** XYLENE

XYLOLOGY *n* study of the composition of wood

XYLOLS > XYLOL

XYLOMA *n* hard growth in fungi

XYLOMAS > XYLOMA

XYLOMATA > XYLOMA

XYLOMETER *n* device for measuring the specific gravity of wood

XYLONIC *adj* denoting an acid formed from xylose

XYLONITE *n* type of plastic

XYLONITES **>** XYLONITE

XYLOPHAGE *n* creature that eats wood

XYLOPHONE *n* musical instrument made of a row of wooden bars played with hammers

XYLORIMBA *n* large xylophone with an extended range of five octaves

XYLOSE *n* white crystalline sugar found in wood and straw

XYLOSES > XYLOSE

XYLOTOMY *n* preparation of sections of wood for examination by microscope

XYLYL *n* group of atoms

XYLYLS > XYLYL

XYST *n* long portico, esp one used in ancient Greece for athletics

XYSTER *n* surgical instrument for scraping bone

XYSTERS > XYSTER

XYSTI > XYSTUS

XYSTOI > XYSTOS

XYSTOS *same as* **>** XYST

XYSTS > XYST

XYSTUS *same as* **>** XYST

Yy

YA _n_ type of Chinese pear
YAAR _n_ in informal Indian English, a friend
YAARS > YAAR
YABA _n_ informal word for 'yet another bloody acronym'
YABAS > YABA
YABBA _n_ form of methamphetamine
YABBAS > YABBA
YABBER _vb_ talk or jabber ▷ _n_ talk or jabber
YABBERED > YABBER
YABBERING > YABBER
YABBERS > YABBER
YABBIE _same as_ > YABBY
YABBIED > YABBY
YABBIES > YABBY
YABBY _n_ small freshwater crayfish ▷ _vb_ go out to catch yabbies
YABBYING > YABBY
YACCA _n_ Australian plant with a woody stem
YACCAS > YACCA
YACHT _n_ large boat with sails or an engine ▷ _vb_ sail in a yacht
YACHTED > YACHT
YACHTER > YACHT
YACHTERS > YACHT
YACHTIE _n_ yachtsman
YACHTIES > YACHTIE
YACHTING _n_ sport or practice of sailing a yacht
YACHTINGS > YACHTING
YACHTMAN _same as_ > YACHTSMAN
YACHTMEN > YACHTMAN
YACHTS > YACHT
YACHTSMAN _n_ person who sails a yacht
YACHTSMEN > YACHTSMAN
YACK _same as_ > YAK
YACKA _same as_ > YACCA
YACKAS > YACKA
YACKED > YACK
YACKER _same as_ > YAKKA
YACKERS > YACKER
YACKING > YACK
YACKS > YACK
YAD _n_ hand-held pointer used for reading the sefer torah
YADS > YAD
YAE _same as_ > AE
YAFF _vb_ bark
YAFFED > YAFF
YAFFING > YAFF

YAFFLE _n_ woodpecker with a green back and wings
YAFFLES > YAFFLE
YAFFS > YAFF
YAG _n_ artificial crystal
YAGE _n_ tropical vine of the Amazon region
YAGER _same as_ > JAEGER
YAGERS > YAGER
YAGES > YAGE
YAGGER _n_ pedlar
YAGGERS > YAGGER
YAGI _n_ type of highly directional aerial
YAGIS > YAGI
YAGS > YAG
YAH _interj_ exclamation of derision or disgust ▷ _n_ affected upper-class person
YAHOO _n_ crude coarse person
YAHOOISM > YAHOO
YAHOOISMS > YAHOO
YAHOOS > YAHOO
YAHRZEIT _n_ (in Judaism) the anniversary of the death of a close relative
YAHRZEITS > YAHRZEIT
YAHS > YAH
YAIRD _Scots form of_ > YARD
YAIRDS > YAIRD
YAK _n_ Tibetan ox with long shaggy hair ▷ _vb_ talk continuously about unimportant matters
YAKHDAN _n_ box for carrying ice on a pack animal
YAKHDANS > YAKHDAN
YAKIMONO _n_ (in Japan) grilled or fried food
YAKIMONOS > YAKIMONO
YAKITORI _n_ Japanese dish consisting of small pieces of chicken skewered and grilled
YAKITORIS > YAKITORI
YAKKA _n_ informal Australian word for work
YAKKAS > YAKKA
YAKKED > YAK
YAKKER _same as_ > YAKKA
YAKKERS > YAKKER
YAKKING > YAK
YAKOW _n_ animal bred from a male yak and a domestic cow
YAKOWS > YAKOW

YAKS > YAK
YAKUZA _n_ Japanese criminal organization
YALD _adj_ vigorous
YALE _n_ mythical beast with the body of an antelope (or similar animal) and swivelling horns
YALES > YALE
YAM _n_ tropical root vegetable
YAMALKA _same as_ > YARMULKE
YAMALKAS > YAMALKA
YAMEN _n_ (in imperial China) the office or residence of a public official
YAMENS > YAMEN
YAMMER _vb_ whine in a complaining manner ▷ _n_ yammering sound
YAMMERED > YAMMER
YAMMERER > YAMMER
YAMMERERS > YAMMER
YAMMERING > YAMMER
YAMMERS > YAMMER
YAMPIES > YAMPY
YAMPY _n_ foolish person
YAMS > YAM
YAMULKA _same as_ > YARMULKE
YAMULKAS > YAMULKA
YAMUN _same as_ > YAMEN
YAMUNS > YAMUN
YANG _n_ (in Chinese philosophy) one of two complementary principles maintaining harmony in the universe
YANGS > YANG
YANK _vb_ pull or jerk suddenly ▷ _n_ sudden pull or jerk
YANKED > YANK
YANKEE _n_ code word for the letter Y
YANKEES > YANKEE
YANKER > YANK
YANKERS > YANK
YANKIE _n_ impudent woman
YANKIES > YANKIE
YANKING > YANK
YANKS > YANK
YANQUI _n_ slang word for American
YANQUIS > YANQUI
YANTRA _n_ diagram used in meditation
YANTRAS > YANTRA
YAOURT _n_ yoghurt
YAOURTS > YAOURT

YAP _vb_ bark with a high-pitched sound ▷ _n_ high-pitched bark ▷ _interj_ imitation or representation of the sound of a dog yapping
YAPOCK _same as_ > YAPOK
YAPOCKS > YAPOCK
YAPOK _n_ type of opossum
YAPOKS > YAPOK
YAPON _same as_ > YAUPON
YAPONS > YAPON
YAPP _n_ type of book binding
YAPPED > YAP
YAPPER > YAP
YAPPERS > YAP
YAPPIE _n_ young aspiring professional
YAPPIER > YAP
YAPPIES > YAPPIE
YAPPIEST > YAP
YAPPING _n_ act of yapping
YAPPINGLY > YAP
YAPPINGS > YAPPING
YAPPS > YAPP
YAPPY > YAP
YAPS > YAP
YAPSTER > YAP
YAPSTERS > YAP
YAQONA _n_ Polynesian shrub
YAQONAS > YAQONA
YAR _adj_ nimble
YARAK _n_ fit condition for hunting
YARAKS > YARAK
YARCO _n_ insulting word for a young working-class person who wears casual sports clothes
YARCOS > YARCO
YARD _n_ unit of length ▷ _vb_ draft (animals), esp to a saleyard
YARDAGE _n_ length measured in yards
YARDAGES > YARDAGE
YARDANG _n_ ridge formed by wind erosion
YARDANGS > YARDANG
YARDARM _n_ outer end of a ship's yard
YARDARMS > YARDARM
YARDBIRD _n_ inexperienced or clumsy soldier
YARDBIRDS > YARDBIRD
YARDED > YARD
YARDER _n_ one who drafts animals to a sale yard
YARDERS > YARDER

y

YARDING n group of animals displayed for sale
YARDINGS > YARDING
YARDLAND n archaic unit of land
YARDLANDS > YARDLAND
YARDLIGHT n light hanging on a pole, used to light a yard
YARDMAN n farm overseer
YARDMEN > YARDMAN
YARDS > YARD
YARDSTICK n standard against which to judge other people or things
YARDWAND same as > YARDSTICK
YARDWANDS > YARDWAND
YARDWORK n garden work
YARDWORKS > YARDWORK
YARE adj ready, brisk, or eager ▷ adv readily or eagerly
YARELY > YARE
YARER > YARE
YAREST > YARE
YARFA n peat
YARFAS > YARFA
YARK vb make ready
YARKED > YARK
YARKING > YARK
YARKS > YARK
YARMELKE same as > YARMULKE
YARMELKES > YARMELKE
YARMULKA same as > YARMULKE
YARMULKAS > YARMULKA
YARMULKE n skullcap worn by Jewish men
YARMULKES > YARMULKE
YARN n thread used for knitting or making cloth ▷ vb thread with yarn
YARNED > YARN
YARNER > YARN
YARNERS > YARN
YARNING > YARN
YARNS > YARN
YARPHA n peat
YARPHAS > YARPHA
YARR n wild white flower ▷ vb growl or snarl
YARRAMAN n Australian word for a horse
YARRAMANS > YARRAMAN
YARRAMEN > YARRAMAN
YARRAN n type of small hardy tree of inland Australia
YARRANS > YARRAN
YARRED > YARR
YARRING > YARR
YARROW n wild plant with flat clusters of white flowers
YARROWS > YARROW
YARRS > YARR
YARTA Shetland word for > HEART

YARTAS > YARTA
YARTO same as > YARTA
YARTOS > YARTO
YAS > YA
YASHMAC same as > YASHMAK
YASHMACS > YASHMAC
YASHMAK n veil worn by a Muslim woman in public
YASHMAKS > YASHMAK
YASMAK same as > YASHMAK
YASMAKS > YASMAK
YATAGAN same as > YATAGHAN
YATAGANS > YATAGAN
YATAGHAN n Turkish sword with a curved single-edged blade
YATAGHANS > YATAGHAN
YATE n type of small eucalyptus tree yielding a very hard timber
YATES > YATE
YATTER vb talk at length ▷ n continuous chatter
YATTERED > YATTER
YATTERING > YATTER
YATTERS > YATTER
YAUD Scots word for > MARE
YAUDS > YAUD
YAULD adj alert or nimble
YAUP variant spelling of > YAWP
YAUPED > YAUP
YAUPER > YAUP
YAUPERS > YAUP
YAUPING > YAUP
YAUPON n southern US evergreen holly shrub
YAUPONS > YAUPON
YAUPS > YAUP
YAUTIA n Caribbean plant cultivated for its edible leaves and underground stems
YAUTIAS > YAUTIA
YAW vb (of an aircraft or ship) turn to one side or from side to side while moving ▷ n act or movement of yawing
YAWED > YAW
YAWEY > YAWS
YAWIER > YAWY
YAWIEST > YAWY
YAWING > YAW
YAWL n two-masted sailing boat ▷ vb howl, weep, or scream harshly
YAWLED > YAWL
YAWLING > YAWL
YAWLS > YAWL
YAWMETER n instrument for measuring an aircraft's yaw
YAWMETERS > YAWMETER
YAWN vb open the mouth wide and take in air deeply, often when sleepy or bored ▷ n act of yawning
YAWNED > YAWN
YAWNER > YAWN
YAWNERS > YAWN
YAWNIER > YAWN
YAWNIEST > YAWN

YAWNING > YAWN
YAWNINGLY > YAWN
YAWNINGS > YAWN
YAWNS > YAWN
YAWNSOME adj boring
YAWNY > YAWN
YAWP vb gape or yawn, esp audibly ▷ n shout, bark, yelp, or cry
YAWPED > YAWP
YAWPER > YAWP
YAWPERS > YAWP
YAWPING > YAWP
YAWPINGS > YAWP
YAWPS > YAWP
YAWS n infectious tropical skin disease
YAWY adj having or resembling yaws
YAY interj exclamation indicating approval or triumph ▷ n cry of approval
YAYS > YAY
YBET archaic past participle of > BEAT
YBLENT archaic past participle of > BLEND
YBORE archaic past participle of > BEAR
YBOUND archaic past participle of > BIND
YBOUNDEN archaic past participle of > BIND
YBRENT archaic past participle of > BURN
YCLAD archaic past participle of > CLOTHE
YCLED archaic past participle of > CLOTHE
YCLEEPE archaic form of > CLEPE
YCLEEPED > YCLEEPE
YCLEEPES > YCLEEPE
YCLEEPING > YCLEEPE
YCLEPED same as > YCLEPT
YCLEPT adj having the name of
YCOND archaic past participle of > CON
YDRAD archaic past participle of > DREAD
YDRED archaic past participle of > DREAD
YE pron you ▷ adj the
YEA interj yes ▷ adv indeed or truly ▷ n cry of agreement
YEAD vb proceed
YEADING > YEAD
YEADS > YEAD
YEAH n answer of yes
YEAHS > YEAH
YEALDON n fuel
YEALDONS > YEALDON
YEALING n person of the same age as oneself
YEALINGS > YEALING
YEALM vb prepare for thatching
YEALMED > YEALM
YEALMING > YEALM
YEALMS > YEALM
YEAN vb (of a sheep or goat) to give birth to (offspring)
YEANED > YEAN

YEANING > YEAN
YEANLING n young of a goat or sheep
YEANLINGS > YEANLING
YEANS > YEAN
YEAR n time taken for the earth to make one revolution around the sun, about 365 days
YEARBOOK n reference book published annually containing details of the previous year's events
YEARBOOKS > YEARBOOK
YEARD vb bury
YEARDED > YEARD
YEARDING > YEARD
YEARDS > YEARD
YEAREND n end of the year
YEARENDS > YEAREND
YEARLIES > YEARLY
YEARLING n animal between one and two years old ▷ adj being a year old
YEARLINGS > YEARLING
YEARLONG adj throughout a whole year
YEARLY adv every year or once a year ▷ adj occurring once a year or every year ▷ n publication, event, etc that occurs once a year
YEARN vb want (something) very much
YEARNED > YEARN
YEARNER > YEARN
YEARNERS > YEARN
YEARNING n intense or overpowering longing, desire, or need
YEARNINGS > YEARNING
YEARNS > YEARN
YEARS > YEAR
YEAS > YEA
YEASAYER n person who usually agrees with proposals
YEASAYERS > YEASAYER
YEAST n fungus used to make bread rise ▷ vb froth or foam
YEASTED > YEAST
YEASTIER > YEASTY
YEASTIEST > YEASTY
YEASTILY > YEASTY
YEASTING > YEAST
YEASTLESS > YEAST
YEASTLIKE > YEAST
YEASTS > YEAST
YEASTY adj of, resembling, or containing yeast
YEBO interj yes
YECCH same as > YECH
YECCHS > YECCH
YECH n expression of disgust
YECHIER > YECHY
YECHIEST > YECHY
YECHS > YECH

y

YECHY > YECH
YEDE *same as* **>** YEAD
YEDES > YEDE
YEDING > YEDE
YEED *same as* **>** YEAD
YEEDING > YEED
YEEDS > YEED
YEELIN *n* person of the same age as oneself
YEELINS > YEELIN
YEESH *interj* interjection used to express frustration
YEGG *n* burglar or safe-breaker
YEGGMAN *same as* **>** YEGG
YEGGMEN > YEGGMAN
YEGGS > YEGG
YEH *same as* **>** YEAH
YELD *adj* (of an animal) barren or too young to bear young
YELDRING *n* yellowhammer (bird)
YELDRINGS > YELDRING
YELDROCK *same as* **>** YELDRING
YELDROCKS > YELDROCK
YELK *n* yolk of an egg
YELKS > YELK
YELL *vb* shout or scream in a loud or piercing way ▷ *n* loud cry of pain, anger, or fear
YELLED > YELL
YELLER > YELL
YELLERS > YELL
YELLING > YELL
YELLINGS > YELL
YELLOCH *vb* yell
YELLOCHED > YELLOCH
YELLOCHS > YELLOCH
YELLOW *n* colour of gold, a lemon, etc ▷ *adj* of this colour ▷ *vb* make or become yellow
YELLOWED > YELLOW
YELLOWER > YELLOW
YELLOWEST > YELLOW
YELLOWFIN *n* type of tuna
YELLOWIER > YELLOW
YELLOWING > YELLOW
YELLOWISH > YELLOW
YELLOWLY > YELLOW
YELLOWS *n* any of various fungal or viral diseases of plants
YELLOWY > YELLOW
YELLS > YELL
YELM *same as* **>** YEALM
YELMED > YELM
YELMING > YELM
YELMS > YELM
YELP *n* short sudden cry ▷ *vb* utter a sharp or high-pitched cry of pain
YELPED > YELP
YELPER > YELP
YELPERS > YELP
YELPING > YELP
YELPINGS > YELP
YELPS > YELP
YELT *n* young sow
YELTS > YELT

YEMMER *southwest English form of* **>** EMBER
YEMMERS > YEMMER
YEN *n* monetary unit of Japan ▷ *vb* have a longing
YENNED > YEN
YENNING > YEN
YENS > YEN
YENTA *n* meddlesome woman
YENTAS > YENTA
YENTE *same as* **>** YENTA
YENTES > YENTE
YEOMAN *n* farmer owning and farming his own land
YEOMANLY *adj* of or like a yeoman ▷ *adv* in a yeomanly manner, as in being brave or loyal
YEOMANRY *n* yeomen
YEOMEN > YEOMAN
YEOW *interj* interjection used to express pain
YEP *n* answer of yes
YEPS > YEP
YER *adj* informal spelling of 'your'
YERBA *n* stimulating South American drink made from dried leaves
YERBAS > YERBA
YERD *vb* bury
YERDED > YERD
YERDING > YERD
YERDS > YERD
YERK *vb* tighten stitches
YERKED > YERK
YERKING > YERK
YERKS > YERK
YERSINIA *n* plague bacterium
YERSINIAE > YERSINIA
YERSINIAS > YERSINIA
YES *interj* expresses consent, agreement, or approval ▷ *n* answer or vote of yes ▷ *vb* reply in the affirmative
YESES > YES
YESHIVA *n* traditional Jewish school
YESHIVAH *same as* **>** YESHIVA
YESHIVAHS > YESHIVAH
YESHIVAS > YESHIVA
YESHIVOT > YESHIVA
YESHIVOTH > YESHIVA
YESK *vb* hiccup
YESKED > YESK
YESKING > YESK
YESKS > YESK
YESSED > YES
YESSES > YES
YESSING > YES
YESSIR *interj* expression of assent to a man
YESSIREE *interj* expression of assent
YESSUM *interj* expression of assent to a woman
YEST *archaic form of* **>** YEAST
YESTER *adj* of or relating to yesterday
YESTERDAY *n* the day before today ▷ *adv* on or

during the day before today
YESTEREVE *n* poetic word meaning yesterday evening
YESTERN *same as* **>** YESTER
YESTREEN *n* yesterday evening
YESTREENS > YESTREEN
YESTS > YEST
YESTY *archaic form of* **>** YEASTY
YET *adv* up until then or now
YETI *n* large legendary manlike creature alleged to inhabit the Himalayan Mountains
YETIS > YETI
YETT *n* gate or door
YETTIE *n* young, entrepreneurial, and technology-based (person)
YETTIES > YETTIE
YETTS > YETT
YEUK *vb* itch
YEUKED > YEUK
YEUKIER > YEUKY
YEUKIEST > YEUKY
YEUKING > YEUK
YEUKS > YEUK
YEUKY > YEUK
YEVE *vb* give
YEVEN > YEVE
YEVES > YEVE
YEVING > YEVE
YEW *n* evergreen tree with needle-like leaves and red berries
YEWEN *adj* made of yew
YEWS > YEW
YEX *vb* hiccup
YEXED > YEX
YEXES > YEX
YEXING > YEX
YEZ *interj* yes
YFERE *adv* together ▷ *n* friend or associate
YFERES > YFERE
YGLAUNST *archaic past participle of* **>** GLANCE
YGO *archaic past participle of* **>** GO
YGOE *archaic past participle of* **>** GO
YIBBLES *adv* Scots word meaning perhaps
YICKER *vb* squeal or squeak
YICKERED > YICKER
YICKERING > YICKER
YICKERS > YICKER
YIDAKI *n* long wooden wind instrument played by some Australian Aboriginal peoples
YIDAKIS > YIDAKI
YIELD *vb* produce or bear ▷ *n* amount produced
YIELDABLE > YIELD
YIELDED > YIELD
YIELDER > YIELD
YIELDERS > YIELD
YIELDING *adj* submissive

YIELDINGS > YIELD
YIELDS > YIELD
YIKE *n* argument, squabble, or fight ▷ *vb* argue, squabble, or fight
YIKED > YIKE
YIKES *interj* expression of surprise, fear, or alarm
YIKING > YIKE
YIKKER *vb* squeal or squeak
YIKKERED > YIKKER
YIKKERING > YIKKER
YIKKERS > YIKKER
YILL *n* ale ▷ *vb* entertain with ale
YILLED > YILL
YILLING > YILL
YILLS > YILL
YIN *Scots word for* **>** ONE
YINCE *Scots form of* **>** ONCE
YINDIE *n* person who combines a lucrative career with non-mainstream tastes
YINDIES > YINDIE
YINGYANG *n* two opposing but complementary principles in Chinese philosophy
YINGYANGS > YINGYANG
YINS > YIN
YIP *vb* emit a high-pitched bark
YIPE *same as* **>** YIPES
YIPES *interj* expression of surprise, fear, or alarm
YIPPED > YIP
YIPPEE *interj* exclamation of joy or pleasure
YIPPER *n* golfer who has a failure of nerve
YIPPERS > YIPPER
YIPPIE *n* young person sharing hippy ideals
YIPPIES > YIPPIE
YIPPING > YIP
YIPPY *same as* **>** YIPPIE
YIPS > YIP
YIRD *vb* bury
YIRDED > YIRD
YIRDING > YIRD
YIRDS > YIRD
YIRK *same as* **>** YERK
YIRKED > YIRK
YIRKING > YIRK
YIRKS > YIRK
YIRR *vb* snarl, growl, or yell
YIRRED > YIRR
YIRRING > YIRR
YIRRS > YIRR
YIRTH *n* earth
YIRTHS > YIRTH
YITE *n* European bunting with a yellowish head and body and brown streaked wings and tail
YITES > YITE
YITIE *same as* **>** YITE
YITIES > YITIE
YITTEN *adj* frightened
YLEM *n* original matter from which the basic elements are said to have been formed

YLEMS > YLEM
YLIKE *Spenserian form of* > ALIKE
YLKE *archaic spelling of* > ILK
YLKES > YLKE
YMOLT *Spenserian past participle of* > MELT
YMOLTEN *Spenserian past participle of* > MELT
YMPE *Spenserian form of* > IMP
YMPES > YMPE
YMPING > YMPE
YMPT > YMPE
YNAMBU *n* South American bird
YNAMBUS > YNAMBU
YO *interj* expression used as a greeting
YOB *n* bad-mannered aggressive youth
YOBBERIES > YOBBERY
YOBBERY *n* behaviour typical of aggressive surly youths
YOBBIER > YOBBY
YOBBIEST > YOBBY
YOBBISH *adj* typical of aggressive surly youths
YOBBISHLY > YOBBISH
YOBBISM > YOB
YOBBISMS > YOB
YOBBO *same as* > YOB
YOBBOES > YOBBO
YOBBOS > YOBBO
YOBBY *adj* like a yob
YOBS > YOB
YOCK *vb* chuckle
YOCKED > YOCK
YOCKING > YOCK
YOCKS > YOCK
YOD *n* tenth letter in the Hebrew alphabet
YODE > YEAD
YODEL *vb* sing with abrupt changes between a normal and a falsetto voice ▷ *n* act or sound of yodelling
YODELED > YODEL
YODELER > YODEL
YODELERS > YODEL
YODELING > YODELLING
YODELINGS > YODELING
YODELLED > YODEL
YODELLER > YODEL
YODELLERS > YODEL
YODELLING *n* type of singing traditional in Switzerland
YODELS > YODEL
YODH *same as* > YOD
YODHS > YODH
YODLE *variant spelling of* > YODEL
YODLED > YODLE
YODLER > YODLE
YODLERS > YODLE
YODLES > YODLE
YODLING > YODLE
YODS > YOD
YOGA *n* Hindu method of exercise and discipline
YOGAS > YOGA

YOGEE *same as* > YOGI
YOGEES > YOGEE
YOGH *n* character used in Old and Middle English to represent a palatal fricative
YOGHOURT *variant form of* > YOGURT
YOGHOURTS > YOGHOURT
YOGHS > YOGH
YOGHURT *same as* > YOGURT
YOGHURTS > YOGHURT
YOGI *n* person who practises yoga
YOGIC > YOGA
YOGIN *same as* > YOGI
YOGINI > YOGI
YOGINIS > YOGI
YOGINS > YOGIN
YOGIS > YOGI
YOGISM > YOGI
YOGISMS > YOGI
YOGOURT *same as* > YOGURT
YOGOURTS > YOGOURT
YOGURT *n* slightly sour custard-like food made from milk that has had bacteria added
YOGURTS > YOGURT
YOHIMBE *n* bark used in herbal medicine
YOHIMBES > YOHIMBE
YOHIMBINE *n* alkaloid found in the bark of a tropical African tree
YOICK *vb* urge on foxhounds
YOICKED > YOICK
YOICKING > YOICK
YOICKS *interj* cry used by huntsmen to urge on the hounds ▷ *vb* urge on foxhounds
YOICKSED > YOICKS
YOICKSES > YOICKS
YOICKSING > YOICKS
YOJAN *n* Indian unit of distance
YOJANA *same as* > YOJAN
YOJANAS > YOJANA
YOJANS > YOJAN
YOK *vb* chuckle
YOKE *n* wooden bar put across the necks of two animals to hold them together ▷ *vb* put a yoke on
YOKED > YOKE
YOKEL *n* simple person who lives in the country
YOKELESS > YOKE
YOKELISH > YOKEL
YOKELS > YOKEL
YOKEMATE *n* colleague
YOKEMATES > YOKEMATE
YOKER *vb* spit
YOKERED > YOKER
YOKERING > YOKER
YOKERS > YOKE
YOKES > YOKE
YOKING > YOKE
YOKINGS > YOKE
YOKKED > YOK
YOKKING > YOK

YOKOZUNA *n* grand champion sumo wrestler
YOKOZUNAS > YOKOZUNA
YOKS > YOK
YOKUL *Shetland word for* > YES
YOLD *archaic past participle of* > YIELD
YOLDRING *n* yellowhammer (bird)
YOLDRINGS > YOLDRING
YOLK *n* yellow part of an egg that provides food for the developing embryo
YOLKED > YOLK
YOLKIER > YOLK
YOLKIEST > YOLK
YOLKLESS > YOLK
YOLKS > YOLK
YOLKY > YOLK
YOM *n* day
YOMIM > YOM
YOMP *vb* walk or trek laboriously
YOMPED > YOMP
YOMPING > YOMP
YOMPS > YOMP
YON *adj* that or those over there ▷ *adv* yonder ▷ *pron* that person or thing
YOND *same as* > YON
YONDER *adv* over there ▷ *adj* situated over there ▷ *determiner* being at a distance, either within view or as if within view ▷ *n* person
YONDERLY > YONDER
YONDERS > YONDER
YONI *n* female genitalia
YONIC *adj* resembling a vulva
YONIS > YONI
YONKER *same as* > YOUNKER
YONKERS > YONKER
YONKS *pl n* very long time
YONNIE *n* stone
YONNIES > YONNIE
YONT *same as* > YON
YOOF *n* non-standard spelling of youth
YOOFS > YOOF
YOOP *n* sob
YOOPS > YOOP
YOPPER *n* young person employed on a former UK government training programme
YOPPERS > YOPPER
YORE *n* time long past ▷ *adv* in the past
YORES > YORE
YORK *vb* bowl or try to bowl (a batsman) by pitching the ball under or just beyond the bat
YORKED > YORK
YORKER *n* (in cricket) ball that pitches just under the bat
YORKERS > YORKER
YORKIE *n* Yorkshire terrier
YORKIES > YORKIE
YORKING > YORK

YORKS > YORK
YORLING *n* as in *yellow yorling* yellowhammer
YORLINGS > YORLING
YORP *vb* shout
YORPED > YORP
YORPING > YORP
YORPS > YORP
YOTTABYTE *n* very large unit of computer memory
YOU *pron* person or people addressed ▷ *n* personality of the person being addressed
YOUK *vb* itch
YOUKED > YOUK
YOUKING > YOUK
YOUKS > YOUK
YOUNG *adj* in an early stage of life or growth ▷ *n* young people in general; offspring
YOUNGER > YOUNG
YOUNGERS *n* young people
YOUNGEST > YOUNG
YOUNGISH > YOUNG
YOUNGLING *n* young person, animal, or plant
YOUNGLY *adv* youthfully
YOUNGNESS > YOUNG
YOUNGS > YOUNG
YOUNGSTER *n* young person
YOUNGTH *n* youth
YOUNGTHLY *adj* youthful
YOUNGTHS > YOUNGTH
YOUNKER *n* young man
YOUNKERS > YOUNKER
YOUPON *same as* > YAUPON
YOUPONS > YOUPON
YOUR *adj* of, belonging to, or associated with you
YOURN *dialect form of* > YOURS
YOURS *pron* something belonging to you
YOURSELF *pron* reflexive form of *you*
YOURT *same as* > YURT
YOURTS > YOURT
YOUS *pron* dialect form of 'you' when referring to more than one person
YOUSE *same as* > YOUS
YOUTH *n* time of being young
YOUTHEN *vb* render more youthful-seeming
YOUTHENED > YOUTHEN
YOUTHENS > YOUTHEN
YOUTHFUL *adj* vigorous or active
YOUTHHEAD *same as* > YOUTHHOOD
YOUTHHOOD *n* youth
YOUTHIER > YOUTHY
YOUTHIEST > YOUTHY
YOUTHLESS > YOUTH
YOUTHLY *adj* young
YOUTHS > YOUTH
YOUTHSOME *archaic variant of* > YOUTHFUL
YOUTHY *Scots word for* > YOUNG
YOW *vb* howl
YOWE *Scot word for* > EWE

YOWED > YOW
YOWES > YOWE
YOWIE n legendary Australian apelike creature
YOWIES > YOWIE
YOWING > YOW
YOWL n loud mournful cry ▷ vb produce a loud mournful wail or cry
YOWLED > YOWL
YOWLER > YOWL
YOWLERS > YOWL
YOWLEY n yellowhammer (bird)
YOWLEYS > YOWLEY
YOWLING > YOWL
YOWLINGS > YOWL
YOWLS > YOWL
YOWS > YOW
YOWZA interj exclamation of enthusiasm
YPERITE n mustard gas
YPERITES > YPERITE
YPIGHT archaic past participle of > PITCH
YPLAST archaic past participle of > PLACE
YPLIGHT archaic past participle of > PLIGHT
YPSILOID > YPSILON
YPSILON same as > UPSILON
YPSILONS > YPSILON
YRAPT Spenserian form of > RAPT
YRAVISHED archaic past participle of > RAVISH
YRENT archaic past participle of > REND
YRIVD archaic past participle of > RIVE
YRNEH n unit of reciprocal inductance
YRNEHS > YRNEH
YSAME Spenserian word for > TOGETHER
YSHEND Spenserian form of > SHEND
YSHENDING > YSHEND
YSHENDS > YSHEND
YSHENT > YSHEND
YSLAKED archaic past participle of > SLAKE

YTOST archaic past participle of > TOSS
YTTERBIA n colourless hygroscopic substance used in certain alloys and ceramics
YTTERBIAS > YTTERBIA
YTTERBIC > YTTERBIUM
YTTERBITE n rare mineral
YTTERBIUM n soft silvery element
YTTERBOUS > YTTERBIUM
YTTRIA n insoluble solid used mainly in incandescent mantles
YTTRIAS > YTTRIA
YTTRIC > YTTRIUM
YTTRIOUS > YTTRIUM
YTTRIUM n silvery metallic element used in various alloys
YTTRIUMS > YTTRIUM
YU n jade
YUAN n standard monetary unit of the People's Republic of China
YUANS > YUAN
YUCA same as > YUCCA
YUCAS > YUCA
YUCCA n tropical plant with lancelike leaves
YUCCAS > YUCCA
YUCCH interj expression of disgust
YUCH interj expression of disgust
YUCK interj exclamation indicating contempt, dislike, or disgust ▷ vb chuckle
YUCKED > YUCK
YUCKER > YUCK
YUCKERS > YUCK
YUCKIER > YUCKY
YUCKIEST > YUCKY
YUCKINESS > YUCKY
YUCKING > YUCK
YUCKO adj disgusting ▷ interj exclamation of disgust

YUCKS > YUCK
YUCKY adj disgusting, nasty
YUFT n Russia leather
YUFTS > YUFT
YUG same as > YUGA
YUGA n (in Hindu cosmology) one of the four ages of mankind
YUGARIE variant spelling of > EUGARIE
YUGARIES > YUGARIE
YUGAS > YUGA
YUGS > YUG
YUK same as > YUCK
YUKATA n light kimono
YUKATAS > YUKATA
YUKE vb itch
YUKED > YUKE
YUKES > YUKE
YUKIER > YUKY
YUKIEST > YUKY
YUKING > YUKE
YUKKED > YUK
YUKKIER > YUKKY
YUKKIEST > YUKKY
YUKKING > YUK
YUKKY same as > YUCKY
YUKO n score of five points in judo
YUKOS > YUKO
YUKS > YUK
YUKY adj itchy
YULAN n Chinese magnolia with white flowers
YULANS > YULAN
YULE n Christmas
YULES > YULE
YULETIDE n Christmas season
YULETIDES > YULETIDE
YUM interj expression of delight
YUMBERRY n purple-red edible fruit of an E Asian tree
YUMMIER > YUMMY
YUMMIES > YUMMY
YUMMIEST > YUMMY
YUMMINESS > YUMMY
YUMMO adj tasty ▷ interj exclamation of delight or approval

YUMMY adj delicious ▷ interj exclamation indicating pleasure or delight ▷ n delicious food item
YUMP vb leave the ground when driving over a ridge
YUMPED > YUMP
YUMPIE n young upwardly mobile person
YUMPIES > YUMPIE
YUMPING > YUMP
YUMPS > YUMP
YUNX n wryneck
YUNXES > YUNX
YUP n answer of yes
YUPON same as > YAUPON
YUPONS > YUPON
YUPPIE n young highly paid professional person ▷ adj typical of or reflecting the values of yuppies
YUPPIEDOM > YUPPIE
YUPPIEISH > YUPPIE
YUPPIES > YUPPY
YUPPIFIED > YUPPIFY
YUPPIFIES > YUPPIFY
YUPPIFY vb make yuppie in nature
YUPPY same as > YUPPIE
YUPPYDOM n state of being a yuppie
YUPPYDOMS > YUPPYDOM
YUPS > YUP
YUPSTER same as > YINDIE
YUPSTERS > YUPSTER
YURT n circular tent
YURTA same as > YURT
YURTAS > YURTA
YURTS > YURT
YUS > YU
YUTZ n Yiddish word meaning fool
YUTZES > YUTZ
YUZU n type of citrus fruit
YUZUS > YUZU
YWIS adv archaic word meaning certainly
YWROKE archaic past participle of > WREAK

y

Zz

ZA n pizza

ZABAIONE n light foamy dessert

ZABAIONES > ZABAIONE

ZABAJONE same as > ZABAIONE

ZABAJONES > ZABAJONE

ZABETA n tariff

ZABETAS > ZABETA

ZABRA n small sailing vessel

ZABRAS > ZABRA

ZABTIEH n Turkish police officer

ZABTIEHS > ZABTIEH

ZACATON n coarse grass

ZACATONS > ZACATON

ZACK n Australian five-cent piece

ZACKS > ZACK

ZADDICK adj righteous ▷ n Hasidic Jewish spiritual leader

ZADDICKS > ZADDICK

ZADDIK n Hasidic Jewish leader

ZADDIKIM > ZADDIK

ZADDIKS > ZADDIK

ZAFFAR same as > ZAFFER

ZAFFARS > ZAFFAR

ZAFFER n impure cobalt oxide, used to impart a blue colour to enamels

ZAFFERS > ZAFFER

ZAFFIR same as > ZAFFER

ZAFFIRS > ZAFFIR

ZAFFRE same as > ZAFFER

ZAFFRES > ZAFFRE

ZAFTIG adj ripe or curvaceous

ZAG vb change direction sharply

ZAGGED > ZAG

ZAGGING > ZAG

ZAGS > ZAG

ZAIBATSU n group or combine comprising a few wealthy families that controls industry, business, and finance in Japan

ZAIBATSUS > ZAIBATSU

ZAIDA n grandfather

ZAIDAS > ZAIDA

ZAIDEH same as > ZAIDA

ZAIDEHS > ZAIDEH

ZAIDIES > ZAIDY

ZAIDY same as > ZAIDA

ZAIKAI n Japanese business community

ZAIKAIS > ZAIKAI

ZAIRE n currency used in the former Zaïre

ZAIRES > ZAIRE

ZAITECH n investment in financial markets by a company to supplement its main income

ZAITECHS > ZAITECH

ZAKAT n annual tax on Muslims to aid the poor in the Muslim community

ZAKATS > ZAKAT

ZAKOUSKA > ZAKOUSKI

ZAKOUSKI same as > ZAKUSKI

ZAKUSKA > ZAKUSKI

ZAKUSKI pl n Russian hors d'oeuvres consisting of tiny sandwiches

ZAMAN n tropical tree

ZAMANG same as > ZAMAN

ZAMANGS > ZAMANG

ZAMANS > ZAMAN

ZAMARRA n sheepskin coat

ZAMARRAS > ZAMARRA

ZAMARRO same as > ZAMARRA

ZAMARROS > ZAMARRO

ZAMBOMBA n drum-like musical instrument

ZAMBOMBAS > ZAMBOMBA

ZAMBOORAK n small swivelling cannon mounted on a camel's back

ZAMBUCK n informal word for a St John ambulance attendant

ZAMBUCKS > ZAMBUCK

ZAMBUK same as > ZAMBUCK

ZAMBUKS > ZAMBUK

ZAMIA n type of plant of tropical and subtropical America

ZAMIAS > ZAMIA

ZAMINDAR n (in India) the owner of an agricultural estate

ZAMINDARI n (in India) a large agricultural estate

ZAMINDARS > ZAMINDAR

ZAMINDARY same as > ZAMINDARI

ZAMOUSE n West African buffalo

ZAMOUSES > ZAMOUSE

ZAMPOGNA n Italian bagpipes

ZAMPOGNAS > ZAMPOGNA

ZAMPONE n sausage made from pig's trotters

ZAMPONI > ZAMPONE

ZAMZAWED adj dialect word describing tea left in the pot to stew

ZANAMIVIR n drug used to treat influenza

ZANANA same as > ZENANA

ZANANAS > ZANANA

ZANDER n European freshwater pikeperch, valued as a food fish

ZANDERS > ZANDER

ZANELLA n twill fabric

ZANELLAS > ZANELLA

ZANIED > ZANY

ZANIER > ZANY

ZANIES > ZANY

ZANIEST > ZANY

ZANILY > ZANY

ZANINESS > ZANY

ZANJA n irrigation canal

ZANJAS > ZANJA

ZANJERO n irrigation supervisor

ZANJEROS > ZANJERO

ZANTE n type of wood

ZANTES > ZANTE

ZANTEWOOD n wood of the zante tree

ZANTHOXYL variant spelling of > XANTHOXYL

ZANY adj comical in an endearing way ▷ n clown or buffoon who imitated other performers ▷ vb clown

ZANYING > ZANY

ZANYISH > ZANY

ZANYISM > ZANY

ZANYISMS > ZANY

ZANZA same as > ZANZE

ZANZAS > ZANZA

ZANZE n African musical instrument

ZANZES > ZANZE

ZAP vb move quickly ▷ n energy, vigour, or pep ▷ interj exclamation used to express sudden or swift action

ZAPATA adj (of a moustache) drooping

ZAPATEADO n Spanish dance with stamping and very fast footwork

ZAPATEO n Cuban folk dance

ZAPATEOS > ZAPATEO

ZAPOTILLA n large tropical American evergreen tree

ZAPPED > ZAP

ZAPPER n remote control for a television, etc

ZAPPERS > ZAPPER

ZAPPIER > ZAPPY

ZAPPIEST > ZAPPY

ZAPPING > ZAP

ZAPPY adj energetic

ZAPS > ZAP

ZAPTIAH same as > ZAPTIEH

ZAPTIAHS > ZAPTIAH

ZAPTIEH n Turkish police officer

ZAPTIEHS > ZAPTIEH

ZARAPE n blanket-like shawl

ZARAPES > ZARAPE

ZARATITE n green amorphous mineral

ZARATITES > ZARATITE

ZAREBA n (in NE Africa) enclosure of thorn bushes around a village or campsite

ZAREBAS > ZAREBA

ZAREEBA same as > ZAREBA

ZAREEBAS > ZAREEBA

ZARF n (esp in the Middle East) a holder, usually ornamental, for a hot coffee cup

ZARFS > ZARF

ZARI n thread made from fine gold or silver wire

ZARIBA same as > ZAREBA

ZARIBAS > ZARIBA

ZARIS > ZARI

ZARNEC n sulphide of arsenic

ZARNECS > ZARNEC

ZARNICH same as > ZARNEC

ZARNICHS > ZARNICH

ZARZUELA n type of Spanish vaudeville or operetta, usually satirical in nature

ZARZUELAS > ZARZUELA

ZAS > ZA

ZASTRUGA variant spelling of > SASTRUGA

ZASTRUGI > ZASTRUGA

ZATI n type of macaque

ZATIS > ZATI

ZAX n tool for cutting roofing slate

z

ZAXES > ZAX

ZAYIN n seventh letter of the Hebrew alphabet

ZAYINS > ZAYIN

ZAZEN n deep meditation undertaken whilst sitting upright with legs crossed

ZAZENS > ZAZEN

ZE pron gender-neutral pronoun

ZEA n corn silk

ZEAL n great enthusiasm or eagerness

ZEALANT archaic variant of > ZEALOT

ZEALANTS > ZEALANT

ZEALFUL > ZEAL

ZEALLESS > ZEAL

ZEALOT n fanatic or extreme enthusiast

ZEALOTISM > ZEALOT

ZEALOTRY n extreme or excessive zeal or devotion

ZEALOTS > ZEALOT

ZEALOUS adj extremely eager or enthusiastic

ZEALOUSLY > ZEALOUS

ZEALS > ZEAL

ZEAS > ZEA

ZEATIN n cytokinin derived from corn

ZEATINS > ZEATIN

ZEBEC variant spelling of > XEBEC

ZEBECK same as > ZEBEC

ZEBECKS > ZEBECK

ZEBECS > ZEBEC

ZEBRA n black-and-white striped African animal of the horse family

ZEBRAFISH n striped tropical fish

ZEBRAIC adj like a zebra

ZEBRANO n type of striped wood

ZEBRANOS > ZEBRANO

ZEBRAS > ZEBRA

ZEBRASS n offspring of a male zebra and a female ass

ZEBRASSES > ZEBRASS

ZEBRAWOOD n tree yielding striped hardwood used in cabinetwork

ZEBRINA n trailing herbaceous plant

ZEBRINAS > ZEBRINA

ZEBRINE > ZEBRA

ZEBRINES > ZEBRA

ZEBRINNY n offspring of a male horse and a female zebra

ZEBROID > ZEBRA

ZEBRULA n offspring of a male zebra and a female horse

ZEBRULAS > ZEBRULA

ZEBRULE same as > ZEBRULA

ZEBRULES > ZEBRULE

ZEBU n Asian ox with a humped back and long horns

ZEBUB n large African fly

ZEBUBS > ZEBUB

ZEBUS > ZEBU

ZECCHIN same as > ZECCHINO

ZECCHINE same as > ZECCHINO

ZECCHINES > ZECCHINE

ZECCHINI > ZECCHINO

ZECCHINO n former gold coin

ZECCHINOS > ZECCHINO

ZECCHINS > ZECCHIN

ZECHIN same as > ZECCHINO

ZECHINS > ZECHIN

ZED n British and New Zealand spoken form of the letter z

ZEDA n grandfather

ZEDAS > ZEDA

ZEDOARIES > ZEDOARY

ZEDOARY n dried rhizome of a tropical Asian plant

ZEDS > ZED

ZEE the US word for > ZED

ZEES > ZEE

ZEIN n protein occurring in maize

ZEINS > ZEIN

ZEITGEBER n agent or event that sets or resets the biological clock

ZEITGEIST n spirit or attitude of a specific time or period

ZEK n Soviet prisoner

ZEKS > ZEK

ZEL n Turkish cymbal

ZELANT alternative form of > ZEALANT

ZELANTS > ZELANT

ZELATOR same as > ZELATRIX

ZELATORS > ZELATOR

ZELATRICE same as > ZELATRIX

ZELATRIX n nun who monitors the behaviour of younger nuns

ZELKOVA n type of elm tree

ZELKOVAS > ZELKOVA

ZELOSO adv with zeal

ZELOTYPIA n morbid zeal

ZELS > ZEL

ZEMINDAR n (in India) the owner of an agricultural estate

ZEMINDARI n (in India) a large agricultural estate

ZEMINDARS > ZEMINDAR

ZEMINDARY same as > ZEMINDARI

ZEMSTVA > ZEMSTVO

ZEMSTVO n council in Tsarist Russia

ZEMSTVOS > ZEMSTVO

ZEN n calm meditative state

ZENAIDA n dove

ZENAIDAS > ZENAIDA

ZENANA n part of Muslim or Hindu home reserved for women and girls

ZENANAS > ZENANA

ZENDIK n (in Islam) unbeliever or heretic

ZENDIKS > ZENDIK

ZENDO n place where Zen Buddhists study

ZENDOS > ZENDO

ZENITH n highest point of success or power

ZENITHAL > ZENITH

ZENITHS > ZENITH

ZENS > ZEN

ZEOLITE n any of a large group of glassy secondary minerals

ZEOLITES > ZEOLITE

ZEOLITIC > ZEOLITE

ZEP n type of long sandwich

ZEPHYR n soft gentle breeze

ZEPHYRS > ZEPHYR

ZEPPELIN n large cylindrical airship

ZEPPELINS > ZEPPELIN

ZEPPOLE n Italian fritter

ZEPPOLES > ZEPPOLE

ZEPPOLI > ZEPPOLE

ZEPS > ZEP

ZERDA n fennec

ZERDAS > ZERDA

ZEREBA same as > ZAREBA

ZEREBAS > ZEREBA

ZERIBA same as > ZAREBA

ZERIBAS > ZERIBA

ZERK n part of a mechanical joint into which grease can be inserted

ZERKS > ZERK

ZERO n (symbol representing) the number 0 ▷ adj having no measurable quantity or size ▷ vb adjust (an instrument or scale) so as to read zero ▷ determiner no (thing) at all

ZEROED > ZERO

ZEROES > ZERO

ZEROING > ZERO

ZEROS > ZERO

ZEROTH adj denoting a term in a series that precedes the term otherwise regarded as the first term

ZERUMBET n plant stem used as a stimulant and condiment

ZERUMBETS > ZERUMBET

ZEST n enjoyment or excitement ▷ vb give flavour, interest, or piquancy to

ZESTED > ZEST

ZESTER n kitchen utensil used to scrape fine shreds of peel from citrus fruits

ZESTERS > ZESTER

ZESTFUL > ZEST

ZESTFULLY > ZEST

ZESTIER > ZEST

ZESTIEST > ZEST

ZESTILY > ZEST

ZESTINESS n quality of being zesty

ZESTING > ZEST

ZESTLESS > ZEST

ZESTS > ZEST

ZESTY > ZEST

ZETA n sixth letter in the Greek alphabet

ZETAS > ZETA

ZETETIC adj proceeding by inquiry ▷ n investigation

ZETETICS > ZETETIC

ZETTABYTE n 10^{21} or 2^{70} bytes

ZEUGMA n figure of speech in which a word is used with two words although appropriate to only one of them

ZEUGMAS > ZEUGMA

ZEUGMATIC > ZEUGMA

ZEUXITE n ferriferous mineral

ZEUXITES > ZEUXITE

ZEX n tool for cutting roofing slate

ZEXES > ZEX

ZEZE n stringed musical instrument

ZEZES > ZEZE

ZHO same as > ZO

ZHOMO n female zho

ZHOMOS > ZHOMO

ZHOOSH vb make more exciting or attractive

ZHOOSHED > ZHOOSH

ZHOOSHES > ZHOOSH

ZHOOSHING > ZHOOSH

ZHOS > ZHO

ZIBELINE n sable or the fur of this animal ▷ adj of, relating to, or resembling a sable

ZIBELINES > ZIBELINE

ZIBELLINE same as > ZIBELINE

ZIBET n large civet of S and SE Asia

ZIBETH same as > ZIBET

ZIBETHS > ZIBETH

ZIBETS > ZIBET

ZIFF n beard

ZIFFIUS n sea monster

ZIFFIUSES > ZIFFIUS

ZIFFS > ZIFF

ZIG same as > ZAG

ZIGAN n Romany dance

ZIGANKA n Russian dance

ZIGANKAS > ZIGANKA

ZIGANS > ZIGAN

ZIGGED > ZIG

ZIGGING > ZIG

ZIGGURAT n (in ancient Mesopotamia) a temple in the shape of a pyramid

ZIGGURATS > ZIGGURAT

ZIGS > ZIG

ZIGZAG n line or course having sharp turns in alternating directions ▷ vb move in a zigzag ▷ adj formed in or proceeding in a zigzag ▷ adv in a zigzag manner

ZIGZAGGED > ZIGZAG

ZIGZAGGER > ZIGZAG

ZIGZAGGY adj having sharp turns

z

ZIGZAGS > ZIGZAG
ZIKKURAT *same as* > ZIGGURAT
ZIKKURATS > ZIKKURAT
ZIKURAT *same as* > ZIGGURAT
ZIKURATS > ZIKURAT
ZILA *n* administrative district in India
ZILAS > ZILA
ZILCH *n* nothing
ZILCHES > ZILCH
ZILL *n* finger cymbal
ZILLA *same as* > ZILA
ZILLAH *same as* > ZILA
ZILLAHS > ZILLAH
ZILLAS > ZILLA
ZILLION *n* extremely large but unspecified number
ZILLIONS > ZILLION
ZILLIONTH > ZILLION
ZILLS > ZILL
ZIMB *same as* > ZEBUB
ZIMBI *n* cowrie shell used as money
ZIMBIS > ZIMBI
ZIMBS > ZIMB
ZIMOCCA *n* bath sponge
ZIMOCCAS > ZIMOCCA
ZIN *short form of* > ZINFANDEL
ZINC *n* bluish-white metallic element ▷ *vb* coat with zinc
ZINCATE *n* any of a class of salts derived from the amphoteric hydroxide of zinc
ZINCATES > ZINCATE
ZINCED > ZINC
ZINCIC > ZINC
ZINCIER > ZINC
ZINCIEST > ZINC
ZINCIFIED > ZINCIFY
ZINCIFIES > ZINCIFY
ZINCIFY *vb* coat with zinc
ZINCING > ZINC
ZINCITE *n* red or yellow mineral
ZINCITES > ZINCITE
ZINCKED > ZINC
ZINCKIER > ZINC
ZINCKIEST > ZINC
ZINCKIFY *same as* > ZINCIFY
ZINCKING > ZINC
ZINCKY > ZINC
ZINCO *n* printing plate made from zincography
ZINCODE *n* positive electrode
ZINCODES > ZINCODE
ZINCOID > ZINC
ZINCOS > ZINCO
ZINCOUS > ZINC
ZINCS > ZINC
ZINCY > ZINC
ZINDABAD *interj* long live: used as part of a slogan in India, Pakistan, etc
ZINE *n* magazine or fanzine
ZINEB *n* organic insecticide

ZINEBS > ZINEB
ZINES > ZINE
ZINFANDEL *n* type of Californian wine
ZING *n* quality in something that makes it lively or interesting ▷ *vb* make or move with or as if with a high-pitched buzzing sound
ZINGANI > ZINGANO
ZINGANO *n* Romany man
ZINGARA *n* Romany woman
ZINGARE > ZINGARA
ZINGARI > ZINGARO
ZINGARO *n* Romany man
ZINGED > ZING
ZINGEL *n* small freshwater perch
ZINGELS > ZINGEL
ZINGER > ZING
ZINGERS > ZING
ZINGIBER *n* ginger plant
ZINGIBERS > ZINGIBER
ZINGIER > ZINGY
ZINGIEST > ZINGY
ZINGING > ZING
ZINGS > ZING
ZINGY *adj* vibrant
ZINKE *n* cornett
ZINKED > ZINC
ZINKENITE *n* a metallic mineral consisting of a sulphide of lead and antimony
ZINKES > ZINKE
ZINKIER > ZINC
ZINKIEST > ZINC
ZINKIFIED > ZINKIFY
ZINKIFIES > ZINKIFY
ZINKIFY *vb* coat with zinc
ZINKING > ZINC
ZINKY > ZINC
ZINNIA *n* plant of tropical and subtropical America
ZINNIAS > ZINNIA
ZINS > ZIN
ZIP *n* fastening device operating by means of two rows of metal or plastic teeth ▷ *vb* fasten with a zip
ZIPLESS > ZIP
ZIPLINE *n* cable used for transportation across a river, gorge, etc
ZIPLINES > ZIPLINE
ZIPLOCK *adj* fastened with interlocking plastic strips ▷ *vb* seal (a ziplock storage bag)
ZIPLOCKED > ZIPLOCK
ZIPLOCKS > ZIPLOCK
ZIPOLA *n* nothing
ZIPOLAS > ZIPOLA
ZIPPED > ZIP
ZIPPER *same as* > ZIP
ZIPPERED *adj* provided or fastened with a zip
ZIPPERING > ZIPPER
ZIPPERS > ZIPPER
ZIPPIER > ZIPPY
ZIPPIEST > ZIPPY
ZIPPILY *adv* in a zippy manner

ZIPPINESS *n* quality of being zippy
ZIPPING > ZIP
ZIPPO *n* nothing
ZIPPOS > ZIPPO
ZIPPY *adj* full of energy
ZIPS > ZIP
ZIPTOP *adj* (of a bag) closed with a zip
ZIPWIRE *same as* > ZIPLINE
ZIPWIRES > ZIPWIRE
ZIRAM *n* industrial fungicide
ZIRAMS > ZIRAM
ZIRCALLOY *n* alloy of zirconium containing small amounts of tin, chromium, and nickel. It is used in pressurized-water reactors
ZIRCALOY *same as* > ZIRCALLOY
ZIRCALOYS > ZIRCALOY
ZIRCON *n* mineral used as a gemstone and in industry
ZIRCONIA *n* white oxide of zirconium, used as a pigment for paints, a catalyst, and an abrasive
ZIRCONIAS > ZIRCONIA
ZIRCONIC > ZIRCONIUM
ZIRCONIUM *n* greyish-white metallic element that is resistant to corrosion
ZIRCONS > ZIRCON
ZIT *n* spot or pimple
ZITE *same as* > ZITI
ZITHER *n* musical instrument consisting of strings stretched over a flat box
ZITHERIST > ZITHER
ZITHERN *same as* > ZITHER
ZITHERNS > ZITHERN
ZITHERS > ZITHER
ZITI *n* type of pasta
ZITIS > ZITI
ZITS > ZIT
ZIZ *same as* > ZIZZ
ZIZANIA *n* aquatic grass
ZIZANIAS > ZIZANIA
ZIZEL *n* chipmunk
ZIZELS > ZIZEL
ZIZIT *same as* > ZIZITH
ZIZITH *variant spelling of* > TSITSITH
ZIZYPHUS *n* jujube tree
ZIZZ *n* short sleep ▷ *vb* take a short sleep, snooze
ZIZZED > ZIZZ
ZIZZES > ZIZZ
ZIZZING > ZIZZ
ZIZZLE *vb* sizzle
ZIZZLED > ZIZZLE
ZIZZLES > ZIZZLE
ZIZZLING > ZIZZLE
ZLOTE > ZLOTY
ZLOTIES > ZLOTY
ZLOTY *n* monetary unit of Poland
ZLOTYCH *same as* > ZLOTY

ZLOTYS > ZLOTY
ZO *n* Tibetan breed of cattle
ZOA > ZOON
ZOAEA *same as* > ZOEA
ZOAEAE > ZOAEA
ZOAEAS > ZOAEA
ZOARIA > ZOARIUM
ZOARIAL > ZOARIUM
ZOARIUM *n* colony of zooids
ZOBO *same as* > ZO
ZOBOS > ZOBO
ZOBU *same as* > ZO
ZOBUS > ZOBU
ZOCALO *n* plaza in Mexico
ZOCALOS > ZOCALO
ZOCCO *n* plinth
ZOCCOLO *same as* > ZOCCO
ZOCCOLOS > ZOCCOLO
ZOCCOS > ZOCCO
ZODIAC *n* imaginary belt in the sky within which the sun, moon, and planets appear to move
ZODIACAL > ZODIAC
ZODIACS > ZODIAC
ZOEA *n* free-swimming larva of a crab or related crustacean
ZOEAE > ZOEA
ZOEAL > ZOEA
ZOEAS > ZOEA
ZOECHROME *same as* > ZOETROPE
ZOECIA > ZOECIUM
ZOECIUM *same as* > ZOOECIUM
ZOEFORM > ZOEA
ZOETIC *adj* pertaining to life
ZOETROPE *n* cylinder-shaped toy with a sequence of pictures on its inner surface which produce an illusion of animation when it is rotated
ZOETROPES > ZOETROPE
ZOETROPIC > ZOETROPE
ZOFTIG *adj* ripe or curvaceous
ZOIATRIA *n* veterinary surgery
ZOIATRIAS > ZOIATRIA
ZOIATRICS *n* veterinary surgery
ZOIC *adj* relating to or having animal life
ZOISITE *n* grey, brown, or pink mineral
ZOISITES > ZOISITE
ZOISM *n* belief in magical animal powers
ZOISMS > ZOISM
ZOIST > ZOISM
ZOISTS > ZOISM
ZOL *n* South African slang for a cannabis cigarette
ZOLPIDEM *n* drug used to treat insomnia
ZOLPIDEMS > ZOLPIDEM
ZOLS > ZOL

z

ZOMBI *same as* > ZOMBIE
ZOMBIE *n* corpse that has been reanimated by a supernatural spirit
ZOMBIES > ZOMBIE
ZOMBIFIED > ZOMBIFY
ZOMBIFIES > ZOMBIFY
ZOMBIFY *vb* turn into a zombie
ZOMBIISM > ZOMBIE
ZOMBIISMS > ZOMBIE
ZOMBIS > ZOMBI
ZOMBOID *adj* like a zombie
ZOMBORUK *n* small swivelling cannon mounted on a camel's back
ZOMBORUKS > ZOMBORUK
ZONA *n* zone or belt
ZONAE > ZONA
ZONAL *adj* of, relating to, or of the nature of a zone
ZONALLY > ZONAL
ZONARY *same as* > ZONAL
ZONATE *adj* marked with, divided into, or arranged in zones
ZONATED *same as* > ZONATE
ZONATION *n* arrangement in zones
ZONATIONS > ZONATION
ZONDA *n* South American wind
ZONDAS > ZONDA
ZONE *n* area with particular features or properties ▷ *vb* divide into zones
ZONED > ZONE
ZONELESS > ZONE
ZONER *n* something which divides other things into zones
ZONERS > ZONER
ZONES > ZONE
ZONETIME *n* standard time of the time zone in which a ship is located at sea
ZONETIMES > ZONETIME
ZONING > ZONE
ZONINGS > ZONE
ZONK *vb* strike resoundingly
ZONKED > ZONK
ZONKING > ZONK
ZONKS > ZONK
ZONOID *adj* resembling a zone ▷ *n* finite vector sum of line segments
ZONOIDS > ZONOID
ZONULA *n* small zone or belt
ZONULAE > ZONULA
ZONULAR > ZONULE
ZONULAS > ZONULA
ZONULE *n* small zone, band, or area
ZONULES > ZONULE
ZONULET *n* small belt
ZONULETS > ZONULET
ZONURE *n* lizard with a ringed tail

ZONURES > ZONURE
ZOO *n* place where live animals are kept for show
ZOOBIOTIC *adj* parasitic on or living in association with an animal
ZOOBLAST *n* animal cell
ZOOBLASTS > ZOOBLAST
ZOOCHORE *n* plant with spores or seeds that are dispersed by animals
ZOOCHORES > ZOOCHORE
ZOOCHORY > ZOOCHORE
ZOOCYTIA > ZOOCYTIUM
ZOOCYTIUM *n* branched stalk connecting the members of the colony of some minute aquatic creatures
ZOOEA *same as* > ZOEA
ZOOEAE > ZOOEA
ZOOEAL > ZOOEA
ZOOEAS > ZOOEA
ZOOECIA > ZOOECIUM
ZOOECIUM *n* part of a polyzoan colony that houses the feeding zooids
ZOOEY > ZOO
ZOOGAMETE *n* gamete that can move independently
ZOOGAMIES > ZOOGAMY
ZOOGAMOUS > ZOOGAMY
ZOOGAMY *n* reproduction involving zoosperm
ZOOGENIC *adj* produced from animals
ZOOGENIES > ZOOGENY
ZOOGENOUS *same as* > ZOOGENIC
ZOOGENY *n* doctrine of the formation of animals
ZOOGLEA *same as* > ZOOGLOEA
ZOOGLEAE > ZOOGLEA
ZOOGLEAL > ZOOGLEA
ZOOGLEAS > ZOOGLEA
ZOOGLOEA *n* mass of bacteria adhering together by a jelly-like substance derived from their cell walls
ZOOGLOEAE > ZOOGLOEA
ZOOGLOEAL > ZOOGLOEA
ZOOGLOEAS > ZOOGLOEA
ZOOGLOEIC > ZOOGLOEA
ZOOGONIES > ZOOGONY
ZOOGONOUS > ZOOGONY
ZOOGONY *same as* > ZOOGENY
ZOOGRAFT *n* animal tissue grafted onto a human body
ZOOGRAFTS > ZOOGRAFT
ZOOGRAPHY *n* branch of zoology concerned with the description of animals
ZOOID *n* any independent animal body, such as an individual of a coral colony

ZOOIDAL > ZOOID
ZOOIDS > ZOOID
ZOOIER > ZOO
ZOOIEST > ZOO
ZOOKEEPER *n* person who cares for animals in a zoo
ZOOKS *short form of* > GADZOOKS
ZOOLATER > ZOOLATRY
ZOOLATERS > ZOOLATRY
ZOOLATRIA *same as* > ZOOLATRY
ZOOLATRY *n* worship of animals
ZOOLITE *n* fossilized animal
ZOOLITES > ZOOLITE
ZOOLITH *n* fossilized animal
ZOOLITHIC > ZOOLITH
ZOOLITHS > ZOOLITH
ZOOLITIC > ZOOLITE
ZOOLOGIC > ZOOLOGY
ZOOLOGIES > ZOOLOGY
ZOOLOGIST > ZOOLOGY
ZOOLOGY *n* study of animals
ZOOM *vb* move or rise very rapidly ▷ *n* sound or act of zooming
ZOOMABLE *adj* capable of being viewed at various levels of magnification
ZOOMANCY *n* divination through observing the actions of animals
ZOOMANIA *n* extreme or excessive devotion to animals
ZOOMANIAS > ZOOMANIA
ZOOMANTIC > ZOOMANCY
ZOOMED > ZOOM
ZOOMETRIC > ZOOMETRY
ZOOMETRY *n* study of the relative size of the different parts of an animal or animals
ZOOMING > ZOOM
ZOOMORPH *n* representation of an animal form
ZOOMORPHS > ZOOMORPH
ZOOMORPHY > ZOOMORPH
ZOOMS > ZOOM
ZOON *vb* zoom ▷ *n* zooid
ZOONAL > ZOON
ZOONED > ZOON
ZOONIC *adj* concerning animals
ZOONING > ZOON
ZOONITE *n* segment of an articulated animal
ZOONITES > ZOONITE
ZOONITIC > ZOONITE
ZOONOMIA *same as* > ZOONOMY
ZOONOMIAS > ZOONOMIA
ZOONOMIC > ZOONOMY
ZOONOMIES > ZOONOMY
ZOONOMIST > ZOONOMY

ZOONOMY *n* science of animal life
ZOONOSES > ZOONOSIS
ZOONOSIS *n* any infection or disease that is transmitted to humans from lower vertebrates
ZOONOTIC > ZOONOSIS
ZOONS > ZOON
ZOOPATHY *n* science of animal diseases
ZOOPERAL > ZOOPERY
ZOOPERIES > ZOOPERY
ZOOPERIST > ZOOPERY
ZOOPERY *n* experimentation on animals
ZOOPHAGAN *n* carnivore
ZOOPHAGY *n* eating other animals
ZOOPHILE *n* person who is devoted to animals and their protection
ZOOPHILES > ZOOPHILE
ZOOPHILIA *n* condition in which a person has a sexual attraction to animals
ZOOPHILIC > ZOOPHILE
ZOOPHILY *same as* > ZOOPHILIA
ZOOPHOBE > ZOOPHOBIA
ZOOPHOBES > ZOOPHOBIA
ZOOPHOBIA *n* unusual or morbid dread of animals
ZOOPHORI > ZOOPHORUS
ZOOPHORIC > ZOOPHORUS
ZOOPHORUS *n* frieze with animal figures
ZOOPHYTE *n* any animal resembling a plant, such as a sea anemone
ZOOPHYTES > ZOOPHYTE
ZOOPHYTIC > ZOOPHYTE
ZOOPLASTY *n* surgical transplantation to humans of animal tissues
ZOOS > ZOO
ZOOSCOPIC > ZOOSCOPY
ZOOSCOPY *n* condition causing hallucinations of animals
ZOOSPERM *n* gamete that can move independently
ZOOSPERMS > ZOOSPERM
ZOOSPORE *n* asexual spore of some algae and fungi that moves by means of flagella
ZOOSPORES > ZOOSPORE
ZOOSPORIC > ZOOSPORE
ZOOSTEROL *n* any of a group of animal sterols, such as cholesterol
ZOOT *n* as in *zoot suit* man's suit consisting of baggy trousers and a long jacket

z

ZOOTAXIES > ZOOTAXY
ZOOTAXY *n* science of the classification of animals
ZOOTECHNY *n* science of breeding animals
ZOOTHECIA *n* outer layers of certain protozoans
ZOOTHEISM *n* treatment of an animal as a god
ZOOTHOME *n* group of zooids
ZOOTHOMES > ZOOTHOME
ZOOTIER > ZOOTY
ZOOTIEST > ZOOTY
ZOOTOMIC > ZOOTOMY
ZOOTOMIES > ZOOTOMY
ZOOTOMIST > ZOOTOMY
ZOOTOMY *n* branch of zoology concerned with the dissection and anatomy of animals
ZOOTOXIC > ZOOTOXIN
ZOOTOXIN *n* toxin, such as snake venom, that is produced by an animal
ZOOTOXINS > ZOOTOXIN
ZOOTROPE *same as* > ZOETROPE
ZOOTROPES > ZOOTROPE
ZOOTROPHY *n* nourishment of animals
ZOOTY *adj* showy
ZOOTYPE *n* animal figure used as a symbol
ZOOTYPES > ZOOTYPE
ZOOTYPIC > ZOOTYPE
ZOOZOO *n* wood pigeon
ZOOZOOS > ZOOZOO
ZOPILOTE *n* small American vulture
ZOPILOTES > ZOPILOTE
ZOPPA *adj* syncopated
ZOPPO *same as* > ZOPPA
ZORBING *n* activity of travelling downhill inside a large air-filled ball
ZORBINGS > ZORBING
ZORBONAUT *n* person who engages in the activity of zorbing
ZORGITE *n* copper-lead selenide
ZORGITES > ZORGITE
ZORI *n* Japanese sandal
ZORIL *same as* > ZORILLA
ZORILLA *n* skunk-like African musteline mammal having a long black-and-white coat
ZORILLAS > ZORILLA
ZORILLE *same as* > ZORILLA
ZORILLES > ZORILLE
ZORILLO *same as* > ZORILLA
ZORILLOS > ZORILLO
ZORILS > ZORIL
ZORINO *n* skunk fur

ZORINOS > ZORINO
ZORIS > ZORI
ZORRO *n* hoary fox
ZORROS > ZORRO
ZOS > ZO
ZOSTER *n* shingles; herpes zoster
ZOSTERS > ZOSTER
ZOUAVE *n* (formerly) member of a body of French infantry composed of Algerian recruits
ZOUAVES > ZOUAVE
ZOUK *n* style of dance music that combines African and Latin American rhythms
ZOUKS > ZOUK
ZOUNDS *interj* archaic mild oath indicating surprise
ZOWEE *same as* > ZOWIE
ZOWIE *interj* expression of pleasurable surprise
ZOYSIA *n* type of grass with short stiffly pointed leaves, often used for lawns
ZOYSIAS > ZOYSIA
ZUCCHETTI > ZUCCHETTO
ZUCCHETTO *n* small round skullcap worn by clergymen and varying in colour according to the rank of the wearer
ZUCCHINI *n* courgette
ZUCCHINIS > ZUCCHINI
ZUCHETTA *same as* > ZUCCHETTO
ZUCHETTAS > ZUCHETTA
ZUCHETTO *same as* > ZUCCHETTO
ZUCHETTOS > ZUCCHETTO
ZUFFOLI > ZUFFOLO
ZUFFOLO *same as* > ZUFOLO
ZUFOLI > ZUFOLO
ZUFOLO *n* small flute
ZUFOLOS > ZUFOLO
ZUGZWANG *n* (in chess) position in which one player can move only with loss or severe disadvantage ▷ *vb* manoeuvre (one's opponent) into a zugzwang
ZUGZWANGS > ZUGZWANG
ZULU *n* (in the NATO phonetic alphabet) used to represent z
ZULUS > ZULU
ZUMBOORUK *n* small swivelling cannon mounted on a camel's back
ZUPA *n* confederation of Serbian villages
ZUPAN *n* head of a zupa
ZUPANS > ZUPAN

ZUPAS > ZUPA
ZUPPA *n* Italian soup
ZUPPAS > ZUPPA
ZURF *same as* > ZARF
ZURFS > ZURF
ZUZ *n* ancient Hebrew silver coin
ZUZIM > ZUZ
ZUZZIM > ZUZ
ZWANZIGER *n* silver coin formerly used in Southern Germany and Austria until the end of the 19th century
ZWIEBACK *n* small type of rusk
ZWIEBACKS > ZWIEBACK
ZYDECO *n* type of Black Cajun music
ZYDECOS > ZYDECO
ZYGA > ZYGON
ZYGAENID *adj* of the burnet moth genus
ZYGAENOID *same as* > ZYGAENID
ZYGAL > ZYGON
ZYGANTRA > ZYGANTRUM
ZYGANTRUM *n* vertebral articulation in snakes and some lizards
ZYGOCACTI *pl n* genus of Brazilian cactuses
ZYGODONT *adj* possessing paired molar cusps
ZYGOID *same as* > DIPLOID
ZYGOMA *n* slender arch of bone on each side of the skull of mammals
ZYGOMAS > ZYGOMA
ZYGOMATA > ZYGOMA
ZYGOMATIC *adj* of or relating to the zygoma
ZYGON *n* brain fissure
ZYGOPHYTE *n* plant that reproduces by means of zygospores
ZYGOSE > ZYGOSIS
ZYGOSES > ZYGOSIS
ZYGOSIS *n* direct transfer of DNA between two cells that are temporarily joined
ZYGOSITY > ZYGOSIS
ZYGOSPERM *same as* > ZYGOSPORE
ZYGOSPORE *n* thick-walled spore formed from the zygote of some fungi and algae
ZYGOTE *n* fertilized egg cell
ZYGOTENE *n* second stage of the prophase of meiosis
ZYGOTENES > ZYGOTENE
ZYGOTES > ZYGOTE
ZYGOTIC > ZYGOTE
ZYLONITE *variant spelling of* > XYLONITE
ZYLONITES > ZYLONITE

ZYMASE *n* mixture of enzymes that is obtained as an extract from yeast and ferments sugars
ZYMASES > ZYMASE
ZYME *n* ferment
ZYMES > ZYME
ZYMIC > ZYME
ZYMITE *n* priest who uses leavened bread during communion
ZYMITES > ZYMITE
ZYMOGEN *n* any of various inactive precursors of enzymes activated by a kinase
ZYMOGENE *same as* > ZYMOGEN
ZYMOGENES > ZYMOGENE
ZYMOGENIC *adj* of or relating to a zymogen
ZYMOGENS > ZYMOGEN
ZYMOGRAM *n* band of an electrophoretic medium showing a pattern of enzymes following electrophoresis
ZYMOGRAMS > ZYMOGRAM
ZYMOID *adj* relating to a ferment
ZYMOLOGIC > ZYMOLOGY
ZYMOLOGY *n* chemistry of fermentation
ZYMOLYSES > ZYMOLYSIS
ZYMOLYSIS *n* process of fermentation
ZYMOLYTIC > ZYMOLYSIS
ZYMOME *n* glutinous substance that is insoluble in alcohol
ZYMOMES > ZYMOME
ZYMOMETER *n* instrument for estimating the degree of fermentation
ZYMOSAN *n* insoluble carbohydrate found in yeast
ZYMOSANS > ZYMOSAN
ZYMOSES > ZYMOSIS
ZYMOSIS *same as* > ZYMOLYSIS
ZYMOTIC *adj* of, relating to, or causing fermentation ▷ *n* disease caused by an enzyme
ZYMOTICS > ZYMOTIC
ZYMURGIES > ZYMURGY
ZYMURGY *n* study of fermentation processes
ZYTHUM *n* ancient Egyptian beer
ZYTHUMS > ZYTHUM
ZYZZYVA *n* American weevil
ZYZZYVAS > ZYZZYVA
ZZZ *n* informal word for sleep
ZZZS > ZZZ

z